WITHDRAWN

WITHDRAWN

W9-CER-266

Ref 920 Wh v.2005-06

Who was who in
America.

NEWARK PUBLIC LIBRARY-NEWARK, OHIO 43055

Feb 2007

Who Was Who in America®

Who Was Who in America®

with world notables

2005-2006
Volume XVII

MARQUIS
Who'sWho ® 890 Mountain Avenue, Suite 4
New Providence, NJ 07974 U.S.A.

Who Was Who in America®

Marquis Who's Who®

Chief Executive Officer	Gene M. McGovern	**President**	James A. Finkelstein
Chief Technology Officer	Ariel Spivakovsky		
Senior Managing Director	Fred Marks		
Senior Managing Director, Special Projects	Jon Gelberg		
Director, Editorial & Product Development	Robert Docherty		
Director, Marketing & Reference Sales	Michael Noerr		
Managing Editor, Research	Kerry Morrison		
Managing Editor, Editorial	Karen Chassie		
Senior Editors	Alison Perruso		
	Sara Randazzo		

Published by Marquis Who's Who LLC.

Copyright © 2006 by Marquis Who's Who LLC. All rights reserved.

No part of this publication may be reproduced, stored in a retrieval system, or transmitted, in any form or by any means—including, but not limited to, electronic, mechanical, photocopying, recording, or otherwise—or used for any commercial purpose whatsoever without the prior written permission of the publisher and, if publisher deems necessary, execution of a formal license agreement with publisher.

For information, contact:
Marquis Who's Who
890 Mountain Avenue, Suite 4
New Providence, New Jersey 07974
908-673-1001
www.marquiswhoswho.com

WHO WAS WHO IN AMERICA® is a registered trademark of Marquis Who's Who LLC.

International Standard Book Number	0-8379-0254-1	(19-volume set)
	0-8379-0255-X	(volume XVII)
	0-8379-0256-8	(Index volume)
	0-8379-0257-6	(volume XVII and Index volume)
International Standard Serial Number	0146-8081	

No payment is either solicited or accepted for the inclusion of entries in this publication. Marquis Who's Who has used its best efforts in collecting and preparing material for inclusion in this publication, but does not warrant that the information herein is complete or accurate, and does not assume, and hereby disclaims, any liability to any person for any loss or damage caused by errors or omissions in this publication, whether such errors or omissions result from negligence, accident, or any other cause.

Manufactured in the United States of America.

Table of Contents

Preface

Marquis Who's Who is proud to present the 2005-2006 Edition of *Who Was Who in America*. This 17th edition features over 4,000 profiles of individuals who had previously been profiled in *Who's Who in America* and other Marquis Who's Who publications, but who have died since the publication of the last edition of *Who Was Who in America* in August, 2004.

Among the notable Americans profiled in this volume are individuals as influential and diverse as Johnny Carson, Arthur Miller, Rosa Parks, William Rehnquist, and Simon Wiesenthal. The impact of these individuals during their lifetimes was enormous and their influence is certain to live on.

Of course, not every person profiled in this volume is a household name. These pages include the profiles of doctors, lawyers, entrepreneurs, researchers, inventors, and other prominent achievers who have died in the last two years.

The biographical information included in the profiles that follow was gathered in a variety of manners. In most cases, those listed had submitted their personal biographical details during their lifetime.

In many cases, though, the information was collected independently by our research and editorial staffs, which use a wide assortment of tools to gather complete, accurate, and up-to-date information.

Who Was Who in America is an important component of the Marquis Who's Who family of publications. Along with *Who's Who in America* and *Who's Who in the World*, Marquis Who's Who also publishes a number of specialized and regionalized volumes. These include *Who's Who of American Women*, *Who's Who in American Law*, *Who's Who in Medicine and Healthcare*, and *Who's Who in the East*, to name a few.

It has been an honor to compile this edition of *Who Was Who in America*. It is our hope that the biographical profiles will do justice to the individuals memorialized on the pages that follow.

Table of Abbreviations

The following abbreviations and symbols are frequently used in this book.

A Associate (used with academic degrees only)

AA, A.A. Associate in Arts, Associate of Arts

AAAL American Academy of Arts and Letters

AAAS American Association for the Advancement of Science

AACD American Association for Counseling and Development

AACN American Association of Critical Care Nurses

AAHA American Academy of Health Administrators

AAHP American Association of Hospital Planners

AAHPERD American Alliance for Health, Physical Education, Recreation, and Dance

AAS Associate of Applied Science

AASL American Association of School Librarians

AASPA American Association of School Personnel Administrators

AAU Amateur Athletic Union

AAUP American Association of University Professors

AAUW American Association of University Women

AB, A.B. Arts, Bachelor of

AB Alberta

ABA American Bar Association

ABC American Broadcasting Company

AC Air Corps

acad. academy, academic

acct. accountant

acctg. accounting

ACDA Arms Control and Disarmament Agency

ACHA American College of Hospital Administrators

ACLS Advanced Cardiac Life Support

ACLU American Civil Liberties Union

ACOG American College of Ob-Gyn

ACP American College of Physicians

ACS American College of Surgeons

ADA American Dental Association

a.d.c. aide-de-camp

adj. adjunct, adjutant

adj. gen. adjutant general

adm. admiral

adminstr. administrator

adminstrn. administration

adminstrv. administrative

ADN Associate's Degree in Nursing

ADP Automatic Data Processing

adv. advocate, advisory

advt. advertising

AE, A.E. Agricultural Engineer

A.E. and P. Ambassador Extraordinary and Plenipotentiary

AEC Atomic Energy Commission

aero. aeronautical, aeronautic

aerodyn. aerodynamic

AFB Air Force Base

AFL-CIO American Federation of Labor and Congress of Industrial Organizations

AFTRA American Federation of TV and Radio Artists

AFSCME American Federation of State, County and Municipal Employees

agr. agriculture

agrl. agricultural

agt. agent

AGVA American Guild of Variety Artists

agy. agency

A&I Agricultural and Industrial

AIA American Institute of Architects

AIAA American Institute of Aeronautics and Astronautics

AIChE American Institute of Chemical Engineers

AICPA American Institute of Certified Public Accountants

AID Agency for International Development

AIDS Acquired Immune Deficiency Syndrome

AIEE American Institute of Electrical Engineers

AIM American Institute of Management

AIME American Institute of Mining, Metallurgy, and Petroleum Engineers

AK Alaska

AL Alabama

ALA American Library Association

Ala. Alabama

alt. alternate

Alta. Alberta

A&M Agricultural and Mechanical

AM, A.M. Arts, Master of

Am. American, America

AMA American Medical Association

amb. ambassador

A.M.E. African Methodist Episcopal

Amtrak National Railroad Passenger Corporation

AMVETS American Veterans of World War II, Korea, Vietnam

ANA American Nurses Association

anat. anatomical

ANCC American Nurses Credentialing Center

ann. annual

ANTA American National Theatre and Academy

anthrop. anthropological

AP Associated Press

APA American Psychological Association

APGA American Personnel Guidance Association

APHA American Public Health Association

APO Army Post Office

apptd. appointed

Apr. April

apt. apartment

AR Arkansas

ARC American Red Cross

arch. architect

archeol. archeological

archtl. architectural

Ariz. Arizona

Ark. Arkansas

ArtsD, ArtsD. Arts, Doctor of

arty. artillery

AS American Samoa

AS Associate in Science

ASCAP American Society of Composers, Authors and Publishers

ASCD Association for Supervision and Curriculum Development

ASCE American Society of Civil Engineers

ASHRAE American Society of Heating, Refrigeration, and Air Conditioning Engineers

ASME American Society of Mechanical Engineers

ASNSA American Society for Nursing Service Administrators

ASPA American Society for Public Administration

ASPCA American Society for the Prevention of Cruelty to Animals

assn. association

assoc. associate

asst. assistant

ASTD American Society for Training and Development

ASTM American Society for Testing and Materials

astron. astronomical

astrophys. astrophysical

ATLA Association of Trial Lawyers of America

ATSC Air Technical Service Command

AT&T American Telephone & Telegraph Company

atty. attorney

Aug. August

AUS Army of the United States

aux. auxiliary

Ave. Avenue

AVMA American Veterinary Medical Association

AZ Arizona

AWHONN Association of Women's Health Obstetric and Neonatal Nurses

B. Bachelor

b. born

BA, B.A. Bachelor of Arts

BAgr, B.Agr. Bachelor of Agriculture

Balt. Baltimore

Bapt. Baptist

BArch, B.Arch. Bachelor of Architecture

BAS, B.A.S. Bachelor of Agricultural Science

BBA, B.B.A. Bachelor of Business Administration

BBB Better Business Bureau

BBC British Broadcasting Corporation

BC, B.C. British Columbia

BCE, B.C.E. Bachelor of Civil Engineering

BChir, B.Chir. Bachelor of Surgery

BCL, B.C.L. Bachelor of Civil Law

BCLS Basic Cardiac Life Support

BCS, B.C.S. Bachelor of Commercial Science

BD, B.D. Bachelor of Divinity

bd. board

BE, B.E. Bachelor of Education

BEE, B.E.E. Bachelor of Electrical Engineering

BFA, B.F.A. Bachelor of Fine Arts
bibl. biblical
bibliog. bibliographical
biog. biographical
biol. biological
BJ, B.J. Bachelor of Journalism
Bklyn. Brooklyn
BL, B.L. Bachelor of Letters
bldg. building
BLS, B.L.S. Bachelor of Library Science
BLS Basic Life Support
Blvd. Boulevard
BMI Broadcast Music, Inc.
BMW Bavarian Motor Works (Bayerische Motoren Werke)
bn. battalion
B.&O.R.R. Baltimore & Ohio Railroad
bot. botanical
BPE, B.P.E. Bachelor of Physical Education
BPhil, B.Phil. Bachelor of Philosophy
br. branch
BRE, B.R.E. Bachelor of Religious Education
brig. gen. brigadier general
Brit. British, Brittanica
Bros. Brothers
BS, B.S. Bachelor of Science
BSA, B.S.A. Bachelor of Agricultural Science
BSBA Bachelor of Science in Business Administration
BSChemE Bachelor of Science in Chemical Engineering
BSD, B.S.D. Bachelor of Didactic Science
BSEE Bachelor of Science in Electrical Engineering
BSN Bachelor of Science in Nursing
BST, B.S.T. Bachelor of Sacred Theology
BTh, B.Th. Bachelor of Theology
bull. bulletin
bur. bureau
bus. business
B.W.I. British West Indies

CA California
CAA Civil Aeronautics Administration
CAB Civil Aeronautics Board
CAD-CAM Computer Aided Design–Computer Aided Model
Calif. California
C.Am. Central America
Can. Canada, Canadian
CAP Civil Air Patrol
capt. captain
cardiol. cardiological
cardiovasc. cardiovascular
CARE Cooperative American Relief Everywhere
Cath. Catholic
cav. cavalry
CBC Canadian Broadcasting Company
CBI China, Burma, India Theatre of Operations
CBS Columbia Broadcasting Company
C.C. Community College
CCC Commodity Credit Corporation
CCNY City College of New York
CCRN Critical Care Registered Nurse
CCU Cardiac Care Unit
CD Civil Defense
CE, C.E. Corps of Engineers, Civil Engineer
CEN Certified Emergency Nurse
CENTO Central Treaty Organization

CEO chief executive officer
CERN European Organization of Nuclear Research
cert. certificate, certification, certified
CETA Comprehensive Employment Training Act
CFA Chartered Financial Analyst
CFL Canadian Football League
CFO chief financial officer
CFP Certified Financial Planner
ch. church
ChD, Ch.D. Doctor of Chemistry
chem. chemical
ChemE, Chem.E. Chemical Engineer
ChFC Chartered Financial Consultant
Chgo. Chicago
chirurg. chirurgical
chmn. chairman
chpt. chapter
CIA Central Intelligence Agency
Cin. Cincinnati
cir. circle, circuit
CLE Continuing Legal Education
Cleve. Cleveland
climatol. climatological
clin. clinical
clk. clerk
C.L.U. Chartered Life Underwriter
CM, C.M. Master in Surgery
CM Northern Mariana Islands
CMA Certified Medical Assistant
cmty. community
CNA Certified Nurse's Aide
CNOR Certified Nurse (Operating Room)
C.&N.W.Ry. Chicago & North Western Railway
CO Colorado
Co. Company
COF Catholic Order of Foresters
C. of C. Chamber of Commerce
col. colonel
coll. college
Colo. Colorado
com. committee
comd. commanded
comdg. commanding
comdr. commander
comdt. commandant
comm. communications
commd. commissioned
comml. commercial
commn. commission
commr. commissioner
compt. comptroller
condr. conductor
Conf. Conference
Congl. Congregational, Congressional
Conglist. Congregationalist
Conn. Connecticut
cons. consultant, consulting
consol. consolidated
constl. constitutional
constn. constitution
constrn. construction
contbd. contributed
contbg. contributing
contbn. contribution
contbr. contributor
contr. controller
Conv. Convention
COO chief operating officer
coop. cooperative
coord. coordinator
CORDS Civil Operations and Revolutionary Development Support
CORE Congress of Racial Equality

corp. corporation, corporate
corr. correspondent, corresponding, correspondence
C.&O.Ry. Chesapeake & Ohio Railway
coun. council
CPA Certified Public Accountant
CPCU Chartered Property and Casualty Underwriter
CPH, C.P.H. Certificate of Public Health
cpl. corporal
CPR Cardio-Pulmonary Resuscitation
C.P.Ry. Canadian Pacific Railway
CRT Cathode Ray Terminal
C.S. Christian Science
CSB, C.S.B. Bachelor of Christian Science
C.S.C. Civil Service Commission
CT Connecticut
ct. court
ctr. center
ctrl. central
CWS Chemical Warfare Service
C.Z. Canal Zone

D. Doctor
d. daughter
DAgr, D.Agr. Doctor of Agriculture
DAR Daughters of the American Revolution
dau. daughter
DAV Disabled American Veterans
DC, D.C. District of Columbia
DCL, D.C.L. Doctor of Civil Law
DCS, D.C.S. Doctor of Commercial Science
DD, D.D. Doctor of Divinity
DDS, D.D.S. Doctor of Dental Surgery
DE Delaware
Dec. December
dec. deceased
def. defense
Del. Delaware
del. delegate, delegation
Dem. Democrat, Democratic
DEng, D.Eng. Doctor of Engineering
denom. denomination, denominational
dep. deputy
dept. department
dermatol. dermatological
desc. descendant
devel. development, developmental
DFA, D.F.A. Doctor of Fine Arts
D.F.C. Distinguished Flying Cross
DHL, D.H.L. Doctor of Hebrew Literature
dir. director
dist. district
distbg. distributing
distbn. distribution
distbr. distributor
disting. distinguished
div. division, divinity, divorce
divsn. division
DLitt, D.Litt. Doctor of Literature
DMD, D.M.D. Doctor of Dental Medicine
DMS, D.M.S. Doctor of Medical Science
DO, D.O. Doctor of Osteopathy
docs. documents
DON Director of Nursing
DPH, D.P.H. Diploma in Public Health
DPhil, D.Phil. Doctor of Philosophy
D.R. Daughters of the Revolution
Dr. Drive, Doctor
DRE, D.R.E. Doctor of Religious Education
DrPH, Dr.P.H. Doctor of Public Health, Doctor of Public Hygiene

D.S.C. Distinguished Service Cross
DSc, D.Sc. Doctor of Science
DSChemE Doctor of Science in Chemical
  Engineering
D.S.M. Distinguished Service Medal
DST, D.S.T. Doctor of Sacred Theology
DTM, D.T.M. Doctor of Tropical
  Medicine
DVM, D.V.M. Doctor of Veterinary
  Medicine
DVS, D.V.S. Doctor of Veterinary Surgery

E, E. East
ea. eastern
E. and P. Extraordinary and Plenipotentiary
Eccles. Ecclesiastical
ecol. ecological
econ. economic
ECOSOC Economic and Social Council
  (of the UN)
ED, E.D. Doctor of Engineering
ed. educated
EdB, Ed.B. Bachelor of Education
EdD, Ed.D. Doctor of Education
edit. edition
editl. editorial
EdM, Ed.M. Master of Education
edn. education
ednl. educational
EDP Electronic Data Processing
EdS, Ed.S. Specialist in Education
EE, E.E. Electrical Engineer
E.E. and M.P. Envoy Extraordinary and
  Minister Plenipotentiary
EEC European Economic Community
EEG Electroencephalogram
EEO Equal Employment Opportunity
EEOC Equal Employment Opportunity
  Commission
E.Ger. German Democratic Republic
EKG Electrocardiogram
elec. electrical
electrochem. electrochemical
electrophys. electrophysical
elem. elementary
EM, E.M. Engineer of Mines
EMT Emergency Medical Technician
ency. encyclopedia
Eng. England
engr. engineer
engring. engineering
entomol. entomological
environ. environmental
EPA Environmental Protection Agency
epidemiol. epidemiological
Episc. Episcopalian
ERA Equal Rights Amendment
ERDA Energy Research and Development
  Administration
ESEA Elementary and Secondary
  Education Act
ESL English as Second Language
ESPN Entertainment and Sports
  Programming Network
ESSA Environmental Science Services
  Administration
ethnol. ethnological
ETO European Theatre of Operations
Evang. Evangelical
exam. examination, examining
Exch. Exchange
exec. executive
exhbn. exhibition
expdn. expedition
expn. exposition
expt. experiment

exptl. experimental
Expy. Expressway
Ext. Extension

F.A. Field Artillery
FAA Federal Aviation Administration
FAO Food and Agriculture Organization
  (of the UN)
FBA Federal Bar Association
FBI Federal Bureau of Investigation
FCA Farm Credit Administration
FCC Federal Communications Commission
FCDA Federal Civil Defense Administration
FDA Food and Drug Administration
FDIA Federal Deposit Insurance
  Administration
FDIC Federal Deposit Insurance
  Corporation
FE, F.E. Forest Engineer
FEA Federal Energy Administration
Feb. February
fed. federal
fedn. federation
FERC Federal Energy Regulatory
  Commission
fgn. foreign
FHA Federal Housing Administration
fin. financial, finance
FL Florida
Fl. Floor
Fla. Florida
FMC Federal Maritime Commission
FNP Family Nurse Practitioner
FOA Foreign Operations Administration
found. foundation
FPC Federal Power Commission
FPO Fleet Post Office
frat. fraternity
FRS Federal Reserve System
FSA Federal Security Agency
Ft. Fort
FTC Federal Trade Commission
Fwy. Freeway

G-1 (or other number) Division of
  General Staff
GA, Ga. Georgia
GAO General Accounting Office
gastroent. gastroenterological
GATE Gifted and Talented Educators
GATT General Agreement on Tariffs and
  Trade
GE General Electric Company
gen. general
geneal. genealogical
geod. geodetic
geog. geographic, geographical
geol. geological
geophys. geophysical
geriat. geriatrics
gerontol. gerontological
G.H.Q. General Headquarters
GM General Motors Corporation
GMAC General Motors Acceptance
  Corporation
G.N.Ry. Great Northern Railway
gov. governor
govt. government
govtl. governmental
GPO Government Printing Office
grad. graduate, graduated
GSA General Services Administration
Gt. Great
GTE General Telephone and Electric
  Company
GU Guam

gynecol. gynecological

HBO Home Box Office
hdqs. headquarters
HEW Department of Health, Education
  and Welfare
HHD, H.H.D. Doctor of Humanities
HHFA Housing and Home Finance
  Agency
HHS Department of Health and Human
  Services
HI Hawaii
hist. historical, historic
HM, H.M. Master of Humanities
HMO Health Maintenance Organization
homeo. homeopathic
hon. honorary, honorable
Ho. of Dels. House of Delegates
Ho. of Reps. House of Representatives
hort. horticultural
hosp. hospital
H.S. High School
HUD Department of Housing and Urban
  Development
Hwy. Highway
hydrog. hydrographic

IA Iowa
IAEA International Atomic Energy Agency
IATSE International Alliance of Theatrical
  and Stage Employees and Moving
  Picture Operators of the United States
  and Canada
IBM International Business Machines
  Corporation
IBRD International Bank for Reconstruc-
  tion and Development
ICA International Cooperation Administration
ICC Interstate Commerce Commission
ICCE International Council for Computers
  in Education
ICU Intensive Care Unit
ID Idaho
IEEE Institute of Electrical and Electronics
  Engineers
IFC International Finance Corporation
IGY International Geophysical Year
IL Illinois
Ill. Illinois
illus. illustrated
ILO International Labor Organization
IMF International Monetary Fund
IN Indiana
Inc. Incorporated
Ind. Indiana
ind. independent
Indpls. Indianapolis
indsl. industrial
inf. infantry
info. information
ins. insurance
insp. inspector
insp. gen. inspector general
inst. institute
instl. institutional
instn. institution
instr. instructor
instrn. instruction
instrnl. instructional
internat. international
intro. introduction
IRE Institute of Radio Engineers
IRS Internal Revenue Service
ITT International Telephone & Telegraph
  Corporation

JAG Judge Advocate General
JAGC Judge Advocate General Corps
Jan. January
Jaycees Junior Chamber of Commerce
JB, J.B. Jurum Baccalaureus
JCB, J.C.B. Juris Canoni Baccalaureus
JCD, J.C.D. Juris Canonici Doctor, Juris
    Civilis Doctor
JCL, J.C.L. Juris Canonici Licentiatus
JD, J.D. Juris Doctor
jg. junior grade
jour. journal
jr. junior
JSD, J.S.D. Juris Scientiae Doctor
JUD, J.U.D. Juris Utriusque Doctor
jud. judicial

Kans. Kansas
K.C. Knights of Columbus
K.P. Knights of Pythias
KS Kansas
K.T. Knight Templar
KY, Ky. Kentucky

LA, La. Louisiana
L.A. Los Angeles
lab. laboratory
L.Am. Latin America
lang. language
laryngol. laryngological
LB Labrador
LDS Latter Day Saints
LDS Church Church of Jesus Christ of
    Latter Day Saints
lectr. lecturer
legis. legislation, legislative
LHD, L.H.D. Doctor of Humane Letters
L.I. Long Island
libr. librarian, library
lic. licensed, license
L.I.R.R. Long Island Railroad
lit. literature
litig. litigation
LittB, Litt.B. Bachelor of Letters
LittD, Litt.D. Doctor of Letters
LLB, LL.B. Bachelor of Laws
LLD, L.L.D. Doctor of Laws
LLM, L.L.M. Master of Laws
Ln. Lane
L.&N.R.R. Louisville & Nashville
    Railroad
LPGA Ladies Professional Golf
    Association
LPN Licensed Practical Nurse
LS, L.S. Library Science (in degree)
lt. lieutenant
Ltd. Limited
Luth. Lutheran
LWV League of Women Voters

M. Master
m. married
MA, M.A. Master of Arts
MA Massachusetts
MADD Mothers Against Drunk Driving
mag. magazine
MAgr, M.Agr. Master of Agriculture
maj. major
Man. Manitoba
Mar. March
MArch, M.Arch. Master in Architecture
Mass. Massachusetts
math. mathematics, mathematical
MATS Military Air Transport Service
MB, M.B. Bachelor of Medicine
MB Manitoba

MBA, M.B.A. Master of Business
    Administration
MBS Mutual Broadcasting System
M.C. Medical Corps
MCE, M.C.E. Master of Civil Engineer-
    ing
mcht. merchant
mcpl. municipal
MCS, M.C.S. Master of Commercial
    Science
MD, M.D. Doctor of Medicine
MD, Md. Maryland
MDiv Master of Divinity
MDip, M.Dip. Master in Diplomacy
mdse. merchandise
MDV, M.D.V. Doctor of Veterinary
    Medicine
ME, M.E. Mechanical Engineer
ME Maine
M.E.Ch. Methodist Episcopal Church
mech. mechanical
MEd., M.Ed. Master of Education
med. medical
MEE, M.E.E. Master of Electrical
    Engineering
mem. member
meml. memorial
merc. mercantile
met. metropolitan
metall. metallurgical
MetE, Met.E. Metallurgical Engineer
meteorol. meteorological
Meth. Methodist
Mex. Mexico
MF, M.F. Master of Forestry
MFA, M.F.A. Master of Fine Arts
mfg. manufacturing
mfr. manufacturer
mgmt. management
mgr. manager
MHA, M.H.A. Master of Hospital
    Administration
M.I. Military Intelligence
MI Michigan
Mich. Michigan
micros. microscopic, microscopical
mid. middle
mil. military
Milw. Milwaukee
Min. Minister
mineral. mineralogical
Minn. Minnesota
MIS Management Information Systems
Miss. Mississippi
MIT Massachusetts Institute of Technol-
    ogy
mktg. marketing
ML, M.L. Master of Laws
MLA Modern Language Association
M.L.D. Magister Legnum Diplomatic
MLitt, M.Litt. Master of Literature,
    Master of Letters
MLS, M.L.S. Master of Library Science
MME, M.M.E. Master of Mechanical
    Engineering
MN Minnesota
mng. managing
MO, Mo. Missouri
moblzn. mobilization
Mont. Montana
MP Northern Mariana Islands
M.P. Member of Parliament
MPA Master of Public Administration
MPE, M.P.E. Master of Physical
    Education
MPH, M.P.H. Master of Public Health

MPhil, M.Phil. Master of Philosophy
MPL, M.P.L. Master of Patent Law
Mpls. Minneapolis
MRE, M.R.E. Master of Religious
    Education
MRI Magnetic Resonance Imaging
MS, M.S. Master of Science
MS, Ms. Mississippi
MSc, M.Sc. Master of Science
MSChemE Master of Science in Chemical
    Engineering
MSEE Master of Science in Electrical
    Engineering
MSF, M.S.F. Master of Science of
    Forestry
MSN Master of Science in Nursing
MST, M.S.T. Master of Sacred Theology
MSW, M.S.W. Master of Social Work
MT Montana
Mt. Mount
MTO Mediterranean Theatre of Operation
MTV Music Television
mus. museum, musical
MusB, Mus.B. Bachelor of Music
MusD, Mus.D. Doctor of Music
MusM, Mus.M. Master of Music
mut. mutual
MVP Most Valuable Player
mycol. mycological

N. North
NAACOG Nurses Association of the
    American College of Obstetricians and
    Gynecologists
NAACP National Association for the
    Advancement of Colored People
NACA National Advisory Committee for
    Aeronautics
NACDL National Association of Criminal
    Defense Lawyers
NACU National Association of Colleges
    and Universities
NAD National Academy of Design
NAE National Academy of Engineering,
    National Association of Educators
NAESP National Association of
    Elementary School Principals
NAFE National Association of Female
    Executives
N.Am. North America
NAM National Association of Manufacturers
NAMH National Association for Mental
    Health
NAPA National Association of Performing
    Artists
NARAS National Academy of Recording
    Arts and Sciences
NAREB National Association of Real
    Estate Boards
NARS National Archives and Record
    Service
NAS National Academy of Sciences
NASA National Aeronautics and Space
    Administration
NASP National Association of School
    Psychologists
NASW National Association of Social
    Workers
nat. national
NATAS National Academy of Television
    Arts and Sciences
NATO North Atlantic Treaty Organization
NATOUSA North African Theatre of
    Operations, United States Army
nav. navigation

X

NB, N.B. New Brunswick
NBA National Basketball Association
NBC National Broadcasting Company
NC, N.C. North Carolina
NCAA National College Athletic Association
NCCJ National Conference of Christians and Jews
ND, N.D. North Dakota
NDEA National Defense Education Act
NE Nebraska
NE, N.E. Northeast
NEA National Education Association
Nebr. Nebraska
NEH National Endowment for Humanities
neurol. neurological
Nev. Nevada
NF Newfoundland
NFL National Football League
Nfld. Newfoundland
NG National Guard
NH, N.H. New Hampshire
NHL National Hockey League
NIH National Institutes of Health
NIMH National Institute of Mental Health
NJ, N.J. New Jersey
NLRB National Labor Relations Board
NM New Mexico
N.Mex. New Mexico
No. Northern
NOAA National Oceanographic and Atmospheric Administration
NORAD North America Air Defense
Nov. November
NOW National Organization for Women
N.P.Ry. Northern Pacific Railway
nr. near
NRA National Rifle Association
NRC National Research Council
NS, N.S. Nova Scotia
NSC National Security Council
NSF National Science Foundation
NSTA National Science Teachers Association
NSW New South Wales
N.T. New Testament
NT Northwest Territories
nuc. nuclear
numis. numismatic
NV Nevada
NW, N.W. Northwest
N.W.T. Northwest Territories
NY, N.Y. New York
N.Y.C. New York City
NYU New York University
N.Z. New Zealand

OAS Organization of American States
ob-gyn obstetrics-gynecology
obs. observatory
obstet. obstetrical
occupl. occupational
oceanog. oceanographic
Oct. October
OD, O.D. Doctor of Optometry
OECD Organization for Economic Cooperation and Development
OEEC Organization of European Economic Cooperation
OEO Office of Economic Opportunity
ofcl. official
OH Ohio
OK Oklahoma
Okla. Oklahoma
ON Ontario

Ont. Ontario
oper. operating
ophthal. ophthalmological
ops. operations
OR Oregon
orch. orchestra
Oreg. Oregon
orgn. organization
orgnl. organizational
ornithol. ornithological
orthop. orthopedic
OSHA Occupational Safety and Health Administration
OSRD Office of Scientific Research and Development
OSS Office of Strategic Services
osteo. osteopathic
otol. otological
otolaryn. otolaryngological

PA, Pa. Pennsylvania
P.A. Professional Association
paleontol. paleontological
path. pathological
PBS Public Broadcasting System
P.C. Professional Corporation
PE Prince Edward Island
pediat. pediatrics
P.E.I. Prince Edward Island
PEN Poets, Playwrights, Editors, Essayists and Novelists (international association)
penol. penological
P.E.O. women's organization (full name not disclosed)
pers. personnel
pfc. private first class
PGA Professional Golfers' Association of America
PHA Public Housing Administration
pharm. pharmaceutical
PharmD, Pharm.D. Doctor of Pharmacy
PharmM, Pharm.M. Master of Pharmacy
PhB, Ph.B. Bachelor of Philosophy
PhD, Ph.D. Doctor of Philosophy
PhDChemE Doctor of Science in Chemical Engineering
PhM, Ph.M. Master of Philosophy
Phila. Philadelphia
philharm. philharmonic
philol. philological
philos. philosophical
photog. photographic
phys. physical
physiol. physiological
Pitts. Pittsburgh
Pk. Park
Pky. Parkway
Pl. Place
P.&L.E.R.R. Pittsburgh & Lake Erie Railroad
Plz. Plaza
PNP Pediatric Nurse Practitioner
P.O. Post Office
PO Box Post Office Box
polit. political
poly. polytechnic, polytechnical
PQ Province of Quebec
PR, P.R. Puerto Rico
prep. preparatory
pres. president
Presbyn. Presbyterian
presdl. presidential
prin. principal
procs. proceedings
prod. produced (play production)

prodn. production
prodr. producer
prof. professor
profl. professional
prog. progressive
propr. proprietor
pros. atty. prosecuting attorney
pro tem. pro tempore
PSRO Professional Services Review Organization
psychiat. psychiatric
psychol. psychological
PTA Parent-Teachers Association
ptnr. partner
PTO Pacific Theatre of Operations, Parent Teacher Organization
pub. publisher, publishing, published
pub. public
publ. publication
pvt. private

quar. quarterly
qm. quartermaster
Q.M.C. Quartermaster Corps
Que. Quebec

radiol. radiological
RAF Royal Air Force
RCA Radio Corporation of America
RCAF Royal Canadian Air Force
RD Rural Delivery
Rd. Road
R&D Research & Development
REA Rural Electrification Administration
rec. recording
ref. reformed
regt. regiment
regtl. regimental
rehab. rehabilitation
rels. relations
Rep. Republican
rep. representative
Res. Reserve
ret. retired
Rev. Reverend
rev. review, revised
RFC Reconstruction Finance Corporation
RFD Rural Free Delivery
rhinol. rhinological
RI, R.I. Rhode Island
RISD Rhode Island School of Design
Rlwy. Railway
Rm. Room
RN, R.N. Registered Nurse
roentgenol. roentgenological
ROTC Reserve Officers Training Corps
RR Rural Route
R.R. Railroad
rsch. research
rschr. researcher
Rt. Route

S. South
s. son
SAC Strategic Air Command
SAG Screen Actors Guild
SALT Strategic Arms Limitation Talks
S.Am. South America
san. sanitary
SAR Sons of the American Revolution
Sask. Saskatchewan
savs. savings
SB, S.B. Bachelor of Science
SBA Small Business Administration
SC, S.C. South Carolina

SCAP Supreme Command Allies Pacific
ScB, Sc.B. Bachelor of Science
SCD, S.C.D. Doctor of Commercial Science
ScD, Sc.D. Doctor of Science
sch. school
sci. science, scientific
SCLC Southern Christian Leadership Conference
SCV Sons of Confederate Veterans
SD, S.D. South Dakota
SE, S.E. Southeast
SEATO Southeast Asia Treaty Organization
SEC Securities and Exchange Commission
sec. secretary
sect. section
seismol. seismological
sem. seminary
Sept. September
s.g. senior grade
sgt. sergeant
SHAEF Supreme Headquarters Allied Expeditionary Forces
SHAPE Supreme Headquarters Allied Powers in Europe
S.I. Staten Island
S.J. Society of Jesus (Jesuit)
SJD Scientiae Juridicae Doctor
SK Saskatchewan
SM, S.M. Master of Science
SNP Society of Nursing Professionals
So. Southern
soc. society
sociol. sociological
S.P.Co. Southern Pacific Company
spkr. speaker
spl. special
splty. specialty
Sq. Square
S.R. Sons of the Revolution
sr. senior
SS Steamship
SSS Selective Service System
St. Saint, Street
sta. station
stats. statistics
statis. statistical
STB, S.T.B. Bachelor of Sacred Theology
stblzn. stabilization
STD, S.T.D. Doctor of Sacred Theology
std. standard
Ste. Suite
subs. subsidiary
SUNY State University of New York
supr. supervisor
supt. superintendent
surg. surgical
svc. service
SW, S.W. Southwest
sys. system

TAPPI Technical Association of the Pulp and Paper Industry
tb. tuberculosis

tchg. teaching
tchr. teacher
tech. technical, technology
technol. technological
tel. telephone
Tel. & Tel. Telephone & Telegraph
telecom. telecommunications
temp. temporary
Tenn. Tennessee
Ter. Territory
Ter. Terrace
TESOL Teachers of English to Speakers of Other Languages
Tex. Texas
ThD, Th.D. Doctor of Theology
theol. theological
ThM, Th.M. Master of Theology
TN Tennessee
tng. training
topog. topographical
trans. transaction, transferred
transl. translation, translated
transp. transportation
treas. treasurer
TT Trust Territory
TV television
TVA Tennessee Valley Authority
TWA Trans World Airlines
twp. township
TX Texas
typog. typographical

U. University
UAW United Auto Workers
UCLA University of California at Los Angeles
UDC United Daughters of the Confederacy
U.K. United Kingdom
UN United Nations
UNESCO United Nations Educational, Scientific and Cultural Organization
UNICEF United Nations International Children's Emergency Fund
univ. university
UNRRA United Nations Relief and Rehabilitation Administration
UPI United Press International
U.P.R.R. United Pacific Railroad
urol. urological
U.S. United States
U.S.A. United States of America
USAAF United States Army Air Force
USAF United States Air Force
USAFR United States Air Force Reserve
USAR United States Army Reserve
USCG United States Coast Guard
USCGR United States Coast Guard Reserve
USES United States Employment Service
USIA United States Information Agency
USMC United States Marine Corps
USMCR United States Marine Corps Reserve
USN United States Navy

USNG United States National Guard
USNR United States Naval Reserve
USO United Service Organizations
USPHS United States Public Health Service
USS United States Ship
USSR Union of the Soviet Socialist Republics
USTA United States Tennis Association
USV United States Volunteers
UT Utah

VA Veterans Administration
VA, Va. Virginia
vet. veteran, veterinary
VFW Veterans of Foreign Wars
VI, V.I. Virgin Islands
vice pres. vice president
vis. visiting
VISTA Volunteers in Service to America
VITA Volunteers in Technical Assistance
vocat. vocational
vol. volunteer, volume
v.p. vice president
vs. versus
VT, Vt. Vermont

W, W. West
WA Washington (state)
WAC Women's Army Corps
Wash. Washington (state)
WATS Wide Area Telecommunications Service
WAVES Women's Reserve, US Naval Reserve
WCTU Women's Christian Temperance Union
we. western
W. Ger. Germany, Federal Republic of
WHO World Health Organization
WI Wisconsin
W.I. West Indies
Wis. Wisconsin
WSB Wage Stabilization Board
WV West Virginia
W.Va. West Virginia
WWI World War I
WWII World War II
WY Wyoming
Wyo. Wyoming

YK Yukon Territory
YMCA Young Men's Christian Association
YMHA Young Men's Hebrew Association
YM & YWHA Young Men's and Young Women's Hebrew Association
yr. year
YT, Y.T. Yukon Territory
YWCA Young Women's Christian Association

zool. zoological

Alphabetical Practices

Names are arranged alphabetically according to the surnames, and under identical surnames according to the first given name. If both surname and first given name are identical, names are arranged alphabetically according to the second given name.

Surnames beginning with De, Des, Du, however capitalized or spaced, are recorded with the prefix preceding the surname and arranged alphabetically under the letter D.

Surnames beginning with Mac and Mc are arranged alphabetically under M.

Surnames beginning with Saint or St. appear after names that begin Sains, and are arranged according to the second part of the name, e.g., St. Clair before Saint Dennis.

Surnames beginning with Van, Von, or von are arranged alphabetically under the letter V.

Compound surnames are arranged according to the first member of the compound.

Many hyphenated Arabic names begin Al-, El-, or al-. These names are alphabetized according to each biographee's designation of last name. Thus Al-Bahar, Neta may be listed either under Al- or under Bahar, depending on the preference of the listee.

Also, Arabic names have a variety of possible spellings when transposed to English. Spelling of these names is always based on the practice of the biographee. Some biographees use a Western form of word order, while others prefer the Arabic word sequence.

Similarly, Asian names may have no comma between family and given names, but some biographees have chosen to add the comma. In each case, punctuation follows the preference of the biographee.

Parentheses used in connection with a name indicate which part of the full name is usually omitted in common usage. Hence, Chambers, E(lizabeth) Anne indicates that the first name, Elizabeth, is generally recorded as an initial. In such a case, the parentheses are ignored in alphabetizing and the name would be arranged as Chambers, Elizabeth Anne.

However, if the entire first name appears in parentheses, for example, Chambers, (Elizabeth) Anne, the first name is not commonly used, and the alphabetizing is therefore arranged as though the name were Chambers, Anne.

If the entire middle name is in parentheses, it is still used in alphabetical sorting. Hence, Belamy, Katherine (Lucille) would sort as Belamy, Katherine Lucille. The same occurs if the entire last name is in parentheses, e.g., (Brandenberg), Howard Keith would sort as Brandenberg, Howard Keith.

For visual clarification:

Smith, H(enry) George: Sorts as Smith, Henry George
Smith, (Henry) George: Sorts as Smith, George
Smith, Henry (George): Sorts as Smith, Henry George
(Smith), Henry George: Sorts as Smith, Henry George

Who Was Who in America®

ABE, KOHEI, electric power company executive; b. Tokyo, Dec. 8, 1923;, Kyoto U., Japan, 1949. Sr. gen. mgr. Chubu Electric Power Co., Nagoya, Japan, 1976-79, dir. acctg., 1979-81, dir., gen. mgr. Gifu office, 1981-83, mng. dir., 1983-89, exec. v.p. dir., 1989-91, pres., CEO, 1991-95, hon. advisor, 1995—2005. Chmn. Fedn. Electric Power Cos., Tokyo, 1993-95, Japan Nuc. Fuel Ltd., Aomori, 1993-95, Ctr. Devel. Power Supply Regions, Tokyo, 1993-95, Overseas Uranium Resources Devel. Co. Ltd., Tokyo, 1993-95; chmn. Chubu Econ. Fedn., Nagoya. Avocations: golf, reading. Died Nov. 8, 2005.

ABELOV, STEPHEN LAWRENCE, marketing executive, consultant; b. NYC, Apr. 1, 1923; s. Saul S. and Ethel (Esterman) Abelov; m. Phyllis S. Lichtenson, Nov. 18, 1945; children: Patricia C., Gary M. BS, NYU, 1945, MBA, 1950. Asst. divsn. mgr. Nat. Silver Co., NY, 1945; sales rep. Angelica Uniform Co., NY, 1945—50, asst. sales mgr., 1950—56, western regional mgr. L.A., 1956—66; v.p. Angelica Uniform Co. of Calif., 1958—66, nat. v.p. sales, 1966—72; v.p. Angelica Corp., 1958—88, cons., 1988—92, group v.p. mktg., 1972—80; exec. v.p., chief mktg. officer Angelica Uniform Group, 1980—88. Vis. lectr. mktg. NYU Grad. Sch. Bus. Adminstrn. Contbr. articles to profl. jours. Vice comdr. Am. Legion; mem. vocational adv. bd. VA; adv. bd. Woodcraft Rangers; bd. dirs. Univ. Temple. With USAF, 1942—44. Mem.: various trade assns., Inst. Environ. Scis., Health Industries Assn. Am. (dir.), Am. Mktg. Assn., Am. Soc. for Advancement Mgmt. (chpt. pres.), Am. Assn. Contamination Control (dir.), U.S. Power Squadron, Coast Guard Aux. (Flotilla comdr., dist. officer), B'nai B'rith (past pres.), St. Louis Coun. on World Affairs, NYU Alumni Assn., Lake of the Ozarks Yachting Assn., Moorings Yacht Club (v.p.), Sales Execs. Club (bd. dirs.), Aqua Sierra Sportsmen Club, NYU Club, Men's Club (exec. v.p.), Town Hall Club, Phi Epsilon Pi (treas.). Home: Saint Louis, Mo. Died Jan. 7, 2006.

ABERNATHY, VIOLA VICTORIA, nurse; b. Halcyondale, Ga., Aug. 15, 1929; d. Horace C. and Alice (Goss) Davis; m. M. Edward Abernathy, Jan. 6, 1990; 1 child, Michael R. Curry. Diploma, St. Joseph's Hosp., 1950; BSN, Armstrong State Coll., 1979. Supr. Forest Hills Nursing Home, Columbia, S.C.; charge nurse ST. Joseph's Hosp., Savannah, Ga., Primus Clinic, Savannah, Ga. Capt. U.S. Army, 1951-56, res. 1956-60. Home: Savannah, Ga. Died Apr. 17, 2005.

ABLE, LUKE WILLIAM, pediatric surgeon, consultant; b. Pt. Arthur, Tex. s. James Levert and Minnie Maude (Branson) A.; m. Mary Beth Able, June 7, 1937 (div. Dec. 1984); children: Luke William, Stephen Smith; m. Margaret Galloway, Dec. 29, 1984 (dec. Dec. 1993); m. Hester Finke, July 14, 1995. BA, U. Tex., 1933, MD, 1940. Diplomate Am. Bd. Surgery and Pediat. Surgery. Extern So. Pacific Hosp., 1939; intern, surg. resident Hermann Hosp., Houston, 1940-43; resident in gen. and cardiovasc. surgery Boston Children's Hosp., 1946-48; pvt. practice Tex., 1948; clin. prof. surgery Baylor Med. Coll., Houston, 1950—2006; surgeon-in-chief, head dept. surgery Tex. Children's Hosp., Houston, 1954-87, surgeon-in-chief, head dept. surgery emeritus, 1987—2006. Active staff/cons. St. Luke's Episcopal Hosp., Meml. Sys., Meth. Hosp., Hermann Hosp., Tex. Children's Hosp.; tchg. assoc. U. Tex., Houston. Author: Siamese Twins, 1968; contbr. numerous articles to surg. and med. jours., chpts. to med. and surg. books. Lt. USNR, 1943-46, PTO. Decorated Purple Heart, Silver Star; named Ky. Col., 1999. Mem. ACS (Outstanding Presentation award), AMA, Am. Med. Soc., Am. Acad. Pediats. (surg. sect. 1949—, Outstanding Presentation award), Am. Pediats. Surg. Assn. (charter), Am. Trauma Assn., Tex. Med. Soc., Tex. Pediat. Soc., Tex. Surg. Soc. (v.p. 1953—, pres. 1987, Comty. Svc. award), Tex. Assn. Pediat. Surgeons (past pres.), Houston Pediat. Soc., Houston Surg. Soc. (pres. 1969-70, Outstanding Surgeon of Yr. 1991, Comty. Svc. award). Harris County Med. Soc. (sec. 1958). Republican. Baptist. Avocations: ranching, forestry. Home: Houston, Tex. Died Mar. 16, 2006.

ABLES, CHARLES ROBERT, lawyer, judge; b. South Pittsburg, Tenn., Sept. 13, 1930; s. William McKinley and Iva (Baldwin) A.; m. Rada B. Edmonds, May 20, 1949; children: Patricia Joan, Barbara Elain. BS, U. Chattanooga, 1964; LLB, U. Tenn., 1965. Bar: Tenn. 1965, U.S. Dist. Ct. (ea. dist.) Tenn. 1965, U.S. Ct. Appeals (6th cir.) 1977. Pvt. practice, South Pittsburg, 1971—; judge Manion County Juvenile Ct., Jasper, Tenn., 1980-90. With USNG, 1948-50. Mem. Lions, Masons. Republican. Presbyterian. Home: South Pittsburg, Tenn. Died Apr. 20, 2005.

ABRAHAM, DONALD EARL, broadcasting executive; b. Carnegie, Pa., July 14, 1931; s. Earl Bede and Helen Elizabeth (Kupski) A.; children: Robert Earl, Karen Elizabeth, Dale Edward, Todd Allen. BS in Bus. Adminstrn., Duquesne U., 1958. Cert. secondary tchr., Pa. Staff acct. Cargill, Inc., Carnegie, 1949-55; office mgr. Louis Hamburg, Inc., Pitts., 1955-56; internal auditor Ea. Gas and Fuel Assn., Pitts., 1956-58; controller, sec. Thurner Constrn., Pitts., 1958-65; asst. supr. bus. affairs Carlynton Sch. Dist., Carnegie, 1965-70; dir. bus. services North Hills Sch. Dist., West View, Pa., 1970-74, Beaver (Pa.) Area Sch. Dist., 1974-75; v.p. fin. Sta. WQED-FM-TV, Pitts., from 1975. Bd. dirs., asst. sec. Met. Pitts. Pub. Broadcasting, 1978—. Mem. Pub. Telecommunications Fin. Mgrs. Assn. (treas. 1983-84), Bus. Fin. Mgrs., Nat. Assn. Accts., Soc. for Advancement Mgrs. Clubs: City, Press (Pitts.). Republican. Methodist. Avocations: golf, tennis, bicycling. Home: Wexford, Pa. Died Sept. 19, 2004.

ABRAHAMS, SAMUEL, writer, retired lawyer; b. N.Y.C., Dec. 3, 1923; s. Isaac and Ida (Ehrman) A.; m. Ida Savitsky, July 8, 1970. BA, Bklyn. Coll., 1945; MA, Columbia U., 1946; JD, Bklyn. Law Sch., 1956; LLM, NYU, 1961; PhD, Heed U., 1993. Bar: N.Y. 1957, U.S. Dist. Ct. (ea. and so. dists.) N.Y. 1962, U.S. Supreme Ct. 1976. Pvt. practice, Bklyn., 1958-90. Arbitrator Civil Ct. N.Y.C., 1982-87; part-time adminstrv. judge parking violations bur., 1976-88; lectr. on fgn. travel, law and politics. Author: Law in Family Conflict, 1970; contbr. articles to profl. and popular jours., newspapers. With U. S. Army, 1942-43. Mem. ABA, North Dade Profls. Jewish Fedn. Grtr. Miami, Bklyn. Coll. Alumni Assn., Internat. Assn. of Jewish Judges and Lawyers, Columbia U. Alumni Assn. Democrat. Avocation: world travel. Home: Miami, Fla. Died Apr. 21, 2004.

ABRUZINO, JOSEPH PAUL, healthcare executive; b. Chgo., Oct. 14, 1946; s. Joseph V. and Carmelia E. (Amato) A.; m. Constance Jacklin, July 14, 1969 (div. Sept. 1976); children: Kimberley Ann, Jeffrey Michael; m. Mary Louise Kenny, May 14, 1986; 1 child, Kristen Michelle. BA cum laude, Northeastern U., 1979; postgrad., John Marshall Law Sch., Chgo., 1971-72, Northwestern U., 1972-73. With profl. managerial sci. office Ill. Dept. Labor, Chgo., 1972-73, methods and procedures advisor, 1973; placement officer Placement Registry Am. Agrl. Econs. Assn., Chgo., 1974-76; exec. dir. Proviso Twp. Mental Health Commn., Melrose Park, Ill., from 1976. Chair Commn. for Coop. Action, Proviso Twp., Ill., 1984-86, Proviso Mental Health Affiliation, 1976—. Organizer Citizens for Bush, LaGrange Park, Ill., 1988; v.p. Proviso Tpw. Mental Health Commn., Westchester, Ill., 1974-75; trustee Proviso Twp. Bd. Trustees, Forest Park, Ill., 1973-76, Village of Bellwood, Ill., 1975-79. Sgt. USMC, 1963-68, Vietnam. Decorated Order of the Gallantry Cross with Palm (Republic of Vietnam). Mem. Ill. Mcpl. League, Proviso Mcpl. League, Ill. Assn. Mental Health Authorities, Coun. Internat. Rels. and UN Affairs, Lions. Republican. Roman Catholic. Avocations: reading, racquetball. Home: La Grange Park, Ill. Died May 24, 2005.

ACKERMAN, ALLAN JAY, accountant; b. N.Y.C., Nov. 1, 1931; s. Samuel and Elizabeth (Roth) A.; m. Doris Lewis Ackerman, Feb. 19, 1955; children: Kenneth R., Michael D., Marc E. Student, NYU, 1949-50; BBA magna cum laude, Pace U., 1955. CPA, N.Y.; cert. fraud examiner. Ptnr. KMG Main Hurdman, N.Y.C., 1955-87, KPMG Peat Marwick, 1987-91; dir. litigation and bankruptcy svcs. Mahoney, Cohen & Co., PC, N.Y.c., from 1993. Mem. AICPA, N.Y. State Soc. CPAs (bd. dirs. 1983-85), Am. Arbitration Assn. (comml. arbitration panel), Am. Acctg. Assn., Am. Bankruptcy Inst., Assn. Cert. Fraud Examiners, Old Oaks Country Club (sec. 1989-95). Avocations: golf, gardening. Home: Palm Bch Gdns, Fla. Died Oct. 8, 2004.

ACKERMAN, PAGE, retired librarian, educator; b. Evanston, Ill., June 30, 1912; d. John Bernard and Florence Page. BA, Agnes Scott Coll., Decatur, Ga., 1933; B.L.S., U. N.C., 1940. Cataloger Columbia Theol. Sem., 1942-43; post librarian U.S. Army, Aberdeen Proving Ground, Md., 1943-45; asst. librarian Union Theol. Sem., Richmond, Va., 1945-49; reference librarian UCLA, 1949-54, asst. univ. librarian, 1954-65, asso. univ. librarian, 1965-73, univ. librarian, 1973-77, prof. Sch. Info. and Library Sci., 1973-77, 82, 83; vis. prof. Sch. Librarianship, U. Calif., Berkeley, 1978, 80. Recipient award of distinction in libr. sci. UCLA Alumnae Assn., 1977, Disting. Career Citation, Assn. Coll. and Rsch. Librs., 1989. Mem. ALA, AAUW (Status of Women award 1973), Calif. Libr. Assn., Coun. on Libr. Resources (bd. dirs. 1975-90). Home: Los Angeles, Calif. Died Feb. 28, 2006.

ADAMS, ALFRED BERNARD, JR., environmental engineer; b. Asbury Park, N.J., Oct. 15, 1920; s. Alfred Bishop and Julia Ruth (Wiseman) A.; m. Claudia Neff, Dec. 28, 1942; children: Alfred B. III, Tamara Adams Harris, Carla Adams York. BSChemE, Ga. Inst. Technol., 1943; postgrad., Wayne State U., 1946-48, U. Ala., Birmingham, 1986-88, Jefferson State C.C., 1989-95. Registered profl. engr., Ala., Mich., Fla., Ga., N.C.; Diplomate in Am. Acad. Environ. Engrs. Project engr. Pennwalt, Wyandotte, Mich., 1946-50; sales mgr., design engr. Goslin-Birmingham Div., Birmingham, Ala., 1950-61; field engr. & Sales Elmco Corp., Birmingham, Ala., 1961-62; prin. engr. Morton-Thiokol Corp., Brunswick, Ga., 1962-64; tech. mgr. Rust Internat., Birmingham, 1964-86; pres., owner Adams Cons. & Engring. Svcs., Birmingham, from 1986. Cons. Goslin divsn. Therma Black Clawson, 1989-98; cons. in field. Contbr. tech. papers to profl. publs. Pres. Woodhaven Lakes Property Owners Assn., Pinson, Ala., 1980-82, Lake Park Neighborhood Assn., 1996-98; mem. Pub. Health Com., Birmingham, 1975-78. 2d lt. U.S. Army Chem. Corps, 1943-53. Mem. Air & Waste Mgmt. Assn., Tech. Assn. Pulp & Paper Industries. Presbyterian. Avocations: travel, photography, golf. Died Jan. 13, 2004.

ADAMS, ELAINE, art agent, publicist, writer; b. L.A., Sept. 15, 1960; d. Mikhael Nikitovich Periev-Shelby and Emma (Davidian) Shelby; m. Peter Seitz Adams, Mar. 12, 1990. BA in Econs. and Math., U. So. Calif., 1982. Stock broker Crowell, Weedon & Co., L.A., 1983-89; art agt., artist rep. Peter Adams Studio, Pasadena, Calif., from 1990. Publicity chmn. Calif. Art Club, Pasadena, 1993; dir. Calif. Art Club Gallery, San Marino, 1999. Editor Calif. Art Club newsletter, 1994—; art reviewer Art-Talk. Assoc. trustee Pacific Asia Mus., Pasadena, 1993, chmn. Festival of Autumn Moon, 1994; bd. dirs. Pasadena Symphony, 1994; co-founder, sec. exec. bd. Calif. Art Acad. and Mus., Pasadena, 1997. Mem. Am. Art Coun. (steering com.). Republican. Russian Orthodox. Avocations: art and antique collecting, gourmet cooking. Died Jan. 20, 2004.

ADAMS, MARK F., industrial engineer; b. Hoquiam, Wash., Aug. 4, 1914; s. Harry John and Nellie Florence (Lamb) A.; m. Ruth L. Zier, June 7, 1942; children: Russel Mark, Charles Francis, Paul David, Sylvia Ruth. AS, Grays Harbor Coll., 1938; BS, Wash. State Coll. (later Wash. State U.), 1940, MS, 1942, PhD, 1951. With state dept. conservation and devel., Olympia, Wash., 1941-45; rsch. chemist Wash. State U., Pullman, 1945-51, head dept. materials engring., div. indsl. rsch., 1945-74; indsl. cons. Consulting Assocs., Inc., Tacoma, from 1974; exec. v.p. Larex Internat. Corp., Tacoma, from 1988. Cons. Norton Corrosion Ltd., Bothell, Wash. Contbr. chpts. to books, articles to profl. jours.; patentee in field. Active Sch. Bd. N. Beach Dist. 64, Copalis, Wash., 1978-82. Invited delegate Citizen Ambassador Program to China, 1986. Mem. Nat. Assn. Corrosion Engrs. (cert., chmn. nat. edn. com. 1961-63), Western Region of Nat. Assn. Corrosion Engrs., N.W. Sci. Assn. (pres. 1969, OUtstanding Scientist 1968), N.W. Coordinating Electrolysis Council (underground elec. distbrn. test steering com. 1973), Am. Chem. Soc., Sigma Xi. Lodges: Kiwanis (lt. gov. Ocean Shores, Wash. club 1977-78). Lutheran. Avocations: singing, woodworking. Died Apr. 8, 2004.

ADAMS, RONALD GENE, communications executive; b. Van Lear, Ky., Dec. 3, 1938; s. James C. and Hazel Marie (Fraley) A.; m. Sherry Gail Johnson, Feb. 26, 1988; 1 child, Ronda Glen. AA, Sinclair C.C., Dayton, Ohio, 1975. Radio operator lic. Radio announcer WBZI, Xenia, Ohio, 1970-72; chief engr. WMWM, Wilmington, Ohio, 1972-73; maintenance supr. GM, Dayton, Ohio, 1965-93; pres. Words for You Publishing and Prodns., Tipp City, Ohio, from 1991. Chief pilot, flight instr. Moraine (Ohio) Airpark, 1975-85; cons. GM, 1994—, flight instr. 1967—. Author: What About Flying!?, 1993; contbr. World Poetry Anthology, 1991; video prodr. Waco Classic, 1996. With USAF, 1957-61. Mem. Quietbirdmen (gov. 1996—), Masons, Profl. Videographers Assoc. Avocation: flying. Died Apr. 13, 2004.

ADCOCK, BETTY-LEE, real estate company executive, real estate broker; b. Waldo, Kans., Nov. 19, 1921; d. Ralph Preston and Hazel (Pangburn) Beatty; m. Charles Warren Adcock, Feb. 17, 1945; 1 dau., Roberta Lee. B.S. in Journalism, Kans. State Coll., 1946; grad. Realtors Inst. Lic. real estate broker, Hawaii; cert. residential specialist, residential broker. Mem. pub. relations staff Boeing Airplane Co., Wichita, Kans., 1942-45; biographical staff AP, N.Y.C., 1945-46; real estate salesman and broker, Honolulu, 1972—; prin. broker, pres., owner Adcock, Ltd., real estate mktg., Honolulu, 1983—2005; retired. Recipient Girl Scout Award of Merit, Kitzingen, Germany, 1960, spl. award Am. Cancer Soc., Middlebury, Vt., 1956. Mem. Nat. Assn.

Realtors. Hawaii Assn. Realtors, Honolulu Bd. Realtors, Honolulu Zool. Soc., Friends of Waikiki Aquarium, Nat. Trust for Historic Preservation, Honolulu Art Acad., Friends of Iolani Palace, Bishop Mus., Hawaii Hist. Soc., Hawaii Humane Soc., Hist. Hawaii Found., Chi Omega. Republican. Episcopalian. Died June 30, 2006.

ADEBIMPE, VICTOR ROTIMI, psychiatrist; b. Iji, Kwara, Nigeria, Nov. 6, 1945; arrived in U.S., 1972; s. Solomon Olawepo and Bolaji Adebimpe; m. Folasade Oluremi Ogunlana, Apr. 29, 1972; children: Oluseyi, Babatunde, Olajumoke. BS, U. Ibadan, Nigeria, 1968; MD, U. Ibadan, 1971. Intern Bapt. Hosp., Ogbomosho, Nigeria, 1971-72; resident Mo. Inst. Psychiatry, St. Louis, 1972-75; attending psychiatrist U. Pitts., 1975-79; med. dir. No. Commn. Mental Health Ctr., Pitts., 1979-82; sr. lectr. U. Ilorin, Ilorin, Nigeria, 1982-84; dir. psychiatry St. Johns Health & Hosp. Ctr., Pitts., 1984-90; med. dir. Charles R. Drew Community Mental Health Ctr., Phila., 1987-92; dir. adult psychiatry Mercy Psychiat. Inst., Pitts., 1990-95, pres. med. staff, 1992-95. Adj. asst. prof. psycniatry Allegheny U. Health Scis., 1996-2005; attending psychiatrist Mercy Providence Hosp., Pitts., 1996-2005; James H. Carter Black History month lectr. Duke U., Durham, N.C., 2005 Contbr. chpts. to books, articles to profl. jours. Med. dir. Glade Run Luth. Svcs., Zelienople, Pa., 1996. Fellow Am. Psychiat. Assn., World Fedn. for Mental Health (life); mem. AAAS, Nat. Med. Assn. Baptist. Home: Pittsburgh, Pa. Died Nov. 15, 2005.

ADWAN, KENNETH OSCAR, surgeon; b. Oklahoma City, Oct. 10, 1924; BS, U. Okla., 1948; MD, U. Tex., 1952. Diplomate Am. Bd. Surgeons. Intern U. Okla. Hosp., 1952-53; resident in surgery Parkland Mem. Hosp., Dallas, 1956-59; fellow in surgery U. Tex. S.W. Med. Ctr., assoc. prof. surgery, 1959-70; mem. staff Drs. Hosp., Dallas; pvt. practice Dallas, 1959—93; ret., 1993. Fellow ACS; mem. AMA. Died Jan. 23, 2006.

AGNE, ROBERT FREDERICK, marketing and advertising consultant; b. Verona, N.Y., Oct. 20, 1919; s. Frederick Lewis and Daphne (Kaiser) A.; m. Jane Julia Scott, Nov. 20, 1948; children: Christine Helen Agne Declercq, Janet Scott. BS in Commerce, N.Y. State Coll. for Tchrs., 1941; MBA, U. Pa., 1948. Mgr. market research Sealright Co., Inc., Fulton, N.Y., 1948-55; sr. market analyst Gilette Safety Razor Co., Boston, 1956-60; dir. market research Harold Cabot and Co. Advt., Boston, 1960-63; dir. market research and planning Stroh Brewery Co., Detroit, 1963-81; prin. Agne Enterprises, Grosse Pointe, Mich., from 1980. Adj. assoc. prof. mktg. Wayne State U., Detroit, 1980-84. Author: Let There Be Light, 1983; contbr. (book) Television and Human Behavior, 1963. Lt. USAAF, 1942-45. Named Prof. of the Day Western Mich. U., 1979. Mem. Am. Mktg. Assn. (pres. Detroit chpt. 1969-70), United Stamp Soc. (pres. 1960-61), Boston Philatelist Soc., Masons. Avocations: stamp collecting/philately, golf, writing. Died June 6, 2004.

AGRAWAL, HARISH CHANDRA, neuroscientist, educator; b. Allahabad, Uttar Pradesh, India; came to U.S., 1964, naturalized, 1982; s. Shambhu and Rajmani Devi A.; m. Daya Kumari Bhushan, Feb. 6, 1960; children— Sanjay, Sanjeev B.Sc., Allahabad U., 1957, M.Sc., 1959, PhD, 1964. Med. research assoc. Thudichum Psychiat. Lab., Galesburg, Ill., 1964-68; lectr. dept. biochemistry Charing Cross Hosp., London, 1968-70; prof. neurology Washington U. Sch. Medicine, St. Louis, 1970—2006. Mem. neurology study sect. NIH, 1979-82 Author: Handbook of Neurochemistry, 1969, Developmental Neurobiology, 1970, Biochemistry of Developing Brain, 1971, Membranes and Receptors, 1974, Proteins of the Nervous System, 1980, Biochemistry of Brain, 1980, Handbook of Neurochemistry, 1984; contbr. numerous papers on various aspects of myelin proteins and their role in demyelinating disrders. Jr. research fellow Council Sci. and Indsl. Research, New Delhi, 1960-62, sr. research fellow, 1963-64; Research Career Devel. award Nat. Inst. Neurol. and Communicative Disorders, 1974-79 Mem. Internat. Soc. Neurochemistry, Internat. Brain Rsch. Orgn., Am. Soc. Neurochemistry, Am. Soc. Biol. Chemists and Molecular Biologists, Am. Soc. Physiology. Home: Aventura, Fla. Died Feb. 3, 2006.

AHERN, JOHN EDWARD, mechanical engineer, consultant; b. Portland, Maine, Apr. 7, 1921; s. Henry Robert and Eva Irene (Legere) A.; m. Cora Marie Wilhelm, Sept. 2, 1950; children: Thomas, Maureen, Corinne, Kathleen, Timothy, Jeannine. BSME, Northeastern U., 1943; MSME, Columbia U., 1952. Registered profl. mech. engr., Calif. Contract engr. Babcock & Wilcox Co., N.Y.C., 1947-52; asst. project engr. Pratt and Whitney Aircraft, East Hartford, Conn., 1952-59; prin. rsch. scientist The Marquardt Corp., Van Nuys, Calif., 1959-67; sr. tech. specialist Aerojet Electro Systems Co., Azusa, Calif., 1967-88; cons. Extech, Glendora, Calif., from 1988. Cons. Douglas Aircraft Co., Long Beach, Calif., 1988-89, Aerojet Electro Systems, Co., Azusa, 1988-91. Author: The Exergy Method of Energy Systems Analysis, 1980; contbr. articles to AIAA Jour. 1st lt. USAAF, 1943-46. Fellow ASME; mem. AIAA. Roman Catholic. Achievements include four patents on cryogenics and heat exchangers. Died Mar. 29, 2004.

AHLGREN, MOLLY O., aquatic ecology educator, researcher; b. Duluth, Minn., Nov. 27, 1957; d. Clifford E. and Isabel (Fulton) A. BS, U. Idaho, 1980; MS, Mich. Tech. U., 1985, PhD, 1989. Asst. prof. aquatic resources Sheldon Jackson Coll., Sitka, Alaska, from 1990. Contbr. articles to profl. jours. Mem. Am. Fisheries Soc., Ecol. Soc. Am., N.Am. Benthalogical Soc., Sitka Consevation Soc., Phi Kappa Phi, Sigma Xi. Died Nov. 30, 2004.

AKERS, SUZANNE SELBERG, social worker; b. San Francisco, Jan. 5, 1947; d. Henry Edward and Barcy Pearl (Allsup) Selberg; m. Scott Roger Akers, Aug. 25, 1973; children: Steven, Michelle. BA, Calif. State U., Chico, 1969; MSW, Calif. State U., San Diego, 1984. Social worker Trinity County Welfare, Weaverville, Calif., 1969-73; hotline dir. Econ. Opportunity Commn., El Centro, Calif., 1974-76; health educator Am. Lung Assn., El Centro, Calif., from 1976. Counselor Am. Inst. Fgn. Study, Greenwich, Conn., 1984— Mem. AAUW, Nat. Assn. Social Workers, Congress of Lung Assn. Staff. Lodges: Order Eastern Star (organist 1981), Native Daughters of Golden West (organist 1984—). Democrat. Methodist. Avocations: writing, photography, travel. Home: Imperial, Calif. Died 2005.

AKINS, GEORGE CHARLES, accountant; b. Feb. 22, 1917; s. Guy Brookins and Eugenie (Swan) A.; m. Jane Babcock, Mar. 27, 1945 (dec. May 3, 2003). AA, Sacramento City Coll., 1941. Acct., auditor Calif. Bd. Equalization, Dept. Fin., Sacramento, 1940—44; contr.-treas. DeVons Jewelers, Sacramento, 1944—73, v.p., contr., 1973—80, v.p., CFO, dir., 1980—84; individual acctg. and tax practice Sacramento, from 1944. Contbg. author: Portfolio of Accounting Systems for Small and Medium-Sized Business, 1968, Portfolio of Accounting Systems for Small and Medium-Sized Business, rev. edit., 1977. Acct., cons. Mercy Children's Hosp. Guild, Sacramento, 1957—77. With USAF, 1942. Mem.: Northwestern Pacific Railroad Hist. Soc., Internat. Platform Assn., Calif. Hist. Soc., Nat. Soc. Accts., Soc. Calif. Pioneers, Mendocino County Hist. Soc. (life), USN League (life), Drake Navigators Guild, Sacramento County Hist. Soc. (life), Crocker Art Mus. (life), Comstock, Commonwealth Club of Calif. Republican. Roman Catholic. Died Feb. 10, 2006.

ALBEE, GEORGE WILSON, psychology professor; b. St. Marys, Pa., Dec. 20, 1921; s. George W. and Maude (Allen) A.; m. Constance Impallaria, Aug. 6, 1955 (dec.); children: Alexander, Luke, Maud, Sarah; m. Margaret Moon-Mui Tong, Dec. 20, 1985. AB, Bethany Coll., 1943, ScD (hon.), 1969; MS, U. Pitts., 1947, PhD, 1949; PhD (hon.), Stirling U., Scotland, 1998. Rsch. psychologist Western Psychiat. Inst., Pitts., 1949-51; asst. exec. sec. Am. Psychol. Assn., Washington, 1951-53; Fulbright prof. Helsinki (Finland) U., 1953-54; assoc. prof. psychology Western Res. U., Cleve., 1954-56, prof., 1957-71, chmn. dept. psychology, 1957-60, 63-66, Ladd disting. prof. psychology, 1959-71; prof. psychology U. Vt., Burlington, 1971-92, prof. emeritus, 1992—2006; courtesy prof. Fla. Mental Health Inst. U. South Fla., Tampa, 1994—2006. Cons. VA, Surgeon Gen. of Army, Pres.'s Com. on Mental Retardation, Peace Corps, 1962-65; vis. fellow Brit. Psychol. Soc., 2003. Author: Mental Health Manpower, 1959, Emerging Concepts of Mental Disorder, 1969, The Uncertain Future of Clinical Psychology, 1970, The Future of Psychology, 1974, The Protestant Ethic, Sex, and Psychotherapy, 1978; editor: Primary Prevention of Psychopathology, 1977; gen. editor: (with Justin M. Joffe) series of books on primary prevention of psychopathology; humor columnist The Longboat Observer. Mem. Vt. Psychology Licensing Bd., 1972-75; dir. task force on manpower Joint Commn. Mental Illness and Health, Cambridge, Mass., 1957-59; program com. Nat. Assn. for Mental Health, 1968-70; dir. task group in prevention Pres.'s Commn. Mental Health, 1977-78; com. on prevention Nat. Mental Health Assn., 1985-86; bd. dirs. Internat. Coun. Psychologists, 1985-88, 98-00; prevention com. World Fedn. Mental Health, 1992-2006, Biennial Albee lectr. on prevention. Recipient Alumni Achievement award in sci. Bethany Coll., 2000. Fellow APA (bd. profl. affairs, coun. reps., bd. dirs. 1965-70, 77-80, pres. div. clin. psychology 1967, nat. pres. 1969-70, policy and planning bd. 1972-75, chairperson com. on human resources 1973-76, mem. com. on sci. and profl. ethics 1990-92, bd. for advancement of psychology in pub. interest 1999-2002, task force on governance 2003, Disting. Profl. Contbn. award 1975, Gold medal for lifetime contbns. in the pub. interest 1993, Presdl. citation 2001. pres. divsn. gen. psychology, 2004-06), Am. Psychol. Soc. (founding fellow); mem. AAAS, AAUP, Am. Bd. Profl. Psychology (bd. dirs. 1975-78, treas. 1976-80), Ea. Psychol. Assn., Midwestern Psychol. Assn., Ohio Psychol. Assn. (pres. 1963-64), Vt. Psychol. Assn., New Eng. Psychol. Assn. (pres. 1978-79, Disting. Contbn. award 1997), Am. Assn. Applied and Preventive Psychology (1st pres. 1990-92, Lifetime Achievement award in prevention psychology 1997), Psychologists for Social Responsibility (pres. 1999, steering com. 2001-06), Soc. for Gen. Psychology (pres. divsn. 1 2005), Phi Beta Kappa, Sigma Xi, Psi Chi. Home: Longboat Key, Fla. Died July 8, 2006.

ALBERT, EDWARD, actor, photographer; b. Feb. 20, 1951; s. Eddie and Margo Albert. Student, UCLA; Merit scholar, Oxford U. Starred in films Butterflies Are Free, 1972, Forty Carats, 1973, Midway, 1976, The Domino Principle, 1977, The Greek Tycoon, 1978, The Day the World Ended, 1980, When Time Ran Out, 1980, Butterfly, 1982, The Squeeze, 1982, A Time To Die, 1983, Ellie, 1984, Easy Prey, Unteachables, Terminal Entry, Distortions, Getting Even, Wild Country, The Rescue, Mind Games, 1989, Fistfighter, 1989, Guarding Tess, 1993; prodn. asst. film Patton, 1970; appeared in TV films Death Cruise, 1974, Killer Bees, 1974, Black Beauty miniseries, 1978, The Millionaire, 1978, Silent Victory: The Kitty O'Neill Story, 1978, The Last Convertible miniseries, 1979; TV appearances include Gibbsville, Orson Welles' Great Mysteries, Kung Fu, Medical Story, The Rookies, Police Story, Ellery Queen; appeared in TV series The Yellow Rose, 1983-84. Died Sept. 22, 2006.

ALBERTSEN, HAROLD LAWRENCE, land use consultant, retired appraiser; b. Port Chicago, Calif., July 9, 1931; s. Richard Hans Christian and Theresa Mary (Maglio) A.; m. Patricia Katherine Herrick, Feb. 4, 1951 (div. 1975); m. Judith Anne McCormick, July 10, 1982; children: Michael, Daniel, Kevin, Kelly. AA, Diablo Valley Jr. Coll., Pleasant Hill, Calif., 1963. Advanced appraisal cert., Calif. Svc. engr. Pacific Tel. & Telegaph, Walnut Creek, Calif., 1955-57; adminstrv. asst. Aerojet Gen. Nucleonics, San Ramon, Calif., 1957-67; sr. appraiser Contra Costa County, Martinez, Calif., 1967-89; ret., 1989; land use cons. A. G. Spanos, Stockton, Calif., from 1990. Founder, pres. Single Hearts Inc., Danville, Calif., 1984-88. Author: One Man's Opinion, 1993; patentee quick fence, roll-a-wall. Founder C.I.M.B.L.-Citizens Involved Means Better Living. With USN, 1951-55. Scholar U. San Francisco, 1949-50. Mem. Navy League (pres. Placer County), World of Poetry, Lions. Republican. Roman Catholic. Avocations: woodworking, woodcarving, piano, fishing, poetry. Died July 29, 2004.

ALBRECHT, WILLIAM MELVIN, research chemist, consultant; b. Hungerford, Pa., Feb. 18, 1926; s. Walter John and Vivian Matilda (Sheffer) A.; m. Kathleen Mae Albrecht, July 3, 1948 (dec. Nov. 1995); children: Gary, Jeffery, Robert, Phillip, Cheryl, Keith, Karen, Marsha. BS in Chemistry, Lebanon Valley Coll., Annville, Pa., 1948; MS in Phys. Chemistry, U. Cin., 1950; Cert., MIT, 1970. Rsch. chemist Battelle Meml. Inst., Columbus, 1950-56, rsch. mgr., 1956-60; R&D chemist IBM, Endicott, N.Y., 1960-66, R&D mgr., 1966-82; cons. chemist Endwell, N.Y., from 1982. Mem. symposium panel Am. Electroplaters Soc., N.Y.C., 1978. Contbr. articles to profl. jours. With U.S. Army, 1944-45. Fellow Sigma Xi. Avocations: saxophone teaching, woodworking, cooking, photography. Died May 16, 2004.

ALBRIGHT, BARBARA JOY, magazine editor; b. Fremont, Neb., July 2, 1955; d. Arthur William and Ruth Ann (Walther) A. BS in Food and Nutrition cum laude, U. Nebr., 1977; MS in Nutrition Communications, Boston U., 1980. Registered dietitian. Dietetic intern San Diego VA Hosp., 1977-78; clin. dietitian Independence (Mo.) Hosp., 1978-79; nutritionist Mktg. Sci. Inst., Cambridge, Mass., 1980; asst. food editor Redbook mag., N.Y.C., 1980-81; free-lance writer, home economist N.Y.C., 1981-82; assoc. food editor Woman's World mag., Englewood, N.J., 1982-83; home economist, dietitian Dudley Anderson Yutzy Pub. Rels., N.Y.C., from 1983; from food editor to editor in chief Chocolatier mag., N.Y.C., 1985—2006. Co-author: Mostly Muffins, 1984, Simply Scones, 1988, Wild About Brownies, 1985; contbr. articles to Los Angeles Times Syndicate, Country Living, other mags. Named Master U. Nebr., 1986, Outstanding Young Alumnus U. Nebr., 1988. Mem. Am. Dietetic Assn., Soc. for Am. Cuisine, Home Economists in Bus. (editor newsletter 1986), N.Y. Women's Culinary Alliance (contbg. editor newsletter 1985-87), Conn. Women's Culinary Alliance (bd. mem. 1989-90), N.Y. Soc. for Nebr. (bd. dirs.), Chi Omega (sec.-treas. 1976-77) Republican. Lutheran. Avocations: aerobics, biking, swimming, knitting, cooking. Home: Darien, Conn. Died July 5, 2006.

ALEXANDER, EDWARD RUSSELL, retired epidemiologist, science administrator; b. Chgo., June 15, 1928; s. Russell Green and Ethelyn Satterlee (Abel) A. PhB, U. Chgo., 1948, BS, 1950, MD, 1953. Intern Cin. Gen. Hosp.; chief surveillance sect. Communicable Disease Center, Atlanta, 1955-57, 59-60; resident, instr. dept. pediatrics U. Chgo., 1954-55, 57-59; asst. prof. dept. preventive medicine and dept. pediatrics U. Wash., Seattle, 1961-65, assoc. prof., 1965-69, prof., 1969-79; chmn. dept. epidemiology U. Wash. Sch. Pub. Health, 1970-75; prof. dept. pediat. U. Ariz., Tucson, 1979-83; dir. rsch. br., venereal diseases control divsn. Ctrs. for Disease Control, Atlanta, 1983-89, asst. dir. sci. sexually transmitted diseases divsn., 1989; chief of epidemiology Seattle King County Dept. Pub. Health, Seattle, 1990-98; prof. dept. epidemiology U. Wash. Sch. Pub. Health, Seattle, 1990-98, prof. emeritus, 1998—2006. Contbr. articles to profl. jours. Markle scholar, 1962-67. Mem. Am. Acad. Pediatrics, Am. Pediatric Soc., Am. Pub. Health Assn. (Abraham Lilienfeld award 1988), Assn. Tchrs. Preventive Medicine, Am. Epidemiol. Soc. (pres. 1986-87), Soc. Epidemiol. Rsch., Internat. Epidemiol. Soc., Am. Venereal Disease Assn. (Thomas Parran award 1984, pres. 1985-87) Died Feb. 26, 2006.

ALEXANDER, JOHN ROBERT, hospital administrator, internist; b. Tulsa, July 28, 1936; s. Hiram Marshall and Roberta Alice (Greene) A.; m. Marjorie Louise Okeson, Aug., 1958; children: Stephanie Maine, Paul Fulton, James Marshall, Cynthia Ann, Karen Louise, Robert Thomas. BS, U. Okla., 1958; MD, U. Okla., Oklahoma City, 1961. Intern St. John's Hosp., Tulsa, 1961-62, 1961-62; resident Meth. Hosp. of Dallas, Tex., 1962-65; resident in internal medicine Methodist Hosp. of Dallas, 1962-65; pres. Tulsa Internists, Ltd., 1974-89, Wheeling Med. Group, Inc., Tulsa, 1989-90; mem. staff St. John Med. Ctr., Tulsa, chief of staff, 1977-78, v.p. med. affairs, from 1991. Vice chmn., bd. dirs. Physicians Liability Ins. Co., Oklahoma City; bd. dirs., mem. adv. coun. Okla. Bd. Nurse Registration and Nursing Edn., Oklahoma City, pres., 1997—; clin. prof. U. Okla. Coll.

Medicine, 1974; mem. Okla. Bd. Med. Licensure and Supervision, Tulsa, 1993—, pres., 1995-96. Editor (report) Med. Edn. in Tulsa County, 1981. Pres. Tulsa County Heart Assn., 1970-71; elder Kirk of the Hills Presbyn. Ch., Tulsa, 1970—; med. dir. Wright City (Okla.) Free Health Clinic, 1975-80; chmn. bd. dirs. Tulsa County Health Dept., 1982; pres. bd. dirs. Tulsa Med. Edn., 1994—. Recipient Disting. Medical Svc. award U. Okla. Alumni Assn., 1995, Disting Svc. award Am. Heart Assn., 1971; named Friends of Nursing, Okla. Nurses Assn., 1990. Fellow ACP; mem. AMA (del. 1985—), Okla. State Med. Assn. (pres. 1989-90), Tulsa County Med. Soc. (pres. 1983), Tulsa Internists Soc.(pres. 1972), U. Okla. Alumni Assn. (pres. 1982-83), Rotary Club Will Rogers (pres. 1973-74), Alpha Omega Alpha. Republican. Avocations: racquetball, photography, golf. Home: Tulsa, Okla. Died May 4, 2004.

ALEXANDER, THOMAS WILLIAMSON, journalist; b. Asheville, N.C., Oct. 16, 1930; s. Thomas Williamson and Judith Barksdale A.; m. Jane Duvall, Sept. 30, 1961; children: Ames Barksdale, Amanda Graves. BA, U. N.C., 1953; MA, NYU, 1960; postgrad., Columbia U., 1965. Reporter Columbus (Ga.) Ledger, 1954-56, Richmond (Va.) News-Leader, 1956-59, Life Mag., N.Y.C., 1960-64; assoc. editor Fortune mag., N.Y.C., 1965-80, bd. editors, 1980-86; freelance writer Maggie Valley, N.C., from 1986. Pres. Cataloochee Ski Area, Maggie Valley, 1990—; chmn. bd. Cataloochee Ranch. Author: Project Apollo, 1963; contbr. articles to numerous jours. (U.S. Steel prize 1974, Nat. Mag. award 1994). Cpl. U.S. Army, 1954-56. Republican. Avocations: woodworking, blacksmithing, hunting, fishing, machining. Home: Maggie Valley, NC. Died Apr. 1, 2005.

ALEXANDER, WILLIAM BROOKS, lawyer, former state senator; b. Boyle, Miss., Dec. 23, 1921; s. William Brooks and Vivien (Beaver) A.; m. Belle McDonald, Mar. 12, 1950; children— Brooks, Becky, John, Jason, Grace. Student, Miss. Coll., 1940-42; LL.B., U. Miss., 1948. Bar: Miss. 1948. Ptnr. Alexander, Johnston & Alexander, Cleveland, from 0198; mem. Miss. Senate, 1960-83, past pres. pro tem. Past pres. Miss. Heart Assn.; bd. dirs. Miss. Coll., Delta Coun., Miss. Econ. Coun.; founder Save a Life, Cleve. Served with AUS, 1942-46 Mem. Miss. Bar Assn. (Outstanding Legislator), Bolivar County Bar Assn., Am. Legion, VFW (past dep. comdr.), Exchange Club, Masons. Baptist. Died Jan. 19, 2006.

ALEXIS, CARL ODMAN, lawyer, geologist; b. Valparaiso, Nebr., Aug. 8, 1918; s. Joseph Emmanual Alexander Alexis and Marjorie Edith Odman; m. May Britt Lennerup, 1954 (div. 1962); children: Carl Erik, Karin Frenze; m. Mildred Craig Bartos, 1966 (dec. 1996); m. Jeanette Strain, Apr. 24, 1999. BS, U. Nebr., 1937; MS, U. Ariz., 1940, PhD, 1949; postgrad., Calif. Inst. Tech., 1939-40, NYU, 1943-44; JD, U. Nebr., 1966. Bar: Nebr. 1966. Chemist Am. Potash and Chem. Corp., 1940-41; mucker Phelps Dodge Corp., Bisbee, Ariz., 1941; instrument man Stanolind Oil and Gas Co., Tulsa, 1941-42; sr. supr. Plum Brook Ordnance Works, Sandusky, Ohio, 1942-43; grad. asst. U. Ariz., Tucson, 1947-48; field engr. Anaconda Copper Corp., Salt Lake City, 1948-49; geologist U.S. Geol. Survey, Washington, 1949-50; phys. sci. adminstr. Office Naval Rsch., Washington, 1950-62; spl. asst. atty. gen. Atty. Gen.-Dept. Rds., 1967-71. Lt. comdr. USN, 1943-46, USNR, 1946-69, ret. Mem. Neb. Bar Assn., Lincoln Bar Assn., Audubon Soc., Am. Legion, Friends of Nebr. State Mus., Nebr. State Hist. Soc., Nebr. Art Assn., Gt. Plains Assn., Rotary (#14), Sigma Xi, Phi Kappa Phi. Home: Lincoln, Nebr. Died Feb. 28, 2005.

ALGER, JOHN RODGERS MEIGS, state representative; b. Boston, Dec. 30, 1927; s. Philip Langdon and Catharine (Jackson) A.; m. Judith Harben, Dec. 22, 1951; children: Louisa, Montgomery, Philip. BS, MS, MIT, 1950; postgrad. in mgmt., Gen. Electric Co., 1953, 60. Registered profl. engr., N.H. Mgr. engring. Gen. Electric Co., Syracuse, N.Y., 1968-70, mgr. hybrid electronics, 1970-72, mgr. strategic planning Louisville, 1972-75, mgr. mktg., 1975-77, mgr. tech. assessment Schenectady, 1977-81, mgr. market evaluation, 1981-87; v.p. fin. services Power Funding Corp. subs. Gen. Electric Co., 1987—88; state rep. dist. Grafton #14 State Reps. (Rep.), Concord, NH, from 1997. Author: Creative Synthesis in Design, 1964; author numerous tech. papers. Trustee 1st Unitarian Soc. of Schenectady, 1984-87; mayor Town of Maryhill Estates, Louisville, 1974-75; treas. Capital dist. World Federalists, Schenectady, 1983-85; sec. Profl. Engrs. Soc. Schenectady, 1983, 84; vice chmn. edn. comm., 2003-, chmn. sci. tech. and energy com., 2005 Mem. IEEE (sr.), ASHRAE, Am. Soc. Engring. Edn., Mt. Washington Observatory, Sigma Xi. Clubs: Appalachian Mountain (Boston). Republican. Avocations: carpentry, home construction, forestry. Died Oct. 11, 2005.

ALLEGRINI, PETER JAMES, portfolio manager; b. Waterbury, Conn., Oct. 13, 1952; M. Joan M. Bowers, May 21, 1977; children: Kathryn, Michael, Steven. BS in Econ., Mt. St. Mary's Coll., Emmitsburg, Md., 1974; MBA in Fin., U. Hartford, 1979. Sr. fin. analyst Travelers Corp., Hartford, Conn., 1978-82; sr. bond analyst, mgr. mcpl. rsch. group Fidelity Investments, Boston, 1982-85, portfolio mgr., from 1985. Mem. Boston Soc. Security Analysts (chmn. mcpl. analyst forum 1987-88), Nat. Fedn. Mcpl. Analysts (bd. govs. 1987-88), Nat. Fin. Analysts Fedn. Avocations: running, skiing, investing, reading, golf. Home: Summit, NJ. Died June 26, 2004.

ALLEN, CLAYTON HAMILTON, physicist, acoustician; b. Whitinsville, Mass., June 2, 1918; s. Charles Aaron and Edith Gertrude (Peck) A.; m. Doris Elizabeth LeClaire, Dec. 7, 1981. BS in Physics, Worcester Poly. Inst., 1940; MS in Physics and Math., Pa. State U., 1942, PhD in Physics and Math., Phys.-Chemistry, 1950. Grad. asst. Pa. State U., 1940-42, grad. assoc. State College, 1945-50; acoustical communications researcher Aircraft Radio Lab., Wright-Patterson AFB, Ohio, 1942-45; ultrasonic researcher Corning (N.Y.) Glass Works, 1950-54; cons. on noise control Bolt Beranek and Newman Inc., Cambridge, Mass., 1954-74; v.p. noise control Sci. Applications Inc., La Jolla, Calif., 1974-75; pres. The Clayton H. Allen Corp., Chebeague Island, Maine, from 1975. Lectr. profl. confs. and meetings. Contbr. articles to Jour. Acoustical Soc. Am., Jr. Cellular and Comparative Physiology, Noise Control, Mech. Contractor, Heating, Piping and Air Conditioning, Am. Indsl. Hygiene Assn., Sound, chpts. to ref. books. Fellow Acoustical Soc. Am.; mem. AAAS, Am. Phys. Soc., Acad. Applied Sci., Innovation Group, Am. Foundrymen's Soc., Nat. Coun. Acoustical Cons., Mass. Coun. Acoustical Cons., Mass. Engrs. Coun., Inst. Noise Control Engring. (past mem. bd. dirs. and bd. examiners), Sigma Xi, Sigma Pi Sigma. Achievements include design of a megawatt acoustic facility for full scale aircraft body component sonic fatigue testing at Wright Patterson AFB, and noise control modifications for: submarines, spacecraft instrumentation, a Brit. gas cooled nuclear reactor, a number of multi-megawatt electric induction heater designs, indsl. plants, hosps., cmty. projects, and the like; 15 patents (some with others) include coverage of high frequency siren designs, apparatus for silencing vibrating machinery, method of fabricating miniature phonograph records, linear and nonlinear hearing protecting devices, and apparatus for alloying metal coatings; other patents pending; engaged in field of applied electronic and mechanical research, design and development. Died Aug. 25, 2004.

ALLEN, DONALD MERRIAM, editor, publisher; b. Muscatine, Iowa, Mar. 26, 1912; s. Paul Edward and Mildred Gertrude (Quinn) A. BA, U. Iowa, 1934, MA, 1935; postgrad., U. Wis., 1941-42, U. Calif., Berkeley, 1947-49. Editor Grove Press, N.Y.C., 1951-53, adv. editor, 1956-63; editor, pub. New Directions, N.Y.C., 1954, Criterion Books, N.Y.C., 1955; pres. Four Seasons Found., San Francisco, from 1964, Grey Fox Press, San Francisco, from 1971. Co-editor Evergreen Rev., 1956-60; editor: (anthology) The New American Poetry, 1960, (book) Frank O'Hara Collected Poems, 1971 (Nat. Book award 1971); translator (drama): Ionesco - 4 Plays, 1958. Lt. USN, 1942-47. Decorated Purple Heart, Bronze Star medal. Avocations: walking, reading. Died Aug. 29, 2004.

ALLEN, JAY PRESSON, playwright, screenwriter, producer, director, actor; b. Ft. Worth, Mar. 3, 1922; d. Albert Jeffry and Willie (Miller) Presson; m. Lewis Maitland Allen, Mar. 12, 1955 (dec., 2003); 1 child, Anna Brooke. Screenplays include Wives and Lovers, 1963, Marnie, 1964, The Prime of Miss Jean Brodie, 1969, Cabaret, 1972 (Academy award nomination best adapted screenplay 1972), Travels with My Aunt, 1972, Funny Lady, 1975; playwright, dir.: Tru, 1989, The Big Love, 1991; playwright: The Prime of Miss Jean Brodie, 1966, Forty Carats, 1968, I and Albert, 1972, A Little Family Business, 1982; screenwriter, exec. prodr.: It's My Turn, 1980, Just Tell Me What You Want, 1980 (David DiDonatello award 1980), Prince of the City, 1981 (Academy award nomination best adapted screenplay 1981, NY Film Critics Circle nomination best screenplay, 1981), Deathtrap, 1982; creator: (TV series) Family, 1976-80; creator, exec. prodr.: (TV series) Hothouse, 1988; exec. prodr. (TV series) Family, 1976-80; actor Celluloid Closet, 1995, The Trouble with Marine, 2000, Rescued From the Closet, 2001; author: (novels) Spring Riot, 1948, Just Tell Me What You Want, 1975. Recipient Humanitas award, 1976, Screenwriters' Guild awards (3), Lifetime achievement award, 1997. Mem. Writers Guild, Dramatists Guild, Acad. Motion Picture Arts and Scis. Died May 1, 2006.

ALLEN, JOHN THOMAS, JR., lawyer; b. St. Petersburg, Fla., Aug. 23, 1935; s. John Thomas and Mary Lita (Shields) A.; m. Joyce Ann Lindsey, June 16, 1958 (div. 1985); children: John Thomas III, Linda Joyce, Catherine Lee (dec.).; m. Janice Dearmin Hudson, Mar. 16, 1987 (div. 2002). BSBA with honors, U. Fla., 1958; JD, Stetson U., 1961. Bar: Fla. 1961, U.S. Dist. Ct. (mid. dist.) Fla. 1962, U.S. Ct. Appeals (5th cir.) 1963, U.S. Ct. Appeals (11th cir.) 1983, U.S. Supreme Ct. 1970. Assoc. Mann, Harrison, Mann & Rowe and successor Greene, Mann, Rowe, Davenport & Stanton, St. Petersburg, 1961-67, ptnr., 1967-74; sole practice St. Petersburg, 1974-95; pvt. practice Allen & Maller, P.A., 1996-98, Gulfport, Fla., from 1998. Counsel Pinellas County Legis. Del., 1974-75; counsel for Pinellas County as spl. counsel on water matters, 1975-98. Mem. Com of 100, St. Petersburg, 1975-98. Mem. ABA, Fla. Bar Assn., St. Petersburg Bar Assn., St. Petersburg C. of C., Lions, Beta Gamma Sigma. Republican. Baptist. Died Dec. 6, 2004.

ALLEN, JULIUS CADDEN, biomedical research educator; b. New London, Conn., Oct. 18, 1938; s. Louis Hyman and Martha (Rosenthal) A.; m. Martha Louise Baird, Aug. 20, 1961; children: Jeffrey Cadden, Matthew Josef. BA, Amherst Coll., 1960; MA, U. Mass., 1962; PhD, U. Alberta, Edmonton, Can., 1967. Asst. prof. biomed. rsch. Baylor Coll. Medicine, Houston, 1971-73, assoc. prof., 1973-83, prof., from 1983; assoc. chief sect. cardiovascular sci., prof. dept. medicine DeBakey Heart Ctr. Cons. ECS study sect. NIH, 1991—; cons. cell C.V. physiol. and pharm. Am. Heart Assn., 1991—; assoc. chief Sect. of Cardiovascular Sci.; dir. grad. program DeBakey Heart Ctr. Mem. editorial bd. Circ. Rsch., J. Pharm. Exptl. Therapeutics; contbr. over 100 rsch. articles to profl. jours. Fellow Am. Heart Assn. (cons., Basic Sci. Coun. Hypertension); mem. Am. Physiol. Soc., Am. Soc. for Pharmacology and Exptl. Therapeutics. Home: Houston, Tex. Died Feb. 10, 2005.

ALLEN, MELVIN LLOYD, psychophysiologist; b. Norman, Okla., Nov. 12, 1949; s. William Lloyd Allen and Mary Ellen Coker Barr; m. Janice Ann Karcher, Aug. 23, 1974 (div. Dec. 1983); m. Gayle Gray Berlioux, Oct. 20, 1989. BA, U. Okla., 1974, MS, 1977, PhD, 1980. Rsch. dir. Inst. for Primate Studies, Norman, 1980-81; project coord. Presbyn. Hosp., Oklahoma City, 1982-86, assoc. dir. G.I. lab., 1983-86, regular staff mem. medicine, from 1984; co-dir. G.I. Lab. HCA Presbyn. Hosp., Oklahoma City, 1986-87, dir. G.I. Lab., 1987-91; rsch. dir. G.I. Presbyn. Med. Ctr., Phila., 1992-96, dir. G.I. motility, 1992-96; adj. assoc. prof. U. Pa., Phila., 1993-96; assoc. prof. Thomas Jefferson U., Phila., from 1996. Reviewer Am. Jour. Primatology, 1981-84, Digestive Diseases and Scis., 1989—, Gastroenterology, 1995—; contbr. articles to profl. jours. With U.S. Army, 1970-71. Fellow Am. Coll. Gastroenterology; mem. AAAS, Am. Motility Soc., Am. Gastroenterol. Assn., Am. Gasteroenterol. Assn. Found. (charter), N.Y. Acad. Scis. Republican. Methodist. Avocations: boating, fishing, billiards, gardening, carpentry. Home: Kansas City, Kans. Died Aug. 6, 2005.

ALLEN, RONALD DUANE, psychotherapist; b. Wardell, Mo., Aug. 10, 1946; s. Ivan W. and Ruth M. (Thompson) A.; m. Donna K. Casey, Aug. 19, 1967; children: Christy, Ron B., Jennifer, Janell. BA, Tenn. Temple U., Chattanooga, 1972; MDiv, Southwestern Sem., Ft. Worth, 1975; MA, Liberty U., Lynchburg, Va., 1989; EdD, U. Sarasota, 1992. Ordained to ministry Bapt. Ch., 1966; lic. profl. counselor. Sr. pastor So. Bapt. Chs., Mo., Tenn. and Tex., 1966-89; therapist, team leader Crittenton Hosp., Kansas City, Mo., 1990-92; case mgr., therapist Prairie Rose Mental Health Ctr., Harlan, Iowa, 1992-93; therapist Royal Oaks Hosp. and Clinic, Windsor, Mo., from 1993. Seminar leader So. Bapt. Conv., Nashville, 1980-85; cons. Mo. Bapt. Conv., Jefferson City, 1980-85. Author: Counseling Those Making Decisions, 1982. Mem. Am. Counseling Assn., Am. Mental Health Counselors Assn., Am. Assn. Marriage and Family Therapists, Nat. Bd. Cert. Counselors. Democrat. Avocations: golf, reading, photography. Home: Lynchburg, Va. Died June 17, 2005.

ALLEN, WILLIAM CECIL, physician, educator; b. LaBelle, Mo., Sept. 8, 1919; s. William H. and Viola O. (Holt) A.; m. Madge Marie Gehardt, Dec. 25, 1943; children: William Walter, Linda Diane Allen Deardeuff, Robert Lee, Leah Denise Rogers. AB, U. Nebr., 1947, MD, 1951; M.P.H., Johns Hopkins U., 1960. Diplomate Am. Bd. Preventive Medicine. Intern Bishop Clarkson Meml. Hosp., Omaha, 1952; practice medicine specializing in family practice Glasgow, Mo., 1952-59; specializing in preventive medicine Columbia, Mo., from 1960; dir. sect. chronic diseases Mo. Div. Health, Jefferson City, 1960-65; asst. med. dir. U. Mo. Med. Ctr., 1965-75; assoc. coordinator Mo. Regional Med. Program, 1968-73, coordinator health programs, from 1969, clin. asst. prof. community health and med. practice, 1962-65, asst. prof. community health and med. practice, 1965-69, assoc. prof., 1969-75, prof., 1975-76, prof. dept. family and community medicine, 1976-87, prof. emeritus, 1987—2005. Cons. Mo. Regional Med. Program, 1966-67, Norfolk Area Med. Sch. Authority, Va., 1965-66; governing body Area II Health Systems Agy., 1977-79, mem. coordinating com., 1977-79; founding dir. Mid-Mo. PSRO Corp., 1974-79, dir., 1976-84. Contbr. articles to profl. jours. Mem. Gov.'s Adv Coun. for Comprehensive Health Planning, 1970-73; trustee U. Mo. Med. Sch. Found., 1976—2004. Served with USMC, 1943-46. Fellow Am. Coll. Preventive Medicine, Am. Acad. Family Physicians (sci. program com. 1972-75, commn. on edn. 1975-80), Royal Soc. Health; mem. Mo. Acad. Family Physicians (dir. 1956-59, 76-82, alt. del. 1982-87, pres. 1985-86, chmn. bd. 1986-87), Mo. Med. Assn., Howard County Med. Soc. (pres. 1958-59), Boone County Med. Soc. (pres. 1974-75), Am. Diabetes Assn. (pres. 1978, dir. 1974-77), Mo. Diabetes Assn. (pres. 1972-73), Soc. Tchrs. Family Medicine, AMA, Mo. Public Health Assn., Am. Heart Assn. (program com. 1979-82), Am. Heart Assn. of Mo. (sec. 1980-81), Mo. Heart Assn. (sec. 1979-82, pres.-elect 1982-84, pres. 1984-86). Methodist. Home: Columbia, Mo. Died Dec. 28, 2005.

ALLNER, WALTER HEINZ, graphics designer, painter, art director; b. Dessau, Germany, Jan. 2, 1909; arrived in U.S., 1949, naturalized, 1957; m. Colette Vasselon, Mar. 8, 1938 (div. June 1951); 1 child, Michel; m. Jane Booth Pope, Apr. 4, 1954; 1 child, Peter. Student, Bauhaus-Dessau, 1927-30. Designer Gesellschafts-und Wirtschafts-Museum, Vienna, Austria, 1929; asst. to typographer Piet Zwart, Wassenaar, Holland, 1930; editorial, painting, and advt. designer Paris, 1932-49; ptnr. Omnium Graphique, Paris, 1933-36; art dir. Formes, Editions d'Art Graphique et Photographique, Paris, 1933-36; Paris editor Swiss art mag. Graphis, 1945-48; founder, editor Internat. Poster Ann., 1948-52; co-dir. Editions Paralleles, Paris, 1948-51; mem. staff Fortune mag., N.Y.C., 1951-74, art dir., 1962-74; mem. faculty Parsons Sch. Design, N.Y.C., 1974-86. Vis. critic, mem. Comite de Parrainage Ecole Superieure d'Arts Graphiques, Paris, 1979—2006; freelance designer, design cons.; lectr., Australia, 1983. Posters for traffic safety campaign, Outdoor Advt. Assn. Am., 1959—60, exhibitions include Salon des Surindependants, Paris, Salon des Réalités Nouvelles, Germany, Austria, U.S., Eng., France, The Netherlands, Switzerland, Latin Am., Japan, others; compiler, editor: A.M. Cassandre, Peintre d'Affiches, 1948; editor: Posters, 1952; corr.: Signes mag., 1990—92; contbg. editor: Design Jour., 1990—92; contbr. articles to profl. jours. Named Laureate 4th Block, Kharkov, Ukraine, 1997; recipient medal Bauhaus-Dessau, German Acad. Architecture, 1979, Bruno Biennale Hon. Membership, Henri award, Alliance Graphique Internat., 1998. Mem.: Alliance Graphique Internationale (internat. pres.), Assn. Italiana Creativi Comunicazione Visiva (hon.). Home: New York, NY. Died July 21, 2006.

ALLWINE, BETTY MAE, critical care nurse, educator; b. Centralia, Wash., May 19, 1926; d. Eugene Irving and Margaret Leah (Simmons) Alvord; m. Kenneth Jerome Allwine, Oct. 21, 1945; children: Marsha, Kenneth Jr., Greg, Suzanne, Eugene, Darel, Joanne, Brenda, Darin. ADN, Lewis Clark State Coll., Lewiston, Idaho, 1982; BSN, Lewis Clark State Coll., 1984; MN, Wash. State U., Pullman, 1992. RN, Wash., Idaho; CCRN. Cardiac rehab. coord. Tri-State Meml. Hosp., Clarkston, Wash., charge nurs ICU; instr. Walla Walla C.C., Clarkston, Wash. Sec. Asotin County Mental Health Bd. Named Outstanding Grad. Student Coll. Profl. Studies, Lewis Clark State Coll., 1984, Outstanding Grad. Student BSN Program, 1984. Mem. AACN. Home: Richland, Wash. Died Mar. 17, 2004.

AL-MAKTUM, SHEIKH MAKTUM BIN RASHID, United Arab Emirian government official, ruler of Dubai; b. 1943; s. Sheikh Rashid bin Said al-Maktoum; married, 1971. Dep. ruler, Dubai, United Arab Emirates; prime min. Govt. of United Arab Emirates, Abu Dhabi, 1971—79, 1991—2006, dep. prime min., 1979-90; v.p. Govt. United Arab Emirates; ruler of Dubai, 1990—2006. Died Jan. 4, 2006.

ALQUIST, ALFRED ERNEST, retired state senator; b. Memphis, Aug. 2, 1908; m. Mai (dec. 1989), 1934; m. Elaine White, 1993; 1 child, Alan. Educated Southwestern U. Former mem. Calif. State Assembly; mem. Calif. State Senate, 1966—96, chmn. fin. com., mem. govt. orgn. and energy and pub. utilities coms. Candidate for lt. gov. State of Calif., 1970; mem. Little Hoover Commn.; mem. Calif. Seismic Safety Commn., Com. Sci. and Tech.; trustee Good Samaritan Hosp. Served with Air-Sea Emergency Rescue Service, USAAF, 1942-44. Mem. Nat. Conf. State Legislators, Am. Legion. Democrat. Clubs: Commonwealth, Elks. Home: San Jose, Calif. Died Mar. 27, 2006.

ALQUIST, LEWIS RUSSELL, art educator; b. Glen Cove, N.Y., Sept. 27, 1946; s. Russell Edward and Marie (Lewis) A. AS, Broward Community Coll., 1966; BFA, Fla. Atlantic U., 1968; MFA, Cranbrook Acad. Art, 1972. Asst. prof. Edinboro (Pa.) State U., 1973-80; vis. artist Sch. of Art Inst. of Chgo., 1980-84; assoc. prof. Ariz. State U., Tempe, from 1984. Artist-in-residence The Exploratorium, San Francisco, 1985-86; cons. Phoenix Arts Commn., 1990, Ariz. Commn. on the Arts, Phoenix, 1988. One-man shows include Weber State U., Ogden, 1990, U. Tex., El Paso, 1989, Randolph State Gallery, Chgo., 1982; curator group exhibition Name Gallery, Chgo., 1982. Visual artist fellowship Ariz. Commn. Arts, 1988, Nat. Endowment for Arts, 1986, Ill. Arts Coun., 1985; artists material grant Contemporary Forum, Phoenix Art Mus., 1988. Avocations: industrial archeology, animated films. Home: Phoenix, Ariz. Died Feb. 24, 2005.

AL-SABAH, SHEIKH JABIR AL-AHMAD AL-JABIR AL-AHMED, Emir of Kuwait; b. Kuwait City, Kuwait, June 29, 1928; s. His Highness Sheikh Ahmad Al-Jabir Al-Sabah; married. Student, Al-Mubarakiyyah Sch. Chief of pub. safety in the al-ahmadi Oil Regions, 1949-59; head Dept. Fin. (then Ministry of Fin. and Economy) Govt. of Kuwait, 1959—62, dep. prime min., 1962—65, prime min., 1965-67; crown prince, 1966-77; Emir of Kuwait, 1978—2006. Chmn. Supreme Def. Council, Kuwait, Supreme Petroleum Coun.; chmn. 5th session Orgn. of Islamic Conf., 1987-; chmn. Supreme Com. for Master Plan and Major projects, Kuwait; delivered speech before the 43rd session of the US General Assembly, September 28, 1988. Chmn. bd. dirs. Kuwait Fund for Arab Econ. Devel.; chmn. Kuwait Found. for Sci. Advancement; chmn. Supreme Com. for Master Plan and Maj. Projects, Kuwait. Home: Amiry Diwan, Kuwait. Died Jan. 15, 2006.

ALSCHULER, JOHN HAAS, architect; b. Chgo., Sept. 19, 1918; s. Alfred Samuel and Rose (Haas) A.; m. Betty Marie Rogers, Sept. 14, 1942 (div. Apr. 1963); children: Jeannie Reed, John Jr., Liora; m. Madge Friedman, Apr. 30, 1965. BArch, MIT, 1943. Lic. architect, Ill, NCARB. Draftsman Perkins & Will, Chgo., 1947-48; ptnr. Friedman, Alschuler & Sincere, Chgo., 1948-62; pvt. practice Chgo., from 1963. Arbitrator Am. Arbitration Assn., Chgo., 1980—. Chmn. code drafting com. sch. safety Ill. Supt. Pub. Instrn., Springfield, 1963-70. Lt. USN, 1943-46. Mem. AIA. Died June 29, 2004.

ALSCHULER, SAM, retired lawyer; b. Aurora, Ill., June 16, 1913; s. Benjamin P. and Lillian (Reinheimer) A.; m. Winifred King, Feb. 8, 1939 (dec. Dec. 1998); children: Albert W., Therese Alschuler Hale. AB, U. Wis., 1933; JD, U. Chgo., 1935. Bar: Ill. 1935, U.S. Supreme Ct. 1953. Pvt. practice, Aurora, 1935; ptnr. Alschuler & Funkey, 1935-84, counsel, 1984-96; ret. Bd. dirs. Weslin Properties, Inc., 1982-93. Mem. Aurora Spl. Svc. Area Com., 1976; pres. bd. dirs. United Cmty. Svc., Aurora, 1959-68; chmn. United Fund Gen. Campaign, 1966; mem. Citizens Cmty. Survey Com., 1964; vice chmn., dir. Kane County Coun. for Equal Opportunity, 1966-69; corp. counsel City of Aurora, 1961-65; pres., trustee Ill. Assn. for the Crippled, 1948-63, pres., 1963; governing mem. Copley Meml. Hosp., dir. Rush-Copley Meml. Hosp., 1942-2004; past pres., hon. bd. dirs. Rehab. Ctr. for So. Kane, Kendall and DeKalb Counties. With AUS, 1944-45. Recipient Copley Caring award Copley Healthcare Found., 1991. Mem. ABA, Ill. Bar Assn., Kane County Bar Assn. (Community Svc. award 1993), Am. Judicature Soc., Greater Aurora C. of C. (pres. 1953-55, dir.), Elks, Moose, Rotary, Sigma Delta Chi, Zeta Beta Tau. Democrat. Home: Aurora, Ill. Died June 25, 2006.

ALTMAN, ARNOLD DAVID, manufacturing executive; b. South Bend, Ind., Dec. 10, 1917; s. David and Goldie (Mooren) A.; children: Daniel Blair, Jonathan Estes. BSEE, U. Notre Dame, 1941. With Newman and Altman, Inc., South Bend, 1946-64; pres. Avanti Motor Corp., South Bend, 1976-82, Nat. Inventory Res., Inc., South Bend, 1980—2006; pres., CEO Rosenstein & Co., South Bend, 1985—2006. Lt. USN, 1942-46. Democrat. Jewish. Home: South Bend, Ind. Died Jan. 7, 2006.

ALVAREZ, LOUIS BASILIO, Spanish language educator; b. Holguin, Oriente, Cuba, June 14, 1927; came to U.S., 1947; s. Luis Apolonio and Amparo (Alfonso) A.; married; 1 child, Maria Cecilia. AA, San Antonio Coll., 1969; BA, Trinity U., San Antonio, 1971; MA, Middlebury (Vt.) Coll., 1973. Enlisted man USAF, 1950, advanced through grades to staff sgt., 1952; assigned to Okinawa, Korea, Ecuador, Panama; ret., 1965; prof. Spanish, Alamo C.C., San Antonio, 1974-88, Miami (Fla.)-Dade C.C., 1991-93; tchr. adult edn. English, Dade County Pub. Schs., Miami, from 1989. Mem. AAUP, Am. Assn. Tchrs. Spanish and Portuguese, Sigma Delta Mu. Republican. Roman Catholic. Avocations: baseball, basketball, wrestling, movies, theater. Home: Miami, Fla. Died Mar. 9, 2004.

ALY, RALPH WILBUR, funeral director; b. Glendale, Ill., Apr. 20, 1926; s. Frank and Floe (Thornton) A.; married, June 22, 1946; children: Charles, Douglas, Jeffrey, Marla. Grad., St. Louis Co. Morturay Sci., 1947. Prin. Aly Funeral Homes, Eddyville, Ill., from 1948, Vienna and Golconda, Ill. Mem. Pope County Bd. Edn., Golconda, ill., 1955-61; chmn. Mill Stone Water Dist., Eddyville, Ill., 1967—; vice-chmn. Lusk Conservance Dist., Golconda, 1968—, Pope County Housing Authority, 1972—; mayor Village of Eddyville, 1968—. With AUS, 1944-46, ETO. Paul Harris fellow, 1987. Mem. Nat. Funeral Dirs. Assn., Ill. Funeral Dirs. Assn., Quad County Funeral Dirs. Assn., Rotary (past pres.), Masons (past sec., present treas.). Democrat. Methodist. Home: Eddyville, Ill. Died Jan. 6, 2004.

AL-ZARQAWI, ABU MUSAB (AHMED FADEL NAZAL AL-KHALAYLEH), international terrorist; b. Zarqa, Jordan, Oct. 30, 1966; s. Fadeel Nazal al-Khalayleh and Um Sayel; m. Jordanian wife; 4 children; m. Palestinian wife, 2001; 1 child. Reached Afghanistan after the Soviets withdrew and became a journalist for a jihadist magazine, Al Bonian al Marsous (The Strong Wall), 1989—92; joined militant Islamic group, Bayaat al Imam, 1992; arrested and jailed in Jordan for having explosives, assault rifles and for plotting against the Monarchy: released on amnesty, 1993—99; moved to Hayatabad in northwestern Pakistan, near the Afghanistan border, 1999; tried in absentia and indicted (with others) for a plot to bomb the Radisson SAS Hotel Amman, Jordan, 1999; returned to Afghanistan where he set up his own training camp, connected to Al Qaeda, in the Western city of Herat, 2000—01; accused of murdering, Laurence Foley, a US diplomat in Amman Jordan, 2002; accused of multiple bombings, beheadings and other murders against civilians in Iraq, 2003—06; widely believed to be the man who beheaded American businessman Nicholas Berg and contractor Eugene Armstrong, 2004. Named one of most influential people, TIME mag., 2005. Died June 7, 2006; killed in an American bombing raid in Diyala Province, Iraq.

AL-ZUBAYDI, MOHAMMED HAMZA, former Prime Minister of Iraq; b. al Imam, Babylon, Iraq, 1938; Mem. Eighth Regional Congress, 1974; alt. mem. Regional Command, 1977; gov. Tamin Governorate, 1977; mem. Eleventh Nat. Congress, Baghdad, 1977; sec. So. Org. Bur., 1979, Ctrl. Region Orgn., 1981; mem. Ninth Regional Congress, 1982-86; adviser to Pres. Saddam Hussein Govt. of Iraq, Baghdad, 1982-86, minister transportation and comm., 1987-92; pres. Coun. of Ministers Govt. of Iraq, Baghdad, 1992; prime min. Govt. of Iraq, Baghdad, 1991—93, dep. prime min., 1994—2001; commander, Central Euphrates Region, 1998—2000. Joined Arab Baath Socialist Party, 1954; elected mem. Ramadi Group, 1962, sec. Ramadi sect. 1964, sec. Arab Baath Socialist Party Ctrl. Euphrates Br., 1964-68; mem. Ninth Nat. Congress, Lebanon, 1968, Counsellor Revolutionary Command Coun., 1966, Mem. External Contacts Bur., dir. gen. Secretariat of the Regional Command, dep. sec. So. Orgn. Bur., dir. gen. RCC Arab Affairs Bur., mem. Baghdad Br. Command, 1974, dep. sec. Ninevah Br. Command. Died Dec. 2, 2005.

AMBROSE, SAMUEL SHERIDAN, JR., retired urologist educator; b. Jacksonville, N.C., Oct. 2, 1923; s. Samuel Sheridan and Beatrice (Collins) A.; m. Betty Stuart Stansbury, Oct. 7, 1950; children: Charles Stuart, Ann Collins, Samuel Bruce. AB in Chemistry, Duke U., 1943, MD, 1947. Diplomate: Am. Bd. Urology, Nat. Bd. Med. Examiners. Intern surgery, then asst. resident urology Duke U. Hosp., 1947—50, resident urology, 1953; instr. physiology Duke U. Med. Sch., 1947, instr. urology, 1953; mem. faculty Emory U. Med. Sch., Atlanta, from 1954, prof. urology, 1972—92, prof. urology surgery emeritus, from 1992, chmn. divsn. urology, 1985—89; mem. staff Emory U. Hosp., 1972—92, chief urology, 1972—91; pvt. practice medicine specializing in urology Atlanta, 1954—71; mem. staff Piedmont Hosp., 1954—72, chief urology, 1960; mem. staff Grady Meml. Hosp., 1954—82, Henrietta Egleston Hosp. for Children, 1956—92; retired, 1992. Contbr. numerous articles to med. jours. Served as officer M.C. USNR, 1950-52. Fellow Royal Soc. Medicine; mem. AMA, ACS, Am. Urol. Assn. (hon. S.E. chpt., pres. S.E. sect. 1974-75, chmn. nat. sci. exhibits com. 1974-83, exec. com. 1983-90, Disting. Svc. award 1990, Gold Cane award 1995, hon. 1996—), Soc. Pediatric Urology (pres. 1971-72), Am. Assn. Clin. Urologists, Am. Acad. Pediat., Am. Assn. Genito-Urinary Surgeons, Soc. Internat. D'Urologie, Pan-Pacific Surg. Assn., Med. Assn. Ga., Ga. Urol. Assn. (pres. 1967), So. Med. Soc. (chmn. urology sect. 1970-71), Fulton County Med. Soc., Atlanta Clin. Soc. (v.p. 1964), Soc. Univ. Urologists, Piedmont Driving Club, Cherokee Town and Country Club (pres. 1968-69), Univ. Yacht Club (commodore 1973), Homosassa Fishing Club (v.p. 1980-81, 92-94). Presbyterian. Home: Atlanta, Ga. Died Aug. 2006.

AMBROSIO, THOMAS JAMES, retired pharmacist, researcher; b. Bklyn., Apr. 20, 1932; s. Pasquale and Fortunata Fetura (Annunziata) A.; m. Antonina Marie Bilello, June 26, 1954; children: Patrick James, Donna Marie. BS in Pharmacy, L.I. U., 1954; MS in Pharm. Sci., Rutgers U., 1966, PhD in Pharm. Sci., 1970. Pharmacist Katz Drug Store, Bklyn., 1954-57; research pharmacist Ortho Research Found., Raritan, N.J., 1957-70, Schering Pharm. Research Co., Kenilworth, N.J., from 1970. Chmn. steering com. packaging sci. and engring. program Rutgers U., New Brunswick, N.J., also moderator ann pharm. packaging conf.; co-adj. prof. Arnold and Marie Coll. Pharmacy, Bklyn., Rutgers U. Grad. Sch. Pharmacy; lectr. in field. Patentee in field. Mem. Somerset County (N.J.) Rep. Com. Served with U.S. Army, 1955-57. Schering research fellow, 1970-71. Mem. ASTM, Tech. Assn. Paper and Pulp, U.S. Pharmacopoeia. Clubs: Somerset Valley Players (Somerville, N.J.) (v.p. 1972-76). Roman Catholic. Avocation: amateur theatre. Home: Somerville, NJ. Died Oct. 31, 2004.

AMER, KENNETH BENJAMIN, helicopter engineer; b. Bklyn., Mar. 23, 1924; s. Harry and Rose (Wolkow) Am; m. Hedie Ankle, Dec. 25, 1946; children: Harold, Les. B Aero. Engring., NYU, 1944; MS in Aero. Engring., MIT, 1947. Rsch. engr. NACA, Langley Field, Va., 1947-53, Hughes Helicopters, L.A., 1953-60, mgr. tech. dept., 1960-85; chief scientist McDonnell Douglas Helicopter Co., L.A., 1985-86; helicopter cons. Rand Corp, Santa Monica, Calif., from 1987. Contbr. articles on helicopters to profl. jours.; patentee helicopter field. McDonnell Douglas Corp. engring. and rsch. fellow, 1986. Fellow Am. Helicopter Soc. (hon., Alexander Klemin award 1976). Home: Los Angeles, Calif. Died June 3, 2004.

AMERO, ROBERT CLAYTON, chemical engineer; b. Rochester, N.Y., Oct. 25, 1917; s. Philip James and Luise (Baumann) A.; m. Grace Kunselman, Nov. 7, 1942; children: Robert Stephen, Sally Ann. BSChemE with distinction, U. Rochester, 1939. Registered profl. engr., Pa. Rsch. engr. Floridin Co., Warren, Pa., 1939-45, asst. tech. dir., 1945-46, v.p., tech. dir., 1946-48; sr. rsch. engr. Johns-Manville Rsch. Ctr., Finderne, N.J., 1948-51; staff asst. Gulf Rsch. and Devel. Co., Harmarville, Pa., 1951-58, acting sect. head fuels, 1958-60, sr. project engr. mktg. tech. div., 1960-65, staff engr. mktg. tech. div., 1965-82; cons. in fuels Glenshaw, Pa., from 1982. Cons. Biennial Fuels and Lubes Conf., Am., British, Canadian, Australian Navies, London, Ottawa, Sydney, Washington, 1967-81. Patentee desulfurizing absorbent, axial intake and exhaust turbine, apparatus for skimming oil from water; contbr. articles to profl. jours. Mem. ASME (chmn. fuels div. 1974-75), Am. Inst. Chem. Engrs., Am. Soc. Energy Engrs. (cert. cogeneration specialist). Republican. Presbyterian. Died Mar. 21, 2004.

AMES, NORMA HARRIET, wildlife consultant, writer; b. Buffalo, Aug. 17, 1920; d. Robert Martin and Flora Mary (Wiener) Knipple; m. Donald Fairbanks Ames, July 8, 1944 (div. 1956); 1 child, Karyn Roberta; m. Richard Allen Rasmussen, Dec. 20, 1991. BA, Smith Coll., 1942; postgrad., Wellesley Coll., 1942, U. Colo., 1964. Asst. chief game mgmt. N.Mex. Dept Game and Fish, Santa Fe, 1956-76, asst. chief pub. affairs, 1976-82; leader Mex. wolf recovery team U.S. Fish and Wildlife Service, 1979-91; wildlife cons. Santa Fe, 1982-87, Colville, Wash., from 1988. N.Mex. rep. Western Regional Environ. Edn. Coun., 1971-74; wolf breeder and researcher Rancho Ma'ii-tsoh, Santa Fe, 1971-87. Author: My Path Belated, 1970, Whisper in the Forest, 1971, (book revs.) Science Books and Films, 1970—; author/illustrator booklets, 1960-82; author/editor: New Mexico Wildlife Management, 1967 (conservation edn. award 1968) Named Conservationist of Yr., Sta. KOB TV and Radio, Albuquerque, 1980; recipient Leopold Conservation award The Nature Conservancy, 1983. Mem. AAAS, The Nature Conservancy, Soc. for Conservation Biology, Defenders of Wildlife, Can. Nature Fedn., Nat. Wildlife Fedn., Am. Livestock Breeds Conservancy, Inland Empire Pub. Lands Coun., N.W. Rivers Coun., AK Wildlife Alliance, The Wildlife Soc. (cert.), Am. Soc. Mammologists, Sierra Club (lectr.), Nat. Audubon Soc. (lectr.), Phi Beta Kappa, Sigma Xi. Avocations: wildlife habitat restoration, minor breed conservation. Died Feb. 4, 2005.

AMLUND, CURTIS ARTHUR, law educator; b. Fargo, N.D., Nov. 29, 1927; s. Arthur Nils Amlund and Corinne Agnes Strand. BA, U. Minn., 1952, PhD, 1959. Instr. U. Minn., Mpls., 1959, U. Oreg., Eugene, 1959-60; vis. lectr. U. Wis., Milw., 1961; from asst. prof. to assoc. prof. N.D. State U., Fargo, 1961-71, prof., 1971—2005. Tchg. asst. U. Minn., Mpls., 1958-59. Contbr. articles to profl. jours. including Oxford, Cambridge Rev., Dalhousie Law Jour. Chair adminstr. screening com. Fargo City Govt., 1986-87. Recipient Outstanding Tchg. in Polit. Sci. award Am. Polilt. Sci. Assn./Nat. Polit. Sci. Honor Soc., 2000—, Disting. Educator award Nat. Blue Key; named Extraordinary Friend of the Ct. award U.S. Dist. Ct. N.D., 2000, Liberty Bell award N.D. Bar Assn., 2001. Mem. AAUP, Phi Beta Kappa. Home: Valley City, ND. Died Oct. 30, 2005.

AMMERAAL, ROBERT NEAL, biochemist; b. Grand Rapids, Mich., Oct. 11, 1936; s. Cornelius and Janet (Kolenbrander) A.; m. Brenda Ferne Bysterveld, June 14, 1966; children: Audrey Jeanne Campbell, Bret Alan, Julia Marie Adamski. BA, Calvin Coll., 1958; PhD, Wayne State U., 1963. Rsch. assoc. U. Chgo., 1962-65; asst. prof. biochemistry U. Ill., Chgo., 1965-67; asst. prof. Trinity Christian Coll., Palos Heights, Ill., 1967-69; rsch. project leader Am. Maize-Products Co., Hammond, Ind., 1969-96. Inventor in field; contbr. articles to profl. jours. and books. Lay preacher Orland Park (Ill.) Christian Reformed Ch.; lay pastor Calvary Reformed Ch., Orland Park, 1990-97. Fellow USPHS, 1963-65; cited for one of Top Ten Med. Discoveries by Time mag., 1966. Republican. Mem. Reformed Ch. Am. Avocations: molecular modeling, producing computer animation and graphics for video, electronic construction. Home: Worth, Ill. Died Feb. 17, 2005.

AMMERMAN, CHARLES R., stockbroker; b. Detroit, Mar. 4, 1942; BS in Bus., Ctrl. Mich. U., 1964, MBA, 1967. Registered investment advisor. Corp. account and mktg. analyst Celanese Corp., Detroit, 1967-75; equity rep., v.p. Merrill Lynch, Louisville, 1979-90; stockbroker PaineWebber Inc., Birmingham, Mich., from 1990. Instr. U. Louisville, 1968-72; bd. dirs. Devaney Svc. Corp., Birmingham. Mem. Cleveland Soc. Fin. Analysts (Mich., bd. dirs. 1985—). Home: Bloomfield Hills, Mich. Died Feb. 11, 2004.

AMOR, SIMEON, JR., photographer; b. Lahaina, Hawaii, Apr. 24, 1924; s. Simeon and Victoria Amor. Grad. high sch., Hilo, Hawaii. Post commdr. Engrs. Post #22, Am. Legion, Honolulu, 1952-53; approp. acct. Hawaii Air Nat. Guard, Honolulu, 1953-64; prodn. control supr. Svc. Bur. Corp., Honolulu, 1964-73; prodn. control computer ops. Bank of Hawaii, Honolulu, 1973-86; owner, propreitor Image Engring., Honolulu, from 1986. Historian VFW Dept. Hawaii, Honolulu, 1987-90, 96-97, First Filipino Infantry Regiment Hawaii Connection; treas. DAV Dept. Hawaii, Honolulu. Tech. advisor: (film documentary) Untold Triumph, Saga of the American Filipino Soldier. Cpl. U.S. Infantry, 1943-46, master sgt. USNG, 1952-64. Recipient Disting. Svc. award Nat. Disabled Am. Vet., 1992-94, Oahu chpt. Disabled Am. Vet., 1992-94. Mem. Am. Photographer's Internat., VFW. Home: Honolulu, Hawaii. Died Mar. 29, 2005.

AMSTER, GERALD STANLEY, electrical engineer; b. N.Y.C., Dec. 27, 1931; s. Isidore and Bella (Harber) A.; m. Edith Amster, Jan. 17, 1972. BSEE, MIT, 1954, MSEE, 1957. Registered profl. engr., N.Y. Elec. engr. Airborne Instruments Lab., Inc., Deer Park, N.y., 1958-69; tech. staff cons. Computer Applications Inc., N.Y.C., 1969-70; sys. analyst Comten Inc., N.Y.C., 1970-71; elec. engr. N.Y.C. Transit Authority, 1971-80; freelance cons. N.Y.C., from 1980. Bd. dirs. Southbridge Towers, Inc., N.Y.C., 1977-82. Achievements include patent in field; developed apparatus for selectively transmitting television images from a plurality of cameras to a monitor; developed software for computer graphics; developed computer program to evaluate the parameters for deterministic models of traffic flow and TIC device handler. Died June 27, 2004.

ANARGYROS, NEDRA HARRISON, cytotechnologist; b. N.Y.C., Dec. 3, 1915; d. Leverette Roland and Florence Martha (Pickard) Harrison; m. Spero Drosos Anargyros, Oct. 21, 1940 (div. 1969). Student, Emerson Coll., 1936; cert. in cytology, U. Calif., San Francisco, 1957. Supr. cytology San Francisco Gen. Hosp., 1957-88; ret., 1988. Mem. DAR (past regent 1990-91, 1st vice regent La Puerta de Ora chpt. San Francisco), Am. Soc. Clin. Pathologists (affil.), Am. Soc. Cytotech. (affil., cert. cytologist), Women Flyers Am., Nat. Soc. Colonial Dames Am. in Calif., Huguenot Soc. Calif., Presidents Mercer U. Club (Macon, Ga.). Republican. Christian Scientist. Home: San Francisco, Calif. Died Sept. 20, 2004.

ANDERSON, ANTHONY LECLAIRE, lawyer; b. Davenport, Iowa, Sept. 15, 1938; s. Frederic Nielsen and Marie Louise (LeClaire) A.; m. Beulah M. Bassham, July 3, 1963; children: Timothy LeClaire, Mark LeClaire, Jonathan Frederic LeClaire. BS with final honors, Washington U., St. Louis, 1967; JD, St. Louis U., 1971. Bar: Mo. 1972, U.S. Dist. Ct. (we. dist.) Mo. 1972, U.S. Dist. Ct. (ea. dist.) Mo. 1972, U.S. Ct. Appeals (8th cir.) 1974, U.S. Ct. Appeals (7th cir.) 1992, U.S. Tax Ct. 1976, U.S. Supreme Ct. 1976. Dir. pub. affairs Key Comm., Inc., St. Louis, 1973-74, Anderson, Wollrab & Wilson, St. Louis, 1974-76, Anderson, Preuss, Mooney & Eickhorst, St. Louis, 1976-82, Anderson, Preuss & Bachman, St. Louis, 1982-87, Anderson & Preuss, St. Louis, from 1987. Dir. Shield Fire Ins. Co., St. Louis, 1976-83. Panel atty. Lawyers Reference Svc., St. Louis, 1972-92; mem. Nat. Rep. Congrl. Com., 1998. Served with U.S. Army, 1962-64. Recipient Law Enforcement Assistance cert. Bd. Police Commrs., 1967, Bi-Centennial Commn., Davenport, Iowa, 1976. Mem. ABA, ATLA, Am. Judicature Soc., Ill. Trial Lawyers Assn., Bar Assn. Met. st. Louis, Press (editor 1968-69), Phi Alpha Delta. Episcopalian. Home: Saint Louis, Mo. Died Feb. 26, 2004.

ANDERSON, DONALD MORGAN, entomologist, researcher; b. Washington, Dec. 27, 1930; s. John Kenneth and Alice Cornelia (Morgan) A. BA, Miami U., Oxford, Ohio, 1953; PhD, Cornell U.l, 1958. Grad. teaching asst. Cornell U., 1954-57; asst. prof. sci. SUNY-Buffalo, 1959-60, rsch. fellow, 1960; rsch. entomologist Dept. Agrl., Washington, 1960-90, rsch. collaborator, from 1990; rsch. assoc. Buffalo Mus. Sci., from 1972, Smithsonian Instn., from 1978. Contbr. articles to profl. jours., chpts to books. Sigma Xi grantee, 1959 Mem. Entomol. Soc. Washington (corr. sec. 1963-65, pres. 1985, hon. mem. 1999—), Entomol. Soc. Am., Coleoperists Soc., Am. Inst. Biol. Sci., St. Andrews Soc. Washington, Clan Anderson Soc. (editor 1979-84, treas. 1985-90, pres. 1990-92), Sigma Xi, Phi Kappa Phi. Died Dec. 27, 2005.

ANDERSON, JACK NORTHMAN, newspaper columnist; b. Long Beach, Calif., Oct. 19, 1922; s. Orlando N. and Agnes (Mortensen) A.; m. Olivia Farley, Aug. 10, 1949; children: Cheri, Lance F., Laurie, Tina, Kevin N., Randy N., Tanya, Rodney V., Bryan W. Student, U. Utah, 1940-41, Georgetown U., 1947-48, George Washington U., 1948. Reporter Salt Lake City Tribune, 1939-41; missionary in So. states for Mormon Ch., 1941-44; war corr. Deseret News, 1945; mem. staff Washington Merry-go-Round column, 1947—2004, co-writer, 1965—69, writer, 1969—2004; Washington editor Parade mag., 1954-68, bur. chief, from 1968. Host, panelist UPI Roundtable. Author: (with Ronald May) McCarthy the Man, the Senator, The Ism, 1952, (with Fred Blumenthal) The Kefauver Story, 1956, (with Drew Pearson) U.S.A. Second Class Power? 1958, Washington Expose, 1966, Case Against Congress, 1968, (with Carl Kalvelage) American Government-Like It Is, 1972, (with George Clifford) The Anderson Papers, 1973, (with James Boyd) Confessions of a Muckraker, 1979, (with Bill Pronzini) The Cambodia File, 1981, (with John Kidner) Alice in Blunderland, 1983, (with James Boyd) Fiasco, 1983, Stormin' Norman, 1991, The Japan Conspiracy, 1993. Sec., trustee Chinese Refugee Relief, from 1962. Served with U.S. Mcht. Marine, 1944-45; with AUS, 1946-47. Recipient Pulitzer Prize for Nat. Reporting, 1972 Mem. White House Corr. Assn. Clubs: National Press (Washington). Died Dec. 17, 2005.

ANDERSON, KEITH, retired lawyer, banker; b. Phoenix, June 21, 1917; s. Carl and Helen (Fairchild) A.; m. Grace R. VanDenburg, 1941 (div. 1957); m. Catherine Huber, 1960; children: Fletcher F., Warren, Nicholas H. AB, Dartmouth Coll., 1939; LLB, Harvard U., 1942. Bar: N.Y. 1942, Ariz. 1946, Colo. 1950. Ret. lawyer. Mem. Univ. Club Denver, Cactus Club. Democrat. Home: Englewood, Colo. Died Oct. 3, 2005.

ANDERSON, KENNETH ARTHUR, minister; b. Worcester, Mass., June 1, 1942; s. John Henry Arnold and Ruth Otellia (Johnson) A.; m. Barbara Michael Prolesky, Apr. 16, 1962 (div. Feb. 1979); children: Kathryn, Kenneth; m. Lisa Gay Goodkowsky, June 14, 1980. BA, Defiance Coll., 1964; MDiv, Pitts. Theol. Sem., 1986, postgrad., from 1991. Ordained to ministry Presbyn. Ch. (U.S.A.), 1986. Pastor Forest Grove Presbyn. Ch., Coraopolis, Pa., 1985-87; owner fin. svcs. bus. Anderson & Assocs., McKees Rocks, Pa., from 1995; dist. sales coord. AFLAC, from 1997. Chmn. Pitts. Presbyn. Div. on Serving, 1989-90; vice chair communication unit Mission Interpretation Stewardship, 1991; chair communication com. Pitts. Presbytery, 1991; pres. bd. dirs. Robinson Emergency Med. Svc., 1993—. Sec. Parkway West Rotary, Pitts., 1988, v.p., 1989, pres. 1990; del. Mayor's Task Force on Hunger, Pitts., 1987-89. Mem. Robinson Assn. Chs. (pres., moderator 1988—). Republican. Home: Monroeville, Pa. Died May 5, 2005.

ANDERSON, MARILYN JOAN, guidance director; b. Denver, Oct. 21, 1935; d. Richard Walter and Dorothy Lela (Clark) Whinnerah; m. Edwin Knowles Anderson, Feb. 12, 1961; children: Kevin Knowles, Cynthia Elizabeth Anderson Schouker. BA, U. Colo., 1958; MA, San Jose State U., 1968. Cert. pupil pers. svcs. grades K-14, Calif.; cert. secondary tchr. life time credential, Calif.; cert. counselor, Va. Tchr. grade 8 M.H. Stanley Intermediate, Lafayette, Calif., 1958-61; sch. psychologist Monroe County, Fla., 1968-69; adjustment counselor Rogers High Sch., Newport, R.I., 1969-70; psychol. examiner Windward Oahu Sch. Dist., Kaneohe, Hawaii, 1970-75; ednl. diagnostician Tri-Svcs. Ctr. for Learning Disabled Student, Chevy Chase, Md., 1978-79; tchr. grades 2 & 3 Shirley Lantham Elem. Sch., Atsugi, Japan, 1980-82; dir. rsch. Tri-Svcs. Ctr., Chevy Chase, 1983-84; counseling psychologist Family Svcs. Ctr./NATO Base, Keflavik, Iceland, 1985-86; guidance dir. George Mason Middle & High Sch., Falls Church, Va., from 1987. Mem. NEA, Va. Tchrs. Orgn., Nat. Assn. Coll. Admissions Counselors, Potomac and Cheseapeke Assn. Coll. Admissions Counselors, Am. Counselors Assn., Va. Counselors Assn., Falls Church Tchrs. Assn. Avocations: windsurfing, cooking, reading. Home: Summerland Key, Fla. Died Dec. 27, 2004.

ANDERSON, MARY R., historian, educator; b. Escanaba, Mich., Apr. 4, 1937; d. Renold Walfred and Alice (Fox) A. BA summa cum laude, Holy Names Coll., Oakland, Calif., 1959; PhD, U. Calif., 1979. Prof. history Holy Names Coll., Oakland, Calif. Author: Art in a Desacralized World, 1984. Grantee Nat. Endowment for the Humanities, 1984; recipient Sears-Roebuck Found. Teaching Excellence and Campus Leadership award, 1991. Mem. Am. Hist. Assn., Western Assn. of Women Historians, Inst. for Hist. Study. Democrat. Roman Catholic. Avocations: opera, symphony, poetry. Home: Alameda, Calif. Died May 9, 2005.

ANDERSON, SHARON LEE, critical care nurse; b. Glasgow, Mont., Jan. 28, 1941; d. W.A. and Mabel (Humphries) Nelson; children: Theresa, Dawn, Brenda, Barbara. AD, Northern Mont., 1984. Cert. advanced cardiac life support. Staff RN intensive/critical care unit Deaconess Mahon Hosp., Glasgow, Am. Lake Vets. Ctr., Tacoma. Died June 9, 2004.

ANDERSSON, STEN, former Swedish government official; b. Stockholm, Apr. 20, 1923; m. Britta A.; 5 children. Student, U. Stockholm. Tchr., courier Worker's Ednl. Assn., from 1944; sec. Internat. Youth Campaign, from 1944; mem. Stockholm City Coun., mem. city exec., fin. and real estate com., 1951-62; dist. rep. Stockholm br. Social Democratic Party, Sweden, from 1953, sec. Stockholm br., 1958-62, nat. party sec., 1963-82, chmn. Stockholm br., from 1975; mem. Swedish Parliament, from 1966; min. of health & social affairs Govt. of Sweden, 1982-85, min. fgn. affairs, 1985-91. Chmn. club br. Social Democratic Youth League, 1982-85, chmn. dist. internat. com., The Olof Palme Meml. Fund for Internat. Understanding and Common Security, Peace Forum of Swedish Labour Movement. Died Sept. 16, 2006.

ANDES, CHARLES LOVETT, marketing executive; b. Phila., Sept. 23, 1930; s. Charles Lovett and Gladys (Stead) A.; m. Dorothea Roberta Abbott, Aug. 25, 1961; children: Elizabeth, Susan, Karen, Page. Student, Swarthmore Coll., 1948-50; BA, Syracuse U., 1952. Pres. Adtech Industries, Phila., 1954-68; exec. v.p., dir. The Franklin Mint Corp., Franklin Ctr., Pa., 1969-73, pres. Pa., 1972-73, chmn. bd., CEO Pa., 1973-85; chmn., CEO The Franklin Inst., Phila., 1985-91, chmn., 1991-93, chmn. emeritus, 1993—2006; pres., CEO Eastern Tech. Coun., 1991-95; chmn., CEO Interactive Mktg. Ventures, 1995-96; CEO Andes, Wickard, McClure, 1997—2006; chmn. The Andover Group, Plymouth Meeting, Pa., 1998—2006. Ptnr. Tech. Leaders Venture Capital Fund; mem. Pa. Tech. Coun.; bd. dirs. Nat. Media Corp. Bd. dirs. Phila. Orch., Am. Music Theater Festival, Nat. Constn., Ctr., Penn Cancer Ctr., Pa. Acad. Fine Arts, Wistar Inst. Mem. Phila. Country Club, Union League, Merion Cricket Club, Johns Island (Fla.) Club. Presbyterian. Home: Haverford, Pa. Died Aug. 17, 2006.

ANDRE, PAUL REVERE, minister; b. Nesbit, Nebr., Oct. 25, 1935; s. George Martin and Iva Elsie (Cassens) A.; m. Anna Katherine Jones, June 7, 1953; children: Paul, Georgia, Iva, Katherine. AA, Cen. Coll., McPherson, Kans., 1957; BA, Greenville (Ill.) Coll., 1959; MDiv, Ashbury Sem., Wilmore, Ky., 1962. Ordained to ministry Free Meth. Ch., 1962. Pastor Free Meth. Ch., Amelia, Nebr., 1962-64, Kearney, Nebr., 1964-66, Colville, Wash., 1966-70, Bellevue, Nebr., 1970-85, MacArthur Free Meth. Ch., Oklahoma City, 1985-90, Cornwall Ave. Free Meth. Ch., Waterloo, Iowa, from 1990. Asst. supt. Nebr. Conf. Free Meth. Ch. N. Am., 1977-79, supt., 1979-83, gen conf. del., 1979, 85. Mem. mayor's commn. on preservation of historic sites City of Bellevue, 1984—. Recipient Outstanding Citizen of Omaha award, 1976. Mem. Nebr. Assn. Evang. (v.p. 1976), Met. Assn. Evangs. Omaha (pres. 1973-76), Greater Omaha Christian Edn. Assn. (pres. 1976-77), Bellevue Ministerial Assn. (v.p. 1971-73, pres. 1973-75, 84—, sec. 1982-83), Rotary (pres. Bellevue 1978-79, Paul Harris fellow, 1981). Died Feb. 10, 2005.

ANDREAS, CAROL, sociologist, educator; b. Newton, kans., Nov. 10, 1933; d. Willis Everett and Hulda Suzanne (Penner) Rich; m. Carl Andreas, May 1951 (div. Aug. 1971); children: Joel, Ronald, Peter. BA, Bethel Coll., 1953; MA, U. Minn., 1954; PhD, Wayne State U., 1967. Lectr. U. Mich., 1967-68; asst. prof. Oakland U., Mich., 1968-71; instr. Oakland C.C., Calif., 1971-72; hon. lectr. U. Colo., Denver, 1978-81; prof. sociology U. No. Colo., Greeley, 1988-94, prof. emeritus sociology, from 1994. Vis. prof. Colorado Coll., summer 1972, U. Nacional del Centro del Peru, 1974-75, U. Oreg., 1986; adj. assoc. prof. U. Colo., Colorado Springs, 1981-84; vis. assoc. prof. Ea. Washington U., 1985; Disting. prof. Simon Fraser U., Vancouver, B.C., Can., summer 1989. Author: Sex and Caste in America, 1971, Nothing Is As It Should Be, 1976, When Women Rebel, 1985, Meatpackers and Beef Barons, 1994. Activist Anti-War Movement, Vietnam and U.S., Women's Movements, U.S. and L.Am., Farmworkers' Unions, Labor and Civil Rights. Mem. Union of Radical Sociologists (founder, jour. The Insurgent Sociologist). Avocations: poetry, journalism, art, music, hiking. Home: Fort Collins, Colo. Died Dec. 8, 2004.

ANDREWS, MARK EDWARD, sportscaster, motivational speaker; b. Detroit, Aug. 9, 1952; s. Paul Edward and Shirley Edith (Guier) A.; m. Margaret May Rees, June 9, 1984 (div.); children: Edward Jay, Hollis Jane; m. Amy Brieden, Apr. 27, 1996. BA in Radio-TV, Wayne State U., 1976. Sportscaster Sta. WBRB, Detroit, 1976-78; sports dir. Sta. WOMC, Detroit, 1978-82; play-by-play announcer Detroit Pistons Basketball, 1981-85; sports dir. Sta. WQBH, Detroit, 1982-83, Sta. WKQI, Detroit, 1983-96; sports reporter Sta. WDIV-TV, Detroit, 1986-87; sports dir. Sta. WXON-TV, Detroit, 1987—88, 1992—2004; sports reporter Sta. WKBD-TV, Detroit, 1988-92, Sta. WOMC, Detroit, 1996—2004; TV play-by-play CCHA Hockey, 1998-99. Sportswriter Detroit Free Press, 1973-75; TV producer Mich. Stags Hockey Club, Detroit, 1974-75; Pub. Address Announcer Super Bowl XVI, 1982. Mem. AFTRA, Nat. Speakers Assn, Detroit Sports Broadcasters, Screen Actors Guild. Lutheran. Home: Grosse Pointe, Mich. Died Feb. 21, 2004.

ANDREWS, MASON COOKE, former mayor, obstetrician, gynecologist, educator; b. Norfolk, Va., Apr. 20, 1919; s. Charles James and Jean (Cooke) A.; m. Sabine Goodman, Sept. 24, 1949; children: Jean, Mason. BA, Princeton U., 1940; MD, Johns Hopkins U., 1943; LLD (hon.), Ea. Va. Med. Sch., 1987. Diplomate: Am. Bd. Ob-Gyn. Intern ob-gyn Johns Hopkins U., Balt., 1944, resident ob-gyn, 1946-50; pvt. practice ob-gyn Norfolk, Va., 1950-70; lectr. Johns Hopkins U. Sch. Medicine, Balt., 1971-72; prof. dept. ob-gyn. Eastern Va. Med. Sch., Norfolk, 1974—90, chmn. dept. ob-gyn., 1974-90. Bd. dirs. First Va. Bank of Tidewater, Chesapeake and Potomac Telephone Co.; mem., dir. Norfolk City Planning Commn., 1963-65, twice chmn., commr., exec. com. mem. Hampton Rds. Planning Dist. Commn., pres. (1971) Planning Coun. of United Communities, Norfolk City Coun., 1974-2000; chmn. Ea. Va. Med. Authority, 1964-70; pres. Am. Assn. Obstetricians Found., 1986-89. Contbr. (numerous articles to sci. jours.). Councilman City of Norfolk, 1974-2000, vice mayor, 1978-82, mayor, 1992-94. Recipient First Citizen citation Norfolk Cosmopolitan Club, 1968, Norfolk citation for outstanding svc., 1964, award for cmty. svc. Med. Soc. Va., AMA, Nat. Brotherhood award Norfolk Conf. Christians and Jews. Fellow Am. Gynecol. and Obstet. Soc. (v.p. 1982-83, pres. 1992-93); mem. South Atlantic Assn. (pres. 1972), Va. Obstet. and Gynecol. Soc. (pres. 1975), Norfolk Acad. Medicine (pres. 1961), Johns Hopkins Soc. Scholars, Harbor Club, Norfolk Yacht and Country Club. Presbyterian. Home: Norfolk, Va. Died Oct. 13, 2006.

ANDREWS, ROBERT ERVIN, JR., microbiology educator; b. Wenatchee, Wash., Jan. 19, 1952; s. Robert E. and Inace M. (McCord) A.; m. Debra J. Maland, Apr. 4, 1993; children: Robert E. III, David N. BS in Bacteriology and Pub. Health, Wash. State U., 1975, MS in Bacteriology and Pub. Health, 1978, PhD in Bacteriology, 1980. Postdoctoral rsch. assoc. Kans. State U., Manhattan, 1980-81; rsch. biologist, project coord. Stauffer Chem. Co., Richmond, Calif., 1981-83; asst. prof. microbiology Iowa State U., Ames, 1983-89, assoc. prof. microbiology, from 1989. Author 2 book chpts.; mem. editl. bd. Applied and Environ. Microbiology; contbr. 30 articles to profl. jours. Recipient Rsch. grant USDA, 1985, 89, 93, 96. Mem. Am. Soc. Microbiology (br. sec. 1978—). Democrat. Avocations: private pilot, wood working. Home: Ames, Iowa. Died July 26, 2005.

ANDRIE, EUGENE STEVEN, conductor, educator; b. Grand Rapids, Mich., Aug. 23, 1914; s. Stephen Frank and Lucy (Kieras) A.; m. Lorraine Evelyn Kloskey, 1937 (dec. 1985); 1 child, Karen. BS, Western Mich. U., 1941; postgrad., U. Mich., 1941; MA, U. Wash., 1951. Prof. music U. Mont., Missoula, 1946-76, prof. emeritus, 1976—2005. Vis. prof. Brigham Young U., Provo, Utah, 1948, U. B.C., Vancouver, Can., 1960; condr. Kalamazoo Jr. Symphony, 1938-41, Mont. All-State Orch., Missoula and Great Falls, 1950-70, Missoula Symphony Orch., 1952-76, Curry Del Norte Chamber Orch., Smith River, Calif., 1989-92; guest condr. Great Falls Symphony Orch., 1965; vol. Friends of Music, South Coast Fisherman STEP Program, 1985-2005; tchr. Suzuki Inst., Rocky Mt. Coll., Billings, Mont., 1989. Author: Violin Student's Source Book, 1980; contbr. to profl. publs. With USN, 1943-46. Recipient Gov.'s Award for Arts, Mont., 1981. Avocations: fishing, hunting, hiking. Home: Harbor, Oreg. Died Nov. 27, 2005.

ANDRYCHUK, DMETRO, retail executive; b. Manitoba, Can., Dec. 10, 1918; came to U.S., 1952; s. Nicholas and Paulene (Kiedyk) A.; m. Eloise Loela Jacksie, Mar. 15, 1944; children: Dennis, Marguerite, Cathy. BA hon., U. Manitoba, 1941, MA, 1942; PhD, U. Toronto, 1949. Physicist Nat. Rsch. Coun., Ottawa, Ontario, Can., 1949-52; spectroscopist Diamond Alkali, Painesville, Ohio, 1952-57; physicist Tex. Instruments, Dallas, 1957-84; owner D.A. Gemstones, Richardson, Tex., from 1962. Cons. Polatomie, Inc., Dallas, 1986—. Author gemstone design math. analysis; patentee gemstone design, 1976. Avocation: gem design. Home: Richardson, Tex. Died Nov. 10, 2004.

ANGELL, JAMES BROWNE, electrical engineering educator; b. S.I., N.Y., Dec. 25, 1924; s. Robert Corson and Jessie (Browne) A.; m. Elizabeth Isabelle Rice, July 22, 1950; children: Charles Lawrence, Carole Corson. S.B., S.M., MIT, 1946, Sc.D. in Elec. Engring, 1952. Research asst. MIT, 1946-51; mgr. solid-state circuit research, research div. Philco Corp., Phila., 1951-60; mem. faculty Stanford U., 1960-95, prof. elec. engring., 1962-89, prof. emeritus, 1990—2006, dir. Solid-State Electronics Lab., 1964-71, assoc. dept. chmn., 1970-89. Cons. to industry and govt., 1960-2006; Mem. electronics adv. group for comdg. gen. U.S. Army Electronics Command, 1964-74; mem. U.S. Army Sci. Adv. Panel, 1968-74; Carillonneur Stanford, 1960-91. Author sect. book. Area chmn. town incorporation com. Portola Valley, Calif., 1963-64; Bd. dirs. Portola Valley Assn., 1964-67. Fellow IEEE (life, chmn. internat. solid state circuits conf. 1964); mem. Am. Guild Organists, Guild Carillonneurs in N. Am. (dir. 1969-75, rec. sec. 1970-75). Died Feb. 13, 2006.

ANGELOV, GEORGE ANGEL, pediatrician, anatomist, teratologist; b. Bulgaria, May 12, 1925; came to U.S., 1978; s. Angel Christov and Maria Angelov; m. Olga Valerie Minkova, Dec. 21, 1952; 1 child, Angel. MD, Sch. of Medicine, Sofia, Bulgaria, 1952. Pediatrician Distric Hosp., Bulgaria, 1952-53; asst. prof. Sch. of Medicine, Sofia, Bulgaria, 1953-64; prof. anatomy and anthropology Sch. of Biology, Sofia, Bulgaria, 1964-77; mgr. reproductive toxicology Lederle Labs., Pearl River, N.Y., 1979-89; cons. reproductive toxicology pvt. practice, Laguna Niguel, Calif., from 1989. Assoc. dean Sch. of Biology, Sofia, 1970-72; vis. scientist Sch. of Medicine, Geneva, 1971, 74. Author: (textbook) Anatomy, 1970; mem. glossary com. Teratology Glossary, 1987-89; reviewer several sci. jours.; contbr. numerous sci. publs. on anatomy, teratology, and growth and devel. of adolescents to profl. jours. Mem. Teratology Soc. USA, European Teratology Soc., Human Biology Coun. USA, Free Union of Univ. Profs. of Anatomy. East Orthodox. Avocations: bridge, chess, history. Died Jan. 2, 2004.

ANGUIANO, RAUL, painter; b. Guadalajara, Jalisco, Mexico, Feb. 16, 1915; s. Jose Anguiano and Abigail V. de A.; 3 children from previous marriage; m. Brigita Anderson, 1977. Studies with Jose Vizcarra and Ixca Farias, Art Students League, N.Y.C., 1941. Founder, mem. Taller de Grafica Popular. Guest tchr., lectr. invited to exhibit works U. West Indies, Kingston, 1970. One-man shows include Mex., Paris, 1962, 65, 67, San Francisco, 1953-65, Havana, 1956, Chile, 1960, Moscow, 1962, Rome, 1965-67, Miami, 1965, San Antonio, 1966, Quito, 1971, Mexico City, 1972, Palm Springs, Calif., 1974; exhibited in group shows in London, Warsaw, Tokyo, Berlin, Prague, Peking, Lille, France, Los Angeles, Lugano, others; works include murals for Hormona Labs., Onyx-Mex. industries and Nat. Mus. Anthropology, Mexico City, mural at Olympia Hotel, Kingston, Jamaica; retrospective exhbn. Salon de la Plastica Mexicana, Mex., 1969. Decorated by Italian Govt., 1977; recipient numerous prizes in field. Died Jan. 13, 2006.

ANSELL, JOSEPH PAUL, director, art educator; b. Bethesda, Md., July 19, 1949; s. Leonard Raymond and Shirley Wolfson Ansell. BA, Knox Coll., 1971; MFA, George Washington U., 1975. From instr. to asst. prof. U. Md., College Park, 1979—91; prof. and chair dept. art Otterbein Coll., Westerville, Ohio, 1991—96; dean of faculty and instrnl. programs Sch. Mus. Fine Arts, Boston, 1996—99; prof. and head dept. art Auburn U., Ala., 2001—06, interim dir. Jule Collins Smith Mus. Fine Art, 2003—04, interim dean Coll. Liberal Arts, 2004—05. Exhbn. cons. U.S. Holocaust Meml. Mus., Washington, 2000—03. Author: Arthur Szyk: Artist, Jew Pole, 2004; contbr. articles to profl. jours. Art auction chair E. Ala. AIDS Outreach, Auburn, 2002, 2003. Mem.: Coll. Art Assn. (chair edn. com. 1992—96, chmn. diversity com. 2004—05). Home: Auburn, Ala. Died June 27, 2006.

ANUTA, MICHAEL JOSEPH, lawyer; b. Pound, Wis., Feb. 4, 1901; s. Michael Anuta and Charlotte Zudnochowsky; m. Marianne M. Strelec; children: Mary Hope Milidonis, Nancy Ellen Beauchamp, Janet Grace Dalquist, Michael John, Karl Frederick. LLB, LaSalle Extension U., 1956; LLD (hon.), Alma Coll., 1960; BS (hon.), San Vicinte De Paul, Maracaibo, Venezuela, 1965. Bar: Mich. 1929, U.S. Supreme Ct. 1932, U.S. Dist. Ct. Mich., U.S. Dist. Ct. Wis., Bar of Interstate Commerce Commn. Traffic mgr. M&M Traffic Assn., Menominee, Mich., 1938-48; pros. atty. Menominee County, Menominee, 1938-48; mcpl. judge City of Menominee, 1958-68; reserve judge Menominee, from 1929. Author: East Prussians from Russia, 1979, Ships of our Ancestors, 1983, History of Rotary Clubs in Wisconsin-Michigan, 1993, Anuta Heritage Register, 1993. Dir., v.p. Mich. Children's Aid Soc.; active Boy Scouts Am., 1945—; moderator Synod Presbyn. Ch. Mich., 1953; chmn. Menominee County Def. Council, WWII, 1953. Lt. col. CAP, Mich. Recipient Silver Beaver award Boy Scouts Am., 1945, Silver Antelope, 1967, Disting. Svc. award community svc. Radio Sta. WAGN, 1963, Disting. citation, Govt. Legislature of Mich., 1989; named Man Yr. Menominee Area C. of C., 1971. Mem. ABA, State Bar Mich., Menominee County Bar Assn., Mich. Prosecuting Attys. Assn. (pres. 1945), Menominee County Hist. Soc. (pres. 1967-74, pres. emeritus), Am. Hist. Socs. Germans from Russia (dir. 1978-81), Hist. Soc. Mich. (dir. 1972-78, award merit 1980, Charles Follow award 1983), Am. Arbitrators Assn., Panel Arbitrators Res. Mich. Judge, Rotary (gov. dist. 1963-64, pres. 1934-35), Shriners, Masons (33 degree). Republican. Avocations: pilot, amateur radio. Died Sept. 9, 2004.

ANZIANO, GALE MARY, guidance counselor, social worker; b. N.Y.C., Dec. 8, 1943; d. Louis and Frances Regina Sileve Rear; m. Samuel Ansiano, Oct. 8, 1978. MS in Edn., Hofstra U., 1969; MSW, Adelphi U., 1975, D of Social Work, 1985. Tchr. English Centrode Estudio, Valencia, Spain, 1965-66; tchr. U. Valencia, 1966; tchr. Spanish East Meadow (N.Y.) Schs., 1966-69; guodance counselor Freeport (N.Y.) Schs., 1969-73; cons. N.Y. State Dept. Social Svcs., N.Y.C., 1980; guidance counselor, social worker Glen Coves (N.Y.) Schs., from 1973. Chmn. Glen Cove Youth Bd., 1979-80, A.S. Pike, Nassau County, N.Y., 1993-97, Youth Commn., Garden City. Mem. NASW, ASPIRE, Kiwanis. Avocations: photography, writing, golf, screenwriting. Home: Garden City, NY. Died Nov. 3, 2004.

APFEL, JEROME B., lawyer; b. Phila., Nov. 6, 1929; s. Irwin and Lillian (Nadich) A.; m. Fanchon Marks, Feb. 26, 1955; children: Sarah, David, Matthew, Ira. BS, Temple U., 1951; JD, U. Pa., 1954, MS, 2000. Law clk. Common Pleas Ct. No. 1, Phila., 1954-55; asst. dist. atty. City of Phila., 1955-61; assoc. Bortin and Apfel, 1955-61; ptnr. Blank, Rome, Comisky & McCauley, Phila., of counsel. Lectr. Temple U. Sch. Law., 1985-92; drafter, promoter guardianship, probate, living will, legislation Pa. Gen. Assembly. Contbr. articles to profl. jours. Bd. mgrs. U. Pa. Law Sch., nat. alumni soc., v.p., 1989-93, pres. 1993-95, assoc. trustee, adv. bd. Annenberg Ctr.; founder, incorporator, bd. dirs. Green Tree Sch., formerly Sklar Sch., Phila., 1955-80, pres. 1965-70; founder, incorporator, trustee Parkway Sch., Phila., 1966-80, pres. 1970-76; founder, incorporator, bd. dirs. Buttonwood Farms, Inc., 1960-63; bd. dirs. League for Emotionally Disturbed Children, Southeastern Pa. chpt., 1955-58, pres. 1957-58; bd. dirs. Nat. Assn. Mentally Ill Children, Southeastern Pa. chpt., 1961-68; pres. Mental Health Assn. Southeastern Pa., 1973-75, v.p., 1967-72, bd. dirs., 1961-72, 73-80, bd. trustees, Mann Music Ctr.; mem. coms. childhood mental illness, public policy Pa. Mental Health, Inc., 1968; hon. mem. Pa. Regional Coun. Child Psychiatrists; mem. profl. adv. bd. Phila. Psychoanalytic Inst.; mem. regulations com. Commonwealth of Pa. Task Force on Mental Health of Children and Youth, 1972-74; pres. Wynnefield Residents Assn., 1965-67, dir. 1963-72, hon. pres., 1967-2006; bd. dirs. Concerto Soloists Chamber Orch. Phila., 1977-89; bd. dirs. Mann Music Ctr.; bd. dirs., advisor Phila. Boys Choir, 1972-87; organizer, sponsor Saturday Night Home Chamber Music Concerts; promotor, sponsor musicians and chamber music concerts Am./Israel Cultural Found.; organizer, sponsor chamber music concert series U Pa. Sch. Music, 1985-88; western divsn. chair Jewish Community Rels. Coun., 1963-65, hon. pres.; trustee Beth David Reform Congregation of Gladwyne, Pa., pres., 1971-72, chmn./mem. every com.; pres. Fedn. Reform Synagogues of Greater Phila. Area, 1969-71; trustee Union Am. Hebrew Congregations, 1969-79, mediator nat. commn. rabbinic-congregational rels., bioethics com.; bd. govs. Reconstructionist Rabbinical Coll., 1971-76. Mem. ABA (adv. bd. 1977-81, mental health advocacy project state hosps., coms. estates, disability law), Pa. Bar Assn.-Pa. Bar Inst. (lectr., chair legal svcs. mentally disabled com. 1986-87, chair legal svcs. older persons com. 1989-92, 94), Phila. Bar Assn. (past mem. exec. com. jr. bar assn., chair mental health com. 1979, 85, various coms., exec. com. probate and trust sect. 1972-75, various coms. probate and trust sect.), Am. Soc. Ancient Instruments (bd. dirs. 1969-79, adv.). Avocations: tennis, opera, chamber music, concerts, cello. Home: Gladwyne, Pa. Died Oct. 16, 2006.

APPEL, KAREL, artist, illustrator; b. Amsterdam, The Netherlands, Apr. 25, 1921; s. Jan and Johanna (Chevallier) A. Ed., Royal Acad. Art, Amsterdam. Numerous one-man shows, most recent being Palais des Beaux-Arts, Brussels, 1983, Gimpel Fits Gallery, London, 1983, St. Mary's Gallery, N.Y.C., 1984, Annina Nosri Gallery, N.Y.C., 1984, Gimpel & Weitzenhoffer Gallery, N.Y.C., 1984; exhibited in numerous group shows including Michael Campbell Fine Art, Scottsdale, Ariz., Jack Rutberg Fine Arts, L.A., Walter-Gilbert Galleries, San Francisco, Michall V. McDonnell, Santa Rosa, Calif., Goldman Kraft Gallery, Chgo., Short Hills (N.J.) Art Gallery, David Anderson Gallery, Buffalo, Am.-European Art Assocs. Inc., N.Y.C., Marisa del Re Gallery, N.Y.C., Stephen Gill Gallery, N.Y.C., Alexander Kahan Fine Arts, N.Y.C., Michelle Rosenfeld Fine Arts, N.Y.C., Argus Fine Arts, Eugene, Oreg.; traveling exhbns. include Palazzo diMedici, Florence, 1985, Japan, 1989, Europe, 1990-92; represented in permanent collections Tate Gallery, London, Mus. Modern Art, N.Y.C., Stedelijk Mus., Amsterdam, Mus. Fine Arts, Boston, also others. Recipient Guggenheim Nat. prize, Netherlands, 1951, UNESCO prize Venice Biennials, 1953, Lissone prize, Italy, 1958, Sal Paulo exhbn. acquisition prize, 1959, Graphique Internat. prize, Ljubljana, Yugoslavia, 1959, Guggenheim Internat. prize, 1961 Died May 3, 2006.

APPIAH, PEGGY, writer; b. England, May 21, 1921; d. Stafford and Isobel (Swithenbank) Cripps; m. Joe E. Appiah, July 18, 1954; children: Anthony, Isobel, Adwoa, Abena. Attended, Whitehall Secretarial Coll. Rsch. asst. British Ministry of Info., London; sec. Racial Unity, London; youth rep. British Coun. Chs., London; chmn. adv. com. Kumasi Children's Home, Ashanti, Ghana, 1968—. Author: Ananse the Spider, 1966, Tales of an Ashanti Father, 1967, The Pineapple Child and Other Tales from Ashanti, 1969, Children of Ananse, 1969, A Smell of Onions, 1971, Why Are There So Many Roads?, 1972, Gift of the Mmoatia, 1973, A Dirge Too Soon, 1976, Ring of Gold, 1976, Why the Hyena Does Not Care for Fish, 1977, Poems of Three Generations, 1978. Home: Kumasi, Ghana. Died Feb. 11, 2006.

APPLE, R.W., JR., (RAYMOND WALTER APPLE, JR.), journalist; b. Akron, Ohio, Nov. 20, 1934; s. Raymond Walter and Julia (Albrecht) A.; m. Betsey Pinckney Brown, July 14, 1982; stepchildren: Catherine Brown Collins, John

Preston Brown. Student, Princeton U., 1952-56; AB, Columbia U., 1961; LHD (hon.), Denison U., 1989; LLD, Knox Coll., 1993, Gettysburg Coll., 1995, Marquette U., 2000; LittD (hon.), U. of the South, 2004. Reporter Wall St. Jour., 1956-57, 59-61; writer, corr. NBC News, 1961-63; mem. staff N.Y. Times, from 1963, Albany bur. chief, 1964-65, Vietnam corr., 1965-66, Vietnam bur. chief, 1966-68, Africa bur. chief, 1969, nat. polit. corr., 1970-76, London bur. chief, 1977-80, 81-85, Moscow bur. chief, 1980-81, Washington bur. chief, 1992-97, chief Washington corr., 1985-97, chief corr., 1998—2006. Assoc. edit. Theodore H. White Meml. lectr. Harvard U., 1989, Joe Alex Morris Jr. Meml. lectr., 1993; Herzberg lectr. Columbia U.; Kent Meml. lectr. Johns Hopkins U., 1990. Author: Apple's Europe, 1986, Apple's America, 2005; contbr. to nat. mags., books. Bd. visitors Western Res. Acad.; chmn. Rhodes Scholarship Com., Mid-Atlantic States. With AUS, 1957-59; judge James Beard Restaurant Awards. Recipient Krout prize history Columbia U., 1961, award NATAS, 1963, George Polk Meml. award, 1967, Overseas Press Club award, 1967, Outstanding Alumnus award Columbia U., 1988, Western Res. Acad., 1976, Weintal award for diplomatic reporting, 1993, Lowell Thomas award for travel writing, Am. Soc. Travel Writers, 1999; Chubb fellow Yale U., 1998. Mem. AFTRA, Am. Inst. Wine and Food, Gridiron Club, Princeton Club, Century Assn. N.Y., Met. Club (Wash.) Home: Washington, DC. Died Oct. 4, 2006.

APPLEMAN, MORRIS, rabbi; b. Yonivel, Poland, Mar. 30, 1922; came to U.S., 1922; s. Dov Berr and Esther Appleman; m. Vivienne Kippelman, Oct. 30, 1949; children: Gaylr, Solomon, Rena Beth, Stuart, Ezra Mordechai. BA, Yeshiva U., 1945; MA, Hofstra U., 1956. Ordained rabbi, 1947. Chaplain Lakehurst Naval Air Sta., Washington, 1949-53; rabbi Toms River, N.J., 1949-53, East Nassau Hebrew Congregation, Syosset, N.Y., from 1954. Author: Isaac Mayer Wise, 1956. Mem. Am. Israel Polit. Action Com. Mem. Rabbinical Coun. Am., L.I. Commn. Rabbis, N.Y. Bd. Rabbis, Nassau Bd. Rabbis, AIPAC. Home: Syosset, NY. Died Mar. 11, 2004.

APPS, WILLIAM, agricultural company executive; b. Herne Bay, Kent, Eng., Apr. 1, 1947; came to U.S., 1966; s. William Apps and Violet May (Rawkins) Daring; m. Patricia Nafis, May 1972 (div. Feb. 1982); 1 child, Christine E.; m. Agatha Durden, Aug. 10, 1985. BA, Armstrong State Coll., 1971. Banking officer Citizens & So. Nat. Bank, Savannah, Ga., 1972-76; account exec. Merrill Lynch, Savannah, 1976-80; corp. v.p. Great So. Savs. Bank, Savannah, 1980-86; pres. Chelsea Plantation, Ridgeland, S.C., from 1986. Served as cadet sgt. Royal Brit. Army, 1964-66. Mem.: Forest City Gun. Episcopalian. Avocations: hunting, tennis. Home: Savannah, Ga. Died June 18, 2004.

ARCHER, CARL MARION, oil and gas company executive; b. Spearman, Tex., Dec. 16, 1920; s. Robert Barton and Gertrude Lucille (Sheets) A.; student U. Tex., Austin, 1937-39; m. Peggy Garrett, Aug. 22, 1939; children— Mary Frances, Carla Lee. Pres., Anchor Oil Co., Spearman, 1959—, Carl M. Archer Farms, Spearman, 1960—; gen. mgr. Speartex Grain Co., Spearman, 1967—, Speartex Oil & Gas Co., 1974—. Mem. Tex. Grain Dealers Assn., Tex. Grain and Feed Assn., Ind. Royalty Owners and Producers Assn., Nat. Grain Dealers Assn., Am. Petroleum Landmen Assn. Mem. Ch. of Christ. Clubs: Perryton, Borger Country, Amarillo. Home: Spearman, Tex. Died Sept. 19, 2004.

ARCHER, GEORGE WILLIAM, professional golfer; b. San Francisco, Oct. 1, 1939; s. Thomas Rowlett and Mary Emily (O'Connor) A.; m. Donna Garman, Sept. 30, 1961; children: Elizabeth Archer Klein, Marilyn Archer Baumgartner. Grad. high sch., San Mateo, Calif., 1958. Winner 13 Profl. Golfers Am. tour tournaments, 1964-89; winner 3 fgn. tournaments, 1968, 80, 81; winner Masters Tournament, 1969, Srs. Tournament, Tournament of Champions, 1990, No. Calif. Open, 1963. Creater, organizer Team Cadillac for Profl. Golfers Am. Srs. Golf Tour. Organizer Diablo Advocates Pro/Am to benefit children's charities, Alamo, Calif., 1980-90. Mem. Profl. Golfers Am. (tour mem.), No. Calif. Golf Assn., Gilroy C. of C. Presbyterian. Avocations: hunting, fishing. Home: Incline Village, Nev. Died Sept. 25, 2005.

ARCHIMEDES, VERDUN JOSEPH, art consultant, mental health nurse; b. San Francisco, Aug. 11, 1942; s. Verdun Joseph and Lena Vivian (Benedetti) A.; m. Jocelyn Peña, Feb. 8, 1996; children: Michael, Verdun J. III, Alexandra. AA, City Coll., San Francisco, 1969, AS, 1983; BA, U. Calif., Berkeley, 1987; postgrad., Yale U., 1987-88, Columbia U., 1988-91; DD honoris causa, Universal Life Ch., 1969. LPN, Calif., Conn., N.Y., Pa. Nursing asst. Mt. Zion Med. Ctr., San Francisco, 1964-70; health coord. Intertribal Med. Svcs., San Francisco, 1970-83; adj. staff nurse San Francisco Gen. Hosp., 1983-87, Yale-New Haven Hosp., 1987-88; nursing practitioner Roosevelt Hosp., N.Y.C., from 1988; founder, dir. Imahj Mesoamerica, N.Y.C., from 1991. Sustaining donor Maya Workshop Found., Austin, Tex., 1991—, Ctr. for Maya Rsch., Washington, 1992—. Bd. mem. Urban Indian Health Ctrs., San Francisco, 1985-87; sponsor Student/Sponsor Partnership, N.Y.C., 1993—. Jacob Toomb scholar U. Calif., Berkeley, 1986-87, Univ. fellow Yale U., 1987-88, Briscoe-Gaines fellow Yale U., 1995—. Mem. AAAS, Archeol. Inst. Am., N.Y. State Nursing Assn., Soc. for Ethnobiology, Disabled Am. Vets., The Cornell Club, Yale U. Alumni Assn. (alumni selection com. 1994—), U. Calif. Alumni Assn. (life). Republican. Roman Catholic. Avocation: classical music. Home: New City, NY. Died Aug. 15, 2004.

ARIS, RUTHERFORD, chemical engineer, educator; b. Bournemouth, Eng., Sept. 15, 1929; came to U.S., 1955, naturalized, 1962; s. Algernon Pollock and Janet (Elford) A.; m. Claire Mercedes Holman, Jan. 1, 1958. B.Sc. (spl.) with 1st class honours in Math, London U., Eng., 1948, PhD, 1960, D.Sc., 1964; student, Edinburgh U., Scotland, 1948-50; D.Sc. (hon.), U. Exeter, 1984, Clarkson U., 1985; DEng honoris causa, U. Notre Dame, 1990; Ch.M., fellow, Inst. Math. Appications, 1992; D Engring. honoris causa, Tech. U., Athens, Greece. Tech. officer Billingham div. I.C.I. Ltd., 1950-55; research fellow U. Minn., 1955-56; lectr. tech. math. Edinburgh U., 1956-58; mem. faculty U. Minn., 1958—2005, prof. chem. engring., from 1963, Regents' prof., 1978-96, Regents prof. emeritus, 1996—2005. O.A. Hougen vis. prof. U. Wis., 1979; Sherman Fairchild Disting. scholar Calif. Inst. Tech., 1980-81; cons. to industry, lectr., 1961—; IXth Centennial lectr. in chem. engring. U. Bologna, 1988; mem. Inst. for Advanced Study, Princeton, 1994. Author: Optimal Design of Chemical Reactors, 1961, Vectors, Tensors and the Basic Equations of Fluid Mechanics, 1962, reprint edit., 1989, Discrete Dynamic Programming, 1964, Introduction to the Analysis of Chemical Reactors, 1965, Elementary Chemical Reactor Analysis, 1969, reprint edit., 1990, (with N.R. Amundson) First-Order Partial Differential Equations with Applications, 1973, reprint 1999, (with W. Strieder) Variational Methods Applied to Problems of Diffusion and Reaction, 1973, The Mathematical Theory of Diffusion and Reaction in Permeable Catalysts, 1975, Mathematical Modelling Techniques, 1978, 2d edit., 1994, Chemical Engineering in the University Context, 1982; co-editor: Springs of Scientific Creativity, 1982, An Index of Scripts for E.A. Lowe's Codices Latini Antiquiores, 1982, (with Amundson and Rhee) First-order Partial Differential Equations, Vol. I Theory and Applications of Single Equations, 1986, Vol. II Theory and Applications of Systems of Quasilinear Hyperbolic Equations, 1986, 2d edit., 2002, Explicatio Formarum Litterarum*The Unfolding of Letterforms, 1990, (with K. Alhumaizi) Surveying A Dynamical System: The Gray/Scott Reaction In A Two-Phase Reactor, 1995, Mathematical Modeling--A Chemical Engineer's Perspective, 1999. Recipient E. Harris Harbison award for disting. teaching, 1969, Alpha Chi Sigma award Am. Inst. Chem. Engrs., 1969, Chem. Engring. lectr. award Am. Soc. Engring. Edn., 1973, Damköhler medal Deutsche Vereinigung fur Chemie und Verfahrenstechnik, 1991, Richard E. Bellman Control Heritage award Am. Automatic Control Coun., 1992, N.R. Amundson award Internat. Symposium on Chem. Reaction Engring., 1998; sr. rsch. fellow NSF, 1964-65, Guggenheim fellow, 1971-72. Fellow Am. Acad. Arts and Scis., Inst. Math. and Applications, Instn. of Chem. Engring. (hon.); mem. NAE, Soc. Nat. Philosophy, Soc. Indsl. and Applied Math., AIChE (R.H. Wilhelm award 1975, Inst. lectr. 1997, Founders award 1999), Mediaeval Acad. Lutheran. Home: Bloomington, Minn. Died Nov. 2, 2005.

ARISS, DAVID WILLIAM, SR., real estate developer, consultant; b. Toronto, Ont., Can., Nov. 29, 1939; s. William H. and Joyce Ethel (Oddy) A.; m. Lillie Ariss, Jan. 26, 1962 (div. 1989); m. Debra Ann Nocciolo, Nov. 17, 1990 (div. 1998); children: Katherine Joyce, David William Jr., Dylan William. BA, Claremont Men's Coll., 1961. Lic. real estate broker. Real estate broker Coldwell Banker, Torrance, Calif., 1971-75; v.p. The Lusk Co., Irvine, Calif., 1975-77; pres. DAL Devel. Co., Corona, Calif., 1977-84; mng. dir. Calif. Commerce Ctr. at Ontario, Ontario, Calif., from 1984. Chmn. Inland Empire Econ. Coun., Ontario, Calif., 1991-92; pres., adv. com. Chaffey Coll., Ontario, 1989; apptd. Calif. World Trade Commn., 1993, 95, 97. Maj. USMC, 1961-70, Vietnam. Decorated Silver Star, Disting. Flying Cross, two Purple Hearts, numerous Air medals. Mem. Urban Land Inst., Nat. Assn. Fgn. Trade Zone, Nat. Assn. Indsl. and Office Parks. Republican. Avocations: skiing, music, reading. Home: Fawnskin, Calif. Died Jan. 31, 2005.

ARIZAGA, LAVORA SPRADLIN, retired lawyer; b. Garvin County, Okla., Apr. 29, 1927; d. Gervase Eugene and Donah Lavorah (Eddings) Spradlin; m. Francisco De-Paula Arizaga, Aug. 10, 1946; children: F.D. III, Lavora Cristina Arizaga Ewan, Rebecca Maria Arizaga Armour, Nicolas Antonio. BA, U. Okla., 1952; JD, U. Houston, 1979. Bar: Tex. 1979. Sole practitioner, Houston, 1979-92. Pres. United Meth. Women, St. Luke's United Meth. Ch., Midland, 1996-98; chmn. Affirmative Action Adv. Bd., City of Houston, 1984-86. Mem. AAUW, LWV (pres. Beaumont, Tex. 1960-61, v.p. Tex. 1983-85, pres. Houston 1985-87, Midland, Tex. 1997-99). Home: Midland, Tex. Died July 10, 2005.

ARMBRISTER, TREVOR, journalist, author; b. Norwalk, Conn., Dec. 4, 1933; s. Geoffrey Campbell and Mary Kemball (Minor) A.; m. Dubos Middleton, Aug. 3, 1958 (div. Sept. 1980); children: Robertson, Alec; m. Judith Anne Cass, June 8, 1985. BA, Washington and Lee U., 1956. Account exec. J. Walter Thompson Co., Washington and N.Y.C., 1958-62; staff writer, bur. chief Saturday Evening Post, N.Y.C. and Washington, 1962-69; sr. staff editor Readers Digest, Washington, 1970-99, contbg. editor, 1999—2003. Author: A Matter of Accountability: The True Story of the Pueblo Affair, 1970, Act of Vengeance: The Yablonski Murders and Their Solution, 1975; co-writer, (with Don Riegle) Congress, 1972, (with Gerald R. Ford) A Time to Heal: The Autobiography of Gerald R. Ford, 1979, (with Dennis Hastert) Speaker: Lessons from Forty Years in Coaching and Politics, 2004. Founder, pres., chmn. Christmas in Apr., Washington, 1982; co-founder, pres., chmn. Christmas in Apr. U.S.A., Washington, 1988-91. Served to 1st lt. U.S. Army, 1956-58. Recipient Community Svc. award, 1985, Journalism award Big Bros./Big Sisters, Phila., 1986, others. Mem. Cosmos Club. Avocation: photography. Died Mar. 22, 2006.

ARMISTEAD, WILLIS WILLIAM, retired academic administrator, veterinarian; b. Detroit, Oct. 28, 1916; s. Eber Merrill and Josephine Brunell (Kindred) A.; m. Martha Sidney Clark, Sept. 17, 1938 (dec. 1964); children: Willis William, Jack Murray, Sidney Merrill; m. Mary Wallace Nelson, 1967. D.V.M., Tex. A&M Coll., 1938; M.Sc., Ohio State U., 1950; PhD, U. Minn., 1955. Diplomate: hon. diplomate; Am. Coll. Veterinary Surgeons, Am. Coll. Veterinary Preventive Medicine. Pvt. practice veterinary medicine, 1938—40; instr. Sch. Veterinary Medicine Tex. A&M U., 1940—42, asst. prof. to prof. Sch. Veterinary Medicine, 1946—53, dean Sch. Veterinary Medicine, 1953—57; dean Coll. Veterinary Medicine Mich. State U., East Lansing, 1957—74; dean Coll. Veterinary Medicine, U. Tenn., Knoxville, 1974—79, chmn. strategic planning adv. com., 1988—89; v.p. agr. U. Tenn. System, 1979—87. Collaborator animal diseases and parasite rsch. divsn. Dept. Agr., 1954-65; cons., adviser commn. veterinary edn. of South So. Regional Edn. Bd., 1953-56; mem. gov.'s sci. adv. bd., 1958-60; nat. cons. to Air Force Surgeon Gen., 1960-62; mem. adv. coun. Inst. Lab. Animal Resources, NRC, 1962-66; pres. Assn. Am. Veterinary Med. Colls., 1964-65, 73-74, Spl. award, 1983; veterinary med. resident investigators selection com. U.S. VA, 1967-70; veterinary medicine rev. com. Bur. Health Professions Edn. and Manpower Tng., HEW, 1967-71; mem. Nat. Bd. Veterinary Med. Examiners, 1970-74; mem. adv. panel for veterinary medicine Inst. Medicine, NAS, 1972-74; mem. bd. agr. and renewable resources NRC, 1976-77; 1st Allam lectr. Am. Coll. Veterinary Surgeons, 1972; Conti Meml. keynote lectr. Ariz.-Calif.-Nev. Veterinary Conf., 1994; mem. curriculum com. Oak Ridge Inst. Continued Learning, 1998-2001. Contbg. author: Canine Surgery, rev. edit, 1957, Canine Medicine, rev. edit, 1959; editor: The N.Am. Veterinarian, 1950-56, Jour. Veterinary Med. Edn, 1974-80; assoc. editor: Jour. Am. Animal Hosp. Assn., 1964-70; contbr. tech. articles to profl. jours. Bd. dirs. Tenn. Farm Bur. Fedn., 1979-87, Tenn. Coun. Coops., 1982-87, Tenn. 4-H Club Found., 1979-87, Tenn. Agrl. Hall of Fame, 1979-87, Tenn. Valley Fair, 1987-2004; mem. Tenn. State Soil Conservation Com., 1979-87; mem. Southwide adv. com. So. Agribus. Forum, 1979-87; mem. adv. bd. Clarence Brown Theater, U. Tenn., 2000-02. Maj. Vet. Corps AUS, 1942—46. Recipient Meritorious Svc. award Selective Svc. System, 1972; hon. alumnus Mich. State U., 1972; recipient Disting. Alumnus award Coll. Vet. Medicine, Tex. A&M U., 1980, 75th Anniversary Achievement award Tex. A&M U. Coll. Vet. Medicine, 1991; named V.P Emeritus, U. Tenn., 1987-2006. Mem. AAAS, U.S. Animal Health Assn., Am. Vet. Med. Assn. (pres. 1957-58, award 1977), Tex. Vet. Med. Assn. (pres. 1947-48), Mich. Vet. Med. Assn. (trustee Edn. and Sci. Trust 1970-74), Fedn. Assns. Schs. of Health Professions (pres. 1975), Tenn. Vet. Med. Assn. (Lifetime Achievement award 1995), Inst. Medicine of NAS, N.Y. Acad. Scis., Rotary (pres. 1987-88), Sigma Xi, Phi Kappa Phi, Alpha Zeta, Phi Zeta, Omega Tau Sigma (nat. Gamma award Ohio State U. 1962), Phi Eta Sigma, Gamma Sigma Delta, Omicron Delta Kappa. Lodges: Rotary. Episcopalian. Home: Knoxville, Tenn. Died Apr. 18, 2006.

ARMSTRONG, BILLIE BERT, retired highway contractor; b. Roswell, N.Mex., Apr. 18, 1920; s. Gayle G. and Murphy (Shannon) A.; m. Betty-Ellen Wilcox, Aug. 16, 1941; children: Billie B. Jr., Judith C., Robert G., Riley A. Student, N.Mex. Mil. Inst., 1935-39, Washington & Lee U., 1939-41. Mng. ptnr. Armstrong & Armstrong Ltd., Roswell, from 1950, G.G. Armstrong & Son, Ltd., Roswell, from 1950. Chmn. bd. dirs. Sunwest Nat. Bank of Roswell, 1967-84; pres. Assoc. Gen. Contractors Am., Washington, 1966-67, Assoc. Contractors N.Mex., Santa Fe, 1952-53, 63; bd. dirs. Southwestern Pub. Svc. Co., Sunwest Fin. Svcs., Inc. Pres. Conquistador Coun. Boy Scouts Am., Roswell, 1981-82, bd. regents N.Mex. Mil. Inst., Roswell, 1960-62. Major U.S. Army, 1942-45. Named Citizen of Yr. Realtors N.Mex., 1969, Roswell, 1968, Jaycees, 1964; recognized for svc. to mankind Sertoma, 1966. Mem. Masons, Shriners, Jesters. Methodist. Avocation: golf. Home: Roswell, N.Mex. Died 2005.

ARMSTRONG, JOHN WILLIAM, JR., retired librarian; b. Portsmouth, NH, July 24, 1920; s. John William and Candace Margie (Garvin) A.; m. Hariot Baker, Apr. 1946 (div. 1951). SB, Harvard Coll., 1942; MSLS, Simmons Coll., 1949. Libr., founder Indsl. Rels. Libr. Grad. Sch. Pub. Adminstrn. Harvard U., Cambridge, Mass., 1946-51; libr., chief acquisitions Air Force Cambridge Rsch. Ctr. USAF, 1951-94; ret. Home: Lexington, Mass. Died June 5, 2004.

ARNESON, DORA WILLIAMS, health science research administrator; b. Fayetteville, Ark., Aug. 4, 1947; d. Harry Wilson and Hazel Marie (Keck) Williams; m. Richard Michael Arneson, Mar. 15, 1973 (div. Apr. 1982). BA in Chemistry, U. Mo., 1967, PhD, 1972. Cert. by Am. Bd. Clin. Chemistry. Instr. biochemistry dept. U. Tenn. Med. Ctr., Memphis, 1972-76; assoc. dir. Inborn Errors of Metabolism Lab., Memphis, 1977-83; sr. project mgr. Midwest Rsch. Inst., Kansas City, Mo., 1984-91, prin. chemist, 1991-92; sect. mgr., from 1992. Mem. genetics screening subcom.

Tenn. Dept. Pub. Health, Nashville, 1982-83. Contbr. articles to profl. publs. Bd. dirs. Nat. Alliance-Ptnrs. of the Americas, Tenn., 1981-83; mem. instl. rev. bd. Meth. Hosp., Memphis, 1982-83. Mem. Am. Chem. Soc., Am. Assn. Cancer Rsch., Drug Info. Assn., Soc. Inherited Metabolic Disorders, Eggs and Issues Club. Home: Kansas City, Mo. Died Apr. 25, 2004.

ARNICK, JOHN STEPHEN, state legislator, lawyer; b. Balt., Nov. 27, 1933; s. John and Josephine (Gaillardo) A. BS, U. Balt., 1956; LLD, U. Balt. Law Sch., 1961. Bar Assn. Magistrate Balt. County, 1966-67; del. Md. Gen. Assembly, Annapolis, 1967-79, 87-94, 1995—2006; atty. pvt. practice, Balt., 1962—2006. Mem. Twin Dist. Dem. Club, Battle Grove Dem. Club, Sons of Italy. Served in USMC, 1956—59. Mem. Ea. Balt. C. of C., Moose Lodge, New 7th Dem. Club, South East Dem. Club. Democratic. Roman Catholic. Home: Baltimore, Md. Died June 13, 2006.

ARNOLD, ERNEST WOODROW, minister; b. White Springs, Fla., Mar. 20, 1914; s. Turner Benjamin and Frances Essie (Wise) A.; m. Mildred Virginia Thomas, Jan. 26, 1945; children: Ernest Woodrow Jr., Cheryl Ruth Arnold Daves. BA magna cum laude, Furman U., 1943; BD, New Orleans Bapt. Theol. Sem., 1948; ThD, Luther Rice Sem., 1965. Ordained to ministry So. Bapt. Conv., 1942. Pastor East Pk. Bapt. Ch., Greenville, S.C., 1950-54, Brentwood Bapt. Ch., Charleston, S.C., 1955-58, Bethel Bapt. Ch., Shelby, N.C., 1958-72, Catawba Bapt. Ch., Rock Hill, S.C., 1972-75, 1st Bapt. Ch., Bostic, N.C., 1975-81, Lily Meml. Bapt. Ch., Shelby, from 1987. Mem. faculty Luther Rice Sem., 1968-76. Author: Truth: Tried and Tested, 1996. With USMC, 1934-38. Recipient commendation USMC, 1935; New Orleans Bapt. Theol. Sem. fellow, 1948-50. Democrat. Home: Boiling Springs, NC. Died Nov. 29, 2004.

ARNOLD, GARY D., banker; b. Tyler, Tex., Sept. 17, 1957; s. Harold D. and Betty J. A.; m. Jennifer L. Palmer, June 18, 1983; children: Abigail, Timothy, Samuel. BBA in Fin., S.W. Tex. State U., 1982; MBA in Fin., U. Tex., 1984. CPA. V.p., controller Bright Banc, Dallas, 1984-88; v.p. Murray Savs. and Loan, Dallas, 1988-90; sr. mgr. KPMG Peat Marwick, Chgo., 1990-96; v.p. First USA, Dallas, 1996-98; sr. v.p. Bank One, Columbus, Ohio, from 1998. Cons. KPMG Marwick, Chgo.; dir. market rsch. studies in field; spkr. in field. Dir. United Cerebral Palsy, Columbus, 1999. Mem. Bank Mktg. Assn., Mortgage Bankers Assn. of Am., Consumer Bankers Assn. Independent. Methodist. Avocations: bicycling, hiking, skiing, camping. Home: La Canada, Calif. Died Mar. 7, 2004.

ARNOLD, THOMAS IVAN, JR., former state legislator; b. Paterson, NJ; s. Thomas Ivan and Marjorie Lewis (Eccles) A.; m. Barbara Jane Phinney, July 25, 1953 (dec. June 1985); children: Thomas I., Barbara J., Edward H., Patricia J., Peter S., Dennis L., Nancy L., Richard B., Susan D., Charles P. ME, Stevens Inst. Tech., Hoboken, N.J., 1950, MS, 1954; PhD, U. Wexford, 1986. Registered profl engr., N.H. Asst. to quality mgr. Curtiss-Wright Corp., Wood Ridge, NJ, 1950-58; mgr. corp. quality control ops. Sanders Assocs., Inc., Nashua, NH, 1958-67; mgr. quality assurance RCA Corp., Burlington, Mass., 1967-72; mgr. product assurance and quality control Compugraphic Corp., Wilmington, Mass., 1972-81; mgr. quality assurance GE, Burlington, 1981-91; mem. N.H. Gen. Ct., 1992—2004, vice chair com. on election laws, 1997-98, mem. com. on sci. tech. and energy, 1999—2004, mem. com. on children and family law, 1999—2004. Moderator Sch. Dist., Brookline, 1960—2004, Town of Brookline, 1976—2004, selectman, 1968-69; chmn. Zoning Bd. Adjustment, Brookline, 1970-82; chmn. Rep. town com.; mem. N.H. State Rep. Com., 1999—2004; mem. EMT Brookline Vol. Ambulance, 1976-86; mem. N.H. Indsl. Heritage Commn., 1995-96; mem. Commn. to Study Child Support and Related Child Custody Issues, 2003-04. With USAAF, 1946-47. Mem.: NRA, Am. Soc. for Quality (sect. chmn. 1964), GO N.H., Mensa, Order of Daedalians. Republican. Episcopalian. Avocations: fixing things, wood working. Home: Brookline, NH. Died May 2006.

ARONSON, RICHARD JAY, real estate broker; b. Pitts., Apr. 3, 1916; s. I. Leonard and Dora M. (Berne) A.: m. Jean Lois Deroy, Aug. 6, 1937; children: Mark B., Steven D., I. Leonard II. BS in Econs., U. Pa., 1937. Pres. U.S. Realty Corp., Pitts., 1951-83; v.p. Realty Growth Co., Pitts., from 1983. Mem. Western Pa. Inst. Real Estate Mgmt. (pres. 1963), United Fund (bd. dirs.), Soc. Indsl. Realtors. Clubs: Westmoreland Country, Concordia (Pitts.) (pres. 1964-65). Lodges: Masons (past master). Avocations: golf, tennis, collecting charles dickens' works. Home: Pittsburgh, Pa. Died Jan. 2, 2004.

ARPON, ROSARIO, community health nurse; b. The Philippines, Apr. 18, 1963; d. Alfredo and Zenaida (Cerdenola) Ragodos; m. Carlito Arpon, Aug. 5, 1989. BSN, Fla. Atlantic U., 1988, postgrad., from 1988. Instr. Palm Beach Community Coll., Belle Glade, Fla.; charge nurse pediatric unit Glades Gen. Hosp., Belle Glade, infection control dir. Mem. Am. Practitioners of Infection Control, Fla. Practitioners of Infection Control (mem. ednl. com.). Home: Ewa Beach, Hawaii. Died Dec. 25, 2004.

ARRINGTON, ANITA, nursing administrator, quality assurance executive; b. Oakland, Calif., Oct. 2, 1944; d. Ethan and June A. (Smith) Newsom; m. Ronnie D. Arrington, Apr. 6, 1986; children: Ray, Sherry, Robert, Sandy. AA, Coll. of the Desert, Palm Desert, Calif., 1978. Cert. profl. in quality assurance. Utilization rev. profl. Hi-Desert Med. Ctr., Joshua Tree, Calif., quality assurance profl., risk mgr.; quality resource svcs. nurse, asst. adminstr. patient care; charge nurse emergency dept. Ea. Okla. Med. Ctr., Pateau. Home: Heavener, Okla. Died June 13, 2004.

ARSENOVIC, ALEXANDAR, physician; b. Beograd, Yugoslavia, Dec. 19, 1928; s. Ilija and Anna (Muk) A.; v. Vukosava Dokovic, Oct. 4, 1954; children: Ilija, Nanka Arsenovic Schneider. MD, U. Beograd, 1953. Diplomate Am. Bd. Family Practice, Am. Bd. Quality Assurance; lic. physician, Pa. Internist/infectologist Univ. Clinics, Beograd, 1954-58; specialist-infectologist, chief of clin. lab. Health Ctr. Vracar, Beograd, 1958-68; resident in family practice Edgewater Hosp., Chgo., 1969-70; internist VA Hosps., various locations, 1970-86; pvt. practice family practitioner and geriatritian Community Med. Ctr. of Burgettstown, Kansas City, Mo., from 1986. Fellow Am. Geriatrics Soc.; mem. Am. Acad. Family Practice. Died Dec. 19, 2004.

ARTINIAN, ARTINE, French literature scholar, collector; b. Pazardjick, Bulgaria, Dec. 8, 1907; came to U.S., 1920, naturalized, 1930; s. Peter and Akaby (Berberian) A.; m. Margaret Willard Woodbridge, June 27, 1936; children: Margaret, Robert Willard, Ellen. AB, Bowdoin Coll., Brunswick, Maine, 1931; diploma, U. Paris, 1932; A.M., Harvard U., 1933; PhD, Columbia U., 1941; Litt.D. (hon.), Bowdoin Coll., 1966; postgrad., U. Grenoble, France, 1931, U. Poitiers, 1932; LHD, Appalachian State U., 2001. Asst. French Bowdoin Coll., 1930-31; ednl. worker dept. correction organizing inmate sch. Welfare Island Penitentiary, NYC, 1934-35; prof. French John Marshall Coll. Law, NJ, 1935-36; chmn. French dept. Bard Coll., Annandale-on-Hudson, NY, 1935-64, chmn. div. langs., lits., 1939-40, 44-45, 56-57, 58-59, 60-64, 'prof. emeritus French, 1964—2005; head instr. French Bard Coll. A.S.T.P. Unit, 1943-44. Prof.-in-charge Sweet Briar (Va.) Jr. Year in France, 1953-55; acting dir. U.S. house Cité Universitaire, Paris, summers 1955, 56, 58; mem. com. examiners (French sect.) Coll. Entrance Exam. Bd., 1962-64; trustee Am. Students Center, Paris, 1954-65; guest of French govt., summer 1946 Compiler extensive Guy de Maupassant collection, also French lit. manuscripts now at U. Tex., Austin; exhibited collection drawings and paintings by French writers, U.S. tour sponsored by French govt., 1968-70; Century and a Half of French Illustrators, Cornell U., Brandeis U., Harvard U., 1968, Tex., 1972, Auckland (N.Z.) Mus., 1977, U.S. Tour, 1980-85, The French Visage, A Century and a Half of French Portraits, Bowdoin Coll. Mus. Art, Hopkins Art Ctr., Dartmouth Coll., others, 1969; Music in Art Henry Morrison Flagler Mus., Palm Beach, Fla., Brandeis U., Wellesley Coll., 1971, Illustrated Letters, Seton Hall U., South Orange, N.J., 1978, French Illustrated Letters, Norton Gallery of Art, West Palm Beach, 1989; over 300 N.C. Self-Portraits donated to Appalachian State U., Boone, N.C.; over 300 Fla. self Portraits donated to Fla. Atlantic U., Boca Raton; also exhibited other collections numerous other univs. U.S. including Columbia, French Inst. N.Y.C., Vassar, U. Va.; Author: Maupassant Criticism in France, 1880-1940, With an Inquiry into His Present Fame and a Bibliography, 1941, 69; editor: La Correspondance inédite de Guy de Maupassant, 1951, Pour et Contre Maupassant, 1955, Complete Short Stories of Guy de Maupassant, 1955, La Queue de la Poire de la Boule de Monseigneur (Flaubert 1st edit.), 1958, Là-Haut (Huysmans 1st edit.), 1963, From Victor Hugo to Jean Cocteau, 1965; Maupassant Biography (with Robert Artinian), 1982; contbr. to profl. jours., books. Mem. chancellor's coun. U. Tex.; philantrophist established scholarship funds, Attleboro, Mass., Sweet Briar Coll., Va., Appalachin State U., Boone, N.C, Bowdoin Coll., Brunswick, Me. Decorated officier d'Academie (France), 1948; Am. Council Learned Socs. fellow, 1943-44; Fulbright research scholar France, 1949-50; Am. Philos. Soc. research grantee Paris, 1960; named to Hon. Order Ky. Cols. Mem. Société des Amis de Guy de Maupassant (v.p. 1950-65), MLA (sec. 19th Century French sect. 1947, chmn. 1948), Am. Assn. Tchrs. French, AAUP (pres. Bard Coll. chpt. 1951-52), Société Littéraire des Amis d'Emile Zola (U.S. rep. bd. dirs. 1954-65), Expressions Paris (hon. pres. 1984—), Theta Delta Chi, Pi Delta Epsilon. Died Nov. 19, 2005.

ARTZ, FREDERICK JAMES, diversified manufacturing company executive; b. Pitts., Dec. 28, 1949; s. Ray Edison and Jean Elizabeth (McClurg) A.; m. Donna Marie Moschella, Dec. 16, 1977; children: James Randall, BrieAnn Elizabeth. BS in Adminstrn. and Mgmt. Sci., Carnegie Mellon U., 1972; MBA, U. Pitts., 1973. Indsl. engr. Spang and Co., Butler, Pa., 1973-74; retail buyer Sun Drug div. Spang Stores, Butler, 1974-79, internal auditor, 1979-82, acctg. mgr., 1982-88, treas., from 1988. Bd. dirs. Spang & Co. Mem. Beta Gamma Sigma. Home: Gibsonia, Pa. Died Oct. 26, 2004.

ARUNASALAM, VICKRAMASINGAM (WILLIE), retired physicist; b. Mathagal, Jaffna, Sri Lanka, Aug. 26, 1935; arrived in U.S., 1958, naturalized, 1973; s. Sithamparapillai and Sithamparam Vickramasingam; m. Saradamani Sivagnanasundaram, Mar. 23, 1968 (dec. Dec. 21, 1997); 1 child, Sharmila. BS, U. Ceylon, Colombo, 1957; MS, U. Mass., 1960; PhD, MIT, 1964. Asst. lectr. U. Ceylon, Colombo, Sri Lanka, 1957—58; instr. U. Mass., Amherst, 1960; from rsch. assoc. to prin. rsch. physicist Princeton (N.J.) U., 1964—80, prin. rsch. physicist, 1980—96; vis. prof. William Paterson U., Wayne, NJ, 1997—97; adj. prof. Rider U., Lawrenceville, NJ, 1999—99; assoc. editor Physics Essays, Ottawa, Quebec, Canada, from 1992. Contbr. 105 articles to profl. jours. Named to Wall of Tolerance, Montgomery, Ala., 2005; recipient Lifetime Achievement award, Ilankai Tamil Sangam USA, 2003, Skanthavarodya Coll. Old Students Assn. of Can., 2003, Tamils Info. and Rsch. Ctr. of Toronto, 2005, World Tamil Movement of Can., 2005, Congratulatory Cert. of Greetings, Can. Govt., 2005. Fellow: Am. Phys. Soc. (sr.); mem.: Sigma Xi. Achievements include research in Plasma Physics and Controlled Thermonuc. Fusion, Quantum Theory, Quantum Electrodynamics, Cosmology, Foundations of Physics, Particle Physics, Condensed Matter Theory, and Quantum Statis. mechanics; works cited as fundamental contributions in many physics books. Home: Princeton Junction, NJ. Died 2005.

ARVIDSON, ROBERT BENJAMIN, JR., geneticist, consultant; b. Lafayette, Ind., June 10, 1920; s. Robert Benjamin Sr. and Ollie Blanche (Ice) A.; m. Rose Janet Gaylord, Sept. 2, 1943 (dec. 2000); children: Cheryl R., James R., Kay E. BSA, Purdue U., 1942, MS, 1950. Poultry genetics staff Hy-Line Internat. Divsn. Pioneer Hi Bred Internat., Des Moines, 1947-50; dir. rsch. Hy-Line Internat., Des Moines, 1951-79, ret., 1979. Cons. World Bank, Washington, 1979-80. Precinct committeeman Rep. Party, Des Moines, 1970. Capt. Q.M.C., U.S. Army, 1942-46. Mem. World Poultry Sci. Assn., Poultry Sci. Assn., Kiwanis (pres. 1979). Methodist. Avocations: golf, fishing, gardening, dahlia growing. Home: Des Moines, Iowa. Died Feb. 22, 2004.

ASCHERMAN, STANFORD WARREN, surgeon; b. Chgo., Aug. 18, 1926; s. Elmer N. and Irma G. (Kapper) A. AB, Stanford U., 1947; BS, U. Ill., 1948, MD, 1950. Lic. physician N.Y., Ill., Calif., Australia. Resident in pathology Cook County Hosp., Chgo., 1950—52; resident in surgery Bellevue Hosp., N.Y.C., Mt. Sinai Hosp., Bronx (N.Y.) Mcpl. Hosp.; pvt. practice San Francisco, from 1959. Endowed chair in elec. engring. Stanford U., 1978, endowed prof. in molecular genetics, 1997. Contbr. articles to profl. jours. Mem. Hadassah Med. Devel., N.S.W. Med. Bd., 1970—. Fellow ACS, Am. Trauma Soc., Nat. Bd. Med. Examiners, Am. Med. Writers Assn., Pan-Am Med. Soc., Internat. Coll. Surgeons, Am. Coll. Legal Medicine; mem. AAAS (life), Pan Pacific Surg. Assn., Australian Med. Assn., Commonwealth Club, Press Club, World Trade Club. Democrat. Died Nov. 24, 2004.

ASCHLIMAN, IDA DELORES, nurse; b. Chgo., Aug. 28, 1929; d. Peter John and Mabelle E. (Shearin) Arns; m. Walter LaVerne Aschliman, Feb. 2, 1951; 1 child, Mark Randall. BS, Coll. St. Francis, 1980; diploma in Nursing, St. Elizabeth Hosp., 1950. Staff nurse Belmont Hosp., Chgo., 1950-54, Elmhurst (Ill.) Meml. Hosp., from 1967. Chmn., organizer Heart Assn. DuPage County Cardiovascular Nurses Commn., Elmhurst, 1970-76; program chmn., organizer ednl. seminars for sr. citizens, 1986-88, commr., 1974—. Mem. Assn. Operating Room Nurses, Am. Assn. Post Anesthesia Nurses, Ill. Assn. Post Anesthesia Nurses. Republican. Methodist. Avocations: fishing, gardening, quilt collecting. Home: Goshen, Ind. Died Mar. 4, 2005.

ASHLEY, HOLT, aerospace scientist, educator; b. San Francisco, Jan. 10, 1923; s. Harold Harrison and Anne (Oates) A.; m. Frances M. Day, Feb. 1, 1947 (wid.). Student, Calif. Inst. Tech., 1940-43; BS, U. Chgo., 1944; MS, MIT, 1948, ScD, 1951. Mem. faculty MIT, 1946-67, prof. aero., 1960-67; prof. aeros. and astronautics Stanford U., Palo Alto, Calif., 1967-89, prof. emeritus, 1989—2006. Spl. rsch. aeroelasticity, aerodynamics; cons. govt. agys., rsch. orgns., indsl. corps.; dir. office of exploratory rsch. and problem assessment and div. advanced tech. applications NSF, 1972-74; mem. sci. adv. bd. USAF, 1958-80, rsch. adv. com. structural dynamics NASA, 1952-60, rsch. adv. com. on aircraft structures, 1962-70, chmn. rsch. adv. com. on materials and structures, 1974-77; mem. Kanpur Indo-American program Indian Inst. Tech., 1964-65, governing bd. Nat. Rsch. Coun., 1988-91; AIAA Wright Bros. lectr., 1981; dir. Rann Inc. Co-author: Aeroelasticity, 1955, Principles of Aeroelasticity, 1962, Aerodynamics of Wings and Bodies, 1969, Engineering Analysis of Flight Vehicles, 1974. Recipient Goodwin medal M.I.T., 1952; Exceptional Civilian Service award U.S. Air Force, 1972, 80; Public Service award NASA, 1981; named one of 10 outstanding young men of year Boston Jr. C. of C., 1956; recipient Ludwig-Prandtl Ring, West German DGLR, 1987, Spirit of St. Louis Medal, ASME, 1992. Fellow AIAA (hon., assoc. editor jour., v.p. tech. 1971, pres. 1973, Structures, Structural Dynamics and Materials award 1969), Am. Acad. Arts and Scis. (Daniel Guggenheim medal 2004), Royal Aero. Soc. (hon.); mem. AAAS, NAE (aeros. and space engring. bd. 1977-79, mem. coun. 1985-91), Am. Meterol. Soc. (profl., 50th Ann. medal 1971), Phi Beta Kappa, Sigma Xi, Tau Beta Pi. Home: Woodside, Calif. Died May 9, 2006.

ASTILL, BERNARD DOUGLAS, environmental health and safety consultant; b. Nottingham, Eng., Feb. 11, 1925; came to U.S., 1952; s. Bernard and Constance (Harriet) A.; m. Norma Sarah Di Lauro, Apr. 9, 1955; children: Paul, Alexandra. BS, U. Nottingham, Eng., 1950, PhD in Organic Chemistry, 1953. Postdoctoral Fulbright fellow U. Rochester, N.Y., 1952-55; biochemist Eastman Kodak Co., Rochester, N.Y., 1955-64; clin. instr. U. Rochester Med. Sch., Rochester, N.Y., 1960-74; rsch. assoc. Eastman Kodak Co., Rochester, 1964-72, supr. biochemistry health & environ. lab., 1972-85, dir. regulatory affairs, life scis., 1985-87; cons. Bernard D. Astill Assocs., Rochester, from 1987.

Cons. in field; com. mem. NAS/NRC Div. Toxicology, Washington, 1980-85, 88-91. Author: (book chpt.) Patty's Toxicology & Indsl. Hygiene, 1981; contbr. articles to profl. jours. Chmn. Rochester Cosmopolitan Club, 1957-59; co-chmn. new mem. campaign Rochester Philharmonic Orch., 1976-78. Petty officer Royal Navy, 1943-46, South Pacific. Mem. Soc. Toxicology, Am. Chem. Soc. (chmn. Rochester sect. 1983), Am. Guild Organists. Avocations: piano, organ, choral dir., gardening, theatre. Died Aug. 5, 2005.

ASTILL, ROBERT MICHAEL, office manager; b. Winchester, Mass., Apr. 11, 1960; s. Kenneth Norman and Hazel Patricia (Lamb) Astill. BA in Psychology, Polit. Sci., Merrimack Coll., 1982. Credit mgr. Kazmaier Internat., Concord, Mass., 1983-90; cons. Astill Group, Winchester, 1990-92; credit mgr. Internat. Ice Cream, Boston, 1992-93; corp. credit mgr. New Eng. Frozen Foods, Southborough, 1993-97; mgr. spl. credit, collection activities Garelick Farms-Lynn divsn, Dean Foods GTL LLC, Lynn, 1997—2000, cons., from 2000. Mem. New Eng. Steamship Found., from 1997, trustee, from 2001; bd. dirs. Friends of Winchester (Mass.) Libr., 1990—94. Mem.: Merrimack Coll. Alumni Assn. (class chair 1999—2000), Nat. Assn. Credit Mgrs. (chmn. exec. bd. wholesale provision 1992—97, sec. exec. bd. restaurant and inst. group 1995—2000, bd. dirs. from 1999), Psi Chi. Roman Cath. Avocations: photography, music, travel. Died June 11, 2005.

ATHY, LAWRENCE FERDINAND, JR., historian; b. Ponca City, Okla., Oct. 6, 1927; s. Lawrence Ferdinand and Helen Elizabeth (Thiel) A.; m. Martha Jane Anthony, May 3, 1952; 1 child, Gayle Lynn. BSME, Rice U., 1950. Registered profl. engr. (ret.), Tex. Roustabout Warren Oil Corp., McLean, Tex., 1950; asst. chief draftsman Wyatt Industries, Houston, 1950-55; mgr. engring. and mfg. Polymer Engring. Corp., Hitchcock, Tex., 1955-57; sr. v.p. Southwestern Mfg. Co., Houston, 1957-79; owner Fluid Power Cons., Houston, 1979-87; historian and epigrapher, Houston, from 1987. Chpt. pres. Fluid Power Soc., Houston, 1970. Author: Captain George Athy of Galway and Maryland and his Descendants, 1987, The Descendants of Corporal John Athy, Continental Line, 1998; contbr. articles to profl. jours.; patentee in field. Precinct chmn. Rep. Party, Houston, 1978-84; election judge Harris County, Houston, 1993-94. With USN, 1945-46. Mem. ASME, The Epigraphic Soc. (ogam archivist 1990—, dir. 1996), Archaeol. Inst. Am., Inst. for the Study Ancient Am. Culture, Archaeol. Conservancy, Victorian Owners Assn. (bd. dirs. 1990), The Briar Club (com. chair 1960), Early Sites Rsch. Soc. Avocations: reading, writing, walking, research. Died Jan. 26, 2004.

ATKINS, IRVIN STANLEY, public relations executive; b. L.A., Mar. 3, 1917; s. Samuel and Fannie A.; m. Ida Mae Miller, Mar. 6, 1940, life ptnr. in major projects. AA, L.A. Jr. Coll., 1936; BA in Mgmt. with honors, U. Redlands, 1986. Assoc. producer People Are Funny (TV show), L.A., 1942-51; dir. People Are Funny, L.A., 1951-62, Linkletter and The Kids, L.A., 1951-62; owner Irvin Atkins Agy., Beverly Hills, Calif., from 1948. Pub. rels agy. clients include Art Linkletter, Carol Channing, Burl Ives, George Hurrell, Art Expo West, Chevron Oil, Milton Bradley, Quaker Oats and Litton Industries; producer L.A. Auto Shows. Producer spoken word recording We Love You, Call Collect, 1969 (Grammy award, 1970); producer TV spls. on all networks, films in Europe, the Mid. East and Asia. Trustee U. Redlands, 1987—, Boy Scouts Am., San Fernando Valley, Calif., 1986—; com. head Childrens Bur. of L.A., 1988—, Childhelp, Inc., 1984—, Family Svc. of L.A., 1988—. Recipient Outstanding Whitehead Alumni award U. Redlands, 1986, City of Hope award, 1983, Disting. Citizen award, U.S. Senate, 1969, Mex. and Am. Found. of the Stars, 1974. Mem. Acad. TV Arts and Scis. (Frank O'Connor Meml. Student TV award, 1985), Acad. Motion Picture Arts and Scis., Dirs. Guild of Am. Avocation: charity work. Died July 14, 2005.

ATKINSON, CLAUDENE DOUGLAS, writer; b. Wichita Falls, Tex., Nov. 17, 1928; d. Walter Claud Jr. and Eula Marguerite (Fletcher) Douglas; married; 1 child, Mark Douglas. BA, U. Houston, 1951; MA, Calif. State U., 1959. Cert. adminstr., counselor, supr., tchr., Tex., Calif. Tchr. English Brazosport Pub. Schs., Lake Jackson, Tex., 1948-51, 54-55; counselor, chair English dept. Houston Pub. Schs., 1955-57, 67-70, Bellflower Pub. Schs., Lakewood, Calif., 1958-63; counselor, instr. Long Beach (Calif.) City Coll., 1965-66; cons. English Houston Pub. Schs., 1970-71; chair humanities divsn. Houston C.C., 1971-77, TV writer, presenter, 1975-77; freelance writer Houston and Ingram, Tex., from 1978. Vis. prof. writing Nat. Coll. Edn., Evanston, Ill., 1979; staff leading woman Alley Theatre, Houston, 1955-57; comms. cons. Byrum Assocs., Houston, 1978-79; speaker conv. Tex. Coun. Tchrs. of English, 1968; presenter conf. Nat. Coun. Tchrs. of English, Las Vegas, Nev., 1971. Field editor lang. textbooks, 1972-77; women's editor: Daily Facts Rev., 1954; contbr. articles to profl. jours.; played leading roles in over 40 theater prodns. Speaker on women's issues, racial equality and lit. various civic, profl. and religious groups, Houston, Long Beach, Honolulu, 1942—; comm. chair United Meth. Ch. Recipient Best Original Short Story award S.W. Writers Conf., 1976, Original Poetry award S.W. Writers Conf., 1977. Mem. AAUW (v.p.). Avocations: reading, photography, theater, films, travel. Died May 8, 2004.

ATKINSON, DON JOSEPH, actor, director; b. Louisville, June 4, 1940; s. Donald Joseph and Eunice Harriet (Sluss) A.; m. Margret Mary Longo, Oct. 11, 1970. Student, New Sch. Social Rsch. Appeared in ten Broadway shows, Off Broadway shows including Grand Tour, Love Me, Love My Children, Off Off Broadway shows, regional shows, stock and dinner theatre, film and TV shows including Love of Life, Lovers and Other Strangers, Zelig, commls. and videos including Dannon Yogurt, Chevy Trucks, Miller Light, East River Savings Bank, Bud Light, Gillette, New York Telephone, video including Peace Sells. Avocations: sailing, primitive weapons expert. Home: New York, NY. Died Jan. 11, 2004.

ATKINSON, EDWARD REDMOND, chemist, consultant; b. Boston, Feb. 15, 1912; s. Joseph and Florence Annie (Bryon) A.; m. Helen Stevenson, Sept. 2, 1935 (dec. Feb. 1943); m. Lorraine Crittendon, Aug. 12, 1944 (dec. July 1991); children: Kathleen, Carol. SB, MIT, 1933, PhD, 1936. Instr. Trinity Coll., Hartford, Conn., 1936-38; prof. U. N.H., Durham, 1938-51; sr. chemist W.R. Grace, Inc., Cambridge, Mass., 1951-57, Arthur D. Little, Inc., Cambridge, 1957-77, ret., 1977. Adj. prof. Northeastern U., Boston, 1951-61. Contbr. over 80 articles to profl. jours. Mem. AAAS, Am. Chem. Soc. (councilor Northeastern sect. 1952-72, chmn. 1956-57), Alpha Chi Sigma (dist. councilor 1949-51). Democrat. Achievements include research in organic and medicinal chemistry, in history of chemistry, and in hazardous chemicals. Home: Amherst, Mass. Died June 25, 2004.

ATKINSON, JANET E., lawyer; b. Detroit, Apr. 30, 1945; d. A.K. and Billie Dorothy Atkinson; m. Robert Joseph Kestell, Aug. 18, 1966 (div. Dec. 1992); children: Jeanette, Elizabeth, Robert, Katherine, Richard. BA, U. Wis., 1967; MLS, U. Md., 1972, JD, 1996. Libr. asst. Madison (Wis.) Pub. Libr., 1967-68; libr. Prince Georges (Md.) County Schs., 1972-74; real estate investor Kent County, Md., 1976-93, Washington, 1979; propr. Creative Cookery, Chestertown, Md., 1979-83; law clk. Shapiro & Olander, Balt., 1996-97; sr. assoc. Ctr. for Support of Families, Chevy Chase, Md., from 1996. Author: (with others) Year 2000 Family Law Update, 1999; contbr. articles to profl. jours. Chair Internat. Orgn. Family Rights Group, Washnigton, 1998-99; bd. dirs. Montgomery County NOW, Md., 1999—; mem. adv. bd. Divorce Roundtable, Montgomery County, 1999—. Mem. ABA (internat. com. chair family law sect. 1999—), Md. Bar Assn., Montgomery County Bar Assn., Women's Bar Assn. Roman Catholic. Home: Bethesda, Md. Died June 1, 2004.

ATZEFF, EFRODITA, fraternal organization administrator; b. Visheni, Kostur, Macedonia, Feb. 12, 1912; came to U.S., 1916; d. Atanas Thomas and Helena (Pandorff) Lebamoff; m. Peter George Atzeff, Oct. 27, 1935 (dec. Sept. 1982); 1 child, Doris Ellen Reynolds. Student, Internat. Bus. Coll., 1931, Ind. U., 1937, 38, 39, 40, Butler U., 1937. Sec. cen. com. Macedonian Patriotic Orgn. of U.S., Can., Australia, Brazil, and Belgium, Ft. Wayne, Ind., 1989-96. Mem. Macedonian Patriotic Orgn. of U.S., Can., Australia, Belgium and Brazil (pres., sec., treas. Kostur chpt. 1934—), Ft. Wayne Philharm. Soc., Ft. Wayne Mus. Art. Avocations: stamp collector, memorabilia. Home: Fort Wayne, Ind. Died Apr. 4, 2004.

AUBINEAU, DIANE, advertising executive; b. Cedar Rapids, Iowa, Aug. 30; d. Myron Julius and Fay (Smith) A. BA, Stanford U. Free-lance portrait painter, San Francisco; designer, editor statewide pubs. U. Calif., Berkeley, Calif.; dir. advt. and sales promotion Addison-Wesley Pub. Co., Menlo Park, Calif.; prin. Aubineau Advt., San Mateo, Calif. Cons. in field. Designer, illustrator: A Family Guide to the San Francisco Bay Area, 1965; rschr. Here Today, San Francisco's Architectural Heritage, 1969; editor, designer: The Secret to Getting Money, 1992. Dir. Vis. Nurse Assn., San Mateo County, Calif., 1980, Stanford Bay Area Singles Club, Stanford, Calif., 1987; mem. sustaining coun. Jr. League San Francisco, 1988—, chair sustainers spring sem., 1996, co-chair sustainers 1999-2000; founder, chair activities Sometimes on Sunday; dir. Woodlake Assn., San Mateo, 1996-98, chair resident rels., 1996, chair nominating com., 1996, sec., 1997-98. San Francisco Art Inst. scholar. Avocation: painting. Home: San Mateo, Calif. Died May 18, 2005.

AUGUSTINE, KATHY MARIE, former state senator, former state official; b. LA, May 29, 1956; d. Philip Blase and Katherine Alice (Thompson) A.; 1 child, Dallas; m. Chaz Higgs, Sept. 12, 2003. AB, Occidental Coll., 1977; MPA, Calif. State U., Long Beach, 1983. Flight attendant Continental Airlines, Houston, 1978-83; crew scheduler Delta Airlines, L.A., 1983-88; tchr. Diocese of Reno/Las Vegas, 1990-96; mem. Nev. Assembly, 1992-94, Nev. Senate, 1994-98; contr. State of Nev., Carson City, 1999—2002. Mem. Nev. State Bd. Fin. Mem. Rep. Women's Club, Las Vegas, Nev., 1992-2006; former coun. of State Govts. West, chair elec. restructuring. Recipient Achievement award Bank of Am., Calif., 1974, Achievement Medallion Am. Legion, 1974, Congressional Internship grantee, Washington, 1975, Disting. Alumni award Calif. State U. Long Beach, 1997, Cmty. Appreciation award Frontier Girl Scout Coun., 1996, Svc. Excellence award Rep. Legis. of Yr., 1998; named Italian Am. of Yr., Augustus Soc. of So. Nev., 2003. Mem.: AAUW, Govt. Finance Officers Assn., Dept. Transp. Exec. Br. Audit Com. (bd. dirs., bd. fin.), Nat. Assn. State Auditors, Comptrollers and Treasurers, Jr. League of Las Vegas. Republican. Roman Catholic. Home: Reno, Nev. Died July 11, 2006.

AURNESS, CRAIG MICHAEL, photographer; b. L.A., Nov. 20, 1946; s. James K. and Virginia (Chapman) A.; m. Daphne Bowen, Feb. 9, 1974; children: Brian, Holly. BA, Prescott Coll., 1970. Freelance photographer Sunset mag., Menlo Park, Calif., 1971-75, Atlantic Richfield, L.A., 1972-78, Nat. Geog., Washington, 1978-88; prin. owner West Light, L.A., from 1978. Photographer, author: (photo books) Iowa: Americas Heartland, 1982, California: the Golden State, 1986, Colorado, 1987. Mem. Picture Agy. Coun. Am., Am. Soc. Mag. Photographers, Nat. Press Photographers Assn. (v.p. local chpt. 1982, Picture of Yr. award 1982), Am. Soc. Travel Writers. Home: Los Angeles, Calif. Died Dec. 14, 2004.

AUSTIN, CHARLES LOUIS, software engineer; b. Seattle, Jan. 26, 1948; s. Louis Claude and Jean (Harbaugh) A. BA, U. Puget Sound, 1970; MBA, Golden Gate U., 1975; postgrad., MIT, 1988. Dep. dir., mobilization systems Office of Sec. of Defense, Pentagon, Washington, 1983-85, dir., mobilization systems, 1986-87, dir., tech. mgmt., 1985-86, dir., program analysis, 1987-89; dir. Command Systems Integration Agy., Pentagon, Washington, 1989-92; program exec. officer Standard Army Mgmt. Info. Systems, Ft. Belvoir, Va., from 1992. Capt. USAF, 1970-77. Mem. Armed Forces Comms. and Electronics Assn., Assn. of the U.S. Army. Achievements include development of numerous state of the art command and control technologies. Died Jan. 7, 2005.

AUSTIN, DAVID LEONARD, II, bishop; b. Tampa, Fla., Nov. 19, 1928; s. David Leonard Sr. and Lula (Thompson) A.; m. Elnora Sanders, Sept. 22, 1956; children: Susan, David Leonard III, Kathy, Bernadett. Student, CCNY, 1948-50; D in Evangelism, Fuller Theol. Sem., 1960. Mem. dept. Evangelism Gen. Ch., 1950, exec. sec., 1950-65, 1st conv. chmn. Evangelism dept., from 1969, 1st v.p.; founder Maranatha Ch., L.A., from 1976, Assemblies of God in Christ, L.A., from 1989. Founder 14 other chs. and missions, 1953—; bishop Cen. Ky. Chs. of God in Christ, 1966-71. Author: Doing the Work of an Evangelism; contbr. articles to profl. jours.; composer ch. music. First presiding bishop, Assemblies of God in Christ. Home: Livermore, Calif. Died Dec. 19, 2004.

AUSTIN, GLENN, retired pediatrician, researcher; b. Richmond, Calif., July 5, 1921; s. Albert Buckley Austin and Laura Roxanne Lakamp; m. Olive Edna Thomas; children: Carla, Linda, Glenn L., Starr. AB, U.Calif. Berkeley, 1943; MD, Stanford U., 1952. Instr. parisitology U.S. Army, San Antonio, 1945; pub. health bacteriologist State of Calif., Berkeley, 1946; gen. practice Mine Worker's Union, Harlan County, Ky., 1952—54; chief resident O.P. Clin. Cin. Children's Med. Ctr., 1954—56; pvt. practice Los Altos, Calif., 1956—2000; ret., 2000. Exec. dir. Nat. Fedn. Pediat. Soc., 1955—60; pres. Family Med. Clinical El Camino, Mt. View, Calif., 1993—2000, Calif. Primary Care Network, Los Altos, Calif., 1995—99. Author: The Parents guide to Child Raising, 1978, The Parents Medical Manual, 1978, Love and Power- Parent and Child, 1988, 2nd, edit., 1993, Grandparenting for the 90's, 1990, An Innovative Proposal for the Health Care Financing System of the United States, 2003; contbr. articles to profl. jour. Chmn. Com. Child Health Financing, 1978—81; alt. del. centra Com. Rep., Santa Clara, Calif., 1998—2000; del. Calif. Med. Assoc., 1978—95. Recipient Santa Clara County Med. Soc. award for Outstanding Contbn. in Cmty. Svc., Cert. of Honor, Am. Acad. of Pediat. Mem.: AMA (del. 1981—83, mem. workgroup costs. health policy agenda 1982—86), Am. Acad. Pediat. (pres. 1981—82). Republican. Presbyn. Died Apr. 11, 2005.

AUSTIN, JAMES ALBERT, healthcare executive, obstetrician-gynecologist; b. Phoenix, Sept. 23, 1931; s. Albert Morris and Martha Lupkin (Mercer) Austin; m. Margaret Jeanne Arnold, July 26, 1952 (div. 1978); children: Cynthia Milee Ludgin, Lauri Jeanne Fuller, Wendy Patrice Rea; m. Sandra Lee Marsh, Jan. 3, 1979 (div. 1992); m. Sharon Marie Reichle, Sept. 9, 1993. BA, U. So. Calif., 1952; MD, George Wash. U., 1956; MBA, Pepperdine U., 1991. Diplomate Am. Bd. Ob-Gyn., Am. Bd. Med. Mgmt. Intern U.S. Naval Hosp., Bethesda, Md., 1956-57, resident in ob-gyn, 1957-60; ob-gyn. Washington Gynecologists, Washington, 1966-69; pres. Ariz. Obstetrics and Gynecology Ltd., Phoenix, 1969-79; chmn. dept. ob-gyn. USN, Agana Hgts., Guam, 1979-81; ob-gyn. Sanger Med. Group, Coronado, Calif., 1981-83; chmn. ob-gyn. FHP Corp., Salt Lake City, 1983-84, assoc. med. dir., 1984-85, hosp. med. dir. Fountain Valley, Calif., 1985-86, assoc. v.p. med. affairs, 1987-90; chief exec. officer Ultra Link Nationwide HMO Network, Costa Mesa, Calif., 1990-93; chief med. officer Downey (Calif.) Community Hosp., 1993-94; sr. advisor FHP Internat. Cons. Group, Costa Mesa, Calif., from 1995; med. dir. So. Calif. Prudential HealthCare Plan of Calif., 1995-97; v.p. Care Continuum, Inc., from 1995; med. dir. Primary Provider Mgmt. Co., Riverside, Calif., 1998—2001, Western Med. Mgmt. LLC, Irvine, Calif., from 2001. Clin. prof. ob-gyn. George Wash. U., Georgetown, Washington, 1966-69; asst. clin. prof. U. Calif. San Diego, 1981-83, U. Utah, Salt Lake City, 1983-85. Ret. rear adm. USN, 1956—88. Fellow Am. Coll. Ob-Gyn.; mem.

AMA (life), Am. Coll. Physician Execs., Ariz. Med. Assn. (bd. dirs. 1978), Am. coll. Physician Execs. Republican. Presbyterian. Home: Sunset Beach, Calif. Died Nov. 12, 2004.

AVERY, KEITH WILLETTE, artist, educator; b. Lansing, Michigan, Dec. 3, 1921; s. Norton Louis and Ruby Mae (Willette) A.; m. Carol Joyce (Haddan), Oct. 10, 1946; children: Carleton Louis, David Keith, Jane Ellen (Avery-)Gray. BS, N. Mex. State U., 1955, LittD (hon.), 1986. Cert. secondary edn. tchr., N.Mex., Ariz., and Mich. Horse trainer, exhibitor A.B. Johnson Chevrolet Co., Grand Rapids, Mich., 1946-47; ranch foreman, horse trainer Lazy U Ranch, Bartlesville, Okla., 1949-50, Mill Iron Lazy 3 Ranch, Carrizozo, N.Mex., 1950-51; artist N.Mex. State U., Las Cruces, 1951-55; instr. and calf roping coach Judson Sch., Scottsdale, Ariz., 1955-59; instr. Lowell High Sch., Mich., 1961-74; artist and horseman Springer, and Roswell, N.Mex., from 1974. Dir. alumni rels., N. Mex. State U., Las Cruces, 1959-60. Author: Ridden Hard and Put Up Wet, 1990, Campfire Echoes, 1994, (biography) Trails of a Wanderer, 1995; Represented in permanent collections Woolaroc Mus., Barttesville, Okla. Served in U.S. Air Force, 1942-46. Named to Cowboy Hall of Fame; recipient Champion Working Stock Horse, Nat. Horse Show Assn., Chgo., 1946, Gold, Silver and Bronze medals, Phippen Invitational Art Show, Prescott, Ariz., 1978, Stetson Hat award, Tex. Cowboy Artist Gold Medal Exhibit, San Angelo, Tex., 1983, Best of Show Painting award, S.W. Regional Art Show, Roswell, 1982, Gov.'s award of excellence and achievement in the arts as dean of N.Mex. cowboy poets and premier painter of the working cowboy, 1994, rep. N.Mex. Cowboy Poetry gathering, NEA, Elko., Nev., 1986, all poetry to archives, Cowboy Hall of Fame, Oklahoma City, 2002, We. Art award, Nat. Cowboy Symposium, Lubbock, Tex., 2003, Am. Cowboy Culture award, Western Art Nat. Cowboy Symposium, Lubbock, Tex., 2003. Republican. Methodist. Home: Roswell, N.Mex. Died June 27, 2005.

AVERY, RONALD DENNIS, school psychologist; b. Passaic, N.J., Oct. 24, 1940; s. George Anthony and Ethel (Nikovits) A.; children: George Anthony Jr., Ronald Dennis. BA in English, Calif. State U., 1970, MA in Secondary Edn., 1972; MS in Psychology, U.S. Internat. U., 1978, PhD in Profl. Psychology, 1977. Cert. psychologist, tchr., Calif. Tchr. reading Lynwood (Calif.) H.S., 1971-78, Lynwood Adult Sch., 1972-74; instr. bus. English and comm. L.A. C.C., 1973-84; tchr., reading specialist Hosler Jr. H.S., Lynwood, 1984-86, 88-94; tchr. Roosevelt Elem. Sch., Lynwood, 1986-87; sch. psychologist Lynwood Unified Sch. Dist., from 1994. Instr. psychology U.S. Internat. U., San Diego, 1975, Calif. Am. U., San Diego, 1976-77; pvt. practice clin. psychology, L.A., 1978—; clin. psychologist Claif. Youth Authority, Southern Reception Ctr., Norwalk, L.A., 1978, 94, Calif., 1980-82; sch. psychologist, Nellis, Whittier and Norwalk, 1993-94; expert witness Calif. Jud. Sys., L.A. and Orange Counties, 1978—. With USAF, 1960-61. Mem. Calif. Assn. Sch. Psychologists (Outstanding Sch. Psychologist Los Angeles County/Region V), Lynwood Tchrs. Assn. (chmn. grievance com. 1974, pres. 1975), KC, Phi Delta Kappa. Republican. Roman Catholic. Avocations: beach activities, fishing, hiking. Died July 14, 2005.

AVILA, ARTHUR JULIAN, metallurgical engineer; b. Hoboken, N.J., July 9, 1917; s. Michael Angel and Caroline Elizabeth (Bauman) A.; m. Mary Noreen DeMartino, Oct. 23, 1948; children: Susan Ekkebus, Philip, Stephen, John. BSCE, NYU, 1946; MS in Metallurgy, Stevens Inst. Tech., 1952. cert. profl. chem. and metall. cons., N.J. Prodn. engr. Western Electric Co., Kearny, N.J., 1943-57, sr. staff engr. Chgo., 1967-72; rsch. supr. W.E. Engring. Rsch. Ctr., Princeton, N.J., 1957-67; tech. dir. TRW Cinch, Chgo., Elk Grove, Ill., 1973-74; cons. Avila Engring. Svcs., Des Plaines, Ill., from 1974. Author: Production Pulse Plating, 1984; co-author: Theory and Practice of Pulse Plating, 1986; patentee in field. Commr. Cub Scouts, Middlesex, N.J. 1970; chmn. Boy Scouts Am., Middlesex, 1971-72; chmn. Cath. Youth Orgn. St. Mary's Parish, Flemington, N.J., 1960-65. Mem. Am. Soc. Metals, Am. Electroplaters Soc. Died Apr. 30, 2005.

AVRAM, HENRIETTE DAVIDSON, librarian, retired federal official; b. N.Y.C., Oct. 7, 1919; d. Joseph and Rhea (Olsho) Davidson; m. Herbert Mois Avram, Aug. 23, 1941; children: Lloyd, Marcie, Jay. Student, Hunter Coll., N.Y.C., George Washington U.; ScD (hon.), So. Ill. U., 1977; DLitt (hon.), Rochester Inst. Tech., 1991; DSc (hon.), U. Ill., 1993. Systems analyst, methods analyst, programmer Nat. Security Agy., 1952-59; systems analyst Am. Rsch. Bur., 1959-61, Datatrol Corp., 1961-65; supervisory info. systems specialist Libr. of Congress, Washington, 1965-67, asst. coord. info. systems, 1967-70, chief MARC Devel. Office, 1970-76, dir. Network Devel. Office, 1976-80, dir. processing systems, network and automation planning, 1980-83, asst. libr. for processing svcs., 1983-89, assoc. libr. Collection Svcs., 1989-92, chmn. network adv. com., 1981-92, chmn. emerita network adv. com., 1992—2006. Chair subcom. 2 sectional com. Z39 Am. Nat. Standards Inst., 1966-80, RECON Working Task F, 1968-73, Internat. Rels. Round Table, 1986-87, subcom. 4 working group 1 on character sets Internat. Orgn. for Standardization, 1971-80; lectr. sch. of info. and libr. sci. Cath. U. Am., Washington, 1973-80, com. mem. strategies for 80's, 1980-81; bd. visitors libr. and learning resources com., 1980; mem. internat. standards coord. com. Info. Sys. Standards Bd., 1983-86; del. to U.S. nat. com. UNESCO/Gen. Info. Program, 1983; chair internat. rels. com. Nat. Info. Standards Orgn., 1983-92. Bd. editors: Jour. Library Automation, 1970-72; contbr. articles to profl. jours. Recipient Superior Svc. award Libr. of Congress, 1968, Margaret Mann citation, 1971, Fed. Woman's award, 1974, Achievement award ALA/Libr. Info. Tech. Assn., 1980, Meritorious Svc. award ANSI, 1992, Disting. Exec. Svc. award Fed. Govt., 1990; co-recipient Rsch. Libr. of Yr. award Assn. Coll. and Rsch. Libr. Acad., 1979. Fellow Internat. Fedn. Libr. Assns. and Instns. (chair working group on content designators 1972-77, chair profl. bd. 1979-81, mem. program mgmt. com. 1983-90, mem. exec. bd. 1983-87, 1st v.p. 1985-87); mem. ALA (bd. dirs., past pres. info sci. and automation div., John Ames Humphrey Forest Press award 1990, Melvil Dewey award 1981, Lippincott award 1988, Hon. Membership award 1997), Am. Soc. Info. Sci. (spl. interest group on libr. automation and networks 1965), Spl. Librs. Assn. (Recognition award 1990), Assn. Libr. and Info. Sci. Edn. (Libr. of Congress disting. svc. award 1992), Assn. Bibliog. Agys. Gt. Britain, Australia, Can. and U.S. (del. 1977-2006). Home: California, Md. Died Apr. 22, 2006.

AXTELL, CLAYTON MORGAN, JR., lawyer; b. Deposit, N.Y., Aug. 4, 1916; s. Clayton Morgan and Olive Aurora (Vosburgh) A.; m. Margaret Williamson Ritchie, Apr. 24, 1943 (dec.); children: Margaret R. Axtell Stevenson, Clayton Morgan III, Karen R. Axtell Arnold, Susan R. Axtell. AB, Cornell U., 1937, JD, 1940. Bar: N.Y. 1940, U.S. Dist. Ct. (no. dist.) N.Y. 1941, U.S. Supreme Ct. 1964. Assoc. Hinman, Howard & Kattell, Binghamton, N.Y., 1940-48, ptnr., from 1948. Former mem. adv. bd. First-City Nat. Bank, Binghamton; bd. dirs. Farmers Nat. Bank, Deposit, N.Y., First City Nat. Bank, Binghamton. Pres. N.Y. State Sch. Bd. Attys., Albany, 1962-63, Broome County Bar Assn., Binghamton, 1967-68, Conrad and Virginia Klee Found., 1977-2003; mem. N.Y. State Rep. Com., Binghamton, 1988-93. 1st lt. US Army, 1942-46 ETO. Decorated Bronze Star U.S. Army, 1945, Croix de Guerre, Govt. of France, 1945; recipient Disting Svc. award U.S. Jr. C. of C., 1942; named Young Man of Yr. Binghamton Jr. C. of C., 1949. Mem. ABA, N.Y. State Bar Assn., Hillcrest -Port Dick Kiwanis (past pres.), Binghamton Club. Republican. Lutheran. Died Dec. 24, 2004.

AYOTTE, GASTON ARTHUR, JR., accountant; b. Woonsocket, R.I., Dec. 30, 1933; s. Gaston Arthur Sr. and Idalie (Donneau) A.; m. Diana Aurore Beauregard, Sept., 26, 1953; children: Paul Charles, Peter John. AS, Bryant Coll., 1975. Cost acct. Whitins Machine Works, Whitinsville, Mass., 1951-56; sales mgr. I. Medoff Co., Woonsocket, 1956-64; salesperson Marcoux Bros. Inc., Woonsocket, 1964-67; pub. acct. Gaston A. Ayotte & Sons, Inc., Woonsocket, from 1968. Mayor City of Woonsocket, 1981-85, mem. city coun., 1961-81, mem. sch. com., 1989-91; gen. chmn. Autumnfest, Woonsocket, 1982-88. Democrat. Roman Catholic. Home: Lincoln, RI. Died Jan. 23, 2005.

AYOUB, ELIA M., pediatrician; b. Haifa, Israel, Apr. 12, 1928; came to U.S., 1956; s. Moussa Assad and Victoria A.; m. Louba Cattan, May 1, 1954; children: Hala, Steven, Gregory, Jeffrey, Paul. BS, Am. U. Beirut, 1949, MD, 1953. Diplomate Am. Bd. Pediats. Physician Trans Arabian Pipeline Co., Beirut, 1953-56; instr. U. Minn., Mpls., 1959-62, asst. prof., 1962-67, assoc. prof., 1967-69; prof. U. Fla., Gainesville, 1969-94, distinguished prof., from 1994. Guest investigator Rockefeller U., N.Y.C., 1963-65; mem. study sect. NIH, Washington, 1985-89; pres. Fla. chpt. Am. Heart Assn., St. Petersburg, 1988-89; adv. commn. UPHS, Washington, 1989-91. Author chpts. in books; contbr. articles to profl. jours. Recipient Gold award Am. Heart Assn., Fla., 1981, Distinguished Svc. award 1989. Fellow Am. Rheumatism Assn., Am. Acad. Pediats.; mem. Am. Pediat. Soc. (coun. chmn. 1982-85), Am. Soc. Clin. Investigators, Am. Soc. Microbiology, Soc. Pediat. Rsch. Home: Gainesville, Fla. Died Apr. 4, 2004.

BABU, SATHYA M., youth services facility administrator; b. Quilon, India, Aug. 23, 1930; s. Madhavan and Gomathy Govindan; m. Michele M., Apr. 21, 1968; two children. BA, U. Kerala, 1950; MA, Banaras Hindu U., 1953, U. Va., 1963; PhD, U. Wis., 1968. Tchr. Sivagiri H.S., India, 1950-51; lectr. S.N. Coll., Quilon, 1953-62; instr. Mt. Mary Coll., Milw., 1966-68; asst. prof. English dept. S.N. Coll., 1968-73; program mgr., interim exec. dir. Urban League, Racine, Wis., 1973-82; bus. cons. Robinson & Assocs., Racine, 1982-84; exec. dir. Taylor Home, Inc., Racine, from 1984. Editor: Perspectives: An Anthology of English Prose, 1970. Mem. Wis. Assn. Families & Children. Home: Racine, Wis. Died Jan. 2, 2004.

BACHE, GERALD MICHAEL, financial planner; b. Bronxville, N.Y., Sept. 20, 1927; s. Frank Semon and Helen Elizabeth (Rosenbaum) B.; m. Eleanor Maria Krout, Jan. 28, 1954; children: Marion Dorothy, Stephen Kenneth, Vivian Louise Quam. BA, Yale U., 1949; LLB, Harvard U., 1952; cert., Coll. Fin. Planning, 1986. Fgn. svc. officer U.S. Dept. of State, 1951-58, 61-82; with Bache & Co., N.Y.C., 1958-61; acct. exec. Prudential-Bache Securities, Washington, 1982-89; v.p. Yosemite Asset Mgmt., Washington & Lavallette, N.J., 1989-92, Hamilton & Bache, Lavallette, from 1992. Author brochure: Ivory Coast: A Market for U.S. Products, 1966. Cellist McLean (Va.) Symphony Orch., 1981-90, Garden St. Philharmonic, Toms River, N.J., 1992—, treas., 1997—. Cpl. U.S. Army, 1946-47. Mem. Diplomatic and Consular Officers Retired, Yale Club. Avocation: cello. Home: Lavallette, NJ. Died Aug. 8, 2005.

BACHMAN, JOHN REED, sales management motivator; b. Cleve., June 6, 1921; s. Reed Ernst Bachman and Ann Augusta Schantz; m. Rosemary Jamison (div. Feb. 1973); m. Charelene Ross, Mar. 29, 1973; children: Nancy Claire, Jamison Reed. BA, U. Mich., 1942. Airline pilot, capt. TACA, San Jose, Calif., 1946, Modern Air, Miami, Fla., 1946-47; salesman Brown & Bigelow, St. Paul, sales mgmt. staff San Diego, Chgo., sales tng. dir. St. Paul, v.p. nat. accounts program. Lt. USN, 1942-45. Mem. LaGorce C.C. (bd. mem. 1975-76), Indian Creek C.C. Republican. Avocations: golf, playing bridge, gin and rummy. Home: Bal Harbour, Fla. Died Aug. 5, 2005.

BACHTEL, ANN ELIZABETH, educational consultant, researcher, educator; b. Winnipeg, Man., Can., Dec. 12, 1928; d. John Wills. and Margaret Agnes (Gray) Macleod; m. Richard Earl Bachtel, Dec. 19, 1947 (dec.); children: Margaret Ann, John Macleod, Bradley Wills; m. Louis Philip Nash, June 30, 1978 (div. 1987). AB, Occidental Coll., 1947; MA, Calif. State U., L.A., 1976; PhD, U. So. Calif., 1988. Cert. life tchr., adminstr., Calif. Elem. tchr. various pub. and pvt. schs., Calif., 1947-50, 64-77; dir. emergency sch. aid act program, spl. projects, spl. art State of Calif., 1977-80; leader, mem. program rev. team Calif. State Dept. Edn., 1981-85; cons. Pasadena Unified Sch. Dist., 1981-85. Cons. Pasadena Unified Sch. Dist., 1981-86; tchg. asst., adj. prof. U. So. Calif.; cons., presenter in field. Editor: Arts for the Gifted and Talented, 1981; author Nat. Directory Programs for Artistically Gifted and Talented Students K-12; contbr. articles to profl. jours. Active legis. task forces; chair resource allocation com. City of Pasadena, 1982-90; mem. Pasadena-Mishima (Japan) Sister Cities Internat. Com., 1983—; asst. chair Pasadena-Jarvenpaa, Finland, 1990-92, chair, 1992-95; asst. chair Pasadena-Mishima, 1996-97; active L.A. World Affairs Coun., Bonita Unified Sch. Dist. Curriculum Coun., 1990-93, Dist. Task Force Fine Arts, 1990-93, Dist. Task Force Tech., 1990-93, Dist. Handwriting Task Force, 1993, Pasadena Hist. Soc., Pasadena Philharm. Com., Womens Com. Pasadena Symphony Assn.; deacon Pasadena Presbyn. Ch., 1989-92, elder, 1997-2000; vice-moderator Presbyn. Women, 2000—; bd. govs. Occidental Coll. Alumni Assn., 2000—04. Emergency Sch. Aid Act grant, 1977-81; named to Bonita Unified Sch. Dist. Hall of Fame, 1990-91. Mem. World Coun. Gifted and Talented Children, Internat. Soc. Edn. Through Art, Nat. Art Educators Assn. (dels. assembly 1988-92), L.A. County Art Edn. Coun., Clan MacLeod Soc. (bd. dirs. So. Calif. chpt.), Phi Delta Kappa, Kappa Delta Pi, Pi Lambda Theta (pres. L.A. chpt. 1991-95, nat. rsch. awards com. 1989-91, chair 1991-95, co-pres. region V 1993-97, Ella Victoria Dobbs Nat. Rsch. award 1989, Outstanding Pi Lambda Thetan in region V 1993-95, Internat. by-laws com. 1999-2003), Assistance League Pasadena. Died Mar. 17, 2006.

BACON, GEORGE HUGHES, JR., retired systems analyst; b. Phila., Mar. 4, 1935; s. George Hughes Sr. and Alice Olive (Campbell); divorced; children: Christopher Scott, Melissa Anne Hinkle. BA in English Lit. and Music, Temple U., 1957; MS in Ednl. Adminstrn., U. Pa., 1968. Computer programmer 1st Pa. Bank, Phila., 1960-62; tchr. Bucks County, Pa., 1962-72; assoc. dir. Kranzley and Co., Cherry Hill, NJ, 1973-74; computer programmer Phila. Nat. Bank, 1975-77; cons. Sci. and Computer Tech. Inc., Malvern, Pa., 1978-79; lead systems analyst Ednl. Testing Svc., Princeton, NJ, 1979-86. Cons., lectr. computer literacy and software Abington (Pa.) Pub. Libr., 1983-84, Jenkintown (Pa.) Music Sch., 1984, Fudan U., Shanghai, China, 1985 Vol. aide Mercer County Geriatric Unit, Lawrenceville, N.J., 1986, Holy Redeemer Hosp., Meadowbrook, Pa., 1988-98, Rydal Park Retirement Home, 1999—; cons. Abington Sch. Bd., 1989-98; tutor Abington Pub. Libr. Literacy Project, 1988; mem. headmaster's coun. Am. Boychoir, Princeton, 1987, Abington Presbyn. Ch. Mem. Temple U. Coll. Arts and Scis. Alumni Assn., U. Pa. Grad. Sch. Edn. Alumni Assn., Phila. Orch. Assn., Friends of Princeton U. Avocations: films, public television and radio, classical music, reading. Home: Rydal, Pa. Died 2006.

BADAL, DANIEL WALTER, psychiatrist, educator; b. Lowellville, Ohio, Aug. 22, 1912; s. Samuel S. and Angelina (Jessen) Badal; m. Julia Lovina Cover, June 1939 (dec. May 1968); children: Petrina Badal Gardner, Julia Badal Graf, Peter C.; m. Eleanor Bosworth Spitler, Sept. 5, 1969 (dec. Feb. 1994). AB, Case Western Res. U., 1934, MD, 1937. Resident in medicine, neurology and psychiatry Peter Bent Brigham Hosp., Mass. Gen. Hosp., Boston City Hosp., 1937-41; fellow in psychiatry and neurology Harvard U., Boston, 1941-45; asst. prof. psychiatry Washington U., St. Louis, 1945; mem. faculty Sch. Medicine Case Western Res. U., Cleve., from 1946, assoc. clin. prof. emeritus psychiatry, from 1983; practice medicine specializing in psychiatry and psychoanalysis Cleve., 1955—2002; ret., 2002. Mem. faculty Cleve. Psychoanalytic Inst., from 1975. Author: Treatment of Depression and Related Moods, 1988, 2d edit., 2006, Treatment of Chronic Depression, 2003, Treating Chronic Depression--Psychotherapy and Medication, 2003; contbr. articles to profl. jours. Fellow NRC Office Sci. R&D, 1941—45. Fellow: Am. Psychiat. Assn. (cert. Excellence Tchg. 1999), Internat. Psychoanlytic Assn. (life); mem.: AMA, Cleve. Psychoanalytic Soc. (pres. 1963), Phila. Assn. Psychoanalysis, Am. Psychoanalytic Soc., Acad. Medicine Cleve., Cleve. Psychiat. Soc., Ohio Med. Assn. Died Apr. 6, 2006.

BAGGER, RALPH WILLIAM, minister; b. Butler, Pa., June 12, 1923; s. Henry Horneman and Margaret (Finck) B.; m. Elizabeth Louise Hodges, Aug. 26, 1950 AB summa cum laude, Muhlenberg Coll., 1948; BD, Luth. Theol. Sem., Phila., 1951; AM, U. Pa., 1951. Ordained to ministry United Luth. Ch. in Am. (now Evang. Luth. Ch. in Am.), 1951. Pastor St. Mark's Luth. Ch., Allentown, Pa., 1951-55, Immanuel Luth. Ch., East Lansdowne, Pa., 1955-59, Friedens Luth. Ch., Hegins, Pa., 1959-68; periodicals and worship editor, bd. publ. Luth. Ch. Am., Phila., 1968-88; trustee Luth. Theol. Sem., Phila., from 1981. Author: (with Elizabeth H. Bagger) Official Summary of Biennial Conventions of United Lutheran Church in America, 1954-60, Official Summary of Biennial Conventions of Lutheran Church in America, 1964-84; editor: Light for Today, 1968-88, The Lessons, 1991. Charter mem. East Lansdowne (Pa.) Civic Assn., 1956-59. Sgt. AUS, 1943-46, ETO, PTO. Mem. Hymn Soc. Am., Omicron Delta Kappa. Home: Allentown, Pa. Died Jan. 18, 2005.

BAHNSEN, SHIRLEY ROESE (JANE BAHNSEN), artist, educator; b. Dayton, Ohio, May 2, 1934; d. Herbert B. and Jane Eloise (Povenmire) Roese; m. Chris J. Bahnsen, June 29, 1969. Student, San Diego State Coll., 1952-53; BA, UCLA, 1957; postgrad., San Diego State Coll., 1960-62; MAT, Ind. U., 1966; postgrad., No. Ill. U. Cert. lifetime secondary teaching credential in Iowa and Calif. Tech. illustrator Convair Astronautics, San Diego, Calif., 1952-53; comml. artist General Dynamics, San Diego, Calif., 1957-59, Tolle Advt. Agy., San Diego, 1959-60; teaching asst. dept. art Ind. U., Bloomington, Ind., 1964-66; comml. artist, tchr. Job Corps, Clinton, Iowa, 1966-68; instr. art Northeast Louisiana State Coll., Monroe, 1968-69; art tchr. The Bishop's Sch., La Jolla, Calif., 1962-64, The La Jolla Mus. of Art, 1962-64; instr. art Mt. St. Clare Coll., Clinton, Iowa, from 1979-. Exhibited fiber art various shows and galleries nationally and internationally, 1957—. Mem. Clinton Art Assn., Surface Design Assn, Am. Crafts Council, Iowa Designer Crafts Assn., Clinton Art Assn. (bd. dirs., nat. exhbn. selection com.). Died Mar. 8, 2005.

BAILEY, AMOS PURNELL, clergyman, journalist, writer; b. Grotons, Va., May 2, 1918; s. Louis William and Evelyn (Charnock) B.; m. Ruth Martin Hill, Aug. 22, 1942 (dec. 1992); children: Eleanor Carol Bailey Harriman, Anne Ruth Bailey Page, Joyce Elizabeth Bailey Richardson, Jeanne Bailey Dodge-Allen; m. Betty Lou Sheffield, Mar. 5, 1994. BA, Randolph-Macon Coll., 1942, DD, 1956; BD, Duke U., 1948; ThM, Union Theol. Sem., 1957; postgrad., Ecumenical Inst., Jerusalem, 1979. Ordained to ministry United Meth. Ch., 1942; pastor Emporia, Va., 1938, Beulah UMC Ch., Richmond, Va., 1938-43, New Kent circuit, 1943-44, Oak Grove United Meth. Ch., Norfolk, Va., 1948-50, Grace United Meth. Ch., Newport News, 1950-54, Centenary Ch., Richmond, 1954-61; supt. Richmond dist. United Meth. Ch., 1961-67; sr. minister Reveille Ch., Richmond, 1967-70; assoc. gen. sec., div. chaplains Bd. Higher Edn. and Ministry United Meth. Ch., Washington, 1970-79; v.p. Nat. Meth. Found., 1979-82; interim minister Herndon Ch., 1985-86; pres., CEO Nat. Temple Ministries, Inc., Fredericksburg, Va., from 1982. Pres. S.E.J. and S.C.U. Comms., 1968-76; dir. Reeves-Parvin Co., 1978-85; v.p. Va. Conf. Bd. Missions, 1955-61, Meth. Commn. Town and Country Work, 1956-67; mem. Meth. Commn. on Higher Edn., 1960-70, Meth. Interbd. Coun., 1960-70; del. Southeastern Jurisdictional Conf., 1964, 68, Gen. Conf., 1964, 66, 68, 70, World Meth. Conf., London, 1966, Denver, 1970, Dublin, 1976, Rio de Janeiro, 1996; exec. com. Congress, 1987-88; fin. com. Nat. Ch. Growth Rsch. Ctr., 1986-89; frequent chaplain U.S. Senate, U.S. Ho. of Reps., Va. Gen. Assembly; mem. coun., exec. com., pres. comms. com. Southeastern Jurisdiction, 1968-76; pres. Joint Comms. Com., 1968-76; vice chmn. Ministry to Svc. Pers. in East Asia, 1972-79; mem. Commn. on Interpretation, Va. Conf. Bd. Ordained Ministry, 1974-82; participant Ednl. Study Mission to Eng., 1988. Author: Daily Bread, 1997, Daily Bread, The Second Slice, 1999; syndicated columnist Daily Bread, 1945— (50th Anniversary award 1995), syndicated radio devotional, 1945-69; condr. weekly radio counseling program The Night Pastor, 1955-69, Sunshine and Shadows, 1967-70; contbr. articles to profl. jours. Mem. exec. com. Va. Conf. Bd. Edn., 1968-72; mem. World Meth. Coun., Va. Commn. Aging; pres. adv. bd. Richmond Welfare Dept., 1956-68, Va. Conf. Bd. Ministry, Richmond Pub. Assistance Com., Richmond Coun. Alcoholism, Citizen Adv. Bd. Duke U. Comprehensive Cancer Ctr., 1995-01; group chmn. industry divsn. Richmond United Givers Fund, 1961; chmn. chaplains adv. coun. VA, Washington; bd. mgrs. Richmond YMCA, 1961-69; bd. dirs. Va. Meth. Advisers; trustee Randolph-Macon Coll., 1960-82, trustee emeritus, 1986; bd. visitors Duke Div. Sch., 1964-70; trustee So. Sem., 1961-76. With Chaplains Corps AUS, 1945-47. Recipient Disting. Alumni award, Duke Div. Sch., 2001, honor for writing Daily Bread daily for 60 years, 2005; scholar A. Purnell Bailey Preministerial, Randolph-Macon Coll., 2002; Two Million Dollar scholar fund, 2002. Mem.: DAV (life), Duke Div. Alumni Assn. (pres.), Meth. Hist. Soc., Kiwanis, Kiwanis Club. Home: Fredericksburg, Va. Died July 16, 2006.

BAILEY, HARLEY EVAN, minister, principal; b. Glenville, W.Va., July 16, 1915; s. Herbert J. and Ervie E. (Stoneking) B.; m. Helen C. Kirkpatrick, June 29, 1935; children: Carolyn Sue Roush, Lynn L. McCormick. BA, Ohio U., 1945; D of Bibliology, Bible Bapt. Sem., 1949; DD, Burton Sem., 1952. Cert. tchr., W.Va., Ohio. Min. First Bapt. Ch., Williamstown, W.Va., 1945-50, Sistersville, W.Va., 1950-55; tchr. Chapmansville (W.Va.) High Sch., 1956-57, Belpre (Ohio) High Sch., 1957-58; prin., tchr. Morristown, W.Va., 1960-61, Alma, W.Va., 1962-63; tchr. Elizabeth, W.Va., 1963-64; min. Jefferson Bapt. Temple, Parkersburg, W.Va., from 1958. Past pres., bd. dirs. Wood County Sch. Bd. Del. Dem. Nat. Convention, 1964, 68, 76, 84; bd. mem. Red Cross, Parkersburg, 1946-48; treas. Community Chest, Williamstown, 1947-48; mem. PTA, Wood County, W.Va., 1991-92; assoc. mem. Fraternal Order of Police, W.Va., 1992. Capt. CAP, 1952-68. Mem. Masons, Order of Ea. Star, Woodmen of the World. Avocations: horse shoe pitching, softball, swimming, fishing, boating. Home: Parkersburg, W.Va. Died May 11, 2004.

BAILEY, LONA M., real estate company executive; b. Mar. 29, 1928; Recipient Real Estate Showcase Cape May County sales awards, 1977-83. Mem. Nat. Assn. Realtors (cert. residential specialist, residential brokerage mgr.), N.J. Assn. Realtors (grad. Realtor's Inst. 1977, Million Dollar Sales award, Gold Sales award 1986), Greater Wildwood-Cape May County Bd. Realtors (treas. 1980, 81, 2d v.p. 1982, 1st v.p., pres.-elect 1983, pres. 1984—). Home: Cape May, NJ. Died Aug. 13, 2005.

BAIRD, CONSTANCE HELEN, hospital administrator; b. Rockville Centre, N.Y., Aug. 23, 1947; d. Henry and Concetta (Carruba) McCArthy; children: Dawn Marie, Cynthia, Kevin. AAS, Suffolk County Community Coll., 1983; BSN, SUNY, Albany, 1984; MS in Nursing, SUNY, Stony Brook, 1986. RN, N.Y. Staff nurse Long Beach (N.Y.) Meml. Hosp., Southside Hosp., Bay Shore, N.Y., A.H.N. in psychiatry. Bd. dirs. Am. Cancer Soc. Mem. Sigma Theta Tau (honored by Matilda Cuomo and Vice Pres. Dan Quayle). Home: Great River, NY. Died Sept. 10, 2004.

BAKER, GEORGE FISHER, III, former investment banker; b. NYC, 1939; m. Marianna Johnson (div.); children: George, Johanna; m. Sarah Jones. AB, Harvard U., 1961, MBA, 1964. Gen. ptnr. Baker Nye Investments LP, N.Y.C., 1967—99; former mng. ptnr. Cambridge Capital Fund LP, N.Y.C.; CEO, chmn. Whitehall Corp., Dallas, 1991—2005. Sr. trustee George F. Baker Trust. Died Dec. 1, 2005.

BAKER, GORDON EDWARD, political science educator; b. Poughkeepsie, N.Y., Dec. 6, 1923; s. Gordon Denzil and Emma (Calhoun) B.; m. June Sharpe, Sept. 2, 1947; children: Jefferson, Leslie Marie. BA, Reed Coll., 1948; MA, U. Wash., 1949; postgrad., Brown U., 1950; PhD, Princeton U., 1952. Mem. faculty U. Calif., Santa Barbara, from 1952, prof. polit. sci., 1965-93, chmn. dept., 1965-71, prof. emeritus, from 1993. Dir. NEH seminars, 1979, 80; spl. cons., Calif., 1973, 91. Author: Rural Versus Urban Political Power, 1955, The Reapportionment Revolution, 1966; co-author: Free Government in the Making, 1985; contbr. chpts. in books and articles to profl. jours. Mem. 20th Century Fund Conf. Rsch. Scholars and Polit. Scientists in Legis. Apportionment, 1962. Served with AUS, 1943-46. Guggenheim fellow, 1969; Social Sci. Rsch. Coun. faculty rsch. fellow, 1962. Mem. Am. Polit. Sci. Assn. (coun. 1968-70, exec. com. 1968-69), Nat. Mcpl. League. Died Jan. 13, 2004.

BAKER, JAY MILTON, obstetrician/gynecologist; b. Honolulu, Oct. 2, 1949; s. Robert Leon and Betty Jo (Hill) B.; m. Susan Helen Hitner (div. June 7, 1993); 1 child, Caryn Allysa; m. Jacinthe Guindon, Apr. 18, 1998. BA, BS, U. Mo., 1977, MD, 1981. Diplomate Am. Bd. Obstetrics and Gynecology. Intern, resident in ob/gyn Naval Hosp., Portsmouth, Va., 1981-85, staff physician med. corps, 1985-92; asst. prof. ob/gyn Ea. Va. Med. Sch., Norfolk, from 1993. Fellow Am. Coll. Obstetrics and Gynecology; mem. Phi Kappa Phi, Alpha Omega Alpha. Avocations: camping, cycling, astronomy, chess, geology. Home: Virginia Beach, Va. Died Oct. 25, 2004.

BAKER, LEE WENDELL, retired public relations consultant; b. Bowen, Ill., Dec. 27, 1919; d. Samuel Albert and Ethel May (Nash) B.; m. George Ann McGreevy, June 9, 1945 (dec. Aug. 1972); Jean Hammond Otto, Nov. 23, 1973. BS, Bradley U., 1942. Pub. relations rep. Allis-Chalmers Corp., Milw., 1945-55, mgr., 1955-65; v.p. Owen King & Assocs., Milw., 1965-67; pres. Lee Baker Assocs., Milw., 1967-83, Denver, 1983-86. Reporter, editor UPI, 1942-45. Author: The Credibility Factor, 1993; contbr. articles to profl. jours.; mem. editl. rev. bd. Jour. Mass Media Ethics. Bd. dirs. Ballet Found. Milw., 1970-79, Artists Series at the Pabst, Milw., 1979-83, Wis. Consumer League, Madison, 1979-83, Colo. Ballet, 1984-90, Denver chpt. Am. Cancer Soc., 1986-93, Colo. divsn. 1993—; bd. dirs., sec. Found. Med. Care Evaluation, Milw., 1978-83; dir. cmty. rels. St. Mary's Acad., Cherry Hills Village, Colo., 1986-89. Mem. Pub. Rels. Soc. Am. (elected Coll. Fellows 1993, pres. Wis. chpt. 1965-66), Milw. Health Assn. (bd. dirs. 1964-77, pres. 1974), City Club Denver (bd. dirs. 1996—), Colo. Authors League. Home: Whitefish Bay, Wis. Died Feb. 12, 2005.

BAKER, ROBERT CARL, food science educator, consultant; b. Newark, N.Y., Dec. 29, 1921; s. Edward William and Frances Ellen (Houghtaling) B.; m. Jacoba Petronella Munson, Oct. 7, 1944; children: Dale, Kermit, Regina, Maureen, Johanna. BS, Cornell U., 1943; MS, Pa. State U., 1949; PhD, Purdue U., 1956. Asst. county agt. Orange County 4-H, 1945-46; asst. prof. poultry husbandry Pa. State U., 1946-49; asst. prof. poultry ext. Cornell U., Ithaca, N.Y., 1949-53, assoc. prof., 1953-56, prof. food sci., 1970-76, dir. Inst. Food Sci., 1956-70, chmn. dept. poultry sci. Cons. food cos. Contbr. numerous articles to sci. jours. Pres. Lansing Retirement Authority, Ithaca, N.Y. Methodist. Home: Groton, NY. Died Mar. 13, 2006.

BAKER, ROBERT K., computer systems consultant; b. Highland Park, Mich., Nov. 10, 1946; Student, Ind. U., 1972-82. Cert. computer programmer. Asst. dept. mgr. Van Camp, Howr & Iron, Indpls., 1974-77; cons. Paramid, Inc., Gaston, Oreg., from 1978; sr. systems programmer Tektronix, Inc., Beaverton, Oreg., 1984-87. Cons. Ind. U., Bloomington, 1979-81, 83-84, IBM, Harrisburg, Pa., 1986-87, UAR Egypt/US State Dept., Cairo, 1987-89, Nike, Inc., Beaverton, 1989-90. Author: (computer software) Paramid OS/2 Utilities, 1988; contbr. articles to profl. jours. Mem. Assn. for Computing Machinery, IEEE, Ind. Computer Cons. Assn., Elks. Died Jan. 21, 2005.

BAKER, RUTH HOLMES, retired secondary education educator; b. Tewksbury, Mass., July 8, 1922; d. William Angus and Anna Martha (Lynch) MacIntyre; m. William Otis Baker; children: Leigh Holmes Flannery, Bruce William, Christopher Doty, Douglas MacIntyre, Deborah Woodbury Black. BA, Tufts U., 1944; postgrad., U. Wyo., 1944-45, Union Theol. Sch., 1947-48, Columbia U., 1947-48. Cert. water safety instr. Instr. swimming ARC, Manchester-by-the-Sea, Mass., 1937-54, Wenham, Mass., from 1954; tchr., athletic dir. Shore Country Day Sch., Beverly, Mass., 1960-71, Gov. Dummer Acad., Byfield, Mass., 1972-79; tchr., coach Manchester-by-the-Sea H.S., Mass., 1980-83; bookstore and snack bar mgr. Pingree Sch., Hamilton, Mass., from 1984. Republican. Episcopalian. Home: Wenham, Mass. Died June 18, 2004.

BALDWIN, WILLIAM HOWARD, retired lawyer, foundation administrator; b. Detroit, Feb. 21, 1916; s. Howard Charles and Ruth E. (Jensen) B.; m. Carol Lees, May 24, 1947; children: Susan, Jeffrey (dec.), Julie, Deborah. BA, Williams Coll., 1938; JD, U. Mich., 1941. Bar: Mich. 1941. Ptnr. Dykema Gossett, Detroit, 1970-77, of counsel, from 1977; chmn., trustee Kresge Found., Troy, Mich., 1963-87. Asst. U.S. prosecutor Nuremburg Trials, 1946. Served with USAAF, 1942-45, lt. col. (ret.). Mem. ABA, Mich. Bar Assn. Republican. Episcopalian. Home: Vero Beach, Fla. Died Nov. 1, 2005.

BALINT, ANNETTE, church administrator; b. Scranton, Pa., July 26, 1948; d. Gerard Salvatore Casciano and Caroline Linda Sanzero; m. Michael Stephen Balint, Apr. 12, 1969. Student, Lacka Jr. Coll., Scranton. Supr. Bell Tel., Scranton, 1966—72; office mgr. Angelica Healthcare, Scranton, 1972—85; coord. Villa St. Joseph Diocese of Scranton, from 1985. Coord. Villa St. Joseph, Dunmore, Pa., 1971—2003. Contbr. articles to local newspapers. Vol. Am. Cancer Soc., 2000—03, Meml. Sloan Kettering, 2000—03; active Altar and Rosary Soc., Scranton, from 1966. Recipient Appreciation award, Am. Cancer Soc., 2003, Attitude award, NRCI, 2003. Mem.: Dem. Women, Cath. Women's Club (bd. mem. from 1982). Home: Scranton, Pa. Died Feb. 6, 2004.

BALL, CURT, actor, writer; b. Corydon, Ky., Sept. 14, 1931; s. Gobel Miller and Nannie Hugh Pirtle (King) B.; m. Belle Schnabel, Dec. 11, 1960. BA, Univ. Evansville, 1965; MA, Ill. State Univ., 1970. Producer, dir. J.B. Rogers Prod. Co., Fostoria, Ohio, 1957-61; freelance actor/writer, from 1951; teaching assoc. Ill. State Univ., Normal, 1969-70; comml. broadcast coach/instr. Mel Blanc & Assocs., Beverly Hills, Calif., 1975. Actor in numerous plays including The Merchant of Venice, The Inspector General, The Man Who Came to Dinner, Summer and Smoke, Idiots Delight, Witness for the Prosecution, Waltz of the Torreadores, Apple of His Eye, Nude With Violin, Once More with Feeling, The Phantom, The Rainmaker, Twelth Night, Antigone, The Goodwoman of Setzuan, The Gazebo, Banners of Steel, The Male Animal, Mary Mary, Barefoot in the Park, Arms and the Man, Marat Sade, Summer Tree, Death of a Salesman, Bus Stop, A Midsummer Night's Dream, Days of Wine and Roses, others; author: poems, fiction and reportage; announcer, actor numerous radio and TV commls; model number mags.; soundtrack recording work; dramatic reader with jazz groups. With USAF, 1951-53. Avocation: sports car racing. Home: Winnetka, Calif. Died Aug. 4, 2005.

BALLARD, ROBERT E., lawyer; b. Center, Tex., Feb. 27, 1936; s. Waymon E. and Effie Mae (Wheeler) B.; m. Eva Lea Oakley, Dec. 23, 1960; children: Lewis Andrew Ballard, Laura Elizabeth Brand-Ballard. BBA, U. Houston, 1960, LLB, 1967. Bar: Tex., U.S. Dist. Ct. (so. and ea. dist.) Tex., U.S. Ct. Appeals (5th cir.), U.S. Supreme Ct. Assoc. Arthur Andersen & Co., Houston, 1960-62; ptnr. Abraham Watkins Nichols Ballard & Friend, Houston, from 1962. Spl. prosecutor State Bar of Tex., Houston, 1993-94. Lt./cpl. USMC, 1960-65. Fellow Tex. Bar Found.; mem. Assn. Trial Lawyers Am., Tex. Trial Lawyers, Am. Bd. Trial Advocates, Houston Bar Assn. Democrat. Baptist. Avocation: motorcycles. Home: Houston, Tex. Died Mar. 10, 2004.

BALLEW, ANTHONY ROBERT, nurse; b. Coffeyville, Kans., July 11, 1952; s. Thomas James Ballew and Sue Ann (Hicks) Faulkner; m. Susan Coleen Turley, Oct. 8, 1955; children: Christopher, Tamara, Sean. Diploma in nursing, Good Samaritan Hosp. Sch. Nsg., Phoenix, 1973; BS in Health Svcs. Adminstrn., U. Phoenix, 1982; postgrad., Calif. Coast U., 1989-92. RN, Ariz. FNP Litton Saudi Arabia Ltd., Jeddah, Saudi Arabia, 1984, health svc. adminstr., 1985, mgr. health svcs., 1986-87; emergency dept. mgr. Mesa (Ariz.) Luth. Hosp., 1988; emergency room nurse practitioner Maricopa Med. Ctr., Phoenix, 1989; chief Emergency Svcs. Ltd., Mesa, Ariz., from 1989. Owner Holbrook (Ariz.) Emergency Med. Svcs., 1978-80; employee health nurse practitioner McDonnell Douglas Helicopters, 1989; pre-hosp. nurse S.W. Ambulance, 1989-90; family nurse practitioner Family Care Assocs., Mesa, 1989-95, Alta MEsa Med. Ctr., 1995—; emergency med. technician instr. Ariz. C.C. Bd., 1979—; contract DUI phlebotomist Mesa Police Dept., 1992—. Diver Maricopa County Sheriff's Office Diver's Posse, Phoenix, 1988-91, asst. tng. officer, 1992—; firefighter Rural/Metro Fire Dept., Scottsdale, Ariz., 1988-94, instr. dive team, 1988-94. Medictr. of Am. scholar, 1972; recipient Mesa Police Dept. Heroism award, 1993; named Citizen of Yr., Holbrook High Sch., 1980. Mem. ANA, Ariz. Nurses Assn., Ariz. Nurse Practitioners Coun. (program planning com. 1990-91, 92-93, sec. 1993—), Profl. Assn. Diving Instrs. (master scuba diver trainer). Republican. Mem. Lds Ch. Avocation: scuba diving. Died July 18, 2005.

BALLOU, LEONARD ROSS, archivist, educator; b. Staten Island, N.Y., May 19, 1926; s. John Jackson and Edna Nelson (De Hart) Ballou; m. Maude LeRita Williams, Feb. 15, 1949 (div. 1975); children: Joyce, Leonard Jr., Ronald-(dec.), Howard, Vicki. BA, Fisk U., 1949; MA, Va. State U., 1964; student, Ea. Sch. Music, 1949, Temple U., 1961—62, Coll. William and Mary, 1968. Mem. faculty Roanoke Theol. Sem., from 1995; organist various chs., 1950—2002; mem. faculty Elizabeth City U., from 1962. Chmn. Albemarle Commn., Hertford, NC, 1996; mem. jury commn. Pasquotank County; chmn. Mayor's Comprehensive Planning Task Force, 2001—02. Named Dir. of Yr., Elizabeth City Boys and Girls Club, 1988, Boss of Yr., Elizabeth City Office Personnel, 1981. Mem.: NC Assn. for Instl. Rsch., Elizabeth City Hist. Preservation Commn. (chmn. 1994—96), N.C. Assn. Instl. Rsch. (life; pres. 1986—87), Alpha Phi Alpha (life named Man of Yr. 1972, 1989). Avocations: coin collecting/numismatics, tropical fish. Home: Elizabeth City, NC. Died Apr. 23, 2004.

BALTUS, RITA KLEIBER, speech and social science educator; b. Escanaba, Mich., Mar. 21, 1925; d. Jay Joseph and Edith (Bailey) K.; m. John Robert, Sept. 14, 1946; children: Mary, John, Margaret, Joseph, Therese. BA, U. Mich., 1947; MA, U. Wis., 1968, PhD, 1983. Tchr. psychology and speech Northcentral Tech. Coll., Wausau, Wis., from 1962. Cons. adult edn., 1983—. Author: Personal Psychology for Life and Work, 1976, rev. edit. 1983, 88, 94. Mem. Am. Vocat. Assn., Wis. Vocat. Assn., Am. Assn. Adult and Continuing Edn., Delta Kappa Gamma, Pi Lambda Theta, Phi Delta Kappa, Sigma Alpha Lambda. Roman Catholic. Avocations: writing, reading, golf. Home: Wausau, Wis. Died Feb. 7, 2004.

BANK, MARJI D., actress; b. Dallas, Sept. 22, 1923; d. John and Rose (Kaufman) Doctoroff; m. Harvey Stuart Bank, Feb. 14, 1954 (dec. Dec. 1980); children: Roanne Bank, Heidi Sue Cairns. AA, U. Chgo., 1940; BS, Northwestern U., 1944. Performed at 24 theatres, including Kennedy Ctr., The Alley, Mo. Rep., Purdue U., Ind. Rep., Goodman Theater, Royal George Theatre, Ivanhoe Theatre, Peninsula Players, Northlight, Candlelight, Forum; lead actress in plays including Plaza Suite, 1973, Gingerbread Lady, 1973, Never Too Late, 1973, Promenade All, 1973, Man-in-the-Moon Marigolds, 1974, One Flew Over the Cuckoo's Nest, 1975, Saturday, Sunday, Monday, 1977, On Golden Pond, 1981, Driving Miss Daisy, 1988, Social Security, 1989, Lost in Yonkers, 1993; supporting credits include Shear Madness, 1982-99 (3350 appearances), The Perfect Ganesh, 1995, Uncle Vanya, 1990, Steel Magnolias, 1988, She Always Said Pablo, 1987, All My Sons, 1987, Les Belles Soeurs, 1982, Buried Child, 1980, The Big Knife, 1977, Hot L Balt., 1975, Streetcar named Desire, 1973, Our Town, 1973, Prisoner of 2d Ave, 1974, House of Blue Leaves, 1972, Cat on a Hot Tin Roof, 1970. Recipient Joseph Jefferson Best Prin. Actress award, 1993. Mem. SAG, AFTRA, Actor's Equity Assn., The Arts Club. Democrat. Jewish. Home: Chicago, Ill. Died May 19, 2006.

BANKS, MELANIE ANNE, nutritionist, biochemist, educator, dietitian; b. McKeesport, Pa., Oct. 27, 1956; d. Raymond Joseph and Emma Dea (Thomas) B. BA in Music, U. Pitts., 1976, BS in Biochemistry, 1977; MS in Chemistry, Duquesne U., 1980; PhD in Nutritional Biochemistry, W.Va. U., 1986. Cert. nutrition specialist; registered dietitian. Clin. rsch. technician Children's Hosp., Pitts., 1979-82; rsch. asst. W.Va. U., Morgantown, 1982-86; rsch. assoc. dept. Pathology U. Pitts., Pitts., 1986-87; rsch. assoc. divsn. respiratory diseases Nat. Inst. of Occupl. Safety and Health, Morgantown, 1987-89; rsch. assoc. dept. food sci. and human nutrition U. Fla., Gainesville, 1989-91; instr. divsn. health sci. Santa Fe C.C., Gainesville, 1989-92; rsch. chemist divsn. food chem. Am. Bacteriol. and Chem. Rsch. Corp., Gainesville, 1991-92; rsch. chemist lipid nutrition lab. USDA, Beltsville, Md., 1992-94; instr. biology Prince George's C.C., Largo, Md., 1993-94; asst. prof. biochemistry Lecom, Erie, Pa., 1994-96; instr. biology and chemistry Notre Dame Coll., South Euclid, Ohio, 1996-97; clin. dietitian Sarah A. Reed Retirement Ctr., Erie, 1998-99; comty. nutritionist Family Health Coun., Erie, 1998-2000; instr. nutrition Jamestown (N.Y.) C.C., 1998-99; asst. prof. nutrician and dietetics Youngstown State U., 1999-2000. Dietetic intern Cleve. Clinic Found., 1996-98; nutrition cons., owner Lake Erie Med. Nutrition Therapy, Erie, 1999—. Capt. M.S.C., USAR, 1990-96. Postdoctoral fellow NRC, 1986, USDA, 1992. Fellow Am. Coll. Nutrition; mem. Am. Chem. Soc., Am. Inst. Nutrition, Am. Dietetic Assn., Sigma Xi. Avocation: musician. Home: West Palm Beach, Fla. Died Feb. 25, 2004.

BANKS, PAUL EDWARD, data processing executive; b. Bingham, Utah, Dec. 20, 1938; s. Merlin Dean and Lillie Eliza (Hodges) Christensen; m. Shirley Ann Sypriano, Feb. 8, 1959; children: Terri, Vicki, Paul, Joseph, Darci. B, Ga. State U., 1981. Computer systems specialist U.S. Air Base, 1955-76; systems analyst LEGGS Data Ctr., Atlanta, 1976-80; mgmt. cons. Bank of Am., San Francisco, 1980-81; dir. MIS ITS Corp., San Diego, 1981-83; data processing mgr. Mitchell, Silberberg & Knapp, L.A., from 1983. Instr. Am. Mgmt. Assn., N.Y.C., 1978-81; speaker Legal Tech., L.A., 1988, L.A. Paralegal Assn., L.A., 1989; cons. SAS Systems, Lakeview Terrace, Calif., 1987—. Contbr. articles to profl. jours. Dir. sch. site coun. Vintage Magnet Sch., 1988. Mem. Data Entry Mgmt. Assn. (v.p. 1979-90, cert.). Home: Sylmar, Calif. Died May 6, 2004.

BANNISTER, BRIAN, retired organic chemist; b. Gateshead, Durham, England, Mar. 10, 1926; came to U.S., 1952; s. Arthur and Margaret Ethel (Spencer) B.; m. Mary Josephine Shea, Dec. 31, 1957. BA with 1st class hons., U. Oxford, Eng., 1947, BSc., MA, U. Oxford, Eng., PhD, 1952. Sr. scientist Upjohn Co., Kalamazoo, Mich., 1954-92. Inventor with numerous patents; contbr. articles to Jour. of Am. Chem. Soc., The Chem. Soc. (Brit.), 1953-92. Recipient Sr. Govett scholarship, New Coll., Oxford, 1947, Mem. Am. Chem. Soc., The Chem. Soc. (Brit.), Sigma Xi. Home: Kalamazoo, Mich. Died Nov. 12, 2004.

BARBA, ROBERTA ASHBURN, retired social worker, writer; b. Morgantown, W.Va., June 23, 1931; d. Robert Russell and Mary Belle (Rogers) Ashburn; m. Harry C. Barba, Jan. 28, 1956 (div. June 1963); 1 child, Gregory Robert; m. Robert Franklin Church, May 10, 1972. BSSW, W.Va. U., 1953; postgrad., U. Conn., Hartford, 1953-54; MSSW, NYU, 1957. Diplomate in Am. Bd. Examiners; lic. N.Y., W.Va. Pvt. practice, W.Va., from 1968; evaluator P.A.C.E., Star City, W.Va., 1973-74; social worker Family Svc. Assn., Morgantown, W.Va., 1974-75, 85-87; human resources asst., social worker Sundale Rest Home, Morgantown, 1977-79; cons., residential svcs. specialist Coordinating Coun. for Ind. Living, Morgantown, 1983-88; provider W.Va. Dept. Welfare, Human Svcs., Morgantown, 1980-87; social worker maternity svcs. Monongalia County Health Dept., Morgantown, 1985-87; social worker Hospice of Preston County, Kingwood, W.Va., 1988-89; shelter worker, field work instr. Bartlett House W.Va. Sch. Social Work, Morgantown, 1986-90; case mgr. Region VI Area Agy. on Aging, Fairmont, W.Va., 1990-92; case mgr. geriatric program W.Va. U., Morgantown, 1992-95; ret., 1995. Author: (with others) Working with Terminally Ill, 1990, (short fiction) Kids Know, 1992, Walk West on Bleecker Street, 1999; freedom writer Amnesty Internat., 1987—. Grantee George Davis Bivens Found., 1953-54. Mem. NASW (charter mem., cert. diplomate), ACLU, NOW, Acad. Cert. Social Workers, W.Va. Human Resources Assn., Phi Beta Kappa. Avocations: gardening, reading, travel. Home: Morgantown, W.Va. Died May 3, 2005.

BARBER, GEORGE RUSSELL, financial consultant; b. Atlanta, Aug. 26, 1914; s. Jesse Oliver and Ara (Bowman) B.; m. Helen Koester (dec. 1979); children: G. Russell, Don W. Student, UCLA, U. So. Calif., 1946-50, Harvard U., 1959-60. Min. Christian Ch.; cons. bus. and fin. G. Russell Barber & Assocs., Whittier, Calif. Cons. non-profit humanitarian orgns. Active in humanitarian activities with numerous orgns. worldwide. Lt. col., chaplain U.S. Army, 1941-45, ETO; with USAF, ret. Mem. Rotary, Masons, Shriners. Died Dec. 17, 2004.

BARBKNECHT, ARNOLD BRUCE, school system administrator; b. Lake Station, Ind., Dec. 18, 1932; s. Adolph William B. and Elsie Sophia (Lindholm) Porter; m. Caryl Cowan, July 22, 1961; children: David Stewart, Matthew Cowan. AB cum laude, Ind. U., 1954, MA, 1957. Cert. adminstr., supr., Ill. Latin and English tchr. Rich Twp. High Schs., Park Forest, Ill., 1958-66, chmn. divsn. humanities, 1966-84; exec. dir. instr., curriculum and personnel devel. Twp. High Sch. Dist. 113, Highland Park, Ill., from 1984. Cons. ABC Cons. and Counseling, Deerfield, Ill., 1990—. Editor: Jour. Action Rsch., 1992—. Sgt. U.S. Army, 1954-56. Named one of Top 100 Best and Brightest Sch. Execs. Exec. Educator, 1990, Leaders of Am. Secondary Edn., 1972. Mem. ASCD (citizen amb. People to People 1993), Instrnl. Supervision Network (assoc. editor 1993—), Nat. Staff Devel. Coun. Lutheran. Avocations: gardening, needlecrafts, reading. Home: Deerfield, Ill. Died May 21, 2004.

BARCUS, NANCY B., art educator, writer; b. Cleve., Nov. 9, 1937; d. Paul and Doris (Garvin) Bidwell; m. James E. Barcus, May 28, 1961; children: Heidi Anne, J. Hans, Jeff Thomas. AB, U. Ky., 1961; MA in English Lit., SUNY Geneseo, 1970; postgrad., Temple U. Cert. tchr., Tex., Ky. Tchr. Suzuki method violin Waco Ind. Sch. Dist., Tex., fine arts specialist at magnet sch.; past asst. dir. pub. rels., writer Baylor U., Waco; asst. prof. English and writing Houghton Coll., NY; co-dir. Ctrl. Tex. Writing Project. Spkr. at workshops and seminars; script writer for media presentations; mag. editor and writer. Author ten books, including The Family Takes a Child, Central Texas Souvenirs; columnist The Wacoan; also feature articles, poems, brochures, newsletters. Named Outstanding Educator, Danforth Found. Assn. Mem.: Suzuki Assn. Am., Nat. Coun. Tchrs. English, Ctrl. Tex. Watercolor Soc., Nat. Writing Project, Phi Beta Kappa. Home: Waco, Tex. Died Oct. 19, 2005.

BARDOLPH, RICHARD, historian, educator; b. Chgo., Feb. 18, 1915; s. Mark and Anna (Veldman) B.; m. Dorothy Corlett, July 28, 1945; children: Virginia Ann (Mrs. George Haskett), Mark III, Richard. BA, U. Ill., 1940, MA, 1941, PhD, 1944; Litt.D., Concordia Coll., 1968; LL.D., Concordia Theol. Sem., 1983. Mem. faculty dept. history U. N.C. at Greensboro, 1944-80, head dept., 1960-80, Jefferson Standard prof., 1970-80; Fulbright lectr. Denmark, 1953-54. Mem. regional selection com. Woodrow Wilson Nat. Fellowship Found.; mem. commn. theology and ch. relations Luth. Ch.-Mo. Synod. Author: Agricultural Literature and Illinois Farmer, 1948, Negro Vanguard, 1959 (Mayflower award 1960), Civil Rights Record, 1849-1970, 1970; Mem. bd. editors: Jour. So. History; Contbr. articles to profl. jours. and encys. Active ACLU, NAACP. Recipient Max O. Gardner award for Outstanding Contbns. to Welfare of Human Race U. N.C., 1979; Ford Found. fellow HArvard U., 1952-53, Guggenheim fellow, 1956-57, sr. fellow NEH, 1971-72. Mem. ACLU, NAACP, Am. Hist. Assn., Orgn. Am. Historians, So. Hist. Assn., Phi Beta Kappa. Died Jan. 25, 2006.

BARDWIL, RICHARD BRIAN, lawyer; b. Salt Lake City, Oct. 24, 1922; s. Said S. and Eva (Boshae) B.; m. Elizabeth J. Helfer, June 10, 1950; children: Steven, Nancy, Robert, Mary, Lori. Student, UCLA, 1940-42, Stanford U., 1942-43; BS, U. So. Calif., L.A., 1949; LLB, Pacific Coast U., L.A., 1952. Bar: Calif. 1952, U.S. Dist. Ct. (so. dist.) Calif. 1952, U.S. Ct. Appeals 1952, U.S. Supreme Ct. 1960. Pvt. practice, L.A., from 1952. Arbitrator Am. Arbitration Assn., L.A., 1960—, Superior Ct., L.A., 1980—. Sgt. U.S. Army, 1942-45. Mem. ABA, Calif. Bar Assn., L.A. Bar Assn., West Hollywood Bar Assn. (pres. 1958-60), Serra Internat. (dist. 82 pres. 1981-83, dist. gov. 1991-93). Avocations: travel, sports, walking. Died Jan. 10, 2004.

BARKER, ELVER AMOS, artist, educator, social change activist; b. Newcastle, Wyo., Jan. 2, 1920; s. Jessie Amos and Opal Rhoada (Roadifer) B. AB, U. Denver, 1943; studied with, Arthur W. Palmer, Thomas Leighton, San Francisco, Daniel Greene, Merlin Enabnit, Ben Konis, Mel Fillerup, George Cherepov. Former elem. sch. tchr.; formerly with Am. Friends Svc. Com., Fellowship of Reconciliation, United World Federalists; instr. art, from 1962. Author: Finger Painting in Oils, 1968. Bd. dirs., mem. editl. bd. Mattachine Soc., San Francisco, 1954-60. Mem. Fellowship of Reconciliation, War Resisters League, Rocky Mountain Skeptics, Human Rights Campaign, Rainbow Vegetarians, Gay and Lesbian Humanist Assn. Home: Denver, Colo. Died Aug. 19, 2004.

BARKER, JESSE COLON, critical care nurse; b. Burlington, N.C., June 18, 1948; s. Joseph Green Jr. and Rebecca Elizabeth (Cates) B.; m. Elizabeth W. Barker, Nov. 22, 1975; children: Joshua Colon, Timothy Loring. Diploma, Rex Hosp., 1970, Duke U., 1972; student, N.C. State U., Raleigh. RN, Md., N.C., N.H. Staff CRNA Sacred Heart Hosp., Cumberland, Md., St. Elizabeth Hosp., Danville, Ill.; chief CRNA Newport (N.H.) Hosp.; freelance anesthetist Durham, N.C. Mem. AANA, NCANA, Anesthesia Patient Safety Found. Home: Sherman, Tex. Died Aug. 28, 2004.

BARKER, ROBERT LOUIS, physician; b. Okinawa, Japan, Dec. 28, 1952; came to the U.S., 1953; s. Robert and Konnie (Maemori) B.; m. Ann D. Hutchinson, Dec. 28, 1975; children: Tanya, Trisha, Justin. BA, Andrews U., 1975; MD, Loma Linda U., 1978. Bd. cert. in internal medicine and critical care medicine. Resident internal medicine Kettering (Ohio) Med. Ctr., 1979-81; fellow in critical care Meml. Sloan Kettering Cancer Ctr., N.Y.C., 1982; assoc. program dir. internal medicine Kettering (Ohio) Med. Ctr., from 1983; pvt. practice South Dayton (Ohio) Acute Care Cons., Inc., from 1983, pres., from 1987. V.p., med. staff Kettering (Ohio) Med. Ctr., 1996, pres. med. staff, 1997. Founding mem. Found. for Critical Care, Washington, 1988; mem. Rep. Senatorial Inner Circle, Washington, 1991-95; chmn. computer integration Spring Valley Acad., Centerville, Ohio, 1994-96; pres. club mem. The Heritage Found., Washington, 1994-96. Clara Wiffenbach fellow Kettering (Ohio) Med. Ctr., 1982. Fellow ACP, Am. Coll. Critical Care Medicine, Am. Coll. Chest Physicians; mem. AMA, Am. Soc. Parenteral and Enteral Nutrition. Seventh-day Adventist. Avocations: computers, biking, racquetball. Home: Centerville, Ohio. Died Feb. 12, 2005.

BARLOW, WALTER JOHN, JR., utilities executive, consultant; b. Bayonne, N.J., Dec. 9, 1948; s. Walter John and Stasia Mary (Ryngiewicz) B.; m. Rebecca Louise Gay, Mar. 19, 1977; children: Jessica, Jennifer, Jan-Michael, Jarrod. BA, St. Anselm's Coll., 1970. Tech. dir. A.C. Lawrence Leather Co., South Paris, Maine, 1970-85, Pownal Tanning, North Pownal, Vt., 1985-88, Engring. Industries, Norway, Maine, 1988-91; gen. mgr. Paris Utility Dept., South Paris, from 1991. Chmn. Paris Budget Commn., South Paris, Maine, 1993—; vice chmn. Paris Planning Bd., South Paris, 1994—; chair bd. trustees Paris Utility Dist., South Paris, 1976-79. Mem. Am. Waterworks Assn., Maine Rural Water Assn. (Best Tasting Drinking Water 1993, 97, Merit of Honor 1996), Maine Water Utilities Assn., Maine Backflow Prevention Assn. (pres. 1997-98), New Eng. Tanners Club (pres. 1982), New Eng. Waterworks Assn., KC (grand knight 1968, award 1974). Republican. Roman Catholic. Avocations: fishing, gardening, youth basketball, lector, hiking. Home: South Paris, Maine. Died Jan. 24, 2005.

BARNES, JEAN FREDENBURGH, educator; b. Milw., Aug. 22, 1923; d. James Lynn and Helene (Neumer) Fredenburgh. BSEd, Milw. State Tchrs. Coll., 1945; MEd, Wis. State Coll., 1952; postgrad, U. Wis., Milw. Cert. tchr., Wis. Cons. Dept. Edn., Agana, Guam, 1964-70, master tchr., 1970-88; asst. prof. English U. Guam, Mangilao; propr. The Beehive, Agana, from 1976. Contbr. articles, poems to profl. publs.; profl. actress, singer, storyteller on radio, TV. Treas. Civic Ctr. Found., 1988—. Grantee Johnson Wax Found.; received recognition 19th Guam Legislature. Mem. NEA, Nat. Coun. Tchrs. English, Higher Edn. Coun., Guam Fire Casualty Marine Ins. Assn. (sec. 1988—). Avocations: radio and tv presentations, needlepoint, music, acting and public speaking. Home: Mangilao, Guam. Died Jan. 9, 2005.

BARNETT, VINCENT MACDOWELL, JR., political science educator; b. Whittier, Calif., Sept. 1, 1913; s. Vincent MacDowell and Ethel (Roper) B.; m. Barbara Brown, June 24, 1939; children: Peter, Deborah Barnett Venman, Stephen, Mary, Wendy Barnett-Mulligan. AB, UCLA, 1935, MA, 1936; PhD, Harvard U., 1938; LL.D., Syracuse U., 1963, Williams Coll., 1963; Litt. D., Union Coll., 1965; L.H.D., Carnegie Inst. Tech., 1965, Hamilton Coll., 1968; D.C.L., Colgate U., 1969. Resident tutor Leverett House and; instr. hist. govt. and econs. Harvard U., 1937-39; instr. polit. sci. Williams Coll., 1939-42, asst. to asso. prof., 1942-48, prof., chmn. dept. polit. sci., 1948-50, David A. Wells prof. polit. sci., 1950-51, A. Barton Hepburn prof. govt., chmn. dept. polit. sci., 1953-62, chmn. grad. center for devel. econs., 1960-62, dean coll., 1957-58; pres. Colgate U., 1963-69; James P. Baxter III prof. public affairs Williams Coll., Williamstown, Mass., 1969-84, prof. emeritus, from 1984—2006. Dir. Harvard U. Devel. Adv. Service, Malaysia Project, Kuala Lumpur, 1971-72, Ford Found. adv. group Ministry of Economy, Cairo, 1976-77; counselor for econ. affairs Am. embassy, Rome, 1958-60; vis. prof. UCLA, summer 1948, Stanford U., summer 1954; exec. dir. Williams Coll. Inst. Am. Studies, 1956-58; tech. dir. 9th Am. Assembly, Columbia U., 1956; project specialist Ford Found., Cairo, 1976-77; spl. asst. to dir. retail trade div. O.P.A., 1942-43; vice chmn. requirements com. W.P.B., 1943-45; chief program div. Spl. Mission to Italy, E.C.A., 1948-50; chief econ. affairs Am. Embassy, Rome, 1951-53, counselor for econ. affairs, 1958-60; U.S. mem. FAO, UN Council, 1959-60, alt. del. conf., 1959, U.S. liaison officer, 1958-60; mem. numerous adv. coms. and commns. Trustee Brookings Instn., Edn. and World Affairs; cons. Prime Minster's Office Brunei, 1986. Contbr. to books, profl. jours; editor: The Representation of the U.S. Abroad, 1956, rev. edit., 1965. Recipient Alumni Profl. Achievement award UCLA, 1968; Superior Service medal State Dept., 1960 Mem. Am. Polit. Sci. Assn., Phi Beta Kappa, Pi Gamma Mu, Pi Sigma Alpha. Home: Williamstown, Mass. Died Feb. 11, 2006.

BARNEY, THOMAS MCNAMEE, lawyer; b. Indpls., Mar. 14, 1938; s. John R. and Helen (Adams) B.; m. Marjorie Joan Eckhert, Sept. 9, 1961; children: Lynn M., Thomas M. Jr., Katherine J. BA, Cornell U., 1960; JD, Ind. U., 1966; LLM in Taxation, NYU, 1967. Bar: Ind. 1966, N.Y. 1967, Fla. 1977. Assoc. Barney & Hughes, Indpls., 1966-67, Dewey, Ballantine, Bushby, Palmer & Wood, N.Y.C., 1967-69, Phillips, Lytle, Hitchcock, Blaine & Huber, Buffalo, 1969-74, ptnr., 1975—99, of counsel, from 2000. Lectr. in taxation SUNY, Buffalo, 1969-82, mem. adv. bd. grad. tax. cert. program, 1981-2000. Author: Major Changes in Estate Tax, 1981. Sec. Upstate N.Y. Synod. Evang. Luth. Ch. Am., Syracuse, 1987-96; bd. dirs. Luth. Theol. Sem., Phila., 1988-91, Niagara Luth. Home Found., 1988—. Lt. (j.g.) USN, 1960-63. Mem. Erie County Bar Assn. (chmn. tax com. 1981-84), Fla. Bar Assn., Ind. Bar Assn., Am. Coll. Trust and Estate Counsel. Home: Angola, NY. Died May 18, 2006.

BARR, CHARLES MILSTEAD, public relations executive; b. Granville, Mo., Feb. 25, 1915; s. Noel Bland and Loyotte Lee (Arnold) B.; m. Mildred Hoyle, Aug. 16, 1936 (dec. Mar. 1987); 1 child, Robert Noel. Student, Texarkana Coll., 1931-34, U. So. Calif., 1957-58. Pub. relations rep. Northrop Corp., Hawthorne, Calif., 1947-52, pub. relations supr., 1952-54, asst. corp. dir. pub. relations Beverly Hills, Calif., 1954-69, corp. dir. pub. relations Century City, Calif., 1969-72; pres. CMB Communications Inc., Rancho Palos Verdes, Calif., from 1981. Mem. Pub. Relations Soc. Am. (accredited), Aviation Space Writers Assn. (assoc.), Nat. Assn. Real Estate Editors. Clubs: Los Angeles Press. Died Sept. 8, 2004.

BARRÉ, CHARLES, small business owner, consultant; b. N.Y.C., Aug. 19, 1950; s. Charles H. and Mildred Eleanor (Kranz) B.; m. Christina Ryan Christiansen, Mar. 12, 1968 (div. 1973); 1 child, Sean Charles; married, 1975 (div. 1991); 1 child, Desirae. AA in Bus. Mgmt., Suffolk Community Coll., 1976. Tractor trailer driver N.Y., N.J., Conn. Trucking Co., N.Y., La., Tex., Mo., Ariz., Wash., 1976-80; clerk, mgmt. SGC Corp., N.Y.C., 1980-82, night crew chief, 1982-87; owner, computer cons. CB Graphics, Selden, N.Y., from 1986. Author: (computer software) Lotto 17, 1988, Wordval, 1989. Avocation: photography. Home: Selden, NY. Died May 19, 2005.

BARSTOW, PAUL ROGERS, theatre studies educator; b. Madison, Wis., Oct. 22, 1925; s. Robbins Wolcott and Dorothy Millard (Rogers) B.; m. Eleanor Talcott Rubsam, June 20, 1953 (div. 1963); children: Victoria Talcott, Julia Robbins, Anthony Edward Chase. Student, Oxford U., Eng., 1945-46; BA magna cum laude, Williams Coll., 1948; MFA, Yale U., 1955; Dipl., Oomoto Sch. Trad. Japanese Art, Kyoto, 1984. Instr. English Williams, Williamstown, Mass., 1948-50; test developer Ednl. Testing Svc., Princeton, N.J., 1950-52; from lectr. to prof. theatre studies Wellesley (Mass.) Coll., 1955-94, emeritus, from 1994. Vis. prof. Thommasat U., Bangkok, Thailand, 1979; vis. lectr. U. Pitts., 1987; actor/dir. Ea. Slope Theatre, 1953, 54, 56, Harvard Summer Players, 1961-64, 75-77, Williamstown Theatre, 1965-66, Provincetown Playhouse, 1967-72, others; actor or dir. many community theatre prodns., film, TV, modeling, commls. Author: Images of Women on Stage, 1975. With U.S. Army, 1943-45; ETO. Danforth fellow. Mem. Actors Equity Assn., Screen Actors Guild, Am. Fedn. Radio and TV Artists, Assn. Asian Performance, Asia Soc., Japan Soc., Japan Soc. Boston, Phi Beta Kappa. Democrat. Shinto. Avocations: acting, travel, gardening, great houses. Home: Uxbridge, Mass. Died Nov. 18, 2004.

BARTEE, STEPHEN WILLIAM, accountant; b. Benkelman, Nebr., Aug. 17, 1950; m. Janet L. Bartee, Mar. 18, 1974; children: Jeremy, Ashley. Degree in acctg., U. Buffalo, 1981; student, Cornell U., 1984; M in Fin., N.Y. Inst. Fin., 1988. Cert. mgmt. acct. Acct., owner Phoenix Assocs., Buffalo, from 1984. Republican. Avocation: chess. Died Apr. 4, 2004.

BARTHEL, HAROLD OSCAR, aeronautical engineering educator; b. Milledgeville, Ill., Sept. 17, 1925; s. Elbert L. and Lucile P. (Keckler) B.; m. Eileen B. Baumeister, Jan. 26, 1962; children: Pamela Sue, Diane Elizabeth. BSME, U. Ill., 1950, MSME, 1951, PhD in Mech. Engring., 1957. Fellow in mech. engring. U. Ill., Urbana, 1950-53, teaching asst., 1953-54, rsch. asst. aero. and astronautical engring., 1954-57, asst. prof., 1957-62, assoc. prof., 1962-91, assoc. prof. emeritus, from 1991. Trustee Wesley Found. U. Ill., Urbana, 1962-68, 74-80, 90—. With USN, 1944-46. Democrat. Methodist. Achievements include creation of model of detonation cell. Home: Urbana, Ill. Died Aug. 3, 2005.

BARTLETT, THOMAS FOSTER, management consultant; b. Oklahoma City, Nov. 28, 1918; s. Martin Johnson and Clara Nell (Mattingly) Bartlett. BS, Harvard U., 1943, MBA, 1948; cert., Sorbonne, Paris, 1987, Oxford (Eng.) U., 1988, Cambridge (Eng.) U., 1989, U. Salamanca, Spain, 1993, U. Genoa, Italy, 1994; grad., US Command and Gen. Staff Coll, Ft. Leavenworth, Kans., 1945. Asst. to pres. Am. Express Co., N.Y.C., 1948-50; export promotion specialist Dept. of State, Paris; mem. U.S. Mission to NATO Dept. Def., London and Paris; econ. cons. Am. Embassy, Rome, 1950-55; exec. asst. to pres. for internat. devel. Kaiser Industries, Oakland, Calif., 1955-56; mktg. specialist Bigelow-Sanford Inc., N.Y.C., 1957-59; pres. Internat. Mgmt. Cons. Thomas F. Bartlett & Assocs., N.Y.C., from 1959. Cons. UN, U.S. Govt., fgn. govts., corps., other orgns.; lectr. in field. Capt. U.S. Army, 1943—46, maj. USAFR. Mem.: Am. Mktg. Assn., Am. Mgmt. Assn., Am. Soc. Profl. Cons., Harvard Club. Avocations: travel, photography. Home: New York, NY. Died July 12, 2006.

BARTNETT, ROBERT ELLIOTT, entomologist, consultant; b. Miami, Fla., July 8, 1929; s. Leslie Robert and Jessie (Pearson) B.; m. Virginia Arlene Hughes, June 18, 1952; children: Cheryl L., Kathleen L., Robert L. BS in Agr., U. Fla., 1951. Registered profl. entomologist; cert. pesticide applicaor; grad. Realtors Inst.; cert. resdl. broker. Dir., entomologist St. Johns County Mosquito Control, St. Augustine, Fla., 1952-64; dir. Plaquemines Parish Mosquito Control, Pointe-a-la-Hache, La., 1964-65; pres. Entomol. Svcs., Inc., Houston, 1973-75, Colonial Am. Real Estate, Inc., Houston, 1973-77; pres., cons. entomologist Bartnett & Co., Houston, from 1977; dir., entomologist Harris County Mosquito Control, Houston, 1965-73 and from 75. Adj. lectr. Rice U., Houston, 1987-90; mem. Biennial Vector Control Conf., Ft. Collins. Contbr. articles to sci. jours. Pub. speaker to civic clubs and mtgs., 1952—; precinct chmn. Harris County Rep. Com., 1980-82; vol. leader United Fund, Houston, 1986-89; adv. mem. Tex. Adv. Com. on Africanized Honey Bee, College Station, 1987-90; chmn. bd. Unity Ch. Christianity, Hosuton, 1990—. Recipient commendation for detecting and stopping St. Louis encephalitis outbreak Harris County Commr.'s Ct., 1987, commendation for stopping encephalitis in Baytown, Baytown (Tex.) City Coun., 1987, Harris County Commrs. Ct. resolution commending pub. svc. and declaring July 31, 1991 "Robert E. 'Bob' Bartnett" Day. Mem. Am Mosquito Control Assn., Entol. Soc. Am., Tex. Mosquito Control Assn. (pres. 1967-68), Fla. Anti-Mosquito Assn. (pres. 1962-63), Am. Soc. Tropical Medicine and Hygiene, Rotary (pres. 1962-63, Paul Harris fellow), Masons (32 degree), Shriners, Phi Sigma, Beta Theta Pi. Avocations: fishing, hiking, camping. Home: Flynn, Tex. Died June 11, 2004.

BARTOL, WALTER W., banker; b. Phoenix, June 24, 1931; s. Walter T. and Nora Mae (Trimble) B.; m. Betty Walker, Sept. 18, 1951; children: Thomas W., Nora Lisa, Walter Lynn. BS, U. Ariz., 1955. Mgr. Walker Feedyards, Glendale, Ariz., 1955-69; v.p. Valley Nat. Bank of Ariz., Phoenix, 1969-88. Pres. Union Devel. Co., Inc., Phoenix, 1965-93; ptnr. B&T Enterprises, 1981—, Union Devel., L.L.C., Phoenix, 1994—. Treas. Ariz. Nat. Livestock Show, Phoenix, 1988-89. Sgt. USAF, 1951-52. Mem. Elks (past exalted ruler 1958-59). Republican. Home: Munds Park, Ariz. Died July 9, 2004.

BARTON, FLORIN EDWARD, retired social services administrator; b. Springfield, Ill., Oct. 4, 1912; s. Roland I. and Rose Ella (Jouett) B.; m. Vivian Gertrude Vancil, Apr. 11, 1937; children: Judith Lee Williamson, JoAnn Steffens. Dist. dir. Muscular Dystrophy Assn., Springfield, 1968-71, regional coord. St. Louis, 1971-77; cons. Cardiac Pulmonary Recussitation Telethon WCIA-TV, Champaign, 1977-79; dir. info. svc. on aging Ill. Presbyn. Home, Springfield, 1979-93; ret., 1993. Mem. Presbytery Great Rivers Task Force on Aging, Peoria, Ill., 1981-91; pres. Springfield Ministry Coun., 1986-89. Author: (booklet) Manual to Assist Congregations in their Ministry to the Elderly, 1981; editor The Informer quar. periodical, 1971-91. Sec. DeMolay Legion of Honor, Springfield, 1976-91; fin. officer Contact Ministries, Springfield, 1983-86; mem. Ill. State DeMolay Found., Collinsville, 1985-91. Mem. Masons. Presbyterian. Avocations: model trains, painting. Home: Springfield, Ill. Died Dec. 1, 2004.

BASS, PERRY RICHARDSON, oil industry executive; b. Wichita Falls, Tex., Nov. 11, 1914; s. E. Perry and Annie (Richardson) B.; m. Nancy Lee Muse, June 28, 1941; children: Sid R., Edward P., Robert M., Lee M. BS in Geology, Yale U., 1937; D. Humanitarian Service (hon.), Tex. Christian U., 1983; LHD (hon.), Yale U., 1993. Chmn. Sid Richardson Carbon & Gas, Ft. Worth, from 1959; pres. Perry R. Bass, Inc., Ft. Worth, 1941—2006, also dir. Pres. Sid Richardson Found., Ft. Worth, 1960—2006, also dir.; dir. Bass Enterprises Prodn. Co., Ft. Worth; mem. ad hoc com. Tex. Energy and Natural Resources Adv. Com.; mem. exec. com. Nat. Petroleum Council, 1961-75, Nat. Oil Policy Commn. on Possible Future Petroleum Problems, 1965; designer, builder fireboats for U.S. Navy Chmn. Tex. Parks and Wildlife Commn., 1977-83, chmn. emeritus, 1988—2006; mem. adv. com. bd. visitors Univ. Cancer Found. of M.D. Andersen Hosp. and Tumor Inst. Recipient Silver Beaver award Boy Scouts Am., 1965, Silver Antelope award, 1969, Silver Buffalo award, 1976; Baden-Powell World fellow World Scout Found., 1988; Golden Deed award Ft. Worth Exchange Club, 1967; Disting. Civic Service award Dallas/Ft. Worth Hosp. Council, 1983, Conservation award Chevron, 1988, Bus. Hall of Fame Tex., 1989, Charles Goodnight award Star-Telegram & Nat. Cutting Horse Assn., 1991, Conservationist of the Yr. Tex. Outdoor Writers, 1992, Humanitarian Newsmaker of the Yr. Ft. Worth Chpt. Soc. Profl. Journalist and Tex. Gridiron Club, 1992, Citizen Conservationist of the Yr. Sportsmen Conservationists of Tex., 1992, medal of honor DAR, 1994, disting. bus. leadership award U. Tex., Arlington, 1994, Chuck Yeager award Nat. Fish & Wildlife Found., 1995, award of excellence Bot. Rsch. Inst. Internat., 2000. Mem. Am. Assn. Petroleum Geologists, Am. Petroleum Inst. (exec. com.), All Am. Wildcatters, Ind. Petroleum Assn. Am., Tex. Mid-Continent Oil and Gas Assn. (exec. com., City Club of Ft. Worth, Ft. Worth Boat Club, River Crest Country Club (Ft. Worth), Petroleum Club of Ft. Worth, N.Y. Yacht Club, Royal Ocean Racing Club (London), Ft. Worth Club. Died June 1, 2006.

BASSETT, JOHN GIBBS, healthcare company executive; b. Long Branch, N.J., Mar. 4, 1948; s. John Jewett and Helen (Gibbs) B.; m. Sara Ludwig, Aug. 30, 1969; 1 child, Ian. BS in Econs., U. Pa., 1970; MBA, SUNY, Albany, 1977. V.p. Hosp. Assn. N.Y. State, Albany, 1977-80, sr. v.p. fin., 1980; v.p. Green Rd. Mgmt. Co., Ann Arbor, Mich., 1980-83; chief exec. officer Commn. on Profl. and Hosp. Activities, Ann Arbor, Mich., 1983-85, sr. v.p., 1985-88, investor, from 1988. Instr. Columbia Sch. Pub. Health, N.Y.C., 1978, Rensselaer Poly. Inst., Troy, N.Y., 1978-80; chmn. Nat. Health Info. Systems, Ann Arbor, 1984-85; cons. L.H.T. Inc., Latham, N.Y., 1990—. Contbr. articles to profl. jours. Mem. campaign bd. United Way of Washington County, Mich., 1982-85; bd. dirs. ARS MUSICA, Ann Arbor, 1983-85. Named one of Outstanding Young Men of Am., 1981—. Avocations: golf, tennis, jogging, reading. Home: Albany, NY. Died Feb. 10, 2004.

BASSUK, DANIEL ELIOT, theatrical storyteller; b. N.Y.C., Oct. 14, 1938; s. Albert and Rose Bassuk; m. Nancy Cathcart, 1963 (div. 1994); children: Andrew, David, Anne; m. Patricia Thomas, Apr. 15, 1995. BS, Columbia U., 1962; PhD, Drew U., 1974; MLS, U. So. Fla., 1983. Founder, pres. Assn. Lincoln Presenters, from 1990. Author (pamphlet) Abraham Lincoln and the Quakers, 1987, (newsletter) Lincarnations, 18 vols., 1991-99. Mem. Lincoln Group N.Y. (awards com. 1988-89), Lincoln Group D.C., Lincoln Fellowship Wis. Mem. Soc. Of Friends. Home: Hillsborough, NJ. Died May 10, 2005.

BAST, KAREN RUTH, sales representative; b. Galveston, Tex., Mar. 9, 1964; BS in Home Econs., Tex. Tech U., 1985. Cert. secondary sch. tchr., Tex. Sales support/tng. Xerox, San Antonio, 1986-89; pharm. sales rep. Abbott Labs., Corpus Christi, Tex., 1989-90, acct. exec. Abilene, Tex., 1990-91, nat. sales trainer Chgo., 1991-92, pharm. sales rep. Ft. Worth, from 1992. Field trainer, product and mktg. cons. Abbot Labs., Ft. Worth, Chgo., 1992—. Mem. Delta Delta Delta (chair collegiate rels. 1988, rush com. 1994—), Pharm. Rep. Assn. (Tarrant County). Republican. Methodist. Avocations: scuba diving, skiing, gardening, travel, entertaining. Died July 15, 2005.

BATSON, DAVID WARREN, lawyer; b. Wichita Falls, Tex., Jan. 4, 1956; s. Warren M. Batson and Jacqueline (Latham) B. BBA, Midwestern State U., 1976; JD, U. Tex., 1979. Bar: Tex. 1980, U.S. Dist. Ct. (no. dist.) Tex. 1981, U.S. Tax Ct. 1981, U.S. Ct. Appeals (5th cir.) 1983, U.S. Ct. Appeals (D.C. cir.) 1983, U.S. Ct. Claims 1984, U.S. Supreme Ct. 1984. Atty. Arthur Andersen & Co., Ft. Worth, 1980-81; tax atty. The Western Co. of N.Am., Ft. Worth,

1981-85; sr. tax atty. Alcon Labs., Inc., Ft. Worth, 1985; gen. counsel Data Tailor, Inc., Ft. Worth, 1985-87; sr. tax atty. Arco, 1988-90; atty. pvt. practice, Wichita Falls, Tex., 1990—99; pvt. practice Stephenville, Tex., from 1999. Lectr. U. of Tex., Arlington, 1984-85; of counsel Means & Means, Corsicana, Tex., 1985-86. Contbr. articles to profl. jours. Speaker A Wish With Wings, Arlington, Tex., 1984-85, Habitat for Humanity (bd. dirs. 1999-). Fellow Tex. Bar Found.; mem. ATLA, Tex. Bar Assn., Christian Legal Soc., Tex. Trial Lawyers Assn., Phi Delta Phi. Avocations: negotiations, camping, self improvement. Died May 23, 2005.

BAUER, WILLIAM HENRY, musician; b. N.Y.C., Nov. 14, 1915; s. Charles Henry and Caroline (Schuessler) B.; m. Marion Veronica Costello, March 7, 1921; children: Pamela Ann, William Greig. Musician various bands, 1939-50; faculty N.Y. Conservatory Modern Music, 1946-49; with Lennie Tristano Trio and Sextet, 1946-49; staff musician NBC, N.Y.C., 1950-57; musician Benny Goodman, from 1958, Sherwood Inn, 1960-62, Ice Capades, 1963-67, Broadway Theatre, 1967-70; owner, tchr. Billy Bauer Guitar Sch., 1970—2005. Musician Woody Herman's First Herd, 1943-46. Author: (autobiography) Sideman, 1996; pub. The Guitar Instructor Reading Music; recorded jazz lines by Lennie Tristano, Lee Konitz and Warne Marsh, (with Lee Konitz) Duet for Saxophone and Guitar. With USO. Recipient Metronome Poll award, 1947-51, Down Beat Poll award, 1949-50. Mem. ASCAP. Avocations: writing mus. backgrounds and basic guitar studies. Home: Albertson, NY. Died June 17, 2005.

BAUM, WILLA KLUG, oral history director; b. Chgo., Oct. 4, 1929; d. Wilhelm Frederick and Dorothy (Hampton) Klug; m. Paul Baum, Aug. 20, 1950 (div. 1979); children: Marc Hampton, Eric Ivan, Rachel Cele, Brandon Drew, Noah Frederick, Anya Josephine. BA, Whittier Coll., 1947; MA, Mills Coll., 1950; student, U. Calif., 1949-54. Dir. Regional Oral History Office U. Calif., Berkeley, 1954—2006. Author: Oral History for the Local Hist. Soc. 1967, 4th rev. edit., 1995, Transcribing and Editing Oral History, 1991; editor: (with David Dunaway) Oral History: An Interdisciplinary Anthology, 1984, 2nd edit., 1996. Mem. Oral History Assn., S.W. Oral History Assn., N.W. Oral History Assn., Calif. Hist. Soc., Am Assn. State Local History. Democrat. Unitarian Universalist. Home: Berkeley, Calif. Died May 18, 2006.

BAUMGARTNER, REUBEN ALBERT, retired school administrator; b. Pearl City, Ill., Dec. 30, 1912; s. Albert Centennial and Laura Anna (Hummermeir) B.; m. Arleigh Camille Mears, June 27, 1942 (dec. Aug. 1969); 1 child, Richard. BA, U. Ill., 1934, MA, 1935; postgrad., U. Iowa, 1938, 41, 55. Math. instr. Polo (Ill.) High Sch., 1935-38, N.D. State U., Fargo, 1938-40; dept. head, math. instr. Freeport (Ill.) High Sch., 1940-56; dir. adult edn. Freeport Pub. Schs., 1949-55; prin. Freeport High Sch., 1956-72; curriculum dir. Freeport Pub. Schs., 1972-77. Contbr. articles to profl. jours. State coord. 55 Alive/Mature Driving, Ill., 1985-88; pres. Stephenson County Sr. Ctr., Freeport, 1975-77; mem. Sec. of State Sr. Adv. Com., Ill., 1985-88. Lt. USN, 1942-46. Mem. Kiwanis (pres. 1954-55, lt. gov. 1975-76). Presbyterian. Avocations: reading, swimming, walking. Home: Freeport, Ill. Died Feb. 16, 2005.

BAUMILLER, ROBERT CAHILL, dean; b. Balt., Apr. 15, 1931; s. Bernard Joseph and Margaret Christine (Sullivan) B. BS, Loyola Coll., 1953; PhD, PhL, St. Louis U., 1961; BTh, Woodstock Coll., 1965. Diplomate Am. Coll. Medical Genetics. Asst. in medicine Johns Hopkins Medical Ctr., Balt., 1962-67; prof. Ob/Gyn Georgetown U., Washington, 1967-90, chief divsn. genetics, 1975-90; distinguished prof. U. Detroit Mercy, 1990-95; assoc. dean, prof. Xavier U., Cin., 1995—2006, adminstr., chmn. instl. rev. bd., 1996—2006, chmn. Goodwyn instnl. rev. bd., 2000—06; asst. in medicine Johns Hopkins Medical Ctr., Balt., 1962-67. Vis. prof. U. Cin., 1997-2006; bd. dir. Bioethics Network Ohio, Cleve. Author: (with others) Encyclopedia of Human Biology, 1997; editor: Services for Special Needs, 1982; contbr. articles to Science, Nature, Am. Soc. Human Genetics. Ordained Roman Cath. priest, 1965. Scholar NSF, Washington, 1959; fellow Nat. Birth Defects Found., N.Y.C., 1960, Kennedy Inst., Georgetown U., Washington, 1972-2006. Fellow Ohio Acad. Sci.; mem. AAAS, Am. Soc. Human Genetics, Am. Coll. Medical Genetics, Soc. of Jesus, Sigma Xi. Home: Cincinnati, Ohio. Died July 13, 2006.

BAXTER, HOWARD H., retired lawyer; b. Cleve., July 31, 1931; s. Harold H. and Bessie (Bovee) B.; m. Ona Mae Miller, June 25, 1955; children: Kevin, Douglas, John, Susan. BS, Iowa State Coll., 1953; JD, Case Western Res. U., 1956. Bar: Ohio 1956, D.C. 1982; U.S. Dist. Ct. (no. dist.) Ohio 1962, U.S. Ct. Appeals (3rd cir.) 1978, U.S. Supreme Ct. 1978, U.S. Ct. Appeals (fed. cir.) 1982. Assoc. McNeal & Schick, Cleve., 1956-60; group counsel Harris Corp., Cleve., 1960-76; sec., gen. counsel Molins USA Inc., Richmond, Va., 1976-79; v.p., gen. counsel The Langston Co., Inc., Cherry Hill, N.J., 1976-79, Cuyahoga County Hosp. System, Cleve., 1979-81; v.p., sec., gen. counsel Macey Machine Co., Inc., Cleve., 1981-88, exec. v.p., 1988-91; ptnr. Kasdan & Baxter Co., Cleve., 1992-2000; pvt. practice Cleve., 2000—02; ret., 2002. Chmn. zoning com. Lakewood (Ohio) Rep. Club, 1959-60; vestry, sr. warden St. Stephens Episcopal Ch., Beverly, N.J., 1977-79, Lakewood, 1981-2004, Ch. of the Ascension, Lakewood, St. Barnabus Epsicopal Ch., 2004—. Mem. NRA, Ohio State Bar Assn., Cleve. Bar Assn., Great Lakes Hist. Soc. (vice chmn. 1981-88, exec. v.p. 1968-76, trustee 1968—, chmn. exec. com. 1982-94), Ohio Gun Collectors Assn., Inc., Edgewater Yacht Club. Avocations: marine history, sailing, shooting sports, scale model railroading. Died Oct. 24, 2004.

BAXTER, NANCY KAY, medical/surgical nurse anesthetist, critical care nurse; b. Haynesville, La., Dec. 29, 1942; d. Willie P. and A. Viola (Morgan) Miller; m. George F. Baxter, Aug. 8, 1959; children: Cynthia, Darryl, G. Kevin, Karen, Rachel. BSN cum laude, Northwestern State U., Natchitoches, La., 1984; M in Health Sci., Tex. Wesleyan U., 1991, postgrad. Cert. registered nurse anesthetist. Staff nurse NICU La. State U. Med. Ctr., Shreveport, 1985; staff RN med.-surg. DeSoto Gen. Hosp., Masnfield, La., 1984, staff nurse CCU Mansfield, La., 1985-86, supr. CCU, 1987-90; cert. registered nurse anesthetist Meml. Med. Ctr., Lufkin, Tex. Named Nurse of the Yr., DeSoto Gen. Hosp., 1986. Mem. Am. Assn. Nurse Anesthetists, Sigma Theta Tau, Phi Kappa Phi. Home: Bella Vista, Ark. Died July 13, 2005.

BAY, JOANN REEDER, financial planner; b. Williamsport, Pa., Sept. 29, 1926; d. Rollin A. and Esther Ellen (Costello) Reeder; m. John William Bay, Sr., Aug. 22, 1948; children: John William Jr., Neil Andrew. BA in English & Psychology, Bucknell U., 1948. Cert.: Inst. Paralegal Tng., Phila. (paralegal) 1973; fin. planner Coll. Fin. Planning. Analyst HAY Assoc., Phila., 1973—75, fin. planning cons., 1975—77; prin., owner J.R. Bay Assoc., Drexel Hill, Pa., 1978—2006. Adv. com. Upper Darby (Pa.) Sch. Bd., 1970—72; exec. v.p. Mother's Group Upper Darby HS, 1970—71, pres. Parent's Group, 1971—72; pro bono work for financially needy women; chmn. investment com. Cmty. Y Ea. Delware County, Upper Darby, 1992—97, Cmty. Y Found., Upper Darby, 1995—97. Named one of 200 Best Fin. Adv. in U.S., Money Mag. Silver Anniversary Issue, 1987. Mem.: Fin. Planning Assn. (llic. practitioner), Delaware County Estate Planning Assn., Philadelphia County Estate Planning Assn., Delaware Valley chpt. IAFP, Women in Transition. Democrat. Presbyterian. Avocations: piano, reading, concerts, museums. Died Feb. 16, 2006.

BAZINET, JACK CHARLES, auto parts company executive; b. Lewiston, Maine, June 30, 1951; s. Albert Joseph and Olivette Elaine (Perrier) B.; m. Jeanette Marie Clark, Oct. 4, 1972; children: Shawn, Shelly, Stephy. AA, Mid. State Coll., Auburn, Maine, 1972. Troubleshooter Johnson Products, Boston, 1966-77; pres. M&P Used Auto Parts Inc., Auburn, from 1978. Mem. Auto Dismantler Recycler Assn., Maine Auto Recyclers (pres. 1988—), Lewiston/Auburn C. of C. Home: Auburn, Maine. Died July 16, 2005.

BEAHRS, OLIVER HOWARD, surgeon, educator; b. Eufaula, Ala., Sept. 19, 1914; s. Elmer Charles and Elsa Katherine (Smith) B.; 1 child, Gean Beahrs Landy; m. Helen Edith Taylor, July 27, 1947; children: John Randolf, David Howard, Nancy Ann Beahrs Oster. BA, U. Calif., Berkeley, 1937; MD, Northwestern U., 1942; MS in Surgery, Mayo Grad. Sch. Medicine, 1949; D of Mil. Medicine honoris causa (hon.), Uniform Svcs. U. Health Sci., 1999. Diplomate Am. Bd. Surgery. Fellow surgery Mayo Grad. Sch. Medicine, Rochester, Minn., 1942, 46-49, prof. surgery, 1966-79; Joel and Ruth Roberts prof. surgery Mayo Med. Sch., 1978-79; prof. emeritus Mayo Grad. Sch. Medicine, Rochester, Minn., 1979—2006; asst. surgeon Mayo Clinic, 1949-50, head sect. gen. surgery, 1950-79, vice-chmn. bd. govs., 1964-75. Bd. dirs. Rochester Meth. Hosp.; trustee Mayo Found.; mem. cancer control and rehab. adv. com. Nat. Cancer Inst., 1975-84; mem. Am. Joint Com. on Cancer, 1975-78, exec. dir., 1980-92; advisory com. Dept.Surgery Uniformed Svcs. U. Health Scis. Editor: Surgical Consultations; editorial bd.: Surgery, Surg. Techniques Illustrated; contbr. over 400 articles to profl. jours. Hon. life, bd. dirs. Am. Cancer Soc., 1975-2006; trustee Rochester Meth. Hosp.; adv. bd. Uniform Svcs. Univ. Health Scis.; med. cons. Pres. and Mrs. Reagan; founder Naval War Coll. Capt. USNR, 1942-64, ret. Recipient Leadership and Humanitarian awards, Am. Cancer Soc., Lifetime Achievement award, Nat. Cancer Awards Trust, 2004. Fellow Royal Coll. Surgery in Ireland (hon.), Royal Australasian Coll. Surgery (hon.); mem. AMA, ACS (mem. exec. com., bd. govs., chmn. cen. jud. com., long-range planning com., chmn. bd. govs., chmn. bd. regents, pres. 1988-89), Am. Group Practice Assn. (sec.-treas. 1974-75), Minn. Surg. Soc. (pres. 1960-61), Am. Thyroid Assn., James IV Assn. Surgeons, Am. Surg. Assn. (pres. 1979-80, chmn. com. on issues 1980-83), So. Surg. Assn., Cen. Surg. Assn., Western Surg. Assn., Soc. Head and Neck Surgeons (pres. 1966-67), Am. Assn. Endocrine Surgeons (pres. 1986-87), Am. Assn. Clin. Anatomists (pres. 1986-87), Soc. Surgery Alimentary Tract, Soc. Pelvic Surgeons (pres. 1983-84), Soc. Surg. Oncology, Am. Assn. Clin. Anatomists (pres.), Philippine Coll. Surgeons (hon.), Hellenic Coll. Surgery (hon.), Assn. Française de Chirurgie Française, Northwestern U. Alumni Assn. (Merit award), Sigma Xi, Phi Kappa Epsilon, Phi Beta Pi, Theta Delta Chi. Republican. Methodist. Home: Rochester, Minn. Died Jan. 7, 2006.

BEAIRD, CHARLES T., former publishing executive; b. Shreveport, La., July 17, 1922; s. James Benjamin and Mattie Connell (Fort) B.; m. Carolyn Williams, Feb. 6, 1943; children: Susan, Marjorie, John. BA, Centenary Coll., 1966; PhD in Philosophy, Columbia U., 1972. Vice pres., asst. gen. mgr. J.B. Beaird Corp., Shreveport, 1946-57; cons. in oil and investments Shreveport, 1957-59; pres. Beaird-Poulan Inc., Shreveport, 1959-73; chmn. bd. Beaird-Poulan div. Emerson Electric Co., 1973-76; pres., pub. Shreveport Jour., 1976-99; pres. Beaird Properties LLC, 2000—06. Dir. Fed. Res. Bank of Dallas, 1972-78, dep. chmn., 1973-78; dir. Winrock Enterprises, Inc., Little Rock; adj. prof. Centenary Coll., Shreveport, 1969-95, prof. emeritus, Mem. Caddo Parish Police Jury, 1956-60; bd. dirs. Woodrow Wilson Nat. Fellowship Found., Princeton, N.J., 1975-78 bd. dirs. Community Found. of Shreveport-Bossier, 1975-85, chmn., 1979-80 Served to capt. USMCR, 1943-46. Mem. Shreveport Club, Cambridge Club. Home: Shreveport, La. Died Apr. 18, 2006.

BEALE, BETTY (MRS. GEORGE K. GRAEBER, ELIZABETH VIRGINIA BEALE), columnist, writer; b. Washington, Nov. 6, 1911; d. William Lewis and Edna (Sims) B.; m. George Kenneth Graeber, Feb. 15, 1969. AB, Smith Coll. Columnist Washington Post, 1937-40; reporter and columnist Washington Evening Star, 1945-81; weekly columnist North Am. Syndicate (formerly Field Newspaper Syndicate), 1953-89; ret., 1989. Lectr. in field. Author: Power at Play: A Memoir of Parties, Politicians and the Presidents in My Bedroom, 1993; columnist Georgetown and Country, 1998-99. Recipient Freedom Found. award, 1969; named Woman of Distinction, Birmingham So. Coll., 1987. Died June 7, 2006.

BEARCE, WINFIELD HUTCHINSON, JR., dean; b. Lewiston, Maine, Oct. 20, 1937; s. Winfield Hutchinson and Martha Marguerite (Murness) B.; m. Gretchen Hildner, June 10, 1961; children: David, Katherine. BA, Bowdoin Coll., 1959; MS, Lawrence U., 1961, PhD, 1964; diploma in Mgmt. Devel. program, Harvard U., 1986. Assoc. prof. Mo. Valley Coll., Marshall, Mo., 1966-71; guest lectr. Peace Corps Kenyatta Tchrs. Coll., Nairobi, Kenya, 1971-73; prof. Chemistry Mo. Valley Coll., Marshall, 1973-79, acad. dean, 1979-82, High Point (N.C.) Coll., 1983-87, Cen. Coll., Pella, Iowa, 1987. Active Svc. Acad. Selection Com. for Congressman, N.C. Mem. Am. Chem. Soc., Coun. for Ind. Colls. Home: Pella, Iowa. Died July 24, 2006.

BEARD, CHARLES EDWARD, library director, consultant; b. New Orleans, July 21, 1940; s. Julius Brown and Lucy Glenn (Dannelly) B.; divorced. BA, U. Ala., 1962; MS in Libr. Sci., Fla. State U., 1964. Adminstrv. officer libr. U.S. Army Command and Staff Coll., Ft. Leavenworth, Kans., 1964-66; head reference dept. Gorgas Libr. U. Ala., Tuscaloosa, 1966-69, head acquisition dept., 1969-70; dir. libr. svc. Judson Coll., Marion, Ala., 1970-71; dir. librs., assoc. prof./coord. edn. libr. media dept. Ga. Coll., Milledgeville, Ga., 1971-78; dir. univ. librs. State U. of West Ga., Carrollton, from 1978. Editor: Solutions to Your Public Relations Problems, 1991, The Ga. Libr., 1975-79; assoc. editor: The Southeastern Libr., 1975-79; contbr. articles to profl. jours. Trustee Freedom to Read Found., Chgo., 1998-2000; co-chair White House Conf. on Librs. and Info. Svc. Task Force, 1991-92; mem. bd. dirs. Positive Response, Inc., Carrollton, 1981—, pres. 1997, 98-2002; v.p. Carrollton County Hist. Soc., 1994-96. Capt. U.S. Army, 1964-66. Recipient Juanita Skelton Disting. Svc. award Ga. Assn. Instrnl. Technologists, 1995, Commendation medal U.S. Army, 1966. Mem. ALA (exec. bd. 1993-97, coun. mem. 1990-97, 1999-2002), Southeastern Libr. Assn. (pres. 1986-88), Ga. Libr. Assn. (exec. bd. 1973-85, 86—, pres. 1981-83, Nix-Jones Disting. Svc. award 1991, Bob Disting. Svc. award 2002), Richardson Libr. (chair), Ga. State Bd. Certification of Librs., Ga. Ctr. for the Book (adv. bd.), Libr. Adminstrn. and Mgmt. Assn. (past mem. exec. com., exec. bd.), Kiwanis (pres. 1975, Outstanding Pres. award 1996), Omicron Delta Kappa (faculty advisor 1990-96), Beta Phi Mu, Phi Alpha Theta. Episcopalian. Avocations: bridge, swimming, gardening, reading. Home: Carrollton, Ga. Died June 2, 2004.

BEASLEY, JAMES EDWIN, lawyer; s. James Edwin and Margaret Ann (Patterson) B.; children: Pamela Jane, Kimberly Ann, James Edwin, Lynn, Nancy. BS, Temple U., 1953, JD, 1956. Bar: Pa. 1956. Law clk. U.S. Dist. Ct. (ea. dist.) Pa., Phila., 1954-56; prin The Beasley Firm, Phila., 1966—2004. Instr. law Temple U., 1976-80, adj. prof., 1994; permanent del. 3d Cir. Jud. Conf.; chmn. standard civil jury inst. Pa. Supreme Ct.; Jud. Ct. of Judicial Discipline, Commnwealth of Pa.; bd. dirs. NATA; past trustee Pop Warner Little Scholars. Author: Products Liability and the Unreasonably Dangerous Requirement; contbr. articles to profl. jours. With USN, 1943-45, USAR, 1951-57. Mem.: ATLA, ABA, Union League, Nat. Air Racing Group, Six Diamonds Aerobatic Flight Team, Aircraft Owners and Pilots Assn. (cert. flight instr. single-multi engine airplane and instrument FAA), Pa. Soc., Temple U. Gen. Alumni Assn. (cert. of honor), Am. Bd. Profl. Liability Attys., Inner Cir. Advs., Pa. Trial Lawyers Assn. (pres. 1969—70), Phila. Trial Lawyers Assn. (pres. 1970—71, Justice Michael Musmanno award), Phila. Bar Assn., Pa. Bar Assn., Nat. Transp. Safety Bd. Bar Assn., Am. Bd. Trial Advs., Am. Law Inst., Am. Judicature Soc., Fed. Bar Assn., QB PhL Hanger. Episcopalian. Home: Villanova, Pa. Died Sept. 18, 2004.

BEATTY, BETTY JOY, library educator; b. Columbus, Ohio, Mar. 25, 1926; d. Lee E. and Gladys (Heffner) Howard; m. James Auerhan Hecht, May 6, 1950 (dec. July 9, 1974); children: James Auerhan (dec.), Timothy Lee, David Arthur; m. Benjamin M. Beatty, Dec. 19, 1975 (dec. Oct. 1997). BFA, Ohio State U., Columbus, 1947, MA, 1948. Branch librarian Warder Public Library (now Clark County Library), Springfield, Ohio, 1957-59; librarian, teacher Shawnee H.S., Springfield, 1959-66; acquisition librarian Wittenberg U., Springfield, 1966-72, head, technical svcs., 1972-84, acting dir. univ. libraries, 1983-84, assoc. prof. emerita, from 1992. Mem. bd. dirs. Faculty Devel. Orgn., Springfield, 1975-78 pres. Wittenberg U. Fed. Credit Union, Springfield, 1979-81, sec. 1984-87; pres. AAUP, Springfield, 1980. Treas. Springfield Symphony Women's Assn., 1974-76; sec. bd. dirs. Touch of Love AIDS Support, Springfield, 1988-95. Mem. Alpha Chi Omega Sorority (pres. 1964-66, sec. 1985-87, 94-96). Democrat. Roman Catholic. Avocations: painting, reading. Home: Springfield, Ohio. Died Nov. 11, 2004.

BECHT, ADELINE CHARLOTTE, retired counseling psychology educator, consultant; b. Muskegon, Mich., Mar. 11, 1937; BA in Psychology, Cascade Coll., 1964; MEd in Counseling and Guidance, Lewis and Clark Coll., 1976; MA in Clin. Psychology, U. Oreg., 1982, DPhil in Counseling and Clin. Psychology, 1982. Founder, dir. corp. blind, deaf, deaf-blind adults Living Rehab. Ctr. Inc., Portland, Oreg., 1971-81; intern in psychology Riverside Hosp. (now named Pacific Gateway Hosp.), Portland, 1980-81; pvt. practice Portland, 1980-89; instr. communications, Am. sign lang. for the deaf Notre Coeur Coll., Portland, 1984-86; adj. prof. counseling psychology Lewis and Clark Coll., Portland, 1987-92; ret., 1992. Vis. lectr., workshop facilitator spl. edn. Lewis and Clark Coll., Portland, 1971-92; cons. on deafness for psychiat. patients Pacific Gateway Hosp., Portland, 1974-92; vis. instr. deaf specialist tng. Western Oreg. State Coll., Monmouth, 1974-80. Contbr. articles to profl. jours. Mem. adv. bd. HEW, 1973-75; bd. dirs. Oreg. Coun. Orgns. Serving the Deaf, 1974-75. Avocations: music from braille, fine arts, knitting, pottery, reading. Home: Milwaukie, Oreg. Died May 30, 2005.

BECK, ANGEL C., columnist, screenwriter, educator, film director; b. Omaha, Aug. 18, 1951; d. James and Aleane (Fitz) Carter; m. Frank J. Beck, May 7, 1977 (div. May 1988); children: Jaman, Angel Marie, Frank J. BGS, U. Nebr., 1975. Sports reporter Oakland (Calif.) Tribune, 1987-88; reporter Shoreline Times/Ft. Worth, 1988-89, Arlington (Tex.) Citizen Jour., 1989-90; talk show host WNET TV, N.Y.C., 1990-91; tchr. Stamford (Conn.) Pub. Schs., from 1990; syndicated columnist Tribune Media Svcs., Chgo., 1996-97, Zwita Prodns. Syndications, Stamford, Conn., from 1997. Adv. I Have a Dream WCBS-TV, N.Y.C., from 1995. Author: History of Black Golfers, 1989, How To Play Bid Whist, 1995; contbr. articles to Black Enterprise jour. Mem.: Nat. Assn. Black Journalists. Avocations: bid whist, jazz. Died Apr. 16, 2004.

BECKER, EDWARD ROY, federal judge; b. Phila., May 4, 1933; s. Herman A. and Jeannette (Levit) Becker; m. Flora Lyman, Aug. 11, 1957; children: James Daniel(dec.), Jonathan Robert, Susan Rose, Charles Lyman. BA, U. Pa., 1954; LLB, Yale U., 1957; LLD (hon.), Temple U., 2003. Bar: Pa. 1957. Ptnr. Becker, Becker & Fryman, Phila., 1957—70; judge US Dist. Ct. (ea. dist.) Pa., 1970—82, US Ct. Appeals (3d Cir.), 1982—98, chief judge, 1998—2003, sr. judge, 2003—06. Counsel Rep. City Com., Phila., 1965—70; mem. task force on implementation of new jud. article Joint State Govt. Commn., 1969; lectr. law U. Pa. Law Sch., 1978—83; mem. edn. adv. com. concerning Comprehensive Crime Control Act Fed. Jud. Ctr., 1981—90, Fed. Jud. Ctr. Com. on Sentencing, Probation and Pretrial Svcs., 1985—90; bd. dirs. Fed. Jud. Ctr., 1991—95; mem. faculty sr. appellate judges seminar Inst. Jud. Adminstrn., N.Y.C., 1992—94. Bd. editors: Manual for Complex Litigation, 1981—90; contbr. articles to profl. jours. Trustee Magna Carta Found., Phila.; vis. com. U. Chgo. Law Sch., 1988—91; chair Rhodes Scholarship Selection Com. Dist. II (Pa., N.Y., Vt., N.H.), 1996—98; bd. mem. Historic Phila., Inc., from 2001; bd. mem., adv. bd. Am. Soc. of Internat. Law, 2000. Mem.: ABA (jud. rep. antitrust sect. 1983—86), Jud. Conf. U.S. (com. on adminstrn. probation sys. 1979—87, chmn. com. on criminal law and probation adminstrn. 1987—90, com. on long range planning 1991—96, exec. com. 1998—2003), Am. Law Inst. (mem. ALI-ABA com. from 1992, chmn. program subcom. 1996—99, adv. com. restatement conflict of laws 2d), Am. Judicature Soc. (Devitt Disting. Svc. award 2002), Phila. Bar Assn., Phi Beta Kappa. Jewish. Home: Philadelphia, Pa. Died May 19, 2006.

BECKER, HERMAN ELI, retired pharmacist; b. N.Y.C., Mar. 27, 1910; s. Abraham Jacob and Esther (Sabin) B.; m. Mina Becker, Sept. 13, 1936; children: Jerome David, Stanley Harold (dec. 1996). Degree in pharmacy, Med. Coll. Va., 1931. RPh, Va. Pharmacist, asst. mgr. Peoples Drug Stores, Richmond, Va., 1931-38; pharmacist Grant Drug Store, Richmond, 1938-40; co-owner, mgr. Blvd. Grant Drug Co., Richmond, 1940-48; pharmacist, asst. mgr. Meadowbridge Pharmacy, Richmond, 1948-67; pharmacist, asst. drug buyer Gem Drug Co., Richmond, 1967-69; pharmacist St. Mary's Hosp., Richmond, 1969-71; pharmacist, asst. mgr. various pharmacies, Richmond, 1971-89. V.p., chmn. bd. Temple Beth El, Richmond, 1963-64, lay reader evening svcs.; bd. dirs. Beth Sholom Home for Aged, Richmond, 1979-84; active Richmond Jewish Ctr., 1990. Recipient Disting. Worker award Temple Beth El, 1965, Samuel Gerson award, 1978, Methuselah award Beth Sholom Home for Aged, 1984. Mem. Richmond Pharm. Assn. (pres. 1957-58, dist. pres. svc. award 1957, human rels. award 1962), Va. Pharm. Assn., Am. Acad. Gen. Pharmacy Practice, B'nai Brith, Masons, Omega Chi. Republican. Home: Richmond, Va. Died Feb. 16, 2004.

BECKER, MICHAEL C(HARLES), plumbing company executive; b. Kansas City, Mo., May 31, 1948; s. Manuel and Taubie (Kleiman) B.; m. Patricia Ann Brown, July 7, 1977; 1 child, Michael David. BSBA, Cen. Mo. State U., 1968. Pres. Chanute Iron & Supply Co., Chanute, Kans., from 1968. Mem. Masons, Shriners. Republican. Jewish. Home: Kincaid, Kans. Died June 3, 2005.

BECKERT, NATALIE A., artist, educator; b. Jamaica, N.Y., May 3, 1937; d. Martin Arthur and Kathryn Elizabeth (Quinn) Myerson; m. James T. Beckert, June 25, 1960; children: Suzanne, Joseph, Jason, Juliane. BA in English, CUNY, 1959; postgrad., West Conn. State U., 1972-77; MFA in Painting, Drawing, Printmaking, Winthrop U., 1990. Tchr., instr. Ctrl. Piedmont C.C., Charlotte, N.C., 1990-94, Winthrop U., Rock Hill, S.C., 1993-94; dir., mgr. Spirit Sq. Print Studio, Charlotte. Solo shows include Mooresville (N.C.) Art League, 1991, Wilkesboro (N.C.) Gallery, 1991, Christa Faut Gallery, Davidson, N.C., 1993, WSOC-TV Lobby, Charlotte, 1994, Pope Gallery, Charlotte, 1994, Union Bldg., Davidson Coll., 1994; represented in collections at Wachovia Bank, Winston-Salem, N.C., 1977, Winthrop U., Rock Hill, S.C., 1989, Nationsbank, High Point, N.C., 1991, others. Judge, registrar Mecklenburg County, N.C., 1988-90; speaker Ctrl. Piedmont C.C., Charlotte, 1990-94; bd. dirs., sec. Friends of Art at Queens Coll., Charlotte, 1990-94. Mem. Phi Kappa Phi. Avocation: gardening. Home: Charlotte, NC. Died May 21, 2005.

BECKETT, EUGENE FRANCIS, engineer, consultant, business owner; b. Detroit, Nov. 27, 1929; s. Howard John and Luelle (Brown) B.; m. Esther May Doss, Sept. 3, 1950; children: Jeffrey, Kelly. BSCE, U. Cin., 1952; MS in Nuclear Engring., USAF Inst. Tech., 1959; JD, George Washington U., 1980. Registered profl. engr., Ohio. Commd. 2nd lt. U.S. Army, 1952, advanced through grades to capt., 1958, resigned, 1963, sr. project engr., 1963, U.S. Atomic Energy Commn., N.Y.C., 1963-66, Bethesda, Md., 1972-74; engring. mgr. Westinghouse Electric Corp., Madison, Pa., 1966-72; project leader U.S. Dept. Energy, 1979-80; licensing mgr. Nuclear Projects, Inc., Rockville, Md., 1974-79, mgr. tech. svcs., 1980-87; sr. exec. cons. NUS Corp., Gaithersburg, Md., 1987; pres. Beckett Assocs., Inc., Rockville, from 1987. Contbr. articles to profl. jours. Decorated Bronze Star. Mem. ASCE (life). Home: Annapolis, Md. Died July 3, 2004.

BECKHAM, EDGAR FREDERICK, educational consultant; b. Hartford, Conn., Aug. 5, 1933; s. Walter Henry and Willabelle (Hollinshed) B.; m. Ria Haertl, Aug. 16, 1958; 1 child, Frederick Hollinshed. BA, Wesleyan U., 1958; MA, Yale U., 1959, postgrad., 1959—61; DHL, Olivet Coll., 1997, Clark U., 2000. Instr. German Wesleyan U., Middletown, Conn., 1961-66, dir. lang. lab., 1963-66, lang. lab. dir., lectr. German, 1967-69, assoc. provost, 1969-73, dean, 1973-90, dean emeritus, 1996—2006; program officer The Ford Found., N.Y.C., 1990-96; coord. Campus Diversity Initiative, 1996-98; sr. fellow Assn. Am. Colls. and Univs., 1998—2006. Lectr. English U. Erlangen, Germany, 1966-67; cons. NEH; mem. Commn. on Instns. Higher Edn., 1981-84; pres. Rockfall Corp., 1985-86; bd. dirs. Assn. Am. Colls., 1985-90; scholar-in-residence Ctr. Am. and World Cultures, Miami U., 2003-04. Chmn. Conn. Humanities Coun., 1979-80, Conn. Com. on Edn. Equity and Excellence, 1994-95, Conn. State Bd. Edn., 1993-95; mem. Dem. Town Com., Middletown, 1972-90; pres. bd. dirs. Conn. Housing Investment Fund, 1981-83; chmn. bd. dirs. Middlesex Hosp., 1983-85, dir. emeritus; trustee emeritus Vt. Acad.; chmn., bd. dirs. Conn. Pub. Broadcasting, 1990-92; chmn. bd. trustees Donna Wood Found.; trustee Mt. Holyoke Coll., 2000-05; bd. dirs. NAFSA, 2001-04; mem. adv. coun. Appalachian Coll. Assn. Inst., mem. Future of Higher Edn. Project, 2001-04. With AUS, 1954-57. Recipient Outstanding Contbn. to Higher Edn. award Nat. Assn. Student Pers. Adminstrs., 1997, Raymond E. Baldwin medal Wesleyan U. Alumni Assn., 1991, Outstanding Svc. award, 1998. Mem. MLA, Am. Assn. Tchrs. German. Home: North Haven, Conn. Died May 24, 2006.

BEDFORD, SYBILLE, writer; b. Berlin, Mar. 16, 1911; d. Maximilian von Schoenebeck and Elizabeth Bernhard; m. Walter Bedford, 1935. Literary journalist, 1930s. Author: A Visit to Don Otavio, 1953, A Legacy, 1956, The Best We Can Do: The Trial of Dr. Adams, 1958, The Faces of Justice, 1961, A Favourite of the Gods, 1968, A Compass Error, 1968, Aldous Huxley: A Biography, vol. 1, 1973, vol. II, 1974, Jigsaw: An Unsentimental Education, 1989, As It Was, 1990, All Titles Republished, Quicksands: A Memoir, 2005. Recipient Order of Brit. Empire, Companion of Lit. Royal Soc. Lit. Fellow Royal Soc. Lit. Avocations: wine, food, reading, travel. Died Feb. 17, 2006.

BEEMAN, JOSIAH HORTON, former ambassador; b. San Francisco, Oct. 8, 1935; s. Josiah Horton and Helen Virginia (Hooper) B.; m. Susan Louise Sturman, Oct. 28, 1995; children: Olivia Louise, Josiah Horton. BA, Calif. State U., 1957. Adminstrv. asst. Congressman Phillip Burton, Washington, 1964-66; mem. San Francisco Bd. Suprs., 1967-68; sec. internat. affairs Presbyn. Ch., N.Y.C., 1969-70, dir. Washington Office, 1970-75; staff dir. Democratic Caucus U.S. Ho. of Reps., Washington, 1975; chief dep. dir. fin. State Calif., Washington, 1975-80; polit. and legis. dir. Am. Fedn. State, County and Mcpl. Employees, Washington, 1980-83; dir. Dem. Nat. Conv., San Francisco, 1983-84; pres. Beeman and Assocs., Washington, Sacramento, 1983-94; U.S. amb. to New Zealand and Samoa US Dept. State, 1994-99; chief of staff U.S. Broadcasting Bd. Govs., 2000-2001. Chmn. Fairfax County Cmty. Svcs. Bd. Democrat. Presbyterian. Died June 14, 2006.

BEER, ALAN EARL, microbiologist, educator; b. Milford, Ind., Apr. 14, 1937; s. Theo and Naoma Marguerite (Speheger) B.; m. Dorothy Gudeman, Aug. 17, 1958; children— Michael, Elizabeth, Margaret, Laura. BS, Ind. U., 1959, MD, 1962. Diplomate: Am. Bd. Ob-Gyn. Resident in Ob-Gyn Hosp. of U. Pa., Phila., 1965-68; USPHS/Ford Found. fellow Dept. Med. Genetics and Ob-Gyn, U. Pa., Phila., 1968-70; asst. prof. dept. Ob-Gyn, U. Tex. Southwestern Med. Sch., Dallas, 1971-73, assoc. prof., 1973-76, prof., 1976-79; Bates prof., chmn. dept. Ob-Gyn, U. Mich., Ann Arbor, 1979-84; prof. Ob/Gyn, dir. Reproductive Immunology Labs., 1984-87; prof. microbiology, immunology, obstetrics and gynecology Chgo. Med. Sch., 1987—2006. Assoc. editor: Jour. Reproductive Immunology, 1979, editor-in-chief, 1979-2006; contbr. articles to profl. jours. Served with USPHS, 1963-65. Recipient Lalor Found. award, 1969; Carl F. Hartman award Am. Fertility Soc., 1970 Mem. Am. Coll. Obstetricians and Gynecologists, Am. Fertility Soc., Internat. Transplantation Soc., AMA, Soc. for Study of Reprodn., Soc. for Gynecol. Investigation, Am. Assn. Ob-Gyn., Am. Soc. Immunology of Reprodn. (pres. 1985). Died May 1, 2006.

BEESON, PAUL BRUCE, physician; b. Livingston, Mont., Oct. 18, 1908; s. John Bradley and Martha Gerard (Ash) Beeson; m. Bartara Neal, July 10, 1942; children: John, Peter, Judith. Student, U. Wash., 1925—28; MD, CM, McGill U., 1933, DSc (hon.), 1971, Emory U., 1968, Albany Med. Coll., 1975, Yale U., 1975, Med. Coll. Ohio, 1979. Asst. Rockefeller Inst., 1937—39, Harvard Med. Sch., 1939—40; asst. prof. medicine Emory U. Med. Sch., 1942—46, prof., chmn. dept., 1946—52; Ensign prof. medicine, chmn. dept. internal medicine Yale Med. Sch., 1952—65; physician-in-chief univ. service Grace-New Haven Community Hosp., 1952—65; Nuffield prof. clin. medicine Oxford (Eng.) U., 1965-74; prof. medicine U. Wash., Seattle, 1974—81. Named Alumnus Summa Laude Dignatus, U. Wash., 1968, hon. knight comdr. Brit. Empire, 1973; recipient 50th Anniversary Gold medal, Peter Bent Brigham Hosp., 1962, Bristol award, Infectious Diseases Soc. Am., 1972, Kober medal, Assn. Am. Physicians, 1973, Abraham Flexner award, Assn. Am. Colls., 1977, Willard Thompson award, Am. Geriat. Soc., 1984, Founders award, So. Soc. Clin. Rsch., 1982, Paul Beeson Scholarship in Aging Rsch., 1995; fellow Berkeley Coll., Yale U., Magdalen Coll. (hon.), Green Coll. (hon.), Oxford U. Master: ACP (John Phillips Meml. award 1976, Disting.Tchr. award 1990); fellow: Royal Coll. Physicians (London), Royal Soc. Medicine (hon.); mem.: NAS, Assn. Physicians Gt. Britain and Ireland, Assn. Am. Physicians (pres. 1967), Am. Soc. Clin. Investigation, Soc. Exptl. Biology and Medicine, Am. Acad. Arts and Scis. Episcopalian. Home: Exeter, NH. Died Aug. 14, 2006.

BEH, WARREN ALBERT, JR., insurance agent, financial planner; b. N.Y.C., May 4, 1932; s. Warren Albert and Henrietta H. (Carll) B.; m. Christine Brosius, June 18, 1955; children: Christine Beh Austen, Ann Beh Wagner. BSBA, U. Del., 1955. CLU, CFP. Sales rep. Sun Life of Can., Wilmington, Del., 1957-77, North Am. Life Assurance Co., Phila., 1977-83, Great-West Life Assurance Co., Phila., 1983-93, AIG Lites, Wilmington, from 1993. Bd. dirs. Home Merciful Rest Soc., Wilmington, 1970-79, Vis. Nurses Assn. Del., Wilmington, 1970-79; v.p. Del. Guidance Svcs. for Youth, Wilmington, 1970-79; bd. dirs. and fin. com. Wilmington Sr. Ctr., 1978—; treas. Roth for Lt. Gov., Wilmington, 1960; life ins. liaison for Rep. candidate for Ins. Commr., Del., 1962, 70, 74, 76; campaign hdqs. mgr. Roth for Congress Com., Del., 1966; mem. U.S. Svc. Acad. Rev. Bd. for Senator Roth, Del., 1975—. With USN, 1955-57. Recipient Nat. Quality award Nat. Assn. Life Underwriters, Washington, 1969—, Charles B. Palmer award New Castle County Life Underwriters, Wilmington, 1974. Mem. Soc. CLUs (Del. chpt., pres. 1974-75), Del. Valley Assn. CFPs, New Castle County Life Underwriters (treas. 1961-70), Estate Planning Coun. Del. (pres. 1978-79), Million Dollar Round Table, Greenville Country Club. Republican. Episcopalian. Avocations: woodworking, landscaping, wilderness canoeing. Home: Wilmington, Del. Died Aug. 28, 2004.

BEHNKE, ROY HERBERT, physician, educator; b. Chgo., Feb. 24, 1921; s. Harry and Florence Alice (MacArthur) B.; m. Ruth Gretchen Zinszer, June 3, 1944; children: Roy, Michael, Donald, Elise. AB, Hanover Coll., 1943; PhD (hon.), 1972; MD, Ind. U., 1946. Diplomate: Am. Bd. Internal Medicine. Intern Ind. U. Med. Center, 1946-47, resident, 1949-51, chief resident medicine, 1951-52; instr. medicine Ind. U. Sch. Medicine, Indpls., 1952-55, asst. prof. medicine, 1955-58, assoc. prof., 1958-61, prof., 1961-72; chief medicine VA Hosp., Indpls., 1957-72; prof. medicine U. South Fla. Coll. Medicine, Tampa, from 1972, chmn. dept. medicine, 1972-95, chmn. dept. head emeritus, from 1995. AMA rep. to residency rev. com. in internal medicine, 1970-75; mem. exec. and adv. com. Inter-Soc. Commn. Heart Disease Resources, 1968-72, chmn. pulmonary study sect., 1969-72; chmn. career devel. com. VA, 1980-83 Mem. Met. Sch. Bd. Washington Twp., 1968-72, pres., 1971; bd. dirs. Southside Community Health Center, 1968; trustee Tampa Gen. Hosp. Found., 1979-85; mem. research coordinating com. Am. Lung Assn., 1983-85, chmn., 1985-87, bd. dirs., 1983-87. Served with AUS, 1943-45, 47-49. Recipient Std. Oil Found. award Ind. U.,

1971, Alumni Achievement award Hanover Coll., 1971; named Hon. Alumnus, USF Coll. Medicine, 1995; John and Mary Markle scholar, 1952, 57. Fellow and master ACP (gov. Fla. chpt. 1980-84, Laureate award 1991); fellow Am. Coll. chest Physicians; mem. AMA, Am. Fedn. Clin. Rsch., Ctrl. Soc. Clin. Rsch., So. Soc. Clin. Rsch., Alpha Omega Alpha. Home: Saint Petersburg, Fla. Died Nov. 4, 2005.

BEIERWALTES, WILLIAM HENRY, physician, educator; b. Saginaw, Mich., Nov. 23, 1916; s. John Andrew and Fanny (Aris) B.; m. Mary Martha Nichols, Jan. 1, 1942; children: Andrew George, William Howard, Martha Louise. AB, U. Mich., 1938, MD, 1941. Diplomate: Am. Bd. Internal Medicine and Nuclear Medicine. Intern, then asst. resident medicine Cleve. City Hosp., 1941-43; mem. faculty U. Mich. Med. Center, 1944-87, prof. medicine, 1959-87, prof. emeritus, from 1987; dir. nuclear medicine, also dir. Thyroid Research Lab., 1952-86, cons., 1987-95. Cons. nuclear medicine depts. St. John Hosp., Detroit, Wm. Beaumont Hosp., Royal Oak and Troy, Mich., 1987-95, The UpJohn Co. Rsch. div., 1952-65, The Abbott Labs. Rsch. div., 1960-67; sr. med. cons. MD (Med. Fedn.), Bagdad, Iraq, 1963; mem. exec. com. Inst. Sci. and Tech., 1963; lectr. Nat. Naval Med. Ctr., 1964-88, Ctr. for Environ. Health Mich. State Dept. Health, 1988-89; Peter Heimann lectr. 34th meeting Internat. Congress Surgery, Stockholm, Sweden, 1991; adv. panel on radionuclide labeled compounds for tumor diagnosis Internat. AEC, 1974-75; mem. Mich. State Radiation Bd., 1980-84; co-chmn. Nat. Coop., Thyroid Cancer Therapy Group, 1978-81 Author: Clinical Use of Radioisotopes, 1957, Manual of Nuclear Medicine Procedures, 1971, Love of Life Autobiog. Sketches, 1996; contbr. numerous articles to profl. jours.; assoc. editor Jour. Lab. and Clin. Medicine, 1954-60; editl. bd. Jour. Nuclear Medicine, 1964-69, assoc. editor, 1975-81; editl. bd. Jour. Clin. Endocrinology and Metabolism, 1963; adv. bd. Annals of Saudi Medicine, 1986-90; patentee for monoclonal antibodies to HCG, and radionuclide in vivo biochem. imaging of endocrine glands, 1951; first to treat a patient for cancer with radio labeled antibodies, 1951; co-inventor radiopharms, 1971; originator of radioimmunodetection of human cancer; first description of cytogenetic evolution of thyroid cancer; first description of fall of serum antithyroid antibodies during pregnancy with rise after delivery, other med. techniques. Guggenheim fellow, 1966-67; Commonwealth Fund fellow, 1967; recipient Hevesy Nuc. Medicine Pioneer award, 1982, Disting. Faculty award U. Mich., 1982, Johann-Geor-Zimmerman Trust for Cancer Rsch. Sci. prize for greatest contbn. to treatment of thyroid cancer, 1983, WWJ 950 Detroit Citizen of Week award, 1994; named Internat. Man of Yr. Internat. Biog. Ctr., Cambridge, Eng., 1992-93. Mem. AMA (Outstanding Scientific Achievement award 1994), ACP, Am. Fedn. Clin. Rsch. (pres. 1954-55), Soc. Nuclear Medicine (pres. 1965-66, Disting. Educator's award 1989, The Best Doctors in Am. award 1993-95), Ctrl. Clin. Rsch. Club (pres. 1958-59), Am. Thyroid Assn. (v.p. 1964-65, 66-67, Disting. Svc. award 1972), Ctrl. Soc. Clin. Rsch. (councillor 1964-67, 67-71), Galens Med. Soc., Assn. Am. Physicians, Mich. Med. Soc., Am. Endocrine Soc., Am. Soc. Clin. Oncology. Home: Petoskey, Mich. Died Aug. 14, 2005.

BEINING, PAUL ROBERT, science educator, priest; b. Pittsburgh, Pa., Feb. 2, 1923; s. William August and Catherine Genoveve Beining. BS, Spring Hill Coll., Mobile, AL, 1949, Licentiate (hon.) Philosophy, 1949; MS, Cath. U., Washington, DC, 1952; Licentiate Theology (hon.), Woodstock Coll., Woodstock, MD, 1954; PhD, Cath. U., Washington, DC, 1962. Instr. biology U. Scranton, Scranton, Pa., 1949—51; asst. prof. biology St. Joseph's Coll., Philadelphia, Pa., 1962—66; chmn. and assoc. prof. biology Wheeling Coll., Wheeling, W.Va., 1966—67; prof. biology U. Scranton, Scranton, Pa., from 1967. Summer guest rschr. Nat. Institutes Health, Bethesda, Md., 1972—81, Food & Drug Adminstrn., Bethesda, Md., 1982—91; functioning cath. priest Soc. Jesus, Baltimore, Md., from 1955, tchr., from 1942. Bd. mem. Retarded Citizens, Lackawanna County, Pa., 2002—02, United Cerebral Palsy, Lackawanna County, Pa., 2002—02, Emergency Med. Svc., Lackawanna County, Pa., 2002—02. Recipient Title VI Higher Edn., Higher Edn. Act Georgetown U., 1969; grantee Equipment Matching grant, NSF U. Scranton, 1964, Personal Rsch. grant, Natinoal Sci. Found. Georgetown U., 1970. Avocations: light airplane piloting, birding. Died Mar. 20, 2004.

BELCHER, EDWARD LORING, manufacturing executive; b. Plymouth, Mass., Mar. 20, 1926; s. Edward Ralph and Helen Loring (Barnes) B.; m. Jacqueline Griebel, Apr. 11, 1953 (div. 1971); m. Gayle Levis, Feb. 29, 1976; children: Gay, Thomas, Sara, Ellen, Martha, Jonathan. BSME, MIT, 1946. Methods engr. ANSCO, Binghamton, N.Y., 1946-48; engr. Chase Brass & Copper, Waterbury, Conn., 1948-53; product engr. Graflex Inc., Rochester, N.Y., 1953-56, product mgr., 1956-59, v.p. mfg., 1959-65, exec. v.p., 1965-75, pres., 1975-90; vice chmn. Caldwell Mfg. Co., Rochester, N.Y., from 1990. Bd. dirs. Voplex Inc., Troy, Mich., Forbes Products Inc., Rochester, Caldwell Mfg. Co. With USN, 1943-45. Democrat. Avocations: volunteering, reading, yard work. Home: Rochester, NY. Died May 3, 2004.

BELKIN, NORMAN, writer; b. Huntington Pk, Calif., Nov. 1, 1924; s. Jacob M. and Rose (Brachman) B.; m. Joanne Rosamund Randall, Oct. 31, 1951 (annulment Mar. 17, 1952); m. Harriet Tauba Eder, Apr. 10, 1966; children: Rifka Rakhel, Calla Natanya. Grad. high sch., L.A., 1942. Freelance writer, L.A., from 1972; actor Circle Theater, L.A., 1947-49. Mem. Lehman Engel Musical Theatre Workshop. Writer book and lyrics including The Money Tree, 1987, Princess and the Frog, 1989, The Perfect Match, 1989, Judge Knott, 1993, Act of Mercy, 1997; writer TV shows including All In the Family, 1974, Maude, 1972-73, The Sandy Duncan Show, 1972, Good Times, 1976, Mary Hartman, Mary Hartman, 1977, animated TV shows including Wait Till Your Father Gets Home, 1972, Smurfs, 1983; contbr. to mags. With USCG, 1943-46. Mem. Writers Guild Am. West, Dramatists Guild, Actors Equity, Screen Actors Guild, Am. Fedn. TV and Radio Actors. Home: West Hollywood, Calif. Died Feb. 13, 2004.

BELL, CAROLYN SHAW, economist, educator; b. Framingham, Mass., June 21, 1920; d. Clarence Edward and Grace (Wellington) Shaw; m. Nelson S. Bell, Aug. 26, 1953; 1 dau. by previous marriage, Tova Maria. AB magna cum laude, Mt. Holyoke Coll., 1941; PhD, London Sch. Econs., 1949; LHD (hon.), Babson Coll., 1983, Denison U., 1988, North Adams State Coll., 1991. Economist OPA, 1941-45; rsch. economist London Sch. Econs., 1946-47, Social Sci. Rsch. Coun., Harvard, 1950-53; mem. faculty Wellesley Coll., 1950-89, prof. econs., 1962-89, chmn. dept., 1962-65, 79-82, Katharine Coman prof. econs., 1970-89, Katharine Coman prof. econs. emeritus, 1989—2006; cons. Lexington, Mass., 1989—2006. Pub. mem. Fed. Adv. Coun. on Unemployment Inc., 1974-77, chmn., 1975-77; bd. econ. advisors Pub. Interest Econ. Ctr.; bd. overseers Amos Tuck Grad. Sch. Bus. Adminstrn., Dartmouth, 1973-79; mem. econs. policy coun. UN Assn., 1976-85, trustee, 1981-90; trustee Joint Coun. Econ. Edn., 1975-83, Tchrs. Ins. and Annuity Assn., 1977-85, Symmes Life Care, Inc., 1994-2001, NEADS, Inc., 1994-2006; mem. NRC Com. for Behavioral & Social Scis., 1977-83; bd. adv. Internat. Labour Rev. Author: Consumer Choice in the U.S. Economy, 1967, The Economics of the Ghetto, 1970; co-author: (with W.W. Cochrane) Economics of Consumption, 1956; co-author: Coping in A Troubled Society, 1974; contbr. articles to profl. jours.; radio and TV commentator; mem. bd. editors Challenge Mag. Mem. Hearing Dog Adv. Coun., 1990-93. Recipient Disting. Achievement award The Boston Club, 1996, WERT award for Tchg. Excellence, 1997, Acad. of Women Acheivers, YWCA, 1997. Mem. AAUP (pres. Wellesley chpt. 1965-66). AAUW (Shirley Farr fellow 1961-62), ACLU, Assn. for Advancement Socio-Econs., Manhattan Inst. (adv. bd.), Am. Econs. Assn. (chmn. com. on status women in econs. profession 1972-74, exec. com. mem. 1975-77), Assn. Evolutionary Econs. (bd. dirs. 1973-75), Ea. Econs. Assn. (exec. bd. 1983-85), Phi Beta Kappa (pres. Eta Mass chpt. 1978-80), Delta Soc. (svc. dog. adv. bd. 1994-95). Died May 13, 2006.

BELL, CORNELIUS, mechanical and aerospace engineer; b. Mpls., July 14, 1946; s. Connie Paul and Lorena (Welch) B.; m. Joyce T. Biles, Jan. 2, 1981 (div. June 1984). AS, Acad. of Aeronautics, Flushing, N.Y., 1968; BS, N.Y. Inst. Tech., 1974; postgrad., Polytech. Inst. Bklyn., 1974-78. Contract engr. Boeing Aerospace Co., Seattle, 1983-84, Babcock & Wilcox Co., Barberton, Ohio, 1984, Hamilton Standard, Farmington, Conn., 1985, Keltec Corp., Ft. Walton Beach, Fla., 1986, Argo Tech, Cleve., 1986-87, Sunstrand Co., Rockford, Ill., 1987, G.E.C. Avionics, Inc., Norcross, Ga., 1987-88, Micro-Tel Div. Adams Russell, Hunt Valley, Md., 1988, Eagle-Picher Industries, Joplin, Mo., from 1989. With U. S. Army, 1968-71, Vietnam. Democrat. Roman Catholic. Avocations: skiing, scuba diving, flying, art. Home: Corona, NY. Died Apr. 6, 2005.

BELL, JAMES FREDERICK, retired lawyer; b. New Orleans, Aug. 5, 1922; s. George Bryan and Sarah Barr (Perry) B.; m. Jill Cooper Arden, Apr. 14, 1951; children: Bradley Cushing, Sara Perry, Ashley Arden. AB cum laude, Princeton U., 1943; LL.B., Harvard U., 1948. Bar: D.C. 1949. Assoc. Pogue & Neal, Washington, 1948-53, ptnr., 1953-88, cons., 1988-89; ret., 1988. Gen. counsel Conf. State Bank Suprs., 1951-87. Chmn. com. on canons and other bus. Episcopal Diocese of Washington, 1960-78; pres. Episc. Ctr. for Children, Washington, 1966-67. Lt. USNR, 1943-46. Mem. ABA, D.C. Bar Assn. Home: Washington, DC. Died 2006.

BELL, RAYMOND JOSEPH, manufacturing executive, engineer; b. Paterson, N.J., July 23, 1949; s. Raymond Joseph Sr. and Mildred Elizabeth (Staiber) B.; m. Nancy Elizabeth Lee, Apr. 22, 1972; children: Aaron, Jocelyn, Colleen, Nathaniel. BA in Chemistry, SUNY, Buffalo, 1971, MS, 1976. Cert. in prodn. and inventory mgmt. R&D engr. Hewlett-Packard Co., Palo Alto, Calif., 1976-83; owner Morris & Lee, Inc., Buffalo, from 1983. Treas., PTO, City Honors Sch., Buffalo, 1989—; chmn. troop 5, Boy Scouts Am., Buffalo, 1990—. Mem. Am. Prodn. and Inventory Control Soc. Avocations: woodworking, classical music, mathematics, economics. Home: Buffalo, NY. Died June 11, 2004.

BELL, ROBERT EUGENE, anthropology educator; b. Marion, Ohio, June 16, 1914; s. Harry Thew and Clara (Stouffer) B.; m. Emily Virginia Merz, Aug. 31, 1938; children— Patricia (Mrs. Paul Lindsey), David Eugene. Student, Ohio State U., 1936-38; BA with honors, U. N.M., 1940; MA, U. Chgo., 1943, PhD, 1947. Asst. prof. anthropology U. Okla., 1947-51, assoc. prof., 1951-55, prof., 1955-69, George L. Cross Research prof., 1969-80, emeritus, from 1980. Chmn. dept., 1947-55, 61-64; head curator Stovall Mus., 1947-85; dir. Mississippi Valley Dendochronology Lab. U. Chgo., 1942-43, 46-47, Oklahoma River Basin Salvage Lab., 1962-78 Author: Oklahoma Archaeology: an Annotated Bibliography, 1969, 2d edit., 1978, The Harlan Site, CK-6, A Prehistoric Mound Center in Cherokee County, Eastern Oklahoma. Archaeol. investigations at site of El Inga, Ecuador, Ferdinandina: Biography of a French-India Trading Community on the Southern Plains, 2004; editor: Am. Antiquity, 1966-70, Bull. Okla. Anthrop. Soc, 1963-66, Prehistory of Oklahoma, 1984. Served with M.C. AUS, 1943-46. Recipient Clarence H. Webb award Outstanding Contbns. to Caddoan Archeology, 1985, Presentation in Recognition of Outstanding Contbn. to Ecuadorian Archeology, Govt. of Ecuador, 1986; subject of Festschrift Okla. Anthrop. Soc., Okla. Archeol. Survey, 1983, Shirk Meml. award for Hist. Preservation, 1987; named to Okla. Hist. Soc.'s Hall of Fame, 1994, Plains Anthropol. Soc. Disting. Svc. award 1994; Fulbright fellow, New Zealand, 1955-56. Mem. Am. Anthrop. Assn., Am. Assn. Phys. Anthropology, AAAS, Okla. Hist. Soc., Am. Ethnol. Soc., Soc. for Am. Archaeology (50th Anniversary award 1985), Mo., Ark., Tex., Kans. archaeol. socs., Inst. Gt. Plains, Southeastern Archaeol. Conf., Polynesian Soc., Soc. for Hist. Archaeology, Soc. for Conservation Archaeology, Explorers Club, Phi Beta Kappa (hon.), Sigma Xi. Home: Norman, Okla. Died Jan. 1, 2006.

BELL, STEPHEN MARTIN, lawyer; b. Bklyn., Feb. 24, 1946; s. Philip and Adele (Tannenbaum) B.; m. Madeline Joan Cohen, Jan. 9, 1947; children: Dawn Jennifer, Jodi Dione. Student, Dade Jr. Coll., 1965-66, U. Miami, Fla., 1967-70; BBA, Memphis State U., 1973. Bar: Fla. 1973, U.S. Dist. Ct. (so. dist.) Fla. 1974. Pvt. practice, Plantation, Fla., from 1973. Avocations: fishing, boating. Died Jan. 31, 2005.

BELLA, ANTHONY, protective services official, educator; b. Pozzallo, Sicily, Italy, Jan. 12, 1933; s. Salvatore Bella and Corradina Gallaro; m. Rosemarie Traola, Sept. 19, 1954; children: Mark Salvatore, Karen Corradina. BS, St. Francis Coll., 1977; MS, L.I. U., 1981. Mcp. police tng. coun. N.Y. state cert. instr. Tng. dir. H.R.A. Police--Peace Officers, N.Y.C., 1968-74; tng. dir., detective Kings D.A. Office--Detective Investigators, Bklyn., 1974-81; tchr. adult edn. S. Shore H.S., Bklyn., 1976-80; pvt. practice criminal investigator Bklyn., from 1987; tchr. N.Y. state security guards L.C. Tng. Ctr., Bklyn., from 1998. Lectr. criminology Tenants Orgn., Bklyn., 1979. Mem. Internat. Police Assn., Soc. Profl. Investigators (chmn. ethics com. 1996, sec. 1998, bd. dirs. 1998—). Roman Catholic. Home: Brooklyn, NY. Died June 29, 2005.

BELLAMY, JOHN CARY, civil engineer, meteorologist; b. Cheyenne, Wyo., Apr. 18, 1915; s. Benjamin Charles and Alice Elizabeth (Cary) B.; m. Josephine Marie Johnston, Sept. 21, 1940; children: John Cary, Agnes Louise, Charles Fulton, William Delaney, Mary Elizabeth. BCE, U. Wyo., 1936; PhM, U. Wis., 1938; PhD in Meteorology, Chgo. U., 1947. Registered profl. engr., Wyo. Ptnr. Bellamy & Sons Engrs., Lamont, Wyo., 1938-42; asst. prof. U. Chgo., 1942-47; assoc. dir. Cook Rsch. Labs., Chgo., 1947-60; dir. NRRI U. Wyo., Laramie, 1960-73, prof. civil engring., 1973-81; prin. Bellamy & Sons Engrs., Laramie, from 1981. Dir. Inst. Tropical Meteorology, U. P.R., 1943-44; spl. cons. U.S. Army Air Corps, Washington, 1944-45; mem. Western Interstate Nuclear Bd., Denver, 1964-75. Contbr. articles to profl. jours.; contbr. to books; patentee in field. Recipient Losey award, Inst. Aero. Sci., 1944, Medal of Freedom, Pres. U.S.A., 1946, Thurlow award Inst. Navigation, 1946. Fellow NSPE (chpt. pres. 1976), Am. Meteorol. Soc. (dir. 1948-52), Inst. Navigation (pres. 1962), Am. Geophys. Union; mem. Wyo. Engring. Soc., Lions (chpt. pres. 1981, 84). Avocations: golf, bowling, computer programming. Died June 5, 2005.

BELLING, DOROTHY IRMA, retired geriatrics and critical care nurse; b. North Tonawanda, N.Y., Dec. 13, 1924; d. George Martin and Josephine (Knoell) B. Diploma in nursing, Millard Fillmore Hosp., Buffalo; BS in Mgmt. and Supervision with honors, U. Buffalo, 1949; MAA in Mgmt. and Supervision with honors, Columbia U., 1959. RN, Md., N.Y. Clin. specialist Heart, Lung and Blood Inst., NIH, Bethesda, Md., 1966-78; night supr. Buffalo VA Hosp., 1959-61; head nurse med.-surg. unit Millard Fillmore Hosp., 1949-52; staff gerontology nurse Carriage Hill Bethesda., 1986-90. Past chmn. task force on nursing practice NIH. Contbr. articles to nursing jours. Recipient nursing rsch. award NIH, 1981. Mem. ANA. Home: Kensington, Md. Died Apr. 11, 2004.

BELSOM, WALTER JOSEPH, JR., accountant, treasurer; b. New Orleans, Feb. 28, 1922; s. Walter J. Sr. and Clara A. (Frye) B.; m. Flora E. Grush, June 12, 1948; children: Donald, Mary, Charles. BA in Acctg., cert. in advanced acctg., Tulane U., 1955; cert. in advanced acctg. Bookkeeper United Fruit Co., New Orleans, 1940-46; acct. S. Zemurray Co., New Orleans, from 1946. Treas., asst. sec. Zemurray Found. Pres. St. Vincent DePaul Orgn., Abita Springs, La., 1983—. Served with USCG, 1942-46, ETO. Mem. Nat. Assn. Accts., New Orleans C. of C. (chmn. agrl. com. 1963). Democrat. Roman Catholic. Avocation: farming. Home: Abita Springs, La. Died Jan. 15, 2005.

BELTZ, GEORGE ALLEN, retired company executive; b. Oak Park, Ill., Feb. 15, 1933; d. George Heinrich and Helen (Allen) B.; m. Merry Belle Kercher, Oct. 14, 1955; children: Jennifer, Sharon, Gregory. BA, Lawrence U., 1954. Various mktg. positions Amoco, 1958-92, coord. jobber rels. Chgo.,

1992; v.p. program devel. Bunker & Bunker Corp., Waltham, Mass., 1993-95; ret., 1995. State del. Rep. Party, 1980. Capt. USAF, 1955-58. Avocations: golf, tennis, travel. Died Oct. 26, 2004.

BENCHLEY, PETER BRADFORD, author; b. NYC, May 8, 1940; s. Nathaniel Goddard and Marjorie Louise (Bradford) Benchley; m. Winifred B. Wesson, Sept. 19, 1964; children: Tracy, Clayton, Christopher. BA cum laude, Harvard U., 1961. Gen. assignment reporter Washington Post, 1963; assoc. editor Newsweek mag., N.Y.C., 1963—67; staff asst. to Pres. White House, Washington, 1967—69; freelance writer, 1969—2006. Mem. Nat. Coun. Environ. Def.; mem. bd. advisors Bermuda Underwater Exploration Inst. Author: (books) Time and a Ticket, 1964, Shark Trouble, 2002, (novels) Jaws, 1974, The Deep, 1976, The Island, 1978, The Girl of the Sea of Cortez, 1982, Q Clearance, 1986, Rummies, 1989, Beast, 1991, White Shark, 1994; co-author: (screenplays) Jaws, 1975 (Brit. Acad. Award nomination), The Deep, 1977, The Island, 1979, Ocean Planet, 1995; writer, narrator, host (episodes) The Am. Sportsman TV show, 1974—83, Galapagos TV spl., 1987, host, narrator Expedition Earth TV series, 1990—93, co-creator Dolphin Cove TV series, 1989, exec. prodr. Beast miniseries, 1996, host, narrator Ocean Reports pub. radio series, 1997—2000, creator, co-exec. prodr. (syndicated TV series) Peter Benchley's Amazon, 1999—2000, co-creator, co-prodr., co-writer, narrator New Eng. Aquarium's World of Water film series, 1998—2006; contbr. articles to newspapers and mags., including Nat-.Geographic, N.Y.Times; freelance writer National Geographic Mag.; contbr. articles to National Geographic Traveler; appeared in, hosted and written and or narrated (several TV documentaries about the sea). With USMCR, 1962—63. Recipient Diver of Yr. award, Sea Rovers Assn., 2002, Lowell Thomas Gold award for adventure-travel writing, Soc. Am. Travel Writers, 2003, 2004, Daniel B. Stone award, N.E. Aquarium, 2005, NOGI award, Acad. Underwater Arts and Sciences, 2005. Mem.: Nat. Bd. of Environ. Def. Died Feb. 11, 2006.

BENNER, GERELD STOKES, chemist; b. Waukegan, Ill., July 27, 1933; s. Kenneth W. Benner and Paula Mae (Stokes) Manning; m. Carol Sue, Nov. 20, 1969 (div. Dec. 1974); children: Jennifer Lynn, Michael Conrad; m. Carole Elaine Gall, Dec. 28, 1976; 1 child, Lori Anne Head. BS, U. N.C., 1961; MS, Ohio State U., 1963, PhD, 1966. Sr. rsch. chemist Goodyear Tire & Rubber Co., Akron, Ohio, 1966-74, M.W. Kellogg Co., Houston, 1974-87; process chemist Merck & Co., Inc., Rahway, N.J., 1989-92; chief chemist MPR Svcs. Inc., Dickinson, Tex., from 1992. Contbr. articles to profl. jours. Bd. dirs. West Meml. Civic Assn., Katy, Tex., 1982-85. With U.S. Army, 1956-58. Mem. Am. Chem. Soc., N.Y. Acad. Scis., SW Catalysis Soc., Sigma Xi, Phi Lambda Upsilon. Presbyterian. Achievements include 7 U.S. (with others) and 3 German patents (deutsche Offentlegungen). Home: Katy, Tex. Died Mar. 6, 2004.

BENNETT, BETTY T., literature educator, former dean; b. N.J. children: Peter, Matthew. BA, Bklyn. Coll., 1962; MA, NYU, 1963, PhD, 1970. Adj. asst. prof. dept. English and comparative lit. SUNY, Stony Brook, 1970-75, asst. chmn. comparative lit., 1971-72, asst. to dean Grad. Sch., 1970-79, adj. assoc. prof., 1975-79; assoc. prof. English and humanities Pratt Inst., Bklyn., 1979-81, prof., 1981-85, dean Sch. Liberal Arts and Scis., 1979-85; dean Coll. Arts and Scis. Am. U., Washington, 1985-97, disting. prof. lit., 1997—2006. Fellowship reader Danforth Found., 1978-79; edn. liaison officer N.Y. State, 1977-80; co-dir. NEH Inst., 1989-90. Author: British War Poetry in the Age of Romanticism: 1793-1815, 1976, The Letters of Mary Wollstonecraft Shelley, Vol. I, 1980, The Letters of Mary Wollstonecraft Shelley, Vol. II, 1983, The Letters of Mary Wollstonecraft Shelley, Vol. III, 1988, Mary Diana Dods: A Gentleman and a Scholar, 1991, Mary Diana Dods: A Gentleman and a Scholar, paperback edit., 1994, Mary Wollstonecraft Shelley: An Introduction, 1998; editor (with Donald H. Reiman and Michael Jaye): The Evidence of the Imagination, 1978; editor: (with Charles Robinson) The Mary Shelley Reader, 1990; editor: Proserpine and Midas and Relation of the Cenci, 1992, The Selected Letters of Mary Wollstonecraft Shelley, 1995; with Stuart Curran Shelley: Poet & Legislator of the World, 1996; editor: Lives of the Great Romantics III: Mary Shelley, 1999; editor: (with Stuart Curran) Mary Shelley in Her Times, 2000; cons. editor and author gen. intro.: The Novels and Selected Works of Mary Wollstonecraft Shelley, 1996, book rev. editor: Keats-Shelley Jour., 1976—94. Keats-Shelley Assn. Am. Disting. scholar, 1992; NEH fellow, 1974-75, Henry E. Huntington Libr. fellow, 1976, Am. Coun. Learned Socs. fellow, 1977-78; Am. Philos. Soc. grant, 1980-81, NEH grant, 1984-87. Mem. MLA, Byron Assn., Keats-Shelley Assn. Am. (bd. dirs.), Soc. for Textual Scholarship (exec. com. 1993—), NYU Alumni Assn., Phi Beta Kappa (founding pres. Zeta chpt. of D.C.). Home: Washington, DC. Died Aug. 12, 2006.

BENNETT, JAMES CHESTER, computer consultant, real estate developer; b. Chico, Calif., May 14, 1932; s. George Clerk and Georgia Mae (James) B.; m. Grace M. Schutrum, Feb. 14, 1955 (div. 1967); children: Ronald, Becky Ann, Todd Bryant. BA in Bus., Calif. State U., Long Beach, 1965. Sgt. USAF, 1947-62; customer engr. IBM, L.A., 1962-70; mgr. computer systems Continental Airlines, L.A., 1970-82; instr. ITT Tech. Inst., Buena Park, Calif., 1982-84; dir. Ramasat Comm., LTD, Bangkok, Thailand, 1984-89; instr. ITT Tech. Inst., San Diego, 1989-90; pres. The Systems Group, Inc., Ramona, Calif., from 1990. Avocations: computer graphics, amature radio. Home: Ramona, Calif. Died Oct. 12, 2004.

BENNISON, ALLAN PARNELL, geological consultant; b. Stockton, Calif., Mar. 8, 1918; s. Ellis Norman Lambly and Cora Mae (Parnell) B.; m. DeLeo Smith, Sept. 4, 1941; children: Victor, Christina, Mary. BA, U. Calif., Berkeley, 1940. Cert. petroleum geologist, cert. profl. geologist. Geology fellow Antioch Coll., Yellow Springs, Ohio, 1940-42; photogrammetrist U.S. Geol. Survey, Arlington, Va., 1942-45; stratigrapher, asst. chief geologist Companias Unidas de Petroleos, Cartagena, Colombia, 1945-49; staff stratigrapher Sinclair Oil & Gas Co., Tulsa, 1949-69; geol. cons. Tulsa, from 1969. Cons. in field. Editor: Tulsa's Physical Environment, 1973; compiler maps; contbr. articles to profl. jours. Fellow AAAS, Geol. Soc. Am., Explorers Club; mem. Am. Assn. Petroleum Geologists (hon., trustee assoc., Disting. Svc. award 1986), Soc. Econ. Paleontologists and Mineralogists (Disting. Svc. award 1990), Tulsa Geol. Soc. (pres. 1965), Tulsa Astronomy Club (v.p. 1965), Explorers Club, Sigma Xi. Republican. Episcopalian. Avocations: photography, astronomy, reading, travel. Died May 5, 2004.

BENSON, PERRY MATTHEW, electronics engineer, educator; b. N.Y.C., Feb. 24, 1926; s. Israel and Helen (Edelman) Benson; m. Edna Switzen, Sept. 10, 1945; children: Ira Jesse, Peter Eric. Electronic technician/engr., Naval Rsch. Lab., 1945; degree, Albert Einstein Coll. Medicine/NYU, 1963—65. Cons. electronics/med. instrument, N.Y.C., 1946—55; engr., tchr., vis. lectr. U. Calif.-San Francisco, NYU, U. So. Calif. Electronics for Medicine, Inc., White Plains, NY, 1955—79; engr., tchr., lectr. U. Calif.-San Francisco, NYU, U. So. Calif. Honeywell Corp., Pleasantville, NY, 1979—85; electronic engr. VA Med. Ctr., Miami Beach, Fla., 1986—88; ret., from 1988. Engring. editor: E for M Bull. in House Jour., 1966. Edn. liaison Civic Assn., N.Y.C., 1953—58; sr. sen. Calif. Sr. Legislature, San Diego County, from 1996; mem. county com. Polit. Party, Scarsdale, NY, 1963—75. ETM 2d class USN, 1944—46. Mem.: Nat. Soc. for Tng. and Devel. (nat. com. participant 1966—84), Calif. Sr. Legislature (chair San Diego caucus 1998—2001, Lt. gov. award 2000). Died July 31, 2004.

BENTON, NICHOLAS, theater producer; b. Boston, Oct. 18, 1926; s. Jay Rogers and Frances (Hill) B.; m. Kate Bigelow, June 5, 1954; children: Frances Hill, Kate, Emily Weld, Louisa Barclay. Grad., Phillips Exeter Acad., 1945; AB, Harvard U., 1951. Promotion writer Life mag., N.Y.C., 1951-55, Fortune mag., N.Y.C., 1955-56; staff writer Time Mag., N.Y.C., 1956-57; advt. promotion mgr. Archtl. Forum, N.Y.C., 1957-64; gen. promotion mgr. Time-Life Books, Alexandria, Va., 1965-68, dir. pub. rels., 1968-83, v.p., 1977-83; lectr. pub. procedures course Radcliffe Coll., 1976-82; producing dir. Am. Kaleidoscope Theatre, 1983-85; pub., editor Middlesex House Press, NY, from 1999. Mem. Nat. Book Awards Com., 1971; co-chmn. Nat. Book Awards Week Com., 1975-79; vice-chmn. Am. Book Awards, 1981-82. Author: A Benton Heritage, 1964, The Call of the Weld, 1999, The Seven Weld Brothers, 2004; co-producer musical Phoenix '55, 1955, Salad Days, 1958, The Golden Age, 1984, the Perfect Party, 1986, Love Letters, 1989, The Heart's a Wonder, 1990; author, dir. (play) Not So Long Ago, 1995. Pres. East 69th St. Assn., 1963-64; 1st v.p. Soc. Meml. Sloan-Kettering Cancer Ctr., 1963-64, asst. treas., 1964-66, treas., 1967-68; exec. com. Friends of the Theatre Collection, Mus. of City of N.Y., 1983-86; pres. Land Owners Assn. Indian Neck, Wareham, Mass., 1993-95; chmn. tutoring program Harvard U., NY H.S., 1991—. With AUS, 1945-46. Recipient Opera Vol. Yr., Opera Guild Internat., 2000. Mem. Pubs. Publicity Assn. (pres. 1970-71), New Eng. Historic Geneal. Soc. (trustee 1979-95, corr. sec. 1982-88, v.p. 1988-93), N.Y. Geneal. and Biog. Soc., Assn. Am. Pubs. (freedom to pub. com. 1979-82), Time-Life Alumni Soc. (bd. dirs. 1994—), Soc. of Colonial Wars (editor newsletter 2005—), Harvard Club (bd. mgrs. N.Y.C. chpt. 1971-73), Bourne Cove Yacht Club (commodore Wareham, Mass. chpt. 1988-91), N.Y. City Opera (bd. dirs. 1995-99, guild pres. 1995-99, editor Tempo newsletter 1993-00). Died Feb. 26, 2006.

BENTSEN, LLOYD MILLARD, JR., former secretary of the treasury, retired senator; b. Mission, TX, Feb. 11, 1921; s. Lloyd M. and Edna Ruth (Colbath) B.; m. Beryl Ann Longino, Nov. 27, 1943; children: Lloyd M. III, Lan, Tina. JD, U. Tex., 1942. Bar: Tex. 1942. Pvt. law practive, McAllen, Tex., 1945-48; judge Hidalgo County, Tex., 1946—48; mem. US Congress from 15th Tex. Dist., 1948—55; pres. Lincoln Consol., Houston, 1955-70; US Senator from Tex., 1971-93; chmn. senate fin. com.; mem. senate commerce, sci., transp. and joint com. on taxation and congl. joint econ. com.; sec. US Dept. Treasury, Washington, 1993-94; ptnr. Verner, Lipfert, Bernhard, McPherson & Hand, 1994—98. Democratic nominee for Vice Pres. U.S., 1988. Served to maj. USAAF, 1942-45. Decorated Disting. Flying Cross, Air Medal with 3 oak leaf clusters; recipient Presdl. Medal of Freedom, 1999. Home: Houston, Tex. Died May 23, 2006.

BERENSTAIN, STANLEY, author, illustrator; b. Phila., Sept. 29, 1923; s. Harry and Rose (Brander) B.; m. Janice Grant, Apr. 13, 1946; children: Leo, Michael. Student, Phila. Coll. Art, 1941-42, Phila. Acad. Fine Arts, 1946-49. Works exhibited in Met. Mus. Art, N.Y.C.; works represented in U. Kans., Kans. State U.; author, illustrator (with Jan Berenstain): The Berenstain's Baby Book, 1951, Sister, 1952, Tax-Wise, 1952, Marital Blitz, 1954, Baby Makes Four, 1956, Lover Boy, 1958, It's All in the Family, 1958, Bedside Lover Boy, 1960, And Beat Him When He Sneezes, 1960, Call Me Mrs., 1961, It's Still in the Family, 1961, Office Lover Boy, 1962, The Facts of Life for Grown-Ups, 1963, Flipsville-Squaresville, 1965, Mr. Dirty vs. Mr. Clean, 1967, You Could Diet Laughing, 1969, Be Good or I'll Belt You, 1970, Education Impossible, 1970, Never Trust Anyone Over 13, 1970, How to Teach Your Children About Sex Without Making a Complete Fool Of Yourself, 1970, How to Teach Your Children About God Without Actually Scaring Them Out of Their Wits, 1971, Are Parents Real?, 1972, What Your Parents Never Told You About Being a Mom or Dad, 1995; author, illustrator (with Jan Berenstain) "Berenstain Bears" series, 1962—; writer TV teleplays include The Berenstain Bears' Christmas Tree, 1979, The Berenstain Bears Meet Bigpaw, 1980, The Berenstain Bears' Easter Surprise, 1981, The Berenstain Bears' Comic Valentine, 1983, The Berenstain Bears Play Ball, 1983, The Berenstain Bears' CBS Show, 1986-87. Recipient Sch. Bell award NEA, 1960, Brit. Book Ctr. honor book, 1968, Best Book award Am. Inst. Graphic Arts, 1970, Silver award Internat. Film and TV Festival, 1980, 82, 87, Young Readers' award Mich. Coun. Tchrs. English, 1981, Children's Classic award Internat. Reading Assn., 1982, 83, 84, 87, Buckeye award Ohio State Libr. Assn., 82, 85, Ariz. Children's Choice Book award nominee, 1985, Ariz. Young Readers award, 1985, Ludington award, 1989; various books named Best Book by U. Chgo. Ctr. for Children's Books, 1972, 74, Honor Book by Phila. Libr. Children's Reading Round Table, 1972, 73, 74, 76, 80, 82, 83, 84, 85, 87, 88, 89, Children's Book of Yr. by Child Study Assn. Am., 1977, 82. Died Nov. 26, 2005.

BERG, G. VIVIAN, artist; b. Worcester, Mass., Feb. 28, 1932; d. Emil Mauritz Mattson and Gunhild Maria Israelson; m. Kenneth George Berg, May 10, 1957; children: Donna Maria, Leah Christine. Tng. cert., Ward Sch. Airline Tng., Worcester, 1951; diploma, Worcester Sch. Bus., 1951. Sec. Ea. Airlines, N.Y.C., 1951-52; legal sec. Office of Russell W. Anderson, Worcester, 1953-61; tchr. art Auburn, 1976-2000. One woman shows include Ogunquit (Maine) Art Ctr., Shore Road Gallery, Boston, Harrison Conf. Ctr., Marlboro, Mass; group shows include Cultural Assembly Portrait Show, UN Conf. Women in Nairobi, 1985; represented in more than 450 permanent, pvt., corp. and pub. collections including Milford (Mass.) Fed. Bank, Milford Savs. Bank, 1st Svc. Bank, Pepperell, Mass., Merrimac Valley Credit Union, North Andover, Mass., Spencer Savs. Bank, Medway (Mass.) Nat. Bank, Unibank for Savs., Hoosac Savs. Bank North Adams, Mass., Medway Co-Operative Bank, Methuen (Mass.) Co-Operative Bank, Am. Eagle Credit Union, Manchester, Conn., TruNorth Fin., North Adams, N.E. Cmty. Credit Union, Haverhill, Mass., Haverhill Co-Op Bank, Falmouth Security Fed., Roslindale Co-Operative Bank, Falmouth Security Fed., Mass., Roslindale Coop., Mass., New Eng. Design Assocs., Worcester, Oxford (Mass.) Free Pub. Libr., Atlantis Gallery Worcester Mass., Shore Rd. Gallery Ogunquit Maine Mem. Am. Soc. Marine Artists, Am. Mensa Ltd., Nat. Mus. Women in the Arts. Episcopalian. Died Oct. 29, 2005.

BERG, ROBERT RAYMOND, geologist, educator; b. St. Paul, May 28, 1924; s. Raymond F. and Jennie (Swanson) B.; m. Josephine Finck, Dec. 20, 1946; children: James R. (dec.), Charles R., William R. BA, U. Minn., 1948, PhD, 1951. Geologist, Calif. Co., Denver, 1951-56; cons. Berg and Wasson, Denver, 1957-66; prof. geology, head dept. Tex. A&M U., from 1967, Michel T. Halbouty prof. geology, 1982-2001, prof. emeritus, 2001—06, dir. univ. research, 1972. Cons. petroleum geology, 1959-2006 Contbr. papers in field. Served with AUS, 1943-46. Recipient Disting. Achievement award, U. Minn., 1992. Fellow Geol. Soc. Am.; mem. Am. Assn. Petroleum Geologists (disting. lectr. 1972, hon. mem. 1985, Sidney Powers Meml. award 1993, Disting. Educator award 2000), Am. Inst. Profl. Geologists (pres. 1971, hon. mem. 1988), Nat. Acad. Engring. Home: Bryan, Tex. Died June 13, 2006.

BERGER, HENRY, physicist; b. Bklyn., Feb. 8, 1936; s. Herman and Lena (Berman) B.; m. Sybil Lois Kagen, June 24, 1964 (div. 1977); 1 child, Mark Kagan. BS in Physics, Poly. Inst. N.Y., 1957, MS, 1959, PhD, 1967; postdoctoral grad. U. Pa., 1972-74. Researcher MIT, Lexington, Mass., 1969-72; cons. Microwave Cons., Massapequa, N.Y., 1974-77; sr. engr. Honeywell, Def. Systems Div., Mpls., 1977-78; program mgr. Dept. Navy, Washington, 1979-89, Dept. Army, Ft. Belvoir, 1989—; faculty math. USDA Grad. Sch., Washington, 1983—. Contbr. articles to profl. jours. Mem. Am. Phys. Soc., IEEE, Sigma Xi. Home: Alexandria, Va. Died Dec. 19, 2004.

BERGER, NEWELL JAMES, JR., retired security professional; b. Pitts., Oct. 26, 1926; s. Newell James and Marjorie Ikler (Herndon) B.; m. Darlene Ingram, Sept. 6, 1950 (dec. Nov. 1990). BS, Mich. State U., 1958; grad., U.S. Army Command and Gen. Staff Coll., 1963, U.S. Army War Coll., 1972; MA, Webster U., 1993. Enlisted man U.S. Army, 1944, advanced through grades to staff sgt., 1948, commd. 2d lt., 1948, advanced through grades to col., 1970, chief corrections hdqrs. Washington, 1970-72, dir. security Office Surgeon Gen., 1972-73, dir. security Health Svcs. Command Ft. Sam Houston, Tex., 1973-78, ret., 1978; security cons. Phoenix and San Diego, 1979-84; chief plant security Teledyne Ryan Aero. Co., San Diego, 1985-86; dep. dir. security BAE Sys. Mission Solutions, San Diego, 1986-99; ret., 1999. Decorated Legion of Merit with two oak leaf clusters. Mem. Internat. Assn. Chiefs Police (life), Am. Soc. for Indsl. Security (life cert. protection profl.). Republican. Episcopalian. Avocations: music, history. Died Feb. 1, 2004.

BERGER, RONALD, real estate investor; b. Chgo., June 30, 1933; s. Albert Erwin and Dorothy (Ginsberg) B.; m. Meta Schwartz; children: Jan Ellen, Louis Alan, Jonathan David. BBA, U. Miami, 1955. V.p. Mid-Am. Appraisal, Chgo., 1959-63; pres. Callner Corp., Chgo., 1963-70; former pres. Berger Fin. Services, Chgo. Bd. dirs. Mid Town Bank, Chgo., Columbia Nat. Bank, Chgo. Mem. Lambda Alpha. Clubs: Standard (Chgo.); Bryn Mawr Country (Lincolnwood, Ill.). Home: Chicago, Ill. Died Apr. 1, 2004.

BERGSTROM, ROBERT WILLIAM, lawyer; b. Chgo., Nov. 8, 1918; s. C. William and Ellen (Anderson) B.; m. Ruth Doyle (dec. 1975); m. Betty Eleanor Howard, 1979; children: Mark Robert, Philip Alan, Bryan Scott, Cheryl Lee, Jeffrey Alan. MBA, U. Chgo., 1947; LLB, Ill. Inst. Tech.-Chgo. Kent Coll. Law, 1940, JD, 1970. Bar: Ill. 1940, Ariz., 1991, U.S. Supreme Ct. 1950. Pvt. practice, Chgo. and Ariz.; founder Ill. Statewide Com. on Cts. and Justice, 1971-85. Bd. dirs. Ill. Com. for Constl. Conv., 1969-70, Ill. Constl. Research Group, 1969, Gov.'s Task Force on Jud. Merit Selection, 1989; spl. counsel Ill. Joint Legislative Com. to Investigate Met. San. Dist. of Cook County, 1967, Ill. Senate Mcpl. Corp. Com., 1970. Co-author: The Law of Competition in Illinois, 1962, Antitrust Developments, 1955-68, Antitrust Advisor, 1985; author Marxism, Senator Sherman, and Our Economic System, 1968, and numerous articles on antitrust, constl. law, and econs.; Editor: Chgo. Bar Record, 1971-72. As chmn. Com. for Legis. Reform, drafted constl. amendment enacted 1980, reducing Ill. Ho. of Reps. by 1/3 and abolishing cumulative voting. Lt. USNR, 1941-46. Named Chicagoan of Yr. in Law and Judiciary, Chgo. Jaycees, 1969; recipient medal Ill. Constl. Conv., 1970, Disting. Pub. Service award Union League Club, 1981; awarded star on Hollywood Walk of Fame, 1993. Mem. ABA, Ill. Bar Assn., Chgo. Bar Assn. (sec. 1969-71), State Bar Ariz., Union League Club (pres. 1971-72). Home: Chicago, Ill. Died June 4, 2006.

BERKSON, SADIE, volunteer; b. Winnipeg, Man., Can., June 18, 1913; came to U.S., 1927; d. Samuel and Minnie (Liss) Finkelstein; m. Isadore J. Berkson, Feb. 3, 1940 (dec. Oct. 1982). Exec. sec. Convenant Club, Chgo., 1929-40. Supr. blood bank ARC, WWII and Six Days War, Israel; past mem. bd. dirs. Fedn. and Jewish United Fund; charter, life bd. dirs. Louis A. Weiss Meml. Hosp., Brandeis Hadassah, B'nai B'rith, Art Inst. Chgo., Friends Chgo. Pub. Libr., Mus. Contemporary Art, Nat. ARC; chmn. 1st Women's Israel Bond Dr., 1948; a founder women's br. Brandeis divsn., Chgo.; co-chmn. 1st women's gift divsn. Jewish Combined Jewish Appeal, 1947; founder 1st spl. women's gift divsn. Crusade of Mercy, 1970; bd. overseers Ill. Inst. Tech.-Chgo.-Kent Coll. Law, 1992—, chmn. Consular Ball, 1993, 94; chmn. Rita Hayworth Ball for Alzheimer's Assn., Chgo., 1987, also bd. dirs. and co-chmn. Chgo. support group, hon. emeritus bd. dirs., 1996—. Recipient award of merit ARC, Woman of Yr. award Crusade of Mercy, 1970, Cartier Disting. Humanitarian award Alzheimer's Assn., 1992, Archtl. award for I.J. Berkson Res. Reading Room, Ill. Inst. Tech.-Chgo. Kent Coll. Law, 1992, Disting. Svc. award Ill. Inst. Tech.-Chgo.-Kent Coll. Law, 1994, honoree Chgo. Rita Hayworth Ball for Alzheimer's, 1997; established, endowed I.J. Berkson Scholarship Fund for Alzheimer's rsch., 1983; endowed I.J. Berkson Res. Reading Room, 1992; seeded, established I.J. and Sadie Berkson Scholarship Fund, Chgo.-Kent Coll. Law, 1992. Mem. Soc. Wills and Endowment for Alzheimer's Assn. (founding). Avocations: painting, golf, tennis, world travel. Died Feb. 1, 2006.

BERLIN, JACOB BORIS, psychotherapist; b. N.Y.C., Apr. 16, 1924; s. Alexander and Martha (Aranow) B.; m. Anne Wright Morris, Apr. 26, 1947; children— Alexander, Ralph, Christopher, Letitia, Deborah. A.B., Harvard U., 1950; M.S.P.H., U. N.C., Chapel Hill, 1951; M.Div., Va. Theol. Sem., 1960; M.A., U. S.C., 1975; DMin Colo. Theol. Sem., 1986. Lic. marriage and family counselor, Ga.; ordained to ministry, Episcopal Ch., 1960. Sanitarian, Near East Found., Iranian area, 1951-57; vicar St. Andrew's Episcopal Ch., Pasadena, Md., 1960-64, St. Anne's Episcopal Ch., Damascus, Md., 1964-69; assoc. dir. pastoral Counseling Ctrs. of Augusta (Ga.), 1969-73; asst. prof. Sch. Nursing, Med. Coll. Ga., 1973-75; dir. St. Paul's Counseling Service, Augusta, 1975—; assoc. rector St. Paul's Episcopal Ch., Augusta, 1975-94; Vicar atonement Episcopal Ch., Augusta, 1994—. Pres., Augusta Area Mental Health Assn., 1976-77; bd. dirs. Sr. Citizens Council, Augusta, 1975-76, Augusta Players, 1969-72, Housing Authority Adjudication Ct., Richmond County, 1973-75. Served with U.S. Army, 1942-45. Named Hon. Citizen of Sarlat, the Dordogne, France in recognition of service as OSS agt. with French resistance in World War II, 1985. Mem. Am. Assn. Pastoral Counselors (diplomate), Am. Assn. Marriage and Family Therapy (approved supr.). Home: Augusta, Ga. Died May 29, 2004.

BERLING, E. GAYLE, nurse practitioner; b. Stillwater, Okla., Oct. 29, 1950; d. William Fred and Mary Glynn (Munger) Cochran; m. Richard Kent Baldwin, Jan. 28, 1971 (div.); m. Gary Wayne Neely, Jan. 23, 1982 (div. June 1985); m. David Thomas Berling, Dec. 2, 1989. Student, Okla. Bapt. U., Shawnee, 1967-71; BSN, Cen. State U., Edmond, Okla., 1973; cert. U. Ariz., 1980. Staff nurse neonatal ICU, U. Okla. Health Scis. Ctr. and Children's Hosp., Oklahoma City, 1973-75; nurse Presbyn. Hosp., Oklahoma City, 1975; pub. health nurse, newborn follow up program Ariz. Dept. Health Svcs., 1975-77; asst. DON Westside Community Hosp., Long Beach, Calif., 1977-78; nurse newborn nursery Desert Samaritan Hosp., Mesa, Ariz., 1978-80; neonatal nurse practitioner Good Samaritan Med. Ctr., Phoenix, 1980-83, 88—, Air Evac, Phoenix, 1980-85; neonatal nurse practitioner Scottsdale (Ariz.) Meml. Hosp., 1984-93; RN auditor Quality, Inc., Dallas, 1987-88; owner NNP Resources Inc., Phoenix, 1992—; nurse practitioner Mead Johnson & Co. grantee, 1980. Mem. Nat. Assn. Neonatal Nurses, Neonatal Nurse Practitioners Ariz. Home: Glendale, Ariz. Died Aug. 5, 2004.

BERLOWE, FREDERIC HERMAN, industrial engineer; b. NYC, Aug. 16, 1930; s. Phillip and Mae (Palmet) B.; m. Sondra Satz, Dec. 27, 1959; children: Amanda Joy, Laura Jane, Peter Emerson. BS in Indsl. Engring., U. Miami, 1952. Registered profl. engr., Fla. Engr. product design, layout Miami Window, Ludman Corp., Miami, 1952-54; engr. mech. contractors Hill-York Dublin Co., Miami, 1955-60; mech. designer Brown and Sells, Coral Gables, Fla., 1960-63; tchr. mech. engring. and refrigeration Miami Dade C.C., 1961-62, U. Miami, Coral Gables, 1960-63; pres. Frederic H. Berlowe Assocs., Inc., Coral Gables, 1963—2005. Village engr. Va. Gardens, Fla., 1964-72. Mem. Nat. Soc. Profl. Engrs. (sr.), Fla. Engring. Soc. (sr.), ASHRAE (sr.), Nat. Acad. Forensic Engrs. (diplomate), Nat. Fire Protection Assn., So. Bldg. Code Congress internat., Internat. Conf. of Bldg. Ofcls., Soc. Automotive Engrs., Masons. Avocations: reading, horseback riding, hunting, boating, woodworking. Home: Miami, Fla. Died Apr. 27, 2005.

BERMAN, LEO, psychotherapist; b. Chgo., Jan. 31, 1917; s. David and Rose (Mahlin) B.; m. Irene Goldstein, May 10, 1944; children: Rena, Janice. D in Metaphys. Sci., U. Metaphys. Sci., L.A., 1981; psychotherapist, Parkside Human Svcs. Inst. Psychotherapy, Park Ridge, Ill., 1982; D of Humanities, U. Metaphys. Sci., 1982. Psychotherapist Luth. Gen. Hosp., Park Ridge, Ill., 1982-84; psychotherapist Ctr. of Concern Inst. Psychotherapy, Park Ridge, 1983-91; psychotherapist ARK, Chgo., 1989-91. Author rsch. papers. With U.S. Army, 1941-44. Mem. AACD, Am. Group Psychotherapy Assn., Am. Assn. Family Counselors and Mediators, Inc., Internat. Acad. Behavioral Medicine Counseling and Psychotherapist, Phobia Soc. Am., Am. Orthopsychiat. Assn., Masons. Avocations: fishing, birdwatching. Home: Des Plaines, Ill. Died Nov. 21, 2004.

BERNARD, JOSEPH, actor, educator; b. N.Y.C., Dec. 12, 1923; s. Bernard and Lena (Kaplan) Fieldman; m. Bina, 1952 (dec. 2001) children: Bella Julie, Sam. Actor on Broadway, N.Y.C., from 1946; tchr. Joseph Bernard Acting Studio, Las Vegas, Nev., from 1979. Playwright Take Off Your Clothes I'll Make You a Star, 1983; screenwriter (film) Bonsetter; actor in numerous Broadway prodns. including A Flag Is Born, 1946, Skipper Next to God, 1947, Mister Roberts, 1948, The Lark, 1955, Candide, 1956, Look Homeward Angel, 1958, Rhinoceros, 1960; actor in regional theatre I'm Not Rappaport, The Sunshine Boys, The Price; (films) Murder, Inc., 1960, Judgement At Nuremburg, 1961, Don't Just Stand There, 1968, Ice Station Zebra, 1968, The Steagle, 1971, The Baby, 1973, Man Who Loved Women, 1983, Fever Pitch, 1985, Heat, 1986, Mikey, 1992, Warlock: The Armageddon, 1993, The Granny, 1995; (TV films) Lost Flight, 1969, The Immortal, 1969, The Challenge, 1970, Quarantined, 1970, The Tattered Web, 1971, Gidget Gets Married, 1972, The Police Story, 1973, The Laughing Policeman, 1973, The Winds of Kitty Hawk, 1978, Pleasure Place, 1980; (TV appearances) The Twilight Zone, 1961, The Defenders, 1964, I Spy, 1967, Star Trek, 1967,. The Big Valley, 1968, It Takes a Thief, 1968, The Flying Nun, 1968, Here Come the Brides, 1969, Get Smart, 1970, The Waltons, 1973, Kaz, 1978, The Rockford Files, 1979. Scholar New Sch. for Social Research, 1940. Home: Las Vegas, Nev. Died Apr. 3, 2006.

BERNARD, WILLIAM BEKKER, retired electronics engineer; b. Chgo., May 31, 1914; s. Frederick and Norma Drucilla (Ziehm) B.; m. Dorothy DeLee King, Aug. 13, 1938; children: Norma Bernard Struch, William Bekker Jr., Robert H. BSEE, U. Fla., 1936. Radio inspector FCC, N.Y.C., 1937-38, Atlanta, 1938-41; commd. ensign USNR, 1938; called to active duty, 1941; advanced through grades to capt. USN, 1957, ret., 1961; sr. engr. Electromech. Rsch., Sarasota, Fla., 1961-71; chief engr. Lampkin Labs., Bradenton, Fla., 1971-76; v.p. engring. Com-Ser Labs., Bradenton, 1976-93; ret., 1993. Contbr. articles to profl. jours.; patentee in field. Republican. Home: Sarasota, Fla. Died July 19, 2004.

BERNDT, WILLIAM O., pharmacology educator, former academic administrator; b. St. Joseph, Mo., May 11, 1933; s. Oscar Emil and Gertrude Ann (Muthig) B.; m. Bonnie Lou Lampe, Aug. 28, 1954; childen; Barbara, Carol, David, Mary Joan, Paul. BS, Creighton U., 1954; PhD, SUNY, Buffalo, 1959. Diplomate Am. Bd. Toxicology. From instr. to prof. pharmacology Dartmouth Med. Sch., Hanover, N.H., 1959-74; prof., chmn. pharmacology and toxicology Med. Ctr. U. Miss., Jackson, 1974-82; prof. pharmacology Med. Ctr. U. Nebr. Med. Ctr., Omaha, from 1982, dean grad. studies and rsch., 1982-96, vice-chancellor academic affairs, 1985-96, interim chancellor, 1991—92, chancellor, 1997—98. Chmn. Cosmetic Ingredient Rev. Expert Panel, Washington, 1987-90, Gordon Rsch. Conf.: Mechanisms of Toxicity, Meriden, N.H., 1991; mem. Am. Bd. Toxicology, 1988-92, pres. 1992. Contbr. chpts. to books and articles to profl. jours. Mem. pharm. study sect. NIH, Bethesda, Md., 1980-84; chmn. Who Task Group Nephrotoxicity Document, Bilthoven, The Netherlands, 1989. Capt. M.C., 1962-63. Fellow Acad. Toxicological Scis.; mem. Am. Soc. Nephrology, Am. Soc. Pharm. and Experimental Therapeutics, Soc. Toxicology, Inst. Soc. Study Xenobiotics, Internat. Soc. Nephrology, Am. Heart Assn. (established investigator 1964-69). Avocations: photography, exercise. Home: Fort Calhoun, Nebr. Died Aug. 31, 2006.

BERRY, BOBBIE CLAYTON, retired secondary school educator; b. Cleveland, Tenn., Oct. 22, 1934; d. Clyde Thomas and Ruth (Witt) Clayton; m. Frederick Harold Berry, Feb. 7, 1955; 1 child, Frederick Clayton. BA, Northeast La. U., 1974, MEd, 1975, EdS, 1985; EdD, Miss. State U., 1989. Cert. spl. edn. tchr. Tchr. Caldwell Parish Sch. System, Columbia, La., 1980-83, assessment tchr., 1983-94; ednl. diagnostician Bossier Parish Sch. Sys., Bossier City, La., 1994—2005, ret., 2005. Adj. instr. Northeast La. U., Monroe, La., 1989, La. Tech. U., Ruston, spring 1995. Mem. Coun. for Exceptional Children, Mid-South Ednl. Rschr. (reviewer 1990-92), La. Ednl. Rschr., Sigma Tau Delta, Phi Kappa Phi, Phi Delta Kappa (sec. 1990-91). Republican. Episcopalian. Avocation: collect ceramic chickens and shoes. Home: Bossier City, La. Died June 25, 2005.

BERRY, EDWARD HENRY, accountant; b. Sikeston, Mo., May 9, 1945; s. Edward H. and Gertrude (Billings) B.; m. Linda Howard, Apr. 9, 1966; children: Keith E., Chris A. BSBA, Semo State U., 1968. CPA, Mo. Staff acct. Berry, Patmor & Co., Sikeston, 1970-76; pres., ptrn. Berry & Heath, Inc., Sikeston, 1977-78; ptnr. Spitzmiller, Hobbs, Clay, Berry, Sikeston, 1978-88; pres., ptnr. Berry & Forbis, P.C., Sikeston, from 1988. Deacon First Christian Ch., Sikeston, 1990—. Sgt. U.S. Army, 1968-70. Mem. AICPA, Sikeston Lions Club (pres. 1987), Sikeston C. of C., Mo. Soc. CPAs, Mo. Edn. Found. (sec. 1991-92), Mo. Soc. CPAs (trustee 1990-92, bd. dirs. 1992—). Democrat. Avocations: golf, hunting, fishing. Home: Galveston, Tex. Died July 31, 2004.

BERRY, JANE MICHIKO, nursing administrator; b. Fresno, Calif., Mar. 6, 1946; d. Sam S. and Kay (Kikue) Hirakawa; m. Monte R. Berry, Sept. 30, 1985; 1 child, Shellie K. Sakamoto. Student, Humboldt State Coll., 1964-65, Calif. State U., Fresno, 1989; AA, Fresno City Coll., 1971. RN, Calif. Indsl. nurse Sperry New Holland, Fowler, Calif.; clin. staff RN Fresno Community Hosp., Valley Med. Ctr., Fresno; dir. nursing San Joaquin Valley Dialysis Ctr., Fresno. Recipient Disting. Svc. award Kidney Found., 1983, 84, 88, 89. Mem. Cen. Valley Kidney Found. (bd. dirs. 1983-90, chmn. dialysis patient picnic 1983-90, chairperson nominating and fin. com. 1988). Home: Fresno, Calif. Died Feb. 15, 2005.

BERRY, LOREN CURTIS, retired lawyer, consultant; b. N.Y.C., Apr. 30, 1912; s. Gordon Lockwood and Katharine Wolcott (Dwight) B.; m. Florence Hoyt Bateson, May 10, 1941; children: Rosina B. Dixon, Roger Wolcott, Lucinda B. AB cum laude, Yale U., 1934; LLB, Columbia U., 1938. Bar: Miss. 1937, N.Y. 1939. Assoc. Rogers & Wells and predecessor firms, N.Y.C., 1939-41, 45-53, ptnr., 1953-83, cons. on estates & trusts, 1983-90, sr. counsel, 1990-2000. Dir. Church & Dwight Co., Inc., 1961-84. Councilman Town of Huntington, N.Y., 1953-57; v.p. Assn. Towns State of N.Y., Albany, 1957-60; del. from 2d senatorial dist. to N.Y. State Constl. Conv., 1967; clerk of vestry St. John's Ch., Cold Spring Harbor, N.Y., 1982-88; mem. Suffolk County N.Y. Rep. Com., 1952-85. With USNR, 1941-45, lt. commdr. 1944-45, WWII Navy Scouting Squadron Assn., counsel, 1994—. Mem. N.Y. State Bar Assn., Suffolk County Bar Assn., Huntington C. of C. (dir. 1958-63), Elks, Union Club N.Y., Tahawus Club. (sec. 1975-95). Home: Hilton Head Island, SC. Died May 3, 2005.

BERRY, ROBERT JOHN, architect; b. Concord, Mass., Nov. 10, 1947; A in Archtl. Engring., Wentworth Inst. Tech., 1967; BArch, U. Ariz., 1971. Registered architect, Mass. Asst. prof. Wentworth Inst. Tech., Boston, 1974-81, 90-94; prin. Robert J. Berry, Architect, Boxborough, Mass., from 1974. Mem. Am. Soc. Archtl. Perspectivists (exhibitor 1986). Avocations: photography, golf, painting. Died Feb. 17, 2004.

BERTOLINO, ANGELA MARIA, educational association administrator; b. Phila., Jan. 27, 1944; d. Peter Jude and Mary Louise (Matero) B. BA, Glassboro (N.J.) State Coll., 1967. Negotiator Willingboro (N.J.) Edn. Assn., 1978-84, pres., 1980-84; assembly del. N.J. Edn. Assn., Trenton, from 1983, mem. polit. action com. Willingboro, from 1983; govt. relations specialist Burlington County Edn. Assn., Willingboro, from 1983, pres., 1980-84; dir. NEA, Washington, 1988-95; vice chmn. Ednl. Info. and Resource Ctr., Sewell, N.J., 1986-89, chmn., 1989-94. Govt. rels. chmn. N.J. Ednl. Assn., 1993—. Mem. NEA, N.J. Edn. Assn., Willingboro Edn. Assn., Burlington County Edn. Assn. Roman Catholic. Avocations: reading, jigsaw puzzles, crossword puzzles, calligraphy, sports. Home: Glendora, NJ. Died July 23, 2005.

BERTOLINO, ELLEN, medical/surgical nurse; b. Pitts., Aug. 27, 1954; d. Thomas L. and helen (Makusenko) Baratta; m. Michael Bertolino, Aug. 17, 1974; 1 child, Angela Michelle. Diploma, Citizen's Gen. Hosp. Sch. Nsg.,

1983; BS in Biology, LaRoche Coll., 1978, postgrad. RN, Pa. Staff nurse Allegheny Valley Hosp., Natrona Heights, Pa. Home: Russellton, Pa. Died Feb. 18, 2005.

BERZON, BETTY, psychotherapist; b. St. Louis, Jan. 18, 1928; d. Irvin and Eva (Zarfas) B. BA in Psychology, UCLA, 1957; MS in Psychology, Calif. State U., San Diego, 1962; PhD in Psychology, Internat. Coll., L.A., 1978. Lic. marriage, family and child counselor, Calif. Rsch. assoc. Western Behavioral Scis. Inst., La Jolla, Calif., 1962-68; dir. group program devel. Human Devel. Inst., Inc. (A Bell & Howell Co.), L.A., 1968-70; dir. rsch., v.p. Kairos, L.A., 1970-72; project dir./program developer Rsch. for Better Schs., Inc., Phila., 1973-76; pvt. practice, tng. cons. L.A., 1970—2006; pvt. practice, psychotherapy, 1970—2006. Guest lectr. ext. divs. UCLA, U. Calif., Riverside, U. Calif., Irvine, U. Calif., San Diego; tng. cons. in field, rsch. projects in field; bd. dirs. Gay and Lesbian Adolescent Social Svcs., L.A. Author numerous books, including Setting Them Straight, 1996, The Intimacy Dance, 1996, Permanent Partners, 1988, Surviving Madness: A Therapist's Own Story, 2002; editor: New Perspectives on Encounter Group, 1972, Positively Gay, 1979, 2d edit., 1992; contbr. articles to profl. jours. Tng. cons. Gay Community Svcs. Ctr., L.A., bd. dirs., 1972-75; tng. cons. Metro Community Ch., 1971-73; bd. dirs. Whitman-Radclyffe Found., 1976-77, exec. v.p., 1976; bd. suprs. West Hollywood Adv. Coun., 1975-77; bd. dirs. Nat. Gay Rights Advs., others. Mem. Gay Acad. Union (nat. pres. 1977-79). Home: Studio City, Calif. Died Jan. 24, 2006.

BESSUNGER, H. JOHN, food importer executive; b. Darmstadt, Hesse, Germany, June 6, 1919; came to U.S., 1949; s. Ernst and Else (Pauly) B.; m. Edith Agnes Brandes, July 21, 1945 (dec. Sept. 1984); m. Kelen Kim Ying Sam Moi, Sept. 19, 1992. BA, Higher Bus. Sch., Darmstadt, 1937. Owner Bessunger Plastic Factory, Ober-Ramstadt/Hesse, 1945-49, Movie Theater, Canaan, N.H., 1950-52; mgr., CEA L.S. Packing Co., Long Island City, N.Y., 1952-53; mgr. J. Reede, N.Y.C., 1953-61; v.p. Carl Christensen Corp., Bklyn., 1961-63, Haram-Christensen Corp., N.Y.C., from 1963, also chmn. bd. Carlstadt, N.J. Lectr. L.I. U. Southampton (N.Y.) campus, 1965—. Author: The Storekeeper's Guide to Imported Cheese, 1966, miscellaneous trade books and jours. Named Hon. Citizen City of Darmstadt, 1988. Mem. Cheese Importer Assn. Am. (past dir.), Lions, Oxford Club. Avocations: music, history, literature, languages. Home: Hampton Bays, NY. Died Feb. 16, 2004.

BEUTEL, BILL (WILLIAM CHARLES BEUTEL), former television news anchor; b. Dec. 12, 1930; m. Adair Beutel; 4 children. Grad., Dartmouth Coll.; student, U. Mich. Law Sch. With various radio/tv stas.; with CBS Radio, N.Y.C., ABC, 1962—2003, anchor, reporter Eyewitness News N.Y.C., 1970—2001, corr., 2001—03, bur. chief, 1968. Host A.M. America, 1975. Prodr. numerous documentaries such as the fall of the Berlin Wall and the integration of East and West Germany, the rise of Hitler and the origins of WW II and the Holocaust; trademark signoff "Good luck and be well". Died Mar. 18, 2006.

BEVER, CHRISTOPHER THEODORE, retired psychiatrist; b. Munich, Mar. 12, 1919; came to U.S., 1936, naturalized, 1943; s. Rudolf Paul and Maria (Bever) Berliner; m. Josephine Jordan Morton, Mar. 12, 1944; children: Christopher Theodore, Caroline Stakpole, Edward Watts, Sarah Sayward. AB cum laude, Harvard U., 1940, MD, 1943; postgrad., Washington Psychoanalytic Inst., 1947-53; diploma, Washington Sch. Psychiatry, 1952; MA in History, U. Md., 1993. Diplomate Am. Bd. Psychiatry. Intern Hartford (Conn.) Hosp., 1944; resident in psychiatry St. Elizabeths Hosp., Washington, 1947-48, psychiatrist, 1948-50, Washington Inst. Mental Hygiene, 1950-51; dir. Montgomery County Mental Hygiene Clinic, 1951-54; assoc. prof. psychiatry U. N.C., 1954-56; pvt. practice specializing psychiatry and psychoanalysis Washington, 1956-96. Dir. Washington Psychoanalytic Clinic, 1983-87; mem. faculty Washington Psychoanalytic Inst., 1954-97, emeritus tchg. analyst, 1997—; mem. faculty Washington Sch. Psychiatry, 1956—; mem. faculty George Washington U., 1957—, clin. prof., 1974-96, emeritus clin. prof., 1996—; cons. Eugene Meyer Treatment Ctr., Washington, 1989-98, Ctr. for Mental Health, Washington, 1990-95, Psychotherapy Referral Network, 1996-98. Bd. dirs. Cmty. Psychiat. Clinic (now CPC Health Corp.), Bethesda, Md., 1956—, pres., 1973-75; bd. dirs. D.C. Inst. Mental Hygiene, 1966-73, pres., 1966-68, trustee, 1973-90; bd. dirs. Washington Sch. Psychiatry, 1983—, Washington Psychoanalytic Found., 1993—; trustee William Alanson White Found., Washington, 1974-84. Recipient Mary W. Allen award Washington Psychoanalytic Soc., 1991, Cmty. Svc. award Washington Psychiat. Soc., 1998. Fellow Am. Psychiat. Assn. (life), Am. Orthopsychiat. Assn. (life); mem. AMA, Am. Psychoanalytic Assn. (life, cert. in psychoanalysis), Columbia (Md.) Study Group. Democrat. Avocations: photography, sailing, computers, history. Home: Glen Arm, Md. Died Dec. 28, 2005.

BEVERS, ROBERT JOE, education company executive; b. Tulsa, Okla., Mar. 17, 1937; s. Victor Glass Bevers and Opal Flossie (Goodwin) Main; m. Joy Arlene Kenter, Aug. 20, 1960 (div. Mar. 14 1986); children: Jana, Nancy; m. Laurel Anne Hyde, June 22, 1986; children: Padraic, Brendan. BA, Rice Inst., 1959, BSCE, 1960. Systems engr. IBM, Houston, 1960-64, sales rep. Austin, 1965-68; v.p. Nat. Western Life Ins. Co., Austin, 1969-70, John Roberts, Inc., Austin, 1972-73; gen. mgr. Control Data Corp., Mpls., 1973-79; pres., founder Logo Dyne, Inc., Mpls., 1979-90; chief exec. officer, co-founder B&H Systems, Inc., Mpls., 1983-90; v.p., chief info. officer United Edn. and Software, Sioux Falls, S.D., from 1989. Avocations: photography, tennis. Died Feb. 22, 2004.

BEYERS, CHARLOTTE KEMPNER, journalist, film producer; b. N.Y.C., Dec. 8, 1931; d. S. Marshall and Charlotte Kempner; m. Gerald Davis (div. 1965); children: Pamela Davis Kivelson, Nancy Davis Stewart, Alan Kempner, Cynthia; m. Robert West Beyers, June 20, 1971. BA in English, Stanford U., 1953, MA in Journalism, 1971. Cert. tchr., Calif. Writer Stanford (Calif.) Med. Ctr., 1965-66, rsch. assoc., 1971-72; free-lance writer Calif., 1969-72; writer Silicon Valley, San Jose, Calif., 1972-80; film producer Peregrine Prodns., Palo Alto, Calif., from 1986. Writer and prodr. videos AIDS in Your Sch., 1987, "A" is for AIDS, 1989, New Crack Facts, 1990, Night Journey to Crack, 1990, Shadow Children, 1991, Working Now, 1992, Women and AIDS: The Greatest Gamble, 1993; prodr. Healing Circles Choices for Back Pain (part of a series), 1996, Healing Circles Choices for Arthritis, 1997. Mem. Am. Soc. Journalists and Authors, Assn. Ind. Video and Film Makers Inc., No. Calif. Assn. Women in Film and TV (head publicity 1990). Avocations: hiking, travel, theater. Home: Palo Alto, Calif. Died Mar. 10, 2005.

BIAS, STEVEN EUGENE, chaplain; b. Pomona, Calif., Sept. 3, 1953; s. Roderick Eugene Bias and Elsie Glennette (Bonds) Joplin; m Jerlene Sue Weil, Aug. 6, 1977; children: Douglas Glen, Bryan Michael. BA in Bible, Cen. Bible Coll., Springfield, Mo., 1975; MDiv, Assemblies of God Theol. Sem., Springfield, 1981; D of Ministry, United Theol. Sem., Dayton, Ohio, 1991. Ordained to ministry Assemblies of God, 1981. Pastor First Assmebly of God Ch., Campbellsville, Ky., 1982-84; chaplain, commd. capt. USAF, Keesler AFB, Miss., 1985-87, chaplain Osan AFB, Republic of Korea, 1987-88, Wright-Patterson AFB, Ohio, from 1988. Contbr. articles to mil. publs. Mem. Air Force Assn. Home: Dayton, Ohio. Died June 22, 2004.

BIBBIE, NELLIE BRASSFIELD, retired eligibility professional; b. Leavenworth, Kans., Jan. 31, 1913; d. Joseph Henry and Hattie (McClanahan) Johnson; m. William Lloyd Bibbie, June 1, 1933; children: Lee-Roy, Carol Ann Bibbie Lewis. AA, Pasadena City Coll., 1964; postgrad., Calif. State U., 1974. Cert. eligibility worker, L.A. County. Key punch operator L.A. County, L.A., 1947-48, Dept. Water and Power, L.A., 1948-56; outside sales profl. Fuller Products, Pasadena, Calif., 1956; eligibility profl. L.A. County, Pasadena, 1956-76; ret., 1976. Author: Duty's Castle, 1997. Mem. Nat. Humane Soc. Democrat. Avocations: reading, collecting classic books. Home: Lancaster, Calif. Died June 30, 2004.

BICKS, RICHARD OSCAR, internist, gastroenterologist; b. Bklyn., May 26, 1927; s. Nathan Hale and Rose (Oseasohn) B.; m. Marcia Bryan, July 31, 1955; children: Nathan A., Steven B., Sharon G. BS, Coll. William and Mary, 1946; MD, SUNY, Bklyn., 1950. Diplomate Am. Bd. Internal Medicine with subspecialty in gastroenterology. Intern Mt. Sinai Hosp., Cleve., 1950-51, resident in medicine, 1951-52; resident in pathology Mallory Inst. Pathology, Boston City Hosp., 1952-53; resident in medicine Beth Israel Hosp., Boston, 1953-54; USPHS fellow in gastroenterology U. Chgo., 1956; teaching fellow in medicine Harvard Med. Sch., Boston, 1953-54; USPHS rsch. fellow U. Chgo., 1956-58; asst. prof. medicine U. Tenn., Memphis, 1958-66, clin. assoc. prof. medicine, 1966-69, clin. prof., from 1969. Contbr. articles to profl. jours., chpts. to books. Pres. Opera Memphis, 1974-77; dir. exch. program Xian Med. U., China, 1978. Lt. comdr. USNR, 1954-62. NIH grantee, 1963-67. Fellow ACP; mem. Am. Gastroenterol. Assn., Am. Soc. Gastrointestinal Endoscopy. Avocations: photography, travel. Home: Memphis, Tenn. Died Feb. 15, 2005.

BIDDLE, DAVID, neurologist; b. Phila., Nov. 17, 1944; s. Benjamin and Anna (Spector) B.; m. Trisha Fae Karagannis, Feb. 14, 1971; children: Erika Lauren, Jeremy Justin. BA, LaSalle Coll., 1966; MD, Jefferson Med. Coll., 1970. Diplomate Am. Bd. Psychiatry and Neurology. Intern L.I. (N.Y.) Jewish Hosp., 1970-71, resident in medicine, 1971-72, resident in neurology, 1974-77; prin. N.Y. Adult Neurology PC, Great Neck, N.Y., from 1977. Adv. bd. L.I. chpt. Myasthenia Gravis Found., 1989—. Contbr. articles to profl. jours. Bd. dirs. Kennilworth Owners' Assn., Kings Point, N.Y., 1988—. Maj. U.S. Army, 1972-74. Fellow Am. Acad. Neurology, Coll. Phila. Physicians; mem. Am Acad. Electodiagnostic Medicine, Royal Soc. Internal Medicine, L.I. Jewish Staff Soc. (pres. 1989-90) Home: Great Neck, NY. Died Mar. 18, 2004.

BIEN, DARL DEAN, business educator, consultant; b. Britton, S.D., July 12, 1940; s. Emil Otto and Clara Marie (Damgaard) B.; m. Bonnie Lee Thaden, Aug. 11, 1963 (div. 1980); children: Erik Neil, Christa Maren. BS, Huron Coll., S.D., 1962; MS, Case Western Res. U., 1966, PhD, 1970. Aerospace engr. Lewis Rsch. Ctr. NASA, Cleve., 1962-71; prof., dept. chair, assoc. dean to dean U. Denver, from 1971. Cons. The Pullman Co., Chgo., 1977-79, Continental Oil Co., Houston, 1979-80, 86, TWA, N.Y.C., 1983-85; various law firms, Colo., N.Mex., Ill., Idaho, 1977-95. Author: Basic Programming, 1975; tech. editor: Decision Sciences, 1975-77; contbr. articles to profl. jours. Pub. rels. profl. Denver Symphony Orch., Colo., 1987; econ. devel. profl. Denver C. of C., 1988. Recipient Achievement award NASA, 1969, 70, Fulbright Hays Exch., Fulbright Found., Eng. 1975-76, Fulbright scholar, Thailand, 1988-89, Macedonia, 1995, Free Enterprise award United Bank Denver, 1987. Mem. Am. Statis. Assn., Decision Sci. Inst., The Inst. Magmt. Sci. Democrat. Avocations: running, reading, gardening. Home: Denver, Colo. Died July 6, 2004.

BIENEMANN, CHARLES EDWARD, JR., lawyer; b. Balt., May 13, 1941; s. Charles Edward and Katherine Walters (Ellis) B.; m. Alison L. Asti, Apr. 20, 1986; chldren: Daniel Andrew Asti, Tracey Ann. BA, Yale U., 1964; JD, U. Md., 1970. Bar: Md. 1970, U.S. Tax Ct. 1977, U.S. Supreme Ct. 1978. Ptnr. Gordon, Feinblatt, Rothman, Hoffberger & Hollander, Balt., 1970-90, Lechowicz & Davis, Annapolis, Md., from 1990. Author: CCH Forms and Planning Aides, 1980, Liabilities of Fiduciaries: Guidelines Estate Planning, 1989; contbr. articles to profl. jours. Mem. ABA, Md. State Bar Assn., Balt. City Bar Assn., Anne Arundel County Bar Assn. Home: Pasadena, Md. Died July 5, 2004.

BIESCHKE, WALTER BERNARD, retired judge; b. Chgo., Jan. 4, 1924; s. Walter John and Margaret Gertrude (Biewald) B.; m. Connie Lee Van Noy, Mar. 17, 1968; children: Walter, Marcus. BA, Notre Dame U., 1950, JD, 1951. Bar: Ill. 1951, U.S. Dist. Ct. (no. dist.) Ill. 1953. Chief trial atty. Owens, Owens & Rinn, Chgo., 1952-62; pvt. practice litigation specialist Chgo., 1962-75; assoc. judge Ill. Cir. Ct. Cook County, Chgo., 1975-77, cir. judge, 1977-96. With U.S. Army Air Corps, 1943-45. Decorated Air medal with 4 oak leaf clusters. Mem. Ill. State Bar Assn., Chgo. Bar Assn. Roman Catholic. Avocations: biking, mountain hiking, fishing, reading, travel. Home: Elgin, Ill. Died Apr. 25, 2005.

BILKEY, EDWARD H., water transportation executive; b. NYC, Apr. 21, 1934; m. Janet Norton (dec.); children: Linda, Carlin, Barbara, Edward Jr.; m. Susan Noyes. BA, Yale Univ., 1956; MA, Fletcher Sch. Law & Diplomacy. Pres. Norton Lilly & Co.; v.p. Maher Terminals, NYC; exec. dir. Dubai Ports Authority, United Arab Emirates, Jebel Ali Free Zone Authority; COO Dubai Port World, Dubai, United Arab Emirates, 2003—06. Served USN. Died July 14, 2006.

BILLE, DONALD ALLEN, nurse, educator; b. Waupun, Wis., Feb. 10, 1943; s. Arthur and Ada (Wellhouse) B.; grad. St. Luke's Hosp. Sch. Nursing, 1964; B.S.N., U. Wis., Madison, 1966, Ph.D., 1975; M.S.N., Marquette U., 1971. Mem. faculty Coll. Nursing, Marquette U., Milw., 1970-72; coordinator intensive care unit VA Med. Center, Wood, Wis., 1973-74; dir. nursing edn. Mercy Hosp., Chgo., 1975-77; asst. prof. U. Ill. Med. Center, Chgo., 1978-79; prof. nursing DePaul U., Chgo., 1979-86; prof. nursing U. Md., Balt., 1986-87; sr. coord. HIV Rsch. Walter Reed Army Med. Ctr., Washington, 1988-90; clin. tng. specialist Kaiser-Permanente Mid-Atlantic Region, Washington, 1990. Served with Nurse Corps, U.S. Army, 1966-70. Mem. Ill. League Nursing (chmn. program com., dir.), Nat. League Nursing, Chgo. Council Fgn. Relations (patron), Assn. Supervision and Curriculum Devel., Am. Soc. Health Edn. and Tng., Phi Delta Kappa, Sigma Theta Tau (Zeta Sigma chpt.) Congregationalist. Author: Staff Development: A Systems Approach, 1982. Editor: Practical Approaches to Patient Teaching, 1981. Mem. editorial bd. Quality Rev. Bull., Jour. Nursing Edn., Nursing Adminstrn. Quar.; editorial bd., book rev. editor Today's OR Nurse; contbr. numerous articles to profl. jours. Died June 1, 2005.

BILLIG, FREDERICK STUCKY, mechanical engineer; b. Pitts., Feb. 28, 1933; s. Thomas Clifford and Melba Helen (Stucky) B.; m. Margaret Rose Pelicano, Nov. 30, 1933; children: Linda Ann Baumler, Donna Marie Bartley, Frederick Thomas, James Richard. B of Engring., Johns Hopkins U., 1955; MS, U. Md., 1958, PhD, 1964. From assoc. engr. to group supr. Applied Physics Lab., Johns Hopkins U., Laurel, Md., 1955-77, asst. dept. supr., 1977-87, assoc. dept. supr., chief scientist, 1987-96; pres., chmn. bd. Pyrodyne, Inc., Glenwood, Md., 1996—2006. Lectr. U. Md., College Park, 1965-96, Space Inst., U. Tenn., Tullahoma, 1965-99, UCLA, 1987-89, Purdue U., 1986-93, SUNY, Buffalo, 1987, Va. Poly. Inst. & State U., 1983-2006, adj. prof., 1987; lectr., adj. prof. hypersonics short course, Munich, London, Paris, Rome, 1988; NATO Adv. Group for Aerospace Rsch. Devel. lectr. Ramjet and Ramrocket propulsion system for missiles short course, Monterey, Calif., London, Munich, 1984; mem. consultants panel Project SQUID, Office of Naval Rsch., 1972-74; cons. propulsion directorate USAF Nat. Aerospace Plane Program; bd. dirs. Croft Leominster. Contbr. articles to profl. jours.; mem. editl. bd. Johns Hopkins APL Tech. Digest, 1981-89; patentee (with others) cooled leading edges, fuel injector pilons, high reactivity fuels for supersonic combustion ramjets, a supersonic combustion missile, translating cowl inlet with retractable propellant injection struts, protellant utilization system. Mem. Joint Army-Navy-NASA-Air Force Working Group on Combustion, 1971-74, U.S. nat. com. Internat. Airbreathing Engines Com., 1972-74, chmn., 1980-98, v.p., 1993-98; mem. hypersonic propulsion peer rev. group NASA, 1980; mem. sci. adv. bd. USAF, 1988-92, sci. adv. bd. aerospace vehicles standing panel, 1988-92. Recipient Silver medal Combustion Inst., 1970, Nat. Aerospace Plane Program Pioneer award, 1989, M. M. Bondaruck award USSR Acad. Sci. and Aviation Sport Fedn., Meritorious Civilian Svc. award Dept. Air Force, 1992, Aviation Week and Space Tech.-Aeronautics and Propulsion Laurels award, 1996; elected to Nat. Acad. of Engring., 1995, Engring. Hall of Fame U. Md., 1997. Fellow AIAA (tech. com. on airbreathing propulsion 1966-68, tech. com. on propellants and combustion 1970-72, membership chmn. coun. nat. capital sect. 1971-73, standing com. on membership 1973-84, treas. nat. capital sect. 1973-74, sec. 1974-75, standing com. on publs. 1974-82, bd. dirs. region 1 1974-81, v.p. bd. dirs. membership svcs. 1981-82, Hugh L. Dryden lectr. in rsch. 1992); mem. NAE, Combustion Inst., Md. Acad. Sci., Pi Tau Sigma, Phi Kappa Phi. Republican. Avocations: golf, fishing, hunting. Died June 1, 2006.

BILLINGS, LETHA MARGUERITE, retired nurse; b. Navina, Okla., June 27, 1909; d. Edgar Hubert and Blanche Edith (Hubbard) Ladner; m. Carroll Humphrey, Aug. 15, 1928 (div. 1931); m. Ralph Melvin Billings, May 19, 1935 (dec. 1981); children: William Edgar, Betty Luella (dec.). Diploma, Okla. Meth. Hosp., Guthrie, Okla., 1929; student, Chgo. Lying-in Hosp., 1931-32, Cook County Hosp., Chgo., 1932. RN, Okla., Calif. Pvt. duty nurse Guthrie Hosp., Wesley Hosp., Oklahoma City, 1930-31; sch. nurse Logan County Schs. and Guthrie Schs., 1932-33; FERA adminstr. Logan County FERA, 1933-35; sch. nurse Guthrie Schs., 1936-38; night supr., mem. obstet. staff Mercy Hosp., Bakersfield, Calif., 1941-44; instr., trainer Home Care, ARC, Woodward, Okla., 1949-55; co-owner Billings Advt. Assn., Woodward, 1950-75; cons. Woodard Nursing Ctr., 1989-91; supr. Woodward Meml. Hosp. and Health Ctr., 1952-84; local coord., long term care Am. Assn. Ret. Persons, Woodward, from 1991. Chmn. Christian Women's Fellowship, First Christian Ch., 1952. del., 1995; del. Rep. County Assn. Wooodward, 1991, White House Conf. on Aging, 1995; mem. Silver Haired Legislature form Dist. 11, Oklahoma City, 1988-92, mem. exec. com., 1990-92; mem. Okla. Health Planning Com., 1969-70; pres. adv. bd. Nutrition Coun.; health advocate, local coord. and long term care State Am. Assn. Retired Persons; mem. Okla. nursing com. ARC; mem. adv. coun. Area Agy. on Aging; vol. Sr. Ctr. Woodward. Named Outstanding Older Oklahoman State Conf. on Aging, 1993. Mem. ANA (econ. and gen. welfare com. 1958-61, study of functions com. 1962-64, chmn. nominating com. 1972, exec. com. pvt. duty sect. 1988-92), Okla. Nurses Assn. (pres. 1958, Nurse of Yr. 1959), Okla. Dist. 18 Nurses Assn., Okla. Fedn. Women's Clubs (past pres. 3rd dist., edn. chmn., health chmn. 1994), Okla. Congress Parents and Tchrs. (pres. 1964-67), PTA (nat., state life mem.), Order Ea. Star (treas., past matron), PEO (chpt. sec.), Ladies Elks. Avocations: bridge, canasta. Died Mar. 24, 2004.

BINDER, MARTIN RANDALL, manufacturing executive; b. Chgo., Dec. 20, 1918; s. Jack Henry Binder and Anna Moses; m. Marjorie Schorr, June 23, 1940; 1 child, Richard. LLB, DePaul U., 1940. Chmn. Abbott-Interfast Corp., Wheeling, Ill., from 1945. Chmn. bd. Bank of Bellwood, Ill., 1985—; chmn. exec. com. 1st Nat. Bank Lincolnshire, 1983—. Chmn. Ill. State Toll Hwy. Authority, 1972; mem. adv. bd. Chgo. Council of Fine Arts, 1986, Ill. Arts Council, 1986; dir. Ill. Devel. Fin. Authority, 1988, Regional Transp. Authority, 1988. Mem.: Masons. Home: Chicago, Ill. Died Apr. 28, 2005.

BINDER, ROBERT HENRI, association executive; b. N.Y.C., Aug. 19, 1932; s. Ernest Robert and Lily (Simmons) B.; m. Mallory Roedy, Dec. 27, 1981 (div. 1991); children: Ainslie, Hilary, Meredith. BA, Princeton (N.J.) U., 1953; JD, Harvard U., 1958. Bar: D.C., N.Y. Atty. Kirlin Campbell & Keating, Washington, 1966-69; asst. sec. policy U.S. Dept. Transp., Washington, 1969-77; prin. Booz Allen & Hamilton, Bethesda, Md., 1978-80; pres. Transp. Assn. Am., Washington, 1981-83; pvt. practice law Washington, 1984-88; membership mgr. U.S. C. of C., Washington, from 1989. With U.S. Army, 1954-56. Mem. Met. Club, Congl. Country Club. Avocations: jogging, tennis, reading, symphony. Home: Jacksonville, Fla. Died Apr. 4, 2004.

BINGHAM, BARRY, JR., (GEORGE BARRY BINGHAM JR.), publishing and broadcasting executive; b. Louisville, Sept. 23, 1933; s. George Barry and Mary Clifford (Caperton) B.; m. Edith Wharton Stenhouse, Nov. 30, 1963; children: Emily Simms, Mary Caperton; adopted children: Philip John, Charles Wharton. AB, Harvard U., 1956. Mgmt. trainee CBS, N.Y.C., 1958-59; researcher, field producer documentaries NBC, N.Y.C., Washington, 1959-62; formerly with Courier-Journal, Louisville Times; with Standard Gravure Corp., WHAS, Inc., Louisville, 1962-86; editor, pub. Courier-Jour. and Louisville Times, 1971-86; vice chmn. bd. WHAS, Inc.; pub. FineLine, 1989-91; owner, pub. Billy Goat Strut Pub., Louisville, 1989—2006. Active Actors Theatre Louisville, 1989-99, Greater Louisville Fund for Arts, Berea Coll., Isaac E. Bernheim Found., Ky. Opera Assn. Capt. USMC, 1956-58. Mem. Harvard Club, River Valley Club. Home: Glenview, Ky. Died Apr. 3, 2006.

BIRD, L. RAYMOND, investor; b. Plainfield, NJ, Jan. 22, 1914; s. Lewis Raymond and Bessie (MacCallum) Bird; m. May Ethel Siercks, June 5, 1949. Student, NYU, 1946—47. With shipping dept. Horn & Hardart Co., 1936—46, control auditor, 1946—49, gen. supt. in commissary, 1949—51; asst. to treas. fin. and legal Lockheed Electronics Co. (formerly Stavid Engring., Inc.), 1951—55, treas., 1955—60; pres., dir. State Bank of Plainfield, NJ, 1960—62; investor, from 1962. Treas. Route Twenty Two Corp. Plainfield area committeeman Young Life Campaign, Inc.; pres. Plainfield Camp of Gideons; chmn. bd. trustees, chmn. exec. com., chmn. fin. and investments com. Barrington Coll.; mem. exec. com., treas. Christian Bus. Men's Com. of Ctrl. NJ; bd. dirs. Child Evangelism Fellowship NJ, Sudan Interior Mission; trustee Evangelistic Com. Newark and Vicinity; bd. dirs., treas. Friends in Christ. Gen. staff officer from pvt. to 1st lt. 6th Armored Divsn., AUS, 1941—45. Mem.: Plainfield Area C. of C., Am. Mgmt. Assn., Internat. Christian Leadership. Baptist. Died 2006.

BIRZON, IRVING, podiatrist; b. Buffalo, June 27, 1923; s. Morris and Nettie Birzon; m. Sandra Edith Friedman, Sept. 2, 1954; children: Mitchell, Peter. Student, U. Buffalo. Podiatrist N.Y. State Podiatric Soc., N.Y.C., 1955-95. With USCG, 1945-49. Democrat. Jewish. Avocations: gardening, tennis. Home: Woodbury, NY. Died Mar. 8, 2004.

BISHOP, LEROY HOWARD, corporate tax manager; b. Chgo., Mar. 9, 1941; s. Norman Leon and Dorothy (Brown) B.; m. Laura Helen Shaw, Aug. 9, 1963; children: Lisa Diane, David Louis, Michael Alan. AA, Prarie State Jr. Coll., 1971; BS, Ariz. State U., 1975. CPA, Ariz. Cost acct. Allan & Garcia Co., Chgo., 1965-67; corp. tax mgr. Bell Atlantic Systems Leasing Internat., Phoenix, from 1967. Chmn. finance Mt. View Baptist Ch., Phoenix, 1985—; chmn. deacons Mt. View Baptist Ch., Phoenix, 1987; trustee Mt. View Baptist Ch., 1983—. Sgt. U.S. Army, 1960-63. Mem. Tax Execs. Inst. (pres. Ariz. chpt. 1985-86), Am. Inst. CPA's, Ariz. Soc. CPA's, Inst. Property Taxation. Republican. Southern Baptist. Home: Henderson, Nev. Died July 9, 2004.

BISHOP, ROBERT LEE, public relations educator; b. Mt. Healthy, Ohio, Aug. 17, 1931; s. Chester Lee and Nova Rhea (McGuire) B.; m. Nadean Bishop, Apr. 19, 1952 (div. Apr. 1976); children: Anita Morrison, Gail Noland, James, Susan. BS, Okla. Bapt. U., 1952; MRE, So. Bapt. Sem., Louisville, 1956; EdD, So. Bapt. Sem., 1960; PhD, U. Wis., 1966. Reporter News Star, Shawnee, Okla., 1950-52; dir. pub. rels. Okla. Bapt. U., Shawnee, 1958-63; asst. then assoc. prof. U. Mich., Ann Arbor, 1965-82; prof., head pub. rels. sequence U. Ga., Athens, from 1982. Aw Boon Haw prof. Chinese U. Hong Kong, 1980-81; cons. in field. Author several books in field, including: Qi Lai! Chinese Communications, 1988, Economics, Politics and Information, 1983; creator three programs for computer-assisted instruction; contbr. over 30 articles to profl. jours. Served as commdr. USNR, 1950-70. Fellow Ctr. for Rshc. on Learning and Teaching, U. Mich., 1975-82. Fellow Pub. Rels. Soc. Am. (bd. dirs. educator's sect., 1984-85); Internat. Communication Assn., Sigma Delta Chi. Avocations: writing, travel. Home: Athens, Ga. Died Apr. 10, 2004.

BITNER, ROBERT LEROY, infosystems specialist; b. Wilton, N.D., Feb. 19, 1934; s. William Robert and Hildur Emma (Stenquist) B.; m Irma Mardella Keller, June 2, 1957; children: Mark, Robyn, Brian, Craig, Keith, Sarah. BSBA, U. N.D., 1957, MS in Guidance, 1967. Interviewer Job Service N.D., Devils Lake, 1959-67, employment counselor, 1967-70, mgr. model cities manpower ctr., 1970-71, employment counselor Bismarck, 1971-72, mgmt. analyst, 1972-75, data systems coord., 1975-89; pvt. practice, infosystems cons. Indsl. Micro Products, Bismarck, from 1989. Author: Interviewer Guide, Terminal Operator Manual, 1975. Chmn. Regional Adv. Com. on Vocat. Rehab., Devils Lake, 1965-67, chmn. Regional Adv. Com. Mental Retardation, 1966-69; officer N.D. State PTA. Avocations: home building, woodworking, lay preaching, supporting missionaries, computer programming. Home: Bismarck, ND. Died Jan. 11, 2004.

BITTAR, EDWARD S., orthopaedic surgeon; b. N.Y.C., June 16, 1942; AB, Rutgers U., 1963; MD, Temple U., 1978; PhD, NYU, 1978. Diplomate Am. Bd. Orthopaedic Surgeons; lic. physician, Va., Fla. Intern in gen. surgery U. Fla. Coll. Medicine, Gainesville, 1978-79, resident in orthopaedics, 1979-82; chief resident Gainesville VA Med. Ctr., 1982-83; fellow in arthroscopy, arthroscopic surgery, sports medicine Orthop. Rsch. of Va., Richmond, Va., 1983; asst. prof. orthop. surgery U. Fla., Gainesville, 1984-87, assoc. prof., 1987-97, assoc. chmn. dept. orthops., 1986-87, dir. med. edn. dept. orthops., 1984-87, co-dir. Orthop. Clinic, Student Health Svc., 1984-87, assoc. clin. prof., from 1989, co-dir. orthop. outreach program, from 1992; pres. Univ. Orthop. Assocs., Gainesville, from 1986; pvt. practice Palm Bay, Fla., from 1987. Adj. prof., U. Fla., 1997—; team physician Fla. Marlins Baseball Club, 1992—, Fla. Manatees, 1993—, Fla. State League Baseball, 1994, U. Fla. Gators, 1984-87, Brevard C.C., 1989—, Fla. Inst. Tech., 1989—, N.Y. Knights, 1992, Melbourne (Fla.) H.S., 1987—; chief orthop. surgery Gainesville VA Med. Ctr., 1984-87; mem. sci. adv. bd. Spinal Cord Rsch. Found., 1986-89; arthroscopy cons. Cabot Med., 1984-87, Laserson-ics Corp., Becton Dickinson; mem. arthroscopy bd. Orthop. and Sports Medicine News, 1989—. Contbr. articles to profl. jours. Grantee VA Hosp., 1989; Meml. Sloan-Kettering Cancer Ctr. scholar. Fellow Am. Acad. Orthop. Surgeons; mem. Arthroscopy Assn. N.Am. (bd. trustees 1995—, psychomotor skills com. 1990—), Am. Bd. Med. Specialties, Fla. Orthop. Soc., Fla. Med. Soc., Brevard County Med. Soc., European Soc. Knee Surgery and Arthroscopy, Am. Soc. Sports Medicine, Internat. Arthroscopy Assn., Mensa. Died May 11, 2004.

BITTER, TWILA HOPE, retired elementary mathematics educator; b. Galatia, Kans., Oct. 31, 1930; d. Pete and Freda (Schwartzkopf) Karst; m. Wilmer Henry Bitter, May 7, 1950; children: Rebecca Hope Bitter Schloemer, Alan, Lynn. BS in Edn., Ft. Hays State U., 1969; MS in Edn., Kans. State U., 1979. Elem. tchr. Dist. 43, Galatia, 1948-50; tchr. 3d grade Lincoln Sch., Great Bend, Kans., 1969; tchr. math. 7th-9th grade Roosevelt Jr. H.S., Great Bend, 1969-74; tchr. 6th grade Joyce Sch., Ulysses, Kans., 1974-77; tchr. 7th grade Kepley Jr. H.S., Ulysses, 1977-94; ret., 1994. Sponsor jr. high youth group Trinity Luth. Ch., Great Bend, 1971-74; tchr. Sunday sch. various chs., Hoisington, Kans., Great Bend. Named Outstanding Educator Unified Sch. Dist. 214, Ulysses, 1984. Mem. NEA, Kans. Nat. Educators Assn., Kans. Assn. Tchrs. Math., Nat. Coun. Tchrs. Math., Phi Delta Kappa (treas. South Winds chpt. 1985-87). Home: Ulysses, Kans. Died May 8, 2005.

BITTRICH, GUSTAV, church musician; b. Morristown, N.J., July 1, 1937; s. Gustav and Margaret Ena (Otway) B.; m. Mary Elizabeth Emery, Dec. 28, 1964. Student, Oberlin Coll., 1955-59. Organist, master of the choristers Christ Ch., Elizabeth, N.J., 1960-64; dir. music. St. James' Episcopal Ch., Bradley Beach, N.J., 1966-68, St. George's Episcopal Ch., Maplewood, N.J., 1969-81, St. Luke's Episcopal Ch., Gladstone, N.J., 1981-85, Bedminster Reformed Ch., Bedminster, N.J., 1985-93; organist Community of St. John Bapt., Mendham, N.J., from 1983. Co-dir. music Diocese Newark 100th Anniversary, 1974, Consecration of Bishop Coadjutor N.J., 1976; treas. Music Commn. Diocese N.J., 1982-95; organ recitalist many local chs.; pvt. piano and organ tchr., 1960—; adminstrv. asst. to v.p. Spa Health Cons., Cranford, N.J., 1986-88; judge Opera at Florham Vocal Competition, 1992; treas. AAM Princeton Conf., 1993. Mem., photographer Washington Crossing Found.; co-owner St. David's Pembroke Welsh Corgis; puppy raiser/trainer The Seeing Eye, 1982-86; co-owner St. Davids's Needlepoint; dir., designer Episcopal Churchwomen All Saints' Chapel Needlepoint Project, 1976; designer St. George's Ch. Diamond Anniversary Needlepoint Project, 1979; mem. liturgical commn. Episcopal Diocese Newark, 1972-77, sec., 1973-77, mem. centennial steering com., 1974, mem. Fellowship Ch. Musicians, 1975-80. Mem. Organ Hist. Soc., Hymn Soc. Am., Assn. Anglican Musicians, Associated Parishes, Royal Coll. Organists, Royal Sch. Ch. Music, Hymn Soc. Am., Assn. Diocesan Liturgical and Music Commns., Am. Guild Organists (Met. N.J. chpt. exec. com. 1969-72, publicity chmn. for 1975 regional conv., chmn. profl. standards com. 1978-81, sec. 1979-82), Pembroke Welsh Corgi Club Am. (charter Garden State chpt.). Episcopalian. Avocations: breeding and showing pembroke welsh corgis, needlepoint, photography, travel. Home: Bedminster, NJ. Died Sept. 30, 2004.

BLACK, CHARLES ALDEN, economist, aquatic engineer; b. Oakland, Calif., Mar. 6, 1919; s. James Byers and Katharine (McElrath) B.; m. Shirley Temple; children: Linda Susan, Charles A. Jr., Lori Alden. BA, Stanford U., 1940, MBA, 1946; postgrad., Harvard U., 1941. Purchasing asst. Castle & Cooke Ltd., San Francisco, 1946-48; asst. to pres. Hawaiian Pineapple, Honolulu, 1948-50; mgr. bus. ops. SRI Internat., Menlo Pk., Calif., 1953-58; mgr. fin. relations Ampex Corp., Redwood City, Calif., 1958-64; v.p., co-founder Pacific Mariculture, Pescadero, Calif., 1964-68; pres., chmn. Mardela Corp., Woodside, Calif., 1969—2005. Co-founder, chmn. bd. Marquest Group, Inc., Pocasset, Mass., 1985-2005, Marine Imaging Systems Inc., Marine Telepresence, Inc. Comdr. USN, 1941-45. Mem. Marine Tech. Soc., World Mariculture Assn., Woods Hole Oceanographic Inst. (mem. corp. bd.), Oceanic Inst., Bohemian Club, Pacific Union Club, Beta Sigma (hon.) Republican. Died Aug. 4, 2005.

BLACK, FRANK ANDERSON, retired military officer; b. Thomaston, Ga., Mar. 31, 1941; s. Theodore and Nellie (Stowe) B.; divorced; children: Sereina Louise, Margot Black Smith. BS, USAF Acad., 1963; MBA, Auburn U., 1971; disting. grad., Air Command and Staff Coll., 1971, Air Wall Coll., 1983. Commd. 2d lt. USAF, 1963, advanced through grades to col., 1981, ret., 1987, tactical reconnaissance pilot 16th tactical recon. squadron Tan Son Nhut AB, Saigon, 1965-66; inspector operational readiness hdqs. USAF Europe, Wiesbaden, Germany, 1968-70; air officer comdg. 24th squadron USAF Acad., Colo., 1971-74; ops. officer 16th tactical recons. squadron USAF, Shaw AFB, S.C., 1974-75, air planner Pacific Air Forces Seoul, Korea, 1976-77, base commdr. tactical air command Moody AFB, Ga., 1980-82, air staff planner hdqs. Washington, 1983-85; joint chiefs of staff, chief strategy divsn. The Pentagon, Washington, 1985-87. Bd. dirs., treas. Upson County Emergency Shelter, Inc., Thomaston, Ga., 1993—; active Thomaston-Upston Arts Coun., 1988—. Decorated Def. Superior Svc. medal, D.F.C., Air medal with 11 oak leaf clusters. Mem. VFW, Air Force Assn. (life), Kiwanis. Avocations: sailing, writing, motorcycles. Home: Gainesville, Ga. Died June 27, 2005.

BLACK, IRA BARRIE, neurologist, educator; b. Bronx, NY, Mar. 18, 1941; m. Janet Linquist (div. 1999); 1 child, Reed. AB, Columbia U., 1961; MD, Harvard U., 1965. Nathan Cummings prof. neurology Cornell U., N.Y.C., dir. divsn. devel. neurology, 1975—90; attending neurologist N.Y. Hosp.; founding dir. Stem Cell Inst. NJ, 2004—06; prof., chmn. neuroscience & cell biology dept. U. Med. & Dentistry Robert Wood Johnson Med. Sch., 1990—2006. Dir. Princeton-Robert Wood Johnson-Rutgers U. Consortium in Neuroscience. Author: Cellular and Molecular Biology of Neuronal Development, The Dying of Enoch Wallace: Life, Death, and the Changing Brain, Information in the Brain: A Molecular Perspective, 1991, The Changing Brain: Alzheimer's Disease and Advances in Neuroscience, 2002. Recipient McKnight Found. award in Neuroscience, Jacob Javits award in Neuroscience, Viktor Hamburger prize, Rita Levi Montalcini award. Mem.: Cure Autism Now

Sci. Advisory Bd., Christopher Reeve Paralysis Found. Advisory Bd., Ctr. Advanced Biotechnology & Med. NJ Sci. Advisory Bd., Soc. Neuroscience N. Am. (pres. 1992). Died Jan. 10, 2006.

BLACK, THEODORE HALSEY, retired manufacturing company executive; b. Jersey City, Oct. 22, 1928; s. Theodore Charles and Mary (Carroll) B.; m. Marilyn Rigsby, 1979; children: Deborah, Theodore Jr., Susan, Zelda, Carol, Brian. BSEE, U.S. Naval Acad., Annapolis, 1953; postgrad., Harvard U., 1974. Salesman, sales mgr. Ingersoll-Rand Co., N.Y.C., 1957-67, gen. mgr. turbo products divsn., 1967-72, v.p., 1972-87, chmn., pres., CEO Woodcliff Lake, 1988-93. Pres., CEO Dresser-Rand Co., Corning, N.Y., 1987-88; bd. dirs. Gen. Pub. Utilities, Parsippany, N.J., Best Foods, Englewood Cliffs, N.J., McDermott Internat., New Orleans. Capt. USMC, 1946-49, 53-59. Recipient Naval Aviator award USN, Corpus Christi, Tex., 1955. Roman Catholic. Avocations: hunting, fishing, tennis, golf. Home: New Canaan, Conn. Died June 28, 2006.

BLACK, WILLIAM ARTHUR (QUAL-LEE-LAH), federal agency administrator; b. Omak, Wash., Feb. 17, 1948; s. Harry and Catherine Leone (Collar) B.; m. Jackie Marie Smith, Nov. 25, 1965 (div. 1988); children: William Arthur Jr., James Wyston, Megan Michelle; m. Patricia Ann Greenslitt, Oct. 2, 1988; children: Bruce Lloyd, Bradley Douglas. Student, U. Wash., Eastern Wash. U., Wenatchee Valley Coll. Enrollment officer Colville Confederated Tribes, Nespelem, Wash., 1969-74, Western Wash. Agy., Everett, 1974-76; tribal operation officer Puget Sound Agy., Everett, 1976-81; mgmt. trainee Dept. Interior, Washington, 1981-82; supt. Spokane Aty., Bur. Indian Affairs, Wellpinit, Wash., 1982-83; tribal ops. officer Juneau (Alaska) Bur. Indian Affairs, 1983; supt. Puget Sound Agy. Bur. Indian Affairs, Everett, from 1983. Nat. coord. Goodwill Games, Bur. Indian Affairs, Washington, 1988—; mem. Am. Indian Trade/Devel. Coun., Everett, 1986—. Trustee Everett Community Coll., 1987—; scoutmaster Evergreen coun. Boy Scouts Am., com. mem.; asst. Congressman Al Swift, Washington; ex-officio mem. Puget Sound Child Protection Team, Am. Indian Goodwill Games Commn. Named Gentleman of Yr., Everett Community Coll. Women's Ctr., 1989. Mem. Assn. Community Coll. Trustees, Colville Confederated Tribes, Elks. Democrat. Avocation: vocal music. Home: Edmonds, Wash. Died Feb. 11, 2004.

BLACKBURN, MICHAEL PHILIP, lawyer; b. East St. Louis, Ill., June 7, 1945; s. Thomas Doyle and Erma Jeanette (Macke) B.; m. Phyllis Ann Macke, Feb. 10, 1972 (div. 1983). BA, So. Ill. U., 1967; JD, Western State U., Fullerton, Calif., 1982. Bar: Calif. 1983, U.S. Ct. Appeals (9th cir.) 1984, U.S. Dist. Ct. (cen. dist.) Calif. 1984, U.S. Tax Ct. 1984, U.S. Supreme Ct. 1992, U.S. Dist. Ct. (no. dist.) Calif. 1992, U.S. Dist. Ct. (ea. dist.) Calif. 1993. Lawyer pvt. practice, Long Beach, Calif., 1983-85; house counsel TransAmerica, Torrance, Calif., 1985-88; assoc. Mercer & Zinder, Orange, Calif., 1988-91, ptnr., 1991, mgr. bay area office Walnut Creek, Calif., 1991-98; v.p. bd. dirs. Zinder, Blackburn, Park, Clements & Keenan, Walnut Creek, Calif., from 1998, v.p., mem. exec. com. Dem. candidate U.S. House Reps., 42nd Congl. Dist., 1986. Capt. USAF, 1967-72. Recipient scholarship So. Ill. Univ., 1963. Roman Catholic. Avocations: pocket billiards, reading. Died May 6, 2004.

BLACKBURN, ROBERT EUGENE, internal auditor, retired; b. Brookville, Ohio, June 28, 1923; s. Harry William and Mary Esther (Wolfe) B.; m. Dorothy Viola Bloom, Aug. 21, 1949; children: Kevin, Kyle. BA, BS, Defiance (Ohio) Coll., 1947; MA, Miami U., Oxford, Ohio, 1951. CPCU. With Motorists Mut. Ins. Co., Columbus, Ohio, from 1952, casualty and property sales mgr., 1968-74, underwriting mgr., 1974-82, internal auditor, 1982-88. Coun. pres. Clinton Heights Luth. Ch., Columbus, 1976; pres. music assn. Centennial High Sch., Columbus, 1978, 79; loaned exec., Franklin County United Way, 1985, 86, 87, 88. With USN, 1943-46, PTO. Mem. Nat. Assn. CPCU (bd. dirs. Columbus chpt. 1981-84), Defiance Coll. Alumni Assn. (bd. dirs. 1982-85). Republican. Avocation: restoring antiques. Home: Columbus, Ohio. Died Feb. 16, 2005.

BLAIR, WILLIAM DRAPER, JR., conservationist; b. Charlotte, N.C., May 3, 1927; s. William D. and Mary-Eula (Mason) B.; m. Jane Fraser Coleman, June 25, 1949; children— Jane C. Blair Gelston, Elizabeth Blair Jones. BA, Princeton U., 1949. Successively reporter, Korean war corr., European corr. Balt. Sunpapers, 1949-53; successively asst. editor, corr., London, chief Bonn (Germany) bur., chief Paris bur. Newsweek mag., 1953-59; with US Dept. State, Washington, 1959-62, dir. Office Media Services, 1962-70, dep. asst. sec. for pub. affairs, 1970-80; pres. The Nature Conservancy, 1980-87. Mem. Nat. Wetlands Policy Forum, 1987-88. Author: Katharine Ordway: The Lady Who Saved the Prairies, 1989. Served with USMCR, 1945-46. Recipient Meritorious Honor award Dept. State, 1964, Superior Honor award, 1967, Disting. Honor award, 1980, Paul Bartsch award Audubon Naturalist Soc., 1987, Chevron Conservation award, 1987, Disting. Svc. award Am. Forestry Assn., 1989. Mem. The Nature Conservancy (gov. 1972-80, chmn. bd. govs. 1975-77, trustee Maine chpt. 1987-94, Oak Leaf award 1988), Audubon Naturalist Soc. Ctrl. Atlantic States (dir. 1966-73, pres. 1968-70), Metropolitan Club, 1925 F St Club, Chevy Chase Club (Washington). Died Aug. 5, 2006.

BLANCHARD, GEORGE SAMUEL, retired army officer; b. Washington, Apr. 3, 1920; s. George S. and Elizabeth (Blanchard) B.; m. Beth Howard, June 9, 1944; children: Kate E. (Mrs. Ronald Hausner), Marylou C. (Mrs. John Hennessey), Deborah E. (Mrs. Eberhard Roell), Blythe H. (Mrs. Charles Watkins). Student, Am. U., 1938—40; BS, U.S. Mil. Acad., 1944; MS, Syracuse U., 1948; grad. Advanced Mgmt. Program, Harvard Bus. Sch., 1966. Commd. 2d lt. AUS, 1944, advanced through grades to gen., 1975; served as co. comdr. and staff officer Europe, 1944-47; adviser Taiwan, 1955—56; with 82d Airborne Div. U.S., 1958-60, Korea, 1961-62; with ADC 1st divsn., c/s 1st Corps Vietnam, 1966-68; comdr. 82d Airborne div. Ft. Bragg, N.C., 1970-72; mem. Pentagon staff, 1962-66, 68-70; comdg. gen. VII Corps U.S. Army Europe, 1973-75; comdr. in chief U.S. Army Europe, 1975—79; ret., 1979. Past pres. World USO, Gen. Analysis, Inc.; bd. dirs. Atlantic Coun. U.S. Contbr. to Ency. Brit. Vice chmn. Literacy Coun. Moore County. Decorated D.S.M. with 3 oak leaf clusters, Silver Star with oak leaf cluster, D.F.C., Bronze Star with oak leaf cluster. Mem. Assn. U.S. Army, Ret. Officers Assn. (past pres.), VFW, U.S. Soc. French Legion of Honor, Nat. Mil. Families Assn. Episcopalian. Home: Fort Belvoir, Va. Died May 3, 2006.

BLANEY, DOROTHY GULBENKIAN, academic administrator; BA in Comparative Lit. with high hons., Cornell U., 1962; Woodrow Wilson Fellow Comparative Lit., U. Calif., Berkeley, 1963; PhD in English, SUNY, Albany, 1971. Asst. prof. English SUNY, Albany, 1968-71; coord. N.Y. State Doctoral Rev. Program, Albany, 1971-73; asst. commr. higher edn. planning and policy analysis N.Y. State Edn. Dept., Albany, 1973-78, dep. commr. higher edn. and professions, 1978-81; cons. Internat. Labor Office, Internat. Mgmt. Inst., Geneva, N.Y.C., Switzerland, U.S., 1981-82; exec. v.p. Pace U., N.Y.C., 1982-88; pres. Cedar Crest Coll., Allentown, Pa., 1989—2006. Co-author (with Ernst R. May): (book) Careers for Humanists, 1981; columnist for Times Mirrors, Morning Call, and, occasionally, U.S.A. Today, Phila. Inquirer, Atlanta Constitution; contbr. articles to mags. and jours. Home: Allentown, Pa. Died July 10, 2006.

BLANK, MYRON NATHAN, theater executive; b. Des Moines, Aug. 30, 1911; s. Abraham Harry and Anna (Levy) B.; m. Jacqueline Navran, Oct. 22, 1935; children: Beverly, Alan, Steven. BA, U. Mich., 1933. With Ctrl. States Theatre Corp., Des Moines, from 1933, pres., from 1950. Founder A.H. & Theo Blank Performing Arts Ctr.; mem., chmn. trust com. Iowa Des Moines Nat. Bank, 1950-82. Salvage chmn. War Prodn. Bd. Polk County, 1940-42; past bd. dirs. Salvation Army, Child Guidance Ctr., YMCA; built Raymond Blank Lodge and Sick Bay, Camp Mitigwa Boy Scout Camp, Anna Blank Hosp. for Child Guidance Ctr., A.H. Blank Park Zoo; chmn. Des Moines United Way dr., 1976; endowed permanent chair for gifted and talented children U. Iowa, permanent scholarship, Weitzmann Inst., Israel; pres. Greater Des Moines Com., 1953, Theatre Owners of Amer., 1957-58; bd. dirs. Iowa Meth. Hosp., Des Moines C. of C., Simpson Coll., Des Moines Club, Wakonda Club; hon. chmn. Variety Club Telethon, 1999. Lt. comdr. USN, 1943-46. Recipient Brotherhood award NCCJ, 1976, Am. Humanitarian award Variety Club Am., 1980, The Iowa award Nat. Soc. for Fund Raising Execs., Disting. Alumni award U. Iowa, 1990, Jr. Achievement Laureate award, 1997; inducted into Midwest Nat. Assn. Theatre Owners Hall of Fame, 2000. Mem. Nat. Assn. Theatre Owners (bd. dirs.), Theatre Owners Am. (pres. 1955, chmn. bd. dirs. 1956-57). Jewish. Avocations: golf, hunting, fishing. Home: Des Moines, Iowa. Died Feb. 26, 2005.

BLAUSTEIN, ALFRED (AL) H., artist, educator; b. N.Y.C., Jan. 23, 1924; s. Sydney and Sophie (Silbersher) Blaustein; m. Lotte Heilbrunn Blaustein, May 5, 1949; 1 child, Marc D. Grad., Cooper Union Art Sch., 1948. Fine arts instr. Albright Art Sch., Buffalo, 1949—52, Skowhegan Sch., Maine, 1950—59, Pratt Inst., Bklyn., 1959—68, prof. fine arts, 1968—2004; vis. prof. Yale U., New Haven, 1959—62. One-man shows include Nordness Gallery, N.Y.C., 1959, 1961, 1963, U. Nebr., 1961, Phila. Art Alliance, 1962, Laeubli Gallery, Zurich, 1962, Phila. Print Club, 1964, Franklin Seiden Gallery, Detroit, 1965, Albany Art Inst., 1965, Randolph-Macon Coll., 1967, Troup Gallery, Dallas, 1968, U. Mo., 1983, Pratt Inst., N.Y.C., 1993, 1994, 1998, one-man shows include retrospective, N.Y.C., 2004, exhibited in group shows at Metro. Mus. of Art, Pa. Acad., Carnegie Internat., Albright-Knox Gallery, Mus. of Fine Arts, Boston, Am. Acad. in Rome, Nat. Acad. of Design, Landmark Gallery, NY, Kent State U., Represented in permanent collections Whitney Mus., Metro. Mus. Art, Libr. of Congress, Chgo. Art Inst., Syracuse U., Washington U., U. Mass., Purdue U., Smithsonian Inst. Pfc USAF. Recipient Eyre medal for Graphics, Pa. Acad., 1959; Rome fellowship, Am. Acad. in Rome, 1954—57, fellowships in painting and printmaking, John Simon Guggenheim Found., 1958—61, grant, Am. Acad. Arts and Letters, 1958, Artist-in-Residence fellowship, Ford Found., 1965. Avocation: bicycling. Home: New York, NY. Died July 15, 2004.

BLEWETT, ROBERT NOALL, retired lawyer; b. Stockton, Calif., July 12, 1915; s. Stephen Noall and Bess Errol (Simard) B.; m. Virginia Weston, Mar. 30, 1940; children: Richard Weston Blewett (dec.), Carolyn Blewett Lawrence. LLB, Stanford U., 1936, JD, 1939. Bar: Calif. 1939. Dep. dist. atty. San Joaquin County, 1942-46; practice law Stockton, 1946-98; ptnr., pres. Blewett & Allen-Garibaldi, Inc., Stockton, 1971-98, ret., 1998. Chmn. San Joaquin County chpt. ARC, 1947-49; v.p. Goodwill Industries, 1967-68; vice chmn. Stockton Sister City Commn., 1969-70; adv. bd. bus. adminstrn. dept. U. Pacific; trustee San Joaquin Pioneer and Haggin Galleries. Fellow Am. Coll. Estate and Trust Counsel, Am. Bar Found.; mem. ABA, Am. Judicature Soc., Am. Law Inst., State Bar Calif. (mem. exec. com. on conf. of dels. 1969-72, vice chmn. 1971-72), Calif. Heritage Coun., Order of the Coif, Rotary (pres. 1987-88), Yosemite Club, San Francisco Banker's Club, Masons, Shriners, Delta Theta Phi, Theta Xi. Republican. Home: Stockton, Calif. Died Dec. 22, 2005.

BLINDER, RICHARD LEWIS, architect; b. N.Y.C., June 14, 1935; s. Maxwell E. and Mona (Wittlin) B.; m. Ellen Rifkind, June 18, 1958; children— Michael, Karen BS in Architecture, U. Cin., 1959; M.Arch., Harvard U., 1960. Registered architect, N.Y., N.J., Fla., D.C., Md. Designer Bellevue Hosp. Project, N.Y.C., 1961-64; project architect Victor Gruen, Architect, N.Y.C., 1964-66, assoc., 1966-68; ptnr. Beyer Blinder Belle, N.Y.C., 1968—2006. Trustee 7th Regiment Armory Conservancy, chmn. Fitch Charitable Trust, 1988-2006. Trustee Montclair Art Mus., 1993-98; mem. Mcpl. Arts Soc., N.Y.C., 1975-2006, Montclair Bd. Adjustment, N.J., 1977-80; trustee Adult Sch. Montclair, 1979-82; chmn. Montclair Redevel. Agy., 1980-84. Recipient Preservation Honor award Nat. Trust for Hist. Preservation, 1980, Tucker award of excellence Bldg. Stone Inst., 1983, Bard award City Club N.Y., 1984, Disting. Achievement award B'nai Brith, 1988, Disting. Alumnus award U. Cin., 1991. Fellow AIA (Disting. Architecture award N.Y. chpt., Design award 1988, Honor award 1988, Presdl. Design award 1988, Nat. AIA Firm award 1995); mem. Real Estate Bd. N.Y. Inc. (zoning com.), Harvard Club (N.Y.C.). Home: New York, NY. Died Sept. 7, 2006.

BLINKEN, ROBERT JAMES, manufacturing and communications company executive; b. NYC, Apr. 18, 1929; s. Maurice Henry and Ethel (Horowitz) B.; m. Jeanne Pagnucco, Mar. 5, 1955 (div. Jan. 1967); children: Robert James, Rachel; m. Allison Matsner, Dec. 14, 1967; children: Anna, Ingrid. Grad., Horace Mann Sch., N.Y.C., 1946; BA cum laude, Harvard U., 1950. Pres. Teleprinter Corp., Paramus, NJ, 1953-61; v.p. Mite Corp., New Haven, 1961-63, pres., 1963-75, chmn., 1975-85, Comm. Network Enhancement, Mountainside, NJ, 1986—2004. Trustee Albright Inst. Archeol. Rsch., N.Y. Blood Ctr. Served to 1st lt. USAF, 1950-53. Home: Bedford Hills, NY. Died Oct. 22, 2005.

BLOCH, DOROTHY, psychoanalyst; b. N.Y.C., Jan. 13, 1912; d. Joseph and Augusta (Singer) B. BA, Hunter Coll., 1931; MA, NYU, 1955. Cert. psychologist, N.Y. Tchr. of English N.Y. Bd. of Edn., 1938-52; psychoanalyst N.Y.C., from 1953; faculty mem., tng. analyst N.Y. Psychol. Assn. for Psychoanalysis, 1955-70, Ctr. for Modern Psychoanalytic Studies, 1970-76; lectr. Mid Manhatten Ctr. for Pscyhoanalysis, 1980-95. Author: "So the Witch Won't Eat Me": Fantasy and the Child's Fear of Infanticide, 1978, reissued, 1984; contbr. articles to profl. jours. Mem. N.Y. Tchrs. Union, 1939-53. Mem. Nat. Psychol. Assn. for PSA, Coun. of Psychoanalytic Psychotherapists, Ctr. for Modern Psychol. Studies. Avocations: painting, travel, gardening, reading, walking. Home: New York, NY. Died Jan. 13, 2005.

BLODGETT, JULIAN ROBERT, small business owner; b. Honolulu, Nov. 21, 1919; s. Harry Hoagland and Esther Julia (Lyons) B.; m. Eleanor Anne Fischer, Nov. 4, 1941 (dec. 1983); children: Eric, Julie, Byron, Paul. BA, UCLA, 1940. Stock clk. Northrop Aircraft Co., Hawthorne, Calif., 1941-42; spl. agt. FBI, Washington, 1942-44, 46-57, Standard Oil Calif., San Francisco, 1945-46; gen. mgr. Western Indsl. Security Co., L.A., 1961-63; chief bur. investigation L.A. Dist. Atty., 1957-61; owner, operator Julian R. Blodgett Investigations, L.A., from 1961, Grey Fox Ltd., from 1995. Chmn., commr. L.A. City Housing Authority, 1963-65. Mem. Former Agts. FBI. Died July 11, 2004.

BLOOM, DAVID L., tool and die designer; b. South Bend, Ind., May 31, 1960; s. Leo William and Deloras (Wawrzynsczk) B. AS in Die Design, Acme Inst. Tech., 1988. Plant mgr., tool and die designer Contour Tool & Die Inc., South Bend, from 1978. Mem. Soc. Mech. Engrs. Roman Catholic. Avocations: coaching little league, softball, outdoors activities. Died Oct. 15, 2004.

BLOOM, MIRIAM KRASNICK, psychoanalyst; b. Chgo., Dec. 22, 1920; d. Sol Harry and Anna (Glick) Krasnick; m. Louis Richard Bloom, Aug. 22, 1942; children: Robert, Fredi Barbara, Steven, Debra. BS, U. Ill., 1941, MA, 1956; postgrad., Union Inst., from 1987. Cert. psychoanalyst; cert. sch. psychologist; cert. tchr.; lic. marriage and family therapist, Colo., Calif. Speech therapist Chgo. Pub. Schs., 1941-42; 9th grade tchr. Champaign (Ill.) Pub. Schs., 1941-43; elem. sch. tchr. Hicksville (N.Y.) Pub. Schs., 1954-57; sch. psychologist various schs., L.I., N.Y., 1957-75, St. Vrain Pub. Schs., Longmont, Colo., 1975-81; founder, dir. Colo. Ctr. Modern Psychoanalytic Studies, Boulder, from 1978; pvt. practice in psychotherapy Westbury, N.Y., 1972-75; pvt. practice in psychoanalysis Boulder, from 1981. Mem. APA, Nat. Assn. for Advancement of Psychoanalysis, Assn. of Modern Psychoanalysts, Colo. Soc. Sch. Psychologist, Colo. Psychol. Assn. Democrat. Jewish. Avocations: swimming, hiking, cooking, reading, crocheting. Died May 6, 2005.

BLOOMBERG, JOYCE ELAINE, nursing educator; b. Johnstown, Pa., July 2, 1939; d. James Elvin and Thelma Elvina (Causer) Colbert; m. Leon Bloomberg, Mar. 10, 1973; children: Lauri Anne, Douglas James. Diploma in nursing, Lankenau Hosp., Phila., 1960; B of Profl. Studies, Elizabethtown (Pa.) Coll., 1973; M in Gen. Edn., Temple U., 1980. Staff nurse obstetrics Lancaster (Pa.) Gen. Hosp.; operating room staff nurse St. Joseph's Hosp., Lancaster; charge nurse Lancashire Nursing Home, Neffsville, Pa.; instr., supr. practical nursing Lancaster County Area Vocat. Tech. Sch., Willow Street, Pa. Mem. Nat. League for Nursing, Lankenau Hosp. Sch. Nursing Alumni Assn. Home: Lancaster, Pa. Died July 11, 2005.

BLOUNT, HELON JACQUELINE, singer, actress; b. Big Spring, Tex., Jan. 15, 1929; d. Ralph E. and Alma Helon (Shipp) B.; m. Keith Gerard Kaldenberg, Dec. 13, 1924 (dec. Feb. 1990); 1 child, Kim Kaldenberg. MusB, U. Tex., 1951, MusM, 1953. Broadway appearances include (Cleo) Most Happy Fella, 1956-58, (Miss Jones) How to Succeed in Business Without Really Trying, 1962-64, (Mrs. McIlhenny) Do I Hear A Waltz?, 1964, (Mother-in-law) Fig Leaves Are Falling, 1970, (Deedee West, Hattie, Stella) Follies, 1971-72, (Stand by Madam Matroppo) Very Good Eddie, 1975-76, (Chair Person, Mop Lady) Woman of the Year, 1981-83; Off-Broadway appearances (Police Matron) Fly Blackbird, 1961, (Wife) My Wife and I, 1966, (Sara/Landlady) Curley McDimple, 1969, (Mrs. Farrell) Riverwind, 1962-64; Chgo. prodn. (Mother Superior) Nunsense, numerous others. Mem. AFTRA, SAG, Actor's Equity Assn. Died Mar. 7, 2005.

BLUM, JAY HERMAN, fabric manufacturing company executive; b. N.Y.C., Dec. 31, 1965; s. Robert Bruce and Leslie (Rogers) B. BA, Trinity Coll., 1988; MS, U. Hartford, 1989. Acct. Coopers & Lybrand, Hartford, Conn., 1988-90; mgr. aircraft div. Craftex Mills, Inc., Blue Bell, Pa., from 1990. Rep. United Way Phila., 1991—. Mem. Union League of Phila. Avocations: sailing, flying, rowing, computers, entrepreneurship. Died July 10, 2005.

BLUMENSON, MARTIN, historian, educator; b. N.Y.C., Nov. 8, 1918; s. Louis and Dorothy (Reicher) B.; m. Genevieve Jeanne Louise Aldebert, May 20. 1947; 1 child, John. AB, Bucknell U., 1939, AM, 1940, Harvard U., 1942; LittD (hon.), Acadia U., 1972, Bucknell U., 1976, U. North Tex., 1988. Instr. history U.S. Merchant Marine Acad., Kings Point, N.Y., 1948-50; sr. historian Office Chief Milit. History, Washington, 1956-66; cons. White House, Washington, 1967-69; chair milit. & strategic studies Acadia U., Wolfville, N.S., Can., 1969-71; King chair Naval War Coll., Newport, R.I., 1971-73; Mark Clark chair The Citadel, Charleston, S.C., 1974-75; Johnson chair Army War Coll., Carlisle Barracks, Pa., 1975-76; prof. George Washington U., Washington, 1976-82. Vis. prof. Nat. War Coll., U. Tex., Austin, 1985, U. North Tex., Denton, 1988. Author: Breakout and Pursuit, 1961, Duel for France, 1963, Anzio: The Gamble that Failed, 1963, Sicily: Whose Victory?, 1964, Eisenhower, 1965, Kasserine Pass, 1967, Bloody River, 1969, Salerno to Cassiuo, 1971, The Patton Papers, 1972, 74, Liberation, 1976, The Vildé Affair, 1979, Patton: The Man Behind the Legend, 1985, The Battle of the Generals, 1986; contbg. editor Army Mag. Lt. col. U.S. Army, 1942-46, ETO, 50-56, Korea. Decorated Bronze Star, 1952; recipient S.E. Morison prize Soc. Milit. Historians, 1995. Mem. Cosmos Club, Colonial Kane Lodge. Home: Washington, DC. Died Apr. 15, 2005.

BLUTH, JOHN FREDERICK, archivist, oral historian; b. Ogden, Utah, Mar. 18, 1944; s. Weyman John and Thelma Lavon Bluth; m. Patricia Harmer, June 1, 1971; 1 child, Sarah. BS, Weber State Coll., Ogden, 1966; MA, Brigham Young U., 1968, PhD, 1978. Cert. archivist. Oral historian Charles Redd Ctr., Provo, Utah, 1973-78; manuscript curator Brigham Young U., Provo, 1979-86; dir. Dalton (Pa.) Libr., 1988-91; archivist Jet Propulsion Lab., Pasadena, Calif., from 1991. Cons. Bur. Land Mgmt., Salt Lake City, 1975-81, Pa. Hist. Commn., Harrisburg, 1986-91; oral historian Kaiser-Permanente, Pasadena, 1994-97. Pres. Project: Art, Scranton, Pa., 1990-91. A.W. Mellon fellow Bentley Libr. U. Mich., 1984, NDEA Title IV fellow, 1968-72. Mem. S.W. Oral History Assn., Soc. Am. Archivists. Mem. Lds Ch. Home: Camarillo, Calif. Died Apr. 19, 2004.

BOARMAN, GERALD JUDE, distribution executive, religious organization administrator; b. Indpls., July 12, 1940; s. John Eldon and Agnes (Dugan) B.; m. Susan Marie Schmalz; children: Gerald II, Jeffrey, Michael, Daniel. Student, Purdue U., 1959, Butler U., 1960, W.Va. State U., 1964. Br. mgr. Dynamic Distbrs., Indpls., 1959-62; paper sales rep. Proctor & Gamble, St. Albans, W.Va., 1963-65, instr. soap salesman Camp Hill, Pa., 1965-66; equipment salesman Breuer Electric Mfg. Co., Camp Hill, 1967-69; v.p. Janitor Supply House, Inc., Harrisburg, Pa., 1969-80; sec. Servo Systems, Inc., Harrisburg, 1977-80; chmn. bd. dirs., founder Bortek Industries, Inc., Mechanicsburg, Pa., from 1980; chmn. bd., founder Multi-Media Ministries, Inc., Mechanicsburg, from 1980; pres., founder World Christian Monetary Fund, Mechanicsburg, from 1987. Chmn. bd. Task Masters, Inc., Mechanicsburg, 1981-87; mem. pres.' coun. advisors Regent U., Virginia Beach, 1987-92. Chmn. adv. bd. Bible Rsch. Ministries, Inc., Nashville, 1990-92; bd. dirs. Kingdom Ministries Internat., 1993—; dep. dir. gen. Internat. Biog. Ctr., Cambridge, Eng.; mem. rsch. bd. advisors Am. Biog. Inst., 1989; speaker Nat. Edn. Ctr. Thompson Inst., Harrisburg, 1984; city fin. mgr. Ams. for Robertson, Washington, 1987; vol. disaster assistance team ARC. Mem. Internat. Sanitary Supply Assn., Internat. Platform Assn. Republican. Avocations: swimming, fishing, boating, scuba diving, parasailing, travel. Home: Mechanicsburg, Pa. Died Mar. 11, 2004.

BOBROWSKY, KIM RUSSELL, lawyer, songwriter, mediator, arbitrator; b. Ann Arbor, Mich., Jan. 1, 1951; d. Alfred R. and Elaine (Elkind) B.; married (div. Apr. 21, 1992); 1 child, Joshua. BA with honors, Penn State U., 1972; JD, Duquesne U., 1976. Bar: Pa. 1976, U.S. Dist. Ct. (we. dist.) Pa. 1977, U.S. Ct. Appeals (3d cir.) 1989, U.S. Supreme Ct. 1992. Plaintiff trial atty. Evans, Ivory & Evans, Pitts., 1976-83; def. trial atty. Continental Ins. Co., Pitts., 1983-90; plaintiff, def. trial atty. Cipriani & Werner, Pitts., 1990-95, of counsel, 1995-96; pvt. practice mediation & arbitration, 1995-96; ptnr. Bowes & Bobrosky, Pitts., from 1996. Adj. cert. settlement judge and arbitrator, U.S. Dist. Ct. Writer (songs) Magic Moments, 1993, My Fantasy, 1993, We've Got This Love, 1993. Mem. Pa. Trial Lawyers Assn., Def. Rsch. Inst., Am. Arbitration Assn. (mem. panel neutrals), Masonic Lodge (past master 1980). Avocations: tai chi, piano, bridge, guitar. Home: Bethel Park, Pa. Died Oct. 24, 2004.

BOCK, NORMA, hospital administrator; b. Gilberton, Pa., Sept. 29, 1925; d. William F. and Kathryn F. (Tregea) McCabe; m. George C. Bock, July 20, 1946 (dec.); children: Linda, Carol, Gretchen. Diploma, St. Luke's Children's Med Ctr., Phila., 1946; BA, Ottowa U., 1979. Cert. nurse adminstrn. ANA. Staff nurse labor and delivery Nazareth Hosp., Phila., head nurse labor and delivery, supr. maternity, dir. maternal/neonatal. Mem. Nurses Assn. of Am. Coll. Ob.-Gyn. (chmnn. nursing practice standards com.), Pa. Perinatal Assn., Pa. Quality Nurse Adminstrs. Home: Levittown, Pa. Died June 18, 2005.

BOCK, RUSSELL SA, writer; b. Spokane, Wash., Nov. 24, 1905; s. Alva and Elizabeth (Mellinger) B.; m. Suzanne Ray, Feb. 26, 1970; children: Beverly A. Bock Wunderlich, James Russell. BBA, U. Wash., 1929. Part-time instr. U. So. Calif., UCLA, 1942-50; with Ernst & Ernst, CPAs, Los Angeles, 1938, ptnr., 1951-69; cons. Ernst & Young, from 1969. Author: Guidebook to California Taxes, annually, 1950—, Taxes of Hawaii, annually, 1964—; also numerous articles. Dir., treas. Cmty. TV So. Calif., 1964-74; dir., v.p. treas., So. Calif. Symphony-Hollywood Bowl Assn., 1964-70; bd. dirs. Claremont McKenna Coll., 1964-70, Cmty. Arts Music Assn., 1974-76, 78-84, Santa Barbara Symphony Assn., 1976-78, Santa Barbara Boys and Girls Club, 1980-93, UCSB Affiliates, 1983-85, Santa Barbara Civic Light Opera, 1995-97. Mem. Am. Inst. C.P.A.s (council 1953-57, trial bd. 1955-58, v.p. 1959-60), Calif. Soc. C.P.A.s (past pres.), Los Angeles C. of C. (dir. 1957-65, v.p. 1963), Sigma Phi Epsilon, Beta Alpha Psi, Beta Gamma Sigma. Clubs: Birnam Wood Golf, Santa Barbara Yacht. Died July 12, 2006.

BOCKHOFF, FRANK JAMES, chemistry professor; b. Tiffin, Ohio, Mar. 26, 1928; s. Cornelius F. and Helen O. (Bormuth) B.; m. Esther I. Camperchioli, Jan. 27, 1951; children— Frank Matthew, Susan Virginia, Celia Marie, James Paul. BS, Case Inst. Tech., 1950; MS, Case Western Res. U., 1952, PhD, 1959. Registered profl. engr., Ohio. Grad. asst. Case Western Res. U., 1950-51; instr. Fenn Coll., Cleve., 1951-54, asst. prof., 1954-60, assoc. prof., 1960-62, chmn. chemistry, 1962-65; prof. Cleve. State U., 1965-90, prof. chemistry, 1983-90, prof. emeritus, from 1990, chmn. dept. chemistry, 1965-83. Tech. cons. Am. Agile Corp., Bedford, Ohio, 1953-56, assoc. dir. research, devel., 1956-61; cons., dir. Signal Chem. Mfg. Co., Bedford, 1960-62, Reox Corp., Cleve., 1962-69; cons. Apex Reinforced Plastics, Cleve., 1961-63 Author: Welding of Plastics, 1959, Elements of Quantum Theory, 1969, 2d edit., 1976; Contbr. articles and revs. profl. jours. Trustee Northeastern Ohio Sci. Fair, 1961-64. Named Outstanding Engring. Tchr. Ohio sect. Am. Soc. E.E., 1960; recipient Tech. Achievement award Cleve. Tech. Soc. Council, 1961; Disting. Faculty award Cleve. State U., 1965; Outstanding Faculty award, 1980 Fellow Am. Inst. Chemists; mem. AAAS Internat. Inst. Conservation of Hist. and Artistic Works, Am. Chem. Soc., Sigma Xi, Tau Beta Pi, Alpha Chi Sigma. Home: Cleveland, Ohio. Died Feb. 2, 2006.

BOCKIAN, JAMES BERNARD, computer systems executive, writer; b. Jersey City, Sept. 16, 1941; s. Abraham and Evelyn (Skner) B.; m. Donna M. Hastings; children: Vivian Shifra, Adrian Adena, Lillian Tova. BA, Columbia U., 1963; MPA, U. Mich., 1965; MA, Yale U., 1967. Vice-consul, fgn. svc. officer Dept. State, Washington, 1967—71; sr. systems analyst J.C. Penney Co., N.Y.C., 1971—77; mgr. systems svcs., head dept. systems projects McDonnell Douglas Automation Co., Florham Park, NJ, 1977—86; prin. JBBA (James B. Bockian & Assocs., Inc.), Morristown, NJ, from 1976. V.p. MIS Thomas Cook, Inc., 1986-90, exec. cons. to Thomas Cook Group; cons. AT&T, major banks and brokerages in project mgmt. systems design and devel., 1997-2001; lectr. in field; cons. in sys. validation to the pharm. industry. Author: Management Manual for Systems Development Projects, 1979, Project Management for Systems Development, 1981, AT&T User Guide to Information Systems Development, 1980; contbr. articles to profl. jours. Mem. Internat. Soc. Pharm. Engrs., AAAS, N.Y. Acad. Scis., Internat. Assn. Cybernetics, Yale Club (N.Y.C.). Home: Morristown, NJ. Died Jan. 3, 2006.

BODDEN, THOMAS ANDREW, lawyer; b. Lafayette, Ind., Dec. 18, 1945; s. William A. and Dorothy B.; m. Irene Bodden; children: Wendee, Todd, Christopher. AB, Cornell U., 1968; JD, U. Miami, 1974. Bar: Hawaii 1975. Assoc. Torkildson, Katz et al, Honolulu, 1975-78, ptnr., 1978-81; pres. Bodden & Temple, LLLC, Maui and Wailuku, Hawaii, from 1981. Author: Taxation of Real Estate in Hawaii, 1979, Taxation of Real Estate in U.S., 1982, Selling DPP Programs, 1983. Pres. Kihei Community Assn., 1984-86. Served to lt. USN, 1969-72. Mem. Am. Coll. Trust and Estate Counsel, Hawaii Bar Assn., Nat. Assn. Realtors/RESSI (pres. 1987), Hawaii Assn. Realtors (pres. 1989). Died Feb. 9, 2004.

BODO, JOHN RAINER, minister; b. Budapest, Hungary, May 10, 1920; s. Charles and Mila Maria DeBodo; m. Jeanne Pfeiffer, Oct. 12, 1950 (div. 1964); children: Erika Bodo Alarcon, Jessica Bodo Wise; m. Mary Lou Lindstrom, June 15, 1974. BD, Union Theol. Sem., 1942; ThM, Princeton Sem., 1943, PhD, 1952. Ordained to ministry Presbyn. Ch., 1942. Pastor First Nassau Presbyn. Ch., Princeton, N.J., 1951-59; prof. practical theology San Francisco Sem., San Anselmo, Calif., 1959-67; chaplain, prof. Macalester Coll., St. Paul, 1967-68; pastor Old First Presbyn. Ch., San Francisco, 1969-76; interim pastor various churches, 1977-87; retired, from 1985. Broadcasting com. Presbyn. Ch., U.S.A., N.Y.C., 1954-57, ch. and soc. coun., 1960-69; com. on ministry Redwoods Presbytery, Novato, Calif., 1990—. Author: The Protestant Clergy & Public Issues, 1812-1848, 1954, Adam & Eve & You, 1977, A Gallery of New Testament Rogues, 1979; contbr. many articles to profl. jours. Democrat. Home: Mountain View, Calif. Died June 30, 2005.

BOGART, DONALD GEORGE, bank executive; b. Buffalo, Aug. 12, 1933; s. Albert Clement and Loretta Marie (Bent) B.; m. Elaine Donna Watson, June 25, 1955 (div. Mar. 1986); children: Kenneth Richard, Michelle Carole Mikolajek. Cert., Am. Inst. Banking, 1965, N.Y. State Banker's Sch. Exec. Devel., 1974. V.p. productivity mgmt. Marine Midland Bank, Buffalo, from 1983, v.p. tech. services Syracuse, N.Y., 1979-83; programming mgr. Marine Midland Services Corp., Buffalo, 1965-71, asst. v.p., mgr. adminstrn., 1975-78; ops. mgr. Marine Midland Banks, Inc., Buffalo, 1951-64, 1972-74. Mem. Am. Soc. Quality Circles, Am. Productivity Mgmt. Assn. Roman Catholic. Avocations: tennis, travel. Home: Buffalo, NY. Died Apr. 16, 2004.

BOGART, LEO, sociologist; b. Poland, Sept. 23, 1921; s. Jacob and Rachel (Blum) B.; m. Agnes Cohen, Aug. 9, 1948. children: Michele, Gregory. BA, Bklyn. Coll., 1941; MA, U. Chgo., 1948, PhD in Sociology, 1950. Instr. English Ill. Inst. Tech., Chgo., 1946-48; pub. opinion rsch. analyst Standard Oil Co., N.J., 1948-51; lectr. in Sociology NYU, 1949-50; dir. account rsch. svc. McCann-Erickson, Inc., N.Y.C., 1952-58; lectr. in sociology Columbia U., N.Y.C., 1953-57; dir. mktg. rsch. Revlon, Inc., N.Y.C., 1958-60; exec. v.p., gen. mgr. Newspaper Advt. Bur., N.Y.C., 1960-89; bus. cons., columnist Presstime mag.; adj. prof. Mktg. NYU, 1990-92. Bd. dirs. Innovation Internat. Media Cons. Group. Author: The Age of Television, 1956, Strategy in Advertising, 1967, Social Research and the Desegregation of the U.S. Army, 1969, Silent Politics, 1971, Premises for Propaganda, 1976, Press and Public, 1981, Polls and the Awareness of Public Opinion, 1985, Project Clear, 1991, Preserving the Press, 1991, Commercial Culture, 1995, Cool Words, Cold War, 1995, Finding Out, 2003, How I Earned the Ruptured Duck, 2004, Over the Edge, 2005; contbr. numerous articles to profl. jours. Past mem. N.Y. adv. bd. City Innovation; past dir. Ctr. for Applied Linguistics, Nat. Safety Coun., Obor Found., Advt. Rsch. Found., Am. Advt. Fedn., Am. Mktg. Assn.; past pres. Soc. for Consumer Psychology. Served with U.S. Army, 1942-46. Decorated 4 Battle Stars; sr. fellow Gannett Ctr. for Media Studies, Columbia U., 1989-90; Fulbright fellow Inst. Nat. d'Etudes Demographiques, Paris, 1951-52; recipient awards from Am. Mktg. Assn., Am. Soc. Newspaper Editors, Internat. Circulation Mgrs. Assn., Internat. Newspaper Promotion Assn., Newspaper Rsch. Coun. Fellow APA, Am. Psychol. Soc., Soc. for Consumer Psychology; mem. Am. Sociol. Assn., Am. Assn. for Pub. Opinion Rsch. (past pres., award), World Assn. for Pub. Opinion Rsch. (past pres.), Market Rsch. Coun. (past pres., award), Radio and Television Rsch. Coun. (past pres.), Overseas Press Club Am., City Club N.Y., Dutch Treat Club. Died Oct. 15, 2005.

BOGEN, JOSEPH ELLIOT, neurosurgeon, educator; b. Cin., July 13, 1926; m. Glenda A. Miksch, 1955; children: Meriel, Mira. AB in Econs., Whittier Coll., 1949; postgrad., U. Cin., 1950, UCLA, 1951; MD, U. So. Calif., 1956. Lic. physician, Calif.; diplomate Am. Bd. Neurol. Surgery. Intern in surgery The N.Y. Hosp., 1956-57, asst. resident in surgery, 1957-58; resident in neurosurgery White Meml. Hosp., 1959-63; asst. in neurology Loma Linda U., 1963; asst. clin. prof. neurosurgery Calif. Coll. Medicine, 1964-68; cons. in neurosurgery Calif. Inst. Tech., 1968; assoc. clin. prof. U. So. Calif., 1973-77, clin. prof. Adj. prof. UCLA, 1984—; vis. prof. Calif. Inst. Tech., 1995. With USNR, 1944-46. Fellow ACS; mem. AAAS, L.A. Soc. Neurol. Psychiatry (bd. dirs. 1975, pres. 1983), So. Calif. Neurosurg. Soc. (pres. 1976), Am. Acad. Neurology, Am. Assn. Neurol. Surgeons, Soc. for Neurosci., Behavioral Neurol. Soc., Western Pain Soc., Am. Pain Soc., Calif. Neuropsychol. Soc., Internat. Neuropsychol. Soc., Acad. of Aphasia (bd. govs. 1976-80). Died Apr. 22, 2005.

BOGER, RICHARD EDWIN, JR., minister; b. Atlanta, May 13, 1952; s. Richard Edwin and Marie Yoder (Leonard) B.; m. Jill Roberta Howard, Apr. 26, 1980; 1 child, John Michael Howard. AB, Lenoir-Rhyne Coll., 1973, Hamma Sch. Theology, 1975; MDiv, Pacific Luth. Theol. Sem., 1978. Ordained to ministry Evang. Luth. Ch. Am., 1980. Intern Vesper Soc., San Leandro, Calif., 1975—76; coord. vols. Care Network, San Leandro, 1978; intern Christ Our Shepherd, Peachtree City, Ga., 1979—80; pastor Luth. Ch. of Our Savior, Jacksonville, NC, 1980—90, Nazareth Luth. Ch., Rural Hall, NC, 1990—98; pastor, webmaster St. Thomas Net Ministry, Winston-Salem, NC, 1999—2004; pastor St. Michael Luth. Ch., Highpoint, NC, 2001—04. Counselor Neighborhood Ch. Clinic, Springfield, Ohio, 1974; pastoral counselor Eden Hayward (Calif.) Pastoral Counseling Svc., 1975-76; mem. Jacksonville Ministerial Assn., 1980-81, Onslow County Ministerial Fellowship, 1984; mem. worship com., music com. N.C. Synod Luth. Ch. in Am., 1982, 84-86, 94, 97-99; assoc. N.C. Chaplains Assn., 1984; pres. Forsyth Luth. Coun., 1992. Pub. Nazareth Luth. Ch. Home Page, 1995. V.p. High Point Ministerial Alliance, 2003—04; bd. dirs. ARC, Jacksonville, 1981—89. Mem. Soc. of the Holy Trinity (founder), Alban Inst., Forsyth Luth. Area Pastors (coord. 1996-98, 2000-2002), Forsyth Luth. Coun., Rural Hall-Stanleyville Mins. Assn. (pres. 1995-97), United Ministry Rural Hall (bd. dirs. 1994-98, sec. 1997). Home: Winston Salem, NC. Died July 21, 2004.

BOGGIO, MARSHALL R., engineering educator; b. Orange, N.J., June 24, 1927; s. Marshall Peter and Margaret (Jandoli) B.; m. Shirley Ann Widejko, June 7, 1953; children: Dawn Ann, Kim Robert, Cindy Lea, Scott Michael. BS in Math. & Physics, Upsala Coll., 1951; MSEE, N.J. Inst. Tech., 1954, MS in Mgmt. Engring., 1967. Registered profl. engr., N.J. Sr. engr. Lockheed Electronics, North Plainfield, N.J., 1954-63, dir. engring., 1984-86; mktg./program mgr. Electronic Assocs., Long Branch, N.J., 1963-84; chairperson engring. sci. Ocean County Coll., Toms River, N.J., from 1986. Patentee in field. Councilperson Governing Body, Point Pleasant, N.J., 1976-83, mayor, 1983-86, chairperson, mem. planning bd., 1990—; v.p. bd. edn. Point Pleasant Sch. Dist., 1974-76. Recipient Coll. Faculty Study award NSF, 1973, Lab. Upgrade award Higher Edn. State of N.J., 1988. Mem. IEEE, Moose, Rotary. Republican. Roman Catholic. Avocations: gardening, golf. Home: Pt Pleasant, NJ. Died Nov. 2, 2004.

BOHMONT, DALE WENDELL, agricultural consultant; b. Wheatland, Wyo., June 7, 1922; s. J.E. and Mary (Armann) B.; m. Marilyn J. Horn, Mar. 7, 1969 (dec. Dec. 2004); children: Dennis E., Craig W. BS, U. Wyo., 1948, MS, 1950; PhD, U. Nebr., 1952; MPA, Harvard U., 1959. Registered investment adv., SEC. Pub. sch. tchr., Rock River, Wyo., 1941-42; from rsch. asst. to head plant scis. U. Wyo., 1946-60; assoc. dir. expt. sta. Colo. State U., 1961-63; dean, dir. agr. U. Nev., Reno, 1963-82, dean, dir. emeritus, 1982—2006; pres. Bohmont Cons. Inc., from 1982; mem. Brucheum Group, Waynesboro, Va., 1984; chief cons. Zygro Corp., 1999. Cons. Devel. & Resources Corp., N.Y.C., 1968-2006, Fredriksen, Kamine & Assocs., Sacramento, 1976, Nev. Agrl. Found., 1986-2006; pres. Enide Corp., Reno, 1974-80, Thermal Dynamics Internat., 1983-87, Cryabis, Inc., Reno, 1993-95; co-chmn. rsch. planning West Divsn. Agr. Expt. Stas., 1975; mem. exec. com., coun. adminstrv. heads agr. Nat. Assn. State Univ. Land Grant Colls., 1975. Author: Golden Years of Agriculture in Nevada, 1989; contbr. articles to profl. jours.; mem. editl. bd.: Crops and Soils, 1962-2006. Pres. Dale W. and Marilyn Horn Found., 1998-2006; Served with USAAF, 1942-45. Fellow AAAS, Agronomy Soc.; mem. Western Soc. Weed Scis. (hon.), Western Crop Sci. Soc. (pres. 1962-63), Nat. Expt. Sta. Dirs. Assn. (chmn. 1967-68), Am. Range Mgmt. Soc., Farm House (dir. 1962-2006), Weed Soc. Am. (hon.), Sigma Xi, Gamma Sigma Delta (pres. 1964-66), Alpha Zeta, Alpha Tau Alpha, Phi Kappa Phi., Lions (v.p. 1985-86, pres. 1986-87, bd. dirs. 1985-2006). Died Mar. 5, 2006.

BOISE, OLA IRENE, music educator; b. Parkersburg, W.Va., Dec. 1, 1946; d. Manford and Ollie Irene (Arthur) B. BA in Fine Arts, Ohio U., 1968, MA in Mus. Edn., 1974. Cert. music edn. elem. through high sch., Ohio. Tchr. music Warren Local Schs., Vincent, Ohio, 1968-69; tchr. elem., music Wood County Schs., Parkersburg, W.Va, 1969-73; tchr. music Amherst (Ohio) Exempted Village Schs., 1974-76, W. Muskingum Local Schs., Zanesville, Ohio, 1976-83, Belpre (Ohio) City Schs., 1983-90; agt. Prudential Ins. Co. Am., 1990; account rep. Washington County News, from 1991. Chmn. bike-a-thon St. Jude's Children's Research Hosp., 1987; mem. exec. bd. Belpre area bi-centennial commn., 1987—. Mem. Belpre Edn. Assn. (exec. council 1986-87), Ohio Music Edn. Assn. (dist. 9 various positions), Belpre Area C. of C. (bd. dirs. 1988—). Republican. Baptist. Avocations: reading, walking, travel. Home: Belpre, Ohio. Died May 30, 2005.

BOLENDER, TODD, dancer, choreographer; b. Canton, Ohio, Feb. 27, 1914; Student, Hanya Holm, N.Y.C.; enrolled, Sch. American Ballet, N.Y.C., 1936. Joined Lincoln Kirstein's Ballet Caravan, 1937; formed Am. Concert Ballet; choreographed 1st ballet, 1943; also danced with Ballet Theatre, 1944 and Ballet Russe de Monte Carlo, 1945, joined Ballet Soc., 1946; prin. dancer N.Y.C. Ballet, 1948-61; dir. ballet, Cologne Opera House, 1963-66, Frankfurt Ballet, 1966-69, Ataturk Oera House, Turkey; artistic dir. State Ballet of Mo., Kansas City, 1981-96, artistic dir. emeritus, 1996-2006. Recipient Mo. Arts Coun. awrd, 1987, W.F. Yates for disting. svc. William Jewell Coll., 1995. Died Oct. 12, 2006.

BOLGER, MARY PHYLLIS JUDGE, special education educator; b. Newark, Aug. 19, 1926; d. Michael Francis and Loretta Margaret (Reinhardt) Judge; m. William Patrick Bolger, Nov. 27, 1948 (dec. May 1973); children: Loretta, Francis, Christopher, Michael. BA, Montclair State U., 1946; MA, Reading Specialist, Seton Hall U., 1973. Cert. reading specialist, tchr. English, social studies, Spanish, and reading, learning disabilities tchr., cons. Tchr. English Bd. Edn., Irvington, NJ, 1946-49; tchr. West Side HS, Newark, 1963-69; reading specialist Roosevelt Jr. HS, West Orange, NJ, 1969-77; learning disability tchr., cons. West Orange HS and Hazel Ave., 1977-91. Tchr. ESL South Orange (N.J.) Maplewood Adult Schs., 1949—64; adj. prof. edn. Seton Hall U., South Orange, 1974—96; cons. dept. curriculum and spl. svcs. West Orange Bd. Edn., 1987—2002, cons., workshop presenter, 2000—01; mem. adv. bd. Prospect Ho., East Orange, NJ, 1994—97; cons. to therapeutic friendship groups for retarded adults, from 1999; cons., workshop presenter Lifelong Learning Inst., Caldwell (N.J.) Coll., 2000—01; freelance lectr., workshop presenter. Editor: (book) Beyond Common Sense: The Art of Intelligent Living, 1992, doctoral dissertations Seton Hall U., 1993—97. Eucharistic min. St. Barnabas Hosp., Livingston, NJ, 1991—2001, Ward Homestead, Maplewood, NJ, 1992—2000; coord. eucharistic ministry to the homebound Our Lady of Sorrows, South Orange, NJ, 1989—2000, Homebound Ministry, 1989—2002. Mem.: Seton-Essex Reading Coun. (pres., v.p.), N.J. Reading Assn. (co-chairperson Reading/Learning Disabilities com.), South Orange Sr. Circle (rec. sec. from 2001), Rosary Altar Soc. Roman Catholic. Avocations: writing, travel, reading, watercolors. Died Aug. 29, 2004.

BOLGER, RICHARD JOHN, small business owner; b. Phila., June 16, 1929; s. Harold Stephen and Edna Florence (Adams) B.; m. Betty Ann Smith, Aug. 4, 1956 (div. 1963); m. Dorothy Elizabeth Evans, June 5, 1965; children: Deborah Elizabeth, David Evans. BSBA, LaSalle U., Phila., 1956. Sales rep. Alan Wood Steel Co., Conshohocken, Pa., 1956-65; sales engr. E.J. Lavino & Co., Phila., 1965-70; account exec. The Pappas Orgn., Wynnewood, Pa., 1970-75; dist. sales mgr. Conners Steel Co., Birmingham, Ala., 1975-83; mgr. installations Frazier Indsl. Co., Long Valley, N.J., 1983-88; mfrs. rep. Linwood, N.J., from 1988. Mem. Egg Harbor Twp. (N.J.) Environ. Commn., 1990—. Mem. Steel Svc. Ctr. Inst., Am. Soc. Metals, Phila. Cricket Club (bd. dirs. 1968-73), Ocean City Yacht Club (fin. sec. 1987-89, bd. dirs. 1982—). Republican. Roman Catholic. Avocations: sailing, squash, tennis, golf. Died Apr. 17, 2004.

BOLING, ELDON AVERY, physician; b. Elma, Wash, Aug. 29, 1925; s. Dawson and Nellie (Beam) B.; m. Lenore Altschule, Feb. 13, 1948; children: Peter, Alice, Lucy, Sarah, Deborah, Eli. BA, Whitman Coll., Walla Walla, Wash., 1946; MD, U. Calif., San Francisco, 1950. Intern San Francisco Gen. Hosp., 1950-51; rsch. fellow Peter Bent Brigham Hosp., Boston, 1952-54; resident in medicine Boston VA Hosp., 1954-57; staff physician Boston VA Med. Ctr., 1959-95, cons. physician, 1995—98. Patentee in field. Lt. comdr. USNR, 1957-59. Avocation: music. Home: Boxford, Mass. Died May 3, 2005.

BOLTZ, GERALD EDMUND, lawyer; b. Dennison, Ohio, June 1, 1931; s. Harold E. and Margaret Eve (Hecky) B.; m. Janet Ruth Scott, Sept. 19, 1959; children: Gretchen Boltz Fields, Eric Scott, Jill Marie. BA, Ohio No. U., 1953, JD, 1955. Bar: Ohio 1955, U.S. Supreme Ct. 1964, Calif. 1978, U.S. Dist. Ct. (cen. dist.) Calif. 1978. Asst. atty. gen. State of Ohio, 1958; atty. spl. investigations unit SEC, 1959-60, legal asst. to commr., 1960-61, sr. trial and spl. counsel Denver, 1961-66, regional adminstr. Ft. Worth, 1967-71, L.A., 1972-78; ptnr. Fine, Perzik& Friedman, L.A., 1979-83; mng. ptnr. Rogers & Wells, L.A., 1983-92; ptnr. Bryan Cave, L.A., 1992—2004. Co-author: Securities Law Techniques. Served with U.S. Army, 1955-57. Mem. ABA, Fed. Bar Assn., L.A. Bar Assn., Ohio Bar Assn., Calif. Bar Assn., Bel Air Bay Club. Presbyterian (elder). Avocations: sailing, piano. Home: Santa Monica, Calif. Died May 10, 2006.

BOLTZ, MARSHA A., nurse practitioner, medical/surgical clinical nurse specialist, educator; b. Akron, Ohio, May 29, 1954; d. Russell G. and E. Ann (Spickard) B. BSN, U. Akron, 1976; student, Andrews U.; MS, U. South Fla., 1990. Staff nurse Akron City Hosp., 1976-81; nurse, diabetes unit Akron Gen. Med. Ctr., 1981-83; pvt. duty nurse Kelly Health Care Staff Builders Med. Pers. Pool, Akron, 1983; ICU-CCU nurse S.W. Gen. Hosp., Middleburg Heights, Ohio, 1983-84; staff nurse critical care unit Sarasota (Fla.) Meml. Hosp., 1984, staff nurse telemetry, 1985-91; clin. nurse specialist Med. Ctr. Ctrl. Ga., Macon, 1991-95; asst. prof. medicine Mercer U. Sch. Medicine, Macon, from 1996. Mem. ANA, Am. Hosp. Assn. (lipid nurse task force), Ga. Nurses Assn., Sigma Theta Tau, Phi Kappa Phi, Alpha Lambda Theta. Home: Macon, Ga. Died Mar. 16, 2004.

BOMIER, JEROME TURNER, lawyer; b. Milw., June 10, 1927; s. Turner Francis and Blanche Elizabeth (Olive) B.; m. Gloria Claire Rogahn, Jan. 28, 1950; children: Kathleen Bomier Emmerling, Jerome T. II, David W., Samuel J. BS, U. Wis., 1949, LLB, 1951. Bar: Wis. 1951. Spl. agt. FBI, Phila., 1951-53; sr. ptnr. Di Renzo and Bomier, Neenah, Wis., from 1953. Bd. dirs. Buckstaff Co., Oshkosh, Wis., J.W. Hewitt Machine, Neenah, Hewitt Transmission Co., Neenah. Trustee, chmn. com. Paine Arboretum and Art Ctr., Oshkosh, 1988—; mem. adv. bd. Neenah-Menasha Vis. Nurse Assn., Neenah, 1986—. With USCG, 1945-46. Mem. ATLA, State Bar of Wis., Winnebago County Bar Assn., Civil Trial Counsel of Wis., Def. Rsch. Inst. Avocations: gardening, reading, travel. Home: Neenah, Wis. Died Jan. 23, 2004.

BOND, THOMAS ROSS, television assistant director; b. Dallas, Sept. 16, 1926; s. Ashley Ross and Margaret (Sauter) B.; m. Pauline Francis Goebel, Apr. 18, 1953; 1 child, Thomas Ross. BA, L.A. State Coll., 1951. Actor Hal Roach Studios, Culver City, Calif., 1932-40, Warner Bros., Burbank, Calif., 1937, MGM, Culver City, 1938, KFWB Radio, Hollywood, Calif., 1937; asst. dir. KFSN-TV, Fresno, Calif., 1975—91; ret., 1991. Producer Emmanuel Luth. Ch., North Hollywood, 1959-72. Appeared in films including Our Gang Comedies, 1932-40, Superman, 1946-48. With USN, 1945-46. Republican. Lutheran. Home: Imperial Bch, Calif. Died Sept. 24, 2005.

BOND, WILLIAM HENRY, librarian; b. York, Pa., Aug. 14, 1915; s. Walter Loucks and Ethel (Bossert) B.; m. Helen Elizabeth Lynch, Dec. 6, 1943 (dec. Jan. 1999); children: Nancy Barbara, Sally Lynch. AB, Haverford Coll., 1937; MA, Harvard, 1938, PhD, 1941. Research fellow Folger Shakespeare Library, 1941-42; asst. to librarian Houghton Library, Harvard, Cambridge, Mass., 1946-48, curator manuscripts, 1948-64, librarian, 1965-82; lectr. bibliography Harvard, 1964-67, prof., 1967-86, librarian, prof. emeritus, from 1986. Asst. keeper manuscripts Brit. Mus., 1952-53; Sandars reader in bibliography Cambridge (Eng.) U., 1981-82. Author: Thomas Hollis of Lincoln's Inn, a Whig and His Books, 1990; editor: (Christopher Smart) Jubilate Agno, 1954, Supplement to Census of Medieval and Renaissance Manuscripts in the United States, 1962, The Houghton Library, 1942-67, 1967, Records of a Bibliographer, 1967, 18th Century Studies in Honor of Donald F. Hyde, 1970, (with Hugh Amory) The Printed Catalogues of the Harvard College Library 1723-1790, 1996. Trustee Emerson Meml. Assn., 1964-89; hon. trustee Concord (Mass.) Free Pub. Library, 1990—; trustee Historic Deerfield (Mass.) Inc., 1965-91, hon. trustee, 1991—, v.p., 1985-88. Served to lt. USNR, 1943-46. Fulbright fellow, 1952-53, Guggenheim fellow, 1982-83 Mem. Bibliog. Soc. Am. (pres. 1974-75), Bibliog. Soc. London (hon. sec. for Am. 1964-93), Grolier Club, Am. Antiquarian Soc. (councillor 1970-91, hon. councillor 1991—), Mass. Hist. Soc., Colonial Soc. Mass. (pres. 1981-93, hon. mem. 1994—), The Johnsonians, Phi Beta Kappa. Home: Concord, Mass. Died Nov. 18, 2005.

BONDS, THYRA VERLE, retired civilian military employee; b. Des Moines, Dec. 1, 1927; d. Charles Christopher and Haley Dell (Evans) Johnson; m. Melvin Bonds, Dec. 26, 1952 (div. 1969); children: Kasandra Verle, Gayle Denyse. AS in Commerce (Bus. Adminstrn.), St. Louis U., 1974; student, Drake U., 1947-52. With Dept. Def., 1957-84; chief program mgmt. Aircraft Surviability Equipment Aviation Command, St. Louis, 1971-84; ret. Aviation Command, St. Louis, 1984. Mentor St. Louis Pub. Schs., 1986—. Contbr. articles to nat. mags. Amb. good will of women Louisville C. of C., 1967-68; vol. Telephone Reassurance Program, St. Louis, 1980; adv. mem. Mo. Commn. Status of Women, 1982—; bd. govs. Army Aviation Scholarship Found., Westport, Conn., 1984-90; mem. Community Adv. Coun., Webster Groves, Mo., 1985-90. Decorated Meritorious Civilian Svc.; recipient Career and Community Svc. award, 1978, Yes I Can award, 1979. Mem. Nat. Army Aviation Assn. Am. (v.p. 1981-83), Coalition 100 Black Women (v.p. 1988-90), Assn. U.S. Army (adv. coun. 1985-90), Nat. Affiliation for Literacy Advance, Nat. Drifters (v.p., treas.), St. Louis Symphony Vols. Assn. (ednl. com.), Order Ea. Star, Phi Chi Theta. Avocations: gardening, tennis. Home: Saint Louis, Mo. Died Aug. 4, 2005.

BONEVA, BONKA, social psychologist; b. Plovdiv, Bulgaria, Nov. 20, 1950; d. Stefan and Lili Stoyanov; m. Kamen Bonev, June 3, 1984; 1 child, Boriana. Diploma, U. Sofia, Bulgaria, 1973; PhD, Bulgarian Acad. Sci., 1988. Asst. prof. U. Sofia, 1985-90, lectr., 1990-93; vis. asst. prof. U. Pitts., 1994-95; rschr. Bulgarian Acad. Scis., from 1976. Vis. scholar Northwestern U., Evanston, Ill., 1988-89. Author: American Theories in Studying Ethnicity, 1994, Being American the Bulgarian Way, 1992; co-author: Balkan Businessmen in Canada, 1993, Linguistic Minorities in Central and East Europe, 1998. NATO fellow, 1993-94, Am. Coun. Learned Socs. fellow, 1988-89. Home: Pittsburgh, Pa. Died Sept. 2, 2004.

BONNEAU, WILLIAM HENRY, JR., president information services; b. New Bedford, Mass., July 3, 1937; s. William Henry and Annette Marriette Yvette; 1 child, Edwin. BBA, Bryant Coll., 1958. Advertiser Am. Tourister, West Warwick, R.I., 1956-58; mktg. dir. Sylvia & Assocs., West Warwick, R.I., 1958-62; world's fair mgr. La. Pavillion, Flushing, N.Y., 1962-63; mgmt. cons. Pan Am./Intercontinental Hotels, N.Y.C., 1963-65, Mauchly & Assocs., Montgomeryville, Pa., 1965-66; mktg. cons. Mktg. Consultants Internat., Jacksonville, Fla., 1966-72; pres. Am. Funding Inc., Jacksonville, Fla., 1972-75, Worldwide Info. Svcs. Inc., Fort Lauderdale, Fla., from 1975. Roman Catholic. Avocations: tennis, boating. Died Apr. 11, 2005.

BONO, JACK ALEX, research laboratory executive; b. Cokeburg Junction, Pa., May 10, 1925; s. Dominick and Maria (Tosi) B.; m. Bette Jackson, Feb. 28, 1946; children: Meri Bono McCarthy, Bette, Steve, John. BS, Northwestern U., 1946. With Underwriters Labs. Inc., Northbrook, Ill., 1946—90, pres., CEO, 1978—90. Served with USNR, 1943-46. Fellow Soc. Fire Protection Engrs., ASTM; mem. Nat. Soc. Profl. Engrs. Clubs: Union League (Chgo.). Episcopalian. Home: Northbrook, Ill. Died Nov. 18, 2005.

BONUTTI, ALEXANDER CARL, design executive; b. Cleve., June 25, 1951; s. Karl Borromeo and Hermina (Rijavec) B. BArch, Ill. Inst. Tech., 1974; MSArch in Urban Design, Columbia U., 1978. Registered architect, Ohio, W.Va., Calif. With William B. Morris, AIA, Shaker Heights, Ohio, 1973; designer Stouffer's Hotels, Cleve., 1974, Ellerbe, Dalton, Dalton and Newport, Bethesda, Md., 1975-76; designer, asst. project mgr. Dalton, Dalton and Newport, Shaker Heights, 1976-79; prin. ACB Design, Cleve., 1980, Kaplan, McLaughlin and Diaz, San Francisco, 1981-91; sr. v.p., mng. prin. Hellmuth Obata Kassabaum, San Francisco, from 1991. Contbr. articles to profl. jours. Bd. dirs. Archtl. Found. San Francisco, 1997—, Architects in Calif. Polit. Action Com., 1996-99. Recipient Honor award Architects Soc. Ohio, Bay Village, 1979. Mem. AIA (steering com. 1989 Monterey Design Conf., Hon. awards U.S. Univ. Health Sci., Naval Facilities Command, Honor award for Pacific Presbyn. Profl. Bldg. 1987, Citation for Excellence, Urban Design Embarcadero Corridor Study, bd. dirs. Calif. coun. 1986-97, chmn. urban design com. San Francisco chpt. 1986-88, v.p., pres.-elect 1989, pres. 1990, chmn. Five Bay Area chpt. leaders forum 1991, Calif. Coun. Bldg. and Constrn. Legis. Commn. 1991), Urban Land Inst. (assoc.), Nat. Trust Hist. Preservation, Inst. Urban Design, Calif. Archtl. Polit. Action Com. (trustee 1997—), Archtl. Found. San Francisco (v.p. 2001—), Phi Kappa Sigma (sec. 1970-71). Democrat. Avocations: jogging, bicycling. Home: Oakland, Calif. Died Feb. 5, 2005.

BOOS, H. GORDON, motion picture director; b. Chgo., Apr. 27, 1958; s. Hans Werner Boos and Lieselotte (Merz) Schweikhofer. Student, U. Chgo., 1977-78, So. Ill. U., 1978-80. Creative dir. Casual Acting Sch. of Hollywood, Calif., from 1981. Asst. dir. (feature films) Valley Girl, 1983, The Ladies Club, 1986, Platoon, 1986, Tucker: The Man and His Dream, 1987, In Country, 1988, The Godfather Part III, 1990, Wilder Napalm, 1993, Cobb, 1994, Tin Cup, 1996, Bogus, 1996, Play It to the Bone, 1999, The Rookie, 2002; dir. (feature films) Red Surf, 1990, Touch Me, 1997, The Vivero Letter, 1998; (TV movies) Perfect Assassins, 1998. Mem. Dirs. Guild Am. (Outstanding Achievement award 1986), The Club Ted (co-founder 1981, Ted of Yr. 1985, 89). Taoist. Avocations: handball, ice hockey. Home: Los Angeles, Calif. Died Apr. 3, 2004.

BORACCI, ANDREW SILVIO, journalist, publisher, editor, playwright; b. Astoria, N.Y., Oct. 1, 1926; s. Enio J. and Maria (Celli) B.; m. Dorothy Kurnik, June 8, 1950 (dec. Mar. 17, 1971); m. Ty Stroudsburg, 1975 (div. 1980). BA in Journalism, Hofstra U., 1950; postgrad., C.W. Post Coll., 1973. News/feature writer Newsday, Hempstead, N.Y., 1947-50; assoc. editor, sr. assoc. editor McGraw Hill Pub., N.Y.C., 1950-55; sr. editor Simmons Boardman, N.Y.C., 1955-57; exec. editor Conover-Nast Pub., N.Y.C., 1957-59; assoc. dir. advt. Holt, Rinehart & Winston, N.Y.C., 1959-61; pres., creative dir. Boracci, Brown & Co., Huntington, N.Y., 1961-73; assoc. dir. comm. L.I. U./C.W. Post Coll., Greenvale, N.Y., 1974-77; editor, pub., owner, founder Eastender Group of Mags., Books, TV, Sag Harbor, N.Y., from 1977. Cons. comm. Edn. Divsn., Borg-Warner, Skokie, Ill., 1973-74, McGraw-Hill, N.Y.C., 1973-74. Playwright: Lisa Stratter, 1950, Baccanalo, 151, one act plays, 1950-54. Bd. advisors coop. edn. Suffolk campus, L.I. U., 1994—; cons. Oakland Cemetary Assn., Sag Harbor, 1993—; glockenspeil player Sag Harbor Community Band, 1990—; chmn. pub. rels. Peconic County Study Group, Southampton, N.Y., 1980—; chmn. 190th anniversary com. Sag Harbor Masons, 1994. With USNR, 1945-47. Mem. Am. Legion, U.S. Power Squadron, Masons (master, 32d degree, dir. comm. 1993—, Wamponsamon Lodge Sag Harbor, Munnakuma chpt. Royal Arch, K.T. Patchogue, mem. publs. com.), K.T. Republican. Roman Catholic. Avocations: jazz piano, boating. Home: Sag Harbor, NY. Died May 7, 2004.

BORDER, GLADYS LOUISE, piano educator; b. Cleve., Feb. 11, 1926; d. Frederick August and Edith Elliot (Spellman) Schnell; m. Tondra Harrison Border, Nov. 16, 1946; children: David, Thomas, Calvin. Diploma, Wilcox Coll. Commerce, Cleve., 1944; student, Baptist Bible Inst., Cleve., 1944-46. Sales clk. part time F.W. Woolworth Co., Cleveland Heights, Ohio, 1942-44; office sec. part time Wilcox Coll. Commerce, Cleve., 1944; sec. Standard Oil Co., Cleve., 1944-47; temporary office work Ballou Svcs., Cleve., 1954; piano tchr. pvt. practice, Cleve., 1955-59, Hollywood, Fla., from 1959; sec. indsl. and pub. rels. Food Fair Offices, Miami, 1961-62; piano tchr. pvt. practice, Hollywood, Fla., from 1997. Ch. pianist First Brethren Ch., Cleveland Heights, Ohio, 1941-46; regular pianist Phi Gamma Fishing Club, Cleve., 1944-46; asst. pianist Youth For Christ, Cleve., 1945; 2nd v.p., corr. sec., awards chmn. Broward County Music Tchrs., Ft. Lauderdale, Fla., 1970-90; pianist in churches Nazarene, Bapt. Hollywood Christian Sch., Cleve., 1947-58; accompanist for band solos McArthur H.S., Driftwood Jr. H.S., Hollywood, Fla., 1961-69; regular pianist 1st Bapt. Choir and Ch., W. Hollywood, Fla., 1971-89, part time 1993—. Author: (life story) On the Life of Gladys Louise (Schnell) Border. Den mother Boy Scouts Am. Cub Scouts, Cleve., 1958-59; Sunday sch. tchr. Ch. of Nazarene, Cleve., 1947-48, 57-58; treas. Band Parents Driftwood Jr. H.S., Hollywood, Fla., 1962, 63; recording sec. Women;s Soc. 1st Meth., Hollywood, Fla., 1962, 64; Sunday Sch. tchr. 1st Meth., Epworth Meth., Hollywood, Fla., 1960, 71; auditions chmn. Nat. Guild Piano Tchrs., 1988-2000; treas. Tues. Morning Musicale, 1994. Recipient Electronic Metronome McArthur High Band Soloists, Hollywood, Fla., 1967, Bowling trophies Bapt. Fellowship League, Hollywood, Fla., 1973-86, music min. plaques (2) 1st Bapt. W. Hollywood, Fla., 1980, 89; named Fairest of the Island Mother's Banquet 1st Bapt. W. Hollywood, Fla., 1994. Mem. Nat. Guild of Piano Tchrs., Jolly Srs., Fla. Fedn. Music Clubs, Broward County Music Tchrs. Assn. Republican. Baptist. Avocations: piano playing, reading, sewing, bowling, writing letters. Home: Hollywood, Fla. Died Aug. 3, 2006.

BORG, STEFAN, industry consultant; b. Brussels, Mar. 31, 1954; came to U.S., 1982; s. Richard Wagner and Marianne (Borg) Hansen; m. Nancy Susannah Schmoe, June 14, 1975; 1 child, Sophia Ashley. MS, U. Copenhagen, 1979; MBA, INSEAD, Fontainebleau, France, 1980. Rsch. asst. U. Copenhagen, 1978-79; sci. asst. Danish Cancer Registry, Copenhagen, 1974-75; mktg. mgr. Boehringer Mannheim GmbH, Vedbaek, Denmark, 1980-82; product mgr. Bethesda Rsch. Labs., Gaithersburg, Md., 1982-84; mgr. bus. devel. Calif. Biotech. Inc., Mountain View, Calif., 1984-86; v.p. bus. devel. Houston Biotech. Inc., The Woodlands, Tex., 1986-90; prin. Borg Biomed. Svcs., The Woodlands, from 1990; gen. ptnr. Batterson, Johnson & Borg Venture Ptnrs., L.P., from 1991. Cons. in field, 1991-93; pres., founder Sunpharm Corp., Jacksonville, Fla., 1991—. Recipient Bronze medal European Pistol Championships, 1974, Gold medal Nordic Pistol Championships, 1976. Mem. Licensing Exec. Soc., Ponte Vedra Inn & Club. Avocations: tennis, riding, hunting. Home: Ponte Vedra Beach, Fla. Died May 3, 2005.

BORING, JOHN EDWARD, civil engineer; b. Kans. City, May 29, 1934; s. Albert Russell and Evelyn Lorena (Carter) B.; m. Dorothy Louise Pelton, Jan. 30, 1955; children: Ramona, Jenna. BSCE, Kans. State U., 1957. Registered profl. engr., Iowa, Colo. Spl. projects engr. Iowa Dept. of Transp., Ames, 1957-61, asst. dist. materials engr. Fairfield, 1961-63; dist. engr. Asphalt Inst., Madison, Wis., 1963-73, Phonenix, 1973-77; materials engr. HKM Assoc., Billings, Mont., 1977-79; asst. divsn. mgr. F.M. Fox & Assoc., Wheat Ridge, Colo., 1979-80; engr. Western Testing Lab., Denver, 1980-82, pres., CEO, 1985-86; engr. Colo. Asphalt Producers Assn., Denver, 1982-84; constrn. inspector Constrn. Mgmt. and Tech. Svcs., Denver, 1988; bldg. cons. R.J. Moore and Assoc., Arvada, Colo., 1989-90; cons. engr. Asphalt Tech., Arvada, 1992, 93-95; quality ctrl. mgr. Profl. Svc. Industries, Denver, 1990-91; constrn. mgr. City of Thronton, Colo., 1991-92; chief engr. H.E. Cons. Ltd., Parker, Colo., 1992-93; support engr. City of Denver, 1993; supr. engr. Parsons Brinckerhoff, Denver, 1995; constrn. insp. City of (Colo.) Englewood, from 1996. Contbr. articles to profl. jours. Fellow Am. Soc. of Civil Engrs. (life); mem. Assn. Asphalt Paving Tech (life), Colo. Soc. Engrs. Achievements include design and performed field rsch. testing of first Full Depth asphalt pavement on interstate sys. Died Mar. 17, 2004.

BORNY, WALTER MICHAEL, lawyer, financial planner, general securities representative, real estate investment consultant, stockbroker, life and disability agent; b. Bklyn., June 23, 1948; s. Walter S. and Dolores (Kaplon) B. Student, Clemson U., 1965-66; AA magna cum laude, County Coll. Morris, Randolph, N.J., 1973; BA magna cum laude, Rutgers U., 1975, JD, 1979. Bar: N.J. 1979; lic. gen. securities rep., real estate agt., life ins. agt., notary pub., Calif. Legal counsel, 2d v.p. Chase Manhattan Bank, Englewood Cliffs, N.J., 1981-83; legal counsel CIS Equipment Leasing Corp., San Francisco, 1983-84; pvt. practice law San Francisco, 1984-85, Borny & Assocs., Foster City, Calif., from 1985; with IDS Fin. Svcs. Corp., Redwood City, Calif., 1992-93, Equitable Fin. Group, San Francisco, from 1994. Active March of Dimes Campaign for Healthier Babies, Make A Wich Found., San Francisco Child Abuse Found., Project Open Hand. Sgt. U.S. Army Security Agy., Vietnam, 1968-69. Decorated Vietnam medal, Vietnamese Cross of Gallantry with Palm; Rutgers Honors Program sr. fellow. Mem. ABA, N.J. State Bar Assn., Nat. Assn. Securities Dealers (cert. gen. securities rep.), Phi Beta Kappa, Phi Alpha Theta. Died Sept. 14, 2004.

BOROWIEC, WILLIAM MATTHEW, lawyer; b. Sierra Vista, Ariz., Dec. 21, 1962; s. Matthew William and Margaret Lynn Borowiec. BA, U. Ariz., 1987; JD, Hamline U., 1989. Bar: Ariz. 1991, U.S. Dist. Ct. Ariz. 1995. Atty. Blaser & Assocs., Tucson, 1991-93, Monroe & Assocs., Tucson, 1993, Felix & Holohan, Tucson, 1993-97; mng. ptnr. Borowiec & Borowiec, PC, Sierra Vista, Ariz., from 1997. Com. mem. Forgach House Charity Tennis Tournament, Sierra Vista. Mem. ABA, Ariz. Trial Lawyers Assn. Avocations: golf, tennis, hunting, fishing. Died Nov. 20, 2004.

BOROWY, FRANK RHINE, lawyer; b. Glen Ridge, N.J., Mar. 2, 1948; s. Frank Stanley and Alenna (Rhine) B.; m. Karen Judith Wallace, Sept. 27, 1975; children: Laura, William. BA, Gettysburg Coll., 1970; JD, U. Conn., 1973. Bar: Conn. 1973, U.S. Dist. Ct. Conn. 1974, U.S. Ct. Appeals (2d cir.) 1975, U.S. Ct. Appeals (fed. cir.), U.S. Supreme Ct. 1977. Ptnr. Nassau, Borowy & Spadaccini, Newington, Conn., from 1980. Asst. atty. Town of Newington, 1985-95. Author: (play) The Way to Philadelphia, 1987. Active Newington Town Coun., 1977-79, Newington Rep. Town Com., 1977—; vice-chmn. Town of Newington Standing Ins. Commn., 1977-79; chmn. Salvation Army Adv. Bd., New Britain, Conn., 1996-99. Mem. Conn. Bar Assn., Conn. Trial Lawyers Assn. Methodist. Home: Newington, Conn. Died Aug. 18, 2005.

BORST, PHILIP WEST, retired academic administrator; b. Fullerton, Calif., Feb. 11, 1928; s. Richard Warner and Beatrice Ione (West) B.; m. Marguerite A. Bruns, Mar. 21, 1959; children— David, Kristin, Pamela; m. Barbara Paul, Oct. 24, 1998. AA, Fullerton Coll., 1947; BA, Stanford U., 1949, MA, 1950; postgrad., U. Calif., 1950-54; PhD (Sch. fellow), Claremont Grad. Sch., 1968. Tchr. history Carlmont High Sch., Belmont, Calif., 1954-57; asst. prof. polit. sci. and history Fullerton Coll., 1957-60, asso. prof., 1960-62, prof., 1962-67, asst. to pres., 1967-70, asst. dean instrn., 1970-72, assoc. dean instrn., 1972-73, v.p. instrn., 1973-77, pres., 1977-94. Mem. Assn. Calif. Community Coll. Adminstrs., Phi Delta Kappa. Democrat. Home: Hemet, Calif. Died May 21, 2006.

BOSTON, WILLIAM CLAYTON, lawyer; b. Hobart, Okla., Nov. 29, 1934; s. William Clayton and Dollie Jane (Gibbs) B.; m. Billie Gail Long, Jan. 20, 1962; children: Kathryn Gray, William Clayton III. BS, Okla. State U., 1958; LLB, U. Okla., 1962; LLM, NYU, 1967. Bar: Okla. 1961. Assoc. Mosteller, Fellers, Andrews, Snider & Baggett, Oklahoma City, 1962-64; ptnr. Fellers, Snider, Baggett, Blankenship & Boston, Oklahoma City, 1968-69, Andrews, Davis, Legg, Bixler, Milsten & Murrah, Oklahoma City, 1972-86; pvt. practice Boston & Boston PLLC, Oklahoma City, 1986—2000. Contbr. articles to profl. jours.; mem. adv. bd. The Jour. of Air Law and Commerce, 1995-2000 Past pres. and trustee Ballet Okla.; past v.p., bd. dirs. Oklahoma City Arts Coun.; past trustee Nichols Hills (Okla.) Methodist Ch.; past trustee, chmn. Okla. Found. for the Humanities; past trustee, vice-chmn., sec. Humanities in Okla., Inc., 1992-95. With U.S. Army, 1954-56. Mem. ABA (former chmn. subcom. on aircraft fin., former chmn. aircraft fin. and contract divsn. forum on air and space law), FBA, Internat. Bar Assn., Inter-Pacific Bar Assn., Okla. State Bar Assn., Oklahoma County Bar Assn. Home: Oklahoma City, Okla. Died 2006.

BOTT, RAOUL, mathematician, educator; b. Budapest, Hungary, Sept. 24, 1923; s. Rudolf and Margit (Kovach) Bott; m. Phyllis Aikman, Aug. 30, 1947; children: Anthony, Jocelyn, Renee, Candace. B Engring., McGill U., Montreal, 1945, M Engring., 1946, DSc (hon.), 1987; DSc, Carnegie Inst. Tech., 1949; DSc (hon.), Notre Dame U., 1979, Carnegie-Mellon U., 1989, U. Leicester, England. Fellow Inst. Advanced Studies, Princeton U., 1949—51, 1955—57; instr. math. U. Mich., Ann Arbor, 1951—52, asst. prof., 1952—55, assoc. prof., 1957—59; prof. Harvard U., Cambridge, Mass., 1959—2005, W. Casper Graustein prof., 1969—99, W. Casper Graustein rsch. prof., 1999—2005. Author: (books and papers) in various branches of math. and its relationship to physics. Recipient Nat. Sci. medal, Pres. of U.S., 1987, Leroy P. Steele prize for Lifetime Achievement, Am. Mathematical Soc., 1990, Wolf prize in math., Wolf Found., Israel, 2000; fellow Sloan fellow, 1956—60, hon. fellow, St. Catharines Coll., 1985. Fellow: Am. Math. Soc. (Veblen prize 1964, Steele prize 1990), Am. Acad. Arts & Scis.; mem.: NAS, French Acad. Sci., London Math. Soc. (hon.). Democrat. Roman Catholic. Avocations: music, nature. Home: Cambridge, Mass. Died Dec. 20, 2005.

BOUCHILLON, CHARLES WESLEY, mechanical engineer; b. Louisville, Miss., July 17, 1931; s. Milton McCulley and Clara Lee (Dempsey) B.; m. Barbara Owens, Sept. 6, 1958; children: Leslie Lynn, Charles Ruston, Milton Scott, David Dink. BSME, Miss. State U., 1953; MSME, Ga. Inst. Tech., 1959, PhD, 1963. Registered profl. engr., Miss. Instr. Ga. Inst. Tech., Atlanta, 1958-62; rsch. asst. Ga. Inst. Tech. Rsch. Found., Atlanta, 1958-62; assoc. prof. mech. engring. Miss. State U., Starkville, 1962-65, prof. mech. engring., 1965-94, assoc. v.p. rsch., 1972-79; former v.p. R&D Fluid Quip, Inc., Springfield, Ohio. Prin. Bouchillon Assocs., Starkville, 1963—. Contbr. articles to profl. jours. 1st lt. U.S. Army, 1954-56. Mem. ASME, TAPPI, Miss. Soc. Mech. Engrs., Lions (pres. 1966). Republican. Methodist. Achievements include 4 patents on hydrocy clones. Died Sept. 13, 2004.

BOUIS, NANCY ELLEN, counselor; b. N.Y.C., Oct. 8, 1946; d. Albert James and Eleanor Harriet (Schoenhaus) Peterson; m. Paul Andre Bouis, June 17, 1967; children: Suzette, Karine, Matthew. AB, Hunter Coll., 1967; MS, U. Tenn., 1972. Cert. tchr., N.Y., N.J., Va., Tex., Tenn., Pa., Md.; cert. reading specialist, N.J., Pa., Tenn.; cert. guidance counselor, Tenn., Pa., Tex. Tchr. reading and elem. Rockbridge County Sch. Dist., Lexington, Va., 1967-68; tchr. reading Hartford County Sch. Dist., Street, Md., 1968-69; tchr. secondary reading and study skills Knoxville (Tenn.) Boro Sch. Dist., 1971-73; remedial reading tchr. Freehold (N.J.) Boro Sch. Dist., 1973-74; tchr. art, Spanish, reading and home econs. Columbia-Brazoria Ind. Sch. Dist., West Columbia, Tex., 1976-86; secondary guidance counselor Colonial Northampton Ind. Unit 20, Nazareth, Pa., 1986-87; jr. high sch. guidance counselor Bangor (Pa.) Area Sch. Dist., 1987-89; dropout prevention counselor Bethlehem (Pa.) Area Sch. Dist., from 1989. Mem. NEA, Pa. Sch.

Counselors Assn., Pa. Counselors Assn., Pa. State Edn. Assn. Roman Catholic. Avocations: tennis, skiing. Home: Bethlehem, Pa. Died Nov. 24, 2004.

BOUMAN, WALTER RICHARD, theology educator; b. Springfield, Minn., July 9, 1929; s. Walter Herman and Cordelia Ilene (Haar) B.; m. Janet Ann Gunderman, Aug. 17, 1957; children: Andrew Arthur, Lukas Lawrence, Gregory Martin. AA, Concordia Jr. Coll., 1948; BA, Concordia Sem., 1951, MDiv, 1954; DTh, Rupert-Carl U., Heidelberg, Fed. Republic of Germany, 1963; DD (hon.), Gen. Theol. Seminary, N.Y.C., 1993. Assoc. prof. Concordia Coll., River Forest, Ill., 1963-71; vis. prof. Evang. Luth. Theol. Sem., Columbus, Ohio, 1971-74, joint prof., 1974-78, Hamma Div. Sch., Springfield, Ohio, 1974-78; prof. systematic theology Trinity Luth. Sem., Columbus, 1978-84, Edward C. Fredt prof. systematic theology, from 1984. Pres. Luth. Acad. for Scholarship, 1975-77; mem. Luth.-Episcopalian Dialogue III, 1983-91; Anglican-Luth. Internat. Commn., 1985—. Author: Christianity American Style, 1970, (with others) Encyclopedia of the Lutheran Church, 1965, The Teaching of Religion, 1965, The New Church Debate, 1983. Pres. Columbus Symphony Youth Orch. Bd., 1980-82; bd. dirs. Jefferson Acad. of Music, Columbus, 1980-83, Columbus Symphony Orch. Bd. Trustees, 1981-83, Luth. Social Svcs., Columbus, 1982-85. Fulbright scholar, 1954-56; Danforth Found. fellow, 1965-71; Luth. Brotherhood Ins. grante, 1979-80, 86-87. Mem. Am. Acad. Religion, Coun. for Ethics and Econs. (bd. dirs. Columbus chpt. 1981-83). Democrat. Avocations: classical music, golf. Home: Columbus, Ohio. Died Aug. 17, 2005.

BOWDITCH, HOEL LAWRENCE, design company executive, consultant; b. Boston, Mar. 4, 1915; s. Henry Ingersoll and Eleanor (Macqueen) B.; m. Mary Hinchman, Oct. 20, 1939; children: Henry I., Wendy L., John L., Peter N. Student, Haverford Coll., 1934-36; grad., Moses Brown Sch., 1934. Registered profl. engr. Restorer Mus. of Fine Arts, Boston, 1936-37; apprentice Mico Instrument Co., Cambridge, Mass., 1937-38; model maker Boston Pattern Works, 1938-39; engr. Foxboro (Mass.) Instrument Co., 1939-59, chief design engr., 1959-79, ret., 1979; pres. Bowditch Creative Design, Foxboro, from 1979. Inventor, holder of 68 industrial instruments patents. Trustee Wonder Mus., 1989-93; chmn. bldg. com. St. Marks Ch., Foxboro, 1960-62, sr. warden, 1964-66; scout master Troop 18 Boy Scouts of Am., 1940, cub master Pack 70, 1962. Recipient 1st Bristol fellow Foxboro Co., 1979. Episcopalian. Avocations: singing, sailing, model making. Home: Foxboro, Mass. Died Apr. 14, 2004.

BOWERS, DOROTHEA ELLEN, retired county auditor; b. Havelock, Iowa, Dec. 15, 1925; d. Elvin Theodore and Lottie Ellen (Muller) Lindstrom; m. Harley Louis Bowers, Apr. 21, 1946 (div. 1978); children: Janice Lee, Bruce Michael, Pamela Ann. Student, Am. Inst. Bus., 1943. Asst. supr. 11th Naval Dist. Disbursing Office, San Diego, 1943-49; payroll, pers. clerk Mefferd Industries, Inc., Laurens, Iowa, 1962-72; acct. clerk Jolliffe's Acct. & Tax, Inc., Laurens, 1972-75; county auditor Pocahontas County, Iowa, 1975-92; ret. Pocahontas Coutny, Iowa, 1992. Pres. Iowa State Drianage Assn, 1980—, Dist. III County Auditors, Iowa, 1978, Dist. III County Offls., Iowa, 1980, Iowa State Assn. County Auditors, 1985. Active Pocahontas County Reps., 1975—, Rep. Party of Iowa; vol. bookkeeper Pocahontas Congregate Meals, Inc., 1990—. Mem. VFW 3533 Aux. Republican. Methodist. Avocations: cross-stitch, ceramics, weaving rag rugs, misc. crafts and sewing. Home: Pocahontas, Iowa. Died June 21, 2004.

BOWES, JOHN, entrepreneur, former toy and outdoor products company executive; b. San Francisco; m. Frances Bowes. Founder, pres. Kransco (sold to Mattel, 1994); owner Yakima Products Inc. (sold to Watermark), Arcata, Calif., 1994—2001, Camelbak outdoor products (sold to Bear Stearns Merchant Banking), 1995—2003. Named one of Top 200 Collectors, ARTnews Mag., 2004. Avocation: Collecting modern and contemporary art. Home: San Francisco, Calif. Died Oct. 26, 2005.

BOWLER, DAVID LIVINGSTONE, electrical engineering educator; b. NYC, June 7, 1926; s. Henry R. and Helen G. (McCron) B.; m. Marjorie H. Cressey, June 5, 1955; children: Bruce C., Margaret W. BS in Elec. Engring., Bucknell U., 1948; MS in Elec. Engring., MIT, 1951; MA, Princeton U., 1958, PhD, 1964. Instr. Bucknell U., Lewisburg, Pa., 1948-49, asst. prof., 1953-55; engr., tech. writer Hazeltine Corp., Little Neck, N.Y., 1951-53; from asst. prof. to assoc. prof. Swarthmore Coll., Pa., 1957-73, prof. elec. engring. Pa., 1973—89. Vis. fellow Bartol Research Found., Swarthmore, 1959-64, Queen's U., Belfast, No. Ireland, 1966-67, U. Fla., Gainesville, 1971, U. Pa., Phila., 1979-80; Fulbright lectr. Univ. Coll., Galway, Ireland, 1984 Co-editor: book series Alternate Energy, 1978—. Mem. Swarthmore Borough Council, 1988—. With USN, 1944-46. IBM fellow, 1956-57 Mem. IEEE, Sigma Xi (pres. chpt. 1981-83), Tau Beta Pi. Democrat. Presbyterian. Died Dec. 22, 2005.

BOWMAN, MARIAN LOUISE, auditor; b. Louisville, Apr. 20, 1921; d. Arthur George and Sadie Louise (Frost) Bodemann; m. Francis Mason Miles, Nov. 27, 1942 (dec. Mar. 1986); 1 child, Joseph Arthur; m. John Russell Bowman, July 3, 1947 (dec. Nov. 1979); 1 child Tracy Leigh. A in Acctg., Clark Coll., 1939-41. Bookkeeper Cissell Mfg. Co., Louisville, 1941-54; office mgr. Apex Wrecking Co., Louisville, 1964-66; bus. mgr. The Lincoln Sch., Simpsonville, Ky., 1966-69; adminstrv. asst. Dept. of Fin./State Govt., Frankfort, Ky., 1970-71; controller Whitney Young Job Corps Ctr., Simpsonville, 1971-80; asst. corp. controller Res-Care, Inc., Louisville, 1980-84, corp. controller, 1984-86; corp. auditor Res-Care Devel. Co., Inc., Louisville, from 1986. Recipient City of Louisville Effort medal, The Louisville Times, 1936; Louisville Collegiate scholar, 1936. Mem. Exec. Women's Internat., Leukemia Soc. (trustee Louisville chpt.), Am. Legion Aux. Lodges: Order Eastern Star. Avocations: reading, crafts, hiking, sewing. Home: Louisville, Ky. Died May 14, 2005.

BOYER, ESTHER EILEEN, school nurse; b. Parsons, Kans., Aug. 7, 1952; d. Gerald Richard and Edith Irene (Raetz) Ellis; m. Roger Boyer, Sept. 5, 1970; children: Angie Lee, Crystal LeeAnn. ADN, Labette Community Coll., Parsons, Kans., 1977; student, Independence Community Coll., Kans., 1975, 88, Coffeyville Community Coll., 1987-88; BSN, Pittsburg (Kans.) State U., 1990. Staff nurse med./surg. Coffeyville Reg. Med. Ctr., 1977-85; office nurse Coffeyville Family Practice Clinic, 1985-87; sch. nurse USD 447, Cherryvale, Kans., from 1987. Lectr. in field. Contbr. articles to profl. jours. Unit mem. Salvation Army, 1988—; mem. Parents as Tchrs. adv. com. Home: Afton, Okla. Died June 25, 2004.

BOYLAN, BERNARD ROBERT, electrical engineer, author; b. Allegan, Mich., July 11, 1927; s. Peter Bernard and Viva (Kitson) B.; m. Phyllis J. Scribano, Nov. 23, 1950; children: Gary, Bonita. BS in Engring, U.S. Naval Acad., 1950. Registered profl. engr., Ill. Dist. engr. GE, N.Y.C., 1954-57, Indpls., 1957-62, regional engr. Chgo., 1962-89, lighting cons., from 1989. Instr. Coll. of DuPage, Glen Ellyn, Ill., 1979-85, U. Notre Dame (Ind.), 1982—. Author: The Lighting Primer, 1987. Past pres. United Fund, Glen Ellyn; area v.p. Met Crusade of Mercy, Chgo., 1972. Lt. USNR, 1950-54. Mem. Illuminating Engring. Soc. (regional v.p. 1976-79, Disting. Svc. award 1985), DuPage Fitness Club. Republican. Roman Catholic. Avocations: racquetball, fishing, golf, genealogy. Home: Glen Ellyn, Ill. Died June 2, 2004.

BOYLAN, BRIAN RICHARD, author, historian, director, photographer, literary agent; b. Chgo., Dec. 11, 1936; s. Francis Thomas and Mary Catherine (Kane) B.; children: Rebecca, Gregory, Ingrid. Student, Loyola U., 1954-58; DD, Universal Ch., 1969. CEO Otitis Media Lit. Agy.; prodr. OTM Prodns.; dir., prodr. Media Medica. Editor: Jour. AMA, Med. World News, Modern Medicine, 1956-77; author: The New Heart, 1969, Infidelity, 1971, The Legal Rights of Women, 1973, Benedict Arnold: The Dark Eagle, 1973, From An Art to a Science, 1975, A Hack in a Hurry, 1980, Final Trace, 1983; works include 16 books, 3 plays, 3 screenplays; book reviewer, critic, 19525; photographer, 19625; theatre dir., 19705; directed works include 31 plays, videotapes and films. Died Oct. 17, 2005.

BOYLAN, WILLIAM JOHN, animal sciences educator; b. Bozeman, Mont., Dec. 25, 1929; s. George L. and Margaret B. (Watson) B.; m. Teresa A. McGee, June 28, 1958; children: Christopher J., John M., Mary Kate, Todd W. Student, U.Calif., Davis, 1954, 57; BS, Mont. State U., 1952; MS, U. Minn., St. Paul, 1959, PhD, 1962. Assoc. prof. quantitative genetics and animal breeding animal sci. dept. U. Man., Winnipeg, Can., 1962-66; prof. quantitative genetics and animal breeding animal sci. dept. U. Minn., from 1966. Researcher Animal Breeding Rsch. Orgn., Edinburgh, Scotland, 1972-73. With U.S. Army, 1955-57, Republic of Korea. NSF rsch. fellow Brown U., Providence, summer 1966; Fulbright (Found.) rsch. scholar U. Alexandria, Arab Republic of Egypt, 1982, Cukurova U., Adana, Turkey, 1988. Mem. Am. Soc. Animal Sci., Am. Genetic Assn. Home: Lake Elmo, Minn. Died Feb. 16, 2004.

BOYNTON, DONALD ARTHUR, title insurance company executive; b. Culver City, Calif., Sept. 6, 1940; s. A.A. and Margaret Lena (Slocum) B.; m. Jean Carolyn Ferrulli, Nov. 10, 1962; children: Donna Jean, Michael Arthur; m. Sharon C. Burns, Nov. 18, 1984; children: Cynthia, David, Sharie. Student, El Camino Jr. Coll., 1960-62, Antelope Valley Jr. Coll., 1963-64, Orange Coast Coll., 1969-72; BA, Bradford U., 1977. With Title Ins. & Trust Co., 1958-63, sales mgr. Santa Ana, Calif., 1980-81; dep. sheriff County of Los Angeles, 1963-65; with Transamerica Title Ins. Co., L.A., 1965-69, state coord., 1981-82; sr. title officer Calif. Land Title Co., L.A. and Orange Counties, 1969-72; asst. sec., systems analyst Lawyers Title Ins. Corp., 39 states, 1972-77; county mgr. Am. Title Co., Santa Ana, Calif., 1977-79; v.p., mgr. Orange County ops. Chgo. Title Ins. Co., Tustin, Calif., 1979-80; pres. Stewart Title Co. of Fresno County, 1985-86; supr. builder svcs. Orange Coast Title Co., Santa Ana, San Diego, 1986-89; sr. title officer TSG dept. Orange Coast/Record Title, Whittier and La Mirada, Calif., 1990-94; sr. title officer, So. Calif. TSG Manager (5 County) State of Calif. for Orange Coast Title, 1993; sr. nat. coord. Chgo. Title and Ins., Irvine, Calif., 1993-96; title officer, claims officer N.Am. Title Ins., Orange, Calif., 1996-97; nat. underwriter/coord. 50 states and Canada LandAmerica/Lawyers Title Ins. Corp., L.A., 1997-98, LandAmerica/Elliptus Techs., Inc., Richmond, Va., from 1998. Mem. Calif. Trustees Assn., Orange County Escrow Assn., Optimists (sec.-treas.), Elks (life, chaplain), Rotary. Home: Richmond, Va. Died Oct. 24, 2004.

BOYNTON, HARRY GENE, chemical engineer; b. Hamilton, Tex., Oct. 19, 1928; s. George Harry and Lucile (Roddy) B.; m. Johnella Sparks, Feb. 16, 1952; children: Amy Denise, Brook David, Kim Elaine. BS, Tex. A&M U., 1949. Rsch. engr. Humble Oil & Refining Co., Baytown, Tex., 1949-58; mkt. devel. engr. Enjay Chem. Co., Elizabeth, N.J., 1958-60; rsch. specialist, assoc. Esso Rsch.& Engring. Co., Baytown, Tex., 1960-68, sr. rsch. assoc., 1968-72, Exxon Chem. Co., Baytown, 1972-74, Baton Rouge, La., 1974-81; sr. engring assoc. Exxon Chem. Ams., Baton Rouge, La., 1981-82; pvt. practice plastics engr. cons. Baton Rouge, 1982-83, Atlanta, from 1983. Sr. tech. advisor Edison Plastics Divsn. of Blessings Corp., Newport News, Va., 1983-94. Ten U.S. patents in chemical engring. field, 1954-62. Mem. Soc. Plastics Engrs. Democrat. Presbyterian. Home: Georgetown, Tex. Died Nov. 20, 2004.

BOYSON, WILLIAM ALBERT, retired obstetrician, gynecologist; b. Gettysburg, Pa., 1920; BA, Gettysburg Coll., 1941; MD, U. Pa., 1950; MS in Ob-Gyn., Baylor U., 1957. Diplomate Am. Bd. Ob-Gyn. Intern Walter Reed Gen. Hosp., Washington, 1950-51; resident obs. Herman Kiefer Hosp., Detroit, 1951; resident gynecology Detroit Receiving Hosp., 1952; resident in ob-gyn. Brooke Gen. Hosp., Ft. Sam Houston, Tex., 1954-57; gynecologist Brooke Army Med. Ctr., San Antonio, 1983-90. Fellow Am. Coll. Surgeons; mem. Am. Coll. Ob-Gyn. Home: San Antonio, Tex. Died Dec. 11, 2005.

BOZMAN, BENNETT, state legislator; b. Norfolk, Va., May 8, 1936; married; 2 children. BS, U. Md., 1961. Pharmacist; del. Dist. 38 Md. State Delegation, 1991—2006, dep. majority whip, 1995—2006, mem. const. and adminstrv. law com., 1991-92, mem. econ. matters com., 1992-93, mem. comm. and govt. matters com., 1994—2006, mem. ways and means com., 1997. Chmn. edn. sub com. Md. State Del., from 2001. Mem. Dem. State Ctrl. Com., Worcester County, 1974-78, Bd. County Commrs., 1978-90, Md. Tourism Devel. Bd., 1994-2006. Mem. Md. Assn. Counties (pres. 1990), Md. Pharm. Assn., Ea. Shore Pharm. Assn., Worcester County Farm Bur., Ocean City VFW, Ocean City Marlin Club, Elks. Died Apr. 27, 2006.

BRACHMAN, MALCOLM KATZENSTEIN, oil company executive; b. Ft. Worth, Dec. 9, 1926; s. Solomon and Etta (Katzenstein) B.; m. Minda Fay Delugach, Sept. 4, 1951 (dec. 2003); children: Lynn, Malcolm K. Jr., Lisa. BA, Yale U., 1945; MA, Harvard U., 1947, PhD, 1949. CLU. Asst. prof. So. Meth. U., Dallas, 1949-50; assoc. physicist Argonne Nat. Lab., Chgo., 1950-53; rsch. staff Tex. Instruments, Inc., Dallas, 1953-54; v.p. Pioneer Am. Ins. Co., Ft. Worth, 1954-61, pres., 1961-73, chmn. bd., CEO, 1973-79; pres. N.W. Oil Co., Dallas, 1956—2005. Chmn. adv. coun. Econ. Growth Ctr. Yale U. Capt. USAF, 1950—57. Recipient Yale Presdl. medal, 1999, Hon. Alumnus award, Tex. Christian U., 1999, Yale medal, Assn. Yale Alumni, 2002. Fellow Am. Phys. Soc., Soc. Petroleum Engrs., Am. Math. Soc.; sr. mem. IEEE, Soc. Exploration Geophysics; mem. Dallas Petroleum Club, Century Assn. (N.Y.C.). Jewish. Avocation: bridge. Home: Dallas, Tex. Died Jan. 11, 2005.

BRACKEN, WILLIAM EARL, JR., lawyer; b. Phila., Jan. 25, 1934; s. William Earl and Etholen Alabell (Terry) B.; m. Sarah Lou Graves, May 31, 1958; children: Elizabeth Louise, Terry Suzanne, Sarah Lynn. BBA, Baylor U., 1956, JD, 1958. Bar: Tex. 1958, U.S. Dist. Ct. (we. dist.), U.S. Ct. Appeals (5th cir.), U.S. Ct. Mil. Appeals, U.S. Supreme Ct. Assoc. Bryan-Maxwell, Waco, Tex., 1961-63; 1st asst. city atty. City of Waco, 1963-67, city atty., 1967-96; pvt. practice Waco, from 1996. Trustee Group Benefits Risk Pool Tex. Mcpl. League, Austin, 1979-81, chmn., 1979—; mem. adv. bd. S.W. Legal Found. Mcpl. Legal Ctr., Richardson, Tex., 1994—; bd. dirs. Evangelia Settlement, Waco; pres. Lake Air Meml. Little League, Waco, 1963-67, The Friends of Waco High Sch., 2000; mem. Tejas Coun. Campfire Bd., 1997; active Bd. Ctrl. Tex. Sr. Ministry, 1997—, chmn., 2000-2001. Lt. USAF, 1958-61, lt. col. USA FR, 1961-84. Recipient Disting. Svc. award Waco Jaycees. Fellow Tex. Bar Found.; mem. Tex. City Atty. Assn. (hon. life, pres. 1969-71), McLennan County Bar Assn., Baylor Law Sch. Alumni Assn. (bd. dirs.). Baptist. Avocations: family, travel, texas rangers baseball, baylor university sports. Home: Waco, Tex. Died Feb. 25, 2004.

BRADEN, ANNE MCCARTY, writer, editor, political organization worker; b. Louisville, July 28, 1924; d. Gambrell N. and Anita (Crabbe) McC.; m. Carl James Braden (dec.), June 21, 1948; children: James, Anita (dec.), Elizabeth. BA, Randolph-Macon Women's Coll., Lynchburg, Va., 1945; DHL (hon.), Trinity Coll., Conn., 1994. Reporter The Anniston (Ala.) Star, 1945-46, Birmingham (Ala.) News & Age-Herald, 1946-47, The Louisville Times, 1947-48; editor publs. consortium of labor unions, Louisville, 1948-51; assorted jobs with various employers Louisville, 1951-57; regional organizer So. Conf. Ednl. Fund, Louisville, New Orleans, 1957-74; regional organizer, editor publs. So. Organizing Com. for Econ. and Social Justice, Birmingham, from 1974. Author: The Wall Between, 1958 (nat. book award runner-up 1958), Southern Freedom Movement, 1965; editor (civil rights newspaper) The Southern Patriot, 1957-74; contbr. numerous articles on civil rights to profl. publs.; creator pamphlets for various social justice groups and religious orgns. Nat. vice chmn. Nat. Com. vs. Repressive Legis. (formerly Nat. Com. to Abolish HUAC), L.A.; bd. dirs. Ctr. for Dem. Renewal (formerly anti-Klan network), Atlanta, Nat. Rainbow Coalition; mem. Racial Justice Working Group, Nat. Coun. Chs. Recipient Mary Rhodes award Sisters of Loretto, Ky., 1982, Ralph Abernathy Community Svc. award SCLC, 1987, Peace and

Justice award Cath. Archdiocese of Louisville, 1989, Roger Baldwin medal of Liberty ACLU, 1990. Democrat. Episcopalian. Home: Louisville, Ky. Died Mar. 6, 2006.

BRADLEY, CLYDE WILLIAM, JR., retail executive; b. Asheville, N.C., Apr. 8, 1920; s. Clyde W. and Annie Boone (Harmon) B.; m. Elizabeth Dial, Dec. 25, 1975; children: Clyde W. III, Brian A., Brenda J. Student, U. Md., 1965. Commd. 2nd lt. USAF, 1942, advanced through grades to col., 1966, ret., 1968; EEO officer Air U., Maxwell AFB, Ala., 1968-80; dir. AF Design Ctr., Montgomery, Ala., 1980-83; sr. tng. officer Civil Air Patrol, Montgomery, 1983-86; prin. Bradley Assocs., Montgomery, from 1986. Author: Leadership, 1965; patentee. Decorated Legion of Merit, Disting. Flying Cross, Air medal, Commendation medal. Mem. Ret. Officers Assn. (pres. 1988—), Am. Ex-POW Assn. (nat. dir. 1986-88, dept. comdr. 1984), Exchange Club (v.p. 1975), Kiwanis, Maxwell AFB (pres.). Democrat. Avocations: golf, outdoor activities, horseback riding. Died May 28, 2004.

BRADLEY, EDWARD WILLIAM, sports foundation executive; b. Milltown, NJ, Aug. 12, 1927; s. William Ernest and Hilda (Schwendeman) B.; m. Eleanor A Massing, Apr. 12, 1952; children: Scott Richard, Gail Sharon Bradley Klewsaat, Lisa June Bradley LaMarca. BE, Panzer Coll., 1950. Dir. athletics, supr. phys. edn. and health Milltown Pub. Schs., 1951—69; owner, pres. The Exec. Health Club, East Brunswick, NJ, 1965—84; chmn., CEO N.J. Fitness and Sports Found., Milltown, 1984—2006; writer Middlesex County Govt., North Brunswick, NJ, 1985—2006; founder Bradley, Walker, Chitwood Group Alliance, 2005. Dir. activities Playboy Club Resort Hotel at Great Gorge, 1972; founder, First Sch. Bicycle Safety Edn. Program Curriculum, State of NJ, 1996; apptd. exec. coun. Cancer Rsch. Inst. Am. Cancer Soc., 1998; served Nat. Coalition Com. Prostrate Cancer, Washington, 2002-06; cons. World WIOC, 2000. Cons. Pres. Kennedy, Johnson, Carter, Nixon, Ford, Reagan, Bush; master cons., adv. Pres.'s Coun. The White House, 1988; meeting with Pres. Clinton (invitation by The White House) nat. project Stay Way, 1994; nat. dir. U.S. Army and NFL, 1993; Chief of Staff Colin Powell meeting at the White House; nat. dir. No-Shows for Charity Shows, 1996; founder Bradley Walker Chitwood Group Internat. Alliance, 2005; dist. coord., cons. Nat. Assn. Disabled Athletes; supt. recreation Borough of Milltown, 1951—64, founder sch. bicycle safety edn. prog. curriculum NJ, 1996; N.J. chmn. Nat. Network on Volunteerism, 1997; regional coord. Winter Olympic Games 2002, Salt Lake City; partnership with Arnold Schwarzenegger's Inner City Games and Mayor Oscar Goodman's Needy Youth Program, Las Vegas, 2003; VIP del. Pres.' Summit, Washington, 1997; apptd. by Gov. Kean chmn. CEO Gov.'s Coun. on Phys. Fitness and Sports, from 1983; mem. Nat. Com. for George W. Bush Pres., 2000; nat. dir., founder sch. Stay Way project Gen. Jones (Pentagon); bd. dirs. Make A Wish Found., NC, 2003; state dir. for fight against abolishing phys. edn. in NJ schs.; chmn., CEO Middlesex County Coun. on Phys. Fitness and Sports divsn. Pres.' Coun. on Phys. Fitness, 1992, NJ Youth Fitness Coalition; mem. NC Prostate Cancer Coalition, 2002; chmn. NJ Olympic XXIII Torch Relay Com., 1984; asst. torch relay U.S. Olympics XXVI, NJ and Atlanta, 1996; state coord. Olympic Torch Relay, Athens, 2004; founder, chmn. Gov.'s Blue Ribbon Panel on Fitness and Sports, David A. Sonny Werblin, pres.; pres. NJ Health Am. Fitness Leaders Award Program; mem. State of NJ Blue Ribbon Com. for Baseball in NJ; dir. Phys. Fitness and Sports for U.S. Job Corps., Edison; state-county coord. Nat. Pk. Svc., NJ Trails Relay, 1996; mem. Mission Possible task NEA-AAPERD; vice chmn., mem. exec. bd. Fairview Food and Clothing Kitchen for Needy Families, 2003; bd. dirs., dir. pub. rels. Safe Haven Shelter for Men, from 2005. Recipient U.S. Outstanding Phys. Leadership award Pres.' Coun. on Phys. Fitness and Sports by Pres. Kennedy and U.S. Jaycees, The White House, 1962, U.S. Healthy Am. Fitness Leaders award Pres.' Coun., U.S. Jaycees and Allstate, 1985, Svc. in Phys. Fitness and Sports award Montclair State Coll., 1988, Phys. Edn. award for Excellence Panzer Coll., Svc. Award Ea. Dist. AAHPERD, NJ Award for People to Watch, 1984, Jerseyan of Week award Newark Star Ledger, 1988, Honor Fellow award NJ Assn. Health, Phys. Edn. and Recreation, 1964, Young Man of Yr. award Milltown Jaycees, 1962, Sports Master award by Pres. Reagan, 1987, Svc. to the Cmty., State and Nation Award, Pres. Bush, 1992, Pres. Clinton, 1997, Pub. Svc. award State NJ and Pres.' Summit, 1997, Daily Point of Light award The White House and Point of Light Found., 1999, Pres.'s Svc. award, The White House, 2000, Outstanding Alumni award Montclair State Coll., 2000, Outstanding Gov.'s award Vol. Svc., Trenton, NJ, 2000, Outstanding Gov.'s award Vol. Svc., Raleigh, NC, 2000; honored guest Pres. Nixon, 1975, Pres. Reagan, 1987, Richard Nixon Libr., 1990-2006, Pres. Reagan Libr., Pres. Bush-the White House, 1991, 92, State of NJ, Pres.' Hist. Summit for 55 Yrs. Pub. Svc., Pres. Clinton, The White House, 1947-2000, Govs. NJ Leadership award Gov. Whitman, 2000, Gov. Vol. award NC Gov. Hunt, 2000, Outstanding Alumni award Montclair State U., 2000, Pres.' Svc. award, Pres. Bush, 2001, Martin Luther King Jr. award for Outstanding Cmty. Svc., 2002; named Leader of NJ State of NJ, 1998; nominated Olympic Torch Relay, Athens, Greece, 2004. Mem.: Internat. Assn. Approved Basketball Ofcls., Nat. Fitness Leadership Assn., Outstanding Phys. Fitness Leadership Congress, NJ/NC Youth Fitness Coalition Pres.' Club (corr. Honored Lifetime citation 2001), Amblers Walking Club, Court Club, Am. Legion, U.S. Jayvees, VFW (NC, NJ). Avocations: bicycling, reading, sports, Volksmarch programs. Died Apr. 24, 2006.

BRADLEY, JAMES HENRY STOBART, meteorologist, consultant; b. London, Mar. 26, 1933; s. John Henry S. and Marjorie Florence Bradley; m. Estella Pauline Bennett, Dec. 27, 1966. BA, Oxford (Eng.) U., 1954, MA, 1997, U. Toronto, 1960; PhD, U. Mich., 1967. Geologist Geol. Survey Can., Ottawa, 1957-59; meteorologist Can. Dept. Transp., Toronto, 1959-63; rsch. asst. U. Mich., Ann Arbor, 1963-67; asst. prof. Pa. State U., University Park, 1968; cons. Govt. of Can., Montreal, 1969-70; rsch. assoc. McGill U., Montreal, 1968-70; asst. prof. Drexel U., Phila., 1970-76; sr. mem. tech. staff Elec. Assocs. Inc., Long Branch, N.J., 1977-83; cons. in pvt. practice N.J., Pa., from 1983. Seconded prof. U. Toronto, 1962-63. Minority inspector Dem. Party, Rose Valley, Pa., 1996—; head of Town Watch, Rose Valley, 1999—. U.S. Nat. Environ. Satellite Svc. grantee, 1968-70, NSF grantee, 1974-76. Mem. Soc. for Computer Simulation (sr.; assoc. editor 1980—, bd. dirs. 1986-94). Democrat. Achievements include work as Canadian member of international working group on solid precipitation and snow on the ground 1961-63. Died Dec. 20, 2004.

BRAME, ARDEN HOWELL, II, herpetologist, genealogist; b. Los Angeles, Mar. 19, 1934; s. Arden Howe and Marguerite Lucile (Adams) B.; m. Susan Diane Bronn, Aug. 23, 1964 (div. June 1969); m. Patricia Louise Verret Reinholtz, Apr. 19, 1970. BA, U. So. Calif., 1957, MS, 1967; student, UCLA, 1956-57. Grad. teaching asst. U. So. Calif., Los Angeles, 1959-65; also student profl. worker in ichthyology-herpetology and vertebrate paleontology Los Angeles County Mus., 1959-65, later research asst. in herpetology; supr. Eaton Canyon Nature Ctr., 1965-68, 70-78; asst. curator sect. herpetology Los Angeles County Mus. of Natural History, 1968-70; instr. genealogy Pasadena (Calif.) City Coll. and Calif. State U., Northridge, from 1977. Mem. citizen nongame adv. com. Calif. Dept. Fish and Game, 1975-79; herpetol. group advisor Survival Service Commn., Internat. Union for Conservation Nature and Natural Resources, Morges, Switzerland, 1974-82. Author: (with Dr. D.B. Wake) The Salamanders of South America, 1963; Systematics and Evolution of the Mesoamerican Salamander Genus Oedipina, 1968; contbr. articles to scholarly and profl. jours.; assoc. pub. TV Facts of Pasadena and Altadena, 1978-79. Served with AUS, 1958. Fellow Herpetologists' League, Augustan Soc. (registered genealogist, pres. 1980-81); mem. Soc. Study Amphibians and Reptiles (bd. dirs. 1967-70, chmn. 1973), Southwestern Herpetologists Soc. (pres. 1971-74), Am. Soc. Ichthyologists and Herpetologists, Brit. Herpetol. Soc., Phila. Herpetol. Soc., N.Y. Herpetol. Soc., Ariz. Herpetol. Soc., N.Mex. Herpetol. Soc., Conn. Herpetol. Soc., Chgo. Herpetol. Soc., Soc. Study of Evolution, Soc. Systematic Zoologists, Ecol. Soc. Am., Western Soc. Naturalists, Biol. Soc. Wash., So. Calif. Acad. Scis., Soc. Tropical Biologists, Pasadena Audubon Soc. (pres. 1971-76), SAR (pres. Pasadena chpt. 1977-83, genealogist Calif. Soc.), S.R., SCV (camp comdr. 1979-83), Gen. Soc. War of 1812, Descendants of the Illegitimate Sons and Daus. of the Kings of Britain, Plantagenet Soc., Sovereign Colonial Soc. Ams. Royal Descent, Soc. Descendanta Knights of the Garter, Colonial Order of Crown, Magna Charta Barons, Order of Washington, Sons of Union Vets. of Civil War, Mil. Order Loyal Legion of U.S., Mil. Order of Stars and Bars (comdr. Calif. chpt.), Dames of Guild of St. Margaret of Scotland (protector), Order of Augustan Eagle, Descents From Antiquity, Order of Armigerous Augustans, Hospitaller Order of St. John of Jerusalem (companion of honor), Noble Co. of Rose, Jamestowne Soc., St. John's Vol. Corps, Sigma Xi, Phi Sigma. Home: Rosemead, Calif. Died Aug. 19, 2004.

BRANDEL, RALPH EDWARD, management consultant; b. Cleve., Sept. 15, 1922; s. Wallace Lester Andrew and Marion (Coulton) B.; m. Dorothy Lucille Alspach, Jul. 14, 1945. BS, U. Md., 1954; MS, Rensselaer Poly. Inst., 1960; postgrad., Am. U., Washington, 1970—72. With USMC, 1942—69, commd. 2d lt., 1944, advanced through grades to col., 1968, inf. officer, 1944, arty. officer, 1945, photointerpretation intelligence officer, 1945, engr. officer, 1949—67; 1S-4 logistics, S-3 ops., 1st Engr. Bn., 1st Marine Divsn. Fleet Marine Force Pacific, 1954—56; asst. prof. naval sci. Rensselaer Poly. Inst., Troy, NY, 1957—60; cmdg. officer 2d MarDiv engrs. Cuban Crisis, 1962—63; tng. plans officer for 4 Korean Armed Forces, 1963—64; Def. Depot Ogden dir. installation svcs., 1964—67; head officer plans HQMC Washington, 1968—69; ret. USMC Hdqrs., Washington, 1969; v.p., sec., treas. Va. Pharms. Co., Inc., Fairfax, 1974—84; cons., 1984—2004. Decorated Joint Svcs. Commendation medal, Navy Commendation medal, Army Commendation medal; recipient Wisdom award of Honor Wisdom Soc.; named Eminent Wisdom fellow Wisdom Hall of Fame, 1998. Mem. VFW (life), Am. Legion (life), Nat. Assn. Atomic Vets. (life), Mil. Officers Assn. of Am. (life), Marine Corps Engr. Assn., Order Internat. Fellowship (life), Toastmasters. Episcopalian. Avocations: furniture restoration, relacquering and gilding antiques, asian art, stamp collecting/philately, photography. Died June 4, 2005.

BRANDES, DORIS, artist, art administrator, journalist; b. N.Y.C., Nov. 20, 1923; d. Robert Ralph Pratt and Grace Isabella Mott; m. Walter A. Spiro, July 24, 1948 (div. May 1971); children: Karen L., Pamela A. Gowers, Paul D., Amy E.; m. Gordon A. Brandes, June 13, 1971 (div. Aug. 1986); m. Tor Bjorn Polfelt, Sept. 11, 1993 (dec. Mar. 30, 2001). BFA, Pratt Inst., Bklyn., 1941; postgrad., Art Students League, 1942-43. Owner, ptnr. Witch Craft, N.Y.C., 1945-48; dir., tchr. Hidden House Creative Workshop, Jenkintown, Pa., 1964-69; printmaker, tchr. Abington Art Ctr., Jenkintown, 1971-79; dir. Cheltenham (Pa.) Art Ctr., 1979-81; founder, pub., editor Art Matters, Phila., 1981-93, dir. projects, 1981-93; founding bd. mem. Michener Art Mus., Doylestown, Pa., 1988—2004. Founding dir. Artsbridge, New Hope, Pa., Lambertville, N.J., 1993-2005; art columnist New Hope Gazette, 1994-2005, Lambertville Beacon, Hunterdon County, N.J., 1996-99; video script and prodn. Art of the River Towns, New Hope, 1996. Author: Artists of the River Towns, 2002; columnist: Artbuzz for Prime Time mag., feature writer: Bucks County Herald. Chairperson Alverthorpe Park Bd., Abington, 1964—65; founding mem. Ptnrs. in Progress, New Hope, 1996—98; adv. bd. Hepatitis B Found., Doylestown, Pa., 1994—99; advisor Artist in Residence, New Hope, 1998; bd. dirs. New Hope Hist. Soc. Recipient R. Tate McKenzie medal for svc. Phila. Sketch Club, 1985, Mayor's Citation City of Phila., 1986, 1st pl. for feature articles Pa. Press Assn., 1999, Cmty. Svc. award New Hope Pub. Libr., 1998. Democrat. Mem. Soc. Of Friends. Avocations: gourmet cooking, knitting, hiking, photography. Died May 17, 2005.

BRANDS, ALVIRA B., mental health nurse; b. Minn., July 9, 1922; d. Benjamin C. and Alma (Linder) Moe; m. Allen J. Brands, Nov. 27, 1972; children: Richard, David. RN, St. Lucas Hosp., Fairbault, Minn., 1943; BSN, U. Minn., 1958, MSN, 1960; DNSc, Cath. U. Am., Washington, 1975. Head nurse, nursing instr. and nursing supr. Anoka (Minn.) State Hosp., 1954-63; chief nursing svcs., div. med. svcs. Minn. Dept. Pub. Welfare, St. Paul, 1963-69; spl. cons. NIMH, USPHS, ADAMHA, DHHS, 1972-74; prog. analyst Mental Health Care and Svc. Fin. Br. Div. Mental Health Svc. Prog., NIMH, ADAMHA, USPHS, DHHS, 1976-79, chief facilities and quality sect., community support br., 1979-83; NIMH project officer for joint interagy. agreement Health Care Fin. Adminstrn., 1976-84; chief mental health sys. improvement and quality assurance Office State and Community Liaison, NIMH, ADAMHA, USPHS, 1983-85, dep. chief mental health resource devel. br. div. edn., 1985-92. Lectr. in field; cons. in field. Contbr. articles to profl. jours. Recipient Adminstrs. Citation, HCFA, 1984, Adminstrs. Meritorious Achievement award, ADAMHA, 1984, Outstanding Svc. award, 1976, 77, others. Mem. N.Y. Acad. Sci., Nat. Assn. Mental Health, Nat. Alliance for Mentally Ill, Assn. Mental Health Adminstrs., Assn. Mil. Surgeons, ANA, Coun. Advanced Practitioners in Psychiat. and Mental Health Nursing, Sigma Theta Tau (Excellence in Nursing award). Home: Scottsdale, Ariz. Died May 7, 2005.

BRANDT, HARRY, mechanical engineering educator; b. Amsterdam, The Netherlands, Nov. 14, 1925; came to U.S., 1946, naturalized, 1962; s. Friedrich H. and Henny (Rous) B.; m. Muriel Ruth Harman, Jan. 24, 1953; children: Joyce Estelle, Marilyn Audrey, Robert Alan. BS, U. Calif.-Berkeley, 1949, MS, 1950, PhD, 1954. Supervising research engr. Chevron Research Co., La Habra, Calif., 1954-64; lectr. UCLA, 1962-64; prof. mech. engring. U. Calif., Davis, from 1964, chmn. dept., 1969-74, 86-91; dir. Internat. Pipeline Techs. Inc., Beaverton, Oreg., 1985-91; chmn. bd. Clean Energy Systems, Inc., 1997—2006. Cons. Lawrence Livermore Nat. Lab., 1969-2006, State of Calif., 1970-87, State of Alaska, 1972, Los Alamos Nat. Lab., 1988-93. Mem. ASME, AIAA, Am. Welding Soc., Sigma Xi, Tau Beta Pi. Presbyterian. Home: El Macero, Calif. Died Jan. 28, 2006.

BRANDT, NANCY G., education educator; b. Joliet, Ill., July 18, 1941; d. Robert Anthony Gordon and Alice Ryan; m. Charles C. Brandt, Oct. 23, 1965; children: Charles III, Elizabeth, Leslie. BS in Edn., St. Francis U., 1980; MS in Edn., Ind. U., Fort Wayne, 1984. Tchr., cons. Whitko Schs., Pierceton, Ind., from 1981. Lector Manchester (Ind.) Coll., 2001; chair NCA, 2001—03. Named Tchr. of Yr., LDIN, 1997. Mem.: Pi Lambda Theta (treas. 1998—2002). Roman Catholic. Avocations: gardening, reading, antiques. Home: Fort Wayne, Ind. Died Feb. 6, 2004.

BRANDT, ROBERT BARRY, lay worker; b. Lebanon, Pa., Nov. 13, 1948; s. Marlin Jay Brandt and Arlene Hilda (Bowman) Gable; m. Ruth Ann Peterson, June 6, 1970; 1 child, Matthew Scot. BA in Sociology, Lebanon Valley Coll., 1971; postgrad., United Theol. Sem., Dayton, Ohio, 1973. Lic. to ministry Meth. Ch., 1968. Min. Ea. Pa. United Meth. Ch., Harrisburg, Pa., 1968-72, deacon Valley Forge, Pa., 1972-76; local ch. lay leader Ridgewood (N.J.) United Meth. Ch., 1985—87, from 2001; dist. lay leader no. dist. North N.J. Conf. United Meth., Paramus, N.J., 1986-89, lay leader ann. conf. Madison, N.J., 1989-96. Chair No. N.J. Bd. of Laity, Madison, 1989-96; chair coun. on ministries Ridgewood United Meth. Ch., 1988-89; mem. bishop's task force No. N.J. United Meth., Madison, 1989, 96-99; mem. Walk to Emmaus Community, 1987—, Disciplined Order of Christ, Nashville, 1988—; v.p. tech. and corp. svcs. Matrix Info. Consulting, Inc., Rochelle Park, N.J., 1987—; mem. gen. coun. on Ministries United Meth. Ch., 1992-96; lay dir. Skylands Walk to Emmaus Cmty., 1996-97. Mem., sec. gen. com. on gen. conf. United Meth. Ch., 1992-2000, del. gen. conf., 1992, 96, 2000; mem. Episcopacy com., N.E. jurisdiction United Meth. Ch., 1991-99, Greater N.J. Conf. United Meth., 1986—; N.E. regional rep. for Internat. Walk to Emmaus, 1998—, internat. steering com., 1998—. Named Layperson of Yr. Northern N.J. Conf., United Meth. Ch., 1993, Man of Yr. Ridgewood United Meth. Ch., 1996. Mem. Nat. Assn. Ann. Conf. Lay Leader. Democrat. Home: Fair Lawn, NJ. Died July 8, 2004.

BRASDA, BERNARD WILLIAM, trust company owner; b. La Crosse, Wis., May 3, 1938; s. George John and Olga Mary Olive (Hanson) B.; m. Carol June Welch, June, 1962 (div. 1979); children: George Allen, Norma Jean. BA, LaSalle Extension U., 1958; PhD (hon.), Juan Hauz U., 1979. Abstractor's asst. Las Cruces (N.M.) Abstract & Title Co., 1963-66; owner Grant County Abstract Co., Silver City, N.M., 1966-69; chief title officer Transam. Title Ins. co., Casa Grande, Ariz., 1969-72; title officer Title Ins. Co., Minn. and Phoenix, 1972-75; owner Brasda Title Service, Phoenix, 1975-76 and from 1979; unit mgr. First Am. Title Ins. Co., Phoenix, 1976-79. Instr. searching techniques, pvt. practice, 1975—. With U.S. Army, 1959-63. Republican. Home: Phoenix, Ariz. Died Aug. 30, 2004.

BRASS, LAWRENCE MITCHELL, neurologist, researcher; b. Bklyn., Apr. 9, 1956; s. Melvin Jay and Joyce Myrna (Friedman) B.; m. Lori Ann Haubenstock, Sept. 12, 1987; children: Zachary Hunter, Schuyler Chapin. BA in Maths., U. Pa., 1978; MD, Tufts U., 1982. Intern Newton-Wellesley Hosp., Newton Lower Falls, Mass., 1982-83; resident Neurological Inst. of N.Y., N.Y.C., 1983-86, chief resident, 1985-86, fellow stroke, 1986-87; asst. prof. neurology Yale U., New Haven, 1987-91, assoc. prof. neurology, 1991-96, assoc. prof. sch. epid. & pub. health, 1995-96, prof. neurology, epidemiology and pub. health, 1996—2006; chief neurology svc. VA Med. Ctr., West Haven, Conn., 1992-95; chief neurology VA Conn., West Haven, 1995—2006. Author: Handbook of Neurological Lists, 1993; editor: Neurobase, 1995. Judge Ann. Barbeque Jack Daniels Distillery, 1993; bd. mem. Am. Heart Assn., Wallingford, Conn., 1995, v.p., New Haven, Conn., 1995; vol. tchr. Sci.-by-Mail, Stamford, Conn., 1995. Recipient Twin Study of Stroke, NIH, 1994, Women's Estrogen for Stoke Trial, 1994, Hemorrhagic Stroke Project Non-Prescription Drug Mfrs. Assn., 1994. Fellow Stroke Coun. Am. Heart Assn.; mem. AMA, Am. Acad. Neurology, Coun. of Epidemiology & Prevention Am. Heart Assn., World Fedn. Neurology (mem. rsch. group on stroke). Avocations: bicycling, sailing, fishing, medical antiques. Home: Woodbridge, Conn. Died Mar. 8, 2006.

BRAUER, ROBERT E., retired bankruptcy judge; b. Staunton, Ill., Apr. 7, 1923; s. Louis H. and Alma E. (Oettel) B.; m. Constance Faye McMichael, Jan. 11, 1945 (div. 1972); m. Billie G. Baker, July 26, 1974. BA, Washington U., St. Louis, 1949, LLB, 1951. Bar: Mo. Assoc. Mattingly, Boas & Richards, St. Louis, 1951-53; asst. U.S. Atty. Eastern Dist. Mo., St. Louis, 1953-60; assoc., ptnr. Rassieur, Long & Yawitz, St. Louis, 1960-61; referee in bankruptcy, U.S. bankruptcy judge U.S. Cts. Ea. and We. Dists. Mo., 1961-86. 2d lt. USAF, 1942-46. Mem. Mo. Bar Assn., St. Louis Bar Assn., Comml. Law League Am., Assn. Bankruptcy Judges, Order of Coif. Avocations: gardening, travel. Home: Bonne Terre, Mo. Died June 8, 2004.

BRAUN, ARTHUR DAVID, music publishing company executive; b. N.Y.C., Nov. 5, 1952; s. Louis and Jean Braun; m. Debbie Tuggle, July 5, 1985; 1 child, Justin. MBA, Pacific Western U., 1990. Pres. Dick James Orgn., N.Y., 1974-82, pres. U.S. ops. Los Angeles, 1985-89, Nashville, 1982-85; pres. U.S. Music Publ. div. TKO Entertainment, Inc., 1989-93; exec. v.p. Drive Entertainment, Inc., 1993-94; pres. Centium Entertainment, Inc., Beverly Hills, Calif., from 1994. 1st chmn. Music Pubs. Forum, N.Y.C. Composer various mus. works. Recipient 12 gold and platinum record awards as pub. Mem. ASCAP, Nat. Acad. Rec. Arts and Scis., Career Inst. of Am., Inc. (former v.p., dir. edn.). Home: Boca Raton, Fla. Died May 23, 2005.

BRAUN, ROBERT FREDERICK, publishing executive; b. Saginaw, Mich., Jan. 7, 1927; s. Martin M. and Edna M. (Ahlgrim) B.; m. Doris M. Veitengruber, July 10, 1948; children: Marsha, Lynn, Judy, Martin. BA, Mich. State U, 1948. Gen. mgr. Braun Builders, Saginaw, 1948-62, Crosland Co., Winston Salem, N.C., 1963-69; investment strategist Integon Corp., Winston Salem, 1969-82; pub. Braun's Sys., Homosassae, Fla., from 1969. With U.S. Army, 1944-46. Lutheran. Avocations: computers, automobiles, history, music. Died Jan. 1, 2005.

BRAVARD, ROBERT STATON, library director; b. Dayton, Ohio, Nov. 2, 1935; s. Elmer Staton and Martha Helen (Schneider) B.; m. Cynthia Ann Buttolph, Aug. 16, 1958; children: Jonathan Staton, Christopher Mark, Thomas Andrew. AB, Wilmington Coll., 1957; MS in Libr. Studies, Syracuse U., 1959. Asst. libr. Findlay (Ohio) Coll., 1959-60, head libr., 1960-63; tech. svcs. libr. Lock Haven (Pa.) U., 1963-70, dir. libr. svcs., from 1970. Cons. Choice, Middletown, Conn. 1964—; chair State System of Higher Edn. Libr. Coun., 1976-78, 82-84; adv. bd. Popular Culture Libr. Bowling Green State U., 1987—. Co-autor: Samuel R. Delany, A Primary and Secondary Bibliography, 1980; editor mag. Lock Haven Internat. Rev., 1987—; mem. editorial bd. The Acquisitions Libr., 1987—. Pres. Ctrl. Pa. Health Systems Agy., Lewisburg, 1982-83, Friends of Ross Libr., Lock Haven, 1983-85; chair Susquehanna Libr. Coop., 1974-76, 92—; mem. Lock Haven City Coun., 1992—. Mem. Phi Beta Delta, Phi Kappa Phi, Beta Phi Mu. Democrat. Avocations: reading, popular culture, comic book collecting. Home: Lock Haven, Pa. Died May 27, 2005.

BRAVERMAN, AARON PHILIP, prinicipal, social science educator; b. Bronx, N.Y., June 27, 1931; s. Samuel Isaac and Clara (Nudel) B.; m. Gloria Anne Levine, Dec. 4, 1955 (dec. Jan. 1973); children: Elyse Braverman Bloom, Gwen Braverman Bloom; m. Arela Alexandrovits Hauser, Dec. 18, 1975; stepchildren: Alan Hauser, Andrew Hauser. BA in Social Scis., Rutgers U., 1949-54; MA in Social Scis., Montclair State Coll., 1956-59; MEd, William Paterson Coll., 1968-72. Tchr. history and econs. Clifton (N.J.) High Sch., 1957-58; tchr. social studies Rochelle Park (N.J.) Midland Sch., 1958-59; spl. agent John Hancock Life Ins. Co., Paterson, N.J., 1959-60; sales rep. Bacon & Graham Co., Paterson, 1960-64; tchr. Paterson Bd. Edn., 1964-70; youth coord. Mayor's Coun. on Youth Opportunity, Paterson, 1970-72; tchr. Paterson Bd. Edn., 1972-74, vice prin., 1974-90; prin. Paterson Pub. Schs., from 1990. Nat. dir. N.J. Jaycees, state v.p., state sec., 1965-68; pres. Paterson Task Force for Cmty. Action, 1970-71, Paterson United Against Drug Abuse, 1972-73. With U.S. Army, 1954-56. Named Outstanding State v.p. N.J. Jaycees, 1966, JCI senator, 1968; recipient Scroll of Honor State of Israel award B'nai B'rith, 1976. Mem. AACD, Nat. Assn. Sch. Prins., N.J. Prins. and Suprs. Assn., Paterson Adminstrs. Assn. (v.p. 1984-90), Paterson Prins. Assn. (chmn. policty com. 1993—), Mended Hearts. Democrat. Jewish. Avocations: reading, contesting. Home: Paramus, NJ. Died Apr. 24, 2004.

BRAVOS, NICHOLAS GEORGE, service executive; b. Alexandria, La., June 29, 1922; s. George Nicholas and Edna (Manteris) B.; m. Voula Skouteris, Jan. 15, 1951; children: George Nicholas, Dee Anastasia. Student, La. State U., 1939-42. Exec. dir. food and beverage Holiday Inns of Am., Memphis, 1962-70; chmn., pres. Internat. Food & Lodging Corp., Memphis, from 1971. Exec. cons. Lotte Fast Food/Lotteria Co., Tokyo, 1971-73, Takashimaya Co. Delica Cafeterias, Osaka, Japan, 1973-75, Washington Hotel Corp., Nagoya, Japan, 1975—. Served with U.S. Army, 1942-46, ETO. Republican. Avocations: swimming, handball. Died June 4, 2005.

BRAWNER, LEE BASIL, retired librarian, consultant; b. Seguin, Tex., May 1, 1935; s. Lee Basil and Thelma (Davenport) B.; m. Nancy Jayne Wallis, Dec. 6, 1958; children: Betsy Lynn, Allen Lee. Student, Tex. A. and M. U., 1953-55; BA, North Tex. State U., 1957; MA, George Peabody Coll. Tchrs., 1960. Head popular libr. and circulation dept. Dallas Pub. Libr., 1958-60, head Lakewood br., 1961-62, chief br. svcs., 1964-67; dir. Waco (Tex.) Pub. Libr., 1962-64; asst. state libr. Tex. State Libr., 1967-71; dir. Met. Libr. System, Oklahoma City, 1971-99; owner Brawner Assocs., L.L.C. Trustee AMIGOS Bibliog. Coun., 1987—90; panelist libr. bldg. awards AIA-ALA, 1990—92; mem. state adv. bd. U. Okla. Sch. Librs. and Info. Studies, from 1994. Co-author: (with Donald K. Beck, Jr.) Determining Your Public Library's Future Size: A Needs Assessment and Planning Model, 1996, Disaster Response and Planning for Libraries, 1998, In Celebration of Intellectual Freedom, 1999. Trustee, v.p. Okla. Ctr. for the Book, 1987-93; trustee Okla. Humanities Com., 1977-78; mem. Leadership Oklahoma City Alumni, 1994-2006; chmn. Okla. Found. for Humanities; trustee Freedom to Read Found., 1982-85, pres., 1985-86; mem. Murrah Fed. Bldg. Meml. Com., 1995-2006. Recipient Alumni award U. North Tex., 1989, First Amendment award Okla. Soc. Profl. Journalists, 1997-98, Downtown Now Pioneer award, 1997, Hugh M. Hefner 1st Amendment award, 1998, Angie Debo Civil Libertarian of Yr. award ACLU Union of Okla. Found., 1999, Libr. Endowment Trust 1st Lee B. Brawner Lifetime Achievement award, 2003; named to 30th Anniversary Honor Roll, ALA Intellectual Freedom to Read Found., 1999. Mem.: ACLU, ALA (coun. 1978—81, intellectual freedom com. 1979—82), Okla. Libr. Assn. (chmn. libr. devel. 1982—83, pres. 1984—85, chmn. legis. com. 1990, chmn. awards com. 1992—93, Disting. Svc. award 1983, SIRS Intellectual Freedom award 1997), Pub. Libr. Assn. (effectiveness com. 1992), Libr. Adminstrn. and Mgmt. Assn. (libr. bldg. awards com. 1987—90, 1992—93, chmn. 1990, chmn. libr. bldgs. and equipment sect. 1992), Sigma Phi Epsilon. Home: Oklahoma City, Okla. Died Feb. 8, 2006.

BRAY, PHYLLIS PETTY, middle school educator; b. Shreveport, La., Sept. 8, 1945; d. Arthur Preston Jr. and Evelyn (Brown) Petty; children: Willard L. III, Beverly E. BA, La. Tech. U., 1967; MA, U. S. Fla., 1982. Cert. tchr., adminstr., supr., Fla. Tchr. Eng. Winnfield (La.) Sr. High Sch., 1967, Zwolle (La.) High Sch., 1967-69, Paxon Sr. High Sch., Jacksonville, Fla., 1969-71, Forest Sr. High Sch., Ocala, Fla., 1971-74, Hudson High Sch., New Port Richey, Fla., 1974-79, 83-84, Gulf Mid. Sch., New Port Richey, 1984-90, reading resource specialist, from 1990. Collegial coach Dist. Sch. Bd. Pasco County, mid. sch. trainer. Co-author: Urchins and Angels, 1989; contbr. articles to profl. jours. Judge, sch.-site portfolios Nat. Bd. for Profl. Teaching Standards, U. Pitts., 1992, 93. Mem. ASCD, Nat. Coun. Tchrs. English, Suncoast Area Tchr. Tng. Program (clin. tchr.), Fla. Profl. Opportunities Program (peer tchr.), Fla. Coun. Tchrs. English, Delta Kappa Gamma (Delta Gamma chpt.). Republican. Baptist. Avocations: writing, painting, needlecrafts, antiques, puzzles. Home: New Prt Rchy, Fla. Died Apr. 17, 2004.

BREGMAN, JACOB ISRAEL, environmental services administrator; b. Hartford, Conn., Sept. 17, 1923; s. Aaron and Jennie (Katzoff) B.; m. Mona Madan, June 27, 1948; children: Janet, Marcia, Barbara. BS, Providence Coll., 1943; MS, Poly. Inst. Bklyn., 1948, PhD, 1951. Rsch. chemist Fels & Co., 1947—48; head phys. chem. labs. Nalco Chem. Co., Chgo., 1950—59; supr. phys. chemistry rsch. sect. Armour Rsch. Found., Chgo., 1959—63; asst. dir. chemistry rsch. Ill. Inst. Tech. Rsch. Inst., Chgo., 1963—65, dir. chem. scis., 1965—67; dep. asst. sec. U.S. Dept. Interior, Washington, 1967—69; pres. Wapora Inc., 1969—82; v.p. Dynamac Corp., 1983—84; pres. Bregman and Co., 1984—2004, CEO, 1984—2004, treas., 2004—06. Chmn. N.E. Ill. Met. Area Air Pollution Control Bd., 1962—63; chmn. Ill. Air Pollution Control Bd., 1963—67; chmn. adv. bd. on saline water conversion NATO Parliamentarians Conf., 1963; chmn. Water Resources Rsch. Coun., 1964—67; profl. lectr. George Washington U., 1980—98. Author: Corrosion Inhibitors, 1963, Surface Effects in Detection, 1965, The Pollution Paradox, 1966, Handbook of Water Resources and Pollution Control, 1976, Environmental Regulations Handbook, 1991, Environmental Impact Statements, 1992, 2d edit., 1999, Environmental Compliance Handbook, 1996, 2d edit., 1999; patentee in field; contbr. 70 articles to profl. jours. Chmn. Montgomery County (Md.) Citizens Task Force on Georgetown Br. Right of Way, 1986—90; mem. Md. Dem. State Ctrl. Com., 1974—78; treas. Montgomery Dem. Ctrl. Com., 1974—76; del. Dem. Conv., 1976; mem. plan commn. Park Forest, Ill., 1956—59; trustee, 1958—62. With AUS, 1943—46, ETO, survivor sunken troop ship "Empire Javelin", 1944. Decorated two Battle Stars, AUS. Fellow: Am. Inst. Chemists; mem.: Am. Chem. Soc., Nat. Def. Ind. Assn. (life), Soc. Am. Military Engrs. (life), VFW, Am. Legion, Phi Lambda Upsilon, Sigma Xi. Home: Saint Petersburg, Fla. Died Jan. 17, 2006.

BREIER, MORTON A., philosopher; b. NYC, June 30, 1934; s. Max M. and Rose (Zucker) Breier; m. Karen M. Sutherland, Mar. 1, 1997; m. Phyllis Benu (div.); children: Nicole C., Damien S., Maximillian D. BSME, CCNY, NYC, NY, 1958. Engr. Gen. Instrument, NYC, 1958—63; dir. advanced design Dortech, Inc., Stamford, Conn., 1967—71; prin./ptnr. Breier Neidle Patrone Assoc., Darien, Conn., 1971—89; pres. Inner Journeys-Outer Worlds, Kailua-Kona, Hawaii, from 1994. Author: (novels) Aleph-Zero, 1976, Masks Mandalas & Meditations, 1996. Pres. New Thought Ctr., Kailua-Kona, Hawaii, from 1998; VP Kona Beth Shalom, Kailua-Kona, Hawaii, from 1999, Habitat for Humanity Kona, Kailua-Kona, Hawaii, from 2000. Home: Kailua Kona, Hawaii. Died Mar. 25, 2004.

BRENNAN, WILLIAM JOSEPH, III, lawyer; b. Newark, Apr. 29, 1933; s. William J. Jr. and Marjory (Leonard) B.; m. Georgianna V. Franklin, Sept. 10, 1960; children: William J. IV, Alexandra V. BA, Colgate U., 1955; LLB, Yale U., 1962. Bar: N.Y. 1963, N.J. 1967, U.S. Dist. Ct. (so. and ea. dists.) N.Y. 1964, U.S. Dist. Ct. N.J. 1967, U.S. Ct. Appeals (1st cir.) 1987, U.S. Ct. Appeals (2nd cir.) 1968, U.S. Ct. Appeals (3rd cir.) 1968, U.S. Ct. Appeals (Fed. cir.) 1991, U.S. Supreme Ct. 1967. Assoc. Breed, Abbott & Morgan, N.Y.C., 1962-67; asst. atty. gen in charge of litigation Office of Atty. Gen. of N.J., Trenton, 1967-68; spl. counsel to gov. Office of the Gov. of the State of N.J., Trenton, 1969; ptnr., mng. ptnr. Smith, Stratton, Wise, Heher & Brennan, Princeton, 1970—2004. Assoc. editor N.J. Law Jour., 1979-2004 Trustee St. Peter's Coll., Jersey City, 1988-94; chmn. bd. dirs. Brennan Ctr for Justice, NYU Sch. Law. Served to 1st lt. USMC, 1956-59. Recipient Award of Distinction, N.J. State Grand Jurors' Assn., 1969, Alumni Achievement award Newark Acad., 1986, Trial Bar award Trial Attys. N.J., 1994. Fellow Am. Coll. Trial Lawyers (chmn. com. on legal ethics 1987-93, chmn. com. on professionalism 1993-97), Internat. Acad. Trial Lawyers, Am. Acad. Appellate Lawyers, Am. Bar Found. (lie, state chmn. 1990); mem. ABA (mem. com. on legal ethics 1989, 3d cir. mem., com. on fed. judiciary 1989-93, ho. of dels. 1986-95), N.J. State Bar Assn. (pres. 1984-85), Assn. of Fed. Bar of State of N.J. (pres. 1992-94), Assn. of Bar of City of N.Y., Yale Law Sch. Assn. N.J., Am. Law Inst. Avocations: scuba diving, flying. Home: Princeton, NJ. Died May 17, 2004.

BRESSLER, BERNARD, lawyer; b. NYC, Jan. 2, 1928; s. Morris and Masha (Roitman) B.; m. Teresa Stern, June 25, 1950; children: Lisa, Jeanette. BA, Rutgers U., 1949; LLB magna cum laude, Harvard U., 1952. Bar: N.Y. 1953, N.J. 1977. Atty. firm Greenman, Shea, Sandomire & Zimet, N.Y.C., 1952-60; ptnr. Bressler, Amery & Ross, N.Y.C., from 1960, Florham Park, NJ, from 1981. Dir., chmn. bd. N.J. Pub. Interest Law Ctr., 1996—; bd. trustees South St. Theatre Co., Morristown, 2003—. Author: (with others) Tax Annotations Nichols Ency. Forms, 1954-59; Editor: (with B. Meislin) New York Lawyers Manual, 1954, Harvard Law Rev., vol. 65. Campaign dir. Summit (N.J.) United Jewish Appeal, 1957-60; chmn. Summit Democrat Club, 1957; trustee Summit Civic Found.; chmn. Summit Area United Negro Coll. Fund, 1979-92. With USNR, 1945-46. Mem.: Lotos (N.Y.C.), Park Ave. Club (N.J.). Home: Morristown, NJ. Died Sept. 17, 2005.

BRESSLER, BERNARD, psychiatrist, educator; b. Milan, Mich., May 22, 1917; s. Sam and Rose (Grossman) B. AB, Washington U., 1938, MD, 1942; grad., Chgo. Psychoanalytic Inst., 1951. Intern St. Louis City Hosp., 1942-43; resident in psychiatry St. Louis City Sanitarium, 1943, Michael Reese Hosp., Chgo., 1943-45; practice medicine specializing in psychiatry Chgo., 1946-53; mem. faculty Duke U. Med. Ctr., Durham, NC, 1955, prof. psychiatry, 1962; pvt. practice Richmond, Va. Asst. dir. U. N.C.-Duke Psychoanalytic Inst., tng. analyst Served with U.A. Army, 1953-55. Fellow Am. Psychiat. Assn. (life); mem. AMA, Am. Psychoanalytic Assn., Psychosomatic Soc., Pan-Am. Med. Assn. Episcopalian. Home: Richmond, Va. Died Nov. 26, 2005.

BRESTIN, STEVEN G., orthopedic surgeon; b. Chgo., Jan. 4, 1945; m. Meredith Dee; children: J.R., John, Sally, Beth, Anne. MD, Ind. U., 1969. Diplomate Am. Bd. Orthopedic Surgery. Intern USPHS Hosp., Seattle, 1969-70, orthopedic surgeon, 1976-80; resident in orthopedic surgery Akron (Ohio) Gen. Med. Ctr., 1972-76; gen. practice USPHS Clin., Portland, Oreg., 1970-72; orthopedic surgeon Kearney (Nebr.) Orthopedic and Fracture, from 1981. Med. dir., chmn. Sentinel Health Care, Kearney, 1994-97. Mem. Plains Physicians Orgn. (pres., chmn. 1994-97). Home: Kearney, Nebr. Died Oct. 16, 2004.

BREWER, FLOYD IRVING, history consultant; m. A. Coleen Hamilton, 1944; children: Jeffrey H., Mark A. Diploma in Elem. Edn., U. No. Maine, Presque Isle, 1942; BS in History and Elem. Edn., U. So. Maine, Gorham, 1944; MA in Vocat. Guidance, Columbia U., 1947, profl. diploma, 1952, EdD, 1956. Asst. prof., coll. adminstr. U. Bridgeport, Conn., 1947-56; coll. adminstr. U. Cin., 1956-66; assoc. prof. edn. SUNY, Albany, 1966-83; history cons. Delmar, N.Y., from 1983. Archaeology apprentice, 1972-80; instr. archaeology Hudson Valley C.C., Troy, N.Y., 1980-83, continuing edn. program Bethlehem (N.Y.) Ctrl. Schs., 1981-85; field dir., editor publs. Bethelhem Archaeology Group, 1981-96; cons. Delmar Place Assisted Living Facility, 1997—. Sr. editor: Bethlehem Revisited, A Bicentennial Story 1793-1993, 1993; sr. author: Bethlehem Diary, Stories and Reflections 1983-1993, 1994; author: A Dutch-English Odyssey: Stories of Brewer and Estey Families in North America 1636-1996, 1997; contbr. articles to profl. jours. With USAF, 1943-46. Mem. N.Y. Archaeol. Assn. Died Nov. 8, 2005.

BRIESE, LEONARD ARDEN, inventor; b. Mpls., Mar. 21, 1933; s. Leonard Albert and Wilma Mrytle (Richards) B.; m. Joan Elaine Ramsay, Dec. 12, 1953; children: Linda Briese Johnson, Leonard Anthony, Leslie Briese Dietlin. Grad. high sch., El Segundo, Calif. Tooling mgr. Altamil Corp., El Segundo, 1954-60; owner, founder Len Briese & Co., El Segundo, 1960-65; pres., chmn., founder Lenco Mfg. Corp., El Segundo, 1965-70; v.p. engring. R & D, Wescal Industries, Inc., El Segundo, 1968-70; v.p., bd. dirs., founder Minipet Electronics Corp., Carson, Calif., 1972-74; pres., chmn., founder Cutters Unltd. Inc., Gardena, Calif., 1975-82; v.p. R & D and engring. Rotary Techs. Corp., Gardena, 1982-86; owner, founder L.A. Briese Co., Gardena, from 1960, Breeze Tool Co., Gardena, CA, 1992-94; v.p. R&D, founder Briese Industrial Tools, Inc., Harbor City, CA, 1994-95, Briese Industrial Technologies, Inc., from 1995. Rsch. cons. Innovative Techs. Inc., Long Beach, Calif., 1986-98, Motivation Inc., Key West, Fla., 1986-98, Mel Fisher, Key West, 1987-98, Mel Fisher Exploration Inc., Key West, 1988-98. Numerous U.S. patents issued or granted in over 50 countries. With USAF, 1952--54, Korea. Mem. VFW (life), Soc. Mfg. Engrs. (sr.), Am. Soc. for Metals, Soc. for Advancement Material and Process Engring, Soc. for Mining, Metallurgy and Exploration, Soc. Plastics Engrs. Republican. Episcopalian. Avocations: motorhome travel, fishing, boating. Died May 12, 2004.

BRIGHT, RICHARD, actor; b. Bklyn., June 28, 1937; s. Ernest and Matilda (Scott) B.; m. Rutanya Alda, June 11, 1977; 1 child, Diane. Studied with Frank Crosano, John Lehne, Paul Mann. Film appearances include Odds Against Tomorrow, 1959, Lion's Love, 1969, The Panic in Needle Park, 1971, The Getaway, 1972, The Godfather, 1972, Pat Garret and Billy the Kid, 1973, Bring Me The Head of Alfredo Garcia, 1974, The Godfather II, 1974, Rancho Deluxe, 1975, Marathon Man, 1976, Looking for Mr. Goodbar, 1977, Handle with Care, 1977, On the Yard, 1978, Hair, 1979, The Idolmaker, 1980, Vigilante, 1983, Two of a Kind, 1983, One Upon A Time in America, 1984, Girls Nite Out, 1984, Crimewaves, 1985, Cut and Run, 1985, Brighton Beach Memoirs, 1986, The Verne Miller Story, 1987, Time Out, 1988, Red Heat, 1988, Ghoul School, 1990, The Ambulance, 1990, The Godfather III, 1990, Ballad of Tina Juarez, 1992, Who Do I Gotta Kill?, 1992, Who's the Man, 1993, The Ref, 1994, Pictures of Baby Jane Doe, 1995, Blue Funk, 1995, Sweet Nothing, 1995, Jaded, 1996, Beautiful Girls, 1996, Night Falls on Manhattan, 1997, The Hotel Manor Inn, 1997, Anima, 1998, O.K. Garage, 1998, Joe the King, 1999, Getting to Know You, 1999, Dead Dog, 2000, The Photographer, 2000, Broke Even, 2000, Trigger Happy, 2001; (TV movies) A Death of Innocence, 1971, The Gun, 1974, Somerset, 1976, Cops and Robin, 1978, Sizzle, 1981, Brass, 1985, Penalty Phase, 1986, There Must Be A Pony, 1986, Houston Knights, 1987, Teamster Boss: The Jackie Presser Story, 1992, Calm at Sunset, 1996, Witness to the Mob, 1998; (TV mini-series) From Here to Eternity, 1979; (TV appearances) Studio One, 1957, The Defenders, 1964, Skag, 1980, Hill Street Blues, 1986, The Equalizer, 1988, Jake and the Fatman, 1991, Law & Order, 1992, 1993, 1997, 2002, Third Watch, 1999, Oz, 2000, 100 Centre St, 2001, The Sopranos, 2002, Law & Order: Criminal Intent, 2002, The Jury, 2004, Law & Order: Special Victims Unit, 2005; (stage) The Balcony, 1959, The Beard, 1968-69, Richard III, 1979-80, A Midsummer Night's Dream, Edward II, A Streetcar Named Desire. Mem. Actors' Equity Assn., Screen Actors Guild, AFTRA. Avocations: bonsai gardening, coin collecting/numismatics, motorcycling. Died Feb. 18, 2006.

BRIGHT, WILLIAM OLIVER, retired linguistics educator; b. Oxnard, Calif., Aug. 13, 1928; s. Oliver Edward and Ethel (Ruggles) B.; m. Elizabeth Halloran, Feb. 2, 1952; 1 child, Susannah; m. Jane Orstan, June 16, 1962; m. Marcia Andersen, Dec. 24, 1964; m. Debra Levy, Sept. 20, 1975; m. Lise Menn, Nov. 28, 1987. AB in Linguistics, U. Calif.-Berkeley, 1949, PhD, 1955. Jr. linguistics scholar Deccan Coll., Poona, India, 1955-57; linguist State Dept., Washington, 1957-58; asst. prof. speech U. Calif. at Berkeley, 1958-59; mem. faculty UCLA, 1959—88, assoc. prof. anthropology, 1962-66, prof. linguistics and anthropology, 1966-88, emeritus prof. linguistics and anthropology, 1988—2006. Adj. prof. linguistics U. Colo., Boulder. Author: The Karok Language, 1957, An Outline of Colloquial Kannada, 1958, Variation and Change in Language, 1976, American Indian Linguistics and Literatures, 1984, Linguistic Variation in South Asia, 1990, A Coyote Reader, 1993, Colorado Place Names, 1993, 1,500 California Place Names: Their Origin and Meaning, 1998, Native American Placenames of the United States, 2004; editor: Studies in Californian Linguistics, 1964, Sociolinguistics, 1966, The World's Writing Systems, 1996, Lang. in Soc. jour., Oxford Internat. Ency. of Linguistics, 1985-92; editorial dir. Malki Mus. Press, 1977-85. Served with AUS, 1952-54. Mem. Linguistic Soc. Am. (pres. 1989, editor jour. Language 1966-88), Am. Anthrop. Assn., Linguistic Soc. India, Soc. Study of Indigenous Langs. of Ams. (pres. 1995). Home: Boulder, Colo. Died Oct. 15, 2006.

BRIGIDA, CARLO JOSEPH, engineering and manufacturing executive; b. N.Y.C., Dec. 22, 1938; s. Joseph and Antonietta (Giordano) B.; m. Genevieve Patricia Marshall, Sept. 28, 1974; children: Joseph C., Victoria A., William T., John M. BSME, Columbia U., 1961; BS, Queens Coll., 1961; MS, Columbia U., 1965. Registered profl. engr., N.Y., N.J. Various positions Foster Wheeler Energy Corp., from 1961; v.p., dir. power systems and condenser ops.; dir. power sys. and condenser ops. Foster Wheeler Energy Corp., 1983, dir. coal water fuel ventures, 1983-84, divsn. v.p. coal-water fuel ventures, 1984-86, divsn. v.p. steam and indsl. products, 1986-88, v.p. comml., 1988-89, v.p. heat transfer products, 1989-93, v.p., from 1993. V.p., pres., bd. dirs. Foster Wheeler Tenn. Inc. Patentee in field; contbr. articles to profl. jours. Mayor Morris Twp., 1989, committeeman, 1989-91, past mem. planning bd.; pres. Neighborhood Assn. Morris Township, 1984-88. Mem. ASME, Heat Exch. Inst. Republican. Roman Catholic. Home: Convent Station, NJ. Died Sept. 23, 2004.

BRINK, NORMA S., performing arts educator, actress; b. Grand Rapids, Mich., Sept. 26, 1928; d. Henry and Helen M. (Seamon) S.; m. Edward H. Brink Jr., Nov. 11, 1950 (div. Oct. 1965); children: John, Mary Teresa, Edward H. III. BA, Western Mich. U., 1949, MA, 1968. Tchr., adminstr. Grand Rapids Pub. Schs., 1949-86; adj. prof. performing arts Davenport Coll., Grand Rapids, from 1986. Condr. comm. workshops for bus. Davenport Entrepreneurial Ctr.; tchr. adult acting Grand Rapids Civic Theatre. Actress profl. theater, radio and TV appearances, numerous cmty. theatre prodns., 1950—. Founder, life bd. dirs. Cmty. Cir. Theatre, Grand Rapids, 1955—; bd. dirs. Kent County Humane Soc., Actors Theatre; vol., past bd. dirs. Grand Rapids Civic Theatre; active LWV; vol. Am. Cancer Soc. Recipient Grand Rapids Arts Coun. award, 1985, other arts awards; named Grand Rapids Vol. of Yr., 1972. Mem. Western Mich. Jazz Soc., French Soc. Home: Grand Rapids, Mich. Died June 12, 2004.

BRINTON, BYRON CHARLES, publishing executive, editor; b. Fessenden, N.D., Jan. 28, 1912; s. Charles Mackay and Elizabeth Rose (Mueller) B.; m. Roberta Lee Wright, Sept. 14, 1935 (dec. Jan. 1993); children: Lynn Ann, Ross Burr, Byron Dorsy, Alice Kathleen, Greg Charles. Jr. cert. with honors, U. Oreg., 1933. Co-owner, co-editor Weekly North Powder News and Haines Record, Haines, Oreg., 1928-34; co-owner, editor Record-Courier, Baker City, Oreg., 1934-57, owner, from 1957, editor, from 1934. Bd. dirs. Oreg. Geographic Names, Oreg. Trail Regional Mus.; pres., organizing exec. Anthony Lakes Ski Area Corp., 1961-64. Active Bonneville Adv. Bd., 1940—, Oreg. State Water Bd., 1958-59; com. sec. City of Baker Mgr. Charter Form Govt., 1950-57; co-founder, dir. Sumpter Valley R.R. Restoration, Baker City, 1980; sec. Hells Canyon Devel. Assn., Baker City, 1944—; mem. devel. com. Oreg. Trail Regional Mus.; mem. emeritus Baker County Mus. Commn. With USN, 1944-46. Recipient Baker County Cattlemens Assn. Svc. plaque, 1993, Outstanding Svc. plaque Baker County Fair, 1993, Oreg. State Coll. Diamond Agr. Achievement Registry award, 1993; named Baker County Man of Yr., 1995. Mem. Oreg. Cattlemens Assn., Baker County Livestock Assn. (Outstanding Svc. plaque), Future Farmers Am. (hon.), Kiwanis (life), Powder River Sportsmens Club (life), Nat. Ski Patrol (charter). Democrat. Baptist. Avocations: skiing, mountain hiking, woodworking, trout fishing, tennis. Home: Baker City, Oreg. Died Mar. 22, 2005.

BRISTOW, CLINTON, JR., academic administrator; b. Montgomery, Ala., Mar. 15, 1949; s. T.C. and Betty Bristow; 1 child, Maya. JD, Northwestern U., 1974, PhD, 1977; postgrad., U. Minn., 1983; MBA, Governor's State U., 1984. V.p. adminstrn. Olive-Harvey Coll., Chgo., 1980-81; dean Coll. Bus. Chgo. State U., 1985-93; pres. Chgo. Bd. Edn., 1990-92, Alcorn State U., Lorman, Miss., 1995—2006. Cons. in field. Contbr. articles to profl. publs. Chmn. Miss. Rhodes Scholarship Com., 1996; bd. dirs. Miss. Agr./Forestry Mus., Jackson, Chgo., Congl. Award Bd., HBCU Capital Fin. Bd.; mem. exec. com. 1890 Coun. Pres. Fellow Northwestern U. Ctr. for Urban Affairs, 1973-74; recipient Role Model award Top Ladies of Distinction, Inc., 1987, Greater Roseland Area Planning, 1990. Mem. Am. Assn. State Colls. and Univs. (state rep.), So. Assn. Colls. and Schs. (exec. com.), Nat. Collegiate Athletic Assn. (bd. of dir.), So. Edn. Found., Miss. Instns. of Higher Learning (coun. of pres.), Southwestern Athletic Conf. (past pres.). Baptist. Avocations: reading, golf, jogging. Home: Alcorn State, Miss. Died Aug. 19, 2006.

BRITT, LOIS GRADY, agricultural executive; b. Duplin County, N.C., Sept. 30, 1935; BS in Home Econs., East Carolina U., 1956; MEd in Adult Edn., N.C. State U., 1969. Mgr. family farm; pub. affairs v.p. Murphy Farms Inc., Rose Hill, N.C. Bd. govs. U. N.C., 1989, 93, 97, sec. bd., standing com. svc., chmn. 1993-98, vice chmn. 1992, sec. 1991, ad hoc com. svc., presdl. search com. 1996-97, co-chmn. com. on tchg. excellence, 1994, com. on inclusion, 1994; chmn. com. on tchg. awards, 1997, issues com. 1996, bd. assessment com., 1995, others; exec. bd. N.C. Agribusiness, pres.-elect 1997, pres. 1998-00. Sunday sch. tchr., adminstrv. bd. Bethel Meth. Ch., Mount Olive, N.C.; life mem. Women of the Ch., N.C. Meth. Conf.; past chmn. Duplin Outdoor Drama Soc.; extension com. on personnel and program devel. USDA. Named Woman of Yr. Bus. and Profl. Womens Club, Tarheel of Week News and Observer; recipient Disting. Svc. awards N.C. Grange 1996, Nat. Assn. of Extension Home Economists, Nat. Assn. of Extension 4-H Agts., Reynolds Extension Agt. award of excellence, Melvin Cording Leadership award Duplin Agri-Bus. Coun., 1998, Order of the Long Leaf Pine, 1991. Mem. Epsilon Sigma Phi, Alpha Zeta. Home: Mount Olive, NC. Died June 4, 2005.

BRITTON, JOHN EDGAR, lawyer; b. Erie, Pa., June 4, 1921; s. Ray W. and Freda (Berlin) B.; married, June 17, 1950; children: Judith B. Bonanno, John W. AB, Bucknell U., 1942; JD, Harvard U., 1948. Ptnr. MacDonald, Illig, Jones & Britton, Erie, Pa., from 1948. Pres. Erie Bottling Corp., 1953-88, Tannetics, Inc., 1969-83; bd. dirs. Eriez Mfg. Co., Efco, Inc.; pres. The Britton Family Found., 1988—. Pres. Hamot Health Systems, Inc., Erie, 1969, trustee 1970-80; founder, dir. Greater Erie Charity Golf Classic, 1970—. 1st lt. USAF, 1942-45. Fellow Am. Coll. Trial Lawyers; mem. Erie County Bar Assn. (pres. 1968, chancellor of the bar 1991), Kahkwa Club, Sanctuary Golf Club. Republican. Lutheran. Avocations: golf, foundation philanthropic work. Home: Erie, Pa. Died Nov. 24, 2004.

BROCK, BERNARD LEE, communication and speech educator; b. Elkhart, Ind., June 15, 1932; s. Ralph Millard and Louise D. (Scamehorn) B.; m. Loree Ann Arthur, Mar. 26, 1961 (div. 1980); children: Arthur C., Leslie C. BA, Ill. State U., 1954; MA, Northwestern U., Evanston, Ill., 1961, PhD, 1965. Tchr. Arlington High Sch., Arlington Heights, Ill., 1954-55, 57-59, Del Mar High Sch., Campbell, Calif., 1960-62; teaching asst. Northwestern U., Evanston, Ill., 1962-64; prof. U. Minn., Mpls., 1965-71; prof. communications Wayne State U., Detroit, 1972—2006. Communications cons. Uniroyal, Detroit, 1979-85, Christian Sch. Ch., Boston, 1965-2006, Gen. Motors, Detroit, 1983-88. Author: Making Sense of Political Ideology: The Power of Language in Democracy, 2006; Co-author: Public Policy Decision Making, 1972; author, editor: Methods of Rhetoric Criticism, 1972, 80, 90, Kenneth Burke and Contemporary European Thought, 1995; editor Speaker and Gavel, 1987; editor: Current Criticism, 1971; contbr. articles to profl. jours. Cpl. U.S. Army, 1955-57. Rsch. grantee Wayne State U., 1980. Mem. Speech Communication Assn. (legis. assembly 1988-91), Cen. States Communication Assn. (chair, vice-chair rhetoric and criticism 1981-83), Kenneth Burke Soc. (program planner conv. 1990-93), Phi Kappa Phi, Delta Sigma Rho-Tau Kappa Alpha. Democrat. Christian Scientist. Home: Novi, Mich. Died Mar. 31, 2006.

BROCKMAN, CHARLES THURSTON, retail executive; b. Indpls., Dec. 8, 1927; s. Charles C. and Dorothy (Hofer) B.; m. Zora Jacobs, Apr. 11, 1966; children: Elizabeth Boester, Robert P. Shields. BSCE with distinction, Purdue U., 1949. Sportscaster Sta. WXLW, Indpls., 1950-54, Sta. WIRE, Indpls., 1954-58; dir. pub. rels. U.S. Auto Club, Indpls., 1958-60; sportscaster Sta. WLW-TV, Indpls., 1960-65, ABC-TV, N.Y.C., 1961-66, MCA Telecast of Ind. 500, N.Y.C., 1964-70; pres. Brockman's Hallmark, Indpls., 1962-85, ret., 1985. Bd. dirs. Indpls. Raceway Park, 1963-79; mem. Mayor's Com. on Drunk Driving, Indpls., 1968-73. 1st lt. U.S. Army, 1949-56. Mem. Country Club of Indpls. (bd. dirs. 1975-78), U.S. Auto Club (bd. dirs. 1961—, pres. 1968-72). Republican. Mem. Christian Ch. Avocations: golf, computer research, stock market. Home: Indianapolis, Ind. Died Jan. 18, 2005.

BROCKMAN, DONALD CHARLES, engineering executive; b. Dixon, Ill., May 1, 1942; s. Walter Henry and Rita Theresa (Kent) B.; m. Carol Lynn Whitehill, Apr. 1, 1967 (div. July 1985); children: Eric Joseph, Amy Elizabeth; m. Mary Ellen O'Donnell, Feb. 22, 1986. B in Indsl. Engring., Gen. Motors Inst., Flint, Mich., 1965. Registered profl. engr., Mich., N.C., S.C., Fla. Foreman Chevrolet Motor div. Gen. Motors Corp., Janesville, Wis., 1960-66; sr. engr. Giffels Assocs., Southfield, Mich., 1966-69; v.p. ENGA, Troy, Mich., from 1969. Mem. Nat. Council Engring. Examiners, Engring. Soc. of Detroit (chmn. credentials com. 1976, 82, chmn. civic affairs com. 1986, constrn. activities com., 1987). Clubs: Atlas Valley Country (Grand Blanc, Mich.). Avocations: golf, hunting, fishing. Home: Drayton Plains, Mich. Died July 2, 2004.

BROCKMAN, STANLEY K., physician, cardiothoracic surgeon, educator; b. Boston, Oct. 11, 1928; s. Harry and Hinder Brockman; m. Yvonne K. Metoxen; children: Eric, Leslie Greenfield, Karen, Douglas. BS, Boston Coll., 1951;

MD, Boston U., 1955. Diplomate Am. Bd. Surgery, Am. Bd. Thoracic Surgery. Surgical intern The John Hopkins Hosp., Balt., 1955-56, asst. resident dept. surgery, 1956-57; sr. asst. surgeon Lab. Cardiovascular Physiology, The Nat. Heart Inst., USPHS, Bethesda, Md., 1957-59; asst. resident dept surgery Vanderbilt U. Hosp., Nashville, 1959-62, chief resident dept. surgery, 1962-63; asst. prof. surgery Vanderbilt U., Nashville, 1963-67, assoc. prof. medicine, 1967-68; dir. divsn. cardiothoracic surgery Michael Reese Med. Ctr., Chgo., 1968-73; assoc. prof. surgery U. Chgo., 1969-70, prof. surgery, 1970-73, Thomas Jefferson U., Phila., 1973-86; dir. thoracic surgical residency tgn. program Thomas Jefferson U. Hosp., Phila., 1974-86; dir. thoracic surgery residency program Hahnemann U. Hosp., Phila., 1986-96, prof. and chmn. dept. cardiothoracic surgery, 1986-96, pres. med. staff, 1992-94, exec. v.p., 1995-96; pres., dir. Likoff Cardiovascular Inst., 1991—98; dir. thoracic surg. resident Allegheny U. Hosp.-Ctr. City, 1996—98, prof., chair, 1996—98, exec. v.p., 1996—98. Editorial bd. Journal of Circulatory Shock, 1974-78; contbr. to profl. jours. Recipient Career Devel. award U.S. Pub. Health Svc., 1963-67; Harvey Cushing fellow The John Hopkins Hosp., 1956-57. Fellow Am. Coll. Cardiology, Am. Coll. Surgeons; mem. AMA, Am. Assn. Thoracic Surgery, Southern Thoracic Surgical Assn., Soc. Thoracic Surgeons, Soc. Vascular Surgery, Soc. Univ. Surgeons, Internat. Cardiovascular Soc., Am. Heart Assn., Southern Soc. Clin. Investigators, Chgo. Surgical Soc., Phila. Acad. Surgery, Pa. Heart Assn., Phila. County Med. Soc., Pa. Assn. Thoracic Surgery, Phila. Acad. Cardiology. Home: Narberth, Pa. Died Dec. 3, 2005.

BROCKMEIER, LOUIS BERRY, physician, consultant; b. Cin., May 13, 1949; s. Frederick and Elaine (Berry) B.; m. Barbara Lou Marple, Sept. 2, 1972; children: David Alexander, Louis Clayborn. AB, Williams Coll., 1971; MD, Ohio State U., 1974. Diplomate Am. Bd. Internal Medicine, Am. Bd. Cardiology. Intern U. Cin., 1974-75, resident, 1975-77, fellowship, 1977-79; staff cardiologist VA Hosp., Cin., 1979-80; pvt. practice Cin., from 1980. Vol. prof. internal medicine/cardiology U. Cin. Coll. Medicine, 1997—. Mem. wellness com. Cin. Pub. Schs., 1991-95; mem. ethics com. Episcopal Diocese of So. Ohio, Cin., 1992-95. Fellow ACP, Am. Coll. Cardiology (pvt. sector com. Ohio chpt. 1992—, legis. com. Ohio chpt. 1997—), Am. Coll. Chest Physicians; mem. AMA (mem. rep. assembly organized med. staff sect. 1994—), Am. Heart Assn. (fellow coun. on clin. cardiology), Ohio State Med. Assn. (ho. of dels. 1996—, vice chair organized med. staff sect. 1997—), Acad. Medicine Cin. (legis. com. 1988—, councillor 1995—), Cin. Soc. Internal Medicine (pres. 1993-94), Glendale Lit. Club (pres. 1993). Avocations: tennis, reading, photography. Home: Cincinnati, Ohio. Died Mar. 31, 2005.

BRODIE, STEVE, record and film production executive; b. Dobznn, Poland, Mar. 1, 1927; came to U.S., 1930; s. Ber and Ester (Schafran) B. Student, U. Rochester, 1947. Salesman Melody Record Distbrs., Buffalo, 1954-57; pres. Best Record Distbrs., Buffalo, 1958-73, Masters Releasing, Inc., N.Y.C., 1958-76, Tupper Pub., Los Angeles, from 1958, Olympic Film Ltd., Los Angeles, from 1976, Thunderbird Records, Los Angeles, from 1976. Pub. (song) Wild Weekend, 1960 (Song of Yr.). Mem. Simon Wiesenthal Holocaust Studies Ctr., Los Angeles, 1982. Served as pvt. U.S. Army, 1945-46, ETO. Recipient Top Ten Rack Jobber award Capitol Records, 1965; named Record Distbr. of Yr. Epic Records, 1967. Mem. Broadcast Music, Inc., ASCAP. Clubs: Hartford (London); Spoast Comm (Los Angeles). Avocations: photography, travel, collecting art. Died Mar. 12, 2004.

BRODL, RAYMOND FRANK, lawyer, consultant, lumber company executive; b. Cicero, Ill., June 1, 1924; s. Edward C. and Lillian (Cerny) B.; m. Ethel Jean Johnson, Aug. 15, 1953; children: Mark Raymond, Pamela Jean, Susan Marie. Student, Norwich U., Northfield, Vt., 1943, Ill. Coll., 1946-48; JD, Loyola U., Chgo., 1951. Bar: Ill. 1951. Atty. law office Joseph A. Ricker, Chgo., 1951-58, Brunswick Corp., Chgo., 1958-62; sec., gen. atty. Edward Hines Lumber Co., Chgo., 1962-84, atty., cons., from 1985, sr. counselor, 2001. Democratic candidate for local jud. office, 1953, 57. Served with AUS, 1943-46. Mem. Ill. Bar Assn. Died May 26, 2005.

BROMFIELD, JOHN FARRON, actor; b. South Bend, Ind., June 11, 1922; s. James Blain and Cecile Martha (Toner) B.; m. Mary Ellen Tillotson, May 5, 1965. Grad., St. Mary's Coll., Moraga, Calif., 1944. Ind. film and TV actor, 1947—2005. Host Chgo. Sportsman and Vacation Show, 1959-83 ann. Actor numerous films including The Furies, Rope of Sand, Sorry Wrong Number, Flat Top, Hot Cars, Revenge of the Creature From the Black Lagoon, Curucu, Crime Against Joe, Easy to Love, Ring of Fear, Hold That Line, Quin Cannon Fronteir Scout, Cimmeron Kid, Manfish, Harpoon, Fronteir Gambler, The Big Bluff, (TV series starring roles) The Sheriff of Cochise, The U.S. Marshall, Fire Side Theater, Schlitz Playhouse of Stars, (guest appearances) Ann Sothern Show, Marie Wilson Show, Lucy-Desi Show, Dick Clark Show, Bob Hope Specials (2), (host) Fisherman's World. Mem. New Bedford Port Soc. (life). Died Sept. 18, 2005.

BROOKE, GEORGE MERCER, JR., retired historian; b. Tokyo, Oct. 21, 1914; (parents Am. citizens); s. George Mercer and Isabel Elsie (Tilton) B.; m. Frances Fleming Bailey, June 13, 1942; children: George Mercer III, Marion Bailey Brooke Philpott. BA in Liberal Arts, Va. Mil. Inst., 1936; MA in History, Washington and Lee U., 1942; PhD in History, U. N.C., 1955. Spl. agent Md. Casualty Co., Balt., 1936-41; history instr. Va. Mil. Inst., Lexington, 1942-43, from asst. prof. to prof., 1948-80, prof. emeritus, from 1980; history instr. Washington & Lee U., Lexington, 1946-47. Author: John M. Brooke, Naval Scientist, 1980, General Lee's Church, 1984, John M. Brooke's Pacific Cruise, 1986; editor: Ironclads and Big Guns of the Confederacy: The Journal and Letters of John M. Brooke, 2002; contbr. numerous articles to profl. publs. Chmn. Citizen-Soldier Meml. Va. Mil. Inst., 1983-84, Sesquicentennial celebration, 1986-89; unit pres. Am. Cancer Soc., 1980-82; pres. Stonewall Jackson area coun. Boy Scouts Am., 1964-67. 1st lt. U.S. Army, 1943-46, PTO. Fulbright rsch. scholar Keio U., 1962-63; Fulbright teaching grantee Nat. Taiwan U., 1963; recipient Silver Beaver award Boy Scouts Am., 1967, Citizen-Scouter of Yr. award, 1989. Mem. SAR, So. Hist. Assn., Assn. for Preservation Va. Antiquities (br. pres. 1975-77), Soc. of the Cin. (standing com. 1984-87), Rockbridge Hist. Soc. (pres. 1960-62, author procs. 1989), English Speaking Union (br. pres. 1980-82), Soc. Mayflower Descs. in Commonwealth of Va., Internat. House of Japan, Am. Legion, Phi Beta Kappa, Kappa Alpha. Republican. Episcopalian. Avocations: travel, reading, walking. Home: Lexington, Va. Died June 16, 2006.

BROOKMAN, ANTHONY RAYMOND, lawyer; b. Chgo., Mar. 23, 1922; s. Raymond Charles and Marie Clara (Alberg) B.; m. Marilyn Joyce Brookman, June 5, 1982; children: Meribeth Brookman Farmer, Anthony Raymond, Lindsay Logan Christensen. Student, Ripon Coll., 1940-41; BS, Northwestern U., 1947; JD, U. Calif., San Francisco, 1953. Bar: Calif. 1954. Law clk. to presiding justice Calif. Supreme Ct., 1953-54; ptnr. Nichols, Williams, Morgan, Digardi & Brookman, 1954-68; sr. ptnr. Brookman & Talbot, Inc. (formerly Brookman & Hoffman, Inc.), Walnut Creek, Calif., 1969-92, Brookman & Talbot Inc., Sacramento, from 1992. Pres. Young Reps. Calif., San Mateo County, 1953-54. 1st lt. USAF. Mem. ABA, Alameda County Bar Assn., State Bar Calif., Lawyers Club Alameda County, Alameda-Contra Costa County Trial Lawyers Assn., Assn. Trial Lawyers Am., Calif. Trial Lawyers Assn., Athenian Nile Club, Masons, Shriners. Republican. Home: Walnut Creek, Calif. Died Dec. 6, 2005.

BROOKS, DORIS BLADE, music educator; b. Camden, N.J., Nov. 1, 1922; d. Emil John and Henrietta Evelyn (Nessen) Blade; m. George Edwin Humphries, Aug. 29, 1947 (div. Jan. 1966; dec.); m. Frederick Manning Brooks, June 3, 1967; children: Hope Carla Humphries, Douglas George Humpries, Randall John Humphries, Leigh Andrea Humphries (now Ariel H. Selano). BS in Music, West Chester State U., 1947, MEd, 1967; MMus, Temple U., 1970. Music demonstration tchr. Camden (N.J.) Bd. Edn., 1947-48; voice/piano tchr. Hegeman Sch. Music, Runnemede, N.J., 1947-67; music tchr. Pyne Poynt Jr. H.S., 1964-68; alto soloist Rodeph Shalom Synagogue, Elkins Park, 1967-80, Ch. of the Saviour, Phila., 1941-80; mem. chorus work Phila. Oratorio Choir, 1959-87; choral dir. Woodrow Wilson H.S., 1968-88; chorus mgr., program chair, state coord. N.J. State Opera Festival, 1978-82; bd. dirs., chair policy com. Camden Sch. Musical Arts Inc., 1997, mem. fundraising and mission statement com., 1997. Founder, pres., charter mem., exec. dir. Camden (N.J.) Sch. Musical Arts, 1986—; mem. com. Camden Carnegie Libr. Redevel. Corp., 1991-92; voice and piano tchr., 1986—. Dir. musical shows, stage prodns.; contbr. articles to profl. jours. Recipient plaque Camden County Cultural/Heritage Com., 1994, Diocese of Pa., Episcopal Ch., 1996. Mem. Phi Delta Gamma (1st and 2d, pres., treas. 1970-90) Democrat. Avocations: singing in choirs, writing a journal, fast walking, movies, gardening. Died June 20, 2005.

BROOKS, JEROME, English language educator, children's book writer; b. Chgo., July 17, 1931; s. Samuel and Rose (Malina) B.; m. Marilyn Glaser, May 27, 1956 (div. Nov. 1970); children: Eliot M. (dec.), Iris Judith (dec.), Elise Beth; m. Kathleen Tucker, Aug. 30, 1980. BA in English, Roosevelt U., 1953; MA in English, George Washington U., 1957. Asst. prof. Fenger Southwest Coll., Chgo., 1958-65, chmn. English dept., 1959-65; prof. English Richard J. Daley Coll., Chgo., 1970-89, Harry S. Truman Coll., Chgo., 1990-92; asst. to pres. Crane Coll., Chgo., 1965-66; dean urban edn. ctr. City Colls. Chgo., 1966-68; acting dean faculty Richard J. Daley Coll., Chgo., 1968-70. Lectr. fiction writing workshop pub. program U. Chgo., 1990—. Author: Uncle Mike's Boy, 1973, The Testing of C. Hammelman, 1977, The Big Dipper Marathon, 1979, Make Me a Hero (named among outstanding young adult novels 1980 ALA Booklist), Naked in Winter, 1990, French translation Ecole des Loisirs, Paris, 1992, Knee Holes, 1992 (Carl Sandburg Lit. award 1992). With U.S. Army, 1953-55. Named Disting. Prof., 1987-88; recipient Excellence in Teaching award U. Houston, 1989. Mem. Author's Guild, Soc. Midland Authors (bd. dirs.), Soc. Children's Book Writers, Children's Reading Round Table Chgo. Died May 28, 2004.

BROTEN, LARRY DUWAYNE, pharmacist; b. Hannaford, N.D., Nov. 25, 1942; s. Harold Vernon and Grace Mabel (Kolberg) B.; m. Patricia Joy Sanders, July 31, 1965; children: Debra, Daniel. BS in Pharmacy, N.D. State U., 1969; postgrad., U. Iowa, 1972-73. Registered pharmacist, Mich., Iowa, Ill., N.D. Dir. store planning Osco Drug, Franklin Park, Ill., 1971-72, asst. store mgr. Elgin, Ill., 1972, store mgr. Cedar Rapids, Iowa, 1972-73, Portage, Mich., 1973-82; staff pharmacist VA Med. Ctr., Battle Creek, Mich., 1982-86, asst. dir. pharmacy svcs., 1986-90, dir. pharmacy svc., from 1990. Adj. instr. Nazareth Coll., Kalamazoo, Mich., 1985, Ferris State U., Big Rapids, Mich., 1990—. With USN, 1962-68, Vietnam. Mem. VFW, Am. Soc. Hosp. Pharmacists, Western Mich. Soc. Hosp. Pharmacists, Sons of Norway. Avocations: woodcarving, woodworking, dog training, fishing, hunting. Home: Galesburg, Mich. Died Apr. 19, 2005.

BROUGHTON, ANNA MARTHA, special education educator; b. Buffalo, N.Y., July 23, 1957; d. Melvin Leo and Madolyn Irene (Royer) B.; m. Louie Ben Henderson, Aug. 18, 1980. BS in Spl. Edn., Mo. Valley Coll., 1979. Cert. spl. edn. tchr., Mo. Spl. edn. tch. Bosworth (Mo.) R-V Sch., 1979-91; spl. edn. tchr. grade 6 Moberly (Mo.) Middle Sch., 1992-93; spl. edn. tchr. grades 7-12 Braymer (Mo.) C-4 Sch., from 1993. Spl. edn. dir. Braymer C-4 Sch., 1994—; cmty. tchr. assn. pres. Bosworth R-5 Sch., 1988-90, chairperson profl. devel. com., 1988-91. Named to Women's Hall of Fame Mo. Valley Coll., 1979. Mem. Mo. State Tchrs. Assn., Coun. for Exceptional Children, Learning Disabilities Assn., Beta Sigma Phi, Gamma Sigma Sigma. Avocations: reading, traveling to historical sites, touring historical homes, collecting porcelain plates. Home: Bosworth, Mo. Died Jan. 10, 2004.

BROWN, ALAN PAUL, physician; b. Paterson, N.J., May 13, 1943; s. Max and Ruth (Saltzman) B.; m. Elizabeth Ann Lubis, Oct. 13, 1946; children: Michele Susan, Andrea Beth. Student, Rutgers U., 1963; MD, Temple U., 1967; postdoctorate, Mayo Grad. Sch. Medicine, 1970-71. Diplomate AM. Bd. Emergency Medicine. Intern Temple U. Hosp., Phila., 1967-68; resident in internal medicine Mayo Clinic, Rochester, Minn., 1970-71; physician Candler Gen. Hosp., Savannah, Ga., 1969-82, med. dir., 1981-82; physician St. Joseph's Hosp., Savannah, 1982-83; med. dir. No. Miss. Med. Ctr., Tupelo, from 1983, also med. dir. flight service. Med. dir. No. Miss. Regional Emergency Med. Service. Lt. comdr. USPHS, 1968-70. Fellow Am. Coll. Emergency Physicians; mem. AMA, No. Miss. Med. Soc. Avocations: car collecting, photography, coin collecting/numismatics. Home: Tupelo, Miss. Died June 9, 2005.

BROWN, ALLAN HARVEY, biological scientist; b. Newark, Sept. 14, 1917; s. Harvey Winfield and Emma Cecil (Abbot) B.; m. Helen Somers, June 14, 1941 (dec. June 1980); children: Bonnie, Kenneth, Janice. BS, U. Md., 1939; MS, U. Rochester, 1941, PhD in Botany, 1944; MS (hon.), U. Pa., Phila. Grad. asst. U. Rochester, N.Y., 1939-42, rsch. asst. in physiology Sch. Medicine and Dentistry N.Y., 1942-44; staff mem. Radiation Lab. MIT, 1944-45; rsch. assoc. chemistry dept. Fels Fund U. Chgo., 1945-47; asst. prof., assoc. prof., prof. botany U. Minn., 1947-63, chmn. dept., 1957-60; prof. biology U. Pa., Phila., from 1963, chmn. dept., 1963-68; dir. Gravitational Plant Physiology Lab. U. City Sci. Ctr., 1972-93. Mem. exec. com. divsn. biology and agr. NRC, 1963-68; bd. trustees Biol. Abstracts, 1966-71, bd. pres., 1971; mem. space sci. bd. NRC, 1962-72; exec. mem. COSPAR Sub-Commn. on Gravitational Biology, 1984-88; mem. Internat. Union of Physiological Scis. Commn. on Gravitational Physiology; mem. NSF Panel for Molecular Biology, 1954-58, NSF Panel for Life Scis. Facilities, 1961-62; cons. NASA, 1961-72; mem. Pa. Gov.'s Sci. Adv. Com., 1965-70; mem. Am. Inst. Biol. Sci./NASA Planetry Quarantine Panel, 1972-75. Editor Plant Physiology, 1957-62; editor Harper and Row series of monographs, 1954-60; mem. editorial bd. Ann. Rev. Plant Physiology, 1962-66. Guggenheim Found. fellow, 1956-57. Fellow AAAS; mem. Am. Inst. Biol. Scis. (adv. com. for Office Naval Rsch. 1953-58), Am. Soc. Plant Physiologists, Bot. Soc. Am., European Low Gravity Rsch. Assn., Japanese Soc. Plant Physiologists, Am. Soc. Gravitational and Space Biology (pres. 1985), Internat. Acad. Astronautics, Sigma Xi. Home: Albuquerque, N.Mex. Died May 24, 2004.

BROWN, CAROLYN SUE, clinical nurse specialist; b. Hobbs, N.Mex., Apr. 18, 1951; BS in Biology, Okla. State U., Stillwater, 1973; BSN, Calif. State U., Chico, 1988; MN, La. State U., 1988. Clin. nurse specialist La.; cert. ACLS instr., cert. BLS instr.; cert. critical care RN. Staff nurse/3-11 charge nurse Samuel Merritt Hosp., Oakland, Calif., 1978-83; staff nurse Jo Ellen Smith Hosp., New Orleans, 1984-86, day charge nurse, 1986-87, staff nurse part-time, 1987-90; nurse clinician part-time O'Neill Surg. Group, Marrero, La., 1988-89; instr. LSUMC Sch. Nursing, New Orleans, 1989-90; staff level III coronary care unit Emory U. Hosp., Atlanta, 1990-91, staff level IV, 1991-93; clin. nurse specialist cardiology Emory U. System of Health Care, Atlanta, from 1993. Presenter in field. Contbr. articles to profl. jours. Recipient Great One Hundred Nurse award New Orleans Dist. Nurses Assn., 1988. Mem. AACN (Atlanta chpt. program com. 1992—, Greater New Orleans chpt. bd. dirs. 1989-90, interim recording sec. 1990), Sigma Theta Tau (Epsilon Nu chpt.). Avocations: cooking, gardening, hiking, bird watching. Home: Decatur, Ga. Died July 21, 2005.

BROWN, CHARLES EARL, lawyer; b. Columbus, Ohio, June 6, 1919; s. Anderson and Ruth (Keeran) B.; m. Mary Elizabeth Hiett, May 23, 1959; children: Douglas Charles, Rebecca Ruth. AB, Ohio Wesleyan U., 1941; JD, U. Mich., 1949. Bar: Ohio 1949. Pvt. practice, Toledo; assoc. Zachman, Boxell, Bebout & Torbet, 1950-53; ptnr. Brown, Baker, Schlageter & Craig (and predecessors), 1953-90, of counsel, 1990-95, Shindler, Neff, Holmes & Schlageter, from 1996. Chmn. steering and exec. coms. Auto Trim Wholesalers div. Automotive Service Industry Assn.,

1960-68 Lucas County Rep. Exec. Com., 1968-92; trustee, sec. Joseph J. and Marie P. Schedel Found., 1963-93, pres., 1993—. Capt. AUS, 1941-46; col. Res. ret. Decorated Bronze Star; recipient John J. Pershing award U.S. Army Command and Gen. Staff Coll., 1963 Fellow Am. Bar Found. (state chmn. 1978-84), Ohio State Bar Found. (trustee 1987-92), Am. Coll. Trust and Estate Counsel; mem. ABA, Ohio Bar Assn. (bd. govs. real property sect. 1953-76, coun. of dels. 1973-84, exec. com. 1984-87), Toledo Bar Assn. (past mem. exec. com.), Sixth Cir. Jud. Conf. (life), Toledo Area C. of C. (past trustee, com. chmn.), Res. Officers Assn., Assn. U.S. Army, Phi Beta Kappa. Congregationalist (past chmn. trustees). Lodge: Masons (32 deg.). Home: Toledo, Ohio. Died June 4, 2005.

BROWN, CHARLES FREEMAN, II, lawyer; b. Boston, Mar. 7, 1914; s. Arthur Harrison and Nellie Abigail (Kenney) B.; m. Caroline Gotzian Tighe, Nov. 12, 1949 (dec. Jan. 1951); m. Pamela Judith Wedd, Nov. 29, 1952; children— Penelope Susan, Nicholas Wedd. AB, Harvard U., 1936, LL.B., 1941. Bar: Mass. 1941. Assoc. atty. Sherburne, Powers & Needham, Boston, 1941-43; asst. gen. counsel, gen. counsel OSRD, Washington, 1943-47; counsel rsch. and devel. bd. and mil. liaison com. US Dept. Def., rep. govt. patents bd., counsel Def. Prodn. Bd., dep. asst. sec. gen. for prodn. and logistics NATO detailed from Washington, London, Paris, 1947-53; asst. to pres. Hydrofoil Corp., Annapolis, Md., 1953-54; asso. gen. counsel CIA, Washington, 1954-60; v.p., treas. Sci. Engring. Inst., Waltham, Mass., 1960-66; dep. gen. counsel NSF, Washington, 1966-73, gen. counsel, 1973-76, chmn. interim compliance panel, 1970-71. Cons., 1976—2006 Trustee Belmont (Mass.) Day Sch., 1963-66; bd. dirs. Hillcrest Children's Ctr., Washington, 1978-87, pres., 1980-83; pres. Cleveland Park Book Club, 1980-83, 91-94; bd. dirs. Cleveland Park Hist. Soc. Recipient Disting. Service award NSF. Mem. Fed. Bar Assn., Cosmos Club. Died Mar. 21, 2006.

BROWN, DAVID LEWIS, lawyer; b. Phila., Aug. 9, 1952; s. Willard W. and Eileen N. (Biener) B. BA, Lehigh U., 1974; JD, Georgetown U., 1977; LLM in Taxation, Temple U., 1980. Bar: Pa. 1977, U.S. Dist. Ct. (ea. dist.) Pa. 1983, U.S. Ct. Appeals (3d cir.) 1983, U.S. Tax Ct. 1981. Ptnr. E.T. Feierstein Assocs., Phila., from 1979. V.p. Lehigh Young Dems., Bethlehem, Pa., 1973-74. Mem. Internat. Assn. Jewish Lawyers and Jurists, Phila. Trial Lawyers Assn., Phila. Bar Assn., Pa. Trial Lawyers assn., Pa. Bar Assn., Assn. Trial Lawyers Am., Meridian Club (bd. dirs. 1988—), Kiwanis (sec.-treas. Germantown chpt. 1984-87, treas. Jenkintown chpt. 1991-96,, 2001—, v.p. 1996-98, pres. 1998-99). Democrat. Avocations: contract bridge, athletics, coin collecting/numismatics. Home: Oreland, Pa. Died Oct. 29, 2004.

BROWN, ELIZABETH A., librarian, multi-media specialist; b. Greensburg, Ind., Dec. 18, 1952; d. Robert Dale Brown and Rachel Hannah Taylor. BA, Purdue U., 1975, MS, 1982; MLS, Ind. U., 1985. Lic. sch. libr. scis. and audiovisual svcs. K-12 Ind. Tchr. Michigan City (Ind.) Area Schs., 1975-76; sch. libr. media specialist Valparaiso (Ind.) HS, from 1976. Coach speech and debate Valparaiso HS, 1989—96. Author: (book) Copyright and You, 1997. Advisor Model UN, 1990—96; mem. Friends of Ind. Dunes. Mem.: NEA, AAUW, ALA, Assn. Am. Sch. Librs., Assn. Ind. Media Educators, Friends of Ind. Dunes, Sierra Club, Alpha Delta Kappa. Avocations: hiking, travel, reading. Home: Valparaiso, Ind. Died Sept. 4, 2004.

BROWN, FRED, virologist; b. Clayton, Eng., Jan. 31, 1925; s. Fred and Jane Ellen (Fielding) B.; m. Audrey Alice Doherty, May 1, 1948; children: Roger, David. ScB in Chemistry, U. Manchester, Eng., 1944, MSc, 1946, PhD, 1948; DSc (hon.), Queen's U., Belfast, Ireland, 1992. Asst. lectr. U. Manchester, 1946-48; lectr. U. Bristol, Eng., 1948-50; sr. sci. officer Hannah Dairy Research Inst., Scotland, 1950-53; sr. research assoc. Christie Hosp., Manchester, 1953-55; head biochemistry Animal Virus Research Inst., Pirbright, Eng., 1955-83; head virology Wellcome Found., Kent, Eng., 1983-90; adj. prof. Yale U., New Haven, 1990-95; former vis. scientist USDA. Editor-in-chief: Jour. Gen. Virology, 1975-80; contbr. sci. papers to various jours. and chpts. to books. Fellow Royal Soc. London (v.p.), Inst. Biology; mem. Soc. Gen. Microbiology (v.p.), Internat. Union Microbiological Socs. Avocations: football, cricket, walking. Home: Old Saybrook, Conn. Died Feb. 20, 2004.

BROWN, GEORGE LESLIE, legal association administrator, consultant, retired manufacturing executive, former lieutenant governor; b. Lawrence, Kans., July 1, 1926; s. George L. and Harriett Alberta (Watson) B.; m. Modeen; children: Gail Brown Chandler, Laura Nicole, Kim Doreen, Cynthia Renee; stepchildren: Ronnie, Carol, Angela, Sharolyn, Nyra. BJ, U. Kans., 1950; postgrad., U. Colo., 1950-51; A.M.P., Harvard Bus. Sch., 1980. Mem. writing staff Denver Post, 1950-65; asst. exec. dir. Denver Housing Authority, 1965-69; exec. dir. Met. Denver Urban Coalition, 1969-75; lt. gov. State of Colo., Denver, 1974-79; v.p. Grumman Corp., N.Y., 1979-90; assoc. Whitten & Diamond (formerly Lipsen, Whitten & Diamond), Washington, 1990-94; dir. Prudential Securities, 1994-97; of counsel Moser and Moser Law Firm, from 1994; v.p. L. Robert Kimball, Archtl. Engrs.; sr. v.p. Greenwich Ptnrs. Bd. dirs. Davis and Elkins Coll., Washington Trade Ctr., Joint Ctr. for Polit. Studies, Boys Choir of Harlem, Coll. Aeros., Air Force Meml. Found. Mem. Colo. Ho. of Reps., 1955, Colo. Senate, 1956-74. Served with USAAF, 1944-46. Recipient Adam Clayton Powell award for polit. achievement, 1975, Opportunities Industrialization Center Nat. Govt. award, 1975; George Brown Urban Journalism scholarship established at U. Kans. William Allen White Sch. Journalism, 1976 Mem. Kappa Alpha Psi. Home: Arlington, Va. Died Mar. 31, 2006.

BROWN, HARRY JOE, JR., real estate developer; b. Beverly Hills, Calif., Sept. 1, 1934; s. Harry Joe Brown and Sally (Eilers); m. Karen Somerville (div.); 1 child, Morgan; m. Katherine Nelson (div.); 1 child, Esme. Studied at, Yale U., Oxford U. Head, develop. 20th Century Fox; pres. Brown Co., NYC. Writer: movie Duffy; prodr.: (plays) Zoo Story, Krapp's Last Tape; co-author (with Richard Meier and Alastair Gordon): (book) American Dream: The Houses at Sagaponac: Modern Living in the Hamptons, 2003. Recipient won final, Paradise Island Pro-Am Backgammon Competition. Achievements include initiating the residential development of "The Houses at Sagaponac" in Southhampton, Long Island, NY. Died Nov. 23, 2005.

BROWN, JACK HAROLD UPTON, physiologist, biomedical engineer, academic administrator; b. Nixon, Tex., Nov. 16, 1918; s. Gilmer W. and Thelma (Patton) B.; m. Jessie Carolyn Schulz, Apr. 14, 1943. BS, S.W. Tex. State U., 1939; Master's degree, U. Tex., 1939—41; PhD, Rutgers U., 1948. Lectr. physics Southwest Tex. State U., San Marcos, 1943—44; instr. physics Rutgers U., New Brunswick, NJ, 1944—45, rsch. assoc., 1944—48; lectr. U. Pitts., 1948—50; head biol. scis. Mellon Inst., Pitts., 1948—50; asst. prof. physiology U. N.C., Chapel Hill, 1950—52; scientist Oak Ridge Inst. Nuclear Studies, 1952; assoc. prof. physiology Emory U. Med. Sch., Atlanta, 1952—58, prof., 1959—60, acting chmn. dept. physiology, 1958—60; lectr. physiology George Washington U. and Georgetown U. med. schs., Washington, 1960—65; exec. sec. biomed. engring. and physiology tng. coms. Nat. Inst. Gen. Med. Scis., NIH, Bethesda, Md., 1960—62; chief spl. rsch. br. div. Rsch. Facilities and Resources NIH, 1962—63, acting chief gen. clin. rsch. ctrs. br., 1963—64, asst. dir. ops. Div. Research Facilities and Resources, 1964—65; acting program dir. pharmacology/toxicology program Nat. Inst. Gen. Med. Scis., NIH, 1966—70, asst. dir. ops., 1965—66, assoc. dir. sci. programs, 1967—70, acting dir., 1970; spl. asst. to adminstr. Health Services and Mental Health Adminstrn., USPHS, Rockville, Md., 1971—72; assoc. dep. adminstr. for devel. Health Svcs. and Mental Health Adminstrn., USPHS, 1972—73; spl. asst. to adminstr. Health Resources Adminstrn., 1973—78; coord. Southwest Rsch. Consortium, San Antonio, 1974—78; prof. physiology U. Tex. Med. Sch., San Antonio, 1974—78; prof. environ. scis. U. Tex. at San Antonio, 1974—78; adj. prof. health svcs. adminstrn. Trinity U., 1975—78; assoc. provost rsch. and advanced edn. U. Houston, 1978—80, prof. biology, 1980—89, prof. emeritus, from 1990; adj. prof. U. Tex. Sch. Public Health, from 1978; prof. public adminstrn. Tex. Women's U., from 1978; adj. prof. community medicine Baylor Coll. Medicine, Houston, 1986—89; vice-chmn. SCORE (Svc. Corps of Retired Execs.), 1993—96; chmn., dist. dir., 1997—2003; regional editor Savant, 1996—2000, dist. mgr., 1997—2002; 69686. Fulbright lectr. U. Rangoon, 1950; cons. health systems WHO, Oak Ridge Inst. Nuc. Studies, Lockhead Aircraft Co., Drexel Inst. Tech., NASA, Vassar Coll., TelTech; mem. adv. bd. Ctr. for Cancer Therapy, San Antonio, 1974—, TelTech; bd. dirs. South Tex. Health Edn. Ctr.; cons. Univ. Tex. Health Sci. Ctr., Houston, Sumitomo Corp., Tokyo; rschr., instr. in radar U.S. Army, Scott Field, Ill. Author: Physiology of Man in Space, 1963, Basic Endocrinology, 1966, 2d edit., 1970, (with S.B. Barker) Future Goals of Engineering in Biology and Medicine, 1968, Advances in Biomedical Engineering, vol. II, 1972, vols. III, IV, 1973, vol. V, 1974, vol. VI, 1976, Vol. VII, 1978, (with J.E. Jacobs and L.E. Stark) Biomedical Engineering, 1972, (with D.E. Gann) Engineering Principles in Physiology, vols. I, II, 1973, The Health Care Dilemma, 1977, Integration and Control of Biol. Processes, 1978, Politics and Health Care, 1978, Telecommunications in Health Care, 1981, Management in Health Care Systems, 1983, A Laboratory Manual in Animal Physiology, 1984, 3d edit., 1988, High Cost of Healing, 1985, (with J. Comolo) Productivity in Health Care Systems, 1987, Guide to Collecting Fine Prints, 1989, Educating for Excellence, 1991, Footsteps in Sci., 1993, Revisions of Starting and Running a Small Business, 1994, Science and Society, 2002; editor: (with Ferguson) Blood and Body Functions, 1966, (with Miller) Exercise Physiology, 1966, Life Into Space, (Wunder), 1968, Nonprofit Institutions, 2002, Scence and the Scientific Society, 2002; contbr. numerous articles on biomed. engring. to sci. jours. Mem. adv. bd. San Antonio Mus. Assn.; mem. spl. effects com. Tex. Sesquicentennial; bd. dirs. Inst. for Health Policy, U. Tex. Health Sci. Ctr. With USN, 1941—42. Recipient cert. appreciation NIH, 1969, 1st pl. award Atlanta Internat. Film Festival, 1970, Achievement award NASA, 1977, spl. team award NASA, 1978, recognition award Emergency Med. Care, 1980, Best Tchr. award Nat. Mortar Bd., 1986, Most Disting. Alumni award S.W. Tex. State U., 1986; Gerard Swope fellow Gen. Electric Co., 1946-48; Fulbright grantee, 1950; Dept. of Def. grantee, 1950-52; NIH grantee, 1950-60; Cancer Soc. grantee, 1958; Damon Runyon Cancer award grantee, 1959; Dept. Energy grantee, 1980-81; NASA grantee, 1987-89. Fellow AAAS, Nat. Acad. Engring., IEEE (life, joint com. engring. in medicine and biology 1966—); mem. Am. Chem. Soc. (sr.), Biomed. Engring. Soc. (founder; pres. 1969-70, dir. 1968-69), Inst. Radio Engrs. (nat. sec. profl. group biomed. engring. 1962-64), N.Y. Acad. Scis., Endocrine Soc., Am. Physiol. Soc. (com. mem. 1959-63, nat. com. on animals in rsch. 1985—), Tex. Print Soc. (founder, pres.), Soc. for Exptl. Biology and Medicine, Svc. Corps Ret. Execs. (vice chmn. 1994-95, chmn. 1995—, dist. mgr. 1996-2002), Sigma Xi (rsch. award 1961, founder, pres. Alamo chpt. 1977-78), Coun. Biology Editors, Soc. Rsch. Adminstrn., Pi Kappa Delta, Phi Lambda Upsilon, Alpha Chi. Clubs: Cosmos. Achievements include invention of of the capsule manometer; respirator for small animals and basal metabolic apparatus for small animals; dust sampler; apparatus for partitioning human lung volumes; laser credit card patient record system; Warburg apparatus calibrator. Home: San Antonio, Tex. Died Oct. 7, 2004.

BROWN, JAMES, financial investment executive; b. Chgo., June 22, 1919; s. James Wilson and Mabel (Brodie) B.; m. Margaret Walter, Oct. 26, 1951; children: Matthew, Joshua, Margaret. AB in Acctg., U. Ill., 1941; MBA, Harvard U., 1947. Acct. Coopers & Lybrand, Chgo., 1941-42; research asst. Harvard Bus. Sch., Boston, 1947-48; investment mgr. Hale & Dorr, Boston, 1949-52, Richardson Vick, N.Y.C., 1952-55; propr. James Brown Cons., N.Y.C., 1956-67; chmn., pres. James Brown Inc., Greenwich, Conn., from 1968, also trustee of retirement trust, from 1968. Served to capt. U.S. Army, 1942-46. Republican. Presbyterian. Avocations: architecture, gardening. Died Nov. 23, 2004.

BROWN, JODI, school nurse; b. Washington, Pa., Sept. 17, 1957; d. Robert and Emma Jean (Turney) Forringer; m. Robert Brown, June 10, 1978; 1 child, Jennifer Ann. Diploma, Cooper Med. Ctr. Sch. Nursing, Camden, N.J., 1978. RN, Va. Psychiat. nurse Camden County Hosps., Lakeland, N.J., Burlington County Meml. Hosp., Mt. Holly, N.J.; sch. nurse Spotsylvania County, Spotsylvania, Va. Mem. policy com. Camden County Hosps. Home: Spotsylvania, Va. Died June 27, 2005.

BROWN, JOHN WILLIAM, truck and trailer dealer; b. Chambersburg, Pa., Jan. 15, 1922; s. C. Earl and Frances S. (Skinner) B.; m. Mildred L. Greenawalt, Oct. 24, 1942; children: Barbara A., Ronald E. Student, Harrisburg (Pa.) Jr. Coll., 1942, Pa. State U., Harrisburg, 1942. Bookkeeper, parts mgr. C. Earl Brown, Inc., Chambersburg, 1945-65, pres. Chambersburg, York, Pa., Hagerstown, Md., from 1965. Bd. chmn. Pa. Truck Dealers. Bd. chmn. C.V. sect. Soc. Automotive Engrs., Hagerstown, Md., 1979-80; bd. dirs. Chambersburg Area Devel. Corp. Staff sgt. U.S. Army, 1942-45, ETO. Mem. Pa. Motor Truck Assn., Md. Motor Truck Assn. (past bd. dirs.), Va. Motor Truck Assn., Pa. Farmers Assn., Pa. Horticulture Soc., Chambersburg C. of C. (bd. dirs.), Rotary, VFW, Elks, Am. Legion, Marine Corps League, Amvets. Republican. Avocations: woodwroking, antique trucks, hunting, gardening. Home: Chambersburg, Pa. Died Feb. 21, 2004.

BROWN, JOY MOSS, oncological nurse; b. Pewee Valley, Ky., Nov. 15, 1949; BA in Psychology, Milligan Coll., 1970; ADN, El Camino Coll., 1983. RN, Calif.; oncology cert. nurse. Nurse cardio-pulmonary unit Harbor-UCLA Med. Ctr., Torrance, Calif., 1984-87; oncology nurse Centinela Hosp. Med. Ctr., Inglewood, Calif., 1987-98, Kaiser Infusion Ctr., Riverside, Calif., from 1999. BLS instr. Am. Heart Assn., Wildomar, 1985—; freefall photographer, Wildomar, 1991—; skydiving instr., Wildomar, 1994—; nurse cons., 1995—; mem. NCLEX rev. panel Nat. RN Bd. Exam. Rev., Princeton, N.J., 1998. Photographer still photos underwater (2nd Place award 1986, 1st Place award 1988), still photos skydiving (2nd Place award 1993); contbr. articles to profl. jours. Mem. U.S. Parachute Assn. (cert. jumpmaster, profl. exhbn. skydiver). Avocations: skydiving, scuba diving, sailing, swimming. Home: Wildomar, Calif. Died Nov. 3, 2004.

BROWN, PAUL FREDERICK, lawyer; b. Ballston Spa, N.Y., July 13, 1931; s. Paul Edgar and Theresa Margaret (Sautter) B.; m. Ifigenia Theodore, Sept. 16, 1956; 1 child, Paul Darrow. BA, Utica Coll. of Syracuse U., 1953; LLB, JD, Syracuse Law Sch., 1957. Bar: N.Y. 1958, U.S. Dist. Ct. (no. dist.) N.Y. 1960, U.S. Ct. Appeals (2d cir.) 1962. Asst. atty. gen. N.Y. State Atty. Gen.'s Office, Albany, 1957-60; town atty. Town of Milton, Ballston Spa, 1960-72 and from 87, supr., 1972-82; chmn. bd. suprs. Saratoga County, Ballston Spa, 1978; ptnr. Brown, Brown & Peterson, Ballston Spa, from 1958. Bd. dirs. Saratoga County Econ. Devel. Corp., Saratoga Springs, N.Y. Town chmn. Town of Milton Rep. Party, 1991—. Mem. ABA, N.Y. State Bar Assn., Saratoga County bar Assn. (mem. exec. com. 1985—, pres. 1985). Avocations: music, fishing, gardening. Home: Ballston Spa, NY. Died Dec. 10, 2004.

BROWN, PHILLIP EDWARD, retired lawyer; b. Portland, Oreg., July 22, 1927; s. Rowland Seth and Bernice Edna (Soule) B.; m. Patricia Diane Flood, June 28, 1952; children: Deborah Anne Brown Robinson, Christopher A., Michael A., Timothy A., Emily A. Student, Oreg. State Coll., 1944-46, George Washington U., 1945, Fu Jen U., 1945; BA, Stanford U., 1949, JD, 1952. Bar: Calif. 1953, U.S. Dist. Ct. (no. dist.) Calif. 1953, U.S. Ct. Appeals (9th cir.) 1953. Assoc. Hoberg & Finger, San Francisco, 1952-58; ptnr. Hoberg, Finger, Brown & Abramson, San Francisco, 1958-75, Hoberg, Finger, Brown, Cox & Molligan P.C., San Francisco, 1975-89. Lectr. Stanford U., U. Calif. San Francisco, 1965-88. Served with USMC, 1945-46, CBI. Fellow Internat. Acad. Trial Lawyers, Am. Coll. Trial Lawyers; mem. Am Bd. Trial Advocates (pres. San Francisco chpt. 1980-81), San Francisco Trial Lawyers Assn.

(pres. 1970-71), Trader Brown soc. Democrat. Methodist. Avocations: carpentry, electrical, plumbing, tile setting. Home: San Rafael, Calif. Died Nov. 9, 2004.

BROWN, RANDALL EMORY, geologist; b. Eugene, Oreg., May 28, 1917; s. Percy Walker and Zula (Correll) B.; m. Helene Kerr, Jan. 21, 1950; children: Derek Jeffrey, Kevin Randall. AB, Stanford U., 1938; MA, Yale U., 1941. Registered geologist. Chief sampler, resident geologist M.A. Hanna Co., Darrington, Wash., 1941; geologist Oreg. Dept. Geology and Mineral Industries, Portland, 1941-42, U.S. Geol. Survey, 1942-45, U.S. Army, Corps Engrs., Portland, 1945-47, Gen. Electric Co. Hanford Works, Richland, Wash., 1947-65; sr. rsch. scientist Battelle Meml. Inst., Richland, 1965-71; asst. prof. Cen. Wash. U., Ellensburg, Wash., 1971-72; instr. Columbia Basin Coll., Pasco, Wash., 1972-73; cons. Pasco, from 1973. Panelist radio and TV sci. program Hanford Sci. Forum, 1954, 56. Contbr. articles to profl. jours. Asst. supr. Franklin County Conservation Dist., Pasco, 1972—. Fellow AAAS, Geol. Soc. Am.; mem. Assn. Ground Water Scientists and Engrs., Nat. Water Well Assn., N.W. Sci. Assn. (pres. 1969-70), Sigma Xi. Republican. Episcopalian (lay reader). Home: Pasco, Wash. Died Mar. 17, 2005.

BROWN, REBECCA ANN, French educator; b. Springfield, Ohio, Dec. 13, 1952; d. Russell Raymond and Virginia Grace (Ingels) Schulte; m. Keith Daniel Brown, June 19, 1976; 1 child, Michael Joseph. BA, Ohio Dominican Univ., 1975; MA, Coll. Mt. St. Joseph, 1988. Cert. tchr. Ohio. Tchr. English Pleasant High Sch., Marion, Ohio, 1975-80, tchr. French, from 1975, advisor fgn. travel with students, from 1976; advisor Nat. Hon. Soc., from 2000. Mem. Ohio Edn. Assn., Ohio Fgn. Lang. Assn., Pleasant Assn. Tchrs. (pres. 1980-81). Avocations: travel, reading, music, art, photography. Home: Delaware, Ohio. Died Aug. 24, 2004.

BROWN, SHELBY JEAN BAILEY, lay worker; b. Gary, W.Va., July 21, 1947; d. Irvin and Hannah (Kennedy) Roberts; m. Garry Lee Bailey, Nov. 9, 1963 (wid. May 1982); children: Patricia Lynn, Larry Lee, Melissa Pauline; m. Freddie L. Brown, June 13, 1992. BA, Bluefield State Coll., 1986; MA, U. W.Va., 1990. Cert. elem. edn. tchr., K-8, specific learning disabilities tchr./spl. edn. K-12, W.Va. Sec./treas. Bethel Assembly of God, Kimball, W.Va., 1965-78, youth dir., 1968-78, Rolfe Pentecostal Holiness Ch., Northfork, W.Va., 1990; tchr. Sunday sch. Bethel Assembly of God and Rolfe Pentecostal Holiness Chs., 1965-91. Sch. tchr. McDowell County Bd. of Edn., Welch, W.Va., 1986-93. Sponsor Fellowship of Christian Students Club, Elkhorn Jr. High, Northfork, W.Va., 1989-91. Home: Christiansburg, Va. Died Jan. 25, 2005.

BROWN, THOMAS ARCHER, artist; b. N.Y.C., Dec. 13, 1917; s. Lowell Huntington and Constance (McKelvey) B.; m. Katherine Jones, Dec. 16, 1940; children: Sara Stuart, Connie Pretti. Student, U. Laussane, Switzerland, N.Y. Sch. Fine and Applied Art, Colorado Springs Fine Arts Ctr, Colo. Represented at The Crespi Gallery, N.Y.C., Little Studio Ltd., N.Y.C., Liona Duncan Gallery, N.Y.C., Sante Fe Art Festival, The Paint Pot, Santa Fe, Contemporayy Art Gallery, N.Y.C., Paull Five Gallery, L.A., The Barn Gallery, Sante Fe, Greenville (S.C.) Mus. Art, Telfair Acad., Savanna, Ga., Ga. Mus. Art, Athens, The Morse Gallery Art, Winter Park, Fal., Fla. Union, Gainesville, Collectors of Am. Art, N.Y.C., William R. Mayer, Riverdale, N.Y.C., others. With U.S. Army, 1945-46. Avocations: sailing, tennis. Home: Santa Fe, N.Mex. Died June 20, 2005.

BROWN, VICTOR HATFIELD, financial executive; b. Phila., Sept. 17, 1929; s. Geary Briwn and Blanche B. (Hatfield) Brown; m. Joan A. Hewitt, Jan. 22, 1955; children: Cynthia Joan, Douglas Victor; 1 child, Paul Arthur. BS in Econ., U. Pa., 1951; MBA, U. Pa., 1954; PhD, U. Buffalo, 1957. Acct. Charles S. Rockey & Co., Phila., 1951—53; instr. acctg. U. Pa., 1953—54; internal auditor Bur. Audits City of Phila., 1954; chmn. acct. dept. U. Buffalo, 1954—58; ptnr. Touche Ross & Co., N.Y.C., 1958—71; contr., v.p. Amoco Corp., Chgo., 1971—81; exec. v.p., chief fin. officer Firestone Tire & Rubber Co., Akron, Ohio, 1981—82; mem. Fin. Acct. Stds. Bd., Norwalk, Conn., 1983—93; prof. George Mason U., Fairfax, Va., 1993—99. Contbr. articles to prof. jours. Mem.: Fin. Execs. Inst. Club Econ., Inst. Mgmt. Accts., Am. Acctg. Assn., Am. Inst. CPA's. Home: Oakton, Va. Died Sept. 11, 2006.

BROWN, WEIR MESSICK, international economist; b. Brighton, Ill., Jan. 27, 1914; s. Spencer Gilson and Nellie Rebecca (Messick) B.; m. Vivian Virginia Bauer, Apr. 24, 1942 (dec. Dec. 1981); children: Suzan L. Meves, Peter D.G. Brown; m. Maxine Glad Stewart, June 4, 1983. AB in Econs., Oberlin Coll., 1936; AM in Econs., Brown U., 1938, PhD in Econs., 1941. Various economist positions, 1938-48; with U.S. Dept. of the Treasury, Washington, 1948; fin. adviser U.S. Marshall Plan mission to the Netherlands The Hague, the Netherlands, 1949-51; chief European div. U.S. Dept. of the Treasury, Washington, 1951-52; fin. attache, Treasury rep. Am. Embassy, Bonn, Fed. Republic Germany, 1952-60; from dep. chief to acting chief U.S. mission Orgn. for Econ. Cooperation and Devel., Paris, 1961-74; fed. exec. fellow The Brookings Inst., Washington, 1974-75; inspector gen. for internat. fin. U.S. Dept. of the Treasury, Washington, 1975-80; pvt. practice econ. cons. Washington, from 1981. Guest scholar The Brookings Inst., Washington, 1985-91; cons. Atlantic Coun. U.S., Washington, 1977-83, U.S. Dept. State, Washington, 1986; vis. prof. econs. dept. U. Ill., Urbana, 1975. Author: Keeping the Central Bank Central, 1987, Bank Lending to Business Borrowers, 1992; contbr. articles to econ. jours., 1948-80; mem. of panel, published reports Atlantic Coun., 1979-83. Mem. steering com. Friends of Music at Smithsonian, Washington, 1982—; mem. bd. Friday Morning Music Club, Washington, 1984-88. Lt. (j.g.) USNR, 1943-46. Recipient Exceptional Svc. award Dept. Treasury, 1974; rsch. fellow Brookings Instn., 1940-41, Social Sci. Rsch. Coun. fellow, 1941. Mem. Am. Econ. Assn., Nat. Economists Club, Cosmos Club. Democrat. Avocations: music, hiking, travel, tennis. Home: Washington, DC. Died May 27, 2004.

BROWNE, HARRY, writer, financial planner; b. NYC, June 17, 1933; s. Edson Bradford and Cecil Margaret (Davis) B.; m. Gloria Frances Maxwell, June 9, 1953 (div. 1964); 1 child, Autumn Lee; m. Pamela Lanier Wolfe, Nov. 2, 1985. Grad. high sch., Van Nuys, Calif. Various sales and advt. positions, L.A., 1956-67; investment advisor U.S., Can. and Switzerland, 1967—2006; dir. pub. policy DownsizeDC.org, currently; cons. Permanent Portfolio, currently; sr. polit. analyst Free Market News Network, currently. Cons. Permanent Portfolio Fund, Austin, Tex., 1982-2006. Author: How You Can Profit from the Coming Devaluation, 1970, How I Found Freedom in an Unfree World, 1973, You Can Profit From a Monetary Crisis, 1974, Harry Browne's Complete Guide to Swiss Banks, 1976, New Profits from the Monetary Crisis, 1978, Investment Rule #1, 1985, Why the Best-Laid Investment Plans Usually Go Wrong, 1987, The Economic Time Bomb, 1989, (with Terry Coxon) Inflation-Proofing Your Investments, 1981, Why Government Doesn't Work, 1995, Fail-Safe Investing, 1999, The Great Libertarian Offer, 2000, A to Z: 872 Libertarian Soundbites You Can Use Right Now, 2004. Libertarian Party cand. for U.S. Pres., 1996. With U.S. Army, 1953-56. Libertarian. Avocations: classical music, opera, reading, sports, television, good food & wine. Home: Franklin, Tenn. Died Mar. 1, 2006.

BROWNING, BERNARD S., business service company executive; b. Browning, Mo., Nov. 7, 1923; s. John Howard and Alma (Lawrence) Browning; m. Adeline Rogers, Aug. 6, 1955; children: Frances Elaine, Virginia Diane, John Scott, Lawrence Rogers. MBA, Harvard U., 1947. Pres. Gen. Bus. Svcs. Inc., 1962—86, chmn, bd. dir., 1962—89, chmn. emeritus, from 1989. With USN, 1943, advaced through grades to rear adm. USNR, 1972. Mem.: Nat. Advisory Coun. Small Bus. Adminstrn. (chmn. 1976—77, Meritorious Svc. award 1977, Adv. of Yr. 1987), Internat. Franchise Assn. (pres. 1974, Hall of Fame 1983), Nat. Small Bus. Assn. (chmn. 1983—85), Rotary Potomac, Md. Republican. Meth. Home: New Market, Md. Died Mar. 22, 2005.

BROWNLOW, DONALD GREY, private school educator; b. Germantown, Pa., Jan. 17, 1923; s. John Charles Victor and Ruth (Hutchinson) B.; m. Sandra Barbara Dobbs, July 16, 1987; children: Kendall Hutchinson, Pamela Cooke, Douglas Grey, Priscilla Dobbs. Student, U. Zürich, 1946-47; BA, U. Pa., 1948, MA, 1949. Rsch. libr. Presbyn. Hist. Soc., Phila., 1949-50; master Am. history and inernat. rels. Haverford (Pa.) Sch., from 1951; dir. Haverford Tours, 1956-75, 81-95. Charter mem. World War II Meml. Soc.; mem. faculty grad. divsn. Pa. State U., 1966—; cons. Imperial War Mus., London. Author: Documentary History of the Paoli Massacre, 1952, Documentary History of the Battle of Germantown, 1955; The Battle of Brandywine, 1957, The Accused: The Ordeal of Rear Admiral Husband E. Kimmel, USN, 1968; Panzer Baron: The Military Exploits of General Hasso von Manteuffel, 1975, Checkmate at Ruweisat: Auchinleck's Finest Hour, 1977, Hell Was My Home, 1983, The Life and Times of Horst Wessel, 1995; author, producer Haverford School Faces the Cold War, Vol. 1, 1962, Vol. 2, 1963. Chmn. Planning Bd. West Nantmeal Twp., 1964-71; mem. Emergency Com. Chinese Refugees, 1962, Com. of One Million; chmn. Zoning Hearing Bd., Warwick Twp., 1976-84; bd. dirs. Gt. Valley Assn., 1959-62; mem. planning bd. Ctr. Teaching Ams., Immaculata Coll., 1961-69; eagle scout Boy Scouts Am., 1939, Quartermaster Sea Scout, 1943; active French and Pickering Creeks Conservation Trust; mem. U.S. Holocaust Meml. Coun.; charter mem. Air Force Meml. Found.; charter mem. WWII Nat. D-Day Mus., New Orleans. Maj. U.S. Army, 1942-84. Recipient Valley Forge Freedoms Found. medal 1962, Suez medal from gov. Suez, UAR, 1966, Diplôme of Appreciation, French Ministry of Def., 2001, Excellence medal US Army Inspector Gen., 2002, Founder's award Hist. Soc. Pa., 2004, Lower Normandy Regional medal, France, 2004, Veteran Medallion, Nat. Def. Found., 2004, 60th Ann. WWII Victory medal Pottstown, Pa., 2005; named Citizen of Honor of Utah Beach, Mayor of Sainte-Marie-du-Mont, France, 1975, name placed on Wall of Liberty by the Battle of Normandy Found., 1994; Cert. of Recognition (Cold War) signed by William J. Cohen, Sec. of Def, Letter of Appreciation and medal Pres. Republic Korea for services in Korean War, 2003, medal and cert. Pa. House of Rep. for WWII svc., 2005 Mem. VFW (life), Am. Hist. Assn. (life), Paoli Meml. Assn. (life), Germantown Hist. Soc., Chester County Hist. Soc., Smithsonian Assocs., Geneal. Soc. Pa., Pa. Soc., Am. Mus. Natural History, Res. Officers Assn. (life), Soc. Am. Magicians, Nat. Wildlife Fedn., Nat. Audubon Soc., Nat. Trust for Hist. Preservation, Libr. Congress Assocs., U.S. Holocaust Meml. Mus., Simon Wiesenthal Ctr., World Wildlife Fund, Pa. Sheriff's Assn., Zool. Soc. Phila., Am. Legion (life), Acad. Natural Scis. Phila., Nature Conservancy, Wilderness Soc., Franklin Inst., Charles Custis Harrison Soc., Reading Pub. Mus., The Colonial Williamsburg Found. Republican. Episcopalian. Home: Elverson, Pa. Died Jan. 11, 2006.

BRUGGER, GEORGE ALBERT, lawyer; b. Erie, Pa., Jan. 19, 1941; s. Albert F. and Georgia V. (Bach) B.; children from previous marriage: Laura, Linda, Mark; m. Ann Rosenberg. BA, Gannon Coll., 1963; JD, Georgetown U., 1967. Bar: Md. 1968, D.C. 2002, U.S. Dist. Ct. Md. 1972, U.S. Supreme Ct. 1972. Law clk. to U.S. asst. atty. gen. U.S. Dept. Justice, Washington, 1963-66; mgr. pub. affairs Air Transport Assn. of Am., Washington, 1966-68; ptnr. Beatty & McNamee, Hyattsville, Md., 1968-75; sr. ptnr., pres. Fossett & Brugger, Chartered, Greenbelt, Md., 1975—2005. Bd. dirs. Prince George's County Fin. Svcs. Corp. Chmn. bd. dirs. Prince George's Econ. Devel. Corp.; pres. Laurel Regional Hosp. Found. Recipient Disting. Alumni award Gannon Coll. Fellow Md. Bar Found.; mem. ABA (chmn. land use regulation com.), Md. Bar Assn. (bd. dirs.), Prince George's County Bar Assn. (pres. 1982), Prince George's Law Found., (bd. dirs.), Prince George's County C. of C. (Disting. Svc. award 1980, 83, 85), Fed. Bar Assn. (dir.). Roman Catholic. Avocations: collecting watches, marine tropical fish. Home: Washington, DC. Died Dec. 5, 2005.

BRUMBAUGH, JOHN A., JR., retired electrical engineer; b. Pittsburg, Kans., Aug. 23, 1927; s. John A. and Leona G. (Finley) B.; m. Shirley Jean Ellis, July 8, 1950; children: Mark Alan, Steven Thomas, Scott Andrew. Design engr. McNally Pitts. Mfg. Co., Pittsburg, 1949—55; plant engr. Morton Salt Co., Hutchinson, Kans., 1955—59, asst. plant mgr. Port Huron, Mich., 1959—65, plant mgr. Grand Saline, Tex., 1965—70, facility mgr. Hutchinson, 1970—84, Morton Salt divsn. Morton Internat., Inc., Rittman, Ohio, 1984—89; ret., 1989. Lt. USNR, 1945-46. Recipient Boss of Yr. award Bus. and Profl. Women, 1979 Mem. Kans. Assn. Commerce, Assn. Commerce and Industry (dir. 1974-84), Tex. Mfrs. Assn., (dir. Dallas chpt. 1966-70), East Tex. C. of C. (dir. 1968-70), Am. Legion, Lions (pres. local club 1964-65). Avocations: golf, hunting, fishing, boating, hiking. Home: Wadsworth, Ohio. Died Jan. 6, 2006.

BRUMFIELD, STEVEN JACK, business executive; b. Royal Oak, Mich., June 18, 1951; m. Jane E.; children: Sara, Elizabeth, Katie, Natalie. BS, Ctrl. Mich. U., 1976. Plant mgr. Plasti-Fiber, Ithaca, Mich., 1976-79, Brown City, Mich., 1979-85; v.p., gen. mgr. Elicon, Madison Hts., Mich., 1985-95; pres. Sidler Inc., Madison Hts., Mich., from 1995. Author: (computer software) Management Consulting. Past pres. Rotary, Brown City. Mem. Automotive Soc. Quality Engring. Avocations: computers, piano. Home: Grand Rapids, Mich. Died Sept. 25, 2004.

BRUNTON, DONNA LEE, secretarial services manager; b. Denver, May 20, 1929; d. Harry Leroy and Myrtle Evelina McCarthy; m. James Ewing Brunton, Aug. 20, 1948 (div. 1979); children: Mark Lionel, Valerie Lee Stotts. Student, Pasadena City Coll., 1963-64; cert. paralegal, U. So. Calif., 1979. Sec. Gray, White & Burkitt, Pasadena, Calif., 1964-79; office mgr. Hill, Gould & Pearson, L.A., 1979-81; owner Quick Response Secretarial Svc., Glendale, Calif., from 1981. Editor: (weekly bull.) Sunrise Rotary, 1993-94. Mem. Rotary Internat., Order of Ea. Star. Republican. Presbyterian. Avocations: gourmet cooking, reading, gardening, walking dog. Home: Altadena, Calif. Died June 12, 2004.

BRUSH, CHARLES FRANCIS, anthropologist; b. Cleve., Apr. 3, 1923; s. Charles Francis and Dorothy Adams (Hamilton) B.; m. Ellen Sparry, July 25, 1958; children: Barbara Brush Wright, Karen Alexandra, Charles Francis. BA, Yale U., 1947, MA, 1948; PhD, Columbia U., 1969. Researcher in anthropology N.Y.C., 1961—2006. Bd. dirs. Brush Wellman Inc., Inst. Noetic Scis.; curatorial assoc. Peabody Mus. Yale U., Yale U. Coun., 1984-90; trustee Sierra Club Found., 1981-87; pres. Am. Scandinavian Soc., 1983-85; rsch. assoc. U. S.C., 1982-87. Excavated earliest ceramics known in Mex., first evidence of deliberate alloying of bronze, 1961. Sec.-treas. Internat. Planned Parenthood Fedn. Western Hemisphere region, 1968-74. Mem. AAAS, Am. Anthrop. Assn., Am. Geog. Soc. (councilor), Soc. Am. Archeology, Explorers Club (bd. dirs. 1971-93, pres. 1978-81), N.Y. Athletic Club, Century Assn. Set altitude record for scuba-diving in the crater lake of volcano Licancábur, 19,300 feet above sea level. Home: Shelter Island, NY. Died June 1, 2006.

BRUUN, EUGENE ROBERT, engineer; b. Phila., Sept. 23, 1934; B of Mech. Engring., CCNY, 1956; MS, Rensselaer Poly. Inst., 1959. Engr. Hamilton United Techs., Windsor Locks, Conn., from 1956. Patentee in field. Mem. AIAA, NSP. Avocation: swimming. Home: Simsbury, Conn. Died Jan. 24, 2004.

BRYAN, DAVID MERLE, travel company executive; b. Peoria, Ill., June 9, 1921; s. Clifford E. and Sibyl Esther (Goyer) B.; m. Margie Esther Casteel, Dec. 23, 1943; children: Margie Ann, Edwyn, David Jr., Daniel. BA with honors, U. Mo., 1944; BD, U. Chgo., 1946; DD (hon.), Phillips U., Enid, Okla., 1964. Sr. min. Jackson Blvd. Christian Ch., Chgo., 1946-49, First Christian Ch., Sedalia, Mo., 1949-56, Univ. Ch., Chgo., 1956-60, First Christian Ch., Topeka, 1960-76; pres., owner Bryan World Tours, Topeka, 1977-80, chmn. bd. dirs., from 1980. CEO Bryan Travel Colls., Topeka and Springfield, Mo., 1980-92. Coauthor: Preaching on Old Testament Themes, 1952, Preaching on Stewardship, 1964; contbr. articles to nat. mags.; prodr., photographer 3 video documentaries; photographer, scriptwriter African movies. Pres. Mo. Coun. Chs., Jefferson City, 1955, Mo. State Conv., Jefferson City, 1956, Mustard Seed, Glendale, Calif., 1970—. Recipient Outstanding Small Bus. award C. of C., Topeka, 1992. Mem. Christian Ch. (Disciples Of Christ). Avocations: amateur radio, scuba and underwater photography, flying, writing. Home: Topeka, Kans. Died Jan. 3, 2005.

BRYAN, FORD RICHARDSON, author, publisher, spectrochemical analyst; b. Mich., May 13, 1912; s. Frederick Charles and Nettie Josephine (Richardson) B.; m. Ellen Juntunen, Apr. 29, 1943 (dec. May 1980). BA, Ea. Mich. U., 1934; BS, U. Mich., 1941. Cert. secondary sch. sci. tchr., Mich. Instr. Lawrence Inst. Tech., Detroit, 1935-36; prin. Port Hope (Mich.) H.S., 1936-41; rsch. engr. Ford Motor Co., Dearborn, Mich., 1941-51; supr. physics Ford Sci. Lab., Dearborn, 1951-74; author, pub., Dearborn, from 1980; with Edison Inst., Dearborn. Author: The Fords of Dearborn, 1987, Beyond the Model T, 1990 (award 1994), Henry's Lieutenants, 1993, Henry's Attic, 1995. Bd. dirs. Dearborn Hist. Soc., 1980—; mem. Dearborn Hist. Commn., 1988-99. Recipient award of merit Hist. Soc. Mich., 1994. Mem. NAS, Optical Soc. Am. (chmn. Detroit sect. 1946-47), Sigma Xi. Home: Dearborn, Mich. Died May 14, 2004.

BRYAN, THOMAS MICHAEL, physician; b. Williamsport, Pa., Mar. 19, 1945; s. Thomas Alfred and Genevieve Theresa (Cole) B.; m. Josephine Marie Gudolonis, May 30, 1970 (div. 1987); children: Thomas Joseph, Kelly Ann. BS, Juniata Coll., 1967; MD, Jefferson Med. Coll., 1971; postgrad., Duke U., 1982-83. Diplomate Am. Bd. Family Practice. Intern Harrisburg (Pa.) Polyclinic Hosp., 1971-72; pvt. practice Harrisburg, 1972-75 and from 90; asst. dir. Family Practice Residency Poly Clinic Hosp., Harrisburg, 1975-78, assoc. dir., 1978-90. Med. cons. Pa. Blue Shield, 1986—; physician advisor Keystone Profl. Rev. Orgn., 1984—. Contbr. articles to profl. jours. Mem. Four Seasons Civic Assn., Harrisburg, 1986; bd. dirs. Pa. Diabetes Acad., 1985—. Fellow Am. Acad. of Family Physicians; mem. AMA, Pa. Acad. Family Physicians (v.p. 1987-88, chmn. 1987-88), Dauphan County Med. Soc. (chmnships, bd. govs. 1986-87). Republican. Roman Catholic. Avocations: travel, gardening, woodworking, cooking. Home: Harrisburg, Pa. Died Aug. 10, 2004.

BRYANT, WILLIAM BENSON, federal judge; b. Wetumpka, Ala., Sept. 18, 1911; s. Benson and Alberta B.; m. Astaire A. Gonzalez, Aug. 25, 1934 (dec. 1997); children: Astaire, William B. AB, Howard U., 1932, LL.B., 1936. Asst. U.S. atty. for D.C., 1951-54; partner firm Houston, Bryant & Gardner, 1954-65; judge U.S. Dist. Ct. Washington, 1965—82, sr. judge, 1982—2005; prof. law Howard U. Sch. Law, 1965-91. Served with AUS, 1943-47. Mem. ABA Died Nov. 13, 2005.

BRYSON, MELVIN JOSEPH, retired biochemist; b. Providence, Utah, June 7, 1916; s. Charles Melvin and Martha Jane Bryson; m. Devona Smart, May 11, 1942; children: Melvin Joseph Bryson, Jr., Betty Sue. BS, Utah State Univ., Logan, UT, 1946; MS, Univ. Utah, Salt Lake City, UT, 1948; PhD, Tex. A&M Univ., College Station, TX, 1952. Asst. dir. Eaton Lab of Norwich, Norwich, NY, 1952—57; rsch. asst. Univ. Utah Sch. of Medicine, Salt Lake City, 1957—59, rsch. asst. prof., 1959—83; lab dir. Inter West Endocrine Lab, Salt Lake City, 1984—94. Maj. US Army, 1941—45, Europe. Home: Salt Lake City, Utah. Died Apr. 14, 2005.

BRZUSTOWICZ, STANISLAW HENRY, dental educator; b. Bklyn., Apr. 30, 1919; s. John Stanislaw and Victoria (Szutarski) B.; m. Wanda Frances Seglow, July 3, 1949; children: Robert, Thomas, Michael, Linda. BS, St. John's U., 1940; DDS, Columbia U., 1943. Pvt. practice, Bklyn., 1947-74, New Hyde Park, NY, 1963-93; prof. clin. dentistry Columbia U. Sch. Dental and Oral Surgery, N.Y.C., 1946-87, prof. emeritus clin. dentistry (operative), 1987—2005; course dir. preclin. operative dentistry, attending dentist Presbyn. Hosp., N.Y.C., 1974—89; spl. lectr. in dentistry, 1990—2005. Bd. dirs., v.p. Prospect Pattern & Machine Works, Inc., Bklyn., 1962-72; bd dirs., sec. to bd. Atlas Savs. & Loan Assn., Bklyn., 1962-94. Contg. author Differential Diagnosis of Mouth Diseases, 1943 Served to capt. U.S. Army, 1943-46 Mem. ADA, N.Y. State Dental Soc., 2d Dist. Dental Soc., Nat. Med. and Dental Soc., Cath. Dentist Guild (joint program dental care for indigent children with Cath. Guardian Soc. 1949-54), Roger Bacon Sci. Soc., Kosciuszko Found., Holy Name Soc., Omicron Kappa Upsilon. Republican. Roman Catholic. Home: New Hyde Park, NY. Died Sept. 28, 2005.

BUCHANAN, JOHN O., civil engineer, construction consultant; b. Asheville, N.C., Oct. 11, 1921; s. Corsey C. and Lilian B. (Barker) B.; m. Helen F. Foote, Dec. 21, 1947; 1 child, Charles Osborne. Student, The Citadel, 1938-43; BS in Civil Engring., Mo. Sch. Mines, 1958, MS in Civil Engring., 1961. Registered profl. civil engr. With Corps of Engrs. U.S. Army, 1943, advanced through grades to lt. col., 1960, ret., 1966; constrn. supr. Dow Chem. Co., Freeport, Tex., 1966-83; civil engr. Lake Jackson, Tex., from 1983. Mem. Am. Arbitration Assn. (at large), Nat. Soc. Profl. Engrs., Tex. Soc. Profl. Engrs. Democrat. Presbyterian. Died Sept. 22, 2004.

BUCHANAN, RANDALL JOHN, theater educator; b. Venice, Utah, May 15, 1930; s. Boyd and Catherine (Boyer) B.; m. Carol Lee Holmes, Jan. 21, 1968 (div. Oct. 1980); children: Kara Elizabeth, Randall John Jr. BA, Brigham Young U., 1954, MA, 1958; PhD, La. State U., 1964. Instr. South Eastern La. U., Hammond, 1960, asst. prof., 1961-64; instr., tech. dir. Midwestern State U., Wichita Falls, Tex., 1960-61; prof., chair div. lang. and lit. So. State Coll., Springfield, S.D., 1964-66; prof., chair communications/TA Tex. A&I U., Kingsville, 1966-81, prof., dir. theatre, from 1981. Critic-judge U. Interscholastic League, Tex., 1967—; adjucator Am. Coll. Theatre Festival, Tex., Ark., La., 1974; pres. Tex. Ednl. Theatre Assn., 1978-81; chmn. Tex. Alliance for Arts Edn., 1980-82; chmn. Univ./Coll. South West Theatre Assn., 1990—. Dir. Majority of One, 1968, Greater Tuna, 1985, Once Upon a Mattress, 1986, Cat on a Hot Tin Roof, 1987 (Weaver award 1988), Light Up the Sky, 1987, Anything Goes, 1988, Tom Jones, 1988, Night Mother, 1989, Carousel, 1989, Musical Comedy Murders of 1940, 1989, Into the Woods, 1990, Amadeus, 1990, Brigadoon. With U.S. Army, 1954-56. Recipient Founders award Tex. Ednl. Theatre Assn., 1985. Mem. Elks. Died May 16, 2004.

BUCKLES, JUDITH ANN, dental educator, program administrator; b. Francisville, Ind., Feb. 15, 1940; d. Lawrence Melvin and Mary Rosella Johnston; m. Edward Donald Buckles, Jan. 27, 1962; children: Dawn Marie, Erica Danielle, Erin Nichole. Cert. dental nurse, Elkhart (Ind.) U. Medicine and Dentistry, 1959; AAS, Purdue U., 1986, BS with honors, 1991. Cert. dental asst. Dental asst. Francis A Jones, DDS, Lafayette, Ind., 1959-69, Raymond Price, DDS, Lafayette, 1969-73; program supr., sr. instr. Ivy Tech. State Coll., Lafayette, 1973—2006; ret., 2006. Religious instr. St. Ann Ch. and Shrine, Lafayette, 1980-95; asst. with fund raising St. Ann Rosary Soc., Lafayette, 1979—, St. Ann Social Club, Lafayette, 1994—, St. Ann Parish Coun., 2000-. Fellow Am. Dental Assts. Assn., Nat. Assn. Dental Assts., Ind. Dental Assocs. Assn., Lafayette Dental Assts. Assn., German-Am. Club, Phi Kappa Phi. Avocations: collecting antique depression glass ware, collecting cookbooks, collecting boyd bears and angels, collecting porcelain dolls, collecting german dishes. Home: Lafayette, Ind. Died May 26, 2006.

BUCKLIN, JANE ROWE, college health nurse; b. New London, N.H., July 24, 1930; d. Earl Edmund and Myra Florence Collins Rowe; m. Elwood Arthur Bucklin, Sept. 21, 1952; children: Cheryl J., Alan E., Denise I. Diploma, Concord Hosp. Sch. Nursing, 1952; BSN, U. N.H., 1982. RN, N.H.; RNC; cert. coll. health nurse. Pvt. duty nurse Portsmouth (N.H.) Hosp., 1968-73; float nurse Exeter (N.H.) Hosp., 1973-74; staff nurse U. N.H. Health Svcs., Durham, 1974-81, nursing supr., from 1981; staff nurse Seaborne Hosp., Dover, N.H., 1987-88. Mem. New England Coll. Health Assn., Am. Coll. Health Assn. Home: Durham, NH. Died July 11, 2004.

BUECHEL, WILLIAM BENJAMIN, lawyer; b. Wichita, Kans., July 27, 1926; s. Donald William and Bonnie S. (Priddy) B.; m. Theresa Marie Girard, Nov. 3, 1955; children: Sarah Ann, Julia Elaine. Student, U. Wichita, 1947-49; BS, U. Kans., 1951; LLB, 1954. Sole practice, Concordia, Kans., 1954-56; stockholder Paulsen, Buechel, Swenson, Uri & Brewer Chartered, Concordia, 1971-75; sec.-treas., 1975-77; pres., 1977-92; of counsel, 1993-95; ret. Bd. dirs. County Bank & Trust, Concordia, 1971-92, mem. trust and adminstrn. com. Citizens Nat. Bank, 1992—. Bd. dirs. Cloud County C.C. Found., 1983-89. Mem. ABA, Kans. Bar Assn. (mem. exec. coun. 1966-68, chmn. adv. sect. profl. ethics com. 1974-76), Cloud County Bar Assn. (pres. 1984-86), Elks, Moose, Rotary. Republican. Methodist. Died Feb. 24, 2005.

BUELL, VICTOR PAUL, marketing educator, author, editor; b. McAlester, Okla., Oct. 18, 1914; s. Victor Paul and Genevieve (Keller) B.; m. Virginia Stevens, May 16, 1942; children: Elizabeth Wilson Buell Barrow, Nancy Trimble Buell Tamms, Victor Paul III. AB, Pa. State U., 1938; grad. advanced tech. tng. bus. adminstn., Harvard U., 1943. Mgr. market research and ops. Real Silk Hosiery Mills, Inc., Indpls., 1938-51; cons. mktg. McKinsey & Co., N.Y.C., 1952-55; mgr. mktg. div. Hoover Co., North Canton, Ohio, 1955-59; v.p. mktg. Archer Daniels Midland Co., Mpls., 1959-64; corp. v.p. mktg. Am. Standard, Inc., N.Y.C., 1964-70; prof. mktg. U. Mass., Amherst, 1970-83, prof. emeritus, 1983—2006, vis. prof., 1985. Cons. to bus., govt., publs. and assns. Author: Marketing Management in Action, 1966, Changing Practices in Advertising Decision-Making and Control, 1973, Organizing for Marketing/Advertising Success, 1981, Marketing Management: A Strategic Planning Approach, 1984; contbg. author: Effective Marketing Action, 1958, The Marketing Job, 1961, Handbook of Business Administration, 1966, Readings in Marketing Research, 1970, Ency. Profl. Mgmt., 1978, Handbook for Professional Managers, 1985, Dictionary of Marketing Terms, 1988, 2d edit., 1995; contbr. articles to mags., mktg. jours.; editor-in-chief Handbook of Modern Marketing, 1970, 2d edit., 1986; editl. bd. Indsl. Mktg.; spkr. mgmt., mktg. groups and seminars; reporter Fleet Beat newspaper. Bd. dirs. Hennepin County United Fund, vice chmn. indsl. campaign; trustee Grad. Sch. Sales Mgmt. and Marketing, Syracuse U.; mem. Amherst Town Bd. Assessors, 1987-89; bd. dirs. Forum for Humanities; subscription mgr. for resident's mag. Fleet Landing Retirement Cmty. Maj., AUS, 1941-46. Recipient award Alpha Kappa Psi, 1975 Mem. Am. Mktg. Assn. (dir. 1957-59, chmn. nat. co. membership com. 1957-58, nat. v.p. 1960-61, pres. 1968-69, chmn. mktg. fund bd., editorial bd. Jour. Mktg.), Home Mfrs. Assn. (dir.), Am. Mgmt. Assn. (mem. nat. planning council), NAM (mktg. com.), Canton Sales Execs. Club (dir. 1956-58, v.p. 1958-59), Sales and Mktg. Execs. Internat., Sales and Mktg. Execs. Western Mass. (dir. 1980-83), Assn. Nat. Advertisers (dir.), Beta Gamma Sigma, Delta Phi (hon.). Congregationalist. Home: Atlantic Bch, Fla. Died Apr. 11, 2006.

BULL, HELEN MAY, artist; b. Sweet Springs, Mo., Apr. 20, 1920; d. John Theodore Langewisch and Ethel Henrietta (Von Berkelo) Butemeyer; widowed; children: Jan Emerson Bull, Guy William Bull. BFA, Otis Art Inst., L.A., 1971; advanced certification Indsl. Rels., UCLA, 1983. Dir. Brazilian Primitive Painting Exhbn., L.A., 1972; pres. Bay West Assn. of Comty Assistance to Homeless Youngsters, L.A., 1973-74; artist, represented by Agora Art Gallery, N.Y.C. Panelist Inst. for Study of Women in Transition, 1976; nursing career devel. con., San. Antonio, Tex., 1978-80. Artist: Spl exhbn. of canvasses in Vista Rm., Faculty Ctr. UCLA, 1973, Art in Permanent Collections includes KTSC-TV, Pueblo, Colo, and framed mural of St. Luke, St. Luke's Luth. Ch., (Gold award 1993); one-person show Agora Gallery, 1999; exhibited group show at Agora Gallery, 1998. Recipient Cert. of merit, UCLA Juried Faculty Exhibit, 1960. Lutheran. Avocations: travel, hiking, coin collecting/numismatics. Home: Aurora, Colo. Died Feb. 5, 2004.

BULLOCH, KATHLEEN LOUISE, educational professional; b. Teaneck, N.J., Feb. 20, 1949; d. Thomas Joseph and Daisy Loretta Oates; m. Clifford Allen Bulloch, June 17, 1972; 1 child, Sean Andrew. BA, William Patterson Coll., 1971; MA, Montclair State Coll., 1972. Cert. speech pathologist Am. Speeh/Lang./Hearing Assn. Chief speech pathologist Barnert Speech Clin., Paterson, N.J., 1971-73; speech/lang. pathologist Brick Town, N.J., 1973-79, Riverside (Calif.) County Office of Edn., 1979-98; mentor tchr. Riverside County Office of Edn., 1992-98, curriculum specialist, 1998-99; intern program supr. Calif. State U., San Bernardino, 1998-99. Ednl. cons. Creative Children's Group, N.Y.C., 1995—; C-FASST Sr. Trainer Calif. State Dept. Edn., Sacramento, 1998; book reviewer Am. Speech/Lang. Assn., Washington, 1996—. Scriptwriter: (children's TV) Bloopy's Buddies, 1997; author: Phantom Tollbooth Unit, 1994, Adventures in Space, 1992; co-author: Adult Aphasia Program, 1977. Named to Outstanding Young Women of Am., 1983. Mem. ASCD, Am. Speech/Lang./Hearing Assn., Calif. Speech/Lang./Hearing Assn., Am. Ednl. Rsch. Assn., Coun. for Exceptional Children. Anglican Catholic. Avocations: reading, writing, exercise, music. Home: Anaheim, Calif. Died May 29, 2004.

BULLOCK, HARVEY READE, screenwriter; b. Oxford, N.C., June 4, 1921; s. Harvey Reade and Vivian Elsie (Murray) B.; m. Betty Jane Folker; children: Kerry, Diana, Courtney, Andrew. AB, Duke U., 1943. Radio, TV, film scriptwriter, producer, from 1947. Lectr. creative writing various colls., seminars. Scriptwriter: (radio) The Abe Burrows Show, 1949, (TV shows) Today with Dave Garroway, Robert Q. Lewis Show, numerous prodns. with R. S. Allen including Salute to Baseball (Random House award), Dick and the Dutchess, McKeever and the Colonel, numerous TV show episodes including The Love Boat, Alice, Hogan's Heroes, The Andy Griffith Show, I Spy, The Danny Thomas Show, The Dick Van Dyke Show, My World and Welcome To It, The Jim Nabors Show, (cartoon series) The Flintstones, The Jetsons, (children spl.) The Red Hand Gang, Poppa and Me (Emmy award nomination), (films) Honeymoon Hotel, Girl Happy with Elvis, Who's Minding the Mint, With Six You Get Egg Roll (Box Office Blue Ribbon award), Don't Drink the Water, Going Coconuts, (TV spls. with Everett Greenbaum) Return To Mayberry; author: The Fat Book, How To Cheat On Your Diet. Mem. Writers Guild Am. Died Apr. 23, 2006.

BULLOCK, THEODORE HOLMES, biologist, educator; b. Nanking, China, May 16, 1915; s. Amasa Archibald and Ruth (Beckwith) B.; m. Martha Runquist, May 30, 1937; children: Elsie Christine, Stephen Holmes. Student, Pasadena Jr. Coll., 1932-34; AB, U. Calif., Berkeley, 1936, PhD, 1940; PhD (hon.), U. Frankfurt, 1988, Loyola U., Chgo., 2000. Research assoc. Yale U. Sch. Medicine, 1942-43, instr. neuroanatomy, 1943-44; instr. Marine Biol. Lab., Woods Hole, Mass., 1944-46, head invertebrate zoology, 1955-57, trustee, 1955-57; asst. prof. anatomy U. Mo., 1944-46; asst. prof. zoology U. Calif. at Los Angeles, 1946, assoc. prof., 1948, prof., 1955-66; Brain Research Inst., U. Calif. at Los Angeles, 1960-66; prof. neuroscis. Med. Sch., U. Calif. at San Diego, 1966-82, prof. emeritus, 1982—2005. Mem. AEC 2d Resurvey of Bikini Expdn., 1948. Author: (with G.A. Horridge) Structure and Function in the Nervous Systems of Invertebrates, 2 vols., 1965; (with others) Introduction to Nervous Systems, 1977; (with W. Heiligenberg) Electroreception, 1986 (with E. Basar) Brain Dynamics, 1989, (with E. Basar) Induced Rhythms in the Brain, 1992, How Do Brains Work?, 1993. Fellow, Ctr. Advanced Study in Behavioral Scis., Palo Alto, 1959—60; Sterling fellow zoology, Yale U., 1940—41, Rockefeller fellow exptl. neurology, 1941—42, Fulbright scholar, Stazione Zoologica, Naples, 1950—51. Fellow AAAS; mem. NAS, Am. Soc. Zoologists (chmn. comparative physiology div. 1961, pres. 1965), Soc. Neurosci. (pres. 1973-74), Internat. Soc. Neuroethology (pres. 1984-86), Am. Physiol. Soc., Soc. Gen. Physiologists, Am. Acad. Arts and Scis., Am. Philos. Soc., Internat. Brain Research Orgn., Phi Beta Kappa, Sigma Xi. Died Dec. 20, 2005.

BULLOUGH, VERN LEROY, sexologist, nursing educator, researcher, historian; b. Salt Lake City, July 24, 1928; s. D. Vernon Bullough and Augusta Rueckert; m. Bonnie Uckerman, Aug. 2, 1947 (dec. 1996); children: David(dec.), James, Steven, Susan, Michael; m. Gwen Brewer, Aug. 15, 1998. BA, U. Utah, 1951; MA, U. Chgo., 1951, PhD, 1954; BSN, Calif. State U., Long Beach, 1981, BA, 1981; DSc (hon.), Buffalo State Coll., 2004. Assoc. prof. Youngstown (Ohio) U., 1954-59; from asst. prof. to prof. Calif. State U., Northridge, 1959—79; dean faculty natural and social scis. SUNY Coll., Buffalo, 1980-89, disting. prof., 1988-93, disting. prof. emeritus, 1993—2006. Prof. Inst. Advanced Study Sexuality, San Francisco, from 1989; adj. prof. U. So. Calif., 1994—2003, Ctr. for Sex Rsch., Calif. State U., Northridge, from 1994; fellow Ctr. for Medieval-Renaissance Studies UCLA, 1995—2006; founder Bonnie and Vern Bullough collection on sex and gender Oviatt Libr., Calif. State U., Northridge; Fulbright prof. Ain Shams U., Cairo, 1966—67; lectr. in field. Author, co-author: more than 55 books; editor (sr. editor): Free Inquiry; mem. editl. bds.: 9 jours., 2003—06; contbr. more than 200 articles to profl. jours., chapters to books. Active in civil liberties and civil rights orgns.; founding mem. first fair housing group in U.S., 1959. With Security Agency U.S. Army, 1946—48. Named Oustanding Prof, Calif Stat Univ sys, Disting Prof, SUNY; recipient numerous other awards for rsch. into sex and gender, history, medicine, nursing and cmty. svcs. Fellow: Coun. for Sci. Medicine and Mental Health, Com. for Sci. Investigation of Claims to the Paranormal, Internat. Humanist and Ethical Union (past pres.), Acad. Humanism (laureate), Soc. Sci. Study Sex (past pres.), Am. Acad. Nursing. Died June 21, 2006.

BUMSTEAD, HENRY, art director, production designer; b. Ontario, Calif., Mar. 17, 1915; s. Lloyd and Emma B. BA, Univ. So. Calif., 1937. Art dir.: (films) Saigon, 1948, The Sainted Sisters, 1948, My Own True Love, 1948, Song of Surrender, 1949, Top o' the Morning, 1949, My Friend Irma, 1949, Streets of Laredo, 1949, The Furies, 1950, No Man of Her Own, 1950, My Friend Irma Goes West, 1950, The Goldbergs, 1950, The Redhead and the Cowboy, 1950, Rhubarb, 1951, Submarine Command, 1951, Jumping Jacks, 1952, The Stars Are singing, 1953, Aaron Slick from Punkin Crick, 1952, Come Back, Little Sheba, 1952, The Stars Are Singing, 1953, Little Boy Lost, 1953, The Bridge at Toko-Ri, 1954, Knock on Wood, 1954, Run for Cover, 1955, Lucy Gallant, 1955, The Man Who Knew Too Much, 1956, That Certain Feeling, 1956, The Leather Saint, 1956, The Vagabond King, 1956, Hollyweood or Bust, 1956, I Married a Monster from Outer Space, 1958, Vertigo, 1958, As Young as We Are, 1958, The Hangman, 1959, The Bellboy, 1961, Conderfella, 1961, The Great Imposter, 1961, Come September, 1961, The Spiral Road, 1962, To Kill a Mockingbird, 1962, The Brass Bottle, 1964, A Gathering of Eagles, 1964, Father Goose, 1964, Bullet for a Badman, 1964,The War Lord, 1965, Gunpoint, 1966, Beau Geste, 1966, Blindfold, 1966, Tobruk, 1966, Banning, 1967, The Secret War of Harry Frigg, 1968, What's So Bad about Feeling Good, 1968, Tell Them Willie Boy Is Here, 1969, A Man Called Gannon, 1969, One More Train to Rob, 1971, Raid on Rommel, 1971, Showdown, 1972, High Plains Drifter, 1973, The Sting, 1973 (Academy award best art direction 1973), The Front Page, 1974, The Great Waldo Pepper, 1975, (TV movies) The Movie Murderer, 1970, McCloud: Who Killed Miss U.S.A.?, 1970, The Birdmen, 1971, The Adventures of Nick Carter, 1972, The Victim, 1972, Honky Tonk, 1974, Don't Push, I'll Charge When I'm Ready, 1977, Amateur Night at the Dixie Bar and Grill, 1979, (TV pilots) Laugh!s, 1990; prodn. designer (films) Topaz, 1969, Slaughterhouse Five, 1972, Family Plot, 1976, Slap Shot, 1977, Rollercoaster, 1977, Same Time Next Year, 1978, House Calls, 1978, The Concorde-Airport '79, 1979, A Little Romance, 1979, Smokey and the Bandit Part II, 1980, The World According to Garp, 1982, Harry and Son, 1984, The Little Drummer Girl, 1984, Warning Sign, 1985, Psycho III, 1986, Funny Farm, 1988, A Time of Destiny, 1988, Her Alibi, 1989, Ghost Dad, 1990, Almost an Angel, 1990, Cape Fear, 1991, Unforgiven, 1992 (Academy award nomination best art direction 1992), A Perfect World, 1993, The Stars Fell on Henrietta, 1993, Absolute Power, 1997, Midnight in the Garden of Good and Evil, 1997, Home Alone III, 1997, True Crime, 1999, Space Cowboys, 2000, Blood Work, 2002, Mystic River, 2003, Million Dollar Baby, 2004, Flags of Our Fathers, 2006, Red Sun, Black Sand, 2006 Home: San Marino, Calif. Died May 24, 2006.

BUNNELL, JOHN BLAKE, lawyer; b. Nashville, Apr. 20, 1958; s. James Crusman Jr. and Virginia Claire (Cross) B.; m. Candace Diane Tucker, Oct. 1, 1982. BS, Austin Peay State U., 1979; MS in Planning, U. Tenn., 1988, JD, 1990. Bar: Tenn. 1991, U.S. Dist. Ct. (mid. dist.) Tenn. 1992, U.S. Dist. Ct. (ea. dist.) Tenn. 1995. Editl. editor, editorialist The All State, Austin Peay State U. Student Newspaper, Clarksville, Tenn., 1975-78; planning intern/adminstrn. Hopkinsville (Ky.)-Christian County Planning Commn., 1978-79; energy tech. analyst Tenn. Energy Authority, Nashville, 1979-80; rsch. asst. U. Tenn. Planning Rsch. Ctr., Knoxville, 1980-83; legal noncommissioned officer 844th Engr. Battalion, Knoxville, 1986-94; asst. dist. atty. gen. Office of Dist. Atty. 21st Dist., Franklin, Tenn., 1991-92; pvt. practice Nashville, 1992; asst. pub. defender Office of Pub. Defender 4th Jud., Newport, Tenn., 1992-96; legal assistance officer U.S. Army Operation Joint Endeavor, Ft. Benning, Ga., 1996-97. Sec., dir. Cumberland Cmtys. Commn., Knoxville, 1991-94, 96—; trial def. counsel Team II, 213th Legal Spt. Orgn., Louisville, 1996-2000; legal assistance atty. 1077th RTU, Oak Ridge, Tenn., 2001—; city atty., Parrottsville, Tenn., 1999—; civil mediator under Rule 31, Tenn. Supreme Ct., 1999—. Author: The Impact of Industrial Revenue Bonds on Job Creation in Tennessee: A Longitudinal Approach. Exec. com. Cocke County ptnrship., 1998-99; pres. Newport/Cocke County C. of C., 1998; mem. Newport Cocke County Econ. Devel. Bd., 1998-99. Sgt. U.S. Army, 1990-91. Mem. Tenn. Assn. Criminal Def. Lawyers, Sevier County Bar Assn., Cocke County Bar Assn., Newport (Tenn.) Kiwanis Club (chmn. retention subcom. 1993-94), Nat. Trust for Hist. Preservation, Order Ky. Cols., Phi Kappa Phi, Pi Kappa Alpha. Methodist. Avocations: archaeology, camping, running, swimming. Home: White Pine, Tenn. Died Jan. 31, 2004.

BUNSHAFT, MARILYN JANOSY, community services specialist; b. N.Y.C., July 27, 1935; d. Albert and Fay Janosy; m. Warren Owen Bunshaft, Aug. 28, 1955; children: Albert J., Jess A., Charles E. BA, Queens Coll., 1957; MS, Hofstra U., 1961. Treas. Crawford Pharmacy, Inc., Roslyn, N.Y., 1978-94; tax preparer pvt. practice, East Meadow, N.Y., 1982-90; cmty. info. specialist East Meadow Pub. Libr., from 1988. Mem. adv. bd. Ctr. for Gerontology, Hofstra U., from 2000. Mem. Adv. Com. on Environ., Hempstead, N.Y., 1980-84; bd. dirs. Nassau Suffolk Lung Assn., N.Y., 1987-96, N.Y. State Lung Assn., 1991-94; mem. allocations com. United Way of Long Island, N.Y., 1991—. Mem. LWV (bd. dirs. Hempstead E., 1961—, pres. 69-70, 76-78); East Meadow C. of C. (bd. dirs. 1992—), Am. Libr. Assn., Pub. Libr. Assn. Avocations: reading, designing clothes, travel, gardening. Home: East Meadow, NY. Died Feb. 6, 2004.

BURCHENAL, JOSEPH HOLLAND, physician; b. Milford, Del., Dec. 21, 1912; s. Caleb E. and Mary E. (Holl) B.; m. Margaret Pembroke Thom, Oct. 15, 1938; m. Joan Barclay Riley, Mar. 20, 1948; children— Mary Holland, Elizabeth Payne, Joan Littlefield, Barbara Fahys, Caleb Wells, David Holland, Joseph Emory Barclay. Student, Princeton U., 1930-33; MD, U. Pa., 1937. Diplomate Am. Bd. Internal Medicine. Rotating intern Union Meml. Hosp., Balt., 1937-38; intern pediatrics N.Y. Hosp.; also research pathology Cornell U., 1938-39; asst. resident medicine Boston City Hosp., 1940-42; spl. fellow medicine Meml. Hosp., N.Y.C., 1946-49, asst. attending physician, 1949-52, attending physician, 1952-83, attending physician emeritus, from 1983, chief chemotherapy service, 1952-64, assoc. med. dir. for clin. investigation, 1964-66, dir. clin. investigation, 1966-83. Research fellow medicine Harvard, 1940-42; research fellow Sloan-Kettering Inst., 1946-48, assoc., 1948-52, mem., 1952-83, mem. emeritus, 1983-2006, v.p., 1964-72, field coordinator human cancer, 1973-80, head Applied Therapy Lab.; asst prof. clin. medicine Cornell U., 1949-50, asst. prof. medicine, 1950-51, assoc. prof., 1951-52; prof. Cornell U. (Sloan-Kettering div.), 1952-55; prof. medicine Cornell U. Med. Coll., 1955-80, emeritus, 1980-2006; spl. cons. clin. panel Cancer Chemotherapy Nat. Service Center, 1955-64; spl. cons. pub. health service, hematology study sect. NIH, 1955-58; cons. Am. Cancer Soc., 1958-64; chmn. U.S. nat. com. Internat. Union Against Cancer, 1960-63, chmn. chemotherapy panel of research commn., 1962-66; chmn. expert com. on cancer chemotherapy WHO, 1961, mem. expert adv. panel on cancer, 1961-79; chmn. chemotherapy adv. com. Nat. Cancer Inst., 1970-71; mem. nat. panel consultants conquest of cancer U.S. Senate Com. Labor and Pub. Welfare, 1970; cons. in oncology Stamford (Conn.), St. Albans (N.Y.) Naval hosps. Assoc. editor: Cancer Research, 1969-74; mem. editorial adv. bd. Cancer. Mem. Rep. Town Meeting, Darien, Conn., 1957-65; Served with M.C., AUS, 1942-45. Recipient Alfred P. Sloan Cancer Research award, 1963, Albert Lasker award in clin. cancer chemotherapy, 1972, prix Lepold Griffuel, 1970, John Phillips award Phillips Exeter Acad., 1974, David A. Karnofsky meml. award Am. Soc. Clin. Oncology, 1974, Jeffrey A. Gottlieb Meml. award, 1980, nat. ann. clin. award Am. Cancer Soc., 1982, others. Mem. Am. Soc. Clin. Investigation, Soc. Exptl. Biology and Medicine, Am. Assn. for Cancer Research (pres. 1965-66), European, Internat., Am. socs. hematology, Am. Soc. Tropical Medicine, Soc. Study Blood, Am. Fedn. Clin. Research, N.Y. Acad. Scis., Harvey Soc., Am. Soc. Pediatric Research (rep. to div. med. scis. NRC 1955-58), Soc. for Pediatric Research, Am. Soc. Clin. Oncology, AMA, ACP, N.Y. County Med. Soc., N.Y. State Med. Soc., Am. Inst. Nutrition, Leukemia Soc. Am. (v.p. med. and sci. affairs 1970-75, chmn. med. and sci. adv. com. 1970-74), James Ewing Soc., Academia Nacional de Medicina de Buenos Aires (corr.), Czechoslovak Med. Soc. (hon.), Brazilian Nat. Acad. Medicine (corr.). Died Mar. 8, 2006.

BURCHFIELD, BRUCE ALLEN, entrepreneur; b. Ft. Dodge, Iowa, Apr. 3, 1947; s. Stanley H. and Bertha (Sampson) B.; m. Mary Ellen Porter, Dec. 15, 1971; children: Shawn, Stewart, Jennifer. BS in Engring., Iowa State U., 1970; MBA, Loyola U., Chgo., 1973. Engr. Reynolds Aluminum, Brookfield, Ill., 1970-73; v.p. First Nat. Bank Chgo., 1973-82; pres. CIRRUS System, Inc. subs. Mastercard Internat., 1982-88; exec. v.p. Mastercard Internat., 1988. Mem. Electronic Funds Transfer Assn. (chmn. 1986-87, bd. dirs.), Medinah Country Club, Bonita Bay Club. Republican. Methodist. Avocations: golf, skiing. Home: Naperville, Ill. Died Feb. 6, 2006.

BURG, JEROME STUART, financial planning consultant; b. N.Y.C., Aug. 2, 1935; s. Norman and Ruth (Schkurman) B.; m. Janis Elaine Lyon, May 26, 1974; children: Jeffrey Howard, David Matthew, Audree, Harriet, Robert, Stephanie. Student, Temple U., 1953-56; CLU, Am. Coll., 1973, chartered fin. cons., 1984; cert. fin. planner, Coll. Fin. Planning, 1983. Pres., CEO Jerome Burg Assoc., Inc., Cherry Hill, N.J., 1963-79, Contemporary Fin. Planning, Scottsdale, Ariz., 1979-89; sr. acct. mgr. Acacia Group, Phoenix, from 1989. Instr. Glendale and Scottsdale C.C., 1983-92, Nat. Inst. Fin., N.J., 1984-90. Host (radio program) Money Talks Sta. KFNN, Phoenix, 1993-98. Pres. N.J. Assn. Life Underwriters, Trenton, 1963-65; instr. Jr. Achievement, Scottsdale, 1985-89; bd. dirs. Phoenix Boys Choir, 1997—; 1st v.p. Pres. Cabinet-Acacia Group, Washington, 1991, 93, co-pres., 1992, mem. pres.' cabinet, 1989—. With U.S. Army, 1956-58. Mem. Internat. Assn. Fin. Planning (bd. dirs. Greater Phoenix chpt. 1982—), Inst. Cert. Fin. Planners. Avocations: golf, skiing. Home: Scottsdale, Ariz. Died May 13, 2004.

BURGENER, JERRY LEE, electronics executive; b. Marceline, Mo., Sept. 4, 1932; s. James Conrad and Bernice Lea (Anderson) B.; m. Carol Joye Koch, Feb. 3, 1954; children: Gala, David, Lori. BBA, Northeast Mo. U., 1950-53. With sales dept. Proctor & Gamble, Kansas City, Mo., 1957-64; regional mgr. Drackett Products, Los Angeles, 1964-67, Newark Electronics, Los Angeles, 1968-71; exec. v.p. Components Ctr., Inc., Fountain Valley, Pa., from 1972. Served as lt. commdr. USN, 1953-56, Korea. Mem. Nat. Electronic Distbrs. Assn. (pres. so. Calif. chpt. 1985, treas. 1982-84, dist. dir. Chgo. Dist. 1986). Avocations: golf, skiing. Home: Las Vegas, Nev. Died Nov. 17, 2004.

BURGESS, DANIEL FRANCIS, television announcer, copy writer; b. Oct. 3, 1925; s. Michael Anthony and Mary (Anania) Bonacci; divorced; children: Terence, Michael, Christian, Tyler. BFA, Ithaca Coll., 1948. Announcer Sta. WKRT, Cortland, N.Y., 1948-49, Sta. WMSA, Massena, N.Y., 1949-55, Sta. WWNY-TV, Watertown, N.Y., from 1955. Pres. Little Theater of Watertown, 1958-61. Author: A Border Case, 1966. Mem.: IT-American (Watertown), K.C. Democrat. Roman Catholic. Home: Watertown, NY. Died May 19, 2005.

BURGESS, JOHN MUIR, management consultant; b. Glasgow, Scotland, Jan. 18, 1937; came to U.S., 1963; s. Gregory Alexander and Mary Kenneth (Muir) B.; m. Barbara Jeffrey Reid, July 24, 1964; children: Victoria Mary, Jennifer Helen. BS, Glasgow U., 1959; MS, Cranfield U., 1961; MMS, Stevens Inst. Tech., 1966. Engr. U.K. Atomic Energy Authority, Aldermaston, 1959-63; mgr. mfg. engring. Curtiss-Wright Corp., Wood Ridge, N.J., 1963-65; dir. planning devel. Gourdine Sys. Inc., Livingston, N.J., 1965-67; prin. McKinsey & Co., N.Y.C., 1967-77; dir. logistics, mgr. mktg. and mfg. Gen. Foods Corp., White Plains, N.Y., 1977-83; pres. Argyll Corp., Stamford, Conn., from 1983. Mem. Inst. Mgmt. Cons., Innis Arden Golf Club, Riverside Yacht Club. Avocations: golf, boating, tennis. Home: Old Greenwich, Conn. Died Jan. 11, 2004.

BURGESS, MADGELENE JONES, social work administrator; b. Florence, Ala., Jan. 3, 1948; d. Grady Earl and Mattie Earlene (Littrell) Jones; m. James Claude Burgess III, June 13, 1983; children: James Claude IV, Nicole Earlene. BA in Humanities, Purdue U., 1969; MS in Social Work, U. Tenn., 1978. Cert. pub. mgr. tng., 1991. Tchr. Lauderdale County Bd. Edn., Greenhill, Ala., 1969-71, Lawrence County Bd. Edn., Lawrenceburg, Tenn., 1971-72; social worker Escambia County Dept. Pensions and Security, Brewton, Ala., 1972-75; supr. Chambers County Dept. Pensions and Security, Lafayette, Ala., 1975-77; dir. Fayette County Dept. Human Resources, Fayette, Ala., 1978-84; asst. dir. Madison County Dept. Human Resources, Huntsville, Ala., 1984-90; reg. mgr. State Dept. Human Resources, Decatur, from 1990. Chmn. InterAgy. Coun., Fayette, 1980-83; bd. dirs. Assn. for Retarded Citizens, Fayette, 1982. Mem. NASW, Nat. Eligibility Workers Assn., Assn. Country Dirs. (treas. 1980-83, v.p. 1988-90). Died Apr. 29, 2004.

BURGH, STEVEN LAWRENCE, record producer; b. Trenton, N.J., Dec. 17, 1950; s. Marvin J. Burgh and Zeldine (Schwartzman) Golden; m. Jamie Allison Reisch, Feb. 26, 1983; children: Louis, Juliet. Prodr., musician Phoebe Snow, N.Y.C., from 1974; producer, musician Steve Forbert, N.Y.C., 1978-82; producer, engr. Baby Monster Studios, N.Y.C., from 1986; prodn., owner Baby Monster Records, from 1997. Musician (album) Phoebe Snow, 1974 (Grammy nominee 1975), Steve Goodman Tribute, 1985 (Grammy 1986); musician aranger platinum album (singer) Gladys Knight, 1973; producer (album) Steve Forbert, 1978, Blend (band), 1997; musician (album) Billy Joel, 1978 (Grammy award), Cyprus Hill, 1995 (Platinum album), Space Hog, 1996 (Gold Album); musician (film) Tender Mercies, 1982 (Oscar 1983), Andy Statman Band, 1996, (TV program) The Edge of Night, 1996 (Emmy award). Mem. Local 802 Am. Fedn. Musicians. Avocation: musical instrument collecting. Died Feb. 7, 2005.

BURIAN, JARKA MARSANO, performing arts educator; b. Passaic, NJ, Mar. 10, 1927; s. Jaroslav Valerian and Olga Marsano Burian; m. Grayce Susan DeLeo, June 15, 1951. BA, Rutgers U., 1949; MA, Columbia U., 1950; PhD, Cornell U., 1955. From asst. prof. to assoc. prof. SUNY, Albany, 1955—59, from assoc. prof. to prof., 1963—93, chair theatre dept., 1971—74, 1977—78, prof. emeritus, from 1993; theatre dir.-prodr. Arena Summer Theatre, Albany, 1959, 1963—64, 1966—68, 1972—73. Author: The Scenography of Josef Svoboda, from 1971 (Spl. award US Inst. for Theatre Tech., 1973), Svoboda: Wagner, from 1983, Modern Czech Theatre, from 2000, Leading Creators of Twentieth-Century Czech Theater, from 2002; editor: The

Secret of Theatrical Space, from 1993 (Golden Pen award, 1995); contbg. editor: Theatre Design and Tech., from 1989; assoc. editor Theatre Jour., 1981—90. Sgt. U.S. Army, 1946—47, sgt. U.S. Army, 1950—51. Recipient Regional Arts award, Albany-Schenectady League of Arts, 1998; fellow Rsch. fellow, NEH, 1974; grantee, US Inst. for Theatre Tech., 2002; Lectr. grant, U.S. State Dept. to Czechoslovakia, 1965, Rsch. grantee, Internat. Rsch. Exch. Bd., 1969, 1974—75, 1993—94, Fulbright Found., 1982, 1988. Mem.: AAUP, U.S. Inst. for Theatre Tech., Internat. Fedn. for Theatre Rsch., Am. Soc. for Theatre Rsch., Theatre in Higher Edn., Phi Beta Kappa. Avocations: travel, swimming. Home: Albany, NY. Died Aug. 25, 2005.

BURK, RONALD LEE, traffic safety professional; b. Peoria, Ill., Mar. 19, 1936; s. Kenneth Marion and Phyllis Lee (Eaton) B.; m. Lila Jean Benham, Aug. 9, 1975; children: Robin Lee, Douglas Joseph, Steven Mathew, Dana Lynn. BA, Butler U., 1958. Cert. pers. cons. Cons. Gen. Emp. Enterprises, Indpls., 1962-70; co-owner, pers. cons. HBS & Assoc., Columbus, Ohio, 1971-83; project mgr., traffic safety Ohio Dept. of Pub. Safety, Columbus, from 1984. Recipient Recognition for Minority Ch. program Ohio State Sentate, 1992, Proclamation for Minority Ch. Program City of Toledo, 1992, Cert. of Appreciation U.S. Dept. Transp., 1992, Outstanding Pub. Rels. award Ohio Dept. of Hwy. Safety, 1990, State Occupant Protection award Gov.'s Traffic Safety Com., 1989, Spel. Recognition award, Ohio Dept. of Hwy. Safety, 1990, Nat. award Am. Coalition for Traffic Safety, 1991; honored by Ronald Burk Day in the City, City of Cleve., 1992. Avocations: golf, collecting, clown painting, Dept. 56 Dickens Village. Home: Columbus, Ohio. Died May 9, 2004.

BURLAND, J(OHN) ALEXIS, psychoanalyst; b. N.Y.C., Sept. 17, 1931; s. Elmer Granville and Catherine Alexander (Dobrushina) B.; m. Patricia Ruth Millar, Mar. 30, 1963. BA, Colgate U., 1952; MD, Columbia U., 1956; MSc, Temple U., 1962. Intern Mary Hitchcock Meml. Hosp., Hanover, N.H., 1956-57; resident in psychiatry Temple U. Hosp., Phila., 1957-58, 60-61; resident in child psychiatry St. Christopher's Hosp., Phila., 1961-63; candidate in gen. and child adolescent psychoanalysis Phila. Psychoanalytic Inst., 1963-72; pvt. practice Bala Cynwyd, Pa., 1963—2004. Assoc. prof. psychiatry Temple U. Hosp., St. Christopehrs Hosp., Phila., 1963-79; clin. prof. Jefferson Med. Coll., Thomas Jefferson U., Phila., 1979-2004; tng. supervising psychoanalyst Inst. Psychoanalytic Ctr. of Phila., 1983-2004, pres., 1991-97. Editor: Rapprochement: Critical Phase of Separation-Individuation, 1980, Self & Object Constancy, 1985. Lt. comdr. USNR, 1958-60. Fellow Am. Psychiat. Assn. (disting. life); mem. Am. Psychoanalytic Assn., Internat. Psychoanalytic Assn., Assn. Child Psychoanalysis, Psychoanalytic Ctr. of Phila. (pres. 1977-80), Union League, Phi Beta Kappa, Delta Upsilon Avocations: classical music, theater, ballet, writing, scuba diving. Died Mar. 20, 2004.

BURNS, GRANT FRANCIS, reference librarian; b. Owosso, Mich., June 18, 1947; s. Francis M. and Marie A. (Olsen) B.; m. Stephanie Winston Voight, Feb. 4, 1972; children: Andrea, Steven. BA in Social Sci., Mich. State U., 1969; AM in English, U. Mich., 1973, MLS, 1976. Ref. libr. U. Mich., Flint, from 1977, asst. dir. Thompson Libr., from 2001. Author: The Atomic Papers, 1984, The Sports Pages, 1987, Affordable Housing, 1989, The Nuclear Present, 1992, Librarians in Fiction, 1998, Email User's Handbook, 2002, Railroad in American Fiction, 2005; contbr. articles to profl. jours. Avocations: reading, gardening. Home: East Lansing, Mich. Died Jan. 5, 2006.

BURNS, MARIE T., retired secondary education educator; b. Nashua, N.H. d. Charles Henry and Eleanor Agnes (Martin) O'Neil; m. Thomas M. Burns; children: Ann Burns Pelletier, Mary Burns Powlowsky, Catherine Burns Patten. BA, Regis Coll.; postgrad., Rivier Coll. Cert. tchr., N.H. Tchr. English Pelham (N.H.) Sch. Dept., City of Nashua. Former trustee, chmn. of house com., sec. bd. dirs. Mary A. Sweeney Home; judge, participant River Coll. Literacy Festival. Mem. Nashua Tchrs. Union (mem. secondary grouping practices com. Nashua Sch. Dist.), N.H. Ret. Tchrs., Nashua Ret. Tchrs. Home: Nashua, NH. Died Feb. 2004.

BURNS, MCARTHUR, social services administrator; b. Ft. Lauderdale, Fla., July 25, 1944; s. Alice Burns; m. Barbara Ann Burns, Apr. 19, 1971; children: Quentin, McArthur, Alice. BS, Fla. A&M U., 1967; MS, Fla. Atlantic U., 1988. Teacher Broward Sch. System, Ft. Lauderdale, 1967-73; counselor State of Fla., West Palm Beach, 1973-78, adminstr., 1978-88, mgr., from 1988. Chmn. One Ch. One Child, 1994. Mem. NAACP, Urban League, Kappa Alpha Psi. Republican. Baptist. Avocations: travel, craftmanship, fishing. Home: Boynton Beach, Fla. Died May 29, 2005.

BURNSTINE, MICHAEL ROBERT, video specialist; b. Richmond, Va., May 25, 1948; s. Jerome Ian and Lillian H. Burnstine. BFA, Va. Commonwealth U., 1975. Cinematographer, reporter Sta. WTVR-TV, Sta. WWBT-TV, Richmond, 1968-73; instr. theater Va. Dept. Correction, Richmond, 1973-77; scout, stills photographer various motion pictures, 1977-81; pres. Talking Pictures Corp., Richmond, 1977-81; instr. Film, Video, TV Am. U., Washington, 1981-83; cons., with depts. prodn., sales Audio Unltd. N.Am., Atlanta; mgr. equipment sales and integration Staging Connections, Atlanta, 1986-90; mgr. sales and mktg. EDS Distance Learning Group, Atlanta, 1990-91; mgr. tech. devel. EDS Video Svcs., Atlanta, from 1990. Died Oct. 8, 2004.

BURRAGE, BRYAN RONALD, humanities educator; b. London, Aug. 30, 1936; s. Ronald John and Winifred Edith Marion (Workman) B.; m. Sylvia Sydney Jarboe, July 6, 1972. AB, U. Kans., 1956; MSc, San Diego State U., 1966; PhD, U. Stellenbosch, 1972. Curator South African Mus., Cape Town, 1969-72; prof. Coll. of the Desert, Palm Desert, Calif., from 1972. Pres. Water Bd. Pinyon, 1974-80. Home: Mountain Center, Calif. Died May 2, 2004.

BURRIS, DUANE, software developer; b. St. Louis, Nov. 27, 1956; s. Hubert Wayne and Marjorie (Graham) B.; m. Brenda Joyce Keegan, Apr. 21, 1978; children: Ashley Keegan Burris, Andrew James Zebadiah Burris. AA in Liberal Arts, Glendale (Ariz.) C.C., 1976; AA in Constrn., Rio Salado Coll., 1981; BS in Computer Sci., Grand Canyon U., 1988. Cert. network engr.; cert. folio cons. Gen. foreman Mardian Constrn., Phoenix, 1978-83, scheduling mgr., 1983-84, info. systems mgr., 1984-90; pres. Witan Industries, Glendale, from 1990. Adj. prof. Grand Canyon U., Phoenix, 1988; cons. Teknow!, Phoenix, 1989. Author (software) XQLLIB, 1989; inventor BNC tool. Foresight N.W. Christian Ch., Phoenix, 1989-92, Sunday sch. tchr., 1980-92; cons. Jr. Achievement, Phoenix, 1989. Recipient Cert. Appreciation Ariz. Alliance of Bus., 1988, 89, Grand Canyon U., 1988; named Outstanding Capenter Ariz. Gov. Bruce Babbit, 1981. Mem. IEEE, Assn. for Computing Machinery, Peoria Econ. Devel. Group, Novell Profl. Developers. Republican. Avocations: ranching, farming, sawmilling. Home: Mayer, Ariz. Died May 21, 2004.

BURROUGHS, JOHN TOWNSEND, lawyer; b. Akron, Ohio, May 27, 1926; s. Ralph and Helen (Townsend) B.; m. Laverne Casey, Nov. 23, 1966; 1 child, Brien C. BA cum laude, Brown U., 1946; MD, Harvard U., 1950; JD with honors, Calif. Western Sch. Law, 1978. Bar: Calif. 1979, U.S. Ct. Claims 1979, U.S. Dist. Ct. (ea. dist.) Wis. 1981, Wis. 1982, Colo. 1986; diplomate Am. Bd. Surgery, Am. Bd. Thoracic Surgery; lic. surgeon, Calif. Intern, then resident Halsted svc. Johns Hopkins Hosp., Balt., 1950-52; fellow in surgery Mayo Clinic, Rochester, Minn., 1954-56; resident in surgery UCLA Med. Ctr., 1956-58, asst. in surgery, 1958-59; asst. prof. dept. surgery UCLA Med. Sch., 1959-63; chief dept. thoracic and cardiovascular surgery Wadsworth VA Hosp.; practice medicine specializing in thoracic and cardiovascular surgery L.A., 1961-72; practice medicine specializing in thoracic, cardiovascular and coronary bypass surgery Milw., 1972-75; staff, chief med. legal research div. dept. legal medicine Armed Forces Inst. Pathology, Washington, 1979-82; ptnr. Joling, Rizzo, Willems, Oleniewski, Stern & Burroughs, S.C., Kenosha, Wis., 1982-85; sole practice Salem, Wis., 1985-88, San Diego, from 1988. Vis. surgeon in cardiovascular surgery U. Free Berlin, 1959; clin. assoc. prof. U. Calif., Irvine, 1963-72; adj. prof. law Antioch Sch., Washington, 1980; chief sect. thoracic surgery VA Hosp., L.A., 1959-63; lectr. on law and medicine, 1979-92; cons. U. Free Berlin, 1959. Contbr. articles to profl. jours. Chmn. Edn. com. Inglewood C. of C., 1968-69, chmn. drug com., 1969-71, bd. dirs. 1970-72; chmn. CPR Tng. Milw. Heart Assn., 1972-74, Community Programs Council, Inglewood, 1970-72, southwestern br. Los Angeles County Heart Assn., 1968-70, CPR Tng. Progam, Los Angeles Heart Assn., 1969-72; med. dir. Program in Inglewood Unified Sch. Dist. on Narcotics and Smoking, 1968-72, Narcotics edn. dist atty.'s advisory council, Los Angeles, 1968-70; trustee Centinela Valley Community Hosp., 1971-72; bd. dirs. Associated Centinela Services, 1971-72. Served to lt. M.C., USNR, 1952-54. Recipient Award of Merit Los Angeles County Heart Assn., 1967-70, Heart Recognition award Los Angeles County Heart Assn., 1971, Disting. Service award Los Angeles County Heart Assn., 1972, Cert. Commendation Los Angeles County, 1972, Cert. Merit Inglewood Unified Sch. Dist., 1969. Fellow ACS, Am. Coll. Cardiology, Am. Coll. Chest Physicians, Am. Coll. Legal Medicine (emeritus); mem. ATLA, Calif. Bar Assn., Wis. Bar Assn. (ret.), Sigma Xi. Home: San Diego, Calif. Died Nov. 10, 2004.

BURROUGHS, LEONARD HARLEE, real estate appraiser, consultant; b. Richmond, Va., Jan. 4, 1930; s. Garrett L. Burroughs and Helen Lee Dixon; m. Momoe Matsuo Burroughs, Jan. 15, 1951 (div. Oct. 1977); children: Arthur, Susan Helen; m. Wanda Faye Fuller, Oct. 15, 1977; children: Michelle Leigh, Tiffany Amber. BGS Mil. Sci., U. Omaha, 1967. Cert. gen. appraiser # 4 Ga. Active duty U.S. Army, 1948—72, advanced through grades to lt. col.; self employed cons. Calhoun, Ga., 1972—74; corp. pilot Cons. Co., Calhoun, 1974—76; western divsn. mgr. Franklin Cons. Co., Battle Mountain, Nev., 1976—82; real estate broker Walraven Realty, Calhoun, 1982—86; real estate appraiser self employed Calhoun, from 1986. County commr. Bd. Commrs. Gordon County, Ga., from 2001. Decorated Disting. Flying Cross, Bronze Star, 4 Air medals, 2 Meritorious Svc. medals, 2 Commendation medals. Mem.: Calhoun Rotary Club. Republican. Avocation: breeding, raising and traning horses. Home: Calhoun, Ga. Died June 21, 2004.

BURTON, GLENN WILLARD, geneticist; b. Clatonia, Nebr., May 5, 1910; s. Joseph Fearn and Nellie (Rittenburg) Burton; m. Helen Maurine Jeffryes, Dec. 16, 1934; children: Elizabeth Ann Fowler, Robert Glenn, Thomas Jeffryes, Joseph William, Richard Bennett. BS, U. Nebr., 1932, DSc (hon.), 1962; MS, Rutgers U., 1933, PhD, 1936, DSc (hon.), 1955. With USDA and U. Ga. at Tifton Exptl. Sta., 1936—2005, prin. geneticist, 1952—2005, chmn. div. agronomy, 1950—64; Univ. Found. prof. U. Ga., 1957. Mem. Tift County Bd. Edn., 1953—58. Recipient 1st Ann. Agrl. award, So. Seedsman Assn., 1950, Sears-Roebuck Rsch. award, 1953, 1960, Superior Svc. award, USDA, 1955, 1st Ford Almanac Crops and Soils Rsch. award, 1962, Disting. Svc. award, 1980, Pres.'s award for Disting. Fed. Civilian Svc., 1981, Nat. Medal of Sci., 1983, named Man of Yr., So. Agriculture Progressive Farmer, 1954, named to Hall of Fame, USDA ARS, 1987, numerous other awards and citations. Fellow: Am. Soc. Agronomy (v.p. 1961, pres. 1962, Stevenson award 1949, John Scott award 1957); mem.: Nat. Acad. Sci., Am. Soc. Range Mgmt., Am. Genetic Assn., Gamma Sigma, Alpha Zeta, Sigma Xi. Home: Tifton, Ga. Died Nov. 22, 2005.

BUSCH, ESTELLE WINSTON, theater director; b. N.Y.C., Aug. 30, 1914; d. Max and Eva Weinberg; m. Ben Busch, Dec. 30, 1942 (dec.); children: Mark, Carolann Carter. Grad., Group Theatre, N.Y., 1935. Founder Pact Theatre, L.A., 1965—70; adminstr. Theatre Alliance, L.A., 1972—78; founder, v.p. Women in Theatre, L.A., 1978—81; exec. dir. Synthaxis Theatre, L.A., 1978—2004, dir., 1984—2004; co-chair MidValley Neighborhood Coun. Theatre, North Hollywood Valley, Calif., 2003—04. Tchr. Valley Store Front, North Hollywood, 2002—03; dir. Collage Improvization Show, 1978—2004. One-woman shows include Edinburgh Theatre Art Festival, 1979—80, Window Panes; dir.: (plays) Emergence of Mel, 2002. Conv. del. AFTRA, LA, 1970—80; active C. of C. North Hollywood, 1993—2003; founder Women in Theater, 1978, bd. dirs., v.p., liaison to AFTRA, SAG, Actors Equity, 1978—81; L.A. rep. Edinburgh Art Festival, 1979; mem. women's coms. SAG, AFTRA, Actors Equity, 1969—79; co-founder Equity Waiver Theatre Scene, L.A., 1969; founder Valley Theatre League, 1993; mem., co-chair No-Ho Theatre Com., 1994—2004; del. AFTRA conv., 1969—79; co-chair theatre com. Neighborhood Coun. North Hollywood, 2003; advocate women's issues Dem. Party, Calif., 1993—2003; bd. dirs. San Fernando Arts Coun., 1982—85. Named 4th dist. Pioneer Woman of Yr., Councilman Tom LaBonge, 2003; named one of 10 Women of Yr., Commn. on Status of Women, 1999; recipient Juanine Clay Life Achievement award, Valley Theatre League, 1979—2000, proclamation of appreciation, L.A. City Coun., 1979—2003, honor, NO-HO News, 1994, certs. of appreciation, State Sen. Richard Alarcon, State Contr. Helen Connor, U.S. Sen. Barbara Boxer, Dist. Atty. Gil Garcetti, letter of congratulation, Pres. Bill Clinton, 1999—2001, Red Carpet award, Women in Theatre, 2004, proclamation in honor of 90th birthday, L.A. City Coun., 2004. Avocations: theater, community involvement. Home: North Hollywood, Calif. Died Mar. 15, 2006.

BUSCH, FREDERICK MATTHEW, writer, educator; b. N.Y.C., Aug. 1, 1941; s. Benjamin and Phyllis (Schnell) B.; m. Judith Burroughs, Nov. 29, 1963; children: Benjamin, Nicholas. BA, Muhlenberg Coll., Allentown, Pa., 1962, LittD (hon.), 1980; MA, Columbia U., 1967. Writer for mags., N.Y.C., and Greenwich, Conn., 1963—66; from instr. to prof. Colgate U., Hamilton, N.Y., 1966-87, Fairchild prof. lit., 1987—2003. Acting dir. Program in Creative Writing U. Iowa, Iowa City, 1978-79; Zell disting. vis. prof. creative writing U. Mich., 2006. Author: 27 books including Sometimes I Live in the Country, 1986, Absent Friends, 1989, Harry and Catherine, 1990, Closing Arguments, 1991, Long Way From Home, 1993, The Children in the Woods: New and Selected Stories, 1994 (PEN/Faulkner award nomination, 1995), Girls, 1997, (essays) A Dangerous Profession, 1998, (novel) The Night Inspector, 1999 (PEN/Faulkner award nomination, NBCC award nomination, 2000); editor: (anthology) Letters to a Fiction Writer, 1997, (stories) Don't Tell Anyone, 2000, A Memory of War, 2003, (novel) North, 2005; numerous other essays and short stories. Recipient Nat. Jewish Book award for fiction, Jewish Book Coun., 1986, Fiction award, AAAL, 1986, PEN/Malamud, 1991, Award of Merit, AAAL, 2001; fellow, Guggenheim Found., 1981—82, Ingram Merrill Found., 1981—82. Mem.: PEN, Am. Acad. Arts and Scis., Authors Guild Am. Home: Sherburne, NY. Died Feb. 23, 2006.

BUSCH, HARRIS, medical educator; b. Chgo., May 23, 1923; s. Maurice Ralph and Rose Lillian (Feigenholtz) B.; m. Rose Klora, June 16, 1945; children: Daniel Avery, Laura Anne Busch Smolkin, Gerald Irwin, Fredric Neal. BS, U. Ill., 1944, MD with honors, 1946; MS, U. Wis., 1950, PhD, 1952. Intern Cook County Hosp., Chgo., 1946-47; asst. surgeon, sr. asst. surgeon USPHS, 1947-49; postdoctoral fellow Nat. Cancer Inst., 1950-52; asst. prof. biochemistry, internal medicine Yale U., 1952-55; assoc. prof., prof. pharmacology U. Ill., 1955-60; prof. biochemistry, chmn. dept. Baylor U. Coll. Medicine, 1960-62, prof. pharmacology, chmn. dept., 1960-98, Michael E. DeBakey disting. svc. prof. and chmn., from 1995, chmn. student promotions com., 1969-72, mem. pres.'s coun., 1972-93, dir. Cancer Rsch. Ctr. Vis. prof. U. Chgo., 1968, 71, Northwestern U., 1968, Ga. Med. Coll., 1971, Washington U., St. Louis, 1972, U. Ala., Birmingham, 1972, Ind. U., Indpls., 1972, U. Nev., Reno, 1978, U. Colo., Denver, 1980; cons. lectr. U. Tenn., U. Tex., San Antonio, 1971; Disting. lectr. SUNY, Buffalo, 1977; Centennial lectr. U. Ill. Coll. Medicine, 1981; Disting. lectr. Tohoku Med. Sch., Japan, 1990, Japan Chemotherapy Soc., 1990, Taiwan, 1992; invited lectr. Vienna, Austria, 1992, George Washington U., 1992, Naples, Italy, 1994, Wilhelm Bernard Workshop, Spa (Liege), Belgium,

1995; mem. adv. com. cell and devel. biology Am. Cancer Soc., 1978-82; cancer chemotherapy study sect. USPHS; mem. Nat. Cancer Planning Com., 1971; mem. bd. sci. counselors to div. cancer treatment Nat. Cancer Inst., 1975. Author: Chemistry of Pancreatic Diseases, 1959, An Introduction to the Biochemistry of the Cancer Cell, 1962, Histones and Other Nuclear Proteins, 1965; co-author: Chemotherapy, 1966, The Nucleolus, 1970; editor: Frontiers in Medical Biochemistry, 1962, The Nucleus of the Cancer Cell, 1963, Jour. Phys. Chemistry and Physics, Methods in Cancer Research, vol. I, 1966, vols. II and III, 1967, vol. IV, 1968, Methods in Cancer Research, vol. V, 1970, vol.VI, 1971, vols. VII-IX, 1973, vol. X, 1973, Methods in Cancer Research, vol. XI, 1975, vols. XII and XIII, 1976, Methods in Cancer Research, vols. XIV, XV, 1978, Molecular Biology of Cancer, 1974, Cell Nucleus, Vols. I-III, 1974, IV-VII, 1978, VIII-IX, 1980; editorial bd.: Jour. Cancer Research and Clin. Oncology, Jour. Biol. Chemistry, Cancer Investigation, New Drugs, Physiol. Chemistry, Phys. Life Scis. Recipient Outstanding Alumnus award for svc. to edn. and rsch. U. Ill., 1977, Disting. Faculty award Baylor Coll. Medicine, 1982, Maimonides award, 1996; Baldwin scholar oncology Yale U. Sch. Medicine, 1952-55; scholar cancer rsch. Am. Cancer Soc., 1955. Mem. Am. Soc. Biol. Chemists and Molecular Biologists, Am. Assn. Cancer Rsch. (pres. elect 1988-89, pres. 1989-90, bd. dirs., sci. and public affairs com. 1987), Am. Chem. Soc., Soc. Pharmacology and Exptl. Therapeutics, Soc. Exptl. Biology and Medicine, Internat. Acad. of Tumor Marker Oncology, Sigma Xi, Alpha Omega Alpha. Home: Houston, Tex. Died Sept. 22, 2006.

BUSH, SPENCER HARRISON, metallurgist, consultant; b. Flint, Mich., Apr. 4, 1920; s. Edward Charles and Rachel Beatrice (Roser) B.; m. Roberta Lee Warren, Aug. 28, 1948; children: David Spencer, Carl Edward. Student, Flint Jr. Coll., 1938-40, Ohio State U., 1943-44, U. Mich., 1946-53. Registered profl. engr., Calif. Asst. chemist Dow Chem. Co., 1940-42, 46; assoc. Engring. Rsch. Inst., U. Mich., 1947-53; research asst. Office Naval Rsch., 1950-53, instr. dental materials, 1951-53; metallurgist Hanford Atomic Products Operation, Gen. Electric Co., 1953-54, supr. phys. metallurgy, 1954-57, supr. fuels fabrication devel., 1957-60, metall. specialist, 1960-63, cons. metallurgist, 1963-65; cons. to dir. Battelle Pacific N.W. Labs., Richland, Wash., 1965-70, sr. staff cons., 1970-83, sr. staff scientist, 1985-2000; pres. Rev. & Synthesis Assocs., cons., from 1983. Lectr. metall. engring. Ctr. for Grad. Study U. Wash., 1953-67, affiliate prof., 1967-78; chmn., mem. com. study group on pressure vessel materials Electric Power Rsch. Inst., 1974-78; cons. U. Calif. Lawrence Livermore Labs., 1975-79, Integral Fast Reactor U. Chgo., 1984-94; chmn. com. on reactor safeguards U.S. AEC, 1971; mem. Wash. Bd. Boiler Rules, 1972-85; mem. spec. adv. com. for Argonne Nuc. Tech. Pgm., U Chgo. 1994-2002; chmn. piping design com. Joint NRC/Pressure Vessel Rsch. Coun., 1982-90, PVRC Peer Rev. on ASME Code Simplification, exec. com., 1982—, mem. steering com. on fatigue, 1992—, hon. emeritus mem., 1999; mem. nuclear safety rsch. rev. com. NRC, 1988-94; mem. high level waste structural integrity panel Dept. Energy Brookhaven Nat. Lab., 1992-97. Contbr. tech. articles to profl. jours. Served with U.S. Army, 1942-46. Recipient Silver Beaver award Boy Scouts Am.; Am. Foundrymens Soc. fellow, 1948-50; Regents prof. U. Calif., Berkeley, 1973-74 Fellow ASME (hon., bd. nuc. codes and stds. 1983-2000, chmn. sec. XI 1985-90, hon. mem. subcom. XI 1995, exec. bd. NDE divsn. 1984-90, chmn. 1987-88, nat. nominating com. 1988-90, Langer award 1983, Melvin R. Green Codes & Stds. medal 1997), ASM (life, chmn. program coun. 1966-67, trustee 1967-69, chmn. fellow com. 1968, trustee found. 2004—), Am. Nuc. Soc. (adv. editl. bd. nuc. applications 1965-77, bd. dirs. 1984-87, Thompson award 1987); mem. AIME (chmn. ann. seminar com. 1967-68), ASTM (Gillette lectr. 1975), Am. Soc. Nondestructive Testing (Mehl lectr.), Nat. Acad. Engring., Sigma Xi, Tau Beta Pi, Phi Kappa Phi. Died Oct. 2, 2005.

BUTCHER, SUSAN HOWLET, sled dog racer, kennel owner; b. Boston, Dec. 26, 1954; d. Charles and Agnes (Young) B.; m. David Lee Monson, children: Tekla, Chisana. Driver 1st dog team to summit Mt. KcKinley, Alaska, 1979; winner among top 10 finishers Long Distance Sled Dog Races, Alaska and Minn., 1978-87; 5th pl. Iditarod Race, Anchorage and Nome, Alaska, 1980, 81, 2d pl., 1988, 90, champion, winner 1st pl., 1986, 87, world record holder, 1986-87; champion, winner 1st pl. Coldfoot Classic Race, Brooks Range, Alaska, 1985; winner Iditarod, Alaska, 1988, Kusho 300, Bethel, Alaska, 1988, Portage 250, Alaska, 1988. Bd. dirs. Iditarod Trail Com., Wasilla, Alaska, 1980-86, ambassador of good will Iditarod Sport of Sled Dog Racing, 1982-2006; mem. nutrition adv. panel Purina Pro Plan, St. Louis, 1986-2006; tech. advisor Allied Fibers, N.Y.C., 1985-2006. Contbr. articles to profl. jours. Hon. chmn. March of Dimes, Anchorage, 1986, Spl. Olympics, Anchorage, 1987. Named Musher of Yr. Team and Trail, N.H., 1987, one of Profl. Sports Women of Yr. Womens Sports Found., N.Y.C., 1987, Sports Woman of Yr., W.S.F, 1988, Sportswomen of Yr. U.S. Sports Acad.; recipient Victor award, Las Vegas, Nev., 1987, 88, legis. commendation States of Alaska and Mass., 1986-87, Moniqo Bedeaux prize French Sport Acad., 1989, Athletic Achievement award Tanguray, N.Y., 1989. Mem. Iditarod Trail Com., Iditarod Trail Blazers (life), Beargrease Race Com., Kuskokwim 300 Race Com. Clubs: Interior Dog Mushers (Manley, Alaska); Nome Kennel; Norton Sound Sled Dog. Avocation: mountain climbing. Died Aug. 5, 2006.

BUTLER, DEBRA SUE, nurse; b. Omaha, Nebr., Dec. 25, 1955; d. James John and Betty Ann (Konopik) Bermingham; m. Thomas J. Butler, Apr. 10 1976; Kara Janelle, Matthew Thomas. Staff nurse Meth. Hosp., Omaha, 1977-78, 89-92; paramedic instr. Creighton U. Omaha Fire Dept., 1978-79; staff nurse Bergan Mercy Hosp., Omaha, 1979-81, Immanuel Hosp., Omaha, 1981-82, St. Joseph (AMI) Hosp., Omaha, 1982-89. Instr. Am. Heart Assn., Omaha, 1978--. Firefighter Millard Fire Dept., 1978-83; Brownie leader, 1987—. Democrat. Methodist. Avocation: cross stiching. Home: Omaha, Nebr. Died Oct. 12, 2004.

BUTLER, DOLORES J., nun, education educator; b. Canton, Mass., Aug. 23, 1930; d. Joseph E. and Helen M. B. BS in Elem. Edn., Villanova U., 1960; EdM in Spl. Edn., St. Louis U., 1968, PhD in Edn., 1973. Prin. St. Michael (Ariz.) Ind. Sch., 1970-73; teaching asst. St. Louis U., 1970-73; rsch. asst. U. Solothurn, Switzerland, 1973-74; prin. Holy Ghost Sch., New Orleans, 1975-80; asst. prof. Xavier U. La., New Orleans, 1981-87, assoc. prof. Grad. Sch. Edn., 1988—91. Early childhood cons. Archdiocese of New Orleans. Mem. NEA, ASCD, Assn. Early Childhood Internat., Nat. Assn. Edn. Young Children, Coun. Exceptional Children, Nat. Cath. Edn. Assn., Phi Delta Kappa. Avocations: cooking, gardening, reading. Died Aug. 11, 2004.

BUTLER, OCTAVIA ESTELLE, writer; b. Pasadena, Calif., June 22, 1947; d. Laurice and Octavia Margaret (Guy) B. AA, Pasadena City Coll., 1968; student, Calif. State U., Los Angeles, from 1969. Free-lance writer, Los Angeles, from 1975. MacArthur fellow, 1995. Author: Patternmaster, 1976, Mind of My Mind, 1977, Survivor, 1978, Kindred, 1979, Wild Seed, 1980, Clay's Ark, 1984, Dawn, 1987, Adulthood Rites, 1988, Imago, 1989, Parable of the Sower, 1993, Bloodchild, 1995, Parable of the Talents, 1998 (Nebula award), Fledgling, 2005; also sci. fiction short stories. Mem. adv. bd. Science Fiction Mus. and Hall of Fame. Recipient fifth prize Writer's Digest Short Story Contest, 1967, Creative Arts Achievement award L.A. YWCA, 1980, Sci. Fiction (Hugo) Best Novelette award World Sci. Fiction Conf., 1985, Best Short Story award World Sci. Fiction Conv., 1984, Nebula Best Novelette award Sci. Fiction Writers Am., 1985, Locus Best Novelette award, 1985, Best Novelette award Sci. Fiction Chronicle Reader, 1985, Nebula award for Best Novel, Sci. Fiction and Fantasy Writers Am., 2000; fellow John D. and Catherine T. MacArthur Found., 1995. Mem. Sci. Fiction Writers Am., Nat. Writers Union. Died Feb. 24, 2006.

BUTTS, JAMES ALVIN, real estate broker; b. Perry, Okla., Nov. 7, 1938; s. Oscar Walter and Laudie (Becquart) B.; m. Mary Schoenborn (div.); 1 child, Jill Marie. BS, Okla. State U., 1961, MS, 1962; postgrad., UCLA, 1972. Asst. dean students U. Tex., Arlington, 1964-65; merchandising mgr. Southland Corp., Dallas, 1965-69; mgr. we. div. Nat. Convenience Stores, Inc., Anaheim, Calif., 1969-73; pres. Minit Market, Inc., Anaheim, 1973-79; exec. v.p. Ladd Liquors, Inc., Santa Ana, Calif., 1979-84; owner Sunset Liquor Store, Tustin, Calif., 1984-88; sales mgr. Tarbell Realtors, Tustin, 1985-87; rep. acquisitions The Southland Corp., Tustin, 1987-88; real estate broker Re/Max, Irvine, Calif., from 1988. Lt. U.S. Army, 1962-68. Mem. Irvine Bd. Realtors (pres., Realtor of Yr. 1991), Nat. Assn. Realtors, Calif. Assn. Realtors. Republican. Roman Catholic. Avocations: shooting, fishing, camping. Home: Irvine, Calif. Died July 22, 2005.

BUTZNER, JOHN DECKER, JR., retired federal judge; b. Scranton, Pa., Oct. 2, 1917; BA, U. Scranton, 1939; LLB, U. Va., 1941. Bar: Va. 1941. Pvt. practice law, Fredericksburg, 1941—58; judge 15th and 39th Jud. Cir. of Va., 1958—62, US Dist. Ct. (ea. dist.) Va., 1962—67, U.S. Ct. Appeals (4th Cir.), Richmond, Va., 1967—98; judge for appointment of ind. counsel U.S. Ct. Appeals (D.C. Cir.), 1988—98. With USAAF, 1942—45. Home: Richmond, Va. Died Jan. 20, 2006.

BUYERS, JOHN WILLIAM AMERMAN, agribusiness and specialty foods company executive; b. Coatesville, Pa., July 17, 1928; s. William Buchanan and Rebecca (Watson) B.; m. Elizabeth Lindsey; children: Elsie Buyers Viehman, Rebecca Watson Buyers-Basso, Jane Palmer Buyers-Russo. BA in History cum laude, Princeton U., 1952; MS in Indsl. Mgmt., MIT, 1963. Div. ops. mgr. Bell Tel. Co. Pa., 1953-66; dir. ops. and pers. Gen. Waterworks Corp., Phila., 1966-68, pres., CEO, 1971-75; v.p. adminstrn. Internat. Utilities Corp., Phila., 1968-71; pres., CEO, dir. C. Brewer and Co., Ltd., Honolulu, from 1975, chmn. bd., from 1982; chmn., CEO D. Buyers Enterprises, LLC, 2001—05. Chmn. Calif. and Hawaiian Sugar Co., 1982-84, 86-90; pres., chmn. bd. Buyco, Inc., 1986-2006; mem. Hawaii Joint Coun. Econ. Edn., Japan-Hawaii Econ. Coun.; bd. dirs. BancWest, First Hawaiian Bank, John B. Sanfilippo & Sons, Inc., ML Macadamia Orchards, L.P. Trustee U. Hawaii Found., 1986-2006; chmn. bd. dirs. Hawaii Visitors Bur., 1990-91; mem. Gov.'s Blue Ribbon Panel on the Future of Healthcare in Hawaii; bd. dirs. Hawaii Sports Found., 1990-95; mem. adv. group to U.S. Dist. Ctr. With USMC, 1946-48. Sloan fellow MIT, 1962-63. Mem. Hawaiian Sugar Planters Assn. (chmn. bd. dirs. 1980-82, dir.), C. of C. Hawaii (chmn. bd. dirs. 1981-2004), Nat. Alliance Bus. (chmn. Hawaii Pacific Metro chpt. 1978), Cap and Gown Club (Princeton), Hilo Yacht Club, Oahu County Club, Pacific Club, Waialae County Club, Prouts Neck (Maine) County Club, U.S. C. of C. (mem. food and agr. com. 1991-2006), Beretania Tennis Club. Presbyterian. Died May 20, 2006.

BYASSEE, MARGARET FOLEY, art educator, poet, vocalist; b. Newport, R.I., Jan. 17, 1922; d. Edward B. and May (Cruickshank) Foley; m. Ivan Byassee, Oct. 1, 1950 (dec.). Student, Wheaton Coll., 1947-49; BA, U. Tenn., Knoxville, 1952; MEd, U. Tenn., Chattanooga, 1984. Cert. tchr. Art tchr. Oak Ridge (Tenn.) City Sch. Sys., 1953-61, Chattanooga (Tenn.) City Sch. Sys., 1962-82, Sweetwater (Tenn.) City Schs., 1984-85, artist-in-residence. Author numerous poems; one-woman shows Gallery 210, Chattanooga, Ariel Galleries, N.Y., among others. Mem. Artist Guild, Newport, R.I., 1998-99, Newport Art Mus., 1998-99; pres. Chattanooga Civic Arts League, Authors and Artists, Chattanooga. Sgt. U.S. Army, 1943-46. Named to Internat. Soc. Poetry Hall of Fame, 1996; recipient Editor's Choice award Nat. Libr. Poetry, 1995, 96, 2000. Mem. Women in the Arts, Internat. Soc. Poetry, Assn. Visual Arts, Chattanooga Tenn. Authors and Artists. Avocations: tennis, golf, camping, soloist with island senior chorus, painting. Home: Portsmouth, RI. Died June 13, 2004.

BYER, DOROTHY ELAINE, artist, designer craftsman, botanist; b. Watkins Glen, N.Y., May 22, 1925; d. Clinton and Edna (Randall) VanVleet; m. Marshall Byer, June 13, 1949; children: Deborah and Judith (twins), Linda. BA, SUNY, Binghamton, 1984. Designer Corning Glass Works, N.Y.C., 1941-43; profl. potter, designer, craftsman, sculptor, from 1953. Bd. dirs. Roberson Mus. Fine Arts Soc., 1959, N.Y. State Craftsmen, 1958-61, 64-67, asst. mgr. fair 1960, mgr. fair 1961, pres. 1964, bd. advisors, 1975. Exhibited shows include Roberson Mus. (award for pottery), Binghamton, 1959, Design Ctr. for Interiors, N.Y.C., 1959, Cooper Union Mus. for Arts of Decoration, 1959, N.Y. State Craft Fair, 1959, 60, Lowe Gallery, 1960, Rundell Gallery, 1960, SUNY-Binghamton, 1961, Cortland, 1961; represented in Sculpture Courtyard, SUNY-Binghamton, 1981. Mem. Am. Fern Soc., Internat. Palm Soc. Died Apr. 25, 2005.

BYRNE, ELEANOR, artist; b. Steubenville, Ohio, Jan. 16, 1921; d. Charles Bachelor and Bertha Droege McGowan; m. Horace Franklin Byrne, Nov. 4, 1948 (dec. Mar. 1999); children: Deborah, Charles, Malcolm. Student, Mount Holyoke Coll., 1943; BA, U. S.C., 1977, MA, 1980, MFA, 1982. Grad. asst. dept. art U. S.C., Columbia, 1977—82; tchr. parent-child workshop Columbia Mus. Art, 1985—90. Exhibited in group shows at S.C. State Fair, 1980—99 (merit awards each yr.), nationally and internationally. Recipient Acad. Palm, French Legion of Honor, 1985. Episcopalian. Avocation: cooking. Died Feb. 6, 2006.

BYRNE, WILLIAM MATTHEW, JR., federal judge; b. LA, Sept. 3, 1930; s. William Matthew Sr. and Julia Ann (Lamb) B. BS, U. So. Calif., 1953, LLB, 1956; LLD, Loyola U., 1971. Bar: Calif. 1956. Ptnr. Dryden, Harrington & Schwartz, 1960-67; asst. atty U.S. Dist. Ct. (so. dist.) Calif., 1958-60; atty. U.S. Dist. Ct. (ctrl. dist.) Calif., Los Angeles, 1967-70, judge, 1971—98, chief judge, 1994—98, sr. judge, 1998—2006; exec. dir. Pres. Nixon's Commn. Campus Unrest, 1970. Instr. Loyola Law Sch., Harvard U., Whittier Coll. Served with USAF, 1956-58. Mem. ABA, Fed. Bar Assn., Calif. Bar Assn., Los Angeles County Bar Assn. (vice chmn. human rights sect.), Am. Judicature Soc. Died Jan. 12, 2006.

CACOSSA, ANTHONY ALEXANDER, Romance languages educator; b. Newburgh, NY, Jan. 29, 1935; s. Salvatore and Franceschina (Scicchitano) C.; m. Anna Iaccino, Apr. 10, 1969. BA, Johns Hopkins U., 1955; MA, Syracuse U., 1956; D Modern Langs., U. Catania, Italy, 1969. Teaching asst. Syracuse (N.Y.) U., 1956-57; asst. prof., chmn. fgn. langs. Coppin State Coll., Balt., 1959-65; asst. prof. to prof. modern langs., coord. Italian studies Towson State U., Balt., 1965-83; adj. prof. Romance langs. and ESL Greenwich U., Hilo, Hawaii, 1989—2000; core faculty advisor in edn. Walden U., Mpls., 1990—96. Vis. tchr. Newburgh (NY) Free Acad., 1956; vis. lectr. Loyola Coll., Balt., 1967; accredited and chartered profl. cons. fgn. lang. edn. and curriculum design, Balt., 1983—; Fulbright lectr. Colombia, 1965, Italy, 1968-69, Costa Rica, 1972-73. Author: A Bergamask Parody of Guarini's Il Pastor Fido, 1972, Italian trans., 1973; contbr. articles to profl. jours. Fellow in Italian NEH, Stanford (Calif.) U., 1979; East European studies fellow Am. Coun. Learned Socs., UCLA, 1986. Mem. AAUP, Sigma Delta Pi (hon.). Died Nov. 22, 2004.

CADDELL, JOHN A., lawyer; b. Tuscumbia, Ala., Apr. 23, 1910; s. Thomas Arthur and Florence Lee (Huff) C.; m. Lucy Bowen Harris, Sept. 1, 1935; children— Thomas A., Lucinda Lee, Henry Harris and John A. (twins). AB, U. Ala., 1931, LLB, 1933, LLD (hon.), 1982. Bar: Ala. bar 1933. Since practiced in, Decatur. Sec., dir. Southeastern Metals Co., Inc., Birmingham, 1946-68; chmn. bd. First Nat. Bank Decatur, 1976-81; City atty., Decatur, 1936-59; counsel com. investigating campaign expenditures U.S. Ho. of Reps., 1944; bd. commrs. Ala. State Bar, 1939-54, Jud. Council Ala., 1946-58; mem. bd. Bar Examiners Ala., 1949, 50 Mem. Ala. Democratic Exec. Com., 1938-50; Trustee U. Ala., 1954-79, also pres. pro tem, 1974-78. Fellow Am. Coll. Trust and Estate Counsel, Am. Coll. Trial Lawyers, Am. Bar Found.; mem. ABA, Ala. Bar Assn. (pres. 1951-52), Morgan County Bar Assn., U. Ala. Alumni Assn. (pres. 1953), Decatur C. of C. (pres. 1943-44), Ala. Acad. Honor, Pi Kappa Alpha, Omicron Delta Kappa, Phi Delta Phi. Democrat (mem. Ala. exec. com. 1938-50). Presbyn. (elder). Clubs: Athletic, U. Alabama, Decatur Kiwanis (pres. 1939). Home: Decatur, Ala. Died Feb. 7, 2006.

CADY, JACK ANDREW, writer, educator; b. Columbus, Ohio, Mar. 20, 1932; s. Donald Victor and Pauline Lucille Cady; m. Carol Orlock. BSc, U. Louisville, 1961. Asst. prof. U. Wash., Seattle, 1968—73; writer-in-residence Pacific Luth. U., Tacoma, 1983—96; ret., 1996. Author: (novels) The Night We Buried Road Dog, 1998, (nonfiction) The American Writer, 2000, The Hauntings of Hood Canal, 2001; contbr. articles to profl. jours. With U.S. Coast Guard, 1952—56. Recipient Nebula award, Nebula Awards Com., 1993, Bram Stoker award, Horror Writers Assn., 1993, Atlantic prize for short fiction, Iowa prize for short fiction, World Fantasy award, award, Nat. Lit. Anthology; fellow fellowship, Nat. Endowment for the Arts. Home: Port Townsend, Wash. Died Jan. 14, 2004.

CALDWELL, CLAUD REID, lawyer; b. Augusta, Ga., Sept. 18, 1909; s. John Mars and Ethel (Bennett) C.; student Acad. Richmond County, 1922-26; m. Josephine F. Clarke, June 30, 1940; children: Claud R., Kathryn C., James W. Bar: Ga. 1932, U.S. Supreme Ct. Ga. 1949, Ga. Ct. Appeals 1949, U.S. Dist. Ct. 1934, U.S. Ct. Appeals (5th cir.) 1953, U.S. Ct. Appeals (11th cir.) 1981, U.S. Supreme Ct. 1968. Pvt. practice, Augusta, 1934-95; ret. 1995; judge Mcpl. Ct., City of Augusta, 1948-49. Pres., Richmond County Ind. Party, 1950-51; bd. dirs. Augusta chpt. ARC, YMCA; chmn. Augusta council Boy Scouts Am., 1949-50. With AUS, 1941-45; ETO; col. USAR (ret.). Recipient Distinguished Pistol Marksman award U.S. Army, 1965. Mem. ABA, Ga. State Bar. Assn., Augusta Bar Assns., Ga. Sport Shooting Assn. (dir., past pres.), Augusta-Richmond County Hist. Mus., Mil. Order World Wars, Nat. Sojourners, Heroes of '96 (Gen. Oglethorpe chpt.), Res. Officers Assn. (Augusta chpt.), Am. Legion, Sons of Confederacy, Assn. U.S. Army, Masons, Augusta Country Club. Presbyn. (deacon). Died 2005.

CALDWELL, LYNTON KEITH, social scientist, educator; b. Montezuma, Iowa, Nov. 21, 1913; s. Lee Lynton and Alberta (Mace) C.; m. Helen A. Walcher, Dec. 21, 1940; children: Edwin Lee, Elaine Lynette. PhB, U. Chgo., 1935, PhD, 1943; MA, Harvard U., 1938; LLD (hon.), Western Mich. U., 1977. Asst. prof. govt. Ind. U., South Bend, 1939-44, dir. advanced studies in sci., tech. and public policy Bloomington, from 1965, Arthur F. Bentley prof. polit. sci., 1971-84, prof. pub. & environ. affairs, 1970—2006; dir. research and publs. Council of State Govts., 1944-47; faculty U. Chgo., 1945-47; prof. polit. sci. Syracuse U., 1947-54; dir. Pub. Adminstrn. Inst. for Turkey and Middle East, UN, Ankara, 1954-55; prof. polit. sci. U. Calif., Berkeley, 1955-56. Mem. environmental adv. bd. C.E.; mem. Sea Grant adv. panel NOAA; panel mem. Office Tech. Assessment; cons. U.S. Senate Com. on Interior and Insular Affairs, 1969—, UN, 1973-74, UNESCO, 1975—, Army Environ. Policy Inst., Nat. Com. on New Directions for Nat. Wildlife Refuge System; mem. Nat. Commn. on Materials Policy, Nat. Acad. Scis. Com. on Internat. Environ. Programs; chmn. com. internat. law, policy and adminstrn. IUCN, 1969-77; mem. Internat. Coun. Environ. Law; mem. sci. adv. bd. Internat. Joint Commn., 1984-91; Franklin lectr. Auburn U., 1972; Disting. Profl. lectr. U. Ala., 1981, William and Mary, 1991, U. Houston, 1992. Author: Administrative Theories of Hamilton and Jefferson, 1944, 2d edit., 1988, Environment: A Challenge to Modern Society, 1970, In Defense of Earth, 1972, Environmental Policy and Administration, 1975, Citizens and the Environment, 1976, Science and the National Environmental Policy Act, 1982, International Environmental Policy: From the 20th to the 21st Century, 1984, 3d edit., 1996, Biocracy: Public Policy and the Life Sciences, 1987, Perspectives on Ecosystem Managment for the Great Lakes, 1988, Between Two Worlds: Science, The Environmental Movement and Policy Choice, 1990, (with K. Schrader-Frechette) Policy for Land: Law and Ethics, 1993, Ecologia: Ciencia y politica medioambiental, 1993, Environment as a Focus for Public Policy, 1995, The National Environmental Policy Act: An Agenda for the Future, 1998; co-editor: Environmental Policy: Transnational Issues and National Trends, 1997, The National Environmental Policy Act: Agenda for the Future, 1999; mem. bd. editors Environ. Conservation Jour., 1973-93, Natural Resources Jour., Sci., Tech. and Soc., 1979-91, Environ. Profl. Jour., 1981-89, Politics and the Life Scis., 1982-96, Colo. Jour. Internat. Environ. Law and Policy, Ambiente y Recursos Naturales (Argentina), Environmental Awareness (India), Duke U. Law and Policy Forum, Environ., 1993-95, Global Environ. Politics. Bd. govs. The Nature Conservancy, 1959-65, Shirley Heinze Environ. Fund., Global Environ. and Energy in the 21st Century. Recipient Sagamore of Wabash award State of Ind., 1980, H. and M. Sprout award Internat. Studies Assn., 1985, Global 500 award UN Environ. Programme, 1991, Disting. Svc. award Ind. U., 2001, Spirit of Philanthropy award Ind. U. Press, 2001; grantee Conservation Found., 1968-69, NSF, Conservation and Research Found., 1969-70, U.S. Office Edn., 1973; guest fellow Woodrow Wilson Internat. Ctr. for Scholars Smithsonian Instn., 1971-72, East-West Ctr. fellow, 1981; named to Royal Order of Crown Thailand. Fellow AAAS; mem. Am. Soc. Pub. Adminstrn. (William Mosher award 1966, Laverne Burchfield award 1972, Marshall E. Dimock award 1981), Nat. Acad. Pub. Adminstrn., Royal Soc. Arts, Nat. Acad. Law and Social Scis. (hon. Cordoba, Argentina chpt.), Internat. Assn. for Impact Assessment (Rose Hulman Inst. Tech. award for outstanding achievement 1989), Am. Polit. Sci. Assn. (John M. Gaus award 1996), Natural Resource Coun. of Am. (Nat. Environ. Quality award 1997), Policy Studies Orgn. (Aaron Wildavsky book award 1996). Home: Bloomington, Ind. Died Aug. 15, 2006.

CALDWELL, SARAH, opera producer, conductor, stage director and administrator; b. Maryville, Mo., Mar. 6, 1924; Student, U. Ark., Hendrix Coll., New Eng. Conservatory, Berkshire Music Ctr., Tanglewood, Mass.; MusD (hon.), Harvard U., Simmons Coll., Bates Coll., Bowdoin Coll. Mem. faculty Berkshire Music Ctr.; dir. Boston U. Opera Workshop, 1953-57; created dept. music theater Boston U.; founded Boston Opera Group (later became Opera Co. of Boston), 1957, served as artistic dir. and condr., 1968—91; disting. prof. dept. music U. Ark., Fayetteville, from 1999. Asst. to Boris Goldovsky in direction of New Eng. Opera Co.; operatic directorial debut with Rake's Progress, Opera Workshop, 1953; operatic debut as condr. with Opera Group of Boston, 1957, Carnegie Hall debut with Am. Symphony Orch., 1974; condr. and/or dir. maj. opera cos. in U.S., including N.Y. Met. Opera, Dallas Civic Opera, Houston Grand Opera, N.Y.C. Opera; condr. with maj. orchs. including: Indpls. Symphony, Milw. Symphony, Am. Symphony, N.Y. Philharmonic; condr. at Ravinia Festival, 1976. Recipient Rogers and Hammerstein award, Nat. Medal Arts, 1997 Achievements include being first woman to appear as conductor with the Met. Opera, N.Y.C., 1976. Died Mar. 23, 2006.

CALENOFF, LEONID, radiologist; b. Vienna, Aug. 24, 1923; arrived in U.S., 1957, naturalized, 1962; s. Albert and Anna (Prover) C.; m. Miriam Arnon, Oct. 30, 1955; children— Jean Zucker, Deborah Lipoff. MD, U. Paris, 1955. Diplomate Am. Bd. Radiology. Intern Jewish Hosp., Cin., 1958; resident in radiology U. Ill. Med. Center, Chgo., 1959-61; asst. radiologist Ill. Research and Ednl. Hosp., Chgo., 1961-64; chief radiology Chgo. State Hosp., 1963-68; dir. radiology Sheridan Gen. Hosp., Chgo., 1964-68; attending radiologist West Side VA Hosp., Chgo., 1963-68, Rehab. Inst. Chgo., 1974-89, chief diagnostic radiology, 1974-86; attending radiologist Northwestern Meml. Hosp., Chgo., 1968—2003, chief outpatient diagnostic radiology, 1979—2003, vice chmn. dept. radiology, 1991-96; chief diagnostic radiology Passavant Pavillion of Northwestern Meml. Hosp., 1972-79; asst. prof. radiology Northwestern U. Med. Sch., 1970-73, assoc. prof., 1973-78, prof., 1978—2003, prof. emeritus, from 2003. Author articles in field, chpts. in books.; Editor: Radiology of Spinal Cord Injury, 1981. Fellow Am. Coll. Radiology; mem. Radiol. Soc. N.Am., Am. Roentgen Ray Soc. Home: Chicago, Ill. Died July 16, 2004.

CALER, WILLIAM ERNEST, research and development engineer; b. Berea, Ohio, Sept. 30, 1955; s. William Eugene and Alice Felicia (Frew) C. BS, U. Wash., 1978; MS, Stanford U., 1984. Research asst. dept. orthopaedics U. Wash., Seattle, 1977-79; research engr. biomechanics, dept. orthopaedics Mass. Gen. Hosp., Boston, 1979-82; research and devel. engr., rehab. research and devel. ctr. Stanford (Calif.) U. and Palo Alto (Calif.) VA Med. Ctr., from 1982. Contbr. articles to profl. jours. Asst. coach Stanford Area Youth Basketball, Palo Alto, 1985, Palo Alto Little League, 1987. Mem. ASME, Am. Soc. Biomechanics, Sigma Xi. Avocation: ind. animation. Home: Mountain View, Calif. Died Apr. 18, 2005.

CALIRI, DAVID JOSEPH, retired lawyer, insurance agent; b. Lawrence, Mass., Dec. 12, 1929; s. Joseph and June Hazel (Rothera) C.; m. Saralou Debnam, Aug. 29, 1958; children: Linda, Donna, Paul, James, John. AB, Harvard Coll., 1951; LLB, Harvard U., 1954. Bar: N.J. Assoc. Gardner & Williams, Passaic, N.J., 1957-59, ptnr., 1959-64, Williams, Gardner, Caliri, Miller & Otley, Wayne, N.J., 1964-71, Williams, Caliri, Miller & Otley, Wayne, 1971-86; N.C. life, health, long-term care and Medicare ins. agt.; in-house counsel Capital Transactions Group, from 2001. Author: The Pine and the Thistle, 1989. Pres. bd. edn., Wayne, 1964-70; chmn., mem. Scholarship and Honors Bd., Wayne, 1972-86; dir. Lenni-lenape coun. Girl Scouts Am., 1970-82; coord. Presbytery of the Palisades, Teaneck, N.J., 1974-76; chmn. Moore County Dem. Party, 1992-97; elder Bethesda Presbyn. Ch., 1988-91, 93-95, mem. gov.'s com. Recognition of State Employees, N.C., 1993—; moderator Outdoor Ministries divsn., 2000-03, Presbytery of Coastal Carolina, 2002. With U.S. Army, 1955-56. Avocations: computers, writing, camping, volunteer work. Died Dec. 28, 2004.

CALKINS, DAVID ROSS, physician, educator; b. Kansas City, Kans., May 27, 1948; s. Leroy Adelbert and Emily Virginia (Kyger) C.; m. Susan Spalding Rice, Sept. 22, 1989; 1 child, Christopher Ross. AB, Princeton (N.J.) U., 1970; MD, MPP, Harvard U., 1975. Diplomate Am. Bd. Internal Medicine. Intern U. Wash., Seattle, 1975-76; resident in medicine Beth Israel Hosp., Boston, 1976-78, from asst. to assoc. in medicine, 1981-96; fellow White House, Washington, 1978-79; spl. asst., dep. exec. sec. HHS, Washington, 1979-81; from instr. to asst. prof. medicine Harvard Med. Sch., Boston, 1981-96; from instr. to asst. prof. Harvard Sch. Pub. Health, Boston, 1985-96, dir. profl. programs dept. health policy and mgmt., 1985-96; chief div. gen. internal medicine, med. dir. ambulatory svc. New Eng. Deaconess Hosp., Boston, 1991-96; assoc. dean for primary care U. Kans. Sch. Medicine, Kansas City, 1996-98, from assoc. prof. to prof. internal and preventive medicine, 1996-99, sr. assoc. dean for edn., 1998-99; assoc. prof. medicine Harvard Med. Sch., Boston, from 1999, assoc. dean for clin. programs, 1999—2003; sr. fellow Inst. Healthcare Improvement, Cambridge, Mass., from 2003; assoc. physician Mass. Gen. Hosp., Boston, from 1996. Died Apr. 7, 2006.

CALKINS, JAMES PHILLIP, ophthalmologist; b. Charlottesville, Va., July 7, 1925; s. LeRoy Adelbert and Mina Marie (Curry) C.; m. Roberta H. Fastje, July 6, 1926; children: Carol Sue, Kenneth, Janet, Robin. BS, U. Kans., 1945; MD, Kans. U., 1948; MS, U. Iowa, 1955. Diplomate Am. Bd. Ophthalmology. Intern Ohio State U. Hosp., Columbus, 1948-49; resident U. Pa., Phila., 1949-50, U. Iowa, Iowa City, 1950-51, 53-55; ophthalmologist pvt. practice, Tucson, Ariz., from 1955. Clin. lectr. ophthalmology U. Ariz., Tucson, 1988—. Capt. USAF, 1951-53. Mem. Ariz. Ophthalmological Soc. (pres. 1967-68), Pima County Med. Assn. Avocation: golf. Home: Tucson, Ariz. Died Oct. 28, 2004.

CALLARD, CAROLE CRAWFORD, librarian, educator; b. Charleston, W.Va., Aug. 8, 1941; d. William O. and Helen (Shay) Crawford; children: Susan Lynne, Annie Laurie. BA in Am. History, U. Charleston, 1963; MLS, U. Pitts., 1966; MA in Social Founds., Ea. Mich. U., 1978; grad., Nat. Inst. for Geneal. Rsch., 1997. Tchr. Blessed Sacrament Sch., South Charleston, W.Va., 1962-64; grad. trainee W.Va. Libr. Commn., Charleston, 1964-65; reference libr. Tompkins County Pub. Libr., Ithaca, N.Y., 1966-69; head libr. U.S. Embassy, Addis Ababa, Ethiopia, 1969-70; head govt. documents Haile Sellassie U., Addis Ababa, 1970-71; br. libr. Ann Arbor (Mich.) Pub. Libr., 1973-83; documents libr. U. Mich., Ann Arbor, 1983-84; pub. svcs. supr. Libr. of Mich., Lansing, 1984-95; depository libr. inspector Govt. Printing Office, 1995-96; libr. Allen Co. Pub. Libr., Ft. Wayne, Ind., 1996-97; specialist Libr. of Mich., Lansing, from 1997; instr. Nat. Inst. for Geneal. Rsch., 1999. Chair around the world, around the campus U. Mich. Faculty Women's Club, Ann Arbor, 1974-76; tchr. genealogy Holt Pub. Schs., Okemos Pub. Schs., 1990-92, Lansing Cmty. Schs., 2000, Washtenaw C.C., 1992-94; judge Mich. history Day, 1991, 93, 94; genealogy chair Abrams Found., 1997—; adj. prof. libr. info. sci. Wayne State U., Mich., 2003-. Author: Index to 150th Anniversary Issue Ithaca Jour., 1967, Guide to Local History, Sources in the Huron Valley, 1980; editor: Sourcebook of Michigan, 1986, Michigan Cemetery Atlas, 1991, Michigan 1870 Census Index, 1991-95, Michigan Cemetery Sourcebook, 1994, Government Documents for Genealogists Historians and Archivists, 1998; column editor Mich. History Mag. and Chronicle; contbr. articles to profl. jours. Membership chair LWV, Ann Arbor; v.p. Geneal. Soc. Washtenaw County, Mich., 1993, pres., 1993-94; v.p. Palatines to Am., 1987-90, Washtenaw Libr. Club, 1982-83; pres. Libr. Staff Assn., Lansing, 1985-86; pres. Govt. Documents Roundtable of Mich., pres., 1992-93; pres. Mich. Data Base Users Group, 1992-93; chmn. book sale Friends of Ann Arbor Pub. Libr. Recipient Notable Document award Govt. Documents Roundtable of Mich., 1991, Paul Thurston Documents award Govt. Documents Roundtable of Mich., 1993, Cert. of Merit Assn. State and Local History, 1995, Mich. Geneal. Coun., Libr. of Mich. Found. and Abrams Found. award, 1996, P. William Filby award for genealogy librarianship, 2003, Profl. Svcs. award, Wayne State U., 2005, Disting. Svc. award, 2005; grantee U. Pitts., 1966, prof. staff grantee Ann Arbor Pub. Schs., 1980, edn. found. grantee Mich. Libr. Assn., 1982. Mem. ALA (Godort state and local documents com., mem. genealogy com. 2000—, instr. genealogy pre-conf. 2001, 02, mem. local history com. 2002-, chmn. genealogy pre-conf. 2003—), AAUW (corr. sec., historian 1973-74, 82-83), DAR (corr. sec. Lansing chpt., 2002-03, libr., 2004—, Sarah Angell Caswell registrar CAR Seimes Microfilm), Children of Am. Revolution, Internat. Soc. Brit. Genealogy (trustee 1994-96), Mich. Libr. Assn. (chmn. govt. documents sect. 1982-84, leadership acad. 1991-93), Spl. Librs. Assn., D.C. Libr. Assn., Va. Libr. Assn., Fedn. Genealogy Socs. (del., corr. sec. 1986-87, v.p. regional affairs 1989-92), Nat. Genealogy Soc. (instr. devel. com. 1988-90, chmn. instns. com. 1992—, archives and libr. com. 1993-94, judge family history writing contest 2005, P. William Filby award 2003), Mich. Geneal. Coun. (ofcl. good will ambassador 1995-), Mid-Mich. Genealogy Soc. (v.p. 2002-03, pres. 2003—), Ingham County Geneal Soc. (v.p 2004—), Beta Phi Mu. Avocations: storytelling, reading, travel, genealogy. Home: Lansing, Mich. Died Dec. 2005.

CALVERT, PATRICIA VIOLA, dietician; b. Richmond, Oreg., Apr. 28, 1940; d. Oliver Raymond Trent and Clara Hester (Brooks) Reynolds; m. Lyle Lavern Calvert, Sept. 9, 1962; children: Lyla Dalene Calvert Keithley. BS, Walla Walla Coll., 1961. Registered dietitian, Oreg. Intern Loma Linda U., 1962; clin. dietitian, chief Good Samaritan Hosp., Portland, Oreg., 1963-68; food and nutrition supr., clin. rsch. dietitian, chief St. Charles Med. Ctr., Bend, Oreg., 1971-95; with Pioneer Meml. Hosp., 1996-98, from 2002; nutrition cons., from 1996. Food and nutrition cons. Pioneer Meml. Hosp., Prineville, Oreg., 1968-74, 87-92, Cen. Oreg. Dist. Hosp., Redmond, 1974-75, Batchelor Butte Nursing Home, Bend, 1968-70, Harney Dist. Hosp., Burns, Oreg., 1987-92; menu cons. Soroptomist Sr. Mealsite, Prineville, Oreg., 1992—. City budget com. Redmond City Coun., 1970, 71; deaconess Powell Butte Christian Ch., 1994-95. Mem. Am. Dietetic Assn., Oreg. Dietetic Assn. (treas., pres.-elect, pres., nominating chair 1963—). Avocations: travel, gardening, reading, crafts, sewing. Home: Redmond, Oreg. Died June 17, 2005.

CALVERT, TERRY LYNN, systems analyst, programmer, computer executive; b. Indpls., July 11, 1950; s. Victor Junior and Annie May (Skaggs) C.; m. Cynthia Ann Matzka, Aug. 29, 1970; children: Derek, Sean, Marc, Ryan. BS, Ill. State U., 1973, MS in Exptl. Psychology, 1977. Ordained to ministry Christian Ch., 1989. Mental health specialist Lincoln (Ill.) State Sch., 1974-77; research asst. Western Carolina Ctr., Morgantown, N.C., 1977-78; unit dir. Eastern Oreg. State Hosp., Pendleton, 1978-79, psychologist, 1980-81; salesman Comrie Olds, Pendleton, 1981-82; pres. Calvert Computer Systems, Athena, Oreg., from 1982. Mayor City of Athena, 1984-85. Mem. Athena C. of C. (pres. 1987-88, v.p. 1999-2000). Republican. Home: Athena, Oreg. Died Mar. 15, 2005.

CALVERT, WILLIAM CARMAN, retired psychologist; b. La Verne, Calif., Dec. 21, 1924; s. George Carman and Birdie Theoda (Alexander) C.; m. Barbara Nadine Mullendore, June 26, 1948; children: Janet Mullendore, Judith Mullendore Ritchie. BA, Pomona Coll., 1947; MA, Stanford U., 1949; PhD, UCLA, 1955. Prof. psychology U. La Verne, Calif., 1956-64, Monmouth (Ill.) Coll., 1964-66, Parsons Coll., Fairfield, Iowa, 1966-67, Upsala Coll., East Orange, N.J., 1968-87; retired, 1987. Asst. dir. Summer Inst. in Contemporary Sci. Psychology, Beloit, Wis. Adv. bd. Calif. State Mental Hygiene Clinic, Covina, 1950-60; 1st v.p. Pomona Valley Mental and Emotional Health Assn., chmn. edn. commn. Lt. (j.g.) USN, 1943-46. Mem. AAAS, Am. Psychol. Assn., Ea. Psychol. Assn., N.Y. Acad. Sci. (advisor commn. instrumentation, 1986—), Sigma Xi. Home: Caldwell, NJ. Died Nov. 12, 2004.

CAMP, JOHN CLAYTON, lawyer; b. Arab, Ala., Sept. 23, 1923; s. Roy Hubert and Alice Mellie (Cox) C.; m. Frances Elizabeth Spencer, Nov. 3, 1944; children: John, Elizabeth Camp Bower, Martha Camp Cox, Charles. Student, Birmingham-So. Coll., 1940-42, U. Ala., 1943, Auburn U., 1944; JD, La. State U., 1948. Bar: La. 1948, U.S. Supreme Ct. 1958, D.C. 1974. Assoc. Thompson, Lawes and Cavanaugh, Lake Charles, La., 1948-55; ptnr. Camp, Carmouche, Barsh, Gray, Hoffman & Gill, Lake Charles, 1955-84, Camp, Barsh & Tate, Washington, 1984-94, Patton Boggs LLP, Washington, 1994—2004. Active Internat. Top Mgmt. Roundtable Confs., London, Milan, Amsterdam, Brussels, Frankfurt, Rome, Dusseldorf, Ditchley Park, Stockholm and Toronto, 1982-87. Mem. Presdl. Trade Commn. to People's Republic of China, 1979; trustee Athens (Greece) Coll., 1985-91; mem. exec. com., vice chmn. Meridian House Internat., 1986-96; past mem. med. ctr. adv. coun. George Washington U. With USAF, 1943-46; bd. advs. Internat. Mgmt. and Devel. Inst., Fowler McCracker Commn. (chmn. policy planning group, 1982-87); pres., mem. exec. com. Metro USO, 1989-92; bd. exec. com. Wolf Trap Found., 1984-91. Mem.: ABA, Nat. Presbyn. Ch., Southwestern La. Bar Assn., La. State Bar Assn., D.C. Bar Assn., Congl. Country Club. Democrat. Presbyterian. Avocations: golf, photography, reading. Home: Silver Spring, Md. Died Nov. 19, 2004.

CAMPBELL, CARROLL ASHMORE, JR., former governor; b. Greenville, SC, July 24, 1940; s. Carroll Ashmore and Anne (Williams) C.; m. Iris Rhodes, Sept. 5, 1959; children: Carroll Ashmore, III, Richard Michael. Student, McCallie Sch., U. S.C.; MA, Am. U.; LLD (hon.), Central Wesleyan Coll.; HHD (hon.), Sherman Coll., Lander Coll.; LLD (hon.), The Citidel, U. S.C.; DLitt (hon.), Coll. Charleston; EdD (hon.), Columbia Coll.; DHL (hon.), Med. U. S.C.; LHD (hon.), Winthrop Coll. Pres. Handy Park Co., 1960-78; mem. S.C. Ho. of Reps., 1970-74, S.C. Senate, 1976, 96th-99th Congresses from S.C. 4th Dist., 1979-87; exec. asst. to gov. State of S.C., 1975, gov., 1987—95; pres., CEO Am. Coun. Life Ins., 1995—2003. Mem. banking, fin. and urban affairs com., com. on House adminstrn., appropriations com., ways and means com., asst. regional whip, Tenn., S.C., Ga. and Fla.; chmn. So. Growth Policies Bd., 1988, Nat. Edn. Goals Panel, 1992; co-chmn. Nat. Edn. Standards and Testing, 1992. Del. Rep. Conv., 1976, 80, 84, 88, 92; mem. Nat. Rep. Congl. Com., Textile Caucus, S.C. Gov.'s Com. on Employment of Handicapped; mem. adv. coun. White House Conf. on Handicapped Individuals; chmn. March of Dimes; hon. chmn. Arthritis Found. Dr.; So. chmn. Bush Pres. Campaign, 1988, So. chmn. and nat. co-chmn., 1992. Recipient Disting. Service award Jaycees; Citizenship award Woodmen of World; K.C. award; Rehab. Assn. Citizenship award; Guardian of Small Bus. award Nat. Fedn. Inst. Bus.; Disting. Service award Ams. for Constl. Action; Watchdog of Treasury award Nat. Associated Businessmen; Humanitarian Service award Rutledge Coll., Leadership award Am. Security Council; Spirit of Am. award Nat. Grocers Assn.; Order of Palmetta, Gov. S.C.; Outstanding Freshman award 96th Club, numerous others, Outstanding Grad. Scholarship award Am. U. Mem. Nat. Gov. Assn. (vice chmn. 1992, chmn. 1993, mem. exec. com. 1992), Nat. Pub. Affairs Honor Soc., Sertoma Club (Citizenship award), Chowder and Marching Club, Masons, Pi Alpha Alpha. Episcopalian. Died Dec. 7, 2005.

CAMPBELL, ELIZABETH PFOHL, association executive; b. Winston-Salem, Dec. 4, 1902; d. John Kenneth and Bessie (Whittington) Pfohl; m. Edmund Douglas Campbell, June 16, 1936; children: Edmund Douglas Jr., Virginia Campbell Holt, Bejamin P., H. Donald. AB cum laude, Salem Coll., 1923, LHD (hon.), 1991; MA, Columbia U., 1924; postgrad., U. Pa., 1929, U. Mich., 1931; DHL (hon.), Washington and Lee U., 1989, Mary Baldwin Coll., 1990, Salem Coll., 1991. Dean of women Moravian Coll. for Women, Bethlehem, Pa., 1928-29; dean Mary Baldwin Coll., Staunton, Va., 1929-36; pres. The Greater Washington Ednl. Telecommunications Assn., Inc., 1957-71, former v.p. community affairs. Elected mem. sch. bd. Arlington County, 1948-56, chair 1950, 55, 61, apptd. 1960-64; former mem. Com. of 100 United Ch. Women; adv. bd. George Mason Coll, 1964-72; bd. dirs. Arlington YMCA, 1965-78; regional chmn. Va. Mental Retardation Planning Coun., 1966-69; bd. trustees YWCA, 1966-70, Salem Coll., Winston-Salem, 1969-73; 1st vice chair Nat. Friends of Pub. Broadcasting, 1970-75; adv. bd. Consortium for Higher Edn. in No. Va., 1973-78, Asia Soc., 1979-83; bd. dirs. Arlington Community TV, 1982-90; mem. Nat. Citizens Com. for Pub. TV; founder, past pres. Dem. Club No. Va. Recipient Golden Mike award Am. Women in Radio and T.V. McCall's, 1967; Centennial Medallion for dedicated nat. svc. DAR, 1991, Esther Van Wagoner Tufty award Washington Leadership in Community Svc. Excellence in Communication, Am. Women in Radio and TV, 1990, First Community Voice and Vision award Arlington Community TV, 1990, Commendation Commonwealth of Va. Gen. Assembly, 1989, Disting. Alumnae award Salem Acad., 1988, The Washington Woman, Lifetime Achievement award 1987, Silver Circle award Nat Acad. TV Arts and Scis., 1986, Bd. Govs. award (Emmy), 1981, First Annenberg Washington Program award Advancement in Comm., 1988, Valiant Woman award Coun. of Ch. Women Arlington, Lifetime Achievement award Met. Area Am. Assn. of Univ. Women, 1993; named Woman of Yr. Marymount Coll., 1967. Mem. AAUW, Acad. TV Arts and Scis., Am. Women in Radio and TV, Nat. Assn. Ednl. Broadcasters, Nat. Friends of Pub. Broadcasting, Quota Club (hon. mem.), 20th Century Club (Washington), Women's Nat. Dem. Club, League Women Voters, Delta Kappa Gamma. Moravian. Home: Arlington, Va. Died Jan. 9, 2004.

CAMPBELL, HELEN WOERNER (MRS. THOMAS B. CAMPBELL), librarian; b. Indpls., Oct. 17, 1918; d. Clarence Julius and Gertrude Elizabeth (Colley) Woerner; student Ind. U., 1935-38; B.S., Butler U., 1967; m. Thomas B. Campbell, Jan. 17, 1942; 1 dau., Martha (Mrs. L. Kurt Adamson). Asst. order librarian Ind. U., Bloomington, 1937-42; librarian Ind. U. Sch. Dentistry, Indpls., 1942-46, cataloger, part-time, 1960-65, asst. librarian, 1965-66, librarian, 1966-80. Mem. Med. Library Assn., Spl. Libraries Assn. (chpt. pres. 1972-73). Home: Indianapolis, Ind. Died June 6, 2006.

CAMPBELL, JOSEPHINE ANNE CONRAD, news service executive; b. Evansville, Ind., Jan. 31, 1927; d. Owen McIntyre and Josephine Anne (Greene) C.; m. Donald Herman Campbell, Mar. 15, 1946 (dec. Mar. 3, 1988); children: Kathleen Mary, Carolyn Margret, Deborah Jean. Cub reporter Daytona Beach (Fla.) News-Jour., 1944-45; copy boy Washington Post, 1945-46; copy editor World Report Mag., Washington, 1946-47; mem. pub. rels. staff AMVETS, Washington, 1952-53; pub. rels. person Govt. Pakistan, Washington, 1953-55; Washington and UN corr. Daily NAWA-I-WAQT, Lahore, Pakistan, 1955-56; writer, editor USIA, 1956-86; founder, CEO Ecotopics Internat. News Svc., Ocean City, Md., 1986-98, Willits, Calif., 1998—2005, Petaluma, Calif., 2005—06. Columnist Prince George's Jour., 1994-2000. Chair White House/Justice Dept. Task Force on Sex Discrimination USIA Press Svc.; active Gov.'s Task Force to Examine State Pension Investment in South Africa, 1987; v.p. Am. Fedn. Govt. Employees, AFL-CIO, Local #1812, 1969—78, del. nat. conv., 1974—76; del. founding conf. Coalition Labor Union Women, 1974; exec. com. Prince George's County NCCJ, 1980—84; rep. Ocean City State Coastal and Watershed Resources adv. Com., 1991—98; steering com., commr. Worcester County Commn. for Women, 1995—98; active Friends of Ocean City Libr., 1988—2006, Friends of Willits Libr., 1999—2006; citizen's adv. bd. Willits News, 1999—2000, op-ed writer, 1999—2006. Jefferson fellow, George Washington U., 1980—81. Mem.: ACLU (Prince George County exec. bd. 1975—81, chair 1985—88, Mendocino County exec. bd. 2003—05), NAACP (3d v.p. Worcester County 1992—98, Sonoma County, Calif. br. 1999—2006), Dog Writers Assn. Am., Nat. Press Club, Nat. Writers Union Local 3, Mendocino County Nat. Women's Polit. Caucus, Women's Inst. Freedom of Press, Conservation Voters, Nat. Resources Def. Coun., Worldwatch, Marine's Meml. Club, Women's Club Ocean City (2d v.p. 1996). Democrat. Roman Catholic. Avocations: photography, poetry writing, political activism. Died Mar. 1, 2006.

CAMPOLI, ELLA FRANCES, mortgage company executive; b. New Castle, Pa., Nov. 5, 1906; d. Domenico and Michelina (Perretta) Faraone; m. James Campoli, May 4, 1925. Student, New Castle Bus. Coll., 1923. Office, traffic mgr. Harper Furniture Co., Cinn., 1948-50; asst. to pres. Harper Furniture co., Cinn., 1951-62; ptnr. Campoli Partnership, Oldsmar, Fla., from 1968-. Mem. Oldsmar City Coun., 1971-76; vice mayor City of Oldsmar, 1975. Mem. AAUW, Am. Bus. Women's Assn. (Women of the Yr. award 1989), Oldmar Civic Club, Pilot Internat. (pres. Cin. chpt. 1961-62, publicity, chairperson 1962—). Democrat. Roman Catholic. Avocations: bowling, whatever can be helpful to mankind. Died Apr. 21, 2005.

CANDELMO, LEE FRANCE, special education educator; b. Orange, N.J., Jan. 17, 1941; s. John and Ruth Claire (France) C.; m. Mary Lariccia, Oct. 20, 1962; children: Robert, Lori, Kristen. BA in English Lit., Rutgers U., 1962; MA in Student Personnel Svcs., Kean Coll., Union, N.J., 1975. English tchr. Bernards Twp. Bd. Edn., Basking Ridge, N.J., 1966-72, counselor, 1972-78; tchr. adult handicapped East Brunswick (N.J.) Bd. Edn., 1978-85, counselor adult and youth handicapped, from 1985. Author: An English Course of Study, 1968, The Intergration of Beadleston Classified Adolescents into a Regular Junior High School, 1975; contbr. book chpt. Recipient award for svc. to disabled persons Nat. Sch. Bd., 1986, U.S. Sec. Edn. award for vocat. edn. for handicapped youth, 1986. Mem. NEA, Rutgers U. Alumni Assn. Presbyterian. Avocations: reading, volunteer work, stamp collecting/philately, photography. Died July 25, 2005.

CANIPELLI, KEVIN V., lawyer; b. Tampa, Fla., Dec. 1, 1944; BBA, Emory U., 1966; JD, Mercer U., 1969. Bar: Fla., U.S. Dist. Ct. Fla., U.S. Supreme Ct., U.S. Ct. Appeals (11th cir.), U.S. Mil. Ct. Appeals. Asst. pub. defender Pub. Defenders' Office, Jacksonville, Fla., 1973-76; pvt. practice Jacksonville, from 1977. 1st lt. U.S. Army, 1971-73. Mem. Jacksonville C. of C., Sertoma Club of Jacksonville (v.p., treas. 1977—). Avocations: biking, sailing. Died Jan. 24, 2004.

CANNON, DOUGLAS E., mayor, retired educator and counselor; b. Zanesville, Ohio, Dec. 23, 1939; s. William Edgar and Margaret Douglass (Worthington) C.; m. Margaret Marie Wright, Dec. 7, 1963; 1 child, Christopher Kem. BS in Edn., Ohio U., 1963, MEd, 1968. Tchr. Zanesville City Schs., 1960-63; tchr., counselor Crooksville (Ohio) Schs., 1963-96; ret., 1996; mayor City of Crooksville, from 1995. Mem., pres. Crooksville Village Coun., 1994-95; sec. Moxahala Watershed Commn., Crooksville, 1996—; trustee Tri-County Cmty. Action Agy., Athens, Ohio, 1996—; mem. Perry County Planning Commn., New Lexington, Ohio, 1996-98, Crooksville Bd. Edn., 1998—, Crooksville Arts Coun., 1998—; bd. dirs. ON-TASC, Youngstown, Ohio, 1997—; pres. Crooksville Hist. Commn., 1998—. Mem. Masons (32d degree, master), Lions. Republican. Methodist. Avocations: camping, fishing, stamp collecting/philately. Home: Crooksville, Ohio. Died Jan. 15, 2005.

CANNON, HUGH, lawyer; b. Albemarle, NC, Oct. 11, 1931; s. Hubert Napoleon and Nettie (Harris) C.; m. Jo Anne Weisner, Mar. 21, 1988. AB, Davidson Coll., 1953; BA, Oxford U., 1955, MA, 1960; LLB, Harvard U., 1958. Bar: N.C. 1958, D.C. 1978, S.C. 1979. Mem. staff U. N.C. Inst. Govt., Chapel Hill, 1959; mem. firm Sanford, Phillips, McCoy & Weaver, Fayetteville, NC, 1960; asst to Gov. of N.C., Raleigh, 1961; dir. adminstrn. State of N.C., 1962-65, state budget officer, 1963; mem., mng. ptnr. Sanford, Cannon, Adams & McCullough, Raleigh, 1965-79; pvt. practice Charleston, SC, from 1979; mem. Everett, Gaskins, Hancock and Stevens attys., Raleigh, from 1990; v.p. gen. counsel Palmetto Ford, Inc., Charleston, from 1979. Author: Cannon's Concise Guide to Rules of Order, 1992. Parliamentarian NEA, 1965—; mem. nat. adv. coun. Am. Inst. Parliamentarians; pres. Friends of Coll., Raleigh, 1963; alt. de. Dem. Nat. Conv., 1964, chief parliamentarian, 1976, 80, 84, 88, 92, 96; bd. govs. U. N.C., 1972-81; trustee Davidson Coll., 1966-74, N.C. Sch. Arts, 1963-72; mem. sch. bd. Charleston County, 2000—. Rhodes scholar, 1955. Mem. Phi Beta Kappa, Omicron Delta Kappa, Phi Gamma Delta. Episcopalian. Home: Charleston, SC. Died Jan. 4, 2005.

CANNON, RAEBURN ANN, manufacturing executive; b. Ft. Atkinson, Wis., July 20, 1910; d. Anthony Edmund and Mary Ann (Williams) O'Malley; m. William Patrick Cannon, June 28, 1941 (dec. July 1984); children: Mary Ann, Catherine, William Patrick Jr., Michael Francis II. AB, Coll. St. Scholastica, 1933; MA, U. Minn., 1936; PhD, U. Mich., 1940. Licensed elem., secondary and coll. tchr. English tchr. Coll. St. Scholastica, Duluth, Minn., 1937-38, Lake Linden (Mich.) High Sch., 1938-41, Frankton (Ind.) Jr. High Sch., 1957-61; pres. Cannon Products, Inc., Elwood, Ind., from 1984. Spanish tutor Culver (Ind.) Acad., 1937-39. Columnist Our Sunday Visitor, 1954-62. Vol. Mercy Hosp., Elwood, 1984—. Named Ind. Woman of Achievement, 1987. Mem. AAUW, Nat. Fedn. Press Women (treas. 1976-80), Women's Press Club (treas. 1982-88, Kate Milner Rabb award 1984). Republican. Roman Catholic. Avocations: needlecrafts, rose gardening, travel, gourmet cooking. Home: Elwood, Ind. Died Mar. 2, 2005.

CANTIN, LUCILLE JULIENNE, education educator; b. Manchester, N.H., Mar. 21, 1939; d. Donat O. and Julienne (Dionne) C. BA, Notre Dame Coll., 1969; MEd with Mid. Sch. Emphasis, U. N.H., 1975; PhD in Curriculum Instruction/Adminstrn., Boston Coll., 1989. Elem. tchr. N.H. Diocesan Schs., 1958-76; prin. Manchester (N.H.) East Cath. Regional Sch., 1976-79; asst. prof. edn. Notre Dame Coll., Manchester, 1979-85, dir. MEd in elem./secondary teaching, 1989-94. Bd. dirs. New Life Dwell Place, Thonotosassa, Fla., 1990—; pres. Sisters of Holy Cross/U.S. Region Inc., Manchester, 1990—. Regional rep. Sisters of Holy Cross, Manchester, 1990—. Mem. ASCD, Assn. Tchr. Educators, Nat. Cath. Edn. Assn., Notre Dame Coll. Concert Choir (soloist 1979—), Alpha Sigma Nu Nat. Jesuit Honor Soc., Phi Delta Kappa Honor Soc. Roman Catholic. Avocations: singing, reading, listening to music. Home: Manchester, NH. Died May 15, 2004.

CANTOR, HAL, biomedical engineer, researcher; b. Farmington Hills, Mich., Aug. 14, 1963; BSChemE, U. Mich., 1984, MS in Biol. Scis. and Biomed. Engring., 1986, PhD in Biomed. Engring., 1994. Dept. head Cybernet Sys. Corp., Ann Arbor, Mich., 1996-97; pres. Advanced Sensor Techs., Inc., Farmington Hills, Mich., from 1997. Grantee Small Bus. Innovation Rsch., Nat. Inst. Health, Nat. Inst. Neural Disorders and Stroke, Defense Advanced Rsch. Projects Agy.; recipient New Investigator award Soc. Study Reproduction, 1993. Died July 13, 2005.

CAPONE, LUCIEN, JR., management consultant, former naval officer; b. Bristol, R.I. s. Lucien and Louise Dolores (Malafronte) C.; m. Charlotte Loretta Lammers, July 22,

1950; children: Lucien, Judith Ann. BS, U.S. Naval Acad., 1949; grad., Naval Postgrad. Sch., 1955, Indsl. Coll. Armed Forces, 1967; MS in Bus. Adminstrn, George Washington U., 1967, postgrad., 1970—71. Commd. ensign USN, 1949, advanced through grades to rear adm., served on destroyers Atlantic Fleet, 1949-54, mem. staff Office Chief Naval Ops. Dept. of Navy, 1955-57, exec. officer U.S.S. Huse, 1957-59, staff, comdr. Mid. East Force Persian Gulf, 1959-61, head plans, programs, and requirements br. Naval Comm. Sys. Hdqrs. Washington, 1961-63; comdg. officer U.S.S. Hammerberg, 1963-64; dep. chief of staff Def. Comm. Agy., Washington, 1964-66; comdg. officer U.S.S. Dahlgren, 1967-69; asst. comdr. plans, programs, requirements Naval Telecom. Command USN, Washington, 1969-72; comdg. officer U.S.S. Richmond K. Turner, 1972-74; dep. dir. nat. mil. command sys. tech. support Def. Comm. Agy., Washington, 1974-76, dir. command and control tech. ctr., 1976-78; dep. dir. command and control Def. Comm. Agy. USN, 1976-78; dir. Inter-Am. Def. Coll., Washington, 1978-79; exec. Booz, Allen & Hamilton, Inc., McLean, Va., 1979-97, v.p., 1983-88, sr. v.p., 1988-97, bd. dirs., oper. coun., 1988-97; cons., from 1997. Decorated Legion of Merit, Def. Superior Svc. medal with oak leaf cluster. Mem. IEEE, AIAA, Armed Forces Comm. and Electronics Assn. (past pres. DC chpt.). Home: Vienna, Va. Died Sept. 25, 2005.

CARBAUGH, JOHN EDWARD, JR., lawyer; b. Greenville, S.C., Sept. 4, 1945; s. John Edward and Mary Lou (McCarley) C.; m. Mary Middleton Calhoun: children: John, Martha, Leacy, Miller. BA, U. South, 1967; JD, U. S.C., 1973, postgrad., 1967—69, Georgetown U., 1977—79. Bar: S.C. 1973, U.S. Ct. Appeals (4th cir.) 1982, U.S. Supreme Ct. 1982. With White House Staff, Washington, 1969—70; campaign dir. re-elect Thurmond campaign Washington, 1970—73; legis. asst. to Senator Jesse Helms U.S. Senate, Washington, 1974—82; pvt. practice Washington, 1982—2006. Bd. dirs. Westech. Internat., Inc., Washington Watch, Inc., Splty. Materials and Mfg., Inc., Tech. Holdings, Inc., The Stealth Corp., Inc.; mem. Pres. Commn. on Econ. Justice, Washington, 1985-87 Author: The Revisionists, 1991, We Need Each Other: U.S.-Japan Relations Approach the 21st Century, 1992; co-author: A Program for Military Independence, 1980; contbr. articles to profl. jours. Rep. Nat. Platform Staff, 1976, 80, 84, 88, 92, 96; Presdl. Transition Team, 1980-81. Sgt. USAR, 1969-77. Mem. Met. Club. Republican. Presbyterian. Avocations: tennis, travel, horticulture. Home: Oakton, Va. Died Mar. 19, 2006.

CARBO, KIMBERLY MONIQUE, public relations executive; b. New Orleans, Aug. 29, 1960; d. Claude Joseph Jr. and Rosina (Dickerson) C. BA in Communications, U. New Orleans, 1981, postgrad., 1982. Editorial asst. La. State U. Med. Ctr., New Orleans, 1980-82; news intern Sta. WDSU-TV affiliate NBC, New Orleans, 1980; customer ops. adminstrv. asst. Cox Cable New Orleans, Inc., 1982, pub. relations asst., 1982-85; mktg. exec. sec., writer Standard Coffee Svc. Co., New Orleans, 1985-86; pub. info. specialist, film liaison Mayor's Office Pub. Info., New Orleans, 1986-87, head pub. info. specialist, film liaison, 1987-88, acting dep. dir., film liaison, 1988-89, dep. dir., film liason, from 1989. Dep. dir., film liaison, 1989—; prodn. asst. Sta. WGNO-TV program Black Is, New Orleans, 1979, Sta. WYES-TV Documentary of New Orleans, 1983; publicity coord. So. Rep. Theatre Festival, New Orleans, 1987; liaison to State Film Commn., New Orleans, 1986—; floor mgr. DRC Prodn., New Orleans, 1986-88. Author various poems and short stories. Vol. numerous polit. campaigns, New Orleans, 1986—, So. Rep. Leadership Conf., New Orleans, 1988; media and hospitality vol. Rep. Nat. Convention, New Orleans, 1988. Mem. Am. Film Inst., New Orleans Assn. Film and Tape Profls. (hon.), New Orleans Film Commn. (staff liaison). Democrat. Roman Catholic. Avocations: writing, music, piano, public relations projects. Home: New Orleans, La. Died July 24, 2004.

CARDWELL, GUY ADAMS, retired language educator; b. Savannah, Ga., Nov. 14, 1905; s. Guy Adams and Ethel Mae (Parmalee) Cardwell; m. Margaret Randolph Bullitt, Dec. 21, 1935 (dec. Oct. 1991); children: Evelyn Bullitt-(dec.), Margaret Randolph, Ethel Parmele(dec.), Lucy Adams; m. Blanche Butler Marshall, May 7, 1992 (dec. Apr. 1995). AB, U. N.C., 1926, PhD, 1936; AM, Harvard U., 1932. Instr., asst. prof. Wake Forest U., 1936-38; asst. prof., prof. Tulane U., 1938-45; prof., head English Dept. U. Md., 1945-49, Washington U., St. Louis, 1949-68; prof. SUNY, Albany, 1968-71. Vis. prof. Duke U., U. N.C., U. Vienna, U. Buenos Aires, Nat. U. Mex., Am. U., Paris, King's Coll., Cambridge U. Author: Twins of Genius, 1953, Der Amerikanische Roman, 1954, Charleston, S.C., Periodicals, 1960, The Man Who Was Mark Twain, 1991; editor: The Uncollected Poems of Henry Timrod, 1942, Readings From the Americas, 1947, Life on the Mississippi, 1968, Mississippi Writings, 1982, The Innocents Abroad; Roughing It, 1984; contbr. articles, poems, essays, stories to profl. jours., quars. Home: Baltimore, Md. Died Sept. 29, 2005.

CAREY, JAMES WILLIAM, communications educator, former dean; b. Providence, Sept. 7, 1934; s. Cyril Joseph and Rita Miriam (Lyons) C.; m. Elizabeth Theresa Gilman, Sept. 7, 1957; children: William, Timothy, Daniel, Matthew. BS, U. R.I., 1957; MS, U. Ill., 1959, PhD, 1963. Prof. U. Ill., Urbana, 1963-67; dir. Inst. Communications Research, U. Ill., Urbana, 1969-76; dean Coll. Communications U. Ill., Urbana, 1979-92; prof. Pa, State U., State College, 1967-68, U. Iowa, Iowa City, 1976-79; CBS prof. Columbia U., N.Y.C., 1993—2006; assoc. mem. Ctr. for Advanced Study, 1975. Bd. dirs. Humanities Coun., Poynter Inst. for Media Studies, Peabody Awards in Broadcasting. Book review editor: Communication Research: An Internat. Quar., 1974-82; cons. and contbg. editor: Jour. Communication, 1981-83, Communication yearbook I, II, III, 1981-83; editor: Sage Ann. Revs. of Communication Research, 1982-87, Communication, 1985-2006; mem. editorial bd.: Journalism Quar., 1974—2006, Journalism Monographs, 1974—2006, Mass Communication Rev., 1974—2006, Studies in the Anthropology of Visual Communication, 1981—2006, Can. Communications Jour., 1980-83; contbr. articles to profl. jours. NEH fellow, 1975, Gannett Ctr. for Media Studies fellow Columbia U., 1985. Mem. Assn. Edn. in Journalism (pres. 1978-79), Assn. Schs. and Depts. Journalism (pres. 1982-83). Democrat. Roman Catholic. Home: New York, NY. Died May 23, 2006.

CARGO, WILLIAM IRA, retired ambassador; b. Detroit, Feb. 27, 1917; s. Ira Wiles and Nina (Lathrop) C.; m. Margaret Grace Ludwig, June 21, 1938; children: David Paul, Ruth. AB, Albion Coll., 1937, LLD, 1963; AM, U. Mich., 1938, PhD, 1941; student Russian lang., Naval Tng. Sch., Boulder, Colo., 1944-45; LLD, Waynesburg Coll., 1970. Instr. polit. sci. U. Mich., 1941-42, Colo. Coll., 1942-43; staff US Dept. State, 1943-78, Bur. UN Affairs, 1946-53, dep. dir. office dependent area affairs, 1952; assigned Nat. War Coll., 1953-54; adviser U.S. delegations Gen. Assembly, Trusteeship Council Sessions, 1946-53; alternate U.S. rep. UN Com. on Non-self-governing Terrs., 1952; U.S. rep. UN vis. mission Trust Terrs. Tanganyika, Italian Somaliland, Ruanda-Urundi, 1951; assigned to U.S. Mission to NATO and European regional orgns. in connection with spl. internat. trade problems, Paris, 1954-57; dep. dir. Office of UN Polit. and Security Affairs, Dept. State, 1957-58, dir., 1958-61; dep. U.S. rep. Internat. Atomic Energy Agy., Vienna, 1961-63; dep. chief of mission, minister-counselor Am. Embassy, Karachi and Rawalpindi, Pakistan, 1963-67; dep. U.S. rep. to NATO minister, Brussels, 1967-69; career minister U.S. Fgn. Service, 1969; dir. policy planning staff US Dept. State, Washington, 1969-73, US amb. to Nepal, 1973—76; sr. insp. Fgn. Service Inspection Corps., Washington, 1976-78, cons., 1979-83; adviser U.S. delegation UN Gen. Assembly, 1957, Gen. Conf. of IAEA, Vienna, 1958, alt. U.S. rep., 1961, 62; adviser U.S. del. Conf. Discontinuance Nuclear Weapons Tests, Geneva, 1959; vice-chmn. U.S. del. Conf. to Amend Single Conv. Narcotic Drugs, Geneva, 1972. Co-author: (autobiography) Wherever the Road Leads, 1997. Served with USNR, 1944-46. Recipient Meritorious Svc. award, Dept. State. Mem. Am. Fgn. Svc. Assn., Diplomatic and Consular Officers Ret., Phi Beta Kappa, Delta Sigma Rho, Phi Mu Alpha. Methodist. Home: Columbia, Md. Died Dec. 13, 2005.

CARLESON, ROBERT BAZIL, public policy consultant, former federal official; b. Long Beach, Calif., Feb. 21, 1931; s. Bazil Upton and Grace Reynolds (Wilhite) Carleson; m. Betty Jane Nichols, Jan. 31, 1954 (div.); children: Eric Robert, Mark Andrew, Susan Lynn; m. Susan A. Dower, Feb. 11, 1984. Student, U. Utah, 1949—51; BS, U. So. Calif., 1953, postgrad., 1956—58. Adminstrv. asst. City of Beverly Hills, Calif., 1956-57; asst. to city mgr. City of Claremont, Calif., 1957-58; sr. adminstrv. asst. to city mgr. City of Torrance, Calif., 1958-60; city mgr. City of San Dimas, Calif., 1960-64, Pico Rivera, Calif., 1964-68; chief dep. dir. Calif. Dept. Pub. Works, 1968-71; dir. Calif. Dept. Social Welfare, 1971-73; U.S. commr. welfare Washington, 1973-75; pres. Robert B. Carleson & Assocs., Sacramento and Washington, 1975-81, chmn. Washington, 1987—93, 2002—06, San Diego, 1993—2001; pres. Innovative Environ. Svcs. Ltd., Vancouver, B.C., Canada, 1992; spl. asst. to Pres. for policy devel. The White House, Washington, 1981-84; prin., dir. govt. rels. KMG Main Hurdman, Washington, 1984-87; dir. transition team US Dept. Health & Human Services, Office of Pres.-Elect, 1980-81; spl. adviser Office of Policy Coordination; sr. policy advisor, chmn. welfare task force Reagan Campaign, 1980. Bd. dirs. Fed. Home Loan Bank of Atlanta, 1987-90, I.E.S., Ltd., Can., Transenviro Co., USA, Churchill Co., USA; adv. com. Fed. Home Loan Mortgage Corp., 1985-87; mem. strengthening family policy coun. Nat. Policy Forum, Washington, 1994. Eagle Scout q.m. sea scout, 1948; lt. gov. Calif. Boys' State, 1948; adv. coun. gen. govt. Rep. Nat. Com., Washington, 1980-81; sr. fellow Free Congress Found., 1994-2006; founder, chmn. Am. Civil Rights Union, 1998-2006; Officer USN, 1953-56, USNR, 1956-67. Mem.: Capitol Hill Club, Army and Navy Club (Washington), Rotary (pres. 1964), Masons. Died Apr. 21, 2006.

CARLIN, MAURICE PATRICK, surgeon; b. Foley, Minn., July 3, 1924; s. John F. and Ida (Philomen) C.; m. Victoria L. Carlin; children: Brian, Barry, Thomas, Tama, Dierdra, Bonnie, Marci MD, Marquette U., Milw., 1946. Diplomate Am. Bd. Neurol. Surgery, Am. Bd. Neurology. Intern Buffalo Gen. Hosp., 1947-48; fellow U. Minn. Grad. Sch., 1948-50; resident neurology Minn. VA Hosp. & Affiliated U. Minn. Hosps., 1948-50, resident, 1953-55; chief resident neurosurgery Ill. Neuropsy. Inst., 1954; pvt. practice neurology and neurol. surgery Santa Rosa, Calif., from 1955. Mem. staff Santa Rosa Meml. Hosp; cons. neurol. and neurol. surgery Sonoma & Mendocino State Hosp, Sonoma Valley Hosp., St. Helena San; Neurol. Surgery Dept. San Diego USN Hosp., 1951-52; clin. ast. neurology and neurol. surgery U. Ill., 1953-55. Lt. USN, 1950-52. Mem. AMA, Am. Assn. Neurology, Am. Assn. Neurol. Surgery, Am. Assn. Physicians and Surgeons, Calif. Neurol. Soc. Died Mar. 1, 2005.

CARLISLE, LILIAN MATAROSE BAKER (MRS. E. GRAFTON CARLISLE JR.), writer, educator; b. Meridian, Miss., Jan. 1, 1912; d. Joseph and Lilian (Flournoy) Baker; m. E. Grafton Carlisle, Jr., Jan. 9, 1933; children: Diana, Penelope. Student, Dickinson Coll., 1929-30, Pierce Coll. Bus. Adminstrn., 1930-31; BA, U. Vt., 1981, MA, 1986, PhD (hon.), 2005. Adminstrv. sec. RAF Ferry Command, Montreal, Can., 1942; exec. staff. mem. in charge collections, research Shelburne (Vt.) Mus., 1951-61; exec. sec. Burlington Area Community Health Study, 1963, coord., 1964; asst. coord. Vt. Mental Retardation Planning Project, 1965; project dir. 4-county Champlain Valley Medicare Alert, 1966; dir. publ. rels. Champlain Valley Agrl. Fair, 1968-77; lectr. U. Vt. Elder Hostel program, 1976-77. Mem. faculty Vacation Coll., 1980-83. Co-author: The Story of the Shelburne Museum, 1955, Profile of the Community, 1964, Environmental and Personal Health of the Community, 1964, Vermont Clock and Watchmakers, Silversmiths and Jewelers, 1970; also numerous catalogs on collections at Shelburne Mus.; editl. cons. Burlington Social Survey, 1967; editor: Historic Guide to Burlington Neighborhoods, 1991, vol. II, 1997, vol. III, 2003; contbr. articles to profl. jours. Pres., Burlington Comty. Coun. for Social Welfare, 1959-61, 1971-73; chmn. bd. Champlain Sr. Citizens, 1977-79, justice of peace, 1979-81; pres. Chittenden County Extension Adv. Com., 1977-78; chmn. publs. com. Vt. Bicentennial Commn., 1974-77; mem. Vt. Ho. of Reps., 1968-70. Recipient Cmty. Coun. Disting. Citizen award, 1978, cert. of award for Excellence in Cmty. Svc. DAR, 1996, Lifetime Achievement award Preservation Burlington, 2004., Lifetime Achievement award Ctr. for Rsch. on Vt., 2005 Mem. Vt. (trustee, chmn. mus. com. 1967), N.Y. (faculty seminar) Chittenden (pres. 1969-72, editor Heritage Series of 10 books about Chittenden County towns 1972-76) hist. socs., Vt. Old Cemetary Assn., Vt. Folklore So., League Vt. Writers (dir. 1962, v.p., pres. 1967-69), Am. Pen Women (pres. Green Mountain br. 1980-82), Order Women Legislators (pres. Vt. br. 1972-74), Meml. Soc. Vt. (pres. 1989-94), Zonta Club (pres. 1964-65), Chi Omega, Conglist. Home: Burlington, Vt. Died July 28, 2006.

CARLISLE, MARGO DUER BLACK, former federal agency administrator; b. Providence; d. Thomas F. Jr. and Margaret MacCormick Black; m. Miles Carlisle; children: Mary Hamilton, Tristram Coffin. BA, Manhattanville Coll. Legis. asst. to Senator James A. McClure US Senate, Washington, 1973, staff mem. budget comm. task force, 1974-75, exec. dir. steering com., 1975-80; staff dir. Senate Rep. Conf., Washington, 1981-84; exec. dir. Coun. for Nat. Policy, Washington, 1985-86; asst. sec. for legis. affairs US Dept. Def., Washington, 1986-89; v.p. for govt. rels. The Heritage Found., Washington, 1989-90; chief staff to Senator Thad Cochran US Senate, Washington, 1991-97; cons. Nat. Security, 1997-98; commr. Commn. to Assess the Orgn. of Fed. Govt. Staff dir. nat. security and fgn. policy subcoms. for Rep. platform, 1984, Washington. Contbr. articles on govt. policy to profl. jours. Trustee Phila. Soc., Washington, 1987-88, 93—95, pres., 1995-96; bd. advisors, Marine Corps U., 1995-2006. Roman Catholic. Avocations: sailing, scuba diving. Died Mar. 28, 2006.

CARLSEN, JANET HAWS, retired insurance company executive; b. Bellingham, Wash., June 16, 1927; d. Lyle F. and Mary Elizabeth (Preble) Haws; m. Kenneth M. Carlsen, July 26, 1952; children: Stephanie L. Chambers, Scott Lyle, Sean Preble, Stacy K., Spencer J. Cert., Armstrong Bus. Sch., 1945; student, Golden Gate Coll., 1945-46. Office mgr. Cornwall Warehouse Co., Salt Lake City, 1950-55, Hansen's Ins., Newman, Calif., 1969-77; owner Carlsen Ins., Gustine, Calif., 1978-97, retired, 1997. Mem. city coun. City of Newman, 1980-82, mayor, 1982-94; bd. dirs. ARC, Stanislaus, Calif., 1982-83, Tosca, 1993-98; bd. dirs. Stanislaus County Area Agy. on Aging, 1995-2000, chairperson, 1996-99; bd. dirs. Calif. state com. TACC Commn. on Aging, 1996-98; grand marshal Newman Fall Festival, 1989; v.p. ctrl. divsn. League of Calif. Cities, 1989-90, pres. 1990, 91; bd. dirs. Sr. Opportunity Svc. Ctr., 1993-96, 97-98, Sr. Opportunity Svc. Program of Stanislaus County, 1995-96; chairperson Ctrl. Valley Opportunity Ctr., 1996-98; mem. Stanislaus County Vision Com., 1997-99; bd. dirs. Gt. Valley Ctr., 1997-99. Named Soroptimist Woman of Achievement, 1987, Soroptimist Woman of Distinction, 1988, Outstanding Woman, Stanislaus County Commn. for Women, 1989, Newman Rotary Club Citizen of Yr., 1993-94, Woman of Yr. Calif. State Assembly Dist. 26, 1994, Ambassador, City of Newman, 1997—, John T. Silver award Newman C. of C., 2000; recipient plaque Ctrl. Valley Opportunity Ctr., 2001. Mem. Booster Club (Newman) Soroptimist Club, Newman Women's Club, Newman Garden Club. Mem. Lds Ch. Home: Newman, Calif. Died Dec. 28, 2005.

CARLSON, CHARLES LONG, controller, accountant; b. Olean, N.Y., Jan. 10, 1917; s. Charles Julius and Edna (Long) C.; m. June Helena Kreamer, Apr. 10, 0148; children: Yvonne, Shaun, Linda, Maria. BS in Bus. Adminstrn., U. Buffalo, 1938. CPA N.Y., Calif. Ptnr. Merle Moore & Co., CPAs, Tucson, 1954—55; sec.-treas., contr. Infilco, Tucson, 1955—64; contr. Traveler Boat divsn. Stanray Corp., Chgo. and Danville, Ill., 1964—65, Dorsett Plastics Co., Santa Clara, Calif., 1966; v.p., sec.-treas. Daniel, Mann, Johnson & Mendenhall, L.A., Calif., 1966—82, bus. cons., sec., from 1982. Dir. numersou subs. Infilco and Daniel, Mann, Johnson & Mendenhall; sec., dir. Infilco (Australasia) Ltd., Infilco (Can.) Ltd., Infilco Mexicana; sec. Gale Separator Co., Tucson, Catalina Constrn. Co., Tucson; sec.-treas. Beach Ocean Inc., from 1985, Honolulu Condo

Inc., 1985—86; bus. mgr. Westwil Ltd., 1986—92, Hampwil Ptnrs., from 1986; asst. treas. Fuller Co., Catasauqua, Pa.; dir. Gen. Steel Co., Ft. Worth, 1960—64; instr. St. Bonaventure U., Olean, 1948. Rep. county committeeman, Olean, 1939; team orgn. chmn. Olean Gen. Hosp. Dr., 1952; gen. chmn. Comty. Chest campaign, Olean, 1950. 2d lt. USAAF, 1944—45. Mem.: AICPA, Tucson C. of C. (tax study com. 1960). Church Of The Nazarene. Died Feb. 26, 2005.

CARLSON, CLAIRE FERGUSON, lawyer; b. Des Moines, Feb. 6, 1927; d. James Clare and Johanna P. (Vanderwaal) Ferguson; m. Raymond D. Carlson, June 24, 1950; children: James D., Mary Christine. BA, U. Iowa, 1949, JD, 1950. Bar: Iowa, 1950, U.S. Dist. Ct. (no., so. dists.) Iowa 1950. Atty. Bastian, Beisser & Carlson, Ft. Dodge, Iowa, 1964-72, Kersten & Carlson, Ft. Dodge, from 1972. Contbr. article to Drake Law Rev. Sec. Webster County Rep. Cen. Com., Ft. Dodge, 1950-52; pres. bd. trustees Blanden Meml. Art Mus., Ft. Dodge; trustee Iowa State Bar Found. Fellow Am. Bar Found.; mem. ABA, Iowa State Bar Assn. (bar study com. on women and minorities' involvement in bar assn. and jud. system of state, grievance com.), Webster County Bar Assn. (pres. 1978-79, grievance com.), Iowa Def. Counsel (pres. 1985), Iowa Assn. Workers Compensation Lawyers (pres. 1979-81), Iowa Indsl. Commn. (adv. com.), Internat. Assn. Def. Counsel, Fedn. Ins. and Corp. Counsel, Def. Rsch. Inst., Iowa U. Law Sch. Found. (trustee), Order of Coif. Republican. Home: Okoboji, Iowa. Died Jan. 3, 2004.

CARLSON, FREDA ELLEN, secondary school educator, educational association administrator; b. Wilmington, Ohio, Jan. 4, 1914; d. Heber W. and Hazel (Reed) Custis; m. Raymond A. Carlson, June 15, 1940; children: Susan Ann Lapp, Philip Reed. MA in Adminstrn., Toledo U., 1967, MA in Teaching and Reading, EdS, 1972. Tchr. elem. Highland Sch., Sylvania, Ohio, 1963-68; from tchr. to supr. Lucas County Schs., Toledo, 1968-76, cons. to tchrs., 1969-76, ret., 1976. Tchr. adult continuing edn. Toledo U., 1961-76. Guardian ad litem Ohio Juvenile Ct., 1976-84: Sarasota County High Sch. Acad. Olympics, 1991—. Recipient Woman of Toledo award St. Vincent Hosp. Guild, 1984. Mem. Internat. Reading Assn. (pres. 1980-81), Nat. Middle Sch. Assn. (sec. 1978-79), AAUW (1st v.p. 1990—), Phi Delta Kappa, Pi Lambda Theta (pres. 1970-72), Delta Kappa Gamma (pres. 1974-76), Phi Kappa Phi. Republican. Lutheran. Died Jan. 17, 2006.

CARLSON, GUSTAV GUNNAR, anthropology educator; b. Gwinn, Mich., Nov. 21, 1909; s. Axel Victor and Brita Christina (Mattson) C.; m. Edith Elizabeth Erickson, Nov. 15, 1933; children: Karen Elizabeth Carlson Ogden, Eric Gustav. AB, No. Mich. U., 1932; MA, U. Mich., 1934, PhD, 1940. Instr. anthropology U. Cin., 1936-40, asst. prof. anthropology, 1940-43, assoc. prof. anthropology, 1946-52, prof. anthropology, 1952-80, head dept. sociology & anthropology, 1961-69, head dept. anthropology, 1969-77, prof. emeritus, 1980—2006; chief ops. intelligence Office of War Info., 1943-46. Vis. prof. U. Yunnan, China, 1945; cons. in field. Rockefeller Found. fellow, 1933; recipient A.B. Cohen award Excellence in Univ. Tchg. U. Cin., 1961-62, Disting. Alumni award No. Mich. U., 1981. Mem. Phi Beta Kappa, Sigma Xi. Avocations: gardening, photography, bread baking. Home: Cincinnati, Ohio. Died June 18, 2006.

CARPENTER, GEORGE ROBERT, artist; b. Boston, Dec. 13, 1928; s. George Gillis and Daisy Winifred Carpenter; m. Virgina A. forsyth, Oct. 14, 1966. One-man shows include Wilkes Coll., Wilkes-Barre, Pa., Rockport (Mass.) Art Assn., Red Piano Gallery, Hilton Head Island, S.C., quadrangle Gallery, Dallas, Hallway Gallery, Washington, Down East Gallery, Washington, Continental Galleries, Ontreal, Que., others; group shows include Acad. Artists Assn., Springfield, Mass., Anchorage Fine Arts Mus., Black Hills State Coll., Spearfish, S.C., cheyenne (Wyo.) Western Galleries, Copley Soc., Boston, Charles and Emma Frye Mus., Seattle, Mainstreams, Marietta, Ohio, Nat. Acad. of Design, N.Y., Rockport Art Assn., Salmagundi Club, N.Y., Wouthwestern Watercolor Soc., Dallas, others; represented in pub. and pvt. collections includingMerck Pharma., Miami U., Ohio, Mills coll., Oakland, Calif., Nat. Steamship Lines, Can., No. Trust Offices, Chgo., others. Mem. adv. bd. Coastal Conservation Assn., Maine, 1997—. Mem. Rockport Art Assn., Watercolor USA Honor Soc., Masons, Shriners, Lions. Avocation: fishing. Died 2006.

CARPENTER, NATHANIEL DENNARD, nursing administrator; b. Phila., Feb. 2, 1959; s. Marvin Dennard and Rose Ann (Heath) Carpenter; m. Jennifer Jones, Mar. 2001; children: Jeffrey Nathan, Eric Randolph; 1 child from previous marriage, Natalie Deneen. Lic. practical nurse, James Martin Sch., Phila., 1982. Staff nurse Med. Coll. Pa., Phila., 1982-85; nursing coord. Hosp. Home Care Greater Phila., 1985-86; staff nurse Kimberly Quality Care, Phila., 1986-90; staff nurse ICU St. Agnes Med. Ctr., Phila., 1987-90; asst. resident health coord. Logan Sq. East, Phila., 1989-92, resident health coord., 1991-94; staff nurse New Ralston House, Phila., 1994—97, asst. primary instr. P&A nursing, from 2003. Author: Vital Signs, 1990. Vol. speaker Planned Parenthood, Phila., 1982-85. With USAF, 1976-77. Avocations: reading, sports. Home: Philadelphia, Pa. Died Feb. 1, 2006.

CARPENTER, PATRICIA, clinical psychologist, poet; b. Detroit, May 16, 1920; d. William Henry and Kathryn Virginia (Dix) Humphrey; m. Warren H. Carpenter, Mar. 29, 1958. AB, Oberlin Coll., 1941; BS in LS, Western Res. U., 1943; MA, Wayne State U., 1958, PhD, 1961. Diplomate in clin. psychology Am. Bd. of Examiners in Psychology. Libr. Detroit Pub. Libr., 1943-49; rsch. libr. United Automobile Workers-CIO, Detroit, 1950-56; rsch. fellow, grad. asst. Wayne State U., Detroit, 1956-58; psychologist Clinic for Child Study, Wayne County Juvenile Ct., Detroit, 1959-63, dir. psychol. svcs., 1963-81; dir. Psychol. Svcs. for Youth, Brighton, Mich., from 1981; cons. Wayne County Juvenile Ct., Detroit, 1981-83. Cons. N. Suburban Counseling Assocs., Mt. Clemens, Mich., 1974-81, Genesee County Child and Adolescent Svc., Flint, Mich., 1980-82; leader intensive jour. workshops Dialogue House, N.Y.C., 1985—. Contbr. articles to profl. jours., poetry to various publs. Avocations: writing, swimming, travel. Home: Howell, Mich. Died Jan. 6, 2004.

CARR, DAVIS, lawyer; b. Elmhurst, Ill., Apr. 1, 1956; s. Harold Dewane and Molly (Wade) C.; m. Kaye Hayes; children from previous marriage: Whitney, Griffin, Jordan; stepchildren: Jeremiah, Aaron, Sarah, Hannah. BA summa cum laude, U. S. Ala., 1976; JD, U. Ala., 1979. Bar: Ala. 1979, U.S. Ct. Appeals (5th cir.) 1980, U.S. Ct. Appeals (11th cir.) 1982, U.S. Supreme Ct. 1984. Ptnr. Hand, Arendall, Bedsole, Greaves & Johnston, Mobile, Ala., 1979-90, Pierce, Carr, Alford, Ledyard & Latta, Mobile, 1990-96, Carr, Alford, Clausen & McDonald, Mobile, Ala., from 1996. Research editor Ala. Law Rev., 1978-79; contbr. articles to profl. jours. Recipient M. Leigh Harrison award; Hugo Black scholar. Mem. ABA (litigation sect.), Ala. Bar Assn., Am. Inns Ct. (Mobile chpt.), Mobile County Bar Assn., Ala. Def. Lawyers Assn. (editor jour. 1986—, pres. 1992-93), Def. Rsch. Inst. (vice chair med. profl. liability sect. 1994—, Ala. state rep., mem. life health and accident sect.), Am. Acad. Appellate Lawyers, Internat. Assn. Def. Counsel, Order of Coif. Republican. Baptist. Home: Fairhope, Ala. Died Feb. 5, 2005.

CARR, JAMES T., transportation company executive; b. Jersey City, Nov. 24, 1924; s. James V. and Augusta E. (Stenecke) C.; m. Helen A. De Tore, Jan. 4, 1948; children: Elaine, James T. Jr., Pamela. BS, NYU, 1950. Notary pub., N.J. Dist. mgr. W.T. Cowan, Inc., Jersey City, 1947-78; terminal mgr. Transcon Lines, Clifton, N.J., from 1978. Trustee I.L.A. 1730 Pension-Welfare Fund, N.Y.C., 1970-78. With AUS, 1943-46, ETO. Mem. N.J. Motor Truck Assn. (chmn. ops. coun.), Delta Nu Alpha. Roman Catholic. Avocations: swimming, basketball, photography, television. Home: Bergenfield, NJ. Died Dec. 23, 2004.

CARRINGER, RITA VIRGINIA, healthcare administrator; b. Boston, Dec. 18, 1929; d. Albert Joseph and Margaret Mary (Carr) Grandmont; m. Robert Warner Carringer, Sr., Feb. 7, 1953; children: Rob, Diane, Lisa, Jay, Elaine. Cert. in nursing, Mt. Auburn Hosp., Cambridge, Mass., 1950. RN; cert. gerontol. nurse ANA, cert. instr.-supr. Ohio Teaching Network. Staff nurse Christ Hosp., Cin.; supr., staff nurse St. Francis Hosp., Cin.; dir. nursing Riverview Community, Cin., inservice dir. Mem. Ohio Gerontol. Soc. Home: Cincinnati, Ohio. Died June 30, 2004.

CARROLL, RONNIE LEE, youth organization administrator; b. Decatur, Ala., Sept. 29, 1945; s. Lee F. and Betty Ruth (Sharp) C.; m. Barbara Elizabeth Lakey, Mar. 10, 1967 (div. 1982); children: Dealana, Adrian; m. Pamela Kay Edwards, June 15, 1986. BS, Miss. State U., 1967. Tchr. head start program, Ashland, Miss., 1966-67; asst. store mgr. W.T. Grant Co., New Orleans, 1967-69; profl. scouter Pine Burr Coun., Boy Scouts Am., Hattiesburg, Miss., 1969-79; scout exec. Cape Fear Coun., Boy Scouts Am., Wilmington, N.C., 1979-85, Cen. Fla. Coun., Boy Scouts Am., Orlando, Fla., from 1985. Contbr. articles to profl. mags. Mem. campaign com. Waller for Miss. Gov., 1971, Finch for Miss. Gov., 1975; mem. campaign com. Gephart for Pres., Fla., 1988. Mem. Nat. Soc. Fundraising Execs. (cert, pres. Cen. Fla. chpt. 1989—, founding pres. Coastal Carolina chpt.), Wilmington Execs. Club, Thalian Assn., Citrus Club, Tuscawalla Country Club, Salem Lodge, Eola Lodge. Republican. Episcopalian. Avocations: camping, gardening, fishing, history, golf. Home: Bethesda, Md. Died Feb. 28, 2005.

CARSOLA, ALFRED JAMES, oceanographer, geologist, educator; b. Los Angeles, Calif., June 6, 1919; s. Thomas and Margaret Rose Carsola; m. Joan Lorraine Breunig, June 21, 1947; children: Marie, Thomas, Timothy, Carol, Margaret, Catherine, Christopher, Paul. BS, UCLA, Los Angeles, CA, 1942; MS, U. of So. Calif., Los Angeles, CA, 1947; PhD, Scripps Instn. of Oceanography, LaJolla, CA, 1953. Oceanographer USN Electronics Lab., San Diego, Calif., 1947—60; scientist Lockheed Aircraft Corp., Burbank, Sunnyvale, Calif., 1960—75; rsch. scientist So. Calif. Coastal Rsch. Project, Los Angeles, Calif., 1971—72; lectr., adj. prof. San Diego State U., San Diego, Calif., 1956—59, 1976—82; lectr. U. of San Diego, San Diego, Calif., 1976—85; adj. prof. Grossmont Coll., El Cajon, Calif., 1974—92, San Diego Mesa Coll., San Diego, Calif., from 1974. Avocation: contract bridge. Home: San Diego, Calif. Died Oct. 23, 2004.

CARSON, BUD (LEON HALDEN CARSON), former professional football coach; b. Brackeridge, Pa. m. Linda Carson; children: Clifford, Dana, Cathi 1 stepchild, Gary Ford. BA in Edn., U. NC, 1952. Head coach Scottsdale (Pa.) HS, 1955—56; freshman coach U. NC, 1957, asst. coach, 1958—63, U. SC, 1965; asst. coach, defensive coord. Ga. Tech., 1966; head coach Ga. Tech. U., 1967—71; defensive coord. Pitts. Steelers, 1972—77, LA Rams, 1978—82, Balt. Colts, 1982—83; defensive coord., defensive backs coach Kans. City Chiefs, 1983—84; defensive coord. NY Jets, 1985-88, Phila. Eagles, 1991—94, St. Louis Rams, 1997—98, defensive cons., 2000; head coach Cleve. Browns, 1988-90. Served in USMC, 1951—53. Died Dec. 7, 2005.

CARY, FRANK TAYLOR, retired business executive; b. Gooding, Idaho, Dec. 14, 1920; s. Frank Taylor and Ida C.; m. Anne Curtis, 1943; children: Marshall, Bryan, Steven, Laura Cary King. BS, UCLA, 1943; MBA, Stanford U., 1948. With IBM Corp., 1948-83, pres., 1971-73, chmn. bd., CEO, 1973-83, chmn. exec. com., 1979-85, also bd. dirs., 1971-91, mem. adv. bd., 1991—2006. Bd. dirs. Celgene Corp., Capital Cities/ABC, Inc., DNA Plant Tech., Inc., ICOS Corp., Lexmark Internat., Inc., Lincare, Inc., Teltrend Inc., Texaco, Inc.; mem. bd. counselors Bechtel Group, Inc.; coun. mgmt. advisers Dean Witter Reynolds Inc.; mem. investment com. MIT, regulatory adv. com. N.Y. Stock Exch., U.S. adv. bd. SpencerStuart. Mem. visiting com. Harvard U. JFK Sch. Govt.; hon. trustee Brookings Instn. Served with AUS, 1944-46. Mem. Am. Acad. Arts and Scis., Bus. Coun. (hon.), Clove Valley Rod and Gun Club, Wee Burn Country Club, Blind Brook Club, N.Y. Yacht Club, Everglades Club, Ocean Club of Fla. Died Jan. 2, 2006.

CASADONTE, MICHAEL JOHN, computer technician; b. Flint, Mich., June 8, 1953; s. John and Pauline E. (Powell) C.; m. Charlotte I. Loveland, Jan. 1, 1985; children: Crystal N., CloAnn. AS in Robotics, Charles Stewart Mott Sch., Flint, Mich., 1984; AS in Fluid Power, Charles Stewart Mott Sch., 1984, AS in Electronics, 1985. Computer technician GM-CLCD, Flint, Mich., from 1990. Consulting Specialize Ins. Svcs. Grand Blanc, Mich., 1985—, Quantum USA, Clio, Mich., 1989—. Home: Clio, Mich. Died July 12, 2005.

CASE, ELIZABETH, artist, writer; b. Long Beach, Calif., July 24, 1930; d. Nelson and Sarah Lee (Odend'hal) C.; children: Walter J. Zwicker Jr., Keith Allen Zwicker, Pat James Cioffi, Susan Cioffi Onopa. Art studies, French Inst., 1946, Art Students League, 1948-49, Elmira Coll., 1949-51, Syracuse U., 1951, Chaffey Coll., Ontario, Calif., 1954. With animation dept. Walt Disney Prodns., Burbank, Calif., 1956-58; mem. faculty Lighthouse Art and Music Camp, 1961; New Hope Art Sch., Pa., 1961; asst. mgr. promotion, copywriter Reinhold Pub. Co., N.Y.C., 1961; copywriter scholary advt. Columbia U. Press, 1963; advt. coord. Orbit Imperial Design Corp., 1964; mem. faculty Ft. Lee (N.J.) Adult Sch., 1975-82; sr. copywriter/designer spl. projects coll. textbook advt. Prentice-Hall, Englewood Cliffs, N.J., 1975-77; mem. promotion and design staff Rutherford Mus. (now Meadowland Mus.), 1979; nat. sales promotion mgr. M. Grumbacher, Inc., 1979-81; typographer and quality control Graphic Tech., Inc., N.Y.C., 1983-90; The Graphic Word, 1990-91; Ace Typographers, N.Y.C., 1991-92; copy editor Times-Beacon Newspapers, Manahawkin, NJ, 1993-94; art review corr. Times-Beacon Islander Mag., 1994—98; editor Leisure West News, Manchester, NJ, from 1998. Prin., dir. Gadfly Prodns., 1969-89, ECHO, 1989—; combat artist USN, GS15, 1974—. One-man show rsch. libr. exhbns. facility Walt Disney Prodns., 1957, 58, Swain's Gallery, New Hope, Pa., 1963, D'Alessio Gallery, N.Y.C., 1963, Gallery 8, N.Y.C., 1969, Ft. Lee Pub. Libr., 1975, Ridgefield Pub. Libr., 1978, Edgewater (N.J.) Nat. Bank, 1983, Edgewater Pub. Libr., 1984, Ea. Va. Med. Ctr. exhbn. facility, Norfolk, 1984, Ocean County Artists' Guild, Island Heights, N.J., 1994, Ocean County Libr., Manchester Br., 1996, Barnegat Br., 1997, Little Egg Harbor Br., 1998, 50-Yr. Retrospective George Waters Gallery, Elmira Coll., 2003; group shows include Friends Ctr., Phila., 1960, Hist. Soc. Ann. Exhbn., Philips Mill, Pa., 1962-63, Englewood Armory show, 1967-68, Hadassah, Paramus, N.J., 1969, Bergen C.C., 1970, traveling exhbn. Bicentennial Am. Freedoms, 1975-76, So. Vt. Art Ctr., 1980, Edgewater Arts Coun., 1982 (1st prize), 1993-94, Bergen County Mus., 1984-85, Noyes Mus., (2nd prize) 1993, Jane Law Long Beach Island Watercolor Ann., 1993-94, 97, 2000-04, Batsto Outdoor Art Show, 1993 (prize), 95 (prize), Jane Law Long Beach Island Ann. Miniature Art Show, 1993-98, Ocean County Art Guild, 1993 (prize), 94, 95 (prize) 1996-2004, Ocean County Coll. Srs. Exhibit, 1993-2005, 95 (2nd prize), 96, N.J. State Show, 1993-2004, Nat. Soc. Mural Painters Centennial exhbn. and Symposium, Art Students League Gallery, 1995, St. Francis Ann. Spring Art Show, Brant Beach, N.J., 1996, Women Oil Painters N.J., Jane Law's Long Beach Island Gallery, 1996 (merit award, 2002); represented in permanent collections Washington Navy Yard Combat Art Collection, Ch. of Christ, Jersey City, Edgewater Pub. Libr., Intrepid Sea-Air-Space Mus. Am. Freedoms Collections (acquired art collection of N.Y.C. sch. sys., Edgewater Pub. Libr. and watercolor purchased by Ocean Grove Hist. Soc. Collection); executed murals at INSCON, San Dimas, Calif., L.A. County Hosp., with Walt Disney team Delaware Canal, New Hope; mural design Allegheny Airlines, Lumberville, Pa., 1960; mural corner Main and 202, New Hope, 1960, Lumberville, Meth. Ch., 1961, swimming pool, Jerico Valley, Pa., 1961, Orbit Imperial Design Corp., N.Y.C., 1965, Fabric Shop, Ft. Lee, 1969, 72, Ch. of Good Shepherd, 1971, The Wrong Elf, Stroke of Color, 1985, Old Bridge Pub. Libr., 1977, reinstalled new libr. bldg., 1995, History of Women Voting (tryptych design) acquired by Elmira Coll., 2003, created for traveling exhbn. Momentous Events in American History, Nat. Soc. Mural Painters, 1980-82, History of Typography, GTI, N.Y.C., 1985 (reinstalled at Bergen County

Tech. Schs. Acad. for Advancement of Sci. and Tech. 1991); writer (poetry) Vanity Druffen In Retrospect, 1958, Pax and Dig Collection, 1968, CD, 2003, Kettlefish Collection, 2003; illustrator cover Bucks County Life, Doylestown, Pa., 1961, Vanity Fair Books, 1962, Am. Scandinavian Rev., 1962, Molecular Kinetic Theory, 1963, Theory of Lanthinides and Chemical Energy, 1963, Harle Publs., 1969-70, Programmed Algebra vols. 1 and 2, 1977, vol. 3, 1979, Use and Misuse of Statistics, 1978; illustrator, designer What Do I Do with a Major in...(Malnig), 2nd edit., 1984, botanical illustrations Trail Guide, Whitesbog Preservation and Trust, 1997; pub. VeggieTree, ltd. ed., 1988—, ECHO posters and Cards, 1988—, ltd. ed., The Wrong Elf, 2002—; contbr. articles to mags. Recipient Spring Concours award Art Students League, 1949, Outstanding Achievement award Elmira Coll., 1976, Merit award Edgewater Coun., 1976; subject of 35-minute film The Wrong Elf, 1978. Mem. Nat. Soc. Mural Painters (publicity chmn. 1973—, sec. 1975, bd. dirs. pub. rels. 1981-83, 92, editor newsletter 1980-81, 95—, author soc brochure and guide, curator bicentennial collection Intrepid Sea, Air, Space Mus. 1993-98, sec. 1995-97). Home: Whiting, NJ. Died Mar. 2006.

CASE, JAMES EDWARD, geologist, geophysicist researcher; b. Mountain View, Ark., Feb. 15, 1933; s. Oris Richard and Juanita (Baxter) C.; m. Peggy Lynn Prejean, Mar. 25, 1954 (div. June 1968); children: Catherine, James, Marian; m. Irma Isaza, Apr. 20, 1972; children: Stephanie, Melanie. BS, U. Ark., 1953, MS, 1954; PhD, U. Calif., 1963. Instr. geology Lamar U., Beaumont, Tex., 1954-55; geologist U.S. Geol. Survey, various, 1955-61, Denver, 1961-66; assoc. prof. geology Tex. A&M U., College Station, 1966-69, U. Mo., Columbia, 1969-71; geophysicist U.S. Geol. Survey, Corpus Christi, Tex., 1971-74, Menlo Park, Calif., 1974-91; ret. Editor: Geology of the Caribbean Region, 1990; contbr. numerous articles to profl. jours. Elected Corr. Mem. Sociedad Colombiana de Geologia, 1973, Academia de Ciencias Exactas, Fisicas, y Naturales, 1975. Fellow AAAS, Geol. Soc. Am.; mem. Am. Geophys. Union, Am. Assn. Petroleum Geologists, Colo. Sci. Soc. (treas. 1963-64), Sigma Xi. Home: Menlo Park, Calif. Died May 22, 2005.

CASEY, JOHN FREDERICK, lawyer; b. Martinsville, Ohio, May 19, 1939; s. Raymond J. and Esther E. (Read) C.; m. Karen S. Bollenbacher, Sept. 2, 1978. BS, Ohio State U., 1961, JD, 1965. Bar: Ohio, 1965, U.S. Dist. Ct. (so. dist.) Ohio 1967, D.C. 1981, U.S. Tax Ct. 1967, U.S. Supreme Ct. 2000. Ptnr. Means, Bichimer & Burkholder, Columbus, Ohio, 1965-70, Chamblin, Snyder & Casey, Columbus, 1971-75; pvt. practice Columbus, 1976-83, 91-93; ptnr., shareholder Wiles, Doucher, Van Buren, Boyle & Casey, Columbus, 1984-85; ptnr. Thompson, Hine & Flory, Columbus, 1986-88, Casey & Christensen, Columbus, 1989, Casey, McFadden & Winner, Columbus, 1990, Harris, McClellan, Binau & Cox, Columbus, 1994; prin. John F. Casey, A Legal Profl. Assn., from 1994. Adv. coun. mem. U.S. Small Bus. Adminstrn., Columbus, 1985-93. Mem. gov.'s Ohio Farmland Preservation Task Force, 1996-97. Mem. Ohio State Bar Assn. (bd. govs. 1990-99, emeritus 2000, estate planning, trust, and probate law sect.), Fin. Planning Assn. Ctrl. Ohio (founding trustee 2000), Columbus Bar Found., Ohio State U. Coll. Law (nat. coun.), Greater Columbus C. of C. Avocations: gardening, golf. Home: Columbus, Ohio. Died Aug. 12, 2005.

CASEY, JOHN L., lawyer; b. Medford, Mass., Jan. 13, 1924; s. John L. and Ruth (Jones) C. AB, Harvard U., 1944, JD, 1948. Bar: N.Y. 1949, U.S. Dist. Ct. (so. and we. dists.) N.Y. 1949, U.S. Ct. Appeals (2d cir.) 1951, Mass. 1969, U.S. Supreme Ct. 1978. Assoc. Simpson, Thacher & Bartlett, N.Y.C., 1948-54; law asst. N.Y. County Surrogates Ct., 1954-56, 56-61; chief counsel Joint Legis. Counsel on Housing, N.Y.C., 1957-59; assoc. Scudder, Stevens & Clark, N.Y.C., 1961-70, sr. v.p., 1969-85, gen. ptnr., 1970-85, mng. dir., from 1985. Bd. dirs. Scudder, Stevens & Clark of Can.; registered rep., v.p., bd. dirs. Scudder Fund Distbrs.; mem. adv. council on pensions to U.S. Sec. Labor, 1981-83. Author: Destroyer 697, 1945; (poems) This Just Man, 1948, Ethics in the Financial Marketplace, 1987; contbr. articles to profl. jours. Pres., trustee St. David's Sch., N.Y.C.; mem. adv. com. Inst. Ethics in Mgmt., Cambridge, Mass., Ctr. for Study of World Religion, Divinity Sch., Harvard U.; nat. chmn. Youth for Eisenhower, 1956. Served to lt. (j.g.) USNR, 1944-45. Mem. ABA, Fed. Bar Assn., Mass. Bar Assn., N.Y. State Bar Assn., Assn. of Bar of City of N.Y., Investment Counsel Assn. Am. (chmn. legal and regulatory com., hon. gov.). Clubs: Harvard (N.Y.C.) (treas., dir.). Died Feb. 9, 2004.

CASOLA, ARMAND RALPH, chemist; b. Newark, N.J., Feb. 21, 1918; s. Ralph and Mary (Caliendo) C.; m. Mary Hewitt, June 5, 1954; children: Mary Grace, William, Neil, Francis, Quentin. BS in Chemistry, CCNY, 1940; MS, Fordham U., 1950, PhD, 1956. Sr. chemist Am. Cyanamid, Bound Brook, N.J., 1954-59; sr. rsch. chemist Strasenburgh Labs., Rochester, N.Y., 1959-65; rev. chemist Bur. of Drugs/FDA, Washington, 1965-66, supr. chemist Rockville, Md., 1966-90, acting chief chemist, 1970-73; cons. Casola Cons. Svcs., Alexandria, Va., from 1990. Contbg. author: Guidelines: Manufacturing and Controls for INDS and NDAs, 1971, Guidelines for Submitting Documentation for Packaging for Human Drugs and Biologics, 1987. Cpl. U.S. Air Corps, 1942-46. Fellow AAAS; mem. Am. Chem. Soc., N.Y. Acad. Scis., Sigma Xi. Roman Catholic. Achievements include work in manufacturing and control of drugs. Home: Alexandria, Va. Died May 1, 2004.

CASSINI, OLEG LOLEWSKI, fashion designer, manufacturer; b. Paris, Apr. 11, 1913; s. Alexander C. and Marguerite (Cassini) Lolewski; m. Merry Fahrney, Sept. 2, 1938 (div. Feb. 5, 1940); m. Gene E. Tierney, June 1, 1941 (div. Feb. 28, 1952); children: Daria, Christina; m. Marianne Nestor, 1971. Grad., Academia Belle Arti, Florence, Italy, 1934; student, Sch. Polit. Sci., Florence, 1932-34. Free lance designer, Paris, 1935; designer-owner dress studio Rome, 1935-36; designer for Jo Copeland, 1936-38, James Rotherberg, Inc., 1938-39; owner studio N.Y.C., 1939-40; designer Paramount Pictures Inc., 1940-41, 20th Century Fox, 1941-42; head wardrobe dept. Eagle-Lion Studios, 1946-47; owner firm Cassini-Dardick, 1947-50; owner firm, pres. Oleg Cassini, Inc., N.Y.C., 1950—2006; named ofcl. White House designer for First Lady Jacqueline Kennedy, 1960-63; established ready-to-wear bus. Milan. Launched signature men's fragrance Cassini for Men, BlackTie by Oleg Cassini; launched signature women's fragrance Cassini. Designer: mus. comedy As the Girls Go; other Broadway plays; author: In My Own Fashion, 1987, A Thousand Days of Magic: Dressing Jacqueline Kennedy for the White House, 1995 Served as 1st lt., cav. AUS, 1942-46. Winner five first prizes Mostra Della Moda, Turin, Italy, 1934; Golden Accolade award; Man of Yr. Men's Fashion, 1980; numerous others. Mem. Council of Fashion Designers Am. Clubs: Tennis (Florence, Italy), Lawn Tennis (Florence, Italy); Parioli (Rome); Town and Tennis (N.Y.C.); Le Club, Deepdale Golf, Nat. Arts. Died Mar. 17, 2006.

CASTELLON, LOURDES, emergency physician; b. Managua, Nicaragua, Dec. 3, 1958; came to U.S., 1983; MD, U. Autonoma de Guadalajara, Jalisco, Mex., 1983. Staff physician Emergency Physicians Inc., Jacksonville, Fla., from 1987. Mem. AMA, Am. Coll. Emergency Physicians, Am. Assn. Women Emergency Physicians, Cambric County Med. Soc., Duval County Med. Soc., Pa. Med. Soc., Fla. Med. Assn. Home: Saint Augustine, Fla. Died Sept. 20, 2004.

CATAPANO, ARTHUR JOHN, game inventor, business owner; b. Nov. 9, 1934; Assoc. in Bus., Quinnipac Coll., 1957. Owner Catapano Sales Co., Wallingford, Conn., 1964. Creator: (board games) Play Ball, 1997, Hoops, 1998, Pigskin, 1998, Spell-A-Name, 1998, Business World, 1998, Make Or Break, 1998. Inductee Lyman Hall H.S. Hall of Fame, 1994. Home: Wallingford, Conn. Died May 5, 2005.

CATCHPOLE, HUBERT RALPH, physiologist; b. London, May 13, 1906; came to U.S., 1930; m. Robin Jane Miller, Dec. 28, 1973 (dec.). BA, Cambridge U., 1928; PhD, U. Calif., Berkeley, 1933. Instr. then asst. prof. physiology Yale U., 1936—43; prof. pathology U. Ill., Chgo., 1950-73, prof. histology, 1973—2005; vis. prof. humanities Rush U., Chgo., 1973—2005. Contbr. over 150 articles to profl. jours. With USN, 1942—46. Commonwealth fellow, 1941-42. Mem. Am. Soc. Physiology, Am. Soc. Anatomy, Am. Soc. Endocrinology, Brit. Soc. Endocrinology, The Chgo. Lit. Club. Democrat. Died Mar. 25, 2006.

CATHERWOOD, HUGH ROBERT, public administration consultant; b. Chgo., July 6, 1911; s. Robert and Lucy Cotton (Morris) C.; m. Frances Maughs, May 31, 1941 (dec. 1963); children: Jane, Nancy; m. Jean Williams, Sept. 5, 1967. BA, Yale U., 1933. Project dir. Griffenhagan Assocs., 1935-42; dir. budget and pers. City of Denver, 1947-53; pres. Western Wood Preserving, Denver, 1954-60, Shannon (Ireland) Repair Svcs., 1960-64; ptnr., pub. adminstrn. cons. Kansas-Denver Assocs., Denver, from 1967. Clients include cities of Houston, Amarillo, El Paso, Texarkana, Tex., Boulder, Colorado Springs, Denver, Colo., states of Mont., La., Mich., Va., numerous counties and individual corps.; chief of party J.L. Jacobs Co., Govt. of Saudi Arabia, Riyadh, 1966-67; arbitrator Fed. Mediation and Conciliation Svc. Contbr. articles and opinion pieces to various publs. Lt. comdr. USNR, 1947—. Mem. Univ. Club N.Y., Univ. Club Chgo., Univ. Club Denver, Denver Country Club, Denver City Club, SCORE (officer), Fed. Fiscal Policy Found. (treas.). Democrat. Episcopalian. Avocation: flying. Died Dec. 26, 2004.

CAVE, HUGH BARNETT, author; b. Chester, Eng., July 11, 1910; came to U.S., 1915; s. Thomas Edward and Edith Mary (Barnett) C.; m. Margaret Long, July 11, 1935; children: Kenneth, Donald. Student, Boston U. Author: The Dagger of Tsiang, 1997, The Door Below, 1997, Escapades of the Eel, 1997, Bitter/Sweet, 1996, Death Stalks the Night, 1995, Magazines I Remember: Some Pulps, Their Editors, and What it Was Like to Write for Them, 1994, Lucifer's Eye, 1991, The Lower Deep, 1990, Conquering Kilmarnie, 1989, Hugh Cave's The Corpse Maker, 1988, Disciples of Dread, 1988, The Voyage, 1988, Shades of Evil, 1982, The Evil, 1981, A Summer Romance and Other Stories, 1980, The Nebulon Horror, 1980, Legion of the Dead, 1979, numerous others; numerous anthologies, short stories; contbr. articles to literary jours. Warr corrs., WWII. Recipient Phoenix award DeepSouth Conv., 1987, World Fantasy award World Fantasy Conv., 1978, Lifetime Achievement award Horror Writers Assn., 1991, Spl. Com. award World Fantasy Conv., 1997, Lifetime Achievemeen award Internat. Horror Guild, 1998. Avocations: photography, gardening. Home: Sebastian, Fla. Died June 27, 2004.

CAWLEY, LEO PATRICK, pathologist, immunologist; b. Oklahoma City, Aug. 11, 1922; s. Pat Bernard and Mary Elizabeth (Forbes) C.; m. Joan Mae Wood, June 20, 1948; children: Kevin Patrick, Karin Patricia, Kary Forbes. BS in Chemistry, Okla. State U., 1948; MD, Okla. Sch. Medicine, 1952. Diplomate Am. Bd. Pathology, Am. Bd. Nuc. Medicine, Am. Bd. Allergy and Immunology, Am. Bd. Med. Lab. Immunology, Am. Bd. Pathology in immunopathology. Intern Wesley Med. Ctr., Wichita, Kans., 1952-53, resident in pathology, 1953-54, Wayne County Gen. Hosp., Eloise, Mich., 1954-56, chief resident in pathology, 1956-57; clin. pathologist, asst. dir. lab. Wesley Med. Ctr., Wichita, 1957-69, dir. sci., 1965-86, dir. labs., 1969-77, dir. clin. immunology, 1979-86; med. dir. Roche Biomed. Lab., Wichita, 1979-86; dir. clin. labs. Vetazyme Corp., Tempe, Ariz., from 1988. Pres. Kilcawley Enterprises, 1986—. Author: Electrophoresis/Immunoelectric Phoresis, 1969; editor series Lab Med Little Brown, 1965-81; contbr. 210 articles to profl. jours. Pfc. USM, 1942-45. Fellow Am. Soc. Clin. Pathologist (bd. dirs. 1968, Disting. Svc. award 1980, Dist. Pathology edn. award 1998), Coll. Am. Pathologist; mem. AAAS, ACS, Am. Assn. Clin. Chemists, Alpha Pi Mu, Phi Lambda Upsilon, Alpha Omega Alpha. Avocations: reading, history. Died Feb. 28, 2005.

CEBROWSKI, ARTHUR K., federal agency administrator, retired military officer; b. Passaic, NJ, Aug. 13, 1942; m. Kathryn Cebrowski; children: Kristin Marie, Julie Anne. BS in Math., Villanova U.; MS in Computer Systems Mgmt., Naval Postgrad. Sch., Monterey, Calif. Dir. Command, Control, Comm. and Computer Systems USN, Washington, dir. Space, Info. Warfare, Command and Control, 1996-98; pres. Naval War Coll, Newport, 1998—2001; dir. Force Transformation US Dept. Def., 2001—05. Comdr. Fighter Squadron 41 and Carrier Air Wing 8, USS Nimitz, comdr. USS Guam, USS Midway, Carrier Group 6, America Battle Group. Mem. CNO Strategic Studies Group; fed. exec. fellow Coun. on Fgn. Rels. Decorated Bronze Star; recipent Def. Disting. Svc. medal, 5 awards Legion of Merit, 2 Meritorious Svc. medals, 10 Air medals, 2 Navy Commendation medals with Combat V, John Paul Jones award for inspiration leadership USN, 1991. Died Nov. 12, 2005.

CERNUTO, MARY ANN, councilwoman, insurance agent, securities analyst; b. Pitts., Jan. 28, 1949; d. Raymond Anthony and Margaret Eva (Gannon) Steppling; m. Joseph Ralph Cernuto III, Dec. 17, 1979; children: Joseph R., Patrick A., Matthew D. ChFC, Nat. Assn. Life Underwriters, 1993; student, Thiel Coll., Greenville, Pa., 1976, Pa. State U., Behrend Campus, 1977. Series 6 securities lic. Owner Cernuto Ins. Agy., Port St. Lucie, Fla., from 1991; ptnr. Home Team Inspection Svc., Port St. Lucie, Fla., from 1994; councilwoman City of Port St. Lucie, from 1994. Pres. Jamac & Sons, Inc.; fellow Life Underwriter's Tng. Coun., 1992—; founder/advisor Econ. Growth Team, Port St. Lucie, 1994—; bd. dirs. Tourist Devel. Coun., St. Lucie County, 1994—, Met. Planning Orgn., Ft. Pierce, Fla., 1994—. Coun. liaison St. Lucie County Sch. Bd.; advisor Civic Liaison, Port St. Lucie, 1993—; mem. Port St. Lucie Rep. Club, 1993—; elected city councilwoman, Port St. Lucie, 1994—; pres. Lincoln Pk. Acad. Band Parents Assn., Ft. Pierce, 1996-97; advisor-trainer St. Elizabeth Ann Seton Cath. Ch., 1992—. Recipient First Place award Jr. Women's Club (Stuart) Fla. Regional Art Juried Show. Mem. Nat. Assn. Security Dealers. Avocations: cooking, writing, working with young adults. Home: Port Saint Lucie, Fla. Died Dec. 5, 2004.

CEROKE, CLARENCE JOHN, engineer, consultant; b. Chgo., Dec. 1, 1921; s. Paul Anthony and Anne (Krieger) C.; m. Violet Marie Lobonc, Sept. 21, 1947; children: Paul, Donald, Robert, Marie, Louise, Karen. BS in mech. Engring., Ill. Inst. Tech., 1943. Reg. profl. engr., Ill. Supr. product devel. U.S.I. Clearing, Chgo., 1969-74; engr. Panduit Corp., Tinley Park, Ill., 1974-75; design engr. Interlake Steel, Chgo., 1975-76; mgr. engring. AFL Industries, West Chicago, 1976-77; design engr. Castle Engring., Chgo., 1977-80; supr. Dreis and Krump, Chgo., 1980-81; project engr. Epstein Process Engring., Chgo., 1981-83; cons. engr. Beacon Engring., Homewood, Ill., 1983-84; engr. Espo Engring., Canton, Ohio, from 1984. Owner Beacon Engring., Homewood, 1978—. Patentee in field; author books. Pres. St. Kilians Holy Name Soc., Chgo., 1960; coach Little League Baseball, Chgo., 1959. With USN, 1943-44. Mem. Mt. Carmel Alumni Assn., Pi Tau Sigma, Hall-Fame Racquet Club. Roman Catholic. Avocations: tennis, contract bridge, in plant safety and environmental research. Died July 7, 2006.

CHABE, ALEXANDER MICHAEL, education educator, photographer; b. Gary, Ind., Jan. 12, 1923; s. Michael Ivanovich and Barbara (Lysak) Chabai; m. Mary Janice Gilbert, Apr. 7, 1951; children: Daniel Stafford, David Gilbert. AB in History, Mich. State U., 1948; MS in Edn., Ind. U., 1950, EdD, 1959; MA in Russian, Norwich U., 1993; postgrad. in Russian, Middlebury Coll., 1949, 85, 91. Tchr. elem. Calumet Twp. Schs., Gary, Ind., 1950-51, San Bruno (Calif.) Sch. System, 1951-52, Benton Harbor (Mich.) Sch. System, 1952-54; elem. sch. supr. Ottawa County Bd. of Edn., Grand Haven, Mich., 1954-56; asst. prof. edn. Park Coll., Parkville, Mo., 1956-58; prof. SUNY, Fredonia, from 1959. Author: Democracy and Communism, 1973, How People Live in France, 1976; author filmstrips in English and Russian, sound slide set; contbr. articles to profl. jours. 1st lt. U.S. Army, WWII. Mem. NEA (life), Am. Assn. Tchrs. of Slavic and Eastern European Langs., Am. Coun. Tchrs. of Russian, Am. Edn. Studies Assn. Russian Orthodox. Avocations: photography, skiing, antiques. Home: Fredonia, NY. Died July 13, 2004.

CHABE, MARY JANICE, secondary school educator; b. Gary, Ind., Nov. 3, 1923; d. Floyd Jacob and Alfretta (Stafford) Gilbert; m. Alexander Michael Chabe, Apr. 7, 1951; children: Daniel Stafford, David Gilbert. BS in Speech and Hearing, SUNY, Fredonia, 1970; MS in Speech and Hearing, SUNY, 1972, postgrad., 1974. Cert. tchr., N.Y. Elem. tchr. Fredonia (N.Y.) Central Sch., 1970-71; tchr. of hearing impaired Bd. Coop. Ednl. Svcs. Chautauqua County, Fredonia, 1972-76; tchr. multiple handicapped Bd. Coop. Ednl. Svcs. Erie, Chautauqua, Cattaraugus Counties, Fredonia, from 1976. Vol. women's auxiliary, Brooks Meml. Hosp., Dunkirk, N.Y., 1964-75; mem. altar guild Trinity Episcopal Ch., Fredonia, 1980-84. Mem. Chautauqua Council N.Y. Internat. Reading Assn. (bd. dirs. 1983—, pres. 1987—), N.Y. Assn. Learning Disabled. Avocations: downhill skiing, developing crafts for handicapped. Home: Fredonia, NY. Died Oct. 29, 2004.

CHAIT, ARNOLD, retired radiologist; b. N.Y.C., Jan. 20, 1930; s. Irving and Tillie (Newman) C.; m. Joan Lois Oppenheim, Mar. 14, 1965; children: Andrea, Elizabeth, Caroline. BA, NYU, 1951; MD, U. Utrecht, Netherlands, 1957; MA (hon.), U. Pa., 1971. Diplomate Am. Bd. Radiology. Intern Kings County Hosp., Bklyn., 1958, resident in radiology, 1959-62; resident in pathology Manhattan Vets. Hosp., N.Y.C., 1959; instr. radiology SUNY, Bklyn., 1962-64, asst. prof. radiology, 1964-67, assoc. prof., 1967; asst. prof. radiology U. Pa., Phila., 1967-70, assoc. prof., 1970-74, prof., 1974-76, clin. prof., 1976-98; chief vascular radiology Hosp. U. Pa., 1969-76, dir. dept. radiology Grad. Hosp., 1976-88, pres. med. staff, 1981-83; prof. radiology Allegheny U. of the Health Scis., 1997—99; ret., 1999. Cons. radiology Bklyn. VA Hosp., 1962-67, Phila. VA Hosp., 1969-76, Phila. Naval Hosp., 1975-76 Contbr. articles to profl. jours. Fellow Coll. Physicians Phila., Am. Coll. Radiology; mem. Pa., Phila. County Med. Socs., Am. Roentgen Ray Soc., Phila. Roentgen Ray Soc. (pres. 1983-84), Radiol. Soc. N. Am., N.Y. Roentgen Soc., AAAS, Assn. U. Radiologists, Soc. Cardiovasc. Radiology Am. Heart Assn. (coun. on cardiovasc. radiology), Soc. Uroradiology, Soc. Cardiovasc. and Interventional Radiology. Home: Narberth, Pa. Died Sept. 12, 2006.

CHALFIN, NORMAN LEONARD, electronics engineer; b. Phila., Oct. 16, 1913; s. Nathan M. and Katherine M. (Tinkelman) C.; m. Ethel Friedman, Jan. 22, 1937; 1 son, Gregory Thomas. Student, NYU, 1931-33; BS, U. Ga., 1936; postgrad., Columbia U., 1936-41; JD, Southwestern U., 1960. Bar: U.S. Patent Office 1955, Can. Patent Office 1955. Instr. communications tng. project Nat. Youth Adminstrn., 1941-42; sr. elec. engr. Western Electric Co., Clifton, N.J., 1942-43; chief radio engring. Crystal Rsch. Labs., Hartford, Conn., 1943; project engr. Am. Type Founders, N.Y.C., 1944; sr. applications engr. N.Am. Phillips Co., Dobbs Ferry, N.J., 1945; sr. devel. engr. Daven Co., Newark, 1946; chief engr. Eastern Ed. Radio News, N.Y.C., 1947-48, Eastern Ed. radio and TV maintenance, 1950; chief engr. Crystal Devices Corp., Freeport, N.Y., 1949-51; tech. editor Hughes Aircraft Co., Culver City, Calif., 1951-52, 1952-57, 58-61; patent engr. Litton Industries, Beverly Hills, Calif., 1957-58; tech. editor Hughes Aircraft Co., Fullerton, Calif., 1958-61; sole practice, 1961-63; instr. Manpower Devel. and Tng. Act courses Solar Electronics Schs., Monrovia, Calif., 1963-64; patent agt. Aerojet Gen. Corp., Azusa, Calif., 1964; instr., coord. Agy. for Internat. Devel. communications tng. project Pasadena (Calif.) City Coll., 1964-66; mem. staff Office of Patent Counsel Jet Propulsion Lab., Pasadena, 1966-77, Office of Patents and Tech. Utilization Calif. Inst. Tech., Pasadena, from 1977, mgr. Office Tech. Utilization, from 1985; mgr. tech. utilization Office Comml. Programs Jet Propulsion Lab., from 1992, tech. transfer specialist, from 1993. Lectr. UCLA, Calif. Inst. Tech. Contbr. articles to profl. jours. Fellow Radio Club Am.; mem. Los Angeles Patent Law Assn. (historian 1966—), IEEE (life), Audio Engring. Soc. (life, chmn. Los Angeles sect. 1959, 69), Am. Radio Relay League, Radio Amateur Satellite Corp. (life). Avocations: photography, video, amateur radio. Home: Pasadena, Calif. Died Mar. 27, 2004.

CHAMBERLAIN, MARY, retired academic administrator, translator; b. Media, Pa., Mar. 26, 1928; d. Lloyd William Chamberlain, Sr. and Marie Gertrude Meloney. BA in Chemistry, Rosemont Coll., 1949; MS in French, Georgetown U., 1957, PhD in Linguistics and Spanish, 1965. Bus. office asst. Dunbarton Coll., Washington, 1950—58; prof. Spanish U. Md. Overseas, Torrejon Airbase, Spain, 1959—61; asst. edn. adviser USAF, Torrejon Airbase, Spain, 1959—61; asst. rschr. Bantu lang. Georgetown U., Washington, 1961—62; prof. Spanish and French Howard U., Washington, 1961—62; chief trainee selection Orgn. Am. States, Washington, 1962—89; ret. Translator: (chronicles) New Norcia Studies No. 9, 2001, New Norcia Studies No. 10, 2002. Roman Catholic. Avocations: music, opera, translations. Died Jan. 22, 2005.

CHAMBERLAIN, OWEN, nuclear physicist; b. San Francisco, July 10, 1920; m. Babette Copper, 1943 (div. 1978); 4 children; m. June Steingart, 1980 (dec.); m. Senta Pugh, 1998. AB (Cramer fellow), Dartmouth Coll., 1941; PhD, U. Chgo., 1949. Instr. physics U. Calif., Berkeley, 1948—50, asst. prof., 1950—54, assoc. prof., 1954—58, prof., 1958—89, prof. emeritus, 1989—2006; civilian physicist Manhattan Dist., Berkeley, Los Alamos, 1942—46. Recipient Nobel prize (with Emilio Segre) in Physics, for discovery of anti-proton, 1959, The Berkeley citation, U. Calif., 1989, Loeb lectr., Harvard U., 1959; fellow Guggenheim, 1957—58. Fellow: Am. Acad. Arts and Scis., Am. Phys. Soc.; mem.: NAS, Berkeley Fellows. Died Feb. 28, 2006.

CHAMBERS, CAROLE ANN, financial consultant; b. Wilmington, Del., Feb. 6, 1941; d. John William and Sally (Himell) Kane; m. Don Quine; children: Robert, James, Sean; m. Jack Cole; children: Tristina, Chris; m. Harold C. Chambers, Dec. 30, 1976. Grad. high sch., Wilmington, 1958. V.p. pub. Chambers Internat. Corp. (formerly Chambers & Assocs.), Boca Raton, Fla., 1982-85; pres. Individual Fin. Consultants, Beverly Hills, Calif., from 1989. Author: Child Support--How to Get What Your Child Needs and Deserves, 1991. Avocations: music composing, water sports, gardening. Home: Los Angeles, Calif. Died Aug. 29, 2004.

CHAMBERS-MCCARTY, LORRAINE, painter, educator; b. Detroit, Aug. 17, 1920; Student, Detroit Art Acad., 1938, Stephens Coll., 1940, Wayne State U., 1942; studied with, Glen Michaels, Emil Weddidge, Robert Wilbert, Guy Palazzola, Ray Fleming, Edgar Yaeger, Hughie Lee Smith, Bertold Schweitz, Thomas Hart Benton, Carol Wald, Adolph Dehn. Mem. faculty Flint Inst. Arts, Mich., 1970-85, Grosse Point (Mich.) War Meml., 1972-90; pvt. tchr. art Royal Oak, Mich.; mem. faculty Muskegon (Mich.) Inst. Arts, 1978-80, Flint Inst. Arts, from 1978; artist in residence Stephens Coll., Columbia, Mo., 1981; now juror, critic, lectr., tchr. pvt. profl. students. Advisor, designer Internat. Women's Air & Space Mus., Ohio, 1986-00, Okla., juror, critic in field, lectr.in field; ofcl. artist USAF, 1981-99; instr. Birmingham Bloomfield (Mich.) Art Assn., Islanders of St. Loud-Workshop Retreats in No. Mich., 1979-94, Paint Creek Ctr. for Arts, Rochester, Mich., Mt. Clemens Ctr. for Arts, Mich., Flint Inst. Arts, Muskegon Mus. of Art, Jesse Besser Mus., Alpena, Ella Sharpe Mus., Jackson, Mich, Ctr. for Creative Studies, Detroit, Art League, Marco Island, Fla., Blue Water Art Assn., Stephens Coll., Mo., Milford Fine Arts Assn., Mich., 1990-00, Sanibel-Captiva Art Assn., Fla. others; cons. Greenfield Village Mus., 1991-00; mentor U. Mich., 1992, Cranbrook Art Acad.; trustee, designer Internat. Women's Air and Space Mus., Cleve., 1997—. Numerous one woman shows including Midland Arts Coun., 1978, Dayton Art Inst., 1978, Flint Inst. Arts, 1980, Nat. Acad. Arts and Letters, 1980, Stephens Coll., 1981; numerous group shows including Women '71, DeKalb, Ill., Butler Mus. Am. Art, Youngstown, Ohio, Detroit Inst. Arts, 1980, Ohio Arts Coun. Nat. Traveling Show, 1982; represented in permanent collections including Smithsonian Nat. Air and Space Mus., Muskegon Mus. Art, Butler Mus. Am. Art, Dow Chem. Co., Midland, Mich., No. Ill. U., DeKalb, K Mart Internat. Hdqrs., Troy, Mich., Capital City Airport, Lansing, R.L. Polk Co., Detroit, Bohn Aluminum and Brass, Southfield, Mich., Jug Pilots P047s, N.Y.C., Am. Natural Resources Hdq., Beech Aircraft, Wichita, Cessna Aircraft Corp., Dennos Mus., Federal Aviation Admintsrn., Flint Inst. Arts, Internat. Women's Air and Space Mus., Mich. Dept. Aviation, Renaissance Ctr.; commns. include murals for Gen. Dynamics Landsystems 1 Mich., Alpena Light & Power Co., art works for Lear Siegler Seating Co., Mich., 4 H Hdqrs., Washington, Trusswall Internat., Mich., R.L Polk Co., Mich., Capitol City Airport, Mich., Gerald Behaylo, Mich., Upjohn Pharm. Hdqs., Mich., Dow Chem. Co., Mich., Internat. Women's Air and Space Mus., Hi-Lex Corp., Mich. and Japan; producer TV series The Artist in You; inventor, designer Artist's Eye: Visual Aid for Artists. Mem. exec. com. Oakland County Cultural Coun. Recipient numerous awards including Purchase prize Butler Mus. Am. Art, 1969, Grand Jury award 16th Ann. Mid-Mich., Best Painting by a Woman award Detroit Inst. Arts, 1971, Disting. Alumnae award Stephens Coll., 1982, 1st place award Nat. Fedn. Local Cable Programmers, 1984; recipient grant Lester Hereward Cooke Found., 1984, Ossabaw Island Project, 1965, 67, 72; named creative artist, Mich. Coun. Arts, 1983, master to apprentice, Mich. Coun. Arts, 1983, artists consultancy, Mich. Coun. Arts, 1983. Mem. Detroit Soc. Women Painters and Sculptors, All Women Transcontinental Air Race Assn., Mich. Watercolor Soc., Artists Equity Assn., Mich. Acad. Arts Sci. Letters. Home: Royal Oak, Mich. Died Oct. 25, 2004.

CHAMBON, CHARLES WILLIAM, electrical engineer; b. Colorado Springs, Colo., Apr. 15, 1954; s. George William and Myrtle Ines (Elliott) C. BSEE, U. Colo., 1982, MSEE, 1985, postgrad., from 1985. Asst. prof. engring. graphic design, instr. physics U. Colo., Colorado Springs, 1981-82; rschr. with Robert Burton and Ronald M. Sega Defense Advanced Rsch. Project, 1979-85; Nasa grad. rsch. fellow, 1991-96. Active Pikes Peak Jaycees, Colorado Springs Jaycees, Colorado Springs Police Dept. Named Community Fund Raiser of Yr., Colo. Jaycees, 1984, Jaycee of Yr., Pikes Peak Jaycees, 1982, 84, Outstanding Young Coloradan, Colo. Jaycees and JCI Senate, 1984, Outstanding Young Man Am., U.S. Jaycees, 1983; recipient Award of Appreciation, Rocky Mountain Multiple Sclerosis Ctr. Denver, 1983, Cert. of Merit, Colo. Engring. Coun., 1982. Mem. IEEE, Acoustics, Speech and Signal Processing Soc. of IEEE, Automatic Control Soc. of IEEE, Aerospace and Electronic Systems Soc. of IEEE, AAAS (disabled resource group 1981—), Am. Radio Relay League, Denver Radio League, Lookout Mountain Repeater Group, Squaw Mountain Ham Club, Pueblo Ham Club, Telstar Ham Club, Amateur Radio Emergency Svc., Pikes Peak FM Assn., Wilderness on Wheels Found., Cheyenne Mountain Repeater Group (pres., founder 1981—), Rocky Mountain Pedals and Chords Organ Club, Eta Kappa Nu (Theta Chi chpt., pres. 1982-83, Beta Tau Pi Sigma Xi, Award of Appreciation 1984). Achievements include research in the targeting of different models with microwaves in the 1 GHz-2 GHz frequency band with 400 watts of power, evaluating encoding techniques including the development and evaluation of "Error Correcting Codes", evaluating an analog disk controller using classical tools, examination of "Single Utterance" and "Continuous Speech" voice recognition systems and the many different strategies used to implement both types, the RADAR sensing of the local terrain, evaluating this local terrain for possible landing locations then by comparing the optimal path to each possible landing location determines and initiates the optimal control to that landing location, The Hankel Transform to solve symmetric integral equations with great ease. Home: Colorado Springs, Colo. Died Apr. 10, 2004.

CHAMP, NORMAN BARNARD, JR., manufacturing executive, committeeman; b. St. Louis, Sept. 20, 1928; s. Norman Barnard and Elizabeth (Trigg) C.; m. Anne Avananden, June 7, 1952 (div. Apr. 1972); children: Deborah Anne, Norman B. III; m. Judith Russell Smith, Oct. 1, 1977; stepchildren: Julie Zander, William A. Zander III. BA, MIT, 1950; MBA, Harvard U., 1952; postgrad., St. Louis U., 1953-57. V.p. ops. Midwest Piping Co., St. Louis, 1953-62; group v.p. Crane Co., N.Y.C., 1962-63; mgr. mfg. St. Louis Car Co., 1963-68; pres. Champ Spring Co., St. Louis, from 1968. Pres., dir. EDMU Realty Co., St. Louis, 1968—; dir. Champ Realty Co., St. Louis, 1968—, pres., 1992—; bd. dirs. Mark Twain Creve Bank, St. Louis. Dem. committeeman Clayton Twp., St. Louis, 1976—; mem. Dem. State Com., 1994—; bd. dirs. South Side YMCA, St. Louis, 1955—, Pilobolus, 1985—; trustee Webster U., 1975—; mem. Nat. Coun. on Arts, Washington, 1978-86; mem. White House Preservation Com., Washington, 1977-81; mem. Mo. Arts Coun., 1994—. Mem. Rotary (St. Louis). Avocations: bridge, hunting. Home: Saint Louis, Mo. Died Jan. 27, 2005.

CHAMPION, JAMES PERRY, JR., management executive; b. Albany, Ga., Sept. 26, 1918; s. James Perry Sr. and Ann Eloise (Stewart) C.; m. Jane Hollis Luthy, Aug. 31, 1941; children: James P. III, Elizabeth Hollis, Wendy C. Baker, Katherine C. Edwards. Student, U. Wis., 1937, U. Ga., 1938-39. Gen. mgr. Albany (Ga.) Warehouse Co., 1946-64, pres., 1964-83, chmn. bd., from 1983. Bd. dirs. 1st Fed. Savs. & Loan, Albany, chmn. bd., 1973—; bd. dirs. 1st State Bank & Trust Co., Albany. City commr. City of Albany, 1963-68; mem. Dougherty County Sch. Bd., Albany, 1956-62, Albany/Dougherty County Historic Area Commn., 1989—. Mem. Ga. Plant Food Assn. (founder and bd. dirs.), Ga. Pecan Growers' Assn., Rotary (pres. 1969-70, fellowship 1978), Am. Legion, Kappa Alpha, Albany C. of C. (bd. dirs.). Methodist. Avocations: local and family history, football. Home: Albany, Ga. Died Apr. 30, 2005.

CHAMPLIN, BLAKE K., lawyer; b. Penn Yan, N.Y., Apr. 3, 1959; s. Keith L. Champlin and Connie M. (Blakesley) Cator; married; children: Tabitha, Joshua. BA in Polit. Sci., U. Hawaii, 1981; JD, U. Tulsa, 1986. Assoc. Shipley & Inhofe, Tulsa, 1985-93; ptnr. Shipley, Inhofe & Strecker, Tulsa, 1993-94, Shipley Jennings & Champlin, Tulsa, from 1995. Contbg author: Oklahoma Environmental Law Handbook, 1997. Bd. dirs. The Astronomy Club of Tulsa, 1986—, Okla. Soc. of Environ. Profls., 1994—. Mem. ABA, Okla. Bar Assn., Okla. Soc. Environ. Profls. Died July 19, 2004.

CHANDLER, OTIS, publisher; b. L.A., Nov. 23, 1927; s. Norman and Dorothy (Buffum) C.; m. Marilyn Brant, June 18, 1951 (div.); children: Norman, Harry, Cathleen, Michael, Carolyn; m. Bettina Whitaker, Aug. 15, 1981. Grad., Andover Acad., 1946; BA, Stanford U., 1950. Joined Times Mirror Co., 1953; pub. Los Angeles Times, 1960-80; chmn. bd., editor-in-chief Times Mirror Co., Los Angeles, 1980-86, chmn. exec. com., 1986—98. Served to 1st lt. USAAF, 1951-53. Mem. Am. Soc. Newspaper Editors, Am. Newspaper Pubs. Assn. Clubs: California. Died Feb. 27, 2006.

CHANG, IRIS SHUN-RU, writer; b. Princeton, N.J., Mar. 28, 1968; d. Shau-Jin and Ying-Ying Chang; m. Bretton Lee Douglas, Aug. 17, 1991, one child, Christopher. BS in Journalism, U. Ill., 1989; MA in Writing, Johns Hopkins U., 1991; Doctorate (hon.), Coll. Wooster, 2002. Author: (books) Thread of the Silkworm, 1995, The Rape of Nanking: The Forgotten Holocaust of World War II, 1997 (N.Y. Times Bestseller, N.Y. Times Notable Book, Bookman Rev. Syndicate Best Books of 1997), The Chinese in America: A Narrative History, 2003. Recipient Peace and Internat. Coop. award John D. and Catherine T. MacArthur Found., 1992, Nat. Woman of Yr. award Orgn. Chinese Am. Women, 1998; rsch. grantee NSF, 1993, Harry Truman Presdl. Libr., 1993. Mem. Com. of One Hundred. Died Nov. 9, 2004.

CHANG, PETER ASHA, JR., lawyer; b. Honolulu, Feb. 1, 1937; s. Peter Asha and Helen (Lee) C.; m. Maybelle Ching, Sept. 3, 1955 (div. Aug. 1982); children: Catherine, Peter III, Christopher. AB, Stanford U., 1958, JD, 1961. Bar: Calif. 1962, U.S. Dist. Ct. (no. and cen. dists.) Calif. 1962, U.S. Ct. Appeals (9th cir.) 1962, U.S. Supreme Ct. 1964. Asst. dist. atty., Monterey, Calif., 1961-66; chief asst. dist. atty., 1966-75; dist. atty. Santa Cruz County, Washington, 1975; pvt. practice Santa Cruz, from 1975. Instr., cons. Calif. Dist. Atty.'s Assn., Sacramento, 1967-74, Nat. Coll. Dist. Attys., 1968-72, Stanford Law Sch., Palo Alto, Calif., 1969-71; faculty mem. Nat. Criminal Def. Coll., Macon,

Ga., 1990—; lectr. in field. Recipient Pros. of Yr. award Calif. Dist. Atty.'s Assn., 1972. Fellow Am. Bd. Criminal Lawyers; mem. ABA, Nat. Assn. Criminal Def. Lawyers (bd. dirs. 1991-96), Calif. Atty. for Criminal Justice. Democrat. Home: Wailea, Hawaii. Died Dec. 11, 2004.

CHANG, YUAN, insurance company executive; b. Beijing, Hebei, July 16, 1934; came to U.S., 1947; s. Chung Fu and Shan Fin (Chen) C.; m. Mary Bernadette Han, Sept. 17, 1960; children: Christine Chang, Timothy Chang, Derek Chang, Leslie Chang. BA in Math., Oberlin Coll., 1956; JD, U. Conn., 1966; postgrad., Harvard U., 1982. Bar: Conn. 1966; cert. actuary. Various mgmt., tech. assignments Travelers Ins. Co., 1956-67, v.p. asset mgmt. & pension svcs., etc., 1968-86; pres., dir. Travelers Corp., Bermuda, 1984-86; v.p. corp. investment strategies, etc. MetLife, 1986-96, bd. dirs. Metric Instl. Realty Advisors, 1990-93, chmn., CEO Greater China Ops. Hong Kong, from 1996. Chmn., commr. pension com. City of Hartford, 1970-86; sr. advisor Minister of Fin., Taiwan, 1971-72; mem. adv. group N.Y. Ins. Dept., 1980-82; mem. Am. Coun. Life Ins. Pension Com., 1983-86, Oberlin investment com., 1987-96, panel on privatization of Social Security, 1996—; advisor N.Y.C. Actuary Office, 1991-96, China Life, 1997—; mem. hon. adv. panel U. Hong Kong, 1998—; trustee edn. found. Peking U., 1998—; mem., bd. trustees Nankai U. Statistical Inst., China, 1996—; vis. prof. Remin U., China, 1997—; consultative prof. Ctrl. China U. Sci. & Tech., 1998—. Author articles, reports. Mem. Am. Acad. Actuaries, Soc. Actuaries (v.p., bd. govs. 1985—). Died Aug. 1, 2005.

CHANH, TRAN CONG, immunologist; b. Go-Cong, South Vietnam, May 12, 1949; came to U.S., 1967; s. Tran C. Dang and Vo Thi Minh; m. Celita de Lacerda Coutinho, Mar. 29, 1974; children: Eric, Tanya. BS in Biology, Am. U., 1971; MS in Microbiology, U. Hawaii, 1976, PhD in Immunology, 1980. Postdoctoral fellow U. Ala., Birmingham, 1980-83; asst. prof. Georgetown U. Med. Sch., Washington, 1983-86; assoc. scientist dept. virology and immunology S.W. Found. for Biomed. Rsch., San Antonio, 1986-90, scientist, from 1990. Grantee U.S. Army Med. R. and D. Command, 1983—, Nat. Heart, Blood and Lung Inst., NIH, 1989—. Home: San Antonio, Tex. Died July 29, 2005.

CHAPPELL, DAVID WELLINGTON, religious studies educator; b. St. John, N.B., Can., Feb. 3, 1940; came to U.S., 1966; s. Hayward Lynsin and Mary Elvira (Mosher) C.; m. Bertha Vera Bidulock, Aug. 23, 1960 (div. Jan. 1976); children: Cynthia Joan, Mark Lynsin David; m. Stella Quemada, July 11, 1981. BA, Mt. Allison U., Sackville, N.B., 1961; BD, McGill U., Montreal, Que., Can., 1965; PhD, Yale U., 1976. Min. United Ch. Can., Elma, Ont., Can., 1964-66; prof. U. Hawaii, Honolulu, 1971—2000, Soka U., Aliso Viejo, Calif., 2000—04; asst. prof. U. Toronto, Toronto, Ont., 1977-78; vis. prof. U. Pitts., 1982; vis. lectr. Taisho U., Tokyo, 1986-88. Former dir. East West Religions Project, Honolulu, 1980-2000, Buddhist Studies Program, U. Hawaii, 1987-92. Author: Unity in Diversity: Hawaii's Buddhist Communities, Buddhist Peacework: Creating Cultures of Peace, 2001; Editor: T'ien-t'ai Buddhism: An Outline of the Four-Fold Teachings, 1983, Buddhist and Taoist Practice in Medieval Chinese Society, 1987; editor Buddhist-Christian Studies jour., 1980-95. Mem. Am. Acad. Religion, Assn. Asian Studies, Internat. Assn. Buddhist Studies, Soc. Buddhist-Christian Studies (past pres.). Democrat. Avocations: interreligious dialogue, tennis. Home: Laguna Hills, Calif. Died Dec. 2, 2004.

CHARTKOFF, MICHAEL MATTHEW, insurance agent; b. New Haven, Conn., Jan. 30, 1937; s. Jean Frederick and Wilma Dorothy (Notkins) C.; m. Hannah Morrison, 1962 (div. 1982); children: John Robert Lawrence, Robin Anna Alexandra; m. Natalie Izzo, June 29, 1983. BA, Parsons Coll., 1959. Pres. Hunter Furniture Corp., Santa Ana, Calif., 1960-67, Chartkoff Ins., Chatsworth, Calif., 1962-67; prin. Chartkoff Ins. Agy., Chatsworth, Calif., 1962-67; photographer Washington, D.C., 1967-70; prin. Chartkoff & Co. Ins., Hamden, Conn., 1970-87; pres. Branford Life & Casualty Agy., Inc., Hamden, Conn., from 1987. Dir. Conn. Ins. Agencts Assn., 1985—. Co-founder Cheshire Conn. Democratic Club, Cheshire, Conn., 1970; founder CHeshire C. of C., 1971; co-chmn. Democrats for Steele, 1973. Mem. Federal Lodge # 17 Ancient Free & Accepted Masons, Meridian Lodge #77 Ancient Free and Accepted Masons, Sphinx Temple Ancient Arabic Order Nobles of the Mystic Shrine, Sphinx Shrine Yacht Club. Democrat. Avocations: flying, sailing, stamp collecting/philately, travel. Home: Meriden, Conn. Died Aug. 13, 2004.

CHASSIE, MARILYN B., nursing educator; b. Kingston, N.Y., Mar. 29, 1944; d. Arthur Kirby and Ellen (Rex) Bache; 1 child, Beth. BSN, Vanderbilt U. Sch. Nursing, 1966; MS, Boston U., 1969; PhD, U. Tex., Dallas, 1984. Dir. nursing affairs Parkland Meml. Hosp., Dallas; asst. dean, nursing practice U. S.C. Coll. Nursing, Columbia, assoc. dean, clin. affairs and community rels., assoc. dean, acad. affairs, assoc. dean advancement and partnerships. Contbr. articles to profl. jours. Bd. dirs., sec. Killingworth Home for Women; mem. congregation coun. Good Shepherd Luth. Ch. Grantee Carolina Rsch. Productive Scholarship, 1986-87, Carolina Venture Fund, 1987-88, USPHS, 1990-94. Mem. ANA, Nat. League for Nursing, So. Nursing Rsch. Soc. Died Aug. 3, 2004.

CHASTAIN, SHIRLEY PERKINS, nursing administrator, medical/surgical nurse; b. Cin., Apr. 28, 1930; d. Warren Langdon Jr. and Ruth Virginia (Washburn) Perkins; m. David Franklin Chastain Jr., Apr. 28, 1956; children: David III, John, Mark, Ann. Diploma, Jewish Hosp. Sch. Nursing, Cin., 1950; BSN, Med. Coll. of Ga., 1977; MS, Ga. State U., 1981. Dir. nurses Inst. for Chronic Illness, Cin., Home for Jewish Aged, Cin., The Jewish Home, Atlanta; nursing supr. Kennestone Hosp., Marietta, Ga., staff nurse oncology unit; ret., 1992. Researcher incidence of urinary tract infrctions in a nursing home setting. Mem. ANA, Ga. State Nurses' Assn., Am. Soc. on Aging, Sigma Theta Tau. Home: Marietta, Ga. Died Nov. 18, 2004.

CHATFIELD, MICHAEL, accounting educator; b. Seattle, June 13, 1934; s. Chester and Thelma (McCormick) C. BA in Bus. Adminstrn., U. Wash., 1957, MBA, 1962; D in Bus. Adminstrn., U. Oreg., 1966. CPA, Wash. Jr. acct. Yergen and Meyer CPAs, Astoria, Oreg., 1957-58; acct. Mill Factors Corp., N.Y.C., 1959; staff acct. R.C. Mounsey and Co. CPAs, Seattle, 1959-61; tchg. asst. acctg. U. Oreg., Eugene, 1962-63, instr. acctg., 1963-65; asst. prof. acctg. UCLA, 1965-72; sr. lectr. acctg. U. Canterbury, New Zealand, 1972-73; prof. acctg. Calif. State U., Hayward, 1973-82, 84-90, Fresno, 1982-84, So. Oreg. U., Ashland, from 1990. Mem. numerous coms. So. Oreg. U., 1991-96; presenter confs. in field. Author: A History of Accounting Thought, 1974 (rev. edit. 1978, Japanese edit. 1979, Korean edit. 1985, Chinese edit. 1989); co-author: (with Denis Neilson) Cost Accounting, 1983, (with Richard Vangermeersch) The History of Accounting: An International Encyclopedia, 1996; editor: Contemporary Studies in the Evolution of Accounting Thought, 1968 (Spanish edit., 1970, 79), The English View of Accountants' Duties and Responsibilities, 1881-1902, 1978; mem. editl. bd. The Acctg. Rev., 1970-72, 74-75, The Accounting Historians Jour., 1976-95; contbr. articles to profl. jours. Mem. Am. Acctg. Assn., Acad. Acctg. Historians (Hourglass award 1974, 96), Beta Alpha Psi. Home: Burien, Wash. Died 2005.

CHEDEKEL, MORRIS ARAN, toxicologist; b. N.Y.C., Feb. 13, 1939; s. Max and Frieda (Schwartz) C.; m. Barbara Sue Genis, Feb. 18, 1960; children: Marcia Lynn Frost, Mark. BS, CCNY, 1961. Mgr. forensic toxicology, supr. substance abuse analysis State N.Y., Bklyn., 1961-88; forensic toxicologist Bendiner & Schlesinger, N.Y.C., 1989-93; pvt. consulting practice Levittown, N.Y., from 1993. Contbr. articles to profl. jours. Co-founder Rochdale-Springfield Vol. Ambulance, Jamaica, N.Y., 1966-70; charter mem., pres. Eleanor Roosevelt Reform Dem. Club, Jamaica, 1964-70. Fellow Am. Acad. Forensic Scis.; mem. Am. Chem. Soc., Am. Assn. for Clin. Chemistry, Soc. Forensic Toxicologists. Democrat. Jewish. Avocation: travel. Died Jan. 9, 2004.

CHENOWETH-HAGE, HELEN P., former congresswoman; b. Topeka, Kans., Jan. 27, 1938; m. Nick Chenoweth (div. 1975), children: Mike, Meg; m. Wayne Hage Sr., 1999 (dec. 2006) Student, Whitworth Coll., 1975-79; cert. in law office mgmt., U. Minn., 1974; student, Rep. Nat. Com. Mgmt. Coll., 1977. Bus. mgr. Northside Med. Ctr., 1964-75; state exec. dir. Idaho Rep. Party, 1975-77; chief of staff to Rep. Steve Symms US Congress, 1977-78; campaign mgr. Symms for Congress Campaign, 1978, Leroy for Gov., 1985-86; v.p. Consulting Assocs., Inc., from 1978; mem. U.S. Congress from Idaho, Dist. 1, Washington, 1995-2001; chairwoman Nev. Live Stock Assn., Hawthorne, Nev., 2003—06; property rights activist. Mem. agriculture, resources, vets. affairs coms., chmn. forest subcom.; bd. dirs. Ctr. Study of Market Alternatives, Mountain States Legal Found.; chmn. bd. America 21. Deacon Capitol Christian Ctr., Boise. Republican. Died Oct. 2, 2006.

CHIARELLI, RONALD DAVID, chemist; b. St. Louis, Apr. 3, 1948; s. Anthony Joseph and Eileen Francis (Whitmore) C.; m. Sandra Sue Brawley, Sept. 6, 1968 (div. May 1984); children: Kenneth David, Dawn Michelle, Michael Anthony; m. Cherly Marie Stephenson, Nov. 22, 1986; 1 child, Matthew Eugene. BS, So. Ill. U., 1970. Lab. trainee Hill-Hentschel Ink Co., St. Louis, 1967-68; shift supr. Richardson Ink Co., St. Louis, 1968-75; plant mgr. Thiele-Engdahl, Inc., St. Louis, 1975-78, A.J. Daw Ink Co., L.A., 1978-79; with tech. svc. div. C.Z. Inks (James River), St. Louis, 1979-86; with tech. sales div. Thiele-Engdahl, Inc., Addison, Ill., 1986-91, I.C.I. Packaging Inks, Neenah, Wis., from 1991. Mem. ASTM, TAPPI. Died Apr. 3, 2004.

CHILD, GARY RICHARD, photographer; b. Portland, Oreg., Sept. 8, 1935; s. Richard P. and Eleanor J. (Johnson) C.; m. Darlene F. Gottfried, Apr. 8, 1956; children: David, Richard, Sarah, Lisa. Student, Portland State U., 1955, Calif. Coast U., 1978. Cert. profl. photographer. Mgr. Bruno Studies, Vancouver & Aberdeen, 1957-59; gen. mgr. Yuen Lui Studios, Portland, 1959-64; pres. G.R. Child, Inc. Child's Photographers, Redmond and Bend, Oreg., from 1964. Named Outstanding Club Pres. Kiwanis Club, 1981; recipient Meritorious Service Citation Oreg. State U., 1968. Mem. profl. Photographers Oreg. (dir. 1966-88, pres. 1979-80), Profl. Photographers Am. Inc., Redmond C. of C. Clubs: Bend Golf and Country. Lodges: Rotary, Elks. Republican. Avocations: golf, gardening. Home: Bend, Oreg. Died Mar. 5, 2004.

CHILL, MYRTLE N., advertising copywriter, promoter; b. Indpls., Apr. 5, 1906; d. Henry and Mathilda (Kuhn) Newman; m. George F. Chill, June 28, 1932. BSJ, Northwestern U., Medill Sch. Journalism, 1927. Editor Armitage News, Chgo., 1927—28; mng. editor The Nor'wester, Chgo., 1928—29; asst. sales promotion editor Sears, Roebuck & Co., 1929—32; head copywriter Goldblatt Bros. Dept. Stores, Chgo., 1932—39; gen. mgr. Substantial Products Co., Chgo., 1939—65; part-time advt. work Edelstein-Nelson, Reich & Kahn; Chicago Bar and Restaurant Supply, Chgo., 1967—2001; promotion mgr. Barbara Newman Designs, Chgo., from 2001. Avocation: genealogy. Home: Chicago, Ill. Died June 2, 2005.

CHIMES, DANIEL, chemical engineer; b. Bklyn., May 23, 1921; s. Alex and Goldie (Nichols) C.; m. Jeanne Hopfenberg, Jan. 12, 1947; children: Arthur, Michael, Nancy. BAChemE, Poly. U., Bklyn., 1942. With quality assurance and product devel. Permacel Tape Corp., New Brunswick, N.J., 1942-55; mgr. product and process devel. Standard Packaging Corp., Clifton, N.J., 1955-58, Rubber & Asbestos Corp., Bloomfield, N.J., 1958-63; v.p. R & D Am. White Cross Labs., Inc., New Rochelle, N.Y., from 1963. Sgt. C.E., U.S. Army, 1944-46. Mem. Am. Chem. Soc. Achievements include research on design and production of surgical dressings using various plastic, cloth, nonwoven and composite webs and design and formulation of adhesives and equipment necessary to produce the finished product. Home: Monroe Township, NJ. Died Apr. 15, 2005.

CHISOLM, BARBARA WILLE, world affairs organization executive; b. Albany, N.Y., Dec. 8, 1936; d. Edmund James and Marian Virginia (Titter) Bowen; m. Roland Frank Wille, July 2, 1969 (dec. July 1988); children: Serena Bowen Wille, Alison Brevard; m. Oliver Beirne Chisolm, Aug. 10, 1991. BA, Smith Coll., 1958; MA, U. London, 1960. Acting dir. rsch. dept. Met. Mus., N.Y.C., 1966-69; dir. Art Gallery of the China Inst., N.Y.C., 1969-71; N.Y.-New Eng. dir., lectr. Nat. Fine Arts Assocs., Washington, 1974-88; former exec. dir., pres. Forum for World Affairs, Stamford, Conn., 1989-2000, bd. dirs.; pres. World Affairs Coun. Am., Washington, 1998—2001, chmn. emeritus, from 2001. Invited guest, Japan, 1992, Hong Kong, 93, NATO, Brussels, 1996, Fgn. Ministry Brazil, 1997, Fgn. Ministry Taiwan, 1999, Singapore, 99, Morocco, 2000, Fgn. Ministry Lebanon, 2002. Dir. Asheville Symphony Orch. Bd., from 2004. Mem.: Fgn. Policy Assn. (bd. dirs.), Women's Fgn. Policy Group. Republican. Episcopalian. Avocations: classical music, skiing, tennis, fly fishing, travel. Home: Asheville, NC. Died Mar. 1, 2005.

CHO, ALFRED C., physicist; b. Shanghai, Dec. 31, 1921; came to U.S., 1948; s. Tuck Kee and Pao-Jen (Wong) C.; m. Louisa Ching, Sept. 14, 1957; children: Christine Seming, Sharlene Sewah. BS, U. Shanghai, 1943; MA, U. Tex., 1950, PhD, 1958. Engr. asst. Shanghai Telephone Co., 1944-48; spl. instr. dept. math. U. Tex., Austin, 1953-57; adj. prof. physics Tex. Christian U., Ft. Worth, 1958-62; sr. structure engr., sr. physicist Gen. Dynamics, Ft. Worth, 1957-62; sr. tech. specialist, supr. N.Am. Rockwell, Downey, Calif., 1962-69; sr. rsch. specialist Lockheed Calif. Co., Burbank, 1969-71; engring. specilist, supr. Litton Ship Sys., Culver City, Calif., 1971-72; mem. tech. staff Hughes Aircraft Co., El Segundo, Calif., 1972-73; sr. engring. specialist Space divsn. Rockwell Internat., Downey, 1973-86; contractor Jet Propulsion lab., Pasadena, Calif., 1986-89; sr. engr. Space divsn. McDonnell Douglas, Huntington Beach, Calif., 1989-92. Mem. Acoustical Soc. Am. (emeritus), Sigma Xi, Sigma Pi Sigma. Home: Hacienda Hgts, Calif. Died Oct. 24, 2004.

CHRAMBACH, ANDREAS C., biochemist, researcher; b. Breslau, Silesia, Germany, Apr. 23, 1927; came to U.S., 1949; s. Richard and Anneliese (Friedlaender) C.; m. Marie Luise Dirksen, 1964 (div. 1979); children: Carla, Monica; m. Birgit Christine An Der Lan, Nov. 7, 1980; children: Adam, Max. PhD, U. Calif., Berkeley, 1960. Rsch. assoc. Inst. for Muscle Disease, N.Y.C., 1959-61; fellow in biophysics Johns Hopkins U. Sch. Medicine, Balt., 1962-64; sr. investigator sect. chief NIH, Bethesda, Md. Author: Practice of Quantitative Electrophoresis, 1985; sr. assoc. editor Electrophoresis. Home: Bethesda, Md. Died Feb. 23, 2006.

CHRENCIK, FRANK, chemical company executive; b. Osage, Iowa, Jan. 6, 1914; s. Tom and Agnes (Walashek) C.; m. Edith Jo Phelps, July 27, 1935; children: Charles Frank, James Phelps (dec.). BS in Chem. Engring, U. Iowa, 1937; grad., Advanced Mgmt. Program, Harvard, 1955. Plant engr., prodn. and constrn. supr. gen. chem. div. Allied Chem. & Dye Corp., 1937-40; mgr. various plants Diamond Shamrock Chem. Co., Cleve., 1946-56, gen. mgr. electrochems. div., 1956-60, co. v.p., sr. officer, 1960-72; dir., chmn. exec. com. Terra Chem. Internat., Inc., Sioux City, Iowa, 1969-72; exec. v.p. chems. and metals group Vulcan Materials Corp., Birmingham, Ala., 1972-77, also bd. dirs., mem. exec. com., vice chmn. bd., 1977-79, dir. emeritus and cons., 1979—2006. Bd. govs. Gulf Coast Devel. Co., Pasadena, Tex., 1955; past mem. adv. council Coll. Engring., U. Iowa.; bd. dirs. Chlorine Inst., 1968-72 Mem. internat. adv. bd.: Ency. of Chem. Processing and Design. Past trustee Nat. Hemophilia Found., N.Y. Served to lt. col. Chem. Corps AUS, 1940-46. Recipient Disting. Alumni Achievement award U. Iowa, 1977; inducted into Acad. of Disting. Engrs., U. Iowa, 1996. Mem. AICE (Outstanding Chem. Engr. award Ala. sect. 1983), U. Iowa Pres.'s Club. Clubs: The Club (Birmingham), Vestavia Country (Birmingham). Home: Birmingham, Ala. Died Feb. 8, 2006.

CHRISTENSEN, DONNA RAY, elementary school educator; b. Chgo., Oct. 26, 1940; d. Raymond and Eleanor Grace (Kuempel) C. BA, Rosary Coll., 1986; MA, Concordia U., 1993. Instr. adult edn. Ctrl. YMCA Coll., Chgo., 1965-68; adminstr. St. James-Christie Acad., Oak Park, Ill., 1969-86; educator Sch. Dist. #89, Maywood, Ill., 1986-91; reading specialist Sch. Dist. #92, Broadview, Ill., 1991-2000. Adj. faculty Concordia U., River Forest, Ill., 1995, Aurora (Ill.) U., 1996, Nat.-Louis U., Evanston, Ill., 2000—, Dominican U., River Forest, 2000—; featured spkr. Ill. Reading Conf., 1993-97, Concordia U. Reading Conf., 1994-2000. Bd. dirs. Oak Park-River Forest Symphony, 1992-94; mem. festival chorus Concordia U., 1988—. Grantee Ill. Math. and Sci. Acad., Olympic Com., 1997-2000. Mem. West Suburban Reading Coun. (bd. dirs. 1994-96), Internat. Reading Assn., Ill. Reading Coun. Avocations: egyptology, writing children's books, collecting royal memorabilia, collecting historic dolls. Home: Forest Park, Ill. Died Jan. 29, 2005.

CHRISTIAN, WINSLOW, lawyer; b. Caldwell, Idaho, Apr. 12, 1926; s. John L. and Bernice (Christian); m. Donna Margaret Hammond, June 12, 1948; children— Megan, Jason, Sidonie. BA, Stanford U., 1947, LL.B., 1949. Bar: Calif. bar 1949. Fulbright teaching fellow (Law Faculty), Rangoon U., Burma, 1950; dep. atty. gen. State of Calif., 1951-52; individual practice law Loyalton, Calif., 1952-54; city atty. Loyalton and Portola, 1952-54; dist. atty. Sierra County, 1954-58; judge Superior Ct., 1958-63; adminstr. Calif. Health and Welfare Agy., Sacramento, 1963-64; exec. sec. to Gov. Edmund G. Brown, 1964-66; justice Calif. Ct. Appeals, San Francisco, 1966-83; sr. v.p., dir. litigation Bank of Am., San Francisco, from 1984; exec. dir. Nat. Center for State Cts., 1971-73; mem. Calif. Jud. Council, 1971-72. Contbr. articles to profl. jours. Pres. Found. for Jud. Edn.; pres., bd. trustees French-Am. Internat. Sch., San Francisco, 1972-76, 86-88. Served with USN, 1944-46. Fellow Am. Bar Endowment; mem. Am. Bar Assn. (chmn. com. implement standards jud. adminstrn. 1975-78, chmn. appellate judges conf. 1979-80), Am. Law Inst. Home: San Francisco, Calif. Died Nov. 15, 2005.

CHRISTIE, WALTER SCOTT, retired state official; b. Indpls., 1922; s. Walter Scott and Nina Lillian (Warfel) C.; m. Betty W. Phelps, Dec. 14, 1991 (dec.); stepchildren: Thomas G. Phelps, Judith Phelps Cummings. BSBA, Butler U., 1948. CPA, Ind.; cert. fin. examiner. With Roy J. Pile & Co., CPAs, Indpls., 1948-56, Howard E. Nyhart Co., Inc., actuarial cons., 1956-62, Ind. Dept. Ins., 1962-92, dep. commr., 1966-74, adminstrv. officer, 1974-79, sr. examiner, 1979-81, adminstrv. asst., 1981-82, chief auditor, 1982-91, ret., 1991. Bd. dirs., sec., treas. Sr. Enterprises. Treas. Delta Tau/Delta House Corp., 1967—, Butler U. With AUS, 1942-45. Named to Hon. Order Ky. Cols. Mem. Ind. Assn. CPAs, Soc. Fin. Examiners (state chmn.), Indpls. Actuarial Club, Nat. Assn. Ins. Commrs. (chmn. zone IV life and health com. 1970-75), Internat. Platform Assn. Episcopalian (assoc. vestryman 1948-60), Optimist Club Downtown Indpls. (bd. dirs., Outstanding Svc. award 1985-87, Optimist of Yr. 1990). Episcopalian (assoc. vestryman 1948-60). Home: Indianapolis, Ind. Died July 29, 2005.

CHRISTY, CHARLES WESLEY, III, industrial engineering educator; b. Chester County, Pa., Apr. 29, 1942; s. Charles Wesley Jr. and Violet R. (Pierpont) C.; m. D. Jean Cullmann, Jan. 25, 1972; children: Richard Townsend, Charles Wesley IV, Michael Pierpont. BS, Widener U., 1973; MBA, Temple U., 1980. Chmn. indsl. engring. tech. Del. Tech. and C.C., Newark, from 1970. Pres. Pierpont Industries, Inc., Wilmington, Del., 1985—; adj. assoc. prof. U. Del., Newark, 1994; examiner Del. Quality Award, Wilmington, 1994. Bd. dirs., past pres. Opportunity Ctr., Inc., Wilmington, 1972—. Mem. Am. Inst. Indsl. Engrs. (bd. dirs. Del. chpt. 1970—, past pres.), Am. Soc. Quality Control. Home: Wilmington, Del. Died Nov. 21, 2004.

CHUHRAN, LINDA, freelance writer, automotive company executive; b. Ypsilanti, Mich., Aug. 28, 1949; m. Terry Edward Chuhran, Feb. 14, 1970; children: Scott Edward, Stacey Lynn. AAS in Cosmetology Mgmt., Schoolcraft Coll., 1980, AAS in Small Bus. Mgmt., 1983, AAS in Mktg. and Applied Mgmt., 1984, AAS in Gen. Bus., 1986, AAS in Gen. Studies, 1987; BA in Social Sci., Madonna Coll., 1988. Lic. cosmetologist, instr.; cert. model. Sr. clk. Allison div. G.M. Detroit, Redford, Mich., 1969; dir. clerical ops. Canton (Mich.) Township Hall, 1984-88; freelance model, photography cons., from 1970; reporter Community Messenger, 1985-87; disbursement analyst GMC, Canton, from 1989. Cons. Photographer and Model Usage Services, Mich., 1976—; del. Southeastern Mich. Councils of Govt., 1984—. Author: Management Study of Michigan General Law Townships and Charter Law Townships, (booklets) 1986 Punch Card Voting System, 1986 Voter Info., Media Relations, 1987, Election Manual for Procedures and Legal Guidelines; creator computer program Absentee Voters, 1986. Adv. bd. Oakwood Hosp., Canton, 1984—; v. chairperson Rep. Forum, Mich., 1986—; mem. Mich. Township Polit. Action Com., Lansing, 1986; advisor Gen. Motors Jr. Achievement, Detroit, 1975-76. Recipient Disting. Advisor award Jr. Achievement of Southeastern Mich., 1975. Mem. NAFE, Schoolcraft Coll. Alumni Bd., Am. Mgmt. Assn., Internat. Records Mgmt. Coun., Bus. and Profl. Women's Orgn., Nat. Hairdressers Assn., Internat. Inst. Mcpl. Clks. Assn. (mem. profl. status com. 1987-88, pub. info. com. 1986-87), Nat. Assn. Govt. Archives and Records Adminstrs., Internat. Platform Assn., Friends Photography, Wayne County Mcpl. and Twp. Clks. Assn. (sec. 1988, treas. 1987-88), Wayne County Realtors Assn., Oakland County Realtors Assn. Avocations: photography, writing, ceramics, drawing, painting. Died Apr. 11, 2004.

CHURCH, ROBERT CHRISTIAN, insurance company executive; b. San Francisco, Feb. 20, 1946; s. James Douglas and Sugna Marie (Urenholt) Britt; m. Sheryl Jean Church, May 22, 1991. Student, Linfield Coll., Portland Coll. Mgr. GAB, Baker, Oreg., 1965-75, Md. Group, Albany, Oreg., 1975-80; claims supr., mgr. Valley Ins., Albany, Oreg., from 1983. Arbitrator Inter-Co. Arbitration Appraisals, Portland, 1975-77. Republican. Avocations: golf, fishing, reading. Home: Albany, Oreg. Died Aug. 23, 2004.

CICCARELLO, ARTHUR T., lawyer; b. Charleston, W. Va., June 7, 1930; s. Joseph Daniel and Carmen Marie (Pacilio) C.; m. Doris Rozala Pauley, Dec. 25, 1951; children: Beverly, Julia, Joseph III. Student, U. Va., 1947-50; LLB, W. Va. U., 1955. Bar: W. Va. Lawyer Legal Aid Soc., Charleston, W. Va., 1955-56; ins. com. counsel State of W. Va., Charelston, 1961; asst. prosecuting atty. Kanawa County, Charelston, 1961-63. 1st lt. USAF, 1951-53. Democrat. Roman Catholic. Died Oct. 15, 2004.

CIHAK, ERWIN FRANK, retired securities trader, real estate developer; b. Chgo., Mar. 22, 1915; s. Louis V. and Mary Anna (Petrak) C.; m. Irene R. Wiktor, Nov. 1, 1943; children: Sandra I., Alan W. Swinger, Pamela R. Paul Maksinovic, Bernadette. BS in Agrl. Edn., U. Ill., 1939. Mktg. mgr. Midwest Grocery, Chgo., 1942-49; owner, pres. Miracle Ham Co., Chgo., 1950-57; owner Custom Beef Co., Chgo., 1957-60; meat broker, buyer P.B.S. Enterprise Inc., Oak Brook, Ill., 1960-70, real estate developer, from 1971. Capt. USAF, ret. Decorated DFC, Purple Heart, Air medal, Predsl. Citiation, Two oak leaf clusters, Pearl Habor survivors medal. Mem. Am. Legion, Disabled Am. Vets., VFW, Pearl Harbor Survivors Assn., 19th Bomb Group-38th Rescue Squad. Avocations: historian, writer, organic gardening, golf. Home: Lombard, Ill. Died Oct. 28, 2004.

CIMO, CRAIG J., domestic commr., lawyer, police officer; b. Alexandria, La., Dec. 16, 1943; s. Joseph P. and Beatrice (Palermo) C.; m. Martha Behrens, May 22, 1966; children: Craig J., Kristen E. BBA, JD, Loyola U., 1967. Bar: U.S. Dist. Ct. (ea. dist.) La. 1968, U.S. Ct. Appeals (5th cir.) 1968, U.S. Supreme Ct. 1979. Pvt. practice law, Gretna, La., 1967—2000; domestic commr. 24th jud. dist. ct., from 2000. Asst. parish atty. Parish of Jefferson, La., 1976-96; magistrate judge City of Harahan, La., 1991-95; legal adv. Harahan Police Dept., 1984-91, 95—, res. police officer, cmdr., 1983—. Mem. La. Bar Assn., Jefferson Bar Assn. Avocations: hunting, fishing, outdoor activities. Died July 6, 2005.

CISTRUNK, ANNIE JANE, English and linguistics educator; b. Montrose, Miss., Mar. 9, 1929; d. Carl Emmitt and Anna (Denson) C.; divorced; children: Hosey C. and James Harold (twins). BA, Tougaloo Coll., 1949; MA, U. No. Iowa, 1960; PhD, Fla. State U., 1973; postgrad., U. Detroit, 1978. Tchr. Harris High Sch., Meridian, Miss., 1949-50, Breisch High Sch., Leland, Miss., 1950-54, Jim Hill High Sch., Jackson, Miss., 1955-56, Jackson Coll., 1960-63, Higgins High Sch., Clarskdale, Miss., 1963-64; sec. U.S. Army, Chgo., 1954-55, Rath Black Hawk Meats, Waterloo, Iowa, 1956-60; instr. Jackson State Coll., 1960-64, Alcorn Coll., Lomran, Miss., 1965-68; asst. prof. Fla. A & M U., Tallahassee, 1968-73; chair English and modern fgn. langs. Jackson State U., 1988, from asst. prof. to prof. English and linguistics, 1973-94. Reader Ednl. Testing Svc., N.J., 1973, 91. Contbr. articles to profl. publs. Supt. Farish St. Meml. Bapt. Ch., Jackson, 1985. Named Tchr. of Yr. Jackson State U. Alumni Assn., 1988. Mem. NAACP, Nat. Coun. Tchrs. English (regional dir. essay contest 1989-92), Coll. Lang. Assn. (chair host com. 1977), Tougaloo Nat. Alumni Assn. (life), Jackson State U. Found. (pres. club 1977-92), Phi Delta Kappa, Zeta Phi Beta, Sigma Tau Delta, Alpha Mu Gamma. Avocations: fishing, sewing, quilting, reading, writing. Home: Jackson, Miss. Died Apr. 4, 2005.

CITRON, MARILYN JANDORF, nursing consultant; b. Pitts., May 21, 1924; d. Robert H. and Sadie (Stern) Jandorf; m. Maurice Citron, Nov. 10, 1946; children: Jo Ann, Amy C. Richman, Carl D. BSN, U. Pitts., 1945, MS in Nursing Edn., 1963, PhD, 1977. Head nurse Magee-Womens Hosp., 1945-47, staff nurse, 1947-48; pvt. duty nurse Western Pa. Hosp., 1948-60; clin. instr. Western Pa. Hosp. Sch. Nursing, 1960-62; instr. nursing Carlow Coll., 1964-67, asst. prof. nursing, 1967-72, assoc. prof. nursing, 1972-81, chairperson dept. nursing, 1972-77, prof. nursing, 1981-85, prof. emeritus, from 1985. Adj. prof. nursing U. Pitts., 1980-85; legal cons. and expert witness, 1986—; curriculum cons. Catholic Assn. Small Colls.; mem. accreditation teams Nat. League for Nurses. Mem. Sigma Theta Tau. Home: Fort Lauderdale, Fla. Died May 6, 2004.

CLAIRE, DENNIS DANIEL, JR., secondary school educator; b. Port Jefferson, N.Y., Aug. 14, 1949; s. Dennis Daniel and Genevieve Claire; m. Janice Marie L'Archévèque, July 17, 1976; children: Dennis Patrick, Ryan J., Patrick J. BA, Marist Coll., Poughkeepsie, N.Y., 1974; MS, L.I. U., 1991; D Arts, St. John's U., 1999. Cert. secondary tchr., N.Y. Tchr. Rhinecliff (N.Y.) Union Free Sch. Dist., 1974-77; prin., master electrician Dennis Clair Electric Co., Mattituck, N.Y., 1977-79; tchr. Greenport (N.Y.) Union Free Sch. Dist., from 1979. Adj. prof. Suffolk County C.C., Riverhead, N.Y., 1998—. Pres. Greenport Tchrs. Assn., 1987-89 (v.p., 1986-87). Mem. World Jewish Congress, N.Y.C., 1995—. Educator of Yr. Suffolk Times, 1990. Mem. MLA, N.Y. State English Coun. (Tchr. of Excellence 1991), L.I. Lang. Arts Coun. Avocations: reading, sailing. Home: Mattituck, NY. Died May 23, 2004.

CLAPPER, GEORGE RAYMOND, retired accountant, computer consultant; b. New Palestine, Ind., June 29, 1931; s. Raymond Henry and Magdalene Barbara (Niedenthall) C.; m. Mary Vaneta Shine, June 29, 1957 (div. 1978); children: Christine M. Dux, Joseph W., Ann T. Wendling, Michael R. BS in Acctg., Ind. U., 1956. With The Upjohn Co., 1956-81, distbn. ctr. mgr. Cin., 1956-57, N.Y.C., 1957-62, Kalamazoo, 1962-66, 68-69, New Orleans, 1966-68, Mpls., 1969; mgr., controller Lab. Procedures, Inc. (name now SmithKline Clin. Labs), King of Prussia, Pa., 1969-72, v.p., gen. mgr., 1972-81, exec. v.p. Kalamazoo, 1981; v.p., gen. mgr. SmithKline Clin. Labs., St. Louis, 1981-82, MDS Labs., Inc., Buffalo, N.Y., 1982-84; COO Specialty Svcs. Group, Phila., 1985-86; pub. acct., computer cons. Indpls., 1987-96. With USMCR, 1947-60. Mem. Am. Legion, KC. Republican. Roman Catholic. Avocations: music, sports, crafts, cooking. Died Mar. 26, 2005.

CLARK, CARL CYRUS, automotive safety company executive, consultant; b. Manila, Apr. 23, 1924; came to U.S., 1926; s. Edward Leeds and Eleanor Frances (Fowle) C.; m. Elizabeth A. Taylor, Dec. 20, 1947; children: Roger, Austen, Andrew, Amy. Studies in mech. engring., Worcester Poly. Inst., 1941-42, BS in Physics, 1944; PhD in Zoology, Columbia U., 1950. Asst. prof. zoology U. Ill., Urbana, 1951-56; head biophysics divsn. Aviation Med. Acceleration Lab. Naval Air Devel. Ctr., Warminster, Pa., 1955-61; mgr. life scis. dept. Martin Co., Balt., 1961-66; chief task group on industry self-regulation Nat. Commn. on Product Safety, 1968-70; head life scis. dept. Worcester (Mass.) Poly. Inst., 1972-74; phys. scientist Nat. Hwy. Traffic Safety Adminstrn., Washington, 1977-90; pres. Safety Sys. Co., Balt., from 1990. Bd. dirs. Millennium Motor Co.; spectroscopy cons. Coca Cola Co., 1947-52; asst. prof. zoology U. Ill., Urbana, 1951-56; rsch. assoc., asst. prof. physiology U. Pa. Sch. Medicine, 1955-61; cons. in life scis. Inst. for Def. Analysis, 1964-66; assoc. chief sci. and tech. divsn., reference dept. Libr. of Congress, 1967-68; guest lectr. sys. safety George Washington U. Sch. Continuing Engring. Edn., 1977-85, lectr. accident reconstrn. and analysis, 1986-91; staff cons. consumer product safety Nat. Bur. Stds., 1970-71; sr. staff Monsour Med. Found., 1974-77; dir. Commn. for Advancement of Pub. Interest Orgns., 1974-75; experimenter Health Satellite Project, NASA, 1975-77; vice chmn. acceleration panel Armed Forces-NRC Com. on Bioastronautics, 1958-62; del. aeromed. panel of adv. group for aero. R&D, NATO, Athens, 1959, Munich, 1965, Opporto, Portugal, 1971; cons. on transp. safety. Patentee retrorocket brake; inventor side airbag, airbag bumper for motor vehicles; co-inventor airbag restraints; contbr. numerous articles to profl. jours. Recipient Civil Servant of Yr. award Phila. Civil Svc. Assn., 1957, Comty. Champion award Civic Justice Found., 1991. Fellow Sys. Safety Soc. (pres. Washington chpt. 1976-78, nat. v.p. 1978-80), Aerospace Med. Assn. (assoc., program com. 1964-65); mem. AAAS, NAS (com. on hearing, bioacoustics, and biomechanics, com. hwy. safety, hwy. rsch. bd. 1965-69), Human Factors and Ergonomics Soc., Pan Am. Med. Assn. (hon., life), Soc. Automotive Engrs., Assn. for Advancement of Automotive Medicine. Died Aug. 24, 2006.

CLARK, EDWIN GREEN, JR., advertising agency executive; b. Roanoke Rapids, N.C., July 14, 1940; s. Edwin Green and Louise (Powell) C.; m. Emily Lamar Harris, Sept. 25, 1976; children: Jordan Pound, Benjamin Harris. AB, Davidson Coll., 1962; JD, U. N.C., 1967. Assoc. Nixon, Mudge, Rose, Guthrie, Alexander & Mitchell, N.Y.C., 1967-70; acct. exec. Benton & Bowles, Inc., N.Y.C., 1970-74; acct. supr. Cole, Henderson, Drake, Inc., Atlanta, 1975-81; pres. Lewis, CLark & Graham, Inc., Atlanta, 1982-92; chmn., CEO Warren, Clark and Graham, Atlanta, from 1992. Served as 1st lt. U.S. Army, 1962-64. Mem. Am. Mktg. Assn., Atlanta Advt. Club, Druid Hills Golf Club, Fripp Island Club. Democrat. Presbyterian. Avocations: family-related activities, reading, writing. Home: Tryon, NC. Died June 19, 2004.

CLARK, HENRY OGDEN, architect; b. Berwyn, Ill., Dec. 29, 1944; s. Charles Dhority and Agnes Theresa (Ogden) C.; m. Susan Jean Longini, Aug. 1967 (div. Aug. 1970); m. Fran Louise Hodges, Aug. 1991; 1 child, Colette Maria. Student, Reed Coll., 1962-64; BArch, U. Mich., 1969; MS in Creative Intelligence, Maharishi European Research U., Weggis, Switzerland, 1980. Registered architect, Ga., Iowa, Wash., Ca., Mich., Del. Intern Anderson, Notter, Boston, 1970-71, Enteleki, Salt Lake City, 1971-73; ctr. chmn. Internat. Meditation Soc., Traverse City, Mich., 1973-75; architect Sizemore Assocs., Atlanta, 1975-79; assoc. prof. art Maharishi Internat. U., Fairfield, Iowa, from 1979; prin. Henry Ogden Clark, Architect, Fairfield, from 1987. V.p., bd. dirs. Merlin's Enterprises Internat., Fairfield, 1985-88; pres. Traverse Bay Group, Fairfield, 1982—, Traverse City, 1988—; bd. dirs. Fairfield Architects and Planners, 1989—; v.p. Maharishi Heaven on Earth Devel. Corp., Malibu, Calif., 1990—; pres., chmn. bd. Maharishi Heaven on Earth Design Corp., Fairfield, 1991—; head architect 7000 Devel. Corp., Fairfield, 1991—; founding mng. ptnr. Real Estate Devel. Svcs., Ltd., 1996—. Co-author: Energy Planning for Buildings, 1978. Dir. Maharishi Sthapatya-Ved Inst. N.Am., 1992—; Natural Law Party candidate for Mich. 11th dist.

U.S. Ho. of Reps., 1996. Recipient State Energy award State of Iowa, 1986. Mem. AIA. Avocations: skiing, swimming, running, sailing, transcendental meditation. Died Dec. 22, 2004.

CLARK, JESSIE DONA, social worker; b. Rochester, N.Y., Feb. 28, 1922; m. James Governeau Banks, Jan. 23, 1943 (div. Nov. 1972); children: James Governeau Banks, Franklin Frazier Banks, David Robert Banks; m. Paul Andrews Clark, Jan. 21, 1973. BA, Howard U., 1947, MSW, 1960. Psychiat. social worker St. Elizabeths Hosp., Washington, 1960-65; family relocation officer D.C. Redey, Land Agy., 1965-73; supr. social worker Dept. Community Mental Health, St. Thomas, V.I., 1975; spl. asst. to comptroller V.I. Housing Auth., St. Thomas, 1975-85. Evaluator, vice chmn. Operation Sisters United, St. Thomas, 1975-83; cons. V.I. Labor Mgmt. Com., St. Thomas, 1984—; cons. human resources dept. U. V.I., 1992—; People to People amb. abroad.; mem. cmty. planning group HIV prevention V.I. Proper to People amb. del. ednl. exch. programs, Russia, 1991, South Africa, 1995, India and Nepal, 1997, China and Hong Kong, 1996, Cuba, 2002, 2003. Bd. dirs. YWCA (Phyllis Wheatley Br.), Washington; commr. Youth Coun., Washington, Vis. Nurses Assn., Washington, Ptnrs. for Health, St. Thomas (editor mo. newsletter 1988-89); mem. Bd. for HIV Prevention, 1999—. Recipient Disting. Lady award Plymouth Congl. Ch., 1967, Outstanding Performance award D.C. Redevelopment Agy., 1971; NIMH fellow 1957-60. Mem. Internat. Assn. Pers. Mgrs. (v.p.), Nat. Assn. Housing and Renewal Ofcls., NASW (pres. V.I. chpt. 1985-87, Social Worker of Yr. award 1983, V.I. Pioneer award 1998), Eta Phi Beta (v.p. 1988-89). Home: St Thomas,. Died Nov. 30, 2005.

CLARK, JOHN ARTHUR, lawyer; b. Glen Ridge, N.J., Dec. 22, 1920; s. Franklin Jones and Eleanor Newhall (Moss) Clark; m. Dorothy Winton Bateson, Apr. 21, 1945 (dec. 1989); children: William F., Margaret W., John R. BA, Haverford Coll., 1942; JD, U. Pa., 1948. Bar: Pa. 1949, N.Y. 1954. Assoc. Moss, Rieser & Bingaman, Reading, Pa., 1948-51; special atty. IRS Regional Counsel, N.Y.C., 1951-53; assoc. Davies, Hardy, Ives & Lawther, N.Y.C., 1953-58, ptnr., 1958-70, Duane, Morris & Heckscher, Phila., 1970-88, of counsel, 1989—2006. Author: How to Save Time and Taxes Handling Estates, 1965; contbr. articles to profl. jours. Trustee Upper Moreland Free Pub. Libr., 1995—97; treas. Met. Christian Coun., Phila., 1980—93. 1st lt. U.S. Army, 1942—46, PTO. Mem.: ABA, Phila. Bar Assn. (vice chmn. com. income estates and trusts ABA taxt sect. 1987—89, chair 1989—91), Pa. Bar Assn., Order of Coif. Home: Blue Bell, Pa. Died Oct. 15, 2006.

CLARKE, SARA MAE, pathologist; b. Ponca City, Okla., Apr. 19, 1936; d. Russell Oldham Jones and Cynthia Marie Tate Jones; m. Walter Frederick Clarke, Oct. 14, 1961; children: Lee Anne, Andrew Frederick. BS in Med Tech., U. Okla., 1959; MA in Biology, U. Colo., 1972; PhD in Exptl. Pathology, U. Colo., Denver, 1977. Chief microbiologist Maryvale Hosp., Glendale, Ariz., 1959-61; chief med. technologist C. Richard Smith, M.D., Clin. Lab., L.A., 1961-63; sr. rsch. scientist Analytical Devel. Corp., Monument, Colo., 1977-78; instr., researcher Ea. Va. Med. Sch., Norfolk, 1978-82; rsch. assoc. AMC Cancer Rsch., Denver, 1983-84; microbiologist USDA-ARS, Denver, 1984-85; devel. assoc. scientist EG&G Rocky Flats, Inc., Golden, Colo., from 1985. Adj. prof. Colo. State U., Ft. Collins, 1989—, rsch. advisor, 1989—; sci. adv. bd. Bioquest Internat., Man., Can., 1988—. Contbr. articles to profl. jours., chpts. to books. NIH fellow, 1973-77. LMem. AAAS, Tissue Culture Soc. Republican. Achievements include discovery of Antibodies to Beryllium in its Oxidized Form using a Novel ELISA Technique; demonstration of loss of fibronectin in chemically transformed cells; development of in vitro system for studying prostate cancer and 1st to make monoclonal antibody against normal prostatic cell component; patent pending. Home: Defuniak Spgs, Fla. Died Mar. 23, 2005.

CLARKSON, ROBERT BRECK, chemist, educator; b. Buffalo, Apr. 19, 1943; s. Elmer W. and Irma A. (Breck) C.; m. Jean L. Patterson, June 12, 1965; children: Jennifer Ann, Geoffrey Lansing, Elizabeth Mansfield. BA with honors, Hamilton Coll., 1965; MA, Princeton U., 1968, PhD, 1969. Asst. prof. Dept. Chemistry U. Wis., Milw., 1969-76; mgr. EPR product Varian Assocs., Palo Alto, Calif., 1976-82; assoc. prof. U. Ill. Sch. Chem. Sci., Urbana, from 1982, assoc. prof. depts. vet. medicine, med. info. sci., bioengri, from 1996. Contbr. chpts. in books and articles to profl. jours. Mem. Internat. EPR Soc. (chair stds. com.), Soc. Magnetic Resonance in Medicine, Am. Chem. Soc., Sigma Xi. Home: Urbana, Ill. Died Aug. 12, 2004.

CLASSEN, JOHN NEWELL, surgeon; b. Balt., Nov. 11, 1916; m. Margaret Taylor Speer, June 21, 1958; children: Henry Ward, John Barthelow, Taylor Speer. AB, Princeton U., 1938; MD, Johns Hopkins U., 1942. Diplomate Am. Bd. Surgery; lic. physician, Md. Rotating intern Union Meml. Hosp., 1942-43, surg. resident, 1946-49, sr. resident, 1949, chief surgery, 1964-72; fellow surgery Lahey Clinic, Boston, 1949-50; chief surgery Union Meml. Hosp., 1964-72; med. dir. A.S. Abell Co., 1956-86. Instr anatomy Johns Hopkins Hosp., 1950-57, instr. surgery, 1950-65, asst. prof., 1965-82, assoc. prof., 1982; sr. cons. surgery Franklin Sq. Hosp., 1950-58; cons. surgeon Hosp. for Women of Md., 1950-64; cons. Greater Balt. Med. Ctr., 1972—, Union Meml. Hosp., 1975, Balt. City Hosp., 1978-79. Contbr. articles to profl. jours. With M.C., USNR, 1943-46. Decorated Purple Heart, Bronze Star. Fellow ACS (chmn. credentials com. State Md., 1975-81); mem. AMA (spl. site visitor, residency rev. com. for surgery), Internat. Cardiovascular Soc., Ea. Vascular Soc., So. Assn. Vascular Surgery, Chesapeake Vascular Soc. (pres. 1981-82), So. Surg. Assn., Ea. Surg. Soc. (pres.-elect 1992, pres. 1993), Southeastern Surg. Congress, So. Med. Assn., Balt. City Med. Soc. (pres. 1970-71), Med. and Chirurgical Faculty Md. Chmn. (med.-legal. com.), Balt. Acad. Surgery (pres. 1976), Elkridge Club. Died Dec. 3, 2004.

CLAWSON, HARRY QUINTARD MOORE, retired business executive; b. N.Y.C., Aug. 8, 1924; s. Harry Marshall and Marguerite H. (Burgoyne) C.; m. Annemarie Korntner, Dec. 1967 (dec. 1988); m. Mary Louise Kirkland, July 1989 (dec. 2004)); m. Elizabeth G. Cantler, Dec. 3, 2005. Student, NYU, 1951-52, New Sch. for Social Rsch., 1953. Supr. transp., liaison with U.S. Army ARC, 1945-46; asst. to dir. pers. UNESCO, Paris, 1947; resident rep. Tex. Co., Douala, French Cameroun, West Africa, 1948-50; asst. dir. overseas bus. svc. McGraw-Hill Pub. Co., 1951-58; dir. client svcs. Internat. Rsch. Assocs., NYC, 1958-61; v.p., sec. Frasch Whiton Boats, Inc., 1961-63; gen. mgr. Sailboat Tng. Facility, 1961-63; pres. Harry Q.M. Clawson & Co., Inc., NYC, 1961-76, Charleston, SC, 1978-2000; dir. planning and adminstrn. splty. chems. div. Essex Chem. Corp., 1976-78; pres. Trident Seafarms Co., Charleston, 1980-85. Contbr. articles to profl. jours. With U.S. Army, 1943-45, ETO. Decorated Bronze Star. Mem. Soc. Colonial Wars, Ex-Mems. Assn. Squadron A., Carolina Yacht Club, 112 Infantry Regiment Assn., Yeamans Hall Club. Home: Charleston, SC. Died Mar. 31, 2006.

CLAYWORTH, JOSEPH FRANCIS, data processing executive; b. Oakland, Calif., July 10, 1942; s. Robert Edgar and Rhoda Gene (Kenney) C.; m. Randy Charline Otto, May 21, 1962 (div. June 1975); 1 child, Elizabeth Jeanne. Student, Santa Rosa Jr. Coll., 1962-63, Portland Community Coll., 1969-71. Police officer Oakland Police Dept., 1963-67; programmer Simon Stores, Oakland, 1967-68; mgr. of programming Service Bureau Corp., Portland, Oreg., 1968-73; mgr. systems devel. Ga.-Pacific Corp., Portland, 1973-80; v.p., data processing Physicians Assn. of Clackamas County, Portland, from 1980. Cons. Clackamas Health Care Consortium, Milwaukie, Oreg., 1983. Served with U.S. Army, 1959-62, Korea. Mem. Model A Ford Club (v.p. 1974-75). Lodges: Elks. Republican. Episcopalian. Avocations: auto restoration, photography, outdoor activities. Home: Lake Oswego, Oreg. Died Oct. 5, 2004.

CLEMENTS, ROBERT W., lawyer; b. Lake Charles, La., Oct. 2, 1934; s. Arthur Joseph and Ruth (Lewis) C.; m. Gay Nell McDonnold, Apr. 14, 1960; children: Robert Scott, Shannon Ruth, Jennifer Gay. BBA, LLB, Tulane U., 1959. Bar: La. 1959, U.S. Dist. Ct. (we. dist.) La. 1959, U.S. Ct. Appeals (5th cir.) 1967, U.S. Dist. Ct. (ea. dist.) La. 1977, U.S. Dist. Ct. (mid. dist.) La. 1984, U.S. Ct. Appeals (11th cir.) 1987, U.S. Dist. Ct. (ea. dist.) Tex. 1992. Law clk. to Hon. E.F. Hunter, Jr., U.S. Dist. Ct. for Western Dist. La., Lake Charles, 1962; assoc. Stockwell, Sievert, Viccellio, Clements & Shaddock, Lake Charles, 1963-66, ptnr., then sr. ptnr., from 1967. Pres., bd. dirs. Lake Charles YMCA, 1973-74. 1st lt. U.S. Army, 1960-61. Mem. ABA, S.W. La. Bar Assn. (pres. 1985), La. Assn. Def. Counsel (bd. dirs. 1973), La. Assn. Hosp. Attys. (pres. 1989), Maritime Law Assn. U.S. Democrat. Presbyterian. Avocations: golf, hunting, photography. Home: Lake Charles, La. Died Mar. 11, 2004.

CLIFFORD, FRANCESCA BISHOP, state official; b. London, May 6, 1959; d. Gabriel Anthony Patrick and Philomena Christina (O'Meara) Bishop; m. Gordon Brian Clifford, Oct. 16, 1982; children: Kennedy Francis Jude, Alexandra Christina Mary. BA in English and Social Svc., U. Portland, 1981. Prodn. coordinator Encore Arts in Performance mag., Portland, Oreg., 1981-83, editor-in-chief, 1983-85; media liaison Portland YWCA, 1983-85; media relations dir. U. Portland, 1985-90; dir. communications Oreg. State System Higher Edn., Portland, from 1990. Freelance mktg. and pub. rels. cons. Newsletter editor Portland Ad-2 Advt. Fedn., 1985-86; author articles. Mem. Women in Communications Inc. (v.p. 1990—), Council for Advancement and Support of Edn. (Bronze award for newswriting 1990), Internat. Assn. Bus. Communicators (Pacesetter 1990). Roman Catholic. Avocations: creative writing, reading, sewing. Home: Portland, Oreg. Died Apr. 16, 2005.

CLINGAN, DONALD FRANK, retired clergyman; b. Atchison, Kans., Feb. 25, 1926; s. Frank E. and Hazel Ellen (Hall) C.; m. Jacqueline Stephenson, Aug. 26, 1952; children: Stephen Frank, Jane Ellen Clingan Reynolds. BA, Phillips U., 1950; BDiv, Tex. Christian U., 1955, MDiv, 1958; DMin, Christian Theol. Sem., Indpls., 1978; Grad. Cert. in Gerontology, U. Oreg., 1976-79. Ordained clergyman, Disciples of Christ. Minister First Christian Ch., Lyons, Kans., 1955-60, sr. minister Manhattan, Kans., 1960-65; dir. of program planning, dept. World Outreach Edn. Disciples of Christ (Divsn. Homeland Ministries), Indpls., 1965-70; exec. dir. dept. svcs. to congregations Nat. Benevolent Assn./Disciples of Christ Ch., Indpls., 1970-80; exec. dir. Nat. Ctr. on Ministry with the Aging, Indpls., 1980-84; sr. minister First Christian Ch., Springfield, Ill., 1984-92. Founding pres. Nat. Interfaith Coalition on Aging, Athens, Ga., 1972-74, exec. dir., 1974-75, bd. dirs.; pres. Inst. on Religion and Aging, Indpls., 1972-84. Author: (camp curriculum) Sincerely Yours, 1964, (curriculum) Christian Living Encounters, 1969, (book) Aging Persons in the Community of Faith, 1975; co-author: Aging: God's Challenge to Church and Synagogue, 1996. Del. White House Conf. on Aging, Washington, 1971, 1995, ofcl. observer, 1981. Sgt. U.S. Army Corps, 1944-46. Recipient George E. David award for Noteworthy Ministry with the Aging, Inst. on Religion and Aging, Indpls., 1984, Nat. Spiritual Well-Being award Nat. Interfaith Coalition on Aging, 1984. Mem. Ill./Wis. Region of the Christian Ch., Kiwanis, Phi Mu Alpha, Blue Key. Democrat. Home: Springfield, Ill. Died Mar. 23, 2004.

CLINGERMAN, JOHN RUFUS, international relations educator; b. Doniphan City, Kans., May 9, 1931; s. Charles E. and Nell R. (Taylor) C.; m. Ruth M. Muilenburg (dec. Aug. 13, 2000), Sept. 3, 1952. BA, Mich. State U., 1953, MA, 1957; grad., U. Paris, 1966, Nat. War Coll., 1976. With U.S. Fgn. Svc., 1957—76; dep. chief mission U.S. Embassy, Lusaka, Zambia, 1976-79; US amb. to Lesotho U.S. Dept. State, Maseru, 1979-81; diplomat-in-residence U. Redlands (Calif.), 1981-83; dir. African affairs U.S. Info. Agy., 1983-86; sr. inspector US Dept. State, Washington, 1986-87; prof. U. Redlands, Calif., 1982—83; prof. internat. rels. Troy State Europe, Germany, England, Greece, 1987-89, Troy State U., Ft. Bragg, N.C., 1989-92. Contbr. articles to profl. jours. Lt. U.S. Army 1953-55 Avocations: golf, tennis, horseback riding, history (france 17th century). Home: Locust Grove, Va. Died May 29, 2004.

CLINTON, TRACY PETER, SR., financial executive, systems analyst; b. Laconia, N.H., Jan. 10, 1948; s. Francis Arthur and Jane Audrey (Ely) C.; m. Sally Carol Dedmon, Apr. 27, 1969 (div. Dec. 1975); children: Tracy Peter Jr., Christopher Mathew; m. Sheryl Ann McPherson, May 6, 1982. BBA in Banking and Fin., U. Ark., 1971. Controller Superior Air Parts, Inc., Addison, Tex., 1971-74; supr., mgr. Levi Strauss & Co., Little Rock, 1975-76, salesperson Columbus, Ohio, 1977; supr. Walter E. Heller Co., Dallas, 1978-79; supr., mgr. Mary Kay Cosmetics, Inc., Dallas, 1980-92; gen. agt. Alt. Fin. Solutions, Inc., 1993; sr. bus. analyst, Tax Outsourcing Project Coord., state coord., audit mgr. 1st Am. Real Estate Tax Svc., Irving, Tex., from 1993. Co-chmn. Citizens for Organized Growth, Lewisville, Tex., 1983; mem. Lewisville Zoning Bd. Adjusters, 1984-86; vice chmn. Lewisville Planning and Zoning Commn., 1984-86; mem. Lewisville City Coun., 1986-92; dir. adult ministries, bd. dirs. 1st Ch. of Nazarene, Lewisville; mem. SSS Bd.; bd. dirs. Denton Ctrl. Appraisal Dist., 1992-97, chmn. Mem. Am. Prodn. and Inventory Control Soc., Am. Mgmt. Assn. Home: Flower Mound, Tex. Died July 2, 2005.

CLONEY, ROBERT DENNIS, chemistry educator, priest; b. Boston, May 6, 1927; s. Thomas Francis and Elinor Beatrice (Driscoll) C. BS, Spring Hill Coll., 1952; PhD, Cath. U. Am., 1957; BTh, Woodstock Coll., 1961. Joined Soc. Jesus St. Andrew-on-Hudson, 1945, ordained priest Roman Cath. Ch., 1960. Instr. chemistry Xavier H.S., N.Y.C., 1952-53; instr. Fordham U., Bronx, N.Y., 1962-64, asst. prof., 1964-71, assoc. prof., from 1971. Dir. of novices Soc. Jesus N.Y. Province, Syracuse, 1982-85. Mem. Am. Chem. Soc., Sigma Xi (local sec. and treas.). Roman Catholic. Died May 4, 2005.

COBB, TIMOTHY LEE, military officer, physician assistant; b. Indpls., Nov. 20, 1948; s. John and Norma Alice (Lacey) C.; m. Sandra Lynn Sleeper, May 10, 1975; children: Elizabeth Anne Cobb, Sarah Ann Cobb. AA, St. Petersburg (Fla.) Jr. Coll., 1972; B of Health Scis. magna cum laude, Duke U., 1977. Cert. physican asst.; cert. orthopedic physician asst. Physician asst. emergency medicine Carteret Gen. Hosp., Morehead City, N.C., 1977-80; commd. 2d lt. USAF, 1980, advanced through grades to major, 1989; physician asst. emergency medicine USAF Hosp., Robins AFB, 1980-83; physician asst. dept. medicine David Grant USAF Med. Ctr., Travis AFB, Calif., 1983-86, resident in othropedic surgery, 1986-87; instr. in surgery Uniformed Svcs. U. of Health Scis., Bethesda, Md., from 1988; orthopedic physician asst. Malcolm Grow USAF Med. Ctr., Andrews AFB, Md., 1987-89, 11th Air Force Regional Hosp., Elmendorf AFB, Anchorage, 1989-93; physician asst. Calallen Orthopaedics, Corpus Christi, Tex., 1994-97, So. Tex. Ctr. for Orthopaedics, Alice, from 1997. Officer-in-charge dept orthopedic surgery Malcolm Grow USAF Med. Ctr., Andrews AFB, 1987-89. Contbr. articles to profl. jours. Decorated Purple Heart, Vietnamese Cross of Gallantry. Fellow Am. Acad. Physician Assts., Am. Coll. Sports Medicine, Soc. Air Force Physician Assts.; mem. Am. Acad. Pain Mgmt. (clin.), Assn. Mil. Surgeons U.S. Avocations: motorcycling, music, movies. Home: Houston, Tex. Died Apr. 25, 2005.

COCKRILL, ROBERT MAURICE, insurance executive; b. Washington, Oct. 18, 1923; s. John and Katherine Eva (Jenkins) C.; m. Virginia Sturges Frier, Nov. 25, 1950; children: Katherine, Michael, Ann, Stephen, John. BS in Econs., Georgetown U., 1950; postgrad., Nat. Law Ctr., Washington, 1950-53. Govt. official U.S. Dept. Def., Washington, 1953-67; ptnr. Coopers & Lybrand, Washington, 1967-84; sr. v.p. Am. Internat. Group, Inc., Washington, 1984—90. Sgt. U.S. Army, 1943-46, CBI. Mem. Washington Golf and Country Club (Arlington, Va.). Republican. Roman Catholic. Avocations: golf, gardening. Home: Mc Lean, Va. Died Apr. 24, 2006.

COFER, BERDETTE HENRY, public management consulting company executive; b. Las Flores, Calif. s. William Walter and Violet Ellen (Elam) C.; m. Ann McGarva, June

27, 1954 (dec. Feb. 20, 1990); children: Sandra Lea Cofer-Oberle, Ronald William; m. Sally Ann Shepherd, June 12, 1993. AB, Calif. State U., Chico, 1950; MA, U. Calif., Berkeley, 1960. Tchr. Westwood (Calif.) Jr.-Sr. High Sch., 1953-54, Alhambra High Sch., Martinez, Calif., 1954-59; prin. adult and summer sch. Hanford (Calif.) High Sch., 1959-60, asst. supt. bus., 1960-67; dean bus. svcs. West Hills Coll., Coalinga, 1967-76; vice chancellor Yosemite Community Coll. Dist., Modesto, 1976-88; pres. BHC Assocs., Inc., Modesto, 1988—2005. Chmn. Valley Ins. Program Joint Powers Agy., Modesto, 1986-88. Contbr. articles to profl. publs. Pres. Coalinga Indsl. Devel. Corp., 1972-74, Assn. for Retarded Citizens, Modesto, 1985; mayor City of Coalinga, 1974-76; foreman Stanislaus County Grand Jury, Modesto, 1987-88. 1st lt. USAF, 1951-53. Recipient Outstanding Citizen award Coalinga C. of C., 1976, Walter Starr Robie Outstanding Bus. Officer award Assn. Chief Bus. Officers Calif. Community Colls., 1988, Humanitarian of Yr. award Stanislaus County Mayor's Com. for Employment of Persons with Disabilities, 1995, Man of Yr. award Am. Legion Post 74, 1999. Mem. Assn. Calif. C.C. Adminstrs. (life), Lions (dist. gov. 1965-66, pres. Lions Eye Found. of Calif.-Nev., Inc. 1999-2001, hon. life dir. Calif.-Nev. Student Spkrs. Found. 2000-05), Phi Delta Kappa (pres. Kings-Tulare chpt. 1962-63), Am. Legion, 40 and 8 (comdr. 1997-98, chef de gare 1999-2000), Sons in Retirement (pres. 1996). Democrat. Avocation: bowling. Died Mar. 26, 2005.

COFFEY, CLARENCE W., treasurer; b. New Orleans, July 10, 1946; s. Clarence W. and Kathyrn (Robinson) C.; m. Saundra Louise Goodson, Feb. 1, 1969; children: Brian, Kimberly. BBA, U. Tex., 1968; MBA, Our Lady of the Lake U., 1994. CPA, Tex. Staff acct. Freeport Sulphur Co., New Orleans, 1968-70, Tenneco Inc., Houston, 1970-73; corp. acct. First City Bankcorp., Houston, 1973-75; v.p., controller ATCO Drilling Ltd., Calgary, Alberta, Canada, 1975-81; controller Goldrus Drilling Co., Houston, 1981-86; sec. treas. Barwil Agys. NA, Inc., Houston, 1986-98; treas. Merichem Co. and Merichem Chems. & Refinery Svcs., Houston, from 1998. Coach Meml. Ashford Little League, Houston, 1981-89, Katy (Tex.) Little Dribblers Little League, 1985-89. Named one of Outstanding Young Men Am., 1977. Mem. AICPA, Delta Mu Delta. Home: Houston, Tex. Died May 11, 2004.

COFFIN, WILLIAM SLOANE, JR., clergyman; b. N.Y.C., June 1, 1924; s. William Sloane and Catherine (Butterfield) C.; m. Eva Anna Rubinstein, Dec. 12, 1956 (div. 1968); children: Amy Elizabeth, Alexander Sloane, David Andrew; m. Harriet Gibney, 1969. Student, Yale Sch. Music, 1942-43, Union Theol. Sem., N.Y.C., 1949-50; BA, Yale U., 1949, B.D., 1956; D.D. (hon.), Wesleyan U.; Ph.D (hon.), Yale U., 2002. With CIA, 1950-53; ordained to ministry Presbyn. Ch., 1956; acting chaplain Phillips Acad., 1956-57; chaplain Williams Coll., 1957-58; univ. chaplain Yale U., 1958-75; sr. minister Riverside Ch., N.Y.C., 1977-87. Author sermons in books, 1962, Once to Every Man, 1977. Bd. dirs. Pres.'s Adv. Council Peace Corps, Operation Crossroads Africa, Am. Freedom of Residence Fund. Served with AUS, 1943-47. Recipient Conn. Valley B'nai B'rith award for Americanism. Died Apr. 12, 2006.

COGSDIL, SARAH ANNELL, retired telephone company executive; b. Ridgeland, S.C., Feb. 1, 1931; d. Robert Lee and Lilly Nell (Boring) Ward; m. James Franklin Fields, Mar. 16, 1950 (div.); m. Calvin Ray Cogsdil, Apr. 13, 1979 (dec.); children: Barbara Gaudin, James Fields, Edward, Gordon; stepchildren: Jimmy Ray, Dennis. Student, Victoria Coll., 1995-97. Operator So. Bell, Jacksonville, Fla., 1948-49; long distance operator Pa. Bell, Oil City, 1949-50; long distance operator, svc. rep. South Ctrl. Bell, Biloxi, Miss., 1969-79; svc. rep. Southwestern Bell, Victoria, Tex., 1982-94, ret., 1994. Mem. Victoria Coll. Art Club (Outstanding Mem. 1997). Democrat. Methodist. Avocations: lapidary, painting, writing, fabric painting, exercising. Home: Gulfport, Miss. Died Nov. 19, 2004.

COHEN, EDWIN SAMUEL, lawyer, educator; b. Richmond, Va., Sept. 27, 1914; s. LeRoy S. and Miriam (Rosenheim) C.; m. Carlyn Labenberg, June 27, 1936 (dec. 1942); m. Helen Herz, Aug. 31, 1944; children: Edwin C., Roger, Wendy. BA, U. Richmond, 1933; JD, U. Va., 1936. Bar: Va. 1935, N.Y. 1937, D.C. 1973. Assoc. Sullivan & Cromwell, N.Y.C., 1936-49; ptnr. Root, Barrett, Cohen, Knapp & Smith (and predecessor firm), N.Y.C., 1949-65; counsel Root, Barrett, Cohen, Knapp & Smith, 1965-69; prof. law U. Va., Charlottesville, 1965-68, Joseph M. Hartfield prof., 1968-69, 73-85, prof. emeritus, 1985—2006, professorial lectr. law, 1994—2006; asst. sec. treasury for tax policy US Dept. Treasury, Washington, 1969-72, under sec., 1972-73; of counsel Covington & Burling, Washington, 1973-77, ptnr., 1977-86, sr. counsel, 1986—2006. Vis. prof. Benjamin N. Cardozo Sch. Law, Yeshiva U., 1987-92, U. Miami Law Sch., 1993, 95-99, chmn. grad. program in taxation and estate planning, 1995-98; mem., counsel adv. group on corp. taxes ways and means com. U.S. Ho. of Reps., 1956-58; spl. cons. on corps. fed. income tax project Am. Law Inst., 1949-54; mem. adv. group Fed. Estate and Gift Tax Project, 1964-68; mem. Va. Income Tax Conformity Study Commn., 1970-71; cons. Va. Income Tax Conformity Study Commn., 1966-68; mem. adv. group to commr. IRS, 1967-68. Author: A Lawyer's Life Deep in the Heart of Taxes, 1994. Recipient Alexander Hamilton award Treasury Dept. Mem. Am. Judicature Soc., ABA (chmn. com. on corporate stockholder relationships 1956-58, mem. council 1958-61, chmn. spl. com. on substantive tax reform 1962-63, chmn. spl. com. on formation tax policy 1977-80, Disting. Svc. award taxation sect. 1997), Va. Bar Assn., D.C. Bar Assn., N.Y. State Bar Assn., Va. Tax Conf. (planning com. 1965-68, 85-95, trustee emeritus 1995-2006), C. of C. of U.S. (bd. dirs., chmn. taxation com. 1979-84), Assn. Bar City N.Y., N.Y. County Lawyers Assn., Am. Law Inst., Am. Coll. Tax Counsel, Order Coif, Raven Soc., Colonnade Club, Boar's Head Club, Farmington Club, City Club, Phi Beta Kappa, Omicron Delta Kappa, Pi Delta Epsilon, Phi Epsilon Pi (Nat. Achievement award - A Living Legend) Home: Charlottesville, Va. Died Jan. 12, 2006.

COHEN, JEREMY BENJAMIN, real estate executive, former professional tennis player; b. Chgo., Feb. 13, 1955; s. Robert Irwin and Shifrette Diane (Bode) C.; m. Marscee Beth Kaden, Oct. 29, 1978; children: Brandon, Jordan. Student, Ariz. State U., 1973-77. Lic. real estate broker, mortgage broker. Profl. tennis player Assn. Tennis Profls., 1977-81; World Team Tennis player Phoenix Sunsets, 1982; sales assoc. The August Group, Scottsdale, Ariz., 1982-85; v.p. Provident Properties, Inc., Tempe, Ariz., 1985-88; pres. Jeremar Corp., Scottsdale, Ariz., from 1988. Instr. Ariz. Sch. Real Estate, Scottsdale, 1983—. Chmn. Fiesta Bowl Invitaional Tennis Tournament. Mem. Nat. Realtor Assn., Ariz. Realtor Assn. Jewish. Avocations: horseback riding, movies. Home: Scottsdale, Ariz. Died Jan. 15, 2004.

COHEN, MELVIN HARRIS, music company executive; b. Salisbury, N.C., Aug. 7, 1946; s. Joseph Aaron and Helen (Wolfert) C. Grad. high sch., Charlotte, N.C. V.p. Reliable Music, Charlotte, N.C., 1963-86, pres., treas., from 1986; ptnr. Cohen Wilson & Bustle, Charlotte, 1979-92. Guest speaker Nat. Assn. Mus. Merchants Conv., Annaheim, Calif., 1992, Atlantic City, 1992. Pres. Walker Woods Homeowners Assn., Charlotte, 1992-95; bd. dirs. Seawatch Homeowners Assn., Surfside Beach, S.C., 1990-92. Named Best Music Store Guitar for the Practicing Musician Mag., 1989, 90, 91, 29th Largest Dealer in Musical Instruments and Sound Reinforcement, Music Trades Mag., 1991, 65th Largest Music Store, 1995, Best Music Store, Creative Loafing, 1992-95, The Apartment Pages, 1994-95, Charlotte's Best Mag., 1994-95; nominated Most Effective Music Store, 1985-96; recipient Best Sound Reinforcement Dealer award Music and Sound Retailer Mag., 1991, 94. Mem. Audio Engring. Soc., Nat. Assn. Musical Merchants. Home: Charlotte, NC. Died Oct. 1, 2004.

COHEN, MYRON, lawyer, educator; b. Paterson, N.J., Feb. 4, 1927; s. Jacob B. and Rose (Stone) C.; m. Nancy Kamin, Nov. 4, 1951 (div. 1960); m. Barbara Levitov, May 12, 1963; children: Peter Fredric, Lee Susan. BEE, Cornell U., 1948; LLB, Columbia U., 1951. Bar: N.Y. 1951, U.S. Dist. Ct. (so., ea. dists.) N.Y. 1955, U.S. Ct. Appeals (2nd cir.) 1960, U.S. Ct. Appeals (Fed. cir.) 1984, U.S. Supreme Ct. 1974. Staff atty. Union Switch and Signal, Swissvale, Pa., 1952-54; assoc. Levisohn, Niner & Cohen, N.Y.C., 1954-56; sr. ptnr. Hubbell, Cohen, Stiefel & Gross, N.Y.C., 1956-85, Cohen, Pontani, Lieberman & Pavane, N.Y.C., from 1985. Adj. prof. N.Y. Law Sch., 1970-2003; vis. lectr. Peking U. Law Sch., 2000—; bd. dirs. Tri Magna Corp.; sec. Medallion Funding Corp., N.Y.C., 1979-86, 86-96. Author: U.S. Patent Law and Practice, 1976, Recent Developments in U.S. Law of Intellectual Property, 1985. Chmn. Mayor's Subway Watchdog Commn., N.Y.C., 1974-76. Lt. j.g. USNR, 1944-57. Mem. ABA, N.Y. State Bar Assn., Assn. Bar City N.Y., N.Y. Intellectual Property Law Assn., Internat. Trademark Assn. Democrat. Jewish. Avocation: skiing. Home: New York, NY. Died Oct. 8, 2005.

COHEN, MYRON, lawyer; b. N.Y.C., July 11, 1927; s. Gershon H. and Rose Mansfield C.; m. Ruth Jaffe, June 24, 1948; children: Jesse Bernard, Mark Jaffe, Lee Jonas, Jonathan TK, Rebecca J. Cohen Muller. LLB, Bklyn Law Sch., 1951. Contracting officer Dept. of Def., Garden City, N.Y., 1951-82; pvt. practice, Bethpage, N.Y., from 1951. Adj. prof. Hofstra U., Uniondale, N.Y., St. Johns U., Flushing, N.Y., 1983. With U.S. Army, 1945-47, Korea. Fellow Nat. Contract Mgmt. Assn. (bd. dirs. 1961-85), Nassau County Bar Assn., N.Y. State Bar Assn., Internat. Assn. of Jewish Lawyers and Jurists, Jewish Lawyers of Nassau. Home: Bethpage, NY. Died Sept. 19, 2004.

COHEN, SELMA JEANNE, dance historian; b. Chgo., Sept. 18, 1920; d. Frank A. and Minna (Skud) C. AB, U. Chgo., 1941, MA, 1942, PhD, 1946. Freelance writer, 1949—2005; editor Dance Perspectives, N.Y.C., 1959-76; founder, dir. Dance Critics Conf., Am. Dance Festival, 1970-72, U. Chgo. Seminars in Dance History, 1974-76; disting. vis. prof. Five Colls., Inc., 1976-77; editor Internat. Ency. Dance, N.Y.C., 1998. Adj. prof. U. Calif., Riverside, 1983-89, disting. scholar, 1990-2005. Author: The Modern Dance: Seven Statements of Belief, 1966, Doris Humphrey, An Artist First, 1972, Dance as a Theatre Art, 1974, Next Week, Swan Lake: Reflections on Dance and Dances, 1982. Founder Selma Jeanne Cohen Fund for Internat. Scholarship on Dance, 1999. Rockefeller Found. grant, 1969; Am. Dance Guild award, 1976; Guggenheim fellow, 1980; Fulbright scholar, 1976; recipient Profl. Achievement award U. Chgo., 1974, award Dance mag., 1981 Mem. Am. Soc. Aesthetics, Am. Soc. Theatre Rsch., Dance History Scholars, Am. Coun. Learned Socs., Internat. Fedn. for Theatre Rsch., World Dance Alliance. Died Dec. 23, 2005.

COHN, DAVID V(ALOR), biochemist, educator; b. NYC, Nov. 8, 1926; s. Ralph and Clara (Schenkman) C.; m. Evelyn Turner, 1947; children: Robert Warren, Emily. BS, CCNY, 1948; PhD, Duke U., 1952; postgrad., Western Res. U., 1953. Faculty U. Kans. Sch. Medicine, Kansas City, 1953-82, prof. biochemistry, assoc. dean rsch., 1974-82; assoc. chief staff for rsch. VA Med. Ctr., Kansas City, Mo., 1953-82; prof. biochemistry U. Mo., Kansas City, 1971-82; v.p. R&D Immuno Nuc. Corp., Stillwater, Minn., 1982; chmn. bd. sci. advisors Endotronics Corp., Mpls., 1983-85; rsch. prof. oral biology and biochemistry U. Louisville Sch. Medicine, Sch. Dentistry, 1984—2002, emeritus prof., from 2002, chmn. dept. oral health, 1989-91, chmn. dept. biol. and biophys. scis., 1992-97, univ. dir. tech. devel., 1996-99; asst. to v.p. rsch. U. Louisville, 1992-95, asst. v.p. econ. devel. and indsl. rels., 1999—2002; CEO, pres. Biomed. Rsch. Cons., Louisville, from 2002. Mem. bd. sci. counselors Nat. Inst. Dental Rsch., Bethesda, Md., 1980-84; bd. dirs. Cambridge Med. Tech., Inc., 1985-86; cons. VA, Washington, 2000—. Editor: Hormonal Control of Calcium Metabolism, 1981, Endocrine Control of Bone and Calcium Metabolism, 1984, Calcium Regulation and Bone Metabolism: Basic and Clinical Aspects, 1987, Calcium Regulating Hormones and Bone Metabolism: Basic and Clinical Aspects, vol. II, 1992; editor in chief Bone and Mineral, 1986-94; contbr. articles to profl. jours. With USN, 1945—46. Grantee USPHS, 1957—, Am. Cancer Soc., 1959-60, VA, 1975-82, Ky. Heart Assn., 1991-93. Mem. AAAS, AAUP (pres. Louisville chpt. 2000—), Internat. Bone and Mineral Soc. (past pres. coun.), Am. Soc. Molecular Biology and Biochemistry, Am. Chem. Soc., Gordon Rsch. Conf. Chem. and Biol. of Bones and Teeth (chmn. 1974). Achievements include research on calcium metabolism, parathyroid gland parathormone/chromogranin biosynthesis and secretion, bone cell growth, differentiation and hormone responsivity, economic development, entrepreneurship, history of science and medicine. Died Feb. 23, 2006.

COHN, ERNST MAX, chemist, columnist; b. Mainz, Hesse, Germany, Mar. 31, 1920; came to US, 1936; s. Martin and Lorle C.; m. Margaret Miller, July 8, 1949 (div. Feb. 1981); m. Doris Brohm, Mar. 31, 1981. BS, U. Pitts., 1942, MS in Chemistry, 1952. Phys. chemist Bur. Mines, Pitts., 1942-52, dmin., phys. chemist coal rsch. Washington, 1953-60; dmin., fuel cells U.S. Army Rsch. Office, Washington, 1960-62; adminstr. NASA, Washington, 1962-76; columnist Energy mag., Norwalk, Conn., from 1977. Author: books; contbr. articles to profl. jours.; patentee in field. Recipient Luff award for rsch. Am. Philatelic. Soc., 1995, medal Féd. Internat. Philatelie, 1985. Mem. Am. Chem. Soc. (emeritus). Avocations: postal history 1870-71, franco-german war. Home: Dothan, Ala. Died Dec. 29, 2004.

COHN, SAMUEL MAURICE, economic and management consultant; b. Phila., Nov. 11, 1915; s. Herman and Bessie (Weisberg) C.; m. Alma Cantor, Oct. 2, 1948; children— Anne L., Richard D. BA, U. Pa., 1936, postgrad., 1936, 38-40. Research asst. Wharton Sch. U. Pa., 1938-39, 41-42; research asst., relocation dir. Phila. Housing Authority, 1939-40; econ. analyst Office War Moblzn. and Reconversion, 1946-47; fiscal economist, chief economist, chief fiscal analysis, dep. asst. dir. for budget rev., asst. dir. for budget rev. Office Mgmt. and Budget and predecessor agy., Exec. Office Pres., Washington, 1947-73; v.p. Robert R. Nathan Assocs., Inc., Washington, 1973-85; dir. Nathan Assocs. Inc., 1986-94. Contbr. articles to profl. jours. Served with AUS; Served with USAAF, 1942-45. Recipient Dir.'s Exceptional Service award Bur. of Budget, 1962; Career Service award Nat. Civil Service League, 1968; Pres.'s award for Distinguished Fed. Civilian Service, 1971; Rockefeller Pub. Service award Princeton U., 1971; Spl. Hon. award Tax Found., Inc., 1976 Fellow Nat. Acad. Pub. Adminstrn.; mem. Am. Statis. Assn. Died Dec. 15, 2005.

COHN, THEODORE ELLIOT, optometrist, educator; b. Highland Park, Ill., Sept. 5, 1941; s. Nathan and Marjorie Cohn; m. Barbara Adler, Nov. 29, 1975; children: Avery Simon, Adrienne Leah, Harris Samuel. SB in Elec. Engring., MIT, 1963; MS in Bioengring., U. Mich., 1965, MA in Math., 1966, PhD in Bioengring., 1969. Asst. prof. U. Calif., Berkeley, 1970-76, assoc. prof., 1976-84, prof., 1985—2006. Vis. fellow John Curtin Med. Sch., Australian Nat. U., Canberra, 1977; vis. scholar U. Calif., San Diego, 1981-90; chair grad. group in bioengring. U. Calif., Berkeley/U. Calif., San Francisco, 2000—03; vice chair grad. affairs, dept. bioengring., U. Calif. Berkeley, 1999-2006. Author, editor: Visual Detection, 1993. Bd. dirs. Berkeley-Richmond Jewish Cmty. Ctr., 1995-2002. Recipient Appreciation award, Aerospace Lighting Inst., 1999. Fellow Optical Soc. Am. (chairvision tech. group 1984-86); mem. IEEE (sr. mem.), Vision Scis. Soc., Human Factors and Ergonomics Soc., Sigma Xi. Home: Kensington, Calif. Died May 25, 2006.

COKER, ROBERT HILTON, construction executive; b. Pensacola, Fla., May 19, 1947; s. Robert H. and Billie (Bennett) C. BS, Fla. State U., 1969. Lic. gen. contr., Calif. Pers. analyst Shell Oil Co., New Orleans, 1969-72; v.p. Coker Industries, Miami, Fla., 1972-74; pers. mgr. Lehigh Portland Cement, Miami, 1974-76; mgr. sales and pers. Hertz Equipment Rental Corp., Tampa, Fla., 1976-78; regional sales mgr. Gelco Space, Tampa, 1978-79, div. v.p., 1979-83; exec. v.p. GE Capital Modular Space, Phila., 1983-91; pres. G.E. Capital Modular Space, Phila., 1992-94; exec. v.p. Space Master Bldg Sys LLC, Atlanta, from 1994. With USAFR, 1970-76. Mem. Modular Office Assn. Democrat. Baptist. Avocation: tennis. Home: Atlanta, Ga. Died Oct. 12, 2004.

COLE, LAWRENCE FREDERICK, minister, counselor; b. Takoma Park, Md., Apr. 27, 1947; s. Kenneth Edward and Grace Mae (Myer) C.; m. Marjorie Suzzanne Fellers, June 28, 1969; children: Traci Lynn, Johnathan Lawrence. BA in Theology, So. Coll., 1983; MA in Counseling Psychology, Bowie State U., from 1983. Technician Xerox Corp., Washington, 1969-70; sr. svc. specialist Saxon Bus. Products, Orlando, Fla., 1970-77; minister Chesapeake Conf. Seventh-day Adventists, Columbia, Md., 1980-84, Potomac Conf. of Seventh_day Adventists, Staunton, Va., from 1984. With USMC, 1965-69, Vietnam. Mem. Am. Assn. for Counseling and Devel., Jaycees (bd. dirs. Jr. Miss Pageant 1975). Democrat. Avocations: woodworking, golf. Died June 15, 2004.

COLISTA, FELICIANO PHILIP, JR., lawyer; b. Detroit, Oct. 14, 1933; s. Feliciano Sr. and Maria (Prugnoli) C.; m. Katherine Louise Barnhart, Oct. 31, 1968; children: Gian A., Celia D., Joseph A. BA, Wayne State U., 1957, JD, 1960. Bar: Mich., U.S. Dist. Ct. (ea. dist., western dist.) Mich., U.S. Ct. Appeals (6th cir.). Sole practice, Detroit, 1961-65, 1970-76; prof. law, asst. dean Sch. Law U. Detroit, 1965-69, acting dean, 1970, dir. urban law program, 1965-69; ptnr. Colista, Green & Adams, Detroit, 1976-84, Colista, Adams, Dettmer & Palmer, Detroit, 1984-90, Colista, Adams & Palmer, Detroit, from 1990. Adj. prof. law Wayne State U., U. Detroit, 1970—; lawyer mem. Mich. Jud. Tenure Commn., 1988—; speaker in field. Referee Civil Rights Commn., Detroit, 1971—; mem. Mich. Judicial Tenure Commn., 1988—, chair, 1993—. Recipient Rights award ACLU, 1968, Detroit Civil Disorders, 1967; named Disting. Alumni award Wayne State U. Law Sch., 1985. Mem. ABA, State Bar Mich. (task force on professionalism 1989—), Detroit Bar Assn. (bd. dirs. 1986—), Am. Judicature Soc., Assn. Trial Lawyers Am. Democrat. Avocations: music, reading. Died July 8, 2004.

COLLINS, DEAN TRACY, psychiatrist; b. Junction City, Kans., Mar. 19, 1928; s. Laurence Edwin and Alverda Patience (Tracy) C.; m. Elisabeth Bartholdi, May 16, 1959. BA, U. Kans., Lawrence, 1950; MD, U. Kans., Kansas City, 1955. Staff psychiatrist Winfield (Kans.) State Hosp. and Tng. Ctr., 1960-62, acting chief dept., supt., 1962-63; cons. psychiatrist Kans. Neurol. Inst., Topeka, 1963-70; staff psychiatrist Menninger Meml. Hosp., Topeka, 1963-70; sect. chief Menniger Meml. Hosp., Topeka, from 1970. Assoc. dir. edn. Menninger Hosp.m 1982—, bd. dir. psychiatry, 1986—. With U.S. Army, 1946-47. Fulbright scholar, 1950-51; A.V. Humboldt scholar, 1957-58. Fellow Am. Psychiat. Assn.; mem. AMA, Kans. Psychiat. Assn. (pres. 1980-82), Shawnee County Med. Soc. (pres. 1975-76). Home: Topeka, Kans. Died Aug. 6, 2004.

COLLINS, MICHAEL EDWARD, religious newspaper editor; b. Columbus, Ohio, Nov. 17, 1938; s. Martin Patrick and Monica Louise (Metzger) C. Student, MIT, 1956-57, Ohio State U., 1957-61. Staff writer Cath. Times, Columbus, 1962-66, news editor, 1966-70, editor, 1970-95, cons. editor, from 1995. Pres. Cath. Men's Luncheon Club, 1972-73, Holy Name Parish Coun., 1972-73; chmn. comm. Diocesan Coun. Cath. Men, 1964-67; chmn. comm. sect. Cath. Conf. Ohio, 1978-80; instr. Gabriel Richard Inst., 1963-69. Contbr. articles to religious jours. Mem. Cath. Press Assn. (mem. various coms.), Soc. Profl. Journalists (pres. Ctrl. Ohio chpt. 1980-82), Mensa, KC. Home: Columbus, Ohio. Died Feb. 11, 2004.

COLOSIMO, KAREN ELIZABETH, academic administrator; b. Lincoln, Nebr., Mar. 5, 1936; d. Glenn Paul and Mildred Evelyn (Carper) Bahr; m. Clark A. Springman (div. May 1972); children: Jeffrey Clark, Jennifer Lynn (dec.), Gregory Andrew, David Stuart; m. William Colosimo, June 23, 1973. Student, U. Nebr., 1954-56, George Williams Coll., Downers Grove, Ill., 1970-71. Adminstrv. asst. State of Nebr., Lincoln, 1954-56; adminstrv. asst. to v.p. George Williams Coll., Downers Grove, 1968-80, dir. devel. rsch., 1980-84; rsch. cons. John Pruehs & Assocs., Naperville, Ill., 1985-88; mktg. asst. Mid Am. Fed., Naperville, 1988-90; dir. advancement scis. Aurora (Ill.) U., 1990-93, dir. donor rsch., from 1993. Mem. Compassionate Friends bd., Hinsdale, Ill., 1978-80, Aurora area Fundraisers, 1989—; mem. adv. bd. Fox Valley Arts Coun., Geneva, Ill., 1990—; mem. DuKane Valley coun., Batavia, 1991—. Mem. Aurora C. of C., Midwest Scottish Deerhound Club Am. (pres. 1990-93, 95-96, bd. dirs. 1991—), Scottish Deerhound Club Am. (pres. 1995-97, bd. dirs. 1997-99). Methodist. Avocations: show Scottish deerhounds, piano, antiques. Home: Oswego, Ill. Died Jan. 8, 2004.

COLVIN, ROBERT E., JR., nursing review coordinator; b. Springfield, Ill., Feb. 18, 1953; s. Robert E. and Anna Pearl (Vanhuss) C.; children: Virginia, Robert, Patrick, Amanda. ADN, NE State Coll., Rainsville, Ala., 1980. RN, Ala. Nurse, infection control practitioner, rev. coord. Jackson County Hosp., Scottsboro, Ala. Chmn. Jackson County AIDS Task Force. Mem. Assn. Practitioners Infection Control, Phi Theta Kappa. Home: Scottsboro, Ala. Died Aug. 28, 2004.

COMBS, PAUL JOSEPH, information technology professional; b. Hamilton AFB, Calif., May 19, 1960; s. Ben Jr. and Velma Ruth (Ward) C.; m. Cairlyn Elaine Bonds, Mar. 22, 1984. BBA in Mgmt. Info. Sys. magna cum laude, U. Ctrl. Okla., 1996. Foreman Rayco Electric, Yukon, 1978-86; owner Current Enterprises, Edmond, Okla., 1986-94, pres., chmn. bd. dirs, 1988-94; owner Combs Distbg. Co., Edmond, 1991-94; computer specialist Oklahoma City Air Logistics Ctr., Tucker AFB, Okla., 1996-99. Vol. Hope Ctr. of Edmond. Mem. Toastmasters (pres. 1994-95), Delta Mu Delta, Alpha Chi, Phi Eta Sigma. Republican. Home: Edmond, Okla. Died Aug. 3, 2004.

COMER, GARY C., retired apparel executive; b. Chgo., Dec. 10, 1927; m. Frances Comer; children: Stephanie, Guy. Copywriter Young & Rubicam, 1950-61, Murphy & Nye, Inc., 1961-63; founder Lands End, Inc., 1963—2002, pres., 1986—90, chmn. bd., 1990—2002. Died Oct. 4, 2006.

COMER, NATHAN LAWRENCE, psychiatrist, educator; b. Phila., Nov. 10, 1923; s. Rubin L. and Fannie (Cassover) C.; m. Rita Ellis, June 19, 1949 (dec. Mar. 1978); children: Robert, Susan Comer Kitei, Debra R., Marc J. BA, U. Pa., 1944; MD, Hahnemann Med. Coll., 1949; postgrad., U. Pa. Diplomate Am. Bd. Psychiatry and Neurology, Am. Bd. Profl. Disability Cons., Sr. Disability Analyst of Am. Bd. Disability Analysts, Am. Bd. Forensic Examiners, Am. Bd. Forensic Medicine. Intern Hahnemann Med. Coll., Phila., 1949-50; resident, NIMH fellow Inst. of Pa. Hosp., Phila., 1951-53, sr. attending psychiatrist, from 1968, resident in psychiatry, 1951-53; chief of psychiatry Ford Rd. campus Thomas Jefferson U. Hosp., Phila., 1978-94; clin. assoc. prof. psychiatry and human behavior Jefferson Med. Coll., Thomas Jefferson U., Phila., from 1994; clin. assoc. prof. psychiatry Drexel U. Coll. Medicine, Phila., from 1978; emeritus attending psychiatrist Hosp. Med. Coll. Pa., from 2000. Pres. med. staff Belmont Ctr. Comprehensive Treatment (formerly Phila. Psychiat. Ctr.), 1975—77, emeritus sr. attending physician, from 1988; pres. med. staff Inst. of Pa. Hosp., 1983—85. Contbr. articles to profl. jours. Bd. dirs. Temple Adath Israel of Main Line, Merion, Pa., 1958-78. Fellow Coll. Physicians Phila., Am. Psychiat. Assn. (disting. life); mem. AMA, Am. Soc. for Adolescent Psychiatry, Hahnemann Med. Coll. Alumni Assn. (pres. 1973-74), B'nai B'rith. Republican. Jewish. Died Nov. 21, 2005.

COMPTON, ASBURY CHRISTIAN, state supreme court justice; b. Portsmouth, Va., Oct. 24, 1929; BA, Washington and Lee U., 1950, LLB, 1953, LLD, 1975. Bar: Va. 1957. Mem. firm May, Garrett, Miller, Newman & Compton, Richmond, 1957-66; judge Law and Equity Ct., City of Richmond, 1966-74; justice Supreme Ct. Va., Richmond, 1974-2000, sr. justice, from 2000. Trustee Collegiate Schs., Richmond, 1972-89, chmn. bd., 1978-80; former chmn. adminstrv. bd. Ginter Park United Meth. Ch., Richmond; former mem. adminstrv. bd. Trinity United Meth. Ch., Richmond; trustee Washington and Lee U., 1978-90. With USN, 1953-56, USNR, 1956-62. Decorated Letter of Commendation. Mem. Va. Bar Assn., Va. State Bar, Bar Assn. City Richmond, Washington and Lee U. Alumni Assn. (past pres., dir.), Omicron Delta Kappa, Phi Kappa Sigma, Phi Alpha Delta. Clubs: Country of Va. Died Apr. 9, 2006.

CONAHAN, FRANK C., retired government executive, educator; b. Wilkes Barre, Pa., Sept. 4, 1933; s. Frank A. Conahan and Loretta A. Cantwell; m. Anne M. Corrigan; children: Frank, Tom, Nancy, Marguerite. BS in Acctg., King's Coll., 1955; postgrad., U. Mich., 1968, Harvard U., 1980; cert., Fgn. Svc. inst., 1972-73. Mem. exec. staff U.S. Gen. Acctg. Office, Washington, 1955-95, dir. European br., 1970s, dir. internat. divsn., 1980-83, asst. comptr. gen., nat. security and internat. affairs, 1983-95; sr. fellow Logistics Mgmt. Inst., Fairfax, Va., 1997-99; adj. faculty mem. Prince George's Coll., Largo, Md., 1997—2005. Testified at over 150 hearings before Congl. coms.; lectr. Brookings Inst., Def. Sys. Mgmt. Coll., Nat. Security Agy., Am. U., Ohio State U., U. Md., George Washington U., Ind. State U. Contbr. over 4,000 reports and testimonies to U.S. Congress. Tchr. Confraternity of Christian Doctrine, 1962-78; chmn. bd. external auditors Orgn. Am. States, 1982-85; sr. player Global War Games, Naval War Coll., 1990s. Served with USNR, 1951-58. Recipient Nat. Pub. Svc. award Nat. Acad. Pub. Adminstrn., 1991. Roman Catholic. Home: Bowie, Md. Died Sept. 28, 2005.

CONGER, JOSEPH HAROLD, III, theater educator; b. Edenton, N.C., Apr. 10, 1948; s. Joseph Harold Jr. and Ruth Bond (Waters) C. BA, U. N.C., Chapel Hill, 1970; MFA, U. N.C., Greensboro, 1976. Asst. prof. U. Montevallo, Ala., 1977-79, U. Md., College Park, 1979-81, U. Fla., Gainesville, 1981-84; assoc. prof. theatre, acting chmn. dept. No. Ky. U., Highland Heights, from 1984. Guest dir. Glassboro (N.J.) Summer Theatre, 1980-85, U. Nebr., Lincoln, 1985-87; guest artist Flatrock (N.C.) Playhouse, 1985—; artistic dir. Jenny Wiley Summer Theatre, Prestonsburg, Ky., 1987—. Dir., choreographer over 50 musicals and operas throughout country. Mem. Southeastern Theatre Conf. (auditions com. 1990), Ky. Theatre Assn. (auditions chmn. 1986-90). Democrat. Episcopalian. Avocations: stamps, dance, bridge. Died Nov. 10, 2004.

CONLEY, KATHERINE LOGAN, religious studies educator; b. Rutherford, N.C., Sept. 3, 1911; d. Claude Joseph and Mary (Beam) Logan; m. Jesse William Conley, Dec. 26, 1942. BS in Edn., Asheville (N.C.) Coll., 1936; postgrad., Presbyn. Ch. Christian Edn., Richmond, Va., 1939-40. Dir Christian edn. Presbyn. Ch., Spartanburg, S.C., 1940-41, Knoxville, from 1941. Chmn. bldg. com. Seventh-Day Adventist Ch., Rutherford, N.C., 1963; lay speaker United Meth. Ch., Rutherfordton, 1973-91. Mem. Genealogical Soc., DAR (regent 1976-78), Amnesty Internat., Am. Bible Soc. (silver). Democrat. Avocations: gardening, arts and crafts, hiking. Home: Rutherfordton, NC. Died Apr. 13, 2005.

CONLEY, RAYMOND LESLIE, English language educator; b. Manhattan, Kans., Feb. 25, 1923; s. Orville Ray and Goldie Gladys (Wallack) Conley. AB with honors, Park Coll., 1947; postgrad., Nebr. U., 1948-50; MA, Northwestern U., Evanston, Ill., 1958; postgrad., Ol Dominion U., 1968. Cert. tchr. speech, English, social scis. Dep. county clk. Nemaha County, Auburn, Nebr., 1942-45; tchr., English, speech St. Edward (Nebr.) High Sch., 1948-50, Oakland (Nebr.) High Sch., 1950-52, Nebraska City (Nebr.) High Sch., 1952-56, Galesburg (Ill.) High Sch., 1956-58, Maine Twp. High Sch. East, Park Ridge, Ill., 1958-65; asst. prof. English, speech Meth. Coll., Fayetteville, N.C., 1966-77; English prof. Campbell U., Buies Creek, N.C., 1980-83, aux. faculty Fort Bragg, NC, 1978—2001. Coach Nebr. State Debate Champs, 1951, 52; mem. Coun. Status Women, Fayetteville, 1965—68; aux. faculty Campbell U., Pope AFB, NC, 1985—2001; speech coach, judge local and sectional contests Toastmistress Club. Actor: Ft. Bragg Vietnam War Tng. Films. Mem. Congress Watch/Pub. Citizen, People for the Am. Way, ACLU, N.C. ACLU, Amnesty Internat.; conservation coord. Sierra Club, 1978; vol. Fayetteville Mus. Art; precinct officer Dem. party, Fayetteville, 1964—68; coord Congrl. Dist. Common Cause, 1978, mem. state program action com., state and gov. bd., 1976—78, 1995—2000, dir. state governance bd., 1995—2000. Recipient Citizenship award, Am. Legion, 1938. Mem.: AAUP, NOW, Inst. So. Studies, Internat. Platform Assn., Ams. United Separation Ch. and State, World Future Soc., N.C. Alliance Democracy, Found. Nat. Progress, Fayetteville Fgn. Film Soc. (co-founder 1967), Lambda Chi Alpha. Presbyterian. Home: Fayetteville, NC. Died Jan. 29, 2005.

CONNELLY, ELIZABETH ANN, retired state legislator; b. NYC; d. John Walter and Alice Marie (Mallon) Keresey; m. Robert Vincent Connelly; children: Alice, Robert, Margaret, Therese. Grad. H.S., Bronx; LLD (hon.), Wagner Coll., 1996. Telephone sales Pan Am. World Airways, N.Y.C., 1946-54; mem. N.Y. State Assembly, Albany, 1973-2000, chair com. on mental health, retardation/devel. disabilities, 1977-92, chair com. on standing coms., 1993-95, speaker pro tem, 1995-2000, chair intern com., 1995-2000; ret., 2000. Chair Legis. Women's Caucus, N.Y. State, 1993-95. Recipient over 350 awards and honors including S.I. Hosp. Vol. of Yr. award, 1972-73, Cert. Appreciation Willowbrook chpt. Benevolent Soc. Retarded Children, 1978, Legislator of Yr. award N.Y. State Coun. on Alcoholism, 1983, Woman of Yr. award Epilepsy Ctr., 1984, Disting. Humanitarian of Yr. award S.I. Ctr. Ind. Living, 1987, Alliance for Mentally Ill of N.Y. State award, 1988, Thomas G. Gilbert Meml. award N.Y. State Mental Health Soc., 1989, Nat. Barrier Awareness Found., 1990, Irish Am. Heritage Mus., 1991, N.Y. State Head Injury Assn. Pub. Policy award, 1994, N.Y. State Cath. Conf. Pub. Policy award 1996, St. John's U. Pres.' medal, 1998, Pres.' medal CUNY Coll. of S.I. Mem. Am.-Irish Legislators' Soc. (pres.). Democrat. Home: Staten Island, NY. Died May 25, 2006.

CONNOR, CECIL MARTIN, hotel administrator; b. Bedford, Va., Sept. 17, 1945; s. William Chester and Annie Lou (Meeks) C.; m. Lieselotte Brigitte Pauli, Aug. 29, 1969; children: Robert Martin, Sascha Michael. BS in Bus Adminstrn., Berea Coll., 1972; MBA in Hotel Restaurant I, Mich. State U., 1983. Asst. mgr. Boone Tavern Berea (Ky.) Coll., 1971-76, mgr., 1976-80, Brook Lodge The Upjohn Co., Kalamazoo, Mich., 1980-90; pres., owner Conference and Meeting Cons., Galesburg, Mich., from 1990. Instr. Ky. Bus. Coll., Lexington, 1975-76, Berea Coll., 1976-80, Transylvania U., 1979; grad. asst. Dale Carnegie Courses, Kalamazoo, Mich., 1986-87; speaker Midwest Univs. Continuing Edn. Assn., Region IV, Kalamazoo, 1989. Vol. instr. Gull Lake Middle Sch., Richland, Mich., 1989. Mem. Soc. for Food Svc. Mgmt., Meeting Planners Internat. Democrat. Mem. Reformed Church of America. Avocations: cooking, interior design, landscaping. Home: Montvale, Va. Died Feb. 3, 2004.

CONOVER, C. ALLAN, electronics executive; b. Plainfield, N.J., Nov. 8, 1938; s. Charles Allan and Sarah (Kane) C.; m. Judy Jane Conover, June 8, 1977; children from previous marriage: Charles Allan III, Christopher Allan. BSEE, LaFayette Coll., 1960. From engr. to engring. mgr. GE, Syracuse and Phoenix, 1960-70; dir., v.p. Honeywell Info. Systems, Phoenix, Boston and Mpls., 1970-80; v.p., group pres. Memorex, Santa Clara, Calif., 1980-87; pres. Optimem, Santa Clara, 1987-89; pres., chief exec. officer Lasertape Systems, Campbell, Calif., from 1989, also bd. dirs. Mem. Eta Kappa Nu. Died Aug. 10, 2005.

CONRAD, NANCY LU, retired podiatrist; b. Chillicothe, Ohio, June 26, 1927; d. Earl Leroy and Mabel Leona (Ellifritt) C. BSc, Capital U., 1949; D of Podiat. Medicine, Ohio Coll. Podiat. Medicine, 1957. Med. technologist Ohio State U. Hosp., Columbus, 1950-53, Cleve. Foot Clinic, 1955-57; pvt. practice podiatry Circleville, Ohio, 1957-95. Judge Amour awards Am. Podiatric Honor Soc., 1974; vis. lectr. Ohio Coll Podiat. Medicine Alumni Assn., 1985-87. Bd. editors: Jour. Am. Podiatric Med. Assn.; contbr. articles to profl. jours. Vis. vol. Clin. Inst., Cleve., 1976-77; bd. dirs., pres. Pickaway County unit Am. Cancer Soc., Cleve.; trustee Pickaway County Hist. Soc., Cleve., 1979; co-instr. defensive driver tng. and babysitting course Bus. and Profl. Women's Club, 1966-68; tutor ops. Boost; instr. sports medicine, bookbinding YMCA, 1982. Recipient Bronze award, Ann. Maxwell Cupshon Sci. Paper award, 1977, Podiatrist of Yr. award State of Ohio, 1988, Editors Recognition award, 1992, Disting. Svc. award Am. Podiatric Med. Assn., 1993; elected to The Ross C. of C. Women's Hall of Fame, 1993. Fellow Royal Soc. Health; mem. Am. Soc. Med. Technologists, Ohio Soc. Med. Technologists, Am. Assn. for Women Podistrists (organizer, 1st pres., editor 1965-82, nomination com. 1983-84, chmn. by-laws com. 1984-85), Am. Coll. Sports Medicine, Can. Podiatric Sports Medicine Acad., Am. Podiatric Med. Writers Assn., Altrusa Internat., NRA, Pi Delta, Delta Phi Alpha (editor alumni mag.). Avocations: music, sports, writing, bookbinding, american indian history. Home: Chillicothe, Ohio. Died July 24, 2005.

CONRATH, ROBERT ROY, insurance agent; b. Indiana, Pa., July 11, 1948; s. Kenneth William and Jean Katheryn (Miller) C.; m. Barbara Frances Finn, June 6, 1970; 1 child, Audrey Jean. AA, Ariz. Western U., 1968; BS, No. Ariz. U., 1970. Career agt. Conn. Mutual Life, Kingman, Ariz., 1970-75; ind. agt. Mohave Ins. Ctr., Kingman, from 1975, pres., from 1979. Ptnr. SHC Properties, Kingman, 1987—. Chmn. Parks and Recreation City Kingman, 1980; councilman City of Kingman, 1982-86. Mem. Ind. Ins. Agts., Nat. Assn. Life Underwriters., Mohave Lions (pres. 1988-89). Republican. Roman Catholic. Avocations: tennis, golf, hunting, photography. Home: Kingman, Ariz. Died Apr. 1, 2005.

CONSADINE, ROBERT CHESTER, electrical engineer; b. Glens Falls, N.Y., Aug. 25, 1937; s. Robert E. and Rose G. (Nolan) C.; m. Dorothy D. Fortin, Aug. 6, 1960; children: Robert J., Janet M., Judith E. BEE, Rensselaer Poly. Inst., 1959; MSEE, Syracuse U., 1967. Design engr. ITT Labs., Nutley, N.J., 1959-61; mfg./test engr. IBM Corp., Poughkeepsie, N.Y., from 1961. Instr. Dutchess Community Coll., Poughkeepsie, N.Y., 1964-70. Pres., coach Wappingers Falls (N.Y.) Pop Warner Football, coach, referee St. Mary's Cath. Youth Athletic Program, Wappingers Falls, 1971-87, football coach Roy C. Ketcham High Sch., Wappingers Falls, 1981-87. Served to 1st lt. U.S. Army, 1960. Recipient Hall of Fame award Sports Mus. of Duchess County, Poughkeepsie, 1984, Community Citizen award Oak Grove Grange #873, 1984. Mem. (sr) IEEE. Democrat. Roman Catholic. Avocations: backpacking, cross country skiing, golf, softball, basketball. Home: Poughkeepsie, NY. Died Jan. 14, 2005.

CONWAY, LOIS LORRAINE, piano teacher; b. Caldwell, Idaho, Oct. 20, 1913; d. William Henry and Auttie Arrola (Bierd) Crawford; m. Edward Owen Conway, June 23, 1934; children: Michael David, Judith Ann, Steven Edward, Kathleen Jean. Degree, Albertson Coll. of Idaho, 1960's; student, Shorwood Music Sch., Chgo., Coll. of Notre Dame, San Francisco. Pvt. piano tchr., Ontario, Oreg., 1940-74, Pendleton, Oreg., 19774-92; ret., 1992. Nat. Guild Piano Tchrs. adjudicator spring auditions Am. Coll. Musicians, Austin, Tex., 1972-96. Author: (poetry) Pacifica-The Voice Within (Semi-finalist 1995). Chmn. Nat. Guild Auditions, Ontario, Oreg., 1959-72, Pendleton, Oreg., 1972-80; v.p., publicity Community Concerts Assn., Ontario, 1960-72, membership work, 1972-75. Democrat. Avocations: gardening, playing piano, bridge, duplicate bridge, motor home travel. Home: Santa Rosa, Calif. Died Nov. 8, 2004.

COOGAN, ALICE, educational association administrator, writer; b. Sao Paulo, Brazil, Mar. 27, 1944; came to U.S., 1947; d. James Alan and Helen (Townsley) C. BA, Stanford (Calif.) U., 1965. Designer Interior Design Collaborative, San Francisco, 1971-75; dep. dir. travel/study programs Stanford Alumni Assn., from 1975. Travel writer, 1984—. Home: Santa Fe, N.Mex. Died Jan. 28, 2004.

COOK, WELLS FRANKLIN, education educator; b. Ovid, Mich., May 20, 1928; s. Wayne Baldwin and Beatrice Cecelia (Stuart) C.; m. Lois Arlene Anderson, Apr. 2, 1930; children: Natalie Ruth Cook Hermes, Annette Jean, Wayne Earl. BS, Cen. Mich. U., 1950; MA, U. Mich., 1955; PhD, Mich. State U., 1974. Tchr. Owosso (Mich.) High Sch., 1950-51; instr. Co. Clk.'s Sch., Ft. Jackson, S.C., 1951-53; tchr. Fenton (Mich.) High Sch., 1953-57; tchr., coord. co-op Royal Oak (Mich.) Pub. Schs., 1957-67; ret., 1967; prof., vocat. tchr. educator, dept. bus. info. sys. Ctrl. Mich. U., Mt. Pleasant, from 1967. Cons., lectr. Mich. Mcpl. League, Ann Arbor, 1979—, Mich. Twps. Assn., Lansing, 1979—; evaluator Career Colls. Assn., Washington, 1979—. Author manuals. Recipient Spl. Recognition award Mich. State Bd. Edn., 1993. Mem. NEA, Mich. Edn. Assn., Nat. Bus. Edn. Assn., Mich. Career Coords. Assn. (pres. 1979-80, Outstanding Svc. awards 1983, 93), Mich. Occupl. Tchr. Educators Assn. (pres. 1988-91), Mich. Vocat. Curriculum Leaders (bd. dirs. 1989-91), Mich. Assn. for Career Edn. (bd. dirs. 1985—), Nat. Assn. Parliamentarians. Methodist. Avocations: singing, reading, collecting mugs, travel, playing piano. Home: Mount Pleasant, Mich. Died June 30, 2005.

COOK, WILLIAM LESLIE, JR., lawyer; b. July 1, 1949; s. William Leslie and Mary Elizabeth (Roberts) C.; m. Mary Jo Dorr, July 17, 1976; children: Leslie Patton, William Roberts, Maribeth Dorr. BA, U. Miss., 1971, JD, 1974. Bar: Miss. 1974, U.S. Dist. Ct. (no. dist.) Miss. 1974, U.S. Dist. Ct. (we. dist.) Tenn. 1986. Assoc. Bailey & Trusty, Batesville, Miss., 1974-79; ptnr. Bailey, Trusty & Cook, Batesville, Miss., 1980-90, Bailey & Cook, Batesville, Miss., 1990-92, Bailey, Cook & Womble, Batesville, Miss., from 1992. Chmn., Miss. Coll. Rep. Clubs, 1973, Panola County March of Dimes, Batesville, 1976-78; Miss. chmn. Nat. Orgn. Social Security Claimants Reps., 1981-82; rep. Honor Coun., U. Miss. Sch. Law, 1974 King Batesville Jr. Aux. Charity Ball, 2000. Paul Harris fellow 1998—. Mem. ABA (torts and ins. practice sect. 1979—, vice chmn. com. on delivery of legal svcs. tothe disabled young lawyers divsn. 1983-85, gen. practice sect. 1985-86), ATLA, Miss. State Bar (state bd. bar admissions 1978-79, mem. ethics com. 1980-83, bd. dirs. Young Lawyers sect. 1980-83, chmn. com. on unauthorized practice of law 1983-86, workers compensation sect., mem. com. on Kid's Second Chance 1992), Panola County Bar Assn. (pres. 1979-80), Miss. Trial Lawyers Assn. (membership com. 1983-84), Ct. Practice Inst. (diplomate), Lawyer-Pilots Bar Assn., Lamar Soc. Internat. Law, Lamar Order-U. Miss., Batesville Jaycees (legal counsel 1975-77), Masons, Shriners, Rotary (pres. 1991-92, 96-97, asst. dist. gov. 1997-99, dist. gov. nominee 1999-2000, dist. gov. 2000-01, multiple Paul Harris fellow, Four Aves. of Svc. Citation, Rotary Found. Dist. Svc. award, Dist. Found. chmn. maj. gifts, del. Coun. on Legislation 2003—), Omicron Delta Kappa, Pi Sigma Alpha, Delta Theta Pi. Methodist. Home: Batesville, Miss. Died Jan. 20, 2004.

COOKE, ROBIN BRUNSKILL (LORD COOKE OF THORNDON), judge, arbitrator; b. Wellington, New Zealand, May 9, 1926; s. Philip Brunskill and Valmai Digby (Gore) C.; m. Phyllis Annette Miller, 1952; 3 children. LLM with honors, Victoria U., Wellington, 1950, LLD (hon.), 1989, U. Cambridge, 1990; MA, PhD, Gonville and Caius Coll., Cambridge, Eng., 1954; DCL (hon.), U. Oxford, 1991. Barrister, Wellington, New Zealand, 1955-72; queen's counsel, 1964; judge New Zealand Supreme Ct., Wellington, New Zealand, 1972-76, New Zealand Ct. of Appeal, 1976-86; pres., 1986-96; mem. House of Lords, Eng., from 1996, Lord of Appeal, 1996-2001. Mem. adv. bd. Justice All-Souls Rev. of Adminstrv. Law, U.K., 1979—88; vis. fellow All Souls Coll., Oxford, 1990; disting. vis. fellow Victoria U., Wellington, from 1996; pres. Ct. Appeal Samoa, 1982, from 1994, Cook Islands, 1981, 82, Kiribati, from 1998; judge Supreme Ct. Fiji, 1995—2001; overseas judge Hong Kong Ct. of Final Appeal, from 1997. Editor: Portrait of a Profession Centennial Book of NZ Law Soc.; editor-in-chief The Laws of New Zealand; contbr. articles to profl. jours. Chmn. Commn. of Inquiry into Housing, 1970-71. Decorated Knight Bachelor, Knight of Brit. Empire; Order of New Zealand; Caius Coll. Hon. fellow, 1982; named Privy counsellor, 1977. Mem. Internat. Commn. of Jurists (commn. mem.), Am. Law Inst., Law Asia (life), Inner Temple (hon. bencher 1985—), Wellington Club, Oxford and Cambridge Club. Mem. Ch. Eng. Avocations: theater, cricket. Home: Wellington, New Zealand. Died Aug. 30, 2006.

COOPER, CHESTER LAWRENCE, research administrator; b. Boston, Jan. 13, 1917; s. Israel and Hannah (Levenson) C.; m. Orah Pomerance, July 23; children: Joan Laurence Gould, Susan Louise Cooper. BS, NYU, 1939, MBA, 1941; PhD, Am. U., Washington, 1960. Asst. dep. dir. CIA, Washington, 1947-62; sr. staff White House/NSC, Washington, 1962-66, U.S. Dept. State, Washington, 1966-70; dir. internat. div. Inst. Def. Analysis, Arlington, Va., 1970-72; fellow Woodrow Wilson Internat. Ctr. Scholars, Washington, 1972-75; dep. dir. Inst. Energy Analysis, Oak Ridge, Tenn., 1975-83; dep. dir., acting dir. Internat. Inst. Applied Systems Analysis, Laxenburg, Austria, 1983-85; coord. internat programs Resources for the Future, Washington, 1985-92; dep. dir. Battelle Pacific N.W. Labs., Washington, 1992-2001, emeritus dir., 2001; dep. dir. emeritus Joint Inst. for Rsch. on Global Change, U. Md./Pacific Northwest Nat. Lab., 2001—05. Cons. Screenscope Films, Washington. Author: The Lost Crusade, 1971 (award 1971), The Lion's Last Roar, 1977, In the Shadows of History, 2005; editor: Growth in America, 1976, Science for Public Policy, 1987. Fellow Woodrow Wilson, Internat. Ctr. for Scholars, 1972—75; scholar, Nat. War Coll., Washington, 1952—53, Internat. Inst. Applied Sys. Analyses, Laxemburg, Austria, 1986. Mem. Coun. Fgn. Rels., Poets, Essayists, Novelists, Cosmos Club. Avocations: fishing, gardening, sculpting, collecting 18th century furniture and silver. Home: Washington, DC. Died Oct. 30, 2005.

COOPER, JOHN JOSEPH, lawyer; b. Vincennes, Ind., Oct. 20, 1924; s. Homer O. and Ruth (House) C.; m. Nathalie Brooke, 1945. AB, Stanford, 1950, LLB, 1951; LLM, U. So. Calif., 1964. Bar: Calif. 1952. Pvt. practice, San Francisco, 1951-54; counsel Shell Oil Co., L.A., 1954-61; gen. counsel, v.p. Varian Assocs., Palo Alto, 1961—90, sr. v.p., 1990. Speaker, lectr. Am. Law Inst., ABA, other legal orgns. Contbr. articles to law revs. and profl. jours. Aviator USNR, 1942-45. Mem. ABA, Calif. Bar Assn. Died Jan. 8, 2006.

COOPER, JOHN RICHARD, electro-forensic engineer, consultant on standards; b. Hutchinson, Kans., June 16, 1926; s. Charles Dudley and Mabel (Fletcher) Cooper; m. Sophia Jane McDonald, Sept. 18, 1949; children: Mary Alice, Elizabeth Jane Peek, Melissa Ann. BSEE, Kans. State U., 1949. Registered profl. engr., Ill. Sales engr. Allis-Chalmers Mfg. Co., Chgo., 1949-59, Marathon Electric Mfg. Co., Chgo., 1959-60; dir. application svcs. S&C Electric Co., Chgo., 1960-91; pres. John Cooper Cons. Svcs., Inc., Wilmette, Ill., from 1991. Chmn. book IEEE Recommended Practice for Protection and Coordination of Industrial and Commercial Power Systems, 1986. Fellow: IEEE (stds. medal 1992, achievement award 1997), Industry Application Soc. of IEEE. Episcopalian. Avocations: travel, fishing. Home: Wilmette, Ill. Died Apr. 11, 2005.

COOPER, MARY JANE, civil volunteer; b. Detroit, Dec. 31, 1926; d. Aloysuis L. and Nora Christina (Van Sumeren) Vermeesch; m. Ernest M. Wiedyk, Feb. 14, 1946 (div. May 1974); children: Ernest Jr., Bernard, John, James, Robert; m. Virgil Cooper, Aug. 14, 1975. Student, Delta Coll., Bay City (Mich.) C.C. Owner/operator Wiedyk Flower Gift, Auburn; alteration/seamtress Hudson's Dept. Store, Saginaw, Mich.; owner/operator D.D.S. of Bay County, Bay City. Vol. Vol. Action Ctr., Bay City, Bay Med. Facility, Essexville, Mich.; pres. Altar Soc., St. Joseph Ch., Auburn, 1968-70; treas. League Cath. Women, Bay City, 1969, Auburn Bus. Assn., 1968. Recipient Vital Action Citizen's award Bay Vol. Ctr., 1991. Republican. Roman Catholic. Avocations: writing, great grandchildren. Home: Auburn, Mich. Died Apr. 25, 2005.

COOPER, MICHAEL DEVON, communications consultant, elementary educator; b. Kewansville, N.C., Sept. 8, 1958; s. Amos Hewry and Anna Lue (GAvin) C.; m. Cynthia Cherry Cooper, Feb. 25, 1984 (div. Dec. 1990). BA in Comm. Arts, Johnson C. Smith U., Charlotte, N.C.; MBA in Bus. Mgmt., Stevens Inst. Tech., Hoboken, N.J.; postgrad, Big Bend Coll., London. Cert. travel agt. Owner Cooper-Paris Travel Agy., Atlanta, 1991-94; mgr. AT&T, Bridgewater, N.J., from 1984. Freelance pianist, musician, N.C., Ga., N.J., Va., S.C., N.Y., Germany, Spain, France; comm. cons. Website/Internet, Newark, 1997. Sgt. U.S. Army, 1981-84. Recipient hon. medal for overseas rels. and German war gravesites Kaiserslautern, Germany, 1984. Mem. Ira Aldridge Dramatic Guild (sec. 1976-80), N.J. Oratorical Soc. (judge). Democrat. Presbyterian. Avocations: exercise, walking, travel, plays, music. Home: Belleville, NJ. Died July 17, 2004.

COOPER, WILLIAM MARION, physician; b. Pitts., Jan. 12, 1919; s. Lardin Monroe and Sophia Antoinette (Swartz) C.; m. Sara Georgia Thomas, Jan. 19, 1942; children: Mikell Lee Cooper Schenck, William Marion, Thomas L., George Robert. BS, Pa. State U., 1939; MD, Hahnemann Med. Coll., 1943; JD, U. Pitts., 1987. Diplomate Am. Bd. Internal Medicine, Am. Bd. Hematology; cert. in Geriatrics. Intern Shadyside Hosp., Pitts., 1943; resident U. Pitts. Sch. Medicine, 1946-48, Cleve. Clin. Found., 1948; practice medicine specializing in internal medicine and hematology Pitts., from 1948; mem. staff Presbyn.-Univ., Shadyside; chief dept. medicine Shadyside Hosp., 1980-91; mem. med. faculty U. Pitts., from 1948, clin. prof. medicine, from 1958, dir. div. continuing edn., 1970-80, assoc. dean continuing edn., 1974-80; dir. continuing edn. Univ. Health Center, Pitts., 1975-80; sr. asst. vice-chancellor Univ. Health Ctr. Pitts., 1979-80. Med. dir. Ctrl. Blood Bank, Pitts., 1951-60, Pitts. Skin and Cancer Found., 1958-65. Contbr. articles to med. jours. Served with M.C. U.S. Army, 1944-45. Mem. AMA, AAAS, ACP (master; bd. govs. 1965-71), Pa. Med. Soc., Allegheny County Med. Soc., Am., Internat. Socs. Hematology, Am. Soc. Internal Medicine, Am. Coll. Legal Medicine, Oakmont (Pa.) Country Club. Home: Pittsburgh, Pa. Died Sept. 12, 2006.

COOPERMAN, ALVIN, television and theatrical producer; b. Bklyn. s. Nathan and Marietta (Steinman) C.; m. Marilyn Frances Fisher; Children: Karen Lynn, Audrey Joan, Margot Jane. Exec. dir. booking Shubert Theatre Enterprises, N.Y.C., 1963-68; v.p. spl. programs NBC, N.Y.C., 1967-68; exec. v.p. Madison Sq. Garden Ctr., Inc., N.Y.C., 1968-72; pres. Madison Sq. Garden Prodns., N.Y.C., 1968-72; CEO Athena Comms. Corp., N.Y.C., 1972—2006. Developed and produced spl. program Wide Wide World, 1955; exec. prodr. Producer's Showcase, 1955-56, Big Event, 1976-77, Screen Gems, 1957-58; prodns. include Dodsworth, Rosalinda, Jack and the Beanstalk, Shirley Temple Storybook, 1956-57, The Untouchables, 1962-63, Bolshoi Ballet Romeo and Juliet (Emmy award nomination 1976), Pele's Last Game, Amahl and the Night Visitors, A Tribute to Toscanini (Emmy award 1980), An Evening with Jerome Robbins (Emmy award 1981), The Life of Pope John Paul II, Ain't Misbehavin, 1985 (Emmy award, Best Musical of the Year award NAACP), My Two Loves, 1986, Safe Passage, 1987, Family Album, 1987, Witness to Survival, 1988-90; prodr./writer animated spl. NBC-TV Fourth King, 1984; prodr./dir./writer TV spl. Mobs and Mobster, 1993; prodr. cable TV show The Higgins Boys and Gruber Show, 1993 (Ace award nominee), ABC movie: Follow the River, 1994; writer: (stage musical) Honky Tonk Heaven, 1995, (ABC spl.) Susan B. Anthony Slept Here, 1995 (Am. Women in Radio and TV Best Documentary award), (feature film) Charity Royall, 1997-98; (play) Thrall, 1999; creator, writer: (websites) The Stork Club, Platinum, 1996; writer, lyricist (musical) The Life and Adventures of Santa Claus, 1998, weathertainment.com, 1999; established Infotainment Internat., Inc., 1999; website developer (with Herman Rush) Weathertainment.com, 1999. Creative cons. Rep. Nat. Conv., 1972; mem., trustee Judy Holliday Meml. Com. for Am. Med. Ctr., Denver; chmn. N.Y. chpt. Arthritis Found.; pres. Broadway Walk Stars Found., 2000. Recipient Peabody award, 1957, Christopher award, 1957, Judy Holliday Humanitarian award, 1972. Mem. Newcomen Soc. N.Am., Am. Theatre Planning Bd., Players Club. Home: New York, NY. Died Aug. 11, 2006.

CORBETT, JOHN RICHARD, retired metals company executive; b. Chgo., Apr. 28, 1928; s. William Fred and Minnie Frances (Heitmann) C.; m. Nancy Reese, June 28, 1952 (div. June 1987); children: Scott R., Douglas R., Mark R., Peter R.; m. Ellen Smith Liesching, Oct. 22, 1988. B.S., U. Wis., 1950, postgrad. U. Wis. Law Sch., 1950-51, 54-55;

J.D., Columbia U., 1956. Atty., ASARCO Inc., N.Y.C., 1955-60, asst. dir. indsl. relations, 1960-64, dir. labor relations, 1964-83, v.p. indsl. relations, 1983-84, v.p. indsl. relations and personnel, 1984-93, ret., 1993; bd. dirs. N.Y.-NJ. Arbitration Group, N.Y.C., Inter-Am. Safety Council, Englewood, N.J., Unemployment Benefits Assn., Washington. Served to lt. (j.g.) USNR, 1951-54. Mem. Nat. Assn. Mfrs. (indsl. relations commn.), Am. Mining Congress (indsl. relations commn.). Presbyterian. Clubs: Wall Street, City Mid-day (N.Y.C.). Home: Saint Helena Is, SC. Died June 22, 2004.

CORDELL, MICHAEL BRAGG, manufacturing executive; b. Ware, Mass., Sept. 15, 1946; s. Arthur Franklin and Helen (Antaya) C.; m. Deborah Susan Christiansen, June 20, 1970 (div. Dec. 1981); 1 child, Geoffrey Michael; m. Barbara Cecelia Vayo, Aug. 31, 1985. Student, John & Wales Jr. Coll., 1974-76. Ptnr. Cordell Machine Corp., Attleboro, Mass., 1969-77; applications engr. Moog Inc., East Aurora, N.Y., 1977-79, regional sales mgr., 1979-82, mfg. engr., 1982-85; mfg. engring. mgr. Parker Hannifin Corp., Irvine, Calif., 1985-90, plant mgr. City of Industry, Calif., from 1990. With USAF, 1966-69. Mem. Soc. Mfg. Engrs. Roman Catholic. Avocations: golf, sailing, flying. Home: Charlotte, NC. Died June 8, 2005.

CORLEY, PAT, actor; b. Dallas, June 1, 1930; s. R.L. and Ada Lee (Martin) C.; m. Iris Carter; children: Troy, Kevin, Jerry, Christina, Michelle, Vickie. Grad., Stockton Coll., 1955. Appearances include TV show Murphy Brown, 1988-96, 20 feature films, numerous Broadway and Off-Broadway plays, residential theatre, musical tents, dinner theatre and over 200 TV shows, 1946-91, theatre dance Stockton Symphony, 1946-49, ballet, 1955-56; (film) Mr. Destiny, 1990; (TV movie) In Defense of a Married Man, 1996, Saved by the Bell: Wedding in Las Vegas, 1994, When Time Expires, 1997. Avocations: golf, tennis, tap dancing. Died Sept. 11, 2006.

CORNELL, DAVID A., research center executive; b. Grand Rapids, Mich., May 17, 1932; s. Frank Hartwell and E. Marie (Angle) C.; m. Linda Joyce Berlien, June 21, 1958; 1 child, Sara Ann. BA, Alma (Mich.) Coll., 1953; MDiv, Western Theol. Sem., Holland, Mich., 1957; MA, We. Mich. U., 1968; ThD, Am. Div. Sch., Chgo., 1970. Tchr. Whitehall (Mich.) High Sch., 1965; instr. Davenport Coll., Grand Rapid, Mich., 1966-69; asst. prof. Adrian (Mich.) Coll., 1969-72; vis. prof. Lake Mich. Coll., Benton Harbor, Mich., 1972-73; exec. dir. Smith Meml. Ctr., Grand Rapids, 1973-81; nursing home cons. Grand Rapids, 1981-82; ch. cons. United Ch. Orgn., Galion, Ohio, 1985-86; research fellow Elizabeth Vera Palmer Inst., Grand Rapids, from 1986. Pastor First congl. Ch., Shelby, Mich., 1960-65, Saugutuck, Mich., 1957-60; lectr. in field. Contbr. articles to profl. jours. Recipient numerous awards. Mem. Am. Philos. Soc. Ethics, Mich. Hist. Soc., Am. Assn. Ret. Persons Tchrs. Assn., Sylvan St. Irregulars, Seagull Found. Avocations: photogaphy, audio recording, hunting, fishing. Home: Grand Rapids, Mich. Died July 18, 2005.

CORNELL, JOHN ALSTON, research and development executive, consultant; b. N.Y.C., Oct. 24, 1922; s. John F. and Jane (Bevan) C.; m. Patricia R. Cornell, June 1952 (div. 1981); children: Diane J., Peter J.; m. Suzanne DeWalt, May 6, 1988. BS, MIT, 1948; MS, Poly. U., Bklyn., 1950. With R & D dept. H.D. Justi & Son, Phila., 1950-56; dir. rsch. Sartomer Resins, Essington, Pa., 1956-70, West Chester, Pa., 1970-76; exec. dir. R & D Westwood (Mass.) Rsch. Lab. Inc., 1976—95. Owner, exec. dir., assoc. Princeton Polymer Lab., Plainsboro, N.J. Contbr. articles to profl. jours.; patentee in field. Bd. dirs., v.p. Citizens Com. for Pub. Edn. in Phila.; 2d lt. AUS, 1943-45, ETO. Decorated Bronze Star, Purple Heart. Mem. AAAS, Am. Chem. Soc., Internat. Dental Rsch. Assn. Avocation: competitive badminton. Home: Kennet Sq, Pa. Died July 18, 2006.

CORNSTUBLE, HERMAN LOGAN, retired industrial engineer; b. Wayne City, Aug. 20, 1921; s. Logan Stephen and Mary Cathern (Feeny) C. A in Indsl. Engring. Mgmt., Washington U., St. Louis, 1966, BS in Indsl. Mgmt., 1988. Mfg. indsl. engr. Boring Mfg. Corp., St. Louis, 1956-91. Cons. to univ. students Boring Mfg. Corp., St. Louis. Cpl. U.S. Army, 1943-45, WWII, China, Burma, India; USN, 1952, Korea. Mem. Assembly of God Ch. Achievements include the manufacturing of the first Mercury Space Capsule used in the first American orbital space flight piloted by Lt. Col. John Glenn who completed three orbits around the world which was considered the forerunner of current Moon flight. Home: Delaware, Ohio. Died June 4, 2004.

CORNWELL, RENDLE LOMAX, pharmaceutical company executive; b. Bolton, Lancashire, U.K., Jan. 27, 1930; came to U.S., 1977; s. George William and Annie (Lomax) C.; m. Dorothy Small, Sept. 17, 1952; children: Nigel Rendle, Bryony Jane, Martin Peter. B in Vet. Sci., U. Liverpool, 1954, M in Vet. Sci., 1960; PhD, U. Liverpool, U.K., 1962, D of Vet. Sci., 1984. Gen. practice vet. med. specializing in large animals, various cities, U.K., 1954-58; lectr. vet. preventive med. U. Liverpool, 1958-62; head parasitol research Pfizer Cen. Research, Sandwich, Kent, U.K., 1962-72, asst. dir. research devel., 1972-77; dir. tech. services agrl. div. Pfizer, Inc., Lee's Summit, Mo., 1977-82, v.p. sci. and tech. N.Y.C., from 1982. Cons. U. Mo., 1986-87. Served as cpl. Brit. Army, 1948-49. Fellow Royal Coll. Vet. Surgeons; mem. Am. Assn. Bovine Practitioners, World Assn. Advancement Vet. Parasitology, Am. Soc. Parasitology. Presbyterian. Avocations: golf, tennis, swimming, singing. Home: New York, NY. Died July 6, 2005.

CORRELL, VIRGINIA LOU, bookkeeper; b. Clearwater, Kans., Nov. 26, 1919; d. William Rogers and Mary O. (Smock) Harrington; m. LeRoy Alfred Correll, July 17, 1948 (dec.); children: Candice, Charlene, Claudia, Catherine, Christina. BS, Panhandle State U., 1942. Instr. jr. high Satanta (Kans.) Grade Sch., 1942-43, prin., coach, 1943-46, grade sch. instr., 1960-82, bookkeeper, lineman, 1942-54; with Santa Fe R.R., Satanta, 1946-47; instr. Liberal (Kans.) High Sch., 1947-48; bookkeeper, asst. coord. Satanta Aging Program, from 1984. Mem. Ret. Tchrs. Assn., Satanta C. of C. (Educator of the Yr. 1979, Sr. Citizen of Yr. 1988). Democrat. Methodist. Avocations: quilt making, rug hooking, reading. Home: Satanta, Kans. Died Mar. 13, 2004.

COSENZA, ARTHUR GEORGE, opera director; b. Phila., Oct. 16, 1924; s. Luigi and Maria (Piccolo) C.; m. Marietta Muhs, Sept. 16, 1950; children: Louis John, Arthur William, Maria. Student, Ornstein Sch. Music, Phila., 1946-48, Berkshire Music Festival, 1947, Am. Theater Wing, N.Y.C., 1948-50. Asso. prof. Coll. Music, Loyola U. of South, 1954-84, dir. opera workshop, 1954-84; dir. Opera Program for City of New Orleans, 1955-73 Appeared in maj. opera houses throughout U.S., Can.; baritone New Orleans Opera, 1954-70, prodr., 1960-74, dir., 1965-98, dir. emeritus, 1998-2006 Served with AUS, 1943-45. Decorated Purple Heart medal; cavaliere Order Star Italian Solidarity; cavaliere Ufficiale dell' Ordine al Merito Italy; officier Ordre des Arts et des Lettres. Mem. Am. Guild Mus. Artists (hon. life), Blue Key. Home: New Orleans, La. Died Dec. 27, 2005.

COSGRIFF, STUART WORCESTER, internist, consultant, educator; b. Pittsfield, Mass., May 8, 1917; s. Thomas F. and Frances Deford (Worcester) C.; m. Mary Shaw, Jan. 23, 1943; children: Mary, Thomas, Stuart, Richard, Robert. BA cum laude, Holy Cross Coll., 1938; MD, Columbia U., 1942, D Med. Sci., 1948. Diplomate Am. Bd. Internal Medicine. Intern Presbyterian Hosp., N.Y.C., 1942-43; asst. resident in medicine, 1943, 46-47; chief resident, 1947-48; instr. in medicine Columbia U., N.Y.C., 1948-50, clin. asst. prof. medicine, 1951-63, clin. assoc. prof., 1963-73, clin. prof. medicine, 1973-83, clin. prof. emeritus, from 1983; attending physician Presbyn. Hosp., N.Y.C., 1948-83, cons. emeritus, from 1984; individual practice medicine, specializing in internal medicine and vascular diseases, from 1948. Cons. in medicine to dir. Selective Svc., N.Y.C., 1957-73, N.Y. Giants Baseball Club, 1951-57, San Francisco Baseball Club, 1958-61; dir. thrombo-embolic clinic Vanderbilt Clinic, N.Y.C., 1948-83. Contbr. articles to med. jours. Served to capt. M.C., U.S. Army, 1943-45, ETO. Fellow ACP, Pan Am. Med. Assn.; mem. Am. Heart Assn., N.Y. Heart Assn., Alpha Omega Alpha Clubs: Knickerbocker Country (Tenafly, N.J.). Roman Catholic. Died Dec. 17, 2005.

COSH, JOHN MORTON, retired bank executive; b. Mimico, Ont., Can., Dec. 28, 1924; s. George Morton and Margaret (Brown) C.; m. Marjorie Bernice Cosh, Apr. 20, 1952; children: George M., John Michael, Jayne Ann, Robert Alan. Cert. banking, U. Wis., 1971. Asst. cashier First Nat. Bank Vista, Calif., 1946-51, escrow officer, asst. mgr., mgr. security, 1951-70; exec. v.p., pres., vice chmn. W. Coast Nat. Bank, 1970-77; pres. Palomar Ind. & Comml. Realtors Inc., 1977-83; v.p. Wells Fargo Bank, 1983-91; ret., 1991. Apptd. to fee arbitration com. Calif. State Bar. Bd. dirs., past pres. Tri-City Hosp.; vice chmn. Oceanside Econ. Devel. Corp.; bd. dirs. Overall Econ. Devel. Commn. San Diego County; past pres. Greater San Luis Rey Council; past bd. dirs., chmn. guarantors fund North County Concert Assn.; vol. Vista Boys Club, founder, past. pres.; pres. Vista Boys Club Found.; life mem. San Luis Rey Council PTA's. Served with USAAF, 1943-46. Recipient Silver Keystone, Golden Boy, Bronze Medallion, Man Behind the Boy awards Boys Clubs Am.; named Disting. Citizen Jaycees, Man of Yr. North County Associated C. of C.'s, 1965, Banker of Yr. Am. Bankers Assn., 1984, Hon. Officer Vista League Cancer Socs. Mem. Vista Hist. Soc., Vista C. of C. (bd. dirs.), Indsl. Devel. Bond Authority (past chmn.), Vista Econ. Devel. Assn. (past chmn.), Elks, Lions, Masons, Rotary. Republican. Presbyterian. Home: Vista, Calif. Died Apr. 16, 2004.

COTTER, GEORGE LOUIS, JR., automotive manufacturing executive; b. Pitts., May 29, 1932; s. George Louis cotter and Lillian Laura (Kerr) Miller; m. Lois Jean Dyer, Oct. 19, 1957; children: Patricia Cotter Wilson, Diane B., George L. III. BS in MechE, U. Mich., 1954; MBA, Harvard U., 1956. Trainee Eaton Corp., Cleve., 1956-57, mgr. factory, 1957-69, asst. gen. mgr. heater div., 1969-71, gen. mgr. climate control div., 1971-79, gen. mgr. axle div., 1979-83, gen. mgr. axle and brake div. Galesburg, Mich., 1983-89, spl. assignment, 1989-90; pres. Indsl. Plastics Co., div. MTD Products, Inc., Valley City, Ohio, from 1990; chmn., treas. Glow Core Corp., Valley City, Ohio, from 1992. Mem. Soc. Automotive Engrs., Tau Beta Pi, Pi Tau SIgma, Phi Eta Sigma. Republican. Mem. United Ch. Christ. Home: Savannah, Ga. Died June 19, 2005.

COTTLE, CRAIG HANSEN, financial executive; b. Lewiston, Utah, July 11, 1943; s. Laurence Glen and Margaret (Hansen) C.; m. Sharon Elizabeth Dooley, June 25, 1969; children: Todd Alan, Sean Glen, Elizabeth Dawn, Jeremy Craig, Timothy Aaron, Darin Shea, Ayssa Shiree. BS, Weber State U., 1969; MBA, Utah State U., 1988. Cert. cash mgr. Tax acct. IRS, Ogden, Utah, 1967-69; staff acct. DelMonte Corp., San Francisco, 1969-71; fin. asst. to pres. Universal Distbg. Co., Sandy, Utah, 1971-72; staff acct. Hans Nievaard, CPA, Salt Lake City, Utah, 1972-73; contr. Master Lease, Inc., Salt Lake City, 1973-74; asst. treas. N.W. Energy Co., Salt Lake City, 1974-86; mgr. fin. resources Iomega Corp., Roy, Utah, 1986-87; asst. v.p. Key Bank of Utah, Salt Lake City, 1988; treas. Price Savers Wholesale Inc., Salt Lake City, 1989-91; pvt. practice fin. mgmt. cons. Kaysville, Utah, from 1992. Exec. v.p., CFO VesCor Capital Corp., Ogden, Utah, 1992-95. Aux. officer Utah Hwy. Patrol, Ogden, 1964-69; vol. fireman North Ogen Fire Dept., 1966-67; troop com. Boy Scouts of Am., Kaysville, 1978-88, explorer com. chmn., 1988-90. Mem. Treasury Mgmt. Assn. (bd. dirs. 1986-89, certification com. 1980-89), Treasury Mgmt. Assn. Utah (founder, pres. 1984-86), Nat. Risk and Ins. Mgmt. Soc., Risk and Ins. Mgmt. Soc. Utah. Republican. Mem. Lds Ch. Avocations: camping, hiking, skiing, rifle and pistol shooting, fishing. Home: Kaysville, Utah. Died Oct. 8, 2004.

COULSON, ROLAND ARMSTRONG, biochemistry educator, researcher; b. Rolla, Kans., Dec. 20, 1915; s. Emmett and Mary Josephine (Armstrong) C.; m. Nancy Kelley, Nov. 16, 1944 (dec. Dec. 1992); children: Thomas Duncan, Carol Melissa. BA, Mcpl. U. Wichita, 1937; MSc, La. State U., 1939; PhD, U. London, 1944. From instr. to assoc. prof. Med. Ctr. La. State U., New Orleans, 1944-54, prof. Med. Ctr., from 1954. Cons. Hotel Dieu Hosp., New Orleans, 1963-79; dean grad. sch. Med. Ctr. La. State U., New Orleans, 1965-74. Co-author: Biochemistry of the Alligator, 1964, Alligator Metabolism, 1983; contbr. articles to profl. jours. With RAF, 1941-44, ETO Rsch. grantee NIH, 1952-68, Schlieder, 1968-71, La. Dept. Wildlife and Fisheries, 1971—. Avocations: bicycling, gun collecting. Home: New Orleans, La. Died Nov. 5, 2004.

COULTER, DAVID CRESWELL, engineer, researcher, executive; b. Fargo, N.D., Apr. 4, 1928; s. John Lee and Phoebe Frost Coulter; m. Winifred Alice Russell, Apr. 4, 1952; children: Douglas Lee, Ann Claire, James Russell. BS in Physics/Math., Am. U., Washington, 1951. Electronic scientist U.S. Naval Rsch. Lab., Washington, 1951-54, electronic engr., 1966-84, Melpar, Inc., Falls Church, Va., 1954-66; rsch. engr. Gallandet U., Washington, 1987-90; prs. Coulter Assocs., Inc., Fairfax, Va., 1978—2004; co-founder Metavox, Inc., Fairfax, 1983—2004, CEO, 1987-98. Cons., engr. Gallaudet U., Washington, 1990-95. Contbr. articles to profl. jours. Deacon Grace Presbyn. Ch., Springfield, Va., 1956-58. Mem. IEEE (sr. mem.), Acoustical Soc. Am. Republican. Achievements include patents for method and apparatus for improving binaural hearing, method and system for speech compression, system for determining consonant formant loci, frequency, amplitude, time plotter with simulated three dimensional display; co-patentee instantaneous detection of human speech pitch pulses. Home: Vienna, Va. Died Oct. 25, 2005.

COUNSIL, WILLIAM GLENN, electric utility executive; b. Detroit, Dec. 13, 1937; s. Glenn Dempsey and Jean Beverly (Rzepecki) C.; m. Donna Elizabeth Robinson, Sept. 10, 1960; children: Glenn, Craig. Student, U. Mich., 1955-56; BS, U.S. Naval Acad., 1960; Advanced Mgmt. Program, Harvard U., 1991. Ops. supr., asst. plant supt. sta. supt. N.E. Nuclear Energy Co., Waterford, Conn., 1967-76; project mgr., v.p. nuclear engring. and ops. N.E. Utilities, Hartford, Conn., 1976-80, sr. v.p. nuclear engring. and ops., 1980-85; exec. v.p. nuclear engring. and ops., electric-generating div. Tex. Utilities Generating Co., 1985-88; vice chmn. Tex. Utilities Electric Co., 1989-93; mng. dir. Wash. Pub. Power Supply System, Richland, 1993-96. With USN, 1956-67. Recipient Outstanding Leadership award ASME, 1986. Republican. Presbyterian. Died Jan. 24, 2006.

COUNTS, WILLIAM EVERETT, financial consultant; b. Washington County, Va., Sept. 5, 1935; s. Edgar Bascom and Maude Flora (Heath) C.; m. Katherine Sue Smith, May 3, 1957; children: Sandra, Susan, Patricia (dec.), William, David. BS, East Tenn. State U., 1957; MEd, U. Va., 1967. CLU, ChFC; registered fin. planner. Life underwriter The Equitable, Richmond, Va., from 1969. Pres. Rockville (Va.) Commun. Ctr., 171-73, Rockville Youth Club, 1972-73. Mem. Am. Soc. CLU and ChFC, Richmond Assn. Life Underwriters, Acca Temple Antique and Classic Car Club (treas. 1990-92, v.p. 1993). Republican. Baptist. Avocations: spectator sports, antique and classic cars, hunting and fishing. Home: Rockville, Va. Died Sept. 1, 2004.

COUPER, RICHARD WATROUS, retired foundation administrator; b. Binghamton, NY, Dec. 16, 1922; s. Edgar W. and Esther (Watrous) C.; m. Patricia Pogue, Sept. 24, 1946; children: Frederick Pogue, Thomas Hayes, Margaret Couper Haskins. AB, Hamilton Coll., Clinton, NY, 1947, LLD (hon.), 1969; AM in Am. History, Harvard U., 1948; LLD (hon.), St.Joseph's Coll., 1982, Wesleyan U., 1986; LHD (hon.), NYU, 1974, William Paterson Coll., 1985, St. Lawrence U., 1986, Hartwick Coll., 1987. With Couper-Ackerman-Sampson, Inc. (and predecessor), Binghamton, NY, 1948-62, treas., 1957-60, v.p., 1960-63; adminstrv. v.p. Hamilton Coll., 1962-65, v.p., 1965-66, acting pres., 1966-68, v.p., provost, 1968-69, trustee, 1959—92; life trustee, from 1992; dep. commr. higher edn. State Edn. Dept., NY, 1969-71; pres., CEO Pub. Libr., NYC, 1971-81, pres. emeritus, 1981—2006; pres. The Woodrow Wilson Nat. Fellowship Found., Princeton, NJ, 1981-90, pres. emeritus, 1990—2006. Capt. U.S. Army, 1942—46. Mem. Orgn. Am.

Hist., Am. Hist. Assn., NY State Hist. assn. (trustee 1979-97), Harvard Club, Century Assn., Lotos Club (NYC), Nassau Club (Princeton, NJ), Grolier Club (NYC), Phi Beta Kappa Fellows. Home: Clinton, NY. Died Jan. 25, 2006.

COUTINHO, JOHN DE S., mechanical engineer; b. Lisbon, Portugal, Aug. 9, 1913; came to U.S., 1917; s. Joaquim de Siqueira and Louise (Valet) C.; m. Eleanor Franciska Burkarth, Sept. 12, 1942; children: Roy, Alan. M. Aero. Engring., NYU, 1942; D. Engring., Tech. U. Berlin, 1970. Registered profl. engr., N.Y., Fla., D.C., Md. From designer to dir. reliability Lunar Module of Apollo Grumman Aero., Bethpage, N.Y., 1939-72; gen. engr. U.S. Army Material Systems Analysis Activity, Aberdeen Proving Ground, Md., from 1972. Organizer 5 nat. engring. confs., 1940—. Author: Advanced System Development Management, 1977; contbr. articles to profl. jours. Recipient Cert. of Appreciation 1st U.S. Army, 1959, Rear Admiral Coates award U.S. Naval Air Systems Command, 1962, Outstanding Svc. award, 1973, Spl. Recognition award Am. Inst. Plant Engrs., 1978, Systems Effectiveness & Safety medal AIAA, 1983. Fellow ASME (life, local and nat. chairs, Centennial medal 1980, Flag award 1989), Am. Soc. for Quality Control (local and nat. chairs, Brambaugh award 1972), N.Y. Acad. Scis. (bd. dirs., Laskovitz Gold medal 1964); mem. Cosmos Club. Roman Catholic. Achievements include introduction of concept of reliability and maintainability into the aerospace industry, quality control of computer software, concept of combat resilience for U.S. Army battlefield systems; performance of first failure mode and effect analysis in the U.S.; establishment of systems reliability requirements for Apollo mission. Died Mar. 4, 2005.

COVER, FRANKLIN EDWARD, actor; b. Cleve., Nov. 20, 1928; s. Franklin Held and Britta (Schreck) C.; m. Mary Bradford Stone, Jan. 30, 1965; children: Bradford Franklin, Susan Henderson. BA, Denison U., 1951; MA, Western Res. U., 1954, M.F.A., 1955. Debut at Cain Park Theatre, Cleve., 1945; mem. acting staff, Cleve. Playhouse, 1954-58; appeared at New York Theatre in Julius Caesar, 1959, Phoenix Theatre (under Ford grant) in Henry IV, She Stoops to Conquer, Plough and the Stars, The Octoroon, Hamlet, 1960-61, Old Globe Theatre, San Diego, in The Old Boy, 1992, The Best of the Jeffersons on Stage, 1993-94; Broadway plays include Giants Sons of Giants, 1961-62, Calculated Risk, 1962-63, Abraham Cochrane, 1964, Any Wednesday, 1965-66, The Investigation, 1966, A Warm Body, 1967, The Freaking Out of Stephanie Blake, 1967, Forty Carats, 1968-70, Applause, 1972, The Killdeer, 1974, Wild Honey, 1986-87, Born Yesterday, 1988-89, MAME Tour, 1994; motion pictures include Mirage, 1964, What's So Bad About Feeling Good, 1966, Such Good Friends, 1969, The Great Gatsby, 1978, The Stepford Wives, 1973, The Day the Bubble Burst, 1980, A Woman Called Golda, 1981, Wall Street, 1987, Likewise, 1987, Lame Ducks, 1991, The Turn, 1996, Almost Heroes, 1998; appeared on television shows The Jackie Gleason Show, 1960s, The Investigation, 1967, Play of the Week, 1960, Edge of Night, 1967, Love of Life, 1960, Trials of O'Brien, 1962, Naked City, 1959, Defenders, 1960, Armstrong Circle Theatre, 1960, The Doctors, 1966, What Makes Sammy Run, 1959, The Secret Storm, 1969, All My Children, 1970, Change at 125th St, 1973, They Came from Outer Space, 1990, Who's the Boss, 1991, In the Heat of the Night, 1991, ER, 1994, Living Single, 1994, Batman: The Animated Series (voice only), 1994, Coach, 1996, Too Something, 1996, Mad About You, 1998, Will and Grace, 1998; appeared in TV movies Shortwalk to Daylight, 1972, Connection, 1973, The Hot House, 1987, Colombo: A Trace of Murder, 1997; performed starring role as Tom Willis in The Jeffersons, 1974-85; performed title role in Macbeth at White House state dinner for Pres. Kennedy, 1961. Vestryman Ch. of the Resurrection, 1970s, warden, 1983, 88-89; hon. trustee Cleve. Playhouse. Lt. USAF, 1951-53. Mem. AFTRA, SAG (bd. dirs.), Equity, Omicron Delta Kappa, Kappa Sigma. Died Feb. 5, 2006.

COWARD, JAMES W., management consultant; b. Buffalo, Mar. 1, 1948; s. Willis G. and Gladys (Woodwell) C.; m. Bonnie K. Heberlig, June 14, 1969 (div. 1985); children: Tracy, Julie. BBA cum laude, Clarkson U., 1970; MBA magna cum laude, Syracuse U., 1972. V.p. Hickman Coward & Wattles, Buffalo, 1972-84; v.p. adminstrn. Air Niagara, Buffalo, 1984; mgmt. cons. Elma, N.Y., 1984-88; pres. CONI, Inc., Glenwood, N.Y., from 1988. Bd. dirs. Niagara Frontier Food Terminal, Buffalo. Served with USNG, 1970-76. Recipient Student Achievement award Wall St. Jour., 1970. Mem. Internat. Food Service Execs. Lodges: Rotary. Republican. Avocations: coaching hockey, snow and water skiing. Died Jan. 31, 2005.

COX, HOWARD WAYNE, publishing executive; b. Lawton, Okla., Apr. 27, 1938; s. George L. and Teresa (Woodward) C.; m. Fay Elliff, Oct. 7, 1962; children: Regina Cox Hogenson, Rhonda Cox. BA, Okla. State U., 1961. Salesperson Southwestern Assocs., Denison, Tex., 1961-64; co-owner Grayson Pub. Co., Denison, 1964-75; owner Cox Pub. Co., Denison, from 1975. Mem. Ind. Free Papers of Am. (pres. 1987-88), Tex. Community Newspaper Assn. (sec. 1989-90). Republican. Episcopalian. Home: Denison, Tex. Died Aug. 14, 2004.

COX, LILLIAN THOMPSON, manufacturing executive; b. Rotan, Tex., Jan. 10, 1918; d. Parker Odus and Sena Belle (Gruben) C.; m. William Truesdale Cox, Apr. 19, 1946 (dec. May 1968); children: Deborah Ann Cox McCleary, Norma Jean Cox Loving, William Truesdale Jr. Asst. mgr. Cox Vending Co., San Antonio, 1946-59; real estate investor San Antonio, from 1950; mgr. Cox Mfg. Co., San Antonio, 1956-59, corp. officer, 1959-68, pres., 1968-82, also chmn. bd. dirs. Republican. Mem. Christian Ch. Home: San Antonio, Tex. Died May 24, 2004.

COX, PETER WINSTON, newspaper editor; b. N.Y.C., Aug. 13, 1937; s. Oscar Sidney and Louise Black Cox; m. Eunice Ann Theodore, Apr. 16, 1965; children: Sara Winston, Anthony Oscar. BA in English, Yale U., 1959. Editor Adirondack Daily Enterprise, Saranac Lake, N.Y., 1961-65, Bath (Maine) Daily Times, 1965-67; mng. editor Bath-Brunswick (Maine) Times-Record, 1967-68; co-founder, pub. Maine Times, Topsham, 1968-86, editor, 1972-86, 92-94; columnist, from 1994. Former pres. Wolfe Neck Farm Found., Freeport, Maine, Maine Civil Liberties Union, Portland, 1985-87; bd. dirs. ACLU, N.Y.C., 1989, Maine Audubon Soc., Falmouth, 1988-92; former mem. steering com. Eco-Eco, Bar Harbor, Maine; former trustee Portland Mus. Art. Recipient Ann. Conv. award Natural Resources Coun., Augusta, Maine, 1980, Mo. medal U. Mo., Columbia, 1976. Avocations: skiing, tennis, gardening, cooking. Home: Georgetown, Maine. Died Nov. 18, 2004.

COZZARELLI, NICHOLAS ROBERT, molecular biologist, educator; b. Jersey City, Mar. 26, 1938; s. Nicholas and Catherine (Meluso) C.; m. Linda Angela Ambrosini, July 28, 1967; 1 child, Laura Amelia. AB, Princeton U., 1960; PhD, Harvard U., 1966. Postdoctoral fellow dept. biochemistry Stanford U. Med. Sch., Palo Alto, Calif., 1966-68; asst. prof. dept. biochemistry U. Chgo., 1968-70, asst. prof. depts. biochemistry, biophysics and theoretical biology, 1970-74, assoc. prof., 1974-77, prof., 1977-82; prof. dept. molecular biology U. Calif., Berkeley, 1982-89, prof., div. biochemistry and molecular biology, dept. molecular and cell biology, 1989—2006, chmn. dept., 1986-89, dir. virus lab., 1986-90. Mem. editl. bd. Jour. Biol. Chemistry, 1988-2006, Cell, 1983-86; mem. editl. adv. bd. Biochemistry, 1982-86; contbr. articles to profl. jours. Mem. NAS (editor Procs. 1995-2006), AAAS, Am. Soc. for Microbiology, Am. Soc. for Biol. Chemistry. Democrat. Avocations: reading, theater. Died Mar. 19, 2006.

COZZOLINO, JOHN MICHAEL, JR., management educator; b. New Haven, Dec. 17, 1940; s. John M. and Lucile (Violante) C.; m. Carol Ann Lombardi, Sept. 7, 1963; children: William John, Stephen Michael. BS, MIT, 1962, MS, 1964, PhD, 1967; MA (hon.), U. Pa., Phila., 1972. Assoc. prof. The Wharton Sch., Phila., 1967-82; prof. decision scis. Coll. Ins., N.Y.C., 1985-86; rsch. dir. Ins. Svcs. Office, N.Y.C., 1986-89; assoc. prof. mgmt. Pace U., N.Y.C., from 1989, dir. Underwriting Edn. Inst. Pleasantville, N.Y., from 1992. Author: Operations Research for Management, 1975, Management of Oil and Gas Exploration Risk, 1977. Home: Norwalk, Conn. Died Mar. 8, 2005.

CRAIG, JAMES ALEXANDER, librarian; b. Toledo, Nov. 26, 1936; s. James Alexander and Marguerite (Murbach) C.; m. Kathleen Geerlings, Aug. 28, 1965. BA, Miami U., 1958; cert., Brunnsvik Folkhogskola, Ludvika, Sweden, 1959; MA, Toledo U., 1966; postgrad., Wayne State U., 1970. Cert. tchr., librarian, Mich. Tchr. Riley Jr. High Sch., Livonia, Mich., 1961-69; librarian Churchill High Sch., Livonia, 1970-71, Traverse City (Mich.) High Sch., from 1971. State com. North Cen. Assn. Schs., Ann Arbor, Mich., 1987—; bd. dirs. Traverse Bay Edn. Credit Union, Traverse City; facilities planning com. Traverse City Schs., 1987-88. Named Outstanding Educator Traverse City C. of C., 1987, Outstanding Person in Edn. M.E.A. Coordinating Council, 1988. Mem. ALA, Mich. Edn. Assn. Media in Edn. Democrat. Presbyterian. Avocations: cross country ski racing, sailing, swimming, tennis, racquetball. Home: Traverse City, Mich. Died Jan. 29, 2005.

CRAIG, ROY PHILLIP, writer, educator, rancher; b. Durango, Colo., May 10, 1924; s. Philip Howard and Anna Dorothea Craig. BA, U. Colo., 1948; MS, Calif. Inst. Tech., 1950; PhD, Iowa State U., 1952. Group leader Dow Chem. Co., Denver, 1952-60; assoc. prof., coord. phys. scis. U. Colo., Boulder, 1961-66, rsch. assoc. UFO study, 1966-67; vis. prof. U. Hawaii, Honolulu, 1968-69; writer, lectr., rancher La Plata County, Colo., from 1969. Cons. Dow Chem. Co., Midland, Mich., 1959; vis. prof. Clarkson Coll. Tech., Potsdam, N.Y., 1962-65, Colo. Coll., Colorado Springs, 1979, State of Ponape, 1981; curriculum cons. U. Hawaii, Honolulu, 1969; spkr. Foresters, Soil Conservationists, Cattlemen's Assn., Bur. Indian Affairs, Colo. LWV, Colo. Edn. Assn., 1971-84; pres. Four Corners Rsch. Inst., Durango, 1975-86. Co-author: Scientific Study of UFOs, 1969; author: UFOs: An Insider's View of the Official Quest for Evidence, 1995; contbr. articles to profl. jours. Pres. La Plata County Landowners Assn., 1974-92. With U.S. Army, 1943-46, ETO. Mem. Four Corners Llama/Alpaca Owners Assn., Phi Beta Kappa, Sigma Xi. Avocations: skiing, white-water rafting, chess. Died Mar. 17, 2004.

CRANKSHAW, JOHN HAMILTON, mechanical engineer; b. Canton, Ohio, Aug. 29, 1914; s. Frederick Weir and Mary (Lashels) C.; m. Wilma Chaffee Thurlow, June 5, 1940; children: Wilma Jean, John H., Geoffrey Thurlow. BSME, MIT, MS, 1940. Registered profl. engr., Pa. Rotating engr. GE, 1940-41; sect. engr. mech. design sect. Motor Engr. divsn. Locomotive Car Equipment, Erie, Pa., 1946-52; exec. engr. J.A. Zurn Mfg. Co., Am. Flexible Coupling Co., 1952-54, v.p. engring., 1954; exec. v.p., dir. Zurn Industries, Inc., mng. dir. R & D divsn., until 1957; pres. Dynetics, Inc., Erie, from 1957, Dynetic Sys., Inc., Erie, from 1970. Expert witness numerous product liability cases. Contbr. articles to profl. jours. Mem. adv. coun. Gannon U.; chmn. Erie Sewer Authority. Maj. Ordnance Dept., AUS, 1941-46. Fellow ASME; mem. ASTM, Soc. Automotive Engrs., Assn. Iron and Steel Engrs., Soc. Exptl. Stress Analysis, Soc. Naval Archs. and Marine Engrs., Am. Soc. Metals, Am. Soc. Lubricating Engrs., Pa. Soc. Profl. Engrs., Erie Engring. Socs. Coun., MIT Club (N.Y.C.), Sigma Xi. Achievements include 25 U.S. and 5 foreign patents; invention and design of main propulsion couplings and clutches for nuclear powered submarines and Navy and Coast Guard surface ships. Died June 15, 2005.

CRANMORE, ROBERT, engineering executive, consultant; b. Bklyn., Oct. 29, 1927; s. George Harlow and Agnes (Bogert) C.; m. Gladys E. Fiske, June 20, 1949 (div. July 27, 1965); children: Patricia E., Donna J., Robert Jr.; m. Dorothea E. Butler, June 15, 1968. Designer Associated Engrs. Inc., Springfield, Mass., 1950-57; design engr. Millers Falls Co., Greenfield, Mass., 1957-64; design engr. lamp div. I.T.T, Lynn, Mass., 1964-70; chief engr. Circle Machine Co., Seabrook, N.H., 1970-72; cons. engr. Concept Engring. Inc., Ft. Lauderdale, Fla., from 1972; owner, cons. engr. Osprey Inc., Ft. Lauderdale, from 1987. Bd. dirs. Lens Care Acquisition Inc., Ft. Lauderdale, 1987—. Patentee in field. With USN, 1944-46. Avocations: swimming, travel, photography, model building. Home: Plantation, Fla. Died July 30, 2005.

CRASSWELLER, ROBERT DOELL, retired lawyer, writer; b. Duluth, Minn., Sept. 17, 1915; s. Arthur Hallifax and Mary Elizabeth (Doell) C.; m. Mildred Elizabeth Clarke, Mar. 21, 1942; children: Peter, Karen Farbman, Pamela Baldino. BA, Carleton Coll., 1937; LLB, Harvard U., 1941. Bar: Minn. 1941, N.Y. 1960. Pvt. practice, Duluth, Minn., 1942-43; econ. warfare posts U.S. Dept. State, Washington, 1943-45; ptnr. McCabe, Gruber, Clure, Donovan & Crassweller, Duluth, Minn., 1946-51; mining exec. West Indies Mining Corp., San Juan, P.R., 1951-53; counsel Pan Am. Airways, N.Y.C., 1954-67; vis. fellow Coun. Fgn. Rels., N.Y.C., 1967-70; vis. prof. Bklyn. Coll., Sarah Lawrence, N.Y.C., 1969-70; staff atty. ITT, N.Y.C., 1970-74, gen. coun. Lat. Am., 1975-81. Author: Trujillo: Life and Times of a Caribbean Dictator, 1966, The Caribbean Community, 1972, Perón and the Enigmas of Argentina, 1986; reviewer (books) for Fgn. Affairs, 1968-81. Dir. Forum for World Affairs, Stamford, Conn., 1986-87. Mem. Internat. Assn. Torch Clubs (Chapel Hill Club v.p. 1994-95), Soc. Automotive Historians. Republican. Avocations: gardening, travel, reading, writing, antique cars. Home: Chapel Hill, NC. Died July 18, 2004.

CRAVENS, JAMES ELLIOT, hospital supply company executive; b. Los Angeles, June 2, 1949; s. James Elliott and Hazel Nelle (Harvey) C.; m. Janice Mary Dziekan, Nov. 29, 1974; children: Mary Nelle, James John. BS, UCLA, 1973. Med. specialist Burroughs-Wellcome Research, Triangle Park, Calif., 1974-77; parenteral specialist Travenol Labs., Deerfield, Ill., 1977-79; chmn. Dealex Hosp. Supply, Brea, Calif., from 1979. Founder, pres. Packaging Techs., Brea, 1982-84; founder, v.p. Pathfinder Group, Horsham, Pa., 1984-88; v.p. sales and mktg. Implant Techs. Inc., Mpls. Bd. dirs. Diamond Bar (Calif.) Community Schs., 1985-86. Mem. Nat. Intravenous Therapy Assn. Democrat. Roman Catholic. Avocations: music, guitar, photography. Home: Fullerton, Calif. Died Jan. 19, 2004.

CRAWFORD, DEAN ERNEST, manufacturing executive, accountant; b. Topeka, Jan. 15, 1940; s. Ernest Percy and Beulah Marie (Jones) C.; m. Peggy Marie Huffman, Nov. 23, 1966; children: Kelly, Karla, Kevin. CPA, Kans. Acct. John Weatherwax, CPA, Lawrence, Kans., 1964-65, Lesh, Bradley and Barrand, CPA's, Lawrence, 1966-72; pvt. practice acctg. Lawrence, 1972-78; comptroller Native Am. Research Co., Lawrence, 1978-80, Compton Industries, Inc., Lawrence, 1980-81; sec. treas, chief fin. officer D and D Tire, Inc., Lawrence, from 1981. Home: Lawrence, Kans. Died July 28, 2004.

CRAWFORD, RUSSELL EUGENE, lawyer; b. Chgo., July 13, 1939; s. Russell E. and Marie (Welter) C.; m. Sandra Kay Tharp, Oct. 1, 1986. BA, U. Iowa, 1961, JD, 1965. Bar: Iowa 1965, Fla. 1973, U.S. Dist. Ct. (mid. dist.) Fla. 1978, U.S. Ct. Appeals (5th cir.) 1980, U.S. Ct. Appeals (11th cir.) 1982, U.S. Dist. Ct. (so. dist.) Fla. 1980, U.S. Ct. Appeals (4th dist.) 1987. Asst. state's atty. 9th Jud. Cir./Orange County, Orlando, Fla., 1974-75; pvt. practice Orlando, from 1975. Faculty mem. Prosecutor/Pub. Defender Tng. Course, 1993-97. Author: Florida Criminal Practice and Procedure, 1994. Chmn. Orange County Rep. Party, Orlando, 1980-88. Capt. USAF, 1965-74. Decorated Bronze Star medal, Air Force Commendation medal with Oak Leaf Cluster, Vietnam Svc. medal. Mem. Fla. Bar Assn. (exec. coun. criminal law sect. 1994-97, criminal rules com. 1995-97), Cen. Fla. Criminal Def. Attys. Assn. (pres. 1978, 90), Tiger Bay Club (pres. 1990). Home: Winter Park, Fla. Died Aug. 23, 2005.

CREER, JAMES READ, financial officer; b. Ogden, Utah, Oct. 26, 1942; s. Harold and Geraldine (Jacobson) C.; m. Ann L. Curran, Aug. 7, 1964 (div. Aug. 1974); children: Wendy, Kellie, Mark, Jennifer; m. Carolyn Rudd, Jan. 11, 1985. BS in Acctg., U. Utah, 1968. CPA. Staff acct. PMM & Co., L.A., 1968-71, sr. acct. Salt Lake City, 1971-72, Haynie, Tebbs & Smith, Salt Lake City, 1972-73; ptnr. Roberts & Creer, Salt Lake City, 1973-74; pvt. practice Salt Lake City, 1974-81; pres., CEO Johnstone Supply, Salt

Lake City, from 1995; v.p., CFO ACW Enterprises Inc., Salt Lake City, from 1989; pres. Creer Corp., from 1995. Acctg. instr. Utah Tech. Coll., Stevens-Henegar Coll. Bus., 1973-76. With USMC, 1960-63. Mem. Children's Justice Ctr. (adv. bd.), Rotary (pres. so. Salt Lake City chpt. 1989-90, Paul Harris fellow 1988). Republican. Mem. Lds Ch. Avocations: hunting, fishing, boating, golf, travel. Home: Salt Lake City, Utah. Died Dec. 8, 2004.

CREMERS, ALBERT LOUIS, manufacturing executive; b. Columbus, Mich., July 16, 1940; s. Albert and Virginia Mary (Fraley) C.; m. Veronica Jean Galvin, May 1, 1965; children: John Albert, Kimberly Ann. Grad. cum. laude, Port Huron Jr. Coll., 1959; BS, U.S. Merchant Marine Acad., 1963; MBA, U. Akron, 1971. Engr. Am. Export, N.Y.C., 1963-64, Burns & Roe, N.Y.C., 1964-65, Western Electric, N.Y.C., 1965-67; program mgr. Babcock & Wilcox, Barberton, Ohio, from 1967. Mem. Jaycees. Lodges: K.C., Elks. Republican. Roman Catholic. Avocations: reading, gardening. Home: Pompano Beach, Fla. Died Mar. 5, 2005.

CRENSHAW, MARILYN JEAN, mathematics educator; b. Stewartsville, Mo., Apr. 27, 1947; d. Gilbert Gale and Mildred Virginia (Thompson) Whiteman; m. James Tiffin Crenshaw, June 20, 1965; children: Amelia Gale, Tiffiny Lee. BA in Edn., U. Mo., Kansas City, 1969; MS, U. Mo., Rolla, 1973. Tchr. Lathrop (Mo.) Sch. Dist., 1969-73, Adult Basic Edn., St. Joseph, Mo., 1971-75; instr. N.W. Mo. C.C., St. Joseph, from 1992. Mem. sch. bd. Lathrop Schs., 1986—, pres. 1990-92, 93—. NSF scholar, 1971-73. Mem. Merchants Assn. (pres. 1979-81). Avocations: sewing, painting, crafting. Home: Lathrop, Mo. Died Aug. 27, 2004.

CRESSEY, DOUGLAS B., insurance company executive; b. Red Oak, Iowa, July 9, 1946; s. William C. and Suzanne (Nelson) C.; m. Cynthia Jill Moyer, Dec. 12, 1987. BS in Social Sci., Colo. State U., 1969. Cert. ins. counselor. Pres., gen. mgr. Fulenwider Insurors, Denver, 1976-79; sr. v.p. VanGilder Ins. Corp., Denver, 1979-89; exec. v.p. Rollins Hudig Hall of Colo., Denver, 1989-91, Rolling Hudig Hall of Ga., Atlanta, 1991-94; pres. Aspen Assocs., Inc., Atlanta, from 1995; dir. risk mgmt., dir. human resources Torrey Homes, Atlanta, 1995-97. Mem. nat. coun. Home Ins. Co., Denver, 1986-90; mem. guest faculty Cont. Legal Edn. Colo., Denver, 1987; mem. com. govt. rels. Ind. Ins. Agents Assn., 1986-89; instr. Bldg. Owners and Mgrs. Assn., Denver, 1985-91. Contbr. articles to profl. jours. Mem. gov.'s task force, tort reform State of Colo., Denver, 1986-87. Recipient Colo. Profl. Ins. Agent of the Yr. Profl. Inst. Agents of Colo., 1986. Mem. Ind. Ins. Agents of Ga., Profl. Ins. Agents Ga., Colo. State U. Alumni (life), Alpha Tau Omega. Avocations: golf, tennis, international travel, scuba diving, photography. Died Jan. 27, 2004.

CREW, WILLIAM LUNSFORD, lawyer; b. Pleasant Hill, N.C., Oct. 29, 1917; s. James Winfield and Texas S. Crew; m. Nancy H. Crew, Nov. 14, 1940 (divorced); m. Dorothy Salter. BA, U. N.C., 1939, LLB, 1941. Pvt. practice, Roanoke Rapids, N.C., from 1941. Atty. Halifax (N.C.) County Dept. Social Svcs., 1972—, City of Roanoke Rapids, 1977-97. State senator State of N.C., 1953-65. Lt. USN, 1943-46. Mem. ABA, N.C. Acad. Trial Lawyers, N.C. Bar Assn. Democrat. Avocations: hunting, fishing. Died Oct. 10, 2004.

CRIPPEN, JUANITA WITHERELL, elementary school educator; b. Burke, N.Y., Oct. 31, 1912; d. George and Nellie (Ennis) Witherell; m. Carter Martin Crippen, Sept. 22, 1944; children: Daniel F., Bonnie J. Crippen Trippany. Tchrs. permanent cert., Potsdam Normal Tchrs. Coll., 1936. Tchr. Local Rural One-Room Dist., Burke and Chateaugay, N.Y., 1931-33, 36-55; first grade tchr. Chateauguay Ctrl. Sch., 1955-77; migrant outreach tutor Migrant Tutorial Outreach, SUNY, Potsdam, N.Y., from 1978. Recipient Presdl. Recognition for 65 years of tchg. Pres. Clinton, 2000; named Oldest Tchr. in N.Y. Still Tchg., N.Y. State United Tchrs. Union, 2000. Democrat. Methodist. Avocations: reading, golf, walking. Home: Burke, NY. Died Aug. 17, 2004.

CRISTOFALO, VINCENT JOSEPH, biochemist, educator; b. Phila., Mar. 19, 1933; s. Charles P. and Adeline A. (Molluro) C.; m. Margaret J. Follet, May 30, 1964; children: Margaret, Jean, Elizabeth, Carolyn, Catherine, Helen. BS in Biology and Chemistry, St. Joseph's Coll., 1955; MA in Physiology, Temple U., 1958; PhD in Physiology/Biochemistry (NSF fellow), U. Del., 1962; MA (hon.), U. Pa., 1982. Asst. instr. in gen. biology Temple U., 1957-58; postdoctoral fellow and research assoc. Temple U. (Fels Research Inst., Sch. Medicine), 1961-63, instr. dept. chemistry, 1962-71; grad. research asst. dept. biol. scis. U. Del., 1958-59, grad. research fellow, 1959-60; asst. prof. biochemistry div. animal biology Sch. Vet. Medicine, U. Pa., 1967-69, asso. prof., 1969-74, prof., 1974-90, prof. emeritus, 1990—2006. Assoc. Wistar Inst., Phila., 1963-69, assoc. prof., 1969-76, prof., 1976-90; research assoc. Phila. Geriatric Ctr.; dir. U. Pa. Ctr. for Study of Aging, 1978-90; dir. Ctr. Gerontol. Rsch. Med. Coll. Pa., Lankenau Inst. for Med. Rsch., 1999-2004; mem. U. Pa. Faculty Arts and Scis.; chmn. Gordon Conf. on Biology of Aging, 1977; mem. com. on med. edn. and geriatrics Inst. Medicine Nat. Acad. Scis., 1977-78; mem. com. on models for biomed. research Nat. Acad. Sci., 1983-85; program chmn. XIII Internat. Congress of Gerontology, 1984-85, 4th Decennial Internat. Rev. Conf. on Cell Culture, 1984-86; mem. ext. rev. com. Burke Rehab. Ctr. Contbr. numerous articles to profl. jours.; editor: (with others) Growth, Nutrition, and Metabolism of Cells in Culture, vol. 1, 1972, vol. 2, 1972, vol. 3, 1977, Pharmacological Interventions of the Aging Process, 1978; editorial bd.: Mechanism of Ageing and Development, In Vitro, Gerontologist, Cell Biology Internat. Reports, 1976-86, Ann. Rev. Gerontology and Geriatrics; interim editor: Jour. Gerontology, 1976-78; editor Jour. Gerontology Biol. Scis.; editorial cons.: (with others) Exptl. Aging Research. Mem. adv. bd. The Ralston House. Fellow AAAS;, USPHS postdoctoral fellow; NIH grantee, 1972-79; recipient Geriatric Leadership Acad. award NIA, 1986-89, 90. Fellow Gerontol. Soc. Am. (chmn. research/edn. com., sect. biology 1974, chmn. pub. policy com. 1986-88, chmn. task force on interorganizational relations, pres. 1990, Kleemeier award 1982, Brookdale award 1983, Keston lectr. 1986); mem. AAAS, Tissue Culture Assn. (exec. bd. 1978-82, chmn. publs. com. 1978-80), Internat. Assn. Gerontology (N.Am. regional com.), Am. Physiol. Soc., Am. Soc. Cell Biology, John Morgan Soc., Soc. Exptl. Biology and Medicine (elected councillor 1987-91), Inst. Medicine Com. to Devel. A Nat. Research Agenda on Aging, Sci. Adv. Bd., Lankenau Med. Research Ctr., Sigma Xi. Home: Narberth, Pa. Died May 8, 2006.

CRNIC, LINDA SMITH, psychobiologist, educator; b. Ft. Wayne, Ind., Mar. 29, 1948; d. Herman Edward and Patricia Ellen (Leeth) Smith; m. David Michael Crnic, June 21, 1969 (div. June 1976); m. Stanley Loyd Wilks, May 3, 1986; 1 child, Michael Smith Wilks. AB, U. Chgo., 1970; MA, U. Ill., Chgo., 1972, PhD, 1975. Postdoctoral fellow U. Colo. Sch. Medicine, Denver, 1975-77, prof., from 1994, asst. prof., 1979-85, assoc. prof., 1985-94. Mem. psychobiol., biol. and neuroscis. subcoms. of the mental health AIDS rsch. rev. com. NIMH, 1989-92; mem. mental retardation rsch. com. NICHD. Contbr. articles to profl. jours. NIH grantee, 1975—; NIMH rsch. career devel. awardee, 1987-92. Mem. Internat. Soc. Devel. Psychobiology (sec.-treas. 1983-86, pres. 1997), Soc. Neurosci. (chmn. Rocky Mountain region group 1983-86), Animal Behavior Soc. Home: Denver, Colo. Died Sept. 11, 2004.

CROCKETT, MARY LOU, real estate broker, city commisioner; b. Inglewood, Calif., Oct. 2, 1938; d. Otto P. and Lorene (Mitchell) Cripps; m. Hugh Crockett, Dec. 26, 1958 (div. 1977); 1 child, Patricia Lee. BA, UCLA, 1959. Licensed Real Estate Broker. Sch. tchr. Orangedale Elementary Sch., Phoenix, 1959-62; ptnr. Cripps Crockett, Realtors, Westchester, Calif., from 1963. Pres., bd. dirs. Venice-Marina del Rey Multiple Listing Svc.; bd. dirs. Venice-Marina del Rey Bd. of Realtors. Contbr. articles to community newspaper. V.p. Westchester Vitalization Corp., 1988-89; co-founder Community Plans, Inc., Westchester, Friends of the Library, Westchester and Loyola Branches; bd. dirs. L.A. Bd. Airport Commrs., 1978-84, pres., 1980-81; hon. mayor Westchester-Playa del Rey, 1988-89; bd. dirs. Bd. Libr. Commrs., City of L.A., pres., 1984. Mem. Calif. Assn. Realtors, Inglewood Bd. of Realtors, Nat. Assn. Realtors, Venice and Marina del Rey Bd. Realtors (bd. dirs.), Calif. Assn. Libr. Trustees & Commrs. (pres. 1990—), Venice-Marina del Rey Bd. Realtors (bd. dirs.) Republican. Christian Scientist. Avocations: clogging, hiking, travel, aviation. Home: Los Angeles, Calif. Died Oct. 15, 2004.

CROSS, TRAVIS, foundation administrator; b. Salem, Oreg., Mar. 23, 1927; s. Henry Alexander and Belvie Loutisha (Gilbert) C.; m. Beverly Jean Briggs, Oct. 30, 1949; children: Craig, Jennifer, Sara, Paul. BA, Stanford U., 1949; D Pub. Svc. (hon.), Willamette U., 1969. Dir. info. and alumni affairs Willamette U., Salem, 1949-50; chancellor's staff Oreg. System Higher Edn., Eugene, 1950-57; asst. to sec. of state State of Oreg., Salem, 1957-59, asst. to gov., 1959-66; pres. Travis Cross & Assocs., Salem, 1966-69; v.p. univ. rels. U. Calif., Berkeley, 1969-71; v.p. exec. rels. Beverly Enterprises, Pasadena, Calif., 1971-75; asst. adminstr. St. Vincent Hosp. & Med. Ctr., Portland, Oreg., 1975-88, asst. to adminstr., 1988-92; trustee Meyer Meml. Trust, Portland, 1982-97. Cons. in field. Transition officer Oreg. Gov.-Elect, Salem, 1966, 79; spl. asst. Romney for Pres., Lansing, Mich., 1967-68; exec. dir. St. Vincent Med. Found., Portland, 1975-81; chmn. Oreg. Commn. Pub. Broadcasting, Portland, 1979-82; mem. Oreg. Jud. Fitness Commn., Portland, 1982-84. Recipient Disting. Svc. award City of Salem. 1968. Home: Portland, Oreg. Died Jan. 1, 2004.

CROSSFIELD, ALBERT SCOTT, aeronautical science consultant, pilot; b. Berkeley, Calif., Oct. 2, 1921; s. Albert Scott and Lucia (Dwyer) C.; m. Alice Virginia Knoph, Apr. 21, 1943; children: Becky Lee, Thomas Scott, Paul Stanley, Anthony Scott, Sally Virginia, Robert Scott. BS in Aero. Engring., U. Wash., 1949, MS in Aero. Sci., 1950; D.Sc. (hon.), Fla. Inst. Tech., 1982. Lic. pilot. Mem. U. Wash. staff charge wind tunnel operation, 1946-50; aerodynamicist, project engr., also pilot research airplanes X-1, X-4, X-5, D-558-I and II, X-F-92, F-102, F-100, F-86, Nat. Adv. Com. for Aeronautics (NACA), 1950-55; participation proposal, design, 1st pilot X-15 research aircraft, design specialist, also chief engring. test pilot Los Angeles div. N.Am. Aviation, Inc., 1955-61, dir. test and quality assurance, space and info. systems div., 1961-66, tech. dir. research and engring., space and info. systems div., 1966-67; v.p. flight research and devel. div. Eastern Air Lines, Miami, Fla., 1967-71, staff v.p. transp. systems devel. Washington, 1971-74; sr. v.p. Hawker Siddeley Aviation Inc., Washington, 1974; tech. cons. House Com. on Sci. and Tech., Washington, 1977-93. Spl. work on the WS-131b, Apollo, Saturn S-II, Paraglider programs. Author: Always Another Dawn, 1960; also articles. Mem. aviation and space hist. preservation com. Calif. Mus. Found., mem. Aerospace Walk of Honor, City of Lancaster, 1990. Lt. USN, 1942-46, WWII, USNR. Recipient Lawrence Sperry award Inst. Aero. Sci., 1954, Octave Chanute award, 1958, Flight Achievement award Am. Astronautics Soc., 1959, Astronautics award Am. Rocket Soc., 1960, Commendation award County L.A. Bd. Suprs., 1960, Internat. Clifford B. Harmon Trophy, 1961, Achievement award Nat. Aeronautics Assn., 1961, Collier Trophy, 1961, Charter award, 1963, Elder Statesman of Aviation award, 1983, Godfry Cabot award Aero Club New England, 1961, John J. Montgomery award Nat. Soc. Aerospace Profls., 1962, Kitty Hawk Meml. award City of L.A., 1969, Al J. Engel award We. Res. Hist. Soc., 1983, Meritorious Svc. to Aviation award Nat. Bus. Aircraft Assn., 1984, Disting. Alumnus award U. Wash., 1986, Crown Cir. award Nat. Congress Aviation and Space Edn., 1988, A. Scott Crossfield Elem. Sch. award Fairfax County Sch. Bd., 1988, Bernt Balchin Trophy, N.Y. State Air Force Assn., 1988, Glenn A. Gilbert Meml. award Air Traffic Control Assn., 1990, Aerospace Walk of Honor, City of Lancaster, Calif., 1990, Disting. Pub. Svc. medal NASA, 1993, Cert. of Appreciation, FAA, 1993, Ho. of Reps., 1993, Gold Air medal Fedn. Aeronautique Internat., Sun City, South Africa, 1995, Ray Lien award Internat. Sport Aviation Mus. and Sun 'N Fun, 1999, Ray Lien award for aviation edn. excellence, 2000, Glenn L. Martin medal, 2000, Lifetime Achievement award Nat. Air & Space Mus., 2000, Crystal Eagle award Aero Club No. Calif., 2002, Gathering of Eagles Recognition USAF, 2003, Aerospace Laureate, Aviation Week and Space Tech., 2004, CAP Disting. Svc. award, 2004; named Lareate for Aeronatics/Propulsion, Aviation Week and Space Tech., 1959, 2003; inducted into Nat. Aviation Hall of Fame, 1983, Internat. Aerospace Hall of Fame, 1963, Internat. Space Hall of Fame, 1988, Va. Aviation Hall of Fame, 1998; AIAA hon. fellow; named One of 100 Pilots of the Century, 2003 Fellow AIAA (hon., chmn. flight test tech. com. 1963-64, Disting. lectr. 1987, 88, 89, Pathfinder award 1999, hon. 1999), Soc. Exptl. Test Pilots (co-founder, chmn. East Coast sect. 1976-77, past exec. advisor, Ivan C. Kincheloe award 1960, Ray E. Tenhoff award 1978), Inst. Aerospace Scis., Aerospace Med. Assn. (hon.); mem. Am. Soc. Qualtiy Control (sect., chmn. L.A. 1964-66, Outstanding Contbn. to Quality Control award 1967), Flying Physicians Assn. (hon., Man of Yr. 1961), Exptl. Aircarft Assn. (hon., Svc. to Sport Aviation award 1979, cert. of appreciation 1982), First Flight Soc. (life), Sterman Alumnus Club, Mustang Pilot Soc. (charter), OX-5 Club, Nat. Aviation Club (pres. 1983, gov. emeritus, Achievement award 1960), Nat. Space Club (Dr. Wernher von Braun Space Flight trophy), Order of Daedalians (hon.), Sigma Xi, Tau Beta Pi. Republican. Episcopalian. Achievements include being the first man to fly the X-15 rocket-powered jet and made aeronautical history in 1953 by becoming the first pilot to fly faster than Mach 2 (twice the speed of sound). Home: Herndon, Va. Died Apr. 20, 2006.

CROSSON, PIERRE ROGER, economist, researcher; b. Dallas, Oct. 28, 1926; s. Earl Theodore and Dena Adalaide (Janelli) C.; m. Carrie Sue West, Sept. 2, 1950; children: David, Anthony, Dena, Amelie. BA, U. Tex., 1948; PhD, Columbia U., 1964. Economist U.S. Dept. Commerce, Washington, 1951-52, U.S. Dept. Interior, Washington, 1952-54, Tenn. Valley Authority, Chattanooga, 1954-55; economist, assoc. dir. econs. Bank of Am., San Francisco, 1955-63; sr. economist Nat. Planning Assn., Washington, 1963-65; sr. fellow Resources for the Future, Washington, from 1965. Cons. Agy. for Internat. Devel. in India and Dominican Republic, Washington, 1978-79; adv. bd. agrl. program Internat. Inst. for Applied Sys. Analysis, Austria, 1981-83. Contbr. chpts. to books and articles to profl. jours. Treas., bd. mem. United Dems. Frederick County, Md., 1994—. Sgt. U.S. Air Corps, 1944-46. Recipient Disting. Svc. award Assn. Environ. and Resource Economists, 1992; resident scholar Rockefeller Found., Bellagio, Italy, 1994. Mem. Am. Agrl. Econ. Assn. Avocations: reading histories, biographies and current affairs, golf, enjoying grandchildren. Home: Frederick, Md. Died Nov. 24, 2004.

CROWE, JOHN FRANCIS, advertising executive; b. Charlestown, Mass., Feb. 14, 1920; s. Michael J. and Margaret (Finn) C.; m. Helen M. Grigas, Mar. 27, 1943; children: Carole Anne Crowe, Michael Charles Crowe, Janice Louise Crowe, Bryan John Crowe. Postgrad., Boston Sch. Commerce, 1941-42, Wentworth Inst.; student, USN War Coll., 1942-45. Stone & Webster Engring. Corp., Boston, 1938-40; spl. searcher FBI, Washington, 1940-42; pres., owner nat. advt. agy. Springfield, Ill., from 1952. Co. comdr. USN, 1942-45. Died Apr. 25, 2005.

CROWE, JOHN JOSEPH (JACK CROWE), journalist; b. Tucson, Oct. 26, 1930; s. George Patrick and Maria Luisa (Ornelas-Diaz) C.; m. Dorothea Maria Greene, Mar. 5, 1957; children: Jacqueline, Dorene, Derek. BA, U. Ariz., 1953; JD, Ariz. State U., 1974. Asst. city editor, reporter Ariz. Republic, Phoenix, 1953-75; asst. prof. journalism U. Ariz., Tucson, 1975-78; sr. policy and procedures specialist Morrison-Knudsen Saudi Arabia Con., King Khalid Military City, Saudi Arabia, 1978-80; info. specialist pub. rels Aramco, Dhahran, Saudi Arabia, 1980-82, planning program analyst tng., 1982-84; assoc prof. No. Ky. U., Highland Heights, 1986-90; publs. specialist Rsch. Inst., King Fahd U. Petroleum and Minerals, Dharan, from 1990. Contbr. articles, columns to newspapers. Named Ky. Col., 1986. Democrat. Roman Catholic. Avocations: reading, writing. Home: Tucson, Ariz. Died June 26, 2004.

CRUMP, THOMAS RICHARD, lawyer; b. Seguin, Tex., Oct. 24, 1945; s. Tom and Helen Margaret (Smith) C.; m. Theresa Frazier, Dec. 24, 1979; children— Tony, Kim, Wade, Val, Jon. B.S. summa cum laude, St. Mary's U., 1969; J.D., 1971. Bar: Tex. 1972, U.S. Tax Ct. 1976. With Petty Geophys., San Antonio, 1966-73; instr. St. Mary's U., San Antonio, 1967-69; sole practice, Seguin, 1973—. Mem. State Bar Tex., San Antonio Bar Assn., Guadalupe County Bar Assn., South Central Tex. Bar Assn., ABA, Tex. Trial Lawyers Assn., Delta Theta Phi. Home: Seguin, Tex. Died Apr. 4, 2005.

CUBBINS, ROBERT FULTON, retired English language educator; b. N.Y.C., May 22, 1929; s. William Robert Cubbins Jr. and Erma Elizabeth (Fulton) Ward; m. Sandra Hope Thornton, July 23, 1977. BA, St. Lawrence U., 1952, MEd, 1955. Cert. Eng. instr. grades 7 through 12, N.Y. Tchr. English Washington Acad., Salem, N.Y., 1955-59, Glens Falls (N.Y.) High Sch., 1959-90. Contbr. outdoor articles to mags. and periodicals, 1963—. Mem. Parent-Tchr.-Student Assn. Coun., Glens Falls, N.Y., 1985. Lt. USMC, 1952-54. Named Tchr. of Yr., Glens Falls Sch. Dist., 1986. Mem. N.Y. State Edn. Assn., Masons, Phi Sigma Kappa. Republican. Episcopalian. Avocations: writing, canoeing, fishing, woodcarving, hunting. Home: Queensbury, NY. Died Apr. 8, 2004.

CULBERT, MICHAEL LEON, communications executive; b. Wichita, Kans., May 9, 1937; s. Otto Leon and Gylah Bess (Buckingham) C. BS, Wichita State U., 1960; DSc (hon.), Sri Lanka Indigenous Health Min., 1985. Journalist various orgns., 1959-65; editor Berkeley Daily Gazette and Richmond Ind., Calif., 1966-75; pres., chmn., editor Com. for Freedom Choice in Medicine Inc., Calif., from 1975; info. dir. AB-Mex. Hosp., Tijuana, Mex., from 1979; v.p. Am. Biologics, Chula Vista, Calif., from 1979; founder, pres. C & C Comm., San Diego, from 1992. Mem. ad hoc com. non-traditional medicine NIH, Bethesda, Md., 1992. Author or co-author 15 books. Formerly with Berkeley Boy Scouts, Berkeley-Sakai Sister City Com., Berkeley-Albany Red Cross, Commn. of Californias. Recipient Man of Yr. award United Reps. Calif., 1969, Editl. award Freedoms Found., 1971, Editl. award Calif. Newspaper Pubs. Assn., 1972. Mem. Commonwealth Club Calif. Avocations: philosophy, religion, astronomy, paranormal phenomena, herbology. Home: San Diego, Calif. Died Sept. 11, 2004.

CULLEN, FRANK W., former government relations consultant; b. Bklyn., June 29, 1926; s. Robert J. F. and Mae E. Cullen; m. Mary Anne Cullen, Sept. 8, 1951 (dec. May 1995); children: Peter J., Frank W. Jr. BS in Bus. Adminstrn., Coll. of the Holy Cross, 1952. Pres. Cullen Pub. Affairs Co., N.Y.C., 1952-59, L.A., 1959-61; campaign asst. Gov. Edmund G. "Pat" Brown, L.A., 1962-63, asst. legis. sec. Sacramento, 1964-66, chief of staff Calif. Beverly Hills, 1967-96; pres. FCA Co., Santa Monica, Calif., from 1967. Founder, bd. advisors, former vice chmn. The Edmund G. "Pat" Brown Inst. Pub. Affairs, Calif. State U., L.A., 1979—; pres., co-founder Indonesian-U.S. Bus. Alliance, L.A., 1979-84. Author: The 80 Proof Cookbook, 1982; commentator (radio/TV) Talking Politics, 1995—. Neighborhood commr. Crescent Bay Area Coun., Boy Scouts Am., 1961-65; commr. State Calif. Econ. Devel. Commn., Sacramento, 1982-91; advisor Dem. Senate Campaign Com., Washington, 1982-92; western regional dir. Harry S. Truman Presdl. Libr., Independence, Mo., 1994-96. With USAF, 1943-46. Recipient Merit award Union U., L.A., 1979, Svc. award Palmer Drug Abuse Program, L.A., 1985, Eagle Outstanding Svc. award Calif. State U., L.A., 1991. Mem. Am. Philatilec Soc. Democrat. Roman Catholic. Avocations: stamp collecting/philately, political items collecting, presidential collecting. Home: Los Angeles, Calif. Died Apr. 3, 2006.

CULLER, ARTHUR DWIGHT, language educator; b. McPherson, Kans., July 25, 1917; s. Arthur Jerome and Susanna (Stover) C.; m. Helen Lucile Simpson, Sept. 14, 1941; children: Jonathan Dwight, Helen Elizabeth. BA, Oberlin Coll., 1938; PhD, Yale U., 1941. Instr. English Cornell U., 1941-42; instr., then asst. Yale U., 1946-55; prof. English, 1958-85; chmn. English dept., 1971-75. Assoc. prof. English U. Ill., 1955-58 Author: The Imperial Intellect; A Study of Newman's Educational Ideal, 1955; Editor: (J.H. Newman) Apologia pro Vita Sua, 1956, (with G.P. Clark) Student and Society, 1959, Poetry and Criticism of Matthew Arnold, 1961, Imaginative Reason: The Poetry of Matthew Arnold, 1966, The Poetry of Tennyson, 1977, The Victorian Mirror of History, 1986 Fulbright fellow in Eng., 1950-51; Guggenheim fellow, 1961-62, 76; NEH fellow, 1979-80 Mem. Am. Acad. Arts and Scis., MLA, Phi Beta Kappa. Home: Hamden, Conn. Died Jan. 27, 2006.

CULLUM, CHARLES GILLESPIE, retired retail food chain executive; b. Dallas, Aug. 26, 1916; s. Ashley Wilson and Eloise (Brooks) C.; m. Garland Mae Chapman, May 6, 1938; 1 child, Lee Brooks BS, So. Methodist U., 1936; LLD, Tex. Coll., 1982. Reporter Dallas News, 1936-37; advt. mgr. Adolphus Hotel, 1937-38; salesman Cullum Cos., Inc., Dallas, 1938-43, v.p., 1946-53, pres., 1953-76, chmn., chmn. emeritus, CEO, 1976-85, chmn. exec. com., 1987—2006. Bd. dirs. Republic Bank of Dallas. Mem. Dallas City Council, 1965-69, mayor, 1967-69; bd. dirs. Dallas Found., State Fair Tex., Cotton Bowl Council, Goals for Dallas, Internat. Linguistic Ctr., Dallas, Assn. Higher Edn., Dallas; mem. Dallas Alliance Ednl. Task Force. Served with USN, 1942-46, PTO Recipient Newton D. Baker award, 1969, Disting. Alumnus award So. Meth. U., 1970, Entrepreneur of Yr. award, 1981 Mem. Tex. Employers Ins. Assn. (bd. dirs.), Food Mktg. Inst. (bd. dirs.), Dallas C. of C. (chmn.) Methodist. Died May 16, 2006.

CUMMINGS, CONSTANCE, actress; b. Seattle, May 15, 1910; d. Dallas Vernon and Kate Logan (Cummings) Halverstadt; m. Benn Wolfe Levy, 1933 (dec.); children: Jonathan, Jemima. Chmn. Young People's Theatre Panel; mem. Arts Council, 1963-69. Broadway debut Treasure Girl, 1928; London debut Sour Grapes, Repertory Players, 1934; film debut Movie Crazy, 1932; appeared on radio, TV, films, theatre; joined Nat. Theatre Co., 1971; appeared in London stage prodns.: Madame Bovary, 1937, Romeo and Juliet, 1939, Saint Joan, 1939, The Petrified Forest, 1942, Return to Tyassi, 1950, Lysistrata, 1957, The Rape of the Belt, 1957, Who's Afraid of Virginia Woolf?, 1964, Justice is a Woman, 1966, Fallen Angel, 1967, Nat. Theatre Co., A Long Day's Journey Into Night, 1972, The Cherry Orchard, 1973, The Circle, 1975, Mrs. Warren's Profession, Vienna, 1976, Wings, U.S., 1978, London, 1979 (Tony award 1979), Hay Fever, 1980, The Golden Age, 1981, The Chalk Garden, N.Y.C., 1982, The Glass Menagerie, N.Y.C., London, 1982, (one woman show) Fanny Kemble, 1986, Crown Matrimonial, 1987, Tête a Tête, Mass., 1989, The Chalk Garden, London, 1992, Uncle Vanya, Chichester Theatre, 1996, others; performed in Claudel-Honnegar oratorio St. John at the Stake, Albert Hall, London, 1949, Peter and the Wolf, Albert Hall, 1955, Wings on Am. pub. TV; dir. Royal Ct. Theatre. Recipient Obie award, 1979, Drama Desk award, 1979; decorated Comdr. Brit. Empire. Mem. Brit. Actors Equity (mem. coun.), Royal Soc. for Encouragement of Arts and Commerce. Mem. Labour Party. Club: Chelsea Arts. Died Nov. 23, 2005.

CUMMINGS, KENNETH ILA, coroner, medical examiner; b. Athens, La., Mar. 14, 1936; s. Otto L. and Idelle (James) C.; m. (div. 1981); children: Alison, Courtney, Kurt, Emily; m. Sandra Tipton Gamble, July 2000. BS in Liberal Arts, La. Tech. U., 1958; MD, La. State U., New Orleans, 1962; M in Dermatology, Tulane U., 1966. Diplomate Am. Acad. Dermatology. Intern Confederate Meml. Med. Ctr., Shreveport, La., 1962-63; resident Tulane U. Charity Hosp. of La., New Orleans, 1963-66; chief resident dermatology La. State U. Sch. Med., New Orleans, 1965-66; clin. prof. dermatology La. State U. Med. Sch., Shreveport, 1968-87; chief resident dermatology Tulane U. Med. Sch., New Orleans, 1965-66, Charity Hosp. La., New Orleans, 1965-66; instr. U.S. Naval Aerospace Med. Inst., Pensacola, Fla., 1966-68; pvt. practice Shreveport, La., 1968-87; coroner, med. examiner Bienville Parish, Arcadia, La., 1987-96. Fed. referee disability cases U.S. Govt., Shreveport, 1972—. Author: (novel) Poppies in the Field, 1998, Next to Nod, 2000; contbr. articles to profl. jours. Lt. comdr. USNR, 1966-68. Recipient Award for Surg. Treatment for Baldness Tex. Med. Assn., 1967, Peterkin prize La. Dermatol. Soc., 1966. Mem. SAG, Am. Acad. Dermatology, La. State Med. Soc., Shreveport Med. Soc., La. Coroners Assn., Screen Writers Guild. Democrat. Episcopalian. Avocations: nusmismatics, fiction writing, movie acting, freelance work. Home: Arcadia, La. Died Apr. 28, 2005.

CUMMINGS-SAXTON, JAMES, chemical engineer, consultant, educator; b. Pitts., Dec. 5, 1936; s. James Allen and Margaret Mary (Helsel) Saxton; m. Carolyn Cummings, Aug. 22, 1959; children: Megan Caitlin Cummings-Krueger, James, Jennifer Aine. B Engring. Sci. in Chem. Engring., Johns Hopkins U., 1959; PhD in Chem. Engring., U. Calif., Berkeley, 1966. Registered profl. engr., D.C. Supr. Bellcomm, Washington, 1964-71; sr. v.p. Internat. Rsch. & Tech., Washington, 1971-79; dep. tech. dir. internat. energy program Argonne (Ill.) Nat. Lab., 1979-83; prin. Indsl. Econs., Inc., Cambridge, Mass., 1983—2004. Instr. chem. engring. Cath. U. Am., Washington, 1974—75, Ill. Inst. Tech., Chgo., 1979—80; rsch. assoc. prof. Clark U., Worcester, Mass., from 1994. Mem.: AIChE (pres. Boston sect. 1993—94), Lions (pres. Nahant, Mass. chpt. 1993—95). Unitarian Universalist. Avocations: hiking, bicycling, reading. Home: Nahant, Mass. Died 2004.

CUMMINS, BRUCE WYNN, power company official; b. South Haven, Mich., Dec. 8, 1947; s. Elmer H. and Dorothy B. Cummins; div.; children: Rexford A. Brunson, Jeffery W. Grad. high sch., South Haven. With J.A. Jones Constrn. Co., D.C. Cook Nuclear Plant, Bridgeman, Mich., 1970-73; heat treatment supr. Auto Spltys., St. Joseph, Mich., 1976-82; mech. repair worker A Palisades Nuclear Plant Consumers Power Co., Covert, Mich., 1982-86, material condition planner Palisades Nuclear Plant, 1986-87, mech. maintenance first line supr. Palisades Nuclear Plant, from 1987. With U.S. Army, 1967-69. Mem. Nat. Brotherhood Machinists and Aerospace Workers (v.p. South Haven 1973), NRA, CPCO Employee Club. Home: South Haven, Mich. Died Jan. 14, 2004.

CUMMINS, MARSHA Z., retired literature educator; b. Detroit, June 21, 1938; d. Ephraim and Bluma Hirsch; m. Herman Z. Cummins, Aug. 18, 1963. BA, Wayne State U., 1959; MA, U. Mich., 1963; PhD, U. Md., 1973. Prof. English Morgan State U., Balt., 1964—71; prof. CUNY, Bronx, 1971—2002, prof. emeritus, from 2003. Author: Writing the Research Paper, 1979, Point of View in the Novels of Jean Rhys, 1985. Mem.: MLA. Home: New York, NY. Died Oct. 8, 2005.

CUNNINGHAM, THOMAS CRAIG, human resources professional; b. Lincoln, Nebr., Aug. 6, 1941; s. Thomas Clelland Cunningham and Helen Estelle (Rouse) Harrell. BA in Edn., Nebr. Wesleyan U., 1963; postgrad., U. Wyo., 1962, 63. Various human resource mgmt. positions Xerox Corp., until 1976; corp. pers. mgr. Loral Vought Sys. and Lockheed Martin Vought Sys., Grand Prairie, Tex., 1976-77; pers. dir. Wilson Food Co. subs. Loral Vought Sys. Corp. divsn. Loral Corp., Grand Prairie, Tex., 1977-79, dir. pers. resources, 1979-84, dir. human resources missiles divsn., 1984-86, v.p. human resources, from 1986. Mem. adv. bd. Ctr. for Human Resources Mgmt., Tex. A&M U.; mem. adv. bd. Student Work Consortium, U. Tex., Arlington. Mem. Phi Kappa Tau (nat. pres. 1979-81, bd. dirs. Found., Alumnus of Yr. award 1975). Died June 21, 2004.

CUOZZI, WILLIAM FRANCIS, JR., lawyer; b. Kearny, N.J., Jan. 4, 1920; s. William F. and Antoinette Russo Cuozzi; m. Domenica A. Baldanza, Nov. 22, 1941; children: Carol, Jo-Ellen, William III. BSc, Seton Hall U., 1942; LLB, Rutgers U., 1945. Bar: N.Y. 1946, N.J. 1967, U.S. Dist. Ct. N.J. 1967. Counsel Dollin Corp., Irvington, N.J., 1946-61, Radiant Lamp, Newark, N.J., 1961-64, Syska Hennesy, N.Y.C., 1964-67; pvt. practice West Orange, N.J., from 1967. Mayor West Orange, N.J., 1974-78, councilman, 1964-74, mcpl. judge, 1992-2003. Mem. Essex County Bar Assn. Democrat. Roman Catholic. Avocations: tennis, golf, theater. Died Apr. 25, 2005.

CURLEY, THOMAS J., JR., lawyer; b. Pittsfield, Mass., Jan. 22, 1957; s. Thomas J. and Elaine Patricia (Lynch) C.; m. Leslie A. Golembeske, Oct. 4, 1986; children: Catherine, Edward, Laura. AB cum laude, Harvard U., 1978; JD cum laude, Suffolk U., 1983. Bar: Mass. 1983, U.S. Dist. Ct. Mass. 1984. Staff mem. Spl. Commn. Concerning State and County Bldgs., Ward Commn., Boston, 1978-80; asst. U.S. atty. Dept. Justice, Boston, 1984-87; assoc. Goodwin, Procter & Hoar, Boston, 1987-89, Campoli & Campoli, Pittsfield, 1989-92, ptnr., from 1992. Chmn. Pittsfield Indsl. Devel. Commn., 1991-93; chmn. Harvard schs. and scholars com. Weston, Mass. region, 1989—; commr. Mass. Turnpike Authority, 1991—; chmn. Pittsfield Rep. City Com., 1989-91, Pittsfield Jail Site Evaluation Com., 1993; mem. Community Devel. Bd., 1993—. Mem. Mass. Bar Assn. Home: Pittsfield, Mass. Died July 28, 2005.

CURNUTT, RONALD COLIN, secondary school educator; b. Vallejo, Calif., Mar. 26, 1947; s. Walter Frank and Harriett Sandra (Martin) C. BA, Cen. State U., 1969, MEd summa cum laude, 1973. Cert. secondary tchr., community coll. tchr., Ariz. Tchr. history Parker (Ariz.) High Sch., Parker Unified Sch. Dist. 27, from 1971, chmn. div. social studies, from 1985, also dist. coord. social studies. Adj. prof. history Ariz. Western Coll. La Paz Ctr., Parker, 1973—, chmn. adv. com., 1985—. Chmn. Parker Trash Rates Com., 1984—, Parker Water Rates Com., 1985—, Parker Trash Appeal Bd., 1986—. Named Outstanding State Am. History Tchr., DAR, 1981, Outstanding Area Educator, Parker C. of C., 1980, Outstanding Social Studies Tchr. of Yr., Parker Unified Sch. Dist., 1990-91. Mem. NEA, Ariz. Edn. Assn., Parker Profl. Educators Assn., Masons (past master), Phi Alpha Theta. Republican. Avocations: painting, military miniatures, photography, golf. Home: Parker, Ariz. Died Nov. 6, 2004.

CURRAM, JAMES WILLIAM THOMAS, farmer; b. Maryville, Mo., Nov. 6, 1946; s. Paul Wellesley and Hilda Pauline (Dalrymple) C.; m. Iva Lou Goff, Apr. 9, 1976. LLB, LaSalle U., 1974. Hortoculturist Kissinger Greenhouses, Maryville, 1964, 66; v.p. Gray Oil & Fuel Co., Maryville, 1971-79; asst. mgr. 71 Cafe, Maryville, 1966-71; pvt. practice law Maryville, from 1970; owner Curram Cattle Co., Maryville, from 1979. Mem. Civil War Roundtable (pres. 1986-88), Grand Lodge of Mo., Knights Templer (past comdr. 1981, dist. dep. grand master 1988—), 7th Cavalry Assn., Masons (high priest 1982, past master Stanberry lodge 1987, Nodaway lodge 1980). Republican. Episcopalian. Home: Maryville, Mo. Died Nov. 1, 2004.

CURRAN, JOHN J., lawyer; b. N.Y.C., Jan. 27, 1931; m. Patricia Curran; children: John, Elizabeth, Joseph, Patricia. BS, Fordham U., 1953, JD, 1961. Bar: N.Y. 1961. Gen. counsel, sec., chmn. exec. com., dir. Prudential Securities, N.Y.C., 1955-87. Arbitrator N.Y. Stock Exch., 1970—, Nat. Assn. of Securities Dealers, N.Y.C., 1968—. Trustee Wilton (Conn.) Libr., 1988-94. Home: Wilton, Conn. Died Dec. 5, 2004.

CURRAN, JOHN ROGER, neurologist; b. Newark, July 7, 1934; s. John Henry and Marion (Law) C.; m. Anne Robinson, Sept. 1, 1956; children: Patrick, Christopher, Andrew, Julia. BS in Pharmacy, U. Mich., 1956; MD, Temple U., 1967. Diplomate Am. Bd. Psychiatry and Neurology. Intern U. Mich., 1967-68, resident in neurology, 1968-71; neurologist Nampa, Idaho, from 1973. Bd. dirs. MRI Ctr. Idaho, Boise, Med. Ventures, San Diego, Idaho Ambulance Ctr., Nampa. Maj. USAF, 1971-73. Mem. AMA, Am. Acad. Neurology, Am. EEG Soc., Idaho Med. Assn., Alpha Omega Alpha. Republican. Presbyterian. Avocations: skiing, biking, golf. Home: Nampa, Idaho. Died Dec. 8, 2004.

CURRY, CATHERINE ANN, retired archivist; b. San Francisco, Feb. 10, 1927; d. John Francis Curry and Mary Agnes O'Donnell. BA in Math., U. Calif., Berkeley, 1948; MA in L.Am. History, Santa Clara U., Calif., 1965; MA in Theology, U. San Francisco, 1979; PhD, Grad. Theol.

Union, Berkeley, 1987. Entered Sisters of the Presentation 1948. Elem. tchr. Archdiocese of San Francisco, 1950—53, Oakland, Calif., 1955—57, Archdiocese of L.A., 1953—55, Montebello, Calif., 1958—59, Archdiocese of Santa Fe, Pecos, N.Mex., 1957—58; secondary sch. tchr. Archdiocese of L.A., 1959—65, 1968—78, Sisters of the Presentation, Berkeley, 1965—68; asst. archivist Archdiocese of San Francisco, Menlo Park, Calif., 1993—2002; ret., 2002. Dir., sec. Calif. Coun. Social Studies, Sacamento, 1971—78; dir. Inst. Hist. Study, San Francisco, 1994—98. Author: Statistical Survey of Religious Women in America in the Nineteenth Century, 1989, Life of Mother Teresa Comerford, 1980; contbr. articles to profl. jours., encys. Mem.: Am. Cath. Hist. Assn., Orgn. Am. Historians, Am. Hist. Assn., History of Women Religious Network, We. Assn. Women Historians, Inst. Hist. Study. Roman Catholic. Avocations: architecture, embroidery, photography, art. Home: San Francisco, Calif. Died Mar. 31, 2004.

CURTIN, FRANCIS MICHAEL, government official, scientist; b. Phila., Sept. 16, 1951; s. John Joseph and Helen (Toole) C.; m. Mary Elizabeth Niles, Mar. 26, 1977. BA in History, BA in Logic-Philosophy, Pa. State U., 1974, MPA, 1976. Rsch. asst. Pa. Transp. Inst., University Park, 1974-76; systems engr. System Devel. Corp., Santa Monica, Calif., 1976-78; systems analyst II, Auerbach Assocs., Rosslyn, Va., 1978-80; chief litigation support and econ. analysis FTC, Washington, from 1980, agy. rep. Office Tech. Assessment, from 1981. Guest lectr. Washington semester program Am. U., Washington, 1985—; cons. on fed. and state info. systems devel. Author: Information Processing for Attorneys and Economists, 1989. Recipient commendation FTC, 1985, Outstanding Productivity award, 1989. Mem. Am. Soc. for Pub. Adminstrn., Am. Soc. for Info. Scis. Roman Catholic. Avocations: marine biology, skiing. Home: Falls Church, Va. Died Oct. 28, 2004.

CURTIS, DANIEL M., film director; b. Bridgeport, Conn., Aug. 12, 1928; m. Norma Mae Klein (dec. Mar. 7, 2006); children: Cathy, Tracy. Student, U. Bridgeport; BA, Syracuse U., 1950. Sales exec. NBC, from 1965, MCA, from 1965; owner, producer CBS Golf Classic, 1963-73; owner Dan Curtis Prodns., from 1965. Dir.: (TV) Dark Shadows, 1966-71, 1990-91; (films) House of Dark Shadows, 1970, Night of Dark Shadows, 1971, Burnt Offerings, 1976; (TV films) The Night Strangler, 1973, The Norliss Tapes, 1973, Scream of the Wolf, 1974, Dracula, 1974, Turn of the Screw, 1974, Melvin Purvis: G-Man, 1974, The Great Ice Rip-Off, 1974, Trilogy of Terror, 1975, The Kansas City Massacre, 1975, Curse of the Black Widow, 1977, Dead of Night, 1977, When Every Day Was the Fourth of July, 1978, The Last Ride of the Dalton Gang, 1979, Mrs. R's Daughter, 1979, The Long Days of Summer, 1980, (TV miniseries) The Winds of War, 1983 (Oscar nomination), War and Remembrance, 1987 (Emmy, Dirs. award, People's Choice award, Golden Globe award). Mem. Dirs. Guild Am. Died Mar. 27, 2006.

CURTIS, DAVID EUGENE, personnel executive; b. Dayton, Ohio, Mar. 10, 1937; s. Haskell and Bertie (Wright) C.; m. Nancy Lee Edwards, Dec. 24, 1959; children: David Edward, Leigh Anne, Bradley Wayne. BS, U. Dayton, 1960. Personnel dir. Dayton Wonder Bread, 1960-65, Toledo Wonder & Hostess Cake, 1965-80, Columbus (Ohio) Wonder & Hostess, from 1980. Pres. Toledo Kennel Club, 1978-80, New Albany-Plain Twp. Hist. Soc., 1982-86, Cen. Ohio Dachshund Club, Columbus, 1984-85; elected ofcl., trustee Plain Twp., 1986-90, 90—, chmn.; mem. adv. bd. Northside Child Devel. Ctr., Columbus. Mem. Cen. Ohio Kennel Club, Golden Retriever Club of Cen. Ohio (corres. sec.). Republican. Methodist. Avocation: breeding and showing dachshunds and golden retrievers. Home: New Albany, Ohio. Died May 26, 2004.

CURTIS, MICHAEL D., flight nurse; b. Hinton, W.Va., June 12, 1959; s. William D. and Mary F. (Bolling) C.; m. Susan J. Curtis, Aug. 25, 1984; children: Erich, Anthony. Assoc. Nursing, La. State U., Eunice. CEN; Cert. Critical Care Nurse, Paramedic. Paramedic Summers County Ambulance Svc., Hinton, W.Va., 1981-83, Acadian Ambulance, Lafayette, La., 1983-85; staff charge nurse Our Lady of Lourdes, Lafayette, 1987-88; flight nurse St. Elizabeth's Hosp., Beaumont, Tex., 1988-90; staff charge nurse emergency rm. Hermann Hosp., Houston, 1990; staff/charge nurse emergencyrm. Meml. S.W. Emergency Rm., Houston, 1991-92; chief flight nurse The Meth. Hosp., Houston, from 1992. Contbr.: What Desert Storm Was Like, 1994, Desert Storm-Line in the Sand, 1995. Staff sgt. U.S. Army, 1990-91, Res., 1983—. Decorated Air medal. Mem. AACN, VFW, Nat. Flight Nurses Assn. Avocations: flying, teaching, photography, computers. Died June 6, 2004.

CURTIS, NANCY RUTH, elementary school educator; b. Mpls., Nov. 3, 1937; d. James Arthur and Helen Ruth (Street) Harris; m. John Harold Curtis, Aug. 26, 1960; 1 child, Nancy Elizabeth. AB, MacMurray Coll., 1959; MEd, Valdosta State Coll., 1976, EdS, 1981. Cert. early childhood edn. Tchr. Pembroke Sch. Dist., Mass., 1959—60, Norwell Sch. Dist., Mass., 1960—62, Kewanee Sch. Dist., Ill., 1963, Toulon Sch. Dist., Ill., 1964—65, Danville Sch. Dist., Danville, Ill., 1967—69, Leon County Sch. Dist., Tallahassee, 1969—71, Lowndes County, Valdosta, Ga., 1971—99. Mem. Ga. Ret. Educators Assn., Delta Kappa Gamma, (corr. sec. 1990-92, 2d v.p. 1992-94, pres. 1994-96), Sigma Alpha Iota (patroness) Democrat. Episcopalian. Avocation: reading. Died Nov. 20, 2005.

CURTIS, ROBERT HARLAND, mining and refining executive, consultant; b. Columbus, Ohio, Jan. 1, 1930; s. Harland Guy and Beatrice Mae (Waltermire) C.; m. Lucy Jovick, Jan. 1, 1953 (div. June 1960); m. Yolanda Ramos, Dec. 19, 1963. Comml. banking degree, Am. Inst. Banking, 1958; Metallurgy degree (hon.), Fresno State Coll., 1974. Asst. cashier and asst. sec. Bank Am. Nat. Trust & Savs. Assn., San Francisco, 1949-60; pres. and mgr. Kaiser Aluminum Acceptance Corp., Oakland, Calif., 1960-65; v.p. Atlas Credit Corp., Oakland and Pitts., 1965-66; sales mgr. Hallman Chevrolet, Reno, Nev., 1966-70; gen. mgr. Fletcher Jones Chevrolet-Mazda, Las Vegas, Nev., 1977-87; pres. U.S. Platinum, Inc., Reno, 1970-77, Internat. Precious Metals, Las Vegas, 1987-89. Pres. and chmn. C&B Salvage and Investment Corp. DBA Curtis Nev. Mines, Las Vegas, 1977—, U.S. Platinum, Inc., 1987—. Author: Off Premisis Banking, 1959; co-editor 23 part series on Philippine Pres. Ferdinand Marcos for Philippine News, 1975-76; contbr. articles to profl. jours. Chmn. and co-founder Comstock Sertoma, Reno, 1968-72. Sgt. airborne inf. U.S. Army, 1947-49. Recipient annual sci. award Calif. Tchr. Assn., Fresno, Calif., 1974. Mem. Nat. Vehicle Lease Assn. (chmn. Las Vegas br. 1983-85), VFW. Republican. Methodist. Avocations: hunting, boating, fishing, treasure hunting. Home: Las Vegas, Nev. Died Jan. 4, 2004.

CURTIS, WILLIAM SHEPLEY, radiologist; b. St. Louis, Sept. 11, 1915; s. Edward Glion and Isabel (Wallace) C.; m. Frances Lois Elmer, Jan. 3, 1942; children: William Shepley Jr., David Jennings, Anne Goodson Curtis Curfman. AB, Dartmouth Coll., 1936; MD, Washington U., St. Louis, 1940. Diplomate Am. Bd. Radiology. Intern St. Luke's Hosp., St. Louis, 1940-41; resident St. Louis Maternity Hosp., 1941, Mallinkrodt Inst. Radiology, 1945-48; radiologist Wasson and Bouslog, Denver, 1948-52; radiologist, ptnr. Boulder (Colo.) Med. Ctr., 1953-83; cons. Wardenburg Student Health Ctr. U. Colo., Boulder, 1953-91. Past trustee Colo. Blue Shield, Denver, cons. Past chmn. Colo. Found. Med. Care, Denver, Boulder County Health Com.; mem. Colo. Health Occupations Adv. Com., Denver; bd. dirs. Boulder Day Nursery. Lt. col. M.C., U.S. Army, 1941-46. Recipient U. Colo. medal, 1992. Fellow Am. Coll. Radiology (emeritus, past councilor); mem. Radiol. Soc. N.Am., Colo. Radiol. Soc. (past pres.), Colo. Med. Soc. (past pres., del.), Boulder County Med. Soc. (past pres.), Boulder Town and Gown, Rotary (past pres. Boulder chpt.). Unitarian Universalist. Avocations: teaching, law, sports. Died Apr. 1, 2004.

CUSHING, RICHARD GOLLÉ, journalist; b. N.Y.C., Apr. 30, 1917; s. Melvin Abbott and Blanche (Goll) C.; m. Nancy Heizer, Mar. 23, 1940; children: Jeffrey, Martha, Lincoln. BA, San Francisco State Coll., 1945; LLD (hon.), U. Havana, Cuba, 1955. Reporter AP, San Francisco, 1935-42, war corr. PTO, 1943-45, bur. chief Shanghai, 1945-46, news editor San Francisco, 1947-49; fgn. svc. officer USIA, Santiago, Chile, 1950-65, Cuba, Nairobi and Caracas, Venezuela, 1953-65; acting dir. Voice of Am., Washington, 1966-69; mem. Sr. Seminar on Fgn. Policy, Washington, 1970-71; San Francisco corr. Voice of Am. USIA, from 1977. Author: Too Pure for the Hyenas, 1976. Mem. grand jury Marin County, Calif., 1984. Mem. World Affairs Coun. (San Francisco chpt.), Commonwealth Club (San Francisco), Press Club San Francisco, Nat. Geog. Soc. Democrat. Avocations: piano, bicycling, international travel. Died July 30, 2004.

CUTLER, JAY B., lawyer, psychiatric association executive; b. N.Y.C., Sept. 7, 1930; s. Murray and Shirley (Salkin) C.; m. Randy Handelsman, Apr. 5, 1952; children: Hollie, Perri. BS, NYU, 1951; JD, Bklyn. Law Sch., 1956; PhD (hon.), So. Coll. Optometry, Memphis, 1978. Bar: N.Y. 1956, D.C. 1958. Atty., pub. affairs TV producer Theodore Granik Law Office, Washington, 1958-68; minority counsel U.S. Senate Health Subcom. Alcoholism and Narcotics, Washington, 1969-77; counsel, staff dir. U.S. Senate Human Resources Com. (Minority), Washington, 1974-77; spl. counsel and dir. govt. relations Am. Psychiatric Assn., Washington, 1977—2003. Tech. cons. on corp. affairs White House Conf. on Children and Youth; lectr. med. grand rounds Downstate Med. Ctr., Bklyn., N.Y. Coll. Medicine, Columbia U. Coll. Physicians and Surgeons, U. Md. Med. Coll., Cleve. Clin., Western Psychiat. Inst., Pitts. Author: Analysis for Comprehensive Health Manpower Training Act in Health/Environment Manpower 1984, Federal Health Care Financing of Mental Illness in the New Economics and Psychiatric Care. Pres. Md. Assn. for Learning Disabled, Coalition for Health Funding, 1978-81,lvice presdl. campaign Hubert H. Humphrey, 1964. With U.S. Army 1951-53. Recipient Award of Excellence Am. Soc. of Assn. Execs., 1985, 87, Appreciation award Puerto Rican Psychiat. Soc., 1993. Fellow Am. Psychiat. Assn. (hon., pres. 1956, Presdl. Commendation 1985). Died Mar. 4, 2005.

CUTLER, TIMOTHY ROCKWOOD, manufacturing executive; b. N.Y.C., Nov. 30, 1931; s. Lloyd Rockwood and Helen (Smith) Cutler; m. Sheelagh R. Riach, Aug. 4, 1953; children: Amanda D., Timothy Rockwood Jr. BBA, Hofstra U., 1960. Sec., fin. v.p. Miracle Adhesives Corp., Bellmore, NY, 1957—64, pres., from 1966. Chmn. Miracle Adhesives Corp., Bellmore, 1983—86. 1st lt. USAF, 1953—56. Home: Oyster Bay, NY. Died May 17, 2005.

CYPHERT, FREDERICK RALPH, retired academic administrator; b. Brookville, Pa., Jan. 4, 1928; s. Ralph Leroy and Bessanna (Nail) C.; m. Lois Florence Grosz, June 1, 1957; children— Stacey Todd, Holly Susan. BS, Clarion State Coll., 1949; MA, Syracuse U., 1950; Ed.D., U. Pitts., 1957. Tchr., curriculum coordinator pub. schs., Penn Hills, Pa., 1950-56; asst. prof. Ball State U., Muncie, Ind., 1956-57; dir. instrn., pub. schs. Torrance, Cal., 1957-59; prof. Ohio State U., Columbus, 1959-65; assoc. dean Ohio State U. (Coll. Edn.), 1965-68; dean U. Va. Sch. Edn., Charlottesville, 1968-74, Ohio State U. Coll. Edn., Columbus, 1974-79, dean emeritus, 1979—2006; dir. Fla. Inst. Edn., 1988. Author: Teaching in America, 1962, Teaching in the American Secondary School, 1964, An Analysis and Projection of Research in Teacher Education, 1965, A Taxonomy of Teacher Classroom Behavior, 1966; Contbr. articles to profl. jours. Mem. Fla. State Libr. Coun. With USAAF, 1946-47. Mem. Ohio Council on Tchr. Edn. (pres. 1966-68), Assn. Colls. and Schs. Edn. in State Univs. and Land Grant Colls. (pres. 1973-75), Assn. Supervision and Curriculum Devel., Am. Ednl. Research Assn., Am. Assn. Colls. Tchr. Edn. (pres. 1976-77), Am. Assn. Sch. Adminstrs., Phi Delta Kappa, Phi Sigma Pi, Pi Gamma Mu. Home: Fort Myers, Fla. Died Nov. 20, 2005.

CYRUS, TERIECE DYER, educational adminstrator; b. West Monroe, La., Feb. 17, 1912; d. Virge Lee and Nora (Green) Ivey; m. Isaac S. Dyer, Oct. 7, 1930; (dec.); children: Virgie Lee, Gwendolyn Marie, Nora Jean; m. Wiliam Cyrus, Dec. 29, 1960. BS, Grambling State U., 1951. Tchr. Quachita Parish Sch. Bd., Monroe, La., 1930-32, 61-71, Webster Parish Sch. Bd., Minden, La., 1940-60; dir. Westside Devel. Ctr., West Monroe, from 1973. Summer dir. Headstart Program, Monroe, 1962-74. Bd. dirs. Quchita Parish Girl Scouts U.S., 1966-73, Sr. Citizen's Ctr., West Monroe, 1979-83; v.p. Mayor's Commn. on Needs of Women, Monroe, 1986—, pres., 1988-89; bd. dirs. Interchurch Conf., State of La., 1988—. Recipient Merit Service award Christian Meth. Ch., 1980. Mem. NEA, LWV (pres. 1980-82), Delta Sigma Theta (treas. 1978-80). Democrat. Avocations: writing, reading, travel. Home: West Monroe, La. Died Mar. 26, 2005.

DAAMS, GERRIT, philosophy professor; b. Alton, Ill., Sept. 4, 1918; s. Lucas and Anthonia D.; m. Harriet Fobes Tilton Daams, June 27, 1952; children: Frederic L., David H., Roderic G. BS, Calif. Inst. Tech., 1940, MS, 1941; PhD, Columbia U., 1952. Lectr. in Physics, CCNY, 1948-56; asst. prof. Philosophy Kent State U., Ohio, 1956-66. Author: Competing Loyalties and Practical Decisions, 1952; contbr. articles to profl. jours. Mem. AAAS, Am. Meteorological Soc., Am. Philosphical Assn., Soc. for Scientific Study of Relig., Mind Assn., Am. Inst. Physics. Avocations: tennis, bicycling, camping, swimming, photography. Died July 11, 2005.

DAILEY, JAMES RICHARD, lawyer; b. Erie, Pa., Aug. 15, 1935; s. Fred and Elinor (Casey) D.; m. Mary Alice Sedelmeyer, July 13, 1963 (dec. Feb. 2001); children: Timothy, Kathleen, Brian. PhilB, U. Detroit, 1957; JD, Dickinson Sch. Law, 1961. Bar: Pa. 1961, U.S. Dist. Ct. (we. dist.) Pa. 1962, U.S. Ct. Appeals (3d cir.) 1968. Asst. Dist. Atty. Office, Erie, Pa., 1966-71, 81-88; sole practitioner Daily Karte & Villella, Erie, from 1968. 2d lt. U.S. Army, 1957-58. Mem. Pa. Bar Assn. Republican. Roman Catholic. Home: Erie, Pa. Died July 9, 2005.

DAILY, CAROLYN JOYCE, public relations and marketing professional; b. Little Rock, Mar. 18, 1939; d. Eugene Joseph and Sarah Jewell (Norris) D.; m. Brendan William O'Connor, Oct. 2, 1982. BS in Journalism, U. Ill., 1961; MA in Communications, Sangamon State U., 1976. Reporter Kansas City (Mo.) Star newspaper, 1961-63; women's editor Kansas City (Kans.) Kansan newspaper, 1963-64; family living editor The Times, Hammond, Ind., 1964-67; account mgr. Martin & Punnett Pub. Rels., Chgo., 1968-69; corp. communications mgr. Ill. Bell, Chgo., 1969-91; pres. CArolyn Daily O'Connor Strategic Comms., Chgo., from 1992. Founding editor UpFront employee newspaper, Ill. Bell, Chgo., 1988-90; v.p. mktg. O'Connor & Assocs., Chgo., 1990—. Author: The Norris Family, 1989. Mem. Nat. Assn. Woman Bus. Owners, Chgo. Speechwriters Forum, Brit. Conservatives Abroad (bd. dirs.), Publicity Club (Silver Trumpet award 1986). Avocations: travel, photography, history, genealogy. Home: Chicago, Ill. Died Aug. 11, 2005.

DAJANI, JARIR SUBHI, retired civil engineer, consultant; b. Jerusalem, Apr. 5, 1940; s. Subhi T. and Lisa (Stori) D.; m. Rihab Dajani, Aug. 23, 1965; children: Jumana, Subhi, Dina. B in Civil Engring., Am. U. Beirut, 1961; MS, Stanford U., 1966; PhD, Northwestern U., 1971. Project engr. Assoc. Consulting Engrs., Lebanon, Saudi Arabia, 1961-65; assoc. prof. Civil Engring. and Policy Scis. Duke U., Durham, NC, 1971—76; assoc. prof. Civil Engring. Stanford (Calif.) U., Calif., 1976-82; cons. Amman, Jordan, 1980-82; adv. Abu Dhabi Fund For Devel., 1982—2004; ret., 2004. Cons. US Agy. for Int. Devel., 1976-82, World Bank, Washington, 1979. Home: Alexandria, Va. Died May 6, 2005.

DALLEMAGNE-COOKSON, ELISE CAMILLE, writer; b. Tarrytown, NY, Mar. 31, 1933; d. Edmund Leo and Irene (Poisson) Cookson; m. Jeremy Gaige, June 6, 1951 (div. June 1955); m. Pierre Georges Dallemagne (dec. May. 1979); children: Pierre E. (dec. May 1994), Paul C. AB, Katherine Gibbs Bus. Sch., 1951; student, NYU, 1951-52, Syracuse U., 1952-54, Fla. Inst. Tech., 1973-75. Publicist, prodn. asst. United Artists, 20th Century Fox, Columbia Pictures, Robert Rossen Prodns., N.Y., Hollywood, Calif., 1955—59; ptnr. Katzka, Farrell, Gaige Films;

pub. affairs officer U.S. Fgn. Svc., 1959—60; farmer Congo and Argentina, 1959-68; internat. hi-tech sales rep. Harris Computers Fla., 1975-78; registered rep. Wall Street various internat. banks, N.Y.C., 1980-89; fgn. lang. tchr. Cherry Valley (N.Y.) Schs., 1989-93. Author: Simplified Swahili, 1970, The Bearded Lion Who Roars, 1995, The Ombu Tree, 1998, The Filmmaker, 2000, The Red-Eye Fever, 2002, Marie Grandin-Sent by the King, 2003, The Jean Tabaud Project, 2005, Marie Grandin-Fille du Roi, 2005; contbr. articles to mags. and features to newspapers. Avocations: farming, teaching. Died Nov. 2005.

D'AMATO, ANTHONY ROGER, recording industry executive; b. NYC, Jan. 21, 1931; s. Agostino and Luisa (Galiani) D'A.; m. Gabrielle Hilton, June 26, 1958; children— Luisa, Jennie, Tania, Joanna, Antonia. BA in Music and English Lit. cum laude (Founders Day award 1956), N.Y. U., 1956; MI.A. (teaching fellow), Brandeis U., 1957. Artist and repertoire dir. stereophonic div. Decca Record Co., Ltd., Eng., 1958-78; pres. TDA Prodns. Ltd., N.Y.C., from 1978; exec. dir. Winnipeg (Man., Can.) Symphony Orch., 1979-80; v.p. artist and repertoire AudioFidelity Enterprises, N.Y.C., 1980-81; mng. dir. Mantovani Prodns., Mantovani Orch., N.Y.C., from 1982. Mng. cons. Leopold Stokowski, 1964-72 Served with USMCR, 1951-53. Recipient Grand Prix du Disque, Charles Cros award rec., 1969 Mem. Assn. Cultural Execs. Can., Winnipeg C. of C., Phi Beta Kappa. Died 2006.

DAMBSKI, JERZY WLADYSLAW, mechanical engineer; b. Vilnius, Poland, Dec. 15, 1931; s. Roman Emilian and Paulina Irma (Gedroyc) D.; m.Anna Izabela Moes-Dambski, Oct. 29, 1960; children: Joanna, Piotr, Pawel, Tomasz. MS, Silesian Politech. Inst., Gliwice, 1956. Registered profl. engr., Calif. Design engr. Design Burs., Warsaw and Gliwice, R.M. Parsons Co., L.A., 1969, Bechtel Power Corp., Norwalk, Calif., 1971, Fluor Engrs. and Const., Irvine, Calif., 1973; engr. scientist McDonnel Douglas (now Boeing-Douglas), Long Beach, Calif., from 1986. Contbr. articles to profl. jours. Lt. Polish mil. Mem. ASME, AIAA, White Eagle Soaring Assn. Died Nov. 30, 2004.

D'ANGELO, FRANCES BONACORSA, educator; b. N.Y.C., May 30, 1914; d. Vito and Francesca Paula (DeLuca) Bonacorsa; m. Carmine John D'Angelo, Aug. 30, 1936. BA, CUNY, 1937, MA, 1942; cert. supr. and prin., NYU, 1963, postgrad., 1950. Cert. tchr., supr. and prin., N.Y. Tchr. St. Joan of Arc Sch., Jackson Heights, N.Y., 1941-43, Union Free Sch. Dist., Franklin Square, N.Y., 1943-60, curriculum coord., asst. prin., 1960-65, reading specialist, 1966-76, prin. summer sch., 1966-74; asst. prin. South Shore Christian Sch., Seaford, N.Y., 1978-81; supr. student tchr. St. John's U., Jamaica, N.Y., from 1983; reading specialist Evangel Christian Sch., L.I., N.Y., from 1987. Chmn. March Dimes, 1970-75, bd. dirs. 1968-75; bd. dirs. Glen Cove Scholarship Fund, 1972—. Recipient Community Svc. award, 1975, Outstanding Svc. award March of Dimes, 1975, Disting. Svc. award Arthritus Found., 1978, Outstanding Contbr. award Am. Com. Italian Migration, 1982. Mem. AAUP, Am. Assn. Retired Persons (v.p. 1980-84), N.Y. State Retired Tchrs., Nat. Italian Am. Found., L.I. Fedn. Women's Clubs, Nassau Fedn. Rep. Women, Lioness Club (2d v.p., Glen Cove chpt. 1989), Ladies Aux. Elks (chaplain 1987-90), Dante Cultural Soc. (pres. 1969-74), Women's Club Glen Cove, Order Sons Italy in Am. (pres. 1981-83). Roman Catholic. Avocations: reading, music, travel, bridge. Home: Glen Cove, NY. Died Jan. 12, 2004.

DANIEL, LEON, journalist; b. Etowah, Tenn., Aug. 8, 1931; s. Oscar Leon and Mary Nancy (Cook) D.; m. Carobel Heidt Calhoun, Oct. 26, 1963 (div.); 1 child, Lillian Fant. Student, U. Tenn., 1949-56. Reporter UP, Nashville, 1956-58; bur. mgr. UPI, Knoxville, Tenn., 1958-61, reporter Atlanta, 1961-66, corr. Saigon, 1966-67, Tokyo, 1967-70, mgr. for Thailand Bangkok, 1970-72, chief corr. for South Asia New Delhi, 1972-74, chief corr. for East Asia Manila, 1974, editor for Asia Hong Kong, 1974-77, editor for Europe London, 1977-80, nat. reporter Washington, 1980-87, mng. editor, internat., 1987-88, sr. editor, columnist, 1989-93; cons., columnist The Ind., Dhaka, Bangladesh, 1995. With USMC, 1950-53, Korea. Decorated Purple Heart. Mem. Phi Gamma Delta, Sigma Delta Chi. Democrat. Episcopalian. Home: Charlottesville, Va. Died Mar. 19, 2006.

DANIEL, MARIAN PHILLIPS, language educator; b. Tulsa, Okla. d. Richard Tevier Daniel Jr. and Aena E. Martin. AA, Stephens Coll., Columbia, Missouri; BA in Romance Langs., U. Ark., 1964, MA in Spanish, 1967. Cert. secondary edn. Tex. Edn. Agy. Editor, translator El Ganadero Internacional, San Antonio, 1967—82; secondary edn. educator South San Antonio Ind. Sch. Dist., 1993—2002, N.E. Ind. Sch. Dist., San Antonio, 2002—04. Mem. Cherokee Nation, Osage Tribe of Indians. Mem.: Tex. Fgn. Lang. Assn. Roman Catholic. Avocations: swimming, scuba diving, travel, sailing. Home: San Antonio, Tex. Died 2006.

DANSER-FISCHER, VICKI LYNN, medical/surgical nurse; b. Parkersburg, W.Va., Dec. 31, 1954; d. Robert Irvin and Mary Anne (Price) Danser; m. Andrew Philip Fischer, May 27, 1990 (dec. May, 2006). Assoc. Nursing with honors, Parkersburg Community Coll., 1975; BS with hon. in Nursing, U. Ky., 1983; BFA with hon., U. Louisville, 1993. Cert. operating rm. nurse, legal nurse cons., 2006. Neonatal ICU staff nurse U. Ky. Med. Ctr., Lexington, 1976-77; staff nurse operating room Meth. Evang. Hosp., Louisville, 1977-78; staff nurse Med. Personnel Pool, Louisville, 1978-79; pvt. duty and staff relief nurse Caretender, Inc., Louisville, 1978-79; supr. oper. rm., infection control nurse, employee health nurse Frontier Nursing Svc., Hyden, Ky., 1979; staff nurse Pattie A. Clay Hosp., Richmond, Ky., 1979-81, U. Ky. Med. Ctr., Lexington, 1981-82; pvt. duty nurse James Whitlock, Lexington, 1982-83; staff nurse Louisville Jefferson County Health Dept., Louisville, 1983-84; surg. nurse Humana Hosp. U. Louisville, Louisville, 1984-88, dir. sterile processing dept., 1988-89; staff nurse Out Patient Surgery Ctr. Suburban Med. Ctr., Louisville, 1989-97; feltmaker, from 1993; legal nurse cons., from 2006. One-woman show The Versatility of Felt, 1999, I Felt A Change, 2002; pvt. collections include Louisville Gas & Elec. Co., The White House, Washington D.C. Active Louisville Visual Art Assn., Adath-Jeshurun Synagogue. Mem. Am. Craft Assn., Louisville Area Fiber and Textile Artists, TAFTA Am. Craft Coun., Louisville Crafters Guild, Golden Key Nat. Hon. Soc. Home: Louisville, Ky. Died May 2006.

DARBY, JOSEPH BRANCH, JR., retired metallurgist, retired federal agency administrator; b. Petersburg, Va., Dec. 12, 1925; s. Joseph Branch and Jessie Catherine (Frazier) Darby; m. Eleanor Lee Daley, Mar. 25, 1951; children: Joseph III, John, Leslie, Peter. BS, Coll. William and Mary, 1948, Va. Poly. Inst., 1951; MS, U. Ill., 1955, PhD, 1958. Chemist Allied Chem. Corp., Hopewell, Va., 1948-49; devel. engr. Union Carbide Corp., Niagara Falls, NY, 1951-53; rsch. scientist Argonne (Ill.) Nat. Lab., 1958-86, assoc. dir. fusion energy program, 1974-78, assoc. dir. ocean thermal energy conversion, 1978-84; program mgr. basic energy scis. Office Energy Rsch., Dept. Energy, Washington, 1986-94; adj. prof. U. Va. Sch. Engring., Charlottesville, 1995-97; ret., 1997. Vis. sr. rsch. fellow U. Birmingham, England, 1970—71. Co-editor: The Electronic Structure of the Actinides and Related Properties, 2 vols., 1974; mem. adv. bd. Jour. Less-Common Metals, 1971—82, Materials Letters, 1988—92; co-editor: Jour. Nuc. Materials, 1971—74; chmn. bd. editors:, 1984—90; mem. adv. bd. Jour. Nuc. Materials, 1990—94; contbr. articles to profl. jours. Mem. nominating com. sch. bd., Wheaton, Ill., 1961—63, Bd. Trustees Coll. DuPage, 1963—65. With A.C. USMC, 1944—46. Recipient Loyalty award, U. Ill., Disting. Editor award, Materials Soc., 1994; Sci. Rsch. Coun. Sr. fellow, 1970—71. Fellow: Am. Soc. Metals (mem. energy coun. divsn., mem. nuc. metallurgy com.); mem.: AAAS, ASTM, Cape Cod Geneal. Soc. (co-pres. 1996—98), Fedn. Materials Socs. (bd. dirs. 1988—94), Am. Inst. Mining, Metall. and Petroleum Engrs., Metall. Soc., Sigma Xi, Sigma Gamma Epsilon, Alpha Sigma Mu, Tau Beta Pi. Presbyterian. Home: Yarmouth Port, Mass. Died Nov. 29, 2005.

DARLING, STANTON GIRARD, lawyer; b. Loudonville, Ohio, Apr. 13, 1920; s. Ira Jay and Pauline Esther (Miller) D.; m. Carolyn R. Miceli, Mar. 21, 1942; children: Stanton Girard II, Kaye Michele. BA, Ohio State U., 1947, JD, 1948. Bar: Ohio 1948, U.S. Dist. Bar (ea. and so. dists.) Ohio. Ptnr. Darling & Keister, Columbus, Ohio, from 1948. Lectr. on real property and condominium law Ohio Bar Continuing Legal Studies, 1964-66. Author: Condominiums in Ohio, 1964. Atty. Heisey Collectors Am., Newark, Ohio, 1970—, North Market Assn., Columbus, 1985—. lst sgt. inf. AUS, 1941-45, ETO. Decorated Purple Heart with oak leaf cluster, Bronze Star with two oak leaf clusters. Mem. Ohio Bar Assn., Columbus Bar Assn. Republican. Avocations: studying antiques, art. Died Feb. 6, 2005.

DARROW, MARIANNE ROSINA, speech pathology/audiology services professional, editor, writer; b. Kingston, NY, Dec. 11, 1925; d. Burton Jacob and Mary Anne Davis; m. H. Van Wyck Darrow, Jr., Nov. 24, 1963 (dec. July 1998); 1 child, Emily Marika. BA in English/Social Studies/Drama cum laude, SUNY, Albany, 1946; MA in Speech/Drama, Columbia U., 1952. Lic. speech-lang. pathologist N.Y., tchr. speech/hearing handicapped N.Y. Copywriter trainee J. Walter Thompson, N.Y.C., 1946—47; dancer Pitts. Ligth Opera Co., 1947, Touring Co., 1947—48; soc. editor Kingston (N.Y.) Daily Freeman, 1953—55; entertainment editor Ulster County Townsman, Woodstock, NY; pre-doctoral assoc. U. Wash. Speech and Hearing Clinic, Seattle, 1957—60; speech and hearing tchr. Kingston City Schs. Consol., 1960—64; speech-lang. pathologist Cerebral Palsy Ctr., Kingston, 1962, therapist, 1967—69; cons. Benedictine and Kingston Hosps., Kingston, 1967—72; speech cons. Ten Broeck Commons, Ulster, 2001—02; with Hutton Nursing Home, Kingston, 2002—03; speech cons. Ulster-Greene ARC, Kingston, NY. Actor: Coach House Players, 1951, Woodstock Playhouse, 1951; contbr. articles to profl. jours., to mags. including The Citizen, Antique Living. Chair pers. com. Kingston City Sch. Bd., 1970—75; founder pres. coun. PTA; chair environ. project Group Against Spraying Pesticides, Hurley, from 1993; founder, mem. prevention group Benedictine Hosp., 1995; dir. entertainment Sapporo, Japan, Nurnberg, Germany, 1948—50. Named Citizen Adv. of Yr., Mid-Hudson Options Project, Inc., 2001. Mem.: AAUW, N.Y. State Speech Hearing Lang. Assn., Am. Speech/Lang./Hearing Assn., Hillside Acres Garden Club. Avocations: gardening, swimming, travel, lecturing. Home: Hurley, NY. Died July 2, 2004.

DART, JACK CALHOON, chemical engineer; b. Concord, Mich., Aug. 14, 1912; s. James Laurance and Ethel Lenore (Calhoon) D.; m. Widder, June 16, 1940, (wid. May 1990); children: Dianne Gibson, Linda Dart, Janis Cook, James. AB, Albion Coll., 1934; BSE, U. Mich., 1935, MSE, 1937. Chem. engr. Pan Am. Ref., Texas City, Tex., 1937-44; chief engr. Esso Labs, Baton Rouge, 1944-47; mgr. rsch. lab. Houdry Process Corp., Phila., 1947-55, v.p., 1955-62; owner J.C. Dart and Assocs., Potomac, Md., from 1962. Mem. Sch. Bd. Nether Providence, Wallingford, Pa., 1961, 62. Recipient Disting. Alumni award Albion (Mich.) Coll., 1982. Fellow Am. Inst. Chem. Engrs. (Disting. Svc. award 1974, founder). Avocations: bridge, photography. Died Feb. 23, 2005.

DART, STEPHEN HOWARD, lawyer, insurance company executive; b. Lansing, Mich., Jan. 17, 1953; s. John Harvey and Margaret Lorraine (Welch) D.; m. Abby Baker, 1986; children: Jackson Carroll, Joseph Baker, Will Stephen, Lily Meredith. BA, Harvard U., 1975; MA, Oxford U., 1977; JD, Harvard U., 1980. Asst. prosecuting atty. Ingham County Prosecutor's Office, Lansing, Mich., 1980-81; dir. devel. Calif. Trial Lawyer's Assn., L.A., 1986-87; ptnr. MacLean, Seaman, Laing & Guilford, East Lansing, Mich., 1987-89; chief oper. officer Mich. Physicians Mutual Liability Co., East Lansing, Mich., from 1989. Pres., CEO Superior Employers Plan, 1993. Died Nov. 4, 2004.

DAS, MOHAN POTTETH, psychiatrist; b. Kerala, India, July 15, 1947; s. V. K. Krishnan Unni and Nanikutty Amma; m. Suma Das, 1979; 1 child, Priya. MD, Med. Coll., Trivandrum, India, 1972. Diplomate Am. Bd. Psychiatry and Neurology. Mem. faculty U. London, Cambridge (Eng.) U., 1976-83, U. Ottawa (Ont., Can.) Health Scis. Ctr., 1984-87; med. dir. Behavioral Health Ctr. Texoma Med. Ctr., Sherman, Tex., from 1989; chief psychiat. svcs. Texoma Med. Ctr.-Behavioral Health Ctr., Sherman, Tex. Contbr. articles to med. jours. Fellow Royal Coll. Physicians; mem. Tex. Med. Assn., Tex. Soc. Psychiatric Physicians, Grayson County Med. Soc., Royal Coll. Psychiatrists. Died Jan. 22, 2005.

DASCENZI, HAZEL MARIE, real estate broker; b. Palestine, Tex., Sept. 6, 1920; d. Calvin Coolidge and Sarah Ethel (Evans) Click; divorced; children: Sharron Marie Beamer, Phillip Chris. Cert. paralegal, So. Calif. Coll. Law, 1990. Lic. real estate broker. Broker, owner Hazel's Realty, Buena Park, Calif., 1959-78, Sunnymead, Calif., 1980-82, San Juan Capistrano, Calif., from 1982; v.p. Harbor View Fin. Svcs., Newport Beach, Calif., 1989—92. Chmn. Silverado Days, Buena Park Gala. Recipient Plaque of Appreciation, Buena Park, Cypress, La Palma Bd. Realtors, 1963, Cert. and Plaque, Women's div. C. of C., Buena Park, 1966-69, Disting. Svc. award Buena Park Jr. C. of C., 1967, Outstanding Chairmanship award and Realtor of Yr. award Calif. Real Estate Assn. Mem. Am. Soc. Disting. Citizens (life). Republican. Mem. Sci. of Mind. Avocations: dance, hiking, reading, cooking. Died July 27, 2004.

DATKA, SHIRLEY F., nurse; b. Elwood, Ind., Nov. 12, 1936; d. Glenn L. and Pauline (Kaiser) Fisher; m. Ronald J. Datka, Dec. 26, 1959; children: Mary Elizabeth, Suzanne Marie, Catherine Mary, Stephen James, John William, Karen Marie. Diploma, Holy Cross Cen. Hosp., 1957. Staff nurse VA Med. Ctr., Salisbury, N.C.; dir. nurses Rowan Manor Nursing Home, Salisbury; office nurse Salisbury Clinic for Women; staff nurse CCU VA Med. Ctr. DD, Augusta, Ga., nurse mgr. intermediate medicine/Hospice 36 bed unit. Instr. Lamaze childbirth. Mem. ASPO, NOVA, Nat. Hospice Orgn., Ga. Nurses Assn. Home: Wilmington, NC. Died Aug. 18, 2004.

DAUER, THOMAS GERALD, marketing executive, consultant; b. Hornell, N.Y., Mar. 23, 1929; s. Raymond and Camilla (Leahy) D.; m. Jacqueline Marie Mitchell, Apr. 1, 1959. BA, Art Ctr. Coll. Design, 1955. Dir. new bus. presentations Hycon Mfg., Pasadena, Calif., 1954-56; art. dir., asst. publ. mgr. AMF Associated Missle Co, Pomona, Calif., 1956-58; art dir. publ. mgr. Martin Marietta Corp., Orlando, Fla., 1958-65; creative dir. Dr. Cortez F. Enloe Medical Advt., N.Y.C., 1964-66; design cons., art dir. Hearst Mags., N.Y.C., 1966-72; advt. mgr., creative dir. Kinro Advt. Co., Atlanta, 1971-74; mktg. services v.p. Amiel Industries SA, Nyon, Atlanta, Switzerland, 1974-79; founder. ultra graphics v.p. Com. Photo Lab, Atlanta, from 1978; pres. Dauer Assocs., Atlanta, from 1978. Cons. Bellsouth China Tech/First Telecomm Sino/Am. Conf., Beijing, 1985-86, Internat. Svc. Systems, N.Y.C., 1990-92, Atlanta Hartsfield Internat. Airport, 1992-93, others. Art dir.: Popular Mechanics mag., 1966-72; dir. The Creation of Commercial Artists / Illustrator. Recipient Civilian Excellence award Army Rocket Guided Missle Agy., 1960. Roman Catholic. Avocations: creating historic paintings, fly fishing. Died Jan. 10, 2004.

DAUGHTREY, WILLIAM HURLEY, financial analyst; b. West Point, Ga., Mar. 13, 1940; s. William Watson and Elsie Marie (Hurley) D.; m. Monnie Elisabeth Roberson, Apr. 7, 1962; children: Cynthia, Sheilah, David, Michele. BS cum laude, North Ga. Coll., 1961; MPH, Emory U., 1979. Investment analyst Citzens and So. Nat. Bank, Atlanta, 1967-70; mgmt. and budget analyst DeKalb County Budget Office, Decatur, Ga., 1970-76; adminstrv. officer DeKalb County Health Dept., Decatur, 1976-83; fin. analyst DeKalb County Fin. Dept., Decatur, from 1983. Adj. lectr. pub. health Emory U., 1984. Contbr. articles to lit. jours.; actor various films, TV commls. Atlanta area. Mem. State Bar Ga. Fee Arbitration Panel, Atlanta, 1985, 87; leader Stone Mountain council Boy Scouts Am., 1982-86; announcer Ga. Radio Readers Service, Atlanta, 1984. Served to capt. U.S. Army M.I. Corps, 1962-67. Mem. Am. Mgmt.

Assn., Govt. Fin. Officers Assn., Mensa. Lodges: Brotherhood St. Andrew (Stone Mountain). Episcopalian. Avocation: community theater. Home: Stone Mountain, Ga. Died Jan. 25, 2005.

DAUPHIN, VERNON MAYFIELD, digital image artist, video producer; b. Jacksonville, Fla., Mar. 31, 1929; s. Vernon M. and Eva May (Hudson) D.; m. Susan L. Helfrich, Feb. 7, 1959; children: William M., Katie Collins. BSEE, BSIE, Ga. Inst. Tech., 1956. Capt., jet fighter pilot USAF, 1951-53; mem. staff command and supervisory control, range safety USAF Missile Test Ctr., Cape Canaveral, Fla., 1956-60; liaison space task group Atlantic Missile Test Range, 1957-60; space sci. engr. NASA, Houston, 1960-87; mng. editor Pixel Press, from 1987; non-linear videographer Dauphin Arts, Jupiter, Fla., from 1992, digital image artist, from 1994. One-man shows include Superclubs, Negril, Jamaica, 1994, 95, 96; exhibited in group shows at Artist Coop. Gallery, Lake Worth, Fla., 1996; prodr.: (video) Safe Cytotoxics, 1992, Safe Handling of Sharps, 1993; prodr., videographer: Lampslight, 1994, Pbmug, 1995. Capt. USAF, 1950-53, with Res., 1954-62. Recipient Crystal Reel award Fla. Motion Picture and TV Assn., Orlando, Fla., 1992, Spl. award Artists Coop. Gallery, Lake Worth, 1996. Mem. Electronic Design Assn., Lighthouse Membership for Parkinson Support (founder, pres. 1988-97), Assn. Fla. Computer Users Groups, Palm Beach MAC Users Group (bd. dirs. 1990-97). Avocation: utilizing computers in media. Home: Lake Worth, Fla. Died Apr. 14, 2005.

DAVID, ANN ANITA, plastering company executive; b. Aintab, Turkey, Jan. 24, 1910; came to U.S., 1922; d. Jack and Yumma Cutler; m. Al David, June 15, 1940; children: Jane Annete David Colletti, Jerry Al. Dress designer Cutler Embroidery Co., L.A., 1932-40; office mgr. Perlite Plastering Co., Inc., L.A., 1972-87, pres., from 1988. Formerly active Girl Scouts U.S.A., Boy Scouts Am., Jobs Daugs., DeMolay; former Sunday sch. tchr., supt., mem. bd. trustees, ch. clk. United Armenian Congl. Ch., Hollywood, Calif., pres. Ladies Aid. Recipient Mother of Yr. award United Armenian Congl. Ch., Trustees award; Mother of Yr. award Armenian Ararat Home for Sr. Citizens. Avocations: sewing, gardening, swimming, jogging, volunteering for convalescent homes and hospitals. Died Apr. 17, 2004.

DAVIDON, ANN MORRISSETT, writer, activist; b. Dayton, Ohio, Aug. 18, 1925; d. Irving Archer and Anna Lee (Rogers) M.; m. William Cooper Davidon (div.); children: Ruth Anna, Sarah Lessie. BA, U. Chgo., 1947; MA, Putney Grad. Sch., 1956. Tchr. English dept. Temple U., 1982-84, Villanova U., 1984-85, So. Conn. State U., 1985-87, St. Joseph's Univ., 1989-90, C.C. of Phila., from 1992, Rutgers U., from 1997. English cons. Fed. Com. for the Environ., Prague, 1991-92; guest English instr. Charles U., Prague, 1991; cons. Am. Friends Svc. Com., Women's Internat. League for Peace and Freedom, Phila., 1970's, 1980's. Author: (with others) Reweaving the Web of Life: Feminism and Nonviolence, 1982, Witness of the Berrigans, 1972; translator: The Priests of Ancient Egypt, 1960; author: (plays) Getting Up and Getting Dressed, 1980, The Magnificent Failure, 1962; contbr. articles to mags. and newspapers. Bd. dirs. SANE/Freeze/Act for Peace, Phila., 1993; exec. com. War Resisters Internat., Hdqrs. London, 1970's; exec. com. War Resisters League, N.Y.C., 1960's, 70's, Nat. Com. War Resisters League, 1995-98; nat. com. Fellowship of Reconciliation, Nyack, N.Y., 1960's. Recipient (with Wm. Davidon) Phila. SANE award, 1973; MacDowell Colony fellow, 1978; Pa. Arts Coun. grantee for scriptwriting, 1997. Mem. Phila. Dramatists Ctr. (founding). Home: Philadelphia, Pa. Died May 7, 2004.

DAVIDSON, NELLIE MCCLEAVE, nurse; b. Lowell, Mass., Nov. 28, 1937; d. Thomas Davidson and Ruth Dale (Ward) Rooney. BS in Nursing, U. Colo., 1959. RN, Mass., Colo., Pa. Head nurse, supr. Boston Lyingpin Hosp., 1959-62; supr. Lawrence Meml. Hosp., Medford, Mass., 1962-63; operating room nurse U. Colo. Med. Ctr., Denver, 1963-65, head nurse, 1965-69; staff nurse Mercy Hosp., Pitts., 1969-76, diabetes educator, 1976-89, case mgr. occupl. medicine, 1989-95, nurse case mgr. Operation Safety Net program, from 1995. Mem. Am. Assn. Diabetes Educators (cert.), Am. Diabetes Assn. Republican. Roman Catholic. Home: Bethel Park, Pa. Died May 3, 2004.

DAVIS, CORALIE GUARINO, librarian; b. New Orleans, Nov. 13, 1926; d. Anthony and Florence Olivia (Ducros) Guarino; m. George Warren Davis, Jr., June 13, 1953 (dec. 1966); 1 child, Mark Jefferson. BFA, Tulane U., 1947; MEd, U. New Orleans, 1975; MLS, La. State U., 1980. Libr. asst. New Orleans Pub. Libr., 1949—50; draftsman Shell Oil Co., New Orleans, 1967—2002; libr. U. New Orleans, 1967—2002; ret., 2002. Author: Index to New Orleans Magazine, 1982, (pamphlet) Selected Bibliography of Works of James Dakin, 1981, (pamphlet) Folk Architecture of Louisiana, a Selected Bibliography, 1985; contbr. articles to profl. jours. Mem. Chalmette Battlefield task force Jean Lafitte Nat. Hist. Park, from 2002. Mem.: DAR (treas. Spirit of '76 chpt. 1974—76), La. Landmarks Soc., St. Bernard Hist. Soc., La. Hist. Soc., New Orleans Mus. Art, La. Colonials (treas. Founders chpt. 1977—79, bd. dirs., chmn. La. history award 1984—85, treas. Founders chpt. 1987—89), Geneal. Rsch. Soc. New Orleans (corr. sec. 1983—84), Chalmette Nat. Hist. Park Assn. (treas. 1978—85), La. State Soc. Daus. of 1812 (pres. 1971—73, registrar 1960—83), Friends of New Orleans Libr. (treas. 1977—2000), Friends of Cabildo, Dames of Ct. of Honor La., Descs. of Founders of New Orleans, U.S. Daus. of 1812 (nat. chmn. pub. rels. 1970—73, chmn. nat. jr. membership 1973—76, 1st v.p.n at. 1976—79, nat. historian 1979—81, pres. Officers Nat. Club 1981—84, hon. v.p. nat. life from 1981, pres. Chalmette chpt. from 2003), Tulane Alumni Assn., UNO Founders Club (sec. 1990—2002), Am. Legion Aux., Beta Phi Mu, Phi Delta Kappa, Phi Kappa Phi. Home: New Orleans, La. Died Oct. 23, 2004.

DAVIS, EDWARD MICHAEL, retired state senator, former police chief; b. Los Angeles, Nov. 15, 1916; s. James Leonard and Lillian (Fox) D.; m. Virginia; children: Michael Edward, Christine Hart, Mary Ellen Burde; m. Aileen Bobbie Nash, Jan. 7, 1984 BS in Pub. Adminstrn. cum laude, U. So. Calif., 1961; LLD (hon.), Western Sierra Law Sch., 1972. With LA Police Dept., 1940—78, chief of police, 1969-78; mem. Calif. State Senate, LA, 1980—92. Adj. prof. U. So. Calif., Los Angeles, 1967-68. Author: Staff One, 1978. Served with USN, 1942-45. Recipient George Washington Honor medal Freedom Found., Flame of Truth award Fund for Higher Edn., 1976; named Man of Yr., B'nai Brith, 1974, Outstanding Am., Los Angeles Philanthropic Found., 1977. Mem. Am. Legion (post 381 commdr. 1968-69), Internat. Assn. Chiefs of Police (pres. 1976-77). Republican. Episcopalian. Home: Chatsworth, Calif. Died Apr. 22, 2006.

DAVIS, JOHN KING, optics scientist; b. Webster, Mass., Nov. 30, 1913; s. Joseph Benjamin and Bertha C. (Rowell) D.; m. Lucy L. McNutt, Nov. 2, 1940; children: John M., Robert B. Student, Bowdoin Coll., 1932-33; AB, Clark U., 1937. Lens designer Am. Optical Corp., Southbridge, Mass., 1939-48, head geometric optics rsch., 1948-62, lens devel. mgr., 1962-71, chief ophthalmic scis., 1971-75; assoc. prof. physiol. optics Pa. Coll. Optometry, Phila., 1975-79, adj. prof., from 1979; cons. in optics Gentex Corp. and Gentex Optics Corp., Dudley, Mass., from 1977. Bd. dirs. Centex Optics Corp. Contbr. articles to profl. publs.; patentee in field. Mem., chmn. Woodstock Bd. Edn., 1955-63; chmn. sunglass subcom. Am. Nat. Standards Inst., 1971. Mem. Nat. Acad. Opticianry (life, bd. dirs. 1976-83, Beverly Myers Nelson Achievement award 1976, Hall of Fame award), Sunglass Assn. Am. (Achievement award 1976, 93), Acad. Optometry (hon. life), Optical Soc. Am. Republican. Congregationalist. Avocation: photography. Home: East Woodstock, Conn. Died May 3, 2005.

DAVIS, JOSEPH LA ROY, horticulurist; b. Pasadena, Calif., June 6, 1932; s. Reading LaRoy and Beulah May (Noble) D.; (dec. Feb. 22, 1988); children: Melissa, Michele, Michael, Myles. BS, Calif. Poly. U., 1958. Lic. pest control advisor. Owner, dir. Joseph L. Davis Cons. Horticulturist, Sierra Madres, Calif., from 1958; prof. Napa (Calif.) Valley Coll., from 1975. Cons. Horticulture, Pest Mgmt., Napa, 1958—, expert witness, 1965—. Author: Horticulture Dictionary, 1988. Apptd. Tree Commn., Napa, 1982-90, Pks. & Recreation Commn., Napa, 1988-90. MSgt. USAFR, 1974-92, Korea. Named Prof. Emeritus, Napa Valley Coll., 1991. Mem. Calif. Agrl. Prodn. (chpt. pres. 1984-85, state dir. 1985-91), Calif. Assn. Nurseryman, Calif. Land Contractors Assn., Internat. Growth Regulator Soc., Am. Soc. Enologists, Pest Control Operators of Calif., Napa County Farm Bur. Episcopalian. Avocations: computer programs for industry, photography, horticulture. Home: Napa, Calif. Died Nov. 30, 2004.

DAVIS, L. CLARICE, artist, consultant, small business owner; b. Akron, Ohio, Jan. 30, 1929; d. Kenneth Fillmore and Ethel (Locken) Davis. BA in Fine Arts, U. Akron, 1955; MLS, UCLA, 1961, MA in Art History, 1968, postgrad. in art history. Lectr. art history Calif. State U., Northridge, 1961—63, 1968—70, Otis Art Inst., L.A., 1969—70; chief mus. libr. Los Angeles County Mus. Art, L.A., 1963—68; acting head art libr. UCLA, 1972—75; propr. Davis Art Books, Santa Monica and L.A., 1971—79; ptnr. Davis & Schorr Art Books, L.A., 1979—91, L. Clarice Davis Art Books, from 1991. Bibliographer, rschr.: Peter Voulkos, Sclupture, 1965, R.B. Kitaj, 1965; author: Annals of Auction Sales, 1976; bibliographer: Theophile A. Steinlen, 1982. Named Samuel H. Kress scholar, UCLA Art Dept., 1971; Howard Campbell scholar, U. Akron, 1954, Deborah King scholar, UCLA Libr. Sch., 1960—61. Mem.: Antiquarian Booksellers Assn. Am., Art Librs. Soc. N.Am. (vice chmn. 1982—83). Died Jan. 29, 2006.

DAVIS, LEANDER M., medical/surgical nurse; b. Guthrie, Okla., Jan. 2, 1958; m. Giles and Virginia (Wade) Davis; m. Gwendolyn Davis, Apr. 25, 1980; children: Shanya, Latrice. LPN, William Beaumont Hosp., El Paso, Tex., 1984; BSN, U. Okla., 1991. Staff nurse LPN Bapt. Med. Ctr., Oklahoma City. With U.S. Army, 1977-86. Home: Oklahoma City, Okla. Died May 16, 2004.

DAVIS, LEWIS, architectural firm executive; b. N.Y.C., July 31, 1925; m. Lynn Mangel (div.); m. Anne Moskovitz. B.Arch., U. Pa., M.Arch, 1948. Adv. to pres. on design and planning U. Pa., 1970—80; founder Davis Brody Bond, LLP, 1952—2006. Vis. critic Harvard, Princeton, Mass. Inst. of Tech., Mass., Univ. of Pa., Pa., RI Sch. of Design, RI, Univ. of Ill., Ill.; Davenport prof. of Arch. Yale Univ. Design, Waterside and Riverbend housing complexes, New York City, US Pavilion in the 1970 World's Fair, Osaka, Japan. Recipient AIA Arch. Firm Award, Louis Sullivan Award for Arch., Nat. Inst. of Arts and Letters' Arnold W. Brunner Award, 3 consecutive nat. awards, Am. Inst. of Arch. Mem.: Cooper Union Sch. of Arch. (faculty mem. for 25 yr.), Bd. of Overseers, Univ. of Pa. Sch. of Design and Planning. He participated in the planning and design of facilities for major corp. such as ARCO, Corning Glass Works, Philip Morris, IBM, AT&T, and Hallmark; hosp. such as New York's Mem. Sloan-Kettering Cancer Center and Mt. Sinai; and Univ. such as Cornell, Cornell Coll. of Vet. Med., Princeton, Brown, Columbia and Harvard Med. Sch. The firm's scope of work has also included the restoration of the Bronx Zoo, and the NY Pub. Libr. Died May 21, 2006.

DAVIS, MAGGIE L., elementary school educator; b. Bastrop, La., July 13, 1939; m. Killion C. Davis II, May 1, 1961. BA, U. Calif, 1982, postgrad.; PhD, Grambling State U., 1961. Cert. elem. tchr. Tchr. Berkeley (Calif.) Unified Sch. Dist., from 1987. Head supr. Willie Youth Field O.E.S., 1983—. Mem. Alpha Kappa Alpha (sec. 1959), NCNW. Lodges: Pride Alameda, O.E.S. (worth matron 1983—), Queen Sheba L.K.T. (fin. sec. 1982—), Queen Adah Grand Chpt. (grand recorder 1984—, fin. sec. 1983—). Democrat. Baptist. Avocations: sewing, reading, solving puzzles, swimming, tennis. Home: Berkeley, Calif. Died June 21, 2004.

DAVIS, MARINA WINN, psychotherapist; b. Laredo, Tex., Aug. 30, 1945; d. Seaborn Lafayette and Lucy Curtis (Winn) Faulk; m. Donnie Fayy Smith, Aug. 21, 1967 (div. Jan. 1988); 1 child, Susan Ellene Smith. BS, U. Montevallo, Ala., 1970; MS, Tex. A&M U., 1991. Lic. prof. counselor, lic. chem. dependency counselor, cert. social work assoc., Tex. Tchr. ACISD, Rockport, Tex., 1989-93; psychotherapist in pvt. practice, Corpus Christi, from 1994. Vol., Family Outreach, Corpus Christi; primary therapist, geropsychiat. unit Columbia Northbay Hosp.; bd. dirs. YMCA New Orlans East, La., 1976, YMCA, Rockport, Tex., 1992. Mem. Phi Delta Kappa, Psi Chi. Methodist. Avocations: collecting aphorisms and illusions, rock climbing. Died Jan. 12, 2005.

DAVIS, RAYMOND, JR., retired physical chemistry professor; b. Washington, Oct. 14, 1914; s. Raymond D. and Ida Rogers (Younger) D.; m. Anna Marsh Torrey, Dec. 4, 1948; children: Andrew Morgan, Martha Safford Davis Kumler, Nancy Elizabeth Davis Klemm, Roger Warren, Alan Paul. BS, U. Md., 1937, MS, 1939; PhD, Yale U., 1942; DSc, U. Pa., 1990, Laurentian U., 1997, U. Chgo., 2000. Chemist Dow Chem. Co., Midland, Mich., 1937-38, Monsanto Chem. Co., Dayton, Ohio, 1946-48; sr. chemist Brookhaven Nat. Lab., Upton, NY, 1948-84; rsch. prof. dept. physics and astronomy U. Pa., Phila., 1984—2005; ret., 2005. Mem., NASA Lunar Sample Review Bd., 1971-73. Contbr. articles to profl. jours. Served with USAAF, 1942-46. Recipient Boris Prejel prize N.Y. Acad. Scis., 1955, award for nuc. applications in chemistry Am. Chem. Soc., 1979, Pontecorvo prize Inst. for Nuclear Rsch., Russia, 2000, Wolf prize in physics, Wolf Found., Israel, 2000, Nat. Medal of Sci., 2001, Nobel prize for physics, 2002, Benjamin Franklin medal for physics, 2003, Enrico Fermi award, US Dept. Energy, 2003. Mem. AAAS, NAS (Comstock prize 1978), Am. Phys. Soc. (Tom W. Bonner prize 1988, W.K.H. Panofsky prize 1992), Am. Geophys. Union, Am. Astron. Soc. (Beatrice M. Tinsley prize 1994, George Ellory Hale prize 1996). Home: Blue Point, NY. Died May 31, 2006.

DAVIS, RONALD FARLANDI, JR., health services facility administrator; b. Arlington, Va., Dec. 10, 1946; s. Ronald Farlandi and Mary Anne (Reynolds) D.; m. Annabella C. Ozbun, Dec. 30, 1965 (div. Nov. 1984); children: Wendy Ann, Kimberly Ann; m. Constance Jeanne Phelps, Feb. 14, 1986. B Health Services, U. Mo., 1982. Fingerprint technician FBI, Washington, 1964-66; enlisted U.S. Army, 1966, advanced through grades to chief warrant officer, 1971, spl. agt. U.S. and Vietnam, 1966-75; adminstr. Sunset Nursing Home, Union, Mo., from 1975. Alderman City of Union, 1977-85; active Franklin County Youth Fair Bd., Union, 1986-88. Named Nursing Home Adminstr. of Yr. ADAPT Inst. Am., 1985. Mem. Am. Health Care Assn., Mo. Health Care Assn. (bd. dirs. 1977-81), Mo. League Nursing Home Adminstrs., Mo. Police Chiefs Assn., Union C. of C., Am. Legion (sgt.-at-arms 1985-88, 1st vice comdr. 1988—), 40 & 8 Club, Mo. League of Nurses, VFW, Rotary (pres. 1979-80, sec. 1985-88). Republican. Roman Catholic. Avocations: instrumental music, flying. Died June 7, 2004.

DAVIS, RUTH LENORE, retired college official; b. Toledo, Ohio, Mar. 24, 1910; d. Thurber Phillips and Ila L. (Andrews) D. BSBA, U. Ariz., 1932, postgrad., 1932-34, U. Mich., 1941-42; DEd, Johnson and Wales Coll., R.I., 1983. Sec. to supt. schs. Tucson Pub. Schs., 1934-35; tchr. Tucson Sr. High Sch., 1935-41; supervising and sr. acct. Jeep Corp., Toledo, 1942-45; v.p. Davis Coll., Toledo, 1941-42, 45-56, pres., 1956-85, pres. emeritus, from 1985. V.p., trustee Davis Jr. Coll. Bd., 1983—. Trustee Epworth United Meth. Ch., Toledo, 1986-89; mem. Com. of 100, Toledo, 1985-88; fin. com. YWCA, Toledo, 1982. Recipient Outstanding Citizenship award, Internat. Inst. Phi Theta Phi, 1987, Outstanding Bus. Educator, 1973, Svc. award Mid-Am. Bank, 1980. Mem. Adminstrv. Mgmt. Soc. (pres. 1973-74, 300 Club award), Ohio Bus. Sch. Assn. (pres. 1946-49), Internat. Pers. Women Toledo (pres. 1975-76), Zonta Club (pres. Toledo 1948-49). Republican. Methodist. Avocations: golf, travel. Home: Sandusky, Ohio. Died Mar. 21, 2005.

DAVIS, THOMAS MYRON, transportation executive; b. Jackson County, Ohio, July 9, 1934; s. Thomas Clarence and Jennie Mae (Williams) D.; m. Carolyn Tucker, May 2, 1959; children: Summer Lea, Todd Joshua. BA in gen. bus., Ohio State U., Columbus, 1956. Sub sta. mgr. The Columbus Citizen Newspaper, Columbus, 1950-56; asst. circulation mgr. The Hartley Pub. Co., Columbus, 1956-57; adminstrn. specialist Military Svc., Fort Manor, 1957-59; asst. buyer F&R Lazarus Fed., Columbus, 1959-61; credit mgmt. Sears Roebuck & Co., Phoenix, 1961-69, Montgomery Ward, 1969-73; mgr. Avon Products, 1973-87; mgmt. quality assurance New Hamton Inc., Newport News, Va., 1987-93; sr. exec. transp. Newport News Inc./Spiegel, from 1993. Mem. exec. bd. Parcel Shippers Assn., Washington, 1993—; mailer tech. adv. coun. U.S. Postal Svc., 1996—; mem. Standard Mail Adv. Coun., 1989—. Advisor Consumer Credit Counseling Svc., Stockton, Calif., 1968. Mem. Tidewater Traffic Club. Avocations: jogging, hiking, stamps. Home: Lanexa, Va. Died Mar. 3, 2005.

DAVIS, WILLIAM MARK, minister; b. Lexington, Ky., June 28, 1963; s. Robert Edward Davis and Helen (Youngman) Lucky; m. Dawna Elaine Davis, July 21, 1990. BA in Psychology, Georgetown Coll., 1986; MDiv, Lexington Theol. Sem., 1989. Ordained to ministry Disciples of Christ Ch., 1989. Assoc. min. Twin Pines Christian Ch., Lexington, 1988-90, South Side Christian Ch., Lima, Ohio, from 1990. Mem. Assn. Christian Ch. Educators, Lima Area Clergy Acad. Died Dec. 25, 2004.

DAWSON, DONALD S., lawyer; b. El Dorado Springs, Mo., Aug. 3, 1908; s. John William and Cora Shelton Dawson; m. Alva Ansley Patten, 1944; 1 child, Diana Star Coyner; m. Ilona Massey, 1955-75; m. Virginia Jenkins Frieldand, 1975; children: Robert Fox, Virginia Fox. BS, U. Mo., 1930; JD, George Washington U., 1938. Bar: D.C., U.S. Supreme Ct., 1938. Enlisted U.S. Army, 1943, advanced through grades to maj., 1946; ret. maj. gen. USAF, 1970; examiner closed bank sect. Reconstrn. Fin. Corp., 1933-39, dir. pers., 1939-43, 46-47; asst. to Jesse H. Jones, Fed. Loan Adminstrn.; spl. exec. asst. to Pres. Harry S. Truman, 1947-53; sr. ptnr. Dawson, Griffin, Pickens, Attys., Washington, 1953-68, Dawson, Riddell, Holroyd, Taylor & Davis, Attys., Washington, 1968-80; counsel Dawson, Riddell, Fox, Holroyd & Jackson, P.C., Washington, 1980-83; pvt. practice Washington, 1983. Asst. to fed. loan adminstr. Fed. Loan Adminstrn., 1939-43; chmn. White House Loyalty Rev. Bd., 1947-53; dir. liaison office for pers. mgmt. Exec. Office of Pres., 1947-53; rep. of U.S. pres. to Inauguration of Pres. Vargas, Brazil, 1951, Inauguration of Pres. Cortines, Mex., 1952. Bd. dirs. Harry S. Truman Libr. Inst. for Nat. and Internat. Affairs, 1980-96, pres., 1991-96, pres. emeritus, 1996; mem. exec. com. Humane Soc. of U.S., 1976—, dir., 1978-84, chmn. nominating com., 1980-84, chmn. bylaws com., 1982—; bd. overseers Coll. of V.I.; mem. centennial com. Dwight D. Eisenhower Soc., 1990; co-founder Am. Friends of Jamaica, 1982, pres. emeritus, 1982-97; mem. exec. bd. Nat. Area coun. Boy Scouts of Am.; dir. Nat. Com. on Playgrounds for Youth of Am., Arthritis and Rheumatism Found. D.C.; trustee Boys Club Washington; hon. trustee U.S. Capitol Hist. Soc. Named Father of Yr., D.C. Sons and Daus. Found., 1962; recipient Martin Luther King award Jamaican Am. Soc., 1996, Harry S. Truman Achievement award, 1984, Disting. Svc. award Dept. Mo., 1984. Mem. Res. Officers Assn. (nat. pres. 1965-66, nat. v.p. for air force 1964-65, exec. com. 1964-67, chmn. air force affairs com. 1960-62, Nat. award), Air Force Assn. (air res. policy com. 1962-64, membership co-chmn. 1973, Gavel award N.Y.C. chpt. 1966), Nat. Dem. Club (founding mem., past pres.), Dwight D. Eisenhauer Soc. (v.p. 1990—), Met. Club, Army and Navy Club (nominating com. 1982, chmn. mgr. selection com. 1980, v.p. 1983-88, pres. 1988-90), Nat. Press Club, Congl. Country Club (hon. mem.), Order of DeMolay (comdr., pres., Legion of Honor), Phi Alpha Delta, Beta Theta Pi. Died Dec. 25, 2005.

DAWSON, EUGENE ELLSWORTH, university president emeritus; b. Kansas City, Kans., Jan. 23, 1917; s. Harold Lambert and Betty Ross Dawson; m. Arlene Wilburma Clark, May 7, 1935; children: Eugene Jr., Clark (dec.), LoLita, Edward, Brent, Deborah. BA, Pittsburg (Kans.) State U., 1940; STB, Harvard U., 1944; PhD, Boston U., 1949; postgrad., U. Chgo., 1953; DHL (hon.), U. Colo., 1967; HHD (hon.), Regis U., Denver, 1967; DLitt (hon.), Keuka Coll., Keuka Pk., N.Y., 1968; DD (hon.), U. Redlands, Calif., 1978; postgrad., St. Elizabeth's Hosp., Washington, 1978-79. Asst. prof. psychology Pittsburg State U., 1946-48, dean of adminstrn., prof. psychology, 1949-57; pres. Colo. Woman's Coll., Denver, 1957-70, U. Redlands, 1970-78, pres. emeritus, 1978—2005. Instr. summer sessions U. Chgo, Kent State U., U. Houston, Western Oreg. U., Iliff Sch. Theology; cons. higher edn. and human svcs.; evaluator grants to univs. and ednl. instns. Contbr. articles to profl. jours., chpts. to books. Bd. dirs. Estes Pk. Ch. of the Air, Qualife Wellness Cmty., Denver, Samaritan Counseling Ctr., Denver; sec. bd. trustees Temple Hoyne Buell Found., Englewood, Colo.; sec. bd. dirs. Buell Devel. Corp., Englewood. Recipient Outstanding Alumni award Pittsburg State U., 1957, Meritorious Svc. award, 1977, Talmud Torah award Congregation Hebrew Edn. Alliance, Denver, 1969. Mem. Colo. Harvard Club, Nebr. PTA (life), Rotary Internat. (Paul Harris fellow So. Calif. divsn. 1972, pres. Denver chpt. 1964-65, dist. gov. 1967-68, Denver Rotary Found.), Phi Delta Kappa, Omicron Delta Kappa. Baptist. Avocations: tennis, hiking, reading, travel. Home: Estes Park, Colo. Died May 31, 2005.

DAWSON, HARRY HOLTON, directional drilling engineer; b. Terrell, Tex., Mar. 23, 1922; s. Harry Francis and Bertha Louise (Haggerty) D.; m. Ruth Lee Case, Aug. 16, 1941; children: Nancy Louise Dawson Sinatra, Harry F., Robert C., Charles Roe, Kimberly K. Dawson McClosky. BSCE, U. Houston, 1949. Directional drilling engr., mgr. Houston Oil and Material Co., Tex., La., 1950-59; directional drilling engr., sales mgr., ptnr. Whipstock Inc., New Iberia, La., 1959-70; directional drilling engr., v.p., ptnr. Cochran-Dean Co., Houston and Lafayette, La., 1979-90; v.p. Sperry-Son-Cochran Dean Co., Houston and New Orleans, 1979-90; pres., engr. Dawson and Assoc. Directional Drilling, New Orleans, from 1990; pres. Crescent Geotech. Svcs., Inc., Belle Chasse, La. Served with USN Aviation, 1942-45, WWII. Mem. Soc. Petroleum Engrs., Am. Assn. Drilling Engrs. Republican. Baptist. Avocations: fishing, boating, designing computer programs. Home: New Orleans, La. Died July 15, 2005.

DAY, MARY, artistic director, ballet company executive; b. Wash., Jan. 25, 1910; Trained by Lisa Gardinier; ArtsD (hon.), Shenandoah Conservatory; DHL (hon.), Mount Vernon Coll. Co-founder Washington Sch. Ballet, from 1944; founder Washington Ballet, 1976, artistic dir., 1976—99. Named Washingtonian of Yr., Washingtonian mag.; recipient Mayor's award, Woman of Achievement award, WETA-TV, Met. Dance award, Founders award, Cultural Alliance, Excellence in Teaching Chautauqua Dance award, sr. Svcs. Disting. award IONA. Died July 11, 2006.

DAY, RALPH LAWRENCE, retired physician, abbot; b. Buenos Aires, Oct. 4, 1923; came to U.S., 1966, naturalized, 1975; s. Rafael Paniagua Tejefor and Maria Atanasia Diaz; m. Betty C. Day, Nov., 7, 1957. BA, U. Buenos Aires, 1952; PhD in Psychotherapy, Sequoia U., 1967, DO in Osteopathy, 1973; ND in Naturopathy, N.A.N.M., Portland, Oreg., 1970; ThD, Bernardean U., 1974; MD, United Am. Med. Coll., 1975; MD, MS, Ch. C. Homeopathy, 1976. Lic. naturopathic physician. With Min. Edn. and Welfare, Argentina, 1949-55; practicant medicine Inst. Burns and Plastic Surgery, Argentina, 1955-62; adminstr. Blood Bank Clinics Hosp., 1956-57; practicant medicine Aviation Mil. Ctrl. Hosp., 1957-58; practicant medicine Children's Ward Inst. Burns and Plastic Surgery, 1958-59, rschr., 1961; asst. prof. lab. techs. course Min. Health, 1961; criminal psychologist Dept. Police, Lima, Peru, 1963-66; founder, abbot Roman Cath. Ch. Soc. St. Benedict, Florence, Colo., 1990. Chief pathologist Inst. for Bio-Social Rsch., Lima, 1963-66; dir., founder Family Clinic, Pocatello, Idaho, 1970-87; with S.S. Cosmas & Damian, Human Life Styling, Clinc, Boise, Idaho and Florence, Colo., 1971-89. Author: Stop Whining and Be a Man, 1996, Psychosomatic Medicine, 1996; co-author: Burns and Repair with Plastic Surgery, 1963; contbr. articles to profl. jours. With Argentinian Navy Aviation, 1942-48. Recipient 1st award, Gold medal Soc. Argentina Cirugia Plastica, 1961; fellow Geigy Labs., 1961. Mem. Am. Assn. Naturopathic Physicians, Am. Naturopathic Assn., Charles F. Menninger Soc., Toastmasters, Lions, Mil. Order of Knights of Temple of Solomon (hon. knight 2002). Avocations: camera music, theology, psychotherapy, meditation. Died 2004.

DAY, WILLIAM ELMER, lawyer; b. Sioux City, Iowa, Mar. 22, 1931; s. Winfred Elmer and Franciska (Croot) D.; m. Shirley J. Lindley, June 2, 1952 (div. 1976); m. H. Joanne Rickord, Aug. 17, 1979; children: Debra, Sue Ellen, David. BS, U. S.D., 1953, JD, 1956. Bar: Iowa 1983. Adjuster State Farm Ins. Co., Sioux City, 1956-82; sole practice Sioux City, from 1982. Served to 1st lt. U.S. Army, 1953-55. Mem.: Kiwanis (pres. Sioux City club 1986—). Republican. Methodist. Home: Spirit Lake, Iowa. Died Aug. 1, 2005.

DAYAL, RAVINDRA, publishing company executive; b. Pilibhit, Uttarpradesh, India, Sept. 6, 1937; s. Bishumber and Savitri (Lal) D.; m. Mala Singh, Dec. 12, 1973; 1 child, Naina. B.A. with honors, St. Stephen's Coll., Delhi, India, 1957, M.A., 1959; B.A. with honors, Univ. Coll., Oxford, Eng., 1961. Asst. mgr. Oxford U. Press, Madras, India, 1962-64, mgr., Bombay, India, 1965-71; chief editor Oxford U. Press, India, Delhi, 1971-76, gen. mgr., 1976—. Contbr. Handbook for Writers in India, 1975, The Craft of Writing, 1978. Contbr. articles to profl. jours. J. N. Tata Endowment scholar, Bombay, 1959; sr. scholar St. Antony's Coll., Oxford, 1961. Club: India Internat. Centre (New Delhi). Avocations: playing Indian musical instruments; archeology; painting; reading and writing; trekking in the Himalayas. Died June 4, 2006.

DEAN, BERNARD SPENCER, data processing specialist; b. Washington, Mar. 14, 1937; s. Joseph S. and Eva A. (Mitchell) D.; m. Muriel A. Dewey, July 16, 1960; children: Anne Dean Spillane, Susan Dean Fullerton, Bernard S. Jr., Karen Dean Sholette, Glenn P., Derek J., Gary M. Student, Villanova U., 1955-58. Computer operator, programmer Nat. Bank of Washington, 1962-65; programmer Army Times, Washington, 1965; programmer, systems analyst Colonial Penn, Phila., 1966-83; software specialist Bull H.N. Worldwide Info. Systems, Marlton, N.J., from 1983. Sec., treas. Cherry Hill (N.J.) Fedn., 1968-71; bd. dirs. Cherry Hill Parks and Recreation Adv. Bd., 1972-77; treas. James H. Johnson Home and Sch. Assn., Cherry Hill, 1977-80. Mem. Camden County Bd. of Realtors (assoc.). Democrat. Roman Catholic. Avocations: tennis, fishing, guitar playing. Home: Bluffton, SC. Died Nov. 1, 2004.

DEAN, JEAN BEVERLY, artist; b. South Paris, Maine, Aug. 23, 1928; d. Henry Dyer and Doris Filena (Judd) Small; m. Samuel Lester Dean. AS, Becker Coll., Worcester, Mass., 1948; AA, Edison Coll., Ft. Myers, Fla., 1980. Artist, Ft. Myers, from 1963. One-woman shows include Edison C.C. Gallery, Ft. Myers, Joan Ling Gallery, Gainesville, Fla., Berry Coll., Mt. Berry Ga., Gallery 10, Asheville, NC, Sanibel Gallery, Fla., 1993, 1995, Barrier Island Group for the Arts, Sanibel, 1994, 1996, Gallery Mido, Belleview Mido Resort, Belleair, Fla., 1996, No. Trust Bank, Ft. Myers, 1996, Lee County Alliance of the Arts, 1996, Art League of Manatee County, Fla., 1996, Naples Libr., 1997, Sy Zy Gy Gallery, Ft. Myers, 1998, 2000, Barnes and Noble, 2000, Captiva Civic Assn., Fla., 2000, So. County Ctr. for the Arts, Ft. Myers, 2000, Viva Gallery, Captiva, Fla., 2000, Broadway Palm Dinner Theatre, Ft. Myers, 2001, Art House, 2002, Tower Gallery, Sanibel, 2002, Alliance for the Arts, Ft. Myers, 2004, exhibited in group shows at S.E. Painting and Sculpture Exhbn., Jacksonville, Fla., Southeastern Ctr. for Contemporary Art, Ybor City, S.W. Fla. Internat. Airport, 1991, 1995, Ctr. Art Show, St. Petersburg, Fla., 1991, Ridge Juried Art Show, Winter Haven, Fla., 1992, Artists Group, Sarasota, 1992, Women's Caucus for Art, 1993, Polk Mus., Lakeland, Fla., 1993, Daytona Mus., Fla., 1994, Women's Caucus Art Nat. Show, San Antonio, 1995, Capitol Gallery, Tallahassee, 1995, Women's Caucus Art State Show, Sarasota, 1995, Women's Caucus for Art, Miami, 1996, 1998, Fla. Artist Group, Winter Haven, 1996, Jacksonville Art Mus., 1998, Edison Coll., Ft. Myers, 1999, Fla. So. Coll., Lakeland, 1999, Art Ctr., St. Petersburg, 1999, Viva Gallery, Captiva, 2000, Charlotte County Nat., Fla., 2000, Nat. Exhibit, Winter Haven, 2000, The Capitol, Tallahassee, 2001, Venice Art Ctr., 2001, Captiva Art Ctr., 2001, Charlotte County National, Fla., 2002, Alliance of the Arts, Ft. Myers, 2002—03, Barrier Island Group for the Arts, Sanibel, 2002, Gallery on Broadway, Ft. Myers, 2002, Florida Gulf Coast U., 2003, Bonita Arts Ctr., Bonita Springs, Fla., 2003, Crossed Palms Gallery, Bookelia, Fla., 2002—04, Art Serve Gallery, Ft. Lauderdale, 2004, Temple Beth El, Ft. Myers, Fla., 2005, Represented in permanent collections Am. Embassy, Madrid, Edison Coll., Ft. Myers, First Fed. Savs. and Loan, Ft. Myers, Naples, Fla., NCNB Bank, Tampa, Health Park, Ft. Myers, Clara Barton House, Washington, Hirshhorn Collection, Porter Goss Collection. Active Lee County Alliance for Arts, 1994-2004; chair invitational com. Barrier Island Group for Arts, Sanibel, 1994-99; founder Open Doors Lee County Alliance of the Arts, Fla., 1990—. Recipient more than 100 awards. Mem. Nat. Mus. Women in the Arts (charter mem.), Fla. Artists Group, Nat. Soc. Experimental Artists. Democrat. Unitarian Universalist. Home: Fort Myers, Fla. Died July 29, 2005.

DEAN, JOE ALAN, controller; b. Granby, Mo., June 13, 1950; s. Gayle L. Moreland and JoAnne (Mitchell) Craig; m. Linda F., Aug. 19, 1972; children: Seth A., Matthew S. BSBA in Acct., Mo. So. State Coll., 1978, BSBA in Mktg., 1979; BSBA Mgmt., Mo. Southern State Coll., 1979. Contr. Mid-Western Machinery Co., Inc., Joplin, Mo., from 1985. Mem. Club of the C. of C. (chmn.), Publicity Nat. Assn. Accts., (dir. 1988), Profl. Devel. Accts. (dir. 1987), Lions Club. Republican. Baptist. Died Mar. 7, 2005.

DEAN, PAMELA LEE, journalist; b. Chgo., Apr. 25, 1959; d. Floyd Andrew and Ruby Lee (Shipp) Jefferson; m. Marc E. Dean, Aug. 23, 1983 (div. 1987); children: Nicholas C., Lea N., Megan A. BA in journalism, Columbia Coll., 1985. Cert. FCC Restricted Radio Telephone Operator. Editl. asst., asst. editor H.H. Backer Assocs., Chgo., 1988; religion editor, investigative reporter Chgo. Daily Defender, 1988-89, asst. editor, night editor, 1990-92; radio announcer, producer Sta: SOUTH 106, Columbus, Ga., 1995-96; radio announcer Sta: FOXIE 105/WOKS, Columbus, 1996-97. Mentor Urban Journalism Workshop Youth Communication Chgo. Ctr., 1989-92; judge communication scholars Archdiocese Chgo., 1989. Author: (play) Resurrection at Daybreak, 1994. Walk coordinator Nat. Multiple Sclerosis Soc. Ga. chpt., Columbus, 1996. Named Woman of Yr. God Never Fails Ministries, Chgo, 1989; honorable mention Reporting Women in Communications, Chgo., 1989. Mem. Nat. Multiple Sclerosis Soc. (Ga. chpt.). Democrat. Roman Catholic. Home: Columbus, Ga. Died Apr. 29, 2004.

DEAN, WAYNE DICKERSON, automotive executive; b. American Fork, Utah, Oct. 31, 1925; s. Owen and Amy (Dickerson) D.; m. Louise Margaret Burge, Nov. 9, 1946; children: Caron Louise Dean Shore, Scott Wayne, Mark Gordon, Kevin George. Grad. high sch., American Fork, Utah. Delivery person Shell Oil Co., Tillamook, Oreg., 1947-49; salesperson Tillamook Motor Co., 1950-51; salesperson, sales mgr. Condit Chevrolet Co., Tillamook, 1951-57; owner Dean Motors, Tillamook, from 1957. Mem. Tillamook County TAC Commn., 1962—; chmn. adv. com. auto dept. Tillamook High Sch., 1987—. Pres. Tillamook Grade Sch. and Jr. High PTA; mem. Tillamook City Planning Commn., 1976-81; mem. Tillamook City Counsel, 1981-82. With USN, 1944-46. Recipient Luther Halsey Gulick award Camp Fire Girls, Inc., 1974. Mem. Nat. Small Bus. United, Nat. Bus. Assn., Nat. Automobile Dealers Assn., Am. Internat. Automobile Dealers Assn., Oreg. Automobile Dealers Assn., Tillamook County Automobile Dealers Assn., Am. Legion. Democrat. Mem. Lds Ch. Avocations: collecting porcelain dolls, figurines, christmas ornaments, hunting. Home: Tillamook, Oreg. Died Oct. 14, 2004.

DEANDA, JAMES, retired federal judge; b. Houston, Tex., Aug. 21, 1925; s. Javier and Mary Louise DeAnda; m. Joyce Anita DeAnda. BA, Tex. A&M U.; LLB, U. Tex., 1950. Bar: Tex. Pvt. practice, Houston, 1951-54, Corpus Christi, 1955-57, 66-68; mem. McDonald, Spann & DeAnda, Corpus Christi, 1957-62, Edwards & DeAnda, 1962-66, 69-74, Flores, Sanchez, DeAnda & Vidaurri, McAllen, 1974-79;

judge US Dist. Ct. (so. dist.) Tex., Houston, 1979-92, chief judge, 1988—92; pvt. practice Houston, 1992—2006. Mem. ABA, Am. Judicature Soc. Roman Catholic. Died Sept. 7, 2006.

DEBAKEY, ERNEST GEORGE, physician, surgeon; b. Lake Charles, La., Feb. 17, 1912; s. Shaker and Raheega DeB.; m. Marsha Lauder, Apr. 8, 1999; 1 child, Elizabeth. BS Pharmacy, Tulane U., 1931, MD, 1939. Diplomate Am. Coll. Surgeons. Intern Charity Hosp., New Orleans, 1939-40, resident, 1941-42, 45-48; resident thoracic surgery Washington U., St. Louis, 1940-41; pvt. practice Mobile, Ala., 1948-93. Prof. emeritus surgery Tulane U., 1949—, U. South Ala., Mobile, 1973—; staff dept. surgery Mobile Infirmary Med. Ctr., Providence Hosp., Springhill Meml. Hosp., USA-Doctors. Chmn. DeBakey Fund Drug Edn. Program, Mobile, 1992—, DeBakey Fund Perioperative Nursing Continuing Edn., 1989—, DeBakey awards excellence perioperative nursing. Major USAF, 1942-45, CBI. Recipient award excellence Mobile Infirmary Med. Ctr., 1993; named Physician of Yr. Mobile County Med. Auxiliary, 1993; dept. surgery Mobile Infirmary Med. Ctr. named DeBakey Surg. Ste. in his honor, 1988, Ernest G. DeBakey Charitable Found., 1997; inducted Ala. Healthcare Hall of Fame, 2001. Fellow Am. Coll. Surgeons; mem. Ala. Thoracic Soc. Republican. Episcopalian. Died July 6.

DECESARIS, GEATON A., JR., construction executive; m. Joanne Nocente, 1974; children: Angela, Maria, Joann, Kristin, Elizabeth. CEO Washington Homes, Inc., Landover, Md., 1988-2000, pres., CEO, 2000—01; pres. Hovnanian Land Investment Group, 2001—06. Died Apr. 15, 2006.

DECHANCE, GLADYS AUDREY, mental health nurse, counselor; b. Margaret, Pa., Dec. 30, 1941; d. Harry E. and Jessie Margaret (Shoop) Claypool; m. Richard Phillip Dechance, Feb. 20, 1965; children: Yvonne René, Richard Phillip Jr. Diploma, Allegheny Valley Hosp., Natrona Heights, Pa., 1962; BA summa cum laude, St. Leo Coll., 1979; MS in Counseling and Human Devel., Troy State U. Ala., 1980. RN, Wash.; cert. child mental health specialist, Wash. RN Ft. Walton Gen. Hosp., Ft. Walton Beach, Fla.; dir. counseling program KJNW Life Mgmt., Spokane, Wash.; psychiat. nurse II Ea. State Hosp., Medical Lake, Wash.; supr., nurse Tamarack Ctr., Spokane; day charge nurse Manor Care Convalescent Ctr., Spokane. 1st lt. Nurse Corp, USAF, 1984-85. Mem. Alpha Gamma, Phi Delta Kappa. Home: Spokane, Wash. Died Nov. 24, 2004.

DECKER, DAVID RANDOLPH, broadcast engineer; b. Searcy, Ark., Feb. 15, 1956; s. Wilbur Albert Decker and Hilda Maxine (Rigg) Decker-Long; m. Jeanine M. Coleman, Nov. 22, 1959 (div. May 1992); children: David Randolph Jr., Zachary A. AA in Broadcast Tech., Parkland Coll., 1978. Gen. class lic. FCC. Broadcast engr. Sta. WCIA-TV, Champaign, Ill., 1977-83; field engring. supr. Sta. KPNX-TV, Phoenix, 1983-97, mgr. tech. ops., from 1997. Co-builder pub. radio sta. Sta. KPCD, Champaign, 1978. Mem. Soc. Broadcast Engrs. Avocations: hunting, fishing, basketball, camping. Home: Peoria, Ariz. Died Jan. 23, 2005.

DECKER, PETER WILLIAM, academic administrator; b. Grand Rapids, Mich., Mar. 20, 1919; s. Charles B. and Ruth E. (Thorndill) D.; m. Margaret I. Stainthorpe, June 10, 1944; children: Peter, Marilyn, Christine, Charles. BS, Wheaton Coll., 1941; postgrad., Northwestern U., 1942-43, U. Mich., 1958-60; DSc, London Inst. Applied Rsch., 1973; LLD, 1975; DSTh, Midwestern Baptist Bible Sem., 1995. Withadvtg. dept. Hotels Windermere, Chgo., 1942; with Princess Pat Cosmetics, Chgo., 1943; market rsch. investigator A.C. Nielson Co., Chgo., 1944-48; pres. Peter Decker Constrn. Co., Detroit, 1948-60; sales mgr. Century Chem. Products Co., Detroit, 1961-62, vice pres., 1962-63, pres., 1963-75; sr. ptnr. G & D Advtg. Assocs., 1967-78; vice pres., treas., exec. dir. Christian Edn. Advancement, Inc., 1975-95; registrar, instr. N.T. Greek Missions and Theology Birmingham Bible Inst., MI, 1973-86; prof. Midwestern Baptist Coll., from 1984, dir. student fin. aid, from 1984. Trustee Midwestern Baptist Coll., 1985—, mem. exec. com., 1984—, asst. to pres. 1985-90, treas. 1991-95; bd. dirs., prof., trusteeMidwestern Bapt. Bible Sem., 1995—, vice pres. Midewestern Bapt. Bible Seminary Grad. Sch., 1998—. Author: Gettin to Know New Testament Greek, Christology, The Pauline Epistles. Scoutmaster, Boy Scouts of Am., 1956-61, neighborhood commr., 1961-66, merit badge counselor, emeritus, 1979—; mem. Bd. Rev. Beverly Hills, Mich., 1957-63; chmn. Bd. Rev. Southfield Twp., Mich., 1964-67; past pres., Beverly Hills Civic Assn., 1956, bd. dirs., 1953-57, pres., 1958-59; trustee, deacon, Birmingham Mich. Bible Inst., instr. Bible Inst.; bd. dirs. Mich. Epilepsy Ctr. and Assn., 1957-71, exec. com., 1962-67. Recipient Arrowhead Honor awd. Boy Scouts Am., 1965. Mem. AAAS, ASTM, Mich. Edn. Assocs., Inc. (exec. com. 1994—, treas. 1994-95), Detroit Soc. Model Engrs. (pres. 1958, 62, bd. dirs. 1955-71), Chem. Splty. Mfg. Assn., Nat. Geog. Soc., Internat. Platform Assn., The Heritage Found., Smithsonian Instn. Assocs., Archaeol. Inst. Am., Bibl. Archaeol. Soc., Bible-Sci. Assn., Creation Rsch. Soc., Mich. Student Fin. Aid Assn., Midwest Assn. Student Fin. Aid Adminstrs. Republican. Avocation: reading. Home: Angola, Ind. Died Jan. 9, 2006.

DEDINI, ELDON LAWRENCE, cartoonist; b. King City, Calif., June 29, 1921; s. Grutly Stefano and Oleta Regina (Loeber) D.; m. Virginia DeSales Conroy, July 15,1944; 1 son, Giulio. AA, Hartnell Coll., Salinas, Calif., 1942; grad., Chouinard Art Inst., Los Angeles, 1942-44. Staff cartoonist: Salinas Morning Post, 1940-41; staff story dept., Walt Disney Studios, Burbank, Calif., 1944-46; staff cartoonist: Esquire mag, Chho., 1946-50, New Yorker mag, N.Y.C., Playboy mag, Chgo.; Author: cartoon album The Dedini Gallery, 1961, A Much, Much Better World, 1985; anthologies of New Yorker, Playboy cartoons. Recipient ann. award for best color Cartoon Playboy, 1978 Mem. Nat. Cartoonists Soc. (Best Mag. Cartoonist award 1958, 61, 64, 89), Cartoonists Guild Inc (2d v.p. N.Y.C. 1970) Home: Carmel, Calif. Died Jan. 12, 2006.

DEDRICK, KENT GENTRY, retired physicist, researcher; b. Watsonville, Calif., Aug. 9, 1923; s. Frederick David and Matilda (Redman) D.; 1 child, Susan Marie. BS in Chemistry and Physics, San Jose (Calif.) State U., 1946; MS in Phys. Scis., Stanford U., 1949, PhD in Theoretical Physics, 1955. Rsch. assoc. U. Mich., Ann Arbor, 1954-55, Stanford U., 1955-62; math. physicist Stanford Rsch. Inst., Menlo Park, Calif., 1962-75; cons. scientist Atty. Gen.'s Office State of Calif., Sacramento, 1976-80; with marine tech. safety dept. State Lands Commn., Sacramento, 1980-81, rsch. specialist, 1981-92; cons. scientist phys. and environ. scis., from 1992. Contbr. articles to profl. jours.; composer instrumental and vocal works, 1978—. Pres. Com. for Green Foothills, Palo Alto, Calif., 1972-74; founding co-chmn. So. Crossing Action Team, San Francisco Bay area, 1970-72, chmn. Bayfront com. Sierra Club, Palo Alto, 1967-72. Mem. Am. Phys. Soc., Am. Geophys. Union, Soc. Wetland Scientists, Sigma Xi. Achievements include co-discovery of mathematical theorem on Lagrange and Taylor series. Home: Sacramento, Calif. Died July 17, 2004.

DEEKENS, ELIZABETH TUPMAN, writer; b. Washington, Aug. 25, 1926; d. William Spencer Tupman and Isabelle McNeil Roberts; m. William Carter Deekens, July 30, 1955 (dec. 1988); children: Arthur Carter, Christine Deekens Old, Catherine Deekens Ward. Student, George Washington U., 1945-49. Parish sec. All Souls Episcopal Ch., Washington, 1951-52; Washington corres. The Living Ch., Mpls., 1951-52; woman's editor Episcopal Churchnews, Richmond, Va., 1952-57; mem. Episcopal Churchwomen Bd., Diocese of Va., Richmond, 1968; mem. Bishop's Liturgical Commn., Diocese of Va., 1975; newsletter editor Vestry, Ch. of Epiphany, Richmond, 1974-82; editor, layreader St. Martin's Ch., Richmond, 1983— Contbr. articles to mags. including Seventeen, Good Housekeeping, features to various newspapers. Mem. publicity staff First Mills Godwin Gubernatorial Campaign, 1965; v.p. corp. comms. Va. Hosp. Assn., 1968-88. Recipient numerous state and nat. writing awards. Fellow Am. Soc. Hosp. Mktg. and Pub. Rels.; mem. Va. Hosp. Mktg. and Pub. Rels. (a founder, bd. dirs. 1969-88, treas. 1975-85), Richmond Pub. Rels. Assn. (pres. 1983-84), Va. Press. Women, Internat. Order of St. Luke the Physicians (sec.-treas. 1989-91, convener Richmond chpt. 1996-98), Stephen Minister Lay Pastoral Care Ministry. Home: Richmond, Va. Died Aug. 18, 2005.

DEEN, JAMES ROBERT, nuclear engineer; b. Dallas, Mar. 1, 1944; s. James Young and Dorothy Faye Deen; m. Katy James Pavlidou, Aug. 14, 1971; children: Dorothy, Christina, David, Joshua, Priscilla, Joy. B in Engring. Sci., U. Tex., 1966, BSME, 1970, PhD, 1973. Registered profl. engr., Calif. Sr. engr. Gen. Electric, San Jose, Calif., 1972-76; asst. nuclear engr. Argonne (Ill.) Nat. Lab, 1976-81, nuclear engr., from 1981. Mem. Am. Nuclear Soc. Republican. Mem. Evang. Free Ch. Avocation: classical music instrn. Home: Bolingbrook, Ill. Died Jan. 29, 2005.

DEER, NONA YAZZIE, nursing administrator; b. Pinon, Ariz., Oct. 16, 1934; d. Jimmy K. and Katherine (Yellowhorse) Yazzie; m. Frederick B. Deer, June 17, 1967; 1 child, Gregury H. Diploma, St. John's Hosp., Tulsa, 1960; BSN, Ariz. State U., 1970; MPH, U. Cal., Berkeley, 1974. Faculty mem. U. Ariz. Coll. Nursing, Tucson, 1975-77; nurse cons. Cal. State Dept. Health, Sacramento, 1977-80; dir. nursing Pub. Health Svc. - Indian Health Svc., Chinle, Ariz., 1984-85; dir. pub. health nursing program USPHS Indian Health Svc., Kayenta, Ariz., 1985-89; dir. pub. health nursing prog. Pub. Health Svc. - Indian Health Svc., Ft. Defiance, Ariz., 1989-90; dir. pub. health nursing program San Carlos, Ariz., from 1990. Mem. Navajo Home Health adv. com., No. Ariz. Health Edn. Ctr. (adv. bd.) Home: Globe, Ariz. Died May 27, 2005.

DEERING, REGINALD A., molecular biologist; b. Brooks, Maine, Sept. 21, 1932; s. Raymond A. and Sibyl L. (Tibbetts) D.; children: Eric, Mark, Linda, Norman. BS, U. Maine, 1954; PhD, Yale U., 1958. Asst. prof. physics So. Ill. U., Carbondale, 1957-58; Fulbright scholar U. Oslo, Norway, 1958-59; rsch. assoc. Yale U., New Haven, 1959-61; asst. prof., then assoc. prof. N.Mex. Highlands U., Las Vegas, 1961-64; assoc. prof. biophysics Pa. State U., University Park, 1964—69, prof. biophysics, 1969—98, prof. molecular & cell biology, 1974—98. Contbr. numerous papers to refereed sci. jours. Grantee NIH. Home: University Park, Pa. Died Jan. 26, 2006.

DEFEUDIS, FRANCIS VINCENT, biochemist, physiologist, consultant; b. Worcester, Mass., Feb. 27, 1938; s. Francis Peter and Josephine Mary (Piccirelli) De F.; m. Patricia Ann Fessenden, May 6, 1964 (div. 1983); 1 child, Francis R. BS in Zoology, U. Miami, 1961; MA in Biology, Clark U., 1964; PhD in Biochemistry, McGill U., Montreal, Que., Can., 1968. NSF teaching fellow Clark U., Worcester, 1962-64; USPHS fellow in biol. scis. Yale U., New Haven, 1968-69; Wellcome Trust fellow Cambridge (Eng.) U., 1969-70; asst. prof. neurochemistry and pharmacology Purdue U., West Lafayette, 1970-74, U. Ind. Sch. Medicine, Indpls., 1971-74; prof. physiology U. Autonoma Madrid Faculty Medicine, 1974-78; prof. biochemistry U. Louis Pasteur Faculty Medicine, Strasbourg, France, 1978-88; pres. Inst. for Biosci., Westborough, Mass., from 1986. Chief sect. neurochemistry Centro Ramon y Cajal, Madrid, 1974-78; organizer, co-organizer internat. meetings, 1972—. Author: Central Cholinergic Systems, 1974, Elements of the Behavioral Code, 1977, Gingko Biloba Extract: Pharmacological Activities and Clinical Applications, 1991, Ginkgo Biloba Extract (EGb 761): From Chemistry to the Clinic, 1998; editor 5 books on biochemistry and pharmacology, 1977-83; mem. editl. bd. Neuropharmacology, Gen. Pharmacology, Neurochemistry Internat., Drug Devel. Rsch.; contbr. over 325 articles to profl. jours. Fellow INSERM, 1978, EMBO, 1978. Fellow Am. Coll. Nutrition, Internat. Coll. Nutrition (pres. 1988); mem. Soc. for Neurosci., Internat. Brain Rsch. Orgn., Brit. Pharm. Soc. Achievements include pioneering research on effects of environment on brain chemistry and behavior, on biochemistry, pharmacology and methodology of GABA receptors, on calcium antagonist drugs; discovery of antagonist action of verapamil on 5-HT2 receptors of blood vessels; research on atherosclerosis. Died Dec. 15, 2004.

DEGNAN, TERRANCE JAMES, lawyer; b. Toledo, Ohio, Apr. 8, 1951; s. Robert Francis and Mary Margaret (Begin) D.; m. Patricia Parker, Sept. 25, 1982; children: Patrick, Caroline. BA, Denison U., 1973; JD, U. Toledo, 1977. Bar: Ohio, 1978; U.S. Dist. Ct. (no. dist.) Ohio, 1978. Assoc. Ritter, Boesel, Robinson & Marsh, Toledo, 1978-79; sr. legal counsel First Nat. Bank of Toledo, 1979-87; chief counsel Nat. City Bank, Northwest (Ohio Citizens Bank), Toledo, from 1987; litigation sect. head Nat. City Corp., Cleve., from 1992. Mem. Toledo Bar Assn. (various coms., chmn. 1978—), Ohio State Bar Assn., Ohio Bankers Assn. Home: Pittsburgh, Pa. Died Sept. 10, 2004.

DEGUERE, PHILIP LEONARD, JR., producer, writer; b. Cin., July 19, 1944; s. Philip Leonard and Cecilia (McLaren) DeG.; m. Karen West, July 23, 1967 (div. 1971); 1 child, Adrienne. BA, Stanford U., 1966. Writer Universal Studios, Universal City, Calif., 1966-69, creative cons. Baretta, 1975, supervising producer Baa Baa Black Sheep, 1976-78, dir. Dr. Strange, 1977-78, exec. producer Simon and Simon, 1979-84; ind. writer Universal City, 1970-75; exec. producer The Twilight Zone CBS, Los Angeles, 1984-86; former pres. Persistence of Vision, Los Angeles. Dir. (documentary) Darkness Darkness, 1970 (Am. Film Festival award 1970). Died Jan. 24, 2005.

DEKKER, JACOB CHRISTOPH EDMOND, mathematician, educator; b. Hilversum, The Netherlands, Sept. 6, 1921; came to U.S., 1947; s. Anton and Maria Magdalena (Zeegers) D.; m. Hedwig Carolina Schemering Reelfs, Dec. 19, 1950. MA, Syracuse U., 1949, PhD, 1950. Instr. U. Chgo., 1951-52, vis. asst. prof., 1955-56; instr. Northwestern U., Evanston, Ill., 1952-54, asst. prof., 1954-55; vis. mem. Inst. for Advanced Study, Princeton, N.J., 1956-58; assoc. prof. U. Kans., Lawrence, 1958-59; from asst. prof. to prof. emeritus Rutgers U., New Brunswick, N.J., from 1959, prof., 1961-86, prof. emeritus, from 1986. Lectr. Nat. U. Mex., Mexico City, 1961; cons. IBM, Poughkeepsie, N.Y., 1958, Endicott, N.Y., 1960. Author: Les Fonctions Combinatoires et les Isols, 1966; contbr. articles to profl. jours. Mem. Am. Math. Soc., Math. Assn. Am., Assn. for Symbolic Logic. Avocation: spanish language and literature. Home: Princeton, NJ. Died Apr. 3, 2004.

DE LANEY, ALLEN YOUNG, retired surgeon; b. Arrington, Tenn., 1917; s. Joseph Peter and Mary Williams (Glover) D.; m. Margaret Duncan, May 30, 1947 (div. Jan. 1978); children: Allen G., Philip Andrew, Bruce Duncan, Mary Elizabeth Johnston; m. Thelma Lou House, Apr. 7, 1979; children: Stewart B. White, Joseph S. White. BS, U. Ark., 1937; MD, Tulane U., 1940. Diplomate Am. Bd. Surgery. Intern Grady Hosp., Atlanta, 1940-41; resident in pathology New Eng. Deaconess Hosp., Boston, 1941; resident in surgery New Orleans VA Hosp., 1948-52; fellow in surgery Tulane U., New Orleans, 1947-50; asst. chief surgeon USS Haven UASA Naval Hosp. Shop Inchon, Pusan, Korea, 1950-51; chief surgeon U.S. VA Hosp., Poplar Bluff, Mo., 1952-53; founder, pres. Gainesville (Fla.) Surg. Group, from 1982; chief of staff Alachua Gen. Hosp., Fla., 1976-78, courtesy staff, from 1987; ret., 1988. Chmn. Alachua County Emergency Medicine Coun., Gainesville, 1975-80. Pres. bd. dirs. Boys Club, Gainesville, 1955, Alachua County Thoracic Soc., Gainesville, 1956; bd. dirs. ARC, United Fund; mem. bus. coun. LWV, 1967-69; mem. Gainesville City Planning Cb., 1961-69; comdr. cons. Gainesville chpt. U.S. Power Squadron, 1985; Disting. mem. pres.'s coun. U. Fla.; founding trustee North Fla. Regional Hosp., Gainesville, 1969-76. Comdr. MC USNR, ret., 1985-86. Recipient medal U. Fla., 2001. Fellow ACS; mem. AMA, Fla. Thoracic Soc. (pres. 1961-62), Fla. Soc. Gen. Surgeons, Fla. Sheriffs Assn. (hon. life), Jocanter Club (co-pres. 1996), Sigma Chi. Home: Gainesville, Fla. Died Mar. 25, 2004.

DELANEY, JEAN MARIE, art educator; b. Jersey City, Nov. 14, 1931; d. John Francis and Genevieve Mary (Boulton) Reilly; m. Donald Kendall Delaney, Dec. 29, 1956; 1 child, Laura Marie. BA in Art Edn., Fairmont (W.Va.) State U., 1954; MA in Clin. Psychology, Loyola

Coll., Balt., 1979; PhD in Art Edn., U. Wis., Milw., 1992. Cert. art tchr., prin., supr., Md. Tchr. English and social studies Reedurban Sch., Stark County, Ohio, 1954-56; art tchr. Perry Hall H.S., Stark County, 1956-57, Margaret Brent H.S., St. Mary's County, Md., 1957-59, Middle River Mid. Sch., Baltimore County, Md., 1959-62; home and hosp. tchr. Harford County (Md.) Bd. Edn., 1968-78; lectr. art appreciation U. Md. Extension, Harford County, 1971-76; art educator Baltimore County Bd. Edn., 1979-93; prof. art edn. S.W. Mo. State U., Springfield, 1993-97, asst. head dept. art and design, 1997-98, full prof. art edn., 1998, ret., 1998. Cons. Salisbury (Md.) State Coll., 1987; adj. prof. art edn. Md. Inst. Coll. Art, Balt., 1988-89; cons. bd. examiners and art edn. Nat. Tchr.'s Exam. test devel. com. ETS, Princeton, N.J., 1988-92. Author: Art Image, 6th Grade Units, 1988; co-author, co-editor: Creating Meaning Through Art: Teacher as Choice Maker, 1998; editor: Art Scholarships, 1988; editor videotape Ernest Goldstein: Art Criticism, 1987; author, editor curriculum guide. Recipient Youth Art Month award of excellence Art and Craft Materials Inst., 1989, grant to coordinate Crayola Dreammakers program for Ctrl. Region U.S. and Can., 1994-96; named Mo. Higher Edn. Art Educator of Yr., 1997. Mem. Nat. Art Edn. Assn. (Eastern Region Art Educator award of yr, 1989, Nat. Secondary Art Educator award of yr. 1990), Md. Art Edn. Assn. (state coun. 1985—, v.p. arts advocacy 1988-89, pres.-elect 1992—, Md. Art Educator of Yr. 1988), Internat. Soc. for Edn. Through Art, Mo. Art Edn. Assn. Home: Bel Air, Md. Died Dec. 28, 2004.

DELAP, JOHN HIRAM, JR., real estate associate, business owner; b. Chgo., Jan. 25, 1932; s. John Hiram Sr. and Ruth (Higginson) DeL.; m. Gloria Susan Gallagher, Aug. 29, 1952; children: John Hiram III, Jay Howard, Dawn Kimberly, George Kevin. B of Pub. Adminstrn., Parkville (Mo.) Coll., 1972. Adminstrv. officer City of Kansas City, Kans., 1968-72; mgr. Geer Real Estate, Kansas City, 1972-78; owner, mgr. Century 21 DeLap & Assocs., Kansas City, 1978-82, Geer Real Estate, Inc., Kansas City, from 1982. Chmn. Wyandotte Community Housing Resource Bd., Kansas City, 1987—. Served to sgt. USMC, 1948-58, Korea. Mem. Wyandotte Assn. Realtors (bd. dirs. Kansas City chpt. 1988—, pres. 1983; recipient numerous awards), Bus. West (pres. 1987-89), Optimist (pres. Kansas City chpt. 1987-88, Disting. Lt. Gov. 1988-89, Disting. Pres. award), Kans. Assn. Realtors (v.p. Topeka chpt. 1988-90). Republican. Episcopalian. Avocation: golf. Home: Kansas City, Kans. Died Nov. 3, 2004.

DELAROSA, KATHLEEN C., lawyer; b. McNary, Ariz., Sept. 5, 1947; d. Hubert Arthur and Juanita Irene (Frazier) McEwen; m. James R. Coughenour, II, Dec. 23, 1973 (div. May 1993); children: Amy M., James R. III, Michael D.; m. Jorge M. DeLaRosa, July 4, 1993. BA Edn., Ariz. State U., 1971, MEd, 1984, JD, 1989. Bar: Ariz., 1989; U.S. Dist. Ct. Ariz., 1989. Assoc. Jennings, Kepner & Haug, Phoenix, 1989-93, Goldstein, Kingsley & McGroder, Phoenix, 1993-95; pvt. practice Phoenix, Ariz., from 1995; rsch./writing cons., from 1993. Author: Ariz. State Law Rev., 1989. Bd. dirs. Ariz. Luth. Outdoor Ministries Assn., Phoenix, 1986-89. Mem. Am. Bar Assn. (tort and ins. sect., mem. editl. bd. Tort & Ins. law jour. 1994-96, long range planning com. 1996—, solo and small firm com. 1995—), Maricopa County Bar Assn. (lawyer referral svc. com. 1989-95, Gold-E-Locks Mock Trial Program 1989-96), Ariz. Women Lawyer's Assn., Ariz. State Bar Assn. (civil jury instr. com. 1990-92). Lutheran. Avocations: snorkeling, travel, fishing, camping. Home: Phoenix, Ariz. Died Sept. 21, 2004.

DELAURENTI, JOHN LEWIS, judge; b. Shelbyville, Ill., May 10, 1933; s. John Charles and Grace Agnes (Broom) D.; m. Leanne Dorothy DeLine, Apr. 9, 1960 (dec. 1991); children: Suzanne L., John R., James L., Elena M.; m. Betty Faye Klenke, Oct. 1, 1992. BA, U. Ill., 1955; JD, Valparaiso U., 1961. Bar: Ill. 1961, Mo. 1968, U.S. Dist. Ct. (so. dist.) Ill. Pvt. practice Jacoby Patton Manns, Alton, Ill., 1961-63; v.p., staff legal counsel Germania S/L, Alton, 1963-67; pvt. practice Roy McGee Firm, Piedmont, Mo., 1967-68, Greenville, Ill., 1968-72; state's atty. Bond County, Greenville, 1968-72; judge State of Ill., Bond County Cir. Ct., 3d Cir., Greenville, Edwardsville, Ill., from 1972. Bd. dirs. Southwestern Ill. Law Enforcement Commn., 1970-77; mem. mng. bd. Ill. State's Atty., 1968-72; del. Ill. Conservation Congress, 1997. Contbr. articles to profl. jours. Active 1st Ill. Conservation Congress, Springfield, 1993, Ill. Wetlands Survey Commn. Ill. Dept. Natural Resource, 1995. Lt. col. USAFR, 1956-82. Recipient Law Enforcement award Ill. Dept. Conservation, 1988. Mem. Ill. Judges Assn. (disciplinary com. 1989-95), Ill. State Bar Assn. (Supreme Ct. rules com. 1992-95, pub. rels. com. 1986-92, environ. law com. 1970-72), Ill. Conservation 3d Congress, Bond County Bar Assn. (pres. 1969-74, 81-85), Madison County Bar Assn., Southwestern Ill. Ret. Officers Assn., Am. Legion, Masons, Rotary. Methodist. Avocations: farming, hunting, fishing. Home: Pocahontas, Ill. Died Aug. 28, 2004.

DELGIORNO, MICHAEL, hotel executive; b. Bklyn., Aug. 18, 1949; s. Robert and Ann (Santori) D.; m. Barbara Musiol, May 21, 1973; children: David, Diane. Student, Southampton Coll., NY, 1967-69. Gen. mgr. Wilmington (Del.) Hilton, 1975-78, Facilities Leasing Corp., Princeton, N.J., 1978-81, Sheraton Univ. Inn, Ann Arbor, Mich., 1981-82, Cleve. Hilton, 1982-83; dir. ops. The Springe Group, Cleve., 1983-85, v.p. ops., from 1985. Mem. Am. Hotel and Motel Assn. (cert.). Clubs: Columbia Hills Country. Avocations: golf, football, music. Died May 15, 2004.

DELLASEGA, JOSEPH LEONARD, financial analyst; b. Parsons, Kans., Jan. 19, 1925; s. Joseph Anthony and Susan Mary (Hayden) D.; m. Marie Yvonne Thornton, June, 11, 1949; children: Paul, Philip, Stephen. MBA, Harvard U., 1958. Various U.S. Naval Officer (Supply Corps), 1945-65; exec. officer, ops. officer Navy Electronics Supply Office, Great Lakes, Ill., 1965-70; mgr. corp. inventory rev. Abbott Labs., N. Chgo., Ill., 1970-74; bus. mgr., treas. Rockhurst Coll., Kans. City; asst. v.p. fin., asst. treas. Loyola Univ. Chgo., from 1979. Mem. Chgo. Coun. Fgn. Rels., Pickwick Golf Club (sec./treas.) Republican. Roman Catholic. Home: Evanston, Ill. Died May 16, 2005.

DELORIA, VINE VICTOR, JR., political science educator, author; b. Martin, S.D., Mar. 26, 1933; s. Vine Victor and Barbara (Eastburn) D.; m. Barbara Jeanne Nystrom, June 1958; children: Philip, Daniel, Jeanne Ann. BS, Iowa State U., 1958; M.Th., Lutheran Sch. Theology, 1963; JD, U. Colo., 1970; D.H. Litt., Augustana Coll., 1971. Staff asst. United Scholarship Service, Denver, 1963-64; exec. dir. Nat. Congress Am. Indians, 1964-67; lectr. West Wash. State Coll., 1970-72; chmn. Inst. for Devel. Indian Law, Washington, 1971-76; lectr. Pacific Sch. Religion, Berkeley, Calif., Summer 1975, New Sch. Religion, Pontiac, Mich., Summer 1976, Colo. Coll., Colorado Springs, 1977, 78; vis. prof. U. Ariz., Tucson, spring 1978, prof. polit. sci., 1978-90, U. Colo., Boulder, 1990—2000. Author: Custer Died for Your Sins, 1969, We Talk, You Listen, 1970, Of Utmost Good Faith, 1972, God Is Red, 1973, Behind the Trail of Broken Treaties, 1974, The Indian Affair, 1974, Indians of the Pacific Northwest, 1977, The Metaphysics of Modern Existence, 1979, Red Man in New World Drama, 1972, American Indians, American Justice, 1983, The Nations Within, 1984, A Sender of Words, 1984, The Aggression of Civilization, 1984, American Indian Policy in the Twentieth Century, 1985. Vice chmn. Am. Indian Resource Assocs., Oglala, S.D., 1973-75; Mem. Bd. Inquiry into Hunger and Malnutrition, 1967-68; mem. exec. council Episcopal Ch., 1969-70. Served with USMCR, 1954-56. Recipient Indian Achievement award Indian Council Fire, 1972, Woodcraft Circle Writer of the Year, 1999, Wallace Stegner award, 2002, Am. Indian Visionary award, 2005 Mem. Am. Judicature Soc. Died Nov. 13, 2005.

DELSON, ELIZABETH, artist; b. N.Y.C., N.Y., Aug. 15, 1932; d. Julius and Emmy (Haas) Pfannmuller; m. Sidney L. Delson, Sept. 10, 1955; children: Karen Lee, Sara Jeanne, Matthew Robert. BA, Smith Coll., 1954; MA, Hunter Coll., 1972. Instr. graphic arts Pratt Inst., 1962—66. Exhibitions include USIA Traveling Exhibit, 1962—64, Bklyn. Mus. Nat. Print Exhbn., 1966, one-woman shows include Hicks Street Gallery, 1964, L.I. U., 1969, 1974, Paerdegat Libr., 1971, 1974, Park Gallery, 1973, Brownstone Gallery, 1974, 1984, Clayton & Liberatore, 2002, exhibited in group shows at Hudson Guild, 1982, 1984, 1988, 1990, 1992, 1998, 2000, Cork Gallery, 1987, 1988, 1989, 1991, 1992, 1994, 1998, 2003, Broome St. Gallery, 1992, 1995, 1996, 2000, 2001, 2002, 2004, 2005, Lever Ho., 1985, 1991, 1998, Millenium Gallery, 2000, Crazy Monkey Gallery, 2004, 2005, Represented in permanent collections N.Y. Pub. Libr., L.I. U., So. Ill. U., Columbia U., Boston Pub. Libr., Bklyn. Mus. Mem.: Artists Alliance East Hampton (co-treas. 2001—04, bd. dir. from 2004), Contemporary Artists Guild (treas. from 1980), Soc. Am. Graphic Artists, Audubon Artists (Medal of Honor, graphics 1961, Gold Medal of Honor 1996, Pen and Brush 1st prize, graphics 2001, Rebecca Borja award 2003). Died Oct. 3, 2005.

DELUCA, ANGELINE F., elementary education educator, reading specialist; b. Sewickley, Pa., May 7, 1949; d. Michael and Maria (Barone) DeL. BS in Edn., Point Park Coll., Pitts., 1971; MEd, Duquesne U., 1979; postgrad., Pa. State U. Cert. elem. tchr., reading specialist, lang. arts tchr. Reading specialist Laughlin Children's Ctr., Sewickley; tchr. St. Peter and Paul Sch., Ambridge, Pa., Our Lady of Fatima Sch., Hopewell, Pa.; reading specialist Ambridge Area Sch. Dist. Mem. ASCD, Internat. Reading Assn., Pa. State Reading Assn., Leotta C. Hawthorne Reading Coun. (treas.), Delta Kappa Gamma (rec. sec. 1994—). Home: Ambridge, Pa. Died Nov. 16, 2004.

DE MARE, GEORGE, author; b. Denver, Nov. 11, 1912; s. J.S. and Marie de Mare; m. Mercedes Moore; children: Gregory, Malcolm, Gilbert, Adrienne. BA, Yale U., 1936. Dir. comms. and publs. Price Waterhouse, 1956-70. Com. on social and econ. improvement White House, 1965. Author: The Empire, 1956, Ruling Passion, 1957, Sybille, 1988, Corporate Lives, 1976 (main selection Fortune Book club), Communicating at the Top, 1986, 101 Ways to Protect Your Job, 1988. Fellow Internat. Assn. of Bus. Communicators (former pres.), N.Y. Assn. of Bus. Editors (former pres.), Indsl. Comms. Coun. (former dir.). Home: Saugerties, NY. Died Jan. 31, 2005.

DE MARTINI, ALFRED E., graphic and industrial designer; b. Camden, N.J., Feb. 25, 1916; s. Frank and Rose (De Rago) De M.; m. Alberta Cianfrani, June 4, 1942; children; Alfred, Nina, Rosemary, Frank, Paul. Student, Phila. Coll. Art, 1937. Pres. De Martini Displays, Camden, N.J., 1935-40; adminstr. War Dept. Suggestion System, Phila., 1940-44; graphic designer Martin & Ladriere, N.Y.C., 1944-48, Parents Inst., N.Y.C., 1948-52; pres. De Martini Assocs., Inc., Phila., 1952-72, De Martini Ednl. Films, Haddon Heights, N.J., 1972-76, De Martini Plaza, Haddon Heights, N.J., 1976, De Martini Assocs., Inc., Haddon Heights, N.J., from 1980. Pubr. Holiday Bazaar, Haddon Heights, 1959-69. Author ednl. film: Oxford: Bastion of Tradition (Gold award 1980); dir., writer film: Shakespeare: Man from Stratford. Chmn. Haddon Hts. Planning Bd. Recipient The Golden Cube Art Dirs. Club, 1968, Gold Medal N.Y. Internat. Film Festival, 1976, V.I. Internat. Film Festival, 1976. Mem. Art Dirs. Club of Phila. (treas. 1955-65, pres.). Avocations: writing, travel. Died Apr. 6, 2005.

DEMARTINI, EDWARD JOHN, lawyer, real estate investor; b. New Orleans, May 30, 1932; s. John and Ethel (McNulty) DeM.; m. Patricia Morgan, Oct. 3, 1953; children: Edward Jr., Margaret S., John, JoAnn. BS, Tulane U., 1953, LLB, 1967; MBA, U. Mich., 1962. Bar: La. 1967, U.S. Dist. Ct. (so. and ctrl. dist.) 1967, U.S. Ct. Appeals (5th cir.) 1968. Officer U.S. Navy, 1953-63; pres. Edsa, Inc., Kenner, La., from 1964; ptnr. Duplantier & DeMartini, New Orleans, 1968-74; sr. ptnr. DeMartini & LeBlanc, Kenner, La., from 1974. Commdr. USNR, 1963-73. Mem. Rotary Club, Elks Club, Am. Judicature Soc., Assn. Naval Aviation, Tailhook. Avocations: coin collecting/numismatics, golf. Home: River Ridge, La. Died Apr. 10, 2004.

DE MARTINO, LYVIA, music publisher; b. N.Y.C., Dec. 8, 1914; d. Antonio and Rosa (Aiello) De M.; children: Rosa, Michael. Diploma in piano and composing, Conservatory of Music, Naples, Italy, 1933. Exec. pres. Italian Book Corp., N.Y.C., from 1963. Appeared on Radio Italia WHBI, 1964-68. Composer various Italian musical compositions. Recipient award Bklyn. Acad. Music Festival, 1963, Zecchino d'Oro award, 1933, 58, 59. Avocations: travel, physical fitness, swimming. Home: Danbury, Conn. Died Aug. 3, 2004.

DEMAY, JOHN ANDREW, III, claim supervisor; b. Pitts., Nov. 11, 1952; s. John Andrew and Helen Louise (Duffy) D. BA in Sociology, St. Vincent Coll., 1978. Claim rep. CNA Ins., Pitts., 1979-83, Md. Casualty Ins., Pitts., 1983-87; claim supr. Gen. Accident Ins., Pitts., from 1987. Sgt. USAF, 1973-77. Died May 5, 2005.

DEMMLER, ALBERT WILLIAM, JR., retired editor, metallurgical engineer; b. Pitts., Feb. 21, 1929; s. Albert William and Hester Louisa (Dye) Demmler; m. Donna Lou Frederick, Feb. 16, 1957 (dec. Nov. 2001); children: Richard Frederick, Keith Alan(dec.), Diane Leslie, Debra Lynn. PhB in Liberal Arts, U. Chgo., 1948; BSMetE, U. Mich., 1951, MSMetE, 1952, PhD, 1955. Rsch. engr. Alcoa Rsch. Labs., New Kensington, Pa., 1955-68; registered rep. Butcher & Singer, Pitts., 1968-74; exec. searcher Reese Assoc., Pitts., 1974-76; assoc. editor Soc. Automotive Engrs. Inc. Mags., Warrendale, Pa., 1976-90, sr. editor, 1990-99, ret., 1999. Patentee in field. Mem. NRA, Soc. Automotive Engrs., Am. Soc. Metals Internat., Hypnotism Soc. Pa., Tarentum Dist. Sportsmens Club, Pa. Rifle and Pistol Assn., Pa. Gun Collectors Assn., Crowfoot Rod & Gun Club, Mensa, Tau Beta Pi, Phi Lambda Upsilon, Sigma Xi. Democrat. Presbyterian. Avocations: competitive rifle, pistol, hypnosis. Home: New Kensington, Pa. Died May 25, 2005.

DENISE, THEODORE CULLOM, philosophy educator; b. Whitewater, Wis., Mar. 9, 1919; s. Malcolm F. and Margaret E. (Lawrence) D.; m. Kathleen W. Cowles, Oct. 4, 1942; children: Patricia Denise White, Theodore Cullom (dec.). BA, U. Mich., 1942, MA, 1947, PhD, 1955. Teaching fellow U. Mich., 1946-48; mem. faculty Syracuse U., 1948—2005, assoc. prof. philosophy, 1959-64, prof. philosophy, 1964-89, prof. emeritus, 1989—2005, chmn. dept., 1959-72, chmn. humanities depts., 1973-76; dir. liberal studies Inst. Univ. Adminstrs., 1961-63; dir. of semester in Italy, 1967-68, 76-77; dir. grad. studies in philosophy, 1976-84; mem. editl. com. Univ. Press, 1972-78. Co-author (editor): Great Traditions in Ethics, 1953, 2d edit., 2005; author: The Social Writings of Bertrand Russell, 1955, Retrospect and Prospect, 1956; co-author: Contemporary Philosophy and Its Origins, 1967; contbr. articles to philos. jours. Served with AUS, 1942-46. Mem. Assn. Symbolic Logic, Am. Philos. Assn., Alpha Kappa Lambda. Home: Easthampton, Mass. Died Nov. 15, 2006.

DENISON, JAMES DICKEY, retired broadcasting executive; b. Clarendon, Tex., July 1, 1926; s. Dallas D. and Gladys (Condron) D.; m. Jo Beth Huser, June 27, 1965; children: Jack D., P. Dianne, Robert Ladd, Kathryn Anne Denison (Kit). Student, McMurry Coll., 1943, student, 1946, U. Tex., 1947—49; BArch, U. Houston, 1952. Contracting engr. Am. Bridge divsn. U.S. Steel, Houston, 1952-60; co-owner, v.p. Globe Equipment Rental, Houston, 1961-67; owner, operator B & B Steel, Hobbs, N.Mex., 1967-73; co-owner, CEO VLA Fabrication divsn. Structures, Inc., Hobbs, 1973-79; owner, operator Denison's Photography, Kingwood, Tex., 1979-82, Sta. KKTC-FM, Brownfield, Tex., 1985-96; ret., 1996. Chmn. N.Mex. State Hwy. Commn., 1974-79; congl. aide U.S. Congressman Harold Runnels, N.Mex., 1971-72. Served with USN, 1944-46, PTO. Mem. Brownfield C. of C., Rotary (v.p. Hobbs club 1971-72). Democrat. Methodist. Avocations: photography, fishing. Home: Brownfield, Tex. Died Nov. 2, 2004.

DENISON, WILLIAM CLARK, mycologist, educator; b. Rochester, N.Y., June 1, 1928; s. Glenn M. and Rhoda T. (Torrance) D.; m. Margaret R. Mellinger, Sept. 11, 1948; children: Robert Ford, Thomas C., Glenn T., Rebecca S. Denison Johnston. BA, Oberlin (Ohio) Coll., 1950, MA, 1952; PhD, Cornell U., 1956. Apprentice millwright Eastman Kodak Co., Rochester, 1944-46; co-dir. Kanawauke Regional Mus., Bear Mtn. (N.Y.) Park, summer 1947;

preparator Dept. Preserved Materials Gen. Biol. Supply House, Chgo., 1948-49; teaching asst. Dept. of Botany Oberlin Coll., 1950-52; teaching asst. Dept. of Plant Pathology Cornell U., 1952-55; asst. prof. Dept. of Biology Swarthmore (Pa.) Coll., 1955-66; assoc. prof. Dept. of Botany & Plant Pathology Oreg. State U., Corvallis, 1966-93, curator, 1966-93, assoc. prof. emeritus, from 1993. Vis. asst. prof. Dept. of Botany U. N.C., Chapel Hill, 1958-59; pres., sr. scientist Northwest Mycological Cons., Inc., Corvallis, 1985—; rsch. in field. Contbr. articles to numerous profl. jours. Co-organizer, counselor Corvallis Draft Info. Ctr., 1968-72; chmn. North Benton County Citizen's Adv. Com., 1974-78; charter mem., firefighter Adair Rural Fire Protection Dept., Adair Village, Oreg., 1975-83; foster parent Children's Svcs. Div. Oreg. Dept. HHS, 1976-79; citizen mem. representing Benton County Benton Govt. Com., 1978-80; pres. Friends of Benton County, 1978-88; founding mem. First Alternative Coop., Corvallis; bd. dirs. Willamette Inst. Biol. Control. Grantee NSF, Am. Philos. Assn. Mem. Internat. Lichenological Assn., AAUP, AAAS, Mycological Soc. Am., Oreg. Natural Resources Coun., Oreg. Pub. Employee Union (assoc.). Home: Corvallis, Oreg. Died Apr. 8, 2005.

DENMAN, ROY, British diplomat; b. June 12, 1924; s. Albert Edward and Gertrude Ann D.; attended St. John's Coll., Cambridge (Eng.) U.; m. Moya Lade, 1966; 2 children. War service, 1943-46; maj. Royal Signals, Joined BoT, 1948; asst. pvt. sec. to successive pres., 1950-52; 1st sec. Brit. embassy, Bonn, W. Ger., 1957-60; mem. U.K. del., Geneva, 1960-61; counsellor, Geneva, 1965-67; under-sec., 1967-70, BoT; dep. sec. DTI, 1970-74, Dept. Trade, 1974-75; 2d permanent sec. Cabinet Office, 1975-77; dir.-gen. for external affairs Commn. of European Communities, Brussels, 1977-82; mem. negotiating del. Commn. European Communities, 1970-72, head del., Washington, 1982—89, bus. fellow, JFK Sch. Govt., Harvard U., 1989-90; mem. Brit. Overseas Trade Bd., 1972-75. Decorated CB, Order of St. Michael and St. George. Club: United Oxford and Cambridge U.; Author: Missed Chances: Britain and Europe in the Twentieth Century, 1996, The Mandarin's Tale, 2002 Died Apr. 4, 2006.

DENNISTON, DOUGLAS, artist, educator; b. Cornwall-on-Hudson, N.Y., Nov. 19, 1921; s. Jesse and Edith (Buchenberger) D.; Patricia Davidson, Oct. 29, 1945; children: Denise, Abigail, Joshua. Two-year cert. Richmond Profl. Inst., Coll. William and Mary, 1942; BFA, U. N.Mex., 1945, MA, 1948. Instr. U. N.Mex., 1947-48, Tex. Western Coll., El Paso, summer 1949, Colo. Women's Coll., Denver, 1948-59; prof. U. Ariz., Tucson, 1959-83, prof. emeritus, from 1983; instr. U. Nev., Reno, summer 1967. Illustrator: Edward Hopper: an Appreciation, 1963, Calendar: A Cycle of Poems (Richard Shelton), 1972; one-man shows include N.Mex. State Mus., Santa Fe, 1946, Acad. Arts, Flint, Mich., 1953, Denver Art Mus., 1954, La Galeria Escondida, Taos, N.Mex., 1954, 55, Johnson Art Gallery, Albuquerque, 1954, Ajo, Ariz., 1958, Colo. Women's Coll., Denver, 1959, Tucson Art Ctr., 1963, Dakota Art Gallery, Rapid City, S.D., 1977, Internat. Mus., McAllen, Tex., 1977, Coll. William and Mary, Williamsburg, Va., 1976, Fine Arts Ctr., Prescott, Ariz., 1986, Local 803 Gallery, Tucson, Ariz., 1995, others; group exhbns. include Va. Mus. Fine Arts, Richmond, 1943, N.Mex. State Fair, Albuquerque, 1944-47 (various prizes), Met. Mus. Art, N.Y.C., 1952, MOMA, N.Y.C., 1953, Denver Arts Mus., 1950, 52 (purchase prize), Denver Art Mus., 1951, 52, 54, 55, 56, 58, 61, 71, Joslyn Art Mus., Omaha, 1952, 54, Butler Art Inst., Youngstown, Ohio, 1954, San Francisco Art Mus., 1954, Tucson Art Ctr., 1961 (award), 66 (purchase), 67, 68, 69, 71, 72, 74, Mus. Fine Arts, Sante Fe, 1962, 76, Phoenix Art Mus., 1962, 69, 70, 73, Wollheim's Rosequist Galleries, Tucson, 1973, Ctrl. Art Collective, 1991, numerous others; represented in permanent collections Va. Mus. Fine Arts, Denver Art Mus., Gilpin County Arts Assn., Ctrl. City, Colo., Jonson Gallery, Albuquerque, Yuma Art Ctr., U. Ariz. Mus. Art, Tucson Airport. Home: Tucson, Ariz. Died May 25, 2004.

DENTON, DENICE D., academic administrator, engineering educator; b. El Campo, Tex. d. Carolyn Mabee; life ptnr. Gretchen Kalonji. BSEE, MIT, MSEE, 1982, PhD in elec. engring., 1987. Asst. prof. dept. elec. & computer engring. U. Wis., Madison, 1987—92, assoc. prof., 1992—95, prof., 1995—96, prof. dept. chemistry, 1995—96, co-dir. NSF Inst. for Sci. Edn., 1995—96; prof. dept. elec. engring. U. Wash., Seattle, 1996—2005, dean Coll. Engring., 1996—2005; vis. scientist Inst. Quantum Electronics, Swiss Fed. Inst. Tech., Zurich, 1991, vis. prof., 1993; chancellor U. Calif., Santa Cruz, 2005—06, also prof. elec. engring. Mem. NAS/NRC Bd. on Engring. Edn., 1991—96, chair, from 1997; mem. adv. bd. Initiatives to Diversify the Professoriate MIT, from 1995; mem. nat. vis. com. NSF Modular Chemistry Consortium U. Calif., Berkeley, from 1995; mem. adv. com. Directorate of Edn. and Human Resources NSF, from 1996, mem. of com. to select recipients of the A.T. Waterman award; mem. nat. adv. com. Mathlinks Consortium Rensselaer Poly. Inst., from 1996; mem. planning com. Nat. Libr. for SME&T Edn. NRC, from 1997, mem. com. on advanced materials and fabrication methods for microelectromechanical systems; mem. steering com. Celebration of Women in Engring. NAE, from 1997; mem. exec. bd. Engring. Deans Coun., from 1997; mem. President's com. to select recipeints of the Nat. Medal of Sci.; mem. vis. com. Calif. Inst. Tech. Divsn. Engring. and Applied Sci.; bd. dir. Silicon Valley Leadership Group, Joint Venture Silicon Valley. Contbr. articles to profl. jours., chapters to books. Recipient Presdl. Young Investigator Award, NSF, 1987, Elec. and Computer Engring. Prof Yr. Award, U. Wis. Madison, 1988, Polygon Outstanding Instructor Award, 1989, Kiekhofer Disting. Tchg. Award, 1990, C.Holmes MacDonald Dist. Young Elec. Engr. Nat. Tchg. Award, Eta Kappa Nu, 1993, Engring. Tchg. Excellence Award, W.M. Keck Found., 1994, Benjamin Smith Reynolds Tchg. Award, U. Wis. Madison Coll. Engring., 1994, Maria Mitchell Women in Sci. award, Maria Mitchell Found., 2006; Hertz Fellow, 1984—87. Fellow: Assn. for Women in Sci., AAAS, IEEE (Prof. of Yr. 1993, Harriet B. Rigas Award 1995); mem.: Am. Soc. Engring. Edn. (AT&T Found. Tchg. award 1991, George Westinghouse Award 1995). Died June 25, 2006.

DEPEW, MARIE KATHRYN, retired secondary school educator; b. Sterling, Colo., Dec. 1, 1928; d. Amos Carl and Dorothy Emelyn (Whiteley) Mehl; m. Emil Carlton DePew, Aug. 30, 1952 (dec. 1973). BA, U. Colo., 1950, MA, 1953. Post grad. Harvard U., Cambridge, Mass., 1962; tchr. Jefferson County Pub. Schs., Arvada, 1953-73; mgr. Colo. Accountability Program, Denver, 1973-83; sr. cons. Colo. Dept. Edn., Denver, 1973-85, ret., 1985. Author: (pamphlet) History of Hammil, Georgetown, Colorado, 1967; contbr. articles to profl. jours. 1971-75. Chmn. Colo. State Accountability Com., Denver, 1971-75. Fellow IDEA Programs, 1976-77, 79-81. Mem. Colo. Hist. Assn., Jefferson County Edn. Assn. (pres. 1963-64), Colo. Edn. Assn. (bd. dirs. 1965-70), Ky. Colonels (hon. mem.), Phi Beta Kappa. Republican. Methodist. Avocations: historical research, writing, travel, collecting antiques. Home: Denver, Colo. Died Aug. 20, 2004.

DERBY, NORMAN CLYDE, manufacturing executive; b. Goffstown, N.H., May 31, 1952; s. Norwin Cedric and Joan (Coombs) D.; m. Evelyn Baxter, June 13, 1977 (div. 1985); 1 child, Christi; m. Cynthia Raines, Nov. 1, 1985. Grad. various trade schs. Retail mgr. Fed Mart Stores, Dallas, 1970-75, Safeway Stores, Dallas, 1970-79; shift supr. Super Sack Mfg. Co., Savoy, Tex., 1979-80, staff asst., 1980-81, plant mgr. Belton, S.C., 1981-84, plant engr. Savoy, from 1984. Cons., Root Control Corp., Oklahoma City, 1988—, East Tex. Lighthouse for the Blind, Tyler, 1988—. Designer assembly line ops. Mem. Am. Inst. Plant Engrs., Partership for Improved Air Travel, Am. Softball Assn. (player, coach Super Sack Softball Team, Sherman, Tex., 1986—). Republican. Episcopalian. Avocations: golf, water-skiing, bowling, softball. Home: Pottsboro, Tex. Died Oct. 14, 2004.

DESCHNER, ELEANOR ELIZABETH, retired biologist, cancer researcher; b. Jersey City, Oct. 18, 1928; BA, Notre Dame Coll., Staten Island, N.Y., 1949; MS, Fordham U., 1951, PhD, 1954. Assoc. prof. medicine & radiology Cornell U. Med. Sch., 1976-92; assoc. radiobiologist Dept. Medicine Meml. Hosp., N.Y.C., 1978-92; head lab of digestive tract carcinogenesis Sloan Kettering Inst. for Cancer Rsch., N.Y.C., 1980-92; ret., 1992. Contbr. numerous articles to profl. jours. Recipient grants from Nat. Cancer Inst., Am. Cancer Soc., Nat. Inst. Health, Am. Coll. of Gastroenterology. Mem. AAAS, Am. Assn. Cancer Rsch., Am. Gastroent. Assn., Royal Soc. Medicine, Am. Soc. Cell Biologists, Cell Kinetics Soc., Genetics Soc., Am. Inst. Biol. Scis., Radiation Rsch. Soc., Am. Soc. Preventive Oncology, Bus. and Profl. Women's Club, Women's Club, Sigma Xi. Republican. Roman Catholic. Home: Jamesburg, NJ. Died May 13, 2005.

DESSAUER, SIDNEY ROBERT, taxicab company executive; b. Chgo., Oct. 9, 1936; s. Herman and Lena (Schwab) D.; m. Sandra Kay Masters, May 12, 1963; 1 child, Helen Victoria. AA in Bus. Adminstrn., Coll. of San Mateo, 1960. Owner, mgr. Alpha Cab Co., San Jose, Calif., from 1977. Chmn. No. Calif. Vets. Employment Com., 1976. Sgt. U.S. Army, 1953-56, Korea. Mem. VFW (life, dist. 12 allstate comdr. 1980-81), AMVETS (life), Am. Legion (life), Mil. Order Cooties (life), Jewish War Vets. (life, dist. comdr. 1976-77, State Man of Yr. award 1976), United Vet. Coun. Santa Clara County (pres. 1976, Man of Yr. award 1981), Hole in One Club. Avocations: stamp and coin collecting, golf. Home: San Jose, Calif. Died May 26, 2004.

DETRUDE, HOWARD JAY, JR., lawyer; b. Pitts., Dec. 15, 1929; s. Howard Jay and Martha Beatrice (Shore) DeT.; m. Lois Jean Witt, July 13, 1952; children: Keith Jay, Beverly Jean, Kevin Lee, Kathleen Ann. BA, Butler U., 1956; JD, Ind. U., 1960. Bar: Ind. 1960, U.S. Ct. Appeals (7th cir.) 1962, U.S. Supreme Ct. 1962. Assoc. Armstrong, Gause, Hudson & Kightlinger, Indpls., 1960-64; ptnr. Kightlinger, Young, Gray & DeTrude, Indpls., 1964-86; v.p., gen. counsel Norris Food Svc., Inc., Beech Grove, Ind., from 1986; gen. counsel The Precedent, Indpls., from 1986. With U.S. Army, 1947-48, 50-52. Mem. ABA, Ind. Bar Assn., Indpls. Bar Assn., 7th Cir. Bar Assn., Am. Coll. Probate Counsel, Lawyers and Pilots Bar Assn., Masons, Shriners. Republican. Lutheran. Home: Indianapolis, Ind. Died Feb. 27, 2004.

DETTINGER, GARTH BRYANT, surgeon, physician, retired military officer, public health service officer; b. Syracuse, NY, Dec. 23, 1921; s. Maurice and Maxine Bryant (giddings) D.; m. Gladys Ruth Hickingbotham, Aug. 5, 1939 (dec. Aug. 1996); children: Holly Maxine Dettinger Dixon-Keane, Ronald Mark, Michael James; m. Jeffa Taylor, July 26, 1997. AB, Harvard U., 1948; MD, Columbia U., 1952; MS in Surgery, Baylor U., 1956. Diplomate Am. Bd. Surgery. B-17 instr. pilot, B-29 aircraft comdr. U.S. Army Air Corps, 1941—45; Commd. officer U.S. Air Force, 1952, advanced through grades to maj. gen., 1977; intern Valley Forge Army Hosp., Phoenixville, Pa., 1952-53; resident in surgery Brooke Army Hosp., San Antonio, 1953-57; chief surgery MacDill Hosp., Tampa, Fla., 1957-59, Elmendorf Hosp., Alaska, 1959-62, Davis-Monthan Hosp., Tucson, 1962-64; hosp. comdr. Roswell, N.Mex., 1964-67; prime recovery helicopter surgeon Project Gemini, Cape Kennedy, Fla., 1964—67; chief profl. services Air Forces Europe, 1967-70; hosp. comdr. Vandenberg, Calif., 1970-72; surgeon Air Force Mil. Personnel Center, San Antonio, 1972-74; command surgeon Air Tng. Command, 1974-75; dir. plans and resources U.S. Air Force, Washington, 1975-77, dep. surgeon gen., 1977-80; asst. health dir. Fairfax County, Va., from 1980. Surg. cons. Surgeon Gen. U.S., CIA, 1978-99; clin. assoc. prof. Georgetown U. Med. Sch., 1983— Editor-in-chief: Surgeons Comments, 1967-70. Recipient Disting. Svc. medal, USAF, 1977. Fellow A.C.S. (bd. govs.); mem. Soc. Med. Cons. to Armed Services, Alpha Omega Alpha. Republican. Episcopalian. Home: Fort Belvoir, Va. Died Mar. 22, 2005.

DEUTSCH, THOMAS FREDERICK, physicist; b. Vienna, Apr. 24, 1932; came to U.S., 1939; s. George and Sabina (Edel) D.; m. Judy Foreman, May 5, 1990. B. Engring Physics, Cornell U., 1955; AM, Harvard U., 1956, PhD, 1961. Prin. rsch. scientist Raytheon Co., Lexington, Mass., 1960-74; staff mem. MIT, Lexington, 1974-84; physicist Mass. Gen. Hosp., Boston, from 1984; assoc. prof. Harvard Med. Sch., Boston, 1987—2006. Contbr. articles to profl. jours.; patentee in field. Recipient of R.W. Wood Prize, 1991, Optical Soc. Am. Fellow Am. Phys. Soc., Optical Soc. Am. (Wood prize 1991), Am. Soc. for Lasers in Medicine; mem. IEEE (sr.). Home: Cambridge, Mass. Died July 17, 2006.

DEVAUGHN, MICHAEL RICHARD, minister, administrator; b. Boston, July 6, 1959; s. Ludie David and Rose Anna Moore DeV.; 1 child, Terrance T. Moody. BA, Ind. U., 1984; MDiv, So. Meth. U., 1988; DDiv (hon.), Faith Inst. Christian Theology, 1994. Ordained elder, CME Ch. Sr. min. Antioch CME Ch., Abilene, Tex., 1988-89, St. Paul CME Ch., Midland, Tex., 1989-91; dean institutional advancement Tex. Coll., Tyler, 1991-93; sr. min. Starrville CME Ch., Tyler, Tex., 1991-93, Carter Chapel CME Ch., Amarillo, Tex., from 1993; exec. dir. Black Hist. Cultural Ctr., Amarillo, from 1996. Bd. dirs. Amarillo (Tex.) Opera, 1994—, United Way, Amarillo, 1994—, Salvation Army, 1994—; city councilman City of Midland, Tex., 1990. Mem. Nat. Soc. Fundraising Execs., Coalition of Black Men, Downtown Lions Club (planning chair), Tex. Lions Camp. Democrat. Methodist. Avocations: reading, gourmet cooking, writing, golf, travel. Home: Amarillo, Tex. Died Oct. 24, 2004.

DE VITO, JOSEPH, psychologist; b. Bklyn., Dec. 19, 1945; s. Salvatore and Rose De Vito; m. Gail Ann Cryan, July 29, 1972; children: Jill, Becky, Gary. BS, Manhattan Coll., 1967; MA, Columbia U., 1973; PhD, Ga. State U., 1978. Cert. psychologist, Conn. Psychologist Wyo. State Hosp., Evanston, 1978-80; dir. Washakie Mental Health Svcs., Worland, Wyo., 1980-82, Inst. for Motivational Devel., Edina, Minn., 1982-83, Morrow-Wheeler-Gilliam Mental Health, Heppner, Oreg., 1984-85; psychologist Washburn Child Guidance Ctr., Mpls., 1985-87, Luth. Social Svcs., International Falls, Minn., 1987-88; psychologist, assoc. Breyer and Cohen, Vernon, Conn., 1988-90; pvt. practice Middletown, Conn., from 1990. Profl. mem. State Conn. Bd. Psychologist Examiners, Hartford, 1996—; adj. faculty Criminal Justice Dept., U. New Haven. With U.S. Army, 1969-70, Korea. Mem. Nat. Assn. Scholars, Nat. Register of Health Svc. Providers in Psychology. Republican. Roman Catholic. Home: Middletown, Conn. Died July 30, 2004.

DEWITT, SALLIE LEE, realtor; b. Ft. Smith, Ark., Oct. 11, 1923; d. Lee and Claudia Cordelia Victoria (Vest) DeWitt. BS, U. Tex., 1944; student, U. Houston, 1971; postgrad. in Computers, Del Mar Coll., 1989. Real estate broker, Tex.; cert. profl. sec. Layout artist, copywriter Corpus Christi (Tex.) Caller-Times, 1945-56; exec. sec. to chief geologist Exxon Co., Houston, 1956-73; adminstrv. asst. to gen. mgr. Valley Telephone Coop., Inc., Raymondville, Tex., 1976-89; owner, mgr. Sallie Lee DeWitt Real Estate, Raymondville, Tex., 1980-89; broker assoc. Alfred Edge Realtors, Corpus Christi, 1990-95; broker, owner Sallie Lee DeWitt Real Estate, from 1996. Property tax cons., Corpus Christi, 1992-94. Mem. Nueces County Hist. Soc., Corpus Christi, 1990—. Mem. AAUW, Women's Coun. Realtors, Corpus Christi Bd. Realtors, C.C. Town Hall, C.C. Bus. and Profl. Women, Civitan Internat., Tropical Trails Investment Club/Harlingen, Tex., Internat. Soc. Poets, Internta. soc. Photographers. Republican. Baptist. Avocations: poetry, piano, art, photography, genealogy. Home: Alamo, Tex. Died June 8, 2005.

DEYO, STEVE, small business owner, speaker, writer; b. Columbus, Ohio, July 26, 1949; s. Harold McKinley and Martha Louise (Brown) D.; m. Graciela Olivia Guerrero, Feb. 15, 1975 (div. June m1994); children: Kevin, Robin, Stephen. BA, Miami U., 1971. Sales rep. Rocky Mountain Mktg., Denver, 1971-72; tax agt. Ohio Dept. of Taxation, Columbus, 1972-75; claims rep. Nationwide Ins., Atlanta, 1975-78; sales mgr. Azrock Industries, Atlanta, 1978-86; acct. exec. Mercer Plastics, Atlanta, 1986-87; acct. mgr. Computer Assocs., Atlanta, 1987-88; editor La Vista de Mexico, Atlanta, from 1988; founder Deyo Comm., Lilburn, from 1991; CEO Aventura Comms., Golden, Colo., from 1994. Spkr. in field. Author: Milestones and Memories: The Art of the Toast. Mem. Toastmasters Internat. (Gwinnett

County pres. 1987-88, Outstanding Spkr. award 1985, 88), Ind. Publishers, Am. Wine Soc., Beta Theta Pi. Republican. Roman Catholic. Avocations: running, backpacking, travel. Died Sept. 6, 2004.

DIBARI, JANET ANN, community health nurse; b. Southampton, N.Y., Aug. 12, 1959; d. Harry E. Jr. and May (Huson) Nugent; m. Nicholar R. DiBari Jr., Sept. 14, 1985; children: Christina Ann, Nicholas Ralph III. AAS in Nursing, Suffolk Community Coll., Selden, N.Y., 1979. RN, N.Y. Pvt. duty nurse, Southampton; office nurse Hamptons Gynecology and Obstetrics, P.C., Southampton; coll. nurse Suffolk C.C.-East, Riverhead, N.Y., from 1984. Contbg. writer For Your Health. Recipient Excellence in Practical Nursing award, 1977. Mem. Suffolk County Assn. Nurses. Home: East Quogue, NY. Died May 7, 2005.

DICKINSON, DAN CALVIN, medical librarian; b. Olden, Tex., Sept. 15, 1920; s. William Calvin and Flossie Stella (Pierce) D.; m. Suzanne Clubb, Feb. 20, 1959. Student, U. Okla., 1938-41, U. Ariz., 1944-45; BA, U. So. Calif., 1949, MS in Bacteriology, 1963. Bacteriology technician U. So. Calif., L.A., 1945-46; chemistry and microbiology instr. Calif. Coll. Mortuary Sci., L.A., 1946-74; substitute libr. Indio (Calif.) H.S., 1975-76; med. libr. John F. Kennedy Meml. Hosp., Indio, from 1976; libr. asst. Desert Hosp., Palm Springs, Calif., 1977-79; libr. tech. Eisenhowen Med. Ctr., Rancho Mirage, Calif., 1978-86. Microbiology chmn. Joint Com. Mortuary Edn., 1955-68; mem. question com. Conf. Funeral Svc. Exam. Bds., Washington, Ind., 1955-74. With U.S. Army, 1942-43. Mem. Med. Libr. Assn., Med. Libr. Group S. Calif. Democrat. Methodist. Avocation: making christmas decorations and other holiday arrangements. Home: Indio, Calif. Died July 31, 2004.

DICKMAN, ROY WILLARD, surgeon; b. Staples, Minn., Apr. 18, 1921; s. Walter Harold and Tilla Carena (Roe) D.; m. Patricia Mae Mauritz, June 15, 1945; children: Pamela, Deborah, Maureen. BS, U. Minn., 1942, BM, 1945, MD, 1946. Diplomate Am. Bd. Surgery. Intern St. Mary's Hosp., Duluth, Minn., 1945-46; resident in surgery NPBA Hosp., St. Paul, 1946; resident in thoracic surgery Mo. State Sanitorium, Mt. Vernon, 1948-49; resident in surgery Mpls. Deaconess Hosp., St. Paul, 1948-49; fellow in gen. surgery U. Minn.-Anker Hosp., St. Paul, 1949-51; mem. staff Meth. Hosp., St. Louis; emeritus U. Minn.; ret. Founder Ind. Physicians Assn. of Meth. Hosp., St. Louis Park, Minn., 1972; co-founder S.W. Clinic of Edina, Minn., 1972. Contbr. articles to profl. publs. Recipient Outstanding Contbn. and Svc. award Meth. Hosp. Ind. Physicians Assn., 1984, Tchr. of Yr. award Family Practice Residency-Surg. Svc., 1980. Home: Edina, Minn. Died Apr. 15, 2004.

DICKSON, ROBERT BRENT, biomedical researcher, educator; b. Washington, June 13, 1952; s. Robert Russell and Marie (Altsheler) D. BS, Coll. William and Mary, 1974; PhD, Yale U., 1980. Postdoctoral fellow molecular biol. lab. Nat. Cancer Inst., NIH, Bethesda, Md., 1980-83, sr. staff fellow medicine br., 1983-88; assoc. prof. anatomy, cell biology, pharmacology Georgetown U., Washington, 1988-93, prof. cell biology and pharmacology, assoc. dir. basic sci. Lombardi Cancer Ctr., 1993—2006, dir. tumor biology PhD program, 1993—99, 2002—06, prof.and vice chmn. dept. oncology Lombardi Cancer Ctr., from 1999, interim chmn. dept. oncology Lombardi Cancer Ctr., 2000—02, Cecilia Fisher Rudman disting. prof. breast cancer rsch. Author: Breast Cancer: Cellular and Molecular Biology (5 volume set), 1988-96, Drug and Hormonal Resistance in Breast Cancer, 1996, Hormones and Growth Factors in Development and Neoplasia, 1998. Died June 24, 2006.

DICKSON, WILLIAM ROBERT, academic administrator; b. Framingham, Mass., Apr. 9, 1935; s. Leo Elwood adn Edith Isabel (McCormick)D.; m. Patricia Ann Lingley, June 30, 1956; children: William Christopher, Jeffrey Lee, Julie Ann. BS, MIT, 1956. Registered profl. engr. Staff engr. Linclon Lab. MIT, Lexington, Mass., 1956-58; assoc. scientist AVCO Corp., Wilmington, Mass., 1958-60; asst. to dir. Phy Plant MIT, Cambridge, Mass., 1960-71, dir. plant, 1971-80, v.p. ops., 1980-82, sr. v.p., 1982. Chmn. bd. examiners City of Cambridge; CEO, chmn., bd. dirs. Harvard Coop. Soc., Cambridge. Served to capt. USAR, 1956-65. Recipient Medal for Excellence, Am. Soc. Mil. Engrs., 1956, Meritorious Svc. award Assn. Phys. Plant Adminstrs., 1980. Mem. Am. Inst. Plant Engrs. (cert. plant engr.), Masons, Algonquin Club. Congregationalists. Home: Framingham, Mass. Died Aug. 14, 2006.

DIEBOLD, JOHN (JOHN THEURER DIEBOLD), management consultant; b. Weehawken, N.J., June 8, 1926; s. William and Rose (Theurer) D.; m. Doris Hackett, Nov. 22, 1951 (div. 1975); 1 dau., Joan; m. Vanessa Vonderporten, June 12, 1982; children: Emma, John. BS (Regtl. Acad. award), U.S. Mcht. Marine Acad., 1946; BA with high honors in Econs, Swarthmore Coll., 1949; MBA with distinction, Harvard U., 1951; LLD (hon.), Rollins Coll., 1965; ScD (hon.), Clarkson Coll., 1965; D of Engring. (hon.), Newark Coll. Engring., 1970; LHD (hon.), Canaan Coll., 1972; DCS (hon.), Manhattan Coll., 1973. With Griffenhagen & Assos. (mgmt. cons.), N.Y.C., also Chgo., 1951-54; owner Griffenhagen & Assocs. (mgmt. cons.), 1957-60, Griffenhagen & Assocs. (merged with Louis J. Kroeger & Assos. to become Griffenhagen-Kroeger, Inc.), 1960; chmn. bd. Griffenhagen-Kroeger, Inc., from 1960; founder Diebold Group, Inc. (mgmt. cons.), N.Y.C., 1954; pres., chmn. bd. The JD Cons. Group, Inc. (formerly Diebold Group, Inc.), from 1954; founder Diebold Europe S.A., 1958, chmn. bd., from 1958; founder, chmn. bd. Mgmt. Sci. Tng. Inst., from 1958; founder John Diebold Inc. (mgmt. and investment), 1967, chmn., 1967—91, DCL Inc. (holding co. of Diebold Computer Leasing, Inc.), 1967-77, Gemini Computer Systems, Inc., 1968-75. Bd. dir., mem. nominating com. Genesco, Prentice Hall, Inc. Author: Automation, The Advent of the Automatic Factory, 1952, republished, 1983, Beyond Automation, 1964, Man and the Computer— Technology as an Agent of Social Change, 1969, Business Decisions and Technological Change, 1970, The Role of Business in Society, 1983, Making the Future Work, 1984, Business in the Age of Information, 1985, Managing Information: The Challenge and the Opportunity, 1985, The Innovators, 1990; editor: World of the Computer, 1973; also articles.; bd. advisors The Jour./The Inst. Socioecon. Studies, 1984—. Mem. Sec. Labor Adv. Com. Manpower and Automation, 1962-66, Pres. Kennedy's Com., Dept. Labor's 50th Anniversary, 1963; mem. U.S. delegation UN Sci. Conf., Geneva, Switzerland, 1963; mem. adv. coun. Soc. for Technol. Advancement of Modern Man, Switzerland, 1963-76; men. com. human values Soc. Advancing Tech., Nat. Council Chs., 1965-68; presdl. appointee nat. adv. council Peace Corps, 1965-70; mem. Com. on 2d Regional Plan for N.Y.C., 1966-70; trustee, treas., mem. exec. com. Nat. Com. on U.S.-China Rels., 1969-92; trustee, sec. Bus. Council for Internat. Understanding, 1970-83; mem. Internat. Inst. Strategic Studies, London, 1971-88; bd. consultants, mem. adv. com. UN We Believe, 1972-86; mem. Adv. Council on Japan-U.S. Econ. Rels., 1972-74; mem. steering com. Atlantic Conf., 1972-82; mem. Coun. on Fgn. Rels., 1967; mem. adv. group developing fgn. affairs program, planning and budgeting system sec. state, 1966-67; Chmn. vis. com. Sch. Bus. Administrn., Clarkson Coll. Tech., 1961-66; vice chmn. vis. com. econs. Harvard U., 1963-69, 70-76, mem. vis. com. engring. and applied physics, 1974-80; vice chmn. Acad. for Ednl. Devel., 1972; adv. coun. Inst. for Crippled and Disabled N.Y.C., 1957-70; mem. U.S. adv. com. European Inst. Bus. Adminstrn., 1965-76; mem. bus. adv. com. Grad. Sch. Indsl. Adminstrn., Carnegie-Mellon U., 1969; chmn. U.S. East Asian History of Sci. Found., 1980-94; trustee Freedom House, 1969-85, mem. adv. bd. 1985, Com. for Econ. Devel., 1970; vice chmn. Am. Coun. on Germany, 1970-80, trustee, 1980-83; trustee Overseas Devel. Coun., 1974-82, mem. adv. bd., 1982; founder, pres. Diebold Inst. Pub. Policy Studies, 1967-2005; trustee Carnegie Instn., Washington, 1975; trustee, vice chmn. legislation com. N.Y. Met. Reference and Research Library Agy., 1974-80; mem. com. for African industrialization Club de Dakar, Paris, 1973-88; pub. mem. Hudson Inst., 1967—; mem. exec. com. Nat. Planning Assn., 1987-90; mem. vis. com. Center for Research in Computing Tech. and Office for Info. Tech., Harvard U., 1971-74; mem. organizing com. on Harvard and East Asia, 1974; founding mem. The Rockefeller Univ. Council, 1973; mem. adv. coun. Grad. Sch. Bus. Adminstrn., Columbia U., 1968-75; mem. vis. com. Grad. Sch. Mgmt., Vanderbilt U., 1969-74; bd. dirs. Young Audiences, 1980-82, Parent Participation TV Workshop Project, 1982; trustee, mem. exec. com. Coun. of Ams., 1971-74; trustee Nat. Planning Assn., 1973; founding mem., mem. exec. com. coun. Rockefeller U., 1973-89; mem. adv. com. ethical and human values of sci. and tech. NSF, 1973-82, indsl. panel on sci. and tech., 1974-84; trustee Overseas Devel. Council, 1974, Found. for Teaching Econs., 1980; mem. Nat. Acad. Sci. Evaluation Panel for Oversight over Inst. Computer Scis. and Tech., Nat. Bur. Standards, 1975-79, 80-84, N.Y. Gov.'s Planning Commn. for Conf. on Libraries, 1976-79, N.Y. Sheriff's Jury, 1976-80; chmn. East Asian History of Sci., Inc., 1980; mem. exec. com. Public Agenda Found., 1981-95; mem. Friends of History of Sci. Harvard U., 1982-94; trustee adv. bd. Found. Student and Communication, Inc., 1983; bd. dirs. U.S. organizing com. Air and Space Bicentennial, 1983-84, mem. ALA Commn. on Freedom and Equality of Access to Info., 1983-86; mem. adv. com. N.Y. in Art, 1983, Deutsches Mus., Munich, Fed. Republic Germany, 1984; trustee The Charles Babbage Found., 1984; mem. corp. com. NEA, 1985; mem. Ctr. for Inter-Am. Rels.; pres. Internat. Com. on Sci. Mgmt. World Mgmt. Coun., 1986-89, chmn., 1986-92; mem. adv. bd. Nat. Exec. Service Corps, 1986; appointed trustee Lehigh U., 1987-94, chair computer sci. and elec. engring. vis. com., 1988, mem. acad. affair com. and research com.; charter mem. grad. sch. of bus. com. Fordham U., 1987-94; mem. adv. bd. Peter F. Drucker Found. for Non-profit Mgmt., 1990. Served with USNR, World War II. Decorated grand officer Order of Istiqlal, Jordan; grand cross Eloy Alfaro Found., Panama; grand cross Order St. Martin, Vienna; commendatore Order Merit, Italy; Order Merit Germany; Chevalier Legion of Honor France; Named one of ten outstanding young men U.S. Jr. C. of C., 1962; recipient Disting. Info. Scis. award Data Processing Mgmt. Assn., 1980; Fellow J. Pierpont Morgan Library, 1973-91. Fellow Internat. Acad. Mgmt.; mem. Internat. Cybernetics Assn. (dir. 1957—), AAAS (chmn. sect. com. on indsl. sci. 1981—), Am. Printing History Assn., U.S.C. of C. (coun. on trends and perspectives 1969-81), Internat. C. of C. (trustee U.S. coun. 1971-74), N.Y. Sci. Policy Assn., Newcomen Soc., Mid-Atlantic Club N.Y., Author's Guild (com. on the 70's 1970-73). Clubs: Harvard Business School, Economic, Union League, Harvard (N.Y.C.); Metropolitan (Washington); Chicago; Bohemian (San Francisco); Reform, Burkes (London). Died Dec. 26, 2005.

DIEDERICH, JOHN WILLIAM, internet publisher; b. Ladysmith, Wis., Aug. 30, 1929; s. Joseph Charles and Alice Florence (Yost) D.; m. Mary Theresa Klein, Nov. 25, 1950; children: Mary Theresa Diederich Evans, Robert Douglas, Charles Stuart, Michael Mark, Patricia Anne Diederich Irelan, Donna Maureen (dec.), Denise Brendan, Carol Lynn Diederich Weaver, Barbara Gail, Brian Donald, Tracy Maureen, Theodora Bernadette Diederich Davidson, Tamara Alice Diederich Williams, Lorraine Angela. PhB, Marquette U., Milw., 1951; MBA with high distinction, Harvard U., 1955. With Landmark Comm., Inc., Norfolk, Va., 1955-90, v.p., treas., 1965-73, exec. v.p. fin., 1973-78, exec. v.p. community newspapers, 1978-82, exec. v.p., CFO, 1982-90, fin. cons., 1990—2006; internet pub. Wide World Web Internat., Incline Village, 1996—2006. Chmn. bd. dirs. Landmark Cmty. Newspapers, Inc., 1977-88; pres. Exec. Productivity Sys., Inc., 1982-88, LCI Credit Corp., 1991-93, Landmark TV Inc., 1991-2006, LTM Investments, Inc., 1991-2006; v.p., treas., KLAS, Inc., 1994-95; v.p. Internet Express, Inc., 1994-2000; pres., bd. dirs. Wide World Web Internat., 1995-06, TWC Holdings, Inc., 1996-2006; instr. Boston U., 1954, Old Dominion U., 1955-59; mgr. No. Neck Newspaper Group LLC, 2002-06; pres. City News Inc., 2004-06. Lt. col. USMC, 1951-53, USMCR, 1953-71. Baker scholar Harvard U., 1955. Mem. SAR, Nat. Assn. Accts., Am. Numismatic Assn., Nat. Geneal. Soc., Wis. Geneal. Soc., Pa. Geneal. Soc., Sigma Delta Chi. Roman Catholic. Died Mar. 27, 2006.

DIGGS, NATALIE VIRGINA, director, headmaster; b. Imperial, Calif., May 18, 1918; d. Jerome Richard and Callie Leovia (Hammond) Collins; m. Orville Singleton Diggs, Dec. 14, 1940; children: Janet Diane, Richard Allen, Denise Gayle. Student, San Bernadino Jr. Coll., 1935-36, Tuskegee Inst., 1937-39; AA, San Bernardino Jr. Coll., 1956; BA, U. Redlands, 1969. Sec. Rialto (Calif.) Edn. Assn., 1972-73; dir. elem. St. Paul A.M.E. Ch., San Bernardino, Calif., 1977-79. Bd. dirs. Rolling Start for the Deaf, San Bernardino, Calif. Access Com. for the Disabled, San Bernardino. Dir. elem. segment Rialto Edn. Assn.; active Girl Scouts Am., 1977-78, mayor's Adv. Council for Sr. Affairs, San Bernardino, 1978-79; bd. dirs. Goodwill Industries Inland County, San Bernardino, 1979-85; mem. Dept. Hwy. Patrol, Sacramento, Calif., 1984-85. Mem. Calif. Tchrs. Assn., AAUW (sec. 1981-83; community awareness chmn. 1985-87; program v.p. 1987-88), nat. Council Negro Women (membership v.p. 1978-80), Cosmos Club (treas. 1981-82). Democrat. African Methodist. Avocations: sewing, bridge, travel. Home: San Bernardino, Calif. Died June 26, 2005.

DIGGS, ROBERT MACLARY, lawyer; b. Tulsa, Jan. 14, 1912; s. James Barnes and Edith (Maclary) D.; m. Clara Curtis, Feb. 19, 1952 (dec. Jan. 1991); children: George, Katherine, Douglas, Jane, Andrew, Lawrence. AB, Hamilton Coll., 1933; LLB, Yale U., 1936. Bar: N.Y. 1937, U.S. Dist. Ct. (we. dist.) N.Y. 1947, U.S. Tax Ct. 1953, U.S. Ct. Appeals (2d cir.) 1959, U.S. Supreme Ct. 1965, U.S. Claims Ct. 1987, U.S. Dist. Ct. (so. and ea. dists.) N.Y. 1989. Assoc. Cravath, Swaine & Moore, N.Y.C., 1936-41; asst. to pres. Hamilton Coll., Clinton, N.Y., 1941-42; assoc. Hornburg, Diggs, Backhaus & Simon, P.C. and predecessor firms, Olean, N.Y., from 1946. Capt. U.S. Army, 1942-46. Republican. Episcopalian. Home: Olean, NY. Died Feb. 22, 2005.

DIGIUSEPPE, ENRICO, tenor, vocal music educator; b. Phila. Studies with Richard Bonelli, Curtis Inst. Music; studies with Hans Heinz, The Juilliard Sch. Leading tenor Met. Opera and N.Y.C. Opera Cos.; instr. voice The Juilliard Sch., N.Y.C., 1985—2006. Performed with maj. opera cos. throughout the U.S., Can., Mex., Europe and the Far East. Died Dec. 31, 2005.

DILL, ROBERT FLOYD, marine geologist; b. Denver, May 25, 1927; s. Robert Kirby and Eldora A. (Fisk) D.; m. Sonia B. Daswick, Dec. 27, 1963; children: Robert F. II, Kathryn Baslee, Marc C., James M. BS in Geology, U. So. Calif., 1950, MS in Geology, 1952; PhD in Marine Geology, U. Calif.-San Diego, La Jolla, 1964. Cert. petroleum geologist. Geologist, oceanographer USN Elec. Lab., San Diego, 1951-72; geologist NOAA, Rockville, Md., 1972-75, 1981-83, U.S. Geol. Survey, Washington, 1975; dir., prof. geology West Indies Lab. Fairleigh Dickenson U., St. Croix, U.S. Virgin Islands, 1975-81, Dept. Interior, Los Angeles and San Diego, 1983-86; cons. Geomarex, San Diego, 1986-87; owner, dir. Dill Geomarine Cons., San Diego, from 1987. Commr. Virgin Island Water Resources Commn., St. Croix, 1979-81; prof. geology U. S.C., 1985—; advisor geology Caribbean Marine Rsch. Ctr., Lee Stocking Island, Bahamas, 1984—. Author: (with others) Submarine Canyons, 1966; producer motion picture Submarine Canyons, 1967, Deeply Submerged Terraces, 1968 (Nat. Ind. Picture Assn. 1969); contbr. 75 articles to profl. jours. Co-chmn. Gorda Ridge Task Force. Served with USN, 1945-47. Recipient Golden Bear award Calif. Resources Agy., 1964. Fellow Geol. Soc. Am.; mem. Am. Assn. Petroleum Geologists, Geol. Soc. Washington, Am. Geophysical Union, Am. Inst. Profl. Geologists & Mineralogists, Soc. Econ. Paleontologists and Minerologists, Marine Tech. Soc., St. Croix C. of C. Republican. Avocations: underwater photography, scuba diving. Home: San Diego, Calif. Died Jan. 25, 2004.

DILLON, MARTIN, musician, educator; b. Portsmouth, Ohio, June 17, 1957; s. Sidney Dillow and Edna Daniels; life ptnr. Dhruv Shravan Kapoor, June 5, 1999. MusB, Cin. Conservatory Music, 1979; MusM, U. Okla., 1984. Asst. prof. music Rutgers U., Camden, NJ, 1990—98, prof. music, from 1998. Dir. theater and musical theater Rutgers U., Camden, from 2000. Dir.: (musical) Man of La Mancha, 2001, 110 in the Shade, 2002; singer (ferrando): (opera) Cosi fan Tutte, 1990; singer: (belmonte) Die Entfuhrung aus dem Serail, 1991; singer: (tamino) Die Zauberflote, 1994;

singer: (don ottavio) Don Giovanni, 1994; singer: (dorvil) La Scala di Seta, 1991; singer: (count almaviva) Il Barbiere di Sevilla, 1993; singer: (beppe) I Pagliacci, 1989; singer: (jaquino) Fidelio, 1988; singer: (florestan), 1997; prodr.(poliuto): (opera) Poliuto, 1998; singer (alfredo): (opera) La Traviata, 1997; singer: (filipeto) I Quattro Rusteghi, 1986; singer: (albert herring) Albert Herring, 1986; singer: (fritz) L'Amico Fritz, 2004; singer: (bomeli) The Tsar's Bride, 1996; singer: (romeo) Romeo and Juliet, 2001; contbr. french recitals Works of Francis Poulenc, 2001 (Friends of French Internat. award, 2001). Dir. Camden Policemen's Choral, 2000—01; hon. capt. Camden Police Assn., 2000—01. Named Texoma Singer of Yr., Nat. Assn. Singing, 1984; recipient 1st Pl. award, Am. Opera Awards, 1989; scholar Benton scholar, U. Okla., 1983, 1984. Democrat. Avocations: travel, languages. Home: New York, NY. Died Aug. 21, 2005.

DILLON, ROBERT JOHN, consumer products manufacturing executive; b. Mpls., Aug. 26, 1919; s. James John and Mary Stella (Hogan) D.; m. Florence Marie Kelley, Jan. 10, 1942; children: Anne, James, Patrick, Thomas, Joan, Mike, Tim. BS in Mining and Metall. Engring., Case Inst. Tech., 1941. Purchasing, sales mgr. The West Bend Aluminum Co., West Bend and Hartford, Wis., 1946-65; v.p., plant mgr. Chrysler Outboard Corp., Hartford, Wis., 1965-68; gen. mfg. mgr. Marine Group Chrysler Corp., Detroit, 1968-79; v.p. Chrysler Outboard Corp., Chrysler Can. Outboard Ltd., 1968-79, Chrysler Boat Corp., 1968-79; v.p. ops. The Eska Co., Dubuque, Iowa, 1979-81, pres., chief exec. officer, vice-chmn. bd., 1981-88, also bd. dirs., indsl. cons., from 1988. Bd. dirs. Southeastern Mich. chpt. ARC, Detroit, 1969-73, Pvt. Industry Council Dubuque and Delaware Counties, Iowa, 1983-85. Served to lt. comdr. USNR, 1941-46, PTO. Mem. Am. Cancer Soc. (pres. Washington County 1956-57), Milw. Archdiocesan Council of Cath. Men (pres. 1963), Hartford C. of C. (pres. 1959). Died Apr. 14, 2005.

DIMES, EDWIN KINSLEY, lawyer; b. Hartford, Conn., Apr. 13, 1923; s. Alfred Eustace and Charlotte (Miller) D.; m. Edwina May Adams, Feb. 3, 1945 (div. 1981); chldren: Martha, Deborah, Kimberley; m. S. Antoinette Morton, Dec. 29, 1990. BA, Conn. Wesleyan U., Middletown, 1947; JD, Yale U., 1950. Bar: Conn. 1950, U.S. Tax Ct. 1960, U.S. Supreme Ct. 1960. From assoc. to ptnr. Wake, See, Dimes and Bryniczka, Westport, Conn., from 1950. State trial referee State of Conn., 1985—. Chmn. bd. fin. City of Westport, 1979-97. 2d lt. USAF, 1943-45. Mem. ABA, Westport Bar Assn., Conn. Bar Assn. (bd. govs.). Republican. Congregationalist. Avocations: boating, tennis. Home: Westport, Conn. Died Mar. 4, 2005.

DINARDO, GEORGE P., bank executive; b. Patterson, N.J., June 4, 1937; s. George V. and Margaret A. (Verhasselt) DiN.; m. Jeanne M. Macolino, Nov. 14, 1959; children: George P., Steven C., Peter J., Michael W., David J. BSME, Rensselaer Poly. U., 1959, MSME, 1962. V.p., mgr. Bankers Trust Co., N.Y.C., 1963-69; exec. v.p. info. mgmt. and research dept. Mellon Bank, Pitts., from 1969. Pres. Upper St. Clair Athletic Assn., Pa., 1987—, adv. bd. Vocat. Rehab. Ctr., Pitts., 1987—, Community Coll. Allegheny County, Pitts., 1987—; bd. dirs. health compensation Presbyn. Univ. Hosp., Pitts., 1982-87. Lt. (j.g.) USNR, 1959-61. Mem.: Duquesne (Pitts.). Republican. Roman Catholic. Home: Pittsburgh, Pa. Died May 5, 2005.

DINDA, MICHAEL W., business executive; b. Mars Hill, Maine, Oct. 5, 1945; Franchise owner Tuff Kote Din, Ft. Huron, Mich., 1979-80; nat. acct. mgr. Control Data Corp. Edn. Divsn., Southfield, Mich., 1981-87; gen. mgr. United Tng. Svcs. Corp., Southfield, from 1988. With U.S. Army, 1967-69. Republican. Roman Catholic. Avocations: bass fishing, billiards. Home: Madison Heights, Mich. Died May 12, 2005.

DINEGAR, ROBERT HUDSON, chemist; b. N.Y.C., Dec. 18, 1921; div. head/sci. and tech., U. N.Mex., Los Alamos, 1992—; chmn. chemistry dept. USN enlisted sci. edn. program San Diego, 1971-74; owner, SYCON, Los Alamos, 1984—; bd. dirs. Shroud of Turin Rsch. Project, Amston, Conn., 1977—. AB in Chemistry, Cornell U., 1942; cert. in meteorology, NYU, 1943; AM in Chemistry, Columbia U., 1947, PhD in Phys. Chemistry, 1951; AB in Theology, Coll. Santa Fe, 1976. Ordained priest Episcopal Ch., 1962. Asst. in chemistry Columbia U., N.Y.C., 1945-50; mem. rsch. staff Los Alamos (N.Mex.) Nat. Lab., 1950-87; ret. Co-inventor low voltage explosive detonator, 1982, high temperature explosive detonator, 1987. Priest The Episc. Ch., Diocese of Rio Grande, 1959—. Comdr. USNR, 1942-75, PTO. Fellow Am. Inst. Chemists (cert.); mem. Am. Chem. Soc., Am. Meteorol. Soc., Baker St. Irregulars, Bros. Three Moriarty, Sigma Xi, Phi Lambda Upsilon. Republican. Home: Los Alamos, N.Mex. Died Apr. 21, 2005.

DIOUM, THERESE ELAINE, human resources executive; b. Indpls., Aug. 19, 1945; d. Bernard and Elaine (Glenn) Wisdom; m. Mamadou Dioum, Jan. 15, 1970 (div. 1979); 1 child, Djenaba. Student, Marian Coll., 1963-64. Regional personnel officer West Africa region Citibank, Abidjan, Ivory Coast, 1977-83; corp. personnel mgr. Amfac, Inc., San Francisco, from 1984. Mem. Am. Soc. Personnel Adminstrs., Northern Calif. Human Resources Council, Bay Area Network Profls. Avocation: creative writing. Home: Fremont, Calif. Died Mar. 9, 2005.

DISKIN, MARSHAL ANDREW, II, editor; b. Glen Cove, N.Y., Sept. 12, 1958; s. Marshal Andrew Sr. and Catherine Elaine (Dragon) D.; m. Marianne Tierney. Student, Brown U., 1977, U. Miami, Fla., 1978, NYU, 1979. Engr. Sta. WKID-TV, Miami, 1976-79, H.B.O. Studio Prodns., N.Y.C., 1979-81; videographer, editor Sta. WPLG-TV, Miami, 1981-83; video tape editor Broadcast Video, Inc., Miami, from 1983. Photographer, editor: TV show Kids Beat mag., 1982 (Emmy 1982); editor: TV spl. Memories-Marv Dolphin Tribute, 1982 (Emmy 1982); editor numerous comml. and shows. Avocations: scuba diver, skiing, water-skiing. Home: Pembroke Pnes, Fla. Died Sept. 28, 2004.

DISS, DAVID MARK, financial company executive; b. Rome, N.Y., Apr. 30, 1953; s. Darell David and Jacquelyn (Humphrey) D.; m. Nancy Muscato, Mar. 17, 1984; children: Laura Elizabeth, David Matthew. Student, Fla. State U., 1975. Cert. planner. Crisis counselor Ft. Worth Crisis Team, 1975-80; dir. counseling United Meth., Ft. Worth, 1980-84; dir. rels. The Damar Group, Inc., Ft. Worth, 1977-84, gen. mgr. Tampa, Fla., 1984-86, chief exec. officer, from 1987. Cons. TSSI, Tampa, 1987-89. Author: The Star System, 1985, Lifting You Higher, 1986, The Revised Star System, 1988. 2d lt. U.S. Army, 1970-71, PTO, Vietnam. Named Top Instr. Book Class, Gen. Markens Assn., Tampa, 197, Outstanding Fellow, Life Crisis Ctr., Tampa, 1988; recipient Best Short Story award Fla. Library Guild, Tallahassee, 1988. Fellow DAMA; mem. LUTC (sr. instr.), Fellowship Christian Athletes, Tampa C. of C. (chmn. edn. 1987-88). Democrat. Mem. Christian Ch. (Disciples Of Christ). Home: Tampa, Fla. Died Feb. 14, 2005.

DIXON, FITZ EUGENE, JR., professional sports team executive; b. Winter Harbor, Maine, Aug. 14, 1923; s. Fitz Eugene and Eleanor Elkins (Widener) D.; m. Edith B. Robb, June 5, 1952; children: George Widener, Edith Eleanor. Student, Harvard U., 1942-43; L.H.D. (hon.), Pa. Mil. Coll., Lafayette Coll., Hahnemann Med. Coll., Cabrini Coll., Pa. Coll. Podiatric Medicine; LL.D. (hon.), Widener Coll., Chestnut Hill Coll.; D.Pub. Service (hon.), Temple U.; Sc.D. (hon.), Spring Garden Coll.; LL.D. (hon.), U. Pa.; LittD (hon.), Drexel U. Ptnr. Phila. Phillies Baseball Team. Life trustee Phila. Free Library, 1974-2006; former pres. Fairmount Park Commn.; trustee Abington (Pa.) Meml. Hosp., 1944-2006, sec. bd., 1947-53, v.p., 1953-68, chmn. bd., 1968-74; chmn. bd. govs. State System Higher Edn.; bd. dirs. Devon Horse Show; trustee Ellis Fund Adv. Com., Newtown, Pa., Episcopal Acad., Merion, Pa., 1961-2006, chmn. bd., 1972-75; trustee Maine Coast Meml. Hosp., Ellsworth, 1951-2006, chmn. bd., 1971-75, hon. chmn. bd., 1975-2006; trustee Phila. Mus. Art, 1979-2006; trustee emeritus Woodlynde Sch.; mgr. emeritus Germantown Hosp. and Med. Ctr.; pres. Soc. of Four Arts, Palm Beach, Fla., Widener Meml. Found. in Aid of Handicapped Children; hon. life trustee Temple U.; chmn. bd. govs. Temple U. Hosp., 1975-77; chmn. bd. Widener U., 1972-2006; co-chmn. American Gold Cup, 1973-2006; hon. trustee Winter Harbor Pub. Library, Nat. Mus. Racing; mem. Phila. Internat. City Coordinating Com., 1979-2006; hon. life dir. U.S. Equestrian Team. Mem. Nat. Steeplechase Assn. (life, past pres.), Am. Horse Show Assn. (life), U.S. Dressage Fedn., Am. Grand Prix Assn. (dir.), Phila. Soc. Promotion Agr., Pa. Hist. Soc., Soc. War of 1812, Phila. Hist. Preservation Corp., Soc. Colonial Wars, Swedish Colonial Soc., Navy League U.S., Maine Maritime Mus., Nat. Trust Hist. Preservation, Pa. Horse Breeders Assn., Inc., Pa. Soc., Thoroughbred Owners and Breeders Assn., Winterthur Mus. and Gardens, Hosp. Assn. Pa., Palm Beach Civic Assn., Preservation Found. Palm Beach, Am. Mus. Britain, Henry Morrison Flagler Mus. Clubs: Athenaeum, Phila., Corinthian Yacht, Phila., Phila. Racquet, Union League (Phila.), Gov.'s of the Palm Beaches; Palm Beach (Fla.) Everglades, Palm Beach Polo & Country, Bath and Tennis, Jockey, Key Largo (Fla.) Anglers, Sunnybrook Golf, Whitemarsh Valley Country, Winter Harbor Yacht (treas. 1948-2006), Bal Harbour (Fla.), Delray Beach Yacht (Fla.), Farmers of Pa., N.Y. Yacht, Marquis Soc. of Lafayette Coll., St. James's Club (London), Pyramid Club (bd. govs.). Episcopalian. Home: Lafayette Hill, Pa. Died Aug. 2, 2006.

DIZENHUZ, ISRAEL MICHAEL, child psychiatrist, educator; b. Toronto, Ont., Can., May 20, 1931; came to U.S., 1957; Student, U. Toronto, 1949-51, MD, 1955. Diplomate Am. Bd. Psychiatry and Neurology. Intern E.J. Meyer Meml. Hosp., Buffalo, 1955-56; resident in psychiatry Hamilton (Ont.) Hosp., 1956-57, U. Cin., 1957-58, fellow in child psychiatry, 1959-60, from instr. to assoc. prof. child psychiatry, 1961-89; prof. emeritus Cin., from 1989; asst. dir. child psychiatry Cen. Psychiat. Clinic, Cin., 1963-66, assoc. dir., 1966-78; psychiatrist cons. staff Children's Hosp., Cin., 1966—2005; sr. assoc. staff psychiatrist, dir. dept. psychiatry The Jewish Hosp., Cin., 1978-87; dir., chief clinician child and adolescent service Cin. Gen. Hosp., 1973-78, attending child psychiatrist, clinician, 1978—2005. Mem. Precocious Pregnancy research team U. Cin., 1959-60, Adolescents in Families of Alcoholics research team Family Service, Cin., 1967-71; co-prin. investigator research project, Cancer Family Care, Cin., 1974-75; lectr. Vol. Training for Community Mental Health Services, Cin., 1963-68; asst. examiner Am. Bd. Psychiatry and Neurology, 1967-2005; cons. Hamilton County Ct. Domestic Relations Conciliation Service, 1974-78, Health Maintenance Plan of Cin., 1976-77; seminar leader Family Service, Cin., 1963-67, Jewish Family Service, Cin., 1963-68; seminar leader, cons. rehab. ctr. program U. Cin., 1973-78; mem. numerous rev. coms. Contbr. articles to profl. jours. Trustee Cin. Ctr. for Devel. Disabilities, 1963-83; trustee Bur. Jewish Edn., 1971-85, v.p. 1974-77. Fellow Am. Psychiat. Assn., Am. Acad. Child Psychiatry (mem. com. on tng. in Child Psychiatry 1972-78); mem. Royal Coll. of Physicians and Surgeons of Ont., Med. Council of Can., Am. Assn. Psychiat. Services for Children (pres. 1971-73), Am. Orthopsychiat. Assn., Ohio Psychiat. Assn., Ohio State Med. Assn., Cin. Soc. Neurology and Psychiatry, Cin. Council Child Psychiatry (pres. 1965-66). Home: Cincinnati, Ohio. Died July 15, 2005.

DJOHAR, SAID MOHAMED, former President of Comoros; b. 1918; Former pres. Supreme Court, Moroni, Comoros; interim pres. Fed. Islamic Republic of the Comoros, Moroni, 1989-90, pres., 1990—95, 1996. Died Feb. 22, 2006.

DOAK, KENNETH WORLEY, research consultant; b. Gallatin, Mo., Jan. 27, 1916; s. Harry Alexander Doak and Sarah Tarwater; m. Mary-Isabel M. Doak, Aug. 11, 1945; children: Kenneth Alexander, Michael Justin, Janice Anne. AB, Cen. Meth. Coll., 1938; PhD, Johns Hopkin's U., 1942. Rsch. chemist U.S. Rubber Co. (UNIROYAL), Passaic, N.J., 1942-55; rsch. assoc. Koppers Co., Inc., Pitts., 1955-60; asst. dir. plastics Dart Industries, Inc., Paramus, N.J., 1961-65, dir. cen. rsch., 1966-70; mgr. plastics rsch. Arco Polymers, Inc., Monroeville, Pa., 1971-77; tech. advisor Arco Chem. Co., Monroeville, 1978-81; freelance cons. Murrysville, Pa., from 1981. Inventor in field; contbr. articles to profl. jours. Elected to Plastics Hall of Fame, 1986; Warner Nat. fellow Johns Hopkins U., 1938-42. Home: Murrysville, Pa. Died May 2, 2004.

DOAN, HERBERT DOW, technical business consultant, former chemical company executive; b. Midland, Mich., Sept. 5, 1922; s. Leland Ira and Ruth Alden (Dow) D.; m. Donalda Lockwood, 1946 (div.); children: Jeffrey W., Christine Mary, Ruth Alden, Michael Alden; m. Anna Junia Cassell, July 16, 1979; 1 child, Alexandra Anne Alden. B Chem. Engring., Cornell U., 1949. Founder, owner Doan Assocs., Midland, 1971-85; chmn., dir. Neogen Corp., Lansing, Mich., 1983-99; pres. Mich. High Tech. Task Force, Lansing, 1981-90; nat. adv. com. dept. engring. U. Mich., Ann Arbor, 1984-95; chmn. Midland Molecular Inst., from 1971; dir. Mich. Materials and Processing Inst., Ann Arbor, 1984-92; trustee, sec. Herbert H. and Grace A. Dow Found., Midland, from 1951; researcher Dow Chem. Co., Midland, 1949-60, exec. v.p., 1960-62, pres., CEO, 1962-71; pres. The Herbert H. and Grace A Dow Found., Midland, 1996—2000, chmn., 2000—06. Dir. Applied Intelligent Systems, Inc., Ann Arbor, Chem. Bank and Trust Co., Arch Devel. Corp., Chgo.; mem. engring. coun. Cornell U., Ithaca, N.Y., 1964-85, emeritus, 1985-2006; mem. Nat. Sci. Bd., Washington, 1976-82, vice chmn., 1981-82; mem. Commn. on Phys. Scis., Math. and Applications, NRC of NAS, Washington, 1987-91; bd. govs. Argonne Nat. Lab., U. Chgo., 1984-90; tech. assessment adv. coun. Office Tech. Assessment, Washington, 1992-95. Staff sgt. USAF, 1942-45; PTO. Mem. Am. Inst. Chem. Engrs., Am. Chem. Soc., Sigma Xi. Home: Midland, Mich. Died May 16, 2006.

DOAN, LARRY EMERY, real estate executive; b. L.A., Dec. 23, 1929; s. Larry Emery and Marie (Cochran) D.; m. Dudley Harbison, Jan. 27, 1951; children: Mary, Terry, Howard, Larry. BA, U. Calif., Berkeley, 1953. Lic. real estate broker. V.p. Harbison Henderson, L.A., 1956-62, McDonnell & Co., L.A., 1962-69; v.p., mgr. DuPont Glore Forgan Co., L.A., 1969-72; v.p. W.E. Hutton Co., L.A., 1972-74; sales assoc. Bliss Keeler Co., San Marino, Calif., 1974-79; pres. Doan Harbison Realty, San Marino, Calif., 1979-88; v.p., ptnr. Podley Caughey & Doan, Pasadena, Calif., from 1988. Lt. (j.g.) USN, 1953-56. Recipient Realtor of Yr. award San Marino/South Pasadena Bd. Realtors, 1985. Mem. San Gabriel Country Club (dir. 1997—). Republican. Avocations: golf, travel. Home: San Marino, Calif. Died July 12, 2004.

DOCHAT, GEORGE RONALD, JR., engineer, research and development executive; b. Akron, Ohio, Mar. 27, 1944; s. George Ronald Sr. and Erma (Page) D.; divorced; children: Rebecca, Scott. AB in Physics, Franklin and Marshall Coll., 1966; MS in Aerospace/Aero. Engring., Ohio State U., Columbus, 1968. Thermodynamic engr. Grumman Aerospace Corp., Bethpage, N.Y., 1968-72; project engr. Gen. Electric Corp., Schenectady, N.Y., 1972-77; program mgr. Mech. Tech. Inc., Latham, N.Y., 1978-83, mgr. space power, from 1983. Contbr. numerous articles to profl. jours. Recipient Plaque, NASA, 1985. Mem. AIAA (tech. com. for aerospace power). Republican. Lutheran. Avocations: tennis, skiing. Home: Aloha, Oreg. Died May 20, 2005.

DODD, ARTHUR VAN ZANDT, climatologist; b. Swarthmore, Pa., Jan. 9, 1924; s. Samuel Morris and Mary Reynolds (Parke) D.; m. Nina Pauline Moss, Nov. 22, 1949; children: Mark Reynolds, Randall Clark. BS, Pa. State U., 1949, MS, 1950; PhD, Boston U., 1964. Climatologist U.S. Army Natick (Mass.) Labs., 1953-68; phys. scis. adminstr., dir. geoscis. divsn. Army Rsch. Office, Durham, N.C., 1968-75, Research Triangle Park, 1975-78; vis. prof. U. N.C., Chapel Hill, 1979-83, lectr., 1984-93. Army rep. climatic design criteria Quadripartite Working Group, U.S., Can., Britain, Australia, 1965-68; Army meteorology steering com. U.S. Army, 1970-78. Contbr. articles to profl. jours. Mem. Town Energy com., Chapel Hill. 1st lt. USAF,

1950-53. Mem. AAAS, Am. Meteorology Soc., Rotary, Sigma Gamma Epsilon. Avocation: energy conservation. Home: Chapel Hill, NC. Died Oct. 12, 2004.

DODD, JOE DAVID, safety engineer, consultant, administrator; b. Walnut Grove, Mo., Jan. 22, 1920; s. Marshall Hill and Pearl (Combs) D.; m. Nona Bell Junkins, Sept. 17, 1919; 1 child, Linda Kay Dodd Craig. Student, S.W. Mo. State U., 1937-39, Washington U., St. Louis, 1947-55. Cert. profl. safety engr., Calif. Office asst. retail credit co., Kansas City, Mo., 1939-42; bus driver City of Springfield, Mo., 1945-47; varous ops., engring. and pers. positions Shell Oil Co., Wood River (Ill.) Refiney, 1947-66; mgr. health and safety dept. Martinez (Calif.) Mfg. Complex, 1966-83; ret., 1983. Exec. dir. Fire Protection Tng. Acad., U. Nev., Reno; rep. Shell Oil Co., Western Oil and Gas Assn., 1970-81. Mem. Rep. Presdl. Task Force. With USMC, 1942-45. Mem. Western Oil and Gas Assn. (Hose Handler award 1972-81, Outstanding Mem. award), Am. Soc. Safety Engrs., Vets. Safety, State and County Fire Chiefs Assn., Peace Officers Assn., Natr. Fire Protection Assn. Presbyterian (elder). Established Fire Protection Tnng. Acad., Stead Campus, U. Nev., Reno. Home: Danville, Calif. Died May 4, 2005.

DOERING, CHARLES HENRY, research scientist, educator, editor, publisher; b. Munich, Jan. 7, 1935; came to U.S., 1950; s. Heinrich and Marianne (Fleischmann) D.; m. Panayiota Maria Thliveris, June 17, 1961; children: Andreanna, Erika, Stefan, Anselm. BS in Chemistry, U. San Francisco, 1956; MS in Organic Chemistry, U. Munich, 1959; PhD in Biochemistry, U. Calif., San Francisco, 1964. Postdoctoral fellow Harvard Med. Sch., Boston, 1964-67; rsch. scientist Stanford (Calif.) U. Sch. Medicine, 1967-76; rsch. assoc. prof. SUNY, Stony Brook, 1976-86; editor Springer Verlag Publs., N.Y.C., 1986-90, Oxford Univ. Press, 1990-91; exec. editor VCH Publs., Inc., 1991-94; sr. editor, mgr. conf. procs. program Am. Inst. Physics, Melville, 1994—2004; ret., 2004. Contbr. over 30 articles to profl. jours. Mem. AAAS, Am. Chem. Soc., Soc. Scholarly Pub. Home: Setauket, NY. Died Oct. 17, 2005.

DOGGETT, BURTON LEE, JR., marketing professional; b. Charlotte, N.C., Sept. 18, 1928; s. Gertrude Franklin (Wadsworth) D.; children: Burton Lee III, David Randolph. BS in Marine Engring., USN Acad., 1951. Comd. ensign USN, 1951, adavanced through grades to lt. comdr., 1963; lt. comd. USNR, 1963-88, ret., 1988; mktg. dir. Aries Corp., Washington, 1961-69; mktg. mgr. Rockwell, Internat., Washington, 1976-85, RCA/GE, 1985-90. Mem. USN League (pres. D.C. coun. 1986-88, nat. dir. 1985—), Alexandria Bus. Club (past pres.), Army & Navy Club. Republican. Epsicopalian. Home: Annapolis, Md. Died Apr. 6, 2005.

DOHMEN, FREDERICK HOEGER, retired pharmaceutical executive; b. Milw., May 12, 1917; s. Fred William and Viola (Gutsch) D.; m. Gladys Elizabeth Dite, Dec. 23, 1939 (dec. 1963); children: William Francis, Robert Charles; m. Mary Alexander Holgate, June 27, 1964. BA in Commerce, U. Wis., 1939. With F. Dohmen Co., Milw., 1939—82, pres., 1952—82, dir., 1947—2004, chmn. bd., 1952-82; ret., 2004. Travel lectr. various orgns., 1980—. Bd. dirs. St. Luke's Hosp. Ednl. Found., Milw., 1965-83, pres., 1969-72, chmn. bd., 1972-73; bd. dirs. U. Wis. Milw. Found., 1976-79, bd. visitors, 1978-88, emeritus mem., 1988—; assoc. chmn. Nat. Bible Week, Laymen's Nat. Bible Com., N.Y.C;., 1968-82, mem. coun. of advisors, 1983—; elder Presbyn. Ch.; bd. dirs. Riveredge Nature Ctr., Newburg, Wis., 1993-94. Mem. Nat. Wholesale Druggists Assn. (chmn. mfr. rels. com. 1962, resolutions com. 1963, bd. control 1963-66), Nat. Assn. Wholesalers (trustee 1966-75), Druggists Svc. Coun. (dir. 1967-71), Wis. Pharm. Assn., Miss. Valley Drug Club, Univ. Club Town Club (Milw.), Beta Gamma Sigma, Phi Eta Sigma, Delta Kappa Epsilon. Home: Mequon, Wis. Died Apr. 2006.

DOLE, VINCENT PAUL, medical research executive, educator; b. Chgo., May 8, 1913; s. Vincent Paul and Anne (Dowling) Dole; m. Elizabeth Ann Strange, May 23, 1942 (div. 1965); children: Vincent Paul III, Susan, Bruce; m. Marie Nyswander, 1965 (dec. 1986); m. Margaret E. Cool, 1992. AB, Stanford U., 1934; MD, Harvard U., 1939. Intern Mass. Gen. Hosp., Boston, 1940—41; mem. staff Rockefeller U., N.Y.C., 1941—83, prof., 1951—83, prof. emeritus, 1983—2006. Developer methadone maintenance treatment program for heroin addiction. Recipient Albert Lasker award, 1988, Gairdner Found. Internat. award, 1970, R. Brinkley Disting. Scientist award, Am. Soc. Addiction Med., 1991. Mem.: Inst. of Med., NAS. Home: New York, NY. Died Aug. 1, 2006.

DOLEZAL, HENRY, retired research chemist; b. San Francisco, June 20, 1925; s. Frank Charles and Teresa (Garcia) D.; m. Lucille Ethel Gregersen, Nov. 29, 1958; children: Carolyn Ann Padgett, Linda Sue Mulcock, Thomas Albert Harrison. AA, City Coll. San Francisco, 1949; BA, U. Calif., Berkeley, 1952. Research chemist U.S. Bur. Mines, Boulder City, Nev., 1952-62, Salt Lake City, 1962-83. Contbr. articles to profl. jours.; patentee in field. Served to 1st lt. U.S. Army, 1943-46. Mem. Am. Legion (treas. Boulder City chpt. 1961—). Lodges: Elks. Democrat. Roman Catholic. Avocations: photography, cooking. Home: Las Vegas, Nev. Died Sept. 16, 2004.

DOLEZAL, VACLAV JAN, retired mathematician, educator; b. Ceska Trebova, Czech Republic, May 21, 1927; arrived in U.S., 1968; s. Vaclav Dolezal and Marie Dolezalova; m. Stana Kabickova, Feb. 22, 1963; children: Tomas, Peter, Zuzana. MEE, Tech. U., Prague, Czech Republic, 1949; CSC in Applied Math., Czech Acad. Sci., Prague, Czech Republic, 1956, DrSc in Applied Math., 1967. Rschr. Rsch. Labs., Prague, 1949—51, Czech Acad. Sci., Prague, 1951—65, 1966—68; vis. prof. SUNY, Stony Brook, 1965—66, prof., 1968—97; ret., 1997. Author: Dynamics of Linear Systems, 1967, Nonlinear Networks, 1977, Monotone Operators, 1979. Grantee, NSF. Home: Port Jefferson, NY. Died June 29, 2004.

DOLGIN, MARTIN, cardiologist, educator; b. NYC, Apr. 12, 1919; s. Samuel and Bertha (Brodsky) D.; m. Jeanne Rydell, Feb. 12, 1950; children: Barbara, Deborah, Stuart. AB, NYU, 1939, MD, 1943. Diplomate: Am. Bd. Internal Medicine; cert. cardivascular disease. Intern, resident in medicine Lincoln Hosp., N.Y.C., 1943, 44; fellow in internal medicine Lahey Clinic, Boston, 1945, 46; fellow in cardiovasc. disease rsch. Michael Reese Hosp., Chgo., 1947; instr. to prof. emeritus NYU, N.Y.C., 1948—2004; attending physician Bellevue Hosp. and Tisch Univ. Hosp., N.Y.C., from 1973; adj. attending physician Montefiore Hosp., N.Y.C., 1948-68; cons. in cardiology Will Rogers Hosp., Saranac Lake, N.Y., Columbus Hosp., N.Y.C., 1960-70; chief cardiology sect. N.Y. VA Hosp., 1955-89, cons. cardiology, from 1989. Editorial bd.: Jour. Electrocardiology; contbr. articles in electrocardiography to publs. Served with M.D. U.S. Army, 1952-54. Fellow ACP, Am. Coll. Cardiology, N.Y. Acad. Sci.; mem. Am. Fedn. Clin. Research, Am. Heart Assn., AAAS, Alpha Omega Alpha Home: Ardsley, NY. Died Feb. 12, 2006.

DOLL, DAVID MICHAEL, journalist; b. West Allis, Wis., Apr. 13, 1933; s. B. Luke and Thelma Nelly (Dings) D.; m. Kathleen Blasi, June 11, 1960; children: D. Michael (dec.), Bernard L., Elizabeth K.M. BS, Marquette U., Milw., 1956, MA, 1958; ABD, U Birmingham, 1960. Instr. Modesto (Calif.) Jr. Coll., 1963-65; asst. prof. tech. dir. Western Ky. U., Bowling Green, 1964-65; asst. prof. Northland Coll., Ashland, Wis., 1967-69; sr. sys. analyst NML, Milw., 1970-72; contbg. writer Sensible Sound, Snyder, N.Y., from 1976; prof. outreach program Mt. Senario Coll., Ladysmith, Wis., 1983-96; contbg. writer, substitute tchr. Racine (Wis.) Unified Sch. Dist. Home: Racine, Wis. Died May 14, 2005.

DOLSON, FRANKLIN ROBERT, columnist; b. N.Y.C., Mar. 22, 1933; s. Harry and Charlotte (Schreiber) D. BS in Economics, U. Pa., 1954. Reporter Sports Illus., N.Y.C., 1955; reporter, desk man Phila. Inquirer, 1955-58, columnist, 1958-75, columnist, sports editor, 1975—95; columnist Phila. Bull., 1975; spl. asst. NY Yankees, 1995—2006. Author: Always Young, 1976; The Philadelphia Story, 1981; Beating the Bushes. Recipient Keystone award Keystone Press Conf., 1967-68; named Sportswriter of Yr., Nat. Sportscasters and Sportswriters, 1972, 73, 74, 76. Mem. Baseball Writers Assn. Am. (dir.), Beta Gamma Sigma. Jewish. Avocations: golf, record collecting. Home: Merion Station, Pa. Died Oct. 8, 2006.

DOMAR, CAROLA ROSENTHAL, social worker; b. Franfurt, Fed. Republic of Germany, Dec. 17, 1919; arrived in U.S., 1940; d. Siegfried and Betty (Warschauer) Rosenthal; m. Evsey David Domar, Apr. 16, 1946; children: Erica Domar Banderob, Alice Domar. BS, Carnegie Inst. Tech., 1947; MSW, Simmons Sch. Social Work, 1968. Cert. social worker; bd. cert. diplomate; lic. social worker, Mass. Social worker Burlington (Mass.) Pub. Sch. System, 1968-73; clin. social worker, dir. retardation svc. Eliot Community Mental Health Clinic, Concord, Mass., 1974-80; pvt. practice Concord, Mass., from 1980. Cons. Acton (Mass.) Pub. Health Nursing Svc., 1981-90, 97—, Nashoba Nursing Svc., Harvard, Mass., 1990-97. Pres. bd. Coun. for Children, Acton, 1975-78; v.p. bd. Dept. Mental Health and Retardation, Concord, Mass., 1985-88; bd. dirs. Dept. Mental Health, Arlington, Mass., 1988-91, Dept. Retardation, Arlington, 1988-95; mem. Acton Family Self-Sufficiency Com., 1997—; Coun. on Aging liaison to Affordable Housing Bd., 1997—. Recipient Cert. of Recognition, Gov. M. Dukakais, Boston, 1983, Cert. of Recognition, Office for Children, Boston, 1985; Ofcl. Citation, Ho. of Reps., Boston, 1983. Mem. NASW, Mass. Assn. Gerontology, Concord Mental Health Assn. (bd. dirs. 1988-89). Died Sept. 24, 2004.

DOMMEN, ARTHUR JOHN, agricultural economist, historian; b. Mexico City, Mex., June 24, 1934; came to U.S., 1940, naturalized, 1958. s. John Henry and Sarah (Hall) D.; m. Phan Thi Hong Loan. B.Sc., Cornell U., 1955; PhD, U. Md., 1975. Mem. staff UPI, 1957-63, bur. chief Saigon, 1959-61, Hong Kong, 1961-63; mem. staff Los Angeles Times, 1965-71; bur. chief Japan, 1965—66, Los Angeles Times, New Delhi, 1966-68, Saigon, Vietnam, 1968-71; agrl. economist Intech, Inc., Silver Spring, Md., 1975-77; mem. AID mission to Tunisia, 1977-79; with USDA, Washington, 1980-96; affiliate prof. Indochina Inst., George Mason U., Fairfax, Va., 1996-98; ind. rschr., 1998—2005. Author: Conflict in Laos, The Politics of Neutralization, 1964, Laos: Keystone of Indochina, 1985, The Indochinese Experience of the French and the Americans, 2001. Served with AUS, 1955-57. Press fellow N.Y. Council Fgn. Relations, 1963-64. Died Dec. 15, 2005.

DONAHO, JOHN ALBERT, management consultant; b. Chgo., Sept. 9, 1917; s. John and Pauline (Langdon) D.; m. Patricia A. Maguire, Sept. 23, 1961. BA, Ctrl. YMCA Coll., 1941; cert. pub. adminstrn., U. Chgo., MA. Asst. to contr. Commonwealth Edison Co., Chgo., 1935—42; asst. dir. work simplification and measurement U.S. Bur. Budget, Exec. Office of Pres., Washington, 1943—47; v.p. devel. Roosevelt U., Chgo., 1947—48; budget dir., city mgr. City of Richmond, Va., 1948—52; pres. John A. Donaho & Assocs. Inc., Reisterstown, Md., 1953—2006. Cons. to Mayor of Balt. and Gov. of Md., 1952-54, 74-87, 88-89; chmn. Md. Local Govt. Ins. Trust, 1987-88; ins. commr. State of Md., 1989-93; lectr., mem. faculty Am. U., Washington, Washington U., Goucher Coll., Balt., Johns Hopkins U., Balt., U. Balt., Fgn. Svc. Inst., Va. Commonwealth U., Roosevelt U., Chgo.; chmn. Va. State Commn. on Uniform Fin. Reporting; cons. UN and Econ Commn., Asia, Far East, 1959-60. Contbr. articles to profl. jours. Pres., dir. Univ. Club, Balt.; dir. United Reisterstown Residents; pres. Lakeview Club, Inc., Reistertown, Civitan Club Balt., Civitan Club Richmond; mem., sec. Balt. City Com. on Workers' Compensation, Balt. City Com. on Ins. and Risk Mgmt.; mem. Md. Gov.'s Task Force on Liability Ins., Md. Gov.'s Blue Ribbon Task Force on Self-Ins., Gov.'s Blue Ribbon Commn. on Ins., Gov.'s Prescription Drug Commn.; chmn. Ad Hoc Com. on Liability Ins. for Md.; mem. Balt. County Restructuring Commn.; trustee Balt. Internat. Culinary Coll., Balt. Street Car Mus.; mem. Baltimore County Redistricting Commn. Fellow Soc. for Advancement Mgmt. (pres. Balt. regional chpt., v.p. Richmond chpt., chmn. round table on work simplification DC chpt.), ASPA (sr. mem., pres. Md. chpt., dir. Olympia chpt.); mem. Nat. Assn. Ins. Commrs. Died Mar. 17, 2006.

DONAHUE, JOEY BURKE, physicist; b. Culver City, Calif., Aug. 5, 1945; s. Paul Alfred and Frances Willard (Shewey) D.; m. Michelle Akiko Mukai, June 28, 1970; children: Stephen, Christopher, John. BA in Physics, U. Calif., Irvine, 1968, MA in Physics, 1971, PhD in Physics, 1975. Rsch. asst. U. Calif., Irvine, 1969-75; rsch. assoc. U. N.Mex., Albuquerque, 1975-77, rsch. prof., 1977-78; staff mem. Los Alamos Nat. Lab., 1978-81, sect. leader, 1981-85, assoc. group leader, 1985-90, dep. group leader, from 1990. Adj. prof. physics U. N.Mex., 1981—; scheduling com. Los Alamos Nat. Lab., 1985—. Contbr. articles to profl. jours. Leader Boy Scouts Am., Los Alamos, 1984—. Recipient Disting. Svc. award Boy Scouts Am., 1989. Mem. Am. Phys. Soc., U.S. Aikido Fedn., World Tae Kwon Do Assn. Achievements include development of facilities fro relativistic atomic physics and neutrino physics at the Los Alamos Meson Physics facility. Home: Los Alamos, N.Mex. Died Mar. 6, 2004.

DONAHUE, JOHN JOSEPH, ships master, shipping officer; b. Bklyn., June 9, 1931; s. Martin J. and Marie H. Donahue; m. Winifred Sullivan, Feb. 9, 1955; children: John T., Thomas J. B in Marine Sci., CCNY, 1953. Cert. master oceans unltd. USCG, C.S.P. Ships officer Farrell Lines Inc., N.Y., 1954-58; terminal mgr. Atlantic & Gulf, N.Y., 1960-61; ships officer Am. Export Lines, N.Y., 1960-66, ops. mgr. N.Y., 1966-70; sr. marine cargo cons. Marsh & McLennan Inc., N.Y., 1970-72; safety dir. United Brands, N.Y., 1972-73; mgr. loss prevention U.S. Industries, N.Y., 1973-76; ship master Energy Transp. Corp., N.Y., from 1976. Honored by UN, 1984. Mem. Am. Soc. Safety Engrs. (profl.), Coun. Am. Master Marines, 7th Rgts. Vets. Assn., Masons. Home: Flushing, NY. Died Aug. 3, 2004.

DONATO, MARY EILEEN, risk management professional; b. San Francisco, July 15, 1943; d. Roy James and Arlynn Lucille (La Bundy) Martin; m. Paul Nicholas Donato, Mar. 18, 1961 (dec. Feb. 1968); children: Nicholas, Arlynn, Anthony, Eddie. BA, U. N.Mex., 1971, MPA, 1985. Cert. assoc. in risk mgmt., Ins. Inst. Classroom tchr. Albuquerque Pub. Schs., 1971-72; claims rep. Allstate Ins. Co., Albuquerque, 1972-76, TransAmerica Ins. Co., Albuquerque, 1978-80, City of Albuquerque, 1980-85; ins./claims mgr., dir. risk mgmt. Albuquerque Pub. Schs., 1985-94; dir. risk mgmt. U. N.Mex., Albuquerque, 1994—2006. Presenter seminar Violence in the Work Place, 1993-94. Vol. tchr. Cmty. Sch., Albuquerque, 1980-82; parent aid All Faiths Receiving Home, Albuquerque, 1982-85; tutor Cath. Social Svcs., Albuquerque, 1996—; vol. office helper St. Charles Borromeo Ch., Albuquerque. Mem. AAUW, Univ. Risk Mgmt. Assn. (conf. chair), Pub. Risk Mgmt. Assn. (v.p. 1990-92), N.Mex. Pub. Risk Mgmt. Assn. (pres. 1996-97), N.Mex. Self Insurers Assn. (pres. 1992-93). Roman Catholic. Home: Albuquerque, N.Mex. Died May 12, 2006.

DONG, FANG ZHONG See TUNG, FONG-CHUNG

DONOGHUE, JOHN PETER, marketing executive; b. Winthrop, Mass., Oct. 3, 1939; s. John Francis and Althea (Hartley) D.; m. Juanita Isabella Sierra, Mar. 16, 1966; children: Daniel, Diane, Patrick. BSME, Tufts U., 1961. Various positions Fiatallis Construction Machinery, Carol Stream, Ill., 1961-80, gen. mgr. eastern div., 1980-82, dir. product mktg., 1982-85, dir. planning and devel., 1985-86, v.p. product support, from 1986. Bd. dirs. Chgo. Metro Hockey League, Northbrook, Ill., 1984-87. Mem. Construction Industry Mfgrs. Assn. (mem. exec. com. Power Crane and Shovel Assn. bur. 1986—, chmn. 1986-87), Barrington Hockey Club (pres. 1985-86, bd. dirs. 1984-87), Barrington Quarterback Club (bd. dirs. 1983-86). Roman Catholic. Avocations: gardening, skiing. Home: Elkhorn, Wis. Died Jan. 5, 2004.

DOOLITTLE, ROBERT FREDERICK, II, high energy astrophysicist; b. Chgo., Dec. 21, 1925; s. Arthur K. and Dortha (Bailey) D.; m. Mary Agnes Parker, Apr. 30, 1955 (dec. Dec. 1972); children: Robert Arthur, Nancy Elizabeth; m. Karen M. Kruse, Dec. 28, 1976. AB, Oberlin Coll., 1948; MS, U. Mich., 1950, PhD, 1958. Asst. prof. physics San Diego State U., 1958-60; sr. scientist TRW Space and Def., Redondo Beach, Calif., 1960-83; various computer programming positions, 1983-95; ret. Cons. Space Tech. Labs., L.A., 1959, Magnesys, Santa Clara, Calif., 1987, 3D Graphics, Pacific Palisades, Calif., 1993, Gilbert Consulting, Pacific Palisades, Calif., 1994-95. Lt. comdr. USNR, 1944-46, 52-54. Mem. Am. Astron. Soc. Home: Pacific Palisades, Calif. Died July 15, 2004.

DORAN, CARTER, academic administrator; b. Galveston, Tex., May 5, 1938; s. Philip Chester and Frances Elizabeth (Carter) D.; m. Constance John Mohr, June 21, 1963; children: Elisabeth Mohr, Meredith Christine. AB, Yale U., 1960; MDiv, Fuller Theol. Sem., Pasadena, 1963; MA, Occidental Coll., L.A., 1966; PhD, U. So. Calif., L.A., 1980. Dean students L.A. Pacific Coll., 1964-65; drama/speech instr. Mt. San Antonio Coll., Walnut, Calif., 1966-68, dir. theatre, 1968-77, dean humanities, 1977-83, dean humanities and social scis., 1983-86; vice chancellor acad. affairs Rancho Santiago Coll., Santa Ana, Calif., 1986-92; asst. supt./v.p. instruction and student svcs. Coll. of the Canyons, Santa Clarita, Calif., 1992-98. Named Outstanding Educator, Mt. San Antonio Friends of the Coll., 1985; Occidental Coll. grad. fellow, 1965-66. Mem. Calif. C.C. Chief Instrn. Officers (pres. 1990-91), Ednl. Leadership Colloquia (facilitator 1987-91). Home: Upland, Calif. Died Mar. 31, 2005.

DORN, CHARLES MEEKER, art educator; b. Mpls., Jan. 17, 1927; s. Melville Wilkinson and Margaret (Meeker) D.; m. Virginia Josephine Coble, July 11, 1947; children: Mary Jan, Charles Meeker. BA, MA, George Peabody Coll. Tchrs., 1950; Ed.D., U. Tex., 1959. Asst. prof. art Union U., Jackson, Tenn., 1950-54; instr. art and edn. Memphis State U., 1954-57; lectr. edn. U. Tex., 1957-59; head art dept. Nat. Coll. Edn., Evanston, Ill., 1959-61; assoc. prof. art No. Ill. State U., 1961-62; exec. sec. Nat. Art Edn. Assn., Washington, 1962-70; prof., chmn. dept. art Calif. State U., Northridge, 1970-72; prof. creative arts Purdue U., Lafayette, Ind., 1972-86, head dept., 1972-76; prof., dir. Ctr. for Arts Adminstrn. Fla. State U., Tallahassee, from 1986, chmn. dept. art edn., 1986-90. Served with AUS, 1945-46. Recipient 25th Anniversary award for disting. service Nat. Gallery Art, 1966. Mem.: Internat. Soc. Edn. Through Art, Nat Art Edn. Assn. (pres. 1975—77), Disting. Svc. award 1979, Disting. fellow 1982, Southeastern Higher Edn. Art Educator award 1990, Higher Edn. award 1990, 1999, Nat. Art Educator of the Yr. 2003), Fla. Art Edn. Assn., Kappa Phi Kappa, Phi Delta Kappa. Home: Tallahassee, Fla. Died June 26, 2006.

DORN, NATALIE REID, consultant; b. N.Y.C. d. John A. and Marianna (Tresenberg) Borokhovich; m. Ed Reid, July 31, 1938 (div. Apr. 1963); children: Michael John, Douglas Paul; m. Robert M. Dorn, Nov. 28, 1964. Student, Bklyn. Coll., 1937-40, Pepperdine Coll., 1969-70. Model Conover Agy., N.Y.C., 1940-54; columnist Westchester (N.Y.) Recorder, 1954-59; ptnr. Dateline, Las Vegas, Nev., 1957-61; mgr., buyer Joseph Magnin, Las Vegas, Nev., 1961-62; ptnr., cons. Personnel Placement Employment Agy. and Conv. Coords., Las Vegas, 1961-63; account exec. John A. Tetley Co., L.A., 1963-65; cons. Sport Ct. Am., Salt Lake City, 1975—2004. Realtor, Va., Calif., 1974--. Exec. v.p. Clark County Mental Health Assn., 1961-63; ednl. chmn. Hollywood Wing, Greek Theatre Assn., 1965, mem. hospitality com. LWV, 1969; co-founder Child Abuse Listening Line, 1973—; sponsor Ashland (Oreg.) Sheakesperean Festival, 1984; concertmaster Sacramento Opera; patron, Davis Art Ctr.; docent Internat. House, Davis, 1987—; bd. dirs. El Macero Niners, Davis Art Ctr. Guild. Mem.: AMA Aux., Crocker Soc., Crocker Art Mus., Nat. Mus., L.A. County Med. Assn. Aux., Nat. Trust for Historic Preservation, Women in Arts, El Macero Country Club. Avocations: painting, writing. Home: El Macero, Calif. Died Apr. 16, 2004.

DORS, JOANNE LEE, public health nurse; b. Greenport, N.Y., Mar. 21, 1946; d. Joseph P. and Stella (Szeszko) Checklick; m. Richard Dors Jr., Aug. 8, 1981. Diploma in Nursing, Mountainside Hosp., Montclair, N.J., 1967; BSN, U. Pa., 1970; MPA, L.I. U., 1985. RN, N.Y. Pub. health nurse Suffolk County Dept. Health Svcs., Bur. Pub. Health, Hauppauge, N.Y., 1974-79, pub. health nurse coord., 1979-81, supervising pub. health nurse, 1981-85, coord. long-term home health care program, 1985-91; ret. Suffolk County Health Svcs., Bur. Pub. Health, Hauppauge, N.Y., 1991. Per diem staff nurse, Ea. L.I. Hosp., Greenport, 1967-70, 74, Hosp. of the U. Pa., Phila., 1968-69, Inst. Pa. Hosp., 1969-70; staff nurse and pvt. duty nurse, Meml. Sloan-Kettering Cancer Ctr., N.Y.C., 1970-74. Roman Catholic. Avocation: crafts. Home: Palm Coast, Fla. Died Aug. 15, 2004.

DOSSMAN, DANIEL, environmental scientist, researcher; b. Cali, Valle, Colombia, Apr. 5, 1949; came to U.S., 1977; s. Daniel and Nelly Dossman; m. Martha C. Sanchez, Mar. 10, 1974; children: Elizabeth, Nicholas. BS in Biology, Univalle, Cali, 1972; MA in Marine Sci., U. Miami, 1979. Asst. prof. Univalle, Cali, 1973-80; environ. specialist Health Reabrilatatre Svcs., Dade County Health Dept., Miami, Fla., 1980-85; environ. officer water resources mgmt. divsn. Broward County Environ. Quality Control Bd., Ft. Lauderdale, Fla., 1986-88; air toxics engr. Broward County Dept. Natural Resource Protection, Ft. Lauderdale, Fla., from 1988. Mem. Fla. Air Toxic Working Group. Avocation: amateur radio operation. Home: Coral Springs, Fla. Died Jan. 26, 2005.

DOTY, HORACE JAY, JR., theater administrator, arts consultant; b. St. Petersburg, Fla., May 25, 1924; s. Horace Herndon and Mabel (Bruce) D.; m. Wanda L. Flory, Dec. 27, 1947; 1 child, Janet. Student, Sherwood Music Sch., Chgo., 1942-43; BA in Music, Pomona Coll., 1950; cert., La Verne Coll., 1969; MA in Edn., Claremont Grad. Sch., 1972. Cert. in Bus. Adminstrn., 1984. Propr. Jay Doty's Inc., Claremont, 1960-68; concert mgr. Claremont Colls., 1968-73; supr. Garrison Theater U. Ctr. Box Office, dir. Auditorium, theater events, coord. programs, 1973-79, 81-90; exec. dir. Flint Ctr. for Performing Arts, Cupertino, Calif., 1979-81. Mem. blue ribbon com. Fox Theater Restoration, Pomona, Calif., 1982; mem. Claremont Bicentennial Com. for Performing Arts, 1975-76; mem. touring adv. panel, cons. and site visitor Calif. Arts Coun.; mem. exec. bd. Calif. Presenters. With inf. AUS, 1943-46. NEA fellow, 1986. Mem. Assn. Coll., Univ. and Cmty. Arts Adminstrs. (dir. 1983-86), Western Alliance Arts Adminstrs. (pres. 1975-77), Internat. Assn. Auditorium Mgrs., Claremont C. of C. (pres. 1965-66). Home: Claremont, Calif. Died Sept. 12, 2004.

DOUGHERTY, ROBERT CHARLES, rubber company executive, consultant; b. Elizabeth, N.J., Apr. 29, 1929; s. Joseph Howard and Marie Louise (Zusi) D.; m. Mary Cecelia Tolbert, June 25, 1956 (div. May 1972); children: Mary, Robert; m. Judy Ann Martinson, June 22, 1972; children: Michael, Shawn, Erin. Student, Stevens Inst. Tech., Hoboken, N.J., 1947-50; BSME, U. Md., 1952, postgrad., George Washington U., CCNY, Am. Univ. Sr. engr., supr. Melpar, Inc., Falls Church, Va., 1954-56; lab. mgr. Emerson Rsch. Lab., Silver Spring, Md., 1956-59; gen. mgr. Materials Testing Co., Bethesda, Md., 1959-65; chief engr. R.E. Darling Co. Inc., Tucson, 1965-75; v.p., gen. mgr. Durodyne, Inc., Tucson, 1975-94; v.p. Darling Industries Inc., Tucson, from 1994. Patentee for 17 inventions in field. Pres. St. Pius X Sch., Bethesda, 1964-69; v.p. Washington Montessori Inst., 1962-69. Capt. USAF, 1954-59. Recipient Apollo Achievement award NASA, Washington, 1969. Mem. Optimists (pres. Tucson chpt. 1985). Republican. Roman Catholic. Avocations: flying, photography, gardening, hunting. Home: Tucson, Ariz. Died Jan. 25, 2005.

DOUGLAS, BRYCE, former pharmaceutical company executive; b. Glasgow, Scotland, Jan. 6, 1924; came to U.S., 1958; s. Alexander and Mary (Turner) D.; m. Joyce M. Flynn, Aug. 24, 1955; children: Alan David, Neal Malcolm, Iain Graham. B.Sc. with honors, Glasgow U., 1944; PhD in Organic Chemistry, Edinburgh U., Scotland, 1948. Chemotherapy researcher, research lab. Royal Coll. Physicians, Edinburgh, 1947-49; research asst. biol. chemistry Aberdeen (Scotland) U., 1949; research fellow in alkaloid chemistry NRC Can., Ottawa, 1949-51; research fellow dept. pharmacology Harvard U., 1952-53; research asso., lectr. Ind. U., Bloomington, 1953-56; vis. research asso. U. Malaya, Singapore, 1956-58; with Smith Kline & French Labs., Phila., 1956-86, v.p. research and devel., 1971-80, pres. research and devel., 1980-81, v.p. sci. and tech., 1981-86. Contbr. articles to profl. jours. Past bd. dirs., v.p. Royal Soc. Medicine Found.; chmn. bd. Beacon Rsch.; mem. bd. overseers U. Pa. Sch. Dental Medicine; past bd. trustees Franklin Inst. of Phila.; past chmn. bd. trustees Beaver Coll., Pa.; mem. adv. coun. Beckman Ctr. for History of Chemistry, U. Pa. Fellow Royal Soc. Chemistry (U.K.), Coll. Physicians Phila.; mem. AAAS, N.Y. Acad. Scis., Am. Chem. Soc., Gulph Mills Golf Club, Stonewall Links Golf Club. Patentee in field. Home: Kimberton, Pa. Died July 29, 2006.

DOUGLASS, WILFORD DAVID, corporate executive; b. Titusville, Pa., July 3, 1927; s. Wilfred Earl Douglass and Madelon Creecraft (Bly) Arthur; m. Audrey Lois Smith, Dec. 28, 1950 (dec. 1973); children: Diane Noel Delio, Patricia Ann Swalm, Erin Marie Douglass Fish; m. Nitaya Tsumjamroon, Sept. 19, 1989. BA, Tulane U., 1958. Enlisted USMC, 1945, commd., 1951, advanced through grades to colonel/chief of staff, 1971, retired, 1975; real estate salesman Evans Realty Inc., Willingboro, N.J., 1975-76; mng. dir. Aeromaritime Internat. Mgmt. Services Ltd., Lagos, Nigeria, 1976-78; v.p. Aeromaritime Internat. Corp. and Aeromaritime Internat. Mgmt. Services Ltd., Washington, 1978-80; pres., chief exec. officer Aeromaritime Investment Co., Fairfax, Va., 1980-92, Acre Ltd., Mass, Inc., Fairfax, 1982-92; dir. Aeromaritime Consolidated Real Estate, Woodbridge, Va., from 1993. Bd. dirs. Marinvest Transport Svcs. Ltd., Rio de Janeiro, Environ. Products Corp., Fairfax, Belgian Overseas Shipping, Antwerp, Belgium; pres. Aeromaritime (Brazil) Ltd., Rio de Janeiro, 1985-91; vice chmn. bd. Dicon Salt PLC, Lagos.; dir. AIMS, Channel Islands; chmn. Cross Group Holdings, AIMS, Liberia, Aeromaritime Investment Co. Decorated Legion of Merit with combat V, Meritorious Service medal, Navy Commendation medal; made African Chief of Otun Ologun by King of Lagos, 1991. Mem. Lagos Caledonian Soc., Lagos Assn. Titled Chieftains. Clubs: Beachland Boat Lagos. Lodges: Masons, Tyrian. Republican. Avocations: boating, deepsea fishing, golf. Home: Lagos, Nigeria. Died Feb. 15, 2004.

DOUTY, ROBERT WATSON, minister, educator; b. Phila., June 20, 1943; m. MarshaLee Wood, Apr. 22, 1972. BA in Psychology, Calif. State U., Long Beach, 1969; MS in Edn., U. Bridgeport, 1974; MDiv, Alliance Theol. Sem., Nyack, N.Y., 1993. Ordained to ministry Am. Bapt. Chs., 1990; teaching cert., N.Y. Tchr. Garrison (N.Y.) Sch., 1980—2003; chmn. bd. deacons 1st Bapt. Ch., Ossining, N.Y., 1980-82, dir. Christian edn., 1985-91, assoc. pastor, 1990-96; dir. Christian edn. St. Philip's Episc. Ch., Garrison, N.Y., 1996-98; pastor Cold Spring (N.Y.) Bapt. Ch., from 1998. Deacon 1st Bapt. Ch., 1973-82, chmn. missions, 1990-95; chaplain Phelps Hosp., Tarrytown, N.Y., 1988—. Author: Star City: A Classroom Management System, 1989; author: (with others) In the Footsteps of Birdy Edwards, 1980; contbr. articles to mags. Victory 94 team leader to elect Gov. George Pataki, 1994. With U.S. Navy, 1962-65. Mem. Baker St. Irregulars (The Priory Sch.). Home: Buchanan, NY. Died May 30, 2006.

DOVER, WILLIAM EDGAR, insulation company executive; b. Marion, N.C., Feb. 14, 1945; s. Harry Talmadge and Catherine (Williams) D.; children: Mardi, Laura, Melanie. BS in BA, Western Carolina U., 1968. Pres. Dover Insulation, Inc., Marion, N.C., from 1972, Dover Insulation Supply Co., Inc., Marion, from 1978; sec.-treas. Western Asbestos, Inc., Hickory, N.C., from 1988. Bd. dirs. First Union Nat. Bank, Marion. Bd. dirs. The McDowell Hosp., Marion, 1987—. Mem. McDowell C. of C. (bd. dirs. 1983-87). Presbyterian. Avocations: hunting, fishing, horseback riding. Home: Marion, NC. Died Nov. 25, 2004.

DOW, AVARD MORTON, SR., investment banker; b. West Baldwin, Maine, July 9, 1916; s. George Wright and Georgia (Harding) D.; m. Katherine Gardner, Oct. 8, 1938; 1 child, Avard M. Jr. Student, U. Maine, N.Y. Inst. of Fin., N.Y.C. Registered Maine guide. Mgr. Burgess & Leith/Advest, Lewiston, Maine, registered rep., v.p. Corporator Mechanics Savings Bank, Auburn, Maine. Bd. Incorporators Cen. Maine Gen. Hosp. Served to cpl. U.S. Army, 1943-46, ETO. Mem. N.Y. Stock Exchange, Maine Game and Fish Assn., Maine Tennis Assn. Lodges: Masons, Shriners. Home: Lewiston, Maine. Died June 24, 2005.

DRAKE, CHESTER LEE, minister; b. New Brunswick, N.J., Dec. 2, 1946; s. Chester LeRoy and Elizabeth (Reed) D.; m. Deborah Jane Smith, July 9, 1977; children: Timothy, Rebekah. BA, Covington Sem., 1982, MA, 1984, DD, 1986, DST, PhD, Covington Sem., 1988; BA, Miami Christian Coll., 1990. Founder, pastor Broward Community Chapel, Ft. Lauderdale, Fla., from 1971; S.E. Regional coord. Moody Bible Inst., Chgo., 1983-88; aftercare counselor T.M. Ralph Plantation funeral Home, Plantation, Fla., from 1990. Chaplain Fla. Funeral Dirs., Tallahasse, 1982—, Christian Funeral Dirs., Pahokee, Fla., 1982—. Author: Helping the Hurting, 1987, Grief Counseling: Lost Art of the Clergy, 1988. Mem. Kiwanis (bd. dirs. 1981-85, treas. 1983-85 Plantation/Jacaranda chpt.). Died June 28, 2005.

DRAPER, THEODORE, author; b. Bklyn., Sept. 11, 1912; s. Samuel and Annie D.; m. Dorothy Sapan, 1935 (div. 1953), 1 child, Roger; m.Evelyn Manacher, 1960 (div.); m. Priscilla Heath Barnum BS, Bklyn. Coll.; LittD (hon.), Emory U., 1992; LLD (hon.), New Sch. Social Rsch., 1997. Writer. Author: The Six Weeks' War: France, May 10 - June 25, 1940, 1944, The 84th Infantry Division in the Battle of Germany, 1946, The Roots of American Communism, 1957, American Communism and Soviet Russia, 1960, Castro's Revolution: Myths and Realities, 1962, Castroism, Theory and Practice, 1965, Abuse of Power, 1967, Israel and World Politics, 1968, The Dominican Revolt, 1968, The Rediscovery of Black Nationalism, 1970, Present History, 1983, A Present of Things Past, 1990, A Very Thin Line, 1991, A Struggle for Power: The American Revolution, 1996; contbr. to mags., others. Fellow Am. Acad. Arts and Scis. Died Feb. 21, 2006.

DRAPP, LINDA A., community health and parish nurse, educator; b. Honolulu, Oct. 29, 1948; d. Linda Ann Guy; m. Daniel Barrett Drapp, Sept. 13, 1969; children: Jennifer Lynn, Andrew Barrett. BSN, Maryville U., St. Louis, 1989. RN, Mo. Foster care parent Mo. Div. Family Svcs., St. Louis; counselor for mentally ill St. Patrick's Ctr., St. Louis, 1989-90; program asst. Young Parents Young People, St. Louis, 1990-93; case mgr. Salvation Army Family Haven Shelter, St. Louis, 1991-93; substitute sch. nurse St. Louis Pub. Schs., 1994; lay health worker educator Sch. Pub. Health St. Louis U., 1994; cmty. health nurse mgr. St. Jane's Cath. Cmty. Svcs., St. Louis, from 1994. Contbr. articles to profl. jours., nursing textbook, newspaper and almanac. Mem. ANA, Mo. Nurses Assn., Maryville U. Alumni Assn., Sigma Theta Tau. Home: Glencoe, Mo. Died Oct. 5, 2004.

DREMIN, LEONARD LONNIE ALEXANDER, risk analyst, insurance agency executive; b. Winnipeg, Manitoba, Can., June 3, 1953; s. Leonard Authur D. and Rose Evelyn (Chorlton) Stuart; m. Virginia Dell Brown Dremin, June 16, 1973 (div. Feb. 1978); m. Charlene Alexandra Smith Dremin, March 20, 1981. Cert., U.S. Army Mil. Police Sch., Fort Gordon, Ga., 1972; AA, Mt. San Antonio Coll., Walnut, Calif., 1978. Auditor ins. Century Nat. Ins. Co., N. Hollywood, Calif., 1976-78; v.p. and bd. dir. Pennant Fin. Ins. Services, Glendora, Calif., 1978-79; Mgr. corp. brokerage CMCI-Cuna Mutual Ins. Group, Pomona, Calif., 1980-81; v.p. mktg. Insureco Ins. Agy., Inc., S. Pasadena, Calif., 1981-83, Crown Valley-A Transam. Co., Orange, Calif., 1983-84; pres., chief exec. officer, founder, and owner Borrowers and Creditors Ins. Services, Inc.,

Loma Linda, Calif., 1984-88. Author: (book) Risk Aware, On-Premise System Manual; inventor on-premise computer tracking system. Sr. plans non-commd. officer Calif. State Mil. Reserve, Norco, 1988; sponsoring mem. 720th Mil. Police Bn. Reunion Assn., Kenosha, Wis., 1988. Served with U.S. Army, 1972-74. Recipient Merit award Boys Scouts Am., Claremont, Calif., 1978, Achievement Ribbon award Calif. State Mil. Reserve, Sacramento, 1986. Mem. Profl. Ins. Agts of Calif. and Nev., Am. Legion, Sierra Club (Chmn. and vice-chmn., 1978-82). Republican. Methodist. Avocations: backpacking, mountain climbing. Home: Rialto, Calif. Died Feb. 25, 2005.

DRESCH, STEPHEN PAUL, economist, former state legislator; b. East St. Louis, Ill., Dec. 12, 1943; s. Lester Wilson Reuben and Leonore Marie (Steege) D.; m. Linda Carol Ness, May 18, 1963; children: Soren K., Stephanie Elizabeth, Phaedra Augusta, Karl Friedrick Johannes. AB Philosophy, Miami U., Oxford, Ohio, 1963; MPhil Econ., NSF fellow, Yale U., 1966, PhD, 1970. Mem. faculty dept. econs. Miami U., Oxford, Ohio, 1963-64; mem. Yale U., New Haven, 1966-67, South Conn. State Coll., New Haven, 1968-69, Rutgers U., New Brunswick, N.J., 1970; researcher Nat. Bur. Econ. Research, N.Y.C. and New Haven, 1969-77; cons. in residence Ford Found., N.Y.C., 1970-72; dir. reserch in econs. of higher edn. Yale U., 1972-75, chmn. Inst. for Demographic and Econ. Studies, from 1975; dean, prof. econs. and bus. Sch. Bus. and Engring. Adminstrn., Mich. Technol. U., 1985-90; mem. from 110th dist. Mich. Ho. Reps., Lansing, 1991—92. Rsch. scholar Internat. Inst. Applied Systems Analysis, Austria, 1983-85; vis. scholar Inst. Econs. and Forecasting of Sci. and Technol. Progress, USSR Acad. of Scis., 1988 Author: Substituting a Value Added Tax for the Corporate Income Tax, 1977, Occupational Earnings, 1967-81, 86, The Economics of Foreign Students, 1987; contbr. articles to profl. jours. Bd. advisors MacKinac Ctr. for Pub. Policy Rsch., Rep. Liberty Caucus. Mem. AAAS, ACLU, Am. Econ. Assn., Fedn. of Am. Scientists, Assn. for Pub. Policy Analysis and Mgmt., Am. Statis. Assn., Sigma Xi. Libertarian. Home: Hancock, Mich. Died Aug. 6, 2006.

DREYER, JOHN EDWARD, lawyer; b. Feb. 22, 1929; s. Felix Edward and Marie Ann (Bungert) D.; m. Shirley Ann Fenhaus, May 29, 1954 (div.); children: Thomas, Laura, Gregory, Michael; m. Nancy A. Mickelson; stepchildren: Karen Mickelson Ortiz, Kevin W. Mickelson. BS, Loyola U., Chgo., 1951; JD, DePaul U., Chgo., 1953. Bar: Ill. 1953, U.S. Dist. Ct. (no. dist.) Ill. 1953, U.S. Ct. Appeals (7th cir.) 1953, U.S. Ct. Mil. Appeals 1954. Jr. ptnr. Sears Streit, Tyler & Dreyer, Chgo. and Aurora, Ill., 1961-63; sr. ptnr. Dreyer, Foote & Streit, Assocs., Aurora, 1963-84, Dreyer, Foote, Streit, Furgason & Slocum, PA, 1984-94, of counsel, from 1994. Dir. Valley Nat. Bank Aurora, 1975-86. Bd. editors DePaul Law Rev., 1952-53. Bd. dirs. Family Support Ctr., Aurora, 1975-86. 1st lt. JAGC, U.S. Army, 1953-56. Mem. ABA, Ill. State Bar Assn. (assembly 1972-78), Kane County Bar Assn., Am. Judicature Soc., Ill. Soc. Trial Lawyers, Nat. Assn. R.R. Trial Counsel, Moose, Phi Alpha Delta, Pi Gamma Mu. Home: Sugar Grove, Ill. Died Oct. 2, 2005.

DREYFUS, RICHARD BAECK, lawyer; b. Galveston, Tex., May 5, 1958; s. A. Stanley and Marianne C. (Berlak) D. BA cum laude, Wesleyan U., Middletown, Conn., 1980; JD, U. Pitts., 1983. Bar: Tex. 1983, Pa. 1984. Assoc. Dibrell & Greer, Galveston, 1983-86, Hirsch & Westheimer, P.C., Houston, 1986-88; atty. Panhandle Ea. Corp., Houston, 1988-90, counsel, 1990-91, sr. counsel, from 1991. Trustee Temple B'nai Israel, Galveston, 1984-86. Mem. ABA, Houston Bar Assn., Houston Young Lawyers Assn. Avocations: travel, sports. Home: Houston, Tex. Died Mar. 12, 2005.

DREYFUSS, PATRICIA, retired chemist, researcher; b. Reading, Pa., Apr. 28, 1932; d. Edmund T. and Anna J. (Oberc) Gajewski; m. M. Peter Dreyfuss, Jan. 30, 1954; children: David Daniel, Simeon Karl. BS Chemistry, U. Rochester, 1954; PhD, U. Akron, 1964. Postdoctoral fellow U. Liverpool, England, 1963—65; rsch. chemist B.F. Goodrich, Brecksville, Ohio, 1965—71; rsch. assoc. Case We. Res. U., Cleve., 1971—73, sr. rsch. assoc., 1973—74; rsch. assoc. Inst. Polymers Sci., U. Akron, Ohio, 1974—84; sr. rsch. scientist, rsch. prof. Mich. Molecular Inst., Midland, 1984—90; ret. Vis. rsch. fellow U. Bristol, 1972; cons. in field, 1974—; vis. prof. Polish Acad. Scis., Poland, 1974; adj. prof. Cen. Mich. U., Mt. Pleasant, Mich. Tech U., Houghton, 1986-92, Mich. Molecular Inst., Midland, 1990-92. Author: Poly (Tetrahydrofuran), 1982; contbr. numerous articles to profl. jours.; co-author books. Flutist West Suburban Philharm. Orch., Lakewood, Ohio, 1969-75, Midland (Mich.) Cmty. Orch., 1990-97; Explorer advisor Explorer post 2069 Boy Scouts Am., Akron, 1975-81; sec., bd. dirs. Adhesion Soc., 1976-88; treas. LWV, 1959-60; mem. ensemble Blessed Sacrament Ch., Midland; occasional flute soloist. Centennial scholar U. Rochester, 1950-54; Sohio fellow U. Akron, 1960, NSF Coop. Grad. fellow, 1961-63, Internat. fellow AAUW, 1964-65, NIH Spl. fellow, 1972-73; recipient Vol. awrd Odyssey of the Mind, Region V, 1999-2000. Mem. Am. Chem. Soc. (cen. region mtg. chmn. 1984-90, loc. sec. chmn., vice chmn., sec. and bd. dirs. Akron chpt. 1974-84, bd. dirs. Midland chpt. 1985-89, Outstanding Leadership Performance award 1981, Disting. Svc. award Akron chpt. 1985, Outstanding Svc. award Midland sect. 2000), AAUW (bd. dirs. Akron chpt.). Achievements include 4 patents in field. Home: Midland, Mich. Died Dec. 6, 2005.

DRINKWATER, ELEANOR C., retired artist; b. Malden, Mas., Feb. 5, 1925; d. George Adolph Drinkwater and Claire Carrie Frederick. Student, Sch. Practical Art, Boston. Art instr., Medford, Mass., Malden, Mass.; sr. tech. artist MIT Lincoln Rsch. Lab., Lexington, Mass.; with Metro. Lith. Co., Everett, Mass. Home: Medford, Mass. Died Jan. 29, 2005.

DRISCOLL, GARRETT BATES, retired telecommunications executive; b. Terre Haute, Ind., July 10, 1932; s. James Edgar and Lorraine Emma (Simmons) D.; m. Suzanne Keder O'Reilly, Apr. 30, 1960 (div. Sept. 1984); children: Garrett Edward, Lorraine Elizabeth Driscoll Veltri; m. Ivy Juanita Bryant, Sept. 24, 1985 (div. Aug. 1995); children: Jennifer Louise, Caroline Margaret; m. Janice Patterson Buckalew, Oct. 25, 1996. AA, Broward C.C., Ft. Lauderdale, Fla., 1973; BA, Fla. Atlantic U., Boca Raton, 1979. Tech. supr. TRT Telecom. Corp., Ft. Lauderdale, 1972-80, asst. mgr. N.Y. ops. N.Y.C., 1980-82; asst. v.p. telecom. 1st Am. Bank, Lake Worth, Fla., 1983-86; dir. telecom. R&D John Alden Sys. Co., Miami, Fla., 1986-97; advisor Jan Gar Enterprises, Lake Wales, Fla., 1997—98; ret., 1998. Lectr. U. Miami, 1988-97. With USAF, 1951-71. Lutheran. Avocations: reading, woodworking, exercise. Died Oct. 5, 2005.

DRIVER, SHARON HUMPHREYS, marketing executive; b. Staten Island, N.Y., Jan. 5, 1949; d. William Edward and Gloria (McCrave) Humphreys; m. William Weston Driver, Jr., June 3, 1972; children: Christopher John, Andrea Nicole. BA, Manhattanville Coll., Purchase, N.Y., 1970; MA, Coll. New Rochelle, N.Y., 1973. Lic. tchr., N.Y. Tchr. Somers (N.Y.) Ctrl. Sch. Dist., 1970-76, Ossining (N.Y.) Village Recreation Dept., 1983-87; media coord., bookkeeper Equation Comm., White Plains, N.Y., 1986-89; media dir. Sims Freeman O'Brien, Elmsford, N.Y., 1989-90; project dir. Rsch. Advantage, Hawthorne, N.Y., 1990-92; asst. v.p. Merson/Greener Assocs., Tarrytown, N.Y., 1992-94; pres. Decision Drivers, Briarcliff, from 1994. Sec. tng. liason, Jr. League, Westchester-on-Hudson, 1982-88; sustainer, trainer-facilitator, Jr. League, Tarrytown, 1988-96; past pres. St. Theresa's Parish Coun., Briarcliff Manor, N.Y.; sec. bd. dirs. Ossining Open Door Health Clinic, 1985-89. Mem. NAFE, Am. Mktg. Assn., Women in Comm. (bd. dirs.), Ad Club of Westchester (bd. dirs.), Qualitative Rsch. Cons. Assn., Sleepy Hollow Toastmasters (charter, sec. exec. com.). Roman Catholic. Avocations: boating, hiking. Home: Briarcliff Manor, NY. Died Jan. 31, 2005.

DRUCK, KALMAN BRESCHEL, public relations counselor; b. Scranton, Pa., Dec. 6, 1914; s. Jacob L. and Mabelle (Breschel) D.; m. Pearl Spiro, Nov. 26, 1936; children: Ellen Druck Mirtz, Nancy Druck Brassem. BS in Journalism, magna cum laude, Syracuse U., 1936. With Hearst Enterprises, 1936-39, Carl Byoir & Assos., 1939-59; pres., vice chmn. Harshe-Rotman & Druck, Inc., N.Y.C., 1960-81; prin. Kalman B. Druck, Inc., from 1981. Supr. courses pub. rels. Baruch Sch. Bus., CCNY, 1939-55; mem. adv. com. schs. communications Syracuse U., Boston U.; adj. prof. Grad. Sch. Communication, Fairfield (Conn.) U., 1987-88. Pub. Public Relations Career Guide, Impact of High Technology on Public Relations. Bd. dirs. Union Am. Hebrew Congregations, 1956-71, N.Y. Fedn. Jewish Philanthropies, 1957-72, Am. Jewish Com., 1979-87; hon. bd. dirs. Palm Beach Civic Assn.; v.p. Palm Beach Com. for Good Govt.; past chmn. civilian pub. affairs adv. com. U.S. Mil. Acad., West Point, N.Y. Recipient Disting. Alumnus Centennial medal Syracuse U., 1970 Mem. Pub. Rels. Soc. Am. (pres. N.Y. chpt. 1953-55, nat. chmn. 1972, chmn. com. on profl. devel. 1979-80, trustee Found. for Pub. Rels. Rsch. and Edn. 1981-86, Gold Anvil award 1966, named Pub. Rels. Profl. of Yr. 1966). Home: Palm Beach Gardens, Fla. Died Mar. 26, 2006.

DRUMMOND, CHESTER HENRY, food manufacturing company executive; b. Camden, N.J., Oct. 29, 1927; s. Chester Henry and Mary Lawrence (Gundlach) D.; m. Mary J. Burt, Jan. 22, 1956; children: H. Robin, David C. Student, U. Pa., 1953-55, Rutgers U., 1957-58. With Campbell Soup Co., Camden, N.J., 1948-60, asst. mgr. ins., 1960-69, mgr. ins., from 1969. Bd. dirs. Triple S, Inc., Washington. Served with USCG, 1945-48. Recipient United Way Service award, 1978. Mem. Ins. Mgrs. Assn., Phila. (gen. chmn. 1981—), Risk and Ins. Mgmt. Soc. (pres. Delaware Valley chpt. 1962-63). Clubs: Niagara Fire Co. (Merchantville, N.J.) (treas. 1982—); Glasstown Antique Fire Brigade (Millville, N.J.). Republican. Avocations: restoration and exhbn. of antique fire vehicles, horology. Home: Merchantville, NJ. Died May 4, 2005.

DRUMMOND, ROBERT J., education educator; b. Newark, Mar. 30, 1929; s. Lester Linwood and Marie Jane (Pester) D.; m. Gloria Drummond, Jan. 1, 1967; children: Heather, Robin. AB, Waynesburg (Pa.) Coll., 1949; AM, Columbia U., 1952, 56, EdD, 1959; postgrad., U. Pitts. Rsch. asst. Tchrs. Coll., Columbia U., N.Y.C.; chmn. dept. psychology and edn. Waynesburg Coll.; prof., coord. field rsch. U. Maine, Orono; prof., program leader U. North Fla., Jacksonville. Author: Appraisal Procedures for Counselors and Helping Professionals, 1988, 3d rev. edit., 1992, Career Counseling, a Developmental Approach, 1995; editor Jour. Employment Counseling, Jour. Rsch. in Edn.; contbr. numerous articles to profl. jours. Recipient Disting. Profl. award U. North Fla., 1987, Dist. Svc. award Nat. Employment Counselors Assn., 1989. Mem. APA (fellow div. edl. psychology), ACA, Nat. Coun. on Measurement in Edn., Nat. Social Sci. Assn., Ea. Ednl. Rsch. Assn., Phi Delta Kappa. Home: Jacksonville, Fla. Died Mar. 14, 2005.

DRYDEN, GALE EMERSON, anesthesiologist, medical products company executive; b. Jefferson County, Ind., June 1, 1922; s. Earl Chester and Mary (Reece) D.; m. Clara Harrell, May 2, 1945; children: Steven, Ellen, Paul, Carla, Earl MD, Cin. Coll. Medicine, 1947. Pvt. practice, Indpls., 1948-51; resident in anesthesiology Marion County Health and Hosp. Corp., Indpls., 1955-57, chief of anesthetics, from 1960; pres. Dryden Corp., Indpls., 1959-1988, Medic Pro, Indpls., from 1965. With USPHS, 1951-54. Home: Indianapolis, Ind. Died Dec. 13, 2004.

DRYDEN, RICHIE SLOAN, physician; b. Robstown, Tex., Apr. 26, 1938; s. Edward Marseille and Lela Frances (Sloan) D.; m. Gladys Coleman, June 13, 1964; children: Warren Edward, Catherine Jeane, Donna Marsielle. BS Zoology, Tex. A&M U., 1960; MD, Baylor U., 1964; MPH, Harvard U., 1968. Commd. USAF, 1965, advanced through grades to col., 1980; intern Ben Taub Hosp., Jefferson Davis Hosp., Houston, 1964-65; resident Harvard Sch. Pub. Health, 1967-68, USAF Sch. Aerospace Medicine, Brooks AFB, Tex., 1968-70; chief aerospace medicine USAF Hosp., Cam Rahn Bay, Vietnam, 1970-71; chief comdr. Howard & Albrook AFB, Panama Canal Zone, 1971-74; chief flight medicine USAF Cons. Svc., Brooks AFB, Tex., 1975-81; chief aerospace medicine Tactical Air Command, Langley AFB, Va., 1981-87; project mgr. systems acquisition Air Force Office Med. Support, 1987-92. Com. chmn. Cub Scouts pack, Howard AFB, Panama, 1974, Brooks AFB, 1975. Decorated Bronze Star, Air medal. Assoc. fellow Aerospace Medicine Soc.; mem. Assn. Mil. Surgeons U.S., Soc. USAF Flight Surgeons. Lutheran. Died June 2, 2004.

DRYE, WILLIAM JAMES, JR., business owner; b. Phila., Aug. 27, 1939; s. William James and Louvenia (Spearman) D.; 1 child, William Bradley. Cert. in acctg., U. Pa., 1966, BBA, 1968. Cert. energy reduction specialist. Clk. U. Pa., Phila., 1957-60, acct., 1960-63, asst. to treas., 1966-67, asst. to bus. mgr., 1967-68, acting comptroller, 1974, asst. comptroller, 1968-81, assoc. comptroller, 1981-83; pres. Delaware Valley Energy Conservation, Phila., from 1983. Mem. Springfield Twp. Town Watch, 1987. Served with U.S. Army, 1963-65. Mem. Am. Mgmt. Assn., Nat. Energy Specialist Assn. (performance award 1987). Avocations: sports, travel, cooking. Died Nov. 29, 2004.

DRZEWIECKI, IRIS M., librarian; b. Buffalo, Nov. 20, 1929; d. Theodore R. and Monica D. (Nagorski) Herrlich; m. Joseph Pileri, May 26, 1951 (dec. Jan. 1974); children: David, Douglas; m. Daniel Drzewiecki, Apr. 3, 1982; stepchildren: Michael, Susan Makowski. BS cum laude, SUNY, Buffalo, 1972; MLS, U. Buffalo, 1974. Cert. libr. media specialist, N.Y. Elem. tchr. Sch. 54, Buffalo, 1972-74; sch. libr. media specialist Ken Ton Sch. Dist., Kenmore, N.Y., 1974-76, Court Street Sch., Lancaster, N.Y., 1976-91, ret., 1991. Contbr. articles to profl. jours. Mem. ALA (nat Newbery awrd com.), Am. Assn. Sch. Librs., N.Y. Libr. Assn., Sch. Librs. Assn. Western N.Y., Assn. for Libr. Svc. to Children. Home: Elma, NY. Died Dec. 5, 2004.

DUBERSTEIN, CONRAD B., federal judge; b. N.Y.C., Oct. 22, 1915; s. Alex N. and Esther (Drucks) D.; m. Anne Saggio, May 11, 1928; 1 dau., Elysa Rice. Student Bklyn. Coll., 1934-38; LL.B., St. John's U., 1941; LLD (hon.), 1990. Bar: N.Y. 1942, U.S. Dist. Ct. (ea. dist.) N.Y. 1945, U.S. Dist. Ct. (so. dist.) N.Y. 1949, U.S. Dist. Ct. (no. dist.) N.Y. 1963; Supreme Ct., 1960, U.S. Ct. Appeals (2d cir.) 1966. Ptnr., Schwartz, Rudin & Duberstein, Bklyn., 1954-60, Schwartz & Duberstein, Bklyn., 1960-70; ptnr. Otterbourg, Steindler, Houston & Rosen, P.C., N.Y.C., 1970-80, sr. atty. insolvency dept.; bankruptcy judge U.S. Dist. Ct. (ea. dist.) N.Y., N.Y.C., 1981—2005, chief judge, 1984-2005. Pres., Levittown (N.Y.) Republican Club, 1960-61; pres. St. John's U. Coun. Served with AUS, 1943-45; ETO. Decorated Purple Heart, Bronze Star medal. Fellow Am. Bar Found., Am. Bankruptcy Inst.; mem. ABA, Fed. Bar Council, Comml. Law League, Nat. Conf. Bankruptcy Judges, Am. Coll. Bankruptcy, N.Y. State Bar Assn., Bklyn. Bar Assn., Am. Legion, Jewish War Vets., Mil. Order of Purple Heart, Hist. Soc. Supreme Ct., DAV, B'nai B'rith. Author: A Broad View of the New Bankruptcy Code, 1979; contbg. author: Bankruptcy Reform Act Manual, Bankruptcy Practice and Strategy. Home: Brooklyn, NY. Died Nov. 18, 2005.

DUBUQUE, GREGORY LEE, medical physicist; b. Louisville, Feb. 6, 1948; s. Lionel Lee Dubuque and Mary Catherine (Bladen) Busija; m. Gloria Sue Horn, June 28, 1969 (div. May 1979); 1 child, Alison Lynn. BS in Physics, Ill. Inst. Tech., 1970; MS, U. Cin., 1972, PhD, 1974. Diplomate Am. Bd. Radiology in Therapeutic Radiology, Am. Bd. Radiology in Med. Nuclear Physics. NASA trainee U. Cin., 1970; instr. radiology U. Colo. Med. Ctr., Denver, 1974-80; chief physicist Nebr. Meth. Hosp., Omaha, 1980-86, Cape Cod Hosp., Hyannis, Mass., from 1986. Clin. instr. U. Nebr. Med. Ctr., Omaha, 1982-86; presenter, chmn. numerous sci. symposia and meetings; reviewer Am. Jour. Roentgenology, Med. Physics. Contbr. articles to sci. and med. jours. Rsch. fellow NSF, 1969-70; fellow Bur. Radiol. Health, 1971-74. Mem. Am. Assn. Physicists in Medicine (pres. Rocky Mountain chpt. 1978-79), Am. Radium Soc., Am. Coll. Radiology Achievements include co-development of SUAR ultrasound phantom test object. Home: West Barnstable, Mass. Died Feb. 2, 2004.

DUDECK, JAMES ROGER, planned giving counsellor; b. Milw., Jan. 19, 1928; s. James and Mabel (Brandt) D.; m. Marie Katherine Klein, Jan. 26, 1958; children: Carla Marie, Martin James. BS in Bus. Adminstrn., Marquette U., 1951; MS in Fin. Svcs., Am. Coll., Bryn Mawr, Pa., 1984. CLU, ChFC. Life underwriter Prudential Ins. Co. Am., Jacksonville, Fla., 1953-65, sr. mktg. cons., 1966-89; planned giving counselor Wycliffe Bible Translators, Huntington Beach, Calif., from 1989. Author, editor: (newsletter) Planned Giving Ideas, 1992-95. With U.S. Army, 1946-47. Fellow Life Mgmt. Inst.; mem. Heartland Estate Planning Coun., Am. Soc. CLU and ChFC (ethics chmn. Imperial Ridge chpt.). Republican. Lutheran. Avocation: church work. Died Mar. 25, 2005.

DUGGAN, DENNIS MICHAEL, newspaper editor; b. Detroit, Oct. 12, 1927; s. Michael and Anne (Judge) D.; divorced; 1 child, Nancy Ellen. AB, Wayne U., Detroit, 1952. Wall St. columnist N.Y. Herald Tribune, 1960-61; asst. real estate editor N.Y. Times, 1961-62; fin. writer N.Y. Daily News, 1967; sr. editor, N.Y. bur. chief Newsday, 1973-83; columnist, 1983—2006. Recipient Meyer Berger award Columbia U. Grad. Sch. Journalism, 1987; co-recipient Pulitzer prize N.Y. Newsday, 1991. Mem. Inner Circle, Soc. Silurians (pres., Peter Kihss award), Dutch Treat Club. Home: New York, NY. Died Apr. 20, 2006.

DUGGAN, SARA CLARK, nurse; b. Lynchberg, S.C., Sept. 4, 1936; d. Thomas Boyle and Gladys Elizabeth (Tenhet) Clark; m. George Michael Duggan Jr., Aug. 15, 1958; children: George Michael III, Patrick Joseph, John James, Daniel O'Connell. RN, St. Francis Xavier Hosp. Sch., Charleston, S.C., 1958. Staff nurse St. Francis Xavier Hosp., 1972-92, supr., 1992-96, ret., 1996. Precinct pres. Rep. party, Charleston, 1994—; mem. Friends of Hampton Plantatcion. Mem. Full Gospel Businessmen's Fellowship Internat., Huguenot Soc. of S.C. Methodist. Avocations: reading, music, piano, choir, sewing. Home: Charleston, SC. Died Nov. 20, 2004.

DULIN, PATRICIA ANN, accountant; b. Muleshoe, Tex., Mar. 24, 1952; d. Woodroe G. and Donna (Radosevich) D. BSBA, U. Nev., Las Vegas, 1975. CPA, Nev. Staff acct. Alex Logan & Co., Las Vegas, 1975, Goussak & Raben, Ltd., Las Vegas, 1976-84, acct., owner, ptnr., 1980-84, Goussak, Raben & Co., Las Vegas, 1984-88, Dulin & Raben, Ltd., Las Vegas, 1988-91; owner Patricia Dulin, CPA, Las Vegas, from 1991. Bd. dirs., officer Frontier coun. Girl Scouts U.S., 1980—; bd. dirs. Jr. League Las Vegas, 1983—, Clark County chpt. ARC, 1987-89, So. Nev. div. Desert S.W. chpt. Multiple Sclerosis Soc., 1989—. Recipient appreciation pin Frontier Coun. Girl Scouts U.S., 1986. Mem. AICPA, Nev. Soc. CPA's, Am. Soc. Women Accts. (bd. dirs. officer 1976-79). Home: Las Vegas, Nev. Died Oct. 10, 2004.

DUMBLETON, DUANE DEAN, academic administrator; b. Shiocton, Wis., May 30, 1939; s. Reginald William and Marguerite Eva (Testin) D.; m. Nancy M. Cavins; children: Laura Layli, Mary Bahiyyih, Rama Ali Sequoyah, Nuriyyih Alexandra, Benjamin Idal. BS, U. Wis., 1962; MA, Syracuse (N.Y.) U., 1969; EdD, U. Ga., 1973. Tchr. geography Hillsborough County Pub. Schs., Tampa, Fla., 1962-63; tchr. English, Geneva (N.Y.) Pub. Schs., 1964-65; tchr. world culture Onondoga County Pub. Schs., Syracuse, 1965-70; tchr. English, Clarke County Pub. Schs., Athens, Ga., 1970-71; mem. faculty Fla. C.C., Jacksonville, from 1973, div. chmn. humanities dept., prof. Asian humanities, edn., 1978-83, campus pres., 1988—2006, dir. staff develop., 1984—87, asst. to pres., 1987—88. Author: Education for American Indians, 1973; contbr. articles to profl. jours. Mem. Jacksonville Cmty. Coun., Inc., 1986—2006; mem. com. Pine Castle, Inc., 1994—99, Sister Cities Assn., Jacksonville, 1989—92, Urban Core Citizens Planning Adv. Com.; mem. com., bd. pres. Interfaith Coun., Jacksonville, 1989—2006; mem. com. Spiritual Assembly of Bahais of Jacksonville, 1974—2000; mem., chair Spiritual Assembly of the Bahais of Clay County, 2001—06. Recipient Svc. award Jacksonville Jaycees, 1978, Clay County Bahai Community, 2000-06. Mem. Cmty. Colls. for Internat. Devel. (bd. dirs., sec. 1988-92), Assn. Bahai's Studies, Fla. Assn. Community Colls., Leadership Jacksonville Alumni Assn., Urban League (bd. dirs.), Learn to Read (bd. dirs. 2000-04), Nat. Conf. of Cmty. and Justice (bd. dirs. 1998-2006, chmn. 2004-05). Avocations: writing poetry and essays, public speaking. Home: Orange Park, Fla. Died Feb. 1, 2006.

DUMOULIN, DIANA CRISTAUDO, small business owner, writer, musician; b. Washington, Jan. 5, 1939; d. Emanuel A. and Angela E. (Cogliano) Cristaudo; m. Philip DuMoulin, May 30, 1964; children: Joanmarie Patricia, John Philip. MA, U. Wis., 1967; BA, Rosary Coll., 1961; cert. in Creative Writing, Piano, Phoenix Coll., 2002. Project mgr. IDC Cons. Group, Framingham, Mass., 1982-84; sr. market analyst Cullinet, Inc., Westwood, Mass., 1984-86; prof. assoc. Ledgeway Group, Lexington, Mass., 1988—93; prin. Customer Mktg. Specialist, Brookline, Mass., 1994—2000; pres. Customer Solutions Internat., Phoenix, from 1994. Adj. faculty Ulster County C.C. Stone Ridge, N.Y., 1967-74; lectr. Boston Coll., Chestnut Hill, Mass., 1976. Author:The Love Pad Dream Journal, 1996, Ourselves in the Garden, 1998; contbr. articles to profl. jours., mags., poetry jours. Pres. LWV, Kingston, N.Y., 1973-74. Recipient Svc. to Young Adults award 70001 Career Assn., 1977, Honorable Mention award Writers Digest Writing Competition, 1996, 98; faculty fellow U. Wis., 1964-66 Mem. Am. Marketing Assn., Nat. Writers Union. Home: Phoenix, Ariz. Died June 28, 2004.

DUNCAN, NANCY KIMMEL, storyteller; b. Terre Haute, Ind., Jan. 2, 1937; d. Harley R. and Emily (Read) Kimmel; m. Harry A. Duncan, June 11, 1960; children: Barnaby Andrew, Lucy Elizabeth, Guy Oliver. BA, Agnes Scott Coll., 1958; MFA, U. Iowa, 1969. Dir. theatre Scattergood Sch., West Branch, Iowa, 1960-72; assoc. dir. Omaha Playhouse, 1973-76; exec. dir. Emmy Gifford Children's Theatre, Omaha, 1976-86; owner Story Performances, Omaha, from 1986. Prodr. (storytelling performance art) Always/Never Coming Home, 1999—. Coord. Storytelling Festival of Nebr., Omaha, 1995—. Mem. Nat. Storytelling Network, Nebr. Arts Coun. Democrat. Home: Omaha, Nebr. Died Sept. 6, 2004.

DUNCANSON, DONALD GEORGE, retired encyclopedia editor; b. L.A., Feb. 26, 1928; s. George H. and Addie (Biddison) D. BA, U. So. Calif., L.A., 1953; MA, Harvard U., 1954; postgrad., U. Chgo., 1954-56. Lexicographer Funk & Wagnalls Inc., N.Y.C., 1956-57; assoc. editor Scott, Foresman & Co., Chgo., 1958-64, Sci. Rsch. Assocs., Inc., Chgo., 1964-67; editor Ency. Britannica, Inc., Chgo., 1967-73, 77-93. With USN, 1946-49. Democrat. Avocations: reading, travel. Home: Franklin Park, Ill. Died Feb. 5, 2004.

DUNHAM, KATHERINE, choreographer, anthropologist, dancer; b. Glen Ellyn, Ill., June 22, 1909; d. Albert Millard and Fanny June (Taylor) Dunham; m. Jordis McCoo (div.); m. John Thomas Pratt, July 10, 1941 (dec. Jan. 1986); 1 child, Marie Christine Pratt. BA in Anthropology, U. Chgo., 1936, MS; PhD, Northwestern U.; LhD (hon.), MacMurray Coll., 1972. Dir., tchr. of own schs. of dance, theatre and cultural arts, Chgo., N.Y.C., Haiti, Stockholm and Paris, from 1931; profl. dancer, from 1934; choreographer for theatre, opera, motion pictures and TV; mem. Chgo. Opera Co., 1935-36; supv. Chgo. City Theatre Project on cultural studies, 1939; dance dir. Labor Stage, 1939-40; prodr., dir. Katherine Dunham Dance Co., from 1945; established dance sch. Port-au-Prince, Haiti, 1961; advisor to First World Festival on Negro Art U.S. Dept. State, 1966; artistic and tech. advisor to Pres. of Senegal, 1966-67; cultural counselor and dir. Performing Arts Tng. Ctr., So. Ill. U., East St. Louis, from 1967; prof. So. Ill. U., Edwardsville, from 1968. Choreographer concerts Tropics, 1937, Schulhoff Tango, 1937, Madame Christoff, 1937, Primitive Rhythms, 1937, Biguine-Beguine, 1937, Florida Swamp Shimmy, 1937, Lotus Eaters, 1937, Haitian Suite, 1937, Peruvienne, 1938, Le Jazz Hot (Boogie-Woogie), 1938, Saludade da Brazil, 1938, Spanish Earth Suite, 1938, Island Songs, 1938, Mexican Rhumba, 1938, L'Ag'Ya, 1938, A Las Montanas, 1938, Bre'r Rabbit an' de Tah Baby, 1938, Bahiana, 1939, Cuidad Maravillosa, 1939, Concert Rhumba, 1939, Cumbancha, 1939, Plantation Dances, 1940, Babalu, 1941, Haitian Suite II, 1941, Honky-Tonk Train (added to Le Hot Jazz), 1941, Rites de Passage, 1941, Tropical Revue, 1943, Callaco, 1944, Choros Nos. 1-5, 1944, Flaming Youth 1927, 1944, Para Que Tu Veas, 1944, Havana 1910/1919, 1944, Carib Song, 1945, Bal Negro, 1946, Motivos, 1946, Haitian Roadside, 1946, Nostalgia (Ragtime), 1946, Batacada, 1947, Bolero, 1947, C'Est Lui, 1947, Rhumba Trio, 1947, Floor Exercises, 1947, La Valise, 1947, Octaroon Ball, 1947, Angelique, 1948, Blues Trio, 1948, Macumba, 1948, Missouri Waltz, 1948, Street Scene, 1948, Veracruzana, 1948, Adeus Terras, 1949, Afrique, 1949, Jazz in Five Movements, 1949, Brazilian Suite, 1950, Los Indios, 1950, Frevo, 1951, Rhumba Jive, 1951, Rhumba Suite, 1951, Spirituals, 1951, Caymmi, 1952, Ramona, 1952, La Blanchisseuse, 1952, Southland, 1952, Afrique du Nord, 1953, Samba, 1953, Cumbia, 1953, Dora, 1953, Honey in the Honeycomb, 1953, Incantation, 1953, Carnaval, 1955, Floy'd Guitar Blues, 1955, Jazz Finale, 1955, Just Wild About Harry, 1955, New Love, 1955, Banana Boat, 1957, Plating Rice, 1957, Sister Kate, 1957, Ti'Cocomaque, 1957, A Touch of Innocence, 1959, Bamboche, 1962, Diamond Thief, 1962, Anabacoa, 1963, theatre The Emperor Jones, 1939, with George Balanchine Cabin in the Sky, 1941, theatre Pins and Needles, 1940, Tropical Pinafore, 1939, Les Deux Anges, 1965, (films) Carnaval of Rhythum, 1939, Pardon My Sarong, 1942, Star Spangled Rhythum, 1942, Stormy Weather, 1943, Casbah, 1948, Boote e Risposta, 1950, Mambo, 1954, Green Mansions, 1958, The Bible, 1966, (Operas) Aida, 1963; author: Katherine Dunham's Journey to Accompong, 1946, Katherine Dunham's Journey to Accompong, rev. edit., 1972; author: (autobiography) A Touch of Innocence, 1959, A Touch of Innocence, rev. edit., 1980; author: Island Possessed, 1969, Kasamance: A Fantasy, 1974; co-author: (plays) Ode to Taylor Jones, 1967—68; author: TV scripts, produced in Mexico, Australia, France, Eng., Italy; contbr. short stories sometimes under pseudonym Kaye Dunn to mags.; consulting editor Dance Scope. Pres. Dunham Fund for Rsch. and Devel. Cultural Arts Inc.; founder Found. Study of Arts and Scis. of Vodun; v.p. Found. Devel. and Preservation Cultural Arts Inc.; bd. dirs. Nat. Inst. Aging, Ill. Arts Coun.; mem. Ill. com. JFK Ctr. Alliance Arts Edn., Am. Coun. Arts in Edn., Arts Worth/Intercultural Coun.; cons. Interamerican Inst. Ethnomusicology and Folklore, Caracas, Venezuela, NEH; mem. rev. com. OAS; mem. adv. bd. Modern Orgn. Dance Evolvement. Decorated Legion of Honor Haiti; named Cmdr., Grand Officer, Hon. Citizen, Port-an-Prince, Haiti, 1957; recipient Merit Chevalier, Haiti, Dance Mag. award, 1968, Eight Lively Arts award, 1969, Disting. Svc. award, So. Ill. U., 1970, East St. Louis Monitor award, 1970, Dance Divsn. Heritage award, AAHPERD, 1972, Nat. Ctr. Afro-Am. Artists award, 1972, Black Merit Acad. award, 1972, Am. Dance Guild award, 1975, 6th Kennedy Ctr. Honors award, 1983, Profl. Achievement award, U. Chgo., Samuel M. Scripps/Am. Dance Festival award, 1986, Nat. Medal Arts, 1989, Capezio Dance award, 1991, Key to City, East St. Louis, Ill., 1968; Julius Rosenfeld Travel fellow, 1936—37, Fulbright fellow, State Dept. Internat. Edn., Mather scholar, Case We. Res. U., 1973. Mem.: AEA, SAG, ASCAP, Lincoln Acad., Royal Anthrop. Soc., Negro Actors Guild, Inst. Black World (bd. dirs.), Black Acad. Arts and Scis., Writers Guild, Am. Fedn. Radio Artists, Am. Guild Music Artists, Am. Guild Variety Artists (bd. govs. 1943—49), Sigma Epsilon. Avocations: horseback riding, cooking, painting, walking. Home: East Saint Louis, Ill. Died May 21, 2006.

DUNLAP, EMMA MAGDALENE, hospital administrator, nurse; b. Greenville, Ohio, Mar. 14, 1933; d. Harvey Curtis and Farris Geneva (Flemings) D. Diploma, Miami Valley Hosp. Sch. Nursing, Dayton, 1954; BS in Edn., U. Cin., 1973, MEd, 1978. RN; cert. diabetes educator. Staff nurse Miami Valley Hosp., Dayton, 1954-55, Wayne Hosp., Greenville, 1955-57, supr., infection control nurse, 1957-73, dir. nursing, inservice edn., 1973-82, coord. patient and community edn., from 1982. Bd.dirs. Darke County Coun. on Aging, Greenville, 1987—. Presbyterian. Home: Greenville, Ohio. Died July 6, 2004.

DUNLAP, JAMES RILEY, SR., former financial executive, credit manager; b. Portland, Oreg., May 21, 1925; s. William Gates and Laura (Riley) D.; m. Betty Towe; children: James R. Jr., Brian Jay, William David. BSBA, U. Oreg., 1950; postgrad., Portland State Coll., 1963-65. Sales rep. Hyster Co., Portland, 1950-61; br. asst. mgr. Reynolds Metals Co., Portland, 1961-71; corp. credit mgr. Burns Bros. Inc., Portland, 1971-79, sec.-treas., 1979-89; ret. Contbr. articles on credit and fin. mgmt. to profl. jours. With USAAF, 1943-46. Melvin Jones fellow. Mem. Nat. Assn. Credit Mgmt. (past pres., bd. dirs.), Internat. Assn. Credit Mgmt. (past pres., bd. dirs., Disting. Svc. award 1985, Herb Barnes Meml. award 1987), Portland Retail Credit Assn. (past pres., bd. dirs.), Oreg. State Cons. Credit Assn. (past pres., lifetime bd. dirs.), Portland Jaycees, Oreg. Motor Supply Credit Assn. (past pres., bd. dirs.), Consumer Counseling Svc. Oreg. (exec. com. 1979-89), Am. Contract Bridge League (past pres. Portland chpt., gold life master), Lions (past pres. host club), Masons (life), Elks, (life), Delta Tau Delta Alumni Assn. (past pres.). Avocations: stamp collecting/philately, bridge, sports. Home: Portland, Oreg. Died Sept. 21, 2004.

DUNN, CHARLES WILLIAM, retired literature and language professor, writer; b. Arbuthnott, Scotland, Nov. 30, 1915; arrived in U.S., 1928, naturalized, 1961; s. Peter Alexander and Alberta Mary Margaret (Freeman) Dunn; m. Patricia Campbell, June 21, 1941 (dec. 1973); children: Deirdre, Peter Arthur; m. Elaine Birnbaum, Oct. 25, 1974; 1 child, Alexander Joseph. BA with honors, McMaster U., 1938; AM, Harvard U., 1939, PhD, 1948; LLD (hon.), St. Francis Xavier U., 1983. Asst. in English Harvard U., 1939-40, tutor, 1940-41, prof. Celtic langs. and lits., chmn. dept., 1963-84, prof. emeritus, 1984—2006, Margaret Brooks Robinson prof. Celtic langs. and lits., 1967-84, master of Quincy House, 1966-81; instr. humanities Stephens Coll., 1941-42; instr. English Cornell U., 1943-46; from instr. to assoc. prof. Univ. Coll., U. Toronto, 1946-56; prof. NYU, N.Y.C., 1956-63. Taft lectr. U. Cin., 1956. Author: Highland Settler: A Portrait of the Scottish Gael in Nova Scotia, 1953, rev. edit., 1991, The Foundling and the Werewolf: A Study of Guillaume de Palerne, 1960 (Chgo. Folklore prize, 1960); author: (with Morton W. Bloomfield) The Role of the Poet in Early Societies, 1989; editor: A Chaucer Reader, 1952, History of the Kings of Britain (Geoffrey of Monmouth), 1958, Chronicles (Froissart), 1961, Romance of the Rose, 1962, Lays of Courtly Love, 1963; editor: (with Edward Byrnes) Middle English Literature, 1973, rev. edit., 1990; contbr. articles, revs. to prof. jours. Recipient Can. award, Fedn. Gaelic Socs., 1955; Dexter fellow, N.S., 1941, Rockefeller fellow, 1942—43, Nuffield fellow, Dublin, Edinburgh and Aberystwyth, 1954—55, Guggenheim fellow, Scotland, Wales and Brittany, 1962—63. Fellow: Soc. Antiquaries Scotland, Am. Acad. Arts and Scis.; mem.: MLA, Mass. Hist. Soc. (resident), Scottish Text Soc., Early English Text Soc., Medieval Acad. Am., Commanderie de Bordeaux Boston (Maitre), Royal Scottish Country Dance Soc., Scots' Charitable Soc. Boston, Odd Volumes Club, Somerset Club, Tavern Club, Comunn Gaidhealach (Scotland), St. Andrews Soc. N.Y., Phi Beta Kappa (hon.). Home: Cambridge, Mass. Died July 24, 2006.

DUNN, ROBERT SIGLER, engineering executive; b. Cin., Aug. 13, 1926; s. John W. and Mirian S. (Sigler) D.; m. Barbara A. Rigdon, June 26, 1949; children: Anne Dunn Stockman, John R., Mark A. BSME, BSEE, Purdue U., 1949. With Collins Radio Co., Cedar Rapids, Iowa, 1949-72, regional v.p., gen. mgr.; v.p. ops. King Radio Corp., Olathe, Kans., 1973-91, also bd. dirs.; pvt. cons., 1991—2005. Mem. Iowa State Bd. Engring. Examiners, 1969-72. Bd. dirs., v.p. Olathe Comm. Hosp., 1982-90; mem. bd. trustees, past chmn. Olathe Health Sys.; chmn. bd. trustees Miami County Med. Ctr.; mem. bd. advisors Kans. U. Sch. Engring., 1979—. Mem. IEEE, NSPE, Am Soc. Quality, Rotary, Pi Tau Sigma, Eta Kappa Nu, Tau Beta Pi. Died Jan. 3, 2005.

DURAN, MIGUEL, electronics engineer; b. Ysleta, Tex., Sept. 30, 1934; s. Matilde and Feliciana (Herrera) D.; m. Emma Luna, Aug. 3, 1955; children: Edsel, Wyatt, Mary, Michael. AS in Elec. Engring., Capitol Radio Engring. Inst., Washington, 1970; BA in Bus. Adminstrn., Upper Iowa U., 1974; BS in Engring. Tech., Southwestern U., Tucson, 1984. Lic. mfg. engring. technologist. Field engr. RCA Svc. Co., Camden, N.J., 1959-67; telemetry systems engr. Lockheed Electronics Co., Houston, 1967-72; systems engr. E-Systems, Inc., Dallas, 1972-84; sr. test engr. Tech. Devel. Corp., Arlington, Tex., 1984-87; sr. mem. tech. staff Electronic Warfare Assocs., White Sands Missile Range, N.Mex., from 1987. Instr. electronic engring. DeVry Inst. Tech., Dallas, 1979-80, Nat. Inst. Tech., Dallas, 1980-87. With USAF, 1955-59. Mem. Am. Soc. for Engring. Edn. Democrat. Roman Catholic. Avocations: reading, electronic projects. Home: Las Cruces, N.Mex. Died Feb. 13, 2004.

DURLAND, JACK RAYMOND, retired lawyer; b. Taylor, Tex., Sept. 21, 1916; s. Den D. and Percy (Langrill) D.; m. June Kathryn Cain, Feb. 5, 1937; children: Jack Raymond, Diane Elizabeth. LLB, U. Okla., 1941. Bar: Okla. 1941. Spl. agt. FBI, 1942-46; sole law practice Oklahoma City, 1946-50; asst. to pres. Cain's Coffee Co., Oklahoma City, 1950-52, pres., 1952-82, Gallery at Nichols Hills Inc., Oklahoma City, 1982-87; ret. Chmn. bd. Nat. Coffee Assn., 1961-62 Bd. dirs. Met. YMCA, Oklahoma City. Mem. ABA, Okla. Bar Assn., World Pres. Orgn. Home: Oklahoma City, Okla. Died Sept. 17, 2005.

DURR, MALCOLM DANIEL, lawyer; b. Bond County, Ill., Apr. 22, 1917; s. Eckard Karol and Bertha (Mitchell) D.; children: Franklin Mitchell, Bradford Karol, Christopher Hubbard. BA, U. Ill., 1938, LLB, JSD, 1940. Bar: Ill. 1940, U.S. Dist. Ct. (so. dist.) Ill. 1940). Pvt. practice, Alton, Ill., from 1940. Counsel Smith, Wesson & Fiocchi, Alton, 1970-73; atty. City of Alton, 1940-41, corp. counselor, 1949-53; asst. state's atty. Madison County, Ill., 1952-56. Maj. USAAF, 1941-51. Decorated DFC (4), Air medals (5), Croix DeGuerre and Etoile D'Argent, France, 1947; recipient Commemorative medal 50th Ann. of WW II, Russia, 1998. Mem. Madison County Bar Assn., Masons. Died June 8, 2005.

DUVICK, DONALD NELSON, plant breeder; b. Sandwich, Ill., Dec. 18, 1924; s. Nelson Daniel and Florence Henrietta (Appel) D.; m. Selma Elizabeth Nelson, Sept. 10, 1950; children: Daniel, Jonathan, Randa. BS, U. Ill., 1948; PhD, Washington U., St. Louis, 1951. With Pioneer Hi-Bred Internat., Inc., Johnston, Iowa, 1951-90, corn breeding coordinator Ea. and So. div., 1965-71, dir. corn breeding dept., 1971-75, dir. plant breeding div., 1975-85, v.p. research, 1985-86, sr. v.p. research, 1986-90, co. dir., 1982-90; affiliate prof. Iowa State U., from 1990. Chmn. nat. plant genetic resources bd. USDA, 1990-91, vice-chmn. nat. genetic resources adv. com., 1992-93; trustee Internat. Ctr. for Maize and Wheat Improvement, 1988-94, trustee Internat. Rice Rsch. Inst., 1996-98; lectr. in field. Assoc. editor: Plant Physiology Jour., 1977-78; contbr. articles to profl. jours. on genetics and plant breeding, devel. anatomy and cytology, cytoplasmic inheritance, quantititive genetics and biodiversity. Pres. Johnston Consol. Sch. Bd., 1965-67. Served with AUS, 1943-46. Pioneer Hi-Bred fellow U. London, 1968; Disting. fellow Iowa Acad. Sci. Fellow AAAS, Crop Sci. Soc. Am. (pres. 1986), Am. Soc. Agronomy (pres. 1992), Iowa Acad. Sci.; mem. NAS, Coun. Agrl. Sci. and Tech. (bd. dirs. 1987-90), The Nature Conservancy (chair bd. trustees Iowa chpt. 1994). Democrat. Mem. United Ch. Christ. Achievements include identification of intra cellular site of zein storage in maize endosperm; research in maize cytoplasmic male sterility, in plant breeding's effects on crop plant genetic diversity, in changes in productivity of hybrid maize since 1930. Home: Johnston, Iowa. Died May 23, 2006.

DWIGGINS, JOHN FREDERICK, comptroller; b. Highland Park, Mich., May 30, 1926; m. Beverly Wolff, May 23, 1952; children: David C., Donald F. BS in Indsl. Mgmt., Ga. Tech. U., 1949. CPA, Ga. Mgmt. cons. Ernst & Whinney, Atlanta, 1952-60; controller Williams Corp., Sumter, S.C., 1960-67; treas., controller Siker Corp., Lakeland, Fla., 1967-76; comptroller, mgr. info. and computer services Holland & Knight, Lakeland, 1976-87; controller Hi Tec Assocs. Inc., Lakeland, 1988. Home: Lakeland, Fla. Died Mar. 12, 2005.

DWORSKY, CLARA WEINER, lawyer, brokerage house executive; b. NYC, Apr. 28, 1918; d. Charles and Rebecca (Becker) Weiner; m. Bernard Ezra Dworsky, Jan. 2, 1944; 1 child, Barbara G. Goodman. BS, St. John's U., N.Y.C., 1937, LLB, 1939, JD, 1968. Bar: N.Y. 1939, U.S. Dist. Ct. (ea. dist.) N.Y. 1942, U.S. Dist. Ct. (so. dist.) Tex. 1993, U.S. Ct. Appeals (9th cir.) 1994, U.S. Ct. Appeals (5th cir.) 1995, U.S. Supreme Ct. 2003. Pvt. practice, N.Y.C., 1939-51; assoc. Bessie Farberman, N.Y.C., 1942; clk., sec. U.S. Armed Forces, Camp Carson, Colo., Camp Claiborne, La., 1944-45; abstractor, dir. Realty Title, Rockville, Md., 1954-55; v.p. Kelley & Dworsky Inc., Houston, from 1960. Appeals agt. Gasoline Rationing Appeals Bd., NYC, 1942; bd. dirs. Southlan Sales Assocs., Houston. Vol. ARC, N.Y.C.; vice chmn. War Bond pledge drive, Bklyn.; vol. Houston Legal Found., 1972-73; pres. Women's Aux. Washington Hebrew Acad., 1958-60, v.p. bd. trustees, 1959-60; co-founder, v.p. S. Tex. Hebrew Acad. (now Beren Acad.), Houston, 1970-75, hon. pres. women's divsn., 1973. Recipient Cert. award, Treas. of U.S., 1943, Commendation, Office of Chief Magistrate of City NY, 1948, Pietas medal, St. Johns U., 1985. Mem.: ABA (chmn. social security com., sr. lawyers divsn. 1989—93, mem. sr. lawyers divsn. coun. 1989—95, chairsubcom. 1993—95, chmn. social security com., sr. lawyers divsn. from 1995, mem. editl. bd. sr. lawyers divsn. pub. Experience), Nat. Assn. Women Lawyers (chmn. organizer Juvenile Delinquency Clinic N.Y. 1948—51), Houston Bar Assn. (sec. social secutiry sect. 1995—96), Fed. Bar Assn. (vice chair programs, sr. lawyers divsn. 1994—96, dep. chair 1996—97, chmn. 1997—98, chair sr. lawyers com. south Tex. chpt. bd. from 1998, co-editor sr. citizens handbook, 2d printing 2002—03, chmn. soc. sec. com., sen. lawyers divsn.), N.Y. State Bar Assn., St. Johns U. Alumni Assn. (coord. Houston chpt. from 1983, pres. 1986), Amit Women Club, Delphians Past Pres.'s Club, Hadassah. Jewish. Home: Houston, Tex. Died Feb. 16, 2006.

DWYER, CORNELIUS J., JR., lawyer; b. New Rochelle, NY, Sept. 3, 1943; s. Cornelius John and Mary Cecelia (McDonough) D.; m. June Forsythe Sonnekalb, Sept. 14, 1968; children: Cornelius William, Colin Micheal. BA, Yale U., 1965; LLB, Harvard U., 1968. Bar: N.Y. 1968, U.S. Dist. Ct. N.Y. 1969. Assoc. Shearman & Sterling, N.Y.C., 1968-76, ptnr., from 1976. Democrat. Roman Catholic. Home: New York, NY. Died May 7, 2005.

DYER, NORRIS WILLIAM, radiologist; b. Ft. Worth, Dec. 13, 1936; s. Herschel O'Dell and Mary Alta (Hiett) D.; m. Martha Ruth Gassei, Aug. 8, 1958 (div. Oct. 1982); children: Jennifer Elizabeth, Mark Richard, John William, Stephanie Victoria, Susanna Mary; m. Dianne Rochelle Hays, June 6, 1984, (dec. May 1996); stepchildren: Ronald Christopher Thompson, Joseph David Thompson (dec. Aug. 1995); m. Paula Jean Schoolcraft, July 12, 1997; stepchildren: Ruth Ann Freeborn, Elizabeth Dorn, Scott Dorn. B in Music Edn., U. Tulsa, 1959; MD, U. Okla., 1969. Diplomate Am. Bd. Radiology. Radiologist Radioloy of Eastern Okla., Inc., Tulsa, 1976-82; pvt. practice Tulsa, 1982-87, Wheeling Med. Group, Tulsa, 1987-92, Met. Radiology, Tulsa, from 1992. Lt. comdr. USN, 1969-73. Mem. Tulsa County Med. Soc., Okla. State Med. Assn., AMA, N.E. Okla. Radiol. Soc., Okla. State Radiol. Soc., Am. Coll. Radiology, Radiol. Soc. N.Am. Republican. Avocation: music. Home: Tulsa, Okla. Died Mar. 16, 2005.

DYMICKY, MICHAEL, retired chemist; b. Synewidsko Wyzhne, Ukraine, Oct. 1, 1920; arrived in U.S., 1949; s. Mykola and Eva (Andrushkiw) Dymicky; m. Olga Zhmurko, Jan. 22, 1943; children: Lida Dymicky Pakula, Oksana Dymicky Matla. Degree in chem. tech., Chem. Tech. Polytechnic, Lwiw, 1943; BS, U. Innsbruck, Austria, 1947, Doctorandum, 1949; PhD, Temple U., 1960. Chemist Am. Sugar Refining Co., Phila., 1949-52; rsch. chemist U. Pa. Med. Sch., Phila., 1952-53, Wyeth Inst. Med. Rsch., Radnor, Pa., 1953-56, 59-62; rsch. chemist Agr. Rsch. Svc. USDA, Phila., 1956-59, 66-89; assoc. prof. Kutztown (Pa.) U., 1962-65. Prof. Kutztown (Pa.) U., 1962—65; gen. sec. Internat. Student Svcs., Innsbruck, 1947—49. Author: Servant of God Metropolitan Andrei Sheptyts'kyi, 1996; contbr. Mem. adv. bd. and chmn. pub. rels. com. Menor Jr. Coll., Jenkintown, Pa., 1976—82. Recipient Citation of Merit, DAV, 1970, Chem. Abstract Svc., 1971, USDA, 1989, Inventor's award, U.S. Dept. Commerce, 1987. Mem.: Ukranian Am. Assn. Univ. Profs., Shevchenko Sci. Soc. (coun. from 1968), Am. Chem. Soc. (student adviser 1963—65). Achievements include patents for amino acid derivatives and anticlostridial agts. Avocation: Avocations: swimming, volleyball, making perfumes. Home: Philadelphia, Pa. Died Feb. 3, 2005.

EARLY, JAMES, education educator; b. Worcester, Mass., Apr. 19, 1923; s. Edward and Rose Shea Early; m. Ann McKenny, Aug. 20, 1949; children: Mark, Edward, Joanne. BA Bowdoin Coll., 1945; MA, Harvard U., 1949, PhD, 1953. Instr. Yale U., 1953—57; asst. prof. Vassar Coll., 1957—64; assoc. prof. SMU, 1964—66, prof., 1966—83, assoc. dean, 1971—77, dean, 1977—80, prof./prof. emeritus, from 1980. Com. on the humanities Tex. Inst. Letters. Author: Romanticism and Am. Architecture, 1965, The Making of Go Down Moses, 1972, Colonial Architecture of Mex., 1994, Presidio, Mission, and Pueblo, 2004. Mem., coun. of planning/preservation City of Dallas, 1970—72. With U.S. Army, 1943—46, ETO. Mem.: Town and Gown Club of Dallas. Home: Dallas, Tex. Died June 20, 2005.

EARLY, WILLIAM TRACY, journalist; b. Scurry County, Tex., Feb. 20, 1934; s. Willis Worley Jr. and Lillian Marian (Walton) E. BA, Baylor U., 1954; BDiv, Southeastern Bapt. Sem., 1958; ThD, Union Theol. Sem., 1963. Ordained minister So. Bapt. Conv, 1957. Pastor Urbanna (Va.) Bapt. Ch., 1964-68; editl. asst. World Coun. Chs., N.Y.C., 1968-69; freelance journalist N.Y.C., 1969—2005. Author: Simply Sharing, 1980. 1st lt., chaplain U.S. Army, 1957-59. Democrat. Home: New York, NY. Died Dec. 16, 2005.

EASTMAN, JAMES THOMAS, dentist; b. South Bend, Ind., Nov. 10, 1923; s. Arthur Andrews and Lydia Georgina (Dittman) E.; m. Daisy Louise Lovejoy, July 17, 1948; children: Gail, Janet, James Jr., Patricia, William. Student, Northwestern U., 1941, 45, Ind. U., 1942-43; DDS, Loyola U. Sch. Dentistry, Chgo., 1949. Gen. practice pediatric dentistry, Elkhart, Ind., from 1949. Chmn. dental adv. com. Dept. Pub. Welfare Elkhart County, 1954-80, Ind. U. at South Bend, 1970-74. Served with USN, 1943-45, to 1st lt. U.S. Army, 1952-53. Recipient Disting. Service award Elkhart County Assn. for the Retarded, 1969, Benefactor award, 1975. Fellow Am. Acad. Pediatric Dentistry; mem. ADA, Ind. Dental Assn. (pres. north cen. dist. 1968-69, trustee 1976-79, Service Recognition award 1979), Am. Soc. Dentistry for children (pres. Ind. chpt. 1973-74), Ind. Soc. Pediatric Dentistry (pres. 1970-71). Clubs: Elcona Country (Elkhart), East Lake Woodlands Golf and Racquet (Palm Harbor, Fla.). Lodges: Elks. Republican. Presbyterian. Avocations: golf, swimming, reading. Home: Elkhart, Ind. Died July 18, 2004.

EATON, CHARLES EDWARD, language educator, writer; b. Winston-Salem, NC, June 25, 1916; s. Oscar Benjamin and Mary Gaston (Hough) E.; m. Isabel Patterson, Aug. 16, 1950. Student, Duke U., 1932-33; AB, U. N.C., 1936; postgrad., Princeton, 1936-37; MA, Harvard, 1940; DLitt (hon.), St. Andrews Coll., N.C., 1998. Instr. English U. Mo., 1940-42; prof. creative writing U. N.C., 1946-51; Am. vice-consul Rio de Janeiro, Brazil, 1942-46. Fellow Bread Loaf Writers Conf., 1941, Boulder Writers Conf., 1942. Author: (poems) The Bright Plain, 1942, The Shadow of the Swimmer, 1951, The Greenhouse in the Garden, 1956, Countermoves, 1963, On the Edge of the Knife, 1970, Colophon of the Rover, 1980, The Thing King, 1983, The Work of the Wrench, 1985, New and Selected Poems, 1942-87, 1985, New and Selected Poems, 1992, 2002, 2003, A Guest on Mild Evenings, 1991, The Work of the Sun: New and Selected Poems, 1991—2002, 2004, The Labyrinth, 1995, (poems) The Country of the Blue, 1994, The Fox and I, 1996, The Scout in Summer, 1999, The Jogger By the Sea, 2000, Between the Devil and the Deep Blue Sea, 2002, (art criticisms) Karl Knaths: Five Decades of Painting, 1973, Robert Broderson: Paintings and Graphics, 1975, (short stories) Write Me From Rio, 1959, The Girl from Ipanema, 1972, The Case of the Missing Photographs, 1978, New and Selected Stories: 1959-89, 1989, (novels) A Lady of Pleasure, 1993, (essays) The Man from Buena Vista. Selected Nonfiction, 1944-2000, 2001; contbr. anthologies including Best American Short Stories, 1952, American Literature: Readings and Critiques, 1961, Epoch Anthology, 1968, Best Poems of the Year, 1955-65, Best Poems of the Year, 1968-70, Best Poems of the Year, 1974-75, O. Henry Prize Stories, 1972, New Southern Poets, 1974, The Poet in Washington, 1977, Contemporary Poetry of North Carolina, 1977, Contemporary Southern Poetry, 1979, Anthology of Magazine Verse, 1980-81, Anthology of Magazine Verse, 1981, Anthology of Magazine Verse, 1985, 1980 Arvon Poetry Competition Anthology, The Direction of Poetry, 1988, 1988, The Courage to Grow Old, 1989, The Rough Ride Home, 1992, N.C. Poetry Soc. Anthology, 1992, Contemporary Authors Autobiographical Series, 1994, Anthology of Magazine Verse, 1997, anthologies Voices from Home, 1997, anthologies The Zeppelin Reader, 1998, anthologies Word and Witness: 100 Years of North Carolina Poetry, 1999, autobiographical/critical essays The Man from Buena Vista: Selected Nonfiction, 1999, New and Selected Nonfiction, 1999-2001. Mem. vis. com. Ackland Mus., U. N.C., 1987-98. Recipient Ridgely Torrence Meml. award, 1951, Gertrude Boatwright Harris award, 1955, Ariz. Quar. award, 1955, 56, 82, Roanoke-Chowan Poetry Cup, 1970, Oscar Arnold Young Meml. award, 1971, Golden Rose award New Eng. Poetry Club, 1972, Alice Fay di Castagnola award Poetry Soc. Am., 1974, Ariz. Quar. award, 1977, 79, Arvon Found. award London, 1980, Brockman award N.C. Poetry Soc., 1984, 86, Hollins Critic award, 1984, Roanoke-Chowan Poetry award, 1987, 91, Fiction award Kans. Quar./Kans. Art Commn., 1987, N.C. award for lit., 1988, Fortner award, 1993. Mem. Am. Acad. Poets, Poetry Soc. Am., New Eng. Poetry Club, N.C. Poetry Soc., N.C. Art Soc., North Caroliniana Soc., Phi Beta Kappa, Sigma Nu. Clubs: Harvard U.; Chancellors U. N.C. Died Mar. 22, 2006.

EATON, CLARA BARBOUR, retired librarian; b. Cleve., Oct. 24, 1930; d. George Willis and Lena Logan (Dulaney) Barbour; m. James Marvin Eaton, July 5, 1952 (div. July 1975); children: Jeffery George, Gary Lee. BS, Western Ky. U., 1952. Cert. librarian, Ky. Librarian Woodford County Schs., Versailles, Ky., 1952, Nortonville (Ky.) Sch., 1952-53, Anton (Ky.) Sch., 1953-54, Ea. Jr. High Sch., Owensboro, Ky., 1962-65, Emerson Elem. Sch., Owensboro, 1968-70, Owensboro Pub. Library, 1975-95. Mem. Ky. Libr. Assn., Green River Libr. Group (pres. 1984-86), Married Ladies' Reading Club (pres. 2005—). Democrat. Episcopalian. Home: Owensboro, Ky. Died May 1, 2006.

EATON, KARL F(RANCIS), insurance executive, consultant; b. Sewal, Iowa, July 16, 1925; s. Stewart E. and Jessie L. (Holmes) E.; m. Martha J. Adams, Mar. 20, 1950; 1 child, Jay A. BA in Math., U. Mo., Kansas City, 1949. Actuarial asst. Bus. Men's Assurance Co., Kansas City, 1948-54, mgr. EDP, 1954-62; contr. Guarantee Mut. Life Co., Omaha, 1962-67; v.p. Employers Reins. Corp., Kansas City, 1967-88; owner, mgr. ins. cons. Eaton Cons. Svcs., Shawnee Mission, Kans., from 1988. Scoutmaster Boy Scouts Am., Prairie Village, Kans., 1966, dist. chmn., Kansas City, Kans., 1982; pres. Truman Med. Ctr. Aux., Kansas City, Mo., 1991-93. Sgt. U.S. Army, 1944-46, ETO. Recipient award of merit Boy Scouts Am., 1979, Silver Beaver award, 1982, Auxilian of Yr. award Truman Med. Ctr. Aux., 1987. Fellow Life Mgmt. Inst.; mem. Life Office Mgmt. Assn. (automation II com. 1963-67), Casualty Actuarial Soc. (assoc.), Am. Acad. Actuaries, Mo. Assn. Hosp. Auxs. (bd. dirs. dist. III 1995-96, 2d v.p. 1997—), Kansas City Actuaries Club (pres. 1955-56). Republican. Presbyterian. Avocation: volunteering. Home: Leawood, Kans. Died Apr. 1, 2004.

EBERLY, WILLIAM SOMERS, financial consultant; b. Toledo, Sept. 25, 1921; s. Somers L. and Clara B. (Valentine) E.; m. Catharine L. Sloan (dec. Nov. 1979); children: Stephen, Michael; m. Elizabeth Eberly, Nov. 28, 1980. BBA, U. Toledo, 1943. Various positions Bklyn. Dodgers Nat. League Baseball team, 1944-52; bus. mgr. Milw. Braves Nat. League Baseball team, 1953-65; promotion mgr. Gladiux Corp., Toledo, 1966; fin. cons., sr. v.p. Salomon Smith Barney, from 1967. Spkr. on evolution of big league baseball, bus. Mem. adv. bd. U. Toledo Ctr. for Women, 1982—. Recipient Blue T award U. Toledo, 1992, Eli Lilly Pharm. award, 1996, New Eng. Deaconess Hosp. Diabetic Achievement award, 1997. Mem. U. Toledo Alumni Assn. (pres., 1972), Toledo Exch. Club (pres.). Home: Toledo, Ohio. Died Mar. 21, 2004.

ECKER, J(ACOB) ALDENE, former social services administrator, consultant; b. Waynesboro, Pa., May 1, 1916; s. Charles Leslie and Effie Pearl (Garnes) E.; m. Martha Elizabeth Andes, June 17, 1944; children: John Leslie, Janine Elizabeth Ecker Duffy. AB, Juniata Coll., 1938; MSW, Case Western Res. U., 1948; BDiv, Bethany Theol. Sem., 1948. Caseworker Ill. Dept. Pub. Welfare, Chgo., 1946-47; caseworker boys ct. svc. Ch. Fedn. of Greater Chgo., 1947-48, dir. boys ct. svc., 1948-52; dir. profl. svcs. family svcs. div. Salvation Army, Chgo., 1952-55; exec. dir. Fox Valley Mental Health Clinic, Elgin, Ill., 1955-82; cons. Ecker Ctr. for Mental Health (formerly Fox Valley Mental Health Ctr.), Elgin, from 1982. Vol. cons. Appalachia Habitat for Humanity, Robin, Tenn., 1986-91, Morgan-Scott Project for Christian Concern, 1987-95; organizing chmn. OEO for Kane County, Elgin, 1965; asst. dir. civilian pub. sc. Ch. of Brethren, Elgin, 1944-46. Recipient Agy. Exec. award Elgin United Way, 1980. Mem. NASW (vice chmn. Fox River Valley chpt. 1961-62, chmn. 1962-64), Mental Health Assn. Tenn. (rep. Cumberland County chpt. 1989-92). Avocations: latch hooking, leaded glass figurines. Home: Mount Morris, Ill. Died Nov. 7, 2004.

ECKERSLEY, RICHARD HILTON, graphics designer, educator; b. Warrington, Lancashire, Eng., Feb. 20, 1941; arrived in U.S., 1980; s. Tom and Daisy Eckersley; m. Dika Jacquette Helène Lagercrantz; children: Nell, Camilla, Sam. BA with honors, London Coll. Printing, 1966; MA, Trinity Coll., Dublin, Ireland, 1962. Asst. designer Percy Lund Humphries, London, 1966—68; freelance designer London, 1969—74; sr. designer Kilkenny (Ireland) Design Workshops, 1974—80, U. Nebr. Press, Lincoln, 1981—2006. Vis. lectr. London Coll. Printing, 1969—74, Cleve. Acad. of Arts, 1979—79; assoc. prof. Tyler Sch. Art, Phila., 1980; sr. critic Yale U. Sch. Design, New Haven, 1995—2006. Author: Glossary of Typesetting Terms, 1994. Named Royal Designer for Industry, Royal Soc. Arts, 1999; recipient award of excellence for book design, Assn. Am. U. Presses, 1982—2001, Am. Inst. Graphic Design, 1985—2001, Silver medal, Leipzig Book Fair, 1989, Carl Herzog prize, U. Tex., 1994. Mem.: Am. Inst. Graphic Arts. Home: Lincoln, Nebr. Died Apr. 16, 2006.

ECKERT, CHARLES ARTHUR, accountant; b. Oakland County, Mich., Oct. 3, 1926; s. Albert August and Margaret Stella (Lockman) E.; m. Wenonah Marie Smith, Nov. 22, 1952 (dec. Jan. 1980); 1 child, Charles Arthur Jr.; m. Bonnie Jean McClanahan Martindale, Apr. 25, 1987; children: Charles C. Martindale, David D. Martindale, George A. Martindale. Car, U. Detroit, 1952; postgrad., U. Mich., Oakland U., Wayne State U., U. Va. CPA, Mich. Acct. Kingsworthy, McGraw & Wright, CPAs, Detroit, 1952-54, Schmeltz & Reick, CPAs, Detroit, 1954-64; owner, mgr. Charles A. Eckert, CPA, Grosse Pointe Woods, Mich., from 1964, Zephyrhills, Fla., from 1990. Substitute tchr. Grosse Pointe Pub. Schs., 1968-70; officer Cloyd Container Corp., Detroit, 1970, Boxcraft Corp., Detroit, 1970. Treas. PTA, Grosse Pointe Woods, 1967-68, pres., 1968-69. With USN, 1945-46. Mem. AICPA, Mich. Soc. CPA's, Elks. Died Nov. 10, 2004.

EDELSTEIN, DAVID SIMEON, historian, educator; b. NYC, Jan. 19, 1913; s. William and Clara (Brener) E.; m. Frances Fisher, June 4, 1939 (dec. Jan. 1990); children: Helen Freedman, Henry, Daniel Louis; m. Gertrude Bernstein, Jan. 5, 1997. BA, CCNY, 1932; MA, Columbia U., 1933, PhD, 1949. Cert. elem. tchr., N.Y. Tchr., adminstr. various sch., NYC, 1934-67; lectr. in-svc. courses Bd. Edn., NYC, 1946-65; lectr. History CCNY, 1947-67; lectr. Edn. U. Colo., 1960, Yeshiva U. Grad. Sch. Edn., 1960-61, Hunter Coll., 1964-65; prof. Edn. Western Conn. State U., Danbury, 1967-83; adj. assoc. prof. History Fordham U., Bronx, NY, 1967-70; instr. in-svc. course Stamford Bd. Edn., Conn., 1970-71; adj. assoc. prof. History CUNY, 1970-75; adj. prof. History Western Conn. State U., Danbury, 1984-85. Lectr. in field. Author: Joel Munsell, Printer and Antiquarian, 1950; author: (with others) M. Stern: editor: Publishers for Mass. Entertainment in the Nineteenth Century, 1980; contbr. biog. sketches Nat. Am. Biography, 1999; contbr. articles to profl. jours. Mem. AAUP, Am. Assn. Sch. Adminstrs., Am. Hist. Assn., Conn. Edn. Assn., Nat. Assn. of Elem. Sch. Prins., N.Y.C. Elem. Sch. Prins. Assn. (life), Nat. Coun. of Local Adminstrs. of Vocat. Edn., Social Studies Coun., Coun. of Chmn. of Acad. Subjects, Nat. Soc. for the Study of Edn., New Eng. Hist. Assn., New Eng. Assn. of Tchr. Educators, Phi Alpha Theta, Phi Delta Kappa. Democrat. Jewish. Home: Yonkers, NY. Died Feb. 25, 2005.

EDGE, DANIEL, artist, educator, consultant; b. Norfolk, Va., June 6, 1940; s. Emmett and Emma Joy (Goddard) Edge. BA, Old Dominion Coll., 1965; BFA, Yale U., 1967, MFA, 1969. Adj. asst. prof. CUNY, 1970—82; adj. assoc. prof. No. Va. C.C., Annandale, Va., 1993—97; adj. prof. of fine arts Tex. State U. System Sul Ross State U., Alpine, Tex., from 2001. Exhibitions include Va. Ann. Exhibit (best-in-show, 1969), Julian Pretto, 1978. Va. Mus. Fine Arts fellow, 1966—67, 1967—68, Tiffany fellow, 1970, Nat. Endowment for the Arts fellow, 1975, Guggenheim fellow, 1978. Mem.: The Mind Assn. Home: Marfa, Tex. Died May 11, 2005.

EDGE, ROBERT WALL, foundation administrator; b. Bethesda, Md., July 7, 1946; s. Cary O. and Geradine (Wall) E.; m. Sharon Kay Harrell, Oct. 17, 1977; children: Gregory Thomas, Elizabeth Liza. Student, U. Richmond, 1964-68; MS, Am. U., Washington, 1985. Child care technician Va. Ctr. for Emotionally Disturbed Children, Richmond, 1966-68; sr. rep. field bodily injury State Farm Ins. Co., Richmond, 1969-73; exec. dir. ADAPTS, Richmond, 1973-85; pres. Devel. Rsch. Assocs., Washington, 1985-89; chmn. bus. dept. Commonwalth Coll., Portsmouth, Va., 1989-91; exec. dir. Physicians For Peace, Norfolk, Va., 1991-93, Cmty. Residences Found., Arlington, Va., from 1993. Named Outstanding Young Man Am., U.S. Jaycees, 1977. Mem. ASTD (com. chair 1992-93), Nat. Soc. Fund Raising Execs. (mentor 1993-94). Unitarian Universalist. Home: Vienna, Va. Died Jan. 19, 2004.

EDWARDS, LARRY LEON, radiological engineer; b. Cooperstown, N.Y., May 14, 1954; s. Robert E. and Dorinne M. (Button) E.; m. Veronica J. Kalaukoa, Mar. 25, 1977; children: Karol. Shereign, Tatyana. AS in Applied Sci. and Tech., Thomas Edison State Coll., 1991, BS in Applied Sci. and Tech., 1993; MBA, Pa. State Great Valley Coll., 2000. Cert. health physicist Am. Bd. Health Physics; registered radiation protection technologist Nat. Registry Radiation Protection Technologists; EMT, Pa. Sr. health physics technician Met. Edison, Middletown, Pa., 1982-84; quality assurance monitor GPU Nuc., Middletown, 1984-93, radiation protection supr., 1993-98, radiol. engr., from 1998. With USN, 1973-81. Mem. Health Physics Soc. (plenary mem.; treas. Susquehanna Valley chpt. 1999—), Phi Theta Kappa. Avocations: motorcycle touring, hunting, fishing. Home: Elizabethtown, Pa. Died July 9, 2004.

EDWARDS, RICHARD GAROLD, optometrist; b. Rock Island, Ill., Dec. 28, 1928; s. Willard Garold and Cora (Graves) E.; m. Iris L. Holmes, Aug. 6, 1955; children: Garold Loren, David Loyd; stepchildren: Gregory Klema, Terry Klema. BS, Ill. Coll. Optometry, 1952, DO, 1953. Pvt. practice optometry, Rock Island, Ill., from 1953. Served with U.S. Army, 1953-55. Mem. Ill. Optometric Assn. Lodges: Kiwanis, Masons. Home: Rock Island, Ill. Died Mar. 20, 2005.

EDWARDS, THOMAS ALLEN, orthopedic surgeon; b. Wrangell, Alaska, June 8, 1929; s. Ellis Hewitt and Lida Scott (McCarty) E.; m. Beata Cecilia Peterson, June 9, 1958; children: Barbara, Nancy, Mary, Thomas (dec.). BA, Williams Coll., 1950; MD, Cornell U. Med. Coll., 1954; MS, Oreg. State U., 1972. Diplomate Am. Bd. Orthopedic Surgery. Pvt. practice orthopedic surgery Salem, Oreg., Lafayette, Ind., Johnson City, Tenn., 1961-88; med. cons. Ins. Inst. Hwy. Safety, Washington, 1988-89; orthopedic surgeon Md., 1990-93; surgeon Alaska Native Hosp., Anchorage, 1993-94. Clin. instr. Oreg. Med. Sch., Portland, 1962-75, Ind. Med. Sch., Indpls., 1976-79; assoc. clin. prof. surgery, East Tenn. Med. Sch., Johnson City, 1979-88. Capt. USAF, 1955-57. Fellow Am. Coll. Surgeons; mem. Am. Acad. Orthopedic Surgeons, Va. Med. Soc., Tenn. Med. Soc., Appalachian Trail Conf. Presbyterian. Avocations: hiking, skiing, travel, music. Home: Salem, Va. Died July 31, 2004.

EDWARDS, VIVIAN, retired humanities educator; b. Bklyn., May 19, 1915; d. L. James and Helen Louise (Gaynor) Joseph; m. Seth Carlyle Edwards, June 21, 1943; children: Seth Carlyle Jr., Jeanne. AB, Bklyn. Coll.-CCNY, 1936; MA, Columbia U., N.Y.C., 1937, EdD, 1959. Instr. English Barber-Scotia Jr. Coll., Concord, N.C., 1937-44; head dept. English Cuttington Coll. (now Cuttington U. Coll.), Suakoko, Liberia, 1949-60, chairperson, 1972-79; head dept. English U. Liberia, Monrovia, 1962-68; dir. freshman English Hampton (Va.) Inst./U., 1969-72; English head divsn. humanities St. Augustine's Coll., Raleigh, N.C., 1979-96; ret., 1996. Sponsor English honor soc. publs.-faculty jour. U. Liberia, 1963-68; mem. faculty jour. staff St. Augustine's Coll., 1985. United Negro Coll. Fund grantee, 1984; recipient poetry award Internat. Soc. Poets, 1994, 95, John Winters award St. Augustine's Coll., 1988. Mem. Sigma Tau Delta (sponsor LambdaLambda chpt. 1979—, medal 1996). Democrat. Avocation: study of folk narratives in liberia. Home: Warwick, RI. Died Aug. 19, 2005.

EGBUFOR, EMMANUEL MICHAEL UKADIKE, accountant, business executive, educator; b. Asaba, Nigeria, July 15, 1941; came to U.S., 1969; s. Francis Okeleke and Comfort Adaeze (Onwuegbuzia) E.; m. Patricia Omaneme Okudah, Dec. 28, 1960; children: Dorothy, Chukwudumebi, Thepiso, Charles. AS in Pub. Acctg., Southeastern U., Washington, 1973, BS in Acctg., 1974, MBPA, 1976; PhD in Acctg., Sussex (Eng.) Coll. Tech., 1979. Gen. mgr. acctg. and fin. depts. Bendix Field Engring. Corp., Columbia, Md., 1974-80; asst. prof. acctg. Rider Coll., Lawrenceville, N.J., 1980-81; assoc. prof. acctg. Trenton (N.J.) State Coll., 1981-84; auditor N.J. State Dept. Higher Edn., 1988-90; teaching fellow Catonsville (Md.) Community Coll., 1990-91; mem. acctg. faculty U. Md., Balt., from 1991; pres., chief exec. officer Emma-Pat Assocs. Ltd., Trenton, from 1985. Fin. advisor internat. div. Found. for Coop. Housing, Washington, 1980; vis. prof. auditing Black Execs. Exch. Program, Nat. Urban Leage, N.Y.C., 1970. Author: Fundamentals of Practical Book-Keeping and Accounting for West Africa, 1991. Fellow Inst. Adminstrv. Acctg. and Data Processing (London); mem. Assn. Cost and Exec. Accts. (London), Brit. Assn. Accts. and Auditors, Brit. Inst. Mgmt., Nat. Assn. Accts. (state assoc. dir. 1979). Avocations: soccer, ping pong/table tennis, boxing, auto racing. Home: Baltimore, Md. Died Aug. 15, 2005.

EGE, HANS ALSNES, securities company executive; b. Haugesund, Norway, Jan. 31, 1924; came to U.S. 1953; naturalized, 1961; s. Sigvald Svendsen and Hilda Svendsen (Hansen) E.; m. Else Mathea Lindstrom, July 11, 1953; children: Elisabeth, Anne Christine. Bus. degree, Oslo Handelsgymnasium, 1946; student spl. bus. courses, City of London Coll., 1947; MBA, Drexel U., 1950. Analyst Alderson & Sessions, Mgmt. & Mktg. Cons., Phila., 1950-51; exec. asst. to U.S. ambassador to Norway Oslo, 1951-53; asst. to pres., asst. v.p. corp. sec. A.M. Kidder & Co., Inc., N.Y.C., 1953-64; stockbroker Reynolds Securities Inc., N.Y.C., 1964-65; mgr. Ridgewood (N.J.) Office, 1965-71; mgr. and resident officer, 1971-77; resident v.p., mgr. Dean Witter Reynolds, Inc., Ridgewood, 1978-82, v.p. investments, from 1983. Trustee, v.p. The Bay Found., N.Y.C., Josephine Bay-Paul & C. Michael Paul Found., N.Y.C. Trustee The Norwegian Seamen's Ch., N.Y.C., Norwegian Immigration Assn., N.Y.C.; mem. Pres.'s Club Drexel U. Served with Norwegian Underground, 1942-45. Decorated War medal. Mem. Am. Scandinaian Found., Norwegian Am. C. of C., Joe Jefferson Club (pres. 1969-70), Saddle River (N.J.) Club, Norwegian Club (N.Y.C.), Tau Kappa Epsilon. Home: Mahwah, NJ. Died Sept. 22, 2005.

EGELSON, POLLY SELIGER, artist, educator; b. Balt., Aug. 6, 1928; d. Robert Victor Seliger and Beatrice Regina (Gordon) Summers; m. Louis I. Egelson, June 6, 1949; children: Robert, Betsy, David, Jane. BA, Radcliffe Coll., 1950. Sculptor, instr. Fuller Mus. Art, Brockton, Mass., 1976-93, Danforth Mus. Art, Framingham, Mass., 1976-79, Cape Mus. Art, Dennis, Mass., 1976-79, Falmouth Artists Guild, Mass., from 1976. Bd. govs. Copley Soc., Boston, 1970-73; pres. New Eng. Sculptors Assn., Boston, 1972-74; chair Newton (Mass.) Cultural Com., 1974-76. Sculpture exhibits include Boston City Hall, 1976, Boston Art Festival, 1978, Ward-Nasse Gallery, N.Y.C., Lincoln Ctr., N.Y.C., 1977, Grand Prix Internat. Art Show, Monaco, 1977-78, Cahoor Mus. Am. Art., Cotuit, Mass.; represented in permanent collections Towson (Md.) State Coll., Cape Mus. Fine Arts, Dennis, Mass., Duxbury (Mass.) Mus. Complex; contbg. artist: (books) Falmouth, A Timeless Legacy, Women Artists in America. Assoc. mem. Nat. Mus. Women, Washington, 1995; panel mem., invited artist Cape Cod Women, Yarmouth, Mass., 1995-96. Recipient Best Sculpture award Attleboro Mus. Art, 1975, Cape Cod Art Assn., 1979, Curators Choice award. Mem. New Eng. Sculptors Assn., New Eng. Monotype Guild (bd. dirs. 1994-96), Falmouth Artists Guild (v.p. 1995), Crazy Quilters Guild (sec. 1990-96). Avocations: swimming, reading. Home: Hadley, Mass. Died Sept. 11, 2005.

EHLER, RICHARD LEE, advertising executive, publisher, consultant; b. Holywood, Kans., July 11, 1930; s. John and Katie Anna (Schmidt) E.; m. Sharon K. DePue, 1959 (div. Apr. 1981); 1 child, Quinton John; m. Barbara J. Decker (div. May 1984). BS in Tech. Journalism, Kans. State U., 1952. Mgr. tech. communications GE, 1955-63; supr. tech. communications Motorola, Phoenix, 1963-64; account exec. Lennen & Newell Inc., San Francisco, 1964-65; v.p. Chace Co. Advt. Inc, Santa Barbara, Calif., 1965-72; account exec. Larson/Bateman Inc., Santa Barbara, 1972-79; owner Richler & Co., Santa Barbara, from 1979. Author: The Print Media Planning Manual, 1991, Directory of Print Media Advertising Resources, Print Media Analysis Tools, Checklists for Print Media Advertising Planning and Buying, 1991. Staff sgt. U.S. Army, 1952-54. Mem. Internat. Assn. of Ind. Pubs., Pubs. Mktg. Assn., Santa Barbara Advt. Club (bd. dir. 1970), Soc. of Tech. Communications (sr., nat. 1963-72), Screenwriters Assn. of Santa Barbara, Toastmasters Internat. (ATM cert. 1984), Elks. Republican. Mem. Unity Ch. Avocations: woodworking, golf. Died Feb. 20, 2004.

EHRICH, FELIX FREDERICK, technical consultant; b. N.Y.C., Oct. 19, 1919; s. Harry and Henrietta (Brenner) E.; m. Ceceil Rinder, July 26, 1953; children: Anne, Elisabeth, Margaret. BS, CCNY, 1939; MS, State U. Iowa, 1940; PhD, U. Md., 1942. Rsch. chemist E.I. Dupont, Newark, 1946-58, rsch. supr., 1958—70, tech. dir. Mexico City, 1970-72, mgr. colors internat. devel., tech. mgr. colors mktg. Wilmington, Del., 1972-82; tech. cons. numerous cos., 1982-98. Cons. numerous cos., 1982—; cons. organic pigment colors, expert witness Connolly, Bove, Lodge, Hutz for Bayer, Inc., 1991-95; arbitrator Better Bus. Bur. of Del., 1983—. Inventor, patentee in field quinacridones, phthalocyanines. Lt. U.S. Army, 1942-46. Mem. Am. Chem. Soc., Sigma Xi. Home: Wilmington, Del. Died Mar. 14, 2004.

EHRLICH, RICHARD, electrical engineer, researcher; b. N.Y.C., Mar. 14, 1925; s. Benjiman M. and Paula (Nilva) E.; m. Bennette Sonya Mann, May 9, 1948; children: Michael Barry, Candice Jo, Alyson Tracy. BSEE, U. Miami, 1949.

Comm. tech. civil aeronautics U.S. Govt., Guantanamo Bay, Cuba, 1945-48, field engr., 1949-50, Western Union, Miami, Fla., 1952-76; rsch. devel. Atmospheric Water, Miami, from 1976. Cons. Atmospheric Water, Miami, 1976—. Patentee in field. With USAF, 1942-45, CBI. Home: Miami, Fla. Died Sept. 2004.

EIFFERT, SYLVIA ANN, elementary educator; b. Eugene, Oreg., Sept. 1, 1940; d. Donald Statton and Helen Mae (Kester) Hendrickson; m. Rex Lee Eiffert, Apr. 3, 1969; children: Matthew, Heather. BA, Westmont Coll., 1963. Elem. tchr. Sch. Dist. 48, Beaverton, Oreg., 1963-68, Dept. Def., Böblingen, Fed. Republic of Germany, 1968-73, Sigonella, Sicily, Italy, 1973-74, Ukiah (Calif.) Unified Sch. Dist., from 1976. Coord. ind. study Ukiah Unified Sch. Dist. Mem. Ukiah Valley Soccer League; elder Presbyn. Ch. Mem. NEA, Calif. Tchrs. Assn., Calif. State PTA, Ukiah PTA, Ukiah Tchrs. Union, Delta Kappa Gamma (rec. sec., pres.). Republican. Home: Ukiah, Calif. Died Apr. 28, 2005.

EIGEL, JAMES ANTHONY, environmental engineer; b. St. Louis, Mar. 1, 1939; s. Edwin George and Catherine Margaret (Rohan) E.; m. Carolyn Margaret Sudheimer, June 10, 1972 (div. 1990); 1 child, Christine. BS, St. Louis U., 1961, postgrad. Ordained to ministry Episcopal Missionary Ch., 1998. Rsch. chemist Falstaff Brewing Corp., St. Louis, 1965-67; rsch. chemist water divsn. City of St. Louis, 1967-71; rsch. chemist Continental Telephone, Hickory, N.C., 1971-75; mgr. main analysis labs. Hoechst Celanese, Spartanburg, S.C., 1975-85; dir. pretreatment/lab. svcs. Macon-Bibb County (Ga.) Water Authority, 1985-89; mgr. tech. svcs. Pima County Wastewater Mgmt., Tucson, Ariz., from 1989. Contbr. articles to profl. jours. Mem. Am. Chem. Soc., Am. Water Works Assn., Water Environ. Fedn., Lions (pres. 1988-89). Mem. Am. Anglican Ch. Achievements include patent for electrical insulation protector. Home: Tucson, Ariz. Died 2005.

EILERS, BRUCE DEAN, music educator; b. Cedar Falls, Iowa, June 7, 1945; s. Charles Wesley Eilers and Barbara Jane Schryver; m. Brenda Joyce Sindt, Dec. 23, 1967; children: Aaron Michael, Rebecca Dianne. BA, U. No. Iowa, 1967, MA, 1974. Cert. permanent profl. tchg. cert. Iowa. Orch. dir. Roosevelt Jr. HS, Cedar Rapids, Iowa, 1967—68, 1970—73, Kennedy HS and Harding Jr. HS, Cedar Rapids, Iowa, 1973—80; pres. Taylor Music Co., Cedar Rapids, Iowa, 1980—85; salesman Cedar Custom Computing, Cedar Rapids, Iowa, 1985—87; orch. dir. Jefferson HS, Cedar Rapids, Iowa, 1987—90, West HS, Waterloo, Iowa, from 1990. Sec., treas. Iowa String Tchrs. Assn., 1990—94; quality edn. com. Waterloo Com. Schs., Waterloo, Iowa, 1991—96; jour. editor Iowa String Tchrs. Assn., 1994—97; 50th all-state music com. Iowa Music Educators Assn., 1994—96; all-state orch. chair Iowa HS Music Assn., 1997—2003; prin. selection com. West HS, Waterloo Comm. Schs., 1997, 99; edn. com. Waterloo Cedar Falls (Iowa) Symphony, 1998—2000. Sgt. U.S. Army, 1968—70, Vietnam. Mem.: Nat. Sch. Orch. Assn., Am. String Tchrs. Assn., NEA, Iowans for Arts Edn. Democrat. Evangelical Lutheran. Avocations: golf, tennis, fishing, bicycling. Home: Waterloo, Iowa. Died June 12, 2005.

EILTS, HERMANN FREDERICK, international relations educator, retired ambassador; b. Weissenfels Saale, Germany, Mar. 23, 1922; came to U.S., 1926; naturalized, 1930; s. Friedrich Alex and Meta Dorothea (Pruser) E.; m. Helen Josephine Brew, June 12, 1948; children: Conrad Marshall, Frederick Lowell. BA, Ursinus Coll., 1942, LLD, 1960; MA, Johns Hopkins U., 1947; postgrad., U. Pa., 1950-51. Joined Fgn. Svc., Dept. State, 1947; 3d sec., vice consul Tehran, Iran, 1947-48, Jidda, Saudi Arabia, 1948-50; consul prin. officer Aden, 1951-53; 2d sec., consul Taiz, Yemen, 1951-53; 2d sec., consul, chief polit. sect. Bahdad, Iraq, 1954-56; officer in charge Baghdad Pact affairs US Dept. State, Washington, 1957-59, officer in charge Arabian Peninsula affairs, 1959-61; 1st sec. Am. Embassy, London, 1962-64, counsellor, dep. chief of mission Tripoli, Libya, 1964-65; US amb. to Saudi Arabia US Dept. State, 1965-70; dep. commandant for internat. affairs, diplomatic adviser U.S. Army War Coll., Carlisle Barracks, Pa., 1970-73; US amb. to Egypt US Dept. State, Cairo, 1973-79; Disting. Univ. prof. internat. rels. Boston U., 1979—2006, chmn. dept. polit. sci., 1982-87, chmn. dept. internat. rels., 1989-93, acad. coord., mil. edn. div., 1990-93, prof. emeritus, 1993—2006. 1st lt. M.I., AUS, 1942-45. Decorated Purple Heart, Bronze Star; recipient Arthur Flemming award, 1958, Disting. Civilian Honor award Dept. Army, 1973, Disting. Honor award Dept. State, 1979, Joseph C. Wilson award, 1979, Disting. Alumnus award Johns Hopkins U., 1980, All-Pa. Coll. Alumni Assn. citation, 1987, Am. Foreign Svc. cup Dept. State, 1992; named Disting. Fellow U.S. Army War Coll., 1991. Fellow Royal Geog. Soc., Royal Asiatic Soc.; mem. Am. Fgn. Svc. Assn., Middle East Inst., Royal Cen. Asian Soc. Mem. Evang. Reformed Ch. Died Oct. 12, 2006.

EISELE, JOHN EVANS, pediatrician; b. Madison, Wis., July 3, 1940; s. Edward Joseph and Dorothy Athalone (Evans) E. BS, U. Wis., Madison, 1962, MD, 1965. Diplomate Am. Bd. Pediatrics. Intern Children's Hosp., Oakland, Calif., 1965-66; resident in pediatrics U. Wis. Hosp., Madison, 1966-68; dir. phys. medicine U.S. Army Hosp., Denver, 1968-70; dir. rehab. Sharp Hosp., San Diego, 1970-78; dir. pediatric rehab. Johns Hopkins U., Balt., 1978-86, East Carolina U., Greenville, N.C., 1986-95. Assoc. prof. East Carolina U., 1986-95, emeritus, 1995—; bd. dirs. Carolina Physicians Health Plan, Raleigh, N.C. Contbr. sci. articles to profl. jours. Maj. U.S. Army, 1968-70. Grantee NIH, 1973-86. Fellow Am. Acad. Pediatrics. Home: Stoughton, Wis. Died Dec. 3, 2004.

EISENHUT, DONNA PARSON, community library manager; b. Valley, Nebr., Aug. 28, 1920; d. Reuben Walter and Alice Victoria (Wicklund) Parson; m. Dale Duane Eisenhut, June 30, 1946 (dec. Sept. 1981); children: Alice Marie, Donna Lynn, Jani Sue. AA, Wayne (Nebr.) State Coll., 1941; student, Creighton U., summer 1943, Sacramento State Coll., summer 1959, 60. Emergency Calif. teaching credential, Nebr. teaching credential. Pub. sch. tchr. Pershing Sch., Omaha, 1941-44; substitute sch. tchr. Avalon (Calif.) Pub. Schs., 1950-80; libr. asst. L.A. County Pub. Libr., Avalon, 1967-80, mgr. L.A. County Cmty. Libr., from 1980. Libr. chmn. Santa Catalina Woman's Club, Avalon, 1980—. Sunday sch. supt. Avalon Cmty. Ch., Avalon, 1952-71; leader Girl Scouts Am., Avalon, 1956-69, Avalon coord., 1969-80; grand marshal 4th of July Parade City of Avalon, 1989. Mem. PTA (hon. life). Avocations: reading, cooking, travel, hiking. Home: Avalon, Calif. Died May 16, 2005.

EKIZIAN, HARRY, civil engineering consultant; b. N.Y.C., July 31, 1921; s. Harry and Nectar (Tatsian) E.; m. Justine Markarian, July 14, 1946 (dec.); 1 child, Michelle Lynne. BSCE, CCNY, 1942. Registered profl. engr., N.Y. Field engr. Johnson-Perini Corp., Chambersburg, Pa., 1942; rsch. engr. Nat. Com. for Aeronautics, Langley Field, Va., 1945-46; civil engr. Dept. Pub. Works, Westchester County, N.Y., 1946; assoc. TAMS Cons., Inc., N.Y.C., 1947-90; cons. engr. Mamaroneck, N.Y., from 1991. Contbr. articles to profl. jours. Pres. Prince Willow Civic Assn., Mamaroneck; co-chmn. tech. com. for constrn. St. Vartan Cathedral, N.Y.C., 1962-64; active various civic and ch. orgns. With U.S. Army, 1943-45. Fellow ASCE; mem. Tau Beta Pi. Achievements include design of ports, transport systems for industerial facilities. Died Jan. 22, 2004.

ELDRIDGE, JOHN CHARLES, medical educator; b. Louisville, Sept. 13, 1955; s. Charles Douglas and Mary (O'Mara) E.; m. Anne Claire Gutman, May 26, 1979; children: Kathryn Elizabeth, Marian Rebecca. BA in Biology, U. Louisville, 1976, MD, 1980. Diplomate Am. Bd. Pediatrics, Am. Bd. Orthopaedics. Intern U. Louisville, 1980-81; resident in pediatrics, 1982-84; resident in surgery, 1984-85; resident in orthopaedics, 1985-89; pvt. practice surgeon Louisville, 1981-82; pvt. practice; fellow in pediatric orthopaedics Hosp. for Sick Children, Toronto, Ont., Can., 1989-90; asst. prof. Sch. of Medicine Emory U., Atlanta, from 1991. Contbr. articles to profl. jours. Fellow Am. Acad. Pediatrics; mem. AMA, Ga. Med. Assn., Med. Assn. of Atlanta, Kelly Soc., Am. Acad. Orthopaedic Surgeons, Pediatric Orthopaedic Soc. of N.Am. Roman Catholic. Home: Atlanta, Ga. Died Apr. 20, 2004.

ELGIN, KATHLEEN, illustrator, writer; b. Trenton, N.J., Jan. 13, 1923; d. Charles Porter and Mary (Poore) E. Student, Dayton Art Inst., 1943. Illustrated 50 children's books; writer, illustrator of 20 children's books, 1950-70; one man shows in N.Y., 1976, Key West, 1985-93. Home: Key West, Fla. Died Jan. 25, 2005.

ELIAS, RAMON JAN, artist, designer; b. North Royalton, Ohio, May 16, 1925; s. Vincent Michael and Catherine Cecelia (Pitonak) E.; m. Margery Halsted Moore, June 6, 1953; children: Eleanor Anne, Ramon J., Jr., Margaret. AB, Brown U., 1947. Analyst Am. Steel & Wire, Cleve., 1948-49; dir., p.r.o. Cleveland Play House, Ohio, 1949-55; designer Holzheimers Int., Cleve., 1955-62; artist, designer Dezign House, Cleve. Numerous pvt. art and design commns.; mem. bd. govs. AID, Cleve., 1958-62. Author: collected short plays, 1970; play Male Chauvanist, 1980, Land Where My Father Died, 1985; artist: one man show of paintings and wallpaper designs Ashtabula Fine Arts Ctr., 1989, twenty-five wallpaper designs in permanent collection of the Biblioteque Forney Mus., Paris; dir: Am. premiere Andre Previn-Johnny Mercer-J.B. Priestly's The Good Companions, 1987; stage design I'm Not Rappaport Ashtabula Fine Arts Ctr., 1988; designer numerous condominium and homes. V.p.Cleve. Play House, 1983, trustee Cleve. play house, 1982--. Lt. U.S. Navy, 1943-47. Mem. Hermit Club. Republican. Roman Catholic. Home: Jefferson, Ohio. Died Mar. 12, 2004.

ELIAS, VICTOR, consulting civil engineer; b. Belgrade, Yugoslavia, May 16, 1937; s. Maurice and Claire (Maissa) E.; m. Beth Geri, Oct. 22, 1966; children: Andrew, Kenneth. BCE, Polytechnic U., Bklyn., 1959, MCE, 1995. Registered profl. engr., Md., N.J., Mass. Staff engr. Woodward Clyde Cons., N.J., 1960-64; supr. soil engr. Storch Engrs., Boston, 1964-70, Green & Assocs., Balt., 1970-74; exec. v.p. Reinforced Earth Co., McLean, Va., 1974-85; pres. V. Elias & Assocs., P.A., Bethesda, Md., from 1985. Contbg. author: Foundation Engineering Handbook, Chpt. 26,. 1991; contbr. articles to profl. jours. Mem. ASCE, NSPE, Am. Arbitration Assn. Died Mar. 29, 2004.

ELKINS, JAMES ANDERSON, JR., banker; b. Galveston, Tex., Mar. 24, 1919; s. James Anderson and Isabel (Mitchell) E.; m. Margaret Wiess, Nov. 24, 1945; children— Elise, James Anderson III, Leslie K. BA, Princeton U., 1941. With First City Nat. Bank, Houston, 1941—88, v.p., 1946-50, pres. then chmn. bd., 1950-82; dir. First City Bancorp., Houston, 1982-88. Bd. dirs. Central Houston Inc. Bd. dirs. Houston Grand Opera; trustee Tex. Children's Hosp., Tex. Med. Ctr., 1991; chmn. bd. trustees Baylor Coll. Medicine; trustee Menil Found.; mem. vestry Christ Ch. Cathedral. Episcopalian. Died Feb. 21, 2006.

ELLEGARD, ROY WHITNEY, real estate appraiser; b. Hartford, Conn., Sept. 16, 1957; s. Roy Taylor and Jeanette (Whitney) E.; m. Bernadette O'Brien, May 22, 1999. BA in Econs., U. Richmond, 1980. Appraiser Stone & Webster, Inc., N.Y.C., 1980-82; cons. Arthur Andersen & Co., N.Y.C., 1983; sr. cons. Arthur D. Little, Inc., Metro Park, NJ, 1984-87; nat. dir. machinery and equipment valuation advisors Ernst & Young LLP, N.Y.C., 1987-98; mng. dir. corp. value consulting Pricewater House Coopers LLP, 1998—2001, Standard & Poor's, 2001—03; ptnr. Ernst & Young, N.Y.C., NY. Mem. Am. Soc. Appraisers (sr., pres. Princeton chpt. 1992-93, 98-99), Kappa Alpha Alumni Assn. (treas. Princeton chpt. 1990-92), Princeton Club N.Y. Republican. Episcopalian. Home: Kent, Conn. Died 2006.

ELLIN, DOROTHY STOTTER, florist, sculptor; b. Chgo., July 26, 1917; d. Max and Lena Rose (Wolfson) Stotter; m. Frederick I. Ellin, Oct. 5, 1940; children: Leon Roland, Marlene B. Student, Wilson Jr. Coll., Chgo., 1936-37, Art Inst. of Chgo. Sec. Bus. Offices Comptometer, Chgo., 1938-41; salesperson Assn. Am. Artists, Chgo. and Fla., 1942-44; florist Designer Flower Shops and Stores, Chgo., 1963-95; wedding cons. Fla., 1965-77; docent Ringling Mus. of Art, Sarasota, Fla., 1975-95. Founding pres., tchr. Art Guild, Skokie, Ill., 1960s; wedding cons., Chgo. Prin. works include Bronze Sculpture In the Beginning, 1964, Bright Future, 1970, Exercise Class, 1985. Bd. dirs. LWV, Skokie, 1960s; chair, organizer various art fairs, 1960s and 70s. Recipient Docent awards Ringling Mus., 1975-95, Sculpture award Longboat Key Art Ctr., 1990. Democrat. Avocations: music, art, design, photography, floral design. Home: Longboat Key, Fla. Died Apr. 7, 2005.

ELLIOTT, GORDON JEFFERSON, retired English language educator; b. Aberdeen, Wash., Nov. 13, 1928; s. Harry Cecil and Helga May (Kennedy) E.; m. Suzanne Tsugiko Urakawa, Apr. 2, 1957; children: Meiko Ann, Kenneth Gordon, Nancy Lee, Matthew Kennedy. AA, Grays Harbor Coll., 1948; BA, U. Wash., 1950; Cert. Russian, Army Lang. Sch., Monterey, Calif., 1952; MA, U. Hawaii, 1968. Lifetime credential, Calif. Community Coll. System. English prof. Buddhist U., Ministry of Cults, The Asia Found., Phnom Penh, Cambodia, 1956-62; English instr. U. Hawaii, Honolulu, 1962-68; dir., orientation English Coll. Petroleum and Minerals, Dhahran, Saudi Arabia, 1968-70; asst. prof., English/linguistics U. Guam, Mangilao, 1970-76; tchr., French/English Medford (Oreg.) Mid High Sch., 1976-77; instr., English Merced (Calif.) Coll., 1977-98, ret., 1998. Cons. on Buddhist Edn., The Asia Found., San Francisco, Phnom Penh, Cambodia, 1956-62; cons. on English Edn., Hawaii State Adult Edn. Dept., Honolulu, 1966-68; conf. on English Edn. in Middle East, Am. U., Cairo, Egypt, 1969; vis. prof. of English, Shandong Tchrs. U., Jinan, China, 1984-85. Co-author: (textbooks, bilingual Cambodian-English) English Composition, 1962, Writing English, 1966, (test) Standard English Recognition Test, 1976; contbr. articles to profl. jours. Mem. Statue of Liberty Centennial Commn., Washington, 1980-86, Heritage Found., Washington, Rep. Presdl. Task Force Founders' Wall, 2001, Lincoln Inst., Am. Near East Refugee Aid, Washington, Rep. Presdl. Task Force, 2001. Sgt. U.S. Army Security Agy., Kyoto, Japan, 1951-55. Tchr. Fellowship, U. Mich., Ann Arbor, 1956; recipient summer seminar stipend, Nat. Endowment For Humanities, U. Wash., Seattle, 1976, travel grants, People's Rep. of China, Beijing, 1984-85. Mem. NRA, Collegiate Press (editorial adv. bd.), Merced Coll. Found., Am. Assn. Woodturners, Elks. Republican. Avocations: swimming, woodturning, classical guitar, stamp/coin collecting, travel. Home: Merced, Calif. Died May 6, 2004.

ELLIOTT, JAMES ROBERT, retired federal judge; b. Gainesville, Ga., Jan. 1, 1910; s. Thomas M. and Mamie Lucille (Glenn) E.; m. Brownie C. Buck, Aug. 3, 1949; children: Susan G., James Robert. Ph.B., Emory U., 1930, LL.B., 1934. Bar: Ga. 1934. Pvt. practice law, Columbus, Ga., 1934-62; judge U.S. Dist. Ct. (mid. dist.) Ga., Columbus, 1962—2000. Mem. Ga. Ho. of Reps., 1937-43, 47-49; Democratic nat. committeeman, 1948-56 Served as lt. USNR, 1943-46, PTO. Mem. Ga. Bar Assn., Kiwanis, Lambda Chi Alpha, Phi Delta Phi, Omicron Delta Kappa. Home: Columbus, Ga. Died June 27, 2006.

ELLIOTT, MARVIN MOORE, personal computer consultant; b. Louisville, Oct. 2, 1934; s. Marvin Moore and Ella Dean (Marshall) E.; m. Carol Elaine Coombs, Dec. 31, 1954; children: Dana Dean Braun, Brian Moore. BA, U. Louisville, 1956. Tchr. Louisville Pub. Schs., 1956-60; master Louisville Country Day Sch., 1960-62; systems engr. IBM Corp., Louisville and Cin., 1962-91; cons., developer Marv Elliott--The Computer Counselor, Inc., Loveland, Ohio, from 1991. Cons., devel. IBM, Cin., 1991—, The Kroger Co., Cin., 1992—. With USMC, 1953. Mem. Masons (master, 32 deg.), Shriners. Republican. Methodist. Avocations: history, theater, vocal music. Home: Loveland, Ohio. Died Apr. 21, 2005.

ELLIOTT, RONALD ALLEN, human resources and financial executive; b. Beatrice, Nebr., Oct. 21, 1945; s. Donald Roy and Catherine Redner (McDonald) E.; m. Joanne Kay Lamp, Dec. 23, 1968; children: Gregory Mark, Jill Catherine. BA, Creighton U., 1967, MBA, 1974. Dir. human resources, fin. Wilson & Co., Engrs. & Architects,

Salina, Kans., 1980-90; dir. human resources and fin. Continental Analytical Svcs., Salina, from 1990. Generalist, mem. functional standards com. Profl. Accreditation Inst., 1989—. Chmn. Salina Human Rels. Commn., 1988-89, Salina Child Care Assn., 1988-89; bd. dirs. Salina Libr., 1990—. Mem. Soc. for Human Resource Mgmt. (pres. Salina chpt., Kans. coun., conf. treas. 1990—), Fin. Mgrs. Group, Domestic Violence Assn. Cen. Kans., Toastmasters (pres. Salinas 1985-86). Avocations: collecting clocks, sailing, automotive crossing. Home: Lincoln, Nebr. Died Nov. 28, 2004.

ELLIOTT, THOMAS JOSEPH, English language educator; b. Boston, Jan. 25, 1941; s. Thomas Joseph and Anne Teresa (Regan) E.; m. Eugenia Marie Coleman, June 18, 1966; 1 child, Christine. AB, Boston Coll., 1963, MA, 1967; PhD, U. Mich., 1970. High sch. English and Latin instr. St. Dominic Savio Coll. Prep. Sch., East Boston, 1963-67; teaching fellow U. Mich., Ann Arbor, 1968-69; asst. prof. to prof. Calif. State Poly. U., Pomona, from 1970. Vis. scholar U. Kent, Canterbury, England, 1984. Translator: A Medieval Bestiary, 1971; contbr. articles to profl. jours. Fellow Southeastern Ctr. for Medieval and Renaissance Studies, Duke U., 1976. Mem. MLA, New Chancer Soc. Democrat. Roman Catholic. Home: Claremont, Calif. Died June 17, 2005.

ELLIS, HAROLD EUGENE, music conductor, songwriter, actor, singer, musician; b. St. Louis, July 5, 1953; AA in Music, L.A. City Coll., 1988. Music pub. ASCAP, Hollywood, Calif., from 1980. Ind. record producer; music arranger specializing in percussion ensemble and string orch. Am. Soc. Music Arrangers, Hollywood. Mem. ASCAP, AFTRA, SAG, NARAS, NAS, Am. Fedn. Music, Am. Soc. Music Arrangers. Democrat. Presbyterian. Avocation: harmonica, kazoo, guitar, women's profl. boxing. Died Feb. 3, 2004.

ELLISON, ROBERT GORDON, thoracic cardiac surgeon; b. Millen, Ga., Dec. 4, 1916; m. Lois Taylor, Feb. 11, 1945; children— Robert Gordon, Gregory, Mark, James, John. AB, Vanderbilt U., 1939; MD, Med. Coll. Ga., 1943. Diplomate Am. Bd. Surgery, Am. Bd. Thoracic Surgery (bd. dirs. 1971-81, chmn. 1979-81). Intern, resident in gen. surgery Univ. Hosp., Augusta, Ga., 1943-46, resident in thoracic-cardiac surgery, 1947-48, resident in pathology, 1949; resident in cardiopulmonary physiology Bellevue Hosp., N.Y.C., 1948; mem. faculty Med. Coll. Ga., 1947-87, chief sect. thoracic surgery, 1955-87, prof. surgery, 1959-87, Leon Henri Charbonnier prof. surgery, 1973-87, Leon Henri Charbonnier prof. surgery emeritus, 1987—2006; chief gen. thoracic surgery VA Med. Ctr., 1987-91. Mem. surgery study sect. NIH, 1969-73; com. cardiovascular disease Ga. Regional Med. Program, 1971-74; cons. area hosps. Author 1 book, chpts. and, papers in field.; Editorial bd.: Annals Thoracic Surgery, 1965-79. Fellow A.C.S. (chmn. local credentials com. 1968-73, gov. 1973-78), Am. Coll. Chest Physicians, Am. Coll. Cardiology (past gov.), Southeastern Surg. Congress; mem. Am. Thoracic Soc. (councilor 1963-66), Soc. Thoracic Surgeons (pres. 1971, historian 1973-92), Thoracic Surgery Dirs. Assn. (exec. com., chmn. in-tng. exam. com. 1976-78), AMA, Soc. Univ. Surgeons, Am. Assn. Thoracic Surgery, Am. Surg. Assn., Am. Physiol. Soc., Am. Soc. Artificial Internal Organs, So. Thoracic Surg. Assn. (pres. 1963-64), So. Surg. Assn., So. Soc. Clin. Investigation, Ga. Heart Assn. (pres. 1974-75), Ga. Thoracic Soc. (pres. 1965-66), Ga. Tb Assn. (pres. 1959), Med. Assn. Ga., Ga. Surg. Soc. (pres. elect 1987, pres. 1988), Richmond County Med. Soc. (v.p. 1968), Richmond County Heart Assn. (trustee 1970—), Augusta Area Tb Assn. (pres. 1954), Augusta Coll. Alumni Assn. (trustee 1969-73, Most Outstanding Alumnus award 1962), Alpha Omega Alpha, Sigma Psi. Methodist. Home: Evans, Ga. Died Jan. 8, 2006.

ELMQUIST, JOHN GUNNAR, plastic and general surgeon; b. Redlands, Calif., July 24, 1936; s. Frans Gunnar and Dagmar Caroline E.; m. Carol Jean Grindahl, Aug. 11, 1962 (div. Apr. 1980); children: Karin, Jon, Thomas; m. Regina Barbara Gatto Allen, Dec. 27, 1992 (div. Oct. 2001). AA, North Park U., 1956; BA, Northwestern U., 1958, MD, 1961. Diplomate Am. Bd. Surgery, Am. Bd. Plastic Surgery. Pvt. practice, W. Palm Beach, Fla., 1971-96; ret., 1996. Capt. U.S. Army, 1966-68. Fellow ACS; mem. Am. Soc. Plastic Surgeons, Am. Soc. Aesthetic Plastic Surgery. Republican. Lutheran. Avocations: travel, golf. Home: Wellington, Fla. Died July 27, 2004.

EL-ZAWAHRY, M.A. MONEIM, retired epidemiologist; b. Hehia, Sharkyia, Egypt, Jan. 17, 1926; s. M. A. El-Karim and Sany'ia M. (Aly) El-Zawahry; m. Grace Ellen Ransdell, Dec. 31, 1956 (dec.); 1 child, A. Sabry. MD, Cairo U., 1952; MPH, U. NC, 1957; MPH, PhD, Johns Hopkins U., 1959. Resident in internal medicine Kings Hosp., Cairo, 1952-53; chief med. officer Rural Tng., Demonstration and Rsch. Ctrs., Cairo, 1953—57; pediatrician cardiac clinic Johns Hopkins Hosp., Balt., 1957-59; demonstrator, lectr., assoc. prof., chair prof. epidemiology High Inst. Pub. Health, Alexandria (Egypt) U., 1957-73; sec., med. rsch. coun. Ministry of Rsch., Egypt, 1961—68; WHO prof. Inst. Medicine, Rangoon, Burma, 1968-75; WHO reg. advisor SEARO, New Delhi, 1975-79; WHO rep. Jakarta, Indonesia, 1979—86; WHO sr. health adviser to UNICEF Hdqs., NYC, 1988; sec. WHO/UNICEF Joint Com. Health Policy, Geneva; ret. Cons. primary health care UN Devel. program and WHO, 1986—87; WHO and UN cons. in Yemen, Egypt, Morocco, Ethiopia, Switzerland, U.S., India, Indonesia, Burma, Thailand, Nepal, Saudi Arabia, and Mongolia, 1987—96; cons. to voluntary health projects, Chillicothe, Ohio, from 1986; guest lectr. internat. health Coll. Medicine and Pub. Health & Children Hosp. Ohio State U., Columbus, from 1987; lectr. HIV/AIDS Ohio U., Chillicothe, from 2001; WHO cons. on HIV/AIDS EMRO, 1990—93; spokesperson Child Immunization Coalition, 1997—2002; mem., chair numerous adv. and rsch. coms. WHO & several countries; keynote spkr. on HIV/AIDS in Africa Hospice Orgn., Zimbabwe, 2004. Co-editor: Egyptian Jour. Pub. Health, 1960—68, author 68 publ.; contbr. over 146 articles sci. reports and WHO documents, 25 WHO publ. Panelist Global Health Forum Ohio State U., Columbus, from 2001; chmn. Polio-Plus and World Cmty. Svcs. Com., Rotary, Chillicothe, 1986—2001; cons. AIDS Task Force, Ross County, Ohio, from 1995; mem. bd. dirs. Family Healthcare, Inc., Chillicothe, Ohio, from 1999. Recipient honors and awards, U.S. Internat. Coop. Adminstrn., Johns Hopkins U., Rockefeller Found., Gold Caduceus pin, Burma Med. Assn., Govt. Indonesia, WHO, U. N.C., Rotary, APHA, Govt. Saudi Arabia, Egyptian Med. Syndicate, Family Healthcare, Inc., others. Mem.: APHA (hon. life, awards), Mass. Med. Soc., Burma Med. Assn. (hon., life), Johns Hopkins Med. and Surg. Assn. (Paul Harris fellow 1986—2004, hon. life), Egyptian Family Planning Assn., Egyptian Assn. Tb and Chest Diseases, Egyptian Pub. Health Assn. (governing coun. 1960—68), Tropical Medicine Soc., Egyptian Med. Syndicate (awards), W.H.O. Network for Future Studies, Johns Hopkins U. Alumni Assn. (life), U. N.C. Alumni Assn. (life), Rotary Internat., Chillicothe Rotary. Avocations: classical music, nature photography, fishing. Home: Chillicothe, Ohio. Died July 30, 2005.

EMERSON, DOROTHY VIRGINIA, retired medical and surgical nurse, administrator; b. Cumberland, Md., Apr. 17, 1923; d. Albert Herman and Lillian Marie (Rosser) Couter; m. Don Allen Emerson, Sept. 21, 1945; 1 child, Dian Margaret Emerson Williams. Diploma, Allegany Hosp. Sch. Nursing, Cumberland, 1945; student, Frostburg (Md.) State U. RN. Exec. dir. Allegany County League for Crippled Children, Cumberland, 1971-86; instr. med.-surg. nursing Meml. Hosp., Cumberland; nursing supr., head nurse med.-surg. Allegany Hosp. (now Sacred Heart Hosp.), Cumberland. Cadet nurse, 1944-45. Recipient numerous awards. Mem. ANA, Md. State Nurses Assn. (pres. Dist. 1 1962-64). Home: Cumberland, Md. Died July 29, 2004.

EMERY, HENRY ALFRED, petroleum engineer; b. Northfield, NH, Feb. 9, 1926; s. Henry A. and Ruth (Trask) Emery; children: Trask, Timothy, Ptarmigan. BA, U. Maine, 1950; diploma in, Colo. Sch. Mines, 1956; MBA, U. Denver, 1966. Registered profl. engr., Colo. With Mobil Pipeline Co., 1950-53, Portland Montreal Pipeline Co., 1956-59; maintenance design engr., planning supr., engring. supt., project mgr. Pub. Svc. Co., Colo., 1959-72; pres. Computer Graphics Co., Denver, 1972-78; divsn. mgr. Kellogg Corp., Littleton, Colo., 1978-82; chmn., CEO Emery DataGraphic Inc., Englewood, Colo., 1982-86; pres. Emery DataGraphic divsn. Harris-McBurney Co., 1987-93, Emery & Assoc., Inc., Greenwood Village, Denver, from 1993. Mem.: Am. Water Works Assn., Urgan Regional Info. Sys. Assn., Geospatial Info. Tech. Assn. (past pres.), Tau Beta Pi. Democrat. Died Jan. 31, 2005.

EMERY, SUSAN WOODRUFF, investment trust official; b. Salt Lake City, Jan. 13, 1923; d. Russell Kimball and Margaret Anglin (McIntyre) Woodruff; m. Terrence John Osborn, May 30, 1959 (div. Dec. 1963); 1 child, John Russell; m. Stephen Earnest Emery, Apr. 7, 1972 (dec. Apr. 1977). BA, U. Utah, 1944. Cashier Merrill Lynch, Pierce, Fenner & Beane, Portland, 1946-51; personal sec. to parents, Portland, 1951-71; co-trustee R.K.-M.M. Woodruff Trust, Portland, from 1971. Vol. driver ARC, Portland, 35 yrs.; mem. Rep. Nat. Com., 1944—, Oreg. Rep. Com., 1944—. Mem. AAUW (life), U. Utah Alumni Assn. (life), Univ. Club, Alpha Delta Pi. Episcopalian. Avocations: travel, theater, concerts, golf. Died Nov. 29, 2004.

EMISON, JAMES WADE, petroleum company executive; b. Indpls., Sept. 21, 1930; s. John Rabb and Catherine (Stanbrough) E.; divorced; children: Catherine Emison Stoick, Elizabeth Ann, Thomas Weston, William Ash; m. Jane Bale Larson, Feb. 14, 1983. BA, DePauw U., 1952, HHD, 2003. Gen. mgr. C&C Oil Co. Inc., Huntington, Ind., 1954-59; pres. May Petroleum Co. Inc., Lima, Ohio, 1959-61; sales mgr. Oskey Bros. Petroleum Corp., St. Paul, 1961—65; v.p. mktg. Nfld. Refining Co. Ltd., N.Y.C., 1965—69; v.p. Oskey Gasoline & Oil Co., Mpls., 1969-76; chmn., CEO Western Petroleum Co. (successor to Oskey Gasoline & Oil Co.), Mpls., 1977—2005. Pres. Western Internat. Trading Co., Eden Prairie, Minn., 1981—2005; bd. dirs. Hydrocarbon Trading & Transport Co., Houston, Community Bank Group, Inc., Eden Prairie, Minn.; ptnr. Bellwood Ptnrs., RBP Realty and RBP Realty II. Trustee DePauw U., Greencastle, Ind., from 1981, former vice chair bd. trustees, co-founder Ctr. for Mgmt. and Entrepreneurship; trustee USMC Marine Corps U. Found. Inc., Quantico, Va., 1984—95; past chair bd. trustees Phi Kappa Psi Endowment Found. Capt. USMC, 1952—54. Recipient Old Gold Goblet, DePauw U., 1987. Mem.: Nat. Assn. Scholars, Nat. Petroleum Coun., Assn. Governing Bds. of Univs. and Colls. (bd. dirs. 1993), Marine Corps Assn. (bd. govs. 1981—84), Minn. Petroleum Assn., Am. Petroleum Inst., Ind. Acad. (hon.), The Continental Soc. Sons of the Indian Wars, Nat. Soc. Sons of Am. Revolution, DePauw U. Alumni Assn. (bd. dirs. 1975—81, pres. 1979—81), Army and Navy Club (Washington), Woodhill Country Club, Spring Hill Country Club, Tralee Golf Club, Ballybunion Golf Club, Monterey Peninsula Country Club, The Minikahda Club, Sagamore of the Wabash, Am. Legion. Republican. Avocations: golf, fly fishing. Home: Wayzata, Minn. Died Dec. 28, 2005.

EMMA, JOAN EMILY, English language and humanities educator; b. Chillicothe, Mo., July 9, 1921; d. Karl and Queen (Bishko) Hirsh; m. Ronald David Emma, Dec. 27, 1948 (dec. Sept. 1988); 1 child, Tania Elizabeth Emma Webb. BA, U. Mo., 1942; MA, U. Mich., 1943. Book reviewer Kansas City (Mo.) Star, 1941-42; instr. English Mt. Holyoke Coll., South Hadley, Mass., 1947-48; journalist for area newspapers Duke U. Bur. Pub. Rels., Durham, N.C., 1952-55; editor tng. manuals U.S. Army Transp. Sch., Ft. Eustis, Va., 1956-58; asst. prof. English Quinnipiac Coll., Hamden, Conn., 1965-66; assoc. prof. English Windham Coll, Putney, Vt., 1967-79; assoc. prof. English and humanities Clarion U. of Pa., 1980-82; adj. prof. English Friends World Coll., Huntington, N.Y., 1989; freelance writer, devel. editor, from 1991. Presenter in field. Contbr. article, rev. to profl. publs. Mem. Oxfam Am., Boston; contbg. mem. Dem. Nat. Com., Dem. Congl. Campaign Com., Washington, 1992—; mem. steering com. Re-elect Pres. Clinton, 1995—. Mem. ACLU, Amnesty Internat., AAUW, Huntington Peace Soc. Democrat. Jewish. Avocation: concerts. Home: East Setauket, NY. Died Apr. 8, 2005.

ENARSON, HAROLD LEROY, retired academic administrator; b. Villisca, Iowa, May 24, 1919; s. John and Hulda (Thorson) E.; m. Audrey Pitt., June 7, 1942; children: Merlyn Pitt Prentice, Elaine, Lisa. BA, U. N.Mex., 1940, L.H.D., 1981; MA, Stanford U., 1946; PhD, Am. U., 1951; L.H.D., Kent State U., 1972, U. Detroit, 1975, Ohio State U., 1981; D.P.S., Bethany Coll., 1975; LL.D., Miami U., Oxford, Ohio, 1978, U. Akron, 1981, Central State U., 1981; Dr. Pub. Service (hon.), U. W. Fla., 1986; LLD (hon.), SUNY, 1987; LHD (hon.), Cleve. State U., 1990, U. Nebr., CCNY, 1993; HHD, No. Mich. U., 1993. Teaching asst., research asst. Stanford U., 1940-41, asst. prof., 1949-50; examiner Bur. Budget, Washington, 1942-43, 46-49; asst. prof. Whittier Coll., 1949; exec. sec. Steel Industry Bd., summer 1949; cons. Nat. Security Resources Bd., summer 1950; spl. asst. White House, Washington, 1950-52; pub. mem. WSB, 1952-53; asst. dir. commerce City Phila., 1953; exec. sec. mayor Phila., 1954; exec. dir. Western Interstate Commn. Higher Edn., 1954-60, sr. advisor, 1981-99; adminstrv. v.p. U. N.Mex., 1960-61, acad. v.p., 1961-66, past project dir.; Internships in Latin Am.; pres. Cleve. State U., 1966-72, Ohio State U., Columbus, 1972-81, pres. emeritus, 1981—2006; Carl Hatch chair pub. adminstrn. U. N.Mex., 1982-83; Regents' prof. U. Calif., San Francisco, spring 1984. Carnegie Corp. adminstrs. fellowship, 1958; mem. Nat. Dental Research Council, 1958-62, surgeon gen.'s cons. group on med. manpower, 1960; cons. Ford Found., Egypt, 1960, C.Am., 1961-63, AID, 1965; dir. edn. svcs. Office Human Resources and Social Devel., 1963-64; nat. adv. health coun. USPHS, 1964-68, task force on reorgn., 1967, Nat. Com. on U.S.-China Rels., 1976—, Nat. Commn. for Coop. Edn., 1968-78, adv. com. U.S. Army Command and Gen. Staff Coll., 1975-78; planning com. Coun. for Fin. Aid to Edn., 1977-81; panelist nat. identification program for advancement women in higher edn. Am. Coun. on Edn., 1977-80, commn. on internat. edn., 1965-67, past mem. commn. on acad. affairs, coun. overseas liaison com., 1977-80, bd. dirs., 1970-73, 79-82; chmn. Inter-Univ. Coun. Ohio, 1979-80; sr. cons. Kellogg Nat. Fellows program W.K. Kellogg Found., 1981-85; pub. mem. U.S. Med. Licensing Exams., 1991-94. Trustee Am. Coll. Testing Program, 1979-82; mem. Nat. Coun. on Ednl. Rsch., 1980-81; mem. nat. sponsors com. Coun. for Internat. Exch. of Scholars, 1981-84; co-chmn. Com. on Future of SUNY, 1984; bd. visitors Air U., 1968-70; chmn. bd. dirs. Acad. Ind. Scholars, 1984-88. With AUS, 1943-46. Recipient Disting. Svc. award Pub. Sector, Assn. of Governing Bds. of Univs. and Colls., 1992. Mem. Nat. Assn. State Univs. and Land-Grant Colls. (chmn. internat. affairs com., mem. com. on financing higher edn., commn. on arts and scis. 1978, chmn. assn. and exec. com. 1980-81), Coun. of Presidents (chmn. 1978-79, mem. exec. com. 1978-79), Nat. Acad. Pub. Adminstrn., Assn. Urban Univs. (pres. 1971-72), Assn. Am. Univs. (health policy joint com. 1978-88), Am. Optometric Assn. (coun. on optometric edn. 1984-88), Rotary. Died July 28, 2006.

ENGEL, JOANNE BOYER, psychology educator; b. Meadville, Pa., Mar. 15, 1944; d. Edward Charles and Wanda Ann (Chasco) Boyer; m. Richard E. Hammer (dec.); 1 child, Cynthia; m. Harold N. Engel, Mar. 12, 1971; 1 child Keith Nichols. BS, Pa. State U., 1965; MEd, U. Sydney, Australia, 1972; MS, Iowa State U., 1978, PhD, 1979. Cert. elem. tchr., Pa., N.J., Ala., Australia. Tchr. Marple Newtown Sch. Dist., Broomall, Pa., 1965-67, Wallingford (Pa.) Sch. Dist., 1967-69, Sydney Pub. Schs., 1969-70; dir. child rsch. lab. Auburn (Ala.) U., 1971-75; instr. human devel. Coll. Home Econs. Iowa State U., Ames, 1975-79; asst. prof. Oreg. State U., Corvallis, 1979-80, assoc. prof., from 1990; from asst. prof. to prof., chair dept. Willamette U., Salem, Oreg., 1980-90. Contbr. articles to profl. jours. Commr. Tchr. Standards and Practice Commn.; mem. sch. reform com. Gov. of Oreg. Mem. Puget Sound English Setter Assn., Oreg. Responsible Dog Breeder Assn., Oreg. Brittany Club (sec., treas. newsletter 1988—), Am. Kennel Club (dog show judge 1991—), Am. Brittany Club, Am. Whippet Club, N.W. Dog Judges Assn., Chintimini Kennel Club (pres. 1992-94), Pacific Rim Golden Retriever Club. Presbyterian. Avocations: dog shows, field trial, dog breeding, horse-back riding. Home: Albany, Oreg. Died Feb. 11, 2005.

ENGELBERG, HYMAN, internist, researcher; b. N.Y.C., Oct. 7, 1913; s. Julius and Tillie (Grebel) E.; children: Michael, Alan, Lon. BA, Cornell U., 1933, MD, 1936. Intern Cedars of Lebanon Hosp., L.A., 1936-37, chief med. resident, 1939-40; asst. resident in medicine Montefiore Hosp., N.Y.C., 1937-38; sr. attending physician Cedars-Sinai Med. Ctr., L.A.; former pres. Calif. Arteriosclerosis Rsch. Found., L.A. Cons. in thrombosis rsch. Stritch Sch. of Medicine, Loyola U., Maywood, Ill. Author: Your Heart's Best Friend--The Untold Story, 1986, Cholesterol: Truth and Humbug, 1991, Heparin and the Prevention of Artherosclerosis: Basic Research and Clinical Application, 1990; contbr. more than 100 articles to profl. jours. 1st lt. USAF, 1940-44. Recipient Honor Achievement award Angiology Rsch. Found, 1969; named hon. mem. Turkish Soc. Hematology, 1987. Mem. N.Y. Acad. Scis. Jewish. Died Dec. 19, 2005.

EPPELE, DAVID LOUIS, columnist, author; b. Jersey City, Apr. 4, 1939; s. Joseph Anton and Lena Marie (Tadlock) E.; m. Gladys Emily Padilla (div. 1975); children: David D., Joseph E.; m. Geneva Mae Kirsch, July 7, 1977. Student, N.Mex. State U., 1958, U. N.Mex., 1966, U. Portland, 1972. Field botanist, SW Deserts and Mex., 1947—2004, N.Mex. Cactus Rsch., Belen, 1953-62; dir. Ariz. Cactus and Succulent Rsch., Bisbee, from 1984; editor Ariz. Cactus News, from 1984; columnist Western Newspapers, from 1987. Columnist: On the Desert, 1986—; author: On the Desert, 1991, On The Desert, vol. 2, 2000; editor: Index of Cactus Illustrations, 1990, Desert in Bloom, 1989. Mem. Mule Mountain Dem. Party, Bisbee, 1978—. With USN, 1958-59. Mem. AAAS, Cactus and Succulent Soc. Am., N.Mex. Acad. Sci., Bisbee C. of C. Avocations: photography, music. Died May 19, 2005.

EPPERSON, ELEANOR LOUISE, retired educator; b. Longmont, Colo., July 15, 1916; d. Fred and Anna Weir (Smith) Dormann; m. John Ira Epperson, July 22, 1944; children: Dirk Alan, Kent John, Glen Scott. BA, U. Denver, 1938, MA, 1978. Cert. diagnostic tchr. Tchr. Denver Pub. Schs., 1938-81. Author: (young teen book) Timberjack and the Chief, 1984; contbr. articles to profl. jours. Legis. rep., state legis. chmn. Delta Kappa Gamma, Denver, 1983-88, active leadership devel. retreat, 1988 (Cert. of Merit 1989, Tribute 1989). Mem. Alpha Gamma Delta (ARC pin 1961). Home: Denver, Colo. Died Apr. 19, 2005.

EPSTEIN, BARBARA, editor; b. Boston, Aug. 30, 1929; d. Harry W. and Helen (Diamond) Zimmerman; children: Jacob, Helen. BA, Radcliffe Coll., 1949. Founder, editor N.Y. Rev. Books, NYC, 1963—2006. Home: New York, NY. Died June 16, 2006.

EPSTEIN, FRED JACOB, pediatric neurosurgeon; b. Yonkers, NJ, July 26, 1937; m. Kathy Candel; children: Samara, Ilana, Jason, Joey, Benjamin. MD, N.Y.U., 1963. Diplomate Am. Bd. Neurological Surgeons. Resident in surgery Montefiore Med. Ctr., N.Y.C.; resident in neurosurgery NYU-Bellevue Med. Ctr.; prof. neurosurgery Albert Einstein Coll. Medicine, 1983—2001; dir. divsn. of pediatric neurosrugery NYU Med. Ctr.; dir. Inst. for Neurology and Neurosurgery Beth Israel Med. Ctr., N.Y.C., 1996—2001, chmn. dept. neurosurgery. Editor-in-chief Jour. of Pediatric Neurosurgery; contbr. articles to profl. jours. Fellowships Am. Coll. of Surgeons, N.Y. Acad. of Medicine, Am. Acad. of Pediatrics; Recipient Lifetime Achievement award, Am. Assn. Neurological Surgeons, 2001 Mem. Internat. Soc. of Pediatric Neurosurgery (pres.), Am. Soc. of Pediatric Neurosurgery (pres.). Died July 9, 2006.

EPSTEIN, JOSEPH ALLEN, neurosurgeon, educator; b. Bklyn., Oct. 3, 1917; m. Natalie Rhoda Jospeh, Nov. 15, 1947; children: Janet, Nancy. BS, CCNY, 1938; MD, L.I. Coll. Medicine, 1942. Diplomate Am. Bd. Neurosurgery. Intern Jewish Hosp. Bklyn., 1943; resident in neurology Mt. Sinai Hosp., N.Y.C., 1947-49; resident in neurosurgery Beth Israel Hosp., N.Y.C., 1949-51; attending neurosurgeon North Shore Cornell Hosp., Manhasset, N.Y., from 1960, L.I. Jewish Hosp., New Hyde Park, N.Y., from 1960; clin. prof. Albert Einstein Coll. Medicine, Bronx, N.Y., from 1986; clin. assoc. prof. North Shore Hosp. divsn. Cornell Med. Sch., from 1970; pvt. practice New Hyde Park, from 1951. Contbr. articles to profl. jours. Capt. M.C., U.S. Army, 1943-46. Recipient Lifetime Achievement award, Am. Assn. Neurol. Surgeons and Congress Neurol. Surgeons, 1993, Disting. Svc. award, Nassau Surg. Soc., 2003. Fellow Cervical Spine Rsch. Soc. (past pres.), Internat. Soc. for Study of Lumbar Spine. Jewish. Home: Old Westbury, NY. Died Jan. 24, 2006.

ERICKSON, RALPH O., botany educator; b. Duluth, Minn., Oct. 27, 1914; s. Charles W. and Stella (Sjostrom) E.; m. Elinor M. Borgstedt, June 17, 1945; children: Diane Erickson Field, Elizabeth Erickson. BA, Gustavus Adolphus Coll., 1935; MS, Washington U., St. Louis, 1941, PhD, 1944. Instr. Gustavus Adolphus Coll., 1935-39; asst. chemist Western Cartridge Co., East Alton, Ill., 1942-44; instr., then asst. prof. botany U. Rochester, NY, 1944-47; mem. faculty U. Pa., Phila., 1947—2006, prof. botany, 1954-85, prof. emeritus, 1985—2006, chmn. grad. group botany, 1957-68, acting dir. divsn. biology, 1961-63, chmn. grad. group biology, 1968-76, acting chmn. dept. biology, 1977-78. Contbr. articles to profl. jours. Guggenheim fellow Calif. Inst. Tech., 1954-55. Mem. AAAS, Bot. Soc. Am., Soc. Devel. Biology (pres. 1959), Am. Inst. Biol. Scis., Sigma Xi. Home: Haverford, Pa. Died Mar. 24, 2006.

ERIKSEN, DAN OLUF, film director; b. Seattle, Sept. 24, 1925; s. Oluf and Esther K. (Andersen) E.; m. Delphina I. Brownlee, Apr. 20, 1954 (div. 1960); 1 child, Lynn Michele. Student, U. Wash., 1946-47. Film dir. numerous feature films and commls.; asst. dir. including The Pawnbroker, 1965, A Thousand Clowns, 1965, Truman Capote's Christmas Memory, 1966, The Group, 1966; dir. A Midsummer Night's Dream, 1966. USMC, 1943-45. Mem. Dirs. Guild Am. Lutheran. Avocations: reading, listening to classical music, walking. Died July 10, 2005.

ERIKSSON, BARBARA DUNLAP, secondary school educator; b. Whittier, N.C., Sept. 11, 1939; d. Lee Wilson and Nellie Grey (Denton) Dunlap; m. Edward N. Eriksson, July 29, 1960; 1 child, Michael N. BA, Stetson U., DeLand, Fla., 1961, MA, 1965; MS, Johns Hopkins U., 1986. Cert. tchr. social sci., adminstrn., supervision. Tchr./libr. Volusia County Bd. of Edn., DeLand, Fla., 1961-63; libr. Newport News Bd. of Edn., 1963-67; adminstrv. asst./travel agt. Kentron Hawaii, Ltd., Honolulu, 1968; tchr. Napa Valley Bd. of Edn., Napa, Calif., 1969-71, Anne Arundel County Bd. Edn., Annapolis, Md., from 1974, social studies dept. chair, from 1984. Owner Homestead Crafts, Cherokee, N.C., Barbara's Attic, Md. Pres. Anne Arundel County Social Studies Coun., Annapolis; sec. faculty coun., interdisciplinary team leader Chesapeake Bay Mid Sch.; active church activities. Ford Found. fellow; Chesapeake Bay Found. Environ. grantee. Mem. AAUW, ASCD, Tchrs. Assn. Anne Arundel County, Ladies of Elks (sec.). Republican. Methodist. Home: Arnold, Md. Died June 23, 2005.

ERINAKES, JANET LEVERNIE, health consulting company owner; b. East Greenwich, R.I., June 15, 1940; d. Norman Samuel and Doris Levernie (Essex) Kettelle; m. Dennis C. Erinakes, June 9, 1962; children: David, Michael. Diploma, Roger Williams Gen. Hosp., Providence, R.I., 1961; student, U. Maine, Pa. State U.; postgrad., Kennedy Western U. RN, Tex., R.I. Asst. head nurse med./surg. Roger Williams Gen. Hosp., Providence, 1961; head nurse pediatrics Kent County Meml. Hosp., Warwick, R.I., 1961-62; asst. head nurse pediatrics Eastern Maine Med. Ctr., Bangor, 1962-65; Lamaze instr. maternal and child health Bangor, 1965-68; Lamaze instr., tchr. maternal and child health State College, Pa., 1974-75; office nurse, surg. asst. Manuel Lagon, M.D., Fort Worth, Tex., 1982-83; from staff nurse to charge nurse dialysis unit Tarrant County Nephrology Ctr., Fort Worth; from asst. head nurse to interim head nurse dept. home dialysis dept. Tarrant County Nephrology Ctr., Ft. Worth, 1990; clin. supr. home health Total Home Health Svcs., Inc., Fort Worth, 1989-90, asst. adminstr. Ft. Worth, 1990-95; owner, pres. Diversified Health Consultants, Inc., Burleson, Tex., from 1995. Lamaze instr., State College, Pa., 1974-75. Home: Burleson, Tex. Died Aug. 23, 2005.

ERMSHAR, LINDA CHARLINE, health services school director; b. L.A., Apr. 29, 1943; d. Herman Jerry and Fern Dorothy (Haynes) Mayer; m. Marvin Carl Ermshar, Dec. 16, 1962; children: Kurt Jerry Douglas, Kimberly Renee, Victoria Rochelle. AA, El Camino Coll., 1964; teaching cert., UCLA, 1973. RN; x-ray tech., std. designated teaching credential and cmty. coll. credential, Calif. Allied health dir. Southland Career Inst., Montebello, Calif., 1969-88; ednl. dir., assoc. dir. Modern Tech. Sch. X-Ray, Anaheim, Calif., from 1988. Mem. med. adv. bd. Brady-Prentice-Hall. RN in charge of students ARC Health Fairs, Whittier, Calif., 1980-87. Recipient Cert. of Recognition Nat. Assn. Trade and Tech. Schs., Washington, 1991. Mem. Am. Assn. Med. Transcription. Republican. Seventh Day Adventists. Avocations: stamp collecting/philately, doll collecting. Home: Anaheim, Calif. Died May 17, 2005.

ERSKINE, KENNETH F., psychotherapist; b. N.Y.C., Nov. 9, 1919; m. Maria C., Feb. 23, 1952; children: Clarke, Lewis. B Social Svcs., CCNY, 1950; MSW, Columbia U., 1952. Cert. social worker; bd. cert. diplomate social work. Intake worker Vets Soc. Ctr., N.Y.C., 1946-50; social worker Family Svc. Bur., Newark, N.J., 1951-53, N.Y.C. Youth Bd., 1953-55; case worker, supr. U.S. VA, Bklyn., 1955-56, social wk. supr., 1956-62; asst. prof. casework Columbia U. Sch. Social Wk., N.Y.C., 1962-69, asst. dir. field work, 1969-74; asst. dir. social work psychiatry dept. Harlem Hosp. Affiliation with Columbia Med. Sch. and Hosp., N.Y.C., 1974-85; psychotherapist Edupsych Assocs., N.Y.C., from 1971. Clin. supr./cons. N.Y. Urban League, Bklyn., 1987—. Bd. dirs. Man Country Sch., Inwood Hts. Housing, others. With USAF, 1943-46. Mem. NASW, Assn. Black Social Workers, Am. Orthopsychiat. Assn. Avocations: drawing, painting, collecting art. Home: New York, NY. Died June 15, 2004.

ESCH, RAYMOND GATES, lawyer; b. Akron, Ohio, May 31, 1940; s. Raymond Gates and Ruth (Durham) E.; m. Janet Louise Allen, June 17, 1962; children: Daniel Allen, Elizabeth Durham, Thomas Gates. BA, Ohio Wesleyan U., 1962; JD, U. Mich., 1965. Bar: Ohio 1965. Assoc. Fuller & Henry P.L.L., Toledo, 1965-71, ptnr., from 1971, mng. ptnr., 1984-87. Spl. counsel to atty. gen. of Ohio, 1995—; mem. Bd. of Commrs. on Grievances and Discipline of Supreme Ct. of Ohio, 1996—. Officer Toledo area coun. Boy Scouts Am., 1982-95; trustee Family Svc. N.W., Ohio, Toledo, 1983-89, chmn. 1986-88; mem. exec. com. Lucas County Rep. Ctrl. Com., Toledo, 1991-96. Mem. ABA, Ohio Bar Assn., Toledo Bar Assn., Toledo Estate Planning Coun., Am. Inns of Ct. (master Waite chpt. 1996—). Episcopalian. Avocations: reading, golf, racquet sports. Home: Maumee, Ohio. Died June 16, 2005.

ESCHENBACH, ARTHUR EDWIN, human factors engineer; b. N.Y.C., Jan. 31, 1918; s. Karl Godfried and Magdelena (Rupert) E.; m. Maria Louise Perez, June 22, 1968; children: Mary Patricia, Karl, Deborah, Charmion, Roxanne. AB, Cornell U., 1947; MA, U. Fla., 1949, PhD, 1955. Lic. psychologist, Fla. Commd. 2nd lt. USAF, 1943, advanced through grades to lt. col., 1965; scientist, human engr. USAF, NASA, U.S., Republic of Korea, 1951-66; ret. USAF, 1966; assoc. prof., dept. head Jacksonville (Fla.) U., 1966-86; pvt. cons., from 1986. Contbr. articles to profl. jours. Home: Jackson, Wyo. Died Dec. 16, 2004.

ESCHENBURG, EMIL PAUL, real estate broker; b. Mt. Clemens, Mich., Dec. 26, 1915; s. Paul Frederick and Ella Sophia (Weise) E.; m. Betty G., June 5, 1943 (div. July 1975); children: Paula E., Emip P., Erich G., Lise Ann; m. Dolly Woar, Dec. 27, 1977. BS with high honors, Mich. State U., 1939; grad., Nat. War Coll., Washington, 1957; MBA, Harvard U., 1960; MA in Internat. Rels., George Washington U., 1971. Cert. real estate residential specialist, real estate investment specialist. With U.S. Army, 1939-70, 2d lt. to brig. gen., 1960-63, asst. comdr. 101st Airborne div., 1963-65; chief joint mil. asst. U.S. Mil. Mission, Ethopia, 1965-67; acting and asst. comdg. gen. 1st inf. div. U.S. Army, 1967-70; salesman real estate Crows Nest Harbor, Washington, 1971-72; salesman Sandy McPherson Realty, Helena, Mont., 1973-80; broker, mgr. Century-21/Heritage Realty, Helena, 1980-89; assoc. broker Ahmann-Heller Realtors, from 1990. Pres. Century-21 Broker's Coun. for Mont., 1988-89. Pres. Helena Bd. Realtors, 1976-77, YMCA, 1988, Helena MLS, 1986; elder Luth. ch., 1981-83; bd. dirs. Mont. State Bd. Realtors, 1977-80, Model Cities Devel. Corp., 1976-80; chmn. Nat. Fund Drive Mont. Vietnam Vets. Meml., Washington, 1983-85; mem. exec. com. Support of the Guard and Reserve, Mont.; mem. Crimestoppers, 1982-83. Attained Top C-21 Real Estate Salesperson award for Top Commissions of All in State of Mont., 1987, Realtor of Yr., 1987; recipient 117 decorations including 77 valor awards. Mem. Nat. Assn. Realtors, Century-21 Investment Soc., Million Dollar Sales Club, Nat. Mktg. Assn., Helena C. of C., DAV, Purple Heart, VFW, Helena Navy League (pres. 1985-86), Kiwanis (disting. pres. Helena chpt. 1980-81, bd. govs. 1983-87, lt. gov. dist. 9 1990), Green Meadow Country, Mont. Club (pres. 1981). Republican. Lutheran. Avocations: golf, family history. Home: Helena, Mont. Died Nov. 26, 2004.

ESHLEMAN, DANIEL SYLVESTER, pastor; b. Hagerstown, Md., Apr. 18, 1937; s. Daniel Irvin and Grace B. (Williams) E.; m. Nancy Louise Stoner; children: Lou Ann, Carol M., Christy S., Daniel P. BA, Grace Coll., 1961; MDiv, Grace Sem., 1964. Ordained to ministry Ch. of the Brethren, 1965. Pastor Findlay (Ohio) Grace Brethren Ch., 1964-68, Grace Brethren Ch., Stratford, N.J., 1968-70, Virginia Beach, Va., 1970-73, Patterson Meml. Grace Brethren Ch., Roanoke, Va., 1973-78, Valley Grace Brethren Ch., Hagerstown, Md., 1978-86, Grace Brethren Ch., Elizabethtown, Pa., from 1986. Moderator Mid-Atlantic Dist. Grace Brethren Ch., 1971, 76, N. Atlantic Dist. Grace Brethren Ch., 1988. Consumer rep. Bd. Examiners of Psychologists, Md., 1981-86. Fellowship Grace Brethren. Mem. Rotary (sec. 1990, v.p. 1991, pres. 1992, Man of Yr. 1986). Home: Elizabethtown, Pa. Died Mar. 22, 2004.

ESPOSITO, BARBARA WAKEFIELD, emergency nurse; b. Huntingdon, Pa., Dec. 16, 1935; d. Chester Wright and Pauline (Whittaker) Wakefield; m. Charles Esposito, Sept. 20, 1958; children: Susan Basalik, Karen Zeltt. Diploma, Pa. Hosp., Phila., 1956. RN Pa., CEN. Staff nurse Pa. Hosp., 1956-58; staff nurse supr. Meth. Hosp., Phila., 1958-68; staff nurse Jeanes Hosp., Phila., 1968-77, supr., 1981; staff nurse Frankford Hosp., Phila., 1977-81, head nurse, emergency room, 1981-86, trauma nurse coord./mgr. emergency care, 1986-88, mgr. trauma program, from 1988. Bd. dirs. Bucks County EHS Coun., Doylestown, Pa.; chairperson Pa. Trauma Nurse Adv. Coun., 1994-95. Contbg. author: A Comprehensive Curriculum for Trauma Nursing, 1992; co-presentor: (poster display) Injuries to Racetrack Employees, 1991, Prognostic Importance of Field Hypotension in Trauma Patients, 1992, Pedestrian Injury, 1993, Rib Fractures in the Elderly, 1994; contbr. articles to profl. jours. Recipient Chapel of Four Chaplains award Girl Scouts of Phila., 1981, Thanks award, 1984. Mem. Emergency Nurses Assn., Am. Trauma Soc., Delaware Valley Trauma Nurse Consortium, Pa. Trauma Systems Found. (mem. standards com. 1989-92), Hosp. Assn. of Pa. (exec. com. 1991-94). Avocations: photography, needlecrafts, reading. Home: Philadelphia, Pa. Died Mar. 19, 2005.

ESSMAN, WALTER BERNARD, endocrinologist; b. N.Y.C., Dec. 25, 1933; s. Louis and Elsie Eve (Eisemann) E.; m. Shirley Sage Glass, June 10, 1962; 1 child, Eric J. BA, NYU, Bronx, 1954; MA, U. N.D., 1955, PhD, 1957; MD, U. Milan, Italy, 1972. Diplomate Am. Bd. Anti-Aging Medicine, Am. Bd. Internal Medicine. Asst. prof. Albert Einstein Coll. Medicine, Bronx, 1961-62; prof. Queens Coll.-CUNY Flushing, 1962-00; resident in medicine L.I. Jewish Med. Ctr., Jamaica, N.Y., 1972-75, fellow in endocrinology, 1975-77, attending physician New Hyde Park, 1977-95; prof. medicine SUNY, Stonybrook, 1977-87; pvt. practice N.Y.C., from 1980. Cons. Sterling-Winthrop, N.Y.C., 1987-97. Author 5 books; editor 21 books; contbr.

over 210 articles to profl. jours. Capt. U.S. Army, 1957-59. Recipient Ambrogino D'Oro, U. Milan, 1972, Gold Medal, Mario Negri Inst., Milan, 1975. Avocation: photography. Home: Glen Cove, NY. Died Sept. 30, 2004.

ESTERSOHN, HAROLD SYDNEY, retired podiatrist, educator; b. Trenton, N.J., Jan. 3, 1927; s. Mathew and Celia (Olitsky) E.; m. Mildred Evins, Dec. 25, 1949; children: Eileen Lisa, Michele Beth, Laura Rene. D of Podiatric Medicine cum laude, Dr. William M. Scholl Coll., Chgo., 1952. Diplomate Am. Bd. Podiatric Surgery. Resident Dr. William M. Scholl Coll. Podiatric Medicine, Chgo., 1952-53; dir. podiatry staff Daus. Israel Home for the Aged, Newark and West Orange, N.J., 1953-73; dir. podiatry residency programs and podiatry externship program St. Michael's Med. Ctr., Newark, 1974-86, established fellowship in lower extremity infectious diseases, 1984-86, dir. podiatric med. edn., 1986-88; assoc. dean podiatry div. Seton Hall U., South Orange, N.J., 1987-88. Cons. Schering Corp., Union, N.J., 1964, Stryker Corp., Kalamazoo, 1972; adj. clin. instr. N.Y. Coll. Podiatric Medicine, Pa. Coll. Podiatric Medicine, Ohio Coll. Podiatric Medicine, Ill. Coll. Podiatric Medicine, Calif. Coll. Podiatric Medicine, 1974-86; podiatry staff South Amboy Meml. Hosp., West Essex Gen. Hosp., St. Vincent's Hosp.; dir. podiatry residency program Hadassah U. Hosp., Ein Karem, Israel, 1987-88; dir. podiatry staff St. Michaels Med. Ctr., 1972-86; staff Doctor's Hosp., Newark, 1958-68, West Essex Gen. Hosp., 1962-80, Newark Beth Israel Med. Ctr., 1963-73, Columbus Hosp. Newark, 1968-76, St. Michael's Med. Ctr., 1972-86, South Amboy Meml. Hosp., 1982-84, St. Vincent Hosp., 1974-80; lectr. in field. Co-author: Current Therapy in Podiatric Surgery, 1989; contbr. articles to profl. jours. Chmn. youth activities Young Israel Synagogue, Newark, 1961-63; podiatry adv. com. N.J. Dept. Instns. and Agys., Trenton, 1969-72; bd. dirs. N.J. affiliate Am. Diabetic Assn., 1975-83, lectr. on diabetic foot, 1974-82. Grantee Schering Corp., 1964, 66, Stryker Corp., 1972; recipient Astra award Astra Pharm. Products, Hershey, Pa., 1985. Fellow Am. Coll. Foot Surgeons (pres. ea. div. 1969-71); mem. Am. Podiatry Assn. (25 Yr. award 1977), N.J. Podiatry Assn. (pres. Ea. divsn. 1959-60, pres. 1967-68), N.J. Podiatry Soc., B'nai Brith (Svc. award 1956). Avocations: golf, tennis, boating, fishing, square dancing. Home: Port Saint Lucie, Fla. Died Apr. 15, 2004.

ESTES, CHARLES BYRON, composer, conductor, author; b. Aurora, Colo., June 17, 1946; s. Byron Sumner and Lillian (Gross) E.; m. Nancy Elizabeth Bliss, Oct. 21, 1978; children: Erich Byron, Matthew Charles, Gretchen Marie. AA, Fullerton Coll., 1966; BA in Comparative Religions, Coll. Idaho, 1969; MA in Composition, Calif. State U., Fullerton, 1979. Keyboardist Paul Zen Quintet, Fullerton, 1971-86; founder, dir. Dir. Image Ensemble, Fullerton, 1974-79; keyboardist PowerVac band, Fullerton, 1975-82; choir dir. Grace Luth. Ch., Anaheim, Calif., 1980-86; composer in residence Grove Shakespeare Festival, Garden Grove, Calif., 1980-93; keyboardist The Domes, Villa Park, Calif., 1985-86; bass soloist 1st United Meth. Ch., Santa Ana, Calif., 1985-86; dir. music Morningside Presbyn. Ch., Fullerton, 1986-91; prof. of counterpoint So. Calif. Coll., Costa Mesa, 1987-88. Author: Music: The Invisible Language, 1993; musical dir. Swansea Project, 1993-2006. Founder Fullerton Hist. Theatre Found., 2001. Recipient Dramalogue Critic's award, 1984-86, 87 (2), 88-90, 91 (3), 92. Mem. Green Party. Home: Fullerton, Calif. Died Mar. 26, 2006.

ESTRIN, FRED MARSHALL, manufacturing executive; b. Los Angeles, Oct. 7, 1940; s. Joseph and Pauline (Fromsky) E.; m. Mildred W. Estrin, Dec. 15, 1963; children: Paula Rae, David Joseph, Matthew Franklin. Student, Calif. State U., Northridge, 1964. Mem. sales staff NCR Corp., Los Angeles, 1965-70; v.p. sales Pharmacy Computer Billing Inc., Encino, Calif., 1971-72; pres. Am. Indsl. Stationers, Canoga Park, Calif., 1972-76; gen. mgr. NBS Systems Inc., Edwardsville, Ill., 1976-84, Bus. Forms div. Stationers Graphics, Los Angeles, 1984-85; sales mgr. Postal Graphics, Los Angeles, 1985-86; v.p. mktg. services Bank Printing Co., Los Angeles, 1986-88; pres., chief operations officer Alpha Network, Santa Fe Springs, Calif., from 1988. Author: Time and Territory Management, 1980. Mem. Econ. Devel. Commn., 1983, Cable TV Commn., 1983 (both Glen Carbon, Ill.). Mem. Nat. Bus. Forms Assn., Printing Industries. Democrat. Jewish. Home: Chatsworth, Calif. Died Feb. 10, 2004.

EUBANKS, RACHEL AMELIA, music educator; b. San Jose, Calif. d. Joseph Sylvester and Elizabeth Amelia (Gant) E. BA, U. Calif., Berkeley, 1945; MA, Columbia U., 1947; DMA, Pacific Western U., 1980. Chmn. music dept. Wilberforce (Ohio) U., 1949-50; founder, pres. Eubanks Conservatory of Music and Arts, L.A., 1951—2006. Author: Musicianship, 1961; composer: Cantata, 1947, Trio, 1977, Symphonic Requiem, 1980, Sonata for Piano, 1992, 5 Interludes for Piano, 1996, Easter Suite for Organ, 1995, Musicianship, Vol. I, II plus tapes, Five Interludes for piano, Vietnamese Love Song for violin and piano, Nocturne, 2006, (cantata for chorus, solo voices, organ, harp, 3 trumpets, 3 flutes and bell choir) The Christmas Story, 2005, chamber music, songs, piano solos. Rosenthal fellow Columbia U., 1946; recipient Cmty. awards City of L.A., 1982, Crenshaw Chamber of Congress, 1986, Calif. Legis. Assembly, 1991, County of L.A., 1991, Phelan award, 1948. Mem. Internat. Alliance of Women in Music, Alpha Mu Honor Soc. Avocation: travel. Home: Los Angeles, Calif. Died Apr. 8, 2006.

EUGENE, JEAN RENOIR, surgeon; b. Haiti, Haiti, Oct. 20, 1964; came to U.S., 1985; s. Gabriel Jasmin and Priscilla Eugene. BSc in Biology, W.Va. Wesleyan U., 1990; DO, Southeastern U., Ft. Lauderdale, Fla., 1994. Diplomate Nat. Bd. Osteo. Med. Examiners; cert. ATLS, ACLS, BCLS. Intern Mich. State U./Botsford Hosp., Farmington, 1994-95; gen. surgery resident St. Barnabas Hosp., Bronx, 1995-99; vascular surgery resident Deborah Heart and Lung Ctr., Browns Hills, N.Y., from 1999. Cons. Haitian Studies for the Area Health Edn. Ctr., Dept. Family Medicine, Southeastern U.; commn. officer U.S. Dept. Health and Human Svcs., summers, 1991, 92; lectr. Area Health Edn. Ctr., U. Miami Sch. Medicine, Nova-Southeastern U. Coll. Osteo. Medicine and U. Fla. Sch. Medicine, 1992-94; lectr. in field. Contbr. articles to profl. jours. Founding mem., exec. dir. Surgeon for the World, 1998—; organizer surg. missions to Haiti in cooperation with Haitian Bapt. Ch. of North Dad, Miami, Fla., 1997, CRUDEM Found. of Cath. Med. Mission, St. Louis, 1998; dir. Haitians for Social Responsibility, 1997-98; exec. dir., pres. Haitian Sociocultural Inst., Ft. Lauderdale, 1990-92; pub. assistance specialist Fla. Dept. Health and Rehab. Svcs., 1989-90. RecipientGolden Citizen award Coun. of Haitian Bapt. Ch. of Greater N.Y., 1996, Resident Achievement award in gen. surgery Am. Coll. Osteo. Surgeons, 1997, Haitian Humanitarian award Haitian Dept. Pub. Health, 1998; named to Outstanding Young Men of Am. Mem. AMA, Am. Osteo. Assn., Am. Coll. Osteo. Surgeons, Assn. of Haitian Am. Physicians. Achievements include research in cross-cultural AIDS prevention, intensive care unit acquired infection, meta-analysis and safety profile (morbidity and mortality) of combined abdominal aoritc aneurysm repair and coronary artery bypass graft, component separation technique for repair of gian incisional hernias: recurrence, morbidity and mortality, sociocultural approach to disease prevention and treatment, sci. value of Haitian traditional/herbal medicine. Died June 25, 2005.

EVANEGA, GEORGE RONALD, medical company executive; b. Cementon, Pa., Feb. 6, 1936; s. George and Helen A. (Cesanek) E.; m. Janet K. Roark, June 16, 1992; children: George C., Veronica A. BS in Engring., Lehigh U., 1957; MS, Yale U., 1958, PhD in Organic Chemistry, 1960. Rsch. scientist Union Carbide, Tarrytown, N.Y., 1962-69; mgr. Pfizer Cen. Rsch., Groton, Conn., 1969-75; dir. Biodynamics, Indpls., 1975-78; Hauptabteilungsleiter Boehringer Mannheim, Tutzing, Fed. Republic Germany, Germany, 1978-79; v.p. product devel. Boehringer Mannheim Diagnostics, Indpls., 1979-81, v.p. mktg. sales, 1981-84, v.p. tech., 1984-88; v.p., chief adminstrv. officer Miles Inc., Elkhart, Ind., 1988-91; pres., COO, Oncor Inc., Gaithersburg, Md., 1991-95; CEO, pres. Gull Labs., Inc., Salt Lake City, from 1995. NIH fellow, 1961. Mem. Am. Assn. Clin. Chemists, Am. Chem. Soc., N.Y. Acad. Sci. Avocations: tennis, golf, oenology. Home: North Salt Lake, Utah. Died May 20, 2005.

EVANS, EILEEN MCKENNA, education educator, research scientist; b. Teaneck, N.J., Sept. 18, 1946; d. Francis Michael and Margaret Cadien McKenna; m. William Davidson Evans, Jr., June 19, 1971; children: William D. III, Carter M., Alexander B. BA in Edn., Fordham U., 1971; MA in Spl. Edn., U. Memphis, 1974; EdD, George Washington U., 1995. Asst. dir. Office Internat. Activities, from 1993; rsch. scientist, exec. dir. George Washington U., from 1996, asst. professorial lectr. Grad. Sch. Edn. and Human Devel., from 1996. Adminstrv. asst. to dean Sch. Edn., Fordham U., N.Y.C., 1970-71; instr., supr., mgr. Lincoln Ctr. for the Performing Arts, N.Y.C.; tchr., cmty. organizer Fla. Dade County Migrant Camps; presenter in field. Contbr. articles to profl. jours. Mem. bd. Alumni Coun. Grad. Sch. Edn. and Human Devel., George Washington U., mem. Child Devel. Day Care Ctr. Com., 1995-96, membership com. univ. faculty club, 1999; trustee Les Passes Rehab. Ctr., Memphis, 1975-82, Jr. League Washington, 1988-90, Mater Dei Sch., Bethesda, Md., 1990-95; trustee, founding mem. Nat. Alliance to End Homelessness, 1983-93, Bright Beginnings, Inc., 1989-94. Recipient Founder's award Nat. Alliance To End Homelessness, 1993, Pres.' award for excellence in volunteerism Jr. League Washington, 1988. Mem. Nat. Assn. Fgn. Student Advisors, Comparative and Internat. Edn. Soc., George Washington Univ. Club (founder, membership com. 1998), Phi Beta Delta (chpt. coord. George Washington U. Beta Omicron chpt., v.p. 1999), Phi Delta Kappa. Roman Catholic. Died Jan. 19, 2004.

EVANS, JANNETTE HELEN, real estate broker; b. Elmhurst, Ill., Apr. 19, 1946; d. Joseph and Marie (Okreszik) Gorka; children: Cassandra Lynn, Tracy Ann. Student, Northwestern U., 1964-66. Office mgr. Albin Industries, Birmingham, Mich., 1967-69; real estate sales assoc. Bassett Assocs., Royal Oak, Mich., 1971-73; pres. Ventura Assocs., Ltd., Huntley, Ill., from 1973. Mem. Nat. Assn. Realtors, Ill. Assn. Realtors, McHenry County Bd. Realtors. Died 2004.

EVANS, JETTA, author, designer educational materials, educator; b. Clarksburg, W.Va., Jan. 19, 1934; d. Forest and Maude L. (Reaser) Rogers; children: David Roach, Barbara Hinman. AB ED cum laude, Fairmont State, 1960; postgrad., Tex. Coll., 1964, Asbury Coll., London, 1971; M in Spl. Edn., West Va. U., 1974. Cert. pub. speaker; cons. in reading, lang., Nat. Edn. Tchr. USERE, Overseas Mil. Schs., Mainze, Germany, New Castle Schs., Del.; owner Victory Learning Ctr., Dayton, Ohio, from 1996. Pres. Jettans Learning Sys., Dayton, Ohio; ednl. cons. in sci. and math. Addison Wesley Pub. Co., Chgo.; cons. in phonics. Author Natural Write to Reading Success, Reading Empowdered. Recipient Tchr. of Yr. award, Elyria, Ohio, 1958. Mem. AEYC, Internat. Reading Assn., Nat. Coun. of Tchrs. of English. Home: Dayton, Ohio. Died Sept. 16, 2004.

EVANS, ROBERT E., bank executive; b. 1940; BS, Ohio No. U., 1962; JD, Capital U., 1967. Bar: Ohio 1967. Chmn. People's Bancorp Inc., Marietta, Ohio, 1980—2005, CEO, 1980—2005. Bd. dirs. McDonough Corp.; trustee Marietta Coll. Mem. ABA. Died June 15, 2005.

EVANS, ROY, small business owner, consultant; b. Oklahoma City, Feb. 13, 1925; m. Sandy Evans; five children. BA in English, So. Meth. U.; MA in Comm., Polit. Sci. and Econs., Corpus Christi State U. From machinist trainee to top machinist and layout person, 1948-56; pres. UAW Local Union Chance Vought Aircraft, 1956-61; pub. rels. dir., sec.-treas., pres. Tex. AFL-CIO, 1961-73; pre-hearing officer, regional mgr. Indsl. Accident Bd., Tex., 1973-80; advisor, liaison U.S. Dept. Labor, Employment Stds. Adminstrn., 1980-90; workers compensation cons., from 1990. Author: Tragedy at Work, 1979; writer, editor union newspapers and newsletters; contbr. articles to profl. jours. Died Dec. 18, 2004.

EVANS, WILLIAM DAVIDSON, JR., lawyer; b. Memphis, Jan. 20, 1943; s. William D. and Maxey (Carter) Evans; m. Eileen McKenna, June 19, 1971 (dec. Jan. 2004); children: William D., Carter M., Alexander B. BA, Vanderbilt U., 1965; JD, U. Tenn., 1968; LLM, Georgetown U., 1985. Bar: Tenn. 1968, D.C. 1988, Md. 1996. Spl. agt. FBI, N.Y.C., 1968-72; ptnr. Glankler, Brown, Gilliland, Chase, Robinson & Raines, Memphis, 1972-82; trial atty. environ. enforcement sect. U.S. Dept. of Justice, Washington, 1982-86; of counsel Washington, Perito & Dubuc, Washington, 1986-91, Graham & James, Washington, 1991-93; ptnr. Rich and Henderson, P.C., Annapolis, Md., 1993-98; sr. asst. county atty. Anne Arundel County Office of Law, Annapolis, from 1998. Editor: Digest Environ. Law of Real Property, 1986—90, Environ. Hazards, 1989—90; contbr. articles to profl. jours. Mem. environ. issues group George Bush for Pres. Campaign, Washington, 1987—88, Robert Dole for Pres. Campaign, Washington, 1995—96. Mem.: ABA, Environ. Law Inst., Md. Bar Assn., D.C. Bar Assn. Republican. Roman Catholic. Home: Washington, DC. Died Oct. 31, 2004.

EVERETT, EUGENIA ZINK, sculptor, educator; b. Loveland, Colo., Nov. 27, 1908; d. Charles Henry and Ruby Olivia (Giddings) Zink; m. Richard Henry Everett, Apr. 2, 1932 (dec. Dec. 1975); children: Jane Carolyn, Fredric Richard. AB, Mt. St. Mary's, L.A., 1929; grad., Claremont Coll., 1958-59; postgrad., Am. U., 1960. Sculptor WPA - FAP, Calif., 1934-38; tchr. Ventura (Calif.) Coll., 1960-69, Sedona (Ariz.) Art Ctr., 1971-92. Author: (poems) Between Silences, 1990. Mem. Internat. Friends Transformative Art, Audubon Soc., Nature Conservancy, Sedona Art Ctr., Sierra Club. Avocations: poetry, gardening. Home: Sedona, Ariz. Died Sept. 1, 2004.

EVERETT, JACQUELIN BROOKS, hospital volunteer administrator; b. Charlottesville, Va., Oct. 30, 1931; d. Grayson Parker and Margaret Lavnenia (McCauley) B.; m. Edgar Merrill Everett, Mar. 6, 1954; children: Jacquelin Everett Gatliff, Patricia Cabell. BS in Edn., Madison Coll., 1953. Cert. hosp. dir. vol. svcs. Tchr. Pub. Schs. Henrico County, Va., 1953-54, Pub. Schs. Chesterfield County, Va., 1954-56; vol. Civic Philantrophic Group, Richmond, Va., 1957-75; substitute tchr. Pub. Schs. Henrico County, Va, 1975-78, Pub. Schs., Glastonbury, Conn., 1978-79; dir. vols. Johnston-Willis Hosps., Richmond, Va., from 1980. Cons. Capitol Area Hosp. Vol. Dirs., Richmond, Va., 1980—. Mem. Va Soc. for Dirs. of Hosp. Vol. Svcs. (pres. 1985-87), Am. Soc. for Dirs. of Vol. Svcs. (membership com. 1988-89), Thomas Jefferson Jr. Woman's Club, Richmond, Va., (pres. 1962-64), Lee Dist. Va. Fed. of Womens' Clubs (pres. 1970-72), Kappa Delta Pi, Sigma Sigma Sigma Soc. Methodist. Avocations: tennis, knitting. Home: Midlothian, Va. Died Mar. 24, 2005.

EVERHART, MARY A., cardiology nurse; b. Kansas City, Mo., Feb. 23, 1934; d. Edwin Morris and Rosie Louise (Comstock) McDonald; 1 child, Twyla. Diploma, Trinity Luth. Sch. Nursing, Kansas City, 1966; student, SMSU, Springfield, Mo. RN Mo., Tenn. Nurse Hosp., Jackson, Tenn.; head nurse, relief supr. Oxford (Miss.) Lafayette Hosp.; nurse Cox Med. Ctr. South, Springfield, Mo. Home: Republic, Mo. Died Mar. 16, 2004.

EVETT, KENNETH WARNOCK, artist, educator; b. Loveland, Colo., Dec. 1, 1913; s. Charles Emery and Sarah (Warnock) E.; m. Bett Schluss, Aug. 16, 1939; children: Daniel, Elisa, Joel. BA, U. No. Colo., 1935; MA, Colo. Coll., 1938. Prof. art Salem Coll., Winston-Salem, N.C., 1945-47, Cornell U., Ithaca, N.Y., 1948-79. One-man shows include (10) Kraushaar Galleries, N.Y., 1948-2005; executed 3 murals Rotunda, Nebr. State Capitol; contbr. articles to profl. jours. Fellow Yaddo Found.; m. Nat. Acad. of Design. Democrat. Avocation: tennis. Home: Ithaca, NY. Died May 28, 2005.

EVINRUDE, FRANCES LANGFORD, singer, actress; b. Lakeland, Fla., Apr. 4, 1913; d. Vasco and Anna Rhea (Barnhill) L.; m. Ralph Erinrude, 1955 (dec. May 1986). Student, So. Coll., Lakeland, Fla., 1920. Appeared in movies Every Night at Eight, Dreaming Out Loud, The Hit Parade of 1937, Born to Dance, Palm Springs, Collegiate,

Radio Stars on Parade, Bamboo Blonde, 1945, All American Coed, Too Many Girls, The RKO Story, Melody Time, Girl Rush, Beat the Band, Broadway Melody of 1936, The Purple Heart Diary, Mississippi Gambler, Career Girl, Dixie Jamboree, Deputy Marshall, Yankee Doodle Dandy, Glenn Miller Story; appeared in TV shows The Bickersons, The Bob Hope Show; radio show appearances include Hollywood Hotel, The Bob Hope Show, Texaco Star Theatre, The Old Gold Show, The Edgar Bergan Show; touring for the U.S.O. with Bob Hope and in Korea and Viet Nam. Died July 11, 2005.

EWELL, WALLACE EDMUND, transportation engineer; b. Fort Worth, Sept. 3, 1942; s. Wallace Mortimer and Claire Eleanor (Kiker) E.; m. Judy Lee King, Sept. 30, 1972; children: George T. Finkle, James Roy, Melissa Anne. BSCE, Tex. A&M U., 1976; MS in Systems Mgmt., U. So. Calif., 1980; MSCE, U. Tex., Arlington, 1984. Registered profl. engr., Tex. Electronics systems maintenance supr. USMC, 1960-76; supr. constrn. subjects USMC Engr. Sch., N.C., 1976-80; constrn. inspector Tex. Dept. Hwys., Fort Worth, 1980-84, bridge inspection supr., 1984-85, roadway design engr., 1985-86; dist. traffic engr. Tex. Dept. Transp., Ft. Worth, from 1986, dir. transp. ops., from 1992. Surface transp. subcom. North Ctrl. Tex. Coun. Govts., 1986—. Contbr. articles to Transp. Quar., 1989, 92, 94 and other jours. on traffic engring. and mgmt. systems. Mem. NSPE, Tex. Soc. Profl. Engrs. Inst. Transp. Engrs. (Tex. sect.). Achievements include supervision of design, construction, operation and maintenance of unique traffic management system in Ft. Worth, an element of the new intelligent-vehicle highway systems. Home: Arlington, Tex. Died June 11, 2004.

EWING, EDGAR LOUIS, artist, educator; b. Hartington, Nebr., Jan. 17, 1913; s. David E. and Laura (Buckendorf) E.; m. Suzanna Peter Giovan, Feb. 12, 1941. Grad., Art Inst. Chgo., 1935; studied, in France, Eng., Italy, 1935-37. Mem. faculty Art Inst. Chgo., 1937-43, U. Mich., Ann Arbor, 1946; asst. prof. fine arts U. So. Calif., 1946-54, assoc. prof., 1954-59, prof., 1959-78, Disting. prof. emeritus, 1978—2006; Mellon prof. Carnegie-Mellon U., Pitts., 1968-69. One-man shows M.H. DeYoung Meml. Mus. Art, San Francisco, 1948, Santa Barbara Mus. of Art, 1952, Long Beach Mus. Art, 1955, Dalzell Hatfield Galleries, Los Angeles, 1954, 56, 58, 61, 63, 65, Hewlett Gallery-Carnegie Mellon U., Pitts., 1969, Nat. Gallery, Athens, Greece, 1973, Los Angeles Mcpl. Art Gallery, 1974, Palm Springs (Calif.) Desert Mus., 1976-77, Fisher Gallery U. So. Calif., 1978, Fisher Gallery, U. So. Calif., 1993-94; group exhbns. Cin Art Mus., Corcoran Gallery Art, Washington, Denver Art Mus., Dallas Mus. Fine Arts, Fort Worth Art Ctr., Met. Mus., N.Y.C.; represented: San Francisco Mus. Art, Dallas Mus. Fine Arts, Ft. Worth Art Ctr., Met. Mus., N.Y.C., Sao Paulo (Brazil) Mus. Art, Wichita Art Mus., Fisher Gallery, U. So. Calif., 1994. Served with C.E., U.S. Army, 1943—46, PTO. Recipient Aberle Florscheim Meml. prize for Oil Painting, Art Inst. Chgo., 1943, Purchase award for oil painting Los Angeles County Mus. Art, 1952, Samuel Goldwyn award, 1957, Ahmanson Purchase award City of Los Angeles Exhbn., 1962, Disting. Prof. Emeritus award U. So. Calif., 1987; Edward L. Ryerson fellow, 1935; Louis Comfort Tiffany grantee, 1948-49, Jose Drudis Fund grantee, Greece, 1967; named one of 100 Artists-100 Yrs., Art Inst. Chgo., 1980. Mem. AAUP, Nat. Watercolor Soc. (v.p. 1952, pres. 1953, Lifetime Achievement award 2003) Democrat. Home: Los Angeles, Calif. Died July 3, 2006.

EWING, RICHARD EVERT, orchard company executive, retired chemist; b. Webster City, Iowa, Dec. 28, 1919; s. Lee Roy and Ruth Elizabeth (Amundson) E.; m. Mildred Ann Ludt, Jan 30, 1943; children: Richard E. Jr., Ronald F., Timothy J. BS, Iowa State U., 1948; MS, U. Idaho, 1952; PhD, Wash. State U., 1958. Sr. scientist Gen. Electric Co., Richland, Wash., 1950-60, Clevite Semiconductor, Palo Alto, Calif., 1960-62; group ldr. Hewlett-Packard Co., Palo Alto, 1962-72; sr. scientist Xerox Corp., Palo Alto, 1972-75; entrepreneur Manson, Wash., 1975-84; pres. Bountiful Orchards, Inc., Manson, from 1984. Sect. Editor Jour. Chem. Abstracts, also contbr. articles to profl. jours; patentee in field. Served with U.S. Army, 1941-45, PTO. Mem. Am. Chem. Soc., Phi Lambda Upsilon. Republican. Mem. Lds Ch. Avocations: woodworking, fly fishing. Died May 27, 2005.

EXNER, JOHN E., JR., psychologist; b. Syracuse, N.Y., Apr. 18, 1928; s. John E. and Jessie Louise (Robedee) E.; m. Doris Elizabeth Castine, Jan. 20, 1951; children: John, Michael, Christopher, James, Andrea. BS, Trinity U., San Antonio, 1953, MS, 1954; PhD, Cornell U., 1958. Adminstr. clin. psychology Rochester (N.Y.) Inst. Tech., 1956-57; from asst. prof. to assoc. prof. DePauw U., Greencastle, Ind., 1957-62; assoc. prof., dir. clin. tng. Bowling Green (Ohio) State U., 1962-69; dir. Office of Selection, Peace Corps, Washington, 1968-69; prof. emeritus L.I. U., 1969-84; exec. dir. Rorschach Rsch. Found., Asheville, N.C., from 1968. Vis. clin. lectr. Ind. U., 1961-62; dir. rsch. Stoney Lodge Hosp., Ossining, N.Y., 1970-85. Author: The Rorschach: A Comprehensive System, Vols. 1-3, 1993, Issues and Methods in Rorschach Research, 1996, A Rorschach Workbook for Comprehensive Systems, 2001. Mem. Better Bus. Bur., Asheville, 1986—. Sgt. USAF, 1945-56. Recipient Trustee award for scholarly achievement L.I. U., 1981. Fellow APA, Am. Psychol. Soc., Soc. for Personality Assessment (pres., Disting. Contbn. award 1980, Walter G. Klopfer award 1990, Marguerite Hertz Meml. Lecture Series award 1993); mem. Internat. Rorschach Soc. (v.p., pres.), Asheville C. of C. Home: Asheville, NC. Died Feb. 20, 2006.

FACCHINELLO, LENA PATRICIA, bank executive; b. Ironwood, Mich., Mar. 8, 1925; d. Anton and Caroline (Schiavetti) Martorelli; m. Louis Facchinello; children: Nancy LeRoux, Mary Schueler. V.p. Security Bank, Milw., from 1955. Pres. West Allis Libr. Bd. dirs. West Allis Fair Housing Bd., West Allis Civic Improvement Found., Inc., West Allis Community Communication Corp., West Allis Meml. Hosp.; adv. bd. mem. SMART Program Milw. Area Tech. Coll.; apptd. mem. West Allis Police and Fire Commn., Pub. Safety Bldg. Task Force. Recipient Citizen of Yr. award West Allis C. of C., 1993. Mem. Fin. Instn. Mktg. Assn., West Allis Expo' 90 Com., West Allis Rotary Club. Roman Catholic. Avocations: walking, biking, gardening. Home: West Allis, Wis. Died Jan. 6, 2005.

FACER, CHARLES RICHARD, conductor; b. Camden, N.J., Sept. 12, 1949; s. Richard Samuel and Ruth Lorraine (Mannschott) F.; m. Barbara Louise Brown, Dec. 18, 1970 (div. May 1985); children: Dana Matthew, Kevin Charles; m. Melissa ann Moseley, July 31, 1988. B Music Edn., Temple U., 1972, MusM, 1974; postgrad., Ind. U., 1980-82. Grad. asst. in choral music and opera Temple U., 1972-73; dir. vocal activities Collingswood (N.J.) Jr. High Sch., 1974-77, Hammonton (N.J.) High Sch., 1977-80; assoc. instr. Ind. U., Bloomington, 1980-82; asst. prof. music, dir. choral activities Drury Coll., Springfield, Mo., 1982-88; mng. artistic dir., conductor Mid-Am. Singers, Springfield, from 1982; choral coord. Springfield Symphony Orch., from 1982; chorus master Springfield Regional Opera, from 1990. Minister of music King's Way United Meth. Ch., Springfield, 1983—; pvt. practice voice tchr., coach, Springfield, 1970—; host, music dir. weekly radio program The Choral Tridition, KSMU-FM, Springfield, 1985—; dir. of music Erlton Bapt. Ch., Cherry Hill, N.J., 1970-74, St. Paul's Evang. Ch., Collingswood, 1974-77; music dir., conductor Glassboro N.J.) Summer Theatre, 1977-84; choral dir. 1st United Meth. Ch., Columbus, Ind., 1981-82; conductor Bloomington Symphony Orch. Chorus, 1980. Composer various choral works; soloist Mid-Am. Singers, Ward Swingle, 1987; singer, actor numerous prodns.; music reviewer The Choral Jour., 1990—. Mem. music adv. panel Mo. Arts Coun., St. Louis, 1984-90. Mem. Am. Soc. Composers, Authors and Publs., Chorus Am. Assn. Profl. Vocal Ensembles, Am. Choral Dirs. Assn. (chair Mo. community choir 1989—), music Educators' Nat. Conf., Phi Mu Alpha Sinfonia (life, pres. Rho Upsilon chpt.). Avocations: cooking, camping, tennis. Home: Springfield, Mo. Died Dec. 6, 2004.

FAHY, JOSEPH THOMAS, lawyer; b. Uxbridge, Mass., July 9, 1919; s. John Francis and Josephine Mary (Rooney) F.; m. Marie C. McOsker, May 7, 1955; children: Margaret Ellen, Joseph Thomas Jr., John Fergus, Mary Celine. AB, Coll. of Holy Cross, 1941; LLB, Harvard U., 1948. Bar: Mass. 1948, U.S. Dist. Ct. Mass. 1954, U.S. Ct. Appeals (1st cir.) 1971, U.S. Supreme Ct. 1971. Assoc. Peabody, Brown, Rowley & Storey, Boston, 1948-56, ptnr., 1957-80; prin. Joseph T. Fahy, P.C., Boston, 1981-92; ptnr. Peabody & Brown, Boston, 1981-92, counsel, 1992-99, Nixon Peabody LLP, Boston, from 1999. Mem. ABA, Boston Bar Assn., Harvard U. Law Sch. Assn., Alpha Sigma Nu, Delta Epsilon Sigma, Holy Cross Club (past bd. dirs.), Harvard Club, K.C. Avocation: american history. Home: Belmont, Mass. Died Oct. 23, 2004.

FAIN, GERALD GENE, government affairs consultant; b. Norwich, Conn., Mar. 20, 1935; s. Yale and Norma Jean (Ritchie) F.; m. Laurel Ruth Reuss, June 22, 1963; children: Stacie L., Rachel L., Kimberly J. BSCE, Tufts U., 1957; JD, U. Conn., 1964. Bar: Conn., U.S. Ct. Claims, U.S. Tax Ct., U.S. Ct. Mil. Appeals, U.S. Supreme Ct. Sales engr. Ingersoll-Rand Corp., St. Louis, 1960-61; atty. U.S. Dept. Justice, Washington, 1964-69; staff atty. Joint Congl. Com. on Atomic Energy, Washington, 1969-72; regional mgr. licensing Gen. Atomic Co., Washington, 1972-75; asst. mgr. then v.p. and mgr. Washington ops. Stone & Webster Engring. Corp., 1975-88; cons. govt. affairs Alexandria, 1989-90; fin. cons., from 1990. Speaker in field. Bd. dirs. Aldersgate United Meth. Ch., Alexandria, Va., 1985-88. Served with USN, 1957-60. Mem. ABA, Fed. Bar Assn. Died Apr. 6, 2005.

FAIR, STEVE EDWARD, pharmaceutical marketing executive; b. Elizabethon, Tenn., Oct. 4, 1957; s. Bill Moody and Georgia Edna (Hart) F. BS in Biology, East Tenn. State U., 1979, postgrad., 1981-82. Radiation monitor supr. Nuclear Fuels Inc., Erwin, Tenn., 1981-89; profl. sales rep. Adria Pharms., Columbus, Ohio, 1990-92; dir. specialty markets Adams Labs. (subs. of Medeva Inc.), Fort Worth, from 1992. Deacon, vice chmn. of bd. dirs. Brick Christian Ch., Watauga, Tenn.; bd. dirs. East Tenn. Christian Home for Children. Recipient Salesmaster's award Adria Labs., 1991. Mem. Free and Accepted Masons #622. Avocations: travel, reading, collecting elvis presley memorabilia, collecting 50s/60s toys. Home: Watauga, Tenn. Died Nov. 15, 2004.

FALK, LESLIE ALLINA, physician; b. St. Louis, Apr. 19, 1915; d. Albert Epstein and Eleanor (Allina) F.; children: Gail, Theodore, Donald, Beth. AB, U. Ill., 1935; PhD, Oxford U., 1940; MD, Johns Hopkins Med., 1942. Resident Johns Hopkins Med. Ctr., Balt., 1942-43; fellow Med. Adminstrn. Svcs., N.Y.C., 1943; staff health subcom. U.S. Sen., Washington, 1943-46; med. dir. U.S. Pub. Health Svc., Atlanta, 1946-47; area med. adminstrn. United Mine Workers Health and Welfare Fund, Pitts., 1948-67; chmn. dept. family and cmty. health Meharry Med. Sch., Nashville, 1967-87. Fellow Am. Acad. of Family Practice, Am. Assn. of the History of Medicine, Am. Coll. of Preventive Medicine, AAUW (Henry Sigerist cir. policy com.); mem. Am. Assoc. of Rhodes Scholars, Health Svcs. Rsch. Forum, Medical History Club. Avocations: tennis, swimming, walking, hiking, writing. Home: Shelburne, Vt. Died Nov. 28, 2004.

FALL, HARRY H., chemical company executive; b. Lucenec, Czechoslovakia, Dec. 8, 1920; m. Agnes Pratt Jett, Sept. 3, 1947; children: Karen Lee, Marcia Lynn, Lisbeth Ann. BS in Chemistry, Pa. State U., 1942, PhD in Chemistry, 1950. Chemist Sylvania Indsl. Corp., Fredericksburg, Va., 1942-44; rsch. assoc. The Upjohn Co., Kalamazoo, 1951-56; sr. rsch. chemist Gen. Tire and Rubber Co., Akron, 1957-64, Goodyear Tire and Rubber Co., Akron, 1964-80; v.p. rsch. Smart Tag Systems Inc., Akron, 1990-97; exec. v.p., v.p. engring. and devel. Houdini Vehicle Security System, Akron, from 1997. Cons. chemist Omnitronics Rsch. Corp., Akron, 1981-83. Contbr. articles to profl. jours. 1st lt. U.S. Army, 1944-46, PTO. Fellow Am. Petroleum Inst., Pa. State U., 1948-50. Fellow Am. Inst. Chemists, Ohio Inst. Chemists (sec.-treas. 1965, chmn. 1967, nat. councillor 1968-88); mem. Am. Chem. Soc. Achievements include various patents, U.S. and fgn.; accomplished the deliberate grafting of saturated polymers. Home: Northfield, Ohio. Died Mar. 12, 2004.

FALLACI, ORIANA, writer, journalist; b. Florence, Italy, June 29, 1930; d. Edoardo and Tosca (Cantini) F. Grad., Liceo Classico Galileo Galilei, Italy; student, U. Florence Faculty Medicine, 1946-48; Litt.D. (hon.), Columbia Coll., Chgo., 1977. Editor, spl. corr. Europeo Mag., Milan, Italy, 1958-77; collaborator with major publs. throughout world, including Look mag., 1977-96, Life mag., 1977-96, The Washington Post, 1977-96, N.Y. Times, 1977-96, London Times, 1977-96; writer, from 1996. Dir. Rizzoli Pubs. Corp. Author: (novels) Penelope alla guerra, 1962 (pub. as Penelope at War, 1966), Lettera a un bambino mai nato, 1975 (pub. as Letter to a Child Never Born, 1976), Un uomo: romanzo, 1979 (pub. as A Man, 1980; Viareggio prize), In'shallah, 1990 (Hemingway prize 1991, Super Bancarella prize 1991), La Rabbia e l'Orgoglio, 2001, La Forza della Ragione, 2004; (non-fiction) I sette peccati di Hollywood, 1958, Il sesso inutile, 1961 (pub. as The Useless sex, 1964), Gli antipatici, 1963 (pub. as The Egoists, 1965), Se il sole muore, 1965 (pub. as If The Sun Dies, 1967), Niente a cosi sia, 1969 (pub. as Nothing, and So Be It, 1972; Bancarella prize 1971), Quel giorno sulla Luna, 1970, Intervista con la Storia, 1974 (pub. as Interview with History, 1976); audio: Oriana Fallaci reads Letter to a Child Never Born, 1993. Recipient St. Vincent award for journalism, 1971, 73. Died Sept. 14, 2006.

FALLIS, HUGH, retired electrical engineer; b. Texarkana, Ark., July 27, 1936; s. Woodson Nash and Hilda Marie (Southern) F.; m. Helga Esser, Apr. 18, 1976. BSEE, Tex. Tech., 1960. V.p. engring. RFE/RL, Inc., Washington, 1982-87, IBS, Inc., Arlington, Va., 1987-92. Author: (book) Public Diplomacy, 1986. Mem. IEEE Avocations: amateur radio, private pilot. Home: Troy, Va. Died Feb. 1, 2004.

FANIZZA, MICHAEL ANTHONY, art educator; b. Killeen, Tex., July 18, 1954; s. Michael and Arleen Fanizza; m. Sanja Softic; 1 child, Olivia Virginia. BA, U. Ill., Chgo., 1981; MFA, Va. Commonwealth U., 1984. Asst. prof. Ohio U., Athens, 1984—86, Chico (Calif.) State U., 1986—88; chair, assoc. prof. Old Dominion U., Norfolk, Va., 1988—99; prof. Mich. State U., East Lansing, from 1999. Prin. Michael Fanizza Designs, Haslett, Mich., from 1999. Artist (graphic design) MF Designs Poster (1st pl. am. Assn. Museums, 1999), Fifteenth Ann. Rosen Sculpture Catalog (Am. Graphic Design award, 2002). Mem.: AIGA, Coll. Art Assn. Home: Haslett, Mich. Died Feb. 26, 2004.

FARBER, SAUL JOSEPH, physician, educator; b. NYC, Feb. 11, 1918; s. Isodor and Mary (Bunim) Farber; m. Doris Marcia Balmuth; children: Joshua M., Beth Mina Farber Loewentheil. AB, NYU, 1938, MD, 1942; PhD (hon.), Tel Aviv U., 1983. Diplomate Am. Bd. Internal Medicine. Intern Sinai Hosp., Balt., 1942—43; rsch. resident Goldwater Meml. Hosp., N.Y.C, 1946—47; resident Bellevue Hosp., N.Y.C, 1947—48; fellow NYU Sch. Medicine, 1948—49, instr., asst. prof. medicine N.Y.C., 1953—62, assoc. prof., 1962—66, prof., chmn. dept. medicine, from 1966, Frederick H. King prof. medicine, from 1978, dean for acad. affairs, 1978—98, acting dean, 1963—66, 1979—81, 1982, dean, 1987—98, provost, 1987—98, chmn., 1998—99. Co-chmn. N.Y. State Health Adv. Coun., 1975—80; chmn. Com. on Resource Requirements of VA Health Care Systems NRC, 1974—77; mem. adv. com. on long term care chronic illness Robert Wood Johnson Found., 1979—2006, co-chmn. clin. nurse scholars adv. com., 1982—2006; mem. med. adv. bd. Hadassah; mem. adv. com. Harold C. Simmons Arthritis Rsch. Ctr., U. Tex. Health Sci. Ctr., Dallas, 1983—86; organizing chmn. Fedn. Coun. Internal Medicine, 1975; splty. advisor Naval Med. Command, Washington, 1985—86. Contbr. articles to profl. jours. Recipient Career Scientist award, Health Rsch. Coun., N.Y.C., 1960—65, Med. Alumni Achievement award, NYU Sch. Medicine Alumni Assn., 1966, Gt. Tchr. award, NYU Alumni Fedn., 1973, Alumni Assn. Achievement award,

Washington Sq. Coll. Arts and Sci., NYU, 1978, Alumni Meritorious Svc. award, NYU Alumni Fedn., 1984, Wise medal, Tel Aviv U., 1990, The Albert Gallatin medal, NYU, 1993, The Abraham Flexner award for Disting. Svc. to Med. Edn., 1995. Master: ACP (pres. 1984—85, regent 1978—86, Disting. Tchr. award 1986, Alfred Stengal Meml. award 1992); mem.: Acad. Health Ctrs. (adv. com. from 1981), Am. Physiol. Assn., Am. Clin. and Climatol. Assn., Inst. Medicine NAS, Interurban Clin. Club, Assn. Am. Physicians, Am. Soc. Clin. Investigation (sec.-treas. 1951—60, councillor 1960—63), Am. Soc. Internal Medicine (Disting. Internist of Yr. award 1976), Sigma Theta Tau (hon.). Died Oct. 11, 2006.

FARCNIK, ALEXANDER, commercial artist, portraitist; b. Hrastnik, Yugoslavia, Sept. 15, 1930; came to U.S., 1968; s. Ivan Anton and Ana (Grgurevic) F.; m. Milka Farenik, 1955; 1 child, Zoran. Student, Piers Coll., L.A., 1973. Draftsman Dor-O-Matic, Milw., 1968-70; comml. artist Am. Art, L.A., 1970-72; draftsman Norolscok, L.A., 1972-74; freelance artist Sacramento, from 1974. Holder 2 patents. Mem. Am. Soc. Portrait Artists. Home: Folsom, Calif. Died June 14, 2005.

FARGHER, JOHN STANLEY WAKELAM, JR., consultant, educator, retired government executive; b. St. Louis, Nov. 13, 1944; s. John Stanley Wakelam and Dorothy Margaret (Huston) F.; m. Eleanor Joyce Schumert, June 18, 1966; children: John Stanley Wakelam III, Cynthia Anne, Elizabeth Anne. BS in Engring. Sci., Mont. Coll. Mineral Sci./Tech., 1969; MEng, Tex. A&M U., 1971; MS in Systems Mgmt., U. So. Calif., L.A., 1979; postgrad., Harvard U., 1986. Chief engr. Iranian A/C Program Mgrs. Office, Tehran, 1975-77; faculty Def. Systems Mgmt. Coll., Ft. Belvoir, Va., 1977-78, prof. acquisition/program mgmt., 1978-81; dep. program mgr. light armored vehicle USMC, Ft. Belvoir, Va., 1981-82; prodn. planning and control dept. head Naval Aviation Depot, Cherry Point, N.C., 1982-84, comptroller and head mgmt. controls dept., 1985-91, bus. planning dept. head, 1991-92, head prodn. engring. dept., 1992-93; instr. dept. indsl. engring. N.C. State U., Raleigh, Md., 1984-85; ind. cons. Raleigh. Examiner Fed. Quality Improvement Prototype award Fed. Quality Inst., 1990, Pres.'s Award for Quality and Product Improvement, 1991; conf. chmn. 1st, 2d and 3d Internat. Symposiums on Productivity in Govt., Washington, 1992, 94, 95; judge Fla. Gov.'s Sterling award, 1992—. Author: Guide for International Programs, 1981, Guide for Joint Service Programs, 1980; editor: Quality in Government, 1992, 2d edit. 1994, 3d edit., 1995; contbr. numerous articles to profl. jours. With U.S. Army, 1963-66. Recipient Navy Civilian Meritorious award Dept. of Navy, 1989. Fellow Inst. Indsl. Engrs. (chmn. spl. productivity projects com. 1990—), Am. Prodn. and Inventory Control Soc. (bd. dirs. 1981—, Mem. of Yr. 1990, charter mem. REMFG specific interest group), Def. Systems Mgmt. Coll. Alumni Assn. (charter mem.), J.F. Kennedy Sch. Govt. Alumni Assn. (chpt. pres. 1986—). Episcopalian. Avocations: hunting, fishing, shooting, writing. Home: Manchester, Mo. Died Dec. 17, 2004.

FARRELL, EDWIN DAVID, trade association executive; b. South Bend, Ind., Aug. 21, 1941; s. James Henry and Mildred Eloise (Swanson) Farrell. BA, Quincy (Ill.) Coll., 1963. Adminstrv. svcs. mgr. Propeller Club U.S., Washington, 1970-77; dep. dir. meetings Am. Psychiat. Assn., Washington, 1977-87; exec. v.p., chief exec. officer Profl. Guides Assn. of Am., Arlington, Va., from 1987. Author: Life Beyond the Grand Ballroom, 1989. Mem. Am. Soc. Assn. Execs., Coun. Hotel, Restaurant and Instnl. Educators, Inter-Industry Coun., Internat. Assn. Tour Mgrs. Episcopalian. Avocations: white water rafting, swimming, boating. Died Apr. 11, 2005.

FARRELL, JOSEPH MICHAEL, water transportation executive; b. Yonkers, N.Y., June 7, 1922; s. Joseph Michael and Mary Elizabeth (Powers) F.; m. Cloatta Grace Pennington, Dec. 6, 1946; children: Cloatta M., Anthony J., Christopher J., Janice E. BS in Marine Transp., U.S. Mcht. Marine Acad., 1943; postgrad., Columbia U., 1948-50, Fordham U., 1947-48. Commd. ensign USNR, 1943, advanced through grades to capt., 1960; ret., 1968; mgr. Great Lakes Svc., States Marine LInes, 1960-62; European mgr. States Marine Lines, Bremerhaven, Germany, 1962-65; exec. v.p. Waterman S.S. Corp., Washington, 1965-95. V.p. Hammond Leasing Corp., Mobile, Ala., 1967-89, Waterman S.S. Co. of Del., 1967-89; pres. Waterman Oceanic Corp., 1974-89; sr. v.p. Ctrl. Gulf Lines, 1993-95; v.p. Internat. Shipholding Corp., 1993-95. Recipient Outstanding Profl. Achievement U.S. Merchant Marine ACad., 1968-88; invested Knight of Malta, 1988. Mem. Propeller Club U.S. (v.p., bd. govs. 1967-68, U.S. Exec. com. 1984-95), Nat. Def. Transp. Ass.n, Navy League, Congressional Country Club, Univ. Club, George Town Club (Washington), Siwanoy Country Club (Bronxville, N.Y.). Home: Chevy Chase, Md. Died Mar. 16, 2006.

FARRELL, LEIGHTON KIRK, minister; b. Hillsboro, Tex., Oct. 13, 1930; s. Aubrey Lee and Lorine (Kirk) F.; m. Charlotte Ann Underwood, May 31, 1952 (div. Feb. 1986); children: Becky Ann Wilson, Scott Gregory; m. Julie Ann Yarbrough, Apr. 25, 1987. BA, So. Meth. U., 1951, MTh, 1953; ThD, Iliff Sch. of Theology, 1956; DHL, Alaska Pacific U., Anchorage, 1983. Ordained elder Meth. Ch. Pastor Edge Park United Meth. Ch., Ft. Worth, 1956-66; adminstrv. asst. to the bishop Dallas-Ft. Worth Area United Meth. Ch., Dallas, 1965-67; sr. minister First United Meth. Ch., Richardson, Tex., 1967-72, Highland Park United Meth. Ch., Dallas, from 1972. Trustee So. Meth. U., Dallas, 1976—; chmn. bd. Meth. Hosps. of Dallas, 1977-83; del. to gen. conf. United Meth. Ch., 1980, 84; bd. dirs. pensions United Meth. Ch. George Washington medal of honor Freedom Founds. Home: Dallas, Tex. Died July 13, 2004.

FARRIOR, GILBERT MITCHELL, metallurgical engineer; b. Raleigh, N.C., Dec. 21, 1923; s. John Alexander and Dora Thorn (Mitchell) F.; m. Patricia Fowler, May 10, 1952; children: Barbara Linda Farrior Kovalsky, Patricia Ann, Marian Louise. BChE, N.C. State U., 1948, MEngr Physics, 1949; MS, U. Tenn., 1962, PhD in Metall. Engring., 1965; grad., Army War Coll., 1973. Registered profl. engr.; cert. logistician. Engr. smelting div. ALCOA, Alcoa, Tenn., 1953-55; rsch. metallurgist U.S. Bur. of Mines, Norris, Tenn., 1959-65, Battelle Meml. Inst., Columbus, Ohio, 1965-68; sr. rsch. metallurgist Kawecki-Berylco, Boyertown, Pa., 1968-81; sr. scientist ALUMAX Engineered Metal Processes, St. Louis, 1981-96, ret., 1996. Cons. Milward Alloys, Lockport, N.Y., 1981-86. Co-author sect. on semisolid metal forming ASM Handbook, Vol. 15, 1988; contbr. articles to profl. jours. Cpl. USMC, 1944-46; sgt. N.C. N.G., 1946-48; lt. ORC, 1948-51; 1st lt. U.S. Army, 1951-53; capt. Tenn. N.G., 1955-64; col. USAR, 1964-78. Mem. Am. Soc. for Metals (sr.), Metall. Soc. (sr.), Sigma Xi. Achievements include research and development of transition metal diborides, thermoelectrics, aluminum grain refiners, and semi-solid metal forming. Home: Saint Louis, Mo. Died Aug. 9, 2005.

FAUGHNAN, JAMES PATRICK, JR., risk management consultant; b. Albany, N.Y., July 18, 1933; s. James P. and Frances (Held) F.; m. M. Gayle Johnson, Jan. 25, 1958; children: James P. III, R. Thomas, Michael A., Suzanne E. Student, Manhattan Coll., 1951-52, Siena Coll., 1952-53, 55-57. Asst. loan mgr. Upstate Loan Co., Delmar, N.Y., 1957-59; asst. treas. West End Savs. & Loan, Albany, 1959-62; field rep. Aetna Casualty & Surety, Albany, 1962-65; exec. v.p. Austin & Co., Inc., Albany, 1965-89; pres. Confirm, Inc., Albany, from 1989. Pres. The Cons. Alliance, Albany, 1990—; bd. dirs. The Eddy, Troy, N.Y., Sr. Care Connection, Troy, LaSalle Sch., Albany, 1991—. Cpl. U.S. Army, 1953-55. Mem. Soc. Risk Mgmt. Cons., Wolferts Roost Country Club (bd. dirs.). Republican. Roman Catholic. Avocations: golf, do-it-yourself projects, reading. Home: Cortland, NY. Died Nov. 24, 2004.

FAY, HELYN, college counselor; b. Fontana, Calif., Sept. 9, 1950; d. James R. Sammon and Patricia J. (Burton) Murarik; m. Ronald E. Fay, Sept. 4, 1971; children: Emily, Timothy. BA in English cum laude, Pasadena Coll., 1972; MS in Counseling with distinction, Calif. Poly. State U., 1991. Tchr. elem. sch. Hickman Mills Sch. Dist., Kansas City, Mo., 1972-75; tchr. asst. Cuesta C.C., San Luis Obispo, Calif., 1984-88; sch. counselor San Luis Coastal Unified Dist., San Luis Obispo, 1990-95; marriage, family and child counselor intern in pvt. practice Barry Martin, Los Osos, Calif., 1992-95; counselor Pt. Loma Nazarene Coll., San Diego, from 1995. Mem. human devel. adv. com. Cuesta Coll., San Luis Obispo, 1993-95; chair eating behavior profl team Pt. Loma Nazarene Coll., San Diego, 1995—. Mem. Am. Assn. of Christian Counselors, Am. Coll. Counselors Assn., Am. Counseling Assn., Calif. Assn. of Marriage & Family Therapists (Clinton E. Phillips scholar 1990), Phi Delta Lambda. Home: San Diego, Calif. Died Jan. 31, 2004.

FEDORS, RAYMOND PETER, chemist; b. Weehawken, N.J., Jan. 16, 1942; s. Peter and Emma Barbara (O'Lenick) F.; children: Laurie Robin, Christina Lynn, Douglas Raymond. Degree in chemistry, Fairleigh Dickinson U., 1964; postgrad., Harvard U., 1990-93. Mgr. R&D Flexabar Corp., Northvale, N.J., 1962-67; corp. staff polymer cons. Becton Dickinson & Co., Hackensack, N.J., 1967-68; pres., chmn. bd. Polymer Rsch. Assocs., Inc., Dumont, Northvale, N.J., 1968-74; with market/product devel. dept. Davis & Geck, Pearl River, N.Y., 1974-75; pres., CEO Raymond P. Fedors & Assocs., Foxboro, Mass., from 1975. Bd. dirs. Compumed, Inc., Suffield, Conn., Strube Industries, Inc., Vestal, N.Y., Sensorsci Co., Foxboro., mng. an investment and new venture capital fund due- diligence on small captial medical device company investments, Raymond P. Fedors & Assocs. Author, prodr., dir., presenter: (TV series) The Business Beat, 1984-87, The Business Beat II, 1987-88, Meditrends, 1986; prodr., writer, presenter, dir.: (seminar series) Entrepreneurs Case Study Public Speaking Workshop, 1982-84. USAF scholar, 1957, scholar North Jersey Sci. and Math. Fair, 1956. Mem. Boston Computer Soc., British Officers Club New England, Soc. Plastics Engrs., Mensa, N.Y. Acad. Scis., T.J. Sokol Slovak Gymnastic Union. Achievements include patent for surgeon's glove and process for making gloves; patents pending for nonstick hypodermic needle, sterile drug delivery system, others; developed nonthrombogenic hydrophilic polymers for blood contact devices and implants. Died Dec. 23, 2004.

FEINBERG, ARTHUR WARREN, medical educator; b. Bklyn., June 17, 1923; BA, Columbia Coll., 1943; MD, Columbia U., 1945. Intern Lenox Hill Hosp., Bklyn., 1945-46; resident Maimonides Hosp., Bklyn., 1948-51; physician pvt. practice, Great Neck, N.Y., 1951-74; attending physician North Shore U. Hosp., Great Neck, N.Y., 1951-74, assoc. dir. dept. medicine, 1975-88, chief geriatric medicine Manhasset; med. dir. Ctr. Extended Care Rehab., Manhasset; prof. clin. medicine NYU Sch. Medicine, N.Y.C., 1996—2005. Bd. dirs. L.I. Alzheimer's Found., N.Y.;Capt. U.S. Army Med. Corps, 1946-48. Fellow N.Y. Acad. Medicine; master ACP; mem. Am. Fedn. Clin. Rsch., Am. Geriatrics Soc., Gerontological Soc. Am., N.Y. Med. Dirs. Assn., Met. Area Geriatrics Soc. (bd. dirs., v.p., pres.). Home: New York, NY. Died Nov. 28, 2005.

FEINSTEIN, MARTIN, performing arts educator, consultant, art director; b. NYC, Apr. 12, 1921; BSS, CCNY, 1942; MA, Wayne State U., 1943; MusD (hon.), Cath. U. Am., 1980, Shenandoah Coll. & Conservatory, 1983; LHD (hon.), Am. U., 1991; DFA, U. Md., 1995. Publicity dir. Hurok Concerts, N.Y.C., 1945-50, v.p., 1950-71; vis. prof. Yale U., New Haven, 1971-73; exec. dir. performing arts John F. Kennedy Ctr., Washington, 1972-80; pres., CEO Nat. Symphony, Kennedy Ctr., Washington, 1980-81; gen. dir. Washington Opera, 1980-95, cons., from 1995; sr. cons. U. Md. Performing Arts Ctr., College Park, 1995-2000, artistic dir., 1998-99, adj. prof., 2000—06. Panelist, onsite visitor Nat. Endowment of the Arts, from 1997. Decorated commendatore Republic of Italy; cross of officer Order Arts and Letters (France); Grand Decoration of Honor for Svcs. (Austria), officer Order of Merit (Germany); recipient medal Nat. Soc. Lit. and the Arts, 1977, award of Contbns. in Field of Dance Am. Assn. Dance Cos., 1979, Townsend Harris medal CCNY, 1977, John Cranko medal, Stuttgart, 1979, Myrtle Wreath award Washington Hadassah, 1982, Amphion award Memphis Symphony, 1983. Home: Potomac, Md. Died Feb. 5, 2006.

FEINSTEIN, ROBERT NORMAN, retired biochemist; b. Milw., Aug. 10, 1915; s. Jacob Feinstein and Jennie Cohen; m. Betty Jane Greenbaum; children: Ann E. Levis, Jean L. Feinstein-Lyon. BS in Chemistry, U. Wis., 1937, MS in BioChemistry, 1938, PhD in BioChemistry, 1940. Asst. scientist toxicity lab. U. Chgo., 1945—49; sr. scientist Argonne (Ill.) Nat. Lab., 1959—80; ret. Contbr. scientific papers to profl. jours., poetry to anthologies. Capt. U.S. Army, 1941—45. Recipient Guggenheim fellowship, 1959—60. Democrat. Jewish. Achievements include patents in field. Avocation: writing light verse. Home: Downers Grove, Ill. Died Sept. 23, 2005.

FELCH, PATRICIA ANNE, lawyer; b. Boston, Mar. 14, 1947; d. William Campbell and Nancy (Dean) F. AA, Pine Manor Coll., Chestnut Hill, Mass., 1967; BA, U. Denver, 1969, MA in Music, 1973, MA in Librarianship, 1973; JD, Loyola U., Chgo., 1987. Bar: Ill. 1987, U.S. Dist. Ct. (no. dist.) Ill. 1987, U.S. Ct. Appeals (7th cir.) 1987, U.S. Trial Ct. 1990, U.S. Ct. Appeals (2d cir.) 1998. Reference/arts libr. Atlanta Pub. Library, 1973-75; music libr. Northwestern U., Evanston, Ill., 1975-81; instr. music Waubonsee Coll., Sugar Grove, Ill., 1978-81; instr. humanities Coll. of DuPage, Wheaton, Ill., 1980-81; law libr. Coffield, Ungaretti, Harris & Slavin, Chgo., 1981-86; weekend libr. Northwestern U. Sch. Law, Chgo., 1981-82; summer assoc. Hosier & Sufrin, Chgo., 1986; assoc. Gessler, Flynn, Fleischmann, Hughes & Socol, Chgo., 1987-92; instr. entertainment law Columbia Coll., Chgo., 1990-93; pres. ARTSLaw Offices of Patricia A. Felch, P.C., Chgo., 1992-96; ptnr. Peterson & Ross, Chgo., 1997-99; instr. entertainment and sports law Loyola U. Chgo., from 1993; ptnr. Banner & Witcoff, Chgo., from 1999. Gen. counsel Orchestral Soc. Ill., Inc., Evanston, 1988—, Neighborhood Svcs., Inc., Chgo., 1992—, Leo Sowerby Found., 1993—, others. Contbr. articles to profl. jours. Bd. dirs. Lawyers for Creative Arts, 1988—, pres., 1994-98; mem. Ill. Alliance for Arts Edn., 1991—, CARPLS, 1994—. Harriet E. Howe scholar U. Denver Library Sch., 1972-73. Mem. ABA, Ill. Bar Assn. (assembly fin. com. 1990-93, chair 1992-93, intellectual property sect. coun. 1990, chair entertainment law com. 1989—, vice chair 1994-95, chair 1995-96, legal edn., admissions and competence standing com. 1985—, vice chair 1991-92, chair 1992-93), Chgo. Bar Assn. (chair entertainment law com. 1992-93, vice chair creative arts com. 1987-88, chair 1988-90), Beta Phi Mu. Avocation: golf. Home: Evanston, Ill. Died Mar. 24, 2005.

FELDMAN, CHESTER, retired editor; b. South Bend, Ind., June 26, 1920; s. Benjamin Hiram and Fannie (Glaser) F.; m. Henrietta Scheib, June 15, 1954; 1 child, Sabra Maya. SB, U. Chgo., 1940, SM, 1941, PhD, 1950. Cons. mathematician Aircraft-Marine Products, Harrisburg, Pa., 1952-53; asst. prof. Purdue U., West Lafayette, Ind., 1953-56, U. N.H., Durham, 1956-58, U. Conn., Storrs, 1958-63; assoc. prof. Kent (Ohio) State U., 1963-68; editor Math. Revs., Ann Arbor, Mich., 1968-79. With U.S. Army, 1942-46, PTO. Fellow AAAS; mem. Am. Math. Assn., Am. Math. Soc., Sigma Xi, Phi Beta Kappa. Avocations: record collecting, reading. Home: Ann Arbor, Mich. Died May 31, 2005.

FELDMAN, EGAL, historian, educator; b. NYC, Apr. 9, 1925; s. Morris and Chaya F.; m. Joan Bischoff, 1992; children: Tyla, Auora, Naomi. BA, Bklyn. Coll., 1950; MA, N.Y. U., 1954; PhD, U. Pa., 1959. Asst. prof. history U. Tex. at Arlington, 1960-66; asso. prof. history U. Wis.-Superior, 1966-68, prof., 1968—94, chmn. dept. history and philosophy, 1973-78, 81-94; dean U. Wis.-Superior (Coll. Letters and Scis.), 1978-81; prof. history emeritus U. Wis.-Superior, 1994—2004. Author: Fit for Men: History of New York's Clothing Trade, 1960, The Dreyfus Affair and the American Conscience, 1895-1906, 1981, The Dreyfus Affair and The Ben Shaan Prints, 1985, Dual Destinies: The Jewish Encounter with Protestant America, 1990, Catholics and Jews in Twentieth-Century America, 2001; contbr. chpts. to books, articles to profl. jours. Recipient Inst. Jewish Rsch. award, 1954, Max Lavine award, 1975, 91, Burlington

Northern Rsch. award, 1991, Kenneth Kingery Book-length Scholarly award Coun. Wis. Writers, 2002; grantee NEH, 1987. Jewish. Home: Superior, Wis. Died Aug. 21, 2004.

FELDMAN, MARTIN JOSEPH, recording studio executive, consultant; b. Taylorville, Ill., Aug. 12, 1939; s. Eli and Blanche (Stewart) F. Drummer with various artists including Stan Getz, Jimmy Smith, Judy Roberts, 1955-70; house drummer London House, Plug Nickel, Mother Blues, Big Johns, 1955-70; sound mixer Saint Lawrence Records, Chgo.; engr. Motown Records, Golden World, Detroit; dir., editor, cameraman Gilbert Altschul Prodns., 1960; founder, pres., prin. rec. engr., producer Paragon Rec. Studios, Chgo., from 1957. Owner, audio cons. Pro Audio; instr. stereo broadcast sound Columbia Coll. Editor (TV series) Wild Kingdom. Mem. Nat. Acad. Rec. Arts and Scis. (nat. trustee, mem. nat. TV com., pres. Chgo. chpt. 1985—), Mayor's Chgo.'s Music Adv. Com. Died Jan. 21, 2005.

FELTON, SAMUEL PAGE, biochemist; b. Petersburg, Va., Sept. 7, 1919; s. Samuel S. and Pearl (Williams) F.; m. Helen Florence Martin, Dec. 31, 1955; 1 child, Samuel Page. BS in Chemistry, U. Wash., 1951, postgrad., 1954. Cert. sr. pharmacist U.S. Army, San Francisco. Chief technician U. Wash., Seattle, 1952-59, rsch. assoc., 1959-62, sr. rsch. assoc., from 1976, dir. ctr. facilities lab. anesthesiology, 1969-73, dir. water quality lab., 1973-83, dir. biochem. lab. sch. of Fisheries, 1983-85; emeritus, micro-nutrition, rsch. and health in salmonids Sch. Aquatic and Marine Scis., U. Wash., Seattle, from 1985; asst. mem., asst. to dir. divsn. biochemistry Scripps Clinic and Rsch. Found., La Jolla, Calif., 1962-66; asst. biochemist Children's Orthopedic Hosp., Seattle, 1966-68. Vis. scientist Va. Inst. Marine Scis. at Coll. William and Mary, Williamsburg, 1985; chief pharmacist Paine Field. Mem. bd. of adjustments City of Edmonds, Wash., Shoreline Mgmt. Commn., Snohomish County, Wash. Sgt. MC, U.S. Army 1941-45. Fellow Am. Inst. Chemists, Am. Inst. Fishery Rsch. Biologists; mem. Am. Chem. Soc., Soc. Exptl. Biology and Medicine. Avocations: sailing, music, travel. Home: Edmonds, Wash. Died July 31, 2004.

FENDER, FREDDY (BALDEMAR HUERTA), singer, actor, writer; b. San Benito, Tex., June 4, 1937; s. Serapio and Margarita (Garza) Huerta; m. Evangalina Muniz, Aug. 10, 1957; children: Baldemar, Tammy, Daniel, Billy, Maria. Student, Del Mar Jr. Coll., Corpus Christi, Tex., 1973-74. Singer (albums) Before the Next Teardrop Falls, 1975, Are You Ready for Freddy, 1975, Since I Met You Baby, 1975, If You're Ever in Texas, 1976, Your Cheatin' Heart, 1976, Rock 'n' Country, 1976, The Best of Freddy Fender, 1977, If You Don't Love Me, 1977, Feliz Navidad, 1977, Swamp Gold, 1978, Tex-Mex, 1979, The Texas Balladeer, 1979, Togerher We Drifted Apart, 1980, The Freddy Fender Collection, 1991, Favorite Ballads, 1991, La Musica de Baldemar Huerta, 2002; (albums with The Texas Tornados) The Texas Tornados, Zone of Our Own, Hangin' on by a Thread, 4 Aces, Live from the Limo, Vol. 1, The Best of the Texas Tornados, Live from Austin,TX; (albums with Los Super 7) Heard it on the X; actor (films) Short Eyes, 1977, She Came to the Valley, 1979, Hacker's Raid, 1988, The Milagro Beanfield War, 1988, Always Roses, 1990, Who Will Sing the Songs, 1990, Mi amigo, 2002; (TV appearances) Great Performances, 1991 Served in USMC, 1954-56 Recipient Grammy, Billboard awards, Outstanding Mexican-Am. award 1977, Best Mexican-Am. Performance, 1990; inducted into Tejano Music Hall of Fame, 1986, European Walk of Fame, 1993, Puda Vida Awards Hall of Fame, 1998; Freddie Fender Lane named in his honor, San Benito, Tex., 1995. Mem. Country Music Assn., AFTRA, Am. Fedn. Musicians U.S. and Can., Broadcast Music Inc. Died Oct. 14, 2006.

FENTON, WAYNE S., psychiatrist; b. Mar. 24, 1953; s. Joseph and Roselyn Fenton; m. Nancy Fenton; children: Kaylan, Amalia, Claire, Nathaniel. BA in Exptl. Psychology, Bard Coll., 1975; MD, George Washington U., 1979. Cert. Am. Bd. Medical Examiners, 1980; cert. Md., Conn., Va.; Diplomate in Psychiatry. Rotating internship, dept. internal medicine Norwalk Hosp., Conn., 1979-80; resident, post doctoral fellow psychiatry Yale U., 1980-83; fellow Inst. Social and Policy Studies, Yale U., 1983-84; staff psychiatrist Yale Psychiat. Inst., Yale U., New Haven, 1983-84, Chestnut Lodge, Rockville, Md., 1984-85; rsch. assoc. Chestnut Lodge Rsch. Inst., Rockville, Md., 1984-90; clin. adminstrv. psychiatrist Chestnut Lodge Hosp., Rockville, Md., 1985-90; dir. rsch. Chestnut Lodge Rsch. Inst., Rockville, Md., 1990—99; asst. clin. dir. Chestnut Lodge Hosp., Rockville, Md., 1990—94, med. dir., 1994—98, CEO, 1994—96; assoc. clin. prof., psychiatry and behavior scis. George Washington U., Washington, from 1990; mem. faculty Washington Sch. Psychiatry, Washington, from 1991; dep. dir. clin. affairs NIMH, 1999—2006, acting dep. dir. Bethesda, 2001—02, associate dir., clinical affairs, 2003—06. Cons. Montgomery County Pub. Defender, Md., 1984-2006, McAuliffe House, Md., 1990-2006. Editl. cons. Schizophrenia Bulletin, 1986-2006, assoc. editor, 1994-2006; editl. cons. Jour. of Nervous and Mental Disease, 1986-2006, Am. Jour. Psychiatry, 1989-2006; contbr. to profl. jours. Recipient nat. rsch. svc. award USPHS, 1983-84, young investigator award NIH, 1989, Nat. Alliance for Rsch. in Schizophrenia and Depression, 1989, Gralnick award Am. Suicide Found., 1992, Md. Schizophrenia Sci. award, 1995. Mem. Am. Psychiat. Assn., Wash. Psychiat. Sopc., Nat. Alliance for Mentally Ill (exemplary psychiatrist 1996), NAPPH. Died Sept. 3, 2006.

FERGUSON, CHARLES SIBLEY, III, independent consultant; b. Chgo., Mar. 6, 1942; s. Charles Sibley Jr. and Jane (Melchert) F.; m. Sandra Louise Rykoff, Nov. 22, 1975; children: Rebecca Jane, Charles Sibley IV. BA, U. Colo., 1966. Personnel mgr. Procon, Inc., Des Plaines, Ill., 1972-74; dir. human resources U.S. League Savs. Instns., Chgo., 1974-81; asst. v.p. adminstrn. Freedon Fed. Savs. Bank, Oakbrook, Ill., 1981-88; ind. cons., from 1988. V.p. Inst. Fin. Edn., Chgo., 1984-85, pres. 1985-86. Served to chief petty officer USCG, 1966-71. Mem. Bus. Forms Mgmt. Assn., Midwest Soc. Profl. Cons. Republican. Congregationalist. Avocations: model railroading, home remodeling. Home: Barrington, Ill. Died Apr. 3, 2005.

FERGUSON, MAYNARD, trumpeter, band leader; b. Montreal, Que., Can., May 4, 1928; came to U.S., 1949. Rec. artist. Trumpet player with Stan Kenton Orch., 1950-53; freelance musician, L.A., 3 yrs.; formed own touring 13-piece orch., 1957-65; formed sextet, 1965; recorded 60 albums, including Maynard '61, 1961, Chameleon, 1974, High Voltage, 1987, Big Bop Noveau, 1990, 91, Live From London, 1992, Footpath Cafe, 1993, These Cats Can Swing, 1995, One More Trip to Birdland, 1996. Recipient Gold record Conquistador, 1978, Grammy award nomination, 1978, 84; voted into Downbeat and Internat. Jazz Educators Hall of Fame, 1992; inducted into Can. Music Hall of Fame, 1997. Died Aug. 23, 2006.

FERGUSON, TOM, author, physician; b. Ross, Calif., July 8, 1943; s. Wallace and Helen (Williams) F.; m. Meredith L. Dreiss, Aug. 22, 1983; 1 child, Adrienne L. Deiss. Student, Reed Coll., 1961-65; BA, San Francisco State U., 1971, MA, 1973; MD, Yale U., 1978. Editor-in-chief Med. Self-Care Mag., Inverness, Calif., 1976-89; pres. Self-Care Prodns., Austin, Tex., 1983—2006. Editor-at-large Self-Care Catalog, 1988-2006 Author: Medical Self-Care: Access to Health Tools, 1980, The People's Book of Medical Tests, 1985, The Smoker's Book of Health, 1987, The No-Nag, No-Guilt, Do-It-Your-Own-Way Guide to Quitting Smoking, 1989, Helping Smokers Get Ready to Quit: A Positive Apprach to Smoking Cessation, 1990, No Deadly Drug, 1992; co-author: Imaginary Crimes: Why We Punish Ourselves and How to Stop, 1990, Hidden Guilt, 1991, What You Need to Know about Psychiatric Drugs, 1991, The Stethoscope Book & Kit, 1991; med. editor: Whole Earth Catalog, 1977-83. Recipient Disting. Achievement award Nat. Ednl. Press Assn., 1978, Lifetime Extension award Com. for Lifetime Extension, 1979. Mem. Nat. Wellness Assn. (adv. bd.), Austin Profl. Writers Group. Avocation: book collecting: modern american fiction. Home: Austin, Tex. Died Apr. 14, 2006.

FERNANDEZ, MORAIMA, accountant; b. Sagua La Grande, Cuba, Feb. 24, 1951; came to U.S., 1967; d. Camilo M. and Maria Z. (Diaz) F. AA, Miami Dade Community Coll.; student, Fla. Internat. U. With accounts payable dept. Green Giant Co., Miami, 1973-75; bookkeeper Atico Mortgage Investors, Miami, 1975-76; comptroller Heavy Duty Parts, Inc., Miami, 1976-78, Equipment Leasing, Inc., Miami, 1978-80; pres. Alphacounts, Inc., Miami, from 1980. Commr. Dade County Commn. on the Status of Women; mem. com. Small and Minority bus. adv. coun.; appointed to Alcohol, Drug Abuse, Mental Health Planning Coun. Recipient Appreciation awards, IRS, Fla. Assn. Ind. Accts., Dade County Pub. Schs., Dade County Elections Dept., Dade County Reps. Mem. Nat. Soc. Pub. Accts., Fla. Assn. Ind. Accts. (v.p., Appreciation award), Internat. Assn. for Fin. Planning, Latin-Bus. and Profl. Women's Club, Am. Soc. Notaries. Republican. Roman Catholic. Died Mar. 31, 2004.

FERNBACH, LOUISE OFTEDAL, physician, educator; b. Fargo, N.D., Dec. 24; d. Sverre and Agnes Lenore (Halland) Oftedal; children: Bertram, Olinda, David, Pamela, Theodore, Robert; m. Alfred Philip Fernbach. BA, Wellesley (Mass.) Coll.; MD, George Washington U. Gen. practice medicine and obstets., Fishersville, Va., 1954-59; psychiatry resident UCLA, 1960; psychiatry fellow Johns Hopkins U., Balt., 1972; dir. mental health U. Fla., Gainesville, 1961-64, U. Ariz., Tucson, 1965-68; asst. prof. psychiatry Sch. Medicine Johns Hopkins U., Balt., 1972-74; dir. Washington Acupuncture Ctr., 1974-81; dir. Orthomolecular Med. Ctr. Linus Pauling Inst., Palo Alto, Calif., 1981-85; pvt. practice of neuropsychiatry and geriatrics Charlottesville, Va., from 1985. Lectr. Physicians for Social Responsibility, 1980—. Author: Acupuncture in Medical Practice, 1980. Fellow Am. Geriat. Soc.; mem. AAAS, AMA (com. on acupuncture), Am. Med. Women's Assn. (Va. state dir. 1991—, Cmty. Svc. award 1994), Am. Psychiat. Assn., Am. Acad. Psychosomatic Medicine, N.Y. Acad. Scis., Am. Acad. Pain Mgmt., World Fedn. for Mental Health. Unitarian Universalist. Avocations: tennis, cooking, painting, writing, golf, swimming. Died Feb. 13, 2005.

FERRARI, MICHAEL DAVID, financial planner, investment advisor; b. Washington, Mo., June 19, 1945; s. David D. and Alma (Farrell) F.; m. Jan Byrne, June 4, l966; l child, Elizabeth A. BS, U. Miami, 1968. CLU; CFP. Asst. mgr. Conn. Gen. Life Ins. Co., Kansas City, Mo., 1968-78; agy. mgr. Equitable Iowa, Kansas City, 1979-83; pres. Ferrari Fin. Ins. and Investment Mgmt., Overland Park, Kans., from 1982. Author, pub. Which Way the Market newsletter, l982—. Contbr. articles to newspapers. Instr. adult edn. area colls., Kansas City, l982—. Mem. Inst. CFPs, Toastmasters (best spkr. award). Republican. Avocations: scuba diving, hiking, restoration of old house, antique cars. Home: Shawnee Mission, Kans. Died May 11, 2005.

FERRO, WALTER, artist; b. N.Y.C., Oct. 6, 1925; s. Joseph Salvador and Mary Elizabeth (Potezna) F.; m. Lore Gausmann, Sept. 20, 1966; children— Elizabeth, Paula. Cert., Bklyn. Mus. Art Sch., 1952. Art cons. One-man exhbns. include Wakefield Gallery, N.Y.C., 1960, Dominican Coll., Racine, Wis., 1962, Kings Coll., Briarcliff, N.Y., 1967, Hiram Malle Meml. Library, Pound Ridge, N.Y., 1988, Gallery L 9, Oberursel, Fed. Republic Germany, 1991; group exhbns. include Bklyn. Mus., 1953, U. Okla., 1959, Jersey City Mus., 1966, Phila. Mus., 1966; represented in permanent collections Met. Mus. Art, Nat. Mus. Am. Art, Smithsonian Instn. Served with USNR, 1942-44. Recipient Kenneth Hayes Miller Meml. award Audubon Artists, 1953; Kate W. Arms Meml. award Soc. Am. Graphic Artists, 1959; Guggenheim fellow, 1972 Died Dec. 27, 2005.

FESSLER, JOYCE ANN, journalist; b. Richmond, Ind., Apr. 15, 1932; d. Olan Dale and Anna G. (Wilbur) Edwards; m. Walter George Fessler, Nov. 15, 1958 (dec. 1979); children: Joseph, MaryAnn, John, Teresa, Christopher, Catherine. BA, Marian Coll., 1953. Eucharistic minister. Reporter Comml. Rev., Portland, Ind., 1953-54; reporter, editor Palladium-Item, Richmond, 1954-58, 72-90, part-time reporter, editor, 1958-72; regional reporter The Criterion, Indpls., 1954-80's; retired, 1990. Vol. soup kitchen. Mem. Soc. Profl. Journalists, Delta Epsilon Sigma. Republican. Roman Catholic. Home: Richmond, Ind. Died Jan. 10, 2005.

FEST, JOACHIM, writer, historian; b. Berlin, Aug. 12, 1926; s. Johannes and Elisabeth (Straeter) F.; m. Ingrid Ascher; children: Alexander, Nicolaus. Degree, U. Stuttgart, Baden, Württemberg, 1981. Editor RIAS, Berlin, Federal Republic of Germany, 1954-61; vice chief editor of play NDR-TV, Hamburg, Federal Republic of Germany, 1961-63, chief editor, 1963-68; freelance writer Federal Republic of Germany, 1968-73; publisher, editor Frankfurter Allgemeine Zeitung, Frankfurt. Author: The Face of the Third Reich, 1963, The Face of the Third Reich: Portraits of the Nazi Leadership, 1970, Hitler: A Biography, 1973, Aufgehobene Vergangeheit, 1981, Im Gegenlicht, 1988, Plotting Hitler's Death: The German Resistance to Hitler, 1933-45, 1996, Speer: The Final Verdict, 2001, Inside Hitler's Bunker: The Last Days of the Third Reich, 2004. Recipient Thomas-Mann-Preis award Thomas Mann Gesellschaft, 1981, Goethe Plakette Stadt Frankfurt, 1987, Premio Mediterraneo award Palermo, 1989. Mem. Max-Planck Soc. (senator). Home: Kronberg, Germany. Died Sept. 11, 2006.

FEUER, CY, film producer, director, theater producer; b. NYC, Jan. 15, 1911; s. Herman and Ann (Abrams) F.; m. Posy Greenberg, Jan. 20, 1946 (dec. 2005); children: Robert, Jed. Student, Inst. Mus. Art Juilliard Found., 1928-32. Head music dept. Republic Pictures, 1938-42, 45-47; partner Feuer and Martin Prodns., N.Y.C., from 1947; mgr., dir. San Francisco & LA Civic Light Opera Assn., 1975-80. Pres. The League of Am. Theatres and Producers, 1989—. Theatrical prodns. include Where's Charley, 1948, Guys and Dolls, 1950, Can-Can, 1953, The Boy Friend, 1954, Silk Stockings, 1955, Whoop-Up, 1958, How To Succeed in Business Without Really Trying, 1961 (Pulitzer prize for drama), Little Me, 1962, Skyscraper, 1965, Walking Happy, 1966, The Goodbye People, 1968, The Act, 1977; producer: motion pictures Cabaret, 1972 (winner 8 Acad. awards), Piaf, 1975, Chorus Line, 1985; author: (autobiography) I Got the Show Right Here, 2003. Inducted into the Theater Hall of Fame, 1994. Died May 17, 2006.

FEUSSNER, ELIZABETH LOBUR, veterinarian, toxicologist; b. New Kensington, Pa., Jan. 28, 1947; d. John Elias and Anna Juliana (Surowski) Lobur; m. James Walter Feussner, July 24, 1971. BS in Animal Sci., Pa. State U., 1969; VMD, U. Pa., 1972. Diplomate Am. Bd. Toxicology. Vet. practitioner Spruce Hill Vet. Clinic, Phila., 1972-74, Evans Animal Hosp., Springfield, Pa., 1974-75, Atlantic Animal Hosp., Pomona, N.J., 1975-76; rsch. scientist, toxicology McNeil Pharm., Fort Washington, Pa., 1976-79, sr. scientist, head of acute toxicology Spring House, Pa., 1979-81; sr. scientist, mgr. of vet. care Argus Rsch. Labs., Inc., Horsham, Pa., from 1982; part-time clin. vet. Thomas Jefferson U., Phila., 1988-92; cons. veterinarian Lankenau (Pa.) Med. Rsch. Ctr., from 1992, Grad. Hosp. Med. Rsch. Ctr., Phila., from 1993. Died Mar. 14, 2005.

FICARRA, BERNARD JOSEPH, former surgeon, legal medicine and bioethics consultant; b. N.Y.C., Jan. 1, 1914; s. Humphrey and Rose Marie (D'Ambra) F.; m. Jean Alice Augustine, Aug. 31, 1966; 1 son, Bernard Thaddeus. BA magna cum laude, St. Francis Coll., 1935, ScB, 1936; MD, Georgetown U., 1939; ScD, U. Steubenville, 1950; LLD, St. Francis Coll., N.Y.; PhD, Minerva U., Milan, Italy, 1960. Diplomate Am. Bd. Surgery. Surg. intern Kings County Hosp. Med. Ctr., Bklyn., 1939-41, resident pathology, 1941-42, resident surgery, 1942-44; fellow surgery Lahey Clin. Found., Burlington, 1946-48; practice medicine specializing in surgery N.Y.C., 1948-60, Greenvale, N.Y., 1953-80; mem. vis. surg. staff Kings County, St. Peters, Holy Family, St. Mary's hosps. Dir. surg. rsch. Ficarra Found., Inc., 1949-69; prof. physiology St. Francis Coll., 1948-51; prof. rsch. physiology St. John's U. Postgrad. Sch., 1951-61; professorial rsch. assoc. L.I. U., Postgrad. Sch., 1961-73; dir. Somerset Enterprises, Ltd., Doric Corp. Author: Diagnostic Synopsis of Acute Surgical Abdomen, 1950; Emergency Surgery, 1953; Thyroid and Parathyroid Diseases, 1958; Surgical and Allied Malpractice, 1968; Medicolegal Handbook, 1983; Medicolegal Examination

Evaluation and Report, 1986, Abortion Analyzed, 1989, Feudal Chateau, 1990, Church on The Hill, 1990, Virtue Lost: Virtue Found, 2000, Evolution: Fact, Fiction, or Fancy, 2001, Real Property: A Perilous Possession, 2001, Bioethics Rise, Decline, and Fall, 2001, Virtue Lost: Virtue Found, 2002, Royal Religious Revolutionaries, 2002, Stemcell Research, 2003, Endless Battle Between Good and Evil, 2003, Thyroid Trauma: Physical and Psychic, 2004, Forensic Science, 2004, Politics and Politicians, 2004, Images of Love, 2004, Arch of Triumph In Decay; mem. emeritus adv. bd. jour. Med. Malpractice Prevention; mem. editl. bd. Jour. Contemporary Health Law and Policy; contbr. 270 articles to profl. jours. Trustee L.I. Ednl. TV Coun. Inc., Sta. WLIW; pres. Cath. Acad. Scis. U.S.A.; cons. Holy Land Christian Charity. Recipient Golden Anniversary Alumni citation, Georgetown U., 1989, Recognition award N.Y. Acad. Sci., N.Y. Acad. Sci.; named to Alumni Hall of Fame St. Francis Prep. Sch., N.Y., 1990; decorated Silver Palm of Jerusalem, 1988, Gold Palm of Jerusalem, Gold medal for Svc. to Holy Land, His Patrimony Rev. Joseph Nazzaro, OFM Custos of the Holy Land, Archbishop Boyle Archdiocesan medal James Cardinal Hickey, 1998, Knight of Merit with Star Sacred Mil. Constantinian Order St. George, Spain. Fellow ICS, Am. Coll. Gastroenterology (com. for legal matters), Am. Coll. Legal Medicine (edn. com.), Am. Coll. Angiology (achievement honor award 1964-65); mem. AMA (Physicians Recognition award 2001, 04), N.Y. State Med. Soc., N.Y. Acad. Medicine, N.Y. Acad. Scis., N.Y. Soc. Med. Jurisprudence, Acad. Templars (Bologna, Italy), Greenvale C. of C., Lahey Clinic Alumni Assn. (coun.), Cath. Acad. Scis. (.U.S. pres.), Alpha Omega Alpha, Pi Alpha, Phi Chi. Lodges: Lions (hon., pres. 1976-78, Knight of Malta, Knight Cmdr. of St. Gregory the Great), Equestrian Order of the Holy Sepulchre of Jerusalem (sect. rep. southeastern lieutenancy Washington, So. Md., No. Va., lt. mid. Atlantic lieutenancy Del., Md., Va., W.Va., Tenn., N.C., Washington, mil. svcs. of USA, Knight Grand Cross, lt. by grand magisterium, lt. of honor Equestrian Order Holy Sepulchre of Jerusalem conferred by Grand Master of Order, Carlo Cardinal Furno, 1998, Golden Palm of Jerusalem for charitable continuous svc. to Holy Land, Vatican City State). Home: Potomac, Md. Died Sept. 15, 2005.

FICKLE, DOROTHY HELEN, museum curator; b. Eliot, Maine, Sept. 27, 1924; d. Chauncey Depew and Sara Katherine (Taudvin) Wentworth; m. Lee Edward Fickle, Sept. 23, 1950; children: Kathleen Anne, Floyd Edward, Susan Aileen. AB, Boston U., 1946, MA, 1947; PhD, U. Pa., 1978. Instr. polit. sci. U. Maine, Orono, 1947-48; tech. REA, Dept. of Agr., Washington, 1948-50; social sci. analyst Census Bur., Dept. Commerce, Washington, 1950-52; tchr. 6th grade Internat. Sch., Bangkok, Thailand, 1962-64; social studies tchr. Dacca (East Pakistan) Am. Sch., 1965-68, Internat. Sch., Bangkok, 1969-70; rsch. fellow Nelson-Atkins Mus. of Art, Kansas City, Mo., 1979-83, curator south Asian art, 1983-93. Guest lectr. Tibetan art U. Kans., Lawrence, 1990-91, guest lectr. Indian art, 1979—; guest lectr. Kansas City Art Inst., 1983—. Author: Life of the Buddha Murals, 1972, Images of the Buddha in Thailand, 1989; contbr. articles to profl. jours. Mem. Friends of the Johnson County Libr., Overland Park, Kans., 1987—. NEH fellow, 1986. Mem. Assn. for Asian Studies, Am. Com. for South Asian Art (sec. 1992—, symposium organizer 1985), Coll. Art Assn., Phi Beta Kappa. Avocations: hiking, reading, theater, concerts. Home: Bainbridge Is, Wash. Died Mar. 2, 2005.

FIDELLE, THOMAS PATRICK, JR., chemical company executive; b. Boston, July 14, 1939; s. Thomas Patrick Sr. and Mary (Fraser) F.; m. Linda Elizabeth Coppersmith, Sept. 18, 1965; children: Meredith Elizabeth, Thomas Alexis. BS in ChemE., Tufts U., 1961; MS in ChemE., U. Mass., 1967, PhD in ChemE., 1969. Mgr. R&D Celanese Corp., N.Y.C., 1969-81, dir. R&D, 1981-83, Great Lakes Chem. Corp., West Lafayette, Ind., from 1983. Vis. prof. U. N.C., Charlotte. Contbr. articles to profl. jours., 1976-89; represented in permanent collection. Pres. New Directions, Inc., Tippecanoe City, 1980; founder, Metrolina Environmantal Concern Assn. Capt. USMC 1961-65. Mem. Flame Retardant Chemists Assn., Soc. of Plastics Engrs. Avocations: golf, flying, sailing, creative photography. Died Apr. 19, 2005.

FIFE, ELAINE HARNER, lawyer, mediator; b. Apr. 22, 1950; d. Orville David and Anna Louise (Mathews) Harner; m. Thomas N. Biehl, June 13, 1971 (div. Sept. 1982); 1 child, Brandon Thomas; m. David Mack Fife, Oct. 9, 1983; 1 child, David Mackie. BA, Ohio State U., 1972; JD, Loyola U., L.A., 1975. Bar: Ohio 1975; U.S. Dist. Ct. (so. dist.) Ohio 1975. Atty. Clinton County Pub. Defender's Office, Wilmington, 1976-77, dir.-atty., 1977-98; pvt. practice Wilmington, 1979-83; ptnr. Fife and Fie, Wilmington, from 1983. Pres., Clinton County Council on Alcoholism, Wilmington, 1985-86; bd. trustees program com. Leadership Clinton, 1986-87; bd. dirs. Ohio Criminal Justice Supervisory Com., 1978-83, Clinton County Cmty. Supervision Program, 1996—; adj. prof. of English So. State Cmty. Coll. Recipient Ohio Pub. Defender award, 1996. Mem. Clinton County Bar Assn. (sec. 1979-80, 86-87, treas. 1985-86, pres. 1988-89), Acad. Family Mediators, Ohio State Pub. Defender Assn. 9bd. dirs. 1977-81), AAUW (pres. 1993-95), Beta Sigma Phi, recipient Silver Beaver Award, Tecumseh Council, B.S.A. Mem. Soc. Of Friends. Died May 25, 2005.

FIGLER, ALAN ANTHONY, medical systems engineer, consultant; b. Rockville Ctr., N.Y., Sept. 17, 1948; s. Edward Leon and Mildred (Aubel) F.; m. Kathleen Backor, June 12, 1971; children: Laura, Brian, Erik. BEE, Rensselaer Poly. Inst., 1970, M in Engring., 1971. Engr. GTE Automatic Electric, Northlake, Ill., 1971-76; group leader Telemed, Inc., Hoffman Estates, Ill., 1976-79; sr. engr. Gould Labs, Rolling Meadows, Ill., 1979-81; mgr. software engring., sr. prin. engr. Baxter Healthcare, Round Lake, Ill., 1981-90; engr. Northgate Rsch., Ind., Arlington Hts., Ill., from 1991. Owner Figler Cons., Crystal Lake, Ill., 1987—. Patentee in field. Recipient award for Outstanding Technical Achievement, Baxter-Travenol Labs., 1986. Mem. Digital Equipment Corp. Users Group, IEEE (chmn. sub com. med. info. bus. Std. 1986—). Lutheran. Avocations: running, railroads, sunbeam sports cars. Home: Woodinville, Wash. Died July 6, 2005.

FILE, JOSEPH, retired research physics engineer; b. Lecce, Italy, May 6, 1923; s. Carlo and Laura (Nuzzi) F.; m. Dorothy Richards, Sept. 2, 1944; children: Joseph C., Laurel M., Jeannette. BME, Cornell U., 1944; MS, Columbia U., 1958, PhD, 1967; D in Physics, U. Lecce, Italy, 1978. Design engr. Petro Chem. Devel. Co., N.Y.C., 1946-56; rsch. sr. Princeton (N.J.) U., from 1956. Advisor N.E. region Fed. Lab. Consortium, 1992—; ofcl. U.S. rep. 2nd Atoms for Peace Conf., Geneva, 1958; Def. Dept. appointee Employer Support for the Guard and Res., 1995. Contbr. articles to profl. jours. Pres. Marine Corps Scholarship Found., 1965-75, chmn. bd. dirs., 1975-94, chmn. emeritus. Col. USMCR, 1942-74; PTO, Korea. Decorated comdr. Order of Italian Republic; Fulbright fellow, 1978. Roman Catholic. Achievements include patent on bending free D, shaped magnetic coils for fusion reactors, and fabrication and operation of world's first sixth order superconducting magnet now used on MRI imaging devices. Home: Skillman, NJ. Died Oct. 15, 2005.

FINCH, EDWIN B., insurance sales executive; b. Carmi, Ill., Nov. 19, 1935; s. Walter E. Finch and Rachel (Boyer) Newcomb; m. Patricia L. Stinnett, June 19, 1934; children: Scott E. finch, Krista K. Pruehs. BS in Ag., U. Ill., 1958; D of bibl. studies, Internat. Coll. Bible Theol., 1996. Commd. 2d lt. U.S. Army, 1958, advanced through grades to capt.; owner Finch Svcs., Carmi, Ill., 1966-76; v.p. Am. Missions Teams, Norris City, Ill., 1994-98; dir. Internat. Coll. of Bible Theology, Norris City, 1994-98; v.p., sec. Marquette Indemnity and Life, St. Louis, 1976-98; pres. Finch Svcs., Inc., Carmi, from 1976. Avocations: playing trumpet, travel. Home: Carmi, Ill. Died May 18, 2005.

FINE, HERBERT HAROLD, lawyer; b. July 30, 1913; s. Jacob Harold and Rebecca (Stern) F.; m. Adelaide Altschuler, Apr. 14, 1940; children: M. Jonathan, Nancy. LLB, Rutgers U., 1934. Bar: N.J. 1934, U.S. Supreme Ct. 1958. Pvt. practice, Red Bank, Middletown, N.J.; assoc. Green & Green, 1934-36; tax cons., 1936-42; assoc. Stein, Stein & Conford, 1942-52; ptnr. Stern & Fine, 1952-63; spl. counsel Widmark and Goldberg, 1963-66. Spl. counsel Township of West Milford, N.J., 1951, City of Passaic, Township of Weehawken, N.J., 1966, City of Hoboken, N.J., 1954-87, City of Union City, N.Y., 1962, 84—, Township of North Bergen, N.J., 1985-97. Mem. Internat. Soc. for Study of Time, Monmouth County Bar Assn. Home: Red Bank, NJ. Died Jan. 14, 2005.

FINEGAN, FRANK JOSEPH, systems engineer; b. N.Y.C., June 26, 1927; s. Frank Joseph and Elizabeth Catherine (Hoenighausen) F.; m. Barbara Grace Brummer, Nov. 26, 1954; children: Susan Finegan Jappell, Sharon Finegan. BSME with high honors, Stevens Inst. Tech., 1952, ME in Applied Mechanics, 1955; Profl. ME, Columbia U., 1960. Registered profl. engr., N.Y. Engr. Otis Elevator, N.Y.C., 1953-54; sr. engr. UNISYS, Great Neck, N.Y., from 1954, lectr., from 1980. Contbr. articles to profl. jours. Served as sgt. U.S. Army, 1945-48. Mem. ASME. Democrat. Roman Catholic. Avocation: golf. Home: Syosset, NY. Died May 2, 2004.

FINKELSTEIN, CLAUDIA MARCELLE, school psychological examiner, jazz vocalist; b. Montreal, Can., Feb. 16, 1944; came to the U.S., 1944; adopted d. Marcel A. and Jeannette C. (Beauchamp) Fugere; d. Juliette Laplante Jobin; m. Martin R. Finkelstein, June 9, 1968; children: Beth, Leah. BA, Colby Coll., 1966; MA, U. Maine, 1973. Cert. psychol. examiner, sch. psychol. examiner. Sch. psychologist Tenn. Sch. for the Deaf, Knoxville, 1968-69; pvt. practice psychol. examiner Portland, Maine, 1976-94; sch. psychol. examiner Portland (Maine) Pub. Schs., from 1994. Vocalist with various jazz ensembles, 1979—; recordings include CD Charlie and Claudia Live! Smooth Singing, 1998. Vol. Dem. Party, Maine, 1964—; chairperson Cape Elizabeth (Maine) Arts Commn., 1992-95. Mem. Maine Psychol. Assn. Jewish. Avocations: camping, reading, movies, writing music, fiction and letters. Home: Cape Eliz, Maine. Died Aug. 2, 2005.

FIREBAUGH, MARCO ANTONIO, former state legislator; b. Baja California, Mexico, Oct. 13, 1966; children: Ariana, Nicolas. BA, U. Calif., Berkeley, 1993; JD, UCLA, 1997. Prin. cons. Latino Legis. Caucus, 1990—95; mcpl. law analyst, 1995—98; mem. Calif. State Assembly, 1998—2004. Democrat. Roman Catholic. Died Mar. 21, 2006.

FISCHER, HENRY GEORGE, Egyptologist; b. Phila., May 10, 1923; s. Henry G. and Agnes Beatrice (Hurdman) F.; m. Eleanor Armstrong Teel, Dec. 15, 1951; 1 dau., Katherine Fraser (Mrs. Woodman Taylor). BA, Princeton U., 1945; PhD, U. Pa., 1955. Instr. English Am. U. Beirut, 1945-48; asst. Egyptian sect. U. Pa. Mus., 1949-56; mem. univ. expdn. to Mit Rahineh, Egypt, 1955, 56; asst. prof. Egyptology Yale Grad. Sch., 1956-58; asst. curator Egyptian art Met. Mus. Art, 1958-63, assoc. curator, 1963-64, curator, 1964-70, Lila Acheson Wallace curator in Egyptology, 1970-79, rsch. curator, 1979-91, curator emeritus, 1992—2005. Adj. asst. prof. fine arts Inst. Fine Arts, N.Y. U., 1962-64, adj. assoc. prof., 1964-66, adj. prof., 1966-80; vis. lectr. art history and archaeology Columbia U., 1960-61; sec.-treas. Am. Com. to Preserve Abu Simbel, 1964-70 Author: Inscriptions from the Coptite Nome: Dynasties VI-XI, 1964, Ancient Egyptian Representations of Turtles, 1968, Dendera in the Third Millennium B.C, 1969, Egyptian Studies I: Varia, 1976, II: The Orientation of Hieroglyphs, Part 1: Reversals, 1977, Ancient Egyptian Calligraphy, 1979, The Renaissance Sackbut and Its Use Today, 1984, L'écriture et l'art de l'Egypte ancienne, 1986 Trustee Am. Research Center in Egypt, 1955-66; bd. dirs. Ams. for Middle East Understanding, v.p. Guggenheim fellow, 1956-57 Mem. Egypt Exploration Soc. (London), Société Française d'Egyptologie, German Archaeol. Inst., Phi Beta Kappa. Home: Sherman, Conn. Died Dec. 11, 2005.

FISCHER, ROBERT H., church history educator emeritus; b. Williamsport, Pa., Apr. 26, 1918; s. M. Hadwin and M. Alice (Gortner) F.; m. Edna Mae Black, Sept. 5, 1942; 1 child, Susan K. Fischer Wade. AB, Gettysburg Coll., 1939; BD, Luth. Theol. Sem., Gettysburg, Pa., 1942; PhD, Yale U., 1947. Pastor Community Parish, Hartland, Vt., 1944-45; asst. pastor Zion Luth. Ch., Sunbury, Pa., 1947-49; prof. ch. history Luth. Sch. Theol., Chgo., 1949-86. Established Luth. tutorship Mansfield Coll., Oxford U., 1957-58; participant Internat. Congresses for Luth. Research; guest prof. Theologische Hochschule, Berlin, 1973, Japan Luth. Sem., Tokyo, 1980. Author: Luther, 1966; editor: Luther's Works, Vol. 37, 1961, Franklin Clark Fry, 1972, A Tribute to Arthur Vööbus, 1977. Sterling doctoral research fellow Yale U., 1945-46; Assn. Theol. Schs. fellow 1964-65. Mem. Soc. for Reformation Research (pres. 1954), Am. Theol. Soc. (pres. midwest div. 1961-62, sec.-treas. 1964-86), Luth. Hist. Conf. (v.p. 1972-76, bd. dirs. 1984—), Phi Beta Kappa, Phi Gamma Delta. Clubs: Sub. Vets. Chorus (accompanist, assoc. dir. 1949-85) (LaGrange). Republican. Avocations: music, sports, handcrafts. Home: Western Springs, Ill. Died July 5, 2004.

FISCHER, THERESE MARIE, special education educator; b. Lead, SD, Mar. 24, 1911; d. Ludwig Henry and Catherine (Volbach) Stadler; m. Carl Michael Fischer, Aug. 12, 1939 (div. Nov. 9, 1970); children: Michael L., Catharine Farrell, John C BA Distinction, San Jose State Coll., 1966; MEd, U. Oreg., 1970. Lic. tchr., Calif. Tchr. spl. edn. Los Altos Sch. Dist., Calif., 1966—76; edn. specialist Los Altos, 1976—85; dir. Coastside Adult Lit., Half Moon Bay, Calif., 1985—91. Bd. dirs. Cmty. Access TV Sta., Coastside, San Mateo County, 1990-2006; tutor Coastside Adult Lit., Half Moon Bay, Calif., 1985-2006; v.p. Friends of Half Moon Bay Libr., 1991-93; founder, chair Hard of Hearing Group, 1994-99; chair Bookclub for Elderly Srs., 2001—. Mem. AAUW (Woman of Excellence 1987, v.p. edn. 1989-91), AARP (bd. dirs. local chpt., Vol. of Yr. 1998). Avocations: travel, reading, clothing design. Home: Half Moon Bay, Calif. Died Apr. 3, 2006.

FISH, JAMES M., investment broker; b. Milw., Aug. 8, 1949; B Fin. and Mgmt., U. Wis., Milw., 1972. Investment broker Braun, Monroe, Milw., 1972-79; sales mgr. F H Hutton, Milw., 1979-88; investment broker A.G. Edwards & Sons Inc., Milw., from 1988. Mem. Athletic Club Milw. Avocation: computer bulletin board (political). Died Dec. 2, 2004.

FISH, STEWART ALLISON, retired obstetrician and gynecologist; b. Benton, Ill., Nov. 4, 1925; s. Floyd Hamilton and Mary Vivian (Fish) F.; m. Patsy June Patterson, Apr. 24, 1957; children: Jayne, Jeffrey, Carolyn, Mary. Student, Va. Poly. Inst., 1943-44, U. Va., 1944-45; MD, U. Pa., 1949. Intern Hosp. of U. Pa., 1949-50; resident obstetrics and gynecology Columbia-Presbyn. Med. Center, N.Y.C., 1950-53; chief resident gynecology Free Hosp. Women, Boston, 1953-54; asst. prof. obstetrics and gynecology Southwestern Med. Sch. of U. Tex., 1954-56; pvt. practice obstetrics and gynecology Dallas, 1956; asst. prof. U. Ark. Med. Sch., 1962-66; prof., chmn. dept. obstetrics and gynecology U. Tenn. Med. Sch., 1966-75; obstetrician and gynecologist in chief City of Memphis Hosps.; mem. staff Bapt. Meml. Hosp.; mem. active staff Nacogdoches (Tex.) Med. Ctr. Hosp., 1975-95; ret., 1995. Cons. U.S. Naval Hosp., St. Joseph Hosp., Meth. Hosp. Contbr. to med. jours. Served to ensign USNR, 1943-46. Recipient Golden Apple award U. Ark., 1966, 75; Bicentennial Silver medal Columbia Coll. Phys. and Surg., 1968 Fellow ACS, ACOG; mem. AMA, Tex. Med. Assn., Ctrl. Assn. Ob-Gyns., Tenn. Ob-Gyn. Soc. (pres. 1972-73), Tex. Assn. Ob-Gyns. (coun.), So. Med. Assn., Sigma Xi, Sigma Chi, Phi Chi. Episcopalian. Home: Nacogdoches, Tex. Died Jan. 1, 2006.

FISHER, EDGAR JACOB, JR., religious organization administrator; b. Istanbul, Turkey, June 3, 1919; came to U.S., 1934; s. Edgar Jacob and Elisabeth Fehr Fisher; m. Mildred Anne Hill, Dec. 18, 1948 (dec. Oct. 1975); m. Constance Fleming Warwick, July 26, 1980; 1 child, Elisabeth Anne. BS, William and Mary Coll., 1942. Adminstrv. asst. Near East Coll. Assn., N.Y.C., 1945-48; dir. Va. Coun. on Health and Med. Care, Richmond, Va., 1948-84; v.p., treas., bd. dirs. Cross-Over Ministry, Richmond, from 1982. Vis. lectr. Ea. Va. Med. Sch., Med. Coll. Va./Va. Commonwealth U., U. Va. Sch. Medicine. Bd. mem., cons. Keep Virginia Beautiful, Richmond, 1960—; bd. mem. Needle's Eye Ministries, Richmond, 1980—, Med. Soc. Va. Found., Ctrl. Va. Health Edn. Ctr., Va. League for Nursing, Va. Thanksgiving Festival, Blue Cross Va., Richmond Area Rehab. Ctr.; sec., bd. mem. Westminster Presbyn. Homes; hon. bd. mem. Easter Seal Soc. Va.; mem. adv. com. Va. Assn. Women and Hwy. Safety Leaders, Va. Solicitation of Contbns. Law; cons. Ea. Va. Med. Sch.; ecumenical rels. divsn. Hanover Presbytery; mem. health info. com. Va. Lung Assn.; active Hunger Task Force for Hanover Presbytery, Engrs. Club Richmond; mem. task force com. on placement svcs. Nat. Health Coun., del.-at-large; mem. investigational rev. bd. Va. Heart Inst.; lay trustee Va. Recreation and Pks. Soc.; elder St. Giles' Presbyn. Ch.; others. Lt. USN, 1942-45. Recipient Disting. Svc. award Med. Soc. Va., Richmond, 1957, Disting. Svc. to Rural Va., Va. Farm Bur. Fedn., 1974, Friends of Nursing award Va. League for Nursing, Richmond, 1972, Cert. Appreciation, Va. Pharm. Assn., 1984, Cert. of Appreciation Am. Cancer Soc.-Va. Divsn., 1977. Mem. Va. Soc. Assn. Execs. (life), Richmond Pub. Rels. Assn. (treas., 2d v.p., 1st v.p., pres.), Kappa Alpha Order, Omicron Delta Kappa. Republican. Avocations: gardening, wood working. Home: Richmond, Va. Died Dec. 11, 2005.

FISHER, HERBERT CALVIN, retired surgeon; b. Denver, July 7, 1910; MD, Cornell U., 1935. Intern St. Luke's Hosp., Denver, 1935-36; resident in surgery U. Minn.; fellow Mayo Found., Rochester, Minn., 1937-40; pvt. practice, 1946-75; ret., 1975. Chief of surg. svc. Children's Hosp.; chief of staff Denver Gen. Hosp., 1971-72; assoc. prof. surgery U. Colo. Sch. Medicine; chief exec. Colo. State Sci. Fair, 1970-75; pres. Internat. Sci. Fair, 1975; chief emergency rm. St Luke's Hosp., 1973-75; assigned Gen. MacArthur's hdqs. in the Philippine Islands, then chief of surg. svc. 315th Gen. Hosp. at Batangao, to 1946; chief surg. svc. Brook Gen. Hosp., 1941-45; county judge, Hinsdale County, 1977-80, 84—; co-founder Lake City Med. Ctr., 1976. Author: A Hole in the Heart; contbr. numerous articles and editls. to profl. jours. Dir. 1st Colo. Health Fair Colo. Md. Soc. Lt. col. M.C., U.S. Army, 1946. Recipient awards for bronze sculpture, 1950-75, Cert. Svc. Colo. Engring. Coun., 1962, 1st prize for bronze sculpture, N.Y.C., 1972. Fellow ACS (life); mem. AMA (life), Am. Bd. Surgery (diplomate, cert.), Cen. Surg. Assn. (elected, life), Am. Heart Assn. (life), Colo. Surg. Assn., Colo. Med. Assn. (life, 3 Top awards for pub. svc. 1950-75). Home: Colorado Springs, Colo. Died July 13, 2006.

FISHER, LINDA ALICE, physician; b. Plainfield, NJ, Dec. 27, 1947; d. Alvin Edwin and Bertha Sophie (Steigmann) F. BA, Douglass Coll., New Brunswick, N.J., 1970; M in Med. Sci., Rutgers U., 1972; MD, Harvard U., 1975; MPH, St. Louis U., 1996. Diplomate Am. Bd. Internal Medicine, Am. Bd. Preventive Medicine. Intern, then resident Jewish Hosp. St. Louis, 1975-78; dir. ambulatory care St. Luke's Hosp., St. Louis, 1978-84; chief med. officer St. Louis County Dept. Health, Clayton, 1984-97, dir. rsch., 1997-2000; project dir. St. Louis STD/HIV Prevention Tng. Ctr., 1995-2000. Chief physician St. Louis Met. Police Dept., 1978-88; clin. instr. medicine Washington U., St. Louis, 1978-94, asst. clin. prof., 1994-2000; asst. clin. prof. medicine St. Louis U., 1979-95, assoc. clin. prof., 1996-2000; adj. faculty health svcs. mgmt. U. Mo., Columbia, 1996, St. Louis U. Sch. Pub. Health, 1993-2000; bd. overseers St. Louis Regional Med. Ctr., 1985-95; cons. Ill. Local Govtl. Law Enforcement Officers Tng. Bd., 1988; dir. Fairfax County Health Dept., 2000-2001. Author short stories; contbr. articles to profl. jours. Chmn. licensure com. Mo. Bd. Registration for Healing Arts, 1983-86; adv. coun. Greater St. Louis Coun. Girl Scouts U.S., 1986-2000. Recipient Disting. Alumni award Douglass Coll., 1992, Publ. award Mo. Pub. Health Assn., 1994, St. Louis Woman of Achievement award KMOX Radio and Suburban Jours., 1995. Fellow ACP; mem. AMA, APHA, Am. Med. Women's Assn. (chpt. pres. 1982-85, Cmty. Svc. award 1992), Am. Med. Writers Assn., Nat. Assn. Med. Communicators (Ken Alvord Cmty. Svc. award 1998), St. Louis Met. Med. Soc. (councilor 1982-84, sec. 1986, editor 1989-90), Med. Soc. No. Va., Internat. Women's Forum, Assn. Documentary Editing. Lutheran. Home: Annandale, Va. Died Jan. 23, 2006.

FISHER, PAUL J., financial consultant; b. Rockford, Ill., Nov. 28, 1930; s. Paul J. and Lorena Sue (Kious) F.; m. Maryhelen Grande, Feb. 4, 1971; children: Tira Jo, Tammy Sue, Jeffrey Paul. BS in Econs., U. Wis., 1952, JD, 1960; LLM, Georgetown U., 1964. Bar: Wash. 1970. Sales staff Hornblower & Weeks, 1955, IBM, 1956; atty. John McLario, Menomonie Falls, Wis., 1960, Donaldson & Hafer, Seattle, 1966-68; pvt. practice Seattle, 1969-85; fin. cons. The Consultants Group, Palm Desert, Calif., from 1985. Segment prodr. Sr. TV. Mem. Econ. Com., Palm Desert, 1997; mem. adv. bd. charitable giving U. Calif., Riverside. Lt. comdr. USN, 1952-54, 61-66. Named Man of the Yr., Kappa Sigma, 1952. Mem. Monterey Country Club, Internat. Assn. Fin. Planners. Avocations: golf, tennis, music. Died Feb. 7, 2005.

FISHER, PHILIP ARTHUR, investment manager; b. San Francisco, Sept. 8, 1907; s. Arthur Lawrence and Eugenia (Samuels) F.; m. Dorothy Whyte, Aug. 14, 1943; children: Arthur, Donald, Kenneth. AB, Stanford U., 1927. Founder, investment mgr. Fisher and Co., San Mateo, Calif., 1931—99. Author: Common Stocks and Uncommon Profits, 1958, Paths to Wealth Through Common Stocks, 1960, Conservative Investors Sleep Well, 1975. Capt. U.S. Army, 1942-45. Home: San Mateo, Calif. Died Mar. 11, 2004.

FISHER, RHODA LEE, psychologist, researcher, consultant; b. Chgo., Oct. 10, 1924; d. Isadore Mordecai and Mary (Margolis) Feinberg; m. Seymour Fisher, Mar. 22, 1947; children: Jerid Martin, Eve Phyllis. B of Music Edn., DePaul U., Chgo., 1947; MA, U. Chgo., 1948, PhD, 1956. Lic. psychologist, N.Y. Intern Elgin (Ill.) State Hosp., 1948-50; with Jewish Vocat. Svc., Houston, 1950-52; psychologist Baylor Med. Coll., Houston, 1952-54; pvt. practice Houston, 1952-61; instr. Syracuse (N.Y.) U., 1962-68; from rsch. asst. to rsch. assoc. SUNY Upstate Med. Sch., Syracuse, 1961-64; rsch. psychologist Syracuse Pub. Schs., 1963-68; pvt. practice Syracuse, 1968—2003. Author: Pretend the World Is Funny and Forever, 1981 (Psychology Today award 1981), What We Really Know About Child Rearing, 1976, 2d edit., 1986, The Psychology of Adaptation to Absurdity: Tactics of Make-Believe, 1993. Mem. Am. Psychol. Assn. (former chair). Avocations: music, humor. Home: Manlius, NY. Died Mar. 21, 2004.

FISHER, SHARON MARY, musician; b. Orange, N.J., Sept. 29, 1944; d. Stanley and Veronica Shirley (Conway) Cozza; m. Andrew Fisher IV, Aug. 16, 1969. B Music Edn., Westminster Choir Coll., 1966; postgrad., Acad. Vocal Arts, 1966—67, Temple U., 1967—69. Cert. music tchr. NJ. Chorister Westminster Choir, Princeton, NJ, 1964-66; music tchr. Phila. Pub. Schs., 1967-69; sect. leader Phila. Boys' Choir, 1969; performer Manhattan Light Opera Co., NY, 1969-70; soprano soloist St. Peter's Ch., Morristown, NJ, 1975-79; organist Ch. of the Saviour, Denville, NJ, 1981-84; performer, lectr., 1986—2006. Performer Scottish Games, Millington, N.J. Albums include Concert Memories, 1991, Ireland: Land of Harp and Song, 1998. Grand marshal Holiday Parade, Denville C. of C., 1991. Recipient Marietta MacLeod award An Comunn Gaidhealach, 1989, Scots award Scottish Club of Twinstates, 1988-89, Harp/Voice trophy O'Carolan Harp Festival, Keadue, Ireland, 1988, Merit award Passaic County Irish Am. Cultural Soc., 1995. Mem. Clarsach Soc. (Edinburgh), Scottish Harp Soc. Am. (Ellice MacDonald grantee 1987), Am. Harp Soc., Nat. Assn. Tchrs. Singing, Nat. Assn. Pastoral Musicians, Internat. Soc. Folk Harpers and Craftsmen, Comhaltas Ceoltoiri Eireann. Avocations: gardening, languages, music. Home: Denville, NJ. Died Feb. 23, 2006.

FISHER, THOMAS EDWARD, lawyer; b. Cleve., Sept. 29, 1926; s. McArthur and Ruth Morgan (Dissette) F.; m. Virginia Moore, June 29, 1957; children: Laura, Linda, John. BS in Naval Sci. and Tactics, Purdue U., 1947, BS in Engring. Law, 1950; JD, Ind. U., 1950. Bar: Ohio 1951, U.S. Dist. Ct. (no. dist.) Ohio 1954, U.S. Supreme Ct. 1955, U.S. Ct. Appeals (Fed. cir.) 1973. Asst. to v.p. Lempco Products, Bedford, Ohio, 1950-51; house counsel Willard Storage Battery Co., Cleve., 1951-54; assoc. Schram & Knowles, Cleve., 1954-55; ptnr. Watts, Hoffmann, Co. LPA and predecessor firms, Cleve., from 1955. Mem. adv. bd. BNA Patent Trademark and Copyright Jour., 1972-2003; mem. adv. panel Franklin Pierce Law Sch., 1987—. Councilman Mentor (Ohio) on the Lake, 1955-57; chmn. ARC, Painesville, Ohio, 1956. Lt. USN, 1944. Mem. ABA (divsn. chair), Cleve. Bar Assn. (trustee), Am. Intellectual Property Law Assn. (chair com., bd. dirs.), Cleve. Intellectual Property Law Assn. (pres.), Cleve. World Trade Assn., Nat. Inventors Hall of Fame (pres.), Nat. Coun. Patent Law Assns. (chair). Avocations: woodworking, fishing, travel, gardening. Home: Chagrin Falls, Ohio. Died Jan. 20, 2005.

FISHWICK, MARSHALL W., education educator; BA, U. Va., 1944; MA history, U. Wis., 1946; PhD am. studies, Yale U., 1950; DLITT (hon.), Dhaka U., Bagladesh, 1983; PhD (hon.), Krakow U., Poland, 1967. Instr. Yale Univ., 1949; prof. Wash. and Lee Univ., 1950—62; vis. prof. Imov. Minn., 1957; dir., cons. Winerthur Mus., 1962—64; disting. vis. prof. U. Wyo., 1963; prof. Lincoln U., 1964—70, Temple U., 1970—76, Va. Tech., 1976—2003; vis. prof. Yale U., 1984. Contbr. chapters to books;, editor to many profl. jour.; adv. editor: Jour. Am. Culture. Grantee Glenn Grant, Wash. and Lee Univ., 1955, Yale Almuni Grant, 1968, 8 Fulbright Grants, Denmark, Germany, Eng., India (2), Bangladesh, Korea, South-East Asia, 1959—85; Sterling Fellow, Rockfeller Found., N.Y., 1948—50. Mem.: Salzburg Adv. Faculty, Am. Culture Assn., Popular Culture Assn., Soc. of Achtl. Hist., Japenese-Am. Studies Assn., Conseils aux Assn., Centro Italiano di Studi Am., Guild to Scholars, Am. Studies Rsch. Ctr., India, European Am. Studies Assn., British Am. Studies Assn., So. Hist. Soc., Va. His. Soc., AAUP, Modern Language Assn., Ogrn. of Am. Hist., Am. Hist. Assn., Am. Studies Assn., Nat. Edn. Assn. Home: Blacksburg, Va. Died May 22, 2006.

FISK, CAROL FRASER, consultant; b. Bklyn., Mar. 2, 1946; d. John M. and Jean C. (Hardman) Fraser; m. Craig Fisk, Nov. 24, 1984. BA, Conn. Coll., 1968; Master in Urban and Regional Planning, Va. Tech., 1972; LHD, Alfred U., 1988. Mgmt. tng. program N.Y. Tel. Co., 1968-70; sr. planner No. Va. Planning Dist. Commn., Falls Church, Va., 1972-77; asst. dir. Arlington (Va.) United Way, 1977-78; coord. Youth Project Arlington (Va.) Svcs. Bd.; sr. rsch. assoc. Nat. Assn. of Counties, Washington, 1979-81; from spl. asst. to dir., regional ops. US Dept. Health and Human Svcs., Washington, 1981-84; US commissioner on aging US Dept. Health and Human Services, Washington, 1984-89; editor Aging Network News, McLean, Va., 1989; cons., 1990; exec. dir. Assisted Living Facilities Assn. of Am., Fairfax, Va., 1990-95; v.p. pub. policy Vols. of Am., Washington, from 1995. Mem. US Delegation to UN World Assembly on Aging, Vienna, Austria, 1982. Mem. Gerontological Soc. Am., So. Gerontol. Soc. Republican. Episcopalian. Home: Falls Church, Va. Died Jan. 7, 2004.

FITE, ROBERT CARROLL, retired cosmetics industry executive; b. Atoka, Tenn., May 14, 1934; s. Russel Neal and Mabel H. (Smith) F.; m. Shirley N. Norwood, Nov. 12, 1973; children: Jeff, Camilla. BS, Memphis State U., 1956. Cert. secondary tchr., Tenn. With City Cosmetics, 1959-60, Revlon Cosmetics, 1960-72, Gerlain Cosmetics, 1972-89; ret., 1989. With U.S. Army, 1956-58. Republican. Presbyterian. Home: Memphis, Tenn. Died Dec. 6, 2004.

FITZGERALD, RUTH MIRIAM, nursing educator; b. Boston, Feb. 14, 1921; d. Gerhardt William and Catherine (Fleming) Lang; m. Joseph T. Fitzgerald, Aug. 30, 1947; children: Brianne, Sean, Kevin, Dennis, Terrence, Gael, Maura, Siobhan. RN, Boston City Hosp., 1942; AB, EdM, Harvard U., 1970, 1972; MBA, Anna Maria Coll., Paxton, Mass., 1983; BSN, Boston State Coll., 1977. Pub. health nurse City of Newton (Mass.) Health Dept., 1974-76; in-svc. educator Aramco, Saudi Arabia, 1978; immunization specialist Mass. Dept. Pub. Health, Boston, 1978-80, health facility inspector, 1980-92; cons. Home Health Agys., from 1992. Ind. pvt. cons. 1st lt. U.S. Army Nurses Corps, 1942-46. Mem. Am. Nurses (del. conv.), Mass. Nurses Assn. (1st v.p.). Died Jan. 11, 2005.

FITZGERALD, WILLIAM HENRY G., former ambassador; b. Boston, Dec. 23, 1909; s. William Joseph and Mary Ellen (Smith) F.; m. Annelise Petschek, July 2, 1943; children: Desmond, Anne. BS, U.S. Naval Acad., 1931; postgrad., Harvard Law Sch., 1934-35; DSc (hon.), Adelphi U., 1962; LLD (hon.), Cath. U. Am., 1990; D in Pub. Svc. (hon.), Regis U., 1999. With Borden Co., N.Y.C., 1936-41; personal bus. interests Mexico, 1946-47; organized Metall. Research & Devel. Co., Washington, 1947, v.p., treas., 1947-56, pres., 1956-58, 60-82, chmn., 1960-82; chmn. bd. Nat. Metallizing Corp., Trenton, NJ, 1956-58; organizer FitzGerald Corp., 1959, pres., from 1980; chmn. bd. The Cottages, Ltd., Jamaica, 1960-70, Linden Corp., Washington, 1962-70, N.Am. Housing Corp., Washington, 1971-88; chmn. Supramar, Ltd., Lucerne, Switzerland, 1963-69, dir., 1970-75; pres. Nat. Media Analysis, Inc., Washington, 1968-70, chmn., 1970-72; ptnr. Hornblower & Weeks, Hemphill-Noyes, Inc., 1970-72, 1st v.p., 1972-77; vice chmn., dir., exec. com. Fin. Gen. Bankshares, Inc., 1977-82; vice chmn. African Devel. Found., 1990-92; U.S. amb. to Ireland, 1992-93. Dir., mem. exec. com. First Am. Bank (N.A.), Washington, 1977-83; dir., mem. exec. com., chmn. investment com. Avemco Corp., Washington, Frederick, Md., 1970-89; Cosmadent, Ltd., Zurich, Switzerland, 1964-75, Chase Fund of Boston, Chase Convertible Fund, Income & Capital Shares Inc., 1970-75, Pyrotector, Inc., Hingham, Mass., 1963-76; cons. to dir. ICA, Washington, 1957; dep. dir. for mgmt. ICA, Dept. State, 1958-60; U.S. conciliator Internat. Center for Investment Disputes, 1975-82; dir. Inst. Inter Am. Affairs, 1958-60; mem. President's Adv. Bd. on Internat. Investments, 1976-78; treas. Presdl. Inaugural Com., 1981; trustee Presdl. Inaugural Trust, 1981-89; mem. nat. adv. com. Internat. Edn., 1982-85. Trustee Fed. City Coun., 1962-90, Wash. Inst. Fgn. Affairs, 1966-2006; bd. dirs. Atlantic Coun. U.S., 1976-2006, treas., 1979-92, mem. exec. com., 1980-2006, vice chmn., 1993-2006; trustee Fgn. Student Svc. Coun., 1963-2006, Oblate Coll. (Cath. U.), 1966-2006; trustee Corcoran Gallery Art, 1977-90, also mem. exec. com., chmn. devel. com.; pres. Soc. for a More Beautiful Nat. Capital, Inc., 1974-77; bd. dirs., mem. exec. com., sr. v.p. Internat. Tennis Hall of Fame, 1964-92, 94—, hon. chmn., 2000-06; nat. chmn. Yorktown Internat. Bicentennial Com., 1981; dir., mem. exec. com. Washington Tennis and Ednl. Found., 1987-2006; U.S. del. Atlantic Treaty Assembly, Reykjavik, Iceland, 1977, Washington, 1979, Rome, 1983, Istanbul, Turkey, 1987, Brussels, 1989, Rome, 1996, sofia, 1997; grand officer Confrèrie des Chevaliers du Tastevin, 1979-2006; grand senechal Sous Commanderie de Washington, 1980-90; trustee White House Preservation Fund, 1979-89, chmn., 1982-89, chmn. emeritus, 1989-90; mem. Nat. Task Force on Prison Industries; trustee, mem. nominating com. U.D.C., 1982-87; mem. nat. com. Vatican Judaica Exhbn., 1987-89; mem. Bretton Woods com., 1992-2006; mem., dir. Coun. of Am. Ambassadors, 1992-2006. Ensign USN, 1931-34; from lt. (j.g.) to comdr., 1941-46. Decorated Orden Militar de Ayacucho Peru, knight grand cross honor & devotion in obedience Order Malta, knight grand cross Sovereign Mil. Order Malta, Equestrian Order Holy Sepulchre, Sacred Mil. Constantinian Order St. George; named to Mid-Atlantic Tennis Hall of Fame, 1997. Mem. Fed. Assn. in U.S.A. Sovereign Mil. Order of Malta (pres. 1975-79), Assn. for Diplomatic Studies and Tng. (dir. 1993-2006), Army-Navy Country Club (Washington), Univ. Club (Washington), Harvard Club (Washington), River Club (N.Y.C.), Met. Club (Washington), Essex Country Club (Manchester, Mass.), Portmarnock Golf Club (Dublin, Ireland), FitzWilliam Lawn Tennis Club (Dublin). Roman Catholic. Died Jan. 5, 2006.

FITZPATRICK, ALAN JOSEPH, deacon, psychologist; b. Needham, Mass., May 16, 1937; s. Joseph Augustine and Julia (Downing) F.; m. Glenda Nadine Pinkley, Oct. 24, 1964; children: Michael, Shaun. BS in Indsl. Engring., Northeastern U., 1962; MEd in Guidance and Counseling, Shippensburg (Pa.) Coll., 1967; PhD in Ednl. Psychology, U. Mo., 1970. Ordained deacon Roman Cath. Ch., 1980; lic. psychologist, Tex. Lay missionary Soc. of Our Lady of

Most Blessed Trinity, Mora, N.Mex., 1962-63; prin., psychologist Northside Ind. Sch. Dist., San Antonio, from 1974. Editor newsletter Archdiocese of San Antonio, 1980—. 1st pres. Tex. State REACT Coun., 1976; mem. exec. com. Bexar County Reps., San Antonio. Lt. col. USAR, 1963-65, 90-91. Home: San Antonio, Tex. Died June 19, 2005.

FIVIZZANI, RICHARD DANTE, finance and management executive; b. Chgo., Aug. 17, 1938; s. Albert John and Rina Marie (Frediani) F.; m. Loretta Ann Stebbins, Apr. 15, 1961; children: Annette Marie, Patti Ann, Maria Rina. AA, Harry S. Thruman Coll., 1964. Cert. purchasing mgr. Purchasing agt. Halo Lighting div. McGraw-Edison, Rosemont, Ill., 1968-72, data processing mgr., 1972-74; materials mgr. Prestige Products div. McGraw-Edison, Chgo., 1974-77; ops mgr. Prestige Products Inc., Bensenville, Ill., 1977-82; mgr. adminstrn. Berman Industries, Chgo., 1983-85, v.p., from 1985. Mem. Purchasing Mgmt. Assn. Chgo. (pres. 1977, Service award 1984), Nat. Assn. Purchasing Mgmt. (asst. v.p. 1979, nat. v.p., 1980, chmn. gen. conf. 1984), St George Alumni Assn. (toastmaster 1983). Avocations: football, golf, home remodeling. Home: Morton Grove, Ill. Died Dec. 30, 2004.

FLANNERY, EDWARD JOSEPH, manufacturing executive; b. Chgo., July 16, 1926; s. Edward J. and Ella (Brennan) F.; m. Dorothy Marie Johnson, May 30, 1953; children: Ann, Kathleen, Michael, Maureen, James, Julie. BSEE, U. Ill., 1950; MBA, U. Chgo., 1959; MSEE, Northwestern U., 1961. Chief engr. Vap Air div. Vapor Corp., Niles, Ill., 1962-69, asst. gen. mgr., 1969-75; v.p., gen. mgr. Raymond Controls, St. Charles, Ill., 1976-83, Brunswick Valve and Control, Morton Grove, Ill., from 1983. Cons. Sundstrand Corp., Rockford, Ill., 1976; bd. dirs. Nireco Corp., Tokyo,, NB Inst. Co., San Francisco. Served with USN, 1944-46. Mem. Instrument Soc. Am. (pres. adv. council 1983—), Valve Mfrs. Assn. Roman Catholic. Home: Park Ridge, Ill. Died Jan. 20, 2005.

FLANNERY, WILBUR EUGENE, health science association administrator, internist; b. New Castle, Pa., June 19, 1907; s. Charles Francis and Mary Catherine (McGrath) F.; m. Ruth Iva Donaldson, June 27, 1929; children: Charles, John, Richard, Harry. Grad., Mercersburg Acad., 1925; BA, Dartmouth Coll., 1929; MA, Oberlin Coll., 1930; MD, Harvard U., 1935. Diplomate Nat. Bd. Medical Examiners. Minister Meth. Ch., New Castle, 1930-31; intern Cleve. City Hosp., 1935-36; resident physician Jameson Meml. Hosp., New Castle, 1936-37; fellowship Cleve. Clinic Found., 1937-40; practice medicine specializing in internal medicine New Castle, from 1940; med. dir. Hospice of St. Francis Hosp., New Castle, from 1987. Chmn. bd. Pa. Blue Shield, Harrisburg, Pa., 1975-80. Contbr. numerous articles to med. jours. Pres. Bd. of Edn., New Castle, 1947-53; former trustee Knoville (Tenn.) Coll.; former pres. of chmn. Lawrence County chpt. ARC, Lawrence County chpt. Pa. Assn. for Blind, Lawrence County Mental Health Clinic, New Castle Exec. Club, Greater New Castle C. of C.; Sunday sch. tchr. Recipient Disting. Citizens award Optimists Club, 1974, United Way Gold award, 1999; named Boss of Yr., Am. Bus. Women's Assoc., 1987; named Outstanding Bus. Person, Hospice of St. Francis, 1999. Mem. AMA (del. 1953-63), Pa. Med. Soc. (pres. 1963-64), Lawrence County Med. Soc. (sec. 1954-55, pres. 1955-56), Am. Soc. Internal Medicine, Am. Med. Writers Assn., Acad. Hospice Physicians (pres. 1990), Internat. Hospice Inst., Internat. Coll. Hospice/Palliative Care, Internat. Platform Assn., Pa. Soc., New Castle Country Club, Univ. Club (Pitts.), Lawrence Club, Youngstown (Ohio) Club, Elks, Lions (pres. New Castle 1943-44 Disting. Svc. award, Melvin Jones fellow 1995). Republican. Presbyterian. Home: New Castle, Pa. Died Mar. 13, 2004.

FLEISCHER, RICHARD O., film director; b. Bklyn., Dec. 8, 1916; BA, Brown U.; M.F.A., Yale U. Former stage dir.; joined RKO Pathe, 1942; pres. Fleischer Studios. Guardian lectr., London, 1981; copyright owner Betty Boop. Dir.: Child of Divorce, 1946, Banjo, 1947, Design for Death, 1948, So This is New York, 1948, Bodyguard, 1948, Make Mine Laughs, 1949, The Clay Pigeon, 1949, Follow Me Quietly, 1949, Trapped, 1949, Armored Car Robbery, 1950, The Narrow Margin, 1952, The Happy Time, 1952, Arena, 1953, 20,000 Leagues Under the Sea, 1954, Violent Saturday, 1955, The Girl in the Red Velvet Swing, 1955, Bandido, 1956, Between Heaven and Hell, 1956, The Vikings, 1958, These Thousand Hills, 1959, Compulsion, 1959, Crack in the Mirror, 1960, The Big Gamble, 1961, Barabbas, 1962,Fantastic Voyage, 1966, Dr. Doolittle, 1967, The Boston Strangler, 1968, Che!, 1969, Tora ! Tora! Tora! (co. dir.), 1970, 10 Rillington Place, 1971, See No Evil, 1971, The Last Run, 1971, The New Centurions, 1972, Soylent Green, 1972, The Don is Dead, 1973, The Spikes Gang, 1974, Mr. Majestyk, 1974, Paris, 1975, Mandingo, 1975, The Incredible Sarah, 1976, Crossed Swords: The Prince and the Pauper, 1978, Ashanti, 1979, The Jazz Singer, 1980, Tough Enough, 1983, Amityville 3-D, 1983, Conan The Destroyer, 1984, Red Sonja, 1985, Million Dollar Mystery, 1987, Call From Space, 1989; Author: Just Tell Me When to Cry. Died Mar. 25, 2006.

FLEISCHNER, ALOIS LEONARD, retired ophthalmologist; b. N.Y.C., Sept. 4, 1913; s. Otto and Frances (Goodman) F.; m. Jean Sokiran, May 1, 1938 (dec. Oct. 1978); children: Mark, Richard. BS, NYU, 1932, MD, 1935. Diplomate Am. Bd. Ophthalmology. Intern, househship eye-ear, nose and throat N.Y.C. Hosp., 1935-39; resident Queens Gen. Hosp., N.Y.C., 1939-40; pvt. practice N.Y.C., 1940-42; pvt. practice ophthalmology, 1946-88; ophthalmologist Bronx (N.Y.) Eye Infirmary, 1946-73, Montefiore Hosp. & Med. Ctr., Bronx, from 1973; cons. ophthalmologist Bronx-Lebanon Med. Ctr., from 1946. Capt. U.S. Army, 1942-46, ETO. Fellow ACS (pres. Bronx chpt. 1963); mem. Am. Acad. Ophthalmology, N.Y. Soc. Clin. Ophthalmology, N.Y. Acad. Medicine. Avocations: golf, art, music. Home: Bronx, NY. Died Jan. 17, 2005.

FLEMING, JOSEPH PATRICK, surgeon; b. Humboldt, Sask., Can., July 5, 1928; s. Harry Fleming and Claire (Kyte) Fleming-Doiron; m. Therese Eccles, Feb. 8, 1931; children: Patti, James, Claire, Harry, Frank, Madeline, Michael, Siobhan. BSc, St. Francis Xavier U., N.S., Can., 1947; MD, Univ. Coll., Dublin, Ireland, 1953. Diplomate Am. Bd. Surgery. Pvt. practice surgery, Vancouver, B.C., Can., 1964-77, Houston, from 1977. Fellow ACS, Royal Coll. Surgeons. Republican. Roman Catholic. Home: Houston, Tex. Died Mar. 27, 2004.

FLETCHER, RAYMOND HAROLD, psychologist, consultant; b. Roxton, Tex., Oct. 14, 1914; s. James A.B. and Leta (Mercer) F.; m. Alma Jo Young, Aug. 24, 1935; children: Jim R., Gwendolyn Jean Fletcher Cotellesse. BS, East Tex. State U., 1935, MS, 1938; PhD, U. Tex., 1944. Asst. supt. Highland Park Ind. Sch. Dist., Dallas, 1945-47; staff cons. Rohrer Hibler & Replogle, Chgo., 1947-48, regional dir., 1948-67, gen. ptnr., 1967-74; v.p. RHR Internat., Chgo., 1974-79, sr. v.p., 1979-80; cons. Exec. Cons. Svcs., Dallas, from 1980. Co-author: Managers for Tomorrow. Mem. Garland (Tex.) Ind. Sch. Dist. Bd. Edn., 1956-61. Recipient Disting. Alumnus award East Tex. State U., 1974. Fellow APA, Am. Psychol. Soc. (charter). Died July 14, 2005.

FLORENCE, MARY ELLEN, mental health nursing educator, therapist; b. Chgo., July 9, 1938; d. Venice E. and June (Summers) Hart; divorced; children: Gregory, John. BSN, Tex. Christian U., 1960; MSN, U. Pa., 1977, PhD, 1983. RN, N.J., Pa. Assoc. prof. Stockton State Coll., Pomona, N.J. Disting. fellow Stockton Found. Mem. ANA (cert. psychiat./mental health nurse), AAMFT (clin. mem., approved supr.), Am. Bd. Sexology (cert. sex therapist). Home: Mays Landing, NJ. Died July 13, 2004.

FLORES, M. JUNE, nursing educator; b. Ogallala, Nebr., June 5, 1935; d. John Y. and Grace A. (Yocom) Brown. Diploma, West Nebr. Gen. Hosp., Scottsbluff, 1956; BS, Metro State Coll., 1979; MSN, U. Colo., Denver, 1981. Dir. nursing svc. Sheridan Manor Nursing Home, Denver; dir. nursing svcs. Meml. Hosp., Guymon, Okla., Trego County Meml. Hosp., Wakeeney, Kans.; satellite coord. Dakota Wesleyan U., North Platte, Nebr.; dir. nursing svc. Linden Manor, North Platte, Walker Post Manor, Oxford, Nebr. Mem. Nebr. State Bd. Nursing. Contbr. articles to profl. jours. Am. Heart Assn. Study grantee. Mem. ANA (dist. pres.). Home: Ogallala, Nebr. Died Apr. 22, 2004.

FLORY, DAISY PARKER, retired educational administrator; b. Charlotte, N.C., Feb. 18, 1915; d. Julius Monroe and Daisy (Kidd) Parker; m. Claude R. Flory, Mar. 26, 1973. BA, Fla. State Coll. Women, 1937; MA, U. Va., 1940, PhD, 1959; D.H.L. (hon.), Fla. State U., 1986. Instr. Leon High Sch., Tallahassee, 1937-42; instr. Fla. State U., Tallahassee, 1942-47, asst. prof., 1947-57, asso. prof., 1957-65, prof. govt., 1965-84, asst. v.p. academic affairs, 1969-73, dean faculties, 1974-84, interim v.p. for academic affairs, 1980-81. Mem. Fla. Gov.'s Study Commn. on Personnel, 1954; pres. Le Moyne Art Found., 1967-68. Mem. Fla. Hist. Soc., Tallahassee Hist. Soc. (past pres.), So. Polit. Sci. Assn. (past sec.), AAUW (pres. local chpt. 1942-43), Phi Beta Kappa, Phi Kappa Phi, Pi Sigma Alpha, Phi Alpha Theta, Mortar Bd. (editor Jour. 1950-56) Home: Tallahassee, Fla. Died Mar. 7, 2006.

FLORY, PHOEBE, artist, educator; b. Cleve., May 14, 1914; d. Walter Leroy and Julia (McCune) F.; divorced. AB in Art, cum laude, Smith Coll., Northhampton, Mass., 1936; student, Cleve. Inst. Art, 1936-38, Art Students' League with, Jean Charlot, Hans Hofman, Florence Cane, N.Y., 1938-39, 40-42, Eliot O'Hara Watercolor Sch., Goose Rocks Beach, Maine, summers 1944-45. Owner The Phoebe Flory Watercolor Sch., Mont Vernon, N.H., from 1970. Adj. prof. Notre Dame Coll., Manchester, N.H., 1989—; tchr. numerous instns. in field including faculty White Pines Coll., Chester, N.H., 1975 and numerous workshops. Author: (books) Portraits in the Making, 1948-49, Watercolor Portraiture, 1949, 65; author/producer: (film) Texture in Painting, 1963 (Golden Eagle award Com. on Internat. Non-Theatrical Film Events 1963); one-woman shows include: Sharon Art Ctr. and First Nat. Bank of Peterborough, N.H., 1987, The Bonfoey Co. at Hathaway Brown Sch., Cleve., 1978, The Am. Stage Festival, Milford, N.H., 1976-77, The Intown Club Gallery, Cleve., 1975, Playhouse 101, Milford, 1971-72, numerous others, 1945—. Grantee The Arthur L. Keyes Meml. Turst, 1973, 74, 75, 77, 78, The Kaley Found., 1975, The N.H. Commn. on Arts, 1975. Fellow Royal Soc. of Arts (London); mem. N.H. Art Assn., Keyes Art Group (founder 1966), others. Democrat. Unitarian-Universalist. Avocations: swimming, gardening, cooking, sketching at theater rehearsals. Died July 30, 2004.

FLOWERREE, ROBERT EDMUND, retired forest products company executive; b. New Orleans, Jan. 4, 1921; s. Robert E. and Amy (Hewes) F.; m. Elaine Dicks, Sept. 22, 1943; children: Ann D., John H., David R. BA, Tulane U., 1942. Vice pres. Georgia-Pacific Corp., 1956-63, exec. v.p. pulp, paper and chem. ops., 1963-75, pres., 1974-76, chmn., CEO, 1976-83, chmn., 1983-84, ret., 1984, Kilgore Corp. Past bd. dirs. Ga. Gulf Corp. Emeritus adminstr. Tulane U., New Orleans; life trustee Lewis and Clark Coll., Portland, Oreg. Served to lt. USNR, 1942-46. Recipient Disting. Alumnus award Tulane U., 1978; inducted into Paper Industry Internat. Hall of Fame, 2001. Mem.: Knights of Malta; Arlington (Portland), Waverley Country (Portland); Boston (New Orleans); Links (N.Y.C.). Died May 1, 2006.

FLOYD, MADGE BLACK, minister, church administrator; b. Atlanta, Sept. 23, 1935; d. William Howard and Nena Madge (Estes) Black; m. Carl M. Floyd Jr., June 14, 1958 (div. May 1981); children: Christine Elizabeth, Carl M. III. AB, Emory U., 1958; MDiv, Pitts. Theol. Sem., 1969; D in Ministry, Boston U., 1978. Ordained to ministry United Meth. Ch. Pastor 1st United Meth. Ch., Greensburg, Pa., 1971-72, Castle Shannon United Meth. Ch., Pitts., 1973-79; exec. dir. TOGETHER Program, United Meth. Ch., Pitts., 1979-84; supt. Pitts. dist. United Meth Ch., from 1984. Stewardship assoc. Gen. Bd. Discipline, United Meth. Ch., Nashville, 1979—, bd. dirs. Gen. Bd. Pensions, Evanston, Ill., 1984—; mem. commn. stewardship Nat. Council Chs., N.Y.C., 1979-84. Fellow Order of St. Luke. Democrat. Avocations: walking, fishing, golf, travel. Home: Pittsburgh, Pa. Died Mar. 10, 2005.

FOELL, J(OHN) DAVID, city manager; b. Dayton, Ohio, June 25, 1931; s. Philip and Margaret (Kaseman) F.; m. Virginia Rae Jansen, Dec. 26, 1954; children: Eric, Janis, Julie. BA, Capital U., Columbus, Oh., 1953; M in Pub. Adminstn., Syracuse U., N.Y., 1954. Asst. city mgr. City of Westerville (Ohio), 1956-58; city mgr. Washington (Ohio) Ct. House, 1958-62, City of Oakwood, Ohio, 1963-93; interim adminstr. City of Urbana (Ohio), 1983; field rep. Ohio Mcpl. League, Dayton, from 1993. Arbitrator employees rels. bd. State of Ohio, 1993—. Served to SP4 Army, 1954-56, Germany. Mem. Internat. City Mgmt. Assn. (v.p. 1972-74), Am. Soc. for Pub. Adminstrn. (local pres. 1970-76, Outstanding Pub. Adminstr. 1976), Ohio Mcpl. League (pres. 1985), Kiwanis (pres. Oakwood chpt. 1989), Rotary (Washington, Ohio chpt.). Republican. Lutheran. Avocation: reading. Home: Dayton, Ohio. Died Sept. 16, 2004.

FOIL, MARY BETH, general surgeon; b. Winston-Salem, Jan. 4, 1954; d. William Charlton and Patricia (Petree) F. BA, U. N.C., 1976; MD, East Carolina U., 1981. Diplomate Am. Bd. Surgery. Resident gen. surgery E. Carolina U., Greenville, 1981-85, chief resident gen. surgery, 1985-86, clin. instr., 1986-87; clin. instr., trauma fellow U. Calif. San Diego Med. Ctr., 1987-88; dir. surg. critical care Pitt County Meml. Hosp., Greenville, from 1988; assoc. dir. trauma svc. E. Caroluna U., from 1988, asst. prof. surgery, from 1988. Co-dir. Adv. Trauma Life Support courses, E. Carolina U. Sch. Medicine, 1989, 90. Contbr. articles to profl. jours. Gov.'s Hwy. Safety Prog. grantee, 1989 Fellow ACS (N.C. chpt.); mem. Am. Trauma Soc. (bd. dirs.), East Carolina U. Med. Alumni Assn. (treas.), Assn. Women Surgeons, Ea. Assn. for Surgeons of Trauma, Am. Coll. Emergency Physicans, Assn. Acad. Surgeons, Soc. Critical Care, Southeastern Surg. Congress., So. Med. Soc., Pitt County Med. AMA, N.C. Med., Am. Assn. Family Physicians, Am. Med. Women's Assn. (v.p. 1989, pres. 1991—), Internat. Soc. for Traumatic Studies (N.C. chpt.). Home: Greenville, NC. Died Feb. 17, 2005.

FOLSOM, JAMES CANNON, psychiatrist; b. Sweetwater, Ala., Oct. 11, 1921; s. Douglas Lawrence and Lillian (Hart) F.; student Livingston State Coll., 1939-41, U. Ariz., 1941, U. Ala., 1942-44; M.D., Washington U., St. Louis, 1946; postgrad. U. Vienna (Austria), 1948; m. Ruth Elizabeth Becton, Aug. 14, 1947 (div. 1950); 1 dau., Ivy Folsom Simpson; m. 2d, Geneva Rose Scheihing, Dec. 29, 1958 (div. 1977); 1 dau., Lisa Folsum Ernst; m. 3d, Barbara A. Foster, July 10, 1982. Intern, Jefferson-Hillman Hosp., Birmingham, Ala., 1946-47; psychiatrist Hill Crest Sanitarium, Birmingham, 1949; resident in psychiatry Timberlawn Sanitarium, Dallas, 1950-52, staff psychiatrist, 1952; resident in psychiatry Menninger Sch. Psychiatry, VA Hosp., Topeka, 1952-53; admission physician VA Hosp., Topeka, 1953-55, chief phys. medicine rehab. svc., 1955-60; clin. dir. Mental Health Inst., Mt. Pleasant, Iowa, 1960-62; chief of staff VA Hosp., Tuscaloosa, Ala., 1962-66, hosp. dir., 1966-71; dep. commr. for hosps. Ala. Dept. Mental Health, also supt. Bryce Hosp., Tuscaloosa, 1971-72; dir. rehab. medicine svc., dept. medicine and surgery VA Cen. Office, Washington, 1972-76; dir. Internat. Ctr. for Disabled, N.Y.C., 1976-84; assoc. chief staff for extended care VA Med. Ctr., Topeka, 1984-86, chief rehab. medicine svc., 1985-88, acting chief intermediate medicine svc., 1986-90; clin. prof. psychiatry Menninger Sch. Psychiatry, 1953-60, 84-90, N.Y. U. Med. Ctr., 1976-84; asso. clin. prof. psychiatry U. Ala. Sch. Medicine, 1963-72, adj. prof. health care mgmt., 1972-76; mem. teaching roster Med. Assn. State of Ala., Montgomery, 1968-72; clin. prof. psychiatry and behavioral scis. George Washington U. Sch. Medicine, 1974-76; cons. Ala. Dept. Mental Health and state hosps., 1969-71; clin. dir. Greil Meml. Psychiatric Hosp., Mongomery, Ala., 1990—. Mem. Interagy. bd. U.S. Civil Svc. Examiners for North Ala., 1966-71; mem. Ala. Gov.'s Com. on Employment of Handicapped, 1967-72; mem. steering com. Comprehensive Mental Health Center Program, Bibb, Pickens and Tuscaloosa counties, 1967-70; mem. adv. coun. Am. Corrective Therapy Assn., 1972—; mem. regional adv. com. Rehab. Rsch. and Tng. Center, George Washington U., 1974-76; mem. adv. bd. Nat. Rehab. Tng. Inst., 1973-74;

chmn. Ala. White House Conf. on Aging, 1971; spl. field rep. Accreditation Council for Psychiat. Facilities, Joint Commn. on Accreditation Hosps., 1973-78; mem. spl. adv. bd. reality orientation tng. project Am. Hosp. Assn., 1973-75, adv. com. for devel. exams. for occupational therapists, 1973-75; mem. med. com. Pres.'s Com. on Employment of People with Disabilities, 1975-86, vice chmn., 1981-86, mem. exec. com., 1976-86, mem. steering com. of exec. com., 1982-86, mem. med., health and ins. com., 1987—; bd. dirs. Ala. Assn. Mental Health, Tuscaloosa County Assn. Mental Health, Tuscaloosa County Boys Club, United Fund Tuscaloosa County, Alzheimer's Disease and Related Disorders Assn., Topeka, 1986-89, Vol. Ctr. of Topeka, 1986-89, Huntington's Disease Soc. Am., 1987-89; nat. project adv. council Boys' Clubs Am., 1977-81; bd. mgmt. Tuscaloosa County YMCA; mem. adv. bd. Tuscaloosa County Salvation Army, Mental Health Bd. Bibb, Pickens and Tuscaloosa counties; mem. bd. advisers Ala. Womens Hall of Fame; trustee Menninger Found., Topeka, 1972—, Wesley Homes Found., Atlanta, 1971-74, The Villages, Topeka, Kans., 1980—. Served to capt. M.C., AUS, 1943-46. Recipient Dir.'s Commendation awards VA Hosp., Topeka, 1960, VA Hosp., Tuscaloosa, 1965, Superior Performance award VA Central Office, 1969, Adminstr.'s Commendation medal VA Central Office, 1969, Achievement award Nat. Rehab. Conf., 1973, John E. Davis award Am. Corrective Therapy Assn., 1974, Meritorious Service award Tex. Assn. Homes for Aging, 1974, others; named Boss of Yr., VA Hosp. Secs. Assn., 1970, also Am. Bus. Women's Assn., Tuscaloosa, 1971; diplomate Am. Bd. Psychiatry and Neurology. Fellow Am. Geriatric Soc., Am. Psychiat. Assn. (com. chmn., editor Newsletter Ala. Dist. br., chmn. nat. rehab. com. 1980-82, chmn. com. on rehab. N.Y. County dist. br. 1979-81, mem. com. on aging 1978-84), Am. Coll. Psychiatrists; mem. AMA, Menninger Sch. Psychiatry Alumni Assn. (editor bull., past pres.; mem. nat. adv. council), Tuscaloosa County Med. Soc., Ala. Acad. Neurology and Psychiatry (past pres.), N.Y. Acad. Medicine (sec. sect. geriatric medicine 1981-82, chmn. 1983-84), N.Y. State Soc. Indsl. Medicine, Assn. Regional Planning Dirs. and Adminstrs., Assn. Med. Supts. Mental Hosps. (pres.-elect 1972), Am. Hosp. Assn. (gov. council psychiat. services sect. 1968, chmn. 1974, del.-at-large to ho. of dels. 1976-80, adv. panel Center for Mental Health and Psychiat. Services 1978-82), Assn. Med. Rehab. Dirs. and Coordinators (hon.), World Psychiat. Assn. (chmn. sect. on psychiat. rehab.), Phi Gamma Delta. Unitarian. Mem. editorial adv. panel Just One Break, 1977; contbr. articles to profl. jours. Died Feb. 4, 2004.

FOOLADI, MIKE M., physician, educator; b. Zolghadar, Iran, Feb. 22, 1937; arrived in U.S., 1960; m. Marjan Fooladi, Aug. 28, 1974; children: Michael, Mark. BS, Baylor U., 1965; MS, Tex. So. U., 1968; PhD, U. So. Miss., 1979; MD, Juarez Med. Sch., 1982; MPH, U. So. Miss., 1997. Lic. Iran, Mex. Prof. chemistry Miss. C.C., Gulfport; prof. biotechnology U. Tehran, Iran; cons. to min. Ministry Agr., Tehran; cons. Shaheed Modaress, Tehran; pres. Fuladi Rsch. Ins., El Paso, Tex., 1985—2001; v.p. Alpina Lab, Bay Minette, Ala.; corp. rsch. dir. Vicksburg (Miss.) & Vertac. Pres. Coosa Chem. Co., Childensburg, Ala., 1978—80. Author: (book) Tal Viva 2021, 1998; contbr. articles to profl. jours. Mem.: AMA, Am. Chem. Soc. Achievements include patents in field. Avocations: walking, horseback riding, reading, writing. Home: Hattiesburg, Miss. Died Apr. 2006.

FOOTE, CALEB, law educator, writer; b. Cambridge, Mass., Mar. 26, 1917; s. Henry Wilder and Eleanor (Cope) F.; m. Hope Stephens, Nov. 17, 1942; children: Robert, Heather, Andrew, Ethan, David. AB, Harvard U., 1939; MA, Columbia U., 1941; LLB, U. Pa., 1953. Bar: Pa. 1956, U.S. Supreme Ct. 1961. Instr. U. Pa., 1953-54; assoc. prof. U. Nebr. Law Sch., 1954-56; prof. U. Pa. Law Sch., 1956-65; Elizabeth Josselyn Boalt prof. law U. Calif.-Berkeley, 1965—88, Elizabeth Josselyn Boalt prof. law emeritus, 1988—2006; Walter E. Meyer vis. Research prof. Harvard U. Law Sch., 1960-61. Co-author: (with R.J. Levy and F.E.A. Sander) Cases and Materials on Family Law, 1966, 3d edit., 1985, (with H. Mayer) The Culture of the University: Governance and Education, 1968, (with R.J. Levy) Criminal Law: Cases and Materials, 1981; editor: Studies on Bail, 1966. Died Mar. 4, 2006.

FOOTE, IRVING FLINT, English language educator; b. Laconia, N.H., Aug. 19, 1930; s. Lewis Ford and Margaret Merrill (Flint) F.; m. Caryl Frances Kenig, 1958 (div. 1961); m. Martha Rush Dowling, 1963 (div. 1966); children: James Murray, Anna Kathleen, Joseph Nathaniel; m. Ruth Anne Quinn, Aug. 30, 1969; children: Samuel Joshua, Lewis Ford II. AB, Princeton U., 1952; MA, U. Conn., 1958. Instr., English U. Conn., Storrs, 1954-56, Arnold Sch., Plymouth, Mass., 1956-57, Ga. Inst. Tech., Atlanta, 1957-61, asst. prof., English, 1961-66; supt. Bernstein Medals Co., Atlanta, 1966-68; asst. prof., English Ga. Inst. Tech., Atlanta, 1968-70, assoc. prof., 1970-92, prof. English, from 1992. Cons. in field. Author: The Connecticut Yankee in the Twentieth Century, 1991; contbr. articles to profl. jours. V.p. Bass Orgn. Neighborhood Devel., Atlanta, 1972-73. Mem. Internat. Assn. for Fantastic in Arts, World Sci. Fiction, Phi Beta Kappa. Home: Dauphin Islnd, Ala. Died Mar. 12, 2005.

FOOTE, RAYMOND EUGENE, video production executive; b. Botwood, Nfld., Can., June 5, 1922; came to U.S., 1946; s. John Henry and Lillian (Manuel) F.; m. Jean Efford, June 3, 1946 (div. Jan. 1960); 1 child, Barbara Ann; m. Elizabeth Koke, Oct. 16, 1965. Student, Nat. Radio Inst., Washington, 1939-40, 42-43, Ampex Video Inst., Elk Grove, Ill., 1971. Sales engr. Westinghouse Elec. Supply, Balt., 1963-65, Trinkle Sales, Inc., Cherry Hill, N.J., 1965-68; gen. mgr. div. indsl. electronics Nationwide Communications, Balt., 1968-70; gen. mgr. high-fidelity house K.M.S. Induries, Balt., 1970-71; mgr. indsl. video Johnson Bros. Radio & TV, Balt., 1971-82; mgr. Regester Audio-Visual Video Systems, Balt., from 1982. Mem. Motion Picture and TV Devel. Adv. Council State of Md., 1983-84; mem. adv. bd. Md. Film Commn., 1982-83. Asst. producer (slide show prodn.) Firearm Safety Training, 1987 (1st place award Am. Soc. for Indsl. Safety 1987). Video producer, worker Com. to Elect Harry Hughes Gov. of Md., Balt. and Annapolis, 1978-79. Served with RAF, 1943-45. Mem. IEEE (assoc.), Royal British Legion. Clubs: Balto Yacht (Middle River, Md.) (hon. commodore). Democrat. Methodist. Avocations: boating, travel, collecting stamps. Home: Baltimore, Md. Died June 11, 2004.

FORBES, ELLIOT, retired music educator; b. Cambridge, Mass., Aug. 30, 1917; s. Edward Waldo and Margaret (Laighton) F.; m. Kathleen Brooks Allen, June 7, 1941; children— Diana, Barbara Anne, Susan. BA, Harvard U., 1941, MA, 1947; MusD, New Eng. Conservatory, 1996; MusD (hon.), Harvard U., 2003. Tchr. Cate (Calif.) Sch., 1941-43; tchr. Belmont Hill Sch., 1943-45; asst. prof. music Princeton U., 1947-54, assoc. prof., 1954-58; Fanny Peabody prof. music, Harvard U., 1961-84, prof. emeritus, 1984—2006; dir. Harvard Glee Club and Radcliffe Choral Soc., Harvard U., 1958-70, prof. music, 1958-61. Editor: Thayer's Life of Beethoven, 1964, rev. edit., 1967, A History of Music at Harvard to 1972, 1988, A Report of Music at Harvard from 1972 to 1990, 1983. Overseer New Eng. Conservatory; trustee Isabella Stewart Gardner Mus. Recipient Alumni medal Harvard U., 1991. Mem. Am. Musicol. Soc., Coll. Music Soc., Am. Acad. Arts and Scis. Home: Cambridge, Mass. Died Jan. 10, 2006.

FORBES, JOHN RIPLEY, museum director, educator; b. Chelsea, Mass., Aug. 25, 1913; s. Kenneth Ripley and Ellen Elizabeth (Barker) F.; m. Margaret Sanders, Dec. 10, 1951; children: Ripley, Anne. Spl. student, U. Iowa, 1933-34, Bowdoin Coll., 1934-35, LHD (hon.), 1987. Founder, dir. Stamford (Conn.) Mus., 1935-37; ornithologist, taxidermist Lee Mus. Biology, Bowdoin Coll., MacMillan-Arctic Expdn., Labrador and Baffin Island, 1937; founder, dir. William T. Hornaday Meml. Found., N.Y., 1938-50; organizer, dir. Kansas City (Mo.) Mus., 1939-41; founder Nashville Children's Mus., 1944, acting dir., 1945-46, trustee for life, 1975; exec. dir. Jacksonville (Fla.) Children's Mus., 1945; founder Fernbank Children's Nature Mus., Atlanta, 1946; organizer, dir. Oreg. Mus. Sci. and Industry, Portland, 1947-49; founder Nat. Found. for Jr. Mus., N.Y., dir. N.Y., 1951-60; founder Sacramento Jr. Mus., dir., 1951-53; co-founder, dir. ops. Nature Centers for Young Am., 1959-60; founder, pres., chmn. bd. Natural Sci. for Youth Found., Conn., from 1961; founder Conservancy Nature Ctr., Naples, Fla., 1959. Organizer Ft. Worth's Children's Mus., 1945. Founder, pres. William T. Hornaday Meml. Trust, Conn., 1961-77; founder Mid-Fairfield County Youth Mus., Westport, Conn., 1958, pres., 1963-66, trustee for life, 1966; founder Am. Assn. Youth Mus., 1964, hon. life mem., 1976; co-founder, v.p. Aspetuck Land Trust, Fairfield County; pres. St. John's on the Lake Assn., N.H., 1963-64; pres. emeritus, trustee John and Anna Newton Porter Found., N.H., 1974-89; founder Outdoor Activity Ctr., Atlanta, chmn., 1977-80; founder Chattahoochee Nature Ctr., Roswell, Ga., pres., 1977-78; founder Reynolds Arboretum and Nature Preserve Morrow, Ga., 1976; founder, pres. Lakes Region Conservation Trust, Meredith, N.H., 1977; founder Forbes Nature Ctr. on Ragged Island Lake Winnipesaukee, N.H., 1979; trustee Hilla Von Rebay Found., 1968; trustee Milford (Pa.) Reservation 1977, pres. 1977-82 1983; founder, pres. Natural Sci. Solar Ctr., Milford, Pa., 1983; founder, trustee Cochran Mill Nature Ctr. and Arboretum, Fairburn, Ga., 1987; founder Autrey Mill Nature Preserve and Heritage Ctr., Alpharetta, Ga., 1988; founder, pres. Big Trees Forest Preserve, Sandy Springs, Ga., 1984; founder Camp Whitley at Lake Careco, Nature Ctr., Austell, Ga., 1992; naturalist, lectr. on Bahia Paraiso, Argentine polar transport ship sunk near U.S. Palmer Base at Arthur Harbor, Antarctic Peninsula, 1989; bd. mem. Environ. Adv. Commn. State of Ga., 1992-94. With M.C., USAAF, 1942-45. Recipient merit award Calif. Conservation Coun., 1953, conservation award Am. Motors, 1971, William T. Hornaday gold medal, 1977, Founder's award Natural Sci. for Youth Found., 1979, Conservationist of Yr. award Ga. Wildlife Fedn., 1991, Nature Educator of Yr. award Roger Tory Peterson Inst., 1995, Cert. Merit, Garden Club of Ga., Inc., 2000, Spl. Appreciation award Friends of Preservation Oaks, 2000; named Hon. Tex. Citizen, Gov. Price Daniel, 1962. Mem. Am. Assn. Mus. (chmn. children's mus. sec. 1965), Nat. Audubon Soc. (life), Am. Nature Study Soc., Nature Conservancy, Wilderness Soc., Am. Ornithologist Union (life), N.Y. Zool. Soc., Am. Birding Assn. (life), Nat. Wildlife Fedn., Conn. Conservation Assn. (pres. 1969-70), Sierra Club, Audubon Soc. N.H. (pres. 1975) Clubs: Explorers (N.Y.C.); Mazamas (Portland, Oreg.). Home: Atlanta, Ga. Died Aug. 28, 2006.

FORBES, RICHARD MATHER, biochemistry professor; b. Wooster, Ohio, Jan. 8, 1916; s. Ernest Browning and Lydia Maria (Mather) F.; m. Mary Medlicott, Feb. 26, 1944; children: Sally Allen, Anne Mather, Stephen Harding. BS, Pa. State Coll., 1938, MS, 1939; PhD, Cornell U., 1942. Instr. biochemistry Wayne State U., 1942; research fellow Cornell U., Ithaca, N.Y., 1942-43; asst. prof. U. Ky., Lexington, 1946-49; assoc. prof. U. Ill., Champaign-Urbana, 1949-55, prof. nutritional biochemistry, 1955-85, emeritus prof., 1985—2006. Contbr. articles to profl. jours. Served to capt. U.S. Army, 1943-46. Recipient H. H. Mitchell award U. Ill., 1981 Fellow AAAS, Am. Inst. Nutrition (Borden award 1984); mem. Am. Soc. Animal Sci. (Gustav Bohstedt award 1968), Sigma Xi. Democrat. Mem. United Ch. of Christ. Clubs: Nat. Exchange, Izaak Walton League. Home: Urbana, Ill. Died June 7, 2006.

FORBES, RODNEY ALLAN, telecommunications analyst; b. Ft. Morgan, Colo., July 8, 1965; s. Leonard Leroy and Dorothy Alice (Harr) F.; m. Sheryl Ann Jamison, July 20, 1985; children: Phillip Keith, Tiffani Lauraine. Student, U. Md., 1987-88, Columbia Coll., 1990-93. Auto mechanic Len's Repair, Centralia, Mo., 1983-84; maintenance man Mt. Zion Bible Sch., Ava, Mo., 1988-89; clerk, cashier Casey's Gen. Store, Hallsville, Mo., 1989; telecommunications analyst A.P. Green Industries, Mexico, Mo., from 1989. Asst. Sunday Sch. supt. Ch. of God, 1990; bd. dirs. Mexico, Ch. of God (Holiness), 1995; mem. exec. com., bd. dirs. United Credit Union, 1995; mem. Pachyderm Club (Reps.), Audrain County, Mo., 1994. With USN, 1984-88 Decorated Good Conduct award USN; Recipient Letter of Commendation, Recruit Tng. Comd., 1984, Presdl. Svc. award White House Communications Agy., 1986. Avocations: flying, riding horses, water-skiing, fishing, hunting. Home: Mexico, Mo. Died Apr. 20, 2005.

FORD, GLENN (GWYLIN SAMUEL NEWTON FORD), actor; b. Que., Can., May 1, 1916; s. Newton and Hannah F.; m. Eleanor Powell, Oct. 23, 1943 (div.); 1 son, Peter Newton; m. Kathryn Hays, March 27, 1966; m. Cynthia Hayward., March 27, 1977; m. Jeanne Baus, March 5, 1993. Acting debut at age 4 in Tom Thumb's Wedding; stage mgr. Wilshire Theater, 1934; stage mgr., actor in The Children's Hour, 1935, Golden Boy; on tour with John Beal in Soliloquy, 1938; actor with Columbia Pictures Corp., 1939-43, 45-53; free lance actor, 1953-55; with Metro-Goldwyn Mayer, 1955—; films include Night in Manhattan, 1937, Heaven with a Barbed Wire Fence, 1939 My Son iIs Guilty, 1939,, Convicted Women, 1940, Men Without Souls, 1940, Babies For Sale, 1940, The Lady in Question, 1940, Blodie Plays Cupid, 1940, So Ends Our Night, 1941, Texas, 1941, Go West, Young Lady, 1941, Screen Snapshots Series 21, No. 6, 1942, The Adventures of Martin Eden, 1942, Flight Lieutenant, 1942, The Desperados, 1943, Destroyer, 1943, Gilda, 1946, A Stolen Life, 1946, Gallant Journey, 1946, Framed, 1947, Return of October, 1948, The Mating of Millie, 1948, The Man From Colorado, 1948, The Loves of Carmen, 1948, The Big Heat, 1953, The Undercover Man, 1949, Lust For Gold, 1949, Mr. Soft Touch, 1949, The Doctor and the Girl, 1949, The White Tower, 1950, The Flying Missle, 1950, The Redhead and the Cowboy, 1951, Follow the Sun, 1951, The Secret of Convict Lake, 1951, The Green Glove, 1952, Young Man with Ideas, 1952, Affair in Trinidad, 1952, Time Bomb, 1953, The Man from the Alamo, 1953, Plunder of the Sun, 1953, Appointment in Honduras, 1953, City Story, 1954, Human Desire, 1954, The Americano, 1955, The Violent Man, 1955, Interrupted Melody, 1955, Blackboard Jungle, 1955, Trial, 1955, Ransom!, 1956, Jubal, 1956, The Fastest Gun Aliver, 1956, The Teahouse of the August Moon, 1956, 3:10 to Yuma, 1957, Don't Go Near the Water, 1957, Imitation General, 1958, The Sheepman, 1958, Cowboy, 1958, Torpedo Run, 1958, It Started With a Kiss, 1959, The Gazebo, 1959, Cimarron, 1961, Cry for Happy, 1961, Pocketful of Miracles, 1961 (also assoc. prodr.), Four Horseman of the Apocalypse, 1962, Experiment in Terror, 1962, The Courtship of Eddie's Father, 1963, Love is a Ball, 1963, Advance to the Rear, 1964, Fate Is The Hunter, 1964, Dear Heart, 1965, The Rounders, 1965, Is Paris Burning?, 1966, Rage, 1966, The Last Challenge, 1967, A Time For Killing, 1967, The Money Trap, 1968, The Day of the Evil Gun, 1968, Heaven With a Gun, 1969, Smith!, 1969, Santee, 1973, Midway, 1976, Superman, 1978, The Visitor, 1979, Day of the Assassin, 1979, Day of Resurrection, 1980, Happy Birthday to Me, 1981, Casablanca Express, 1989, Border Shootout, 1990, Raw Nerve, 1991; appeared in TV series Cade's County, 1971-72, Jarret, 1973, The Family Holvak, 1975; movies for TV include The Brotherhood of the Bell, 1970, Punch and Jody, 1974, The Greatest Gift, 1975, The Disappearance of Flight 412, 1975, The 3,000 Mile Chase, 1977, No Margin For Error, 1978, Evening in Byzantium, 1978, The Sacketts, 1979, The Gift, 1979, Beggarman, Thief, 1979, My Town, 1986, Law at Randado, 1989, Final Verdict, 1991; TV miniseries Once An Eagle, 1976; narrator documentary America, 1971; host TV series When Havoc Struck, 1978; appeared in TV spl. The Dick Powell Show, 1963, Police Story: No Margin for Error, 1978, Our Hollywood Education, 1992; prodr. (TV Series) The Faith of Our Children, 1953; composer, editor The Animated Kid's Bible, 2005 Served with USMCR, 1942-45. Named Number One Box Office Star in Am., ann. poll. Motion Picture Herald, 1958. Died Aug. 30, 2006.

FORESTIER, EMMANUEL ADRIEN, banker; b. Lyon, France, May 12, 1953; s. Claude and Claude (Thierry) Forestier; m. Helene Brault, Sept. 8, 1979; children: David, Virginie, Benjamin. Ingenieur agronome, Inst. Nat. Agronomique, Paris, 1977; M in Econs., Pantheon Sorbonne U., Paris, 1977, PhD in Econs., 1980. With World Bank, Washington, 1979-80, with young profls. program, 1980-84, economist, 1985-87, sr. economist, 1987-92, prin. pvt. sector specialist, 1994-97, mgr. telecomms. divsn. Paris, from 1997; sr. banker European Bank for Reconstruction and Devel., London, 1992-94. Mem. French Assn. of Agrl. Econs., Polo de Paris. Avocations: skiing, golf, tennis, shooting. Home: Bethesda, Md. Died Dec. 21, 2004.

FORLINI, FRANK JOHN, JR., cardiologist; b. Newark, Mar. 30, 1941; s. Frank Sr. and Rose Theresa (Parussini) F.; m. Joanne Marie Horch, July 19, 1969; children: Anne Marie, Victoria, Frank III, Anthony. BS in Biology, Villanova U., Pa., 1963; MD, George Washington U., 1967. Diplomate Am. Bd. Internal Medicine, Am. Bd. Cardiovascular Disease. V.p., bus. agt. Cooks, Countermen and Cafeteria Workers Union Local 399 AFL, 1960-61; intern Bklyn.-Cumberland Med. Ctr., N.Y., 1967-68, resident in internal medicine N.Y., 1968-70; fellow in cardiology Inst. Med. Sci. Pacific Med. Ctr. Presbyn. Hosp., San Francisco, 1970-72; practice medicine specializing in cardiology Rock Island, Ill., 1974—2000; sr. ptnr. Forlini Med. Speciality Clinic, Rock Island, 1974—2000. Owner Forlini Farm and Forlini Devel. Enterprises; assoc. prof. pharmacy L.I. U., Bklyn., 1969-70; pres., CEO U.S. Oil & Transp. Co., Inc., 1966-89; pres. Profl. and Execs. Ins. Assocs., 1973-89, Profls. Assocs., 1973-89; med. and exec. dir. Cardiovasc. Inst. Northwestern Ill., 1984—; exec. dir., owner Franksoft Pub., 1988—; Shelter for Abused Women and Children, Rock Island, 1992-94, pres., chmn., 1994, chmn. capital campaign com., 1994; bd. dirs. Rescue Missions and Christian Family Care Ctr., 1992-94, pres., 1994. Contbr. articles to profl jours. Dep. registrar County of Rock Island, from 1985; trustee South Rock Island Twp., Rock Island County, 1987—97, Twp. Intergovtl. Agy., 1993—97, Friends of Twp. Govt. of Rock Island County, chmn., from 1995; alderman City of Rock Island, Rock Island County, from 1997, mayor pro tem, 2000—01; mem. Rock Island Comml. Indsl. Revolving Loan Fund, from 1998, mem. health care com., from 2001; mem. exec. com. Rock Island County Rep. Cen. Com., 1992—94; chmn. fin. com. Life and Family Ednl. Trust, 2001—02; mem. Sunset Marina Steering Com., from 2002, Mayor's Quad City Transit Task Force, from 2003; del. Ill. Mcpl. League, 1998, 2002—03, Nat. League Cities, 2000; mem. nat. com. Coll. Young Reps., 1965—66; mem. Physicians for Reagan-Bush, 1980, 1984; chmn. D.C. Coll. Young Reps., 1965—66; mem. exec. com. Rep. Cen. Com., Washington, 1965—66; vice chmn. Rock Island Reps., 1985—90, precinct committeeman, 1985—90, 1992—93; del. Ill. State Rep. Conv., 1992; pres. parish coun. St. Thomas Roman Cath. Ch., San Antonio; bd. dirs. Life and Family Ednl. Trust, 2000—03. Maj. USAF, 1972—74. Nat. Inst. Heart Disease NIH-USPHS grantee, 1964-66, 70-72; Fellowship of Cath. Scholars, 1994—. Fellow: N.Am. Soc. Pacing and Electrophysiology, Am. Coll. Cardiology; mem.: KC (3d deg. from 1994), AMA, Soc. Cath. Social Scientists, Rock Island County Twp. Assn. (v.p. 1994, pres. 1994—95, mem. exec. com. 1994—97), Western Ill. Ind. Physicians Assn. (bd. dirs. from 1995, sec. 1996—97, mem. exec. com. from 1996, treas. from 1997), Rock Island County Med. Soc. (chmn. com. on ins. from 1990), Ill. State Med. Soc., Univ. Faculty for Life. Home: Rock Island, Ill. Died Apr. 30, 2004; Rock Island.

FORMAN, HOWARD IRVING, lawyer, former federal agency administrator; b. Phila., Jan. 12, 1917; s. Jacob and Dora (Moses) F.; m. Ada Pressman, Aug. 2, 1938; children: Kenneth J., Harvey R. BS in Chemistry, St. Joseph's Coll., 1937; LLB, Temple U., 1944; MA, U. Pa., 1949, PhD, 1955. Bar: D.C. 1945, Pa. 1973. Rsch. chemist Frankford Arsenal, Dept. Army, Phila., 1940-44, patent atty., 1944-46, chief patents br., 1946-56; asst. dir. Pitman-Dunn Rsch. Labs., 1955-56; lectr. polit. sci. Temple U., 1956-63; from patent atty. to trademark and internat. corp. counsel Rohm and Haas Co., Phila., 1956-76; dep. asst. sec. U.S. Dept. Commerce, Washington, 1976-81; also dir. Office of Product Standards Policy; chmn. interagy. com. on standards policy Weiser, Stapler & Spivak, Phila., 1974-76; head. U.S. dels. to UN internat. confs., Geneva, 1976-81; sec., dir. Rohm & Haas Asia, Inc., 1973-76; v.p., gen. counsel, dir. Brilliant Internat., Inc., Bala-Cynwyd, Pa., 1974-83; sec., dir. Far East Chem. Services, Inc., Wilmington, Del., 1973-76, Rohm and Haas GmbH, Zug, Switzerland, 1975-76; dir. U.S. Pharm. Corp., 1975-83; pvt. practice Phila., 1981—2005. Advisor to asst. sec. for econ. affairs relative to internat. intellectual property matters Dept. State, 1968-72; orginator Internat. Lab. Accreditation world-wide biennial confs. (ILAC), 1977-2005; chmn. ANSI accredited stds. com., Z21, on performance and installation gas burning appliances and accessories, 1981-97. Author: Inventions, Patents and Related Matters, 1957, Patents-Their Ownership and Administration by the U.S. Government, 1957; Editor: Patents, Research and Management, 1961, The Law of Chemical, Metallurgical and Pharmaceutical Patents, 1967; author plays: The Birth of the American Patent System, 1976, The Birth of the American Patent and Copyright Systems, 1990.; contbr. to publs. in field. Bd. dirs. Lower Moreland Twp. Sch. Bd., Montgomery County, Pa., 1969-75; bd. dirs. Eastern Montgomery County Vocat.-Tech. Sch., 1969-75, sec., 1970-75; bd. dirs. Warminster (Pa.) Gen. Hosp., 1983-91; emeritus dir. Allegheny United Hosps., Inc., 1991-94; life trustee Med. Coll. Pa. and Hahnemann U. Hosps., 1994-98. Recipient Robert J. Painter Meml. award Stds. Engring. Soc.-ASTM, 1978, Leo B. Moore award Stds. Engring. Soc., 1981. Fellow Am. Inst. Chemists; mem. ABA, FBA, AAAS, ASTM (hon. life, bd. dirs. 1985-87), Internat. Assn. Protection Indsl. Property, Am. Nat. Stds. Inst. (bd. dirs. 1977-80, Finegan Stds. medal 1996), Nat. Coun. Patent Law Assn. (chmn. 1967-68), Am. Chem. Soc., Sci. Rsch. Soc. Am., Am. Assn. Lab. Accreditation (dir. 1983-91), Am. Patent Law Assn. (bd. mgrs. 1970-73), Am. Coll. Legal Medicine, Phila. Bar Assn. (sec. 1973-74, com. on jurimetrics, tech. and patents, v.p. 1975), Phila. Patent Law Assn. (pres. 1964-66), Licensing Execs. Soc., Stds. Engring. Soc. (Robert J. Painter Meml. award 1978, Leo B. Moore award 1981), Franklin Inst. (vice chmn. Futures Ctr. campaign), Nat. Lawyers Club, Gas Appliance Mfrs. Assn. (meritorious svc. award 1996), Am. Soc. Gas Engrs. (hon.), Sigma Xi. Achievements include being the principal draftsman, prime mover in devel. original OMB Circular A-119 which established nat. policy calling for primary dependence of Fed. Govt. on private sector standards orgns. for devel. of standards required for procurement and regulatory purposes by govt. agencies. Home: Huntingdon Valley, Pa. Died Dec. 5, 2005.

FORREST, JOSEPH MICHAEL, manufacturing company executive, consultant; b. Hancock, Mich., May 24, 1946; s. George William and Mary Ann (Halonen) F.; m. Debra Kay Jarrett, Nov. 24, 1968 (div. June 1983); children: Laura Jennifer, Kathryn Elizabeth, Jarrett Michael; m. Lynn Marie Wentela, Jan. 6, 1984. BS, No. Mich. U., 1971. Registered profl. engr., Mich. Supr. Fed.-Mogul Corp., Greenville, Mich., 1971-76, gen. foreman, 1976-77, supt. Blacksburg, Va., 1977-84; quality assurance mgr. Automotive Products Co., Sterling Heights, Mich., 1984-86, Machining Industries, New Baltimore, Mich., 1986-87, FitzSimons Mfg. Co., Big Rapids, Mich., from 1987. Author: Quality Assurance Manual, 1986, 87. Mem. Greenville Sch. Bd., 1976-77. Sgt. U.S. Army, 1967-68, Vietnam. Mem. Am. Soc. Quality Control. Democrat. Roman Catholic. Died July 7, 2005.

FORSTER, FRANCIS MICHAEL, neurologist, educator; b. Cin., Feb. 14, 1912; s. Michael Joseph and Louise Barbara (Schmid) F.; m. Helen Dorothy Kiley (dec. 2004), June 15, 1937; children— Denis, Susan, Kathleen, Mark, Gabrielle. Student, Xavier U., Cin., 1930-32, LL.D., 1955; BS, U. Cin., 1935, B.M., 1936, MD, 1937; D.Sc. hon., Georgetown U., 1982. Diplomate: Am. Bd. Psychiatry and Neurology (dir.). Rotating intern Good Samaritan Hosp., Cin., 1936-37; house officer neurology and neurosurgery Boston City Hosp., 1937-38, resident neurology, 1939-40; fellow psychiatry Pa. Hosp., Phila., 1938-39; asst. neurology Harvard Med. Sch., 1939-40; Rockefeller Found. research fellow physiology Yale Sch. Medicine, 1940-41; instr. neurology Boston U. Sch. Medicine, 1941-43; asst. prof. neurology Jefferson Med. Sch., 1943-47, assoc. prof. neurology, 1947-50; prof. neurology, dir. dept. Georgetown U. Sch. Medicine, 1950-58, dean Sch. Medicine, 1953-58; prof., chmn. dept. neurology U. Wis. Sch. Medicine, 1958-78, prof. emeritus, 1978—2006; dir. Epilepsy Center, VA Hosp., Madison, Wis., 1977-82. Cons. neurology. Author: Synopsis of Neurology, 1962, 66, 73, 78, Reflex Epilepsy, Behavioral Therapy and Conditional Reflexes, 1977; editor: Modern Therapy in Neurology, 1957, Evaluation of Drug Therapy, 1961. Mem. AMA (chmn. nervous and mental diseases sect. 1952-53), AAAS, D.C. Med. Soc. (chmn. sect. neurology and psychiatry 1955-56, pres. 1958), Am. Acad. Neurology (chmn. survey com. 1948-51, pres. 1957-59), Am. Neurol. Assn. (chmn. com. internat. collaboration 1954-55), Am. Epilepsy League (pres. 1951-52), Assn. Rsch. Nervous and Mental Diseases, Am. Physiol. Soc., Am. Assn. Electroencephalographers, Med. Soc. Wis., Cosmos Club (Washington), Sigma Xi, Alpha Omega. Clubs: Cosmos (Washington). Died Feb. 23, 2006.

FORSYTHE, HENDERSON, retired actor; b. Macon, Mo., Sept. 11, 1917; s. Cecil Proctor and Mary Catherine (Henderson) F.; m. Dorothea Maria Carlson, May 26, 1942; children: Eric, Jason. Student, Culver-Stockton Coll., 1935-37; BA, State U. Iowa, 1939, M.F.A., 1940. Mem. faculty, dir. U. Iowa, summers 1953-55 Numerous appearances Broadway and off-Broadway plays, TV and film prodns., 1955-2006; sheriff in U.S. and London prodns. Best Little Whorehouse in Texas (Tony award); prin. role in TV series Eisenhower and Lutz, CBS, 1987-88, Nearly Departed, 1989; appeared in running role in daytime TV drama As the World Turns, 1960-91; prin. role in 110 in the Shade, N.Y.C. Opera, 1992; lead in Quarrel of Sparrows, 1993; TV comml./Col. Sanders for Kentucky Fried Chicken, 1994. Served with U.S. Army, 1941-46. Mem. Actors Equity Assn., AFTRA, Screen Actors Guild, ANTA. Presbyterian. Home: Williamsburg, Va. Died Apr. 17, 2006.

FORTUNE, ROBERT RUSSELL, financial consultant; b. Collingswood, N.J., Nov. 22, 1916; s. Colin C. and Minnie M. (Brown) F.; m. Christine E. Dent, Nov. 10, 1956. BS in Econs., U. Pa., 1940. CPA, Pa. With Haskins & Sells (C.P.A.s), 1940-42, 46-48; with Pa. Power & Light Co., Allentown, 1948-84, v.p. fin., 1966-75, exec. v.p. fin., dir., 1975-84. Chmn., CEO Assoc. Electric and Gas Ins. Svcs. Ltd., 1984-93, Chestnut St. Exch. Fund, chmn., 1994—. Tech. adv. com. on fin. FPC, 1974-75. Treas. Allentown Sch. Dist. Authority, 1963-85, Lehigh-Northampton Airport Authority, 1985-94. With USN, 1942-46. Mem. Fin. Execs. Inst., Am., Pa. insts. CPAs. Clubs: Lehigh Country. Republican. Home: Allentown, Pa. Died Apr. 25, 2006.

FOSS, KARL ROBERT, auditor; b. Aug. 26, 1938; s. Robert Henry and Ethel Caroline (Huston) Foss. Student, U. Wis., 1956-59, 62; BS, Madison Bus. Coll., 1961. Auditor Wis. Dept. Revenue, Madison, 1962-95; owner, mgr. LIST, Middleton, Wis., 1968-76. Pub.: Suppliers List, 1968, Suppliers List Directory, 1989. Bd. dirs. Middletown Hist. Soc., 1976—93, v.p., 1980; mem. legis. adv. Old Car Hobby, from 1971. Co-recipient Spl. Interest Autos Appreciation award, 1971. Mem.: Contemporary Hist. Vehicle Assn., Acctg. and Mgmt. Assn., Model T Ford Club Am., Vintage Chevrolet Club Am., Antique Automobile Club Am., Studebaker Drivers Club, Oldsmobile Club Am. (nat. bd. dirs. 1973—85, treas. 1981—85), Wis. Automobile Clubs Assn. Inc. (co-founder 1971, bd. dirs. from 1971, pres. 1972—74, 1977—78, 1980, 1986—87, v.p. 1975—76, 1979, 1985, from 1995). Died Apr. 2006.

FOSTER, CAR M., educational facility executive, consultant; b. Harodsburg, Ky., Dec. 5, 1925; s. Mark D. and Mattie (Roberts) F.; m. Jewell Lovett, m. Sept. 14, 1946; children: Sharon, Carolyn, Mark. BS, U. Ky., 1949; MS, Ind. U., 1957; PhD, Purdue U., 1965. Lic. psychologist, Ky. Tchr. Ind. pub. schs., 1949-57, prin., 1957-64; instr. Purdue U., Lafayette, Ind., 1964-65; prof. U. Ky., Louisville, 1965-69; asst. supt. Louisville pub. schs., 1969-72; prin. Jefferson County Schs., Louisville, 1972-86; pres. The Learning Connection, Inc., Louisville, from 1986. Mem. Ind. Gov.'s Sci. Com.; book reviewer, lectr. and cons. in field. Creator 4 ednl. films; contbr. articles to profl. jours. Mem. Student-Parent Advocacy Resource Ctr., Jefferson County; chmn. T.J. Unitarian Ch. Served with USN, 1944-46. Named Ind. Tchr. of Yr.; grantee in field. Mem. Think Tanks (co-chmn.). Avocations: racquetball, tennis, bridge, woodworking. Died Mar. 4, 2004.

FOSTER, ELIZABETH L., nursing administrator; b. Waterville, Maine, July 4, 1946; d. Edward Albert and Norah Douglas (Putnam) Lewis; m. Robert Nicholas Foster, July 7, 1984. BSN, Boston U., 1968, MS, 1978. Chief exec. officer Bar Harbor (Maine) Pub. Health Nursing Assn.; independent community health nurse Red Bird Mission United Meth. Ch., Red Bird Valley, Ky.; chief exec. officer Greater Lynn (Mass.) Vis. Nursing Assn.; asst. prof. RN to BSN nursing program U. So. Maine, Bangor; asst. prof. nursing Husson Coll./Ea. Maine Med. Ctr., Bangor; dir. clin. care Kno-Wal-Lin Home Health Care, Inc. Mem. Nat. League Nursing, Sigma Theta Tau. Home: Palermo, Maine. Died Sept. 7, 2004.

FOSTER, GEORGE MCCLELLAND, JR., anthropologist, educator; b. Sioux Falls, SD, Oct. 9, 1913; s. George McClelland and Mary (Slutz) F.; m. Mary Fraser LeCron, Jan. 6, 1938; children: Jeremy, Melissa Bowerman. BS, Northwestern U., 1935; PhD, U. Calif., Berkeley, 1941; DHL (hon.), So. Meth. U., 1990. Instr. Syracuse U., 1941-42; lectr. UCLA, 1942-43; vis. prof. U. Calif.-Berkeley, 1953-55, prof. anthropology, 1955-79, prof. emeritus, 1979—2006, chmn. dept., 1958-61; acting dir. Mus. Anthropology, 1955—58; lectr. pub. health, 1955-64. Anthropologist Inst. Social Anthropology, Smithsonian Instn., 1943-52, dir., 1946-1952; field rsch. Calif. Indians, 1937, Spain, 1949-50, Mexico, 1940—2004; adviser AID, India-Pakistan, 1955, Afghanistan, 1957, Zambia, 1961, 62, Nepal, 1965, Indonesia, 1973-74, WHO, Sri Lanka, 1975, Malaysia, 1978, India, 1979, 80, 81, Manila, 1983; adviser UNICEF, Geneva, 1976 Author: Traditional Cultures and the Impact of Technological Change, 1962, Tzintzuntzan: Mexican Peasants in a Changing World, 1967, Applied Anthropology, 1969, (with B. Anderson) Medical Anthropology, 1978, Hippocrates' Latin American Legacy, 1993, others, also monographs and articles. Recipient Berkeley citation, 1979; Guggenheim fellow, 1949; fellow Center for Advanced Study in Behavioral Scis., 1969-70 Fellow Am. Anthrop. Assn. (pres. 1970, Disting. Service award 1980); mem. Southwestern Anthrop. Assn. (Disting. Research award 1981), Nat. Acad. Scis., Am. Acad. Arts and Scis., Soc. Applied Anthropology (Malinowski award 1982) Clubs: Cosmos (Washington). Home: Berkeley, Calif. Died May 18, 2006.

FOSTER, WILLIAM ANTHONY, management consultant, educator; b. Washington, Nov. 26, 1929; s. Willard Hill and Evelyn Marie (Serrin) F.; m. Donna Roy Hayden, Feb. 5, 1955 (div. July 1985); children: Serrin M., Donna L., Shickel, Laura A. Valentine; m. Frances Christian Meacham, Dec. 6, 1995. BS in Bus. and Pub. Adminstrn., U. Md., 1956; MSPA, Nova Southeastern U., 1975, DPA, 1977. Registered profl. engr., Calif. Dir. indsl. engring. Washington region U.S. Postal Svc., 1969-71, mgr. indsl. engring. and plant maintenance Ea. Region, 1971-72, mgr. indsl. engring. Washington, 1972-80, nat. coord., 1980-83, program mgr. tng., 1983-86; pres., educator, trainer, cons. William A. Foster Assoc., Washington, from 1986. Educator, trainer, cons. U.S. Postal Svc., Washington, 1983-86, Embry-Riddle U., Daytona Beach, Fla., 1993, U. D.C., Washington, 1977-83, Southeastern U., 1980; dir., mgr. ops. U.S. Postal Svc., Washington, 1962-83. Author exec. tng. books; moderator TV show (Inaugural award 1991). Charter mem. Charleston Assn., Springfield, Va., 1968-84. Mem. ASTD (com. mem. 1986—), Am. Inst. Indsl. Engrs. (govt. liaison 1976-80, Nat. award for excellence 1969), Am. Soc Pub. Adminstrn. (cons. 1980-84), D.C. Coun. Engring. and Archtl. Socs. (chmn., PBS chair 1979-81, Outstanding Svc. award 1981, Bicentennial Engring. and Archtl. award 1976). Republican. Roman Catholic. Avocations: public speaking, american history, travel. Home: Reston, Va. Died Apr. 24, 2005.

FOUSHI, JOHN ANTHONY, cost engineer; b. Chicago Heights, Ill., June 13, 1928; s. John Anthony Sr. and Clara (Bachtle) F.; m. Betty L. Schofield, Oct. 21, 1950; children: John H., Debora A., David A. BSME, Ill. Inst. Tech., 1950. Supervising cost engr. Inland Steel Co., East Chicago, Ind., 1950-85; cons. Foushi & Assocs., Chicago Heights, from 1985. Sch. bd. mem. Bd. Edn. Sch. Dist. #170, Chicago Heights, 1968-84. Cpl. U.S. Army, 1951-53. Recipient medal of merit for cmty. svc. George M. O'Brien 4th Congl.

Dist. Ill., Chicago Heights, 1984. Fellow AACE Internat. (cert. cost engr., life mem., pres. 1981-82, award of merit 1995). Home: Chicago Heights, Ill. Died Oct. 20, 2005.

FOUT, MARY JANE, librarian, educator; b. East St. Louis, Oct. 26, 1937; d. William Pomeroy and Phebe Georgia (Anderson) Eaton; m. John Calvin Fout, Feb. 26, 1960 (div. May 1973); children: Justine Alyss, Elizabeth, John Eric. BA in German and History, U. Omaha, 1959, MA in History, 1963; M of Libr. and Info. Sci., U. Calif., Berkeley, 1977. Cert. tchr., Nebr., N.Y., Calif. Tchr. Indian Hills Jr. H.S., Omaha, 1959-60, Tech. Jr. High Sch., Omaha, 1962-64, Heidelberg Jr. H.S., Germany, 1964-65; archivist intern Social Welfare History Archives, U. Minn., Mpls., 1965-67; lectr. history U. Nebr., Omaha, 1967-68; interlibr. loan libr. Bard Coll., Annandale-on-Hudson, N.Y., 1971-73; career ctr./attendance clk. Armijo High Sch., Fairfield, Calif., 1974-76, career ctr./English Libr. libr., 1976-82, tchr. fgn. lang. and pub. svc., 1982-89, libr., from 1989. Summer youth employment tng. program counselor, summers 1980—. Contbg. author: Social Welfare History archives Collection, 1972. Mem. AAUW (past pres.), World Affairs Coun. No. Calif., Calif. Media Libr. Educators Assn. (charter), Am. Field Svc. (dist. rep., past pres. chpt., Pat Lawrence award 1990), Overseas Brats, Commonwealth Club, Alpha Xi Delta, Delta Kappa Gamma. Democrat. Avocations: reading murder mysteries, spectator sports, travel. Home: Fairfield, Calif. Died Oct. 19, 2004.

FOWLER, DENNIS F., insurance, employee benefits executive; b. Sept. 3, 1960; BA, U. Ky., 1982. Dist. mgr. Am. Gen., Nashville, 1986-96; sales exec. Mut. of Omaha, Nebr., from 1998. With USAF, 1982-86. Home: Rush, Ky. Died July 31, 2005.

FOWLER, KENNETH BRUCE, financial company executive; b. Paterson, N.J., Feb. 10, 1935; s. Kenneth Leon and Marie Theresa (Spinnato) F.; m. Elizabeth Aston, Nov. 2, 1957; children: Bruce Aston, Laurie Ann Fowler Bodner. BA, Miami U., 1959. Agt. Lincoln Nat. Life Co., Cin., 1964-65; v.p. Mariemont Ins., Inc., Cin., 1965-76; pres. Kenneth B. Fowler & Assoc., Inc., Cin., 1976-82; pres., chief exec. officer Profl. Planning Assocs., Inc., Cin., from 1982. Contbr. articles to profl. jours. With U.S. Army, 1957-59, Fed. Republic of Germany Mem. Ohio Assn. Life Underwriters (pres. 1980), Cin. Assn. Life Underwriters (pres., bd. dirs. 1970, Hall of Fame award), Million Dollar Round Table Ilife.), Assn. Advanced Life Underwriters. Nat. Assn. Life Underwriters, Top of Table Million Round Rable (charter). Republican. Home: Cincinnati, Ohio. Died Feb. 13, 2004.

FOWLES, JOHN, author; b. Essex, Eng., Mar. 31, 1926; s. Robert and Gladys (Richards) F.; m. Elizabeth Whitton, Apr. 2, 1954 (dec. 1990); m. Sarah Smith, Sept. 3, 1998. Degree in French (hon.), Oxford U., 1950; LittD (hon.), Exeter U., 1983, U. East Anglia, 1997. Author: The Collector, 1963, The Aristos: A Self-Portrait of Ideas, 1964, The Magus, 1966, The French Lieutenant's Woman, 1969, Poems, 1973, The Ebony Tower, 1974, Shipwreck, 1977, Daniel Martin, 1977, Islands, 1978, The Tree, 1979, The Enigma of Stonehenge, 1980, Mantissa, 1982, A Short History of Lyme Regis, 1983, A Maggot, 1985, Wormholes, 1998, John Fowles, Journals, Vol. 1, 2005. Lt. Royal Marines. Hon. fellow New Coll., Oxford U., 1997. Died Nov. 5, 2005.

FOX, FRANCES JUANICE, retired librarian, educator; b. Vicksburg, Miss., Aug. 17, 1916; d. Willie Amercy Thaxton and Fannye Lou (Spell) Hepfer; m. Leonard John Fox, Feb. 25, 1937; children: Frances Juanice, L. John Jr., Kenneth L., Robert T., William E., Elizabeth Jean. AA, Phoenix Coll., 1959; BS in Edn., Ariz. State U., 1963, MS in Edn., Libr., 1972. Cert. kindergarten, primary, and elem. tchr., cert. libr., cert. religious edn. Diocese of Phoenix. Substitute tchr. Eseambia County Sch. Dist., Pensacola, Fla., 1936-38; kindergarten tchr. Lollipop Ln. Sch., Phoenix, 1960-61, 1st United Meth. Day Sch., Phoenix, 1961-62; tchr. grade 3 Wilson Elem. Sch., Phoenix, 1962-63; summer libr. R.E. Simpson Elem. Sch., Phoenix, 1964, 65; preschool tchr. Jewish Community Ctr., Phoenix, 1967-68; libr. Audio Visual Ctr. Sts. Simon and Judge Elem. Sch., Phoenix, 1969-82. Cataloger First United Meth. Ch. Libr., Phoenix, 1963, Baker Ctr. Ariz. State Univ. Meth. and Hillel Students Libr., Tempe, 1969; tchr. ch. sch., 1942-69, ret., 1969. Contbr. poetry to varius publs., including Nat. Libr. Poetry, 1995, Poetic Voices of Am., 1990, 95, World Book of Poetry. 1990; co-compiler: (libr. manual) Diocese of Phoenix, 1980-81. Organizer, leader Girl Scouts USA, Birmingham, Ala., 1951, 52, Phoenix, 1976-83; leader cub scouts Boy Scouts Am., Birmingham, 1950-52, Phoenix, 1952-55; swim instr. ARC, Fla., Ariz., 1933, 34, 53, 54; dance instr. Circle Game and Beginning Dance, Wesley Cmty. Ctr., Phoenix, 1966, 67; sch. tchr. Meth. Ch., 1939-69. Scholar Phoenix Coll., Ariz. State Coll., 1959; recipient Gold Poet award World Book of Poetry, 1990, Honorable Mention Poetic Voices of Am., 1990, Internat. Twentieth Century Achievement award Cambridge Edn., 1994. Mem. ALA, Ariz. State Libr. Assn. (com. on continuing edn. 1979-81), Gold Star Wives of Am. Inc. (pres. 1993-94, nat. parlementarian 1990-91), DAV Aux. (life), Ariz. PTA (life mem., organizer, v.p.), Phi Theta Kappa, Iota Sigma Alpha Honor Soc. Methodist. Avocations: dance, photography, genealogy, sewing, music composition. Home: Phoenix, Ariz. Died Aug. 18, 2005.

FOX, ROBERT RICHARD, arts administrator, writer; b. Bklyn., Feb. 2, 1943; s. Charles and Mary (Wilkes) F.; m. Aug. 20, 1967; children: Joshua Wilkes, Jessica Sara. BA, Bklyn. Coll., 1967; MA, Ohio State U., 1970. Lectr. English Rider Coll., Lawrenceville, N.J., 1971-72; asst. editor Ohio U. Publs., Athens, 1973-77; lit. coord. Ohio Arts Coun., Columbus, from 1977. Mem. steering com. Ohio Ctr. for the Book, Columbus, 1987—. Author: Destiny News, 1977, novels Tlar, 1987, Codpol, 1987. Recipient PEN Syndicated Fiction award, 1987. Mem. Ohio Library Assn. (bd. dirs. Columbus chpt. 1985-90; Citation 1982). Home: Columbus, Ohio. Died Mar. 4, 2005.

FOXWORTH, JO, advertising agency executive; b. Tylertown, Miss. Grad. in Journalism, U. Mo. With McCann-Erickson, Interpub. Group of Cos., 1955—68; founder Jo Foxworth Inc., N.Y.C., 1968—2006. Author: Boss Lady, 1979, Wising Up: The Mistakes Women Make in Business and How to Avoid Them, 1981, Boss Lady's Arrival and Survival Plan, 1986, The Bordello Cookbook, 1997, Murder Under Wraps, 2002. Named to AAF Hall of Fame, 1997. Died Feb. 2, 2006.

FOY, BETTY LANTZ, retired educator; b. Oakland, Md., July 24, 1930; d. Harold Loren and Mabel Blanche (Hayes) Lantz; m. James Dewey Foy, June 11, 1949 (div. July 1958); 1 child, Marilyn Sue. BS, Frostburg (Md.) State Coll., 1960; MA, W.Va. U.-W.Va. Wesleyan Coll., 1967. Cert. tchr., Md. Tchr. Garrett County Bd. Edn., Oakland, Md., 1960-90. Tutor Oakland Literacy Coun., 1990-92; leader jr. choir Bethel United Meth. Ch., Mountain Lake Park, Md., 1970-71, Sunday sch. tchr., 1973-75; pres. United Meth. Women, 1990-93; sec. Am. Heart Assn. Western Md., 1990-93. Recipient Dependability award Am. Heart Assn. Western Md., 1991. Mem. AAUW (sec. 1991-92), Garrett County Tchrs. Assn. (publicity chmn. 1963-65, sec. 1970-72), Am. Assn. Ret. Persons (tax aide Garrett County 1990-92, instr. driving 1991-92, pres.), Order Ea. Star (worthy matron 1981-82, sec. 1982—). Republican. Avocations: reading, sewing. Home: Mtin Lk Park, Md. Died June 16, 2005.

FRANCIOSA, ANTHONY (ANTHONY PAPALEO), actor; b. NYC, Oct. 28, 1928; s. Anthony and Jean (Franciosa) Papaleo; m. Shelley Winters (div.), m. Beatrice Bakalyar (div.), m. Judy Kanter (div.), 1 child, Nina, m. Rita Thiel, 1970; children: Christopher, Marco. Studied drama with Joseph Geiger; scholarship Dramatic Workshop, New Sch. Social Rsch.; studied Actor's Studio. Worked with drama groups including Off Broadway, Inc., N.Y. Repertory Theatre; internat. tour Grand Hotel, 1990-91, Love Letters, 1992-95; appeared in Broadway prodns. End as a Man, 1953, Wedding Breakfast, 1954-55, A Hatful of Rain, 1955 (Tony award nomination 1956, Daniel Blum's Theatre World award for best leading actor 1956, Acad. award nomination 1957); film appearances include A Face in the Crowd, 1957, This Could Be the Night, 1957, Long Hot Summer, 1958, Naked Maja, 1959, Career, 1960 (Golden Globe award), Story on Page One, 1960, Go Naked in the World, 1960, Senilita, 1961, Period of Adjustment, 1962, Assault on a Queen, 1966, A Man Could Get Killed, 1966, The Swinger, 1966, Fathom, 1967, A Man Called Gannon, 1968, The Sweet Ride, 1968, In Enemy Country, 1968, Across 110th Street, 1972, Ghost in the Noonday Sun, 1973, The Drowning Pool, 1975, Firepower, 1979, The World is Full of Married Men, 1979, Death Wish II, 1982, Soot gli occhi dell'Assassino, 1982, Tenebrae, 1983, Avitami ai Sognare, 1984, La Cicala, 1985, Death House, 1988, La Morte e di Mona, 1990, Backstreet Dreams, 1990, Double Threat, 1992, City Hall, 1995; (TV mini-series) Aspen, 1974, Wheels, 1975; (TV movies) Fame Is the Name of the Game, 1970, Earth II, 1971, The Deadly Hunt, 1974, Hide and Go Seek, 1975, The Catcher, 1976, This Is the Week That Was, 1977, Sideshow, 1979, The Black Widow, 1980, Matt Helm, 1982, Till Death Do Us Part, 1983, Stagecoach, 1987, Ghost Writer, 1990; star TV series Valentine's Day, 1964-65, The Name of the Game, 1968-72, Search, 1972-73, Matt Helm, 1975-76, Finder of Lost Loves, 1984-85; narrator A Lincoln Portrait with St. Louis Symphony Orch., 1971, conducted by Andre Previn. Recipient Count Volpe Di Misurata cup Venice Film Festival for Hatful of Rain, 1958, Critics Outer Circle award, 1956, Goledn Globe award for best motion picture actor in drama for film Career, World Foreign Press, 1960. Died Jan. 19, 2006.

FRANCIS, ALBERT W., elementary school educator; b. St. Louis, Jan. 9, 1952; s. Joseph T. and Alberta M. (Hoeltge) F. BS in Elem. Edn., SE Mo. State U., 1974. Cert. elem. edn. Elem. tchr. Warren County R-III, Warrenton, Mo., 1974-79, Montgomery County R-II, New Florence, Mo., from 1980. Pres. PTO. Mem. ASCD, Mo. Tchrs. Assn., Montgomery County CTA (pres., v.p.). Home: Saint Ann, Mo. Died Nov. 2, 2004.

FRANCK, FREDERICK SIGFRED, artist, writer, oral surgeon; b. Maastricht, The Netherlands, Apr. 12, 1909; came to U.S., 1939, naturalized, 1945; s. Daniel and Helen (Foyer) F.; m. Claske Berndes Franck, July 15, 1960; 1 son, Lukas van Witsen Franck. Student, U. Amsterdam, 1926-31; Chirurgien Dentiste, Antwerp Dental Sch., 1935; LDS, Royal Coll. Surgeons, Edinburgh, Scotland, 1937; DMD, U. Pitts., 1942, DFA (hon.), 1963; ArtsD (hon.), Mt. St. Mary Coll., 1994. Practice dentistry, London, 1937-39; resident oral surgery U. Pitts., 1942-44; anaesthetist Elizabeth Steel Magee Hosp.; staff Children's Hosp., Pitts., 1942-44; service cons. Netherlands East Indies govt., 1944-46; dentist N.Y.C., 1946-66; vis. staff Albert Schweitzer Hosp., 1958-60. Chief mission Med. Internat. Coop., 1958; research fellow Nanzan U., Nagoya, 1981. Author: Open Wide, Please, 1957, Au Pays de Soleil, 1958, Days with Albert Schweitzer, A Lambarene Landscape, 1959, reissued 1992, (juvenile) My Friend in Africa, 1960, reissued 1995, African Sketchbook, 1961, My Eye is in Love, 1963 (Art Am. 50th Anniversary spl. citation 1963), Au Fil de L'Eau, 1964, Outsider in the Vatican, 1965, Met Het Oog Op Het Vatikaan, 1965, Au Pays Du Soleil, 1965, I Love Life, 1967, Exploding Church, 1968, Open Boek, 1967, Au Fil De L'Eau, 1968, Croquis Parisiens, 1969, Tutte le Strade portano a Roma, 1969, Le Paris de Simenon, 1969, Simenon's Paris, 1970, Tussen Broek en Brooklyn, 1971, The Zen of Seeing, 1973, Pilgrimage to Now/Here, 1973, (play) Inquest on a Crucifixion, 1975, An Encounter with Oomoto, 1975, The Book of Angelus Silesius, 1976, Zen and Zen Classics, 1977, EveryOne, The Timeless Myth of Everyman Reborn, 1978, The Awakened Eye, 1979, Art as a Way, A Return to the Spiritual Roots, 1981, The Buddha Eye, An Anthology of the Kyoto School, 1982, reissued, 2004, The Supreme Koan, Confessions of a Journey Inward, 1982, Messenger of the Heart, The Book of Angelus Silesius, 1982, 2005, De Zen van het Zien, 1983, 92, Echoes from the Bottomless Well, 1985, De Droomzolder--Oog in Oog met Venetie, 1985, Life Drawing Life, 1989, Little Compendium on that Which Matters, 1989, reissued 1993, 2004, To Be Human Against All Odds, 1991, reissued 1996, Zen Seeing, Zen Drawing: Meditation in Action, 1993, Fingers Pointing Toward the Sacred, 1994, The Tao of the Cross, 1996; co-author What Does It Mean to be Human?, 1998, 2000, Beyond Hiroshima, 1999, Watching the Vatican, 2000, Pacem In Terris A Love Story, 2000, Moments of Seeing, 2000, Seeing Venice: An Eye in Love, 2002, A Passion for Seeing, 2003, A Zen Book of Hours, 2003, What Matters, 2004, Ode to the Human Face, 2004, The Icon Reborn, 2005, The Inner Journey: Views from the Buddhist Tradition, 2005; contbg. editor Parabola Quar.; rsch. editor Nanzan Monograph Series; contbr. articles, drawings to various mags. and periodicals; one-man shows include Contemporary Arts Gallery, Lilienfield Galleries, Passedoit Gallery, Albert Landry Gallery, (all N.Y.C.), 1959-60, Saginaw (Mich.) Mus., Doll & Richards Gallery, Boston, Ringling Mus. Art, M.H. De Young Mus., San Francisco, Waddell Gallery, Far Gallery, both N.Y.C., Foster-White Gallery, Seattle, 1976, U. Puget Sound Gallery, Seattle, 1977, Thorpe Intermedia Gallery, N.Y.C., 1977, The Inter-Faith Ctr., N.Y.C., 2000, others; shows in Paris, Amsterdam, Geneva, London, Rotterdam, Brussels, Rome, Tokyo, Kyoto, 1971, U. Maine, 1970-72, Melbourne, Australia, 1972, Interchurch Ctr. Gallery, 1972, Greater Middletown Arts Coun., 1973, Far Gallery, 1973, Singer Meml. Mus., The Netherlands, 1986, Pa. State U., 1989, Cathedral of St. John the Divine, N.Y.C., 1993, Albert Schweitzer Ctr., Great Barrington, Mass., 1993, Quinnipiac Coll., Hamden, Conn., 1994, Amber Gallery, Leiden, The Netherlands, 1994, Van Rijn Gallery, Maastricht, The Netherlands, 1994, Oude Kerk, Amsterdam, The Netherlands, 1994, Paul Mellon Arts Ctr. Choate Rosemary Hall, Wallingford, Conn., 1996; touring exhbn. Drawings of Lambarene, Albert Schweitzer's Hospital in Action, 1995, 96, 97, 98, Cathedral of St. John the Divine, N.Y.C., Newark, 1996, Weimar Gallery, Germany, 1999, Vanderbilt Gallery U. Tenn., Interfaith Ctr., N.Y.C., 2000-2001, Rider U., Princeton, 2001, Albert Shahinian Fine Art and Poughkeepsie Art Mus. Galleries, 2003-06, Yale Inst. Sacred Music, 2004, The Cathedral of St. John the Divine, 2005, The N.Y. Open Ctr., 2005; group shows include Met. Mus., Whitney Mus., Corcoran Biennale, Indpls. Mus., Mpls. Mus., Nanzan U. Mus., Nagoya, Japan, 1981; represented in permanent collections including M.H. De Young Mus., Fogg Art Mus., San Francisco Mus. U. Ill., Mus. Modern Art, The Vatican, Witherspoon Gallery, Raleigh, N.C., Tokyo Nat. Mus., Nat. Collection Fine Arts, Washington, Santa Barbara, Amsterdam, Eindhoven, Maastricht, N.Y. Pub.Libr., Seattle Mus., Dartmouth Coll., Cornell U., AschenbachFound., Ga. Mus., Whitney Mus., N.Y.U., State Capitol Mus., Wash., Fordham U. Lowenstein Gallery, Roanoke Mus. Fine Arts, Cathedral of St. John the Divine, N.Y.C., U. Nymegen, The Netherlands, U. Pa.,Kans. State U., New Harmony, Ind., Cath. Ctr., Stedelijk Mus., Bonnefanten Mus., Musées Nationaux Français, Nanzan U., Santa BarbaraMus., others; traveling exhbn. to 12 univs. and colls., 1970-72, to The Netherlands and Belgium, 1991, 92; drawing exhbn. Amber Gallery, Leiden, Holland, 1999; built Pacem in Terris Trans-religious Sanctuary, Warwick, N.Y., 1966; steel sculptures commd. Genesis Farm, N.J., 1990, Omega Inst., N.Y., 1991, Pa. State U., 1991, Ch. of Saviour, Washington, 1991, Wainwright House, Rye, N.Y., 1991, Fondacion Elpis, Buenos Aires, 1991, Cath. St. John the Divine, N.Y.C., Bucknell U., Peace Garden, Harrisburg, Pa., Hengelo, The Netherlands, 1993, Sarajevo, 1994, Belgium, 1995, Antwerp, 2003, New Cmty. Corp., Newark, 1995, Choate Rosemary Hall, Wallingford, Conn., 1995, Sequoia, Calif., 1995, Ittoen Found., Kyoto, Japan, 1997, Assisi, Italy, 1999, Dandelion Trust, England, Bosnia, Mt. Saviour, Elmira, NY, 2001, Gannon U., Erie, Pa., 2001, Pitts, 2002, Antwerp, Belgium, Buenos Aires, Devonshire, Eng., San Rafael, Calif., 2003, Megen, Netherlands, Yale U. Inst. for Sacred Music, 2005, St. Francis Friary Loretto, Pa. Recipient award of Excellence, Chapmen U. and Albert Schweitzer Inst., 1995, purchase prize, U. Ill., Am. Inst. Arts Letters, Living Arts Found., 1st prize Garnegie Inst., prize, Musees Nationaux Francais, medal for drawings, Pope John XXIII, 1963, Revered Citizen award, Orange County, N.Y., 2000, Ruth Bayley Peace award, PeaceLinks, 2000, Disting Citizen award, Warwick, N.Y., 2000, Ut Diligatis Invicem award, Gannon U., 2001, World Citizen award, Nuclear Age Peace Found., Santa Barbara, Calif., 2001, Spirituality and Health award, 2001, Ressurection Cross, Antwerp, Belgium, Buenos Aires, Devonshire, Eng. and San Rafael, Calif.

Fellow Internat. Inst. Arts and Letters, Soc. for Arts, Religion and Contemporary Culture (dir.), Knighthood Order of Orange Nassau; mem. Artists Equity Assn. (hon. dir. N.Y.), P.E.N. Home: Warwick, NY. Died June 5, 2006.

FRANCYK, WILLIAM PETER, radiologist; b. Bklyn., June 26, 1939; s. Martin Peter and Rose (Newman) F.; m. Joan Crosby, Feb. 18, 1961 (div. July 1992); children: Tara Wells, Peter D., David Martin. AB, Cornell U., 1961; MD, SUNY, Bklyn., 1965. Diplomate Am. Bd. Radiology. Intern U. Utah, 1965-66; resident U. Wis. Hosps., 1966-69; staff radiologist U.S. Great Lakes (Ill.) Naval Base, 1969-71, LDS Hosp., Salt Lake City, 1971-77, St. Benedicts Hosp., Ogden, Utah, 1977-89, FHP Hosp., Salt Lake City, 1993-96, locum tenens, from 1996. Lt. comdr. USN, 1969-71. Avocations: skiing, hiking, cultural events. Died July 11, 2005.

FRANK, ISAIAH, economist, educator; b. NYC, Nov. 7, 1917; s. Henry and Rose (Isserles) F.; m. Ruth Hershfield, Mar. 23, 1941 (dec. 2004); children: Robert E., Kenneth D. B in Social Sci., CCNY, 1936; MA in Econs., Columbia U., 1938, PhD in Econs., 1960. Rsch. assoc. in econs. Columbia U. Council for Research in Social Scis., 1936-39; tchg. fellow, instr. econs. Amherst Coll., 1939-41; Carnegie fellow Nat. Bur. Econ. Rsch., 1941-42; cons. WPB, 1942; sr. economist OSS, 1942-44; various positions U.S. Dept. State, 1945-63; dir. Office Internat. Trade, 1957-59, Office Internat. Financial and Devel. Affairs, 1961-62, dep. asst. sec. for econ. affairs, 1962-63; William L. Clayton prof. internat. econs. Sch. Advanced Internat. Studies, Johns Hopkins U., 1963—2006. Mem. Industry-Govt. Iron and Steel Mission to Europe, 1947; adviser U.S. del. Econ. Commn. for Europe, 1948; dep. dir. fgn. resources div. Pres.'s Materials Policy Commn., 1951-52; head U.S. del. Conf. on Dollar Liberalization, OEEC, Paris, 1955-56; chmn. U.S. del. GATT, Geneva, 1958; alt. U.S. rep. Fourth Meeting Devel. Assistance Group, London, 1961; chmn. U.S. del. to prep. com. UN Conf. Trade and Devel., Geneva, 1963—; U.S. rep. Spl. Trade Conf. OAS, Alta Gracia, Argentina, 1964; exec. dir. Pres.'s Commn. on Internat. Trade and Investment Policy, 1970-71; adv. com. UN Trade and Devel. Bd.; dir. internat. econ. studies Com. Econ. Devel.; mem. adv. council Inst. for Latin Am. Integration; mem. adv. com. Inst. Internat. Econs.; cons. World Bank; chmn. adv. com. on internat. investment State Dept.; mem. svcs. policy adv. com. U.S. Trade Rep.; mem. adv. com. on internat. econ. policy U.S. Dept. State. Author: The European Common Market: An Analysis of Commercial Policy, 1960, Foreign Enterprise in Developing Countries, 1980, Finance and Third-World Economic Growth, 1988, Breaking New Ground in U.S. Trade Policy, 1991, U.S. Trade Policy Beyond the Uruguay Round, 1994, U.S. Economic Policy Toward the Asia-Pacific Region, 1997; co-author, editor: The Japanese Economy in International Perspective, 1975; contbr. articles to profl. publs. 1st lt. AUS, 1944-45. Recipient Rockefeller Pub. Svc. award, 1959-60 Mem. Coun. Fgn. Rels., Am. Econ. Assn., Cosmos Club, Phi Beta Kappa. Home: Washington, DC. Died May 26, 2006.

FRANK, REUVEN, former broadcast executive; b. Montreal, Que., Can., Dec. 7, 1920; came to U.S., 1940, naturalized, 1943; s. Moses Zebi Reichenstein and Anna (Rivenovich) F.; m. Bernice Kaplow, June 9, 1946; children: Peter Solomon, James Aaron. Student, Univ. Coll., U. Toronto, 1937-40; BS in Social Scis, Coll. City N.Y., 1942; MS in Journalism, Columbia, 1947. Reporter Newark Evening News, 1947-49, night city editor, 1949-50; mem. staff NBC News, 1950-67, exec. v.p., 1967-68, pres., 1968-72, 1982-84, exec. producer, 1972-82, editorial adv., 1984-85, exec. producer, from 1985; news editor Camel News Caravan, 1951-54; producer polit. conv., 1956; polit. convs. and elections, 1960; elections, 1962; producer Huntley-Brinkley Report, 1956-62, exec. producer, 1963-65; exec. producer polit. convs. and elections, 1964. Writer-producer: Berlin-Window on Fear, 1953, The Road to Spandau, 1954, Outlook; series, 1956-59, Time Present, 1959-60, Chet Huntley Reporting, 1960-63, Israel The Next Ten Years, 1958, The S-Bahn Stops at Freedom, 1958, The American Stranger, 1958, The Requiem for Mary Jo, 1959, The Big Ear, 1959, Our Man in the Mediterranean, 1959, Where is Abel, Your Brother?, 1960, Our Man in Hong Kong, 1961, The Land, 1961, The Many Faces of Spain, 1962, Our Man in Vienna, 1962, Clear and Present Danger, 1962, The Tunnel, 1962, A Country Called Europe, 1963, The Problem with Water is People, 1963; exec. producer: series Weekend, 1974-79; exec. producer, co-writer: If Japan Can...Why Can't We?, 1980, America Works When America Works, 1981, The Biggest Lump of Money in the World, 1985, The Japan They Don't Talk About, 1985, Nuclear Power, in France it Works, 1987. Trustee Edwin E. Aldrin Fund State of N.J., 1970-73. Recipient Sigma Delta Chi award news writing for TV, 1955; Robert E. Sherwood award, 1958, 59; George Polk award L.I. U., 1961; Columbia Journalism Alumni award distinguished service, 1961; First Person award Inst. Edn. by Radio-TV, Ohio State U., 1963; Emmy award best news program, 1958, 59, 60, 61, 62, 64; best documentary program, 1963; program of year, 1963; George Foster Peabody award, 1976, Alfred I. Dupont award Columbia U., 1980; Martin R. Gainsbrugh award Fiscal Policy Council, 1980; Headliners award, 1981; others.; Poynter fellow Yale, 1970, AAAS-Westinghouse Sci. Writing award, 1987, Assn. Sci. Writers award 1987. Mem. Writers Guild Am. (organizing com. 1954-56), Am. Newspaper Guild (Newark News organizing com. 1948-50) Died Feb. 5, 2006.

FRANK, SIDNEY E., liquor company executive; b. Montville, Conn., Oct. 2, 1919; s. Abraham and Sarah Frank; m. Louise Rosenstiel, 1945 (dec.); 2 children; m. Marian Frank. Student, Brown U., 1937—38. With Schenley Industries, 1945—70; founder Sidney Frank Importing Co., New Rochelle, NY, 1972, chmn., CEO; founder Frank Media LLC, 2005. Owner Travel Savvy Mag., Bus. Traveler Mag.; chmn. bd. Sidney and Louise Frank Found. Chmn. bd. Sidney and Louise Frank Found.; former bd. mem. Riverdale Country Sch. Avocations: golf, art collecting. Died Jan. 10, 2006.

FRANKEL, ALAN DAVID, educational association administrator; b. N.Y.C., June 19, 1950; s. Morris Moses and Sylvia (Schwartz) F.; m. Robyn Leslie Ruina, Aug. 31, 1984. BA, CCNY, 1971; BS, Mercy Coll., 1979; MS in Edn., L.I. U., 1979, MA in Psychology, 1980; PhD, Fordham U., 1990. With Sears, Roebuck & Co., Bronx and White Plains, N.Y., 1968-74, dept. mgr., 1970-75; substitute tchr. Lakeland (N.Y.) Sch. Dist., 1974-77, Yorktown Hebrew High, 1978, Temple Beth-El, 1976-82; reading specialist coll. opportunity program Mercy Coll., Dobbs Ferry, N.Y., 1977-82, prof. psychology, 1982-86; dean acad. affairs MTI Bus. Sch., N.Y.C., 1986-87; dir. Am. Hi Tech, N.Y.C., 1987; v.p. ops Am. Tour Mgmt. Inst., N.Y.C., 1988, dir., from 1989. Cons. for reading diagnosis AT&T, 1984. Author: Teacher's Guide to Aware Bear Series, 1986, Structural Analysis, 1981; mng. editor Instrnl. Software Rev. Recipient Morton Gotschall award CCNY, 1970. Mem. Assn. Supervision and Curriculum Devel., Western Coll. Reading Assn., N.Y. Coll. Learning Skills Assn., Psi Chi. Jewish. Home: Peekskill, NY. Died Jan. 25, 2005.

FRANKEL, HERBERT A., corporation executive; b. N.Y.C., Oct. 25, 1925; s. Samuel and Sadie (Seidenberg) F.; m. Ruby Stein, Mar. 13, 1949 (div. Nov. 1970); children: Marsha Ann, C. David, Laurence Joseph, Barnett; m. Eve Rubin, Mar. 2, 1975. BS, MIT, 1950. V.p. Foseco, Inc., N.Y.C., 1950-53; pres. Sonicor Instrument Corp., Copiague, N.Y., 1966-94, chmn., from 1994. Jewish. Died Jan. 29, 2005.

FRANKFORT, JAMES, artist; b. Brussels, May 11, 1930; s. Jack and Hillegonda (Frank) F.; children: Michelle, Jacob, Daniel, Reina. Grad., Parson's Sch. Design. Freelance artist, from 1953. Mem. Visual Arts Ctr., 1993—. With U.S. Army, 1952-53. Home: Waldport, Oreg. Died July 21, 2005.

FRANKLIN, BENJAMIN ARTHUR, editor, reporter; b. N.Y.C., Nov. 12, 1927; s. Benjamin A. and Zilpha C. Franklin; m. Jane Burrage, June 10, 1950; children: Abigail, Elizabeth, Clare. BA, U. Pa., 1948; MS in Journalism, Columbia U., 1950. Reporter Evening Star, Washington, 1948—50, ABC Radio News, Washington, 1953—59, N.Y. Times, Washington, 1959—91, Nucleonics Week, Washington, 1991—93; editor Washington Spectator. Lt. (j.g.) USCG, 1950—53, N. Atlantic. Recipient Weatherford award, Berea Coll., Ky., 1970, Disting. Svc. award, Soc. Profl. Journalists, 1973, Honors award, Environ. Policy Inst., Washington, 1974. Mem.: Washington Nat. Press Club. Democrat. Episcopalian. Died Nov. 19, 2005.

FRANKLIN, LEONARD LORING, lawyer; b. Brookline, Mass., Apr. 13, 1928; s. Phil and Mollie (Slonimsky) F.; m. Deborah S. Wildenberg, Sept. 10, 1950; children: Susanna, Daniel. LLB, UCLA, 1948; JD, Bklyn. Law Sch., 1956. Bar: N.Y. 1956, Tex. 1961. Pvt. practice, Austin, Tex., 1961-75; house counsel U.S. Surg. Corp., N.Y.C., 1975-77; pvt. practice N.Y.C., 1977-87; estate tax atty. IRS, N.Y.C., 1987-94; pvt. practice N.Y.C., from 1994. City judge City of Westlake Hills, Tex., Austin; mem. commdr. divsn. ADR, N.Y. State Supreme Ct. Sch. bd. pres. Westlake Independent Sch. Dist., Austin; impartial hearing officer N.Y.C. Bd. Edn. Mem. N.Y. County Lawyers Assn. Democrat. Jewish. Avocations: flying, computer. Died May 10, 2004.

FRANKLIN, ROBERT DRURY, oil industry executive, lawyer; b. Mead, Okla., June 6, 1935; s. Sam Wesley and Frankie Marjorie (Gooding) F.; m. Barbara Jean Bellis, May 30, 1958 (div. 1973); children: Philip Foster, Elizabeth Jean. BS in Petroleum Engring., U. Okla., 1957; JD, So. Methodist U., 1964. Registered profl. engr., Tex. Petroleum engr. Mobil Oil Corp., Denver City, Tex., 1957-59; prodn. mgr. Bayview Oil Corp., Dallas, 1959-65; sec., dir. Siboney Corp., Dallas, 1965-70; pres., dir. Northland Oils Ltd., Dallas, 1970-89, Costa Resources, Inc., Dallas, from 1972; v.p., dir. Internat. Oil & Gas Corp., Dallas, 1979-84; with Tex. Legal Svcs. Ctr. Mem. Rep. Eagles, Washington. Mem. State Bar Tex., Ind. Petroleum Assn. Am., Soc. Petroleum Engrs., Am. Petroleum Inst., Energy Club of Dallas, Mensa, Willow Bend Polo Club, Midland Country Club. Presbyterian. Avocations: polo, tennis, skiing. Home: Canyon Lake, Tex. Died Aug. 7, 2004.

FRANTZ, PAUL LEWIS, lawyer; b. Bozeman, Mont., Sept. 11, 1955; s. Walter Kirke and Charlotte Catherine (Caldwell) F. BS in Bus./ Fin., Mont. State U., 1978; JD, U. Mont., 1983; M in Internat. Mgmt., Am. Grad. Sch. Internat. Mgmt., 1985; LLM in Transnational Bus. Practice, McGeorge Sch. Law, 1992. Bar: Mont. 1983, U.S. Dist. Ct. Mont. 1983, U.S. Ct. Internat. Trade 1984, U.S. Ct. Appeals (9th cir.) 1986, N.Y. 1994, Minn. 1996. Law clk. to U.S. magistrate, Billings, 1983-84; law clk. to judge U.S. Dist. Ct., Helena, 1985; with Morrow, Sedivy & Bennett, P.C., Bozeman, 1986-91, Church, Harris, Johnson & Williams, P.C., Great Falls, 1992; pvt. practice Bozeman, 1993-95; assoc. prof. Coll. Bus. Adminstrn. Calif. State U., Long Beach. Pres. Mont. Coun. for Internat. Visitors, 1990. Mem. State Bar Mont., Kiwanis. Died Mar. 5, 2005.

FRANZ, JOHN JOSEPH, manufacturing and consulting engineer; b. Chgo., July 22, 1927; s. John Joseph and Anna May (Sholtz) F.; m. Ethel Kalas, July 14, 1951; children: Gail, Andrew, Thomas, Elaina. BA, Calif. State U.-Fullerton, 1975. Registered profl. engr., Calif. Project engr. Beckman Instruments Co., Fullerton, 1964-70; tooling mgr. Weiser Co., South Gate, Calif., 1970-74; mfg. engr. Clemar Corp., Azusa, Calif., 1976-79, Keyboard Co., Garden Grove, Calif., 1980-82; sr. mech. engr. Optical Radiation Corp., Azusa, 1979-80; sr. mfg. engr. Weslock Corp., L.A., from 1980. Patentee rotor and shaft assembly for variable resistor. With USN, 1945-48, PTO. Fellow Nat. Soc. Profl. Engrs., Calif. Soc. Profl. Engrs.; mem. Soc. Mfg. Engrs. (2d vice chmn. 1979-80), Am. Soc. for Metals, Melody Rounders Dance Club. Republican. Roman Catholic. Avocations: travel, dance, golf, gardening. Home: La Puente, Calif. Died June 2, 2004.

FRAZER, MARILEE HELEN, prosecutor, pathologist; b. Wilmington, Del., Nov. 20, 1953; d. August Henry and Christine (Hoover) F. BA in Biol. Scis., U. Del., 1975; MD, Jefferson Med. Coll., 1978; JD, Wayne State U., 1989. Diplomate Am. Bd. Anatomic Pathology, Am. Bd. Forensic Pathology. Dep. coroner Cuyahoga County Coroner's Office, Cleve., 1983-84; asst. med. examiner Wayne County Med. Examiner's Office, Detroit, 1984-89; atty. Mich. Ct. Appeals, Detroit, 1989-90; asst. prosecuting atty. Wayne County Prosecutor's Office, from 1990. Fellow Am. Coll. Pathology; mem. Nat. Assn. Med. Examiners, Am. Acad. Forensic Scis. Home: Dearborn, Mich. Died Jan. 30, 2004.

FRAZER, WILLIAM JOHNSON, JR., economics educator; b. Greenville, Ala., Oct. 15, 1924; s. William Johnson Frazer and Margaret Thompson Winkler; m. Mary Ann Burford, Nov. 12, 1949 (div. 1982); children: William J. Frazer III. BA, Huntington Coll., 1950; postgrad., U. Tex., 1950-51; MA, Columbia U., 1953, PhD, 1968. Instr. of econs. Pratt Inst., Bklyn., 1953-54, Rensselaer Poly. Inst., 1954-56; economist Fed. Res. Bank of N.Y., 1956-57; sr. economist Fed. Res. Bank of Chgo., 1966-67; asst. prof. U. Fla., Gainesville, 1957-64, assoc. prof., 1964-68, prof., from 1968. Faculty fellow Harvard U., 1959-60, U. Pa., 1964-65; mem. faculty Fla. State U. program, London, 1989-90, 92; prof. London Sch. Econs., 1994. Author: (with William Yohe) The Analytics and Institutions of Money and Banking, 1956, The Demand for Money, 1967, Crisis in Economic Theory, 1973, Power and Ideas: Milton Friedman and the Big U-Turn Vol. I, The Background, and Vol. II, The U-Turn, 1988, The Legacy of Keynes and Friedman, 1994, The Central Banks, 1994, (with John Guthrie) The Florida Land Boom: Money, Speculation, and the Banks, 1995, The Friedman System: Economic Analysis of Time Series, 1997, Central Banking, Crises, and Global Economy, 2000, Business Conditions, Logging, and Sharecropping: A South Alabama Trade Area with European and Birmingham Connections, 2002; contbr. articles to profl. jours. and encyclopedias. Monetary and fin. advisor City of Gainesville, 1980—, chmn. pension rev. com., 1981-82. With USN, 1943-46. Republican. Methodist. Home: Gainesville, Fla. Died Oct. 24, 2004.

FRECH, BRUCE, mathematician; b. Norristown, Pa., Dec. 11, 1956; s. Henry and Ruth (Derstein) F.; m. Toni Fredette, May 19, 1991. BS, Rensselaer Poly. Inst., 1978; PhD, U. Va., 1983. Asst. prof. math. Lehigh U., Bethlehem, Pa., 1984, U. Scranton, Pa., 1986-88, Colby Coll., Waterville, Maine, 1988-90; mathematician Pacer Systems, Horsham, Pa., 1985; tech. advisor Tailwind Bicycles, Schwenksville, Pa., 1990-92; engr. Am. Elec. Lab., Lansdale, Pa., from 1992. Coach bicycle racing team Colby Coll., 1988-90. Mem. Am. Math. Soc., U.S. Cycling Found. Avocation: bicycling. Home: Schwenksville, Pa. Died Jan. 29, 2005.

FREDERICKSON, ARTHUR ROBB, physicist; b. Rahway, N.J., July 5, 1941; s. Arthur Raymond and Bertine Lavinia (Beecher) F.; m. Christine Magnuson, June 6, 1970; children: Timothy R., Nathan B., Julie H. BSc, Rensselaer Poly. Inst., 1965; PhD, U. Mass., Lowell, 1991. Physicist Cambridge Rsch. Labs., Bedford, Mass., 1967-80, Rome Air Devel. Ctr., Bedford, 1980-87, Air Force Geophysics Lab., Hanscom AFB, Mass., 1987-91, Air Force Phillips Lab., Hanscom AFB, Mass., 1992-97, Calif. Inst. Tech. Jet Propulsion Lab., Pasadena, 1997—2004. Mem. spl. topics rev. groups, panels Dept. Def., 1980—. Author: Spacecraft Dielectric Material Properties, 1986; contbr. articles to profl. jours. Chmn. Town Ctr. Com. Planning Bd., Stow, Mass., 1974-75; adult leader Carlisle (Mass.) area Boy Scouts Am., 1981-90. Mem. IEEE (sr., chmn. Boston sect. nuclear and plasma soc. 1983-92), Am. Phys. Soc., Sigma Xi. Achievements include patent on device to aid centering of high-energy beams, method and system for secondary emission detection, charge accumulation gamma radiation detector, process for prevention of spontaneous discharging in irradiated insulators. Home: Pasadena, Calif. Died Apr. 5, 2004.

FREDRICKS, A. L., retired secondary educator; b. Cleve., Oct. 15, 1935; s. Fred and Naomi Lucille (Bernhard) F.; m. Phyllis Clara Gerth, Aug. 20, 1960 (div. Oct. 1972); children: Michelle Marie Fredricks Swanson, Kim Therese, Jeffrey Alan, Denise Anne, Scott Matthew; m. Carolyn M. Noguerola, July 16, 1992. BA in Biology, Western State Coll., 1961, MA in Sci., 1966. Lic. tchr., N.Mex. Prodn. checker and auditor G.F. Swift & Co., Denver, 1961-64;

seed potato cert. insp. Mont. Potato Improvement Assn., Mont. State U., Bozeman, 1966-68; faculty asst./instr. Wis. State U., La Crosse, 1968-70; sanitarian technician La Crosse County Health Commn., La Crosse, 1971-73; tchr. Gallup (N.Mex.)-McKinley County Schs., 1973-93; retired, 1993. Mem. Am. Inst. Biol. Scis., N.Mex. Acad. Sci., Am. Fedn. Tchrs., McKinley County Fedn. Tchrs. Home: Gallup, N.Mex. Died Jan. 9, 2004.

FREED, JAMES INGO, architect; b. Essen, Germany, July 23, 1930; arrived in U.S., 1939, naturalized, 1948; s. Michael and Dora Freed; m. Hermine Gerberg, May 28, 1967; 1 child, Dara Michaella. BArch, Ill. Inst. Tech., 1953; DHL (hon.), Hebrew Union Coll.-Jewish Inst. Religion, 1995, N.J. Inst. Tech., 1995, Ill. Inst. Tech., 1998. Registered N.Y., D.C., Ill., Ohio, Nebr., Mo., Wis., Calif., Tex., Ark., Ariz., Minn., Colo., Va., N.J., Conn. Designer archtl. divsn. Webb & Knapp, Inc., 1950—55; practice architecture Danforth & Speyer, Chgo., 1951—52, Michael Reese Planning Assn., Chgo., 1952—53; designer Mies Van der Rohe, N.Y.C., 1955—56, I.M. Pei & Assocs., N.Y.C., 1955—66, I.M. Pei & Ptnrs., N.Y.C., 1966—80, ptnr., 1980—89, Pei Cobb Freed & Ptnrs., N.Y.C., 1989—2005. Prof. architecture, dean Coll. Architecture, Planning and Design Ill. Inst. Tech., 1975—78; adj. prof. architecture Columbia U., 1984; Eero Sarrinen prof. archtl. design Yale U., 1985; adj. instr. design Cooper Union, 1958—59, 1965—69; vis. critic Cornell U., 1963, 67, RISD, 1983; bd. mem. Creative Time, N.Y.C., 1974—84, Bright New City, Chgo., 1976—78; jury mem. Reynolds Award, 1975; mem. steering com. Coun. on Tall Bldgs. and Urban Habitat, 1982—2005; mem. Assn. Collegiate Schs. Arch. Jury, 1981, chmn., 82; critic, jury mem. various universities; lectr. in field. Prin. works include Gray Gallery, Chgo., 1976, Walter Kelly Gallery, 1977, Graham Found., 1978, Walker Art Ctr., Mpls., 1978—79, The New Sch., N.Y.C., 1982, U. Calif., Berkeley, 1982, Whitney Mus., N.Y.C., 1984, San Francisco Mus. Modern Art, 1985, Cleve. Ctr. for Contemporary Art, 1985, NAD, 1987, Am. Acad. and Inst. Arts and Letters, 1987, Ill. Inst. Tech. Exhbn., Chgo., 1988, N.Y. Architects, 1987—88, Chgo. Antheneum, 1993—94, Century Assn., N.Y.C., 1994, Kips Bay Plz. Apts., 1962 (City Club N.Y. Albert S. Bard award, 1965), NYU Towers, 1969 (Concrete Industry Bd. award, 1966, AIA Honor award, 1967, City Club N.Y. Albert S. Bard award, 1967), Univ. Plz. (AIA Honor award, 1967), 88 Pine St., NY Fin. Dist., N.Y.C., 1973 (R.S. Reynolds Meml. award, 1974, AIA Honor award, 1975), FAA Air Traffic Control Towers, various cities, 1965—72, Nat. Bank Commerce, Lincoln, Nebr., 1976 (Concrete Reinforcing Steel Inst. award, 1977), West Loop Plz., Houston, 1980, Gem City Savs. and Home Savs., Dayton, Ohio, 1981, 499 Park Ave, Manhattan, N.Y., 1981, Warwick Post Oak, Houston, 1982, Jacob K. Javits Conv. Ctr., N.Y.C., 1986, 1988 (AIA Honor award, 1988, Concrete Industry Bd. award of merit, 1988), Potomac Tower, Rosslyn, Va., 1990, First Bank Pl., Mpls., 1992, 1299 Pennsylvania Ave., Washington, 1993, LA Convention Ctr., 1993 (Art/LA Internat. Arts award for architecture, 1993), U.S. Holocaust Meml. Mus., Washington, 1993 (AIA Honor award, 1994), San Francisco Main Libr., 1996, Ronald Reagan Bldg. and Internat. Trade Ctr., Washington, 1998, The Washington House, Alumni Ctr. at Ball State U., 1998, Science and Engring. Quad at Stanford U., 1999, Roman L. Hruska U.S. Courthouse, Omaha, Nebr., 2000, Air Force Meml., Air Force Meml. Found., Arlington, Va., 2003, Broad Ctr. for the Biol. Sciences, Calif. Inst. Tech., numerous others; published (books and articles). Archtl. commr. Art Commn. of N.Y.C., 1983—91; archtl. commn. U. Washington, Seattle, 1984—91; bd. dirs. Creative Time, N.Y.C., 1974—84, Bright New City, Chgo., 1976—78, Art in Pub. Places, Chgo., 1976—78, 1980—2005; mem. N.Y. Mcpl. Arts Soc., 1983—2005, Syracuse U. Adv. Com., 1983—88, Archtl. Commn. U. Wash., Seattle, 1984—91; bd. dirs. Regional Plan Assn., NY, 1995—98, NJ, 1995—98, Conn., 1995—98; mem. steering com. Coun., on Tall Bldgs. and Urban Habitat; jury mem. Assn. Collegiate Schools Architecture, 1981, chmn., 1982. C.E. U.S. Army, 1953—55. Named one of "The Twelve Most Fascinating People of 1993", Barbara Walters Special, 1993; recipient R.S. Reynolds Meml. award, 1974, Poses Creative Arts award medal for arch., Brandeis U., 1981, Chgo. Arch. award, Ill. Coun. Am. Inst. Architects, 1985, Men of Industry award, Concrete Industry Bd. Inc., 1987, Sixth Ann. Jewish Cultural Achievement award, Nat. Found. for Jewish Culture, 1994, Internat. Arts award for Architecture, ART/LA, 1993, Tucker award, Bldg. Stone Inst., 1994, Nat. Arts medal, NEA, 1995, Outstanding Achievement in Design for the Govt. of the U.S., 1997, Award for Design Excellence, Presdl. Design Awards, 1997, Interfaith Lifetime Achievement award, Interfaith Com. Remembrance, 1998. Fellow: AIA (nat. com. on design 1972—73, vice chmn. nat. com. on design 1974, chmn. nat. com. on design 1975, Chgo. Architecture award Ill. Coun. 1985, medal of honor N.Y. chpt. 1987, Nat. Honor award 1988, 1st ann. Thomas Jefferson award for Pub. Architecture 1992, Nat. Honor award 1994, Presdl. Citation for Lifetime Achievement 1998, award of merit N.Y. state 1999), Am. Acad. Arts and Scis.; mem.: NEA (tilted arc adv. panel 1987), Am. Acad. Design, Mcpl. Art Soc. N.Y., Am. Acad. Arts and Letters (com. for prizes in arch. 2000, Arnold W. Brunner Meml. prize in Architecture 1987, Presdl. Design award 1997), Nat. Acad. Design (assoc.), N.Y. Mcpl. Arts Soc., N.Y. Soc. Architects (Lifetime Achievement award 1992, Architectural Achievement award 1994), Archtl League N.Y. Died Dec. 15, 2005.

FREEDMAN, JAMES OLIVER, former academic administrator, lawyer; b. Manchester, NH, Sept. 21, 1935; s. Louis A. and Sophie (Gottesman) Freedman, Louis A. and Sophie (Gottesman) Freedman; m. Bathsheba Freedman; 2 children. AB, Harvard U., 1957; LLB, Yale U., 1962; LLD (hon.), Cornell Coll., 1982; LLD (hon.), So. Meth U., 1988; LLD (hon.), Mt. Holyoke Coll., 1988, Vt. Law Sch., 1992, U. N.H., 1992; LHD (hon.), St. Ambrose U., 1984, Colby-Sawyer Coll., 1995, Dartmouth Coll., 1998, Hebrew Union Coll., 1998, Brown U., 1999, Whitman Coll., 1999; LHD (hon.), U. Rochester, 2002. Bar: N.H. 1962, Pa. 1971, Iowa 1982. Prof. law U. Pa., 1964—82, assoc. provost, 1978, dean, 1979—82, univ. ombudsman, 1973—76; pres., disting. prof. law and polit. sci. U. Iowa, 1982—87; pres. Dartmouth Coll., Hanover, 1987—98, pres. emeritus, 1998—2006; pres. Am. Acad. Arts and Scis., 2000—01; Henry N. Rapaport lectr. Jewish Theol. Sem., 2001. 8th ann. Roy R. Ray lectr. So. Meth. U. Sch. Law, 1985; Tyrell Williams lectr. Washington U. Sch. Law, 1984; Francis Greenwood Peabody lectr. MIT, 1999; W.E.B. du Bois lectr. U. Md.-Balt. County, 1999; bd. dirs. Houghton Mifflin Co., 1991—2001; Howard R. Bowen lectr. Claremont Grad. U., 1997; Simon H. Rifkind lectr. CCNY, 2000. Author: Crisis and Legitimacy: The Administrative Process and American Government, 1978, Idealism and Liberal Education, 1996; contbr. Bd. govs. Am. Jewish Com., from 1999; mem. Phila. Bd. Ethics, 1981—82; chmn. Pa. Legis. Reapportionment Commn., 1981, Iowa Gov.'s Task Force on Fgn. Lang. Studies and Internat. Edn., 1982—83; trustee Jewish Pub. Soc., 1979—88, Brandeis U., from 2000, Hebrew Union Coll., from 2001; bd. dirs. Am. Coun. on Edn.; bd. dirs. Jacob K. Javits fellows program U.S. Dept. Edn., 1993—97; bd. dirs. Salzburg Seminar Am. Studies, 1988—92, 1994—97. Recipient Am. Book award, 1990, William O. Douglas First Amendment award, Anti-Defamation League, 1991, Gilda Radner award, Wellness Cmty. Greater Boston, Frederic W. Ness award, Assn. Am. Coll. and Univ., 1997; fellow, NEH, 1976—77; scholar Pa. chpt., Order of Coif, 1981, vis., Phi Beta Kappa, 1999—2000. Mem.: Am. Phil. Soc., Am. Acad. Arts & Scis. (pres. from 2000), Am. Law Inst., Clare Hall Cambridge U. (life). Home: Cambridge, Mass. Died Mar. 21, 2006.

FREEMAN, JOHN CLINTON, meteorologist, oceanographer; b. Houston, Aug. 7, 1920; s. John Clinton and Ann (Dotson) Freeman; m. Marjorie Schaefer, June 14, 1947; children: John C. III, Walter H., Jill F. Hasling, Cathryn F. Disch, Helen, Paul D. BA, Rice U., 1941; MS, Calif. Inst. Tech., 1942; postgrad., Brown U., 1946—48; PhD, U. Chgo., 1952. Commd. 2d lt. USAF, 1941, advanced through grades to lt. col., 1970; weather officer U.S. Army, 1941-46; math. rschr. grad. divsn. applied math. Brown U., Providence, 1946-48; rschr. in meteorology U.S. Weather Bur., Washington, 1948-49, Inst. Advanced Study, Princeton, NJ, 1949-50, U. Chgo., 1950-52; rschr. in meteorology and oceanography, prof. Tex. A&M, College Station, 1952-55; meteorology and oceanography rschr. Gulf Cons.-NESCO, Houston, 1955-66; prof., chmn. and dir. rsch. Inst. Storm Rsch.-U. St. Thomas, Houston, 1957-88; dir. rsch. Weather Rsch. Ctr., Houston, from 1988, past pres. Convenor, chmn. Internat. Conf. Coastal Engring, Houston, 1984; presenter in field. Contbr. chapters to books. Fellow: Am. Meterology Soc. (chmn. com applied meteorology 1975—76, Meisinger award 1950, Spl. award Tex. Tornado Radar Network 1961, award for outstanding contbn. advancement of applied meteorology 2003); mem.: Marine Tech. Soc. (local chmn. 1970), Am. Geophys. Union. Democrat. United Ch. Of Christ. Achievements include co-discovery of orbital effect on the sun and the earth forming the link between the disturbances on the sun and disturbances in the earth's atmosphere. Avocation: dog training. Home: Houston, Tex. Died Nov. 18, 2004.

FREEMAN, MURIEL MESSINGER, freelance writer; b. N.Y.C., July 21, 1920; d. Samuel and Elsie (Marshall) M.; m. Leslie Sherwood Freeman, (dec. May 18, 1987); children: Edward Phillip, Deborah Freeman Lubin. BSin History and Economics, NYU, 1941, postgrad., 1948-52, New Sch. Soc. Research, 1948-52. Writer The Plainfield Courier-News, N.J., 1964-71, Somerset Messenger-Gazette, Somerville, N.J., 1971-78, The N.Y. Times, New Jersey Section, N.Y.C., 1972-79, The Tribune, N.Y.C., 1978, The Courier-News, Bridgewater, N.J., from 1979, The Princeton Packet, N.J., from 1980, Forbes Newspaper, from 1990. Writer--interviewed over 300 celebrities in fields of dance, opera, theater, music, literature including Malcolm Forbes, Dr. George Gallup, Upton Sinclair, Edward Villella, Merce Cunningham, Peter Benchley, Celeste Holm, Mary Lea Johnson (producer La Cage Aux Folles, Sweeney Todd, Charles Schribner, Jerome Hines, Frederica Von Stade), Milton Babbitt, Alvin Ailey, Congresswoman Millicent Fenwick. Publicity chair Columbia Mgmt. Community Concert Assn., 1960-70, chair Bi-Centennial Art Inventory of Smithsonian Inst., 1976, chairperson Music and Art Appreciation, Office of Aging, Somerset County, N.J., 1986—; chmn. book and author luncheons Somerset County Libr., 1991. Avocations: attending dance, opera, theater, concerts, swimming. Home: Bridgewater, NJ. Died Jan. 8, 2004.

FREIDELL, HUGH VERNON, internist, nephrologist; b. Santa Barbara, Calif., June 21, 1923; s. Hugh Fredrick and Selina Maria (Saari) F.; m. Anna Mae Davis, Apr. 6, 1952; children: Kathy Ann Freidell Day, Susan Lee Freidell Mosby, Sharon Maria Freidell Paratte, Debra Mary Freidell Babai. MD, Baylor U., 1948. Diplomate in internal medicine and nephrology Am. Bd. Internal Medicine; diplomate Am. Bd. Forensic Examiners. Intern Highland-Alameda Hosp., Oakland, Calif., 1948-49; resident Santa Barbara (Calif.) Cottage-County Hosp., 1949-50, Univ. Hosp. of Nebr., Omaha, 1950-52; fellow artificial unit Cleve. Clinic, 1958; practiced medicine/nephrology Santa Barbara, 1954—97. Chmn. dept. internal medicine Santa Barbara Cottage Hosp., 1961-62, 87-88, med. dir. acute renal unit, 1959-85; co-med. dir. Santa Barbara Cmty. Dialysis Ctr., 1975-91. With U.S. Army, 1943-46, capt. M.C., USAF, 1952-54. Fellow ACP; mem. Calif. Med. Assn., Santa Barbara County Med. Soc. (pres. 1971), Aquatic Med. Soc., Am. Soc. Nephrology, Masons, Shriners. Republican. Presbyterian. Avocations: scuba diving, flying, horseback riding, fishing, water sports. Home: Santa Barbara, Calif. Died Dec. 20, 2005.

FREIDIN, JACK, architect; b. N.Y.C., Jan. 16, 1930; m. Marta Neufeld Freidin, Feb. 3, 1966. BArch, Pratt Inst., 1951; M of Planning, Columbia U., 1954; Postgrad. in Computer-Aided Design, Harvard U. Registered architect N.Y., N.J., Conn. Former designer Marcel Breuer; design critic Pratt Inst., 1959-70; sr. ptnr. Freidin Bolcek Assocs., N.Y.C., from 1956. Lectr. numerous profl. seminars. Contbr. articles to profl. jours., newspapers. Recipient numerous awards in field, including design honors from Nat. Assn. Home Builders, The Queens County C. of C., Ponderosa Pine Wood Co., Mus. of Modern Art. Mem. AIA, Nat. Coun. Archtl. Registration Bds., Am. Arbitration Assn. Died Feb. 14, 2004.

FRENCH, KENNETH EDWARD, retired mechanical engineer; b. Elyria, Ohio, Apr. 16, 1929; s. Kenneth and Marguerite Frances (Willems) F.; m. Stella Rogers Wallace, 1958 (div. 1981); children: Robyne Horn, Catherine Curcuruto, Marion Korte; m. Mary Lyons McEvoy, Oct. 23, 1982. BS in Engring., Calif. Inst. Tech., 1953; MS in Mech. Engring., MIT, 1957; degree in Mech. Engring., U. Santa Clara, 1968. Registered profl. engr., Calif., Tex. From jr. engr. to design engr. A Lockheed Aircraft Corp., Burbank, Calif., 1952-55; sr. engr. Sandberg-Serrell Corp., Pasadena, Calif., 1956-57; chief engr. Irvin Air Chute Co., Glendale, Calif., 1957-58; from rsch. engr. to program engr. Lockheed Missiles and Space Co., Sunnyvale, Calif., Huntsville, Ala., Austin, Tex., 1981-88; ret., 1989. Lectr. mech. engring. San Jose (Calif.) State U., 1974-79. Contbr. articles to profl. jours. including AIAA Jour., Jour. Spacecraft and Rockets, Textile Rsch. Jour., Jour. Aircraft, Unmanned Sys. With U.S. Army, 1946-48. Mem. AIAA, ASME (chmn. Santa Clara Valley sect. 1974, Centennial Medallion 1980), SAR, Mensa. Achievements include design of design, development and test of parachute used to recover US recoverable space vehicle-Discoverer; research in parachute technology. Avocations: reading, walking, writing articles on local/family history. Home: Seal Beach, Calif. Died Mar. 31, 2005.

FRERICHS, EDWIN NATHAN, retail planning consultant; b. Buffalo Center, Iowa, Feb. 3, 1926; s. Onno H. and Elmina Ann (Davis) F.; m. Elizabeth A. Ryals, Dec. 23, 1948; children: Lori, Derek. BA in Art & Indsl. Design, U. Iowa, Iowa City, 1950. Registered Interior Designer, Realtor. Interior designer Adleta Showcase Co., Dallas, 195-63; retail planning cons. Rya Retail Design, Dallas, 1963-69, Frerichs Assn., Dallas, 1965-71; dir. store planning constrn. McRaes Dept. Stores, Jackson, Miss., 1971-72; v.p. prodn. dir. RYA Retail Design, Dallas, 1972-79; retail planning cons. RE Assocs., Dallas, 1979-83, ENF Design Group, Dallas, 1983-88; store design project mgr. J.C. Penney Co, Dallas, 1988-92; retail planning cons. ENF Design Group, Dallas, from 1992. Sgt. U.S. Army, 1944-46, 50-51, Korea. Mem. Am. Inst. Interior. Mem. Christian Ch. Avocations: photography, woodworking, wine making, private pilot. Home: Dallas, Tex. Died Aug. 16, 2005.

FRESH, JAMES HENRY, pastor; b. Cumberland, Md., July 1, 1922; s. Frank Lee and Evelyn Manon (Lingle) F.; m. Betty M. Beem, Aug. 3, 1945; children: David L., J. Douglas, Sue A. Fresh Tasker. BA, Gettysburg Coll., 1944; MST, Chgo. Luth. Theol. Sem., 1946; MSW, Loyola U., Chgo., 1953. Ordained to ministry Evang. Luth. Ch. Am. Pastor St. Matthew Luth. Ch., Princeton, Ill., 1946-52; exec. dir. Luth. Welfare, Chgo., 1952-56; pastor 1st Luth. Ch., Galion, Ohio, 1956-66, St. Mark Luth. Ch., Dunedin, Fla., 1966-89; chmn. bd. St. Mark Village Inc., Palm Harbor, Fla., from 1978, dir. stewardship and planned giving, from 1989. Pres. Social Welfare of Luth. Chs. of Ohio, Columbus, 1960-66; pres. Dunedin Ministerial Assn., 1970-73; mem. ch. bd. appeals City of Dunedin, 1975. Recipient Legion of Honor award Demolay, 1959; named Trustee of Yr., Am. Assn. of Aged, 1990. Mem. Masons, Shriners, Rotary (past-pres. Galion chpt., Paul Harris fellow 1982). Republican. Home: Palm Harbor, Fla. Died Mar. 12, 2004.

FREUD, NICHOLAS S., lawyer; b. NYC, Feb. 6, 1942; s. Frederick and Fredericka (von Rothenburg) F.; m. Elsa Doskow, July 23, 1966; 1 child, Christopher. AB, Yale U., 1963, JD, 1966. Bar: N.Y. 1968, Calif. 1970, U.S. Tax Ct. 1973. Ptnr. Chickering & Gregory, San Francisco, 1978-85, Russin & Vecchi, San Francisco, 1986-93, Jeffer, Mangels, Butler & Marmaro, LLP, San Francisco, from 1993. Mem. joint adv. bd. Calif. Continuing Edn. of Bar, chair taxation subcom. 1987-87; mem. fgn. income adv. bd. Tax Management Internat. Jour., mem. bd. advs. The Jour. of Internat. Taxation; mem. adv. bd. NYU Inst. on Fed. Taxation; academician Internat. Acad. Estate and Tax Law; mem. tax commn., Union Internat. des Avocats. Author: (with Charles G. Stephenson and K. Bruce Friedman) International Estate Planning, rev. edit., 1997; contbr. articles to profl. jours. Fellow Am. Coll. of Tax Counsel; mem. ABA (tax sect. vice chair adminstrn. 2000-02, coun. dir. 1995-97, chair com. on U.S. activities of foreigners and tax treaties 1989-91, vice chair 1987-89, chair subcom. on tax treaties 1981-87), Calif. State Bar Assn. (taxation sect. exec. com. 1981-85, vice chair 1982-83, chair 1983-84, vice chair income tax com. 1981-82, chair 1982-83, vice chair personal income tax subcom. 1979-80, chair 1980-81, co-chair fgn. tax subcom. 1978-79, cert. specialist in taxation law), N.Y. State Bar Assn. (taxation sect., mem. com. on U.S. activities of fgn. taxpayers and fgn. activities of U.S. taxpayers), Bar Assn. of San Francisco, Bar Assn. of City of N.Y., San Francisco Tax Club (pres. 1988), San Francisco Internat. Tax Group. Died Aug. 18, 2006.

FREYTAG, RICHARD ARTHUR, banker; b. Chgo., Oct. 26, 1933; s. Elmer Walter and Mary Louise (Mayo) F.; m. Pamela Burge, Feb. 11, 1989; children: Richard Christopher Hughes Freytag, Bliss Louise Mayo Smith. AB, Trinity Coll., Hartford, Conn., 1955; MBA, Harvard U., 1961; MS, MIT, 1971. Map salesman Rand McNally & Co., Chgo., 1955-56; internat. salesman Diversey Corp., Chgo., 1959-60; with Citibank, Japan, Taiwan, Korea, 1962-70, v.p., sr. credit officer, 1971-73, sr. officer Hong Kong, China, Vietnam, 1973—76, investor rels. and problem loan recovery mgmt. N.Y.C., 1977-84; pres. Citicorp Holdings, Inc., Citibank Overseas Investment Corp., 1984-96, vice chmn., dir., 1996-98; pres., CEO Citicorp Banking Corp., New Castle, Del., 1984-96, vice-chmn., dir., 1996-98; pres. Citibank Del., 1989-96, vice-chmn., dir., 1996-98. Vice-chmn. Far East Bank, Ltd., Hong Kong, 1973-76, sr. ptnr. Washington Capital Ptnrs., 1999-2002; bd. dirs. Citicorp Capital Investors Europe Ltd., The Thomas Group, Inc., Irving, Tex.; mem. Expanded Sr. Panel on N.E. Asian Ltd. Nuclear Arms Agreement, 1992-2005. Trustee Med. Ctr. of Del.; bd. visitors Nat. Def. U., 1988-93, 2002-05; chmn. Nat. Def. U. Found., 1993-99, chmn. emeritus, 1999-2005; mem. Gov.'s Coun. on Banking, 1994-97. 1st lt. USAF, 1956-59, maj. gen. USAFR, 1986-93, fighter pilot operational in F-100 "supersabre", 1956-59. Decorated Air Force DSM, 1993, Medal for Disting. Pub. Svc. Dept. Def., 2000; recipient Brooks prize MIT, 1971; Alfred Sloan fellow The Nat. City Found., N.Y.C., 1969. Mem. Nat. Air Force Salute Found. (pres. 1988-90, chmn. 1990-92), Air Force Assn. (Iron Gate chpt. pres. 1988-90, chmn. 1990-92, Ira Eaker fellow 1991, Medal of Merit 1990, Exceptional Svc. award 1989), Coun. on Fgn. Rels., Falcon Found. (trustee), Del. Bankers Assn. (dir., pres. 1992-97), Del. Bus. Roundtable (vice chmn. 1994-96). Episcopalian. Died July 4, 2005.

FRIAR, GEORGE EDWARD, lawyer, state official; b. Coxton, Ky., Aug. 18, 1916; s. George Allen and Ida Mae (Crutchfield) F.; m. Margaret Ellen Riggin; children: George Edward Jr., Cynthia L. Smith, Elizabeth Ralston. Student, Maryville Coll., Princeton U., Vanderbilt U., U. Tenn. Sch. Law. Chmn. bd., pres. Corporate Concepts, Inc.; sec. of state State of Tenn. Gen. counsel So. Govs. Conf. With USN, World War II. Mem. ABA (ho. of dels.), Nat. Assn. Bar Execs. (pres.). Home: Sarasota, Fla. Died June 18, 2005.

FRIEDAN, BETTY, women's rights advocate, writer; b. Peoria, Ill., Feb. 4, 1921; d. Harry and Miriam (Horwitz) Goldstein; m. Carl Friedan, June 1947 (div. May 1969); children: Daniel, Jonathan, Emily. AB summa cum laude, Smith Coll., 1942, LHD (hon.), 1975, SUNY, Stony Brook, 1985, Cooper Union, 1987; Doctorate (hon.), Columbia U., 1994. Rsch. fellow U. Calif., Berkeley, 1943; lectr. feminism univs., women's groups, bus. and profl. groups in US and Europe; co-founder NOW, 1966, 1st pres., 1966-70, chairwoman adv. com., 1970-72, mem. bd. dirs. legal def. and edn. fund; founding mem. Nat. Women's Polit. Caucas, 1971; organizer Internat. Feminist Congress, 1973, First Women's Bank, 1973, Econ. Think Tank for Women, 1974; co-founder Nat. Abortion Rights Action League (NARAL), v.p., 1970-73. Disting. vis. prof. sch. journalism and studies of women and men in soc., U. So. Calif., 1987; vis. prof. sociology Temple U., 1972, Queens Coll., 1975; vis. lectr. Calhoun Coll., fellow Yale U., 1974; lectr. New Sch. Social Research, NYC, 1971; sr. research assoc. Ctr. Social Scis., Columbia U., NYC, 1979-81; bd. dirs. NOW Legal Defense and Education fund; co-chmn. Nat. Comms. Women's Equality; del. White House Conf. on Family, 1980; del. UN Decade for Women Confs. in Mexico City, Copenhagen, Nairobi; mem. LORAN Commn. Harvard Community Health Plan; vis. scholar U. South Fla., Sarasota, 1985; Disting. vis. prof. Sch. Journalism and Social Work Sch. U. So. Calif., Cornell U., Sch. Industrial and Labor Rels, Ithaca, NY, 1998—2006; dir. New Paradigm Program, Inst. for Women and Work, 1998-2006. Author: The Feminine Mystique, 1963, It Changed My Life: Writings on the Women's Movement, 1976, The Second Stage, 1981, The Fountain of Age, 1993, Beyond Gender: The New Politics of Family and Work, 1998, Life So Far, 2000; mem. editl. bd. Present Tense mag.; contbg. editor McCall's mag., 1971-74; contbr. Atlantic Monthly; contbr. articles to NY Times, Cosmopolitan, Saturday Rev., Family Circle, Good Housekeeping, McCall's, Newsweek, The New Republic, The New Yorker, Harpar's Mag., American Behavioral Scientist, Social Policy, and others; papers being collected by Schlesinger Libr. Harvard U. Mem. exec. com. Am. Jewish Congress, co-chair nat. commn. women's equality, 1984-85; mem. nat. bd. Girl Scouts USA, 1976-82; mem. NY County Democratic Com. Recipient Humanist of Yr. award, 1974, Eleanor Roosevelt Leadership award, 1989; Inst. Politics fellow Kennedy Sch. Govt., Harvard U., 1982, rsch. fellow Ctr. Population Studies, Harvard U., 1982-83, Chubb fellow Yale U., 1985, Andrus Ctr. Gerontology fellow U. So. Calif., 1986, guest scholar Woodrow Wilson Ctr. for Internat. Scholars, 1995-96, disting. vis. prof. George Mason U., 1995, Mt. Vernon Coll., 1996; Ford Found. grantee, 1998. Mem. AFTRA, PEN, Author's Guild, Women's Ink, Women's Forum, Mag. Writers, Am. Soc. Journalists and Authors (1st recipient Mort Weisinger award for outstanding mag. journalism 1979, Author of Yr. 1982), Assn. Humanistic Psychology, Am. Sociology Assn., Gerontol. Soc. Am., Cosmos Club, Nat. Press Club, Phi Beta Kappa. Died Feb. 4, 2006.

FRIEDMAN, BRUCE, management consultant; b. S.I., N.Y., June 3, 1936; s. David and Mary (Perricone) F.; m. Diane Hilja Simenson, Aug. 25, 1961; 1 child, Aaron Craig. BA, U. Chgo., 1962, MBA, 1964. Cert. mgmt. cons.; chartered life underwriter. Asst. mgr. The Prudential Inst. Co. of Am., Chgo., 1962-69; mgr. KPMG Peat Marwick, Chgo., 1969-74; cons. Towers, Perrin, Chgo., 1974-75; dir. human resources consulting Coopers & Lybrand, Chgo., 1975-80; owner, pres, chief exec. Bruce Friedman and Assocs., Champaign, Ill., from 1980. With U.S. Army, Army Security Agy., 1954-56. Fellow Life Mgmt. Inst.; mem. Inst. Mgmt. Cons., Am. Arbitration Assn. (arbitrator 1983—). Republican. Avocation: reading. Home: Champaign, Ill. Died Apr. 26, 2005.

FRIEDMAN, EDWARD DAVID, lawyer, arbitrator; b. Chgo. s. Jacob C. and Bessie (Levison) F.; m. Mary Louise Melia, Nov. 1, 1947 (dec. Feb. 1997); children: Michael, Daniel, Mary Eleanor, Elizabeth; m. Carol Green, Nov. 26, 1999. AB with honors, U. Chgo., 1935, JD cum laude, 1937. Bar: Ill. 1937, U.S. Ct. Appeals 1950, D.C. 1969, U.S. Supreme Ct. 1969. Law clk. to fed. master in chancery, Chgo., 1937-38; assoc. Rosenberg, Toomin & Stein, Chgo., 1938-39; gen. counsel staff SEC, 1939-42; chief counsel OPA, 1942-43; spl. asst. to dep. solicitor and solicitor Dept. Labor, Washington, 1943-48, dep. solicitor of labor, 1965-68, acting solicitor of labor, 1969; ptnr. Bernstein, Alper, Schoene & Friedman, Washington, 1969-75, Highsaw, Mahoney & Friedman, Washington, 1975-80, Friedman & Wirtz, 1980-90; chief law officer 5th regional office, also asst. gen. counsel NLRB, 1948-60; labor counsel to Senator John F. Kennedy, 1960-61, Senator Wayne Morse, 1961-65, U.S. Senate Labor and Pub. Welfare Com., 1961-65; counsel to majority and minority floor mgrs. Senators Clark and Case on Title VII of Civil Rights Bill, 1964; spl. asst. sec. labor fgn. farm labor program, 1965; counsel compaign conduct adminstrv. com. United Steelworkers Am., 1980-89. U.S. del. to OECD, Paris, 1968. Mem. editl. bd. U. Chgo. Law Rev, 1936-37. Mem. town coun., Garrett Park, Md., 1954-58, mayor, 1960-66; mem. Truro (Mass.)Zoning Bd. Appeals, 1999—. U. Chgo. James Nelson Raymond fellow, 1937. Mem. ABA, D.C. Bar Assn., Fed. Bar Assn., Order of Coif, U. Chgo. Alumni Club. Home: Truro, Mass. Died Apr. 4, 2006.

FRIEDMAN, STANLEY MARCUS, psychiatrist; b. N.Y.C., May 19, 1925; s. Morris Albert and Celia (Walker) F.; children: Jennifer, Steven, William. BS, CCNY, 1946, MS, 1947; PhD, Case Western Res. U., 1950; MD, NYU, 1954. Rsch. cons. Port of N.Y. Authority, N.Y.C., 1951-58; pvt. practice N.Y.C., from 1958; with Mt. Sinai Hosp., N.Y.C., from 1958, clin. asst. prof. Sch. Medicine, 1975-81, clin. assoc. prof. Sch. Medicine, from 1981. Contbr. articles to profl. jours. Lt. (j.g.) USMS, 1943-46, USNR. Founds. Fund for Rsch. in Psychiatry grantee, 1958-59, NIMH grantee, 1964-65. Mem. Am. Psychiat. Assn., Am. Psychoanalytic Assn., N.J. Psychoanalytic Soc. Home: Tenafly, NJ. Died May 19, 2004.

FRIERSON, WILLIAM MANTON, philosophy and religion educator; b. Farmville, Va., May 12, 1933; s. William Joseph and Ione (Livingstone) F. BA in History and Modern Fgn. Langs., Emory U., 1954, PhD in Philos. Theology, 1977; BD in Biblical Studies, Union Theol. Sem., 1958; ThM, Princeton Theol. Sem., 1963. Ordained to ministry Presbyn. Ch., 1958. Asst. pastor Univ. Presbyn. Ch., Baton Rouge, La., 1958-60, pastor, 1961-62, Norcross (Ga.) Presbyn. Ch.; assoc. pastor, then pastor First Presbyn. Ch., Lafayette, La., 1966-71; univ. chaplain Emory U., Atlanta, 1977-79; instr. in philosophy Eureka (Ill.) Coll., 1979-80; from asst. prof. to assoc. prof. philosophy and religion Valdosta (Ga.) State Coll., from 1980. Mem. faculty senate Valdosta State Coll., 1991—, mem. various coms. Editor: Faculty Handbook, Valdosta State Coll., 1992, author: (with others) Code of Ethics, Valdosta State Coll., 1988-90. Preacher, tchr., mem. coms. Christ Episcopal Ch., Valdosta, 1980—. Fulbright grantee U. Utrecht, Holland, 1954-55. Mem. Am. Acad. Religion, Ga. Philos. Soc., Soc. Christian Philosophers. Democrat. Avocations: gardening, music, stamps, canoeing, travel. Home: Valdosta, Ga. Died June 1, 2005.

FRISTACKY, NORBERT, computer engineering educator, researcher; b. Puchov, Czechoslovakia, Nov. 8, 1931; s. Eduard and Anna (Janasova) F.; m. Hilda Matejcikova, Feb. 21, 1937; 1 child, Tomas. Dipl.-Ing., Slovak Tech. U., Bratislava, Czechoslovakia, 1954, PhD, 1964. Asst. prof. Slovak Tech. U., 1955-62, 63-70, assoc. prof., 1971-85, full prof., from 1985, head dept. computer engring., 1978-90, mem. sci. coun., 1988-92. Rschr. Krizik Rsch. Inst., Prague, Czechoslovakia, 1962; vis. lectr. Salford (Eng.) U., 1970-71; vis. prof. Tech. U., Dresden, Germany, 1986; mem. supervisory com. R&D Inst., VUVT Engring., Zilina, Czechoslovakia, 1990-91. Author: Programmable Logic Controllers, 1981 (Czechoslovakia Tech. Nat. Soc. prize 1981), Logic Circuits, 1986, 90 (Slovak Lit. Fund prize 1986), Digital Computers (Slovak Lit Fund prize, 1994), 1993; editor Elec. Engring. Jour., 1991-2002; mem. editl. bd. Jour. Computing and Informatics, 1981—. Rector Slovak Tech. U., 1990-91. Mem.: IEEE (chmn. Slovak com., Computer Soc. IEEE award Computer Pioneer 1996), Slovak Acad. Soc., Internat. Fedn. Info. Processing (Slovak nat. com., tech. com., working group), Slovak Informatics Soc., Czechoslovak Elec. Engring. Soc. (chmn. spl. interest group in informatics sci. and engring. 1977—92), Slovak Soc. Cybernetics and Informatics (v.p. 1991), Slovak Acad. Scis. (sci. com. electronics and cybernetics 1988—96), Am. Czechoslovak Soc. (hon.). Home: Bratislava, Slovakia. Died July 5, 2006; Bratislava.

FRITZ, HENRY EUGENE, historian, educator; b. Garrison, Kans., June 20, 1927; s. Frank Alfred and Esther (Anderson) Fritz; m. Dolores Ileen Moeller, Sept. 3, 1950; children: Esther Anne, Malin Eugenia, Marie Louise. BS, Bradley U., 1950, MA, 1952; PhD of History, U. Minn., 1957. Instr. history U. Wis. Milw., 1956—58; asst. prof. St. Olaf Coll., Northfield, Minn., 1958—62, assoc. prof., 1962—68, prof. Am. History, 1968, chmn. history dept., 1969—84. Founder, dir. Am. Minorities Studies St. Olaf Coll., Northfield, 1970—72; faculty fellow Newberry Libr., Chgo., 1968—69; expert witness on Indian rights to mineral and timber lands U.S. Dept. Justice. Author: The Movement for Indian Assimilation, 1860-1890, 1963; contbr. articles to profl. jours. With AUS, 1945—46, ETO. Louis and Maude Hill fellow, Hill Found. St. Paul, 1965. Mem.: We. History Assn. (hon.; chmn. local arrangements 24th ann. meeting 1984, chmn. local arrangements 37th ann. meeting 1997, awards of merit com. 1981—84, Award of Merit 1997), Orgn. Am. Historians (life), Kiwanis. Republican. Lutheran. Avocations: farming, horses, beef cattle, horticulture. Home: Northfield, Minn. Died Nov. 13, 2005.

FRODSHAM, OLAF MILTON, music educator; b. Bournemouth, Eng., Oct. 25, 1915; came to U.S., 1921; s. Sydney Herbert and Oline Magarethe (Espersen) F.; m. Grace Elaine Bessey, Aug. 17, 1946; 1 child, Lance Philip. AB, U. Redlands, 1937, MA, 1938; postgrad., Royal Sch. London, 1962, Exeter U., 1967. Cert. life gen. secondary credential, life gen. jr. coll., life gen. elem. Tchr. Porterville HS, Calif., 1938-41, Kamehameha Sch., Honolulu, 1941-42; instr., dir. choral music Long Beach City Coll., Calif., 1946-50; assoc. prof. Occidental Coll., LA, 1950-78; dir. choral music. Calif. Inst. Tech., Pasadena, Calif., 1953-82; dir. music St. Bede the Venerable Sch., LaCanada, Calif., 1982-92, Santa Clara Elem. Sch., Oxnard, Calif., 1992-95, Luth. Ch. of Our Redeemer, Oxnard, Calif., 1994-99. Adj. asst. prof. Long Beach State U., 1948-52. Dir. choral recs. God of Abraham Praise, 1978; Liszt: Messe fur Vierstimmigen Männerchor, 1979-80. Staff sgt. U.S. Army, 1942-46, PTO. Recipient Leadership in Edn. Athenaeum award U. Redlands, 1972; named Hon. Alumnus, Calif. Inst. Tech., Pasadena, 1970. Mem. Am. Choral Dirs. Assn., Music Educators Assn., Choral Conductors Guild, Pacific Southwest Choral Assn. (sec.-treas. 1970-78, pres. 1978-79), Calif. Tchrs. Assn. Roman Catholic. Avocations: weight training, cooking, singing. Home: Pasadena, Calif. Died June 27, 2005.

FROHNSDORFF, GEOFFREY JAMES CARL, physical chemist; b. London, Feb. 4, 1928; came to U.S., 1960; s. Stanley George Carl and Adeline May (Lee) F.; m. Doris Helen Keen, Aug. 10, 1956 (div. July 1989); children: Katharine Ann Carney, Gregory James Carl, Elizabeth Susan Conolly. BSc, U. St. Andrews, Scotland, 1951, BSc with honors, 1953; MS, Lehigh U., 1956; PhD, Imperial Coll., London, 1959. Postdoctoral fellow Royal Mil. Coll., Kingston, Ont., Can., 1959-60; asst. dir. R&D Am. Cement Corp., Riverside, Calif., 1960-65, mgr. R&D, 1965-70; group leader Gillette Co. Rsch. Inst., Rockville, Md., 1970-73; sect. chief bldg. materials Nat. Inst. Stds. and Tech., Gaithersburg, Md., 1973-81, divsn. chief bldg. materials, 1981—2002. Mem. internal adv. bd. Ctr. for Sci. and Tech. of Advanced Cement-Based Materials, Northwestern U.; chmn. ISO TC59/SC3/WG9 on Design Life of Bldgs., Geneva. Editor: Blended Cements, 1986. Pres. Jurupa Mountains Cultural Ctr., Riverside, Calif., 1967-70. With RAF, 1947-49. Recipient Silver medal US Dept. Commerce, 1982. Fellow ASTM (hon. mem., P.H. Bates award com. on cement 1978, Award of Merit 1993, W.H. Cavanaugh Meml. award 1995), Am. Concrete Inst. (Delmar Bloem award 1985), Am. Ceramic Soc. Achievements include initiation of computer simulations of the performance of cement and concrete, many activities concerned with prediction of service life of building materials. Home: Gaithersburg, Md. Died Mar. 5, 2006.

FROLIO, JEFFREY LYNN, photojournalist, musician; b. Omaha, July 10, 1958; s. Joseph Sebastian and Clella Grace (Giberson) F.; m. Marianne Hartman, Oct. 15, 1982; children: Nicole Jo, David Jeffrey, Carly Anne. BA, U. Nebr., Omaha, 1982. Photojournalist KSFY-TV, Sioux Falls, S.D., 1982-84, KETV-TV, Omaha, from 1984. Keyboard player Bakersfield Band. Author: (melodrama plays) Egad, You Cad, 1992, Dazed in Florence, 1993, Rock Bottom, 1994. Bd. dirs. Florentine Players, Omaha, 1992. Recipient Janus award Mortgage Bankers Assn., 1986; named best actor Florentine Players, 1979, 88, 89, 90, 92, 93. Mem. Nebr. News Photographer Assn. (runner-up Nebr. News Photographer of the Year, 1992), Omaha Press Club. Home: Omaha, Nebr. Died June 10, 2004.

FRY, LOUIS EDWIN, JR., architect; b. Prairie View, Tex., Sept. 11, 1928; s. Louis Edwin and Obelia (Swearingen) F.; m. Genelle Wiley, Nov. 7, 1955; children— Jo Nisa, Louis Edwin, Vicki-Lynn, A'lexa AB, Howard U., 1949; B.Arch., Harvard U., 1953, M.Arch., 1954, M.Arch. in Urban Design, 1962. Registered profl. architect, D.C., Va., Md., N.J. Arch. McGowan & Johnson, Washington, 1955-59, Fry & Welch Assoc. PC, Washington, 1959—2006. Vis. critic Harvard U., Cambridge, Mass., 1970-74; bd. dirs. Mid Atlantic NCARB, Washington, 1979-81; pres. D.C. Arch. Registration Bd., 1979-84; mem. Redevel. Land Agy., 1978—2006; mem. design com. Harvard U., 1980—2006, vis. mem. Grad. Sch. Design Mem. Shepherd Park Community Assn., Washington, Georgia Ave. Profl. and Civic Assn., Washington Fulbright fellow, Holland, 1954-55 Fellow AIA; mem. Nat. Orgn. for Minority Architects, Omega Psi Phi Democrat. Avocation: breeding salt-water fish. Home: Washington, DC. Died Mar. 7, 2006.

FULLER, HAROLD WAYNE, retired chemist, biochemist; b. Chgo., Sept. 4, 1925; s. Garle Manning Fuller and Carol Barendt; m. Mary Agnes Huisinga, Aug. 30, 1952; children: Anne, John, Kathleen, Barbara, Jane. AB, Kalamazoo Coll., 1950. Owner Fuller Foto, Gainesville, Fla., 1956-62; tchr. sci. Trenton (Fla.) High Sch., 1964-65, Melrose (Fla.) High Sch., 1965-66; chemist I U. Fla., Gainesville, 1966-79; chemist III Fla. Dept. Transp., Gainesville, 1979-90; lab. mgr., dept. physics Santa Fe C.C., Gainesville, 1990-98; ret., 1998. With U.S. Army, 1944-45, Italy. Decorated Bronze Star, Purple Heart. Fellow Am. Inst. Chemist; mem. Royal Soc. Chem. (charter), Mayflower Soc. Republican. Lutheran. Achievements include the development of procedures for the Florida Department of Transportation to chemically test cement. Home: Gainesville, Fla. Died June 18, 2005.

FULLER, SARAH BETSY, lawyer; b. Washington, Feb. 26, 1946; d. Stanley Edward and Marjorie Thelma (Barth) Cohen; m. Ronald G. Fuller, Oct. 3, 1975; children: Jonah B., Cecily B., Eli Gabriel. BA, Cornell U., 1968; MS, U. Wis., 1971; JD, Stanford U., 1974. Bar: Calif. 1975, Ariz. 1978, N.Y. 1978, U.S. Dist. Ct. (we., no. and so. dists.) N.Y. 1995, U.S. Ct. Appeals (2d cir.) 1995. Gen. atty. U.S. Dept. Justice, Civil Rights Divsn., Washington, 1974-77; mng. atty. DNA-Navajo Legal Svcs., Tuba City, Ariz., 1977-78; lectr. Cornell U. Law Sch., Ithaca, N.Y., 1978-88; staff atty. Prisoners Legal Svcs. N.Y., Ithaca, from 1988. Former adj. prof. law Cornell U. Law Sch. Co-author: Brown U. Board of Edn.: Equal Schooling for All, 1994. Jewish. Avocations: birding, camping. Died Apr. 21, 2004.

FULLER, TERRY RAY, lawyer; b. Canadian, Tex., Feb. 22, 1953; s. Raymon F. Fuller and Wanda J. (Grant) Smith; m. Jennifer L. Behrens, Sept. 24, 1974; children: Jacqueline, Aubrey-Anne. BA, Ft. Hays State U., 1976; JD, Washburn U., 1978. Bar: Kans. 1979, U.S. Dist. Ct. Kans. 1979. Sole practice, Kinsley, Kans., from 1979; county atty. Edwards County, Kinsley, 1980-88. Chmn. Edwards County Dem. Cen. Com., 1982-87. Mem. Kans. Bar Assn. Democrat. Avocations: history, music. Home: Kinsley, Kans. Died Oct. 28, 2004.

FULLER, VINCENT JOHN, lawyer; b. Ossining, N.Y., June 21, 1931; s. John Vincent and Rose (Croke) Fuller; m. Beatrice Fuller; children: Kenwyn, Beatrice, Alison, Vincent, Anthony. BA, Williams Coll., 1952; LLB, Georgetown U., 1956, LLD, 1988. Bar: D.C. 1956, N.Y. 1957, U.S. Dist. Ct. (so. dist.) N.Y. 1964, U.S. Ct. Appeals D.C. 1956, U.S. Ct. Appeals (2d cir.) 1965, U.S. Ct. Appeals (5th cir.) 1967, U.S. Ct. Appeals (6th cir.) 1969, U.S. Ct. Appeals (7th cir.) 1977, U.S. Supreme Ct. 1962. With Williams & Connolly, ptnr. Washington. With USN, 1952—54. Fellow Am. Coll Trial Lawyers; mem. ABA, DC Bar Assn., NY State Bar Assn., The Barristers, Am. Bd. Criminal Lawyers. Avocation: history. Died July 26, 2006.

FULMER, SCOTT GORDON, environmental planner, archaeologist; b. Lawton, Okla., Mar. 30, 1950; s. Richard Proctor and Evelyn Marie (Westlind) F. BA in Anthropology, U. Calif., Santa Barbara, 1975; postgrad., San Diego State U., 1981-83; profl. cert. hazardous materials mgmt., U. Calif., San Diego, 1990. Rsch. archaeologist Mimbres (N.Mex.) Found., 1976; prin., v.p. ASM Inc., San Diego, 1977-78; archaeologist cons. to govt. and industry, Calif., 1979-82, Calif. Dept. Pks. and Recreation, San Diego, 1982-83, CALTRANS, San Diego, 1983-84; environ. mgmt. specialist County of San Diego, 1984-85; environ. analyst Port of San Diego, 1985-89; project mgr. RECON, San Diego, from 1990. Program chair Soc. Calif. Archaeology annual meeting, San Diego, 1983. Contbr. articles to profl. jours. Judge San Diego Sci. Fair, 1985-90; juror AIA community design award, San Diego, 1989. Mem. Nat. Assn. Environ. Profls., Nat. Trust Hist. Preservation, Soc. Profl. Archaeologists (cert.), Soc. Am. Archaeology, Assn. Environ. Profls. (chpt. officer 1987-89). Home: San Diego, Calif. Died Jan. 24, 2004.

FUMAGALLI, ORAZIO, sculptor, art history educator; b. Taranto, Italy, Feb. 21, 1921; e$D; s. Francesco and Luisa Emilia (Friscira) F.; m. Barbara Merril Ellison; children: Luisa, Piera, Elio. BA, U. Iowa, 1948, MFA, 1950, PhD, 1963. Asst. prof./ednl. curator U. Minn., Duluth, 1954-60, assoc. prof. art history/dir. Tweed Gallery, 1960-64; chmn./founder art dept. U. Wis.-Stout, Menomonie, 1964-79, prof. art, 1965; exch. tchr. sculpture Thurrock Tech. Coll., Essex, Eng., 1979-80; prof. emeritus U. Wis.-Stout, from 1986. One-man and group shows in U.S. and Italy, 1949—; exhibited in (solo ehibitions) Tweed Mus. Art, Tiergarten 105 Skulpturen (Germany), Paine Art Ctr., Sioux Art Ctr., Polk County Heritage Gallery, Des Moines Iowa, U. Wis., Oskosh, Reeve Meml. Union, Winona State U., Furlong Gallery Fifty Years in Art, 1986, Wis. Acad. Scis. Arts and Letters, Madison, A Wisconsin Master, 1989, Scherzi & Lobgesänge, 1990, Hanover (Germany), Sommer Gala, Skulpturen, Fallingbostel-Walsrode, (Germany), Kultur Amt, Salzwedel (Germany), Orazio Fumagalli, Rzeźba, Pita and Pozan, (Poland), Figure Fragments: Songs of Praise, Univ. Louisville, among others, (group exhibitions) Charles A. Wustum Mus. Fine Arts, U. Chgo., Circle Ctr. Gallery: Invitational Sculpture Exhibit, Wis. and Ill. Figurative Art, Neville Pub. Mus., One Yr. Traveling Exhibition, Twelve Wis. Masters, The Milw. Inst. Art and Design, Wis. Sculpture: Look to the 1990's, Zeitgenössische Kunst Aus Italien, 1990, Grossburgwedel (Germany), and various others; featured artist Edgewood-Orchard Gallery, Door County, Wis. With USCG, 1942-46. Fulbright Scholarship U.S. Govt., 1950-51; Belgian Am. Found. fellowship, 1955. Mem. Am. Assn. Mus. (program com.), Nat. Endowment for the Arts (cons.). Home: Menomonie, Wis. Died Apr. 10, 2004.

FUNK, JOHN CALVIN, service organization executive; b. Olympia, Wash., Oct. 21, 1941; s. Orlo Vernon and Geneva (Dowdy) F.; m. Barbara Ann Hutcherson, July, 12, 1963; children: Maria, Bobby, Timmy, Angela. AA, Phoenix Coll., Ariz., 1961; BS, Portland (Oreg.) State U., 1965. Sales Standard Ins. Co., Portland (Oreg.) and Phoenix, 1965-69; various positions Dow Chem. Co., Phoenix and L.A., 1969-85; v.p. health care bus. devel. Penn Corp. Fin., 1985-87; pres., chief exec. officer PPO Alliance, Woodland Hills, Calif., from 1987. Mem. editl. staff PPO Letter. Chmn. trustees Calif. Bapt. Coll., Riverside, 1986; trustee Golden State Sem., 1991; local com. chmn. Gideons Internat., Thousand Oaks, Calif., 1986-90; chmn. ch. council, chmn. deacons First So. Bapt. Ch., West Hills, Calif., 1987, deacon, chmn., 1988. Mem. Am. Assn. Preferred Provider Orgns. (pres. 1990-91, nat. bd. dirs.), Adaptive Bus. Leaders Orgn. (exec. coun.), Healthcare Forum, Am. Mktg. Assn. Avocations: church activities, golf. Home: Westlake Vlg, Calif. Died Nov. 6, 2004.

FUNK, LISA AVERILL, state transportation planner; b. Macomb, Ill., Aug. 21, 1957; d. Bruce J. and Phyllis (Reichle) Averill; m. Stephen Lawrence Funk, Nov. 30, 1985; children: Kelly Michelle, Jason Stephen. BS, Mich. State U., 1979. With scheduling and publs. office Mich. State U., East Lansing, 1977-79; caseworker Friend of the Ct., Saginaw, Mich., 1979-80; instr. Jazzercise Inc., Lansing, Mich., from 1983; transp. planner Mich. Dept. Transp., Lansing, from 1980. Active donations Mich. State U. Ralph Young Fund, Sta. WKAR TV Auction, East Lansing, 1985—. Mem. Coun. on Environ. Strategy SE Mich. Coun. of Govts. Home: Lansing, Mich. Died July 3, 2004.

FUNK, PATRICIA ANN, health facility administrative assistant; b. Coatesville, Pa., Dec. 14, 1934; d. Daniel Jsoeph and Mary Helen (Wolownik) Burns. AN, Coatesville Sch. Nursing, 1955; BS, West Chester (Pa.) State Coll., 1975; MEd, West Chester U., 1979. Staff nurse Coatesville Hosp., 1955-56, head nurse emergency rm., 1956-57, student nurse recruiter, 1957-59, adminstrv. asst., 1959-75, in-svc. educator, 1975-79; in-svc. coord. Pottstown (Pa.) Med. Ctr., 1979-81, dir. ednl. svcs., from 1981. Editor newsleter Sepashet, 1986. Bd. dirs. Am. Heart Assn., 1989—, Am. Cancer Soc., 1981—. Recipient Outstanding Vol. award Am. Cancer Soc., 1985. Mem. Hosp. Assn., Pa. Soc. Health Mgrs. (sec., bd. dirs. 1991—), Berks-Pottstown Arthritis Assn. (bd. dirs. 1982—), Soc. Health Edn. Trainers (bd. dirs. Southeastern Pa. chpt. 1984—), Tri-County Bus. and Edn. Coun. (bd. dirs. 1984—). Republican. Avocations: crafts, skiing, reading, music. Home: Pottstown, Pa. Died July 15, 2004.

FUQUA, JOHN BROOKS, retired consumer products and services company executive; b. Prince Edward County, Va., June 26, 1918; s. J.B. Elam and Ruth F.; m. Dorothy Chapman, Feb. 10, 1945; 1 son, John Rex. Grad. high sch., Prospect, Va.; LLD (hon.), Hampden-Sydney Coll., 1972, Duke U., 1973, Fla. Meml. Coll., 1982, Oglethorpe U., 1986; LHD (hon.), Queens Coll., 1987, Longwood Coll., 1990; LLD (hon.), U. Tulsa, 1991, Mercer U., 1991; DHL (hon.), Queens Coll., Charlotte, 1995; D in Adminstrn. (hon.), Cumberland Coll., 1995. Chmn. Fuqua Industries, Inc., Atlanta, 1965-89. Mem. adv. bd. Norfolk So. Corp.; established Ctr. for USSR Mgr. Devel., tng. program for top Soviet mgrs. at Fuqua Sch. Bus. Duke U., 1990. Author: Fuqua-A Memoir, 2002. Mem. Augusta Aviation Commn., 1945-67; past mem., fin. chmn. Augusta Hosp. Authority; past mem. Ga. Sci. and Tech. Commn.; mem. Ga. Ho. of Reps., 1957-62, chmn. House Banking Com., 1959-63; mem. Ga. Senate, 1963-65, chmn. Senate Banking and Fin. Com., Dem. Party and Exec. Com. Ga., 1962-66; bd. visitors Emory U., 1970-76; former mem. adv. council Ga. State U.; former trustee Ga. State U. Found.; trustee Duke U., 1974-87; trustee Hampden-Sydney Coll., 1976-91; bd. dirs. Horatio Alger Assn. Disting. Americans; bd. dirs. Lyndon B. Johnson Found; bd. visitors Fuqua Sch. Bus., Duke U.; past dir. Atlanta C. of C.; donor $10 million to found Fuqua Sch. Bus., Duke U., 1980, $5.5 million to build the Dorothy Chapman Fuqua Conservatory, Atlanta Bot. Gardens, 1989, $10 million to establish Fuqua Sch., Va., 1993, $3 million to establish the Fuqua Heart Ctr. of Atlanta at Piedmont Hosp., 1995, $1.5 million to Atlanta Com. for Spl. Games, 1996, $4 million to Jr. Achievment Internat., 2001, $1 million to PACE Acad., Atlanta, 2002, $1 million to The Wesley Woods Found., 2002, $1 million to The Nuc. Threat Initiative, 2002; established Fuqua Internat. Christian Comm., Crystal Cathedral, 1991, Fuqua Orchid Ctr. for Conservation and Edn., 1997, Fuqua Ctr. Late-Life Depression at Wesley Woods Geriatric Ctr., 1997, J.B. Fuqua chair pub. speaking, Pace Acad., 1999. Recipient Horatio Alger award, 1984, award U. Pa. Wharton Grad. Sch. Bus., 1985, Disting. Entrepreneurship award, 1985, Free Enterprise medal Entrepreneur of Yr. Shenandoah Coll., 1991, Pinnacle award Sales and Mktg. Execs. Internat. Acad. Achievement, 1993, Fellow of the Coll. award Capitol Coll., 1994, Shining Light award Atlanta Gas Light & WSB, 2000, Disting. Georgian award Augusta State U., 2002, Philanthropist of the Yr. award Bus. to Bus. Mag., 2003; named Boss of Yr. Augusta Jaycees, 1960, Broadcaster-Citizen of Yr. Ga. Assn. Broadcasters, 1963, Broadcast Pioneer of Yr., 1979, Outstanding Bus. Leader Northwood Inst., 1986, Mktg. Statesman Sales and Mktg. Execs. Internat., 1986, Bus. Statesman Harvard Bus. Sch. Club Met. Atlanta, 1987, Georgian of Yr., 1989, Philanthropist of Yr. Ga. chpt. Nat. Soc. Fund Raising Execs., 1989, Philanthropist of Yr. Nat. Assn. Fund Raising Execs., 1993, Entrepreneur of Yr. Stanford Bus. Sch. Alumni Assn., 1992; The Fuqua Heart Ctr. of Atlanta at Piedmont Hosp. named in his honor; inducted into J. Mack Robinson Coll. of Bus. Hall of Fame, Ga. State U., 2001, Atlanta Bus. Hall of Fame, Jr. Achievement Ga., 2002, Bus. Hall of Fame, Jr. Achievement Nat., 2002. Mem.: Chief Exec. Orgn. Home: Atlanta, Ga. Died Apr. 5, 2006.

FURMAN, SEYMOUR, surgeon; b. Bronx, N.Y., July 12, 1931; s. Joseph and Bertha Kellert Furman; m. Evelyn Mae Katz, June 1, 1957 (dec. Sept. 9, 2002); children: Bruce, Gary, Neil. Degree, NYU, 1951; MD, SUNY, Bklyn., 1955, DSc (hon.), 2001. Diplomate Am. Bd. Surgery, Am. Bd. Thoracic Surgery. Intern Montefiore Hosp., Bronx, 1955—56, surg. resident, 1956—60, attending surgeon, 1963—2006; thoracic surg. resident Baylor U. Affiliated Hosps., Houston, 1962—63; attending surgeon Jack D. Weiler Hosp., Bronx, 1963—2006; attending cardiologist Montefiore Med. Ctr., Bronx, 1994—2006. Presenter in field; founder NASPExAM; founder, editor Heartweb, Pacing and Clin. Electrophysiology, Electricity and the Heart website; vis. prof. Ben Gurion U., Israel, 1992; disting. vis. scholar The Bakken Mus., Mpls., 2004. Author (with D.J.W. Escher): Principles and Techniques of Cardiac Pacing, 1970, Cardiac Pacing and Pacemakers: Medcom Famous Teachings in Modern Medicine, 1973, Modern Cardiac Pacing-A Clinical Overview, 1975; author: (with M. Schaldach) Advances in Pacemaker Technology, 1975; author: (with D.J.W. Escher) Cardiac Pacing and Pacemakers: Part I: Fundamenals: Medcome Famous Teachings Modern Medicine, 2d edit., 1982; author: Cardiac Pacing and Pacemakers: Part II: Dual Chamber Pacing: Medcom Famous Teachings in Modern Medicine 2d edit., 1983; author: (with D.L. Hayes and D.R. Holmes) A Practice of Cardiac Pacing, 1986, 2d edit., 1989, 3d edit., 1993; author: Procs. of IX World Symposium on Cardiac Pacing and Electrophysiology, 1991; contbr. articles to profl. jours., chpts. to books. Lt. comdr. USNR, 1960—62. Recipient Disting. Svc. award, Inter-Soc. Commn. for Heart Disease Resources, 1971, Pioneer in Cardiac Pacing award, Cardiostim '88, Monte Carlo, Monaco, Disting. Alumnus award, Montefiore Staff and Alumni Assn., 1990, Disting. Scientist award, Am. Coll. Cardiology, 1996, award for contbns. to cardiac pacing, Europace '97, Plate of Merit, Citta di Ferrara and Arcispedale "S. Anna" di Ferrara, Italy, 1997. Fellow: Israel Heart Soc. (hon.); mem.: Argentinian Soc. Elec. Stimulation (hon., corr.), Heart Rhythm Soc., N.Am. Soc. Pacing and Electrophysiology (pres. 1981—82, founder, founder oral history program, Disting. Svc. award 1989, Disting. Achievement award 1996, Heart Rhythm Soc. Founders award 2004), Internat. Cardiac Pacing and Electrophysiology Soc. (founder), Internat. Cardiac Pacing Soc. (founder), Latin Am. Soc. Pacing (hon.), Brazilian Soc. Cardiac Pacing (hon.), Brit. Cardiac Soc. (hon.), Argentine Soc. Cardiac Stimulation (hon.), Chilean Cardiol. Soc. (hon.). Achievements include development of transvenous cardiac pacing; demonstration of prolonged patient survival with transvenous cardiac pacing; development of strength duration curve of human cardiac stimulation; relation of electrode size to stimulation threshold; development of transtelephone pacemaker monitoring; design of pacemaker management of Bradycardia Tachycardia Syndrome; development of three position pacemaker code; database and statistical definition of pulse generator and lead quality; delineation of dual chamber pacemaker mediated tachycardia; development of oral history of cardiac pacing, implantable cardiac defibrillation and clinical cardiac eletrophysiology. Home: Bronx, NY. Died Feb. 20, 2006.

FURST, ARTHUR, toxicologist, educator; b. Mpls., Dec. 25, 1914; s. Samuel and Doris (Kolochinsky) F.; m. Florence Wolovitch, May 24, 1940; children: Carolyn, Adrianne, David Michael, Timothy Daniel. AA, L.A. City Coll., 1935; AB, UCLA, 1937, AM, 1940; PhD, Stanford U., 1948; ScD, U. San Francisco, 1983. Mem. faculty, dept. chemistry San Francisco City Coll., 1940-47; asst. prof. chemistry U. San Francisco, 1947-49, assoc. prof. chemistry, 1949-52; assoc. prof. medicinal chemistry Stanford Sch. Medicine, 1952-57, prof., 1957-61; with U. Calif. War Tng., 1943-45, San Francisco State Coll., 1945; rsch. assoc. Mt. Zion Hosp., 1952-82; clin. prof. pathology Columbia Coll. Physicians and Surgeons, 1969-70; dir. Inst. Chem. Biology; prof. chemistry U. San Francisco, 1961-80, prof. emeritus, from 1980, dean grad. div., 1976-79. Vis. fellow Battelle Seattle Research Center, 1974; Michael vis. prof.

Weizmann Inst. Sci., Israel, 1982; cons. toxicology, 1980—; cons. on cancer WHO; mem. com., bd. mineral resources NRC; emeritus mem. scientific advisory bd. Golden Neo Life Diamite Internat., Fremont, Calif. Author: Toxicologist as Expert Witness, 1997, 151 Myths in Everyday Science, 2004; contbr. over 300 articles to profl. and ednl. jours. Recipient Klaus Schwartz Commemorative medal Internat. Toxological Congress, Tokyo, 1986, Profl. Achievement award UCLA Alumni Assn., 1992, Henry Hall Clay award U. San Francisco, 1977; ann. lectureship named in his honor Stanford U. Health Libr. Fellow Acad. Toxicological Scis. (diplomate), AAAS, Am. Coll. Nutrition, Am. Coll. Toxicology (nat. sec., pres. 1985, Lifetime Contbn. award 2001), N.Y. Acad. Scis., Am. Inst. Chemists; mem. Am. Soc. Pharmacology and Exptl. Therapeutics, Am. Chem. Soc., Am. Assn. Cancer Rsch., Soc. Toxicology (Lifetime Achievement award 2004), Sigma Xi, Phi Lambda Upsilon. Achievements include research activities on organic synthesis, chemotherapy cancer, carcinogenesis of metals and hydrocarbons. Home: Cupertino, Calif. Died Dec. 1, 2005.

FURST, GRETA LENETSKA, entertainer, writer, travel agent; b. N.Y.C., May 15, 1932; d. Harry and Heloise (Altschul) Lenetska; m. Lionel A. Furst, June 15, 1967; children: Valeri Furst Wauschek, Larry M. Student, UCLA, 1951-54. Sales clk. Saks Fifth Ave., N.Y.C., 1950-51, credit and control clk. Beverly Hills, Calif., 1951-53; asst. chief insp. Hoover Electric, West Los Angeles, Calif., 1953-54; office mgr. Craig & Randall Constrn., L.A., 1954-59; restaurant owner The Coffee Palace, L.A., 1958-61; internat. performer, singer in worldwide tours USO, L.A., 1960-63; performer, singer, actor self employed; profl vol. L.A. Free Clinic, others. Prodr., dir. Beverly Hills Follies, Beverly Hills C. of C., 1992; regular performer Srs. Entertaining Srs. Composer songs; painter portraits; one-woman show Here I Go Again, 1999. Bd. dirs., pres. Friends of the L.A. Free Clinic; trustee L.A. West Mosquito Abatement Dist., 1978-83; mem. Bverly Hills Traffic and Parking Commn., 1992-2000, chair, 1995; mem. adv. com. Access Svcs. Recipient Agy. Leadership award United Way Greater L.A., 1995, Frances Helfman award L.A. Free Clinic, 1998, resolution Calif. State Assembly, 1998, Lenny Somberg award, 2005. Mem. NATAS, SAG, AFTRA, AGVS, Srs. Entertaining Srs., Bronx H.S. of Sci. West Coast Alumni. Democrat. Jewish. Avocations: portraiture, travel, reading, community service. Died June 1, 2005.

FUZEK, JOHN FRANK, chemical consultant; b. Knoxville, Tenn., Dec. 21, 1921; s. John and Maria (Pucher) F.; m. Bettye Lynn Bean, May 31, 1943; children: Mary Ann, Mark Lynn, Martha Elizabeth. BS in Chem. Engring., U. Tenn., 1943, MS in Phys. Chemistry, 1945, PhD in Phys. Chemistry, 1947; post PhD fellow, Office Naval Rsch., 1947-48. Chemist Hercules Powder Co., Wilmington, Del., 1943-44; research chemist N. Am. Rayon Corp., Elizabethton, Tenn., 1948-55; head research physics dept. Beaunit Fibers, Elizabethton, 1955-66; sr. research chemist Tenn. Eastman Co., Kingsport, 1966-70; research assoc. chemicals div. Eastman Kodak Co., Kingsport, 1970-86; cons. Kingsport, from 1986. Author: (with others) (chpt.) Clothing Comfort, 1977, Water in Polymers, 1980; contbr. articles in Jour. Am. Chem. Soc., I&EC Product R&D, ASTM Standard News; patents dyeable polypropylene fibers, process for spinning viscose, silk-like polyester fiber, silk-like textile fiber; contbr. articles to profl. jours. Recipient Sci. Research award Oak Ridge (Tenn.) Inst. of Nuclear Studies, 1950. Fellow AAAS, ASTM (vice chmn. com. D-13 on textiles 1984-90, Cert. of Appreciation 1983, Merit award 1990), Am. Inst. Chemists (pres. Tenn. chpt. 1971-72); mem. Am. Chem. Soc. (nat. councilor 1964-66, chmn. N.E. Tenn. chpt. 1957-58, nat. alt. councilor 1978-80, Speaker of Yr. 1979), Fiber Soc. (Lectr. of Yr. 1980-81), Coblentz Soc., Am. Crystallographic Assn., Am. Assn. Textile Chemists and Colorists, Sigma Xi. Republican. Presbyterian. Avocations: solar eclipse chasing, ballroom dancing, photography. Home: Kingsport, Tenn. Died June 23, 2005.

FYLER, PATRICIA ANN, legal nurse consultant, small business owner; b. Pittsfield, Mass., Aug. 20, 1928; d. Clarence Augustus and Elaine Agnes (Carruthers) McConkey; m. Robert Parmelee Fyler, Oct. 4, 1949; children: Deborah, Rebecca, Pamela, Nancy, Cynthia. Student, Bishop Meml. Nursing Sch., 1949, St. Francis, 1954-56; BS, U. Redlands, 1985. CEN. Staff to head nurse Berkshire Med. Ctr., Pittsfield, 1949-54; staff nurse, operating room St. Francis Hosp., Lynwood, Calif., 1954-57, St. Jude Hosp., Fullerton, Calif., 1958-62, relief charge nurse, 1962-67, charge nurse, 1967-78, asst. supr. emergency dept., 1978-80, mgr. emergency dept. Yorba Linda, Calif., 1980-89; owner, pres. Fyler Assocs./Multi-Specialty Legal Nurse Cons., Brea, Calif., from 1990; staff RN St. Jude Med. Ctr., Fullerton, from 1989. Active cont. learning program, PTA, youth orgns., continuing learning experience; past pres. Orange County, Calif.; pres. L.A. Mem. Am. Assn. Legal Nurse Cons. (past pres. Orange County, past pres. Los Angeles County), Emergency Nurses Assn. (numerous offices). Home: Oceanside, Calif. Died Feb. 5, 2005.

GABBARD, LUCINA PAQUET, literature and language professor, actress; b. New Orleans, Jan. 16, 1922; d. Algernon Wernet and Cordelia Owens Paquet; m. Earnest Glendon Gabbard, Jan. 29, 1942; children: Krin Ernest, Glen Owens. BA, La. State U., 1942; MA, U. Iowa, 1947; PhD, U. Ill., 1974; LittD (hon.), Ea. Ill. U., 1994. From instr. to prof. English Ea. Ill. U., Charleston, 1950—84. Author: The Dream Structure of Pinter's Plays, 1972, The Stoppard Plays, 1982; contbr. articles to profl. jours.; actor: (plays) Grapes of Wrath, The Gift, Divided States, Buckets o' Beckett: End Game, A Summer Remembered, Steel Magnolias, Driving Miss Daisy, Close of Play, Another Part of the Forest, The Octette Bridge Club, The Government Inspector; (films) Prelude to a Kiss, 1992, Groundhog Day, 1993, Blink, 1994, My Best Friend's Wedding, 1997, Redemption, 2000, Novocaine, 2001, Children on their Birthdays, 2002, Sin City, 2005; (TV series) Early Edition, Cupid, Turks, Missing Persons, The Untouchables, America's Most Wanted, Grapes of Wrath; also numerous commls., indsl. films. Mem.: AFTRA, SAG, Actors Equity Assn., Phi Kappa Phi, Delta Delta Delta. Home: Houston, Tex. Died May 23, 2006.

GABLE, JOHN ALLEN, historian, educator; b. Rockford, Ill., Nov. 14, 1943; s. Allen Herman and Mary Jane (Kirkpatrick) G. AB, Kenyon Coll., 1965; PhD in History, Brown U., 1972. Asst. prof. history Briarcliff Coll., Briarcliff Manor, N.Y., 1974-77; exec. dir. Theodore Roosevelt Assn., Oyster Bay, N.Y., from 1974; adj. assoc. prof. C.W. Post L.I. U., Greenvale, N.Y., 1977-89; adj. prof. New Coll. Hofstra U., Hempstead, N.Y., from 1989. Editor, founder Theodore Roosevelt Assn. Jour., 1975—; author, editor 6 books in field; contbr. articles to profl. jours. Vestry Christ Ch., Oyster Bay, 1979-2002. Mem. Orgn. Am. Historians. Episcopalian. Home: Glen Cove, NY. Died Feb. 18, 2005.

GABRIEL, EDWIN ZENITH, consulting engineer; b. Union City, N.J., Aug. 26, 1913; s. Enoch H. and Louise Beatrice (Seraydarian) G. BSME, N.J. Inst. Tech., 1936, ME, 1939, MSEE, 1952; postgrad., MIT, 1949-50. Registered profl. engr. N.J.; lic. Am. Bd. Profl. Engrs. and Land Surveyors. Heating systems engr. Webster-Talmadge Co., N.Y.C., 1938-39; efficiency engr. Prudential Ins. Co. of Am., Newark, 1939-41; mech. and elec. engr. U.S. Govt., 1941-52; project engr. Wright Aeronautical Corp., Caldwell, N.J., 1952-53, Kearfott (Singer Corp.), Clifton, N.J., 1953-55; asst. prof. elec. engring. Lehigh U., Bethlehem, Pa., 1955-56, Villanova (Pa.) U., 1956-60, Fairleigh Dickinson U., Teaneck, N.J., 1960-62; assoc. prof. weapons and engring. dept. U.S. Naval Acad., Annapolis, Md., 1962-64; electronic engr. Avionics Lab, Fort Monmouth, N.J., 1965-73. Presenter papers at profl. confs. Author: Automatic Control Systems, 1965, Computer Cookbook Approach to Digital Circuits and Computers, 1984, Cookbook Approach to Analog Circuits, 1985; numerous patents on computers and handling equipment in U.S., Can., Australia. Cubmaster, asst. scoutmaster Boy Scouts Am., Eatontown, N.J., 1946-48; sec. men's club Community Ch., Eatontown, 1946-48; founder, leader Search for Truth by Youth, Ocean Grove, N.J., 1985-87; Bible study tchr., Asbury Park, 1987-89; Bible tchr. Drop-in-Ctr., Thornley Chapel, Ocean Grove, 1989-90. With AUS, 1943-45. Recipient cert. of merit Internat. Inventor's Expn., 1965; grantee NSF, Stevens Inst. Tech., 1962, U. Notre Dame, 1963. Mem. IEEE (life), ASME (acting sec. materials handling div. 1939-42), Am. Helicopter Soc., N.J. Inst. Tech. Alumni Assn. Republican. Baptist. Achievements include patents for on aircraft and boat crash avoidance systems; patents pending for on auto collision avoidance and protection systems. Avocations: photography, choir singing, bible study leader, exercising. Died Feb. 16, 2004.

GAGLIANO, VINCENT, diversified consumer products manufacturing company executive; b. Chgo., Jan. 17, 1931; s. Salvatore and Phyllis Rose (Monaco) G.; m. Janet Rose Terrafino, Sept. 25, 1954; children: Phyllis Marie, Madeline Rose. Student, U. Ill., Chgo., 1948-49, Wright Jr. Coll., 1950-51; BS in Indsl. Engring., Indls. Engring. Coll., Chgo., 1956. Indsl. engr. U.S. Steel Corp. (now called USX Corp.), Chgo., 1954-56, Motorola Corp., Chgo., 1956-58; dir. procurement Webcor Dormeyer Corp., Chgo., 1958-62; div. v.p. Thomas Div. Whirlpool, Sepulveda, Calif., 1962-81; v.p. ops. Forecast Lighting Co., Inglewood, Calif., 1982-85; group v.p. Kidde Consumer Durables Corp., Compton, Calif., 1985-87; pres. Vigon Lighting Co. subs. Kidde Corp., from 1987, Dalme, Inc. Automobile Security Systems Mfg., Canoga Park, Calif., from 1987. Chmn. Elk Grove (Ill.) Cancer Soc., 1970; pres. Jaycees, Elk Grove, 1959-60. Lifetime bd. mem. (hon.) Elk Grove Boys Baseball, 1968. Mem.: Porter Valley Country. Republican. Roman Catholic. Avocation: golf. Home: Northridge, Calif. Died Sept. 7, 2004.

GAGNON, PAUL A., historian, researcher; b. Springfield, Mass., Jan. 6, 1925; s. Joseph Eugene and Alice Tougas Gagnon; m. Mona Ann Harrington, May 21, 1960; children: Eliza, Benjamin, Thomas. BA in History and Govt., U. Mass., 1950; MA in History, Harvard U., 1951, PhD in History, 1960. Dean faculty U. Mass., Boston, 1965—71, prof. history, 1971—89; chief staff Bradley Com. on History in Schs., Cleve., 1987—88; historian in residence Am. Fedn. of Tchrs., Washington, 1987—88; dir. First U.S. Dept. of Edn., Washington, 1991—93; sr. assoc. Nat. Com. on Time & Learning, Washington, 1993—94; sr. rsch. assoc. Boston U. Sch. of Edn., Boston, 1995—2005. Cons., editor Calif. History Project, L.A., 1989—91; writer Paideia Group, Chgo., 1984—91; cons., writer Achieve, Inc., Washington, from 1999. Author: (book) France Since 1789, 1972, Democracy's Untold Story, 1987, Educating Democracy, 2003. With USN, 1942—46. Mem.: Nat. Coun. for Hist. Edn. (trustee from 1992). Avocations: sailing, European travel. Home: Cambridge, Mass. Died Apr. 28, 2005.

GALANTE, ANN MURIEL, municipal official; b. N.Y.C., May 20, 1929; d. Johnson D. and Anna Francis (Donavan) Boyd; m. James Vincent Galante, June 25, 1949; children: Patricia, Ann, James, Margaret, Joseph. BS in Pub. Adminstrn., SUNY, Old Westbury, 1986; MA in Liberal Studies, Empire State Coll., SUNY L.I. Ctr., 2000. Trustee Village of Mineola, N.Y., 1982-85, mayor N.Y., 1985-91; receiver of taxes Town of North Hempstead, Manhasset, N.Y., from 1992. Mem. N.Y. State Gov.'s Task Force on State Mandates, N.Y.C., 1989-90, N.Y. State Gov.'s Task Force on Sexual Harassment, N.Y.C., 1993-94. Active numerous cmty., ednl., religious, sr. citizen, youth and women's orgns.; past pres. Mineola Welcome Wagon (now Friends and Neighbors); former mem. bd. dirs. Am. Heart Assn.; mem. citizenship com. Nassau County 4-H Clubs, Plainview, N.Y., 1983-87; com. mem. Nassau County Dem. Com., Carle Place, N.Y., 1991—; del. 19th Dist. Jud. Conv., Hauppauge, N.Y., 1992—; Presdl. elector N.Y. State Electoral Coll., Albany, 1996; mem.-at large bd. dirs. Shelter Rock dist. Boy Scouts Am., 1996-97; co-founder Mineola Homebound Svc.; eucharistic min. Corpus Christi Ch., Mineola, 1981—, also past chmn. justice and peace com., renew 2000 com., 100th anniversary com.; trustee Mineola Hist. Soc., 1990—; active Mineola Mustang Run Com., Mineola Bicentennial of Constn. Com.; charter mem. Circle of Friends Soc., Girl Scouts U.S.A., Nassau County; co-founder Mineola Friends of A. Holly Patterson Nursing Home, Mineola Homebound Svc.; mem. master plan and planning com. Village of Mineola, Pres.'s Coun. L.I. Womens Agenda; mem. steering com. L.I. Railroad Mineola Downtown Revitalization Study; co-chair N.H. com. against domestic violence; del. Dem. Nat. Conv., 2000. Named hon. fire chief Mineola Fire Dept., 1985, Outstanding Friend, Corpus Christi Sch., 1996, Disting. Grad., Empire State Coll., 1996, Woman of Yr., Mineola Welcome Wagon; recipient numerous awards for cmty. svc., including Mother of Yr. award Southeastern Dist. Elks Club, Humanitarian award Nassau County Dem. Com. Mem. Tax Receivers and Collectors Assn., N.Y. State Assn. Towns, Soroptimists Internat. of Nassau County (past pres., Woman of Distinction award 1995), Am. Assn. Ret. Persons, Rotary. Roman Catholic. Avocations: travel, theater, women's history research, walking, swimming. Home: Mineola, NY. Died Nov. 30, 2004.

GALBRAITH, JOHN KENNETH, retired economist; b. Iona Station, Ont., Can., Oct. 15, 1908; s. William Archibald and Catherine (Kendall) Galbraith; m. Catherine Atwater, Sept. 17, 1937; children: Alan, Peter, James. BS, U. Guelph, 1931, LLD (hon.); MS, U. Calif., 1933, PhD, 1934; postgrad., Cambridge (Eng.) U., 1937—38; LLD (hon.), Bard Coll., U. Calif.; LLD (hon.), Miami U.; LLD (hon.), U. Mass., U. Mysore, Brandeis U., U. Toronto, U. Sask., U. Mich., U. Durham, R.I. Coll., Boston Coll., Hobart and William Smith Colls., Albion Coll., Tufts U., Adelphi Suffolk Coll., Mich. State U., Louvain U., Oxford U., U. Paris, Carleton Coll., U. Vt., Queens U., Moscow State U., Harvard U., Smith Coll. London Sch. Economics, others. Rsch. fellow U. Calif., 1931—34; instr. and tutor Harvard U., 1934—39; asst. prof. econs. Princeton U., 1939—42; econ. adviser Nat. Def. Adv. Commn., 1940—41; asst. adminstr. in charge price div. OPA, 1941—42, dep. adminstr., 1942—43; mem. bd. of editors Fortune Mag., 1943—48; lectr. Harvard U., 1948—49, prof. econs., 1949—75, Paul M. Warburg prof. econs., 1959—75, ret., 1975. Hon. fellow Trinity Coll., Cambridge U.; hon. prof. U. Geneva; U.S. amb. to India, 1961—63. Author: numerous books including, American Capitalism, 1952, A Theory of Price Control, 1952, The Great Crash, 1955, The Affluent Society, 1958, The Liberal Hour, 1960, Economic Development, 1963, The Scotch, 1964, The New Industrial State, 1967, Indian Painting, 1968, Ambassador's Journal, 1969, Economics, Peace and Laughter, 1971, A China Passage, 1973, Economics and the Public Purpose, 1973, Money: Whence It Came, Where It Went, 1975, The Age of Uncertainity, 1977; author: (with Nicole Salinger) Almost Everyone's Guide to Economics, 1978; author: Annals of an Abiding Liberal, 1979, The Nature of Mass Poverty, 1979, A Life in Our Times, 1981, The Anatomy of Power, 1983, The Voice of the Poor: Essays in Economic and Political Persuasion, 1983, A View From the Stands, 1986, Economics in Perspective: A Critical History, 1987; author: (with Stanislav Menshikov) Capitalism, Communism and Coexistence, 1988; author: (novels) The Triumph, 1968, A Tenured Professor, 1990, The Culture of Contentment, 1992, A Journey Through Economic Time, 1994, A Short History of Financial Euphoria, 1993, The Good Society, 1996, Name-Dropping From F.D.R. on, 1999, The Essential Galbraith, 2001, The Economics of Innocent Fraud, 2004; contbr. to econ. and sci. jours. Dir. U.S. Strategic Bombing Survey, 1945, Office of Econ. Security Policy, State Dept., 1946. Recipient Medal of Freedom, 2000; fellow, Social Sci. Rsch. Coun., 1937—38. Fellow: Am. Acad. Arts and Letters (pres. 1984—87); mem.: AAAS, Ams. for Dem. Action (chmn. 1967—68), Am. Agrl. Econ. Assn., Am. Econ. Assn. (pres. 1972), Saturday, Century. Home: Cambridge, Mass. Died Apr. 29, 2006.

GALEHOUSE, LAWRENCE DAVID, lawyer; b. Akron, Ohio, July 29, 1946; s. John Frederick and Gertrude Agnes (Baker) G. BA, Georgetown U., 1968; JD, U. Ga., 1975. Bar: Ga. 1975, U.S. Ct. Mil. Appeals 1975, U.S. Supreme Ct. 1980. Commd. 2d lt. U.S. Army, 1968, advanced through grades to lt. col., 1983, def. atty. Ft. Benning, Ga., 1975-77, appellate def. supr. Falls Church, Va., 1978-80, trial judge Falls Church and Germany, 1980-86, chief law instr. Ft. McClellan, Ala., 1986-89; asst. dist. atty. Office Dist. Atty., Augusta, Ga., 1989-92; pvt. practice Augusta, from 1992. Home: Lexington, Mass. Died Sept. 8, 2005.

GALLAGHER, PATRICK FRANCIS, anthropologist, educator; b. Wilkinsburg, Pa., Apr. 18, 1930; s. Hugh Vincent and Mary Caroline (Denne) G.; m. Mary Ann Bridge, 1954 (div. 1965); children: Patrick Francis III, John Vincent, Lisa Bridge; m. Mary Ann Hammerel, Sept. 16, 1971 (div. 1979); children: Molly Alison, Kingman Cruxent. BA summa cum laude, U. Pitts., 1957; PhD in Anthropology, Yale U., 1964; student, Washington Sch. Psychiatry, 1968. From asst. prof. to prof. George Washington U., Washington, 1961-69; prof., dean Coll. of the Potomac, Washington, 1971-72; assoc. prof. Cerro Coso C.C., Ridgecrest, Calif., 1973-75; prof. anthropology Universidad Nacional Francisco de Miranda, Venezuela, 1979-81; lectr. Chapman Coll. Ctrs., Palmdale, Calif., 1973—2006. Lectr. Smithsonian Instn., Washington, 1966-68, 73, Davis & Elkins Coll., Elkins, W.Va., 1990-91. Author: La Pitia: An Archaeological Sequence in Northwestern Venezuela, 1976; asst. editor: Abstracts of New World Archaeology, 1961-62; illustrator: Sons of the Shaking Earth, 1959, The Entry of Man into the West Indies, 1960, Man Takes Control, 1961, Conservatism among the Iroquois at the Six Nations Reserve, 1961, Mexico, 1962; contbr. articles to profl. jours. NSF grantee, 1965, 67-68. Fellow AAAS, Royal Anthropol. Inst. of Gt. Britain and Ireland, Am. Anthrop. Assn.; mem. Asociacion Venezolana Para el Avance de la Ciencia, Archeol. Assn. Venezuela (corr.), Anthropol. Soc. Washington (coun. 1967-69), Soc. Am. Archaeology (treas.-elect 1968), Phi Beta Kappa, Sigma Xi. Home: Fort Bragg, Calif. Died July 29, 2006.

GALLAGHER, ROBERT E., risk management marketing company executive; b. 1923; m. Isabel Gallagher; 4 children. Grad., Cornell U., 1947. Pres. Arthur J. Gallagher & Co., Itasca, Ill., 1963—90, CEO, 1963-94, chmn. bd., 1990—2006. Founder Robert E. Gallagher Charitable Trust. Recipient Elizabeth Ann Seaton award, Nat. Catholic Ednl. Assn., 2001. Died Aug. 30, 2006.

GALLINGER, LOIS MAE, medical technician; b. Hibbing, Minn., Sept. 5, 1922; d. Clarence Adolph and Dorothy Mae (Stoller) Belanger; m. Ben Elton Gallinger, Sept. 1, 1956; children: Carol Elda, Gregory John. BS, U. Minn., 1946; Med. Tech. Intern, Coll. St. Scholastica, 1948-49. Cert. med. technologist. X-ray technologist Leigh Clinic, Grand Forks, N.D., 1946-47, Nicollet Clinic, Mpls., 1947-48; med. technologist Little Traverse Hosp., Petoskey, Mich., 1949-52; med. and x-ray technologist Lakeside Med. Ctr., Duluth, Minn., 1952-60; med. technologist St. Mary's Med. Ctr., Duluth, 1961-87; retired, 1987. Treas. Benedictine Health Ctr. Aux., Duluth, 1984-97, Women's Assocs. Duluth Symphony, 1986-99; cookie chmn. No. Pine Girl Scouts USA, Duluth, 1969; bd. dirs. St. Paul's Episc. Women's Club, Duluth, 1970s, greeter's chmn., 1970s, corr. sec., 1990-94, publicity chmn., 1994, asst. treas., 1997-98, treas., 1998-2002; vol. Am. Cancer Soc., 1993—, Am. Lung Assn., 1993, Am. Diabetic Assn., 1996, Am. Leukemia Assn., 1996, 98, Mothers March of Dimes, 1997. Mem. AAUW, Am. Soc. for Clin. Lab., Minn. Soc. for Clin. Lab. (regional historian 1969). Avocations: music, reading, politics. Home: Duluth, Minn. Died Dec. 31, 2005.

GALLO, JOSEPH EDWARD, retired electrical engineer, former city councilman; b. Bklyn., July 18, 1917; s. Frank and Mary Lucy (Richard) G.; m. Ida Selma Winzinger, Apr. 13, 1941 (dec. 1989); children: Jonathan, David, Jane; m. Mary Jean Nelson, May 3, 1991. BS in Elec. Engring., NYU, 1937; MS in Engring., U. Pa., 1963. Elec. engr. Brewster Aero Corp., N.Y., Pa., 1940-44; chief systems engr. Curtiss-Wright Elecs., Carlstadt, N.J., 1944-58; project engr. RCA Corp., Burlington, Mass., Moorestown, N.J., 1958-83, Camden, N.J., 1958-83; retired, 1983. Cons., H.H. Aerospace Co., Lexington, Mass., 1974-76, Esscube Engring. Inc., Marlton, N.J., 1983. Inventor, patentee flight simulator field, 1950's. Mem. Am. Radio Relay League, IEEE, Aircraft Owners Pilots Assn. Republican. Roman Catholic. Avocations: amateur radio, flying, hiking. Home: Prescott, Ariz. Died Mar. 22, 2005.

GALPERIN, LEONID BORIS, petroleum engineer, chemical engineer, researcher; s. Boris Mark Galperin and Kathy Ykov Kuperman; m. Irina Zalman Faynberg, Feb. 20, 1975; 1 child, Andrew Abraham. PhD in chem. engring., Petrochemical Rsch. Inst, 1964—68. Chemical engineer, Tech. Inst., St Peterburg, Russia, 1961. Sr. rschr. Petrochemical Rsch. Inst., St. Peterburg, Russia, 1969—78; devel. specialist UOP LLC, Des Plaines, Ill., 1985—92. Sr. rschr. UOP LLC, Des Plaines, Ill., 1993—98, r & d assoc., from 1999. Mem.: Internat. Zeolite Assn. (assoc.). Achievements include 23 US patents; 5 US patents are pending; 10 European and Russian patents. Home: Wilmette, Ill. Died June 21, 2004.

GALVIN, NOREEN ANN, nurse, educator; b. New Haven, Dec. 9, 1943; d. John Joseph and Helen Jane (Doherty) G.; divorced; children: Eileen M., Paula T., Beth A. Diploma in Nursing, Hosp. St. Raphael Sch. Nursing, 1964; BSN, Cath. U. Am., 1967, MSN, 1979. Staff nurse Greater S.E. Community Hosp., Washington, 1970-72, asst. head nurse, 1972-75; nurse assoc. Guy W. Gargour, M.D., Bethesda, Md., 1975-76; lectr. Prince George's Community Coll., Largo, Md., 1975-78; asst. dir. nursing So. Md. Hosp. Ctr., Clinton, 1977-82, dir. planning, 1982-85; nursing adminstr. Parkwood Hosp., Clinton, 1985-86; staff nurse Phsycians Meml. Hosp., La Plata, Md., 1986-88; prof. Charles County C.C., La Plata, from 1988. Nurse cons. Nancy C. Taber, Ft. Washington, Md., 1983-85. Pres. Brandywine (Md.) Dem. Club, 1979, 88, Brandywine Heights Citizens Assn., 1980—; vice chmn. So. Md. Health Systems Agy., Clinton, 1985-90. St. Raphaels Hosp. scholar, 1964. Mem. ANA, Acad. of Med.-Surg. Nursing, Orgn. for the Advancement Assoc. Degree Nursing, Md. Nurses Assn. (bd. dirs. 1989—, dist. 9 sec. 1995—), Lioness (3d v.p. Brandywine chpt. 1985-86, pres. 1994—), Sigma Theta Tau. Roman Catholic. Avocations: crocheting, dance. Home: Brandywine, Md. Died June 17, 2005.

GAMMON, REGINALD ADOLPHUS, arts and humanities educator, artist; b. Phila., Mar. 31, 1921; s. Reginald Adolphus and Martha Mahtilda (Brown) G.; m. Janice Barbara Goldberger, Sept. 13, 1974; children: Regina Lee, Patrick L. King. Grad., Phila. Mus. Coll. Art, 1949, Tyler Sch. Fine Arts, 1951. Artist in residence SOMPSEC, Bklyn., Bd. Edn., N.Y.C., 1969; prof. arts and humanities Western Mich. U., Kalamazoo, 1970-90, prof. emeritus, 1991—2005. Free lance artist, N.Y.C., 1962-69; lectr. in field. Exhibited in group shows at Kalamazoo Black Fine Arts Competition (1st prize 1990), Krasl Art Ctr. Kalamazoo Area Pastel Soc., Carnegie Ctr. for the Arts. With USN, 1944-46, PTO. Mem. Kalamazoo Black Arts and Cultural Com. (cons. 1987—2005), Arts Coun. Greater Kalamazoo (creative artists grant 1990-2005). Episcopalian. Avocations: photography, dance, volleyball. Home: Albuquerque, N.Mex. Died Nov. 3, 2005.

GANSKOPP, WILLIAM FREDRICK, oil company executive; b. Nanticoke, Pa., July 24, 1915; s. Herman and Ida Helene (Hecht) G.; m. Neale Irene Crosby, July 9, 1942; children: Jennifer Winell, Daryl Stephen. AB in Physics, Lafayette Coll., 1938; diploma in advanced mgmt., Northwestern U., Caracas, Venezuela, 1960. Engr. Standard Oil Co. of N.J., Elizabeth, 1938-42; capt. 703d engrs., Africa, Italy, 1942-45; gas engr. Creole Petroleum Corp., Caracas, Venezuela, 1946-51, mgr. gas sect., 1954-62, drilling engr. Jusepin, Venezuela, 1952-54; natural gas dept. head Esso Nederland, Hague, The Netherlands, 1962-65; natural gas exec. Esso Ea., Sydney, Australia, 1965-68; pres. Gan-Ed, Inc., Columbus, N.C., 1970-78, chief exec. officer, 1978-81; dir., cons. Owosso Gan, Inc., Gainesville, Fla., from 1981. Author: Despite The Odds, 1998; patentee self-propelled golf cart; patentee in Can., Japan and Mex. Recipient Barge Math. award Lafayette Coll., Easton, Pa., 1936, citation MTO, Livorno, Italy. Mem. Ret. Officers Assn. (life, program chmn. 1981-82), Gainesville Golf and Country Club, Masons. Republican. Lutheran. Avocations: golf, tennis, bridge, chess. Died Jan. 29, 2004.

GARBARINO, ROBERT PAUL, retired dean; b. Wanaque, N.J., Oct. 6, 1929; s. Attillio and Theresa (Napello) G.; m. Joyce A. Sullivan, June 29, 1957; children: Lynn, Lisa, Mark, Steven. BBA cum laude, St. Bonaventure U., 1951; JD with highest class honors, Villanova U., 1956. Bar: Pa. 1956, U.S. Dist. Ct. (ea. dist.) Pa. 1956, U.S. Ct. Appeals (3d cir.) 1962, U.S. Supreme Ct. 1962, U.S. Tax Ct. 1966, U.S. Ct. Internat. Trade 1966. Law clk. U.S. Dist. Ct. (ea. dist.) Pa., Phila., 1956-57; asst. counsel Phila. Electric Co., Phila., 1957-60, asst. gen. counsel, 1960-62; ptnr. Kania & Garbarino & predecessor firm, Phila. and Bala Cynwyd, Pa., 1962-81; assoc. dean adminstrn. Sch. Law Villanova (Pa.) U., 1981-96. Right-of-way cons. Edison Electric Inst., N.Y.C., 1960—62; trustee reorgn. Tele-Tronics Co., Phila., 1962—64; mem. bd. consultors Law Sch. Villanova U., 1967—81, mem. bd. consultors (life mem.), 1996—2003, chmn., vice chmn. bd. consultors, 1971—76; chmn. Profl. Sports Career Counseling Panel Villanova U.; mem. pres.'s adv. coun. St. Bonaventure U., NY, 1975—86, chmn., 1976—78. Contbr. articles to profl. jours.; 1st editor-in-chief Villanova U. Law Rev., 1954. Mem. community leadership seminar Fels Inst. Local and State Govt., 1961. Staff sgt. USMC, 1951-53. Mem. ABA, Phila. Bar Assn., Order of Coif. Home: Devon, Pa. Died Mar. 8, 2005.

GARCIA, HOWARD ALEXANDER, physicist; b. Denver, May 4, 1929; s. Seneca Barrios and Susan Josephine (Martinez) G.; m. Nancy Jean Porter, May, 1954 (div. 1958); children: Steven, Mark; m. Doris Lorraine Rock, Sept. 24, 1960; children: Britt, Lorraine. BS in Civil Engring., U. Colo., 1952; PhD in Astronomy, Georgetown U., 1970. Engr. Autometric Ops. Raytheon, Alexandria, Va., 1960-70, Martin Marietta Aerospace, Denver, 1970-76; physicist Space Environment Lab., Boulder, from 1976. Contbr. articles to Solar Physics, Geophysical Rsch. Letters, Astron. Jour., Ad vanced Space Rsch. and others. Lt. U.S. Coast and Geodetic Survey, 1952-60. Mem. Am. Astron. Soc., Am. Geophys. Union (treas. Front Range Br. 1989-90). Democrat. Home: Boulder, Colo. Died July 25, 2005.

GARDNER, JERRY LOUIS, JR., lawyer; b. New Orleans, Oct. 25, 1932; s. Jerome Louis and Marguerite F. (Marcour) G.; m. Gayle June Gardner, Dec. 27, 1958; children: Ylon M., Kevin M. BA, Tulane U., 1954, JD, 1960. Bar: La. 1960, U.S. Dist. Ct. (mid., ea., and we. dists.) La. 1960, U.S. Ct. Apls. (5th cir.) 1960, U.S. Ct. Apls. (D.C. cir.) 1974, U.S. Ct. Apls. (11th cir.) 1981, U.S. Supreme Ct. 1973. Atty. NLRB, 1960-67; ptnr. Barker, Boudreaux, Lamy, Gardner & Foley, New Orleans, 1967-84; ptnr. Gardner, Robein & Urann, 1984-92; mediator U.S. arbitration and mediation Gulf South, Inc., 1992—; lectr. Tulane U., Loyola U., La. State U.; co-chmn. continuing legal edn. com. La. State Bar, past chmn. labor law sect. Served to capt. USAF, 1954-57. Mem. ABA (council labor and employment law sect.), La. Bar Assn., New Orleans Bar Assn. Roman Catholic. Home: New Orleans, La. Died Apr. 28, 2005.

GARDNER, ROBERT HARRY, public relations consultant; b. Chgo., May 21, 1913; s. Harry Montgomery and Virginia Robinson (Jones) G.; m. Jean Seymour, Dec. 2, 1950; children: George S., Elizabeth M. BA, Amherst Coll., 1936. Radio writer Ruthrauff & Ryan Advt., Chgo., 1938-42; account exec. Mitchell McKeown Orgn., Chgo., 1942-47; ptnr. Gardner & Jones, Chgo., 1947-60; chmn. Gardner, Jones & Co., Inc., Chgo., 1960-79; sr. cons. Hill and Knowlton, Inc., Chgo., from 1979; owner Spl. Assignment Pub. Rels., Chgo., from 1980. Author: (with W. Lloyd Pressel) Supervision for Empowered Workers, 1992, The New Creators of Empowered Workers, 1993. Trustee Symphony of Oak Park and River Forest, Ill., 1990—. With AUS, 1943-46. Fellow Pub. Rels. Soc. Am. (accredited, chmn. accreditation bd. 1975, chmn. counselors acad. 1973); mem. Publicity Club Chgo. (v.p. 1962), Univ. Club Chgo. (sec. 1971). Home: Holland, Mich. Died Apr. 2, 2005.

GARFIELD, GENIE MAY, rancher; b. Forsyth, Mont., June 28, 1921; d. Malcolm Kenneth and Edith May (Cox) Philbrick; m. Russell Merritt Garfield, May 11, 1943 (wid. Oct. 1982); 1 child, Debra Garfield Bangs. Student, Mont. State U., 1938-40. Admissions asst. Carleton Coll., Northfield, Minn., 1940-41; sec. 2d Air Force Hdqrs., Spokane, Wash., 1941-45; rancher, from 1972. Bd. dirs. 1st INterstate Bank, Colstrip, Mont., 1985 --. Bd. dirs. Hinsdale (N.H.) Sch. Bd., 1958-69, No. Plains Resource Coun., Billings, Mont.; chmn. Bottom Line Rider, 1984—, Hinsdale Nursing Assn., 1968-72; active Rosebud Co. Planning Bd. Forsyth, Mont., 1974-81, Hinsdale Woman's Club, 1953-73. Recipient Conservation Achievement award Soil Conservation Dist. Rosebud Co., Forsyth, Mount., 1990. Died Apr. 20, 2004.

GARFINKLE, LOUIS ALAN, screenwriter; b. Seattle, Feb. 11, 1928; s. Louis and Golda (Himelhoch) G.; m. Audrey Elyse Alpert, Aug. 6, 1958; children: Wendy Cane, Luane Davis, Gwynne. BA, U. So. Calif., Los Angeles, 1948. Writer Sta. KOMO, Seattle, 1945, Sta. KMPC, L.A., 1948; screenwriter, producer Allied Artists, L.A., 1956-58, United Artists, L.A., 1957; TV writer Selmur Prodns., Inc., L.A., 1958-66; screenwriter Rosamond Prodns., Inc., L.A., 1971-74, Am. Internat., L.A., 1973, EMI, Beverly Hills, Calif., 1974-80, Won Five, Inc., L.A., from 1978. Co-founder Collaborator Systems Inc., 1989. Screenwriter films The Young Guns, 1957, I Bury the Living, 1958, Face of Fire, 1959, A Minute To Pray, A Second To Die, 1967, The Doberman Gang, 1971, Little Cigars, 1973, The Deer Hunter, 1978 (Acad. award nominee); playwright Broadway musical Molly, 1973, one-man show I Shall Return, 1975; co-developer Collaborator computer software screenplay elements. With Signal Corps, U.S. Army, 1950-52. Mem. Writers Guild Am., Acad. Motion Picture Arts and Scis., Dramatists Guild, Acad. TV Arts and Scis., PEN. Democrat. Jewish. Died Oct. 10, 2005.

GARNETT, WILLIAM A., photographer; b. Chgo., 1916; Student, Art Center Sch. of Los Angeles, 1937-38. Freelance advt. and mag. photographer, including aerial photography, 1938—. Prof. design U. Calif.-Berkeley, 1968-84, prof. emeritus, 1984-2006; fellow Ctr. for Advanced Visual Studies, MIT, 1967; appeared on TV programs The Pursuit of Happiness, NBC, 1976, From Here to There, CBS, 1980, Evening Mag, CBS, 1981; illustrator, collaborator: The American Aesthetic (Nathanial Owings), 1968; author, photographer: The Extraordinary Landscape, 1982, William Garnett Aerial Photographs, 1994. Exhibited in one-man shows including George Eastman House, Rochester, N.Y., 1955, numerous group shows in U.S. and abroad including Mus. Modern Art, N.Y.C., Met. Mus. Art, San Francisco Mus. Art, White House, 1979, Smithsonian Instn. Air and Space Mus. of Aerial Photography, Washington, 1979, also at several world fairs; represented in permanent collections George Eastman House, Mus. Modern Art, Smithsonian Instn., Polaroid Collection, Cambridge, Mass., Met. Mus. Art, N.Y.C., Gilman Paper Co., N.Y.C.; works include: photo mural for Wrigley Stadium, Los Angeles, 1938, two essays on beauty of America as seen from the air for Life Mag., 1965, numerous mag. articles. Recipient award Am. Soc. Mag. Photographers, 1983 Home: Napa, Calif. Died Aug. 24, 2006.

GARRETY, FRANCES, poet; b. York, Pa., Sept. 27, 1962; d. David and Mary Jo Garrety. Contbr. (poetry and artwork) Many Voices Mag., Survivorship Mag., (poetry to anthologies) Poetic Voices of America, 1990, Mirrors of the Mind, 1998 (3d pl. award), Ages and Stages Anthology, 1999, Best Poems and Poets of 20th Century, 2000; contbr.: poetry to CD Sounds of Poetry, 2003. Recipient Editor's Choice award, Nat. Libr. of Poetry, 1998. Mem.: Internat. Soc. Poets (Poet of Merit award, medal and silver cup 2002, Outstanding Achievement in poetry silver cup and medal 2003). Avocations: writing, artwork, sock monkeys. Home: Bellefonte, Pa. Died July 30, 2004.

GARRIS, JACK JOHN, lawyer; b. N.Y.C., Oct. 16, 1919; s. John and Constance (Maniatakos) Garatzogeane; m. Helen Cazepis, Sept. 26, 1948; children: Michael Jack, Jacalen J., Steven Zachary. BA, U. Mich., 1946; JD, George Washington U., 1951. Cir. ct. commr. Washtenaw County, Ann Arbor, Mich., from 1951. County supr. Ann Arbor, 1955—; cand. for Mayor, Ann Arbor, 1969. Sgt. USAF., 1942-46. Mem. Mich. Hellenic Bar Assn. (past pres.), Am.

Trial Lawyers Assn., Mich. Trial Lawyers Assn. (bd. dirs. 1985), Washtenaw County Bar Assn. Republican. Mem. Greek Orthodox Ch. Home: Ann Arbor, Mich. Died Feb. 21, 2005.

GARRISON, DAVID LACEY, JR., oil industry executive; b. Houston, July 12, 1945; s. David Lacey and Marie Bel (Gardiner) G.; m. Pamela Jean Reid Adger, Mar. 7, 1970 (div. July 1975); 1 child, James Gardiner; m. Robin Childers, Apr. 2, 1977; children: Robert Adam, Susan Alexandra. LLD, La Academia Mexicana, Mexico City, 1991. Landman Chapman Oil Co., Houston, 1978; ptnr. J.A. Bel et al, Lake Charles, La., 1964—2006; pres. Garrison Oil Co., Houston, 1979—84, Lakeside Exploration Corp., Houston, 1984—2006. V.p., bd. dirs. Lacassane Co., Inc., Lake Charles, 1990—. La. commr. of Indian Affairs, Baton Rouge, 1972—75; vice-chmn. Sam Houston Area coun. Boy Scouts Am., from 1995, bd. dirs. So. Region, from 1999; bd. dirs. Nat. Cath. Com. on Scouting, 1997—2001. Decorated knight comdr. Pontificial Order St. Gregory the Gt. (Vatican City), knight grand cross Equestrian Order of the Holy Sepulchre, knight grand cross with gold star with collar Sacred Mil. Constantinian Order of St. George, knight sovereign Mil. Order of Malta (Rome), knight of justice Most Venerable Order of St. John (U.K.). Roman Catholic. Avocations: hunting, fishing. Home: Houston, Tex. Died Jan. 25, 2006.

GARRY, MICHAEL JOSEPH, dentist; b. Terre Haute, Ind., Sept. 29, 1953; s. Robert Francis and Betty Lou (Lagemann) G.; m. Patricia Lynn Baker, May 18, 1975; children: Jennifer Lynn, Sarah Marie, Joseph Ryan. BS cum laude, Ind. State U., 1975; DDS, Ind. U., Indpls., 1979. Gen. practice dentistry, Terre Haute, Ind., 1979-87, Greenwood, Ind., from 1988. Teaching clinician extramural programs Ind. U. Dental Sch., Indpls., 1979—; mem. dental audit com. Union Hosp., Terre Haute, 1980-86. Vol. dentist Indigent Care Program, Vigo County, Ind., 1979-86, League of Terre Haute, 1979-87. Mem. ADA, Western Ind. Dental Soc. (bd. dirs. 1985—), Ind. Dental Assn., Indpls. Dist. Dental soc. Lodges: Elks. Democrat. Baptist. Avocations: golf, tennis, fox hunting. Home: Greenwood, Ind. Died May 10, 2005.

GARTNER, CHARLES HARRISON, retired obstetrician, gynecologist; b. Covington, Ky., June 24, 1942; s. Joseph Charles and Mary Aleen (Stamper) G.; m. Eileen Shirlee Mann, Jan. 26, 1968 (div. Jan. 1974); 1 child, Gayle Marie. BS, Xavier U., 1964; MD, Northwestern U., 1968. Diplomate Am. Bd. Ob-Gyn. Practice medicine specializing in ob-gyn, Denver, from 1972. Fellow Am. Coll. Obstetricians Gynecologists, Am. Assn. Gynecol. Laparoscopists, Am. Fertility Soc.; mem. Colo. Med. Soc., Clean Creek Valley Med. Soc. Democrat. Home: Denver, Colo. Died Nov. 13, 2004.

GARY, NANCY ELIZABETH, nephrologist, academic administrator; b. NYC, Mar. 4, 1937; d. Walter Joseph and Charlotte Elizabeth (Sayer) G. BS, Springfield Coll., Mass., 1958; MD, Med. Coll. Pa., 1962. Diplomate Am. Bd. Internal Medicine, Am. Bd. Nephrology. Resident Nassau County Med. Ctr., East Meadow, N.Y., 1962-64, St. Vincent's Hosp. and Med. Ctr., N.Y.C., 1964-65, chief renal sect., 1967-74; fellow in nephrology Georgetown U. Med. Ctr., Washington, 1965-67; instr. medicine NYU Sch. Medicine, N.Y.C., 1968-74; asst. prof. U. Medicine and Dentistry of N.J.-Rutgers Med. Sch., Piscataway, 1974-76, assoc. prof., 1976-81, prof., 1981-88, assoc. dean, 1981-87, exec. assoc. dean, 1987-88; dean Albany (N.Y.) Med. Coll., 1988-90; sr. med. adv. to adminstr. health care financing HHS, Washington, 1990-92; clin. prof. medicine George Washington U. Sch. Medicine, from 1991; prof. medicine Uniformed Svcs. U. Health Scis., Bethesda, Md., from 1992, exec. v.p., dean Sch. Medicine, 1992-95, dean emeritus, 1996—2006; clin. prof. Howard U. Coll. Medicine, Washington, 1992—2006; pres., CEO Ednl. Commn. Fgn. Med. Grads., Phila., 1995—2001. Contbr. chpts. to books, articles to profl. jours. Robert Wood Johnson Health Policy fellow NAS Inst. Medicine, 1987-88; recipient Joseph F. Boyle, M.D. award for Disting. Pub. Svc., Am. Soc. Internal Medicine, 1992, Meritorious Svc. award, George Washington U. Sch. Medicine, 1995 Mem. ACP (Master), AMA, Nat. Kidney Found., Alpha Omega Alpha. Home: Washington, DC. Died May 31, 2006.

GASPER, LOUIS, sociology educator; b. Lorain, Ohio, Feb. 10, 1911; s. Daniel and Matilda (Cinders) G.; m. Nellie Mabel Kremer, Mar. 27, 1943. DGB, Moody Bible Inst., 1940; BA cum laude, Bowling Green State U., 1947, BS in Edn. cum laude, 1947, MA, 1949; BDiv, Findlay Coll. Grad. Sch. Divinity, 1954; PhD in Am. culture, Case Western Res. U., Cleve., 1958; AMEd, U. So. Calif., 1962; MAc Arts and PhD, Am. Coll. Acupuncture, 1966; MDiv, Winebrenner Theol. Sem., 1968. Ordained to ministry, Bapt. Ch., 1940. With U.S. Steel Corp., 1929-38; minister various chs., Ill., Ohio, 1939-57; tchr. Fostoria (Ohio) High Sch., 1945-47; assoc. prof. history Bluffton Coll., 1949-50; assoc. prof. Florence (Ala.) State U. (name changed to Northern Ala. U.), 1957-58; tchr. L.A. City Schs., 1958-59; assoc. prof. Humboldt State U., Calif., 1959-60; assoc. prof. sociology dir. elem. edn. L.A. Pacific Coll. (name changed to Azusa Pacific Coll.), 1961-63; prof. sociology, chair. dept. sociology L.A. Pierce Coll., 1963-76, emeritus prof., dept. chair, from 1976. Prof. sociology, chair dept. philosophy edn. and sociology, 1967-76; pres. faculty assn., 1967-68; chair acad. senate, 1967-68; sr. mem. curriculum com., 1973-76; asst prof. Calif. State U., Northridge, part-time, 1964-67; assoc. prof. Calif. State U., L.A., 1967-71, Long Beach, 1971-73, mem. Emeriti and Retired Family, 1989; mem. rsch. staff U. So. Calif., 1965-68; marriage, family and child counselor, 1963—; intern Am. Inst. Family Rels., Hollywood, Calif., 1963-65, asst. staff assoc., 1965—; coord. Acupuncture Rsch. Inst., sec., dir., 1977—, others; pres. L.A. Internat. U, Samuel Hahnemann Sch. Homoeopathic Medicine. Author: The Fundamentalist Movement, 1963, Introduction to Sociology, 1965, Fundamentals of Sociology, 1966, 2d edit. 1969, Vital Social Problems, 1967; co-author: Harry Elmer Barnes Learned Crusader, 1968, Sociology Syllabus and Readings in Sociology, 1964; contbg. author chpts. to books; contbr. articles to profl. jours. Dual ministerial rel. with United Ch. of Christ, 1962, ARC; com. mem. in formation of the Advanced Med. Aide Corps Cuyahoga County Civil Def. and Cleve. Acad., 1956; Red Cross disaster trainer NASA in Reynoldlite Aluminum Rocket Plant, Tuscumbia, Ala., 1957; appointed by Gov. Wilson Calif. Blue Ribbon Com. for Scope of Practice for acupuncture, 1992. Mem. United Acupuncturists of Calif. (English speaking chmn. bd., 1978—), Am. Sociol. Assn. (emeritus), Acupuncture Rsch. Inst. Alumni Assn. (editor A.R.I. Meridian), Homoepathic Med. Assn. Am. (pres. 1985), Am. Assn. Acupuncture and Oriental Medicine (founder 1981), Calif. Assn. Marriage Counselors (charter, life), Pierce Coll. Faculty Assn. (pres. 1967-68), Group Psychotherapy Assn., So. Calif. Book and Motor Soc. (Bowling Green State U.), Gold Card Peace Officers Assn. (life), Phi Kappa Phi, Alpha Kappa Delta, Kappa Delta Pi. Home: Monterey Park, Calif. Died Dec. 16, 2004.

GASTLER, HAROLD LEE, railroad executive; b. Wellsville, Mo., May 16, 1927; s. Leo J. and Thelma L. (Oliver) G.; m. Joyce D. Isman, Sept. 13, 1952; 1 son, Kim Leigh. BS in Engring., U. Mo., 1951; grad., Advanced Mgmt. Program, Harvard U., 1962. With Frisco R.R., 1951-66, v.p. staff, 1962-63, gen. mgr., 1963-66; pres. Toledo, Peoria & Western R.R., Peoria, Ill., 1966-67; v.p. ops. Chgo. & Northwestern R.R., Chgo., 1968-73; pres., chief operating officer Missouri-Kansas-Texas R.R. Co., Dallas, 1973—88, also bd. dirs. Served to ensign USN, 1945-46. Democrat. Lutheran. Died Dec. 25, 2005.

GATCH, FRANCES ANNE, retired small business owner; d. Owen Thomas King and Mary Allie Foster; m. Ronald Vernon Gatch, Sept. 25, 1976 (div. June 6, 2002); 1 child, Diane Michelle. AA, Daytona Beach Jr. Coll., Fla., 1975—79. Bus. co-owner AiReed Filter Products, Daytona Beach, 1972—2000; ret. Author: (genealogy record) The Gatch Family of South Carolina. Mem., pres., state dir. Daytona Beach Jaycee Aux., 1974—82; mem., v.p., sec. Bonner Elem. PTA, Daytona Beach, 1986—92; mem., pres. Halifax River Toastmistress Club, Daytona Beach, 1978—81. Named Woman of the Yr., Daytona Beach Jaycee Aux., 1977, Jayceette of the Yr., Daytona Beach Jaycees, 1979, Outstanding Young Women of Am., 1980; recipient Outstanding Aux. award, Daytona Beach Jaycee Aux., 1979, Today's Woman Essay award, Fla. Jaycee Aux., 1979, Golden Apple award, Bonner Elem. PTA, 1991, Outstanding Young Women of Am., 1980. Mem.: Phi Theta Kappa. Avocations: needlepoint, reading. Home: Chattanooga, Tenn. Died Sept. 17, 2004.

GATES, CARMEN JEAN WEGENER, animal behaviorist; b. Bismarck, N.D., Aug. 20, 1940; d. John Berry and Claribel Ruth (McGoon) Wegener; m. Wayne Robert Gates, July 7, 1962; children: Paul Brian, Stacy Lynn, Michael Wayne. Student, Madison Coll., 1958-59, Am. U., 1960-61, No. Va. C.C., 1985-86, student, 2000. Cert. behavior cons. Auburn U. Coll. Vet. Medicine, 2003. Dental asst. pvt. practice dental offices, Arlington, Va., 1961-64; vet. technician pvt. practice vet. office, Springfield, Va., 1965-66, Fairfax, Va., 1966-67; obedience instr. Dulles Gateway Obedience Club, Sterling and Herndon, Va., 1971—2001; floral designer various florists, Fairfax, Va., 1987-89; obedience instr., animal behavior cons. Dulles Gateway Kennels, Chantilly, Va., 1990—93, Old Mill Kennels, Leesburg, Va., 1991—93; tchr. obedience classes, animal behavior cons., dog trainer, Gt. Falls, Va. Expert witness in animal behavior cases, Fairfax County; instr. obedience No. Va. C.C., Annandale, 1990—91, Herndon Cmty. Ctr., 1990—91, South Run Recreation Ctr., Burke, Va., 1989-93, Pender Vet. Clinic, Fairfax, 1992—97; tng. dir. Old Dominion Animal Health Ctr., McLean, Va., 1997-2001; lectr. in field; cons. in field. Mem. chancel choir Great Falls (Va.) Meth. Ch. Recipient Companion Dog Degree Am. Kennel Club, 1971, 73, 83, Companion Dog Excellent degree Am. Kennel Club, 1972, 77, 89. Mem. Nat. Assn. Dog Obedience Instrs., Assn. Pet Dog Trainers, Assn. for Behavior Analysis (trainers forum), Dulles Gateway Obedience Tng. Assn. (v.p. 1972, bd. dirs. 1973, tng. dir. 1980). Avocations: bowling, golf, gardening, training show dogs. Home: Great Falls, Va. Died Oct. 11, 2004.

GAUGHAN, JOHN JAMES, radiation oncologist; b. Leetonia, Ohio, May 14, 1922; s. Michael Joseph and Jessie J. (Gallagher) G.; m. Alma Marie; children: Marcia, Sharon, Patricia, Kathleen, Maureen. BS, Adelbert Coll. of Case Western Res. U., Cleve., 1943; MD, St. Louis U., 1946. Diplomate Am. Bd. Radiology. Intern St. John's Hosp., Cleve., 1946-47; resident Chile VA Hosp., Cleve., 1949-52; radiologist Lakewood (Ohio) Hosp., 1952-57, St. John Hosp., 1957-81; radiation oncologist Med. Ctr. Radiologists Luth. Med. Ctr., Cleve., from 1981. Chmn. bd. dirs. Physician Ins. Co. Ohio and subs. cos., Pickerington; bd. dirs. Fla. Physician Ins. Co., Jacksonville, Fla. Physician Ins. Co., Indpls. Served to capt. AUS, 1947-49, PTO. Fellow Am. Coll. Radiology; mem. AMA (del.), Am. Soc. Radiation Oncologists, Radiol. Soc. N.Am., Eastern Radiol. Soc., Ohio State Med. Assn. (pres. 1978-79), Acad. Medicine of Cuyahoga County, Acad. Medicine of Cleve. (pres. 1973-74). Clubs: Westwood Country (Rocky River, Ohio). Avocations: golf, bridge. Home: Cleveland, Ohio. Died Jan. 23, 2004.

GAUTHIER, MARY ELIZABETH, librarian, researcher, secondary education educator; b. Tudor, Alta., Can., May 17, 1917; d. Harold Bertram and Mary Evelyn (Foley) Bliss; m. Louis Lyons Gauthier, May 31, 1947 (dec. 1976). PhB, Northwestern U., 1970; MA in Edn., Lewis U., 1976; EdD, Pacific States U., London, 1979. Clk. LaGrange (Ill.) Pub. Libr., 1956-57; package libr. AMA, Chgo., 1958-60; staff libr. Duff, Anderson & Clark, Chgo., 1960-63; libr./tchr. Fremont Sch. Dist. 79, Mundelein, Ill., 1970-75; substitute tchr. Valleyview Sch. Dist. 365-U, Romeoville, Ill., 1978-89; dormitory dir./tchr. Project Upward Bound, Romeoville, Ill., 1984-94, enrichment studies, 1991-94; ind. researcher South Bend, Ind., 1990-94. Instr. Joliet (Ill.) Jr. Coll., 1986-89; cons. Wash. High Sch.; bd. of advisors Ivy Tech. Coll., Southbend, 1993 Author: Some Basic Principles of New Scientific Attitudes in Education, 1980, Communication: Roots of Tradition, 1986; contbr. monograph and articles to profl. jours. Active Manor Pk. Community Assn., Ottawa, Can., 1953. With RCAF, 1943-45. Recipient Gold medal Internat. Symposium on the Mgmt. of Stress, Monte Carlo, 1979; grantee Ill. State Bd. Edn., 1985, Ind. U. South Bend, 1992. Mem. AAAS, N.Y. Acad. Scis. Died Jan. 18, 2004.

GEE, JIMWAH, aerospace eineer; b. Canton, People's Republic of China, May 15, 1926; came to U.S., 1941; s. George Yow and Kay Hing (Wong) G.; m. Helen Borhun Chan, Jan 28, 1951; children: Kelvin Wellman, Dolly Maizie. BS in Aerospace Engring., Northrop Inst. Tech., 1953. Cert. supersonic aerodynamics, computer graphics. Analyst wind tunnel, missile devel. divsn. Rockwell Internat., L.A., 1954-64, wind tunnel test engr. rocketdyne divsn. Canoga Park, 1964-66, engr., computing space divsn. Downey, Calif., 1966-70, escape system aero-engr. Los Angeles, 1971-79; acting tech. dir. Rockwell Internat. Advt. in Taiwan and China, Pitts., from 1978; space shuttle test engr. space transp. system divsn. Rockwell Internat., Downey, 1979-82, weapon separation aero-engr. North Am. A/C ops. divsn. El Segundo, Calif., from 1982; sr. engr. Rockwell Internat. Corp., L.A., from 1986. Contbr. articles to profl. jours. Chmn. bd. dirs. Chinese-Am. Welfare Council, L.A., 1976-78; vice-chmn. Community Welfare Com., L.A., 1973-74. With USNR, 1944-46, Iwo Jima. Recipient Indo-China Refugee Sponsorship award U.S. Dept. State, 1975-76. Mem. Rockwell Mgmt. Assn., Inst. Aeronautical Sci., Chinese-Am. Engrs. and Scientists Assn. So. Calif. (acting pres. 1971-72), Gee Poy Kuo Assn. (scholarship chmn. 1984—, Service award 1976), Am. Legion (life). Democrat. Mem. Confucian Ch. Home: La Puente, Calif. Died Oct. 28, 2004.

GEER, DAISY GEE, retired women's health nurse; b. Marks, Miss., July 22, 1933; d. Harry and Chong (See) Joe; m. Lawrence W.Y. Eng, July 28, 1956 (div.); children: Lawrence Phillip, Katherine Eng Gillentine, Curtis, Linda Eng Cox; m. F. George Geer, Feb. 28, 1975 (dec. May 1979). BSN, U. Houston, 1955; postgrad., Tex. Woman's U.; cert. in nursing, Harris County Community Coll., Houston, 1989. Float nurse Baylor U. Med. Ctr./Women & Children's Hosp., Dallas, 1961-64; relief charge nurse Yale Clinic & Hosp., Houston, 1969-78; office nurse Dr. Paul McGuff, Houston, 1978-79; pvt. duty nurse Personal Care Home Health Agy., Baytown, Tex., 1990-91; with Exxon Food Mart, 1991-92, ret., 1992. Died Mar. 12, 2004.

GEGELIYA, DMITRIY ILICH, chemist, researcher; b. Tbilisi, Republic of Georgia, May 24, 1933; came to U.S., 1993; s. Ilia Gegeliya and Ketevan Dahulabishvili; 1 child, Ketevan; m. Tamara Boguslavskaya, April 21, 1987. Engr., Tech. U., Tbilisi, 1958; PhD, Postgrad. Cours, Moscow, 1974. Engr. Road Project Inst., Tbilisi, 1958-61; sr. engr. Phys. Chem. Inst., Moscow, 1961-63; sr. rschr. Road Rsch. Inst., Moscow, 1963-80, lab. chief, 1980-83, dep. dir. Tbilisi, 1983-93. Prof. Peninsula Inst., Mountain View, Calif., 1995. Author: Asphalt Concrete Pavement for Roads, Bridges and Airports, 1978 (Gold medal 1981), Directions for Optimal Regime of Asphalt Concrete Production, Storage and Transportation, 1989. Mem. Ho. of Scientists (pres. 1996), Internat. Acad. Scis., Edn. Industry & Arts (pres. 1997). Roman Catholic. Avocations: wood decoration, inlay. Home: San Francisco, Calif. Died Dec. 9, 2004.

GEISEL, SAMUEL GEORGE, systems analyst; b. Banks Twp., Pa., Feb. 24, 1944; s. William James and Kathryn Louise (Tyger) G.; m. Ruby Eileen Snyder, Nov. 2, 1968; children: Katrena Evon, Kara Elena. AA, SUNY, Albany, 1973; BA, U. Md. European Div., 1984. Enlisted man U.S. Army, 1966, advanced through grades to chief warrant officer Vietnam and other sites, 1978, ret., 1986; systems analyst Cordatum, Inc., Bethesda, Md., 1986-87, Systems and Applied Scis. Corp., Rockville, Md., 1987-89; sr. programmer, analyst DelTek Systems, Inc., McLean, Va., from 1989. Mem. Assn. U.S. Army, Ret. Officers Assn., Am. Legion, Mensa, Intertel. Republican. Home: Woodbridge, Va. Died Jan. 19, 2005.

GEIST, ELTON WERNER, metal processing executive, metallurgist; b. Hyde County, S.D., Mar. 5, 1921; s. Samuel Edwin and Ethel May (Mesick) G.; m. Doris Virginia

Roeser, July 9, 1941; children: Gregg D., Daille C. Geist Pettit. BS in Metall. Engring., S.D. Sch. Mines and Tech., 1947. Registered profl. engr., Ohio. Miner Homestake Mining Co., Lead, S.D., 1941-42; metall. engr. Nat. Lead Co., Tahawus, N.Y., 1947-49; plant supt. Telluride (Colo.) Mines, Inc., 1949-51; mgr. M.A. Hanna Co., Cleve., 1951-66; pres. Midland Standard, Inc., Cleve., from 1966, also bd. dirs. Bd. dirs. Mineral Services, Inc., Cleve. Author: (technical papers) Beneficiation Plant Design, 1968, Magnetic Separation, 1983, Magnetic Separator Design, 1986. Pres. Iron Mountain-Kingsford C. of C., Iron Mountain, 1962; elder Old Stone Ch., Cleve., 1982. Recipient 100 Centennial award S.D. Sch. Mines and Tech., Rapid City, 1985. Mem. Colo. Mining Assn., Soc. Mining Engrs., Can. Inst. Mining and Metallurgy, AIME (chmn. Upper Peninsula chpt., Iron Mountain, Mich. 1958), Greater Cleve. Growth Assn. Clubs: Six Continents (N.Y.C.); University (Cleve.). Republican. Home: Cleveland, Ohio. Died July 29, 2004.

GELFAND, M. DAVID, law educator; b. Buffalo, N.Y., Aug. 12, 1949; m. Mary Fondren, Dec. 26, 1971; 1 child, Katherine Marie BA, Columbia U., 1971, JD, 1976; M.Phil., Oxford U., Eng., 1974. Bar: Fla. 1977, N.Y. 1979, U.S. Ct. Appeals (3d, 5th, 11th and fed. cirs.), U.S. Supreme Ct. Cons. practice, La., Fla. and N.Y., from 1977; instr., spl. lectr. Law Sch. U. Miami, Fla., 1977-78; prof. law Tulane U., New Orleans, 1978—2005, C.J. Morrow research prof., 1984-85; vis. assoc. prof. Pace U., White Plains, N.Y., 1981-82; exec. dir. Ctr. Legal Studies on Intergovtl. Rels., New Orleans, 1982-89; dir. Appellate Advocacy Program Tulane U., 1988-92; vis. scholar Nuffield Coll. Oxford U., Eng., 1983; spl. master in voting rights U.S. Dist. Ct., New Orleans, 1983, U.S. Dist. Ct. (so. dist.) Fla., 1992. Lectr. on civil rights, aging, local govt. finance in U.S., Asia, Africa, Europe; panelist at field hearing U.S. Ho. of Reps. Select Com. on Aging, 1985; witness at field hearing Citizens' Commn. on Civil Rights, Phoenix, 1985; Fulbright sr. lectr. in constnl. law, Japan, 1987; expert witness mcpl. fin., 1987, 90; lead cons. on voting rights issues to N.Y.C. Charter Revision Commn., 1987-89; expert witness on civil rights, 1992, land use, 1992; court appointed ind. expert reapportionment Congl. Dists. Fla. U.S. Dist. Ct. No. Dist. Fla., 1992. Author: Federal Constitutional Law and American Local Government, 1984; co-author: State and Local Taxation and Finance, 1985. Editor: State and Local Government Debt Financing, 3 vols., 1985, plus ann. supplements; A Half Century of Municipal Decline, 1985; contbr. articles to profl. publs. Mem. due process com. ACLU, 1976-84; New Orleans City Planning Commn., 1986-87; mem. La. commn. on Bicentennial of U.S. Constn., 1986-90; pres. Adv. Ctr. for Elderly and Disabled, 1989—. Kellett fellow, 1972-74; Prince von Thurn und Taxis guest prof. Regensburg Univ., Germany, 1983 Fellow Eason-Weinmann Ctr. Comparative Law; mem. Assn. Am. Law Schs. (pres. local govt. sect. 1988-90), Nat. Assn. Bond Lawyers, South Shore Yacht Club (founding bd. dirs.). Unitarian Universalist. Died Sept. 25, 2005.

GENTILE, MELANIE MARIE, record producer, marketing and public relations consultant, writer; b. N.Y.C., Apr. 27, 1944; d. Frank Joseph and Jean Ferreri; m. R.P. Gentile, Apr. 4, 1964 (div. 1982); children: Robert, Jessica. Student, Calif. State U., 1967-70. Pres. U.S. venture Yasu Corp. of Tokyo, 1971-86; cons. in mktg., 1986-89; exec. prodr. and pres. Schrimshaw Prodn. Co. and Record Co., Nashville, from 1975; owner Triad Music, from 1996. Account exec., creative cons. Erwin Wasey Advt. Corp.; freelance creative cons. Jacques Yves Cousteau, 1968—. Author: Look Back But Don't Stare, Out of the Mouths of Babes; co-author: Essays of the Heart-What Our Youngest Really Think of the World We've Given Them. Mem. ASCAP (CMA award Acad. of Country Music, Billboard mag.). Died Feb. 3, 2005.

GENTNER, DONALD RICHARD, human interface designer, psychology researcher; b. Gowanda, N.Y., Jan. 20, 1940; s. Richard Francis and Florence Agnes (Winter) G.; m. Dedre Dariel Cooke, Aug. 17, 1968 (div. 1975); m. Judith Stewart, May 10, 1986. BS in Chemistry, Rensselaer Poly. Inst., 1961; PhD in Phys. Chemistry, U. Calif., Berkeley, 1967. Fellow Ctr. Advanced Study in Theology and Scis., Chgo., 1967-68; lectr. U. Ghana, Legon, 1968-70; med. researcher U. Calif., San Diego, 1971-72, psychology researcher, 1972-85; sr. researcher Philips Labs., Briarcliff Manor, N.Y., 1986-88; human interface designer Apple Computer, Cupertino, CA, from 1989. Contbr. numerous articles to profl. jours.; patentee in field. Mem. Assn. Computing Machinery, Computer Profls. for Social Responsibility, Sigma Xi. Avocations: hiking, woodworking, travel, genealogy. Home: Palo Alto, Calif. Died June 12, 2005.

GEOFFROY, CHARLES HENRY, retired retail executive; b. Longford, Ireland, Sept. 25, 1926; came to U.S., 1927, naturalized, 1945; s. Francis Louis and Kathleen Elizabeth (Fetherston) G.; m. Alida Baird McClenahan, Apr. 24, 1954; children: Evan Lloyd, Mark Lee, Douglas Baird. BA, Haverford Coll., 1949; postgrad., U. Pa., 1950. With GM Ins. Corp., Phila., 1950-51; mgr. rsch. dept. Ward Wheelock Co., Phila., 1951-54; assoc. rsch. dir., account exec. Lennen & Newell, Inc., N.Y.C., 1954-59; account exec. Young & Rubicam, Inc., N.Y.C., 1959-64, v.p. L.A., 1965-67; pres., mng. dir. Young & Rubicam, Ltd., Toronto, Ont., Canada, 1968-74; pres., dir. J.K. Gill Co. Ltd., Portland, Oreg., 1974-80; pres., chief operating officer Grantree Corp., Portland, 1980-83; pres. Rathcline Corp., Portland, 1984-86; chmn. Wide Travel Internat., Portland, 1986-94, ret., 1994. With AUS, 1945-46. Fellow Inst. Can. Advt.; mem. Portland Execs. Assn., Waverley Country Club, Arlington Club, Huguenot Soc. Great Britain and Ireland, Rotary. Home: Portland, Oreg. Died Oct. 31, 2005; in Portland, Oreg.

GEORES, RONALD JOSEPH, dance educator; b. Samboy, N.J., Oct. 7, 1939; s. Eric G. and Gertrude (O'shea) G.; m. Clementine Monti, Aug. 6, 1960; children: Heidi, Heather. Student, Union Coll., 1960. Dancer Elsa Greenwood Sch. Dance, Newark, N.J., Arthur Murray Group, Hollywood, Fla., 1957-68; with Fred Astaire Dance Studios, N.J., 1968-84; dir. The Ballet Sch., Summit, N.J., Dancemakers, Summit, from 1984. Adjudicator U.S. scholarship championship Mexico City, Anchorage, Alaska, Honolulu, 1993; nat. dance dir., examiner U.S. Ind. Dance Coun., Montgomery, Ala., 1993—; master scrutineer Winner's Circle dance events. Past editor ballroom and ballet dance N.J. Mag. of Music and Arts, past bd. advs. Past judge disco contest Soap Facytory; past adjudicator Miss Jr. Miss N.J. Contest; organizer ballroom dancing competitions N.J. Invitaitional. Mem. U.S. Terpichore, Inc., Dance Educaters Am., Nat. Dance Coun. Am., Pan-Am. Dance Tchrs., Inc. Home: Westfield, NJ. Died Dec. 22, 2004.

GEORGES, LYNNE, critical care nurse; b. Pitts., Aug. 8, 1958; d. Raymond Eugene and Elizabeth Louise (Cabalik) G. BSN, U. Pitts., 1980, MSN, 1990; student, Shadyside-McKeesport Hosp., Pitts., 1982-84, California (Pa.) U., 1982-84. RN, Pa. Nurse aide South Hills Health System, Jefferson Hosp., Pitts., 1976-80; staff nurse med.-surg. unit St. Clair Meml. Hosp., Pitts., 1980-81, staff nurse emergency dept. relief charge nurse, 1981-84; staff nurse ICU-CCU, charge relief nurse South Side Hosp., Pitts., from 1986; nursing skills lab. instr. Carlow Coll., Pitts., 1991-94, clin. instr. med.-surg., 1992-94; clin. nurse specialist Medbridge, Pitts., 1994-95. Mem. Assn. Clin. Nurse Specialists, Assn. Rehab. Nurses, Sigma Theta Tau. Home: Pittsburgh, Pa. Died Jan. 2, 2004.

GERBER, ABRAHAM, economic consultant, executive; b. N.Y.C., Dec. 19, 1925; s. Morris and Rose (Levy) G.; m. Beverly Kulkin, Dec. 23, 1948 (dec. 1966); children: Douglas K., Judith E.; m. Ilene Pomerantz, Sept. 28, 1967; children: Barbara J. Nakazawa, Gary L. AB, Columbia Coll., 1948; MA, Columbia U., 1950; postgrad. New Sch. for Social Rsch., 1950-51. Economist U.S. Dept Commerce, Washington, 1951, U.S. Dept. Interior, Washington, 1951-53; economist, asst. to pres., sec. system devel. com. Am. Electric Power Svc. Corp., N.Y.C., 1953-67; sr. v.p. Nat. Econ. Rsch. Assoc., White Plains, N.Y., Palm Beach, Fla., 1967-89; pres. Econ. Rsch. Inc., West Palm Beach, Fla., 1989—; bd. dirs. Regent Bank, Davie, Fla.; cons. Pres.'s Cabinet Com. Energy, Washington, 1953; mem. adv. com. U.S. Dept. Interior Office Coal Rsch., Washington, 1961-69; chmn. com. Energy Econ. Growth, Nat. Acad. Engring. Com. on Power Plant Siting, Washington, 1971-72. Contbr. articles to profl. jours. Mem. exec. com. Pub. Utility Rsch. Ctr. U. Fla., Gainesville, 1982—; panel mem. Nuclear Regulatory Commn. State Regulatory Activity, Washington, 1977. Served with USAAF, 1943-45. Mem. IEEE (sr.), AAAS, Am. Econ. Assn., Am. Nuclear Soc. Internat. Conf. Large High Voltage Electric Systems, Govs. Club, Frenchman's Creek Club. Jewish. Avocations: tennis, swimming, theater, opera. Home: Palm Beach Gardens, Fla. Died Mar. 18, 2004.

GERBNER, GEORGE, communications educator, former dean; b. Budapest, Hungary, Aug. 8, 1919; came to U.S., 1939, naturalized, 1944; s. Arpad and Margaret (Muranyi) G.; m. Ilona Kutas, Oct. 8, 1946 (dec. Dec. 8, 2005); children: John C., Thomas J. Student, U. Budapest, 1937-38, UCLA, 1940-41; BA, U. Calif.-Berkeley, 1943; MS, U. So. Calif., 1951, PhD, 1955; LHD (hon.), LaSalle Coll., Phila., 1980, Emerson Coll., 1989, Worcester State Coll., 1992. Reporter, asst. fin. editor The Chronicle, San Francisco, 1942-43; engaged in free-lance publicity, 1947-48; instr. Pasadena (Calif.) Jr. Coll., 1948-51, El Camino Coll., Los Angeles, 1951-56; asst. prof., then assoc. prof. U. Ill., Urbana, 1956-64; prof. communications Annenberg Sch. Communications, U. Pa., 1964—2005, dean, 1964-89, dean emeritus, 1989—2005; Bell Atlantic Prof. of Telecomms. Temple U., Phila. Founder, dir. Cultural Indicators Project, 1968-2005; founder, pres. Cultural Environment Movement, 1993-2005; vis. prof. Temple U., Phila., 1997-2005, U. Budapest, 1993, Salesian U., Rome, 1992; Disting. vis. prof. Am. U., Washington, 1995, 96; vis. lectr. U. Athens, 1996, Am. U., 1995-96, Temple U., 1997, Villanova U., 1997-2000. Author numerous articles and books in field.; editor Jour. of Communication, 1974-91; chmn. editorial bd. Internat. Ency. of Communications. 1st lt. inf., AUS, 1943-46, ETO. Decorated Bronze Star; grantee U.S. Office Edn., 1959, NSF, 1962, 80, 83, NIMH, 1958, 71-82, Internat. Sociol. Assn., 1963, UNESCO, 1963, 83, 85, Nat. Commn. Causes and Prevention Violence, 1969, Surgeon Gen.'s Sci. Adv. Com., 1970, White House Office Telecomm. Policy, 1977, U.S. Adminstrn. on Aging, 1978, AMA, 1979, Com. on Religious Rsch., 1983, Nat. Inst. Drug Abuse, 1985-86, W. Alton Jones Found., 1987-88, Hoso Bunka (Japan) Found., 1990-91, U.S. Commn. on Civil Rights, 1991, Nat. Cable TV Assn., 1992, SAG, AFTRA, 1992-93, Turner Broadcasting Sys., 1993, AARP, 1994, Ark. Trust, 1994, Ctr. for Substance Abuse Prevention, 1994, Robert Wood Johnson Found., 1995-97, Sloan Found., 1997, SAG, 1999-2001; recipient Excellence in Media award Internat. TV Assn., 1992. Fellow Internat. Communication Assn.; mem. Am. Sociol. Assn., Internat. Assn. Mass Communication Research (hon. life), Assn. Edn. Journalism (Paul J. Deutschman award for excellence in rsch. 1996). Died Dec. 24, 2005.

GEREAU, MARY CONDON, political corporate executive; b. Winterset, Iowa, Oct. 10, 1916; d. David Joseph and Sarah Rose (Stack) Condon; m. Gerald Robert Gereau, Jan. 14, 1961. Student, Mt. Mercy Jr. Coll., 1935-37; BA, U. Iowa, 1939, MA, 1941. Program dir. ARC, India, 1943-45; dean of students Eastern Mont. Coll., 1946-48; supt. pub. instrn. State of Mont., 1948-56; sr. legis. cons. NEA, 1967-73; dir. legis. Nat. Treasury Employees Union, 1973-76; legis. asst. to Senator Melcher US Senate, Mont., 1976-86; pres. Woman's Party Corp., 1991—2006. Cochmn. Truman Commerative Com. Contbr. articles on state govt. and edn. to profl. jours. Nat. chmn. Equal Rights Ratification Coun.; pres. Coun. Chief State Sch. Officers, 1956; exec. bd. Rural Edn. Assn., 1953—56; mem. campaign staff Kennedy, Johnson, Humphrey, Jackson; v.p. Nat. Women's Party, 1984—91; mem. Westmoreland Dem. com.; bd. dir. Coun. Chief State Sch. Officers, 1953—56. Named Conservationist of Yr. Mont. Conservation Coun., 1952, Roll Call Cong. Staffer of Yr., 1985; recipient Disting. Svc. State Sch. Officers, 1956, medal of honor Vet. Feminists of Am., 2000. Mem. U.S. Congress Burro Club (pres. 1983-84), Mont. State Soc. of Wash. Home: Colonial Beach, Va. Died Feb. 12, 2006.

GERLACH, THURLO THOMPSON, electrical engineer; b. Sparta, Ill., Oct. 30, 1916; s. Kenneth Frederick and Golda M. (Thompson) G.; m. Ellen Marie Kuhn, July 14, 1946 (dec. Nov. 24, 2004). BEE, Tri-State U., 1937; grad., Air Force Command and Staff, 1952. Registered profl. engr., Ill., Mont. Dist. engr. Ill. Power Co., Centralia, 1937-40, area engr. Sparta, 1940-41, Granite City, Ill., 1946-48; engr. U.S. Bur. Standards, Washington, 1948-50, Fed. Power Commn., Washington, 1953-56, Bur. of Reclamation, Billings, Mont., 1950-51, 56-77; cons. Billings, from 1977. Del. heavy engr. constrn. program Citizen Amb. Program, Peoples Republic of China, 1990, USSR, 1991, Panama, 1996. Active People to People Internat., Kansas City, Mo., 1989—. Major USAF, 1941-46, 51-53. Mem. NSPE, IEEE, U.S. Com. Large Dams, Elks, Masons. Methodist. Achievements include participation in development, construction and operation of Missouri River Basin power system. Home: Vero Beach, Fla. Died Nov. 5, 2005; Arlington Nat. Cemetery, Va.

GERNON, ROBERT L., state supreme court justice; b. Sabetha, Kans., July 29, 1943; children: Rebecca Gernon Wilson, Kristin Gernon Olson. BSBA, U. Kans.; JD, Washburn U., 1969; LLM in Jud. Process, U. Va., 2001. Asst. atty. Shawnee County, presentence investigator; probation officer; pvt. practice, 1970—79; atty., county counselor Brown County, 1971—75; judge 22d Dist., 1979—88, adminstrv. judge, 1981—88; mem. Ct. Appeals, 1988—2002; justice Kans. Supreme Ct., Topeka, from 2003. Trial advocacy instr. U. Kans. Sch. Law; chmn., program coord. ann. program Ann. Survey of Law Com.; faculty advisor Nat. Jud. Coll.; spkr. in field; mem. task force on permanency planning U.S. Supreme Ct. Fellow: Kans. Bar Found., Am. Bar Found.; mem.: Kans. Dist. Judges' Assn. (mem. legis. com.), Kans. Bar Assn. (continuing legal edn. com. from 1986, mem., past chair pub. info. com., mem. com. on professionalism, Outstanding Svc. award 1991, Professionalism award 2001). Died Mar. 2005.

GERRISH, MARTIN FREDERIC, theater executive, retired drama instructor; b. Madison, Maine, Aug. 4, 1926; s. Charles E. and Emma Margaret (Knapp) G.; m. Elaine Francis Terrill, Sep. 5, 1949; 1 child, Edward Kenneth. BFA, U. Ariz., 1955, MFA, 1957. Drama instr., dir. U. Louisville, 1957-58, Reedley (Calif.) Coll., 1958-61, Grossmont Coll., El Cajon, Calif., 1961-86; pres., dir. Octad-One Prodns., Inc., Spring Valley, Calif., from 1976. Actor Old Globe Theatre, San Diego, 1961-82, Mission Playhouse, San Diego, 1962-86. Appeared in plays The Runner Stumbles (Atlas award), 1976-77, The Lion In Winter (Atlas award), 1976-77; dir. The Runner Stumbles, 1976-77. Pres. Associated Community Theatres (v.p. 1987-88), San Diego County, Calif., 1988-89. Sgt. USAF, 1945-46. Recipient Aubrey awardsAssociated Community Theatres, San Diego County, Calif., 1986, 89, 90 Mem. Calif. Retired Tchrs. Assn. Home: Spring Valley, Calif. Died Feb. 19, 2004.

GETSINGER, KEITH ROBERT, financial consultant; b. Detroit, Apr. 4, 1964; s. Kenneth William and Shirley Jean (Mayernick) G. BA, U. Mich., 1985; MBA, U. Chgo., 1991. Cons. Data Resources, Inc., Pitts., 1985-87, sr. cons. Chgo., 1988-90; industry analyst J.D. Power and Assocs., Agoura Hills, Calif., 1990; sr. cons. Ibbotson Assocs., Chgo., 1991-94; pvt. cons. Reseda, Calif., 1994-95; product mgr. Transamerica Investors, L.A., from 1995. Home: San Anselmo, Calif. Died Feb. 24, 2004.

GETTY, GERALD WINKLER, lawyer; b. Chgo., June 17, 1911; s. Oliver and Pearl (Winkler) G.; m. Helen Brennan, Oct. 2, 1938 (dec. 1966); children: Michael, Muriel, Marie; m. Gracia Gibbs, June 3, 1967. JD, DePaul U., 1938, JD (hon.), 1972. Bar: Ill. 1938, Ind. 1938, U.S. Supreme Ct. 1960. Lawyer U.S. Govt., Chgo., 1938-42; pub. defender Cook County, Chgo., 1942-72; ptnr. Getty and Getty, Dolton, Ill., 1972-83; prin. Gerald W. Getty and

Assocs., Dolton, from 1983. Author: Public Defender, 1972, Theory of Condominium and Cooperative Apartment Law, 1993. Mem. Elks. Died Feb. 29, 2004.

GEWERTZ, MARTIN ANSON, lawyer; b. Dallas, Dec. 3, 1948; s. Irving David and Anita Rose (Indin) G.; m. Sharon Gay Abelman, Mar. 11, 1973; 1 child, Nevin Merrill. BA, U. Tex., 1970; JD, U. Houston, 1972. Bar: Tex. 1973, U.S. Dist. Ct. (we. dist.) Tex. 1976, U.S. Ct. Appeals (5th cir.) 1976, U.S. Supreme Ct. 1976. Pvt. practice, San Antonio, from 1973. Prof. Law San Antonio Coll., San Antonio, 1980—; 2d asst. city prosecutor City of Leon Valley, Tex., 1980-81. Mem. editorial bd. The Houston Law Review, U. Houston, 1971-72. Mem. Leon Valley Zoning Bd., 1979-80. Recipient Am. Jurisprudence award Bancroft Whitney Co., 1971. Mem. San Antonio Subrogation Assn., Comml. Law League Am., Bankruptcy Bar Assn., San Antonio Bar Assn., Order of the Barons, Phi Delta Phi, Zeta Beta Tau. Jewish. Avocations: karate blackbelt, travel, skiing, photography, swimming. Died Sept. 26, 2005.

GHORBAL, ASHRAF A., former ambassador; b. Alexandria, Egypt, May 1925; B.S. with honors, Cairo U.; Ph.D., Harvard U., 1949; m., 2 children. Joined Diplomatic Service, 1945; mem. Egyptian del. UN, 1949, then assigned to Paris and London, to 1956; head Egyptian interests sect. Indian embassy, Washington, 1968-73; press adviser to Pres. Sadat, 1973; amb. of Egypt to U.S., 1973—84; participant Camp David meetings resulting in Camp David framework for peace, 1978; mem. Egyptian del. to peace negotiations to draft peace treaty with Israel, Blair House, Washington, 1978. Died Nov. 29, 2005.

GIAIMO, ROBERT NICHOLAS, former congressman, lawyer; b. New Haven, Oct. 15, 1919; s. Rosario and Rose (Scarpulla) G.; m. Marion F. Schuenemann, May 17, 1945; 1 child, Barbara Lee. A.B., Fordham Coll., 1941; LL.B., U. Conn., 1943; Bar: Conn. 1947, Washington, 1979; practiced in New Haven, 1947-80, Washington, 1981-91; mem. US Congress from 3d Dist. Conn., 1959-81 chmn. budget com., 1977-81, sr. mem. com. on appropriations, also subcom. on def.; chmn., Pers. Appeals Bd., State of Conn. 1955-58; mem. North Haven Bd. Edn., 1949-55; Served as 1st lt. AUS, World War II; capt. JAGC, USAR. Democrat. Died May 24, 2006.

GIBBES, EMILY V., religion educator; b. N.Y.C., Aug. 14, 1915; d. George Edward and Genevieve (Anderson) G. BA, Hunter Coll., N.Y.C., 1936; MA, NYU, 1947; DHL, Mary Holmes Coll., Westpoint, Miss., 1981. Field dir. United Presbyn. Ch. USA, 1950-68; assoc. gen. sec. Div. Edn., Ministry Nat. Coun. Chs., 1972-80; prof. religious edn. N.Y. Theol. Sem., N.Y.C., 1981-88, dean religious edn. program, 1981-88; ret. Mem. Religious Edn. Assn. (pres. 1974-77). Home: Doylestown, Pa. Died Mar. 22, 2004.

GIBBONS, JOHN MARTIN, JR., physician, educator; b. NYC, Feb. 25, 1933; s. John Martin and Mary Frances (Darr) G.; m. Mary Therese Peyser, Dec. 26, 1955; chidlren: Catherine Way, Mary Sloan, John M. III, Fredericka Kerr, Myles. AB, Holy Cross Coll., 1954; MD, Georgetown U., 1958. Diplomate Am. Bd. Ob-Gyn., Am. Bd. Maternal and Fetal Medicine. Intern and resident ob-gyn Saint Vincent's Hosp., N.Y.C., 1958—63; from asst. to assoc. prof. ob-gyn. U. Conn., Farmington, 1970—78, prof. ob-gyn., 1978—2006. Chief dept. ob-gyn. Fordham Hosp., N.Y.C., 1968-70; dir. dept. ob-gyn. Saint Francis Hosp. and Med. Ctr., Hartford, Conn., 1970-93, sr. v.p. for med. affairs, 1993-99; mem. adv. coun. Nat. Inst. Child Health and Human Devel., NIH, 2001-05. Mem. Capital Area Health Consortium Bd., 1978-2000; mem. exec. com. Combined Hosps. Fund, 1978-82, Mt. Sinai Hosp. Bd., 1990-95; mem. Bristol Hosp. Bd., 1997-2004, 2005-06; mem. Hartford Ballet Bd., 1978-83, hon. mem., 1983-95, v.p., 1993-95, pres., 1995-97; mem. Hartford Stage Bd., 1999-2003; mem. Med. Delivery Sys., Inc., 1985-88, Greater Hartford Arts Coun., 1988-92, 95-97; corporator Wadsworth Atheneum, 1987-97; overseer Bushnell Meml. Hall, 1990-2006. Capt. USAR, 1961-68. Fellow ACOG (dist. treas. 1987-91, dist. vice chmn. 1991-94, nat. fin. com. 1992-00, dist. chmn. 1994-97, nat. treas. 1997-00, pres.-elect 2002-03, pres. 2003-04, immediate past pres. 2004-05), ACS, Soc. Maternal-Fetal Medicine, Obstet. Soc. Boston; mem. Conn. State Med. Soc. (sec. ob-gyn., vice chmn. 1979-82, chmn. 1982-85), Hartford Med. Soc., Hartford Golf Club, Harvard Club of N.Y.C., Lotos Club (N.Y.C.). Home: Hartford, Conn. Died July 22, 2006.

GIBBS, RAYMOND WELDON, surgeon; b. Boston, Aug. 1, 1920; s. Raymond T. and Elizabeth (Weldon) G.; m. Dorothy Dawson; children: Virginia, Raymond W., Janet. SB, Boston U., 1943; MD, N.Y. Med. Coll., 1951. Instr. surgery Yale Med. Sch., 1953-54; sr. clin. instr. surgery Tufts Med. Sch., 1960-70; instr. Harvard Med. Sch., 1961-89; surgeon Harvard U. Dept. Athletics, 1957-90. Surgical cons. Boston, 1957—. Fellow ACS, Am. Coll. Sports Medicine, Am. Burn Asn., Boston Surgical Soc., Mass. Med. Soc. Home: West Roxbury, Mass. Died Feb. 7, 2005.

GIBNEY, FRANK BRAY, publishing executive, foundation administrator; b. Scranton, Pa., Sept. 21, 1924; s. Joseph James and Edna May (Wetter) G.; m. Harriet Harvey, Dec. 10, 1948 (div. 1957); children: Alex, Margot; m. Harriet C. Suydam, Dec. 14, 1957 (div. 1971); children: Frank, James, Thomas; m. Hiroko Doi, Oct. 5, 1972; children: Elise, Josephine. BA, Yale U., 1945; DLitt (hon.), Kyung Hee U., Seoul, Korea, 1974. Corr., assoc. editor Time mag., N.Y.C., Tokyo and London, 1947-54; sr. editor Newsweek, N.Y.C., 1954-57; staff writer, editorial writer Life mag., N.Y.C., 1957-61; pub., pres. SHOW mag., N.Y.C., 1961-64; pres. Ency. Brit. (Japan), Tokyo, 1965-69, TBS-Brit., Tokyo, 1969-75, vice chmn., 1976-99; v.p. Ency. Brit., Inc., Chgo., 1975-79; vice chmn., bd. editors Ency. Brit., Chgo., 1978—2006; pres. Pacific Basin Inst., Pomona Coll., Claremont, Calif., 1979—2006. Prof. Pomona Coll., 1997-2006; bd. dirs. U.S. Com. for Pacific Econ. Cooperation, 1988-2006, v.p., 1993-95; cons. com. on space and aeros. U.S. Ho. of Reps., Washington, 1957-59; vice chmn. Japan-U.S. Friendship Commn., 1984-90, U.S.-Japan Com. Edn. and Cultural Interchange, 1984-90. Author: Five Gentlemen of Japan: Portrait of a Nation's Power, 1953, 3d edit., 2004, The Frozen Revolution, 1959, (with Peter Deriabin) The Secret World, 1960, The Operators, 1961, The Khrushchev Pattern, 1961, The Reluctant Space Farers, 1965, Japan, The Fragile Super-Power, 1975, 3rd edit., 1996, Miracle by Design, 1983, The Pacific Century: America and Asia in a Changing World, 1992, Korea's Quiet Revolution: From Garrison State to Democracy, 1993; co-author: The Battle for Okinawa, 1995; editor: The Penkovskiy Papers, 1965, Senso, 1995, Unlocking The Bureaucrats' Kingdom, 1998, The Nanjing Massacre, 1999, Rising Sun; Morning Calm, 2004. Served to lt. USNR, 1942-46. Decorated Order of the Rising Sun 3d Class Japan, Order of Sacred Treasure 2d Class Japan. Mem. Council on Fgn. Relations, Tokyo Fgn. Corr. Club, Japan-Am. Soc., Century Assn., Yale Club. Roman Catholic. Home: Santa Barbara, Calif. Died Apr. 9, 2006.

GIBSON, MICHAEL ALFRED, composer, conductor; b. Wilmington, Del., Sept. 29, 1944; m. Ellen Alexandra Haight, Apr. 16, 1984; 1 child, Andrew. Student, Harvard U., 1962-64, Berklee Sch. Music, 1966-67. Freelance instrumentalist, Boston and N.Y.C., 1960-75; freelance arranger and orchestrator N.Y.C. and Hollywood, Calif., 1970—2005; freelance composer, 1975—2005. Orchestrator (Broadway mus.) Over Here!, 1975, Peter Pan, 1978, Barnum, 1978, Woman of the Year, 1981, My One and Only, 1983 (Drama Desk award 1983), Anything Goes, 1987 (Drama Desk nomination), Cabaret, 1987; composer, condr.: (film and LP) Grease, 1978 (Platinum LP 1978); arranger: (record) Kathleen Battle Christmas LP, 1987; arranger, contbr. (film) Billy Bathgate, 1991. Mem. N.Y. Arrangers and Orchestrators Com. (co-chmn. 1983-2005). Avocations: flying, travel, chess, astronomy. Died July 15, 2005.

GIBSON, VIVIAN LOUISE, retired nursing consultant; b. Raymond, Mont., June 17, 1918; d. August A. and Rose (Bandar) G. Diploma, Columbus Sch. Nursing, 1940; BSEd, Hunter Coll., 1955; MA in Adminstrn., NYU, 1958. Asst. dir. nursing edn. HEW Pub. Health Svc. Hosp., San Francisco; dir. nursing HEW Fed. Bur. Prisons, Alderson, W.Va.; nursing cons. HEW Indian Health Svc., Window Rock, Ariz.; retired. Capt. USPHS, 1945-52. Mem. ANA, Calif. Nurses Assn., Mont. League Nursing (treas., bd. dirs.), Nat. League Nursing, Nat. Pub. Health Assn., Mont. Pub. Health Assn., Nat. Mental Health Assn., Mont. Mental Health Assn. (v.p., pres.-elect), Mental Health Assn. Sheridan County (v.p., pres.), Hosp. Home Health Svcs. Sheridan County (bd. dirs.). Home: Outlook, Mont. Died Nov. 19, 2004.

GIDEZ, LEWIS IRWIN, biochemist, publications director; b. Boston, Jan. 27, 1927; s. Max and Ida (Burgin) G.; m. Margaret Mary Powers (dec. 2001), Feb. 19, 1955; children: John Paul, Gregory, J. Reed, Christopher, Maura. BS, Iowa State U., 1948; PhD, Harvard U., 1953. Assoc. med. scientist Brookhaven Nat. Lab., Upton, N.Y., 1952-58; asst. prof. biochemistry Albert Einstein Coll. of Medicine, Bronx, N.Y., 1958-69, assoc. prof. biochemistry, 1969-86. Dir. pubs. Fedn. Am. Socs. for Exptl. Biology, Bethesda, Md., exec. editor jour., Bethesda, 1988-97; exec. editor FASEB Jour. of Lipil Rsch., Bethesda, 1970-2000 Pres. Demarest N.J. Bd. Edn., 1972, 73, 76, 80, 81. Served to lt. cmdr. USNR, 1945-47. Fellow Council on Arteriosclerosis Am. Heart Assn.; mem. Am. Chem. Soc., Am. Soc. for Biochemistry and Molecular Biology, Council of Biology Editors (former treas.). Democrat. Home: Rockville, Md. Died Mar. 20, 2005.

GIDWITZ, GERALD S., retired hair care company executive; b. Memphis, 1906; m. Jane; 5 children. PhB, U. Chgo., 1927. Co-founder, chmn. bd. and chmn. exec. com. Helene Curtis Industries, Inc., Chgo., 1952—96. Trustee Roosevelt U., Auditorium Theatre Coun.; bd. dirs. Chgo. Crime Commn., Jamestown Found.; founder learning for earning that educates adults on pub. aid and gets them jobs at no cost to the students, 2001-. Mem. Ill. Mfg. Assn. (past bd. dirs.). Home: Chicago, Ill. Died July 11, 2006.

GILBERT, EDWARD WILLIAM, safety specialist; b. Rochester, N.Y., Jan. 29, 1938; s. Charles F. and Bertha (Faddis) G.; m. Ruth Hallows, Dec. 26, 1964; children: Cheryl A., Glena A. Student, Roberts Wesleyan Coll., 1957-59. Group leader Eastman Kodak Co., Rochester, 1959-74, safety technician, 1974-86, safety specialist, from 1986. Mem. Environ. Speakers Team, Rochester, 1989—, Rochester Safety Coun., Nat. Safety Coun. Adv. bd. Project Outreach, Rochester; v.p. Brockport (N.Y.) Cen. Sch. Bd. Edn., 1988—; chmn. Monroe County Sch. Bd. Labor Rels. Com., 1991. Mem. Monroe County Sch. Bd. Assn., Environ. Info. Coun. Rochester. Home: Spencerport, NY. Died Sept. 7, 2004.

GILBERT, SHARON, artist; b. Bklyn., Feb. 15, 1944; m. Vyt Bakaitis, Jan. 23, 1970; children: Elena Bakaitis, Ellery Bakaitis. BFA, Cooper Union, 1966. Author: Three Mile Island Reproductions, 1979, Waste, 1980, '80 Faces, 1980, A Nuclear Atlas, 1982, Poison America, 1988, Green the Fragile, 1989, Urgent Life, 1990, Action Poses, 1991, Urban Renewal, 1992, Working Time, 1994, Chemical Ways, 1997, Police (State) USA, 2001, So Quiet, 2003, Seeing Amsterdam, 2004; one-woman shows include Printed Matter, N.Y.C., 1980, Resnick Gallery, LI U., 1990, Rutgers U., New Brunswick, N.J., 1992, PABA Gallery, New Haven, 1999, Ctr. Book Arts, N.Y.C., 2002, Kanaal 10, Amsterdam, 2004, exhibited in group shows at Albert-Ludwig U., Freiburg, Germany, 1980, Ctr. George Pompidou, Paris, 1985, Mus. Modern Art, N.Y.C., 1988—90, Vasarely Mus., Budapest, Hungary, 1990, Bklyn. Mus. Art, 2004, Corcoran Gallery Art, Washington, 2005, others. Grantee, Carl Schurz Hans German-Am. Inst., Freiburg, 1980, Women's Studio Workshop, 1982, N.Y. Found. Arts, 1989, Artists Space, 1990, Puffin Found., 2005. Home: Brooklyn, NY. Died June 9, 2005.

GILBOA, NISAN, physician; b. Balachna, Russia, Feb. 12, 1945; came to U.S. 1973; s. Schmuel and Mina (Lapp) G.; married, 1967; children: Amit, Noam, Keren. MD, Hebrew U., Jerusalem, 1973. Resident U. Oreg. Med. Sch., Portland, 1973-75; fellow U. Colo. Med. Sch., Denver, 1975-77; asst. prof. Union U. Med. Sch., Albany, N.Y., 1977, to 1990; assoc. prof. medicine U. Pitts., from 1990. Cons. Genentech Co., San Francisco, 1985; peer rev. com. Am. Heart Assn., 1985-89. Referee, reviewer med. and sci. jours.; contbr. articles to profl. jours. Am. Heart Assn./Am. Kidney Found. grantee, 1980-91. Home: Pittsburgh, Pa. Died Mar. 11, 2004.

GILL, FRED LEE, city official; b. Shelby, N.C., May 7, 1947; s. Edward Sanders and Vernie Gill; m. Bettye Jean Arnold, Aug. 3, 1969; children: Brendalyn Katrell, Fred, Kenneth Ashley, Kevin Arnold. AA in Pre-Laww, Morristown (Tenn.) Jr. Coll., 1967; BA in History, Barber-Scotia Coll., Concord, N.C., 1969; postgrad., John Marshall Law Sch., Atlanta, 1974, Ga. State U., 1976. Manpower dir. I CARE, Inc., Statesville, N.C., 1969-70; pers. officer Econ. Opportunity Atlanta, Inc., 1972-74; conciliator U.S. EEOC, Atlanta, 1974-76; equal opportunity specialist USDA, Atlanta, 1976-79; dir. pers. City of Durham, N.C., 1979-80; pers. dir. City of Winston-Salem, N.C., 1980-84; mgr. classification and compensation City of Atlanta, from 1984. Speaker, lectr., condr. or participant numerous workshops at numerous orgns. and sch. systems; mem. adv. com. Atlanta Area Tech. Sch. Bd. dirs. Atlanta Feed the Hungry, John F. Kennedy Work Activity Ctr. Sgt. U.S. Army, 1970-72, Vietnam. Decorated Army Commendation medal; recipient Mgr. of Yr. award Atlanta Bur. Personnel and Human Resources, 1986. Mem. Am. Compensation Assn., Ga. Local Govt. Pers. Assn., Nu Beta Epsilon, Omeg a Psi Phi. Died Aug. 25, 2004.

GILLEN, HOWARD WILLIAM, neurologist, medical historian; b. Chgo., Nov. 25, 1923; s. John Howard and Emily Elizabeth (Bayley) G.; m. Corinne V. Neese, July 24, 1948. BS, U. Ill., 1947; MD, U. Ill., Chgo., 1949. Hon. active neurologist New Hanover Regional Med. Ctr., Wilmington, N.C., 1973-93, emeritus neurologist, from 1993; cons. neurologist Cape Fear Meml. Hosp., Wilmington, 1973-93; clin. prof. neurology U. N.C., Chapel Hill, 1973-93, clin. prof. emeritus, from 1993. Adj. prof. biol. sci. U. N.C., Wilmington, 1986—; rsch. assoc. I.R.I.S.C., Wilmington, 1989-93, sr. investigator, 1993-99. Capt. USNR, ret. Home: Wilmington, NC. Died Sept. 3, 2004.

GILLES, DOROTHY KATHLEEN, community organizer, arts/play therapist; b. Chgo., Nov. 12, 1936; d. John William and Margaret Kathleen (Schueller) Cordes; m. Peter Edmund Gilles, Oct. 6, 1956 (div. Aug. 1985); children: Peter Alan, John Harry, Mark David. BME, Northwestern U., 1971; MEd, Nat. Coll. Edn., 1972; PhD, St. Louis U., 1978. Diplomate Nat. Inst. Expressive Therapy; cert. reality therapist Inst. Reality Therapy. Spl. edn. educator Met. Sch., St. Louis, 1974-75; music tchr. Granite City (Ill.) Sch. Dist., 1976-77; univ. instr., asst. prof. So. Ill. U., Edwardsville, 1979-82; ednl. diagnostician, music tchr. Spl. Sch. Dist., St. Louis, 1983-85; spl. edn. tchr. L.A. Unified Sch. Dist., 1985-86; instr. Nat. U., San Diego, 1986-88; spl. edn. tchr. South Bay Union Sch. Dist., Imperial Beach, Calif., 1988, Francis Howell Sch. Dist., St. Charles, Mo., 1989-97; arts therapist Opening Doors, Edwardsville, St. Charles, St. Louis, from 1990; music therapist Hawthorn Children's Psychiat. Hosp. Program co-chair Very Spl. Arts Festival, So. Ill. U., Edwardsville, 1979, insvc. workshop leader, 1979-82, coord. acad. credit, chair evaluation com., 1982; invited spkr. 2d Internat. Symposium Music Edn. for Handicapped, 1981. Contbr. articles on music edn. for spl. children to profl. jours. including Outlook, Music Therapy Perspectives, Procs. of Internat. Symposium Music Edn. for the Handicapped, Edn. for the Handicapped. Den mother Boy Scouts Am., Evanston, Ill., 1962; program chair PTO, Evanston, 1965; youth choir dir. Presbyn. ch., Edwardsville, 1973. Recipient Alumni Achievement award Nat. Coll. Edn., 1979. Mem. Nat. Expressive Therapy Assn. (cert. expressive therapist), Nat. Guild Hypnotists (cert. hypnotherapist), St. Louis Psychol. Assn., Mental Health Assn. Greater St. Louis, Midwest Reality Therapy Assn., Profl. Women's Alliance, Sigma Alpha Iota (pres. 1962-64, Sword of Honor), Kappa Delta,

Pi Kappa Lambda. Democrat. Religious Science. Avocations: piano playing, swimming, travel, gourmet cooking, spanish. Home: Edwardsville, Ill. Died Dec. 11, 2004.

GILLIES, PATRICIA ANN, biologist; b. Berkeley, Calif., Sept. 23, 1929; d. William W. and Barbara (Weddle) Myers; m. Robert W. Gillies, Sept. 17, 1948 (div. 1968); children: Catherine I. Barton, Coila L. McGowan. AB, Calif. State U., Fresno, 1954; MA, Calif. State U., 1961. Tchr. Parlier (Calif.) Unified Sch. Dist., 1955-56; inspector U.S. Dept. Agr., Fresno, 1956-58; teaching asst. Fresno State Coll., 1958-59; pub. health biologist Dept. Health Svcs., State of Calif., Fresno, 1959-93; retired, 1993. Dir. Consolidated Mosquito Abatement Dist., Selma, Calif., 1974—. Contbr. articles to profl. jours. Mem. Soc. Vector Ecologists, Am. Mosquito Control Assn., Calif. Mosquito and Vector Control Assn. Democrat. Episcopalian. Avocations: handcrafts, gardening. Home: Fresno, Calif. Died May 11, 2004.

GILMAN, FRANCES M., genealogist, librarian; b. Cleve., Jan. 4, 1921; d. Christopher and Frances (Hitchcock) Magee; m. Stanley Hugh Gilman, Sept. 6, 1941 (div. May 1980); children: Robert Hugh, Wylie Burke, Andrew Magee, Kate Kane. BA, Sarah Lawrence Coll., 1941; MS in Libr. Sci., Columbia U., 1975. Libr. Clinton (Conn.) Hist. Soc., from 1988. Spkr. geneaol. issues to various groups including Friends of the Clinton Libr., DAR chpts., among others. Contbr. articles to profl. jours. Mem. Conn. Profl. Genealogists Coun., from 2002; orgn. chair Dem. Party, White Plaines, NY, 1986—87; bd. dirs. Godfrey Libr., Middletown, Conn., from 1998, Gov. Jonathan Trumbull House, Lebanon, Conn., 1998—2000. Democrat. Avocations: tennis, work on family pedigrees. Home: Clinton, Conn. Died Feb. 11, 2005.

GILMAN, NORMAN WASHBURN, organic chemist; b. Augusta, Maine, June 6, 1938; s. Frank A. Gilman and Helene D. (Washburn) Dorr; m. Diane P. Poulin, July 12, 1958; children: Craig S., Jennifer K. PhD, Princeton U., 1967. Rsch. investigator Hoffmann-LaRoche Inc., Nutley, N.J., from 1968. Cpl. USMC, 1956-59. Mem. AAAS, Am. Chem. Soc., Sigma Xi, Alpha Chi Sigma. Home: Pine Brook, NJ. Died Aug. 1, 2005.

GILMORE, DAVID L., judge; b. Washington, Pa., Oct. 28, 1944; s. Charles Jean and Dorothy (Beck) Gilmore; m. Janice Lynn Kughn, June 21, 1969; children: Melissa K., Thomas J. BS, California U. of Pa., 1966; JD, Duquesne U., Pitts., 1970. Bar: Pa. 1971, U.S. Dist. Ct. (we. dist.) Pa. 1972. Pvt. practice, Washington, Pa., 1970—87; asst. dist. atty. Washington County, Washington, Pa., 1972—73, asst. county solicitor, 1973—74, county solocitor, 1974—75, county commr., 1976—83; judge Ct. of Common Pleas, Washington, from 1984, pres. judge, from 2003. Cpl. USMCR, 1966—72. Democrat. Presbyterian. Avocation: cooking. Home: Washington, Pa. Died Sept. 30, 2004.

GILMORE, VOIT, travel company executive; b. Winston-Salem, NC, Oct. 13, 1918; s. John Merriman and Helen (Hensel) G.; m. Kathryn Kendrick, Jan. 21, 1945 (div. 1975); children: Kathryn, Geraldine, Susan, Peter, David.; m. Tatiana Dominick, July 4, 1982 (div. 1990); m. Josephine Baldwin, Nov. 23, 1990. BJ, U. N.C., 1939, M in Geography, 1985, PhD in Geography, 1987; grad., Nat. Inst. Pub. Affairs, Washington, 1940. Cert. travel counselor Inst. Cert. Travel Agts. Asst. to div. mgr. Pan Am. Airways, Miami, Fla., 1940-41; personnel mgr. Pan Am. Airways-Africa Ltd., Accra, Gold Coast, 1942-43; pub. relations dir. Pan Am. Airways, San Francisco, 1946-48; pres. Storey Corp. and affiliated cos., 1948-61, 64-83, Four Seasons Travel Service, Inc., 1971-95. Dir. U.S. Travel Svc., Washington, 1961-64, So. Nat. Bank of N.C., 1980-95; news corr. to Arctic, 1958, Antarctic, 1958, 60, 61, 63; mem. adv. coun. U.S. Travel and Tourism Adminstrn., 1990-96. Contbr. articles on polar exploration to newspapers, mags. Mem. town coun., mayor, Southern Pines, N.C., 1953-57; mem. N.C. Senate, 1965-69, N.C. Bd. Conservation and Devel., 1957-61; trustee U. N.C., Fayetteville, 1981-87; mem. Gov.'s Adv. Com. on Travel and Tourism, 1982, N.C. Forestry Adv. Com., 1986; candidate for U.S. Congress from 8th Dist. N.C., 1968; bd. dirs. U. N.C. Sch. Journalism Found., Chapel Hill; chmn. Clean N.C. 2000, 1999-01. Lt. (j.g.) USN, 1943-46, PTO. Recipient European Tourism Golden Helm award, West Berlin, 1986, Parker award Travel Coun. NC, 1997, Order of Long Leaf Pine award Gov. NC, 2003, NC Pub. Svc. award Gov. NC, 2004; named to Travel Industry Assn. Hall of Leaders, 1988. Fellow Royal Geog. Soc. (life), Explorers Club (life); mem. Am. Soc. Travel Agts. (pres. 1988-90), Assn. of Am. Geographers, Am. Forestry Assn. (pres. 1973-75), Soc. Am. Travel Writers, Travel Coun. N.C. (pres. 1969-71), Bohemian Club, Cosmos Club, Country Club N.C., Heidelburg Prince Club. Died Oct. 2005.

GINZBURG, RALPH, editor, writer; b. Bklyn., Oct. 28, 1929; s. Raymond and Rachel G. (Lipkin) G.; m. Shoshana Brown, Dec. 16, 1958; children— Bonnie, Shepherd, Lark. BBA, Coll. City N.Y., 1949; postgrad., Bklyn. Coll., 1950; diploma, Henry George Sch. Econs., 1951. Copyboy NY Daily Compass, 1949-50; re-write man Washington Times-Herald, 1950-51. Freelance writer, photographer for mags. including Parade, others, 1951-53; staff writer, NBC, 1954-55; mng. bd. Look mag, 1955-56; articles editor Esquire, 1956-58; articles editor Eros, 1962-63, Fact, 1964-68, Avant-Garde, from 1969, Moneysworth, from 1971, Am. Business, from 1976, EXTRA!, 1977—, Better Living, from 1980, Uncle Sam, from 1981; author: 100 Years of Lynching, 1961, An Unhurried View of Erotica, 1956, Eros on Trial, 1964, Castrated: My Eight Months in Prison, 1973; freelance journalist NY Times, NY Post, NY Daily News, Newsday, AP, UPI, Reuters, Agence-France Presse, 1986-90. Served with AUS, 1950-51. Recipient Page One award for photography Am. Newspaper Guild, 1989. Mem. ACLU, Sierra Club, Wilderness Soc., Friends of Earth, Urban Coalition, Fellowship of Reconciliation, War Resisters League, N.Y. Ramblers, Adirondack Mountain Club, Common Cause, Quaker Action Group, Scenic Hudson Preservation Soc., Audubon Soc., Green Mountain Club, World Wildlife Fund, Am. Youth Hostels, Greenpeace, Ams. for a Safe Israel, Friends of Animals Died July 4, 2006.

GIPSON, JEFFERY, chemistry professor; b. Waco, Tex., Aug. 7, 1922; s. Jeffery and Johnnie (Donahue) G. BS, Tillotson Coll., 1944; MS, Howard U., 1949; PhD, U. Tex., 1955. Assoc. prof. chemistry So. U., Baton Rouge, 1954-59; prof. chemistry, chmn. dept. St. Augustine's Coll., Raleigh, N.C., 1959-76; prof. chemistry Va. Union U., Richmond, from 1981. Vis. prof. chemistry Met. State coll., Denver, 1974; vis. prof. sci. U. Va., Charlottesville, summer 1985; cons. USAID, Bangalore, India, 1965, 67; rsch. scientist DNA Lawrence Radiation Lab., Livermore, Calif., summer 1970; rsch. trichina Los Alamos (N.Mex.) Sci. Lab., summer 1971; mem. colloid chem. conf. U. So. Calif., L.A., summer 1983; environ. scientist U.S. EPA, Arlington, 1987, Chgo., 1988, Phila., 1989, 91, 92, Research Triangle Park, N.C., 1990, Phila., 1991-92. Editor: Experiments in Physical Science, 1989; contbr. articles to profl. jours. Sgt. U.S. Army, 1944-46, PTO, 50-51. Mem. AAAS, AAUP, Am. Assn. Retired Profs., Nat. Space Acad. Am. Legion. Avocations: walking, create science crosswords. Home: Richmond, Va. Died Feb. 5, 2006.

GIRAUD, RAYMOND DORNER, retired language professional; b. N.Y.C., Aug. 26, 1920; s. Gabriel and Mabel (Dorner) G.; m. Lise Kurzmann, Feb. 1, 1948. BA, Coll. City N.Y., 1941; MA, U. Chgo., 1949; PhD, Yale, 1954. Instr. English and French Ill. Inst. Tech., 1946-49; instr., then asst. prof. French Yale U., 1952-58; mem. faculty Stanford U., 1958—2006, prof. French, 1962—86, chmn. dept. French and Italian, 1968-72, prof. emeritus, 1986—2006. Author: The Unheroic Hero, 1957, Flaubert, A Collection of Critical Essays, 1964. Served with AUS, 1942-45. Decorated Chevalier, Ordre des Palmes Acadēmique, 1967; Guggenheim fellow, 1961-62. Home: Palo Alto, Calif. Died June 17, 2006.

GIROD, ERWIN ERNEST, internist; b. L.A., Oct. 1, 1944; s. Dudley Leonard and Rena Merl (Hudson) G.; m. Jill Louise Johnson, Dec, 16, 1967; children: Jeffrey Johnson, Janette Renee. BA, Calif. State U., L.A., 1966; MD, U. Calif., Irvine, 1970. Diplomate Am. Bd. Internal Medicine. Med. intern L.A. County-U. So. Calif. Med. Ctr., 1970-71, resident in internal medicine, 1971-73; ward med. officer, dir. med. ICU, adminstrv. chief critical care U.S. Naval Hosp., San Diego, 1973-75; dir. ICU Christian Med. Coll., Brown Meml. Hosp., Ludhiana, Punjab, India, 1976-77; asst. prof. medicine Punjab U., 1976-77; chief gen. medicine, asst. chief dept. medicine Loma Linda VA Hosp., 1978-80; pvt. practice Pasadena, Calif., 1981-86; internal medicine specialist Hanson Med. Group, Inc., San Gabriel, Calif., 1986—93; ind., from 1993. Asst. prof. dept. medicine Loma Linda U., 1978-80; mem. staff Huntington Meml. Hosp., Pasadena, 1981—, St. Luke Med. Ctr., Pasadena, 1982-2002; assoc. staff mem. Meth. Hosp. So. Calif., Arcadia, Calif., 1986—; lectr. in field. Contbr. articles to profl. publs. Bd. dirs. Lifewater, Internat., Baldwin Park, Calif., 1984-89; med. advisor Overseas Missionary Fellowship, Orange, Calif., 1988-92. Lt. comdr. USN, 1973-75. Fellow ACP, Am. Biographical Inst., Internat. Biographical Ctr. (life); mem. Calif. Med. Assn., Christian Med.-Dental Soc., Ephebian Soc. L.A., Gideons Internat. (chaplain Pasadena camp 1992-95), World Inst. Achievement (Internat. Cultural Diploma of Honor 1989, World Decoration of Excellence Medallion 1989, Disting. Leadership award 1989), Phi Kappa Phi, Alpha Gamma Omega (Legion of Honor). Republican. Congregationalist. Avocations: swimming, music, roses. Home: Pasadena, Calif. Died Oct. 4, 2004.

GIROIR, LEO JEAN JR., accountant; b. New Orleans, Nov. 5, 1941; s. Leo Jean and Evelyn Gerhardt G.; children from previous marriage: Lisa Marie, Wendy Ann Giroir-Colson; m. Louise Moore. BBA, Loyola U., 1963. CPA, Calif., La. Staff acct. Haskins & Sells CPAs, New Orleans, 1966-71; ptnr. Ross Landis & Pauw CPAs, Riverside, Calif., 1971-79, Easley & Giroir CPAs, Colton, Calif., 1979-81, McGladrey Hendrickson CPAs, Colton, 1981-84; shareholder Leo J. Giroir Jr. CPA, APC, Riverside, from 1984. Chair bd. dirs. Riverside Arts Found., 1991-97, Riverside County ARC, 1997—; treas. Riverside Ballet Theatre, 1991-92; bd. dirs. BBB, So. Calif., 1981—. Served in U.S. Army, 1964-66. Republican. Roman Catholic. Avocations: cooking, fishing. Died July 1, 2005.

GITTLER, STEVEN, lawyer, educator; b. Breslau, Germany, May 21, 1926; m. Antonia Brne, Aug. 7, 1954; 1 child, Jean Elizabeth. Diploma, City Colls. Chgo., 1946—47; BA, Lake Forest Coll., 1948; MA, Wash. State U., 1949; attended, U. Ill., 1951, U. Mich., 1954—55; EdD, SUNY, Buffalo, 1961. Bar: NY 1981. Instr. Mich. State U., East Lansing, 1953—54; prof. edn. Buffalo State Coll., 1955—95; mgr. residence hall, rsch. instr. in edn. Kent State U.; arbitration panelist, U.S. Dist. Ct. (We. Dist. NY) Supreme Ct. State NY., Am. Arbitration Assn., Buffalo, from 1999. Lt. col. med. svc. corps, Us.army Res., Ret.; mediator & factfinder Nys Pub. Employment Rels. Bd., NY, from 1973; dir. Edn. Law Assn., formerly Nat. Assn. of Legal Problems in Edn. (NOLPE), 1967—69. Hearing officer City Ct. of Buffalo, NY State Supreme Ct., Erie, NY, 1993—2003. Pvt. first class U.S. Army, 1944—46. Mem.: Bar Assn. of Erie County (life), Mason (32nd Degree Mason 1965). Achievements include admitted to the U.S. Supreme Court, 1984. Died Mar. 12, 2004.

GIVENS, DOUGLAS RANDALL, archaeologist, historian, educator; b. St. Louis, May 4, 1944; s. Glenn Stuart and Helena Katherine (Neff) G.; m. Linda Louise West, Mar. 29, 1969; 1 child, Clayton West. BA, MA, So. Ill. U., 1972; PhD, Washington U., 1986. Instr. anthropology St. Louis Community Coll.-Meramec, St. Louis, 1973-75, asst. prof. anthropology, 1975-78, assoc. prof. anthropology, 1978-88, prof. anthropology, from 1988; adj. prof. anthropology U. Mo., St. Louis, 1989-96; rsch. assoc. Peabody Mus. of Archaeology and Ethnology, Havard U., from 1996. Editor Bull. of History of Archaeology, 1991—; assoc. editor obituaries/history of archaeology Am. Antiquity, 1990-94; author: Alfred Vincent Kidder and the Development of Americanist Archaeology, 1992; contbr. articles to profl. jours. With USAF, 1967-70. Wenner-Gren Found. for Anthropol. Rsch. grantee, 1990-91, 93-94. Fellow Am. Anthropol. Assn.; mem. Soc. Am. Archaeology (mem. task force on curation 1992-96), History of Sci. Soc., Internat. Soc. for the Study of Time, Mo. Archaeol. Soc., AAAS, Brit. Assn. for Advancement of Sci. Avocations: woodworking, classical organ, piano, tennis. Home: High Ridge, Mo. Died May 22, 2004.

GIVHAN, EDGAR GILMORE, physician, writer; b. Montevallo, Ala., Aug. 6, 1935; AB in German Lit., Washington and Lee U., 1956; MD, Washington U., St. Louis, 1960. Diplomate Am. Bd. Internal Medicine. Intern Vanderbilt U., 1960, resident in internal medicine, 1965, instr. in hematology, 1965-66, Auburn U. Sch. Lab. Tech., 1967-85; co-owner Commercial Garden Design, Montgomery, Ala., from 1982. Pres. med. staff Montgomery Bapt. Hosp., 1974-75; cons. physician Ala. Medicaid Program, 1982-86; bd. dirs., cons. Humana Hosp. East Montgomery; med. dir. Humana Ins. Co. Ala.; chmn. bd. Direct Care, 1995—; horticulture lectr. Author: (guide and video) How to Grow Great Southern Gardens, 1992, Flowers for South Alabama Gardens, 1980, Conversations with a Southern Gardener, 1999, (with others) Heritage Gardens, 1992, Alabama Gardens Great and Small, 2002; contbr. articles to profl. jours. Chmn. bd. South Montgomery YMCA, 1973; bd. dirs. ARC, Montgomery, 1970-73, med. dir. blood processing ctr., Montgomery, 1973-80; bd. dirs. Montgomery Symphony Orch., Blue Cross and Blue Shield Ala., 1979-85, Montgomery C. of C., 1980-84; bd. vis. for the humanities Auburn U. Capt. USAF, 1962-64. Vanderbilt U. fellow, 1965-66. Fellow ACP; mem. AMA, Ala. Soc. Internal Medicine, Montgomery Soc. Internal Medicine (pres. 1970), Montgomery County Med. Soc. (pres. 1976), Ala. Soc. Clin. Oncology (v.p. 1982), Am. Soc. Hematology, So. Garden History Soc. (pres., bd. dirs.), Phi Beta Kappa. Died Nov. 15, 2004.

GLADDEN, JOSEPH FITZGERALD, tax office manager, writer; b. Richmond, Va., July 4, 1974; s. Henry Stanley and Mary Elizabeth Gladden. Office tax mgr. S&R Gladden Taxes, Greensboro, NC, from 1996. Bd. dirs. S&R Gladden, from 1996. Author: (poetry book) Secrets From My Heart, 2003, (novels) Deception, Lies & Betrayal, 2004. Democrat. Pentecostal. Avocations: travel, music, sports, writing. Home: Greensboro, NC. Died June 23, 2005.

GLASBERG, MEYER SAMUEL, lawyer, accountant; b. Phila., Dec. 16, 1916; s. Harry and Mary (Cooper) G.; m. Jean Carlin, Dec. 13, 1942 (dec. Apr. 1991); 1 child, Mark R. Student, Temple U., 1939, BSc, JD, Temple U., 1979. Bar: Pa. 1979, U.S. Dist. Ct. Pa. 1979; CPA, Pa. Pvt. practice acctg., pvt. practice, Phila., 1944-67; acct. Brown and Co., Phila., 1967-73, J.K. Lasser and Co., Phila., 1973-77, Touche Ross and Co, Phila., 1977-79; pvt. practice in law pvt. practice, Phila., from 1979. Mem. Pa. Bar Assn., Phila. Bar Assn. Home: Atlantic City, NJ. Died July 24, 2005.

GLATTFELDER, CALVIN FUGARD, pulp and paper company executive; b. Fairfield, Iowa, Aug. 19, 1924; s. Homer Franklin and Florence Angeline (Fugard) G.; m. Martha Elizabeth Wilson, July 5, 1947; children: Calvin, Nancy. BS in Forestry, Pa. State U., 1949; student, Iowa State U., 1942-43. Registered profl. forester, Md. Svc. and research forester Pa. Dept. Forests & Waters, Mont Alto, Pa., 1949-52; forester The Glatfelter Pulp Wood Co. subs. P.H. Glatfelter Co., Fredericksburg, Va., 1952-56, mgr. So. div., 1956-65, v.p., 1965-73, v.p., gen. mgr. Spring Grove, Pa., 1973-88, dir. woodland ops., 1988-90; also bd. dirs., from 1956. Mem. adv. com. State & Pvt. Forestry, U.S. Dept. Agr., Washington, 1975-78. Chmn. adminstrv. bd. United Meth. Ch., Fredericksburg, Va., 1972-73; mem. Goddard Chair Com. Pa. State U., 1982—; mem. Citizens Adv. Coun. to Pa. Dept. Environ. Resources, Harrisburg, 1985-90. With USN, 1943-47. Recipient Forestry Achievement award, Pa. State U., 1982, Outstanding Leadership award No. Logger, 1988; named Conservationist of the Yr. Pa. Forestry Assn., 1988. Mem. Am. Pulpwood Assn. Inc. (chmn. bd. dirs. 1988-90), Soc. Am. Foresters, Am. Forestry Assn., Pa. Forestry Assn., PT Boats Inc., Country Club York, Kiwanis, Masons, Pinehurst Country Club, Countryside Golf Club, Xi Sigma Pi, Sigma Nu. Republican. Methodist. Avocations: golf, tennis, photography, travel. Home: York, Pa. Died May 14, 2004.

GLAZER, ANDREW NORMAN SHAFRON, lawyer; b. Amityville, N.Y., Dec. 8, 1955; s. Edward Lewis Glazer and Shirley (Nagelberg) Shafron. BGS cum laude, U. Mich., 1977; JD, Emory U., 1980. Bar: Ga. 1980, U.S. Ct. Appeals (5th and 11th cirs.) 1980. Assoc. atty. Goodman & Bush, Atlanta, 1980-81; jud. clk. Hon. Dorothy T. Beasley, Atlanta, 1981-82; pvt. practice Atlanta, 1982-84; dir. edn. Nat. Ctr. Paralegal Tng., Atlanta, 1985-87; pres. Found. Profl. Edn., Atlanta, 1988-89; v.p. Nat. Ctr. Group, Atlanta, 1989-90, exec. v.p., chief oper. officer, 1990-92; pres. The Foundation Group, from 1992. Author: Pre-law Orientation Seminar Manual, 1988; exec. producer video to accompany book, 1988. Mem. State Bar Ga. (Continuing Legal Edn. Com.). Avocations: tennis, backgammon, writing. Died July 4, 2004.

GLAZIER, LYLE, writer, educator; b. Leverett, Mass., May 8, 1911; s. Harry Lee and Mertie Abby (Briggs) G.; m. Amy Louise Niles July 15, 1939 (dec. Mar. 1987); children: Laura, Susan, Alis. AB, Middlebury Coll., 1933, MA Bread Loaf Sch. of English, 1937; PhD, Harvard U., 1950; postgrad. in word processing, Vt. C.C., 1993-94. Prin. Northfield Mass. Ctr. Graded Sch., 1934-35; housemaster Mt. Hermon Sch. for Boys, Gill, Mass., 1935-37; instr. English, Bates Coll., Lewiston, Maine, 1937-42, Tufts Coll., Somerville, Mass., 1942-44; asst. in Shakespeare, Harvard U., Cambridge, Mass., 1944-45; tchg. fellow Harvard U. and Radcliffe Coll., Cambridge, Mass., 1945-47; asst. prof. English, U. Buffalo, 1947-52, assoc. prof., chmn. Am. studies, 1952-63; prof. English and Am. studies SUNY, Buffalo, 1965-72, prof. emeritus, from 1972. Fulbright chair Am. studies U. Istanbul, 1961-63, Fulbright Lectr. Hacettepe U., Ankara, Turkey, 1968-69, vis. prof., 1970, 71; lectr. U. Madras, India, 1970, 71; cons. thematic studies CUNY, 1973-75; vis. prof. Sana'a U., North Yemen, 1980; vol. adj. prof. So. Vt. Coll., Bennington, 1984-86; USIS vol. expert Am. lit., India, 1971; vol. prof. Miles Coll., Birmingham, 1967. Author: (novel) Summer for Joey, 1987, Stills from a Moving Picture, 1974, (poetry) Orchard Park and Istanbul, 1965, You Too, 1969, Voices of the Dead, 1971, The Dervishes, 1971, Two Continents, 1976, Azubah Nye, 1988, Recalls, 1986, Prefatory Lyrics, 1991, Searching for Amy, 1993, 2d edit. 2000 (criticism) American Decadence and Rebirth, 1971, Great Day Coming, 1988, Bennington Politics and Schools, 1986, Included in Reflections on a Gift of a Watermelon Pickle and Other Modern Verse (children's poetry anathology selected by children), 1966, 95, Contemporary Authors Autobiography Series, 1996; contbr. poems and articles to profl. and lit. jours.; contbr. to Festschrift for S.M. Pandeya, Banaras Hindu U., 1996. Exec. com. Friends of Bennington Free Libr., 1990-92; mem. sch. bd., vice chmn. Orchard Park (N.Y.) Sch. Dist., 1952-58; mem. Town Charter Commn., Bennington, 1987-89; mem. Gamaliel Painter's Cane Soc., Middlebury Coll., 1990—, mem. founders soc. Founders Soc., 1998—, mem. exec. com. Friends of Libr., Middlebury Coll., 1987-89, Abernethy Poetry/Rare Book Collection, Starr Libr., Middlebury, 2000; mem. Ret. Srs. Vol. Program, 1973—; mem. Bennington County Dem. Com., 1984-87; mem. exec. com. Bennington Area AIDS Project, 1990—; mem. nat. steering com. Clinton/Gore 1996, 1995-98, Gore 2000, 1999—; mem. Bennington Area Art Coun., 1990—; mem. Bennington Area Home Health Assn., 1990—, Bennington Counseling Svc., 1990; mem. Bennington County Chorus, 1973-79, patron, 1980—; mem. Grad. Students Middlebury Gay Lesbians, 1995, Vt. Mountain Pride Media, 1999; mem. Acad. of Am. Poets, ACLU, Bennington Mus. Found. Libr. of Congress Assocs., S.W. Vt. Regional Cancer Ctr., Rattlesnake Gutter Trust, Bread Loaf Writers' Conf. Fellow Am. Coun. Learned Socs., 1951-52. Mem. MLA, Bennington Robert Frost Soc., Vt. Coun. on Arts, League Vt. Writers, Poets and Writers, Am. Assn. Ret. Persons, Edmund Hayes Soc., North Bennington Artists Soc., Bennington County Humane Soc., Vt. Hist. Soc., Nat. Trust for Hist. Preservation, New England Artists Trust. Avocation: music. Home: Amherst, Mass. Died Oct. 21, 2004.

GLEASON, HARRIET HALL, nurse; b. Otranto, Iowa, May 11, 1923; d. Roy Francis Sr. and Amy Ruth (Read) G. RN, Kahler Sch. Nursing, Rochester, Minn., 1947; BS, BA, Hartwick Coll., 1956. RN, N.Y. Office nurse Mayo Clinic, Rochester, 1947-53, various hosps., Oneonta, N.Y.C., 1953—56; instr. Fairview Hosp., Mpls., 1956-57; clin. instr. Swedish Hosp., Mpls., 1958-59; supr. sick children unit Mt. Sinai Hosp., 1959-60; ward nurse various temp. agys., N.Y.C., 1960-82; gen. and spl. duty nurse various vol. assignments, Morgantown, W.Va., from 1982. Author: (cookbooks) Therapeutic Diets, 1980, Be Brave, 1994, (essays) I Understand, 1994. Active ARC; membership com., vol. Rep. Party Caucus, Mpls., N.Y.C. and W.Va., 1960-82, 92, 93. Mem. AAUW, Tri Beta, Zeta Tau Alpha (Pan Hellenic rep.). Lutheran. Avocations: reading, spectator sports, volunteer work, music appreciation. Died Jan. 23, 2004.

GLEASON, STEPHEN CHARLES, physician; b. Leon, Iowa, June 30, 1946; s. Charles Gerald and Ferne Louise (Pollard) Gleason; m. Lisa Ann Corcoran, Aug. 22, 1981; children: Julia K., Alex K., Michael John, Timothy Charles, Christian Kelly, Sean Patrick, Keriann Louise, Julia, Alex. BS, Iowa State U., 1971; DO summa cum laude, Coll. Osteo. Medicine and Surgery, 1974; PhD, Washington U., 1999. Diplomate Am. Bd. Family Practice, Bd Cert. Addiction, Medicine, Toxicology. Resident in family practice Meml. Med. Ctr., Corpus Christi, Tex., 1974—75; family practice medicine Des Moines, 1975-93; chief of staff to Gov.Tom Vilsack State of Iowa, 2002—05. Chmn. dept. family practice Mercy Hosp. Med. Center, Des Moines, 1979-82; pres., CEO chief med. officer Mercy Clinic System, 1984-97; mem. papal med. security team Pope John Paul's Am. Pilgrimage, 1979; asst. prof. Mayo Grad. Sch. Medicine, 1996—. Chmn. Iowa CARES Med. Found., 1987, Nat. Health Policy Coun., 1989-98; bd. dirs. Family Health Plan, HMO, 1985, Securecare PSD, Inc., 1990-99; White House health advisor, 1992-94; v.p. med. ops. Cath. Health Initiatives, 1997-98; sr. health adv. Pres. Clinton Campaign, 1996; sr. med. advisor Health Care Financing Adminstrn., 1998-99; dir. Dept. Pub. Health, State of Iowa, 1999-2002; pres. deligate World Health Orgn., 2000; active med. mission in El Salvador during earthquake disaster, 2001. Recipient Outstanding Young Iowan, 1982, Iowa Physician of Yr., 1990. Mem. AMA, Am. Acad. Family Physicians, Sigma Alpha Epsilon, Sigma Sigma Phi. Democrat. Home: Des Moines, Iowa. Died Mar. 25, 2006.

GLESER, GOLDINE COHNBERG, psychologist; b. St. Louis, June 15, 1915; d. Julius and Lena (Goldberg) Cohnberg; m. Sol Morris Gleser, June 4, 1936; children: Leon Jay, Malcolm Anthony, Judith Augusta. AB, Washington U., 1935, MS in Math., 1936, postgrad., 1936-38, PhD in Psychology, 1950. Instr. math. Washington U., St. Louis, 1947-49, rsch. asst. psychol. svcs., 1949-50; rsch. asst. to assoc. Washington U. Coll. Medicine, St. Louis, 1950-54; asst. to assoc. prof. U. Cin. Coll. Medicine, 1956-64; rsch. asst. to assoc. prof. U. Ill., Urbana, 1957-63; prof. psychology U. Cin., 1964-79, dir. psychol. div. dept. psychiatry, 1967-79, prof. emerita, from 1979. Cons. Dept. Edn., U. Ill., 1951-55, Malcolm Bliss Rsch. Lab., Washington U., 1954-56, Traumatic Stress Study ctr., U. Cin., 1981-91; cons. on evaluation Shiawassee County Community Mental Health Ctr., Ososso, Mich., 1972-85; mem. adv. com. on clin. drug evaluation NIH, Washington, 1960-61, reviewer devel. behavioral sci. rsch. grants, 1972-75; mem. joint com. to revise edn. and psychol. test standards APA/AERA, 1981-83. Author: (with Cronbach) Psychological Tests and Personnel Decisions, 1965, (with Gottschalk) Measurement of Psychological States, 1969, (with others) The Dependability of Behavioral Measurements, 1972, Prolonged Psychosocial Effects of Disaster, 1981, (with Ihilevich) Evaluating Mental-health Programs: The Progress Evaluation Scales, 1982, Defense Mechanisms: Their classification, correlates and measurement with the Defense Mechanisms Inventory, 1986, Defenses in Psychotherapy: The Clinical Application of the Defense Mechanisms Inventory, 1991, The Defense Mechanisms Test, 1968, others. Grantee Found. Fund for Rsch. in Psychiatry, U. Cin., 1959-65, NIMH, 1975-77; recipient Rieveschl award U. Cin., 1979, Lifetime Achievement award Ohio Women in Psychology, 1988, award for Traumatic Stress Studies, 1990. Fellow APA (rep. to coun. 1976-78, award 1985), Am. Statis. Assn., Am. Psychol. Soc., Ohio Psychol. Assn.; mem. Midwest Psychol. Assn., Cin. Psychol. Assn. (pres. 1957-58, 65-66, award 1988), Psychometric Soc. (trustee 1966-69), Soc. of Multivariate Exptl. Psychology (pres. 1977-78). Avocations: needlecrafts, fishing, computer games. Died Nov. 24, 2004.

GLICKMAN, SYLVIA ROBERTA, music educator, pianist, composer, publisher; b. N.Y.C., Nov. 8, 1932; d. Morris and May (Jacobs) Foodim; m. Harvey Glickman, Sept. 2, 1956; children: Lisa, Nina, Peter. BS, Juilliard Sch. Music, 1954, MS, 1955. Instr. piano New Eng. Conservatory Music, 1956-58; dir. chamber music Haverford (Pa.) Coll., 1967-84; artist, tchr. piano Franklin and Marshall Coll., Lancaster, Pa., 1985-89; pres. Hildegard Pub. Co., from 1988. Vis. prof. piano Rubin Acad. Music, Jerusalem, 1967-68. Composer: Emily Dickinson Songs, (for chorus, soloists and piano) Seven Deadly Sins, (Commd. Pa. Coun. on the Arts 1986), (for chamber orch.) The Walls are Quiet Now, (for bass and seven instruments) Am I a Murderer?; anthologist: Piano Music of Amy Beach, 1982, Four Piano Sonatas--Alexander Reinagle (1756-1809), 1988, Dances & Entertainment piano (Commd. Network for New Music), 1990, American Keyboard Music 1865-1909, 1990; musician (recs.) Bartok: Piano Quartet, 1981, Reinagle: Piano Sonatas, 1982; editor: (keyboard sect.) Books for College Libraries, 1987; co-editor: Women Composers: Music Through the Ages, 12 vols., 1996-2000. Bd. dirs. Montgomery (Pa.) Bicentennial Commn., 1976, Main Line Reform Temple, Wynnewood, Pa., 1985-89; dir. youth festival Tri-County Concerts, 1989-90. Recipient Solo Artist award Nat. Endowment for the Arts, 1982, Unique Contbn. to Music award Womens' Way, 1987; Fulbright grantee, 1955-56; licentiate Royal Acad. Music, London, 1956. Mem. Am. Music Ctr., Sonneck Soc., Internat. Congress on Women in Music, Citizens for the Arts in Pa., Coll. Music Soc., Pa. Composers Forum, Internat. Alliance for Women in Music (bd. dirs.). Democrat. Jewish. Avocation: reading. Home: Bala Cynwyd, Pa. Died Jan. 16, 2006.

GLOVER, ALBERT DOWNING, retired veterinarian; b. Newark, Mo., Dec. 4, 1907; s. Albert D. and Mattie O. (Downing) G.; m. Mildred Elva Haselwood; children: Allen, Gary, Janet. BS in Agr., U. Mo., 1932; DVM, Colo. State Coll., 1936. Former chmn. City Coun., Canton, Mo., other civic activities. Mem. Mo. VMA (pres. 1951, legis. commn.), AVMA (v.p. 1952), Mo. Vet. Examining Bd., Am. Legion (past comdr.), Shriners, others. Home: Canton, Mo. Died Feb. 16, 2004.

GLUCKSMAN, LEWIS L., investment company executive; m. Loretta Brennan; children: Mary, Jane. Grad., Coll. William & Mary, NYU. Ptnr. Lehman Brothers, N.Y.C., 1966—84, CEO; vice chmn. Smith Barney Inc., N.Y.C. Co-founder Glucksman Ireland House, 1993. Died July 5, 2006.

GLUSHIEN, MORRIS P., lawyer, arbitrator; b. Bklyn., Oct. 15, 1909; s. Isaac and Minnie (Hoffman) G.; m. Anne Williams, Nov. 18, 1945; children: Minna Taylor, Ruth Wedgwood. AB with honors, Cornell U., 1929, JD with honors, 1931. Bar: N.Y. 1932, U.S. Supreme Ct. 1940. Pvt. practice, Bklyn., 1932-38; mem. faculty Cornell Law Sch., 1938-39, New Sch. for Social Rsch., 1977-78; chief U.S. Supreme Ct. sect., assoc. gen. counsel NLRB, 1939-47; gen. counsel Internat. Ladies Garment Workers Union, AFL-CIO, 1947-72; arbitrator, 1972—2006; spl. master fed. ct., 1976-78. Mem. Nat. Acad. Arbitrators; mem. arbitration panels Am. Arbitration Assn., Fed. Mediation and Conciliation Service, various state and city agys. Editorial bd.: Cornell Law Quar, 1930-31; Contbr. legal periodicals. Bd. dirs. Nat. Legal Aid and Defender Assn., 1954-72. Served with AUS, as cryptanalyst, 1942-45. Mem. ABA (past chmn. labor law sect.), N.Y. State Bar Assn. (labor rels. com.), Assn. of Bar of City of N.Y. (past chmn. com. labor and social security legis.), Indsl. Rels. Rsch. Assn., Practicing Law Inst., Am. Jewish Congress (com. law and social action), Am. Judicature Soc., AFL-CIO (past mem. nat. legis. coun.), Civil Svc. Reform Assn. (exec. com.), N.Y. Com. for Modern Cts. (past v.p., bd. dirs.), Nat. and N.Y. State Against Discrimination in Housing Coms., ACLU (com. free speech and assn.), Ams. for Dem. Action, NYU Conf. on Labor, Curia, Phi Beta Kappa, Phi Kappa Phi. Home: Los Angeles, Calif. Died May 19, 2006.

GLYNN, ERNEST B., civil and environmental engineer; b. Cambridge, Mass., Dec. 19, 1911; s. Frederick Stanley G. and Maude Lillian Landers; m. Beatrice Beverly Bakerink, Jan 27, 1951; children: Nancy Belva, Priscilla Beverly. Diploma Structural Design, MIT, 1939; BS, U. Md., 1956. Registered profl. engr., Washington. Archtl. engr. Office Chief of Engrs. U.S. Army, Washington, 1942, 45-47, archtl. engr. Hq. 2nd Army Balt., 1947-48, ports engr. bd. engr. river and harbors Washington, 1948-51, engr., intelligence specialist, asst. chief of staff G-2, 1951-63; sr. engr. rsch. specialist Def. Intelligence Agy., Washington, 1963-73; pvt. practice Washington, 1973-85, Alexandria, Va., from 1985; prof. engring. George Washington U., Washington, 1982-85. Presenter, lectr. in field. Contbr. over 30 articles to profl. jours. Mem. Mt. Vernon dist. Fairfax (Va.) Falls Ch., 1959-65; mem. citizen adv. com. Met Wash COG, Washington, 1965-96. Served in U.S. Army, 1942-45. Decorated Croix de Guerre with palm, France; recipient two presdl. citations. Fellow Am. Soc. Civil Engrs. (chair solid waste com. 1950, 51); mem. Am. Acad. Environ. Engr. (diplomate), Va. Soc. Profl. Engrs., Nat. Soc. Profl. Engr. (pres. George Washington chpt. 1976, outstanding engr. 1976, engr. of yr. award 1984), Solid Waste and Environ. Protection, Masons (master lodge 4 Washington). Died Apr. 2, 2006.

GODDARD, RAY, lawyer; b. Cin., Nov. 6, 1925; s. Paul and Christine (Quinton) G.; m. Betty Ainsworth, July 21, 1946 (div. 1973); children: Ray Q. Stephen, Denise; m. Carmella J. Pino, Sept. 14, 1973. LLB cum laude, U. Balt., 1954. Bar: Md. 1954, U.S. Supreme Ct. 1958, U.S. Ct. Claims 1962. Dep. dist. counsel U.S. Army C.E., Balt., 1955-64; spl. trial counsel U.S. Dept. Justice, Washington, 1964-81; fed. adminstrv. law judge HHS, Portland, Maine, 1981-84; sr. assoc. Max E. Greenberg, Cantor & Reiss, N.Y.C., 1984-88; ptnr. Blodnick, Pomeranz, Reiss, Shultz & Abramowitz, N.Y.C., 1988-89; sr. ptnr. Goddard & Blum, N.Y.C., 1989-92, Goddard, Ronan & Dineen, N.Y.C., from 1992. Lectr. profl. orgns. and ednl. instns. Author monographs on constrn. contract law. Recipient U.S. Dept. Justice award, 1980. Mem. ABA. Avocation: photography. Home: New York, NY. Died Jan. 23, 2004.

GOEDICKE, PATRICIA, poet, educator; b. Boston, June 21, 1931; d. John Bernard and Helen Victoria (Mulvey) McKenna; m. Leonard Wallace Robinson, June 3, 1971. BA, Middlebury Coll., 1953; MA, Ohio U., 1965. Lectr. Ohio U., Athens, 1963—68, Hunter Coll., N.Y.C., 1969—71; assoc. prof. U. Guanajuato, Mexico, 1972—79, U. Mont., Missoula, 1983—90, prof., 1991—2003, prof. emerita, 2003—06. Vis. writer Kalamazoo Coll., 1977; guest poet Sarah Lawrence Coll., Bronxville, NY, 1980-81; vis. poet U. Mont., 1981-83; adv. bd. Calapooya Collage, Salem, Oreg., 1987-98, Hellgate Writers, Missoula, 1989-97; judge Oreg. Lit. awards, Portland, 1995; resident artist Rockefeller Found., 1993, faculty San Miguel Poetry Week, 2003, faculty Skagit River Poetry Project, 2004. Author: (poetry) Between Oceans, 1968, For the Four Corners, 1976, The Trail That Turns on Itself, 1978, The Dog That Was Barking Yesterday, 1980, Crossing the Same River, 1980, The King of Childhood, 1984, The Wind of Our Going, 1985, Listen, Love, 1986, The Tongues We Speak, 1989, Paul Bunyan's Bearskin, 1992, Invisible Horses, 1996, As Earth Begins to End, 2000; author numerous poems; contbr. articles to profl. jours.; consulting editor Eastern Wash. State U. Press, Cheney, 1995. Recipient award NEA, 1969, Strousse award Prairie Schooner, 1987, Edward Stanley award, 1992, Walter Hall award Hubbub, 1995, Ohioana poetry award, 2002, H.G. Merriam award disting. contbns. Mont. lit., 2003, Stout award Hubbub, 2003; Nat. Endowment Arts fellow, 1976, Creative Writing fellow NEA, 1976-77; Duncan Frazier prize, 1976, Coordinating Coun. Lit. Mags. prize, 1976, William Carlos Williams prize New Letters, 1977, Pushcart Prize, 1977-78, Carolyn Kizer poetry prize Monmouth Inst., 1987, Chad Walsh poetry prize, 2002; Spl. commendtion Arvon Internat. Poetry Competition, 1987; Rsch. grantee U. Mont., 1989; disting. scholar, Mont., 1991; residency Rockefeller Ctr., Bellaggio, Italy, 1993; named Disting. Alumna, Ohio U., 2002. Fellow: MacDowell Colony; mem.: Poets Editors Novelists West, Poets Editors Novelists USA, Assoc. Writing Programs, Poetry Soc. Am. (Ohioana Poetry award 2002, H.G. Merriam award 2003), Acad. Am. Poets (assoc.). Democrat. Avocations: music, downhill skiing, reading, dance. Home: Missoula, Mont. Died July 14, 2006.

GOLD, WILLIAM, microbiologist; b. Buffalo, Jan. 2, 1923; s. Paul and Merle (Stirberg) G.; m. Aida Sara Frank, Dec. 21, 1952; children: Avram Reuben, Morris Samuel, Rebecca Rose, Hannah Star. BS, Cornell U., 1943; MS, U. Wis., 1948, PhD, 1950. Fellow Rutgers (N.J.) U., 1950-51; research assoc. E.R. Squibb, New Brunswick, N.J., 1951-57; microbiologist Bzura, Inc., Keyport, N.J., 1957-63; supr. biochemistry dept. Beechnut/Lifesavers Co., Portchester, N.Y., 1963-67; asst. prof. NYU Coll. Dentistry, N.Y.C., 1967-73; mgr. pharmacology Cooper Labs., Mountain View, Calif., 1973-81; supr. devel. of biologics Baxter Microscan, Sacramento, 1982-94. Contbr. articles to profl. jours.; patentee in field. Served with U.S. Army, 1943-46, ETO. Grantee John Hartford Found., NYU Coll. Dentistry, 1968-73. Mem. Am. Chem. Soc., Am. Soc. Microbiology, Sigma Xi. Jewish. Avocation: religious studies. Home: Elizabeth, NJ. Died May 24, 2004.

GOLDBERG, ERWIN B., advertising and marketing executive; b. Bklyn., Apr. 20, 1945; s. David and Adele (Littenberg) G.; m. Diane Burko, Sept. 4, 1966 (div.); 1 child, Jessica Burko-Goldberg. Dir. advt. Life Assurance Corp. Pa., Phila., 1976-77; sales promotion mgr. Nat. Liberty Corp., Valley Forge, Pa., 1977-80; v.p. McAdams & Ong Advt., Phila., 1980-81; pres. Arau & Goldberg Advt., Phila., 1982-85; v.p., gen. mgr. Lefton Direct, Phila., 1985-92; pres. Goldberg Advt. and Direct Mktg., Phila., from 1992. Bd. dirs. Phila. Child Guidance Clinic, 1987-90. Mem. Direct Mktg. Assn., Phila. Direct Mktg. Assn. Democrat. Jewish. Died Nov. 5, 2004.

GOLDBERG, GLENN ALAN, advocacy organization administrator; b. New Haven, Conn., Dec. 1, 1947; s. Herbert B. and Lillian Grace (Chauser) G.; m. Kari Zeh; 1 child, Jesse Zeh. BA with honors, U. Conn., 1969; JD, Columbia Law Sch., 1972. Bar: Conn. 1979, D.C. 1979. Trial atty. Bur. of Consumer Protection, FTC, Washington, 1972-74; instr. in law George Washington U., Washington, 1974-75; gen. counsel Action on Smoking & Health, Washington, 1974-75; adj. prof. Antioch Sch. of Law, Washington, 1975; exec. dir. Nat. Ctr. for Law & the Deaf, Gallaudet U., Washington, 1975-77, Deaf Counseling, Advocacy & Referral Agy., Oakland, Calif., 1978-80; non profit cons. Goldberg & Assocs., Pacific Grove, Calif., 1980-86; exec. dir. NorCal Ctr. on Deafness, Sacramento, Calif., from 1986. Bd. dirs. Sacramento Community Cable Found. (chmn. fundraising com.), 1987—. Contbr. articles to profl. jours. Coord. Students for Ribicoff, Storrs, Conn., 1974; Senate Intern Senator Abraham Ribicoff, Washington, 1968; congressional intern Rep. Joseph Monahan, Washington, 1968. Mem. Nat. Assn. of the Deaf, Calif. Assn. of the Deaf, Self Help for Hard of Hearing People, Phi Beta Kappa. Democrat. Jewish. Avocations: jazz clarinet, alto saxophone, sign language, bridge, tv game shows. Home: Port Angeles, Wash. Died Dec. 19, 2004.

GOLDBERG, HILARY THAM, poet; b. Kelang, Malaysia, Aug. 20, 1946; arrived in US, 1971; d. Sun Hong Tham and Tuck Khoon Oo; m. Joseph Ray Goldberg, May 20, 1945; children: Ilana P., Shoshana M., Rebecca S. BA in English Lit., U. Malaysia, 1971. Poet-in-residence Howard County Poetry & Literacy Soc., Columbia, Md., 1993-94; artist-in-edn. Va. commn. Arts, Richmond, from 1990, The Kennedy Ctr. for Performing Arts, N.Y.C., from 1999; poet-in-residence Arlington-Fairfax (Va.) Jewish Congregation, from 2000; poetry editor Potomac Rev., Port Tobacco, Md., from 1995; editor-in-chief The Word Works, Inc., Washington, from 1995. Panel judge Va. Commn. Arts, 1994-98, Md. Arts Coun., Balt., 1986-97, N.J. Grants Mid-Atlantic Arts Found., Balt., 1997-98. Author: (memoir) Lane With No Name: Memoirs and Poems of a Malaysian-Chinese Girlhood, 1997, also 9 volumes of poetry including No Gods Today, 1969, Paper Boats, 1987, Bad Names for Women, 1989, Tigerbone Wine, 1992, Men & Other Strange Myths, 1994, Counting, 2000, The Tao of Mrs. Wei, 2003. Chair Coalition for Resettlement IndoChinese Refugees, Arlington, 1979-80; pres. sisterhood Arlington-Fairfax Jewish Congregation, 1988-89, pres., 1990-93, v.p., 1992-96. Artist-in-Edn. grantee Va. Commn. Arts, 1990-2001. Mem. Writer's Ctr. Avocations: painting, travel. Home: Arlington, Va. Died June 24, 2005.

GOLDBERG, MYRON ALLEN, physician, psychiatrist; b. Bronx, June 4, 1942; s. Marcus and Rose (Spiegel) G. AB, Hunter Coll., 1965; MD, Universidad del Noreste, Tampico, Mexico, 1979. Staff psychiatrist, forensic unit Bronx-Lebanon Hosp., Bronx, N.Y., 1985-86, team leader inpatient unit, 1986-88, chief physician geriatric svcs., dept. psychiatry, from 1986; clin. instr. Albert Einstein Coll. of Medicine, Bronx, from 1986, team leader inpatient unit, 1991-92, team leader inpatient svc., from 1992. Inventor fluid pressure relief valve, 1973. Judicial del. Dem. Coop City Club, Bronx, 1986; exec. com. Dem. Club, Bronx, 1987-88 and other offices. Recipient recognition Crotona Park Community Mental Health Ctr., 1986. Mem. Am. Psychiatric Assn., AMA. Democrat. Jewish. Avocations: tropical fish, science fiction, woodworking. Home: North Bergen, NJ. Died Mar. 20, 2004.

GOLDBERG, STEVEN SELIG, education law educator; b. Bklyn., Jan. 8, 1950; s. Harry Louis and Ruth (Bartnofsky) Goldberg; married. BA, SUNY, Binghamton, 1970; JD, Bklyn. Law Sch., 1973; MA, Columbia U., 1976; PhD, U. Pa., 1985. Bar: Pa. 1974, US Dist. Ct. (ea. dist.) Pa. 1976, US Ct. Appeals (3d cir.) 1976, Nebr. 1980. Atty. Camden Regional Legal Svc., NJ, 1976, Edn. Law Ctr., Phila., 1976-80; fellow law psychology grad. tng. program U. Nebr., Lincoln, Nebr., 1980-81; pvt. practice Phila., 1982-85; asst. prof. edn. law U. ND, Grand Forks, ND, 1986-88; assoc. prof. Arcadia U., Glenside, Pa., 1988-93, prof., 1993—2006; adj. prof. edn. sch. U. Pa., Phila., 1990—2006; adj. prof. edn. law Rutgers Law Sch., Camden, NJ, 1995—2006; adj. prof. ednl. law U. Pa. Law Sch., Phila., 2002—06. Appellate officer Pa. Spl. Edn. Appeals Panel, 1995-2006; editl. adv. bd. West's Edn. Law Reporter, 1987-2006; mem. profl. adv. bd. Montgomery County (Pa.) Assn. for Children with Learning Disabilities, Pa. Assn. Children with Learning Disabilities, 1976-80; cons. right to edn. assistance group Pa. Dept. Edn. Author: Special Education Law, 1982; editor: Readings on Equal Education, 1991; (with P. Zirkel) Digests of Supreme Court Cases in Education, 1995, 4th edit., 2001; co-host, prodr. show Sta. KFJM Pub. Radio U. ND, 1987; prodr. videotapes; contbr. articles to profl. jour. Mem. ABA (dispute resolution sect., co-chair edn. com. 1997), Phila. Bar Assn., Am. Ednl. Rsch. Assn (chmn. edn. law 1989-90), Edn. Law Assn. (bd. dir. 2000-06), Soc. for Profl. Dispute Resolution (co-chmn. edn. sector). Jewish. Home: Philadelphia, Pa. Died Feb. 1, 2006.

GOLDEN, DONALD MICHAEL, writer, inventor; b. Springfield, Mass., June 5, 1953; s. Donald Leon and Marilyn Ruth (Bush) G.; m. Agnes Bozena Meduna, Nov. 13, 1971; children: Steven Frank, Tina Marie Golden Weaver, Tiffany Lynn. Owner, mgr. painting co., Ashford, Conn., 1971-94; writer, inventor, Colorado Springs, Colo., from 1994. Author: (juvenile) Mulligan Stew Gang, 1996, also various others; author: (poetry) Sparrowgrass Poetry Forum, 1998; inventor magic fingers, painter's mate. Rep. Goodwill industries charity functions, Bridgeport, Conn., 1966-67. Recipient Editor's Choice award Nat. Libr. Poetry, 1997. Avocations: fishing, gold panning, woodworking, artistry, drawing comics. Died Oct. 26, 2004.

GOLDEN, GARY J., dean; b. Lowville, N.Y., Apr. 3, 1952; s. Glenn A. and Gladys (Burkhard) G.; m. Kathy Jo Sellmeyer, Nov. 28, 1991; children: Eric Joseph, Gregory Joseph. BS, Rutgers U., 1974; MS, SUNY, Brockport, 1978; EdS, U. N.Mex., 1981. Leadership cons. Delta Upsilon Fraternity, Indpls., 1974-75, leadership devel. dir., 1975-76; resident dir. SUNY, Brockport, 1976-78; asst. dean of students U. N.Mex., Albuquerque, 1978-87, assoc. dean of students, 1987-91; dean student svcs. San Juan Coll., Farmington, N.Mex., 1991—2004. Active Rotary Club, Albuquerque and Farmington, 1986-94 (scholarship 1985); bd. dirs. U. N.Mex. Alumni Assn., Albuquerque, 1993-2004. Mem. Am. Assn. Coll. Registrars and Admission Officers, Nat. Assn. Campus Activities. Home: Farmington, N.Mex. Died Nov. 25, 2004.

GOLDEN, HERBERT HERSHEL, retired language educator; b. Boston, Nov. 1, 1919; s. Max and Minnie (Turetzky) G.; m. Hilda Rachel Lazerow, June 13, 1943 (dec. May 1964); children: Robert Sherman, Barry Allen (dec. Aug. 2003), Steven Eliot; m. Evelyn Pauline Sowa, Oct. 7, 1965. BA, Boston U., 1941, MA, 1942, Harvard U., 1947, PhD, 1951. Lectr. Spanish and French, Boston U., 1945-49, instr. Romance langs., 1949-53, asst. prof., 1953-57, assoc. prof., 1957-63, prof., 1963-85, prof. emeritus, from 1985. Cons. for NDEA lang. insts. U.S. Office Edn., HEW, Washington, 1955-56; asst. to mng. editor Modern Lang. Jour., Nat. Fedn. Modern Lang. Tchrs. Assns., Boston, 1955-58; instr. French and Italian, Harvard U. Ext., Cambridge, Mass, 1960-79; mem., editor, mem. adv. com. on fgn. langs. Mass. Dept. Edn., Boston, 1960-69; Fulbright lectr. U. Rome, 1962-63. Co-author: Modern French Literature and Language: A Bibliography of Homage Studies, 1953, reprinted 1971, Modern Iberian Language and Literature: A Bibliography of Homage Studies, 1958, reprinted 1971, Modern Italian Language and Literature: A Bibliography of Homage Studies, 1959, reprinted 1971, Histoire de France à Travers les Journaux du Temps Passé (1715-1789). Lumières et Lueurs du XVIII Siècle, 1986; editor: Studies in Honor of Samuel Montefiore Waxman, 1969, Giulio Bertoni and the Aesthetic Factor in Linguistics, 1969; contbr. articles and revs. to profl. jours. With U.S. Army, 1942-45, ETO. Decorated Purple Heart, Bronze Star, Gold medal of cultural merit (Italy); recipient diploma of merit Internat. Assn. for Study Italian Lang. and Lit., 1973, diploma of appreciation, France, 2001; Rsch. fellow Marion and Jasper Whiting Found., 1979-80. Mem. MLA (steering com. fgn. lang. program 1956-59), Am. Soc. for 18th Century Studies (editor Festschriften: 18th Century Bibliography), Am. Assn. Tchrs. Italian (sec.-treas. 1959-64, pres. 1964-66), French Soc. 18th Century Studies, Masons, Phi Beta Kappa (pres. Mass. Epsilon chpt. 1970-72, cert. disting. merit 1985). Avocations: classical music, collecting French films on video, reading. Home: Brookline, Mass. Died July 23, 2006.

GOLDENBERG, PHILIP THEODORE, physician; b. Hartford, Conn., Aug. 17, 1920; s. Joseph and Esther (Taylor) G.; m. Gloria Rose Lavitt, Jan. 20, 1952; children; Jeffrey, Andrew, Lori. BA, Cornell U., 1943; MD, Boston U. Sch. Med., 1946. Diplomate Am. Bd. Internal Medicine. Physician, Hartford, from 1952. Pres. Hartford Med. Soc., 1977. Capt. U.S. Army, 1947-49, Germany. Fellow ACP. Home: Bloomfield, Conn. Died Apr. 15, 2004.

GOLDENBERG, SAMUEL, optometrist, school administrator; b. N.Y.C., Dec. 6, 1920; s. Marcus and Anna (Kantrowitz) G.; m. Renee Weiss, Mar, 30, 1950; 1 child, Ilene. OD, So. Coll. Optometry, Memphis, 1942; BA, Drew U., 1944; MA, Seton Hall U., 1955; PhD, NYU, 1967. Cert. optometrist, N.J.; cert. tchr., ednl. adminstr., sch. prin., N.J. Optometrist, Convent Station, N.J., from 1943; tchr. Rockaway Twp. (N.J.) Pub. Schs., 1951-62, Morris Twp. (N.J.) Pub. Schs., 1962-68, prin., 1968-71, asst. supt., 1971-72; prin. Morristown (N.J.) Pub. Schs., 1972-78, sch. adminstr., from 1978. Cpl. USAF, 1944-45. Recipient citation USAF, 1945. Mem. N.J. Prins and Suprs. Assn., Morris Sch. Dist. Adminstrs. Assn., N.J. Adminstrs. Assn. Avocation: home repairs. Home: Morristown, NJ. Died Jan. 7, 2004.

GOLDRICK, KAREN GOUVIS, art educator; b. Chgo., Dec. 31, 1953; d. Arthur Angelo and Marion Gene (Malevitis) G.; m. Jack Goldrick, July 17, 1976; children: Katherine Marisa, Stacy Marie. BS in Psychology, Loyola U., 1975; MS in Early Childhood, Chgo. State U., 1979; BFA, Sch. of the Art Inst., Chgo., 1987. Cert. art tchr., Ill. Tchr. Chgo. Pub. Schs., 1975-89, Wilmette (Ill.) Park Dist., from 1991; vis. tchr. The Sch. of the Art Inst. of Chgo.-Basic Program, 1990-94; faculty Sch. of the Art Inst. of Chgo., from 1994. Recipient Tchr. of the Yr. award Holden Sch., 1988. Mem. Nat. Art Edn. Assn., Ill. Allaince for Art Edn. Home: Chicago, Ill. Died July 31, 2005.

GOLDSCHMIDT, KARL, psychotherapist; b. Nuremberg, Bavaria, Fed. Rep. of Germany, May 29, 1923; came to U.S., 1933; s. Siegfried and Gertrude (Loewensohn) G.; m. Lori Finclaire; children: Wendy, Kim. BEE, Columbia U., 1948, MEE, 1956; MSW, Fordham U., 1981. LCSW, N.J. Mem. tech. staff Bell Telephone Labs., N.Y., N.J., 1948-79; sch. social worker Long Branch (N.J.) Schs., 1981-82; psychotherapist The Consultation Ctr., Freehold, N.J., 1982-83, Family & Community Svcs., Red Bank, N.J., 1983-89; pvt. practice and workshop facilitator Tinton Falls, N.J., from 1985. Mgmt. cons. Bus. Effectiveness Cons., Tinton Falls, 1985—. Designer 15 workshops including Self-Therapy, Stress Mgmt., Time Mgmt., Getting Well Again, 1981—; inventor in telephony field, 1950-70. Tchr., recreation leader Monmouth Folk Dancers, Red Bank, 1961—. With U.S. Army, 1943-46. Pulitzer scholar Columbia U., 1941. Mem. IEEE, NASW, Acad. Cert. Social Workers. Avocations: dance, hiking, biking, playing music, cross country skiing. Died Aug. 25, 2004.

GOLDSTEIN, CHARLES IRWIN, research mathematician; b. N.Y.C., Nov. 21, 1940; s. Emil and Fay (Greenberg) G.; m. Joyce Kluback, May 31, 1975; children: Andrew, Roger. BS, CCNY, 1962; MS, NYU, 1964, PhD, 1967. Rsch. mathematician Brookhaven Nat. Lab., Upton, N.Y., from 1967; adj. prof. math. SUNY, Stony Brook, from 1986. Vis. rsch. mathematician, U. Wis., Madison, 1971, NASA Langley Rsch. Ctr., Hampton, Va., 1978, U. Calif.-Berkeley and Lawrence Berkeley Lab., 1979, Naval Rsch. Lab., Washington, 1983. Contbr. rsch. articles to jours. and books. Courant Inst. rsch. fellow, NYU, 1962-67. Mem. Soc. Indsl. and Applied Math., Am. Math. Soc., Sigma Xi. Jewish. Achievements include development, analysis and implementaion of numerical methods for solving partial differential equations and wave propagation problems. Home: Nesconset, NY. Died Oct. 5, 2004.

GOLDSTEIN, HARRIS SIDNEY, psychiatrist; b. Chgo., Mar. 6, 1934; s. Herman Bendorf and Lillian (Sain) G.; m. Brigitte Maria Wolbert, Dec. 6, 1961; children: Marcel, Michael, Nicole, Sharon. BS, U. Ill., Urbana, 1955; MD, U. Ill., Chgo., 1959; MLA, Johns Hopkins U., 1966; DSc, SUNY, Bklyn., 1971. Cert. psychiatry, child psychiatry. Intern Cook County Hosp., Chgo., 1959-60; resident in psychiatry Sheppard-Pratt Hosp., Towson, Md., 1963-66; rsch. fellow SUNY, Downstate Med. Ctr., Bklyn., 1966-68, asst. prof., 1968-73, assoc. prof., 1973-75; assoc. prof. Robert Wood Johnson Med. Sch. U. Medicine and Dentistry N.J., Piscataway, 1975-95; dir. tng. child and adolescent psychiatry, 1993-95. Contbr. articles to profl. jours. Capt. U.S. Army, 1960-62. Mem. Am. Psychiat. Assn., Am. Acad. Child and Adolescent Psychiatry, Phi Beta Kappa. Jewish. Died July 30, 2005.

GOLDSTEIN, PAUL ROBERT, management company executive, consultant; b. Indpls., May 13, 1928; s. Harry and Belle Witcovski Goldstein; m. Nancy L. Fink, Dec., 18, 1955 (div. May 1969); children: Lynne G. Throop, James H. BS, Ind. U., 1948; postgrad., NYU, 1948, Purdue U., 1954. Registered money mgr. SEC. Rsch. corr. Merrill, Lynch, Pierce, Fenner & Smith, N.Y.C., 1950, account exec. trainee, 1953; account exec. Merrill, Lynch, Pierce, Fenner & Reaves, Indpls., 1954—61, DuPont, Glore, Forgan, Indpls., 1961-73, Paine, Webber, Jackson & Curtis, Indpls., 1973-78; dep. assessor Marion County, Indpls., 1978-83; mgr. margin dept. C.L. McKinney & Co., L.A., 1985-86; CEO PRG Mgmt. Co., Indpls., from 1987. Columnist I.U. Daily Student, 1945-46. Commdr. post #114 Jewish War Vets., Indpls., 1994; regional adv. bd. Anti-Defamation League, Indpls., 1962-66; ward chairperson Dem. Cen.

Com., Indpls., 1978-82; mem. vet. adv. bd. Roude Bush VA Hosp., 1996-98. Sgt. Corps. of Engrs., 1950-52, Korea. Recipient 50 Yr. Gold Cir., Sigma Alpha Mu, 1995. Mem. Am. Legion, Greater Indpls. Progress Com. (sec., profl. sports sub-com. 1966-68), B'nai B'rith (pres. lodge # 58 1961-62). Democrat. Jewish. Avocations: collecting art and rare books, tennis, golf. Home: Indianapolis, Ind. Died Feb. 14, 2006.

GOMES, EDWARD CLAYTON, JR., construction company executive; b. Terre Haute, Ind., Nov. 15, 1933; s. Edward Clayton Sr. and Jewel Margaret (James) G.; m. Pamela Thompson, Jan. 11, 1958; children: Hilary T., Valerie C. BBA, Washington U., St. Louis, 1955, MBA, 1968. Pres. Mo. Petroleum Products Co., St. Louis, 1969-80; pres., CEO Lionmark, Inc., St. Louis, 1980—2002. Bd. dirs. Martin K. Eby Constrn., Inc., Wichita, Magna Bank, St. Louis, Rightchoice Managed Care, Inc.; internat. dir. Young Pres.'s Orgn., N.Y.C., 1975-80; trustee Blue Cross Blue Shield Mo., 1991-94. Bd. dirs. Acad. of Sci., St. Louis, 1977-80; trustee St. Louis Art Mus., 1988-92, The Hawthorne Found., Jefferson City, Mo., 1983-86; commr. St. Louis Sci. Ctr., 1980-83. Mem. World Bus. Coun., Chief Execs. Orgn. (bd. dirs.), Whittemore House, St. Louis Club, Beta Gamma Sigma. Episcopalian. Avocations: swimming, tennis, reading, travel. Home: Saint Louis, Mo. Died Oct. 12, 2005.

GONGAWARE, WILLIAM RALPH, utilities executive; b. Ft. Wayne, Ind., Oct. 30, 1940; s. Francis Lutillus and Anna Velma (Puff) G.; m. Betty Jean Sanders; children: Christopher, Gregory, Stacey. BSEE, N.C. State U., 1967; MSME, Naval Postgrad. Sch., Monterey, Calif., 1976. Commd. ensign USN, 1968, advanced through grades to lt. comdr., 1978, electronics mgr., missile officer CG-12 N.Y.C., 1968-71, lt., engring. and exec. officer USS Sumner DD-692, 1971-73, lt. comdr., first lt. USS Pensacola LSD-38 Norfolk, Va., 1976-79, lt. comdr. Naval Sea Systems Commd. Washington, 1979-80, resigned, 1980; supr. mech. equipment Va. Power, Richmond, 1980-83, dir. reliability, quality engr., 1983-87, productivity coord., 1985-87, maintenance engr., 1987-89; asst. prof. J. Sargeant Reynolds C.C., Richmond, Va., from 1989; electronics engring. tech. program head, from 1991; tech. prep project dir., from 1992. Assoc. prof., 1993—. Mem. Am. Soc. Engring. Edn., Internat. Poets Soc. Democrat. Lutheran. Home: Richmond, Va. Died Aug. 1, 2004.

GONZALEZ, FRANK, JR., engineering educator; b. Tampa, Fla., July 16, 1948; s. Frank Sr. and Aida (Prida) G.; m. Sara Roquemore, Feb. 16, 1974; children: Ryan, Sean, Erin. BS, U. Fla., 1970, MS, 1971, PhD, 1974. Rsch. assoc. U. So. Calif., L.A., 1975-78, U. Wash., Seattle, 1979-81; asst. prof. engring. U. Wis., Wausau, 1981-87, assoc. prof. engring., from 1987. Contbr. articles to profl. jours. Mem. Am. Soc. for Engring. Edn., Soc. for Mfg. Engring. Avocations: piano, racquetball. Home: Wausau, Wis. Died Jan. 19, 2004.

GOOD, BARBARA J., foreign service officer; b. Oakland, Calif., Oct. 31, 1927; d. Ralph Allen and Charlotte (O'Connor) G. BA, U. Calif., Berkeley, 1950. Cryptographer U.S. Dept. State Fgn. Svc., Rome, 1951-53, sec. La Paz, Bolivia, Buenos Aires, Kobe, Japan, and Paris, 1953-64, recruiter, 1965-70, program officer U.S. Nat. Commn. for UNESCO, 1970-79, dir. internat. women's affairs, alt. del. UN Commn. Status of Women Washington, 1979-80; cultural affairs officer U.S. Info. Svc., Calcutta, India, 1981-83; NGO liaison officer U.S. State Dept., 1984; cultural affairs officer U.S. Info. Svc., Amman, Jordan, 1985-87. NGO officer Coalition Against Trafficking in Women, Washington, 1990—; bd. dirs. Am. Fgn. Svc. Assn. First v.p. Nat. Woman's Party, Washington, 1989—. Recipient Accolade for Professionalism in Comm., Advt. Comm. Times, Phila., 1980; Honor award Women's Action Orgn., 1980; disting. honoree and recipient, UN Human Rights award Nat. Woman's Party, Washington, 1988. Mem. UN Assn., NCA (bd. dirs., mem. exec. bd. 1990), Nat. Coun. Women (exec. bd. 1992), Women's Inst. for Freedom of Press (assoc.), Internat. Abolitionist Fedn. (bd. dirs. 1994). Democrat. Avocations: health clubs, skiing, golf, swimming. Home: Pebble Beach, Calif. Died May 13, 2004.

GOODBERRY, DIANE JEAN (DIANE OBERKIRCHER), retired mathematics educator, accountant; b. Buffalo, June 24, 1950; d. Ralph Arthur and Muriel Carol (Glaeser) O.; m. Lawrence D. Goodberry, Sr. BS in Math. Edn., State Univ. Coll., Brockport, N.Y., 1972, MS in Ednl. Adminstrn., 1974; grad., Nat.Tax Tng. Sch., Monsey, N.Y., 2000. Cert. in secondary math. edn., N.Y. Uni-Pay clk. Marine Midland Bank, Buffalo, 1968-72; asst. registrar State Univ. Coll., Brockport, 1972-74; home instrn. tutor Clarence Ctrl. Sr. H.S., Sweet Home Sr. H.S., NY, 1974-75; part-time inst. Erie C.C., Buffalo, 1975-86; instr. math. Ednl. Testing Methods, Buffalo, 1984-90, Buffalo Pub. Sch. System, from 1974. Mem. curriculum devel. com. Buffalo Pub. Schs., 1988, 92—, yearbook advisor 1994—, math. intervention coord., 2002—; cooperating tchr. BRIET-U. Buffalo, 1990-96; owner Taxes by Diane; CEO, Larry's GrassRoots Landscaping Inc.; cons. Nat. Tax Tng. Sch., 1999—; AIS coord., Buffalo Pub. Sch. Sys., 2002—. Vol., World Univ. Games, Buffalo, 1993. Mem. AAUW, Nat. Assn. of Female Execs., Women Tchrs. Assn. (bd. dirs., v.p. 1993-94, pres. 1994-96, rec. sec. 1996-98, treas. 1998), Assn. Math. Tchrs. N.Y. State (conf. spkr.), Theodore Roosevelt Rough Riders, Nat. Coun. Math. (conf. spkr.), Assn. Curriculum Devel. and Supervision (Top 2000 scholar of 20th Century award, named one of 2000 Outstanding Scholars of 20th Century Winner in Math). Republican. Methodist. Avocations: crafts, reading, travel, sports. Home: Holland, NY. Died Dec. 1, 2004.

GOODE, JANE KINNEY, artist; b. Mpls., July 22, 1919; d. Edwin Cyril and Irene Francis (Woodruff) Kinney; m. Howard Joseph Charles La Perriere, Oct. 15, 1948 (div. Aug. 1949); 1 child, Bonnie; m. Calvin Morris Goode, Oct. 17, 1959. Student, Terry Art Sch., Miami, Fla., 1941, Art Workshops, from 1973. Pvt. sec. to col. U.S. Army Corps. of Engrs., Miami, 1942-45; mem. singing trio USO, 1945-48; staff mem. Little River Shopper, Miami, 1949-50; sales WTSP Radio Station and St. Petersburg Times, St. Petersburg, Fla., 1950-55; acct. exec. Adcraft Adv. Agy., Corpus Christi, Tex., 1955-74; exec. dir. Paisano Girl Scout Coun., Corpus Christi, Tex., 1974-86; artist Corpus Christi, Tex., from 1986. Mem. Pres. team to hire the Handicapped, 1962-63; mem. pub. rels. United Way, 1964; bd. dirs. Corpus Christi Press Club, 1960-61; pres. Corpus Christi Advt. Club, 1961-62; mem. and adv. mem. Mcpl. Arts Commn., Corpus Christi, 1987—; fin. com. YWCA, 1988-90; bd. dirs. Early Childhood Devel., 1988-91, Art Ctr. Corpus Christi, 1998—. Named Women of Yr. Advt. Club, 1961; recipient Thanks Badge award Paisano Girl Scout, 1979, The Silver Medal award Advertising Fedn., 2001; named one of 7 Women in Careers, YWCA, 2003. Mem. Art Mus. of Corpus Christs, Art Ctr. of Corpus Christi. Home: Corpus Christi, Tex. Died Oct. 31, 2004.

GOODELL, JOHN DEWITTE, electromechanical engineer; b. Omaha, Nebr., Sept. 20, 1909; s. Edwin Dewitte and Vera May (Watts) G.; m. Bernadette Michel, Apr. 27, 1943; children: Mary, Greg, Thomas, Caroline, Daniel. Cons. engr., N.Y.C., 1931-41; tech. dir. U.S. Army Detroit Signal Lab., 1941-43; dir. engring. Minn. Electronics, St. Paul, 1946-57; mgr. new product design CBS Lab., Stamford, Conn., 1957-60; dir. engring. Robodyne, U.S.Industries, Silver Spring, Md., 1960-61; corp. tech. dir. U.S. Industries, N.Y.C., 1962-63; producer Goodell Motion Pictures, St. Paul, 1964-75; cons. engr. New Product Design, St. Paul, 1976-90; exhibit prototyper Sci. Mus. of Minn., St. Paul, 1990-93; dir. engring. Tomorrow's World, St. Paul, from 1993. Author: The World of Ki, 1967; writer, dir. (motion picture) Always a New Beginning, 1973, (acad. nominated best documentary 1973), (TV documentary) Wisdom and Change, 1992; dir. Challenge for Tomorrow, 1964 (indsl. Oscar); inventor: automatic mail handler, automatic manipulator, magnetic pulse controlling device, conditioned reflex teaching machines and others, 1954-2004; editor Jour. of Computing Systems, 1965-70. With U.S. Navy, 1943-46, S. Pacific. Recipient Master Design award, Product Engring., 1962. Mem. IEEE (sr.), Soc. Motion Picture and TV Engrs. Avocations: Oriental Game of Go (capt. U.S team 2nd place winners Internat. Go Cong., 1964). Died Apr. 4, 2004.

GOODMAN, FELICITAS DANIELS, anthropologist; b. Budapest, Hungary, Jan. 30, 1914; came to U.S., 1947; d. Nikolaus and Maria (Uhlig) Daniels; m. Glenn H. Goodman, Mar. 27, 1937 (div. 1967); children: Nicolas, Frederick, Susan, Beatrice. M., U. Heidelberg (Germany), 1936; MA, Ohio State U., 1968, PhD, 1971. Instr. German dept. Ohio Wesleyan U., Delaware, 1947-50; sci. translator Battelle Meml. Inst., Columbus, Ohio, 1951-58; multilingual abstractor Chem. Abstracts/Ohio State U. Med. Sch., Columbus, 1958-64; lectr. German dept. Ohio State U., Columbus, 1962-68; assoc. prof. dept. sociology-anthropology Denison U., Granville, Ohio, 1968-79; dir. Cuyamunque Inst., Santa Fe County, N.Mex., from 1979. Author: Speaking in Tongues, 1972, The Exorcism of Anneliese Michel, 1981, How About Demons?, 1988, Ecstasy, Ritual, and Alternate Reality, 1989, Where the Spirits Ride the Wind, 1990, Trance (in German), 1992. V.p. sec. sociology-anthropology Ohio Acad. Sci., Columbus, 1977-78. Fellow AAAS, Am. Anthropol. Assn. Home: Columbus, Ohio. Died Mar. 30, 2005.

GOODRICH, DONALD FRANKLIN, II, lawyer, educator; b. Covington, Ky., June 6, 1954; s. Donald Franklin and Margaret Jean (Schwartz) G.; m. Holly Ann Wendling, Aug. 29, 1980 (div.); 1 child, Donald Franklin III. Student, Oxford U., Oxfordshire, England, 1974-75; BA, No. Ky. U., 1975; MA in History, Eastern Ky. U., 1976; MPA, Ky. State U., 1977; JD, No. Ky. U., 1983. Bar: Ky. 1984, U.S. Dist. Ct. (ea. dist.) Ky. 1984. Research asst. to dist. service No. Ky. U., Highland Heights, 1972-73; teaching asst. dept. history Eastern Ky. U., Richmond, 1975-76; asst. to dean Sch. Pub. Affairs Ky. State U., Frankfort, 1976-77; reference law librarian Coll. Law U. Cinn., 1983; assoc. Lyons and Fries, Cinn., 1980-84; prin. Goodrich and Assocs., Newport, Ky., from 1984. Prof. Coll. Arts and Letters, Polk C.C., Winter Haven, Fla. Mem. exec. com. Ky. Republicans, Frankfort, 1981-83; legis. aide Minority Leader Ky. Ho. of Reps., Frankfort, 1983; Rep. candidate state rep. 67th Legis. Dist., 1986. Fellow HEW, 1977. Mem. ABA (book award local govt. law 1983), Trial Lawyers Assn. Am., Am. Judicature Soc., No. Ky. Bar Assn., Phi Alpha Theta. Episcopalian. Died June 26, 2004.

GOODRICH, NORMA LORRE (MRS. JOHN H. HOWARD), literature and language professor; b. Huntington, Vt., May 10, 1917; d. Charles Edmund and Edyth (Riggs) Falby; m. J.M.A. Lorre, Dec. 10, 1943 (div. June 1946); 1 son, Jean-Joseph; m. John Hereford Howard, Jan. 20, 1964. BS cum laude, U. Vt., 1938; postgrad. (U. Vt. fellow), U. Grenoble, France, 1938-39; PhD (Ellis fellow), Columbia U., 1965; LittD, U. Vt., 1993. Tchr. high schs., Vt., 1939-43, Bentley Sch., N.Y.C., 1943-47; owner dir. Am. Villa in Normandy, Trouville, France, 1947-53; tchr. Fieldston Sch., N.Y.C., 1954-63; asst. prof. French U. So. Calif., 1964-66, assoc. prof., 1966-71; dean faculty Scripps Coll., Claremont, Calif., 1971-72; prof. French and comparative lit. Claremont Colls., 1972—82, prof. emeritus, 1982—2006. Vis. scholar Calif. Luth. Coll., 1965, Isle of Man, U.K., 1986, Claremont McKenna Coll., 1986; vis. prof. John Carroll U., Cleve., 1987, Calif. State U., Long Beach, 1986, 87, 88, Cal Arts, Pasadena, 1989, Calif. Poly. U., Pomona, 1992, Southwestern Coll., 1993, Riverside Bapt. Coll., 1994, Scripps Coll., Claremont, 1994; lectr. Arthurian Soc., Carlisle, Cumbria, Eng., 1994, 96, 97, Santa Anita (Calif.) Ch., 1995, Trinity Episc. Ch., Redlands, Calif., 1996. Author: Ancient Myths, 1959, rev. edit., 1977, 94, Medieval Myths, 1960, rev. edit., 1977, 94, Doctor and Maria Theresa, 1961, Myths of the Hero, 1961, Ways of Love, 1963, Charles of Orleans: A Study of Themes in His French and English Poetry, 1967, Giono: Master of Fictional Modes, 1973, Afterword for the Man Who Planted Trees (Jean Giono), 1985 (New Eng. Book award), London edit., 1989, King Arthur, 1986, 2d edit., 1989, Merlin, 1987, 2d edit., 1989, Il Mito della Tavola Rotonda (transl. of King Arthur), 1989, Le Roi Arthur, 1989, Die Ritter von Camelot, 1994, 95 (transl. of King Arthur), Castle Epstein (transl. of Alexander Dumas), 1989, Priestesses, 1989, Guinevere, 1991, The Holy Grail, 1992, Il Mito di Merlino, 1992 (transl. of Merlin), Heroines, 1993, Il Mito di Ginevra (transl. Guinevere), 1995; editor: Bullfinch Mythology, The Age of Fable, 1995, Bullfinch Mythology, The Age of Chivalry, 1995, Il Santo Graal, 1997, (boxed edit.) Hors Commerce, 1997; contbr. articles to internat. profl. jours.; guest appearances various TV and radio shows, Eng., 1986, 94, U.S., 1986-90, 93, 94. Mem. pub. rels. staff Worthington Corp., N.Y.C., 1953-54; bd. dirs. patron West End Opera Assn., 1973-74, program dir., 1975-76; guest lectr. Flower Festival, Arthuret Ch., Longtown, Cumbria, Eng., 1991, guest preacher, 1992. Recipient Good Citizen medal SAR, 1989, Martha Washington medal, 1992, Wallace award Am. Scottish Found., 1990; invested as Dame Knights Templar, Commandery of Nova Scotia, in the Rosslyn Chapel, Scotland, 1990; reinvested as Knight Templar, Dame and Officer with the rank of comdr. in Teampull of Sion, Edinburgh, Scotland, 1990, St. Mary's Cath., Edinburgh, Order of St. George, 1993, Mil. Order Fgn. Wars, 1994, Calif. Commandery medal, 1997. Fellow Soc. Antiquarians, Nat. Inst. Social Scis.; mem. Assn. Study of Dada and Surrealism (sec. 1970-72), Philol. Assn. Pacific Coast (nominating com. 1971-72), MLA (mem. del. assembly's election com. 1975), The Prehistoric Soc., Am. Assn. Tchrs. French, Medieval Assn. Pacific, Medieval Acad. Am., Nat. Soc. DAR (vice-regent 1996-97), Columbia U. Alumni Assn., Dante Soc., Pierport Morgan Libr., Clan MacArthur, Clan MacKay (hon.), 78th Fraser's Highlanders 2d Bn. of Foot Am. (lt.), Tordarroch Trust (Scotland and U.S.), Met. Opera Guild, Order of the Crown of Charlemagne in the U.S.A. (life), Phi Kappa Phi. Avocations: gymnastics, gardening, dress making, travel. Home: Claremont, Calif. Died Sept. 19, 2006.

GOODWILLING, PHILIP LOUIS, psychical research professional; b. Feb. 11, 1935; m. Arline S. Martin; 3 children. Student, Washington U., St. Louis, 1956-59. Comptr. to nat. labor orgn., 1961-85; ret., 1985; pres., psychic investigator Haunt Hunters, St. Louis, from 1985. Adminstr. Housing for Elderly project, HUD, St. Louis. Author: To Catch a Ghost; co-author: Haunt Hunters Handbook for the Psychic Investigator. Mem. Psychic Sci. Inst. (v.p.), Parapsychol. Svcs. Inst. Died Nov. 27, 2004.

GOODWIN, GLENN LAVERN, accountant; b. Hayward, Wis., Oct. 2, 1931; s. Vernon Willis and Violet Helen (Markstedt) G.; m. Rosemary Badger, Aug. 29, 1955; children: Mark, Catherine, Ruth, Alysha, Christine. BS, Brigham Young U., 1956. Sr. acct. Arthur Young & Co., Los Angeles, 1959-63; ptnr. Joseph Bentley & Co., Los Angeles, 1963-69, B.D.O. Seidman, Grand Rapids, Mich., from 1969. Contbr. articles to profl. jours. Pres. area Boy Scouts Am., Mich., 1984-88; stake pres. Ch. Jesus Christ of Latter-day Sts., Grand Rapids, 1975-85. Capt. USAF, 1956-59. Recipient Silver Beaver award Boy Scouts Am., 1972, Silver Antelope award Boy Scouts Am. 1982. Mem. Am. Inst. CPA's, Mich. Assn. CPA's, Nat. Assn. Accts. (nat. dir. 1982-84), Gov. Fin. Officers Assn. (spl. rev. com. 1985—), Assn. Govt. Accts., Grand Rapids C. of C., Rotary (dist. treas. Grand Rapids club 1984-85). Republican. Mem. Lds Ch. Avocations: genealogy, camping, hiking, gardening. Home: Nauvoo, Ill. Died Apr. 27, 2005.

GORDAN, ANDREW LEB, aerospace engineer; b. Cleve., Dec. 11, 1923; m. Clina Ann DeLa Mater, July 2, 1945; children: Pamela, Edward, Judith, Andrew. BS in Engring., Case Western Res. U., 1953; grad., Indsl. Coll. of Armed Forces, 1974; MS in Engring., Calif. Inst. Tech., 1976, PhD in Engring., 1978. Project engr. The Cross Co., Detroit, 1953-58; sr. rsch. engr. Goodyear Aircraft Co., Akron, Ohio, 1958-60; mgr. rsch. and devel. The Curtis Wright Corp., Cleve., 1960-64; sr. engr., tech. advisor NASA-Lewis Rsch. Ctr., Cleve., 1964-88; v.p. engring. Analytical Engring. Corp., North Olmsted, Ohio, 1988—90; chief engineered NASA programs Loral Aerospace, 1990—93; cons. PMLG, Inc., from 1994. Cons. Clevite Corp., Dania, Fla. Patentee in field; contbr. articles to profl. jours. Pres. Old Brooklyn Civic Orgn., Cleve., 1968; chief sci. humanitarian project Western Res. Med. Sch. and VA Hosp., Cleve., 1972. With

USN, 1941-45. Mem. Internat. Elec. Electronic Electromech. Soc., Nat. Geographic Soc., Am. Astron. Soc., Soc. Automotive Engrs. Roman Catholic. Avocation: painting. Died June 18, 2006.

GORDON, FORREST LYLE, minister; b. Rich Hill, Mo., Feb. 4, 1926; s. Fay Ward and Martha Blanche (Caton) G.; m. Onie Elizabeth Orr, Sept. 11, 1946; children: Carol Diane Gordon Kobe, David Ward. CLU, Am. Coll., 1977. Lic. as min. First Bapt. Ch., 1976; ordained to ministry Evang. Ch. Alliance, 1987. Capt. (ret.) L.A. City Fire Dept., 1951-62; pastor of adminstrn. and missions First Bapt. Ch., Reseda, Calif., from 1986. Mem. fin. com. S.W. Bapt. Conf., West Covina, Calif., 1987-90. Author: Church Safety, 1990. Chmn. Reseda Cen. Bus. Dist. Citizens Adv. com., 1987-89. With USCG, 1943-46. Fellow Nat. Assn. Ch. Bus. Adminstrn.; mem. Christian Mgmt. Assn., Reseda C. of C. Republican. Home: Hemet, Calif. Died June 21, 2005.

GORDON, GERD STRAY, retired historian, educator, writer; b. Stavanger, Norway, Nov. 15, 1912; came to U.S., 1948; d. Johannes and Ella (Stray) Johansen; m. Johan Vogt (div.); children: Mette Wernøe, Gerd Ada Vogt, Christina Isaksen; m. Raymond Gordon; 1 child, Karen Allyn. Student, Oslo U., 1937-41; BA, Fla. State U., 1960; MA, U. Pitts., PhD, 1978. Cert. tchr., Fla., Pa. Accredited corr. Aftenposten-Norsk Dameblad, Oslo, 1948-55; tchr. Panama C.Z. Schs., Panama Episc. Sch., 1960-61, Am. Coop. Sch., Tunis, Tunisia, 1962-64, Am. Internat. Sch., Bangkok, 1965-68, Djakarta, Indonesia, 1968-69, Am. Sch., New Delhi, 1969-70, Pitts. Pub. Sch. Sys., 1970-83; freelance lectr., from 1983. Lectr. Slippery Rock (Pa.) U., U. Kans., Lawrence, Vanderbilt U., Nashville; presenter Symposium of Scandinavian Historians. Author: Kvinnen Idag (Woman Today), 1952; contbr. articles to numerous publs including Dictionary of Scandinavian History, 1986. Dem. ofcl., Denver, 1952-57, election judge, 1954-58; bd. dirs., rep., Planned Parenthood, Denver and Pitts., 1952-89; participant Citizen Day Com. signed S.P. Kinney II Denver Woman's Press Club, 1965, Senate of Pa., 1985. Resistance worker during German occupation of Norway, World War II. Recipient Outstanding Citizen award Norwegian Resistance; Ella Lyman Cabot Trust grantee U. Pitts. Mem. Denver Women's Press Club (bd. dirs. 1952—), Pitts. U. Historian Alumnae Orgn., Fla. State U. Alumnae Assn., AAUW (bd. dirs. Pitts. chpt. 1984—), LWV (past bd. dirs. Denver and Pitts. chpts.), Countryside Garden Club (bd. dirs. 1970—). Avocations: gardening, quilting, skiing, swimming, yoga. Home: Pittsburgh, Pa. Died Nov. 5, 2004.

GORDON, JACK DAVID, foundation administrator, real estate company officer; b. Detroit, June 3, 1922; s. A. Louis and Henrietta (Rodgers) G.; m. Myra L. MacPherson; children: Andrew Louis, Deborah Mary, Jonathan Henry; stepchildren: Leah Siegel, Michael Siegel. BA, U. Mich., 1942. Engaged in real estate and ins. businesses, Miami Beach, Fla., 1946-52; founding dir., pres., chief mng. officer Washington Savs. & Loan Assn., Miami Beach, 1952-80, vice chmn. bd., 1980-81; founding dir. Jefferson Nat. Bank of Miami Beach, 1962-77, past chmn. exec. com.; dir. Inst. Pub. Policy and Citizenship Studies Fla. Internat. U., now the Jack D. Gordon Inst.; pres. The Hospice Found. of Am., Miami. Mem. Fla. State Senate, 1972-92, pres. pro tempore, 1982-84, majority leader, 1988-90; housing fin. cons. Dept. State and; expert cons. UN Tech. Assistance Program in Costa Rica, Nicaragua, Panama, Ethiopia, Somali Republic, Nigeria, 1959-63; cons. to ROCAP, 1962-64, Eastern Nigerian Housing Corp., 1963; contract supr. AID Housing Guaranty Program in Latin Am., 1966-69; chmn. Miami Beach Housing Authority. 1947-56. Author: (with others) A Survey of New Home Financing Institutions in Latin America, 1969. Mem. Dade County Bd. Pub. Instrn., 1961-68. Served with AUS, 1943-46. Mem. Am. Jewish Congress, Am. Friends of Hebrew U., ACLU. Democrat. Home: Miami, Fla. Died Dec. 16, 2005.

GORDON, KENNETH HICKOK, psychiatrist; b. Altoona, Pa., Dec. 18, 1924; s. Kenneth Hickok Sr. and Ines Frae (McClellan) G.; m. Janice Taylor, June 16, 1951; children: Deirdre, Pamela, Sheila. MD, Temple U., 1948, MS in Psychiatry, 1956. From instr. to assoc. prof. Temple U., Phila., 1954-61, from asst. to assoc. prof., 1961-66, prof., adj. prof., 1966—2005; assoc. dept. psychiatry Lankenau Hosp., Phila., 1971—2005; clin. prof. psychiatry and human behavior Jefferson Med. Coll., Phila., 1979—2005; attending physician Jefferson U. Hosp., Phila., 1979—2005. Chmn. Advs. for Children of Pa., Phila., 1979-82; bd. dirs. Emily Bacon Child Psychiatry Clinic, Phila. Contbr. articles to profl. jours.; producer video tape Comprehensive Treatment of Spinal Cord Injuries, 1982. Co-founder Main Line Mental Health and Mental Retardation Ctr., Phila., 1966; pres. World Federalists Assn., Phila., 1971-87, Citizens for Valley Forge, Pa., 1975-78; chmn. Valley Forge Land Use Task Force, 1974-77; bd. dirs. Crossroads Sch., Paoli, Pa., 1989-96; pres. bd. dirs. Tabor Children's Svcs., Phila. Fellow Am. Psychiat. Assn. (life), Phila. Coll. Physicians, Am. Acad. Child and Adolescent Psychiatry; mem. AMA, Am. Soc. for Adolescent Psychiatry, Spinal Injury Assn., Regional Coun. Child Psychiatry (pres. 1977-79, 91-93), Franklin Inn Club, Delaware Valley Ornithol. Club, Alpha Omega Alpha. Avocations: ethology, horticulture, sculpture. Died July 25, 2005.

GORDON, LARRY DEAN, elementary school educator; b. Greentop, Mo., Oct. 24, 1938; s. Aubrey T. and Oletha F. (Lay) G.; m. Dolores M. Overstreet, Aug. 23, 1959; children: Sheila, David, Shelly. BSE, N.E. Mo. State U., 1959, MA, 1962; EdS, George Peabody Coll., 1968; EdD, Mo. U., 1971. Tchr. Riverview Gardens Sch. Dist., St. Louis, from 1959; instr. grad. program N.E. Mo. State U., Kirksville, from 1974. Pres. Nat. Edn. Assn. Riverview Gardens, St. Louis, 1978. Mem. Phi Epsilon Kappa (Disting. Svc. award, pres. 1975-76, 90-91), Phi Delta Kappa. Avocations: reading, travel, music, sports. Home: Ballwin, Mo. Died July 13, 2005.

GORDON, MICHAEL D., electronics engineer, nurse, air force officer; b. St. Louis, Dec. 30, 1946; s. Hardin G. and Lola D. (Wadlow) G.; m. Karen Lynn Minor, May 17, 1967 (dec. Oct. 1967); m. Debra Horton, Nov. 5, 1995; adopted children: Li Nin, Maria, Tina, Johnathan. Diploma in respiratory therapy, U. Calif., San Diego, 1970; BSN, UCLA, LA, 1973; BA in Theology, NCA Coll. & Sem., Gatlinburg, Tenn., 1981; BS, MS in Electronic Engring., UCLA, 1989. RN, Calif.; cert. electronics engr., respiratory therapy tech., physician's asst. Respiratory therapist USAF, from 1970; RN, pediatrics, gen. nursing USAF, UNICEF, from 1973; commd. officer USAF, 1973, advanced through grades to brig. gen., 1993; chaplain, counselor USAF, UNICEF, from 1981; elec. engr. USAF, from 1989. Flight nurse; emergency nurse; helicopter pilot; cons. Muscular Dystrophy Assn., N.Y.C., 1982—, Children's Hosp., L.A., 1982—; chief bd. dirs., founder Children of AN LOC Found., 1970; contbr. devel. Internat. Electronics Comm. Sys. UNICEF and WHO, telecomputer sys. Children's Hosp. Goodwill amb. Muscular Dystrophy Telethon, 1974—, Holt Internat. Children's Svcs., 1974—, children's hosps., 1982—, UN, UNICEF, 1982—; vol. nurse, chaplain ARC; vol. Oklahoma City Bombing Disaster Team, 1995 Recipient UNICEF Hall of Fame award, 1980, Disting. Svc. award, 1981, Disting. Electronics award, 1995, Disting. Commendation award Children's Hosp., 1997. Mem. VFW, ANA, Nat. Chaplain's Assn. (life, Legion of Honor, Chaplain's medal of honor 1981, named to Chaplains Hall of Fame 1983), Am. Assn. Respiratory Care, Am. Legion, Phi Beta Kappa, Alpha Psi Omega. Baptist. Achievements include research on improvement of avionic computer electronic systems for air craft helecoptors. Home: Choctaw, Okla. Died June 11, 2004.

GORDON, MORTON LAWRENCE, rabbi; b. Putnam, Conn., Oct. 17, 1924; s. Solomon Z. and Florence (Bloch) G.; m. Anna S. Lesser, Jan. 4, 1948; children: Jonathan, Sandra. BS, NYU, 1946, MA, 1971, D. Hebrew Letters, 1974; Rabbi, Yeshiva U., 1947. Ordained rabbi, 1947. Rabbi Degel Israel Synagogue, Watertown, N.Y., 1947-50, House of Peace Synagogue, Columbia, S.C., 1950-54, Sons of Zion Synagogue, Putnam, 1954-62, Jewish Ctr. of Mt. Vernon (N.Y.), 1962-68, Temple Torah, Little Neck, N.Y., from 1968. Pres. L.I. (N.Y.) Commn. Rabbis, 1975-77; pres. L.I. Bd. Rabbis, 1981-83. Contbr. sermons to religious publs. Recipient Horowitz award Fedn. Jewish Philanthropies, 1980. Mem. Am. Assn. Marriage and Family Therapists (clin.), Rabbinical Coun. Am. (bd. dirs.), N.Y. Bd. Rabbis (bd. dirs.), Internat. Synagogue (bd. dirs.), Masons (chaplain). Home: Great Neck, NY. Died Mar. 11, 2005.

GORDON, NANCY MOREHOUSE, humanities educator, forester; b. Chgo., Jan. 21, 1926; d. Edward Ward and Anna Mason (Ely) Morehouse; m. Harold J. Gordon Jr., Sept. 10, 1949 (dec.); children: Elizabeth, Edward, Richard. BA, Bryn Mawr Coll., 1947; MA, Yale U., 1948, PhD, 1955; MS, U. Mass., 1988. Lic. forester, Maine. Lectr. history Chatham Coll., Pitts., 1955-57, U. Pitts., 1958, Carnegie Inst. Tech., Pitts., 1959, U. Mass., Amherst, 1960-65, 66-68, tchg. asst. forestry, 1984-86. Vis. lectr., asst. prof. Mt. Holyoke Coll., South Hadley, Mass., 1962, 1968-69; vis. lectr., assoc. prof. Westfield (Ma.) State Coll., 1981-82; cons. forester Anson, Maine, 1989—. Author, editor: The Austrian Empire, 1974; editor: Innovation & Achievement in the Public Interest, 1966; co-author: Stepping Back to Look Forward, 1998. Elected mem., rep. Town Meeting of Amherst, Mass., 1964-68, 1975—; chair cogeneration com. Town of Amherst, 1980-81, mem. Overall Econ. Devel. Program com., 1981-84; mem. adv. com. chpt. 32 Mass. Dept. Environ. Mgmt., Boston, Mass., 1989-92. Fellow AAUW, 1958-59, Am. Philosophy Soc., 1969-70; Fulbright-Hays Travel grant Fulbright, 1965-66. Mem. Mass. Forestry Assn. (bd. dirs. 1988-92, 96—), Soc. Am. Foresters, Forest History Soc., Soc. Hist. Tech., Northeastern Forest Economists, New England Hist. Assn., Amherican Hist. Assn. Home: Amherst, Mass. Died July 20, 2005.

GORDON, RONALD CLAYTON, biomedical engineer; b. Petersburg, Va., Aug. 13, 1933; s. Robert Lee and Georgia Frank (Clayton) G.; m. Vivian Verdell, Jan. 27, 1957 (div. 1987); children: Ronald Jr., Susan; stepchildren: Yasmin, Taslim, Karim; m. Zarina Watkin, Mar. 27, 1989. BS, Va. State Coll., 1955, MS, 1968; PhD, U. Va., 1978. Physicist Nat. Bur. Standards, Washington, 1957-64; rsch. engr. McDonnell Douglas, Santa Monica, 1964-68; asst. prof. U. Va. Sch. Medicine, Charlottesville, 1979-82; fgn. sci. technologist U.S. Army, 1982-92; asst. prof. U. Va. Sch. Medicine, 1992-94; commr. Dept. Rehab. Svc., Richmond, Va., 1994-95; dir. Va. Neuro Trauma, Crozet, 1995—97. NIH fellow, 1972-76. Died Aug. 14, 2004.

GORENSTEIN, SAMUEL, retired mathematician, educator; s. Isidore and Bessie Gorenstein; m. Shirley Slotkin, July 3, 1948; children: Ethan Ezra, Gabriel William. PhD, N.Y. U., 1968. Sr. mathematician Sys. Devel. Corp., Paramus, NJ, 1959—63; mathematician advisor IBM, Armonk, NY, 1963—89. Adj. prof. Poly. Inst. N.Y., N.Y. U., N.Y.C., 1968—83. Contbr. articles to profl. jours. Vol. math tutor Union Settlement Cmty. Ctr., N.Y.C., 1997—2000. 2nd lt. navigator Army AC, 1943—45, European Theatre of Operations. Fellow, NASA, 1966. Mem.: Ops. Rsch. Soc. (chair computer sci. sect. 1975—81). Achievements include development of constructed price index for total cost of computing systems. Home: New York, NY. Died 2005.

GORLIN, ROBERT JAMES, medical educator; b. Hudson, N.Y., Jan. 11, 1923; s. James Alter and Gladys Gretchen (Hallenbeck) G.; m. Marilyn Alpern, Aug. 24, 1952; children: Cathy, Jed. AB, Columbia U., 1943, postgrad., 1947-50; DDS, Washington U., St. Louis, 1947; MS, State U. Iowa, 1956; DSc (hon.), U. Athens, Greece, 1982, U. Thessalonike, 1993, U. Md., 1999, U. Minn., 2002, U. Copenhagen, 2003. Oral pathologist VA Hosp., Bronx, NY, 1950-51; instr. dentistry Columbia U., N.Y.C., 1950-51; dental dir., pathologist Op. Blue Jay, Thule, Greenland, 1951-52; mem. exec. faculty, chmn. oral pathology and genetics Sch. Dentistry U. Minn., Mpls., 1956-90, assoc. prof. div. oral pathology Sch. Dentistry, 1956-58, prof. Sch. Dentistry, 1958-93, prof. pathology and dermatology Sch. Medicine, Sch. Dentistry, 1971-93, prof. pediatrics, ob-gyn, otolaryngology Sch. Medicine, 1973-93, Regents' prof. oral pathology Mpls., 1978-93; Fulbright exch. prof., Guggenheim fellow Royal Dental Coll., Copenhagen, 1961; 1st Lingamfelter lectr. dermatology U. Va., 1971; 1st Boyle lectr. Case Western Res. U. Med. Ctr., Cleve., 1972; vis. prof. UCLA-Harbor Gen. Hosp., 1972; asst. chief dental service Glenwood Hills Med. Ctr., 1959-61, chief, 1962-64, cons., 1969-73; Regents' prof. emeritus U. Minn. Sch. Dentistry, Mpls, 1994—2006. Mem. Minn. Adv. Bd. Human Genetics, 1959—73; Minn. mem. U.S. Congl. Liaison Com. for Dentistry, 1963—80; mem. Ctr. Histologic Nomenclature and Classification of Odontogenic Tumors and Allied Lesions WHO, 1966—80; mem. adv. com. periodontal disease and soft tissue study NIH, 1967—78, mem. dental sect., 1970—73; mem. adv. com. Nat. Found. Clin. Rsch., from 1974; vis. prof. Tel Aviv U., 1980, Sch. Dentistry, Jerusalem, 1981; 2nd Edward Sheridan lectr., Dublin, 89; Windemere lectr. Brit. Paediatric Assn., 1990; founder, bd. dirs. Found. for Devel. and Med. Genetics, 1994; lectr. in field; cons. in field. Author: (with M. Cohen) Syndromes of the Head and Neck, 1964, 76, 90, 2001 (with R. Goodman) The Face in Genetic Disorders, 1970, 77, The Malformed Infant and Child, 1983, (with B. Konigsmark) Genetic and Metabolic Disorders, 1977, Hereditary Hearing Loss and Its Syndromes, 1995; co-contbr.: Computer Assisted Diagnosis in Pediatrics, 2d edit., 1971; editor: (with H. Goldman) Thoma's Oral Pathology, 1970, Chromosomes and Human Cancer (J. Cervenka and B. Koulischer), 1972; editorial cons. Jour. Dental Rsch., Geriatrics, Archives of Oral Biology, Jour. Pediats., Pediats., Am. Jour. Diseases of Children, Syndrome Identification, Radiology; editor oral pathology Oral Surgery, Oral Medicine, Oral Pathology, Clin. Pediats.; assoc. editor Am. Jour. Human Genetics, 1970-73, Jour. Oral Pathology, 1972-83, Jour. Maxillofacial Surgery, 1973-2006, Cleft Palate Jour., 1976-2006, Clin. Pediat., 1985-2006; mem. bd. Excerpta Medica, 1976-80, Jour. Craniofacial Genetic Devel. Biology, 1980-2006, Jour. Clin. Dysmorphology, 1982-86, Gerodontics, 1984-86, Birth Defects Ency., 1986-2006, Dysmorphology Clin. Genetics, 1987-2006; cons. editor Stedman's Med. Dictionary, 1959-2006; contbr. numerous articles to profl. jours. Bd. dirs. Minn. div. Am. Cancer Soc., 1959-60, mem. nat. clin. fellowship com., 1962-65; With U.S. Army, 1943-44; lt. USNR, 1953-55. Recipient Fredrick Birnberg Rsch. award, Columbia U., 1987, Lifetime Achievement award, March of Dimes, 1989, award, Am. Cleft Palate Assn., 1993, Disting. Alumni award, Washington U., 1997, Goldhaber award, Harvard U., 1997, Premio Anni Verdi award, Spoleto, Italy, 1997; fellow, Columbia U., 1947—48, NIH, 1948—49, Nat. Insts. Dental Rsch., 1949—50. Fellow: Royal Soc. Surgeons of Eng., Royal Soc. Surgeons of Ireland, Am. Acad. Oral Pathology (v.p. 1957—58, sec. 1958—64, v.p. 1964—65, pres. 1966—67, award 1993, diplomate), Am. Coll. Med. Genetics (hon.), Am. Bd. Oral Pathology; mem.: Triology Soc., Am. Skin Assn. (Lifetime Achievement award 2005), Inst. Medicine, ADA (Norton Ross prize 1995, Gold medal 2003), Skeletal Dysplasia Soc. (hon.), Nat. Inst. Medicine NAS (sr.), Internat. Assn. Oral Pathology (hon.), Hollywood Acad. Medicine (hon.), Internat. Soc. Craniofacial Biology (bd. dirs. 1966—67, v.p. 1967—68, pres. 1969—70), Internat. Skeletal Soc., Royal Soc. Medicine London (Burrough Wellcome fellow 1991, R. Abercrombie award in med. genetics 1994, Disting. lectr. 2001), Am. Soc. Human Genetics (Disting. lectr. 2001, Excellence in Human Edn. award 2004), Minn. Soc. Pathologists, Internat. Assn. Dental Rsch. (sec. Minn. divsn. 1958—59, pres. 1959—60, Crones Facial Biology Rsch. award 1997), Nat. Trust Medicine (sr.), Omicron Kappa Upsilon, Sigma Xi. Home: Golden Valley, Minn. Died Aug. 29, 2006.

GOSSAGE, WAYNE, library director, management consultant, entrepreneur; b. Bellingham, Wash., June 13, 1926; s. Coy Dell and Sadie Fay (Campbell) G.; m. Grace Villella, July 3, 1950; children: Leslie Anne, Gordon; m. Muriel Regan, Sept. 8, 2003. BS, U. Wash., 1947; MS, Columbia U., 1951, MA, 1969. Asst. head adult svcs. East Orange Pub. Libr., East Orange, NJ, 1951—54; head adult svcs. Levittown Pub. Libr., Levittown, NY, 1954—55; dir. Warner Libr., Tarrytown, NY, 1956—63; asst. libr. Tchrs. Coll. Columbia U., N.Y.C., 1964—67; dir. Bank St. Coll. Edn. Libr., N.Y.C., 1967—80; pres. Gossage Regan Assocs., Inc., N.Y.C., 1980—2000; chmn. Gossage Sager Assocs. LLC, N.Y.C., 2000—03; ret., 2003. Libr. search cons. Gossage Regan Assocs., Inc., N.Y.C., 1980-2000, Gossage Sager Assocs., LLC, N.Y.C., 2000-06; 1st exec. search cons. dirs. pub. libr. sys., u. deans librs., 1983. Contbr. articles to profl. jours. Vice pres. Hist. Soc. Tarrytown, 1960-61; trustee Harvard Libr., N.Y., 1978-2000; mem. alumni trustee nominating com. Columbia U., 1974-76; bd. advisors Pratt Inst. Sch. Info. and Libr. Sci., 1988-2001. With USNR, 1944-46. Coun. on Libr. Resources fellow, 1978-79; recipient Disting. Community Svc. award Tarrytown, 1962. Mem. ALA (notable books coun. 1961-62, ACRL bd. dirs. 1975-76, chmn. edn. and behavioral scis. sect. 1975-76, Ralph Shaw award for libr. lit. jury 1975-76, chmn. Wilson indexes com. 1978-81, Mudge citation com. 1985-87), N.Y. Libr. Assn. (v.p. resources and tech. svcs. sect. 1974-75, legis. com. 1974-75, pres. coll. and univ. librs. sect. 1978-79), N.Y. Libr. Club (pres. 1990-91), Spl. Libr. Assn. (chmn. div. social sci. 1975-76), Columbia U. Sch. Libr. Svcs. Alumni Assn. (sec.-treas. 1974-76, pres. 1977-78), Archons of Colophon (convenor 1989-90). Achievements include first personnel firm to provide library temporary services; first personnel firm to provide nationwide library executive search services. Avocations: reading, writing, walking, travel. Home: Carlsbad, N.Mex. Died Mar. 2, 2006.

GOSSELIN, PETER PAUL, electronics company executive, consultant; b. Boston, Feb. 10, 1941; s. Robert Louis and Margaret Regina (Tahmezian) G.; m. June D. Anderson, Jan. 14, 1960 (div. Sept. 1985); children: Julie, Sharon, Lynda, Valerie. BS in Mgmt., Northeastern U., 1973. Product mgr. ITT Semicondrs., Lawrence, Mass., 1963-72; plant mgr. Semicon, Inc., Lawrence, Mass., 1972-75; pres., chief exec. officer Park Electronic Products, Salem, N.H., 1975-85, Parkwest Microcomponents, Inc., Pacentia, Calif., from 1985-. Cons. Caluctta, India, 1979-81, Iskra, Zagreb, Yugoslavia, 1983-86. Mem. Am. Electronics Assn., K.C., The Exec. Com. Roman Catholic. Avocations: golf, racquetball, tennis. Home: Trabuco Canyon, Calif. Died July 4, 2005.

GOSSETT, KATHRYN MYERS, language professional, educator; b. Baltimore, Ohio; d. Charles Edgar and Vera Mae (Good) Myers; m. William Thomas Gossett, June 30, 1984. BA summa cum laude, Ohio U., 1931, MA, 1936. Cert. tchr., Ohio, Pa., Mich. Latin and English tchr. Beccaria Twp. High Sch., Coalport, Pa., 1931-32; French, Latin and English tchr. Buford (Ohio) High Sch., 1932-36; tchr. fgn. langs. Oak Hill (Ohio) High Sch., 1936-42; critic tchr. Ohio U. and Athens High Sch., 1942-43; English and Spanish tchr. Eastern High Sch., Lansing, Mich., 1943-45; French tchr. Kingswood/Cranbrook Pvt. Sch., Bloomfield Hills, Mich., 1945-55, chmn. fgn. lang., 1955-75. Fulbright tchr. Lycée de Jeunes Filles, Annecy, France, 1953-54. Contbr. articles to profl. jours. Decorated chevalier des Palmes Academiques (France); recipient Cranbrook Founders medal, 1976; U. Besancon (France) scholar. Mem. AAUW, Am. Assn. Ret. Persons, Eastern Star, Bloomfield Hills Country Club, The Ocean Club of Fla. (Ocean Ridge), The Little Club (Gulf Stream, Fla.), The Village Club (Bloomfield Hills), Phi Beta Kappa. Republican. Episcopalian. Avocations: art, music, history. Home: Bloomfield Hills, Mich. Died June 4, 2005.

GOSSETT, OSCAR MILTON, retired advertising executive; b. N.Y.C., May 27, 1925; m. Anna C. Scheid, May 29, 1949; children: Susanne, Michael, Thomas, Lorraine, James M. Student, Stevens Inst. Tech., 1943-44, 46-47, Columbia U., 1947-48. With Compton Advt., Inc., 1949-86, pres., 1968-86, chmn. bd. & CEO, 1971-83; chmn. bd., CEO Compton Communications Holding Co., 1982, Saatchi & Saatchi Compton Worldwide, 1982-86; co-chmn., formerly co-CEO Saatchi & Saatchi Advt. Worldwide, formerly exec. dir., dir. N.Am. ops., chmn. emeritus, 1992-2006. Nat. chmn. Religion in Am. Life; bd. dirs. Eye Bank for Sight Restoration, Nat. Ctr. for Health Edn.; mem. dean's adv. coun. Harvard Sch. Pub. Health. Served as officer USNR, 1943-46. Mem. Am. Advt. Fedn. (bd. govs.), Advt. Women of N.Y. (1st hon. male mem.). Methodist. Inventor mobile of solar system. Died Mar. 1, 2006.

GOTT, JERRY D., soil scientist; b. West Plains, Mo., Mar. 21, 1940; s. James S. and Sybil L. (Karr) G.; m. Karen Sue Budd, Oct. 13, 1966; 1 child, Rodney Dean. BS, S.W. Mo. State U., 1967. Soil scientist Mark Twain Nat. Forest USDA Forest Svc., Winona, Mo., 1967-71, forest soil scientist Mark Twain Nat. Forest, 1971-73, Rolla, Mo., 1973-98. Cons. 1998—. Mem. Mo. Assn. Profl. Soil Scientists (exec. bd. 1977-80), Am. Soc. Agronomy, Am. Registry Cert. Profls. in Agronomy, Crops and Soils. Home: Rolla, Mo. Died Mar. 12, 2005.

GOTTLIEB, RONALD SAUL, cardiologist; b. Phila., Jan. 13, 1940; m. Gloria Gottlieb, 1962; children: Mark, Neil. BA, Franklin and Marshall Coll., 1961; MD, U. Pa., 1965. Diplomate Am. Bd. Internal Medicine with subspecialty in cardiovasc. disease; lic. physician, Pa. Intern in medicine Thomas Jefferson U. Hosp., Phila., 1965-66, resident in medicine, 1966-67, fellow in cardiology, 1971-73; resident in neurology Hosp. of U. Pa., Phila., 1967-68, resident in medicine, 1970-71; pvt. practice Graduate Cardiology Cons., Inc., Phila. Instr. medicine Thomas Jefferson U. Hosp., 1973-75, asst. prof., 1975-79, assoc. prof., 1979-87, adj. assoc. prof., assoc. dir. cardiac catheterization lab., 1977-80; clin. assoc. prof. medicine in assoc. faculty Sch. Medicine, U. Pa.; former dir. interventional cardiology The Grad. Hosp.; physician adv. bd. Advanced Cardiovascular Sys., Inc., Devices for Vascular Intervention, Inc.; lectr. in field. Contbr. numerous articles and abstracts to profl. jours. With U.S. Army, 1968-71. Fellow ACP, Am. Coll. Cardiology, The Soc. for Cardiac Angiography and Interventions, Phila. Coll. Physicians; mem. AMA, Am. Heart Assn. (fellow on clin. coun.), Pa. Med. Soc., Phila. County Med. Soc., Phila. Acad. Cardiology, Southeastern Pa. Heart Assn., Soc. Interventional Cardiologists (tri-state area governing body). Home: Ambler, Pa. Died July 18, 2004.

GOULD, SAMUEL HALPERT, pediatrics educator; b. Balt., June 14, 1922; s. Herman and Theresa Gould; m. June Linda Walter, June 17, 1952; children: Hallie, Phyllis, Cynthia, Nancy. MD, State U. Iowa, 1951. Diplomate Am. Bd. Pediat. Intern Balt. City Hosp., 1951-52, Johns Hopkins Hosp., Balt., 1952-53; resident U. Iowa Hosps., Iowa City, 1953-54; pvt. practice, Benton Harbor, Mich., 1957-86; assoc. prof. pediat. U. Chgo., from 1986, chief sect. gen. pediat., 1993-99. Mem. Alpha Omega Alpha. Home: Chicago, Ill. Died June 23, 2005.

GOULD, WILLIAM MAX, graphic designer, artist; b. Lafayette, Ind., May 5, 1939; s. William Elijah and Gail Louise (Goddard) G.; m. Lois Evelyn Rivers (div.); children: Scott M., Heather L. Diploma, Ringling Sch. Art, 1962. Apprentice Truline Studios, Chgo., 1963-64; package designer Diamond Nat. Corp., Chgo., 1964-66; dir. art and design Hirsh-Arrons Design, Chgo., 1966-70; art dir., designer James Sweeton Assocs., Chgo., 1970-72, Henning Rasmussen Assoc., Chgo., 1973-76; pres. William M. Gould Advt. Design, Chgo., from 1976. Recipient Letterhead of Yr. award Asp&l Publ., 1966, Best Illustration award Soc. for Tech. Communication, 1980, Advt. award Foodservice Product News, 1982, Advt. award The Mil. Engr., 1988. Home: Scottsdale, Ariz. Died Mar. 9, 2005.

GOULD, WILLIAM RICHARD, retired utility company executive; b. Provo, Utah, Oct. 31, 1919; s. William Gilbert and Pauline Eva (Faser) G.; m. Erlyn Arvilla Johnson (dec. 1992), Mar. 20, 1942; children: Erlyn Sharon, William Richard, Gilbert John, Wayne Raymond.; m. Millie Johnson, 1994, 1 child, Wayne BS in Mech. Engring, U. Utah, 1942; postgrad., MIT, UCLA, U. Idaho. Registered profl. engr., Utah, Calif. With So. Calif. Edison Co., from 1948, mgr. engring., 1962-63, v.p. engring., constrn., planning, 1963-67, sr. v.p., 1967-73, exec. v.p., 1973-78, pres., 1978—84, chmn. bd., CEO, 1980-84, chmn. bd. emeritus, 1984—2006. Bd. dirs. Union Bank, Kaiser Steel Corp., Energy Services, Inc., Mono Power Co., Electric Systems Co., Project Mgmt. Corp., Breeder Reactor Corp., Associated So. Investment Co., Beckman Instruments., Sci. Applications Internat. Corp., Ecolaire, Inc., Joy Techs., Inc.; chmn. Calif. Tech. Services Adv. Council Pres. U.S. nat. com. Internat. Congress Large Electric Systems; past chmn. bd. Atomic Indsl. Forum.; mem. sci. and engring. com. U. Redlands; bd. councilors Sch. Engring., U. So. Calif.; mem. energy adv. bd., trustee Calif. Inst. Tech.; exec. com. Assembly Engring.; mem. nat. adv. bd. U. Utah; mem. adv. com. electric certificate program UCLA; trustee Long Beach Community Hosp.; bd. dirs. Nat. Energy Found.; former chmn. and dir. Electric Power Research Inst., Eyring Research Inst., Los Angeles World Affairs Council, Los Angeles Philharm. Assn. Served to lt. USN, 1942-47. Recipient George Westinghouse Gold Medal award Assn. Mech. Engrs., 1979; recipient Disting. Alumni award U. Utah, 1981, Disting. Contbn. award Inst. Advancement Engrs., 1982, Engring. award for Disting. Mgmt. U. So. Calif., 1983; named Electric Industry Man of Yr. Electric Light and Power Mag., 1983; Centennial medal IEEE, 1984; co-winner Calif. Industrialist of Yr. award, 1984. Fellow ASME (Centennial award for service 1980), Inst. Advanced Engring. (chmn. bd., Engr. of Year 1970); mem. Nat. Acad. Engring., Newcomen Soc. N.Am., Edison Electric Inst. (dir., chmn. exec. adv. bd. policy com. on nuclear power, mem. policy com. on research), Los Angeles Council Engrs. and Scientists (adv. com.), Pacific Coast Elec. Assn. (dir.), Los Angeles C. of C. Mem. Ch. of Jesus Christ of Latter-day Saints. Club: California. Home: Long Beach, Calif. Died Mar. 11, 2006.

GOWDY, CURT (CURTIS EDWARD GOWDY), sportscaster; b. Green River, Wyo., July 31, 1919; m. Jerre Dawkins, June 1949; children: Cheryl Ann, Curtis, Trevor. BS, U. Wyo., 1942, LLD, 1972. Radio sta. broadcaster, Cheyenne, Wyo., Oklahoma City; with Mel Allen broadcast N.Y. Yankees Baseball Team games, 1949-51; announcer for Boston Red Sox Baseball Team games, 1951-66; broadcaster Am. Football League games, from 1961; sports broadcaster NBC-TV, Major League Baseball Game of Week, World Series, Profl. Game of Week, Rose Bowl, Super Bowl, 1961-79; sports broadcaster NFL Football, Sports Spectacular CBS-TV, from 1979; host Am. Sportsman Outdoor Series for ABC-TV; owner radio stas. KOWB, Laramie, Wyo. Pres. Basketball Hall of Fame; overseer Boston Mus. Fine Arts. Served with USAAF, 1942-43. Named Sportscaster of Yr., Nat. Assn. Sportwriters and Sport Broadcasters, 1965, 67; named to Sports Broadcasters Hall of Fame, 1981, Baseball Hall of Fame, 1984, Am. Sportscasters Hall of Fame, 1985, Okla. Sports Hall of Fame, 1992, Pro Football Hall of Fame, 1993, Boston Red Soc Hall of Fame, 1995; recipient George Foster Peabody award, 1970, 6 Emmy awards as host and co-prodr. Am. Sportsman, Ford C. Frick award, Baseball Hall of Fame, 1984, Fisherman of Yr. award Sport Fishing Inst. Washington, 1991, Life Time Achievement award NATAS, 1992, Pete Rozelle award, Pro Football Hall of Fame, 1993. Died Feb. 19, 2006.

GOZENPUT, MIKHAIL, physician assistant; b. Bobruysk, USSR, Nov. 5, 1953; came to U.S., 1989; s. Semen and Maya (Gayster) G.; m. Margarita Tseyflin, Sept. 1, 1979; children: Yeugeny, Ernest. MD, Pediatric Med. Sch., Leningrad, USSR, 1977; Physician Asst., Cornell U., 1992. Cert. physician asst. Attenting Ear, Nose and Throat Emergency Hosp., Belarus, USSR, 1977-89; physician asst. Maimonides Med. Ctr., N.Y.C., from 1992, Kings Brook Jewish Med. Ctr., N.Y.C., from 1992. Mem. Am. Assn. Physician Assts. Republican. Avocations: sports, music, gardening. Home: Fair Lawn, NJ. Died Apr. 27, 2004.

GRADISAR, HELEN MARGARET, academic administrator; b. Bridgeville, Pa., July 1, 1922; d. Frank Luke and Elizabeth Helen (Pogacnik) G. BSBA, Duquesne U., 1944. Jr. acct. Carnegie-Ill. Steel Corp., Pitts., 1943-50; asst. dir. alumni rels. Duquesne U., Pitts., 1950-67, exec. sec. alumni assn., 1963-67; registrar Rosemont (Pa.) Coll., 1967-68, Carlow Coll., Pitts., 1968-74, asst. dean, registrar, 1974-77, registrar, dir. instl. rsch., 1977-78, 85-88, dir. instl. rsch., 1978-85 and from 88. Bd. dirs. Bridgeville Pub. Libr., 1988—; sec. Chartiers Valley Joint Sch. Dist. Authority, Bridgeville, 1990—. Mem. Am. Assn. Collegiate Registrars and Admissions Oficers, Cath. Daus. of the Ams., N.E. Assn. for Instl. Rsch., Assn. for Instl. Rsch., Duquesne U. Alumnae Assn. (past pres.), Duquesne U. Century Club, Epsilon Eta Phi (past pres.). Democrat. Avocations: music, antiques, collectibles, travel. Home: Bridgeville, Pa. Died Mar. 15, 2005.

GRAFFIS, DON WARREN, agronomist; b. Royal Center, Ind., Feb. 17, 1928; s. Warren and Rose Blanche (Daily) G.; m. Nancy Eaton Newman, May 31, 1956; children: Gwenith L., Dale W., Judy M. BS, Purdue U., 1950, MA in Agronomy, 1956; PhD in Agronomy, U. Ill., 1960. Tchr. Van Buren Twp., Star City, Ind., 1950; tech. rep. Swift & Co., Hammond, Ind., 1952-53; tchr. Noble Twp., Union Mills, Ind., 1953-55; rsch. asst. U. Ill., Urbana, 1956-60, extension and rsch. agronomist, from 1966; extension agronomist Rutgers U., New Brunswick, N.J., 1960-63; instr. Ohio State U., Columbus, 1963-66. Co-author: Approved Practices in Pasture Management, 1985. Sgt. U.S. Army, 1950-52. Fellow Am. Soc. Agronomy, Crop Sci. Soc. Am.; mem. Ill. Forage and Grassland Coun. (exec. sec. 1977—, Outstanding Contbn. award 1981), Am. Forage and Grassland Coun. (chmn. affiliate couns. 1982, Merit cert. 1984, Cooper Ext. Svc. U. Ill. Sustained Excellence in Programs and Svc. 1988), Epsilon Sigma Phi (Cert. of Appreciation 1988), Gamma Sigma Delta. Avocations: gardening, photography, golf, fishing, carpentry. Home: Ionia, Mich. Died Nov. 13, 2004.

GRAFTON, EDWIN GULLEDGE, ophthalmologist, educator; b. Austin, Tex., May 4, 1916; s. Edwin G. and Lula (Sullivan) G.; m. Lila Christine Laubenthal, Oct. 1, 1946; children: Lila G. Hanson, Linda G. Barton, Edwin G. Jr. BA, U. Tex., 1936; MD, Harvard U., 1940. Diplomate Am. Bd. Ophthalmology. Intern The Johns Hopkins Hosp., 1940-41, resident, 1941-42, 46; pvt. practice Dallas, from 1947. Former assoc. prof. U. Tex. Health Sci. Ctr., Dallas. Major USAF, 1942-46. Mem. Tex. Soc. Ophthalmology (pres. 1972), Tex. Ophthal. Assn. (pres. 1971). Home: Dallas, Tex. Died May 6, 2004.

GRAHAM, MARILYN ANNE, nursing administrator; b. Sault St. Marie, Mich., May 23, 1932; d. Alvin H. and Mary A. (Christ) Fabry; m. Jack A. Graham, Aug. 7, 1954; children: Mark, Charles. Diploma, Mercy Cen. Sch., Grand Rapids, Mich., 1953; BA, Siena Heights Coll., Adrian, Mich., 1988. Cert. occupation health nurse, audiometric technician, first aid instr. Emergency rm. staff Mercy Hosp., Bay City, Mich.; staff nurse VA, Saginaw, Mich.; med. staff nurse Midland (Mich.) Hosp.; nursing supr. The Dow Chem. Co. Mem. Am. Assn. Occupational Health, Inc. (bd. dirs. 1982-84). Home: Sanford, Mich. Died Jan. 16, 2004.

GRAHAM, WILLIAM B., pharmaceutical company executive; b. Chgo., July 14, 1911; s. William and Elizabeth (Burden) G.; m. Edna Kanaley, June 15, 1940 (dec. 1981); children: William J., Elizabeth Anne, Margaret, Robert B.; m. Catherine Van Duzer, July 23, 1984. SB cum laude, U. Chgo., 1932, JD cum laude, 1936; LLD, Carthage Coll., 1974, Lake Forest Coll., 1983; LLD (hon.), U. Ill., 1988; LHD, St. Xavier Coll. and Nat. Coll. Edn., 1983; LHD (hon.), Barat Coll., 1997, DePaul U., 1998. Bar: Ill. 1936. Patent lawyer Dyrenforth, Lee, Chritton & Wiles, 1936-40; mem. Dawson & Ooms, 1940-45; v.p., mgr. Baxter Internat., Inc., Deerfield, Ill., 1945-53, pres., 1953-71, CEO, 1960-80, chmn. bd., 1980-85, sr. chmn., 1989-95, chmn. emeritus, 1995—2006. Prof., chair Weizmann Inst. Sci., Rehoboth, Israel, 1978; lectr. U. Chgo., 1981-82. Pres. Lyric Opera Chgo. 1984-92, co-chmn. 1992-2002, chmn. emeritus, 2003-06; Big Shoulders, Wendy Will Care Fedn., Chgo. Hort. Soc.; trustee Orchestral Assn., U. Chgo., Evanston (Ill.) Hosp.; past pres. Cmty. Fund of Chgo. Recipient V.I.P. award Lewis Found., 1963, Disting. Citizen award Ill. St. Andrew Soc., 1974, Decision Maker of Yr. award Am. Statis. Assn., 1974, Marketer of Yr. award AMA, 1976, Found. award Kidney Found., 1981, Chicagoan of Yr. award Chgo. Boys Club, 1981, Bus. Statesman of Yr. award Harvard Bus. Sch. Club Chgo., 1983, Achievement award Med. Tech. Svcs., 1983, Disting. Fellows award Internat. Ctr. for Artificial Organs and Transplantations, 1982, Chgo. Civic award DePaul U., 1986, Internat. Visitors Golden Medallion award U. Ill., 1988, Chgo. medal U. Chgo., 1992, Laureate award Lincoln Acad. Ill., 1992, Lyric Opera Carol Fox award, 1992, Good Scout award N.E. Coun. Boy Scouts Am., 1993, Making History award Chgo. Hist. Soc., 1996; recognized for pioneering work Health Industry Mfrs. Assn., 1981; inducted Jr. Achievement Chgo. Bus. Hall of Fame, 1986, Modern Healthcare Hall of Fame, 1994, Art

Alliance Legend award Dreihaus Found., 2000. Mem. Am. Pharm. Mfrs. Assn. (past pres.), Ill. Mfrs. Assn. (past pres.), Pharm. Mfrs. Assn. (past chmn., award for spl. distinction leadership 1981), Chgo. Club (past pres.), Commonwealth Club, Comml. Club, Indian Hill Club, Casino Club, Old Elm Club, Seminole Club, Everglades Club, Bath and Tennis Club, Links Club, Phi Beta Kappa, Sigma Xi, Phi Delta Phi. Home: Kenilworth, Ill. Died Jan. 24, 2006.

GRAHAM, WILLIAM ERRETT, clinical social worker; b. Tucson, Oct. 1, 1947; s. Kenneth Errett and M. Natalie (Koehler) G.; m. Mary Catherine Grenier, June 14, 1973; children: Matthew, Joseph. BA in Psychology, U. Ariz., 1975; MSW, Ariz. State U., 1977. Clin. social worker Ariz. Children's Home, Tucson, from 1977; pvt. practice psychotherapy Tucson, from 1985. Mem. youth services adv. com. Pima Coll., Tucson, 1979—; field instr. Sch. Social Work, Ariz. State U., Tempe, 1979—. Workshop chmn. Am. Assn. Psychiat. Services for Children Conv., Chgo., 1979; sports ofcl. Ariz. Interscholastic Assn., Tucson, 1982; bd. dirs. Enrichment for Parents, Tucson, 1986. Named Outstanding Field Instr. Sch. Social Work Ariz. State U., 1985. Mem. Nat. Assn. Social Workers (cert., diplomate, registered clin. social worker). Avocations: high sch. sports ofcl. Home: Tucson, Ariz. Died Mar. 30, 2005.

GRAMMER, MAURINE PARKER, educator, writer, appraiser; b. Kansas City, Mo., Dec. 7, 1903; d. John Henry and Julia (West) Parker; m. David Allen Grammer, Nov. 27, 1925 (dec. Feb. 1959); 1 child, David Allen Jr. BS in Art, U. N.Mex., MA in Anthropology, 1957; student, Wyo U., Stephens Coll. Tchr. Albuquerque Pub. Schs., 1927-68; appraiser estates, art and antiques, especially Indian art, from 1943. Author: The Bear that Turned White, 1991, The Navajo Brothers and the Stolen Herd, 1992, Little Huggy Bear Goes to Albuquerque, 1996; author unit of study on Native Ams. for Columbia Tchrs. Coll.; contbr. articles to profl. jours.; loom patentee. Precinct chair Republican Party, Albuquerque, 1960-79. Inducted into Sr. Found. Hall of Fame, Albuquerque, 1996; named Tchr. of Yr., Kirtland AFB, 1968. Mem. NEA, N.Mex. Educators Fed. Credit Union, Pi Lambda Theta, Delta Kappa Gamma. Avocations: native american culture, indian art and antiques. Home: Albuquerque, N.Mex. Died June 20, 2004.

GRANDSTRAND, RUTH HELENA, retired community health and gerontology nurse; b. Shafer, Minn., Jan. 28, 1916; d. Gustav Furman and Edna Gertrude (Paulson) Hawkinson; m. Clifford J. Grandstrand, Aug. 28, 1943; children: Mark Clifford, Lois Ruth, Gail Louise (dec.) Diploma, Bethesda Sch. Nursing, St. Paul, 1937; postgrad., U. Minn., 1938-39. Cert. in hospice mgmt. Surg. nursing supr. Asbury Hosp., Mpls., 1939-41; instr. nursing arts Bethesda Hosp., 1941-43; dir. insvc. edn. Margaret S. Parmly Residence, Chisago City, Minn., 1977-85; home care nurse Meml. Enterprises, Freeport, Ill., 1985-94; ret., 1994. Home care nurse, Freeport. Vol. Ret. Sr. Vol. Program. 2d lt. Army Nurse Corps, 1941-43. Mem. Minn. Nurses Assn., Ill. Nurses Assn. Home: Freeport, Ill. Died Apr. 24, 2005.

GRANSTROM, MARVIN LEROY, civil and sanitary engineering educator; b. Anaconda, Mont., Sept. 25, 1920; s. Carl August and Alida Sophia (Eckstrom) G.; m. Ruth Maybelle Olsen, Jan. 1, 1944; children— David Marvin, Kay Ruth, Chris Carl. BS, Morningside Coll., 1942; BS in Civil Engring, Iowa State Coll., 1943; MS in San. Engring, Harvard, 1947, PhD, 1955. Engring. aide Soil Conservation Service, Whiting, Iowa, 1939; cons. engr. Sioux Falls, SD, 1946; instr. civil and san. engring. Case Inst. Tech., 1947-49; assoc. prof. san. engring. U. N.C., 1949-58; prof. civil engring. Rutgers U., New Brunswick, NJ, 1958-83, prof. emeritus, 1983; research participant Oak Ridge Nat. Labs., 1954; cons. Nat. Engring. Sch., Lima, Peru, 1955-57, WHO, from 1966. Cons. in hydrology, 1970— Author articles in field. Served with USMCR, 1943-46 Research grantee N.C., 1953; Research grantee NIH, 1954-58; Research grantee NSF, 1954-63; Research grantee Army Chem. Center, 1961-64; Research grantee surgeon gen. U.S. Army, 1962; Research grantee Office Water Resources Research, Dept. Interior, 1965-76; Research grantee N.J. Dept. Environ. Protection, 1957—; fellow Nat. Found., 1946-47; fellow USPHS, 1952-53 Mem. Am. Chem. Soc., ASCE, Am. Water Works Assn., Am. Water Resources Assn., Am. Acad. Environ. Engrs., Tau Beta Pi, Sigma Xi, Delta Omega, Chi Epsilon. Home: Middletown, NJ. Died Nov. 26, 2006.

GRANT, GEORGE CLARENCE, lawyer; b. Monroe County, Ga., Oct. 16, 1917; s. Joseph Clarence and Nannie (Smarr) G.; m. Frances Barnes, Nov. 16, 1947; children: Fran B., Martha Grant Clark. JD, Mercer U., 1938. Bar: Ga. 1938, U.S. Dist. Ct. (mid. dist.) Ga., U.S. Ct. Appeals (11th cir.), U.S. Supreme Ct. Assoc. Martin, Martin & Snow, Macon, Ga., 1938-48; ptnr. Martin, Snow, Grant and Martin, Snow, Grant & Napier, Macon, Ga., 1948-92; retired Martin, Snow, Grant & Napier, 1992. Pres. Macon Jr. C. of C., 1948-49. Lt. comdr. USN, 1941-46. Fellow Am. Coll. Trial Lawyers, Am. Bar Found., Ga. Def. Lawyers Assn. (pres. 1983-84, bd. dirs. 1981-99). Independent. Baptist. Home: Macon, Ga. Died May 5, 2004.

GRANT, GEORGE CLIFFORD, retired marine biology educator; b. Medford, Mass., Aug. 13, 1929; s. George Arland and Beatrice (Chadwick) G.; m. Eileen Margaret O'Connor, Apr. 20, 1952; children: Shelley Ann Damian, George Charles. BS, U. Mass., 1956; MA, Coll. William and Mary, 1962; PhD, U. R.I., 1967. Fishery rsch. biologist U.S. Bur. Comml. Fisheries, Millville, Del., 1956-60; assoc. marine scientist Va. Inst. Marine Sci., Gloucester Point, 1967-77, sr. marine scientist, 1977-81, asst. dir., 1982-86; asst. prof. U. Va., Gloucester Point, 1967-78, Coll. William and Mary, Gloucester Point, 1967-78, assoc. prof., 1977-81, prof., 1981-92; prof. emeritus, from 1993. Contbr. some 35 articles to profl. jours. including Fish. Bull. With U.S. Army, 1948-52. NDEA fellow U.S. Dept. Def., U. R.I., 1964-65. Fellow Am. Inst. Fishery Rsch. Biologists; Coll.William and Mary Alumni Service Award, 2002, Sigma Xi. Home: Gloucester Point, Va. Died Apr. 2, 2005.

GRANT, GERALD SEYMOUR, accountant; b. N.Y.C., Feb. 15, 1924; s. Harry and Rae (Vischoff) G.; m. Dorothy Bogard, Sept. 1, 1946; children: Barbara E., Joanne S. Grant Overly. BS, NYU, 1949, MA, 1951. CPA, Nebr. Sr. acct. S.D. Leidesdorf, N.Y.C., 1955-62; mgr. Peat, Marwick, Mitchell & Co., Lincoln, Nebr., 1962-65; ptnr. Trachtenbarg Grant, Lincoln, 1965-70, Johnson, Grant & Co., Lincoln, 1971-85, Baird, Kurtz, Dobson, Lincoln, from 1985. Instr. U. Nebr., Lincoln, 1968-84, 85. Pres. Congregation Tifereth Israel, Lincoln, 1968-72; pres. Jewish Welfare Fedn., Lincoln, 1978-80. Served with U.S. Army, 1943-46, PTO. Mem. Am. Inst. CPA's, Nebr. Soc. CPA's (treas. 1971-72), Am. Acctg. Assn., Lincoln C. of C. (bd. dirs. 1983-86). Clubs: University (Lincoln) (bd. dirs. 1985—). Democrat. Avocation: golf. Home: Lincoln, Nebr. Died Jan. 31, 2005.

GRASSHOFF, JURGEN MICHAEL, research chemist, environmental consultant; b. Berlin, May 7, 1936; came to U.S., 1965; s. Erich J. and Melitta (Frank) G.; m. Marianne Aebi, Sept. 21, 1963 (dec. Sept. 26, 1986); children: Sibylle, David, Michaela; m. Tuyet Pham, May. 18, 1989. Diploma in Chemistry, Tech. U. Hanover, 1961; PhD, Eidgenoessische Technische, 1965. Cert. in environ. waste mgmt. Lab. supr. Steding & Co., Hannover, Germany, 1961-62; rsch. chemist Pennwait Corp., King of Prussia, Pa., 1965-67; scientist Polaroid Corp., Cambridge, Mass., 1967-75, sr. scientist, 1975-95. Inventor: Synthesis of Amino Monomers, 1975, Polymeric Thiols, 1979, Novel dye Receptors, 1988, Thermal Acid Genecrating Polymers, 1994, Thymine Polymers, 1995. Mem. Am. Chem. Soc. Avocations: music, swimming, skiing, running. Died May 3, 2005.

GRAVEL, CAMILLE FRANCIS, lawyer; b. Alexandria, La., Aug. 10, 1915; s. Camille F. and Aline Delvaille G.; m. Katherine Yvonne David, Nov. 26, 1939 (dec. 1979); children: Katherine Ann Gravel Vanderslice, Mary Eileen Gravel Cappel, Martha Louise Antoon, Camille Francis III (dec.), Grady David, Eunice Holloman Gravel, Virginia Maureen Gravel Carbo, Margaret Lynn, Mark Alan, Charles Gregory, Richard Alvin (dec.); m. Evelyn Gianfala, 1980. BA, U. Notre Dame, 1935, La. State U., 1935-37, Cath. U. Am., 1937-39; LLD (hon.), Loyola U., New Orleans, 1976. Bar: La. 1940, U.S. dist. ct. La. 1940, U.S. Ct. Appeals (5th cir.) 1953, U.S. Supreme Ct. 1954. Asst. dist. atty. 9th Jud. Dist., Rapides Parish, La., 1942; atty. State Inheritance Tax Collector, Rapides Parish, 1943-45; asst. city atty. Alexandria (La.), 1946-48; atty. La. Tax Commn., 1948-52. Mem. Gov.'s Commn. on Higher Edn. Svcs., 1978-82; mem. Gov.'s Adv. and Rev. Commn. on Asst. Dist. Attys., 1979-88, exec. counsel, 1976-80, exec. asst., 1984-88 to gov. La.; mem. bd. suprs. La. State U. and A&M Coll., 1975-90, chmn. bd., 1981-82. Mem. U.S. Capitol Police Force, 1937-39. Invested Knight of St. Gregory by Pope Pius XII, 1954; hon. fellow Harry S Truman Library Inst., 1975. Fellow Internat. Acad. Trial Lawyers, Internat. Soc. Barristers; mem. AAUP, ABA, Nat. Assn. Criminal Def. Lawyers, La. Bar Assn., Alexandria Bar Assn. (pres. 1949-50), Notre Dame Law Assn., La. Trial Lawyers Assn., Lamar Soc., Am. Assn. Ret. Persons, Am. Heart Assn., Cath. U. Am. Alumni Assn. (nat. bd. govs. 1977), Alexandria-Pineville C. of C., Am. Legion, Elks (past exalted ruler), KC, Order of Coif, Phi Delta Phi, Kappa Sigma. Roman Catholic. Died Dec. 23, 2005.

GRAVES, BELLE L., accountant; b. Lincoln, Nebr., July 1, 1914; d. Fred T. and Hermina (Ruckert) G. BS in Bus., U. Nebr., 1937; MA, Columbia U., 1953. Cost acct. Woods Bros. Constrn. Co., Lincoln, 1937-40; comptroller Ben Simon & Sons, Lincoln, 1941-51; acctg. tchr. Lincoln Sch. Commerce, 1952-57; owner Graves Printing Co., 1958-69; acct. Nebr. Book Co., 1969-85; tax and fin. advisor Lincoln, from 1985. Bd. dirs., treas. Alzheimers Lincoln/Greater Nebr.; treas. generally yours Lincoln Gen. Hosp. Aux. Gift Shop; curator Gladys Lux Hist. Gallery, 1988—; state pres. Woman's Wesleyan Ednl. Coun, 1995-96; treas. Lincoln Cmty. Playhouse Guild, 1991—; pres. United Meth. Women, 1996. Recipient Friend of the Coll. of Human Resources and Family Scientist award, 1995; named Vol. of Yr. by United Way, 1991, Vol. of Month, Lincoln Gen. Hosp. Aux. Mem. Nat. Soc. Pub. Accts., Nebr. Pub. Accts., C. of C. of Lincoln (v.p. women's div. 1938-39), Toastmasters, Lincoln Doll Club (pres. 1986-88), Does, Kappa Phi. Republican. Methodist. Avocations: photography, travel, church activities. Died Apr. 23, 2005.

GRAVES, H. BRICE, retired lawyer; b. Charlottesville, Va., Sept. 1, 1912; BS, U. Va., 1932, MS, 1933, PhD, LL.B., 1938. Bar: N.Y. 1940, Va. 1949. Assoc. Cravath, Swaine & Moore, N.Y.C., 1938-42, 45-48; ptnr. Hunton & Williams, Richmond, Va., 1949—2005, ret., 1976. Planning com. U. Va. Ann. Tax Conf., 1971-82, trustee emeritus, 1989—; lectr. in field Contbr. articles to profl. jours. With USNR, 1942—45. Mem. Richmond Bar Assn., Va. Bar Assn. (chmn. taxation com. 1971-73), ABA (chmn. com. exempt orgns. tax sect. 1963-65, com. mem. 1975-77), Am. Law Inst., Richmond Estate Planning Council, Am. Coll. Tax Counsel Home: Richmond, Va. Died Oct. 12.

GRAVES, STEPHEN MATTHEW, executive; b. Potstown, Pa., Apr. 7, 1955; s. John Henry and Marjorie Ann (Kuolt) G.; m. Joann Erb, Mar. 1, 1985; children: Erika, Ian. BA in Criminology, Fla. State U., 1977; BA in Asia Studies, U. Md., Tokyo, 1982; MA in Internat. Bus., Sophia U., Tokyo, 1989. Market analysis GM, Tokyo, 1984-85; mktg. mgr. Bridgestone Corp., Tokyo, 1985-91, territory mgr. Seattle, from 1991. Lectr. Internat. Mgmt. Devel. Studies, Tokyo, 1988-91. Died Feb. 15, 2005.

GRAY, BRIAN MARK, lawyer, researcher; b. Detroit, Dec. 21, 1939; s. Joseph Clay and Mary Jane (Bond) G.; m. Patricia Kay Gillett, Aug. 19, 1967; children: Diana Lisa, Amy Noel. BA, U. Mich., 1961, JD, 1964; postgrad., U. London, 1965, U. Brussels, 1966. Bar: Mich. 1967, U.S. Dist. Ct. Mich. 1967, U.S. Ct. Customs and Patent Appeals 1981, U.S. Ct. Appeals (fed. cir.) 1985, U.S. Supreme Ct. 1974. Assoc. Butzel, Eamon, Long, Gust & Kennedy, Detroit, 1964; sr. rsch. clk., chief judge Mich. Ct. Appeals, Grand Rapids, 1967-68; ptnr. Krueger, Gray & Lesica, Muskegon, Mich., 1967-74; pvt. practice Anchorage, from 1975. Of counsel in patent matters; cons. in field. Author: Your Estate Plan, 1980, European Community Corporate Mergers. Del. U.S.-Japan Bilateral Session Legal and Econ. Rels., 1988; del. designate Moscow Conf. Law and Econ. Rels., 1990. Rsch. grantee U. London, 1965. Mem. ABA, Mat-Su Borough Bar Assn., Mich. Bar Assn., Alaska Bar Assn., Soc. Gray's Inn (life), Phi Alpha Delta, Phi Beta Kappa. Lutheran. Avocations: breeding and training arabian horses, building and flying experimental aircraft. Died July 1, 2004.

GRAY, STEPHEN MARK, pharmacist and natural medicine specialist, consultant; b. Sacramento, Apr. 11, 1955; s. Leo Joseph and Helen Marie (Halbur) G. BS in Pharmacy, Idaho State U., Pocatello, 1978. Registered pharmacist, Calif. Staff pharmacist Meth. Hosp. of So. Calif., Arcadia, 1978-80, Raleys Drug/Grocery Chain, West Sacramento, Calif., 1981-82, Valley Med. Ctr., San Jose, Calif., 1983-84, Manor Drug, Sacramento, 1985-87; mng. pharmacist Raleys Drug/Grocery Chain, 1987-95; founder, mgr. Herbal Pharm. Resource, Sacramento, from 1994. Mem. Am. Pharm. Assn., Calif. Pharm. Assn., Assn. natural Medicine Pharmacists, Herb Rsch. Found., Am. Homeopathic Pharm. Assn. Republican. Avocations: outdoor sports, personal and spiritual growth, health. Home: Sacramento, Calif. Died Aug. 19, 2004.

GRAYSON, RICHARD ANDREW, aerospace engineer; b. Silver Spring, Md., Aug. 5, 1966; s. Benson Lee and Helen Marie (Donovan) G. BS in Aerospace Engring., U. Va., 1988; MBA, U. Ga., 1995, PhD in Fin., 2001. Engr. Army Rsch. Lab., Aberdeen Proving Ground, Md., 1989-95; engr., rschr. Terry Coll. Bus./U. Ga., Athens, 1995-99; vis. prof. fin. U. Del., Newark, 1999-2000, U. Ga., Athens, from 2001; asst. prof. Loyola Coll. Md., Balt., from 2001, asst. prof. fin., from 2001. Mem. Joint Tech. Coordinating Group Air Sys., Wright-Patterson AFB, Ohio, 1990-95; leader PATRIOT Assessment Team, Riyadh, Saudi Arabia, 1991-92. Advisor youth group Episcopal Ch., McLean, Va., 1988-94. Recipient comdr.'s award for civilian svc. Dept. Army, 1991. Mem. Am. Helicopter Soc., Internat. Platform Assn., Source Selection Evaluation bd., Army LHX helicopter. Achievements include leader of on-site investigations in Saudi Arabia and at Ballistic Rsch. Lab, to assist in evaluating PATRIOT lethality against SCUD-B tactical ballistic missiles fired in Operation Desert Storm; performed AH-64 and UH-60 crew station vulnerability tests. Home: Athens, Ga. Died Mar. 16, 2005.

GREASER, BARBARA L., elementary school educator; b. Charles City, Pa., Apr. 26, 1948; d. Edward and Marguerite Lucille (Peterson) Curtis; m. Charles Edward Greaser, Feb. 1, 1980. BS, Sioux Falls (S.D.) Coll., 1970; MEd, Temple U., 1972; Cert. in Reading, Lehigh U., Allentown, Pa., 1975. Tchr. Souderton Area Sch. Dist., Harleysville, Pa., from 1970. Mem. Nat. Sci. Tchrs. Assn., Pa. Sci. Tchrs. Assn., MCSTA, SAEA (mem. Adopt-a-Hwy. com. 1993-95). Republican. Baptist. Avocation: cooking. Home: Harleysville, Pa. Died Nov. 10, 2004.

GREBLE, THOMAS CHARLES, lawyer; b. N.Y.C., Oct. 27, 1949; s. George W. Greble and Jocelyn M. (Hough) Sheldon; m. Diane Joan Metzger, Feb. 14, 1974; children: Emily, Matthew, Julia. BA, Villanova U., 1971; JD, Fordham U., 1974. Bar: N.Y. 1975; U.S. Supreme Ct. 1980; U.S. Dist. Ct. (so. and ea. dists.) N.Y. 1975; U.S. Ct. of Appeals (2nd cir.) 1978, U.S. Ct. Appeals (D.C. cir.) 1982, U.S. Ct. Appeals (11th cir.) 1984. Asst. corp. counsel honors program N.Y.C., 1974-76; assoc. gen. counsel N.Y. State United Tchrs., N.Y.C., 1976-79; assoc. Jackson, Lewis, Schnitzler & Krupasn, N.Y.C., 1979-80; sr. assoc. Roberts & Finger, N.Y.C., 1980-83, ptnr., 1983-86, sr. ptnr. and mgmt., from 1986. Adj. prof. law, Fordham Law Sch., N.Y.C., 1986-87, NYU, N.Y.C., 1987—; gen. counsel N.Y. Assn. of Temporary Svcs., Inc., N.Y.C., 1991—; legal commentator. Author: Manager's Guide to Employment Law, Americans with Disabilities Act Guide, 1993; author tech. publs. Basketball coach New Castle Rel. League. Recipient Helbig Meml. scholarship Fordham Law Sch., N.Y.C., 1971-73. Mem. The Birchwood Club. Avocations: duplicate bridge tournaments, tennis. Home: Chappaqua, NY. Died June 16, 2005.

GREBNER, EUGENE ERNEST, biochemist, educator; b. Pitts, Feb. 6, 1931; s. Eugene Eduard and Carolina (Fuerst) G.; m. Mary Alice Wagner, Nov. 26, 1955; children: Lisa J., Matthew E. AB, Hiram Coll., 1952; PhD, U. Pitts., 1964. Postdoctoral fellow NIH, Bethesda, Md., 1964-67; asst. mem. Albert Einstein Med. Ctr., Phila., 1967-75; assoc. prof. Thomas Jefferson U., Phila., 1975—96; prof. emeritus Thomas Jefferson U, Phila., 1996—2006; assoc. dir. Div. of Med. Genetics, Thomas Jefferson U, Phila., 1990—96. Dir. Tay-Sachs Prevention Program of Delaware Valley. Contbr. articles to sci. jour. Bd. dir. Upper Moreland Pub. Libr., Willow Grove, Pa., 1976-81. Sgt. US Army, 1952-54, Korea. Mem. Nat. Tay-Sachs and Allied Diseases Assn. (mem. sci. adv. com. 1987-2006). Democrat. Home: Willow Grove, Pa. Died May 11, 2006.

GRECO, STELLA MARY, women's health nurse; b. Hartford, Conn., Apr. 28, 1936; d. Raffaele and Anna M. (Cicerchia) G. Diploma, St. Francis Hosp. Sch. Nursing, 1958; cert. in ob./gyn., Mt. Sinai Hosp., 1983; cert. in counseling, U. Conn. Health Ctr., 1985, cert. in health rev., 1986. NP, Conn. Pvt. duty and charge nurse St. Francis Hosp. & Med. Ctr., Hartford, 1965-88; office mgr., head nurse Drs. Fishman & Zmijeski, Hartford, 1971, head nurse, office mgr., 1977-78; coord. women's health svc. Bristol (Conn.) Hosp. State of Conn. scholar, 1955. Mem. St. Francis Hosp. Sch. Nursing Alumni Assn. (exec. bd.). Home: Hartford, Conn. Died Sept. 18, 2004.

GREEN, GERALD, author; b. Bklyn., Apr. 8, 1922; s. Samuel and Anna Ruth (Matzkin) Greenberg; m. Maria Anna Pomposelli, Nov. 9, 1950 (dec. Nov. 1979); children: Nancy Green Wohl, Theodore Samuel, David Nicholas; m. Marlene Medjuck Eagle, Oct. 19, 1980. AB, Columbia U., 1942; MS, Columbia U. Sch. Journalism, 1947. Editor Internat. News Service, 1947-50; writer, prodr. NBC-TV News, N.Y.C., 1950-64; freelance writer N.Y.C., 1964—2006. Council mem. Writers Guild Am., East N.Y.C., 1985-87. Prodr: Today show with Dave Garroway, Wide Wide World, Chet Huntley Reporting; prodr., writer various TV documentaries; author: (with Lawrence Klingman) His Majesty O'Keefe, 1948, The Sword and the Sun, 1950, The Last Angry Man, 1957, The Lotus Eaters, 1959, The Heartless Light, 1961, The Portofino PTA, 1962, The Legion of Noble Christians, 1965, (with Drew Pearson) The Senator, 1968, To Brooklyn With Love, 1968, The Artists of Terezin, 1969, Faking It, 1971, The Stones of Zion: A Novelist's Journal in Israel, 1971, Blockbuster, 1972, Tourist, 1973, The Hostage Heart, 1974, My Son, the Jock, 1975, An American Prophet, 1975, Girl, 1976, Holocaust, 1978 (Prix Internat. Dag Hammarskjold award 1979), The Healers, 1978, Cactus Pie, 1979, The Chains, 1980, Murfy's Men, 1981, Karpov's Brain, 1982, Not in Vain, 1984, East and West, 1986; screenwriter: (TV movies) The Last Angry Man, 1959, Holocaust, 1978 (Emmy award outstanding writing in a drama series 1978), Kent State, 1980, Tourist, 1980, Wallenberg: A Hero's Story, 1985 (Emmy award nomination outstanding writing in a limited series 1985). Served with U.S. Army, 1942-46, ETO. Recipient Alumni award Columbia U. Sch. Journalism, 1957, Emmy nominations, 1967, 72. Mem. Writers Guild Am. (council), Authors League of Am., Am. PEN Club, Am. TV Acad. Arts and Scis., Phi Beta Kappa. Democrat. Jewish. Avocation: travel. Died Aug. 29, 2006.

GREEN, JANICE STRICKLAND, emergency services nurse; b. Norfolk, Va., Nov. 13, 1939; d. William H. and Naomi Strickland; m. Benny H. Green, 1962. Diploma in nursing, DePaul Hosp., Norfolk, Va., 1960; BS in Healthcare Admin., St. Joseph's Coll., North Windham, Maine, 1981. Staff nurse Cabbarus Meml. Hosp., Concord, N.C., 1963, DePaul Hosp., Norfolk, Va., 1963-64, head nurse, 1964-85; dir. emergency svcs. DePaul Med. Ctr., 1985-91; adminstr., govt. svcs. dir. PHP Healthcare Corp., 1991-96, regional dir., 1996-98. Mem. Am. Coll. Healthcare Eecs., Am. Assn. Ambulatory Care Nurses, Health Care Adminstrs. Tidewater. Home: Norfolk, Va. Died Apr. 26, 2004.

GREEN, JAY NELSON, lawyer; b. Kilgore, Tex., Jan. 11, 1958; s. James Perry and Ouida Norris G.; m. Ellen Elizabeth Bradley, Aug. 16, 1980; children: Cullen, Mason, Weston. BBA, Baylor U., 1979, JD, 1982. Bar: Tex.; U.S. Dist. Ct. (ea. dist. Tex.) 1983; U.S. Ct. Appeals (5th cir.) 1983; cert. Tex. Bd. Legal Specialization, assoc. Am. Bd. Trial Advs., Tex. Bar Found. Mem. staff Potter, Minton, Roberts, Davis & Jones, Tyler, Tex., 1982—2002; pvt. practcie, from 2002. Pres. Tyler Teen Ct, Inc., 1990-91; v.p. Smith County Young Lawyers, Tyler, 1985; instr. Tyler Jr. Coll., 1987; adj. prof., assoc. Baylor Sch. Law. Mem. steering com. Bush Re-election for Smith County, Tyler, 1998; chmn. Smith County, Tom Phillips Campaign, Tyler, 1988. Named Smith County Outstanding Young Lawyer, 1991. Baptist. Avocation: golf. Died Jan. 3, 2004.

GREEN, LYLE DAVID, mathematics educator; b. White Clay, Nebr., Apr. 25, 1909; s. Frank Leslie and June Jennie (Addie) G.; m. Doris Margaret Collins, Mar. 9, 1935; 1 child, Frank Warren. BS, Chadron State Coll., 1932; MA, Colo. No. U., 1946; postgrad. in math., Mich. State U., 1947-51. Prin. pub. schs., Sheridan County, Nebr., 1934-39, Lyman, Nebr., 1939-42; asst. dean Independence, Kans., 1946-47; instr. Mich. State U., East Lansing, 1947-51; assoc. rsch. engr. U. Mich., Ann Arbor, 1951-71. Author: My World War II Experience Revisited, 1996. Sgt. U.S. Army, 1942-45, Okinawa. Congregationalist. Avocations: duplicate bridge, exercise, gardening, word processing. Home: Chelsea, Mich. Died May 16, 2005.

GREEN, MARY ELOISE, nutrition and food management educator; b. East Liberty, Ohio, June 10, 1903; d. Milton M. and Sylvia M. (Creviston) G. BS, Ohio State U., 1928, MS, 1933; PhD, Iowa State U., 1949. Elem. tchr. Perry Twp. Sch., East Liberty, 1923-26; high sch. tchr. Monroe Twp. Sch., West Liberty, Ohio, 1928-37, Brown Twp. Sch., Kilbourne, Ohio, 1937-39; instr. Ohio Wesleyan U., Del., 1937-39; from instr. to prof. Ohio State U., Columbus, 1939-72, prof. emeritus, from 1972. Fellow AAAS; mem. Am. Dietetic Assn., Am. Assn. Family and Consumer Scis., Inst. of Food Technologists, Pi Lambda Theta, Sigma Delta Epsilon, Iota Sigma Pi, Kappa Omicron Nu, Am. Assn. Univ. Women, Order of Eastern Star. United Methodist. Home: Columbus, Ohio. Died Sept. 16, 2005.

GREEN, STANLEY JOSEPH, chemical engineer, researcher; b. N.Y.C., Mar. 11, 1920; s. Maurice and Ada (Silverstein) G.; m. Alice B. Denenholz, Apr. 8, 1951; children: David P., Douglas M., Ronald F. BSChemE, CCNY, 1940; MSChemE, Drexel Inst. Tech., 1953; PhD-ChemE, U. Pitts., 1968. Registered profl. engr., Pa. Assoc. chem. engr. U.S. Bur. Mines, College Park, Md., 1942-45; chem. engr. Fercleve Corp., Oak Ridge, Tenn., 1945, Acme Coppersmithing & Machine Co., Oreland, Pa., 1945-54; mgr. reactor devel. and analysis Bettis Atomic Power Lab. div. Westinghouse, West Mifflin, Pa., 1954-77; dir. steam generator project Electric Power Research Inst., Palo Alto, Calif., from 1977. Contbr. articles to profl. jours. Recipient Donald Q Kern award Am. Inst. Chem. Engring., 1985. Fellow ASME (chmn. ditto-heat transfer div. 1973, centennial medallion 1980). Democrat. Jewish. Home: Palo Alto, Calif. Died Aug. 10, 2004.

GREENBLATT, SEYMOUR, lawyer; b. Chgo., Apr. 7, 1918; s. Max And Ida Greenblatt; m. Belle Greenblatt, June 4, 1942; children: Elaine Winslow, Richard, Debra, Michael. BA with high honors, U. Ill., 1938, JD with highest honors, 1940. Pvt. practice, Newburgh, N.Y., 1941-48; lawyer Greenblatt & Greenblatt, Newburgh, 1948-54, Greenblatt & Neuman, Newburgh, 1954-61, Greenblatt Forester & Neuman, Newburgh, 1961-70, Greenblatt Crain & Winslow, Newburgh, 1970-80, Greenblatt & WInslow, Newburgh, from 1980. Pres. Newburgh Jewish Com. Ctr., 1950-51; master Masons, Newburgh, 1954; spl. prosecutor Orange County Rep. Orgn., 1972-74. Sgt. U.S. Army, 1942-45, PTO. Order of Coif, U. Ill., 1947. Avocations: handball, tennis, baseball, running. Home: Newburgh, NY. Died May 6, 2004.

GREENE, ANITA JENKINS, elementary school educator; b. Eatonton, Ga., July 2, 1938; d. George Oliver and Agnes Juanita (Jefferson) Jenkins; 1 child, Antonio Bernard. AB in English, Morris Brown Coll., 1958; MA in Reading, Atlanta U., 1974; postgrad., Dartmouth Coll., Hanover, N.H., 1986; cert. supr., Ga. State U., 1991. Tchr. Twiggs County Bd. Edn., Jeffersonville, Ga., 1958-60, Greene County Bd. Edn., Greensboro, Ga., 1960-62, Franklin County Bd. Edn., Carnesville, Ga., 1963-64, Atlanta Bd. Edn., 1964-65; mail clk. U.S. Postal Svc., Atlanta, 1965-67; tchr. Cherokee County Bd. Edn., Canton, Ga., 1968-72; reading specialist Atlanta Pub. Schs., 1973-91, curriculum specialist, from 1991. Mem. ASCD, Internat. Reading Assn., Nat. Assn. Edn., Nat. Coun. Tchrs. English, Ga. Assn. Edn., Atlanta Assn. Edn., Morris Brown Coll. Alumni Assn. (Profl. award 1991, Alumna of Yr. 1993). Democrat. Baptist. Avocations: reading, travel, playing scrabble, pinochle. Home: East Point, Ga. Died Jan. 24, 2004.

GREENE, JEROME ALEXANDER, minister, public administrator; b. Welch, W.Va., Mar. 12, 1941; s. Emanuel and Savannah (Eldridge) A.; m. Aurelia Henry, Apr. 18, 1975; children: Rhonda Sobers, Russell Sobers. BA, CCNY, 1964; MA in Counseling Psychology, Bowie (Md.) State U., 1983, cert. in family counseling, 1984; postgrad., NYU, 1985-86, Billy Graham Sch. Evangelism, 1988, Moody Bible Inst., from 1991. Cert. principal/administr., N.Y. State; ordained to ministry Independent Charismatic Ch., 1983. Evangelist Bethel Gospel Tabernacle, Jamaica, N.J., 1961-63; exec. dir. People's Devel. Corp., Bronx, from 1979; founder, pastor Bronx (N.Y.) Christian Charismatic Prayer Fellowship, Inc., from 1983. Prof. Touro Coll., N.Y.C., 1982-86. Composer over 120 religious songs. Pres. Morrisania Edn. Coun., Bronx, 1968—, Dist. Community Sch. Edn. Bd., Bronx, 1975-86; chairperson Community Planning Bd., Bronx 4, 1986-91; dir. funded programs Community Sch. Dist. 5, N.Y.C., 1975-77; bd. dirs., fellow mem. Morrisania Neighborhood Family Care Ctr., 1987-91; elected Dem. dist. leader 76th Assembly Dist., Bronx, 1988, 90—; coord. Bronx Project Antioch Coll., 1975-76; pres. 1071 Franklin Ave. Housing Devel. Fund Corp., 1984—. Recipient Outstanding Leadership award Morrisania Ednl. Coun., 1981, citation N.Y. State Assembly, 1985, Civic Leadership award N.Y.C. Mission Soc., 1988. Mem. Coun. Black Elected Officials, Bronx Unity Dem. Club, Inc. (pres. 1978—). Home: Bronx, NY. Died Aug. 23, 2004.

GREENE, RICHARD THADDEUS, retired bank executive; b. Charleston, S.C., July 18, 1913; s. Richard and Martha (Black) G.; m. Virginia L. Lea; children: Cheryll Y., Richard I. Jr. BS, Hampton U., 1938; D in Comml. Scis. (hon.), St. Johns U., 1992. Asst. treas. Citizen's & Southern Bank & Trust Co., Phila., 1938-41; rep., bus. mgr. Assoc. Pubs., Inc., N.Y.C., 1945-58; nat. advt. rep., sec./bus. mgr. Interstate United Newspapers, N.Y.C., 1958-60; exec. asst. to pres. Carver Fed. Savs. Bank, N.Y.C., 1960, mgr. Bklyn. office, 1961, asst. sec., mgr. Bklyn. office, 1961-63, asst. v.p., mgr. Bklyn. office, 1963-66, v.p., mgr. Bklyn. office, 1966-68, exec. v.p., 1968, pres., 1969-95, chmn., 1995—97. Bd. dirs. finance com. HUDC, Fin. Svcs. Corp., Harlem Urban Devel. Corp., N.Y.C. Partnership Inc., Thrift Assns. Svc. Corp., Fed. Home Loan Bank N.Y.; bd. advisors Black Enterprise. Former bd. dirs. Am. Savs. & Loan League, Inc., Queens Coun. on the Arts, Uptown C. of C., United Way of Tri-State, N.Y. Urban League, Inc.; trustee George E. Meares Meml. Scholarship Fund; former trustee Citizen's Budget Commn., N.Y.C.; Bd. dirs., chmn. fin. com. Apollo Theatre Found.; elder Westminster Presbyn. Ch. Maj. U.S. Army, 1941-45. Recipient Outstanding Citizen award N.Y. Recorder, Citizenship award Bklyn. HOme for the Aged, Achievement award for contbn. to community Cornerstone Bapt. Ch., Bklyn., Black Bank Pres. award Westminster Presbyn. Ch., Jamaica, N.Y., Citation of Appreciation award Abyssinian Bapt. Ch., N.Y.C., Professionalism & Excellence in Banking award Urban Bankers Coalition Inc., Banking award Harlem Commonwealth Coun., Booker T. Washington award N.Y. Hampton Alumni Club Inc. Mem. N.Y. League of Savs. Insts. (legis. com.), Harlem Bus. Alliance, Nat. Freedom Day Assn., One Hundred Black Men Inc., N.Y. Hampton Alumni Club, Omega Psi Phi (Man of Yr. award, Citizen of Yr.), Sigma Pi Phi. Home: Brooklyn, NY. Died Aug. 3, 2006.

GREENFIELD, BRUCE HAROLD, lawyer, merchant banker; b. Phila., Mar. 12, 1917; s. William I. and Bertha (Kauffman) Greenfield; m. Adele Gersh, Sept. 18, 1955; children: Gregory Richard, Elizabeth Susan, Margaret Alison. BA, Duke U., 1938; JD, Yale U., 1941. Bar: Pa. 1941. Atty. Office Tax Legis. Counsel, Treasury Dept., 1941-48; partner firm Folz, Bard, Kamsler, Goodis & Greenfield, Phila., 1949-53; v.p. Bankers Securities Corp., Phila., 1953-59, exec. v.p., 1959-70, pres., 1970-82; v.p., treas., dir. Sta. WSMB, Inc., New Orleans, 1957-82; ret., 1982. Pres., bd. dirs. Albert M. Greenfield & Co., Inc.; lectr. NYU, Tulane U., Am. U. Tax Insts. Contbr. articles to profl. jours. Trustee Albert M. Greenfield Found.; bd. dirs. Am. Jewish Com., Phila., Girl Scouts U.S., 1978—87. Served to maj. USAAF, 1942—46. Mem.: Phi Beta Kappa. Democrat. Died Nov. 8, 2005.

GREENWOOD, JOHN, optometrist; b. Altenburg, Germany, Dec. 2, 1922; s. Abraham Adolf Daniel and Bettina B.B. (Alt) G.; m. Elsie Brownwald, Sept. 2, 1951; children: Deborah J., Judith E., Lucy R. OD, Ill. Coll. of Optometry, 1952; MS in Forensic Sci., George Washington U., 1975. Bd. cert. optometrist, Md., Ariz.; cert. in diagnostic pharm. drugs. Optometrist Dr. John Greenwood, Washington, 1952-85, Optometric Assn., Chevy Chase, Md., 1985-87; staff optometrist Kaiser Permanente Med. Ctr., Kensington, Md., from 1988. Pres. Optometric Soc. of D.C., 1961-62, Internat. Assn. Bds. of Examiners in Optometry, Washington, 1975-76; mem. peer rev. Medicaid, Pub. Health Dept., Washington, 1975-77. Editor Grand Lodge Procs., 1969-73; contbr. articles to profl. jours. V.p. Citizens Assn., Arlington, Va., 1953-54; lectr. hwy. safety Met. Police Dept., Washington, 1961-73; mem. Hackers Lic. Appeals Bd., Washington, 1969-74, Citizens Traffic Bd., Washington, 1969-79; pres. exec. chpt. City of Hope Nat. Med. Rsch. Ctr., Washington, 1978. Named Optometrist-of-Yr., Optometric Soc. D.C., 1968, 70; recipient Disting. Svc. award Govt. D.C., 1969, fellowship Superior Profl. Stature, APHA, 1970, Grand Lodge Disting. Svc. medal Grand Lodge FAAM, 1990; 33rd degree Supreme Coun. Scottish Rite, So. Jurisdiction, 1991. Fellow Am. Acad. Optometry, Nat. Eye Rsch. Found. (Named for Outstanding Contbn. to Eye Care 1970), Rotary Internat.; m. Allied Masonic (sovereign master 1994-95), Grand Royal Arch of D.C. (grand master 2nd veil, high priest 1994-95), Masonic and Eastern Star Home (grand lodge rep. 1992-96), Scottish Rite D.C. (lt. uniformed unit 1979—), Pythagoras Lodge of Rsch. (sr. master 1967). Avocation: music. Died May 27, 2004.

GREGG, ERIC EUGENE, umpire; b. Phila., May 8, 1951; m. Romona Camilo, Dec. 31, 1974; children: Eric, Kevin, Ashley, Jamie. Umpire N.Y.-Pa. League, Fla. State League, Ea. League, Dominican Republic League, Pacific Coast League, Major League Baseball, 1975—99. Died June 5, 2006.

GREGORY, HASKELL DON, videographer; b. Corpus Christi, Tex., Nov. 13, 1959; s. Haskell Emerson and Mildred Mel (Bates) G. BAS, Nicholls State U., 1986. Chief videographer prodn. dept. Vision Cable, Houma, La., 1985-86; producer, writer KALB-TV, Alexandria, La., 1986-89, chief videographer, from 1989. Freelance disc jockey, Alexandria, 1986—. Appeared in The Taming of the Shrew, 1985, various cabaret prodns., 1986-90. Recipient Sr. Media award Thibodaux Lions, 1985, Spl. Recognition award Cerebral Palsy La., 1982-85. Mem. Cen. La. Press Club, Cen. La. Ad Club (Bronze award 1989). Republican. Mem. Ch. of Christ. Avocations: sports, music, walking, books. Died Apr. 24, 2004.

GREMMEL, GILBERT CARL, family physician; b. Robstown, Tex., Nov. 29, 1922; s. Albert Henry and Tennie Elizabeth Gremmel; m. Helen Kistler, 1949 (div. 1965); children: Gilbert Jr., Shirley, Rebecca, Susan, Curtis, James; m. Ilse Elizabeth Schreiber Bell, Apr. 23, 1969; children: Erika Barbara, Albert Henry, Heidi. MD, U. Tex., Galveston, 1951; BA, U. Tex., San Antonio, 1978, BBA in Fin., 1982. Diplomate Am. Bd. Family Practice. Intern U.S. Army, San Antonio, 1951-52; pvt. practice Boerne, Tex., 1955-64, San Antonio, 1964-82, Sonora, Tex., 1982-86, Halletsville, Tex., 1986-88; family physician Med. Networks, Houston, 1988, Med. Clinic, Mabank, Tex., 1988-90;

pvt. practice Shamrock, Tex., 1990-92, Seminole, Tex., from 1992; chief of staff Meml. Hosp., Seminole, Tex., from 1995. Emergency physician S.W. Med. Assocs., Rockport, Tex., 1990—. Trustee Boerne County Line Ind. Sch. Dist., 1959-62; pres. San Antonio Community Dept. of Family Practitioners, 1980. With U.S. Army, 1943-46, 51-53. Mem. Am. Assn. Family Practitioners, Five-County Med. Soc. (v.p. 1993, pres. 1994). Republican. Avocations: classical music, history, archaeology. Home: Seminole, Tex. Died Apr. 5, 2004.

GREN, JACK E., speaker, educator; b. Ft. Wayne, Ind., Dec. 27, 1923; s. Elmer C. and Emma (Geske) G.; m. Joan M. Pequignot, Sept. 9, 1948; children: Joni J., Jeffrey J. BS in Bus., Ind. U., 1949; HHD (hon.), Burton, 1964; LLD (hon.), U. Findlay, 1986. Merchandising, promotion, writer Time Inc., Life mag., N.Y.C., 1949-50; nationwide cons., conv. speaker, seminar leader, from 1950; dir. Investment Mgmt. Co., from 1954; prof. Ind. U., Ft. Wayne, 1967-71. Author: Executive Guide to Successful Speechmaking, 1969, Who Are the Veterans of World War Two?, Designated National Salute to All WWII Veterans (Freedoms Found./George Washington Hon. medal); contbg. editor Why Give It Away When You Can Sell It, 1962, E-Z Tenscript, 1950; speeches and articles read into Congl. Record and selected for placement in Libr. of Congress; contbr. feature articles to nat. publs. Mem. Mayor's Adv. Bd. Ft. Wayne; v.p., mem. Econ. Devel. Commn., Ft. Wayne; life mem., v.p. Jaycees, Ft. Wayne. With USAF, 1943-46, USAFR. Named Sagamore of the Wabash, Disting. Citizen and Ambassador of Goodwill, Gov. of Ind., Admiral of Chesapeake Bay, State of Md., Brigadier Gen. State Wash., Col., Aide-de Camp Gov. of N.Mex., Col. Aide-de-Camp Gov. of Tenn., Lt. Col., Aide de Camp Gov. of Ala., Admiral of Tex. Navy, Order of Paul Revere Patriots, State of Mass., Hon Citizen, State of Nebr., State of. Mont., Hon. Tar Heel, State of N.C., Ky. Col., hon. Sheriff, Ind., Knight, Soverignity of Zante; recipient Civic Citation for Meritorious Achievement, Award of Appreciation S.C., Freedoms Found. award, Key to Ft. Wayne; Gren Park, Ft. Wayne named in his honor, 1984. Mem. Acad. Arts, Letters, Sci. and Culture, Internat. Am. Inst., Air Commandos of WWII, 5th and 10th AF (hon. life), 11th Armored Div. 3rd Army/Ind. Warbirds (hon.). Avocations: antique cars, flying, physical fitness. Home: Fort Wayne, Ind. Died Apr. 26, 2005.

GRIEST, JEFFERY WILLING, construction management engineer, consultant; b. Gettysburg, Pa., May 9, 1927; s. Frederic Erle and Eleanor (Prickett) G.; m. Lindley C. Boyer, June 1954 (div. Aug. 1955); m. Margaret N. Calder, July 7, 1956; children: Julia Ann, Daniel Martin. Student, U.S. Naval Acad., 1946-48; BS in Civil Engring., Swarthmore (Pa.) Coll., 1950; MS, Drexel U., 1954; postgrad., U. Calif., Berkeley, 1955-56. Registered profl. engr., Pa., Fla., Ga., N.J. Job foreman Atlantic Refining Co., Phila., 1950-53; asst. to supt. Conduit & Found. Corp., Phila., 1953-54; project engr., design engr. Creole Petroleum Corp., Venezuela, 1956-61; design engr., resident engr. Ralph M. Parsons Co., L.A. and Cape Kennedy, Fla., 1962-65; resident engr. N.Am. Aviation, Cape Kennedy, 1965-66; project engr. Barclay White & Co., Phila., 1966-67; project engr., project mgr. Robert E. Lamb Inc., Valley Forge, Pa., 1967-78; site project mgr. Gen. Pub. Utilities Forked, River N.J. Nuclear Plant, 1978-81; v.p., mgr. indsl. divsn. Hensley-Schmidt, Atlanta and Chattanooga, 1981-85; sr. project mgr., sr. engr. O'Brien-Kreitzberg & Assocs., Atlanta and Pennsauken, N.J., 1985-94; self-employed constrn. mgmt. cons., Cinnaminson, Kennett Sq., N.J., Pa., from 1994. Clk., property com. Moorestown (N.J.) Monthly Meeting of Quakers, 1993-2000. Cpl., U.S. Army, 1954-55. Mem. ASCE (life), NSPE, Am. Legion. Republican. Avocations: scuba diving, bicycling, hunting, bridge. Home: Kennett Square, Pa. Died Mar. 20, 2004.

GRIFFIN, GLORIA JEAN, retired elementary school educator; b. Emmett, Idaho, Sept. 10, 1946; d. Archie and Marguerite (Johnson) G. AA, Boise (Idaho) Jr. Coll., 1966; BA, Boise Coll., 1968; MA in Elem. Curriculum, Boise State U., 1975. Cert. advanced elem. tchr., Idaho. Tchr. music, tutor, Boise, Idaho; sec. Edward A. Johnson, atty., Boise, Idaho; tchr. Head Start, Boise, Idaho; elem. tchr. Meridian Sch. Dist., Idaho, 1968—2002, ret. Idaho, 2002. Developer multi-modality individualized spelling program; co-developer program for adapting curriculum to student's individual differences. Author: The Culture and Customs of the Argentine People As Applied to a Sixth Grade Social Studies Unit, violin and piano composer of Lament, 2005. Sec. PTA. Named Tchr. of Yr., Meridian Sch. Dist., 1981. Mem. Actor's Guild, Alpha Delta Kappa (rec. sec.). Died Aug. 4, 2006.

GRIFFIN, SHANNON, middle school principal; b. Northfield, Minn., Mar. 27, 1937; d. Burnett Harrison and Beulah Theodora (Forstrom) Voss; m. Bromley Griffin, Dec. 15, 1959 (div. July 1984); children: Hayley, Kyle Bromley. BA, Carleton Coll., 1959; postgrad., St. Cloud State U., 1983, U. Minn., 1983. Cert. tchr. English 7-12, math. 7-12, cert. h.s. prin., supt., Minn. Tchr. math., Wausau, Wis., 1959-60; remedial math. tchr. Wackernheim, Germany, 1960-61; tchr. math. and English, St. Anthony Village H.S., 1961-66; tchr., supr., coord. Onamia Ind. Sch. Dist., 1967-68, 78-86; asst. prin. Sanford Jr. H.S., 1986-90, Roosevelt H.S., 1990-91, Washburn H.S., 1991-94, Edison H.S., 1991-95; prin. Olson Mid. Sch., 1995—2002; ret. Contbr. to editl. page Star Tribune. Named Mpls. Secondary Prin. of Yr., 1998, Carleton Coll. Disting. Alumni, 1999; scholar U. Minn. Coffman Alumni scholar, 1986. Mem. ASCD, Nat. Assn. Secondary Sch. Prins., Phi Kappa Phi. Mem. Dem. Farmer Labor Party. Mem. United Ch. of Christ. Avocations: golf, walking, weightlifting, tennis, gardening. Died Mar. 20, 2004.

GRIFFITH, G. LARRY, lawyer; b. Keokuk, Iowa, Mar. 6, 1937; s. Charles Floyd and Lillian Mae (McClinton) G.; children: Randall Dale, Kristin Lin, Barry Wynn BA, DePauw U., 1959; JD, U. Iowa, 1962. Bar: Iowa 1962, Minn. 1963. Ptnr. Dorsey & Whitney, Mpls., 1962—2000, chair real estate dept., 1991—95, of counsel, 2001—04. Instr. modern real estate trans. U. Minn., Mpls., 1970-71; bd. dirs. Brock-White Co Comment editor U. Iowa Law Rev., 1961-62 Scout master Boy Scouts Am., Mpls., 1965-69; bd. dirs. Jr. Achievement, 1991-2005 Rector scholar De Pauw U., 1955-59 Mem. ABA, Minn. Bar Assn., Hennepin County Bar Assn., U.S. Ski Assn. (Alpine competition com. ctrl. divsn. 1981-87, chmn. region I 1984-86), Mpls. Athletic Club, Burnsville Athletic Club (bd. dirs., legal advisor 1980-92), Phi Alpha Delta Avocations: skiing, tennis, hunting, scuba diving, golf. Died Jan. 13, 2006.

GRIGSBY, ROBERT S., lawyer, educator; b. Mars, Pa., Jan. 26, 1926; s. Jess C. and Elizabeth D. (Shomaker) G.; m. Jean R. Reber, June 16, 1950; 1 child, Pamela S. McCready. BS, U. Pitts., 1950; LLB, Duquesne U., 1955. Bar: Pa. 1956, U.S. Dist. Ct. (we. dist.) Pa. 1955, U.S. Ct. Appeals (3rd cir.) 1957, U.S. Supreme Ct. 1965. From assoc. to ptnr. Dalzel, McFalls, Breden & Martin (and predecessor firms), Pitts., 1958-85; judge Ct. Common Pleas of Allegheny County, Pitts., 1978-79; dir., ptnr. Cohen & Grigsby, P.C., Pitts., from 1985. Adj. prof. U. Pitts. Sch. Law, from 1981; bd. dirs. Pa. Continuing Legal Edn. Solicitor, contr. Allegheny County, Pitts., 1976-78. With USN, 1944-46. Fellow Am. Coll. Trial Lawyers; mem. ABA, Internat. Assn. Def. Counsel, Maritime Law Assn., Product Liability Adv. Coun., Pa. Bar Inst., Pa. Bar Assn., Allegheny County Bar Assn., Acad. Trial Laywers Allegheny County, Fedn. Ins. and Corp. Counsel. Avocations: gardening, golf, fishing. Home: Sewickley, Pa. Died Aug. 26, 2004.

GRIM, FREDERICK EARL, mechanical engineer, consultant; b. Atlanta, Nov. 8, 1946; s. Raymond George and Dorothy Valentine (Sherman) G.; m. Iris Delia Arroyo, Mar. 16, 1970; children: Priscilla, Frederick II, Gregory. BME, Ga. Inst. Tech., 1972; MBA, Ga. State U., 1974. Registered profl. engr., Tenn. Design engr. Robert & Co., Atlanta, 1972-74; sr. engr. Westinghouse Electric Co., Pitts., 1974-78; mgr. R&D Samsonite Corp., Murfreesboro, Tenn., 1978-81; pres. F.E. Grim, P.E., Murfreesboro, from 1981. Chmn. Bd. Adjustment and Appeals Bldg. Code, Murfreesboro, 1987—; scoutmaster Murfreesboro area Boy Scouts Am., 1988—. Capt. U.S. Army, 1966-70, Vietnam. Decorated 4 Bronze Star awards, 2 Purple Heart awards, Air medal, Cross of Gallantry (Republic Vietnam). Mem. NSPE, Tenn. Soc. Profl. Engrs., Nat. Fire Protection Assn., Soc. Automotive Engrs. Avocations: photography, backpacking, canoeing. Home: Murfreesboro, Tenn. Died Aug. 5, 2005.

GRIMM, JAMES C., university administrator; b. Euclid, Ohio, May 7, 1932; s. Eugene Charles and Delores Maud (Lowrie) G.; m. M. Margery Low, June 17, 1961; children: Karel Jo, Deborah Ann. BS in Edn., Bowling Green (Ohio) State U., 1954, MS in Edn., 1955. Head resident Bowling Green State U., 1957-58, asst. dean men, 1958-59, dir. residence svc., 1959-62; dir. residence halls U. Miami, Coral Gables, Fla., 1962-71, assoc. dean students, 1971-77; dir. housing U. Fla., Gainesville, from 1977. Del. 6th Internat. Mtg. Univ. Adminstrs., College Park, Md., 1989; cons. Rollins Coll., Winter Park, 1987-88, Tex. Tech. U., 1989. Co-author: Bibliography of Housing, 1987; editor monograph: Housing Security, 1991. 1st lt. U.S. Army, 1955-57. Mem. Assn. Coll. and Univ. Housing Officers (exec. bd., pres. 1984-85, internat. com. chmn. 1987-91, pres. Found. 1991-92, Charles Beene Award for Outstanding Svc. 1986, Housing Officers Leadership award 1990), Conf. Univ. Adminstrs. of U.K., Assn. Univ. Accommodations Officers U.K. Avocations: travel, camping, hiking, tennis, woodworking. Home: Gainesville, Fla. Died Sept. 26, 2004.

GRINER, NORMAN, retired film director and graphic designer; b. N.Y.C, July 11, 1932; s. Samson and Rosa (Hien) G.; m. Barbara Helen Bankoff (div. 1964); m. Jane Conway Dillard, 1966; children: Julia Louise Griner, Joanna Laura Griner. BFA, Cooper Union, 1952. Art dir., designer The Macmillan Co., N.Y.C., 1952-53, 55-56, Esquire Mag., N.Y.C., 1956-57, The N.Y. Times, N.Y.C., 1957; art dir. CBS-TV, N.Y.C., 1957-59; designer, photographer, owner, dir. Horn/Griner, Inc., N.Y.C., 1957-74; dir., owner Griner/Cuesta & Schrom, N.Y.C., 1974-94, ret., 1994. Dir., producer Oye Willie, 1981. Bd. dirs. York Theatre Co., N.Y.C.; mem. Cen. Park Conservancy, N.Y.C., Civitas, N.Y.C., Carnegie Hill Neighbors, N.Y.C. Cpl., U.S. Army, 1953-55. Recipient numerous awards Art Dirs. Club, Cannes Film Festival, Clio awards, etc. Mem. Dirs. Guild Am., Cooper Union Advancement Soc., Nat. Arts Club, Cooper Union Alumni Assn. (bd. dirs. 1967-71). Avocations: horticulture, photography, travel. Home: New York, NY. Died Apr. 17, 2004.

GRISWOLD, PAUL MICHAEL, clinical psychologist, consultant; b. Milw., Sept. 26, 1945; s. Willard Matthew and Evelyn (Haerle) G.; m. AnnMari Gerardine La Valle, Aug. 2, 1969; children: Matthew Paul, Jennifer Jean. BA, Marquette U., 1967, MS, 1969; PhD, Kent State U., 1972. Sr. staff psychologist Wis. Div. Corrections, Milw., 1972-83; pvt. practice clin. and cons. psychology Menomonee Falls, Wis., from 1973. Lectr. Mount Mary Coll., Milw., 1973-78; faculty Wis. Sch. of Profl. Psychology, Milw., 1981—; cons. Ethan Allen Sch. Wis. Div. Corrections, Wales, Wis., 1984—1989. Contbr. articles to profl. jours. Mem. Am. Psychol. Assn., Wis. Psychol. Assn., Milw. Area Psychol. Assn. Avocations: old cars, sailing, ice boating. Home: Hubertus, Wis. Died June 22, 2004.

GROOMER, CINDY LEE, county government official; b. Amarillo, Tex., July 27, 1956; d. L. Leroy and Doris (Mashburn) Carroll; children from previous marriage: Jessica, Jon. Student, Amarillo Coll, 1983-84, Amarillo Coll., from 1989-. Sec. Amarillo (Tex.) Globe News, 1982-84; ptnr. Raynbo Video Prodns., Amarillo, Tex., 1982-87; sec. TXO Prodn. Corp., Amarillo, Tex., 1984-86; dist. clk. Potter County, Amarillo, Tex., from 1986. Sec. Potter County Bail Bond Bd., Amarillo, 1987—; mem. Regional Edn. Com. for Non-Traditional Employment. Service unit dir. Girl Scout Council, Amarillo, 1986-87, chairperson Juvenile Diabetes Found., Amarillo, 1987—, Amrillo ISD Vocat. Edn. Adv. Com., 1987—, founding mem. exec. sec., Potter County Rep. Party, Amarillo, 1980—, founding mem. Amarillo Young Rep., 1980-82; bd. dirs. High Plains Food Bank, 1988—. Mem. Downtown Kiwanis, Toastmasters. Baptist. Home: Amarillo, Tex. Died June 29, 2005.

GROSS, GEORGE, lawyer, publishing executive; b. Vari, Hungary, May 1, 1934; s. David and Julia (Klien) G.; m. Marcy A. Lynn, May 6, 1966 (div. 1980); children: Julian A., Alexandra L. BA, U. Conn., 1959; LLB, Boston U., 1962. Bar: Conn. 1962, D.C. 1963. Counsel housing, urban devel. subcom. Ho. of Reps., Washington, 1969-74, exec. dir. budget com., 1974-78; dir. fed. rels. Nat. League of Cities, Washington, 1978-84; adminstr. N.Y.C. Human Resources Adminstrn., 1984-86; exec. dir. N.Y. State Fin. Control Bd., N.Y.C., 1986-88; v.p. govt. affairs Mag. Pubs. Am., Washington, 1989—98; city mgr. City of Bridgeport, Conn., 2003. With U.S. Army, 1959-61. Mem. River Bend Golf and Country Club (Great Falls, Va.). Democrat. Avocation: golf. Home: Bethesda, Md. Died Nov. 10, 2004.

GROSS, STANISLAW, environmental sciences educator, activist; b. Lodz, Poland, Nov. 27, 1924; came to U.S., 1960; s. Oskar and Janina (Gundelach) G.; children: Krzysztof, Zbigniew, Richard. BChemE, Tech. U., Lodz, 1947, MChemE, 1949; PhD in Organic Chemistry, U. London, 1961. Dep. mgr. organic dyestuffs Boruta, Zgierz, Poland, 1946-50; assoc. prof. Inst. for Indsl. Medicine, Lodz, 1950-58; biochemical cancer rschr. Chester Beatty Rsch. Inst., London, 1958-62; sr. scientist plant tumor rsch. Boyce Thompson Inst., Yonkers, N.Y., 1962-66; assoc. mem., head molecular biology divsn. Inst. for Muscle Diseases, N.Y.C., 1966-74; rsch. assoc. prof. biochemistry N.Y. Med. Coll., Valhalla, 1973-78; vis. prof. biochemistry Lódź (Poland) Med. Sch., 1979-81; founder, first dir. environ. health scis. program N.Y. Med. Coll. Grad. Sch. Health Scis., Valhalla, 1982-93, adj. prof., 1982-95. Chair N.Y. Acad. Sci. com. organizing USA Celebrations of Centennary of Radioactivity, 1996-98. Contbr. over 45 articles to profl. jours. Tech. advisor to Congressman from N.Y., 1985-2002. Mem. N.Y. Acad. Scis. (founding mem. Lyceum Club), Biophys. Soc., Polish Inst. of Arts and Scis. of Am, Radiation Rsch. Soc. Home: Tarrytown, NY. Died Feb. 16, 2005.

GROSSBERG, MANUEL, advertising professional; b. Bklyn., Mar. 9, 1927; s. Isadore and Rose (Schmertzler) G.; m. Arista Baltronis; children: Mitchell Cary, Robert Harris. BA, NYU, 1950. Sr. art dir. Batten, Barton, Durstine & Osborne, N.Y.C., 1962-68; v.p., assoc. creative dir. Warwick, Welsh and Miller Advt., Inc., N.Y.C., 1968-78; creative cons. Manuel Grossberg Assocs., Inc., N.Y.C., 1978-82; creative dir., bd. dirs. Grossberg & Tudanger Advt., Inc., N.Y.C., 1982-85; pres., creative dir. Sixthsense, Inc., N.Y.C., from 1986. Served with U.S. Army, 1944-46, ETO. Recipient Andy awards, 1969, Clio awards, 1968, Best Local Radio award, Big Apple Broadcasters, 1978, hon. mention AD Club NYC, 1982. Mem. Graphic Artists Guild. Democrat. Avocation: photography. Home: New York, NY. Died Feb. 23, 2004.

GROSSMAN, LAWRENCE, biochemist, educator; b. Bklyn., Jan. 23, 1924; s. Isidor Harry and Anna (Lipkin) G.; m. Barbara Meta Mishen, June 24, 1949; children: Jon David, Carl Henry, Ilene Rebecca. Student, Coll. City N.Y., 1946-47; BA, Hofstra U., 1949; PhD, U. So. Calif., 1954; postdoc., Johns Hopkins U., 1954-56. Scientist NIH, Bethesda, Md., 1956-57; asst. prof. biochemistry Brandeis U., Waltham, Mass., 1957-62, assoc. prof., 1962-67, prof., 1967-75; E.V. McCollum prof. and chmn. dept. biochemistry Johns Hopkins Sch. Hygiene and Pub. Health, Balt., 1975-89, Disting. Svc. prof., 1989—2004. Mem. sci. adv. com. Am. Cancer Soc.; adviser in biochemistry NIH; U.s. rep. to Internat. Union of Biochemistry, NAS. Author: Method in Nucleic Acids, 12 vols.; exec. editor Nucleic Acids Research; assoc. editor Cancer Rsch.; mem. editorial bd. Jour. Biol. Chemistry, Mutation Rsch.-DNA Repair, cancer rsch.; contbr. articles to profl. jours. Trustee Brandeis U. Lt. USNR, 1942-45. Decorated DFC (2), Air medal; recipient USPHS Career Devel. award, 1964-76, Merit award NIH, Stebbins medal Pub. Health Edn.; named M. Katz lectr. in atmospheric chemistry, 1994; Dept. Energy rsch. grantee; Commonwealth fellow, 1963, Guggenheim fellow, 1973, Burroughs-Wellcome fellow, 1989. Mem.

AAAS (program com.), Am. Soc. Biol. Chemistry and Molecular Biology, Am. Chem. Soc., Am. Soc. Photobiology, Environ. Mutagen Soc. Home: Baltimore, Md. Died Jan. 13, 2006.

GROTH, JON QUENTIN, management consultant; b. Washington, Aug. 29, 1941; s. Quentin Neil and Rena Gladys (Lund) G.; m. Karrell Sue Keeney, Sept. 5, 1985; children: Jennifer, Kristen, Kendall. Student, Ohio U., 1959-60, 62-63, Baldwin-Wallace Coll., 1964. Asst. mgr. Ins. Co. of N. Am., Phila., 1966-72; regional mgr. Ryan Ins. Group, Chgo., 1972-79; asst. sec. Cin. Ins. Co., 1979-85; exec. v.p., chief ops. officer Cin. Equitable Ins. Co., 1985-90; chmn., CEO Metanoia Assocs., Inc., Cin., from 1991; COO, CEO Concept 3 Ins. Agy., Inc., from 1996; COO Concept 3 Fin. Svcs., Inc., from 1996. Chmn., CEO Metanoia Ministries. Avocation: amateur radio. Died Aug. 22, 2004.

GROTT, JOAN, librarian; b. Hanna, Alta., Can., July 30, 1946; d. Justin and Audrey (Ford) G.; m. Joel Azerrad, 1982. BA, Pace U., 1969; MLS, St. John's U., 1972. Ref. and young adult libr. Warner Libr., Tarrytown, N.Y., 1971-81, asst. dir., 1977-81; dir. Nyack (N.Y.) Libr., 1981-88, Mamaroneck (N.Y.) Pub. Libr. Dist., from 1988. Named Citizen of Yr., Mamaroneck LWV, 1993. Mem. Pub. Libr. Dirs. Assn. N.Y. State (pres. 1990), Pub. Libr. Dirs. Assn. Westchester (pres. 1990), Pub. Libr. Dirs. Assn. the Ramapo Catskill Libr. System (pres. 1984-86), Rotary (pres. Mamaroneck chpt. 1993-94). Home: Briarcliff Manor, NY. Died July 18, 2005.

GROZEA, COSTEL BERNARD, motion picture company executive; b. Bucharest, Romania, Apr. 15, 1924; came to U.S., 1962; s. Bernard and Cici (Phillips) G.; m. Wanda Giordano, March 9, 1944 (div. 1966); children: Bernard Ilario, Filip. Student, Southampton U., Eng., Sorbonne, France. Lic. Explosives Engr., Calif.; U.S. Lic. Firearms and Ammunitions, High-Low Explosives. Dir. spl. effects Quo Vadis Metro Goldwyn Mayer, Rome, 1950-51, The Crimson Pirate Warner Bros., Island Ischia, Italy, 1951-52, Helen of Troy Warner Bros., Rome, 1952-53, War and Peace Paramount Pictures Internat., Rome, 1953-54, A Farewell to Arms 20th Century Fox, Rome, 1956-57, Sergeant X Les Films Marceaux, France, 1957-58, Battle of Austerlitz Compagnie Francaise des Prodn. Internat., France, Yugoslavia, 1958-59, The Tartars Metro Goldwyn Mayer and Lux Films, Italy, Yugoslavia, 1960-61, Constantine the Great Theodora Prodns., Yugoslavia, 1962-63; owner, motion picture cons. Cygnet Enterprises, Los Angeles, Yucca Valley, Calif., from 1963. Served to 2d lt. British Army, 1941-48. Decorated African Star (Eng.). Mem. Soc. Motion Picture and TV Engrs., Nat. Rifle Assn. Republican. Roman Catholic. Home: Yucca Valley, Calif. Died July 28, 2004.

GRUBBS, CONWAY E., marine company executive; b. Tribbey, Okla., Mar. 26, 1918; s. Harvey Kendrick and Ida Irene (Wright) G.; m. Clyde Laverne Mason, Aug. 23, 1941; children: Jimmy Conway, Barri Lynn. Student, Northeastern Okla. A&M Coll., 1937-38. Mgr. ops., mgr. mktg., gen. mgr, v.p., dir. Caribbean, Ctrl. and So. Am. Chgo. Bridge & Iron Co., Oakbrook, Ill., 1955-69, asst. mgr. marine ops., dir. underwater welding rsch., 1969-76, mgr. worldwide underwater constrn. Prairieville, La., 1976-79; pres., owner D&W Underwater Welding Svc., Inc., Baton Rouge, 1979-84; dir. underwater welding R & D Global Divers and Contractors, Inc., Lafayette, La., from 1984. Cons. U.S. Nat. Rsch. Coun., U.S. Dept. Interior; chmn. exec. com. Joint Industry Underwater Welding Devel. Program. Contbr. articles to profl. jours. With USAAF, 1941-44. Recipient award in recognition of significant achievements in comml. diving, Assn. Diving Contractors Internat. Mem. Am. Welding Soc. (chmn. coms., tech. rep., Meritorious Award for Outstanding Achievements in the Sci. of Welding 1987), Internat. Inst. Welding (chmn., del.). Achievements include patents for Method of Underwater Welding Using Pressurized Welding Electrode Transfer Capsule and Dry Welding Electrode Insitu Storage, Viewing Scope for Turbid Environment and Use in Underwater Welding, and Method of Underwater Welding Using Viewing Scope; major advancements in underwater 'wet' welding. Died June 12, 2004.

GRUSON, MICHAEL, lawyer; b. Berlin, Sept. 17, 1936; came to U.S., 1962; s. Rudolf and Barbara Gruson; m. Hiroko Tsubota, July 11, 1964; children: Rudolf, Andreas, Sebastian, Matthias, Florian, Konrad. LLB, U. Mainz, 1962; M in Comparative Law, Columbia U., 1963, LLB, 1965; Dr. iur, Freie U., 1966. Bar: N.Y. 1969, U.S. Ct. Appeals (2d cir.) 1969, U.S. Dist. Ct. (so. dist.) N.Y. 1971, U.S. Supreme Ct. 1977. Assoc. Shearman & Sterling, N.Y.C., 1966—73, ptnr., 1973—2000, of counsel, 2000—06. Bd. dirs. Mizuho Corp. Bank. Author: Die Bedurfniskompetenz, 1967; co-author: Sovereing Lending: Managing Legal Risk, 1984, Legal Opinions in International Transactions, 4th edit., 2003, Regulation of Foreign Banks, 3 vols., 4th edit., 2005, Acquisition of Shares in a Foreign Country, 1993; contbr. articles to profl. jours. Mem. Am. Law Inst., Internat. Bar Assn. (past vice chmn. com. banking law, past chmn. subcom. on legal opinions), N.Y. State Bar Assn. (com. internat. banking, securities and fin. trans., internat. law and practice sect.), Internat. Law Assn. (com. on internat. monetary law, hon. treas. Am. br.). Home: Hopewell Junction, NY. Died Dec. 20, 2005.

GRYNA, FRANK MICHAEL, engineering educator, director of quality; b. N.Y.C., Aug. 29, 1928; s. Frank A. and Madeline M. (Dyer) G.; m. Doris Anne MacIntosh, June 9, 1957; children: Wendy, Derek, Gary. BS in Indsl. Engring., NYU, 1948, MS in Indsl. Engring., 1950; PhD, U. Iowa, 1970. Registered profl. engr.; cert. quality engr., reliability engr. Instr. NYU, 1950-52; asst. prof. Rutgers U., New Brunswick, N.J., 1952-54, 56-57; analyst ops. research Esso Rsch. and Engring. Co., Linden, N.J., 1957-58; mgr. reliability and quality assurance Space Systems Div. Martin Co., Balt., 1958-62; disting. prof. indsl. engring. Bradley U., Peoria, Ill., 1962-82; pvt. practice cons. Peoria, 1962-82; sr. v.p. Juran Inst., Inc., Wilton, Conn., 1982-91; prof., dir. Ctr. for Quality U. Tampa, Fla., 1991-94, Disting. prof., from 1994. Author: Quality Circles, 1980 (Book of Yr. award Inst. Indsl. Engrs./Joint Pubs. 1980), (with others) Quality Planning and Analysis, 1993; assoc. editor: Quality Control Handbook, 1988. With U.S. Army, 1954-56. Named Engr. of Yr. Peoria Engring. Socs., 1976. Fellow Am. Soc. Quality Control (Edwards medal 1993, E.L. Grant award 1979), Indst. Indsl. Engrs. (Annual Excellence award 1976), Inst. for Quality Assurance, Zeta Psi. Republican. Roman Catholic. Avocations: swimming, music. Home: Chesterfield, Mo. Died Feb. 22, 2005.

GUARRIELLO, MICHAEL LAURENCE, manufacturing company executive, educator; b. Elizabeth, N.J., Feb. 16, 1940; s. Andrew Vincent and Lannie (Caprio) G.; m. Maryjane Anes, June 27, 1964; children: Michael Andrew, Christopher Robert. BS, Stevens Inst. Tech., 1961. V.p. Westmore Inc., Fanwood, N.J., 1962-64; dept. chief Western Electric Co., Kearny, N.J., 1964-75; asst. mgr. Teletype Corp., Little Rock, 1975-84; mgr. AT&T, Little Rock, 1984-89; pres. Mgmt. Gen. Inc., Little Rock, from 1990. Mem. faculty U. Ark. Grad. Inst. Tech., Little Rock, 1990—, chmn. adv. bd. Coll. Sci. and Engring. Tech., 1987-90. Mem. Am. Prodn. and Inventory Control Soc. (cert. in prodn. and inventory mgmt.), Ark. Assn. Entrepreneurs, KC (adv. 1989—). Republican. Roman Catholic. Avocations: golf, fishing. Home: Dallas, Tex. Died Nov. 21, 2004.

GUEST, BARBARA, author, poet; b. Wilmington, NC, Sept. 6, 1920; d. James Harvey and Anna (Hetzel) Pinson; m. Lord Stephen Haden-Guest, 1948 (div. 1954); 1 child, Hon. Hadley; m. Trumbull Higgins, 1954 (dec.); 1 child, Jonathan van Lennep. AB, U. Calif., Berkeley, 1943. Editorial assoc. Art News, 1951-59. Author: (plays) The Ladies Choice, 1953, The Office, 1961, Port, 1965; author: (with Kevin Killian) Often, 2000; author: (poems) The Location of Things, 1960, Poems, 1963, The Blue Stairs, 1968, Moscow Mansions, 1973; author: (with Sheila Isham) I Ching: Poems and Lithographs, 1969; author: The Countess from Minneapolis, 1976, The Türler Losses, 1980, Biography, 1981, Quilts, 1981, Fair Realism, 1989; author: (with June Felter) Musicality, 1989; author: (with Richard Tuttle) The Altos, 1991; author: Defensive Rapture, 1993, Selected Poems, 1995, Stripped Tales, 1995, Quill Solitary Apparition, 1996, Rocks on a Platter: Notes on Literature, 1999, If So, Tell me, 1999, The Confetti Trees: Motion Picture Stories, 1999; author: (with Laurie Reid) Symbiosis, 2000; author: Miniatures and Other Poems, 2002, (novels) Seeking Air, 1978, reprint, 1997, The Red Gaze, 2005, (biographies) The Poet H.D. and Her World, 1984, Herself Defined, 2002, (essays) Forces of Imagination: Writing on Writing, 2003, Dürer in the Window, 2003; editor: (poetry) Partisan Rev. Recipient Longview award, Longview Found., 1960, Laurence Lipton prize in lit., 1990, San Francisco State U. award for poetry, 1994, Fund for Poetry award, 1995, 2005, The America award, 1996, Pen West Josephine Miles award, 1996, Robert Frost medal, Poetry Soc. Am., 1999, Lifetime Achievement award, Small Press Traffic, San Francisco, 2003; grantee, Nat. Endowment for the Arts, 1978; Yaddo fellow, 1958. Died Feb. 15, 2006.

GUEST, C. MAYNARD, physician; b. Bronxville, N.Y., May 9, 1917; s. Carroll Maynard and Gladys (Tooker) G.; m. Frances Eldridge, Sept. 12, 1940 (dec. May 1982); m. Loviscie Kinne, July 17, 1983. BA, Amherst Coll., 1939; MD, U. Pa., 1943. Diplomate Am. Bd. Internal Medicine. Instr. medicine Albany (N.Y.) Med. Coll., 1950-68, clin. asst., prof. medicine, 1968-72, clinic assoc., prof. medicine, from 1972; attending physician in medicine Albany Med. Ctr. Hosp., 1950-83, St. Peter's Hosp., Albany, 1950-83. Exec. sec. N.Y. State Bd. for Profl. Med. Conduct, 1983—. Served as lt. (j.g.) USNR, 1944-45; to maj. USAR, 1953-55. Fellow ACP. Clubs: Ft. Orange (Albany). Republican. Home: Clifton Park, NY. Died Sept. 10, 2004.

GUEVARRA, MANUEL ROBINSON, sculptor; b. San Roque, Cavite, The Philippines, June 17, 1931; s. Jose Andico and Frances (Robinson) G.; m. Carol Ann Bennett, June 15, 1963; children: Mark Bennett, Christian Benjamin. AA, Valencia Coll., 1979. Actor Cor-Qui Films Inc., Manila, 1950-51; enlisted USN, 1953, advanced through grades to chief petty officer, ret., 1976; procurement specialist Naval Tng. Ctr., Orlando, Fla., 1977-79; supr. dist. ops. USPS, Orlando and Lake Mary, Fla., 1979-97; sculptor Crealde Sch. of Arts, Winter Park, Fla., from 1997. Prin. works include The General, 1997, bronze life-size bust of Gen. MacArthur (donated to Pacific War Meml., Phillippines), 2002; Winston Churchill, 1997, George Patton, 1997; works exhibited at Art-Works Gallery and Studio, Oviedo, Fla. Assoc. mem. Orlando Mus. of Art, mem. Crealde Sch. of Art; com. mem. St. Stephen's Ch., Winter Springs, Fla., 1989-90; counselor Boy Scouts Am., Winter Park, 1976-78. Recipient Hon. Mention award, Williams and Jenkins Gallery, 2002. Mem. Fleet Res. Assn., Nat. Assn. Postal Suprs., Fil-Am. Club of Ctrl. Fla. (auditor, v.p. 1976-78). Democrat. Roman Catholic. Avocations: sculpture, stamp collecting/philately, coin collecting/numismatics, gardening, carpentry. Home: Winter Springs, Fla. Died Nov. 12, 2004.

GUGGENHEIMER, JOAN, lawyer; b. Apr. 22, 1952; m. Peter Guggenheimer; children: Laura, Eric. BA, State U. of NY at Binghamton, 1973; JD, Columbia U., 1979. Bar: NY 1979. Law clerk Murray I. Gursein US Ct. Appeals (2d Circuit), 1979, law clerk to Honorable Amalya L. Kerne, 1980; assoc. counsel Davis Polk and Wardwell, 1980—85; staff lawyer Smith Barney, 1985; head of diversity Smith Barney (now Citigroup), 1985—2003; deputy gen. counsel Smith Barney, 1993—95; gen. counsel Smith Barney Capital Markets, 1995—97; sr. deputy gen. counsel Smith Barney, 1997—99; gen. counsel global corp. and investment bank Citigroup, 1999—2003, co-gen. counsel, 2001—03; chief legal officer Bank One Corp., Chgo., 2003; gen. counsel, exec. v.p. J.P. Morgan Chase. Editor: Law Review Columbia U. Home: Scarsdale, NY. Died July 30, 2006.

GUILES, RONALD DAVIS, biochemist, educator; b. San Mateo, Calif., Nov. 23, 1951; s. Richard Charles and Doris May Guiles. PhD, U. of Calif., 1988. Post-doctoral rsch. assoc. U. of Calif. San Francisco, San Francisco, 1988—91; asst. prof. U. of Md., Baltimore, Md., 1991—96, assoc. prof. Md., from 1996, U. of Md. Biotechnology Inst., 1996—2003. Mem.: Am. Chem. Soc. Home: Columbia, Md. Died Jan. 9, 2005.

GUILFORD, ROBERT E., lawyer; b. Cleve., Apr. 14, 1933; s. Isadore H. and Malvene G.; m. Edel Singer, 1960 (div. 1963); 1 child, Steven; m. Judith Cagen, May 5, 1990. BA in Philosophy with honors, U. Va., 1955; JD, Harvard U., 1958. Bar: Calif. 1959, U.S. Dist. Ct. (cen. dist.) Calif. 1959, U.S. Dist. Ct. (no. dist.) Calif. 1964, U.S. Dist. Ct. (no. dist.) N.Y. 1996, U.S. Ct. Appeals (9th cir.) 1959. Asst. U.S. atty. US Dept. Justice, L.A., 1958-59; legal staff MCA Universal, Universal City, Calif., 1959-65; gen. counsel World Horizons Inst., Newport Beach, Calif., 1965-70; ptnr. Bryant, Maxwell, Guilford & Sheahan, 1970-75; outside counsel Home Savings & Loan Assn., Beverly Hills, Calif., 1975-80; pvt. practice Santa Monica, Calif., 1980-85; gen. counsel Mus. of Flying, Santa Monica, Calif., 1985-90; assoc. counsel Am. Golf Corp., Santa Monica, Calif., 1987-90; pvt. practice, 1990—93; shareholder Baum, Hedlund, Profl. Corp., L.A., 1993—2006. V.p., chief pilot, trustee Mus. Flying, Santa Monica; v.p. Supermarine Aviation Ltd., Liberty Aero Corp., NATO Aviation. Mem. State Bar Calif., Lawyer-Pilot's Bar Assn., Aircraft Owners and Pilots Assn., Exptl. Aircraft Assn., Classic Jet Aircraft Assn. (chmn. bd. dirs.), Warbirds Am. (co-founder), Hunter Flight Test Ltd. (v.p.), Nat. Air Disaster Found. (Safety award 2002), Mustang Pilots Club (founder, pres.), Phi Eta Sigma. Avocation: pilot. Died July 16, 2006.

GULLEY, CAROLE GRACE, health facility administrator; b. Rarden, Ohio, Feb. 25, 1935; d. William J. and Beulah P. (Daulton) Somerset; m. Donald G. Gulley, July 11, 1953 (dec.); children; Roxanne, Rucilla, Jnita, Tabitha, Harry, Joshua. ADN, Ohio U., Portsmouth, 1972; BSN, Ohio U., 1984; MS, Wright State U., 1992. RN, Ill., Ohio.; cert. orthopedic nurse specialist. Head nurse So. Hills Hosp., Portsmouth; supr. So. Ohio Correctional Facility, Lucasville; infection control, quality assurance coord. Pike Community Hosp., Waverly, Ohio; supr. Med.-Tech. Svcs., Columbus, Ohio; nurse mgr. Holzer Med. Ctr., Gallipolis, Ohio; DON Oak Hill (Ohio) Community Med. Ctr. Clin. instr. Hocking Coll., Rio Grande U. Recipient Profl. Traineeship award, 1991-92. Mem. Assn. for Practitioners Infection Control, Nat. Assn. Quality Assurance Profls., Quality Rev. Coords. Ohio, Sigma Theta Tau. Home: Gallipolis, Ohio. Died July 9, 2004.

GUNNELS, THOMAS CURTIS, seminar company executive; b. Cameron, Tex., Aug. 1, 1929; s. Thomas Pitts and Alice (Jones) G.; m. Sue Lee Gunnels, June 3, 1959 (dec. Aug. 1965); children: Susan, Sandra; m. Frankie Regas, Aug. 16, 1970. BBA, So. Meth. U., 1954. CLU, LUTCF. Pers. mgr. State Farm Ins. Co., Murfreesboro, Tenn., 1954-58, dir. agy. tng., 1958-59, agy. mgr. Knoxville, Tenn., 1959-95; CEO Seminar Co., from 1995. Chmn. Nat. Conf. Christians/Jews, Knoxville, 1989-91; pres. Better Bus. Bur., Knoxville, 1973-75, Conv. Bur., Knoxville, 1970-71. Author: Keep Your Lights On, 1998; contbr. articles to profl. jours. S/Sgt. USAF, 1946-49. Named Man of the Yr., Knoxville Rotary Club, 1991, Brotherhood award, 1995, The Nat. Conf. of Christian and Jews, 1995. Mem. Knoxville Assn. Life Underwriters (pres. 1990-91, Man of the Yr. 1990). Republican. Episcopalian. Avocations: tennis, profl. speaking, writing. Died Nov. 11, 2004.

GUPTA, AYODHYA PRASAD, entomologist, immunologist, cell biologist; b. Menhadawal, India, July 1, 1928; came to U.S., 1960; s. Badri Prasad and Prakashvati Gupta: m. Godaveri Rawat, June 26, 1967; children: Rajeew, Anita. MS in Entomology, U. B.C., Vancouver, Can., 1961; PhD, U. Idaho, 1964. Rsch. assoc. Rutgers U., New Brunswick, N.J., 1964-65, asst. prof., 1966-68, assoc. prof., 1968-73, prof., from 1973, dir. grad. program, 1981-86. Cons. Food & Agrl. Orgn., UN, Rome, 1974, UN Devel. Program, N.Y.C., 1982; founder Disting. Internat. award in Insect Morphology and Embryology, 1984; organizer program in morphology Internat. Congress Entomology, China, 1992, Florence, Italy, 1996. Founder, editor-in chief Internat. Jour. Insect Morphology and Embryology, 1970, Comparative Arthropod Morphology, Physiology and Devel., 1991; editor Entomology in the U.S.A., 1976; subject reviewer,

reviewer Thesaurus of Entromology, 1977; author, editor 10 books; contbr. articles, papers to profl. jours. Pres. Assn. Indians in Am. N.J. chpt., 1972-74. Inducted into U. Idaho Alumni Hall of Fame, 1991; recipient recognition award for svc. to entomology Coll. Agr. U. Idaho, 1991, Pride of India award B.S. Sanstha, Queens, N.Y., 1993, Jewel of India award Non-resident Indian Soc. India, 1995; fellow U. Idaho, 1961; insect species Colyphus guptai named in his honor, 1977. Fellow Royal Entomol. Soc. London; mem. AAAS, Entomol. Soc. India (life), Entomol. Soc. Am. (numerous offices), Arthropodan Embryol. Soc. Japan (hon.), Idaho Acad. of Scis., N.Y. Acad. Scis. Achievements include research on insect blood cells, cellular immunity and insect morphology. Home: Somerset, NJ. Died Aug. 14, 2005.

GUST, JOHN DEVENS, lawyer; b. Phoenix, Aug. 31, 1918; s. John Lewis and Ada Lee (Rebstock) G.; m. Mary Elizabeth Montgomery, Sept. 1, 1942; children— John Devens, Morgan M. A.B., Stanford U., 1940, J.D., 1942. Bar: Ariz. 1943. Ptnr., Gust, Rosenfeld, Divelbess & Henderson, Phoenix, 1946-86, sr. ptnr., 1968-86; sr. counsel, 1986—; dir. Valley Nat. Bank Ariz. Served to lt. j.g. USNR, 1941-46. Mem. ABA, State Bar Ariz. (past pres., dir.), Maricopa County Bar Assn. (past pres., dir.). Republican. Club: Ariz. Home: Mule Creek, N.Mex. Died July 30, 2006.

GUTHRIE, ROBERT BAXTER, insurance agent; b. McCredie, Mo., Sept. 1, 1920; s. McKamey Phillips and Mabel (Pratt) G.; m. Jane Ann Cooper, Apr. 18, 1954; children: Jan Elizabeth Lee, Jeannie Lynn McKinnon, James McKamey Guthrie. BA, Westminster Coll., 1941. CLU, ChFC. Farmer, livestock feeder Sunbright Farms, Kingdom City, Mo., 1936-68; founder, regional v.p. Family Benefit Life Ins. Co., Jefferson City, Mo., from 1964; also bd. dirs. Bd. dirs. Family Benefit Investment Co., 1968-80; v.p. Mo. Farm Bur. Fedn., 1969. Co-author: (position paper) Why and How Presbyterians Make Social Policy Witness, 1992. Pres. Fulton Bd. Coll. Assocs., 1965; chmn. Callaway County ARC drive, 1955; moderator Mo. Union Presbytery, 1965, '92; pres. Callaway United Way, 1977, Callaway County Ecumenical Ministries, 1982, Kingdom of Callaway Award Banquet, 1970; elder Old Auxvase Presbyn. Ch., 1945—. Recipient Alumni Achievement award Westminster Coll., 1977. Mem. Am. CLU, ChFC Soc. (pres. Ctral. Mo. chpt. 1976-77), Audrain County Life Underwriters (pres. 1983-84), Kingdom of Callaway Life Underwriters (bd. dirs. 1987—), Million Dollar Roundtable, Fulton Kiwanis Club (pres. 1991), Alpha Delta Alumni Assn., Omicron Delta Kappa. Republican. Avocations: gardening, farm mgmt., timber mgmt., running (most trophies earned after 65th birthday). Home: Kingdom City, Mo. Died Aug. 29, 2004.

GUTMANN, REINHART BRUNO, priest, social worker; b. Munich, May 1, 1916; came to U.S., 1942, naturalized, 1946; s. Franz and Berta G.; m. Vivian Carol Brunke, Oct. 7, 1944 (dec. Jan. 2003); children: Robin Peter Edward, Martin Francis. Student, History Honours Sch., Manchester U., Eng., 1936-38; MA in Social Scis, St. Andrews U., Scotland, 1939; postgrad., Coll. of Resurrection, Eng., 1939-41, Coll. Preachers, Washington, 1948, 52, U. Wis., summer, 1951, St. Augustine's Coll., Eng., 1964. Ordained deacon Ch. of Eng., 1941, ordained priest, 1942; curate St. Michael's Parish, Golders Green, London, 1941-42; rector St. Mark's Parish, Green Island, NY, 1944-45, St. Andrew's Parish, Milw., 1952-54; chaplain and mem. faculty Hoosac (N.Y.) Sch., 1943-45; founder, exec. dir. Neighborhood House and Episcopal City Mission, Milw., 1945-60; exec. dir. Friendship House, Washington, 1960-62; cons. Indian Social welfare Exec. Council of Episcopal Ch., N.Y.C., 1962-64; exec. sec. div. community services Exec. Council of Episcopal Ch., 1964-68, exec. for social welfare and field services, 1968-71; part-time priest-in-charge St. Thomas of Alexandria, Pittstown, NJ, 1968-75; hon. asst. priest St. Martin's Ch., Pawtucket, RI, 1980; pres. Cedar Brook Cons., Inc., 1982—86; ret., 1987. Priest-in-charge St. Peter's Mission, North Lake, Wis., 1958-60, hon. asst. priest St. Ambrose Parish, Fort Lauderdale, Fla., 1984-98, asst. priest emeritus, 1996, hon. asst. priest emeritus, 1998-2006; mgr. spl. projects Human Resources Adminstrn., NYC, 1971-72, spl. asst. to asst. adminstr., 1972-73, dir. mgmt. office cmty. svcs., 1973, spl. asst. to dep. adminstr. social svcs., 1973-75; nat. exec. dir. Foster Parents Plan, Inc., Warwick, R.I., 1975-82. Organizer Gordonstoun Am. Found., 1983, exec. sec., 1983-87; chmn. dept. Christian social relations Province of Midwest, Episcopal Ch., 1954-60; chmn. social edn. and action Nat. Fedn. Settlements, 1960-62; hon. canon All Saints Cathedral, Milw., 1971; founder Silver Spring Neighborhood Ctr., Milw., 1958; founder Northcott Neighborhood House, Milw., 1959. Mem. Acad. Cert. Social Workers, Nat. Assn. Social Workers. Democrat. Home: Tuscaloosa, Ala. Died May 16, 2006.

GUTTERMAN, MILTON M., operations research analyst; b. N.Y.C., Nov. 5, 1927; s. Benjamin and Gussie (Rothchild) G.; m. Joan Helen Levey, Nov. 30, 1952; children: Gail Rosemary, Allen Bernard. BS, CCNY, 1948; MS, U. Chgo., 1949. Researcher Inst. for Air Weapons Rsch., Chgo., 1952-54; rsch. engr. IIT Rsch. Inst., Chgo., 1954-66; sr. ops. rsch. cons. Amoco Corp., Chgo., 1966-92; pvt. practice cons., 1992-93. Rsch. cons. in field. Editor: (book) Computer Applications 1962, 1964; assoc. editor Transactions on Math. Software, 1975-80; asst. editor ORSA Jour. on Computing, 1987-91. With U.S. Army, 1946-47. Mem. Ops. Rsch. Soc. Am. (chmn. computer sci. tech. sect. 1989-91), Math. Programming Soc., Soc. for Indsl. and Applied Math., Assn. for Computing Machinery, Am. Rose Soc., No. Chicagoland Rose Soc., Am. Contact Bridge League (life master). Jewish. Died June 1, 2005.

GWYN, PATRICIA D., human resources specialist; d. William Mark Dougherty and Antona Marie Varels-Dougherty; 1 child, Kenneth R. Jr. (dec.). Author: (handbook) Arizona State Monitor's Guide, 1993. Mem.: Nat. Mus. Women in Arts. Avocations: drawing, painting, interior decorating. Home: Mesa, Ariz. Died June 9, 2005.

HAAS, PETER E., SR., apparel company executive; b. San Francisco, Dec. 20, 1918; s. Walter A. and Elise (Stern) H.; m. Josephine Baum, Feb. 1, 1945; children: Peter E., Michael Stern, Margaret Elizabeth; m. Mimi Lurie, Aug., 1981; stepchildren: Ari Laurie, Daniel Lurie Student, Deerfield Acad., 1935-36; AB, U. Calif., 1940; IA cum laude, Harvard, 1943. With Levi Strauss & Co., San Francisco, 1945—2005, exec. v.p., 1958-70, pres., 1970-81, CEO, 1976-81, chmn. bd., 1981-89, chmn. exec. com., 1989—2005; chmn. exec. com., bd. dirs. Levi Strauss Assocs. Inc. Holding Corp. Bd. dirs. Levi Strauss & Co., 1970-81; dir. emeritus AT&T. Trustee San Francisco Found., 1984-2005; assoc. Smithsonian Nat. Bd., 1988-2005; bd. dirs. No. Calif. Grantmakers, 1989-2005; former mem. exec. com. Strive for Five; former mem. Golden Gate Nat. Recreation Area Adv. Com.; pres. Jewish Welfare Fedn., 1976-78, chmn. 1953, 1964, 1975; former trustee Stanford U.; former dir., vice chmn. San Francisco Bay Area Council; gen. campaign mgr., United Way of San Francisco Bay Area, 1969, pres. 1972, chmn. bd. trusteees, 1973; former pres. Aid to Retarded Children; former bd. govs. United Way of Am. Recipient Alexis De Tocqueville Soc. award, United Way Am., 1985; named CEO of Yr., Fin. World mag., 1981, Bus. Statesman of Yr., Harvard Bus. Sch., 1982, Alumnus of Yr., 1996; Baker scholar, 1940. Died Dec. 3, 2005.

HABECK, DANIEL ERNEST, minister; b. Minocqua, Wis., Mar. 25, 1932; s. Irwin John and Dorothy Bertha (Seefeldt) H.; m. Carol Mae Asp, June 14, 1957; children: Cheryl, Charis, Dania, Jana. BA, Northwestern Coll., Watertown, Wis., 1954; MST, Wis. Luth. Sem., Mequon, 1957. Ordained minister in Luth. Ch., 1957. Pastor Grace Luth., Muskegon Heights, Mich., 1957-64, Zion Luth., Toledo, 1964-71, Martin Luther Luth., Oshkosh, Wis., from 1971. Bd. control Mich. Luth. Sem., Saginaw, 1963-71; chmn. No. Wis. Dist. Bd. for Parish Edn., 1982-88; cir. pastor Mich. Dist. No. Wis. Dist., 1968—. Home: Oshkosh, Wis. Died July 3, 2004.

HACKETT, SYLVIA LAVADA, lawyer; b. Hagerstown, Md., Mar. 22, 1938; d. Alfred Mobray and Hazel Virginia (Sard) H. BA, Wake Forest U., 1959; JD, U. Balt., 1972. Bar: Md. 1972, D.C. 1981. Caseworker Dept. of Social Services, Towson, Md., 1959-67; probation officer Cir. Ct., Towson, 1967-72; atty., supr. support & custody div. Balt. County Cir. Ct., Towson, 1972-91; sole practice Baltimore County, from 1972. Bd. dirs. Samuel Ready Scholarships, Inc., Balt. Mem. adv. com. on adoption State of Md., Balt., 1977-91; regional del. diocesan council, Episcopal Diocese Md., 1983-86, chmn. program and budget, 1985-86; mem. Gov.'s Task Force to Study Adoption Laws, 1985-87. Fellowship Nat. Endowment for the Humanities, U. Iowa, 1978. Mem. ABA, Md. Bar Assn., Women's Bar Assn. Md., D.C. Bar Assn., Assn. Family and Conciliation Cts., Acad. Family Mediators, U. Balt. Alumni (bd. govs.), Iota Tau Tau. Republican. Died Mar. 13, 2005.

HADEN, BILLY HARPER, research biochemist; b. Jackson, Miss., Mar. 8, 1940; s. Billy Sunday and Fannie Lou (Ware) H.; m. Linda Lee Mims, Feb. 23, 1963; children: Billy, Stacey, Andrew. BS in Chemistry, Miss. State U., 1963; MS in Chemistry, U. Notre Dame, 1968, postgrad., 1968-71, Mich. State U., 1971-72. Researcher Ames Co. div. Miles Labs., Inc., Elkhart, Ind., 1963-68, assoc. research biochemist, 1968-72; applications and customer service chemist Analytical Systems Mktg. div. Bausch and Lomb, Rochester, N.Y., 1972-74; mgr. devel. applications Syva Co., Palo Alto, Calif., 1974-77; mgr. applications and clin. investigations Beckman Instruments, Inc., Brea, Calif., 1977-94; dir. tech. and regulatory Reagents Applications, San Diego, 1994-95; mgr. devel. Med. Analysis Systems, Camarillo, Calif., 1995-99; v.p. sci. and regulatory Precision Systems Inc, Natick, Mass., from 1999. Patentee in field; contbr. 150 articles to profl. jours. Advisor Boy Scouts Am./Cub Scouts, Elkhart and Rochester, 1971-74;chief, asst. chief Y Indian Guides/Princesses, Elkhart and Rochester, 1970-82, com. mem., 1972-73; v.p. bd. dirs. Elkhart Civic Theater, 1969-72. Recipient Career Devel. award Syntex Corp., Palo Alto, 1975, Mgmt. Supervisory Devel. U. Calif., 1982, Excellence in Leadership award Beckman Instruments, Inc., Brea, Calif., 1985. Mem.: Am. Assn. Clin. Chemists (treas. N.E. sect.), Am. Chem. Soc. Avocations: outdoor activities, travel, coin collecting/numismatics. Home: Southborough, Mass. Died Nov. 2004.

HADZI, DIMITRI, sculptor, educator; b. N.Y.C., Mar. 21, 1921; s. Theodore and Christina H.; m. Cynthia Hoyle; children: Christina, Stephen. Student, Bklyn. Poly. Inst., 1940-43, Cooper Union, 1946-50; MA (hon.), Harvard U., 1977; DFA (hon.), Lawrence U., 1987. Prof. Harvard U., Cambridge, Mass., 1975—89, prof. emeritus, 1989—2006. One-man shows, Galleria Schneider, Rome, 1958, 60, Galerie Van de Loo, Munich, 1961, 95, Radich Gallery, N.Y.C., 1961-62, MIT, 1963, Richard Gray Gallery, Chgo., 1972, 87-88, 96, Mekler Gallery, L.A., 1978, Gruenebaum Gallery, N.Y.C., 1978, 84, Fogg Mus. Harvard U., 1981, 84; group shows include, Venice Biennale, 1956, 58, 62, Guggenheim Mus., N.Y.C., 1979, Kouros Gallery, N.Y.C., 1995, Long Point Gallery, Provincetown, Mass., 1996, Richard Gray Gallery, Chgo., 1997; represented in permanent collections, Mus. Modern Art, N.Y.C., Guggenheim Mus., Whitney Mus., N.Y.C., Hirshhorn Mus., Washington, Yale U. Gallery, Fogg Art Mus., Phila. Mus. Art, Dallas Mus. Art, UCLA, Albright-Knox Art Gallery, Buffalo; archtl. Commns. include Bronze doors, St. Paul's Ch., Rome, 1962-76, Fed. Res. Bank, Mpls., 1971-73, Johnson Wax, Racine, Wis., 1978-79, fountain, Owens-Illinois, Toledo, 1982, fountain, Copley Pl., Boston, 1984, Harvard Square, Cambridge, Mass., 1985, Pine Manor Coll., Boston, 1987, City of Appleton, Wis., 1987, Embacadero Ctr., San Francisco, 1989, Fed. Courthouse, Birmingham, 1991. Served with USAAF, 1942-46. Recipient Louis Comfort Tiffany award, 1954, St. Gaudens award, The Cooper Union, 1987; fellow Fulbright, Athens, 1950—51; John Simon Guggenheim Found. Fellowship, 1957. Home: Cambridge, Mass. Died Apr. 16, 2006.

HAELTERMAN, EDWARD OMER, veterinary microbiologist, educator; b. Norway, Mich., Oct. 14, 1918; s. Omer and Hortanse Agnes (Smith) H.; m. Violet Marie Raiche, Aug. 10, 1946. D.V.M., Mich. State U., East Lansing, 1952; MS, Purdue U., 1955; PhD, 1959; PhD Doctor Honoris Causa, State U. Ghent, Belgium, 1974. Instr. Purdue U., West Lafayette, Ind., 1952-59, asso. prof., 1959-64, prof. microbiology, 1964-84, prof emeritus, 1984. Asst. dean Sch. Vet. Medicine, 1958-61; Vis. investigator Rockefeller U., 1958; research officer East African Vet. Research Orgn., 1967-68 Contbr. articles to profl. jours. Served with USNR, 1942-45. Mem. Am. Soc. Microbiology, AVMA, AAAS, AAUP, U.S. Animal Health Assn., Sigma Xi, Phi Kappa Phi, Phi Zeta, Gamma Sigma Delta. Clubs: Torch. Lodges: Kiwanis. Democrat. Home: West Lafayette, Ind. Died Jan. 9, 2005.

HAGEMIER, HERMAN FREDERICK, chemist; b. Linton, Ind., Oct. 23, 1908; s. Clarence Frederick and Estella (Davidson) H.; m. Georgia Emmiline Tracy, Jan. 28, 1939 (dec. 1966); children: Evelyn Louise, Frederick Louis; m. Loueva Elizabeth Stoner Helton, Nov. 4, 1971. BS in Botany and Chemistry, Butler U., 1953. Independent researcher, 1962-2000. Author: Magnetic Double Helix, 1992, Magnetic Double Helix II, 1996, Magnetic Double Helix III, 1998. Home: Pendleton, Ind. Died June 7, 2004.

HAGEN, YVONNE BORN FORREST, writer; b. Ile Aux Moines, Morbihan, France, Aug. 14, 1920; came to U.S., 1929; d. Wilbur Studley and Floss May (Springer) Forrest; m. Karl-Victor Hagen, Sept. 15, 1940 (dec. July 1948); children: Nina, Karen, Anthony; m. N.H. Stubbing, May 10, 1983 (dec. Oct. 1983). Student, Fontainbleau Sch. of Fine Arts, Columbia U., 1940-41. Interviewer Am. Mag. Art, NY, 1946-48; art reviewer European edit. N.Y. Herald Tribune, 1954-61; art critic Art Aujourdhui, monthly mag., 1957, 58, 59; dir. Modern Art Munich, 1967-71. Advisor to numerous galleries in Europe and Calif.; dir. New Art Liaison. Author: (autobiography) From Life to Art and Back, 2005, also monographs; contbr. forewords and articles to art mags.; editor catalogs on modern art. Mem. Lindisfarne (assoc.). Democrat. Avocations: enjoy seeing chinese art, travel, chamber music. Home: Sagaponack, NY. Died Nov. 28, 2005.

HAIN, WALTER E., health care professional; b. Waukegan, Ill., Oct. 11, 1939; s. Walter P. and Doris E. (Kull) H.; m. Maria Jane Villaneuva, oct. 8, 1970; children: Reynaldo, Catalina. Cert. hosp. corpsman, Naval Sch. Health Sci., 1965, cert. ind. duty tech., 1983; BS in Health Sci., George Washington U., 1984. Cert. med. coder, med. ins. billing, nurse asst., Calif.; cert. advanced lab., oper. rm. tech., field med. tech. Enlisted USN, 1965; served as computer data supr. Naval Res. Readiness Command 9, Millington, Tenn., 1982-84; patient affairs supr. Marine Corps Air Station, Tustin, Calif., 1988; supr. med. records Naval Tng. Ctr., San Diego, 1974-77; med. unit clk. Gen. Hosp., Riverside, Calif., from 1990; ret. USN, 1988. Home: Riverside, Calif. Died May 4, 2005.

HAINES, ROBERT EMMETT, technical writer, vocational educator; b. East St. Louis, Ill., Aug. 18, 1931; s. William McIllvain and Fonnie LaFont (Radford) H.; m. Mozelle Jay Hood, Jan. 9, 1959; 1 child, Mindy Ilene. BS in Edn., So. Ill. U., 1974. Cert. tchr., Ill. History tchr. Althof H.S., Belleville, Ill., 1974-76; constrn. tech. instr. Lewis and Clark Jr. Coll., Godfrey, Ill., 1977-80, ARAMCO, Saudi Arabia, 1981-82, tech. writer, 1983-85, ednl. devel. specialist, 1986-91. Author: Bob's View, 1995, (poetry collection) What's a Redneck and Other Poems, 1992. Mem. VFW, Masons, Shriners, Phi Theta Kappa. Republican. Avocations: writing, novels. Died May 11, 2004.

HAIR, GILBERT MARTIN, foundation administrator; b. Manila, Philippines, Mar. 16, 1941; came to U.S., 1945; s. Jack and Jane McMahon Hair; m. Joanne Walsh, June 1966 (div.); m. Susan Christian, Apr. 5, 1969 (div. 1979); 1 child, Nicole. BA, Am. U., 1966; postgrad., San Fernando Valley Coll. Law, 1973-74. Cert. travel counsel, cert. Cruise Line Internat. Assn., Calif. Landscape Contractors Assn. With CIA, 1963-66; sales rep. Pan Am. World Airways, N.Y.C., 1966-71; dir. mktg. Continental Airlines, L.A., Micronesia, 1972-79; sr. v.p. mktg. Air North Am., Pasadena, Calif., 1979-83; instr., program dir. Jostens, Inc., L.A., Ventura, Calif., 1982-87; stockbroker, investment banker Thousand

Oaks, Calif., 1987-93; pres., exec. dir. The Ctr. for Internee Rights Inc., Newbury Park, Calif., 1990—92, Miami Beach, from 1992. Mem. Rep. Nat. Com., Washington, from 1964; pres. Conejo Valley (Calif.) Rep. Action Com., from 1992. With USMC, 1960—63. Mem.: Admiral Nimitz Found., Philippine Scouts Heritage Soc. (life), Coalition Retired Mil. Vets. (life), Am. Ex POW Assn. (life), Am. Defenders of Bataan and Corregidor (life), Disabled Am. Vets. (life), Marines' Meml. Club, Explorers Club, Westlake Tennis and Swim Club, Royal Bangok Sports Club (life), Am. Legion (life). Roman Catholic. Avocations: golf, tennis, fishing, travel, politics. Home: Miami Beach, Fla. Died Sept. 15, 2004.

HALBERSTEIN, JOSEPH LEONARD, retired editor; b. Piqua, Ohio, Mar. 10, 1923; s. David and Mollie (Oberferst) H.; m. Lillian Friedman, Aug. 9, 1964; children: Richard Martin, Howard Louis. BA in Journalism, Ohio State U., 1944; postgrad., Pa. State U., 1976. Sportswriter Columbus (Ohio) Citizen, 1943-44; sports editor Lima (Ohio) News, 1944-49; circulation mgr. Town and Village, N.Y.C., 1950-52; sports editor, mng. editor Wilmington (Del.) Sunday Star, 1952-54; wire editor, sports editor Gainesville (Fla.) Sun, 1955-71; mng. editor, assoc. editor Bucks County Courier Times, Levittown, Pa., 1971-93, ret., 1993. Lectr. various univs. Contbr. articles to profl. jours. Bd. dirs. ARC, Langhorne, Pa., 1971-80, Congregation Beth El, Levittown, 1978-85. Recipient 2d Pl. best column Nat. Newspaper Assn., 1961, 1st Pl. best column Keystone Press Assn., 1976, 2d Pl. best game story Basketball Writers Assn. Mem. Fla. Sportswriters Assn. (pres.), Pa. AP Mng. Editors Assn. (pres.), Soc. of Profl. Journalists (greater Phila. chpt. pres. 1981-82), Pa. Soc. of Newspaper Editors, Sigma Delta Chi. Avocations: walking, travel, computers. Home: Levittown, Pa. Died May 30, 2006.

HALDEMAN, GLORIA SHAPIRO, small business owner; b. Kansas City, Mo., May 21, 1935; d. Samuel S. Shapiro and Dorothy Lillian (Eisberg) Shapiro Amdur; children: Sanford, Harris, David, Pankin; married, Mar. 1997. AB, U. Mich., 1957. Cert. tchr., Mich., Calif. Owner, operator CEO, pres. Alpha Buttons, Escondido, Calif., from 1991. Substitute tchr. Vista (Calif.) Unified Schs., 1991-96. Membership chmn., ways and means com., regional officer comty svcs., children's programs Parents Without Ptnrs., St. Louis, 1974-81; v.p. ways and means Escondido Panhellenic, 1995-96; active Women in the Arts Mus., 1993; vol. PSI World Children's Seminar, 1992—. Mem. Hidden Valley Obedience Club (founder, dir. tng. 1986, treas. 1992), Therapy Dogs, NAFE, Sigma Delta Tau Alumni Assn. (pres. 1995). Jewish. Avocations: dog obedience, genealogy. Home: Escondido, Calif. Died Sept. 17, 2005.

HALE, LEONARD PETER, III, instrumentation and electrical engineer; b. Cuero, Tex., Nov. 29, 1945; s. Joe Karbosky and Geneva (Hale) Johnson. AAS in Elec. Engring., Tex. State Tech. Inst., 1972; BS in Elec. Engring. Technology, U. Houston, 1976. Lic. radio telephone operator FCC. Electronics technician Tektronix, Houston, 1972-77; elec. engr. Daniel Industries, Houston, 1977-85, Morco, Inc., Corpus Christi, Tex., 1985-86; instrumentation engr. Ebasco Engring., Houston, 1986; elec. engr. S.W. Tube, Sandsprings, Okla., 1987; R&D technician T.D. Williamson, Tulsa, 1987-88; controls technologist Parsons SIP, Houston, 1988-89; instrumentation and elec. engr. Elf Atochem, Houston, from 1989. Sgt. USAF, 1965-69, Vietnam. Mem. Instrument Soc. of Am., VFW (trustee), Moose. Republican. Avocations: hunting, fishing. Home: Houston, Tex. Died Jan. 15, 2005.

HALE, LYLE A., retired fuel supply company executive; b. Afton, Wyo., Mar. 18, 1922; s. Louis Holbert and Lois Angela (Allred) H.; m. Jeanette Seibold, Aug. 3, 1950; children: Debra, Linda, Shawna, Karen, Fred, Larry, Ronald, Jerron. BS in Petroleum Geology, Utah State U., 1948; MA in Petroleum Geology, U. Wyo., 1950. Cert. petroleum geologist. Field geologist Amerada Petroleum Corp., Tulsa, 1948-51; exploration geologist Mountain Fuel Supply Co., Rock Springs, Wyo., 1951-67, rsch. geologist Salt Lake City, 1967-68, chief geologist, 1968-69, mgr. of exploration, 1969-70, v.p., mgr., 1970-75; cons. geologist May Petroleum and AAMinerals, Rocky Mountain region, 1975-87; owner, operator Rainbow Ranch, Star Valley, from 1987. Asst. geologist U.S. Geol. Survey, Anchorage, summer 1947. Editor: Idaho Phosphate Deposits, Geology, Reserves etc., 1967; co-editor: Geology-Oil and Gas Fields of Wyoming, 1962. Mem., bd. dirs. Rotary Club, Bountiful, Utah, 1973-74; v.p. Utah Petroleum Assn., Salt Lake City, 1969-71. Named Oil Man of Month, Western Oil Reporter, Denver, 1971. Mem. Am. Assn. Petroleum Geologists, Rocky Mountain Assn. Geologists (Explorer of Yr. 1974, Best Paper award 1973). Republican. Mem. LDS Church. Avocations: trout fishing, ranching. Home: Bountiful, Utah. Died July 23, 2004.

HALITSKY, JAMES, meteorologist; b. N.Y.C., Oct. 18, 1919; s. Joseph John and Sarah (Katznelson) H.; m. Sylvia Heitler, Mar. 11, 1944; children: Julie Anne, David James. B Mech. Engring., CUNY, 1940; M Aero. Engr., NYU, 1952, PhD in Meteorology and Oceanography, 1970. Aero. engr. Edo Aircraft Corp., L.I., N.Y., 1940-48; rsch. scientist NYU, 1948-70; assoc. prof. U. Mass., Amherst, 1970-75; cons. Croton-on-Hudson, N.Y., from 1975. Lectr. Pa. State U., College Station, 1955, 67; adj. prof. NYU, 1979-84, CCNY, 1979-91; grant reviewer USPHS, Washington, 1967-70. Contbr. articles to profl. jours. Grantee USPHS 1957-65, U.S. Weather Bur. 1963-64, U.S. Atomic Energy Commn. 1965-71, U.S. Army Electronic Rsch. & Devel. Lab. 1961-65. Mem. Am. Meteorol. Soc., NY Acad. Scis., Sigma Xi. Achievements include initiation of research into and developing design procedures for environmentally-safe disposal of building-generated waste gas into the atmosphere. Died May 7, 2005.

HALL, DEWEY EUGENE, stock brokerage executive; b. Marion, Ind., Feb. 17, 1932; s. C. Dewey and Edith P. (Nelson) H.; m. Diana Diggs, Dec. 26, 1955; children: John Stephen, Janet Susan. BS, Ball State U., 1954; postgrad., George Washington U., 1957-58; grad. securities program, U. Pa., 1969. Registered rep. N.Y. Stock Exchange. Ins. underwriter Govt. Employees Ins. Co., Washington, 1957-59; dist. mgr. Field Enterprises, Birmingham, Ala., 1960, ter. mgr., 1961-64; sales mgr. Philip A. Hunt Chem. Co., Washington, 1965-66; registered rep. Ferris & Co., Washington, 1967-69; br. mgr. Hornblower-Weeks, Hemphill, Noyes, Buffalo, N.Y., 1970-75, Buffalo and Harrisburg, Pa., 1970-75; v.p., mgr. Bache & Co., Buffalo, 1976-81, Prudential Bache Securities, Columbus, Ohio, 1981-88; v.p., br. mgr. J.C. Bradford & Co., Columbus, Ohio, 1989-91; 1st v.p., mgr. Stifel, Nicolaus and Co., Inc., Wichita, Kans., from 1992; sr. v.p. McDonald and Co. Securities, 1994-96; pres. Jaminson Assocs., Columbus, Ohio, from 1996. Instr. Cath. U. Am., Washington, 1967-69. Capt. United Way, Columbus, 1986; bd. dirs. NCCJ, Buffalo, 1974, Industry/Edn. Coun., Buffalo, 1979-81; mem. Columbus Coun. World Affairs, 1987—. Capt. USAF, 1954-57. Mem. Nat. Security Dealers Assn. (chmn. dist. bus. conduct com. 1987, adv. coun. 1987), Soc. Cert. Fin. Planners, Newcomen Soc. Am., Worthington Hills Country Club, Columbus Athletic Club, Capital Club, Ohio State U. Faculty Club, Dayton Racquet Club, Kiwanis, Sigma Phi Epsilon. Republican. Methodist. Avocations: boating, sports, travel, music, theater. Home: Skillman, NJ. Died Jan. 26, 2005.

HALL, KERMIT LANCE, academic administrator, historian, educator; b. Akron, Ohio, Aug. 31, 1944; s. Kermit Hall and Katherine Lois Galbraith; m. Phyllis Anne Moke, May 1, 1944. BA, U. Akron, 1966; MA, Syracuse U., 1967; PhD, U. Minn., 1972; MSL, Yale U., 1980. Prof. history Vanderbilt U., Nashville, 1972—76, Wayne State U., Detroit, 1976—81; prof. law and history U. Fla., Gainesville, 1981—92; dean Henry Kendall Coll. Arts and Scis., prof. law and history U. Tulsa, 1992—94; exec. dean Coll. Arts and Scis., dean Coll. Humanities, prof. history and law Ohio State U., Columbus, 1994—99; provost, vice chancellor, prof. history N.C. State U., Raleigh, 1999—2000; pres., prof. history Utah State U., Logan, 2000—04, SUNY Albany, 2004—06. Dir. Am. Coun. on Edn., Washington, 2000—06; adv. dir. Wells Fargo Bank of No. Utah, Salt Lake City, 2002—06; mem. exec. adv. com. SCT Corp., Phila., 2001—06; dir. Nat. Assn. State Univs. and Land Grant Colls., 2002—06, Regence Blue Cross Blue Shield of Utah, 2003—04. Author: (book) The Magic Mirror: Law in American History; editor: The Oxford Companion to the Supreme Court of the United States (Main Selection, History Book Club, 1992), The Oxford Companion to the Supreme Court of the United States, revised 2nd edit., 2005, The Oxford Guide To Supreme Court Decisions (Main Selection, History Book Club, 1999), The Oxford Companion to American Law. Mem. John F. Kennedy Assassination Records Rev. Bd., Washington, 1994—98; dir. Rsch. Triangle Inst., Raleigh, NC, 1999—2000, Utah Festival Opera, Logan, 2000. 1st lt. U.S. Army, 1968—69. Decorated Air Medal; named George E. Knepper Disting. Lectr., U. Akron, 2000, Utah's Best Hands On Leader, Salt Lake Mag., 2001, Simon E. Sobeloff Lectr., U. of Md. Coll. of Law, 1996; recipient James Madison award, ALA, 1996, Outstanding Achievement award, Logan and Cahce Valley, Utah C. of C., 2003, Silver Gavel award, ABA, 1993, Outstanding Reference Work award, ALA, 1992, Hon. Fellow, Ctr. for Gt. Plains Studies, 1992; fellow Earhart Found., 1979—80, Legal History fellow, Am. Bar Found., 1980—81, Lectr. in Finland, Fulbright-Hayes Found., 1987; grantee Minority Scholars in History grantee, Pew Charitable Trust, 1991—94, Rsch. in Selection of Judges grantee, NSF, 1984—86, History Tchg. Alliance grantee, Rockefeller, Exxon, and Hewlett Founds., 1984—87, Defining the Core of Citizenship grantee, NEH, 1993—94, Native Ams. and Higher Edn. grantee, Coca Cola Found., 1994—96; vis. scholar Am. Bar Found., 1986—87, U. No. Iowa, 1996. Fellow: Am. Coun. Learned Socs.; mem.: ABA (com. on pub. edn. about the law from 2001, Silver Gavel award 1993), Am. Hist. Assn., Am. Soc. for Legal History (assoc.; bd. dirs. 1994—97), Orgn. of Am. Historians (life), Rotary Internat. (assoc.). Democrat. Avocations: salt water fishing, hiking, reading, strength conditioning. Home: Albany, NY. Died Aug. 13, 2006.

HALL, MARY HUGH, retired secondary school educator; b. Sumter, S.C., Apr. 15, 1937; d. Hughson Perry and Virginia Dare (Owens) Matthews; m. James Wallace Hall Sr., July 2, 1960; 1 child, James Wallace Jr. BA in Social Studies and French, Columbia Coll., 1959; postgrad., West Ga. Coll., 1975-79. Tchr. Arlington (Ga.) Schs., Inc., 1959-61; tchr., chair French dept. Douglas County H.S., Douglasville, Ga., 1965—97; ret., 1997. Mem. steering com. West Ga. Alliance, Carrollton, 1992—. Recipient Outstanding Officer award Jaycees, 1970, 71. Mem. NEA, Douglas County Assn. Educators, Ga. Assn. Educators. Avocations: dance, reading, cooking, wood crafts. Home: Douglasville, Ga. Died June 22, 2005.

HALLER, KURT, theoretical physics educator; b. Vienna, May 6, 1928; came to U.S., 1939, naturalized, 1945; s. Benjamin and Regina (Katz) H.; m. Lottie Schlegel, Aug. 2, 1952; children: Paul Bret, Geoffrey Scott. AB, Columbia U., 1949, PhD, 1958. Instr. Newark Coll. Arts and Scis., Rutgers U., 1953-54; instr. Newark Coll. Engring., 1954-56; rsch. asst. Columbia U., N.Y.C., 1956-57; rsch. assoc. Washington U., St. Louis, 1957-59; asst. prof., assoc. prof. physics NYU, N.Y.C., 1959-64; assoc. prof. U. Conn., Storrs, 1964-70, prof., from 1970, acting dept. head, 1981-82, 92-93, interim dept. head, 1986, mem. senate, 1987-93. Vis. physicist lectr. cir. Am. Inst. Physics, 1968-69; chmn. steering com. Ea. Theoretical Physics Conf., 1972; Fulbright-Hays sr. lectr., vis. prof. Inst. for Theoretical Physics, U. Graz, Austria, 1973-74. Editor: Proc. of Storrs Meeting of Div. Particles and Fields of Am. Phys. Soc., 1988; contbr. articles to Phys. Rev., Physics Letters, Jour. Math. Physics, also others. Rsch. grantee Dept. Energy, 1979—. Fellow Am. Phys. Soc. (chmn. organizing com. 4th meeting div. particles and fields 1987-88). Achievements include research on quantum field and elementary particle theories. Home: Storrs Mansfield, Conn. Died May 2004.

HALMOS, PAUL RICHARD, retired mathematician; b. Budapest, Hungary, Mar. 3, 1916; came to U.S., 1929; s. Alexander Charles and Paula (Rosenberg) H.; m. Dorothy Moyer, Jan. 1, 1934 (div. Mar. 1945); m. Virginia Templeton Pritchett, Apr. 7, 1945. BS, U. Ill., 1934, MS, 1935, PhD, 1938; DSc (hon.), U. St. Andrews, Scotland, 1984; D Math. (hon.), U. Waterloo, Can., 1990. Instr. U. Ill., Urbana, 1938-39, assoc., 1942-43; fellow, asst. Inst. for Advanced Study, Princeton, N.J., 1939-42; asst. prof. Syracuse (N.Y.) U., 1943-46; from asst. prof. to prof. U. Chgo., 1946-61; prof. U. Mich., Ann Arbor, 1961-68; prof., chmn. dept. U. Hawaii, Honolulu, 1968-69; prof., then Disting. prof. Ind. U., Bloomington, 1969-85; prof. Santa Clara (Calif.) U., 1985-96, prof. emeritus, 1996—2006. Author: Finite Dimensional Vector Spaces, 1942, Measure Theory, 1950, Algebraic Logic, 1962, A Hilbert Space Problem Book, 1967, I Want to Be a Mathematician, 1985, others. Mem. Math. Assn. Am. (Haimo award for Dist. Coll. & Univ. Teaching of Mat., 1994), Am. Math. Soc., others. Avocations: photography, walking. Home: Los Gatos, Calif. Died Oct. 2, 2006.

HALPERIN, DONALD MARC, retired state senator; b. Bklyn., July 25, 1945; s. Charles and Gladys (Solomon) H.; m. Brenda Stibel, June 22, 1969; children: Jeremy Nehemiah, Rebecca Ruth. BA in Sociology, Rutgers U., 1967; JD, Bklyn. Law Sch., 1970, Tel Aviv U., 1978. Bar: N.Y. 1972, Fla. 1975. Counsel Fuchsberg & Fuchsberg, N.Y.C., 1974-80; Gaffin & Mayo, 1981-83; Seiden, Stempel & Bennett, 1983—2006; mem. NY State Senate, N.Y.C., 1971—93; commr. Housing & Community State of NY, 1993—95; ptnr. Kantor Davidoff Wolfe Mandelker & Kass. Mem. Legis. Commn. on Expenditure Rev., Pub. Auth. Control Bd. Recipient Masada award State of Israel Bonds, 1974, Pub. Service award N.Y. State Jewish Wars Vet., 1975, Cert. of Achievement, Nat. Dist. Atty. Assn., 1976. Mem. Nat. Fedn. Italian Am. Orgns. (hon.), Nat. Conf. Ins. Legislators (past pres.). Democrat. Jewish. Home: Brooklyn, NY. Died June 26, 2006.

HALPERIN, ROBERT M., lawyer; b. Boston, Mar. 11, 1954; s. Meyer H. and Libby (Shoer) H.; m. Candace J. Kaller, July 5, 1981; 1 child, Sarah. BA, Harvard U., 1976; MA in Pub. Policy, Duke U., 1980, JD, 1980. Assoc. Crowell and Moring LLP, Washington, 1980—83, ptnr., 1984—2006; assoc. Thelen, Martin, Johnson and Bridges, San Francisco, 1983-84. Dir. Galerie de Tours Fine Arts, Ltd., Bethesda, Md. Mem. D.C. Bar Assn., Calif. Bar Assn., Fed. Communications Bar Assn., ABA. Home: Bethesda, Md. Died July 13, 2006.

HALPIN, THOMAS S., military antiques dealer; b. Jamaica, N.Y., May 27, 1941; s. Thomas S. Halpin and Millicent May Shaw; m. Barbara Jean Kirk, May 20, 1982. BA in Econs., Tusculum Coll., 1964. Asst. mgr. F. W. Woolworth Co., Franklin Sq., N.Y., 1964-65; asst. mfr.'s rep. New Hyde Park, N.Y., 1965-66; sales rep. Gen. Binding Corp., Northbrook, Ill., 1966-72; proprietor Mil. & Naval Antiquities, Mineola, N.Y., 1972-98, Las Vegas, Nev., from 1998. Editor, 1975-87, 88-98; contbr. articles to profl. jours. Commiteeman N.Y. Conservative Party, 1978—. With USNR, 1962-65. Recipient Marie Moore award, Grand Ctrl. Coin Conv., 1988. Mem. Navy League U.S. (life), N.E. Orders & Medals Soc. (pres. 1972-74, Best of Show 1967), L.I. Coin Club (v.p., sec. 1988-94, pres. 1994-98, Spl. Presentation plaque 1998). Episcopalian. Home: Las Vegas, Nev. Died Oct. 29, 2005.

HAM, GARY MARTIN, psychologist; b. Lincoln, Nebr., Feb. 6, 1940; s. Wendell E. and Sally Bertha (Lind) H.; children: Jeffery M. BS in Psychology, Wash. State U., 1963, MS in Psychology, 1965; PsyD, Newport U., 1988. Diplomate Am. Psychotherapy Assn., Am. Bd. Psychol. Spltys. in Med. Psychology; lic. psychologist, Calif.; cert. tchr., Calif, counselor. Clin. psychologist Riverside (Calif.) County Dept. Mental Health, from 1967. Tchr., cons., pub. speaker, researcher Riverside County Dept. Mental Health, 1967—; instr. U. Calif. Riverside, Chapman U. Clin. psychologist Riverside County, Critical Incidents Disaster Response Team, 1985—, ARC Disaster Team. 1st lt. USAF, 1964-67. Mem. AAS, AAAS, APA, ASCD, Am. Mental Health Counselors Assn., Am. Critical Incident Stress

Found., Calif. Psychol. Assn., Air Force Soc. Psychologists, Am. Coll. Forensic Examiners, Psi Chi, Sigma Phi Epsilon. Home: Redlands, Calif. Died Feb. 2004.

HAMBLETON, THOMAS EDWARD, theatrical producer; b. Towson, Md., Feb. 12, 1911; s. Thomas Edward and Adelaide (McAlpin) H.; m. Caroline L. Hoysradt, 1936 (dec. 1947); children— Anne Crawford (dec.), Caroline Lucinda, Susan Sherwood; m. Merrell Hopkins, Feb. 1949; children— Thomas Edward, Mary, Mark. Student, St. Paul's Sch., Concord, N.H.; BA, Yale U., 1934; student, Yale Sch. of Drama, 1957. Cons. theatre N.Y. Festival of Performing Arts, 1988. Producer plays Once Upon A Mattress; mng. dir. plays Phoenix Theatre, N.Y.C., 1953-82; where prodns. include Chemin de Fer; also numerous works by Shakespeare, Shaw, Gilbert and Sullivan, O'Neill, Chekov A Memory of Two Mondays, 1975-76, Ladyhouse Blues, Canadian Gothic/American Modern, Marco Polo, A Sorrow Beyond Dreams, G.R. Point, Scribes, 1976-77, Hot Grog, Uncommon Women and Others, Elusive Angel, One Crack Out, City Sugar, 1977-78, Getting Out, Later, Says I, Says He, Big and Little, Chinchilla, 1978-79, Winter Dancers, Shout Across the River, The Trouble With Europe, Save Grand Central, Second Ave. Rag, 1979-80, Bonjour La, Bonjour, Beyond Therapy, The Captivity of Pixie Shedman, Meetings, Isn't It Romantic, 1980-81; mng. dir. Theatre, Inc., Phoenix, 1953-82, v.p., dir., Center Stage Balt.; producer Cole Porter benefit Carnegie Hall, 1985; exec. producer Theatre of Nations, Balt., 1986 Pres. bd. dirs. Hampden-Booth Theatre Collection and Libr.; bd. dirs. Farrar, Straus & Giroux, Peale Mus., Balt. City Life Mus., Balt. Center Stage, Balt. Theatre Devel. Fund, Balt. Festival of Arts. Lt. comdr. USNR, World War II. Named to, Theatre Hall of Fame, 2002; recipient Tony award, Theatre Wing and League of Am. Theatres, 2002. Mem. ASCAP (popular awards panel), League N.Y. Theatres (gov.), First Am. Congress of Theatre (pres.) Home: Cockeysville, Md. Died Dec. 17, 2005.

HAMBLETT, STEPHEN, retired newspaper publishing executive; b. Nashua, NH, 1934; m. Julie Hamblett (dec.); m. Jocelin Hamblett; 3 children. BA, Harvard U., 1957. With Providence Jour. Co., 1957—2000, various sales and mgmt. positions, 1957-69, asst. v.p., 1974-79, from v.p. mktg. corp. devel. to exec. v.p., 1979-85, pres., asst. pub., 1985-87, pub., chief exec. officer, 1987-98, chmn., 1987—2000. Bd. dir. AP, 1991—99. Died Dec. 13, 2005.

HAMBURG, SUSAN LYNNETTE, surgical, oncology and neuropsychiatry nurse; b. Portland, Oreg., May 30, 1956; d. Claude Wayne and Marie Annette (Hilderbrand) Wallace; m. Eric B. Hamburg, Sept. 2, 1981. ADN, Portland Community Coll., 1987. Cert. epidural nurse. Charge nurse Holladay Park Med. Ctr., Portland, from 1987. Home: Portland, Oreg. Died Jan. 18, 2004.

HAMBY, MARILYN S., critical care nurse; b. Richmond, Ind., Nov. 14, 1957; d. Roy Andrew and Virginia (Rowlfs) Schucha; m. Joe Hamby, Sept. 29, 1980; 1 child, Christopher. AS, Gadsden (Ala.) State Coll., 1990. Surg. intensive care nurse, Gadsden. Home: Gadsden, Ala. Died July 10, 2005.

HAMILTON, ALLEN EMERSON, JR., electrical contractor; b. Eugene, Oreg., June 1, 1935; s. Allen Emerson and Lillian Theresa (Dippert) H.; m. Barbara Lee Killian, Sept. 17, 1960; children: James A., Karen L., Kurt M. BS, U. Oreg., 1957; MS, NYU, 1958. Gen. mgr. Hamilton Electric, Inc., Eugene, 1960-89; mktg. mgr. Cherry City Electric, Inc., Eugene, 1989-92; exec. mgr. Nat. Elec. Contractors Assn., Eugene, 1992-95, exec. dir. western region, from 1995. Owner Neal & Hamilton, Eugene, 1980-90. Campaign chair Larry Campbell for State Rep., Eugene, 1977-94; pres. Eugene/Springfield Conv. Bur., 1980-81, Lane County Fair Bd., Eugene, 1991-93. 1st lt. USAF, 1958-60. Recipient Leadership award Jr. Achievement, 1975; named No. Calif. Constrn. Man of Yr. San Francisco Elec. Contractors, 1988. Mem. Nat. Elec. Contractors Assn. (v.p. 1981-85, dir. Oreg. Pacific Cascade chpt. 1976-91, nat. pres. 1986-89, James H. McGraw award 1978, L.K. Comstock award 1989), Coun. Indsl. Rels. (co-chair 1986-89), Eugene Execs. Assn. (pres. 1969), Acad. Elec. Contractors (chair 1990-93), Eugene Area C. of C. (pres. 1977-78), Masons. Republican. Avocation: travel. Home: Eugene, Oreg. Died Jan. 1, 2004.

HAMILTON, CHARLES EDWARD, physician; b. Altus, Okla., Oct. 26, 1924; s. Harvey Leslie and Mary Edna Duke Hamilton; m. Janice Elaine Hargis, Aug. 11, 1963; children: Charles (dec.), Carol, Mark, Mary Elizabeth. Student, U. So. Calif., L.A., 1942-45; MD, Tulane U., 1949; MS in Healthcare Adminstrn., U. Colo., 1988. Diplomate Am. Bd. Pediat., Am. Coll. Physician Execs. Commd. officer USN, 1949, advanced through grades to capt., ret., 1972; chair dept. pediat. Hamilton Med. Group, Lafayette, La., 1954-88; field rep. physician Joint Commn. on Accreditation of Healthcare Orgns., Oakbrook Terrace, Ill., from 1989. Mem. Phi Beta Kappa. Republican. Episcopalian. Avocations: rosarian, travel. Home: Lafayette, La. Died Oct. 22, 2004.

HAMILTON, EDWARD SYLVESTER, minister; b. The Dalles, Oreg., July 10, 1939; s. Lester Sharp and Dorothy Ann (Jurgensmeier) H.; m. Myrlene Louise Jacobson, Nov. 15, 1981; children: Kim Michelle, Tami Leigh. BS in Psychology, Lewis & Clark Coll., Portland, Oreg., 1962; MDiv, Fuller Sem., 1985, DMin, 1996. Ordained Presbyn. Ch., 1986. Purchasing mgr. various cos., Portland, Oreg., 1966-71; owner, ptnr. United Pub. Co., Boise, Idaho, 1971-80; owner Peninsula Dry Cleaners, Gig Harbor, Wash., 1981-82; intrn Fircrest (Wash.) Presbyn. Ch., 1983; staff intern Associated Ministries, Tacoma, Wash., 1984; co-pastor Eagle River (Alaska) Presbyn. Ch., 1986-88; co-pastor (interim) Community Presbyn. Ch., Redmond, Oreg., 1988-90; co-pastor First Presbyn. Ch., Marysville, Calif., 1990-93; organizer, co-pastor Morning Star Presbyn. Ch., Bayville, N.J., from 1993. Bd. dirs. Alaska Housing Ministries, Anchorage, 1986-88; organizing bd. chmn. Eagle River Food Bank, 1986-88, founding pres. Eagle River Clergy Assn., 1986-88; chmn. Congregational Renewal Com., Sacramento (Calif.) Presbytery, 1990-92 Chaplain Yuba County Sheriff's Dept., Marysville, Calif., 1990-93; chmn. Yuba County Substance Abuse Com.; chaplain Ocean Gate (N.J.) Borough Police Dept., 1997—; bd. trustees Ocean Mental Health Svcs., Bayville, 1997—. Home: Bayville, NJ. Died Jan. 24, 2004.

HAMILTON, GEORGE WESLEY, agronomist, educator; b. Williamsport, Pa., May 29, 1961; s. George Wesley and Sarah Jane (Stryker) H.; m. Rebecca Sue Renn, July 16, 1983; children: Natalie Jane, Julia Louise. BS, Pa. State U., 1983, MS, 1990, PhD, 2001. Rsch. technologist Pa. State U., University Park, 1983-86, sr. rsch. aide, 1986-90, supr., 1990-91, instr., from 1991, sr. lectr., 1996—2002, asst. prof., 2002—04. Author: Fate and Significance of Pesticides in Urban Environments, 1992, Science and Golf II, 1994. Named Innovator of Yr., N.E. Weed Sci. Soc., 1994, 97. Mem. Am. Soc. Agronomy, Soil Sci. Soc. Am., Crop Sci. Soc. Am. Achievements include patents for calibration for granular broadcast spreaders and pelletized mulch for turf-grass establishment. Home: State College, Pa. Died July 9, 2004.

HAMILTON, JAQUELINE HALEY, artist, landscaper; b. Nov. 22, 1936; AA, Stephens Coll., 1954-56; student, Marshall U., 1956-58, Prince Georges U., 1984-86. Juried artist Torpedo Factory Art Ctr., Alexandria, Va., from 1989; pvt. practice Clinton, Md., from 1993. Exhibited in group shows at Gallery West, 1989, 90, Prince George's C.C., 1991, Md. nat. Capital Park and Planning Show, 1991, Newberry Farms Art Gallery, 1991-92, Doctor's Hosp. Art Show, 1992, 96, Bread and Chocolate, 1993-94, 1994-96, Am. Water Soc., 1996. Recipient Nyborg award Mid-Atlantic Regional, 1990, Dick Blick award 1991, Silver Medal award 1996. Home: Clinton, Md. Died Mar. 25, 2005.

HAMILTON, LOIS ANN, math educator, consultant; b. Bonners Ferry, Idaho, Oct. 29, 1939; d. Harry Powers and Wilma Eileen (Magart) Copeland; m. John Alexander Hamilton Jr., July 21, 1956 (div. Aug. 1987); foster children: Linda Singer, Theodore Alan Osterhout. BA, Wilkes U., 1969; MS, Elmira Coll., 1974; postgrad., Cornell U., 1976-77, SUNY, Cortland, 1991-92. Cert. nursery and elem. tchr. 1969. Sec. to Rev. John A. Hamilton Jr., Pa., N.Y., 1963-70; elem. tchr. Watkins Glen (N.Y.) Cen. Schs., 1969-71; summer sch. tchr. Odessa-Montour N.Y. Sch. Dist., 1970, 71; transition elem. tchr. Addison (N.Y.) Cen. Sch., 1971-74, elem. tchr., 1974-80, kindergarten tchr., 1980-81, remedial math. tchr., 1981-94; ret., 1994. Tchr. Fun with Math. Addison Community Sch., 1987-92; co-chmn. A.C.T.I.O.N. Grant Com., Alfred, NY, 1988-89; advisor math clubs, Addison, 1987-89, 5th and 6th Grade Math. Clubs, 1987-92; coord. 3rd and 4th Grade Math. Clubs, 1990-92, author, bound 3rd and 6th grades, P.E.P. Test Analyses, Addison Ctrl. Sch., 1983-93, chmn. student of month com., 1987-92; cons., lectr., presenter in field Vol. Red Cross, Elmira, NY, 1972; vol. design, print certs. Horseheads Christian Sch., 1995-, Baptist Christian Sch. Assn. NY State, 2000-; vol. sec. Pastor Sidney S. Aldrich, Horseheads, NY, 1995—; vol. caregiver, Horseheads, NY, 1991-95; vol. Horseheads Christian Sch., 1995—; vol. tchrs. asst. HorseheadsChristian Sch., 1995-96, vol. math and reading tutor, 1996—; vol. Christian counselor, Horseheads, 1999—. Mem. Nat. Coun. Tchrs. Math., Assn. Math. Tchrs. N.Y. State (program com. ann. meeting 1990), Oreg. Coun. Tchrs. Math., Conceptually Oriented Sci./Math. Integrated Curriculum Inst. (pilot tchr. 1991-92). Republican. Baptist. Avocations: singing, reading, poetry, writing. Died Nov. 2005.

HAMILTON, PERRIN C., lawyer, state official; b. Phila., Oct. 15, 1921; m. Bette J. Shadle; children— Deborah, Maribeth, Perrin Jr. Student Dickinson Coll., 1943, LLB, 1948. Bar: D.C., PA. 1949. Spl. counsel U.S. Senate, 1953; sr. ptnr. Hepburn Willcox Hamilton & Putnam, Phila., from 1980; commr. Crime Victims Bd., Del. River Port Authority; bd. dirs. Valley Forge Mil. Acad., Freedoms Found. Bd. advisors Dickinson Coll., State of Pa. Cabinet Ofcl.; pres., bd. advisors Salvation Army. Lt. USNR, World War II. Decorated Order of Merit, Italy; recipient Freedoms Found. award, 1970. Mem. ABA, Pa. Bar Assn., Phila. Lawyers Club (past pres.), Union League Club (pres.), Merion Cricket Club. Episcopalian. Died Dec. 16, 2005.

HAMILTON, WILLIAM VICTOR, tool manufacturing executive; b. Terre Haute, Ind., May 17, 1931; s. Clyde Abraham and Helen Elizabeth (Camp) H.; m. Betty Lou Haynes, Dec. 4, 1955; children: Kimberly Cameron, Mark Haynes. BA in Bus. Econs., U. Nebr., 1961; MBA, George Washington U., 1973. Commd. 2d lt. USAF, 1953, chief data processing br. SAC hdqrs. Omaha, 1964-67, ops. analyst SAC hdqrs., 1967-69; chief ops. data processor USAF The Pentagon, Washington, 1969-71, retired, 1971; asst. pres. Morris Cafritz Hosp., Washington, 1971-74; mgmt. cons. W.V. Hamilton Assn., Arlington, Va., 1974-83; pres. Am. Machine Systems Corp., Albany, Ind., from 1983. Cons. Polaris Data Systems, Arlington, 1974; cons. govt. mktg. Blue Shield Assn., Washington, 1975-77, Optimum Systems Corp., Santa Clara, Calif., 1977; cons. mktg. research Fabergé, N.Y.C., 1979-80. Analyst, Connelly for Pres., Washington, 1980. Mem. Soc. Mfg. Engrs. (treas.), Kiwanis (dir., v.p.), Muncie C. of C. Policy Com., Unitarian Universalist Fin. Com. (bd. dirs.). Lodges: Masons. Avocations: flying, fishing, bridge. Home: Muncie, Ind. Died Oct. 24, 2004.

HAMMER, JOHN RICHARD (DICK), pension plans administrator; b. Plainfield, N.J., Dec. 21, 1922; s. Einar and Katherine V. (Collins) H.; m. Hannah Martin Davis; children: Katherine, John R. Jr., Johannah, Elizabeth, Nathaniel, William. BA, U. N.C. CLU. Sales mgr. Am. Book Co., N.Y.C., 1949-55; salesman, supr. Provident Mut. Life Ins. Co., Phila., 1955-62; mgr. State Mut. Cos., Worcester, Mass., 1962-74; asst. prof. ins. sales N.W. Mo. State U., 1974-76; brokerage mgr. Prin. Fin. Group, Des Moines, 1976-87; retirement benefits mgr. Guilford Mills, Inc., Greensboro, N.C., from 1987. Chmn. Gov.'s Community Resource Coun. Prisons, N.C., 1986—; co-leader charismatic prayer group, Greensboro, 1978—. 1st lt. USAF, 1942-58. Mem. N.C. Life Underwriters (past pres.), N.C. Chartered Life Underwriters (pres. Greensboro chpt. 1959—), Sherwood Park Swim and Racquet Club (pres. 1969-71), Greensboro C. of C. (life), Yokefellows Internat. Republican. Roman Catholic. Avocations: tennis, golf, racquetball, swimming, bridge. Home: Greensboro, NC. Died Mar. 3, 2004.

HAMMOND, CALEB DEAN, JR., cartographer, publisher; b. Orange, N.J., June 24, 1915; s. Caleb Dean and Alice (Lindsley) H.; m. Patricia Treacy Ehrgott, July 20, 1940; children— Beth Lynn, Wendie Harrison, Caleb Dean 3d. BS, Worcester Poly. Inst., 1937. Sales engr. Texas Co., N.Y.C., 1937-39; prodn. mgr. Hammond, Inc. (formerly C.S. Hammond & Co.), Maplewood, N.J., 1939-42, v.p. charge sales and mgmt., 1945-48, pres., 1948-67, chmn. bd., 1968-80, 85-95, chmn. emeritus, 1995—2006. Trustee emeritus Worcester Poly. Inst. Served from cadet to engring. lt. USCG, 1942-45. Mem. Assn. Am. Pubs., Am., Royal geog. socs., Phi Gamma Delta. Clubs: Baltusrol Golf (Springfield, N.J.). Home: Maplewood, NJ. Died June 4, 2006.

HAMMOND, CHARLES ROBERT, astronomer, educator; b. Table Grove, Ill., Nov. 7, 1915; s. Thomas Arthur and Julia Berniece (Parmenter) H.; m. Jean Marguerite Jones, Nov. 16, 1946; children: Robert Arthur, Philip Warner. AB in Astronomy, UCLA, 1938. Tchg. asst. astronomy UCLA, 1936-38; co-dir. La Crescenta (Calif.) Obs., 1938-40; organizer, libr., edn. dept. Lockheed Aircraft Corp., Burbank, Calif., 1940-41; chief libr. Vega Aircraft Corp. (subs. Lockheed), Burbank, Calif., 1941-42; contract technicist, assoc. physicist, chief libr. divsn. Naval Ordnance Lab., Washington, Silver Spring, Md., 1942-46; mgr. tech. publs., mgr. office svcs., libr. Hartford-Empire Co. (Emhart Corp.), various cities, Conn., 1946-78; instr. and lectr. astronomy U. Hartford (Hillyer Coll.), Conn., 1957-72. Instr., lectr. astronomy St. Joseph Coll., West Hartford, Conn., Tunxis C.C., Bristol, Conn., and Ctrl. Conn. State U., New Britain, 1960-82; adj. prof. astronomy Trinity Coll., Hartford, 1981—. Contbr. sect. on chem. elements to Chem. Rubber Co. Handbook of Chemistry and Physics, 46th-85th edits., 1964-; contbr. articles to profl. jours. Historian First Ch. Christ Congl., West Hartford, 1982-92. Mem. Soc. for Rsch. on Meteorites, Meteoritical Soc., Astron. Soc. of Pacific, Brit. Astron. Assn., Royal Astron. Soc. Can., Astron. Soc. Greater Hartford (hon., former pres., Astronomer of Yr. 1993), Civitan Club Hartford (former pres.), Sigma Xi. Achievements include being first to identify positively both meteorites that fell in Wethersfield, Conn., 1971, 82. Home: West Hartford, Conn. Died Nov. 13, 2004.

HAMPTON, ADELE VIVIENNE BELL, school system administrator; b. Cleve., July 13, 1927; d. William Lee and Mary Elizabeth (Gaither) Bell; m. Gabriel Edward Hampton Jr., Aug. 19, 1950 (wid. Feb. 1989); children: Gayle Lisa, Gabriel Edward II, Andrea Elaine. BS, Ohio State U., 1950; MA in Edn., Case Western Res. U., 1965. Cert. elem. edn. adminstr. Tchr. elem. edn. Cleve. Bd. Edn., 1957-62, tchr. gifted edn., 1962-67, adminstr., from 1967. Contbr. articles to profl. jours. Aldersgate United Meth. Ch., Warrensville Heights, Ohio, chairperson edn. com., pres. Chancel Choir, 1961—; adv. bd. Youth Devel. Ctr., 1986—; mem. CCAS, 1980—. Recipient award Project Perform, Gund Found., Cleve., 1983-88; effective schs. grantee Ohio Bd. Edn., Columbus, 1985-87. Methodist. Avocations: art, music. Home: Cleveland, Ohio. Died June 29, 2004.

HAMPTON, STEPHEN DREW, law clerk; b. Jacksonville, Fla., July 20, 1952; s. James Jarrel and Margaret Francis (Bell) H. BA, Duke U., 1973; MA, U. Nev. Las Vegas, 1979; JD, Southwestern U., 1991. Law clk. Kegal Tobin Harriety & Truce, L.A., 1989-91; legal writer Mark Oring, L.A., 1992-94; law clk. Dena Patti & Assocs., Las Vegas, 1994-95, Paul Kirst & Assocs., Las Vegas, from 1996. Mem. county ctrl. com. Dem. Party Nev., 1984-88, del. to state conv., 1984, 88, del. to county conv., 1984, 86, 88. Avocations: chess, bicycling, swimming. Home: Las Vegas, Nev. Died June 2, 2005.

HANDLER, DELORES ANNE, artist; b. Chicago Heights, Ill., Aug. 23, 1947; d. Ivan John and Marie (Engbard) Frank; adoptive parents Anton J. Petroski and Carrie L. Engbard; m. Adrian L. Shipley, Oct. 30, 1965 (div. Oct. 1975); m. Mark J. Handler, Feb. 25, 1989; children: Anne Marie, Anthony Adrian. Degree in Liberal Arts, Bellevue Coll., 1982; degree in Comml. Art, North Light Art Sch., Cin., 1989; degree in Floral Design, Lifetime Career Sch., Bellevue, Nebr., 1992. Portrait artist, wall muralist, calligrapher, illustrator, Omaha, Nebr., from 1975; artist crafts Miami, Fla., 1992; display mgr. Sears/Homestead (Fla.) Plaza. Dir. Aardvark and Calico Cat Galleries, Sumter, Council Bluffs, Iowa, dee Haudler Studios. Author, illustrator: (book) The Great Nebraska Fly, 1990, There Are All Kinds of Grandmas, 1993; exhibitor Women in the Arts gallery, Washington, so. Fla. region including the Fla. Keys, Homestead AFB, Miami, others; commissioned portraiture and wall murals Omaha, Nebr. and Council Bluffs; regional art work thoughout N. Dakota, S. Dakota, Kans., Ill., Iowa and Nebr. Recipient Award for Excellence, Poetry.com, 2004. Mem. Am. Soc. Portrait Artists, Women in the Arts (charter), Oil Pastel Assn. Republican. Roman Catholic. Avocations: people, the human condition, dog breeding, floral design, Native Am. studies. Home: Council Bluffs, Iowa. Died Apr. 7, 2005.

HANHAUSEN, EDWARD HENRY, ophthalmologist; b. Jersey City, Aug. 18, 1926; s. Edward and Louise (Bechtle) H.; m. Ethel Doris Ashworth, June 17, 1950; children: Sheryl Ann, Jeffrey Edward. BS, Ursinus Coll., 1946; MD, U. Pa., 1950. Intern Temple U. Hosp., Phila., 1950-51, resident, 1951-54, instr. ophthalmology, 1954-55, from instr. to assoc. prof., 1958-80; sr. attending ophthalmologist Bryn Mawr (Pa.) Hosp., 1958—2004; pvt. practice Wayne, Pa., 1958—2004. Capt., U.S. Army, 1956-58, ETO. Home: Villanova, Pa. Died June 29, 2004.

HANNA, JONI MARIE, special education administrator; b. Twin Falls, Idaho, Sept. 15, 1949; d. H.B. and Virginia (Martin) Hurst; m. John C. Hanna, Mar. 24, 1972 (dec.); children: Jesca, Jathan, Jalyse. BEd with honors, U. Nev., Las Vegas, 1972; MA in Spl. Edn. with honors, Seattle Pacific U., 1987. Cert. elem. tchr., spl. edn. tchr., Wash. Spl. edn. resource room tchr., spl. edn. tchr. Clark County Sch. Dist., Las Vegas, 1972-74; ednl. therapist Bellevue (Wash.) Christian Sch., dir. spl. acad. svcs., from 1984. Adj. prof. Columbia (S.C.) Bible Coll., 1987—, Seattle Pacific U., 1992—; instr., cert. therapist Nat. Inst. for Learning Disabilities, 1989—. Mem. Coun. for Exceptional Children, Orton Dyslexia Soc., Learning Disabilities Assn., Christian Schs. Internat. Home: Bellevue, Wash. Died July 6, 2004.

HANNA, SHARON LYN, social sciences educator, writer; b. Cozad, Nebr., Oct. 7, 1940; d. Eldred Reynolds and Lorane Mae (Casselman) H.; m. Larry Luther Patterson, June 17, 1962 (div. June 1977); children: Lisa Ann, Lyn Kathleen; m. Robert George Dinkel, Dec. 26, 1978. BA, Nebr. Wesleyan U., 1962; MS, U. Nebr., 1980. Tchr. Lincoln (Nebr.) Pub. Schs., 1962-65, 79-80, Fair Lawn (N.J.) Pub. Schs., 1965-66; dir., tchr. Early Childhood Edn. Ctr., Freeport, Ill., 1970-77; dept. chair and instr. social sci. S.E. Cmty. Coll., Lincoln, from 1980. Presenter numerous city, state and nat. groups. Author: Person to Person, 1995, Career Development by Design, 1998; contbr. articles to profl. jours. State pres. Stepfamily Assn. Am., 1980-88, nat. chmn. nat. conf., 1987, nat. v.p., 1988-90, nat. pres., 1990-92. Recipient Disting. Internat. Citizen award Alpha Gamma Delta, 1993. Mem. APA, AAUW, Nat. Coun. Family Rels., Midwest Sociol. Assn., Faculty Assn. Avocations: travel, reading, bicycling, fishing, golf. Home: Lincoln, Nebr. Died Aug. 5, 2004.

HANNEMANN, NORMAN ALBERT, retired pastor; b. Dimock, S.D., Sept. 15, 1924; s. Walter Frederick and Edna Pearl (Stainbrook) H.; m. Dorothy Luella Moh, June 6, 1948; children: Phillip, Daniel, Rebecca, Mark. BA, Concordia Sem., 1948. Ordained to ministry Luth. Ch., 1948. Pastor St. John Luth. Ch., Newcastle, Nebr., 1948-52, Immanuel Luth. Ch., Lidderdale, Iowa, 1952-57, Our Savior Luth. Ch., Cheyenne, Wyo., 1957-63, Faith Luth. Ch., York, Nebr., 1963-82, Christ Luth. Ch., Norfolk, Nebr., 1982-91. Mem. Iowa Dist. West Luth. Ch. Mo. Synod (youth bd. 1953-57), So. Nebr. Dist. Luth. Ch. Mo. Synod (mission bd. 1960-70), Nebr. Dist. Luth. Ch. Mo. Synod (Evangelism bd. 1970-78, constn. com. 1978—). Home: Norfolk, Nebr. Died Sept. 27, 2004.

HANSEN, ERWIN GUNTHER, mechanical engineer, consultant; b. Ventnor, Isle Wight, Eng., Apr. 2, 1913; came to U.S., 1954; s. Albert Bernard and Mary Claire (Selwyn) H.; m. Alice Wenzel, June 19, 1946 (dec. Dec. 1952); 1 child, Doreen Mary-Christine Hansen-Kelley; m. Anna Germaine Merle, Sept. 22, 1962. BA with honors, Cambridge (Eng.) U., 1939, MA in Mech. scis., 1952. Registered profl. engr., N.Y., Calif., Mass., N.J., Pa., Vt. Engr. S.A. Caliqua, Paris, 1946-54; dept. head Midland-Ross Corp., N.Y.C., 1954-62; v.p. Syska & Hennessy Inc., N.Y.C., 1962-86; cons. mech. engr. Winter Park, Fla., from 1986. Lectr. in field. Author: Hydronic System Design and Operation, 1985; contbr. articles to profl. jours. Fellow ASHRAE; mem. ASME, N.Y. Acad. Scis., Univ. Club of Winter Park. Republican. Roman Catholic. Achievements include 4 patents. Died Apr. 14, 2004.

HANSEN, MICHAEL ROY, chemist; b. Bremerton, Wash., July 27, 1953; s. Roy Vernon and Bonnie Jean (St. Cyr) H.; m. Valerie Jean Paulson, Feb. 14, 1984 (div. Aug. 14, 1987); 1 child, Ryan Ernest. BS in Chemistry, BS in Molecular Biology, U. Wash., 1978. Rsch. scientist Weyerhaeuser, Federal Way, Wash., from 1987. Chemistry instr. Highline Community Coll., Des Moines, Wash., 1991—. Patentee in field. With U.S. Army, 1972-75. Mem. AAAS, Am. Chem. Soc., Soc. Plastics Engrs., N.Y. Acad. Soc. Achievements include 23 patents and 15 patents pending. Home: Seattle, Wash. Died May 28, 2004.

HANSEN, OLIVER KEITH, human factors scientist, ergonomist; b. Ogden, Utah, Oct. 2, 1929; s. Jesse Ray and Pansy Mabel (Williams) H.; m. Venita Flitton, 1955; children: Brian K., Jeffery S., Christopher R. AA in Engring. Sci., Weber State Coll., Ogden, 1952; BS in Psychology and Anthropology, U. Utah, 1957, MS in Psychology, 1959. Psychometric technician U. Utah, Salt Lake City, 1956-58; rsch. psychologist USAF Aeromed. Labs., Dayton, Ohio, 1958-59; rsch. engr. autonetics divsn. N.Am. Aviation, Anaheim, Calif., 1959-62; scientist Northrop Nortronics, Anaheim, 1962-66; mem. tech. staff Rockwell Internat., Anaheim, 1966-80; cons. Hughes Aircraft Co., Fullerton, Calif., 1980; owner, dir. Hedcon, Inc., Villa Park, Calif., from 1980. Cons. U.S. Army, USN, 1980-87, Northrop Aircraft and Rockwell Internat., 1980-85. Author: Human Factors Design: Objectives for Automotive Displays, 1992; contbr. over 5o articles on human factors engring. rsch. and design to profl. publs., chpts. to books. With U.S. Army, 1948-49. Pre-doctoral rsch. fellow NIH. Fellow Human Factors and Ergonomics Soc.; mem. Soc. for Info. Display, Orange County Astronomers. Avocations: skiing, tennis, fishing, writing, poetry. Home: Villa Park, Calif. Died June 25, 2004.

HANSON, BRUCE EUGENE, lawyer; b. Lincoln, Nebr., Aug. 25, 1942; s. Lester E. and Gladys (Diessner) H.; m. Peggy Pardun, Dec. 25, 1972 (dec. Nov. 1989). BA, U. Minn., 1965, JD, 1966. Bar: Minn. 1966, U.S. Dist. Ct. Minn. 1966, U.S. Tax Ct. 1973, U.S. Ct. Appeals (8th cir.) 1973, U.S. Ct. Appeals (fed. cir.) 1983, U.S. Supreme Ct. 1970. Shareholder Doherty, Rumble & Butler, P.A., St. Paul, 1966-99; ptnr. Oppenheimer, Wolff & Donnelly, LLP, Mpls., from 1999. Dir., sec. Am. Saddlebred Horse Assn.; bd. trustees, chair United Hosp., 1996-98. Mem. ATLA, Hennepin County Bar Assn., Minn. State Bar Assn., Am. Health Lawyers Assn., Minn. Soc. Hosp. Attys., North Oaks Golf Club, Order of Coif, Phi Delta Phi. Home: Saint Paul, Minn. Died Oct. 5, 2004.

HANSON, MARY LOUISE, retired social services administrator; b. Walsenburg, Colo., Nov. 8, 1928; d. Norman Francis and Ellen Matilda (Peterson) Kastner; m. Peter R. Hanson, Sept. 1, 1951 (dec. Dec. 1991); children: Sherod Day, Janell Marie, Kari Annette. BA, U. Wyo., 1951, MA, 1958. Bookkeeper Rawlins Nat. (Wyo.) Bank, 1948-49; scholarship sec. U. Wyo., Laramie, 1962-64; dist. counselor Vocational Rehab., Laramie, 1964-71; exec. dir. Laramie Sr. Ctr., 1973-92; ptnr. First St. Gallery, Laramie, from 1996. Pres. Laramie Sr. Housing, Inc., 1982-92, Laramie Housing, Inc., 1988—. Developed 1st counseling and tng. programs for vocat. rehab. Albany and Platte Counties, Wyo., 1964-71; dir. renovation hist. bldgs., Laramie, 1973-92. Fed. and Wyo. State grantee, 1964-71, Divsn. Aging., 1973-92. Mem. Albany County Hist. Soc., Laramie Plains Mus., U. Wyo. Alumni Assn. Achievements include developing 24 units of Regency Apartments for seniors in 1996. Home: Laramie, Wyo. Died Feb. 13, 2004.

HANSON, OLIVIA NADINE, physical science technician, secretary, counselor; b. Dott, W.Va., Mar. 21, 1943; d. Ewell Blake and Eleanor Ruth (Breeden) Bailey; m. Walter Wayne Radford (dec. Mar. 1989); children: Donald Wayne Radford, Donna Jayne Radford-Baez, Adam Keith Radford; m. John Winton Radford (dec. July 1990); 1 child, John Blake Radford; m. John Charles Hanson, Feb. 10, 1995. Grad., The Exec. Sec. Sch., Bluefield, Va., 1973. Legal asst. Edwin Wiley, Princeton, W.Va., 1973-74; typesetter Princeton Times, 1973-74; inspection recording clk. Dept. Labor, Princeton, 1974-86, phys. sci. technician, 1974-95. Bookkeeper DAR, Washington, 1961-62; aerobic instr. Figure Trim, Princeton, 1980-86; sales rep. Shaklee Chrp., San Francisco, 1982-95, Sarah Coventry, N.Y.C., 1974-80; counselor Civil Rights, Princeton, 1990-95. Chmn. for St. Jude Children's Rsch. Hosp., Memphis, 1986; tutor Lit. Vol. Am., Princeton, 1988-95; counselor Equal Employment Opportunity, Pitts., 1990-95; sec. Fed. Women's Program, Mt. Hope, W.Va., 1993-95. Named Mother of Yr., Willowbrook Bapt. Ch., 1973. Democrat. Avocations: reading, writing poems and children's books, dance, crafts, sewing. Home: Virginia Bch, Va. Died Jan. 22, 2005.

HANUSEY, RICHARD DMYTRO, library director; b. Phila., Nov. 30, 1945; s. Richard and Adela Francias (Mackunas) H.; m. Kathleen Mary Morrow, Oct. 2, 1971; children: Keala, Amanda. Student, E. Stroudsburg State U., 1971; Diploma in Libr. Sci., U. Hawaii, 1973. Cert. libr. Libr. asst. dept. planning State of Hawaii, Honolulu, 1973-75; libr. Picatinny Arsenal, Dover, N.J., 1975-77; adminstrv. libr. U.S. Army Area Spt. Group, Livorno, Italy, 1977-80; libr. dir. U.S. Army, Norddeutschland, Bremerhaven, Germany, 1980-86; adminstrv. libr. Fort Drum/10th Mt. Divsn., Watertown, N.Y., 1986-88; libr. dir. U.S. Army, Pacific, Schofield Bar, Hawaii, from 1988. Chmn. mng. info systems U.S. Army/Dept. Community Action, Fort Shafter, Hawaii, 1992—; mem. army libr. com. dept. info. resources, U.S. Army, Washington, 1991—, libr. career planning bd., 1991—; mem. joint army-state ednl. schs. adv. coun., Honolulu, 1992—. Mem. Parent's Sch. Assn., Honolulu, 1994. Fellow Hawaii Libr. Assn., ALA. Avocations: surfing, running. Home: APO,. Died Nov. 21, 2004.

HAPSHE, ELAINE MARIE, gerontological clinical nurse specialist, educator; b. Lawrence, Mass., Aug. 29, 1941; d. Nicholas A. and Loretta (Marchand) H. Diploma in Nursing, Lowell (Mass.) Gen. Hosp., 1962; BS in Biology and Chemistry, Marymount Manhattan Coll., 1973; MS, Ariz. State U., 1976; PhD in Nursing, Tex. Woman's U., 1994. Staff nurse Long Beach (Calif.) Cmty. Hosp., 1962-64; asst. head nurse, staff nurse Univ. Hosp., N.Y.C., 1964-66, med.-surg. head nurse, 1966-68, adminstrv. med.-surg. supr., 1968-74; asst. dir. CNS St. Anthony Hosp., Oklahoma City, 1976-79; asst. prof. U. Okla., Oklahoma City, 1977-93; assoc. prof. Ga. So. U., Statesboro, from 1994. Cons. Presbyn. Hosp., Oklahoma City, 1986-90; mem. career leader com. Okla. Tchg. Hosp., Oklahoma City, 1987-89; mem. neuro rehab. com. Bapt. Med. Ctr., Oklahoma City, 1990-92; cons. Vis. Nurses Assn., Oklahoma City, 1990-94, mem. profl. adv. bd., 1989-94; mem. advanced practice adv. com. Okla. Bd. Nursing, Oklahoma City, 1992-93. Recipient Excellence in Nursing award U. Okla. Grad. Nurses Assn., 1991. Mem. AACN (bd. dirs. 1978-80, sec.), Okla. Assn. Clin. Nurse Specialists (founding pres., 1993-94), Midwest Nursing Rsch. Soc., Okla. Nurses Assn. (mem. Okla. health care reform 1993-94), Sigma Theta Tau (Beta Delta chpt., adminstrv. v.p. 1991-93, 1st v.p. 1993-95, Storga award 1993, Tina award 1994), Phi Kappa Phi. Avocations: arts and crafts, biking, walking, wood restoration. Home: Statesboro, Ga. Died Mar. 25, 2005.

HARCUM, LOUISE MARY DAVIS, retired elementary school educator; b. Salisbury, Md., May 1, 1927; d. E. Linwood and Dora Ellen (Shockley) Davis; m. W. Blan Harcum, Sr., Sept. 5, 1944; children: W. Blan, Jr., Angie E., Lee P., R. Linwood. BS, Salisbury State U., 1962, MEd, 1969; grad., Inst. Children's Lit., 1995. Cert. tchr. 9-10 English, Md. Tchr. Wicomico County Bd. Edn., Salisbury, Md., 1962—93, subs. tchr., 1994—96; tchr. English evening H.S. Bd. Edn. Salisbury, Md., from 1995. Columnist Daily Times, 1985-87; tchr. cons. Eastern Shore Md. Writing Project; ptnr., owner Beechnut Farms, Md. Co-author: Wicomico County History, 1981; author: Behavior Modification, 1989-92. Co-coord. Rep. Party Campaign, Wicomico County, Md., 1992; vice chmn. Zoning Appeals Bd.; pres. Wicomico County Farm Bur. Women, 1993, leader Olympians-Mardela 4-H Club, 1994-1997; mem. New Cmty. Singers, 1975-95, Sen. Richard Colburn's Scholarship Com., Wicomico County; chmn. senatorial com. for Colburn, 1996-2003. Mem. AAUW (pres. 1970-72, pres. Salisbury Branch 1994-96), Third Time Around-Salisbury Studio of Dance, County Rep. Women's Club (chmn. 1999-2001, state cmty. chmn. 2001, Rep. Fedn. 2000 Caring for Am. com. 1999-2001, established Cmty. Tutorial Ctr. in San Domingo 1998), Wicomico County Rep. Women (pres. 1998-2000), Wicomico Rep. Club, Ret. Tchrs. Wicomico County (pres. 1996-98). Republican. Methodist. Avocations: gardening, writing, dance. Home: Mardela Springs, Md. Died Nov. 3, 2005.

HARDT, GERALD EUGENE, law enforcement administrator; b. Elkhorn, Wis., May 27, 1944; s. David and Elsie Louise Hardt; children: David D., Gerald E. Jr.; m. June Alice Bosetti, July 8, 1973 (div. Dec. 1997); children: Jean Hawkins, Richard Hawkins, Angela Hawkins; m. Kathryn Thompson Green, May 24, 1999. AA, Glendale (Ariz.) C.C., 1968; BS, Ariz. State U., 1970, MPA, 1990. Dep. chief Maricopa County Sheriff's Office, Phoenix, 1970-91; release officer Oreg. Ct. Sys., Salem, 1992-95; program mgr. Ariz. Criminal Justice Commn., Phoenix, from 1995. Mem. Maricopa Pub. Safety Pers. Retirement Sys. Bd., Phoenix, 1988-91. Pres. Ariz. FBI Nat. Acad. Grads., 1991. Sgt. USAF, 1962-66. Mem. Fraternal Order Police (life), Masons (3rd degree), El Zaribah Temple Shrine, York Rite Freemasonary. Republican. Lutheran. Avocations: travel, reading. Home: Glendale, Ariz. Died Apr. 1, 2005.

HARKEY, IRA BROWN, JR., newspaperman, educator, author; b. New Orleans, Jan. 15, 1918; s. Ira Brown and Flora Broad (Lewis) H.; m. Marie Ella Gore, 1939 (div. 1963); children: Ira Brown III, Meg Harkey Walters, Erik G., Maybin, Amelie Harkey Foster, William Millsaps; m. Marion Marks Drake, Dec. 10, 1963 (div. 1976); 1 child, Katherine B.; m. Virgia Quin Mioton, Feb. 24, 1977. Grad., Isidore Newman Sch.; BA, Tulane U., 1941; MA in Journalism, PhD in Polit. Sci., Ohio State U. Reporter, feature writer Times-Picayune, New Orleans, 1939-42, 46-48; editor, pub., pres. The Chronicle, Pascagoula, Miss., 1948-63; pres. Gulf Coast Times, Ocean Springs, Miss., Advertiser Printing Inc., Pascagoula, 1948-63; mem. faculty Ohio State U., 1965-66; Carnegie vis. prof. U. Alaska, 1968-69; profl. lectr. journalism U. Mont., 1970; Allen lectr. U. Oreg., 1972; sec., v.p., dir. Okla. Coca-Cola Bottling Co., Inc., Oklahoma City, 1965-80, Gt. Plains Industries, 1979-80; pres. Indian Creek Co., Inc., 1981-93. Author: The Smell of Burning Crosses, 1967, The Story of Noel Wien, 1974, repub., 1991, repub. 1999, (pamphlet) Dedicated to the Proposition..., 1963; co-author: Alton Ochsner, Surgeon to the South, 1990; contbr. articles to mags. Bd. dirs. Human Rels. Coun., Upper Arlington, Ohio, 1965-68; mem. planning commn. Millsaps Coll., 1991. Served to lt. USNR, 1942-46. Recipient Pulitzer prize for disting. editorial writing, 1963, Sidney Hillman Found. award, 1963, Sigma Delta Chi nat. award for disting. pub. service in newspaper journalism, 1963, Media award NCCJ, 1963, Hall of Fame Miss. Press Assn., 1993, Civil Libertarian of Yr. award

Miss. chpt. Civil Liberties Union, 1992. Mem. AAUP, Am. Polit. Sci. Assn., Authors Guild, La. Club (new Orleans), Boston Club (New Orleans), Phi Beta Kappa, Delta Kappa Epsilon, Kappa Tau Alpha, Pi Sigma Alpha. Died Oct. 8, 2006; New Orleans.

HARKINS, HERBERT PERRIN, otolaryngologist, educator; b. Aug. 13, 1912; s. Percy Stoner and Myra (Perrin) H.; Anna Catherine Shepler, July 16, 1938; children: Herbert P., Sally Anne, Nancy Shepler. BS, Lafayette Coll., 1934; MD, Hahnemann Med. Coll., 1937; MSc, U. Pa., 1942. Res. Diplomate Am. Ba. Otolaryngology. Lectr. otolaryngology Hahnemann Med. Coll., 1939-44; assoc. prof., 1944-51; prof. head dept. otolaryngology, 1951; asst. prof. otolaryngology Grad. Sch. Medicine, U. Pa., 1951—2006. Sr. staff otolaryngology Lankenau Hosp. Bd,. Studies in Higher Edn. Contbr. numerous articles on ear, nose and throat to med. jours. Trustee Lafayette Coll. Comdr. USN, 1945—48. Fellow ACS, Am. Otolaryngology Soc. Plastic Surgery; mem. Am. Soc. Ophthalmic and Otolaryngologic Allergy (pres.), Am. Pa. acads. ophthalmology and otolaryngology, Coll. Physicians Phila., Phila. Laryngol. Soc., Phila. County Med. Soc., AMA, Am. Laryngol., Rhinol. and Otol. Soc. Clubs: Union League, Phila. Country Bachelors Barge. Home: Gladwyne, Pa. Died July 4, 2006.

HARKINS, RICHARD ERLE, design studio executive; b. Tulsa, Nov. 18, 1932; s. Erle Wellington and Jessie Aleece (Hamly) H.; m. Marilyn Aldridge, June 14, 1958; children: Richard Scott, Christopher Bart, Melanie Renee. BA, U. Okla., 1954, MA, 1958. Exec. dir. Internat. Supreme Coun., Order of DeMolay, Kansas City, Mo., 1958-78; ptnr., pres. Seville Cons., Kansas City, from 1979; pres. B-C One Inc., Kansas City, 1980-85, Innovative Designs, Inc., Kansas City, from 1985. Mem. Gov.'s Coun. on Phys. Fitness and Health, Jefferson City, Mo., 1982-86, former mem. adv. bd.; bd. dirs. Mid-Continent coun. Girl Scouts U.S., 1967-74; past pres., treas. South Suburban Jr. Baseball Assn., Kansas City; bd. dirs. Kansas City Sports Commn.; mem. exec. bd. U.S. Olympic Com., 1982-89. Lt. (j.g.) USN, 1954-57. Mem. Pub. Rels. Soc. Am. (Greater Kansas City chpt. pres. 1973, treas. 1988-90, assembly del.), Amateur Athletic Union U.S. (sec. 1967-81, v.p. 1981-84, pres. 1984-88, Vol. Hall of Fame 1988, past pres., sec.-treas. Mo. Valley Assn.), USA Track and Field (sec.-treas. Mo. Valley Assn.), USA Amateur Boxing Fedn. (sec.-treas. Mo. Valley Assn.), Masons (master 1965). Avocations: sports, travel, photography. Home: Raymore, Mo. Died Apr. 18, 2004.

HARLEY, RALPH LEROY, JR., art and photo historian, educator; b. Des Moines, Oct. 20, 1934; s. Ralph Leroy and Athena Katherine (Himmel) H.; m. Joanna Lindgren, May 29, 1960. BFA in Art and Art Edn., Drake U., 1957; Diploma, McCormick Sem., 1961; MA in Art History, U. Wis., Madison, 1965; PhD in Art History, U. N.Mex., 1984. Assoc. prof. art history Kent (Ohio) State U., 1986, asst. prof., 1969-86, instr., 1967-69, asst. dir., 1972-74, coord. div. art history, 1982, 87-88; vis. instr. U. Ky., Lexington, 1967. Instr. workshops/seminars in field including Frederick Sommer Photographic Workshop/The Sch. of the Arts at Sun Valley, 1976, Ansel Adams Workshop on the Art History and Criticism of Photography, The Ctr. for Creative Photography, U. Ariz., Tucson, 1975, others. Contbr. articles/photographs to profl. jours., art catalogs; contbr. The Dictionary of Art.; works include modern prints from vintage negatives for pub. and pvt. collections including Maxwel Mus., U. N.Mex., contbr. replicas and reconstructions for exhbn., U. Archives and Am. History Rsch. Ctr., Kent State U. Libr., Mawel Mus., U. N.Mex.; contbr. ltd. edit. black and white projections documenting the exhbn. "Avant-garde Photography in Germany: 1919-1939", San Francisco Mus. Modern Art, others. Contbr. to profl. publs. Recipient numerous rsch. travel grants, Kent State U., 1989, Univ. Rsch. Coun. 1985-87, Coll. of Fine and Profl. Arts, 1986, others. Mem. Midwest Art History Soc., Photographic Hist. Soc., European Soc. History of Photography, Scottish Soc. History of Photography, Assn. Art Historians. Avocation: photography for reconstruction of vintage imagery and video for paradigm analysis. Home: Kent, Ohio. Died June 7, 2005.

HARMON, ROBERT JOHN, child psychiatrist; b. Cleve., June 7, 1946; s. William Clare and Roberta (Held) Harmon; m. Darlene K. Harmon, July 11, 1969; children: Jaeda, Ian. AB magna cum laude, Miami U., Oxford, Ohio, 1967; MD summa cum laude, U. Colo., Denver, 1971. Lic. physician, Colo., Md.; diplomate Am. Bd. Psychiatry and Neurology, cert. gen. psychiatry, child psychiatry and addiction psychiatry. Psychiatry resident U. Colo. Sch. Medicine, Denver, 1971-73, child psychiatry resident, 1976-78; rsch. assoc. social and behavioral scis. NIMH, Bethesda, Md., 1973-76; postdoctoral faculty developmental psychobiology rsch. grp. U. Colo. Sch. Medicine, Denver, from 1979, asst. prof. child psychiatry, 1978-82, assoc. prof. child psychiatry, 1982-92, prof., from 1992, head Div. Child Psychiatry, 1984—2002; dir. Kempe Therapeutic Presch., 1992—2005, dir. Irving B. Harris Program, from 1996; psychiat. dir. women's and children's residential svcs. The Haven, from 2001; med. dir. Ctr. for Dependancy, Addiction & Rehab., from 2005. Examiner Am. Bd. Psychiatry and Neurology, Evanston, Ill., from 1988; program chair Am. Acad. Child and Adolescent Psychiatry, from 2004; mem. diaqgnostic classification task force Zero to Three, Washington, from 1987, bd. dirs., from 1986, chair, 2003, DCO-3 tng. task force, from 2003. Co-editor: The Development of Attachment, 1982, Continuities and Discontinuities in Development, 1984; contbr. articles to profl. jours. Grantee John D. and Catherine T. MacArthur, 1984-86, NIMH, 1980-83, Harris Found., 1996—; Rsch. Scientist Devel. awardee, 1980-85. Fellow Am. Acad. Child and Adolescent Psychiatry; mem. Colo. Child and Adolescent Psychiatric Soc. (exec. com. 1983-87), Devel. Psychobiology Rsch. Grp., Am. Psychiatric Assn. (disting.fellow), World Assn. for Infant Mental Health, Am. Acad. Addiction Psychiatry, Am. Coll. Psychiatrists, Am. Soc. Addiction Medicine. Home: Denver, Colo. Died Feb. 24, 2006.

HARMS, CARL, actor; b. Chgo., Aug. 30, 1910; s. August and Lili (Vonder Heit) H.; m. Marianne Appel, Feb. 14, 1960 (dec. 1988); children: Sarah Kleeman, Margaret Merrill Piera. Grad. high sch., Chgo. Chmn., sec. bd. dirs. Equity-League Pension & Health Fund; pres. Equity Real Estate Corp. Appeared in Fritz Leiber Shakespeare Repertory Theater, 1930, Circuit Theatre, 1934-35, Fed. Theatre, 1936-38, Great No. Theatre, Bil Bairds Marionette Theatre, 1940-75, (Broadway) Flahooley Broadhurts Theatre, 1951, Much Add About Nothing Music Box Theatre, 1952, Girl on The Via Flamina 48 St. Theatre, 1954, and in numerous TV prodns. Trustee Clarence Derwent Awards Found. Mem. Actors Equity Assn. (coun. mem. 1957, sec. 1961, 1st v.p. 1973), Actors Equity Found. (pres.). Home: New York, NY. Died Aug. 11, 2005.

HARNETT, JOEL WILLIAM, marketing executive, magazine publisher; b. N.Y.C., Dec. 3, 1925; s. Sydney G. and Dorothy (Barnett) H.; m. Lila Beverly, Oct. 1, 1951. BA, U. Richmond, 1945. Retired U.S. Army, 1965; v.p., asst. to pres., dir. mktg. Look Mag., N.Y.C., 1951-69; chmn., chief exec. officer, founder Media Horizons, Inc., N.Y.C., 1969-88; chmn., owner Phoenix Home/Garden, Scottsdale Scene, Harnett's Sports Ariz. mags., Phoenix, 1988—2006. Chmn. Phoenix Home/Garden Co. Author: The Devil's Own Politics: The Explosive Political Rise and Fall of the Evangelical Movement, 2006; Pub. Arizona Monthly mags.; culture and sports writer and columnist Chmn. exec. com. Council on Mcpl. Performance, N.Y.C., 1985-86; bd. dirs. Nat. Civic League; past pres. Valley Citizen's League; bd. dirs. Cronkite Sch. Journalism, Ariz. State U. Maj., U.S. Army. Mem. Mag. Pubs. Assn. (mgmt. com. 1980-85), Town Tennis Club (pres.), Ariz. Club, City Club of N.Y. (past chmn.), University CLub, Phi Beta Kappa. Democrat. Jewish. Avocations: tennis, poetry, reading. Died Aug. 11, 2006.

HARPER, MARY STARKE, retired psychologist, sociologist; b. Ft. Mitchell, Ala., Sept. 6, 1919; d. Champ and Lillie Starke; widowed; 1 child, Willie Louise. Diploma, Tuskegee U., 1941, DSc (hon.), 1994; BS, U. Minn., 1950, MA, 1952; PhD, St. Louis U., 1963; LLD (hon.), St. Joseph Coll., 1998; DSc (hon.), U. SC, 2003. DON edn. US Dept. Vets. Affairs, Brecksville, Ohio; dir. mental health program for minorities NIH/NIMH, Rockville, Md., 1972—78, coord. long-term care mental health, 1978—81, dir. long term care, 1995; dir. office policy devel. and rsch. White House Conf. on Aging, Washington, 1981—86; ret., 1995. Adv. mental health and aging White House, Washington, 1981—86; geropsychiatric rsch. cons. Johnson & Johnson Rosalyn Carter Inst., Americus, Ga., 2000—06; adv. panel women's health US Dept. Health and Human Svcs., Washington; adv. panel mental health women US Surgeon Gen. Commn., Washington; faculty U. Minn., Mpls., UCLA, 1954, Va. Polytech., 1994; faculty dept. sociology St. Joseph Coll., NYC, 1968; chair health care reform Mental Health/Pub. Sector, 1993. Editor: Management and Care of the Elderly, Minority Aging: Essential Health Curricula Content for Selected Health Professionals and Allied Health, Behavioral Social and Mental Health Aspects of Aging, Mental Illness in Nursing Homes: An Agenda for Research, Older Women: Mental Health in Rural Areas; contbr. articles to profl. jours. Active Grant Makers in Aging, Atlanta, 2004; coalition mental health and aging DC Dept. Health, Washington, 1990—95, medicaid adv., 2000; sec. Internat. Assn. Aging; bd. dirs. Urban League, Peekskill, NY. Recipient award, Nat. Assn. Hist. Black Coll., 2000. Fellow: Am. Acad. Nursing; mem.: Nat. Assn. Mental Health Commn. (com. chair 2000), Am. Psychol. Assn. (adv.), Chi Eta Phi. Roman Catholic. Avocations: gardening, antiques, crocheting, reading. Home: Columbus, Ga. Died July 27, 2006.

HARPER, THOMAS BUCKMAN, III, lawyer; b. Phila., Jan. 21, 1925; s. Thomas Buckman Jr. and Grace (Everman) H.; m. Frances McCarron, Oct. 6, 1951; children: Patricia, Sallyanne, Catherine, Elizabeth, Thomas, Mary Frances. BA in Econs., La Salle Coll., 1948; JD, U. Pa., 1951. Bar: Pa. 1952, U.S. Dist. Ct. (ea. dist.) Pa. 1951, U.S. Ct. Appeals (3rd cir.) 1952, U.S. Supreme Ct. 1987. Assoc. Stradley, Ronon, Stevens & Young, Phila., 1951-80, adminstrv. ptnr., 1980-83, ptnr., 1983-89, sr. ptnr., 1989—95. Trustee, chmn. campus devel. com., mem. bus. affairs com. Community Coll. Phila.; bd. dirs. Holy Redeemer Vis. Nurse Agy. N.J., Holy Redeemer Found., St. Mary's Manor, Lansdale, Pa.; bd. dirs., mem. membership and bylaws com. Gwynedd-Mercy Coll.; mem. coun. mgrs. and instl. svcs. Archdiocese of Phila., mem. bd. edn., 1975-82; mem. pres.'s coun. Chestnut Hill Coll. With inf. AUS, 1943-46, ETO. Mem. ABA, Pa. Bar Assn., Phila. Bar Assn., Philopatrian Lit. Inst. (past bd. dirs.), Whitemarsh Valley Country Club (bd. govs., sec.), Vespers Club, Peale Club, Sierra (past pres. Phila. chpt.), KC. Avocations: golf, literature, art. Home: Lafayette Hill, Pa. Died Jan. 21, 2006.

HARRINGER, OLAF CARL, architect, museum administrator; b. Hamburg, Germany, Apr. 29, 1919; came to U.S., 1927; s. Henry Theodore and Anke (Berger) H.; m. Helen Ehrat Hedges, Dec. 20, 1975; children— Carla, Brita, Eric. Student, Evanston Acad. Fine Arts, The New Bauhaus, 1937-38, Ill. Inst. Tech., 1942-45. Designer Raymond Loewy Assos., Chgo., 1946-49, H. Allan Majestic Assos., Chgo., 1949-51, Dickens, Inc., Chgo., 1951-52, Olaf Harringer and Assos. (architects/designers), Chgo., 1952-62; account exec. several exhibit firms Chgo., 1962-68; dir. exhibits Mus. Sci. and Industry, Chgo., 1957-60, 68-80; prin. Olaf Harringer Assos., Chgo., 1981-95. Mem. AIA (emeritus). Home: Hollywood, Fla. Died Mar. 31, 2006.

HARRIS, CHRISTIE LUCY, author; b. Newark, Nov. 21, 1907; d. Edward and Matilda (Christie) Irwin; m. Thomas A. Harris, Feb. 13, 1932; children: Michael, Moira, Sheilagh, Brian, Gerald. Tchrs. cert., Provincial Normal Sch., Vancouver, B.C., Can., 1925. Tchr., B.C., 1925-32; free-lance scriptwriter Canadian Broadcasting Corp. radio, 1936-63; women's editor B.C. News Weekly, Abbotsford, 1951-57. Author: Raven's Cry, 1966, 92, Mouse Woman books (3), 1976, 77, 79, The Trouble With Princesses, 1980, Something Weird Is Going On, 1994, others. Decorated Order of Can., 1981; recipient Can. Book of Yr. medal for Children's book, 1967, 77; Can. Council Children's Lit. prize, 1981; recipient Lifetime Achievement award BC Gas, 1998. Mem. Writers' Union Can. (life). Died Jan. 2.

HARRIS, HOWARD HUNTER, retired oil industry executive; b. Cushing, Okla., Dec. 7, 1924; s. Oscar Hunter and Gertie Lee (Stark) H.; m. Gwendolyne J. Moyers (died July 26, 2003), Dec. 31, 1945; children: Howard Sidney, Rodney Craig. BS in Bus. Adminstrn., U. Okla., 1949, JD, 1949; postgrad. in advt. mgmt., Stanford U., 1971. Atty. Emery & Harris, Cushing and Stillwater, Okla., 1949-50; staff atty. Sun Oil Co., Tulsa, 1950-54; div. atty. Marathon Oil Co., Tulsa, 1954-63; staff atty Marathon Internat. Oil Co., Findlay, Ohio, 1963-65; mgr. legal affairs Deutsche Marathon Petroleum Gmbh., Frankfurt and Munich, 1965-70; mktg. aty. and assoc. gen. counsel Marathon Oil Co., Findlay, Ohio, 1970-74, v.p. corp. external affairs, 1974-86, ret., 1986. Pres. Gainey Ranch Cmty. Assn., 1995-98. Served with AUS, 1943-45. Decorated Bronze Star Mem. Am. Petroleum Inst., ABA, Ohio Bar Assn., Okla. Bar Assn., Order of Coif, Beta Gamma Sigma. Lodges: Masons. Republican. Episcopalian. Home: Scottsdale, Ariz. Died Oct. 4, 2005.

HARRIS, PETER ANGELO, accounting executive; b. Boston, July 19, 1918; widower; 1 child, Donna Harris. BBA, Northeastern U., 1943; MBA, Babson Coll., 1969. Sec.-treas. southwest Hardware Co., L.A., 1965-69; comptroller Mal's Dept. Stores, Newton, Mass., 1969-73; with Zayre Corp. div. Bell Nugent, Framingham, Mass., from 1973; comptroller, tax and acctg. specialist S.J. Balsama Corp., Brockton, Mass., from 1973. Lt. USNR, 1943-47. Mem. Nat. Soc. Pub. Accts., AHEPA, Am. Legion (vice comdr., chaplain). Home: Waltham, Mass. Died Apr. 12, 2004.

HARRIS, RONALD RICHARD, psychotherapist; b. St. Louis, Feb. 9, 1950; s. Harold Cedric and Maxine Doris (Aufdenberg) H.; m. Nancy Jean Jones, Nov. 26, 1980; 1 child, Aaron Richard. BS, Southeast Mo. State U., 1979; MA, Regis U., 1998. Lic. profl. counselor. Sales rep. Ga. Pacific Corp., Cape Girardeau, Mo., 1979-80; mgr. K-Mart Corp., Grand Island, Nebr., 1980-82, Gen. Nutrition, Inc., St. Louis, 1982-86, Walmart Stores, 1986-88; counselor Mental Health Ctr., Canon City, Colo., 1988-96, Harris Counseling & Cons., Canon City, Colo., from 1996. Cons. in field. Sgt. USAF, 1972-78. Mem. ACA, Nat. Cert. Counselors, Colo. Assn. Psychotherapists, Scottish Rite (pres. 1998-2000), Masons (master Mason), Shriners. Died Jan. 11, 2004.

HARRIS, THEODORE EDWARD, mathematician, educator; b. Phila., Jan. 11, 1919; s. Julius and Hazel (Rosenfield) H.; m. Constance Ruth Feder, June 29, 1947; children: Stephen Joel, Marcia Faye. Student, So. Meth. U., 1935-37; BA, U. Tex., Austin, 1939; MA, Princeton U., 1946, PhD, 1947; D of Tech. (hon.), Chalmers Inst. of Tech., Gothenburg, Sweden, 1989. With Rand Corp., 1947—66, chmn. dept. math., 1959—66; prof. math. U. So. Calif., 1966—89, prof. emeritus, from 1989. Vis. asst. prof. UCLA, 1949-50; vis. assoc. prof. Columbia, 1953; vis. prof. Stanford U., 1963; lectr. U. So. Calif., 1989-97. Author: The Theory of Branching Processes, 1963; Editor: Annals of Math. Statistics, 1955-58. Served to maj. USAAF, 1942-45. Recipient Albert S. Raubenheimer disting. faculty award, 1985, disting. emeritus award U. So. Calif., 1990. Fellow AAAS, Inst. Math. Stats. (pres. 1966-67); mem. Am. Math. Soc., Nat. Acad. Scis., Phi Beta Kappa, Sigma Xi. Jewish. Home: Beverly Hills, Calif. Died Nov. 3, 2005.

HARRIS, WAYNE MANLEY, lawyer; b. Dec. 28, 1925; s. George H. and Constance M. Harris; children: Wayne, Constance, Karen, Duncan, Claire. LLB, U. Rochester, 1951. Bar: N.Y. 1952, U.S. Supreme Ct. 1958. Ptnr. Harris, Chesworth & O'Brien (and predecessor firms), Rochester, NY, from 1958. Drafter 5 laws passed in State of N.Y. Pres. Adopt-A-Stream program Delta Labs, Inc., from 1971; pres. Friends Bristol Valley Playhouse Found., 1984—87, Monroe County Conservation Coun., Inc., 1956—61, v.p., 1984—87, Powder Mills Pk. Hatchery Preservation, Inc., 1993—95, pres., 1995—2002. With U.S. Army, 1944—46, Germany. Decorated Bronze Star; named Vol. Conservationist of the Yr., N.Y. State Conservation Coun. Inc., 2000; recipient Sportsman of the Yr. award, Genesee Conservation League, Inc., 1960, Conservationist of the Yr. award, Monroe County Conservation Coun., Inc., 1961, N.Y. State Conservation Coun. Nat. Wildlife Fedn. Water Conservation, 1967, Kiwanian of the Yr. award, Kiwanis Club, 1965, Livingston County Fedn. Sportsmen award, 1967, Hon. Fellowship award, Rochester Acad. Sci., 1970, Meritorious Leadership in Civic Devel. award, Rochester C. of C., 1972, Svc. award, Rochester Against Intoxicated Drivers, 1989, Conspicuous Svc. cross, N.Y. State, 2000, N.Y. Senate Resolution 241 award, 2001. Mem.: ATLA, Indsl. Mgmt. Coun., AIDA Reins. and Arbitration Soc., N.Y. State Trial Lawyers Assn., Wild Turkey Fedn. Home: Mendon, NY. Died 2006.

HARRISON, CHARLES WAGNER, JR., applied physicist; s. Charles Wagner and Etta Earl (Smith) H.; m. Fern F. Perry, Dec. 28, 1940; children: Martha R., Charlotte J. Student, U.S. Naval Acad. Prep. Sch., 1933-34, U.S. Coast Guard Acad., 1934-36; BS in Engring., U. Va., 1939, EE, 1940; SM, Harvard U., 1942, M of Engring., 1952, PhD in Applied Physics, 1954; postgrad., MIT, 1942, 52. Registered profl. engr., Va. Engr. Sta. WCHV, Charlottesville, Va., 1937-40; commd. ensign U.S. Navy, 1939, advanced through grades to comdr., 1948; research staff Bur. Ships, 1939-41, asst. dir. electronics design and devel. div., 1948-50; research staff U.S. Naval Research Lab., 1944-45, dir.'s staff, 1950-51; liaison officer Evans Signal Lab., 1945-46; electronics officer Phila. Naval Shipyard, 1946-48; mem. USN Operational Devel. Force Staff, 1953-55; staff Comdg. Gen. Armed Forces Spl. Weapons project, 1955-57; ret. U.S. Navy, 1957; cons. electromagnetics Sandia Nat. Lab., Albuquerque, 1957-73. Instr. U. Va., 1939-40; lectr. Harvard U., 1942-43, Princeton U., 1943-44; vis. prof. Christian Heritage Coll., El Cajon, Calif., 1976. Author: (with R.W.P. King) Antennas and Waves: A Modern Approach, 1969; contbr. numerous articles to profl. jours. Fellow IEEE (Electronics Achievement award 1966, best paper award electromagnetic compatibility group 1972); mem. Internat. Union Radio Sci. (commn. B), Electromagnetics Acad., Famous Families Va., Sigma Xi. Home: Albuquerque, N.Mex. Died July 18, 2006.

HARRISON, SAUL ISAAC, child psychiatrist, educator; b. N.Y.C., Nov. 4, 1925; MD, U. Mich., 1948. Diplomate Am. Bd. Psychiatry and Neurology, Am. Bd. Child and Adolescent Psychiatry. Prof./dir. child/adolescent psychiatry edn. U. Mich., Ann Arbor, 1956-83; prof./dir. child/adolescent psychiatry Harbor UCLA, Torrance, 1984-92. Author/editor 9 books; contbr. over 100 articles to profl. jours., chpts. to books. Lt. USNR, 1943-45, 48-50, 52-54. Commonwealth Fund Fellow, London, 1966; recipient McGavin award Am. Psychiat. Assn. for career accomplishment in child/adolescent psychiatry, 1992. Died Feb. 13, 2004.

HARRISON, SHIRLEY WANDA, volunteer; b. Patchogue, N.Y., Oct. 18, 1923; d. Frederick Edward and Sadie (Schaefer) Sexauer; m. David Paul Harrison, June 21, 1946; children: Thomas, Joan, Roger. AB, Barnard Coll., 1944; AM, Columbia U., 1946; PhD, CUNY, 1970. Asst. prof. Manhattan C.C., N.Y.C., 1972-76; assoc. prof. Nassau C.C., Garden City, N.Y., 1978-89; rsch. assoc. Hunter Coll., N.Y.C., 1978-78, 1983-84, Queens Coll. CUNY, Flushing, N.Y., from 1990. Contbr. articles to profl. jours. Active PTA, Bayside, N.Y., 1961-70. Mem. Am. Phys. Soc., Assn. Women Sci., Nat. Women's Political Caucus. Democrat. Episcopalian. Avocations: computers, travel. Home: Bayside, NY. Died May 23, 2004.

HARRISON, STEPHEN MURRAY, electronics executive; b. Fall River, Mass., July 24, 1948; s. Raymond Robert and Dorothy Elizabeth (Murray) H.; m. Heather Nancy Hall, Nov. 9, 1974; children: Blake, Devon. BS in Bus. Mgmt., Providence Coll., 1971; MS in Fin., U. Mass., 1973. Sr. gen. acct. Hewlett Packard, Waltham, Mass., 1973-75, cost acctg. mgr. Andover, Mass., 1975-78, acctg. mgr., 1978-80, br. bus. mgr. Lexington, Mass., 1980-81; controller Bytex Corp., Southborough, Mass., 1981-83, v.p. fin., from 1983. Democrat. Home: Medford, Mass. Died Aug. 6, 2004.

HARRON, PAUL FRANCIS, broadcast executive.; b. Phila., Jan. 19, 1942; s. Paul Francis and Margaret Elizabeth (Harper) H.; B.S. in Acctg., Holy Cross Coll., Worcester, Mass., 1959; m. Katherine Joyce Crowley, Sept. 13, 1979. Account exec. Sta. WKTV, Utica, N.Y., 1965-66; regional salesman/mgr. Sta. KAUZ-TV, Wichita Falls, Tex., 1966-67; nat. sales mgr. Mid. N.Y. Broadcasting Corp., Phila., 1967-69; v.p. Harron Communications Corp., Phila., 1971-77, pres., dir., 1977-81, pres., chmn. bd., Paoli, Pa., 1982—99; Served with M.C., USAR, 1964-70. Mem. Phila. Cable Club, Nat. Assn. Broadcasters. Clubs: Vesper Boat (dir. 1981-82); Seaview Country (Absecon, N.J.); Atlantic Country (Northfield, N.J.); Indian Creek Country (Miami Beach, Fla.); Aronimink Country (Newton Square, Pa.); N.Y. Athletic (N.Y.C.). Home: Malvern, Pa. Died Dec. 8, 2005.

HART, BRUCE, screenwriter, director; b. N.Y.C., Jan. 15, 1938; s. Lou S. and Dorothy (Feins) H.; m. Carole Ruth Strickler, April 30, 1943. AB, Syracuse U., 1959; JD, Yale U., 1962. Bar: N.Y. 1963. Writer, lyricist Sesame Street, N.Y.C., 1969; producer, writer Psychology Today Film Series, Los Angeles, 1970; writer, lyricist Free To Be You and Me, N.Y.C., Los Angeles, 1973; dir, writer, lyricist Sooner or Later, N.Y.C., 1978; exec. producer, writer Hot Hero Sandwich, N.Y.C., 1979; writer Leap of Faith, N.Y.C., 1988. Producer, writer (ednl. film) Developmental Psychology, 1970 (CINE Golden Eagle, 1970); author: (with others) Sooner or Later, 1978, Waiting Games, 1981, Oh, Boy! Babies!, 1982 (Christopher award, Mass Media award, 1982), Breaking Up Is Hard To Do, 1986, Cross Your Heart, 1988, Now or Never, 1991. Served to lt. USNR, 1962-65. Recipient 2 Emmy awards, 1969, 73. Mem. Writers Guild Am., Dirs. Guild Am., Authors Guild, ASCAP. Home: New York, NY. Died Feb. 21, 2006.

HART, CLARICE REID, retired reading specialist, English educator; b. Norfolk, Va., Mar. 1, 1927; d. William and Ella Elizabeth (Doswell) Reid; m. Marvin Lee Hart, Feb. 10, 1982 (dec. Feb. 1996); 1 child, Maria Endira. BS, W.Va. State U., 1953; tchg. cert., Old Dominion U., 1954; reading cert., Virginia Beach (Va.) City Sch., 1965. Tchr. 6th grade Virginia Beach City Schs., 1963-73, chpt. I reading specialist, 1973-92; English instr. Upward Bound Norfolk (Va.) State U., 1992-98. Author: (poetry) Nightfalls, 1996 (Internat. Reading Soc. plaque 1996). Tutor Cmty. Svc., Virginia Beach, 1995-98; Sunday sch. tchr. United House Prayer, Virginia Beach, 1998. Recipient Apple for Tchr. award Iota Phi Lambda Sorority, Norfolk, 1990. Outstanding Aux. Mem. award United House Prayer, 1997. Mem. AARP (regional rep. 1995-98), NEA (mem.-at-large 1992-98), Virginia Beach Edn. Assn., Concerned Women Am., Democratic Women Am., L&J Gardens Civic League, Phi Delta Kappa (profl. storyteller 1980-98, pub. rels. chair 1996-98, Outstanding Cmty. Svc. award 1997), Delta Sigma Theta. Avocations: singing, water aerobics, walking, reading, travel. Home: Upper Marlboro, Md. Died Mar. 30, 2005.

HART, LYLE CORDELL, audio-visual producer; b. Alliance, Nebr., Aug. 2, 1931; s. Clarence Cordell and Hazel (Leslie) H.; m. LeJean Dow, July 8, 1960; children: Thomas, T. Scott, Jenny. Student, Nebr. State Tchrs., 1949-51, 54-55; BA, U. Iowa, 1958. Cameraman, editor Barbre Prodns., Denver, 1956, 60, Hawkins Prodns., Denver, 1959; dir. photography United Film Industries, Denver, 1961-62; cameraman Centron Corp., Lawrence, Kans., 1962-70; sr. audio-visual producer Deere & Co., Moline, Ill., from 1970. With USAF, 1951-54. Episcopalian. Avocations: photography, travel, reading. Home: Geneseo, Ill. Died Sept. 28, 2004.

HART, SHIRLEY A., nurse; b. Chattanooga, Dec. 29, 1946; d. William Yural and Helen Louise (Hillhouse) H. Cert. in nursing, Riverside Hosp. Sch. Nursing, 1969. Lic. practical nurse, Tenn. Obstetrics and staff nurse Riverside Hosp., Nashville, 1967-69; staff and med. nurse Women's Hosp., Chattanooga, 1972-76; psychiat. nurse Valley Psychiat. Hosp., Chattanooga, 1977-78; head nurse Life Care Nursing Home, Collegedale, Tenn., 1978-79; staff nurse Diagnostic Hosp., Chattanooga, 1979-83; pvt. duty nurse Quality Care Home Health Agy., Chattanooga, 1983-87, Contin-U-Care Home Health Agy., Chattanooga, 1987-93; night infirmary nurse Baylor Prep. Sch., Chattanooga, from 1986. Camp nurse Camp Illahee, Brevard, N.C., summer 1992. Contbr. poems to profl. publs. Counselor Chattanooga Rape Crisis Ctr., 1975-76; bd. dirs. Orchard Park Seventh Day Adventist Community Ctr., Chattanooga, 1993—. Recipient Trophy, World of Poetry, 1984. Mem. NAFE, Tenn. Poetry Soc., Tenn. Writers Alliance, Inc. Democrat. Seventh-Day Adventist. Avocations: drawing, writing short stories, novels, poetry, arts and crafts. Home: Chattanooga, Tenn. Died Nov. 1, 2004.

HART, STANLEY V., banker; b. Owen County, Ind., Nov. 22, 1942; s. Delbert L. and Geneva (Beatty) H.; m. Kay Dalton, Apr. 14, 1962; children: Lisa, Della, Brian. Student, U. Wis., 1973, student, 1978. Asst. cashier Terre Haute (Ind.) First Nat. Bank, 1968-73, asst. v.p., br. adminstr., 1974-77, v.p., ops., 1978-89, sr. v.p. ops., from 1989; v.p., chief ops. officer First Famers State Bank, Sullivan, Ind., from 1988, bd. dirs. Instr. Am. Inst. Banking, 1968—; bd. dirs. Index (Ind. Automated Clearing House). Mem. Clay County Sch. Bldg. Corp., 1986—. With USAR, 1960-66. Home: Clay City, Ind. Died Feb. 28, 2004.

HARTMAN, ROBERT WILLIAM, retired federal official; b. N.Y.C., Jan. 7, 1938; s. Eugene and Ella (Schweitzer) H.; m. Rhona Cohen, Jan. 31, 1960; children: Peter Adam, Michael Gordon. BA, Queens Coll. N.Y., 1958; AM, Harvard U., 1961, PhD, 1964. Tchr. Upward Bound program Brandeis U., Waltham, Mass., 1966, asst. prof. econs., 1963-68; Brookings econ. policy fellow HEW, Washington, 1968-69; rsch. assoc., sr. fellow Brookings Instn., Washington, 1969-82; sr. analyst for budget process Congl. Budget Office, Washington, 1982-91, acting dep. dir., 1987-91, asst. dir. spl. studies divsn., 1991—96. Vis. lectr. Grad. Sch. Pub. Policy, U. Calif., Berkeley, 1975-76; mem. budget group Carter-Mondale Transition Staff, Washington, 1976-77. Author: Credit for College, 1971, Reforming School Finance, 1973, Setting National Priorities, 1974, 75, Pay and Pensions for Federal Workers, 1983. Recipient Excellence in Teaching award Brandeis U.; Univ. fellow Harvard U., Earhart Found. fellow. Mem. Assn. for Pub. Policy Analysis and Mgmt. (policy coun. 1986-90, chmn. nominating com. 1990, treas., assoc. eidtor Jour. of Policy Analysis and Mgmt.). Home: Washington, DC. Died Sept. 1, 2006.

HARVESTER, JAMES VERNON, retired minister; b. Meridian, Miss., Aug. 9, 1921; s. Isaac Uriah and Mary Jane (Allen) H.; m. Helen Grace Griffin, July 3, 1944; children: James V. Jr., Bryan Allen, Charles Lee, Michael Raymond, Eric Thomas, Paulette. BA, Fla. So. Coll., 1947; MDiv, Emory U., Atlanta, 1949; MA in Pub. Adminstrn., George Washington U., 1959. Ordained to ministry, United Meth. Ch., 1949. Pastor The United Meth. Ch., various locations, 1946-51, 70-92, Thonotosassa (Fla.) United Meth Ch., 1979-92; ret. Bd. dirs., sec. Fla. United Meth. Credit Union, Lakeland, 1983—; fin. cons. Tampa, 1979—. Instr. AARP Tax Aide Program, Tampa, 1979—. Col. U.S. Army, 1940-45, 51-70. Decorated Legion of Merit with oak leaf cluster, Army Commendation Medal with 2 oak leaf clusters; recipient Silver Beaver, Boy Scouts Am., 1963; named Mil. Bus. exec. of the Yr., N.Y. Fed. Bus. Assn., 1969. Mem. Rotary (dir. 1974-77). Avocations: photography, reading, furniture refinishing. Home: Tampa, Fla. Died July 19, 2005.

HARVEY, DAVID EUGENE, construction company executive; b. Wilmette, Ill., Feb. 6, 1922; s. Frank William and Helen Geraldine (McJunkin) H.; m. Patricia Meany, Sept. 2, 1950; children— Jerome, Michael, David Eugene, Barbara, Donna, Janice, Brian, Mary Ann, Frank, Eileen, Patricia. BS in Archtl. Engring, U. Ill., 1951. Architect Ragnar Benson Constrn. Co., Chgo., 1951-52; engr., estimator W.S. Bellow Constrn. Co., Houston, 1952-53, Benson Co. Builders, Houston, 1953-58; founder, chmn., CEO Harvey Constrn. Co., Houston, 1958—2006. Dir. Galleria Bank, Houston. Served with USAAF, 1943-46. Recipient award excellence Urban Land Inst., 1979 Mem. Asso. Gen. Contractors (sec. Houston chpt. 1981), Houston C. of C. Clubs: K.C. (3 deg.). Republican. Roman Catholic. Home: Houston, Tex. Died Feb. 15, 2006.

HARVIN, CHARLES ALEXANDER, III, state legislator, lawyer; b. Sumter, S.C., Feb. 7, 1950; s. Charles Alexander Harvin, Jr. m. Cathy Jane Brand; 1 child, Mary Franklin; Grad. in history and polit. sci. Baptist Coll., Charleston, S.C., 1972, Augusta Law Sch., 1976; hon. degree Sherman Chiropractic Coll., Spartanburg, S.C., 1979, Francis Marion Coll., 1986; LLD (hon.) Charleston So. Univ., 1988. Mem. S.C. Ho. of Reps., 1976—, asst. majority leader, majority whip, 1978-82, majority leader, 1982—, mem. ways and means com., vice chmn. rules com., majority leader Emeritus Ho. of Reps., S.C., 1987—. Pres. Bapt. Coll. Young Dems., 1970-72; officer Charleston County Young Dems., 1971-72; chmn. 6th Congl. Dist. Young Dems., 1975-76; life mem. S.C. Young Dems.; chmn. Clarendon County Dem. Com.; vice chmn. S.C. Dem. Com., 1976-78, also mem. exec. com.; del. Dem. Nat. Conv., 1984; mem. S.C. Gov.'s Agr. Study Com.; U.S. Constn. Bicentennial Commn., 1985—; trustee S.C. Hall of Fame; vice chmn. alumni bd. Bapt. Coll., 1975-76; bd. visitors Clemson U., 1977-78,.Med. Univ. S.C., 1986-87, Charleston So. Univ., 1988-90. Maj. USNG. Recipient Outstanding Service award Charleston County Young Dems., 1972, S.C. Young Dems., 1977; Disting. Service award S.C. Dem. Com., 1981; appreciation award S.C. Tech. Edn. Colls., 1981; Legislator of Yr. award S.C. Young Dems., 1982, S.C. Student Legislature, 1981, S.C. State Library Bd., 1982, S.C. Assn. for Deaf, 1985; award S.C. Coun. for Exceptional Children, 1982, S.C. Agrl. Cmty., 1982; Outstanding Legislator Service award United Parcel Svc., 1984; Disting. Svc. award Bapt. Coll. of Charleston Alumni Assn., 1984, also numerous other awards and commendations. Mem. ABA, Am. Judicature Soc., S.C. Trial Lawyers Assn., Clarendon County Farm Bur., Clarendon County Hist. Soc. (v.p. 1983-84, pres. 1985-86), S.C. State Employees Assn., NAACP, Huguenot Soc. of S.C., First Families of S.C., Alpha Phi Omega (life). Lodges: Masons, Shriners. Home: Summerton, SC. Died Oct. 11, 2005.

HARWOOD, WILLIAM TENER, writer; b. Paterson, N.J., Sept. 29, 1921; s. William Smith and Sarah Cambridge Harwood. BS, Columbia Pacific U., 1983, MS, 1986, PhD, 1988. Cert. energy engr., Ga. Engring. asst. Wright-Aero Corp., Woodridge, N.J., 1965-69. Cons. Nuclear Regulatory Commn., Washington; speaker Nat. Energy Conf., 1978. Author: First Cause. Served with U.S. Army, 1942-43. Mem. Assn. Energy Engrs., Assn. Environ. Engrs. and Mgrs. Inst., N.Y. Acad. Scis. Avocations: boxing, swimming, mountain climbing. Home: Port Angeles, Wash. Died Sept. 2, 2004.

HASERICK, JOHN ROGER, retired dermatologist; b. Mpls., Sept. 23, 1915; s. Ernest B. and Addie (Swanson) H.; m. Jane Margaret Fleckenstein, May 10, 1941; children: John Roger, Jane. BA, Macalester Coll., 1937; MD, U. Minn., 1941, MS in Dermatology, 1946. Diplomate: Am. Bd. Dermatology (pres. 1975). Intern Ancker Hosp., St. Paul, 1940-41; resident in medicine Univ. Hosps., Mpls., 1941—42, resident in dermatology, 1945-46; med. svc. 26th Gen. Hosp., 1943—45; pvt. practice Pinehurst, NC, 1970-87; head dept. dermatology Cleve. Clinic, 1948-67; prof. Case Western Res. U., Cleve., 1967-70; clin. prof. medicine and dermatology Duke U., Durham, NC, 1970-85; with Pinehurst Dermatology Clinic, 1970-87; clin. prof. dermatology U. Minn., 1997—2006. Author: LE Primer, 1972, The Wolves Club, 2002; contbr. 75 articles to med. jours.; author: (CD-ROM) Consultations in Lupus Erythematosus, 2003. Mem. Vols. in Medicine, Martin County Med. Soc., Stuart, Fla., 1997—; bd. dirs. Moore County Free Care Clinic, 2004—. Recipient Discovery award Dermatology Found., 1999. Fellow ACP; mem. AMA (Hektoen Silver award 1952), Am. Acad. Dermatology (pres. 1974), Am. Soc. Dermatopathology (pres. 1975, Founder's award 1996), N.C. Med. Assn., Am. Soc. Investigative Dermatology, Am. Dermatol. Assn., Country Club of N.C. (Pinehurst), Wolves Club (Pinehurst, pres. 1983). Achievements include discovering LE factor (antinuclear) in blood of patients wih lupus erythematosus. Home: Southern Pines, NC. Died May 1, 2006.

HASH, CHARLES PATTON, JR., association executive; b. Hattiesburg, Miss., May 24, 1965; s. Charles Patton and Barbara (Bilbo) H. Dep. dir. S.C. Hist. Soc., Charleston, 1990-2000; exec. dir. Palmetto Soc. Charleston, 1994-2000; dir. of devel. Nat. Lesbian and Gay Journalists Assn., Washington, from 2000. Co-editor: Charleston—Alone Among the Cities, 2000; contbr. articles to profl. jours. Mem. NSFE, S.C. Hist. Soc. Episcoplian. Avocations: gardening, bicycling, research. Home: Washington, DC. Died Feb. 8, 2005.

HASHIMOTO, RYUTARO, former Prime Minister of Japan; b. July 29, 1937; Grad., Keio (Japan) U. Mem. Japanese Ho. of Reps. from Okayama, 1963—2005; chmn. com. on social and labor affairs, 1976; min. health and welfare, 1970; min. transport, 1986-87; min. fin., 1987-91; chmn. Rsch. Commn. on Fundamental Policies for Med. Care, Liberal Dem. Party, 1984, chmn. Rsch. Commn. on Pub. Adminstrn. and Fin., 7 yrs., sec. gen., from 1989; prime min., 1996-98. Died July 1, 2006.

HASKINS, ERIC WILBUR, electrical power engineer; b. Eugene, Oreg., Aug. 8, 1947; s. Wilbur Calvin and Mary Louise Haskins; m. Kathleen Salay, Mar. 17, 1973 (div. June 1987); children: Bradee Rae, Matthew Eric. BS in Elec. Power Engring., Oreg. State U., 1969. Registered profl. engr., Oreg. Mfrs. rep. McGraw Edison Power Sys. Divsn., Pitts., 1969-79; mgr. engring. svcs. Edison Elec. Inst., Washington, 1979-91; mgr. utility partnership program U.S. Energy Assn., Washington, from 1991. Bd. dirs. Utilities Telecomm. Coun., Washington, 1979-91; mem. adv. com. utility comms. architecture Elec. Power Rsch. Inst., Palo Alto, Calif., 1988-91; co-founder Power Engring. Edn. Found., Washington, 1990, Nuclear Employee Data Sys., Washington, 1987. Author booklet: Working at a Nuclear Plant - Why the Hassle?, 1983; co-author reference manual EEI Guide to Effective Drug and Alcohol Policy Development, 1985; contbr. articles to profl. publs. Mem. IEEE, Profl. Engring. Soc. Presbyterian. Avocations: golf, skiing, music, reading, target shooting. Home: Fairfax, Va. Died Jan. 3, 2005.

HASS, KENNETH C., physicist; b. Flushing, N.Y., May 7, 1958; s. Joseph J. and Alberta M. (Simons) H.; m. Nancy M. Magnani, Nov. 12, 1983; children: Andrew J., Christopher E. BA in Physics and Math., CUNY, Flushing, N.Y., 1979; AM in Physics, Harvard U., Cambridge, Mass., 1980, PhD in Physics, 1984. Postdoc. MIT Harvard, Cambridge, Mass., 1984-87; rsch. scientist Ford Motor Co., Dearborn, Mich., from 1987. Panel mem. Nat. Rsch. Coun. Panel on Diluted Magnetic Semiconductors, Washington, 1988-89; chair Am. Phys. Soc. Com. on Edn., College Park, Md., 1999-00. Editor: Computing in Science and Engineering, 1999—; contbr. articles to profl. jours. Fellow Nat. Sci. Found., 1979-82. Mem. ACS, AAAS, Am. Phys. Soc., Materials Rsch. Soc., Sigma Xi. Home: Ann Arbor, Mich. Died June 1, 2005.

HASSANALI, NOOR MOHAMED, President of the Republic of Trinidad and Tobago; b. San Fernando, Trinidad and Tobago, Aug. 13, 1918; s. Ashraph and Rasulan (Ramjohn) H.; m. Zalayhar Mohammed, May 17, 1952; children: Khalid, Amena. BA in Law honors, U. Toronto, Can., 1947; barrister-at-law, Gray's Inn, Eng., 1948. Pvt. practice law, Republic of Trinidad and Tobago, 1948-53; magistrate, 1953-59; sr. magistrate, 1960; sr. crown counsel Office of Attorney General, Republic of Trinidad and Tobago, 1961-64; sr. law officer Office of Atty. Gen., Republic of Trinidad and Tobago; solicitor gen. Ministry of Legal Affairs, Republic of Trinidad and Tobago, 1965; judge of the High Court Supreme Ct. of Judicature, Republic of Trinidad and Tobago, 1966-77, judge of Court of Appeal, 1978-84; President of the Republic of Trinidad and Tobago, 1987-97. Master of the Moots Hugh Wooding Law Sch., 1985-86; mem. jud. and legal service commn., 1985-86, Trinidad and Tobago Def. Force Commns. Bd., 1985-86. Exec. mem. Scout Assn. Tidad and Tigo, Trinidad and Tobago, 1965-86; mem. bd. control Naparima Coll., San Fernando, 1948-60. Avocations: walking, football, soccer, cricket, theater. Died Aug. 25, 2006.

HAUER, ANN, retired elementary school educator; b. Braddock, N.D., Sept. 19, 1942; d. Ray Joseph and Mildred Elizabeth (Kippes) Splonskowski; m. Jim Hauer, June 26, 1965; children: Todd, Melissa. BA, Mary Coll., 1969; MA in Ednl. Adminstrn., U. N.D., 1981. Cert. elem. prin. Elem. tchr. Richholt Sch., Bismarck, N.D., 1970-74, tchr., asst. prin., 1974-76; tchr. Roosevelt Sch., Bismarck, 1976-95; elem. rep. Bismarck Pub. Schs. Curriculum Steering Com., developer curriculum metrics, nutrition, career edn., chmn. dist. social studies standing com., chmn. social studies curriculum com., mem to revise curriculum to add outcomes-based edn., 1993. Tchr. rep. N.D. adv. bd. Project Wild. Recipient Tchr. Yr award C. of C., 1987; named Educator of Yr., 1990, Project WET, 1989. Mem. NEA, N.D. Edn. Assn., Bismarck Edn. Assn. (govt. relations com., elem. negotiator, profl. rights and responsibilities chmn., pres. 1983-84, 1987—, health curriculum evaluation and standing com.), Assn. Supervision and Curriculum Devel., Bismarck C. of C. (Tchr. of Yr. award 1987, edn. com.), Phi Delta Kappa (v.p. 1985-86). Roman Catholic. Lodge: Elks. Home: Bismarck, ND. Died July 27, 2004.

HAUF, JOHN GEORGE, real estate broker; b. N.Y.C., July 19, 1939; s. George John and Rose Cecelia Hauf; children: Jason, Susan. BSBA, Fordham U., 1961; MBA in Econs., NYU, 1966. Cert. real estate broker, appraiser. Mktg. assoc. SCM Corp., N.Y.C., 1964—66; rsch. assoc. Daniel Yankelovich, Inc., Phila., 1966—69; mktg. dir. Dun & Bradstreet, Inc., N.Y.C., 1969—77, Rural Transport, New Brunswick, NY, 1977—80; real estate broker Edward S. Gordon Co., N.Y.C., 1980—85, Richar Ellis & Co., N.Y.C., 1985—91, Coldwell Banker, Washington Cross, Pa., from 1991. Mem. com. Real Estate Bd. of Bucks County, Doylestown, Pa., from 1995; mem. hwy. com. Upper Makefield Twp., Washington Crossing, from 2000; pres. Upper Makefield Hist. Soc., Washington Crossing; mem. trail com. Upper Makefield Twp., Washington Crossing, from 2001; mem. Friends of Delaware Canal, New Hope, Pa., from 1997. Mem.: Upper Makefield Businessman's Assn., Phi Theta Kappa. Avocations: historical preservation activities, sailing, painting, skiing, reading. Home: Washington Crossing, Pa. Died July 4, 2004.

HAUGH, EDWIN ALBERT, editor, publications specialist; b. Wilmington, Del., Sept. 6, 1936; s. Edwin Albert and Margaret Edna (Warfel) H.; m. Mary Galloway, Oct. 2, 1965 (div. Sept. 1989); children: Christopher, Timothy, Jonathan. BA, U. Del., 1958. Tech. editor Thiokol Chem. Corp., Elkton, Md., 1958-64, Scott Paper Co., Phila., 1970-72, JRB Assocs., McLean, Va., 1975; publs. supr. Atlantic Rsch. Corp., Alexandria, Va., 1964-70; chief Tech. Info. Ctr., Frederick (Md.) Cancer Rsch. Ctr., 1972-74; med. editor Nat. Cancer Inst., Bethesda, Md., 1976-80; mng. editor Jour. Nat. Cancer Inst., Bethesda, Md., 1980-87; publs. specialist Nat. Cancer Inst., Bethesda, Md., from 1988. Recipient Disting. Tech. Comm. award Soc. for Tech. Comm., 1987. Mem. Lions (pres. 1978-79, Melvin Jones fellow 1994). Republican. Roman Catholic. Home: Frederick, Md. Died June 14, 2004.

HAUGHEY, CHARLES JAMES, former Prime Minister of Ireland; b. Castlebar, County Mayo, Ireland, Sept. 16, 1925; s. John and Sarah Ann (McWilliams) H.; m. Maureen Lemass, Sept. 18, 1951; children: Eimear, Conor, Ciaran, Sean B.Commerce, Univ. Coll., Dublin; B.L., Kings Inns, Dublin. Ptnr. Haughey Boland & Co., chartered accts., 1950-60; called to bar, 1948; bloodstock breeder, from 1950; mem. Dublin Corp., 1953-55, Irish Parliament for Dublin (Artane) Constituency, from 1957; parliamentary sec. to minister justice, 1960-61; min. justice Govt. of Ireland, Dublin, 1961-64, min. agr., 1964-66, min. fin., 1966-70, min. health & social welfare, 1977-79, prime min., 1979-81, 82, 1987—92; chmn. Irish Parliamentary com. on EEC, 1973-77; pres. European Coun., Lan-Lane, 1990. Leader opposition party, 1981-82, 82-87; pres. Fianna Fail Party Fellow Inst. Chartered Accts. Ireland; mem. Royal Hibernian Acad. Arts (hon.). Clubs: St. Stephens Green, Ward Union Hunt. Died June 13, 2006.

HAUSER, TED HENRY, cameraman; b. N.Y.C., May 27, 1933; s. Benjamin and Claire Gertrude (Zucker) H.; m. Sheila Ava Alpert, Aug. 12, 1956.; 1 child, Bryan. Student, City Coll., 1956-58, Sch. Radio and TV, N.Y.C., 1959. First asst. cameraman Internat. Photographers Motion Picture Industries, Local 644, N.Y.C., from 1962, Internat. Photographers Guild, Local 659, Calif., from 1985. Served with USN, 1952-55. Democrat. Jewish. Avocations: motion pictures, video. Home: Van Nuys, Calif. Died June 8, 2005.

HAVAS, HELGA FRANCIS, microbiologist, immunologist; b. Vienna, Nov. 26, 1915; came to U.S., 1940; m. Peter Havas, 1939; children: Eva Catherin, Stephen Walter. MA, Columbia U., 1943; PhD, Lehigh U., 1950. Rsch. chemist Cornell U., Ithaca, N.Y., 1945-46; rsch. fellow Lehigh U., Bethlehem, Pa., 1947-50; rsch. assoc. Inst. Cancer Rsch., Phila., 1950-63; assoc. prof. dept. microbiology Temple U. Sch. Medicine, Phila., 1963-72, prof. dept. microbiology, 1972-84, prof. emeritus, 1984—2004. Internat. Student Svc. fellow Lyon (France) U., 1938-39: Abbott Labs fellow Columbia U., N.Y.C., 1940-41; Katherine Comstock Thorne fellow Lehigh U., 1947-50; spl. fellow USPHS, Temple U. Sch. Medicine, Phila., 1964-66; recipient Career Devel. award USPHS-NIH, 1967-71. Mem. Am. Assn. for Cancer Rsch., Am. Soc. Microbiology, Am. Assn. Immunologists, Sigma Xi. Home: Jenkintown, Pa. Died Aug. 26, 2004.

HAWLEY, JAMES F., mathematics educator; b. Ft. Scott, Kans., July 6, 1938; s. F. Hale and K. Marie (Sanderson) H.; m. M. Marie Brillhart; children: Ryan, Barbara, David. BA, Pittsburg (Kans.) State U., 1960, MA, 1961; PhD, U. Iowa, 1979. Instr. math. Pittsburg State U., 1961-62, U. Mo., Columbia, 1962-63; asst. prof. math. Kans. Wesleyan U., Salina, 1963-64; asst. prof., assoc. prof., now prof. math. Graceland Coll., Lamoni, Iowa, from 1964, coord. academic computing, from 1965, prof., from 1980. Pastor Reorganized Ch. of Jesus Christ LDS Ch. Mem. Iowa Coun. Tchrs. Math., Am. Statis. Assn. Avocation: farming. Home: Lamoni, Iowa. Died Oct. 1, 2004.

HAWLEY, MONES EDGAR, physicist; b. Casper, Wyo., June 14, 1923; s. Edgar Emmett and Brenda (Anderson) H.; m. Natalie Anne Farone, Dec. 22, 1945 (div. 1980); children: Nathan, Mark, Nancy, Monica, Matthew; m. Eunice Ann Gould, Sept. 20, 1980. BS in Physics, U. Rochester, 1947, MS, 1948. Jr. physicist Stromberg-Carlson Co., Rochester, N.Y., 1947-48; engr. Radio Corp. Am., Camden, N.J., 1948-55, engring. mgr. Moorestown, N.J., 1955-62; gen. mgr., dir. rsch. Planning Rsch. Corp., Washington, 1962-73; v.p. Profl. Svcs. Internat., L.A., Washington, 1973-77; exec. v.p. Jack Faucett Assocs., Bethesda, Md., from 1977. Cons. in acoustics, Moorestown, Washington, 1955—. Author: The Coal Industry in America, 1985; editor: Coal: Social, Economic, Environmental Aspects, 1977, Coal: Scientific and Technical Aspects, 1978; chair, prin. author (Am. Nat. Standard) Measurement of the Intelligibility; editor: Speech Intelligibility and Speaker Recognition, 1989. Active zoning bd., Moorestown, 1960-62; fellow Corcoran Gallery Art, Textile Mus.; founder Folger Shakespeare Libr., gov., 1967-70; active Walters Gallery Art, Balt. Mus. Art. Tech. sgt. USAAF, 1942-45. Fellow Acoustical Soc. Am.; mem. Octagon Soc. Am Archtl. Found., IEEE (life sr.), Nat. Acad. Sci. Com. on Hearing and Broacoustics (emeritus). Achievements include patents for noise-cancelling headset, active ear defender, third-order pressure gradient microphone, universal stage microphone, directional microphone, indirect panel lighting system, envelope threader, magnetothermal microphone, sequential testing of analysis of variance, noise shield, and microphone implant. Home: Washington, DC. Died June 5, 2004.

HAWORTH, CHARLES RAY, lawyer; b. Little Rock, June 23, 1943; s. Clarence Frederick and Vinita Leona (Bowers) H.; m. Nancy Anne Patterson, Aug. 16, 1970; 1 child, Alan. BA, U. Tex., 1965, JD, 1967. Bar: Tex. 1967, U.S. Dist. Ct. (no. dist.) Tex. 1968, U.S. Dist. Ct. (we. and so. dists.) Tex. 1988, U.S. Dist. Ct. (ea. dist.) Tex. 1989, U.S. Ct. Appeals (5th cir.) 1968, U.S. Ct. Appeals (11th cir.) 1982, U.S. Supreme Ct. 1971; bd. cert. civil trial law Tex. Bd. Legal Specialization. Law clk. U.S. Ct. Appeals (5th cir.), Houston, 1967-68; assoc. Coke & Coke, Dallas, 1968-71; prof. law Washington U. Sch. Law, St. Louis, 1971-79; ptnr. Johnson & Gibbs, Dallas, 1979-85, Andrews & Kurth, Dallas, 1985-92; mng. ptnr. Scott, Douglass, Luton & McConnico, L.L.P., Dallas, 1992-95; ptnr. Owens, Clary & Aiken, L.L.P., Dallas, 1995—2006. Vis. prof. U. Va. Sch. Law, Charlottesville, 1975-76, U. Tex. Sch. Law, Austin, 1977; cons. Dept. Justice, Washington, 1978. Editor: Congress and the Courts, 1977; contbr. numerous articles to profl. jours. Bd. dirs. Dallas Opera, 1991—2000. Grantee Dept. of Justice, 1978; named Tex. Super Lawyer Tex. Monthly, 2003, 04, 05. Mem.: Dallas Bar Assn. (chair bus. litigation sect. 2002), Tex. Bar Assn. Republican. Avocation: fishing. Home: Dallas, Tex. Died Nov. 22, 2005.

HAYDEN, JAMES WALWORTH, emergency physician, director; b. Gardner, Ma., Apr. 25, 1942; s. Robert Hawley and Dorothea Wallace (Ward) H.; m. Lauren Shanks, Dec. 10, 1982; children: David Ward, Mark Stevenson. BS in Chemistry, U. N.C., 1963; PhD in Organic Chemistry, U. Kans., 1968; MD, U. Tex., Houston, 1977. Bd. cert. Am. Bd. Forensic Examiners, Am. Bd. Med. Examiners; cert. Am. Assn. Med. Rev. Officers, Am. Soc. Addiction Medicine; cert. ACLS provider and instr., advanced trauma life support provider, BLS instr., pediat. advanced life support provider. Rsch. chemist Shell Devel. Co., Emeryville Rsch. Ctr., Houston, 1968-72; asst. to the dir. Inst. Clin. Toxicology, Houston, 1973-75; sr. rsch. assoc. U. Tex. Med. Sch., Houston, 1975-76; intern and resident Baylor Coll. Medicine, Houston, 1977-78; program physician Inst. Clin. Toxicology Ctrl. Methadone Clinic, Houston, 1978-79, med. dir., 1979-80; emergency dept. physician Gulf Coast Emergency Physicians, St. Luke's Episcopal Hosp., Houston, 1978-79, Houston Emergency Physicians Assocs., Meml. Hosp. Sys., Houston, 1979-80; med. dir. Chem. Dependence Assocs. and Huntsville (Tex.) Clinic, Houston, 1980-87; emergency dept. physician S.E. Tex. Emergency Physicians, West Houston Med. Ctr., 1986-87, Newport (Wash.) Cmty. Hosp., 1989-90; exec. dir. Chem. Dependence Assocs., Priest River, Idaho, from 1987; emergency dept. physician Emergency Physician Svcs., Holy Family Hosp., Spokane, Wash., from 1989; assoc. med. dir., med. rev. officer Cascade Transp. Svcs., Spokane, from 1994. Adj. instr. dept. pharmacology U. Tex. Med. Sch., Houston, 1973-77, adj. asst. prof. dept. pharmacology, 1981-88, clin. instr. family practice and cmty. medicine, 1981-88; presenter in field. Contbr. articles to profl. jours. Fellow Am. Acad. Family Physicians; mem. Am. Coll. Emergency Physicians, Assn. Emergency Physicians, Am. Soc. Addiction Medicine, Am. Assn. Med. Rev. Officers, Tex. Med. Assn., Idaho Med. Assn., Bonner County Med. Soc., Wilderness Med. Soc. Home: Priest River, Idaho. Died July 29, 2005.

HAYES, JOSEPH ARNOLD, author; b. Indpls., Aug. 2, 1918; s. Harold J. and Pearl (Arnold) H.; m. Marrijane Johnston, Feb. 18, 1938 (dec. 1991); children: Gregory J., Jason H., Daniel D.; m. Pauline Knox, Jan. 2, 1994. Student, Ind. U., 1941, D.H.L., 1970. Free-lance writer, from 1943. Asst. editor: Samuel French Plays, 1941-43; co-producer, dir.: (play) The Happiest Millionaire, 1956; author: (plays) Leaf and Bough, 1949, The Midnight Sun, 1959, Calculated Risk, 1962, Impolite Comedy, 1976, Come Into My Parlor, 1987, (book, play and motion picture) The Desperate Hours, 1954 (Lit. Guild, Readers Digest book clubs selection, 2 Antoinette Perry awards 1954-55), (novels) The Hours After Midnight, 1959, Bon Voyage, 1956, Don't Go Away Mad, 1963, The Third Day, 1964, The Deep End, 1967, Like Any Other Fugitive, 1971, The Long Dark Night, 1974, Missing and Presumed Dead, 1977, Island on Fire, 1979, Winner's Circle, 1980, No Escape, 1982, The Ways of Darkness, 1985, Act of Rage, 1989; also numerous screenplays, (with 1st wife) 18 plays; author: (play) Come Into My Parlor, 1986; contbr. short stories to nat. mags. Home: Sarasota, Fla. Died Sept. 11, 2006.

HAYES, RICHARD ALVIN, public school administrator; b. Cherokee, Okla., Aug. 8, 1948; s. Leonard Steffen and Winifred Cleo (McVay) H.; m. Patricia Cecilia Koetting, Dec. 27, 1978; children: Claire, Deirdre, Martha, Richard, Bunny, Robert. BA in Edn., N.W. Okla. State U., 1970; MS in Edn., Ft. Hays State U., 1985. Tchr., coach Newkirk (Okla.) Pub. Schs., 1970-71, Hominy (Okla.) Pub. Schs., 1971-74, Tyrone (Okla.) Pub. Schs., 1974-76, Mankato (Kans.) Unified Sch. Dist. # 278, 1976-78, Carmen (Okla.) Dacoma Pub. Schs., 1978-81; dist. mgr. Auto Club of Am., Oklahoma City, 1981-84; tchr., coach Fargo (Okla.) Pub. Schs., 1984-85; prin., coach Unified Sch. Dist. 455 - Hillcrest Schs., Cuba, Kans., 1985-87; prin. Unified Sch. Dist. 358 - Oxford (Kans.) Schs., from 1987. All-Star Coach 8-Man Coaches Assn./Football, Alva, Okla., 1978, N.W. Coaches Assn./Basketball, 1981; All-League Coach, Orient Conf. Coaches/Basketball, 1981. Mem. United Sch. Adminstrs., Nat. Assn. Second. Sch. Prins., Kans. Assn. Secondary Sch. Prins., Kans. 8-Man Coaches Assn. (treas. 1987), Coaches Assn. (pres. 1978-81, other offices). Democrat. Roman Catholic. Avocations: golf, farming, children's activities. Home: Oxford, Kans. Died Nov. 30, 2004.

HAYNES, JAMES EDWARD, philosopher, educator, computer scientist; b. Washington, Apr. 4, 1943; s. Harry Willard and Olverta Agnes (Humphries) H.; m. Julia Florence Moody, Aug. 31, 1963 (div. 1974); 1 child, Irene Ella. BA, Gallaudet U., 1977; MA, Md. U., 1983, postgrad., from 1988. Tech.writer eastern adminstrv. dir. U.S. Dept. Agr., Hyattsville, Md., 1963-68, computer programmer Beltsville, Md., 1968-74, Gallaudet U., Washington, 1974-83, sr. computer programmer, 1983-89, asst. prof. philosophy, from 1989. Mem. AAUP, Am. Philos. Assn., Royal Inst. Philosophy, Spl. Interest Group on Artificial Intelligence, Digial Equipment Corp. Users Soc. Home: Bowie, Md. Died Dec. 13, 2004.

HAYS, CONSTANCE L., reporter; b. NYC, Apr. 8, 1961; d. John Laibe and Ann (Davis); m. John Hays, 1986. BA in Asian studies, Harvard U., 1983. Food and beverage reporter NY Times. Author: The Real Thing: Truth and Power at the Coca-Cola Company, 2004. Died Dec. 4, 2005.

HAYTON, RICHARD NEIL, retired military officer, writer, publisher; b. Pine Bluff, Ark., Nov. 25, 1916; s. Richard Raymond and Ruth Naomi (Owens) H.; m. Virginia Ann Ridenour, Apr. 18, 1943 (dec. July 1994); children: Richard Neil Jr., Stephen Brian; m. Bertha Tellez, May 10, 1996; 1 child, Louann Vinci. BS, U. Md., 1955; MA in Govt., George Washington U., 1956. Commd. 2d lt. USAF, 1942, advanced through grades to maj. Fla., from 1960, ret., 1960; freelance writer, pub. Fla., from 1960. Author: (pen name Thomas Starling) The King and the Cat, 1975, The Garlic Kid, 1978, Jethrow's Cabin, 1982, Peter Paladine of the Great Heart, 1995. Avocations: publishing, writing, travel, computers. Home: Rockledge, Fla. Died Oct. 1, 2004.

HAYZLETT, ROBERT RALPH, publishing company executive; b. Loup City, Nebr., Mar. 22, 1921; s. Gilbert Warren and Maude Viola (Johnson) H.; m. Glendelle Mary Jaedike, Oct. 12, 1945; children: Robert Glen, Mark Randal. Student, Pasadena (Calif. City Coll., 1947-49; B in Engring., U. So. Calif., 1951, MBA, 1965. Engr. Navaho Missile Project North Am. Aviation Inc., L.A., 1951-53; asst. prodn. mgr. Union-Tribune Pub. Co., San Diego, 1953-56; chief indsl. engr. rsch. inst. Am. Newspaper Pubs. Assn., Easton, Pa., 1956-57; prodn. mgr. News & Courier and Evening Post Pub. Co., Charleston, S.C., 1957-59, Savannah (Ga.) News-Press, Inc., 1959-60; bus. mgr. Los Angeles Evening Herald-Express, L.A., 1960-61; prodn. mgr. Sam Fernando Valley Times Co., North Hollywood, Calif., from 1961. Sec.-treas., gen. mgr. K and B Nameplate Mfg. Inc., L.A., 1963—; corp. indsl engr. Continental Graphics Inc., 1967—; ops. dir. Beacon News, Copley Press Inc., Aurora, Ill., 1971-75; gen. mgr. Daily Tribune, Royal Oak, Mich., 1975—; cons., lectr. printing processes. Contbr. articles to profl. jours. Maj. USAAF, 1942-45; lt. col. res. Decorated Disting. Flying Cross. Mem. Los Angeles C. of C., Am. Inst. Indsl. Engrs., Alumni Assn. U. So. Calif., Deauville Country Club. Died Apr. 26, 2004.

HAZELKORN, HERBERT MARKUS, dentist, public health educator; b. N.Y.C., Mar. 14, 1924; s. Joseph and Sadie (Messing) H.; m. Ila Augenlicht, Dec. 20, 1947 (dec. June 1974); children: Ellen Sue, Bruce Jay; m. Barbara Lois Markus (dec.), June 22, 1975. BS in Chemistry, U. Ill., Urbana, 1943; BS in Dentistry, U. Ill., Chgo., 1947, DDS, 1949, MSPH, 1984, PhD, 1989. Lic. dentist, Ill. Rsch. chemist Ill. Geol. Survey, Urbana, 1943-45; gen. practice dentistry Chgo., 1949-53, suburban Chgo., 1955-84; asst. prof. dentistry U. Ill., Chgo., 1951-72, instr. pub. health, 1985-89, assoc. prof. pub. health, 1989-2001, assoc. prof. emeritus, 2001—04. Chmn. bd. Chicagoans Against the Anti-ballistic Missile, 1967, Alliance to End Repression, Chgo. 1970-72; bd. dirs. Ams. for Dem. Action, Washington, 1978-2004. Served to lt. USN, 1953-55. Mem. ADA, Chgo. Dental Soc., Am. Pub. Health Assn., Ill. Pub. Health Assn., Sigma Xi, Delta Omega. Avocations: carpentry, bicycling. Home: Glencoe, Ill. Died Dec. 7, 2004.

HAZEN, ELIZABETH FRANCES, retired special education educator; b. Lamar, Colo., May 27, 1925; d. Otis Garfield and Cora B. (Baker) McDowell; children: H. Ray, Bobby D., Anita K. Iezza, Gloria G. Gill. AA, Lamar Jr. Coll., 1946; BS in Edn., Southwestern Okla. U., 1967, MS in Edn., 1969; postgrad., Ea. Ky. U., 1983. Cert. speech-hearing therapist, reading specialist, learning and behavior disorders, Ky. Elem. tchr. Granada (Colo.) Sch., 1946-51, South Ctrl. Elem. Sch., Lamar, Colo., 1951-52; lead tchr. Tom Thumb Pre-Sch., Ellsworth AFB, S.D., 1961-62; math. and sci. tchr. Elk City (Okla.) Elem. Sch., 1966-67; beginning speech tchr. Sayer Jr. Coll., Okla., 1967-68; speech and hearing therapist Burns Flat (Okla.) Schs., 1967-69, Maconaqueh Sch. Corp., Bunker Hill, Ind., 1969-72; reading specialist Myers Mid. Sch., Louisville, Ky., 1972-76; tchr. Core Westport Jr. H.S., Louisville, 1977-79, chmn. Core dept., 1978-79; learning disabled resource tchr. Jeffersontown H.S., Louisville, 1979-80, Waggoner Mid. Sch., Louisville, 1980-81, Westport Mid. Sch., Louisville, 1981-94; ret., 1994. Chmn. exceptional children's edn. dept. Westport Mid. Sch., Louisville, 1983-91; speech and hearing therapist Burns Flat (Okla.) Bd. Edn., 1967-69. Bd. dirs. Westport Middle Schs. PTA/Student Assn., 1989-90. Named Outstanding Tchr. of Disadvantaged, State of Okla., 1969. Mem. NEA (ret.), Ky. Mid. Sch. Assn., Ky. Edn. Assn. (ret.), Ky. Ret. Tchrs. Assn., Jefferson County Tchrs. Assn. Died May 8, 2005.

HAZZLEDINE, PETER MEREDITH, metallurgist, consultant; b. Beeston, Notts, Eng., Feb. 13, 1940; came to U.S., 1991; s. Philip Douglas and Lorna (Thomas) H.; m. Marion White, Jan. 6, 1976 (div. Nov., 1993); children: Thomas, Helen; m. Joyce Weaver, Feb. 14, 1994. MA, U. Cambridge, Eng., 1965, PhD, 1966, ScD, 1994. Lectr. Oxford (Eng.) U., 1968-91; prin. scientist UES, Inc. Mem. The Materials Soc., Materials Rsch. Soc. Avocation: woodwork. Home: Yellow Springs, Ohio. Died Jan. 14, 2005.

HEACOX, RUSSEL LOUIS, mechanical engineer; b. Big Timber, Mont., Feb. 7, 1922; s. Charles Lewis and Gladys Ellen (Gibson) H.; m. Jacqueline J. Jewett, Sept. 22, 1944 (dec. 1974); children: William J., Teri Bertoli; m. Ketty Hansine Jorgenson, Dec. 22, 1976; m. Arlene Krause, 1997. BSME, U. Wash., 1950. Registered profl. engr., Calif. Equipment design engr. P & Z Co. Inc., South San Francisco, Calif., 1966-74; owner Heacox Engring. Designs, Tiburon, Calif., from 1974. Capt. USMC, 1943-46, PTO. Mem. NSPE, Crane Certification Assn., Scottish Rite Shrine Assn., Masons. Achievements include patent for Slurry Trench Excavation Bucket and Spotter Assembly, for Diesel Pile Driver Muffler System. Died Feb. 22, 2005.

HEAD, GREGORY ALAN, mechanical engineer, consultant; b. Dallas, Mar. 2, 1955; s. A. Lee and Georgia M. Head. BSME, Brigham Young U., 1981; MS in Engring. Mgmt., U. Alaska, Anchorage, 1988; postgrad., U. Tex., Arlington, 1990-98. Registered profl. engr., Tex. Engr. tech. Hercules Aerospace, Inc., Salt Lake City, 1978-79, LTV Aerospace Inc., Dallas, 1979-80; engr. Hercules Aerospace Inc., Sale Lake City, 1980-82, CMH-Vitro, Anchorage, 1982-84; petroleum engr. Arco Alaska, Anchorage, 1984-87; cons. FAH World Wide Photographers, Anchorage and Dallas, from 1987; sr. v.p. systems divsn. D.C. Systems, Denton, Tex., 1988-94, pres. Sanger, from 1994. Cons. Alaska Mountaineering Assn., Anchorage, 1990—; capt. Arctic Adventurers, 1988-98. Author: Arctic Lands and Uses, 1989. Missionary, Ch. of Jesus Christ of Latter Day Saints, Washington, 1975-77; mem. Mountain Rescue Team, Anchorage, 1989-96; emergency med. technician State of Alaska, 1987-97. Named Photographer of the Yr., FAH Worldwide Photo, Inc., 1990. Mem. ASME, Nat. Geog. Soc., Nat. Assn. Pvt. Enterpreneurs, Am. Soc. Profl. Photographers, Brigham Young U. Football Alumni Assn., Suzuki Moto Cross Team. Republican. Avocations: international expeditionary hiking, mountain/rock climbing, enduro motor bike racing, civic activities, international travel. Home: Sanger, Tex. Died July 3, 2004.

HEADY, FERREL, retired political science educator; b. Ferrelview, Mo., Feb. 14, 1916; s. Chester Ferrel and Loren (Wightman) H.; m. Charlotte Audrey McDougall, Feb. 12, 1942; children— Judith Lillian, Richard Ferrel, Margaret Loren, Thomas McDougall. AB, Washington U., St. Louis, 1937, AM, 1938, PhD, 1940; degree (hon.), Park Coll., 1973, John F. Kennedy U., 1974, U. N.Mex., 1993. Jr. adminstrv. technician, also adminstrv. asst. Office Dir. Personnel, Dept. Agr., 1941-42; vis. lectr. polit. sci. U. Kansas City, 1946; faculty U. Mich., 1946-67, prof. polit. sci., 1957-67; dir. Inst. Pub. Adminstrn., 1960-67; acad. v.p. U. N.Mex., Albuquerque, 1967-68, pres., 1968-75, prof. pub. adminstrn. and polit. sci., 1975-81, prof. emeritus, 1981—2006. Asst. to commr. Com. Orgn. Exec. Br. of Govt., 1947-49; dir., chief adviser Inst. Pub. Adminstrn., U. Philippines, 1953-54; mem. U.S. del. Internat. Congress Adminstrn. Scis., Spain, 1956, 80, Germany, 1959, Austria, 1962, Poland, 1964, Mexico, 1974; exec. bd. Inter-Univ. Case Program, 1956-67; sr. specialist in residence East-West Center, U. Hawaii, 1965; mem. Conf. on Pub. Service, 1965-70; chmn. bd. Assoc. Western Univs., 1970-71; commr. Western Interstate Commn. Higher Edn., 1972-77; mem. commns. on bus. professions and water resources, mem. exec. com. Nat. Assn. State Univs. and Land Grant Colls., 1968-75 Author: Administrative Procedure Legislation in the States, 1952, (with Robert H. Pealy) The Michigan Department of Administration, 1956, (with Sybil L. Stokes) Comparative Public Administration: A Selective Annotated Bibliography, 1960, Papers in Comparative Public Administration, 1962, State Constitutions: The Structure of Administration, 1961, Public Administration: A Comparative Perspective, 1966, rev. edit., 1979, 6th edit., 2001, One Time Around, 1999; contbr. profl. jours. Chmn. state affairs com. Ann Arbor Citizens Coun., Mich., 1949-52; mem. exec. com. Mich. Meml.-Phoenix Project and Inst. Social Rsch., 1960-66; mem. Gov. Mich. Constl. Revision Study Commn., 1960-62; schs. and univs. adv. bd. Citizens Com. for Hoover Report, 1949-52, 54-58; cons. to Ford Found., 1962; chmn. Coun. on Grad. Edn. in Pub. Adminstrn., 1966; mem., vice chmn. N.Mex. Gov.'s Com. on Reorgn. of State Govt., 1967-70; mem. N.Mex. Am. Revolution Bicentennial Commn., 1970-73, N.Mex. Gov.'s Com. on Tech. Excellence, 1969-75, Nat. Acad. Pub. Adminstrn.; mem., vice chmn. N.Mex. Constl. Revision Commn., 1994-95. Served to lt. USNR, 1942-46. Recipient Faculty Disting. Achievement award U. Mich., 1964, N.Mex. Disting. Pub. service award, 1973, award of distinction U. N.Mex. Alumni Assn., 1975, Outstanding Grad. Tchr. award U. N.Mex., 1981-82, Fulbright sr. lectureship, Colombia, 1992, Waldo award for career contbns. to lit. and leadership of pub. adminstrn., 1994. Mem. Am. Polit. Sci. Assn., Am. Soc. Pub. Adminstrn. (pres. 1969-70), AAUP (chmn. com. T 1957-61), Am. Council Edn. (mem. commn. on fed. relations 1969-72), Phi Beta Kappa, Phi Kappa Phi. Presbyterian. Home: Albuquerque, N.Mex. Died Aug. 17, 2006.

HEALEY, MYRON DANIEL, actor; b. Petaluma, Calif., June 8, 1923; s. Robert Daniel and California Myrtle (Penney) H.; m. Dorothy Ann Pemberton, Dec. 26, 1944 (div. June 1949); 1 child, Christine Ann Healey Dickerson; m. Elizabeth Mary D'Errico, Dec. 3, 1966 (div. Sept. 2, 1970); 1 child, Mikel Derrica. U.S. Army Coll. Tng. Cert., East Cen. Tchrs. Coll., 1943. Freelance actor, writer, dialogue dir., drama coach, Hollywood, Calif., N.Y.C., Bombay, Honolulu, Manila, from 1941. Dir. Santa Monica (Calif.) Theater Guild, 1949. Author: (tng. manual) Info. Officers Guide, 1955; screenwriter: Colorado Ambush, 1951, Texas Lawman, 1951. Capt. USAFR, 1943-46, ETO. Decorated Air medal with Cluster; Golden Boot award Motion Picture & Television Fund, 2000 Mem. Screen Actors Guild, AFTRA, Writers Guild of Am. West, Am. Film Inst. Avocations: photography, archtl. design, swimming, cycling, camping. Died Dec. 21, 2005.

HEALEY, ROBERT MATHIEU, theologian, educator; b. N.Y.C., June 1, 1921; s. James Christopher and Catherine (Mathieu) H.; m. Edith Louise Welle, June 20, 1953; children: Christopher Leon (dec.), Paul David. AB, Princeton U., 1942; MFA, Yale U., 1947, BD, 1955, MA, 1956, PhD, 1959. Ordained to ministry Presbyn. Ch. (USA), 1956. Faculty U. Dubuque Theol. Sem., Iowa, from 1956, prof. Am. ch. history Iowa, 1966-74, prof. ch. history Iowa, from 1974, head div. history and theology Iowa, 1968-70, 81-90; interim acad. dean U. Dubuque-Theol. Sem., Iowa, 1970-71, faculty sec. Iowa, 1982-85, 87-90. Vis. prof. U. Paris, 1965-66, Hebrew U. and Hebrew Union Coll., Jerusalem, 1973-74, U. Edinburgh, 1980-81; theologian in residence Am. Ch., Paris, 1965-66; adminstrv. coun. Sch. Theology, Dubuque, 1968-71; coun. theol. edn. United Presbyn. Ch., 1966-69, cons. gen. coun. of gen. assembly, 1972; cons. Am.-Holy Land project Hebrew U., 1973-74; resident scholar Ecumenical Inst. Advanced Theol. Studies, Jerusalem, 1973-74; guest mem. Ecumenical Theol. Rsch. Fraternity, Jerusalem, 1973-74 Author: Jefferson on Religion in Public Education, 1962, The French Achievement: Private School Aid, A Lesson for America, 1974, A Workbook for the History of the Early and Medieval Church from Pentecost to the High Middle Ages, 1988, A Workbook for the Reformation and Modern Church: A Survey of Church History from 1300 to the Present, 1988; contbr. articles to profl. hist. and religious jours. Mem. adv. bd. Dubuque Area Sheltered Workshop, 1971; mem. Handicapped Persons, Inc., 1977—, governing bd., 1977-80; mem. Iowa Gov.'s Com. on Employment of Handicapped, 1978-82, vice chmn., 1978-80 Named Handicapped Iowan, 1977; faculty fellow Am. Assn. Theol. Schs., 1957-58, 65-66, rsch. fellow, 1980-81 Mem. Am. Acad. Religion, Am. Soc. Ch. History, Assn. Theol. Sems. Iowa (bd. dirs. 1967-71, 76—), Assn. Faculty Theol. Edn. Profls. (pres. U. Dubuque chpt. 1973, 75-77, 81-83), Dubuque County Hist. Soc., Presbyn. Hist. Soc., Sixteenth Century Studies Soc. Home: Saint Paul, Minn. Died Apr. 16, 2004.

HEALEY, ROBERT WILLIAM, school system administrator; b. Charleston, Ill., Sept. 29, 1947; s. William Albert and Ruth M. (Wiedenhoeft) H.; m. Sharon Barbara Grande, Aug. 7, 1982; children: William Robert, Steven Anthony. BS in Elem. Edn., Ea. Ill. U., 1970, MS in Ednl. Adminstrn., 1972; EdD in Curriculum and Supervision, No. Ill. U., 1977. Cert. elem. teaching K-9, gen. adminstrv. K-12, Ill. Prin. Glidden Elem. Sch., De Kalb, Ill., 1972-74, Lincoln Elem. Sch., De Kalb, 1974-83, Littlejohn Elem. Sch., De Kalb, 1983-84, Littlejohn and Cortland Elem. Schs., De Kalb, 1984-85; prin., dist. coord. testing and evaluation Jefferson Elem. Sch., De Kalb, 1986-96; dir. personnel DeKalb Sch. Dist., 1996—98, dir. HR, 1999—2001, asst. to supt., 2001—03; interim prin. Brooks Elem. Sch., DeKalb, 2002. Dir. Title I Elem. and Secondary Edn. Act., Pre-Sch. Base Line Program, 1972-74; dir. gifted edn. Bd. Edn. Negotiating Team, 1974-81, coordinator dist. testing and evaluation, 1981-84, coordinator spl. edn., 1984-86; mem. adv. bd. Evanston (Ill.) Educators Computer Software, 1983—; dir. testing DeKalb Sch. Dist. 428, 1986—; treas. No. Ill. Commn. for Gifted Edn., Oakbrook, 1980-82; mem. various elem. sch. planning and program councils, De Kalb, 1973-2003; coordinator numerous sch. programs, De Kalb, 1973-2003; leader numerous workshops DeKalb, 1976-85; sec. De Kalb Sch. Bd. Study com. on sch. lunch programs, 1976-77; cons. Scholastic Testing Service, 1980-83; chmn. dist. reading com., De Kalb, 1986—; mem. bd. edn. collective bargaining team, 2001—. Coordinator 10 yr. study of student achievement in DeKalb Schs., 1980-83;

author numerous presentations, 1975-84; co-author: DeKalb School District Parent Handbook, 1986; contbr. articles to profl. jours; inventor multi-purpose table and stage. Chmn. Task Force I DeKalb Sch. Dist., 1973-75; treas. No. Ill. Planning Commn., 1980-82; active Supts. Task Force on Spl. Edn., DeKalb, 1976-79, Mayor's Commn. DeKalb Planning Commn. for Yr. of Child, DeKalb, 1979, Dist. Computer Com., DeKalb, 1980-83, Dist. Revenue and Donations Com., 1980-83, Ill. PTA. Recipient Disting. Program award Nat. Assn. for Tchr. Educators, Chgo., 1978; named Citizen of Day, Sta. WLBK, De Kalb, 1983; Reading is Fundamental grantee Lincoln Sch., 1980-83, Ill. Ctr., 1980-83, Ill. Arts Coun., Littlejohn Sch., 1984, Jefferson Sch., 1986; named master, Ill. Adminstrs. Acad., 1995. Mem. NEA (life), ASCD, NAESP (Nat. Disting. Prin. award representing Ill. 1995), Ill. Prins. Assn. (Prin. of Yr. award 1995, Herman Graves award 1998), Ill. Assn. for Superv-sion and Curriculum Devel., Soc. Am. Inventors, Ill. Coun. Gifted Edn. Avocations: swimming, computer, home. Home: Dekalb, Ill. Died Oct. 27, 2004.

HEALEY, WILLIAM JOHN, III, electronics company executive; b. Boston, Aug. 19, 1940; s. William John Healey Jr. and Ava Maria deCordova. BA, New Coll., Oxford, England, 1958, MA in lit., 1961. Divisional supr. domestic corp. tax div. 1st Nat. City Bank, N.Y.C., 1962-64; officer, office mgr. packing & friction materials div. Johns Manville Corp., N.Y.C., 1969-72; mgr. Orange Bay Estates, Ltd., Montego Bay, Jamaica, West Indies; chmn. Ascarib Ltd., San Francisco. Mem. Ridley Coll. Debating Team, Can. Serve dwith Royal Reserve Corps, Can. Mem. Royal Hist. Assn. Clubs: Hanover Polo (Jamaica). Republican. Roman Catholic. Home: Montego Bay, Jamaica. Died June 6, 2004.

HEALY, ROBERT DANFORTH, manufacturing executive; b. Northhampton, Mass., Apr. 17, 1939; s. Frederick Clark and Myrtle Frances (Clark) H.; m. Mary Jane Guilcher, Apr. 22, 1978. Machinist Pratt and Whitney Aircraft, E. Hartford, Conn., 1963-67; plant mgr. Ridge Tool Co., Cromwell, Conn., 1967-71; owner CVS Industries, Chesterfield, Mass., 1971-73; v.p., ptnr. Quabbin Industries Inc., Chicopee, Mass., 1972-92; pres. Seth Alden Healy's Sons, Inc., Williamsburg, Mass., from 1992. Ptnr. Indsl. Airpark Assn., Chicopee, 1981—, Am. Gravure Engraving, Holyoke, Mass., 1985-91, Pro-Mac Engring. Inc., Chicopee, 1987-92, Quabbin Internat. Inc., Richmond, Calif., 1987-92; dir. Tubbs Showshoe Co., Stowe, Vt. Mem. ASME. Republican. Died June 29, 2004.

HEALY, WILLIAM PAUL, lawyer, business consultant; b. Chgo., Feb. 3, 1916; s. Earl Thompson and Nora Helen (O'Connor) H.; m. Miriam Louise Streed, June 12, 1948; children: Susan Ruth, Elizabeth Healy Phipps. Student, Loyola U., Chgo., 1936-39; JD, John Marshall Law Sch., Chgo., 1942; postgrad., Ill. Inst. Tech., 1942-44. Bar: Ill. 1942. Assoc. dir. Borg-Warner Rsch. Ctr., Des Plaines, Ill., 1956-61; dir. spl. projects Litton Industries, Inc., Beverly Hills, Calif., 1961-66; v.p. Gulton Industries, Inc., Metuchen, N.J., 1966-68; pres., CEO Microtenna Corp., Coral Gables, Fla., 1968-70; sr. v.p., COO Columbia Gen. Corp., Chgo., 1970-72; dir. Coral Ridge Properties, Inc., Coral Springs, Fla., 1972-75; ptnr. Record, Healy, Finney & Jankowicz, Decatur, Ill., 1975-85; chmn., CEO Aloe Creue Cosmetics, Inc., 1976-80; regional dir. small bus. Fla. Internat. U., Dania, from 1985; prin. MHK Assocs., Coral Springs, from 1992; of counsel Lewis & White, Attys. at Law, Tallahassee, Fla., from 1995. Cons. Katy Industries, Inc., 1968-84, CRL, Inc., Des Plaines, 1978-91, Internat. Diagnostics, Ltd., Plantation, Fla., 1987—. Judge Miami (Fla.)-Herald Small Bus. Awards, 1990, 91, Blue Chip Enterprise Initiative, Hartford, Conn., 1992, 93, 94, 95. With U.S. Army, 1943-46. Recipient cert. and plaque Ft. Lauderdale (Fla.) Coll., 1986, cert. Broward County Housing Authority, Ft. Lauderdale, 1991. Mem. Chgo. Bar Assn., Fla. C. of C. (mem. econ. affairs com. 1992, 93, other coms.), Broward Econ. Devel. Coun. (bd. dirs. 1996—). Avocations: community service, travel, reading. Home: Fort Lauderdale, Fla. Died Feb. 28, 2005.

HEARST, JAMES ELDON, compensation consultant; b. Toronto, Ont., Can., June 2, 1930; s. John Eldon and Beatrice Margaret (Way) H.; m. Mary Carol Dressel, Aug. 7, 1953 (div. 1969); children: John Eric, Caryl Lee; m. Betty Ann Robinson Arbaugh, May 27, 1972; 1 stepchild, Randolph Bradford Arbaugh. BA, Albion Coll., 1953. Salary analyst Chrysler Corp., Detroit, 1957-60; compensation analyst, then labor rels. rep. Brunswick Corp., Chgo., 1960-65; mgr. indsl. rels. Owens Yacht Co., Balt., 1966-69; personnel mgr. Rixon Electronics, Silver Spring, Md., 1969-71, Arundel Corp., Balt., 1972-74; compensation cons. Comml. Credit Corp., Balt., 1974-75; mgr. compensation, benefits Blue Cross/Blue Shield, Balt., 1975-78, Dillingham Corp., Honolulu, 1979-84, Hawaiian Electric, Honolulu, 1984-86; asst. v.p., mgr. compensation and benefits Bank of Hawaii, Honolulu, 1986-89. Speaker in field. Chmn. personnel mgmt., Hawaii chpt. Am.Heart Assn., 1986—, Vol. Info. and Referral Svcs., Honolulu, 1986—. Mem. Am. Compensation Assn., Elks. Died Feb. 12, 2004.

HEARTHWAY, MARY ANN, occupational health nurse; b. Snow Hill, Md., Jan. 14, 1948; d. Lester Vincent and Mildred Ellen (Shockley) Hearthway; 1 child, Jonathan Vincent Johnson. AA, St. Mary's Coll. of Md., 1968; BSN, W.Va. Wesleyan Coll., 1971. Cert. occupl. health nurse. Staff nurse surg. St. Joseph's Hosp., Towson, Md., 1971-73, staff nurse ICU-CCU Lancaster, Pa., 1973-75; staff nurse pediatric ICU I'I DuPont Inst., Wilmington, Del., 1975-77; clin. instr. Salisbury (Md.) State Coll., 1977-80; staff nurse surg. ICU-CCU Peninsula Gen. Hosp., Salisbury, 1977-80; DON Hartley Hall Nursing Home, Pocomoke City, Md., 1980-86; occupl. health nurse Perdue Farms, Inc., Salisbury, from 1986. Mem. Md. Seneca Valley Assn. Occupl. Health Nurses, Soroptomist (sec.-treas., bd. dirs.). Methodist. Avocations: reading, travel, gardening. Home: Salisbury, Md. Died Nov. 1, 2004.

HEATH, JOHN CHARLES, lawyer; b. Louisville, Ga., Oct. 12, 1947; s. William E. and Cornelia (Ledbetter) H.; m. Beverly M. Wright, June 21, 1975; children: Andrew John, Ryan Scott. AB in Econs., Ga. State U., 1970; JD, Emory U., 1975. Bar: Ga. 1975, Tenn. 1983, U.S. Dist. Ct. (no. dist.) Ga. 1975, U.S. Dist. Ct. (mid. and so. dists.) Ga. 1976, U.S. Dist. Ct. (mid. dist.) Tenn. 1983, U.S. Dist. Ct. (ea. dist.) Tenn. 1987, U.S. Supreme Ct. 1979. Assoc. Herbert Shafer, Atlanta, 1975-76, Lazarus & Stokes, Atlanta, 1977-78; sole practice Atlanta, 1978-80, Celina, Tenn., 1984-90, Livingston, Tenn., from 1990; ptnr. Jonap & Heath, Atlanta, 1980-83; assoc. York & York, Celina, 1983-84. Judge City of Celina, 1985-88, City of Livingston, 1994—. Cub master Cub Scouts Boy Scouts Am., Celina coun., 1985-90; chmn. Clay County Parks and Recreation Bd., Celina, 1987-90; elder Christian Ch., 1997—. Mem. Upper Cumberland Trial Lawyers Assn. (pres. 1996-97), Lions (pres. Livingston club 1997—). Democrat. Home: Livingston, Tenn. Died Jan. 17, 2005.

HEBERT, CAROL ANNE, foundation director; b. Greenville, S.C., Sept. 6, 1946; d. Calvin Edward and Margaret Anne (Rowland) Kennedy; m. James R. Harley, Aug. 26, 1973 (div. May 1982); children: Padraic, Zobeida; m. Cyril W. Hebert, Dec. 10, 1983. BBA, Western Internat. U., 1985, MBA, 1986. Dir. program ops. Ariz. Recovery Ctrs. Assn., Phoenix, 1976-78; regional dir. Women in Community Service, Dallas, 1978-81; exec. dir. Ariz. Women's Employment Edn., Phoenix, 1982-86, Crime Victim Found., Phoenix, from 1987. Cons. Ctr. for Non-Profit Devel., Dallas, 1978-81, Maricopa Pvt. Industry Council, Phoenix, 1986—; chair steering com. Women of Achievement, Phoenix, 1986. Author: The Bottom Line. Mem. task forces on welfare to work, women and poverty State of Ariz., Phoenix, 1985-86, task force on women, welfare, and work U.S. Dept. Labor, San Francisco, 1985-86; chairperson mayor's task force on self-sufficiency, Phoenix, 1985—; bd. dirs. Ariz. Women's Town Hall, Phoenix, 1987—. Named one of Women Who Care Gov. of Ariz., 1985. Mem. Nat. Orgn. for Victim Assistance, nat. Soc. Fund Raising, Execs., Wider Opportunities for Women (coordinator Ariz. chpt. 1985-86). Democrat. Home: Phoenix, Ariz. Died Dec. 1, 2004.

HECHT, CHIC, ambassador, former senator; b. Cape Giradeau, Mo., Nov. 30, 1928; m. Gail Hecht; children: Lori, Leslie. BS, Washington U., St. Louis, 1949; postgrad., Mil. Intelligence Sch., Ft. Holibird, Mo., 1951. Mem. Nev. State Senate, 1966-74, Rep. minority leader, 1968-72; U.S. Senator from Nev., 1982-89; mem. Banking, Housing and Urban Affairs Com.; chmn. housing and urban affairs subcom.; mem. Energy and Natural Resources Com.; mem. Senate Select Com. on Intelligence; US amb. to The Bahamas US Dept. State, Kingston, 1989-93. Served with U.S. Army, 1951-53. Mem. Nat. Counter Intelligence Corps. (past pres.), Nat. Mil. Intelligence Assn. Home: Las Vegas, Nev. Died May 15, 2006.

HECK, ALBERT, JR., broadcasting executive; b. Wilkes-Barre, Pa., Jan. 25, 1927; s. Albert and Ethel (Wilcox) Gould; m. Jane M. Heck, Dec. 1975; children: Bruce Craig, Scott. Grad. high sch., Asbury Park, N.J. Mgr. Walter Reade Theatres, Asbury Park; promotion mgr. Asbury Park Press; sales mgr. House Beautiful Mag., N.Y.C.; N.Y. sales mgr. Look Mag., N.Y.C.; dist. sales NBC Radio Network, N.Y.C.; v.p. mktg. sales Radio Advt. Bur., N.Y.C.; pres. Radio Network Assn., N.Y.C. Avocations: sailing, photography, painting. Died Mar. 30, 2005.

HECK, RICHARD T., tree farmer; b. Madison, Ind., Sept. 16, 1924; s. Richard Charles and Virginia (Tevis) H.; m. Ruth Irwin Heck, June 27, 1948; children: Richard Gregory, Rebecca Jeanne. Student, Admiral Farragut Naval Acad., Pine Beach, N.J., 1942-43, Hanover Coll, 1947-48. Tree farmer, Hanover, Ind., from 1943. Vol. firefighter, 1946—; mem. arson investigation team Jefferson County, Ind., 1983-90, Hanover Twp. Vol. Fire Co., 1956—; trustee Hanover Coll., 1991-2000. With USN, 1944-54, WWII, Korea. Named to Hon. Order of Ky. Cols., 1971, Sagamore of Wabash, 1973; named Ind. Outstanding Tree Farmer, Ind. Tree Farm Commn., 1983, Nat. Outstanding Tree Farmer Am. Forest Found., 1984, Good Steward award Nat. Arbor Day Found., 1984, North Ctrl. Region Outstanding Tree Farmer, 1984, Ind. Conservationist of Yr., Ind. Dept. Natural Resources, 1985, Forest Conservationist of the Yr. Ind. Wildlife Fedn., 1987. Mem. Soc. Am. Foresters (hon.), Nat. Forestry Assn. (life), Ind. Foresty and Woodland Owners Assn. (bd. dirs. 1984-95, Ind. state tree farm com. 1984—), NRA (life), Ind. Vol. Firemans Assn. (life), Nat. Muzzle Loading Rifle Assn. (life), Internat. Assn. Arson Investigators, Inc., Nat. Eagle Scout Assn., Soc. Ind. Pioneers, Am. Legion, Wahpanipe Muzzle Loading Rifle Club, Connor Prairie Rifles Club, Masons, Elks. Republican. Presbyterian. Avocations: hunting, fishing, hiking, collecting indian artifacts, competitive muzzle loading shooting. Died Sept. 6, 2005.

HECKENKAMP, ROBERT GLENN, lawyer; b. Quincy, Ill., June 29, 1923; s. Joseph Edward and Ethel E. (Requet) H.; m. Jean E. Duker, June 22, 1946 (dec. 1983); children: Gae Kelly, Joy Heckenkamp-Roate; m. Wilma E. Dobbs, Nov. 15, 1985. BS, Quincy Coll., 1947; JD, DePaul U., 1949. Bar: Ill. 1949, U.S. Dist. Ct. (cen. and so. dists.) Ill. 1949, U.S. Ct. Appeals (7th cir.) 1952, U.S. Supreme Ct. 1965. Sr. ptnr. Heckenkamp, Simhauser & Zerkle, Springfield, Ill. Fellow Am. Coll. Trial Lawyers (com. chmn. 1983-86), Internat. Acad. Trial Lawyers; mem. ATLA, ABA, Ill. State Bar Assn. (pres. 1980-81), Sangamon County Bar Assn., Ill. Trial Lawyers Assn. (pres. 1977-78). Soc. Trial Lawyers. Avocations: hunting, fishing. Home: Springfield, Ill. Died June 11, 2005.

HECKER, HENRY C., audiologist; b. Szeged, Hungary, Jan. 9, 1934; came to U.S. 1957; s. Henrik and Margaret (Baade) H.; m. Ruth Rutherford, Aug. 20, 1962; children: Janene, Eric B. BA in Molecular Biology, U. Utah, 1965, MA in Audiology, 1968. Staff audiologist Baylor Coll. Medicine, Houston, 1968-70; chief audiologist Riverside Hosp., Newport News, 1970-74; pvt. practice audiology H.E.N.P.A., Inc., Newport News, from 1974; dir. audio/vestibular lab. Mary Immaculate Hosp., Newport News, from 1974; faculty Ea. Va. Med. Sch., Norfolk, from 1973, Med. Coll. Va., Richmond, from 1976. Cons. audiologist VA Hosp., Hampton, Va., 1971-75. Contbr. articles to profl. jours. Vice chmn. Bd. Examiners for Audiology, State of Va., Richmond, 1973-75; pres., bd. dirs. New Beginnings Boys Foster Home, Churchview, 1971-79; bd. dirs. Hed Injury Found. of Va., Newport News, 1989—. With Hungarian Army, 1954-56. Named Audiologist of the Yr., Audiol. Resource Assocs., 1985, DiCarlo award for clin. achievement, ASHA-SHAV, Washington, 1987, Service award, Lions, 1980, Kresge Rsch. Lab. & KAM's Fund award for rsch., 1991. Mem. Am. Speech and Lang. & Hearing Assn., So. Audiol. Soc. (pres. 1985), Audiol. Resource Assn. (pres. 1984), Acad. of Dispensing Audiologists (fellow), Internat. Torch Clubs (pres. 1975-76). Republican. Methodist. Achievements include research in ultrahigh frequency hearing ability and on the feasibility of supersonic hearing capability. Home: Newport News, Va. Died May 12, 2004.

HEDLUND, CHARLES JOHN, oil industry executive, conservationist; b. Appleton, Minn., Nov. 3, 1917; s. William Martin and Sophia Stickney Hedlund; m. Helen Marie Thorstenson, Aug. 30, 1940; children: Susan Louise, Patricia Jo, Ann Elizabeth, Christopher Charles. B Chem. Engring., B Bus. Adminstrn., U. Minn., 1940; LLD (hon.), Am. U., Cairo, 1993. Refinery engr. Std. Oil Co. La., Baton Rouge, 1940-46; with coord. and econs. dept. Std. Oil Co. (N.J.) (now Exxon), N.Y.C., 1947-52; dir. program Petroleum Adminstrn. for Def., Washington, 1952-53; mgr. coord. and econ. dept. Std. Oil Co. (N.J.), NY, 1954-59; exec. v.p. Esso Std. Italia, Genoa, Italy, 1960-61; pres. Svenska Esso AB, Stockholm, 1962-66; v.p. mktg. Esso Europe, London, 1967; v.p. Exxon, pres. Esso Mid. East, NY, 1968-80. Mem. exec. com. Arabian Am. Oil Co., Dhahran, Saudi Arabia, 1968-80; chmn. petroleum working group NATO, Paris, 1952-53. Chmn. Anglo Am. Sch.-Stockholm, 1962-66; trustee The Nature Conservancy, 1978-87(chmn. 1984-85), N.Y. adv. bd. Salvation Army, 1970-80, Am. Mus. Natural History, 1979-89, Conservation Internat., 1987— (founding chmn. 1987-95), Am. U. Cairo, 1976— (chmn. 1980-92). Named to Order of Arts and Scis. 1st Class, Govt. Egypt, 1993. Mem. Baltrusol Golf Club (N.J.), Country Club Fla., Ocean Club Fla. (trustee 1997-99), The Little Club, Century Assn. (N.Y.), Lansdowne Club (London), Tau Beta Pi, Beta Gamma Sigma, Phi Lambda Upsilon. Republican. Episcopalian. Avocations: conservation, education, golf, tennis. Home: Village Of Golf, Fla. Died July 2005.

HEER, CLIFFORD V., physics educator, consultant; b. Archbold, Ohio, May 31, 1920; s. Nelson Veer and Minnie May (Leu) H.; m. Esther Jean Leonard, Dec. 17, 1949; children: Barbara Jean, Deborah Ann, Daniel Nelson. BSc in Physics, Ohio State U., 1942, PhD, 1949. From asst. prof. to assoc. prof. Ohio State U., Columbus, 1949-61, prof., 1961-90, prof. emeritus, from 1990. Cons. in field; cons. Space Tech. Lab., L.A., 1959-64. Author: Statistical Mechanics Kinetic Theory and Stochastic Processes, 1972; contbr. numerous articles to profl. jours. With Signal Corps, U.S. Army, 1942-46. Recipient William A. Fowler award for disting. work in physics, 1990. Fellow Am. Phys. Soc. Republican. Methodist. Avocations: canoeing, hiking. Home: Columbus, Ohio. Died July 8, 2004.

HEFELFINGER, DAVID CHARLES, pediatrician, educator; b. Asbury Park, N.J., Mar. 19, 1938; s. Charles Moses and Claire Josephine Hefelfinger; m. Virginia Mauney, Aug. 25, 1962; children: David C. Jr., Michael Wray, Ashley. BS, U. N.C., 1961, MD, 1965. Diplomate Am. Bd. Pediat. Intern Vanderbilt U. Sch. Medicine, Nashville, 1966-67, resident, 1967-68; chief resident U. Tex. Med. Br., Galveston, 1968; pediatrician Pensacola, Fla., 1971-73; chmn. dept. pediats. Coll. Cmty. Health Scis. U. Ala., Tuscaloosa, from 1973, assoc. dean for clin. affairs, 1978-80. Contbr. more than 30 articles to profl. jours. including Jour. Med. Assn. State Ala., Resident and Staff Physician, Jour. Chronic Disease, Ala. Pediatrician. Maj. comdr. U.S. Army, 1968-71. Recipient Outstanding Commitment to Tchg. award U. Ala. Soc., 1997. Mem. Am. Acad. Pediats. (fed. coord. 1992-95), Med.

Assn. State Ala., Tuscaloosa County Med. Soc., West Ala. Pediat. Soc. (pres. 1984—), Phi Kappa Phi. Avocations: golf, skiing, wine, reading, writing. Home: Tuscaloosa, Ala. Died July 19, 2005.

HEFFERN, CLARA BERNARD, cultural organization administrator; b. Wahpeton, N.D., Aug. 18, 1910; d. Arnold and Gertrude (Schiller) Bernard; m. Marion Cadwell Heffern, June 25, 1935; children: Barbara J., Gertrude A., Nancy C., Mary M., Kathryn S. Student, N.D. State Sch. of Sci., 1926-28; BS, U.N.D., 1930; postgrad., Vassar Coll., 1955, Coll. of Great Falls, 1955-56. Tchr. Fairmount (N.D.) High Sch., 1930-32, Wahpeton (N.D.) High Sch., 1932-35, Ursuline Acad., Great Falls, Mont., 1954-64; dir., curator Cascade County Hist. Mus., Great Falls, 1976-80; interviewer N.W. Ursuline History Found., Great Falls, from 1987. Con. Paris Gibson Sq., Great Falls, 1976-88; bd. dirs. Cascade County Hist. Soc., Coll. of Great Falls Guild. Active Citizen's Involvement Com. Preservation of Hist. Bldg., Great Falls, 1975-76; cons. Great Falls Genealogy Soc., 1976-88. Mem. AAUW, Coll. Great Falls Pres.' Council (fund raising com. 1975-88), Alpha Chi Omega, Ursuline Assn., 20th Century Book Club (pres. 1967-68). Roman Catholic. Avocations: antiques, research, swimming, walking, family history. Home: Helena, Mont. Died Apr. 20, 2005.

HEIL, ROBERTA VICKIE, educational consultant; b. Rockford, Ill., July 4, 1950; d. Roland Earl and Margaret Elaine (White) Palmer; m. William Heil; children: Alicia, Aaron. BA in Psychology, DePauw U., 1972; MS in Edn., U. Kans., 1986, PhD, 1989. Cons. The Computing Sch. House, Stanley, Kans., 1982-89; researcher U. Kans., Lawrence, 1985-88; cons. The Learning Continuum, Stanley, from 1989. Adj. prof. U. Kans., 1989. Died Dec. 19, 2004.

HEILKER, VINCENT DE PAUL, musician, educator; b. Balt., July 17, 1924; s. Clement Augustus and Teresa Odell (Walter) H.; m. Mary Catherine Wood, June 14, 1954; children: Phyllis Ann, Paul Vincent, Karen Roberta. Diploma, The Juilliard Sch. Music, 1951; BS, Columbia U., 1955, MA, 1957. Cert. music edn. tchr. Tchr. music Henry Whitehorn Jr. High Sch., Verona, N.J., 1957-58, Bellmore (N.Y.)-Merrick Cen. High Sch. Dist. 3, 1958-84, Hebrew Acad. of Suffolk, Hauppauge, N.Y., 1984-86. Performer various clubs, U.S., 1940—; performer with Louis Prima, Tony Pastor, Tex Beneke, Jeffrey Wald, 1940-55; arranger of acts for various theaters and shows, 1951-70; pvt. tchr. music, N.Y.C., 1957—; mus. dir., arranger, performer The Huntsmen band, Nassau County, N.Y., 1965-75; mus. dir., arranger Nassau County Dixie Cops, Mineola, N.Y., 1984—. Composer numerous pop songs, 1965-75. Mus. dir. Jerusalem Avenue Jr. High Dance Band, Bellmore, 1958-84. Served as cpl. USAAF, 1945-46. Recipient Lifetime Achievement Membership award N.Y. State Congress Parents and Tchrs., Inc., Bellmore, award of Appreciation Bd. Edn., Supt. Schs. and Bellmore-Merrick Cen. High Sch. Dist. 3, 1958-84. Mem. Am. Fedn. Musicians, Bellmore-Merrick United Sec. Tchrs. (Dedication, Service and Professionalism Community award 1984). Democrat. Roman Catholic. Avocations: travel, camping, walking, bicycling, music. Home: De Lancey, NY. Died Apr. 18, 2005.

HEIMANSON, DORIAN, electrical engineer; b. Riga, Latvia, June 11, 1938; s. Zvulon and Roza (Kitai) H.; m. Ana Kugan, Mar. 26, 1960; children: Zeev, Shelly. Elec. Engr., Polytech. Inst., Riga, 1960; PhD in Solid State Sci., Univ. Moscow, 1971; PhD in Physics, Univ. Tel-Aviv, 1979. Project mgr. Israel Aircraft Industry, 1974-80; prin. engr. Electronic materials Corp., Azusa, Calif., 1981-82; gen. mgr. Nanofilm, Westlake Village, Calif., 1982-85; R&D mgr. Sigmatron Nova, Thousand Oaks, Calif., 1985-91; cons. Thin Film Engring., Woodland Hills, Calif., 1988-91; chief scientist CUC, Rochester, N.Y., from 1991. Patentee in thin film equipment and technology. Home: Foster City, Calif. Died July 28, 2004.

HEINECKEN, ROBERT FRIEDLI, artist, educator; b. Denver, Oct. 29, 1931; s. Friedli Wilhelm and Mathilda Louise (Moehl) H.; m. Janet Marion Storey, Jan. 7, 1955 (div. 1980); children—Geoffrey Robert, Kathé Marie, Karol Leslie. AA, Riverside Coll., 1951; BA, UCLA, 1959, MA, 1960. Vis. faculty Harvard U., 1972, San Francisco Art Inst., 1970, Art Inst. Chgo., 1970, Internat. Museum Photography, Rochester, N.Y., 1967, vis. faculty SUNY, 1969; prof. art UCLA, 1960-90, prof. emeritus, 1990—2006, with oral history program, 1997—2006. One-man shows include Light Gallery, N.Y.C., Witkin Gallery, N.Y.C., Pasadena Art Mus., Focus Gallery, San Francisco, Madison (Wis.) Art Ctr., Friends of Photography Gallery, Carmel, Calif., Internat. Mus. Photography, Foto Forum, Universitat Kassel, Gallery Min, Tokyo, Art Inst. of Chgo.; exhibited in group shows at Mus. Modern Art, N.Y.C., Whitney Mus., N.Y.C., Nat. Gallery Can., Ottawa, Camden Arts Ctr., London; represented in permanent collections Internat. Mus. Photography, Rochester, Mus. Modern Art, N.Y.C., Fogg Art Mus., Cambridge, Mass., San Francisco Mus. Art, Oakland (Calif.) Mus. Art, Libr. of Congress, Washington, Pasadena Mus. Art; represented by Pace/MacGill Gallery, N.Y.C., Archive at Ctr. for Creative Photography, U. Ariz. Trustee Friends of Photography, Carmel, 1974-75. Served with USMCR, 1953-57. Guggenheim fellow, 1975; Nat. Endowment for Arts grantee, 1977, 81, 86. Mem. Soc. for Photog. Edn. (chmn. bd. dirs. 1970-72) Home: Albuquerque, N.Mex. Died May 19, 2006.

HEINEMANN, HEINZ, chemist, educator, researcher, consultant; b. Berlin, Aug. 21, 1913; came to U.S., 1938; s. Felix and Edith (Boehm) H.; m. Elaine Patricia Silverman, Feb. 12, 1948 (dec. Dec. 1993); children: Susan Carol, Peter Michael; m. Barbara A. Tenenbaum, Apr. 23, 1995. Diploma, U. Berlin, 1935; PhD, U. Basel, Switzerland, 1937. Rsch. chemist Danciger Oil & Refineries, Pampa, Tex., 1940-41, Attapulgus Clay Co., Phila., 1941-48; sect. chief Houdry Process Corp., Marcus Hook, Pa., 1948-57; dir. chem. & engring. rsch. M.W. Kellogg Co., N.Y.C., 1957-69; mgr. catalysis rsch. Mobil R & D Corp., Princeton, N.J., 1969-78; disting. scientist Lawrence Berkeley Lab., U. Calif., 1978—2005; lectr. in chem. engring. U. Calif., Berkeley, 1979-90. Pres. Internat. Congress on Catalysis, 1956-60; cons. numerous chem. and petroleum cos., 1978-2005. Editor Catalysis Revs. jour., 1966-86; author 130 publs. on catalysis and fuel chemistry; contbr. 6 chpts. to books, numerous articles to publs. Mem. Flood Control Commn. Princeton Twp., 1970-75, Gov's. Adv. Coun. Rsch., Trenton, N.J., 1976-78; dir. Princeton Art Assn. Recipient Phila. Catalysis Soc. award, 1976, Disting. Scientist award U.S. Dept. Energy, 1978, Homer H. Lowry award U.S. Dept Energy, 1994; Advances in Catalysis Chemistry II symposium held in his honor, Salt Lake City, 1982. Fellow AAAS; mem. Am. Chem. Soc. (Indsl. and Engring. Chem. award 1972, numerous offices), Catalysis Soc. N.Am. (Applied Catalysis award 1975), Nat. Acad. Engring., Internat. Congress Catalysis (pres. 1956-60), Ret. Chemists Group (pres. 2001). Achievements include over 50 patents in field; invention of and participation in commercialization of 16 industrial processes. Home: Washington, DC. Died Nov. 23, 2005.

HEINS, ROBERT WILLIAM, health facility administrator; b. N.Y.C., Jan. 20, 1933; s. Fred August and Clara G. (Johnson) H.; m. Anna Sabatello, Jan. 14, 1956 (div. Nov. 1982); children: Kurt, Tom, Margie, Bill; m. Deanna McCandless, Dec. 1982; stepchildren: Myla, Sara. Patient accounts mgr. Childrens Hosp. of L.A., 1963-67, UCLA Hosp. & Clinics, Westwood, Calif., 1967-69; dir. fin. U. Calif. Hosps. & Clinics, San Francisco, 1969-72; cons. Herman Smith Assocs., Hinsdale, Ill., 1972-73; dir. fin. N.C. Meml. Hosp., Chapel Hill, 1973-74; dir. med. svc. plan U. Mich. Sch. of Medicine, Ann Arbor, 1974-76; exec. dir. med. svc. plan U. N.C. Sch. of Medicine, Chapel Hill, 1976-78; dir. med. svc. plan U. Tex. Health Svcs. Ctr., Dallas, 1978-85; med. sch. cons. Shared Med. Systems, Malvern, Pa., 1985-86; assoc. dean fiscal affairs Tex. Tech. U. Sch. of Medicine Health Svcs. Ctr., Lubbock, 1986-89; adminstr. Laconia (N.H.) Clinic, 1989-90; asst. v.p. bus. affairs Childrens Nat. Med. Ctr., Washington, 1990-91; adminstr. Laconia Clinic, from 1991. Bd. dirs. Lakes Region Mental Health, Inc. Sgt. USMC, 1950-54, Korea. Mem. Med. Group Mgmt. Assn. (chmn. govt. rels. com. 1984-89), Healthcare Fin. Mgmt. Assn., Am. Hosp. Assn., Rotary. Lutheran. Avocation: music. Died Dec. 16, 2004.

HELDRICH, GERARD CHARLES, JR., lawyer; b. Perth Amboy, N.J., Mar. 20, 1933; s. Gerard Charles Sr. and Gertrude L. (Murphy) H.; m. Constance B. Heldrich, Nov. 26, 1955 (div. Nov. 1991); children: Gerard Charles III, Philip J., Michael G., Constance Ann; m. Jenny Heldrich Lee, Dec. 21, 1991; 1 child, Scott J. Czerniejewski. BA, Trinity Coll., Hartford, Conn., 1955; JD, IIT Chgo.-Kent Coll. Law, 1961. Bar: Ill. 1961. Asst. gen. counsel Combined Ins. Co. Am., Chgo., 1961-67; mem. faculty Chgo.-Kent Coll. Law, 1967-70; spl. asst. atty. gen. State of Ill., Chgo., 1970-74; counsel, dir. Heldrich Gutman & Assocs., Chgo., 1967—2005. Bd. dirs. Lincoln Park Savs. Bank, Chgo. Author: Painting of Elmer, 1989. Sec. Northbrook (Ill.) Civic Found., 1980-82. Cpl. USMCR. Recipient Wall St. Jour. Student Achievement award; Trinity Coll. U. Chgo. law scholar. Mem. ABA, ATLA, Ill. State Bar Assn., Chgo. Bar Assn, Fed. Trial Bar (sr. counsel), Delta Phi. Baha'i' Faith Avocations: fishing, golf, inventing, writing. Died Mar. 31, 2005.

HELGESON, DUANE MARCELLUS, retired librarian; b. Rothsay, Minn., July 2, 1930; s. Oscar Herbert and Selma Olivia (Sateren) H. BS, U. Minn., 1952. Libr. Chance-Vought Co., Dallas, 1956-59, Sys. Devel. Corp., Santa Monica, Calif., 1959-62, Lockheed Aircraft, Burbank, Calif., 1962-63, C.F. Braun Co., Alhambra, Calif., 1963-74; chief libr. Ralph M. Parsons Co., Pasadena, Calif., 1974-79; pres. Mark-Allen/Brokers-in-Info., L.A., 1976-80; phys. sci. libr. Calif. Inst. Tech., Pasadena, 1980-84; corp. libr. Montgomery Watson, Pasadena, 1985-94; ret., 1994. Mem. adv. bd. L.A. Trade Tech. Coll., 1974-79, U. So. Calif. Libr. Sch., 1974-79. Editor: (with Joe Ann Clifton) Computers in Library and Information Ctrs., 1973. With USAF, 1952-54. Mem. Spl. Librs. Assn. (chmn. nominating com. 1974). Home: Fergus Falls, Minn. Died Jan. 20, 2005.

HELLER, LAWRENCE AARON, business owner, association executive; b. Pitts., May 24, 1937; s. Joseph and Lillian (Levin) H.; m. Doreen A. Dorsey; children: Jonathan D., Jennifer A. BA, U. Pitts., 1958, MA, 1964, PhD, 1976. Dir. student union U. Pitts., 1963-66; assoc. dean student activities SUNY, Binghamton, 1964-66; dir. student union/activities Oberlin (Ohio) Coll., 1966-72; lectr. U. Pitts., 1973-76; mgmt. exec., dir. edn. Shea Mgmt., Inc., Pitts., 1976-84; exec. dir. Am. Coll. Mental Health Adminstrn., Pitts., from 1989, TechLaw Group, Inc., Pitts., from 1987; exec. v.p. West Pa. Higher Edn. Coun., Pitts., 1986-98; owner Lawrence A. Heller Assocs., Pitts., from 1984. Pres. Fernwold Reproductions Inc., Pitts., 1997—; pres. Atrium Condominium Assn., 1997—; cons. NIR Sys., Silver Spring, Md., 1991; edn. cons. Infac, Indpls., 1981-86; conf. planning cons. Penton Pub., Cleve., 1983-86; conf. coord. Pa. Inst. Behavioral Healthcare, 1994-96; staff support svcs. Healthcare Mgmt. Assn., 1994—; planning cons. Am. Assn. Psychiat. Adminstrs., 1996, Biotech. Med. Mgmt. Assn., 1998—. Pres. Edgewood (Pa.) Found., 1990-94, v.p., 1984-90; founding bd. dirs. Edgewood Symphony Orch., 1988-92, Edgewood Theater Co., 1991-94. Mem. Inst. Assn. Mgmt. Cos., Am. Soc. Assn. Execs., Pitts. Soc. Assn. Execs., SMC/PA Small Bus. Jewish. Avocations: acting, directing, needlecrafts. Home: Pittsburgh, Pa. Died May 3, 2005.

HELMAN, EVE, artist; b. N.Y.C., Jan. 18, 1911; d. Philip and Meta (Belinky) Levitzki; m. Morris J. Helman, Dec. 31, 1935 (dec.); children: David, Ira. BA in Art, Hunter Coll., 1932; MA in Art, Columbia U., 1934. Paintings, collages are included in pvt., pub. collections. Named to Hunter Coll. Alumni Hall of Fame, 1973; recipient Knickerbocker Artists award, 1974. Mem. Nat. Assn. Women Artists (awards chairwoman 1978—, awards 1975, 78, 81, 83, 87, 96-2000, 1st prize 2000), Am. Soc. Contemporary Artists (membership chairwoman 1984—), N.Y. Artists Equity. Avocations: bridge, golf, needlepoint, knitting (original designs). Home: New York, NY. Died Mar. 14, 2005.

HELMER, RICHARD GUY, nuclear physicist; b. Homer, Mich., Feb. 19, 1934; s. Hurshul Guy and Edith Maude (Putnam) H.; m. Mary Joan Scrivens, June 10, 1956; children: Gary Allen, Carl William. BS, U. Mich., 1956, MS, 1957, PhD, 1961. Physicist Phillips Petroleum Co., Idaho Falls, Idaho, 1961-65, Idaho Nuclear Co., Idaho Falls, 1965-70; sr. scientist Aerojet Nuclear Co., Idaho Falls, 1970-76; prin. scientist EG&G Idaho, Idaho Falls, from 1976. Mem. task group on gamma-ray energies Internat. Union Pure and Applied Physics, 1972—; chmn. working group on gamma and beta-ray spectrometry Internat. Commn. on Radionuclide Metrologie, 1985-91. Mem. editorial bd. Nuclear Instruments and Methods Jour., Uppsala, Sweden; author book on gamma-ray spectrometry; contbr. articles to profl. jours. Bd. dirs. Child Devel. Ctr., Idaho Falls, 1968-74, Regional Council Christian Ministry, 1970—; trustee Sch. Dist. 91, Idaho Falls, 1979-85. Fellow Am. Phys. Soc.; mem. AAAS, Am. Nuclear Soc., N.Y. Acad. Scis. Avocations: photography, racquetball, hiking, cross country skiing. Home: Idaho Falls, Idaho. Died Jan. 16, 2005.

HEMMETT, GORDON MELVILLE, lawyer; b. Rochester, N.Y., Aug. 5, 1940; s. Gordon M. and Marion C. (Call) H.; m. Carolyn Miller, Aug. 1963 (div. 1976); children: Edward, Jeffrey, Elizabeth; m. Monica C. Bombard, Aug. 3, 1985. BA, Allegheny Coll., 1962; JD, Syracuse U., 1965. Bar: N.Y. 1965. Assoc. various law firms, Glens Falls, N.Y., 1965-69; claims counsel Glens Falls Ins. Co., 1969-71; pvt. practice Hudson Falls, N.Y., 1971-86; dist. atty. Washington County, Hudson Falls, N.Y., 1982-89; judge Washington County Ct., Salem, N.Y., from 1990. Mem. N.Y. State Bar Assn., Washington County Bar Assn. (v.p. 1989—), Hudson Falls C. of C. (past pres.), Rotary (past pres.). Republican. Avocations: walking, boating, hunting, fishing, bicycling. Home: Hudson Falls, NY. Died Feb. 23, 2004.

HENDREN, LINDA SUE, secondary school educator; b. Bethany, Mo., Aug. 16, 1953; d. Ira I. and Twillia Melseen (Melson) Turner; m. Joel Tenney Hendren, May 25, 1975; children: Julie, Beth. BS in Edn., N.W. Mo. State U., Maryville, 1975, MS in Edn., 1996. Cert. tchr. home econs. and English, Mo. Tchr. home econs. Cainsville (Mo.) R-1 Sch., 1975-80; tchr. English North Harrison R-III Sch., Eagleville, Mo., 1985-97, tchr., tech. coord., from 1997. Chmn. Career Ladder Com., Eagleville, 1993—. Recipient Mo. Incentive grants Mo. Dept. Edn., 1995, 96, Tech. Literacy Challenge grant, 1996, 97. Methodist. Avocations: reading, camping, computers. Home: Bethany, Mo. Died July 7, 2005.

HENICK, NITA HALPERN, retired social worker; b. N.Y.C., Mar. 4, 1925; d. Robert A. and Fanny (Wenick) Halpern; m. William Henick, Sept. 11, 1948; children: Daniel M., Arthur R., Susan L. BA, Queens Coll., CUNY, 1945; student, U. Pa., 1946—48; postgrad., CUNY, 1985. Lic. social worker, N.Y.; cert. social worker. From social worker to social work supr. Coler Meml. Hosp., Roosevelt Island, NY, 1967-90, ret. Co-chair N.Y.C. PACE, 1988-89; bd. dirs. Health Svc. Agy., N.Y.C., 1977-90, chmn. task force on long term care, 1988-90; mem. women's rights groups and environ. conservation groups. Fellow Brookdale Inst. on Aging, N.Y.C., 1985; recipient recognition awards N.Y.C. PACE, 1989. Mem. NASW (pres. N.Y.C. chpt. 1988-90, Recognition award 1990), Acad. Cert. Social Workers (N.Y.C. Coun. citation 1990) Democrat. Jewish. Avocations: travel, reading, walking, lobbying. Home: Long Island City, NY. Died Aug. 14, 2004.

HENNESSY, GERALD THOMPSON, lawyer; b. Boston, May 5, 1913; s. Gerald Joseph and Mary Agatha (Thompson) H.; m. Blanche Louisa Male, Sept. 14, 1947 (dec. Apr. 27, 1991). LLB, Albany Law Sch., 1950. Asst. supr. acctg. Gen. Electric Co., Schenectady, N.Y., 1946-47; spl. agt. OPS, U.S. Govt., Albany, N.Y., 1951-52; pvt. practice Schenectady, from 1952. Lt. Col. U.S. Army, 1941-45, Res., 1945-66, ret. Mem. ABA, N.Y. State Bar Assn., Schenectady County Bar Assn. (pres. 1979-80). Home: Schenectady, NY. Died Feb. 15, 2005.

HENRICSON, BETH ELLEN, microbiologist; b. Johnson City, N.Y., Apr. 22, 1947; d. Clifford Lyle and Margaret Addison (Moore) Hevenor; m. Lawrence Karl Henricson, Aug. 9, 1969; children: Erik Karl, Karen Jeanette. BS in Microbiology, Pa. State U., 1969; postgrad., U. Rochester, 1969-70; MEd, Boston U., Sechenheim, Germany, 1987; PhD in Biomed. Sci., Uniformed Svcs. U. Hlth. Scis., 1992. Registered clin. pub. health microbiologist Am. Acad. Microbiologists. Med. technologist Dept. of Army, Ft. Hood, Tex., 1981-84; microbiologist, med. technician Dept. of Army 5th Gen. Hosp., Stuttgart, Germany, 1986-87; predoctoral rsch. fellow USUHS, Bethesda, Md., 1987-92; NRC fellow FDA Ctr. Biol. Evaluation & Rsch., NIH, Bethesda, Md., 1992-93; postdoctoral rsch. fellow Henry M. Jackson Found., Bethesda, Md., 1993-95; microbiologist supr., quality assurance coord. Va. Dept. Agr. and Consumer Svcs., Warrenton, 1995—2002; adminstrv. officer Vet. Med. Assistance Team-2, Nat. Disaster Med. Sys., from 2000. Contbg. author: Endotoxin Research, 1990, Bacterial Endotoxins, 1995, Bioterrorism Agents: Implications for Animals, 2001, author, editor: VDACS Office of Animal Industry Lab. Svcs. Quality Assurance Guidance Manual; contbr. articles to profl. jours. Leader Boy Scouts Am., Germany, 1978—85, Girls Scouts Am., Germany, 1982—87, Boy Scouts Am., Hawaii, 1978—85, Boy Scouts Am., Tex., 1982—87, Girls Scouts Am., Tex., 1982—87; vol. Washington AIDS Ride, 1996. Scholar N.Y. State Regents, 1965. Mem.: AAUW, ACLU, LWV, AAAS, Am. Acad. Vet. Disaster Medicine, Am. Chem. Soc., Nat. Environ. Health Assn., Internat. Endotoxin Soc., Am. Soc. Microbiology, U.S. Animal Health Assn., Assn. Vet. Microbiologists (v.p. Colonial States chpt. 1996—98, pres. 1999—2001), N.Y. Acad. Scis., Am. Assn. Vet. Lab. Diagnosticians (life; Bacteriology, Mycoplasmology, Mycology steering com. from 1998, subcom. for antimicrobial susceptibility testing from 1998, co-chair lab. biosafety com. 2002), Phi Kappa Phi, Phi Beta Kappa, Phi Sigma, Iota Sigma Pi. Achievements include research in cellular and molecular mechanism of endotoxic shock and early endotoxin tolerance; systemic inflammatory response to endotoxin analogs; lipopolysaccharide, inducible gene expression; systemic inflammatory response syndrome; acyloxyacyl hydrolase contribution to LPS detoxification; LPS and Taxol or paclitaxel activation of Lyn Kinase autophosphorylation and LPS-induced cytokine production; contribution of C. diphtheriae to wound infection in an equine; contribution in agents of bioterrorism: consequences in animals; contribution in NCCLS antimicrobial QC for aqua culture. Died Mar. 4, 2004.

HENRY, ERNESTYNE ETHEL THATCH, educational association administrator; b. St. Louis, July 19, 1917; d. Clarence Hardwill and Evelena (Thompson) Thatch; m. Horace McKinley Henry, Sept. 1, 1942; children: John Harvey McKinley, Joan Marcille Vernadette. U. Ark., 1938, 1936; BS, 1940; MS, U. Ill., 1950; postgrad. various colls. including, U. N.Mex., U. Colo., Colo., State U., U. Santa Clara, U. Denver, 1954-84. Tchr. Ft. Smith (Ark.) pub. schs., 1940-42; with Civil Svc., Denver, 1942-43; tchr. East St. Louis (Ill.) pub. schs., 1947-52; diagnostic and prescriptive coordinator Denver pub. schs., 1952-84; ret., 1984; asst. prin. Fairview Elem. Sch., Denver, 1961-62; founder, dir. Thatch Enterprises, Denver, from 1989. Lectr. U. Colo., summer 1959. Contbr. articles to profl. jours. Precinct com. Dem. Party, Denver, 1953-78, voter registration staff, 1952—. Mem. U. Ark. Pine Bluffs Alumni Assn. (bd. dirs. 1978—, Outstanding Alumni), AAUW (v.p. 1986-87), Nat. Coun. Negro Women (v.p.), United Teaching Profession (bldg. rep. 1980-84), Internat. Rels. Club (treas. 1970-89), Opera Colo., Top Ladies of Distinction (charter pres. 1989—), U. Ill. Alumni Assn., Lioness Club (treas. 1990), Phi Delta Kappa, Sigma Gamma Rho (bd. dirs. 1963-65, 69-75). Democrat. Methodist. Avocations: travel, drama, bridge. Home: Denver, Colo. Died July 16, 2004.

HENRY, HOMER C., railroad company executive; b. LaFollette, Tenn., July 1, 1950; s. John David and Mabel Ann (Davis) H.; m. Julia Gallagher, Aug. 17, 1968 (div. Mar. 1986); m. Donna Lee Watson, July 19, 1986. BS in Econs., U. Calif., Riverside, 1972, MBA, 1980; Internat. Bus. Econs. deg. (hon.), U. So. Calif., Los Angeles, 1985. Lic. comml.-instrument pilot. Pilot USAF, Norton AFB, Calif., 1973-80; locomotive engr. Santa Fe Ry., San Bernadino, Calif., 1974-80, road foreman of engines Barstow, Calif., 1980-84, gen. road foreman of engines L.A., 1984-87, system road foreman of engines, 1987-88, system dir. train operating practices Chgo., from 1988. Mem. Internat. Ry. Operating Officers Assn. (regional cons.). Republican. Avocations: aviation, hist. research, tennis, fine dining. Home: Naperville, Ill. Died Jan. 27, 2004.

HENRY-LEWIS, SABRINA NORINE, computer systems analyst; b. Springfield, Ohio, Dec. 14, 1954; d. Karl Leo Francis and Jane Delores (Spivey) Henry; m. Glenn Anthony Lewis, Sept. 25, 1986. BSBA, Cen. State U., Wilberforce, Ohio, 1979. Coop. edn. computer programmer Naval Air Engring. Ctr., Lakehurst, N.J., 1978-80, computer systems analyst, from 1980. Cons. in field. Vice chmn. Fed. Women's Program Com., 1982—; conselor Fed. Equal Employment Opportunity, 1987; sec. Upward Bound adv. com. Georgian Ct. Coll., Lakewood, N.J., mem., 1987; sec. correspondence NAACP, Lakewood, 1982; leader Ocean County Girl Scouts Assn., Lakewood, 1986—. Mem. Civilian Recreation and Welfare Assn., Phi Gamma Nu. Home: Lakewood, NJ. Died Nov. 23, 2004.

HENSARLING, LARRY REID, petroleum and gas geologist; b. Bryan, Tex., May 5, 1933; s. Philip Hirem and Grace (Reid) H.; m. Joan Menefee, July 30, 1955; children: Reid, Tod, Ann, Neal. BS, U. Tex., 1956. Geologist Sunray Mid Continent Oil Co., Shreveport, Lafayette, La., 1956-63, Morris & Burk, Lafayette, 1964-66; geologist, owner Petroleum Futures, Inc., Lafayette, 1967-78, Tee Oil Inc., Lafayette, 1979-91, Dove Resources, Inc., Lafayette, 1992-94; v.p., founder Gulf Coast Exploration, San Antonio, Tex., from 1995. Adv. mem. Geology Found. U. Tex. Austin, 1982-95, Am. Assn. Petroleum Geologists Found., Tulsa, 1981-95; mem. Bill Clinton Energy Team, Houston, 1992—; bd. dirs. Gulf Coast Exploration, Okla. City. Author: (book) Oil and Gas Fields: Southwest Louisiana; speaker and lectr. in field. Bd. dirs. Oakbourn Comty. Coll., Lafayette, City Club, Lafayette, 1980's. Larry Hensarling professorshp U. S.W. La. named in his honor, 1981. Mem. Am. Assn. Petroleum Geologists. Roman Catholic. Achievements include discovery or co-discovery of 35-40 different areas of production for oil or gas or both. Home: San Antonio, Tex. Died Sept. 18, 2004.

HENSHAW, BARBARA LOUISE HANBY, retired psychology tester, counselor; b. Washington, Apr. 5, 1926; d. Chauncey Bayard and Margarethe Elizabeth (Frederick) Hanby; m. Edmund Lee Jr., Aug. 5, 1950; children: Lynne Pope, Richard, Scott. AB, George Washington U., 1948, AM, 1952. Asst. to registrar George Washington U., Washington, 1950-52; psychometrist Langly Sch., McLean, Va., 1965-73, Burgundy Farms Sch., Alexandria, Va., 1965-73; husband-clerk U.S. Ho. Reps., 1975-83. Vol., precinct chmn. Dem. Party, Fairfax, Va., 1956-87. Mem. Phi Beta Kappa. Episcopalian. Avocations: travel, hiking, fishing, swimming. Died Feb. 7, 2005.

HENSON, DAVID B., biology professor; b. Orlando, Fla. m. Earlene V. Ovletrea; children: Mary, Charles. BS in Biology, Fla. A&M U., 1961; MSEd in Chemistry, Tuskegee U., 1968; PhD in Biochemistry, U. Iowa, 1972. Acting chmn. dept. biochemistry, asst. dean student affairs Howard U. Coll. Medicine, assoc. prof. biochemistry; dean student affairs, assoc. dean Yale Coll.; lectr. molecular biophysics and biochemistry, fellow Timothy Dwight Coll., Yale U.; provost, prof. chemistry Fla. Atlantic U., Broward; vice chancellor acad. svcs./student support svcs. U. Colo., Boulder; pres., prof. chemistry Ala. A&M U., Huntsville; v.p. student svcs. Purdue U., West Lafayette, Ind.; pres., prof. biochemistry Lincoln U., Jefferson City, Mo., 1997—2005. Contbr. articles to profl. publs. Treas. Coun. on Pub. Higher Edn. Mo.; bd. dirs. Jefferson City C. of C.; bd. govs. Capital Region Med. Ctr.; mem. steering com. River Rendezvous. Diabetes rsch. fellow U. Tex. Med. Sch., Houston, fellow Am. Coun. Edn. Mem. Sigma Xi, Beta Kappa Chi, Alpha Phi Alpha. Home: Jefferson City, Mo. Died Oct. 29, 2005.

HENSON, JOHN DENVER, international management consulting firm executive; b. Fairmont, W.Va., Feb. 28, 1921; s. Denver Clair and Achsa Elizabeth (Martin) H.; m. Jitka Dondova, Feb. 14, 1947 (div. Jan., 1962); children: John Donda, Mark Denver; m. Lydia Cuan-Perez, June 3, 1966. Student Liberal Arts, Phoenix Coll., 1940-42; student Fin., Econs., Am. U., Biarritz, France, 1945; student pharmacy, U. New Mex., 1946-47; grad. cert. Internat. Trade, Am. Grad. Sch. Internat. Mgmt, 1948. Commd. 2d lt. U.S. Army, 1942, advanced through ranks to capt., 1946, active duty., 1942-46, 49-58, wartime svc. ETO and Korea; lt. col. AUS; asst. gen. svcs. officer Internat. Coop. Adminstrn., Kabul, Afghanistan, 1959-61, chief supply mgmt. br., sr. supply mgmt. advisor to Cambodian Govt. Phnom Penh, Cambodia, 1961-64; chief procurement mgmt. br. Agy. for Internat. Devel. State Dept., Saigon, Vietnam, 1964-66, chief office of Korea/Vietnam affairs Seoul, Korea, 1966-68; dep. chief supply mgmt. divsn. U.S. AID, State Dept., Jakarta, Indonesia, 1968-71; chief E. Asia Bur. comml. import programs, dep. Cambodia desk officer AID, Washington, 1971-72; chief procurement mgmt. divsn., sr. supply mgmt. advisor to Vietnamese govt. U.S. AID Saigon, 1972-75; chief logistics divsn. Bangkok, Thailand, 1975; pres. J.D. Henson & Assocs. Internat. Mgmt. Cons., Miami, Fla., from 1976; sr. v.p. U.S. Gulf Holdings Corp., Fla. and Guyana, from 1995; pres. Here Comes Grandma, Inc., Miami, from 1996. Pres. Nat. Industries and Consol. Energy Corp., Dallas and Miami, 1987-91; v.p. internat. ops. Diversified Internat. Directions, Inc., Miami and Costa Rica, 1984-87, Miami, 1986-88; bd. dirs. Mandel Enterprises, Inc., Miami, Zane Internat. Mktg., Inc., Miami, House of Cuan, Inc. Oriental Imports, Miami; dir. internat. affairs U.S. Gulf Holdings Corp., Fla. and Guyana, 1995—; v.p., sec., treas. Sabrine Ballroom Shoes, Inc., Miami, 1991—; spl. advisor to Sec. Commerce, State of Fla., Miami, 1987-92; exec. guest lectr. U. Miami Grad. Sch. Internat. Bus., Miami, 1978—. Mem. Founding Task Force, The Beacon Coun., Miami, 1985; spl. advisor to Fla. Vol. Orgn. Internat. Commerce Execs., Miami, 1987-92; dir. Internat. Ctr. Fla. (now World Trade Ctr.), Miami, 1978—; v.p., dir. Fla. Exporters and Importers Assn., 1978-86; asst. to civilian aide to Sec. of War for Ariz., 1940-42; founder, 1st commdr. citizens military tng. camps, Assn. the U.S., Ariz., 1940-42; chmn. Maricopa County C.M.T.C. War Dept., 1940-42; observer Rep. Nat. Conv., Chgo., 1944; del. Ariz. Rep. State Conv., Phoenix, 1946, 48; chmn. Govs. Coord. Com. for Civic and Vet. Orgns., 1946-48, adv. bd. Miami Dade C.C. Endowment Found., 1987—; pres. Cambodia Gourmat Soc., Phnom Penh, 1963. Recipient medaille de la France Liberées, French Ministry of Vets. Affairs, Perigueux, France, 1955, Vietnam Civilian Svc. medal U.S. Dept. State, Washington, 1966, Chong My Boi Tinh Pub. Svc. medal Pres. Vietnam, Siagon, 1974, Vietnam Spl. Svc. medal Office of Prime Min., Saigon, 1975, Pres.'s E awards for Export Promotion, U.S. Dept. Commerce, Washington, 1981, 83. Mem. VFW (life mem., judge advocate Ariz. 1946-47, nat. membership com. 1979-80, 80-81), Fla. Coun. of Internat. Devel., Am. Health Industries World Trade Assn. (v.p., sec., treas., bd. dirs. 1983—), World Trade Ctr., Am. Fgn. Svc. Assn., Health Coun. South Fla., Mil. Order of World Wars (life), Res. Officers Assn. (life), Ret. Officers Assn. (life), Nat. Assn. Ret. Fed. Employees (life), Am. Philatelic Soc. (life), Soc. IndoChina Philatelists, Fla. C. of C. (internat. devel. com. 1991-94), Alliance Francais, The Chosin Few, Am. Legion (life), Asia-Am. Assn., Elks. Republican. Unitarian-Universalist. Avocations: mineralogy, stamp collecting/philately, aviculture, tennis, swimming. Home: Miami, Fla. Died Aug. 24, 2005.

HENZLER, CAROLYN JEAN, artist; b. Bryan, Tex., Dec. 29, 1944; d. Melvin Charles and Mildred Pearl (Novosad) H.; m. Terrence Day, Oct. 19, 1974. AB, U. Calif., Berkeley, 1974. One-woman shows include The New Gallery of the Ednl. Alliance, N.Y.C., 1990, 91, 92, Ernest Rubenstein Gallery, N.Y.C., 1995, Ocean County C.C., Toms River, N.J., 1997; two-person shows include The New Gallery of the Ednl. Alliance, N.Y.C., 1988, 93; exhibited in group shows at 80 Washington Sq. East Gallery, N.Y.C., 1985, Circlework Visions Gallery, N.Y.C., 1987; internet on-line show, 1995. Recipient Exhibition grants Artists Space, 1988, 90, 91. Mem. Manhattan Graphics Ctr. Democrat. Avocation: tai chi. Home: Long Beach, Calif. Died Jan. 13, 2004.

HEPWORTH, DEREK GRAHAM, financial company executive; b. Beverly, Mass., Dec. 7, 1935; s. Joseph Wood and Dorothy Elizabeth (Goodwin) H.; m. Elaine Marie MacDuff, Aug. 11, 1956; children: David Derek, Suzanne Judith, Douglas Jon, Dennis Paul, Derek Thomas. AB, Amherst Coll., 1958; MBA, Babson Coll., 1980. Chartered fin. analyst. Sales rep. Mobil Oil Corp., Boston, 1958-62, Johnson & Johnson, Chgo., 1962-64; mktg. coordinator John Hancock Fin. Svcs., Boston, 1964-68, conf. planner, 1968-71, cons. internal mgmt., 1971-77, securities analyst, 1977-82; v.p. Independence Investment Assocs., Boston, 1982-88; sr. v.p., dir. mktg. Peregrine Capital Mgmt., Mpls., from 1988. Fellow Life Mgmt. Inst.; mem. Am. Arbitration Assn. Republican. Roman Catholic. Avocations: golf, fishing, travel. Home: Swampscott, Mass. Died Apr. 17, 2005.

HERBERT, ANNE TIMBROOK, interior design executive; b. Elizabeth, N.J., May 13, 1934; d. Richard Elson and Marguerite Helen (Cawthorne) Timbrook; m. Norman Theodore Herbert, June 20, 1953 (div. Dec. 1980); children: Glenn, Jean, Janet. BFA, Syracuse U., 1955. Cert. interior design profl. Designer, draftsman Modern Kitchens of Syracuse, N.Y., 1955-57; designer, cons. Ouaquaga, N.Y., 1957-77; prin. Elson Assocs., Endwell, N.Y., from 1977. Substitute tchr. in art, indsl. arts Jr. High and High Sch., Windsor, N.Y., 1968-69. Mem. Windsor Civic Club, 1960-70, pres., 1964; mem. Old Onaquaga Hist. Soc., Harpursville, N.Y., 1964—, pres., 1966-68, v.p. 1970-87; mem. Broome County Bicentennial Commn., Binghamton, N.Y., 1973-76; bd. dirs. Broome County Hist. Soc., Binghamton, 1974—. Mem. Am. Soc. Interior Designers (profl. bd. dirs. N.Y. Upstate/Can. East chpt. 1982-89, 92—, chpt. sec. 1984-85, Presdl. Citation for Disting. Svc. 1983), Univ. Singles, Inc. (pres. 1985-86, bd. dirs. 1983-90), Tau Sigma Delta, Phi Kappa Phi. Republican. Avocations: horses, sailing, exploring hist. sites. Home: Endwell, NY. Died Jan. 14, 2005.

HERETH, LYLE GEORGE, electrical engineering technologist; b. Everett, Wash., Oct. 14, 1947; s. L. Walter and Alvina Katharina (Weber) H.; m. Margaret Sue Brewer, Dec. 19, 1978; children: Christopher, Walter, Emilie, Jennifer, Jacob. BS in Elec. Engring. Tech., Weber State Coll., 1975; M of Engring. Adminstrn., U. Utah, 1981. Quality engr. Nat. Semiconductor, Salt Lake City, 1975-78, Beehive Internat., Salt Lake City, 1978-80; quality mgr. Sperry Univac, Salt Lake City, 1980-82; sys. devel. mgr. LDS Ch., Salt Lake City, 1982-85, dir. tech., arch., 1985-90, asst. coord., 1990-93, cons. emerging tech., 1993-99, mgr. info. tech., from 1999. Mem. Internat. Coun. on Archives com. current records in electronic environment, chmn. info. sys. VIM, CDC Corp., Minn., 1984-89; project mgr. geneal. sys. FamilySearch, 1987 (Smith award 1992, 95). Chmn. planning and zoning South Salt Lake City Govt., 1986-94; chaplain South Salt Lake Police and Fire Depts. Recipient Pub. Svc. awards South Salt Lake Govt., 1983, 94. Mem. Assn. for Info. and Image Mgmt. Mem. Lds Ch. Avocations: reading, camping, cooking, acting. Home: S Salt Lake, Utah. Died June 16, 2005.

HEROLD, JOSEPH HERMAN, educatinal institution executive; b. Union, N.J., Mar. 11, 1936; s. Joseph H. and Marie (Russo) H.; m. Carreen C. Rogers, June 29, 1963; children: Lisa Lee, Scott Samuel. BA, Western New Mex. U., 1965; MA, Trenton State Coll., 1976. Acctg. mgr. McGraw Hill Book Co., Highstown, N.J., 1966-69; exec. assoc. Ednl. Testing Svc., Princeton, N.J., from 1969. Adj. prof. bus. Mercer County Community Coll., Trenton, N.J., 1968-87, Bucks County Community Coll., 1974-76, Trenton State Coll., 1989; speaker in field. Contbr. numerous articles to profl. jours. With U.S. Army Counterintelligence Corp., 1958-60. Mem. World Future Soc., Bus. Adv. Coun. (chmn. 1978), Nat. Bus. Edn. Assn., Cen. Jersey Computer

Club, Phi Delta Kappa, Delta Pi Epsilon, Gamma Beta. Democrat. Avocations: personal computing, golf. Home: Trenton, NJ. Died July 15, 2005.

HERR, KING G., bank executive; b. Cedar County, Iowa, Sept. 6, 1907; s. Herbert and Catharine (King) H.; m. Julia Hansen, June 29, 1936 (dec. Apr. 1970); children: Catharine Van Nostrand, Susan Engberg, John; m. Margaret Schrock Alton, May 26, 1989. BS, U. Iowa, 1930. Sr. v.p. Interstate Fin., Dubuque, Iowa, 1930-67; v.p. Am. Trust and Savs. Bank, Dubuque, 1967-88. Nat. dir. rural community devel. SCORE, Iowa City, 1988—. Mem. Rotary (dist. gov. 1977-78). Presbyterian. Home: Iowa City, Iowa. Died Mar. 9, 2005.

HERREN, DONALD RAY, minister; b. Corbin, Ky., May 2, 1930; s. Oscar K. and Viola (Shotwell) H.; m. Patricia Eads, Aug. 21, 1951; children: Thomas K., Mark R. AB, Union Coll., Barbourville, Ky., 1951, DD (hon.), 1969; BD, Lexington (Ky.) Theol. Sem., 1955; postgrad., Northwestern U., from 1961. Ordained to ministry United Meth. Ch., 1955. Min. 1st United Meth. Ch., Lexington, 1952-59; sr. min. So. Hills United Meth. Ch., Lexington, from 1959. Leader groups to Middle East, USSR, Europe, Hawaii, Japan, People's Republic China. Bd. dirs. Good Samaritan Hosp., Lexington, 1964—; mem. Fayette County (Ky.) Bd. Edn., 1968-80 (steering com. for tax referendum), Ky. Bd. Edn., 1981—; vice chmn. Paul Miller Ford Found.; bd. dirs. Blue Grass Boys' Ranch, Lexington YMCA, Day Treatment Ctr. for Juveniles, Cen. Ky. chpt. ARC, Fayette United Community fund; mem. Ky. Crime Commn., Met. Pks. and Recreation Bd., Nat. Pks. and Recreation Bd., Task Force on Edn., State of Ky., Adv. Coun., Voc. Edn., State of Ky., Mem. NCCJ (bd. dirs. Blue Grass chpt.), Urban League (bd. dirs. Lexington chpt.), Greater Lexington Area C. of C. (bd. dirs.), Kiwanis (past pres.). Home: Lexington, Ky. Died Dec. 4, 2004.

HERRIN, STEPHANIE ANN, retired aerospace and astrobiotical engineer; b. Oakland, Calif., May 13, 1950; d. Thomas Edgar Herrin and Mary Teresa Silva; m. Este Stovall, May 20, 1989. BSc, U. Pacific, 1976; MSc, Columbia Pacific U., 1978; PhD in Engring. & Applied Scis., U. Bradford, West Yorkshire, U.K., 1994. Reliability engr. Applied Tech. Litton Industries, Sunnyvale, Calif., 1979-80; sr. reliability engr., reliability project mgr. ESL, Inc., Sunnyvale, 1980-84; sr. reliability and quality assurance engr. Martin Marietta, Balt., 1984-85; lead, sr. reliability engr. Los Alamos Tech. Assn., Albuquerque, 1985-86; sr. reliability engr. Boeing, Houston, 1987-89; sr. sys. engr., knowledge capture engr. Astrobiology Inst. NASA-Ames Rsch. Ctr., Moffett Field, Calif., 1988-99; marine capt. pvt. personal yacht, from 1999; sr. systems/astrobiotical engr. biology lab. Space Sta. Freedom. Cons. Lawrence Livermore Labs., Livermore, Calif., 1985-87; failure analysis engring. radiographer, analyst Ford Aerospace & Comm. Corp., Palo Alto, Calif., 1973-79; owner, analyst Fail Safe Radiography, Palo Alto, 1975-81. Contbr. articles to profl. jours. Recipient U.S. govt. Manned Flight Awareness award, 1994, 96-97, 2000 Outstanding Scientists of 20th Century medal, Cambridge, Eng., 2000, Cambridge U. Sch. Honor Scientist of Yr., Queen Elizabeth II; named Internat. Scientist of Yr. Cambridge U., 2001; NASA grantee, 1987-89, 90-93, 94-95; recipient numerous fellowships and lifetime awards. Mem.: AAUW, IEEE (reliability and maintainability soc., engring. in medicine and biology computer soc., info. theory, sys., man and cybernetics, oceanic engring. soc.), Nat. Assn. Ret. Fed. Employees. Achievements include patent for Real-time Automated Diagnosis and Intelligent Utility for Maintainability (RADIUM). Home: Redwood City, Calif. Died June 24, 2005.

HERRON, THOMAS J., academic dean; b. Phila., Sept. 8, 1947; s. Thomas J. and Mary M. (Welsh) H. BA, St. Charles Sem., Overbrook, Pa., 1969; MDiv, 1973; SSL, Biblical Inst., Rome, 1979; STD, Gregorian U., Rome, 1986. Asst. pastor St. Albert the Great, Huntingdon Valley, Pa., 1973-76; tchr. Arch. Kennedy Highschool, Conshohocken, 1979-82; staff Congregation for the Doctrine of the Faith, Rome, 1982-88; academic dean St. Charles Sem., Overbrook, Pa., from 1988. Chmn. Archdiocesan Med. Moral Com., Phila., 1989—, censor librorum Archdiocese of Phila., 1989—, chaplain Phila. Chpt. of Legatus, 1989—. Author: Most Probable Date of First Clement, 1987; editor: Catholic Priest as Moral Teacher, 1990; contbr. articles in profl. jours. Papal Chamberlain, Holy See, Vatican City, 1987; Prelate of Honor of His Holiness, Vatican City, 1991. Mem. Cath. Bibl. Assn., Cath. Theol. Soc., Assn. of Theol. Schools, Middles States Accrediting Agy. Roman Catholic. Home: Wynnewood, Pa. Died May 2, 2004.

HERSH, JOSEPH H., physician; b. N.Y.C., July 26, 1909; s. Samuel and Minnie (Gurfein) H.; m. Lillian Berk, June 20, 1934; children: Stephen P., Marc J. BS in Chemistry, NYU, 1933; MD, NYU Coll. Medicine, 1935. Cert. Asst. attending surgeon Kings County Hosp., Bklyn., 1938-45, Sea View Hosp., Staten Island, N.Y., 1938-45, N.Y. Post-grad. Med. Sch. and Hosp., N.Y.C., 1945-49; assoc. attending surgeon NYU Med. Ctr., N.Y.C., from 1949, Bellevue Hosp., N.Y.C., from 1949; attending surgeon French Hosp., N.Y.C., 1952-72, Lebanon Hosp., N.Y.C., 1955-85. Clin. prof. head and neck surgery NYU Med. Sch., 1952—. Contbr. articles to profl. jours. Fellow ACS, Am. Soc. Head and Neck Surgery, Am. Acad. Allergy, Am. Soc. Study Headaches, Am. Acad. Otolaryngology/Head and Neck Surgery, Am. Soc. Facial Reconstruction Surgery, N.Y. Acad. Medicine. Home: Chevy Chase, Md. Died Aug. 7, 2005.

HERTZBERG, ARTHUR, rabbi, educator; b. Lubaczow, Poland, June 9, 1921; s. Zvi Elimelech and Nehamah (Alstadt) H.; m. Phyllis Cannon, Mar. 19, 1950; children: Linda, Susan. AB, Johns Hopkins U., 1940; MHL, Jewish Theol. Sem., 1943; PhD, Columbia U., 1966; DD, Lafayette Coll., 1970; DHL (hon.), Balt. Hebrew Coll., 1974, Jewish Theol. Sem., 1987, Balt. Hebrew U., 1997, Boston Hebrew Coll., 1999, Hebrew Union Coll., Cin., 2000, CUNY Grad. Ctr., 2001, Johns Hopkins U., 2005. Rabbi, 1943; Hillel dir. Mass. State and Smith Coll., 1943-44; rabbi Congregation Ahavath Israel of Oak Lane, Phila., 1944-47, West End Synagogue, Nashville, 1947-56, Temple Emanu El, Englewood, NJ, 1956-85, rabbi emeritus, 1985—2006; prof. religion Dartmouth Coll., 1985-91, prof. emeritus, 1991—2006. Lectr. Columbia U., 1961-68, adj. prof. history, 1968-90; vis. scholar Mideast Inst., 1991-2006; vis. assoc. prof. Jewish studies Rutgers U., 1966-68; lectr. religion Princeton U., 1968-69; vis. prof. history Hebrew U., Jerusalem, 1970-71; vis. prof. Ecole des Hautes Etudes, Paris, 1989; vis. scholar St. Antony's Coll., Oxford, 1989; pres. Conf. Jewish Social Studies, 1967-72; mem. exec. com. World Zionist Orgn., 1969-78, Jewish Agy. for Israel, 1969-71, bd. govs., 1971-78; pres. Am. Jewish Congress, 1972-78, Am. Jewish Policy Found., 1978-2006; v.p. World Jewish Congress, 1975-91, co-chmn. adv. coun., 1991-2006; vis. prof. humanities NYU, 1991-2006. Author: The Zionist Idea, 1959; (with Martin Marty and Joseph Moody) The Outbursts that Await Us, 1963, The French Enlightenment and the Jews, 1968, Being Jewish in America, 1979, The Jews in America: Four Centuries of an Uneasy Encounter, 1989, Jewish Polemics, 1992; (with Aron Hirt-Manheimer) Jews: The Essence and Character of a People, 1998, A Jew in America, 2002, The Fate of Zionism, 2003; editor: Judaism, 1961, 2d rev. edit., 1991; introduction author At Home Only With God, 1992; sr. editor: Ency. Judaica, 1972; contbr.: Ency. Britannica, 1975. Vice pres. bd. dirs. Meml. Found. for Jewish Culture, 1965-98. Served 1st lt., chaplain USAF, 1951-53. Recipient Amram award, 1967, award for Lifetime Achievement Present Tense, 1989, Jewish Cultural Achievement award Nat. Found., 2001, Book award N.J. Coun. for Humanities, 2003, Book award Jewish Book Coun., 2003; Inst. Advanced Studies fellow, Jerusalem, 1982 Jewish. Home: Englewood, NJ. Died Apr. 17, 2006.

HERVEY, HOMER VAUGHAN, retired federal agency administrator; b. Texarkana, Tex., Sept. 27, 1936; s. Charles Ethelbert and Ambolyn (Vaughan) H.; m. Nancy McDonald, July 7, 1962; children: Nancy Vaughan, H.V. Jr. BS in Social Scis., Georgetown U., 1958, MA, 1962. Executive trainee Riggs Nat. Bank, Washington, 1958-61, U.S. Govt. Office of Edn., Washington, 1961-63; program officer Exec. Office of the Pres., Washington, 1963-73, Dept. of the Treasury, Washington, 1973-77, Fed. Preparedness Agy., Washington, 1977-79, Fed. Emergency Mgmt. Agy., Washington, 1979-85, asst. assoc. dir., dir. ops., from 1985, ret., 2001. Mem. exec. com. Georgetown U. Library, Washington, 1982—. Mem.: Chevy Chase. Avocations: motion pictures, tennis, golf, reading. Home: Chevy Chase, Md. Died Feb. 16, 2005.

HESS, EMERSON GARFIELD, lawyer; b. Pitts., Nov. 13, 1914; AB, Bethany Coll., 1936; JD, U. Pitts., 1939. Bar: Pa. 1940. Sr. ptnr. Hess, Reich, Georgiades, Wile & Homyak and predecessor firm Emerson G. Hess & Assocs., Pitts., 1940-92; of counsel DeMarco & Assocs., Pitts., from 1992. Solicitor Scott Twp. Sch. Bd., 1958-65; legal counsel Judiciary com. Pa. Ho. of Reps., 1967-69; solicitor Scott Twp., 1968-69, Crafton Borough, 1974-78, Authority for Improvements in Municipalities of Allegheny County, 1977-80. Bd. dirs. Golden Triangle YMCA, Pitts., 1945—, WQED Ednl. TV, Pitts., 1952-68; pres., dir. Civil Light Opera Assn., Pitts., 1967-68; mem. internat. com. YMCA World Svc., N.Y.C., 1968-78; trustee, chmn. Cen. Christian Ch., Pitts., 1962-63; pres. Anesthesia and Resuscitation Found., Pitts., 1964-88, Pa. Med. Rsch. Found., 1960-88. Mem. ABA, Pa. Bar Assn., Allegheny County Bar Assn. Home: Pittsburgh, Pa. Died Nov. 11, 2004.

HESS, ROBERT HALDEMAN, state agency administrator; b. Bareville, Pa., Dec. 1, 1937; s. Titus Myer and Anna Mae Ginder (Haldeman) H.; m. Carol Jean Kesler, June 8, 1963; children: Karin Lynnae, Bradley Shane. BA in Philosophy, McPherson Coll., 1963; MDiv, Bethany Theol. Sem., 1967; MS in Ednl. Adminstrn., Purdue U., 1976. Probation officer Cook County Juvenile Ct., Chgo., 1967-68; assoc. pastor Stone Ch. of the Brethren, Huntingdon, Pa., 1968-70; project dir. Devel. for Ch. of the Brethren, Ft. Wayne, Ind., 1970-73; tng. instr. Ft. Wayne State Hosp. and Tng. Ctr., 1973-76; dir. orgnl. devel. Ft. Wayne State Devel. Ctr., from 1976. Assoc. prof. Purdue U., Ft. Wayne, 1976-79; cons., trainer to numerous health and mfg. orgns., 1985—. Pres. Consumer Ctr., Ft. Wayne, 1977; mem. campaign coun. United Way, Ft. Wayne, 1989. Mem. ASTD (local officer 1975-80, regional pres. 1980-82, nat. bd. dirs. 1982-89 Torch award 1984, Vince Miller award 1989), Pers./Indsl. Rels. Assn., Ft. Wayne C. of C. (mem. com. 1988—). Avocations: racquetball, volleyball, travel, gardening, designing/building solar home system. Home: Fort Wayne, Ind. Died May 5, 2005.

HETLAGE, ROBERT OWEN, lawyer; b. St. Louis, Jan. 9, 1931; s. George C. and Doris M. (Talbot) H.; m. Anne R. Willis, Sept. 24, 1960; children: Mary T., James C., Thomas K. AB, Washington U., St. Louis, 1952, LLB, 1954; LLM, George Washington U., 1957. Bar: Mo. 1954, U.S. Dist. Ct. (ea. dist.) Mo. 1954, U.S. Supreme Ct. 1957. Ptnr. Hetlage & Hetlage, 1958-65, Peper, Martin, Jensen, Maichel & Hetlage, St. Louis, 1966-97, chmn., 1994-97; of counsel Blackwell Sanders Peper Martin LLP, St. Louis, from 1998. 1st lt. U.S. Army, 1954-58. Fellow Am. Bar Found. (life, v.p. 2002-04, pres. 2004—2006); mem. ABA (chmn. real property, probate and trust law sect. 1981-82), Bar Assn. Met. St. Louis (pres. 1967-68), Mo. Bar (pres. 1976-77), Am. Coll. Real Estate Lawyers (pres. 1985-86), Anglo-Am. Real Property Inst. (chmn. 1991). Died June 16, 2006.

HETRICK, JOAN WILLETTE, critical care nurse, administrator; b. Oct. 14, 1959; d. Wilbert D. Sproul and Lois Diane (Wilson) Pinette Anderson; m. Charles Vance Frum, May 4, 2002. B in Health Scis., Fla. Atlantic U., 1996; ASN, Miami-Dade Med. Ctr., 1998. RN, Fla., Ga. Adminstrv. asst., cons. Holiday Prime Foods, 5 Star Mktg. Group, Davie, Fla., 1996—2002; RN critical care Aventura (Fla.) Hosp., 1999; RN Meml. Reg. Hosp., Hollywood, Fla., 1999, Hollywood Med. Ctr. Telemetry and Prog. Care, 1998-99; charge nurse Hallandale Rehab. Ctr., 2000—02; ER nurse Plantation Gen. Hosp., 2001—02; RN specialist Agy. for Health Care Adminstrn., Fla., 2001—02; RN Agy., 2002—03; oncology nurse Kennestone Hosp., Ga., 2003—04; gynecol. oncology nurse Northside Hosp., from 2004; oncology nurse Atlanta Med. Ctr., from 2004, oncology, from 2004. Health instr. Miami Book Fair Internat., Miami-Dade C.C., 1997; health care rschr. for 104th Congress, 1995. Mem. Oncology Nurses Soc., Internat. Thespian Soc., Fla. Nurses Assn., Oncology Nursing Soc., Kappa Delta Pi, Alpha Phi Omega. Republican. Avocations: critical care nursing studies, business studies, real estate studies, pets, surfing the internet. Home: Kennesaw, Ga. Died Oct. 12, 2005.

HEULER, LEROY AUGUST, construction company executive; b. Milw., Apr. 28, 1931; s. Lester Arthur and Florence Ella (Spalsbury) H.; m. Patricia Ann Grayson, Sept. 13, 1952; children: Cheryl, James, John, Lisa. BSBA, Marquette U., 1953. Treas. Glendale Tiles, Inc., Milw., 1953-58; pres. Heuler Tile Co., Wauwatosa, Wis., 1958-89, chmn., from 1990. Pres. Hepatha Luth. Ch., Milw., 1958-60, Elm Grove (Wis.) Luth. Ch. Found., Inc.; bd. dirs. Elm Grove Luth. Ch., 1968-74. Mem. Assn. Tile Contractors Milw., Milw. Assn. Commerce, Luth. Layman's League, Delta Sigma Pi. Clubs: Westmoor Country (bd. dirs., pres.), Concordia Century. Republican. Home: Elm Grove, Wis. Died June 7, 2005.

HEVERLY, RICHARD CHARLES, marketing consultant; b. Waterloo, Iowa, Oct. 10, 1928; s. Harold A. and E. Margaret (Pullen) H.; m. Janice Boquist, Aug. 11, 1951; children: Kathleen Heverly Patrick, Steven C., Mary Heverly Poulos. BS, Macalester Coll., St. Paul, 1953. CLU. Agt. Mass. Mut. Life, St. Paul, 1953-60; gen. agt. Washington Nat. Ins. Co., Cedar Rapids, Iowa, 1960-64, regional dir. Evanston, Ill., 1964-68, regional v.p., 1968-72, v.p., 1972-74, v.p., dir., 1974-88; pres. Heverly Fin. Group, Lake Forest, Ill., from 1988. Elder Presbyn. Ch. U.S.A. Sgt. U.S. Army, 1946-48. Fellow Life Mgmt. Inst.; mem. Nat. Assn. Life Underwriters, Am. CLUs, Iowa Game (past pres.), Kiwanis Club of Evanston. Republican. Avocations: golf, travel. Home: Tucson, Ariz. Died July 6, 2005.

HEWES, HENRY, drama critic; b. Boston, Apr. 9, 1917; s. Henry Fox and Margaret (Warman) H.; m. Jane Fowle, Aug. 21, 1945; children: Henry Fox, Tucker Fowle, Havelock. BS, Columbia, 1948. Staff writer N.Y. Times, 1949-51; drama editor Saturday Review, 1952-73, drama critic, 1954-77, critic-at-large, 1977; drama critic Internat. Theatre Yearbook, 1978-80. Lectr. Sarah Lawrence Coll., 1955-56, Columbia, 1956-57, Salzburg Seminar in Am. Studies, 1970, New Sch. for Social Rsch., 1972-79; exec. sec. Bd. Standards and Planning for Living Theatre, 1956-66, Am. Theatre Planning Bd., 1966-90; mem. Pulitzer Prize Jury for Drama, 1968, 81, 84, 89, chmn., 1985; chmn. Margo Jones Award Com., 1967-88, Joseph Maharam Award Com., 1965-86; cons. Bicentennial World Theatre Season, 1974; bd. dirs. Am. Theatre Wing; mem. adv. council Theater Hall of Fame, Tony awards nominating com., 1966-70, 79-85, Tony awards adminstrn. com. Adapter: play La Belle Aventure (produced as Accounting for Love), London, 1954; adaptor, dir.: play Tennessee Williams' Three Players of a Summer Game, Westport, Conn., 1955, (with Siobhan McKenna) Exptl. Hamlet, N.Y.C., 1957, Our Very Own Hole in the Ground, N.Y.C., 1972; adapter, dir. play Watergate version Measure for Measure, Gt. Lakes Shakespeare Festival, 1974; moderator: (1976-84) Am. Theatre Wing TV Seminars; Editor: The Best Plays of 1960-61, 61-62, 63-64; editor Famous American Plays of the 1940s. Served as tech. sgt. USAAF, 1941-45. Recipient Spl. award Outer Critics Circle, 1985, Margo Jones Citizen of the Theatre medal, 1993. Mem. N.Y. Drama Critics Circle (v.p. 1969-71, pres. 1971-73), Drama Desk (pres. 1967-74), Am. Theatre Critics Assn. (founder, exec. sec. 1973-85), ANTA (exec. dir. Greater N.Y. chpt. 1953-58), Internat. Assn. Theatre Critics, New Drama Forum, Critics Circle, London. Died July 18, 2006.

HEWITT, BENJAMIN ATTMORE, psychologist, consultant; b. Westerly, R.I., Dec. 20, 1921; s. Benjamin Henry and Anne Mildred (Wangelin) H. BA, Yale U., 1943, MA,

1950, PhD, 1952. Lic. psychol., Conn. Dean Mitchell Coll., New London, Conn., 1948-51; dir. counseling Wesleyan U., Middletown, Conn., 1952-53; pres. Psychol. Svcs., Inc., New Haven, Conn., 1958-70; rsch. assoc. Yale U., New Haven, 1960-68; cons. psychologist New Haven, 1969-92; furniture cons. Wakefield, R.I. Guest curator Work of Many Hands; Card Tables in Fed. Am. Yale U. Art Gallery, New Haven, 1981-82; furniture researcher, 1965—. Author: The Work of Many Hands: Card Tables in Federal America, 1982. With U.S. Army, 1943-46, PTO. Mem. APA, Conn. State Psychol. Assn. (coun. 1960-64, ethics com. 1983-84), Friends of Am. Arts at Yale (sec. 1969-83, exec. com. 1969-92). Avocations: gardening, furniture collecting, boating. Home: Wells, Maine. Died Apr. 13, 2006.

HEWITT, GEORGE EDWARD, investment executive; b. N.Y.C., July 2, 1921; BME, Columbia U., 1943; cert. radar UHF techniques, MIT, 1943; postgrad., UCLA extension; student, Orange Coast Coll. Registered profl. engr., Calif.; licensed real estate agt., Calif. Mem. staff radiation lab. MIT, Boston, 1943-45; engr., project engr. Gilfillon Bros., Inc., 1946-48; founder, v.p., gen. mgr. Canoga Corp. merged with Underwood Olivetti, 1948-58; founder, pres. V-N Mfg. Co., 1949-60; founder, gen. ptnr. Airad Co., 1950-59; pvt. practice personal estate mgmt., from 1970. Founder, pres., chmn. The George E. Hewitt Found. for Med. Rsch., 1980—; mem., trustee U. Calif. Coll. Medicine, Irvine; bd. dirs. Ctr. Health Ednl. Meml. Med. Ctr., Long Beach; chief exec. officer Irvine Imaging Internat., Calif. Mem. World Affairs Coun.; bd. dirs. Beckman Laser Inst. Mem. Nat. Soc. Immunology, U. Calif. Med. Research and Edn. Soc., Orange County Performing Arts, Internat. Oceanographic Found., Am. Def. Preparedness Assn., Navy League, Newport Found., Newport Harbor Art Mus. Clubs: Lido Island Yacht, Balboa Bay, Hoag 552, Exchange (bd. dirs.). Died June 10, 2005.

HEWLETT, JOAN LOOMIS PLASKOFF, women's health nurse; b. Omaha, Apr. 19, 1938; d. Benjamin John Kingcome and Ottillie Amalia (Krugman) Hewlett; children: Rebecca, Jeffrey, Roger Loomis, David Hewlett, Nancy Lynn Hewlett Plaskoff. ADN, Cerritos Coll., Norwalk, Calif., 1970; BSN, Phoenix U., 1981, postgrad., Andrews U., Berrian Springs, Mich., from 1990. Cert. ACLS, neonatal ICU nurse, maternal child nurse; cert. pub. health nurse, Calif. Instr. clin. labor and delivery nursery Neonatal ICU Long Beach (Calif.) City Coll., 1977-78; charge neonatal ICU, ob-gyn. labor and delivery nursery St. Jude's Hosp., Fullerton, Calif., 1970-73; charge labor and delivery, neonatal ICU newborn nursery St. Mary's Hosp., Long Beach, Calif., 1972-74; clin. instr., lectr. Ctrl. C.C., Grand Island, Nebr., 1988-89; float nurse, skilled care St. Francis Hosp., Grand Island, Nebr., 1989-90. Clin. instr. Cerrites Coll., Calif., 1992-93, Long Beach City Coll., 1993; float nurse 3 Registries Kelly Home Care, 1973-82; clin. instr., lectr. Concorde Career Inst., 1994. Mem. disaster team ARC, 1968—; vol. Make-A-Wish FOund., Grand Island, 1990—; foster mother, 1957-77. Recipient Internat. Nursing Contbns. award Cerritos Coll., 1990. Mem. NAFE, ANA, Nebr. Nurses Assn. Died Apr. 20, 2005.

HEYWOOD, CHARLES WILLIAM, former dean, history professor; b. Pitts., Apr. 24, 1921; s. Charles Edwin and Marie Louise (Shrawder) H.; m. Vivian Eleanor Yergey, June 30, 1950; children: Philip Edwin, Ann Marie, James Eric. BA, Earlham Coll., 1943; MA, U. Pa., 1946, PhD, 1954; LHD (hon.), Cornell Coll., 1987. Instr. Coll. of Wooster (Ohio), 1949-53; asst. prof. Cornell Coll., Mt. Vernon, Iowa, 1954-57, assoc. prof., 1957-61, prof., 1961-87, dean, 1983-87, dean emeritus, 1987—2005. Mem. Commn. on Insts. of Higher Edn., North Ctrl. Assn., 1971-75 (cons. evaluator 1974-83). Contbr. articles to profl. jours. Mem. Mt. Vernon Bd. Edn., 1965-71, pres., 1967-71; mem. Mt. Vernon's City Coun., 1990-96; trustee Cornell Coll., 1993-2005. Mem. AAUP (nat. coun. 1960-63, 1st v.p. 1966-68, com. on acad. freedom 1963-72), Orgn. Am. Historians, Latin Am. Studies Assn., Phi Beta Kappa. Home: Mount Vernon, Iowa. Died Nov. 16, 2005.

HIATT, DEAN ROBERT, retired air force officer, real estate agent; b. Arkansas City, Kans., Sept. 1, 1921; s. Dean Brian and Leland (Taylor) H.; m. Elizabeth Jan Sekerak, June 7, 1946; children: Joan Elizabeth, John Dean. Commd. 2d lt. USAF, from 1942, advanced through grades to lt. col., 1967; navigator 90th Bomb Group B-24, New Guinea, 1943-44; radar navigator 11th Bomb Wing B-36, Carsiwell AFB, Tex., 1950-59; mem. standardization bd. radar navigation B-52, 42nd Bomb Wing, Loring AFB, Maine, 1959-66; radar navigator 4200 Strategic Recon Wing SR-71, Beale AFB, Calif., 1966-67; asst. exec. officer Nat. Guard, Pentagon, 1967-70; exec. officer 90th Strategic Missile Wing, F.E. Wabbon AFB, Wyo., 1970-72, ret., 1973; salesperson Gulf Oil Corp., Ft. Worth, Tex., 1944-49; real estate salesperson Jim Duncan Century 21, Weatherford, Tex., from 1973. Precinct chmn. Rep. Party, Weatherford, 1974—. Decorated Air Medal, DFC, Air Force Commendation medal. Avocations: old airplanes, old songs, fishing. Home: Weatherford, Tex. Died Apr. 2, 2004.

HIBBARD, EUGENE JOSEPH, graphic illustrator, photographer; b. Chgo., Dec. 10, 1932; s. Eugene Melvil and Florence Myrtle (Simpson) H.; m. Janet Grace Shaw; children: Teri M., Cori R., Lindsay E. BFA, Wayne State U., 1962. Indsl. illustrator Ford Motor Co., Dearborn, Mich., 1960-72; graphic illustrator Traverse Bay News, Traverse City, Mich., 1972-74; graphic illustrator, cartoonist, photographer Traverse City (Mich.) City Record-Eagle, from 1975. Speaker, instr. in field. Cartoonist for "Local Scene" cartoon panels, 1975—; cartoonist: (book) A Boy, A Bike & Buster, 1994. With USAF, 1952-56. Mem. Am. Assn. Editorial Cartoonists, Nat. Press Photographers Assn. Republican. Avocations: art, photography, travel. Home: Traverse City, Mich. Died July 1, 2005.

HICKMAN, JAMES CHARLES, finance educator, dean; b. Indianola, Iowa, Aug. 27, 1927; s. James C. and Mabel L. (Fisher) Hickman; m. Margaret W. McKee, June 12, 1950; children: Charles Wallace, Donald Robert, Barbara Jean. BA, Simpson Coll., 1950; MS, U. Iowa, 1952, PhD, 1961. Actuarial asst. Bankers Life Co., Des Moines, 1952-57; from asst. prof. to assoc. prof. dept. stats. U. Iowa, 1961—67, prof., 1967-72; prof. bus. and stats. U. Wis., Madison, 1972-93, dean Sch. Bus., 1985-90, emeritus prof. and dean, from 1993; Warren prof. U. Man., 1990; Bowles prof. George State U., 1996. Mem. panel cons. social security fin. Senate Fin. Com., Ho. Ways and Means Com., 1975—76; mem. adv. com. Joint Bd. Enrollment Actuaries, 1976—78; mem. Actuarial Stds. Bd., 1985—92; dir. Mems. Capital Advisors; vis. prof. Nankai U., Tianjin, China, 1993, 96. Mem. editl. bd. N.Am. Actuarial Jour., from 1997. Mem. bd. pensions Presbyn. Ch. U.S., 1989—2003. With USAAF, 1945—47. Recipient Alumni Achievement award, Simpson Coll., 1979, David Halmstad award for actuarial rsch., Actuarial Ednl. Rsch. Fund, 1979, 1981, Disting. Alumni award, U. Iowa, 1993; Coll. Liberal Arts Alumni fellow, 1999. Fellow: Soc. Actuaries (bd. govs. 1971—74, v.p. 1975—77, bd. govs. 1991—94, J. E. O'Connor Disting. Svc. award 2000); mem.: Nat. Acad. Social Ins., Am. Statis. Assn., Swiss Assn. Actuaries (corr.), Casualty Actuarial Soc. (assoc.), Am. Acad. Actuaries (Jarvis Farley award for svc.), Actuarial Found. (trustee 1994—2000), Beta Gamma Sigma (bd. govs. 1988—92). Presbyterian. Home: Madison, Wis. Died Sept. 10, 2006.

HICKS, JAMES LEON, city official; b. Soperton, Ga., Nov. 25, 1922; s. Edmond and Gertrude (Gillis) H.; m. Gwendolyn Horton, Sept. 22, 1950. AB, Morehouse Coll., 1950; postgrad., Atlanta U., 1950-70. Prodn. supr. Ga.-Lockheed Co., Marietta, 1952-65; tchr., counselor Atlanta Bd. Edn., 1965-68; urban planner City of Atlanta, 1969-73, ctr. dir., from 1973. Sgt. F.A., U.S. Army. Mem. G G Club (pres.), Bus. and Law Club, Masons, Omega Psi Phi. Democrat. Episcopalian. Avocations: golf, dance, basketball, football, baseball. Home: Atlanta, Ga. Died Oct. 18, 2004.

HICKS, ROGER ANDREW, minister; b. Joliet, Ill., Nov. 3, 1957; s. Hershal and Lela Valentine (Letterman) H.; m. Sarah Jane Haviland, Jan. 17, 1981; children: Jenny, Rachel, Glorya, Andrew, Jeremiah. BA, SE Bapt. U., Bolivar, Mo., 1982. Ordained to ministry So. Bapt. Conv. Pastor 1st Bapt. Ch., Niangua, Mo., 1979-81, West Finley Bapt. Ch., Fordland, Mo., 1981-84, Calvary Bapt. Ch., Marshfield, Mo., from 1984. Farmer Oakbrook Farms Inc., Niangua. Home: Marshfield, Mo. Died Aug. 3, 2004.

HIEBER, DOUGLAS MARTIN, librarian director; b. Waterloo, Iowa, Apr. 25, 1933; s. Leroy Edward and Mina Marguerite (Martin) H.; m. Wanda Glorine Rosdail, Aug. 10, 1963; children: Caroline, Paul, Jane. BA, Cornell Coll., Mt. Vernon, Iowa, 1955; MSLS, U. Ill., 1959. Art libr. U. Iowa Libr., Iowa City, 1959-62; head circulation U. Iowa Libraries, Iowa City, 1962-67; curator Herbert Hoover Presidl. Libr., West Branch, Iowa, 1962-67; head circulation U. No. Iowa Libr., Cedar Falls, from 1967. Chmn., bd. trustees Met. Transit Authority, Black Hawk County, Iowa, 1979—, Iowa Credit Union League, Des Moines, 1985-86. With USN, 1956-57. Mem. Iowa Libr. Assn. (pres. 1976-77), Am. Libr. Assn., Elks. Democrat. Methodist. Home: Granite Bay, Calif. Died July 29, 2005.

HIGGINBOTHAM, LLOYD WILLIAM, mechanical engineer; b. Haydentown, Pa., Nov. 24, 1934; s. Clarence John and Nannie Mae (Piper) H.; m. Genevieve Law, Oct. 17, 1953 (div.); 1 child, Mark William; m. Mary Bannaian, July 23, 1966; 1 child, Samuel Lloyd. With rsch. and devel. TRW Inc., Cleve., 1953-57; pres. Higginbotham Rsch., Cleve., 1957-64, Higginbotham Assocs., Woodland Hills, Calif., from 1964; founder, CEO Engrs. of World, Woodland Hills, Calif., from 1993; founder, pres., CEO, Enhance Engring. Edn. Found., Inc., Woodland Hills, from 1993, Engrs. Jt. Coun., Inc., from 1999. Pres., CEO Engrs. Coun., 1993—; cons. grad. engring. programs UCLA, Calif. State U., L.A., U. So. Calif.; pres. adv. com. Pierce Coll., L.A.; adv. com. So. Calif. Productivity Ctr.; cons. various Calif. legislators. Mem. Town Hall Calif. Recipient Community Svc. award City of Downey, Calif, 1974, Archimedes award NSPE, Outstanding Contbr. Recognition, 1986, Outstanding Leadership Recognition, 1987, William B. Johnson Meml. Internat. Interprofl. award, 1992. Fellow Inst. Advancement Engring. (class of 1982, exec. dir., exec. mgr. 1984-93); mem. Soc. Carbide and Tool Engrs. (chmn., 1974-76), Soc. Mfg. Engrs. (chmn. San Fernando Valley chpt. 1977-79, numerous awards), San Fernando Valley Joint Coun. Engrs. (now Engrs. Coun., Inc., advisor, pres. 1981-82, 92-94), San Fernando Valley engrs. Coun. (pres., CEO 1992—), Profl. Salesmen's Assn., Am. Soc. Assn. Execs., L.A. Coun. Engrs. and Scientists (exec. mgr. 1984-93), N.Y. Acad. Scis., L.A. Area C. of C., Toastmasters, Masons. Republican. Avocations: golf, spectator sports. Home: Woodland Hills, Calif. Died Mar. 20, 2004.

HIGGINS, JON STANLEY, investment company executive; b. Chgo., Sept. 4, 1941; s. Stanley John and Helen Francis (House) H.; m. Janet Kathryne Moore, June 17, 1967; children: Jon Samuel, Rebecca Jane. Student, Whitman Coll., 1959-60; AA, Menlo Coll., 1961; BS cum laude, UCLA, 1968, MBA, 1969. Br. mgr. Freed Fin. Co., Las Vegas, Nev., 1963-66; mgmt. cons. Cresap, McCormick & Paget, San Francisco, 1969-74; planning mgr. Bechtel Group, San Francisco, 1974-77, chief auditor, 1979-80, mgr. mgmt. info., 1983-86, sr. regional rep. Seoul, Republic of Korea, 1980-83; exec. asst. to pres. Bechtel Investments, San Francisco, 1986-88, CFO, from 1988. Chmn. bd. Petro Source Corp., Houston; bd. dirs. Fremont Investment Advisors, San Francisco, BecField Drilling Svcs., Houston, J. P. Morgan S.E. Asia, Ltd., Singapore. Pres. Las Vegas Lenders Exch., 1964, Westminster Assn. Retail Bus., Westminster, Calif., 1966; dir. Am. C. of C., Seoul, 1982-83. Mem. World Trade Club, World Affairs Coun., Commonwealth Club, Fin. Execs. Inst. Home: Alamo, Calif. Died Jan. 7, 2004.

HIGGS, J. JEFFREY, retired physician and medical director; b. Jersey City, Nov. 23, 1919; s. Joseph J. and Margaret S. (Edmonds) H.; m. Julia Bertha Smith, Apr. 9, 1944 (div. 1977); children: Gregory David, Maggie Higgs Blackburn; m. Geraldine Agnes Sherman, Dec. 28, 1978. BA, Lincoln (Pa.) U., 1939; MD, Howard U., 1943. Rotating intern Harlem Hosp., N.Y.C., 1943-44; resident in internal medicine Provident Hosp., Balt., 1944-45; staff physician Tewksbury (Mass.) State Hosp., 1945-46; mcpl. physician St. Croix, Christiansted, V.I., 1946-48; attending family practice physician Huntington (N.Y.) Hosp., 1948-68, emergency physician, 1968-75; staff physician Union Carbide Corp., Texas City, Tex., 1978-84, med. dir., 1984-90. Counselor N.Y. State chpt. Am. Coll. Emergency Physicians, 1960s and 70s; bd. dirs. Alcoholism Referral project U. Tex. Med. Br., Galveston, 1986. Past pres. local chpt. NAACP, Huntington, 1950s; chmn. Huntington Housing Authority, 1960s; bd. dirs. Suffolk County br. ARC, 1960s, other civic activities. Fellow Am. Coll. Occupational and Environ. Medicine; mem. Galveston County Med. Soc. (life). Avocations: gardening, swimming, bicycling, jogging. Home: Houston, Tex. Died June 26, 2005.

HIGGS, MARY PHIL EGERTON, editor; b. Richmond, Va., July 14, 1928; d. William Graham Egerton and Rebecca Crenshaw White; m. Barnie Allen Higgs, June 14, 1948; children: Janet Anne, Graham Egerton, David Allen, Mary Virginia Higgs Beach Higgins. BA with highest honors, U. Tenn., 1973. Missionary United Meth. Ch., 1949; tchr., adminstr. Rhodesia Ann. Conf. (now Zimbabwe Ann. Conf.), 1949—66; Rhodesia editor Africa Christian Advocate, 1951—64; program dir. Rhodesia Ambassadors Quartet tour to U.S., 1958—60; assoc. editor Vanderbilt U. Publs., Nashville, 1968—78, editor, dir., 1978—93. Democrat. Episcopalian. Home: Hermitage, Tenn. Died Feb. 28, 2005.

HILDEBRAND, ALICE GRACE, physician; b. Omaha, June 24, 1913; s. Carl Herbert and Effie Jane (Levoy) H. BS in Medicine, U. Nebr., Omana, 1932; MS in Medicine, U. Minn., Mpls., 1940; MD, U. Nebr., Omaha, 1936. Cert. Am. Bd. Internal Medicine, 1947. Pvt. practice, Seattle, 1942-94; retired capt. USPHS. Assoc. prof. clin. medicine U. Washington Sch. Medicine, Seattle, 1947-80. Capt. USPHS, ret. Fellow ACP. Home: Olympia, Wash. Died June 30, 2004.

HILL, DEAN ALLEN, retail executive, real estate developer; b. McGill, Nev., Feb. 3, 1934; s. Allen Glen and Eula Mae (Fister) H. AA, San Bernardino Valley Coll., 1954; BA in Psychology, U. Calif., Berkeley, 1957. Buyer Bullocks Stores, Inc., Los Angeles, 1960-67; buyer, div. mgr. Goldwaters Stores, Inc., Phoenix, 1967-70, Webbs Dept. Stores, Glendale, Calif., 1970-78; owner, mgr. various apt. bldgs. Glendale, Van Nuys, Calif. and Los Angeles, 1975-79, Casa Colina Restaurant, San Clemente, Calif., 1979-82; ops. mgr. Builders Emporium subs. Wickes, Inc., from 1982. Comml., residentia interior designer various offices, stores and residences. Served to lt. (j.g.) USN, 1957-60. Recipient Cert. of Merit City of San Clemente, 1981. Died June 9, 2005.

HILL, HENRY FORREST, investment company executive; b. Newark, May 17, 1917; s. George Warren and Elsa Elise (Von Zirkel) H.; m. Ruth Ann Hayes, June 28, 1947. BSCE with distinction, Purdue U., 1938. Civil engr. Armco Internat Corp., Central and South America, 1939-43; pres. Armco Venezoland, S.A., Caracas, Venezuela, 1944-45, Tropical Isle Holdings, Key Biscayne, Fla., 1950-54; ptnr. Construciones Elndustrias, S.A., Puerto La Cruz, Venezuela, 1945-46, Mass Electric, S.A., Venezuela, 1946-50; independent researcher Miami, Fla., 1955-65; ptnr., engr. U.S. Mfg. and Galvanizing Corp., Miami, 1966-72; mng. dir. Hill Internat. Ltd., Miami, from 1973. Author: (poems) Rhymes Without Reason, 1989; contbr. poetry to newspapers, mags. Bd. overseers Sloan Kettering Cancer Ctr., N.Y.C., 1988—; bd. dirs. Greater Miami Crime Commn., 1970-83. Mem. 200 Club, Snapp Creek Lakes Club (pres. 1975, 81), Riviera Country Club, Tau Beta Pi. Home: Miami, Fla. Died May 2, 2004.

HILL, JAMES STANLEY, computer company executive, consultant; b. Merrickville, Ont., Can., July 24, 1914; m. Doris C. Huelster, 1938; children: George, Janice, Mary, Beverly, Richard. With Minn. Life Ins. Co., 1930-69; sr. v.p., 1966-69; pres. Digiplan, Inc., White Bear Lake, Minn., 1969—2006, Red Oak Press, 1994—2006. Bd. dirs., chmn. audit com. Hadco Inc., 1981-98; pub. spkr., 1994-2006.

Author: Confessions of an 80 Year Old Boy, 1994, Almost Immortal, 1996. Treas. Minn. State H.S. Math. League, 1984-2004; bd. dirs. United Hosp., 1972-99. Fellow Soc. Actuaries (bd. govs., v.p.). Died Dec. 25, 2005.

HILL, LAWRENCE SIDNEY, finance educator; b. Gary, Ind., Nov. 10, 1923; m. Evelyn Honig, Mar. 22, 1964; 1 child, Robert J. BSE, Purdue U., 1947; cert. in Indsl. Hygiene, Ga. Inst. Tech., 1948; MBA, U. So. Calif., 1960, MSIE, 1962, Engr., 1965, PhD, 1968. Registered profl. engr., Calif. Asst. indsl. engr. USX Corp., Gary, 1947, indsl. engr., 1951—52; engr. indsl. hygiene Ill. Dept. Pub. Health, Chgo., 1948—51; sr. engr. Nat. Safety Coun., Chgo., 1953; sr. indsl. engr. Martin Marietta Co., Balt., 1953—55; group head McDonnell Douglas Co., Santa Monica, Calif., 1955—57; sr. mem. staff Rand Corp., Santa Monica, 1957—71; prof. mgmt. sci, Calif. State U., L.A., 1969—97; cons., prin. engr. Ralph M. Parsons Co., Pasadena, Calif., 1973—82; v.p. Calif. Tech. Sys., Inc., Pasadena, 1979—82; cons., sr. mem. tech. staff TRW Inc., Redondo Beach, Calif., 1982—90; cons., environ. mgr. USN, Long Beach, Calif., 1991—94. Lectr. U. So. Calif., 1964—70; vis. lectr. Ops. Rsch. Soc. Am./Inst. Mgmt. Scis., 1973—95; expert witness in safety, mgmt., from 1986. Contbr. articles to profl. jours., chapters to books. Mem.: Alpha Iota Delta, Alpha Pi Mu. Avocation: sports. Home: Malibu, Calif. Died Oct. 2005.

HILLARD, GARY EDWARD, metal products executive; b. New Brighton, Pa., Mar. 16, 1951; s. Robert Edward and Vada Virginia (Burkhart) H.; m. Diana Lynn Sheets, Aug. 20, 1971; children: Gary Edward Jr., Tracie Lynn. BA, U. Pitts., 1973; MS, Robert Morris Coll., 1980. Cert. in prodn. and inventory mgmt., cert. in integrated resource mgmt. Scheduling supr. Crucible Steel, Inc., Midland, Pa., 1973-82; prodn. and inventory control supr. Magnetics, Inc., Butler, Pa., 1982-86; materials mgr. Hunt Value Co., Salem, Ohio, 1986-89, Kennametal, Inc., Roanoke Rapids, N.C., from 1989. Mem. Am. Prodn. and Inventory Control Soc. (v.p. membership 1990-92, Mem. of Yr. 1990). Avocations: flower gardening, travel. Home: Goldsboro, NC. Died Sept. 16, 2004.

HILLARY, E. MILES, marine engineer; b. Bklyn., Mar. 3, 1922; s. Edwin M. and Florence (Donaldson) H.; married, 1944; children: Sandra Lou Hillary Kunz, Donna Mrie Hillary Cipolla, Thomas Miles, Brendan Miles, Ryan Thomas. BS in Marine Engring., U.S. Mcht. Marine Acad., Kings Point, N.Y., 1943; postgrad., Hofstra Coll., NYU. Pres., chief exec. officer Hill-Pak, Inc., Aston, Pa., from 1966. Vice chmn. Packaging Inst., Phila. Served to lt. (s.g.) U.S. Mct. Seamen, 1942-45. Mem.: High 12 (pres. Media, Pa. chpt. 1988), Masons, Shriners. Republican. Presbyterian. Avocations: boating, fishing. Home: Media, Pa. Died Aug. 28, 2004.

HILLER, STANLEY, JR., manufacturing executive; b. San Francisco, Nov. 15, 1924; s. Stanley and Opal (Perkins) Hiller; m. Carolyn Balsdon, May 25, 1946; children: Jeffrey, Stephen. Student, Atuzed Prep. Sch., U. Calif., 1943. Pres. Hiller Aircraft divsn., Kaiser Cargo, Inc., Berkeley, Calif., 1944—45; organized Hiller Aircraft Corp. (formerly United Helicopters, Inc.), Palo Alto, Calif., 1945, pres., CEO, 1950—64; (co. bought by Fairchild Stratos 1964); mem. exec. com. Fairchild Hiller Corp., 1965; chmn. bd., CEO Reed Tool Co., Houston, Bekins, 1980, York Internat., 1985, Baker Internat. Corp., 1975, Keytronic Corp., from 1992; ptnr. Hiller Investment Co. Named 1 of 10 Outstanding Young Men U.S., 1952; recipient Fawcett award, 1944, Disting. Svc. award, Nat. Def. Transp. Soc., 1958. Fellow: Am. Helicopter Soc. (hon.); mem.: Am. Soc. of Pioneers, Am. Inst. Aeros. and Astronautics, Phi Kappa Sigma. Died Apr. 20, 2006.

HILLJE, BARBARA BROWN, lawyer; b. Carlisle, Pa., Dec. 18, 1942; d. R. Morrison and Gladys M. (Lauver) Brown; m. John W. Hillje, Mar. 23, 1968. AB, Vassar Coll., 1964; BS in Edn., Ind. U. Pa., 1965; MA, Temple U., 1971, ABD, 1977; JD, Villanova U., 1984. Bar: Pa. 1984, U.S. Dist. Ct. (ea. dist.) Pa. 1984, N.J. 1985, U.S. Dist. Ct. N.J. 1985, U.S. Supreme Ct. 1990. English tchr. Council Rock Sr. High Sch., Newtown, Pa., 1965-68; assoc. Harry J. Agzigian and Assocs., Levittown, Pa., 1985-87; pvt. practice Langhorne, Pa., 1987—2006. Contbr. articles to profl. jours. Bd. dirs., pres. bd. Children of Aging Parents, Levittown, 1985-93; mem. facility ethics com. Statesman Health & Rehab. Ctr., Levittown, Pa., 1996-2006; bd. dirs. D'Youville Manor, 2001-06. Recipient Women Helping Women award Soroptimists of Indian Rock, Inc., 1995; named Woman of Yr., Lower Bucks AAUW, 1985, Neshaminy BPW, 1987, Legal Humanitarian of Yr., Bucks County United Way, 1994, Consumer Connection award, 1996. Mem. AAUW (bd. dirs., legis. cons. Pa. divsn. 1990-92), Middletown-Newtown LWV (bd. dirs. 1983-89, citizen campaign watch adv. panel 1992, 94, 96), Pa. Bar Assn., Nat. Acad. Elder Law Attys., Older Women's League (legis. chair 1984-94, Women of Worth award 1993). Home: Levittown, Pa. Died Mar. 14, 2006.

HILTON, JAMES ARTHUR, clergy member; b. Salem, Ind., June 6, 1937; s. Walter Francis and Bernice Frye (Dawalt) H.; m. Carolyn June Sprecher, June 19, 1960; children: Mark Alan, Holly Anne Hamer. BA, Butler U., 1959; MDiv, Christian Theol. Sem., 1962; DMin, Emory U., 1979. Ordained to ministry Christian Ch., 1963. Pastor First Christian Ch., Rensselaer, Ind., 1963-73; sr. pastor Tropical Sands Christian Ch., Palm Beach Gardens, Fla., 1973-87, Fairview Christian Ch., Lynchburg, Va., 1987-90, First Christian Ch., Tampa, Fla., 1990-96, Ctrl. Christian Ch., Clearwater, Fla., from 1996. Dir. Global Mission, Christian Ch., 1990-93; v.p. Christian Ch., Indianapolis, 1972; chmn. New Congregation Com., Christian Ch., Orlando, Fla., 1982-86. Author: Congregational Administration, 1979, God's Word Interpreted, 1992. Mem. adv. bd. Planned Parenthood, Palm Beach, Fla., 1985-86; congl. witness on sch. prayer U.S. Congress, 1995; trustee Lexington Theol. Sem., 1996—. Recipient Neighbor award St. Joseph's Coll., Rensselaer, 1973, Brotherhood award B'nai B'rith, Palm Beach, 1985. Mem. Rotary Club. Avocations: reading, swimming, history. Home: Clearwater, Fla. Died Jan. 5, 2005.

HILTON, ROBERT PARKER, SR., national security affairs consultant, retired naval officer; b. Atlanta, Mar. 17, 1927; s. William Linwood and Elizabeth Shumate (Parker) H.; m. Joan Maxine Mader, Sept. 3, 1955; children: Robert Parker, Wendy Hilton-Jones. BA, U. Miss., 1948; postgrad., Naval War Coll., 1961, Nat. War Coll., 1968; MA in Russian Affairs, Georgetown U., 1964; postgrad., Sino-Soviet Inst. George Washington U., 1964-68. Commd. ensign U.S. Navy, 1948, advanced through grades to rear adm., 1972; svc. all operational fleets cruisers/destroyers Korea, Japan, Vietnam, Italy, Belgium; asst. chief staff logistics CINCSOUTH, Naples, Italy, 1972-74; dep. dir. force devel. and strategic plans Office Joint Chiefs Staff, 1974-76; dir. East Asia and Pacific region Office Sec. Def., Washington, 1976-77; dir. strategy plans and policy div. OPNAV (OP60), 1977-78; asst. dep. CNO, Plans and Policy, 1979; dep. asst. chief staff Plans and Policy SHAPE, 1979-81; vice dir. ops. Office Joint Chiefs Staff, 1981-83; retired USN, 1983; sole proprietor Hilton Assocs., Alexandria, Va., 1984-98. Cons. nat. security affairs, also nat. security and def. matters Inst. Def. Analyses, Alexandria, Va., 1984-94, mem. rsch. staff, 1994-2004 Decorated Def. D.S.M., Navy D.S.M., Def. Superior Svc. medal, Legion of Merit, Bronze Star, Joint Service Commendation medal. Mem. Coun. Fgn. Rels., Councillor Atlantic Coun. (sr.), U.S. Naval Inst., Nat. Trust Historic Preservation, Pi Sigma Alpha, Pi Kappa Phi, Phi Delta Theta. Clubs: Masons, Army Navy Country. Episcopalian. Home: Alexandria, Va. Died Apr. 28, 2004.

HIMELSTEIN, MONROE, retired surgeon, educator; b. Lebanon, Conn., Jan. 18, 1924; s. Max A. and Dorothy J. (Malkin) H.; m. Faith Freedman, Apr. 26, 1953; children: Mary H. Cohn, Jane H. Sheehan. AB, Wesleyan U., Middletown, Conn., 1947; MD, Columbia U., 1951. Diplomate Am. Bd. Surgery, Nat. Bd. Med. Examiners. Intern Hartford (Conn.) Hosp., 1951-52, surgical resident, 1952-56, clin. asst. to sr. surgeon, from 1956; asst. clin. prof. Dartmouth Med. Sch., Hanover, N.H., from 1984; assoc. clin. prof. surgery U. Conn. Sch. of Medicine, Farmington, from 1970. Cons. in surgery Inst. for Living, Hartford, 1977—, Rocky Hill Vet.'s Hosp., Rocky Hill, Conn., 1968—; bd. dirs. Capital Area Health Consortium, Hartford; chief of staff Hartford Hosp., 1986-89, bd. dirs. and exec. com., corporator; lectr. in field. Contbr. articles to profl. jours. Lt. (j.g.) USNR, 1943-46, PTO. Fellow Am. Coll. Surgeons; mem. Conn. Soc. Am. Bd. Srugeons, New Eng. Surgical Soc. (sr. mem.), AMA, Conn. Med. Soc., Hartford County Med. Assn. (bd. dirs. 1986-92), Hartford Med. Soc. (chmn. bd. censors and adv. bd.). Jewish. Avocations: golf, gardening, furniture refinishing. Died Mar. 2, 2005.

HIMES, GEORGE ELLIOTT, pathologist; b. Huntington, W.Va., Jan. 5, 1922; s. Connell Bradley and Elizabeth (Skeans) H.; m. Rita T. Wasniewski (dec. July 1993); children: Rita Ann Brust, Susan Ruth Burger, George Elliott Jr., Brent Lee; m. Barbara A. Cunningham, Dec. 21, 1994. Student, U. Cin., 1939-42; DO, Chgo. Coll. Osteo. Medicine, 1942-45. Intern Lamb Mem. Hosp., Denver, 1945-46; resident pathology Chgo. Osteo Hosp., 1946-48; asst. prof. pathology Chgo. Coll. Osteo Med., 1948-56; asst. lab. dir. Chgo. Osteo Hosp., 1948-51; dir. of labs Flint (Mich.) Osteo Hosp., 1951-87, dir. of labs and nuclear med., 1957-80, dir. sch. med. tech., 1975-85; assoc. prof. pathology Coll. Osteo Med., Des Moines, 1968-89; adj. prof. pathology Coll. Osteo. Medicine Mich. State U., East Lansing, Mich., 1974-84, clin. prof. pathology Coll. Osteo. Medicine; mem. adv. coun. on diabetes Genesys Regional Med. Ctr., 2003, mem. Type II diabetes. Mem. radiation, chem. & biol. safety com. Mich. State U., 1978—; mem. Am. Osteo. Bd. Pathology, 1959-68, Am. Osteo. Bd. Nuclear Medicine, 1974-84. Bd. dirs. ARC, Flint, 1963-74, United Way, 1964-72; pres. Flint Civitan Club, 1954. Mem. AMA, AAAS, Am. Osteo. Coll. Pathologists (past pres. and sec.-treas. 1954-72), Am. Osteo. Assn., Am. Assn. Blood Banks, Mich. Osteopathic Assn., Coll. Am. Pathologists, Am. Soc. Clin. Pathologists, Soc. Nuclear Medicine, Mich. Soc. Pathologists, Genesee Country Osteo. Assn., Nat. Assn. Photoshop Profls., Flint Golf Club (past pres.). Avocations: golf, stamps, computing sciences. Died Feb. 18, 2004.

HIMES, KENNETH ALAN, retired marketing executive; b. Phila., Nov. 2, 1937; s. Kenneth Elwood and Thelma Frances (Dieffenbacher) H.; m. Diane Margaret Zurinsky, Sept. 14, 1959; children: Christine Ann Himes Daly, Susan Leigh. BS in Bus., Lycoming Coll., 1959. With Woolrich (Pa.) Inc., 1959-90, sales rep., 1960-85, sr. v.p. mktg., 1985-90. Founder, sec. Woolrich Vol. Fire Co., 1960; trustee Lycoming Coll., 1987-95, Williamsport Hosp. and med. Ctr., 1988-95; fire commr. Bluffton Twp., 1995-2003; cochmn. Fire Commn., 1997-98. Named Outstanding Alumnus Lycoming Coll., 1987. Mem. Nat. Assn. Men's and Boys' Apparel, Somerset Hills Jaycees, Masons, Rotary, Sigma Pi (treas. 1957). Republican. Methodist. Avocations: golf, travel, fishing. Home: Hilton Head Island, SC. Died Oct. 22, 2004.

HIMMELFARB, MILTON, retired editor; b. Bklyn., Oct. 21, 1918; s. Max and Bertha (Lerner) H.; m. Judith Siskind, Nov. 26, 1950; children: Martha, Edward, Miriam, Anne, Sarah, Naomi, Dan. BA, CCNY, 1938, MS, 1939; B.Hebrew Lit., Jewish Theol. Sem. Coll., 1939; diplôme, U. Paris, 1939; postgrad., Columbia U., 1942—47. Dir. information and research Am. Jewish Com., N.Y.C., 1955-86; editor Am. Jewish Year Book, N.Y.C., 1959-86; contbg. editor Commentary mag., N.Y.C., 1960-86. Vis. prof. Jewish Theol. Sem., N.Y.C., 1967-68, 71-72; vis. lectr. Yale, 1971; vis. prof. Reconstructionist Rabbinical Coll., Phila., 1972-73. Author: The Jews of Modernity, 1973. Mem. U.S. Holocaust Meml. Coun., 1986-89. Home: White Plains, NY. Died Jan. 4, 2006.

HINCKLEY, TED C., historian, educator, writer; b. NYC, Oct. 4, 1925; s. Theodore Charles and Eunice Marguerite (Platt) H.; m. Caryl Fay Chesmore, June 17, 1948; children: Susan Platt Hinckley Koester, Deborah Christine Hinckley Brooks. BA in Bus. Adminstrn., Claremont McKenna Coll., Claremont, Calif., 1950; BS in History, N.W. Mo. State U., Maryville, 1951; MA in Edn., U. Mo., Kansas City, 1953; PhD in History, Ind. U., 1961. Jr. exec. Chesmore Seed Co., St. Joseph, Mo., 1950; tchr. history Barstow Sch., Kansas City, Mo., 1951-53; asst. to pres. Claremont McKenna Coll., 1953-55; headmaster St. Katharine's Sch., Davenport, Iowa, 1955-57; tchg. asst. Ind. U., Bloomington, 1957-59; prof. history San Jose State U., Calif., 1959-90; adj. prof. Western Wash. U., Bellingham, from 1991. Lectr. Fulbright Assocs., Yogyakarta, Indonesia, 1994—95; PACE lectr. USS Boxer, 1997, USS A. Lincoln, 1998, USS Leyte Gulf, 1999, USS Nicholas, 2001; ACCL lectr. SS Grande Mariner, 2001; AP reader Hist., from 2000. Author: John G. Brady, 1982, The Canoe Rocks, 1995, War, Wings...1945, 1996, The Americanization of Alaska, 1972; mem. editl. bd. Pacific N.W. Quar., 1974-93, Alaska History, 1984-2000, Jour. of the West, 1977—. Mem. Calif. Hist. Preservation Commn., Sacramento, 1980—85; assoc. Danforth Found., St. Louis, 1962; playwright Four Women, Webb Sch., Knoxville, 2001; elder Saratoga Presbyn. Ch., Calif., 1968—70. With USN, 1943—46, 2d lt. USAR, 1950—53, ensign USNR, 1953—56. Huntington Libr. summer fellow, 1971, Alaska Hist. Commn. fellow 1983-84; grantee Am. Philos. Soc., 1962, 66. Mem.: Fulbright Assn., Alaska Hist. Soc., Western Hist. Assn. (coun. 1987—90), Am. Hist. Assn., Phi Beta Kappa. Christian. Avocations: play writing, gardening, carpentry. Home: Sedro Woolley, Wash. Died Sept. 5, 2004.

HIRSCHFELD, ABRAHAM JACOB, real estate developer, municipal official; b. Rymanov, Poland, Dec. 20, 1919; s. Simon and Sara (Simon) H.; m. Zipora Teicher, July 4, 1943; children: Rachel, Elie. PhD (hon.), Seminarius Lutherensus Espiscopus Americannus, 1961. Pres. Farlands Enterprises Inc., N.Y.C., Radio City Parking, Inc., N.Y.C., Vertical Club Corp., N.Y.C., Hirschfeld Realty, N.Y.C.; ptnr. New York Penta Hotel, N.Y.C., 1983—2005; former commr. City of Miami Beach, Fla. Organizer First Women's Bank; developer of the Chm. Bank Bldg.; builder Hirschfeld Theatre, 1988; former chmn., pub. N.Y. Post, Open Air Newspaper. Author Accidental Wedding, 1986. Mem. U.S. Electoral Coll., 1968-76, Pub. Devel. Corp., N.Y.C., 1970, Tri-State Regional Planning Commn., N.Y.C., 1979-82; treas. Dem. State Com., N.Y., 1972; pres. Dems. for Reagan, N.Y.C., 1980; trustee Fifth Ave. Synagogue, N.Y.C., 1982—, Daytop Found., N.Y.C., 1982; chair Keter Abraham Synagogue, Miami, Fla., 1987; mem. Tony awards com. League Am. Theatres and Prodrs., Inc. Recipient Ben Gurion award State of Israel Bonds, 1975. Mem. Friar Club (N.Y.C.), High Ridge Country Club (Palm Beach, Fla.), Univ. Club. Democrat. Jewish. Died Aug. 9, 2005.

HIRSCHHORN, HERBERT HERMAN, lawyer; b. Bklyn., Apr. 13, 1909; s. Bernard and Rae (Greenberg) H.; m. Rose Berger, July 10, 1968. BA, NYU, 1930, JD, 1932, D in Jud. Sci., 1934, MA, 1937. Bar: N.Y. 1934, U.S. Supreme Ct. 1959, U.S. Dist. Ct. (so. and ea. dists.) N.Y. 1962, U.S. Dist. Ct. (we. dist.) N.Y. 1964, U.S. Ct. Appeals (2d cir.) 1966. Assoc. Gair Gair Conason Steigman & Mackauf and predecessor firms, N.Y.C., from 1932. Dir. emeritus NYU Alumni Fedn.; dir. Coll. Arts & Sci., Sch. Law & Grad. Sch. Arts 7 Sci. Alumni Assn., NYU. Recipient Alumni Meritorious Svc. award NYU, 1982, Disting. Svc. award NYU and Washington Sq. Coll., 1992, Judge Edward Weinfeld award NYU Law Ctr., 1993; inscribed on the Wall of Honor, NYU Sch. of Law 1996. Mem. ABA, N.Y. State Bar Assn., N.Y. County Lawyers Assn., Am. Judicature Soc., Assn. Trial Lawyers Am., Soc. Med. Jurisprudence, Met. Women's Bar Assn., N.Y. Women's Bar Assn., Internat. Assn. Jewish Lawyers and Jurists, N.Y. State Trial Lawyers Assn. (dir. 1954-80, dir. emeritus 1982—). Home: New York, NY. Died May 22, 2006.

HIRSCHMAN, ALBERT, histology and cell biology educator; b. N.Y.C., Oct. 20, 1921; s. Harry and Pauline (Stadler) H.; m. Mildred Laura Gottschall, July 18, 1943; children: Beverly, Sally Alice, Robert Steven. BS, CUNY, 1942; MS, Poly. U., 1946, PhD, 1952. Chem. technician Jewish Hosp. of Bklyn., 1942-43, sr. technician, 1943-47; instr. L.I. Coll. of Medicine, Bklyn., 1947-52; asst. prof. SUNY Health Sci. Ctr., Bklyn., 1952-62, assoc. prof. histology and cell biology, from 1962. Cons., adj. prof. Touro Coll. Ctr. for Biomed. Edn., Dix Hills, N.Y., 1980—;

vis. prof. Rockefeller U., N.Y.C., 1961-62, Hebrew U., Jerusalem, Israel, 1981-82. Contbr. over 30 sci. articles to profl. jours. Univ. devel. com. United Univ. Professions, Albany, N.Y., 1989—, governing bd., 1989—. Grantee NIH, 1955-73. Mem. AAAS, Am. Chem. Soc., N.Y. Acad. Scis., N.Y. Bone and Tooth Discussion Group (exec. dir. 1965—), Am. Assn. Anatomists. Avocation: computers. Home: Flushing, NY. Died June 6, 2004.

HIRSH, JAMES BAKER, education educator; b. Chgo., July 23, 1949; s. Bernard Louis and Regina (Baker) H.; m. Pat Moore, Dec. 1, 1974 (div. Mar. 1990); children: James E., Erin R. BA, U. Denver, 1971, MA, 1973, PhD, 1976. Dean continuing edn. Muhlenberg Coll., Allentown, Pa., 1976-86; project dir. Nat. Univ. Continuing Edn. Assn., Washington, 1986-87; former dir. continuing edn. Delaware Valley Coll., Doylestown, Pa.; v.p. student affairs Emporia State Univ., Emporia, Kans., 2000—04. Sec. Van Savn Ramsey & Van Houten, Chalfont, Pa., 1989-90; former prin. Adult Edn. Mktg. Svcs., Quakertown, Pa. Editor: Jour. H.E. Mgmt. Bd. dirs. Allentown Libr., 1986; v.p. Allentown Sch. Bd., 1986. Mem. Nat. Univ. Continuing Assn., Assn. Continuing Higher Edn. Democrat. Avocations: reading, writing. Home: Emporia, Kans. Died Nov. 17, 2004.

HITE, LARRY RAY, electrical engineer; b. Aberdeen, S.D., Oct. 3, 1939; s. Erwin R. and Hazel E. (Ives) H.; m. Beverly J. Sombke, Oct. 1, 1961; children: Douglas T., Teresa R. ASEE, Cen. Tech. Inst., Kansas City, Mo., 1961; BSEE, So. Meth. U., Dallas, 1981. Electronics technician Tex. Instruments Inc., Dallas, 1961-74, engr. elec. design, 1974-87, mem. group tech. staff, 1987-98, sr. mem. tech. staff, from 19;98. Contbr. articles to profl. jours.; patentee in field. Mem. IEEE, Experimental Aircraft Assn. Republican. Lutheran. Avocations: sport aviation, antique and classic cars. Home: Dallas, Tex. Died Dec. 14, 2004.

HITE, MARK RICHARD, industrial engineer; b. Marshalltown, Iowa, Aug. 14, 1949; s. Billy Eugene and Doris Rae (Storjohann) H. AA, Boone Jr. Coll., Iowa, 1969; BS, Iowa State U., 1971. Corp. project engr. Ruan Cos., Des Moines, 1973-81, corp. maintenance engr., 1981-83, engring. mgr., from 1983. Councilman 2d ward City of Madrid, Iowa, City of Carlisle, Iowa. Mem. Soc. Automotive Engrs. Republican. Baptist. Home: Carlisle, Iowa. Died Jan. 8, 2005.

HO, ANDREW K. S., pharmacology educator; b. Hong Kong, Apr. 22, 1939; came to U.S., 1967; s. Kaak-Yan and Han-Li (Li) H.; m. Ju-Chang Wei, Nov. 8, 1969; children: Shirley Ann-Fun, Allan An-Li. BSc and MSc, U. Melbourne, Victoria, Australia, 1963; PhD, Monash U., Victoria, Australia, 1967. Postdoctoral fellow NYU Med. Ctr., N.Y.C., 1968-70; rsch. specialist II Mendocino State Hosp., Ukiah, Calif., 1970-72; rsch. assoc. U. Calif., San Francisco, 1970-71; asst. prof. Wayne State U., Detroit, 1972-75; assoc. prof. Coll. of Medicine U. Ill., Peoria, 1975-85, prof. Coll. of Medicine Peoria and Urbana, from 1985. Vis. scientist NIMH, Bethesda, Md., 1972; vis. prof. Heritage Found. of Alta., U. Calgary, Can., 1984-85. Contbr. over 70 articles to profl. jours. Mem. community adv. bd. Chem. Dependence Ctr., Proctor Community Hosp., Peoria, 1980-84. Grantee Am. Heart Assn., 1976, NIH, 1978-91. Mem. ASPET, Assn. Med. Edn. and Rsch. in Substance Abuse, Internat. Soc. for Biomed. Rsch. on Alcoholism. Achievements include patent for alcohol aversion process by enzyme inhibition. Home: Downers Grove, Ill. Died Nov. 22, 2004.

HOBACK, FLORENCE KUNST, retired psychiatrist; b. Grafton, Wv., Oct. 26, 1922; d. G H A and Mary (Conaway) Kunst; m. John Holland Hoback, Oct. 27, 1945 (dec.); children: Holly Hoback Clark, Conaway K. AB, W.Va. U., 1944; MD, U. Md., Balt., 1948. Pvt. practice medicine, Huntington, W.Va., 1950-55; internal medicine VA Hosp., Huntington, 1955-60; resident psychiatry Med. Coll. VA, Richmond, 1960-65; pvt. practice psychiatry Huntington; ret., 1988. Police commn. City of Huntington, 1975-77. Fellow Am. Psychiatric Assn., mem. AMA, W.Va. Med. Assn., Am. Women's Med. Assn. Avocations: gardening, history. Home: Huntington, W.Va. Died Mar. 2, 2005.

HOBBS, MAX EDWARD, lawyer; b. Decatur, Ind., Nov. 20, 1931; s. Joseph Ernest and Helen Marjorie (Fletcher) H.; m. Holley Johnson, Aug. 27, 1957; children: John Maxwell, Thomas Fletcher. BS, Ind. U., 1954, JD, 1960. Bar: Ind. 1960, U.S. Dist. Ct. (no. and so. dists.) Ind., U.S. Ct. Appeals (7th cir.), U.S. Supreme Ct. Assoc. Hasley & Eggers, Ft. Wayne, Ind., 1960-62; ptnr. Willis, Hobbs & Connor, Ft. Wayne, 1962-82; pvt. practice Ft. Wayne, 1982-92; with Hobbs & Swihart, Ft. Wayne, from 1992. Assoc. city atty. City of Ft. Wayne, 1962-64; gen. counsel Hosp. Authority of City of Ft. Wayne, 1975—; cert. mediator, State of Ind. Pres. Allen County Hist. Soc., Ft. Wayne, 1970-73; bd. dirs. Historic Ft. Wayne, Civic Theater, Ft. Wayne. Maj. USAF, 1954-57. Mem. ABA, Allen County Bar Assn. Democrat. Avocations: sailing, gardening, woodworking, acting. Home: Fort Wayne, Ind. Died Apr. 3, 2005.

HODGE, CHARLES FRANKLIN, entertainer, writer; b. Decatur, Ala., Dec. 14, 1934; s. George Elbert and Mattie Pearl (Hawkins) H. Grad. high sch., Decatur. Tenor Pathfinders, Columbus, Ohio, 1953-54; lead tenor Foggy River Boys, Springfield, Mo., 1954-58; singer, musician, arranger Elvis Presley, Memphis and Los Angeles, 1960-77; film actor, tech. advisor Elvis Dick Clark Prodns., Hollywood, Calif., 1979; comic Chris Beards Onan Prodns., Santa Monica, Calif., 1980; ind. lectr., entertainer, author Decatur and Los Angeles, 1980—2006. Author: Me 'n' Elvis, 1984. Served as pvt. U.S. Army, 1958-60. Mem. Screen Actors Guild, AFTRA, Am. Fedn. Musicians. Lodges: Eagles. Avocations: boating, watching old movies on tv. Home: Decatur, Ala. Died Mar. 3, 2006.

HODGE, ERNEST EDWARD, physician; b. Galveston, Tex., Nov. 20, 1951; s. Myrle Claude and Ethel Jane (Lyon) H.; m. Betsy Jo Bocskey, Nov. 26, 1977. BS in Chemistry, U. Tex., 1973, MA, 1975; MD, U. Tex., San Antonio, 1979. Intern. U. Tex. Health Sci. Ctr., San Antonio, 1979-80, resident in urology, 1980-85, clin. instr. dept. surgery, div. urology, 1986-87; staff urologist, transplant surgeon Humana Hosp., San Antonio, 1986-87; staff urologist SW Tex. Meth. Hosp, St. Luke's Luth. Hosp., San Antonio, 1986-87; cons. urology Audie Murphy V.A. Hosp., San Antonio, 1986-87; fellowship Cleve. Clin. Found. Renal Transplantation and Renovascular Surgery, 1985-86; mem. dept. urology Cleve. Clinic Found., from 1987; staff urologist, dir. renal transplant program Charleston (W.Va.) Area Med. Ctr., 1987-91; head sect. renal transplant Cleve. Clinic Found., from 1991. Mem. adv. bd., sci. com. South Tex. Organ Bank, San Antonio, 1986-87; med. dir. W.Va. div. Va. Organ Procurement Agy., pres., 1990. Contbr. 18 articles to profl. jours. Mem. ACS, AMA, So. Med. Assn., Bexar County Med. Soc., Tex. Med. Assn., Kanawha Med. Soc., Nat. Kidney Found., Am. Soc. Nephrology, Urologic Soc. Transplantation and Vascular Surgery, W.Va. State Med. Soc. Assn., W.Va. Urologic Soc. Republican. Avocations: sports, bowling. Home: Austin, Tex. Died Jan. 24, 2004.

HODGES, MARGARET MOORE, writer, educator; b. Indpls., July 26, 1911; d. Arthur Carlisle and Anna Marie (Mason) Moore; m. Fletcher Hodges, Jr., Sept. 10, 1932; children: Fletcher III, Arthur Carlisle, John Andrews. AB with honors, Vassar Coll., 1932; MLS; Carnegie Libr. Staff scholar, Carnegie Inst. Tech., 1958. Lectr. U. Pitts. Grad. Sch. Library and Info. Services, 1964-68, asst. prof., 1968-72, assoc. prof., 1972-75, prof., 1975-77, prof. emeritus, 1977—2005 (Children's libr., radio and TV storyteller) Carnegie Library Pitts., 1953—64, (story specialist) Pitts. Pub. Schs., 1964—68, (storyteller) WQED Schs. Svcs. Dept NIT network., from 1965; author: (juvenile books) One Little Drum, 1958, What's for Lunch Charley?, 1961, Club Against Keats, 1962, Tell It Again, 1963, Secret in the Woods, 1963, Wave, 1964, Hatching of Joshua Cobb, 1967, Constellation, a Shakespeare Anthology, 1968, Sing Out, Charley!, 1968, Lady Queen Anne, 1969, Making of Joshua Cobb, 1971, Gorgon's Head, 1972, Hopkins of the Mayflower, 1972, Fire Bringer, 1972, Persephone and the Springtime, 1973, Baldur and the Mistletoe, 1974, Freewheeling of Joshua Cobb, 1974, Knight Prisoner, The Tale of Sir Thomas Malory and His King Arthur, 1976, The High Riders, 1980, The Little Humpbacked Horse, 1980, The Avenger, 1982, If You Had a Horse, 1984, Saint George and the Dragon, 1984, Making a Difference, 1989, The Voice of the Great Bell, 1989, The Arrow and the Lamp, 1989, The Kitchen Knight, 1990, Buried Moon, 1990, Brother Francis and the Friendly Beasts, 1991, Saint Jerome and the Lion, 1991, Hauntings, 1991, Don Quixote and Sancho Panza, 1992, Of Swords and Sorcerers, 1993, St. Patrick and and the Peddler, 1993, The Hero of Bremen, 1993, Hidden in Sand, 1994, Gulliver in Lilliput, 1995, Comus, 1996, Molly Limbo, 1996; co-editor: Elva S. Smith's The History of Children's Literature, 1980, The True Tale of Johnny Appleseed, 1997, Silent Night, the Song and Its Story, 1997, Up the Chimney, 1998, Joan of Arc, the Lily Maid, 1999, The Boy Who Drew Cats, 2002, The Legend of St. Christopher, 2002, Merlin and the Making of the King, 2004. Mem. ALA (Newbery-Caldecott com. 1960), Pa. Library Assn., Am. Assn. Library Schs., Pitts. Bibliophiles, Zonta Internat., Distinguished Daus. Pa. Republican. Episcopalian. Home: Verona, Pa. Died Dec. 13, 2005.

HODGSON, RICHARD SARGEANT, marketing executive; b. Breckenridge, Minn., Oct. 18, 1924; s. Lorin Baird and Ruth Frances (Sargeant) H.; m. Lois Marjorie Hogan, Jan. 19, 1952; children: Susan Rolfing, Steven, Scott, Lisa. AA, N.D. State Sch. Sci., 1943; student, Gustavus Adolphus Coll., 1943-44, Western Mich. Coll., 1944, Northwestern U. Assoc. editor Billboard Pub. Co., Chgo., 1946-47, Tide mag., Chgo., 1947-48; dir. pub. relations N.D. State Sch. Sci., Wahpeton, 1948-50; exec. editor Advt. Publs., Inc., Chgo., 1952-59; pres. Am. Mktg. Services, Boston, 1960-62; div. dir. R.R. Donnelley & Sons Co., Chgo., 1962-72; v.p. Franklin Mint, Franklin Center, Pa., 1972-75; pres. Sargeant House, Westtown, Pa., 1975—2004. Bd. dirs. Foster & Gallagher, Inc., Peoria, Ill. Author: Direct Mail Showmanship, 1961, Direct Mail and Mail Order Handbook, 1964, Direct Mail in the Political Process, 1976, Greatest Direct Mail Sales Letters, 1986, Complete Guide to Catalog Marketing, 1991. Lt. col. USMC, 1942-67. Recipient Jesse H. Neale award Am. Bus. Press, 1959, Dartnell Gold medal, Dartnell Pub. Co., 1964, Ed Meyer award Direct Mktg. Ednl. Assn., 1985; named Mktg. Communications Man of Yr. Mktg. Communications Execs. Assn., 1973. Mem. Direct Mktg. Assn. (bd. dirs. 1962-75), Chgo. Assn. Direct Mktg. (pres.), Westtown-Goshen Rotary (pres. 1991-92). Home: West Chester, Pa. Died Jan. 26, 2006.

HODSON, PHILLIP HARVEY, microbiologist; b. Springville, Utah, July 25, 1931; s. LeRoy Ainsworth and Iva (Phillips) H.; m. Maxine Reinhardt, July 1, 1955; children: Phillip Max, Marian, Elaine, Cheryl. AA, Snow Jr. Coll., 1951; BS, Brigham Young U., 1953, MS, 1957; PhD, U. Tex., 1962. Lab. technician Utah Valley Hosp., Provo, 1955-57; rsch. scientist U. Tex., Austin, 1957-61; researcher and prodn. Monsanto Co., St. Louis, 1962-72; fermention microbiologist Eli Lilly and Co., Indpls., 1972-93; retired, 1993. Contbr. articles to profl. jours.; patentee in field. Cpl. U.S. Army, 1953-55. Mem. Am. Soc. Microbiology, Soc. Indsl. Microbiology, Am. Chem. Soc., Sigma Xi. Mem. Lds Ch. Avocations: photography, auto repair. Home: Indianapolis, Ind. Died Jan. 5, 2005.

HOEHLER, FRED KENNETH, JR., retired labor studies institute administrator; b. Cin., Nov. 18, 1918; s. Fred Kenneth and Dorothy Scovil (Stevens) H.; m. Lisa G. Portman, Apr. 27, 1979; children: Fred Kenneth III, Daniel Price. BS, U. Ariz., 1942; MA, U. Chgo., 1947. Asst. prof. pub. adminstrn. U. P.R., 1947-49; asst. prof. polit. sci. Pa. State U., 1949-54; asst. dir. social security dept. AFL-CIO, Washington, 1954-56; prof., assoc. dir. Sch. Labor and Indsl. Relations, Mich. State U., East Lansing, 1956-70; dir. George Meany Ctr. for Labor Studies, Washington, 1969-85. Edn. dir. United Steelworkers Am., Pitts., 1965-67; faculty mem. Salzburg Seminar in Am. Studies, 1978; mem. Gov.'s Study Commn. on Workmen's Compensation, Lansing, 1960-62; mem. Nat. Commn. on Higher Edn. Issues, 1981-82; cons. community action orgn. OEO, 1964-65; advance study program Brookings Instn., 1962-71 Mem. adv. com. Grad. Sch. Social Work Portland State U.; trustee U. Mid-Am., 1976-82; chmn. bd. dirs. Am. Open U.; Served with USAAF, 1943-46. Received citation pub. service U. Chgo., 1971 Mem. Univ. Labor Edn. Assn. (chmn. 1961), Nat. Inst. Labor Edn. (bd. dirs. 1961-65) Clubs: City of Portland (program com.). Home: Bellingham, Wash. Died Jan. 4, 2006.

HOEHN, MARGARET MAIER, neurologist; b. San Francisco, Nov. 24, 1930; d. Peter Paul and Eva Till Maier; children: Robert Anthony Till, Margaret Eve Maier Hanan. BA, U. Sask., Saskatoon, Can., 1950; MD, U. B.C., Vancouver, Can., 1954; postgrad., U. B.C. and Nat. Hosp. Neurol. Diseases, London, 1954—60. Asst. in neurology Boston U., 1961-62; asst. prof. Columbia U., NYC, 1963-70; clin. prof. U. Colo., Denver, from 1970, dir. Parkinson's disease and movement disorder clinic, from 1984. Clin. rschr. Parkinson's Disease and other movement disorders; cons. in clin. rsch., lectr. in field. Contbr. over 100 articles to profl. jours.; developer Hoehn and Yahr Scale as a measure of severity of Parkinson's disease. Fellow ACP, Royal Coll. Physicians Can., Am. Acad. Neurology; mem. Am. Neurol. Assn., Movement Disorder Soc., Colo. Soc. Clin. Neurology, Alpha Omega Alpha. Avocations: travel, bridge, swimming, reading, theater. Died July 16, 2005.

HOENACK, AUGUST FREDERICK, architect; b. N.Y.C., Apr. 1, 1908; s. Hugo H. and Hulda (Kilian) H.; m. Mary Margery Course, June 14, 1939; children— Stephen A., Judith (Mrs. Paul Schultz), Francis A., August Jeremy. B.Arch., Pratt Inst., 1938; student, Columbia, 1930-31; postgrad., George Washington U., 1940-41. Architect PBA, Washington, 1938-41; asso. architect hospital facilities USPHS, Washington, 1942-46, asst. chief, 1946-55, chief architecture, engring. equipment br., 1955-68; v.p. firm Jensen & Halstead (Architects, Engrs. & Consultants), Chgo., 1968-73; asso. Dalton, Dalton, Little, Newport, Bethesda, Md., 1973-80. Contbr. profl. jours. Recipient Superior Service award HEW, 1967, Outstanding Alumnus award Pratt Inst., 1968 Fellow AIA (mem. health environment com. 1960-67), Am. Assn. Hosp. Planning (Distinguished Service to Hosp. Design award 1967), Am. Hosp. Assn., Internat. Hosp. Fedn. Home: Madison, Conn. Died Mar. 11, 2006.

HOEPRICH, PAUL DANIEL, internist, educator; b. Alliance, Ohio, Jan. 3, 1924; s. Michael and Katharina (Wagner) H.; m. Muriel Lucy Blackwell, July 11, 1948; children: Martha Sue Kennedy, Paul Daniel Jr., Thomas Eric, Kurt Lincoln. Student, Harvard Coll.; MD, Harvard Med. Sch., 1947. Diplomate Am. Bd. Internal Medicine. Instr. medicine Johns Hopkins Sch. Medicine, Balt., 1956; instr. epidemiology Johns Hopklns Sch. Hygiene & Pub. Health, Balt., 1956; asst., assoc. prof. medicine U. Utah Coll Medicine, Salt Lake City, 1957-67, asst., assoc. prof. pathology, 1959-67; prof. medicine U. Calif. Sch. Medicine, Davis, 1967-91, emeritus, from 1991, prof. pathology, 1968-86, chief infectious and immunlogic diseases, 1967-80, chief med. mycology, 1986-91. Cons. physician in field. Editor, author: The Fluids of Parenteral Body Cavities, 1959, Infectious Diseases, Edits. 1-5, 1972-94; editor The Infectious Diseases Newsletter, 1985-90; contbr. chpts. to books and articles to med. and scientific jours. Capt. U.S. Army M.C., 1950-53. Recipient Soma Weiss award Harvard Med. Sch., 1947, Disting. Faculty award U. Calif. Davis Med. Ctr., 1986; Fogarty sr. fellow NIH, 1976. Fellow ACP, Infectious Disease Soc. Am. (founding); mem. AAAS, Am. Soc. Clin. Investigation, Assn. Am. Physicians. Home: Fairfax, Va. Died Sept. 16, 2004.

HOFELDT, JOHN W., retired lawyer; b. Elkhart Lake, Wis., Sept. 6, 1920; s. Johann Heinrich and Matilda A. (Kuester) H.; m. Marion Ruth Meyer, Nov. 27, 1943; children: Nancy R. Hofeldt Werley, William A., Mark R. Ph.B., U. Wis.-Madison, 1943, LL.B. (editor Law Rev. 1946-47), 1947. Bar: Wis. 1947, Ill. 1948. Since practiced in, Chgo.; ptnr. Haight & Hofeldt (and predecessors), 1955—89; ret., 1989. Lectr. John Marshall Grad. Sch., Chgo., 1971-91. Mem. Ill. Sch. Dist. 194 Bd. Edn., 1964-72.

Served with USN, 1943-46. Mem. ABA, Wis. Bar Assn., Ill. Bar Assn., Patent Law Assn. Chgo., Masons, Shriners Union League Club (Chgo.). Republican. Home: Madison, Wis. Died Feb. 28, 2006.

HOFFMAN, ELAINE JANET, artist; b. Oak Park, Ill., Aug. 19, 1925; d. Dewitt Alexander and Magda Catherine (Christensen) Patterson; m. Carl Rudolph Hoffman; children: Clayton, Lynda Hoffman Snodgrass, Byron. Degree, Averett U., Danville, Va., 1945; BA, Marylhurst U., Lake Oswego, Oreg., 1978; grad., Northwest Watercolor Sch., Chgo., 1965, North Light Art Sch., Oreg., 1990. Active Lake Oswego Arts Devel. Com., 1989—, Lake Oswego Adult Ctr., 1989—; deacon Lake Grove Presbyn. Ch., Lake Oswego, 1982—. Mem. Art Inst. Oreg., Portland Critique Group, Portland Watercolor Group, Watercolor Soc. Oreg., Colored Pencil Soc. Am. (v.p. 2001), Lake Area Artists (pres 1967-68, 71-72, 72-73). Avocations: golf, church activities, music, genealogy. Home: Lake Oswego, Oreg. Died Nov. 1, 2005.

HOFFMAN, HOWARD STANLEY, experimental psychologist, educator; b. NYC, May 23, 1925; s. Melvin Leo and Henrietta (Rosenthal) H.; m. Alice Marie Cruikshank, June 7, 1961; children: Randall, Gwendolyn, Russell, Franklin, Daniel, Martha. BA, New Sch. for Social Research, N.Y.C., 1952; MA, Bklyn. Coll., 1953; PhD, U. Conn., 1957. Rsch. fellow in auditory perception U. Conn., 1953-56, instr. dept. stats., 1956-57; asst. to prof. psychology Pa. State U., 1957-70; prof. psychology Bryn Mawr Coll., 1970-92, prof. emeritus, 1992—2006. Bd. editors: Jour. Exptl. Analysis Behavior, 1966-69, Jour. Exptl. Psychology, Animal Behavior Processes, 1974-84; reviewer: Jour. Comparative and Physiol. Psychology. Served with AUS, 1943-45. Fellow AAAS, Am. Psychol. Assn., Am. Psychol. Soc.; mem. Eastern Psychol. Assn., AAUP, Sigma Xi, Phi Kappa Phi, Psi Chi. Home: Haverford, Pa. Died Aug. 31, 2006.

HOFFMAN, JOHN RALEIGH, physicist; b. Evansville, Ind., July 7, 1926; s. John Henry and Ruth Margaret (Bryant) H.; m. Phyllis Christine Reindel, July 5, 1950; children: John Russell, Gary Paul. BS, U. Richmond, 1949; MS, U. Fla., 1951, PhD, 1954. Rsch. asst. U. Fla., 1950—54; rsch. scientist Sandia Corp., Albuquerque, 1954—57; supr. project Kaman Nuc. Co., Colorado Springs, 1957—68; v.p. Kaman Scis. Corp., Colorado Springs, 1968—86, sr. v.p., 1986—90, exec. v.p., 1990—92; gen. mgr. Kaman Instrumentation Corp., 1989—90; ret. Kaman Scis Corp., 1992; tech. and mgmt. cons., from 1992. Mem. nominating com. Colo. Supreme Ct., 1998-2004; bd. dirs. Red Spot Paint and Varnish Co., U. Club U. Colo., Colo. Springs Served with USNR, 1944-46. Mem. IEEE, Am. Phys. Soc. Republican. Presbyterian. Died Jan. 12, 2006.

HOFFMAN, ROBERT KENNETH, restaurant owner, former beverage company executive; b. Oklahoma City, July 18, 1947; s. Edmund M. and Adelyn Hoffman; m. Marguerite Steed; 1 child, Katherine; children: Hannah, Augusta. Grad., Harvard U., 1970, MBA, 1972. Co-chmn. Coca-Cola Bottling Group SW, until 1998, Custom Food Group; co-owner Abacus restaurant, Dallas, 1999—2006. Co-founder National Lampoon, 1969, mng. editor, 1970. Founding chmn. The Dallas Plan; donated $150 million contemporary art collection and a $20 million endowment to Dallas Mus. Art, 2005. Named one of Top 200 Collectors, ARTnews mag., 2004, 50 Most Generous Philanthropists, BusinessWeek, 2005; recipient Inst. Human Relations Award, Am. Jewish Com., 1995, Gertrude Shelburne Humanitarian Award, Planned Parenthood of Dallas and N.E. Tex., 1996, Linz Award, Zale Corp. & Dallas Morning News, 1996. Avocation: Collector postwar Am. and European art, Chinese monochromes. Died Aug. 20, 2006.

HOFFMAN, STANLEY J(OHN), JR., drafting and systems manager; b. Buffalo, Aug. 4, 1945; s. Stanley John Sr. and Helen (Rachwal) H.; m. Mary Margaret Carducci, Dec. 29, 1964; 1 child, Christina Marie. Grad. high sch., Buffalo. Registered profl. engr., N.Y., Fla. Draftsman Buffalo Tool & Die, 1963-67; design draftsman Superior Design, Buffalo, 1967-73, Moog Inc., East Aurora, N.Y., 1973-87, sr. design draftsman, 1980-87, drafting supr. Clearwater, Fla., from 1987. Bd. dirs. Moog Employees Credit Union, East Aurora, 1985-87. Mem. Am. Soc. Tolerance Engrs. Achievements include patent for servovalve, fixed fail safe. Home: South Wales, NY. Died Mar. 22, 2005.

HOLASH, LISE MARIE HÉLÉNE, secondary school educator; b. Montreal, Que., Can., Aug. 18, 1941; came to U.S., 1981; d. Georges Henri and Cécile (Codère) Mercier; m. N. J. Holash, June 15, 1966 (div. 1985); children: Claire S., Mark N. Diploma, Montreal Mus. Fine Arts, 1961; BA, Universite de Montreal, 1962; diplome superieur, Institot Catechetique, France, 1964; MA, Fordham U., 1967; BE in Music, U. Sask., Can., 1968. Cert. tchr., Fla. Tchr. Montreal Cath. Schs., 1963-64; asst. prof. Fordham U., N.Y.C., 1964-65; prof. Institut de Pastorale, Bruges, Belgium, 1965-66; tchr. Regina (Can.) Cath. Schs., 1966-68, 76-80; prof. Notre Dame Coll., Wilcox, Sask., Can., 1968-73, Royal Can. Mounted Police Tng. Depot Div., Regina, 1973-76; tchr. Ottawa (Can.) Cath. Schs., 1980-81; dir. adult edn. Archdiocese Miami, Fla., 1981-84; tchr. La Salle High Sch., Miami, 1984-86, Dade County Pub. Schs., Miami, from 1986. Bd. dirs. Oxfam Can., Toronto, 1975-78, South Fla. Youth Symphony; sponsor French Club/French Honor Soc., Classical League, Le Soleil Couchant Miami Sunset Sr. High Sch., 1986—. Mem. Am. Assn. Tchrs. French, Dade County Fgn. Lang. Tchrs. Assn. Avocations: langs., computers, music, reading. Died Feb. 19, 2004.

HOLDEMAN, HELEN FRANCES, nursing educator; b. Salunga, Pa., June 6, 1925; d. George Washington and Frances Hostetter (Nissley) Cutrell; m. Paul Howard Holdeman, June 27, 1948; children: Bonita Jean, Timothy Cutrell, Mark Alan, Priscilla Frances. BSN, Goshen Coll., 1948. RN, Colo; cert. occupational health nurse. Staff nurse Gates Rubber Co., Denver, 1949-50; instr. nurse aides Gulfport (Miss.) Hosp., 1953-54; staff nurse Denver Gen. Hosp., 1955, Sanford Hosp., Perryton, Tex., 1956-59, Loveland (Colo.) Meml. Hosp., 1959; office mgr. LR Sanford MD, Loveland, Colo., 1960-69; occupational health nurse Hewlett-Packard Co., Loveland, Colo., 1969-82; dir. svcs. Larimer County Hospice, Loveland, Colo., 1982-83; dir. edn. Eu Luth. Good Samaritan, Loveland, Colo., 1983-93; instr. nursing Front Range C.C., Ft. Collins, Colo., from 1993. Mem. hosp. dist. bd. Larimer County, Colo., 1973—; mem. adv. bd. Thompson Valley Hosp. Dist., 1973—, McKea Med. Ctr., 1976-78, Healthy Beginnings, Larimer County, 1991—, Good Samaritan, Loveland, 1993—. Named Profl. Woman of Yr., Loveland, 1965. Mem. Colo. Nurses Assn. (pres., sec. 1972-74, bd. dirs. 92-94), Occupational Health Nurses (pres., sec. 1975-77, bd. dirs.) Democrat. Home: Loveland, Colo. Died Mar. 29, 2004.

HOLDER, BARBARA JUNE, secondary school educator; b. Bklyn., June 24, 1941; d. Nathan and Sarina Kent; m. Alex A. Weiner, Dec. 9, 1963 (div. 1970); 1 child, Deborah Anne Goldman; m. Alan Holder, Sept. 12, 1972. BA magna cum laude, Columbia U., 1973, MA with hons., 1975, MPh, 1981. Pvt. practice dance tchr., 1970-78; adj. assoc. prof. Pace U., Pleasantville, N.Y., 1978-93; jour. cons. Dialogue House, N.Y.C., from 1987; instr. in creative writing Ridgefield (Conn.) Adult Edn., from 1998; instr. lit. Ridgefield Libr., 1998. Leader poetry workshops various librs., cultural ctrs., N.Y. 1990—, organizer and host poetry reading Pace U., Pleasantville, N.Y., 1981-90. Author: (book of poems) Black Birds White Stones, 2005; contbr. poems to anthologies. Recipient fellowships Columbia U., 1968-73, 1973-75; nominee Pushcart prize, 2005. Mem. Poets and Writers Guild, Phi Beta Kappa. Home: West Redding, Conn. Died 2005.

HOLLAND, ENDESHA IDA MAE, playwright, educator; b. Greenwood, Miss., Aug. 29, 1944; d. Ida Mae H.; 1 child, Cedric Lamar. BA, U. Minn., 1979, MA, 1984, PhD, 1985. Founder, dir. Women Helping Offenders, Inc., Mpls., 1971-75; founder, chmn. Nat. Assn. Women Helping Offenders, Inc., Bloomington, Minn., 1975-77; instr., womens studies program U. Minn., Mpls., 1982-85; assoc. prof. Am. studies SUNY, Buffalo, 1985—2006. Ajudicator (play-screen) Ill. Arts Coun., Chgo., 1989, N.Y. State Arts Coun., N.Y.C., 1990; planning com. First Internat. Womens Playwrights Conf., Buffalo, 1986-88. Playwright: (play) Second Doctor Lady, 1981 (Nat. Lorraine Hansbery award), The Reconstruction of Dossie Ree Hemphill, 1981, From the Mississippi Delta, 1988 (Pulitzer prize nominee), Miss Ida B. Wells, 1982, Parader Without a Permit, 1985; (TV script) Requiem for a Snake, 1984; Author: From the Mississippi Delta, 1997 Recipient Spotlight award Nat. Coalition Black Women, Buffalo, 1989, Star award Jackson State U. Alumni, N.Y.C., 1989, Disting. Lectr. award Calif. State U. Dominguez Hills, 1989. Mem. African-Am. Theatre Conf. (exec. mem., pub. rels.), Nia Writers Workshop, The Dramatists Guild, Minority Faculty Staff (exec. mem., rec. sec.) Died Jan. 25, 2006.

HOLLEY, JAMES RICHARD, JR., data processing executive; b. Amarillo, Tex., Sept. 28, 1944; s. James R. and Vera V. (Canady) H.; m. Judy Carol Dear, June 5, 1965; children: David C., Raymond N. Student, La. State U., Alexandria, 1962-63, La. Coll., Pineville, 1963-64; BA in Math., U. Tex., Austin, 1966. Cert. data processor. Computer programmer Keystone Steel & Wire, Peoria, Ill., 1966-68, programming supr., 1969, mgr. computer systems, 1970-72, mgr. systems and programming, 1976-82; adminstrv. mgr. Keystone Consolidated Industries, Peoria, 1973-75; mgr. systems and programming Foster & Gallagher, Peoria, from 1983. Mem. adv. bd. Ill. Central Coll., East Peoria, Ill., 1988—. Mem. Data Processing Mgmt. Assn. (treas. 1978-80, v.p. 1991—, individual performance award 1981, chpt. devel. award 1989). Presbyterian. Avocation: fishing. Home: East Peoria, Ill. Died Sept. 13, 2004.

HOLLOWAY, JOHN THOMAS, physicist, consultant; b. Cape Girardeau, Mo., June 19, 1922; s. Herbert Henry and Addie Mae (Cahill) H.; m. Kay Vickers, Nov. 11, 1965; children: Linda, Kim (dec. Jan. 1999). AB, Millikin U., Decatur, Ill., 1943; PhD, Iowa State U., 1957. With nuclear physics br. Office Naval Research, Washington, 1946-53, head br., 1951-52; research asst. Ames Lab., AEC, Iowa, 1954-57; with Office Dir. Def. Research and Engring., Washington, 1958-61; dep. dir. Office of Sci. Dir. Def. Research and Engring., 1959-61; with NASA, 1961-68, dep. dir. grants and research contracts, 1961-67, chief advanced programs and tech., space applications div., 1967-68; dir. Nat. Hwy. Safety Research Center, Dept. Transp., 1968-69; v.p. research Ins. Inst. Hwy. Safety, 1969-72; asso. dir. ops. Interdisciplinary Communications Program, Smithsonian Instn., 1972-77, program mgr. internat. program population analysis, 1972-77, research and devel. cons. in hwy. safety, biomed. electronics, energy conservation, 1977-78; sr. staff officer bd. on radioactive waste mgmt. Nat. Acad. Scis.-NRC, 1978-85; cons. on radioactive waste mgmt., hwy. safety, from 1985. Mem. conf. com. Nat. Conf. Advancement Research, 1971-75 Author papers in field; adviser documentary films. Served with USNR, 1944-46. Mem. Am. Phys. Soc., Sigma Xi. Clubs: Cosmos (Washington); Army-Navy Country (Arlington, Va.). Home: Washington, DC. Died Dec. 9, 2005.

HOLM, BERTIL K., science administrator, consultant, secretary; b. N.Y.C., Aug. 24, 1925; s. Oscar and Edith S. Holm; m. Evelyn Alice Heining, June, 1951 (dec. Aug. 1987); children: Alicia, Jeffrey; m. Winnie Mellema, June 10, 1988. ASAS, Tech. U., 1947; BS in Agr., Rutgers U., 1952, MA in Bus., 1953. Owner Charlotte Valley Poultry Farms, Charlotteville, 1953-60; with sales dept. Hales and Hunter, Chgo., 1960-63; with nat. account dept. Sterwin Chems., N.Y.C., 1963-69, Pfizer, Chgo., 1969-71; gen. mgr., sec. Coop. Rsch. Farms, Charlotteville, from 1971. Bd. dirs. Farms Internat., Inc., N.Y.C. Author: Agricultural Banking Agri Banking, 1964. Deacon 1st Summit Bapt. Ch., Charlotteville, 1965, youth dir., 1967; mem. Holm Scholarship Found., 1988. With USN, 1943-45, ETJO. Mem. Alpha Gamma Rho (pres. New Brunswick, N.J. chpt. 1950-52). Republican. Home: Charlotteville, NY. Died Apr. 15, 2004.

HOLMAN, WILLIAM BAKER, surgeon, coroner; b. Norwalk, Ohio, Mar. 22, 1925; s. Merlin Earl and Rowena (Baker) Holman; m. Jane Elizabeth Henderson, June 24, 1951; children: Craig W., Mark E., John S. BS, Capital U., 1946; MD, Jefferson Med. Coll., 1950. Intern St. Luke's Hosp., Cleve., 1950—51, resident in gen. surgery, 1951—52, 1955—57; practice medicine specializing in surgery Norwalk, 1957—92; coroner Huron County, Norwalk, 1962—95, health commr., 1985—95; asst. clin. prof. surgery Med. Coll. Ohio at Toledo, 1984—92. Mem. Norwalk City Sch. Bd. Edn., 1962—78, pres., 1964, 1967—71, 1978; mem. exec. com. Huron County Rep. Com., Norwalk, 1980; bd. dirs. REMSNO, Toledo, 1974—92, Norwalk Profl. Colony, 1983—92, Fisher-Titus Med. Ctr., 1977—82, chmn., 1982; bd. dirs. Norwalk Area Health Svcs., Inc., 1987—92, from 1994; chmn. Norwalk Area Health Svcs., from 2003; vice chmn. Fisher-Titus Found., 2003; mem. bd. Bellevue Hosp., from 2003. Served to 1st lt. U.S. Army, 1952—54. Fellow: ACS; mem.: AMA, Nat. Assn. Med. Examiners, Ohio State Coroners Assn., Huron County Med. Soc. (pres. 1978), Ohio State Med. Assn. Lutheran. Avocations: boating, photography, stamp collecting/philately, gun collecting. Home: Pickerington, Ohio. Died Feb. 14, 2004.

HOLMES, BARRY TREVOR, business and cross cultural development consultant; b. Letchworth, England, Sept. 23, 1933; came to U.S., 1985; s. Edwin George and Marian (Jones) H.; children from previous marriage: Katharine, Alison, Joanne; m. Sherie Shortridge Bell, Mar. 27. 1992; 1 child, Kelly Campbell Shortridge. Diplomat, U.K., 1950-92; bus. and cross cultural devel. cons. Atlanta, from 1992. Bd. dirs. Br. Am. Bus. Group, Atlanta, 1994—. Capt. Br. Army, 1953-55. Mem. Atlanta C. of C. (internat. com. 1994—), Atlanta Rotary, English Speaking Union (pres. 1996-97). Presbyterian. Avocations: chess, walking, reading spy novels. Home: Atlanta, Ga. Died Nov. 17, 2004.

HOLMES, DAVID CHARLES, broadcasting company executive; b. Spokane, Wash., Aug. 18, 1919; s. Charles Clark and Maud Emily (Bunce) H.; m. Virginia Marie Therese Romar, June 15, 1944; children: Dian Holmes Moulin, David Charles Jr. BS, U.S. Naval Acad., 1942. Commd. ensign USN, 1942, advanced through grades to capt., 1962; naval aviator, guided missiles project officer Bur. Aero., 1954-57; mgr. U.S. space tracking network Advanced Rsch. Projects Agy., 1958-62; with NATO, Oslo, 1963-65; dir. Naval Weapons Engring. Support Activity, 1968-72; aerospace cons. Naval Rsch. Lab., Washington, 1972-82; pres. Encore Broadcasting Corp., Annapolis, Md., from 1989; sec. Silver Queen Media, Inc., from 1990. Trustee Providence Trust, 1980—; gen. ptnr. Providence House Ltd. Partnership 1980—; bd. dirs. Kernco, Inc., Annapolis Nat. Bank. Author: (fiction) The Signpost, 1944, No Time for Marriage, 1951, Frenchie, 1953, The Velvet Ape, 1955; (nonfiction) On the Wings of the Wind, 1954, The Story of Weather, 1956, What's Going On in Space?, 1958, Why Shoot the Moon?, 1960, The Search for Life on Other Worlds, 1965, NAVSTAR, Navigation for the Future, 1974, TEMPUS, Time Via Satellite, 1978. Mem. AIAA, Authors Guild, Mystery Writers Am., Authors League, Nat. Press Club, Annapolis Yacht Club, Army Navy Country Club, Naval Acad. Officers and Faculty Club, Sigma Xi. Home: Annapolis, Md. Died June 26, 2004.

HOLSINGER, RALPH LEE, author; b. Covington, Ohio, July 14, 1918; s. Frederick Martin and Mary Vannas (Inman) H.; m. Elizabeth Vornholt, Jan. 18, 1958. BA, Ohio Wesleyan U., Delaware, 1941. Mgmt. trainee RCA Mfg. Co., Camden, N.J., 1941-42; reporter Piqua (Ohio) Daily Call, 1945-46, Dayton (Ohio) Daily News, 1946-47; adminstrv. asst. Rep. William M. McCulloch, Washington, 1947-48; reporter, Washington corr. Dayton (Ohio) Jour. Herald, 1949-60; mng. editor Cin. Enquirer, 1960-64; prof. journalism Ind. U., Bloomington, 1965-89, prof. emeritus, from 1989. Editing cons. various newspapers, Ind., Ill., Ky.; expert witness libel cases newspapers, Duluth Minn., Muncie, Ind., Ft. Wayne, Ind., Indpls.; regent AP Mng. Editors, 1984. Author: Media Law, 1987. Sgt. U.S. Army, 1942-45, ETO. Named to Ind. Journalism Hall of Fame, Ind. Soc. Profl. Journalists, 1989. Mem. Soc. Profl. Journalists, Assn. Edn. in Journalism, Phi Beta Kappa. Republican. Home: Ashton, Md. Died Dec. 8, 2004.

HOLSTON, A. FRANK, retired commentator, communications educator; b. Balt., Feb. 25, 1928; s. Arthur F. Sr. and Sara A. Holston; m. Marianne B. Holston, Dec. 27, 1953; children: William Carroll, Sara Anne, Jeanne Marie. BS, U. Ala., 1951; MA, Mich. State U., 1962. Radio and TV broadcaster, sports dir., Balt., 1944-72; announcer ABC-TV, ESPN, N.Y.,Conn., 1974-88; prof. comm. C.C. Balt., 1956-88; ret., 1988. Chmn. faculty senate exec. com., Balt., 1969—70; gen. mgr. Liberty Campus, Balt., 1968—69, WBJC-FM, 1968—69; pres., bd. dirs. Shearwater, Inc., 1996—98; track ofcl. U.S. Naval Acad., from 1998; spkr. in field. Bd. dirs. Annapolis (Md.) Bur. Recreation, 1993—, Broadcast Edn. Assn., Washington, 1985-89, Ecumedia, Balt., 1975-76; v.p. Rep. Ctrl. Com., 1991-97, pres., 1995-97; chmn. '51 reunion U. Ala., 2001; pres. Feddayes, Boumi Temple Shrine, 1967-68. With USN, 1945, USNR. Ford Found. scholar, Northwestern U., 1958, News Am. fellow, Syracuse U., 1960. Mem.: Shriners (pres. Annapolis club 1960—61). Presbyterian. Home: Annapolis, Md. Died Feb. 10, 2006.

HOLZEMER, ROBERT LISZT, marketing consultant; b. Columbus, Ohio, Feb. 26, 1913; s. John Francis and Evelyn Pearl (Winters) H.; m. Barbara McCampbell, Nov. ll, l938; children: Robert, Katharine, Barbara, John, James, Stephen, Daniel, Thomas. BSBA, Ohio State U., 1937. Salesman, gen. sales mgr. Williams Mfg. Co., Portsmouth, Ohio, 1937-62; dir. mgmt. devel. Genesco Inc., Nashville, 1962-75; v.p. Blue Bell Inc.-Wrangler Boots, Nashville, 1975-77; pres. Robert L. Holzemer Co., mktg. cons., Nashville, 1978-82, Portsmouth, from 1982. Vol. speaker various mil. and civilian early retirement groups, Nashville, l977-8l; vol. instr. Nashville Vo-Tech. Sch., 1978-79; mem. Internat. Exec. Svc. Corps, Svc. Corps Ret. Execs., SBA. Author: (manual) Sales Division Management, l965, Santa's Christmas Tree, 1969. Precinct committeeman Portsmouth Rep. Com., l949-53; v.p. bd. dirs. Mercy Hosp., Portsmouth, l958-6l; bd. dirs. Goodwill Industries, Nashville, l975-78; mem. Shade Tree Commn., Portsmouth, l988-89. Lt. USNR, l944-46, PTO. Recipient Disting. Svc. award Portsmouth C. of C., l948, award of excellence Notre Dame High Sch., Portsmouth, l957, svc. award Svc. Corps Ret. Execs., l987. Mem. Ohio State U. Alumni Assn., K.C. (pres. 1950-51, hon. life mem.), 4th degree, past faithful navigator), Rotary (bd. dirs. Portsmouth l955-56, fellow), Am. Legion (life mem.), Elks. Roman Catholic. Avocations: golf, fishing. Died Jan. 29, 2005.

HOMMELL, ADRIENNE ELIZABETH, secondary school educator; b. Englewood, N.J., Aug. 4, 1934; d. Adrien B. and Adele Jessie (Thomass) H. BA, Tusculum Coll., 1956. Cert. elem. tchr., N.J. Media specialist Eastampton Twp. Elem. Sch., Mt. Holly, N.J., from 1968. Vice-chair person Eastampton Twp. Zoning Bd. Adjustment, 1981—. Mem. AAUW, N.J. Edn. Assn., NEA, Eastampton Twp. Edn. Assn. Home: Mount Holly, NJ. Died July 16, 2004.

HONDERICH, BELAND HUGH, publisher; b. Kitchener, Ont., Can., Nov. 25, 1918; s. John William and Rae Laura (Armstrong) H.; m. Florence Irene Wilkinson, Oct. 1943; John Allen, Mary Elizabeth, David Beland; m. Agnes Janet Hutchinson (Oct. 1969). Ed., pub. schs., Baden, Ont.; LL.D. (hon.), York U., 1976, Wilfrid Laurier U., 1977; D Litt (hon.), Carleton U., 1989. Reporter Toronto Star Ltd., Ont., 1943-45, fin. editor Ont., 1945-55; editor in chief Daily Star and Star Weekly, 1955-66, pres., pub., 1966-88; chmn. Toronto Star Newspapers, 1976-94, Torstar Corp., 1977-93. Died Nov. 8, 2005.

HONEYCUTT, JERRY LEE, sales executive; b. Dayton, Ohio, Sept. 12, 1946; s. Walter O. and Hazel L. (Reed) H.; m. Linda Romback, Feb. 17, 1966 (div. Nov. 1971); 1 child, Kerry Ann; m. Diane Dreyfus, Nov. 24, 1972; children: Tori Diane, Darin Gregory. BBA, No. Mich. U., 1968. Regional mgr. Airtemp div. Chrysler Corp., Dayton, 1968-78; zone mgr. Westinghouse Electric, Norman, Okla., 1978-81; sales mgr. Sun Dial div. Square D Co., Dallas, 1981-85; nat. sales mgr. Suburban Mfg. Co., Dayton, Tenn., from 1985. Dir. cool com. Westinghouse Electric, Norman, 1980. Served to sgt. USAF, 1964-68. Lutheran. Avocations: remodeling, construction, travel. Home: Hixson, Tenn. Died July 10, 2005.

HONIGMAN, ROBERT DAVID, lawyer; b. Detroit, Feb. 2, 1939; s. Alfred George and Helen Rose (Henig) H. BBA, U. Mich., 1958; JD, Wayne State U., 1961. Bar: Mich. 1962. Bus. law instr. Mich. State U., Lansing, 1961-63; civil svc. examiner Detroit Civil Svc., 1964-70; ptnr. Honigman, Miller, Schwartz & Cohn, Detroit, 1970-72; house counsel Seligman & Assocs., Southfield, Mich., 1972-74; pvt. practice Fraser, Mich., 1974-88, Birmingham, Mich., from 1988. Bus. law instr. Wayne State U., Detroit, 1980-86. Author: University Secrets, 1997; contbr. essays to profl. publs. With USNR, 1963-69. Mem. Mensa, Birmingham Bloomfield Art Assn., Alliance Francaise de Detroit, Brazilian Cultural Club of Detroit (treas. 1995-98). Avocations: tennis, painting. Home: Birmingham, Mich. Died Mar. 8, 2005.

HONIKMAN, LARRY HOWARD, pediatrician; b. Washington, Feb. 16, 1936; s. Zuse and Frances (Deckelbaum) H.; m. Elaine Honikman; children: Sheryl, Julie, Amy. BA, U. Va., Charlottesville, 1957, MD, 1961. Intern Royal Victoria Hosp., McGill U., Montreal, Que., Can., 1961-62; resident in pediats. Children's Hosp. Med. Ctr.-Harvard Med. Sch., Boston, 1964-66, fellow in medicine, 1966-68; asst. prof. in medicine Harvard Med. Sch., Boston, 1968-73, rsch. fellow in medicine, 1969-70; pvt. practice pediatrics, 1973—2000. Tchr. Boston U. Sch. Medicine, 1977-2006, Harvard U. Sch. Medicine, 1977-2006, Tufts U. Sch. Medicine, 1982-2006; mem. staff pediatrics dept. Children's Hosp. Med. Ctr., 1973-2006, Brigham and Women's Hosp., Boston, 1976-2006, Cardinal Cushing Hosp., Brockton, Mass., 1975-2006, Carney Hosp., Dorchester, Mass., 1977-2006; lectr. in field.; cardiac cons. dept. pub. health, div. maternal and child health svcs. Commonwealth of Mass., 1968-75. Contbr. articles to profl. jours. including Jour. of Am. Med. Assn., Pediatrics, Am. Jour. Disease Children, Circulation. Capt. U.S. Army, 1962-64. Mem. AMA, AAAS, APHA, Am. Heart Assn., Mass. Heart Assn. (chmn. rheumatic fever adv. com. S.E. chpt. 1973-74, mem. state rheumatic fever svcs. com. 1968-71, co-chmn. rheumatic fever workshop 1966), Mass. Med. Soc., Nutrition Today Soc., N.Y. Acad. Scis., Collegium Internationale Angiologae, Phi Beta Kappa. Home: Norton, Mass. Died Feb. 1, 2006.

HONTS, GEORGE EDWARD, III, judge; b. Eagle Rock, Va., Feb. 20, 1940; s. George Edward Jr. and Louise (Bair) H.; m. Patricia Helen Arthur, Aug. 17, 1968; children: G.E. IV, Joel G. BA, Washington and Lee U., 1962, JD, 1968; MJS, U. Nev., 1988. Bar: Va. 1968. Ptnr. Carter Roe Emick & Honts, Fincastle, Va., 1968-83; commr. accounts Cir. Ct. Botetount County, Fincastle, 1970-83; judge 25th Judical Cir., Fincastle, from 1983. Substitute judge 25th Judicial Dist., Va., 1972-83. Bd. visitors Radford U., 1982-83; sr. warden St. Mark's Episcopal Ch., Fincastle, 1990-91. Mem. Am. Judicature Soc., Jud. Conf. Va. (chmn. compensation com. 1984-91, sentencing guidelines com. 1990-94, com. on commrs. of accounts 1993-95, criminal sentencing guidelines commn., 1994—, exec. com. 1995—), Phi Alpha Delta, Omicron Delta Kappa. Home: Fincastle, Va. Died Mar. 23, 2004.

HOOD, EDWARD, data processing executive; b. L.A., Nov. 5, 1954; s. Thomas Leslie and Mary (Jewell) H.; m. Carmenita Feu. AA in Adminstrn. of Justice, L.A. City Coll., 1977; BA in Phys. Edn., Calif. State U., L.A., 1980. Ordained to ministry, Bapt. Ch., 1983. Dir. pub. rels. and fin. Greater Revelation Bapt. Ch., L.A., 1979-83, assoc. minister, 1981-92, Gospel Truth Ch., L.A., 1981-84; owner Compusys, L.A., from 1989; chmn. and pres. Video Documentary, L.A., from 1988; asst. prin. and tchr. Grace Luth. Christian Elem. Sch., L.A., 1990-91; pastor Bright and Morning Star Cmty. Christian Ch., San Bernardino, from 1992. Athletic and audio-visual equip. person Nat. Youth Sports Program, summers 1983-90; athletic equip. attendant II, Calif. State U., L.A., 1981-90, part-time lectr., 1989-90; substitute instructional aide San Bernardino County, Calif., 1992—. Author: The Philosophy "Paradoxism:; creator "Black Jesus or Compassion collection"; inventor Airskate. Pres. Menlo Ave. Block Club Neighborhood Watch, L.A., 1984-87; asst. coach "B" football, instr. K-coll., Manual Arts High Sch., 1979. With USMC, 1972-74. Mem. NAACP. Democrat. Avocations: reading, swimming, tennis, piano, polo. Home: Fontana, Calif. Died Dec. 12, 2004.

HOOD, JAMES, internist, consultant; b. Leslie, Fife, Scotland, Sept. 5, 1930; came to U.S., 1966; s. James and Mary J. (Keith) H.; m. Margaret Ferguson Goodman, Aug. 21, 1953; children: James Derek, Margaret Lesley. M.B., Ch. B., U. of Edinburgh, Scotland, 1952. Diplomate Am. Bd. Internal Medicine, Am. Bd. of Nutrition, Am. Bd. Physician Nutrition Specialists. Registrar in medicine and chest diseases Newmarket Gen. Hosp., Suffolk, Eng., 1958-60; med. registrar, clin. tutor Edinburgh Ea. Gen. Hosp., 1960-62; sr. med. registrar Hampstead Gen. Hosp., Royal Free Hosps. Med. Sch., London, 1962-63; clin. researcher Med. and Biol. Rsch. div. Sandoz Inc., Basle, Switzerland, 1964-66; fellow in clin. nutrition, instr. in medicine U. Hosps., Iowa City, Iowa, 1966-70; staff internal medicine St. Luke's and Mercy Hosps., Cedar Rapids, Iowa, 1970-88, Mid Mich. Med. Ctr., Midland, from 1989; assoc. Midland Internal Medicine Assocs., 1989-93; internist, consultant pvt. practice, Midland, Mich., from 1993. Advisor drug evaluations AMA, Chgo., 1971. Author: (with others) Current Therapy, 1975; contbg. editor: Nutrition Revs., 1967-70; contbr. articles to New Eng. Jour. Medicine, Am. Jour. Clin. Nutrition, Jour. Clin. Investigation, Vitamins and Hormones, Am. Jour. Hosp. Pharm. Surgeon lt. Royal Naval Vol. Res., 1954-56. Fellow ACP, 1970, Royal Coll. of Physicians of Edinburgh, 1971, Am. Coll. Nutrition, 1988. Mem. Am. Soc. Internal Medicine, Soc. for Exptl. Biology and Medicine, Am. Soc. for Nutritional Scis., Am. Soc. Clin. Nutrition, Am. Fedn. Clin. Rsch., Mich. Med. Soc., Midland County Med. Soc., Rotary. Presbyterian. Avocation: research in vitamin deficiency and drug bioavailability. Home: Midland, Mich. Died Oct. 8, 2004.

HOPEWELL, HARRY LYNN, JR., financial and investment advisor; b. Portsmouth, Va., Dec. 19, 1937; s. Harry Lynn and Charlotte Ross (Mathews) H.; m. Carolyn Jean Lawrence, Oct. 19, 1955 (div. Sept. 1976); children: Harry Lynn III, Frank Mathew; m. Leslie Ann Lindsay, Oct. 9, 1976; 1 child, Stewart Lindsay. AA, Coll. of William and Mary, 1958; BS, Va. Poly. Inst., 1961; MBA, Harvard U., 1968. Cert. fin. planner. Prin. The Monitor Group, Inc., Fairfax, Va., 1980—2006. Contbg. editor Fin. Planning mag.; editor: Jour. Fin. Planning; contbr. articles on personal fin. planning to profl. jours. Vestryman, sr. warden St. James Episcopal Ch.; bd. dirs. Fauquiet Hist. Soc.; chmn. bd. trustees Wakefield Sch., The Plains, Va., 1990-91; mem. Architecture Rev. Bd., Warrenton, Va., 1990-94; mem. gov.'s commn. on Champion Schs., 1994-95. Mem. Inst. Cert. Fin. Planners, CFP Bd. Stds., State Coun. Higher Edn. (Va., vice chmn. 1996-2006) Avocation: civil war history. Home: Warrenton, Va. Died Mar. 28, 2006.

HOPFE, HAROLD HERBERT, retired chemical engineer; b. Ware, Mass., Apr. 21, 1936; s. Herbert Henry and Lottie Maud (Senecal) H.; m. Winifred Ann Dorsey, June 29, 1957; children: Peter Harold, William David, Susan Elizabeth Haryasz. BSChemE, U. Mass., 1958, MSChemE, 1970. Registered profl. engr., N.Y. Devel. engr. Monsanto Co., Indian Orchard, Mass., 1961-82, corp. fellow, 1982-98; ret., 1998; CEO U.S. Wave Energy, Inc., Longmeadow, Mass., from 1995; pres. Polystress Co., Longmeadow, from 1988. Author: (software), tech. editor: Stress/Strain in Polymers, 1993; patentee ocean wave power generators, polymer processing systems. Children's story author/reader Pub. Libr., Longmeadow, 1989, Shriners Hosp., Springifeld, Mass., 1989. Recipient Centennial award Boston Edison, 1986. Mem. Soc. Am. Inventors. Avocation: computer software devel. Home: Longmeadow, Mass. Died Jan. 30, 2004.

HOPKINS, ALFRED ARCHIBALD, former mayor; m. Marion Mrlik, 1947; children: Barbara, Kathleen, Mark. Mem. city coun. City of Annapolis, Md., 1961—89, mayor, 1989—97. Died June 22, 2006.

HORD, PAULINE JONES, primary school educator; b. Memphis, Apr. 18, 1907; d. Samuel Anderson and Loretta (Hall) Jones; m. Andrew Frank Hord, Mar. 30, 1940 (div. Oct. 1946). BA, Southwestern Coll., Memphis, 1929; EdD (hon.), Crichton Coll., Memphis, 1991, Rhodes Coll., 1999. Tchr. Memphis City Sch. System, 1929-67; nat. cons. Phonovisual Products, Inc., Bethesda, Md., 1967-77; freelance cons., workshop dir. Memphis, 1978-87; dir. sing spell read and write model Memphis Sch. System, 1987-95. Dir. TV Lit. Program WKNO-TV, Memphis, 1955-60; acting dir. Primary Day Sch., Bethesda, Md., 1960-61; lit. TV Specialist with Peace Corps., Colombia, S. Am., 1963-64; dir. Heads Up Lit. Program, State Correctional Inst., Parchman, Miss., 1986-96. Author: Praying for the President, 2003, The Master Design, 2003. Lit. tchr. Heads Up Lit. Program, Parchman Penetentiary, 1987-92; bd. mem. Second Chance Prison Min., Tenn., Miss., 1988-92. Recipient Leadership Adult Edn. award Ford Found., 1958, Disting. Col. Christian Svc. award Miss. State Penetentiary, Parchman, 1987, Memphis Comml. Appeal award, 1989, 95th Daily Point of Light award, 1990, Person of Vision award Alliance for the Blind and Visually Impaired, 1993, Disting. Alumni award Rhodes Coll., 1998; named one of Outstanding Bus. Women of Yr., Women's Exec. Coun., Memphis, 1959, Sr. Citizen of Yr., Shelby County Coun. on Aging, 1988. Republican. Mem. United Meth. Avocations: reading, creating educational games, leading prayer groups. Home: Memphis, Tenn. Died May 5, 2005.

HORN, LEIF, physiology educator; b. Tromsö, Norway, Mar. 15, 1925; came to U.S., 1957; s. Rolf Tonnes and Agnes (Einarsen) H.; m. Anne Barger-Nielsen, Aug. 2, 1949 (div. 1972); 1 child, Dag; m. Sabine Friedericke Pulz, Feb. 27, 1979; children: Hans, Eva. Cand. philos., Oslo U., 1946-47, PhD, 1956. Instr. of surgery and biophysics Med. Coll. Va., Richmond, 1957-58, asst. prof. of biophysics, 1958-60; asst. prof. pathology and exptl. surgery NYU Med. Sch., N.Y.C., 1960-64; assoc. prof. of physiology N.Y. Coll. of Medicine, N.Y.C., 1964-67, Coll. of Medicine and Dentistry N.J. Med. Sch., Jersey City, 1967-68; prof. of physiology U. Medicine & Dentistry of N.J., Newark, from 1968. 2d lt. Norwegian Air Force, 1945. NIH spl. fellow, 1959-62, Angiology Rsch. Found. fellow, Perdue Frederik Co. fellow; recipient Angiology award, 1964. Home: Summit, NJ. Died July 9, 2005.

HOROWITZ, LEWIS JAY, stock exchange executive; b. N.Y.C., Feb. 13, 1935; s. Jack and Ethel Lahn (Wartur) H.; children: Jay B., Stephen G.; m. Jo-Ann Malkin, Jan. 13, 1983. BA, Brown U., 1956. Arbitrage broker, N.Y.C., 1959; ptnr. Bernard, Berk & Co., N.Y.C., 1958-65; mem. firm Silver, Barry and Van Raalte; ptnr. successor firm Phelan, Silver, Vesce & Barry & Co., 1965-82; pres., CEO N.Y. Futures Exchange (subs. N.Y. Stock Exchange), N.Y.C., 1983-88, chmn., CEO, 1988-93; exec. v.p. equity sales, mem. mgmt. com. N.Y. Stock Exchange, 1989—95, also past chmn. mktg. info. program. Bd. dirs. Intermarket Clearing Corp. subs. Options Clearing Corp., Chgo.; bd. mgrs. N.Y. Cotton Exch., 1993-2005. Bd. dirs. N.Y. Downtown Beekman Hosp., 1993-2005, Jewish Bd. Guardians, 1970-78; bd. dirs. Ramapo Anchorage Camp, Rhinebeck, N.Y., pres., 1973-78; participant Jr. Achievement N.Y.C. pub. schs., 1988-89; trustee Lynchburg Coll., Va., 1989; active Brown U. Alumni Assn. Mem. Nat. Futures Assn. (bd. dirs., mem. exec. com. 1989-2005). Home: New York, NY. Died Nov. 25, 2005.

HOROWITZ, RAYMOND J., lawyer, director; b. NYC, May 7, 1916; s. Israel S. and Sadye (Freiman) H.; m. Margaret Goldenberg, Sept. 22, 1940; 1 dau., Judith. AB, Columbia U., 1936, LL.B., 1939. Bar: N.Y. 1939. Pvt. practice, N.Y.C., 1939-41; asst. corp. counsel City of N.Y., 1941-43; assoc. Meyer, Wallach & Silverson, N.Y.C., 1943-46; ptnr. McGoldrick, Dannett, Horowitz & Golub and predecessors, N.Y.C., 1946-69; former mem., now of counsel firm Graubard Miller and predecessors, from 1969. Cons. Nat. Housing Agy, 1946-47, Office Housing Expediter, 1947, Temporary State Housing Rent Commn., 1950-51 Author: (with others) Building Regulation in New York City, 1944. Chmn. trustees' vis. com. on Am. paintings and sculpture Met. Mus. Art. Mem. Assn. Bar City N.Y., N.Y. County Lawyers Assn., Phi Beta Kappa. Clubs: Century Assn. Home: New York, NY. Died Sept. 20, 2005.

HORTON, HAMILTON COWLES, JR., state senator; b. Winston-Salem, N.C., Aug. 6, 1931; m. Evelyn Horton; 1 child, Rosalie. AB, U. N.C., 1953, LLB, 1956. Atty., 1960—2003; mem. N.C. Ho. of Reps., Raleigh, 1969-70, N.C. State Senate, Raleigh, 1971—75, 1995—2006. Joint caucus leader gen. assembly N.C. State Senate, 1973, adminstrv. asst. for Senator Jessie Helms, 1976-78, vice chair bd. on state goals and policies, 1985-89, chair recreation and natural heritage trust. With USN, 1956-60. Mem. N.C. Bar, Environ. Def. Fund, Inst. Polit. Leadership, N.C. Environ., Rotary. Moravian. Republican. Died Jan. 31, 2006.

HORTON, JOHN ERNEST, motion picture industry consultant; b. Davenport, Iowa, Jan. 3, 1919; s. Leroy Francis and Beatrice Olga (Abramson) H.; m. Drucie Snyder, Jan. 26, 1950; children: Evlyn Spencer, Elizabeth Snyder, Jon Dru. B Pub. Adminstrn., U. Mo., 1940. Location mgr. Warner Bros. Pictures, Burbank, Calif., 1946-48; chief motion pictures Dept. Army and Dept. Def., Washington, 1948-50; mil. aide to Pres., The White House, Washington, 1949-50; Washington rep. Universal Pictures Co., 1950-55, prodn. exec., prodr. Universal City, Calif., 1955-59; cons. to motion picture industry John E. Horton Assocs., Washington, from 1959; v.p., bd. dirs. Doremus and Co., Washington, 1971-80. Cons. to def. industry Ryan Aero./Continental Motors, Washington, 1965-72; cons. EduCap Inc., Washington; Washington rep. Alliance Motion Picture and TV Prodrs., 1987-95. Chmn. pub. rels. U.S. Olympic com., 1968-72; cons. on pub. affairs Pres.'s Coun. on Pub. Fitness and Sports, Washington, 1973-90; co-chmn. 21st Century Fund, Harry S Truman Libr. Inst., Independence, Mo., 1993-96, bd. dirs.; trustee Charleston Mus., v.p. bd. trustees; bd. dirs. Harry S. Truman Libr. Inst., 1996-2000. Lt. col. inf. U.S. Army, 1940-46, MTO, col. Res., 1961. Recipient commendation res. forces policy bd. US Dept. Def., 1956, cert. of achievement Dept. Army, 1961. Mem. Acad. Motion Picture Arts and Scis., Met. Club Washington, Burning Tree Club (Bethesda, Md.), Seabrook Island Club, Phi Gamma Delta. Episcopalian. Avocations: golf, writing, literature, travel, personal computers. Home: Johns Island, SC. Died June 4, 2006.

HORTON, ODELL, retired federal judge; b. Bolivar, Tenn., May 13, 1929; s. Odell and Rosa H.; m. Evie L. Randolph, Sept. 13, 1953; children: Odell, Christopher. AB, Morehouse Coll., 1951; cert., U.S. Navy Sch. Journalism, 1952; JD, Howard U., 1956; HHD (hon.), Miss. Indsl. Coll., 1969; LLD (hon.), Morehouse Coll., 1983. Bar: Tenn. 1956. Pvt. practice law, Memphis, 1957-62; asst. U.S. atty. (We. Dist.) Tenn. US Dept. Justice, Memphis, 1962-67; dir. div. hosp. and health services City of Memphis, 1968; judge Criminal Ct. Shelby County, Memphis, 1969-70; pres. LeMoyne-Owen Coll., Memphis, 1970-74; commentator Sta. WREC-TV (CBS), Memphis, 1972-74; judge U.S. Dist. Ct. (we. dist.) Tenn., 1980—97, chief judge, 1987. Mem. Jud. Conf. of U.S. Com. on Defender Svcs.; chair com. to establish a Death Penalty Resource Ctr., Nashville. Bd. mgrs. Meth. Hosp., Memphis, 1969-79; bd. dirs. Family Svc. Memphis, United Negro Coll. Fund, N.Y.C., 1970-74. With USMC, 1951-53. Recipient Disting. Alumni award Howard U., 1969, L. M. Graves Meml. Health award Mid-South Med. Ctr. Coun., Memphis, 1969, Bill of Rights award West Tenn. chpt. ACLU, 1970, Disting. Service award Mallory Knights Charitable Orgn., 1970, Disting. Service award Smothers Chapel C.M.E. Ch., 1971, Outstanding Citizen award Frontiers Internat., 1969, Ralph E. Bunche Humanitarian award Boy Scouts Am., 1972, Outstanding Educator and Judge award Salem-Gilfield Bapt. Ch., 1973, Spl. Tribute award A.M.E. Ch., 1974, United Negro Coll. Fund award, 1974, Humanities award Citizens Com. Coun. of Memphis, 1969, Shelby County Penal Farm award, 1974, Disting. Service award LeMoyne-Owen Coll., 1974, Disting. Service award Lane Coll., 1977, Dedicated Community Service award Christian Meth. Episc. Ch., 1979. Mem. NAACP, ABA (sr., chair conf. fed. trial judges, jud. adminstrn. divsn., chair exec. com. nat. conf. fed. trial judges 1994-95). Home: Memphis, Tenn. Died Feb. 22, 2006.

HORTON, PATRICIA SANDRA, priest; b. Asheville, N.C., Oct. 3, 1947; d. Charles Dwight and Edith (Greer) H. BS in Edn., Western Carolina U., 1969; MEd, U. Ga., 1973; MDiv, U. of the South, 1986. Ordained to ministry Episcopal Ch. as priest, 1987. Asst. to rector St. David's Ch., Roswell, Ga., 1986-90; rector St. Francis Episcopal Ch., Macon, Ga., from 1990. Mem. commn. on ministry Diocese of Atlanta, 1987-90, mem. liturgy and music com., 1986-90, mem. consultation commn., 1989—, gen. conv. dep., 1991, Macon (Ga.) convocation dean, 1990—. Mem. Nat. Episcopal Clergy Assn. Democrat. Home: Birmingham, Ala. Died Jan. 13, 2004.

HORVATH, RICHARD G(EORGE), finance company executive; b. Trenton, N.J., Feb. 22, 1933; s. Stephen John Sr. and Anna (Chlaupek) H.; m. Eleanor Barbara Maziekien, June 13, 1953; children: Richard G. Jr., Doreen A. BS in Bus. Mgmt., Fairleigh Dickinson U., 1955; MBA, Rutgers U., 1960. CLU. Various pos. Prudential, Newark, 1957-67; mgr. Prudential Ins. Co., Newark, 1967-69, assoc. gen. mgr., assoc. treas., 1969-71, gen. mgr., assoc. treas., 1971-73, gen. mgr., 1973-74, v.p. corp. svcs., 1974-78, v.p., 1978-84, v.p., head govt. health programs Millville, N.J., 1984-87; pres. Prudential Trust Co., Ft. Washington, Pa., 1987-91; sr. v.p. Prudential Asset Mgmt. Co., Florham Park, N.J., from 1987. Bd. dirs. Mgmt. Inst., 1984-87, chmn., 1986-87. Pres. Boys and Girls Clubs Newark, 1979-80, chmn., 1990-91; bd. dirs. BBB, Newark, 1980-83; trustee Newark Mus., 1982—; bd. trustees Boys' and Girls' Clubs Newark, 1978—. With U.S. Army, 1955-57. Recipient Man and Boy award Boys & Girls CLubs of Newark, 1981; inducted into Garfield (N.J.) Hall of Fame, 1992. Mem. Fairleigh Dickinson U. Alumni Assn. (1st. v.p. 1991-93, pres.-elect 1993-94, trustee), Beta Gamma Sigma. Avocations: sports, travel, movies, reading. Died Feb. 9, 2005.

HOTZ, ROBERT BERGMANN, editor, publisher; b. Milw., May 29, 1914; s. Harry Phillip and Emma (Bergmann) H.; m. Joan Willison, Nov. 18, 1944; children: George, Michael, Robert Lee, Harry II. BS, Northwestern U., 1936. Reporter, Paris edit. N.Y. Herald Tribune, 1936-37; reporter, editor Milw. Jour., 1938-41; news editor McGraw-Hill Pub. Co., Washington, 1946-49; dir. pub. relations Pratt & Whitney Aircraft, Hartford, Conn., 1950-52; editor Aviation Week and Space Tech. mag., N.Y.C., 1953-80, pub., 1976-80; editor Space Tech. Internat., 1958-80; editorial cons. McGraw-Hill, Inc., 1980-84. Author: With General Chennault, the Story of the Flying Tigers, 1943, Pratt and Whitney Aircraft Story, 1950, Both Sides of Suez, 1975, The Promise of the Space Age, 1980; editor: Way of a Fighter, Memoirs of Claire Lee Chennault, 1949. Mem. gen. adv. com. ACDA, 1982-92; mem. Presdl. Commn. on Shuttle Challenger Accident, 1986. Served from 2d lt. to maj. USAAF, 1942-46. Decorated Air medal with oak leaf cluster; recipient Airpower award Air Force Assn., 1958; Paul Tissandier diploma Fedn. Aeronautique Internationale, 1958; Press award Nat. Space Club, 1965; Strebig and Ball trophies Aviation/Space Writers Assn., 1972; Pub. Service award Am. Astronautical Soc., 1974; Lauren D. Lyman award Aviation/Space Writers Assn., 1974; 11th Crain award Am. Bus. Press Assn., 1978; Meritorious Service award Nat. Bus. Aircraft Assn., 1981 Mem. AIAA (Pendray Aerospace Lit. award 1981), 14th Air Force Assn., Royal Aero. Soc. (companion), Nat. Press Club, Caterpillar Club, RAF (London), Explorers Club (N.Y.C.). Home: Middletown, Md. Died Feb. 9, 2006.

HOTZE, CHARLES WAYNE, publishing executive; b. Moline, Ill., Feb. 19, 1919; s. Charles Edmund and Nellie (Gibbs) H.; m. Hazel Ann Tebbens, Dec. 20, 1956; children: Karen Ann, Carla Ann. BA, U. Ill., 1941. Pres., chmn. bd. Fowle Printing Co., Milw., 1953-55; pres. Pub. Clin. Med., Northfield, Ill., from 1954, Med. Digest, Inc., from 1955, C. W. Hotze Bldg. Corp., from 1956, Pediatrics Digest, Inc., from 1962, Psychiatry Digest, from 1962, Dermatology Digest, from 1963, Ob/Gyn Digest, from 1964, Urology Digest, from 1964, Cardiology Digest, 1966, Med. Comm., Inc., from 1968; chmn. bd. Lake County Press, Inc., Waukegan, Ill., 1971-78; pres. K&C Land Devel. Corp., from 1993. O.R.L. Digest, 1971—, Ophthalmology Digest, 1971—, Orthopedics Digest, 1973—, Pharmacy Digest, 1978—, Veterinary Digest, 1978—, Radiology Digest, 1979, Anesthesiology Digest, 1981—. Served to 1st lt. Infantry, AUS, 1942-44. Mem. Soc. Acad. Achievement, Am. Med. Writers Assn., Pharm. Advt. Club, Midwest Pharm. Advt. Club, Ams. Armorial Ancestry, Mayflower Soc., SAR, Am. Legion, Benevolent and Protective Order of Elks, Psi Upsilon. Clubs: Sunset Ridge (Northfield, Ill.). Home: Northfield, Ill. Died June 10, 2006; Ill.

HOUGARDY, ROBERT GRAY, investment specialist; b. Feb. 24, 1931; s. Oscar Daniel and Evelyn Mildred Hougardy; m. Jeanne Rae Grove, Dec. 28, 1957; children: Peter, Nevin, Elizabeth, Matthew. Student, Air U., 1954; BBA, Woodbury U., 1955; postgrad., N.Y. Inst. Fin., 1967-68; MS in Fin., Adam Smith U., 1996. Cert. fin. planner, Calif.; registered investment counsel. Market analyst Frito-Lay, L.A. and San Jose, Calif., 1955-67; stockbroker Michum Jones & Templeton, Santa Cruz, Calif., 1967-70, Dean Witter-Reynolds, Santa Cruz, 1970-79; stockbroker, br. mgr., fin. planner Smith Barney, Santa Cruz, 1979-95; sole proprietor R. Hougardy Investment Counseling, Santa Cruz, Calif., from 1996. Bd.dirs. Clinch Found., Monterey, Calif.; mem. fin. bd. dirs. Monterey Diocese Roman Cath. Ch., 1994. Pres. Soquel Union Sch. Dist., Santa Cruz, 1972-76; mem. Rep. Ctrl. Com., Santa Cruz. Maj. N.G., AUS, 1947-52, Korea, 1983-87. Mem. Calif. N.G. Assn., Res. Officers Assn., KC (3d degree). Avocation: tennis. Died June 20, 2005.

HOUGHAM, NORMAN RUSSELL, diversified financial services company executive; b. Correctionville, Iowa, Sept. 28, 1937; s. Russell Lowell and Geneva Marie (Lafferty) H.; m. Evelyn Joy Foley, Apr. 10, 1960; 1 child, Jill. Student, Am. Inst. Banking, 1969; diploma, Sch. Bank Adminstrn., 1980. Clk. Earlham (Iowa) Savs. Bank, 1959-60; cashier Capital City State Bank, Des Moines, 1960-76; v.p. Brenton Nat. Bank, Des Moines, 1976-82; sr. v.p. Am. Fed. Savs. and Loan, Des Moines, 1982-90; mng. agt. Resolution Trust Corp., 1990-94; CFO Midwest Fin. Svcs. Ltd., from 1995. Bd. dirs. Earlham Swim Pool Devel. Corp., 1972; mem. bd. edn. Earlham Sch., 1986; bd. dirs., treas. Pioneer Pl. Retirement Homes, Earlham, 1998—; bd. dirs., chmn. fin. com. Earlham Ch. of Christ, 1999; trustee Earlham Pub. Libr., 1990. Recipient Bd. Dirs. award Des Moines chpt. Am. Inst. Banking, 1972, Instr. Appreciation award Inst. for Fin. Edn., 1983, award of merit Earlham Bd. Edn., 1986, Spl. Achievement award FDIC, 1992, Cert. of Appreciation RTC, 1992. Mem. Masons. Republican. Avocations: reading, teaching. Home: Earlham, Iowa. Died Sept. 4, 2005.

HOUK, VICTOR CALDWELL, electronics manufacturing executive; b. Knoxville, Tenn., July 12, 1920; s. Frederick C. and Ada Minerva (Caldwell) H.; m. Lucy Barker, Jan. 30, 1925; children: Susan, Steven, Jeffrey. BEE, U. Tenn., 1942; MS in Indsl. Mgmt., MIT, 1954. Mktg. rep. RCA Corp., 1950-84; mgr. various depts. Harrison, N.J., 1950-59; mgr. mktg. various depts. Lancaster, Pa., 1959-72; mgr. mktg. closed circuit TV, 1972-84; v.p. mktg. Am. Dynamics, Orangeburg, N.Y., from 1984, also bd. dirs. Bd. dirs. Xybion Corp., Ceder Nolls, N.J. Served to capt. Signal Corps U.S. Army, 1942-45, CBI. Sloan fellow, 1954. Mem. Tau Beta Pie. Republican. Baptist. Avocations: golf, flying, sports. Home: Santa Barbara, Calif. Died Mar. 6, 2004.

HOWARD, EDWARD EARLE, marketing executive; b. Phillipsburg, N.J., Sept. 28, 1928; s. Elston M. and Freida M. (Hamlen) H.; m. Phyllis Ann Bonstein June 6, 1953; 1 child, Leslie Ann. Student, Lafayette Coll., 1946-48. Asst. nat. advt. mgr. The Express, Easton, Pa., 1962-64, nat. advt. mgr., 1964-68, dir. advt. and promotion, 1968-72, dir. sales and mktg., 1972—; gen. mgr. The Free Press, Phillipsburg, 1975—. Chmn. United Fund, Easton, 1969-70; chmn. membership drive YMCA, 1971; chmn. Lafayette Coll. Bus. Campaign, 1978, Northampton County Drug and Alcohol Commn., Pa., 1978-81. Mem. Internat. Newspaper Advt. and Mktg. Execs. (mem. sales and mktg. com. 1980-82), Internat. Newspaper Promotion Assn. (pres. Eastern region 1969-70), Easton Area Sales and Mktg. Execs. (bd. dirs. 1970-72, 87—), Easton Area C. of C. (pres. 1974). Republican. Avocations: reading, handball. Home: Easton, Pa. Died Mar. 24, 2005.

HOWARD, GAIL FRANCES, artist, educator, author; b. Spokane, Wash., Jan. 18, 1946; d. Harold Elvis Stallings and Gladys S. (Klee) Jewett; Garnett James Howard, May 31, 1967; 1 child, Jan Carin. Student, Wash. State U., 1964-66, East Wash. State U., 1965-67, 72-73, U. Wash., 1966, U. Washington D.C., 1974-75; BA in Psychology and Human Svcs., Marymount U., 1977. Info. and reference specialist Arlington County, Va., 1976-77; cons. Identity Rsch., Inc., 1978-80; art history tchr. Children's House, 1984; art tchr., cons. Our Saviour Luth. Schs., 1985-86; tchr. art and writing gifted and talented program Papillion LaVista Sch. Dist., from 1986. Educator, cons. Hawaii Pub. Sch. Leaward Dist., 1986, ASSETS Sch. for Gifted, Honolulu, 1985-86; tchr. Arapahoe County Pks. and Recreation Dist., 1989; artist-in-residence, cons., tchr. Peabody Elem. Sch., Littleton, Colo., 1989; condr. seminars Grad. Study Continuing Edn., Chapman Coll.; tchr. watercolor Littleton Community Srs. Ctr.; mem. ednl. adv. com. Littleton Sch. Dist.; ind. rep. Excel Telecomm., 1996—. Represented in exhbns., including Omaha Children's Mus., Hawaii Ronald McDonald House, Manoa Gallery, Hawaii Children's Mus., Sta. KHET-TV, East Wash. State U.; author, artist: (book) Me and My Pencil: I Can Draw, 1985; (art instruction booklet) Exploring Shapes in Space, 1985; promotor, artist; Spectacular Color Works, Honolulu, 1985-86, Colo. Arts Sampler, Littleton, 1989; feature artist Hawaii pub. TV program Spectrum, 1986; represented by Colburn's Gallery, Spokane, Wash., A Frame of Mind, Coeur d'Alene, Idaho; author Small Biz Cash Machine, 1999, Memoirs: Beginning at the End, 2006. Rep. community bd., Leaward Dist., Hawaii, 1981-83; pres., Palehua Community Assn., Honolulu, 1980-82; v.p., Palehua Vista Community Assn., 1980-82; mem. Ewa Neighborhood Bd., Honolulu, 1980-82; sec., treas. Arapahoe County Cultural Coun., 1989—; mem. Hangman Creek Stream Team, 1996—; chair Latch/Hangman Valley Neighborhood Coun., 1998-99. Work selected by Hawaii Watercolor Soc., 1986. Mem. Wild Flower Soc. and Creations (founder, creator 1989). Died June 1, 2006.

HOWARD, LAURENCE WEBB, JR., brokerage house executive; b. Jacksonville, Fla., Nov. 26, 1929; s. Laurence Webb and Eleanor (Lytle) H.; m. Lanessa Turner McMillan, June 1, 1962; children: John F., Carol Howard Hulsey, Laurence W. III, Robert McMillan. BA, Dartmouth Coll., 1951. Pres. Howard Feed Mills, Inc., Jacksonville, 1954-79; 1st v.p. Dean Witter Reynolds, Jacksonville, 1979-84; v.p. Prudential Bache, Jacksonville, from 1984. Episcopalian. Home: Ponte Vedra Beach, Fla. Died June 14, 2004.

HOWE, RAYMOND BRADLEY, security systems consultant; b. N.Y.C., Aug. 25, 1920; s. Herbert R. and Ruth (Bradley) H.; m. Faye M., Aug. 6, 1950 (div. Sept. 1978); children: Anthony, Carolyn, Chris, Mary Ellen, Jennifer, John, Charles; m. Joy R. Throckmorton, Sept. 21, 1978; 1 child, Tracy. BS, U. Md., 1949. Research scientist USDA, Beltsville, Md., 1949-50; spl. agt. FBI, Washington, 1950-78; pres. Ray Howe & Assocs., Lees Summit, Mo., from 1978. Chmn. Lynwood Racing Stables, Lees Summit, 1985—. Author: (cartoon book) Fall Semester '84, 1984; contbr. articles in field to Ripples mag., 1983-84. Chmn. Security Com., Village of Lakewood, Mo., 1983. Served to capt. A.C., U.S. Army, 1942-46, ETO. Decorated Air medal with clusters. Mem. Soc. Former Spl. Agts. FBI (chmn. Kansas City chpt. 1986), Cartoonists Guild, Thunderbolt Assn., VFW (vice comdr. 1986). Clubs: Lakewood Country (Lees Summit). Republican. Avocation: owning and training thoroughbred race horses. Home: Lees Summit, Mo. Died June 19, 2005.

HOWELL, JEANETTE DORIS RATHBURN, elementary school educator; b. Cazenovia, N.Y., July 10, 1936; d. Adelbert Wallace Rathburn and Erna Joan Matilda Reetz; m. Louis A. Howell, Sept. 16, 1963; children: William Henry, Joan Elizabeth Howell Loyd. AB Gen. Home Econs.,

Brenau Coll. U., 1960; BA in Edn., U. Ga., 1964. Tchr. fourth grade Hall County Bd. Edn., Gainesville, Ga., 1961-62, Oconee County Bd. Edn., Watkinsville, Ga., 1964-65; part-time tchr. Clarke County Bd. Edn., Athens, Ga., 1979—96. Mem. bd. edn., Oglethorpe County, Ga., 1996-2003, mem. Edn. Com. Athens, Ga., 1993-94; active Athens 1996 Olympic Com., 1994— Jeannette Rankin Found., Athens. Recipient awards AAUW, 2000-01, Girl Scouts U.S.; Brenau Coll. scholar. Mem. AAUW (Am. Fellowship award 1993), LWV, Order Eastern Star (2d v.p. membership, Outstanding Officer award 1993-94), Red Hat Soc., Phi Delta Kappa. Republican. Lutheran. Avocations: coin and stamp collecting, music, dance, travel. Home: Watkinsville, Ga. Died Nov. 14, 2005.

HOWELLS, WILLIAM WHITE, anthropology educator; b. NYC, Nov. 27, 1908; s. John Mead and Abby MacDougall (White) H.; m. Muriel Gurdon Seabury, June 15, 1929 (dec. 2002); children— Gurdon Howells Metz, William Dean SB, Harvard U., 1930, PhD, 1934; DSc (hon.), Beloit Coll., 1975, U. Witwatersrand, 1985. From asst. prof. to prof. anthropology U. Wis., 1939-54, prof. integrated liberal studies, 1948-54; prof. anthropology Harvard U., 1954-74, prof. emeritus, from 1974. Hon. fellow Sch. Am. Research, 1975 Author: Mankind So Far, 1944, The Heathens, 1948, Back of History, 1954, Mankind in the Making, 1959, rev. edit., 1967, The Pacific Islanders, 1973, Cranial Variation in Man, 1973, Evolution of the Genus Homo, 1973, Skull Shapes and The Map, 1989, Getting Here: The Story of Human Evolution, 1993, Who's Who in Skulls, 1995; editor: Early Man in the Far East, 1949, Ideas on Human Evolution, 1962, Paleoanthropology in the People's Republic of China, 1977, Am. Jour. Phys. Anthropology, 1949-54; assoc. editor Human Biology, 1955-74. Served as lt. USNR, 1943-46 Recipient Viking Fund medal in phys. anthropology, 1954 Fellow AAAS, Indian Anthrop. Assn. (fgn.), Am. Acad. Arts and Scis., Am. Anthrop. Assn. (pres. 1951, Disting. Service award 1978), Soc. Antiquaries London; mem. NAS, Austrian Acad. Scis., Mass. Hist. Soc., Am. Assn. of Physical Anthropologists (sec., treas. 1939-41, Charles R. Darwin Lifetime Achievement award 1992); corr. mem. Geog. Soc. Lisbon, Anthrop. Soc. Paris (Broca prix du Centenaire 1980), Anthrop. Soc. Vienna, Royal Soc. South Africa (fgn.), Soc. for Biol. Anthropology Spain (corr.), Harvard Faculty Club Died Dec. 20, 2005.

HOWES, MELINDA SUE, marketing executive; b. Weston, W.Va., Nov. 16, 1947; d. John Everett and Eloise (McNemar) H. BA in Communications, Columbia Union Coll., Takoma Park, 1969. Assoc. program dir. WGTS-FM Radio, Takoma Park, Md., 1967-69; asst. pub. rels. dir. Nat. Recreation & Parks Assn., Washington, 1970-71, Washington Med. Ctr., 1971-72; dir. pub. rels. and audiovisual communication Washington Adventist Hosp., Takoma Park, 1972-74; news reporter WTAP-TV & Radio, Parkersburg, W.Va., 1974-76; features editor The Daily Times, Marietta, Ohio, 1976-79; v.p. mktg. Fla. Hosp. Med. Ctr., Orlando, 1979-82; pres., owner Mktg. Support Group, Orlando, from 1982. Chair promotion com. Fla. Hosp. Capital Campaign, Orlando, 1991-96; mem. pres.'s coun. Fla. Hosp. Found., Orlando, 1988-96, mem. Golden Circle of Friends, 1983-96. Recipient Telly award, 1990, Addy award, 1982, 89, 90, Touchstone award Am. Hosp. assn. Mktg. and Pub. Rels. Soc., 1985, 86, MacEachern award Am. Hosp. Assn., 1982, Nurse Recruiting Retention award, 1981, many others for articles, reports. Mem. Orlando Area Ad Fedn. Republican. Seventh-day Adventist. Avocations: reading, writing, sports, photography. Home: West Union, W.Va. Died May 29, 2005.

HRIBAR, JOHN PETER, SR., engineering administrator, consultant; b. Cleve., Jan. 1, 1936; s. John Frank and Virginia C. (Vito) H.; m. Francine Marie Stepic, Oct. 3, 1964; children: John P. Jr., Wendy M., Tammy J., Tommie J., Francine A. BS in Civil Engring., U. Notre Dame, Ind., 1958. Registered profl. engr., Ohio, Ill., Ind., Wis., Ariz., Calif., Nev. With Howard Needles Tammen & Bergendoff, 1958-92, dep. dir. adminstrv. svcs. Milw., 1977-85, dir. engring. Phoenix, 1990-92; tech. dir., chief civil engr. Frederic R. Harris, Inc., San Pedro, Calif., from 1993. Contbr. articles to profl. jours. Mem. St. Joseph Athletic Assn., Milw., 1981-87, pres. 1986; mem. parish coun. Community of Blessed Sacrament, 1990-93, chmn. 1992-93. Fellow ASCE (exec. com. engring. mgmt. div. 1987-90, chmn. 1989), Am. Pub. Works Assn. Roman Catholic. Avocations: reading, travel. Home: Scottsdale, Ariz. Died Jan. 17, 2005.

HSIEH, HAZEL TSENG, retired elementary and secondary educator; b. Beijing, Nov. 4, 1934; came to U.S., 1947; naturalized, 1968; d. Hung-tu and Man-lone (Huang) Tseng; m. Hsueh Ying Hsieh, July 1, 1961; children: Durwynne, Timothy. Student, Adelphi U., 1954-56; BS, Tufts U., 1958; postgrad., Harvard U., 1959, U. Hartford, 1962-64; MA, Columbia U., 1977. Cert. tchr., N.Y. Tchr., asst. dir. Parents Nursery Sch., Cambridge, Mass., 1957; tchr. Sch. for Young Children, St. Joseph Coll., West Hartford, Conn., 1958-63; dir. Ctr. Nursery Sch., Yorktown Heights, N.Y., 1967-68; tchr. Yorktown Ctrl. Schs., Yorktown Heights, 1968-97; ret., 1997. Substitute Visiting Day Nursery, N.Y.C., summer 1953-57; co-chair adv. com. Lakeland-Yorktown BOCES Mass Comm. Project, Yorktown Heights, 1982-87; mem. Internat. Faculty, Challenger Ctr. Space Sci. Edn., Alexandria, Va., 1990—. Author: Living in Families, 1991; editor: Honor Society Competition Directory of Nominations, 1985-89. Past mem. Yorktown Schs. Dist. Mission State Com.; mem. Dist. Acad. Stds. Com., 1994-97, Dist. Task Force on Gifted and Talented Edn., 1995-97, Mohansic Shared Decision Making Coun., Yorktown Heights, 1992-97, Mohansic Literacy Com. 1992-96, Tech. Sci. Coms., 1992-97, Wee Deliver Com., 1993-94, Dem. Party; curriculum coord. Ch. Good Shepherd, Granite Springs, N.Y., 1967-69; organizer Parent Orgn. for Arlington Symphony Orch., 1982-84, Mohansic Space Day, 1993, 97; tchr. rep. PTA, 1977-78; founder Internat. Young Astronaut chpt 27796, 1990, leader, 1990-97; coord. project Marsville, Hudson Valley, 1992—; vol. crafts, space sci. workshops, 1990—. Recipient Kohl Internat. Teaching award, Wilmette, Ill., 1991; Challenger Seven fellow, 1990; Challenger Ctr. Internat. Faculty, 1990—; grantee NASA, 1989, N.Y. State Electric and Gas Co., 1987, PTA, 1987, No. Westchester Tchr. Ctr., 1988, Pi Lambda Theta, 1991, IBM, 1992, Readers Digest Found. and Westchester Edn. Coalition, 1995-97. Mem. Am. Fedn. Tchrs., Yorktown Congress Tchrs. (sr. bldg. rep. 1977-78), Union Concerned Scientists, Save the Redwoods League, Nature Conservancy, Sierra Club, Pi Lambda Theta (chair curriculum innovation award com. Westchester Area chpt. 1985-93, chpt. pres. 1991-95, 1st v.p. 1989-91, 2d v.p. 1987-89, corr. sec. 1983-87, advisor 1995—, region 1 sec. and exec. bd. 1996-98, mem. region 1 awards com. 1992-98, chair 1994-96, region 1 comm. chair 1998—, Westchester area chpt. comm. chair 1998—, grantee 1991, Outstanding Chpt. 1991-92). Avocations: downhill skiing, tennis, chinese culture and crafts. Died Aug. 20, 2005.

HSU, ENRICO YUN PING, manufacturing executive; b. Shanghai, Apr. 13, 1926; came to U.S., 1966; s. Joachim and Magdalena (Shen) H.; m. Magdalena Weiyin Lee, Nov. 16, 1957; children: Joachim, Dave, Felix, Calvin. BS, Aurora U., 1948; MS, Columbia U., 1959; PhD, Rutgers U., 1987. Mgr. distbn. planning Ingersoll-Rand, Phillipsburg, N.J., 1968-73, dir. info. systems Woodcliff Lake, N.J., 1973-83; pres. Ridgewood Info. Resource Ctr., Glen Rock, N.J., from 1983. Mem. Assn. Computing Machinery, Nat. Council Phys. Distbn. Mgmt., Am. Prodn. and Inventory Control Soc. (exec. v.p. local chpt.). Roman Catholic. Home: Mahwah, NJ. Died Apr. 19, 2005.

HUANG, THOMAS TSUNG-TSE, naval architect, mechanical engineer; b. Taoyuan, Taiwan, Sept. 1, 1938; s. Chuang and Shih (Lin) H.; m. Suiteh Kuo, Apr. 29, 1942; children: Margaret Wenying, Mitchell Tseng-Teh. BS, Nat. Taiwan U., 1961; MS, Iowa State U., 1964; PhD, Cath. U. of Am., 1968. Registered profl. engr., Va. Assoc. rsch. scientist Hydronautics, Inc., Laurel, Md., 1963-68; rsch. sr. naval architect David Taylor Model Basin NSWCCD, W. Bethesda, Md., 1968-94, chief hydrodynamist, 1994-98; prin. scientist Newport News (Va.) Shipbuilding, from 1998. Recipient David Taylor award U.S. Navy, 1979; named Engr. of Yr., David Taylor Rsch. Ctr. U.S. Navy, 1986. Fellow ASME; mem. Soc. Naval Archs. and Marine Engrs. Achievements include patent on appendage produced preswirl. Home: Reston, Va. Died May 10, 2005.

HUBBARD, MICHAEL JAMES, lawyer; b. N.Y.C., Dec. 8, 1950; s. William Neil and Elizabeth (Terleski) H. AB, U. Mich., 1976; JD, Marquette U., 1979. Bar: Wis. 1980, Mich. 1980. Assoc. Kidston, Peterson P.C., Kalamazoo, 1980, Barbier, Goulet & Petersmarck, Mt. Clemens, Mich., 1981; pvt. practice Detroit, 1982-86, Belleville, Mich., 1990-98; assoc. Lawrence J. Stockler, P.C., Southfield, Mich., 1987; staff atty. Hyatt Legal Svcs., Southgate, Mich., 1988; assoc. Dunchock, Linden & Wells, Coruna, Mich., 1989. Mem. State Bar Mich. (criminal law, negligence, gen. practice sects.) Republican. Died June 12, 2004.

HUBER, VIDA SWARTZENTRUBER, nursing educator; b. West Liberty, Ohio, Mar. 27, 1937; d. L.L. and Nanna V. (Bender) Swartzentruber; m. Harold E. Huber, June 6, 1970; 1 child, Heidi Marie. Diploma, Milford Meml. Hosp., 1959; BSN, Eastern Mennonite Coll., 1961; MA in Nursing Edn., Columbia U., Tchrs. Coll., 1966, EdD, 1970. Staff nurse Milford Meml. Hosp., Del., 1959-60; nursing supr. County Rest Home, Greenwood, Del., 1959-60, 61-65; instr. nursing Milford Meml. Hosp., Del., 1961-64, ednl. dir. Del., 1964; chmn., prof. Eastern Mennonite Coll., Dept. Nursing, Harrisonburg, Va., 1967-84; vis. prof. U. Va. Sch. Nursing, Charlottesville, Va., 1984-86; exec. dir. Va. Soc. Profl. Nurses, Harrisonburg, Va., 1987-88; prof., head nursing dept. James Madison U., Harrisonburg, Va., 1988-99, interim assoc. dean Coll. Integrated Sci. and Tech., 1999—2001, assoc. dean, from 2001, dir. Inst. for Innovation in Health and Human Svcs., from 2001. Speaker in field; bd. dirs. County Rest Home, Greenwood, Del., 1970-81, pres., 1980-81; bd. dirs. Alley Alias Network, 1989—, Harrisonburg Free Clinic, Va., 1990-2005. Contbr. articles to profl. jours. Named Outstanding Young Women Am., 1973, Outstanding Educator AM. 1973, 75, one of Outstanding Nurses in Va., Va. Nurses Assn.; recipient Women's Caucus Award for Svc., 1992, James Madison Citizenship awrd, 2002. Mem. ANA, Am. Assn. Colls. Nursing, Nat. League Nursing, Va. Assn. Colls. Nursing, Mennonite Nurses Assn. (project dir. 1988), Kappa Delta Pi, Pi Delta Kappa, Pi Lambda Theta, Sigma Theta Tou. Home: Harrisonburg, Va. Died Nov. 20, 2005.

HUBERT, MARVIN H., construction consultant; b. N.Y.C., June 8, 1925; s. Jack W. and Dorothy (Goldweitz) H.; m. Barbara Joan; children: Robynne, Bambi, Jason. BS in Indsl. Engring., Lehigh U., 1947. Pres. Barlen Constrn. Cons., N.Y.C., 1960-83, Hubert Tech. Industries, Boca Raton, Fla., from 1983. Author estimating manual in field, 1978, 79; contbr. articles to profl. jours. Mem. NSPE, ASME, Profl. Engring. in Pvt. Practice, Am. Soc. Cost Engring., Polo Club of Boca Raton (asst. treas.). Avocations: computers, photography. Died Jan. 12, 2005.

HUDGINS, HERBERT CORNELIUS, JR., education educator, department chairman; b. Trotville, N.C., Oct. 9, 1932; s. Herbert Cornelius and Lucille Dixie (Simpson) H. AB, High Point Coll., 1954; MEd, U. N.C., Chapel Hill, 1959; EdD, Duke U., 1966. Cert. tchr., prin., N.C. Tchr. Thomasville (N.C.) City Schs., 1954-59, 1959-64; asst. prof. U. N.C., Greensboro, 1966-69, prof., 1985-88; assoc. prof. Temple U., Phila., 1969-74, prof., 1974-80, No. Ill. U., DeKalb, 1980-85; prof. edn., chmn. dept. ednl. leadership East Carolina U., Greenville, N.C., 1988-94. Author: The Warren Court and the Public Schools, 1970; co-author: Law and Education, 1979, 3d edit., 1991, 4th edit., 1995, Liability of School Officials and Administrators for Civil Rights Torts, 1982. Recipient Lindback teaching award Temple U., 1975, Benjamin Rosner teaching award, 1977. Mem. Nat. Orgn. on Legal Problems Edn. (E.C. Bolmeier award 1989), Nat. Assn. Secondary Sch. Prins., N.C. Profs. Ednl. Leadership, Kappa Delta Pi, Phi Delta Kappa. Democrat. Methodist. Avocations: gardening, refinishing furniture, trivia. Home: Greenville, NC. Died July 3, 2004.

HUDY, JOHN JOSEPH, psychologist; b. Milw., June 10, 1956; s. Jack Donald and Florence Rosemary (Harlow) H. BA in Psychology, U. Wis., Milw., 1979; MA in Exptl. Psychology, U. South Fla., 1981, PhD in Indsl. Psychology, 1985. Chief of manpower City of Clearwater (Fla.), 1982-87; project mgr. CORE Corp., Pleasant Hill, Calif., 1987-91; rsch. psychologist Acumen Internat., San Rafael, Calif., from 1991. Pres. Mgmt. Systems Inc., Alameda, Calif., 1991—; bd. dirs. U.S.F. Psychology Found., Tampa, Fla., 1982-87. Reviewer Acad. Mgmt. Rev. jour.; contbr. articles to profl. jours. Speaker, writer Zero Population Growth, Berkeley, Calif., 1987-91. Recipient Kemper-Knapp Found. scholarships U. Wis. Milw., 1975, 76. Mem. Am. Psychol. Soc., Acad. Mgmt. Achievements include rsch. on computerized expert-system mgmt. assessment and feedback systems, data from U.S., France, Japan, Great Britain showing trait distributions relevant to effective performance. Home: Mill Valley, Calif. Died Mar. 18, 2004.

HUERTA, BALDEMAR See FENDER, FREDDY

HUFF, ROSEMARY BOWERS, music and voice educator; b. Krebs, Okla., Dec. 14, 1924; d. Harvey Henry and Hilda Magdalene (Kiple) Bowers; m. Howard Farmer Huff, June 10, 1951 (dec. Sept. 16, 2001); children: Carol Celeste Huff Hicks, Angela Kay, Gloria Ann Huff Graham, Craig Kenton. AB in Music Edn., Park Coll., 1947; M Sacred Music, Union Theol. Sch. Sacred Music, N.Y.C., 1951. Ordained to ministry Christian Ch. (Disciples of Christ), 1951. Tchr. music Harper-Maize (Kans.) Pub. Sch., 1947-49; music educator divsn. overseas ministries Christian Ch. (Disciples of Christ), Tokyo, 1951-62; min. music Willow Rd. Christian Ch., Enid, Okla., 1963-69, Ctrl. Christian Ch., Enid, 1970-80; organist, choir dir. Phillips Theol. Sem., Enid, 1968-80; min. music Bethany Christian Ch., Tulsa, 1980-89; pvt. tchr. piano and voice, Enid, 1965-80, Tulsa, from 1980. Judge Tri-State Music Festival, Enid, 1970-99. Recipient Honored Min.'s award Christian Ch. (Disciples of Christ), 1992. Mem. Assn. Disciple Musicians (planning coun. 1986-89), Hymn Soc. Am., Nat. Music Tchrs. Assn., Okla. Music Tchrs. Assn. (cert. piano and voice tchr.), Tulsa Accredited Music Tchrs. Assn. (dir. accreditation 1986-89), Hyechka Music Club. Democrat. Avocations: music, art. Home: Tulsa, Okla. Died Aug. 5, 2005.

HUFFMAN, MARY FRANCES, retired secondary school educator; b. Montgomery, Ala., Apr. 30, 1911; d. Mary Huffman; m. Alexander Lee, June 28, 1936 (div. Aug. 1938); 1 child, Patricia Day Smoke. BS, Ala. State U., 1951, MEd, 1961; postgrad., So. U., Baton Rouge, La., 1960, Beloit Coll., 1963, Talladega Coll., 1963—64. Cert. elem. and secondary tchr. Ala. Tchr. Elem. Schs., Troy, Ala., 1929-30, Prattville, Ala., 1930-32, Lowndes County, Ala., 1932-42, Union Springs, Ala., 1943-45, Montgomery, 1945-73, ret., from 1973. Sec. Nat. Caucus & Ctr. Black Aged, Congress Christian Edn., from 1955, Montgomery County Multi-Black Caucus; counselor Montgomery-Antioch Dist., Ala. State Women; me. program com. YMCA, 1969; treas. Alonzo Mitchell OES 636, Montgomery, 1980; Sunday sch. tchr. Holt St. Bapt. Ch., sec. matrons cir.; with Lilly Baptist Ch., 2002. Mem.: AARP, NEA, AAUW, Montgomery County Ret. Tchrs. Assn., Assn. Ret. Tchrs. Am., Twelve Tribes (rec. sec. Montgomery). Avocation: travel. Home: Charlotte, NC. Died Aug. 22, 2004.

HUGHES, BARNARD, actor; b. Bedford Hills, N.Y., July 16, 1915; s. Owen and Madge (Kiernan) H.; m. Helen Stenborg, Apr. 19, 1950; 2 children. Student, Manhattan Coll., DHL (hon.), 1989. Stage debut with Shakespeare Fellowship Co. in The Taming of the Shrew, N.Y.C., 1934; actor (plays) including Please, Mrs. Garibaldi, 1939, Herself, Mrs. Patrick Crowley, 1939, The Ivy Green, 1949, Dinosaur Wharf, 1951, The Teahouse of the August Moon, 1956, A Bell for Adano, 1957, Home of the Brave, 1957, The Will and The Way, 1957, Enrico IV, 1958, A Majority of One, 1959, Advise and Consent, 1960, Rosmersholm, 1962, A Doll's House, 1963, The Advocate, 1963, Nobody Loves and Albatross, 1963, Hamlet, 1964, I Was Dancing, 1964, Generation, 1965, Hogan's Goat, 1965, How Now Dow Jones, 1967, The Wrong-Way Light Bulb, 1969, Sheep on the Runway, 1970, Line, 1971, Abelard and Heloise, 1971, Older People, 1972, Hamlet, 1972, Much Ado About

Nothing, 1972 (Tony nomination 1973), Uncle Vanya, 1973, The Good Doctor, 1973, The Merry Wives of Windsor, 1974, Pericles, Prince of Tyre, 1974, All Over Town, 1974, The Three Sisters, 1977, The Devil's Disciple, 1977, 78, Da, 1978 (Tony award Best Actor 1978, Outer Critics Circle award 1978), Homeward Bound, 1980, Iceman Cometh, 1981, 85, Translations, 1981, Tartuffe, 1982, Angels Fall, 1982, 83, End of the World, 1984, The Sky is No Limit, 1984, You Can't Take It With You (Abbey Theatre, Dublin, Ireland), 1989, Prelude to A Kiss, 1990, Da, 1999, (Olympia Theatre, Dublin, Ireland) 1993, Waiting in the Wings, 1999, (films) including The Young Doctors, 1961, Hamlet, 1964, Midnight Cowboy, 1969, Where's Poppa?, 1970, Deadhead Miles, 1970, The Pursuit of Happiness, 1971, The Hospital, 1971, Cold Turkey, 1971, Rage, 1972, Sisters, 1973, Oh God!, 1977, First Monday in October, 1981, Tron, 1982, Best Friends, 1982, Maxie, 1985, Where are the Children?, 1986, The Lost Boys, 1987, Da (Olymoia Theatre, Dublin, Ireland), 1988, Doc Hollywood, 1991, Sister Act II: Back in the Habit, 1993, Odd Couple II, 1997, The Cradle Will Rock, 1998, (TV movies) including Guilty or Innocent: The Sam Sheppard Murder Case, 1975, 1975, Tell Me My Name, 1977, See How She Runs, 1978, Homeward Bound, 1980, The Sky's No Limit, 1984, Agatha Cristie's A Carribean Mystery, 1983, Night of Courage, 1986, A Hobo's Christmas, 1987, Day One, 1989, Home Fires Burning, 1989, Guts and Glory: The Rise and Fall of Oliver North, 1989, The Incident, 1990, Miracle Child, 1993; star: (TV series) Doc, 1975-76, Mr. Merlin, 1981-82, The Cavanaughs, 1986-87, Blossom, 1991-93. With U.S. Army, 1943-45, No. Africa, Italy. Recipient St. Clair Bayfield award, 1973; elected to Theatre Hall of Fame, 1991. Died July 11, 2006.

HUGHES, DICKSON, actor, composer, producer; b. Akron, Ohio, Dec. 14, 1922; s. William Richard Hucks and Bessie Mercedes (Sullivan) Laird. BA, U. Redlands, Calif., 1948. Music dir. The Sacramento (Calif.) Light Opera, 1966-72; music lectr. The Leigh Bur., Princeton, N.J., 1968-80; actor Tamara Internat., Los Angeles, from 1984; entertainer, writer, from 1949; owner, producer, creator The Dickson Line, N.Y.C., 1962-83, Los Angeles, from 1983. Music lectr. Writer musical score: Orinoco (winner ASCAP award, 1987); lyricist numerous songs. Served with USN, 1943-47, PTO. Mem. Am. Soc. Composers, Authors, and Publishers, Actors Equity Assn., Am. Fedn. TV and Radio Artists, Screen Actor's Guild. Avocations: painting, poetry, swimming, skiing. Died June 18, 2005.

HUGHES, MICHAEL PEYTON, chemist; b. Lufkin, Tex., Sept. 9, 1938; s. James A. and Flora (Aldredge) H.; m. Mary Eloise Copeland, Jan. 30, 1960; children: Mary Elizabeth, David. C., Michael Scott. BA in Chemistry, Tex. Christian U., 1960, MA in Chemistry, 1961; PhD of Organic Chemistry, Rice U., 1964. Chemist Celanese Chem. Co., Corpus Christi, Tex., 1964-73; chief rsch. chemist El Paso Products Co., Odessa, Tex., 1973-84, mgr. R&D, 1984-88; v.p. environ. regulatory affairs Rexene Corp., Dallas, 1988-92, dir. R&D Odessa, from 1993. Patentee in field. Fellow Rotary Internat.; mem. Am. Chem. Soc., Soc. Plastics Engrs., Sigma Xi, Alph Chi, Phi Lambda Upsilon. Methodist. Home: Mayhill, N.Mex. Died May 28, 2004.

HUGO, NANCY, county official, alcohol and drug addiction professional; b. Cedar Rapids, Iowa, May 4, 1944; d. Roger S. and Phyllis Anita (Wenger) Conrad; m. Marshall G. Hugo (div.), Apr. 5, 1968; 1 child, Andrea. BS, Drake U., 1966; MS, Pepperdine U., 1987; adminstrn. credential, U. Calif., Irvine, 1989. Cert. adminstr., middle sch. educator, Calif. Tchr., asst. prin. Ocean View Sch. Dist., Huntington Beach, Calif., 1966-90; coord. alcohol and drug prevention edn., tobacco use prevention edn., sch. crisis response, program mgr. juvenile ct. schs. drug and alcohol programs Orange County Dept. Edn., Costa Mesa, Calif., from 1990, coord. phys. edn., 1991-93, coord. bus. edn. partnership, 1993-95. Author: No Butts...About Quitting Tobacco Use, A Tobacco Cessation Program, 1995; co-author: Snuff Out Teen Tobacco and Nix Spit, 1994. Mem. ASCD, NEA, Assn. Calif. Sch. Adminstrs., Calif. Edn. Assn., Calif. Assn. Health Phys. Edn. Recreation and Dance, Calif. Tchrs. Assn. Home: Henderson, Nev. Died Feb. 27, 2004.

HUHN, WALTER PAUL, JR., sales executive, metallurgical consultant; b. Pitts., Nov. 19, 1925; s. Walter Paul H. and Mary Elizabeth Lynch; m. Dorothy Marie Quinn, Feb. 4, 1950; children: Debra Blythe, Patricia, Kerry Paul. BS, Carnegie Tech., 1950. Laborer, metall. observer Jones & Laughlin Steel, Pitts., 1946-50; melt shop metallurgist Crucible Steel Co., Midland, Pa., 1950-61; metall. sales technician Am. Potash Kerr-McGee, Cleve., 1961-76; metallurgical sales technician Diamond Shamrock, Cleve., 1976-79, Foote Mineral Co., Cleve., 1979-85; regional sales mgr. Polymet Alloys Inc., Cleve., 1985-99; mktg. mgr. Pickands-Mather, Cleve., from 1999. Presenter in field. Lt. USN, 1943-46. Mem. Am. Soc. Metals, Am. Inst. Metallurgical Engring. Republican. Roman Catholic. Avocations: video, electric trains, computer programs. Home: Bay Village, Ohio. Died Mar. 10, 2004.

HUIZENGA, EDWARD RICHARD, mortgage banker; b. Monterey, Calif., Dec. 2, 1931; s. Jake Dick and Brenda (Schofield) H.; m. Ida Theresa Yeme, Nov. 18, 1954; 1 child, Cindy Ann Huizenga. Student, Monterey (Calif.) Peninsula, 1951, Calif. Poly., 1954-55. Office mgr. Dept. HUD, Fresno, Calif., 1970-85; builder account mgr. All Valley Mortgage, Fresno, 1986-88, Commonweath United Mortgage, Fresno, 1989-92, N.Am. Mortgage, Fresno, from 1992. Named to Calif. Builders Hall Fame, 1997. Mem. Builders Industry Assn. (dir. SJV chpt., life dir. ctrl. coast chpt., Oscar Spano award 1994, Pres.'s award 1988, 94, Assoc. of Yr. award 1989), Nat. Assn. Home builders (housing fin. com.), CBIA (dir.). Republican. Roman Catholic. Avocations: duck hunting, skiing, golf. Home: Fresno, Calif. Died Dec. 13, 2004.

HUMPHREY, MARY FRANCES, historian, writer, retired health care recruiter; b. Lowell, Mass., May 19, 1927; d. Frederick Vincent and Elizabeth Theresa Lynch; m. Keith Nelson Humphrey; children: Sharon Elizabeth Humphrey-Mason, Nancy Ellen Griffin, Janet Lynn Stephenson. Degree in Library Svcs., U. Maine, Presque Isle, 1977. Cert. librarian in charge. Payroll clerk Presque Isle AFB, 1944-46; sec. Maine Potato Growers, Inc., Presque Isle, 1946-52, U.S. Congressman Clifford G. McIntire, Washburn, 1954-58; librarian Washburn Meml. Library, 1970-73; librarian, sch. sec. Maine Sch. Adminstrn. Dist. # 45, Washburn, 1967-79; employment mgr.-recruiter The Aroostook Med. Ctr., Presque Isle, 1980-90; proofreader Echoes-No. Maine Jour., Caribou, from 1992; historian, author, from 1990. Trustee Washburn Meml. Libr., 1973—, Washburn Regional Health Ctr., 1978-88; sec. Aroostook County Sch. Libr. Assn., Presque, 1968-79. Vol. Well Baby Clinic, Washburn, 1954-60; leader Little Sisters 4-H Club, Washburn, 1960-65; mem. chair P.I. Cmty. Concert Assn., Presque Isle, 1952-64; mem. & officer Washburn PTA, 1965-73, Washburn Women's Ext., 1952-80; officer and fundraiser Dollars For Scholars, Washburn, 1969-75; mem. Pool Study Com., Washburn, 1995—, 911E Study Com., Washburn, 1995—. Recipient Hon. Alumni award Washburn Dist. H.S. Alumni, 1970, Plaque Washburn Regional Health Ctr. Bd., 1988. Mem. Salmon Brook Hist. Soc. (officer 1980), Friends of Aroostook County Hist. Ctr. Avocations: reading, quilting, attending elderhostel programs. Home: Washburn, Maine. Died June 23, 2005.

HUMPHREYS, DONALD WAYNE, environmental engineering educator; b. Iowa Falls, Iowa, Mar. 14, 1931; s. Wayne B. and Alta B. (Hyde) H.; m. Constance S. Severaid, June 12, 1954; children: Janet Krasner, Eric, Ann Sellers, Paul. BA, U. No. Iowa, Cedar Falls, 1953, MA, 1964; PhD, U. Iowa, Iowa City, 1972. Vis. prof. Ind. U., Bloomington, 1972-74; prof. sci. edn. Temple U., Phila., 1974-82, prof. environ. engring., 1982—2000, dir. undergrad. studies, 1996—2006, prof. emeritus, 2000—06. Materials devel. NSF, Washington, 1990-92; environ. cons., Gilbertsville, 1974-95. Author: Aguide to Freshwater Protists and Metazoans, 1977. Dir., chair Berks/Mont Mcpl. Authority, Gilbertsville, 1978-88. With U.S. Army, 1953-55. NSF grantee, Washington, 1968-69; fellow Inst. Math. and Sci., Temple U., 1985-2000. Mem. APHA, Nat. Biology Tchrs. Assn. (dir. 1963-2006), Am. Soc. Engring. Edn. Home: Gilbertsville, Pa. Died Mar. 17, 2006.

HUNKINS, LINDA SUE, publisher; b. Denver, Jan. 3, 1948; d. Harvey Donald and Helen Marie (Steele) H. BA, Hasting (Nebr.) Coll., 1970; MA, Princeton (N.J.) U., 1973. Advanced to sr. v.p. ATE Enterprises, Cin., 1976-85; v.p. U.S. Ecology, Louisville, Ky., 1985-88; pres. Am. Hazmat, San Diego, 1988-90; pres., owner Amboy Assocs., San Diego, from 1990. Democrat. Avocation: camping. Home: San Diego, Calif. Died Jan. 23, 2004.

HUNN, MAX W., freelance/self-employed photojournalist; b. Rock Island, Ill., Dec. 10, 1914; s. Wilbur Bennett and Wilhelmina Mary Hunn; m. Beatrice Desjardin Hunn, Aug. 17, 1984; 1 child, Sandra Fo Piano; children: Linda Bair, Sandra Peters. BA in Journalism History, Grinnell Coll., 1937. Reporter Daily Dispatch, Moline, Ill., 1937—40, chief photographer, 1940—42; photo editor Pan Am. World Air, Miami, Fla., 1946—55; freelance photojournalist Fla., from 1955. Lt. USN, 1942—46. Mem.: WWII USN Armed Guard. Presbyterian. Avocations: travel, fishing. Home: Inverness, Fla. Died Dec. 10, 2004.

HUNT, JAMES MUNSON, management consultant; b. New Britain, Conn., Sept. 16, 1947; s. Stanley Mills and Dorothy Adams (Kinkade) H. BA, Bates Coll., 1969; JD, Willamette U., 1976. Bar: Calif. 1976. Pvt. practice, Oakland, Calif., 1976-80; ptnr. Legal Productivity Resources, Cambridge, Mass., 1981-86, Found. for Integrating Systems and Human Resources, Cambridge, Mass., from 1983, Heller and Hunt, Legal Cons., Brookline, Mass., from 1986. Author Practicing Law and Managing People: How to Be Successful, 1988; editor Heller and Hunt Law Practice Mgmt. Report, 1987—. Active in Boston Youth at Risk Program, 1986—; bd. dirs. Berkeley Ecology Ctr. 1971-72, 1976-77. Served alt. mil. duty nat. service, 1969-71. Mem. Mass. Bar Assn. Democrat. Avocations: marathon running, singing. Home: Somerville, Mass. Died Dec. 29, 2004.

HUNT, JOHN MEACHAM, retired petroleum geochemist; b. Cleve., Dec. 1, 1918; s. Raymond Edward and Marguerite (Meacham) H.; m. Doris Press, Apr. 10, 1947 (div. June 1973); children: Randall Keith, Lawrence Lee; m. Phyllis Laking, Sept. 1, 1973. BA in Chemistry, Western Res. U., 1942; MS in Petroleum Chemistry, Pa. State U., 1943, PhD in Organic Chemistry, 1946. Instr. chemistry Pa. State U., University Park, 1947; rsch. chemist Jersey Prodn. Rsch. Co., 1948-55, head geochem. rsch., 1956-63; chmn. dept. chemistry and geology Woods Hole (Mass.) Oceanographic Inst., 1964-67, chmn. chemistry, 1967-74, sr. scientist, 1974-84, scientist emeritus, from 1984. Chief scientist Red Sea Expdn., 1966, Black Sea Expdn., 1969; mem. U.S. del. petroleum geochemists to USSR oil fields and petroleum labs., 1962; vice chmn. workshop on inputs, fates and effects petroleum in marine environ. NAS, 1973, mem. U.S. nat. com. for geochemistry, 1974-76; chmn. Gordon Rsch. Conf. on Organic Geochemistry, 1976; Crosby lectr. dept. earth scis. MIT, 1981; mem. organizing com. 8th Internat. Congress on Organic Geochemistry, Moscow, 1977; lectr. numerous countries. Author: Petroleum Geochemistry and Geology; chmn. editorial bd. Organic Geochemistry, 1985-89; also over 100 articles. Recipient Karcher medal 3d Ann. Karcher Symposium, 1979. Mem. Am. Chem. Soc., Am. Assn. Petroleum Geologists (lectr. continuing edn. com. 1970-82, disting. lectr. 1964, assoc. editor Bull. 1964-85), Geochem. Soc. (Treibs medal 1982), European Assn. Organic Geochemists, Sigma Xi. Home: Falmouth, Mass. Died July 23, 2005.

HUNTER, BARBARA DUNN, mathematics educator; b. N.Y.C., Oct. 16, 1935; d. Henry Joseph and Ethel Marie (Barry) Dunn; m. James Richard Hunter, June 6, 1959; children: Francis Joseph Hunter, Mary Elizabeth Hunter West. BA, Marian Coll., 1957; MA, Butler U., 1959, Ball State U., 1973. Tchr. Sacred Heart High Sch., Indpls., 1957-59, Anderson (Ind.) Community Schs., from 1970, chairperson math. dept., from 1991; coach acad. teams. Republican. Avocations: needlecrafts, travel, volunteer work. Home: Anderson, Ind. Died Apr. 1, 2005.

HUNTER, CARL GLENN, retired commissioner; b. Little Rock, Aug. 30, 1923; s. Robert Weir and Jewel Monette Hunter; m. Mary Anid Scott, Jan. 20, 1945; children: Carl Scott, David Albert. BS in Agr., U. Ark., 1945. Cert. hon. master gardener U. Ark. Ext. Svc., biologist The Wildlife Soc., instr. Ark. Law Enforcement Acad., Prescott Coll., ARiz., U. Ark. Little Rock. Asst. chief game mgmt. Ark. Game and Fish Commn., Little Rock, 1942—57, asst. dir., 1977—87; gen. mgr. Wingmead Plantation, Stuttgart, Ark., 1957—77. Agt., author Ozark Soc. Found., Little Rock, 1984—2001; horticulturist Wildflowers of Ark., Little Rock, 1987—2001; rep. Ark. Conservation Coalition, Little Rock, 1990—2001. Author: Wildflowers of Arkansas, 1984, Trees, Shrubs & Vines of Arkansas, 1989, This Cup, 1991, Autumn Leaves & Winter Berries in Arkansas, 1995, The Piano Player, 1997, Poems & Pieces, 2003; contbr. articles to profll. jours. Named Outstanding Alum, U. Ark., 1998. Mem.: Ozark Soc., Ark. Native Plant Soc. Avocations: photography, botany, gardening, landscaping, music. Home: Alexander, Ark. Died Mar. 23, 2005.

HUNTER, MEL, artist; b. Oak Park, Ill., July 27, 1927; s. Milford Joseph and Lucille (Clarkson) H.; m. Nancy Sue O'Connor, July 1969 (div. Mar. 1986); children: Lisa, Scott, Amy; m. Susan Harriet Smith, Sept. 7,. 1986. Student, Northwestern U., Evanston, Ill. Founder Smith-Hunter Gallery, 1988—; pres. Aquagraphics Portfolio, Inc., Ferrisburgh, Vt., 1991—, Polaris Press, Inc., Ferrisburgh, 1992—. Author: The New Lithography, 1984, The Current Sad State of the Print World, 1993; pub. The Mylar Manifesto, 1979, (periodical) PRINTthoughts, 1995; printer of original lithographs; drawings and paintings appeard in Nat. Geographic, Life, Collier's Newsweek (cover), Ency. Americana, Time-Life; watercolor originals include Birds of the Northeast. Recipient Best Aviation Book of Yr. award Aviation and Space Writers Assn., 1962. Mem. True Original Printmakers Assn. (co-founder). Originator of mylar lithographic process; created more than 150 original lithographics edits; co-developed mezzographic fine art print process. Died Feb. 20, 2004.

HURLBURT, CHARLES ARTHUR, disability issues consultant; b. Middletown, Conn., Jan. 11, 1963; s. Charles Arthur Sr. and Mary Ann (Macca) H. AS in Human Svcs., Mitchell Coll., 1983; BS in Human Svcs., N.H. Coll., 1988; postgrad., So. Conn. State U., from 1988. Community living instr. Bethphage Luth. Svcs., Wethersfield, Conn., 1985-90; counselor disability issues Disability Counseling Svcs., Rocky Hill, Conn., from 1988; project coord. Ptnrs. in Policymaking Program U. Conn. Health Ctr., Farmington, 1990-91. Conducted various presentations, 1989-91. Mem. AACD, Coun. Exceptional Children, Assn. Persons with Severe Handicaps, Conn. Coalition Families of Persons with Disabilities (bd. mem. 1989-91), Conn. Traumatic Brain Injury Assn., Middletown Com. Concerning People with Disabilities (co-chairperson 1990—). Democrat. Avocation: reading. Home: Rocky Hill, Conn. Died Apr. 10, 2005.

HYATT, ROSEMARY JANE, community mental health nurse; b. Johnson City, N.Y., Oct. 4, 1949; d. Robert and June (Adams) Clute; m. Harold Hyatt, May 31, 1981; children: Robert, Jaime. AAS, Ulster Community Coll., Stone Ridge, N.Y., 1981; BSN, SUNY, New Paltz, 1984; MSN in Community Health Nursing, Pace U., 1987. RN, N.Y. Staff nurse Kingston (N.Y.) Hosp., 1981-84; health/nutrition coord. Ulster Cmty. Action-Head Start, Kingston, 1984-87; cmty. mental health nurse Ulster DDSO-Taconic, Kingston, 1987-99; nurse administr. N.Y. State Office Mental Retardation and Devel. Disabilities, Taconic, 1990-91. Mem. Office Mental Retardation and Devel. Disabilities Nurses; PRI assessor, screener N.Y. State Mini fellowship in Aging and Devel. Disabilities. Mem. surrogate decision making com. panel for N.Y. State, 1995-97. Mem. ANA (cert. in devel. disabilities nursing), N.Y. State Nurses Assn., Sigma Theta Tau. Home: Kingston, NY. Died Dec. 11, 2004.

HYMAN, EDWARD SIDNEY, physician, consultant; b. New Orleans, Jan. 22, 1925; s. David and Mary (Newstadt) H.; m. Jean Simons, Sept. 29, 1956; children: Judith, Sydney, Edward David, Anne. BS, La. State U., 1944; MD, Johns Hopkins U., 1946. Diplomate: Am. Bd. Internal Medicine, Intern Barnes Hosp., Washington U., St. Louis, 1946-47; fellow in medicine Stanford U., San Francisco, 1949-51, asst. resident in medicine, 1950-51, Peter Bent Brigham Hosp., Boston, 1951-53; teaching fellow in medicine Harvard U., Boston, 1952-53; practice medicine specializing in internal medicine, New Orleans, 1953—; dir. kidney unit Charity Hosp., New Orleans, 1953-55; investigator Touro Research Inst., New Orleans, 1959; dir. Hyman Corp.; mem. staff Sara Mayo Hosp., 1954-79, chief of staff, 1968-70, trustee, 1970-78; mem. staff Touro Infirmary, New Orleans, St. Charles Hosp.; panelist Pres.'s Commn. on Health Needs of Nation, 1952; cons. water quality New Orleans Sewerage and Water Bd., 1978; mem. research adv. com. Cancer Assn. New Orleans, 1976-81, La. Bd. Regents, 1983. Contbr. articles to profl. jours. NIH grantee, 1960-81; Am. Heart Assn. grantee, 1962-65. Fellow ACP; mem. Am. Fedn. Clin. Rsch., Am. Soc. Artificial Internal Organs, Am. Physiol. Soc. Biophys. Soc. (chmn. local arrangements 1971, 77, 81, 87), Am. Soc. Microbiology, AAAS, Pvt. Drs. Am. (co-founder 1968, v.p. 1968-84, Dist. Svc. award 1981), Orleans Parish Med. Soc. (gov. 1972-80), La. State Med. Soc. (ho. of dels. 1970-81), Surfaces in Biomaterial Found. Jewish. Subspecialties: Internal medicine; Biophysics. Current work: Clincial internal medicine, biochemistry, biophysics, nephrology, artificial organs, water quality, government in medicine, cause of death in renal failure, significance of bacteria in urine. Isolated aldosterone, 1949; patentee sheet plastic oxygenator (artificial heart), oil detection device; inventor telephone transmission of electrocardiogram, early data transmission; inventor hydrogen platinum detection of heart shunts, Method for detection of bacteria in urine, Systemic Coccal Disease (SCD), Desert Storm Syndrome (following the Persian Gulf War) as a bacterial disease (SCD), grantee treatment of Gulf War Syndrome as a form of SCD, Silicone Implant Disease as a bacterial disease, as a manifestation of Systemic Coccal Disease. Died Mar. 9, 2004.

HYMAN, ELAINE, artist; b. NYC, Aug. 24, 1925; d. Harry and Dora (Himelstein) Lubart; m. Julian Bennett Hyman, Oct. 18, 1950; children: Steven E., Mona Rubin, Harvey A. BA, NYU, 1945; postgrad., Syracuse U. Grad. instr. Syracuse (N.Y.) U., 1946-47. Trustee Bergen Mus., Paramus, N.J., curator of art, 1985, 86, 87. Solo shows include Adelphi U., 1969, Bodley Gallery, N.Y.C., 1973, 78, 82, Bergen County Mus., 1974, Moore Gallery, Aspen, Colo., 1976; exhibited in group shows at Caravan House, N.Y.C., 1971, World Trade Ctr., N.Y.C., 1978, Lever House, N.Y.C., 1979, 81, Walker-Kornbluth Gallery, Fairlawn, N.J., 1984-2003, others; represented in permanent collections Snite Mus., Notre Dame U., Fordham U. Law Ctr., Norfolk (Va.)-Chrysler Mus., U. Scranton, Montclair Art Mus., N.J., also pvt. collections in U.S. and Europe. Bd. dirs. Innovative Print Com. of Rutgers U. Mem.: Print Club N.Y. (trustee 1993—2003). Democrat. Jewish. Avocations: art collection, travel, museums, galleries, reading. Died Sept. 2006.

HYMAN, IRWIN A., psychologist; b. Neptune, N.J., Mar. 22, 1935; Henry Meltzer and Harriet (Greenitz) H.; m. Nada Pospishil (div.); children: Nadine, Deborah; m. Susan Brown, June 16, 1985; 1 child, Rachael. BA, U. Maine, 1957; MEd, Rutgers U., 1961, EdD, 1964. Lic. psychologist, N.J., Pa.; cert. sch. psychologist, N.J., Pa. Tchr. Millstone Twp. (N.J.) Schs., 1957-61; sch. psychologist Lawrence Twp. (N.J.) Schs., 1962-66; chief of clin. svcs. Tng. Sch. at Vineland, N.J., 1966-67; prof. spl. edn., chief clin. psychologist Keane Coll., Union, N.J., 1967-68; prof. sch. psychology Temple U., Phila., 1968—2005, dir. Nat. Ctr. for Study of Corporal Punishment, 1977—2005. Cons. sch. psychologist Pennington (N.J.) Sch., 1986-95; cons. childrens mag., 1986-89, ACLU, U.S. Ho. Reps., Washington, 1990, U.S. Senate, Washington, 1984; tech. specialist Chinese Univs. Project, World Bank, 1987. Author: Reading Writing and the Hickory Stick, 1990, The Case Against Spanking, 1997, School Discipline and School Violence, 1997, Dangerous Schools, 1999; co-editor: Corporal Punishment in American Education, 1979, School Consultation; cons. editor Sch. Psychology Review, 1985-87; contbr. articles to profl. jours. Recipient Pres.'s award Nat. Assn. Sch. Psychologists, 1994, Award for Disting. Contbns. to Sci. and Profession of Psychology, Pa. Psychol. Assn. Fellow Am. Acad. of Sch. Psychology and Clin. Psychology (pres. 1999-00), Am. Psychol. Assn. (pres. div. 16 1977-78, Disting Svc. to Sch. 1986), Internat Soc. for Rsch. on Aggression; mem. Nat. Assn. for Advancement of Sci., Soc. for Traumatic Stress Studies, Coun. for Exceptional Children, Am. Ednl. Rsch. Assn., Phi Delta Kappa. Democrat. Jewish. Avocations: spearfishing, skiing, running. Home: Southampton, Pa. Died Feb. 7, 2005.

ILCHMAN, ALICE STONE, retired foundation, academic, and federal agency administrator; b. Cin., Apr. 18, 1935; d. Donald Crawford and Alice Kathryn (Biermann) Stone; m. Warren Frederick Ilchman, June 11, 1960; children: Frederick Andrew Crawford, Alice Sarah. BA, Mt. Holyoke Coll., 1957; MPA, Maxwell Sch. Citizenship, Syracuse U., 1958; PhD, London Sch. Econs., 1965; LHD, Mt. Holyoke Coll., 1982, Franklin and Marshall Coll., 1983. Asst. to pres., mem. faculty Berkshire C.C., 1961-64; lectr. Ctr. for South and S.E. Asia Studies U. Calif., Berkeley, 1965-73; prof. econs. and edn., dean Wellesley (Mass.) Coll., 1973-78; asst. sec. ednl. and cultural affairs US Dept. State, 1978; assoc. dir. ednl. and cultural affairs Internat. Comm. Agy., 1978—81; advisor to sec. Smithsonian Instn., 1981; pres. Sarah Lawrence Coll., Bronxville, NY, 1981-98; chmn. bd. Rockefeller Found., N.Y.C., NY, 1995—2000. Dir. Jeannette K. Watson Fellowship, 1999-2006; intern, asst. to Sen. John F. Kennedy, 1957; dir. Peace Corps Tng. Program for India, 1965-66; chmn. com. on women's employment NAS; sr. advisor Thomas Watson Found., 1999-2006; bd. dirs. NYNEX, Seligman Group of Investment Cos. Author: The New Men of Knowledge and the New States, 1968, (with W.F. Ilchman) Education and Employment in India, The Policy Nexus, 1976, The Lucky Few and the Worthy Many: Scholarship Competitions and The Future Leaders, 2004. Trustee Mt. Holyoke Coll., 1970-80, Mass. Found. for Humanities and Pub. Policy, 1974-77, East-West Ctr., Honolulu, 1978-81, Expt. in Internat. Living, The Markle Found., The Rockefeller Found., chmn. bd. dirs., acting pres., 1998, Chamber Music Soc. Lincoln Ctr.; former trustee The U. of Cape Town, South Africa, Corp. Adv. Bd., Hotchkiss Sch.; mem. Smithsonian Coun., Yonkers Emergency Fin. Control Bd., 1982-88, Am. Ditchley Found. Program Com., Internat. Rsch. and Exch. Bd., Com. for Econ. Devel., The Masters Sch., Save The Children; bd. dirs. Pub. Broadcasting Corp., 2000-06. Hon. fellow Wadham Coll., Oxford U. Mem. NOW Legal Def. Edn. Fund, Coun. Fgn. Rels., Century Assn. (N.Y.C.), Bronxville Field Club. Home: Bronxville, NY. Died Aug. 11, 2006.

ILIFF, WARREN JOLIDON, zoo administrator; b. Madison, Wis., Nov. 5, 1936; s. Warren Jolidon and Wilma Marie (Lowenstein) I.; m. Ghislaine de Brouchoven de Bergeyck, Feb. 13, 1970. AB, Harvard U., 1958. Helicopter pilot, crop duster, Central Am., 1962-66; dir. planning Air Transport Assn., Washington, 1966-67; spl. asst. to dir. Nat. Zoo, Washington, 1967-71; exec. dir. Friends of Nat. Zoo, 1971-73; asst. dir. Nat. Zoo, 1973-75; dir. Washington Park Zoo, Portland, Oreg., 1975-84, Dallas Zoo, 1984-91, Phoenix Zoo, 1991; pres., CEO Long Beach Aquarium of the Pacific, Long Beach, Calif., 1996—2002. Bd. dirs. Wildlife Preservation Trust Internat., 1985—2006, Jane Goodall Inst., 1985-2006; Served with USMC, 1958-62. Mem. Am. Assn. Zool. Parks and Aquariums (past pres.), Internat. Union Dirs. Zool. Gardens. Home: Long Beach, Calif. Died Aug. 5, 2006.

IMAMURA, SHOHEI, film director; b. Tokyo, Sept. 15, 1926; Dir., instr. Broadcasting and Movie Tech. Sch., Yohohama, Japan; former asst. dir. Yasujiro Ozu. Dir. (films): Stolen Desire, 1958, In Front of West Ginza Station, 1958,Endless Desire, 1958, My Second Brother, 1959, Pigs and Battleships, 1961, Insect Woman, 1963, Vengeance is Mine, 1979, Why Not?, 1981, The Ballad of Narayama, 1983, Zegen, 1988, Black Rain, 1990, The Eel, 1997, Dr. Akagi, 1998, Warm Water Under a Red Bridge, 2001 September 11, 2002 Winner Japanese Acad. award for best film (Ballad of Narayama), 1983, Cannes Film Festival's Golden Palm award, 1983. Died May 30, 2006.

INFIELD, MARTHEA MAE, mental health service executive; b. Cleve., Dec. 31, 1929; d. Neil Edward and Freda Margaret (Schray) Bowler; m. Dwight Hosak Infield, Nov. 14, 1953; children: Susan, Dwight David, Donald, Elisabeth. BBA, Fenn Coll., 1952; MSSA, Case Western Res. U., 1970. Asst. to overseas div. mgr. Goodyear Tire & Rubber, Akron, Ohio, 1953-54; social worker Lucas County Welfare Dept., Toledo, 1964-65; social worker protective svcs. Cuyahoga County Welfare Dept., Cleve., 1967-68; crisis counselor Crisis Intervention Team, Cleve., 1970-72, coord., 1972-74, exec. dir., founder CIT Mental Health Svcs. (now NE Ohio Health Svcs.), 1974—. Republican. Presbyterian. Home: Cleveland, Ohio. Died Apr. 7, 2005.

INGALL, MICHAEL ALEXANDER, psychiatrist, educator; b. Boston, July 8, 1940; s. Morris and Bessie (Gottler) I.; m. Carol Linda Krepon, June 18, 1961; children: Marjorie Beth, Andrew Morris. AB, Harvard U., 1961; MD, Chgo. Med. Sch., 1966. Diplomate Am. Bd. Psychiatry and Neurology, Am. Bd. Geriatric Psychiatry. Straight med. intern Univ. Hosp., Boston, 1966-67; resident in psychiatry Boston U. Med. Ctr., 1967-68, 70-72, fellow in child psychiatry, 1971-72; med. dir. Providence Mental Health Ctr., 1972-84; chief psychiat. svcs. Harvard Community Health Plan/N.E., Warwick, R.I., 1984-93; clin. assoc. prof. of psychiatry Brown U. Med. Sch., Providence, from 1978. Forensic psychiatrist Atty. Gen.'s Office of R.I., Pub. Def. Office of R.I.; cons. psychiatrist Whitmarsh House, Providence. Singer: Providence Singers, 1987—, R.I. Civic Chorale, 1986-88; East Coast Editor, The Fessenden Review, 1988-89; author of several scientific and popular articles. Physican Traveler's Aid Homeless Van, Providence, 1987-92; bd. dirs. Solomon Schechter Sch. Providence, 1980-88, R.I. Youth Guidance Ctr., Providence, 1976-80. Lt. comdr. USN, 1968-70. Recipient Alumni Assn. award Chgo. Med. Sch. 1966, Roche Award, 1966, disting. psychiatrist award Alliance for the Mentally Ill., 1996. Fellow Am. Psychiatric Assn. (Falk Fellowship award 1972); mem. Am. Group Psychotherapy Assn., Physicians for Soc. Responsibility, R.I. Psychiatric Soc. (pres. 1979-80), Alpha Omega Alpha. Home: Providence, RI. Died Aug. 12, 2004.

INGLEFIELD, JOSEPH THACHER, JR., allergist, immunologist, pediatrician; b. Duquesne, Pa., Apr. 29, 1930; m. Effie Carothers, 1951 (dec. 1995); children: Jody, Candy, Dave, Wendy, Gretchen, Jimmy; m. Kate Lane (separated). Grad., Washington & Jefferson Coll., 1952; MD, U. Rochester, 1957. Diplomate Am. Bd. Allergy & Immunology, Am. Bd. Pediatrics. Intern William Beaumont Army Hosp., El Paso, Tex., 1957-58; resident Tripler Army Hosp., Honolulu, 1958-60; fellow in pediatrics and allergies Children's Hosp., Washington, 1969-72; with Fairfax Hosp., Falls Church, Va. Mem. AMA, MSV, Am. Acad. Pediatrics, Assn. Am. Physicians, North Va. Pediatric Soc. Died Jan. 30, 2006.

IRVING, DONALD C., English educator; b. Watseka, Ill, Mar. 11, 1938; s. Carl Richard and Magdalene Louise (Martin) I.; m. Janet Kay O'Neal, June 27, 1964 (div. Nov. 1993); children: Kathleen, Michael. BA, U. Ill., 1960; MA, So. Ill. U., 1962; PhD, Ind. U., 1969. Instr. English Ctrl. Mo. State U., Warrensburg, 1962-64; from instr. to prof. emeritus of English and Am. Studies Grinnell Coll., Iowa, 1968—2003, assoc. dean faculty Iowa, 1983-88, chmn. Am. studies Iowa, 1974-76, 84-86, chmn. English dept. Iowa, 1972-74, 90-92, dir. off-campus studies Iowa, 1983-88. Mem. initial planning com. DARE, Grinnell, 1980-82. Home: Grinnell, Iowa. Died Aug. 5, 2004.

IRVIS, K. LEROY, former state legislator; b. Saugerties, N.Y., Dec. 27, 1919; s. Francis H. and Harriet (Cantine) I.; m. Cathryn L. Edwards; children: Reginald, Sherri. AB summa cum laude, N.Y. State Tchrs. Coll., 1938; MA, SUNY, Albany, 1939; MEd, SUNY, 1986; LLB, U. Pitts., 1954, JD, 1968; DL, Lincoln U., 1979. Tchr. Balt. Pub. Schs., 1938-40; civilian attache War Dept., 1940-45; dir. pub. realtions Urban League, Pitts., 1945; news commentator and writer Pitts.-Courier Radio Sta.; asst. dist. atty. Allegheny County, 1957; lawyer, from 1957; mem. Pa. Ho. of Reps., Harrisburg, 1958, speaker, 1977-78, 83-84, 85-86 and from 87, dem. leader, 1979-82, majority caucus chmn., minority whip, then majority leader. Del. Dem. Nat. Convs. 1968, 72, 76, 84; vice chmn. Dem. Nat. Conv., 1980; mem. Dem. Nat. Com., 1982. Bd. dirs. United Balck Front, Community Action Pitts., Neighborhood Assistance Adv. Bd., Three Rivers Improvement and Devel., Greater Pitts. Bus. Devel. Corp., Post Gazette Dapper Dan Club, Bidwell Cultural and Tng. Ctr., WQED Pub. TV, NAACP; trustee U. Pitts. Med. Sch. Adv. Com.; bd. vis. CArngeie-Mellon U. Sch. of Urban and Pub. Affairs. Recipient awards from numerous orgns. including: Conf. on Black Basic Edn., U. Pa., Pa. Jewish Coalition. Mem. NAACP (life, Com. to Civil Rights award). Avocations: wood sculptor, painter, writer, model airplane enthusiast, poet. Home: Pittsburgh, Pa. Died Mar. 16, 2006.

IRWIN, STEVE (STEPHEN ROBERT IRWIN), animal scientist, television personality; b. Victoria, Australia, Feb. 22, 1962; s. Bob and Lyn Irwin; m. Terri Raines, June 4, 1992; children: Bindi Sue, Robert Clarence. Dir. Australia Zoo, Beerwah, Queensland, Australia, 1991—2006. Died after being stung by a stingray barb that went through his chest off Australia's north coast while filming an underwater documentary. Host: (TV series) The Crocodile Hunter, 1996—2006; host (TV series) The Crocidile Hunter's Croc Files, 1999, The Crocodile Hunter Diaries, 2002; actor: The Ten Deadliest Snakes in the World, 1998, Island of Snakes, 2004, Ice Breaker, 2004, Search for a Super Croc, 2004, Crocs in the City, 2004, Confessions of the Crocodile Hunter, 2004, Tigers of Shark Bay, 2004; (films) Dr. Doolittle 2, from 2001, The Crocodile Hunter: Collision Course, 2002, The Wiggles: Wiggles Safari, 2002; guest appearances Rosie O'Donnell Show, 1999, Rove Live, 2002, Oprah Winfrey Show, 2003, Late Night with Conan O' Brien, 2004, 2005, Tonight Show with Jay Leno, 2003, 2004, 2005, 2006, Sunrise, 2006, and several others. Died Sept. 4, 2006.

ISBERG, REUBEN ALBERT, radio communications engineer; b. Chugwater, Wyo., Dec. 11, 1913; s. Albert Gust and Laura Carolina (Thun) I.; m. Dorothe Louise Hall, Feb. 23, 1936; children: Jon Lewis, Barbara Louise Isberg Johnson, Edward Russel. AB in Phys. Sci., U. No. Colo., 1935. Registered profl. engr., Calif. Radio and TV engr. W2XBS/WNBT-NBC, N.Y.C., 1939-42; electronic devel. engr. div. war rsch. Columbia U., Mineola, N.Y., 1942-46; chief engr. KRON-TV, San Francisco, 1946-52; ind. cons. TV engr. various locations, 1952-54; sr. engr. Ampex Corp., Redwood City, Calif., 1954-60; statewide communications engr. U. Calif., Berkeley, 1960-67; ind. cons. radio communications engr. Berkley, from 1967. Chair sub-com. for FM radio stereo standards NSRC, Washington,1 960-61; mem. com. for establishing 2500 MHz instrnl. TV svc., FCC, 1965-67. Contbr. to profl. publs. Named Honored Alumnus, U. No. Colo., 1993. Fellow IEEE (chair awards com. vehicular tech. soc. 1984-90, Avant Garde medal and cert. 1991), Audio Engring. Soc., Soc. Motion Picture and TV Engrs., Radio Club Am.; mem. Acoustical Soc. Am., Soc. Cable TV Engrs., Inst. Radio Engrs. (chair San Francisco sect. 1951). Republican. Congregationalist. Achievements include work on guided radio communications in subways, mines, ships and buildings, U.S. and Can. patents for tunnel distributed antenna system with signal taps coupling approximately the same amount of energy. Died Apr. 13, 2004.

ISDANER, LAWRENCE ARTHUR, accountant; b. Phila., June 6, 1934; s. Irving and Frances (Ford) Isdaner; m. Audrey Goldstein, Apr. 4, 1957; children: Scott Alan, Bart Matthew. BS, U. Pa., 1956. CPA Pa. Founder, mem. Isdaner & Co. LLC, CPAs, Bala Cynwyd, Pa., 1967—2005. Founding dir., chmn. bd. dirs. Allegiance Bank N.Am., from 1998. Author: Army Industrial Fund and Cost Accounting Manual, 1958. Internat. bd. dirs. Pop Warner Little Scholars,

Phila., from 1992; bd. dirs. Golden Slipper Club, Phila., from 1974, pres., 1977; mem. investment adv. bd. Curtis Inst. Music. With U.S. Army, 1957—59. Mem.: AICPA, Pa. Inst. CPAs, Desert Mountain Club, Germantown Cricket Club, Kiwanis. Avocation: tennis. Home: Bala Cynwyd, Pa. Died Dec. 26, 2005.

ISEMAN, JOSEPH SEEMAN, lawyer; b. N.Y.C., May 29, 1916; s. Percy Reginald and Edith Helene (Seeman) I.; m. June Lorraine Bang, Dec. 10, 1966; children: Peter A., Frederick J., Ellen M.; stepchildren: Anne Hamilton, Susan E. Hamilton, William C. Hamilton. BA magna cum laude, Harvard U., 1937; LLB, Yale U., 1941; LHD (hon.), Am. U. of Paris, 1997. Bar: N.Y. 1941, D.C. 1970, France, 1986. Investigator, clk. Comml. Factors Corp., 1937-38; atty. WPB, 1941-42; mng. dir. Iranian Airways Corp., 1946; assoc. Chadbourne, Wallace, Parke & Whiteside, N.Y.C., 1946-50, Paul, Weiss, Rifkind, Wharton & Garrison, N.Y.C., 1950-53, ptnr., 1954-86, counsel, 1987—2006. Counsel Charles F. Kettering Found., 1965-84. Author: A Perfect Sympathy, 1937; contbr. articles to profl. jours. Trustee Bennington Coll., 1969—81, acting pres., 1976; bd. dirs. Acad. for Ednl. Devel., Safe Horizon, 1980—2006, also chmn.; bd. dirs. The Hastings Ctr., from 1999, Am. U., Paris, 1987—2000, also vice chmn. Capt. USAF, 1942—46. Woodrow Wilson vis. fellow Coll. William and Mary, 1977, Ripon Coll., 1979, Rollins Coll., 1980, De Pauw U., 1980, Fisk U., 1981, Albright Coll., 1982, Hood Coll., 1983, Southwestern U., 1984. Mem. ABA, N.Y. State Bar Assn., Assn. of Bar of City of N.Y., Century Assn., Coveleigh Club, Phi Beta Kappa. Democrat. Home: New York, NY. Died Apr. 25, 2006.

ISOKANE, SAM SETSUO, real estate company executive, consultant; b. Honolulu, Feb. 11, 1925; s. Matsujiro and Shige (Yano) I.; m. Teruko Gono, Nov. 25, 1968 (div. Jan. 1975); 1 child, Lisa Yukari. BA, U. Hawaii, 1943; cert., Nat. Installment Banking Sch., U. Colo., 1971; postgrad. Japan mgmt. program, Japan-Am. Inst. Mgmt. Sci., 1975-76. Lic. realtor, Hawaii; cert. real estate appraiser (CREA). Commodity specialist commerce and industry br. Okinawa Mil. Gov., 1949-51; field rep. Japan div. Coca-Cola Export Corp., Okinawa and Yokohama, 1951-54; v.p., mgr. Svc. Fin. Ltd., Honolulu, 1968-73; real estate broker Palisades Properties, Inc., Honolulu, 1978-84; owner, CREA, prin. broker Sam S. Isokane, Realtor, Honolulu, from 1985. Treas. Hawaiian Leanders Exchange, Ltd., Honolulu, 1960; mgmt. cons. Fukuyama Piano Co., Ltd., Tokyo, 1973-74. Mem. Liliha-Kapalama Neighborhood Bd., Honolulu, 1981-83; trustee Hawaii Vets. Meml. Fund, Honolulu, 1983—; precinct chmn. Honolulu Dem. Com., 1984. With M.I., AUS, 1943-46, PTO. Mem. Nat. Assn. Realtors, Honolulu Bd. Realtors, Hawaii Consumer Fin. Assn. (pres. 1962), Hawaii Econ. Study Club (pres. 1970), MIS Vets Club (1st v.p. 1987-88). Buddhist. Home: Honolulu, Hawaii. Died Feb. 27, 2005.

ISRAELSTAM, ALFRED WILLIAM, lawyer; b. Chgo., Nov. 8, 1908; s. Adolph and Tillie Block Israelstam; m. Beatrice Ruden, Oct. 29, 1934; children: David M., Frances. JD, U. Chgo., 1933. Bar: U.S. Dist. Ct. (no. dist.) Ill. 1934. Sole practice, Chgo., 1934-98, Buffalo Grove, Ill., from 1998. Bd. dirs. Erect-A-Tube Inc., Harvard, Ill. Author: Verses for 21st Century, 1997. Jewish. Avocation: poetry—sonnet writing. Died Apr. 15, 2005.

IVAN, FRANCIS M., sales executive, writer; b. Greeley, Colo., Dec. 14, 1926; s. Godfrey A. and Esther Ann Ivan; m. Joan Carol Waidtlaw, May 27, 1962; 1 child, Kathleen. At, Jones Real Estate Coll., Denver, 1971—73. Lic. real estate broker Colo., Nev. Ptnr. Oldsmobile franchise, Burlingame, Calif., 1959—71, gen. mgr., 1959—71; owner and broker Money Land Co., Denver, 1971—84; owner and COO Pacific Equipment Brokers, San Diego, 1981—84; indsl. broker Reno (Nev.) Realty, from 1993. Mem. Bd. of Realtors, Denver, 1971—84. Author: (books) Why Not?, 2002, Who Knows?, 2002. With USN, 1943—47, PTO. Republican. Avocations: skiing, golf. Died Oct. 23, 2004.

IVY, RICHARD F., retired minister; b. Boston, Apr. 27, 1928; s. Earl Arnett and Dorothy Ellen (Whitmarsh) I.; m. Hatsuko (Lily) Kanazawa, May 28, 1954; children: J. Timothy, Rose Ann Ivy Cogan. BA in Govt. Adminstrn., Coll. William and Mary, Newport News, Va., 1975. Ordained minister. Commd. U.S. Army, Japan, 1946—66, France, 1946—66; pastor Shadygrove Bapt. Ch., Figure Five, Ark., 1953—54. Author: (biography) Abraham Eustis: Artillery General, 1993. Organizer Dandy Citizens Assn., Inc., York County, Va., 1983, pres.; chair Yorktown Tercentenary Celebration, York County, 1990—91, York County Hist. Com., 1988—93. Recipient Comdr. award for civilian svc., Dept. of Army, 1983, County Pts. of Light, Nat. Assn. Counties, 1991, Outstanding Vol., York County, 1991. Mem.: Ft. Eustis Hist. and Archeol. Assn. (pres. 1993—97), Peninsula Caged Bird Soc. (chmn. from 1983), Bird Clubs of Va. (adminstrn. coord. from 1983), Bird Clubs Am. (dir. edn. and mgmt. from 1994, chair). Baptist. Avocations: breeding exotic birds, publishing education. Home: Yorktown, Va. Died June 11, 2004.

IWAKI, HIROYUKI, conductor; b. Tokyo, Sept. 6, 1932; m. Kaori Iwaki. LLD (hon.), Monash U., 1986; student, Tokyo U. Fine Arts. Conducting debut Nihon Housoce Kyoukai (Japan Broadcasting Corp.) Symphony Orch., Hong Kong, 1956, condr., 1963, Berlin Philharm. Orch., Vienna Philharm. Orch., Royal Concertgebouw Orch., Gewandhaus Orch., Liepzig, Melbourne (Australia) Symphony Orch., 1973—89, condr. laureate (life), 1987—2006. Fellow faculty of arts Monash U., 1991. Recipient Iwaki Auditorium named in his honor, Melbourne Symphony Orch., 1995, Grand Prix Disque, NHK Broadcasting Culture award, Japanese Broadcasting Corp., 1993, Medal of Honor with Purple Ribbon, Emperor of Japan, 1996. Mem.: Order of Australia (hon.). Died June 13, 2006.

JACKS, THOMAS JEROME, research chemist, consultant; b. Chgo., Jan. 24, 1938; s. Alexander Stephan and Mildred Katherine Jacks; m. Audrey Radcliff, Feb. 29, 1989. AB, Case Western Res. U., 1961, PhD, 1965. Mem. faculty Case Western Res. U., Cleve., 1963-65; rsch. chemist USDA, New Orleans, from 1965. Contbr. numerous articles to profl. jours., chpts. to books; inventor synthesis of conjugual acid, 7-acyloxy-4-methyl-compounds. Mem. Am. Oil Chemists Soc. (assoc. editor jour. 1973—), Am. Soc. Plant Physiology, Am. Chem. Soc. Avocations: fishing, boating. Home: Metairie, La. Died Aug. 3, 2004.

JACKSON, BILLY MORROW, retired artist, educator; b. Kansas City, Mo., Feb. 23, 1926; s. Alonzo David and Opal May (Morrow) Jackson; m. Blanche Mary Trice, June 12, 1949 (div. Jan. 1988); children: Lon Allan, Robin Jackson Todd, Aron Drew, Sylvia Marie; m. Siti Mariah Mansor, Feb. 1988. BFA, Washington U., St. Louis, 1949; MFA, U. Ill., 1954. Prof. art U. Ill., Champaign, 1954-87; ret., 1987; prin., owner Jackson Studios, Inc., Champaign, from 1991. One-man shows include Jane Haslem Gallery, Washington, 1990, Popoff Art Gallery, Paris, 2002, Represented in permanent collections Smithsonian Inst., Washington, Nat. Art Gallery, NASA Archives, Union League Club Chgo., Boston Pub. Libr., Met. Mus. Art, N.Y.C., Mus. Legion of Honor, San Francisco, Libr. of Congress, Washington, Springfield (Mo.) Art Mus., Conn. Acad. Fine Arts, Hartford, Artist's Guild, St. Louis, Phila., Free Libr., Evansville (Ind.) Mus. Arts & Scis., Joslyn Art Mus., Omaha, Norfolk Mus., Reading (Pa.) Pub. Libr. and Art Gallery, Lakeview Ctr. Art, Peoria, Ill., Butler Inst. Am. Art, Youngstown, Ohio, Civic Ctr. Art Collection, Springfield, Ill., N.Y. Hilton, N.Y.C., Ill. State Mus., Springfield, World Book Ency., Chgo., Rockefeller Ctr., Dulin Gallery Art, Knoxville, Tenn., Swope Mus., Terre Haute, Ind., Bur. of Peclamation, Washington, EPA, Krannert Art Mus., U. Ill., Champaign, Wichita (Kans.) Art Mus., Gov.'s State Coll., Park Forest South, Ill., Sheldon Meml. Gallery Art, U. Nebr., Lincoln, Busey First Nat. Bank, Champaign, 1st Nat. Bank, Swanlund Bldg., Bechmann Inst., U. Ill., Kedan (Malaysia) State Art Gallery, Nelson-Atkins Mus. Art, Kansas City, Mo., R.I. Sch. Art and Design, Providence, Abraham Lincoln Presdl. Libr. and Mus., Springfield, Ill., Jack and Shirley Lubeznik Ctr. for Arts, Michigan City, Ind., commd. mural, state Capital Bldg., Springfield, Ill., Mara Inst. Tech., Malaysia, Ill. Sch. Deaf, Jacksonville, Quincy (Ill.) Vet. Hosp. and Home, Carle Hosp. Edn. Bldg., Urbana, Ill., Mural Agr. Libr., U. Ill., Champaign, Ill. State Police, 2002, Project 500, U. Ill., 2003; subject of book Billy Morrow Jackson: Interpretation of Time and Light (Howard E. Wooden), 1990, In Our Time (retrospective), 1997, Krannert Art Mus., Champaign; author (with Siti Mariah Jackson): On This Island: An Artistic View of Martha's Vineyard, 2005; numerous exhibitions. With USMC, 1944—46, PTO. Democrat. Home: Champaign, Ill. Died June 16, 2006.

JACKSON, HARRY ALLEN, naval architect, marine engineer; b. Saginaw, Mich., Dec. 7, 1916; s. Allen D. and Ina Ruth (Lorimer) J.; m. Mary Rebecca McElroy, Apr. 15, 1944; children: Harry Allen Jr., Lisle Ann. BS, U. Mich., 1940. Profl. engr., N.H., Wash., Conn. Commd. capt. U.S. Navy, 1935, naval architect, 1941-69, ret., 1969; pvt. practice in engring. Groton, Conn., from 1969. Dir. SEA Inc., San Diego, Calif., 1978—; sr. lectr. MIT, Cambridge, Mass., 1971—. Author: (textbook) Submarine Design Notes, 1982; contbr. tech. papers to profl. jours. Fellow Soc. Naval Architects and Marine Engrs. (David. W. Taylor medal 1993), Royal Inst. Naval Architects; mem. Am. Soc. Naval Engrs. (hon. Harold E. Saunders award 1980). Avocations: sailing, metal and wood working. Died Apr. 10, 2005.

JACKSON, MARY, actress; b. Milford, Mich., Nov. 22, 1910; d. Thomas E. and Lela (Stephens) J.; m. Griffing Bancroft, Jr., July 4, 1937. BA, Western Mich. U., 1932. Appeared on: Broadway in Kiss and Tell, 1943-45, Eastward in Eden, 1947, The Flowering Cherry, 1950, The Trial of the Catonsville Nine, 1970; appeared in: West Coast presentations of Desk Set, 1956, Birthday Party, 1965, The Fifth of July, 1979; film appearances include Friendly Persuasion, 1956, Targets, 1966, Airport, 1970, Wild Rovers, 1971, The Trial of the Catonsville, 1972, Terror House, 1972, Kid Blue, 1973, Blume in Love, 1973, Our Time, 1974, Fun with Dick and Jane, 1977, Audrey Rose, 1977, Coming Home, 1978, Some Kind of Hero, 1982, Big Top Pee Wee, 1988, Skinned Alive, 1989, The Exorcist III, 1991, Leap of Faith, 1992, Ozone, 1993, A Family Thing, 1996; (TV movies) Do Not Go Gentle Into That Good Night, 1967, The Failing of Raymond, 1971, Columbo: Try and Catch Me, 1977, Letters from Frank, 1979, The Two Lives of Carol Letner, 1981, A Small Killing, 1981, A Wedding on Walton's Mountain, 1982, Between Two Brothers, 1982, A Day for Thanks on Walton's Mountain, 1982, My Town, 1986, Meet the Munceys, 1988, The Case of the Hillside Stranglers, 1989, A Walton Wedding, 1995, A Walton Easter, 1997; (mini-series) Space, 1985; (TV series) The Waltons, 1972—81, Harcastle & McCormick, 1983, Parenthood, 1990; (TV appearances) The Philco Televisio Playhouse, 1952, Robert Montgomery Presents, 1955, 56, Alfred Hitchcock Presents, 1956, General Electric Theater, 1960, The Barbara Stanwyk Show, 1960, My Three Sons, 1961, Route 66, 1961, Hazel, 1961, Stoney Burke, 1962, The Fugitive, 1964, 65, 66 The Outer Limits, 1964, The Andy Griffith Show, 1964, 66 The F.B.I., 1965, 66, 67, Please Don't Eat the Daisies, 1965, The Invaders, 1967, 68, Insight, 1967, The Second Hundred Years, 1967, Lancer, 1969, Room 222, 1970, Mary Tyler Moore, 1971, The Name of the Game, 1971, Cannon, 1971, Barnaby Jones, 1973, 77, The Rookies, 1974, The Manhunter, 1974, The Bionic Woman, 1977, The Rockford Files, 1979, Hart to Hart, 1981, Quicy, 1982, Family Ties, 1982, Magnum P.I., 1983, The Jeffersons, 1985, Scarecrow and Mrs. King, 1985, Highway to Heaven, 1986, Stingray, 1987, Hill Street Blues, 1987, Hunter, 1987, L.A. Law, 1989 Mem. Los Angeles adv. com. Actors Fund Am. Recipient Disting. Alumna award Western Mich. U., 1976 Mem. Acad. Motion Picture Arts and Scis., Acad. TV Arts and Scis., Actors Equity Assn. Democrat. Presbyterian. Home: Los Angeles, Calif. Died Dec. 10, 2005.

JACKSON, NANCY MORRISON, architect; b. Pitts., Aug. 15, 1922; d. Robert Kirk and Marcella Genevieve (Pfendler) Morrison; m. George Clark Jackson, Aug. 25, 1945; children: Ellen Jackson Rudy, Robert Clark, Mary Jackson Porter. BArch, Carnegie Mellon U., 1946. Arch. Prack & Prack, Pitts., 1942, Kaiser, Neal & Reid, Pitts., 1943—44, Marks & Simboli, Pitts., 1947, Edward C. Roock, Syracuse, NY, 1958, Austin-Mead, Hartford, Conn., 1967—70, Kane Farrel White, 1970—72; pvt. practice Farmington, Conn., 1972—78; gen. svcs. adminstrn. Washington, 1978—2005. Mem. Nat. Archtl. Accrediting Bd.; citations U.S. State Dept. Mem. admissions coun. Carnegie Mellon U.; mem. Cath. Family Svcs., Commn. for Ecumenical Affairs, Conn. Mem.: AIA (Masterspec rev. com.), Am. Arbitration Assn. (constrn. industry arbitrator), Conn. Soc. Arch. Bd., Arts Club of Washington, Kappa Alpha Theta. Roman Catholic. Died Oct. 22, 2005.

JACOBS, ALFRED JACK, financial services executive; b. Providence, R.I., Sept. 24, 1925; s. Samuel and Sylvia (Reuter) J.; m. Jeanne Sclore, Dec. 21, 1928; 1 child, Marc Robb Jacobs. BSME, U. R.I., 1948; MBA, Marquette U., 1967. Registered profl. engr., N.H., R.I. Design engr. Allied Chem. & Dye, Hopewell, Va., 1948-50, Enginaire, Inc., Providence, 1950-55, Allstates Design and Devel., Inc., Trenton, N.J., 1955-58; sales engr. Norman Engring. Co., Chgo., 1958-64, Miller Fluid Power, Bensenville, Ill., 1964-66; assoc. prof. Milw. Sch. Engring., 1966-68; pres. Jemal Assocs., Milw., 1968-91, Asset Mgmt., Inc., Milw., from 1991. Contbr. articles to profl. jours. Pres. Gifts from the Heart, Milw., 1992, bd. dirs. 1988-92; bd. dirs. Hist. Keyboard Soc., Milw., 1989-92, Milw. Chamber Orch., 1979-85; officer YMCA Indian Guide Program, 1966-73. Home: Milwaukee, Wis. Died Apr. 11, 2004.

JACOBS, ALLYN, management company executive; b. Bklyn., June 7, 1953; Owner Taco Tah Inc., L.A., 1977-80, La Adelita Food Inc., L.A., 1980-83; mgr. R.T.M. Inc., L.A., 1983-85, tng. mgr., 1985-89, KFF Mgmt. Inc., Encino, Calif., 1989-90, dir. tng. L.A., from 1990. Avocation: coin and stamp collector. Home: North Hollywood, Calif. Died May 10, 2005.

JACOBS, BRUCE MARRIN, lawyer; b. Oakland, Calif., July 21, 1926; s. Allen Walter and Celia Teresa (Marrin) J.; m. Jane Gray, June 26, 1954; children: Tracy Ann, Brian G., Nancy C. Fleming. AB, U. Calif., Berkeley, 1947; JD, U. San Francisco, 1953. Bar: Calif. 1953. Assoc. Law Office Robert K. Byers, Gilroy, Calif., 1953-56; ptnr. Byers & Jacobs, Gilroy, 1957-67, Jacobs & Biafore, Gilroy, 1967-74, Jacobs & McDonald, Gilroy, 1974-95; retired, 1995. Dir. Nat. Fiberglass, Gilroy. Bd. pres. Gavilan Community Coll., Gilroy, 1963, trustee, 1963-73; city atty. City of Gilroy, 1968-91. Lt. (j.g.) USN, 1944-49, PTO. Mem. State Bar Calif., Gilroy C. of C. (pres. 1958), Gilroy Rotary (pres. 1957, 59), Gilroy Elks. Republican. Presbyterian. Avocations: travel, photography, flying. Home: Gilroy, Calif. Died Feb. 8, 2004.

JACOBS, FLORA GILL, former museum director, writer; b. Washington, Dec. 22, 1918; d. Morris Hilliard and Dora (Seidenman) G.; m. Ephraim Jacobs, Sept. 8, 1940; 1 child, Amanda Bolling. Student, George Washington U., 1936-40. Asst. editor woman's/fashion pages Washington Times-Herald, Washington, 1940-42, editor woman's/fashion pages, 1942-43; founder, dir. Washington Doll's House and Toy Mus., Washington, 1975—2004. Author: (nonfiction) A History of Dolls' Houses, 1953, rev. edit., 1965, A Book of Dolls and Doll Houses, 1967, Doll's Houses in America, 1974, Victorian Dolls' Houses and Their Furnishings, 1978, Doll's Houses in America: Historic Preservation in Miniature, 1979, The Small World of Antique Dolls: Six Decades of Collecting Mansions, Cottages, Shops, Stables, Theaters, Churches-Even A Zoo, 2005; (fiction) The Dolls' House Mystery, 1958, The Toy Shop Mystery, 1960, The Haunted Birdhouse, 1970 Recipient Crystal award Internat. Guild Miniature Artisans 1991. Mem. Mystery Writers of Am., Author's Guild, Children's Book Guild of Washington (past pres.), Nat. Press Club, Newswoman's Club. Democrat. Home: Chevy Chase, Md. Died May 31, 2006.

JACOBS, JAMES PAUL, retired insurance executive; b. Augusta, Ark., May 14, 1930; s. James Leonard and Ida Lee (Taylor) J.; m. Joan Gillum, Aug. 18, 1956; 2 children: LeAnn, Caryl Lynn Watson. Student, Louis A. Allen Mgmt., 1970; Assoc. in mgmt., Ins. Inst. of Am., 1971. Underwriter trainee Ins. Co. of N. Am., Phila., 1954-55, underwriter Richmond, Va., 1955-58, supervising underwriter, 1958-64, underwriting mgr., 1964-68, Detroit, 1968-71; casualty mgr. Montgomery & Collins, Inc., L.A., 1971-73; ptnr. Tabb Brockenbrough & Ragland, Richmond, Va., 1973-1995, ret., 1995. Mem. agts. adv. coun. Comml. Union Ins. Co., Boston, Gt. Am. Ins. Co. Cin., Cigna Cos. Phila., Pa. Mfrs. Assn. Ins. Co., Phila., ITT Hartford, Conn., Jonathan Trumbell Assocs., Md. Ins. Group Agts. Forum, U.S. Fidelity and Guaranty Co.; bd. dirs. "All Industry" Va. "I" Day Corp., Richmond; instr. U. Richmond, 1965-78. Contbr. articles to profl. jours. Active in Colonial Williamsburg Assocs., Friends of Kennedy Ctr., Smithsonian Assocs.; bd. dirs. Daily Planet, Richmond (non-profit orgn. for aiding the homeless), 1988-1998, pres., 1995-97; mem. Reveille United Meth. Ch., pastor parish com., Sunday sch. supt.; mem. Pulaski Heights United Meth. Ch., Little Rock. Capt. USMC, 1951—54. Mem. CPCU (bd. dirs. 1979-82, regional v.p. 1981, chpt. officer 1976-79). Republican. Methodist. Avocation: sports fan. Died July 23, 2005.

JACOBS, JANE, author; b. Scranton, Pa., May 4, 1916; d. John Decker and Bess Mary (Robison) Butzner; m. Robert Hyde Jacobs, Jr., May 27, 1944 (dec. 1996); children: James Kedzie, Edward Decker, Mary Hyde. Author: Downtown Is For People in The Exploding Metropolis, 1959, The Death and Life of Great American Cities, 1961, The Economy of Cities, 1969, The Question of Separatism, 1980, Cities and the Wealth of Nations, 1984, Systems of Survival, 1992, The Nature of Economies, 2000, Dark Age Ahead, 2004, (juvenile) The Girl on the Hat, 1989, editor, commentator: A Schoolteacher in Old Alaska: The Story of Hannah Breece, 1995. Died Apr. 25, 2006.

JACOBS, SUZANNE, author; b. Phila., Nov. 29, 1934; d. Robert and Evelyn (Segal) Gold; m. Barry Stephen Jacobs, June 12, 1952; children: Lynda Beth, Bonnie Dee, Ellen Merle (dec.). Student, Lower Merion Nigh Sch. Owner Offbeat Press, Merion, Pa.; currier Pa. Endocrine Lab., Phila.; dir. Temple Israel Nursery Sch., Phila. Author: Early One Saturday Morning, 1994 (Silver Poet award), World of Poetry, 1995 (Golden Poet award), Twisted Tales, 1996, The Last Tear, 1999; writer polit. commentary for Main Line Times. Coagulator Rep. Party, Phila., 1996; writer, asst. Brith Sholom, 1994-96; writer, dir. plays, entertainment organizer Duke DFC, 1985-90. Recipient KFC Cols. Way award, 1997, Pa. Arts award. Avocations: antiques, collecting art. Home: Philadelphia, Pa. Died July 8, 2005.

JACOBSEN, FREDERICK MARIUS, psychiatrist, psychopharmacologist; b. Ames, Iowa, Jan. 19, 1954; s. Frederick Marius and Maude Elizabeth (Battle) J.; m. Lillian Comas-Díaz, Sept. 24, 1983. AB in Biol. Scis. cum laude, Cornell U., 1976; MPH, U. Ill., 1978, MD, 1980. Diplomate Nat. Bd. Med. Examiners, Am. Bd. Psychiatry and Neurology. Intern medicine Greenwich Hosp., Greenwich, Hosp., 1980-81; postdoctoral fellow in psychiatry dept. psychiatry Yale U. Sch. Medicine, New Haven, 1981-84; chief resident psychiatry Yale New Haven Hosp., New Haven, 1983-84; med. staff fellow clin. psychobiology br. NIMH, Bethesda, Md., 1984-86, sr. staff fellow clin. psychobiology br., 1986-87, med. officer lab. clin. sci. & clin. psychobiology br., 1987-88, guest researcher clin. psychology, 1988-89, guest researcher lab. clin. sci., from 1988; asst. clin. prof. psychiatry and behavioral sci. George Washington U. Sch. Medicine, Washington, 1985-91, assoc. clin. prof., 1991—98, clin. prof., from 1998; med. dir. Transcultural Mental Health Inst., Washington, from 1986; assoc. prof. psychiatry Georgetown U. Sch. Medicine, Washington, from 1991. Cons. psychiatrist VOCA Corp., Washington, 1987-88; cons. in sleep disorders Nat. Capital Sleep Ctr., MDG, Bethesda, 1985-86; quality assurance com. NIH, Bethesda, 1985-87; research psychiatrist Whiting Forensic Inst., Middletown, Conn., 1983-84; quality assurance com. Yale-New Haven Hosp., 1983-84; cons. psychiatry and geriatric psychopharmacology Sound View-Specialized Care Ctr., W. Haven, Conn., 1983-84, New Haven Convalescent Ctr., 1983-84; presenter in field. Co-author: Melatonin in Humans, 1985, (with N.E. Rosenthal) Depression and Mania, 1988, Clinical Guidelines in Cross-Cultural Mental Health, 1988, Biorhythms and Stress in the Physiopathology of Reproduction, 1988, Affective Disorders, 1988, Seasonal Affective Disorders and Phototherapy, 1989; contbr. articles to profl. jours.; abstrator in field. Med. advisor Capital Area Depressive and Manic Depressive Assn., Washington, 1987—; cons. psychiatry Immigration and Naturalization Svc., Washington, 1985-87; grad. edn. com. dept. psychiatry Yale U., New Haven, 1982-83. Scholar Am. Field Svc., Sao Paulo, Brazil, 1971-72, James scholar U. Ill. Sch. Medicine, Chgo., 1977, Cornell U. Biol. Research scholar, 1975-76, acad. scholar U. Ill. Sch. Pub. Health, 1978; fellow Calhoun Coll. Yale U., 1981-82; NIMH Tng. grantee dept. psychiatry U. Ill. Sch. Medicine, 1978, 79. Fellow APA; mem. AAAS, AMA (Physicians Recognition award 1987, 90, 94), Soc. Biol. Psychiatry, Am. Psychiat. Assn., Math. Assn. Am., World Psychiat. Assn., N.Y. Acad. Sci. (life), Med. Soc. D.C., Washington Psychiat. Soc. (sec. com. internat. affairs), Found. for Advanced Edn. in the Scis., Soc. for Study Psychiatry and Culture, Am. Soc. Clin. Endocrinology, Am. Soc. Clin. Pharm. Therapeutics, Am. Coll. Clin. Pharmacology, Am. Soc. Clin. Psychopharmacology (charter), Am. Coll. Women's Health Care Physicians (founding mem.), Soc. for Light Treatment and Biol. Rhythms (charter), Am. Sleep Disorders Assn., Delta Omega. Home: Washington, DC. Died June 7, 2004.

JACOBSEN, JUDITH EVA, author, lecturer, consultant; b. Miami Beach, Fla., Dec. 27, 1952; d. Lyman William Jacobsen and Carolyn Elise (Comins) Burnham; m. John William Firor, Oct. 15, 1983. BA in Polit. Sci., U. Maine, 1975; JD, Coll. William & Mary, 1978; PhD in Geography, U. Colo., 1989. Bar: Va. 1979. Exec. dir. Carrying Capacity, Inc., Washington, 1981-82; sr. researcher Worldwatch Inst., Washington, 1982-83; asst. prof. U. Wyo., Laramie, 1989-93; adj. prof. environ. policy and mgmt. program Univ. Denver, from 1993. Cons. Am. Embassy, Lagos, Nigeria, summers 1984-85, President's Coun. on Sustainable Devel., Population and Consumption Task Force, 1994-95. Author booklets U.S. Carrying Capacity, 1982, Promoting Population Stabilization, 1983, Population Change, Resources and Environment, 1983; contbr. articles to profl. publs., chpts. to books. Trustee Zero Population Growth, Washington, 1984-92, mem. exec. com., 1985-90, pres. bd., 1986-89; v.p. bd., chmn. fundraising Boulder Valley Women's Health Ctr., Boulder, Colo., 1985-87; trustee High County News, 1992—. Mem. Assn. Am. Geographers. Democrat. Home: Boulder, Colo. Died Aug. 28, 2004.

JACOBSON, HAROLD, physical chemist, pharmaceutical executive; b. N.Y.C., Jan. 15, 1929; s. Aaron and Lillie (Berman) J.; m. Charlotte Schindler, May 20, 1952 (dec. Nov. 1970); children: Eric M., David G.; m. Joyce Reznick, Feb. 11, 1973; 1 child, Michael L. BS, CCNY, 1950; PhD, Poly Inst Bklyn., 1959. Chemist Good Housekeeping Mag., N.Y.C., 1950-52, Nat. Bur. Standards, Washington, 1952-55, Nat. Cash Register Co., Dayton, Ohio, 1959-61; mem. tech. staff Bell Telephone Labs., Murray Hill, N.J., 1961-63; sr. scientist, analyst R & D E.R. Squibb & Sons, New Brunswick, N.J., 1963-77, dept. head quality control, 1977-87; dir. regulatory affairs Bristol-Myers Squibb, Princeton, N.J., from 1987. Adj. prof. Middlesex County Coll., Edison, N.J., 1967-70; chmn. Packaging Group Conf., New Brunswick, 1990; lectr. various tech. mtgs. Author: (with others) Pharmaceutical Dosage Form: Tablets, 1980, 2d edit., 1989, Analysis of Antibiotics, 1985; contbr. articles to profl. sci. jours. Mem. Am. Assn. Pharm. Scientists (chmn., bd. dirs. N.E. Ann. Mtg. Group 1978-81), Am. Chem. Soc., N.Y. Acad. Sci., Parenteral Drug Assn. Home: East Brunswick, NJ. Died Jan. 30, 2004.

JACOBY, THOMAS S., cultural organization administrator; b. Konigsberg, Fed. Republic Germany, May 13, 1935; came to U.S., 1939; s. Berthold and Anni (Pfingst) J.; m. Adrienne Zacansky, Apr. 14, 1962; children: Michael, Melissa. BS in Edn., West Chester U., 1958; EdM, Temple U., 1961. Cert. health, phys. edn. tchr. Tchr. Sch. Dist. of Phila., 1958-69, dept. head, athletic dir., 1969-71, supr. health and phys. edn., 1971-90, curriculum coord. phys. edn. and athletics, 1990-93, adminstrv. asst. to regional supt., 1993-95, adminstrv. asst. student svcs., 1995-97, dir. svcs. to students with disabilities, 1997-99; ednl. cons., 1999-2000; exec. dir. Phila. Reads, 2000—05. Adj. asst. prof. Temple U., Phila., 1976-2005; cons. Tech. Adv. Svc. for Attys., Blue Bell, Pa., 1977-2005; bd. dirs. Lake Owego Camp for Boys, Greeley, Pa. Author: (pamphlets) Physical Education for the Bicentennial, 1976, Street Games of Philadelphia, 1985; contbg. editor: Unique Games and Sports Around the World, 2001. Pres. Phila. Coun. B'nai B'rith, Phila., 1985, Jewish Cmty. Rels. Coun., 1998-2000, co-chmn. edn. com. Jewish Coun. on Pub. Affairs, 2001-05. Mem. AAHPERD (2003 conv. mgr., Honor award 2002), Pa. State Assn. Health, Phys. Edn., Recreation and Dance (pres. 1980, conv. mgr. 1975, 79, exhibits mgr. Ea. Dist. 1988-92, pres. Ea. Dist. 1994, Profl. Honor awards 1973, 90, Elmer B. Cottrell award 1984), ASTM, ASCD, Am. Assn. Sch. Adminstrs., Am. Camping Assn., Phi Delta Kappa. Died June 15, 2005.

JAFFE, RONA, author; b. N.Y.C., June 12, 1932; d. Samuel and Diana (Ginsberg) J. BA, Radcliffe Coll., 1951. Sec., N.Y.C., 1952; assoc. editor Fawcett Publs., N.Y.C., 1952-56; founder Rona Jaffe Found., 1995. Author: The Best of Everything, 1958, Away From Home, 1960, The Last of the Wizards, 1961, Mr. Right Is Dead, 1965, The Cherry in the Martini, 1966, The Fame Game, 1969, The Other Woman, 1972, Family Secrets, 1974, The Last Chance, 1976, Class Reunion, 1979, Mazes and Monsters, 1981, After the Reunion: A Novel, 1985, An American Love Story, 1990, The Cousins, 1995, 5 Women, 1997 The Road Taken: A Novel, 2000, The Room-Mating Season: A Novel, 2003. Died Dec. 30, 2005.

JAFFE, SAMUEL ZELMEN, rabbi, educator; b. N.Y.C., Dec. 15, 1922; s. Morris and Toby (Sharlin) J.; m. Edythe Judith Golin, Aug. 1952; children: Arvin, Joshua, Michele. BA, Yeshiva U., 1943; MA, Columbua U., 1946; M. Hebrew Lit., Hebrew Union Coll., 1948, DD (hon.), 1973; ThD, Burton Sem., 1962. Ordained rabbi, 1948. Dir. B'nai Brith Hillel Found., U. Fla., Gainesville, 1949-52; rabbi Congregation Beth Sholom, Park Forest, Ill., 1954-58, Temple Beth El, Hollywood, Fla., 1958-91. Assoc. prof. Barry U., Miami Shores, Fla., 1975—; v.p. Holacaust Documentation and Edn., Miami, Fla., 1982—; bd. dirs. Jewish Family Svc., Broward County, Fla., 1990. Bd. dirs. Henderson Mental Health Ctr., Ft. Lauderdale, Fla., 1985—; pres. Jewish Nat. Fund, Miami Beach, 1989—. 1st lt. U.S. Army, 1952-54. Rabbi Samuel Z. Jaffe Chair in Jewish Studies named in his honor Bar Ilan U., Israel, 1990; recipient Appreciation award City of Hollywood. Mem. Greater Miami Rabbinical Assn. (past pres.), South Broward Coun. Rabbis (past pres.), S.E. Assn. Cen. Conf. Am. Rabbis (past pres., exec. bd.), Zionist Orgn. Am., B'nai Brith. Home: Boca Raton, Fla. Died Aug. 20, 2004.

JAGGERS, VELMA MARY LEE, foundation administrator, educator; b. McAlester, Okla., Dec. 12, 1919; d. John Jaggers; m. O. Lee Jaggers, June, 1957; 1 child, Robin. Student, U. of World Ch., 1965; MA, Nat. Eccles U., London, 1970; PhD, DLitt. Ordained to ministry. Pres. Arch Elder's Commn. Internat., Inc., L.A., Miss Velma's Found., Inc., L.A.; univ. tchr. L.A. Contbr. articles to profl. publs. Recipient citation Pres. of U.S., V.P. of U.S., various govs., mayors, fgn. potentates. Died 2004.

JAGIELLO, WALTER EDWARD, communications executive, entertainer; b. Chgo., Aug. 1, 1930; s. John and Katherine (Mirek) J.; m. Jeanette Lazarz, June, 1950 (div. 1970); children: Edward, Julianna, James; m. Jeanette Anna Kozak, Mar. 17, 1972. Radio broadcaster, 1949—2006; owner, pres. Jay Jay Record Co., Chgo., 1951-64, Miami, Fla., 1964—2006, Jay Jay Pub. Co., Miami, 1959—2006, Walters Music, Miami, 1962—2006, Li'l Wally Music Prodns., Miami, 1964—2006, Specialty Distbn., Inc., Miami, 1960—2006. Composer (album) Polish Feelings, 1985 (Grammy nomination), over 2000 songs; performer over 140 albums, 3 appearances Lawrence Welk Show. Recipient citation Nat. Ballrooms Assn., 1969; mus. works exhibited at World's Fair, Poznan, Poland, 1966; elected into Polka Hall of Fame; invited performer at Vatican Audience Hall for Pope John Paul II, 1984; 50 Yrs. of Entertaining banquet held in his honor, 1988. Mem. Nat. Acad. Rec. Arts and Scis. (life; co-founder Chgo. chpt.), Polish Culture Soc., Internat. Polka Assn. Clubs: Polish Am. (Miami), Polka Ambassadors (Pa.). Roman Catholic. Avocations: swimming, cooking. Home: Miami, Fla. Died Aug. 17, 2006.

JANDL, JAMES HARRIMAN, internist; b. Racine, Wis., 1925; MD, Harvard U., 1949. Diplomate Am. Bd. Internal Medicine. Successively intern, asst. resident, research fellow, research assoc., asst. physician, assoc. physician, dir. Thorndike Meml. Lab.; assoc. vis. physician, physician, dir. Harvard Med. unit Boston City Hosp., 1961-74; cons. physician Mt. Auburn Hosp., 1968—2006; sr. physician Beth Israel Deaconess Med Ctr., 1975—2006; mem. faculty Harvard Med. Sch., from 1952, assoc. prof. medicine, 1964-68, prof. medicine, 1968—2006, George R. Minot prof. medicine, 1968—2006; sr. cons. in medicine Brigham & Women's Hosp., 1987—2006. Vis. prof. MIT, 1973-74. Author: Blood: Textbook of Hematology', 1987, Blood: Pathophysiology, 1991. Served with USNR, 1950-52. Mem. Am. Fedn. Clin. Research, Am. Soc. Clin. Investigation, Assn. Am. Physicians. Home: Concord, Mass. Died July 17, 2006.

JAROS, ARTHUR GEORGE, accountant; b. Chgo., Apr. 13, 1922; s. George Arthur and Sylvia (Kovarik) J.; m. Dawn Lillian Vachta, Nov. 19, 1949; children: Arthur G. Jr., Wesley A., Randall S. NS, Northwestern U., 1943. CPA, Ill. Staff acct. Frazer and Torbett, Chgo., 1946-48; pvt. practiceacctg. and ins. Chgo., 1948-87; v.p., treas. Family Fed. Savs. Ill., Cicero, from 1955, also chmn. bd. dirs. Lectr. career program for students J. Sterling Morton High Sch., Cicero, 1970. Chmn. profl. div. Community Chest, Cicero, 1965. Served as lt. USN, 1943-46, ETO, PTO. Mem. VFW, U.S.S. Jeffers Reunion Group, Elks (exalted ruler 1953-54, bd. trustees 1955—). Avocations: music, sports, stamp and coin collecting, travel. Home: Riverside, Ill. Died Apr. 22, 2004.

JASION, ARTHUR RAYMOND, plastic surgeon; b. Balt., Jan. 18, 1936; widowed; children: Edward, Robert, Arthur W. BS, U. Md., 1957, MD, 1959. Diplomate Am. Bd. Plastic Surgery. Pvt. practice, Timonium, Md., from 1967; active staff Franklin Square Hosp., Balt., from 1968; cons. Mercy Hosp., Balt. Home: Luthvle Timon, Md. Died July 3, 2004.

JASKIEWICZ, LEONARD ALBERT, retired lawyer; b. Norwich, Conn., Aug. 25, 1927; s. Michael and Eleanor C. (Smigiel) J.; m. Ruth Evelyn Lalor, Jan. 31, 1953; children: Jon Michael, Barbara Joan, Virginia Ruth. BA, U. Conn., 1949; MA, Syracuse U., 1950; JD, George Washington U., 1954. Bar: D.C. 1954, U.S. Supreme Ct. 1961. Fiscal mgmt. ofcl. U.S. Dept. Navy, Washington, 1950-53; from assoc. to ptnr. Dow, Lohnes and Albertson, 1954-64; ptnr. Grove, Jaskiewicz & Cobert, 1964-93; ret., 1993. Served with AUS, 1946-47, USAR, 1950-62. Mem. ABA, D.C. Bar Assn., Transportation Lawyers Assn. Lodges: Masons, Shriners. Died Sept. 20, 2006.

JASMON, ROBERT LAWRENCE, transportation executive; b. Springfield, Ill., Dec. 14, 1936; s. Lawrence G. and Helen L. (McReynolds) J.; m. Norma J. Sexton, Oct. 22, 1955; children: Michael, Mark, Richard, Joseph. BA, Bradley U., Peoria, Ill., 1958. Engring. designer Sangamo Electric Co., Springfield, Ill., 1958-63; fieldman, exec. sec. Tri-State Trucking Assn., Springfield, 1963-65; salesman Charles Bruning div. A-M Corp., Springfield, 1965-68; asst. mgr. Nat. Elect. Contractors Assn., Springfield, 1968-69; purchasing agt. office of Sec. of State State of Ill., Springfield, 1969-72; exec. v.p. Mid-West Trucking Assn., Springfield, from 1972. Industry advisor Nat. Gov.'s Conf. Washington, 1984-87; mem. trucking safety task force State of Ill., Springfield, 1987. Mem. exec. com. Sangamon County Rep. Cen. Com., Springfield, 1976—; trustee Capitol Twp., Springfield, 1977—. Mem. Am. Soc. Assn. Execs., Ill. Soc. Assn. Execs. (pres. 1979), Am. Trucking Benevolent Assn. (treas. 1980-86), Springfield Jr. C. of C. (v.p. 1960-61), Springfield C. of C. (transp. com. 1980—). Clubs: Am. Bus. Club. Baptist. Home: Springfield, Ill. Died Apr. 1, 2004.

JAYNE, CYNTHIA ELIZABETH, psychologist; b. Pensacola, Fla., June 5, 1953; d. Gordon Howland and Joan (Rockwood) J. AB, Vassar Coll., 1974; MA, SUNY, Buffalo, 1978, PhD, 1983. Lic. psychologist, Pa. Instr. dept. psychiatry Temple U. Sch. Medicine, Phila., 1982-84, asst. prof., 1984-85, asst. dir. outpatient svcs., asst. dir. residency tng., 1982-85, clin. asst. prof., 1985—2003; pvt. practice psychology Phila., 1985—2004. Adj. prof. Chestnut Hill Coll., 1994-98. Contbr. articles to profl. jours. Soc. for Sci. Study Sex scholar, 1981; Sigma Xi grantee, 1981, Kinsey Inst. Dissertation award, 1983. Mem. Pa. Psychol. Assn., N.Am. Soc. Psychosocial Obstetrics Gynecology, Soc. for Sci. Study Sex (bd. dirs. 1984-86). Died June 3, 2004.

JEFFERIS, PAUL BRUCE, lawyer; b. Barnesville, Ohio, Jan. 11, 1952; s. Maurice D. and Ruth C. (Rinehart) J.; 1 child Paul M. BA, Ohio State U., 1977; JD, U. Akron, 1980. Bar: Ohio 1980. Asst. prosecutor Belmont County, St. Clairsville, Ohio, 1981-83; pvt. practice, Barnesville, from 1983. Bd. dirs. St. Clairsville Drug and Alcohol Coun., 1982—. With USN, 1975-77. Mem. ABA, Belmont County Bar Assn., Am. Legion, Moose. Roman Catholic. Avocations: reading, hunting. Died June 26, 2005.

JEFFERSON, EDWARD GRAHAM, chemical company executive; b. London, July 15, 1921; came to U.S., 1951, naturalized, 1957; s. Edward Hemmings and Margaret Agatha (Graham) J.; m. Naomi Nale Love, June 27, 1953; children: Edward Graham, Charles David, Peter Love (dec.), Andrew McKinley. PhD, King's Coll., U. London, 1951. With E.I. du Pont de Nemours & Co., Wilmington, Del., from 1951, asst. dir. Research & Devel. div., 1964-66, dir. Fluorocarbons div., 1966-69, asst. gen. mgr. plastics dept., 1969-70, asst. gen. mgr. explosives dept., 1970-72, asst. gen. mgr. polymer intermediates dept., 1972, v.p., gen. mgr. film dept., 1972-73, sr. v.p., dir., 1973-79, mem. exec. com., 1973-86, pres., COO, 1980-81, chmn., CEO, 1981-86, chmn. fin. com. Dir. AT&T, Chem. N.Y. Corp./Chem. Bank., Seagram Co. Ltd. Mem. Bus. Com. for Arts; bd. dirs. Nat. Action Council for Minorities in Engring., 1980-83; vice-chmn. bd. trustees U. Del., U. Pa., 1984-86; trustee U.S. Council Internat. Bus., Tuskegee U., 1982-87, Acad. Natural Sci.; mem. Bus. Com. for Arts, Bus. Council; mem. vis. com. Med. Sch. and Sch. Dental Medicine Harvard U.; bd. govs. Joseph H. Lauder Inst. Mgmt. and Internat. Studies, U. Pa., 1983-86; mem. Pres.'s Export Council, 1985-87; chmn. adv. bd. Sch. Internat. and Pub. Affairs Columbia U., N.Y.C, bd. tustees Winterthur Mus. and Gardens; Served to capt. Brit. Army, 1942-47. Fellow King's Coll., U. London.; Mem. AAAS, Bus. Roundtable (policy com.), Am. Chem. Soc., Am. Inst. Chem. Engrs., Soc. Chem. Industry (Am. sect.), Conf. Bd. (vice chmn.), Dirs. of Indsl. Research. Episcopalian. Died Feb. 9, 2006.

JEFFERY, JOHN EDWARD, retired research chemist; b. Winnipeg, Man., Can., June 21, 1915; came to U.S., 1920; s. Isaac and Margaurite Elizabeth (Giles) J.; m. Ruth Norine Settergren, Jan. 2, 1942; children: Lynn, Robert, Jill, Sherry. BS in Chemistry, U. Wash., 1938, MS, 1941. Rsch. chemist Atlas Powder Co., Tamaqua, Pa., 1941-45; rsch. chemist, analytical group leadder ITT Rayonier Inc., Shelton, Wash., 1945-78; ret., 1978. Contbr. articles to profl. jours.; patentee delay electric blasting. Pres. Shelton Sch. Bd., 1952, Shelton Hosp., 1956. Mem. Am. Chem. Soc., Kiwanis, Moose, Elks. Episcopalian. Avocation: travel. Home: Shelton, Wash. Died Dec. 27, 2004.

JEFFREDO, JOHN VICTOR, aerospace engineer, manufacturing company executive, inventor; b. LA, Nov. 5, 1927; s. John Edward and Pauline Matilda (Whitten) J., m. Elma Jean Nesmith (div. 1958); children: Joyce Jean Jeffredo Ryder, Michael John; m. Doris Louise Hinz, (div. 1980); children: John Victor, Louise Victoria Jeffredo-Warden; m. Gerda Adelheid Pillich, 1980. Grad. in aero. engring., Northrop U., 1949; AA in Machine Design, Pasadena City Coll., 1951; grad., Ordnance Sch. U.S. Army, 1951; postgrad, U. So. Calif., 1955—58, Palomar Coll., 1977—96; MBA, La Jolla U., 1980, PhD in Psychology, 1984. Design engr. Douglas Aircraft Co., Long Beach and Santa Monica, Calif., 1955-58; devel. engr. Honeywell Ordnance Corp., Duarte, Calif., 1958-62; cons. Honeywell Devel. Labs, Seattle, 1962-65; supr. mech. engring. dept. aerospace divsn. Control Data Corp., Pasadena, Calif., 1965-68; project engr. Cubic Corp., San Diego, 1968-70; supr. mech. engring. dept. Babcock Electronics Co., Costa Mesa, Calif., 1970-72; owner, operator Jeffredo Gunsight Co., Fallbrook, Calif., 1971-81; chief engr. Western Designs, Inc., Fallbrook, Calif., 1972-81, exec. dir., 1981-88, CEO, 1988-96, owner, operator, 1981-87, Western Design Concepts, Inc., 1987-94; exec. dir. JXJ, Inc., San Marcos, Calif., 1981-88, CEO, from 1988. Mgr. Jeffredo Gunsight divsn., 1981-94, chief engr. JXJ, Inc., 1987-92 (merger JXJ, Inc. and Western Design Concepts, Fallbrook, Calif.), prin. 1992—, owner, mgr., Energy Assocs., San Diego, 1982-86, pres. Jeffredo Internat., 1984-88, founder, CEO John-Victor Internat., San Marcos, Calif., Frankfurt, Fed. Rep. Germany, 1988-99, The Jeffredo Solution, Fallbrook, 1996—; pres., CEO, Maritime Shoshone, Inc., 2000-01, chmn., CEO, 2001—; engring. cons. Action Instruments Co., Inc., Gen. Dynamics, Alcyon Corp., Systems Exploration, Inc. (all San Diego), Hughes Aircraft Co., El Segundo, Allied-Bendix, San Marcos, Santa Barbara Rsch., Goleta, Calif.; bd. dirs. Indian World Corp., JXJ, Inc., John-Victor Internat.; owner, operator Maritime Shoshone, Inc., 2000—; chmn. bd. The Badger Creek Studio, Fallbrook, 1997—. Author: Gabrieleño, New Perspective on the Island Gabrielino, The Ocean People, Wildcatting, Then There Were None, 1999; contbr. articles to profl. jours. and mags.; guest editl. writer Town Hall, San Diego Union; narrator: (film) The Sacred Desert, 1994; spkr. in field; patentee agrl. frost control, vehicle off-road drive system, recoil absorbing system for firearms, telescope sight mounting system for firearms, breech mech. sporting firearm, elec. switch activating system, 37 others, others pending. Active San Diego County Border Tsk Force on Undocumented Aliens, 1979-80, 81-82, mgr., rep. Island Gabrieleno Group, NAGPRA repatriation project, 1995—, historian Maritime Shoshone, 1995—, spokesman Island Shoshone, 1995—; bd. dirs. Nat. Geographic Soc., 1968. With U.S. Army, 1951-53. Recipient Superior Svc. Commendation award U.S. Naval Ordnance Test Station, Pasadena, 1959. Mem. AIAA (sr.), NRA (life), Calif. Rifle and Pistol Assn. (life), Soc. Automotive Engrs., San Diego Zool. Soc., The Wilderness Soc., Catalina Island Conservancy, The Nature Conservancy, Clan Stewart Soc. Am., Ducks Unlimited, Pechanga Band of Luiseno Indians (life), Cova, Catalina Island Mus. Soc., The Planetary Soc., Soc. for Calif. Archaeology, Skeptics Soc., North County Scots. Avocations: chess, music, archaeology, painting, sculpting. Home: Bonsall, Calif. Died Jan. 21, 2004.

JEFFRESS, JAMES VAN BUREN, JR., newspaper editor; b. Alhambra, Calif., Nov. 8, 1934; s. James Van Buren Sr. and Mildred Mae (Paine) J.; m. Mary Jane Jackson, Mar. 24, 1962; children: Laurie Jane, Jean Louise. Student, East L.A. Jr. Coll., 1957-58, L.A. State Coll., 1959-60. Make-up editor Brawley (Calif.) News, 1961-62; mng. editor Victor Press, Victorville, Calif., 1962-67; copy chief Daily Report, Ontario, Calif., 1967-71; copy editor, People editor Mercury News, San Jose, Calif., from 1972. Served with U.S. Army, 1953-56, Korea. Avocation: reading. Died Nov. 17, 2004.

JELLICO, JOHN ANTHONY, artist; b. Koehler, N.Mex., June 26, 1914; s. Michael and Matilda (Saban) J.; children: Janice, Carol, Kenneth. Diploma, Art Inst. Pitts., 1937; cert., Phoenix Art Inst., 1939. Illustration dept. head Art Inst. of Pitts., 1946-50, asst. dir., 1950-56; dir. Colo. Inst. of Art, Denver, 1956-62, pres., 1962-75. Co-owner art gallery, Santa Fe, N.Mex. Contbg. editor Am. Artist, N.Y.C., 1969-81; assoc. editor Southwestern Art, Austin, 1974-77; author: How to Draw Horses, 1946, 5 text books; executed murals St. Patrick's Ch., Raton, N.Mex., 1937, 3d Air Force Chapels, 1942-46. Staff sgt. USAF, 1942-46. Scholarship Art Inst. of Pitts., 1935; invited to hang four paintings at White House, 1975-77. Avocations: fishing, hiking, travel. Home: Littleton, Colo. Died May 20, 2004.

JELLINEK, MILES ANDREW, lawyer; b. Dec. 27, 1947; s. Alfred Marquis and Rena Elizabeth (Felberg) J.; m. Annabelle Francis O'Leary, Apr. 9, 1976; children: Beth Elise, Laura Anne. BA, U. Pa., 1969, JD, 1974. Bar: Pa. 1974, N.J. 1987. Law clk. Ct. Common Pleas, Phila., 1974-75; sr. mem. Cozen O'Connor, Phila., 1975—2006. Adj. instr. dept. legal studies Temple U., 2001—06; instr. Ins. Soc. Phila., 2005—06. Mem.: Germantown Cricket Club. Democrat. Jewish. Avocations: tennis, squash, golf, singing. Home: Merion Station, Pa. Died June 27, 2006.

JENNINGS, JERRY D., federal agency administrator; b. Flint, Mich., July 2, 1940; s. C. Oren and Retha S. (Wood) J.; m. Misako Sonoda, Oct. 10, 1976; children: Catherine, Victoria, Elizabeth. Student, Mott Community Coll., Flint, Mich., 1958-59, U. Mich., 1960; BS, Ea. Mich. U., 1961; student, John Jay Coll., CUNY, 1970-71, Harvard U., 1987. Intelligence officer CIA, Washington and S.E. Asia, 1965-68; spl. agt. FBI, Memphis, N.Y.C., 1968-72; spl. asst. to dir. Office Nat. Narcotics Intelligence Dept. Justice, Washington, 1972-73; staff mem. NSC, Washington, 1973-82; exec. dir. Office of Sci. and Tech. Policy and White House Sci. Coun., Washington, 1982-86; acting dir. Selective Svc. Sys., Washington, 1987, dep. dir., 1988—90; acting dir. Fed. Emergency Mgmt. Agy., Washington, 1990, dep. dir., 1991-92; chmn., chief exec. officer Phoenix Comm. and Rsch. Co., McLean, Va., 1993—2000; deputy asst. sec. def and dir. Def. POW/Missing Personnel Office, 2001—05. Served to Capt. USMC, 1961-65. Mem.: SAR, VFW (life), Mil. Order Carabao, Am. Legion (life), Army and Navy Club (Washington). Baptist. Avocations: tennis, skiing, chess. Home: Vienna, Va. Died July 22, 2006.

JENNINGS, TODD KYLE, investment banker; b. L.A., Mar. 10, 1949; s. William Randolph and Jeanne Burton (Englemann) J.; m. Mary Mallory Kountze, June 30, 1973; children: Barton, William, Mary Mallory. AB, Harvard Coll., 1971; MBA, Harvard U., 1973. Investment banker E.F. Hutton & Co. Inc, N.Y.C., 1973-82, group head, investment banking, mktg., 1982-87, dep. head, corp. fin. dept., 1987; pvt. practice investment banking N.Y.C., from 1988; co-owner The Alternate Network, Inc./Info./Entertainment Mktg., Cons., Old Greenwich, Conn., from 1989. Mem.: Round Hill (Greenwich, Conn.), Wianno (Osterville, Mass.). Home: New York, NY. Died Mar. 1, 2004.

JENSEN, HARLAN ELLSWORTH, veterinarian, educator; b. St. Ansgar, Iowa, Oct. 6, 1915; s. Bert and Mattie (Hansen) J.; m. Naomi Louise Geiger, June 7, 1941; children: Kendra Lee Jensen Belfi, Doris Eileen Jensen Futoma, Richard Harlan. DVM, Iowa State U., 1941; PhD, U. Mo., 1971. Diplomate: Charter diplomate Am. Coll. Vet. Ophthalmologists (v.p. 1970-72, pres. 1972-73). Vet. practice, Galesburg, Ill., 1941-46; small animal internship New Brunswick, N.J., 1946-47; small animal practice Cleve., 1947-58, San Diego, 1958-62, Houston, 1962-67; mem. faculty U. Mo., Columbia, 1967-80, chief ophthalmology, 1967-80, prof. emeritus Vet. Sch., from 1980, assoc. prof. ophthalmology Med. Sch., 1972-80. Cons. in vet. ophthalmology to pharm. firms; guest lectr., prof. ophthalmology Vet. Sch. U. Utrecht, The Netherlands, 1973; tchr., lectr. various vet. meetings; condr. seminar World Congress Small Animal Medicine and Surgery, 1973, 77. Author: Stereoscopic Atlas of Clinical Ophthalmology of Domestic Animals, 1971, Stereoscopic Atlas of Ophthalmic Surgery of Domestic Animals, 1974; co-author: Stereoscopic Atlas of Soft Tissue Surgery of Small Animals, 1973, Clinical Dermatology of Small Animals, 1974; contbr. articles to profl. jours. Recipient Gaines award AVMA, 1973 Mem. Am. Vet. Radiology Soc. (pres. 1956-57), Am. Vet. Ophthalmology Soc. (pres. 1960-62), Farm House Frat., Rotary (pres. Pacific Beach, Calif. 1960-62, pres. Columbia 1977-78), Sigma Xi, Phi Kappa Phi, Phi Zeta, Gamma Sigma Delta. Mem. Bible Ch. Achievements include invention of instrument for ear trimming in dogs, 1949, breathing apparatus, 1953; designer sound proof animal hosps.; developer 3-D study program for vet. ophthalmology, 1969. Home: Fort Worth, Tex. Died Dec. 30, 2005.

JESSUP, JOE LEE, business educator, management consultant; b. Cordele, Ga., June 23, 1913; s. Horace Andrew and Elizabeth (Wilson) J.; m. Janet Amis, Apr. 16, 1989. BS, U. Ala., 1936; MBA, Harvard U., 1941; LLD (hon.), Chung-Ang U., Seoul, Korea, 1964. Sales rep. Proctor & Gamble, 1937-40; liaison officer bur. pub. rels. U.S. War Dept., 1941; spl. asst. and exec. asst. Far Ea. div. and office exports Bd. Econ. Warfare, 1942-43; exec. officer to chief of staff Svcs. of Supply-Europian Theatre, 1943-44; exec. officer, office deptl. adminstrn. Dept. State, 1946; exec. sec. adminstr.'s adv. coun. War Assets Adminstrn., 1946-48; v.p. sales Airken, Capitol & Service Co., 1948-52; assoc. prof. bus. adminstrn. George Washington U., 1952, prof., 1952-77, prof. emeritus, from 1977, asst. dean Sch. Govt., 1951-60; pres. Jessup and Co., Ft. Lauderdale, Fla., 1957—2002. Bd. dirs. Giant Food, Inc., Washington, mem. audit com., 1971—75; bd. dirs. Hunter Assn. Labs., Fairfax, Va., mem. exec. com., 1966—69, exec. v.p., 1967, coord. Air Force Regources Mgmt. program, 1951—57; del. in edn. 10th Internat. Mgmt. Conf., Sao Paulo, Brazil, 1954, 11th Internat. Mgmt. Conf., Paris, 1957, 12th Internat. Mgmt. Conf., Sydney and Melbourne, Australia, 1960, 13th Internat. Mgmt. Conf., Rotterdam, The Netherlands, 1966, 14th Internat. Mgmt. Conf., Tokyo, 1969, 15th Internat. Mgmt. Conf., Munich, 1972; mem. Md. Econ. Devel. Adv. Commn., 1973—75. Mem. Civil Svc. Commn., Arlington County, Va., 1973—75; trustee Tng. Within Industry Found., Summit, NJ, 1954—58; mem. bd. overseers Lynn U., Boca Raton, Fla., 1991—2002; mem. adv. bd. Youth Automotive Tng. Ctr., Hollywood, Fla., from 1993; trustee Philharm. Orch., Fla., 1986—91; mem. nat. adv. coun. Ctr. Study of Presidency, 1974—99; mem. Atlanta regional panel selection of White House fellow, 1990—95, mem. Miami regional panel. Decorated Bronze Star; recipient cert. of appreciation Sec. of Air Force, 1957 Mem.: Royal Palm Yacht and Country Club, Univ. Club (Washington), Harvard Club (N.Y.C.). Home: Boca Raton, Fla. Died Jan. 31, 2006.

JIMENEZ, LUIS ALFONSO, JR., sculptor; b. El Paso, Tex., July 30, 1940; s. Luis Alfonso and Alicia (Franco) J.; m. Susan Brockman; children: Elisa Victoria, Luis Adan, Juan Orion, Sarah Alicia Xochil. BS in Art and Architecture, U. Tex., Austin, 1964; postgrad., Ciudad U., Mexico City, 1964. Exhibited in one-man shows, including, Graham Gallery, N.Y.C., 1969-70, O.K. Harris Works of Art, N.Y.C., 1972-75, Contemporary Arts Mus., Houston, 1974, Mus. of N.Mex., Santa Fe, 1980, Frumkin Struve, Chgo., 1981, Adeliza's Candy Store Gallery, Folsom, Calif., 1983, Phyllis Kind Gallery, N.Y.C., 1984, Moody Gallery, Houston, 1995, 2002, Scottsdale Cultural Arts Ctr., retrospective Nat. Mus. Am. Art, Washington, 1994, Marsha Mateyka Gallery, Washington, 1994, Adair Margo Gallery, El Paso, Tex., 1995, A.C.A. Galleries, N.Y.C., 1998, Working Class Heroes: Images from the Popular Culture, traveling retrospective, opened Dallas, Dallas Mus. Art 1997, Palm Springs Mus. Art, 1998, Blaffier Mus., Houston, Mex. Fine Arts Ctr. Mus., 2000, Man on Fire retrospective Albuquerque Mus. Art, 1994; exhibited in group shows, including, Human Concern Personal Torment, Whitney Mus., N.Y., 1969, Nat. Mus. Am. Art, Washington, 1980, Albuquerque Mus., 1980, Edinburgh (Scotland) Festival, 1980, Walker Art Center, Mpls., 1980, U. Minn., Mpls., 1981, Roswell Mus. and Art Ctr., N. Mex., 1984, Albright-Knox Art Mus., Buffalo, N.Y., Hirshhorn Mus. and Sculpture Garden, Smithsonian Instn., Washington, Hispanic Art in the U.S., 1988, Hispanic Arts in the U.S. traveling show, 1987-89, Latin Am. Spirit in the U.S., 1989, Committed To Print, Mus. Modern Art, N.Y.C., 1989, Whitney Biennial, N.Y.C., 1991, New Mus., N.Y.C., Art of the Other Mex. traveling exhibit, 1993, 20 Yrs. of Landfall Prints, Whitney Mus., 1997, Arte Latino, traveling Smithsonian Inst. exhibit, 2000-06; represented in permanent collections, Smithsonian Am. Art Mus., Anderson Mus. Contemporary Art, Roswell N.M., Witte Mus., San Antonio, Long Beach (Calif.) Mus., New Orleans Mus. Art, Roswell (N. Mex.) Mus. and Art Center, Sheldon Meml. Gallery, Lincoln, Nebr., Art Inst. Chgo., Met. Mus. Art, N.Y.C., Smithsonian Instn., Mus. Modern Art, Albuquerque Mus. Art, Fed. Reserve Bank, Dallas, Fine Arts Mus., Santa Fe, U. Texas, San Antonio, U. N.Mex., Albuquerque, Whitney Mus., also pvt. collections; works include Vaquero Sculpture, Moody Park, Houston, 1977; Nat. Endowment for Arts and City of Houston Sodbuster sculpture, Fargo, N.D., 1977; Southwest Pietà, Nat. Endowment for Arts commn. Art in Pub. Places, City of Albuquerque, 1981; Steel Worker, Nat. Endowment for Arts, La Salle Sta., Buffalo,

N.Y.; Niagara Frontier, Transp. Authority Commn.; Howl, Wichita State U., Kans., 1983; Border Crossing, Otis Art Inst. of Parsons Sch. Design, Los Angeles, 1984; Fiesta Dancers, Gen. Services Adminstrn., Otay Mesa, Calif., 1986; sculpture commn. NEA and City of El Paso, 1986, Plaza de los Lagartos, Horton Plz., San Diego, 1986, City of Las Vegas, 1989, New Denver Airport, 1991, Firefighters, Cleve., 1996, sculpture commn. U. OK, Norman, OK, 1998. Recipient Steuben Glass award 1972, Hassam Fund award Am. Acad. Arts and Letters, 1977, Awards in Visual Arts, 1985, Greenburger Found. award, 1987, Showhegan sculpture award, 1989, Gov.'s award State of N.Mex., 1993, Award of Distinction Nat. Coun. of Art Adminstrs., 1995; named goodwill amb. City of Houston, 1993, 98, Tex. Artist of Yr., Houston Art League, 1998, Distinguished Alumni, Univ. Tex. and Austin; fellow Nat. Endowment Arts, 1987, 88, Am. Acad. in Rome, 1979, La Napoule Art Found. and Nat. Endowment Arts residency fellow, 1990; S.W. Pieta sculpture designated U.S. Nat. Treasure, 1999; grantee Fund for Am. Culture, 1999. Died June 13, 2006.

JOHNSON, ALICE ELAINE, retired academic administrator; b. Janesville, Wis., Oct. 9, 1929; d. Floyd C. and Alma M. (Walthers) Chester; m. Richard C. Johnson, Sept. 25, 1948 (div. 1974); children: Randall S., Nile C., Linnea E. BA, U. Colo., 1968. Pres., administrator Pikes Peak Inst. Med. Tech., Colorado Springs, Colo., 1968-88. Mem. adv. com. to Colo. Commn. on Higher Edn., 1979-80, State Adv. Coun. on Pvt. Occupational Schs., Denver, 1978-86; mem. tech. adv. com. State Health Occupations, 1986-88; bd. dirs. All Souls Unitarian Ch., Colorado Springs, 1990-96, mem. celebration team, 1990-91, pres. bd. trustees, 1991-93. Mem. Colo. Pvt. Sch. Assn. (pres. 1981-82, bd. dirs. 1976-88, Outstanding Mem. 1978, 80), Phi Beta Kappa. Democrat. Unitarian Universalist. Avocations: writing, travel, reading. Home: Hays, Kans. Died Feb. 17, 2004.

JOHNSON, BURDETTE AUSTIN, utilities executive, consultant; b. Hampton, N.H., Oct. 6, 1905; s. Joseph Austin and Annie Abbie (Shaw) J.; m. Helen Eunice Richardson, June 26, 1929 (dec.); children: Burdette Austin Jr. (dec.), Laurie Bertha McCanne. AB, Harvard, Cambridge, Mass., 1927; degree in Advanced Utility Mgmt., U. Mich., Ann Arbor, 1957. Treas. White Mt. Power Co., Meredith, N.H., 1929-37; with Commonwealth Energy System, Cambridge, from 1937, fin. v.p., 1958-75, mem. bd. trustees, 1975-81, officer and dir., 1949-75, cons., from 1981. Chmn. USICO Ins. Co., Bermuda, 1968-81; dir. Delta Dental Ins., Medford, Mass., 1975—; pres. New England Gas Assn., Needham, Mass., 1966-67, Fin. Exec. Inst. Boston, 1955-56, Treas.'s Club of Boston. Author: History of the Commonwealth Energy System, 1982; contbr. articles to jours. in field. Chmn. and dir. Am. Congregational Assn., Boston, 1984—; pres. Rotary Internat., Meredith, N.H., 1935, Cambridge, 1975; chmn. Cambridge Partnership for Pub. Edn., 1985; pres. Cambridge YMCA, 1973-75. Recipient Hon. Mem. award Treasurer's Club of Boston, 1975, Disting. Svc. award Cambridge C. of C., 1985, SMB award Cambridge YMCA, 1993. Mem. Fin. Execs. Inst. (pres., Boston treas.), Harvard Club of Boston, Harvard Club of N.Y.C., Masonic Orgns. (chmn. investment com.), Salvation Army (past chmn., Others award 1984), Harvard Faculty Club. Republican. Avocations: gardening, y exercising. Home: Weston, Mass. Died Jan. 2, 2005.

JOHNSON, BYRON, lawyer; b. Rochester, N.Y., June 17, 1915; s. Byron Arthur Johnson and Marjorie Huntington (Gardner) Sallisbury; m. Cynthia Montgomery Hogle Little, June 7, 1941 (div. Jan. 1971); children: Cynthia Montgomery Johnson Goulard, Winthrop Dow; m. Jane Evans Hartwell, Mar. 22, 1973. AB, Hamilton Coll., 1936; JD, Yale U., 1939; MBA, Harvard U., 1939. V.p. and gen. mgr. E.W. Edwards & Son dept. store, Rochester, Syracuse, Buffalo, N.Y., 1956-61; pres. 1st Nat. Bank of Rochester, N.Y., 1967-68; ptnr. Johnson Mullan Brundage PC and predecessor firms, Rochester, N.Y., from 1940; pres. Johnson, Mullen, Brundage, PC and predecessor firms, Rochester, N.Y., from 1970. Bd. trustees Rochester Inst. Tech., 1958—; pres. Boy Scouts Am. Oletiono Coun., ochester, 1958-59. Lt. comdr. USN, 1941-45, ETO, PTO. Mem. N.Y. Bar Assn., Fla. Bar Assn., Pa. Bar Assn., Monroe County Bar Assn. Home: Rochester, NY. Died July 3, 2005.

JOHNSON, CHARLES ALLEN, surgeon; b. Hickory, N.C., Feb. 19, 1938; s. Robert Lee and Daisy (Sain) J.; children: Charles Allen Jr., Tracy Elaine, David Ted. AB in Chemistry, Duke U., 1959, MD, 1964. Diplomate Am. Bd. Surgery, Am. Bd. Thoracic Surgery. Intern in surgery Washington U. Sch. Medicine Barnes Hosp., St. Louis, 1964-65, resident in surgery, 1965-69, chief resident cardiothoracic and cardiovascular surgery, 1968-69; practice medicine specializing in gen., thoracic and cardiovascular surgery Sarasota, Fla., 1969-80; sr. resident thoracic cardiovascular surgery Charlotte (N.C.) Meml. Hosp. and Med. Ctr., 1981; practice medicine specializing in cardiac, thoracic and vascular surgery Huntsville, Ala., 1982, Sarasota, from 1982. Chmn., mem. Sarasota County Pub. Hosp. Bd., 1975, 76, 85; bd. dirs. Fla. Life Care, Inc.; trustee West Cen. Fla. PSRO, Sarasota, 1978-81. Fellow ACS, Am. Coll. Cardiology, Am. Coll. Chest Physicians; mem. AMA, The Soc. Thoracic Surgeons, So. Thoracic Surg. Assn., Fla. Soc. Thoracic and Cardiovascular Surgeons, Am. Heart Assn. (mem. council on cardiovascular surgery), Soc. Clin. Vascular Surgery, Sarasota County Med. Soc. Clubs: Field (Sarasota). Republican. Methodist. Avocations: tennis, flying. Home: Sarasota, Fla. Died June 11, 2004.

JOHNSON, CRANE, writer, lawyer; b. Bayard, Nebr., June 30, 1921; s. Carl Arthur and Pearl (Haskins) J. MA, U. So. Calif., 1948; postgrad., Stanford U., 1949; PhD, Case We. Res. U., 1960; LLB, N.Y. Law Sch., 1960; LLM, NYU, 1968. Bar: N.Y., 1962. Vol. legal aid lawyer. Author: Past Sixty, 1953, The Withered Garland, 1956, Seven Short Plays, 1965, Tiger In Crystal, 1966, Seven Shorter Plays, 1966, Seven Strange Plays, 1966, Twenty-Five One Act Plays, 1966, Ten One Act Plays, 1967, Thirty-Five One Act Plays, 1967, Venus Preserved, 1971, The Locusts, 1971, Dracula, 1976, Presque Isle Village, 1995, Three Jacumba Tales, 1998, Ten Stories, 1999, Twelve Jacumba Tales, 1999, Jacumba Heidi, 2000, Buckboard to Jacumba, 2001, Mountain Springs Saga, 2002, Seven Jacumba Tales, 2003, Letters From Miss Ellen, 2004, El Meson de Los Naranjitos, 2005; author of over 50 plays. U.S. rep. at ednl. confs. in London and Vienna. Served with AUS, WWII. Mem. N.Y. Bar Assn. Died Feb. 2006.

JOHNSON, DAVID PITTMAN, psychotherapy consultant, social work educator; b. Nashville, July 29, 1936; s. Calvin Leonard (Count de Valona) and Charles Bernice (Cagle) J. (Countess de Valona); m. Edna Marie Wooten; 1 child, Michael David; m. Linda June Russell; 1 child, Christopher David Leonard. BS, Huntingdon Coll., 1963; MSW, Tulane U., 1966, DSW, 1972. Clin. social worker Montgomery (Ala.) Mental Health Center, 1966-69; dir. Christian Counseling Center, New Orleans, 1971-72; dir. outpatient svcs. Montgomery Area Mental Health Authority, 1972-75; pvt. practice psychotherapy clin. cons., Montgomery and Tuscaloosa, Ala., 1974—; assoc. prof. clin. social work U. Ala., 1975—. Former editor: Armiger's News; editor: The Heraldic Register of Am., Orthodox Chivalry. Fellow Am. Coll. Heraldry (founder, bd. govs. 1972—); mem. Heraldry Soc. (Eng.) Heraldry Soc. Scotland, Nat. Soc. SAR (nat. geneal. com.), St. Andrew's Soc. of Tuscaloosa (founding pres.), Sovereign Greek Order St. Dennis of Zante, Knightly Assn. St. George the Martyr, Order of St. John of Jerusalem, Holy Orthodox Order of St. Basil the Great, Order Constantini Magni, Noble Co. Rose. Clan Johnston-e of Am. Democrat. Mem. Orthodox Ch. in Am. Home: Tuscaloosa, Ala. Died Mar. 8, 2004.

JOHNSON, EDITH SCOTT, language educator, writer, consultant; b. Nashville, Ga., Mar. 25, 1943; d. James O'Leary and Edith Scott (Strother) Fuller; m. David James Moore, Feb. 4, 1962 (div. Sept. 1968); children: Meg Moore Bragdon, Marijim Moore Reeves; m. James Carter Johnson, Nov. 22, 1969 (div. June 1975); 1 child, James Carter III. BA in Art and English, Valdosta (Ga.) State Coll., 1968; MA in English, U. Nev., Reno, 1990; PhD in English, Ga. State U., Atlanta, 1997. Test code writer Westinghouse Air Brake Co., Lexington, Ky., 1962-64; rsch. asst. U. Ky., Lexington, 1964-67; songwriter, recording artist Dove and Commanchee Records, Nashville, 1967-74; adminstrv. coord. devel. studies Ga. State U., Atlanta, 1976-80; asst. dir. PACE program U. Nev., Reno, 1985-88, asst. dir. writing ctr., 1988-90, adj. instr. English, 1989-91; asst. prof. English Abraham Baldwin Coll., Tifton, Ga., from 1991; instr. English Moultrie (Ga.) Tech. Coll., from 2002. Writing cons. Crisp Area Arts Alliance, Cordele, Ga., 1996-97; resident poet Abraham Baldwin Coll., 1995-97; rschr. Ga. State U., Atlanta, 1991-97. Author: Driftwood and Wintergreen, 1996 (Internat. Poet award Internat. Soc. Poets), Cold Hearts and Glass Eyes, 1997 (1st class award Ga. State U.), Images of Love and Ice, 1998, The Evening Wolves, 1998, The Toolbox, 2002; contbg. poet: World of Poetry, 1985 (Golden Poet award 1985), Iliad Press, 1995-96 (Poet of Yr. award 1995-96); performer Arts Experiment Sta., Tifton, 1996-97; poetry reader The Magpie Shop, Art Dept. Cornwall (Eng.) Coll., 1996. Tchr. bible Trinity United Meth. Ch., Tifton, 1997. Collected works dedicated in her honor Crisp Area Arts Alliance, Cordele, 1997. Mem. Nat. Coun. Tchrs. English, Nat. Assn. for Devel. Edn. (presenter, presider 1991-97), Nat. Authors' Registry. Avocations: dulcimer, piano, guitar, singing, landscape and portrait art. Home: Moultrie, Ga. Died Apr. 30, 2004.

JOHNSON, GARY PAUL, education educator; b. Seattle, Feb. 5, 1944; s. Paul Johnson and Dorothy (Gravert) Bullock; m. Teresa Mantz; children: Joy, Jay. BA, Central Wash. State U., 1966; MA, SUNY, Buffalo, 1968; DEd, W.Va. U., 1972. Dir. mgmt. and adminstrv. studies Appalachian Ctr., W.Va. U., Morgantown, 1970-71; asst. prof., then assoc. prof. Pa. State U., University Park, 1971-81; assoc. prof. St. John's U., Jamaica, N.Y., 1981-84, Ark. State U., Jonesboro, 1985-88, Bowling Green (Ohio) State U., 1988-91, Miss. State U., Starkville, from 1991. Sch. fin. cons. to various govtl. orgns. and assns. Collaborator Educating for Careers, 1977; mem. editorial adv. bd. Jour. Edn. Fin., 1977-80, spl. publs. editor, 1981-83; contbr. articles to profl. jours. Mem. Am. Ednl. Fin. Assn., Am. Ednl. Rsch. Assn., Ohio Assn. Sch. Bus. Officials, Nat. Ctr. for Effective Schs., Buckeye Assn. Sch. Adminstrs., Phi Delta Kappa. Avocations: fishing, photography, racquetball. Died Mar. 23, 2005.

JOHNSON, GENE ALLEN, retired municipal environmental administrator; b. Nashville, Nov. 6, 1936; s. Percy Allen and Elizabeth (Russell) J.; m. Melba Sue Wallace, Dec. 24, 1955 (div. 1965); 1 child, Gene A. Jr. (dec.); m. Mary Lynn Whittle, May 25, 1967; 1 child, Elizabeth L. B in Engring., Vanderbilt U., 1957. Diplomate Am. Acad. Environ. Engrs.; profl. engr., Tenn.; registered land surveyor. Sanitary engr. Tenn. Dept. Health, Nashville, 1957-61; cons. engr. Hickerson, Adams & Johnson, Nashville, 1961-63; wastewater treatment engr. dept. water and sewer services Met. Govt. Nashville, 1963-73, chief engr., 1973-80, asst. dir., 1980-88, assoc. dir., 1988-94, A/E contract adminstr. dept. fin., 1994-96, ret., 1996; pres. Consol. Engring. Techs., Waverly, Tenn., 1996-98; dir. water and wastewater dept. City of Dickson, Tenn., from 1998. Mem. Am. Waterworks Assn., Water Environ. Fedn. Baptist. Avocations: hunting, fishing. Died Mar. 26, 2005.

JOHNSON, HAROLD CUMINGS, educator, music director, retired air force officer; b. Lansing, Mich., Dec. 12, 1933; s. Harold Eugene and Mary (Cumings) J.; m. Marion Frye, Aug. 21, 1954; children: Robin Ann, Gary Cumings, Gregory Harold. MusB, U. Mich., 1955, MusM, 1957; postgrad., U. Dayton, 1985-86. Cert. elem. and secondary tchr., Ohio. Commd. 2nd lt. USAF, 1952, advanced through grades to lt. col., 1957; comdr. 3d USAF Band, London, 1959-63, Mil. Airlift Command Band, Scott AFB, Ill., 1965-69, USAF Europe Band, Wiesbaden, Fed. Republic Germany, 1969-75, USAF Band of Flight, Wright Patterson AFB, Ohio, 1975-85; ret. USAF, 1985; instr. Sinclair Community Coll., Dayton, Ohio, from 1985; minister of music First Presbyn. Ch., Fairborn, Ohio, from 1985; tchr. Mary Help of Christians Sch., Fairborn, from 1986. Instr. music theory USAF 661st Band, Wright Patterson AFB, 1987—. Author: Dazzler, 1966; composer band concert pieces; arranger band music USAF, 1965-85. Mem. Dayton Choirmasters; pres. Tecumseh coun. Boy Scouts Am., 1987-89; sec. First Frontier, Inc., Xenia, Ohio, 1987—. Recipient Silver Beaver award Boy Scouts Am., 1982. Mem. Nat. Band Assn., Ohio Music Educators Assn., Music Educators Nat. Conf., Dayton Musicians Assn., Rotary (pres. 1985-86), Masons. Home: Wichita, Kans. Died July 26, 2004.

JOHNSON, JOSEPH EDWARD, microcomputer sales and services executive; b. Mt. Holly, N.J., Apr. 30, 1932; s. James Edward and Christine DeKalb (Hatcher) J. BSEE, Rutgers U., 1954; postgrad., Cornell U. Engr. Bell Telephone Labs., Inc., Whippany, N.J., 1955-64, Holmdel, N.J., 1972-82, Bellcomm., Inc., Washington, 1964-72; v.p. Bit Processing, Inc., Princeton, N.J., from 1982. Editor: (mag.) Rutgers Engineer, 1953 (Gold R award 1954). Recipient NASA Apollo Achievement award, 1969. Mem. AIAA, World Future Soc., Tau Beta Pi, Eta Kappa Nu. Republican. Episcopalian. Avocations: astrophysics, investing, geopolitics, travel, sports. Home: Spring Lake Heights, NJ. Died Jan. 6, 2004.

JOHNSON, KEITH RONALD, obstetrician/gynecologist; b. Chgo., Mar. 19, 1929; s. Clarence Albert and Alma Alice (Semrad) J.; m. Esther Louise Rieve, June 26, 1954; children: Robert, Jeffrey, Cynthia. BS, U. Ill., 1950; MD, U. Ill., Chgo., 1954. Diplomate Am. Bd. Obstetrics and Gynecology. Intern L.A. City Hosp., 1954-55; resident in ob/gyn San Diego County Gen. Hosp./Mercy Hosp., 1957-60; pvt. practice specializing in ob/gyn. La Mesa, Calif., from 1960. Lt. USNR, 1955-57. Fellow Am. Coll. Obstetricians and Gynecologists, Internat. Coll. Surgeons; mem. Calif. Med. Assn., San Diego Med. Assn., Am. Assn. Gynecol. Laparoscopists, Rotary. Republican. Avocations: tennis, gardening, model railroading, sailing. Home: El Cajon, Calif. Died May 6, 2005.

JOHNSON, KENNETH MICHAEL, sociology and demography educator; b. Flint, Mich., June 23, 1950; s. Delmar Lawrence and Gloria Marie (Swanson) J.; m. Brenda Gail Pierce, Aug. 14, 1976; children: Christopher Michael, Matthew James. BA, U. Mich., 1972; MA, U. N.C., 1975, PhD, 1980. Instr. Loyola U. Chgo., 1976-79, asst. prof., 1980-85, assoc. prof. sociology and anthropology, 1986-93; prof., from 1993; pres. Applied Demographic Rsch. Group, Inc., from 1989. Demographic cons. McDonald's Corp., Oak Brook, Ill., 1981-89, Budget Rent a Car Corp., Chgo., 1981-89. Author: The Impact of Demographic Change on Rural Business, 1985; contbr. articles to profl. jours. Grantee U.S. Dept. Agr., 1990-92, 92-94. Mem. Population Assn. Am., Am. Sociol. Assn., Rural Sociol. Soc. Home: Arlington Heights, Ill. Died Feb. 29, 2004.

JOHNSON, M. EARL, clergyman, administrator; b. Kandiohy, Minn., Feb. 11, 1928; s. Alvin Victor Emmanuel and Rose Evangeline (Peterson) J.; m. Darliene Joyce Morken, June 7, 1949; children: Billy Bryant, Jacque Lynn, Robert Anthony, Wendi Lee. Diploma, North Ctrl. Bible Coll., Mpls., 1950; postgrad., U. Oreg., 1954-58. Ordained to ministry Assemblies of God Ch., 1950. Pastor Assemblies of God Ch., Pelican Rapids, Minn., 1950-52, Granada, Minn., 1952-54; coll. tchr. Open Bible Standard, Eugene, Oreg., 1954-58; min. of music Bethel Temple, Assemblies of God, Sacramento, 1958-65; pastor Assemblies of God, Downey, Calif., 1965-68, Bethel Ch. Assemblies of God, Redding, Calif., 1968-82; exec. officer No. Calif./Nev. Dist. Coun., Inc. Assemblies of God, Santa Cruz, Calif., from 1982. Trustee Bethany Coll., Santa Cruz, 1978—, Am. Indian Bible Coll., Phoenix, 1983—; chmn. bd. trustees Asian Pacific Bible Sch., L.A., 1989—. Republican. Avocations: computers, physical fitness. Died Jan. 16, 2004.

JOHNSON, MARVIN RICHARD ALOIS, architect, consultant; b. Humphrey, Nebr., Aug. 13, 1916; s. Otto Henry and Reenste (Berends) J. AB, U. Nebr., 1943, BA in Architecture, 1943; M.Architecture, Harvard U., 1948. Designer, draftsman firm Clark & Enersen, Lincoln, Nebr., 1946-47, 48-50; cons. architect div. sch. planning N.C. Dept. Public Instrn., Raleigh, 1950-80; architect, cons. ednl. facilities, from 1981. Cons. HEW, Washington, 1960 Contbr. articles to profl. jours. Served with USNR, 1943-46. Fellow AIA (recipient Distinguished Service citation N.C.

chpt. 1960, v.p. N.C. chpt. 1977-78, pres.-elect 1979, pres. 1980); mem. Council Ednl. Facility Planners, Am. Assn. School Adminstrs., Phi Beta Kappa. Democrat. Lutheran. Home: Lincoln, Nebr. Died Jan. 30, 2006.

JOHNSON, MARY TEEL, pianist, educator; b. Warsaw, Ind., Sept. 28, 1921; d. William Rollin and Leona Gladys (Haines) Teel; m. Delman Howard Johnson, June 1, 1946; 1 child, Spencer Teel. BA in Piano and Music Edn., Wash. State U., 1943; M in Piano, L.A. Conservatory, 1951-52; studies with Madame Rosina Lhevinne, L.A., 1951-52. Jr. high music and Am. history tchr. Tacoma (Wash.) Pub. Sch. System, 1943-44; pvt. piano tchr. Tacoma, 1944-50, San Gabriel, Arcadia, Calif., 1950-63, Mpls., 1963-84; musician, writer Monterey, Calif., from 1984. Am. history vol. Monterey Peninsula Unified Sch. Dist., 1985-88; speaker Minn. Music Tchrs. Assn., Mpls, 1986, Steinway & Sons, N.Y.C., 1987, Calif. Music Tchrs. Assn., Monterey, 1987, 88, AZ Music Tchrs. Assn., Phoenix, 1990. Author: Keys to Successful Piano Lessons, 1986. Solicitor, presenter commemorative prints of Statue of Liberty and Signing of Constitution to all pvt. and pub. schs. on Monterey Peninsula, 1987. Recipient State and Nat. Am. Heritage award DAR, 1986, Best Chpt. Program award, DAR, 1987, Resolution of Appreciation Bd. Edn. Monterey Peninsula Unified Sch. Dist., 1986. Mem. DAR, Monterey County Symphony Guild (officer 1984—). Republican. Avocations: reading, piano, writing, speaking to orgns. Home: Monterey, Calif. Died Mar. 8, 2004.

JOHNSON, MICHAEL JOSEPH, military officer; b. Deerbourne, Mich., Apr. 5, 1963; s. Harry Willis and Susannah Teresea (Burns) J.; m. Joan Elizabeth Becker, Apr. 21, 1990; 1 child, Michael Joseph Johnson Jr. BS in Aviation Mgmt., Met. State Coll., 1985; postgrad., Averett Coll. Commd. 2d lt. USMC, 1985, advanced through grades to capt., 1991; bat. liaison officer, platoon comdr., co. exec. officer Co. I, 3rd Bat., 1st Marines, 1992-94; exec. officer Hdqrs. Co. 1st Marines, 1990, comdg. officer, 1990-91; S-3A for ops., platoon comdr., leadership officer 148th officer candidates course; acad. officer Officer Candidates Sch., Quantico, Va., 1991-94. Republican. Epsicopalian. Avocations: volleyball, rugby, harley-davidson. Home: Quantico, Va. Died July 18, 2004.

JOHNSON, OLIN CHESTER, education educator; b. Phila., Sept. 19, 1941; s. Benjamin F. and Eva M. Johnson; m. Vernetta Dudley, Nov. 22, 1964; children: Quanda, Olin Jr. BS, Cheyney State Coll., 1965; MEd, Temple U., 1969; MS, U. Pa., 1972. Cert. elem. edn., social studies, elem. prin., secondary prin., supt., Pa. Tchr. Phila. Sch. Dist., 1965-68, supr., 1968-72, dir., coord. urban career ednl. ctr., 1973-75, prin., from 1976, William Bryant Sch., 1977-80, Charles R. Drew Sch., from 1981. Mem. secondary sch. com. U. Pa., Phila.; adj. asst. prof. Drexel U., Phila., 1989—, mem. ednl. adv. com. Chmn. Cmty. Concern 13, Inc., 1970—, B.F. Johnson Scholarship Fund, 1971—; vice-chmn. Phila. M.H. Multi-Purpose Learning Ctr., 1975-85; bd. dirs. Open Door Bapt. Ch.; exec. adminstr. B.F. Johnson Found., 1989—. Recipient award Nat. Tchr. Corp., 1970, Four Chaplains Cmty. Svc. award, 1971, 73, Phila. Prin. Merit award Phila. Sch. Dist. #1, 1978, OIC commendation, 1973, Pa. Dept. Edn. Planning and Testing citation, 1987, Prin. Outstanding Leadership C.R. Drew award, 1987, Strawbridge Civic award, 2001; Ford Found. fellow U. Pa., 1971-74. Mem. Am. Assn. Sch. Adminstrs., Pa. Congress Sch. Adminstrs., Phi Delta Kappa, Kappa Alpha Psi. Died Mar. 10, 2004.

JOHNSON, PATRICIA HARDY, early childhood specialist pre-school provider; b. Washington, Sept. 14, 1933; d. Dennis and Ira Bell (McGarrah) Hardy. BS, Miners Tchrs. Coll., Washington, D.C., 1955; MA, NYU, 1962; EdD, U.S. Internat. U., San Diego, 1989. Cert. tchr. elem. physically handicapped, mentally handicapped, learning handicapped, supervision, sch. psychologist, adminstrn. Resource specialist L.A. Unified Sch. Dist., 1981-84; asst. prin. L.A. Child Guidance Clin., 1984-86, prin., 1986-89; owner, pres. Raintree Inn, Inc., L.A., from 1985. Author: Raintree Inn Incorporated's Complete Child Care Center's Curriculum Guide, 0-27 Months; contbr. articles to profl. jours. Mem. usher bd. and hospitality com. Eternal Promise Bapt. Ch., L.A. Spl. Edn. grantee State of Calif.; numerous fellowships received from Univs. Mem. NAFE, Am. Assn. Ret. Persons, NYU Alumni, UCLA Alumni, Beta Pi Sigma, Gamma Theta Upsilon. Democrat. Avocations: gourmet cooking, travel. Home: Huntington Park, Calif. Died July 4, 2005.

JOHNSON, PHYLLIS, retired engineering draftsman; b. Seneca, Kans., June 5, 1923; d. Paul Eugene and Emily (Burger) J. BA, U. Wash., 1950. With Boeing Airplane Co., Seattle, from 1942, jr. engr., 1945-51, drafter, 1951-88. Mem. Seattle Profl. Engring. Employees Assn., Boeing Employees Travel Club (sec. 1974-76). Republican. Avocations: reading, travel. Home: Seattle, Wash. Died Feb. 11, 2005.

JOHNSON, RICHARD JAMES VAUGHAN, retired publishing executive; b. San Luis, Potosi, Mex., Sept. 22, 1930; s. Clifton Whatford and Myrtle Louise (Hinman) Johnson; m. Belle Beraud Griggs, Aug. 6, 1955; children: Shelley Beraud, Mark Hinman. BBA, U. Tex., Austin, 1954. Asst. to exec. dir. Tex. Daily Newspaper Assn., 1955—56; with Houston Chronicle Pub. Co., 1956—2002, chmn., 2000—02, ret., 2002. Chmn., CEO, dir. Robert A. Welch Found.; bd. visitors M.D. Anderson Cancer Ctr.; bd. dir. Tex. Med. Ctr. With U.S. Army, 1952—54. Mem.: Am. Newspaper Pubs. Assn, (past pres. and chmn.), Tex. Daily Newspaper Assn. (pres. 1978), Houston Club, River Oaks Country Club. Unitarian Universalist. Died Jan. 14, 2006.

JOHNSON, ROBERT ALAN, chemical engineer; b. Salt Lake City, Apr. 4, 1923; s. J. Herman and Hazel Florence (Woodruff) J.; m. Helen Patricia Colberg, July 23, 1948; children: Brian W., Cynthia A. Johnson Smalley, David S. BSChemE, U. Nebr., 1947. Registered profl. engr., Calif. Employee Standard Oil Co., Whiting, Ind., 1947-50, Casper, Wyo., 1950-57, project chem. engr. Whiting, Ind., 1957-61; prin. process engr. CF Braun & Co., Alhambra, Calif., 1961-88; chief process engr. RM Parsons Co., Pasadena, Calif., from 1988. Deacon, ruling elder La Canada Presbyn. Ch., 1975. Mem. Am. Inst. Chem. Engrs., Am. Chem. Soc., Casper Engrs. Club (founder 1954, pres. 1957), Sigma Xi, Sigma Phi Epsilon, Pi Mu Epsilon. Home: La Canada Flintridge, Calif. Died July 11, 2005.

JOHNSTON, MARSHA M., neuro-medical-cardiology nurse; b. Fargo, N.D., May 20, 1955; d. Edward Glenn and Anna Boyd (Masterson) Masterson. BA in Social Work, Jamestown (N.D.) Coll., 1973; diploma, St. Luke's Hosp. Sch. Nursing, Fargo, 1983; BSN, U. of Mary, Bismarck, N.D., 1990. RN, N.D. Primary nurse neuro-med.-cardiology ICU, St. Luke's Hosp. Mem. ANA, N.D. Nurses Assn. (sec. dist. 4, chmn. profl. nurse adv. coun.). Home: West Fargo, ND. Died Feb. 6, 2004.

JONAS, GILBERT, public relations and fund raising executive; b. July 22, 1930; s. Harry and Mitzi (Rosenstein) J.; m. Barbara L. Selby, Sept. 1953 (div. Nov. 1961); 1 child, Susan; m. P. Joyce Theise, Dec. 27, 1964; children: Jillian, Stephanie. BA, Stanford U., 1951; grad. cert. Chinese studies, Columbia U., 1953, MA in Internat. Affairs, 1955. Pub. rels. counsel African Independence movements and East Asian govts., 1955-67; exec. sec. Am. Friends of Vietnam, N.Y.C., 1956-57; v.p. Harold L. Oram, Inc., N.Y.C., 1958-61; exec. sec. Am. Med. Ctr. for Burma, N.Y.C., 1959-61; cons., acting dir. Far East, Peace Corps, Washington, 1961; pres., owner Gilbert Jonas Co., Inc., N.Y.C., 1962—2003. Author: One Shining Moment-A History of the Student World Federalist Movement, 1942-1953, 2000, Freedom's Sword: The NAACP and the Struggle Agaist Racism in America, 1909-1969, 2004. Dir. pub. info. N.Y. Youth for Stevenson, 1956; mem. exec. com. N.Y. Com. for Dem. Voters, 1959-62; pres. Reform Ind. Dem. of N.Y., 1958-59; mem. civil rights staff Nat. Citizens for Kennedy-Johnson, 1960; devel. and pub. rels. counsel NAACP, 1965-95, mem. exec. com. Mid-Manhattan br., 1997-2000, life mem.; mem. steering com. N.Y. Citizens for Humphrey-Muskie, 1968; nat. coord. Biracial Democrats Miss. Democratic Convention, 1968, Charles Evers for Gov. Miss., 1971; co-founder N.Y.C. Reform Movement, Dem. party, 1958-63; bd. dirs. Am. Com. on Africa, 1955-59, League Indsl. Democracy, 1972-91, Harlem Youth Devel. Found., 1998—2002; nat. coord. Holy Land Conservation Fund, 1977-82; cons. Internat. Civil Rights Ctr. and Mus., Greensboro, N.C., 1996-97, Chinese Dissidents; founding bd. mem., treas. The Wei Jingsheng Found., 1998-2002; chmn. World Federalist Assn. Greater Metro N.Y., 2001-2002; mem. nat. bd. World Federalist Assn., 2002-04; mem. coun. World Federalist Movement, 2001-03. With U.S. Army, 1953-55. Recipient Ann. Freedom award Miss. NAACP, 1970, Ann. Humanitarian award Manhattan NAACP, 1989, Non-Fiction Onyx award African-Am. Acad. Arts and Letters, 2004. Mem. Phi Beta Kappa, Sigma Delta Chi. Home: New York, NY. Died Sept. 21, 2006.

JONASSON, OLGA, surgeon, educator; b. Peoria, Ill., Aug. 12, 1934; d. Olav and Swea C. (Johnson) J. MD, U Ill., Chgo., 1958; DSc, Newberry (S.C.) Coll., 1982. Diplomate Am. Bd. Surgery (bd. dirs. 1988-94). Intern and resident U. Ill. Rsch. & Ednl. Hosps., 1959-64; prof. surgery U. Ill., 1975-87; chief of surgery Cook County Hosp., Chgo., 1977-86; chmn., prof. dept. surgery Ohio State U., Columbus, 1987-93; mem. staff U. Ill. Hosps., Chgo., 1993—2006, dir. edn. and surg. dept., 1993—2006. Markle scholar John & Mary Markle Found., 1969. Fellow ACS; mem. Am. Surg. Assn. Died Aug. 30, 2006.

JONES, BOBBY EUGENE, state agency administrator, educator; b. Briceville, Tenn., Sept. 12, 1932; s. Lawrence John and Minnie (Chadwick) J.; m. Alta Roddy, Apr. 5, 1956 (dec. Sept. 17, 1966); 1 child, Bobby Eugene, Jr.; m. Retha Branam, Oct. 5, 1967 (div. Aug. 15, 1979); 1 child, William Thomas. LLD, U. Balt., 1958; BS, E. Tenn. State U., 1980; MS, U. Tenn., 1982, DEd, 1983. Cert. in accident reconstruction U.S. DOT. Gen. mgr. surg. equipment co., Tampa, Fla., 1959-65; gen. mgr., owner med. supply co., Knoxville, Tenn., 1966-79; team leader U.S. DOT, Knoxville, Tenn., 1980-83; exec. dir. Criminal Justice Adminstrn., Knoxville, Tenn., from 1985. Mem. adv. bd. Tenn. Drug Abuse, Knoxville, 1995-96; cons. State Ct. Judges, Knoxville, 1991-96. Author: Self-Sustained Misdemeanor Probation, 1979. Dist. mgr. Anderson County Rep. Party, Clinton, Tenn., 1967-96; v.p. Neighborhood Watch, Briceville, Tenn., 1992-96. Served in USN, 1950-54, Korea. Mem. C. of C., Masons. Republican. Baptist. Avocations: golf, fishing, volunteering in alcohol and drug program. Died Sept. 24, 2004.

JONES, CAROL PYLE, artist; b. Concord Twp., Pa., June 15, 1911; d. Irwin W. and Gertrude (Martin) Pyle; m. Russell B. Jones, Oct. 1, 1932; children— Russell B., Richard I.G. One person exhbn. Newman & Saunders Galleries, Wayne, Pa., 1983; exhibited Smithsonian Instn., Phila. Art Alliance, Wilmington Art Center, Chester County Art Center, Am. Watercolor Soc.; represented in permanent collections Wilmington Soc. Fine Arts, U. Del., also pvt. collections. Recipient Gold medal Am. Penwomen Regional Show, 1957, 59; Best in Show, Smithsonian Instn., 1960; 1st prize Chester County Art Assn., 1962; Phila. Regional Council Art Centers, 1962. Mem. Nat. Acad. Design (asssoc., 1974, academician, 1994). Died July 25, 2004. Died July 25, 2004.

JONES, CHARLES E., SR., psychiatric and mental health services professional; b. Howre de Grace, Md., Sept. 2, 1934; s. Arthur M. and Frazelia E. (Lassiter) E. Jones; m. Nellie N. Jones, Sept. 20, 1960; children: Charles Jr., Angelia. Cert., 1956; AA, Harford Community Coll., 1968; student, West Tex. State U., from 1976. Cert. in psychiat. nursing, mental health counseling. Diabetic coord. VA Hosp., Perry Point, Md., head nurse, psychiat. supr., staff nurse Ft. Lyon, Colo. With USAF, 1954-58. Mem. Md. Nurses Assn., Psychiat. Nurses Assn. Home: Fort Lyon, Colo. Died May 29, 2005.

JONES, CHARLES J., wood products manufacturing executive; b. Marshfield, Oreg., Jan. 29, 1940; s. Charles J. Cotter and Lois C. (Smith) Meltebeke; m. Sharon S. Madsen, Mar. 29, 1969; children: Mary E., Judith A., Kari C., April M., Autumn C. AS in Fire Sci. Tech., Portland Community Coll., 1974; BS in Fire Adminstrn., Eastern Oreg. State Coll., 1983; diploma, Nat. Fire Acad., 1983, 85; MPA, Lewis and Clark Coll., 1989. Cert. class VI fire officer, Oreg., hazardous materials instr., fire instr. I; lic. real estate agt. From firefighter to capt. Washington County Fire Dist., Aloha, Oreg., 1964-74, battalion chief, 1974-81, dir. comms., dir. research and devel., 1981-85, dir. strategic planning, 1986-88; cons. Tualatin Valley Fire & Rescue, Aloha, 1989-90; pres., CEO Palletoys, from 1989. Basic and advanced 1st aid instr. ARC, 1965-80; cons. Washington County Consol. Communications Agy., 1983-86, chmn. 9-1-1 mgmt. bd., 1982-83; mem. adv. bd. Washington County Emergency Med. Svcs., 1981-83; owner/instr. Internat. Vocat. Inst. and Family Tree Learning Ctrs. Jones Internat., Ltd., 1990-95. Editor local newsletter Internat. Assn. Firefighters, 1970; contbr. articles on fire dept. mgmt. to jours. Active Community Planning Orgn., Washington County, 1979-90, chmn. 1988-89. With USAF, 1957-59. Mem. Oreg. Fire Chiefs Assn. (chmn. seminar com. 1982-83, 89, co-chmn. 1981, 84, 86, 87, 88). Republican. Mem. Congl.Ch. Avocations: photography, genealogy, antique auto restoration, travel, writing. Died Feb. 15, 2004.

JONES, DORIS W., performing company executive; b. Malden, Mass. Dir. Capitol Ballet Co., 1961—82. Died Mar. 21, 2006.

JONES, FRANKLIN DEL, psychiatrist, consultant; b. Hereford, Tex., Sept. 22, 1935; s. Oren William and Augusta Virginia (Morris) J.; m. June Suk Kim, Nov. 30, 1957; children: Gregory, Geoffrey, Gresham, Giselle. Student, Baylor U., 1957; MD, Southwestern Tex. U., 1961. Diplomate in psychiatry and in addiction psychiatry Am. Bd. Psychiatry and Neurology. Commd. 2nd lt. U.S. Army, 1961, advanced through grades to col., ret., 1988; pvt. practice Rockville, Md., 1988-98. Cons. Fairfax County Mental Health, Annandale, Va., 1968-98, Montgomery County Addictions, Rockville, 1972-98; cons. in psychopharmacology and behavior therapy Walter Reed Army Med. Ctr., 1988-98. Editor: War and Its Aftermath, 1983, Military Psychiatry, 1994, War Psychiatry, 1995, Rehabilitation Methods in Neuropsychiatry, 1996. Pres. Md. Soc. for Autistic Adults and Children, Annapolis, 1984-86; v.p. Cmty. ACTS, Annapolis, 1988-94. Decorated Bronze Star, Legion of Merit. Fellow Am. Psychiat. Assn., Behavior Therapy and Rsch. Soc.; mem. World Psychiat. Assn. (chmn. 1977-83, sec. 1983-89, hon. pres. 1989-93). Avocation: detective and science fiction stories. Died Feb. 22, 2005.

JONES, J. L., clergyman; b. Fountain, Colo., Sept. 27, 1962; s. James Lee and Norma Janet (Smades) J.; m. Lora Ann Webb, May 25, 1985; children: Janessa Ann, Jayden Lee. BS, Kans. state U., 1985; MDiv, Midwestern Bapt. Theol. Sem., 1989. Ordained to ministry Bapt. Ch., 1989. Summer missionary Hill City (Kans.) Bapt. Ch., 1984; pastor Concordia (Kans.) So. Bapt. Fellowship, 1989-91, Calvary Bapt. Ch., Clay Ctr., Kans., 1986-93, Immanuel Bapt. Ch., Grand Island, Nebr., from 1993. Moderate Platte Valley Bapt. Assn., 1995—. Mem. Ministerial Alliance Clay Ctr. (pres. 1991), Smoky Hill Bapt. Assn. (dir. discipleship tng. 1989-90, dir. stewardship 1991-92, vice-moderator 1992). Avocations: fishing, restoring vehicles. Home: Miami, Okla. Died Nov. 23, 2004.

JONES, LOVANA S., state legislator; b. Mansfield, Ohio, Mar. 28, 1935; 2 chilren. BA, Ohio State U. Mem. from 5th dist. Ill. Ho. of Reps., 1987—2006, formerly asst. majority leader. Mem. children and family law com., edn. fin. elections com., pub. safety and infrastructure appropriation-coms., chmn. reapportionment com., mem. state govt. com. Supr. anti-gang program Chgo. Intervention Network. Died May 8, 2006.

JONES, MARIE REINHART, editor; b. Phila., June 5, 1925; d. Henry Joseph and Kathryn Frances (Finn) Reinhart; m. Charles Nicholas Jones Jr., June 27, 1953; children: Charles J., Maryalice Jones May, Christopher Henry, Kathleen M. BA magna cum laude, Chestnut Hill Coll., 1947. Reporter Chestnut Hill Local newspaper, Phila., 1963-68, assoc. editor, 1968-72, co-editor, 1972-79, editor, from 1979. Lectr. in field. Founding dir. Cascade Aphasia Ctr., Phila., 1976—; mem. adv. council La Salle U., Phila., 1979-81, Spring Garden Coll. Archtl. Sch.; bd. dirs. N.W. Unit Am. Cancer Soc., Phila., 1980-87; cons. Chestnut Hill Community Assn., Phila, 1987. Recipient first place feature award Keystone Press, 1982. Mem. Nat. Assn. Newspaper Editors, Pa. Newspaper Editors Assn., Pa. Newspaper Pubs. Assn., Great Books Found. (discussion leader), Sigma Delta Chi, Kappa Gamma Pi, Delta Epsilon Sigma. Avocation: travel. Home: Philadelphia, Pa. Died Jan. 26, 2004.

JONES, MARY LOU, occupational health nurse; b. Akron, Ohio, Sept. 30, 1931; d. Robert M. and Mabel O. (Rhoades) Ellis; m. John David Jones, Aug. 16, 1953; children: Randall, Stephen, Susan. Diploma, Christ Hosp. Sch. of Nursing, Cin., 1953; BSN, U. Cin., 1989; BSPA, St. Joseph's Coll., North Wendom, Maine, 1980; postgrad. in nursing/health, U. Cin. Cert. occupational health nurse. Coord. The Christ Hosp. Downtown Med. Ctr., Cin. Mem. AAOHN, OAOHN, SWOAOHN (past pres., v.p.). Home: Cincinnati, Ohio. Died Jan. 6, 2004.

JONES, ROBERT EMMET, language and humanities educator; b. N.Y.C., Sept. 16, 1928; s. Robert Emmet and Lois Kathryn (UpdeGrove) J. AB, Columbia U., 1948, PhD, 1954; certificat de phonetique Sorbonne, Paris, 1949. Vis. instr. French Columbia U., 1953-54; asst. prof. French U. Ga., Athens, 1954-61, U. Pa., 1961-67; assoc. prof. French and humanities M.I.T., 1967-71, prof. French and humanities, 1971-92, prof. emeritus, 1992—2006; tchr. French cooking, 1976—2006. Author: The Alienated Hero in Modern French Drama, 1961, Panorama de la nouvelle critique en France, 1968, Gerard de Nerval, 1974, H.R. Lenormand, 1984, Botticelli's Face, 2002; contbr. articles to profl. jours. Mem. MLA, Am. Assn. Tchrs. French, French Library Boston. Clubs: St. Anthony, St. Botolph. Episcopalian. Home: Boston, Mass. Died June 3, 2006.

JONES, R(OGER) KENT, civil engineer, educator; b. Streator, Ill., Sept. 5, 1926; s. Thales Winsor and Dorothy Lucille (Smith) J.; m. Pauline Rose Bartkoski, Sept. 13, 1947 (div. Jan. 1972); children: Michael, Dorothy, Raymond, Margaret, Virginia, Charles, Teresa, Stanley; m. Agnes Chaesun Baek, Feb. 6, 1972 (div. Apr. 1995); children: Edgar Kim, Sara Su. BCE, Marquette U., 1952. Registered profl. engr., Ill., Tex., Mo. Product engr. Southwestern Petroleum, Ft. Worth, 1963-66; constrn. engr. Ambursen Engring. Co., Houston, 1966-67; facilities engr. VA Hosp., Houston, 1967-68; prin. civil engr. Metro. Water Reclam Dist., Chgo., 1968-94; commr. edn. Esperanto League N.Am., Chgo., 1994—2002, also bd. dirs.; dir. Aviation Lang. Devel. Project, from 1998. Instr. civil tech. U. Houston, 1967-68; tech. advisor Harold W. Coll., Chgo., 1992. Adminstr. translation: General Chemistry, 1990 (prize 1994); editor: The Esperanto Language in Elementary Schools, 1997. Candidate Ft. Worth City Coun., 1959; mem. Cath. Interracial Coun., Ft. Worth, 1961-66; coord. Am. Disabled Accessible Pub. Transit, Chgo., 1983-84. Electronic technician USN, 1944-49. Recipient Appreciation award Am. Assn. Tchrs Esperanto, 1996. Avocation: piano. Died Feb. 3, 2004.

JONES, ROSEMARY, college official; b. Washington, Pa., Aug. 15, 1951; d. Roy F. and Grace Vivian (Beton) J. BA in Sociology, Ohio State U., 1974, MA in Pub. Adminstrn., 1977. Mgmt. analyst office planning studies Ohio State U., Columbus, 1974-76; staff assoc., edn. rev. com. Ohio Gen. Assembly, Columbus, 1977-78; from adminstr. to asst. dir. info. systems and rsch. Ohio Bd. Regents, Columbus, 1978-90; from project dir. instl. rsch. to dir. rsch. planning Lakeland C.C., Mentor, Ohio, 1990-93; from dist. dir. instl. planning evaluation to exec. dir. Cuyahoga C.C., Cleve., from 1994. NPECSS planning com. Dept. Edn., 1994-96, NPEC student outcomes data working group, 1996, NCES coop. sys. fellows program, 1996; com. on revising info. sys. for higher edn. Ohio Bd. Regents, Columbus, 1994-96, subsidy consultation com., 1996, 2002, cons., 1990-91, com. on resource analysis revision, 1994-96, 2002, vice-chair higher edn. info. adv. com., 1996-98, chair, 1999-2001, chair subcom. on data access and reporting, 1998-99; mem. Ohio Awards for Excellence Coun., 1999-2001; com. on performance Ohio Bd. Regents, 2000-2004. Consumer adv. bd. United Health Plan, Columbus, 1978-82, chair, 1980-82; vol. Ronald McDonald House, Columbus, 1989, operating bd. mem., 1989; bd. dirs. Netcare Found., Columbus, 1988; state and regional conf. chair ASPA, Columbus, 1981, 83-84; steering com. Ctrl. Ohio Salute to Pub. Employees, Columbus, 1983; mem. strategic planning com. Mentor Pub. Libr., 1998-2003. Recipient Pres.'s award of achievement Cuyahoga C.C., 2000. Mem. Assn. Instl. Rsch., Ohio Conf. for Coll. and Univ. Planning (two-yr. campus coun. rep. 1997-99), Ohio Assn. Instl. Rsch. (two-yr. campus coun. rep. 1994-96), Cleve. Planning Forum, Soc. for Coll. and Univ. Planning, Cleve. Commn. on Higher Edn. Strategic Planning Com. (temp. chair 1991), Ohio Assn. C.C.s (performance measurement study team 1999-2001), Oxford U. Roundtable. Home: Mentor, Ohio. Died Mar. 10, 2006.

JONES, WALTER HARRISON, chemist, educator; b. Griffin, Sask., Can., Sept. 21, 1922; s. Arthur Frederick and Mildred Tracy (Walter) J.; m. Marion Claire Twomey, Oct. 25, 1959 (dec. Jan. 1976); m. Dorothy-Lynne Byrne, 1979 (div. 1981, remarried 1994, div. 1997). BS with honors, UCLA, 1944, PhD in Chemistry, 1948. Rsch. chemist Dept. Agr., 1948—51; AEC fellow UCLA, 1954, vis. rsch. chemist, from 1994; sr. rsch. engr. N.Am. Aviation, 1954—56; rsch. chemist Los Alamos Sci. Lab., N.Mex., 1951—54; mgr. chemistry dept. Ford Motor Co., 1956—60; sr. staff and program mgr., chmn. JANAF-ARPA-NASA Thermochem. panel Inst. Def. Analyses, 1960—63; head propulsion dept. Aerospace Corp., 1963—64; sr. scientist, head advanced tech. Hughes Aircraft Co., 1964—68; prof. aero. sys., dir. Corpus Christi Ctr. U. West Fla., Pensacola, 1969—75, prof. chemistry, 1975—95. Vis. prof. U. Toronto, 1979, 92, U. Queensland, 1998; cons. pvt., fed. and state agys.; active Atomic Energy Commn. Author: (novels) Prisms in the Pentagon, 1971; contbr. articles to tech. jours., chpts. to books. Mem. Gov.'s Task Force on Energy, Regional Energy Action Com., Fla. State Energy Office, adv. com. Tampa Bay Regional Planning Coun.; judge regional and state sci. fairs. Fellow, UCLA, 1954; grantee, NSF, from 2000; fed. and state grantee, rsch. corp. grantee. Fellow ASEE/ONR, NATO, Am. Inst. Chemists; mem. AIAA, AAUP, AAAS, Am. Astron. Soc. (propulsion com.), Am. Chem. Soc. (chmn. Pensacola sect.), NY Acad. Scis., Am. Phys. Soc., Internat. Solar Energy Soc., Combustion Inst. World Assn. Theoretical Organic Chemists, Am. Ordnance Assn., Air Force Assn., Philos. Soc. Washington, Pensacola C. of C., Phi Beta Kappa, Sigma Xi (pres. local chpt.), Pi Mu Epsilon, Phi Lambda Upsilon (sec. local chpt.), Alpha Mu Gamma, Alpha Chi Sigma (pres. local chpt.). Achievements include patents in field. Died Mar. 28, 2006.

JONES, WILLIAM JENIPHER, pastor; b. Spring Hill, Md., Oct. 27, 1912; s. Richard Edward and Margret Sadie (Brown) J.; m. Pauline Payne, Oct. 30, 1946; children: William Edward, William David. AA, Tenn. Christian Coll., 1975; BD, Tenn. Christian U., 1977; MA, Fla. State Christian Coll., 1980. Ordained to ministry Internat. Coun. Community Chs., 1961; cert. notary pub., Ill. Asst. min. St. John Community Ch., Robbins, Ill., 1969-86, pastor, from 1986. Former operator, sta. transp. clk. Chgo. Transit Authority; del. United Coun. Community Chs., Birmingham, Ala., 1991; mem. conf. unification ministry Internat. Religious Found., Korea and Japan, 1987; mem. Pioneer Orgn., Martin Luther King Coll. Mins., Morehouse Coll., Atlanta, 1986-89. Pres. Better Govt. Party, Chgo., 1986; former trustee Village or Robbins, also former police and fire commr.; bd. dirs. Family Health Ctr. Clinic; former chmn. South Suburban Mayors Planning Group. Staff sgt. U.S. Army, 1944-46. Mem. Internat. Religions Assn. Am. Christian Ministry, Ill. Sheriffs Assn., Ill. Police Assn., Ill. Fire and Police Commrs. Assn., Am. Legion (post comdr. Robbins 1965-68), Elks (exalted ruler Robbins 1957-58), Masons (master Robbins 1952-54), Alpha Psi Omega (bd. dirs. 1977—). Democrat. Home: Robbins, Ill. Died Mar. 31, 2005.

JONES, WILLIAM RANDOLPH, history professor; b. Little Rock, Apr. 6, 1930; s. John Riley Jones and Jewell Esther Spears; m. Anne Steed, Nov. 13, 1960; children: Anne, Brantley, Mark, Adam. AB in History and Lit., Harvard Coll., 1951; MA in History, Harvard U., 1952, PhD of History, 1958. Prof. Ga. State U., Atlanta, 1956—58, Coll. Charleston, SC, 1958—59, Ohio Wesleyan U., Delaware, 1959—62, U. N.H., Durham, 1962—95, Armstrong Atlantic State U., Savannah, Ga., 1997—2000. Cons. Testing Svc., Princeton, N.J., 1975-82; cons. in world history and silk road projects UNESCO, Paris, 1978-95; mem. seminar on legal history Columbia Law Sch., 1975-82; founder, co-dir. Internat. Conf. Group on China and Europe in the Middle Ages, 1988-95. Author: Relations of the Two Jurisdictions: Studies in Medieval and Renaissance History, 1970; contbr. articles to profl. jours. With U.S. Army, 1955-58. French Govt. fellow U. Paris, 1951, Fulbright fellow King's Coll., London U., 1958. Democrat. Home: Tucson, Ariz. Died Dec. 6, 2005.

JORDAN, GARY BLAKE, electrical engineer; b. Urbana, Ill., Feb. 3, 1939; s. Robert Leslie and Lois Evelyn (Schildhammer) J.; m. Gloria Jean Heppler, Mar. 21, 1969; children: Gareth Kylae, Glynis Jerelle. BSEE, Ohio U., 1961; DEE, Pacific So. U., 1977; PhDEE (hon.), Sussex Coll. Tech., Eng., 1977. Exec. v.p. Electronic Warfare Orgn., Hermosa Beach, Calif., 1968-78; sr. program mgmt. engr. Ford Aerospace and Comm. Corp., Palo Alto, Calif., 1974-79; program mgr. ESL/TRW Inc., Sunnyvale, Calif., 1979-88; dir. Nat. Intelligence Agy., Sunnyvale, Calif., 1975-81, Jordan & Assoc., 1988-95, electronic engr. analysis and tech., from 1995. Contbr. sci., engring., tech. articles to profl. jours. and mags. Non-Resident fellow Wash. Acad. Scis. Fellow Am. Biog. Inst., Lambda Xi Pi (life); mem. Soc. Scholarly Pub. (charter), AAAS, IEEE, Am. Def. Preparedness Assn., Soc. Tech. Communication., Armed Forces Communications Electronics Assn., U.S. Naval Inst., Internat. Amateur Radio Club. Home: Poway, Calif. Died Mar. 11, 2004.

JORDAN, LOIS HEYWOOD, real estate developer; b. Salem, Oreg., Apr. 22, 1913; d. Frank Hall and Winnifred E.(Heywood) Reeves; m. Edmund A. Jordan, Nov. 19, 1936 (dec. Dec. 1982); children: Jolie Mae, E. Andrew Jr., Jennifer Loie Student, Oreg. State U., 1931-33, N.W. Sch. of Art, Portland, Oreg. Dress designer, Portland, 1933-36; real estate developer, from 1955; pres. Jordan Developers, Portland, from 1987. Pres. Alameda Sch. PTA, Portland, 1960; v.p. Ainsworth Sch. PTA, Portland, 1964; pres. Alameda Garden Club, Portland, 1956, Women's Convalescent Home, Portland, 1957; v.p. sec. SW Hills Residential League, Portland, 1968; v.p. Friends Marquam Ravine, Portland, 1976; bd. dirs. Friendly House, Portland, 1986. Mem. Sons and Daus. of Oregon Pioneers (bd. dirs.), Multnomah Athletic Club, Pi Beta Phi (mgr. Oreg. State chpt. 1932-33). Republican. Presbyterian. Avocation: art. Home: Portland, Oreg. Died Feb. 29, 2004.

JORDAN, RAYLENE O., insurance agent; b. Avon Lake, Ohio, Aug. 7, 1948; d. Chester Barr and Grace Lucille McCurdy Barr Current, Paul Coleman Current (Stepfather); m. Thomas Michael Jordan, Oct. 12, 2001; children: Kelley Anne Doyle Mayes, John Allan Doyle, Jeffery Thomas Doyle, James Robert Doyle. Student, Redlands Coll., El Reno, Okla., 1986—87; B in Computer Sci., Okla. State U., 1995; cert. in med. terminology, Austin CC, 1997; BusB, 2003. Group I ins. lic. Tex.; notary pub. Tex. Bus. owner BB Inc., Cedar Park, Tex., 1995—98; case mgr. Hammerman & Gainer, T.P.A., Austin, 1998—99; examiner J.S. List & Assocs., Austin, 1999—2000, Amil Internat. Ins. Co., Austin, 2000—01. Mem.: NAFE (hon.), Internat. Assn. Female Execs. Roman Catholic. Avocations: travel, cooking, horses, black labrador retrievers, exercise. Home: Cypress, Tex. Died Dec. 6, 2004.

JORDING, CATHY SUE, education educator; b. Sullivan, Ind., Dec. 31, 1945; d. Fred D. and Adda (Bush) Kite; m. Marvis L. Jording, June 15, 1968; children: Kyla Michele, Brent Allan. BS, Ind. State U., Terre Haute, 1967; MA, U. Evansville (Ind.), 1972; EdS, Western Ky. U., Bowling Green, 1989; EdD, U. Ky., 1996. Cert. adminstr., supr., elem. prin. Tchr. South Knox Pub. Schs., Vincennes, Ind., 1967-68, Daviess County Schs., Owensboro, Ky., 1970-73, 87-90; founder, dir. Peace Luth. Presch./Kindergarten, Owensboro, 1975-87; dir. edn. Peace Luth. Ch., Owensboro, 1977-81; early childhood edn. cons. Luth. Ch.-Mo. Synod, Ft. Wayne, Ind., 1978-87; pvt. early childhood edn. cons. Owensboro, from 1987; prin. Hancock County Schs., Hawesville, Ky., 1990-96; asst. prof.- coord. ednl. leadership U. Tex., Permian Basin, from 1997. Early childhood edn. cons. Green River Comprehensive Care, Owensboro, 1989—. Author: Management Guide for Early Childhood Programs, 1990. Mem. NEA, ASCD, Nat. Assn. Edn. Young Children, Nat. Assn. Secondary Sch. Prins. (cert. prin. assesor), Ky. Assn. Children Under Six, So. Assn. Children Under Six, Audubon Assn. Children Under Six, Assn. Childhood Edn. Internat., Ky. Assn. Sch. Adminstrs., Ky. Assn. Elem. Sch. Prins., Hancock County Edn. Assn. Lutheran. Home: Statesboro, Ga. Died Aug. 31, 2004.

JOSEPH, WILLIAM GERARD, state supreme court administrator; b. Johnstown, Pa., July 13, 1954; s. William and Helen (Liszczak) J. BS, U. Pitts., 1976; JD, Duquesne U., 1982. Bar: Pa. 1982, U.S. Dist. Ct. (we. dist.) 1982. Staff atty. Supreme Ct. Pa., Pitts., from 1983. Advisor Statewide Com. on Ct. Automation, Pitts., 1985—; legal systems adminstr. Supreme Ct. Pa., Pitts., 1988—. Democrat. Antiochian Orthodox. Avocations: sports, automobiles, computers, sailing, flying. Home: Pittsburgh, Pa. Died May 15, 2004.

JOSEPHSON, ALAN SAMUEL, medical educator; b. Bronx, N.Y., Nov. 30, 1930; s. Max and Mildred (Berk) J.; m. Adeline Goldberg, Dec. 24, 1955; children: Michelle, Neil, Debra. AB, NYU, 1952, MD, 1956. Diplomate Am. Bd. Medicine, Allergy and Immunology, Diagnostic Lab. Immunology. Intern III med. div. Bellevue Hosp., N.Y.C., 1956-57, med. resident, 1957-58, chief med. resident, 1960-61; USPHS trainee NYU, 1958-60; instr. Coll. of Medicine U. Cin., 1961-63; asst. prof. SUNY, N.Y.C., 1963-67, assoc. prof., 1967-75; prof. SUNY Downstate Med. Ctr., Bklyn., from 1975. Dir. div. allergy and immunology SUNY, Bklyn., 1970—. Fellow ACP, Am. Acad. Allergy and Immunology. Home: Brooklyn, NY. Died Jan. 30, 2004.

JOSEPHSON, DIANA HAYWARD, not-for-profit executive; b. London, Oct. 17, 1936; came to U.S., 1959; d. Robert Hayward and Barbara Bailey. BA with honors, Oxford U., Eng., 1958, MA, 1962; M in Comparative Law, George Washington U., 1962. Bar: Eng. and Wales 1959, D.C. 1963. Assoc. Covington & Burling, Washington, 1959-68; asst. dir. Office of the Mayor, Washington, 1968-74; exec. dir. Nat. Capital Area ACLU, Washington, 1975-78; dep. asst. adminstr. policy and planning, satellites NOAA, US Dept. Commerce, Washington, 1978-82; pres. Am. Sci. and Tech. Corp., Bethesda, Md., 1982-83, Space Am., Bethesda, Md., 1983-85; v.p. mktg. Arianespace, Inc., Washington, 1985-87; v.p. Martin Marietta Comml. Titan Inc., Washington, 1987-89; dir. bus. devel. Martin Marietta Advanced Launch Systems, Denver, 1989-90, Martin Marietta Civil Space and Communications Co., Denver, 1990-93; dep. under sec. oceans & atmosphere, NOAA U.S. Dept. Commerce, Washington, 1993-97; prin. dep. asst. sec. for installations and environ. Dept. Navy, Washington, 1997-2000; sr. v.p. Environ. Def., N.Y.C., 2000—04; assoc. dir. societal-environ. rsch. & edn. Nat. Ctr. Atmospheric Rsch., 2005—06. Mem. adv. coun. Nat. Ctr. for Atmospheric Rsch., 2003-05; mem. Space Applications Bd., NRC, 1988-89, Comml. Space Transp. Adv. Commn., U.S. Dept. Transp., Washington, 1984-85; mem. adv. bd. Washington Space Bus. Roundtable, 1985-87. Mem. D.C. Law Revision Commn., Washington, 1975-78, D.C. Internat. Women's Yr. State Coordinating Com., 1977. Mem. Am. Astronautical Soc. (bd. dirs. 1985-88), Nat. Space Club (bd. govs.), Women in Aerospace, Washington Space Bus. Roundtable (adv. bd. 1985-87). Avocations: sailing, reading. Home: Boulder, Colo. Died Mar. 6, 2006.

JOSLYN, DENNIS J., genetics educator; b. Chgo., Apr. 29, 1947; BS, Ill. Benedictine Coll., 1969; MS, U. Ill., 1973, PhD, 1978. Asst. rsch. scientist U. Fla., Gainesville, 1976-79; asst. prof. genetics Rutgers U., Camden, N.J., 1979-85, assoc. prof., 1985-93, prof., 1993—2006, assoc. dean faculty, 1993—2006. Vis. scientist Merck Sharp & Dohme Rsch. Labs., West Point, Pa., 1990-2006. Contbr. more than 30 articles to profl. jours. Rsch. grantee N.J. Dept. Environ. Protection, 1980-91, Merck Sharp & Dohme Rsch. Labs., 1990-92. Mem. N.Y. Entomol. Soc. (pres. 1988-90, trustee 1990-91). Achievements include research in chromosomes during transformation in cultured cells, in distinguishing between induced versus spontaneous tumors, in development of self-marking techniques for insects, in evolution of chromosomes in insects, and in development of genetic control strains of mosquitos acting as vectors of malaria and encephalitis. Died Mar. 1, 2006.

JOYCE, MICHAEL STEWART, foundation executive, political science educator; b. Cleve., July 5, 1942; s. William Michael and Anna Mae (Stewart) J.; m. Mary Jo Olsen, June 2, 1989; children from previous marriage: Mary Therese, Martin Michael BA, Cleve. State U., 1967; PhD, Walden U., 1974. Intake clk. Cuyahoga County Welfare Dept., Cleve., 1961-64, unit supr., 1964-65; tchr., athletic dir. St. Adelbert Sch., Berea, Ohio, 1965-67; tchr., coach St. Edward High Sch., Lakewood, Ohio, 1965-67; social sci. research assoc. Ednl. Research Council Am., Cleve., 1970-73, asst. dir. social scis., 1973-74, asst. to pres., 1974-75; instr. polit. sci. Baldwin-Wallace Coll., 1972-73; exec. dir. Morris Goldseker Found., Balt., 1975-78, Inst. for Ednl. Affairs, N.Y.C., 1978-79, John M. Olin Found., N.Y.C., 1979-85; pres. Lynde and Harry Bradley Found., Milw., from 1985, also bd. dirs. Trustee John M. Olin Found., N.Y.C., 1982-85, Pinkerton Found., N.Y.C., Found. for Cultural Rev., N.Y.C., Md. Acad. Scis., Balt., 1976-78, Md. Hist. Soc., Balt., 1977-78; sec. Inst. for Ednl. Affairs, Washington; panelist NEH grant rev., Washington, 1983, 84; chmn. Philanthropy Roundtable; mem. selection com. Clare Booth Luce Fund; bd. dirs. Blue Cross/Blue Shield United of Wis. Author: (textbook) Youth and the Law, 1973; contbg. editor: (8 vols. textbook series) The Human Adventure, 1971, (2 vols. textbook series) The American Adventure, 1975; contbr. articles to profl. jours. and chpts. to books Mem. Nat. Commn. Civic Renewal, Cardinal's Com. on Laity Archdiocese N.Y., 1983; mem. commn. Catholic Social Teaching and U.S. Economy, 1984-85; nat. co-chmn. Scholars for Reagan-Bush, 1984; mem. exec. com. Pres.'s Pvt. Sector Study Cost Control the Grace Commn.; exec. com. Caths. for Bush, 1988; mem. adv. bd. USIA for Internat. Ednl. Exchange; mem. Eastern Regional Selection Panel on White House Fellowships; asst. to chmn. Nat. Productivity Adv. Com., 1982; mem. Presdl. task force on Pvt. Sector Initiatives, 1981; mem. Presdl. transition team, 1980-81; trustee N.Y. Foundling Hosp., 1982-86, Orch. Piccola, Balt., 1976-78; mem. Nat. Commn. on Civil Renewal; bd. dirs. Blue Cross Blue Shield, 1996, United of Wis. Mem. Mt. Pelerin Soc., Sovereign Mil. Order Malta, Union League Club (N.Y.C.), Milw. Club., University Club. (Milw.). Republican. Roman Catholic. Died Feb. 24, 2006.

JUDD, THOMAS ELI, electrical engineer; b. Salt Lake City, Apr. 12, 1927; s. Henry Eli Judd and Jennie Meibos; m. Mary Lu Edman, June 21, 1948; children: Shauna, Kirk E., Blake E., Lisa. BSEE, U. Utah, 1950. Registered profl. engr., Utah. Mech. engr. Utah Power & Light Co., Salt Lake City, 1950-55; chief engr. Electronic Motor Car Corp., Salt Lake City, 1955-56, Equi-Tech Corp., Salt Lake City, 1978-79; hydraulic devel. engr. Galigher Co., Salt Lake City, 1956-58; pres. Toran Corp., Salt Lake City, 1958-71, T M Industries, Salt Lake City, 1971-78; chief exec. officer, mgr. Ramos Corp., Salt Lake City, from 1979. Project cons. Eimco Corp., Salt Lake City, 1966; design cons. to tech. cos. Patentee in field in U.S. and fgn. countries; contbr. editor U.S. Rail News, 1982—. Cons. Nat. Fedn. Ind. Bus., 1983—. With USNR, 1945-46, PTO. Mem. Tau Beta Pi. Republican. Mem. Lds Ch. Avocation: flying. Home: Salt Lake City, Utah. Died Aug. 10, 2004.

JUDGE, THOMAS LEE, management consultant, former governor; b. Helena, Mont., Oct. 12, 1934; s. Thomas Patrick and Blanch (Guillot) J.; m. Suzie Koch, June 27, 1981; children: Tommy, Patrick. BA, U. Notre Dame, 1957; student, U. Louisville, 1958-60. Sales exec. Nat. Starch Products & Chem. Co., Louisville, 1957-58; merchandising dir. Louisville Courier-Jour., 1958-60; owner, pres. Judge Advt.-Pub. Relations, Helena, 1960-72; lt. gov. State of Mont., Helena, 1969-73, gov., 1973-81; mng. partner Mountain States Mgmt. Co., 1981—2006. Chmn. Nat. Conf. Lt. Govs., 1972; mem. exec. com. Nat. Govs. Conf., 1979-80; chmn. Western Govs. Policy Office, 1978 Chmn. Old West Region Commn., 1973; chmn. Fedn. Rocky Mountain States, 1974; Mem. Mont. Ho. of Reps., 1960-65, asst. minority leader, 1962; mem. Mont. Senate, 1967-69; Bd. dirs. YMCA, 1962-64. Served with AUS, 1958-59. Eisenhower fellow Taiwan, 1981; Named Notre Dame Man of Year for Mont., 1966, 1 of 100 Outstanding Young Men Am. Time mag., 1974 Mem.: KC, Elks, Eagles. Democrat. Home: Helena, Mont. Died Sept. 8, 2006.

JUST, HAROLD, advertising agency executive; b. N.Y.C., Jan. 7, 1925; s. Max and Anna (Margolies) J.; m. Beverly Hecht (div. June 1963); children: Riki, Helayne; m. Judith Zambler, June 8, 1977. Student, Mus. of Modern Art, N.Y.C., 1939-41, Pratt Inst., 1941-43, Art Students League, N.Y.C., 1950-52. V.p. creative dir. BJB Graphics, Inc., N.Y.C., 1948-78, N.E. Advt., N.Y.C., 1978-80, Just, Inc., N.Y.C., from 1980. Advt., pub. relations cons. Guilford Mills, Allied Fibers, NBC-TV, Am. Cancer Soc., Fairchild Publs.; guest lectr., tchr. advt. various schs., 1974—. Illustrator numerous books for McGraw-Hill, Crown Pub., Holt Pub., Hougton-Mifflin; contbr. polit. satire to N.Y. Times, Forbes, Newsweek, Bus. Week, Fortune, others; works included in one-man shows including Angeleski Gallery, Artz Gallery, Mt. Vernon Soc. of Art, Soc. of Illustrators; works included in collections including Atlanta State Mus., Fla. State Mus., Wash. State Mus., also corp. and pvt. collections. With U.S. Army, 1942-45. Recipient 5 promotional design awards from printing industry, 1982-87; scholar Mus. of Modern Art, N.Y.C., 1939. Mem. Soc. of Illustrators. Avocations: tennis, chess. Home: East Hampton, NY. Died July 11, 2005.

KAESS, KEN, advertising executive; married; 2 children. BA in Psychology, Vassar Coll., 1976. Acct. exec. Doyle Dane Bernbach (DDB), 1977; mgmt. supervisor job Jordan, Case & McGrath, 1981—83, v.p., 1984—86; sr. v.p., mgmt. supervisor DDB, LA, 1986—88; v.p. children's programming New World Entertainment, LA, 1986—90; exec. v.p., pres. entertainment div. DDB, LA, 1990—93; mng. ptnr. DDB New York, 1994; pres. US operations DDB Worldwide, 1997, pres. N. Am. ops., 1998, pres. NYC, 1999—2006, CEO, 2001—06. Mem.: Ad Coun. (bd. dirs.), Am. Assn. Advt. Agys. (chmn.). Died Mar. 27, 2006.

KAHN, DAVID, dermatologist, educator; b. Bay City, Mich., Sept. 21, 1912; s. Alexander and Augusta (Dreyer) K.; m. Carrol Mae Green, Apr. 6, 1941; children: Wendy, Susan. AB, U. Mich., 1934, MD, 1938; MS in Dermatology, U. Chgo., 1942. Diplomate Am. Bd. Dermatology. Intern Harper Hosp., Detroit, 1938-39; resident U. Chgo. Clinics, 1939-41, resident inst. dermatology, 1941-42; practice medicine specializing in dermatology Lansing, Mich., 1946-88; prof. Mich. State U., East Lansing, 1973-96. Contbr. articles to profl. jours.; co-author landmark article describing skin marker for pancreatic cancer (glucagonoma), 1942, republished in centennial issue Archives Dermatology, 1982. Bd. dirs. Cmty. Svcs. Coun., Lansing, 1952-58, Cmty. Chest, Lansing, 1955-61. Served to maj. U.S. Army, 1942-46, ETO. Fellow Am. Acad. Dermatology; mem. Mich. Dermatol. Soc. (pres. 1964), Ingham County Med. Sco. (pres. 1961). Jewish. Died Dec. 2004.

KAHN, DAVID, physicist, researcher; b. Peoria, Ill., Feb. 4, 1926; s. Abe and Sophia (Brand) K.; m. Dorothy Gwon, Jan. 6, 1957; children: Alan, Edward, Harold. BS, U. Ill., 1945; PhD, U. Chgo., 1953. Scientist NASA, Cleve., 1953-56; sr. scientist Martin-Marietta Corp., Balt., 1956-70; rsch. assoc. AMP Inc., Harrisburg, Pa., 1980-86, mem. tech. staff II, 1986-87, sr. mem. tech. staff, 1987-97, sr. tech. advisor, 1997-98. Lt. USNR, 1944-46. AEC fellow U. Chgo., 1950-52, rsch. fellow Am. Cancer Soc., 1954-55. Mem. Am. Soc. for Metals Internat., Am. Phys. Soc., Materials Rsch. Soc., Fgn. Policy Assn. (pres. 1985-88), Torch Club (sec. 1983—). Achievements include seven patents. Home: Harrisburg, Pa. Died Mar. 11, 2004.

KAHN, HOWARD DALE, optometrist, consultant; b. Norfolk, Va., July 5, 1925; s.Louis and Bertha (Leon) K.; m. Dorothy Helen Mollen, July 14, 1946; children: Norman, Nancy Kahn Eberhardt. Student, U. Va., 1943-44, U. Richmond, 1944-45; OD, Pa. Coll. Optometry, Phila., 1950. Pvt. practice optometry, Virginia Beach, Va., 1951-66; ptnr. Drs. Kahn and Toscano, Virginia Beach, 1966-79; ptnr. (with son) Drs. Kahn and Kahn, Virginia Beach, 1979-90, cons., from 1990. Author: Video Display Terminals and Vision, 1989; assoc. editor: Current Optometric Information and Terminology, 1974, 2d edit. 1975; contbg. author Nursing mag., 1974. Advisor, hon. life mem. All Vol. Rescue Squad, Virginia Beach, 1952—; key man Virginia Beach Civitan Club, pres., 1962; life bd. dirs. Temple Emanuel, pres., 1967. Lt. (j.g.) USNR, 1943-46; PTO. Recipient Safety Coun. award City of Virginia Beach, 1993. Fellow Coll. Optometrists in Vision Devel., Va. Acad. Optometry (pres. 1970); mem. Am. Optometric Assn. (chmn. edn. com. 1965-68, Edn. Recognition award 1979—), Va. Optometric Assn. (prs. 1965, Disting. Achievement award 1993, Optometrist of Yr. 1967), Tidewater Optometric Assn. (Contbn. to Field of Devel. Optometry award 1989), Virginia Beach Jaycees (life, pres. 1958), Kiwanis (life). Avocations: tennis, bowling, fishing. Home: Virginia Bch, Va. Died Mar. 21, 2005.

KAHN, IRWIN WILLIAM, industrial engineer; b. N.Y.C., Feb. 3, 1923; s. Milton and Clara (Clark) K.; BS, U. Calif.-Berkeley, 1949; student Cath. U., 1943-44; m. Mildred Cross, May 14, 1946 (dec. May 1966); children: Steven Edward, Michael William, Evelyn Ruth, Joanne Susan; m. Marajayne Smith, Oct. 9, 1979. Chief indsl. engr. Malsbary Mfg. Co., Oakland, Calif., 1953-57, Yale & Towne Mfg. Co., San Leandro, Calif., 1957-60; sr. indsl. engr. Eitel McCulloch, San Carlos, Calif., 1961-62, Lockheed, Sunnyvale, Calif., 1962-69; v.p. Performance Investors, Inc., Palo Alto, 1969-74; with Kaiser-Permanente Svcs., Oakland, 1974-76; nat. mgr. material handling Cutter Labs., Berkeley, Calif., 1976-83; sr. mgmt. engr. Children's Hosp. Med. Ctr., Oakland, 1983; sr. indsl. engr. Naval Air Rework Facility, Alameda, Calif., 1983-85, Naval Supply Ctr., Oakland, 1985-88; vis. lectr. U. Calif., Berkeley, 1986; tchr. indsl. engring. Laney Coll., Oakland, 1967—, Chabot Coll., Hayward, Calif.; pres. East Bay Table Pad Co., 1990. Chmn. Alameda County Libr. Adv. Commn., 1965—. Served with AUS, 1943-46. Registered profl. engr., Calif. Mem. Am. Inst. Indsl. Engrs. (chpt. pres. 1963-64, chmn. conf. 1967 nat. publ. dir. aerospace div. 1968-69), Calif. Soc. Profl. Engrs. (pres. chpt.), Toastmasters (dist. gov. 1960-61). Died Jan. 5, 2006.

KAITZ, HASKELL A., retired lawyer and accountant; b. Chelsea, Mass., Nov. 25, 1922; s. Isidor and Anna G. (Cohen) K.; m. Bettie Kahan, Nov. 19, 1944; children: Merrill A., Gary M. BSBA, Boston U., 1943; JD, Suffolk U., 1969. Bar: Mass. 1970, U.S. Tax Ct. 1970, U.S. Supreme Ct. 1979; CPA, Mass., Fed. Dist. Ct. 1982. Ptnr. Kaitz, Levine and Ilacqua and predecessors, CPA's, Boston, 1943-2000. Contbr. articles to profl. jours. Mem. AICPA (40-yr. hon.), Mass. Soc. CPA's, Mass. Bar Assn. Avocation: computer programming. Died May 28, 2004.

KAMHOLZ, ROBERT LOUIS, JR., lawyer; b. Cary, Ill., July 5, 1953; s. Robert L. Sr. and Helen G. (Sabatke) K.; m. Peggy A. Hunsberger, Aug. 2, 1975; children: Erika L., Amelia A., Susan C., Robert L. III. BA in Polit. Sci. summa cum laude, Ill. Wesleyan U., 1975; JD magna cum laude, U. Mich., 1978. Bar: Wis. 1978, U.S. Dist. Ct. (ea. and we. dists.) Wis. 1978, U.S. Tax Ct. 1978. Assoc. Godfrey & Kahn, S.C., Milw., 1978-85, ptnr., from 1985. Lectr. on estate planning, taxation and marital property; mem. uniform probate code rev. com. State Bar of Wis., 1994—. Pres. Divine Savior Luth. Ch., Hartford, Wis., 1989-93. Mem. ABA, State Bar Wis., Milw. Bar Assn., Milw. Estate Planning Coun. Lutheran. Avocations: fishing, genealogy. Home: Slinger, Wis. Died May 29, 2005.

KAMMEYER, VICKI L., critical care nurse; b. Huntington, Ind., Sept. 29, 1942; d. Clem L. and Lolita F. (Casey) Pinney; m. Herbert L. Kammeyer, Feb. 15, 1979; children: David, Kathy, Daniel, Penny, Matthew. Diploma, Parkview Meth. Sch. Nursing, 1963; BS in Health Arts, Coll. of St. Francis, Joliet, Ill., 1988. Cardiovascular surgery coord. St. Joseph Med. Ctr., Ft. Wayne, Ind.; nurse telemetry unit Lawnwood Regional Med. Ctr., Ft. Pierce, Fla. Mem. Assn. of Operating Rm. Nurses. Home: Naples, Fla. Died July 12, 2005.

KAMSLER, HAROLD MILTON, rabbi; b. N.Y.C., Dec. 10, 1911; s. Samuel S. and Annie (Levy) K.; m. Etta Seymans, Dec. 5, 1937; children: Joel, David. BA, NYU, 1932, MA, 1935; MHL, Jewish Inst. Religion, 1936; DD (hon.), Jewish Theol. Sem., 1975. Ordained rabbi, 1936. Rabbi Hillside Hollis Hebrew Ctr., N.Y., 1936-43, Oyster Bay (N.Y.) Jewish Ctr., 1980-85, Bnai Jacob Congregation, Phoenixville, Pa., from 1985; rabbi, exec. dir. Jewish Community Ctr., Norristown, Pa., 1943-80. Chmn. Nat. Youth Commn., United Synagogue Am., N.Y., 1960-65. Contbr. articles to profl. publs. Pres. Norristown Pub. Libr.; mem. Norristown Human Rels. Commn., Montgomery County TB Soc., Norristown Community Chest. Recipient Chapel of Four Chaplains award, 1977. Mem. Rabbinical Assembly (exec. com. 1958-61), N.Y. Bd. Rabbis, Phila. Bd. Rabbis, B'nai Brith, Masons. Home: Phoenixville, Pa. Died Feb. 21, 2005.

KANE, LOWELL H., urologist; b. N.Y.C., June 18, 1930; s. Eugene and Ruth K.; m. 1961 (div. 1970); 3 children. BA, Drew U., 1951; MD, N.Y. Med. Coll., 1955. Diplomate Am. Bd. Urology. Intern Bronx Mcpl. Hosp., 1955-56; resident Bronx Veteran's Hosp., 1958-59, Beth Israel Hosp., 1959-62; urologist Queens, N.Y., from 1962. Mayor Village North Hills, N.Y., 1978-91. Lt. (s.g.) USN, 1956-58. Fellow Am. Coll. Surgeons. Avocations: golf, computers, fishing, photography. Home: Albertson, NY. Died Nov. 16, 2004.

KANTER, L. ERICK, public relations executive; b. New Ulm, Tex., Dec. 15, 1942; s. Lawrence and Wilma A. (Kellner) K.; m. Mary Anne Meadows, Feb. 28, 1970. Staff reporter, Newsweek Mag., Houston, 1965-66, Newsweek Mag., Boston, 1970-71. Dir. media rels. U.S. Pay Bd. and Cost of Living Coun., Washington, 1971-74; dep. dir. pub. affairs NOAA, Washington, 1974-77; dir. pub. affairs White House Conf. on Econ. Devel., Washington, 1977-78, Presdl. Commn. on Coal Industry, Washington, 1978-80; cons. Energy Concepts, Inc., Washington, 1980-84; v.p. pub. info. and mktg. Investment Co. Inst., Washington, 1984-95; with Kanter & Assocs., Arlington, Va., from 1995. Co-author: Four Days, Forty Hours, 1970; editor: Final Report, White House Conference, 1978, Final Report, President's Commission on Coal, 1979. Lt. (j.g.) USN, 1967-69, Vietnam, the Pentagon. Mem. Nat. Press Club, Soc. Profl. Journalists, U.S. Navy Pub. Affairs Alumni Assn. Avocations: photography, fishing. Died Nov. 23, 2004.

KAPLAN, ABRAHAM IRVING, retired psychiatrist; b. N.Y.C., Dec. 25, 1914; s. Max and Rose (Perlstein) K.; m. Shirley B. Bercovici, Jan. 18, 1942; children: Martin Paul, Richard David. BA, NYU, 1934; MD, Anderson Coll. Med., Glasgow, Scotland, 1939. Diplomate Am. Bd. Psychiatry and Neurology. Internship Jewish Meml. Hosp., N.Y.C., 1940-41; resident Post-Grad. Hosp., N.Y.C., 1942-43; pvt. practice psychiatry Queens Village, N.Y., 1946-51; resident Creedmore State Hosp., Queens, N.Y., 1951-52, Hillside Hosp., Queens, 1952-53; analytic tng. N.Y. Med. Coll., N.Y.C., 1953-56, clin. instr., 1956-58; asst. clin. prof. Med. Sch. Cornell U., N.Y.C., 1970-85; attending psychiatrist L.I. Jewish-Hillside Med. Ctr., Queens, 1965-86, North Shore U. Hosp., Manhasset, N.Y., from 1970. Maj. AUS, 1943-46. Fellow Am. Psychiat. Assn.; mem. Nassau Psychiat. Soc. (pres. 1976-77). Jewish. Avocations: reading, tennis, music. Home: Palm Beach, Fla. Died July 7, 2005.

KAPLANSKY, IRVING, mathematician, educator, research institute director; b. Toronto, Ont., Can., Mar. 22, 1917; came to U.S., 1940, naturalized, 1955; s. Samuel and Anna (Zuckerman) K.; m. Rachelle Brenner, Mar. 16, 1951; children— Steven, Daniel, Lucille. BA, U. Toronto, 1938, MA, 1939; PhD, Harvard, 1941; LLD (hon.), Queen's U., 1969. Instr. math. Harvard, 1941-44; mem. faculty U. Chgo., 1945-84, prof. math., 1956-84, chmn. dept., 1962-67, George Herbert Mead Distinguished Service prof. math., 1969-84; dir. Math. Scis. Research Inst., Berkeley, Calif., 1984-92; dir. emeritus, 1992—2006. Mem. exec. com. div. math. NRC, 1959-62 Author An Introduction to Differential Algerbra, 1957, Commutative Rings, 1970, Lie Algebras and Locally Compact Groups, 1971, Field and Rings, 2nd edit., 1972, Infinite Abelian Groups; contbr. tech. papers. Guggenheim Fellow. Mem. Nat. Acad. Scis., Am. Acad. Arts & Sciences, Am. Math. Soc. (mem. coun. 1951-53, v.p., 1975, pres. 1985-86, served on the com. on translations from Russian and other Slavic Languages, 1949-58; mem. editl. bd. of the following for the Soc. Bulletin, 1945-47, 1979-85, Transactions, 1947-52, Proceedings, 1957-59; recipient Leroy P. Steele Career award, 1989), London Math. Soc. (hon.) Died June 25, 2006.

KAPP, RICHARD P., conductor, arts administrator; b. Chgo., Oct. 9, 1936; s. Paul and June Tamara (Raff) K.; m. Nancy Walz, Mar. 24, 1964 (div. Dec. 1979); children: Joanna E. de Seyne, Alexandra D. Horner; m. Barbara A. Borders, Sept. 9, 1981; 1 child, Madeline W. BA, The Johns Hopkins U., 1957; student, Staatl. Hochschule für Musik, Stuttgart, Germany, 1957-59; JD, NYU, 1966. Korrepetitor, Kapellmeister Stadttheater, Basel, Switzerland, 1960-62; nat. music dir. Young Audiences, Inc., N.Y.C., 1965-67; dir. Ctr. for Regional Arts Devel., Manchester, N.H., 1967-68; program officer The Ford Found., N.Y.C., 1969-78; v.p. Gen. Music Publ. Co. Inc., Dobbs Ferry, N.Y., 1978-82; former music dir. Philharmonia Virtuosi, N.Y.C.; former pres., owner Essay Recordings, Dobbs Ferry. Guest condr. orchs. U.S., Euro pe, 1972-2006. Composer musicals Bibi, 1960, Teddy and Alice, 1988. Home: Danbury, Conn. Died June 4, 2006.

KAPPA, MARGARET MCCAFFREY, retired resort hotel consultant; b. Wabasha, Minn., May 14, 1921; d. Joseph Hugh and Verna Mae (Anderson) McCaffrey; m. Nicholas Francis Kappa, Sept. 15, 1956; children: Nicholas Joseph, Christopher Francis. BS in Hotel Mgmt., Cornell U., 1944; grad., Dale Carnegie course, 1978. Cert. hospitality housekeeping exec. Asst. exec. housekeeper Kahler Hotel, Rochester, Minn., 1944; exec. housekeeper St. Paul Hotel, 1944-47, Plaza Hotel, N.Y.C., 1947-51; exec. housekeeper, personnel dir. Athearn Hotel, Oshkosk, Wis., 1952-58; dir. housekeeping The Greenbrier, White Sulphur Springs, W.Va., 1958-84, cons., 1984—2003, ret., 2003. Tchr. housekeeping U.S. and fgn. countries; cons.; vis. lectr. Cornell U.; hotel cons. Grand Hotel, 1984-2002. Author: (with others) Managing Housekeeping Operations, 1989. Pres. St. Charles Borromeo Parish Assn., White Sulphur Springs, 1962, v.p. 1980, 82; tech. adv., host 2 ednl. videos Am. Hotel and Motel Assn., 1986; host Kappa on Kleaning for video Spectra Vision AHMA Ednl. Inst., 1994. Recipient diploma of honor Société Culinaire Philanthropique, 1961, Lamp of Knowledge award for promotion of professionalism Am. Hotel and Motel Assn., 1995. Mem. AARP, Cornell Hotel Soc. (pres. 1980-81, exec. com. 1981-82, First Women Pres.), Nat. Exec. Housekeepers Assn. (pres. N.Y. chpt. 1950), N.Y.U. Hotel and Restaurant Soc. (hon. life), Nat. Woman's Quota (charter mem. Greenbrier County), St. Charles Parish Assn., White Sulphur Springs Busy Bees, AARP. Independent. Roman Catholic. Died May 8, 2006.

KARLOVITZ, BELA, mechanical engineer, consultant; b. Papa, Hungary, Nov. 9, 1904; came to U.S., 1938; d. Adolf and Helen (Hanauer) K.; children: Bela A. Marie, Les. BSME, Tech. U., Budapest, Hungary, 1926; MEE, Eidyenossishe Techniche Hochschule, Zurich, Switzerland, 1928. Registered profl. engr. Head engr. Electric Pub. Utility, Budapest, 1928-38; research engr. Westinghouse Electric Co., Pitts., 1938-47, U.S. Bur. Mines, Pitts., 1947-53; cons. engr. Combustion and Explosives Research, Inc., Pitts., 1953-86; cons. Energy Systems Assocs., Pitts., from 1987. Patentee in field. Recipient gold medal Combustion Inst., 1970, Faraday Meml. medal Internat. Magnets Hydrodynamics Group, 1986. Mem. Am. Physical Soc., the Combustion Inst. Home: Pittsburgh, Pa. Died Feb. 29, 2004.

KARNEY, IRVING HYMAN, construction company executive; b. Bklyn., Dec. 1, 1923; s. Meyer and Lena (Feldman) K.; m. Reba Krell, June 21, 1947; children: Robert Lloyd, Mark Howard. BS in Constrn. Mgmt., Columbia U., 1956. Archl. draftsman Kahn & Jacobs, Archs., N.Y.C., 1946-52; asst. arch. N.Y.C. Bd. Edn., 1952-54; constrn. adminstr. Uris Bldgs. Corp., N.Y.C., 1954-63; v.p. constrn. Goodrich Constrn. Corp., N.Y.C., 1963-67; constrn. project mgr. Tishman Realty & Constrn. Corp., N.Y.C., 1967-69; v.p. constrn. The Frouge Corp., N.Y.C., 1969-72; constrn. project mgr. Litwin & Swarzman, Owner-Builders, N.Y.C., 1972-75; v.p. constrn. Cohen Bros. Realty & Constrn., Inc., N.Y.C., 1975-77, 79-91; constrn. project mgr. Rose Assocs., Inc., N.Y.C., 1977-79. Adv. bd. The Frouge Corp., N.Y.C., 1970-72. With U.S. Army, 1943-46. Recipient Master Builder award Builders Assn. Greater N.Y., 1960, Excellence in Constrn. award N.Y. Soc. Archs., 1977; completion of tallest apt. building in N.Y.C., Park Ave. Assn., 1979. Avocations: tennis, biking, swimming, arts and crafts, handball. Home: Brooklyn, NY. Died Feb. 13, 2005.

KARP, ROBERT, surgeon, educator; b. L.A., Feb. 6, 1934; s. Jacob Hamilton and Myrtle (Aronson) K.; m. Sondra Gayle Price, May 24, 1960; children: Andrew and Gillian (twins). BS, Stanford U., 1954; MD, U. Calif., San Francisco, 1958. Diplomate Am. Bd. Surgery, Am. Bd. Thoracic Surgery. From instr. to prof. surgery U. Ala., Birmingham, 1967-83, assoc. prof. surgery, 1971-74, prof. surgery, 1974-83, U. Chgo., 1983—2000, chief cardiac surgery, 1983—98; interim CEO Aspen Valley Hosp., 2004. Editor-in-chief Jour. Cardiac Surgery, Advances in Cardiac Surgery. Capt. U.S. Army, 1960-62. Fellow ACS, Am. Coll. Cardiology; mem. Am. Heart Assn., Soc. Univ. Surgeons, Am. Surg. Assn. Avocations: skiing, fly fishing. Home: Snowmass, Colo. Died May 18, 2006.

KARR, MARGARET PHELAN, lawyer; b. Fort Dodge, Iowa, June 13, 1918; d. Daniel Edward and Mary Lucille (Madden) Phelan; m. Lloyd Karr, May 14, 1938 (dec. 1990); children: Janet Karr Essig, Richard Lloyd. Bar: Iowa 1943, U.S. Dist. Ct. (no. dist.) Iowa, U.S. Supreme Ct. 1957. County atty. County of Hamilton, Iowa, 1943-46; ptnr. Karr, Karr & Karr, Webster City. Fellow Am. Coll. Trust and Estate Counsel; mem. Hamilton County Bar Assn., Iowa State Bar Assn., ABA. Republican. Roman Catholic. Home: Webster City, Iowa. Died Jan. 5, 2004.

KARR, MICHAEL B., real estate and financial consultant; b. Russia, Aug. 30, 1920; came to U.S., 1923, naturalized, 1930; s. Sam and Dina (Flanzbaum) Karpoff; student Cornell U., 1941; B.S., Ohio State U., 1943, postgrad. Grad. Sch. Agrl. Econs. and Real Estate; Dr. Bus. Appraisal, Pacific Western U., 1978; m. Pauline W. Medert, Sept. 1973; children— Lisa B., Keith M., Melissa B., Elisabeth S. Real estate broker, 1940—; pres., chief exec. officer numerous corps., 1945—; instr. real estate Bliss Coll., Columbus, 1973-75; vis. lectr. real estate appraisal Franklin U., Columbus, 1974; past pres. Columbus Recreation and Parks Commn. Past pres. Columbus and Franklin County Met. Park Dist., Vision Center Central Ohio, Franklin County Forum; past pres., past dir. bds. and commns. sect. Ohio Parks and Recreation Assn.; trustee Columbus Zool. Assn.; past trustee Franklin County unit Am. Cancer Soc.; chmn. bd. Columbus Charity Solicitation Bd.; mem. adv. bd. Ohio Capital Planning and Improvement Bd.; past chmn. Ohio Underground Parking Commn.; mem. Columbus Dist. adv. council SBA; mem. hon. alumni com. Ohio State U. Sch. Natural Resources; past pres. Sight Savers Columbus. Named Ky. col., 1970. Mem. Nat. Inst. for Real Estate Cons.'s, Am. Soc. Appraisers, Frat. Order Police Assocs., Frat. Order Dep. Aux., Columbus Maennerchor. Republican. Jewish. Clubs: Columbus Elks (life), Masons, Shriners (pres. Morgan Horse patrol 1981, Shrine Jesters Ct. #8), Agonis, Columbus Downtown Lions (past pres.), Athletic of Columbus, Press of Ohio, Columbus Feed (past sec.-treas.). Home: Columbus, Ohio. Died Nov. 3, 2004.

KARR, TIMOTHY RAY, medical technician; b. Bad Axe, Mich., Aug. 22, 1952; s. Rodney Karr and Dolores (Sowden) Karr Baker; m. Evelyn M. Roth, Mar. 25, 1978; children: David Ashley, Sarah Elizabeth, Michael John. BS in Edn., Cent. Mich. U., 1974. Tchr. Alma (Mich.) Pub. Schs., 1974-75, trainer, supr. aide, 1976-77, tchr., trainer, 1977-78; EMT Gratiot County EMS, Alma, 1974-79; athletic trainer Alma Coll., 1974-82; trainer Flushing (Mich.) High Sch., 1979-80; EMT specialist Gratiot County EMS, Alma, from 1982, instr., from 1985. Mem. Mich. Assn. EMT's, Soc. Mich. EMT Inst., Am. Trauma Soc., Mich. Athletic Trainers Soc., Nat. Athletic Trainers Assn. Home: Alma, Mich. Died May 24, 2005.

KASTELIC, ROBERT L., education educator; b. July 2, 1949; BA in Edn., Ariz. State U., MEd; EdD, Columbia U. Tchrs. Coll., 1993. Educator, Scottsdale, Ariz.; asst. prof. Pacific U., Oreg.; dir. rsch. & devel. Southwest Ednl. Rsch. Svcs., Scottsdale, Ariz. Home: Cave Creek, Ariz. Died Feb. 19, 2005.

KASTEN, MELVIN CHARLES, surgeon; b. Jackson, Mo., May 9, 1924; s. John Martin Carl and Adena Wilhemenia (Lowes) K.; m. Mary Alice Critchlowe, June 19, 1949; children: Mark, Mike, Margaret. BS, Southeast Mo. State U., 1948; BS in Medicine, U. Mo., 1949; MD, U. Pitts., 1951. Diplomate Am. Bd. Surgery. Surgeon Cape Surgical Clinic, Inc., Cape Girardeau, Mo. Mem. Cape Girardeau City Coun., 1992—. Fellow Am. Coll. Surgeons; mem. AMA (alt. del. Chgo. 1974-77, del. 1977—), Mo. State Surgical Soc. (pres. elect, pres. 1983, 84), Southe Hosp. Assn. (trustee, 2nd v.p. 1991, 92), Mo. State Med. Assn. (chmn. coun. 1991, 92, pres. elect 1992-93, pres. 1993-94), Cape Girardeau C. of C. (bd. dirs.). Republican. Lutheran. Avocations: hunting, fishing. Died Apr. 15, 2004.

KASTLE, DAVID ANTHONY, lawyer; b. L.A., Apr. 22, 1957; s. Howard Jean and Sandra Nancy Kastle; 1 child, Jackson James. BA, U. Calif., Santa Cruz, 1979; JD, Gonzaga U., 1983. Bar: Wash. 1983. Sole propr., Lynnwood, Wash., from 1983. Died Jan. 25, 2005.

KATZ, MAX, psychiatrist; b. Rosthern, Sask., Can., Feb. 16, 1919; naturalized U.S. citizen, 1964; m. Ellen Speiser; children by previous marriage: Lawrence, Andrea, Shirley, Elaine. BA, U. Sask., 1939; MD, U. Manitoba, Winnipeg, Can., 1942. Pvt. gen. practice, B.C., Can., 1946-53; resident psychiatry Temple U. Hosp., Phila., 1953-56. Clin. assoc. prof. psychiatry Temple U., Phila. Capt. Royal Can. Army Med. Corps, 1943-46. Mem. Am. Psychiat. Assn., Am. Psychoanalytic Assn., AMA, Phila Psychoanalytic Soc. Died Apr. 14, 2004.

KATZENSTEIN, THEA, art gallery director; b. NYC, Mar. 30, 1927; d. Carl E. and Lillian (Rosenblatt) Schustak; m. William Katzenstein, Sept. 10, 1950; children: Leo, Ranee. Student, Sarah Lawrence Coll., 1948-50; BS, Columbia U., 1962, MA, 1967. Pres. Gallery A., N.Y.C., 1967-71, Melita, N.Y.C., 1972-77, TK Studio, Miami Beach, Fla., from 1977. Adj. prof. of jewelry Fla. Internat. U., 1989-90; enamelling instr. U. Miami, 1991. Author: Early Chinese Art and The Pacific Basin, 1967; represented in pvt. collections Trustees Miami Metro Zoo, 1994-2000, dir. 2000—; founder Mt. Sinai Hosp., 1996—, U. Miami, 1999; dir. Circle Lowe Mus., U. Miami, 1999; resident coun. Hyatt-Aventura, 2003 Mem. Soc. N.Am. Goldsmiths, Enamel Guild South (sec. 2001—), Nat. Enamelist Guild, Fla. Soc. Goldsmiths (pres. S.E. chpt. 1988-91, 94-98, v.p. state bd. 1998-2000, treas. 2000—), Fla. Craftsmen, Zonta (sec. Coral Gables chpt. 1989-90), Women in the Visual Arts, Womens Jewelry Assn. Democrat. Jewish. Died July 14, 2005.

KATZIN, LEONARD ISAAC, chemist, consultant; b. Eau Claire, Wis., Jan. 18, 1915; s. Morris and Ida Golda (Stein) K.; m. Alice Ginsburg, Sept. 2, 1938 (dec. Sept. 1984); children: Ruth N. Johnston, Martha R. Simon, Lisbeth E. Unger, Judith H. Katzin-Kaplan. AB, UCLA, 1935; PhD, U. Calif., Berkeley, 1938. Asst. aquatic biologist USPHS, Washington, 1940-42; fellow in radiology U. Rochester Med. Sch., N.Y., 1942-43; asst. sect. chief Manhattan Project U. Chgo., 1943-46; sr. scientist, group leader Argonne (Ill.) Nat. Lab., 1946-78; pres. Cons. Services, Port Hueneme, Calif., from 1978. Vis. prof. U. Chgo., 1956-57, Hebrew U., Jerusalem, 1969-70, U. Tel Aviv, 1969-70; extension lectr. U. Ill., Chgo., 1961. Author/editor: Production and Separation of U233, 1951; contbr. articles to profl. jours.; patentee in field. Mem. AAAS, Am. Chem. Soc. (councillor 1962-64, Chemist of Yr. 1964), Am. Phys. Soc. Avocations: golf, photography, fishing. Died July 24, 2005.

KAUFFMAN, JOSEPH FRANK, retired academic administrator; b. Providence, Dec. 2, 1921; s. Frank J. and Lena (Andelman) K.; m. Gladys Davidson, June 20, 1943; children— Marcia Lee, Glenn Frank. A.B., U. Denver, 1948; M.A., Northwestern U., 1951; Ed.D., Boston U., 1958. Dr. Pedagogy (hon.), U. R.I., 1973, R. I. Coll., 1977. Asst. to pres. Brandeis U., Waltham, Mass., 1952-56, dean students, 1956-60; exec. v.p. Jewish. Theol. Sem. of Am., N.Y.C., 1960-61; dir. tng. U.S. Peace Corps, Washington, 1961-63; staff assoc. Am. Council on Edn., Washington and dir. higher edn. services Am. Personnel and Guidance Assn., Washington, 1963-65; dean student affairs U. Wis., Madison, 1965-68; pres. R.I. Coll., Providence, 1968-73, pres. emeritus, 1987-2006; exec. v.p. U. Wis. Systems, Madison, 1980-83, exec. v.p. emeritus, 1987-2006; prof. dept. ednl. adminstrn. U.Wis.-Madison, 1973-87, prof. emeritus, 1987-2006; commr. North Central Assn. Colls. and Schs., Chgo.; mem. Commn. on Leadership Devel., Am. Council on Edn., Washington; Author: Education, 1968; The Selection of College Presidents, 1974; At the Pleasure of the Board, 1980; co-editor: The College and the Student, 1965. Trustee St. Norbert Coll., De Pere, Wis.; Served with U.S. Army, 1942-45; ETO. Mem. Am. Assn. for higher Edn. (chmn.-elect 1985), Assn. for Study of Higher Edn. (pres. 1981-82). Democrat. Jewish. Home: Madison, Wis. Died Sept. 27, 2006.

KAUFMAN, JERRY, public relations executive, writer; b. N.Y.C., July 3, 1927; s. Mark Kaufman and Lillian (Seltzer) Smith. Student, NYU, 1944-48. Gen. asst. WOR Artist Bur., N.Y.C., 1945-48; pub. rels. asst. Edward L. Bernays, N.Y.C., 1948-50; show publicity dir. DuMont TV, N.Y.C., 1950-51; pub. rels. account exec. Arthur Schmidt Pub. Rels., N.Y.C., 1951-54, Grey Advt., N.Y.C., 1954-59, Palmer & Codella, N.Y.C., 1959-61, J.M. Mathes, N.Y.C., 1961-72, Turkheimer & Ryan, N.Y.C., 1972-83; pvt. practice pub. rels. N.Y.C., from 1983. Also freelance and pvt. practice pub. rels., N.Y.C., 1970-96; shopping ctr. promotions for car and boat industries; free boat dealer display setups for dealers in U.S. and Can., including coordinating Nat. Marine Mfrs. Assn., Chgo., Can. Marine Mfrs. Assn., Toronto. Writer indsl. films Hershey Chocolate, Samsonite Luggage, radio plays on WNYC/NY, others; scripts appeared on Hotel, ABC-TV series; writer one-act plays N.Y.C., Washington and Virginia Beach Play Festivals. Recipient 20-Yr. Vol. Citation, Recordings for Blind. Mem. Playformers, Dramatists Guild/Authors League, Am. Renaissance Theatre. Democrat. Jewish. Died Dec. 9, 2004.

KAUFMAN, JESS, communication, financial and marketing consultant; b. Bklyn., June 12, 1920; s. Samuel and Alice (Simon) K.; m. Selma Helen Bruckner, June 20, 1948; children: Steven, David, Susan. BS, NYU, 1949, also postgrad. Staff tax dept. G.A. Saxton & Co., N.Y.C., 1938-41; chief acct. 3d Naval Dist., 1943-46; comptroller, ast. treas. Hytron divsn. CBS, N.Y.C., 1946-48; v.p. mktg. Contel, Jericho, N.Y., 1948-81; cons. Weinrich-Zitzmann-Whitehead Inc. Fin. Svcs., 1981-84; pres. Kaufman Assocs. Internat., 1981-94; chmn. bd., CEO Express Telecom Inc., 1983-84; fin. cons. Stratford, Conn., 1985-88; dir. sr. observer program Nass Am. C.C., Garden City, N.Y., 1989-94; cons. exec. info. sys. Conn., 1991-96; cons. telecom., electronics, computer data transmission Rubbins Eye Ctrs. and Ambulatory Surg. Ctrs., Monroe, Ansonia, Bridgept,

Conn. Surrogate for Pres. Clinton's Health Reform Act, N.Y.; guest lectr. Grad. Sch. Pub. Health, NYU, Grad. Sch. Pub. Health Columbia U., N.Y.C., Grad. Sch. Pub. Health, Yale U., New Haven, Army Surgeon Gen. Inst. for Rsch., Washington, Sch. of Architecture, Stanford (Calif.) U., Am. Hosp. Assn. Inst. on Elec. and Mech. Engring. Design for Hosps., Chgo.; cons. comms. and med. electronics AID, industry interface Exec. Br. of U.S. Govt.; participant in confs.; vis. lectr. hosp. comm. systems andhealth care to various hosp. assns. Contbr. articles on hosp. comms. to profl. publs. Participant Gov.'s Conf. on Aging, State of N.Y.; bd. dirs. Producers Coun., Inc., Washington. Served with USN, 1941-43. Decorated Purple Heart; elected to Student Hall of Fame, NYU. Fellow APHA, AAAS, Royal Soc. Health; mem. AMA, Assn. Mil. Surgeons U.S., Internat. Hosp. Fedn., Am. Hosp. Assn., Fgn. Policy Assn., Am. Mgmt. Assn., Pub. Health Assn. N.Y., NYU Alumni Assn. (mem. fund campaign com.), Alpha Phi Sigma. Home: Stratford, Conn. Died Aug. 28, 2004.

KAUFMAN, YORAM JANUSZ, scientist; b. Wroclaw, Poland, June 1, 1948; s. Anatoli Abraham and Balka K.; m. Jean Bracha Eshkoli, July 2, 1949; children: Nadav, Daphne. PhD, Tel Aviv U., 1979. Sr. scientist NASA/GSFC, Greenbelt, Md., 1992—2006. Project scientist EOS-Terra mission NASA, 1996-2000. Contbr. articles to profl. jours. Lt. Israeli Army, 1973-78. Mem. AAAS, AMS, Am. Geophys. Union Home: Silver Spring, Md. Died May 31, 2006.

KAVANAU, LAWRENCE LEWIS, systems engineering executive; b. Detroit, Oct. 16, 1926; s. George and Bessie (Leitson) K.; m. Shirley Buckler, Dec. 28, 1947 (dec.); children: Jerard Irving, Laura Sue, Sandra Lee; m. Dorothy Weil Sherby, Oct. 28, 1973 (div.). BS in Math., BS in Aero. Engring., U. Mich., 1948, MS in Aero. Engring., 1949; PhD in ME, U. Calif., Berkeley, 1955. Cold weather test engr., guided missile div. USAAF, 1945-46; aerodynamic researcher U. Mich., 1947-49; head wind tunnel ops. Jet Propulsion Lab., Calif. Inst. Tech., 1949-51; rarified gas dynamics researcher U. Calif., Berkeley, 1951-54; head aerodyns. and thermodynamics, research and devel. lab., missile systems div. Lockheed Aircraft Corp., 1954-56; mgr. research, planning, spl. projects, vehicle devel. and aerospace scis. Aeronutronics div. Ford Motor Co., 1956-61; spl. asst. for space, dir. def. research engring. Dept. Def., 1961-63; exec. v.p. space and info. systems div. N.Am. Aviation, Inc., 1963-65, asst. to pres. and chmn. bd., 1965-66; founder, pres. Systems Assocs., Inc., Long Beach, Calif., 1966-75; pres. Kavanau & Assocs., Long Beach and LaJolla, Calif., from 1975; founder, pres. SKC Research, Inc., Long Beach, 1978-85; pres. Wanlass Corp., Salt Lake City and San Diego, 1985; founder, pres. Venture Mgmt., San Diego, 1985-87; chmn. bd., chief exec. officer Team Austin, Inc., San Diego, 1987-89, also bd. dirs. Bd. dirs. SYS (formerly Systems Assoc., Inc.), San Diego, 1966—. Recipient Flemming award 1963, U. Mich. Sesquicentennial award 1967. Mem. AIAA, ASME, IEEE, Long Beach C. of C. (pres. 1973-74), Sigma Xi. Died Feb. 19, 2005.

KAY, JOHN DAVID, communications executive; b. Chgo., Feb. 27, 1937; s. John and Sylvia (Bloom) K.; m. Margaret Priscilla Showalter, Oct. 26, 1963; children: Laura Suzanne Holmes, James Gilmer. BA in Journalism, U. Colo., 1962. Dir. consumer mktg. Nat. BankAmericard, San Francisco, 1975-76; v.p. mktg. and sales Olson-Travelworld Orgn. subs. Gen. Mills Co., L.A., 1977-78; pres. High-Yield Mktg., Inc., Glen Ellyn, Ill., 1978-80; dir. mktg. and sales On TV Subscription TV, Chgo., 1980-82; v.p., regional gen. mgr. Multicom, Inc./Pactel Corp. & Comm. Industries, Chgo., 1983-88, Pactel Paging/Pactel Corp., Dallas, 1988-89; div. v.p., gen. mgr. PageMart, Inc., Dallas, 1990-92; cons. in field Plano, Tex., from 1992. Cons., mktg. advisor Internat. Creative Group, Chgo., 1978-80. With U.S. Army, 1958-60. Named Hon. Citizen, Gov. of Wash., 1959. Republican. Presbyterian. Avocations: scuba diving, jogging, biking, golf. Home: Dallas, Tex. Died Jan. 22, 2004.

KAYE, ROBERT, pediatrics educator; b. NYC, July 17, 1917; s. Harry and Anna (Brisk) K.; m. Ellen Eskin, Nov. 16, 1960; children: Elizabeth, Margaret, Hillary, Sanford, Anthony. BA, Johns Hopkins U., 1939, MD, 1943. Intern Johns Hopkins Hosp., Balt., 1943, resident, 1944-45; instr. pediatrics Johns Hopkins Med. Sch., Balt., 1945; assoc. physiology Harvard Sch. Pub. Health, 1946-48; prof. pediatrics U. Pa., 1964-73, 86-88; prof., chmn. pediatrics Hahnemann Med. Coll. and Hosp., Phila., 1973-86; chmn. dept. pediatrics Med. Coll. Pa., Phila., 1988-92, prof., 1992-95; prof. emeritus Med. Coll. Pa., U. Pa., Hahnemann Med Coll., Phila., 1995—2006. Contbr. articles to profl. jours. With U.S. Army, 1942—46. Nat. Found. Infantile Paralysis fellow, 1946-48. Mem. AAAS, Am. Pediatric Soc., Soc. Pediatric Rsch., Am. Diabetes Assn., Brodhead Forest and Stream Assn., Bala Golf Club. Jewish. Died July 14, 2006.

KEATING, LOUIS JEREMIAH, lawyer; b. Chgo., Jan. 1, 1930; s. Louis Joseph and Catherine Rita (Dowd) K.; m Mary B. English, June 30, 1956; children: Moira, Celeste, Brian, Thomas, Christopher. JD, DePaul U., 1952. Bar: Ill. 1952. Assoc. Kirkland & Ellis, Chgo., 1954-62, ptnr. Chgo, 1962-89. Dir. Peoria Jour. Star, Inc., 1983; asst. prof. Northwestern U., fall 1977 Served to lt. j.g. USN, 1952-54. Recipient John Courtney Murray award, DePaul U. Ctr. for Church State Studies, 1997. Mem. Chgo. Bar Assn., Ill. State Bar Assn., ABA, Inter-Am. Bar Assn., Phi Gamma Mu Clubs: Flossmoor Country. Home: Wilmette, Ill. Died Feb. 1, 2006.

KECK, CHERYLE, newscaster; d. Charles Dotson Jr. Keck. B in Speech Comm., U. NC, Wilmington, 1987. With Sta. WNCT-TV, Greenville, NC, Sta. WZZM-TV, Grand Rapids, Mich.; anchor, reporter Sta. WDSU-TV, New Orleans, Sta. WKYC-TV, Cleve.; anchor Sta. KTRK-TV, Houston, 1998—2004. Died Jan. 17, 2006.

KEEBLER, LOIS MARIE, elementary school educator; b. Jasper, Ala., Nov. 24, 1955; d. Roosevelt T. and Marie (Smiley) K. Student, Cen. State U., Wilberforce, Ohio; cert., North Ala. Regional Hosps., 1981. Cert. tchr., Ala. Tchr. Mamani Vallied Children Devel. Ctr., Dayton, Ohio. Vol. pub. schs. Democrat. Baptist. Avocation: bowling. Home: Jasper, Ala. Died July 2, 2005.

KEEFE, EDWARD FRANCIS, gynecologist, educator; b. N.Y.C., June 11, 1910; s. Edward Francis and Ellen (DeForest) K.; m. Harriette Malley, June 28, 1952 (dec. 1990); 1 child, Mart Maria. BS, CCNY, 1931; MD, Cornell U., 1935. Internship St. Luke's Hosp., N.Y.C., 1936, St. Luke's Hosp. and St. John's Hosp., Bklyn., 1936-38; asst. resident Meml. Hosp., N.Y.C., 1938-39, Sloane Hosp. for Women, N.Y.C., 1939-40; mem. attending staff St. Vincents Hosp., N.Y.C., 1940-75. Adj. prof. N.Y. Med. Coll., Valhalla, 1991—; pres. Forest Industries Inc., Greenwich, Conn., 1971—. Inventor Ovulindex thermometer. Passed asst. surgeon USPHS, 1942-46. Decorated knight Sovereign Mil. Order of Malta. Fellow Am. Coll. Obstetricians and Gynecologists. Roman Catholic. Avocation: book collector. Home: Greenwich, Conn. Died Sept. 20, 2004.

KEESING, DONALD BEAUMONT, economist; b. London, Nov. 11, 1933; came to U.S., 1934; s. Felix Maxwell and Marie Margaret (Martin) K.; m. Joanne Marie Donovan, July, 1959 (div. Aug. 1963); m. Madeleine Polk Sidle, Aug. 30, 1963; children: Audrey Elizabeth, Donald Felix. AB magna cum laude, Harvard Coll., 1954; MA, Harvard U., 1956, PhD, 1961. Economist Inst. Def. Analyses, Washington, 1961-64; asst. prof. econs. Columbia U., N.Y.C., 1964-68; assoc. prof. econs. Stanford (Calif.) U., 1968-72; prof. econs. U. N.C., Chapel Hill, 1972-75; sr. economist research and ops. World Bank, Washington, 1976-88; former prin. economist trade policy div. Vis. prof. econs. Williams Coll., Williamstown, Mass., 1974-75. Co-author: Textile Quotas Against Developing Countries, 1980; contbr. articles to profl. jours. Served to sgt. USAR, 1958-64. Postgrad. fellow Latin Am. studies Am. Coun. Learned Socs., Social Sci. Rsch. Coun., 1966-68. Mem. Phi Beta Kappa. Avocations: aerobics, jogging, walking, yoga, snorkeling. Home: Washington, DC. Died Apr. 25, 2004.

KEGELES, S. STEPHEN, behavioral science educator; b. Manchester, N.H., June 2, 1925; s. Alex and Jennie (Wilder) K.; m. Jane Ainsworth, Jan. 3, 1948; children: Susan, Martha, Nancy, Robert, Dorothy. BA, Drake U., 1949; MA, Boston U., 1951, PhD, 1955. Rsch. psychologist Boston Psychopathic Hosp., 1950-52, USPHS, Washington, 1954-56; chief social psychol. studies sect. Div. Pub. Health and Resources, USPHS, 1957-62; chief social studies br. Divsn. Pub. Health and Resources, USPHS, 1960-62; rsch. assoc., lectr. U. Mich., 1962-65, assoc. prof. pub. health, asst. dir. pub. health practice, 1965-66, co-dir., doctoral tng. program in pub. health adminstrn., 1966-69, prof. dept. behavioral scis. and community health, 1969-95, prof. emeritus, from 1995; prof. U. Calif. Sch. Pub. Health, Berkeley. Sr. rsch. scientist Ctr. for the Environ. and Man, Inc., Hartford, Conn., 1970-71; assoc. dir. Conn. Cancer Control Rsch. Unit at Yale, 1986-89; head, behavioral scis., 1986-89; expert cons. WHO, 1969-79; tech. advisor surgeon gens. adv. com.; adv. com. Conn. State Dept. Health Svcs. Contbr. articles to profl. jours., chpts. to books. With USN, 1943-45. Recipient Disting. Sr. Sci. award Behavioral Scientists in Dental Rsch., 1988, numerous grants from various orgns. Fellow Acad. Behavioral Medicine Rsch.; mem. Internat. Assn. Dental Rsch., Am. Assn. Dental Rsch., Am. Pub. Health Assn., Am. Psychol. Assn. Died May 1, 2005.

KEISER, STANLEY THOMAS, musician, producer; b. L.A., Apr. 4, 1950; s. Gordon Leroy and Marcella Amelia K.; m. Ann Shear Wynnette, July 4, 1982; children: Danielle Irissa, Matthew Evan. AA, Pierce Coll., 1967-69; postgrad., U. Calif., Berkeley, 1969-71; BMus, Calif. State U., Northridge, 1995. Ind. bandleader, musician, Los Angeles, from 1970; songwriter Gold Hill Music, North Hollywood, Calif., 1975-79; producer Wild Talent Music, Encino, Calif., from 1984; co-producer, engr. Supreme Enterprises, Inc., Santa Monica, Calif., 1986-87. Engr. Wild Talent Studios, Encino, 1984—; leader Hollywood Argyles, 1993-94. Artist, producer, engr. Sleeping Giant Music/Prestige Records Ltd., 1991—, Bohebiam Holiday, Prestige Records, 1991; artist Secret Island, Clarity Recordings, 1994. Recipient NARAS Student Music awards, 1989. Mem. Am. Fedn. Musicians, Broadcast Music, Inc., Screen Actors Guild, AGVA. Democrat. Lutheran. Avocations: softball, weight tng., surfing. Died June 23, 2005.

KELLER, CHARLES DALE, secondary school educator; b. Forrest City, Ark., Feb. 5, 1946; s. Hugh Alvin Keller, Sr. and Mary Evelyn (Moore) Starr; m. Brenda Sue Adams, Aug. 7, 1950; 1 child, Megan. BSE, Ark. State Coll., 1966; MSE, Ark. State U., 1970; postgrad., Ark. State U., U. Nev. Grad. asst. Ark. State U., Jonesboro, 1966-67; tchr. Jonesboro H.S., 1967-68, South Pemiscot H. S., Steele, Mo., 1968-69, Beatty (Nev.) H.S., 1969-72; internat. tchg. fellow Echuca H.S., Victoria, Australia, 1972-74; ednl. devel. and tng. officer Royal Melbourne Inst. of Tech., Australia, 1975-76; tchr. Eagle Valley Jr. High, Carson City, Nev., 1990-93, Carson H.S., 1993-95, dean of students, 1995-99, asst. prin. alt. edn. divsn., from 1999. Pres. Seminar and Counseling Svcs., Carson City, 1988-90; dir. Citizen Outreach, Carson City, chmn. joint svcs. coun. Chmn. Joint Svc. Coun., Carson City, 1988-90; elder First Presbyn. Ch., Carson City, 1990-93; adv. bd. Carson City Children's Mus., Carson City, 1990-95; mem. Nev. Day Com., 1988-93. Recipient Internat. Tchg. Fellowship, Victoria Dept. Edn., Australia, 1972-73. Mem. Australian Coll. Edn., Ormsby County Edn. Assn., Kiwanis (Kiwanian of Yr. 1988-89, 91-92, Disting. Lt. Gov., Calif./Nev., Hawaii, 1991-92, life mem.). Home: Carson City, Nev. Died Mar. 11, 2005.

KELLER, HARRY ALLAN, electronics technician; b. Columbus, Nebr., Dec. 19, 1943; s. Guy and Charlotte (Cameron) K. Degree in electronic technology, Radio Engring. Inst., Omaha, 1965; cert. of tng., Sears Ext. Inst., Dallas, 1969. Lead electronic technician Dale Electronics, Columbus, 1965-70; electronic mech. technician Sears & Roebuck, Columbus, 1969-70; electronic technician Ed's TV, North Bend, Nebr., 1970-73, P&K Electronics, Columbus, 1973-77; electronic mechanic Wards, Columbus, 1977-79; electronic mech. technician Becton Dickinson, Columbus, from 1979. Active State of Nebr. R.A.C.E.S., Civil Def. Nebr. Races Network, Colfax County, 1992. Recipient Speech Craft Cert. Toastmasters Internat., 1970. Mem. Inst. Electronics Engrs. Inc., Am. Radio Relay League (v.p. local club 1976-79). Republican. Methodist. Avocations: amateur radio, car club. Home: Rogers, Nebr. Died May 24, 2005.

KELLER, SHIRLEY INEZ, accountant; b. Ferguson, Iowa, Sept. 15, 1930; d. Adelbert Leslie and Inez Marie (Abbey) Hilsabeck; m. Earl Wilson Keller, Feb. 2, 1957 (dec. 1987); children: Earl William, Cynthia Marie, Eric Walter, Kenneth Paul. Student, U. Iowa, 1949-51; AS, Cameron U., 1971, BS, 1973; postgrad., Arapahoe Community Coll., 1986. High speed radio operator U.S. Army Signal Corps, N.Y.C., Japan, 1951-57; auditor U.S. Dept. Justice, Washington, 1973-76, U.S. Dept. Energy, Oklahoma City, 1976-83, U.S. Dept. Interior, Albuquerque, 1983-86, acct. Denver, 1986-95, ret., 1995. Seminar instr. U.S. Dept. Interior, Denver, other cities, 1989-94. Author: Oil and Gas Payor Handbook, 1993. Scorekeeper Boy's Baseball, Lawton, Okla., 1964-72; den mother Boy Scouts Am., Lawton, 1965-66. Sgt. U.S. Army, 1951-57. Decorated Merit Unit Commendation, U.N. Commendation, Korean Svc. medal. Mem. Toastmasters Internat. (sec. Buffalo chpt. 1991, sgt.-at-arms Buffalo chpt. 1992, Competent Toastmaster 1993). Democrat. Roman Catholic. Avocations: gardening, water aerobics, physical fitness, making chocolate truffles. Home: Lakewood, Colo. Died June 3, 2005.

KELLER, STEPHEN WAYNE, director development, consultant; b. West Chester, Pa., May 18, 1965; s. Robert William and Jane Josephine (Shahade) K.; 1 child, Louis Marley Moses. BA in History, Ind. U., Pa., 1987; MA in Labor Rels., Ind. U., 1989; PhD in Am. Studies, SUNY, Buffalo, 1994. Asst. to dir. Pa. Ctr. for Labor Rels., Indiana, 1987-89; instr. State Univ. Coll., Buffalo, 1994; co-dir. Grad. Group on Indsl. Heritage Policy, Buffalo, 1990-94; dir. devel. West Side Community Svcs., Buffalo, 1993-94; dir. grants and resources City of Buffalo, from 1994. Cons. Nat. Park Svc., 1991-93. N.Y. State bargaining rep. Grad. Student Employees Union, Comm. Workers of Am. affiliate, Buffalo, 1992-93. Recipient Cmty. Svc. recognition Chevy Chase Cmty. Ctr., Indiana, Pa., 1989, Cert. of merit Cultural Programs for Autonomy, Bluefields, Nicaragua, 1991, numerous rsch. grants from pub. and pvt. sources, 1990-94. Mem. Am. Hist. Assn., Orgn. of Am. Historians, Oral History Assn., Am. Studies Assn., Tri-State Conf. Maronite Catholic. Home: Buffalo, NY. Died June 17, 2005.

KELLEY, BRUCE DUTTON, pharmacist; b. Hartford, Conn., Jan. 4, 1957; s. Roger Weston and Elizabeth Morrill (Atwood) K.: m. DawnReneé Cinocco, Jan. 19, 1990. Student, U. Hartford, 1975-77; BS in Pharmacy, U. Colo., 1985; diplomas in Russian, Moscow U., Moscow, 1993, 95; BA in Russian, U. Colo., 1995. RPh, Colo. Pharmacist King Soopers, Inc., Boulder, Colo., from 1990; asst. tour leader in Russia U. Tex., El Paso, 1991. Russia asst. guide, U. Ariz., Tucson, 1992 (summer). Vol. Warderburg Student Health Ctr., U. Colo., Boulder, 1981-83, Am. Diabetes Assn. Mem. NRA (life), Nat. Eagle Scout Assn. (life), Am. Legion, Boulder Cosmopolitan Club, Niwot Optimist Club. Republican. Avocation: hiking. Home: Vancouver, Wash. Died Sept. 6, 2005.

KELLEY, CHARLES RAY, psychologist; b. Enid, Okla., Sept. 25, 1922; s. Charles G. and Estella F. (Hogan) K.; m. Barbara Crane, Sept. 1954 (div. 1966); children: Kathleen, John Tim; m. Erica Jean Smith, Mar. 1966; children: Eric, Kevin. BA, U. Hawaii, 1949; MA, Ohio State U., 1950; PhD, New Sch. for Social Research, 1958. Diplomate Am. Bd. Sexology. Asst. prof. N.C. State U., Raleigh, 1952-57; chief scientist Dunlap & Assocs., Santa Monica, Calif., 1957-70; dir., founder Radix Inst., Ojai, Calif., 1970-86; freelance tchr., writer Vancouver, Wash., from 1987. Vis. scientist NATO div. Sci. Affairs, European Univs. and Rsch. Ctrs., 1962-70; vis. prof. U. Ill., Urbana, 1970. Author: (books) Manual and Automatic Control, 1967, Education in Feeling and Purpose, 1970, The Science of Radix Processes, 1992, (course study) Science and the Life Force, 1990, Radix Personal Growth Work, 1993, Now I Remember: Recovered Memories of Sexual Abuse, 1994; contbr. articles to profl. jours. Sgt. USAF, 1942-46. Fellow APA, Am. Psychol. Soc. Unitarian Universalist. Died Apr. 30, 2005.

KELLEY, LOIS ELIZABETH, arts administrator, consultant; b. Peoria, Ill., Jan. 20, 1922; d. Doran A. Dieter and Sylvia Irene Huntington; m. George Thomas Edwards (div. 1949); children: George Thomas Jr., William Clarke; m. Russell Eugene Kelley (dec. June 1981); 1 child, Kathleen Lee. Student, Miss Brown's Bus. Sch., Milw., 1941, U. Ala., Tuscaloosa, 1941; cert. in arts adminstrn., Golden Gate U., 1976. Flight attendant Pan Am. World Airways, 1943-45; legal sec. Helliwell & Clarke, Miami, Fla., 1948; arts adminstr. San Mateo County Fair Arts, San Mateo, Calif., 1972-90; gallery chmn. Foster City (Calif.) Arts and Culture Commn., 1974-93; arts adminstr., pres. Peninsula Art Assn., from 1994. Chmn. Foster City Bicentennial Commn., 1974-78; vice chmn. San Mateo County Arts Coun., 1972-76; pres. Women's Caucus for Art, San Mateo, 1992-93; pres. bd. dirs. San Mateo County Fair and Expn., 1985-86; mem. No. Calif. arts adv. bd. to CAL-EXPO, 1972-94; founder Foster City Art League; jr. leader Girl Scouts U.S.A., Foster City, 1968; initiator, establisher Redwood Grove at San Mateo County Fairgrounds, 1985. Recipient award of appreciation San Mateo County Fair Assn., 1977, 91, Gavel award, 1986; outstanding svc. award dist. IV, Calif. Parks and Recreation Soc., 1992, Outstanding Dedicated Svc. award City of Foster City Arts, 1992. Home: Foster City, Calif. Died June 23, 2004.

KELLEY, ORBY G., JR., administration and labor relations executive; b. Norfolk, Va., July 31, 1931; s. Orby G. Sr. and Mary Frances (Rawls) K.; m. Mary Elizabeth Briggs, June 7, 1950 (div. July 1983); children: Orby III, Mary Louise, Leigh Anne; m. Georgeanne Olin, Apr. 2, 1990. BA, Old Dominion U., 1958; LLB, U. Va., 1964; MBA, UCLA, 1980. Journalist Virginian-Pilot, Norfolk, 1958-61; dir. graphic arts Virginian-Pilot/Ledger Star, Norfolk, 1964-67; dir. pers. Landmark Comms., Norfolk, 1967-73, Providence (R.I.) Jour. Co., 1973-80; v.p. human resources Warner Comms., N.Y.C., 1980-86; v.p. adminstrn. and labor rels. Adelphia Comms., Coudersport, Pa., from 1986. Author: Unintentional Discrimination in Employment Interviewing, 1980; contbr. articles to profl. jours. Lt. (j.g.) USN, 1951-55, ETO/PTO. Mem. Soc. Human Resources Mgmt., Soc. Profl. Journalists. Republican. Baptist. Avocations: photography, history, travel. Home: Coudersport, Pa. Died Aug. 4, 2004.

KELLOGG, JACK LORENZO, fundraising executive, lawyer; b. Frankfort, Ind., Mar. 7, 1933; s. Oscar and Lucille Estella (Cline) K.; m. Patricia A. Rossworn, Oct. 24, 1959 (div. 1976); children: John Rossworn, Patrick Dilworth, Peter Cline; m. Ann Marie Hill, Nov. 10, 1979. AB, Wabash Coll., Crawfordsville, Ind., 1955; JD, NYU, 1958. Bar: N.Y. 1959. Pvt. practice, N.Y.C., 1959-80; pub. Princeton (N.J.) Community Phone Book, Inc., 1980-88; dir. planned giving Arthritis Found., Inc., Pompano Beach, Fla., 1988-89; dir. devel., mem. exec. com. Red Cloud Sch., Inc., Pine Ridge, S.D., 1990-95; v.p. Cath. Charities Archdiocese of Denver, from 1996. Mem. Nat. Soc. Fund Raising Execs. (bd. dirs. Fla. chpt. 1989), Wabash Coll. Alumni Assn. (alumni bd. 1971-73). Died July 18, 2005.

KELMAN, IRVING G., financial planner, insurance agent; b. N.Y.C., Aug. 7, 1926; s. Morris and Matie (Ovrutsky) K.; m. Arlene Eisenberg, Aug. 14, 1949 (div. Sept. 1976); 1 child, Lori G. Kelman Seely; m. Nina H. Kelman, Sept. 13, 1981. BS, U. R.I., 1950; MBA, NYU, 1953. Pub. acct. various orgns., 1965-68; controller, CFO various mfg., electronics and pharm. cos., 1968-86; ind. fixed income instnl. sales agt. New Rochelle, N.Y., from 1986. Capt., bd. dirs. United Fund, White Plains, N.Y., 1972. Sgt. USAF, 1943-46. Mem. Fin. Execs. Inst. (life, pres. 1946-47). Avocations: coin collecting/numismatics, crossword puzzles. Died Jan. 21, 2004.

KELTNER, JOHN WILLIAM, mediation, arbitration consultant; b. Literberry, Ill., June 20, 1918; s. Claude Eugene and Geno Blanche (Lewis) K.; m. Alberta Isabelle Cochran, Jan. 1, 1941 (div. 1972); children: Mary Jean, Lewis Dean; m. Maria Leigh Steinhauer, June 3, 1979. B.Ed., Ill. State U., 1940; MA, Northwestern U., 1943, PhD, 1947. Cert. secondary tchr., Ill. Various acad. teaching positions, 1940-46; asst. prof. speech Iowa State Tchrs. Coll. (now No. Iowa U.), 1946-48; assoc. prof. speech U. Okla., 1949-54; head dept. speech Kans. State U., 1954-58; commr. Fed. Mediation and Conciliation Svc., 1958-63, tng. officer, 1960-63, ad hoc mediator, 1963-71; dept. head speech comm. Oreg. State U., 1963-71, prof. speech communication, 1963-86; founder, dir. Self Awareness and Interpersonal Communication Workshops, 1972-92; prin. Consulting Assocs., Corvallis, Oreg., from 1964. Mediator in family and divorce disputes, 1975—; prof. emeritus speech comm. Oreg. State U., 1987—; arbitrator, mediator in lab.-mgmt. rels. et al., 1963—; pres. SAIC, Inc., 1985-90; bd. dirs. Linn-Bentcam County Ct. mandated mediation com., 1991—; bd. dirs. Cmty. Mediation and Dispute Resolution Svcs. Benton County, 1993; adv. coun. Neighborhood Dispute Resolution Svcs., 1991—. Author: Group Discussion Processes, 1957, Interpersonal Speech Communication, 1970, Elements of Interpersonal Communication, 1973, Instructor's Manual, Interpersonal Speech Communication, 1970, Instructor's Manual, Elements of Interpersonal Communication, 1973, Mediation: Toward A Civilized System of Dispute Resolution, 1987, The Management of Struggle: Elements of Dispute Resolution through Negotiation, Mediation, and Arbitration, 1994, others; editor: Reading and Resource Book on Self Awareness and Interpersonal Communication, 1981, 82, 83, 84, others; TV prodr. Mem. Neighborhood Dispute Resolution, Corvallis, 1992—. Mem. Soc. Profls. in Dispute Resolution (Svc. award 1981), Am. Arbitration Assn., Speech Comm. Assn., Ctrl. States Speech Assn. (pres. 1951), Western Speech Comm. Assn. (pres. 1971-73, hon. award 1988). Avocations: reading, writing, community services. Home: Corvallis, Oreg. Died Jan. 13, 2005.

KENDALL, SUSAN HAINES, library director; b. Greenville, Ohio, Nov. 5, 1952; d. Kenneth Edward and Zelda Lucille (Delk) Haines; m. John Leroy Sweigart, May 25, 1974 (div. 1986); m. Patrick William Kendall, Nov. 28, 1986. BS in Edn., Wright State U., 1977; MLS, Ball State U., 1981. Cert. tchr. Ohio, libr. Ohio. Libr. clk. Greenville (Ohio) Pub. Libr., 1971-77; libr. asst. Flesh Pub. Libr., Piqua, Ohio, 1977-78, Amos Meml. Pub. Libr., Sidney, Ohio, 1978-81; libr. dir. Preble County Dist. Libr., Eaton, Ohio, from 1981. Tech. task force Ohio Pub. Libr. Info. Network, Columbus, 1993-95, bd. dirs. 1995-2003. Editor Preble's Pride quar., 1986—; contbr. to Ohio Librs., 2000. Bd. dirs. Preble County Hist. Soc., 2000—. Mem. ALA, Ohio Libr. Assn. (mem. coun. S.W. chpt. 1984-86, asst. coord. 1986-87, coord. 1988-89), Miami Valley Librs. (coun. 1981—, v.p. 2002-2003), Commodore-Preble DAR, Preble County Genealogy Soc. (v.p. 2003-04, pres. 2005—), Eaton/Preble County C. of C Republican. Methodist. Avocations: genealogy, motorcycling. Home: Eaton, Ohio. Died Apr. 22, 2005.

KENNEDY, DAVID BURL, physician; b. Indpls., Jan. 26, 1950; s. Robert Dean and Esther Evelyn (Stephani) K.; m. Barbara Anne Ehrgott, Jan. 6, 1973; children: Elizabeth Anne, Jeffrey Townsend, Catherine Patricia, Marissa Rose. B.S., Ind. U., 1972, M.D., 1975. Diplomate Am. Bd. Psychiatry and Neurology. Intern, resident Ind. U. Med. Ctr., Indpls., 1975-78; cons. psychiatrist Psychiat. Clinics of Ind., Anderson, 1977, Four County Mental Health Ctr., Logansport, Ind., 1980-86; staff psychiatrist Regional Mental Health Ctr., Kokomo, Ind., 1978-80; pres. David B. Kennedy, M.D., Inc. and Kennedy Clinics, Indpls. and Kokomo, 1980—; clin. prof. psychiatry Ind. U. Sch. Medicine, Indpls., 1978—; active staff St. Vincent Stress Ctr., Indpls.; assoc. med. dir. Logansport St. Hosp.,1994-2001; med. dir., 2002-.Mem. AMA, Ind. State Med. Assn., Marion County Med. Soc., Am. Psychiat. Assn., Ind. Psychiat. Soc., Phi Beta Kappa. Club: Columbia, Skyline (Indpls.). Avocations: boating, computers. Home: Cicero, Ind. Died Dec. 20, 2005.

KENNETT, WILLIAM ERIC, geologist, consultant; b. San Francisco, May 30, 1914; s. John Dennis and Gerda (Johanson) K.; m. Frances Louise Archer, May 31, 1942; children: Karen Kennett Sanders, Kathryn Kennett Torrington. AA in Sci., Modesto Jr. Coll., 1935; BA in Geology, U. Calif., Berkeley, 1938. Registered geologist, Calif.; registered petroleum engr., Calif. Geologist U.S. Geol. Survey, Medford, Oreg., 1938; from geologist to geol. supr. The Superior Oil Co., Calif., 1939-56; geol. mgr. Calif. Phillips Petroleum, L.A., Santa Barbara, Calif., 1956-70, chief exploration geologist USA Bartlesville, Okla., 1970-72; chief geologist Phillips Petroleum Far East, Singapore, 1972-76; v.p. Phillips Petroleum New Zealand, Wellington, 1976-79; v.p. ops. Ogle Resources, Santa Barbara, 1980-88; cons. water resources pvt. practice, Santa Barbara, from 1988. Mem. Santa Barbara Com. on Foreign Rels., 1981—, Downtown Parking Com., City of Santa Barbara, 1989—, Allied Neighborhood Assn., Santa Barbara, 1991—; pres. Braemar Ranch Homeowners' Assn., Santa Barbara, 1989—. Mem. U. Calif. Alumni Club (v.p. Santa Barbara), 1992—. Republican. Methodist. Avocations: geol. rsch., golf, deep sea fishing, travel. Died Jan. 30, 2005.

KENNY, WILLIAM DENNIS, finance company executive; b. Gibbon, Okla., Aug. 16, 1937; s. Bernard J. and Dorothy (Hicks) K.; married; children: Timothy, Denise, Ann, Kathleen. Grad. high sch., Lamar, Colo. Electrician various cos., Denver, 1954-74; pres. Kenny Electric, Denver, 1974-84, Hayes West, Denver, 1984-87; pvt. practice Littleton, Colo., from 1986. Bd. dirs. MegaBank, Englewood, Colo. Mem. various homeowners' bds. Englewood, Littleton, 1977—; bd. dirs. Arapahoe County, Littleton, Colo., 1985—. Mem. Assn. Gen. Contractors (nat. dir. 1985-86). Lodges: K.C. Republican. Roman Catholic. Avocations: golf, travel. Home: Denver, Colo. Died Aug. 4, 2004.

KENT, IRWIN I., consulting actuary; b. Bayonne, N.J., May 15, 1923; s. John and Bessie (Handelman) K.; m. Marian Kavrell, Nov. 28, 1948; 1 child, Kenneth Alan. BS, U. Iowa, 1942; postgrad., U. N.Mex., 1942-43, Calif. Inst. Tech., 1943-44, U. Mich., 1946-47. Cons. actuary, v.p. Pension Planning Co., N.Y.C., 1947-61; cons. actuary, pres. Actuarial Svcs., Inc., Union, N.J., 1961-86; v.p. Alexander & Alexander Cons. Group, Inc., Lyndurst, N.J., 1986-91, Kent Cons., Lyndhurst, 1991-95, Irwin Kent Cons., Boca Raton, Fla., from 1996. Cons. actuary; lectr. in field. Commr. Twp. of Cranford, N.J., 1961-69, 72. 1st lt. USAF, 1943-46. Fellow Conf. Actuaries in Pub. Practice (pres. 1989-90); mem. Am. Acad. Actuaries, Soc. Actuaries, Enrolled Actuaries Meeting Com. (chmn. 1986-87). Republican. Avocations: tennis, golf, jogging, snorkeling, bridge. Home: Boca Raton, Fla. Died Feb. 2, 2005.

KEOGH, JAMES, journalist, former federal official; b. Platte County, Nebr., Oct. 29, 1916; s. David James and Edith (Dwyer) K.; m. Verna Pedersen, May 17, 1940; children— Kevin, Katherine Ann Ph.B., Creighton U., 1938. Reporter Omaha World-Herald, 1938-48, city editor, 1948-51; contbg. editor Time mag., 1951-52, assoc. editor, 1952-56, sr. editor, 1956-61, asst. mng. editor, 1961-68, exec. editor, 1968; spl. asst. to Pres. The White House, 1969-70, head speechwriter, 1970—73; freelance writer, 1971-72; dir. USIA, 1973-77; exec. dir. The Business Roundtable, 1977-86. Author: This is Nixon, 1956, President Nixon and the Press, 1972, Centennial in Belle Haven, 1989, One of a Kind, 1995, Living By Our Wicks, 1999; editor: Corporate Ethics: A Prime Business Asset, 1988. Bd. dirs. The Phila. Fund, 1987-2003. Recipient Distinguished Nebraskan award, 1972 Mem.: Belle Haven (Greenwich, Conn.) (pres.-commodore 1967-68, 84). Home: Greenwich, Conn. Died May 10, 2006.

KEOUGH, WILLIAM RICHARD, English language educator; b. Boston, June 20, 1942; s. William Alexander and Rita Frances (Minahan) K. Prof. English, 1969-97. Pub. Tara West, Fitchburg, 1988—. Author: Punchlines, 1990; (poetry) Any Such Greenness, 1992. Active Literacy Vols., Mass., 1980—. Mem. NEA (grantee 1979), MLA, Am. Conf. Irish Studies, Multi-Ethnic Lit. of U.S. Democrat. Avocations: writing, biking. Home: Fitchburg, Mass. Died July 16, 2005.

KEPHART, ROBERT DENNIS, publisher; b. Denver, Sept. 9, 1934; s. Robert Tennis Kephart and Myra Louise Wilson; m. Mary Sue Pair, Dec. 7, 1959 (div. 1975); 1 child, Patrick Neil. Student, U. Colo., 1953-54. Pub. Human Events, Washington, 1964-74, Libertarian Rev., Washington, 1969-72; pres., pub. Kephart Comms., Inc., Washington, 1974-81; mng. dir. Caribbean Overseas Enterprises, Largo, Fla., from 1981; dir. Agora Pub., Balt., from 1997. Recipient Lifetime Achievement in Civil Liberties award Thomas Szasz Awards Com., 1998. Mem. Newsletter Assn. Am. (Mktg. and Editl. Excellence award 1978, 79), Belleair Country Club. Avocations: painting, archaeology. Home: Belleair Shrs, Fla. Died June 8, 2004.

KERN, EDITH, Romance languages and literature educator; b. Dusseldorf, Germany, Feb. 7, 1912; d. L.G. Berg and J. Bison. BA, Bridgewater Coll., 1942; MA, Johns Hopkins U., 1944, PhD in Romance Lang. and Lit, 1946; LHD (hon.), Bridgewater Coll., Va., 2002. Asst. prof. modern langs. U. Md., U. Kans.; dir. Ford Foun. TV project U. Pa., 1946-60; prof. French Grad. Sch., St. Johns U., N.Y.C., 1960-65; prof. Romance lit. and comparative lit. Grad. Sch. U. Wash., Seattle, 1965-72; Doris Silbert prof. humanities, chmn. comparative lit. program Smith Coll., Northampton, Mass., 1972-77, prof. emeritus, 1977—2005; John Cranford Adams prof. Hofstra U., 1977-81; faculty New Sch. for Social Rsch., N.Y.C., 1986—2005. Vis. prof. UCLA, 1962, SUNY-Buffalo, 1965, Stanford U., 1970, U. Warwick, Eng., 1978, Brandeis U., fall 1978, SUNY at Binghamton, spring 1979, Colgate U., 1982; disting. prof. Purdue U., 1984; dir. NEH Summer Seminar, 1975; 79, experimental year-long NEH Seminar for Coll. Tchrs., 1977-78; elected. Coun. Scholars for Libr. of Congress, 1983-86; mem. faculty New Sch. Social Rsch., 1985-2005; docent Met. Mus. Art, 1984-2002. Author: French Dramatic Theory, 1949, Sartre, 1962, Existential Thought and Fictional Technique, 1970, The Absolute Comic, 1980; contbg. author: Disciplines of Criticism, 1968, Boccaccio, 1974, Moliere, 1975, Beckett, 1983, Writing in a Modern Temper, 1984, Literary Theory and Criticism, 1985, Waiting For Godot, 1987, Aesthetics and the Literature of Ideas, 1990, Carrefour de Cultures, 1993; mem. editl. bd. Twentieth Century Lit., 1972-2005; founding editor Dada/Surrealism; contbr. articles to profl. jours. Bollingen Found. fellow, 1967; Nat. Endowment for Humanities fellow, 1972; Guggenheim fellow, 1975-76; Radcliffe-Harvard Fellow, 1975-76; Rockefeller Found. Fellow, 1982 Mem. MLA (v.p. 1975-76, pres. 1977-78), Comparative Lit. Assn. (nat. exec. coun. 1973—2005), Nat. Soc. Lit. and Arts, Am. Comparative Lit. Assn., Internat. Comparative Lit. Assn., Renaissance Soc. Am., PEN. Home: New York, NY. Died Sept. 29, 2005.

KERR, CLARENCE FRANCIS, retired police sergeant, private detective; b. Chgo., Aug. 28, 1929; s. Michael Harry Kerr and Rose Mary (Kryzanowski) Nicpon; m. Marion Elaine Green, June 10, 1949 (div. June 1985); children: Karen Kerr Hoffman, Edward, Frances Kerr Weiser. AA, Wright Jr. Coll., 1957. Patrolman, detective Chgo. Police Dept., 1954-92, sgt., 1960-80, watch commander, 1965-80; pres., prin. Clarence Kerr Detective Agy., Chgo., from 1980. With U.S. Navy, 1946. Recipient Hero award Chgo. Tribune, 1955, Lambert Tree medal Chgo. City Coun., 1955, Hamilton Watch award, 1956; named Outstanding Police Officer, Am. Legion, Chgo., 1956. Fellow Lambert Tree, Carter Harrison Honor Soc. (pres. 1980-88); mem. Fedn. of Police, Chgo. Police Sgts. Assn., Ill. Police Assn. Democrat. Roman Catholic. Avocations: travel, hiking, reading. Home: Chicago, Ill. Died Dec. 23, 2004.

KERSHAW, ANNIE ELIZABETH, school administrator, educator; b. Orlando, Fla., Aug. 20, 1966; d. Ralph James and Louiza (Peyton) K.; m. Stephan Michael Rogers, Nov. 2, 1991 (div. Aug. 1994). AA, U. Fla., Gainesville, 1988, BA, 1989; MA, Chgo. State U., 1995. Lic. Sch. Adminstr. Ind., Ill. Primary LD tchr. Rockway Elem. Sch., South Miami, Fla., 1989-90; patent bus. svcs. Cedars Med. Ctr., Miami, Fla., 1990-91; ED/LD resource tchr. Dist. One Middle Sch., Chgo., 1991-94; program coord., dept. dir. Austin Spl. Sch., Chgo., 1991-94; family counselor II Children's Home Aid Soc., Chgo., 1994-95; edn. coord., sch. adminstr. Willowglen Acad., Gary, Ind., from 1995. Author: (book-journal) Resources in Edn., 1995. Mem. AAUW, ASCD, Ill. Coun. Children with Behavior Disorders, Coun. for Exceptional Children. Avocations: decorating home, cooking, reading, sewing, computer games. Home: Merrillville, Ind. Died July 16, 2005.

KERT, BERNICE GALANSKY, writer; b. St. Louis, Oct. 4, 1923; d. Gus D. and Mary (Katanik) Galansky; m. Morley J. Kert, Jan. 14, 1945 (dec. May 1990); children: Elizabeth, Kathryn Green, Charles. BA, U. Mich., 1944. Teaching fellow dept. English U. Mich., Ann Arbor, 1946-47. Editl. bd. The Hemingway Rev., Moscow, Idaho, 1992-2005. Author: (biographies) The Hemingway Women, 1983, re-issue, 1999, Abby Aldrich Rockefeller, 1993. John Simon Guggenheim Meml. Found. fellow, N.Y.C., 1988; scholar-in-residence Bellagio (Italy) Study Ctr., 1991. Mem. J.B. Berland Found., The Hemingway Soc., Hillcrest Country Club, Authors Guild. Democrat. Jewish. Avocations: music, films, literature, travel. Home: Beverly Hills, Calif. Died July 23, 2005.

KERVER, THOMAS JOSEPH, editor, consultant; b. Cleve., Nov. 9, 1934; s. William F. and Hope M. (Roberts) K.; m. Elizabeth G. Galloway, Apr. 12, 1969 (div. Apr. 1990); children: Kenneth, Stephen, Suzanne, Sarah. BA, Xavier U., 1956; M of Mil. Arts and Scis., U.S. Army Gen. Staff Coll., 1968; MA in Polit. Sci., U. Wis., 1972, MA in Journalism, 1972. Commd. 2d lt. U.S. Army, 1956, advanced through grades to lt. col., 1976; pres. Kerver People, Ft. Collins, Colo., 1976-80; dir. communications, publicity Colo. Bankers Assn., Denver, 1980-82; sr. editor Cardiff Pub. Co., Englewood, Colo., 1982-90; bus. editor Cablevision Mag., Denver, from 1990. Prof. journalism Colo. State U., Ft. Collins, 1978-80; vice chmn. Larimer County Budget Adv. Com., Ft. Collins, 1978-79; chmn. Larimer Conty Pvt. Industry Coun., Ft. Collins, 1979-80; adv. bd. Nat. Cable TV Mus. Inst.; instr. telecomms. fin. U. Denver. Contbr. articles to profl. jours. Organizer Larimer County Dem. Party, Ft. Collins, 1976-80; cons. Nat. Urban Indian Coun., Denver, 1980-81; organizer, affiliate Clinton for Pres. Campaign, Denver, 1992. Decorated Bronze Star (4), Legion of Merit (2); recipient Presdl. Citation award Pres. Jimmy Carter, 1980, Cert. of Distinction award Nat. Alliance Bus., 1980, Morton Margolin award Disting. Nat. Bus. Reporting, 1993, 94, 1st prize Best Editl. Dept., Chilton Publs., 2nd prize Assn. Bus. Press Editors, 1996. Mem. Cable/Satellite Broadcasters Assn. Asia (chartered), Soc. Satellite Profls. Roman Catholic. Avocations: wine, classical music, opera, cooking. Home: Denver, Colo. Died Apr. 8, 2004.

KESSLER, SANDRA S., elementary school educator; b. Oneida, N.Y., Apr. 15, 1937; d. Henry Cornelius and Estelle (Cmaylo) Schoeneck; m. Douglas K. Kessler, June 24, 1961; children: Hans D., Joel C., Eric S. BS, SUNY, Cortland, 1959; MS, Nazareth U., Rochester, N.Y., 1976; EdD, Syracuse U., 1990. Tchr. secondary phys. edn. New Hartford (N.Y.) Ctrl. Sch., 1959-61; secondary tchr. Rush Henrietta Sch., Henrietta, N.Y., 1961; elem. tchr. Pittsford (N.Y.) Ctr. Sch., from 1971. Created mentor program/workshop Women Helping Girls with Choices. Mem. adv. bd. YMCA, Rochester, 1989-95; chair tchr. ctr. policy Pittsford Ctrl. Sch. Tchr. Ctr., 1980-95; mem. dist. planning team Pittsford Ctrl. Sch., 1994-96. Recipient Lifetime award Pittsford Parent-Tchr.-Student Assn. Mem. AAUW, Delta Kappa Gamma, Phi Delta Kappa. Roman Catholic. Avocations: skiing, hiking, biking, reading. Home: Pittsford, NY. Died May 13, 2005.

KETHLEY, JOHN BRYAN, museum curator; b. Passaic, N.J., Oct. 18, 1942; s. Thomas William and Jane Darnaby (Moore) K.; m. Judith Dianne Townsend, June 14, 1968. BS, U. Ga., 1964, PhD, 1969. NIH postdoctoral trainee Acarology Lab., Ohio State U., Columbus, 1969-70; asst. curator Field Mus. Natural History, Chgo., 1970-75, assoc. curator, from 1975, head div. insects, 1974-77, 80-84. Lectr. Summer Inst. Acarology, Ohio State U., 1974—; lectr. com. on evolutionary biology U. Chgo., 1976—. Mem. editorial bd. Internat. Jour. Acarology, 1976-81; contbr. articles to profl. publs. NSF grantee, 1978-86, 89—. Mem. Acarological Soc. Am. (governing bd. 1977-82), Entomol. Soc. Am., Entomol. Soc. Washington, Ga. Entomol. Soc., Soil Ecology Soc., Sigma Xi, Phi Kappa Phi. Home: Clinton, Tenn. Died Apr. 29, 2004.

KETTLEWELL, CHARLES W., lawyer; b. Belmont County, Ohio, Oct. 21, 1941; BS, Ohio State Univ., 1964, JD, 1971. Bar: Ohio 1971, Oreg. 1991, US Dist Ct. (so. dist.) Ohio 1972, US Supreme Ct. 1973. Law clerk Ohio Supreme Ct., 1971—73; private practice, 1973—77; asst. counsel Ohio Office Disciplinary Counsel, 1977—83; ptnr. Kettlewell & Kettlewell LLC, Columbus, Ohio, from 1985. Adj. prof. law, legal ethics Ohio State Univ., from 1977. Capt. JAG Corps USNR. Recipient ABA Michael Franc Profl. Responsibility award, 2003. Fellow: Columbus Bar Assn., Ohio State Bar Assn., ABA; mem.: Assn. Profl. Responsibility Lawyers (founder, pres. 1990—92), Nat. Organization of Bar counsel (pres. 1982—83). Died Feb. 21, 2005.

KEVINS, DAVID VINCENT, financial investment consultant; b. Toronto, Ont., Can., Apr. 5, 1954; came to U.S., 1956; s. Francis and Edith Kathleen (O'Hara) K.; m. Karen Alice Millar, Aug. 9, 1986. BS, U. So. Calif., 1976, PharmD, 1981. Profl. harness racing driver, trainer U.S. Trotting Assn., Columbus, Ohio, 1977-83; pharmacy mgmt. Better Drugs of Calif., Inc., Glendale, 1983-86; chief exec. officer D&K Inc., L.A., from 1986; founder Dago Drug Store Investments, Bellflower, Calif., from 1989. Cons. JNJ Millar Legal Inc., San Diego, 1986—; cons. Aversa & Uversa Ltd., Monterey Park, Calif., 1985—; owner, chief exec. officer D&K Inc., Hermosa Beach, Calif., 1986—. Vol. L.A. Mission, 1984—; contbr. Christian Childrens Fund, Richmond, Va., 1982—. Recipient Attridge award for musical performance, U. So. Calif. Sch. Music, 1972; Calif. State U. scholar. Mem. Am. Assn. Investors., Sports Connection, Manhattan Beach. Democrat. Roman Catholic. Avocations: basketball, racquetball, skiing, travel, making money. Died Sept. 29, 2004.

KEYES, I(RVONA) MARY, health care facility executive; b. Mason City, Iowa, May 27, 1936; d. Irvin John Witte and Bonnie Marie (Broers) Westphal; m. Thomas Robert Keyes, Oct. 17, 1959 (div. Jan. 1976); children: Teresa, Michael, Kerry, Maureen. RN diploma, St. Mary's Sch. Nursing, Rochester, Minn., 1957. Head nurse neurology St. Mary's Hosp., Rochester, 1957-59; asst. dir. nurses Walker Meth. Health Care, Mpls., 1967-68; dir. nurses Chateau Care Ctr., Mpls., 1968-76; coordinator health care Chanassen (Minn.) Treatment Ctr., 1976-77; staff nurse Abbott-Northwestern Hosp., Mpls., 1977-79; assoc. dir. chem. dependency programs Golden Valley Hosp., Mpls., 1979-83; program dir. Warren Eustis House for Adolescents, Eagan, Minn., 1983-84; chief exec. officer The Gables Extended Treatment Program for Chemically Dependent Women, Rochester, 1984-88, Choices for Women Extended Treatment Program for Women, Palm Springs, CA, from 1988. Speaker chem. dependency numerous profl. confs. and community groups, 1985—. Contbr. articles on chem. dependency to profl. jours., 1986—. Mem. Minn. Women's Forum on Chem. Health, Mpls., 1984—; mem. task force Olmsted County Chem. Dependency Planning Com., Rochester, 1986—; officer Human Services adv. Council to Minn. Commr. Health, 1974-81. Recipient Service award Mayor of Rochester, 1986, Women's Forum on Chem. Health, 1986; named Outstanding Mem. Adv. Bd. Minn. Commr. Health, 1979. Mem. Minn. Chem. Dependency Assn. (officer bd. dirs. 1986-87), Inst. Chem. Dependency Profls. Minn. (cert.), St. Mary's Sch. Nursing Alumni Assn. Democrat. Roman Catholic. Avocation: playing violin/viola for Mayo Civic Chamber Orch./Quartets. Died July 7, 2005.

KEYES, JAMES LYMAN, JR., diesel engines distributor company owner; b. Peru, Ind., Apr. 27, 1928; s. James Lyman and Mary Edith (Weigle) K. AB, Wabash Coll., 1950; MBA, Harvard U., 1952; LLD (hon.), Wabash Coll., 1987. Mgr. Cummins Diesel Sales Corp., Columbus, Ind., 1959-61; dir. mktg. svcs. Cummins Engine Co., Inc., Columbus, 1962-65, gen. sales mgr., 1966-67, v.p. OEM sales, 1968-70, v.p. nat. accounts, 1971-73, v.p. indsl. mktg., 1974-76; chmn., CEO, owner Cummins Ohio, Inc., Columbus, Ohio, 1976-94, from 1994. Bd. dirs. Ohio Trucking Assn., 1980—. Mem. Newcomen Soc., Columbus, Ohio, 1984—, Coun. for Ethics in Econs., Columbus, Ohio, 1987—, Rotary Internat., Columbus, Ohio, 1983; chmn. Mayor's Econ. Devel. Coun., Columbus, Ohio, 1982-84; pres. Columbus (Ohio) Landmarks Found., 1976-77; bd. dirs. Columbus (Ohio) Coun. on World Affairs, 1982—; bd. trustees Wabash Coll., Crawfordsville, Ind., 1980—, v.p., 1990—, chmn. exec. com., 1987-89; elder Presbyn. Ch., 1979-82; mem. commn. Columbus Met. Airport and Aviation, 1989-91. 1st lt. USAF, 1952-54. Recipient Christopher Columbus Achievement award City of Columbus (Ohio), 1987. Mem. Nat. Assn. Wabash Coll. Men (pres. 1974-76), Ind. Assn. for Retarded Children (pres. 1965-68), Nat. Assn. for Retarded Children (v.p. 1968-72), Univ. Club (Columbus, Ohio), Masons, Shriners, Kappa Sigma. Republican. Avocations: golf, travel. Home: Columbus, Ohio. Died June 4, 2004.

KHATTER, PRITHIPAL SINGH, radiologist; b. Ferozepore Cant, Punjab, India, Feb. 1, 1936; came to U.S., 1976; s. Harnam Singh and Jagjit Kaur; m. Kamal Jit Kaur Chahal; children: Avinash, Boldy. MB BChir, Med. Coll., Amritsar, Punjab, 1959; diploma in radiology, GSVM Med. Coll., Kanpur, 1961, diploma in clin. pathology, 1962, MD in Radiology, 1965. Diplomate Am. Bd. Radiology. Resident in diagnostic radiology VA Med. Ctr., Dallas, 1976-78; radiologist, clin. pathologist Jit & Pal X-Rays (P) Ltd., Moradabad, India, 1965-76; radiologist, chief VA Med. Ctr., Huntington, W.Va., 1978-90; clin. faculty radiology, from instr. to assoc. prof. Marshall U. Sch. Medicine, Huntington, 1978-90; radiologist Radiology, Inc., Huntington, 1980-90, Davis Meml. Hosp., Elkins, W.Va., 1990-96, Radiol. Cons. Assn., Fairmont, W.Va., 1996-98, Radiology Physicians Assocs., from 1998. Named Hometown Hero, Town of Elkin, 2002. Fellow Indian Med. Assn.; mem. Indian Radiology Assn. Avocations: reading, music, tennis, badminton. Home: Phoenix, Ariz. Died June 28, 2004.

KIEFFER, JAMES MARSHALL, lawyer; b. Buffalo, June 10, 1940; s. Elveus Francis and Marjorie (Marshall) K.; m. Judith Ann Fee, Aug. 6, 1965; children: Eric Corwin, Knight Darrow. BA, Colgate U., 1962; JD, U. Mich., 1965. Bar: N.Y. 1966, U.S. Dist. Ct. (we. dist.) N.Y. 1969, U.S. Ct. Appeals (2nd cir.) 1980, U.S. Supreme Ct. 1980. Assoc. Ohlin, Damon, Morey, Sawyer & Moot, Buffalo, 1965-72; ptnr. Damon & Morey, Buffalo, 1972-93, Feldman Kieffer and Hermann LLP, Buffalo, from 1993. Tchr. SUNY Med. Sch. & Law Sch., Buffalo. Bd. dirs. People, Inc., Buffalo, 1972-79. Fellow Am. Coll. Trial Lawyers; mem. ABA, Erie County Bar Assn. (bd. dirs. 1991-94), Western N.Y. Trial Lawyers Assn. (pres. 2000), Def. Trial Lawyers Assn. of Western N.Y. (pres. 1991-92), N.Y. State Bar Assn., Def. Rsch. Inst. Avocations: tennis, squash, skiing. Home: Buffalo, NY. Died June 21, 2005.

KIEP, JOHN WILLIAM, finance executive; b. Joliet, Ill., Feb. 11, 1930; s. John Michael and Anne Mary (Kaffer) K.; m. Marjery June Seppi, Jan. 24, 1953; children: Michael John, Julia Anne. BA in Acctg., St. Ambrose Coll., 1953; MS, No. Ill. U., 1967. Controller Amax Aluminum Extrusions, Inc., St. Charles, Ill., 1955-68; chief fin. officer B.W. Constrn. Co., Chgo., 1968-71; v.p., treas. Kaiser Ducett Corp., North Aurora, Ill., 1971-77, Kaiser Ducett Internat. Inc., San Juan, P.R., 1976-77; fin. mgr. Ill. State Toll Hwy. Authority, Oak Brook, 1978-92, spl. asst. to exec. dir., 1978-80, acting exec. dir., 1980-81; fin. cons., prin. Wheaton, Ill., from 1992. Active Wheaton (Ill.) Housing Commn., 1973-78, chmn., 1978; mem. Wheaton Plan Commn., 1978-85; bd. dirs. Marianjoy Rehab. Hosp., Wheaton, 1978-86, chmn., 1980-82. Served with U.S. Army, 1953-55. Mem. Am. Pub. Works Assn., Mun. Fin. Officers Assn., Internat. Bridge, Tunnel and Turnpike Assn. Lodges: KC. Roman Catholic. Avocations: golf, fishing, gardening, painting. Home: Wheaton, Ill. Died Oct. 13, 2004.

KIERNAN, JOHN ROBERT, broadcast executive; b. Paterson, N.J., May 8, 1947; s. John Henry and Marion (Vanderhoff) K. Grad. H.S., Kinnelon, N.J. Disc jockey WDHA-FM, Dover, N.J., 1967-70, WEEX Radio, Easton, Pa., 1970-71, WAEB, Allentown, 1972-74; owner WKTC, 1973-76; ops./asst. gen. mgr. WACM Radio, Freeland, Pa., 1976-77; ops. mgr. WCNR Radio, Bloomsburg, Pa., 1977-80; ops./corp. program dir. WNNJ/WIXL FM, Newton, N.J., 1982-87; gen. mgr. WPSC FM, Wayne, N.J., from 1987. Cons. KAA Prodns., Montville, N.J., Satellite Shack, Montville. Democrat. Avocations: travel, fishing. Home: Shamrock, Tex. Died Nov. 2, 2004.

KILBANE, ANNE L., judge; b. Cleve., Sept. 22, 1941; d. Thomas Bryan and Nora (Coyle) K. BA in Chemistry, Seton Hill Coll., Greensburg, Pa., 1963; JD, Cleve. Marshall Coll. Law, 1976. Bar: Ohio 1977, U.S. Dist. Ct. (so. dist.) Ohio 1977, U.S. Dist. Ct. (no. dist.) Ohio 1978), U.S. Ct. Appeals (6th cir.) 1978, U.S. Supreme Ct. 1985. Sr. chemist Dept. of Health City of Cleve., 1963-66; chief brewing chemist, asst. quality control mgr. Carling Brewing Co., Cleve., 1966-71; chemist, plant mgr. Phillips Syrup Corp., Parma, Ohio, 1971-75; asst. to dir. law City of Cleve., 1975-77; assoc. Kilbane & Kilbane, Columbus, Ohio, 1977-78, Nurenberg, Plevin, Heller, Cleve., 1978-86, ptnr., 1986-99; judge Ohio Ct. of Appeals (8th dist.), Cuyahoga County, Ohio, from 1999. Lectr. in field. Mem. Ohio State Bar Assn. (negligence subcom.), Ohio Women's Bar Assn. (founding), Ohio Jud. Conf., Ohio Ct. Appeal Judge's Assn., Cuyahoga County Bar Assn. (appellate sect.), Cleve. Bar Assn. (appellate sect., commn. on women in the law), Nat. Lawyers Assn., 6th Cir. Jud. Conf. (life), Cleve. Marshall Alumnae Assn. (life), Am. Chem. Soc. Home: Lakewood, Ohio. Died Nov. 23, 2004.

KILGOUR, FREDERICK GRIDLEY, librarian, educator; b. Springfield, Mass., Jan. 6, 1914; s. Edward Francis and Lillian Bess (Piper) K.; m. Eleanor Margaret Beach, Sept. 3, 1940; children: Martha, Alison, Meredith. AB, Harvard U., 1935; student, Columbia Sch. Library Service, summers 1939-41; LLD (hon.), Marietta Coll., 1980, Coll. of Wooster, 1981; DHL (hon.), Ohio State U., 1980, Denison U., 1983, U. Mo., Kansas City, 1989. Staff Harvard Coll. Library, 1935-42, OSS, 1942-45; dep. dir. office of intelligence collection and dissemination U.S. Dept. State, 1946-48; librarian Yale Med. Library, 1948-65; asso. librarian for research and devel. Yale U. Library, 1965-67; mng. editor Yale Jour. Biology and Medicine, 1949-65; lectr. in history of sci. Yale U., 1950-59, lectr. history of tech., 1961-67; fellow Davenport Coll., 1950-67; pres., exec. dir. Online Computer Library Ctr., OCLC, Inc., 1967-80, vice chmn. bd. trustees Online Computer Library Ctr., 1981-83; founder trustee Online Computer Libr. Ctr., 1984—95; Disting. rsch. prof. U. N.C., Chapel Hill, 1990—2000. Author: Library of the Medical Institution of Yale College and Its Catalogue of 1865, 1960, The Library and Information Science CumIndex, 1975, The Evolution of the Book, 1998; co-author: Engineering in History, 1956, 90; author: Collected Papers, 3 vols., 1984; editor: Book of Bodily Exercises, 1960, Jour. Library Automation, 1968-71; contbr. articles to profl. jours. Served as lt. (j.g.) USNR, 1943-45, overseas duty. Decorated Legion of Merit; recipient Margaret Mann citation in cataloging and classification, 1974, Melvil Dewey medal, 1978; Acad./Research Librarian of Year, 1979, Lifetime Achievement award, Sch. Info. and Libr. Scis., 2004; Library Info. Tech. award, 1979, numerous others Mem. ALA, Am. Soc. Info. Sci. (Merit award 1979), Cosmos Club. Home: Chapel Hill, NC. Died July 31, 2006.

KIM, CHARLOTTE CHUNG-SOOK, retired librarian, administrator; b. Seoul, Korea, Apr. 15, 1940; came to U.S., 1963; d. Soon Kyung and Un Yun (Kim) Hong; m. Samuel C. Kang, Dec. 19, 1964 (div. Aug. 1976); Ben H. Kim, Nov. 17, 1985; children: Patricia Jean, Claudia Suk-Jin. BA, Yonsei U., 1962; MEd, Duquesne U., 1967; MLS, U. Pitts., 1968. Children's libr. Whitehall (Pa.) Pub. Libr., 1965-67, Carnegie Libr. Pitts., 1969-71, br. head, 1971-76, divsn. head, 1976-85; br. head Chgo. Pub. Libr., 1986-88, chief N.W. dist., 1989-90, asst. commr., 1990—2004, ret., from 2004. Bd. trustees North Cen. Coll., Naperville, Ill., 1995-2001. Bd. dirs. YWCA Met. Chgo., 1996-97, Korean Am. Scholarship Found., Chgo., 1992—, Chgo. Libr. Sys., 1991-96; v.p. Korean Am. Sr. Ctr., Chgo., 1994-98, pres., 1998—; v.p. Korean Am. Comty. Svcs., Chgo., 1990-93, Korean YWCA Chgo., 1997-98, bd. pres., 1999-2003, pres.; mem. adv. coun. Dem. and Peaceful Unification Korea, 1999-

2003, v.p.; del. White House Conf. on Libr. and Info. Svcs., 1991; pres. Korean Women's Internat. Network (ctrl. chpt. U.S. East region). Recipient Outstanding Pub. Svc. award Friends of Chgo. Pub. Libr, 1987, Disting. Pub. Svc. award Asian Human Svcs. of Chgo., 1992, Outstanding Comty. Svc. award Korean Am. Assn. Chgo., 1995, Asian Libr. of Yr. award Sec. Ill. State/Ill. State Libr., 1998, Outstanding Achievement Cmty. Leadership award YWCA Met. Chgo., 1998, Korean Presdl. award 1999, 2002, Kathy Osterman Superior Pub. Svc. award City of Chgo., 2003; named Man of Yr., Korea Cen. Daily of Chgo., 1988, One of 100 chgo. Women Making Difference, Today's Chgo. Woman, 1998. Mem. ALA (internat. rels. com. 1992—, councilor 1993-97), ALA/Ethnic Materials and Info. Exch. Round Table (bd. dirs. 1994-96), Ill. Libr. Assn., Asian/Pacific Am. Librs. Assn. (past pres. 1991-92). Democrat. Methodist. Avocations: travel, reading, opera, concerts, plays. Home: Chicago, Ill. Died May 1, 2005.

KIM, TONG RIM, art foundation administrator; b. Seoul, Korea, Jan. 20, 1916; came to U.S., 1964; d. Kuk Sun and Yoo Dang; m. Whanki Kim, May 1, 1944 (dec. July 1974); 1 child, Wha Young. Student, Ewha U., Seoul, 1934-36, U. Sorbonne, Paris, 1955-56, Ecole du Louvre, 1956-58. Dir. Whanki Found. Fine Arts for Young Artists, N.Y.C., 1979-99. Author: Life & Work, 1992, also essays. Founder Whanki Mus., Seoul. Home: New York, NY. Died Feb. 29, 2004.

KIMBALL, JAMES N., corporate media executive; b. LaVerkin, Utah, Oct. 27, 1934; s. Abram Noble and Louise (James) K.; m. Joan C. Kimball, Dec. 28, 1959; children: Ted, John, Amy. BS, U. Utah, 1959, MS, 1961. V.p. Terracor, Salt Lake City, 1969-73, Ivory & Co., Salt Lake City, 1978-80, Boyer Co., Salt Lake City, 1980-84, Morris/Ask Mr. Foster, Salt Lake City, 1986-89; pres. Kimbal Travel Cons., Salt Lake City, 1971-86, Kimbal Incentives, Salt Lake City, 1986-89; dir. media rels. Huntsman Chem. Corp., Salt Lake City, from 1989. Dir. Phlcorp, Inc., Phila. Columnist Deseret News, Utah Holiday mag. Mem. Dem. State Cen. Com., Salt Lake City, 1965-70; dep. dir. dept. devel. services of Utah, Salt Lake City, 1966-68; mem. instnl. council Dixie Coll., St. George, Utah, 1972-74; commr. Utah State Pub. Service Commn., Salt Lake City, 1978-80. Mem. Soc. Incentive Travel Execs., Meeting Planners Internat. Mem. Lds Ch. Avocations: scuba diving, mountain climbing, marathon running. Home: Salt Lake City, Utah. Died May 16, 2004.

KIMBRELL, JACQUELINE ANN, geriatrics nurse; b. Sweetwater, Tex., Aug. 15, 1953; d. Don V. and Peggy L. (Oliver) Nichols; m. Ted Kimbrell, May 20, 1971; children: Tracy, Marc. Student, Oscar B. Jones, 1978, Western Tex., 1990. Charge nurse Rolling Plains Hosp., Sweetwater; in-svc. coord. Loraine (Tex.) Nursing Ctr., charge nurse, dir. nursing; charge nurse Roscoe Nursing Ctr. Mem. ANA, NFLPN, Thi Pheta Kappa. Home: Sweetwater, Tex. Died July 24, 2004.

KIME, JOHN WILLIAM, retired military officer; b. Greensboro, N.C., July 15, 1934; m. Valerie Jean Hiddlestone., Aug. 5, 1980; 1 child, James. Grad., Balt. City Coll., 1951, USCG Acad., 1957, Indsl. Coll. Armed Forces, 1977; MS, MIT, 1964. Registered profl. engr., Mass. Commd. ensign USCG, 1957, advanced through grades to adm., 1990, ret., 1994; with CGC Casco, Loran Sta. Wake Island, 1960, CG Hdqs., Washington; prin. U.S. negotiator Internat. Maritime Orgn., London; 1st engring. officer CGC Boutwell, Boston; asst. chief merchant marine tech. divsn. CG Hdqs., Washington, 1977-78, dep. chief Office Marine Environ. & Systems, 1981-82, chief Office Marine Safety, Security and Environ. Protection, 1984-88, comdt., 1990-94; commdg. officer Marine Safety Office, Balt., 1978-81; chief ops. divsn. 7th CG Dist., Miami, 1982-84; comdr. 11th CG DIst., Long Beach, Calif., 1988-90; chmn., CEO Interocean Ugland Mgmt. Group, Voorhes, NJ, 1994—2005. Decorated Def. DSM, Transp. DSM, Army DSM, Navy DSM, Air Force DSM, CGDSM, Def. Superior Svc. medal, Legion of Merit. Fellow Soc. Naval Archs. and Marine Engrs. (hon. life, pres. 1992-94, Vice Adm. Jerry Land medal 1990, UN World Maritime prize 1993); mem. Am. Soc. Naval Engring., Tau Beta Pi, Sigma Xi. Died Sept. 14, 2006.

KIMMEL, ROBERT IRVING, communication systems design consultant, former state government official; b. Uniontown, Pa., Jan. 28, 1922; s. Andrew Filson and Dorothy Jean (Walker) K.; children: Donna Jean, Robert Filson, LuAnna Pat, Kevin Normaine, Gregory Paul. Student, Bucknell U., 1940—41, student, 1943—44, Washington U., St. Louis, 1942, Pa. State U., 1972. Self-employed entertainer, 1944; mgr. Cassiday Theaters, Midland, Mich., 1945—56; engring. illustrator Dow Chem. Co., Midland, 1956—59; engring. mgr. Radio Comm. Co., Bloomsburg, Pa., 1959—64; chief electronics Pa. State Police, Harrisburg, 1964—74, dir. comm. divsn., 1974—79; chmn. Pa. Law Enforcement Telecom. Planning Com., 1976—79; design cons. Comm. Sys. Design Assocs., Harrisburg, from 1979; v.p. Partnership, Inc., from 1980; mgr. Paxton Herald and Paxton Herald West newspapers, from 1981. Cons., lectr. in field. Contbr. articles to profl. jours. Mem. task force Cultural Ctr., Harrisburg, 1975-76; head coach Lakevue Midget Baseball Assn., 1976-78; pres. coun. St. Mark's Luth. Ch., Harrisburg, 1975-79; bd. dirs. Harrisburg Performing Arts Co., 1979, Emergency Health Svcs. Fedn., 1984-86; v.p., bd. dirs. Am. Lung Assn. Ctrl. Pa., 1987—, treas., 1989—; bd. dirs. Am. Lung Assn. Pa., 1988-92; chmn. LP Customer Postal Coun., 1992—; bd. dirs. Salvation Army Rehab., 1992—, John Heinz Sr. Ctr., 1994—, mng. dir., CEO, 1996; bd. dirs. United Negro Coll. Fund, 1994—; exec. dir. John Heinz Harrisburg Sr. Ctr., 1996-99; exec. dir. Pa. Assn. Sr. Ctrs., 1999-2001; instr. Dancers Workshop, 1979-86; sec.-treas. Susquehanna Valley Assn., 1984—; co-chmn. customer adv. coun. U.S. Postal Svc., 1991-93; co-chmn. United Negro Coll. Fund Ctr. Pa. Spl. Com., 1993—; exec. dir., constrn. cons. Greater Edgemont Sr. Ctr., 2001—; tech. adviser Ctrl. Pa. Sickle Cell Counsel, 2001—; tech. cons. Comm. Sys. Design Assocs., 2001—. Served with USAAF, 1942-43. Recipient various pub. svc. awards, certs. of merit. Fellow Radio Club Am.; mem. Assn. Pub. Safety Comm. Officers (pres. 1978-79), Pa. Chiefs Police Assn. (life; chmn. frequency adv. com. 1967-79), Engrs. Soc. Pa. (pres. 1978-79), Nat. Assn. Dance and Affiliated Artists (past v.p.), Greater Harrisburg Arts Coun. (dir.), Internat. Platform Assn. Achievements include developing vehicle location system, elec. security systems. Emails. Home: Harrisburg, Pa. Died July 20, 2005.

KIMWELI, DAVID MUTUA, psychologist; b. Machakos, Kenya, Jan. 17, 1955; came to U.S., 1984; s. Samson Kimweli and Alice (Waiu) Mutunge.; m. Joyce Kamanthe Kitoka, Apr. 18, 1981; children: David, Faith Sally. BA, Johnson Bible Coll., Tenn., 1985; MA, W. Ga. U., 1989; PhD, U. Ky., 2002. Headmaster Maiani Secondary Sch., Yoani, Machakos, Kenya, 1977-79; acct. Ministry of Water Devel., Embu, Eastern Province, Kenya, 1979-83; pres. Reach and Touch, Inc., Carrollton, Ga., from 1984; dir. Psychol. Learning Cons., Lexington. Dir. World Missions, Atlanta, 1990, Reach Kenya, Douglasville, Ga., 1992 Author: Spiritual Fullment, 1988, Gender-Role Development, Educational Level and Subjective Well-Being Among Appalachians, 2002. Recipient Athletic Championship Machakos Dist, Nunguni Macha Kos, 1974; named Best Sunday Sch. Tchr., A.I.C. Ch., Mukaa, 1975. Mem. Am. Psychol. Assn., Ky. State Bd. of Psychologists. Republican. Avocations: golf, tennis, soccer, reading, boating, running. Died May 9, 2004.

KIMZEY, JOHN HOWARD, chemical and aerospace engineer; b. New Orleans, Mar. 21, 1922; s. John Harrison and Mary Howard (Mallett) K.; m. Mary Eugenia Knight, Sept. 27, 1944; children: Carol Eugenia, Kaye Ellen, Mary Virginia, William Howard. AA, William and Mary Coll., Norfolk, Va., 1956; BS, Va. Poly., 1958. Registered profl. engr., Tex. Chem. engr. Nval Mine Engring. Facility, Yorktown, Va., 1958-62; aero. engr., mem. various publ. revs. Lyndon B. Johnson Space Ctr., Houston, 1962-86, subsystem mgr. spacecraft materials, 1985-86; engring. cons. Eagle Engring., Houston, from 1986. Author: Flammability as Related to Spacecraft Design and Operations, 1990, Material Selections for Spacecraft Applications, 1993; contbr. articles to profl. jours. Charter pres. Bay Area Lions Club, Houston, 1964. Lt. USN, 1943-53. Mem. NFPA (hyperbaric chambers com.). Baptist. Achievements include research in Skylab experiment M-479, Zero Gravity Flammability. Home: Nassau Bay, Tex. Died Aug. 30, 2004.

KINDERMAN, A. SANDFORD, manufacturing executive; b. Phila., June 26, 1943; s. Srully and Petty (Miller) K.; m. Judy Zucker, Jan. 30, 1972; children: Dori Jane, Karen, Richard. BA, Lake Forest Coll., 1965. With Brite Star Mfg. Co., Inc., Phila., from 1965, owner, chmn., 1980—2006. Patentee in field. Home: Gladwyne, Pa. Died Mar. 29, 2006.

KINDMAN, JERRY, lawyer, accountant; b. N.Y.C., Jan. 24, 1937; s. Harry and Dorothy (Rosengarten) K.; m. Gloria Ruth Katz, Dec. 10, 1946; children: Hillary, Jennifer. BS in Acctg., Queens Coll., 1960; JD, NYU, 1963, LLM in Taxation, 1967. Bar: N.Y.; CPA. Staff acct. Laventhol & Horwath, N.Y.C., 1960-61, Ernst & Ernst, N.Y.C., 1962-63; tax atty. Hertz Corp., N.Y.C., 1964-65, Am. Metal Climax, N.Y.C., 1965-67, Liggett & Myers, N.Y.C., 1967-71; lectr. City U. N.Y., N.Y.C., 1968-77; ptnr. Schmall & Kindman, N.Y.C., 1972-82; pres. Jerry Kindman & Co., P.C., N.Y.C., from 1983. Bd. dirs. The Radio Found., Sutton House, N.Y.C. Bd. dirs. N.Y. Young Rep. Club, N.Y.C., 1961-67. Served to Specialist 4th class U.S. Army, 1956-63. Mem. Am. Inst. CPA's, N.Y. State Soc. CPA's. Home: East Hampton, NY. Died Nov. 12, 2004.

KING, CLARENCE LEROY, JR., lawyer; b. Salina, Kans., Apr. 5, 1932; s. Clarence L. Sr. and Margaret R. (Swift) K.; m. Doris I. Altman, Aug. 18, 1951; children: Jeffrey E., Joni D. BA, Kansas Wesleyan U., Salina, 1954; JD, Washburn U., 1957. Bar: Kans. 1957; U.S. Dist. Ct. 1957, U.S. Dist. Ct. 10th Cir., 1987; U.S. Supreme Ct. 1972. Sole practice, Salina, 1957-58; ptnr. King & Stokes, Salina, 1958-73, King, Stokes, Knudson & Nitz, Salina, 1974-81, King, Adrian & King, Salina, 1981-82, King, Adrian, King & Brown, Salina, 1982-91; with Hampton, Royce, Engleman & Nelson L.C., Salina, from 1991. Faculty Kans. Coll. Trial Advocacy, mem. Govs. Regional Com. on Criminal Adminstrn., 1969; regional chmn. White House Conf. on Children and Youth, Kans. del., mem. exec. com., 1970; Kans. Hwy. Commr. 1974-75. Author (with others) Kansas Workers Compension Manual, 1978; contbr. articles to profl. jours. Active Univ. Meth. Ch.; active against juvenile delinquency; del. Dem. Nat. Conv., 1968; mem. state platform com., 1968, 70, 76; mem. adult chpt. Fellowship Christian Athletes; mem. Kans. Citizens for the Arts Com.; life mem. PTA; pres. local PTA 1966-67; sec. youth com. YMCA, 1972-73; trustee Kans. Wesleyan U.; organizer, hon. bd. dirs. Big Bros. and Big Sisters, Salina Youth Care Home Found., Inc.; bd. dirs. Children's Spl. Edn. Ctr.; chmn. bd. dirs. Cen. Kans. Mental Health Ctr., 1964-65. Named Outstanding Young Man of Salina, 1961, Outstanding Young Alumnus, Kans. Wesleyan U., 1965; recipient St. Francis Disting. Service to Youth award, 1971, Patriot of Today award NAACP, 1976, Masters in Trial award Am. Bd. Trial Advs., 1995. Mem. ABA, Am. Trial Lawyers Assn., Am. Bd. Trial Advs. (adv., nat. exec. com. 1985, 1987, chpt. pres. 1983-84, nat. pres. 1991), Kans. Bar Assn. (mem. various coms., chmn. litigation sect. 1983-85, outstanding svc. award, 1984, Phil Lewis Medal of Distinction, 1994, bd. dirs.), Northwest Kans. Bar Assn., Kans. Trial Lawyers Assn., Salina County Bar Assn. (mem. various coms., pres. 1973), Kans. Young Lawyers (v.p. 1959, pres. 1964), Def. Research Inst. (exceptional performance citation, 1988), Kans. Def. Council (bd. dirs. 1978-83, pres. 1987-88), Kans. Coll. Ofcls. Assn., Salina C. of C. (bd. dirs. 1977-79, mem. various coms., outstanding young man award), Kans. Wesleyan U. Alumni Assn. (pres. 1959-60), Am. Coll. Legal Medicine (assoc. in law). Avocations: horses, antiques. Home: Salina, Kans. Died Jan. 17, 2004.

KING, CLARK CHAPMAN, JR., lawyer; b. Quincy, Ill., May 18, 1929; s. Clark Chapman and Miriam Doris (Decker) K.; m. Joyce Jepson Jones, Jan. 5, 1955; children: Clark Chapman III, Jeffrey L., Stephen D., Carolyn Ann. BA cum laude, Amherst Coll., 1951; LLB, Harvard U., 1954. Bar: Ill. 1955, U.S. Dist. Ct. (no. dist.) 1955, (mid. dist.) Ill. 1960, U.S. Ct. Appeals (7th) 1957, (5th) 1982, (11th) 1985, (6th) 1984, U.S. Supreme Ct. 1977. Asst. atty. gen. State of Ill., Springfield, 1954, spl. asst. atty. gen., 1957-60; assoc. Robertson, Kepner, Springfield, 1957-60, Hough, Young & Coale, Chgo., 1960-61; ptnr. Lord, Bissell & Brook, Chgo., 1961-94, of counsel, 1994—2006. Active Northbrook Civic Assn.; vice-chmn. Cook County Young Reps., Chgo., 1960; area chmn. Northfield Twp. Rep. Orgn., 1960-70. Sgt. U.S. Army, 1954-57. Mem. Chgo. Bar Assn., Internat. Bar Assn., Agrl. Bar Assn. Avocations: fishing, hunting. Home: Northbrook, Ill. Died Mar. 6, 2006.

KING, CLARK ELMER, utilities executive; b. Sunderland, Iowa, July 24, 1934; s. Elmer E. and Willma (Clark) K.; m. Margaret Thompson, Dec. 2, 1960; children: Ronald Clark, Kathy Kay. BSEE, Finlay Engring. Coll., Kansas City, 1954. Engr. trainee/service engr. Pub. Service Co. of Okla., Tulsa, 1954-65, project. engr., 1965-67, sales supr., 1967-73, dir. area devel., 1973-74, div. asst. mgr., 1974-76, dist. mgr. Lawton, 1976-78, mgr. rates Tulsa, 1978-81, div. mgr. McAlester, 1981-83, v.p. mktg. ops. Tulsa, from 1983. Dir. Ark. Basin Devel. Auth., Tulsa, 1986—. With U.S. Army, 1957-59. Avocation: golf. Home: Punta Gorda, Fla. Died June 17, 2004.

KING, CORETTA SCOTT, civil rights advocate, educational association administrator, writer; b. Heiberger, Ala., Apr. 27, 1927; d. Obidiah and Bernice (McMurray) Scott; m. Martin Luther King, Jr., June 18, 1953 (dec. Apr. 4, 1968); children: Yolanda Denise, Martin Luther III, Dexter Scott, Bernice Albertine. AB, Antioch Coll., 1951; Mus.B., New Eng. Conservatory Music, 1954, Mus.D., 1971; L.H.D., Boston U., 1969, Marymount-Manhattan Coll., 1969, Morehouse Coll., 1970; H.H.D., Brandeis U., 1969, Wilberforce U., 1970, Bethune-Cookman Coll., 1970, Princeton U., 1970; LL.D., Bates Coll., 1971. Voice instr. Morris Brown Coll., Atlanta, 1962; commentator CNN, Atlanta, 1980—2006; lectr., writer; founding pres., CEO Martin Luther King Jr. Ctr. for Nonviolent Social Change Inc., 1968—2006. Chairwoman Martin Luther King, Jr. Fed. Holiday Commn.; mem. Black Leadership Forum, Black Leadership Roundtable. Author: My Life With Martin Luther King, Jr., 1969, The Words of Martin Luther King, 1983; contbr. articles to mags.; syndicated newspaper columnist N.Y. Times Syndication Sales Corp., 1986-90, United Features Syndicate, 1990-94; concert debut, Springfield, Ohio, 1948; numerous concerts throughout U.S., concerts, India, 1959, performances, Freedom Concert; freelance journalist. Del. to White House Conf. Children and Youth, 1960; sponsor Com. for Sane Nuclear Policy, Com. on Responsibility, Moblzn. to End War in Viet Nam, 1966, 67, Margaret Sanger Meml. Found.; mem. So. Rural Action Project, Inc.; pres. Martin Luther King, Jr. Found.; chmn. Commn. on Econ. Justice for Women; mem. exec. com. Nat. Com. Inquiry; co-chmn. Clergy and Laymen Concerned about Vietnam, Nat. Com. for Full Employment, 1974; pres. Martin Luther King Jr. Center for Nonviolent Social Change; co-chairperson Nat. Com. Full Employment; mem. exec. bd. Nat. Health Ins. Com.; active YWCA; bd. dirs. So. Christian Leadership Conf., Martin Luther King, Jr. Found. Gt. Britain; trustee Robert F. Kennedy Meml. Found., Ebenezer Bapt. Ch. Recipient Nat. Coun. Negro Women Ann. Brotherhood award, 1957, Outstanding Citizenship award Montgomery (Ala.) Improvement Assn., 1959, Merit award St. Louis Argus, 1960, Distinguished Achievement award Nat. Orgn. Colored Women's Clubs, 1962, Louise Waterman Wise award Am. Jewish Congress Women's Aux., 1963, Myrtle Wreath award Cleve. Hadassah, 1965, award for excellence in field human relations Soc. Family of May, 1968, Universal Love award Premio San Valentine Com., 1968, Wateler Peace prize, 1968, Dag Hammarskjold award, 1969, Pacem in Terris award Internat. Overseas Service Found., 1969, Leadership for Freedom award Roosevelt U., 1971, Martin Luther King Meml. medal Coll. City N.Y., 1971, Internat. Viareggio award, 1971, Eugene V. Debs award, 1982, numerous others; named Woman of Year Utility Club N.Y.C., 1962, Woman of Year Nat. Assn. Radio and TV Announcers, 1968, UAW Social Justice award, 1980. Mem. Nat. Council Negro Women (Ann. Brotherhood award 1957), Women Strike for

Peace (del. disarmament conf. Geneva, Switzerland 1962, citation for work in peace and freedom 1963), Women's Internat. League for Peace and Freedom, NAACP, United Ch. Women (bd. mgrs.), Alpha Kappa Alpha (hon.) Baptist (mem. choir, guild adviser). Club: Links (Human Dignity and Human Rights award Norfolk chpt. 1964). Died Jan. 31, 2006.

KING, EDMUND LUDWIG, retired language educator; b. St. Louis, Jan. 10, 1914; s. William Frederick B. Seifert and Lydia (Ludwig) King; m. Willard Mae Fahrenkamp (dec. 2004), Jan. 29, 1951. BA, U. Tex., 1933, MA, 1934, PhD, 1949. Instr., asst. prof. modern langs. Miss. State Coll., 1936-41; instr. English U. Tex., Austin, 1946; instr. Spanish Princeton (N.J.) U., 1946-50, asst. prof. Spanish, 1950-57, assoc. prof., 1957-66, prof. Spanish, 1966—82, Carpenter prof. Spanish, 1976—82, prof. emeritus, 1982—2005. Chmn. romance langs. Princeton U., 1966-72, corp. pres. Internat. Inst. in Spain, Boston, Madrid, 1975-82, resident dir. 1982-83. Author: Becquer: From Painter to Poet, 1953; translator: The Structure of Spanish History, 1953; editor: El Humo Dormido, 1991; cons. American Heritage Larousse Spanish Dictionary, 1986. Maj. U.S. Army, 1941-46. Mem. MLA, Hispanic Soc. Am. (corr.), Internat. Inst. in Spain (hon. dir.). Democrat. Episcopalian. Avocations: music, gardening. Home: Princeton, NJ. Died Dec. 24, 2005.

KING, JAMES AMBROS, tenor; b. Dodge City, Kans., May 22, 1925; s. Howard Willis and Hettie Lenora (Shaffer) K.; married; children: David, Daniel, Ruth, Thomas, Elisabeth. Mus.B., La. State U., 1950; MA, U. Kansas City, Mo., 1952; Litt.D. (hon.), U. Ky., 1978; L.H.D. (hon.), U. Mo., 1980; voice studies with, Dallas Draper, Martial Singher, Max Lorenz, William Hughes. Prof. music U. Ky., Lexington, 1952-61. Debut, Deutsche Oper, Berlin, 1962, Salzburg (Vienna) Festival, 1962, Bayreuth Festival, 1965, Vienna State Opera, 1963, Met. Opera, 1966, appearances, Kammersanger, Hamburg, Berlin, Munich, Zurich, and Vienna state operas, LaScala, Milano, Opera de Paris, Bolshoi Theater, Moscow, San Francisco Opera, Salzburg Festival, Covent Garden, London, Tokyo Opera, Met. Opera, N.Y.C., Deutsche Oper Berlin, Teatro Colón, Buenos Aires, Chgo. Opera, Stuttgart Opera, others; leading roles in: German film prodns. of operas and Fidelio; various appearances, European TV, 25 major recs., including 14 complete operas. Served with AC USN, 1943-45. Winner Am. Opera Auditions Cin., 1961; named Alumnus of Yr. La. State U., 1979, 80; awarded title of Kammersänger cities of West Berlin, Munich, and Vienna. Mem. Phi Mu Alpha Sinfornia, Omicron Delta Kappa. Baptist. Died Nov. 20, 2005.

KING, M. JEAN, association executive; b. Cleve., May 5, 1930; BS in Med. Tech., U. Del., 1960, MS in Microbiology, 1960. Med. technologist Del. Hosp., Wilmington, 1950-60; staff microbiologist Wilmington Gen. Hosp., 1960-61, Episcopal Hosp., Phila., 1961-68; mem. faculty dept. microbiology Temple. U. Med. Sch., 1966-68; staff microbiologist Crozier Chester (Pa.) Med. Ctr., 1969-71; pres., founder Ind. Dogs, Inc., Chadds Ford, from 1984; designer Parkinson's Walker Dog Pilot Program, U. Pa. Hosp., Phila., 1997. Pres. Akbash Dogs Internat., 1987; speaker rehab. hosps., svc. orgns., self help groups, radio and TV. Theater pipe organ concert artist Longwood Gardens, Kennett Square, Pa., Dickenson Theater Organ Soc., Wilmington, Del., Sunnybrook Ballroom, Pottsdown, Pa., Marietta (Pa.) Theater, Phoenixville (Pa.) Theater. Founder Parkinsans Walker Dog Pilot Program, U. Pa. Hosp. Recipient award Delta Soc., Am. Animal Hosp. Assn., Gaines Dog Food, 1987-88, Work with Handicapped Population citation Pres. George Bush, 1990, Poor Richard Pro Bono award, 1994; named to Hall of Fame, U. Del., 1988. Mem. Am. Akbash Dog Assn. (pres. emeritus), Delta Soc., Del. County C. of C., Beta Beta Beta. Home: Chadds Ford, Pa. Died Oct. 12, 2005.

KING, MARCIA JONES, artist, physicist, photographer; b. Oak Park, Ill., May 17, 1934; d. Walter Leland Jones and Florence W. (Dull) Anderson; m. James Craig King, Nov., 1953 (div. 1966); 1 child, James Craig King, Jr. BS, Johns Hopkins U., 1960, PhD, 1969. Elec. engr. Electronic Comm., Inc., Timonium, Md., 1959-63; rsch. assoc. theoretical particle physics Syracuse (N.Y.) U., 1969-72; asst. editor Phys. Rev. Brookhaven Nat. Lab., Upton, N.Y., 1972-74; physicist Argonne (Ill.) Nat. Lab., 1974-78; pvt. practice potter and physicist Syracuse, N.Y., from 1978. Contbr. articles to profl. jours.; exhibitor pots throughout Ctrl. N.Y.; one-woman photography shows in Ctrl. N.Y. and So. Calif.; author: Nature's Telling: Anza-Borrego Desert, 1996. Mem. AAAS, Am. Phys. Soc., Syracuse Ceramic Guild (pres. 1982-84), Phi Beta Kappa, Sigma Xi. Democrat. Died Oct. 24, 2004.

KING, NAOMI MINNIE, artist, educator; b. L.A., June 5, 1913; d. Leander Leroy and Minnie M. (Dodge) Breard; m. Francis Hartford; 1 child, Margaret Mary Hartford Weintraub; m. John M. Riley; 1 child, John Martin Riley; m. J. Deane King. Fashion designer, Milw., Dallas, L.A., 1945-62; owner Piccolinos, Glendale, Calif., 1962-73; curator pub. art Descanso Gardens, La Canada, Calif., 1979-81; artist, tchr. continuing edn. Santa Barbara (Calif.) City Coll., 1990-98. One woman shows include Descanso Hospitality House, 1981, Faulkner Gallery East, Santa Barbara, 1984, The Astra Gallery, 1985, 86, Downey Mus. Art, 1991, Alley Gallery, 1994; exhibited in group shows at Cabrillo Art Ctr., 1980, 85-98, Reynolds Gallery, Santa Barbara, 1993, others; slides of works included in archives of Nat. Mus. Women in the Arts, 1993-98. Home: Culver City, Calif. Died Mar. 14, 2004.

KING, RICHARD ALLEN, lawyer; b. St. Joseph, Mo., July 4, 1944; s. Allen Welden and Lola (Donelson) K.; m. Deedee Gershenson, Apr. 19, 1986; children from previous marriage: Mary, Suzanne, Allen. BA, U. Mo., Columbia, 1966, JD cum laude, 1968. Bar: Mo. 1968. Law clk. Office of Chief Counsel, IRS, 1967; assoc. Reese, Constance, Slayton, Stewart & Stewart, Independence, Mo., 1968—73; ptnr. Constance, Slayton, Stewart & King, Independence, 1973—80, Cochran, Kramer, Kapke, Willerth & King, Independence, 1980—81; exec. asst. to gov. State of Mo., Jefferson City, 1981—82, dir. revenue, 1982—85; ptnr. Smith, Gill, Fisher and Butts, Inc., Kansas City, Mo., 1985—87, Wirken & King, Kansas City, 1988—93; chmn., CEO King Hershey, Kansas City, Mo., from 1993. Asst. city counselor City of Independence, 1968—69, mayor, 1974—78; vice chmn. Nat. Conf. Rep. Mayors, 1975—77; chmn. Mo. Gov.'s Task Force on Cmty. Crime Prevention, 1975—76, Kansas City Pub. Improvements Adv. Com., 1991—96, KC Team Effort, 1991—95; pres. Good Govt. League, Independence, 1972—73; mem. Mo. Commn. Human Rights, 1973—74; bd. dirs. Multistate Tax Commn., 1983—85, Chrisman Sawyer Bank, 1989—95. Contbr. articles to profl. jours. Bd. dirs. Am. Cancer Soc., Independence, 1973-79, chmn. crusade, 1973; bd. dirs. Independence Boys Club, 1972-79, Independence Cmty. Assn. Arts, 1973-76, Independence Sanitarium and Hosp., 1974-78, Jefferson City Meml. Hosp., 1981-85, NE Jackson County Mental Health Ctr., 1978-80, Greater Kansas City Nat. Coun. on Alcoholism, 1978-81, Am. Legion Boys State Mo., Jefferson City United Way, 1982-85, Multi-State Tax Commn., 1982-85, Jackson County Hist. Soc., Nat. Frontier Trails Mus.; pres. Friends U. Mo. Truman Campus, 1979-80, Kansas City Consensus, 1989-90; trustee Harry S Truman Scholarship Found., 1975-78, Kansas City U., 1979-80, Andrew Drumm Inst., 1990—, pres. bd. trustees, 1992-94; bd. vis. Park U., 2005-. Capt. U.S. Army, 1969—72. Recipient Outstanding Young Man of Mo. award Mo. Jaycees, 1975, award Mo. Inst. Pub. Adminstrn., 1983 Mem.: ACLU (bd. dirs. Kans. chpt. from 2006, bd. dirs. We. Mo. chpt. from 2006), ABA, Independence C. of C. (pres. 1980—81), Mo. Econ. Devel. Fin. Assn. (bd. dirs. from 1990, pres. 1999—2001), Kansas City Bar Assn., Internat. Assn. Gaming Attys., Nat. Assn. Bond Lawyers, Kansas City Bar Assn. (chmn. real estate law com. 1988—89), Ea. Jackson County Bar Assn., Mo. Bar Assn., Order of Coif, Beta Theta Pi, Phi Delta Phi. Unitarian Universalist. Home: Kansas City, Mo. Died Aug. 24, 2006.

KING, RONOLD WYETH PERCIVAL, physicist, educator; b. Williamstown, Mass., Sept. 19, 1905; s. James Percival and Edith Marianne Beate (Seyerlen) K.; m. Justine Merrell, June 22, 1937 (dec. Aug. 1990); 1 son, Christopher Merrell; m. Mary M. Govoni, June 1, 1991. AB, U. Rochester, 1927, S.M., 1929; PhD, U. Wis., 1932; student, U. Munich, Germany, 1928-29, Cornell U., 1929-30. Asst. in physics U. Rochester, 1927-28; Am.-German exchange student, 1929-30; White fellow in physics Cornell U., 1929-30; U. fellow in elec. engring. U. Wis., 1930-32, research asst., 1932-34; instr. physics Lafayette Coll., 1934-36, asst. prof., 1936-37; Guggenheim fellow Berlin, 1937-38; with Harvard U., 1938, successively instr., asst. prof., assoc. prof., 1938-46, prof. applied physics, 1946-72, prof. emeritus, 1972—2006. Cons. electromagnetics and antennas, 1972—2006. Author: Electromagnetic Engineering, Vol. 1, 1945, 2d edit, Fundamental Electromagnetic Theory, 1963, Transmission Lines, Antennas and Wave Guides, (with A.H. Wing and H.R. Mimmo), 1945, 2d edit., 1965, Transmission-Line Theory, 1955, 2d edit., 1965, Theory of Linear Antennas, 1956, (with T.T. Wu) Scattering and Diffraction of Waves, 1959, (with R.B. Mack and S.S. Sandler) Arrays of Cylindrical Dipoles, 1968, (with C.W. Harrison, Jr.) Antennas and Waves: A Modern Approach, 1969, Tables of Antenna Characteristics, 1971, (with G.S. Smith et al) Antennas in Matter, 1981 (with S. Prasad) Fundamental Electromagnetic Theory and Applications, 1986, (with M. Owens and T.T. Wu) Lateral Electromagnetic Waves Theory and Applications to Communications, Geophysical Exploration and Remote Sensing, 1992 (with G. Fikioris and R.B. Mack) Cylindrical Depole Arrays, 2002; also articles in field. Guggenheim fellow Europe, 1937, 58, IBM scholar Northeastern U., 1985; recipient Disting. Service citation U. Wis., 1973, Pender award U. Pa., 1986. Fellow IEEE (Centennial medal 1984, Grad. Edn. award 1997, Disting. Educator award 2001), AAAS, Am. Acad. Arts and Scis., Am. Phys. Soc.; mem. IEEE Antennas and Propagation Soc. (Disting. Achievement award 1991, Chento Tai Disting. Educator award 2001), AAUP, Internat. Sci. Radio Union, Bavarian Acad. Sci. (contbg. mem.), Phi Beta Kappa, Sigma Xi. Home: Winchester, Mass. Died Apr. 10, 2006.

KING, VIRGINIA, librarian; b. Akron, Ohio, May 12, 1917; d. Wilson Reed and Eunice Mina (White) King. BS in Mus. Edn., Greenville Coll., 1939, BA, 1941; MusM, U. So. Calif., 1954, MLS, 1967. Tchr. music L.A. Pacific Coll., 1943—45, Greenville Coll., Ill., 1945—46, L.A. Pacific Coll., 1946—65; prof. music, libr. Azusa Pacific U., Calif., 1965—82, libr. music and periodicals, 1982—89; ret., 1989. Home: Stanwood, Wash. Died Feb. 25, 2006.

KINNEY, CAROL NAUS ROBERTS, real estate broker; b. Mpls., May 7, 1923; d. Edward Paul and Esther (Colwell) Naus; m. Thomas R. Roberts, May 2, 1942 (dec. Feb. 1968); children: Thomas Naus Roberts, Margaret Elizabeth Roberts, Shelley Roberts; m. Harry E. Kinney, Aug. 30, 1970 (div. Aug. 1988); life ptnr. Allan L. Levine, Feb. 1998. Student, Mt. Holyoke Coll., 1940-42; BA in Bacteriology magna cum laude, U. Minn., 1946. Mem. staff Los Alamos Scientific Lab., 1964-70; co-owner Harry E. Kinney Gen. Contractor, Albuquerque, 1977-81, 86; real estate broker Christopher Webster, Albuquerque, 1992-94, Kate Southard Real Estate, Albuquerque, 1994-98, Carol Kinney Real Estate, Albuquerque, from 1998. City Councillor Los Alamos, N.Mex., 1968-70; chair 100 Yr. Cmty. Outreach U. N.Mex., Albuquerque, 1986-89; chair bd. of ethics and campaign practices City of Albuquerque, 1990-94; bd. N.Mex. Gov.'s Mansion Found., 1988-92, 96—. Honored as Albuquerque Vol. Jr. League of Albuquerque, 1985; entered into Albuquerque Sr. Hall of Fame, 1989—; Albuquerque's First Lady, 1974-78, 81-85. Mem.: Rio Grande Nature Ctr. (trustee 1984—86, from 1988), N.Mex. Symphony (trustee 1992—2001, exec. com. 1998—2001, emeritus trustee from 2001), The Nature Conservancy (trustee 1976—90, 1992—2000, Disting. trustee from 2001), Phi Beta Kappa, Beta Sigma Phi. Republican. Unitarian Universalist. Avocations: skiing, camping, contractor/foreman for building own home. Died Dec. 16, 2005.

KINNISON, HARRY AUSTIN, retired transportation engineer; b. Springfield, Ohio, Oct. 2, 1935; s. Errett Lowell and Audrey Muriel (Smith) K. BSEE, U. Wyo., 1964; M. in Transp. Engring., Seattle U., 1983; PhD in Civil Engring., U. Tenn., 1987. Enlisted USAF, 1958, commd. 2d lt., 1964, advanced through grades to capt., 1968, released from active duty, 1968; electronics engr. 1839th Electronics Installation Group, Keesler AFB, Biloxi, Miss., 1972-77; staff engr. Casper (Wyo.) Air Facilities Sector FAA, 1977; test engr. Boeing Aerospace Co., Seattle, 1977-81; grad. rsch. engr. U. Tenn. Transp. Ctr., Knoxville, 1983-87; avionics engr. Boeing Comml. Airplane Co., Seattle, 1981-83, 87-90, maintenance programs engr. customer svcs. divsn., 1990-2000; ret., 2000. Adj. asst. prof. aviation mgmt. Embry-Riddle Aero. U. Ext. Republican. Mem. Christian Ch. Home: Kent, Wash. Died July 10, 2004.

KINT, ARNE TONIS, industrial and mechanical engineer; b. Tallinn, Harjumaa, Estonia, Nov. 2, 1932; came to U.S., 1957; s. Tõnis and Salme (Redlich) Kint; m. Saima Kärp, Aug. 30, 1964. BSME, Stockholm Tekniska Inst., 1954; BS in Indsl. Engring., Ga. Inst. Tech., 1960; MS in Indsl. Engring., U. Calif., 1963. Registered profl. indsl. engr., Calif.; cert. profl. materials handling and mgmt., Mich. Mech. engr. Philips Neon Co., Stockholm, 1954-57; student indsl. engr. Weirton (W. Va.) Steel Co., 1959; plant, foundry engr. H.C. Macaulay Foundry Co., Inc., Berkeley, Calif., 1960-67; indsl. engring. project leader Matson Navigation Co., San Francisco, 1967-69; area indsl. engr. Interpace Corp., Pitts., 1969-72; cons. indsl. engr. Oakland, Calif., 1972-73; work design, analysis supr. Truck Divsn. Internat. Harvester Co., Inc., San Leandro, Calif., 1973-75; sr. systems project engr. Engineered Sys. & Devel. Corp., Santa Clara and San Jose, Calif., 1975-89; cons. ind. engr. Applied Engring. and Design, Inc., San Jose, Calif., 1989-90; project engr. Jacobs Engring. Group, Martinez, Calif., 1990-92; cons. ind. engr. Indsl. Engring. USA, Oakland, Calif., 1992-98; cons. to pres. Fabricated Metals, Inc., San Leandro, Calif., 1998-99; project mgr. Mason West, Inc., San Francisco, Calif., 1999-00. Bd. dirs. Estonian Info. Ctr., Stockholm, 1946-75; pres. Estonian League of Liberation, San Francisco, 1968-73. Decorated Gold Svc. medal Estonian Nat. Found., 1971. Mem. Estonian Soc. San Francisco (pres. 1962-63), Swedish Am. C. of C., Estonian Ski Club. Avocations: skiing, boating, hunting, travel, fishing. Home: Oakland, Calif. Died Aug. 2, 2005.

KINZELL, LA MOYNE B., health facility administrator, nursing educator; b. Melstone, Mont., May 4, 1930; d. William Edward and Iro Millicent (Keeton) Berger; m. Les Kieth Kinzell, Sept. 18, 1954; children: Yvette Li Goins, Anitra Elise Chew, Antony Mikhail Kinzell. BS, Mont. State U., 1954; MA, Calif. State U., Northridge, 1982. RN Calif. Instr. surg. nursing Mont. Deaconess Hosp., Great Falls, 1954-55; instr. nursing arts St. Patrick's Hosp., Missoula, Mont., 1957-59; instr. sci. Palmdale (Calif.) Sch. Dist., 1966-86, dir. health svcs., 1986-2000. Adv. bd. facilitator Palmdale Healthy Start, 1992-2000; com. mem. Am. Cancer Soc., 1986—, United Way, 1991—; bd. dirs. A.V. Ptnrs. in Health, 2000—. Mem. Citizen Amb. Sch. Nursing Del. to Europe, 1994; treas. campaign sch. bd. mem., Palmdale, 1989, 93, 97; bd. dirs. A.V. Symphony Orch. and Master Choral, 2000—, A.V. Light Found., 2001-. Recipient Tchr. of Yr. award Palmdale, 1985-86, Los Angeles County Sheriffs Dept. award, 1985, Nat. Every Child by Two, Immunization Ptnrs. award, 1995; grantee Drug, Alcohol and Tobacco Edn., 1987, Healthy Start Planning, 1994, 95, Healthy Start Operational award, 1996, 98. Mem. Am. Heart Assn. (bd. dirs. 1997-2001), Am. Lung Assn. (chair edn. 1988-94), Calif. Sch. Nurse Orgn. (sec. 1992-95), Health Careers Acad. (adv. com. 1995—), Phi Kappa Phi, Alpha Tau Delta, Sigma Theta Tau, Delta Kappa Gamma (area IX chair legislature 1993-95, area IX dir. 1995-97, area IX sec. 2001-, mem. Chi state expansion com. 1997-99, leadership com. 1999-2001, chair leadership com. 2001-03, profl. affairs com., 2003-05. scholarship com., 2005-07) Democrat. Episcopalian. Avocations: travel, gardening, geology, marine biology, swimming. Home: Palmdale, Calif. Died Apr. 14, 2006.

KIRSCHENBAUM, TERRY, lawyer; b. Bronx, Jan. 6, 1947; s. Paul and Goldie (Schuesty) K. BA in Math., CUNY, 1974, MS in Environ. Health, 1982, JD, 1986. Bar: N.Y. 1987, N.J. 1987. Pvt. practice, North Tarrytown, N.Y., from 1987; asst. scientist N.Y.C. Dept. Health, from 1982. Mem. ABA, Assn. Bar City N.Y. Avocation: amateur radio. Died May 27, 2004.

KISTLER, RICHARD EDWIN, operations research analyst; b. Ludington, Mich., June 20, 1931; s. Samuel Edwin and Jewel Marguerite (Loree) K.; m. Marianne McKeown, Mar. 21, 1959. BA, Lewis & Clark, 1952; MEd, U. Portland, 1956; PhD, Stanford U., 1964. Ins. underwriter Phil Grossmayer Co., Portland, Oreg., 1954-59; ford found. fellow Stanford U., Palo Alto, Calif., 1959-61, instr., 1961-62; analyst Naval Weapons Ctr., China Lake, Calif., 1962-75, comptroller, 1975-87, planner, from 1987. Contbr. articles and papers to profl. jours. Recipient Superior Civilian Svc. award Chief of Naval Material, 1984, Meritorious Civilian Svc. award Naval Weapons Ctr., 1991, Michelson Lab. award, 1967, Spl. citation, 1986. Democrat. Avocations: gardening, restoring old cars. Home: Ridgecrest, Calif. Died May 3, 2005.

KITNER, HAROLD, artist, educator; b. Cleve., May 18, 1921; s. Isaac and Frieda Kitner; m. Joyce Lapaz, Nov. 30, 1946; children: Jon, Ann, Kathi. MA, Case Western Res. U., 1947; postgrad., Cleve. Inst. Art, Ohio U., Cleve. Coll., Washington and Lee U.; D Equivalency, Kent State U., 1949. Chmn. fine arts Kent (Ohio) State U., 1950-74, dean Honors Coll., 1970-72, prof. emeritus, 1980. One-man shows include Cleve. Mus., Kent State U. Mus., Libr. Congress; represented in permanent collections at Akron Art Mus., Canton Art Inst., Cleve. Mus., Dayton Art Inst., Akron U., Kent State U. Negotiator, pres. faculty union AAUP, Kent., 1977-80; founder Blossom Festival Sch., Cleve., 1967. Jewish. Home: Charleston, SC. Died Jan. 3, 2004.

KIYASU, JOHN YUTAKA, biochemist, educator; b. San Francisco, Dec. 25, 1927; s. Kunisada and Sadako (Kiyasu) K.; m. Lily Y. Nomura; children: Patricia Kiyasu Blossom, Anne Kiyasu Murdock, Lynn Kiyasu Hartwell, John T. BA, U. Calif., 1950, MA, 1951, PhD, 1955. Registered profl. chemist. USPHS postdoctoral fellow U. Calif., Berkeley, 1955-56, U. Chgo., 1956-57; asst. prof. biochemistry U. Rochester (N.Y.) Sch. Medicine, 1960-63; assoc. prof. chemistry Adelphi U., Garden City, N.Y., 1963-67; rsch. biochemist Nassau County Med. Ctr., East Meadow, N.Y., 1967-70; dir. biochemistry St. Lukes-Roosevelt Med. Ctr., N.Y.C., 1970-83; pres. Serapine Labs., Inc., Garden City, 1983-90; chief chemist Brookdale Hosp. Med. Ctr., Bklyn., 1990-91; aquaculturalist Serapine Farms, Mill River, Mass., from 1994. Assoc. prof. pathology Columbia U., N.Y.C., 1974-94, prof. emeritus, 1994—; prof. emeritus chemistry Adelphi U. Contbr. articles to profl. publs. Bd. dirs. Japanese Am. Citizens League, N.Y.C., 1985-87, Garden City C. of C., 1985-88. Prin. investigator grantee NIH, 1960-67; postdoctoral fellow Nat. Heart Inst. Congregationalist. Achievements include patents in early detection of heart attacks. Home: Garden City, NY. Died May 2006.

KLARE, GEORGE ROGER, retired psychology professor; b. Mpls., Apr. 17, 1922; s. George C. and Lee (Launer) K.; m. Julia Marie Price Matson, Dec. 24, 1946; children: Deborah, Roger, Barbara. Student, U. Nebr., 1940-41, U. Minn., 1941-43, U. Mo., 1943; BA, U. Minn., 1946, MA, 1947, PhD, 1950. Instr. U. Minn., 1948-50; staff psychologist Psychol. Corp., N.Y.C., 1950-51; research assoc. U. Ill., 1952-54; asst. prof. dept. psychology Ohio U., Athens, 1954-57, assoc. prof., 1957-62, prof., 1962-79, Disting. prof., 1979-89, Disting. prof. emeritus, from 1989, chmn. dept., 1959-63, acting dean Coll. Arts and Sci., 1965, 85-86, dean, 1966-71, media coordinator, 1972-75, acting assoc. provost for grad. and research programs, 1986-87; research assoc. Harvard U., 1968-69; vis. prof. State U. N.Y. at Stony Brook, 1971-72, U. Iowa, 1979-80. Staff mem. N.Y.C. Writers Conf., 1956-57; cons., lectr. Nat. Project Agr. Communication, 1957-59, Com. on World Literacy and Christian Lit., 1958-62; exec. asst., sr. rsch. engr. Autonetics, 1960-61; cons. Resources Devel. Corp., 1962-65, Boston Pub. Sch., 1968, D.C. Heath Co., 1971, Western Electric, 1973, Westinghouse, 1975, Human Resources Rsch. Orgn., 1978-79, U.S. Navy, 1975, Armed Svcs. Readability Rsch., 1975, Center for Ednl. Exptl., Devel. and Evaluation, 1978-79, 81, U.S. Army, 1979, Bell System Center for Tech. Edn., 1975-80, Time, Inc., 1977-79, AT&T, 1979-81, 83,84, Coll. Osteo Medicine, Ohio U., 1987-89; lectr. Open Univ., Eng., 1975, NATO Conf. Visual Presentation of Info., The Netherlands, 1978, Beijing Normal U., 1990. Author: (with Byron Buck) Know Your Reader, 1954, The Measurement of Readability, 1963, (with Paul A. Games) Elementary Statistics: Data Analysis for the Behavioral Sciences, 1967, A Manual for Readable Writing, 1975, 4th edit., 1980, How to Write Readable English, 1985, Assessing Readability-Citation Classic, 1988; mem. editorial bd. Info. Design Jour., 1979—, Instrl. Sci., 1975-93, Reading Tchr., 1981-82, Reading Rsch. and Instrn., 1985-87, The Literacy Dictionary, 1993 (invited essay 1995). Served to 1st lt. USAAF, 1943-45. Decorated Air medal, Purple Heart; Fulbright travel grantee U.S.-U.K. Ednl. Commn. to Open U., 1977-81 Fellow Am. Psychol. Assn.; mem. Nat. Reading Conf. (invited address 1975, Oscar Causey award for outstanding contbns. to reading research 1981), Internat. Reading Assn. (elected to Hall of Fame 1997), Am. Ednl. Research Assn., Phi Beta Kappa, Delta Phi Lambda, Psi Chi, Phi Delta Kappa. Died Mar. 3, 2006.

KLEBER, BROOKS EDWARD, military historian; b. Trenton, N.J., Apr. 15, 1919; s. Brooks Charles and Eleanor Bennett (Stoddard) K.; m. Mae Emaline Stacey, Mar. 23, 1946. PhB, Dickinson Coll., 1940; MA, U. Pa., 1948, PhD, 1957. Asst. chief historian U.S. Army Chem. Corps, Army Chem. Ctr., Md., 1950-63; chief historian U.S. Continental Army Command, Ft. Monroe, Va., 1963-73, U.S. Tng. and Doctrine Command, Ft. Monroe, Va., 1973-80; dep. chief historian U.S. Ctr. Mil. History, Washington, 1980-84, asst. chief mil. history, 1984-87; ret. Cons. Time-Life WWII Series, Prisoners of War vol., 1981. Co-author: Chemicals in Combat in the U.S. Army in World War II, 1966; contbr. Dictionary of American Military Biography, 1984, The D-Day Encyclopedia, 1994. Capt. U.S. Army Inf., 1941-46, ETO (prisoner of war, Germany). Decorated Bronze Star, Combat Inf. badge, Meritorious Svc. medal; recipient two Dept. Army awards for civilian svc., 1983, 87, and one for exceptional civilian svc., 1993; named to Inf. OCS Hall of Fame, Ft. Benning, Ga., 1982. Fellow U.S. Army Mil. Inst.; mem. Soc. Mil. History (bd. trustees), Va. Res. Officers Assn. (pres. 1966-67). Avocation: birds. Home: Newport News, Va. Died Nov. 9, 2004.

KLEIN, DANIEL SIMON, physician; b. Yonkers, N.Y., Feb. 27, 1944; s. Charles William and Miriam (Cantor) K.; m. Lorraine Saulino, Mar. 15, 1976; children: Victoria, Elizabeth, Alexandra. BA, Harvard U., 1966; MD, Einstein Med. Coll., 1970. Diplomate Am. Bd. Internal Medicine. Intern Lincoln Hosp., N.Y.C., 1971; resident Montefiore Hosp., N.Y.C., 1973-74; attending physician Morrisonia Family Care Ctr., Bronx, 1975-76; pvt. practice Rawlins, Wyo., 1976-89; pub. health officer Albany County, Wyo., from 1996; pvt. practice Laramie, Wyo., from 1989. Adj. faculty U. Wash. Med. Sch., 1998—; clin. faculty family practice/internal medicine/nursing U. Wyo., 1995; clin. asst. prof. dept. medicine U. Wash. Med. Sch., 2000—. Sr. asst. surgeon USPHS, 1973-75. Recipient St. George award Am. Cancer Soc., 1998. Fellow: ACP-ASIM (gov. Wyo. chpt. 1996—2000); mem.: Wyo. Med. Soc. (trustee from 1994, Physician of the Yr. 1998). Democrat. Avocations: bicycling, skiing, spanish literature. Home: Laramie, Wyo. Died Feb. 15, 2004.

KLEIN, MARK PAUL, real estate developer; b. Champaign, Ill., Apr. 27, 1943; s. George and Mary Klein; m. Libby Klein; children: Marnee, Meredith. BBA, U. Pa., Phila., 1976; MBA, Drexel U., 1979. Owner Klein Real Estate, Newtown Square, Pa., from 1977. Prof. St. Joseph U., Phila., 1981, Pa. State U., Media, 1986, Polley U., Newtown Square, 1988-97. Comdr. CAP, 1970; bd. dirs. Buxmont Ballet Co., New Hope, Pa., 1980, Simon Milles Sales Co., Phila., 1987, Victoria Mills Co., Springfield, Pa., 1996. With USN, 1966-68. Avocations: sailing, skiing. Home: Newtown Square, Pa. Died Jan. 5, 2004.

KLESPER, NANCY LEE, nurse; b. Bridgeport, Conn., Oct. 7, 1947; d. Frederick William and Philomena Ann (Simmons) K.; m. Russell Bayles, June 14, 1974 (div. Sept. 1978). Student, Sacrad Heart U., 1975-77; grad., St. Vincent's Nursing Sch., Bridgeport, 1974; BA in Psychology, Bridgeport Nurse Anesthesia Sch.; MA in Psychology, Profl. Sch. Psychol. Studies, postgrad., from 1987. registered nurse anesthetist, N.C.; cert. hypnotist in psychology. Nurse operating room Norwalk (Conn.) Hosp., 1974-77, 79-80; asst. dir. nursing Roncelli Inst., Bridgeport, 1978-79; nurse psychiat. staff Conn. Mental Health, New Haven, 1979; nurse anesthetist St. Mary's Hosp., Waterbury, Conn., 1982-86; freelance anesthetist San Diego, La Jolla, Calif., from 1986. Mem. Am. Assn. Nurse Anesthetists, Calif. Assn. Nurse Anesthetists, Calif. Assn. Marriage and Family Therapists. Clubs: Sterling House Ski (Stratford, Conn.). Republican. Roman Catholic. Avocations: travel, swimming, writing, singing, education. Died Sept. 14, 2004.

KLIEVER, LONNIE DEAN, religion educator; b. Corn, Okla., Nov. 18, 1931; s. David R. and Amanda W. Kliever; m. Arthiss Marie Laughman, Aug. 14, 1964; children: Launa Natale, Marney. BA, Hardin-Simmons U., 1955; MDiv, Union Theol Sem., 1959; PhD, Duke U., 1963. Prof. philosophy U. Tex., El Paso, 1962-65; prof. religion Trinity U., San Antonio, 1965-69; prof. religious studies U. Windsor (Ont., Can.), 1969-75, So. Meth. U., Dallas, from 1975. Author: H. Richard Niebuhr, 1978, The Shattered Spectrum, 1981, The Terrible Meek, 1987, Dax's Case, 1989. Mem. Am. Acad. Religion, Soc. for Sci. Study of Religion, Can. Soc. for Study of Religion, Am. Cultural Assn., AAUP. Methodist. Home: Dallas, Tex. Died July 7, 2004.

KLIGERMAN, MORTON M., radiologist; b. Phila., Dec. 26, 1917; s. Samuel and Dorothy (Medvene) K.; m. Barbara B. Coleman, Mar. 14, 1956; children: Hilary, Thomas A., Valli á Court. BS, Temple U., 1938, MD, 1941, MSc, 1949; MA (hon.), Yale U., 1958; D.F.A. (hon.), New Sch. Music, 1985; MA (hon.), U. Pa., 1986. Instr. radiology Temple U., Phila., 1947-48, Columbia U., N.Y.C., 1948-50, asst. prof. radiology, 1950-53, assoc. prof., 1953-58; Robert E. Hunter prof. radiology, chmn. dept. radiology Yale U., New Haven; also radiologist-in-chief Yale-New Haven Hosp., 1958-72; dir. Cancer Research and Treatment Center U. N.Mex., Albuquerque, 1972-80, prof. radiology, 1972-80; asst. dir. for radiation therapy Los Alamos Sci. Lab., 1972-80; chief divsn. radiation oncology Bernalillo County Med. Center, Albuquerque, 1972-80; prof. radiation oncology U. Pa., Phila., 1980—2006, Henry K. Pancoast prof. research oncology, 1984-88, prof. emeritus, 1988—2006. Cons. on staff Presbyn. Hosp., Lovelace-Bataan Med. Center, St. Joseph Hosp., VA Hosp., all Albuquerque, Los Alamos Med. Center. Contbr. articles to profl. jours. Bd. dirs. Santa Fe Opera, 1975-80, mem. nat. adv. bd., 1980-89; bd. dirs. Santa Fe Opera Found., 1976-80, also pres.; bd. dirs. N.Mex. divsn. Am. Cancer Soc., 1972-76, Phila. divsn., 1985-89, Pa. Ballet, 1985-89; bd. advisors Annenberg Ctr., U. Pa., 1987-2001, bd. overseers, 2001-03, Phila. Scholar Fund, 1992—. With M.C., U.S. Army, 1944-47. Recipient Disting. Alumni award Temple U., 1964; Silver Medallion Columbia U., 1967; Grubbe Gold Medal award Chgo. Med. Soc.-Chgo. Radiol. Soc., 1976; Disting. Alumnus award Temple U. Med. Sch., 1986; named Med. Alumnus of Yr. Temple U. Med. Sch., 1989; Morton M. Kligerman endowed chair radiation oncology U. Pa. Med. Sch., 2003. Fellow Am. Coll. Radiology, Coll. Physicians Phila.; mem. Pa. Med. Soc., Philadelphia County Med. Soc., Am. Assn. Cancer Rsch., Am. Radium Soc. (v.p. 1976-77, pres. 1982-83, Janeway medal 1981), Am. Soc. Therapeutic Radiologists (pres. 1968-69, Gold medal 1982), Am. Legion, Alpha Omega Alpha. Home: Philadelphia, Pa. Died June 7, 2006.

KLINKSICK, CHARLES THEODORE, minister; b. Toledo, Ohio, June 12, 1916; s. Theodore George and Alma Marie (Kuhlman) K.; m. Lois Julia Jahnke, Jan. 10, 1945; children: James E., Carolyn R. Kaylor, Dale E., Joann M. Peters. BA, Capital U., Columbus, Ohio, 1938; MDiv, Trinity Luth. Sem., Columbus, Ohio, 1942; DMin, Josephinum Sem., Worthington, Ohio, 1976. Ordained to ministry Am. Luth. Ch., 1943. Founding pastor Christ Meml. Luth. Ch., Detroit, 1943-55; co-pastor Univ. Luth. Ch., E. Lansing, Mich., 1955-62; sr. pastor Clinton Hts. Luth. Ch., Columbus, Ohio, 1962-78; pastor Hope Luth. Ch., Hubbard lake, Mich., 1978-82; interim supply pastor chs. Grace Luth., 1st Presbyn., Alpena, Trinity Luth., Barton City, Mich., 1984-91; min. N.W. Mich. Synod, Evang. Luth. Ch. Am., Lansing, from 1982. Chmn. Luth. Housing Corp. of Alpena, Mich., 1983-91. Writer newspaper religious column, Life Lines, 1985—; author sermons in Selected Sermons, 1974, 75, 76; contbr. International Lesson Annual, 1991-92. Grantee, Ohio Synod of Am. Luth. Ch., 1942, 73, 75; inducted into Hall of Fame Woodward H.S., Toledo, Ohio, 1999. Mem. Kiwanis (bd. dirs. 1962, v.p., prog. chmn. 1975). Republican. Died Feb. 16, 2005.

KLOOSTER, JUDSON, retired dean; b. La Combe, Alta., Can., Dec. 24, 1925; s. Henry J. and Evelyn Mae (Eglin) K.; m. Arlene Jean Madsen, Nov. 28, 1948; children: Cherylin Klooster Peach, Lynette Carol Tibbetts, Terrill Ann Klooster McClanahan Hannum. Student, Andrews U., 1942-43, Pacific Union Coll., 1943—44; DDS, U. of the Pacific, 1947; MMS, Tulane U., 1968; D of Pub. Svc. (hon.), U. of the Pacific, 1992. Pvt. practice dentistry, San Francisco, 1947-49, Escondido, Calif., 1949-67; part-time mem. faculty Loma Linda (Calif.) U. Sch. Dentistry, 1956-67, full-time prof. restorative dentistry, 1967—97, dir. continuing edn., 1968-72, dean, 1971-94, dean emeritus, 1994—2004, emeritus prof. dentistry, 1997—2004. Mem. faculty U. Pacific Sch. Dentistry, 1947—49; cons. USPHS, VA. Treas. Am. Fund for Dental Health, 1987-89, v.p. 1990-91, pres., 1992-93. Lt. Dental Corps USNR, 1953-55. Fellow Am. Coll. Dentists, Internat. Coll. Dentists (councillor 1993-97, Lifetime Achievement award 2004); mem. ADA, Calif. Dental Assn. (chmn. coun. dental edn. 1972-75), Tri-County Dental Soc. (ex officio dir. 1971-94, pres.-elect 1978-79, pres. 1979-80), Rotary (pres. San Bernardino South club 1977-78), Xi Psi Phi. Republican. Mem. Seventh Day Adventist Ch. (elder 1969-2004). Home: Loma Linda, Calif. Died Oct. 31, 2004.

KLOSE, JULES ZEISER, physicist; b. St. Louis, Aug. 7, 1927; s. Julius Harry and Florence (Zeiser) K.; m. Evelyn Yvonne Brady, Jan. 22, 1958; children: Linda Marie, Jules Stephen, Charles David, James Michael. AB in Physics, Washington U., 1949; MS, U. Rochester, 1953; PhD, Cath. U. of Am., 1958. Physics aid U.S. Naval Gun Factory, Washington, 1948; instr. Dunford Sch., St. Louis, 1949; asst. prof. physics U.S. Naval Acad., Annapolis, Md., 1953-58, assoc. prof. physics, 1959-61; physicist Nat. Inst. Standards and Tech., Gathersburg, Md., 1961-88, contractor, 1989-90. Guest scientist Nat. Inst. Standards and Tech., Gaithersburg, 1991—; rsch. assoc. and lectr. U. Mich., Ann Arbor, 1960-61. Author: (book) Radiometric Standards in Vacuum Ultraviolet, 1987; contbr. articles to profl. jours. Basketball coach St. Mary's Elem. Sch., Annapolis, 1969-86; pres. Anne Arundel County Tennis Assn., Annapolis, 1970-71; soccer coach St. Mary's High Sch., Annapolis, 1978-79. With AUS, 1946-47, PTO. Mem. Am. Phys. Soc., Optical Soc. Am., Coun. for Optical Radiation Measurements, Severn Valley Racquet Club, Sigma Xi. Achievements include devel. of modern method of measuring lifetimes of atomic and molecular excitations; rsch. on vacuum ultraviolet radiometry, atomic transition probabilities, ultrasonics, thermal relaxation in gases, cosmic rays, space instruments. Home: Annapolis, Md. Died Aug. 8, 2004.

KLÜVER, JOHAN WILHELM (BILLY KLÜVER), electrical engineer, writer; b. Monaco, Monaco, Nov. 13, 1927; came to U.S., 1954; s. Johan Wilhelm and Greta (Lundborg) K.; m. Olga Adorno, 1965 (div. 1975); children: Maja, Kristian Patrik; m. Julie Breyer Martin, 1983. Degree in elec. engring., Royal Inst. Tech., Stockholm, Sweden, 1951; MSEE, U. Calif., Berkeley, 1955, PhD in Elec. Engring., 1957; DFA (hon.), New Sch. Social Rsch., 1998. Asst. prof. U. Calif., 1957-58; mem. tech. staff Bell Telphone Labs., Murray Hill, N.J., 1958-68; former pres. Experiments in Art and Tech., Inc., N.Y.C. Curator in field; prodr. 9 Evenings: Theatre and Engring., 1966; commr.

Pepsi Pavilion, Expo 70, Osaka, Japan, 1970; commr. U.S. contbn. to Paris Biennale for Young Artists, 1969; lectr. in field. Author: Un Jour avec Picasso, 1994, A Day With Picasso, 1997; co-author: Kiki's Paris, 1989; editor: Pavilion, 1972; co-editor: Kiki's Memoirs, 1996; contbr. articles to profl. jours. Mem. IEEE, Am. Phys. Soc., Am. Optical Soc., Soc. for Info. Display, Royal Order of Vasa, Phi Beta Kappa, Sigma Xi. Died Jan. 11, 2004.

KNEEPKENS, THOMAS JOHN, accountant, financial planner; b. Appleton, Wis., July 20, 1951; s. Sylvester Anthony and Beverly June (McGoey) K.; m. Linda Jean Otte, July 23, 1971; children: Andrea Jean, Anthony Thomas. BBA, U. Wis., Oshkosh, 1976. CPA, Wis.; cert. fin. planner; personal fin. specialist. Sr. acct. Clifton Gunderson CPA's, Oshkosh, Wis., 1976-79; contr. Pepsi Cola Bottling Co., Oshkosh, Wisconsin Rapids, Wis., 1979-82; pvt. practice Kneepkens & Co., Oshkosh, Wis., from 1982. Sgt. USAF, 1970-74. Mem. AICPA, Nat. Assn. Tax Preparers, Wis. Inst. CPAs, Inst. CFPs, Winnebago County Estate Planning Coun. Avocations: sky diving, football, baseball, soccer, reading. Died Jan. 22, 2005.

KNEPPER, WILLIAM EDGAR, editor; b. Kansas City, Kans., Aug. 4, 1929; s. Edgar Morford nad Ethel Viginia (Powell) K.; m. Virginia S. Steven, Sept. 3, 1956, (div. Dec. 1985); children: Christopher, Michael; m. Alberta R. Cohen, Oct. 3, 1987. BA in Econs., U. Kans.; MA in Econs., Harvard U., MPE in Polit. Economy. Economic analyst Bur. Analysis and Rsch., 1956-58; consulate officer to comml. officer U.S. Consulate Gen., Monterrey, Mex., 1958-61; assignments specialist Bur. Pers., 1961-62; staff asst. to Sec. of State Rusk, 1962-64; with Latin Am. area tng. Stanford U., 1964-65; econ., fin. officer U.S. Embassy, Santo Domingo, Dominican Republic, 1965-67, counselor for econ. and comml. affairs Montevideo, Uruguay, 1967-71; sr. tng. Harvard U., 1971-72; dir. office Regional Econ. Affairs Bur. Inter-Am. Affairs, 1972-75; internat. economist U.S. Delegation to the Multilateral Trade Negotiations, Geneva, 1975-78; alt. dir. Office of Andean Affairs Bur. Inter-Am. Affairs, 1978-80; dir. office Analysis for Inter-Am. Republics Bur. Analysis and Rsch., 1980-83, dep. asst. sec. state, 1984-85; prof. internat. rels. Indsl. Coll. of the Armed Forces, 1985-86; state dept. rep., mem. econs. faculty Inter-Am. Def. Coll., Ft. McNair, Washington, 1986-88; editor Washington Report, from 1988. V.p. St. Georges Corp., Consumers for World Trade, 1988—; assoc. Global Bus. Access, 1991. Lt. USN, 1952-54. Mem. Cosmos Club, Harvard Club, Nat. Press Club. Home: Oakland, Calif. Died Nov. 4, 2004.

KNIGHT, ROBERT HUNTINGTON, lawyer, former bank executive; b. New Haven, Feb. 27, 1919; s. Earl Wall and Frances Pierpont (Whitney) K.; m. Rosemary C. Gibson, Apr. 19, 1975; children: Robert Huntington, Jessie Valle, Patricia Whitney, Alice Isabel, Eli Whitney. Grad., Phillips Acad., Andover, Mass., 1936; BA, Yale, 1940; LL.B., U. Va., 1947, LLM, 1949. Bar: N.Y. bar 1950. With John Orr Young, Inc. (advt. agy.), 1940-41; asst. prof. U. Va. Law Sch., 1947-49; assoc. firm Shearman & Sterling & Wright, N.Y.C., 1949-55, ptnr., 1955-58; dep. asst. sec. def. for internat. security affairs US Dept. Def., 1958-61; gen. counsel US Dept. Treasury, 1961-62; ptnr. firm Shearman & Sterling, N.Y.C., 1962-80, sr. ptnr., 1980-85, of counsel, 1986—2006; dep. chmn. Fed. Res. Bank N.Y., 1976-77, chmn., 1977-83. Counsel to bd. United Technologies Corp., 1974-85; dir. internat. bd. Owens-Corning Fiberglas Corp.; dir. I-Corps, Nat. Leadership Bank, Mercator, Inc., Citizen Exchange Coun.; mem. Intelsat Arbitration Panel, 1971-91. Bd. dirs. Internat. Vol. Services; chmn. bd. dirs. U. Va. Law Sch. Found., 1970-90; bd. dirs. Asia Found. Served to lt. col. USAAF, 1941-45. Mem. ABA, Fed. Bar Assn., Internat. Bar Assn., Inter-Am. Bar Assn., Assn. of Bar of City of N.Y., N.Y County Lawyers Assn., Internat. Law Assn., Washington Inst. Fgn. Affairs, Council Fgn. Relations, Pilgrims Club, Links Club, World Trade Ctr Club, River Club (N.Y.C.), Army and Navy Club, Met. Club (Washington), Round Hill Club (Greenwich, Conn.), Ocean Club (Ocean Ridge, Fla.), Farmington Club (Va.). Died Sept. 28, 2006.

KNILANS, JAMES CARTER, small business owner; b. Elkhorn, Wis., Aug. 15, 1939; s. James K. and Loraine (Carter) K.; m. Nancy Jo Windhorst, Oct. 19, 1967; children: Joseph C., Jami A. Student, Parkside Coll., 1972; MBA, Lake Forest (Ill.) Coll., 1982. With Gimbels, Milw., 1960-61; mgr. Marc's Big Boy, Milw., 1961-65; salesperson Met. Life Ins. Co., Milw., 1965-68, Western Pub. Co., Champaign, Ill., 1968-79, nat. account exec. Racine, Wis., 1979-83; owner, mfr.'s rep. Knilans & Assocs., Racine, from 1983. With USN, 1957-60. Mem. Midwest Toy Assn. Died Dec. 5, 2004.

KNISELY, WILLIAM HAGERMAN, anatomical sciences educator emeritus, retired university dean; b. Houghton, Mich., Feb. 3, 1922; s. Samuel Henry and Flora Belle (Hagerman) K.; m. Marguerite Marie Labasse, Jan. 18, 1947; children: Chantal Patton, Marc, Paul, Colette, Philip. PhB, U. Chgo., 1947, BS, 1950; MS, Med. Coll. S.C., 1952, PhD, 1954; LittD (hon.), Coll. of Charleston, 1977; LHD (hon.), Lander Coll., 1982. Orderly, night clk. U. Chgo. Hosp., 1946-49; research asst. Med. Coll. S.C., Charleston, 1949-54; from instr. to assoc. prof. Duke U., Durham, N.C., 1954-59; prof., chmn. dept. anatomy U. Ky., Lexington, 1959-63; prof., dir. Inst. Biology and Medicine Mich. State U., East Lansing, 1963-70; prof., vice chancellor for health affairs U. Tex. System, Austin, 1970-75; pres. Med. U. S.C., Charleston, 1975-82; exec. assoc. dean Coll. Medicine U. Okla., Oklahoma City, 1982-87; assoc. dean rsch. affairs, 1987-89; assoc. dean Coll. Grad. Studies U. Okla., Oklahoma City, 1982-89; prof. anat. scis. emeritus, from 1989; sr. program assoc. biomed. and health care ethics program U. Okla. Health Sci. Ctr., 1989-93. Chmn. program planning com. Physician Manpower div. Nat. Adv. Council on Edn. for Health Professions, 1970-72; mem. steering com. for edn. devel. Mass. Gen. Hosp., 1978-80; cons. Dept. Medicine and Surgery VA, 1974. Commr. Navajo Health Authority, 1972-76; chmn. Tex. coordinating bd. Higher Edn. Task Force on Med. and Dental Edn., 1972-74. Served with U.S. Army, 1943-46, ETO. Recipient Sesquicentennial Disting. Alumnus award Med. U. S.C., 1974, Honors of the Soc. award Am. Soc. Allied Health Professions, 1984, Amicus Medicinae award U. Okla. Med. Alumni Assn., 1992; William Knisely award named in his honor U. Ky., 1981; Am. Heart Assn. rsch. fellow, 1955-57; USPHS sr. rsch. fellow, 1957-59. Fellow Royal Microscopical Soc. London; mem. Am. Assn. Anatomists, Am. Assn. for History of Medicine, AMA (affiliate), So. Hist. Assn., Am. Dietetic Assn. (hon. 1976—). Avocations: reading, geology. Home: Austin, Tex. Died May 3, 2004.

KNOBLER, NATHAN, art educator; b. Bklyn., Mar. 13, 1926; s. Solomon Harry and Edna (Rothenberg) K.; m. Lois Jean Mandell, Sept. 3, 1950; 1 child, Adam. BFA, Syracuse U., 1950; MA, Fla. State U., 1951. Asst. prof. U. Conn., Storrs, 1959-62, assoc. prof., 1962-67, prof., 1967-77, head art dept., 1962-68, prof. emeritus, 1977—2006; dean of faculty Phila. Coll. Art, 1977-79, dean acad. affairs, 1979-82; prof. grad. studies U. of Arts, Phila., 1982—2004. Vis. prof. Tech. U., Delft, The Netherlands, 1990. Author: The Visual Dialogue, 1967, 3d edit., 1981; exhibited paintings, sculpture and prints. Mem. AAUP, Internat. Soc. Ecol. Psychology, Coll. Art Assn. Home: Philadelphia, Pa. Died Feb. 3, 2006.

KNORTZ, WALTER ROBERT, accountant, retired insurance company executive; b. Bklyn., July 15, 1919; s. John Walter and Elizabeth Anna (Grotyohann) K.; m. Muriel Clancy, Oct. 14, 1950 (dec.); children: Deborah Ann, Kenneth Robert, Pamela Jane; m. Dorothy E. Lauterborn, Nov. 17, 1962. BBA, St. Johns U., 1942; MBA, N.Y. U., 1949. Acct. Consol. Edison Co., N.Y.C., 1936-45; mng. acct. S.D. Leidersdorf & Co., N.Y.C., 1945-53; with Equitable Life Assurance Soc. of U.S., N.Y.C., 1953-82, 2d v.p., 1969-73, v.p., assoc. controller, 1973-75, v.p., fin. officer investment ops., 1975-82; asst. treas., treas. Equitable Life Holding Corp., 1971-75; comptroller Equitable Life Mortgage & Realty Investors, 1970-75; v.p., treas. Equitable Life Community Enterprises Corp., 1970-75, Student Life Funding, Inc., 1970-75; v.p., dir. Equico Lessors, Inc., Mpls., 1974-78; v.p. Equico Securities, Inc., 1970-80, Planters Devel. Corp., St. Louis, 1972-81. Mem. Phila. Stock Exch., Inc., 1971-78. Pres. Leisure Towne Civic League, 1983-84, treas., 1985-86; mem. bldg. fund com. Holy Eucharist Ch., chmn. fin. com., 1984-89. Served with AUS, 1942-45. Mem. AICPA, Tax Execs. Inst., Fin. Execs. Inst., Beta Rho Kappa, Delta Mu Delta. Roman Catholic. Home: Southampton, NJ. Died May 17, 2006.

KNOT, ALVAN PAUL, lawyer; b. Kalamazoo, Nov. 24, 1949; s. Bert and Adeline (Ruster) K.; m. Francesca E. Robles; children: Jonathan, Jason, Danielle, Andrea, Alli. BA with high distinction, U. Mich., 1973; JD cum laude, Thomas M. Cooley Law Sch., 1976. Bar: Mich. 1976, U.S. Dist. Ct. (we. dist.) Mich. 1976, U.S. Ct. Appeals (6th cir.) 1985, U.S. Supreme Ct. 1988. Assoc. Allen, Worth & Hatch, Marshall, Mich., 1977-79; asst. city atty. Lansing (Mich.) City Atty.'s Office, 1979-84, chief asst. city atty., 1984-87, city atty., 1987-93; ptnr., shareholder Alvan P. Knot, P.C., from 1993. Adj. prof. law Thomas M. Cooley Law Sch., Lansing, 1979-83. Chair Mich. Controlled Substance Adv. Commn., 1990-92; mem. Jud. Evaluation Com. Ingham County, 1991—. Mem. Fed. Bar Assn., Ingham County Bar Assn. (com. chmn. 1988), Mich. Mcpl. Lawyers Assn. (mem. uniform traffic com. 1988, mcpl. liability com. 1992—), State Bar Mich. (pub. corp. coun. 1991—, charter revision commn., 1992—). Died Mar. 26, 2005.

KNOTTS, DON (JESSE DONALD KNOTTS), actor; b. Morgantown, W.Va., July 21, 1924; s. William Jesse and Elsie L. (Moore) K.; m. Kathryn Metz, Dec. 27, 1947 (div. 1964); children: Karen Ann, Thomas Allen; m. Loralee Czuchna, Oct. 12, 1974 (div. 1983). BA, W.Va. U., 1948. Appeared on Broadway in No Time for Sergeants, 1955-56; other stage appearences include A Good Look at Boney Kern, Last of the Red Hot Lovers, Mind with the Dirty Man; with Steve Allen Show, 1956-61; (radio) portrayed Windy Wales on Bobby Benson, 1949-55; (soap opera) Search for Tommorrow, 1953-55; (TV series) played Barney Fife Andy Griffith, 1960-65 (5 Emmy awards for Outstanding Performance in a Supporting Role), also Don Knotts Show, 1970-71, Laugh Back, 1975, Three's Company, 1979-84, What A Country!, 1987, Doug, 1991, recurring role in series Matlock, 1988-92; (TV movies) The Man Who Came to Dinner, 1972, I Love a Mystery, 1973, Return to Mayberry, 1986, Matlock: The Picture, 1991, Quints, 2000, Hermie: A Common Caterpillar, 2003; film appearances include No Time for Sergeants, 1958, Wake Me When It's Over, 1960, The Last Time I Saw Archie, 1961, It's a Mad, Mad, Mad, Mad World, 1963, Move Over Darling, 1963, The Incredible Mr. Limpet, 1964, The Ghost and Mr. Chicken, 1966, The Reluctant Astronaut, 1967, The Shakiest Gun in the West, 1968, The Love God?, 1969, How to Frame a Figg, 1971, The Apple Dumpling Gang, 1975, No Deposit, No Return, 1976, Gus, 1976, Herbie Goes to Monte Carlo, 1977, Hot Lead, Cold Feet, 1978, The Prize Fighter, 1979, The Apple Dumpling Gang Rides Again, 1979, Private Eyes, 1981, Cannonball Run II, 1984, Big Bully, 1996, Pleasantville, 1998; author: The Barney Fife Guide to Life, Love, and Self-defense, 1993; (voice) The Little Troll Prince, 1985, Pinocchio and the Emperor of the Night, 1987, Timmy's Gift: Precious Moments Christmas, 1991, Cats Don't Dance, 1997, 101 Dalmatians: The Series, 1997, Jingle Bells, 1999, (video) Tom Sawyer, 2000, Hermie & Friends, 2004-2005, Chicken Little, 2005, Robot Chicken, 2005; (voice-video game) Scooby-Doo: Night of 100 Frights, 2002; TV guest appearances Many Loves of Dobie Gillis, 1959, The Andy Williams Show, 1962-69, The Joey Bishop Show, 1964, Mayberry R.F.D., 1968, The Bill Cosby Show, 1970, The New Scooby-Doo Movies, 1972, Here's Lucy, 1973, The Captain and Tennille, 1976, The Late Summer Early Fall Bert Convy Show, 1976, Fantasy Island, 1978, 1979, Love Boat, 1979, Disneyland, Inspector Gadget, 1985, She's the Sheriff, 1988, Step by Step, 1993, Burke's Law, 1994, The Andy Griffth Show Reunion: Back to Mayberry, 2003, 8 Simple Rules...for Dating My Teenage Daughter, 2003, Las Vegas, 2005, 3rd Ann. TV Land awards, 2005, others. With U.S. Army, 1943—46. Decorated World War II Victory Medal, Philippine Liberation Medal, Asiatic-Pacific Campaign Medal (with four bronze stars), Army Good Conduct Medal, Marksman Badge (with Carbine Bar). Died Feb. 24, 2006.

KNOX, RICHARD EVERT, clergyman; b. Quinlan, Tex., Aug. 17, 1917; s. Thomas Booth and Zana (Neighbors) K.; m. Mildred Pigg, June 7, 1939 (dec. Feb. 1975); children: Norma Sandra Peters, Matilda Ann Edens; m. Martha Pearl Hayden, Dec. 10, 1978. AA, Wesley Coll., Greenville, Tex., 1938; BA, East Tex. State, 1942, MA, 1956. Lic. radio operator. Supt. intermidates Sunday sch. First Bapt., New Boston, Tex., 1947-73, deacon, from 1956; pres. Bowie County Broadcasting Co. Inc., New Boston, from 1974, FGBMFI, New Boston, from 1974; operator Sta. KNBO Christian Radio, New Boston, from 1977. Field rep. Full Gospel Bus. Men, northeast Tex., 1989—; disc jockey Sta. KNBO Radio Christian, New Boston, 1977—, daily techr., 1977—, pres., 1972—; internat. advisor Flame Fellowship Internat., 1984—; area advisor N.E. Tex. Area Womens Aglow Fellowship, 1976-85. With U.S. Army, 1945-46. Mem. New Boston C. of C., Lions (held all offices), Masons (master), Order of Ea. Star (worthy advisor). Home: New Boston, Tex. Died July 30, 2005.

KNUTSON, JOHN A., lawyer; b. San Francisco, Dec. 10, 1945; s. Robert Nelson and Louise Marie (Urrére) K.; m. Suzanne Sheryl, Aug. 5, 1972; children: Michelle Louise, Adam Robert. BA, San Francisco State U., 1971; JD, U. Calif., San Francisco, 1974. Bar: Calif. 1974. Assoc. Law Office G. McEnerney, San Francisco, 1974-79, Fisher & Hurst, San Francisco, 1979-82, ptnr., 1982-87, mng. ptnr., 1987-90; founding & mng. ptnr. Kenney, Burd, Knutson & Markowitz, San Francisco, 1991-94; v.p. legal/sr. gen. counsel and sec. Plantronics Inc., Santa Cruz, Calif., from 1994. Sgt. USAR, 1966-72. Mem. ABA, State Bar Calif., Meadow Club (pres. 1991, bd. dirs. 1989-91). Avocations: golf, reading, travel, computers, the arts. Died Jan. 25, 2004.

KOBAYASHI, GEORGE SHOICHIRO, mycologist; b. San Francisco, Nov. 25, 1927; s. Yoshiro and Tomeki (Hashimoto) K.; m. Mariko Tomita; children: Patricia F., Dale K., Kimi L., Scott D. BS, U. Calif., Berkeley, 1952; PhD, Tulane U., 1963. Wine chemist Roma Wine Co., Lodi, Calif., 1952-53; sr. lab. technician U. Calif., Berkeley, 1953-59; USPHS predoctoral trainee Tulane U., New Orleans, 1959-63; instr. Washington U. Sch. Medicine, St. Louis, 1963-66, asst. prof., 1966-71, assoc. prof., 1971-77, prof., from 1977. Mem. study sect. NIH, Washington, 1978-84; mem. adv. bd. Am. Type Culture Collection, Washington, 1989—. Mem. editorial bd. Antimicrob Ag Chemother, 1977—; contbr. over 150 articles to profl. jours. With U.S. Army, 1946-47. Rsch. grantee NIH. Fellow Infectious Diseases Soc. Am., Am. Acad. Microbiology; mem. Am. Soc. Microbiology (chmn. med. mycology div. 1980-81), Med. Mycology Soc. Ams. (pres. 1977-78, Rhoda Benham medal 1989), Am. Soc. Microbiology (found. lectr. 1986). Achievements include rsch. in fungi. Died Apr. 19, 2005.

KOBBEROE, BIRTHE, corporate financial executive, accountant; b. Copenhagen, June 17, 1937; arrived in U.S., 1983, permanent resident, 1996; d. Gustav Carl Andersen and Britta Madsen; m. John Kobberoe, Mar. 4, 1961; children: Michael, Lise. Student, Nelholt & Son, 1954—58; diploma, Copenhagen Trade Sch., Denmark, 1955; diploma in English, Berlitz Sch. Lang., 1956, U. Nev., Las Vegas, 1984. Acct. Hoffman & Sons, Copenhagen, 1958, Jens Pedersen Forwarder, Copenhagen, 1958—59, Nordic Antenna Man, Copenhagen, 1959—63; acct., CFO Ratel Radio, Copenhagen, 1963—83, Ratel Radio, Cons., Las Vegas, from 1983. Editor bi-monthly Danish Am. newspaper; pub. (CD with Poems), 2002; author: (book of poetry) A Lifetime of Poetry, 2003, The Silence Within, 2004, Diamond Pearls, 2004, Eternal Portraits, 2004, The Colors of Life, 2004, Invoking the Muse, 2005. Culture leader Scandinavian Club of Las Vegas, 1986—90. Recipient Nat. Libr. Poetry Editor's Choice award, 1997, 2001—03, Internat. Poet of Merit award, 2002, Congl. Order of Merit, 2003. Mem.: The Great Book Found., Nev. State Garden Club (environment chmn. 1988—90, auditor), Sunset Garden Club. Republican. Lutheran. Avocations: swimming, painting, writing books, poetry, piano. Died Sept. 22, 2005.

KOBERT, NORMAN NOAH, asset management consultant; b. N.Y.C., Apr. 15, 1929; s. Murray Hyman Kobert and Rose Winger; m. Natalie Toby Tanhauser, Nov. 23, 1955; children: Robyn Beth, Roy Scott, Jay Stuart, Lisa Ellen. B in Indsl. Engring., NYU, 1949; MBA, Marquette U., 1959; D in Comml. Sci. (hon.), London Sch. Econs., 1973. Chief indsl. engring. Consol. Ldries, Newark, 1949-52; chief mgmt. engring. svcs. Picatinny Arsenal, Dover, N.J., 1953-55; mgr. mgmt. engring. svcs. Ordnance Corps U.S. Army, Washington, 1955-57; asst. dir. Mgmt. Ctr. Marquette U., Milw., 1957-61; v.p. Bayer, Kobert & McElrath, Detroit, 1961-64; exec. v.p. Stevenson, Jordan & Harrison, N.Y.C., 1965-72; prin. N. Kobert & Assocs., Ft. Lauderdale, Fla., from 1972. Bd. dirs. Lexington Industries, N.Y.C.; dir. Entourage Broward Ctr. for Performing Arts. Author: Aggressive Management Style, 1980, Inventory Strategies, 1980, Managing Time, 1981, Managing Inventory for Cost Reduction, 1992, Cut the Fat Not the Muscle, 1995, Improving Management of the Manager's Time, 1996; editor-in-chief (newsletter) Workstyle; contbg. editor, columnist Inventory Outlook, Purchasing mag., Newton, Mass., 1989-92; mem. productivity panel Bottom Line Bus., 1979-84. Recipient Brampton Productivity Improvement award, 1995; Cyril Vanes grantee Indonesia Bjonct, Jakarta, 1978. Mem. Am. Inst. Indsl. Engrs., Soc. Advancement of Mgmt., Am. Prodn. and Inventory Soc., Harbor Beach Surf Club, Entourage (v.p.), Alpha Pi Mu, Beta Gamma Sigma. Jewish. Avocations: golf, dance, trap-shooting, tennis, chess. Died Nov. 17, 2004.

KOBLER, JOHN F., priest, researcher; b. Chgo., June 16, 1925; s. Leo Peter Kobler and Ella O'Donnell. MA, St. Louis U., 1957. Ordained Passionists, Louisville, 1954; cert. tchr. h.s. Mo., 1957. Sem. lector in Latin and Greek Mother of Good Coun. Sem., Warrenton, Mo., 1956—65; tchr. Latin Bellarmine Coll., Louisville, 1965—67; superior Immaculate Conception monastery, Chgo., 1968—71, Immaculate Conception Monastery, Chgo., 1975—79; fund raiser CP missions, Birmingham, Ala., 1972—75, pres. Province Senate, 1973—76; rschr. Vatican II Chgo., from 1979. Tchr. med. ethics St. Mary's Infirmary, St. Louis, 1956—57, St. Mary's and Elizabeth Hosp., Louisville, 1966; cons. Nat. Method Inst., Charlottenburg, Denmark, 1963—67; chaplain Fort Leonard Wood, Whiteman AFB, Fort Knox; superior, founder province devel. office CP Monastery, Chgo., 1975—79; assoc. editor Soc. Justice Rev., St. Louis, from 2001; assoc. dir. Holy Cross Retreat House, Cin., 1971; mem. extraordinary chpt. acad. formation and fin. com. Senate of Holy Cross Province, 1969; trustee Cath. Theol. Union, Chgo., 1970—71. Author: Vatican II and Phenomenology, 1985, Vatican II, Theophany and Phenomenon of Man, 1991; contbr. more than 80 articles to profl. jours. here and abroad. Recipient Golden Heart award, Immaculate Conception Monastery, 1975. Mem.: Am. Cath. Philos. Assn., Soc. Cath. Social Scientists, Fellowship of Cath. Scholars, C.G. Jung Inst. of Chgo., Lumen Christi Inst. Cath. Faith, Thought and Culture, The Acton Inst. Study of Religion and Liberty, Cath. Hist. Soc., The Metaphysical Soc. Am. Achievements include research in use of a phenomenological style in Vatican II's reflection. Avocation: philosophy. Died May 15, 2005.

KOCH, KATHLEEN JANE, geography educator; b. Toledo, Dec. 19, 1953; d. Joseph Marion and Nancie Jane (Penske) K. BS, Ball State U., 1976, MA, 1988. Cert. secondary tchr., Ind., Mo. Tchr. phys. sci. Lake Cen. High Sch., St. John, Ind., 1978-79; tchr. sci. Avalon Redistricted II Sch., Tina, Mo., 1979-81, Hale (Mo.) Redistricted I Sch., 1981-84, St. Louis Cath. Sch., Batesville, Ind., 1984-85; tchr. earth sci. and geography Randolph Cen. Sch. Corp., Winchester, Ind., from 1986; coord. social studies dept. Winchester (Ind.) Community High Sch., 1990-91; basic skills instr. Ind. Vocat. Tech. Coll. Region 9, Richmond, Ind., from 1992. Coord. Ea. Ind. Acad. Competition League, Winchester, 1987—. V.p. Carroll-Livingstone County Coop. Tchrs. assn., Hale, 1982-83; sec. Assn. for Children with Learning Disabilities, Chillicothe, Mo., 1982-83. Mem. Hoosier Assn. Tchrs. of Sci., Inc., Ind. State Tchrs. Assn., nat. Sci. Tchrs. Assn., Randolph Cen. Tchrs. Assn., Geography Edn. network of Ind., Nat. Coun. Geog. Educators, Winchester/Ind. Jaycees, Phi Delta Kappa. Roman Catholic. Avocations: clown, writing, rock collecting, trivia master, historical research. Home: Winchester, Ind. Died Oct. 14, 2004.

KOCHEL, TIMOTHY FRANK, cable television executive, consultant; b. Lemmon, S.D., Dec. 17, 1933; s. Samuel Frank and Louise (Seidel) K.; m. Patsy Arlene Heier, Nov. 2, 1962; children: Dawn Marie, Michael Frank, Gillian Lucy. Cert. in mechanics, N.D. State Sch. Sci., 1951, cert. electronic tech., 1959. Transmitter engr. Sta. KOTA-TV, Rapid City, S.D., 1959-61; with electronic dept. Northrop Corp., Hawthorne, Calif., 1961-62; owner Stateline Electronics, Lemmon, 1964-82; chief engr. Sta. KBJM-AM, Lemmon, 1969-80; v.p., chief engr. Mott (N.D.) Cable Systems, Inc., 1979-82; pres., chief engr. Lemmon Cable Systems, Inc., 1979-82; treas., sec., chief engr. Western Dakota Cable, Inc., Elgin, N.D., from 1982. Cons. engr. Sta. KNDC-AM, Hettinger, N.D., 1970—. Served as cpl. U.S. Army, 1954-55, Korea. Mem. Am. Legion (comdr. Lemmon Post 1980-82, dist. vice comdr. 1983-87), VFW. Republican. Home: Mott, ND. Died July 18, 2004.

KOCIVAR, BEN, aviation specialist, journalist; b. N.Y.C., Apr. 13, 1916; s. Izidor and Rebecca (Ladman) K.; m. Thelma Levine, Aug. 30, 1941; children: Karl, Carol, Jane. BS in Social Sci., CCNY, 1938; MA in Journalist, U. Mo., 1941. Info. specialist War Dept., Washington, 1941-45; sr. editor Look Mag., N.Y.C., 1945-69; pub. rels. mgr. N.Y. Airways, N.Y.C., 1971-79, Crossair Airlines, Zurich, 1985-88; cons. Pan Am. Airlines, N.Y.C., 1969-72, Agusta Helicopter USA, Houston, 1981-85, SAAB Aircraft, Washington, 1984-88; aviation editor Popular Sci., N.Y.C., 1971-88; aviation tech. specialist FAA, Washington, 1986-95; tech. specialist Joseph Del Balzo Assoc., Washington, from 1994. Contbr. articles to profl. publs. Candidate North Castle (N.Y.) Town Bd., 1983. Recipient Aviation/Space Writers award All Am. Cities, 1975. Mem. AIAA, Nat. Sci. Writers Assn., N. Am. Airline Pub. Rels. Assn. (chmn.), Am. Soc. Journalists, Wings Club (N.Y.C.), Aero Club (Washington), Helicopter Club of Am. Home: Kihei, Hawaii. Died July 22, 2005.

KOENIG, NORMA EVANS, retired religious studies educator; b. Bloomfield, Ind., Feb. 10, 1922; d. Alexander Robert and Della E. (Stein) Evans; m. Robert Emil Koenig, July 18, 1943; children: Elsa K. Weber, Robert Evans, Richard Alexander, Martha K. Stone, Thea K. Burton, Laura K. Godinez. AM, U. Chgo., 1947. Cert. clergy United Ch. Christ, United Presbyn. Ch. Counselor Elmhurst Coll., Elmhurst, Ill., 1946—47; editor Chgo. Bapt. Assn., Chgo., 1947—48; editor, writer divsn. Christian edn. United Ch. of Christ, 1954—65; instr., asst. prof. U. Ill., Chgo., 1948—54; editor, bd. chair United Presbyn. Ch., Phila., 1968—70; editor JED Share Mag., 1970—90; interim assoc. prof. Lancaster Theological Seminary, 1989—90. Developer ElderNet. Author: All About Arthur, 1961, One Night, 1961, Tell Me the Stories of Jesus, 1957; author: (packets) Ch. & the Kindergarten Child, 1955; Ch. & the Nursery Child, 1956. Pres. Lower Merion (Pa.) HS Parents Assn., 1964—66, Interschool Coun., Lower Merion, 1967—69, Penn Wynne Libr. Bd., Lower Merion, Twp. Libr. Assn. and Bd., Lower Merion. Recipient Florence James Adams Poetry Reading award, Chgo., 1947, Children and Ch. award, St. Louis, 1992, Best Children's Bk of Yr., 1961. Democrat. Avocations: music, drama, public speaking. Home: Havertown, Pa. Died Apr. 9, 2006.

KOENIG, PIERRE, architect, educator; b. San Francisco, Oct. 17, 1925; s. Harold Rudolph and Blanche Jeanne (Chigé) K.; m. Merry Sue Thompson, July 10, 1954 (div. Sept. 1959); 1 child: Randall Francis; m. Gaile Carson, July 10, 1962 (div. Sept. 1975); 1 child: Jean Pierre; m. Gloria Gladys Kaufman, Oct. 28, 1984. BArch, U. So. Calif., 1952. Registered architect, Calif. Pvt. practice, L.A., 1952—2004; from asst. to prof. architecture Sch. Architecture U. So. Calif., L.A., 1964-97, prof. architecture, 1997—2004, disting. prof. arch., 1998—2004, asst. dir. Inst. Building Rsch., 1969-72, dir. Chemehuevi Planning Program, 1972-78. Guest lectr. CCNY, 1963, Pratt Inst., N.Y., 1963; vis. instr. and lectr. Yale U., New Haven, Conn., 1963; lectr. Art Ctr. Sch., Pasadena, Calif., 1991-94; guest spkr. San Francisco Mus. Modern Art, 1990, UCLA Design Ctr., Santa Monica, Calif., 1993; spkr. and panelist Mus. Contemporary Art, L.A., 1990; spkr. L.A. County Mus. Art, 1996. Exhibited in group show at the Mus. Modern Art, L.A., 1989-90. Prin. works include Lamel house, Glendale, Calif., 1950, also numerous other exposed steel and glass and prefabricated houses in Calif. Corp. U.S. Army, 1943-46. Recipient Sao Paulo Biennial Exhbn. award, 1957, AIA House and Home Mag. award, 1957, 1960, 1962-63, AIA Sunset Mag. Honor award, 1959, 1961-62, Western Constrn. Honor award, 1959, Am. Inst. of Iron and Steel award, 1963, Best Exhbn. Bldg. award, 1964, L.A. Grand Prix award, 1964, AIA L.A. Fiesta award, 1967, 36 Best Bldgs. in L.A. since 1945 award, 1967, AIA Olympic Arch. award, 1984, L.A. Dept. of Cultural Affairs award, 1989, AIA 100 Archs./100 Yrs. award, 1995, AIA Calif. Council 25 Year award for Excellence in Design, 1996, AIA Calif. Coun. Maybeck award for Outstanding Lifelong Achievement in Archtl. Design, 1996, Lifetime Achievement in Arch. award Pacific Design Ctr., 1998. Fellow AIA (Gold medal for arch. L.A. chpt. 2000). Avocations: photography, running, music, miniatures, computers. Died Apr. 4, 2004.

KOFFLER, STEPHEN ALEXANDER, investment banker; b. Providence, R.I., Sept. 22, 1942; s. Irving I. and Jessie Lillian (Seltzer) K.; m. Enid Freya Mellion, June 15, 1963; children: Samara Rachel, Debra Lyn. BMetE, Rensselaer Poly. Inst., 1964, MS, 1967, PhD, 1968. Security analyst Auerbach Pollak & Richardson, N.Y.C., 1968-70; asst. v.p. investment banking A.G. Becker, Inc., N.Y.C., 1970-72; v.p., treas. Mattel, Inc., Hawthorne, Calif., 1972-74; sr. v.p., chief fin. officer Audio Magnetics, Inc., Gardena, Calif., 1974-75; cons. Koffler & Co., L.A., 1975-81; mng. dir. Becker Paribas, Inc., L.A., 1981-84, Merrill Lynch, L.A., 1984-91; exec. v.p., dir. investment banking divsn. Sutro and Co., Inc., L.A., 1991-94; mng. dir. Smith Barney Inc., L.A., 1994-96; pres. Koffler & Co., L.A., 1996—2003; mng. dir. Barrington Assocs., LP, L.A., 2004. Bd. dirs. Sandel Med. Industries, St. John's Health Ctr. Bd. dirs. L.A. Music Ctr. Opera, 1989—96, Greater L.A. Zoo Assn. Mem. Am. Soc. for Metals, Nat. Assn. Securities Dealers Inc. (mem. corp. fin. com. 1994-95), Riviera Tennis Club, Regency Club, Teton Pines Country Club, Brentwood Country Club. Avocations: tennis, golf, hiking, opera. Home: Pacific Palisades, Calif. Died Nov. 5, 2004.

KOFFSKEY, GEORGE CHESTER, JR., retired sales representative; b. New Orleans, Sept. 26, 1921; s. George Chester and Edna Marie (Coulonge) K. BS in Pharmacy, Loyola U., New Orleans, 1943, PharmD, 1982. Registered pharmacist, La. Med. sales rep. Norwich Eaton Pharm. Co., New Orleans, 1947-87; ret., 1987. Dir. choir and music dept. Salem United Ch. of Christ, New Orleans, 1951—, pres. ch., 1980—. Lt. (j.g.) USNR, 1943-46. Mem. La. Hosp. Pharmacists Assn., Am. Guild Organists (past dean New Orleans chpt.), Blue Key, Masons, Rho Chi. Democrat. Avocations: music, sports. Home: New Orleans, La. Died June 1, 2005.

KOFORD, KENNETH JOHN, economics educator; b. Hollywood, Calif., Dec. 30, 1948; s. Kenneth Harold and Theresa Amelia (Sutton) K.; m. Blagovesta Dimitrova. BA, Yale U., 1970; MA, UCLA, 1973, PhD, 1977; D honoris causa, Sofia U., Bulgaria, 2001. Asst. prof. econs. Vassar Coll., Poughkeepsie, N.Y., 1976-78; vis. asst. prof. Conn. Coll., New London, 1978-79; asst. prof. econs. U. Del., Newark, 1979-85; vis. assoc. prof. Washington U., St. Louis, 1985; vis. assoc. Calif. Inst. Tech., Pasadena, 1987; assoc. prof. econs. and polit. sci. U. Del., Newark, 1985-94, prof. econs. and polit. sci., 1994—2004, prof. legal studies, 1997—2004, dir. legal studies program, 2000—04. Resident scholar Jerome Levy Econs. Inst., Annandale-on-Hudson, N.Y., 1991; instr., dir. in A.I.D. program, Bulgaria, 1991-92; Fulbright lectr. Sofia U., Bulgaria, 1997; bd. dirs. Ea. Econ. Assn. Editor: Keynes Economic Legacy, 1986, Social Norms and Economic Institutions, 1991, Eastern Econ. Jour., 1998-2004; contbr. articles on econs. and polit. sci. to profl. jours. Mem. Am. Econ. Assn., Am. Polit. Sci. Assn., Econometric Soc., Pub. Choice Soc. Home: Newark, Del. Died Oct. 25, 2004.

KOFRANEK, ANTON MILES, floriculturist, educator; b. Chgo., Feb. 5, 1921; s. Antonin J. and Emma (Rehorek) K.; children— Nancy, John A. BS, U. Minn., 1947; MS, Cornell U., 1949, PhD, 1950. Asst. prof. to prof. U. Calif., Los Angeles, 1950-68, prof. hort. dept. Davis, 1968-87, ret. prof. emeritus, 1987. Vis. prof. U. Wageningen, Netherlands, 1958, Cornell U., 1966, Hebrew U., Rehovot, Israel, 1972-73, Lady Davis fellow, 1980; vis. prof. Glasshouse Crops Research Inst., Littlehampton, U.K., 1980, AID, Egypt, 1978-82, FAO-UN, India, 1985 Co-author: (with Hartmann, Rubatzky and Flocker) Plant Science— Growth, Development and Utilization of Cultivated Plants, 2d edit., 1981; co-editor: (with R. A. Larson) U. Calif. Azalea Manual, 1975; contbr. articles to profl. jours. Served with AUS, 1942-45, ETO; Served with AUS, PTO. Recipient rsch. awards of merit Calif. State Florist Assn., 1966, Garland award 1974; named Young Man of Yr. Westwood Jr. C. of C., 1956; recipient rsch. and tchng. award Soc. Am. Florists, 1993. Fellow Am. Soc. Hort. Sci (dir., sectional chmn. 1973-74); mem. Sigma Xi, Pi Alpha Xi. Home: Davis, Calif. Died Mar. 29, 2006.

KOGON, IRVING CHARLES, chemist; b. Bklyn., Aug. 8, 1923; s. Charles and Sophie Kogon; m. Rita Lois Handelman, Nov. 28, 1927; children: Gary Bruce, Jay Stuart. BEE, Pa. State U., 1944; AB, Bklyn. Coll., 1948, MA, 1951; PhD, N.Y. Poly. U., 1954. Post-doctoral position U. Wis., Madison, 1953-54; scientist EI DuPont, Wilmington, Del., 1954-82; polyurethane and polymer cons. Wilmington, from 1983. Cons. Fortune 500 cos., 1982—. Staff sgt. U.S. Army, 1943-46, NATOUSA. Mem. Am. Chem. Soc., Polyurethan Mfrs. Assn. Avocations: stamp collecting/philately, repairing old items. Died Aug. 5, 2004.

KOHL, HAROLD, missionary, educator; b. Linden, N.J., Dec. 13, 1923; s. Herman and Martha (Sperber) K.; m. Beatrice Minniebelle Wells, Mar. 21, 1946; children: Loren, Loretta, Lyndon. BA, Monmouth Coll., 1962; MA in Edn., NYU, 1968, postgrad., 1974; ThD in English Bible, Internat. Bible Inst., 1980. Ordained to ministry Assemblies of God Ch., 1948. Pastor, evangelist Assemblies of God Ch., W.Va., Md., 1944-50, pres. youth ministries Potomac Dist. Coun., 1947-48, fgn. missionary Colombo, Sri Lanka, 1950-56; pastor Assemblies of God Chs., N.J., 1956-61; missionary, tchr., educator Assemblies of God Ch., Far East, Pacific, Europe, 1961-94, ednl. cons. Far East, Pacific, 1980-83; assoc. pastor Hayfield (Va.) Assembly of God, 1995-2000; ret., 2000. Pres. Bethel Bible Coll., Manila, 1963-68; pres., founder Far East Advanced Sch. Theology (now Asia Pacific Theol. Sem., Baguio City, The Philippines), Manila, 1964-73; adj. prof. Baguio City, 1991-2000; dean coll. divns. Internat. Corr. Inst. (now named Global U., Springfield, Mo.), Brussels, 1973-78, Belgium, 1983-88, Rhode St. Genese, Belgium, 1988-99, mem. external faculty, Brussels/Irving, Tex., 1988-94. Mem. Soc. Pentecostal Studies, Religious Edn. Assn., Phi Delta Kappa, Phi Theta Kappa. Republican. Avocations: photography, reading, walking. Home: Winchester, Va. Died Feb. 20, 2005.

KOLB, GWIN JACKSON, language educator; b. Aberdeen, Miss., Nov. 2, 1919; s. Roy Rolly and Nola Undine (Jackson) K.; m. Ruth Alma Godbold, Oct. 11, 1943; children: Gwin Jackson II, Alma Dean. BA, Millsaps Coll., 1941; MA, U. Chgo., 1946, PhD, 1949; LHD, Millsaps Coll., 1991. Editorial asst. Modern Philology, 1946-56; mem. faculty U. Chgo., 1949-89, prof. English, 1961-77, Chester D. Tripp prof. humanities, 1977-89, prof. emeritus, 1990—2006, chmn. dept., 1963-72, chmn. coll. English staff, 1958-60, head humanities sect. in coll., 1960-62. Vis. assoc. prof. Northwestern U., winter 1958, Stanford U., spring 1960; vis. prof. U. Wash., summers 1967, 73, Ohio State U., spring 1987, Peking U., fall 1994, U. Evansville, winter, spring 1996, Huntingdon Coll., winter, spring 1997, U. Ga., winter 1998, Berry Coll., winter, spring 2000. Co-author: Dr. Johnson's Dictionary, 1955, Reading Literature: A Workbook, 1955; editor: (Samuel Johnson) Rasselas and Other Tales, 1990; co-editor: A Bibliography of Modern Studies Complied for Philological Quarterly, 1951-65, 3 vols., 1962, 72, Modern Philology, 1973-89, Approaches to Teaching the Works of Samuel Johnson, 1993. Served with USNR, 1942-45. Frederick A. and Marion S. Pottle fellow Beinecke Libr. Yale U., 1993; recipient Quantrell award U. Chgo., 1955, Medal of Honor U. Evansville, 1992, Alumni award Millsaps Coll., 1967; Guggenheim fellow, 1956-57; grantee Am. Coun. Learned Socs., 1961-62. Mem. MLA, Midwest MLA (pres. 1964-65), Johnson Soc. Ctrl. Region (pres. 1965-66), Nat. Coun. Tchrs. English (bd. dirs. coll. sect. 1966-68), Am. Soc. 18th Century Studies (exec. bd. 1973-76, pres. 1976-77), The Johnsonians, Assn. Depts. English (pres. 1968), Caxton Club, Quadrangle. Home: Kenilworth, Ill. Died Apr. 3, 2006.

KOLKO, PHILIP, manufacturing executive; b. N.Y.C., Aug. 5, 1935; s. David and Rose (Suchenky) K.; m. Arleen Powdermaker, June 5, 1957 (div. 1975); children: Richard, David, Beth; m. Yuriko Tanabe, Oct. 26, 1986. BA, Duke U., 1956. Mgr. software devel. IBM Corp., Kingston, N.Y., 1960-80, mgr. network svcs. White Plains, N.Y., 1981-83, mgr. communications strategy Asia Pacific group Tokyo, 1983-87; mgr. network svcs. Hawaiian Airlines, Honolulu, 1988-89; dir. mgmt. info. Verifone Inc., Costa Mesa, Calif., from 1989. Chmn. bd. dirs. Trans Pacific Mgmt. Corp., Denver, 1986—; prin. P. Kolko Cons., San Francisco, 1987—; sec. Hawaii High Tech. Adv. Com., 1988-90. Contbr. articles to profl. jours. Active Pres. Coun. U. Fla., Gainesville, 1986—; bd. dirs. Mid Hudson Sci. Ctr., Poughkeepsie, N.Y., 1981-83; chmn. Boy Scout com., Poughkeepsie, 1983-84; v.p. Hale Kaheka Assn., Honolulu, 1988-90. Lt. USN, 1957-61. Mem. Honolulu Telecommunications Assn., Japan Am. Soc., Am. Mgmt. Assn., Duke U. Alumni Assn., Nobiru Kai of San Francisco, Tokyo Am. Club, Commonwealth Club Calif., Masons. Democrat. Avocations: writing, skiing, running. Home: San Francisco, Calif. Died June 27, 2004.

KOLODNY, ABRAHAM LEWIS, physician; b. Norfolk, Va., July 2, 1917; s. William and Jennie (Eisenberg) K.; m. Mildred Fiske, Aug. 10, 1942; children: William (dec.), David Greene, Sukie, Douglas Merrill, Peggy Lee. Grad., U. Va., 1941. Intern South Balt. Gen. Hosp., 1941-42; residency Ashburn Army Arthritis Ctr., McKinney, Tex., 1944-46; with Arthritis Clinic/Sinai Hosp., Balt., 1948-70; chief, rheumatology N. Charles Hosp., Balt., 1951-90; co-chief, rheumatology Franklin Square Hosp., Balt., 1970-95; commr. Md. Commn. Rheumatic Diseases, 1987-91; ret., 1999. Pres. North Charles Gen. Hosp., 1963-67; staff mem. Franklin Sq. Hosp., 1970-95; state commr. Arthritis and Related Diseases, 1986-91; ret. chief rheumatology Homewood Hosp. Ctr.; formerly active Johns Hopkins Med. Health Systems. Contbg. author textbooks in field, articles to profl. jours. Maj. U.S. Army, 1942-47, CBI. Decorated Bronze Star, Combat Med. badge, Presdl. Unit citation, Victory medal, Chinese Victory medal, others. Fellow Am. Coll. Rheumatology, N.Y. Acad. Scis.; mem. AMA, Am. Soc. Clin. Pharmacology, Md. Arthritis Found. (bd. dirs. 1975-91), Md. Soc. for Rheumatic Diseases (co-founder), So. Med. Assn. Home: Brooklandville, Md. Died June 3, 2005.

KONING, DIRK W., media specialist, writer; b. Zuni, N.Mex., Jan. 30, 1957; s. Stanley Earl and Margaret Mae K.; m. Virginia Marie Lane, July 17, 1977; children: Shaun, Kelly. BA in Comm., Mich. State U., 1980. Writer Sta. WGVU TV PBS, Allendale, Mich., 1979-80; mgr. Grand Rapids (Mich.) C.C., 1980-81; exec. dir. Cmty. Media Ctr., Grand Rapids. Pres. Alliance for Comms. Democracy, Washington; bd. dirs. ACLU. Mem., advisor Sch. Comm. Grand Valley U., Allendale, Mich., 1997-99. Home: Lowell, Mich. Died Feb. 10, 2005.

KONRAD, AGNES CROSSMAN, retired real estate agent, retired educator; b. Rutland, Vt., Nov. 26, 1921; d. Warren Julius and Susan Anna (Cain) Crossman; children: Suzanne Martha, Dianna Marie; m. Henry Konrad, Nov. 27, 1954. Assoc. degree in Edn., Castelton Coll., 1943; BS in Edn., Castelton State Coll., 1951; postgrad., SUNY, New Paltz, 1969-70, Fla. Atlantic U., 1973; grad., Realtors Inst. Fla., 1981. Cert. realtor. Tchr. 1st to 8th grades Pittsford (Vt.) Pub. Schs., 1943-44, tchr. 1st grade, 1950-52; tchr. 3d grade Ralph Smith Sch.-Hyde Park (N.Y.) Ctrl. Schs., 1952-69, Violet Ave. Sch.-Hyde Park Sch. Sys., 1969-73; realtor Four Star Realty of Boca Raton (Fla.), 1974-93; ret., 1993. Inducted into Golden Alumni Soc. of Castleton State Coll., 2001. Mem. AAUW (life), N.Y. State Ret. Tchrs. Assn. (life), Castleton Vt. State Coll. Alumni. Avocations: painting, travel, reading, poetry, computer art painting. Home: Boca Raton, Fla. Died Mar. 20, 2005.

KOOISTRA, WILLIAM HENRY, clinical psychologist; b. Grand Rapids, Michigan, May 20, 1936; s. Henry P. and Marguerite (Brinks) K.; m. Jean (Heynen), Aug. 24, 1957 (div. Dec. 1984); children: Kimberly Lynn, William Peter, Kristin Jean, Allison Carol; m. Carol Sue (Smitter), Mar. 9, 1985. BA, Calvin Coll., 1957; PhD, Wayne State U., Mich., 1963. Diplomate Am. Bd. Psychology, Am. Bd. Forensic Examiners. Intern psychology Lafayette Clinic, Detroit, 1961—62; chief psychologist Pine Rest Christian Hosp., Grand Rapids, Mich., 1964—67; clin. psychologist Mental Health Professionals of West Mich., Grand Rapids, from 1967. Instr. Wayne State U., 1959-63, Hope Coll. Holland, Mich., 1964, Calvin Coll. Grand Rapids, Mich., 1964-81, Grand Valley State U., 1987-92. Founder Project Rehab., Grand Rapids, 1968, (bd. dir., 1969—, pres., 1972-74); mem. Kent County Dem. Exec. Com., 1969-73, 79-82, 86—; mem. governing bd. Fountain Street Ch., 1989-95, (pres. 1994); rep. 3d dist. Presl. Electoral Coll., 1992. Mem. Am. Psychol. Assn. (council rep. 1982-85); Am. Soc. Psychologists in Pvt. Practice (sec. 1973-75); Mich. Psychol. Assn.(pres. 1979); Mich. Soc. Forensic Psychology; Grand Rapids Area Psychol. Assn (pres. 1968). Avocations: golf, tennis, sailing. Home: Grand Rapids, Mich. Died Nov. 30, 2004.

KOPEC, JOHN WILLIAM, research scientist; b. Chgo., Nov. 5, 1936; s. John Frank and Marie Eva (Wreshnig) K.; m. Jean Elois Prather, Dec. 28, 1958 (div. June 1977); children: Brian More, Vaune Estra. AA, Chgo. City Coll., 1974; student, Ill. Inst. Tech., Chgo., 1974-80. Systems analyst Motorola, Chgo., 1959-61; asst. exptl. engr. Ill. Inst. Tech. Rsch. Inst., Chgo., 1961-68, extpl. engr., 1968-74, lisison engr. Chgo. and Geneva, Ill., 1974-81; supr. Riverbank Acoustical Labs., Ill. Inst. Tech. Rsch. inst., Chgo. and Geneva, Ill., 1986-94, lab. mgr., from 1994, ret., 1998. Author: The Sabines at Riverbank, 1997; contbr. articles to Jour. Acoustical Soc. Am.; paper reviewer, contbr. articles Internat. Noise Control Engrs. With USAF, 1955-59. Fellow: Acoustical Soc. Am. (chmn. archives and history 1992—94, sec. tech. com. 1991—94, mus. curator 1985—98, co-chmn. tech. program 2001, Silver cert. 2002); mem.: ASTM (chmn. awards com., sec. E 33.01 1980—98, appreciation award 1994), Can. Acoustical Soc., Soc. Automotive Engrs. (task group, paper reviewer), N.Y. Acad. Scis. Achievements include one of first smokeless fires for firefighters of U.S. Navy and U.S. Air Force; one of first to discover ionization of turbulent flow in a hypersonic wind tunnel; discovered Wallace Clement Sabine files previously thought destroyed; developed one of first rapid transit speech noise floor's, also an industrial colored noise floor map. Home: Chicago, Ill. Died Oct. 14, 2004.

KOPPELMAN, JULIUS, financial consultant; b. N.Y.C., Aug. 30, 1916; s. Louis and Lena (Vogel) K.; m. Dorothy Barocas, Oct. 30, 1943; children: Estelle, Vicki, Marcia, Nancy. BS in Bus. Acctg., NYU, 1947. Controller tube div. RCA, Harrison, N.J., 1963-69, v.p. fin. N.Y.C., 1969-71, v.p., gen. mgr. computer div. Framingham, Mass., 1971-73; pres. RCA Svc. Co., Cherry Hill, N.J., 1974-76; group v.p. RCA, 1976-77, exec. v.p., dir. N.Y.C., 1977-81; chmn. bd. Harding Svcs. Inc., Morristown, N.J., from 1982. Bd. dirs. Gibson Greeting, Inc., Cin., Heekin Can Co., Cin., Lincoln Food Svc. Inc., Ft. Wayne, Ind., Outlet Communications, Inc., Providence, Alley & Gargano Advt., N.Y.C. Bd. govs. Am. Jewish Com., N.Y.C., 1988; bd. trustees Rider Coll. Laurenceville, N.J., 1981, Princeton United Jewish Appeal, 1989. Philip Furman Human Rels. awardee, Am. Jewish Com., 1988. Mem. Fin. Execs. Inst. Home: Princeton, NJ. Died Dec. 3, 2004.

KORNFELD, JUDITH R., product marketing consultant; b. Oklahoma City, July 31, 1948; d. Samuel and Ida (Charetsky) K. BA in Linguistics, U. Chgo., 1969; PhD in Linguistics/Psychology, MIT, 1974. Sr. systems engr. SofTech, Inc., Waltham, Mass., 1978-81, Higher Order Software, Cambridge, Mass., 1978-81; mem. tech. staff AT&T Bell Labs., Short Hills, N.J., 1981-84; project mgr. ALPHATECH, Burlington, Mass., 1984-85; product mgr. Fed. Systems Group Mktg. Symbolics, Inc., Cambridge, 1985-87; product mgr. fed. sys. mktg. Sun Microsystems, Mountain View, Calif., 1987; ind. cons. in product mktg. Menlo Park, Calif., from 1987. Mem. ACM, Sigchi, Bay Area Human Factors Soc. Died Mar. 16, 2005.

KOROS, AURELIA MARIE CARISSIMO, immunology educator, researcher; b. Boston, Aug. 28, 1934; d. Nino and Josephine (Sciacca) Carissimo; m. Peter Joseph M. Koros, June 1, 1957; children: Nina, Alicia, Sonya, Beatrice, Ariel. AB, Radcliffe Coll.-Harvard U., 1956; MS, U. Pitts., 1960, PhD, 1965. Rsch. assoc. Allegheny Gen. Hosp., Pitts., 1976-79; supr. virology lab. Allegheny County Health Dept., Pitts., 1979-82; asst. prof. Sch. Medicine, U. Pitts., 1965-75, asst. rsch. prof. Grad. Sch. Pub. Health, from 1980. Contbr. articles to sci. jours. Mem. AAAS, Am. Soc. Hematology, Am. Assn. for Cancer Rsch., Am. Assn. Immunologists, Marine Biol. Assn. U.K., Soc. for Biol. Therapy, Internat. Assn. for the Study of Lung Cancer. Home: Pittsburgh, Pa. Died Jan. 18, 2005.

KOSKELLA, LUCRETIA C., real estate broker, appraiser; b. Newburgh, N.Y., Aug. 29, 1928; d. Vincent George and Josephine Anita (Gross) Canadé; m. John Archie Koskella, June 13, 1954 (div. May 1961); 1 child, Judith Ann. Grad. h.s., Newburgh. Lic. real estate, N.Y., lic. real estate broker, N.Y., lic. real estate appraiser, N.Y. Real estate salesperson, 1961-71; real estate broker, from 1971. Chair adv. bd. real estate appraisal L.K.R.B., Newburgh, 1971—; active C.L.E.A.N. Chadwick Lake, Newburgh, 1980-96. Contbr. poetry to mags. Charter mem., organizer Scenic Hudson, Newburgh, 1980-96; Orange County Rep. committeewoman Rep. Party, 1980-92; campaign mgr., chmn., coord. local, state, and nat. campaigns, N.Y., 1980-96; publicist senate campaigns, Orange County and Newburgh, 1980-96; mem. exec. bd., speechwriter, spkr. Orange County Rep. Com., 1992-94; active Orange County Chpt. N.Y. Fedn. Rep. Women; vol. Am. Cancer Soc., Heart Assn., March of Dimes, PTA, Am. Diabetes Assn. Recipient Dedication Contest winner Water and Light Poetry Mag., 1994. Mem. NRA, NOW, Nat. Mus. Women in Arts, N.Y. State Sheriffs Assn. (bus. mem.). Avocations: golf, art, poetry, swimming, computers, skeet shooting. Died June 20, 2005.

KOSOW, IRVING LIONEL, editor, author, retired engineering educator; b. N.Y.C., Jan. 14, 1919; s. Morris Aaron and Yetta (Strassberg) K.; m. Ruth Cooper, Jan. 11, 1942; children: Sonia Kosow Guterman, Julia Kosow Grosberg. BS, CCNY, 1939; MS, NYU, 1952, PhD, 1960. Naval ordnance engr. U.S. Naval Shipyard, Bklyn., 1939-46; assoc. prof. N.Y.C. Tech. Coll., Bklyn., 1946-56; prof., head dept. elec. engring. Coll. S.I., CUNY, 1956-76, assoc. dean, 1966-69; editor elec. engring. tech. John Wiley and Sons, N.Y.C., 1976-79; prof. elec. engring. So. Coll. Tech., Marietta, Ga., 1979-86. Editor elec. engring. and tech. Prentice-Hall, Inc., Englewood Cliffs, N.J., 1956-72. Author: Electric Machinery and Control, 1964, Electric Machinery and Transformers, 1972, 2d edit., 1991, Control of Electrical Machines, 1973, Study Guides in DC/AC, 1977, Circuit Analysis, 1988; former contby. editor and author McGraw-Hill Ency. Sci.; former contby. reviewer CHOICE; patentee constriction machine, cutoff valve. NSF grantee, 1960, 67, 73, 74, 75. Mem. IEEE (sr., life), AAAS, AAUP, Am. Soc. Engring. Edn. (life), Kappa Delta Pi. Avocations: photography, tennis, classical music. Home: Marietta, Ga. Died Jan. 1, 2004.

KOSTELANETZ, BORIS, lawyer; b. St. Petersburg, Russia, June 16, 1911; came to U.S., 1920, naturalized, 1925; s. Nachman and Rosalia (Dimschetz) K.; m. Ethel Cory, Dec. 18, 1938; children: Richard Cory, Lucy Cory. B.C.S., N.Y. U., 1933, BS, 1936; JD magna cum laude, St. John's U., 1936, LL.D. (hon.), 1981. CPA N.Y.; bar: N.Y. 1936. With Price, Waterhouse & Co., C.P.A.'s, N.Y.C., 1934-37; asst. U.S. atty. (so. dist.) NY US Dept. Justice, confidential asst. to U.S. atty, 1937-43, spl. asst. to atty. gen. U.S., 1943-46, chief war frauds sect., 1945-46; spl. counsel com. investigate crime in interstate commerce U.S. Senate, 1950-51; ptnr. Kostelanetz Ritholz Tigue & Fink, N.Y.C., 1946-89, of counsel, 1990-94, Kostelanetz & Fink, N.Y.C., 1994—2006. Instr. acctg. N.Y. U., 1937-47, adj. prof. taxation, 1947-69; Mem. com. on character and fitness Appellate div. Supreme Ct. N.Y., 1st dept., 1974—2006, chmn., 1985-98. Author: (with L. Bender) Criminal Aspects of Tax Fraud Cases, 1957, 2d edit., 1968, 3d edit., 1980; Contbr. articles to legal, accounting and tax jours. Chmn. Kefauver for Pres. Com. N.Y. State, 1952. Recipient Meritorious Svc. award NYU, 1954, John T. Madden Meml. award, 1969, Pietas medal St. John's U., 1961, medal of honor, 1983, James Madison award, 1988, Torch of Learning award Am. Friends of Hebrew U. Law Sch., 1979, N.Y.U. Presdl. citation, 1990, N.Y. State Bar Assn. Fifty-Yr. Lawyer award, 1990, ABA Sect. Taxation Distinguished Svc. award, 1999. Fellow Am. Coll. Trial Lawyers, Am. Coll. Tax Counsel, Am. Bar Found.; mem. ABA (coun. sect. taxation 1978-81, ho. of dels. 1984-89), Fed. Bar Assn., Internat. Bar Assn., Soc. King's Inn, Ireland (hon. bencher 1995), N.Y. State Bar Assn., N.Y. State CPAs, N.Y. County Lawyers Assn. (v.p. 1966-69, pres. 1969-71, bd. dirs. 1958-64, 66-69, 71-74, chmn. judiciary com. 1965-69), Assn. of Bar of City of N.Y., NYU Sch. Commerce Alumni Assn. (pres. 1951-52), NYU Alumni Fedn. (pres. 1989-92), St. John's U. Law Sch. Alumni Assn. (pres. 1955-57). Home: New York, NY. Died Jan. 31, 2006.

KOSTER, KENNETH CLAYTON, financial executive; b. Clayton, Mo., Feb. 6, 1964; s. Kenneth Keith and Georgia Carolyn Koster; m. Kimberly England, Oct. 26, 1991; children: Emily Claire, Bradley Keith. BS in Econs. and Bus. Adminstrn., Culver-Stockton Coll., 1986; MBA in Fin. and Mktg., U. Tenn., 1994. Field svc. dir. Edward Jones & Co., St. Louis, 1986-92; trust investment officer, v.p. 1st Tenn. Bank, Knoxville, 1994-97; sr. portfolio mgr., sr. v.p. Bank of Am., Des Moines, from 1997. Republican. Mem. Evangelical Free Ch. Avocation: music. Home: Brentwood, Tenn. Died Apr. 6, 2005.

KOSZTOLNYIK, ZOLTAN JOSEPH, retired history professor; b. Heves, Hungary, Dec. 15, 1930; came to U.S., 1949; s. Zoltan and Irene (Koenig) K.; m. Penelope South, June 15, 1966; children: Karen Penelope, Elizabeth Irene. BA, St. Bonaventure U., 1959; MA, Fordham U., 1961; PhD, NYU, 1968. Fulbright scholar U. Vienna, Austria, 1963-65; instr. medieval history Tex. A&M U., College Station, 1967-68, asst. prof., 1968-72, assoc. prof., 1972-81, prof., 1981—2003, prof. emeritus, 2003—06. Author: Five Eleventh Century Hungarian Kings, 1981, From Colomon the Learned to Bela III (1095-1196), Hungarian Domestic Policy and Its Impact Upon Foreign Affairs, 1987, Hungary in the Thirteenth Century, 1996; contbr. articles to profl. jours., chpts. to books including: Great Lives in History, Ancient and Medieval, 1989, Triumph in Adversity: Studies in Hungarian Civilization, 1988, Vorlesungen des II Internationalen Kongresses for Hungarologie, Wien, 1986, 89, others, in jours. including Ch. History, 1977, 80, 88, Cath. Hist. Rev., 1973, 93, Annuarium historiae conciliorum, 1984, 90, Cithara: Essays in Judaeo-Christian Tradi-Szazadok, 1992. With M.I., U.S. Army, 1955-57. Recipient Founder's Day award NYU, 1969, TAMU Disting. Tchg. award, 1995; rsch. grantee Tex. A&M U., Vienna, 1986. Mem. Am. Hist. Assn., Am. Cath. Hist. Assn., Phi Kappa Phi. Home: Bryan, Tex. Died Apr. 28, 2006.

KOTEEN, JACK, management consultant, writer; b. N.Y., Aug. 22, 1919; s. Meyer and Eva (Gitlin) K.; m. Gloria Rogoff, Oct. 9, 1949; children: Glenn Michael, Douglas Evan. BA, NYU, 1940, attended John Hopkins Sch. for Advanced Internat. Studies. Mgmt. analyst Exec. Office of Pres. Fed. Govt. Agy., 1941-42; dir. devel. adminstrn., chief African tech. assist. in pub. and bus. adminstrn. in agy. for internat. devel. U.S. Dept. State, 1955-74; v.p. Assocs. for

Mgmt. and Evaluation, 1975-79; ind. cons., 1980-90; dir. Strategic Mgmt. Ctr.; instr. U. Md., Am. U., USDA. Author: (book) Strategic Management in Public and Non-profit Organizations, 1989, 91, 2d edit., 1997. Chair bd. dirs. Internat. Program for Human Resources Devel., Bethesda, Md., 1981-85. 1st Lt. Army Air Corps, 1942-45. Named Hon. Paramount Chief Mpelle People, N. Liberia, 1960; recipient Superior Honor award U.S. Dept. of State, 1974. Avocations: african art, golf. Home: Boynton Beach, Fla. Died Apr. 4, 2005.

KOURAKIS, EMANUEL MICHAEL, osteopathic physician; b. Chgo., Aug. 26, 1934; s. Manoussos Emanuel and Evangelia (Manoussakis) K.; m. Themis Ianthe Soter, Aug. 27, 1959; children: Stephen Michael, Thomas Michael, Anna Michelle. BS, De Paul U., Chgo., 1956; DO, Coll. Osteopathic Medicine and Surgery, Des Moines, 1963. Diplomate Am. Bd. Internal Medicine, Am. Bd. Nuclear Medicine. Intern Detroit Osteo. Hosp., 1963-64; resident Grandview Hosp., Dayton, Ohio, 1964-67; osteoapthic physician specializing in internal medicine Milw. Bd. dirs. Northwest Gen. Hosp., Milw., 1981—. Mem. Am. Osteopathic Assn., Am. Coll. Osteopathic Internists Physicians and Surgeons, Soc. Osteo. Physicians and Surgeons (Milw. dist.), Wis. Assn. Osteo. Physicians and Surgeons. Mem. Greek Orthodox. Avocations: photography, chess, archery. Home: Wauwatosa, Wis. Died May 19, 2004.

KOUTSTAAL, CORNELIS W., university administrator; b. Rotterdam, The Netherlands, May 10, 1935; came to U.S., 1961; s. Arie and Martina (Leentvaar) K.; m. Murilyn E. Graves, June 21, 1961; children: Robbart Willem, Stanley Wellington. Diploma, Inst. Gehrels, The Hague, The Netherlands, 1957, Logopedic Acad., 1960, Acad. Pedagogy, 1958, Clarke Sch. Deaf, 1963; MS, Springfield Coll., 1963; PhD, Western Res. U., 1966. Lic. speech pathologist, audiologist. Tchr. Effatha Sch. Deaf, Voorburg, The Netherlands, 1958-61, Clarke Sch. Deaf, Northhampton, Mass., 1961-63; fellow Western Res. U., Cleve., 1963-66; prof. Bowling Green (Ohio) State U., 1966-74; chmn., prof. CUNY, Bklyn., 1974-79; dean, prof. Ithaca (N.Y.) Coll., 1979-87; exec. dir. Delano Med. Mgmt. Corp., Pacific Palisades, Calif., 1987-91; prof. head divsn. human potential and performance Truman State U., Kirksville, 1991—2001; prof. emeritus, 2002. Lectr. U. Louvain, U. Groningen, 1969, Rotary Internat. project dir. for hearing impaired, Belize, 1997-2000. Author: Back to Basics, 1987; editorial cons. Williams and Wilkins Pub., Phila., 1975-80; editor-in-chief Spine Print Newsletter, Delano, 1987-90; contbr. 42 articles to profl. jours., also 2 films. Bd. dirs. Boy Scouts Am., Rye, N.Y., 1975, N.E.M.O. Health Coun., Chariton Valley Assn. for Handicapped Citizens, Continuing Med. Edn. Coney Island Hosp., Bklyn., 1974-78. Grantee NSF, 1967, NIH, 1979-81, U.S. Office Edn., 1970, 74-76, pvt. founds., 1979-86, corps., 1979—, Carl P. Miller Discovery Grant, 1996, Rotary Internat. matching grant, 1997-2000. Mem. APA, Am. Speech and Hearing Assn., Acoustical Soc. Am., Am. Assn. Phonetic Scis. (charter), Kirksville C. of C., Rotary (Paul Harris fellow), Phi Kappa Phi, Sigma Xi Rsch. Soc. Am. Avocations: music, reading, sports, travel. Home: Kirksville, Mo. Died Mar. 16, 2005.

KOZIOL, RICHARD DANIEL, municipal building and zoning director; b. Chgo., June 16, 1935; s. Frank Albert and Phyliss (Cygnar) K.; m. Gerrie Lou Lyster, Apr. 12, 1958 (div. May 1984); children: Ken, Karen Koziol Keth, Linda Koziol Dickens. cert. bldg. official Council Am. Bldg. Officials. Bldg. inspector Village of Skokie, Ill., 1962-67; dir. bldg. and zoning Village of Downers Grove, Ill., 1967-68, Village of Glenview, Ill., from 1968. Leader Boy Scouts Am., Rosemont, Ill., 1966-72. Served to master sgt. U.S. Army, 1957-61. Mem. Internat. Conf. Bldg. Officials, Nat. Fire Protection Assn., Bldg. Officials and Code Adminstrs. Internat., Ill. Council Code Adminstrs. (pres. 1982-83), Suburban Bldg. Officials (pres. 1981, William F. Bartell Meml. award 1984), N.W. Bldg. Officials (pres. 1973). Clubs: Radio Control Model (Chgo.), Model Aeronautics (Washington). Roman Catholic. Avocations: sailing, bicycling, canoeing, water-skiing, cross country skiing. Home: Chicago, Ill. Died Feb. 14, 2004.

KOZLOWSKI, STEVEN C., secondary education educator, administrator, consultant; b. Oak Park, Ill., Oct. 1, 1966; s. Chester S. and Elizabeth M. (Nickel) K. BS in Chem. Engring., Ill. Inst. Tech., 1989; MS in Edn. Adminstrn., Ill. State U., 1993. Cert. secondary tchr., Ill. Process engr. Quantum Chem. Co., Morris, Ill., 1986-90; applications engr. Nalco Chem. Co., Naverville, Ill., 1990-92; tchr., chmn. dept. math, sci., computer sci. St. Benedict H.S., Chgo., from 1993; tchr. Ida Crown Jewish Acad., Chgo., from 1994. Tchr. Sylvan Learning Ctrs., Oak Park, 1993—; ind. tutor, Cicero, Ill., 1994—. Exec. dir. Cicero Jr. High Planning Com., 1992; bd. dirs. J. Sterling Morton H.S., Cicero and Berwyn, Ill., 1989-93. Edn. Policy fellow Inst. Ednl. Leadership, Washington, 1992. Mem. NSTA, ASCD, Nat. Coun. Tchrs. Math., Am. Assn. Sch. Adminstrn. Republican. Roman Catholic. Avocation: computer technology. Home: Cicero, Ill. Died Feb. 15, 2005.

KRACHMALNICK, SAMUEL J., music conductor, educator; b. St. Louis; s. Abe and Jennie Krachmalnick; m. Gloria Lane, 2 children Diploma, Juilliard Sch. Music, 1950. Assoc. music dir. Met. Opera Nat. Co., 1965-67; prof., dir. symphony and opera U. Wash., Seattle, 1971-76; dir. symphony and opera UCLA, 1976—91. Music dir. Harkness Found., 1970-76. First conductor Zurich Stadtheater, 1961-63. Died Apr. 1, 2005.

KRAMER, JOHN ROBERT, law educator, dean; BA, Harvard Coll., 1958; LLB, Harvard Law Sch., 1962. Law clk. U.S. Ct. Appeals (9th cir.), 1962-63; asst. U.S. atty. US Dept. Justice, Washington, 1963-65; pvt. practice Shea & Gardner, Washington, 1966-69; exec. dir. Nat. Coun. on Hunger & Malnutrition, 1969-75; prof. Georgetown U. Law Ctr., 1971-86, assoc. dean, 1976-86; dean Tulane U. Law Sch., 1986-96, prof., 1986—2006. Edn. counsel Com. on Edn. & Labor U.S. Ho. of Reps., 1965-66, cousel Agrl. and Ways & Means Coms., 1975-81, spl. counsel to Thomas Foley, 1981-86; chmn. Law Access, Inc., 1993-96; counsel to parliamentarian on the Dem. Conv., Atlanta, 1988; chmn. Ctr. on Budget and Policy Priorities, 1980-2002. Editor: Hunger USA, 1969; author: Hunger USA Revisited, 1972. Pres. Field Found., 1981-91. Recipient Fulbright scholarship, 1958-59. Mem. Am. Assn. Law Schs. (chmn. congl. rels. com. 1976-86). Died Mar. 7, 2006.

KRAUSE, ROBERT MORTIMER, banker, mechanical engineer; b. Glenwood, Ill., Dec. 15, 1908; s. William and Charlotte (Bright) K.; m. Eleanor Driese, July 31, 1936; children: Marjorie N., Robert W., Bette B., Bryant W. BS in Mech. Engring., Ill. Inst. Tech. (name formerly Armour Inst.), 1931. Registered profl. engr., Ill. Chief levelman U.S. Coast and Geodetic Survey, Urbana, Ill., 1933-34; spl. engr. to mill mgr. Container Corp. Am., Chgo., 1934-54; pres. Homewood (Ill.) Fed. Savs., 1954-80, also bd. dirs. Bd. dirs. Homewood Svc. Corp., Homewood Fed. Savs. Trustee Village of Homewood, 1951-65, Village of Glenwood (Ill.), 1932-34; commr. Homewood Park Bd., 1947-51; engr. engring. com. Village of Homewood, 1943-47; pres. Homewood-Flossmoor C. of C., 1959-61. Mem. ASME (pres. Chgo. sect. 1946), Western Soc. Engrs. (chmn. mech div. 1945), Paper Industry Mgmt. Assn., Tau Beta Pi, Pi Tau Sigma, Theta Xi. Lutheran. Avocations: woodworking, gardening. Died June 13, 2004.

KREBS, CAROL MARIE, architect, psychotherapist; b. St. Louis, May 6, 1958; d. Festus John and Virginia (Klohr) K. B in Environ. Design, U. Kans., 1982; MA in Edn. Counseling, St. Louis U., 1995. Archtl. intern GSA, Kansas City, Mo., 1980-81, Old Post Office Renovation, St. Louis, 1980-81; free-lance archtl. designer St. Louis, 1981-84; archtl. designer Interior Space, St. Louis, 1984, Gina Ward and Assoc., St. Louis, 1984-85, Michael Fox and Assoc., St. Louis, 1985—88; mgr. facility design and constrn. Southwestern Bell Telephone, St. Louis, 1988—90; mgr. int. arch. and design exec. facilities Southwestern Bell Corp. Asset Mgmt., St. Louis, 1989-94; psychiat. therapist DePaul Health Ctr., St. Louis, 1994—98, Comtrea, Inc. Therapist St. Mary's Health Ctr., Mo. Dept. Mental Health, Dept. of Developmental Disabilities, 1998-99, MCI WorldCom, 1999-2001, Generation D.; instr., counselor St. Louis C.C. Active Big sister Big Bros./Big Sisters of Greater St. Louis, 1986—; mem. Operation Food Search. Mem. AIA. Home: Saint Louis, Mo. Died July 15, 2005.

KREIMES, PAUL ALLEN, biblical studies educator; b. Lackawanna, N.Y., July 31, 1945; s. Harvey James and Margaret Genevieve (Erdmann) K. BA, Sacred Heart Sem., Detroit, 1968; MA, U. Detroit, 1973; MDiv, St. John's Sem., Plymouth, Mich., 1975; SSL, Pontifical Bibl. Inst., Rome, 1986. Acad. dean S.S. Cyri and Methodius Sem., Orchard Lake, Mich., 1986-88; dean students, asst. prof. O.T. Sacred Heart Major Sem., Detroit, from 1988. Mem. Cath. Bibl. Assn. Am., Soc. Bibl. Lit., Nat. Assn. Profs. Hebrew. Roman Catholic. Avocations: music, reading, tennis, travel. Home: Detroit, Mich. Died Jan. 30, 2004.

KREMPEL, RALF HUGO BERNHARD, writer, artist, art gallery owner; b. Groitzsch, Saxony, Germany, June 5, 1935; came to U.S., 1964; s. Curt Bernhard and Liesbeth Anna Margarete (Franz) K.; m. Barbara von Eberhardt, Dec. 21, 1967 (div. 1985); 1 child, Karma. Student, Wood and Steel Constrn. Coll., Leipzig, German Democratic Republic, 1955. Steel constructor, worldwide, 1955-73; co-owner San Francisco Pvt. Mint, 1973-81; prin. artist San Francisco Painter Magnate, from 1982; dir. Stadtgalerie Wiprechtsburg Groitzsch, Germany, from 1991, Museumsgalerie am Markt, Groitzsch, from 1994. Exhbns. Centre Internat. d'Art Contemporain, 1985, Art Contemporain Cabinet des Dessins, 1986, Galerie Salammbo-Atlante, 1987 and others, Retrospective Mus.-gallery Borna, 1993; inventor, designer Visual Communication System, utilizing colors instead of letters to depict and transmit messages; Arrivalution as the Origin of Species; 6 Order of the Universe registrations, Arrivalution as the Origin of Species, Libr. of Congress, Washington, 1991—; Trilogy-Codex for the Coxmos: Arrivalution*Avivalu*Deflooration on CDROM, 2005—. Avocations: art research, photography. Home: San Francisco, Calif. Died June 24, 2005.

KRIVETSKY, ALEXANDER, aeronautical engineer, consultant; b. N.Y.C., June 28, 1914; s. Egnatz and Antonina (Mankiewicz) K. BSME, NYU, l935, MS in Aero. Engring., l936; postgrad., U. Buffalo, l950-54, MIT, l953. Registered profl. engr., N.Y. Project stress engr. Curtis-Wright Corp., Buffalo, 1936-45; chief advanced structural tech., staff engr. Bell Aerospace Co., Buffalo, 1945-75; engr. McMahon Engring., Buffalo, 1975-81; cons. engr. Koch Metal Spinning Co., Inc., Buffalo, from 1981. Tech. designer Bell Aerosystems Co., Buffalo, l96l-63. Contbr. articles to profl. jours. Mem. ASCE, ASME, AIAA (past officer). Republican. Avocations: woodworking, photography. Home: Buffalo, NY. Died June 30, 2004.

KRIZMIS, RENA PANCHERI, psychologist, educator; b. Schram City, Ill., May 1, 1923; d. Louis and Laura (Dalla Piazza) Pancheri; m. William James Krizmis, Sept. 3, 1945; children: William James Jr., Laura Jean. BA, Roosevelt U., 1965; MA, U. Chgo., 1967, cert. advanced studies, 1970; PhD, Loyola U., 1978. Tchr. Thornton Twp. H.S., Harvey, Ill., 1965-66; prof. Chgo. State U., from 1967. Acting dir. Coun. Ctr. Chgo. State U., 1981-84. Mem. Toastmasters Internat., Inc. Avocations: poetry, yoga. Died Jan. 28, 2004.

KROGSTAD, ROBERT WELLINGTON, financial services consultant; b. Muskegon, Mich., Sept. 9, 1919; s. John Endre and Ella (Olsen) K.; m. Barbara Cutler, Jan. 20, 1946 (div. 1968); children: John Gifford, Jane Cutler, Barbara Ann; m. Marie-Agnes Sourieau, Feb. 23, 1979; children: Mathieu-Pierre, Astrid Madeleine. BSME, Mich. State U., 1941; postgrad., Calif. Inst. Tech., 1943. Plant supt., chief engr. Grand Haven (Mich.) Stamped Products Co., 1946-49; plant mgr. EKCO, Inc., Byesville, Ohio, 1949-50; asst. plant mgr., chief engr., v.p. engring. Thomas Industries, Inc., Ft. Atkinson, Wis., 1950-57; exec. v.p., chief operating officer Carnes Corp., Verona, Wis., 1957-68; pres., co-owner Leer Mfg. Co., New Lisbon, Wis., 1969-73; pres., chief exec. officer E.D. Coddington Mfg. Co., Milw., 1976-85, Milw. Heat Tools, Inc., 1985-87; chmn. The Wellington Group, Charlottesville, Va., from 1987. Mem. adv. bd. Univ. Bus. Innovation Ctr., Charlottesville, 1987—. Patentee in field. Fin. chmn. Dane County Republican party, Madison, Wis., 1963-67; fin. chmn. 2d dist., Knowles for Gov. campaign, Madison, 1965-66; co-chair Rockefeller for Pres. campaign, Madison, 1966-67; co-chmn. fin. Milw. County Rep. party, 1981-84; mem. Rep. State Fin. Com., Milw., 1979-84; trustee Am. Scandinavian Found., N.Y.C., 1979—. Lt. USN, 1943-46. Mem. Young Businessmen's Club, Pres.'s Club Mich. State U., Masons, Scottish Rite, Shriners. Episcopalian. Avocations: fly fishing, bird shooting, farming, travel. Home: Charlottesville, Va. Died July 10, 2005.

KRONIK, JOHN WILLIAM, language educator; b. Vienna, May 18, 1931; arrived in U.S., 1939, naturalized, 1944; s. Bernard and Melanie (Hollub) K.; m. Eva Kronik, Dec. 26, 1955; children: Theresa J., Geoffrey B. BA, Queens Coll., 1952; MA, U. Wis., 1953, PhD, 1960; DHL, Ill. Coll., 1979. Asst. prof. Romance lang. Hamilton Coll., Clinton, 1958-63; assoc. prof. Spanish, U. Ill., Urbana, 1963-66; prof. Romance studies Cornell U., Ithaca, NY, 1966-2000, prof. emeritus, 2001—06. Vis. prof. Columbia U., 1968, Middlebury Coll., Vt., 1979, 80, 86, 91, Brigham Young U., 1982, U. Colo., 1989, U. Calif., Berkeley, 91, U. Calif., Irvine, 1994, U. Calif., L.A., 1999, 2000, U. Calif., Riverside, 2003; cons. NEH, 1973-92, Guggenheim Found., 1988-2006; corporator Internat. Inst. in Spain, Madrid, 1972-2006. Author: La farsa y el teatro espanol, 1971; co-editor: La familia de Pascual Duarte, 1961, Textos y Contextos de Galdos, 1994, Intertextual Pursuits: Literary Mediations in Modern Spanish Narrative, 1998; series editor Prentice-Hall, 1962-75; mem. editl. bd. MLA, N.Y.C., 1983-85; editor PMLA, 1985-92, Anales Galdosianos, 1986-90; contbr. articles to profl. jours. With U.S. Army, 1953—55. Fulbright fellow, 1960-61, 87-88; Rockefeller Found. rsch. resident, 1975; Guggenheim fellow, 1983-84; ACLS grantee, 1983-84. Mem. MLA, Internat. Assn. Hispanists, Internat. Galdos Assn. (pres.), Am. Assn. Tchrs. Spanish and Portuguese. Home: Ithaca, NY. Died Jan. 22, 2006.

KROP, STEPHEN, retired pharmacologist; b. N.Y.C., Sept. 24, 1911; s. Dmetro Pantele Krop and Mary Badewko; m. Mary Lulick, July 28, 1934; children: Elaine, Marianne, Paul, Thomas. BS, George Washington U., 1939; MS, Georgetown U., 1940; PhD, Cornell U., 1942. Diplomate Fed. Exec. Inst., 1970. From asst. to instr. pharmacology Cornell U. Med. Coll., Ithaca, NY, 1939—44; chief pharmacology dept. reserach divsn. Ethicon Inc., 1957—63; chief drug pharmacology br. rsch. divsn. Bur. Sci. Rsch., 1963—79; cons. toxicologist EPA, others, Washington, 1979—85; from instr. to asst. prof. pharmacology Yale U. Sch. Medicine, 1944—46; chief pharmacology sect. med. divsn. CWS, U.S. Army, 1946—48; pres. Ethicon Rsch. Found., 1957—63; head pharmacodyamics dept. Squibb Inst. Med. Rsch., 1948—49; dir. pharmacology divsn. Warner Inst. Therapeutic Rsch., 1949—51; rsch. assoc. Chemical-Biological Coordination Ctr. NRC, 1951—52, asst. and acting dir., 1951—52; coord. physiology divsn. Med. Rsch. Labs., 1952—57; mil. chemicals rsch. and asst. chief divsn. physiology U.S. Army Chem. Warfare Med. Labs., 1952—57. Advisor grain infestation Nat. Grain Sanitation Conf., Kansas City, Kans., 1956—56; health edn. exch. scientist Polish Health Ministry, Poland, 1978—78; ret., 1979; ann. Stephen and Mary Krop lectr. Georgetown U. Med. Ctr. First editor Military Chemicals Safety Manual. Fellow: Wash. Acad. Scis., NY Acad. Sciences; mem.: Am. Indsl. Hygiene Assn., Am. Physiol. Soc., Am. Soc. Pharmacology and Exptl. Therapeutics, The Harvey Soc., Soc. Exptl. Biology and Medicine, Am. Assn. Advancement Sci., Cosmos Club (Washington), Soc. Sigma Xi. Catholic. Achievements include research in Treatment Of Nerve Gas Poison; Treatment Of Hexachlorophene Poisoning. Avocations: music, genealogy, memoirs, history. Died July 6, 2005.

KRUEGER, JAMES HERBERT, SR., sales specialist; b. Milw., Jan. 5, 1943; s. Herbert W. and Lily A. (Kuphall) K.; m. Sherry L. Stein, Apr. 18, 1965 (dec. Nov. 1987); children: Kenneth J., Kelly L., Kristin L., James H. II, Jason F. MS in Fin. Svcs., Am. Coll., 1980, MS in Mgmt., 1985. Dist. rep. Aid Assn. for Luths., Appleton, Wis., 1965-83, gen. agt., from 1983. Speaker various fin. orgns. Fundraiser, vol. Luth. Ch. Mem. Nat. Assn. Life Underwriters (chmn. pub. rels. com. Washington chpt. 1980-84, 82-83), Wis. Assn. Life Underwriters (pres. Madison chpt. 1981-82, vice chmn. pub. svc. com. 1990—, Disting. Svc. award 1989), Million Dollar Round Table (life). Republican. Home: Appleton, Wis. Died May 10, 2005.

KRUEGER, LESTER EUGENE, pyschology educator; b. Chgo., Nov. 6, 1939; s. Carl and Helen (Milanowski) Krueger. PhD, Harvard U., 1969. Asst. prof. CCNY, 1969—72, assoc. prof., 1973—74; asst. prof. psychology Ohio State U., Columbus, 1974—76, assoc. prof., 1976—80, prof., from 1980. Cons. editor: Memory & Cognition, 1977—99, assoc. editor: Perception & Psychophysics, 1987—98; contbr. articles to profl. jours. With U.S. Army, 1957. Grantee NIH grantee, 1970—76, NIMH grantee, 1979—80. Fellow: Am. Psychol. Soc., Am. Psychol. Assn.; mem.: AAUP, Psychonomic Soc., Sigma Xi. Home: Columbus, Ohio. Died Mar. 21, 2005.

KRUEGER, ROBERT ALLEN, general manager; b. Oak Park, Ill., Dec. 29, 1935; s. Clarence A. and Edna A. (Polke) K.; m. Carol I. West, June 21, 1959; children: Jeffrey, Jerald, Thomas. AB, Knox Coll., 1957; PhD, Kans. State U., 1965. Dir. R & D B.F. Goodrich Chem., Independence, Ohio, 1975-78, v.p., 1978-80, sr. v.p., 1980-85; gen. mgr. ICI Resins U.S., Wilmington, Mass., from 1985. Pres. ICI Resins Can., Brandtford, Ont., 1988—; bd. dirs. Image Polymers Co., Wilmington, Associated Industries of Mass., Boston. Editor: Research Management, 1976-79; patentee in field; contbr. articles to profl. jours. Mem. Am. Chem. Soc., Nat. Paint and Coatings Assn., Nat. Petroleum Refiners Assn. (bd. dirs. 1981-85), Indsl. Rsch. Assn. Avocation: sailing. Home: Gilford, NH. Died Apr. 17, 2004.

KRUEGER, RONALD L., communications executive; b. Pitts., July 12, 1930; s. Carl F. and Alyce (Kennedy) K. Student, Carnegie Tech. Inst., Pitts., 1948-54, Franklin Coll., 1950-52. Program dir. Stas. KDKA-TV/WDTV-TV, Pitts., 1948-58; v.p. Banner Films, Chgo., 1958-60, TV Stas., Inc., N.Y.C., 1960-64, Sta. KATZ-TV, N.Y.C., 1964-68, HRP, Inc., N.Y.C., 1968-79; pres. TV Cons. Svcs. (formerly TelCom Assocs.), L.A., from 1979. Contbr. articles to profl. jours. Served as sgt. U.S. Army, 1950-53. Mem. Hollywood Fgn. Press Assn. (assoc.), Hollywood Heritage Soc. (assoc.). Roman Catholic. Died Aug. 10, 2005.

KRUIDENIER, DAVID, retired newspaper executive; b. Des Moines, July 18, 1921; s. David S. and Florence (Cowles) K.; m. Elizabeth Stuart, Dec. 29, 1948; 1 child, Lisa. BA, Yale U., 1946; MBA, Harvard U., 1948; LLD, Buena Vista Coll., 1960, Simpson Coll., 1963; LittD, Luther Coll., 1990; DHL, Drake U., 1990. With Mpls. Star and Tribune, 1948-52; with Des Moines Register and Tribune, 1952-85, pres., pub., 1971-78, CEO, 1971-85, chmn., CEO, 1982-85; with Cowles Media Co., 1983-93, pres., CEO, 1983-84, chmn., CEO, 1984-85, chmn., 1985-97. Trustee Gardner and Florence Call Cowles Found., Drake U., Des Moines Art Ctr., Grinnell Coll. Greater Des Moines Found. With USAAF, 1942-45. Decorated Air medal with three clusters, D.F.C. Mem. Coun. on Fgn. Rels., Des Moines Club, Mpls. Club, Sigma Delta Chi, Beta Theta Pi, Beta Gamma Sigma. Home: Des Moines, Iowa. Died Jan. 9, 2006.

KRUSE, MAX LEE, controller; b. Oakley, Kans., July 18, 1961; s. A.B. and Mary Ann Kruse. BS in Acctg., Kans. State U., 1984. CPA, Mo. Acct., auditor Arthur Andersen & Co., Kansas City, Mo., 1984-87; asst. contr. Hoyt Co., Kansas City, 1987-88, Xtra Corp., Liberty, Mo., from 1988. Mem. Mo. Soc. CPAs, Meadowbrook Country Club. Republican. Avocations: golf, softball, reading, travel. Home: Leawood, Kans. Died Jan. 24, 2005.

KUBE, HAROLD DEMING, retired financial executive; b. Buffalo, Wyo., June 16, 1910; s. Carl Christen and Inez (Mather) K.; m. Shirley Smith; children: Robert Ford, Thomas Smith. BS, U. Nebr., 1932; MBA, Harvard U., 1934. Owner Beef Cattle Farm, Warrenton, Va., from 1950; co-owner Resources Devel. Assocs., 1965-80; dir. emeritus Jefferson Savs. and Loan Assn., Warrenton, from 1980, Greater Washington Investors, Inc., from 1987. Bd. dirs. A & K Land and Cattle Corp., Warrenton. Co-author: Manufacturing Distribution in U.S., 1938. With USN, 1944-46. Mem. Am. Econ. Assn. Episcopalian. Avocation: golf. Died June 18, 2004.

KUCHEL, GAYLON LYLE, criminal justice educator, consultant; b. Kingsley, Iowa, June 27, 1924; s. Philip Arthur and Minnie Marie (Lage) K.; m. Wanda Mae Bowden, Sept. 14, 1945; children: Wade Philip, Kimberly Ann Kuchel Klein. BA, U. Iowa, 1949, MA, 1950. From asst. prof. to prof. criminal justice U. Nebr., Omaha, 1962-94, prof. emeritus, from 1994. Expert witness in civil and criminal trials. Contbr. articles to profl. jours. Mem. Nebr. State Parole Bd., Lincoln, 1967-69, Omaha City Pers. Bd., 1968-72, Nebr. Crime Commn., Lincoln, 1968-89, 90-92; treas., bd. dirs. Nebr. Patrol Found.; bd. dirs. Nat. Law Enforcement Edn. Program, Washington; mem. Nebr. State Drug and Violent Crime Policy Bd., Lincoln, 1988—; chmn. Citizen's Rev. Bd., City of Omaha, 1993—. Avocations: reading, fishing, gardening. Home: Omaha, Nebr. Died May 31, 2005.

KUELTHAU, PAUL STAUFFER, lawyer; b. West Bend, Wis., Mar. 31, 1912; s. George Herman and Marie Louise (Rix) K.; m. Laura Parish, Aug. 16, 1937; children: Karen Allan, Marline Holmes. AB, U. Wis., 1934, JD, 1936. Bar: Wis. 1936, U.S. Ct. Appeals (10th cir.) 1941, U.S. Ct. Appeals (7th cir.) 1947, Mo. 1953, U.S. Dist. Ct. (ea. dist.) Mo. 1954, U.S. Ct. Appeals (8th cir.) 1962, U.S. Dist. Ct. (so. dist.) Ill. 1964, U.S. Supreme Ct. 1973, U.S. Ct. Appeals (D.C. cir.) 1974. Regional atty. NLRB, various locations, 1939-46, chief counsel to chmn. Washington, 1946-53; assoc. Lewis, Rice, Tucker, Allen & Chubb, St. Louis, 1953-62; ptnr. Moller, Talent, Kuelthau, & Welch, St. Louis, 1962-88. Contbr. articles to profl. jours. Mem. ABA, Mo. Bar Assn., Bar Assn. St. Louis, Indsl. Relations Research Assn. Presbyterian. Home: Woburn, Mass. Died Jan. 27, 2005.

KUENNE, ROBERT EUGENE, economics professor; b. St. Louis, Jan. 29, 1924; s. Edward Sebastian and Margaret (Yochum) K.; m. Janet Lawrence Brown, Sept. 7, 1957; children: Christopher Brian, Carolyn Leigh Jeppsen. Student, Harris Jr. Coll., St. Louis, 1941-42; B.J., U. Mo., 1947; AB, Washington U., St. Louis, 1948, A.M., 1949, Harvard, 1951, PhD, 1953; PhD (hon.), Umea U., 1985. Asst. prof. econs. U. Va., 1955; mem. faculty Princeton (N.J.) U., from 1956, assoc. prof., 1960-69, prof. econs., from 1969. Cons. U.S. Naval War Coll., 1954, 55, Inst. Def. Analyses, Arlington, Va., 1968—2001, Inst. for Energy Analysis, Washington, 1978-82; vis. prof. mil. systems analysis U.S. Army War Coll., 1967-85; mem. sci. and mgmt. adv. com. U.S. Army Computer Systems Command. Author: The Theory of General Economic Equilibrium, 1963, The Attack Submarine: A Study in Strategy, 1965, The Polaris Missile Strike: A General Economic Systems Analysis, 1966, Monopolistic Competition Theory: Studies in Impact, 1967, Microeconomic Theory of the Market Mechanism, 1968, Eugen von Böhm-Bawerk, 1971, Rivalrous Consonance, 1986, Economics of Oligopolistic Competition, 1992, General Equilibrium Economics, 1991, Economic Justice in American Society, 1993, Price and Nonprice Rivalry in Oligopoly: The Integrated Battleground, 1999. Served with AUS, 1943-46. Named Oliver Ellsworth Bicentennial preceptor, 1975-60; fellow European Econs. and Fin. Ctr., 1992—; Fulbright fellow, 1991. Mem. Princeton Club (N.Y.C.). Home: Princeton, NJ. Died Nov. 5, 2005.

KUERTI, ROSI, educator; b. Vienna, July 8, 1905; d. Karl and Betty Jahoda. PhD, U. Vienna, 1928. Tchr. U. Istanbul, Turkey, 1937-38, Buckingham Sch., Cambridge, Mass., England, 1938-39; prof. Hathaway Brown Sch., Cleve., 1939-40, Case Western Res. U., Cleve.; tchr. John Raper Sch., Cleve. Died July 27, 2004.

KUHL, WALTER JAMES, JR., physician; b. Portland, Oct. 28, 1922; s. Walter James and Naomi (Billeter) K.; m. Olive Christine Ellithorpe, Dec. 18, 1948; children: James O., Sarah J., John W., Ann E. AB cum laude, Whitman Coll., 1944; MD, Johns Hopkins U., 1947. Intern, resident Bellevue Hosp., N.Y.C., 1947-49; fellow in medicine, 1949-51; instr. medicine NYU Coll. Medicine, N.Y.C., 1953-55; asst. prof. Northwestern U. Med. Sch., Chgo., 1955-60; chief metabolism sect. med. svc. VA Rsch. Hosp., Chgo., 1955-60; clin. asst. prof. medicine U. Oreg., Portland, 1960-74; physician McLean Clinic, Oregon City, Oreg., 1960-65; dir. med. edn. Emanuel Hosp., Portland, 1965-73; physician VA Hosp., Vancouver, Wash., 1973-80. Chmn. cont. med. edn. Oreg. Regional Med. Program, Portland, 1971-74. Contbr. articles to profl. jours. Pres. Clackamas County Mental Health Coun. 1964; mem. Clackamas County Cmty. Coun., 1965; mem. citizens adv. com. Surface Water Mgmt. Clackamas County, 1992-2002; bd. dirs. Lower Tualatin Valley Homeowners Assn., 1988-97. 1st lt. U.S. Army, 1951-53. Henry Strong Denison scholar, 1945. Fellow Am. Coll. Physicians; mem. Oreg. Soc. Internal Medicine (pres. 1970-71), Am. Diabetes Assn., Endocrine Soc., Ctrl. Soc. Clin. Rsch., Phi Beta Kappa, Nu Sigma Nu, Phi Delta Theta. Home: West Linn, Oreg. Died Feb. 22, 2005.

KUHN, DONALD MARSHALL, marketing professional; b. Miami, Fla., Nov. 2, 1922; s. Paul Carlton Kuhn and Helen (Merrick) Bond; m. Jane Emma Williams, Dec. 24, 1948 (dec. 1988); children: Marshall Merrick, Richard Williams, Diane Joan, Paul Willard; m. Kay Bardsley, Feb. 25, 1990 (div. March 2, 2004). BA in Journalism and Drama, U. Miami, 1949. Cert. fundraising executive. Advt. copywriter Sears Roebuck and Co., Chgo., 1949-50; dir. pub. relations Tb Inst. Chgo. and Cook County, 1950-54; dir. fundraising Dade County Tb Assn., Miami, 1955-59, Minn. Tb and Health Assn., St. Paul, 1959-60, Mich. Lung Assn., Lansing, 1960-68, Am. Lung Assn., N.Y.C., 1968-78; nat. founder, dir. regional fin. program Rep. Nat. Com., Washington, 1978-79; exec. v.p., dir. fundraising div. Walter Karl, Inc., Armonk, N.Y., 1979-90, cons., 1990-93, May Devel. Svcs., Greenwich, Conn., from 1993. Mem. direct mktg. task force Am. Red Cross, Washington, 1983-84; mem. direct mail task force Am. Heart Assn., Dallas, 1982. Editor: Non-profit Council Info. Exchange, 1987-90; contbr. articles to Fundraising Mgmt. Mag. and other publs. Bd. dirs. Isadora Duncan Internat. Inst., N.Y.C., 1987-2003. Mem. Assn. Fundraising Profls. (bd. dirs. 1978-80), Direct Mktg. Assn. (mem. operating com., non-profit coun. 1987-90, recipient non-profit coun. fundraising achievement award 1991). Republican. Congregationalist. Avocations: personal computers, croquet. Died Nov. 18, 2005.

KUHNS, CRAIG SHAFFER, business educator; b. Spokane, Wash., Apr. 14, 1928; s. Theodore Lewis and Audrey Grace (Shaffer) K. BS, U. Calif., Berkeley, 1950, BA, 1954, MBA, 1955. Analyst Standard Oil Co. of Calif., San Francisco, 1955-57; bus. educator U. Calif./San Jose State U., 1958-63, City Coll. of San Francisco, from 1963. Adj. faculty U. San Francisco, 1977-90. 1st lt. U.S. Army, 1951-52, col. Mil. Intelligence USAR, 1953-80, col. AUS, ret. Mem. Calif. Alumni Assn., U.S. Army War Coll. Alumni Assn., Res. Officers Assn,. Japan Soc. Republican. Avocation: travel. Home: San Francisco, Calif. Died Apr. 30, 2004.

KULCZYNSKI, EDWINA MARY, secondary school educator; b. Camden, N.J., May 15, 1935; d. Witold and Florence (Praiss) Zebrowski; m. Henry Theodore Kulczynski, Sept. 29, 1957; children: Mark, Damian, Edwina, Karen. BS, Immaculata Coll., 1957; student, Rutgers U., 1958. cert. tchr., Phila., 1958. Tchr., dept. head St. Joseph's Sch., Camden, 1958-63; buyer Jacob Reed's Mens Clothing, Cherry Hill, N.J., 1975-78; tchr., dept. head Paul VI High Sch., Haddonfield, N.J., 1978-88; co-owner Flories Inc., Westmont, N.J. Chairperson Middle States Evaluation of Paul VI High Sch., Westmont, 1986-88. Author: Second Chance, Cookbook; producer: gourmet product, Flories, 1983—. Bd. dir. Parent Tchrs. Assn., Westmont, 1975-77. Mem. Am. Assn. of U. Women, Camden County Home Econs. Avocations: painting, piano, collecting recipes, swimming. Home: Collingswood, NJ. Died Jan. 28, 2004.

KUMAR, ANAND, management executive, consultant; b. Agra, India, Dec. 11, 1950; came to U.S., 1972; s. Dharma Deo and Shanti Sharma; m. Abha Sharma, Jan. 21, 1977; children: Amit, Anshul. BS (hon.), Aligarh (India) U., 1970, MA, 1972; MBA, L.I. U., 1975. From trainee to mktg. analyst Met. Life, Pitts., 1975-77; mktg. and econ. officer Swiss Industries Fedn., N.Y.C., 1977-80; dir. market and strategic planning Bulova Watch Co., Jackson Heights, N.Y., 1980-84; pres. Kumar Assocs., Inc., Ft. Lee, N.J., from 1985. Adj. prof. L.I. U., Bklyn., 1988—; bd. dirs. MA Holding Co., Inc., Ft. Lee. Democrat. Hindu. Avocations: model railroads, gourmet food. Home: West New York, NJ. Died Sept. 23, 2004.

KUNERT, PAUL CHARLES, lawyer; b. Hankinson, N.D., Jan. 14, 1935; s. Harry Firdinand Kunert and Mary Bernice Sisson; m. Sandra Kathryn Rood, Nov, 19, 1962 (dec. June 1994); children: Melissa, Kathryn, Miles Joseph; m. Paricia Joan McGraw, Oct. 11, 1997. Student, St. John's U., 1954-55; BA, U. Minn., 1957, JD cum laude, 1960. Bar: Minn. 1961, U.S. Dist. Ct. Minn. 1972. Assoc. Robins, Davis & Lyons, St. Paul, 1961-66; ptnr. Sahr, Kunert & Tambornino, Mpls., 1967-96, Kunert, Tambornino & Kuhar, Mpls., 1996-2000; sole practice Minnetonka, Minn., from 2000. Mem. Minn. Def. Lawyers Assn., Hennepin County Bar Assn. Home: Edina, Minn. Died Feb. 6, 2004.

KUNITZ, STANLEY JASSPON, poet, editor, educator; b. Worcester, Mass., July 29, 1905; s. Solomon Z. and Yetta Helen (Jasspon) K.; m. Helen Pearce, 1930 (div. 1937); m. Eleanor Evans, Nov. 21, 1939 (div. 1958); 1 dau., Gretchen; m. Elise Asher (dec.), June 21, 1958. AB summa cum laude, Harvard U., 1926, MA, 1927; LittD (hon.), Clark U., 1961, Anna Maria Coll., 1977, St. Mary's Coll., Md., 1994; LHD (hon.), Worcester State Coll., 1980, SUNY, Brockport, 1987. Editor Wilson Library Bull., 1928-43; lit. faculty Bennington Coll., 1946-49; prof. English Potsdam (N.Y.) State Tchrs. Coll., 1949-50; dir. seminar Potsdam Summer Workshop in Creative Arts, 1949-53; lectr. The New Sch., 1950-57; vis. prof. poetry U. Wash., 1955-56; vis. prof. English Queens Coll., 1956-57, Brandeis U., 1958-59; dir. poetry workshop Poetry Center YMHA, N.Y., 1958-62; Danforth vis. lectr. various Am. colls., 1961-63; lectr. Columbia U., 1963-66, adj. prof. writing Grad. Sch. Arts, 1967-85. Editor Yale Series Younger Poets, 1969-77; vis. prof. poetry Yale U., 1970, Rutgers U. at Camden, 1974; vis. prof., sr. fellow in humanities Princeton U., 1978, Vassar Coll., 1981; cons. poetry Libr. of Congress, 1974-76; founder Fine Arts Work Ctr., Provincetown, Mass., Poets House, NYC. Author: (verse) Intellectual Things, 1930, Living Authors, 1931, Authors Today and Yesterday, 1933, Junior Book of Authors, 1934, British Authors of the 19th Century, 1936, American Authors, 1600-1900, 1938, Twentieth Century Authors, 1942, First Supplement, 1955, Passport to the War, 1944, British Authors Before 1800, 1952, Selected Poems, 1928-1958, 1958 (Pulitzer prize), Poems of John Keats, 1964, European Authors, 1000-1900, 1967, The Testing-Tree, 1971, The Terrible Threshold, 1974, The Coat Without a Seam, 1974, A Kind of Order, A Kind of Folly: Essays and Conversations, 1975, The Poems of Stanley Kunitz 1928-1978, 1979, The Wellfleet Whale and Companion Poems, 1983, Next-To-Last Things: New Poems and Essays, 1985, The Essential Blake, 1987, Interviews and Encounters, 1993, Passing Through: The Later Poems, 1995 (Nat. Book award), Collected Poems, 2000, The Wild Braid: A Poet Reflects on a Century in the Garden, 2005; editor (with David Ignatow) The Wild Card, Selected Poems, Early and Late, of Karl Shapiro, 1998, The Collected Poems, 2000; translator: (with others) verse Antiworlds (A. Voznesensky), 1966, Antiworlds and The Fifth Ace, 1967, Stolen Apples (Y. Yevtushenko), 1971, (with Max Hayward) Poems of Akhmatova, 1973, Story Under Full Sail (A. Voznesensky), 1974; Editor, co-translator: Orchard Lamps (Ivan Drach), 1978. With AUS, 1943-45. Recipient Garrison medal for poetry Harvard, 1926, Oscar Blumenthal prize, 1941, Guggenheim fellow creative writing, 1945-46, Amy Lowell traveling fellow for poetry, 1953-54, Levinson prize for poetry, 1956, Harriet Monroe award U. Chgo., 1958, Pulitzer prize in poetry, 1959, Brandeis Creative Arts Poetry award, 1964, Lenore Marshall award for poetry, 1980, Nat. Endowment Arts sr. fellow, 1984, Bollingen prize, 1987, Montgomery fellow Dartmouth Coll., 1991, Centennial medal Harvard U., 1992, Nat. Medal Arts, 1993, Shelley Meml. award, 1995, Nat. Book award, 1995, award St. Botolph Club Found., 1996, Robert Frost medal Poetry Soc. Am., 1998, Courage Conscience award Peace Abbey, 1998; grantee Ford Found., 1958-59, Nat. Inst. Arts and Letters, 1959; named N.Y. State Poet, 1987-88, Walt Whitman Birthplace Poet, 1989, Barnes and Noble Writers for Writers award Poets and Writers, 1999, Literary Arts award Nat. Coun. for Jewish Culture, 2000, US Poet laureate, 2000. Mem. Acad. Am. Poets (fellowship award 1968, chancellor 1970-95); mem. AAAL (sec. 1985-88), Poets House N.Y. (founding pres. 1985-90), Fine Arts Work Ctr. in Provincetown (founding mem., bd. dirs. 1968-2006, medal for disting. svc. in arts 1997), Phi Beta Kappa. Died May 14, 2006.

KURILOFF, EFFIE HANNAH, education educator; b. Bklyn., Mar. 31, 1931; d. Morris and Nora Kuriloff; m. Bert Schwarzschild, Aug. 5, 1956 (div. 1986); children: David Mark, Nomi, Daria Ida. BS, N.J. Coll. for Women, 1952; MS, Bank St. Coll., 1954. Cert. tchr., N.Y., Calif. Tchr. Walden Sch., N.Y.C., 1954, Bedford Elem. Sch., Westport, Conn., 1955-56, San Francisco Unified Sch. Dist., 1956-65; instr. child devel. and family studies City Coll., San Francisco, from 1965. Dir., parent educator Mission Cooperative Nursery Sch./Rocky Mountain Participation Nursery Sch., San Francisco, 1965—; cons. in field, 1977—. Author: Maya: A Pre-schooler Meets the Death of Her Father, 1993; featured in documentary film The Tricycle Solution: Teachable Moments for Parents and Preschoolers, 2002. Chair Seward St. Mini-Park, San Francisco, 1975, Mural Project Eureka Valley Promotion Assn., San Francisco, 1977, Children's Fair Castro St. Fair, San Francisco, 1982; homeless educator Episc. Sanctuary Shelter, San Francisco, 1992-99. Recipient Ventures Beneficial to the Cmty. award Mayor of San Francisco, 1976. Mem. Nat. Assn. for Edn. Young Children. Democrat. Jewish. Avocations: pottery, singing, gardening, painting, hiking. Home: Oakland, Calif. Died Feb. 26, 2004.

KURKE, MARTIN IRA, psychologist, consultant; b. Bklyn., Jan. 9, 1924; s. Jacob William and Miriam (Vexler) K.; m. Joy B. Edinger, Aug. 26, 1951 (div. Dec. 1971); children: Kathy Ann, David S.; m. Patricia Lee Crutchfield, Dec. 27, 1971; children: Harold T. Hedges Jr., Kathleen Youngblood, Leslie B. O'Shaughnessey. BA, NYU, 1949; MA, U. of Buffalo, 1953; PhD, Am. U., 1963; LLB, LaSalle Extension U., Chgo., 1974. Lic. psychologist, Va., Md., D.C.; diplomate in forensic psychology and indsl. and orgnl. psychology Am. Bd. Profl. Psychology; diplomate Am. Bd. Forensic Examiners; cert. human factors profl. Bd. Cert. in Profl. Ergonomics. Engring. psychologist, ops. rsch. analyst Bell Aircraft Corp., Buffalo, N.Y., 1952-54; rsch. psychologist U.S. Army Human Engring. Lab., Aberdeen Proving Ground, 1954-57; sr. human factors psychologist Dunlap & Assocs., Washington, 1957-61; sr. ops. rsch. analyst, prin. staff scientist Tech. Ops., Inc., various cities, Va., 1961-68; sr. rsch. assoc. Human Scis. Rsch., Inc., McLean, Va., 1968-69; dir. rsch. Aries Corp., McLean, 1969-70; rsch., later chief psychologist, chief drug control div. Bur. Narcotics and Dangerous Drugs, Washington, 1970-73; sci. officer Select Com. on Narcotics Abuse and Control U.S. Ho. of Reps., Washington, 1983-85; chief spl. studies Drug Enforcement Adminstrn., Washington, 1973-78, asst. to pers. dir., 1980-83, exec. asst. Office Info. Systems, 1985-88, ops. rsch. analyst Lorton, Va., 1988-94. Vis. prof. psychology George Mason U., Fairfax, Va., 1979-80, adj. prof., 1980-88, rsch. adj. prof., 1993—; cons. on indsl. and orgnl. psychology and forensic human factors to various orgns. and firms, 1964—. Author books, including Psychology in Product Liability and Personal Injury Litigation, 1986, Police Psychology Into the Twenty-First Century, 1995; editor: Forensic Reports, 1987-92; contbr. articles to profl. publs., chpts. to books. Mem. Fairfax County Dem. Com., 1966-70; bd. dirs. Koinonia Found., Springfield, Va., 1967-68, Pinewood Lake Homeowners Assn., Alexandria, Va., 1980-85. With AUS, 1943-46, ETO. Decorated Bronze Star with V clasp and oak leaf cluster; recipient numerous letters of commendation and appreciation, citations and awards from various mil. and govtl. orgns., 1960-85; grand prize Aero Digest Design Forum, 1955, cert. of acclamation Ops. Rsch. Soc. Am., 1975. Fellow AAAS, APA, Am. Psychol. Soc., Am. Psychology and Law Soc., Human Factors and Ergonomics Soc., Soc. Applied Exptl. and Engring. Psychologists, Am. Acad. Forensic Psychology, Psychologists in Pub. Svc. (pres. CJ sect. 1984, Disting. Svc. award 1991), Cons. Psychologists; mem. Soc. Indsl. and Orgnl. Psychology, Soc. Police and Criminal Psychology (diplomate), Va. Psychol. Assn., Va. Applied Psychology Acad., Sigma Xi, Psi Chi, also others. Avocation: writing. Died Mar. 31, 2005.

KURZ, ALAN SCOTT, retired small business owner; b. N.Y.C., N.Y., May 8, 1951; s. Marvin Roy Kurz and Barbara Yarmus; m. Kathleen Turmer, Sept. 8, 1976 (div. Sept. 2, 1981). BA, Boston U., 1974. Owner Travel in Style (5 agys.), Great Neck and Little Neck, NY, 1974—79, Galaxy Travel (28 agys.), L.A., 1980—88; gen. mgr. Oasis Reservations, Miami, 1989—96; owner Askme Computers, Miami, 1996—2001; ret., 2001. Cons. to travel agys., tour opers., computer bus., Fla., from 1997; keynote spkr. Am. Soc. Travel Agts. Avocations: reading, scuba diving, skiing. Died June 4, 2004.

KYKER, GRANVIL CHARLES, JR., physics educator; b. Greensboro, N.C., Dec. 2, 1938; s. Granvil C. and Mary Agnes (Garrett) K.; m. Penelope Scott Reynolds, June 28, 1958; children: Margaret Reynolds, Dorothy Anne. ScB in Physics, Brown U., 1959; PhD in Physics, Duke U., 1964. Rsch. assoc. Duke U., Durham, N.C., 1964-67, instr., 1967-68; asst. prof. Oakland U., Rochester, Mich., 1968-74, Rose-Hulman Inst. Tech., Terre Haute, Ind., from 1975. Author: Study Guide to Accompany Physics, 1976, 2d edit., 1982, Study Guide to Accompany College Physics, 1986; contbr. articles to profl. jours. Mem. AAUP, Am. Phys. Soc., Am. Assn. Physics Tchrs., Am. Soc. for Engring. Edn., Health Physics Soc., Sigma Xi. Democrat. Baptist. Avocations: singing, photography, chess. Home: Terre Haute, Ind. Died Mar. 9, 2005.

LABBE, ARMAND JOSEPH, curator, anthropologist; b. Lawrence, Mass., June 13, 1944; s. Armand Henri and Gertrude Marie (Martineau) L.; m. Denise Marie Scott, Jan. 17, 1969 (div. 1972). BA in Anthropology, Univ. Mass., 1969; MA in Anthropology, Calif. State U., 1986; lifetime instr. credential in anthropology, State Calif. Curator collections Bowers Mus., Santa Ana, Calif., 1978-79, curator anthropology, 1979-86, chief curator, 1986—2005, dir. rsch. and collections, 1991—2005. Instr. prof. Santa Ana Coll., 1981-86, U. Calif., Irvine, 1983, 87, 91, 93, Calif. State U., Fullerton, 1982-83, 88, 97-, faculty, appt. rsch. assoc. dept. anthropology, 1997-2005, Calif. State U., Fullerton; trustee Balboa Arts Conservation Ctr., San Diego, 1989-97, Ams. Found., Greenfield, Mass., 1985-94, Quintcentenary Festival Discovery, Orange County, Calif., 1990-91, Mingei Internat. Mus., La Jolla, Calif., 1993-2005, treas. bd. dirs. 1996-2003, vice-chmn. bd. dirs., 2003; inaugural guest lectr. Friends of Ethnic Art, San Francisco, 1988. Author: Man and Cosmos, 1982, Ban Chiang, 1985, Colombia Before Columbus, 1986 (1st prize 1987), Leigh Wiener: Portraits, 1987, Colombia Antes de Colón, 1988 (honored at Gold Mus. Bogotá, Colombia, 1988), Images of Power: Master Works of the Bowers Museum of Cultural Art, 1992, Guardians of the Life Stream: Shamans, Art and Power In Prehispanic Central Panama, 1995, Shamans, Gods, and Mythic Beasts: Colombian Gold and Ceramics in Antiquity, 1998, Prehistoric Thai Ceramics, 2002; co-author: Tribute to The Gods: Treasures of the Museo del Oro, Bogotá, 1992; contbg. author: What Is A Shaman: Shamans and Medicine Men From A Western Point of View, 1999, Companions in Day, Figurative Sculpture from Ancient Am., 2004. Hon. bd. dirs. Ethnic Arts Coun. L.A.; cons. Orange County Coun. on History and Art, Santa Ana, 1981-85; mem. Task Force on County Cultural Resources, Orange County, 1979; cons., interviewer TV prodn. The Human Journey, Fullerton, 1986-89; treas., bd. trustees Mingei Internat. Mus., San Diego, 1996-2005; art bd. Orange County 46th Congl. Dist., 1997-2005. With USAF, 1963-67. Recipient cert. of Recognition Orange County Bd. Suprs., 1982, award for outstanding scholarship Colombian Community, 1987, Distinguished Citizens for the Arts award NAACP, 1999, cert. of recognition Calif. State Senate, 1999; honored for authorship Friends of Libr., 1987, 88; grantee Nat. Endowment for Arts, 1994, NEH, 2000. Fellow Am. Anthrop. Assn.; mem. AAAS, Am. Assn. Mus., N.Y. Acad. Scis., S.W. Anthrop. Assn. Avocations: photography, travel. Home: Costa Mesa, Calif. Died Apr. 2, 2005.

LABEN, DOROTHY LOBB, volunteer nutrition educator, consultant; b. Yonkers, N.Y., Mar. 7, 1914; d. John David and Edna Lyall (Klein) Lobb; m. Robert C. Laben, Nov. 29, 1946; children: John Victor, Robert James, Elizaeth Jean Cunningham, Catherine Lyda Baldwin. AB, Wellesley Coll., 1935; MS, Conn. Coll. for Women, 1937. Cert. med. technologist Am. Soc. Clin. Pathologists. Med. technologist Carl H. Wies M.D., New London, Conn., 1937-40; rsch. chemist Hixon lab. U. Kans. Med. Sch., Kansas City, 1940-41; med. technologist chemistry Blodgett Meml. Hosp., Grand Rapids, Mich., 1941-43; grad. researcher chemistry Cornell U. (Nutrition), Ithaca, N.Y., 1943-45; researcher U.S. Plant, Soil and Nutrition Lab. Cornell U., Ithaca, 1944-45; researcher food composition Bur. Human Nutrition and Home Econs., USDA, Washington; lab. asst. and instr. chemistry dept. Okla. A&M U., Stillwater, 1947. Cons. Yolo County Coalition Against Hunger, Davis, Calif., 1970—. Bd. dirs. Econ. Opportunity Commn. of Yolo County Calif., 1970-75. Recipient Brinley award City of Davis, 1985; named Woman of Yr. Calif. State Senate, Sen. Pat Johnston, Sacramento, 1991. Mem. LWV, UN Assn. (bd. dirs. 1986-88). Presbyterian. Home: Davis, Calif. Died Aug. 7, 2005.

LABOVITZ, DEBORAH ROSE RUBIN, occupational therapist, educator; b. Phila., Oct. 13, 1942; d. Samuel Frank and Clara (Blank) Rubin; m. Judah Isaiah Labovitz, June 3, 1962; children: Gail Susan Labovitz Seligman, Bruce Joel, Daniel Mark. BS in Occupational Therapy, U. Pa., 1963, Ma in Sociology, 1974, PhD in Sociology, 1979. Lic. occupl. therapist Nat. Bd. for Cert. of Occupl. Therapy. Dir. occupational therapy Mercy Douglas Hosp., Dept Psychiatry, Univ. Pa., Phila., 1963-66; adj. lectr. U. Pa., Phila., 1967-69, adj. instr., 1971-72, instr., 1972-76, asst. prof., 1976-80; prof. and chair dept. occupational therapy NYU, N.Y.C., 1980—2000. Cons. Ea. Pa. Psychiatric Inst., 1967-69, to pres. Beaver Coll., Phila., 1980; adj. lectr. U. Pa., 1980-81; mem. NYU Faculty Senate (acad. affairs com. 1987-88, faculty coun. exec. com. 1988-89, acad. affairs com. 1989-90, mandatory retirement subcom., 1988-92, fin. affairs com., 1988-90), Faculty Resource Network, Minority Conf. Com., 1991-92; Sch. of Edn. Budget Adv. Com., 1985-2006, chair 1992-93; Sch. of Edn. Instl. Planning and Devel. Com., 1986-2006, chair 1992-93; chair Sch. of Edn. Senate and Faculty Coun.; other coms. and offices. Author: Ordinary Miracles: True Stories About Overcoming Obstacles and Surviving Catastrophes, 2003; co-author (with Patricia Winstead-Frye) Ordinary Miracles in Nursing, 2005; Contbr. articles to profl. jours.; presenter at numerous profl. confs. and ednl. meetings. Alt. del. Dem. Nat. Conv., Miami Beach, Fla., 1972. Grantee: N.Y.C. Bd. Edn., 1990-93, 93-96, MCH grant project, RSA long term tng. grantee, 1984-87, AOA, 1988-90, NYU Challenge grant, 1990, and others. Fellow Am. Occupational Therapy Assn. (vice chair commn. on edn. steering com. 1991-93; reviewer conf. papers, rsch. grants, postdoctoral fellowships, various books and articles, many other coms. and com. offices, Svc. award 1986, 89, 93, Cert. of Appreciation 1991); mem. AAUP, Pa. Occupational Therapy Assn. Dist. V., World Fedn. of Occupational Therapists, N.Y. State Occupational Therapy Assn. (mem. chief's group met. N.Y. dist., Cert. Appreciation 1987). Home: Elkins Park, Pa. Died July 14, 2006.

LACY, WALTER JEROME, real estate executive, farmer; b. Troup, Tex., Jan. 29, 1930; s. Curby Jerome and Opal Frankie (Tankersley) L.; m. Dolores Marie Carle, Aug. 8, 1959; children: Deborah Ann, Karen Marie, Michael Jerome. BS, Stephen F. Austin U., 1957. Cert. tchr., Tex.; lic. real estate broker, Tex. Tchr. Tex. Pub. Schs., San Antonio, Webster, 1956-85; owner mobile home park, Alvin, Tex., from 1965, tree farm, Jacksonville, Tex., from 1960. Patentee in field of athletic and pipe cleaning equipment. Mem. Alvin planning commn., 1970-82, charter rev., 1994. With USAF, 1951-55. Mem. Tex. Forestry Assn., Harris County Landowners Assn. Democrat. Roman Catholic. Avocations: hunting, fishing, tv, reading. Home: Alvin, Tex. Died Aug. 2, 2004.

LADEFOGED, PETER NIELSEN, phonetician; b. Sutton, Eng., Sept. 17, 1925; came to U.S., 1962; s. Niels Nielsen and Marie Frances (Foucard) L.; m. Jennifer Macdonald, Dec. 19, 1953; children: Lise, Thegn, Katie. MA, U. Edinburgh, Scotland, 1951, PhD, 1959; DLitt (hon.), U. Edinburgh, 1993. Lectr. U. Edinburgh, 1953-61, U. Ibadan, Nigeria, 1959-60; rsch. fellow West African Langs. Survey, Nigeria, 1961-62; asst. prof. phonetics UCLA, 1962-63, assoc. prof., 1963-65, prof., 1965-91, prof. emeritus, 1991—2006, rsch. linguist, 1991—2006; team leader East African Survey Lang. Use and Lang. Teaching, Uganda, 1968. Author: A Course in Phonetics; others. Served with Brit. Army, 1943-47. Fellow Acoustical Soc. Am. (Silver Speech Comm. medal 1994), Am. Speech and Hearing Assn., Am. Acad. Arts and Scis., Am. Speech Lang. and Hearing Assn.; mem. Linguistic Soc. Am. (pres. 1978), Internat. Phonetic Assn. (pres. 1986-91). Home: Aliso Viejo, Calif. Died Jan. 24, 2006.

LADER, LAWRENCE, writer; b. N.Y.C., Aug. 6, 1919; s. Ludwig and Myrtle (Powell) L.; m. Jean MacInnis, Aug. 24, 1942 (div. Jan. 1946); m. Joan Summers, Sept. 27, 1961; 1 dau., Wendy Summers. AB, Harvard U., 1941. With press dept. ABC, 1941-42; contbg. editor Coronet mag., 1946; feature editor Glamour mag., 1953; lectr. NYU, 1957-59, Philips Brooks Assn., Harvard, from 1962; regular contbr. Am. Heritage, Reader's Digest, N.Y. Times mags., others, from 1941; exec. dir. Hugh Moore Fund, 1966-67; fgn. corr. Arab-Israel War, 1948, other overseas assignments, 1951, 55, 57; adj. assoc. prof. journalism NYU, 1967-72. Author: Margaret Sanger, 1955, The Bold Brahmins, New England's War Against Slavery, 1961, Abortion, 1966, juvenile Margaret Sanger, 1969, Breeding Ourselves to Death, 1971, Foolproof Birth Control, 1972, Abortion II: Making the Revolution, 1973, Power on the Left: American Radical Movements since 1946, 1979, Politics, Power and the Church, 1987, RU 486, 1991, A Private Matter, 1995, Ideas Triumphant, 2003. Chmn. exec. com. Nat. Abortion Rights Action League, 1969-72, chmn. bd., 1972-76; pres. Abortion Rights Mobilization, 1976—. Served to lt. AUS, 1942-46; officer-in-charge N.Y. Troop Information, Armed Forces Radio Service. Recipient Benjamin Franklin Mag. award, 1969, Cert. Distinction, NOW, 1989; named Feminist Majority Feminist of Yr., 1992. Mem. Authors Guild. Clubs: Harvard, Century Assn. (N.Y.C.). Home: New York, NY. Died May 7, 2006.

LAFFERTY, JOYCE G. ZVONAR, retired elementary school educator; b. Balt., July 9, 1931; d. George S. and Carolyn M. (Bothe) Greener; children: Barbara Z. Gunter, John G. Zvonar, David A. Zvonar. BS, Towson State U., 1963; M equivalent, Md. Inst. Coll. Art, 1978. Cert. tchr., Md. Tchr., dept. chmn. Hampstead Hill Jr. High Annex, Balt.; tchr. Forest Park Sr. High, Balt.; tchr., dept. chmn. Roland Park Mid. Sch., Balt. Mem. Nat. Art Edn. Assn., Internat. Soc. Artists, Balt. Tchrs. Union. Home: Austin, Tex. Died Oct. 1, 2005.

LAFOE, BARBARA S., retired primary school educator, principal; b. Chgo., Apr. 20, 1931; d. Harold Ulysses and Olivia Jeanette (Robinson) Strickland; m. Jay B. Lafoe, Apr. 24, 1954 (div. Apr. 1964). BE, Chgo. Tchrs. Coll., 1951; MA, Roosevelt U., 1974. Cert. elem. tchr., sch. prin., Ill. Tchr. Chgo. Pub. Schs., 1951-83, prin., adminstr., 1983-90. Mem. Chgo. Prins. Assn., Alpha Kappa Alpha (grad. advisor 1949—). Mem. United Ch. Christ. Avocation: organist. Home: Chicago, Ill. Died Nov. 1, 2004.

LAI, JENG YIH, surgeon; b. Rep. China, Dec. 5, 1941; came to U.S., 1968; s. Ting-Zo and See-Mae (Lee) L.; m. Su Kao, July 19, 1944; children: Stephen, Christina, Monica. MD, Nat. Taiwan U., 1967. Diplomate Am. Bd. Surgery, Am. Bd. Thoracic Surgery. Intern St. Francis Gen. Hosp., Pitts., 1968-69, resident in gen. surgery, 1969-73; fellow in cardiovascular surgery Rush-Presbyn.-St. Luke's Med. Ctr., Chgo., 1973-74; resident in cardiovascular and thoracic surgery St. Paul Hosp., Dallas, 1974-76; fellow in cardiovascular surgery Tex. Heart Inst., Houston, 1976-77; surgeon cardiovascular and thoracic surgery St. Francis Regional Med. Ctr., Wichita, Kans., from 1977; pvt. practice specializing in cardiovascular and thoracic surgery Wichita, 1981-88. Clin. asst. prof. in surgery U. Kans., Wichita. Bd. dirs. Wichita Indochinese Ctr., 1985-86. Served as lt. surgeon China Army, 1967-68. Fellow Am. Coll. Surgeons, Denton A. Cooley Cardiovascular Soc.; mem. AMA, Am. Heart Assn., Med. Soc. Kans., Sedgwick County Med. Soc., Wichita Asian Assn. (pres. 1985-86). Avocations: tennis, travel, reading. Home: Foster City, Calif. Died July 14, 2004.

LAING, DONA MARTIN, perioperative services nurse; b. Cleve., Aug. 24, 1949; d. Daniel Roy and Rosemary (Geschke) Martin; m. Bruce Naylor Laing, Nov. 25, 1971; children: Scott Martin, Mitchell Naylor. BS in Edn., Kent State U., 1971; diploma in nursing, Cleve. Met. Gen. Hosp., 1982; BSN, Bowling Green State U., 1991; MSN, Kent State U., 1998. Cert. instr. trauma nursing, emergency nursing pediatric course; CNOR, CEN. Staff nurse burn ICU Cleve. Met. Gen. Hosp., 1982-84; charge nurse surg. ICU Brentwood Hosp., Warrensville Hts., Ohio, 1984; charge nurse emergency rm./trauma St. Luke's Hosp., Cleve., 1984-87, staff nurse oper. rm., 1987-91; trauma nurse coord. Meridia Huron Hosp., Cleve., 1991-93; nurse USAFR, from 1990; clinical coord. emergency dept. U. Hosps. of Cleve., 1993-94, clin. nurse operating rm., 1994-99; clin. nurse specialist perioperative svcs. MetroHealth Med. Ctr., Cleve., from 1999. Instr. emergency nurses pediat. course; mem. Cuyahoga County Critical Incident Stress Debriefing Team. Capt. nurse corps USAFR. Mem. Assn. Oper. Rm. Nurses (cert., Joan Gowin scholar 1990, 96), Emergency Nurses Assn. (cert. trauma nursing core course instr., emergency nursing pediatric course instr., course dir. for course in advanced trauma nursing), Greater Cleve. Safe Kids Coalition, Sigma Theta Tau. Home: Bedford, Ohio. Died July 17, 2005.

LAKE, JAMES EDWIN, radio and marketing consultant; b. Grand Rapids, Mich., Feb. 24, 1923; s. James Harrison and Beulah Joy (Dugger) L.; m. Gracile Forster, Sept. 16, 1948; children: James Harold, David Forster. BA in Radio/TV, U. Ala., Tuscaloosa, 1953, postgrad., 1953-54. Account exec. Radio Stas. WSGN, WAPI, WBRC, Birmingham, Ala., 1954-58; gen. sales mgr. Sta. WYDE-Radio, Birmingham, 1958-61; mgr. Sta. WNPT-Radio, Tuscaloosa, Ala., 1962-64; announcer, programmer Sta. WCOA-Radio, Pensacola, Fla., 1970-84; advt. cons. Stas. WMEZ (FM), WBSR(AM), Pensacola, 1977-89. Cons. All Saints United Episcopal Ch., Pensacola, 1983—, Thomas A. Buchanan, Pensacola, 1985—, Kury Investment Group, Pensacola, 1986—, Saltmarsh, Cleaveland & Gund, CPA's, Pensacola, 1986—. Author: Don't Waste Your Money in Advertising, 1987; producer Pensacola Symphony Orch., 1974; record producer Pensacola Symphony Orch., 1974. Active Pensacola Symphony Orch., 1970-85, pres. 1972-73; founder Pensacola Community Concerts Assn., 1974. Served to 1st lt. U.S. Army, 1943-46, PTO. Recipient Excellence in Broadcasting award Broadcasting Assn., 1974, 80, Diploma of Honor, Internat. Robert Stolz Soc., 1987. Mem.: Lions, Sertoma. Republican. Avocations: genealogy, history, travel, music. Home: Pensacola, Fla. Died Feb. 14, 2005.

LALLY, VINCENT EDWARD, atmospheric scientist; b. Brookline, Mass., Oct. 13, 1922; s. Michael James and Ellen Teresa (Dolan) L.; m. Marguerite Mary Tibert, June 5, 1949; children: Dennis V., Marianne Baugh, Stephen J. BS in Meteorology, U. Chgo., 1944; BSEE, MIT, 1948, MS in Engring. Adminstrn., 1949. Engr. Bendix-Friez, Balt., 1949-51; chief metall. equip. devel. Air Force Cambridge Rsch. Labs., Bedford, Mass., 1951-58; rsch. dir. Teledynamics, Phila., 1958-61; dir. Nat. Sci. Balloon Facility Nat. Ctr. for Atmospheric Rsch., Boulder, Colo., 1961-66, sr. scientist, 1966-91, sr. scientist emeritus, from 1991. Contbr. articles to sci. jours., chpt. to handbook in field. 1st lt. USAAC, 1942-46. Fellow Am. Meteorol. Soc. (Cleveland Abbe award 1990); mem. Inst. Navigation, Sigma Xi. Achievements include 7 patents for space inflatables, superpressure balloons, rocket instruments, communications techniques; made first balloon flight around the world, longest balloon flight; pioneered technology in measurements from radiosondes, aircraft and rockets. Home: Loveland, Colo. Died Sept. 20, 2005.

LAMAR, DONOVAN EUGENE, educator; b. Detroit, Feb. 9, 1956; s. Charles Jr. and Delgreta (Dobbs) LaM.; divorced; 1 stepchild, Kathryn LyNae Cameron. A Gen. Studies, Glendale Coll., 1983; BA, Ottawa U., 1988, MA, 1992; postgrad., No. Ariz. U., from 1992. Cert. tchr., C.C. tchr., Ariz. Asst. mgr. ITT Grinell Corp., Phoenix, 1978-80; student advisor, program advisor, evening adminstr. Gateway C.C., Phoenix, from 1981; program advisor, specialties coord., dir. peer assistance South Mountain C.C., Phoenix, from 1981. Substitute tchr. Issac Jr. H.S. Dist., Phoenix, 1988-89; cons., mgr. humanreosurces D.E.L.Cons. Phoenix, 1986—, co-op. faculty coord. South Mountain C.C., 1991-93, adj. faculty, 1994—; exec. dir., founder Minority Male Leadership Inst., 1994—. Mem. Valley Citizens League, Phoenix, 1989; adv. mem. New Turf Gang Prevention Program, Phoenix, 1991; bd. dirs. Jr. Achievement Cen. Ariz., 1992, mem. curriculum com., Phoenix, 1991—; bd. dirs. Black Bd. Dirs., Phoenix, 1991—. With USNG, 1981-87. Recipient Innovator of Yr. award League of Innovations in C.C., 1991-92. Mem. Nat. Coun. on Black Am. Affairs. Avocations: basketball, swimming, scuba diving, hunting, fishing. Home: Phoenix, Ariz. Died Feb. 14, 2004.

LAMARCHE, PAULINE JULIA, computer specialist, educator; b. Worcester, Mass., Feb. 8, 1942; d. John Michael and Hilda Ella (Simmler) McKeon; children: Charles Jr., Steven, Michael, Jennifer. BS, Worcester State Coll., 1964, MA in Computer Sci., 1987. Cert. tchr., Mass. Math. tchr. Worcester Pub. Schs., 1964-65, Auburn (Mass.) Pub. Schs., 1977-83, computer specialist, 1983-92; system mgr. Town of Auburn, 1988-92. Math. instr. Assumption Coll., Worcester, 1986-88; vis. scholar Mass. Acad. Math. & Sci., Worcester, 1992-93, master tchr., 1993—; computer instr. Anna Maria Coll., Paxton, Mass., 1992; computer sci. instr. Worcester Poly. Tech. Inst., 1992-94. Pres. Mother of Twins, Worcester, 1969-72; news editor S. Worcester County Assn. Retarded Citizens, Southbridge, 1973-75. Coach of N.E. Div. All-Stars, Am. Computer Sci. League, Auburn High Sch., 1990, coach of Nat. Grand Prize, Multi-Media/Computer Learning, 1990. Mem. Mass. Computer Using Educators (treas. 1990—), Boston Computer Soc. (newsletter editor 1987-90), Auburn Edn. Assn., Mass. Tchrs. Assn., Nat. Tchr. Assn., Merrimac Edn. VAX Consortium, New Eng. Pentamation Users Group. Democrat. Roman Catholic. Avocations: sports, movies, travel. Home: Worcester, Mass. Died Sept. 2, 2004.

LAMB, BILL (WILLIAM JOSEPH LAMB), television executive; b. N.Y.C., Oct. 29, 1929; s. Vincent Daly and Donna (Rendina) L.; children: Diane, William Jr., Matthew. BA, Hofstra Coll., 1953; MBA, Harvard U., 1956. Prodn. mgr. NBC-TV, N.Y.C., 1956-62; sr. v.p. WNET-TV, N.Y.C., 1962-70, 1981-85; pres. Sterling Manhattan Cable TV, N.Y.C., 1971-72; sr. v.p. KCET-TV, L.A., 1974-80; pres. Polymuse, Inc., N.Y.C., 1985-90, Variel, Inc., Encino, 1995-96. Cons. Rosner/Lamb Inc., N.Y.C., 1973-74, Ford Found., N.Y.C., 1971-75, Internat. Bus. Machines, N.Y., 1972-73; advisor/panelist N.E.H., N.E.A., Washington (D.C.), 1976-77; bd. dirs. Varitel TV, Connors Investor Svcs. Prodn. exec. documentaries Cosmos, 1980, Heritage (Peabody award, 1985), 1984, The Brain, 1984; TV plays Fifth of July, 1982, Skin Of Our Teeth, 1984; TV mini-series Parnell, 1990; exec. producer/devel. TV documentary Sea Powers, 1989, TV drama Parnell, 1990. Died June 17, 2006.

LAMB, ELIZABETH SEARLE, freelance writer, poet; b. Topeka, Jan. 22, 1917; d. Howard Sanford and Helen Baker (Shaver) Searle; m. F. Bruce Lamb, Dec. 11 1941 (dec. Dec. 1992); 1 child, Carolyn. BA, U. Kans., Lawrence, 1939, BMus, 1940. Canon City corr. Pueblo (Colo.) Chieftan, 1957-59; editor Frogpond: Quar. Haiku Jour./Haiku Soc. Am., N.Y.C., 1984-91, 94. Author: Today and Every Day, 1970, Inside Me, Outside Me, 1974, In This Blaze of Sun, 1975, Picasso's Bust of Sylvette, 1977 (HSA Merit Book award), 39 Blossoms, 1982 (HSA Merit Book award), Casting into a Cloud: Southwest Haiku, 1985 (HSA Merit Book award), Lines for My Mother, Dying, 1988, (in Chinese) The Light of Elizabeth Lamb: 100 American Haiku, 1993, Ripples Spreading Out, 1997, (in Polish/English) Petals of Iris, 1998, Across the Windharp: Collected and New Haiku, 1999 (HSA Merit Book award); assoc. editor Haiku S.W., Santa Fe, 1993; author numerous poems. Bd. dirs. Pub. Libr., Canon City, 1957-58; sec. Friends of the Pub. Libr., Santa Fe, 1979-82; 1st hon. curator Am. Haiku Archive, Calif. State Libr., Sacramento, 1996-97. Recipient 2d place award Ruben Dario Meml. Poetry Contest, OAS, 1967, awards Nat. League Am. Pen Women, Haiku Soc. Am., Mus. Haiku Lit., Tokyo, Mainichi Daily News, Tokyo, Poetry Soc. Japan, 55th Ann. Basho Festival, Ueno, Japan, numerous others. Mem. Haiku Soc. Am. (pres. 1971), Poetry Soc. Am., Haiku Internat. Assn. (Japan), Haiku Can. Democrat. Christian. Avocations: chamber music, harp. Home: Santa Fe, N.Mex. Died Feb. 21, 2005.

LAMBERT, ABBOTT LAWRENCE, retired accountant; b. N.Y.C., Mar. 19, 1919; s. Woolf W. and Estelle (Wittcover) L.; m. Natalie Rosenberg, Mar. 19, 1950 (dec.); m. Lois H. Ribman, Oct. 9, 1958 (dec.); children: Nancy Lambert Rodgers, Jane Lambert Peck. BA, Columbia U., 1940, MS in Acctg., 1946. CPA, N.Y. Acct., N.Y.C., 19440-42, 46-48; v.p. Chopak Mills, Inc., N.Y.C., 1948-71; pres. Carthage Fabrics Corp., N.C., 1964-71; pres., dir. 1025 Fifth Ave. Corp., N.Y.C., 1965-71, dir., 1975-78, 81-82. Trustee Associated Camps, 1972—, v.p., 1985—, Fedn. Jewish Philanthropies N.Y., 1958-75, life 1975-86; founding mem. coun. Overseers UJA Fedn., N.Y., 1986; life rep. assembly Domestic Affairs Divsn. UJA Fedn., 1986—; trustee Assn. Jewish Sponsored Camps, 1964—, pres., 1964-67, 76-79, hon. pres., 1990—. Capt. AUS, 1942-46. Decorated Bronze Star. Mem. N.Y. State Soc. CPAs, Zeta Beta Tau. Home: New York, NY. Died 2004.

LAMBERT, NADINE MURPHY, psychologist, educator; b. Ephraim, Utah; m. Robert E. Lambert, 1956; children: Laura Allan, Jeffrey. PhD in Psychology, U. So. Calif., 1965. Diplomate Am. Bd. Profl. Psychology, Am. Bd. Sch. Psychology. Sch. psychologist Los Nietos Sch. Dist., Whittier, Calif., 1952-53, Bellflower (Calif.) Unified Sch. Dist., 1953-58; research cons. Calif. Dept. Edn., Los Angeles, 1958-64; dir. sch. psychology tng. program U. Calif., Berkeley, 1964—2004, asst. prof. edn., 1964-70, assoc. prof., 1970-76, prof., 1976—99, prof. grad. sch., 1994—2006, assoc. dean for student svcs. Berkeley, 1988-94. Mem. Joint Com. Mental Health of Children, 1967-68; cons. state depts. edn., Calif., Ga., Fla.; cons. Calif. Dept. Justice; mem. panel on testing handicapped people Nat. Acad. Scis., 1978-81. Author: School Version of the AAMD Adaptive Behavior Scale, 3d edit., 1993; co-author: (with Wilcox and Gleason) Educationally Retarded Child: Comprehensive Assessment and Planning for the EMR and Slow-Learning Child, 1974, (with Hartsough and Bower) Process for Assessment of Effective Functioning, 1981, (with Windmiller and Turiel) Moral Development and Socialization -- Three Perspectives, 1979; assoc. editor Am. Jour. Orthopsychiatry, 1975-81, Am. Jour. Mental Deficiency, 1977-80, (with McCombs) How Students Learn-Reforming Schools Through Learner-Centered Education, 1998, (with Hylander and Sanoval) Consultee-Centered Consultation, 2004, others. With Hartsough and Sandoval Children's Attention and Adjustment Survey, 1990. Recipient Dorothy Hughes award for outstanding contbn. to ednl. and sch. psychology NYU, 1990, Tobacco Disease Related Rsch. award U. Calif., 1990-94, NIDA, 1994-2001; grantee NIMH, 1965-87, Calif. State Dept. Edn., 71-72, 76-78, NHSTE Dept. Transp., 1995. Fellow APA (coun. reps. divsn. sch. psychologists, bd. dirs. 1984-87, mem. bd. profl. affairs 1981-83, bd. ednl. affairs 1991-94, chmn. 1992-94, exec. com. divsn. sch. psychology 1994-96, mem. commn. for recognition of specialities in psychology 1993-97, 2004-06, Disting. Svc. award 1980, award for disting. profl. contbns. 1986, award for disting. career contbns. of applications of psychology to edn. and tng. 1999, Div. Sch. Psychologists sr. scientist award 2005), Nat. Assn. Sch. Psychologists (hon.; Legend in Sch. Psychology 1998), Am. Orthopsychiat. Assn.; mem. NEA, Calif. Assn. Sch. Psychologists (pres. 1962-63, Sandra Goff award 1985), Soc. for Sci. Study of Sch. Psychology. Home: Berkeley, Calif. Died Apr. 26, 2006.

LAMBRINIDES, JAMES IOAKIM, art and design educator; b. Eressos, Lesbos, Greece, July 28, 1920; came to U.S., 1952; s. Vasilios and Xantha (Iatopoulos) L.; m. Alice Galactides, Feb. 14, 1975; 1 child, Antigoni. BArch, Chgo. Tech. Coll., 1956; BFA, Am. Acad. Art, Chgo., 1960. Draftsman Western Engring., Chgo., 1958; designer Chgo., 1960; mural painter, 1960-70; artist, from 1970; instr. Chgo. colls., from 1992. Designer restaurants, Chgo., 1960, chs., Chgo., Greece, 1963; painter icons, chs., Chgo., Greece, 1963—. Designer, painter: icons including Madonna and Child, 1976; creator icons, murals including The Hunting of Diane, 1965. Mem. St. Andrew's Greek Orthodox Ch. Mem. Chgo. Outdoor Sketching Club (pres. 1972), Palette & Chisel Acad., Island of Lesbos Assn. Democrat. Avocation: swimming. Home: Chicago, Ill. Died Dec. 18, 2004.

LAMKINS, ROBERT GERALD, fundraising executive; b. Medicine Lodge, Kans., Nov. 13, 1938; s. Charles Nelson and Thelma Fanelle (Peterie) L.; m. Marcia Lane Johnson, June 23, 1962; children: Carla Elaine, Martha Elizabeth. BA, Friends U., 1960; MS, Boston U., 1966. Dir. alumni rels. Friends U., Wichita, Kans., 1961-64; dir. devel. William Woods Coll., Fulton, Mo., 1965-70; dir. ann. giving Calif. Inst. Teach., Pasadena, 1970-78; pres. Little Co. of Mary Hosp. Found., Torrance, Calif., 1978-93; regional v.p. Western region J. Donovan Assocs., Inc., Salem, Mass., from 1993. Pres., corr. sec. Nat. Cons. Group Inc., Marina Del Rey, Calif., 1984-92; bd. dirs., v.p. Vol. Ctr., Torrance. Fellow Assn. for Healthcare Philanthropy (regional dir. 1990-92); mem. So. Calif. Assn. for Hosp. Devel. (pres. 1983), Nat. Soc. Fund Raising Execs., Rotary (pres. Palos Verdes chpt. 1988-89, Chmn. of Yr. 1991, Rotarian of Yr. 1993), Kiwanis, Toastmasters (treas. local chpt. 1992, Competent Toastmaster 1992). Republican. Avocations: old time radio, stamp collecting/philately. Home: Rncho Pls Vrd, Calif. Died Aug. 5, 2005.

LAMMER, LYNN MARIE, business owner; b. Menomonie, Wis., Mar. 14, 1951; d. John Francis and Willa Barbara (Rayburn) Lammer; m. E. Peter Matrejek (div. May 1986); m. Gregory J.L. Schmidt, Jan. 1, 1987 (div. 1998); children: Tara, Richard, Tiffany. BA, U. Wyo., 1973; JD, William Mitchell Coll. Law, 1984. Law clk. 10th Jud. Dist. Ct. Minn., Stillwater, Minn., 1984-87; dir. mail mgr. West Pub. Co., St. Paul, 1987-88, mktg. coord., 1988-90; pres., CEO ENCO, Stillwater, 1988-93; CEO EnviroHealth Cons., Inc., Stillwater, 1993-95; homeopathic cons., from 1996; pres. Homeopathic Cons., Inc., from 1997. Bd. dirs. L-Mark Shopping Ctr.; cons. H.E.A.L., Atlanta, 1990-92. Mem. Sch. Bd. Ind. Sch. Dist. 834, Stillwater, 1990-93, sec., 1990-91, treas., 1991-92, trustee, bd. dirs., 1990—; officer Minn. Women's Polit. Caucus, St. Paul, 1990-93, cons., 1989—; bd. dirs. Valley Co-Op, 1987-90, St. Croix Valley Arts Coun., 1993-96, Growing Cmties. for Peace, 1997—. Mem. AAUW, Minn. Homeopathic Assn. (bd. dirs. 1997—), Stillwater C. of C., Rotary, Alpha Chi Omega. Avocations: kaleidoscopes, dog training, skiing. Died Jan. 20, 2004.

LAMMOT, THEODORE RESSIG, III, orthopaedic surgeon; b. Phila., Oct. 11, 1928; s. Theodore Ressig II and Edith Colquhoun (Taylor) L.; m. Adrienne Treene (dec. 1973); children: Alison, Theodore IV, Elizabeth, Anne, James; m. Susanne Elizabeth Meagher, May 31, 1993; children: Kevin, Christina, Thomas, Daniel. BA, Williams Coll., 1950; MD, U. Pa., 1954. Diplomate Am. Bd. Orthopedic Surgery. Intern and resident U. Mich., Ann Arbor,

1954-59; asst. prof. U. Pa., Phila., 1961-66; assoc. surgeon Children's Hosp., Phila., 1961-66; assoc. prof. Temple U., Phila., 1966-71; chief orthopaedic surgery St. Christophers Hosp. for Children, Phila., 1966-71; assoc. surgeon Shriners Hosp., Phila., 1966-71; orthopaedic surgeon Ft. Collins, Colo., 1971-79, Ventura, Calif., from 1979. Cons. Polio Found., Pa. and Colo., 1961-71, 71-79, Calif. Crippled Children, Ventura, 1979-91, Childrens Heart Hosp., Phila., 1961-71, Children's Seashore House, Atlantic City, N.J., 1961-71; chief orthopaedics Gateway Ctr., Fort Collins, 1971-79. Author: Textbook of Pediatrics, 9th edit.; contbr. articles to profl. jours. Sch. bd. St. Pauls Sch., Ventura, 1981-84, 93—. Capt. U.S. Army, 1959-61. Mem. Am. Acad. Orthopaedic Surgeons, Calif. Orthopaedic Assn. (bd. dirs.), Eastern Orthopaedic Assn. (founder), Masons. Republican. Episcopalian. Avocations: sailing, skiing, hiking. Home: Ventura, Calif. Died Dec. 17, 2004.

LAMOND, RAY EDWARD, soil scientist; b. Emporia, Kans., Sept. 8, 1951; s. Duane F. and Leona (Bishop) L.; m. Rebecca A. Davis, May 19, 1973; children: Monte R., Michael D. BS in Agronomy, Kans. State U., 1973, MS in Agronomy, Soils, 1975, PhD in Agronomy, Soils, 1979. Soils rsch. Kans. State U., Parsons, 1979-82, soils and crops specialist Manhattan, 1982-85, soil fertility specialist, from 1985. Contbr. articles to profl. jours. Recipient Award of Recognition, Nat. Fertilizer Solutions Assn., 1982, 83, Pottawatomie County Ext. Coun., 1989; grantee, Kans. Agrl. Expt. Sta., 1991, USDA-CSRS Water Quality Program, 1990—, Farmland Ind., 1990—. Mem. Am. Soc. Agronomy, Soil Sci. Soc. Am., Sigma Xi, Gamma Sigma Delta. Achievements include research on nitrogen placement as a critical factor in maximizing N efficiency in no-till grain sorghum production. Home: Wamego, Kans. Died July 24, 2004.

LAMPROSE, SOCRATES LEO, civil engineer; b. Silvis, Ill., June 14, 1924; s. Leonidas and Mary (Maroungas) L.; m. Constance Callas, Feb. 3, 1946 (div. Dec. 1977); 1 child, Niki; m. Nancy Lee Askins, Apr. 15, 1978; children: Leesl, Eric, David. BS in Civll Engring., U. N.Mex., 1948. Registered profl. engr. La. Asst. resident engr. East Bay Mcpl. Utility Dist., Oakland, Calif., 1948-49; sr. engr. Bechtel, Inc., Saudi Arabia, 1949-50; engr. Can. Bechtel, Vancouver, B.C., 1950-51, Bechtel Corp., N.Y.C., 1952; chief field engr. The Lummus Co., New Orleans, 1952-54; v.p. Big River Inds., Baton Rouge, La., 1954-58; real estate developer Sanda Terrare, Inc., Houston, 1958-60, Baton Rouge, 1958-60, Oklahoma City, 1958-60; sr. engr. Aeroject-Gen., Sacramento, 1960-63; v.p. Brown & Root, Inc., Anchorage and Houston, 1963-77; bus. devel. rep., sr. bus. devel. mgr. R.M. Parsons & Procon Corp., Pasadena, Calif. and Houston, 1978-81; bus. devel. mgr. McClelland Engrs., Houston, 1981-86; v.p. Woodword-Clyde Cons., Houston, 1986-87; sr. v.p. Jay Kim Engrs., Diamond Bar, Calif., 1987-90; v.p. Allied Enviro Engring., North Hollywood, 1990-91; pvt. practice as cons., 1991-93; sales rep. Calif. AquaTec, Inc., Rockford, Ill., from 1993; lab. sales mgr. Am. Analytics, Chatsworth, Calif., from 1993. Chmn. bd. dirs. Water Control Dist. #50, Harris County, Tex., 1964-67. With USNR, 1942-45. Mem. NSPE, Soc. Am. Mil. Engrs. (bd. dirs.). Greek Orthodox. Avocations: golf, swimming, tennis. Died Oct. 20, 2004.

LANCASTER, EDMUND CLIFTON, retired banker; b. Spartanburg, S.C., Nov. 19, 1912; s. Samuel Theron DeJarnett and Ada (Smith) L.; m. Clara Moss, June 13, 1936; children: Clara Louise Lancaster Stevens, Alice Angela Lancaster Muckenfuss. AB, Wofford Coll., 1933. With C & S Bank, Spartanburg, 1933-41, Arkwright Mill, Spartanburg, 1941-44; sr. v.p., cashier, trust officer Piedmont Nat. Bank, Spartanburg, 1947-58; exec. v.p. Lake Region Bank Commerce, Winter Haven, Fla., 1958-60; pres., trust officer Ga. Nat. Bank of Albany, 1960-70; pres., trust officer, vice chmn. Security Bank & Trust Co., Albany, from 1970, bd. dirs., from 1969, now ret. Chpt. chmn. ARC, Spartanburg, 1956; vice chmn. Spartanburg Bd. Edn., 1956; trustee Albany Hosp. Bd., 1967-74. Lt. (j.g.) USNR, 1944-46, PTO. Mem. Doublegate Country Club, Kiwanis (pres. Albany 1965). Republican. Presbyterian. Avocations: gardening, golf. Home: Spartanburg, SC. Died Apr. 21, 2004.

LANCOUR, KAREN LOUISE, secondary school educator; b. Cheboygan, Mich., June 2, 1946; d. Clinton Howard and Dorothy Marie (Passeno) L. AA, Alpena Community Coll., 1966; BA, Ea. Mich. U., 1968, MS, 1970. Teaching asst. Ea. Mich. U., Ypsilanti, 1968-70; tchr. sci. Utica (Mich.) Community Schs., 1970-98, ret., 1998. Resource agt. NASA Chandra Project, from 2003. Editor Sci. Olympiad Nat. Dir.'s Man., 2000—. Nat. event supr. Sci. Olympiad, from 1986, mem. nat. rules com., from 1987, Mich. state event supr., from 1986, regional dir., 1987, state bd., from 1998. Recipient Disting. Svc. award Nat. Sci. Olympiad, 1995. Mem. Nat. Sci. Tchrs. Assn., Mich. Sci. Tchrs. Assn., Nat. Assn. Biology Tchrs., Met. Detroit Sci. Tchrs. Assn. (Outstanding Sci. Educator award 1997), Smithsonian Inst., Nat. Geographic Soc., Edison Inst., Mortar Bd., Internat. Biograph. Soc., Am. Biograph. Inst. Rsch. Assn. (dep. gov.), Internat. Platform Assn., Phi Theta Kappa, Kappa Delta Phi. Home: Alpena, Mich. Died Feb. 2006.

LANDAU, FREDERICK JAY, television producer, news consultant; b. Bklyn., Apr. 13, 1951; s. Major L. and Natalie Landau. BS in Journalism, U. Md., 1973. Morning air personality, sports announcer Sta. WIPS, Ticonderoga, N.Y., 1973-74; sports dir., newscaster Sta. WWCO, Waterbury, Conn., 1974-76; dir. pub. rels., public address announcer Conn. Falcons, women's profl. softball, Meriden, 1976-77; news dir., morning anchor Sta. WADS, Ansonia, Conn., 1977-82; assignment editor, reporter Sta. WTXX-TV, Hartford and New Haven, 1982, news dir., anchor, 1982-86; freelancer, fill-in Sta. WWCO, Waterbury, 1986-87; dir. broadcast ops. Primo Newsvc., Inc., Old Greenwich, Conn., from 1987, prodr., writer, tape editor Newsworthy, from 1990. Sportscaster, fill-in anchor Sta. WATR, NBC, Waterbury, 1981-82; color commentator Yale U. men's basketball telecasts Sta. WTXX-TV, 1982-83, host ann. Big East Basketball Conf. preview show, 1983-84. Mem. Soc. Profl. Journalists. Home: Norwalk, Conn. Died Apr. 29, 2004.

LANDAUER, ELVIE ANN WHITNEY, humanities educator, writer; b. Detroit, Dec. 10, 1937; d. Augustus and Leona (Green) Moore; m. Thomas Whitney, 1963 (div. 1978); m. Ernest Landauer, Dec. 31, 1987. BA, Calif. State U., L.A., 1978; MA, San Francisco State U., 1989; postgrad., U. N.Mex. Dep. dir. Calif. Arts Coun., Sacramento, 1976-79; exec. dir. Mothers Emergency Svc., Sacramento, 1979-82; assoc. dir. San Francisco Cmty. Bds., 1982-83; adminstr. San Francisco Rsch. Project, 1983-86; exec. dir. East Bay Ctr. for Performing Arts, Richmond, Calif., 1987-89; instr. English Calif. C.C.s, Pittsburg, Fremont & Hayward, 1990-93; instr. Am. studies U. N.Mex., Alburg, 1993-94; instr. humanities New Coll., San Francisco, 1994-95. Rschr. LA Cmty. Arts Alliance, 1972; bus. owner, pres., pub. Academics of Course, Inc., Vallejo, Calif., from 1997. Author: (drama anthology) The Disinherited, 1971, The Uptown Mrs. Carrie, 1989; prodr.: Meat Theater Co., 1970—72. Bd. dirs. Richmond (Calif.) Arts Coun., 1986-89; workshop coord. L.A. Writers Workshop, 1966-69, Sacramento Civic Theater, 1980; project coord. City Spirit Project, Pasadena, Calif., 1972-75. With USN, 1958-61. Recipient Woman of Yr. award Iota Phi Lambda, Sacramento, 1981. Home: Vallejo, Calif. Died May 25, 2006.

LANDE, JAMES AVRA, retired lawyer; b. Chgo., Oct. 2, 1930; s. S. Theodore and Helen C. (Hamburger) L.; m. Ann Mari Gustavsson, Feb. 21, 1959; children: Rebecca Susanne, Sylvia Diane. BA, Swarthmore Coll., 1952; JD, Columbia U., 1955. Bar: N.Y. 1958, Calif. 1967. Assoc. Rein, Mound & Cotton, N.Y.C., 1957-59; atty. VA, Seattle, 1959-61, Weyerhaeuser Co., Tacoma, 1961-63, Lande Assocs., San Francisco, 1963-67, NASA, Ames Rsch. Ctr., Moffett Field, Calif., 1967-70; house counsel Syntex Corp., Palo Alto, Calif., 1970-73; dir. contracts dept. Electric Power Rsch. Inst., Palo Alto, Calif., 1973-81; corp. atty., dir. contracts Lurgi Corp., Belmont, Calif., 1981-82; contracts mgr. Bechtel Corp., San Francisco, 1982-92; sr. contract mgr. Bay Area Rapid Transit Dist., Millbrae, Calif., 1992—2004; ret. Adj. prof. U. San Francisco Sch. Law, 1972-73; lectr. law U. Santa Clara Sch. Law, 1968-82; pres. Syntex Fed. Credit Union, 1971-72. Served with U.S. Army, 1955-57. Mem. Calif. Bar Assn., Nat. Contract Mgmt. Assn. (past pres., dir. Golden Gate chpt.), Lawyers Club San Francisco. Home: San Francisco, Calif. Died June 21, 2006.

LANE, PATRICIA BAUMGARTNER, medical office manager; b. Scottsbluff, Nebr., Mar. 15, 1927; d. Casper and Myrtice A. (Edwards) Baumgartner; m. James A. Lane, Sept. 4, 1949; children: Leann Keller, Rene Rickabaugh. BBA, U. Denver, 1949. Sec. Edwin Shields Hewitt & Assocs., Chgo., 1949-51, C. of C., Newcastle, Wyo., 1951, Newcastle Sch. Dist., 1952-53; office mgr. Dr. James A. Lane, Newcastle, from 1970, optometric technician, from 1980. Pres. Wyo. Assn. Retarded Citizens, 1976-77; nat. bd. mem. Assn. Retarded Citizens, 1978-80, regional nat. v.p., 1980-84; bd. mem. United Fund of Weston County, Wyo., 1976-78; bd. trustees United Meth. Ch., Newcastle. Named Vol. of Yr. Assn. Retarded Citizens, Wyo., 1977. Mem. PEO Sisterhood, Wyo. Optometric Aux. (pres. 1960), 20th Century Club (treas. 1976—), Order Eastern Star. Republican. Avocations: reading, kniting. Home: Newcastle, Wyo. Died Apr. 30, 2005.

LANE, VICKI See MANOCCHIO, VIVIENNE CINDA

LANEY, HOWARD ELIMUEL, clergyman; b. Maiden, N.C., Sept. 8, 1925; s. Charlie Ivy and Lottie Mae (Huffman) L.; m. Margie Ree Abernathy, May 29, 1943; children: Carolyn (Mrs. Joe Wells), Ricky Allen, Debra Lynn. Student, Gardner-Webb Coll., 1949-51, Furman U., Lenoir-Rhyne Coll., 1955-56, Sch. Pastoral Care, Winston Salem, N.C., 1958. Ordained to ministry Bapt. Ch., 1949. Pastor Faith Bapt. Ch., Lincolnton, N.C., 1951-56, Liberty Grove, Roaring River Chs., North Wilkesboro, N.C., 1956-60, Starnes Cove Bapt. Ch., Asheville, N.C., 1960-67, Providence (N.C.) Bapt. Ch., 1967-69, Anderson Grove Bapt. Ch., Albemarle, N.C., 1969-77, Fairplains Bapt. Ch., North Wilkesboro, 1977-88; supply pastor Ctr. Bapt. Ch., North Wilkesboro, 1988-89; pastor Boiling Springs Bapt. Ch., Purlear, N.C., from 1989. Chaplain Chevrolet Co., Asheville; coroner North Wilkesboro, 1990—. Mem. adv. bd. Campbell Coll., Buies Creek, N.C., 1981—; bd. dirs. Deafness Ctr, North Wilkesboro, 1956—, Rest Home, Crime Stoppers, Mulberry Fairplains Fire Dept., 1967—(Fireman of Yr. 1984), First Responders, 1986—. Mem. Stone Mountain Bapt. Assn. (moderator 1979), Wilkes Ministerial Assn. (treas. 1989—). Home: North Wilkesboro, NC. Died Sept. 12, 2004.

LANG, WALTER H.J., retired minister; b. Omaha, Nov. 3, 1913; s. Victor Cornelius and Martha (Rath) L.; m. Valeria Ruth Wessler, Aug. 13, 1940; children: Robert Paul, Philip. Diploma, Concordia (Mo.) Coll., 1932; Bachelor's degree, Concordia Seminary, St. Louis, 1937; postgrad., various univs. Pastor St. Philip's Luth. Ch., St. Louis, 1937-39; sch. tchr. Tex., 1939-40; pastor St. Paul Luth. Ch., Denton, Tex., 1940-42, Holy Cross Luth. Ch. and Mt. Calvary Luth. Ch., Houston, 1942-50, St. Paul Luth. Ch., Winslow, Nebr., 1950-55, Grace Luth. Ch., Caldwell, Idaho, 1959-66; dir. Bible Sci. Assn., 1963-83, Genesis Inst., Richfield, Minn., 1983-97, Seattle, from 1997. Author: Job and Science, 1991; author numerous pamphlets and publs. on creation; editor: (newsletter) Ark Today. Republican. Avocation: travel. Home: Seattle, Wash. Died July 10, 2004.

LANGEVIN, EDGAR LOUIS, retired humanities educator; b. Hanover, N.H., Dec. 8, 1929; BS, Worcester State Coll., 1952, MEd, 1955; MA, Assumption Coll., 1960; MBA, Anna Maria Coll., 1979, paralegal cert., 1993; Cert. of Advanced Grad. Study, U. Mass., 1989. Substitute tchr. Worcester (Mass.) Pub. Schs., 1953-57; tchr. Providence St. Jr. High, 1957-63, Burncoat High, Worcester, 1963-69; assoc. prof. Framingham (Mass.) State Coll., 1969-96; ret., 1996. Chair Career Day Fgn. Lang. Majors, Framingham State Coll., 1975; prof. emeritus Framingham State Coll., 1996. Active Worcester Dem. City Com., 1992—. Mem. Elks. Home: Worcester, Mass. Died Nov. 30, 2004.

LANGSAM, NORBERT, investor; b. Vienna, Sept. 16, 1925; s. Isak and Lea Rywa (Kandel) L.; m. Iva Morelli, June 24, 1925 (dec. Feb. 1988); 1 child, Michael. BA, U. Rome, Italy, 1945; BS in Chemistry, Technion, Haifa, Israel, 1947; MBA, Haifa U., 1948. CLU. Operation mgr. Baden Mfg., N.Y.C., 1960-65; v.p. Radio Ctr. Statiy, N.Y.C., 1966-78; pres. Ridgewood House, Queens, N.Y., 1978-83; investor Middle Village, N.Y., from 1983. Cons. various companies, N.Y.C., Chgo., 1978—. Major U.S. Army, 1945-46. Jewish. Avocations: travel, swimming, hunting, fishing. Died Jan. 14, 2005.

LANGSTAFF, JOHN MEREDITH, musician; b. Bklyn., Dec. 24, 1920; s. Bridgewater Meredith and Esther Knox (Boardman) Langstaff; m. Diane Guggenheim; 1 child, Carol; m. Nancy Graydon Woodbridge, Apr. 3, 1948; children: John Elliot, Peter Gerry, Deborah Graydon. Student, Curtis Inst. Music, Juilliard Sch. Music, Columbia U. Founder, dir. emeritus Revels, Inc., Watertown, Mass. Mem. faculty Simmons Coll., Boston, 1970—86, Wheelock Coll., Boston, 1974—79, Mass. Coll. Art, 1977, Boston Coll., 1979, U. Conn., 1977—79, Lesley Coll., 1978—99; artistic dir. Young Audiences Mass., 1972—81, adv. bd. mem., 1981—2005; lectr. in field. Author: Frog Went a-Courtin', 1955, Over in the Meadow, 1957, On Christmas Day in the Morning, 1959, The Swapping Boy, 1960, Ol' Dan Tucker, 1963, Hi! Ho! The Rattlin' Bog, 1969, Jim Along, Josie, 1970, Gather My Gold Together, 1971, The Golden Vanity, 1971, Soldier, Soldier, Won't You Marry Me?, 1972, The Two Magicians, 1973, Shimmy, Shimmy Coke-a-pop!, 1973, St. George and the Dragon, 1973, A-Hunting We Will go, 1974, A Season for Singing, 1974, Sweetly Sings the Donkey, 1976, Hot Cross Buns, 1978, The Christmas Revels Songbook, 1985, Sally Go Round the Moon, 1986, What a Morning!, 1987, Climbing Jacob's Ladder, 1991, I Have a Song to Sing-O, 1994; author: (foreword) Old Christmas, 1996; co-author: Celebrate the Spring, 1998, Celebrate the Winter, 2001, Making Music, 2003; co-author: (film) The Lively Art of Picture Books; recitals: rec.: Odeon-Capital, Jupiter, RCA-Victor, Nixa, Renaissance, CRI, Tradiiton, HMV, Desto, Weston Woods, Revels Records, Minstrel Records; soloist: Cantata Singers, N.Y. Philharmonic, Nat. Symphony, Montreal Symphony Orch., Little Orch. soc., N.Y. Oratorio Soc., Collegium Musicum, Stratford Shakespeare Festival, Mpls. Symphony Orch.; video: Making Music in the Classroom, 1995; Let's Sing!, Let's Keep on Singing!, 1997; Making Music with Children, 1999; dir-.(music dept.): Potomac Sch., 1953—68, Shady Hill Sch., 1969—72. 1st lt. inf. AUS, WWII. Recipient Hope S. Dean Meml. award, Found. for Children's Books, 1991, citation, Boston Theater, 1996, award, Kodaly Music Inst., 2001, Country Dance and Song award, 2005. Mem.: English Folk Song Soc. (founder, dir. Christmas Revels 1956, 1957, 1966, 1970—2000, dir. Spring Revels 1972—97, dir. Sea Revels 1983—94), Actors Equity, Internat. Folk Music Coun. Home: Cambridge, Mass. Died Dec. 13, 2005.

LANS, CARL GUSTAV, architect, economist; b. Gothenburg, Sweden, Oct. 19, 1907; came to U.S., 1916; s. Carl and Ida Carolina (Schon) L.; m. Gwynne Iris Meyer, Dec. 21, 1935; children: Douglas C., C. Randolph. Student, CCNY, 1925-26, Sch. Architecture, Columbia U., 1926-30. Registered architect, Calif. Architect with Harry T. Lindeberg, N.Y.C., 1930-32; architect Borgia Bros. Ecclesiastical Marble, N.Y.C., 1932-34; with architects Paist & Stewart, Miami, Fla., 1934-35; chief engr. insp. Dept. Agr., 1936-38; asst. tech. dir. FHA, 1938-48; tech. dir. Nat. Assn. Home Builders, Washington, 1948-52; with Earl W. Smith Orgn., Berkeley, Calif., 1952-56; architect, economist Huntington Beach, Calif., from 1956; ptnr. John Hans Graham & Assocs. Architects, Washington, 1947-55. Spl. adviser Pres. Rhee, Republic of Korea, 1955-56; guest lectr. various univs., 1949-52. Author: Earthquake Construction, 1954. Chmn. bd. edn. adv. com., Arlington, Va., 1948. Recipient Outstanding and Meritorious Svcs. citation Republic of Korea, 1956. Mem. AIA (citation), Nat. Acad. Scis. (bldg. rsch. adv. bd. dirs.), S.W. Rsch. Inst., Seismol. Soc. Am., Prestressed Concrete Inst., Urban Land Inst., Nat. Press Club. Died Mar. 30, 2004.

LANZA, FRANK C., electronics executive; b. San Francisco, Nov. 6, 1931; BS, Heralds Engring. Coll., 1956. Project engr. Philco Western Devel. Labs., 1957-59; v.p.

Textron Corp., Providence, 1960-72; with Loral Corp., N.Y.C., 1972-97, v.p., 1973-79, exec. v.p., 1979-81, corp. pres., COO, 1981-97; co-founder, chmn., CEO L-3 Communications Holdings Inc., N.Y.C., 1997—2006. Served with USCG, 1953-55. Died June 6, 2006.

LAPHAM, LOWELL WINSHIP, physician educator, researcher; b. New Hampton, Iowa, Mar. 20, 1922; s. Percy Charles and Altha Theresa (Dygert) L.; m. Miriam Amanda Sellers, June 22, 1945 (div. 1982); children: Joan, Steven, Judith, Jennifer. BA, Oberlin Coll., 1943; MD cum laude, Harvard U., 1948. Diplomate Am. Bd. Pathology in neuropathology, Am. Bd. Psychiatry and Neurology in neurology. Instr. Case Western Res. U. Sch. Medicine, Cleve., 1955-57, asst. prof., 1957-64, assoc. prof., 1964, U. Rochester (N.Y.) Sch. Medicine, 1964-69, prof., 1969-92; prof. emeritus, from 1992. Cons. neuropathology Cleve. Met. Gen. Hosp., 1957-64, Cleve. VA Hosp., 1957-64, Genesee Hosp., Rochester, 1966-92, Rochester Gen. Hosp., 1966-92. Contbr. numerous articles to profl. jours. 1st lt. USAR, 1951-53. Fellow Nat. Multiple Sclerosis Soc., 1957-59; rsch. grantee NIH, USPHS. Mem. Am. Assn. Neuropathologists. Unitarian Universalist. Avocations: music, travel. Home: Oberlin, Ohio. Died 2006.

LAPPERRE, JOHN HUBER, marketing professional, accountant; b. Chgo., Mar. 11, 1911; s. John and Caroline Mary (Huber) L.; m. Grace Burchard, Sept. 4, 1937 (dec. Feb. 1974); m. Anna Ruth Bloem, May 17, 1975. BS in Commerce, Northwestern U., 1949. Accountant Keeshin Motor Express, Chgo., 1935-46; contr. Barrett-Cravens Co., Chgo., 1946-49, Borden Co., Chgo., 1949-52; accountant Pullman-Standard, Chgo., 1952-61, plant contr. Bessemer, Ala., 1961-65, market rsch. Chgo., 1965-72, dir. planning, 1972-76. Contbr. articles to profl. jours. Lt. Col. U.S. Army, 1942-46, ETO. Mem. Nat. Multiple Sclerosis Soc. (trustee, treas., vice-chmn., chmn., Hope Chest award 1964, 80, Disting. Svc., chmn. 1981, 88), Nat. Assn. Accts., Ret. Officers Assn., Northwestern U. Alumni Assn. (class rep.). Republican. Episcopalian. Avocation: travel. Home: Evanston, Ill. Died Mar. 28, 2004.

LARKEY, BETTY BRAY, writer; b. Henning, Tenn., Jan. 6, 1937; d. Cyrus Lawson and Melba Irene (Olds) Bray; m. Kenneth Clayton Larkey, Jr., July 11, 1963 (div.); children: Jennifer Scott, Margaret Cunningham Larkey Dow. BS, Howard Payne U., 1958; MA, U. Memphis, 1969. Freelance consulting, Memphis, 1989-95; mgr. product documentation, tech. writer Cortelco Sys., Inc., Memphis, from 1995. Adj. instr. English and speech State Tech. Inst., Memphis; instr. speech U. Memphis. Author: Planting the Faith: A History of St. John's Episcopal Church, Memphis, TN, 1996; editor: The Two Clubs of Menasha, 1994. Treas. Memphis Symphony League, 1968-69; cmty. arts chmn. Jr. League Memphis, 1973-74; pres. Etude Music Club, Memphis, 1983-84, Memphis Concert Ballet, 1985-87; bd. dirs. Theatre Memphis, Memphis Coll. Art, Memphis Vocal Arts Ensemble; bd. dirs. Theatre Memphis, Memphis Coll. Art, Memphis Arts Coun., Memphis Symphony League, Memphis Concert Ballet, United Way, Am. Cancer Soc., others. Mem. Soc. for Tech. Communicators, Alpha Chi. Republican. Presbyterian. Avocations: music (piano, choir, composition), flower arranging, theater, art, tennis. Home: Memphis, Tenn. Died Jan. 1, 2005.

LARRICK, NANCY, writer, editor, lecturer; b. Winchester, Va., Dec. 28, 1910; d. Herbert S. and Nancy (Nulton) L.; m. Alexander L. Crosby (dec. 1980). AB, Goucher Coll., 1930; MA, Columbia U., 1938; EdD, NYU, 1955; LLD (hon.), Goucher Coll., 1975; LittD (hon.), Lehigh U., 1980. Classroom tchr. Winchester Pub. Schs., 1930-42; editor children's mags. Young Am., N.Y.C., 1946-50; edn. dir. children's books Random House Inc., N.Y.C., 1952-60; freelance writer, from 1960. Adj. prof. edn. Lehigh U., 1963-73. Author: Parent's Guide to Children's Reading, 1958, 65, 69, 75, 82 (Edison Found. award 1958), Parent's Guide to Children's Education, 1963, Let's Do A Poem!, 1992; editor 20 anthologies of poetry for children; contbr. articles to profl. jours. Recipient Award for Contbns. to Literacy, Ind. U., 1982. Mem. Internat. Reading Assn. (pres. 1956-57, Citation of Merit 1977), Nat. Coun. Tchrs. of English, Reading Hall of Fame (pres.). Home: Winchester, Va. Died Nov. 14, 2004.

LARSEN, ALVIN HENRY, chemical engineer; b. Salt Lake City, June 22, 1939; s. Henry Victor and Marie (Bartholomew) L.; m. Sharon Leila Branch, Aug. 20, 1966; children: Reed Henry, Adrian Platt, Cherry Ann, Elliott Kimball, Cameron McKay, Katrina Joy. BSChE with honors, BA, U. Utah, 1965; PhD, Calif. Inst. Tech., 1969. Registered profl. engr., Mo. Sr. mathematician Monsanto Co., St. Louis, 1968-70, sr. engr., 1970-72, engring. specialist, 1972-77, engring. supt., 1979-85, prin. engring. specialist, 1977-79, 86-93, prin. engr., from 1993. Chmn. Tech. Community of Monsanto, St. Louis, 1982; v.p. Fluid Properties Rsch., Inc., Stillwater, Okla., 1977-78. Author: Physical Property Data Book, 1975, 77; contbr. articles to profl. jours. Fellow AIChE (chmn. data compilation 1979-85, Design Inst. Phys. Property Data Mgmt. award 1986); mem. Am. Chem. Soc., Sigma Xi. Mem. Lds Ch. Achievements include development of correlation library of physical property programs in Monsanto; of new liquid enthalpy model for process simulation. Home: Saint Louis, Mo. Died June 23, 2004.

LARSEN, JEANETTE LENORE, insurance safety consultant; b. Fresno, Calif., Mar. 3, 1955; d. William Hans and Barbara Jean (Busch) L.; m. David Wagenleitner, Nov. 8, 1980. BA, Calif. State U., Fresno, 1977; A in Risk Mgmt., Ins. Inst. Am., Malvern, Pa., 1986, A in Loss Control Mgmt., 1988. CPCU, cert. safety profl. Health planner City of San Joaquin, Calif., 1977-78; safety cons. Fireman's Fund Ins. Co., Fresno, from 1978. Bd. dirs. San Joaquin Health, 1978—. Mem. Am. Soc. Safety Engrs., Cen. Calif. Safety Soc. (pres. 1980-81), Fresno Art Mus., Fresno Zool. Soc., Merced Soc. Prevention of Cruelty to Animals, Toastmasters (chpt. pres. 1985, 86, 92), Phi Mu Alumnae (scholarship chmn., del., 1987-88). Republican. Avocations: backpacking, skiing. Home: Fresno, Calif. Died Mar. 10, 2004.

LASH, WILLIAM HENRY, III, law educator, former federal agency administrator; b. Jersey City, Jan. 21, 1961; s. William H. Jr. and Vivian G. Lash; m. Sharon K. Zackula, Dec. 31, 1992; 1 child, William H. IV. BA, Yale U., 1982; JD, Harvard U., 1985. Bar: N.J. 1986, Washington 1988. Law clk. to Justice Alan B. Handler NJ Supreme Ct., Trenton, 1985-86; assoc. Fried, Frank, Harris et al, Washington, 1986-88, 88-89; counsel to chmn. U.S. Internat. Trade Commn., Washington, 1988; asst. prof. law Western New Eng. Coll., Springfield, Mass., 1989-90, St. Louis U., 1990-93; prof. law George Mason U., Arlington, Va., 1994—2001, 2005—06; asst. sec. for markey access & compliance US Dept. Commerce, Washington, 2001—05. U.S. econ. commr. Orgn. for Security and Cooperation in Europe, 2001-05; dir. Nostalgia TV Network, Washington, 1993-98, Carlton Maritime Fund; mem. adv. bd. World TV Program, Washington, 1998; disting. sr. fellow Ctr. for Study of Am. Bus., St. Louis, 1993-2006; bd. dirs. Virtual Credit Svcs.; adj. fellow Citizens for a Sound Economy, 2000-01. Author: Regulating Securities, 1996, International Trade Law, 1998. Bd. dirs., treas. Internat. Law Students Assn., 1996-2001; vice chmn. fin. instns. Federalist Soc., Washington, 1997-2001; mem. Va. Commn. for Environ., Richmond, 1996; bd. dirs. Trade Policy Ctr. Cato Inst.; adj. fellow Citizens Sound Economy. Mem. ABA (editl. bd. Bus. Law for Today 1997-2000), Yale Club N.Y.C. Republican. Lutheran. Died July 15, 2006.

LASSITER, CATHERINE SPARKS, internal auditor; b. Augusta, Kans., Apr. 22, 1922; d. Robert Isaac and Bessie Evelyn (Kidwell) Sparks; m. E.E. Lassiter, Aug. 12, 1945 (dec. Jan. 1978); 1 child, Sara Catherine. Cert., La. Sch. for Supr. Tng., 1979, Am. Inst. of Banking, Longview, Tex., 1982, So. Meth. U., 1986. Asst. cashier First State Bank, Hallsville, Tex., 1970-82, adminstrv. officer, 1982-84; v.p., internal auditor Community Nat. Bank, Longview, from 1984, bd. dirs., 1984-91; retired, 1991. Mem. Order of Eastern Star (Hallsville chpt. 995 worthy matron 1975-76), Beta Sigma Phi (preceptor Kappa Sigma chpt., treas. 1975—). Baptist. Avocations: amateur photography, square dancing, knitting, flower garden, reading. Home: Longview, Tex. Died Mar. 1, 2004.

LATZ, DAVID MURRAY, dentist; b. Indpls., June 12, 1936; s. Walter Henry and Lucile (Murray) L.; m. Barbara Ann Fisher, Sept. 8, 1956; children: Michael Thomas, Lisa Ann, Mark David. BS, Ind. U., 1958, DDS, 1961. Instr. Ind. U. Sch. Dentistry, 1961-62, honorary faculty, 1978-82. Pres. Prentice Little League, Indpls. 1974, coach CYO, Indpls. 1953-79, Brebeuf Preparatory Sch., Indpls. 1980. Mem. ADA, Ind. Dental Assn., Indpls. Dist. Dental Assn. Roman Catholic. Avocations: race driver, sports car, golf, tennis. Home: Zionsville, Ind. Died Nov. 28, 2004.

LAUDEMAN, ARTHUR NEAL, lawyer; b. Balt., July 24, 1936; s. R. Douglass and Dorothy I. (Remington) L.; m. Janet S. McGriff, Aug. 5, 1961; children: Kirk W., Craig M., Julia A. BS in Acctg., U. Ill., 1959; JD, John Marshall Law Sch., 1967. Bar: Ill. 1967, U.S. Dist Ct. (so. dist.) Ill. 1967, U.S. Ct. Appeals (7th cir.) 1970, U.S. Tax Ct. 1968, U.S. Ct. Claims 1969. Lawyers Arthur N. Laudeman Ltd., Bloomington, Ill., from 1968. Mem. Bloomington Rotary Club (pres. 1980-81). Republican. Presbyterian. Home: Bloomington, Ill. Died May 3, 2004.

LAUGHLAND, JOHN CHARLES, civil engineer; b. Kingston, Ont., Can., Sept. 5, 1936; s. Milton and Norah Marie (O'Connor) L.; m. Alice Margaret Strong, Oct. 14, 1961 (div. Mar. 1990); children: Mary-Eileen, Patriac James Fergus, Andrea Vidal; m. Billie V. Willis, Mar. 30, 1990; children: Sarah Margaret, Connor Willis, Gavin O'Neill. BSCE, U. Wash., 1958; cert. in hwy. traffic, Yale U., 1965. Registered profl. engr., N.J., Md., W.Va., Va. Hwy. engr. U.S. Bur. Pub. Rds., 1958-66; sr. traffic engr. Roy Jorgensen Assoc., Inc., Gaithersburg, Md., 1966-75; pvt. practice cons. civil engr. Frederick, Md., from 1975; county engr. Jefferson County Commn., Charles Town, W.Va., from 1987. Coauthor: Methods for Evaluating Highway Safety Improvements, 1974, Engineer's Guide to Alternative Energy Sources, 1978. Candidate for commr. Frederick County, 1986. Staff sgt. USNG, 1954-60. Recipient Hon. Mention for Hwy. Safety Rsch., Nat. Safety Coun., 1967. Fellow Inst. Transp. Engrs. Republican. Avocations: violin, choral directing, singing tenor, long distance running, carpentry. Home: Frederick, Md. Died May 7, 2004.

LAUGHLIN, STANLEY IRA, lawyer; b. N.Y.C., Oct. 2, 1924; s. Michael Francis and Florence (Kennedy) L.; m. Edith Brown, Sept. 3, 1949; children: David Alvin, Sheryl Laughlin Mihopulos. BEE, Pratt Inst., 1949; MSEE, Poly. Inst., Bklyn., 1963; JD, N.Y. Law, 1970. Lic. profl. engr., N.Y.; bar: N.Y. 1971, U.S. Dist. Ct. (ea. dist., so. dist.) 1973, U.S. Ct. Appeals (2nd cir.) 1975, U.S. Ct. Appeals (fed. cir.) 1986, U.S. Supreme Ct. 1986. Load dispatcher L.I.L.C.O., Hicksville, N.Y., 1949-57; engr. Sperry Gyroscope, Lake Success, N.Y., 1957-64; patent engr. A.I.L., Div. Cutler-Hammer, Deer Park, N.Y., 1964-70; patent agt. U.S. Philips Corp., Briarcliffe Manor, N.Y., 1970-73; sole proprietor North Babylon, N.Y., from 1971. Mem. Suffolk County Bar Assn. Christian Scientist. Died Apr. 2, 2004.

LAUR, GEORGE CHARLES, II, training consultant; b. Balt., May 2, 1946; s. George Charles and Mary Ruth (Shea) L.; m. Margaret Hardy Smith, 1997. BA in Social Sci., U. Balt., 1971. Basketball coach Loyola, Calvert Hall, Balt., 1970-83; sales mgr. Schaefer & Strohminger Olds, Balt., 1983-85; trainer, cons. Hammond & Assocs., Balt., 1985-90; owner, trainer, cons. Laur Assocs., Balt., from 1990; coord. Careerpath Svcs., Balt., from 1996. Founder, dir. Balt. Basketball Clinic, 1966-71, Wes Unseld Basketball Camp, Balt., 1971-83. Author: The Player's Notebook, 1972. Com. chmn. Mt. Carmel Sch. Accreditation, Balt., 1982; candidate Pres. of U.S., 1995—. Avocations: coaching, writing, politics. Died Aug. 6, 2005.

LAURENT, JOHN LOUIS, artist; b. Bklyn., Nov. 27, 1921; s. Robert and Marie (Caraes) L.; children: Brehon, Bret. BFA, Syracuse U., 1948; cert., L'Acad. de la Grande Chaumiere, Paris, 1949; MFA, Ind. U., 1954. Bd. dirs. Barn Gallery Assocs., Ogonquit, Maine, 1988—, Ogonquit Mus. Art, 1988—. One-man shows and group exhbns. include Payson-Weisberg Gallery, N.Y.C., 1983, Midtown Gallery, 1984-86, Que.-Labrador Found., Ipswitch, Mass., 1985, Nat. Acad. Inst. Arts and Letters, N.Y.C., 1986, Barridoff Gallery, Portland, Maine, 1988, Blackthorn Gallery, Portsmouth, N.J., 1988, Fitchburg (Mass.) Mus., 1989; retrospective exhbn. Ogunquit Mus. Art, 1991; represented in numerous pub. and pvt. collections; contbr. illustrations to catalog; represented by Frost Gully Gallery, Portland. With USN, 1942-46, PTO and ATO. Autusta Hazard fellow, 1948; grantee Louis Comfort Tiffany Found., 1956, Nat. Coun. Art, 1966-67. Democrat. Anglican. Home: Ogunquit, Maine. Died Apr. 14, 2005.

LAURENT, ROBERT DENIS, economist, educator; b. San Francisco, Dec. 22, 1939; s. Denis Albert Laurent and Tina Rose (Anzini) Cunningham; m. Laurette Janet Selig, Sept. 14, 1968 (div. 1984); children: Micheline, Paul. BA, U. Calif., Berkeley, 1962; PhD, U. Chgo., 1970. Sr. economist Fed. Res. Bank of Chgo., from 1968. Instr. econs. Lake Forest Grad. Sch. Mgmt. Contbr. articles to profl. jours. With USCG, 1962-63. Mem. Am. Econs. Assn. Home: Glenview, Ill. Died June 30, 2005.

LAVENGOOD, LAWRENCE GENE, management educator, historian; b. Tulsa, June 30, 1924; s. Lawrence Wilbur and Elizabeth (Gardner) L.; m. Gloria M. deLeon, Aug. 27, 1947; children: Jessica, Abigail, Timothy, Rachel. MA, U. Chgo., 1947, PhD, 1953. Asst. prof. bus. history Northwestern U., Evanston, Ill., 1953-59, assoc. prof., 1959-69, chmn. dept. policy and environ., 1980-82, prof. bus. history and policy and environ., 1970-94, prof. emeritus, 1994—2006. Mem. Com. on Ethics in Bus. Edn., 1977-79; cons. on mgmt. devel. edn. U.S. and European corps.; U.S. faculty coord. Sasin Grad. Inst. Bus. Adminstrn., Chulalongkorn U., Bangkok, 1983-95; chmn. bd. dirs. ctr. for ethics Garrett-Evang. Theol. Sem., Evanston, 1995-2002. Editor, contbr.: Moral Man and Economic Enterprise, 1967. Mem. Bd. Edn. Ill. elem. dist. 65, Evanston, 1967-72, 75-78; bd. dirs. Evanston Comm. Found., 1996—2001. Recipient Ann. Kellogg Alumni Choice award, 1992. Democrat. Presbyterian. Home: Evanston, Ill. Died July 12, 2006.

LAVER, GERALD EBY, management and financial consultant; b. Elyria, Ohio, May 19, 1924; Edmond Ray and Edith Lucille (Eby) L.; m. Edna Frances Dumont, Apr. 25, 1948; children: Cheryl Ann, Diana Laver Bowman, Christian Eby. Student, Fenn Coll., 1942-43, Baldwin Wallace U., 1943-44, Columbia U., 1944, Harvard U., 1944-45; BBA, Cleve. State U., 1947. With Dun & Bradstreet, Inc., Cleve., 1947-53; builder sales mgr. Columbia Gas System Dist. Cos., Columbus, Ohio, 1953-70; gen. ptnr. Dumont Bus. Cons., Statesville, N.C., from 1957. V.p. builder svcs. Galbreath Mortgage Co., Columbus, 1970-73; chmn. bd. dirs. Marconi Bldg., Inc., Columbus, 1973-76, Am. Standard Coal Co., Reno, 1974-85; sec. Lendor Holdings Corp., 1994—; v.p. ops. Ultimate Resources, Inc., Columbus, 1975-78; pres. bd. trustees Friendship Village Columbus, Inc., 1974-84; trustee Friendship Village Dublin, Inc., 1979-84. Author: Money, Money, Money, 1985. Co-advisor 4-H, 1940-42; treas. 125th Anniversary Celebration, Elyria, Ohio, 1957; chmn., bd. dirs., Washington Ave. Christian Ch., Elyria, 1955, elder, 1952-55, 56-59, deacon, 1948-62; mem. bldg. com. Salvation Army, 1955; pres. Jr. C. of C., 1957; pres. Lorain County Home Builders Assn., 1957-80; chmn. bd. dirs. Northwest Christian Ch., Columbus, 1964-65; mem. Ohio Builders Com., Am. Gas Assn.,1964-70; mem. Producer's Coun., Columbus, 1960-70, Builder's Exchange, Columbus, 1960-70, Columbus Homebuilders' Assn., 1959-70; health care adv., Tenn., 1989-90. Staff officer USN, 1943-46, PTO. Decorated 3 combat medals USN; named Elyria Young Man of Yr., Jaycees, 1965, Elyria Outstanding Young Man, Ohio Jr. C. of C., 1961. Mem. Univ. Lodge F & Am, Scottish Rite, Shriners, Civitan, Gideon, Acad. Hill Historic. Dist. Garden Club. Republican. Methodist. Avocations: ecology, organic gardening, stamp collecting/philately, city beautification, stock analysis. Died Apr. 2, 2005.

LAVIN, EDWIN, osteopathic family physician; b. Phila., Sept. 26, 1927; s. Benjamin and Rose (Chernoff) L.; married, Oct. 26, 1952; children: Jordan Scott, Tracey Sue Lavin Kahana. BSc in Phys. Edn. cum laude, Temple U., 1950; postgrad., La Salle Coll., 1951, U. Pa., 1952; DO, Phila. Coll. Osteo. Medicine, 1958. Tchr. health and phys. edn. Phila. Sch. System, 1950; phys. therapist Jefferson Hosp., Phila., 1951-52, VA, Phila., 1952-54; intern Bristol (Pa.) Hosp., 1958-59; pvt. practice Somerton, Pa., 1959-87; quality assurance physician Humana So. Fla., Palm Beach County, 1989; ship's surgeon Royal Caribbean Lines, Miami, Fla., 1989-91; cruise physician Premier Cruise Lines, Port Canavaral, Fla., 1990; mem. staff internal medicine VA Hosp., Miami, from 1990. Mem. staff Warminster (Pa.) Hosp., 1986-87; cons. Arthritis Group, Ft. Lauderdale, Fla., 1991—; compensation evaluator VA Hosp., Miami, 1992—; organizer confs. in field, Dade County, Fla., 1993. Contbr. articles to profl. publs. Active Phila. Rep. Com., 1984. Sgt. USAAF, 1944-45. Fellow Am. Acad. Family Practice; mem. Am. Osteo. Assn., Fla. Osteo. Assn., Dade County Family Practice Assn., One Island Place Conf. (pres. 1993-94), Kappa Phi Kappa. Republican. Jewish. Avocations: aviation, flying, tennis, financial advising. Home: Aventura, Fla. Died Oct. 17, 2004.

LAVINE, LEROY STANLEY, orthopedist, surgeon, consultant; b. Jersey City, Oct. 28, 1918; s. Max and Katherine (Miner) L.; m. Dorothy Kopp, Feb. 14, 1946; children: Michael, Nancy. AB, NYU, 1940, MD, 1943. Diplomate Am. Bd. Orthopedic Surgery. Intern Morrisania City Hosp., Bronx, N.Y., 1944; resident Jewish Hosp., Bklyn., 1949-51, Ind. U. Med. Ctr., Indpls., 1951-52; emeritus dir., prof. orthopedic surgery Health Scis. Ctr., SUNY, Bklyn., 1964-80; hon. orthopedic surgeon Mass. Gen. Hosp., Boston, from 1983; emeritus dir. rehab. svcs. Spaulding Rehab. Hosp., Boston, from 1983. Prof. emeritus Health Scis. Ctr., SUNY, Bklyn., 1980—; lectr. Harvard Med. Sch., Boston, 1983—; mem. adv. panel FDA, Rochville, MD, 1988-91, cons. 1992-95; cons. Dept. Health and Human Svcs., NIH, Bethesda, Md., 1992—. Contbr. more than 100 articles to profl. jours. Mem. coun. MIT, Cambridge, 1991—. Capt. U.S. Army, 1946-48. Grantee NIH, 1968-80, AEC, 1968-80. Fellow AAAS, ACS, N.Y. Acad. Scis., Am. Acad. Orthopedic Surgeons; mem. Cosmos Club. Achievements include initial performance clinical case of elec. bone stimulation. Died July 25, 2005.

LAW, ORLEY THOMAS, retired neuroscientist, educator, consultant, poet; b. Clarksburg, W.Va., July 9, 1925; s. Orley T. Law and Genevieve Kate Roberts; m. Reinette Clark, July 15, 1976; children: Daniel Keith, Michael Brian. BA, U. Mich., 1949; MA, U. Mich, 1950, PhD, 1952. Rsch. assoc. U. Mich., Ann Arbor, Mich., 1954—59, sr. rsch. engr. minuteman guidance sys., 1959—60; prof. Claremont Graduate Sch., Claremont, Calif., 1960—75; ret., 1976. Adv. Alzheimers Assn., Grover Beach, Calif., 1998—2001; cons. in field. Author: The Long Good Night, 2001; co-author: Where Poets Gather vol. I, 1999, vol. II, 2000. Candidate Mich. State Senate, Ann Arbor, 1958. With USN, 1943—46, Pearl Harbor. Fellow, NSF, 1953—55; grantee 4 Rsch. grants, NIMH, 1960—65. Avocations: writing, elder-care, motorcycles. Home: Los Osos, Calif. Died Dec. 13, 2004.

LAW, ROGER ALAN, lawyer; b. Grand Rapids, Mich., July 25, 1933; s. R. Dale and Esther S. (Johnson) L.; m. June B. Howe, Dec. 29, 1956; children: David, Diane Smith, James, Charles. BS, U. Mich., 1954, LLB, 1957. Bar: Mich. 1957, U.S. Dist. Ct. (we. dist.) Mich. 1957. Ptnr. Law, Weathers & Richardson, Grand Rapids, 1957-92. Mem. Mich. Bar Assn., Grand Rapids Bar Assn. (pres. 1983-84). Avocations: piano, golf, mathematics, billiards. Died Aug. 29, 2004.

LAWLER, ROBERT EUGENE, radiologist; b. Munfordville, Ky., Sept. 14, 1939; s. William Roscoe and Bonnie Katherine (Crouch) L.; m. Lavona Sue Munden, Dec. 17, 1966; children: Robert Eugene, David Michael, Richard Edward, Deborah Elizabeth. BS, Western Ky. U., 1960; MD, Vanderbilt U., 1964. SB Intern, Butterworth Hosp., Grand Rapids, Mich., 1964-65; resident Vanderbilt Hosp., Nashville, 1965-68; pvt. practice medicine specializing in radiology, Wuesthoff Hosp., Rockledge, Fla., 1970-84, Radiology Offices, Inc., Rockledge, 1978-88; v.p. Radiology Offices, Inc., Fla.; staff radiologist Ctr. for Health Imaging, Merritt Island, Fla., 1990—. Asst. producer movie China Run, 1986; exec. producer movie Vietnam Run, 1988; assoc. producer movie The Cu Chi Tunnels, 1988. Served with USAF, 1968-70. Mem. AMA, Fla. Med. Assn., Brevard Med. Soc., Am. Coll. Radiology, Fla. Radiol. Soc., Soc. Nuclear Medicine. Republican. Mem. Ch. of Christ. Inventor of radiol. technique caliper, 1970. Home: Cocoa, Fla. Died Dec. 30, 2004.

LAWRENCE, MARC, actor, director; b. N.Y.C., Feb. 17, 1913; s. Israel Simon Goldsmith, Minerva Norma (Sugarman) G.; m. Fanya Foss (dec. 1995), Oct. 7, 1942; children— Michael, Antoinette; Student CCNY, 1928-30; Films appearances include: Dr. Socrates, 1935, I Am the Law, 1939, Johnny Appollo, 1940, The Great Profile, 1940, The Ox-Bow Incident, 1940, Cloak and Dagger, 1946, I Walk Alone, 1947, Key Largo, 1948, Asphalt Jungle, 1950, White Slavery, 1951, The Man with the Golden Gun, 1976, Marathon Man, 1977, A Piece of the Action, 1977, Foul Play, 1978, Revenge of the Pink Panther, 1978, Goin' Coconuts, 1979, Hot Stuff, 1979, Swap Meet, 1979, Cataclysm, 1980, Super Fuzz, 1980,Cat and Dog, 1982, Night Train to Terror, 1985, The Big Easy, 1987, Blood Red, 1989, Newsies, 1991, Ruby, 1991, Four Rooms, 1995, From Dusk Til Dawn, 1996, End of Days, 1999, The Shipping News, 2001, Looney Tunes: Back in Action, 2003; (TV movies) Switch, 1975, Terror at Alcatraz, 1982, Donor, 1990, Gotti, 1996; dir. television programs, 1959-61; writer, prodr., dir., star film Daddy's Girl, 1973; cons. Ursus Prodn. Co., Marina del Rey, Calif. Columnist The Dream Makers, 1977. Recipient award Hollywood Achievement Soc., 1982. Mem. AFTRA, Screen Actors Guild, Dir.'s Guild Am., Acad. Motion Picture Arts and Scis. Died Nov. 28, 2005.

LAWRENCE, PHENIS JOSEPH, commercial artist; b. Brookville, Ind., Aug. 11, 1926; s. Phenis Woodson Lawrence and Rose (Miller) Lawrence Pattie.; m. Lillian Warnock, Aug. 25, 1956; children: Melody Rose, Timothy Lee, Beverly Vida, Robert Phenis, David Warnock. BAA, U. Fla., 1950. Staff artist Bacon, Hartman & Volbrecht, Inc., St. Augustine, Fla., 1950, art dir. Jacksonville, Fla., 1961-62; silk screen artist RICH's Dept. Store, Atlanta, 1950-51; staff artist Quick & Sacrey, Louisville, Ky., 1951; illustrator, supr. Tng. Facilities NATTC, NAS, Jacksonville, 1951-56; art dir. Miller Press, Inc., Jacksonville, 1956-60; owner, designer P.J. Lawrence Artist, Jacksonville, from 1960; art & prodn. mgr. Prudential Ins. Co., Jacksonville, 1984. Freelance artist, Jacksonville, 1960—; corresponding rep. Nat. Soc. Art Dirs, N.Y.C., 1962-66. Art dir., designer, artist, prodn. mgr. numerous comml. works including (slide) Speak up for Value, 1963 (First Place award Advt. Fedn Am., 1964), (logo) Coffee Delite, 1963, (Merit award plaque Art Dirs. Club Jacksonville, 1964), (letterhead) Antique Bottle Collector's Club of Jacksonville, 1973. Chmn. Jr. C. of C. Jacksonville, 1958-60 (Del. Nat. Conv., 1960, cert. of Merit, 1958, Man of Month award, 1960). With USN, 1944-46. Mem. Sigma Phi Epsilon Alumni Assn. (treas. 1966-79), KC (3d and 4th deg.). Democrat. Roman Catholic. Avocations: collecting coins and stamps, hunting, fishing, golf, photography. Home: Jacksonville, Fla. Died Aug. 10, 2005.

LAWRENCE, RALPH WALDO, manufacturing executive; b. Mineola, N.Y., Sept. 10, 1941; s. Ralph Waldo and Gertrude (Ingles) L.; m. Judith Alice Frost, June 20, 1964; children: Susan, Carolyn. BA, W.Va. Wesleyan Coll., 1963; M in Pub. Adminstrn., Western Mich. U., 1979. Pres. Lawrence Mfrs., Columbus, Ohio, 1970-85; chief automated info. systems contract svcs. Systems Automation Ctr., Columbus, 1980-87, chief plans and mgmt. div., 1987-88; chief ops. Constrn. Supply Ctr., Columbus, 1988-89; chief Info. Ctr. DLA Systems Automation Ctr., Columbus, Ohio, 1989-92, DISA Office of Tech. Integration, Columbus, 1992-93; dep. of def. integration mgr. CALS, Blacklick, Ohio, 1993-95; prin. info. engr. Boeing Info. Systems, Columbus, 1995; bus. mgr. Computer Scis. Corp., Moorestown, N.J., 1995-97; owner Lawrence Mfrs., Westerville, Ohio, from 1997. Bus. mgr. Computer Scis. Corp., 1995-97; prin., Lawrence Mfrs., 1998—. Served to capt. U.S. Army, 1963-66. Mem. Data Processing Mgmt. Assn. (pres. Columbus chpt. 1987, program dir. Columbus chpt. 1985, bd. dirs 1987-88), Masons. Republican. Presbyterian. Avocations: golf, sailing. Home: Crossville, Tenn. Died Dec. 16, 2005.

LAWRENCE, WILLIAM PORTER, retired military officer, former academic administrator; b. Nashville, Jan. 13, 1930; s. Robert Landy and Tennie (Brewer) L.; m. Diane Wilcox, 1974; children: William Porter, Laurie, Fritz, Wendy. BSEE, U.S. Naval Acad., 1951; MS in Internat. Affairs, George Washington U., 1974; LHD (hon.), Fisk U., 1980. Commd. ensign U.S. Navy, 1951, advanced through grades to vice adm., 1980, designated naval aviator, 1952; test pilot, service in Korea and Vietnam; prisoner-of-war Vietnam, 1967-73; dir. aviation programs div. Navy Dept., Washington, 1975-78; supt. U.S. Naval Acad., 1978-81; comdr. U.S. 3d Fleet, 1981-83; chief naval pers. Dept. Navy, Washington, 1983-86; ret., 1986; former chair leadership U.S. Naval Acad. Author poem Oh Tennessee My Tennessee (composed as prisoner-of-war, designated state poem of Tenn.), 1970, Tennessee Patriot (memoir), 2005. Decorated D.S.M. with 3 oak cleaf clusters, Silver Star with 2 oak leaf clusters, D.F.C., Air medal, Bronze Star with oak leaf cluster, Purple Heart with oak leaf cluster; recipient Gold medal Nat. Football Hall of Fame, 1979, Theodore Roosevelt award Nat. Collegiate Athletic Assn., Liberty Bowl's Disting. Svc. award, 1984, Tenn. Outstanding Achievement award, 1986, Citizen of Yr. award Mil. Chaplains Assn., 1986; first Naval Aviator to fly twice the speed of sound, Mercury Astronaut candidate. Mem. VFW, Assn. Naval Aviation (pres.), Naval Inst., Am. Legion, Rotary. Methodist. Home: Crownsville, Md. Died Dec. 2, 2005.

LAY, KENNETH LEE, former diversified energy company executive; b. Tyrone, Mo., Apr. 15, 1942; s. Omer and Ruth E. (Reese) L.; m. Linda Ann Phillips, July 10, 1982; children: Robyn Anne, Mark Kenneth, Todd David, Elizabeth Ayers, Robert Ray. BA, U. Mo., 1964, MA, 1965; PhD, U. Houston, 1970. Economist, corp. planning dept. Exxon Corp., Houston, 1965-68; asst. prof. & lectr. in economics George Washington U., Washington, 1969-73; tech. asst. to commr. & vice chmn. Fed. Energy Regulatory Commn. (formerly Fed. Power Commn.), Washington, 1971-72; dep. under sec. for energy US Dept. Interior, Washington, 1972-74; v.p. Fla. Gas Co. (now Continental Resources Co.), Winter Park, Fla., 1974-76, pres., 1976-79; exec. v.p. The Continental Group, 1979-81; pres., COO Transco Energy Co., Houston, 1981-84; chmn., CEO Houston Natural Gas Corp., Houston, 1984-85; pres., COO Enron Corp. (formerly HNG/InterNorth), Houston, 1985—86, CEO, 1986—2001, 2001—02, chmn., 1986—2002; pres. Lay Interests LLC, 2002—04. Bd. dirs. Eli Lilly & Co., Trust Co. West, Compaq Computer Corp.; past chmn. Greater Houston Partnership; indicted on charges of accounting fraud, 2004; convicted on fraud and conspiracy charges, 2006. Former chmn. bd. regents U. Houston; bd. trustees The H. John Heinz III Ctr. for Sci., Econs. & the Environment, The Bus. Coun., Am. Enterprise Inst.; Houston Host Com. for 1992 Rep. Nat. Conv.; co-chmn. 1990 Houston Econ. Summit Host. Com.; trustee Howard U.; active Resources for the Future. Decorated Navy Commendation medal, Nat. Def. Svc. medal; recipient Pvt. Sector Coun. Leadership award, 1997, Horatio Alger award, 1998; N.A.M. fellow; State Farm fellow; Guggenheim fellow; named one of 25 Top Mgrs. in the World, Bus. Week., 1999; named to Tex. Bus. Hall of Fame, 1997. Mem. Nat. Petroleum Coun., River Oaks Country Club, Phi Beta Kappa. Republican. Methodist. Died July 5, 2006.

LAZERATION, JONI LYNN, critical care nurse; b. Astoria, N.Y., Dec. 12, 1955; d. John and Mary Fay (Judd) L. RN, Montefiore Hosp., Pitts., 1976. Staff nurse Conemaugh Valley Meml. Hosp., Johnstown, Pa. Mem. Am. Assn. Critical Care Nurses (chpt. bd. dirs.). Home: Nanty Glo, Pa. Died Feb. 19, 2004.

LEAHY, JOHN AUSTIN, pastor; b. Cleve., May 27, 1931; s. Joseph F. and Helen F. (Roberts) L. MA in History, John Caroll U., 1960, MEd, 1961; PhD in History, Case Western Res. U., 1988. Prof. Borromeo Coll., Wickliffe, Ohio, 1960-64; prin., dir. St. Vincent High Sch., Akron, Ohio, 1964-65; supt. elem. schs. Diocese of Cleve., 1965-73, ednl. cons., 1973-83; dir. Parmadale, Parma, Ohio, 1970-83; pastor St. Bartholomew Ch., Middleburg Heights, Ohio, from 1983. TV commn. Middleburg Heights, 1986—; bd. dirs. Cath. Counseling Ctr., Cleve., 1969—, trustee, 1973—. Mem. Nat. Cath. Edn. Assn. Died Mar. 29, 2005.

LEAKE, CHARLES ROBERT, systems analyst, educator; b. NYC, Apr. 23, 1930; m. Rita I. Leake, Feb. 10, 1968; children: Anna M., Charles R. Jr.; 1 child from previous marriage, Robert J. BS in Math., NYU, 1963, MS in Math., 1965, PhD in Math. Edn., 1969. Shipping clk. Gilliams and Rubin, NYC, 1951-63; math instr. Fords Jr. HS, NJ, 1964-65; asst. prof. math. Wagner Coll., NYC, 1965-70; asst. prof. math Bronx C.C., NY, 1970-73; ops. rsch./sys. analyst Dept. of Def., US Army, 1975—2004. Adj. faculty Univ. Coll. U. Md., Am. Mil. U., Greenwich U. Author: Linear Algebra, 1970, Pre Algebra Mathematics, 1973. With U.S. Army, 1951. Fellow NYU, 1963-64. Mem. AAAS, Operational Rsch. Soc., Mil. Ops. Rsch. Soc., Washington Evolutionary Sys. Soc., Ancient Mystical Order Rosae Crucis, Mensa. Lutheran. Died Oct. 24, 2004.

LEAVELL, WILLIAM A., publisher, editor; b. Montgomery, Ala., Apr. 12, 1923; William A. and Myrtle I. (Watson) L.; m. Patty J. Shobe, June 24, 1927; William A. III, Melissa I. BA, U. Ala., 1945; MA, George Washington U., 1947, PhD, 1949. Owner Leavell & Assoc., Belleair, Fla., 1950-62; columnist "Keep Off The Grass" syndicated column, 1963-73; editor, pub. Washington Report, Editor Release Svcs. (Washington Report), St. Petersburg, Fla., 1974-97. Regular guest on several radio and TV stas. Author: (novel) As Honest As Times Permit, 1974. Adminstrv. asst. Congressman Arthur Winstead Washington 1947-49. With USAF 1944-45. Home: Saint Petersburg, Fla. Died Apr. 5, 2005.

LEAVITT, HENRY ALAN, health care consultant; b. Cambridge, Mass., July 7, 1940; s. Benjamin and Fannie (Freedman) L. BA, U. Mass., 1962, MA, 1966; MPhil, George Washington U., 1971; MBA, U. Pa., 1979. Pub. health adminstr. U.S. Govt., Washington, 1966-79; v.p. Health Sector Mgmt., Bethesda, Md., 1979-83; nat. dir. HMO devel. Am. Med. Internat., Beverly Hills, Calif., 1984-86; dir. spl. projects Affordable Health Care Concepts, Sacramento, 1986-88; pres. Managed Healthcare Strategies, L.A., from 1989. Mem. accreditation standards task force Assn. of U. Programs in Health Adminstrn, Washington, 1980-81; tech. cons. USAID Reform Project, Moscow and Kiev, 1995-96, 95-98. Editor (CD ROM) Managed Care Issues, 1995; contbr. articles to profl. jours. Scout master Boy Scouts Am., Palos Verdes, Calif., 1985-89. George Washington U. tchg. fellow, 1969-71. Mem. U. Mass. Alumni Assn. Died Aug. 9, 2005.

LEAVITT, MARY JANICE DEIMEL, special education educator, civic worker; b. Washington, Aug. 21, 1924; d. Henry L. and Ruth (Grady) Deimel; m. Robert Walker Leavitt, Mar. 30, 1945; children: Michael Deimel, Robert Walker, Caroline Ann Leavitt Snyder. BA, Am. U., 1946; postgrad., U. Md., 1963-65, U. Va., 1965-67, 72-73, 78-79, George Washington U., 1966-67. cert. spl. edn. tchr. 1968. Tchr. Rothery Sch., Arlington, Va., 1947; dir. Sunnyside Children's House, Washington, 1949; asst. dir. Coop Sch. for Handicapped Children, Arlington, 1962; dir. Arlington and Springfield, Va., 1963-66; tchr. mentally retarded children Fairfax (Va.) County Pub. Schs., 1966-68; asst. dir. Burgundy Farm Country Day Sch., Alexandria, Va., 1968-69; tchr., substitute tchr. specific learning problem children Accotink Acad., Springfield, Va., 1970-80; substitute tchr. learning disabilities Children's Achievement Ctr., McLean, Va., 1973-82, Psychiat. Inst., Washington and Rockville, Md., 1976-82, Home-Bound and Substitute Program, Fairfax, Va., 1978-84. Asst. info. splst. Ednl. Rsch. Svc., Inc., Rosslyn, Va., 1974-76; docent Sully Plantation, Fairfax

County (Va.) Park Authority, 1981-87, 88-94, Children's Learning Ctrs. Vol. Honor Roll, 1987, Walney-Collections Fairfax County (Va.) Park Authority, 1989-97; sec. Widowed PersonsSvc., 1983-85, mem., 1985-90; mem. ednl. subcom. Va. Commn. Children and Youth, 1973-74; den mother Nat. Capital Area Cub Scouts, Boy Scouts Am., 1962; troop and fundraising chmn. Nat. Capitol coun. Girl Scouts U.S.A., 1968-69; capt. amblyopia team No. va. chpt. Delta Gamma Alumnae, 1969; vol. Prevention of Blindness, 1980-95; fund raiser Martha Movement, 1977-78; mem. St. John's Mus. Art, Wilmington, N.C., 1989—, Corcoran Gallery Art, Washington, 1989-90, 94—, Brunswick County Literacy Coun., N.C., 1989—; Sunday sch. tchr. St. Andrews Episcopal Ch., Burke, Va., 1995-99, mem. search com., 1996, libr. project, 1999; mem. World Affairs Coun. Washington DC, 1998—. Recipient award Nat. Assn. Retarded Citizens, 1975, Sully Recognition gift, 1989, Ten Yr. recognition pin Honor Roll, 1990. Mem. AAUW (co-chmn. met area mass media com. DC chpt. 1973-75, v.p. Alexandria br. 1974-76, fellowship co-chmn., historian Springfield-Annandale br. 1979-80, 89-94, 94-95, name grantee ednl. found., 1980, cultural co-chmn. 1983-84), Assn. Part-Time Profls. (co-chmn. Va. local groups, job devel. and membership asst. 1981), Older Women's League, Nat. Mus. Women in the Arts (charter), Libr. Congress Assocs. (nat.), Mil. Dist. Washington Officer's Clubs (McNair, Ft. Myer), Delta Gamma (treas. No. Va. alumnae chpt. 1973-75, pres. 1977-79, found. chmn. 1979-81, Katie Hale award 1989, treas. House Corp. Am. U. Beta Epsilon chpt. 1994-97). Episcopalian. Home: Springfield, Va. Died July 14, 2006.

LEBOWITZ, MARSHALL, publishing company executive; b. Boston, Mar. 4, 1923; s. Max Nathan and Rissah (Zangwill) L.; m. Charlotte Lily Meyersohn, Aug. 7, 1949; children: Wendy Ann, Marian Kay, Mark Louis. AB, Harvard U., 1942. Statis. analyst U.S. WPB, Washington, 1942-43; periodicals mgr. J.S. Canner & Co., Inc., Needham Heights, Mass., 1946—67, gen. mgr., 1967—96, v.p., 1967—96, Plenum Pub. Corp., 1967—96. Mem. Natick (Mass.) Planning Bd., 1964-69, chmn., 1968-69; mem. Natick Town Meeting, 1954—, chmn. town by-laws revision com., 1965-67; pres. Greater Framingham Mental Health Assn., 1963-64, dir., 1954-63; mem. Greater Framingham Mental Health Area Bd., 1972-78, v.p., 1974-75, pres., 1975-77; mem. Regional Drug Rev. Bd., 1973; chmn. Natick Regional Vocat. Sch. Planning Com., 1974-77; mem. Natick Sch. Com., 1978-81, clk., 1979-81; chmn. legis. impact study commn. Town of Natick, 1980; chmn. town commn. to rev. by-laws and mcpl. charter, 1980-90; mem. trustees adv. coun. Leonard Morse Hosp., 1973-91, vice chmn., 1974-77, mem. mental health adv. com., 1972-91; chmn. Natick Land-Use Com., 1983—; mem. Mcpl. Charter Rev. Com., 1985-88, Framingham-Natick Golden Triangle Planning Com., 1988-93; trustee Morse Inst. Libr., 1989—, pres., 1996—; bd. dirs. Framingham-Natick Cemetery Assn., 1991—; mem. Mcpl. Facilities Planning, 1994-96. With AUS, 1943-46. Named Natick Sr. Man of Yr., 1997; recipient Geshelin Humanitarian award, Temple Israel of Natick. Jewish (fin. sec. temple 1954-56, treas. 1952-54, vice-chmn. bd. 1958-59). Home: Natick, Mass. Died Dec. 17, 2005.

LEDUC, BENJAMIN ARTHUR, retired obstetrician, gynecologist; b. La Habra, Calif., Aug. 1, 1929; s. Benjamin Philip LeDuc and Erma Izola Jondahl; m. Mona Rae Slaybaugh, Dec. 23, 1956; children: Lori, Ronald. BS, La Sierra Coll., 1953; MD, Loma Linda U., 1961. Diplomate Am. Bd. Ob-gyn. Rotating internship Glendale (Calif.) Adventist Hosp., 1961—62; resident in ob-gyn. White Meml. Med. Ctr., L.A., 1962—65; practice of ob-gyn. Policlinica Bella Vista, Mayaguel, PR, 1965—99; mem. med. staff Bella Vista Hosp., Mayaguel, PR, 1965—2001, med. dir., 1973—2003; ret., 2003. Bd. dirs. Antillian Union of Seventh-Day Adventists, San Juan, PR, 1973—85. With U.S. Army, 1953—55. Fellow: Am. Coll. Obstetrics and Gynecology. Avocations: sailing, orchids, photography. Died May 19, 2005.

LEE, AMY FREEMAN, artist, educator; b. San Antonio, Oct. 3, 1914; d. Joe and Julia (Freeman) Freeman; grad. St. Mary's Hall, 1931; student U. Tex., 1931-34; student Incarnate Word Coll., 1934-42, Litt.D. (hon.), 1965; m. Ernest R. Lee, Oct. 17, 1937 (div. Jan., 1941). Art critic San Antonio Express, 1939-41; staff art critic radio sta. KONO, 1947-51; lectr. Eng. dept., Incarnate World Coll., San Antonio, Tex., lectr. on art humanities dept. Trinity U., San Antonio, 1954-56, San Antonio Art Inst., 1955-56; lectr. art Our Lady of Lake Coll., San Antonio, 1969-71, The Humane Soc., Am. Inst. Architects, Washington, numerous others, 1991—; elected to San Antonio Women's Hall of Fame, 1991, Ark. chpt. Am. Inst. Architecture, Hot Springs, 1991, Austin, Tex., 1993, Inst. Tex. Cultures, 1993, Ann. Windcrest Christmas Contest, San Antonio, others; lectr. to colls., us., museums, art, civic and humane orgns. One man shows, 1947—, including U. Tex., 1970, 73, Tex. Tech. U., 1970, Del Mar Coll., Corpus Christi, Tex., 1970, Southwestern U., Georgetown, Tex., 1971, 79, Pioneer Meml. Libr., Fredricksburg, Tex., 1971, U. Tex. Student Union, 1972, Ojo del Sol Gallery, El Paso, 1972, Shook-Carrington Gallery, San Antonio, 1972, 1st Repertory Theatre, San Antonio, 1974, Sol del Rio Galleries, San Antonio, 1976, 87, 89, Oakwell Libr., San Antonio, 1976, U. Central Ark., Conway, 1977, NE La. State U., Monroe, 1978, Our Lady of the Lake U., San Antonio, 1978, Univ. Art Gallery, N. Tex. State U., Denton, 1979, L & L Gallery, Longview, Tex., 1980, 93, Meredith Long Galleries, Houston, 1980, Incarnate Word Coll., San Antonio, 1981, St. Mary's Hall, San Antonio, 1981, Sol del Rio Gallery, San Antonio, Tex., 1987, 1989, 35th Anniversary Exhbn. Art, A.C., Monterrey, Mex., 1990, McNay Art Mus., 1991, others, Tex. and Calif.; exhibited works in numerous group shows U.S. and Europe, including Nat. Soc. Painters in Casein, N.Y.C., 1969-79, Tex. Watercolor Soc., San Antonio, 1974-77, Nat. Watercolor Soc., 1978, 79, Silvermine Guild, New Canaan, Conn., 1974-75, Art Mus. S. Tex., Corpus Christi, 1975-76, Nat. Tour Am. Drawings, Smithsonian Instn., 1965-66, S.W. Tex. Watercolor Soc., 1976, 79, Tex. Watercolor Soc., 1980, Silvermine Guild Artists, New Canaan, Conn., 1980, Sol del Rio Gallery, San Antonio, 1982, 83, 85, McNay Art Mus., San Antonio, 1983, 85, Incarnate Word Coll., San Antonio, 1984, 85, Bright Shawl Gallery, San Antonio, 1985, also ann. exhbns. San Antonio Art League, 1986, St. Mary's Hall Libr., 1988, Arte, A.C., Monterrey, 1992, L&L Gallery, Longview, Tex., 1993, nat. art socs., galleries, confs.; represented in permanent collections. Pres., mem. exec. bd. San Antonio Blind Assn.; jury mem. children's poetry contest San Antonio Libr. System, apptd. by mayor libr. found., 1983-84; judge numerous art and lit. competitions; elected lifetime chmn. Young Pegasus Poetry Contest Jury, 1984, judge 1992-93; elected mem. adv. bd. Mex. Cultural Inst., San Antonio, 1990; elected mem. adv. coun. The Tex. Ctr. for Legal Ethics and Professionalism, 1991; apptd. by the Supreme Ct. of Tex. to Tex. Lawyer Discipline Commn., by gov. Tex. to Tex. Com. on Humanities, 1992; hon. chair San Antonio State Hosp. Centennial; chmn. bd. trustees Incarnate Word Coll., San Antonio; bd. dirs., nat. sec., mem. adv. bd. Gulf States Regional Office; nat. trustee, nat. sec. Humane Soc. U.S.; judge San Antonio Public Schs., 1987, lectr. in field; bd. dirs. Man and Beast, Inc.; fine arts adv. coun. U. Tex.; pres. Friends San Antonio Public Libr., 1969-70; mem. com. on grievance oversight Tex. State Bar, 1979-90; designated dir. emeritus Man and Beast Inc., San Antonio, 1986, hon. pres., 1980, hon. dir., 1985-87; mem. steering com. 100th Anniversary Celebration Healy-Murphy Ctr., 1988; trustee Inst. Humanities at Salado, Tex., 1993, Tex. Ctr. Legal Ethics and Professionalsim, Austin, 1993. Recipient awards, 1960—, including: 1st prize Contemporary Artists Exhbn., San Antonio, 1973; Women in Art awardSan Antonio Bus. and Profl. Women's Club, 1975; Drought awardLocal Artists Exhbn., San Antonio, 1977, drawing award, 1978, M.J. Kaplan award Nat. Soc. Painters in Casein and Acrylic, 1978; numerous other art awards; Hon. Stagescrew award, drama dept. San Antonio Coll., 1975; Service award Providence High Sch., San Antonio, 1976; Gold medal Incarnate Word Coll., San Antonio, 1978; Disting. Alumna medal St. Mary's Hall, 1981, Spl. recognition award Tex. Ednl. Theater Assn., 1982, Arts and Letters award Friends of San Antonio Library, 1985, The Joseph Wood Krutch medal Humane Soc. of U.S., 1985, Harold Vagtborg award Council of Research and Acad. Libraries (San Antonio), 1986, Hors de Concourt award Tex. Watercolor Soc., 1989, Spirit of Am. Women award J.C. Penny, 1990, citiation City of San Antonio, 1991; named Woman of Distinction, Baylor U., 1967, Texas Art Collector, McNay Mus., 1991, Tex. Women's Hall Fame, Gov.'s Tex. Commn. for Women, 1984, Hon. RN-Nursing Divsn. San Antonio Coll., 1992; Amy Freeman Lee AAUW Ednl. Found. Fellowship named, 1973; honored for 45 yrs. of disting. service to Madonna Ctr., San Antonio, 1986. Fellow Tex. Art Edn. Assn. (charter mem.), 1993; mem. Am. Fedn. Arts, Nat. Soc. Painters in Casein, Artists Equity Assn., Boston Soc. Ind. Artists (Smith Coll. purchase prize 1950), San Antonio Art League (adv. bd. of presidents, 6th v.p.), Nat. Soc. Arts and Letters, San Antonio Chamber Music Soc. (dir.), Philos. Soc. Tex., Defenders of Wildlife, Am. Anti-Vivisect. Soc. (life), World Fedn. for Protection Animals (life), Nat. Assn. for Advancement Humane Edn., Tex. Art Educators, Humane Soc. U.S. (v.p. Earthkind, 1992), Woman's Aux. Santa Rosa Hosp. (founder), St. Mary's Hall Alumni Assn., San Antonio Conservation Soc., Poetry Soc. Am., Am. Soc. for Aesthetics, Assn. Internationale des Critiques d'Art, Paris, Contemporary Artists Group San Antonio (dir.), Southwest Watercolor Soc. (purchase prize 1967, Harwood K. Smith award 1969), Tex. Watercolor Soc. (founder, pres., dir., purchase prize 1963, 64, 69, 74, 79, 80, emeritus charter mem. 1994), Nat. Watercolor Soc. (Figure painting award 1967), Calif., Los Angeles, San Antonio watercolor socs., Tex. Art Edn. Assn., Coll. Art Assn. Am., Silvermine Guild Artists, S. Tex. Print Soc., Tex. Fine Arts Assn. (adv. council), Tex. Art Alliance, Artists Fellowship of N.Y., Assn. Governing Bds. Univs. and Colls., Internat. Platform Assn., Bus. and Profl. Women's Club (hon.), AAUP, AAUW, Internat. Soc. for Edn. Through Art, Cum Laude Soc. (hon.), Kappa Pi (hon.), Delta Delta Delta, Tau Sigma Delta (hon.), Delta Kappa Gamma (hon.), numerous other groups. Author: Hobby Horses, 1940; A Critic's Notebook, 1943; Remember Pearl Harbor, 1945; contbg. editor S.A. mag. and Radio Sta. KTSA, San Antonio, 1977. Died July 20, 2004.

LEE, ANNA, actress; b. Sevenoaks, Eng., Jan. 2, 1913; came to U.S., 1939; d. Bertram Thomas and Edith Maude (Digby) Winnifrith; m. Robert Stevenson, Dec. 1934 (div. 1944); children: Venetia Stevenson, Caroline Stevenson, John Stafford, Stephen Stafford, Jeffrey Byron.; m. Robert Nathan, Apr. 5, 1970 (dec. 1985). Film actress RKO, MGM, Twentieth Century Fox, Paramount, Warner Bros., Hollywood, Calif., 1940-75; TV actress ABC, Hollywood, 1978—2004. Actress appearing in movies including Flying Tigers, 1940, My Life With Caroline, 1940, How Green Was My Valley, 1941, Hangmen Also Die, 1941, Flesh and Fantasy, 1942, Fort Apache, 1943, Bedlam, 1944, Summer Storm, 1944, The Sound of Music, 1966, TV series General Hospital, 1978-2004 (winner Soap Opera awards 1982, 83, 87), Port Charles, 1997-2003. Chmn. Royal Oak Found. of Calif., 1977-89. Designated Mem. of the Most Excellent Order of the British Empire, Queen Elizabeth, London, 1982. Died May 14, 2004.

LEE, DIANE B., printing company owner; b. South Bend, Ind., Aug. 31, 1954; d. Richard Thomas and Iola (Keller) B. BS, Purdue U., 1974; MA, Johns Hopkins U., 1978; MBA, U. Mich., 1980. Asst. to v.p. comml. devel. Genex Corp., Gaithersburg, Md., 1980-81, mgr. mktg., 1981-82, dir. tech. mktg., 1982-84, dir. corp. devel., 1984-85, dir. comml. devel., 1985; officer indsl. devel. UN Indsl. Devel. Orgn., Vienna, Austria, 1986; mgr. assoc. Schering-Plough Corp., Kenilworth, N.J., 1986-87, product mgr., 1987-90; Venture Capital Bus. Search, 1990-91; pres. Robert J. Young Printing, Inc., Nashville, from 1991; owner Venture Capital Bus. Search, Madison, N.J. Mem. Phi Beta Kappa. Methodist. Avocations: ch. activities, music. Home: Brentwood, Tenn. Died June 25, 2005.

LEE, EDWARD BROOKE, JR., real estate executive, fund raiser; b. Silver Spring, Md., Oct. 25, 1917; s. E. Brooke Lee and Elizabeth (Wilson) Aspinwall; m. Brenda Baker Puderbaugh, Feb. 12, 1998; stepchildren: Thomas Ance Puderbaugh, Shawn Michael Puderbaugh, Shannon Lee Puderbaugh. AB, Princeton U., 1940; student, The Infantry Sch., 1942; postgrad. bus. sch., Harvard U., 1957. Cert. real estate broker Md., D.C., Va. Various indsl. positions to nat. account mgr. Scott Paper Co., Phila., 1940-62; comml. broker Shannon and Luchs, Washington, 1962-83, Merrill Lynch Comml. Realty, Washington, 1983-89, Prudential Preferred Properties, Bethesda, Md., 1989-95; pres. E. Brooke Lee Properties, Inc., Montgomery County, Md., from 1979; fund raiser key gifts Nat. Found. for Cancer Rsch., Bethesda, Md., 1985-95. V.p. Ga. Ave. Properties, Montgomery County, Ga.-Conn., Inc., Montgomery County, Conn. Aspen, Inc., Montgomery County, 1962—; sec.-treas. Brooke Lee Family, Inc., Montgomey County, 1962—. Contbr. articles to profl. jours. Chmn. Drug Action Coalition, Inc., fin. v.p., bd. dirs., 1966-70; rep. candidate for Mayor of Washington, 1982, rep. primary candidate for U.S. Senate, State of Md., 1986. Served to capt. airborne inf. U.S. Army, 1943-45, ETO. Named Realtor Assoc. of Yr., Washington Bd. of Realtors, 1984. Mem. Harvard Bus. Sch. Club (pres. 1962, exec. v.p. 1975), Princeton Club of Washington (sec., bd. dirs. 1970-75), Princeton Club of N.Y., Nat. Account Mktg. Assn. (founder, pres. 1959-62). Clubs: Metro, Chevy Chase Country (Washington). Lodges: Kiwanis. Republican. Episcopalian. Avocations: tennis, hunting, swimming, sailing, skating. Died Aug. 20, 2004.

LEE, ELLEN FAITH, insurance company associate; b. Portland, Oreg., Sept. 30, 1951; d. Ira Lawrence Harris and Doris Louise Landis; married, July 13, 1983. Cert. med. aide Okla. Bd. Nursing. Aide Williamette Residential, Eugene, Oreg., 1982-84; med. aide Oak Hills Nursing Home, Jones, Okla., 1984-85; group leader, computer problem solver Plasma Alliance, Oklahoma City, 1985-95; computer cons. Jericho Corrections, Oklahoma City, 1995-96; assoc. Bituminous Ins., Oklahoma City, from 1996. Avocation: barrell racing. Home: Oklahoma City, Okla. Died Aug. 11, 2005.

LEE, IN, physician; b. Seoul, Korea, Apr. 7, 1943; m. Sari Lee, Oct. 30, 1970; children: Ben H., Tami Eo, Chery H. MD, Yonsei U. Coll. Medicine, 1967. Pres. N.J. Med. Group, Ft. Lee, from 1996. Lt. Korean Mil., 1967—70. Mem.: Am. Coll. Physicians. Republican. Methodist. Died May 10, 2005.

LEE, JONG-WOOK, World Health Organization Director General; b. Apr. 12, 1945; married; 1 child. MD, Seoul Nat. U. Med. Sch. of Medicine; M in pub. health, U. Hawaii, Sch. Pub. Health. With LBJ Tropical Med. Centre, Am. Samoa; leprosy cons. in South Pacific World Health Org., 1983, team leader, leprosy control South Pacific, 1984, with regional leprosy control programme Western Pacific Regional Office Manila, Philippines, 1986, regional advisor chronic diseases, dir. polio eradication initiatives Western Pacific, 1990—94, dir. global program for vaccines and immunization Geneva, 1994—98, exec. sec. children's vaccine initiative, sr. policy advisor to the Dir. Gen., 1998, dir. gen., 2003—06. Named one of World's 100 Most Influential People, Time Mag., 2004; recipient Disting. Alumni award, U. Hawaii, 2005. Achievements include increased funding from $15 million to $70 million for global programme for vaccines and immunization from 1994 to 1998. Died May 22, 2006.

LEE, LANSING BURROWS, JR., lawyer; b. Augusta, Ga., Dec. 27, 1919; s. Lansing Burrows and Bertha (Barrett) Lee; m. Natalie Krug, July 4, 1943; children: Melinda Lee Clark, Lansing Burrows III, Bothwell Graves, Richard Hancock. BS, U. Va., 1939; postgrad., U. Ga. Sch. Law, 1939-40; JD, Harvard U., 1947. Bar: Ga. 1947. Pvt. practice, Augusta, Ga., 1947—2006; corp. officer Ga.-Carolina Warehouse & Compress Co., Augusta, 1957-89, pres., CEO; co-owner Ga.-Carolina Warehouse. Chmn. bd. trustees James Brice White Found., from 1962; sr. councillor Atlantic Coun. U.S.; sr. warden Episcopal Ch., chancellor, lay min. Capt. USAAF, 1942—46. Fellow: Am. Coll. Trust and Estate Counsel; mem.: Med. Coll. Ga. Found. (bd. dirs.), U.S. Supreme Ct. Hist. Soc., State Bar Ga. (former chmn. fiduciary law sect.), Augusta Bar Assn. (pres. 1966—67), Ga. Bar Found., U. Va. Thomas Jefferson Soc. Alumni, Harvard U. Law Sch. Assn. Ga. (pres. 1966—67),

Pres.'s Club Med. Coll. Ga., Harvard Club Atlanta, Augusta Country Club, Internat. Order St. Luke the Physician, Soc. Colonial Wars Ga. Home: Augusta, Ga. Died Nov. 2, 2005.

LEE, MELVIN JOSEPH, minister; b. New Orleans, Dec. 25, 1929; s. John and Isabelle (Green) L.; m. Dorothy Peterson, June 5, 1971; children: Betty, Barbara, Joseph, Edward. BS in Chemistry, So. U., New Orleans, 1970; MDiv, Union Bapt. Theol. Sem., New Orleans, 1988, ThM, 1989. Ordained to ministry Bapt. Ch., 1984. Assoc. min. 3d Missionary Bapt. Ch., St. Bernard, La., 1984-87, pastor, from 1987, chair deacon bd., 1974-84; coroner's investigator Orleans Parish, New Orleans, 1982—2000. Bd. dirs. So. Gen. Missionary Bapt. Assn., New Orleans, 1987—, chmn. bldg. com., 1988-92. Author: What Baptists Should Know, 1991; contbr. articles to profl. jours. Chmn. St. Bernard Cmty. Devel. Corp., 1988-93. Sgt. USAF, 1947-52. Democrat. Home: New Orleans, La. Died Apr. 20, 2005.

LEE, PATSY RUTH, retired elementary education educator; b. Mangum, Okla. d. Caswell Jay Franklin and Elizabeth H. (Epperson) Hinds; m. J. L. Lee, Mar. 4, 1951; children: Scot Franklin, Mark David. BS in Home Econs., Okla. Coll. for Women, 1948; MA in Elem. Edn., Ctrl. Mich. U., 1970. Cert. tchr., Mich. Dietetic intern U. Okla. Hosp., Okla. City, 1950; dietitian Elk City (Okla.) Coop. Hosp., 1949-51; dietician Bay County Hosp., Panama City, Fla., 1955-56; dietitian cons. Shawnee (Okla.) Gen. Hosp., 1958-59; dietitian Paxton (Ill.) Gen. Hosp., 1961-65; tchr. Oscoda (Mich.) Area Schs., 1965-91. Sec., chair Oscoda (Mich.) Planning Commn., 1991-99; trustee, vice-chair, treas. Oscoda (Mich.) Sch. Bd., 1995-97; vice chair, sec. Iosco Dem. Party, Iosco County Mich.; bus. chair sect., edn. chair United Way of Oscoda, Mich. Mem. Mich. Assn. Ret. Sch. Personnel (pres. 2000—), Oscoda Lioness Club (pres., sec., treas. Lioness of Yr.), Huron Shores Bus. and Profl. Women (legis. chair, Woman of Yr. 1978), Delta Kappa Gamma (pres. chpt. 1982-84). Democrat. Meth. Avocations: reading, crafts, entertaining, community service. Home: Oscoda, Mich. Died Nov. 20, 2004.

LEE, ROBERT W(ILLIAM), journalist, researcher; b. Salt Lake City, June 19, 1937; s. William Orme Jr. and Golda Alice (Anderson) L.; m. Karen Brinkerhoff, Nov. 24, 1958; children: Michael Don, Gary Dean, William Reed, Robert Bruce, Lawrence Alan. BS, U. Utah, 1960. Pres. Thermotech, Inc., Salt Lake City, 1960-65; adminstrv. asst. John Birch Soc., Washington, 1965-72, Washington rep., 1972-77; adminstrv. asst. Salt Lake County Commn., 1979-81; contbg. editor Am. Opinion Mag., Belmont, Mass., 1981-85, Rev. of the News Mag., Belmont, 1969-85, Conservative Digest Mg., Ft. Collins, Colo., 1985-89; talk-show host Radio Sta. KTKK, Salt Lake City, 1989-94; contbg. editor The New Am. Mag., Appleton, Wis., from 1985. Author: The United Nations Conspiracy, 1981; co-author: A Taxpayer Survey of the Grace Commission Report, 1984, Flight 007: Were There Survivors?, 1986; editor/pub. newsletter Comments and Corrections, 1981—. Mem. Lds Ch. Avocations: golf, chess, bowling, sport shooting, books. Home: Murray, Utah. Died Nov. 3, 2004.

LEE, ROTAN EDWARD, lawyer, entrepreneur; b. Phila., Oct. 18, 1948; s. Rotan and Bessie (Hart) L. BA with high honors, U. Md. Eastern Shore, Princess Anne, 1971; JD with high honors, Antioch Sch. Law, Washington, 1979. Bar: Pa. 1979, U.S. Dist. Ct. (ea. dist.) Pa. 1980. Sr. legal asst. to congl. office U.S. Ho. of Reps., Washington, 1978-79; chief legal counsel to subcom. Small Bus. Com., U.S. Ho. of Reps., Washington, 1978-79; pres. Alcon/Unified Internat., Inc., 1975-79; sr. project mgr. energy and small scale tech. Mark Battle & Assocs., Inc., 1979-82; dir., chief counsel Minority Bus. Legal Def. and Edn. Fund, Washington, 1979-85; founding ptnr. Burrell, Waxman, Donaghy & Lee, Phila., 1985-88; ptnr. Fox, Rothschild, O'Brien & Frankel, Phila., 1988-94; sr. exec. v.p., COO, dir. RMS Techs., Inc., Marlton, N.J., 1994-96; ptnr. Sherr, Joffe & Zuckerman, P.C., West Conshohocken, Pa., 1994—2006; vice chmn. Genesis Teleserv Corp., West Conshohocken, 1996—2006. Affiliate prof. Sch. Bus. and Mgmt., Temple U., Phila., 1995, adj. prof. Coll. Edn., 1993-94; chmn. bd. dirs. Phila. Gas Works, 1994-97, Talleyrand Atlantic, LLC, 1997; dir. law, pub. policy, edn., strategic planning and energy Mellon Bank Corp., Mellon PSFS; speaker in field. Contbr. articles to profl. jours. Bd. dirs. Urban League Phila., 1989, Phila. Child Guidance Ctr., 1995-96, Phila. Orch. Assn., 1991-94; chmn. Cultural Diversity Inst., 1991-95; mem. Bd. Edn., Sch. Dist. Phila., pres., 1992-94. Recipient Paul Porter award Antioch Sch. Law, 1976-79, Learned Hand award Am. Jewish Com., 1993, Brotherhood/Sisterhood Cmty. award NCCJ, 1995, others; Rose Walt scholar, 1969-71. Mem. Beta Kappa Chi, Alpha Kappa Mu, Sigma Tau Delta. Died Apr. 24, 2006.

LEE, SHENG YEN, writer; b. Xinyang, Henan, China, Dec. 28, 1924; s. Yi-San and Qin-Yuan (Gan) L.; m. Winnie Cho, Aug. 25, 1949; 1 child, Yin May. BS in Chemistry, Nat. Northeastern U., 1946; PhD in Chemistry, U. Colo., 1964. Chemist inspector Agrl. Inspection Bur., Taiwan, 1948-51; lang. interpreter Chinese Army, Taiwan, 1951-53; chem. engr. Agrl. Chem. Works, Kaohsiung, Taiwan, 1953-59; chemist Polymer Corp., Ltd., Sarnia, Ontario, Can., 1965-68; chemist, supr. Harry Diamond Labs., U.S. Army, Adelphi, Md., 1969-79; chemist Goddard Space Flight Ctr., NASA, Greenbelt, Md., 1979-91; editor Chinese Am. Forum, Inc., Silver Spring, Md., 1984-99. Prof. hon. Xinyang Tchrs. Coll., 1991. Founder, bd. chmn. Chinese Am. Forum, 1984-2000; patentee in field; contbr. sci. papers to profl. publs. Named Inventor-of-the-yr. finalist NASA, 1990. Avocations: reading, travel, swimming, writing. Home: Silver Spring, Md. Died July 20, 2005.

LEEDY, JACK JOSEPH, psychiatrist; b. Pitts., Apr. 30, 1921; s. David Lipschutz and Stella (Brown) L.; m. Norma Milman, July 19, 1959; children: Ronna, David, Sondra, Cheryl, Janet. BS, U. Pitts., 1941, MD, 1944; postgrad., Western Psychiat. Inst., 1946, Columbia U., 1952. Diplomate Am. Bd. Psychiatry and Neurology in Psychiatry. Intern Montefiore Hosp., Pitts., 1944-45; resident in psychiatry Massilon (Ohio) State Hosp., 1945-46, Cleve. State Hosp., 1947-49; res. in neuropsychiatry N.Y. City Hosp. Welfare Island, 1949-50; sr. psychiatrist, dir. Cumberland Hosp., Bklyn., 1957-77; sr. psychiatrist VA, Bklyn., 1977-87; staff psychiatrist Luth. Med. Ctr., Bklyn., from 1987. Author, editor: Poetry Therapy, 1969, Poetry the Healer, 1973, Poetry as Healer, 1985, Psyching Up for Tennis, 1977. 2d lt. U.S. Army, 1943-44. Mem. Nat. Assn. Poetry Therapy (pres. emeritus 1981—, registered poetry therapist), Assn. Poetry Therapy (founder 1960). Avocations: poetry, tennis. Home: Brooklyn, NY. Died Mar. 24, 2004.

LEFEVER, MAXINE LANE, music educator; b. Elmhurst, Ill., May 30, 1931; d. Thomas Clinton and Georgia Marie (Hampton) Lane; m. Orville Joseph Lefever, Aug. 18, 1951 (div.); m. Geoffrey Ashe, Dec. 8, 1992. Student, Ill. Wesleyan U., 1949-51; BA, Western State Coll., 1958; MS, Purdue U., 1964, postgrad., 1965. Elem. sch. tchr. Leaf River (Ill.) Pub. Schs., 1953-54, Mancos (Colo.) Pub. Schs., 1954-56; elem./jr. hs tchr. Cortez (Colo.) Pub. Schs., 1956-60; instr. bands Purdue U., Lafayette, Ind., 1965-79, asst. prof., 1980-88, prof. emerita, 1989. Cons. numerous festivals and contests; pres., dir. Am. Mus. Ambs., from 1967. Contbr. articles to profl. jours.; composer: percussion ensembles. Hon. mem. USN Band, from 1970. Recipient Disting. Pinnacle award, Purdue U., 2003, Excellence citation, NBA, 1976, award, John Philip Sousa Found., 1984. Mem.: Big Ten Band Dirs. Assn., Percussion Ats Soc., Coll. Band Dirs. Nat. Assn., Nat. Band Assn. (exec. sec., citation of excellence), Music Educators Nat. Conf., Inc. Music Educators Assn., John Philip Sousa Found. (v.p., exec. sec., Star of Order of Merit), Tau Beta Sigma, Delta Omicron, Alpha Lambda Delta, Phi Sigma Kappa (hon.), Kappa Kappa Psi (hon.). Died June 20, 2004.

LEHMANN, GARY LAWRENCE, mechanical engineering educator; b. Ithaca, N.Y., Sept. 13, 1957; s. Lawrence Frank and Mary (Lovelace) L. BSME, Clarkson U., 1979, MS, 1981, PhD, 1985. Engr. Eastman Kodak Co., Rochester, NY, 1980-81; rsch. asst. Clarkson U., Potsdam, NY, 1982-85; assoc. prof. SUNY, Binghamton, NY, 1985—2005. Union Carbide fellow, 1983-85; Gen. Electric Co. rsch. grantee, 1987, IBM Corp. rsch. grantee, 1988, 89. Mem. ASME (com. on cooling electronics, tech. biblicographer com. 1988-2005), AIAA. Home: Binghamton, NY. Died June 23, 2005.

LEIGHLY, HOLLIS PHILIP, JR., metallurgical engineering educator, researcher; b. St. Joseph, Ill., May 28, 1923; s. Hollis Philip and Bessie (Haworth) L.; m. Elizabeth Marie Petersen, Aug. 31, 1951; children: Karen, David. BS, U. Ill., 1948, MS, 1950, PhD, 1952. Registered profl. engr., Calif.; chartered engr. U.K. Rsch. metall. Bendix Corp. Rsch. Labs., Detroit, 1952-54, Denver Rsch. Inst., 1954-60; chmn. metall. dept. U. Denver, 1957-60; assoc. prof. to prof. U. Mo., Rolla, from 1960. Referee 13th Internat. Symposium on Influence of Radiation on Material Properties, 1987; vis. prof. Benjamin Meaker Found., U. Bristol, 1991. Contbr. articles to profl. jours. With U.S. Army, 1943-46, ETO. Olin Industries fellow Univ. Ill., 1951-52, NATO fellow Univ. Guelph, Ont., Can., 1974, British Sci. & Engring. Rsch. Coun. fellow Univ. East Anglia, 1979-80. Mem. Sigma Xi (chp. pres. 1959, 64). Achievements include research in defects in metals and alloys using positron annihilation. Home: Rolla, Mo. Died Aug. 28, 2004.

LEIPHART, CLARENCE DARON, ophthalmologist; b. York County, Pa., Aug. 20, 1915; s. Charles Taylor and Elsie May (Daron) L.; m. S. Isabelle Manifold, Oct. 15, 1944; 1 child, Ann Louise Unholz. BS, Temple U., Phila., 1938, MD, 1941. Diplomate Am. Bd. Ophthalmology. Pvt. practice gen. medicine, Hellam, Pa., 1946-59; pvt. practice ophthalmology Lancaster, Pa., from 1962. Physician advisor Ke Pro Peer Rev., Lemoyne, Pa., 1987—. Asst. surgeon USPHS, 1943-46. Fellow Am. Acad. Ophthalmology; mem. Rotary, Masons. Republican. Presbyterian. Avocation: gardening. Died Feb. 6, 2005.

LEITH, EMMETT NORMAN, electrical engineer, educator; b. Detroit, Mar. 12, 1927; s. Albert Donald and Dorothy Marie (Emmett) Leith; m. Lois June Neswold, Feb. 17, 1956; children: Kim Ellen, Pam Elizabeth. BS, Wayne State U., 1950, MS, 1952, PhD, 1978; DSc (hon.), U. Aberdeen, Scotland, 1996. Mem. rsch. staff U. Mich., 1952—2005, prof. elec. engring., 1968—2005. Cons. several indsl. corps. Contbr. articles to profl. jours. With USNR, 1945—46. Named Man of Yr., Indsl. Rsch. mag., 1966; recipient Gordon Meml. award, SPIE, 1965, citation, Am. Soc. Mag. Photographers, 1966, Achievement award, U.S. Camera and Travel mag., 1967, Excellence of Paper award, Soc. Motion Picture and TV Engrs., 1967, Daedalion award, 1968, Stuart Ballantine medal, Franklin Inst., 1969, Alumni award, Wayne State U., 1974, cited by Nobel Prize Commn. for contbns. to holography, 1971, Holley medal, ASME, 1976, Nat. medal of Sci., 1979, Russel lecture award, U. Mich., 1981, Denins Gabor medal, Soc. Photo-Instrumentation Engrs., 1983, Gold medal, 1990, Mich. Trailblazer award, 1986. Fellow: IEEE (Liebmann award 1967, Inventor of Yr. award 1976), Optical Soc. Am. (Wood medal 1975, Herbert Ives medal 1985), The Royal Photographic Soc. of Great Britain (hon.), Engring. Soc. Detroit (hon.); mem.: NAE, Sigma Pi Sigma, Sigma Xi. Achievements include patents in field; first demonstrating (with colleague) capability of holography to form high-quality 3-dimensional image. Home: Canton, Mich. Died Dec. 23, 2005.

LEM, STANISŁAW, writer; b. Lvov, Poland, Sept. 12, 1921; s. Samuel L.; m. Barbara Leśniak, 1953; 1 child, Tomek. Student, Lvov Med. Inst., 1393-41, 44-45, Jagiellonian U., Cracow, 1946-48; PhD (hon.), U. Wrocław, 1981. Asst. Sci. Circle Jagiellonian U., 1947-49. Contbr. Życie Nauki mag., 1947-49; lectr. U. Cracow. Author: (fiction) Człowiek z Marsa, 1946, Astronauci, 1951, Sezam i inne opowiadania, 1954, Obłok Magellana, 1955, Dzienniki gwiazdowe, 1957 (pub. as The Star Diaries, 1976, Memoirs of a Space Traveller: Further Reminiscences of Ijon Tiehy, 1982), Czas nieutracony: Vol. I: Szpital przemienienia, Vol. II: Wśród umarłych, Vol. III: Powrót, 1957 (pub. as Hospital of the Tranfiguration, 1988), Śledztwo, 1959 (pub. as The Investigation, 1974), Inwazja z Aldebarana, 1959, Eden, 1959, Powrót z gwiazd, 1961 (pub. as Return from the Stars, 1980), Solaris, 1961, Pamiętnik znaleziony w wannie, 1961 (pub. as Memoirs Found in a Bathtub, 1973), Księga robotów, 1961, Noc Ksiezycowa, 1963, Niezwyciężony i inne opowiadania, 1964 (pub. as The Invincible, 1973), Bajki robotów, 1977, Cyberiada, 1965 (pub. as The Cyberiad, 1974), Polowanie, 1965, Wysoki zamek, 1966, Ratujmy Kosmos i inne opowiadania, 1966, Głow pana, 1968 (pub. as His Master's Voice, 1983), Opowieśći o pilocie Pirxie, 1968 (pub. as Tales of Pirx the Pilot, 1979, More Tales of Pirx the Pilot, 1982), Opowiadania, 1969, Bezsenność, 1971 (pub. as The Futurological Congress, 1974), Doskonała próznia, 1971 (pub. as A Perfect Vacuum, 1979), Opowiadania wybrane, 1973, Wielkość urojona, 1973 (pub. as Imaginary Magnitude, 1984), Maska, 1976, Suplement, 1976, Katar, 1976 (pub. as The Chain of Chance, 1978), Mortal Engines, 1977, Powtórka, 1979, Golem XIV, 1981, The Cosmic Carnival of Lem, 1981, Wizja lokalna, 1982, Biblioteka XXI wieku, 1986 (pub. as One Human Minute, 1986), Fiasko, 1987 (pub. as Fiasco, 1987), Dzienniki gwiazdowe, 1991; (play) Jacht Paradise, 1951; (other writings) Dialogi, 1957, Wejście na orbitę, 1962, Summa technologiae, 1964, Filozofia przypadku: literatura w świetle empirii, 1968, Fantastyka i futurologia, 1970, Rozprawy i szkice, 1975, Prowokacja, 1984, Microworlds: Writings on Science Fiction and Fantasy, 1984, Pokój na ziemi, 1987, Rozmowy ze Stanisławem Lemem, 1987, Ciemność i pleśń, 1988. Recipient Polish Ministry of Culture award, 1965, 73, Polish State prize for literature, 1976, Austrian State prize for fgn. literature, 1985, Alfred Jurzykowski Found. award, 1987, Kafka award (Austria), 1991. Mem. Polish Astronautic Soc., Polish Acad. of Scis. (Poland 2000 Com.), Sci. Fiction Research Assn., Sci. Fiction Writers Am. Died Mar. 27, 2006.

LEMAY, CHARLOTTE ZIHLMAN, physics educator; b. Ft. Worth, June 30, 1919; m. Jack Evans LeMay, July 29, 1944; children: Douglas Russell, Lawrence Bruce, Caroline Adelia LeMay Salvati. AB in Physics, Chemistry, Math., Tex. Christian U., 1940; MA in Physics, Mt. Holyoke Coll., 1941; PhD in Physics, La. State U., 1950. Engr. Tex. Instruments, Inc., Dallas, 1952-53, 1955-57; rsch. physicist Stanford Rsch. Inst., Menlo Park, Calif., 1953-54; engr. Westinghouse Electric Corp., Pitts., 1957-60; rsch. physicist IBM, Kitchawan, N.Y., 1960-63; prof. physics Western Conn. State U., Danbury, 1963-89, prof. physics emiritus, 1990. Chmn. dept. physics Western Conn. State U., 1970-78, chmn. promotions and tenure com., 1982-83, chmn. dept. physics and astronomy, 1985-89. Contbr. articles to profl. jours.; patentee in field. Otis Skinner fellow Mt. Holyoke Coll., 1940-41; Univ. Faculty scholar Western Conn. State U., 1983; grantee NSF, 1971-72, 74-75, 77-78, 82, Western Conn. State U., 1983-84, Conn. State U., 1986. Mem. IEEE (sr. life), Am. Phys. Soc., Am. Assn. Physics Tchrs., Am. Soc. Engring. Edn., Optical Soc. Am. (life, bd. dirs. S.W. Conn. sect. 1983-84, treas. 1993—), Soc. Women Engrs. (sr.), Soc. for Photog. Edn., Soc. Photo-Optical Instrumentation Engrs., DAR, Sigma Xi. Home: Nokomis, Fla. Died May 12, 2004.

LEOMPORRA, TULLIO GENE, federal judge; b. 1923; m. Palma Anuzelli; children: Mark Tully, Tully Gene Jr., Licia, Palma, Dean Justin. BA, U. Pa.; postgrad., U. Ill.; JD, Georgetown U. Bar: Pa. Pvt. practice, 1951-71; magistrate judge U.S. Magistrate Ct. (Ea. dist.) Pa., Lafayette Hill, 1971—93, chief magistrate, 1985—93, sr. magistrate, 1993—2004. U.S. commr., 1966-71; adj. prof. MBA program LaSalle U., Phila., 1983-92. With U.S. Army, 1943-46. Died Mar. 20, 2006.

LEONARD, JAMES JOSEPH, physician, educator; b. Schenectady, June 17, 1924; s. James Joseph and Helena (Flood) L.; m. Helen Louise Mitchell, Oct. 24, 1953; children: James Joseph, W. Jeffrey, Paul Mitchell, Kathleen Marie. MD, Georgetown U., 1950. Intern medicine Georgetown U. Hosp., 1950-51, jr. asst. resident, 1951-52, fellow cardiology, 1953-54; asst. resident medicine Boston City Hosp., 1952-53; resident pulmonary diseases D.C. Gen. Hosp., 1954-55, med. officer, 1955-56; instr. medicine Georgetown U. Med. Sch., 1955-56, Duke Med. Center, 1956-57; asst. prof. medicine, dir. div. cardiology Georgetown U. service D.C. Gen. Hosp., 1957-59; asst. prof. medicine U. Tex. Med. Br., Galveston, 1959-62; asso. prof. medicine Ohio State U. Med. Sch., 1962-63; dir. div. cardiology U. Pitts. Med. Sch., 1963-70, asso. prof. medicine, 1963-67, prof. medicine, 1967-77, acting chmn. dept., 1970, chmn. dept., 1971-77; prof., chmn. dept. medicine Uniformed Services U. of Health Scis., from 1977. Master ACP; mem. So. Soc. Clin. Investigation, Am. Clin. and Climatol. Assn., Central Soc. Clin. Research, Assn. Am. Physicians, Assn. Profs. Medicine, Assn. U. Cardiologists. Home: Washington, DC. Died Dec. 16, 2005.

LEONARD, JERRIS, lawyer, former federal agency administrator; b. Chgo., Jan. 17, 1931; s. Jerris G. and Jean Marie (Reville) L.; m. Mariellen C. Mathie, Aug. 22, 1953; children: Mary Leonard Ralston, Jerris G., John E., Kathleen Ann, Francis X., Daniel J. BS, Marquette U., 1952, JD, 1955. Bar: Wis. 1955, D.C. 1973. Practice in, Milw., 1955-69; mem. firm Michael, Best & Friedrich, 1964-69; asst. atty. gen. civil rights divsn. US Dept. Justice, Washington, 1969-71; adminstr. Law Enforcement Assistance Adminstrn., 1971-73; ptnr. Leonard & McGuan, P.C., Washington, 1973—75, Manatt Phelps Rothenberg & Evans, Leonard, Ralston, Stanton & Danks, Washington, 1988—96. Mem. Wis. Assembly from Milwaukee County, 1957-61; mem. Wis. Senate, 1961-69, senate majority leader, 1967-69; pres. Wis. Agys. Bldg. Corp., 1963-69; chmn. Wis. Legislative Council, 1967-69; Rep. candidate for U.S. Senate, 1968; sr. adv. presdl. transition team, 1980-81. Named 1 of 5 Outstanding Young Men Wis. Jaycees, 1965 Mem. ABA, Wis. Bar Assn., D.C. Bar Assn., Fed. Bar Assn., Am. Judicature Soc., Alpha Sigma Nu, Delta Sigma Pi, Sigma Nu Phi. Home: Bethesda, Md. Died July 27, 2006.

LEONARD, NELSON JORDAN, retired chemistry professor; b. Newark, Sept. 1, 1916; s. Harvey Nelson and Olga Pauline (Jordan) L.; m. Louise Cornelie Vermey, May 10, 1947 (dec. 1987); children: Kenneth Jan, Marcia Louise, James Nelson, David Anthony; m. Margaret Taylor Phelps, Nov. 14, 1992. BS in Chemistry, Lehigh U., 1937, DSc, 1963, Oxford U., Eng., 1983; DSc (hon.), U. Ill., 1988; BSc, Oxford U., Eng., 1940; PhD, Columbia U., 1942; D. (hon.), Adam Mickiewicz U., Poland, 1980. Fellow and rsch. asst. chemistry U. Ill., Urbana, 1942-43, instr., 1943-44, assoc., 1944-45, 46-47, asst. prof., 1947-49, assoc. prof., 1949-52, prof. organic chemistry, 1952-73, head div. organic chemistry, 1954-63, prof. chemistry and biochemistry, 1973-86, R.C. Fuson prof. chemistry, mem. Ctr. for Advanced Study, 1981-86, R.C. Fuson prof. emeritus, 1986—2006. Investigator antimalarial program Com. Med. Research, OSRD, 1944-46; sci. cons. and spl. investigator Field Intelligence Agy. Tech., US Army and US Dept. Commerce, 1945-46; mem. Can. NRC, summer 1950; Swiss-Am. Found. lectr., 1953, 70; vis. lectr. UCLA, summer 1953; Reilly lectr. U. Notre Dame, 1962; Stieglitz lectr. Chgo. sect. Am. Chem. Soc., 1962; Robert A. Welch Found. lectr., 1964, 83; Disting. vis. lectr. U. Calif.-Davis, 1975; vis. lectr. Polish Acad. Scis., 1976; B.R. Baker Meml. lectr. U. Calif., Santa Barbara, 1976; Ritter Meml. lectr. Miami U., Oxford, Ohio; Werner E. Bachman Meml. lectr. U. Mich., Ann Arbor, 1977; vis. prof. Japan Soc. Promotion of Sci., 1978; Arapahoe lectr. U. Colo., 1979; Tanabe rsch. lectr. Scripps Rsch. Inst., La Jolla, Calif., 1993; mem. program com. in basic scis. Arthur P. Sloan, Jr. Found., 1961-66; Philips lectr. Haverford Coll., 1971; Backer lectr., Groningen, Netherlands, 1972; FMC lectr. Princeton U., 1973; plenary lectr. Laaxer Chemistry Conf., Laax, Switzerland, 1980, 82, 84, 88, 90, 92; Calbiochem-Behring Corp. U. Calif.-San Diego Found. lectr., 1981; Watkins vis. prof. Wichita State U. (Kans.), 1982; Ida Beam Disting. vis. prof. U. Iowa, 1983; Fogarty scholar-in-residence NIH, Bethesda, Md., 1989-90; Sherman Fairchild Disting. scholar Calif. Inst. Tech., 1991; Syntex. disting. lectr. U. Colo., 1992; faculty assoc. Calif. Inst. Tech., 1992—; mem. adv. com. Searle Scholars program Chgo. Community Trust, 1982-85; ednl. adv. bd. Guggenheim Found., 1969-88, mem. com. of selection, 1977-88. Editor: Organic Syntheses, 1951-58, mem. adv. bd., 1959-2006, bd. dirs., 1969-2006, v.p., 1976-80, pres., 1980-88; editorial bd. Jour. Organic Chemistry, 1957-61, Jour. Am. Chem. Soc., 1960-72; adv. bd. Biochemistry, 1973-78, Chemistry International, 1984-91, Pure and Applied Chemistry, 1984-91; contbr. articles to profl. jours. Recipient medal Synthetic Organic Chem. Mfrs., 1970, Wheland award U. Chgo., 1991, creativity award U. Oreg., 1994, Arthur C. Cope Scholar award Am. Chem Soc., 1995; named to Mt. Vernon (N.Y.) H.S. Hall of Fame, 1985; fellow Rockefeller Found., 1950, Guggenheim fellow, 1959, 67. Fellow Am. Acad. Arts and Scis. (v.p. 1991-93); mem. NAS, AAAS, Polish Acad. Scis. (fgn.), Ill. Acad. Sci. (hon.), Am. Chem. Soc. (award for creative work in synthetic organic chemistry 1963, Edgar Fahs Smith award and lectureship Phila. sect. 1975, Centennial lectr. 1976, Roger Adams award 1981, Paul G. Gassman Disting. Svc. award divsn. organic chemistry 1994, A.C. Cope rsch. scholar award 1995), Am. Soc. for Biochemistry and Molecular Biology, Chem. Soc. London, New Swiss Chem. Soc., Internat. Union Pure and Applied Chemistry (sec. organic chemistry divsn. 1989, v.p. 1989-91, pres. 1991-93), Pharm. Soc. Japan (hon.), Am. Philos. Soc., Phi Beta Kappa, Phi Lambda Upsilon (hon.), Tau Beta Pi, Alpha Chi Sigma. Achievements include patents on synthesis of sparteine; esters of pyridine dicarboxylic acid as insect repellents; fluorescent derivatives of adenine- and cytosine-containing compounds. Home: Pasadena, Calif. Died Oct. 9, 2006.

LEONARD, WILLIAM F., lawyer; b. Quincy, Fla., Sept. 4, 1926; s. Charles E. and Zula (Lookabill) L.; m. Elizabeth Roberts, Jan. 5, 1949; children: William Robert, C. Glenn, Elizabeth Leonard Booth. Pre-law, Fla. State U., 1949; JD, U. Fla., 1951. Bar: Fla. Sr. ptnr. Leonard & Morrison, Ft. Lauderdale, Fla., from 1953. Mem. 4th Dist. Ct. of Appeal Judicial Nominating Com., 1987-90. Bd. of govs. Nova Law Sch., Ft. Lauderdale, Fla., 1975—; chmn. bd. trustees Holy Cross Hosp., Ft. Lauderdale, 1975—; regent State of Fla., 1982-87; bd. dirs. Bonnet House, Ft. Lauderdale, 1985-93; bd. dirs. Ft. Lauderdale Hist. Soc., 1985—, U. Fla. Found.; hon. mem. Fla. Blue Key. Mem. ABA, Fla. Bar Assn. (bd. govs. 1975-79), Broward Couty Bar Assn. (pres. 1974-75), Phi Delta Phi, One Hundred Club of Broward (pres. 1981-82), Fla. Coun. of 100. Democrat. Baptist. Avocations: sports, travel. Home: Fort Lauderdale, Fla. Died Aug. 7, 2005.

LEOPOLD, LUNA BERGERE, geology educator, engineer, meteorologist; b. Albuquerque, Oct. 8, 1915; BS in Civil Engring., U. Wis., 1936, DSc (hon.), 1985; MS in Physics and Meteorology, UCLA, 1944; PhD in Geology, Harvard, 1950; D Geography (hon.), U. Ottawa, 1969; DSc (hon.), Iowa Wesleyan Coll., 1971, St. Andrews U., 1981, U. Murcia, Spain, 1988. With Soil Conservation Service, 1938-41, U.S. Engrs. Office, 1941-42, U.S. Bur. Reclamation, 1946; head meteorologist Pineapple Research Inst. of Hawaii, 1946-49; hydraulic engr. U.S. Geol. Survey, 1950-71, chief hydrologist, 1957-66, sr. research hydrologist, 1966-71; prof. geology U. Calif. at Berkeley, 1973—87, prof. emeritus, 1987—2006. Author (with Thomas Maddock, Jr.): The Flood Control Controversy, 1954; author: Fluvial Processes in Geomorphology, 1964, Water, 1974; author: (with Thomas Dunne) Water in Environmental Planning, 1978; author: A View of the River, 1994, Water, Rivers and Creeks, 1997, also tech. papers. Capt. air weather svc. USAF, 1942—46. Recipient Disting. Svc. award, US Dept. Interior, 1958, Veth medal, Royal Netherlands Geog. Soc., 1963, Cullum Geog. medal, Am. Geog. Soc., 1968, Rockefeller Pub. Svc. award, 1971, Busk medal, Royal Geog. Soc., 1983, Berkeley citation, U. Calif., David Linton award, Brit. Geomorphol. Rsch. Group, 1986, Linsley award, Am. Inst. Hydrology, 1989, Caulfield medal, Am. Water Resources Assn., 1991, Nat. Medal Sci., NSF, 1991, Palladium medal, Nat. Audubon Soc., 1994, Joan Hodges Queneau Palladium medal, Am. Assn. Engring. Socs., 1994, Benjamin Franklin medal in Earth and Environ. Sci., Franklin Inst., 2006. Fellow: Calif. Acad. Sciences; mem.: Am. Philos. Soc., Am. Acad. Arts and Scis., Am. Geol. Inst. (Ian Campbell medal), Am. Geophys. Union (Robert E. Horton medal 1993), Geol. Soc. Am. (pres. 1972, Kirk Bryan award 1958, Disting. Career award geomorphological group 1991, Penrose medal 1994), ASCE (Julian Hinds award), NAS (Warren prize), Cosmos Club (Washington), Phi Kappa Phi, Sigma Xi, Chi Epsilon, Tau Beta Pi. Home: Berkeley, Calif. Died Feb. 23, 2006.

LEPORIERE, RALPH DENNIS, retired quality engineer; b. Elizabeth, N.J., Nov. 8, 1932; s. Maximo and Christian (Lello) L.; m. Judith Louise Crowhurst, Nov. 19, 1960; children: Bonnie Ann, David Anthony. BS in Chemistry, Rutgers U., 1954. Registered profl. engr., Calif. Chemist N.Y. Quinine & Chemical Works, Newark, 1954-55; asst. to chief quality control C.D. Smith Pharmacal Co., New Brunswick, N.J., 1955-56; asst. supr. quality control White Labs., Kenilworth, N.J., 1958-60; statistician Calif. and Hawaiian Sugar Co., Crockett, Calif., 1960-2000; ret., 2000. Instr., chmn. quality control dept. Laney C.C., Oakland, Calif., 1967-87; asst. prof., chmn. quality control dept. John F. Kennedy U., Martinez, Calif., 1967-72; instr., mem. adv. com. ann. statis. short course U. Calif., Davis, 1969-94 Pres. PTA Napa Junction Elem. Sch., Napa County, Calif., 1971-73; mem. early childhood com., program adv. com. Napa Valley Unified Sch. Dist., Napa County, 1972-76; v.p. Am. Canyon County Water Dist., American Canyon, Calif., 1971-73, pres., 1973-83, gen. mgr., 1981. Recipient Hon. Service award Calif. State PTA, 1973. Fellow Am. Soc. Quality Control (cert. quality engr., chmn. San Francisco sect., founder East Bay Subsect. 1970-71); mem. Soc. Mfg. Engrs. (sr.), Am. Statis. Soc., Am. Chem. Soc. Republican. Roman Catholic. Home: American Canyon, Calif. Died Jan. 3, 2005.

LESH, MICHAEL JOSEPH, accountant; b. Hamburg, Ark., Sept. 22, 1929; s. Michael Lesh and Mary (Herlevic) Wallesh; m. Georgiann Agnes Egloff, June 16, 1951; children: Mark Kenneth, Carolyn Lesh Rowley, Mary Kathryn (dec.). BS, U. Ill., 1955. CPA, Ill., Washington, D.C. Supr. auditing Peat, Marwick, Mitchell & Co., Chgo., 1955-62; asst. controller Chgo. & Eastern Ill. R.R. Co., Chgo., 1962-66; cons. project dir. Booz, Allen & Hamilton, Chittagong, Bangladesh and Tehran, Iran, 1966-69; mgr. budgets and cost acctg. Atchison, Topeka & Santa Fe R.R. Co., Topeka, 1969-74; controller Santa Fe Natural Resources Inc., Chgo., 1974-81; asst. to v.p. acctg. Atchison, Topeka & Santa Fe R.R. Co., Topeka, from 1984; controller Santa Fe Energy Co. div. Santa Fe Natural Resources, Chgo., Amarillo, Tex., 1974-84. Sustaining mem. Nat. Rep. Com., 1981—. Roman Catholic. Avocations: reading, bridge, golf, travel. Home: Topeka, Kans. Died Aug. 10, 2004.

LESSER, JULIAN (BUD LESSER), film producer, historian; b. San Francisco, Jan. 18, 1915; s. Sol Leonard and Fay (Grunauer) L.; m. Genee Kobacker, 1938 (div. 1952); m. Betsy Bamberger, Jan. 24, 1955 (div. Jan. 1980); children: Stephen, Belinda, David; m. Helene Feinberg, Aug. 8, 1983. BA, Stanford U., 1936; postgrad. Grad. Sch. Bus., Harvard U., 1937. Salesman J.E. Brulatour & Co., Eastman Raw Films, Hollywood, Calif., 1937-39; chair Def. Coun. Film Bur., L.A., 1941-42; v.p. Sol Lesser Prodns., L.A., 1947-58; pres. Royal Prodns., L.A., 1950-80. Presenter in field. Journalist/historian niche periodicals Maj. USMCR, 1942-49. Mem. USMC Combat Corrs. (bd. dirs. 1996-98, pres. L.A. chpt. 1999&, Dickson award 1994). Died Mar. 22, 2005.

LESSOFF, HOWARD, physicist, chemist; b. Boston, Sept. 23, 1930; s. Alexander and Frances (Palenofsky) L.; m. Vera Schlosberg, June 21, 1959; children: Victor W., Steven C. BS, Northeastern U., Boston, 1953, MS, 1957. Lectr. Lincoln Coll., Northeastern U., Boston, 1957-70; staff scientist Bell Telephone Lab, North Andover, Mass., 1960-61; sr. scientist RCA Material Rsch. Ctr., Needham, Mass., 1957-60, 61-64; sect. head NASA Electronic Rsch. Ctr., Cambridge, Mass., 1964-70; branch head Naval Rsch. Lab, Washington, from 1970. Author: Civil War with Punch, 1984; contbr. articles to profl. jours.; inventor on field. Served with U.S. Army, 1953-55. Recipient Presidential Commendation, Washington, 1988. Fellow Washington Acad. Sci., mem. IEEE, Am. Assn. Crystal Growth, Sigma Psi. Avocations: photography, writing, music. Home: Rockville, Md. Died Feb. 18, 2004.

LESTER, URBAN ALEXANDER, retired lawyer, educator; b. Tenn., Aug. 24, 1929; s. Norbert John Canutus and Margaret Delia (Johnson) L.; m. Juliette Noone, Nov. 16, 1968. BA, Cath. U., 1954, JD, 1959. Bar: D.C. 1962. Assoc. Ford, Larson, Greene and Horan, Washington, 1963-65; spl. counsel State of Alaska, 1967-68; ptnr. Lester and Contrucci, 1968-78; lectr., disting. lectr. Cath. U., Washington, 1972-78, asst. prof. law, 1978-84, assoc. prof. law, 1984—2003; of counsel Alvord and Alvord, Washington, 1979—2003. Program dir. tchr. tng. Nat. Inst. for Trial Advocacy, Harvard U., Cambridge, Mass.; pres. acad. senate Cath. U., Washington, 1983-85. Asst. editor Cath. U. Law Rev., 1955-56. Capt. USAF, 1954-58. Recipient Robert E. Oliphant Svc. to Nat. Inst. Trial Advocacy award, 2003. Mem. ABA, Fed. Bar Assn., Army-Navy Club. Home: Washington, DC. Died May 22, 2006.

LEVAN, ARTHUR BERNARD, obstetrician-gynecologist; b. Chgo., Dec. 31, 1912; s. Samuel Albert and Sarah (Salk) L.; m. Elfriede Horst, May 29, 1944 (dec. July 1979); children: Kathryn, Peter. BS, U. Ill., Champaign and Chgo., 1934; MD, U. Ill., Chgo., 1936, MS in Pathology, 1937. Diplomate Am. Bd. Ob-Gyn. Chmn. dept. ob-gyn Resurrection Hosp., Chgo., 1956-58, Holy Family Hosp., Des Plaines, Ill., from 1964; staff Luth. Gen. Hosp., Park Ridge, Ill. Clin. assoc. in ob-gyn, U. Ill. Chgo. Served to maj. U.S Army Med. Corps., 1941-46. Fellow ACS, Am. Coll. Ob-Gyn; mem. AMA, Chgo. Gynecol. Soc. Avocations: golf, swimming, horsemanship. Home: Hoffman Est, Ill. Died Jan. 31, 2005.

LEVENDOSKY, CHARLES LEONARD, journalist, poet; b. Bronx, N.Y., July 4, 1936; s. Charles Leonard and Laura (Gregorio) L.; m. Charlotte Ann Jaeger, July 15, 1962 (div. Nov. 1997); children: Alytia, Ixchel. BS in Physics, U. Okla., 1958, BA in Math., 1960; MA in Edn., NYU, 1963. Tchr. Christiansted H.S., V.I., 1963-65; tutor Kyoto (Japan) U., 1965-66, Elizabeth Irwin H.S., N.Y.C., 1966-67; asst. prof. English NYU, N.Y.C., 1967-71; poet in schs. arts couns. of N.Y., Ga., N.J., 1967-71; poet-in-residence Wyo. Arts Coun., Cheyenne, 1972-82; editl. page editor Casper (Wyo.) Star-Tribune, 1982—2004; columnist The New York Times Wire Svc., 1995—2004. Co-dir. Bill of Rights seminar, Casper, 1991; chmn. Ad Hoc Com. for Judicial Fellowship, Casper, 1991-94. Author: Hands and Other Poems, 1986, Circle of Light, 1995; editor: Ucross: The First Ten Years, 1992; contbr. articles to profl. jours.; creator, editor Casper Star-Tribune's First Amendment Web site-FACT (Editor and Pub. award for best original feature for newspaper's online svcs. 1996), First Freedom Op-Ed Svc., ALA, 1995. Panelist First Amendment Congress, Williamsburg, Va., 1986, del., 1991, 97; adv. bd. Wyo. St. Hist. Records, Cheyenne, 1992; bd. trustees Freedom to Read Found., 1993-97, Freedom to Read Found., 2000-04. Appointed Poet Laureate of Wyo., Cheyenne, 1988-96, Humanities scholar Humanities Coun. in Pub. TV series, Wyo., 1991-97; recipient Intellectual Freedom award ALA, 1987, First Amendment award Hugh M. Hefner Found., 1987, H.L. Mencken award Free Press Assn., 1988, Print Media award Wyo. chpt. Am. Bd. Trial Advocates, 1992, Silver Gavel award ABA, 1994, H.L. Mencken award Balt. Sun, 1994, First Amendment award Soc. Profl. Journalists, 2000. Mem. ACLU, PEN, Ams. United for Separation of Ch. and State, Freedom to Read Found., Nat. Coalition Against Censorship. Home: Casper, Wyo. Died Mar. 14, 2004.

LEVIN, BARRY SHERWIN, physician; b. Dec. 17, 1940; BS in Hisotry, U. Wis., 1962; MD, U. Ill., 1966. Diplomate Am. Bd. Internal Medicine, Am. Bd. Nephrology. Intern then resident U. Ill. Rsch. and Edn. Hosp., Chgo., 1966-68; resident U. Calif., San Francisco, 1967-68, asst. clin. prof. medicine, 1975-82; fellow Peter Brent Brigham Hosp., Boston, 1969-71; asst. prof. medicine U. Chgo., 1974-75; med. dir., chmn. dept. transplantation Calif. Pacific Med. Ctr., San Francisco, from 1979. Med. dir. Calif. Transplant Donor Network, 1987-88; staff physician Andrews AFB, Md., 1971-73, Washingotn Hosp., Calif. Pacific Med. Ctr., San Francisco, 1975—; assoc. attending physician, dir. Michael Reese Hosp., Chgo., 1974-75. Contbr. articles to profl. jours. Fellow NIH, 1969-71. Mem. Am. Soc. Nephrology, Am. Soc. Transplant Physicians (pres. 1988-89), Internat. Soc. Nephrology, Transplantation Soc., Alpha Omega Alpha. Home: San Rafael, Calif. Died June 21, 2005.

LEVINE, AARON, executive; b. Boston, Aug. 5, 1918; s. Isaac William and Sybil (Mannis) L.; m. Estelle Malloy, Sept. 7, 1941 (dec. Mar. 1988); children: Joseph, Deborah, Jonathan (deceased); m. Nancy Goldstein, Nov. 16, 1991; children: Larry, Blaine, Jeffrey. AB, Harvard U., 1940, MA, 1941; DHL (hon.), U. Cin., 1996. With Fed. Dept. Stores, Cin., 1956-82; fin. officer Hebrew U. Coll., 1982-88; co-dir., founder Inst. for Learning in Retirement, U. Cin., 1989-96, emeritus, from 1996. Named to Ohio State Sr. Citizens Hall of Fame, 1996. Home: Cincinnati, Ohio. Died June 2004.

LEVINE, HELEN GAWRONSKI LACATIS, communications specialist; b. Detroit, May 31, 1931; d. Mitchell T. and Elizabeth (Korzeniewski) Gawronski; m. John Lacatis, June 30, 1956 (div. 1977); children: Laura Elizabeth, Monica Dorothy, Audrey Vernelle; m. Ethan Levine, 1982. Diploma, Detroit Conservatory of Music, 1954; BA, Wayne State U., 1970, MA, 1977. Adminstr. asst. Wayne State U., Detroit, 1968-70; dir. vol. svc. and community rels. Rehab. Inst., Detroit, 1971-82; dir. vol. svc. DePaul Hosp., Cheyenne, Wyo., 1982-83; v.p. pub. rels. Wyo. Hosp. Assn., Cheyenne, 1983-84; air talent Sta: KLEN-FM, Cheyenne, 1984-86; field rep. Am. Heart Assn., Wyo., 1985-86; pub. info. officer Dept. Health State of Wyo., 1986-97. Cons. U. Chgo., 1968; found. officer Laramie County Libr., Cheyenne, 1985-86; mem. faculty Preston U., Park Coll. Featured columnist Casper Star Tribune; contbr. articles to profl. jours. Mem. Cmty. it Interagy. Bd., Cheyenne, 1982-86, Gov.'s Com. on Older Am., Cheyenne, 1983-85, Mayor's Coun. for People with Disabilities, Cheyenne, 1984-91, United Way Allocations Com., Cheyenne, 1984-86, Wyo. Diabetes Coun. 1995—; bd. dirs. Cheyenne Symphony, 1989-91; cons. Save Orch. Hall Found., Detroit, 1970-71. Mem Pub. Rels. Soc. Am., Wyo. Press Assn., Wyo. Press Women, Nat. Fedn. Press Women, AAUW. Avocations: golf, reading, camping, hiking. Home: Cheyenne, Wyo. Died Jan. 4, 2005.

LE VINE, JEROME EDWARD, retired ophthalmologist; b. Pitts., Mar. 23, 1923; s. Harry Robert and Marian Dorothy (Finesilver) L.; m. Marilyn Tobey Hiedovitz, Apr. 14, 1957; children: Loren Robert, Beau Jay, Janice Lynn. BS, U. Pitts., 1944; MD, Hahnemann Med. Sch., Phila., 1949; postgrad. in ophthalmology, U. Pa., 1951-52. Diplomate Am. Bd. Disability Cons., Am. Bd. Quality Assurance & Utilization Rev. Intern St. Francis Hosp., Pitts., 1949-50; resident in ophthalmology Jefferson U. Med. Sch. Hosp., Phila., 1952-54; ophthalmologist Leech Farm VA Hosp., Pitts., 1955-59; chief eye dept. Stanocola Clinic, Baton Rouge, 1959-64; sole practice medicine specializing in ophthalmology Baton Rouge, 1959-86; ret., 1986. Cons. La. State U., East La. State Hosp. Infirmary, Villa Feliciana Geriatric Hosp., disability dept. Social Security Adminstrn., div. blind La. State Pub. Welfare dept.; mem. staff Our Lady of the Lake Hosp., Baton Rouge Gen. Hosp., Women's Hosp.; instr. spl. edn. U. Southeastern La., 1971. Mem. Am. Bd. Quality Assurance and Utilization Rev., 1990. With MC, AUS, 1942-44. Fellow Am. Geriatric Soc., Royal Soc. Health; mem. AMA, La. State Med. Soc., East Baton Rouge Parish Med. Soc., 6th Dist. Med. Soc., New Orleans Acad. Ophthalmology, So. Med. Assn., La. Med. Soc., Baton Rouge Parish Med. Soc., Pi Lambda Phi, Phi Delta Epsilon. Democrat. Jewish. Home: Baton Rouge, La. Died Feb. 26, 2006.

LEVINE, MARILYN ANNE, artist; b. Medicine Hat, Alta., Can., Dec. 22, 1935; came to the U.S., 1973; d. Herman Rutherford and Annie Louise Hayes; m. Sidney Levine, Sept. 30, 1959 (div. 1977). BSc, U. Alta., Edmonton, 1957; MSc, U. Alta., 1959; MA, U. Calif., Berkeley, 1970, MFA, 1971. Tchg. fellow dept. chemistry U. Alta., Edmonton, 1957-59; chemist I Geology Survey Can., Ottawa, 1959-61; chemistry instr. Campion Coll., U. Sask., Regina, Can., 1962-64; ceramics instr. dept. ext. U. Regina, Sask., 1966-69, 1971-73. Vis. art instr. U. Calgary, Alta., summers 1968, 71; lectr. in art U. Calif., Davis, 1972; visual arts lectr. U. Regina, 1972-73; asst. prof. art U. Utah, Salt Lake City, 1973-76; vis. asst. prof. art-sculpture U. Calif., Berkeley, 1975-80; vis. art lectr. Calif. State Coll., Hayward, 1981. One-woman shows include Hansen Fuller Gallery, San Francisco 1971, 75, 80, 83, Norman Mackenzie Art Gallery, Regina, 1974, O.K. Harris Works of Art, N.Y.C. 1974, 76, 79, 81, 84, 85, 91, Inst. Contemporary Art, Boston, 1981, Galerie Alain Blondel, Paris, 1981, Rena Bransten Gallery, San Francisco, 1990. Mackenzie Art Gallery, Regina, also traveling, 1998-99; group exhibits include Nat. Mus. Modern Art, Kyoto, 1971, Sidney Janis Gallery, N.Y., 1972, Musee d'Art de la Ville de Paris, 1973, Whitney Mus. Am. Art Downtown Br., N.Y., 1974, Mus. Contemporary Crafts, N.Y., 1975, Australian Nat. Gallery, Canberra, 1977, Everson Mus. Art, Syracuse, N.Y., 1979, Denver Art Mus., 1979, Pa. Acad. Fine Arts, Phila., 1981-83, Mackenzie Art Gallery, U. Regina, 1980, Abbaye Saint-Andre, Meymac, Correze, France, 1983, Am. Craft Mus., N.Y., 1986-92, Philbrook Mus. Art, Tulsa, 1987-89, Scripps Coll., Claremont, Calif., 1994-96; represented in permanent collections U. Art Mus., Berkeley, Can. Coun. Art Bank, Australian Nat. Gallery, Canberra, Mus. Contemporary Art, Chgo., Nelson-Atkins Mus. Art, Kansas City, Mo., Nat. Mus. Modern Art, Kyoto, Montreal Mus. Fine Art, Va. Mus. Fine Arts, Richmond, San Francisco Mus. Modern Art, Everson Mus. Art, Syracuse, Philbrook Mus.

Art, Tulsa, Mus. Contemporary Ceramic Art, Shigaraki, Japan, Mint Mus. Craft and Design, Charlotte, N.C., Ichon World Ceramic Ctr., Icon, Korea. Recipient David P. Gardner Faculty Rsch. grantee U. Utah, Salt Lake City, 1975, Sr. Arts Grant award Can. Coun., Ottawa, Ont., Can., 1976; Visual Artists Fellowship grantee Nat. Endowment for the Arts, Washington, 1976, 80. Home: Oakland, Calif. Died Apr. 2, 2005.

LEVINE, MELVIN CHARLES, lawyer; b. Bklyn., Nov. 12, 1930; s. Barnet and Jennie (Iser) Levine. BCS, NYU, 1952; LLB, Harvard U., 1955. Bar: N.Y. 1956, U.S. Supreme Ct. 1964. Assoc. Kriger & Haber, Bklyn., 1956-58, Black, Varian & Simon, N.Y.C., 1958; pvt. practice N.Y.C., from 1959. Devel. multiple dwelling housing; dir. Am. ORT, mem. nat. campaign com.; trustee Bramson ORT Coll.; del. World ORT Gen. Assembly; mem. housing ct. adv. coun. N.Y. State Unified Ct. Sys.; mem. ind. Dem. jud. screening panel N.Y.C. civil ct. judges; mem. Character and Fitness Com. Trustee Jewish Ctr. Hamptons. Recipient Cmty. Achievement award, N.Y. ORT Scholarship Fund. Mem.: Assn. Bar City of N.Y. (adj. mem. jud. com.), N.Y. County Lawyers Assn. (dir., mem. civil ct. com., mem. housing ct. com., mem. uniform housing ct. rules com., liaison Assn. Bar City N.Y. selection housing, civil, criminal judges, mem. com. jud., mem. task force tort reform, co-chair civil ct. practice sect., Civil Ct. Practice Sect. Disting. Svc award). Democrat. Jewish. Died Sept. 6, 2005.

LEVINE, OSCAR, lubricant coatings company executive; b. Bklyn., Feb. 6, 1923; s. Benjamin and Celia (Richman) L.; m. Betty Lee Palais, Sept. 12, 1948; children: Douglas Stewart, Jan Louise. BS, CCNY, 1943; AM, Columbia U., 1948; PhD, Georgetown U., 1958. Rsch. scientist Lewis Flight Propulsion Lab., Cleve., 1948-52, U.S. Naval Rsch. Lab., Washington, 1952-58, Gillette Co., Boston, 1958-85; owner RO-59, Inc., Pembroke, Mass., from 1985. Contbr. rsch. papers to profl. publs. With U.S. Army, 1944-46. Avocations: golf, tennis, swimming, reading, research. Home: Stoughton, Mass. Died Dec. 20, 2004.

LEVISAY, SUZANNE BAKER, counselor; b. Oklahoma City, Apr. 15, 1947; d. Robert and Helen (Lischalk) Baker; m. David Levisay, June 1, 1972; 1 child, Michael Ethan. BA, U. North Tex., 1969, MA, 1972; MSSW, U. Tex., Arlington, 1979. Lic. master social worker, advanced clin. practitioner, ind. practitioner in social work, Tex. Treatment coord. children's residential svcs Tarrant County MHMR, Ft. Worth; outpatient therapist Denton County MHMR, Denton, Tex.; pvt. practice counselor Denton. Mem. NASW, Am. Orthopsychiat. Assn., Acad. Cert. Social Workers. Home: Denton, Tex. Died Mar. 9, 2005.

LEVIT, EDITHE JUDITH, physician; b. Wilkes-Barre, Pa., Nov. 29, 1926; m. Samuel M. Levit, Mar. 2, 1952; children: Harry M., David B. BS in Biology, Bucknell U., 1946; MD, Med. Coll. Pa., 1951, DMS (hon.), 1978; DSc (hon.), Wilkes U., 1990. Grad. asst. in psychology Bucknell U., 1946—47; intern Phila. Gen. Hosp., 1951—52, fellow in endocrinology, 1952—53, clin. instr., assoc. in endocrinology, 1953—57, dir. med. edn., 1957—61, cons. med. edn., 1961—65; asst. dir. Nat. Bd. Med. Examiners, Phila., 1961-67, assoc. dir., sec. bd., 1967—75, v.p., sec. bd., 1975—77, pres., CEO, 1977—86, pres. emeritus, life mem., bd. dirs., 1987—2006. Adv. coun. Inst. for Nuclear Power Ops., Atlanta, 1988—93; cons. in field. Contbr. articles to profl. jours. Bd. sci. counselors Nat. Libr. Medicine, 1981—85; bd. dirs. Phila. Gen. Hosp. Found., 1964—70, Phila. Council for Internat. Visitors, 1966—72. Recipient award for outstanding contbns. in field of med. edn., Commonwealth Com. of Woman's Med. Coll., 1970, Alumni award, Bucknell U., 1978, Disting. Dau. of Pa. award, 1981, Spl. Recognition award, Assn. Am. Med. Colls., 1986, Disting. Svc. award, Fedn. State Med. Bds., 1987. Master: ACP; fellow: Coll. Physicians of Phila.; mem.: AMA, Phila. County Med. Soc., Pa. Med. Soc., Inst. Medicine Nat. Acad. Scis., Phi Sigma, Alpha Omega Alpha, Phi Beta Kappa. Home: Philadelphia, Pa. Died Oct. 18, 2006.

LEVITT, THEODORE, marketing educator; b. Vollmerz, Germany, Mar. 1, 1925; came to U.S., 1935, naturalized, 1940; s. Boris and Recha (Gruenebaum) L.; m. Joan Levy, 1948; children: John M., Frances B., Kathryn L., Laura C., Peter K. BA, Antioch Coll., 1949; PhD in Econs., Ohio State U., 1951. Mem. faculty Grad. Sch. Bus. Adminstrn. Harvard U., Boston, 1959—84, prof. bus. adminstrn., 1964—84, head mktg. area, 1977-84. Bd. dirs. AM Internat., Consol. Natural Gas Co., Lifetime Corp., Melville Corp., Sanford C. Bernstein Inc., Saatchi & Saatchi Co. PLC, The Stride Rite Corp.; cons. in field. Author: Innovation in Marketing, 1962, Industrial Purchasing Behavior: A Study in Communications Effects, 1965, The Marketing Mode: Pathways to Corporate Growth, 1969, The Third Sector: New Tactics for a Responsive Society, 1973, Marketing for Business Growth, 1976, The Marketing Imagination, 1983, Thinking About Management, 1990; co-author: Marketing: An Introductory Analysis, 1964, Marketing: A Contemporary Analysis, 1972; editor Harvard Bus. Rev., 1985-89; contbr. articles to profl. jours. Recipient Charles Coolidge Parlin award as Mktg. Man of Yr., 1970, Geoge Gallup award for Mktg. Excellence, 1976, Paul D. Converse award Am. Mktg. Assn., 1978, William M. McFeely award Internat. Mgmt. Coun., 1989, Outstanding Bus. Book of Yr. award Acad. Mgmt., 1962. Died June 28, 2006.

LEVY, LEONARD WILLIAMS, history professor, writer; b. Toronto, Ont., Can., Apr. 9, 1923; s. Albert and Rae (Williams) L.; m. Elyse Gitlow, Oct. 21, 1944; children: Wendy Ellen, Leslie Anne. BS, Columbia U., 1947, MA, 1948, PhD (Univ. fellow), 1951; LHD, Brandeis U., 1987; DHL (hon.), Claremont Grad. Sch., 1991, Ripon Coll., 1996. Research asst. Columbia U., 1950-51; instr., asst. prof., assoc. prof., prof. Brandeis U., Waltham, Mass., 1951-70, first incumbent Earl Warren chair constl. history, 1957-70, dean Grad. Sch. Arts and Scis., 1958-63, dean faculty arts and scis., 1963-66; Andrew W. Mellon prof. humanities, history, chmn. grad. faculty history Claremont Grad. Sch., Calif., 1970-90, prof. emeritus Calif., 1990—2006; Disting. scholar in residence So. Oreg. State Coll., 1990—2000. Reiser lectr. U. Chgo. Law Sch., 1964; Gaspar Bacon lectr. Boston U., 1972; Elliott lectr. U. So. Calif. Law Sch., 1972; Hugo Black lectr. U. Ala., 1976; Bicentennial lectr., City of St. Louis, 1976; disting. lectr. U. Cin., 1978, U. Idaho, 1991. Author: The Law of the Commonwealth and Chief Justice Shaw, 1957, Legacy of Suppression: Freedom of Speech and Press in Early American History, 1960, Jefferson and Civil Liberties; The Darker Side, 1963, Origins of the Fifth Amendment: The Right Against Self-Incrimination, 1968 (Pulitzer Prize in history 1969)(reprinted with new preface, 1999), Judgments: Essays on American Constitutional History, 1972, Against The Law: The Nixon Court and Criminal Justice, 1974, Treason Against God: History of the Offense of Blasphemy, 1981, Emergence of a Free Press, 1985, Constitutional Opinions, 1986, The Establishment Clause: Religion and the First Amendment, 1986, Original Intent and the Framers' Constitution, 1988, Blasphemy: Verbal Offense Against the Sacred, from Moses to Salman Rushdie, 1993, Seasoned Judgments, 1994, A License to Steal: The Forfeiture of Property, 1996, Origins of the Bill of Rights, 1999, The Palladium of Justice, 1999, Ranters Run Amok, 1999, The Bill of Rights, 2004, The Fourth Amendment, 2004, Facets of Freedom, 2004, A Bookish Life, 2003; editor: Major Crises in American History, 1962, The American Political Process, 1963, The Presidency, 1964, The Congress, 1964, The Judiciary, 1964, Parties and Pressure Groups, 1964, Freedom of the Press from Zenger to Jefferson, 1966, American Constitutional Law, 1966, Judicial Review and the Supreme Court, 1967, Freedom and Reform, 1967, Essays on The Making of the Constitution, 1969, rev. edit. 1987, The Fourteenth Amendment and the Bill of Rights, 1970, The Supreme Court Under Earl Warren, 1972, Jim Crow in Boston, 1974, Essays on the Early Republic, 1974, Blasphemy in Massachusetts, 1974, The Framing and Ratification of the Constitution, 1987, The American Founding, 1988, American Constitutional History, 1989; co-editor: Ency. Am. Presidency, 4 vols., 1993; gen. editor: Am. Heritage Series, 60 vols., Harper Documentary History of Western Civilization, 40 vols.; editor-in-chief Ency. Am. Constn., 4 vols., 1986, supplement, 1991; gen. editor: Bicentennial History of the American Revolution; adv. bd.: Revs. in Am. History, John Marshall Papers, Salmon P. Chase Papers; contbr. articles to profl. jours. Mem. nat. bd. Commn. on Law and Social Action, Am. Jewish Congress; mem. U.S. Bicentennial Commn. Am. Revolution, 1966-68; mem. exec. council Inst. for Early Am. History and Culture; mem. nat. adv. council ACLU, Pulitzer prize juror, chmn. biog. jury, 1974, history jury, 1976. With AUS, 1943-46. Recipient Sigma Delta Chi prize for journalism history, 1961, 86, Frank Luther Mott prize Kappa Tau Alpha, 1961, Commonwealth Club prize for non-fiction, 1975, Oboler Meml. Prize of Am. Library Assn. for Intellectual Freedom, 1986, Cert. Merit ABA, 1986, Henry L. Mencken award Free Press Assn., 1986, Dartmouth Medal ALA, 1987, 95; Guggenheim fellow, 1957-58; Center For Study Liberty in Am. History fellow Harvard, 1961-62, Am. Bar Found. sr. merit fellow, 1973-74, Am. Coun. Learned Socs. fellow, 1973, NEH sr. fellow, 1974. Mem. Am. Hist. Assn. (Littleton-Griswold com. legal history), Orgn. Am. Historians, Am. Soc. Legal History (dir.), Am. Antiquarian Soc., Soc. Am. Historians, Inst. Early Am. History and Culture (exec. coun.), Mass. Hist. Soc., Kappa Delta Pi. Democrat. Died Aug. 24, 2006.

LEVY, S. WILLIAM, dermatologist, educator; b. San Francisco, Sept. 28, 1920; s. Joseph and Dora (Taylor) L.; m. Elisabeth Rellstab, Mar. 17, 1974; children: David Lewis, Ann Louise. BS, U. Calif., San Francisco, 1943, MD, 1949. Practice medicine specializing in dermatology, San Francisco; research dermatologist Biomechanics Lab., U. Calif., San Francisco; mem. staff Children's Hosp. of the Calif.-Pacific Med. Ctr., Mt. Zion Hosp. and Med. Center. Cons. to Letterman Army Hosp.; central med. adv. Calif. Blue Shield, San Francisco; clin. prof. dermatology U. Calif.; cons. in field. Author: Skin Problems of the Amputee, 1983; co-author: The Skin in Diabetes, 1986, Dermatology, 3rd edit., 1992, Dermatology in General Medicine, 5th edit., 1998, Atlas of Limb Prosthetics, 2d edit., 1992, 3d edit., 2004, Cutis, 1995, Biomechanics, 1999, In Motion-Amputee Coalition of America, 2000; lectr. on skin problems of amputees, skin problems of diabetics, landmines and effects on soc., 2001-03. Served with USN, 1943-46. Recipient Lehn and Fink Gold Medal award. Fellow Am. Acad. Dermatology (life, Gold medal); mem. San Francisco Dermatol. Soc. (pres.), Pacific Dermatologic Assn. (v.p.), AMA, Calif. Med. Assn. (sci. council 1977-84), San Francisco Med. Soc. Home: Kentfield, Calif. Died May 6, 2005.

LEWINE, SIDNEY, healthcare administration executive; b. Atlantic City, N.J., Mar. 31, 1915; s. Oscar and Yetta (Liberman) L.; m. Leanore Gittelman, Feb. 27, 1937 (dec. 1978); children: David, Mark, Barbara; m. Betty Marks, May 1980. BS, U. Pa., 1935, MA, 1936. Pers. worker govt., social agys. and industry, 1937-50; asst. dir. Mt. Sinai Hosp., Cleve., 1950-52, dir., 1952-77; dir. Ctr. for Urban Hosp. Am. Hosp. Assn., Chgo., 1978-80; lectr. Cleve. State U., 1983-87, vis. assoc. prof., 1987-91, exec. in residence, from 1991. Trustee U. Circle Inc., Cleve., 1981—; bd. dirs., exec. com. Health Sys. Agy. North Ctrl. Ohio, Cleve., 1988—; bd. dirs. Montefiore Home, Cleve., 1986—. Fellow Am. Coll. Health Care Execs. (life); mem. Am. Hosp. Assn. (life), Assn. Med. Colls. (Disting. Svc. Mem. 1981—), Greater Cleve. Hosp. Assn. (Disting. Svc. award 1992, Cleve. Med. Hall of Fame 1997). Home: Cleveland, Ohio. Died July 1, 2004.

LEWIS, ALBERT DALE MILTON, retired civil engineering educator; b. Paoli, Ind., May 20, 1920; s. Edward Hon and Josephine (Hancock) L.; m. Eleanora Gertrude Irons, Apr. 13, 1946; 1 child, Linda Lee Lewis Raney. BSCE, Purdue U., 1941, MSCE, 1951. Registered profl. engr., Ind. Field engr. The M.W. Kellogg Co., N.Y.C., 1941-44, 46-47, Gulf Oil Corp., Toledo and Cin., 1947-49; design engr. Standard Oil Co. Calif., San Francisco, 1952-54; instr. structural engring. Purdue U., West Lafayette, Ind., 1950-52, assoc. prof., 1954-85, prof. emeritus, from 1985. Chmn. com. on steel bridges Transp. Rsch. Bd., 1985-90. Contbr. articles to profl. jours. and procs. With USN, 1944-46. Fellow ASCE (chmn. com. on exptl. analysis and analogues 1965-67, com. on electronic computation 1977-80); mem. NSPE, Am. Concrete Inst., Am. Soc. for Engring. Edn., Soc. for Exptl. Mechanics, Assn. for Computing Machinery, Am. Ry. Engring. Assn. (chmn. com. on systems engring. 1982-84), Am. Radio Relay League, Ind. Soc. Profl. Engrs. (Ind. Engr. of Yr. award 1986), Full Gospel Bus. Men's Fellowship. Presbyterian. Avocations: amateur radio, personal computers. Home: West Lafayette, Ind. Died June 12, 2004.

LEWIS, CARL PHILLIP, medical research executive; b. Redondo Beach, Calif., June 18, 1934; s. Carl Potter and Ollie Elizabeth (Spears) L.; m. Litiana Tayaga Vuibureta, Oct. 8, 1971; children: Inia, Tina Maraia, Leilani Seniua. BS in Chemistry, UCLA, 1956; PhD in Analytical Chemistry, Stanford U., 1960; MD, Johns Hopkins U., 1970. Med. lic. Md. Fellow in clin. pharmacology Johns Hopkins U., 1968-70; instr. chemistry Stanford U., Palo Alto, Calif., 1959-61; chemist Olin Mathieson Corp., New Haven, 1961-63; clin. rsch. mgr. The Upjohn Co., Kalamazoo, Mich., 1970-75, 80-91; lectr. biochemistry Fiji Sch. Medicine, Suva, 1976-80; exec. dir. Bristol Myers Squibb, Wallingford, Conn., from 1992. Contbr. articles to profl. jours. Mem. AMA, Hawaiian Malacological Assn. Avocations: malacology, mineralogy, sailing, hiking, fishing. Home: Henderson, Nev. Died Feb. 6, 2005.

LEWIS, DAVID, lawyer, accountant; b. Bklyn., Aug. 15, 1929; s. George and Florence (Bierman) L.; m. Annette Greenberg, Sept. 27, 1955 (div. Feb. 1971); children: Lori E. Weiner, Gwen B. Simon; stepchildren: Stacy K. Semel, Marc S. Hanellin; m. Joan F. De Mov, Apr. 29, 1973. BBA, CCNY, 1950; JD, Bklyn. Law Sch., 1958. Bar: N.Y. 1966; CPA, N.Y. Staff acct. Ronis & Liebowitz, CPAs, Bklyn., 1949-51, A.L. Eolis & Co., CPAs, Joseph S. Herbert & Co., CPAs, N.Y.C., 1953-57, Abraham Polakoff, CPA, David Goodkind & Co., CPAs, N.Y.C., 1957-63; ptnr. Blumenkranz & Lewis, CPAs, N.Y.C., 1963-64, Auslander, Gordon & Lewis, CPAs, Mineola, N.Y., 1964-69, Wolinetz, Paskowitz & Co., CPAs, N.Y.C., 1969-73; pvt. practice acctg. N.Y.C., 1973-80; pvt. practice acctg. and law Ft. Lee, N.J., 1980-87; pvt. practice law and acctg. White Plains, N.Y., from 1987. With U.S. Army, 1951-53. Mem. AICPA, N.Y. State Soc. CPAs. Jewish. Avocations: travel, golf, book and art collecting, reading. Home: Long Beach, NY. Died Apr. 14, 2004.

LEWIS, DAVID PAUL, accountant, auditor; b. Erie, Pa., June 1, 1956; s. Norbert Ronald and Patricia (Anthony) L. BS in Acctg., Pa. State U., 1978; JD, Cleve. Marshall Coll. Law, 1987. CPA, Ohio; Bar: Ohio 1987. Internal auditor Roadway Express, Akron, Ohio, 1978-81, Broadview Savs. & Loan, Cleve., 1981-82, U.S. Truck Lines, Cleve., 1982-85; audit mgr. Nat. City Bank, Cleve., from 1986. Mem. Am. Inst. CPA's, Ohio Soc. CPA's, Cleve. Bar Assn., Ohio Bar Assn. Republican. Roman Catholic. Avocations: athletics, music, Italian food, Pa. State U. football. Home: Cuyahoga Falls, Ohio. Died June 3, 2005.

LEWIS, FLORENCE WIRSCHING, mathematics educator; b. Hoboken, N.J., Dec. 25, 1924; d. Otto Julius and Kathe Anna (Luedecke) Wirsching; m. Richard Lowell Lewis, June 17, 1951 (dec. Oct. 1974); children: Martha, Jonathan, Ruth, Paul. BA summa cum laude, Montclair State Coll., 1944; MA, Northwestern U., 1949. Instr. math. Purdue U., West Lafayette, Ind., 1946-51, 53-55; supt. Julian (Nebr.) Pub. Schs., 1951; tchr. Fitzgerald High sch., Detroit, 1952; instr. algebra An Indsl. Corp., Benton Harbor, Mich., 1957-58; tchr. St. Joseph (Mich.) High Sch., 1962-63; instr. Lake Mich. Coll., Benton Harbor, 1963-66; pvt. tutor South Bend, Ind., from 1978; pvt. math. tutor, from 1978. Cons. South Bend Sch. Corp., 1986; tchr. Ind. Univ. South Bend, Ind., 1993. Pres. Stevensville (Mich.) Elem. Sch. PTA, 1957-58. Tuition scholar Montclair State Coll., 1942-44, grad. scholar Northwestern U., 1945; NSF fellow Vanderbilt U., 1966. Mem. AAUW (chmn. excellence in edn. study group), Pi Mu Epsilon, Sigma Delta Epsilon (nat. treas. 1952-53). Lutheran. Avocations: bibycling, swimming. Died Apr. 20, 2004.

LEWIS, GOLDY SARAH, real estate developer, executive; b. West Selkirk, Man., Can., June 15, 1921; d. David and Rose (Dwor) Kimmel; m. Ralph Milton Lewis, June 12, 1941; children: Richard Alan, Robert Edward, Roger Gordon, Randall Wayne. BS, UCLA, 1943; postgrad., U. So. Calif., 1944-45. Pvt. practice acctg., L.A., 1945-57; law office mgr., 1953-55; dir., exec. v.p. Lewis Homes, Upland, Calif., from 1955, Lewis Construction Co. Inc., Upland, from 1959, Lewis Bldg. Co., Inc., Las Vegas, from 1960, Republic Sales Co., Inc., from 1956, Kimmel Enterprises, Inc., from 1959; mng. partner Lewis Homes of Calif., from 1973; mng. ptnr. Lewis Homes of Nev., from 1972, Western Properties, from 1972, Foothill Investment Co., from 1971, Republic Mgmt. Co., from 1978. Contbr. articles to mags., jours. Mem. Dean's Coun. UCLA Grad. Sch. Architecture and Urban Planning; mem. UCLA Found., Chancellor's Assocs.; endowed Ralph and Goldy Lewis Ctr. for Regional Policy at UCLA, 1989, Ralph and Goldy Lewis Hall of Planning and Devel. at U. S.C., 1989, others. Co-recipient Builder of Yr. award, Profl. Builder Mag., 1988, Housing Person of Yr. award, Nat. Housing Conf., 1990, Entrepreneur of Yr. award, Inland Empire, 1990; named Ralph and Goldy Lewis Sports Ctr. in their honor, City of Rancho Cucamonga, 1988, also several other parks and sports fields including Lewis Park in Claremont; named one of Women of Yr., Calif. 25th Senate Dist., 1989, (with husband Ralph M. Lewis) Disting. CEO, Calif. State U., San Bernadino, 1991, Mgmt. Leaders of the Yr., Univ. Calif., Riverside, 1993; recipient 1st award of distinction, Am. Builder mag., 1963, Homer Briggs Svc. to Youth award, West End YMCA, 1990, Spirit of Life award, City of Hope, 1993, Builder of Century award, Bldg. Industry Assn., Baldy View chpt., 1999. Mem. Nat. Assn. Home Builders, Bldg. Industry Assn. So. Calif. (Builder of Yr. award Baldy View chpt. 1988), Internat. Coun. Shopping Ctrs., Urban Land Inst. Home: Claremont, Calif. Died 2006.

LEWIS, JOSEPH MARTIN, infosystems specialist; b. Cin., Feb. 6, 1924; s. Joseph J. and Sophia (Peters) L.; m. Mary Ruth Obryan; children: Robert J., Patrick F., Bryan M., Kathleen, Michelle. BS, U. Cin., 1948. Data processing mgr. Kroger Co., Cin., 1960-59; cons. Pullman Inc., Chgo., 1959-61; data processing mgr. Thiokol Chem., Brigham City, Utah, 1961-62; data processing cons. Gen. Electric, Schenectady, N.Y., 1963-65; corp. dir. Atlas Chem. Ind., Wilmington, Del., 1965-66; mgmt. infosystems mgr. City and County of Denver, from 1966. Pres. GMIS, Denver, 1979-80, 85-86; bus. advisor computer tng. for handicapped Community Coll. of Denver, 1979—. Advisor Emily Griffith Opportunity Sch., Denver, 1980-86. Named Employee of Yr. Gen. Electric, 1964. Avocation: handcrafts. Home: Plano, Tex. Died Dec. 16, 2004.

LEWIS, LAURA HESTER SHEPHERD, clinical psychologist, consultant; b. Rulo, Nebr., Nov. 18, 1921; d. Ernest Charles and Marian Eloise (Cook) Shepherd; divorced, 1978; 1 child, Ellen Lewis Anderson. RN, N.E. Meth. Hosp., Omaha, 1942; BS, Nebr. Wesleyan U., 1959; PhD, U. Nebr., 1967. Lic. psychologist, Nebr., N.Mex.; diplomate Am. Bd. Profl. Psychology. Asst. staff psychologist U. Nebr. Psychol. Clinic, Lincoln, 1961-64; from asst. clin. psychologist to staff psychologist Lincoln State Hosp., 1964-65; intern Nebr. Psychiatric Inst., Omaha, 1964-65; practicum supr. field placement child psychiatry fellows and residents Lincoln Regional Ctr. Nebr. Psychiat. Inst., Omaha, 1966-67; dir. training for paraprofessionals children's and adolescent psychiat. unit Lincoln Regional Ctr., Nebr., 1966-70; psychology practicum supr. dept. psychology U. Nebr., Spring 1967; coord. clin. svcs. children's/adolescent psychiat. unit Lincoln Regional Ctr., 1966-69, acting dir., 1969-70; dir. inpatient psychiatric svcs. Children's Meml. Hosp., Chgo., 1972-74, dir. tng. psychology divsn. of child psychiatry, 1970-74; asst. prof. clin. psychiatry & pediatrics Northwestern U. Med. Sch., Chgo., 1973-74; dir. Harbor City (Calif.) Outpatient Clinic, 1974-78; clin. adminstr., clin. child psychologist So. Calif. Permanente Med. Group-Kaiser Divsn., Lomita, 1974-78; pvt. practice, cons. Calif., 1978-92, Las Vegas, N.Mex., 1992-94; contract instr. Calif. Sch. Profl. Psychology, L.A., 1978-79; instr. clin. psychology Calif. State U., Dominguez Hills, Spring 1978; asst. clinical prof. dept. psychiatry L.A. Harbor Gen. Hosp. L.A. Harbor-UCLA Sch. Medicine, Torrance, Calif., 1980-89; clinical prof. psychology Fuller Theol. Sem., Pasedena, Calif., 1981; pvt. practice N.Mex., 1993-94; mem. med. staff Northeastern Regional Hosp., from 1994. Vis. lectr. psychology Nebr. Wesleyan U., Lincoln, 1969-70; cons. telephone hot line, Village of Oak Park, Ill., 1974, UCLA Sch. Medicine, 1976, Rivera Hall, Redondo Beach, Calif., 1978, Rehab. Svcs., Bay Harbor Hosp., Harbor City, Calif., 1993, Project for Prevention of Sexual Abuse of Presch. Children, Children's Svcs. Dept. Psychiatry, Harbor-UCLA Sch. Medicine, Torrance, 1993; bd. dirs. Harbor View House, San Pedro, Calif.; delegate People-to-People Program, People's Rep. of China, 1989, USSR, 1991; speaker presentations and seminars at hospitals, religious centers, corps., 1973-91; cons. adminstrn. Northeastern Regional Hosp., 1994—. Author: (with others) Group Therapy with Children and Adolescents: A Treatment Manual, 1985; contbr. articles to profl. jours. Mem. Nebr. Little White House Conf. on Children and Youth, 1968; mem. health svcs. task force Village of Oak Park, Ill., 1974. 1st lt. U.S. Army Nurse Corps, 1942-45, PTO. Fellow Acad. Clin. Psychology; mem. APA (divsn. 12, sect. 1), Soc. Personality Assessment, N.Mex. Psychol. Assn., Nebr. Psychol. Assn. (com. legis. affairs and profl. relationships 1969), Sigma Xi. Democrat. Methodist. Avocations: birding, fishing, hiking, rock hounding, reading. Home: Las Vegas, N.Mex. Died Feb. 5, 2005.

LEWIS, NORMAN, retired English language educator, writer; b. N.Y.C., Dec. 30, 1912; s. Herman and Deborah (Nevins) L.; m. Mary Goldstein, July 28, 1934; children—Margery, Debra BA, CUNY, 1939; MA, Columbia U., 1941. Instr., lectr CUNY, N.Y.C., 1943-52; assoc. prof. English NYU, N.Y.C., 1955-64; instr. Compton Coll., Calif., summers 1962-64, UCLA, 1962-69; prof. English Rio Hondo Coll., Whittier, Calif., 1964-91, chmn. communications dept., 1964-75. Author: (with others) Journeys Through Wordland, 1941, Lessons in Vocabulary and Spelling, 1941, (with Wilfred Funk) Thirty Days to a More Powerful Vocabulary, 1942, rev. edit., 1970, Power with Words, 1943, How to Read Better and Faster, 1944, rev. edit., 1978, The Lewis English Refresher and Vocabulary Builder, 1945, How to Speak Better English, 1948, Word Power Made Easy, 1949, rev. edit., 1978, The Rapid Vocabulary Builder, 1951, rev. edit., 1980, 3d edit., 1988, How to Get More Out of Your Reading, 1951, Twenty Days to Better Spelling, 1953, The Comprehensive Word Guide, 1958, Dictionary of Correct Spelling, 1962, Correct Spelling Made Easy, 1963, rev. edit. 1987, Dictionary of Modern Pronunciation, 1963, New Guide to Word Power, 1963, The New Power with Words, 1964, Thirty Days to Better English, 1964, The Modern Thesaurus of Synonyms, 1965, RSVP-Reading, Spelling, Vocabulary, Pronunciation (books I-III), 1966, 77, See, Say, and Write! (books I and II), 1973, Instant Spelling Power, 1976, R.S.V.P. for College English Power (books I-III), 1977-79, R.S.V.P. with Etymology (books I and II), 1980-81, Instant Word Power, 1980, New American Dictionary of Good English, 1987; editor: New Roget's Thesaurus of the English Language in Dictionary Form, 1961; also numerous articles in nat. mags. Died Sept. 8, 2006.

LEWIS, PATRICIA MARIE, critical care nurse, educator; b. Jamaica, N.Y., July 17, 1946; d. Philip Patrick and Caroline (Stubben) Clarke; children: Catherine A., Marie A. BSN, Niagara U., 1968; MS, U. Rochester, from 1996. CCRN; cert. ANCC acute care nurse practitioner, ACLS. Staff nurse med. ICU, critical care unit North Shore Hosp., Manhasset, N.Y., 1968-69; staff nurse med. ICU, surg. ICU, CCU Strong Meml. Hosp., Rochester, N.Y., 1969-70, Rochester Gen. Hosp., 1973-77, staff nurse med. ICU, CCU, 1977-78, team coord. med. ICU, 1977-79, nurse mgr. med. ICU, CCU, 1981-90, critical care educator, 1990-94, project nurse medicine, 1994-96, nurse practitioner, stroke care unit, from 1997. Lectr. CCRN certification rev. course AACN, 1991—; lectr. Ohio State U. Critical Care Nursing Conf., 1997, state conf. N.Y. State Post-Anesthesia Nurses Assn., 1994; presenter poster Practice Partnerships in Critical Care Partnerships in Health Care Symposium, U. Rochester, 1992; lectr. RN refresher course Roberts Wesleyan Coll., 1994; preceptor U. Rochester, nurse practitioner program, 1996-98. Rochester Gen. Hosp. grantee, 1994-95. Mem. AACN (pres. Greater Rochester area Finger Lakes chpt. 1993-94, bd. dirs. 1992-95), Sigma Theta Tau, Internat. Honor Soc. (Xi Episolon chap.). Avocation: photography. Home: Webster, NY. Died May 28, 2005.

LEWIS, WILLIAM HAROLD, bank executive; b. Mena, Ark., Jan. 25, 1937; s. Charles Allen and Nellie Mae (Robison) L.; m. Lillian Elaine Maracle, Apr. 9, 1960; children: Kellie Deanne, Jonathan William. Student, Syracuse U., 1966-68, U. Wis., 1968-70. Asst. comptroller Mchts. Nat. Bank, Syracuse, N.Y., 1963-72; corp. planning officer United Carolina Bank, Whiteville, N.C., from 1972. Cons., instr. Ind. Bankers Ga., Atlanta, 1980, N.C. Savs. Guaranty Corp., Raleigh, 1982-83. Treas. Rescue Mission Alliance, Syracuse, 1968-72; trustee Columbus Pvt. Schs. Inc., Whiteville, 1974-80. Served with USAF, 1959-63. Mem. Bank Adminstrn. Inst. (v.p. Eastern N.C. chpt. 1977-78, pres. 1978-79, state dir. nat. office 1980-82, regional dir. 1982-84). Home: Whiteville, NC. Died Jan. 23, 2005.

LEYSE, CARL FERDINAND, nuclear engineer; b. Kewaunee, Wis., Feb. 11, 1917; s. Henry and Emilie (Duescher) L.; m. Rhodora Adeline Stearns, Sept. 7, 1946; children: Karen Elizabeth, Dale Robert. BS in Mech. Engring., U. Wis., 1948; postgrad., Ill. Inst. Tech., 1949-50. Nuclear design engr. Argonne (Ill.) Nat. Lab., 1948-51; chief reactor projects engring. sect. Nat. Reactor Testing Sta., Idaho Falls, 1951-56; tech. dir., pres. Internuclear Co., Clayton, Mo., 1956-59, 61-63; mgr. nuclear sci. and engring. dept. Curtiss-Wright Corp., Quehanna, Pa., 1959-60; mgr. nuclear safety Aerojet Nuclear Systems Co., Sacramento, 1963-72; mgr. internal rsch. and dir. programs Idaho Nat. Engring. Lab., Idaho Falls, 1972-84; cons. Idaho Falls, from 1985. Contbr. papers to profl. jours. Master sgt. USAF, 1942-45. Mem. Am. Nuclear Soc., AIAA, Nat. Space Soc. Republican. Achievements include patents for radial flow nuclear thermal rocket, engineering test reactor, food irradiation reactor, high flux reactor, flux trap research and testing nuclear reactor. Died Nov. 24, 2004.

LI, LILIA HUIYING, journalist; b. Hunan, China, June 14, 1932; d. Chun-chu and Sol-ran (Chang) Li.; m. Ma Luk Son, May 18, 1953 (dec. Feb. 1963); 1 child, Blanche; m. George Oakley Totten III, July 1, 1976; children: Vicken Yuriko, Linnea Catherine. MA (equivalent grad. study), Hong Kong U., 1958. Mng. dir. Oriental Evening News, Hong Kong, Midday News, Hong Kong, Tsuwan Daily News, Hong Kong, 1958—68; gen. mgr. Angelican Ch. Guest House, Hong Kong, 1962-68; spl. corr. UN, N.Y.C., 1975; dir. L.A. br. The Mirror Monthly, Hong Kong, from 1988, The Depingxian Montly, Hong Kong, from 1998. Leader delegation of Hong Kong Businesswomen to Conf. on Commerce, Beijing, 1956; speaker First Internat. Women's Conf., Mexico City, 1975; organizer Internat. Women's

Year Arts Festival, N.Y.c., 1975-77; vis. lectr. East Asian Studies Ctr. U. So. Calif., L.A., 1976, fellow, 1976—; invited participant Soc. for the Promotion of Chinese Cultural Unity, Taiwan, 1995, Kunming, China, 1999, ceremonies at Hand Over of Hong Kong to People's Republic of China, 1997; founder, pres. China Seminar-forum for peace across the Taiwan straits, 1985-2004, a forum for good rels. across the Taiwan straits, 1991-2004. Author: Unforgettable Journey, 1957, Nine Women and Other Writings, 1959, Li Huiying's Writings, 1979, Sidelights on World Affairs, 1985, Expanded Edition of Collected Writings, 1988, Farewell 20th Century!, 2001, revised edit. 2004; contbr. numerous articles to periodicals. Mem. China Soc. People's Friendship Studies, Beijing, Chinese Am. Alliance in Am. for China's Peaceful Reunification, Chgo., 2002, (pres.); mem. St. John's Episcopal Ch., L.A., L.A.-Guangzhou Sister City Assn. Designated Outstanding Bus. Woman in Hong Kong by South China Morning Post, 1962, Peace ambassador St. John's Episcopal Ch., L.A., 2003; recipient of award. from US China People's Friendship Assn., 1981; award. from The L.A. Guangzhou Sister City Assn., 1984; made First Hon. Reporter, Xinmin Evening News, Shanghai, 1999, recipient of plaque for 27 years of svc., East Asian Studies Cmty., Los Angeles, 2003. Mem. Asian-Am. Journalists Assn., Assn. for Asian Studies. Avocations: photography, calligraphy, gardening, flower arrangement, interior decorating. Died Nov. 7, 2004.

LIBONE, JOYCE MARIE, nurse; b. Bridgeport, Conn., Sept. 13, 1927; d. George Robert and Margaret M. (Gaffney) Roland; m. Donato D. Libone, Jan. 29, 1949; children: John J., Ralph D. Diploma St. Vincent's Hosp., 1948. Oper. rm. supr. Mary Shiels Hosp., Dallas, 1949-51, Community Hosp., Dallas, 1970-73; pediatrics nurse Dr. Piranio, Dallas, 1951-54; orthopedic nurse, asst. supr. St. Paul's Hosp., Dallas, 1973-78; oper. rm. nurse Morton Hosp., Dallas, 1978-81; med. reviewer Blue Cross Blue Shield Ins., Dallas, 1983-86; utilization coord. and discharge planner Labouré Care Ctr., Dallas, 1986—; nurse liaison Family Practice Physicians, Southwestern Med. Sch. and St. Pauls Hosp., 1986-90. Vol. nurse Cath. Sch. System. Mem. Oper. Rm. Nurses Assn. Roman Catholic. Clubs: Cath. Daughters Am. (1st vice regent), Alhambra (sec.-treas.). Home: Dallas, Tex. Died July 7, 2005.

LIBOWITZ, GEORGE GOTTHART, materials science consultant; b. Bklyn., June 18, 1923; s. Simon Libowitz and Blanche (Rosenberger) Libowitz Greenbaum; m. Mildred Appel, June 11, 1949 (dec. 1982); children: Skona Brittain, Steven M. BA in Chemistry, Bklyn. Coll., 1945, MA in Chemistry, 1950; PhD in Chemistry, Cornell U., 1954. Rsch. assoc. chemistry dept. Tufts U., Medford, Mass., 1954-57; sect. leader solid state chemistry Atomics Internat. div. NAA, Canoga Park, Calif., 1957-61; head crystal defects sect. Aerospace Corp., El Segundo, Calif., 1961-63; staff scientist Ledgemont Lab. Kennecott Corp., Lexington, Mass., 1963-73; mgr. solid state chemistry Allied Corp., Morristown, N.J., 1973-80; sr. scientist Allied-Signal Corp., Morristown, 1980-86; pres. G. G. Libowitz, Inc., Morristown, from 1986. Mem. adv. com. U.S. ERDA Nat. Workshop, 1977; mem. internat. steering com. Metal Hydride Symposia, world wide, 1980-92; chmn. Gordon Rsch. Conf., Tilton, N.H., 1983; cons. Brookhaven Nat. Lab., Upton, 1982-83. Author: Solid State Chemistry of Binary Metal Hydrides, 1965; editor: Metal Hydrides, 1968, Materials Science in Energy Technology, 1979; assoc. editor Solid State Ionic Jour., 1980-85, Materials Letters Jour., 1982-88; contbr. over 70 articles to sci. jours.; editorial adv. bd. Jour. Solid State Chemistry, 1967-88, Jour. of Less-Common Metals, Lausanne, Switzerland, 1982-90. Fellow Am. Phys. Soc.; mem. Am. Chem. Soc., N.Y. Acad. Sci., Soc. Sigma Xi. Jewish. Achievements include patents in applications of metal hydrides; introduced use of lattice defect theory to study of metal hydrides; first to characterize hydrides of intermetallic compounds; growth of first single crystal of a metal hydride; first to propose use of metal hydrides for heat storage; initiation of first program on interaction of hydrogen with metallic glass alloys. Home: Morristown, NJ. Died Mar. 25, 2005.

LIDDLE, NANCY HYATT, retired museum director; b. Martinsville, Ind., Aug. 27, 1931; d. Ralph Romeo and Gladys Cain Hyatt; m. Charles M. Liddle III, Sept. 17, 1955; children: Christopher, Matthew, Sara. AB, Ind. U., 1953. Co-dir. 327 Gallery, Albany, N.Y., 1960-65; art critic Knickerbocker News, Albany, 1965-67; asst. dir. U. Art Gallery, SUNY, Albany, 1967-77, dir., 1977-92. V.p. Coun. of SUNY Exhbn. Dirs., 1981—87, 1994—2002; bd. dirs. Albany Inst. of History and Art. Curator, dir. various exhibits. Bd. dirs. Historic Albany Found., 1973-76, Albany Acad. for Girls, 1980-91, Upper Hudson Planned Parenthood, Albany, 1992-98; com. mem. Mayor's Strategic Planning for Arts, Albany, 1990. Mem. Cosmopolitan Club (N.Y.), Fort Orange Club (Albany). Home: Albany, NY. Died Apr. 16, 2004.

LIEBERMAN, ALVIN, manufacturing executive; b. Chgo., June 14, 1921; s. Louis and Jennie (Kuznetsky) L.; m. Tillie Bess Lavin, Aug. 24, 1947; children: Gary M., Harold A. BA, Cen. YMCA, Chgo., 1942; BS in Chem. Engring., Ill. Inst. Tech., 1948, MS in Chem. Engring., 1949. Research assoc. Alfred (N.Y.) U., 1949-51; mgr. engring. section IIT Rsch. Inst., Chgo., 1951-68; research and devel. dir. Royco Instruments, Menlo Park, Calif., 1968-83; tech. specialist Particle Measuring Systems, Boulder, Colo., 1983-85 and from 87; chief scientist HIAC div. Royco Instrument, Menlo Park, 1985-87. Cons., Menlo Park, 1968—. Contbr. articles to profl. jours. Served with U.S. Army, 1942-45, PTO. Mem. Am. Chem. Soc., Am. Inst. Chem. Engrs., Inst. Environ. Sci. (Whitfield award 1985), Fine Particle Soc. (pres. 1977-78, Hausner award 1983, regional editor Powder Tech.), Sigma Xi. Avocation: classical music. Home: Mountain View, Calif. Died Jan. 13, 2005.

LIEBERMAN, MILTON, food distribution company executive; b. N.Y.C., Nov. 20, 1921; s. Samuel and Dora (Miller) L.; m. Charlotte Kahn, Jan. 23, 1943; children: Mona Elayne Lieberman Levine, Jay Ira. BS, NYU, 1943. Office mgr. Liebmor Dairy Co., N.Y.C., 1942-54, ptnr., 1954-60; pres., chief exec. officer Liebmor Foods, Inc., N.Y.C., 1960-65, Dynamic Food Distbrs., Inc., N.Y.C., 1965-73; mgr. Jet Food Products, Garfield, N.J., 1973-77; pres., chief exec. officer New Amsterdam Cheese Corp., N.Y.C., 1977-82; sales mgr. Ruby Nash Distbrs., Inc., N.Y.C., from 1982. Mem.: B'nai B'rith (treas. 1968—). Jewish. Avocation: building and repairing household items. Home: Delray Beach, Fla. Died May 7, 2005.

LIEBMAN, SHIRLEY ANNE, analytical research scientist; b. Boston, Sept. 4, 1934; d. John A. and Fay Glazier; m. Harmon L. Liebman, June 23, 1956; children: Robert C., David J. BS, Northeastern U., Boston, 1956; PhD, Temple U., Phila., 1969. Lab. technician MIT, 1953-55; jr. engr. Boeing Co., Seattle, 1956-58; rsch. chemist Monsanto Rsch. Corp., Everett, Mass., 1958-61; sr. rsch. scientist Armstrong World Ind., Lancaster, Pa., 1969-80; mgr. application and contract rsch. Chem. Data Systems, Oxford, Pa., 1980-83; sr. assoc. NRC-Ballistic Rsch. Lab., Aberdeen, Md., 1984-86; sr. scientist Geo-Ctrs., Inc., Aberdeen, 1986-91; v.p., dir. contract rsch. and applications CCS Instrument Systems, West Grove, Pa., 1991-93. Sr. adv. bd. Environ. Rsch. Ctr., U. Nev., Las Vegas, 1990-95; cons. Computer Chem. Sys., Inc., Avondale, Pa., 1986-91, The CECON Group, Inc., Wilmington, Del., 1991—; founder and v.p. LL Sci. & Tech. Alliance, Inc., 1995-96; exec. Internat. Exec. Svc. Corps, 1995—; bd. Army Sci. and Tech., 2001—. Co-editor: Pyrolysis and GC in Polymer Analysis, 1985; contbr. over 170 articles to profl. jours., chpts. to books. Citizens adv. coun. Lancaster Housing and Redevel. Authority, 1986—. Mem. AAAS, Am. Chem. Soc., Soc. for Applied Spectroscopy, Royal Soc. Chemistry (London). Republican. Unitarian Universalist. Achievements include patents in field; research in major disciplines of physical/analytical organic chemistry, chemical engineering and computers, polymer characterization, materials and environmental sciences, and the integrated intelligent instrument approach to analytical sciences. Home: Holtwood, Pa. Died Jan. 7, 2004.

LIEBOW, JOANNE ELISABETH, poet and freelance publicist; b. Cleve., May 15, 1926; d. Arnold S. and Rhea Eunice (Levy) King; m. Irving M. Liebow, June 30, 1947 (div. Jan. 1972); children: Katherine Ann Liebow Frank, Peter. Student, Smith Coll., 1944-47; BA, Case Western Res. U., 1948. Cleve. reporter Fairchild Publs., N.Y.C., 1950-51; pub. info. specialist, mktg. comms. coord. Cuyahoga C.C., Cleve., 1979-99. Founder, pres. Mt. Sinai Jr. Women's Aux., Cleve., 1948-50; pres. PTA, Bryden Elem. Sch., Beachwood, Ohio, 1964; bd. dirs., pres. Beachwood Bd. Edn., 1968-76. Recipient Exceptional Achievement award Coun. for Advancement of Edn., 1982, Citation award, 1982, Grand prize, 1983, Cleve. Communicator's award Women in Comms. Inc., 1982; Sophia Smith scholar Smith Coll., 1946. Home: San Jose, Calif. Died May 3, 2004.

LIEBZEIT, MERLIN ELROY, restaurant franchise owner; b. Plymouth, Wis., Nov. 10, 1920; s. Henry Gottleib and Ella (Dassow) L.; m. Erna Julia Holdorf, Nov. 26, 1941; children: Larry, Beverly, Dennis (dec.), Betty, Steven. Owner Dairy Queen Prodn. Co., Hilbert, Wis., 1940-57, Dairy Queen, Appleton, Wis., from 1950, Merlin's Coupon Magic, from 1981. Served with U.S. Army, 1944-46, ETO. Mem. Internat. Fedn. of Dairy Queen Store Owners (pres. 1971-77, 79), Wis. Dairy Queen Store Owners Assn. (pres. 1971-76). Republican. Lutheran. Avocations: world travel, photography. Died Apr. 18, 2005.

LIGETI, GYORGY SANDOR, composer; b. Dicsoszentmarton, Romania, May 28, 1923; s. Sandor Ligeti and Ilona Somogyi; m. Vera Spitz, 1957; 1 child. Student Budapest Acad. Music, 1945-49. Tchr., Budapest Acad. Music, 1950-56; guest prof. Stockholm Acad. Music, 1961-71; composer-in-residence Stanford U., Calif., 1972; with Electronic Studios, Cologne, Fed. Republic Germany, 1957-59; prof. composition, Hamburg Music Acad., 1973-89. Composer: numerous orchestral and instrumental pieces, including: String Quartet #2, 1968, Melodien, 1971, Monument, Selbstportrait, 1976, Le Grand Macabre, 1977, Trio, 1982, Piano Concerto, 1988. 9 Piano Etudes, 1985-89, Nonsense Madrigals for 6 singers, 1988, others. Recipient Grawemeyer award U. Louisville, 1986, Wolf prize in arts (music) Wolf Found., Israel, 1994/5. Home: Vienna, Austria. Died June 12, 2006.

LILLARD, LOUISE DAVIS, lawyer; b. St. Louis, Mar. 4, 1919; d. Louis Ensenore and Maude Adele (Clamorgan) D.; m. Laurence E. Dunn, Dec. 25, 1941 (div. 1948); m. Richard G. Lillard, Aug. 27, 1949; 1 child, Monique. AB, UCLA, 1940, MA, 1941, JD, 1985. Bar: Calif. 1985; cert. tchr., Calif. Tchr. French Beverly Hills (Calif.) High Sch., 1941-76; supr. student tchrs. in fgn. langs. Calif. State U., Northridge, 1969-82; assoc. Law Offices Christopher Dieterich, Santa Monica, Calif., 1985—2005; freelance writer, editor L.A., 1976—2005. Co-author French textbook: L'Hexagone, c'est la France, 1983; contbr. articles to various publs. Mem. ABA, Calif. Bar Assn., Am. Assn. Tchrs. of French, Phi Beta Kappa. Democrat. Died July 17, 2005.

LIMMER, EZEKIEL, retired federal agency administrator, economist; b. Galatz, Romania, May 1, 1912; came to U.S., 1920; s. Morris Solomon and Peppy (Ernowitz) L.; m. Evelyn Ifshin, Aug. 10, 1947; children: Beverly Limmer Greenberg, Leslie Sue Limmer. AB, Brown U., 1933; MA, Columbia U., 1934; PhD, Am. U., Washington, 1942. Statistician ICC, Washington, 1935-38; economist U.S. Dept. Agr., Washington, 1938-42, 48-51; statistician War Assets Adminstrn., Washington, 1946-48, Office of Salary & Stabilization, Washington, 1951-53; chief domestic cargo rates sect. Civil Aeronautics Bd., Washington, 1956-80; ret., from 1980. Lectr. Am. U., Washington, 1948-59, U. Md., Washington, 1965-77. Author: Agricultural Exemptions From Motor Carrier Regulation, 1941; author numerous reports. Trustee United Jewish Appeal, Washington, 1970-71. Capt. U.S. Army Transp. Corps, 1942-46, ETO Mem. Bnai Brith (trustee 1962-65, v.p. Silver Springs, Md. chpt. 1980-85), Phi Beta Kappa. Democrat. Jewish. Avocation: bridge. Home: Coconut Creek, Fla. Died Aug. 3, 2004.

LINCOLN, EUGENE, religious organization executive; b. Marion, Ind., Oct. 5, 1923; s. Albert and Glenora Agnes (Townsend) L.; m. Darlene Jacqueline Boatwright, July 4, 1947; children: David Lee, Michael Eugene, Angelita Karolene, Jonathan Wayne. BS, Marion Coll., 1948; MA, Andrews U., 1973. Credentialed missionary Seventh-day Adventists, 1979. Editor The Sabbath Sentinel, Fairview, Okla., 1960-85; copy editor Rev. and Herald Pub. Assn., Hagerstown, Md., 1974-89; lst v.p. Bible Sabbath Assn., Fairview, 1976-88, pres., from 1988. Bd. dirs., mem. adv. bd. Seventh-day Adventist Missionary Found., Phoenix, 1980—. Author: Right Face, 1976, The High Cost of Loving, 1979, Understanding the Power of Prayer, 1984; contbr. articles to various pbuls. Democrat. Home: Hagerstown, Md. Died July 17, 2004.

LINDBLOOM, KENNETH DEAN, investment company executive; b. Denver, Sept. 26, 1946; s. Edward Monroe and Priscilla (Johnson) L.; m. Sherrilee Graham, Dec. 27, 1967; children: Ken, Stephanie, Edward, Shelley, Sara, Sydney, Robert, Stacy. BS, Met. State Coll., Denver, 1972; MS, So. Oreg. State U., 1987. Various law enforcement positions, 1968-76; dir. security Aurora (Colo.) Pub. Schs., 1976-78; investment exec. Shearson Am. Express, Medford, Oreg., 1979-80, Edward D. Jones, Medford, 1980-85; br. mgr., v.p. investments AG Edwards & Sons, Medford, from 1985. Bd. dirs. Oreg. Health Edn. and Cultural Facilities Authority, Portland, 1990—, So. Oreg. Drug Awarness, Medford, 1990—, Medford Sch. Dist., 1986—, So. Oreg. Regional Svcs. Inst., Medford, 1982—, Medford Civic Theater, 1982-85, Hosp. Facilities Authority, Medford, 1983-87; gov. Oreg. Sch. Study Coun., Eugene, 1987—; mem. budget com. City of Medford, 1983-87; mem., coord. Citizens for a Safe Jackson County, Medford, 1989-90. Mem. C. of C., Mensa, Rotary (dir. Bear Creek Valley chpt. 1987—). Republican. Mem. Lds Ch. Home: Medford, Oreg. Died May 26, 2004.

LINDEN, LYNETTE LOIS, bioelectrical engineer; b. Cheyenne, Wyo., Feb. 5, 1951; d. Byron Nels and Mary Ann (Savage) L. BA with honors, U. Calif., Santa Cruz, 1972; MS, MIT, 1974, PhD, 1988. Asst. engr. Burroughs Corp., Pasadena, Calif., 1969-70, engr., cons. La Jolla, Calif., 1971-73; teaching asst. U. Calif., Santa Cruz, 1974-76, MIT, Cambridge, Mass., 1973-75, tutor, 1976-79; engr. Lincoln Labs., Lexington, Mass., 1979-80; asst. prof. engring. Boston U., from 1980; ind. rsch. sci. Watertown, Mass., from 1990. Contbr. articles to profl. jours. Mem. AAAS, Am. Chem. Soc., N.Y. Acad. Scis., Soc. Women Engrs., Sigma Xi. Achievements include research in dimensionality constraints on color perception, application of group theory to computational models of neurons, visual perception, sensory systems, living systems, and biophysics of sensory systems. Analos design of dechmir circuits for arithmetic communication, and sensor processing of signals. Died Apr. 21, 2004.

LINDER, STU (STEWART BRIDGEWATER LINDER), film editor; b. Geneva, Il, Nov. 8, 1931; m. Cathy Fitzgerald, 1981; children: Stewart, Raymond. Student, Pepperdine U. Editor: (films) Grand Prix, 1966, Blue, 1968, The Fortune, 1975, (with Susan Martin) First Family, 1980, My Bodyguard, 1980, Six Weeks, 1982, Diner, 1982, The Natural, 1984, Young Sherlock Holmes, 1985, Code Name: Emerald, 1985, Good Morning, Vietnam, 1987, Tin Men, 1987, Rain Man, 1988 (Academy award nomination for best film editing 1988), Avalon, 1990, Bugsy, 1991, Toys, 1992, Quiz Show, 1994, Disclosure, 1994, Slepers, 1996, Wag the Dog, 1997, Sphere, 1998, Libert Heights, 1999, An Everlasting Piece, 2000, Bandits, 2001, Envy, 2004. Served in U.S. Army. Died Jan. 12, 2006.

LINDO, J. TREVOR, psychiatrist, consultant; b. Boston, Feb. 12, 1925; s. Edwin and Ruby Ianty (Peterson) L.; m. Thelma Elaine Thompson, Sept. 22, 1962. BA, NYU, 1946; cert. in pre-clin. studies, U. Freibourg, Switzerland, 1953; MD, U. Lausanne, Switzerland, 1957. Lic. psychiatrist, N.Y., Conn. Clin. instr. Columbia U., N.Y.C., 1965-75, asst. clin. prof., 1975-82, assoc. clin. prof., 1982-85; attending psychiatrist Bedford-Stuyvesant Cmty. Mental Health Clinic, Bklyn., 1976-86, med. dir., from 1986. Attending psychiatrist Harlem Hosp. Ctr., N.Y.C., 1964-75; vis. psychiatrist Interfaith Hosp., Bklyn., 1976-85; psychiat. cons. Bklyn. Bur. Cmty. Svc., 1980, Marcus Garvey Manor, Bklyn., 1982-86; candidate Nat. Bd. Forensic Examiners, 1995. Co-chairperson com. Dr. Thomas Matthew, N.Y.C., 1974. With U.S. Mcht. Marine, 1947-51. Fellow Am. Coll. Internal Physicians; mem. Nat. Med. Assn., Am. Psychiat. Assn., Provident Clin. Soc. (v.p. 1980-82, parliamentarian 1982—), Bklyn. Psychiat. Soc., Black Psychiatrists of Am. Avocations: travel, african art, sailing, swimming. Died Mar. 2, 2004.

LINDSEY, ANNE WEST, writer; b. Carterville, Ill., Mar. 29, 1914; d. Jett J. and Lillian Mae (Davis) West; m. Harold L. Zimmerman, Nov. 24, 1959 (dec. 1970); m. Wyatt Allen Lindsey, Dec. 9, 1981 (dec. Nov. 1990). BA, So. Ill. U., 1935; postgrad., U. Mo., 1937. Tchr. Marion Ill. High Sch., 1935-36; newspaper reporter various newspapers, 1937-44; tchr. profl. writing Grad. Sch. So. Ill. U., Carbondale, 1956-60. Pres. coun. So. Ill. U.; lectr., speaker in field. Contbr. fiction and articles to 147 nat. mags. including Saturday Evening Post, Holiday, Good Housekeeping, Mademoiselle, Readers' Digest, Ford Times, also fgn. publs., TV dramas for Alcoa Theatre, Fireside Theatre, Robert Montgomery Presents. Bd. dirs. Marion Cultural and Civic Ctr., 1979-90; exec. com., dir., trustee Nat. Friends of Pub. Broadcasting; founder, chmn. bd. dirs. Friends of WSUI-WUSI TV, Carbondale, Olney, Ill.; bd. dirs. State of Ill. Humanities Coun.; mem. adv. bd. Morris Libr., Carbondale, 1961-86; gov. exec. com. So. Ill. U. Found. Bd.; mem. humanities adv. bd. John A. Logan Coll., Carterville, Ill.; mem. State of Ill. Six-Man Steering Com. for the Arts; bd. dirs. Lovejoy Libr., Edwardsville, Ill.; writers aide Nat. Hospitalized Veterans. Recipient Booster award WSUI-TV, 1978, Delta award So. Ill. U., 1982, Alumni award So. Ill. U., 1983, Golden Friend award Morris Libr., 1989, Disting. Svc. award So. Ill. U., 1991, World Affairs Forum, 1992. Avocations: theatre work, travel, swimming, art, circuses. Home: Benton, Ill. Died Oct. 29, 2005.

LINDSEY, JEFFERSON FRANKLIN, III, electrical engineering technology educator; b. East St. Louis, Oct. 9, 1942; s. Jefferson Franklin Jr. and Helen Lucile (Sullenger) L.; m. Sandra S. Skalnik, Dec. 22, 1962; children: Laura L., Jefferson F. IV. BSEE, U. Tex., 1964; MSEE, U. Houston, 1967; DEng, Lamar U., 1976. Registered profl. engr. Elec. engr. NASA, Houston, 1964-68; researcher McDonnell Douglas, Houston, 1974-80, St. Louis, 1985-90; prof. U. Houston, Carbondale, Ill., 1968-80; owner Lindsey Assocs., Carbondale, Ill., from 1976; prof. So. Ill. U., Carbondale, from 1980. Patentee in field; contbr. over 50 articles to profl. jours., chpts. to books, conf. proceedings and tech. reports to profl. publs. Troop com. Boy Scouts of Am., Carbondale, 1980-86; comms. cons. Vol. Fire Dept., Energy, Ill., 1980-83. Recipient Award of Distinction for Ind. Rsch., McDonnell Douglas, 1987, NASA Shuttle Approach and Landing Test award, 1978, Cert. of Merit, NASA, 1971, 76. Mem. IEEE (sr.), Soc. for Advancement Materials and Processes Engring. Avocations: amateur radio, walking. Home: Carbondale, Ill. Died Aug. 21, 2005.

LINDSEY, RUTH, retired education educator; b. Kingfisher, Okla., Oct. 26, 1926; d. Lewis Howard and Kenyon (King) L. BS, Okla. State U., 1948; MS, U. Wis., 1954; D in Phys. Edn., Ind. U., 1965. Registered kinesiotherapist, 1970. Instr. Okla. State U., Stillwater, 1948-50, Monticello Coll., Alton, Ill., 1951-54, DePauw U., Greencastle, Ind., 1954-56; prof. Okla. State U., Stillwater, 1956-75; vis. prof. U. Utah, Salt Lake City, 1975-76; prof. phys. edn. Calif. State U., Long Beach, 1976-88, prof. emeritus, from 1988; ret. Cons. in field. Co-author: (originally titled Body Mechanics) Fitness for the Health of It, 6 edits., 1969-89, Concepts of Physical Fitness, 9 edits., 1997, Fitness for Life, 1st edit., 1979, 4th edit., 1997, Concepts of Physical Fitness and Wellness, 1st edit., 1994, 2d edit., 1997, The Ultimate Fitness Book, 1984, Survival Kit for Those Who Sit, 1989, A Menu of Concepts: Physical Fitness Concepts, Toward Active Lifestyles and Fitness and Wellness Concepts, Toward Healthy Lifestyles, 1996, Fundamental Concepts of Fitness and Wellness, 2000; contbg. author: Exercise and the Older Adult, 1998; editor, pub.: Why Don't You Salt the Beans, 1997, Kenyon's Songs, 1998; editor: Perspectives: Jour. of Western Soc. for Phys. Edn. Coll. Women, 1988-95; contbr. articles to profl. jours. Mem. Commn. on Aging, City of Westminster, 1998-2001. Amy Morris Homans scholar, 1964; recipient Disting. and Meritorious Svc. Honor award Okla. Assn. Health, Phys. Edn. and Recreation, 1970, Meritorious Performance award Calif. State U., 1987, Julian Vogel Meml. award Am. Kinesiotherapy Assn., 1988, Texty award Text and Acad. Authors Assn., 1997, William Holmes McGuffey award Tex. and Acad. Authors Assn., 1998. Fellow AAHPERD, Am. Kinesiotherapy Assn., Calif. Assn. Health, Phys. Edn., Recreation and Dance, Nat. Coun. Against Health Fraud, Western Soc. for Phys. Edn. of Coll. Women (Hon. Mem. award 1995), Phi Kappa Phi. Democrat. Baptist. Avocations: golf, travel, writing. Home: Albuquerque, N.Mex. Died May 29, 2005.

LIPKA, LEONARD NORMAN, contracting company executive; b. N.Y.C., June 29, 1932; s. Morris and Genesse (Levine) L.; m. Leonore Baer (div. 1985); children: Hilary, Jordan, Susan; m. Patricia Elizabeth Joyce. BA, NYU, 1962. V.p. Gen. Sheet Metal, Bronx, 1960-73; gen. mgr. Sevenoars, Bronx, 1973-83, Igloo, Miami, Fla., 1983-86; pres. Condex, Inc., Ft. Lauderdale, Fla., from 1986. Antiques cons., Bronx, 1972—. Chmn. young rep. com. Village Rep. Party, N.Y.C., 1965-66; candidate N.Y. State Assembly, N.Y.C., 1966—. With U.S. Army, 1951-53. Mem. ASHRAE, Tower Club, NYU Club. Republican. Avocations: reading, astronomy, antiques. Home: Dania, Fla. Died Oct. 20, 2004.

LIPNER, LEE DAVID, film editor; b. Chgo., Oct. 10, 1943; s. Paul Nathan and Edna (Sweeney) L.; m. Pearl Carón Rozner, May 29, 1965; 1 child, Lisa Anne. BS, Ill. Inst. Tech., 1965. Chemist Desoto Chem., Chgo., 1965-66; high sch. math tchr. Chgo. Bd. Edn., 1966-67; chemist, plant mgr. Superior Paint Co., Chgo., 1967-68; technician, mgr. Technicolor, Chgo., 1968-72; lab. mgr. Filmmakers Lab., Lansing, Mich., 1972-73; technician Producers Color Service, Detroit, 1973-78; pres. Image Express, Detroit, from 1978. Mem. Am. Chem. Soc., Soc. Motion Picture & TV Engrs., Detroit Producers Assn. Jewish. Avocation: guitar playing. Home: Southfield, Mich. Died Apr. 17, 2004.

LIPPERT, ALLAN LEONARD, geographer, educator; b. Chgo., Aug. 1, 1941; s. Elmer Louis Lippert and Lucille (Cappetto) Kocharski; m. Wanda Danette Connell, Mar. 19, 1976 (div. 1983); m. Alice Jane Berry, Dec. 20, 1986 (div. 1994). AA, Manatee Jr. Coll., Bradenton, Fla., 1964; LLB, JD, Blackstone Law Sch., Chgo., 1970; BA, U. South Fla., 1972, MA, 1973; PhD, Columbia U., 1998. Adj. prof. U. South Fla., Tampa, 1970-74; tchr. S.E. High Sch., Bradenton, Fla., 1974-78; prof., geographic impact planner Manatee C.C., Bradenton, from 1978; adj. prof. Bethune-Cookman Coll., Bradenton, from 1988. Cons. Tchr. Edn. Commn., Tallahassee, 1987—; mem. adv. coun. Post-Secondary Environ. Edn., Tallahassee, 1991—; mem. adv. bd. Fla. Geog. Alliance, Tallahassee, 1987—; pres. Rsch. Assocs., Bradenton, 1987-91. Author: Western Civilization, 2 vols., 1980; author, editor: Exploring Sociology, 1980, Topics in Sociology, 1984, Classical and Contemporary Social Issues, 1991, 2d edit. 1994, Sociology Through Fact and Fiction, 1997; contbr. articles to profl. jours. Bd. dirs. South Fla. Chess Conf., Bradenton, 1975-78; judge Student Sci. Fairs, 1980—; cons. Ringling Museums, Sarasota, Fla., 1980-81. Maj. U.S. Army, 1965-70, Vietnam. Decorated Purple Heart, Air medal with 3 oak leaves, Commendation medal, Cross of Gallantry with Palm Republic of Vietnam. Mem. Fla. Soc. Geographers (v.p. 1985-86, pres. 1986-87), Manasota Geog. and Anthropologic Soc. (advisor), Assn. Am. Geographers, Am. Legion. Roman Catholic. Avocation: egyptology. Home: Bradenton, Fla. Died Dec. 13, 2004.

LITTLE, ROBERT ANDREWS, architect, artist; b. Brookline, Mass., Sept. 9, 1915; s. Clarence Cook and Katherine Day (Andrews) L.; m. Ann Murphy Halle, Dec., 27, 1940; children: Sam Robertson, Revere (dec.). AB cum laude, Harvard U., 1937, M.Arch., 1939. Designer G.H. Perkins, Cambridge, Mass., 1939-41; architect U.S. Navy, Washington, 1941-43; ops. analyst Air Staff Intelligence, Washington, 1943-45; prin. Robert A. Little & Assos., Cleve., 1946-58, 67-69; partner Little & Dalton, Cleve., 1958-67; dir. design Dalton-Dalton-Little-Newport, Cleve., 1969-78; owner Robert A. Little, Design and Architecture, from 1978. Tchr., lectr. Harvard, U. Pa., Carnegie Inst. Tech., U. Mich., Smith Coll., U. Notre Dame, Kent State U. Exhibited art and graphics in Cleve., Phila., Boston., since 1970; works include Air Force Mus., Dayton, Ohio; one-person shows in Ohio, Maine, Mass. Trustee Cleve. Mus. Sci., 1952-56, Cleve. Inst. Music, 1956-58; mem. Cleve. Fine Arts Com. Served with U.S. Army, 1940. Fellow AIA (pres. Cleve. chpt. 1966-68, nat. and state design awards), Harvard Sch. of Design Alumni Assn. (past pres., internat. dir. of devel.) Home: Cleveland, Ohio. Died Aug. 1, 2005.

LITTON, ROBERT CLIFTON, marine engineer, consultant; b. Banner Elk, N.C., Jan. 11, 1934; s. Hailey Clifton and Edna (Walsh) L.; m. Michele Louise Gennette, July 1, 1961. B in Mech. Engring., U. Va., 1957; MS in Mech. Engring., Rensselaer Polytech. Inst., 1963. Commd. ensign USN, 1957, advanced through grades to capt., ret., 1984; pvt. practice marine engring. cons. Great Falls, Va., 1985-94; sr. cons. engr. Mech. Tech., Inc., Latham, N.Y., 1988-95; program mgr. Innovative Tech., Inc., McLean, Va., 1988-89, Sachse Engring. Assocs., Inc., San Diego, 1989-90; bus. area mgr. naval engring. RGS Assocs., Arlington, Va., 1994-96; v.p. ops. New Dawn Universal Power Corp., Arlington, from 1996. Mem. Soc. Naval Archs. and Marine Engrs., Am. Soc. Naval Engrs., U.S. Naval Inst., Naval Sub. League. Republican. Avocations: personal computers, audio and video systems, golf. Died Aug. 14, 2005.

LITWIN, BURTON LAWRENCE, entertainment industry executive, theatrical producer, lawyer; b. N.Y.C., Jan. 1, 1931; s. Samuel G. and Eleanore (Kos) L.; m. Dorothy Beth Lefkowitz, Nov. 18, 1956; children: Richard Seth, Robert Aron, Kenneth David. BA, Washington and Lee U., 1951; LLB, NYU, 1953. Bar: N.Y. 1954, U.S. Dist. Ct. (so. dist.) N.Y. 1958, U.S. Ct. Appeals (2d cir.) 1964. Assoc. Wilzin and Halperin, N.Y.C., 1956-64; ptnr. DaSilva and Litwin, N.Y.C., 1964-65; sole practice, N.Y.C., 1965-67; v.p., dir. bus. affairs Belwin-Mills Pub. Corp., N.Y.C., 1967-74, v.p., gen. mgr., counsel, 1975-86; pres., CEO Newcal Properties and Prodns., Ltd., Newcal Music Co., Dobbs Ferry, N.Y., 1986—; bd. dirs. Nat. Teaching Aids, Inc., Garden City Park, N.Y. Producer: (theatrical works) Sophisticated Ladies, N.Y.C., Tokyo, Paris, Moscow, Leningrad, L.A., Washington 1980—, Poppy, London, 1982-83, Stardust, N.Y.C., 1986—. Pres. Temple Beth Abraham, Tarrytown, N.Y., 1982-83; bd. dirs. Creative Arts Rehab. Ctr., N.Y.C., 1983-84. Served to sgt. U.S. Army, 1953-55. Recipient Tony award nomination League of N.Y. Theatres, 1982; ann. Image award NAACP, 1982, Outer Critics Circle award, 1987, Ivor Novello award nomination Brit. Acad. Songwriters, Composer and Authors, 1983. Mem. ASCAP (bd. appeals 1981-83, adv. com. 1985-87), N.Y. State Bar Assn., Copyright Soc. USA, League of Am. Theatres and Producers., Friars Club, B'nai B'rith. Avocations: photography, traveling, golf, tennis. Died Aug. 27, 2005.

LIU, BINYAN, author; b. Changchun City, Jilin, People's Republic China, Jan. 15, 1925; s. Fengming and Yaqin (Shen) L; m. Hong Zhu, May 18, 1929; children: Dahong, Xiaoyan. Tchr., Tianjin, People's Republic China, 1944-46; youth worker Harbin, People's Republic China, 1946-50; journalist China Youth News, Beijing, 1951-58; editor translations of fgn. philos. works Beijing, 1978-79; sr. reporter People's Daily, Beijing, 1979-87; writer Beijing, 1987-88; Nieman fellow Harvard U., Cambridge, Mass., 1988-89; writer-in-residence Trinity Coll., Hartford, Conn., 1989—2005. Vis. prof. UCLA, 1988. Author: Tell the World, 1990, (collection of reportage in English) Men or Monsters?, 1982, 11 collections of lit. reportage. Hon. fellow Iowa U., 1982. Mem. China Writer's Assn. (vice-chmn. 1985-90, Nat. Award for Lit. Reportage 1981, 85, 87). Died Dec. 5, 2005.

LIU, XU-DONG, mathematics educator; b. Shanghai, Mar. 7, 1962; s. Kai-Ben Liu and Xiu-Feng Yang; m. Xiaohui Lu, Aug. 8, 1987; 1 child, Evan. MA, UCLA, 1990, PhD in Applied Math., 1993. Vis. mem. Courant Inst. of Math. Scis., NYU, 1993-96; assoc. prof. U. Calif., Santa Barbara, from 1996. Contbr. articles to profl. jours. including Jour. of Computational Physics. Grantee NSF, 1998—. Home: Goleta, Calif. Died Oct. 19, 2005.

LIVZIEY, JAMES GERALD, secondary school educator; b. Buffalo, July 30, 1927; s. James Ephlyn and Helena Charlote (Kiener) L.; m. June Ellen Andersen, July 25, 1955; children: Naomi Lynn, Patricia Ellen. AA, Southwestern Jr. Coll., 1970; BA, San Diego State U., 1972. Enlisted U.S. Navy, 1945, advanced through grades to lt. comdr., 1967, ret., 1969; high sch. instr. SWHS Dist., Chula Vista, Calif., from 1972. Recipient award Freedoms Found., 1991; fellow Taft Inst., 1977, Pacific Acad. Advanced Studies, 1978. Fellow Alpha Gamma Sigma; mem. Naval Inst. USN, Masons, Knight Comdr. Ct. Honor (32d degree). Avocations: golf, reading, educational reasearch. Home: Chula Vista, Calif. Died May 25, 2004.

LLOYD, GARY EVAN, academic administrator, consultant; b. Somerville, Mass., Feb. 8, 1936; s. Aubrey Burnell and Edith (Mountain) L.; m. Nella Fischer (div. 1981); 1 child, Gwynne; m. Carol Thomas; children: Catherine Edith, Andrew Thomas. BS, Babson Coll., 1958; MBA, Am. U., 1965. Asst. prof. U. So. Calif., L.A., 1968-71; asst. dir. Am. U., Washington, 1971-72, dir. bus. coun. for Internat. Understanding Inst., from 1972. Lt. comdr. USNR, 1958-68. Mem. U.S. Gen. Acctg. Office (adv. com. internat. div. Washington chpt., symposium pub. diplomacy), Am. Assn. Collegiate Sch. of Bus. (mem. editorial bd. Washington chpt.), Bus. Edn. and Tng. Ams. for Bus. Edn. with Japan, Japan Soc. Sietar Internat. (bd. of govs.), ASPA Internat., Babson Club, New Hampton Club. Republican. Avocations: boat building, fishing, hunting, travel, reading. Home: Washington, DC. Died July 7, 2004.

LLOYD, JOSEPH WILSEY, minister, chaplain; b. Oconomowoc, Wis., Jan. 24, 1940; s. John George and Sevilla Mary (Wilsey) L.; m. Hope Marie Willie, Aug. 25, 1962; children: John David, Judith Lynn, Christine Marie Lloyd-Cagle, Elizabeth Sevilla. Student, Cedarville (Ohio) Coll., 1961-64; BA, Bishop Coll., Dallas, 1973; postgrad., Wheaton (Ill.) Coll., 1974-75; MDiv, No. Bapt. Theol. Sem., Lombard, Ill., 1976. Ordained to ministry Am. Bapt. Chs. in U.S.A., 1977. Min. Christian edn. Morgan Park Bapt. Ch., Chgo., 1973-76; pastor E.C.H.O. Bapt. Parish, Humeston, Iowa, 1976-80, 1st Bapt. Ch., Alliance, Nebr., 1980-84, Mt. Olive Bapt. Ch., Cherokee, Iowa, 1984-88, 1st Bapt. Ch., Ft. Madison, Iowa, from 1988. Chaplain dist. 13, Iowa State Patrol, Des Moines, 1985—; mem. region pers. com. and area program bd. Mid-Am. Bapt. Chs., Des Moines, 1988—. Columnist Pastor's Paragraphs, New Era, Humeston, 1976-80. Jackson del. Iowa Dem. Conv., 1988; religious counselor The Crossing Point, Ft. Madison. Recipient cert. of commendation Iowa State Patrol, 1986, Law Enforcement award Optimist Internat., 1988. Mem. Internat. Conf. Police Chaplains, Mid-Am. Bapt. Mins. Coun., Am. Bapt. Mins. Coun., Tri State Gun Club (Montrose, Iowa). Home: Hedrick, Iowa. Died July 10, 2005.

LOCK, JAMES SIDNEY, minister; b. Starkeville, Miss., Aug. 25, 1927; s. James and Sidney (Chambers) L.; m. Jo Thornton, June 6, 1951; children: Sidney L. Caldwell, James Stephen. BS, Auburn U., 1949; MDiv, Duke Divinity Sch., 1952; DMin, Drew Theol. Sch., 1984. Ordained to ministry Meth. Ch., 1954. Pastor White Meml./Wesley Charge, Henderson, N.C., 1951-52, Ashford Charge, Ala. West Fla. Conf., Ashford, Ala., 1952-57, Hartford (Ala.) First Meth. Ala. West Fla. Conf., 1957-61, Kingswood Meth. Ch. Ala. West Fla. Conf., Mobile, Ala., 1961-66; assoc. dir. Ala.-West Fla. Conf. Coun., Andalusia, Ala., 1966-71; pastor First United Meth. Ch., Atmore, Ala., 1971-76, Dalraida United Meth. Ch., Montgomery, Ala., 1976-84, First United Meth. Ch., Ft. Walton Beach, Fla., from 1984. Mem. bd. edn. Ala. West Fla. Conf., 1956-64, 71-72, bd. evangelism, 1964-66, Blue Lake commn., 1964-70, coun. on finance and adminstrn., 1972-80; chairperson bd. missions Ala. West Fla. Conf., 1984-88, resource person task force on prison ministries and prison reform, 1975-76; ministerial adv. bd. to Birmingham So. Coll. Ala. West Ala. Conf., 1975—, chairperson, 1975-81. Mem. Loop Lions Club, 1963-66; pres. Atmore Rotary Club, 1972-73; bd. dirs. Deep South coun. Girl Scouts Am., 1972-76; bd. dirs. Atmore United Fund, 1974-76, pres., 1976; v.p. NW Fla. Health Coun., 1990-91; bd. dirs. Cath. Social Svcs., Okaloosa County, 1989—. Mem. Kiwanis (Ft. Walton Beach club, bd. dirs. 1990-91, chairperson spiritual aims com. 1990-91). Home: Andalusia, Ala. Died Aug. 12, 2004.

LOCK, JOHN RICHARD, lawyer; b. Baton Rouge, Dec. 24, 1941; s. John Henry Lock and Julia (Hooker) Sturdivant; m. Sidney Brient, Dec. 28, 1965; children: Julia Corrine, Elizabeth Ann. BBA, Tex. A&M U., 1964; JD, U. Tex., 1967. Bar: Tex. 1967, U.S. Tax Ct. 1973, U.S. Dist. Ct. (we. dist.) Tex. 1974, U.S. Ct. of Appeals (5th cir.), U.S. Supreme Ct.; CPA, Tex. Atty. John Lock & Assocs., Austin, Lock & Virr, P.C., Austin. Mem. ABA, AICPA, Travis County Bar Assn., State Bar Assn. of Tex. (cert. estate planning, probate law, and tax law), Tex. Soc. of CPAs. Home: Austin, Tex. Died Jan. 21, 2004.

LOCKLIN, WILBERT EDWIN, management consultant, former academic administrator; b. Washington, Apr. 2, 1920; s. Wilbert Edwin and Margaret Mae (Franklin) L.; m. Olga Maria Osterwald, June 28, 1947; children: Kenneth, Patricia, Randall. BS, Johns Hopkins U., 1942; LLD, George Williams Coll., 1966; DHum, Springfield Coll., 1994. Vice-pres. Nat. Bur. Pvt. Schs., N.Y.C., 1947-49; account exec. Reuel Estill & Co., N.Y.C., 1949-51; asst. dir. admissions Johns Hopkins, 1945-47, asst. to pres., 1955-65; v.p. Johns Hopkins Fund, 1960-65; pres. Springfield (Mass.) Coll., 1965-85, Locklin Mgmt. Services, 1985—2006. Chmn. bd. dirs., mem. exec. com., salary com., charitable funds com.; chmn. trust com. Bay Bank Valley Trust Co., 1966-91; mem. exec. com. Assn. Ind. Colls. and Univs. in Mass., 1971-83; founding mem. Cooperating Colls. of Greater Springfield.; pres. Cooperating Colls. of Greater Springfield, 1982-83; mem. exec. com., bd. dirs. Business Friends of Arts. Bd. dirs. Springfield Symphony Orch., 1973-83; campaign dir. Elms Coll., 1992-94; sr. advisor Mass. Soc. for Prevention of Cruelty to Animals, 1995-99, Loomis Communities, 1998-2006; Served with USAAF, 1942-45. Decorated DFC, Air medal. Home: Fort Pierce, Fla. Died Mar. 4, 2006.

LOCKWOOD, FRANK JAMES, manufacturing executive; b. San Bernadino, Calif., Oct. 30, 1931; s. John Ellis and Sarah Grace (Roberts) Lockwood; m. Crystal Marie Miller, 1986; children from previous marriage: Fay, Frank, Hedy, Jonnie, George, Katherine, Bill, Dena. Student, Southeast City Coll., Chgo., 1955, Ill. Inst. Tech., 1963-64, Bogan Jr. Coll., Chgo., 1966. Foreman Hupp Aviation, Chgo., 1951-60; dept. head UARCO, Inc., Chgo., 1960-68; pres. XACT Machine & Engring., Chgo., 1986—2005. Chmn. bd. dirs., pres., bd. dirs. Lockwood Engring., Inc., Chgo., Ill. Nat. Corp., Chgo.; cons. engr., Chgo. Participant Forest Land Mgmt. Program; mem. Ill. Ambs.; commr. Econ. Devel. Commn., Mt. Vernon, Ill., 1985; mem. bd. Jefferson County, Ill., from 1992; mem. exec. com., mem. legis. com. Ill. County Bds. Coun. Named Chgo. Ridge Father of the Yr., 1964. Mem.: Ill. Drivers' Assn., Shriners (past master 2), Masons (32 degree). Achievements include patents for printing equipment; beverage cans; gasoline pump dispenser "Super Pin"; business forms equipment. Home: Texico, Ill. Died Sept. 4, 2005.

LOCKWOOD, LOIS MINIELY, animal hospital executive; b. Boise, Idaho, Nov. 23, 1924; d. Howard John and Margaret E. (Danielson) Miniely; m. Robert W. Lockwood, Jan. 19, 1945; children: Linda K. Lockwood Johnson, Craig H. BA in Social Welfre, U. Calif., Berkeley, 1949. V.p. Diversified Baby Products, Covina, Calif., 1984-88; prin. Commonwealth Animal Hosp., Fullerton, Calif., from 1987. Pres. H.S. and grade sch. PTA, West Covina, Calif., 1966-70, LWV, West Covina, 1966-68; leader Girl Scouts U.S.A. and Boy Scouts Am., West Covina, 1960-65; fund raiser Dorothy Chandler Pavilion; mem. West Covina Planning Coun., 1965. Named Citizen of Yr., West Covina C. of C., 1964. Mem. AAUW (pres. West Covina 1966-68). Home: West Covina, Calif. Died Dec. 10, 2004.

LODWICK, MICHAEL WAYNE, lawyer; b. New Orleans, Sept. 21, 1946; s. Frank Tillman Jr. and Grace Evelyn (Hilty) L.; children: Sarah Peirce, Jane Durborow, Elizabeth Hilty; m. Mary League, June 15, 1991. BA, La. State U., 1968; MA, Tulane U., 1972, PhD, 1976; JD, Loyola U., New Orleans, 1981. Bar: La., U.S. Dist. Ct. (ea. dist.) La. 1981, U.S. Ct. Appeals (5th cir.) 1981, U.S. Ct. Appeals (D.C. cir.) 1982, U.S. Ct. Appeals (11th cir.) 1986, U.S. Ct. Appeals (9th cir.) 1990, U.S. Ct. Appeals (2d cir.) 1996, U.S. Ct. Appeals (4th cir.) 1996, U.S. Supreme Ct., 1987, Calif. 1990, U.S. Dist. Ct. (ctrl., no. and so. dists.) Calif. 1990. Instr. to asst. prof. Tulane U., New Orleans, 1976-78; assoc. Barham & Churchill, New Orleans, 1981-83, O'Neil, Eichin & Miller, New Orleans, 1983-87, ptnr., 1987-89, Fisher & Porter, 1989-97, Porter, Groff & Lodwick, from 1997. Editor, co-founder and pub. Plantation Soc. in Americas jour., 1979-83, 86—; editor-in-chief Loyola Law Rev., 1980-81; contbr. articles to profl. jours. Mem. New Orleans Symphony Chorus, 1985-89, Pacific Chorale, 1989—. Tulane U. fellow, 1970-72; recipient Loyola U. Law Rev. Honor award, 1981, Loyola Law Alumni award, 1981. Mem. ABA, La. State Bar Assn., State Bar Calif., Fed. Bar Assn., Assn. Transp. Law, Logistics and Policy, Maritime Law Assn. U.S. Home: Huntington Beach, Calif. Died May 21, 2004.

LOEFFLER, JAMES JOSEPH, lawyer; b. Evanston, Ill., Mar. 7, 1931; s. Charles Adolph and Margaret Bowe L.; m. Margo M. Loeffler, May 26, 1962; children— Charlotte Bowe, James J. BS, Loyola U.; JD, Northwestern U. Bar: Ill. 1956, Tex. 1956. Assoc. Fulbright & Jaworski, Houston, 1956-69, ptnr., 1969—82, sr. ptnr., 1982—86, Chamberlain, Hrdlicka, White, Johnson & Williams, Houston, 1986-90; pvt. practice law Houston, 1990-2000. Mem. Ill. Bar Assn., Tex. Bar Assn., Houston Country Club. Died May 2, 2006.

LOEVINGER, ROBERT, retired research physicist; b. St. Paul, Minn., Jan. 31, 1916; BA, U. Minn., 1936; MA, Harvard Coll., 1938; PhD, U. Calif., Berkeley, 1947. Asst. physicist The Mt. Sinai Hosp., N.Y.C., 1947-56; asst. prof. Stanford U. Med. Sch., Palo Alto, Calif., 1957-65; chief dosimetry sect. Internat. Atomic Energy Agy., Vienna, 1965-68; dosimetry group leader Nat. Inst. Stds. and Tech., Washington, 1968-88. Recipient William D. Coolidge award Am. Assn. Physicists in Medicine, 1995. Home: Rockville, Md. Died Nov. 6, 2005.

LOEWEN, ROLAND PHILLIP, metal products executive; b. Hillsboro, Kans., Nov. 23, 1913; s. Peter C. and Kathrine (Riesen) L.; m. Lorraine Polson, Nov. 23, 1941. BSChemE, U. Kans., 1941. From engr. to asst. plant mgr. Montsanto Co., Anniston, Ala., 1941-52; asst. plant mgr. Tenn. Products and Chem. Co., Chattanooga, 1952-58; plant mgr., v.p. Tenn. Tex. Alloy Corp., Houston, 1958-78; co-owner Alchemy, Baytown, Tex., from 1978. Author: How to Refine Gold and Silver, 1984; contbr. articles to profl. jours.; lectr. on gold refining, U.S.,Israel, Eng. Mem. Wardens and Commonality of the Mystery of Goldsmiths of the City of London (assoc.). Avocation: restoring old unusual cars. Died Apr. 8, 2005.

LOFTUS, JOSEPH PHILIP, JR., former federal agency administrator; b. Chgo., Aug. 31, 1930; s. Joseph P. and Margaret Mary (Boland) L.; m. Barbara Ellen Pohner, June 27, 1959; children: Diana, William, Joseph P., Sean, James, Patrick. BA, Cath. U., Washington, 1953; MA, Fordham U., Bronx, N.Y., 1956. Aerospace technologist L.B. Johnson Space Ctr., Houston, 1961-62, mgr. ops. integration, 1963-69, mgr. program engring. office, 1969-75, chief tech. planning office, 1976-85, asst. dir., 1985—2001. Editor: Orbital Debris from Upper Stage Breakups, 1989; contbr. articles to profl. jours. Capt. USAF, 1956-65. Recipient Exceptional Svc. medal NASA, Houston, 1974, 84, Outstanding Leadership medal, 1991; named Sloan fellow Stanford U., Palo Alto, Calif., 1975-76. Assoc. fellow AIAA (chmn. space transp. 1984-87); mem. AAAS, HFS, APA, Internat. Acad. Astro. (corr. mem.). Roman Catholic. Home: Friendswood, Tex. Died Sept. 4, 2005.

LOGAN, FRIEDA MAE, painter, educator; b. Springfield, Mo., Apr. 30, 1929; d. Carl and Anna Julia Elizabeth (Hollingshead) Oberlander; m. Glenn Woodrow Logan, Dec. 9, 1951; children: Glenn Kerry, Leslie Logan Stapinski. BA, Kansas City Art Inst., 1951, postgrad., 1980, Penn Valley Coll., 1982-84. Stylist Ricemor Coats & Suits, Kansas City, Mo., 1951-52; stylist, designer Brand & Puritz Inc., Kansas City, Mo., 1952; designer Dan-Deb Mfrs., Kansas City, Mo., 1953-58; freelance illustrator for various retail cos., Kansas City, Mo., 1958-75, 79-84; staff artist Ray Advt., Kansas City, Mo., 1976-77, Macy's, Kansas City, Mo., 1977-79; ind. painter Springfield, Mo., from 1984. Mem. Pub. Sch. Com. to Evaluate Curriculum for Visual Arts, Springfield, 1993; exhibits dir. Image Point Gallery, 1996-97; tchr. watercolor classes Springfield Art Mus., 1996-99; tchr. pvt. studio classes, 1996-99. Exhibited works in numerous nat. and regional exhibits; contbr. articles to art mags. Mem. Springfield Visual Arts Alliance (membership dir. 1995-96, exhibits dir. 1996-98). Avocations: needlecrafts, photography. Home: Springfield, Mo. Died May 15, 2004.

LOGAN, J. MURRAY, investment manager; b. Balt., Mar. 15, 1935; s. Lloyd and Helen Mildred (Gilbert) L.; m. Mary Page Cole, June 19, 1987 (dec. Sept. 1993); 1 child by previous marriage, Maria Charlotte. BA, Johns Hopkins U., 1959. Securities analyst Merrill Lynch Pierce Fenner & Smith, N.Y.C., 1959-62; ptnr. Wood Struthers & Winthrop, N.Y.C., 1962-70; v.p. EFC Mgmt. Corp., L.A., 1970-73, Faulkner, Dawkins & Sullivan, Inc., N.Y.C., 1973-75; chmn. investment policy com. Rockefeller & Co., Inc., N.Y.C., 1975-97; mng. ptnr. L-R Global Ptnrs., N.Y.C. Bd. dirs. World Trust Fund, Luxembourg, Berkshire Opera Co., Camphill Found., Camphill Village, U.S.A., past pres. Trustee Johns Hopkins U., Balt., 1984-91. With USCG, 1954-56. Mem.: Mashomack, The Leash. Home: New York, NY. Died Jan. 2006.

LOKEY, FRANK MARION, JR., broadcast executive, consultant; b. Ft. Worth, Oct. 15, 1924; s. Frank Marion Sr. and Corinne (Whaley) L. Student, Smith-Hughes Evening Coll., 1955-59. Announcer, newscaster, disc jockey, morning personality Stas. WAPI, WBRC and WSGN, Birmingham, Ala., 1941-52; pres. Sta. WRDW-TV, Augusta, Ga., 1952-55; asst. gen. mgr., mgr. sales, news anchor Sta. WLW-A TV (now WXIA-TV), Atlanta, 1955-66; co-owner, gen. mgr. Sta. WAIA, Atlanta, 1960-62; S.E. news corr., talk show host CBS News N.Y., N.Y.C., 1960-66; asst. to owner, gen. mgr. Sta. WBIE-AM-FM, Atlanta, 1962-64; asst. to pres., gen. mgr. Stas. KXAB-TV, KXJB-TV, KXMB-TV, Aberdeen, Fargo, Bismarck, S.D., N.D., 1966-67; exec. v.p., gen. mgr. St. WEMT-TV, Bangor, Maine, 1967-70; pres., gen. mgr. Stas. KMOM-TV, KWAB-TV, Odessa-Midland, Big Spring, Tex., 1970-75; exec. v.p., gen. mgr. Sta. KMUV-TV (now named KRBK-TV), Sacramento, Calif., 1975-77; CEO Lokey Enterprises, Inc., Sacramento, L.A., El Centro, Calif., from 1977, also chmn. bd. dirs. Cons., troubleshooter 18 TV stas. nationwide, 1977—; cons., actor 6 movie prodn. cos., Hollywood, Calif., 1980—; cons., outside dir. Anderson Cons., Manhattan, L.I., N.Y., 1981—; network talk show host/news corr. for 7 news orgns. worldwide, 1984—; bd. dirs. Broadcast Audience Behavior Rsch., Manhattan, 1986—, mem. inner circle, 1986—; mem. bd. advisors Men of Achievement, Cambridge, Eng.; owner/franchiser The Party Place; motivational spkr. Creator, originator approach to real estate mktg.; prodr. swing/ballroom dance parties, LA., Palm Spring, Calif., Las Vegas, Nev., London, Paris, Dublin, Ireland, Sydney Australia. Hon. mem. Imperial County Bd. Suprs., El Centro, 1986—, El Centro City Coun., 1987—. Mem. Am. Legion. Baptist. Avocations: producer big bands parties, movie acting, ancient history, tracing family tree. Died Apr. 25, 2004.

LONDON, SHIRLEY L., retired social worker; b. Cleve., Dec. 26, 1920; d. Isaac and Lena (Neiman) L. BA, Western Res. U., 1949; MSW, Columbia U., 1951, 3rd Yr. Cert., 1957. Bd. cert. diplomate social work, clin. social worker. Social worker Babies Hosp./Columbia-Presbyn. Med. Ctr., N.Y.C., 1952-57; chpt. social worker, cons. Muscular Dystrophy Assn. of Am., Bklyn., 1957-59; sr. assoc. Albert Einstein Coll. Medicine, Bronx, N.Y., 1959-89; chief social worker Bronx Mcpl. Hosp. Ctr./Pediatrics, 1959-79, dir., staff devel. and quality assurance, Dept. Social Work, 1979-89; cons., pvt. practice, 1989-91. Contbr. articles to profl. jours. With WAAC/WAC, 1942-45, ETO. Fellowship NIMH; grantee Pfeifer Found. Mem. NASW, Columbia Univ. Alumni Assn. Home: Novelty, Ohio. Died Mar. 27, 2005.

LONG, DAVID MICHAEL, JR., biomedical researcher, cardiothoracic surgeon; b. Shamokin, Pa., Feb. 26, 1929; s. David Michael and Elva (Christ) L.; m. Donna Rae Long, Feb. 26, 1954; children: Kurt, Raymond, Carl, Grace, Carolyn, Ruth. BS magna cum laude, Muhlenberg Coll., Allentown, Pa., 1951; MS, Hahnemann U., Phila., 1954, MD, 1956; PhD, U. Minn., 1965. Lic. physician, Calif.; diplomate Nat. Bd. Med. Examiners, Am. Bd. Surgery, Am. Bd. Thoracic Surgery; cert. trauma provider, advanced life support; advanced cardiac life support. Intern Hahnemann U. Hosp., Phila., 1956-57; resident in surgery U. Minn., Mpls., 1957-65, fellow in surgery, 1957-61, 63-65, fellow in physiology, 1959-61; pres., chmn. bd. Long Labs., San Diego, 1984-85; chmn., dir. rsch. Fluoromed Pharm., Inc., San Diego, 1985-89; chmn., dir. sci. Alliance Pharm. Corp., La Jolla, Calif., 1989-91; pres., chmn. Abel Labs., Inc., Spring Valley, Calif., from 1991; CEO, chmn. Biofield Corp., Spring Valley, from 2000. Mem. faculty Hahnemann U., 1953-54, U. Calif., San Diego, 1973-92, U. Minn., 1959-61, 63-64, Naval Med. Sch., 1962, Chgo. Med. Sch., 1965-67, Cook County Grad. Sch. Medicine, 1965-73, U. Ill., 1967-73; cons. Chgo. State Tuberculosis Sanitarium, 1967-72; asst. dir. dept. surg. rsch. Hektoen Inst. for Med. Rsch. of Cook County Hosp., 1965-68, dir., 1968-73, assoc. attending staff, 1965-73; attending staff West Side VA Hosp., 1966-73, U. Ill. Hosp., 1967-73, Villa View Hosp., 1973-85, AMI Valley Med. Ctr., 1973-85, Grossman Dist. Hosp., 1973-85, Alvarado Cmty. Hosp., 1973-85, Sharp Meml. Hosp., 1973-84; head divsn. cardiovasc. and thoracic surgery U. Ill., 1967-73; cons. continuing med. edn. com. Grossmont Dist. Hosp., 1985—; mem. continuing med. edn. com. Sharp Healthcare Sys., 1994—; cons. Docent Corp., 1975-76; com. mem. consensus devel. com. Thrombolytic Therapy in Thrombosis, NIH/FDA, 1980; trustee N.Y. Acad. Art, N.Y.C., 1997—; bd. govs., chmn. Hahnemann U. Hosp./Tenet Healthcare, Phila., 1999—. Contbr. numerous articles and abstracts to profl. jours., chpts. to books; editl. bd. Current Surgery, 1967-89; co-editor Hematrix, 1982-85. Bd. dirs. Rsch. Assocs. of Point Loma Nazarene Coll., San Diego, chmn., 1984-85; trustee Muhlenberg Coll., Allentown, Pa., 1992-2002, chmn., 1994-2002; bd. dirs. Grossmont Hosp. Found., Grossmont Hosp., La Mesa, Calif., 1992—; co-chmn. Calif. divsn. of campaign of Muhlenberg Coll., 1992-93; chmn. Campaign of Grossmont Hosp. Found. for David and Donna Long Cancer Treatment Ctr. and Cardiac Diagnosis Ctr., 1992-94; co-chmn. Campaign for Health Ctr., Point Loma Nazarene Coll., San Diego, 1992-94. Rsch. fellow Heart Assn. Southeastern Pa., 1953-54, Student Senate of Hahnemann U., 1955; trainee Nat. Cancer Inst., 1957-58, Nat. Heart Inst., 1958-60, 63-64; spl. rsch. fellow Nat. Heart Inst., 1960-61; established investigator Minn. Heart Assn, 1964-65; Muhlenberg Coll. scholar, 1947-51, Hahnemann U. scholar, 1952-55, Luth. Brotherhood Leadership scholar, 1951 Fellow ACS, Am. Coll. Chest Physicians (sec. cardiovascular surgery com. 1976-78), Am. Coll. Cardiology; mem. AAAS, AMA, Am. Assn. Thoracic Surgery, Am. Assn. Anatomists, Internat. Cardiovascular Surgery Soc., Internat. Soc. for Artificial Cells and Immobilization Biotechnology, Am. Heart Assn., Am. Physiol. Soc., Am. Thoracic Soc., Assn. for Advancement of Med. Instrumentation, Cajal Soc. Neuroanatomy, Calif. Med. Assn., Internat. Soc. Surgery, Internat. Soc. Hemorheology (founding mem.), N.Y. Acad. Sci., San Diego County Med. Soc., Soc. Thoracic Surgeons, Soc. Univ. Surgeons, Warren H. Cole Soc., Western Thoracic Surg. Soc. Lutheran. Achievements include 17 U.S. patents and 11 fgn. patents. Died Apr. 8, 2006.

LONG, EMMETT THADDEUS, retired communications educator; b. Kaufman, Tex., Dec. 31, 1923; s. Emmett Thaddeus Sr. and Ruth Eliza (Jones) L.; m. Marjorie Ruth Harris, Feb. 22, 1946; children: David Alan, Steven Harrison. BA, Pepperdine U., 1945, U. Calif., Berkeley, 1946, MA, 1948; EdD, U. So. Calif., L.A., 1965. Asst. prof. Pepperdine U., L.A., 1948-54, dir. admissions, 1954-57; admissions officer Calif. State Poly. U., Pomona, 1957-59; assoc. dean Calif. State U., Fullerton, Calif., 1959-72, assoc. dean office of chancellor L.A., 1972-75, prof. Fullerton, 1975-86, prof. emeritus, from 1986. Author: (legis. report) School Relations in California, 1969; editor: Liberal Studies in Communication. Parliamentarian United Ch. of Christ Conf., 1975-97. Named for Disting. Svc., Pi Kappa Delta, 1958, Articulation Conf., Calif., 1975. Mem. Calif. Faculty Assn., Univ. Club Claremont (pres. 1993-94), Calif. State Emeritus Assn. (pres. 1993-97), Phi Delta Kappa. Democrat. Avocations: travel, speaking. Home: Claremont, Calif. Died Mar. 10, 2005.

LONG, JAMES HARVEY, JR., electronics executive; b. Johnson City, Tenn., Sept. 14, 1944; s. James H. and Beulah (Anderson) L.; m. Laura Stone, Nov. 25, 1988; children: Robert Michael, Christopher William. BS in Chemistry, U. Tenn., 1965, PhD in Chemistry, 1968. Rsch. chemist Shell Chem. Co., Houston, 1968-73, process mgr., 1973-77, staff engr., 1977-81, venture devel. mgr., 1981-84, supt. Geismar, La., 1984-86, venture mgr. Houston, 1986-87; v.p. Supercondr. Techs., Santa Barbara, Calif., 1987-93; pres., CEO UNIAX Corp., Santa Barbara, from 1994. Mem. Am. Electronics Assn., Assn. Old Crows, Soc. Photo Optical Instrument Engrs. Avocations: flying, flight instruction, travel. Died Sept. 20, 2004.

LONG, JESSE PAUL, lawyer; b. Punxsutawney, Pa., Mar. 22, 1912; s. Jesse C. Long and Florence E. Shadle; m. June 28, 1939; children: David W., Sarah Long O'Brien. BA, U. So. Calif., L.A., 1933; JD, Dickinson Sch. Law, 1935. Bar: Pa. 1935, Pa. Superior Ct. 1936, U.S. Dist. Ct. (we. dist.) Pa., U.S. Ct. Appeals (3rd cir.) 1945, U.S. Ct. Claims 1954, U.S. Tax Ct. 1969, Commonwealth Ct. Pa. 1971, U.S. Dist. Ct. (mid. dist.) Pa. 1971. Pvt. practice law, Punxsutawney, from 1935. Pres. Punxsutawney Bank/Keystone Nat. Bank, 1971-74. Died Jan. 11, 2005.

LONG, JOHN VANDERFORD, lawyer; b. Tulsa, June 11, 1920; s. Clarence Ray and Odie Deata (McLaughlin) L.; m. Nicole Jeanne Denier, Sept. 27, 1946; children: Olivier Denier, Sylvia Vanderford. BA, U. Chgo., 1943, JD, 1950; postgrad., Georgetown U., Université de Paris. Bar: D.C. 1951, U.S. Supreme Ct. 1961, Md. 1975. Legal advisor to chmn. NLRB, Washington, 1953-55; assoc. Cooper, Ostrin, DeVarco & Ackerman, Washington, 1955-58, Sher, Oppenheimer & Harris, Washington, 1958-62; ptnr. Bridgeman & Long, Washington, 1963-75, Long & Long, Bethesda, Md., 1975-89; of counsel Kuder, Smollar, Friedman, Washington, from 1990. Author: Marriage and Family Law Agreements, 1978, (with Judge Jouce Hens Green and Roberta Murawski) Dissolution of Marriage, 1986; contbr. articles to profl. jours. Fellow Internat. Acad. Matrimonial Lawyers (founding); mem. ABA (family law sect. 1983-95), D.C. Bar (chair family law sect. 1984-89, labor law sect. 1984-89), Am. Acad. Matrimonial Lawyers (com. internat. support laws). Died Nov. 28, 2004.

LONGACRE, RICHARD DAWSON, brokerage house executive; b. Medina, Ohio, Sept. 17, 1921; s. Leland Dawson and Genevieve (Nichols) L.; m. Marjorie Ann Fournier, Mar. 13, 1964; children: Sandra Moore, Deanne Longacre, Larraine Thompson. BA, Dartmouth Coll., Hanover, N.H., 1942. Mgr. Longacre & Son, Medina, Ohio, 1946-56; v.p. Paine Webber, Miami, Fla., from 1957. Securities arbitrator N.Y. Stock Exchange, Miami, 1985-90, Nat. Assn. Securities Dealers, Miami, 1990, Am. Assn. Arbitrators, Miami, 1990. Pres. Medina (Ohio) City Sch. Bd., 1964. Lt. comdr. USN, 1942-45. Mem. Key Biscayne C. of C. (pres. 1975), Dartmouth Alumni Club, Mahi Shrine, Key Biscayne Yacht Club, Lions Club (pres. 1954). Republican. Congregationalist. Avocations: golf, tennis. Home: Key Biscayne, Fla. Died Feb. 11, 2005.

LONGINOTTI, MARY ANGELA, secondary school educator; b. Chattanooga, Jan. 8, 1949; d. James Casbin and Mary Nell (Smith) Johnson; m. Carl Joseph Longinotti, Aug. 15, 1980; children: Carey, Scott, Kelly, Jamie, John. BS in Math., U. Ark., 1970; MEd in Math., U. Cen. Ark., 1991. Math. tchr. Dover (Ark.) High Sch., 1970-71, Mil. Edn. Program, Ansbach, Germany, 1972-74, St. Mary's High Sch., Little Rock, 1979-80, St. Joseph's High Sch., Conway, Ark., 1980-85, Greenbrier (Ark.) High Sch., from 1985. Tchr. Johnson & Johnson Cooperative Learning, 1991. Mem. Nat. Coun. Tchrs. Math. Roman Catholic. Home: Conway, Ark. Died May 12, 2004.

LOOMIS, BERNARD, toy licensing and design company executive; b. N.Y.C., July 4, 1923; s. Louis and Mary (Garfinkle) L.; m. Lillian Prince, Dec. 22, 1946; children: Merrill Nan, Debra Jan. Student mktg. and engring., NYU, 1940-57; exec. mgmt. program, UCLA, 1964. With Mattel Toys, Hawthorne, Calif., 1961-71, div. v.p., 1969-71; pres., chief exec. officer Kenner Products Co. div. Gen. Mills Corp., Cin., 1971-78; v.p. Gen. Mills Corp., 1973-78, group v.p. Toy Group div., 1978-81; pres. mktg. and design services Gen. Mills Toy Group, N.Y.C., 1981-84; pres. GLAD Toy Design and Devel., N.Y.C., 1984-87, Bernard Loomis, Inc., N.Y.C. Served with USAAF, 1943-45. Mem. Toy Mfrs. Am. (chmn. 1981-82, mem. adv. com.) Died June 2, 2006.

LOOSBROCK, CAROL MARIE, information management professional; b. Dubuque, Iowa, Aug. 21, 1936; d. Julius Carl and Elizabeth Cecilia (Kurz) L. BA, Clarke Coll., 1958; postgrad., Art Inst. Chgo., 1959-63; MS, Am. U., 1979. With Dept. Def., Washington, from 1968, specialist, from 1979. Mem. AAAS, Assn. Computing Machinery (Washington D.C. symposium steering coms. 1980-81, exec. coun. 1981-84); N.Y. Acad. Scis. (life), Am. Mgmt. Assn., Am. Security Coun. Found. (U.S. congl. adv. bd. 1984—, coalition for peace through strength leadership award, coalition for Desert Storm, coalition for internat. security), Am. Mus. Natural History. Republican. Home: Washington, DC. Died Apr. 6, 2004.

LOPEZ, NILO C., writer; b. Key West, Fla., Sept. 21, 1919; s. Juan Nepomuceno Lopez, Herminia Alonzo; m. Onelia Fernandez Lopez, Oct. 29, 1943. Author: (book) Memories of Old Key West, 1997, Thirties and Later Years, 1998, The Key West Hemingway Loved, 2000. Democrat. Roman Catholic. Avocations: reading, sports. Home: Key West, Fla. Died Mar. 14, 2005.

LORE, IRVING ALLAN, lawyer; b. Milw., Feb. 28, 1916; s. Michael and Jean (Dinerstein) L.; m. Clarissa Lerner, Feb. 4, 1940; children: Nancy Einhorn, Eileen Gosman. BA, U. Wis., 1935, JD, 1937. Bar: U.S. Supreme Ct., 1942. Sole practice, Milw., 1937-79; of counsel Saichek & Hertel, Milw., from 1979. Sec.-treas. Midwest Research Technologies, Inc., Immunotronics, Inc. Editor: U. Wis. Law Rev., 1935-37; also articles. Bd. dirs. Milw. Sch. Engring., 1966—, United Way Greater Milw., 1971-80; mem. bd. Met. Milw. Assn. Commerce, 1962-75, Milw. Found., 1971-74, assoc., 1975—; trustee Walter Schroeder Scholarship Fund Marquette U., Milw., 1963—, Mt. Sinai Med. Ctr., Milw., 1972—; chmn. Profl. div. United Way Campaigns, 1971-72. Served to lt. (j.g.) USN, 1943-45, PTO. Recipient Humanitarian award State of Wis. Nat. Conf. Christians and Jews, 1976. Mem. ABA, Assn. Trial Lawyers Am., Wis. Bar Assn., Wis. Acad. Trial Lawyers, Milw. Bar Assn., Order of the Coif, Artus. Clubs: Milw. Athletic, University. Lodges: Masons, Consistory, Shriners. Jewish. Avocations: bowling, bridge. Home: Milwaukee, Wis. Died Apr. 11, 2004.

LORIMER, CLARK D., small business owner; b. Williamsport, Pa., Feb. 27, 1947; s. Clark and D. Jean Lorimer; children: Craig A., Duane C. Owner AGS Electrical, Williamsport, Muncy, Pa., from 1968. With USNR, 1965-68. Mem. NRA (life). Avocations: fishing, boating, hunting. Home: Hughesville, Pa. Died Apr. 2, 2005.

LOSSAU, CARL SHIPLEY, education educator, consultant, planner; b. Chgo., Oct. 13, 1931; s. George William and Ella Carolyn (Busch) L.; m. Sarah Carolyn Heatherly (dec. 2001), Dec. 20, 1958; children: Kathleen Sarah, Michael William. BA, Northwestern U., 1953, MS, 1954, PhD, 1961. Planner City of Chgo., 1959-61, City of St. Louis, 1961-62; prof. geography So. Ill. U., Edwardsville, 1962—94, chair dept. geography, 1991—2006, prof. emeritus, 1994—2006. Alderman City of Edwardsville, 1977-85. Methodist. Home: Edwardsville, Ill. Died Jan. 16, 2006.

LOTTES, PATRICIA JOETTE HICKS, foundation administrator, retired nurse; b. Balt., Aug. 18, 1955; d. James Thomas and Linda Belle (Cadd) Hicks; m. Jeffrey Grant Gross, Aug. 18, 1979 (div. 1981); m. William Melamet Lottes, Sept. 10, 1983 (div. 1997). Diploma in practical nursing, Union Meml. Hosp., 1978. Staff nurse Union Meml. Hosp., Balt., 1978-79, critical care nurse, 1979-81; vis. critical care nurse Balt., 1981-84; head nurse Pharmakinetics, Inc., Balt., 1984-85; dir. Arachnoiditis Info. and Support Network, Inc., Ballwin, Mo., 1991—2001, dir. nat. support groups, from 1992. Nat. support group leader Arachnoid, 1993-2002. Sec., treas. O'Fallon (Mo.) Elks Ladies Aux., 1989-91, treas., 1991-92, incorporator, 1991, bd. dirs., 1991-94; co-chairperson 303d Field Hosp., U.S. Army Family Support Group, St. Louis, 1990-94. Mem. Nat. Disaster Med. Systems (assoc.), Elks Benevolent Trust, Elks Nat. Home Perpetual Trust. Republican. Baptist. Avocation: quilting. Home: O'Fallon, Mo. Died June 15, 2004.

LOTZ, JOAN THERESA, public relations company executive; b. N.Y.C., Feb. 22, 1948; d. Andrew J. and Joan (McCartney) L. BA, Lehman Coll., 1970. Libr. asst. Met. Mus. Art, N.Y.C., 1969-74; office mgr. York Cable Corp., Inc., N.Y.C., 1974-77, Mobile Communications, Inc., N.Y.C., 1977-78; lease mgr. Major Muffler Ctrs., Inc., N.Y.C., 1978-81; v.p., asst. to chmn. Rowland Worldwide, N.Y.C., 1981-93; pres. JL Enterprises, N.Y.C., from 1993. N.Y. State Regent's scholar, 1965-69. Mem. Nat. Scholastic Soc. Democrat. Roman Catholic. Avocation: ballet. Died Dec. 16, 2004.

LOUGHLIN, JOHN LEO, painter; b. Worcester, Mass., Apr. 11, 1931; s. John Joseph and Margaret Bernadette (Ford) L.; m. Elsa Maria Farinelli; children: Suzanne Mary, John Jospeh II. Cert., Worcester (Mass.) Art Sch., Mass., 1954; AB in Fine Arts, Clark U., 1957; MEd, Bridgewater State Coll., 1964. Illustrator, cartographer Nat. Geog. Mag., Washington, 1958-60; illustrator, head art dept. U.S. Naval War Coll., Newport, R.I., 1964-68; art dir. Sta. WSBE-TV, Providence, 1968-88; freelance painter Lincoln, R.I., from 1988. 1st lt. U.S. Army, 1952-53. Recipient numerous awards including gold medal, medal of honor. Mem. Guild of Boston Artists, New Eng. Watercolor Soc., Allied Artists of Am., Hudson Valley Art Assn., Providence Art Club, R.I. Watercolor Soc. (pres.). Avocation: fishing. Died May 23, 2004.

LOVE, BENTON F., banker; b. Paris, Tex., Nov. 19, 1924; s. Benton F. and Nell Peyton (Scott) L.; m. Margaret Janelle McKean, Sept. 20, 1947; children: Jeffery Benton, Janelle Margaret, Julie McKean. BBA, U. Tex., 1948. Founded paper mfg. firm which merged with Gibson Greeting Card Co., 1962; pres. River Oaks Bank and Trust Co., Houston, 1965-67; sr. v.p. Tex. Commerce Bank Nat. Assn., 1967-68, exec. v.p., 1968-69, pres., 1969-72, chmn. bd., CEO, 1972-80; pres. Tex. Commerce Bancshares Inc., 1971-72, chmn. bd., CEO, 1972-89, dir., cons.; pres. Assn. Res. City Bankers, 1981, hon. mem.; dir. Internat. Monetary Conf., 1986-88,; bd. dirs. Burlington No. Inc., Cox Enterprises Inc., Enterprises, Inc., Eli Lilly and Co., Proler Internat. Corp., Mitchell Energy and Devel. Corp. Author: People and Profits: A Bank Case Study, 1968. Chmn. council of overseers Jesse H. Jones Grad. Sch. Adminstrn., Rice U. Capt. 8th Air Force, USAAF, 1943-45. Decorated 11 combat decorations including D.F.C.; recipient Disting. Alumnus award U. Tex., 1975; named Houston's Cultural Leader of Yr., 1977, Key Houstonian of Yr., 1982, Tex. Bus. Exec. of Yr., 1983; named to Tex. Bus. Hall of Fame, 1989. Presbyterian. Died Jan. 13, 2006.

LOVE, SIDNEY IRWIN, psychologist, psychotherapist; b. N.Y.C., Feb. 12, 1922; s. Irving Daniel and Dora (Sokol) L.; m. May 9, 1948; children: Carolyn Beth, Jeanine Deboral. BS, CCNY, 1946; MSW, Columbia U., 1948; PhD, Heed U., 1978. Lic. psychologist, N.Y.; lic. social worker, N.Y. Assoc. therapist Child Guidance Inst. Jewish Bd. of Guardians, N.Y.C., 1948-61; asst. prof. dept. edn. Stony Brook br. SUNY, L.I., 1961-64; founder, mem. faculty Ctr. for Modern Psychoanalysis in N.Y., N.Y.C., 1971-81; founder, gen. dir. seminars Riverdale (N.Y.) Seminars in Modern Analytic Psychotherapy, from 1981. Pvt. practice, N.Y.C. and Riverdale, 1952—. Contbr. articles to profl. jours. Sgt. U.S. Army, 1942-45, World War II, ETO. Decorated Bronze Star, Purple Heart. Fellow Am. Orthopsychiat. Assn. (life); mem. Nat. Psychol. Assn. for Psychoanalysis, NASW, Coun. for Health Svc. Providers in Psychology. Home: Bronx, NY. Died Feb. 11, 2004.

LOVETT, CHESTER, lawyer; b. Charleston, W.Va., Oct. 18, 1922; s. Benjamin and Anna (Schwartz) L.; 1 child from previous marriage, Joseph; m. Sharon Wood, Jan. 19, 1980. AB, W.Va. U., 1946, JD, 1949. Bar: W.Va. 1949, U.S. Ct. Appeals 1967, U.S. Supreme Ct., 1973. Pvt. practice, Charleston, W.Va., 1949-84; ptnr. Lovett, Cooper & Glass, Charleston, from 1984. Bd. trustees B'nai Jacob Synagogue, Charleston; bd. dirs. W.Va. Symphony. With U.S. Army, 1943-46, ETO. Am. Acad. Matrimonial Lawyers, W.Va. Trial Lawyers Assn., W.Va. State Bar (family law com.), Charleston Chamber Music Soc. (bd. dirs.). Jewish. Avocation: photographer. Home: Charleston, W.Va. Died Aug. 14, 2005.

LOWES, NORMAN MALCOLM, investor, retired sales executive; b. Yonkers, N.Y., July 12, 1928; s. Norman Harper and Mary Elizabeth (McMahon) L.; m. Elizabeth Therese Norton, Oct. 24, 1949; children: Mary, Patricia, Kathleen, Elizabeth, Suzanne. Student, NYU, 1948-50; BS, Adelphi U., 1958. V.p. sales Gibson Greeting Cards, Cin., 1952-72; v.p. C.M. Paula Co., Cin., 1972-90; owner, investor Apt. Mgmt. Co., Cin., from 1990. Sgt. USMC, 1946-48. Mem. Am. Mgmt. Assn. Republican. Roman Catholic. Avocations: swimming, boating, golf, tennis. Home: Cincinnati, Ohio. Died Mar. 10, 2005.

LOWREY, ANNIE TSUNEE, retired cultural organization administrator; b. Osaka, Japan, Mar. 3, 1929; naturalized U.S. citizen, 1963; d. Shigeru Takahata and Kuniko Takahata Takahashi; m. Lawrence K. Lowrey, Mar. 17, 1953; children: Kristine K. Ricci, Jay. BS in Lit., Wakayama (Japan) Shin-Ai, 1949; BS in Art Edn., Kans. State U., 1967; MA in Indsl. Tech., Wichita State U., 1976. Cert. instr. Wichita-Tchr. Assessment and Assistance Program, 1987. Tchr. Minoshima Elem. Sch., Wakayama, Japan, 1945-46, Wakayama Jr. H.S., 1948-49, Truesdell Jr. H.S., Wichita, Kans., 1967-69; tchr., coord. dept. fine arts Wichita H.S. East, 1969-92, instr. Japanese, 1991-92; lectr. dept. art and indsl. tech. Wichita State U., 1974-88, instr. computer applications in industry, 1990-91; tchr. Woodman Elem. Sch., Wichita, summer 1987; instr. art appreciation Butler County C.C., McConnell and Wichita, 1988-92; dir. edn. and exhbn. Wichita Ctr. for Arts, 1992-95; ret., 1995. Asst. to fine arts photographer Charles Phillips, Wichita, spring 1989; judge Sister City Art Contest, 1991, Wichita Botanica Photography Competition, painting competition Wichita Painter's Guild, design competition Kans. Aviation Mus., 1991-92; instr. art instrnl. strategy to elem. and secondary art tchrs. Ft. Collins and Loveland, Colo. sch. dists., 1989; presenter many profl. confs. and workshops, most Nat. Art Edn. Conf., Phoenix, 1992, Kans. Accessible Arts, 1994, Kans. State U., 1994. Chairperson writing team for Kans. Plan for Indsl. Edn.-TV, 1974-75; co-author tech. edn. curriculum Kans. State Bd. Regents, 1989. Judge Miss Asia contest 10th Ann. Asian Festival, Wichita, 1990; pres. pub. art adv. bd. City of Wichita, 1991—. Carnegie grantee for development of inter-disciplinary program on cultural literacy, 1984, Matsushita Electronic Co. grantee for curriculum devel., 1986; inductee Kans. Tchrs. Hall of Fame, 1994.

Mem. NEA (presenter nat. conv. 1985), ASCD, Nat. Art Edn. Assn.Western Region Outstanding Educator of Yr. 1988), Kans. Alliance for Arts Edn. (bd. dirs. 1987-89), Phi Delta Kappa (pres. Wichita State U. chpt. 1983-84), Delta Phi Delta. Home: Wichita, Kans. Died Aug. 16, 2005.

LOWY, ROBERT RALPH, physician; b. Berlin, Nov. 22, 1929; came to U.S., 1947; s. Hans and Greta (Gans) L.; m. Beverly Frances Katz, Dec. 27, 1957; children: Laurence, Monica. BA, NYU, 1955; MD, SUNY, Bklyn., 1959. Resident in internal medicine Bklyn. VA Hosp., 1960-61; intern Montefiore Hosp., Bronx, N.Y., 1959-60, resident in internal medicine, 1962-63, fellow in gastroenterology, 1962-63; chmn. dept. medicine Little Neck (N.Y.) Cmty. Hosp., from 1974, chief divsn. gastroenterology. Asst. prof. medicine SUNY, Stony Brook, Albert Einstein Coll. Medicine, Bronx. Fellow Am. Coll. Gastroenterology, Am. Gastroenterol. Assn.; mem. N.Y. State Soc. Medicine, Queens Med. Soc. Died Feb. 23, 2004.

LOY, RICHARD NELSON, insurance company executive; b. Corpus Christi, Tex., Sept. 2, 1945; s. Franklin Everett and Adelia Melita (Gibbons) L.; m. Carla Diane Combs, Nov. 28, 1969; children: Eric, Brandon. BSBA, Western Ky. U., 1969. CLU. Exec. v.p. Southeastern States Securities, Lexington, Ky., 1969-71; exec. g.a. Am. Family Securitiy Ins. Co., Lexington, 1971-75, exec. v.p., 1975-83; dir. mktg. Ky. Ctrl. Life Ins. Co., Lexington, from 1983. Trustee Cardinal Hill Hospital, Lexington, 1977-86, treas., 1979-81, adv. trustee, 1986—. Mem. Am. Soc. CLU (chmn. 1973-75), Gen. Agents and Mgrs. Assn. (chmn. 1971-75), Lexington Life Underwriters Assn. (chmn. 1971-75), Bluegrass Estate Planning Coun., Western Ky. U. Alumni Assn., U. Ky. Alumni Assn., U. Ky. Wildcat Club (pres. 1984-85). Avocations: football, basketball, gourmet cooking. Home: Lexington, Ky. Died Oct. 14, 2004.

LUBECK, SALLY, educator; b. St. Louis, May 12, 1945; d. Lambert Walter and Erma Jean (Gilbert) Roy; children: Julie Rebecca, Aaron David. BA, Washington U., St. Louis, 1967, MAT in English, 1969, MA in Edn., 1969; EdD, U. Mo., St. Louis, 1984. Postdoctoral felloww Grad. Sch. Edn., Harvard U., 1984-85; postdoctoral fellow U. N.C., Chapel Hill, 1985-86, coord. Bush Inst. for Child & Family Policy, 1986-88, sr. investigator Frank Porter Graham Child Devel. Ctr., 1988-91, asst. prof. Sch. Edn., 1988-91; asst. prof. U. Mich., Ann Arbor, from 1991. Author: Sandbox Society, 1985 (Outstanding Acad. Book award 1987); cons. editor Internat. Jour. Qualitative Rsch. in Edn., 1987—; editor Theory into Practice, winter 1989. Recipient Disting. Alumni award U. Mo., St. Louis, 1988; Spencer fellow, 1986-88. Mem. Am. Ednl. Rsch. Assn. (asst. chmn. div. D 1989-90), Am. Anthrop. Assn. (bd. dirs. coun. on anthropology and edn. 1987-91). Avocations: tennis, travel. Died Apr. 10, 2004.

LUCA, MARK, retired art educator; b. San Francisco, Oct. 14, 1918; s. Angelo and Jessey (Dorr) L.; 1 child, Angelo. BA with honors, San Francisco State Coll., 1940; MA, Columbia U., 1948; PhD, U. Calif. Berkeley, 1958. Cert. elem., secondary educator, Calif. Art instr. State Coll., Potsdam, N.Y., 1948-50; supr. edn. U. Calif., Berkeley, 1958-78; ret., 1978; exch. prof. U. London, 1969; art instr. Calif. Coll. Arts and Crafts, Oakland, 1978-88; edn. instr. Hayward State U., 1984-87, 89-90; instr. Columbia Pacific U., from 1986. Art supr. (part-time) Castro Valley (Calif.) schs., 1964-65; coord. child art U. Calif. Ext., Berkeley, 1965; asst. dir./curator/edn. dir. Museo Italo-Americano, San Francisco, 1978-81. Artist: (painting and printmaking) exhibits of work in U.S., Mexico, South Am.; co-author: (textbook) Understanding Children's Art, 1967, Art Education, 1968; author: (state guides) Teaching Gifted Children Art Grades 1-12, 1973; contbr. articles to profl. jours. Cons. art and multi-ethnic edn. San Mateo County schs., 1970; radio readings Sta. KPFA-FM, Berkeley, 1970-71; art judge San Francisco pub. schs., 1969, 70, 71; cons. statewide humanities framework, Sacramento, 1970; bd. dirs. Youth-in-Arts, San Rafael, 1987-92, Rohnert Park Assn. for the Arts 1994-95 (dir. visual arts FTA gallery 1996-97); mem., exhibits coord. North Bay Italian Cultural Found., 1995-97. Recipient mural scholarship Columbia U., 1948, internat. fellowship Mexican govt. Instituto Politecnico Mexico, D.F., 1951, U.S. govt. grants for E.P.O.C.H. project, 1968-72; named Outstanding Art Educator Calif. Art Edn. Assn., 1978. Mem. Calif. Tchrs. Assn. (life), Calif. Soc. Printmakers (founding, sec. 1968-98, historian 1972-73), Calif. Writers Club (pres. Berkeley br.). Democrat. Unitarian Universalist. Avocations: art, writing, walking, theater, music. Home: Rohnert Park, Calif. Died June 26, 2005.

LUCAS, LINDA LUCILLE, dean; b. Stockton, Calif., Apr. 22, 1940; d. Leslie Harold Lucas and Amy Elizabeth (Callow) Farnsworth. BA, San Jose State Coll., 1961, MA, 1969; EdD, U. San Francisco, 1982; JD, John F. Kennedy U., 2002. Dist. libr. Livermore (Calif.) Elem. Schs., 1962-64; libr. Mission San Jose High Sch., Fremont, Calif., 1964-69; media reference libr. Chabot Coll., Hayward, Calif., 1969-75; asst. dean instrn. Chabot-Las Positas Coll., Livermore, 1975-91; assoc. dean instrn. Las Positas Coll., Livermore, 1991-94, dean acad. svcs., 1994-2000, dean emeritus, from 2000; atty. at law, 2003. Participant Nat. Inst. for Leadership Devel., 1991. Bd. dirs. Tri-Valley Community TV, Livermore, 1991-98, Valley Choral Soc., 1993-98, Chabot-Las Positas Colls. Found., Pleasanton, Calif., 1991-94; mem. needs assessment com Performing Arts Coun., Pleasanton. Mem. ALA, Coun. Chief Librs., Assn. Calif. Community Coll. Adminstrs., Calif. Libr. Assn., Calif. Bar Assn. Avocations: choral music, photography. Home: Pleasanton, Calif. Died Sept. 22, 2004.

LUCAS, RUTH FRANCES, elementary school educator; b. Lubbock, Tex., May 13, 1929; d. Wendell and Irma Belle (Stevens) Phillips; m. Harvey Dean McGehee, July 22, 1951 (div. July 1968); children: Buckley Ray, Claude Allen, Karen Allene, Dena Jane; m. Harvey Franklin Lucas, June 14, 1974. Student, Victoria (Tex.) Jr. Coll., 1947-49; BS, Abilene (Tex.) Christian Coll., 1951. Cert. elem. tchr., Mo., Ark., Tex. Tchr. Ft. Worth Pub. Schs., 1951-52, Tulsa Pub. Schs., 1960-61, Greenville (Tex.) Pub. Schs., 1961-64, Gentry (Ark.) Pub. Schs., 1964-76, Colcord (Okla.) Pub. Schs., 1976-77, Gravette (Ark.) Pub. Schs., from 1977. Mem. NEA, DAR, Ark. Edn. Assn., Ark. Ret. Tchrs., Ark. Assn. Univ. Women. Democrat. Mem. Ch. of Christ. Avocations: travel, needlecrafts. Home: Gravette, Ark. Died Mar. 15, 2004.

LUCE, GORDON COPPARD, retired savings bank executive; b. San Diego, Nov. 21, 1925; m. Karen Turnbow, 1955, children: Randall, Kelly, Andrew BA, Stanford U., 1950, MBA, 1952. Sec. of Bus. & Transp. State of Calif., 1967-69; former sr. v.p. branches mktg. & adminstrn. Home Fed. Savs. & Loan Assn., San Diego; pres. Great Am. Bank, San Diego, 1969-79, CEO, 1969—90; chmn. Great Am. First Savs. Bank, San Diego, 1979—90. Mem. Pres.'s Commn. on Housing, 1981; alt. del. with rank amb. 37th Gen. Assembly UN, 1982-83; del. Internat. Conf. on Pvt. Sector Initiatives, Paris, 1986; mem. Presdl. Bd. Advisors Pvt. Sector Initiatives, 1985-88; mem. Pres.'s Fgn. Intelligence Adv. Bd., 1988, 89. Trustee Ronald Reagan Presdl. Found., 1986-88. Served with U.S. Army, 1944-46. Decorated Bronze Star. Died Aug. 21, 2006.

LUCK, HERMAN DAVID, physician; b. N.Y.C., May 10, 1925; s. Julius Alexander and Ruth (Field) L.; m. Frances Jean Wingfield, Jan. 22, 1950; children: Rebecca Jean, Jennifer June. BS, Bates Coll., 1945; MD, Case Western Reserve U., 1949. Diplomate Am. Bd. Family Practice. Intern Harris Meml. Hosp., Ft. Worth, 1949-50; intern internal medicine U. Ark. Med. Scis., Little Rock, 1953; pvt. practice Arkadelpia (Ark.) Med. Assn., from 1953. Asst. prof. medicine U. Ark. Med. Sci., Little Rock, 1970. Trustee Henderson State U., Arkadelphia, 1971-83; chmn. Ark. State Bd. of Higher Edn., Little Rock, 1988—. Lt. USN, 1949-53. Named Man of Yr., Arkadelphia Jr. C. of C., 1962. Fellow Am. Acad. Family Practice; mem. AMA, Arkadelphia C. of C. (pres. 1961). Democrat. Presbyterian. Avocations: golf, writing. Home: Arkadelphia, Ark. Died Jan. 3, 2005.

LUDLAM, JOEL AUGUST, optometrist, researcher; b. Phila., Mar. 7, 1948; s. John Joseph Ludlam and Helen Louise Paczulla; m. Delphine Ludlam, Oct. 10, 1981 (div. Dec. 2000); children: Kasandra, Uwe, Michele. BS in Biology, Wake Forest U., 1970; BS in Visual Sci., Pa. Coll. Optometry, 1972, OD, 1974; PhA, Mythologics U., Tucson, 2000. Lic. optometrist, Ariz.; cert. oral therapeutics, topical pharms., Ariz. With Indian Hosp. USPHS-DHEW, Shiprock, N.Mex., 1974-79. Optometrist Ariz. Industries for the Blind, Phoenix, 1986-91. Maj. USPHS, 1974-79. Recipient medal of honor Navajo Nation, Window Rock, Ariz., 1985. Fellow www.mythologics.com (v.p. 1996). Republican. Avocations: gardening, bird watching, canoeing. Home: Mesa, Ariz. Died Jan. 15, 2004.

LUEGGE, WILLARD ARTHUR, chemist, consultant; b. Oak Park, Ill., Mar. 19, 1931; s. Theodore Wilhelm and Irma Minnie (Schoepfer) L.; m. Joanna Carleen Wechter, Sept. 1, 1951; children: Sherylene, Lynette. BA, Ind. U., 1953; postgrad., Ind. U., U. Louisville, UCLA, 1954-64. Rsch. chemist Louisville Cement Co., Speed, Ind., 1956-60; quality control chemist Cal Portland Cement Co., Mojave, Calif., 1960-61; chemistry tchr. Palmdale (Calif.) High Sch., 1961-90; owner-dir. PM Labs, Lancaster, Calif., 1968-89; cons. extractive metallurgical chemistry Lancaster, from 1989. Sci. dept. chmn. Palmdale High Sch., 1964-79; mem. Calif. Assn. Chemistry Tchrs., 1963-89; rsch. chemist USAF Rocket Propulsion Lab., Edwards AFB, summers, 1966, '67, '68; bd. dirs. Bryman Refining Co., Inc. Inventor assay kit, 1970. Recipient Tchr. of the Yr. award Am. Chem. Soc., 1967; NSF grantee, 1963, 64. Mem. Western Mining Coun., Western States Pub. Lands Coalition. Presbyterian. Avocations: travel, jazz, basketball, baseball, football. Died Mar. 6, 2005.

LUND, ANDERS EDWARD, consultant, timber expert; b. Luverne, Minn., Sept. 26, 1928; s. Anders Edward and Hulda Marie (Anderson) L.; m. Terry Frances Froehlin, Dec. 31, 1992. BS, Colo. State U., 1955; MF, Duke U., 1956, D of Forestry, 1964. Registered forester in wood sci. & tech., S.C. Sr. scientist Koppers Co., Inc., Monroeville, Pa., 1958-66; assoc. prof. Clemson (S.C.) U., 1966-67; prof. Tex. A&M U., College Station, 1967-73; head Tex. Forest Products Lab., Lufkin, 1967-73; dir. Inst. Wood Rsch. Mich. Tech. U., Houghton, 1974-84; cons. Anders E. Lund, Inc., Farmington Hills, Mich., from 1984; timber expert Mich. Dept. Transp., Lansing, from 1984. Contbr. over 35 articles to profl. jours.; around 40 patents in field. Mem. Mich. Gov.'s Task Force, Lansing, 1982-84. Fellow Duke U., 1958; recipient assistantship U.S. Forest Svc., 1956. Fellow ASTM (vice chmn. com. D-7 1991—), Inst. Wood Sci.; mem. Am. Wood Preservers' Assn. (v.p.), Soc. Wood Sci. & Tech., Internat. Assn. Wood Anatomists, Internat. Rsch. Group Wood Preservation. Home: Farmington Hl, Mich. Died Feb. 11, 2005.

LUNDE, ANDERS STEEN, demographer; b. Bridgeport, Conn., Dec. 10, 1914; s. Anders and Cecilia (Steen) L.; m. Eleanor Sheldon, Sept. 9, 1939; children: Erik Sheldon, Peter Steen, Anne Louisa. BA, St. Lawrence U., 1938, MDiv, 1942; MA, Columbia U., 1947, PhD, 1955. Ordained to ministry Unitarian Ch., 1942. Lectr. Rutgers U., New Brunswick, N.J., 1948-51; assoc. prof. St. Lawrence U., Canton, N.Y., 1951-55; prof. Gallaudet Coll., Washington, 1955-58; chief natality statis. br. Nat. Ctr. for Health Statis., Washington, 1962-64, asst. dir. nat. vital statis. div., 1964-67, dir. Office of State Svcs. Research Triangle Park, N.C., 1967-74, assoc. dir. Washington, 1974-77; adj. prof. biostatis. Sch. Pub. Health U. N.C., Chapel Hill, from 1977. Cons., author Internat. Inst. Vital Registration and Statis., Bethesda, Md., 1977-80. Author: Whirligigs: Design and Construction, 1982, reprinted (under title Easy-to-Make Whirligigs), 1996, More Whirligigs: Large Scale and Animated Figures, 1984, 2d edit., 1998, reprinted (under title Making Animated Whirligigs), 1998, Whirligigs in Silhouette, 1989, Whirligigs for Children: Young and Old, 1992, reprinted (under title Whimsical Whirligigs and How to Make Them), 2000; artist (permanent collection) Smithsonian Instn., Washington, D.C.; contbr. numerous articles to profl. jours. Minister Old Ship Ch., Hingham, Mass., 1941-43, First Unitarian Ch., Phila., 1958-62; mem. adv. com. Ret. Sr. Vol. Program, Chapel Hill, 1983-89; bd. dirs., treas. N.C. Art Soc., 1978-82; bd. dirs., 1st v.p. N.C. Botanical Garden Found., 1984-90. Capt. U.S. Army, 1943-46/ Recipient First award Durham (N.C.) Art Guild, 1982, Hon. Mention, N.C. Mus. History, 1983. Fellow AAAS, APHA, Am. Statis. Assn.; mem. Am. Population Assn. (sec.-treas. 1965-68, bd. dirs. 1968-71). Democrat. Episcopalian. Avocation: wood sculpture. Home: Pittsboro, NC. Died Apr. 12, 2004.

LUNDIN, BRUCE THEODORE, engineer, management consultant; b. Alameda, Calif., Dec. 28, 1919; s. Oscar Linus and Elizabeth Ellen (Erickson) L.; m. Barbara Ann Bliss, July 27, 1946 (wid. Feb. 1981); children: Dianne, Robert, Nancy; m. Jean Ann Oberlin, Mar. 22, 1982. BSME, U. Calif.-Berkeley, 1942; D of Engring. (hon.), U. Toledo, 1975. Chief engine research NASA Lewis Ctr., Cleve., 1952-58, asst. dir., 1958-61, assoc. dir., 1961-68, dir., 1969-77; dep. assoc. adminstrn. NASA, Washington, 1968-69. Adv. U.S. Air Force Sci. Adv. Bd., Washington, 1961-77; mem. Aerospace Safety Adv. Bd., Washington, 1961-72; staff dir. Pres.'s Commn. on the Accident at Three Mile Island, 1981; mem. TM1-2 Safety Adv. Bd., 1981-89; chmn. Rockwell Internat. Safety Oversight Panel, 1988-89. Pres. Westshore Unitarian Ch., Rocky River, Ohio, 1967-68; trustee Southwest Gen. Hosp., Berea, Ohio, 1970-75. Recipient Outstanding Leadership medal NASA, 1965, Pub. Service award NASA, 1971, 75, Disting. Service medal NASA, 1971, 77, Engineer of the Year award Nat. Space Club, 1975 Fellow AIAA; mem. Nat. Acad. Engring. Avocations: sailing, skiing, fishing. Home: North Olmsted, Ohio. Died Jan. 24, 2006.

LUNDY, GARY DAVID, journalist, sports writer; b. Madison, Tenn., Dec. 31, 1954; s. David Lee Lundy and Joan Marie (Groth) Delosh; m. Cynthia Ross, Aug. 12, 1978. BS in Journalism, U. Tenn., 1977, BS in Fin., 1987. Sports editor The Daily Beacon/U. Tenn., Knoxville, 1976-77; sports writer The Cleve. (Tenn.) Banner, 1977; sports editor The Roane County News, Kingston, Tenn., 1977-79; sports writer The Knoxville Jour., 1979-91, The Knoxville News-Sentinel, from 1992. With Tenn. Sports Writers Assn. (Tenn. Sports Writer of Yr. 1990), U.S. Basketball Writers Assn. (1st place Features 1990). Recipient 1st place Sports Reporting, Tenn. AP Mng. Editors, 1990, 6-time finalist Writing award AP Sports Editors, 1988-91, 1st place Enterprise Reporting, 1989, Green Eyeshade award for Sports Commentary, Atlanta Soc. Profl. Journalists, 1989, 1st place All Media in S.E., 1989. Methodist. Died Nov. 22, 2004.

LUPO, ANDREW BRITTON, restaurant management company executive; b. Columbus, Ga., Aug. 23, 1944; s. Harvey Eugene and Margaret (Kennon) L.; m. Barbara Shier, Dec. 15, 1976; children: Margaret Ruth, Sarah Brittiny. M Hotel Supply, Am. Hotel-Motel Assn. Sch., Chgo., 1988. Sec.-treas. Mary Mac's Ltd., Atlanta, from 1962; pres. Interhost Corp., from 1989. Cons. Underground Atlanta, 1987-89. Active Jackson for Mayor Campaign, Atlanta, 1989. Mem. Ga. Hospitality and Travel Assn. (bd. dirs., trade show com. 1987—), Atlanta C. of C. (chmn. bus. after hours, chmn. entrepreneur of yr. com. 1987-89), East Lake Country Club, Flat Creek Country Club. Republican. Roman Catholic. Home: Fayetteville, Ga. Died July 12, 2004.

LUPO, THOMAS J., mortgage banker, real estate developer; b. Jan. 28, 1922; m. Alvena Florence Smith; children: Robert E. Smith, Mrs. Norris Smith Lupo Williams. BS in Arch., Tulane U., 1942. Owner Tommie Lupo Realtor, Robert E. Smith Real Estate. Former chmn. corp. devel. Pelican Homestead and Savings Assn.; chmn. bd. dirs. Hedwig Inc., Noroaltom Devel. Co., Zephyr Inc., South Pines Inc., Lakeshore Shopping Ctr., Harrison Ave. Shopping Ctr., Noro Plaza Office Bldg. Complex, New Orleans Land Co., Wulu Enterprises, B.V., Pirates Cove Ltd., Robert E. Smith Ctr., Smith Lupo Ctr. Former trustee Kirkwood Trust, H.S. Smith Trusts, A.S. Lupo Trust, Police and

Firearm Tragedy Fund Inc., 'Commodore' Thomas J. Lupo Found., U.S.S. Fanshaw Bay Found.; sponsor Thomas J. Lupo award for Archtl. Excellence Tulane U.; former chmn. Nat. Org. Regional Planning Councils and Commns.; former pres. New Orleans Area Health Planning Coun.; former v.p. La. State Regional Planning Coun.; commr. Municipal Yacht Harbor, New Orleans, 1950. Served with Navy. Named to Internat. Bus. Hall of Fame, 1956, one of Ten Outstanding Businessmen in Am. Harvard U., 1958. Died Dec. 27, 2004.

LUQUETTE, WILLIAM JOSEPH, alcohol/drug abuse services professional; b. Corpus Christi, Tex., Nov. 23, 1957; s. Aurillian Joseph Luquette and Margurite Elizabeth Luquette-Estrada. BA, West Tex. A&M U., 1992; MAT, S.W. Tex. State U., 1996; postgrad., Tex. A&M U., from 2002. Lic. chem. dependency counselor. Grad. teaching asst. S.W. Tex. State U., San Marcos; case mgr. Austin/Travis County MHMR, 1994—95; LCDC counselor intern Travis TTC House, 1995—97, Austin Drug & Alcohol Program, 1997—98; intake coord. Parks & Assocs., Amarillo, 1998—99; clin. supr. Recovery Camp of Tex., Corpus Christi, from 2000. Profl. advisor Coastal Ben ICRC, Corpus Christi. Mem.: Tex. Assn. Addiction Profls. (treas. 1999—2001, coord. from 2000), Psi Chi, Alpha Kappa Delta. Democrat. Roman Catholic. Avocation: mountain biking. Home: Corpus Christi, Tex. Died Aug. 16, 2004.

LUSK, ROBERT EDWARD, lawyer, airline executive; b. Rapid City, S.D., June 17, 1929; s. Edward Franklin and Ruby Mae (Wheeler) L.; m. Maxine May Schwabe, Mar. 25, 1952; children: Ted, Sally, Mary Kay. BS in Acctg., U. Mo., 1951, AB in Econs., 1954, JD, 1957. Bar: Mo. 1957, U.S. Dist. Ct. (we. dist.) Mo. 1957, U.S. Supreme Ct. 1962. Law clk. Smith & Williams, Springfield, Mo., 1956; instr. acctg. U. Mo., Columbia, 1956-56; atty. Mann, Walter, Powell & Weathers, Springfield, 1957-59; in govt. affairs Trans World Airlines, San Francisco-Kansas City, Mo., 1966-83; atty. U.S. Dept. Agr., Kansas City, Mo., 1959-66, 83-94. Mem. bd. editors Law Rev., U. Mo., 1956-57. Chmn. Bd. Zoning Adjustments, Platte County, Mo., 1986-94; mem. Planning and Zoning Commn., Platte County, 1983-86; bd. dirs Mid Am. Health Network, 1984-91; v.p. Spelman Meml. Hosp., 1978-91. Col. U.S. Army, 1951-53, Korea, Res., 1953-81. Decorated Bronze Star; recipient County Citizen of Yr., Platte County Bus. and Profl. Assn., 1983, Order of Coif. Mem. MIl. Order of World Wars (chpt. comdr. 1992), VFW (post commdr. 1994), Lions Club. Episcopalian. Home: Sun City West, Ariz. Died May 20, 2005.

LUSSENDEN, DONALD ALLAN, personnel executive; b. Flint, Mich., June 10, 1921; s. Charles Wesley and Bernice Marie (Booher) L.; m. Helen Jane Lipsey, Aug. 10, 1946 (div. Mar. 27, 1961); children: Kendrick, Garrett, Patricia; m. Lucille Helen Kalusniak, Jan. 20, 1962; 1 child, Debra. BA in Sociology, Wayne State U., 1949. Prodn. worker Ford Motor Co., Dearborn, Mich., 1939-41, 46-50, warranty processor, 1952-55, personnel recuriter, 1955-65, personnel coordinator, 1965-80, recruiting cons., from 1983. Served to 1st lt. U.S. Army, 1941-46, 50-52. Avocations: archaeology, history, genealogy. Home: Livonia, Mich. Died June 9, 2004.

LUTWAK, LEO, retired physician, educator; b. N.Y.C., Mar. 27, 1928; s. Herman and Charlotte (Safirstein) L.; m. Cecile Kroshinsky, Dec. 23, 1950 (dec. 1976); children: Mark Steven, Diane Ellen, Paul Jonathan, Jean Rachel, Robert Ira; m. Victoria Jones, July 21, 1976; children: David Morris, Aviva Ruth. BS, City Coll. N.Y., 1945; MS, U. Wis., 1946; PhD, U. Mich., 1950; MD, Yale U., 1956. Biochemist Brookhaven Nat. Lab., 1950-52; dept. surgery Yale, 1952-56; intern medicine Duke Hosp., 1956-57; clin. assoc. NIH, 1957-59, sr. investigator, 1960-63; resident medicine USPHS Hosp., San Francisco, 1959-60; asst. clin. prof. medicine Georgetown U., 1961-63; Jamison prof. clin. nutrition, prof. univ. health services, also dir. clin. nutrition unit Cornell U., 1963-72; prof. medicine U. Calif. at Los Angeles Med. Sch.; also prof. nutrition Sch. Pub. Health, 1972-76; chief sect. endocrinology, nutrition and metabolism VA Hosp., Sepulveda, Calif., 1972-76; chmn. dept. medicine Akron (Ohio) City Hosp., 1976-78; prof. medicine, prof. and program dir. nutritional scis. NE Ohio Univs. Coll. Medicine, 1976-84; med. officer FDA, 1992—2006. Adj. prof. Akron U., 1977-84; NRC sr. rsch. fellow Ames Rsch. Lab., NASA, Calif., 1970-71; vis. prof. medicine Stanford Med. Sch., 1970-71; spl. rsch. endocrinology, bone physiology, obesity; cons. adv. panel NIH, 1964-68, Gerontol. Soc., 1964; cons. NASA, 1964-92, Tompkins County Hosp., 1963-72. Author articles in field. Pres. Ithaca Assn. Jewish Studies, 1964. Fellow Am. Inst. Chemists, Am. Coll. Nutrition, A.C.P.; mem. Soc. Exptl. Biology and Medicine, AAAS, Am. Fedn. Clin. Research, Am. Bd. Nutrition (dir., v.p. 1980-81, pres. 1981-82), Am. Inst. Nutrition, Am. Physiol. Soc., Am. Diabetes Assn., Ala. Diabetes Assn. (bd. dirs. 1986-89), Akron Diabetes Assn. (dir. 1976-83), Am. Soc. Clin. Nutrition, Pan Am. Med. Assn., Western Soc. Clin. Research, Endocrine Soc., N.Y. Acad. Scis., Phi Beta Kappa, Sigma Xi, Phi Lambda Upsilon. Home: Silver Spring, Md. Died Feb. 23, 2006.

LUTZ, CHARLENE JOYCE, special education educator, consultant; b. Santa Monica, Calif., Feb. 16, 1947; d. Frederick Pusant and Margaret Jane (Vartian) Samuelson; m. Arnold Anthony Lutz, Jan. 4, 1980 (div. Mar. 1987); children: Stara Lynn, Mista Lea; m. Gerard Anthony Howells, June 23, 1967 (div. June 1976); 1 child, Russell Allen Howells. BA in Psychology, UCLA, 1973; MEd, Calif. State U. LA, 1974; JD, U. West Los Angeles, 1994. Cert. tchr., tchr. learning handicapped, c.c. tchr., psychology resource specialist Calif. Tchr. spl. edn. Los Angeles County Office Edn., Downey, Calif., 1975—83; tchr. master tng. Calif State U., L.A., 1976—79; tchr. spl edn., resource specialist Centinela Valley Union H.S. Dist., Lawndale, 1983—85, program spl. coord., 1985—91; tchr. spl. edn. L.A. Unified Sch. Dist., 1991—95, resource specialist, 1995—2002. Cons. expert witness, LA, from 1994; tchr. master training Nat. U., Inglewood, Calif., 2001—02; career transition coord. LA Unified Sch. Dist., 2002. Author: Quick 'N' Easy Learning Tasks, 1986. Mem. Nat. Taxpayer's Union, Washington, from 1995, Howard Jarvice Taxpayer's Assn., L.A., from 1995. Mem.: NEA, Calif. Tchrs. Assn., United Tchrs. L.A., Pi Lambda Theta, Phi Delta Kappa. Libertarian. Avocations: gardening, walking, travel, cooking. Home: Playa Del Rey, Calif. Died Apr. 22, 2004.

LYKKEN, DAVID THORSON, psychology educator; b. Mpls., June 18, 1928; s. Henry Gilman Lykken Sr. and Francis Hamilton; m. Harriet S. Betts, 1952 (dec. Nov. 8, 2005); children: Jesse H., Joseph D., Matthew A. BA, U. Minn., 1949, MA, 1952, PhD, 1955. NSF postdoctoral fellow U. London, 1954-55; NIH postdoctoral fellow U. Minn., Mpls., 1955-57, asst. prof., 1957-59, assoc. prof., 1960-65, prof., 1965—98, prof. emeritus, 1998—2006; fellow Inst. Study Behavioral Scis., Stanford, Calif., 1959-60. Former series editor Acad. Press, Inc., N.Y. Author: A Tremor in the Blood, 1981; contbr. articles to sci. profls. Fellow Am. Psychol. Assn. (disting. contbns. to psychology in pub. interest award 1990), AAAS; mem. Soc. for Psychol. Rsch. (pres. 1980-81), Behavior Genetics Soc., Internat. Soc. for Twin Rsch., Am. Psychol. Soc. Home: Minneapolis, Minn. Died Sept. 15, 2006.

LYNCH, ANDREW PARKHURST, II, international trade advisor; b. Evanston, Ill., Feb. 22, 1925; s. Josiah Parkhurst Lynch and Virginia (Stillwell) Cole; m. Patricia A. Rayhill, Aug. 1964 (div. June 1973); m. Barbara Ann McCall, Sept. 6, 1973 (dec. July 1989). BA, Northwestern U., 1949. Sales rep. Farah Mfg. Co. Inc., El Paso, Tex., 1952-64; founder, chief exec. officer Pro Temp, S.A. de C.V., Mexico City, 1964-70; Chgo. met. mktg. mgr. Batesville (Ind.) Casket Co., 1970-74; dir. mktg. Major Casket Co. Calif., L.A., 1974-78; dir. internat. fin. Walter E. Heller & Co., Chgo., 1978-84; founder, chief exec. officer AP Lynch Fgn. Svcs. Corp., Chgo., Rotterdam, Netherlands, and Hong Kong, from 1984. Cons., speaker U.S. Dept. Commerce; liaison person various trade assns. and univs; adviser to fgn. govts. Author: Exporting, a Three-Ring Circus, 1987, Anatomy of an International Transaction. Mem. U.S. Polo Assn. Republican. Avocations: polo, large game, fishing. Home: Wheaton, Ill. Died Mar. 22, 2005.

LYNCH, SISTER FRANCIS XAVIER, nun, development director; b. Watertown, N.Y., Oct. 21, 1918; d. George Francis and Sarah Emma (Nicholson) L. BS in Nursing, Cath. U. Am., 1944, MS in Adminstrn., 1948, postgrad. in chemistry, 1949-51; Dr. Humane Letters (hon.), Long Island U., 1967. Tchr. St. Leo Sch., N.Y.C., 1939-40, Holy Angels Sch., Buffalo, N.Y., 1940-41; operating room supr. Champlain Valley Hosp., Plattsburgh, N.Y., 1941-42; instr. Biology & Biol. Scis. D'Youville Coll., Buffalo, N.Y., 1944-48, head dept. Biology, 1948-51, dean Sch. of Nursing, 1951-62, pres., 1962-68; initiator expansion program Grey Nuns Motherhouse, Yardley, Pa., 1969-71; dir. devel. Grey Nuns of the Sacred Heart, Yardley, Pa., 1971-92; vol. patient rep. Capital Health Sys., Trenton, N.J., from 1993. Cons. to Hosps. operated by Grey Nuns and their schs. of Nursing, 1955-62; mem. N.Y. State Bd. Nurse Examiners (Regents), 1952-64. Bd. dirs. A. Barton Hepburn Hosp., Ogdensburg, N.Y., 1976-88, dir. emeritus, 1988—; mem. Capital Health Sys. Mem. Nat. Cath. Devel. Conf. (charter, v.p., bd. dir., Disting. Svc. award), Phila. Mus. Art, Ctr. for Study of the Presidency, World Affairs Coun. Republican. Avocations: reading, travel, nature study. Home: Yardley, Pa. Died Jan. 28, 2005.

LYNCH, JONATHAN DAVID, publishing executive; b. Lawrence, Mass., Sept. 21, 1930; s. Harry B. and Rae R. L. BS, Yale U., 1952, MS, 1958. Sr. cons. McKinsey & Co., N.Y.C., 1958-67; dir. corp. plans CBS, Inc., N.Y.C., 1967-71; cons. Lynch & Assocs., N.Y.C., Boston, 1971-83; dir. advanced computer lab. U. Miami, Coral Gables, Fla., 1983-89; chmn. AI Week, Inc., Atlanta, from 1989; sr. v.p. Intelligent Ventures, Inc., Miami, from 1989. 1st lt. USAF, 1952-54. Home: Boynton Beach, Fla. Died June 27, 2005.

LYON, JANE MAUREEN MAHAN, mental health nurse; b. Jersey City, May 19, 1931; d. James John and Jane Francis (McGovern) Mahan; m. David Lockwood Lyon, Jan. 17, 1953; children: Jenny M., John W. RN, Jersey City Med. Ctr., 1952. Cert. psychiat. and mental health nurse. Home: Kerrville, Tex. Died June 30, 2004.

LYON, RICHARD KIRSHBAUM, lawyer; b. Washington, Apr. 24, 1912; s. Simon and Minnie Rose (Kirshbaum) L.; m. Marjorie Hausman, Aug. 26, 1948 (dec. Aug. 1955); children: Simon M., Richard H.; m. Dorothy Weisberg, Feb. 7, 1960; 1 child, Jon W. AB, Dartmouth Coll., 1933; JD, Georgetown U., 1936. Bar: D.C. 1936, U.S. Supreme Ct. 1939. Assoc. Lyon & Lyon, Washington, 1936-41; sole practice Washington, 1946—2005. Commr. D.C. Jud. Disabilities and Tenure Commn., Washington; gen. counsel Better Bus. Bur. Met. Washington, 1954-89, gen. counsel emeritus, 1989-2005. Vice chmn. D.C. Dem. com., 1966; gen. counsel, legis. chmn. Johnson-Humphrey Inaugural com., Washington, 1965. Served to comdr. USNR, 1941-46. Mem. D.C. Bar Assn. (past v.p. and bd. dirs.), D.C. Organized Bar. Jewish. Died Dec. 18, 2005.

MABLEY, JACK, columnist, educator; b. Binghamton, N.Y., Oct. 26, 1915; s. Clarence Ware and Mabelle (Howe) M.; m. Frances Habeck, Aug. 29, 1940; children: Mike, Jill, Ann, Pat, Robert. BS, U. Ill., 1938. With Chgo. Daily News, 1938-61, reporter, writer, columnist, 1957-61; columnist Chgo.'s Am., 1961-69, asst. mng. editor, 1966-69; asso. editor Chgo. Today, 1969-73; columnist Chgo. Today, Chgo. Tribune, 1973-74, Chgo. Tribune, 1974-82, Daily Herald, Arlington Heights, Ill., 1987—2004; pres. Mabley & Assocs., Corp. Communications, Glenview, Ill., 1982. Lectr. journalism Northwestern U., 1949-50; Author: Halas, Hef, the Beatles and Me, 1972 Pres. Village of Glenview, Ill., 1957-61, Skokie Valley Community Hosp., Skokie, Ill., 1977-79. Served from ensign to lt. USNR, 1941-45. Recipient Media award Nat. Assn. for Retarded Citizens, 1977 Died Jan. 7, 2006.

MACDONALD, ALEXANDER DANIEL, retired physics consultant; b. Sydney, N.S., Can., Apr. 8, 1923; came to U.S. 1960; s. Daniel Malcolm and Alexandrina (MacLeod) MacD.; m. Lois Roberta Stevenson, May 1, 1946; children: Muriel Ruth, Susan Lex, Robert Bronson, Daniel Rufus. BSc, Dalhousie U., Halifax, N.S., 1945, MSc, 1947; PhD, MIT, 1949. Prof. physics Dalhousie U., Halifax, 1949-60, head div. applied math., 1962-65; sr. scientist G.T.E. Microwave Physics Lab., Palo Alto, Calif., 1960-62; sr. mem. rsch. lab. Lockheed Missile & Space Ctr., Palo Alto, Calif., 1965-73, dir. comm. and electronics lab., 1973-78; sr. scientist Lockheed Space Systems Div., Sunnyvale, Calif., 1978-81; cons. in physics MacDonald Cons., Palo Alto, 1981-96; ret., 1996. Mem. space rsch. com. NRC-Can., 1958-60; cons. radiation physics V.O. Hosp., Halifax, 1953-60. Author: Microwave Breakdown in Gases, 1966, Russian translation, 1969; contbr. articles to profl. jours. Fellow Am. Phys. Soc. Democrat. Mem. Soc. Of Friends. Home: Menlo Park, Calif. Died Feb. 5, 2005.

MACDONALD, KEVIN JOHN, artist; b. Washington, July 2, 1946; s. Lawrence and Frances Ellen (Quinn) MacD. Student, Montgomery Coll., 1964-66; B.F.A., George Washington U., 1969; postgrad., Corcoran Sch. Art, 1969. Exhbns. include, Corcoran Gallery Art, Washington, 1974, 76, 79, 80, Md. Biennial, Balt. Mus., 1976, 78, 80, Phillips Collection, Washington, 1977, Lunn Gallery, Washington, 1976, 77, 79, 80; represented in permanent collections, Met. Mus., N.Y.C., Corcoran Gallery, Phillips Collection, Nat. Mus. Am. Art., Hirshhorn Mus. and Sculpture Garden. Died June 2, 2006.

MAC DONALD, MARGARET CLARK, retired real estate agent; b. Lewiston, Maine, Dec. 20, 1929; d. Arthur Bailey and Blanche (Plummer) Clark; m. John Edward Mac Donald, June 16, 1951 (dec. July 1988); children: Cornelia Ann Roberts (dec.), Edward Clark, Susan Mac Donald Moynahan. BS, Skidmore Coll., 1951. Bus. rep. N.Y. Bell Co., N.Y.C., 1951-52; show room mgr. Bonnie Doone, N.Y.C., 1952-53; interior decorator Susan Wang, N.Y.C., 1953-54; designer Maggie Mac Donald Interiors, Miami, Fla., 1960-64; owner, sec. Atlantic Millwork, Inc., Miami, 1964-88; assoc. realtor Keyes Co. Realtors, Miami, 1995-98. Pres. Homemaker Svc. Dade County, Cmty. Vol. Svc. Bur., 1967-68; pres. Jr. League Miami, Inc., 1969-70, chmn. sustaining mems., 1982; pres. Vis. Nurse Assn. Dade County, Fla., Inc., 1975-77; pres., past treas. Metropolitans, 1983-84; second v.p., spl. events chmn. The Vizcayans, 1984-85; pres. Dade County Nat. Soc. Colonial Dame Am., 1988-89; pres. Colonial Dame of Am. XVII, 1989-90, rec. sec., 1998-99. Mem. Nat. DAR (Biscayne chpt., del. conf. Washington, corr. 1998-99), Daus. Colonial Wars, Founders and Patriots (v.p. 2000). Avocations: reading, tennis. Home: Bristow, Va. Died Sept. 25, 2004.

MACEY, EARL CHRISTOPHER, osteopathic physician and surgeon; b. Richmond, Mo., Mar. 10, 1909; s. Henry Christopher and Lucy Ann (Penny) M.; m. Dorothy Belle Gstrein, July 2, 1939; children— Martha Ann, Earl Christopher. Student Central Coll., Fayette, Mo., 1928-29; D.O., Kirksville Coll. Osteo. Medicine, Mo., 1933; postgrad. Coll. Physicians and Surgeons, Los Angeles, 1946-47, U. Mex., Mexico City, 1948, U. Nebr. Med. Sch., 1979. Intern Laughlin Hosp., Kirksville; tng. in proctological surgery Mayo Clinic, Rochester, Minn., 1944; practice osteo. medicine and surgery, Marshall, Mo.; del. seminars, Nassau, Bahamas, 1972, Bermuda, 1974, Tokyo, 1976. Author: Poliomyelitis, 1938; Hypertension, 1940; Biblical Medicine, 1975. Mem. West-Central Mo. Assn. Osteo. Physicians and Surgeons (pres. 1941), Am. Osteo. Assn. (life), Mo. Assn. Osteo. Physicians and Surgeons (life). Democrat. Methodist. Lodges: Kiwanis (v.p. 1975), Optimist (pres. 1957). Home: Gainesville, Fla. Died Dec. 1, 2004.

MACFARLANE, LOUELLA SHIRLEY, writer; b. L.A., June 7, 1908; d. Louis Emanuel and Helen Irene (Shirley) Bamberger; m. David Dimeley MacFarlane, July 28, 1924 (dec. 1979); 1 child, Robert Michael. Writer short stories, 1926-45; screenwriter Hollywood, Calif., 1945-76; sculptor, painter Palm Springs, Calif., from 1976. Mem. Writer's Guild Am. Died Dec. 9, 2004.

MACK, FLOSSIE PHILLIPS, elementary school educator; b. Mayodan, N.C., Aug. 22, 1944; d. Lewis H. and Hattie O. Phillips. BS, N.C. A&T State U., Greensboro, 1969; MEd, Rutgers U., 1973. Cert. early childhood tchr., bus. edn. tchr. Typist Capitol Collection Bur., 1964-65; receptionist U. N.C., Greensboro, 1969-70; legal sec. Smith & Patterson Law Firm, 1970-71; tchr. Greensboro City Schs., from 1973. State Tuition grantee; Work-Aid scholar; recipient LCH Civil award. Mem. NANBPWC, Tau Gamma Delta. Home: Greensboro, NC. Died Mar. 28, 2005.

MACKAMAN, DONALD HAYES, lawyer; b. Des Moines, Oct. 29, 1912; s. Frank Hindes and Eva (Hayes) M.; children: Linda, Bert, Donald Jr. BA, Drake U., 1933, JD, 1935. Sec., v.p., gen. counsel Campbell Taggart, Inc., Dallas, 1933-77; of counsel Gardere Wynne Sewell LLP, Dallas, from 1977. Mem. Order of Coif, Phi Beta Kappa. Home: Dallas, Tex. Died June 1, 2004.

MACKEY, GEORGE WHITELAW, mathematician, educator; b. St. Louis, Feb. 1, 1916; s. William Sturges and Dorothy Frances (Allison) M.; m. Alice Willard, Dec. 9, 1960; 1 child, Ann Sturges Mackey. BA, Rice Inst., 1938; A.M., Harvard U., 1939, PhD, 1942; MA, Oxford, 1966. Instr. math. Ill. Inst. Tech., 1942-43; faculty instr. math. Harvard U., 1943-46, asst. prof., 1946-48, assoc. prof., 1948-56, prof. math., 1956-69, Landon T. Clay prof. math. and theoretical sci., 1969-85, prof. emeritus, 1985—2006. Vis. prof. U. Chgo., summer, 1955, UCLA, Summer, 1959, Tata Inst. Fundamental Rsch., Bombay, 1970-71, U. Calif., Berkeley, 1984; Walker Ames vis. prof. U. Wash., summer, 1961; Eastman vis. prof. Oxford (Eng.) U., 1966-67; assoc. prof. U. Paris, 1978; vis. rschr. Math. Sci. Inst., Berkeley, 1983; lectr. U. Heidelberg, Germany, 1988, CUNY, 1987, U. Iowa, 1988, Kings Coll. of U. London, 1991; invited lectr. U. Munich, Germany, 1994, U. Heidelberg, 1995; vis. lectr. U. Tainjin, U. Beijing, U. Shanghai,. U. Hong Kong, 19911 mem. Inst. Advanced Study Princeton U., 1978. Author: Mathematical Foundations of Quantum Mechanics, 1963, Lectures on the Theory of Functions of a Complex Variable, 1967, Induced Representations and Quantum Mechanics, 1968, The Theory of Unitary Group Representations, 1976, Unitary Group Representations in Physics, Probability and Number Theory, 1978, The Scope and History of Commutative and Noncommutative Harmonic Analysis, 1992; contbr. articles math. jours. Served as civilian, operational research sect. 8th Air Force, 1944; applied math. panel NDRC, 1945. Recipient Humboldt prize Max Planck Inst., Bonn, Fed. Republic of Germany, 1985-86; Guggenheim fellow, 1949-50, 61-62, 70-71; Vis. scholar Catalan U., Bellaterra, Spain, 2000. Mem. Am. Math. Soc. (v.p. 1964-65, Steele prize 1974), Nat. Acad. Scis., Am. Philos. Soc., Am. Acad. Arts and Scis., Phi Beta Kappa, Sigma Xi. Died Mar. 15, 2006.

MACLAURY, ROBERT E(THAN), language educator; b. Oceanside, Calif., May 24, 1944; s. Richard and Margaret MacLaury; m. Maria Isabel MacLaury. BA, U. of the Ams., Mexico City, 1967, MA, 1970; PhD, U. Calif., Berkeley, 1986. Vis. prof. U. Ariz., Tucson, 1988—90, U. Regina, Canada, 1993, George Washington U., Washington, 1993—95; de Carle lectr. U. Otago, Dunedin, New Zealand, 1998. Author: (book) Color and Cognition in Mesoamerica, 1997; co-editor: (book anthology) Language and the Cognitive Construal of the World, 1995; editor: (spl. jour. issue) Vantage Theory, 2002. Fellow, Fulbright Found., 1978, Wenner Gren fellow, 1990. Achievements include research in Mesoamerican color survey; Zopotec language description; vantage theory. Avocation: hiking. Home: Beverly Hills, Calif. Died Feb. 18, 2004.

MACLEISH, RODERICK, writer, television producer, scriptwriter; b. Bryn Mawr, Pa., Jan. 15, 1926; s. Norman Hillard and Lenore (McCall) MacL.; m. Diana S. Chapin, May 1, 1950 (div. June 1971); children: Cynthia Sumner, Roderick Jr. Student, U. Chgo., 1944-45; DHL (hon.), Washington-Jefferson Coll., 1958. Copy boy, TV script editor ABC, N.Y.C., 1945-51; news dir. WBZ-Westinghouse Broadcasting Co., Boston, 1951-57; Washington bur. chief Westinghouse Broadcasting Co., 1957-59, chief fgn. corr. London, 1959-66, sr. commentator Washington, 1966-71; commentator CBS, Washington, 1971-76, NPR, Washington, 1976-90; commentator, TV prodr. Monitor Radio-TV, Washington, 1990-97; ret., 1997. Writer, narrator (PBS 3-hr. spl.) The Hermitage, 1994-95; author: The First Book of Eppe, 1985, Prince Ombra, 1987, Crossing At Ivalo, 1989. Pres. Assn. Am. Corrs. in London, 1964. Mem. Cosmos Club (Washington). Episcopalian. Died July 1, 2006.

MACLEOD, DOUGLAS DONALD, senior mechanical engineer; b. Port Washington, N.Y., Apr. 21, 1930; s. Donald and Ceanie (Pollock) MacL.; m. Joan May Stockvis, June 27, 1959; 1 child, Robert Douglas. B in Marine Engring., SUNY, Throgs Neck, 1952; postgrad., Columbia U., 1954-56. Licensed marine engr., N.Y. Assoc. engr. Portsmouth (N.H.) Naval Shipyard, 1952-53; engr. Sperry Gyroscope Co., Lake Success, N.Y., 1953-65; sr. engr. Perkin Elmer Optical Tech. Div., Danbury, Conn., 1965-68, Sperry Systems Mgmt. Div., Lake Success, 1968-74, Naval Weapons Sta. Earle, Colts Neck, N.J., 1975-89; program mgr. U.S. Army Communications Electronics Command, Ft. Monmouth, N.J., from 1990. Chmn. advancement com. Boy Scouts Am., Little Silver, N.J., 1987—. Mem. Friends of Photography (Long Branch, N.J.). Home: Surfside Bch, SC. Died Feb. 16, 2004.

MAC LOW, JACKSON, poet, composer, writer; b. Chgo., Sept. 12, 1922; s. Jackson and Fannie (Baskin) Mac L.; m. Iris Lezak, Feb. 3, 1962 (div. Oct. 19, 1973); children: Mordecai-Mark, Clarinda; m. Anne Tardos, Jan. 20, 1990. AA, U. Chgo., 1941; AB in Classical Greek cum laude, Bklyn. Coll., 1958. Instr. NYU, Am. Lang. Inst., 1966-73; instr. English Mannes Coll. of Music, N.Y.C., 1966; short-term residencies, from 1966; poet, composer, writer, performer, freelance editor, tchr. N.Y.C., from 1973; instr. SUNY, Albany, 1984, Binghamton, 1989, Buffalo, 1989, 97, Temple U., Phila., 1989, Naropa Inst., Boulder, Colo., 1975, 91, 94, Schule für Dichtung in Wien, Vienna, Austria, 1992, 93, Bard Coll., Annandale-on-Hudson, N.Y., 1994, Brown U., Providence, 1994; Regents' lectr. U. Calif., San Diego, 1990; instr. U. Pa., Phila., 1997. Multimedia performances, concerts and readings, 1960-2004; multimedia performance artist with Anne Tardos, 1979-2004, including FluxusVirus, Cologne, 1992, Flux Attitudes, New Mus., N.Y., 1992, Days of Silence, Warsaw, 1993, Rolywholyover A Circus, Mus. of Contemporary Art, L.A., 1993, Fluxus Vivus, Arts Club, Chgo., 1993, Miami-Dade C.C., 1993; verbal music performance artist with Pauline Oliveros, 1995. Author: The Twin Plays: Port-au-Prince & Adams County Illinois, 1963, 2d edit. 1966, The Pronouns-A Collection of 40 Dances-For the Dancers, 1964, 2d edit. 1971, 3d edit. 1979, Verdurous Sanguinaria, 1967, August Light Poems, 1967, 22 Light Poems, 1968, 23d Light Poem: For Larry Eigner, 1969, Stanzas For Iris Lezak, 1972, 4 trains, 1974, 36th Light Poem: In Memoriam Buster Keaton, 1975, 21 Matched Asymmetries, 1978, 54th Light Poem: For Ian Tyson, 1978, A Dozen Douzains for Eve Rosenthal, 1978, phone, 1978, Asymmetries 1-260, 1980, Is That Wool Hat My Hat, 1982, From Pearl Harbor Day to FDR's Birthday, 1982, 2nd edit., 1995, Bloomsday, 1984, French Sonnets, 1984, 2d edit., 1989, The Virginia Woolf Poems, 1985,Eight Drawing-Asymmetries, 1985, Representative Works: 1938-85, 1986, Words nd Ends from Ez, 1989, Twenties: 100 Poems, 1991, Pieces o'Six: Thirty-three Poems in Prose, 1992, 42 Merzgedichte in Memoriam Kurt Schwitters, 1994, Barnesbook, 1996, 20 forties, 1999, Struggle through, 2001; CD: Open Secrets, 1993; cassette tapes include The Black Tarantula Crossword Gathas, 1975, Homage to Leona Bleiweiss and Shorter Simultaneities, 1977, Songs and Simultaneities with Anne Tardos, 1985; records include 1st Milarepa Gatha, 1978, Concert at the Kitchen 1980, 1983; paintings, drawings, collages, assemblages, musical and performance scores exhibited internationally; works appear in 83 anthologies and other collections. Recipient fellowship for Multimedia, N.Y. State's Creative Artists Pub. Svc. Program, 1973-74, for Poetry, 1976-77, Creative Writing fellowship NEA, 1979, Guggenheim fellowship for Poetry, 1985, San Francisco State U. Poetry Ctr.'s Book award, 1985, Fulbright Travel grant New Zealand, 1986, Composer's grant The Queen Elizabeth II Arts Coun. of New Zealand, 1986, Fellowship in Poetry, N.Y. Found. for Arts, 1988, grants The Fund for Poetry, N.Y.C., 1988, 91. Buddhist. Died Dec. 8, 2004.

MACMINN, ALEENE MERLE B(ARNES), newspaper editor, columnist, educator; b. Salt Lake City, Sept. 19, 1930; d. Harold Sansom and Allie (Rasmussen) Barnes; m. Fraser K. MacMinn (dec. 2000), July 28, 1961; children: Margaret A., Gregor Geordie. AA, Glendale Coll., 1950; BA, U. So. Calif., L.A., 1952. Women's page reporter Glendale (Calif.) News-Press, 1948-52, L.A. Times, 1953-57, asst. family editor, 1957-60, asst. TV editor, 1960-65, exec. TV editor, 1965-69, asst. entertainment editor, 1969-72, TV Times editor, 1972-91, asst. Calendar editor, entertainment columnist, 1989-93. Sr. lectr. U. So. Calif. Sch. Journalism, 1979-92. Mem. Women in Communications, Alpha Gamma Delta. Mem. Lds Ch. Home: Glendale, Calif. Died Mar. 5, 2006.

MADIGAN, ROBERT A., former state senator; b. Lincoln, Ill., Nov. 28, 1942; m. to Connie Madigan; two children. BS, Millikin U., 1966. Mem. from Dist. 45 Ill. State Senate, Springfield, 1987—2002. Mem. agr. and conservation, labor and commerce, elem. and secondary edn., pensions and licensed activities, welfare and corrections, pub. health, welfare and corrections coms., Ill. Senate; mem. joint coms. on intergovernmental cooperation, regulation of professions and occupations, consumer banks, Ill. pension funds in Northern Ireland; bd. dirs. Comprehensive Health Ins. Plan, Geologic Map Task Force. Died May 4, 2006.

MADSEN, DON RAY, dentist; b. Cleburne, Tex., Sept. 3, 1946; s. Raymond Woodrow and Georgialee (Stephens) M.; m. Susan Cort Webster, 1966 (div. Sept. 1979); m. Lori Ann Smith, May 10, 1980; children: Colin Jamison, Alexandria Reese. BS, Tex. Wesleyan Coll., 1973; DDS, Baylor U., 1977. Pres., owner Don R. Madsen, DDS, Inc., Ft. Worth. Cons. Prudential Ins. Co., Houston, 1986—. With U.S. Army, 1966-69. Mem. ADA, Tex. Dental Assn., Ft. Worth Dist. Dental Soc., Acad. Gen. Dentistry, Am. Med. Athletic Assn., Am. Acad. Implant Dentistry, Am. Acad. Prosthetic Dentistry, Jr. C. of C. Republican. Episcopalian. Avocations: running, skiing, golf, scuba diving (master diver). Home: Fort Worth, Tex. Died Nov. 20, 2004.

MAES, JOHN LEOPOLD, theologian, psychologist, educator; b. Watertown, Mich., Aug. 6, 1923; s. John and Mary (Cornwell) M; m. Mary M. Johnson, Aug. 28, 1942; children: Barbara (dec.), John David. BTh, Owosso Coll., 1948; AB, Mich. State U., 1954, MA, 1957, PhD, 1963. Ordained to ministry United Meth. Ch., 1963, United Ch. Christ, 1976; lic. health care provider in psychology Nat. Registry Health Care Providers in Psychology, Mass., Maine, lic. psychologist, Mass., Maine. Pastor, Houghton Lake, Mich., 1948-52, Francestown, NH, 1977-80; assoc. prof. Sch. Theology Boston U., 1963-72, adj. prof. Colls. Liberal Arts, Edn. and Theology, exec. dir. Danielsen Inst., 1982-89, prof. emeritus, cons., from 1989; prof., acad. dean Franklin Pierce Coll., Rindge, NH, 1972-75; cons., pvt. practice, 1975-82; bd. govs. Danielsen Inst., 1967-82; min. couns. 1st Congl. United Ch. Christ, Bradenton, Fla., from 1999. Dir. counseling ctr. Boston U., 1967—72, acting assoc. dean student affairs, 1970—72; writer pastoral counselor's licensure exam. State of Maine, 1991; guest lectr., vis. prof. Caribbean Grad. Sch. Theology, 2001. Author: Suffering: A Caregiver's Guide, 1990; (with others) Fathering: Fact or Fable, 1977, Maturity and the Quest for Spiritual Meaning, 1988, Psychological Perspectives and the Religious Quest, 1999; contbr. articles to profl. jours. John L. Maes grad. scholar established in honor Boston U., 2001. Mem. APA, Am. Assn. Pastoral Counselors (diplomate, bd. govs. 1966-71, chmn. ctrs. and tng. com. 1967-71, mem. pastoral counselors exam. bd. 1994-98), Am. Mental Health Counselors Assn. Democrat. Died Oct. 19, 2005.

MAGNUSON, SUSAN MARIE FARR, human resources professional; b. Grand Rapids, Mich., Oct. 15, 1949; d. Norman B. and Faye Deane (Baker) Farr; m. David Scott Magnuson, May 7, 1971; children: Keith, Kari. Student, U. Ala., 1978-79. Clk. Wyoming (Mich.) Police Dept., 1968-76; pers. asst. Western Supermarkets, Birmingham, Ala., 1976-79; coord. employee benefits, pers. asst. S.E. Ala. Med. Ctr., Dothan, 1979-84; mgr. human resources Rexham Laminex Inc., Charlotte, N.C., 1984-93, D&K Laminex, Charlotte, from 1993. Condr. workshops on career devel. and team bldg. skills; asst. in devel. mng. career workshop. Mem. Soc. for Human Resources Mgmt., Employers Assn. Carolinas, Charlotte Area Pers. Assn., Charlotte Area Compensation Coun., Arrowood Employers Assn. Republican. Methodist. Home: Concord, NC. Died June 9, 2005.

MAHAFFEY, MARYANN, retired councilwoman; b. Burlington, Iowa, Jan. 18, 1925; m. Herman Dooha; 1 child, Susan. BA, Cornell Coll., 1946, LHD (hon.), 1995; MSW, U. So. Calif., 1951. Legis. rep., chair Mich. Social Work Coun., 1965-68; founder, chair City of Detroit Task Force on Hunger & Malnutrition, 1969-74; council member City of Detroit, 1974—2005, pres. pro tem, 1978—82, 1998—2001, pres., 1990—98, 2002—05; prof. emeritus Wayne State U., Detroit, 1990—2006. Pres. Detroit City Coun., 1991-98. Del. founding conv. Nat. Women's Polit. Caucus, 1971-73; chair, founder Mich. Statewide Nutrition Commn., 1973-83; designer, initiator Detroit Police Dept. Rape Crisis Ctr. and Family Trouble Clinic of Detroit, Family Svc. and Police, 1974-75; del. IWY, Mexico City, 1975, Houston, 1978; dep. chair U.S. Conf. on Families, 1979-81; chair human devel. com. Nat. League of Cities, 1992, chair Mich. del. to UN Conf. Women, Beijing, 1995; summer recreation dir. Nat. Intercollegiate Christian Coun. in Concentration Camp for Japanese Ams., 1945; trainer, integrator Brownie Troop Indpls. Girl Scouts, 1951-52; organizer Welfare Rights, Detroit, 1961; founder Nat. Peace and Disarmament Com. NASW, 1962-69, pres., 1975-77; founder Women in Social Welfare, 1972-74; author policy of women's rights, Internat. Fedn. Social Workers, 1987; mem. exec. com. Internat. Fedn. Social Workers, 1984-86. Mem. NAACP (life), Am. Orthopsychiat. Assn. (pres. 1984-85), Japanese Am. Citizens League, Women in Mcpl. Govt. (pres. 1995, adv. bd., mem. NLC policy adv. coun.), Nat. Coun. Negro Women (life). Died July 27, 2006.

MAHAFFY, TELFAIR, safety scientist; b. Jacksonville, Fla., Jan. 26, 1936; s. Conrad Brickwedel and Mary Willard (Telfair) M.; m. Nancy A. Scheurer, Oct. 23, 1959 (div.); children: Anne, Michael. AB in English, U. N.C., 1958; postgrad., Yale U., 1958-60. Mortgage broker The Travelers, Jacksonville, Fla., 1960-64, Norton Realty, Jacksonville, Fla., 1964-68; v.p. Haughton & Co., Jacksonville, Fla., 1968-72; pres., onwer Fla. Mortgage Exch., Jacksonville, 1972-87; safety dir. Holmes Lumber Co., Jacksonville, 1987-99. Bd. dirs. Jacksonville Athletic Charities, 1988-93, v.p. Mem. Fla. Hunter-Jumper Assn. (pres. 1978), North Fla. Hunter-Jumper Assn. (pres. 1976), Osprey Club (bd. dirs. 1998—). Republican. Episcopalian. Avocations: swimming, horse show jumping. Home: Jacksonville, Fla. Died May 31, 2005.

MAHER, JOHN EDWARD, economist; b. Utica, N.Y., Dec. 26, 1925; s. William Roscoe and Isabel (Knight) M.; m. Naomi Sargent Berg, Jan. 30, 1947 (div. June 1983); children: Howard, David, Sean; m. Merna Lois Habhegger, June 17, 1983. AB cum laude, Harvard U., 1948; MS, U. Wis., 1949; PhD, Harvard U., 1955. Asst. prof. DePauw U., Greencastle, Ind., 1954-57; asst. prof. Wesleyan U., Middletown, Conn., 1957-61; Assoc. prof. Oakland U., Rochester, Mich., 1961-64; sr. economist Joint Coun., N.Y.C., 1964-70; prof. So. Conn. State U., New Haven, 1970-87, dean, 1982-83; cons. Maher Crakes & Assocs., Hamden, Conn., from 1987. Cons. State of Conn., Hartford, 1960-61, Huanghe U., Zhengzhou, People's Republic of China, 1986; adj. prof. Hohai U. Nanjing, China, 2000—. Author: What is Economics, 1969, Labor and Economy, 1965; co-author: Economics in the Curriculum, 1971, Thinker, Sailor, Brother, Spy, 1995; mng. editor Jour. Econ. Edn., 1967-70, editorial bd.; author essays in field. Lt. comdr. (ret.) USN, 1943-89. Guest scholar Brookings Inst., 1977; Mellon fellow Yale U., 1978. Economists for Arms Reduction. Avocation: satirical writing. Home: Prior Lake, Minn. Died Feb. 15, 2005.

MAHFOUZ, NAGUIB (NAGĪB MAHFUZ), author; b. Gamaliya, Cairo, Dec. 11, 1911; s. Abdel Aziz Ibrahim and Fatma Mostapha Mahfouz; m. Attiyat Allah, 1954; children: Om Kolthoum, Fatima. Grad. in philosophy, Secular U., Cairo, 1930. Civil servant, 1934; sec. U. Cairo, 1936-38;

with Ministry of Waqfs, 1939-54, Dept. Arts and Censorship Bd., 1954-59; dir. Found. for Support of Cinema State Cinema Orgn., Cairo, 1959-69; cons. cinema affairs Ministry of Culture, Cairo, 1969-71. Staff mem. Ar-Risāla; contbr. Al-Hilāl, Al-Ahrām. Author: (fiction) Hams al-junun, 1938, 'Abāth al aqdār, 1939, Radubis, 1943, Kifah Tība, 1944, Al-Qāhira al-jadīda, 1945, Khān al-Khalīli, 1946, Zuqāq al-Midaqq, 1947 (pub. as Midaq Alley, 1966), Al-sarāb, 1948, Bidāya wa-nihāya, 1949 (pub. as The Beginning and the End, 1985), Al-thulāthiya: Vol. I: Bayn al-Qasrayn, 1956 (pub. as Palace Walk, 1989; Egyptian State prize 1956), Vol. II: Qasr al-shawq, 1957 (pub. as Palace of Desire, 1991), Vol. III: Al-Sukkariya, 1957 (pub. as Sugar Street, 1992), Awlād hāratina, 1959 (pub. as Children of Gebelawi, 1981, Children of our Alley, 1996), Al-lis wa-l-kilāb, 1961 (pub. as The Thief and the Dogs, 1984), Al-sammān wa-l-kharīf, 1962 (pub. as Autumn Quail, 1985), Dunya Allah, 1962 (pub. as God's World, 1988), Al-Tarīq, 1964 (pub. as The Search, 1987), Al-shahhāz, 1965 (pub. as The Beggar, 1986), Bayt sayyi' al-sum'a, 1965, Tharthara fawq al Nīl, 1966 (pub. as Adrift on the Nile, 1993), Miramār, 1967 (pub. as Miramar, 1978), Khammārat al-qitt al-aswad, 1969, Taht al-midhalla, 1969, Hikāya a bi-la bidāya wa-la nihāya, 1971, Shahr al-'asal, 1971, Al-marāya, 1972 (pub. as Mirrors, 1977), Al-hubb tahta al-matar, 1973, Al-jarīma, 1973, Al-Karnak, 1974, Hikāyāt hāratina, 1975 (pub. as Fountain and Tomb, 1988), Qalb al-layl, 1975, Hadrat al-muhtaram, 1975 (pub. as Respected Sir, 1986), Malhamat al harāfīsh, 1977 (pub. as The Harafish, 1994), Al-hubb fawqa Hadabat al-Haram, 1979, Al-shaytān ya'iz, 1979, 'Asr al-hubb, 1980, Afrā al-qubbah, 1981 (pub. as Wedding Song, 1984), Layāli alf laylah, 1982 (pub. as Arabian Nights and Days, 1995), Ra'aytu fīma yara al-na'im, 1982, Al-bāqi min al-zaman sā'ah, 1982, Amāma al'arsh, 1982, Rihlat Ibn Fattumah, 1983 (pub. as The Journey of Ibn Fattouma, 1992), Al-tandhīm al-sirri, 1984, Al-ā'ish fī al-haqīqah, 1985 (pub. as Akhenaton: Dweller in Truth, 1998), Yawm qutila al-za'īm, 1985 (pub. as The Day the Leader was Killed, 1997), Hadīth al sabāh wa-al-masā, 1987, Sabāh al-ward, 1987, Qushtumor, 1988, Al-Fajr al-Kadhib, 1988, Asda' al-Sira al-dhatiya, 1996 (pub. as Echoes of an Autobiography, 1997), The Seventh Heaven, 2005. Recipient Nat. prize for Letters (Egypt), 1970, Collar of the Republic, 1972, Nobel prize for lit., 1988; named to Egyptian Order of Ind., Order of the Republic. Mem. Am. Acad. and Inst. Arts and Letters (hon.), Am. Acad. and Inst. Arts and Scis. (hon.). First Arab writer to win the Nobel Prize in Literature. Died Aug. 30, 2006.

MAHOLTZ, MICKEY, physics educator; b. Jersey City, N.J., Sept. 17, 1941; s. Nicodemus S. and Dinah (Morelli) M.; m. Helen M. Leonard, Sept. 26, 1964; children: Micheal, Jay, Nicole. BSEE, Pa. State U., 1962; BS in Physics, Clarion U., 1964; MST in Physics, U. Wis., Superior, 1976. Sci. dept. head Curwensville (Pa.) Schs., from 1964. Owner Penfield (Pa.) Cable TV, 1972—. Author: Castle Electricity Program, 1992. Pres. Huston Twp. Alumni, Penfield. Recipient Presdl. award Nat. Sci. Tchrs., Washington, 1990, Kevin Burns award Chemistry Soc., Pitts., 1995. Mem. Am. Assn. Physics Tchrs., Pa. Jr. Acad. Scis. (dir. 1966—), Pa. State Edn. Assn. Republican. Methodist. Home: Penfield, Pa. Died Feb. 27, 2004.

MAHON, ELDON BROOKS, former federal judge; b. Loraine, Tex., Apr. 9, 1918; s. John Bryan and Nola May (Muns) M.; m. Nova Lee Groom, June 1, 1941; children: Jana, Martha, Brad. BA, McMurry U., 1939; LLB, U. Tex., 1942; LLD (hon.), McMurry U., 1974; HHD (hon.), Tex. Wesleyan U., 1990. Bar: Tex. 1942. Law clk. Tex. Supreme Ct., 1945-46; county atty. Mitchell County, Tex., 1947; dist. atty. 32d Jud. Dist. Tex., 1948-60, dist. judge, 1960-63; v.p. Tex. Electric Service Co., Ft. Worth, 1963-64; mem. firm Mahon Pope & Gladden, Abilene, Tex., 1964-68; U.S. atty. U.S. Dist. Ct. (no. dist.) Tex., Ft. Worth, 1968-72, judge, 1972-89, sr. judge, 1989—2002. Com. on the budget Judicial Conf. the U.S., 1975-83, 5th cir. judicial coun., 1984-89. Pres. W. Tex. council Girl Scouts U.S.A., 1966-68; former trustee McMurry U.; past bd. dirs. Harris Meth. Hosp. With USAAF, 1942-45. Named an Outstanding Tex. Prosecutor, Tex. Law Enforcement Found., 1957; recipient Disting. Alumnus award McMurry U., 1987. Em. ABA, FBA, Ft.-Worth-Tarrant County Bar Assn. (Silver Gavel award 1998), Am. Judicature Soc., Dist. and County Attys. Assn. Tex. (pres. 1954-55), Tex. Bar Found. (life, Samuel Pessarra outstanding jurist award 1998). Methodist. Died Dec. 3, 2005.

MAIER, HENRY B., environmental engineer; b. Yonkers, N.Y., July 11, 1925; s. Henry and Adelaide (Boyce) M.; m. Elizabeth A. Maier, May 4, 1968. BA, Columbia U., 1947; postgrad., Adelphi U., Hofstra U. Prin. Maier Solar Developments, Hempstead, N.Y. Author: Techniques for Seascape Painting. Mem. AIAA, Am. Chem. Soc., N.Y. Acad. Scis. Achievements include patents for elapsed time indicator, multiple reflecting solar collecting system, electroresponsive coatings, fusion power pellets, and fusion power; design of initial stage of work for aerospace vehicle, comet flyby study; development of rapid method for perspective visualizations, for views of engineering and design concepts; definition of geometrics for placement of measuring points by approximation; research on inorganic sulfur and chlorine pollutants from combustion of fossil fuels and from incinerator processes, and their interactive roles in the progressive deterioration of the stratospheric ozone shield previously blocking frequencies in the infrared, far infrared and microwave frequencies, with particular regard to the prediction and pattern formation of major North Atlantic storm systems; study for a comet detecting telescope; design study for single span, steel beam highway bridge for enhanced safety from emerging situations of high-speed trucks, severe weather conditions and limited maintenance; study of architectural modern design, Y2K study. Home: Hempstead, NY. Died Feb. 28, 2005.

MAIN, PATRICIA ENGLANDER, investor; b. London, Apr. 8, 1931; d. Harry Norman and Eve (Roth) Englander; m. Arnold M. Singer, June 11, 1950 (div. May 1963); m. Frank Graham Main, Apr. 30, 1966 (div. Apr. 1981); m. Franklin Walter Mohney, Aug. 10, 1981 (dec. May 1991); children: Lisa Nicole Kelly, Susan Jennifer Kerschner, Jacqueline Eve Singer. Student, Mt. Holyoke Coll., 1948-50. Dir. pub. rels. Contemporary Arts Mus., Houston, 1962-64; relocation sales assoc. Paul Reinke Corp., Cherry Hill, N.J., 1964-69; account exec. Relocation Realty Svc. Corp., N.Y.C., 1972-76, v.p. ops., 1976-79; owner Patricia Mohney Gallery, Reading, Pa., 1981-84; v.p. Venture Components Corp., N.Y.C., 1984-92; pvt. investor N.Y.C., from 1992. Trustee, bd. mem. Reading Art Mus., 1980-83; mem. bus. and profl. com. N.Y.C. Ballet, 1985-95; mem. com. denominational affairs All Souls Ch., N.Y.C., 1998—. Mem. Mt. Holyoke Coll. Alumnae Club (bd. dirs. 1969-77, pres. 1977-79). Home: New York, NY. Died May 14, 2005.

MAISEL, MELVIN LEO, employee benefit and insurance consultant; b. Bklyn., May 15, 1924; s. Abraham and Ida (Ravitch) M.; m. Selma Abramsky, June 8, 1946; children: Marc, David, Naomi Maisel Duker. BS in Bus. Mgmt., NYU, 1947. V.p. Fiberoid Doll Products Corp., N.Y.C., 1947-58; agt. New Eng. Mut. Ins. Co., 1958-67; pres. Stabilization Plans for Bus., Inc., White Plains, N.Y., from 1964; v.p. Nat. Pension Service, Inc., White Plains, N.Y., from 1968; chmn. First Nat. Bank of Stamford, Conn., from 1986. Past chmn. adv. com. Iona Coll. Tax Inst.; guest lectr. AICPA, N.Y. State Soc. CPAs, Mount Vernon and Queens County Bar Assns., also industry and trade assns. Author: The S Corporation Pension Trap, How to Use Disability Planning to Guarantee Your Business Interest and Income; co-author: How to Save Taxes and Increase Your Wealth With a Professional Corporation, How to Use Tax Shelters Today, Lurie's Commentaries on Pension Design, The Problem That Won't Go Away, Intercorp-A Business Trade Jour. of Connecticut-Westchester County, Coping With Taxes on the Second Death, Evaluating Survivorship Life Insurance, Using a Profit Sharing Plan as an Estate Planning Tool, CPA Jour.; contbr. articles to profl. jours. Served with U.S. Army, 1943. Mem. Assn. Advanced Life Underwriting, Nat. Assn. Life Underwriters (charter and qualifying mem. of Internat. Forum, Top of the Table, Million Dollar Round Table, Nat. Quality award, 1961—, Nat. Sales Achievement awards, 1966—), Profl. Planners Forum Ltd. (charter), Estate Planning Council West Chester (charter) (pres. 1969). Home: Greenwich, Conn. Died Mar. 6, 2005.

MAITLEN, FRANK BARTLETT, financial consultant; b. Albany, Ind., Apr. 4, 1923; s. Harry L. and Letha Floss (Sutton) M.; m. Mary Evelyn Mock, June 19, 1943; children: Marsha Ann, Nancy Jo, David Leroy, Franklin Bruce. BS, Purdue U., 1949; MEd, Rollins Coll., 1974. Cert. high sch. and jr. coll. tchr. Vocat. tchr. Noble Twp. Schs., Wolflake, Ind., 1949-59; mgr. 4 farms Albion, Ind., 1954-59; sci. tchr. Brevard County Schs., Titusville, Fla., 1959-82; farm mgr., tax preparer Brevard County, State of Fla., Titusville, from 1959. Freelance fin. cons., Titusville, 1982—. Cpl. USAF, 1943-45, ETO. Decorated Bronze Stars (5). Democrat. Avocations: golf, boating, dance, athletics, travel. Died June 28, 2005.

MAKINS, CHRISTOPHER JAMES, foreign policy institute administrator; b. Southampton, N.Y., July 23, 1942; s. Roger Mellor and Alice Brooks (Davis) M.; m. Wendy Whitney, July 26, 1975; 1 child, Marian Whitney. BA, Oxford U., Eng., 1963; MA, Oxford U., 1971. From 3rd to 1st sec. Her Majesty Diplomatic Svc., London, Paris, Washington, 1964-75; dep. dir. Trilateral Commn., N.Y.C., 1975-76; sr. assoc. Carnegie Endowment for Internat. Peace, Washington, 1977-79; sr. scientist, asst. v.p. Sci. Applications Internat. Corp., Washington, 1979-89; dir. internat. security programs Roosevelt Ctr. Am. Policy Studies, Washington, 1985-89; v.p., exec. v.p. Aspen Inst., Washington, 1989-97; pres. Atlantic Coun. U.S., Washington, 1999—2005. Sr. adviser German Marshall Fund U.S., Washington, 1997—99; mem. internat. adv. bd. ICL Ltd., London, 1999—2000, 2005—06; bd. dirs. New Star Enhanced Income Trust, 2001—03. Contbr. articles to profl. jours. Mem. coun. Non-Profit Sector Rsch. Fund, Washington, 1997—2001; bd. dirs. Washington Concert Opera, from 1987, chmn., 1993—97; trustee The Phillips Collection, Washington, 1991—98, Greater Washington Ednl. Telecomms. Assn., 1980—88, Gov. Ditchley Found., from 2004. Fellow All Souls Coll., Oxford, 1963-70; mem. Coun. Fgn. Rels., Internat. Inst. Strategic Studies, Pratts Club, Met. Club, Alibi. Avocations: tennis, squash, boating, opera. Home: Washington, DC. Died Jan. 28, 2006.

MALAMUD, HERBERT, physicist; b. N.Y.C., June 28, 1925; s. Max and Anna (Mintzer) M.; m. Sylvia Kolkin, Oct. 27, 1951; children: Ronni Sue Jillions, Marc David, Kathi Jan Knill. MS, U. Md., 1951; PhD, NYU, 1958; MS, C.W. Post Coll., 1976. Diplomate Am. Bd. Sci. in Nuclear Medicine. Rsch. asst. U. Md., College Park, 1950-53, NYU, Bronx, 1953-57; adv. rsch. engr. Sylvania Elec. Prodn. Co., Bayside, N.Y., 1957-59; sci. rsch. engr. Republic Aviation Corp., Farmingdale, N.Y., 1959-64; head rsch. sect. Sperry Gyroscope Co., Great Neck, N.Y., 1964-65; dir. physics Radiation RSch. Corp., Westbury, N.Y., 1965-67; v.p. Plasma Physics Corp., Hicksville, N.Y., 1967-70; physicist Queens Hosp. Ctr., Jamaica, N.Y., 1970-79; tech. dir. Nuclear Assocs., Carle Place, N.Y., 1979-89; hosp. physicist Nassau County Med. Ctr., East Meadow, N.Y., from 1989. Adj. instr. physics CCNY, 1958-59; adj. prof. physics Hofstra U., 1960-61, Poly. Inst. Bklyn., 1961-64, N.Y. Inst. Tech., 1966-67; adj. prof. mgmt. engrng. C.W. Post Coll., 1975—; adj. prof. computer sci. Westchester C.C., 1978; asst. prof. medicine SUNY, Stony Brook, 1975—; cons. North Shore U. Hosp., 1973-78, VA Hosp., Bronx, 1977-78. Contbr. over 20 articles to physics jours.; referee Jour. Nuclear Medicine; reviewer Am. Scientist, Clin. Nuclear Medicine. Mem. radioisotope and radiation safety com. L.I. Jewish/Hillside Med. Ctr.; mem. com. human rsch., radiation protection and pubs. North Shore U. Hosp. Cpl. U.S. Army, 1943-46, ETO. Mem. AAAS, Am. Physic Soc., Am. Inst. Physics, Am. Assn. Physicists in Medicine, soc. Nuclear Medicine, Sigma Xi, Sigma Pi Sigma. Achievements include patents for Medical Accessory Equipment. Home: Mc Lean, Va. Died Aug. 14, 2005.

MALANCA, ALBERT ROBERT, lawyer, mediator; b. Tacoma, Apr. 25, 1927; s. Albert and Caroline (Mencarelli) M.; m. Jeannine Marian O'Halloran, June 13, 1952 (dec. Sept. 1993); children: Rand (dec.), Gina M., Warren A.; m. Glenna Lee Bradley-House, Jan. 1, 1994; 1 child, Chaise. BA, U. Wash., 1949, JD, 1950. Bar: Wash., U.S. Dist. Ct. (we. and ea. dists.) Wash., U.S. Supreme Ct. Assoc. Goodwin Eastvold & Hicks, Tacoma, 1951-54; ptnr. Goodwin Hicks & Malanca, Tacoma, 1954-55, Goodwin Hicks Malanca & Hager, Tacoma, 1955-57, Carnahan Gordon & Goodwin, Tacoma, 1957-60, Gordon Goodwin Sager Hicks & Thomas, Tacoma, 1960-62, Gordon Goodwin Sager & Thomas, Tacoma, 1962-66, Gordon Sager Honeywell Malanca & Peterson, Tacoma, 1966-68, Gordon Honeywell Malanca Peterson & Johnson, Tacoma, 1968-70, Gordon Thomas Honeywell Malanca Peterson O'Hern & Johnson, Tacoma, 1970-76, Gordon Thomas Honeywell Malanca Peterson & O'Hern, Tacoma, 1976-85; sr. ptnr. Gordon Thomas Honeywell Malanca Peterson & Daheim, Tacoma, 1985—2005. Mediator and arbitrator, Tacoma/Seattle, 1985-2005 Author, speaker legal seminars. Patron, Tacoma Art Mus., 1998. Fellow Am. Coll. Trial Lawyers (state chmn. 1985-86), Am. Bar Found. (life); mem. ABA, Wash. State Bar Assn., Fed. Bar Assn. (pres. 1980-81), Tacoma-Pierce County Bar Assn. (trustee 1975-77). Episcopalian. Avocations: boating, skiing, fishing, hunting, golf. Home: Gig Harbor, Wash. Died Jan. 19, 2005.

MALARA, ANTHONY CARMELO, retired broadcast executive; b. Watertown, N.Y., Sept. 11, 1936; s. Anthony J. and Florence (Gorri) M.; m. Mary Frances Dacey, Aug. 8, 1959; children— Elizabeth, Margaret, Anthony J. Student, Syracuse U., 1954-55. Gen. mgr. broadcast div. Sta. WWNY-TV, Watertown, 1971-78; v.p. sta. services CBS-TV Affiliate Relations, N.Y.C., 1978-80, affiliate relations v.p., 1980-81; v.p., gen. mgr. CBS-TV Network div. CBS Inc., N.Y.C., 1981-82, pres. CBS-TV Network div., 1982-86, sr. v.p. distbn. and affiliate relations CBS-TV Network div., 1986-88, pres. affiliate relations div., 1988—95. Recipient Disting. Service award Syracuse U., 1984 Mem. Internat. Radio and TV Soc. (bd. govs.), N.Y. State Broadcasters Assn. (pres. 1978-79) Clubs: Bronxville Field (N.Y.). Roman Catholic. Home: Sarasota, Fla. Died Aug. 24, 2006.

MALAY, MARCELLA MARY, nursing educator, administrator; b. Nashua, N.H., Mar. 18, 1948; d. John H. and Helyn (Sullivan) M. BSN, U. Del., 1970; MS, Boston U., 1977; postgrad., Mass. Coll. Pharmacy, Boston. RN, Mass. Instr. Faulkner Hosp., Boston, 1973-76, New England Deaconess Hosp., Boston, 1975-87; asst. prof. Mass. Coll. Pharmacy, Boston, from 1987; edn. specialist New Eng. Bapt. Hosp., Boston, 1987-93, DON, 1993-95, dir. edn., quality improvement and rsch., 1996-97, sr. dir. organization and improvement, from 1997. Mem. teleconf. adv. com. Tufts Med. Sch. Mem. ANA, Mass. Nurses Assn., Sigma Theta Tau. Home: Norwood, Mass. Died Mar. 21, 2004.

MALCOLM, JOHN LOWRIE, soil scientist, consultant; b. Westfield, N.J., July 30, 1920; s. John. L. and Adelaide (Allardice) M.; m. Janet May, Nov. 27, 1946; children: Martha J., Frieda L., David L. BSc, Rutgers U., MS, 1945, PhD, 1948. Soil chemist Sub Tropical Experiment Sta., U. Fla., Homestead, 1948-59; soil fertility advisor Internat. Cooperation Adminstrn., San Salvador, El Salvador, 1959-63; fertilizer specialist U.S. AID, New Delhi, 1963-68; project mgr. Food and Agriculture Orgn., Accra, Ghana, 1969; soil advisor Agy. for Internat. Devel., Washington, 1970-96; pvt. practice cons. Mc Lean, Va., from 1996. Fellow AAAS; mem. Am. Soc. Agronomy (chairperson internat. div. 1988), Soil Sci. Soc. Am., Am. Chem. Soc. Episcopalian. Died Mar. 23, 2005.

MALLER, OWEN, clinical psychologist; b. Bklyn., Jan. 27, 1930; s. Randolph Guggenheim and Edith M.; m. Alma Maller, Aug., 1974. BS, U. Ill., 1952, PhD, 1964; MA, So. Meth. U., Dallas, 1955. Cert. Nat. Register Health Svc. Providers in Psychology. Rsch. psychologist VA Hosp. and U. Pa., Phila., 1966-76; assoc. chief rsch. Dept. Army U.S. Army Lab, Natick, Mass., 1976-90; head edn. Am. Cancer Soc., Bryn Mawr, Pa., 1990-94; therapist Psych Resource Assn., Bala Cynwyd, Pa., 1994-99; clin. psychologist Cummings & Tannenbaum & Assocs., Narbeth, Pa., 1999—2005. 1st lt. U.S. Army, 1952-54. USPHS post doctoral fellow U. N.C.--Raleigh, 1964-66; post doctoral fellow Duke U., 1966-67. Mem. APA, Pa. Psychol, Sigma Xi (chair 1985, award 1987). Home: Haverford, Pa. Died Aug. 23, 2005.

MALLOVE, EUGENE FRANKLIN, science writer, astronautical engineer; b. Norwich, Conn., June 9, 1947; s. Mitchel Noah and Gladys (Alexander) M.; m. Joanne Karen Smith, Sept. 6, 1970; children: Kimberlyn Beth, Ethan Armstrong. SB in Aero./Astronautical Engring., MIT, 1969, SM in Aero./Astronautical Engring., 1970; ScD in Environ. Health Scis., Harvard U., 1975. Cons. engr. Hughes Rsch. Labs., Malibu, Calif., 1970-77; engr. Harvard Air Cleaning Lab., Boston, 1975-77, Analytic Scis. Corp., Reading, Mass., 1977-79; pres., founder Astronomy New England Inc., Holliston, Mass., 1979-85; author, freelance sci. writer Holliston, Mass and Bow, N.H., from 1982; engr. MIT Lincoln Lab., Lexington, 1983-85; sci. writer, broadcaster Voice of Am., Washington, 1985-87; adj. prof. Boston U. Sch. Communication, 1988-90; chief sci. writer news office MIT, Cambridge, 1987-91, lectr. in sci. journalism, from 1990. Author: The Quickening Universe, 1987, The Starflight Handbook, 1989 (Astron. Soc. of Pacific award 1989), Fire From Ice, 1991; contbr. articles to local and national newspapers. Fellow British Interplanetary Soc.; mem. AIAA, AAAS, Nat. Assn. Sci. Writers, Inst. on Religion in an Age of Sci., Sigma Xi, Tau Beta Pi. Republican. Jewish. Avocations: amateur astronomy, camping. Died May 14, 2004.

MALONE, CORINNE, mental health nurse; b. Bklyn., Oct. 24, 1929; d. Patrick and Estelle (Evans) M. Diploma, St. Catherine's Hosp., Bklyn., 1953; BSN, Adelphi U., 1963; student, U. Rochester, 1967. Cert. assessor Office of Health Systems Mgmt. Nurse St. Catherine's Hosp., Winthrop Univ. Hosp., Mineola, N.Y.; supr., pub. health nurse Nassau County (N.Y.) Dept. Health; nurse Brunswick Hosp., Amityville, N.Y. Home: Woodbury, NY. Died Sept. 14, 2004.

MALONEY, CHARLES GARRETT, bishop; b. Louisville, Sept. 9, 1912; s. David J. and Imelda Mary (Shea) M. Student, St. Joseph Coll., Rensselaer, Ind., 1926-32; Ph.B., S.T.L., Gregorian U., Rome, 1938; J.C.L., Catholic U. Am., 1942. Ordained priest Roman Cath. Ch., 1937; chaplain St. Thomas Orphanage, Louisville, 1938; asst. pastor St. Frances of Rome, Louisville, 1939; chaplain St. Joseph Infirmary, Louisville, 1942-46; sec., asst., chancellor Archdiocese of Louisville, 1946-55, vicar gen., 1954, aux. bishop, 1954—88, ret. aux. bishop, 1988, aux. bishop emeritus, 2006; titular bishop of Capsa, 1954; ordained titular bishop of Capsa, 1955; first titular bishop Bardstown, Ky., 1995—2006. Mem. Vatican Council II. Died Apr. 30, 2006.

MALONEY, J. PATRICK, minister, educator, seminary administrator; b. Pitts., Feb. 19, 1929; s. James Deasy and Helen (Crouse) M.; m. Bettie Jean Silvus, Dec. 1, 1953; children: Sharon Shakespeare, Lori Spencer, Mitzi Kelley, Patricia Hawkins, Kathleen Brown (dec.), James D. Maloney. BA, Jacksonville U., 1961; BD, New Orleans Bapt. Theol. Sem., 1964; PhD, St. Marys Sem. and U., Balt., 1973. Ordained to ministry So. Bapt. Conv., 1960. Pastor Fairfield Bapt. Chapel, Jacksonville, Fla., 1958-61, 1st Bapt. Ch., Thomas, La., 1963-64, Hayne Boulevard Bapt. Ch., New Orleans, 1964-67, Kent Bapt. Ch., Landover, Md., 1969-77, Fisher Rd. Bapt. Ch., 1977-83, Mission Oaks Bapt. Ch., East Ridge, Tenn., from 1983. Prof. Sem. Extension So. Bapt. Conv., Nashville, 1973—; acad. v.p. Oxford Grad. Sch., Dayton, Tenn., 1982-86. Mem. Cath. Theol. Soc. Am., Evang. Theol. Soc., Oxford Soc. Scholars. Home: Chattanooga, Tenn. Died Oct. 26, 2004.

MALONEY, THOMAS J., anthropologist, educator, writer; b. Arlington, Mass., Nov. 16, 1922; s. Thomas Joseph and Doris Eleanor (Edwards) M.; m. Elizabeth Gartner, Feb. 7, 1948; children: Susan, Margaretha, Elizabeth, Thomas Jefferson. BSChemE, Northeastern U., 1948; STB, Harvard U., 1952; AM in Sociology, Wash. U., St. Louis, 1956; PhD in Anthropology, Wash. U., 1966. Chem. engr. Gen. Aniline & Film Corp., Easton, Pa., 1948, U. Colo. Experiment Sta., Boulder, Colo., 1948-49, Aircraft Gas Turbine divsn. GE, Boston, 1950-52; min. Unitarian Ch., Davenport, Iowa, 1952-53, Quincy, Ill., 1953-56; tech. pers. assoc. Bettis Atomic Power divsn. Westinghouse Electric Corp., Pitts., 1956-57; part-time instr. dept. anthropology U. Colo., Boulder, 1957-59; min. Unitarian Ch., Boulder, 1957-62; asst. prof. N.Mex. Highlands U., Las Vegas, 1962-67; assoc. prof. anthropology and sociology Ripon (Wis.) Coll., 1967-69; prof. anthropology So. Ill. U., Edwardsville, 1969-87, prof. emeritus, from 1987. With U.S. Army, 1942-44, with USMC, 1944-46; 1st lt. USAR, 1949-52. Fellow AAAS, Am. Anthrop. Assn. Died May 6, 2005.

MALVERN, DONALD, retired aircraft manufacturing company executive; b. Sterling, Okla., Apr. 22, 1921; s. George Michael and Anna Francesca (Elsass) M.; m. Ruth Marie Vogler, June 4, 1949; 1 son, Michael John. BSME, U. Okla., 1946. Engr. Victory Architects and Engrs., Clinton, Okla., 1943, Douglas Aircraft Co., Santa Monica, Calif., 1943; with McDonnell Aircraft Co., St. Louis, 1946-88, exec. v.p., 1973-82, pres., 1982-86; v.p. McDonnell Douglas Corp., 1973-88; aerospace cons. St. Louis, 1988—2006; pres. McDonnell Douglas Services, Inc., 1978-82. Trustee Falcon Found., 1983-2006; bd. visitors Def. Sys. Mgmt. Coll., 1983-86, U. Okla. Coll. Engring., 1988-91; pres. Wings of Hope, 1989-92, chmn., 1992-2004, dir. emeritus, 2004-06; 1st lt. USAAF, 1943-46; capt. Mo. Air NG, 1946-51. Inducted into Okla. Aviation and Space Mus.'s Hall of Fame, 1987; recipient Disting. Alumni award U. Okla., 1999, Unsung Hero award United Way of St. Louis, 2000. Fellow AIAA (Tech. Mgmt. award 1968, Reed Aeros. medal 1980); mem. Am. Def. Preparedness Assn. (pres. St. Louis chpt. 1979-80), Navy League U.S. (life), Nat. Aeros. Assn., Air Force Assn., Armed Forces Mgmt. Assn., Pi Tau Sigma, Tau Beta Pi, Tau Omega, Sigma Tau Beta. Clubs: Bellerive Country, St. Louis. Home: Chesterfield, Mo. Died Jan. 19, 2006.

MANARY, RICHARD DEANE, retired manufacturing executive; b. Des Moines, Nov. 11, 1944; s. Robert Claude and Veronica (Cornwell) M.; m. Eileen Cecile, Aug. 16, 1986; children: Erica (dec.), Matthew, Stephen, Lauren. AA in Indsl. Engring., Southwestern Coll., 1976; BA in History, Calif. State U., San Diego, 1967, BS in Edn., 1973; grad., Stanford U. Bus. Ext., 1991; MBA, Nat. U., 1993. Registered profl. engr., Calif.; cert. elem. tchr., Calif. Mfg. engr. Rohr Industries, San Diego, 1967-78, chief R&D divsn. Riverside, Calif., 1978-80, project mfg. mgr., 1980-84, dep. program mgr. Wichita, Kans., 1984-87, mgr. Titan 3d, Titan IV missile programs Riverside, 1987-89, program mgr. MD-11, 1989-91, gen. program mgr. Boing mil. programs Chula Vista, Calif., 1991-95, gen. mgr. space products divsn., 1995-97; program mgr. tactical mil. fighters Goodrich, Chula Vista, 1997-99; dir. ops. B.F. Goodrich, Chula Vista, 1999-2000; plant mgr. Goodrich Co., Dallas, 2000—01, ops. dir. Riverside, Calif., 2001—02, dir. plant facilities, environ. and indsl. engring., from 2002; ret. Contbr. articles to profl. jours. Chmn. employee and community assistance program Rohr Industries, Riverside, 1981-85; adv. Riverside chpt. Jr. Achievement, 1978-79. Mem. Soc. Mfg. Engrs. (sr., assoc., chmn. 1978-79), Soc. Automotive Engrs., Soc. Material and Process Engrs., Am. Soc. Metals, Nat. Mgmt. Assn. (chmn. 1980-81), Aerospace Industries Assn. (space com.), Air Force Assn., San Diego Port Tenants Assn., San Diego Regional C. of C., ChoLa Vista City C. of C., KC. Super Bowl Host Comm., Regional Chamber of Commerce. Democrat. Roman Catholic. Avocations: backpacking, skiing, stamp collecting/philately, travel, boating. Home: Bonita, Calif. Died July 26, 2004.

MANCHESTER, ARTHUR HERSCHELL, English and foreign language educator; b. Aberdeen, Wash., July 25, 1933; s. Forrest E. and Annie (Nuttall) M.; m. Barbara Jane Sanford, Aug. 10, 1962; children: Vance Arthur, Eric Andrew. AB, N.W. Nazarene Coll., Nampa, Idaho, 1955; MA, U. Colo., 1958. Cert. in secondary edn., Oreg. Teaching asst. U. Colo., Boulder, 1957-58; prof. N.W. Nazarene Coll., 1958-60; tchr. R.E. Bennett Jr. H.S., Chehalis, Wash., 1960-62, Gresham (Oreg.) Union H.S., 1962-91; home instr. Multnomah County (Oreg.) Pub. Schs., 1996; home and hosp. tchr. Portland (Oreg.) Pub. Schs., from 1991; tchr. Gresham (Oreg.,) Sam Barlow H.S., 1996-97. Analytical writing scorer Multnomah County and State of Oreg. Schs., 1987—. Author: Math Puzzles and Games, 1977, 2d edit., 1994. Recipient Dankstipendium, Deutscher Akademischer Austauschdienst, 1956-57, summer stipend NDEA, 1963, Honorarium, NEH, 1978. Mem. NEA, Oreg. Edn. Assn., Confedn. Oreg. Fgn. Lang. Tchrs. (pres. 1981-82, bd. dirs. 1978-80, 82-83). Republican. Nazarene. Avocations: walking, reading, word puzzles. Home: Portland, Oreg. Died Sept. 3, 2004.

MANCINI, LOIS JEAN, elementary school educator; b. Pitts., May 1, 1944; d. Edward Walter and Margaret Jane Freidhof; m. George John Mancini, July 7, 1967; children: Robin Jennifer, Lori Jean. MEd, Rutgers U., 1988. Cert. elem. tchr. N.J., prin. N.J. Tchr. Moorestown (N.J.) Bd. Edn., Cinnaminson (N.J.) Bd. Edn., Andover (N.J.) Bd. Edn. Author: Mortimer Goose, 1998. Pres. Westampton N.J. Bd. Edn., 1993—. Named Tchr. of Yr., State of N.J., 1996. Mem. NEA, N.J. Edn. Assn., N.J. Sch. Bds. Assn. (pres. bd. dirs. 1993). Presbyterian. Avocations: reading, travel. Home: Mount Holly, NJ. Died Sept. 12, 2004.

MANCINI, ROCCO ANTHONY, civil engineer; b. Prezza, Abruzzi, Italy, Aug. 16, 1931; came to U.S., 1940; s. Salvatore and Bambina (Tulliani) M.; m. Eileen Clifford, Apr. 11, 1959; children: Charles V., Ann Marie, Linda E., Donna. BSCE, MIT, 1953; cert. in transp. engring., Yale U., 1958. Registered profl. engr., Mass. Supr. devel. planning Mass. Bay Transp. Authority, Quincy, 1966-68, project mgr. traffic engring., devel., 1976-79, mgr. transp. systems mgmt. projects, 1979-80, acting dir. program devel., 1980-82, rep. to Met. Planning Orgn., 1982-87, project mgr. constrn. office, 1987-89, asst. dir. constrn., 1989-92, asst. dir. design and constrn., from 1992. Cons. spl. transp. projects, City of Honolulu, 1968-69, Sao Paulo, Brazil, 1968-69; prin. transp. engr. Wilbur Smith and Assocs., 1969-70; New Eng. regional mgr. Tippetts-Abbett-McCarthy-Stratton, 1970-76. Contbr. articles to profl. publs. Mem. Milton (Mass.) Town Meeting, active various town coms. With U.S. Army, 1954-55. Automotive Safety Found. fellow Yale U., 1957-58. Fellow Inst. Transp. Engrs. (pres. New Eng. sect. 1965-66)); mem. ASCE (transp. com. 1953—). Achievements include development, design and supervision of transportation construction projects. Died Aug. 7, 2005.

MANDELKERN, LEO, biophysics professor, physical chemist; b. N.Y.C., Feb. 23, 1922; s. Israel and Gussie (Krostich) M.; m. Berdie Medvedoff, May, 1946; children: I. Paul, Marshal, David. BA, Cornell U., 1942, PhD, 1949. Postdoctoral rsch. assoc. Cornell U., Ithaca, NY, 1949-52; phys. chemist Nat. Bur. Standards, Washington, 1952-62; prof. chemistry and biophysics Fla. State U., Tallahassee, from 1962, R.O. Lawton Disting. prof., from 1984. Vis. prof. U. Miami (Fla.) Med. Sch., 1963, U. Calif. Med. Sch., San Francisco, 1964, Cornell U., 1967; mem. biophysics fellowship com. NIH, 1967-70; mem. study panel crystal growth and morphology NRC, 1960; cons. in field. Author: Crystallization of Polymers, 1964, An Introduction to Macromolecules, 1972, 1983, Crystallization of Polymers, Vol. 1, 2002, Vol. 2, 2004; contbr. numerous articles to profl. jours. 1st lt. USAAF, 1942-46, PTO. Recipient Meritorious Svc. award U.S. Dept. Commerce, 1957, Arthur S. Fleming award Washington Jaycees, 1958, Mettler award N.Am. Thermal Analysis Soc., Phila., 1984, Disting. Svc. in Advancement of Polymer Sci. award Soc. Polymer Sci., Japan, 1993, Outstanding Achievement award Soc. Plastic Engrs., 2005. Fellow: AAAS, Biophys. Soc., Am. Phys. Soc. (Outstanding Educator of Am. 1973, 1975), Am. Chem. Soc. (Polymer Chemistry award 1975, Fla. award 1984, Rubber divsn. Whitby award 1988, Applied Polymer Sci. award 1989, Charles Goodyear medal 1993, Disting. Svc. in Advancement of Polymer Sci. 1993, Polymer Divsn. P.J. Flory award 1994, Polymer Materials Sci. & Engring. Divsn. Coop. Rsch. award 1995, Herman F. Mark award 2000), Polymer Soc. Japan (sr.; sr.), Cosmos Club Washington, Alpha Epsilon Pi; mem.: Soc. Plastic Engrs. (Outstanding Achievement award 2005). Home: Tallahassee, Fla. Died May 31, 2006.

MANERS, WENDELL R., music minister; b. Clanton, Ala., Sept. 24, 1955; s. R.P. and Alice (Cleckler) M.; m. Nancy Lynne DeVaughn, Nov. 1, 1974; children: Jared Wendell, Jenna Lynne. B in Music Edn., Troy State U., 1981; MRE, Southwestern Bapt. Theol. Sem., 1984. Lic. to Gospel ministry, 1981. Minister music Shiloh Bapt. Ch., Clanton, Ala., 1975-76; minister music and youth Collins Chapel Bapt. Ch., Jemison, Ala., 1976-78, Southside Bapt. Ch., Greenville, Ala., 1978-82, First Bapt. Ch., Oxford, Ala., 1984-87; minister music and activities Hepzibah Bapt. Ch., Talladega, Ala., from 1987. Recipient Ministerial scholarship Chilton Ministerial Assn., Clanton, Ala., 1976. Mem. Jaycees, Ala. Singing Men. Avocations: golf, fishing, painting, hunting. Died Jan. 7, 2004.

MANETH, ALVIN LEE, financial planning company executive; b. Great Bend, Kans., June 12, 1934; s. Henry J. and Lena (Hlavaty) M.; m. Jolene Clara Schremmer, June 9, 1959; children: Darrin, Tamee, Danielle. BS, Fort Hays State U., 1960. Indsl. engr. Boeing Corp., Wichita, Kans., 1962-63; owner Maneth Constrn., Wichita, 1962-72, from 1972, A&J Co., Phoenix, 1972-91, Direct Fin., Scottsdale, Ariz., from 1983; bus. specialist Realty Internat., Scottsdale, 1988-89; pres., chief exec. officer Freedom Inc.; owner, gen. mgr. Profl. Cons. Am., Scottsdale. Author: How to Sell U.S. Real Estate to Hong Kong Investors, 1986, Sell It and Get the Cash, 1987. With U.S. Army, 1954-57. Mem. Optimists (pres. Wichita chpt. 1970, lt. gov. 1971), Scottsdale C. of C/ Republican. Roman Catholic. Avocation: collecting and restoring antique cars. Home: Phoenix, Ariz. Died Feb. 5, 2005.

MANGAN, JOSEPH F., data processing executive; b. N.Y.C., July 5, 1943; s. James F. and Anna F. (Farrell) M.; m. R. Elizabeth Donaldson, Oct. 17, 1970. BBA cum laude, Coll. of Ins., N.Y.C., 1974. CPCU. Claims adjuster Gt. Am. Ins. Cos., N.Y.C., 1968-69; underwriter Comml. Union Ins. Cos., N.Y.C., 1969-71; sr. underwriter Crum & Forster Ins. Co., N.Y.C., 1971-75; asst. prof. The Coll. of Ins., N.Y.C., 1975-81; asst. to pres. GNY Ins. Co., N.Y.C., 1981-87; project mgr., internal cons. Best's Underwriting Guide A. M. Best Co., Oldwick, N.J., from 1987. Cons. Empire Blue Cross & Blue Shield, 1980, 85, City of N.Y., 1980, John P. Tilden & Co., Inc., 1981-81, U.S. Atty., Mineola, N.Y., 1981. Author, editor: Best's Underwriting Newsletter; contbr. column Best's Review mag.; cons. editor: Werbel's General Insurance Guide. Lector St. Bartholomew Ch., Scotch Plains, N.J., 1983—. Sgt. U.S. Army, 1966-68, viet Nam. Mem. VFW, DAV, Soc. CPUs (underwriting sect. northeast region governing com.), Soc. Ins. Rsch., Viet Nam Vets Am., MOPH. Avocations: photography, swimming. Home: Scotch Plains, NJ. Died Nov. 4, 2004.

MANGAN, WILLIAM J., physician; b. Niagara Falls, N.Y., July 25, 1933; s. John Gerald and Catherine (McAndrew) M.; m. Joan Marie Barr, Aug. 26, 1961; children: David F., John G., James P., Brian M. BS, Coll. of Holy Cross, Worcester, Mass., 1955; MD, U. Buffalo, 1959. Diplomate Am. Bd. Internal Medicine. Pvt. practice, Buffalo, 1968-83; physician Buffalo Med. Group, 1983-95. Assoc. clin. prof. SUNY, Buffalo. Capt. USNG. Mem. Western N.Y. Soc. Internal Medicine (pres. 1982), N.Y. State Soc. Internal Medicine (pres. 1985, award of merit 1989), Am. Soc. Internal Medicine (chmn., ins. com.), Buffalo Acad. Medicine. Roman Catholic. Avocations: skiing, hunting, golf, gardening, running. Home: Williamsville, NY. Died Apr. 26, 2005.

MANHEIM, WERNER, language educator; b. Berlin, Feb. 17, 1915; came to U.S., 1937; s. Martin and Else (Schindler) M.; m. Eliane Housiaux, Aug.18, 1951 (dec. 1994). BEd, U. Berlin, 1935; MusB, Cin. Conservatory Music, 1940, MusM, 1941; DFA, Chgo. Musical Coll., 1950; LittD (hon.), World Acad. Arts & Culture, 1993. Asst. prof. Ind. U., E. Chgo., 1947-54; rsch. asst. Inst. for Sex Rsch., Bloomington, Ind., 1955-58; from asst. prof. to prof. French and German Ind. U., Fort Wayne, from 1958. Instr. music St. Francis Coll., Fort Wayne, 1969-77. Author 20 vols. poetry; contbr. articles to profl. jours. With U.S. Army, 1941-45. Recipient medal studiosis humanitatis, 1979, Poetenmünze zum Halbenbogen, 1980, certificate of merit Cambridge Adolf Bartels Commemoration honor, 1980, Dr. Heinrichmock medal, 1982, Eminet Poet Internat. Poets Acad., 1986, Golden Poet award, 1989, 90, 91. Mem. Internat. Authors Plesse, Internat. Culture Coun. (sec.), World Poetry Soc., German Haiku Soc. (hon.). Avocation: piano. Home: Fort Wayne, Ind. Died Apr. 21, 2005.

MANN, ALFRED, musicology educator, choral conductor; b. Hamburg, Germany, Apr. 28, 1917; came to U.S. May 2, 1939, naturalized, 1943; s. Wilhelm and Edith (Weiss) M.; m. Carolyn Owens, Aug. 23, 1948; children: Adrian, John, Timothy Cert., State Acad. Music, Berlin, Germany, 1937, Royal Conservatory, Milan, Italy, 1938; diploma, Curtis Inst. Music, Phila., 1942; MA, Columbia U., 1950, PhD, 1955; MusD (hon.), Whitworth Coll., 1947, Baldwin-Wallace Coll., 1984, Muhlenberg Coll., Allentown, Pa., 1985. Instr. State Acad. Music, Berlin, 1937-38; instr. Scuola Musicale, Milan, 1938-39; research asst. Curtis Inst. Music, Phila., 1939-42; chmn. to prof. emeritus Rutgers U., New Brunswick; prof. emeritus musicology Eastman Sch. Music/U. Rochester, 1980—2006. Condr. Cantata Singers, N.Y., 1952-59, Bach Choir, Bethlehem, Pa., 1970-80, recs. G.F. Handel, Chandos Anthems, 3 vols., 1964, 65, 66, 1998 (CD); dir. publs. Am. Choral Found., Phila., 1962-98. Author: Study of Fugue, 1958, Theory and Practice, 1987 (re-issued as The Great Composer as Teacher and Student, 1994), Bach and Handel: Choral Performance Practice, 1992, Handel, The Orchestral Music, 1996; editor vols. for Complete Works of Handel, Mozart, Schubert, 1965—, J.J. Fux, Gradus ad Parnassum, 1938, 43, 85, Messiah critical edit. of Handel's conducting score, 1959, 65, 89, Am. Choral Rev., 1962-98. Bd. dirs. G.F. Handel Gesellschaft, Halle, Germany. Served with CIC, U.S. Army, 1943-45 Guggenheim fellow, 1958. Fellow Am. Coun. Learned Soc., Am. Philos. Soc., Nat. Found. Humanities; mem. Am. Musicological Soc., Internat. Musicological Soc., Am. Bach Soc. (sec. 1972-92), Am. Handel Soc. (hon., bd. dirs.), Internat. Bach Soc. (hon.), Internat. Schuetz Soc. (bd. dirs. Am. chpt.), Bach Riemenschneider Inst. (hon.). Home: Fort Wayne, Ind. Died Sept. 21, 2006.

MANN, HAROLD EARLE, physician; b. Phila., Mar. 8, 1920; s. Louis and Jeanette Ruth M.; m. Muriel Mann, July 25, 1948; children: Deborah Hoffman, Carol Mann, Lisa Ricketts Mann, Jennifer Mann. BA, U. Pa., 1940, MD, 1944. Cert. psychiatry, child psychiatry, psychoanalysis. Intern Michael Reese Hosp., Chgo., 1944-45; resident-psychiatry Worcester (Mass.) State Hosp., 1945-46, Boston State Hosp., 1946-47; resident in child psychiatry Judge Baker Ctr., Boston, 1947-51; capt. U.S.P.H.S., Washington, 1951-53; pvt. practice San Francisco, 1953-58, Berkeley, Calif., from 1958. Mem. East Bay Psychiat. Assn. (pres. 1971), No. Calif. Psychiat. Soc. (pres. 1973), Am. Coll. Psychiatrists, Am. Coll. Psychoanalysts, others. Home: Walnut Creek, Calif. Died May 10, 2005.

MANN, ROBERT PAUL, retired lawyer; b. Pitts., July 24, 1929; s. O. Paul and Floy Melinda (Foster) M.; m. Dorothy Neeld, Sept. 4, 1953; children: Robin Duvall Francik, Stewart Neeld Mann. BS, U. Md., College Park, 1951; JD, U. Md., Balt., 1953. Bar: Md. 1954, U.S. Dist. Md. 1965, U.S. Tax Ct. 1976. Pvt. practice, Ruxton, Md., 1956-96; ret., 1996. Trial magistrate, 1957-59. Past pres. Artists Equity, Timonium Rotary, Towson Libr.; active wildlife orgns.; art donor to numerous major mus. Mem. Omicron Delta Kappa, Delta Theta Phi, Sigma Chi. Episcopalian. Home: Ruxton, Md. Died Apr. 6, 2006.

MANN, ROBERT WELLESLEY, biomedical engineer, educator; b. Bklyn., Oct. 6, 1924; s. Arthur Wellesley and Helen (Rieger) M.; m. Margaret Ida Florencourt, Sept. 4, 1950 (dec. 2002); children: Robert Wellesley, Catherine Louise. SB, MIT, 1950, SM, 1951, ScD, 1957. With Bell Tel. Labs., NYC, 1942-43, 46-47, U.S. Army Signal Corps, 1943-46; rsch. engr. MIT, 1951-52, rsch. supr., 1952, mem. faculty, 1953—2006, prof. mech. engring., 1963-70, Germeshausen prof., 1970-72, prof. engring., 1972-74, Whitaker prof. biomed. engring., 1974-92, Whitaker prof. emeritus, sr. lectr., 1992—2006, head systems and design divsn., mech. engring. dept., 1957-68, 82-83, founder, dir. engring. projects lab., 1959-62; founder, chmn. steering com. Ctr. Sensory Aids Evaluation and Devel., 1964-86, chmn. divsn. health scis., tech., planning and mgmt., 1972-74, founder, dir. Newman biomechanics and human rehab. lab., 1975-92; dir. bioengring. programs Whitaker Coll. MIT, 1986-89; dir. Harvard-MIT Rehab. Engring. Ctr., 1988-93. Mem. exec. com. Divsn. Health Scis. and Tech. Harvard U. MIT, 1972-85; prof., 1979-2006, mem. Com. on Use of Humans as Exptl. Subjects MIT, 1984-93, co-chair Pub. Svc. Ctr., 1988-92; lectr. engring. Faculty of Medicine, Harvard U., 1973-79; rsch. assoc. in orthop. surgery Children's Hosp. Med. Ctr., 1973-2006; cons. in engring. sci. Mass. Gen. Hosp., 1969-2006; cons. in field, 1953-2006; mem. Nat. Commn. Engring. Edn., 1962-69; com. prosthetics rsch. and devel. NRC, 1963-69; chmn. sensory aids subcom., 1965-68, com. skeletal sys., 1969; mem. com. interplay engring. with biology and medicine NAE, 1969-73; mem. bd. health scis. policy Inst. Medicine, 1973-74, 82-86; mem. com. on nat. needs for rehab. physically handicapped NAS, 1975-76; mem.-at-large confs. com. Engring. Found., 1975-81; chair sensory aids panel scis. merit rev. bd. Rehab., R & D Svc., Dept. Vets. Affairs, 1983-95, 99-2006, mem. Visual/Hearing Impairment Rehab. Panel, 1999-2006; mem. Commn. on Life Scis. NRC, 1984-88, Com. on Strategic Tech. for U.S. Army, NRC, 1989-93; NRC Com. on Space Biology and Medicine, 1992-95. Consulting editor: Ency. Sci. and Tech., 1962-67; assoc. editor: IEEE Trans. in Biomed. Engring., 1969-78, ASME Jour. Biomech. Engring., 1976-82; mem. editl. bd. Jour. Visual Impairment and Blindness, 1976-80, SOMA, 1986-92; mem. editl. adv. bd. new liberal arts program Alfred P. Sloan Found., 1986-92; contbr. over 400 articles to profl. jours. Mem. scientific adv. coun. United Cerebral Palsy Rsch. & Edn. Found., 2006; pres., trustee Amanda Caroline Payson Scholarship Fund, 1965—86; trustee Nat. Braille Press, 1982—2006, pres., 1990—94; trustee Mary Flannery O'Connor Charitable Trust, 2002—06; bd. dirs. Carroll Ctr. Blind, 1967—74, pres., 1968—74; mem. corp. Perkins Sch. Blind, 1970—2000, Mt. Auburn Hosp., 1972—2000, mem. bd. overseers, 2000—06; mem. Cardinal's adv. com. on social justice Archdiocese of Boston, 1993—96; bd. overseers St. Marguerite D'Youville Found., Youville Lifecare Inc., 1994—98; chmn. Flannery O'Connor-Andalusia Found., Inc., 2002—06; sci. adv. coun. United Cerebral Palsy Rsch. and Edn. Found., 2006. Recipient Sloan award for Outstanding Performance, 1957, Talbert Abrams Photogrammetry award, 1962, Assn. Blind of Mass. award, 1969, IR-100 award for Braillemboss, 1972, UCP Goldenson Rsch. for Handicapped award, 1976, New Eng. award, 1979. Fellow Am. Acad. Arts and Scis., Am. Inst. Med. and Biol. Engring., IEEE (mem. editl. bd. Spectrum 1984-86), AAAS, ASME (gold medal 1977, H.R. Lissner award for biomed. engring. 1977); mem. NAS, Inst. Medicine NAS, NAE, Biomed. Engring. Soc. (bd. dirs. 1981-84), Orthop. Rsch. Soc., Rehab. Soc. N.Am., MIT Alumni Assn. (pres. 1983-84, Alumni Fund Bd. 1978-80, bd. dirs. 1980-86, 93-95, corp. joint adv. com. 1983-84, chair nat. selector com. 1985-88, awards com. 1992-94, chmn. 1994, bd. Tech. Rev. 1986-95, chmn. 1993-95), Sigma Xi (nat. lectr. 1979-81), Tau Beta Pi, Pi Tau Sigma, Sigma Xi. Roman Catholic. Achievements include patents on missile power units, founding of computer aided design in 1963, earliest braille translation software and hardware in 1962, cybernetic amputation prosthesis, 1966, in vivo measurements of human cartilage pressures, 1984. Home: Lexington, Mass. Died June 16, 2006.

MANNING, BROWN ROTHWELL, physician assistant; b. Knoxville, Tenn., Jan. 2, 1951; s. Robert Cooper and Mary Elizabeth (Robertson) M.; m. Deborah Hansen, Sept. 24, 1977 (div. Oct. 1994); children: Christopher Brown, Andrea Deborah; m. Dianne K. Binzel, Oct. 20, 1995. BS, U. Ga., 1974; B of Med. Sci., Emory U., 1975; MPH, U. Ala., Birmingham, 1985. Cert. physician asst. Clin. physician asst. Jefferson Clinic, P.C., Birmingham, Ala., 1976-86; dir. Emory U. physician asst. program Emory U., Atlanta, 1986-90; instr. U. Fla. physician asst. program U. Fla., Gainesville, 1990-92; clin. physician asst. Jefferson Clinic, P.C., Birmingham, Ala., from 1992. Chmn. Accreditation Rev. Com. on Edn. for Physician Assts., Marshfield, Wis., 1990-95; mem. adv. com. Ga. State Bd. Med. Examiners, Atlanta, 1987-90, Ala. Bd. Med. Examiners, Montgomery, 1995—; cons. Fla. Correctional Med. Authority, Tallahassee, 1991-95. Commr. Commn. on Accreditation of Allied Helath Edn. Programs, Chgo., 1994—. Fellow Am. Acad. Physician Assts., Ala. Soc. Physician Assts. (pres. 1984-85, Outstanding Mem. award 1986), Epsilon Delta. Episcopalian. Avocations: hiking, home remodeling, softball, biking. Home: Birmingham, Ala. Died July 16, 2004.

MANOCCHIO, VIVIENNE CINDA (VICKI LANE), vocalist, composer; b. Bklyn., Mar. 11, 1949; d. Victor David and Victoria (Allawas) M. Student, U. Miami (Fla.), 1967-69. Internat. singer appeared with Bob Hope, Don Rickles, Merle Haggard, Lou Rawls, others; performed in Japan, S.Am., N.Am., Europe; performed for Presidents Ronald Reagan and Jimmy Carter; actress, singer, dancer summer stock theater, 1961-65; mem. Jackie Gleason Dancers, 1965-70; singer Boca Raton (Fla.) Symphonic Pops, London Philharm., 1989; albums Vicki Lane, With Love, Off the Top of My Head, Pompadour; composer Madame de Pompadour; composer, featured in Lincoln Mercury TV comml. Performer Multiple Sclerosis TV Telethon, Cerebral Palsy Telethon, Parkinson's Disease Telethon. Named Miss Italian Am. Italian Am. Orgn., 1965, Miss Treadway World Miss World Contst, 1970. Roman Catholic. Avocations: health spa, swimming, dance, theater. Home: Hollywood, Fla. Died July 31, 2005.

MANOS, JOHN MICHAEL, federal judge; b. Cleve., Dec. 8, 1922; m. Viola Manos; 4 children. BS, Case Inst. Tech., 1944; JD, Cleve.-Marshall Coll. Law, 1950. Bar: Ohio 1950. Asst. plant mgr. Lake City Malleable Iron Co., Cleve., 1946-50; atty. Manos & Manos, 1950-63; law dir. City of Bay Village, 1954-56; industries rep. Cleve. Regional Bd. of Rev., 1957-59; judge Ohio Ct. Common Pleas, Cuyahoga County, 1963-69, Ohio Ct. Appeals, Cuyahoga County, 1969-76, U.S. Dist. Ct. (no. dist.) Ohio, Cleve., 1976-91, sr. judge, 1991—2006. With USN, 1942-45. Named Phi Alpha Delta Man of Yr., 1972, Outstanding Alumnus Cleve.- Marshall Law Alumni Assn., 1976. Mem. ABA, Fed. Bar Assn., Ohio State Bar Assn., Nat. Lawyers Club (hon.), Bar Assn. Greater Cleve., Cuyahoga County Bar Assn., Delta Theta Phi (Man of Yr. 1970). Died July 6, 2006.

MANTON, THOMAS JOSEPH, former congressman; b. NYC, Nov. 3, 1932; m. Diane Schley; children: Cathy, Tom, John, Jeanne. BBA, St. John's U., 1958, LLB, 1962. Mem. N.Y.C. Police Dept., 1955-60; mktg. rep. IBM, 1960-64; pvt. law practice, 1964-84; mem. US Congresses from 9th (now 7th) N.Y. Dist., Washington, 1984-98; ptnr. Manton, Sweeney, Gallo, Reich & Bolz, N.Y.C., 1999—2006. Mem. N.Y.C. Council, 1970-84; chmn. exec. com. Queens County Dem. Orgn.; Served with USMC, 1951-53; mem. N.Y. State Dem. Com. Democrat. Died July 22, 2006.

MAPES, RICHARD MATHER, SR., minister; b. New Haven, Sept. 7, 1925; s. Milton Crawford and Gladys Merwin (Blakeslee) M.; m. Marianne Fenner, June 16, 1951; children: Cynthia, Richard Mather Jr., Catherine, Carolyn. AB, Yale U., 1949; BDiv, Yale Divinity Sch., 1952; DD, Tougaloo (Miss.) Coll., 1982. Sr. minister Olmsted Community Ch., Olmsted Falls, Ohio, 1952-61; asst. conf. minister Ohio Congl. Chs., Cleve., 1961-63; dir. field edn. Oberlin & Vanderbilt Divinity Sch., Nashville, 1963-67; minister Trinity Congl. Ch., Pepper Pike, Ohio, 1967-71; sr. minister First Ch. Congl., Painesville, Ohio, 1971-76, Naples (Fla.) United Ch. of Christ, 1976-91, 1st Congl. Ch., Branford, Conn., from 1991. Bd. dirs. Uplands Retirement Village, Pleasant Hills, Tenn. Bd. dirs. Collier County Sch. Bd., Naples, 1982-84, Alcohol, Drug and Mental Health Bd. Dist. 8, Ft. Myers, Fla., 1988-91, United Way of Collier County, Naples, 1988-90. Staff sgt. inf. U.S. Army, 1943-46, ETO/PTO. Mem. Naples Ministerial Assn. (pres. 1980-81), Kiwanis (pres. Naples chpt. 1982-83). Democrat. Home: Branford, Conn. Died June 21, 2005.

MARAFIOTI, DOMINICK, small business owner; b. Rochester, N.Y., Apr. 10, 1926; s. Pasquale and Carmela (Parisi) M.; m. Marie Ricciardi, Jan. 19, 1957; children: Mary Ann, Dominic Jr., Bernadette. Mgr. Waring Theatre, Rochester, 1958-60; owner Cleaning Bus., Rochester, from 1961. Nat. chief Buck Jones Rangers of Am., Rochester, 1980—. Founder, Boys and Girls Safety Patrol Club, Rochester, 1945. Pfc. U.S. Army, 1943-45. Decorated Bronze Star; recipient letter of commendation Pres. Eisenhower, 1959, Iron Eyes Cody peace medal, 1990; hon. sheriff Monroe County, medallion and flag; Am. Flag, DAR. Avocations: collect 16mm western features, western memorbilia. Died Sept. 8, 2004.

MARBURY, WILLIAM ARDIS, banker; b. Ruston, La., July 22, 1917; s. William Ardis Sr. and Leola (Ridgdill) M.; m. Virginia Lomax, Sept. 5, 1943; children: Rebekah, Caroline. BA, La. Tech. U., 1936, LLD (hon.), 1987. Pres., chmn. Bankers Life of La., Ruston, from 1959; pres. Ruston State Bank & Trust Co., 1972-81; also bd. dirs. Bankers Life of La., Ruston, from 1959. Bd. dirs., chmn. Ruston State Bank & Trust Co., La. Tech Univ. Found. Bd. dirs., pres. Lincoln Gen. Hosp., Ruston, 1962-82. Recipient Silver Beaver award Boy Scouts Am., Washington, 1979, Alumnus of Yr. award La. Tech. U., Ruston, 1976, Disting. Svc. award Kiwanis, Ruston, 1990. Mem. Ruston C. of C. (pres. 1955, Robert E. Russ award 1990). Republican. Episcopalian. Home: Ruston, La. Died 2005.

MARCINKUS, PAUL C., archbishop; b. Cicero, Ill., Jan. 15, 1922; Ordained priest Roman Catholic Ch., 1947. Served in Vatican secretariat, Rome, from 1952; ordained titular bishop of Orta, 1969; ordained titular archbishop of Orta, 1981; sec. Inst. for Religious Works (Vatican Bank), 1968—71, pres., 1971—89; named pro-pres. Pontifical Commn. for Vatican City State, 1981—90. Died Feb. 20, 2006.

MARCUS, JULES ALEXANDER, physicist, researcher; b. Coytesville, N.J., May 10, 1919; s. Alexander and Julia Hollister (Parks) M.; m. Ruth Charlotte Barcan, Aug. 28, 1942; children: James S., Peter W., Katherine H., Elizabeth P. BS, Yale U., 1940, PhD, 1947. Physicist Johns Hopkins U., Balt., 1944-46; instr. physics Yale U., New Haven, 1942—43, rsch. asst., 1946-47; postdoctoral fellow U. Chgo., 1947-49; asst. prof. physics Northwestern U., Evanston, Ill., 1949-61, prof. physics, 1961-89, prof. emeritus physics, from 1989. Contbr. articles to profl. jours. Union Carbon and Carbide fellow, U. Chgo., 1947-49; NSF rsch. grantee, 1952-75. Fellow Am. Phys. Soc.; mem. Am. Assn. Physics Tchrs., N.Y. Acad. Scis., Sigma Xi. Achievements include first observation of quantum oscillations in magnetic properties of ordinary metals; spin-density wave modification of electronic structure of antiferromagnetic chromium; research in low-temperature solid-state physics. Home: Higganum, Conn. Died Nov. 5, 2005.

MARDER, JOHN G., real estate investor, marketing consultant, rancher, corporate financial executive; b. N.Y.C., Dec. 27, 1926; s. Joseph T. and Rhea Marder; m. Barbara Sand, 1956 (div. 1971); children; Jonathan A., Susan Zelouf, Jane Martin; m. Joan Kron, 1971. Student, Cornell U., 1944-45; BS in Bus., Columbia U., 1950. Merchandising exec. Macy's, N.Y.C., 1951-56; exec. v.p. Grey Advt. Inc., N.Y.C., 1956-86; real estate investor-developer Miami Beach, Anguilla B.W.I., 1986—2004; ptnr. buffalo ranch and mktg. enterprise Belle-Air Farms, Thompson, Pa., 1999—2005. Bd. dirs. several profit, not-for-profit and ednl. corps. Served as radio officer U.S. Maritime Service, U.S. Army Transport Service, 1945-46; 2d Lt. Q.M.C. U.S. Army, 1951-53. Home: New York, NY. Died Dec. 10, 2005.

MARDIN, ARIF, music industry executive, musician; b. Istanbul, Turkey, Mar. 15, 1932; m. Latife Mardin; children: Joe, Julie. Grad., Istanbul U.; postgrad., London Sch. Econs., Berklee Coll. Music, 1961, D (hon.). With Atlantic Records, NYC, 1963—2001, v.p., 1969, sr. v.p.; with Manhattan Records, NYC, 2001—04. Prodr.: The Young Rascals, Dusty Springfield, Aretha Franklin, Roberta Flack, Donny Hathaway, Hall & Oats, John Prine, Willie Nelson,

The Average White Band, The Bee Gees, Phil Collins, Bette Midler, Judy Collins, Carly Simon, Laura Nyro, Dionne Warwick, Culture Club, Howard Jones, George Benson, Melissa Manchester, Chaka Kahn, others; (albums) Saturday Night Fever, 1978 (Grammy award for Album of Yr., 1979), Queen of Soul: The Atlantic Recordings, 1992 (Grammy award for Best Album Notes, 1993), Smokey Joe's Cafe, 1995 (Grammy award for Best Musical Show Album, 1996), Come Away With Me, 2002 (2 Grammy awards for Album of Yr. & Best Pop Vocal Album, 2003), A Little Moonlight, 2003 (Grammy award for Best Jazz Vocal Album, 2004); (songs) Be Bop Medley, 1983 (Grammy award for Best Vocal Arrangement, 1984), Wind Beneath My Wings, 1989 (Grammy award for Record of Yr., 1990), Don't Know Why, 2002 (Grammy award for Record of Yr., 2003). Named to NARAS Hall of Fame, 1990; recipient Grammy award for Prodr. of Yr., 1975, 2002, Man of Yr. award, Assembly Turkish Am. Assns., 1990, Shofar of Peace award, Sephardic Hebrew Acad., 1992, Trustees award, Grammy Awards, 2002; Quincy Jones scholar, 1958. Achievements include accumulating 12 Grammy awards and producing over 40 gold and platinum albums. Died June 25, 2006.

MARGULIES, HERMAN, artist, educator; b. Boryslaw, Poland, Dec. 7, 1922; came to U.S., 1951; s. Aron and Mina (Rinzler) M.; 1 child, Alan Margulies. Student, Royal Acad. Fine Arts, Brussels, 1947-49. Tchr. pastel painting Washington (Conn.) Studio, from 1986. Juror El Paso, Tex. Mus. of Art Exhbn. 1989, Kans. Pastel Soc. Nat. Exhbn., Wichita, 1989, Conn. Pastel Soc., 1993, Acad. Artists Assn., Mass., 1994. Artist: pastel paintings, Bergen, N.J. Mus. (Best in Show 1983), Pastel Soc. of Am. (Exceptional Merit 1983, 1986), Audubon Artists (Isenberg Award 1989); paintings in many collections including Yad Vashem Mus., Mktg. Corp. of Am., Conn. Bank & Trust Co., Xerox, Pepsico. Recipient more than 100 awards including award of Excellence Middlesex Mus., North Brunswick, N.J., 1985, Spaulding award Hudson Valley Art Assn., White Plains, N.Y., 1986, 88, 90. Fellow Am. Artists Profl. League (1st pastel award 1987, The Claude Parson Meml. award 1998); mem. Pastel Soc. Am. (bd. dirs. 1983-85, Master Pastelist 1985, 5 awards, 1987, 92), Hudson Valley Art Assn. (bd. dirs. 1984-89, Salmagundi Club award 1999), Knickerbocker Artists N.Y. (pres. 1985-90, award 1983-84, Gold medal for disting. achievemnet 1991), Allied Artists Am. (bd. dirs. N.Y. 1989—, Pastel Soc. Am. awards 1987, 92, Mary Lou Fitzgerald Meml. award 1990, Doris Mina Mora Meml. award 1995, Silver Medal of Honor award 1996, Janet Lippman award 1998, Hahnemuhle Pastel Paper award 1999), Audubon Artists (Savoir-Faire Fa briano Paper award 1997), Nat. Arts Club, Salmagundi Club (Ogden Pleisner award 1991). Home: Washington Depot, Conn. Died July 15, 2004.

MARIEN, ROBERT, producer, director, naturalist, photographer, designer; b. San Juan, P.R., Oct. 3, 1952; came to U.S., 1980; s. Jorge Marién and Conchita Hernáiz. BS, U. Sacred Heart, Santurce, P.R., 1976; MS, U. P.R., 1978; MFA, Calif. Inst. Arts, 1982. Producer Dept. Natural Resources, San Juan, 1976-77; film editor Guastella Film Producers, Inc., San Juan, 1977-78; dir. photography Publi Co-Op, San Juan, 1978-79; photographer Expo-Foto 80, San Juan, 1980; prodn. photographer M3 Effects, Inc., North Hollywood, Calif., 1982-83; film research Dennis Film Services, Inc., Hollywood, Calif., 1983-84; cinema coordinator XXIII Olympic Games, Los Angeles, 1984; host spl. shows Universal Studios Tour, Inc., Universal City, Calif., 1984-86; prodn. asst. Columbia Picture Industries, Inc., Burbank, Calif., 1984-86; cameraman Jerry Kramer Prodns., Inc., Hollywood, Calif., 1986; prof. basics of filmmaking Art Ctr. Coll. Design, Pasadena, Calif., 1986-87; producer promotions, copywriter Sta. KVEA-TV, Glendale, Calif., 1986-88; contractor, producer Spanish TV/radio spots The Disney Co., from 1989. Owner, photographer Stock Photo Agy., Rom-Ma Stock Images, Pasadena, Calif., 1989—; prof. cinema and scis., documentary prodr. Columbia Coll., Hollywood, 1989-95; owner Paraiso Gardens, 2001—; designer, builder Water Gardens, 2001—. Producer, dir., editor: (documentaries) Marine Environments, 1977, The Forests of Puerto Rico, 1978 (Environmental award 1979), (visual essay) Sojourn Earth, 1982 (Gold medal 1982, Filmex 1983, Golden Halo 1984, Gold Lone Star award Houston Internat. Film & Video Festival, 1988); producer, cameraman The VIII PanAmerican Games in Puerto Rico, 1979; producer, cameraman Through the World of Nutrition, 1979; dir. photography, cameraman Chef's Delight, 1983; dir. photography The Puerto Rican Cuatro, 1978, Celebrity On Course, 1985; camera asst. The Computer Question, 1983. Home: Pasadena, Calif. Died June 24, 2005.

MARINO, CHARLES JOSEPH, freelance/self-employed arbitrator; b. Gillespie, Ill., May 30, 1926; s. Joseph and Lucille (Valerio) M.; m. Laura Donadon, Apr. 15, 1950; 1 child, Charles Joseph Jr. BS in Commerce, St. Louis; BA in Mgmt., Webster U., MA, 1978. Indsl. rels. Kroger Co., St. Louis, 1946-47; dir. pers. St. Louis U., 1949-67; dir. manpower mgmt. Blue Cross Hosp. Svcs. Inc., St. Louis, 1967-75; exec. asst. to the dir. health and hosps. City of St. Louis, 1975-77; cons. to exec. dir. Urban League St. Louis, 1977-79; auditor dept. revenue State of Mo., 1979-85; pvt. practice, from 1979; arbitrator ABA, St. Louis, 1994. Panel mem. Fed. Mediation and Conciliation, 1979—; panel arbitrator dist. 12 United Mine Workers of Am. and Consol. Coal Cos., 1994—. Chmn. compliance divsn. St. Louis Coun. on Human Rels., 1968-76; mem. adv. bd. Minority Econ. Devel. Assn., 1970-77; bd. dirs. Opportunities Industrializatio O.I.C., 1972-75; bd. dirs. Consumer Credit Counseling Svc., 1977-78; mem. labor and indsl. rels. com. State of Mo., 1972-75; mem. adv. com. Bd. Edn. Work-Study PRogram, 1972-75; bd. dirs., exec. com. nominating com., fin. and endowment com., chmn. pers. policy com. Urban League of St. Louis, 1968-77. With U.S. Navy, 1944-46. Mem. Internat. Rels. Rsch. Assn., Am. Arbitration Assn., Internat. Pers. Mgmt. Assn., Nat. Assn. Accts., Indsl. Rels. Rsch. Assn., Am. Soc. for Pers. Adminstrn., Am. Mgmt. Assn., Am. Arbitration Assn., St. Louis Pers. and Guidance Assn., Am. Inst. of Mgmt., Met. St. Louis Bar Assn. (arbitrator devel. 1981). Roman Catholic. Avocations: chess, golf. Home: Saint Louis, Mo. Died July 17, 2004.

MARK, PHYLLIS BLAUFARB, sculptor; b. N.Y.C., Jan. 20, 1921; d. Jacob and Bessye (Klein) Blaufarb; m. Alan Mark; children: Pamela Mark-Whitley, Ira Stuart. Student, Ohio State U., NYU; studied with Seymour Lipton, New Sch., N.Y.C. Co-pres. SOHO 20 Gallery, N.Y.C., 1993-94, also bd. dirs. Bd. dirs. Artists Representing Environ. Art, N.Y.C., Sculptors Guild, N.Y.C. One-woman shows include Carl Schurz Park, N.Y.C., 1973, Images Gallery, Toledo, 1974, DuBose Gallery, Houston, 1974, Gallery 99, Fla., 1975, Guild Hall, East Hampton, N.Y., 1977, John Edwards Hughes, Inc., Dallas, 1978, Art Fiero, Bologna, Italy, 1978, Elaine Benson Gallery, Bridgehampton, N.Y., 1980, 91, 93, Fontana Gallery, Bala Cynwyd, Pa., 1981, Friedberg Gallery, Long Boat, Fla., 1981, Sculpture Ctr., N.Y.C., 1983, Houston-Bowery Outdoor Exhbn. Space, 1987, Soho 20 Gallery, 1987, 89, 92, Bi-Coastal Sculpture Exhibit, San Francisco, 1989, Shidoni Outdoor Gallery, Tesque, N.Mex., 1989, Manhattan C.C., 1992, Cast Iron Gallery, 1992, Landmark at Tarrytown, N.Y., 1996; exhibited in group shows including the Morris Mus., Morristown, N.J., 1972, Hudson River Mus., Westchester, N.Y., 1972, N.Y.C. Cultural Ctr., 1973, Bklyn. Mus. Art, 1975, 77, Guggenheim Mus., N.Y.C., 1976, Huntsville (Ala.) Mus., 1978, L.A. Mus., 1978, Albright-Knox Mus., Buffalo, 1980, Barbara Gilman Gallery Miami, Fla., 1980, Theo Portnoy Gallery, N.Y.C., 1980, Payson Weisberg Gallery, N.Y.C., 1982, Mus. Graphic Arts, Bilbao, Spain, 1982, Muscarelle Mus., Williamsburg, Va., 1982, 84, Desert Botanical Garden, Phoenix, Ariz., 1983, Phila. Art Alliance, 1987, Kulturforum, Monchengaldbach, Germany, 1989, South Vt. Art Ctr., 1991, Fed. Reserve Bank, Phila., 1992, Guild Hall, East Hampton, N.Y., 1983 (hon. mention 1983), 92, 93; represented in permanent collections including Corcoran Gallery of Art, Washington, Fort Wayne (Ind.) Mus. Art, Syracuse U. Permanent Collection, Allentown (Pa.) Mus. Art, Lowe Mus., Fla., Cornell Univ., Ithaca, N.Y., Merryman Collection, Stanford U., Calif., Am. Collection, Galveston, Tex., RCA Collection, Fla., and N.Y.C., Tupperware Collection, Fla., Southampton (N.Y.) Hosp., Dancer, Fitzgerald & Sample Agy., N.Y.C., Orlando (Fla.) Conv. Ctr. and Civic Ctr., AT&T, Gulf and Western Inc., CIGNA Corp., Phila., Golden Nugget Hotel, N.J., Royal Palace Collection, Brunei Sultanate, Borneo, Fujiya Co. Ltd., Japan. Recipient sculpture installation Assn. Better N.Y., 1973, N.Y.C. Dept. Cultural Affairs, 1973, Montgomery Coll., Rockville, Md., 1984; grantee Nat. Endowment of Arts/Ind. Arts Coun., 1979. Mem. Sculptors Guild (v.p. pubs., editor 1986—, exec. v.p. 1993-94). Home: New York, NY. Died May 23, 2004.

MARKEY, HOWARD THOMAS, former dean, retired federal judge; b. Chgo., Nov. 10, 1920; s. Thomas Joseph and Vera Marie (Dryden) M.; m. Elizabeth Catherine Pelletier, Mar. 17, 1942; children: Jeffrey, Christopher, Thomas (dec.), Jennifer Catherine. JD cum laude, Loyola U., Chgo., 1949; M. Patent Law, John Marshall Law Sch., 1950; LL.D. (hon.), N.Y. Law Sch., 1977, Western State U., 1982, Dickinson Sch. Law, 1982; DSc (hon.), Worcester Poly. Inst., 1982; LL.D. (hon.), Loyola U., Chgo., 1983. Bar: Ill. 1950. Practiced law, Chgo., 1950-72; ptnr. Parker & Carter, 1949—50, Parker, Markey & Plyer, 1905—72; chief judge U.S. Ct. Customs and Patent Appeals, 1972-82, U.S. Ct. Appeals (Fed. Cir.), Washington, 1982-91; dean John Marshall Law Sch., Chgo., 1991—94. Lectr. on jets, rockets, missiles and space, 1946-50, on U.S. Constn.; instr. patent law Loyola U., 1970-71. Bd. advisers Loyola U. Sch. Law. Served to lt. col. USAAF, 1941-46; to lt. col. USAF, 1950-52; pioneer jet test pilot 1944-46; maj. gen. Res. Decorated Legion of Merit, D.F.C., Soldier's medal, Air medal, Bronze Star (U.S.); Mil. Merit Ulchi medal (Korea); Recipient George Washington Honor medal Freedoms Found., 1964. Fellow Am. Bar Found.; mem. ABA, Fed. Bar Assn., Am. Judicature Soc., Am. Legion (post comdr.), Air Force Assn. (pres. 1960-61, chmn. 1961-62). Republican. Roman Catholic. Died May 3, 2006.

MARKEY, ROBERT GUY, lawyer; b. Cleve., Feb. 25, 1939; s. Nate and Rhoda (Gross) Markey; m. Nanci Louise Brooks, Aug. 25, 1990; children: Robert Guy, Randolph. AB, Brown U., 1961; JD, Case Western Res., 1964. Bar: Ohio 1964. Ptnr. Baker & Hostetler, Cleve., from 1983. Died Jan. 21, 2006.

MARKHAM, WILLIAM, county official; b. Pitts., Feb. 11, 1940; s. Charles Robert and Madolyn Jeanette (Pickett) M.; m. Sharon Rhodes, Nov. 22, 1972; children: James Rhodes, Robert William. BA, Ctr. Coll. of Ky., Danville, 1962; D in Commerce (hon.), Ft. Lauderdale (Fla.) Coll., 1982. Cert. Fla. Appraiser, Am. Sr. Appraiser. Mem. mktg. staff Am. Oil Co., Atlanta, 1963-67; property appraiser (elected) Broward County, Ft. Lauderdale, Fla., from 1968. Sgt. USMC Res. Recipient Good Govt. award Jaycees, Disting. Svc. award; recipient Damon award Knights of Pythias, Am. Sportsman award Nat. Football Hall of Fame, Great Am. Traditions award B'nai B'rith, 7 nat. awards for outstanding work in assessment profession; named Man of Yr. City of Hope Margate chpt. 1148. Mem. Internat. Assn. Assessing Officers (bd. dirs. 1974—, exec. bd. 1982-84), Tax Assessors' Assn. Fla. (pres. 1972-73). Home: Sea Ranch Lks, Fla. Died Mar. 8, 2004.

MARKIEWICZ, JAMES EDWARD, manufacturing executive; b. Chgo., Sept. 14, 1932; s. Edward James and Eugenia Elizabeth (Formanski) M; m. Mary Lou Henneberg, June 7, 1952; 1 child, Sharon Markiewicz Schnider. Student, U. Ill., Chgo., 1950-51, Northrop Areo. Inst., 1951-52, DeVry Inst. Tech., 1952-54. Various positions Precision Extrusions Inc., Bensenville, Ill., 1950-70, v.p. mfg., from 1970. Patent quenching apparatus for extruded articles; contbr. articles to profl. jours. Served with USNR. Mem.: Medinah (Ill.) Country (bd. dirs. 1985-87). Roman Catholic. Home: Roselle, Ill. Died Feb. 12, 2005.

MARKLE, SHARON LEA, psychotherapist, school counselor; b. Parkersburg, W.Va., Aug. 20, 1945; d. Everett Dewayne and Opal Ruth (Smith) Gates; m. Michael Bruce Markle, June 5, 1964 (div. 1990), remarried Mar. 1, 1991; children: John Matthew, Joseph Bruce. AA, W.Va. U., 1979; BA in Edn., Glenville State Coll., 1981; MA in Counseling, Marshall U., 1990. Lic. profl. counselor; nat. cert. counselor. Instr. Wood County Bd. Edn., Parkersburg, W.Va., 1981-89; faculty mem. W.Va. U., Parkersburg, 1990; instr. Wood County Bd. Edn., Parkersburg, 1990-91; psychotherapist Counseling Assocs., Washington, WV, from 1991; sch. counselor Ritchie County Bd. Edn., W.Va., from 1991. Vol. cons. West Dist. Guidance Ctr., Parkersburg, 1989—. Author: His Mysterious Ways, 1990; contbr. articles to profl. jours. Mem. Ritchie County chpt. Am. Cancer Soc. Mem. NEA, ACA, NAFE, W.Va. Counseling Assn., Am. Sch. Counselor's Assn., W.Va. Sch. Counselor's Assn., Profl. Women's Assn., W.Va. Edn. Assn., Chi Sigma Iota, Ritchie County Bd. Edn. Assn., Phi Theta Kappa, Delta Kappa Gamma. Republican. Methodist. Died Jan. 18, 2005.

MARKOS, WILLIAM G., investment advisor; b. Ipswich, Mass., Sept. 2, 1934; s. George J. and Mary (Nickolakakis) M.; m. Prudence Torrumeo, Dec. 1, 1968. BA, Harvard U., 1956, MBA, 1960. Registered investment advisor. Sales v.p. Smith Barney & Co., Boston, 1960-86; pres. Ipswich Investment Mgmt. Co., Boston, from 1986. Bd. dirs. Muro Pharm., Tewksbury, Mass.; former chmn. Ipswich Fin. Com. Trustee Hellenic Coll., Brookline, Mass., Ipswich Hist. Soc.; pres. Logganino Benefit Soc., Ipswich. With Res., 1957-58. Mem. Am. Hellenic Progressive Assn., Am. Hellenic Bus. Inst., Harvard Club Boston, John T. Heard Lodge, Alpha Omega Coun., Inc. (bd. dirs., pres.). Republican. Greek Orthodox. Avocations: tennis, boating, gardening. Home: Ipswich, Mass. Died June 17, 2005.

MARKS, ADIE, advertising executive; b. Waco, Tex., Dec. 29, 1914; s. Eli and Sadye (Friedlander) M.; m. Jeanette Ginsburg, Oct. 26, 1937 (div. 1954); children: Marian, Ronald; m. Jo Alessandro, Nov. 24, 1955; children: Dena, Paul, Dale. BA in Journalism, U. Tex., 1936. Pres. Gulf State Advt. Agy., Houston, 1940-76, vice chmn. bd., 1986-95; founder Adie Marks Advt., 1995—2005. With USN, 1943-46. Democrat. Jewish. Avocation: horse racing. Home: Houston, Tex. Died Aug. 31, 2006.

MARKS, LEONARD HAROLD, lawyer; b. Pitts., Mar. 5, 1916; s. Samuel and Ida (Levine) M.; m. Dorothy Ames (dec. 2001), June 3, 1948; children: Stephen Ames, Robert Evan. BA, U. Pitts., 1935, LL.B., 1938. Bar: Pa. 1938, D.C. 1946. Asst. prof. law U. Pitts. Law Sch., 1938-42; prof. law Nat. U., 1943-55; asst. to gen. counsel FCC, 1942-46, ops. counsel, 1986—2006; ptnr. Cohn & Marks, Washington, 1946-65, 69-86. Chmn. exec. com. Nat. Savs. and Trust Co., 1977-85; chmn. Internat. Conf. on Comm. Satellites, 1968-69; Am. del. Internat. Broadcasting Confs., 1948-69; pres. Internat. Rescue Com., 1973-79, Honor Am. Com., 1977-86; chmn. U.S. Adv. Commn. on Internat. Ednl. and Cultural Affairs, 1973-78; chmn. Fgn. Policy Assn., 1981-87, exec. com., 1987-96; head U.S. del. Internat. Telecom. Union, 1983, 87; chmn. U.S. del. to London Info. Forum, Commn. on Security and Cooperation in Europe, 1989. Mem. ABA (ho. of dels. 1962-64), Fed. Comm. Bar Assn. (pres. 1959-60), Bar Assn. D.C., Acad. Diplmacy (chmn. exec. com. 2000—), World Affairs Council Washington (chmn.), Cosmos Club, Metropolitan Club (v.p., gov.), Federal City Club, Broadcasters Club (pres. 1957-59), Alfalfa Club (Washington), Order of Coif, Phi Beta Kappa, Omicron Delta Kappa, Sigma Delta Chi. Clubs: Cosmos, Metropolitan, Federal City, Broadcasters, (pres. 1957-59), Alfalfa (Washington). Home: Washington, DC. Died Aug. 11, 2006.

MARLER, ROBERT FRANKLIN, JR., English language educator; b. Winston-Salem, N.C., Apr. 18, 1932; s. Robert F. and Eliza (M.) M.; m. Janet Marie Brown, June 22, 1986; 1 child, Mary Elizabeth. BSCE, Princeton U., 1954; MA in English & Am. Lit., George Washington U., 1961, PhD in Am. Lit., 1970. Mech. engr. Shell Oil Co., 1954-55, 57-58, H.D. Nottingham & Assocs., Arlington, Va., 1959-62; instr. George Washington U., 1963-66, Temple U., Phila., 1966-70, asst. prof., 1970-74, assoc. prof., 1974-80, prof., 1980-94, prof. emeritus, 1994—2006, chmn. dept. English, 1974-75. Founder, dir. Am. studies program Temple U., 1972-75, dir. internat. studies program, chmn. coun. internat. studies Inst. for Langs. and Internat. Studies, Coll. Arts and Scis.,

1988-90, founder, dir. coun. program devel. and funding, 1980-83, founder Am. studies program in Japan, 1983-84, acting assoc. provost for continuing edn., 1975-76; founder, pres. The Phila. Area Cultural Consortium, 1974-80; cons. and lectr. in field. Co-author, Fishing the Delaware Valley, 1997; Contbr. articles to profl. jours. With U.S. Army, 1955-57. Grantee NEH, 1972, 77, Nat. Am. Studies Faculty, 1973-76, Phila. Area Cultural Consortium, 1976, Pa. Pub. Com. for Humanities, 1976-80. Mem. MLA, N.E. MLA, Am. Studies Assn., Walt Whitman Assn. (bd. dirs. 1990-94), Franklin Inn. Home: Benton, Pa. Died Sept. 1, 2006.

MARLIN, ARTHUR DAVID, executive; b. Cambridge, Mass., Sept. 29, 1934; s. Myer and Blanche (Tobin) M.; m. Lois Ann Bernstein, Sept. 11, 1960; children: Myra Jane, Susan Harriet, Robert Paul. BSBA, Northeastern U., 1960. Jr. acct. Cabot Corp., Boston, 1956-60, sr. acct., 1960-62, from credit asst. to corp. credit mgr., 1962-88; exec. v.p. NACM-New Eng., Inc., Arlington, Mass., from 1988. Chmn. chem. div. Nat. Chem. Credit Assn., N.Y.C., 1974-75, chmn. internat. div., 1975-76, chmn. exec. bd., 1976-78; chmn. Rubber Industries Credit Assn., N.Y.C., 1972-74, 84-86, Raw Material Credit Assn., N.Y.C., 1987-88; treas. NACM-New England Inc., 1976-78, v.p., 1978-79, pres. 1979-81. Pres. Beth El Temple Ctr., Belmont, Mass., 1975-77. Home: Mashpee, Mass. Died June 12, 2005.

MAROTTE, NANCY CLARKE, journalist, educator; b. Arkadelphia, Ark., Sept. 18, 1942; d. Russell Byron and Martha (Clarke) Woodell; m. Leonard Ernest Marotte, June 20, 1965; children: Melanie, Jeffrey. BA in English, So. Meth. U., 1966; MA in Teaching English, CCNY, 1971. Cert. tchr., Kans. Substitute tchr. Wichita (Kans.) Pub. Schs., from 1978; reporter Metro Pub. Co., Wichita, from 1987. Instr. composition B.C. Community Coll., 1989—. Originator Hobby Harvest, Wichita, 1975; co-chmn. founding com. East Heights United Meth. Presch., Wichita, 1977; tutor ESL, Cath. Charities, Wichiita, 1983-84. Mem. Kans. Press Women, Celebration Singers, Sigma Delta Chi. Democrat. Methodist. Avocation: photography. Home: Wichita, Kans. Died Dec. 24, 2004.

MARR, HENRY L. (HANK MARR), music educator, pianist, organist, composer; b. Columbus, Ohio, Jan. 30, 1927; s. John and Flora Ethel (Hogg) M.; m. Beatrice Jackson, Mar. 19, 1954 (div. Apr. 1972); children: Henry L. Jr., Herman L., Herbert L., Harold L. MusB, Ohio State U., 1954. Musician, sideman Charlie Brantley's Honeydippers, Tampa, Fla., 1948-50; sideman Sammy Hopkins Trio, Columbus, 1951-52, Rusty Bryant with Nancy Wilson, Columbus, 1952-56; leader Hank Marr Trio and Quintet on tour, U.S., Can., Europe, 1958-68; condr., pianist, arranger George Kirby, Las Vegas, Nev., 1968-77; tchr. music Ft. Hayes Career Ctr., Columbus, 1977-79; instr. music, performer Capital U., Columbus, 1981-88, Denison U., Granville, Ohio, 1981-88, Ohio State U., Columbus, 1981-88, asst. prof., 1988-93, assoc. prof., from 1993. With U.S. Army, 1945-48. Recipient award of excellence Sta. KBLE-TV Ohio Inc., 1978. Mem. Nat. Assn. Jazz Educators (cert. of appreciation 1984), Columbus Fedn. Musicians (bd. dirs. 1983—), Jazz Arts Group Columbus (arranger 1982—), Black Jazz Music Caucus. Avocations: collecting hammond organs, softball, ping pong/table tennis, television. Home: Columbus, Ohio. Died Mar. 16, 2004.

MARRINER, CHERYL MARIE, producer, director; b. Chgo., Sept. 20, 1962; d. Russell Allen Marriner and Elaine Marie (Brennecke) Jensen. BA, Columbia Coll., 1985. Producer, dir. promotions Sta. KGET-TV, Bakersfield, Calif., from 1986. Producer, dir. various commls. and pub. service announcements. Mem. Bakersfield Advt. Club (1st, 2d, 3d place awards). Died Apr. 18, 2005.

MARSHALL, JAMES ANDREW, civil engineer, real estate developer; b. Chgo., May 27, 1932; s. William Emmet and Margaret (Fitzgerald) Marshall. BSCE, Ill. Inst. Tech., 1955, MS in City and Regional Planning, 1960. Registered profl. engr., Ill. Civil engr. Hoyer-Schlesinger-Turner, Chgo., 1973-76, Harza Engrs., Chgo., 1990-91. Mem. Ill. and Mich. Canal Nat. Hist. Corridor, Lockport, Ill., from 1993. Exhibitions include Am. Indian architecture, Ill. Inst. Tech., Chgo., 1982, Hero, Hawk and Open Hand, Art Inst. Chgo., 2004—05; author: booklets. With U.S. Army, 1955—57. Mem.: Owasippe Staff Assn. Boy Scouts Am., Chgo. Area Orienteering Club, Chgo. Lit. Club. Democrat. Achievements include discovery of mathematical knowledge of prehistoric Native Americans. Avocation: surveying and mapping Indian mounds and earthworks. Died Apr. 1, 2006.

MARSHALL, JOHN DAVID, retired librarian, author; b. McKenzie, Tenn., Sept. 7, 1928; s. Max Cole and Emma (Walpole) M. BA, Bethel Coll., McKenzie, 1950; MA in Libr. Sci., Fla. State U., 1951, postgrad., 1951-52, Oxford (Eng.) U., summer 1989. Grad. asst. Sch. Libr. Sci. Fla. State U., 1951-52; ref. libr. Clemson (S.C.) U. Libr., 1952-55; head ref. dept. Auburn (Ala.) U. Libr., 1955-57; head acquisitions divsn. U. Ga. Libr., Athens, 1957-67; libr., assoc. prof. Mid. Tenn. State U., Murfreesboro, 1967-76, univ. bibliographer, assoc. prof., 1976-80, prof., 1980-93, prof. emeritus, from 1994; Mary Ball Holmes lectr. Bethel Coll., 1999. Book rev. staff Libr. Jour., 1953-64. Contbg. editor So. Observer, 1953-66; gen. editor Contributions to Library Literature series, 1963-78; book rev. editor Jour. Libr. History, 1966-76, Southeastern Librarian, 1979-82; author: Books in Your Life, 1959, Louis Shores: A Bibliography, 1964, A Fable of Tomorrow's Library, 1965, Louis Shores, Author-Librarian: A Bibliography, 1979, One Librarian's Credo, 1986, Lizzie Borden and the Library Connection, 1990, Churchill's Fulton Speech, 1994, Books are STILL Basic, 1994, And Now Buzz Off: Wit and Wisdom of Sir Winston S. Churchill, 2000; co-editor: Books-Libraries-Librarians, 1955; editor: Of, By, and For Librarians (1st series), 1960, An American Library History Reader, 1961, In Pursuit of Library History, 1961, Mark Hopkins' Log and Other Essays by Louis Shores, 1965, Approaches to Library History, 1966, The Library in the University, 1967, Of, By, and For Librarians: Second Series, 1974, Southern Books Competition at Twenty-Five: A Silver Anniversary Tribute, 1980, Books are Basic: The Essential Lawrence Clark Powell, 1985. Bd. govs. Friends of Linebaugh Pub. Libr., Murfreesboro, Tenn., 1994-2002, pres., 1984, treas., 1996; mem. Murfreesboro City Libr. Bd., 1985-93, treas., 1990-93; mem. Highland Rim Reg. Libr. Bd., 1989-95, treas., 1993-95, Rutherford County Libr. Br., 1989-95; bd. govs. Winston Churchill Meml. Libr., 1989—. Recipient Disting. Alumni award Sch. Libr. and Info. Sci., Fla. State U., 1989, Alumni Achievement award Bethel Coll., 1989, Disting. Alumni Svc. award, 1992; Churchill fellow Westminster Coll., 1982 Mem. ALA (membership com. 1953-55, libr. history round table 1956—, sec. 1969-72), Assn. Coll. and Rsch. Librs. (pubs. com. 1957-62), Southeastern Libr. Assn. (hon. life, chmn. awards com. 1986-88, Outstanding Author Award com. 1990-92, 96-2002, Mary Utopia Rothrock award 1994), Tenn. Libr. Assn. (chmn. intellectual freedom com. 1968-70, 84-85, mem. Tenn. History Book Award com. 1985-2003, chmn. 1985-86, Frances Neel Cheney award 1984, Honor award 1992), Internat. Churchill Soc., Phi Kappa Phi, Beta Phi Mu. Avocations: reading, writing/editing, collecting Churchilliana. Home: Murfreesboro, Tenn. Died June 6, 2005.

MARSHALL, NANCY JEAN, women's health nurse; b. Randall, W.Va., Feb. 23, 1935; d. William Samuel and Elizabeth Lee (Mance) Gardner; m. Charles Henry Marshall, July 2, 1955; children: Charles Keith, Barbara Kim, Thomas Kevin. Diploma, Upshur County Sch. Nursing, 1985. Staff nurse Stonewall Jackson Meml. Hosp., Weston, W.Va., from 1985. Adv. bd. mem. Fred Eberle Sch. Practical Nursing, Buckhannon, W.Va., 1988—. Mem. Nat. Assn. Practical Nursing Edn. and Svcs., LPN W.Va. (newsletter chairperson 1985—), Dist. #19 LPN (sec. 1986—), Concerned Nurses W.Va. (bd. dirs. 1988—), Nat. League Nursing, Fedn. and Nursing Edn. Licensure. Republican. Avocations: reading, camping, continuing education. Home: Weston, W.Va. Died Feb. 7, 2004.

MARSHALL, PAUL, JR., music educator, composer; b. Cin., Nov. 26, 1927; s. Paul and Addie Mae (Brannon) M.; m. Sylvia Reed, Mar. 15, 1957; children: Elliott, Orrin, David, Jonathan. MusB, Ohio State U., 1954, MA in Music, 1955, BS in Music Edn., 1960. Cert. music tchr., N.Y., Ohio, N.J. Asst. prof. Claflin Coll., Orangeburg, S.C., 1958-59; music instr. pub. schs., Springfield, Ohio, 1961-65, Ringwood, N.J., 1965-68; prof. music Bergen Community Coll., Paramus, N.J., from 1968, chmn. dept. fine arts, 1972-81. Composer, arranger Glenn Miller Orch., N.Y.C., 1964-74; arranger, keyboard Muse Records, N.Y.C., 1977—; pianist Phoenix Records, N.Y.C., 1978—. Composer: (opera) The Mink Stockings, 1961, (symphony) The Free Spirit, 1963, (song cycle) Soprano and Piano, 1980, (electronic music) Annihilation II, 1992. Bd. trustees John Harms Theater, Englewood, N.J., 1987; dir. High Sch. Equivalency Program, Paramus, N.J., 1969-72. Sgt. U.S. Army, 1947-49. Mem. NAACP, NEA, Am. Fedn. Musicians, Music Educators Nat. Conv., N.J. Edn. Assn. Avocations: chess, computer/electronic music. Home: Englewood, NJ. Died Oct. 18, 2004.

MARSHALL, VALOYCE JEANNE PEARCE, nursing administrator, rehabilitation nurse; b. Rogers, Ark., Jan. 8, 1942; d. Walter Madden and Verba Jo (Dean) Pearce; m. James E. Marshall; children: Charlotte, James, Matthew. Diploma, Sparks Sch. Nursing, Ft. Smith, Ark., 1964; student, Ft. Smith Jr. Coll., 1961-62, Cottey Coll., 1960-61. Cert. nursing adminstrn., cert. rehab. RN. Admistrv. supr. Ctr. for Disability & Rehab., Comanche County Meml. Hosp., Lawton, Okla., unit supr., adminstrv. supr., nursing dir. Mem. Assn. Rehab. Nurses, Okla. Assn. Rehab. Nurses (pres. 1990). Home: Lawton, Okla. Died Jan. 11, 2004.

MARSI, KENNETH LARUE, chemist, educator; b. Los Banos, Calif., Dec. 13, 1928; s. Sam and Wilma Evelyn (Soper) M.; m. Gertrude Irene Gutschenritter, Mar. 5, 1955; children: Marianne, Kenneth Scott, Brian Geoffrey, Teresa Jeanne. AB, San Jose State U., 1951; PhD, U. Kans., 1955. Sr. research chemist The Sherwin-Williams Co., Chgo., 1955-57; from asst. prof. to assoc. prof. chemistry Kans. State U., Ft. Hays, 1957-61; from asst. prof. to prof. Calif. State U., Long Beach, 1961-96, part time faculty, 1996—2002. Cons. chemist Douglas Aircraft, Santa Monica, Calif., 1964-67; cons. S-cubed, San Diego, 1983-2005. Author: Problems in Organic Chemistry, 1968; reviewer Prentice-Hall, Inc., Englewood Cliffs, N.J., 1961-2005; abstractor Chem. Abstracts, Columbus, Ohio, 1958-67; contbr. articles to profl. jours. Named Outstanding Prof. Calif. State U.,Long Beach, 1984, Trustees Outstanding Prof. Calif. State U. System, 1985. Mem. Am. Chem. Soc., Organic Sect. Am. Chem. Soc., Phi Beta Kappa, Sigma Xi (treas. Kans. chpt. 1954-55), Phi Lambda Upsilon (pres. 1954). Democrat. Episcopalian. Avocations: gardening, reading, biking, backpacking, genealogy. Home: Monarch Beach, Calif. Died Aug. 20, 2005.

MARTIN, ALBERT CAREY, architect; b. Los Angeles, Aug. 3, 1913; s. Albert Carey and Carolyn Elizabeth (Borchard) M.; m. Dorothy Virginia Dolde, Nov. 15, 1937; children— Albert Carey III, David Charles, Mary Martin Marquardt, Claire, Charles Dolde. B.Arch. cum laude, U. So. Calif., 1936. Registered architect, Calif. Architect Albert C. Martin and Assocs., L.A., 1937-42, ptnr., 1942-97; ptnr. emeritus AC Martin Ptnrs., L.A., 1997—2006. Dir. Rancho Los Alamitos Found. Prin. works include Los Angeles Dept. Water and Power, ARCO Twin Towers, St. Basil's Ch., Union Bank Sq. Trustee Los Angeles Orthopaedic Hosp.; bd. dirs. Long Beach Mus. Art Found. Recipient Annual Spirit of Los Angeles award Los Angeles Hdqrs. City Assn., 1980, Brotherhood award NCCJ, 1980, Asa V. Call Achievement award U. So. Calif. Alumni Assn., 1984, Boy Scouts Am. Good Scout award L.A. Area Coun., 1989; named Constrn. Man of Yr. Los Angeles C. of C., 1971. Fellow AIA (past dir., pres. So. Calif. chpt., past v.p. Calif. Coun.); mem. U. So. Calif. Archtl. Guild (advisor, disting. alumnus 1990), L.A. C. of C. (past pres.), Calif. C. of C. (past dir.), Lambda Alpha, Automobile Club of So. Calif. Clubs: California, Jonathan (Los Angeles). Republican. Roman Catholic. Avocation: sailing. Home: Arroyo Grande, Calif. Died Mar. 30, 2006.

MARTIN, DAVID J., lawyer; b. Buffalo, 1937; m. Mimi McLaughlin; children: John, David, Cammy, Mary Faith, Julia, Kathleen. BA, Canisius Coll., 1959; LLB, Cath. U. of Am., 1962. Bar: N.Y. 1962, Pa. 1971. Assoc. Dewey, Ballantine, Bushby, Palmer & Wood, N.Y.C., 1966-68, Bond, Schoeneck & King, Syracuse, N.Y., 1968-70; counsel CoreStates Fin. Corp., Phila., 1970-91, exec. v.p., chief counsel, 1991-95; of counsel Bryn Mawr Capital Mgmt. Inc., 1995—2006. Died Sept. 6, 2006.

MARTIN, DORIS ELLEN, publisher, management consultant; b. Chgo., Oct. 26, 1927; d. John L. and Marie (Miller) Martin; m. Morton Rosenberg, Dec. 15, 1963 (div. 1964). BS, NYU, 1952; MS, Boston U., 1958; EdD, Columbia U., 1964. Instr. Colby Coll., Waterville, Maine, 1952-54; dir. edn. dept. YWCA, Honolulu, 1954-59; dir. The Conf. Ctr., U. Hawaii, Honolulu, 1960-65; dir. spl. projects and assoc. prof. NYU, N.Y.C., 1965-66; dir. of spl. project state plan Dept. Planning/Econ. Devel., State of Hawaii, Honolulu, 1966-69; spl. asst. George Washington U., Washington, 1970; mgmt. cons. Dr. D. Martin Assocs., Wailuku, Hawaii, from 1980. Editor, pub. Martin Mgmt. Books, Wailuku, Hawaii, 1985—; author 13 books. Mem. Rep. Nat. Com., 1975—. Mem. Pubrs. Mktg. Assn. Died July 14, 2005.

MARTIN, JACK, lawyer; b. Bklyn., Jan. 19, 1929; s. Alfred and Ioa Martin; m. Edith Martin, Dec. 11, 1948 (div. Aug. 1961); children: Steven Lawrence, Glenn David. LLB, Bklyn. Law Sch., 1953. Bar: N.Y. 1954, U.S. Dist. Ct. (ea. and no. dists.) N.Y. 1956. Mem. ATLA, N.Y. State Trial Lawyers Assn. Democrat. Jewish. Died Dec. 1, 2004.

MARTIN, JAMES HENRY, bluegrass musician; b. Sneedville, Tenn., Aug. 10, 1927; s. Lee Ease and Sarah (Burchett) M.; children: James Jr., Ray Willard, Lisa Sarah, Lee Ease. Lead singer, emcee Bill Monroe, 1949-53; leader Jimmy Martin and the Sunny Mountain Boys, from 1953; band leader, entertainer Sta. WJR Barn Dance, Detroit, 1953-57, La. Hayride, Shreveport, 1957-60, World's Original Jamboree, Wheeling, W.Va., 1960-63. Rec. artist: Widow Maker (Citation of Achievement Broadcast Music, Inc. 1964), Sunny Side of the Mountain (Outstanding Song award ASCAP 1965), Will the Circle Be Unbroken (Grammy nomination 1972), I'd Rather Have America. Recipient Gold Guitar award C.M.R. mag., 1963, Cert. Appreciation Music of Bluegrass Assn., Met. Award of Honor City of Nashville, 1964, Disting. Citizin award City of Nashville, 1964, Americana award Sta. WENO, Nashville, 1968, Bluegrass Festival award Mr. Ralph Stanley, 1971; named Bluegrass Entertainer of Yr., Bluegrass Unlimited mag., 1973. Died May 14, 2005.

MARTIN, LYNN GARY, minister; b. Roswell, N.Mex., Dec. 1, 1936; s. Hubert C. and Vera Edith (Jordon) M.; m. Betty Jewell Russell, May 16, 1953; children: Steven Lynn, David Alan. Grad. high sch., Modesto, Calif. Ordained to ministry Pentecostal Ch. of God, 1956. Tchr. high sch. Pentecostal Ch. of God, Ukiah, Calif., 1960-70, pastor Sebastopol, Calif., 1970-71; tchr. religion Piner High Sch., Santa Rosa, Calif., 1971; pastor Pentecostal Ch. of God, Modesto, Calif., 1971-73, Visalia, Calif., 1973-81; tchr. religion Coll. of Sequoias, Visalia, Calif., 1979-80; evangelist Pentecostal Ch. of God, Fresno, Calif., from 1989. Dist. dir. home missions, chmn. bd. Pentecostal Ch. of God, Roseville, Calif., 1962-69. Author: Beware Your Facade Is Showing, 1990. Died June 18, 2004.

MARTIN, MICHAEL J., psychologist, therapist; b. Covington, Ky., Dec. 13, 1946; BS in Psychology, St. John's U., 1982, MS in Clin. Hypnotherapy, 1987. Lab. technician Sheperd Chem. Co., Cin., 1967-69; liaison, analyst H.S. Crocker Co., Cin., 1969-79; supr. Exhibit Group of Cin., 1979-82; therapist, cons., from 1982. Author: Eureka, 1944. Died Apr. 8, 2005.

MARTIN, RICHARD N., retired electronics executive; b. Clifton Springs, N.Y., Aug. 22, 1922; s. Douglas and Evelyn (Hilton) M.; m. Hutson Weber, Dec. 26, 1949 (div. Dec. 1958); children: Jeffrey, Peter, Bradford; m. Barbara E. Hener, Oct. 24, 1963; 1 child, Lisa. Student, Alfred U., 1940-41; BA, Hofstra U., 1948; MS, Syracuse U., 1950.

Chief lab. tech. Westlake Hosp., Melrose Park, Ill., 1950-51; immunologist B.H. Kean M.D., N.Y.C., 1951-53, St. Francis Hosp., Poughkeepsie, N.Y., 1953-57; dir. tech. services Am. Hosp. Supply, Miami, Fla., 1957-68; v.p. internat. Coulter Electronics Inc., Hialeah, Fla., 1968-92. Cons., dir. numerous cos. world-wide. Contbr. numerous articles in field. Mem. parish council St. John's Ch., Harpenden, Eng., 1980-83, local council Harpenden Village, 1980-82. With USN, 1942-45, PTO. Recipient Queen's Award to Industry Govt. U.K., 1970, 71. Mem. AAAS, Am. Inst. Biol. Scis., Am. Assn. Blood Banks, Am. Soc. Microbiology, N.Y. Acad. Scis., Am. Horticulture Soc., Royal Brit. Horticulture Soc. Republican. Episcopalian. Avocations: music, gardening, wine tasting. Home: Daleville, Va. Died Dec. 6, 2004.

MARTIN, STEELE WADE, minister; b. Chgo., Aug. 31, 1926; s. Leon Wade and Eleanor Marie (Pickel) M.; m. Priscilla Fallis Clark, May 28, 1953; 1 child, Candace Clark Martin Mittman. BA, Northwestern U., 1947; MDiv, Gen. Theol. Sem., 1951, MST, 1956. Ordained to ministry Episcopal Ch., 1951. Fellow and tutor Gen. Theol. Sem., N.Y.C., 1951-53; assoc. St. Margaret's Ch., South Bronx, N.Y., 1953-54; rector St. Mary's Ch., East Providence, R.I., 1954-59; teaching missionary Brazil, 1959-62; rector St. Michael's Ch., Brattleboro, Vt., 1962-74, Christ Ch., Quincy, Mass., 1974-88; interim rector St. Stephen's Ch., Providence, R.I., from 1988. Fellow Coll. Preachers, Washington; dir. Gen. Theol. Libr., Boston, 1970—; trustee Mass. Bible Soc., Boston, 1979-85; dir. Enablement, Inc., Boston, 1984—; dep., mem. staff Gen. Conv. of Episcopal Ch., 1969-76. Author: Blue Collar Ministry, 1989. Protestant chaplain Quincy Fire Dept., 1978-88. Mem. Interim Ministry Network, Boston Mins. Club, Providence Art Club. Home: Providence, RI. Died Apr. 14, 2005.

MARTIN, WALTER, retired lawyer; b. Crookston, Minn., Nov. 7, 1912; s. Frederick and Rosalie (Mertz) M.; m. Catherine Mary Severin, May 1, 1942 (dec. May 1979); children: Frederick H., Jacqueline K., Patricia, Priscilla, Walter Jr., John E. BA, Albion Coll., 1937; JD, U. Mich., 1939. Bar: Mich. 1939, U.S. Dist. Ct. (fed. dist.) 1939, U.S. Ct. Appeals (6th cir.) 1947, U.S. Supreme Ct. 1958. Ptnr. Martin & Martin, Saginaw, Mich., 1939-94; ret., 1994. Fellow Mich. Bar Assn., Saginaw County Bar Assn. (pres. 1958). Lutheran. Avocations: hunting, fishing. Home: Saginaw, Mich. Died July 11, 2004.

MARTINEZ, ANDREW TREDWAY, lawyer; b. New Orleans, Oct. 24, 1930; s. Andrew Richmond and Mary Leslie (Tredway) M.; m. Margaret Leslie Buchan, June 7, 1952; children: Andrew, Leslie, Margaret. BA, Tulane U., 1952, LLB, 1956. Bar: La. 1956, U.S. Dist. Ct. (ea. dist.) La. 1956, U.S. Ct. Appeals (5th cir.) 1962, U.S. Supreme Ct. 1971. Ptnr. Terriberry, Carroll and Yancey, New Orleans, 1956-2001. Assoc. editor Am. Maritime Cases, 1989-2001; adv. editor Tulane Maritime Jour., 1976-2001. Lt. (j.g.) USN, 1952-54. Mem. ABA, Maritime Law Assn. U.S., Assn. Average Adjusters U.S., La. Bar Assn., New Orleans Bar Assn. Home: New Orleans, La. Died Apr. 23, 2005.

MARTINO, DONALD JAMES, composer, clarinetist, educator; b. Plainfield, NJ, May 16, 1931; s. James Edward and Alma Ida (Renz) M.; m. Mari Rice, Sept. 5, 1953 (div. June 1968); 1 child, Anna Maria; m. Lora Harvey, June 5, 1969; 1 child, Christopher James. BMus, Syracuse U., 1952; MFA, Princeton U., 1954; MA (hon.), Harvard U., 1983. Instr. music Princeton U., 1957-59; asst. prof. theory music Yale U., 1959-66, assoc. prof., 1966-69; chmn. dept. composition New Eng. Conservatory Music, Boston, 1969-80; Irving Fine prof. music Brandeis U., 1980-82; prof. music Harvard U., from 1983, Walter Bigelow Rosen prof. music, 1989-93; Walter Bigelow Rosen prof. emeritus, 1993—2005. Tchr. composition and theory Yale Summer Sch. of Music and Art, 1960-63; tchr. composition Berkshire Music Ctr., summers, 1965-67, 69; composer in residence Berkshire Music Ctr., 1973, Composers' Conf., Johnson, Vt., summer 1979, May in Miami, 1994, Festival Internat. Musica de Morelia, Mex., 1996, Composers' Conf., Wellesley, Mass., 1997, Ernest Block Music Festival Composers Conf., Newport, Oreg., summer 1998; vis. lectr. Harvard U., 1971; Maurice Abravanel vis. disting. composer U. Utah, 1994, Mary Duke Biddle disting. composer Duke U., 1995; master artist-in-residence Atlantic Ctr. for the Arts, 1997; BMI composer in residence Vanderbilt U., 1998. Composer: Separate Songs, 1951; for high voice and piano, Sonata for Clarinet and Piano, 1951, Piano Quartet, 1951, With Little Children In Mind, 1951, String Quartet No. 2, 1951, The Bad Child's Book of Beasts, 1952, Suite of Variations on Medieval Melodies cello sonata, 1952; String Quartet No. 3, 1953, sonata for Violin and Piano, A Set for Clarinet, 1954, Quodlibets for Flute, 1954, Three Dances for Viola and Piano, 1954, String Trio, 1954, Three Songs, 1955, Portraits; a secular cantata for chorus, soloists and orch., 1955, Sette Canoni Enigmatici, 1956, Contemplations for Orch. (commd. by Paderewski Fund), 1956, 24 Tin Pan Alley Tunes, 1956, Quartet for Clarinet and Strings, 1957, After Lennie, Canon Ball, Cathy, Three Way, Late In The Day (performed by Core Ensemble with Martio clarinet soloist, Boston and on tour 1991-97), Mac Fugal, Lover Come Bach, 1957, Piano Fantasy, 1958, Trio for violin, clarinet and piano, 1959, Cinque Frammenti, 1961, Two Rilke Songs, 1961, Fantasy-Variations for violin, 1962, Concerto for Wind Quintet (commd. by Fromm Found. and Berkshire Music Center), 1964, Parisonatina Al'Dodecafonia; for cello solo, 1964, Concerto for Piano and Orch. (commd. by New Haven Symphony), 1965, B, a, b, b, it, t; for clarinet, 1966, Strata; for bass clarinet, 1966, Mosaic for grand orch. (commd. for Chgo. Symphony by U. Chgo.), 1967, Pianississimo; sonata for piano, 1970, Seven Pious Pieces, 1971, Concerto for Violoncello and Orch., 1972, Augenmusik, 1972, Notturno, 1973 (Naumburg Chamber Music award commn., Pulitzer prize in music 1974), Paradiso Choruses for Chorus, Soloists, Orch. and Tape, 1974 (Paderewski Fund commn., Classical Critics citation Record World mag. 1976), Ritorno for Orch. (Plainfield Symphony Bicentennial commn.), 1975, Triple Concerto for Clarinet, Bass Clarinet and Contrabass Clarinet with Chamber Ensemble (N.Y. State Council on Arts and Andrew W. Mellon Found. commn.), 1977, Impromptu for Roger; piano solo, 1977, Quodlibets II (Am. Music Ctr. commn.); flute solo, 1980, Fantasies and Impromptus, piano solo (Koussevitzky Found. commn.), 1981, Divertisements for Youth Orch. (Groton, Mass. Arts Ctr. Commn.), 1981, Suite in Old Form, piano solo, 1982, String Quartet (Elizabeth Sprague Coolidge Commn., winner 1st prize Kennedy Ctr. Friedheim Awards 1985), 1983, Canzone e Tarantella, clarinet and cello, 1984, The White Island, for chorus and chamber orc. (Boston Symphony Centennial Commn.), 1985, Concerto for Alto Saxophone and Chamber Orch. (Nat. Endowment Consortium commn.), 1987, From the Other Side, Divertimento for Flute, Cello, Percussion and Piano (commd. by Flederman New Music Ensemble for the Australian Bicentennial, 1988), 12 Preludes (commd. Meet the Composer-Readers Digest), 1990, 15, 5, '92 AB for Carinet solo, 1992, Three Sad Songs, 1993, Viola and Piano (Elizabeth Sprague Coolidge commn.), Concerto for Violin and Orchestra (Nat. Endowment Commn.), 1997, Variazioni sopra un soggetto cavato, cl. solo, 1998, Serenata Concertante (Koussevitzky Found. Com.), 1999, Piccolo Studio, Alto Saxaphone solo, 1999, Romanza, Violin solo, 1999, Sonata for Violin Solo (Naumburg commn.), 2002, Trio for Cello Clarinet & Piano (NY New Music Ensemble Commn.), 2003, Soliloquy for Vibraphone (Michael Parola Commn.), 2003, Trio for Cello, Viraphone and Piano (Core Ensemble Commn.), 2003, Concertino for Clarinet and orch., 2003, String Quartet No. 5, 2004, Sonata No. 2 for Violin and piano, 2004, numerous others; contbr. articles to profl. jours. Recipient BMI Student Composer awards, 1952-53; Bonsall fellow, 1953-54; Kosciuszko scholar, 1953-54; Nat. Fedn. Music Clubs award, 1953; Kate Neal Kinley fellow U. Ill., 1954-55; Fulbright grantee Florence, Italy, 1954-56; Pacifica Found. award, 1961; Creative Arts citation Brandeis U., 1963; Morse Acad. fellow, 1965; Nat. Inst. Arts and Letters grantee, 1967; Guggenheim fellow, 1967-68, 73-74, 82-83; Nat. Endowment on Arts grantee, 1973, 76, 79, 89, Mass. Council on Arts grantee, 1973, 79, 89; recipient Pulitzer prize in music, 1974, Kennedy Ctr. Friedheim Awards 1st prize, 1985, Mark M. Horblit award Boston Symphony Orch., 1987, Paul Revere award for mus. autography Music Publ. Assn., 1990-92. Mem. AAAS, AAAL, Coll. Music Soc., Am. Composers Alliance, Broadcast Music Inc., Am. Music Ctr., Internat. Soc. Contemporary Music (a founder New Haven chpt. 1964, dir. U.S. sect. 1961-64), Am. Soc. U. Composers (founding mem., exec. com. 1965-66, trustee 1965-2005), Internat. Clarinet Soc. Home: Newton, Mass. Died Dec. 8, 2005.

MARVICK, ELIZABETH WIRTH, retired political scientist; b. Chgo., Oct. 4, 1925; BA, U. of Chgo., 1944, MA, 1946; PhD, Columbia U., 1968. Lectr. in polit./social sci. CUNY, 1947—51; lectr. in polit. sci. UCLA, 1974—90. Author: The Young Richelieu, A Psychoanalytic Approach to Leadership, 1983, Louis XIII, the Making of a King, 1986. Rsch. grantee, tchg. fellow, Am. Coun. Learned Socs., Fulbright Commn., 1974, 1975, 1976. Mem.: Internat. Polit. Sci. Assn. (rsch. com. chair 1978—91), Western Soc. French History (coun.), Internat. Soc. Polit. Psychology (coun.). Avocation: tennis. Home: Reno, Nev. Died May 19, 2005.

MARX, ANNE (MRS. FREDERICK E. MARX), poet; b. Germany; came to U.S., 1936, naturalized, 1938; d. Jacob and Susan (Weinberg) Loewenstein; m. Frederick E. Marx, Feb. 12, 1937; children: Thomas J., Stephen L. Student, U. Heidelberg, U. Berlin. Mem. staffs N.Y.C. Writers Conf., 1965, Iona Coll., 1964, 65, 70, Wagner Coll., 1965, Poetry Workshop, Fairleigh Dickinson U., 1962, 63, 64, Poetry Soc. Am. Workshop, 1970-71, 78-79; Bronxville Adult Sch. Lecture Series, 1972; bd. dir. poetry series Donnell Library Ctr. (N.Y. Pub. Library), 1970-74; poetry day chmn. Westchester County, 1959—; Poetry Day Workshop, Ark., 1966, 70, Ark. Writers Conf., 1971, South and West Conf., Ark., 1972; vis. poet So. U., 1979; tchr., poetry readings, Jakarta, Indonesia, summer 1979; poetry workshop leader Scarsdale Cultural Ctr., 1981-82; conv. speaker Nat. Fedn. State Poetry Socs., 1974, 81, 82; condr. symposium Immigrant Voices, Pa. State U., 1986; judge Chapbook Award Nat. Federation of Poetry Socs., 1994, 1996-97; judge various nat. poetry contests; ongoing project: Selected Poems from Half a Century, 1997—. Poet over 1500 poems pub. in nat. mags., anthologies, lit. jours. and newspapers; author: Ein Buechlein, 1935, Into the Wind of Waking, 1960, The Second Voice, 1963, By Grace of Pain, 1966, By Way of People, 1970, A Time to Mend; selected poems, 1973; A Conversation with Anne Marx; 2 hour talking book for blind, 1974; Hear of Israel and Other Poems, 1975, 40 Love Poems for 40 Years, 1977, Face Lifts for All Seasons, 1980, 45 Love Poems for 45 Years, 1982, Holocaust: Hurts to Healings, 1984, German edit. Wunden und Narben, 1986; A Further Semester, 1985, Love in Late Season (New Poems by Anne Marx), 1993, Selected and New Poems, 2003, Full Circle, 2004; co-editor: Pegasus in the Seventies, 1973; contbr. to American Women Poets Discuss Their Craft, 1983, The Courage to Grow Old, 1989, A Collection of Essays by Ballantine Books, 1989; nat. editor poetry recs., Lamont Library at Harvard, stas. WFAS, WRNW, WEVD, WRVR, Voice of Am., The Pen Woman, 1986-88, Christian Sci. Monitor Anthology of Poems, 1989, Canadian Anthology, 1991, Irish Anthology, 1991, M. Rukeyser Anthology, 1999. Named Poet of Yr., N.Y. Poetry Forum, 1981, winner Chapbook competition, Crossroads Press, 1984; recipient Am. Weave Chapbook award, 1960, Nat. Sonnet, 1959, 1967, 1981, award, World Order Narrative Poets, 1959, 1967, 1981—85, prizes, Nat. Fedn. Women's Clubs, 1959, 1960, Nat. Fedn. State Poetry Socs., 1962, 1965, 1966, 1973, 1980—83, South and West Publn. award, 1965, Greenwood prize Eng., 1966, 2d Ann. Viola Hayes Parsons award, 1977, award, Delbrook Center Advanced Studies, 1978, Ann. Writer's Digest award, 1983—90, 1st prize, Nat. Essay Competition, 1990, N.Y. State Outstanding Writer award, 1991, N.Y. State 1st prize for Poetry, 1995. Mem. Poetry Soc. Am. (life, exec. bd. 1965-70, v.p. 1971-72, 2 fellowships, Cecil Hemley Meml. award 1974), Poetry Soc. Gt. Britain, Nat. League Am. Pen Women (pres. Westchester county br. 1962-64, North Atlantic regional chmn. 1964-66, nat. letters bd. 1972-74, biennial poetry workshop leader, nat. poetry editor 1974-78, N.Y. State lit. chmn. 1979-80, N.Y. State pres. 1982-84, 2d nat. v.p. 1984-86, nat. editor Pen Woman mag. 1986-88, contbg. editor 1990—, Biennial Book award 1976, Biennial awards (4), 1982, (2), 1984, Writer of Yr. 1991, N.Y. State Poetry award 1996, 1st prize Biennial Conv. 1998, established Anne Marx Sestina award 1998, judge poems Anne Marx Sestina award fund 2006, Helen Sutton Booth Spl. Biennial award 2002), Acad. Am. Poets, Poet Soc. Pa., Composers, Authors and Artists Am., Inc. (poetry editor mag. 1973-78), Poets and Writers, Inc., N.Y. Poetry Forum (life). Achievements include being subject of story "An American by Choice, A Poet's Credo" pub. in The PEN Woman mag., Nov. 1988, The Courage to Grow Old, 1989, N.Y. Times interview "Finding Poetry in All of Life's Events," 1993; collected works N.Y. Pub. Libr.: Anne Marx Archives, 1992, early German material added to collection, 1994, Juvenile Diaries, 2000, collection updated, 2005. Home: Hartsdale, NY. Died Apr. 16, 2006.

MARX, MELVIN H., psychologist, educator; b. Bklyn., June 8, 1919; m. Kathleen Kendall, Sept. 5, 1948; children: Diana, Christine, Ellen, James. AB, Washington U., 1940, MA, 1941, PhD, 1943. Instr. to prof. U. Mo., Columbia, 1944-84; sr. rsch. scientist Ga. State U., Atlanta, 1985-89; vis. prof. Fla. Inst. Tech., Melbourne, from 1990; disting. vis. prof. Western Carolina U., Cullowhee, N.C., from 1991. Author: Introduction to Psychology: Problems, Procedures, Principles, 1976; co-author: Systems and Theories in Psychology, 1963, 4th edit., 1987; editor: Psychological Theory, 1951; co-editor: Fundamentals and Applications of Learning, 1977. Recipient numerous Rsch. grants NIMH U. Mo., 1950-84, NSF U. Mo., USAF U. Mo., Army Rsch Inst., 1974-82. Fellow APA (mem. council), Am. Psychological Soc.; mem. Midwest Psychological Assn. (pres. 1965), Psychonomic Soc., Sigma Xi. Home: Fort Pierce, Fla. Died May 9, 2005.

MASCIA, JOSEPH SERAFINO, banking, economics and finance educator; b. Astoria, N.Y., Mar. 18, 1939; s. Peter and Lucy (Grodio) M.; m. Ritva A. Halinen, Dec. 14, 1966; 1 child, Mark Joseph. BA, CCNY, 1960; MBA, NYU, 1964, MS, 1973, MPA, 1977. Rsch. assoc. 1st Nat. City Bank, N.Y.C., 1962-66; dir. rsch. N.Y. State Bankers Assn., N.Y.C., 1966-69, 72-73; asst. v.p. Marine Midland Banks, Inc., N.Y.C. and Buffalo, 1969-71; fin. economist Dept. Treasury, Washington, 1971-72; dir. rsch., economist Irving Bank Corp., N.Y.C., 1973-76; instr. Montclair State Coll., Upper Montclair, N.J., 1977-78; asst. prof. economics Marist Coll., Poughkeepsie, N.Y., 1978-79; assoc. prof. banking, econs. and fin. Adelphi U., Garden City, N.Y., from 1979, chmn. dept., 1992-95, prof. emeritus, from 2000. Arbitrator Mcpl. Securities Rulemaking Bd., Nat. Futures Assn., 1991, N.Y. Stock Exch., N.Y.C., 1990—, Nat. Assn. Securities Dealers, N.Y.C., 1990—. Contbr. articles to profl. jours. 1st lt. USAR, 1961-68. Mem. Am. Econ. Assn., Am. Fin. Assn. Roman Catholic. Avocation: amateur musician. Home: Bronxville, NY. Died May 12, 2004.

MASCOLA, RICHARD F., former medical association administrator; Degree in prosthodontics, N.Y.U. Coll. Dentistry, 1962. Pres. ADA, 2001—02. Recipient Albert L. Borish Award, 2001. Died May 28, 2005.

MASLOWSKI, WALTER CASPER, oral and maxillofacial surgeon; b. Camden, N.J., May 9, 1929; s. Casper Mayer and Cecilia May (Walinski) M.; m. Beatrice Jacquelyn Cross, June 24, 1960; children: Kassia, Trina. BS, LaSalle Coll., 1949; DDS, U. Md., 1953; MS, Ohio State U., 1960. Diplomate Am. Bd. Oral and Maxillofacial Surgery. Practice dentistry specializing in oral and maxillofacial surgery, Lima, Ohio, from 1965; chief dept. oral and maxillofacial surgery St. Rita's Med. Ctr., Lima, from 1965. Cons. Oakwood Forensic Ctr., Lima, 1960—; medical missionary and clinician, Poland, 1983-86. Served to capt. USAF, 1953-60, Korea. Fello Internat. Assn. Oral Surgery (founding mem.), Am. Assn. Oral and Maxillofacial Surgeons; mem. Am. Dental Soc. of Anesthesiology (del. 1965-78, adv. bd. 1987), Ohio Dental Soc. of Anesthesiology (Outstanding Service award 1978), Lima Acad. Dentistry (pres. 1977-78), Morgan Allison Soc. Oral Surgeons. Lodges: Rotary (bd. dirs. Lima chpt. 1980-83), Serra Internat. Republican. Roman Catholic. Avocations: photography, tennis, racquetball, travel, fishing. Home: Lima, Ohio. Died May 12, 2005.

MASON, DONNA M., mental health nurse, administrator; b. Miss., July 4, 1955; d. Clifton and Mae (Martin) M. Student, Hofstra U., 1974-77; diploma, Med. Career Inst., Chgo., 1981, St. Luke's Sch. Nursing, Racine, Wis., 1984. Hospice home care nurse Vis. Nurse Assn., Racine; charge nurse Addiction Ctr. of Racine; clin. nurse mgr. St. Luke's Meml. Hosp., Racine. Bd. dirs. Racine Women's Resource Ctr.; charter mem. St. Paul Bapt. Ch. Nurses Guild, Racine. Home: Racine, Wis. Died Dec. 28, 2004.

MASON, GERALD RAY, lawyer; b. Augusta, Kans., Oct. 23, 1939; s. Clarence Walter and Dorothy Hazel (Mann) M.; m. Emma Louise While, Mar. 9, 1943; children: Shari Lynn, Kathryn Marie, Douglas James. AS, No. Okla. Jr. Coll., 1960; JD, U. Wyo., 1964. Bar: Wyo. 1964, U.S. Dist. Ct. Wyo. 1964, U.S. Ct. Appeals (10th cir.), 1979, U.S. Supreme Ct. 1986. Ptnr. Sievers & Mason, Pinedale, Wyo., 1964-74; sole practice Pinedale, 1974-78; pres. Mason & Refior P.C., Pinedale, 1978-81, Mason & Twichell P.C., Pinedale, 1981-89; pvt. practice Pinedale, 1989-91; ptnr. Mason & Graham, P.C., from 1991. Bd. dirs. Wyo. Trial Lawyers Assn., Cheyenne. Atty. Sublette County Sch. Bd., Pinedale, 1980—. Mem. Am. Trial Lawyers Assn., Wyo. State Bar Assn. (mem. bd. commrs. 1990-93, v.p. 1993-94, pres.-elect 1994-95, pres. 1995-96). Republican. Baptist. Avocations: hunting, fishing, golf, flying. Home: Pinedale, Wyo. Died July 6, 2005.

MASON, JOE BEN, retired prison mission executive; b. Texhoma, Tex., Oct. 24, 1910; s. Lloyd Elliot and Lillie Mae Mason; m. Helen Sutton, May 1936 (dec. 1971); 1 child, Joe Lawrence; m. Ada Giebelhaus, Mar. 25, 1972. 2-yr. cert., Amarillo Coll., 1932; student, U. Tex., 1933, Biola U., L.A., 1954; ThD (hon.), Faith Bible Coll. and Sem., Lagos, Nigeria, 1988. Ins. adjuster Md. Casualty Co., El Paso, Tex., 1935-36, FCAB Co., El Paso and Lubbock, Tex., 1937-41; owner, mgr. Mason Claim Svc., Phoenix, 1945-54; founder, dir. Prison Mission Assn., Inc., Weatherford, Tex., 1955-90, dir. ermitus, from 1990; founder, dir. Pen Pal Fellowship, Riverside, Calif., from 1990. Dir. emeritus Prison Mission Assn. Inc., Weatherford, Tex., 1990—. With USN, 1943-45. Mem. Marketplace Ministries. Republican. Avocations: reading, travel. Home: Sun City, Ariz. Died Apr. 23, 2005.

MASON, MARCELLA JUNE, legal assistant and secretary; b. Cannelton, Ind., Jan. 19, 1934; d. Maurice and Catherine (Brunner) M. BA, Ind. U., 1956. Reporter, photographer Porter County Pub. Co., Inc., Hebron, Ind., 1956-61, with advt. dept., reporter, 1963-65, reporter, photographer, 1969-80; asst. mgr. Valparaiso (Ind.) Lic. br. Bur. Motor Vehicles, 1961-63, 1965-69, dist. supr. Indpls., 1968-69; legal sec./asst. Petry, Fitzgerald & Shanahan, Hebron, from 1969. Vol. Porter County Red Cross, 1962-97; bd. dirs. Porter County Coun. on Aging, 1980-85; clk.-treas. Town of Hebron, 1971-79, 90-96; v.p. Ind. Young Dems., 1961-63; spl. asst. to pres. Young Dem. Clubs Am., Washington, 1964-65; v.p. Porter County Dem. Cen. Com., 1965-70; bd. dirs. Am. Cancer Soc. Porter County; sec. Lake of the Four Seasons Property Owners Assn., 1977—; sec.-fin. clk. Lake Eliza Area Conservatory Dist., 1978—. Mem. Nat. Assn. Legal Secs., Ind. Assn. Legal Secs. (pres. 1988-90, nat. dir. 1990-92, legal sec. of yr. 1981), Ind. Dem. Editorial Assn. (pres. 1973, exec. sec. 1981-93, award of merit 1983), Porter County Legal Secs. Assn., Order Ea. Star. Methodist. Avocations: reading, crossword puzzles, swimming, politics. Home: Hebron, Ind. Died July 18, 2005.

MASRY, EDWARD LOUIS, lawyer; b. Patterson, N.J., July 29, 1932; m. Jacqueline Wilson (separated 1974); children: Louanne, Louis, Nichole; m. Joette Levinson, 1992; adopted children: Christopher, Timothy. Student, Valley Jr. Coll., 1950—52, U. Calif., Santa Barbara, UCLA, U. So. Calif.; JD, Loyola U., L.A., 1960. Bar: Calif. 1961, U.S. Dist. Ct. Calif. 1961, U.S. Ct. Appeals (9th cir.) 1961, U.S. Supreme Ct. 1961. Pvt. practice, L.A., 1961—75, San Fernando Valley, Calif., 1975—82; ptnr. Masry & Vititoe, San Fernando Valley, 1982—97, Westlake Village, Calif., 1997—2005. Corp. dir. Gabriel Olsen Volkswagen, 1969—73, Merlin Olsen Porsche Audi, 1970—88; chmn., CEO Save World Air, Inc., 2001—05. Mem. adv. bd. Boys & Girls Club, Conejo, Calif., Las Virgenes, Calif.; mem. Thousand Oaks City Coun., Calif., 2000; mayor City of Thousand Oaks, 2003—05. With U.S. Army, 1952—54, Korea. Recipient U.S. Congl. award Outstanding Lawyer of the Yr., 1982, 1988, 1990, cert. of appreciation, Las Virgenes Unified Sch. Dist., 2002, cert. spl. congl. recognition, Def. Ctr. Commitment Environment Justice, 2002, Environ. Hero award, 2002, award, Nat. Jewish Fund, 2002, Santa Monica Mountains Recreational Area, Calif. Dept. Pks. and Recreation Angeles Dist., Mountains Restoration Trust, others. Mem.: ATLA, ABA, Consumer Attys. Assn. L.A., Los Angeles County Bar Assn., Ventura County Bar Assn., Consumer Attys. Calif., Trial Lawyers Pub. Justice (Acad. Justice award 2001), Phi Alpha Delta (justice, L.A. alumni justice). Achievements include being renown for his legal collaboration with Erin Brockovich in the $333 settlement against Pacific Gas & Electric Co. for the contamination of the water supply of Hinkley, California, 1997. Died Dec. 5, 2005.

MATANKY, ARNIE, publisher; b. Oak Park, Ill., June 25, 1930; s. Harry and Mary (Jakobowsky) M. AA, Wright Coll., 1950; postgrad., U. Chgo., 1954-55. City desk asst. Chgo. Sun, 1947; with Chgo. Jour. of Commerce, 1948; editor radio news Community News Service, Chgo., 1948-51; news editor CBS News, Chgo., 1953-59; owner, operator Info. Cons., Chgo., 1959-71 and from 80; dir. pub. info. Chgo. Park Dist., 1971-80; pub. Near North News, Chgo., from 1956. Contbg. editor Public Relations, 1970; editor Africa File. Pres. Lincoln Park Villas Condominium Assn., Chgo., 1978-91, Park Synagogue, Chgo., 1970-72, Sandburg Village Coun., Chgo., 1970-72; chmn. 18th Dist. Community Police Coun., Chgo., 1969-71; bd. dirs. Internat. Visitors Ctr., 1972-82; bd. overseers Nat. Ctr. for Freedom of Info. Studies. Sgt. 1st class U.S. Army, 1951-53. Mem. Am. Legion (comdr. 1958-59, vice chmn. fgn. rels. coun., vice comdr. dept. of France, treas. Fgn. and Outlying Depts. and Posts), Nat. Am. Vets. Press Assn. (pres. 1977-79), Internat. Press Club Chgo. (pres. 1991—), Chgo. Coun. on Fgn. Rels., Libr. of Internat. Rels., Psywar Soc. (U.K.), Jewish War Vets., Am. Topical Assn., Am. Philatelic Soc., UN Philatelists, Brit. Am. Postal Cover Soc., Amnesty Internat., Assn. of Former Intelligence Officers, Hugo's Companions (pres. 1991), Arthur Conan Doyle Soc., Chinese Passenger Traffic Club (v.p.), Travelers Century Club, Kiwanis (pres. Near North Chgo.), B'nai B'rith (pres. 1965-67), Near North Assn. Condominium Pres. (sec. 1990-95). Home: Chicago, Ill. Died Jan. 5, 2004.

MATASOVIC, MARILYN ESTELLE, manufacturing executive; b. Chgo., Jan. 7, 1946; d. John Lewis and Stella (Butkauskas) M. Student, U. Colo. Sch. Bus., 1963-69. Owner, pres. UTE Trail Ranch, Ridgway, Colo., from 1967; pres. MEM Equipment Co., Mokena, Ill., from 1979; sec./treas. Marlin Corp., Ridgway, from 1991, v.p., sec.-treas., from 1991, pres., from 2003; sec.-treas. Linmar Corp., Mokena, 1991-93, pres., from 2003; ptnr. Universal Welding Supply Co., New Lenox, Ill., 1964-90; v.p. OXO Welding Equipment Co, Inc., New Lenox, 1964-90; ptnr. Universal Internat., Mokena, Ill., 1990—2003, owner, from 2003; ind. travel agt. Ideal Travel Concepts, Mokena, 1994—2003; mgr. Hereford Works Warehouse, Mokena, from 1997, owner, from 2001, Barnyardblvd.com, from 2001; ptnr. OXO Hereford Ranches, Ridgeway, Colo., from 2003. Co-editor newsletters. U.S. rep. World Hereford Conf., 1964, 68, 76, 80, 84, 96. Recipient Outstanding Hereford Woman award, 1999. Mem. Am. Hereford Aux. (charter, bd. dirs. 1989-94, historian 1990-92, v.p. 1992, pres.-elect 1993, pres. 1994), Am. Hereford Women (charter, pres. 1994, bd. dirs. 1994-96, award 1999), Am. Agri-Women, Colo. Hereford Aux., Ill. Hereford Aux. (sec. 1969-70, publicity 1970-72), U. Colo. Alumni Assn., Ill. Agri-Women, Las Vegas Social Register. Avocations: showing cattle, computers, travel. Home: Mokena, Ill. Died May 25, 2004.

MATHENY, ROBERT DUANE, retired clergyman; b. Long Beach, Calif., Nov. 17, 1924; s. Harry and Ethel Mae (Brothers) M.; m. Norma Elizabeth Cheverton, June 22, 1949; children: Sarah Elizabeth, Paul Duane. BA, Tex. Christian U., Ft. Worth, 1945; MDiv, Tex. Christian U., 1949; postgrad., Princeton Theol. Sem., 1960, U. Chgo., 1952, Pacific Sch. Religion, 1955. Ordained to ministry Christian Ch. (Disciples of Christ), 1950; cert. grief counselor. Minister 1st Christian Ch., Conroe, Tex., 1948-50, First Christian Ch., Center, Tex., 1950-53, Jacksonville, Tex., 1953-63, sr. minister Richardson, Tex., 1963-68, Covenant Christian Ch., Tucker, Ga., 1968-70, Winter Park Christian Ch., Winter Park, Fla., 1970-76, First Christian Ch., Bay City, Tex., 1976-80, Oaks Christian Ch., Houston, 1980-83; sr. minister, pastor St. Charles Ave. Christian Ch., New Orleans, 1983-89; outreach grief cons. Lake Lawn Metairie Funeral Home, New Orleans, 1986-95, St. Bernard Meml. Funeral Home, Chalmette, La., 1988-95. Contbr. articles to profl. jours. Pres. Civic Music Assn., Jacksonville, Tex., 1958-63. Mem. AACD, Tex. Conf. Chs. (pres. 1965), Greater New Orleans Fedn. Chs. (exec. bd. 1987-89), La. Interchurch Conf. (v.p. 1987-90), Assn. for Death Edn. and Counseling, Fostick Soc. Retired Christian Ch. Disciples, Masons, Rotary, Alpha Psi Omega. Democrat. Avocations: opera, drama, walking, history. Home: Louisville, Ky. Died July 7, 2005.

MATHER, GEORGE ROSS, clergy member; b. Trenton, N.J., June 1, 1930; s. Samuel Wooley and Henrietta Elizabeth (Deardorff) M.; m. Doris Christine Anderson, June 28, 1958; children: Catherine Anne Mather-Grimes, Geoffrey Thomas. BA, Princeton U., 1952; MDiv, Princeton Theol. Sem., 1955; DD, Hanover Coll., 1986. Ordained to Ministry, 1955. Asst. pastor Abington (Pa.) Presbyn., 1955-58; pastor 1st Presbyn. Ch. Ewing, Trenton, 1958-71; sr. pastor 1st Presbyn. Ch. Ft. Wayne, Ind., 1971-86; interim pastor 3d Presbyn. Ch. Ft. Wayne, Ind., 1987-95. Author: Frontier Faith: The Story of the Pioneer Congregations, 1992, The Best of Fort Wayne, vol. 1, 2000, vol. 2, 2001; co-editor: On the Heritage Trail, 1994; contbr. articles to profl. jours. Pres. Allen County Libr. Trustees, Ft. Wayne, Allen County Libr. Found., Ft. Wayne, Clergy United for Action, Ft. Wayne; trustee Hanover (Ind.) Coll.; chmn. Bicentennial Religious Heritage Commn., 1994; bd. dirs. Smock Found., 1971-85. Mem. Ind. Religious History Assn. (bd. dirs.), Allen County Ft. Wayne Hist. Soc. (bd. dirs.), The Quest Club (pres.). Avocations: tennis, travel, hiking, canoeing. Home: Fort Wayne, Ind. Died Sept. 30, 2004.

MATHESON, MAX SMITH, physical chemical researcher; b. McGill, Nev., May 24, 1913; s. Henry Thompson and Ethel (Smith) M.; m. Gladys Mulchahey, Sept. 30, 1939 (div. 1965); children: Linda J., Marc E.; m. Georgine M. Modica, Apr. 29, 1967 (dec. Dec. 1995); 1 child, Jean S. Fornango. AB, U. Utah, 1936; PhD, U. Rochester, 1940. Rsch. chemist Gen. Labs., U.S. Rubber Co., Passaic, N.J., 1940-50; assoc. chemist Argonne (Ill.) Nat. Lab., 1950-52, sr. chemist, 1952-79, dir. chem. div., 1965-71, group leader, 1971-79, cons., 1979-90, temporary employee Lemont, Ill., 1990-97. Adj. prof. U. Utah, Salt Lake City, 1982-85; chmn. Gordon Conf. Radiation Chem., New Hampton, N.H., 1960; vis. prof. Hebrew U., Jerusalem, 1972. Author: (with others) Photocatalysis in Organized Assemblies, 1989; contbr. articles to profl. jours. Fellowship Guggenheim Found., 1960-61. Mem. AAAS, Am. Chem. Soc. (com. internat. activities 1968-73), Am. Phys. Soc., Radiation Rsch. Soc. (council 1975-78), Phi Beta Kappa, Phi Kappa Phi. Achievements include first to prepare XeF_2; research on measurement rate constants free radical polymerization, on kinetics dihalide ions-first observation, on pulse radiolysis, on rate constants in ionizing irradiated aqueous solutions, on picosecond measurements of hydrated electron and OH in irradiated solutions, on photochemistry of potential solar energy conversion systems on chemistry in radioactive wastes. Home: Chesterfield, Mo. Died Jan. 26, 2005.

MATHIAS, BOB (ROBERT BRUCE MATHIAS), Olympic athlete, former congressman; b. Tulare, Calif., Nov. 17, 1930; s. Charles Milford Mathias and Lillian Elsie (Harris); m. Gwen Haven Alexander, 1977; children: Romel, Megan, Marissa, Alyse, Reiner. AB, Stanford U., 1953. Olympic athlete; founder Bob Mathias Sierra Boys Camp, 1962—77; mem. US Congress from Calif., 1967—75; dep. dir. US Selective Svc., 1975; dir. US Olympic Training Ctr., Colorado Springs, 1977—83; pres. Am. Kids Sports Assn., 1988—91, Bob Mathias, Inc. Actor: It Happened in Athens. Served in USMC, 1954—56 USMC Reserves, 1956—65. Named to Nat. Track and Field Hall of Fame, 1974,San Francisco Bay Area Hall of Fame, 1981, US Olympic Hall of Fame, 1983; recipient Sullivan award, Theodore Roosevelt award, NCAA, 1995 Achievements include gold medal in decathlon Olympic Games, 1948, 52; youngest individual athletics champion. Died Sept. 2, 2006.

MATHIAS, MERVIN A., retired surgeon; b. Phila., 1917; MD, Temple U., 1942. Diplomate Am. Bd. Surgery. Intern Jewish Hosp., Phila., 1942-43, resident in pathology, 1946-47; resident in surgery West Jersey Hosp., Camden, N.J., 1948-50; surgeon in pvt. practice, to 1982. Mem. Am. Occupl. Medicine Assn., Internat. Med. Assn. Home: San Mateo, Calif. Died 2006.

MATSEOANE, CAROL, social worker; b. N.Y.C., July 10, 1944; d. Joseph Daniel Taylor and Nannie Lee Winborne; m. Stephen Matseoane, Jan. 21, 1968; children: Dara, Joyce, Karen. BA, Hunter Coll., 1966, MSW, 1970; PhD, Walden U., 1992. Cert. social worker, N.Y. Social worker Spl. Svcs. for Children Protective Svcs., N.Y.C.; psychotherapist-counselor O. Quentin Hyder MD, N.Y.C.; social work supr. JHMCB Ctr. for Nursing and Rehab./Long Term Home Care Prog., Bklyn.; clin. dir. Lamb's Counseling Ctr., New Hope Counseling Ctr. Recipient Apple Polisher award, Women's Inner Circle of Achievement award. Mem.: NAFE, NASW, Am. Bd. Med. Psychotherapists (life). Home: New York, NY. Died Jan. 28, 2006.

MATTHEWS, JAMES GORDON, JR., obstetrician, gynecologist; b. Bridgeport, Conn., Jan. 22, 1916; s. James G. and Sue Gay (Short) M.; m. Gladyce Lorraine Carlberg, Apr. 4, 1942; children: Suzanne, James III, Barbara, William, Christine, Thomas. BS, Ea. Mich. U., 1937; DO, Kirksville Coll Osteo Mecidine, 1942. Diplomate ob-gyn. Am. Osteo. Bd. Intern-resident ob-gyn. Detroit Osteo. Hosp., Highland Park, Mich., 1942-45, sr. ob-gyn., chmn., 1947-68; chmn. ob-gyn. Bicounty Community Hosp., Warren, Mich., 1970; sr. attending ob-gyn. Doctor's Hosp., Columbus, Ohio, 1971-75, chair ob-gyn., 1974-75, Dallas Ft. Worth Med. Ctr., Grand Prairie, Tex., 1975-90; clin. prof. ob-gyn. Tex. Coll. Osteo. Medicine, Ft. Worth, from 1975, Okla. State U. Coll. Osteo. Medicine, Tulsa, from 1984; dir. resident tng. ob-gyn. Dallas Ft. Worth Med. Ctr., Grand Prairie, 1984-94; retired, 1994. Lectr. in field; cons. sex edn. Bd. Edn., Berkley, Mich. Contbr. articles to profl. jours. Mem. Grand Prairie YMCA Bd. Mgmt., 1977—; sustaining campaign chmn. YMCA, Grand Prairie, 1989; pres. Rotary Club, Grand Prairie, 1988-89. Named Pub. Servant of Yr., Grand Prairie C. of C., 1988, Vol. of Yr., Dallas Met. YMCA, 1989, Physician of Yr., Dallas/Ft. Worth Med. Ctr. Found., 1990. Fellow Am. Coll. Osteo. Ob-Gyn. (disting., pres. 1964); mem. Am. Osteo Assn. (life), Am. Menopause Soc., Am. Bd. Sexology (diplomate), Tex. Osteo. Med. Assn. (life), Assn. Reproductive Health Profls., Grayline Game Club (pres.), Red Run Golf Club (life), Mich. Inter-Club Swimming Assn. (pres.), Rotary Internat. (Paul Harris fellow). Methodist. Avocations: golf, sailing, skiing. Home: Grand Prairie, Tex. Died July 27, 2005.

MATTHEWS, PAUL WILLIAM, savings and loan executive; b. American Falls, Idaho, Dec. 21, 1954; s. William Hulme and Joan (McLean) M.; m. Becky Turner, Dec. 30, 1976; children: Melissa, Austin, Cody, Trevor. BA, U. Utah, 1980. Mgr. trainee First Fed. Savs., Twin Falls, Idaho, 1981-83, br. mgr. Burley, Idaho, 1983-88, v.p., from 1988. Chmn. Burley Area Devel. Commn., 1988—. Mem. Inst. Fin. Edn., Burley Area C. of C. (bd. dirs. 1983—, v.p. 1985—, pres. 1987, chmn. 1988—), Kiwanis (bd. dirs. Burley chpt. 1982-83, treas. 1983-86, chmn. fundraising com. 1986-87, pres. 1991-92). Republican. Mem. Lds Ch. Avocations: reading, golf, home improvement activities. Home: Burley, Idaho. Died Aug. 26, 2005.

MATTISON, JOEL, plastic surgeon; b. Arcadia, Fla., Dec. 29, 1931; s. William L. and Millie B. Mattison; m. Jean Morris, June 5, 1955; children: Lewis, Karl. AB, Davidson Coll., 1951; MDiv, Princeton Sem., 1954; MD, Duke U.,

1961. Diplomate Am. Bd. Plastic Surgery, Am. Bd. Quality Assurance and Utilization Rev. Physicians. Intern surgery Duke U. Med. Ctr., Durham, N.C., 1961; resident plastic surgery U. Fla., Gainesville, 1964-69; practice medicine specializing in plastic surgery Tampa, Fla., 1969-95; clin. prof. surgery U. South Fla., Tampa. Frequent lectr. on med. ethics. Contbr. articles on med. ethics, Am. antiques and decorative arts to profl. jours. Recipient Disting. Alumnus award Princeton Sem., 1991. Fellow ACS; mem. Am. Soc. Plastic Surgeons, Southeastern Soc. Plastic Surgeons (Outstanding Achievement award 1985, Pickrell award 1999), Fla. Soc. Plastic Surgeons, Rotary. Presbyterian. Home: Tampa, Fla. Died Mar. 30, 2004.

MATUG, ALEXANDER PETER, lawyer; b. Chgo., May 25, 1946; s. Alexander J. and Marianne (Paszek) M.; m. Jeanne Marie Buker, Aug. 16, 1969; children: Alexander W., Krista E., Thomas E. BA, St. Mary's Coll., Minn., 1968; JD, Loyola U., Chgo., 1972. Bar: Ill. 1972, U.S. Dist. Ct. (no. dist.) Ill. 1972. Pvt. practice, Palos Heights, Ill., from 1972. Bd. dirs. Am. Heritage, Sertoma, Palos Heights, 1991—; profl. adv. bd. Sertoma Speech and Hearing Ctr., Palos Hills, Ill., 1991—. Mem. Ill. Bar Assn., S.W. Suburban Bar Assn. Roman Catholic. Home: Palos Park, Ill. Died Sept. 3, 2004.

MAUCK, HENRY PAGE, JR., medical and pediatric educator; b. Richmond, Va., Feb. 3, 1926; s. Henry Page and Harriet Hutcheson (Morrison) M.; m. Janet Garrett Horsley, May 14, 1955; children— Henry Page III, John Waller. BA, U. Va., 1950, MD, 1952. Diplomate: Am. Bd. Internal Medicine. Intern Henry Ford Hosp., Detroit, 1952-53; resident Med. Coll. Va., Richmond, 1953-56, asst. prof. medicine and pediatrics, 1961-66, assoc. prof., 1966-72, prof., from 1972. Fellow in cardiology Am. Heart Assn., 1956-57; cons. cardiology Langley Field Air Force Hosp., Hampton, Va., McGuire's VA Hosp., Richmond. Contbr.: chpt. to Autonomic Control of Cardiovascular System, 1972; contbr. articles to sci. jours. Served with U.S. Army, 1944-46. Fellow ACP, Am. Coll. Cardiology (former gov. Va.); mem. Am. Physiol. Soc., So. Soc. Clin. Investigation, Am. Fedn. Clin. Research, So. Soc. Clin. Research. Presbyterian. Home: Richmond, Va. Died Sept. 2, 2006.

MAURICE, DON, personal care industry executive; b. Peoria, Ill., Aug. 29, 1932; s. Imajean (Webster) Crayton; m. Cindalu Jackson, Aug. 31, 1990. Student, Loma Linda U., 1984-86; cert. paralegal studies, Calif. State U., San Bernardino, 1994. Lic. hair stylist, skin therapist; cert. paralegal, notary pub. Owner 2 schs. in advanced hair designs, San Diego, 1962-64, D & M Enterprises, Advt. Agy., 1964-78; now cons. D&M Enterprises Advt. Agy.; dist. mgr. AqRo Matic Co. Water Purification Systems, San Diego, 1972-75; profl. sales educator Staypower Industries, San Diego, 1972-76, 3d v.p., 1975-76; regional bus. cons. Estheticians Pharmacology Rsch., Garden Grove, Calif., 1975-81; owner, operator Don Maurice Hair Designs, Hemet, Calif., 1980-83; dir., operator Hair Sytles by Maurice, Loma Linda, Calif., 1984-88; owner, pres. Grooming Dynamics, Redlands, Calif., from 1988. Bus. cons. Yogurt Place, Paradise Valley, Ariz., 1978-79, others; regular guest Channel 6/Channel 8, San Diego, 1968-78; cons. infomercial Pre-Paid Legal Svcs., Inc., 1994—; undercover criminal investigator, 1955-59, 1999—. Author: The New Look For Men, 1967, The Art of Men's Hair Styling, 1968 (accepted by Library of Congress), Baldness, To Be or Not To Be, 1989. Promoter Spl. Olympics, Hemet, 1981. Sgt. U.S. Army, 1950-53, Korea. Decorated Purple Heart, 1952; named Leading Businessman in His Profession, Union and Evening Tribune, 1969. Mem. Internat. Platform Assn., Christian Businessmen's Assn. Avocations: writing, sculpting, art, sports, music. Died Mar. 12, 2004.

MAWHINNEY, EUGENE ALBERTO, social science educator; b. Jonesboro, Maine, Oct. 14, 1921; s. Bert and Estella (Whitney) M.; m. Anne Dowling, Aug. 24, 1946; children: Meredith Anson, Mark Allen. BS, U. Maine, 1947, MA, 1949; PhD in Polit. Sci., U. Ill., 1955. Assoc. prof. polit. sci. NE Mo. State Coll., 1951-55; mem. faculty Elmira (N.Y.) Coll., 1955-59, prof. polit. sci., 1958-59, head dept. social sci., 1956-59; mem. faculty U. Maine, from 1959, prof. polit. sci., 1963-90, Disting. Maine prof., 1982-90, prof. emeritus polit. sci., 1990—2006, head dept., 1966-75. Mem. Maine Task Force Govtl. Reorgn., 1967-68, 76-77, Maine Jud. Council, 1965-77, 80—2006, Maine Commn. Senate Apportionment, 1966-67, 71, Maine Commn. House Apportionment, 1971-72, Maine Task Force Regional and Dist. Govt., 1977-78, Maine Commn. on Relocation of Supreme Jud. Ct., 1985-86, Maine Bar Assn. Commn. on assignment of Counsel, 1985-86 cons. N.Y. State Commn. Constl. Revision, 1957-58; exec. dir. Maine Mgrs. Inst., 1960-65 Author: Profile of Metropolitan Elmira, 1958, Maine Legislative Apportionment, 1967, (with others) Downeast Politics: The Government of Maine, 1975. Trustee Washington Acad., 1969-91. Served with AUS, 1942-46. Recipient Disting. Service award Maine Bar Assn., 1987. Mem. Am. Polit. Sci. Assn., New Eng. Polit. Sci. Assn. (pres. 1974-75), Kappa Delta Pi, Kappa Delta Phi, Phi Kappa Phi, Pi Sigma Alpha. Lodges: Masons (32 deg.); Shriners. Congregationalist. Home: Orono, Maine. Died June 24, 2006.

MAYER, ENDRE AGOSTON, physicist, engineer; b. Ercsi, Fejer, Hungary, Feb. 17, 1929; came to U.S., 1949; s. Otto and Iren (Nilgesz) M.; m. Jean Yost (dec. 1988); children: Susan J., Sandra J., Warren E. Student, U. Innsbruck, 1946-49; BS in Physics, Denison U., 1951. Registered profl. engr., Mich. Test engr. Consumers Res., Washington, N.J., 1951-54; devel. engr. Swartwout Co., Cleve., 1956-59; research physicist Bell Aerospace, Cleve., 1959; sr. devel. engr. TRW, Cleve., 1959-62; engring. mgr. Bendix Corp., Southfield, Mich., 1962-81, Schenck Pegasus Corp., Troy, Mich., 1981-95, HEM Data, Troy, from 1995. Tech. editor Fluidics Quarterly jour., 1968—; contbr. numerous articles to profl. jours.; patentee in field. Vice chair Bd. Zoning Appeals, Birmingham, Mich., 1978-88. Served with U.S. Army, 1954-56. Recipient Westinghouse Corp. medallion, 1958. Mem. ASME, NSPE, AIAA, Soc. Automotive Engrs., Am. Rocket Soc. Baptist. Avocations: photography, woodworking, flying. Home: Troy, Mich. Died Sept. 1, 2004.

MCADAMS, H. T., statistician, researcher; b. Carrollton, Ill., Apr. 23, 1918; s. Hiram Ulysses Grant McAdams and Myrtle Mae Sherman; m. Catherine Conlee Jouett, Dec. 31, 1938; children: Constance, Dennis, Kay. EdB, Ill. State U., 1940; MA in Math., SUNY, Buffalo, 1956; postgrad., N.C. State U., 1961—62. Rsch. physicist Western Cartridge Co., East Alton, Ill., 1941—46; rsch. chemist Aluminum Co. Am., East St. Louis, Ill., 1946—53; prin. physicist Cornell Aeronautical Lab., Inc., Buffalo, 1953—64; spl. assignment engr. Bethlehem (Pa.) Steel Corp., 1964—65; staff scientist Calspan Corp., Buffalo, 1965—76; sr. rsch. analyst Falcon Rsch., Buffalo, 1976—81; pvt. statis. cons. Buffalo, 1981—86, Argenta, Ill., 1986—96, Carrollton, 1996—2004. Contbr. articles to profl. jours. Pres. bd. edn. Bethalto (Ill.) Pub. Schs., 1950—51; mgr. statis. survey Argenta Civic Club, 1990—91. Mem.: Am. Statis. Assn. Achievements include patents for air data computer system; method and apparatus for determining surface characteristics incorporating a scanning electron microscope; differential rate screening; agglomeration process using sewage sludge as a fuel; research in generalization of the Moebius Strip; method for precise control of size distributions of particulate material; means for maximizing packing density of aggregates; application of stochastic process theory to manufacturing processes, particularly metal cutting by grinding; off-road trafficability of the earth's surface; trafficability and visibility of the lunar surface; physicogeometric properties of surfaces affecting surface integrity; improved algorithm for cross-impact analysis; development of mathematical model for characterizing emissions and fuel economy of automotive vehicles; research in refinement and extension of random balance methodology; refinement of principal component regression. Avocations: music, poetry, creative writing, songwriting, gardening. Home: Carrollton, Ill. Died Nov. 18, 2005.

MCALLISTER, ROBERT DALE, judge; b. St. Louis, Oct. 8, 1930; s. Hudson William and Marie Edna (Gross) McA.; m. Sondra Sue Faupel, July 6, 1960 (div. 1970); m. Julianne States, Dec. 12, 1970; children: Terry Sue, David Lee, Melissa Ann, Jennifer Marie. BA in Elem. Edn., Harris Tchrs. Coll., 1953; JD, St. Louis U., 1965. Bar: Mo. 1965, Iowa 1965. Asst. city atty. City of Des Moines, 1965-70; ptnr. Spaulding & McAllister, St. Louis, 1970-78; judge 21st Jud. Ct. Mo., St. Louis, from 1979. Author: Murphy's Law, 1990, The College, 1992. With U.S. Army, 1953-55. Mem. United Ch. of Christ. Avocations: tennis, golf, acting, writing. Home: Chesterfield, Mo. Died Aug. 5, 2005.

MCARTHUR, JOHN ALFRED, oil company executive; b. Bklyn., Aug. 30, 1937; s. John Percival and Julia Alice (Monahan) McA.; m. Elizabeth JoAnn Shields, Feb. 11, 1961; children: Julia, John, Joan. BSChemE, Pa. State U., 1959. Oper. foreman Chevron Oil, Salt Lake City, 1962-66; sr. analyst Sun Co., Inc., Phila., 1966-72, environ. specialist, 1972-74, mgr. operational planning, 1974-76, info. specialist Radnor, Pa., 1976-77, mgr. internal analysis, 1977-80, dir. planning svcs., 1980-84, dir. corp. planning, from 1984. Mem. benefits plans investment com., Sun Co., 1988—. Driver Townwatch, Berwyn, Pa., 1988. Avocations: backpacking, tennis. Home: Golden, Colo. Died Mar. 31, 2004.

MC BEATH, WILLIAM HENNINGER, physician, association executive; b. Leitchfield, Ky., Feb. 26, 1931; s. Bishop Henninger and Annie DeJarnette (English) McB.; m. Shirley Ann Nickell, June 1, 1959; children: Elizabeth Angela, Rebecca Susan, William Henninger, Jr. BS, Georgetown Coll., 1953; MD, U. Lousiville, 1957; M.P.H., U. Mich., 1964. Intern Jefferson Davis Hosp., Houston, 1957-58; resident in community health USPHS Career Devel. Program, U. Ky./Ky. State Dept. Health, 1961-62; dir. div. med. care Ky. State Dept. Health, Frankfort, 1962-66; dir. Ohio Valley Regional Med. Program Lexington, Ky., 1966-73; exec. dir. Am. Public Health Assn., Washington, 1973—93. Asso. prof. community medicine, spl. asst. to v.p. U. Ky. Med. Center, Lexington, 1962-73; lectr. in med. care orgn. U. Mich. Mng. editor: Am. Jour. Public Health; exec. editor: Nation's Health. Diaconate chmn. First Bapt. Ch., Washington; mem. exec. com. D.C. Bapt. Conv.; mem. gen. bd. Am. Bapt. Chs. USA. Served as capt. M.C. USAF, 1958-61. Fellow Am. Public Health Assn.; mem. Am. Soc. Assn. Execs., World Fedn. Public Health Assns. (dir.), Am. Assn. World Health (dir.), Assn. Tchrs. Preventive Medicine, Am. Bapt. Fgn. Mission Soc. (dir.), Georgetown Coll. Alumni Assn. (pres. 1970-72), Soc. Amateur Cinematographers, Pi Kappa Alpha, Phi Chi, Delta Omega. Clubs: Rotary. Democrat. Home: Rockville, Md. Died May 15, 2006.

MCBRIDE, ELIZABETH ANNE, retired academic advisor; b. Hong Kong, Aug. 5, 1933; d. Andrew Howie and Anne Hotchkies (Stewart) McB.; divorced; 1 child, Ramón Berguer. BA in English and French, U. Western Australia, 1954; diplome Sorbonne, Paris, 1955; BA Honors (French), U. Western Australia, 1956. Cert. translation/interpretation in French and Spanish. Instr. English U. Barcelona (Spain), 1960-61; adminstrv. asst., asst. editor European Office of UN, Geneva, 1961-67; adminstrv. asst. langs. dept. Wayne State U., Detroit, 1967-76; acad. advisor Wayne State, Detroit, 1976-93; ret., 1993. Speaker, presenter in field. Mem. NAFSA, Assn. Internat. Educators (presenter on study abroad in Latin Am. 1977-93, tng. grantee 1983, 87, 89). Home: Albuquerque, N.Mex. Died Feb. 6, 2004.

MCCABE, CHARLES KEVIN, lawyer, author; b. Springfield, Ill., Nov. 2, 1952; s. Charles Kenneth and Betty Lou (Williams) McC. BS in Aero. and Astronautical Engring. magna cum laude, U. Ill., 1975; JD, U. Mich., 1978. Bar: Ill. 1978, U.S. Dist. Ct. (no. dist.) Ill. 1978, U.S. Ct. Appeals (7th cir.) 198o. Engring. co-op. student McDonnell Aircraft, St. Louis, 1972-74; chief aerodynamicist Vetter Fairing Co., Rantoul, Ill., 1974-75; with Lord, Bissel & Brook, Chgo., from 1978. Author: Qwiktran: Quick FORTRAN, 1979, FORTH Fundamentals, 1983, Steam Locomotive Fundamentals, 1999; co-author: 32 BASIC Programs, 1981; contbr. articles on aviation, computers to various mags., 1974—. Pres., dir. Ill. Railway Mus, 1992—. Nat. Merit scholar U. Ill., Urbana, 1970. Mem. Chgo. Bar. Assn. Home: Winfield, Ill. Died Oct. 11, 2004.

MCCABE, JOHN LEE, engineer, educator; b. Fond du Lac, Wis., Mar. 26, 1923; s. Arthur Lee and Florence Gertrude (Molleson) McC.; m. M. Leora Harvey, Mar. 17, 1946; 1 child, Steven Lee. Student, Western Mich. U., 1941-42, U. Colo., 1946-47, C.C. Aurora, 1984-85. Designer project assignments, Denver, 1947-50; archtl. engr. The Austin Co., Denver, 1950-52; resident engr. Peter Kiewit Sons Co., Portsmouth, Ohio, 1953; dist. mgr. Hugh J. Baker Co., Evansville, Ind., 1953-56; engr. Lauren Burt Inc., Denver, 1956-58; project mgr. Denver Steel Products Co., Commerce city, Colo., 1958-66; pres. corp. McCabe and Co., Aurora, Colo., 1966-75; master tchr. h.s. Sch. Dist. 50, Westminster, Colo., 1975-83; tchr. Aurora Pub. Schs., 1983-92; subs. tchr. Lawrence (Kans.) Pub. Schs., 1993-99; math. instr. Lawrence Career Coll., 1999-2000. Writer Kans. Sr. Press Svc., 1996—. Columnist Lawrence Jour.-World, 1997-99; author: Word Problems Simplified, 1986, Everyday Algebra, Everyday Geometry, 1987, Everyday Mathematics-A Study Guide, 1988, Mathematics Workbook series for Technical Schools, Drafting, Machine Shop, Auto Body, Welding, Horticulture, 1987-88, Mathematics Workbook series for Middle Schools, Problem Solving, 1987, Whole Numbers, Fractions-Decimals-Percents, 1989, Measurments, Metrics, 1990, Basic Algebra, Basic Geometry, 1991, Everyday Metrics, 1992, How to Get Started as a Contractor, 2d edit., 1992, Essentials of Algebra, 1993, Applying Algebra, 1994, Metrics at Work, 1994, Basic Trigonometry, 1994, Algebra Word Problems, 1994, Personal Finance, 1995, Applied Trigonometry, 1996 (novel) The Survivors, 1998. With USAF, PTO, WWII. Mem. Colo. Soc. Engrs. (life), 20th Air Force Assn., Am. Legion. Roman Catholic. Home: Lawrence, Kans. Died Dec. 17, 2004.

MCCABE, KEVIN FRANCIS, chiropractor, biologist; b. Madison, Wis., Feb. 8, 1959; s. Robert Albert and Marie Elinor (Stanfield) McCabe; m. Laurie Ann Dimond, June 27, 1987. BA, U. Wis., 1981; MS, S.D. State U., 1984; D in Chiropractic, Palmer Coll. Chiropractic, Davenport, Iowa, 1989. Cert. chiropractice sports practitioner, animal chiropractor, registered Am. Chiropractic Rehab. Grad. rsch. asst. dept. wildlife and fisheries scis. S.D. State U., Brookings, 1982-84; agrl. rsch. technician B dept. wildlife Va. Poly. Inst. and State U., Blacksburg, 1984-85; profl. aide S.D. Dept. Game, Fish and Parks, Rapid City, 1985; pvt. practice Ames, Iowa, 1989-90; pres., ptnr. Chiropractic Assocs. Svc. Corp., West Allis, Wis., 1991-97; co-owner HealthRite Chiropractic, LLC, Wauwatosa, Wis., from 1996, Burleigh Rd. Animal Hosp., from 2002. Named Outstanding Young Men Am., 1987, 1988. Mem.: Am. Vet. Chiropractic Assn., Wis. Chiropractic Assn., Am. Chiropractic Assn. (coun. phys. therapeutics and rehab.), Mensa, Palmer Coll. Chiropractic Alumni Assn., Wildlife Soc., S.E. Wis. Master Gardners, Lewiston Outing Club, Chir Rho Theta. Democrat. Avocations: racquet sports, hunting, dog training, golf, photography. Home: Wauwatosa, Wis. Died Apr. 16, 2004.

MCCAIN, SHARON TEAGUE, learning specialist; b. Birmingham, Ala., Oct. 21, 1941; d. Claxton Harles and Rebeckah Almeda (Young) Teague; m. Douglas Owens McCain, June 12, 1964; children: Matthew, Michael, Melissa, Marc, Jeanette. BA English/Speech, U. Montevallo, 1964; MS Adminstrn./Supervision Curriculum, Nova U., 1975. Tchr. Five Points (Ala.) High Sch., 1964-65, Okeechobee (Fla.) High Sch., 1965-68, Vero Beach (Fla.) High Sch., from 1968. Author: Poems of the Heart, 1982. Lay minister United Meth. Ch., Vero Beach, 1985—. Named to Outstanding Young Women of Am., 1978. Mem. Nat. Coun. Tchrs. English, Fla. Coun. Tchrs. English, Delta Kappa Gamma (pres. 1980-82). Democrat. Methodist. Avocations: reading, poetry, needlepoint. Home: Vero Beach, Fla. Died Feb. 9, 2004.

MCCANN, ANDREW HUGHES, dance consultant, journalist; b. San Antonio, June 3, 1933; s. Hughes Sanford and Marie (Andrew) McC.; m. Alice Carolyn Hamlin (div.); children: Steven Andrew, Stephanie Alicia; m. Kristal Sue Fitzgerald. Registered adjudicator Nat. Dance Coun. Am. Dance dir. Dale Dance Studios, Phoenix, 1955; co-mgr. Fred Astaire Studios, Dallas, 1964, Tyler, Tex., 1965, mgr. Memphis, 1968, Arthur Murray Studios, Arlington, Va.,

1977; nat. dance dir. Dance World USA Studios, Inc., 1978; regional devel. coord. Md. area Fred Astaire Internat., Inc., 1980. Contbr. DanScene mag., Ballroom Dancing USA mag., Dance Action Internat. mag.; columnist Amateur Dancer. Soloist Arlington (Va.) 7th Day Adventist Ch.; judge Va. Commonwealth Games, Roanoke, 1995-96. With U.S. Navy, 1950-54, Korea. Mem. Dance Educators Am., U.S. Ind. Dance Coun., Profl. Dancers Fedn., N.Am. Dance Tchrs. Assn. Democrat. Avocations: tropical fish, chess, gardening, jazz music. Died Aug. 23, 2004.

MCCANTS, MALCOLM THOMAS, chemical engineer; b. Houston, Jan. 17, 1917; s. John Thomas and Julia Adele (Yeatman) McC.; m. Flora Olivia Jackson, Feb. 25, 1941; children: Michael, Julianne. BA, Rice Inst., 1937, BSChemE, 1939; MSChemE, MIT, 1940. Registered profl. engr., Tex., Calif. Chem. engr. Humble Oil & Refining Co., Baytown, Tex., 1940-43; asst. chemist Great. So. Corp., Corpus Christi, Tex., 1943-47, gen. supt., 1950-53; process engr. Fluor Corp., L.A., 1947-50; plant mgr. Great. No. Oil Co., St. Paul, 1954-56; cons. engr. Petroleum Technologists, Houston, 1957-94; sr. v.p. Basic Equipment Corp., Houston, from 1994. Mem. Sigma Tau. Achievements include 5 U.S. patents and 3 foreign patents; responsible for building the first BTX plant, refinery in Minn., Crude Unit in Bolivia, Crude Unit in Chile, Crude Unit in Russia. Home: Humble, Tex. Died May 7, 2004.

MCCARROLL, HELEN, community health nurse, critical care nurse; b. Gary, Ind., May 10, 1926; d. Robert Edward and Emma Jane (Jenkins) Lee; m. Davis McCarroll, Apr. 15, 1951; children: Linda, Karen, Frederick, Shirley. Diploma, Tuskegee U., 1948; diploma in psychiat. nursing, Ind. U. N.W., 1978. RN; CCRN; cert. pscyhiat./social work nurse. Nurse ICU St. Mary's Med. Ctr., Gary, Ind., staff RN, staff RN coronary care, retired, 1985. Contbr. articles to profl. jours. Vol. critical care area St. Mary's Med. Ctr. Home: Gary, Ind. Died Feb. 12, 2005.

MCCARTER, NEELY D., seminary president; s. Robert William and Nell (Dixon) McC.; m. Jean Maxwell, May 28, 1954; children: Robert Sidney, Robin Jeanette, Shirley Jean. AB, Presbyn. Coll., 1950, LittD, 1983; BD, Columbia Theol. Sem., 1953; postgrad., Columbia U., 1968; ThM, Union Theol. Sem., 1958; MA, Yale U., 1959, PhD, 1961. Ordained to ministry Presbyn. Ch. U.S., 1953. Pastor U. Fla., Gainesville, 1953-58; prof. Christian edn. Columbia Theol. Sem., Decatur, Ga., 1961-66; Robert and Lucy Reynolds Critz prof. Christian edn. Union Theol. Sem., Va., 1966-73, dean Va., 1973-79; pres. Pacific Sch. Religion, Berkeley, Calif., 1979-91, pres. emeritus, 1991—2006. Author: Hear the Word of the Lord, 1964; co-author: The Gospel on Campus, 1959, Help Me Understand, Lord, 1978; co-editor: Preaching In and Out of Season, 1990. Died May 10, 2006.

MCCARTHY, EUGENE JOSEPH, writer, former senator; b. Watkins, Minn., Mar. 29, 1916; s. Michael John and Anna (Baden) McC.; m. Abigail Quigley, June 1945 (separated); children— Ellen Anne, Mary Abigail, Michael Benet, Margaret Alice. AB, St. John's U., Collegeville, Minn., 1935; AM, U. of Minn., 1939. Tchr. pub. schs., 1935-40, 45; prof. econ. edn. St. John's U., 1940-42; civilian tech. work with Mil. Intelligence Div., US Dept. War, 1944; instr. sociology and econs. St. Thomas Coll., St. Paul, 1946-48; mem. 81st-85th Congresses from 4th Minn. dist., 1949-59, mem. ways and means com.; U.S. senator from Minn., 1959-70; mem. senate finance, fgn. relations and govt. ops. coms.; Adlai Stevenson prof. polit. sci. New Sch. for Social Research, 1973-74; syndicated columnist, from 1977. Dir. Harcourt Brace Jovanovich, Inc. Author: Frontiers in American Democracy, 1960, Dictionary of American Politics, 1962, A Liberal Answer to the Conservative Challenge, 1964, The Limits of Power, 1967, The Year of the People, 1969, Other Things and The Aardvark, 1970, Up 'Til Now, 1987, The Hard Years, 1975, Mr. Raccoon and His Friends, 1977,(with James J. Kilpatrick) A Political Bestiary, 1978, America Revisited, 1978, Ground Fog and Night, 1979, The Ultimate Tyrany, 1980, Gene McCarthy's Minnesota: Memories of a Native Son, 1982, Complexities and Contraries: Essays of Mild Discontent, 1982, The View from Rappahannock, 1984, Up 'Til Now: A Memoir, 1987, Required Reading A Decade of Political Wit and Wisdom, 1988, The View from Rappahannock II, 1989, (with William McGaughey) Nonfictional Economics: The Case for Shorter Hours of Work, 1989, Up Til Now, 1991, A Colony of the World: The United States Today, 1993, Required Reading, 1994, Eugene J. McCarthy: Selected Poems by Eugene J. McCarthy, 1997, No Fault Politics, 1999, An American Bestiary, 1999, 1968: War & Democracy, 2000, Hard Years: Antidotes to Authoritarians, 2001, Parting Shots From My Brittle Bow: Reflections on Am. Politics and Life, 2005. Roman Catholic. Achievements include candidate for presdl. nomination of Dem. Party, 1968, 1972, 1976, 1988, 1992. Died Dec. 10, 2005.

MCCASLIN, NELLIE, writer; b. Cleve., Aug. 20, 1914; d. Paul Giles and Nellie (Wagner) McC. BA, Case Western Res. U., 1936, MA, 1937; PhD, NYU, 1957; HHD (hon.), Ferrum Coll., 1986. Tchr. Tudor Hall Sch., Indpls., 1937-44; prof. Nat. Coll. Edn., Evanston, Ill., 1944-56, Mills Coll. Edn., N.Y.C., 1957-72; prof. dept. communications arts and sci. NYU, N.Y.C., 1972-90, adj. prof. Adj. prof. drama Tchrs. Coll. Columbia, N.Y.C., 1960-early 1970's; adv. bd. Puppetry For Early Childhood, N.Y.C., Creative Theatre, Inc., Princeton, N.J., Pact, Inc., N.Y., Police Athletic League, N.Y.C. Author: Creative Drama in the Classroom, 1968, 2d edit., 1974, 3d edit., 1980, 4th edit., 1984, 5th edit., 1990, 6th edit., 1996, Children and Drama, 1975, 2d edit., 1981, 3d edit., 1997, Creative Drama in the Elementary Grades, 1987, Historical Guide to Children's Theatre in America, 1987, Theatre for Young Audiences, 1989, Children's Theatre in the United States, a History, 2d edit., 1997; contbr. articles and plays to profl. jours. and forewards to books; appeared on World/Net, 1987. Vol. animal shelter Bide-a-Wee Home Assn. Recipient Newton D. Baker award Case Western Res. U. Alumni, 1985, Outstanding Rsch., Am. Alliance Theatre and Edn., 1987, Life Achievement award 1996, Great Tchr. award NYU, 1986; Am. Theatre Assn. fellow, 1979. Mem. Am. Alliance Theatre and Edn., Internat. Assn. Theatre for Children and Youth, Am. Assn. Theatre and Youth, Children's Theatre Assn. Am. (past pres.), Am. Theatre Assn. Democrat. Presbyterian. Avocations: animals, humane education. Home: New York, NY. Died Feb. 28, 2005.

MCCAULEY, FLOYCE REID, psychiatrist; b. Braddock, Pa., Dec. 30, 1933; d. John Mitchel and Irene (Garner) Reid; m. James Calvin McCauley, July 15, 1955; children: James Stanley, Lori Ellen. BSN, U. Pitts., 1956; DO, Coll. Osteopathic Medicine, Phila., 1972. Diplomate Am. Bd. Forensic Medicine, Am. Bd. Forensic Examiners, bd. eligible in child and adult psychiatry. Intern Suburban Gen. Hosp., Norristown, Pa., 1972-73; resident in adult psychiatry Phila. State Hosp. and Phila. Mental Health Clinic, 1973-75; fellow Med. Coll. of Pa. and Ea. Pa. Psychiat. Inst., Phila., 1975-78; Chief child psychiatry inpatient unit Med. Coll. Pa., Phila., 1978-80; med. dir. Carson ValleySch., Flourtown, Pa., 1980-82; dir. outpatient psychiat. clinic Osteopathic Med. Ctr. Phila., 1980-86; staff psychiatrist Kent Gen. Hosp., Dover, Del., 1986-89; psychiat. cons. Del. Guidance Svcs. for Children, Dover, 1986-91; clin. dir. children's unit HCA Rockford Ctr., Newark, 1991-93; with Kid's Peace Nat. Hosp. for Kids in Crisis, 1993-95; staff psychiatrist St. Lukes Quakertown Hosp., 1996-98; cons. Interact Phila., 1996-98; staff psychiatrist Del. Guidance Svcs. for Children and Youth, Dover, 1998—2001. Psychiat. cons. Cath. Charities Day Treatment Program 3-6 Yr. Olds, Dover, Del., 1990—2003, Seaford (Del.) Br. New Eng. Fellowship Rehab., 1991—93; cons. Del. Guidance Day Treatment Program, 1990—2002; mem. Mental Health Code Rev. Com., Del., 1991; staff psychiatrist Kids Peace Nat. Hosp. for Kids in Crisis, 1993—95, Penn Found., 1995—98; cons. psychiatrist Valley Day Sch., Morrisville, Pa., from 2000, Children's Svcs., Inc., Phila., from 2002. Mem. Mayor's Com. for Mental Health, Phila., 1983. Named to Chapel of Four Chaplains, Phila., 1983. Mem.: Am. Osteopathic Assn. Democrat. Methodist. Avocations: sewing, decorating, playing classical guitar, drawing, singing with copper penny players. Home: New Hope, Pa. Died Dec. 18, 2005.

MCCLATCHY, JAMES BRIGGS, newspaper publisher, editor; b. Sacramento, Calif., Dec. 17, 1920; s. Carlos K. and Phebe (Briggs) McC.; m. Susan Brewster; children: Carlos F., William B. BA, Stanford U.; MS, Columbia U. Chmn. The McClatchy Co., 1980—87, 1989—2005; pub. McClatchy Newspapers, 1987—89, 1995—2005. Past pres., dir. InterAm. Press Assn.; dir. Capital Region Inst., Sacramento; pres. Ctrl. Valley Found. Died May 26, 2006.

MCCLELLAN, JAMES PAUL, law educator, educational administrator, editor; b. Erie, Pa., June 26, 1937; s. James Charles and Florence (Turner) McC.; m. Molly Denver Synon, Oct. 2, 1976; children: Graham, Susannah, Margaret, Duncan, Angus, Douglas. BA, U. Ala., 1960; PhD, U. Va., 1964, JD, 1981. Asst. prof. polit. sci. U. Ala., Tuscaloosa, 1964-65, Emory U., Atlanta, 1965-69; assoc. prof. govt. Hampden-Sydney (Va.) Coll., 1969-74; legis. asst. U.S. Senate, Washington, 1974-76; minority counsel Subcom. Separation Powers, U.S. Senate Jud. Com., Washington, 1976-78, chief counsel, staff dir., 1981-83; pres. Ctr. Jud. Studies, Cumberland, Va., from 1983. Founder, editor Benchmark, 1983—; founder, pres. Joseph Story Soc., 1986—; mgr. Goshen Berry Farm; mem. Adminstrv. Conf. U.S., 1984-87. Author: Joseph Story and the American Constitution, 1971; (with others) The Political Principles of Robert A. Taft, 1967, Federal Regulation of Consumer Creditor Relations, 1981; bd. editors Jour. Politics, 1974-78, Modern Age, 1976—; founder, co-editor Polit. Sci. Reviewer, 1971-74; founder, editor Benchmark, 1983—. Justice of Peace, Prince Edward County, Va., 1972-76; Rep. candidate Va. Ho. Dels., 1985; trustee Benjamin Franklin U., 1985-87, James Monroe Meml. Found., 1985—. Served with USMCR, 1958-64. Rsch. grantee NEH, 1984, Earhart Found., 1969, 87, Liberty Fund, 1979. Mem. Va. Bar Assn. (spl. issues com.), Ruritan (Cumberland, Va.). Episcopalian. Died Jan. 28, 2005.

MCCLENDON, JOHN HADDAWAY, retired botanist, biology educator; b. Mpls., Jan. 17, 1921; s. Jesse Francis and Margaret (Stewart) McC.; m. Betty Morgan, June 27, 1947; children: Susan, Lise, Natalie. BA, U. Minn., 1942; PhD, U. Pa., 1951. Asst. prof. agrl. biochemistry U. Del., Newark, 1953-64; assoc. prof. botany U. Nebr., Lincoln, 1965-86, prof. biol. sci., 1987-89, ret., 1989. Contbr. articles to profl. jours. 1st lt. M.I., U.S. Army, 1942-45, CBI. NSF grantee, 1960, 65. Mem. Am. Soc. Plant Physiologists, Native Plant Soc. Oreg., Zero Population Growth, Bot. Soc. Am., Audubon Soc., Wilderness Soc., Sigma Xi. Democrat. Home: Ashland, Oreg. Died June 22, 2004.

MCCLINTICK, DURSTYNE WILLIAMSON, retired program analyst, accountant; b. Nacogdoches County, Tex., Feb. 27, 1921; d. John Hardy Williamson and Nannie Alma Fountain; m. Dwight Sterl McClintick, May 10, 1973 (dec. Oct. 1996); 1 child, Kay Lynne Fehr. BBA, Ga. State U., 1969. CPA, Ga. Appellate auditor IRS, Birmingham, Ala., 1958-63, Atlanta, 1963-68, appeals officer, 1968-70, program analyst Washington, 1970-77; ret., 1977. Treas. Edna Frazier-Cromnell Scholarship Fund, Washington, 1986—, Friends of Meridian Hill, Washington, 1993—, Washington Parks & People, 1998—; treas., coun. mem. Constituent Svc. Fund Frank Smith, Washington, 1996-98; ward 1 chair Cmty. Adv. Com. Comprehensive Plan, Washington, 1984. Democrat. Avocations: genealogy, community outreach, travel. Home: Washington, DC. Died June 10, 2004.

MCCLINTON, CURTIS ORR, statistician; b. Birmingham, Ala., Jan. 15, 1937; s. Clarence Paul and Martha Eugenia (Orr) McC.; m. Nancy Margaret Trucks, Aug. 18, 1963 (dec. Apr. 1982); children: Michael and Steven (twins). Student, Auburn U.; BS in Indsl. Mgmt., Samford U., 1959; postgrad., U. Ala., Birmingham, 1960-65; spl. tng., Applied Statistics Tng. Inst., 1975-86, Jefferson State Jr. Coll., from 1987. Jr. acct. Stockholm Valves, Birmingham, 1959-60; cost acct. Reynolds Metals Co., Birmingham, 1960-65, Rust Engring., Hunstville (Ala.) and Birmingham, 1965-72; adminstrv. analyst City Council and City Clk. Depts. City of Birmingham, 1972-75; statistician Jefferson County Health Dept. Bur. Vital Statistics, Birmingham, 1975-89; statis. analyst Jefferson County Health Dept. Environ. Health Bur., Birmingham, from 1990. Exec. v.p., coach South Roebuck Pony Baseball Little League, Birmingham, 1977-84; bd. dirs. East Side Swim Club, Birmingham, 1981-83; adv. bd. William J. Christian Community Schs., Birmingham, 1986; tchr., deacon, coach Sunday Sch., also supt. fin. com. and Royal Ambassador leader. Mem. Health Workers Assn. (bd. dirs.), Ala. Pub. Health Assn., Assn. Huntsville Area Contractors (bd. dirs. 1968), Toastmasters (local treas. 1960), Lions (chmn. mem. and scholarship com.), Alpha Kappa Psi. Republican. Baptist. Home: Birmingham, Ala. Died July 13, 2004.

MCCLURE, HAROLD MONROE, veterinary pathologist; b. Hayesville, N.C., Oct. 2, 1937; s. Elmer S. and Willie S. (Davenport) McC.; m. Joan V. Cunningham, June 7, 1958; children: Michael, Michelle, Barry. BS, N.C. State U., 1963; DVM, U. Ga., 1963. Postdoctoral fellow in pathology U. Wis., Madison, 1963-66; vet. pathologist Yerkes Primate Ctr., Emory U., Atlanta, from 1966, chief div. pathology, from 1979, assoc. dir., from 1982, asst. prof. pathology, from 1981. Mem. rev. com.s NIH, bethesda, Md.; cons. Am. Assn. Accreditation of Lab. Animal Care, Rockville, Md., 1989—; mem. AIDS adv. com. NIAID, Bethesda, 1989-91. Contbr. articles to sci. publs. Recipient numerous grants NIH, USDA, NASA. Mem. Am. Soc. Microbiology, Internat. Acad. Pathology, Phi Kappa Phi, Phi Zeta, Gamma Sigma Delta. Republican. Baptist. Achievements include patent on acutely lethal simian immunodeficiency virus. Home: Atlanta, Ga. Died Oct. 23, 2004.

MCCOLLUM, ODELL, minister; b. Reidsville, N.C., Feb. 16, 1926; s. Roy Sr. and Carrie Lee (Hodge) McC.; m. Margaret Mae Adkins, Aug. 7, 1948; children: Larry Odell and Tresa Lynette. DD (hon.), United Christian Coll., N.C., 1974; D of Sacred Letters (hon.), United Christian Coll., N.Y., 1979. Ordained to ministry United Holy Ch. Am., Inc., 1958. Pastor House of Prayer, Warren, Ohio, 1957-65, Gospel Tabernacle, Columbus, Ohio, from 1964; bishop United Holy Ch. of Am., 1972. Pres. N.W. Dist. United Holy Ch., 1980-96; 2nd v.p. United Holy Ch. of Am., 1980-92, v.p., 1992-96, pres., 1996; bd. dirs. One Church, One Child, Columbus. Program chmn. 100th Anniversary Jour., United Holy Ch. of Am., Inc., 1986. With U.S. Army, 1944-46. Democrat. Home: Gahanna, Ohio. Died Aug. 16, 2005.

MCCONNELL, ROBERT EASTWOOD, architect, educator; b. Spokane, Wash., July 15, 1930; s. Robert Ervie and Alma (Eastwood) Mc C.; m. Beverly Ann Vincent, Sept. 12, 1953; children: Kathleen Ann, Karen Eileen, Terri Lynn. B in Archtl. Engring., Wash. State U., 1952; MArch, Mass. Inst. Tech., 1954. Project architect John W. Maloney (Architect), Seattle, 1956-62; asst. prof. architecture Ariz. State U., Tempe, 1962-66, asso. prof., 1966-67; prof. U. Kans., Lawrence, 1967-69; prof., head dept. art and architecture U. Idaho, Moscow, 1969-71; prof. U. Ariz., Tucson, 1971-92, dean Coll. Architecture, 1971-77, prof. emeritus, dean emeritus Tucson, from 1992, acting assoc. dean, 1994; partner McConnell & Peterson, Architects, Tempe, 1963-66; pvt. practice architecture, 1962-96. Author, project dir.: Land Use Planning for Ariz., Ariz. Acad, 1974; Contbr. articles to profl. jours. Chmn. Idaho Gov.'s Awards Program in Arts and Humanities, 1970; project dir. Rio Salado Conceptual Study, Phoenix, 1966; bd. dirs. Tucson Regional Plan, 1972-79. Served with USAF, 1954-56. Fellow AIA (awards 1969, 76, pres. So. Ariz. chpt. 1975-76, bd. dirs. 1971-77); mem. AIA Ariz. (mem. coun. of dels. 1971-77, chmn. honor awards jury 1975), Phi Kappa Phi, Scarab, Tau Beta Pi, Sigma Tau. Home: Oro Valley, Ariz. Died Oct. 22, 2005; Vet. Meml. cemetary, Cave Creek, ariz.

MCCORD, JOAN, sociologist, educator, rsearcher; b. NYC, Aug. 4, 1930; d. Robert and Mildred Lucile (Stern) Fish; m. William Maxwell McCord, Mar. 17, 1951 (div. 1965); children: Geoffrey Sayre McCord, Robert Maxwell McCord; m. Carl Avrom Silver, June 24, 1970 (dec. July 1998). BA, Stanford U., 1952, PhD, 1968. Tchr. Concord

(Mass.) Pub. Schs., 1952-55; rsch. asst. Harvard U., Cambridge, Mass., 1955-56; rsch. assoc. Stanford (Calif.) U., 1959-65; from asst. prof. to prof. Drexel U., Phila., 1968-87; prof. criminal justice Temple U., Phila., from 1987. Sr. assoc. U. Montreal, Quebec, 1987-94, Johns Hopkins U., Balt., 1986-97; co-chair NRC Panel on Juvenile Crime: Prevention, Treatment and Control. Contbg. author: Straight and Devious Pathways From Childhood to Adulthood, 1990, At the Treshold: The Developing Adolscent, 1990, Ency. Marriage and the Family, 1995, Understanding Aggressive Behavior in Children, 1996, Nebraska Symposium on Motivation, 1997, Ency. Mental Health, 1998, Where and When: Historical and Geographical Aspects of Psychopathology, 1999, Social Dynamic of Crime and Control: New Theories for a World in Transition, 2000, Handbook of Law and Social Science: Youth and Justice, 2001, Crime and Social Orgn.: Advances in Criminological Theory, 2002, Lessons of Criminology, 2002, Violent Crime: Assessing Race and Ethnic Differences, 2003; editor: Facts, Frameworks and Forecasts: Advances in Criminological Theory, 3, 1992; editor: Coercian and Punishment in Long-Term Perspectives, 1995, Violence and Childhood in the Inner-City, 1997; co-editor: Juvenile Crime/Juvenile Justice, 2001; contbr. articles to profl. jours. Josiah Royce fellow Harvard U., 1957, Stanford Wilson fellow Stanford U., 1962-63, fellow NIMH, 1965-68, Am. Soc. Criminology, 1982, Internat Soc. for Rsch. on Aggression, 1984, U. Pa., 2003-04. Fellow Am. Acad. Exptl. Criminology (vice chair 2001-03); mem. NSF (adv. bd. 1987-91), NAS (vice-chair NRC law and justice com. 1990-96), Internat. Soc. Criminology (bd. dirs., v.p. 1995-2004, Prix Emile Durkheim award 1993), Am. Soc. Criminology (pres. 1988-89, Herbert Block award 1991, Edwin L. Sutherland award 1994), Soc. for Rsch. on Adolescence (Social Policy Best Jour. award 2002), Am. Sociol. Assn. (chair sect. on crime law and deviance 1989-90), Soc. for Life History Rsch. (chair 1990-92). Home: Narberth, Pa. Died Feb. 24, 2004.

MC CORMICK, RICHARD PATRICK, history professor; b. N.Y.C., Dec. 24, 1916; s. Patrick Austin and Anna (Smith) McC.; m. Katheryne Crook Levis, Aug. 25, 1945; children: Richard Levis, Dorothy Irene. BA, Rutgers U., 1938, MA, 1940, LittD (hon.), 1982; PhD, U. Pa., 1948. Historian, Phila. Q.M. Depot, 1942-44; instr. U. Del., 1944-45; mem. faculty Rutgers U., 1945—2006, univ. historian, 1948—2006; dean Rutgers Coll., 1974-77, prof. history, 1977-82, prof. emeritus, 1982—2006. Research adviser Colonial Williamsburg, 1953-61; Fulbright lectr. Cambridge (Eng.) U., 1961-62; Commonwealth lectr. U. London, 1971; chmn. N.J. Hist. Commn., 1967-70 Author: Experiment in Independence, 1950, History of Voting in N.J, 1953, N.J. From Colony to State, 1964, Second American Party System, 1966, Rutgers: a Bicentennial History, 1966, The Presidential Game, 1982, The Black Student Protest Movement at Rutgers, 1990; co-author: The Case of the Nazi Professor, 1989. Mem. N.J. Tercentenary Commn., 1958-60, Am. Revolution Bicentennial Commn., 1971-74. Social Sci. Research Council fellow, 1956-57 Mem. Am. Hist. Assn. (scholarly distinction award 2003), Soc. Historians of Early American Republic (pres. 1988-89), N.J. Hist. Soc. (pres. 1950-57), Phi Beta Kappa. Died Jan. 16, 2006.

MCCRAW, GLORIA JANE, elementary school educator; b. Shelby, N.C., May 24, 1947; d. Robert Lee and Neressa Marie (Humphries) Turner; m. Roger Dale McCraw, June 13, 1969; children: Sharon Leslie, Lisa Dayle, Lee David. AA, Gardner Webb, 1967; BS, Appalachian State U., 1969; MA, U. N.C., 1978. Cert. tchr., N.C. Tchr. 2d, 3rd and 4th grades Elizabeth Elem. Sch., from 1970. Recipient Vincent J. Colombo Creative Tchr. award Cleveland County Schs., Shelby, 1978. Mem. Assn. Childhood Educators Internat. (treas. 1987-89, publicity chmn. 1989-92), Alpha Delta Kappa (corr. sec. 2001-02) Democrat. Baptist. Avocations: making dried flower wreaths, water color painting, quilting. Home: Shelby, NC. Died Aug. 18, 2005.

MCCUE, ARTHUR BERNARD, city government official; b. Providence, June 27, 1926; s. Daniel Lawrence and Mary Ellen (O'Malley) McC.; m. Helen Elizabeth Flynn, Apr. 24, 1954; children: Gerald, Brian, Timothy, Julie, Joan, Marie, Joseph, Jeanette. BS, Boston Coll., 1950; LLB, Boston U., 1953; LLM, Suffolk U., 1961; MEd, U. Mass., Boston, 1985. Bar: Mass. 1955, U.S. Dist. Ct. (fed. dist.) 1957, U.S. Ct. Appeals (1st cir.) 1959, U.S. Supreme Ct. 1959, U.S. Ct. Claims 1960, U.S. Ct. Mil. Appeals 1969. Enlisted U.S. Army, 1944; advanced through grades to lt. USNR, from 1965; trial counsel Md. Casualty Co., Boston, 1968-78, chief trial counsel, 1978-86; asst. city clk. City of Somerville, Mass., 1986-88, city clk. Mass., from 1988. Mem. Mass. Def. Lawyers Assn., Def. Rsch. Inst. Roman Catholic. Avocation: physical fitness activities. Home: Somerville, Mass. Died May 13, 2004.

MCCULLOUGH, THOMAS FRANCIS, retired educator; b. L.A., Nov. 12, 1922; s. Thomas E. and Margaret (Babbitt) McC. BSChemE, U. Notre Dame, 1948, MS in Chemistry, 1949; PhD, U. Utah, 1955. Joined Brothers of Holy Cross, Roman Cath. Ch., 1957. Field test lab. staff Ariz. State Hwy. Dept., Flagstaff, 1949—50; analytical chemist Union Oil Co., Wilmington, Calif., 1950—51; chemistry tchr. St. Edwards U., Austin, Tex., 1958-93; retired, 1994. Rschr. SUNY, Syracuse, 1974—75. Contbr. articles to profl. jours. With U.S. Army, 1943-46. Rsch. grantee NSF, 1960, 1964-65. Mem. Austin Tex. Stamp Club (v.p., pres.). Avocations: hiking, stamp collecting/philately. Home: Austin, Tex. Died Oct. 17, 2004.

MCCUNE, EDWARD ALLISON, general surgeon; b. Tahlequah, Okla., Nov. 3, 1930; s. Edward Henry and Vera (Allison) McC.; m. Margaret Douglas Rucks, Jan. 29, 1960; children: Allison, Joe, Evelyn, Louisa. Student, Westminster Coll., Fulton, Mo., 1948-50, Northeastern State U., Tahlequah, 1950-51; MD, U. Okla., Oklahoma City, 1955. Diplomate Am. Bd. Surgery. Resident in surgery Univ. Hosp., Oklahoma City, 1955-60; pvt. practice, Enid, Okla., 1962-64 and from 67, Oklahoma City, 1965-67. Mem. staff St. Mary's Hosp., Enid, 1962-64, 67—, chief surgery, chief staff, trustee, past pres.; mem. staff Bass Hosp., Enid, 1962-64, 67—, chief staff; mem. staff Presbyn. Hosp., Oklahoma City, 1965-67. Mem. Enid City Coun., 1983-87. Capt. USAF, 1960-62. Mem. ACS (pres. Okla. chpt.), Okla. Surg. Assn. (past pres.), Southwestern Surg. Congress, Soc. Am. Gastrointestinal Endoscopic Surgeons, Rotary. Republican. Presbyterian. Avocations: golf, flying, hunting, plectrum banjo. Home: Enid, Okla. Died May 15, 2005.

MCCUNE, ELLIS E., retired academic administrator, education educator, consultant; b. Houston, July 17, 1921; s. Ellis E. and Ruth (Mason) McC.; m. Hilda May Whiteman, Feb. 8, 1946; 1 son, James Donald. Student, Sam Houston State U., 1940-42; BA, UCLA, 1948, PhD, 1957; LHD, Golden Gate U., 1994. Teaching asst. UCLA, 1949-51; from instr. to assoc. prof. polit. sci. Occidental Coll., Los Angeles, 1951-59, chmn. applied politics and econs. curriculum, 1951-56; asst. prof. Calif. State U., Northridge, 1959-61, assoc. prof., chmn. dept. polit. sci., 1961-63, prof., 1963, dean letters and sci., 1963; dean acad. planning Calif. State Univs. and Colls., 1963-67; pres. Calif. State U., Hayward, 1967-90, pres. emeritus, 1991—2006; acting chancellor The Calif. State U. System, 1990-91, ret., 1991. Cons. govtl. units and agys.; lectr., panelist; mem. Calif. State Scholarship and Loan Commn., 1964-68, chmn., 1967-68; pres. Govtl. Adminstrn. Group Los Angeles, 1959; chair planning com., mem. exec. com., bd. dirs. Eden Med. Ctr. Found., 1994-2003, pres.-elect, 1995-97, pres., 1997-99. Chmn. univs. and colls. div. United Bay Area Crusade, 1969-70, 73-74; bd. dirs. Oakland (Calif.) Museum Assn., 1974-77, 86-88, Hayward Area Hist. Soc., 1998-2004; vice chmn. higher edn. div., East Bay United Way, 1989-90; mem. arts adv. council, 1986-87, devel. com., 1988-89, Bay Area Urban League, bd. trust Calif. Coun. Econ. Edn. No. sect., Emergency Shelter Program Adv. Coun., Hayward Area Hist. Assn., NAACP Hayward chpt.; trustee Calif. Council Econ. Edn.; sec. bd. dirs. Eden Community Found., 1978-79; rsch. fellow Haynes Found, 1957. With USAAF, 1942-46. Mem. Am. Coun. Edn. (adv. com. 1970-72, inst. coll. & univ. adminstrs. 1973-74, bd. dirs. 1985-86), Western Assn. Schs. and Colls. (accrediting commn. sr. colls. and univs. 1974-78, chmn., 1978-82, pres. 1979-81), N.W. Assn. Schs. and Colls. (commn. colls. 1974-80), Assn. Am. Colls. (bd. dirs. 1972-75, vice chmn. 1975-76), Assn. Western Univs. (bd. dirs.), Coun. Postsecondary Accreditation (bd. dirs. 1977-88, exec. com. 1979-88, chmn. 1985-87, immediate past chmn., 1988-89, chmn. com. recognition 1982-84), Am. Assn. State Colls. and Univs. (chmn. accreditation com. 1983-86, com. acad. pers. and acad. freedom 1987-88, com. on acad. affairs 1988-91), Calif. Coun. Edn. (trustee), Western Polit. Sci. Assn. (exec. coun. 1958-61), Hayward C. of C. (dir. 1968-71, 73-76, 77-80, 82-85, 86-90), Regional Assn. East Bay Colls. and Univs. (exec. com. 1974-90, sec. 1975-76, 87-88, vice chmn. 1976-77, 84-85, chmn. 1977-79, 85-86), Rotary, Phi Beta Kappa, Pi Gamma Mu, Pi Sigma Alpha. Clubs: Bohemian (San Francisco). Home: Palm Desert, Calif. Died Apr. 18, 2006.

MCDANIEL, PAUL WILLIAM, physicist, researcher; b. Robards, Ky., Jan. 1, 1916; s. Leslie Elbert and Lillie (Ligon) McD.; m. Loreen Webb, June 4, 1937 (div. Aug. 1975); m. Kathryn Mitchell, Aug. 16, 1975. BS, Western Ky. U., 1936; MA, Ind. U., 1938, PhD, 1941. Dep. dir. rsch. AEC, Washington, 1950-60, dir. rsch., 1960-72; pres. Argonne U. Assn., Washington and Argonne, Ill., 1973-75, ret., 1975. Maj. U.S. Army, 1942-45. Home: Glendale, Ariz. Died May 31, 2004.

MC DERMOTT, ROBERT FRANCIS, retired insurance company executive; b. Boston, July 31, 1920; BS, U.S. Mil. Acad., 1943; MBA, Harvard U., 1950. Commd. USAF, 1943, advanced through grades to brig. gen.; dean faculty USAF Acad., 1956—68; pres., chmn. United Svcs. Auto. Assn., San Antonio, 1968—93. CEO, pres. La Cantera Devel. Co., La Cantera Hospitality, Inc., Fiesta Tex. Showpark, Inc., HTO, Inc. Author articles in field. Died Aug. 28, 2006.

MCDEVITT, BRIAN PETER, historian, poet; b. Jersey City, Dec. 29, 1944; s. Bernard Aloysius and Veronica Sabina (Decker) McD.; m. Dorothy Helen Gilligan, Oct. 19, 1968; children: Peter David, Timothy Bernard. BS, Seton Hall U., 1966; MA, Columbia U., 1971; DLitt, Drew U., 2004. Tchr. history St. Patrick's High Sch., Elizabeth, N.J., 1966-68, Vail Deane High Sch., Elizabeth, N.J., 1968-70; fed. grant writer Alexian Bros. Hosp., Elizabeth, N.J., 1970-72, Union County Coll., Cranford, N.J., 1972-76; prin., owner Ednl. Svcs., Westfield, NJ, 1976—88; pub. Libr. Sales NJ, from 1988. Adj. prof. history Union County Coll., Cranford, N.J., 1976-2002; adj. prof. classics Montclair (N.J.) State U., 1990-2002. Author: The Irish Librists, 1988, The Irish Librists and the Scrolls of Aristotle, 1993, A Historian's Thematic Study of Western Civilization, 1994, Evidence of an Ancient Greek Navigation System, 1995, The Irish Librists and The Vatican Library Mystery, 1996, A Definition of Western Civilization, 1997, Ancient Greeks: First Navigators, 2000, Ten Historical Odes, 2001, Twenty-Three Sonnets, 2001, Arthur Brooke's Poem: The Tragic HIstory of Rome and Juliet, revised, 2002, (video) The Minoans According to Sir Arthur Evans, Experiments in Odes asnd Sonnets, 2003, The Trirewie Experiment (video), 2004; contbr. articles to profl. jours. N.J. Dept. Higher Edn. grantee. Mem. Trireme Trust U.S.A. (internat. rowing team 1990), Friends of Trireme (London), Soc. Naval Architects and Marine Engrs., Assn. Ancient Historians, Soc. Ancient Greek Philosophy, Assn. Muslim Social Scientists, Classical Assn. of Atlantic States, Keats-Shelley Meml. Assn. (London and Rome), Am. Soc. Naval Engrs., Westfield United Fund, Westfield P.A.L., Westfield Basketball Assn., Westfield Baseball Assn., Boy Scouts Am, US Naval Inst. Roman Catholic. Avocations: golf, rowing, basketball, playing piano, stamp collecting/philately. Died Aug. 3, 2005.

MCDONALD, CHARLES EDWARD, lawyer; b. El Paso, Tex., Nov. 13, 1957; s. Carlos and Armida (Adauto) McD.; 1 child, Miranda Lee. BA in Philosophy, U. St. Thomas, Houston, 1980; JD, South Tex. Coll. Law, 1985. Bar: Tex. 1985, U.S. Ct. Appeals. (5th cir.) 1991, U.S. Supreme Ct. 1992. Prin. Law Office Charles E. McDonald, El Paso, 1985-2000, McDonald and Assocs, El Paso, from 2000. Comms. liaison Coleman Re-election Congl. Campaign, El Paso, 1984, 86. Mem. ATLA, Tex. Trial Lawyers Assn., State Bar Tex., El Paso County Bar Assn. (ethics com. 1997-98, rules com. 1997-98, clin. law coun. 1997-98), Nat. Assn. Cave Divers. Roman Catholic. Avocations: cave diving, chess, travel, foreign language (spanish). Died June 1, 2005.

MCDONALD, DONALD BURT, environmental engineering educator, consultant; b. Salt Lake City, Utah, Mar. 5, 1932; s. Donald T. and Dorthea (Miller) McD.; m. Marilyn Pratt, June 19, 1954 (div. 1967); children: Barbara, Karen, Donald; m. Ardis J. Brower, July 23, 1977 (dec. May 1988); m. Barbara Haslam, Nov. 25, 1988. BS, U. Utah, 1954, MS, 1956, PhD, 1962. Project dir. Utah Fish & Game Dept., Salt Lake City, 1958-60; instr. Carbon Coll., Price, Utah, 1960-62; prof. U. Iowa, Iowa City 1962-92, prof. emeritus, 1992—; cons. various utilities and engring. firms. Served to sgt. U.S. Army, 1949-52, Korea. Mem. Water Pollution Control Fedn., Am. Water Works Assn., Am. Soc. Testing Materials. Avocations: skiing, backpacking. Home: Iowa City, Iowa. Died Apr. 30, 2004.

MCDONALD, JOHN CECIL, lawyer; b. Lorimor, Iowa, Feb. 19, 1924; s. Cecil F. and Mary Elsie (Fletcher) McD.; m. Barbara Joan Berry, May 8, 1943; children: Mary Elisabeth (Mrs. Dell Richard), Joan Frances (Mrs. Andrew Ackerman), Jean Maurine. Student, Simpson Coll., 1942, So. Ill. U., 1943; JD, Drake U., 1948. Bar: Iowa 1948, U.S. Ct. Mil. Appeals 1956, U.S. Supreme Ct. 1956. Practiced in, Dallas Center, Iowa, from 1948; sr. ptnr. McDonald, Brown & Fagen and predecessor firms, from 1971; county atty. Dallas County, 1958-62; asst. county atty., 1963-69; city atty. Dallas Center, 1956-80. Mem. Simpson Coll. Alumni Council, pres., 1977-80; legal adviser Dallas Community Bd. Edn., 1953-69, pres., mem., 1968-76; nat. adv. com. Cen. Coll.; alt. del. Iowa Coordinating Council for Post-High Sch. Edn.; finance chmn. Dallas County Rep.Cen. Com., 1954-63, chmn., 1963-68; chmn. Iowa 7th Congl. Dist. Rep. Cen. Com., 1968-69, Iowa Rep. Cen. Com., 1969-75; mem. Rep. Nat. Com., 1969-88, mem. exec. com., 1973—; mem. Rule 29 com., com. on reform; mem. Gov. Iowa's inaugural com., 1969, 71, 73, 75, 79; del. Rep. Nat. Conv., 1964, 72, 76, 80, 84, chmn. com. on contests, 1976, 80, 84, 88, chmn. com. on credentials, 1976, 80, 88, mem. com. on arrangements and exec. com. of com. on arrangements, 1976, 80, 84, mem. rules rev. com., 1977-84; chmn. Midwest Rep. State Chairmen's Assn., 1973-75, Nat. Rep. State Chairmen's Adv. Com., 1973-75; hon. co-chmn. Vice Pres.'s Inaugural, 1981; trustee Dallas County Hosp., Perry, Iowa; bd. visitors U.S. Air Force Acad., 1975-78, chmn., 1977-78; trustee Simpson Coll., 1978—; bd. dirs. Iowa Student Loan Liquidity Corp., 1987-99; mem. Iowa Coll. Aid Commn., 1989—; mem. Iowa Bd. Regents, 1981-87, pres., 1985-87; bd. dirs. Iowa Public Broadcasting Network, 1981-85; U.S. commr. Am. Battle Monuments Commn., 1982-94. Served with USAAF, 1942-46; Col. USAF, 1951-52, ret. Recipient Alumni Achievement award Simpson Coll., 1974; Disting. Service award Drake U., 1978 Mem. ABA, Iowa Bar Assn. (past chmn. spl. com. on mil. affairs, mem. mil. affairs com.), Dallas County Bar Assn. (past pres.), Am. Legion, Farm Bur., Blackfriars, Drake U. Law Sch. Alumni Assn. (class officer), Comml. Club (past pres.) (Dallas Ctr.), Hillcrest Country Club (past pres.) (Adel, Iowa), Des Moines Club, Masons (32 degree), Shriners, Rotary (past pres. Dallas Ctr.), Alpha Tau Omega, Delta Theta Phi, Alpha Psi Omega. Clubs: Des Moines. Lodges: Masons (32 deg.), Shriners, Rotary (pas pres. Dallas Ctr.). Presbyterian. Home: Dallas Center, Iowa. Died Dec. 2, 2005.

MCDONALD, MARGUERITE FULLER, secondary school educator; b. Arlington, Mass., July 2, 1911; d. Walton Boutelle and Mary Florence (Dow) Fuller; m. Victor A. George, June 16, 1938 (dec. June 1960); children: Victor Walton, Francis Fuller; m. Harry J. McDonald, July 28, 1968. BS, Edinboro (Pa.) U., 1933. Art tchr., Aliquippa, Pa., 1933-39, Beaver (Pa.) Area Sch. Dist., 1956-73; tchr. adults Pa. State U., Monaca, Pa., 1964-68; drawing tchr. pvt. sch. Sanibal, Fla., 1976-77, Sanibel Captiva Art League, 1976-80, ret., 1980. Tchr. art history, art for elem. tchrs. Geneva (Pa.) Coll. extension, East Liverpool, Ohio, 1964-68. Bazaar chmn. Tusca-Ridge Garden Club, Beaver, 1973-86. Mem. AAUW. Avocations: doll house restoration, horticulture, flower arranging. Home: Lutz, Fla. Died May 22, 2005.

MCDONALD, PAUL KIMBALL, lawyer, investment executive; b. Worcester, Mass., June 8, 1932; s. Irving Thomas McDonald and Marie Agnes Haggerty; m. Sally Lou Kirkendall, Oct. 26, 1957; children: Katrina Louise Greenly, Linda Marie Bennett, Heidi Ann Bishop. AB, Harvard U., 1953, LLB, 1956, JD, 1957. Asst. to pres. W.R. Grace & Co., N.Y.C., 1956-65; pres. Paul McDonald & Co., N.Y.C., 1965-89. Bd. dirs. several corps. Trustee St. Vincent's Hosp., N.Y.C., 1967-74, N.Y. Foundling Hosp., 1967-74, others. Home: Greenwich, Conn. Died July 21, 2005.

MCDONALD, STEPHEN EUGENE, forest services administrator; b. Orofino, Idaho, Apr. 25, 1940; s. Eugene Maurice and Sundy Carolyn (Crum) McD.; m. Janet (Jill) Ilene Lawrence; children: Kenneth Frederick, Robert Norman. BS in Forestry, U. Idaho, 1962, MF, 1975; PhD in Forestry, Colo. State U., 1981. Forester U.S. Forest Svc. Clearwater Nat. Forest, Orofino, 1962-65; supr. forester U.S. Forest Svc. Coeur D'Alene (Idaho) Nat. Forest, 1965-75; western nursery specialist U.S. Forest Svc. Region 2, Denver, 1975-80; nursery, tree improvement staff U.S. Forest Svc. Chief's Office, Washington, 1980-83; dir. U.S. Forest Svc., Broomall, Pa., 1983-84; rsch. biologist U.S. Forest Svc. Timber Mgmt., Washington, 1984-87; supr. rsch. biologist, asst. dir. U.S. Forest Svc. Rocky Mountain Sta., Ft. Collins, Colo., from 1987. Mem. Soc. Am. Foresters, Xi Sigma Pi, Sigma X, Phi Kappa Phi. Home: Manassas, Va. Died Sept. 12, 2004.

MCDOUGAL, IVAN ELLIS, artist; b. Lometa, Tex., June 29, 1927; s. Ellis and Bertha (Robbins) McD.; m. Gloria Deal, Dec. 17, 1949; children: Dana Marlene, Celia Annette, Lea Elaine. Student, Schreiner Inst., 1947-48, Trinity U., 1948-49, Am. Acad. Art, 1949-50. Illustrator Express-News, San Antonio; advtsg. art dir. San Antonio Light, 1954-74, advtsg. promotion mgr., 1974-84. Featured in The Texas Hill Country Interpretations, 1981, Pecos to the Rio Grande Interpretations by 18 Artists, 1983, La. Watercolor Soc. (World Trade Ctr. Purchase prize, 1996); permanent collections include McNay Art Mus., San Antonio; contbr. articles to profl. jours. Founding mem. Watercolor Gang, 1964. With USN, 1945—47. Recipient Best of Show award 1st We. Fedn. Exhbn., 1976, Top 100 Nat. Arts for the Parks Exhbn., 1990, 92. Mem. Tex. Watercolor Soc. (7 awards 1972-91, Founders Meml. award 2001), San Antonio Watercolor Group (3 awards 1980-84), San Antonio Art League (Artist of Yr. 1978, 8 awards 1965-98). Avocation: golf. Home: San Antonio, Tex. Died Nov. 26, 2005.

MCDOUGALL, GERALD DUANE, lawyer; b. Hammond, Ind., Sept. 18, 1931; s. John and Carol Maxine (Lind) McD.; m. Ingrid Rosina Kempf, Jan. 26, 1960 (dec. 2000); children: Manfred, James. JD, Mercer U., 1971. Bar: U.S.V.I. 1972, Colo. 1973, Germany 1973, Tex. 1985. Atty. US V.I. Dept. Labor, St. Thomas, 1971-72; pvt. practice, Denver, 1972-74, 76-84, Heilbronn, Neckar, Germany, 1974-76, Amarillo, Tex., from 1985. Precinct committeeman Rep. Ctrl. Com., Denver, 1978-84. Sgt. U.S. Army, 1951-54, ETO, 61-67, Vietnam. Mem. Tex. Bar Assn., Tex. Criminal Defense Lawyers Assn., Amarillo Bar Assn. Home: Amarillo, Tex. Died Nov. 14, 2004.

MCENTEE, JAMES PATRICK, SR., human relations executive; b. Oakland, Calif., Apr. 9, 1931; s. James and Mary (Kelly) McE.; m. Ann J. Mainland, Aug. 18, 1973; children: Mona, Jesse, Maria Elena, Dianne, James, Chinecy, Amy K., Peter M. BA, St. Joseph's Coll., 1957; MDiv., St. Patrick's Sem., 1973; AA, San Jose City Coll., 1979. Pastoral assoc. Roman Catholic Archdiocese of San Francisco, 1957-73; exec. dir. Vol. Action Ctr., San Jose, Calif., 1973-76; dir. human rels. County of Santa Clara, San Jose, Calif., from 1976. Counselor A&J Assoc., San Jose, 1974-94. Pres. Calif. Assn. Human Rights Orgn., 1986-90; chairperson Mexican Am. United for Progress, Morgan Hill, Calif., 1969-73. Recipient Commendation award NAACP, 1990, Commendation award Asian Law Alliance, 1984, Commendation award Am. Indian Ctr., 1989; named Family of Yr. B'Hai Cmty., San Jose, 1994. Democrat. Roman Catholic. Avocations: walking, swimming. Home: San Jose, Calif. Died Sept. 13, 2004.

MCFADDEN, ROBERT CLYDE, real estate broker; b. Fullerton, Calif., Oct. 22, 1949; s. John W. and Beverly (Cross) McF.; m. Tina McFadden, Oct. 20, 1991 (div. Oct. 1995); children: Julie, Robert C., Carson, Shawnee. AA, Western Nev. C.C. Real estate broker Champions, Inc., Carson City, Nev., from 1978, mobile home dealer, from 1985. Restored 1862 St. Charles hotel across from Nev. capitol, 1995, Mills Mansion, 1998, home used in The Shootist, last John Wayne movie, 1991. Candidate for mayor of Carson City, 1992, 96. With U.S. Army, 1970-72. Mem. Nev. Art Mus., Nev. Mus., Nev. Hist. Soc. Republican. Achievements include donation of $30,000 to Va.-Truckee R.R. reconstruction; designing of 30-mile running trail around Carson City, 1996. Home: Carson City, Nev. Died Nov. 17, 2004.

MCFARLAND, GARY LANE, fire protection engineer, consultant; b. Memphis, Apr. 21, 1952; s. Jasper Anderson Jr. and Maxine (Hardy) McF.; m. Terry Lorraine Moore, Aug. 20, 1970 (div. July 1984); children: Joshua, Jeremy, Justin. Student, Air Force C.C., Gulfport, Miss., 1985-86, Nat. Inst. for Cert. in Engring. Techs., Memphis, 1988-89. Electrician AC Electric, Memphis, 1970-72; owner, mgr. McFarland & Son, Hickory Valley, Tenn., 1973-81; draftsman McFarland & Assocs., Memphis, 1981-85, cons., from 1991; engr. LASCO Fire Protection, Memphis, 1986-88; owner, engr. Bi-Mac Cons., Memphis, 1988-89; engr. Grinnell Fire Protection Corp., Memphis, 1989-90, salesman, 1990-93, dist. mgr., from 1993. Cons., Jones, MAH, Gaskil, Rhodes Architecture, Memphis, 1988—, Belz Investment Corp., Memphis, 1987—, Boyle Investment Corp., Memphis, 1991—. Sec. Ruritan Civic Club, Hardeman County, Tenn., 1981; rep. Small Farmers Am., Bolivar, Tenn., 1975. Staff sgt. Tenn. Army N.G., 1985-92. Mem. Soc. Fire Protection Engrs., Nat. Fire Protection Assn., Comml. and Indsl. Assn., Memphis C. of C., Memphis Zool. Soc. Republican. Avocations: photography, civil war history, wildlife art, painting, antique weaponry. Home: Memphis, Tenn. Died Apr. 2, 2004.

MCFARLAND, NAOMI LOUISE, school system administrator; b. Chillicothe, Ohio, Feb. 19, 1947; d. William Harrison and Vera Marie (Hott) Smith; m. John Alfred Immell, Aug. 29, 1970 (div. 1974); 1 child, Jon; m. John Allen McFarland, July 10, 1976; children: Jamie, Lisa. Student, Ohio U., Chillicothe, 1965-66, Mata Coll., Columbus, Ohio, 1967. Supr. Reynolds Aluminum Co., Ashville, Ohio, 1970-77; bus driver Westfall Local Schs., Williamsport, Ohio, 1983-92, dir. transp., from 1992, tchr., 1985-93. Orgn. advisor 4-H Club, Circleville, Ohio, 1988-95. Recipient cert. of achievement Ohio Dept. Edn., 1991, safe driving award Franklin County Bd. Edn., 1992, 93. Mem. Ohio Assn. for Pupil Transp., Ohio Assn. Sch. Bus Ofcls. (chairperson Ohio Sch. Bus ROAD-E-O, ctrl. region, judge regional and state sch. bus road E-O 1996). Methodist. Avocations: reading, travel, music, sports, gardening. Home: New Holland, Ohio. Died Feb. 17, 2004.

MC FEE, THOMAS STUART, retired federal agency administrator; b. Delafield, Wis., Nov. 19, 1930; s. Leon Worrick and Margurette Ella (Morris) McFee; m. Mary Virginia Butler, June 7, 1952; children: Richard Stuart, John Worrick, Charles Paxton. BS, U. Md., 1953, postgrad., 1956-60. Mathematician math. computation divsn. David Taylor Model Basin, Navy Dept., Washington, 1956-58, dir. sys. analysis br. ops. rsch. divsn., 1958-62; project leader weapons sys. evaluation group U.S. Dept. Def., 1962-65; tech. asst. to dir. Sci. and Tech. Office, Exec. Office of Pres., White House, 1965-66; dir. sys. devel. HEW, 1967-69, dep. asst. sec. for program sys., planning and evaluation, 1969-71, dep. asst. sec. for mgmt. planning and tech., 1971-77, dep. asst. sec. for mgmt., 1977-78; asst. sec. for pers. adminstrn. US Dept. Health & Human Services, 1978-95. With USAF, 1954-56. Mem. Am. Soc. Pub. Adminstrn., Am. Consortium for Internat. Pub. Adminstrn., Nat. Acad. Pub. Adminstrn. (elected). Home: Ashton, Md. Died June 14, 2006.

MCGAHERN, JOHN, writer; b. Dublin, Nov. 12, 1934; s. John and Susan (McManus) McG.; m. Madeline Green, 1973. DLitt (hon.), Dublin U., Ireland, 1991, Galway U., 1993. Tchr. St. John the Baptist Boys Nat. Sch., 1956-63; rsch. fellow U. Reading, 1968-71; O'Connor prof. Colgate U., 1969, 72, 77, 79, 83. Author: (novels) The Barracks, 1963 (A.E. Meml. award 1962), The Dark, 1965, The Leavetaking, 1974, The Pornographer, 1979, The Rockingham Shoot, 1987, Amongst Women, 1990 (GPA Book award, Irish Times award, shortlisted Booker Prize, 1990), The Power of Darkness, 1991, By the Lake, 2003; (short stories) Nightlines, 1970, Getting Through, 1978, High Ground, 1985, The Collected Stories, 1992; (memoir) All Will Be Well, 2006; (radio plays) Sinclair, 1971; (teleplays) Swallows, 1975, The Rockingham Shoot, 1987. British No. Arts fellow, 1974-76; McCauley fellow, 1964; recipient Soc. of Authors award, 1967, British Arts Coun. award, 1968, 70, 73, 81, Am. Irish Found. Lit. award, 1985, Galway Festival Tenth Anniv. award, 1987, Irish Times-Aer Lingus Lit. prize, 1990; decorated Chevalier Ordre des Arts et des Lettres, 1989, GPA Literature award, 1992, Prix de Literature Etrangere Ecureuil, 1994. Mem. Aosdana Irish Acad. Letters. Died Mar. 30, 2006.

MCGARIGLE, WILLIAM JOHN, video producer, camera operator; b. Boston, Jan. 16, 1932; s. John Edward and Florence Irene (Dalton) McG.; m. Gretchen Jean Ritter, July 31, 1965 (div. Oct. 1990); children: Jennifer Elisa, Carolyn Jo. AA, El Camino Coll., 1959; BA, Calif. State U., Long Beach, 1962, MA, 1964. Cert. jr. coll. tchr., Calif. Assoc. prof. English Riverside (Calif.) City Coll., 1964-67, Ventura (Calif.) Coll., 1967-69; freelance writer, 1969-78; instr. radio-TV Univ. La Verne (Calif.), 1979-81, dir. dept. radio-TV, pres. Univ. La Verne Prodns., Inc., 1981-84; v.p., producer Ultimate Video, Glendora, Calif., 1984; pres., producer Bill McGarigle Prodns., Claremont, Calif., from 1984. Relief cameraman, field engr. Eye Witness News Sta. KABC-TV, Los Angeles, 1981. Co-producer, dir. (video documentary) Tale of New Cities, 1981; producer, dir., co-writer TV history series The Story of Orange County, Part III, 1989. Fellow Phi Kappa Phi; mem. Internat. Documentary Assn., Am. Film Inst., Nat. Assn. Broadcasters and Technicians, Internat. Photographers Guild. Avocation: sailing. Home: Claremont, Calif. Died July 13, 2005.

MCGAVIN, DARREN, actor, director, producer; b. Spokane, Wash., May 7, 1922; s. Reid Delano Richardson and Grace (Bogart) McG.; m. Melanie York, March 20, 1944 (div. 1969), children: York, Megan, Bridget, Bogart; m. Kathie Browne (dec. Apr., 8, 2003), Dec. 31, 1969 Student, U. Pacific, 1 year, Neighborhood Playhouse, 6 months; BFA, Actors Studio. Pres., chief exec. Taurean Films (S.A.), Tympanum Corp. Plays include Captain Brassbound's Conversion, The Rainmaker, Tunnel of Love, My Three Angels, Dinner at Eight, The Innkeepers, The King and I (revival, Lincoln Ctr., N.Y.C.; Film appearances include A Song to Remember, 1945, Counter-Attack, 1945, Kiss and Tell, 1945, She Wouldn't Say Yes, 1945, Fear, 1946, Queen for a Day, 1951, Summer Madness, 1955, The Court Martial of Billy Mitchell, 1955, The Man with the Golden Arm, 1956, The Delicate Delinquent, 1957, Beau James, 1957, The Case Against Brooklyn, 1958, Bullet for a Badman, 1964, The Great Sioux Massacre, 1965, African Gold, 1966, Mission Mars, 1968, Anatomy of a Crime, 1969, Love American Style, 1970, Mrs. Pollifax, Spy, 1970, The Petty Story, 1972, B Must Die, 1973, The Poetry Story, 1974, 43: The Richard Petty Story, 1974, Hay que matar a B, 1975, Crackle of Death, 1976, The Demon and the Mummy, 1976, No Deposit, No Return, 1976, Airport '77, 1977, Hot Lead and Cold Feet, 1978, Repo, 1980, Zero to Sixty, 1980, Hangar 18, 1980, Firebird 2015 AD, 1981, A Christmas Story, 1984, The Natural, 1984, Raw Deal, 1985, Turk 182!, 1985, Flag, 1986, From the Hip, 1986, Dead Heat, 1988, Captain America, 1990, Blood and Concrete, 1990, In the Name of Blood, 1990, Happy Hell Night, 1992, Billy Madison, 1995, Still Waters Burn, 1996, Small Time, 1996, Pros and Cons, 1999; (TV series) Crime Photographer, 1951-52, Mike Hammer, 1958-59, Riverboat, 1959-61, The Outsider, 1968-69, The Night Stalker, 1974-75, Small and Frye, 1983, Murphy Brown, 1990 (Emmy award), Miracles & Other Wonders; (TV mini-series) Ike, 1979, The Martian Chronicles, 1980, Freedom to Speak, 1982, Arounf the World in 80 Days, 1989,; (TV films) The Legend of Jud Starr, 1967, The Outsider, 1967, The Forty-Eight Hour Mile, 1970, The Challenge, 1970, Tribes, 1970, The Berlin Affair, 1970, Tribes, 1970, Banyon, 1971, Mrs. Pollifax--Spy, 1971, The Death of Me Yet, 1971, The Night Stalker, 1972, Something Evil, 1972, The Rookies, 1972, Here Comes the Judge, 1972, Say Goodbye, Maggie Cole, 1972, The Night Strangler, 1973, The Six Million Dollar Man, 1973, Law and Order, 1976, Brink's: The Great Robbery, 1976, The Night Stalker, 1977, The Users, 1978, A Bond of Iron, 1979, Donovan's Kid, 1979, Not Until Today, 1979, Love for Rent, 1979, Waikiki, 1980, The Baron and the Kid, 1984, The Return of Marcus Welby, M.D., 1984, My Wicked, Wicked Ways...The Legend of Errol Flynn, 1985, Tales From the Hollywood Hills, 1987, Inherit the Wind, 1988, The Diamind Trap, 1988, Kojak: Its Always Something, 1990, Child in the Night, 1990, By Dawn's Early Light, 1990, Clara, 1991, Perfect Harmony, 1991, Mastergate, 1992, The American Clock, 1993, A Perfect Stranger, 1994, Fudge-A-Mania, 1995, Derby, 1995; (TV appearances) Tales of Tomorrow, 1952, Goodyear Television Playhouse, 1952, Short Short Dramas, 1953, Danger, 1952, 1953, The Revlon Movie Theater, 1953, The Philco Television Playhouse, Suspense, Campbell Playhouse, Mama, 1954, Kraft Television Theater, 1954, Alfred Hitchcock Presents, 1955, Armstrong Circle Theatre, It's Always Jan, 1956, Climax, 1956, Robert Montgomery Presents, 1956, The Alcoa Hour, 1957, Studio One, Decision, 1958, The Islanders, 1961, Stagecoach West, 1961, Death Valley Days, 1961, Route 66, 1961, Rawhide, 1961, Purex Summer Specials, 1962, The United States Steel Hour, 1964, The Alfred Hitchcock Hour, 1964, The Nurses, 1964, The Defenders, 1964, Bob Hope Presents the Chrysler Theatre, 1964, Ben Casey, 1964, The Rogues, 1965, Dr. Kildare, 1965, Confidential for Women, 1966, Court Martial, 1966, Felony Squad, 1966, Gunsmoke, 1966, The Virginian, 1967, The Man From U.N.C.L.E., 1967, Mission: Impossible, 1967, Custer, 1967, Mannix, 1970, The Name of the Game, 1970, Braken's World, 1970, Matt Lincoln, 1970, Cade's County, 1971, The Bold Ones: The Lawyers, 1971, Police Story, 1974, Owen Marshall: Counsellor at Law, 1974, Shaft, 1974, The Evil Touch, 1974, Win, 1980; The Love Boat, 1980, Nero Wolfe, 1981, Magnum P.I., 1981,Disneyland, 1982, Tales of Unexpected, 1983, The Hitchhiker, 1985, Tales From the Darkside, 1985, Worlds Beyond, 1986, Highway to Heaven, 1988, Monsters, 1989, Civil Wars, 1992, Sibs, 1992, Murder, She Wrote, 1992, Burke's Law, 1995, Sisters, 1995, Gargyles, 1995, The Commish, 1995, Grace Under Fire, 1996, Touched by an Angel, 1997, Millenium, 1997, The X Files, 1999, Night Stalker, 2005; actor, dir. (films) Happy Mother's Day-...Love, George, 1973; dir., writer (films) American Reunion, 1976. Mem. Screen Actors Guild, Actors Equity Assn., Dirs. Guild Am., Writers Guild Am., AFTRA Died Feb. 25, 2006.

MCGEE, PAMELA J., secondary school educator; b. Loraine, Tex., May 1, 1952; d. Printis J. and Estelle Ward McGee. BS, La. Tech. U., 1973, MA, 1992. Cert. tchr. Tex., La. Tchr. Port Arthur (Tex.) Ind. Sch. Dist., 1975—78; adminstr. law firm, Houston, 1978—90; tchr. Union Parish Schs., Farmerville, La., 1991—92, Marshall (Tex.) Ind. Sch. Dist., from 1992; adj. faculty Panola Jr. Coll., Carthage and Jefferson, Tex., from 1992, Tex. State Tchrs. Coll., Marshall, from 1992. Dept. chair, spl. edn. Marshall High Sch., from 1997. Recipient Outstanding Spl. Edn. Tchr. award, Rotary Internat., 1999. Mem.: Tex. Classroom Tchrs. Assn., Alpha Delta Kappa. Baptist. Home: Marshall, Tex. Died June 19, 2004.

MCGEE, (WILLIAM) SEARS, state justice; b. Houston, Sept. 29, 1917; s. James Butler and Alice (Sears) McG.; m. Mary Beth Peterson, Mar. 8, 1941; children— James Sears, Mary Gray McGee Neilson, Claire Logan McGee Holmes, Alice Gray (Mrs. Bob Ruckman), George Sears, Erwin Smith. Student, Rice Inst., 1934-36; LL.B., U. Tex., 1940. Bar: Tex. bar 1940. Judge County Ct. Law, Harris County,

1948-54, 151st Dist. Ct., Harris County, 1954-55; practice Houston, 1955-58; judge 55th Dist. Ct., Harris County, 1958-69; justice Tex. Supreme Ct., from 1969. Instr. civil law procedure U. Houston Coll. Law, 1950-52; Sec.-treas. Houston Jr. Bar, 1947 Bd. dirs. central br. YMCA, Houston; mem. Houston Community Council; pres. Houston Council Deaf Children. Served to lt. USNR, 1943-46. Mem. Tex. State Bar. (dir., mem. legislative com. jud. sect.), Tex. Bar Found., Am. Bar Assn., Am. Judicature Soc., Sons of Herman, Phi Delta Theta. Home: Austin, Tex. Died 2006.

MCGHEE, AGNES, real estate broker, educator; b. Halifax, Va., Sept. 14, 1940; d. Harvey B. and Edna G. Barksdale; m. Robert J. McGhee, Mar. 24, 1962; childrenL Richard J., David B. BS in Med. Tech., Stratford Coll., Danville, Va., 1962. Lic. real estate sales, Va.; grad. Realtors Inst.; cert. residential appraiser. Bacteriologist Hampton (Va.) Gen. Hosp., 1972-77; sales mgr. real estate Lotz Realty, Newport News, Va., 1977-81; v.p. Hedgepeth Realty, Grafton, VA., 1981-84, Hedgepeth-McGhee Realty, Grafton, 1984-86; broker, owner, pres. McGhee Manor Realty, Grafton, 1986-90; tng. dir. Atlantic Homes Realty, Newport News, Va., 1990-97; real estate educator McGhee Seminars, from 1997; mng. broker Long & Foster Realtor, Williamsburg, Va., from 1999. Adj. prof. Christopher Newport U. Mem. York County Bd. Zoning Appeals, 1988-97. Recipient numerous awards; named to Outstanding Young Women of Am.; named Outstanding Bus. Woman of Yr. Mem. Nat. Assn. Realtors, Va. Assn. Realtors (bd. dirs. 1997-99, chmn. edn. 1998-99), Va. Peninsula Assn. Realtors (bd. dirs. 1983-85), Williamsburg Area Assn. Realtors (bd. dirs. 1998—, exec. bd. sec. 1999—, chmn. edn. com. 1998), York County Bus. Assn. Died Aug. 23, 2005.

MCGOVERN, FRANCES, retired lawyer; b. Akron, Ohio, Apr. 18, 1927; d. Bernard Francis and Pauline A. (Menegay) McG. AB, U. Akron, 1948; LLB, Case Western Res. U., 1949. Bar: Ohio 1949, U.S. Dist. Ct. (no. dist.) Ohio 1951, U.S. Supreme Ct. 1963, U.S. Ct. Appeals (6th cir.) 1975. Pvt. practice, Barberton, Ohio, 1949-52; assoc. Motz, Morris, Wilson & Quine, Akron, Ohio, 1952-55; ptnr. Quine & McGovern, Akron, 1955-60, 63-65; atty. Ohio Edison Co., Akron, 1965-78, sr. atty., 1978-88, assoc. gen. counsel, 1988-89. Author: Written on the Hills--The Making of the Akron Landscape, 1996, Fun, Cheap and Easy--My Years in Ohio Politics 1949-1964, 2001. Mem. Ohio Gen. Assembly, 1955-60, chmn. judiciary com., 1959-60; mem., chmn. Ohio Pub. Utilities Commn., 1960-63; mem. Dept. Labor Employment Security Bd., Washington, 1963-68; vice-chmn. Charter Commn. Summit County, 1969-70; del., platform com. Dem. Nat. Conv., 1960, del. 1964; trustee N.E. Ohio Coll. Medicine, Rootstown, 1979-81, U. Akron, 1973-82; pres. United Way, 1987-89, bd. dirs.; sec. Employee Spl. Svcs. Commn., 1974-91; bd. dirs. Med. Edn. Found. N.E. Ohio U. Coll. Medicine, 1982-97, trustee emeritus, 1997-2003, Archbishop Hoban H.S., 1977-90, U. Akron Found., 1973-97, Summit County Hist. Soc., 1997-2003, Progress Through Preservation, 1996-2003, Access, 1999-2002; chmn. county charter com. Akron Regional Devel. Bd., 1990-92; active LWV, Akron Edn. Found., 1993-96, Summit 2000. Recipient Achievement award Kappa Kappa Gamma, 1962, Akron Beacon Jour., 1968, Disting. Svc. award United Way, Akron, 1969, Disting. Alumni award U. Akron, 1989, others. Mem. Akron Bar Assn. (St. Thomas More award 1997). Democrat. Died Feb. 6, 2004.

MCGOWAN, JOHN PATRICK, retired university librarian; b. N.Y.C., May 11, 1926; s. Patrick and Nora (Naughton) McG.; m. Eileen Durkin, Nov. 4, 1950; children—Carol, Joanne, John, Deirde, Malcolm AB in English, Hunter Coll., 1950; A.M.L.S., Columbia U., 1951; B.E. in Indsl. Engring., NYU, 1956. Librarian NYU, N.Y.C., 1951-56; librarian Tech. Inst., Northwestern U., Evanston, Ill., 1956-59; dir. library Franklin Inst., Phila., 1959-66; assoc. univ. librarian Northwestern U., Evanston, 1966-71, univ. librarian, 1971—92, Charles Deering McCormick univ. librarian, 1987. Named Rsch. Librarian of the Yr. Assn. of Rsch. Librs., 1990. Avocation: sailing. Home: Winnetka, Ill. Died Feb. 4, 2006.

MCGRIFF, ERLINE P., nursing educator; b. Petersburg, Va., Feb. 18, 1924; d. Thomas Dunlop and Bessie May (Webb) Perkins; m. Vern H. McGriff, Sept. 22, 1965. Diploma, Sibley Meml. Hosp., 1945; BSNE, Cath. U. Am., 1950, MSNE, 1953; EdD, Columbia U., 1967. RN, N.J., N.Y. From staff nurse to clin. instr. Sibley Meml. Hosp., Washington (D.C.), 1945-46; assoc. dir. nursing svcs., asst. prof. nursing Med. Coll. Va., Richmond, 1956-63; profl. staff asst. ANA, N.Y.C., 1965-67; lectr. Tchrs. Coll. Columbia U., N.Y.C., 1967-69; from asst. to assoc. prof., dir. continuing edn. nursing NYU, 1969-73, prof., from 1975, head div. nursing, 1975-82; prof., dept. head Trenton (N.J.) State Coll., 1973-75. Project dir. Va. Dept. Edn., Richmond, summer 1956; chmn. nursing subcom. Health Professions Edn. Adv. Coun. Dept. Higher Edn. State N.J., 1973-75; commr. Dept. Nursing N.Y.C. Tech. Coll., 1979—. Manuscript reviewer Jour. Profl. Nursing, 1987—. McLeod-Smith fellow Va. Nurses Assn., 1963, 1964, Isabel Hampton Robb fellow Nurses' Ednl. Funds, Inc. 1965; Clara Strasburger scholar Columbia U., 1964; recipient Sister Mary Alma Disting. Leader Nursing award Felician Coll., 1984; grantee USPHS, 1971-74, 1977-80, W.K. Kellogg Found, 1985-88, NIMH, 1986-89, NYU, 1987-90. Fellow Am. Acad. Nursing, ANA (vice chmn. task force 1971-72); mem. Nat. League Nursing (accreditation visitor 1977—), AAUP, AAUW, Soc. Advancement Nursing, Inc. (pres. 1984—, v.p. and editor of newsletter 1983-84), Nursing Edn. Alumni Assn. Tchrs. Coll. Columbua U. 1971-72), Nursing Edn. Alumni Assn. Tchrs. Coll. Columbia U. (life mem., Disting. Achievement award Nursing Svc. 1973, pres. 1974-76), Sigma Theta Tau, Pi Lambda Theta, Kappa Delta Pi. Home: New York, NY. Died Dec. 24, 2004.

MC INERNEY, DENIS, lawyer; b. NYC, May 31, 1925; s. Denis and Anne (Keane) McI.; m. Mary Irene Murphy, Nov. 14, 1953; children: Kathleen Mc Inerney O'Hare, Denis J., Maura Mc Inerney Romano. BSS, Fordham U., 1948, JD cum laude, 1951, LLD (hon.), 1996. Bar: N.Y. 1951, D.C. 1961. Instr. philosophy Fordham U., 1948-51; assoc. Cahill Gordon & Reindel, N.Y.C., 1951-61, ptnr., 1961-90, sr. counsel, 1991—2006. Vice chmn. Com. Character and Fitness Admission State Bar N.Y., 1st Jud. Dept., 1979-97, chmn. Departmental Disciplinary Com., 1st Jud. Dept., 1997-2003; lectr. in field. Co-author: Practitioners Handbooks for Appeals to the Appellate Divisions of the State of New York, 1979, and to the Court of Appeals of the State of New York, 1981. Bd. dirs. Vols. of Legal Svc., Inc., 1985-2001, Cath. Youth Orgn.; mem. adv. bd. St. Vincent's Hosp., Westchester, N.Y.; chmn. bd. visitors Fordham Law Sch.; trustee Fordham U., 1988-94. Sgt. 82d Airborne Divsn. U.S. Army, 1943-46, ETO. Decorated Knight of Malta, Knight of the Holy Sepulcher; recipient Achievement in Law award Fordham U., 1977, St. Thomas More award Archdiocese NY Cardinal's Com. of Laity Lawyers' Divsn., 2001, Second Harvest award Fordham U. Sch. Law, 2003. Fellow Am. Coll. Trial Lawyers (state chmn. 1980-82); mem. ABA, N.Y. State Bar Assn., Bar Assn. City N.Y., New York County Lawyers Assn. (pres. 1982-84), N.Y. County Lawyers Assn. Inn of Ct. (pres. 1996-2002), Fordham U. Law Alumni Assn. (pres. 1968-72, medal of achievement 1975). Clubs: Westchester Country, Univ. Roman Catholic. Home: Rye, NY. Died Feb. 2, 2006.

MCINTOSH, DONALD EDWARD, anesthesiologist; b. Detroit, Jan. 13, 1930; s. Charles Louis and Mary Margaret (McKanna) McI.; m. Norene Marie O'Connor, July 3, 1954; children: Bruce John, Mikail Marie, Sharon Rose. PhB, Marquette U., 1951; MD, Med. Coll. Wis., 1960. Diplomate Am. Bd. Anesthesiology. Clin. clerkship in anesthesiology Kans. U. Med. Ctr., 1962; resident in anesthesiology Kansas City Gen. Hosp., 1964-66; fellow in pediatric anesthesiology St. Louis Sch. Medicine, 1966; pvt. practice medicine Parsons, Kans., 1961-64; practice medicine specializing in anesthesiology Rsch. Med. Ctr., Kansas City, Mo., from 1966, chief dept. anesthesiology, 1971-78, pres. med. staff, 1982; chief dept. anesthesiology Cox Med. Ctr., Springfield, Mo., 1984-86; ret., 1986. Clin. prof. anesthesiology U. Mo., Kansas City, 1978—, v.p., 1981-82, 91-92; v.p. Mo. State Med. Assn., 1981-82, 91-92. Served to capt. U.S. Army, 1951-53, 60-61. Fellow Am. Geriatric Soc.; mem. AMA, Mo. State Med. Assn. (v.p. 1981-82), Jackson County Med. Soc. (pres. 1979, Cert. of Merit, 1983), Nat. Fedn. Cath. Physicians (pres. 1988-89), Elks, KC. Republican. Roman Catholic. Avocations: sailing, fishing. Home: Lees Summit, Mo. Died Jan. 15, 2004.

MCKAY, JOHN PHILLIP, JR., international marketing professional; b. Tulsa, Sept. 26, 1957; s. John Phillip and Sheila Verdine (Liles) McK.; m. Paula Sue Turner, April 16, 1983; 1 child, Ross Alexander. BS in Bus. Adminstrn., Okla. State U., 1979; MA in Internat. Mgmt., Am. Grad. Sch. of Internat. Mgmt., Ariz., 1980. Competition mktg. rsch. analyst Hilti Inc., Tulsa, 1981-83; supr., internat. mktg. AT&T Commn., Morristown, N.J., 1984-87; merchandising mgr. Laufen Internat., Tulsa, 1988; v.p. Data & Mgmt. Counsel, Inc., Chadds Ford, Pa., from 1989. Alumnus ednl. counselor Am. Grad. Sch. Internat. Mgmt., Ariz., 1981—. Tng. coord. pre-marital counseling program Asbury United Meth. Ch., Tulsa, 1994. Mem. Am. Mktg. Assn., Clan MacKay Soc. of the USA, Okla. State U. Alumni Assn. Republican. Mem. United Meth. Ch. Avocations: genealogy, foreign language, travel, reading, weight training. Home: Tulsa, Okla. Died Aug. 3, 2005.

MCKEITHEN, WALTER FOX, state official; b. Columbia, La., Sept. 8, 1946; s. John Jesse and Marjorie (Funderburk) McK.; m. Yvonne May; children: Marjorie, Marianne, Rebecca, John Jesse. B in History and Social Studies, La. Tech. U., 1972. Owner, operator Apparel Mart Dept. Store, Columbia, 1974-83, McKeithen Chem. & Cementing, Columbia, 1979-88; mem. appropriation, natural resources and joint budged coms. La. Ho. of Reps., Baton Rouge, 1983-87; sec. state State of La., Baton Rouge, 1988—2005. Tchr., coach Caldwell Parish High Sch., Grayson, La., 1975-78; past mem. La. Assn. Educators. Past v.p. Caldwell Parish Jaycees; trustee La. Sch. Employees' Retirement System; mem. La. Tourist Devel. Commn.; second injury bd. La. Workmen's Compensation; mem. State Bd. Election Supervisors and State Bond Commn., La. Farm Bur., Am. Petroleum Inst.; administrv. bd. Broadmoor Meth. Ch. Recipient Outstanding Legislator award La. Assn. Educators, 1985, Golden Apple award La. Fedn. Tchrs., 1986. Republican. Methodist. Died July 16, 2005.

MCKELVEY, ALAN CURTIS, pharmacist; b. Dayton, Ohio, Mar. 29, 1958; s. Paul Laverne and Julia Curtis McKelvey; m. Linda Beckley, May 21, 1983; children: Jennifer, David. BS, Ohio No. U., 1981. Registered pharmacist Ohio, cert. smoking cessation facilitator Am. Lung Assn. Pharmacist Revco Drug Store, Xenia, Ohio, 1981—82, Wright State U., Fairborn, Ohio, from 1982. Pharmacist Howards Pharmacy, Huber Heights, Ohio, 1989—97, CVS, Huber Heights, Ohio, 1997—2002, Wal-Mart Pharmacy, Beavercreek, Ohio, 2002—03, from 2002; part-time pharmacist Walgreens, Kettering, Ohio, from 2002; pharmacy and therapeutics com. United Healthcare Ohio, Centerville, 1993—99; externship site preceptor Ohio No. U., Fairborn, from 1991, U. Cin. Coll. Pharmacy, from 1994, Ohio State Coll. Pharmacy, Fairborn, from 1999. Officer YMCA Indian Princesses, Kettering, Ohio, 1990—96; youth soccer coach YMCA, Kettering, 1995—2001; pharmacy advisor Reach Out Montgomery County, Dayton, from 1999. Named Pharmacist of the Yr., Miami Valley Pharm. Assn., 1986. Republican. Nazarene. Avocations: marching band pit crew member, swimming, gardening. Home: Kettering, Ohio. Died Apr. 18, 2006.

MCKENZIE, WESLEY MELVIN, JR., music educator, composer; b. LaGrange, Ga., Sept. 17, 1945; s. Wesley Melvin McKenzie, Sr. and Gladys Thompson McKenzie; m. Karen Sue Nichols, July 11, 1988; m. Sydney Rosalie Boone, Jan. 15, 1965 (div. Apr. 3, 1970); children: Dawn Elizabeth Rivera, Kimberley Sue, Eric Lee Riggs, Daniel Wesley. MusB, U. of Ga., 1963—66, MFA, 1966—68; Mus D in Composition, Fla. State U., 1974—78. Cert. tchr. Ga. State Bd. Edn., 1972, Fla. State Bd. Edn., 1974, Nev. State Bd. Edn., 1994. Dir. of bands Dawson County H.S., Dawsonville, Ga., 1968—69; assoc. dir. of bands Cairo H.S., Ga., 1969—71, dir. of bands, 1972—74; gen. music, beginning band instr. Washoe County Sch. Dist., Reno, 1994—98; assoc. dir. of bands Edward C. Reed H.S., Sparks, Nev., 1997—99; dir. of bands Edward C. Reed H.S., 1999—2004. Profl. performer Wes McKenzie Music Inc., Fla., 1974—98, Ga., 1974—98, Calif., 1974—98, Nev., 1974—98. Composer: (chamber music) Quintet for Brass, Sonatina for Alto Saxophone and Piano, (doctoral dissertation) Concerto for Alto Saxophone & Wind Band, (concert band composition) La Playa; editor: (music theory workbook) Basic Music Theory by Charles Douglas. Mem.: Internat. Assn. of Jazz Educators, Nev. Music Educators Assn. (nev. all-state jazz band chmn. 1998—99), NEA. Achievements include Led Outstanding Nevada Jazz Band, Reno Jazz Festival, 2000; Led Reed High School Wind Ensemble to Command Performance, Northern Nevada Band Festival, 2000; Guest Conductor, Northern Nevada Zone Honor Jazz Band, 2000. Avocations: scuba diving, computers, music performance. Home: Reno, Nev. Died Sept. 4, 2004.

MCKEON, SISTER MARGARET MARY, parochial school administrator; b. Ridgewood, N.Y., Feb. 28, 1924; d. James Stephen and Mary Anastasia (Sawey) McK. BS in Edn., Trinity Coll., Washington, 1962; MS in Edn., Hunter Coll., 1971, profl. cert. adminstrn. and supr., 1974; post-grad., Ga. State U., 1977. Cert. tchr., adminstr., Ga. Elem. tchr. various parochial schs., N.Y., N.C., Ga., Va., Md., 1944-73; tchr. remedial reading St. Joachim & Anne Sch., Queens, N.Y., 1973-74; mem. adminstrv. team Holy Rosary Sch., S.I., N.Y., 1975-76, tchr. remedial reading, 1975-76, asst. prin., 1976-77; prin. St. Thomas More Cath. Sch., Decatur, Ga., from 1977. Mem. ASCD, Nat. Cath. Edn. Assn. (Prin. award 1987-88), Ga. Ind. Sch. Assn., Atlanta Assn. Ind. Schs. Avocations: sewing, crocheting, needlepoint, quilting. Home: Decatur, Ga. Died June 20, 2005.

MCKERNS, KENNETH WILSHIRE, science educator, researcher; b. Hong-Kong, Mar. 5, 1919; s. Frederick William McKerns and Daisy Peel; m. Dorothy Vivian McDuffe, Feb. 12, 1943; children: Maureen Kendra, Leslie Allison. BSc, U. Alta., Edmonton, Can., 1942, MSc, 1946; PhD, McGill U., Montreal, Quebec, Can., 1949. Chief biochemist Can. Packers Ltd., Toronto, Ontario, Canada, 1950—54; lectr. St. Andrews U., Saint Andrews, Scotland, 1954—55; group leader Lederle Labs., Pearl River, NY, 1955—60; assoc. prof. U. of Fla., Gainesville, Fla., 1960—63, prof., coll. medicine, 1960—63; grad. rsch. prof. Univerisity of Fla., Gainesville, Fla., 1963—79; pres. Internat. Found. Biochemical Endocrin, Trenton, Maine, from 1979. Artist Guild, Boca Raton Mus. of Art, Fla. Capt. Royal Can. Arty., 1942—45, Europe. Fellow, Nat. Res. Coun. Can., 1959—60, NIH, 1969—70, Harvard Med. Sch., 1970—71. Achievements include patents for Inventor, Isolation & Purification ACTH; US Patent 4,193,915 18 Mar. 1980: Inhibitory & Antibody Generating Peptides for Contraception & Cancer Inhibition; Pre patent application, August, 1999, Inhibition Prostate Cancer by Unique Synthetic Peptides. Avocations: professional artist, coastal sailing. Home: West Palm Beach, Fla. Died July 10, 2005.

MCKINNEY, JERRY WAYNE, media company executive; b. Esperanza, Texas, Sept. 17, 1937; s. Lee Parker McKinney and Elsie Margaret Haass; m. Violet Elizabeth Davenport, Oct. 1959 (div. Oct. 1969); m. Valda Kay Cooper, Feb. 12, 1972; children: Kathleen Low, Ellen. Announcer, comml. mgr. Sta. KVOU Radio, Uvalde, Tex., 1959-62; announcer Sta. K-SIX Radio, Corpus Christi, Tex., 1962-66; reporter, editor Corpus Christi Caller-Times, 1966-74; polit. editor Albuquerque Tribune, 1974-79; mgr. pub. rels. Mountain Bell Telephone, Albuquerque, 1979-80; press sec. Congressman Joe Skeen Washington, 1980-85; Tokyo bur. chief Voice of Am., Washington, 1993-95, corr., 1985-93, 95-99, mng. editor news divsn., 1999—2001, ret., 2001; press sec. Congressman Joe Skeen, Washington, 2001—02; pres. McKinney Media LLC. Mem. exec. com. Rep. Party N.Mex., Albuquerque, 1979-80; mem. exec. com. Chaparral chpt. Girl Scouts Am., Corpus Christi, 1972-74. With USN, 1955-59. Mem. Soc. Profl. Journalists (past pres. N.Mex. profl. chpt., past dep. dir. region 9),

Corpus Christi Press Club (pres. 1971-72), Overseas Press Club Am., Fgn. Corr. Club Japan (hon. mem., fgn. corr.). Avocations: reading, travel. Home: Albuquerque, N.Mex. Died May 26, 2006.

MCKINNEY, RICHARD ISHMAEL, philosophy educator; b. Live Oak, Fla., Aug. 20, 1906; s. George Patterson and Sallie Richard (Ellis) McK.; m. Phyllis Vivian Kimbrough, June 27, 1933 (dec. May 1965); children: George Kimbrough, Phyllis Zanaida McKinney Bynum; m. Lena Roberta Martin, Aug. 5, 1967. BA, Morehouse Coll., 1931; BD, Andover Newton Theol. Sch., 1934, STM, 1937; PhD, Yale U., 1942; DD, St. Paul's Coll., Lawrenceville, Va., 1978. Pastor Pond St. Bapt. Ch., Providence, 1933-35; asst. prof. philosophy and religion Va. Union U., Richmond, Va., 1935-42, dean Sch. of Religion, 1942-44, acting v.p., 1978-79; pres. Storer Coll., Harpers Ferry, W.Va., 1944-50; chmn. dept. philosophy Morgan State U., Balt., 1951-76, acting dean Coll. Arts and Scis., 1977-78; disting. scholar in philos. theology Coppin State Coll., Balt., 1983. Vis. prof. U. Pa., Phila., spring 1972, U. Ife, Ile-Ife, Nigeria, spring 1974. Author: Religion in Higher Education Among Negroes, 1945, History of First Baptist Church of Charlottesville, Va., 1863-1980, 1981, History of the Black Baptists of Florida, 1850-1985, 1987, Mordecai-The Man and His Message: The Story of Mordecai Wyatt Johnson, 1998; contbr. articles to profl. jours. Bd. dirs. Balt. Urban League, 1958-59, Luth. Hosp., Balt., 1963-65, Am. Cancer Soc., Balt., 1965-70, Enoch Pratt Libr., Balt. Mem. AAUP, NEA, Am. Philos. Assn., Soc. for Values in Higher Edn., Soc. for Existential Philosophy and Phenomenology, Phi Beta Kappa, Omega Psi Phi, Sigma Pi Phi (nat. pres. 1986-88), Phi Sigma Tau (nat. pres. 1959-62). Democrat. Avocation: cabinet maker. Home: Baltimore, Md. Died Oct. 28, 2005.

MCKINNEY, ROBERT JOE, retired accountant; b. Greenville, S.C., May 29, 1936; s. Frank Earl and Connice Phyllis (Dawkins) McK.; m. Mary Jackson, June 15, 1958; children: Harold D., DeAngela M. Assocs. Degree, Lewis Bus. Coll., Detroit, 1968; programming cert., Honeywell Inst., 1972. Clk. U.S. Postal Svc., Detroit, 1961-68; field tax auditor Mich. Dept. Treasury, Detroit, 1968-72; computer programmer GM, Detroit, 1972-74; field tax auditor Mich. Employment Security Commn., Detroit, 1974-79, field audit supr., 1979-97; ret., 1997. Chairperson supervisory com. Mich. Employment Security Credit Union, Detroit, 1986—. Inventor of board game. With U.S. Army, 1959-61. Mem. Am. Legion, Northwestern H.S. Men's Club (treas. 1971-91). Democrat. Home: Detroit, Mich. Died June 27, 2005.

MCKNIGHT, H. BRENT (HAROLD BRENT MCKNIGHT), federal judge; b. Mooresville, N.C., Feb. 20, 1952; BA, U. N.C., 1974, JD, 1980; MA, Oxford U., 1977. Bar: N.C. Asst. dist. atty State of N.C., 1982—88; judge N.C. State Dist. Ct., 1988-93, US Magistrate Ct. (we. dist.) N.C., Charlotte, 1993—2003, US Dist. Ct. (we. dist.) N.C., 2003—04. Rhodes scholar, 1977. Died Nov. 27, 2004.

MCKNIGHT, WILLIAM BALDWIN, physicist, educator; b. Macon, Ga., July 4, 1923; s. Gilbert Franklin and Exie (Baldwin) McK.; m. Helen Mabel Bowling, Oct. 1, 1955; children: Tandy Ringoringo, Linda McKnight Gibson. BS, Purdue U., 1950; PhD, Oxford U., 1968. Physicist Underwater Sound Reference Lab., Orlando, Fla., 1952-53, U.S. Army Missile Command, Redstone Arsenal, Ala., 1953-61, supervisory rsch. physicist, 1961-74; cons. Ballistic Missile Def. Advanced Tech. Ctr., 1975; rsch. prof. physics U. Ala., Huntsville, from 1974; pres. Tech. Rsch. Assocs. Inc., from 1984. Contbr. articles to profl. jours. V.p. Cotaco Cmtys. League, Somerville, Ala., 1964-65; active Madison County Rep. Exec. Com., Ala. Silver-Haired Legislature, 2001-02; mgr. Gordo Area C. of C., 1993-97; chmn. transp./infrastructure com. Pickens County Strategic Planning, 1994-96; active North-South Hwy. Corridor, West Ala. Coalition Task Force, 1995-96; chmn. Citizens for the Improvement of Pickens County, 1997—, Gordo Area Indsl. Devel. Authority; chmn. adv. coun. Pickens County Commn.; bd. dirs. West Ctrl. Partnership of Ala.; pres. Gordo Area Cmty. Devel. Found.; citizens adv. com. West Ala. Rural Planning Orgn. Decorated D.F.C., Air medal with three oak leaf clusters, Presdl. Unit Citation with oak leaf cluster; recipient Research and Devel. award U.S. Army, 1961, 64; named Gordo Vet. of Yr., Gordo Rotary Club and Gordo C. of C., 2004; Sec. of Army fellow, 1966-67. Fellow Optical Soc. Am.; mem. IEEE (sr.), Am. Phys. Soc., Rotary (pres. Gordo club 1997-98), Oxford and Cambridge Club, Tuscaloosa Univ. Club, Sigma Xi, Sigma Pi Sigma. Mem. Ch. of Christ. Home: Gordo, Ala. Died Dec. 7, 2005.

MCKOWN, RICHARD GEORGE, artist, educator, writer; b. Cambridge, Mass., Nov. 30, 1947; s. Joseph Maxwell and Miriam (Barker) McK.; m. Deborah J. Berry, Aug. 10, 1969. BA in Studio Arts, U. N.H., 1969; MA in Photography, U. Iowa, 1971, MFA in Photography, 1972. Dir. media svcs. Emerson Coll., Boston, 1973-75; acting dir. Provincetown (Mass.) Group Gallery, 1976; real estate broker Foster and Foster, Inc., Acton, Mass., 1979-81; photography instr. Decordova Mus. Sch., Lincoln, Mass., 1979-81; artist-in-residence Cultural Edn. Collaborative Inst. for the Arts, Boston, 1983-88; instr. visual arts Middlesex Community Coll., Bedford, Mass., from 1984; instr. photography No. Essex C.C., Haverhill, Mass., from 1988. Artist-in-residence Mass. Cultural Coun., 1991—; computer coord. Concord-Carlisle Regional H.S., 1994—. One-man shows include Abbott Meml. Libr., Emerson Coll., Boston, 1974, 75, Tirca Karlis Gallery, Provincetown, Mass., 1976, Photoworks Gallery, Boston, 1977, Photographic Gallery, Mid. Tenn. State U., Murfreesboro, 1978, Grey Gallery, Antioch Coll., Yellow Springs, Ohio, 1979, 417 Gallery, Prairie State Coll., Chgo. Heights, Ill., 1980, Concord (Mass.) Free Pub. Libr., 1981, Andover (Mass.) Gallery, 1985, Meridien Hotel, Boston, R.J. Grey Art Gallery, Acton, 1988, New East End Gallery, 1989, Cherrystone Gallery, Wellfleet, Mass., 1993, Fire-house Ctr. for Arts., Newbury, Mass., 1993, Merrimack Coll., North Andover, Mass., 1994, Middlesex C.C., Bedford, Mass., 1994, William-Scott Gallery, Provincetown, 1997, Bangs St. Gallery, Provincetown, 1998; group shows include Danforth Mus., Framingham, Mass., 1987, J.L. Becker East End Gallery, Provincetown, Mass., 1988, Hudson River Mus., Yonkers, N.Y., 1989, No. Essex Community Coll., Haverhill, Mass., Middlesex Community Coll., Burlington, Mass., Inst. de Bachillerato Federico Garcia Lorca, Granada, Spain, 1990, Berta Walker Gallery, Provincetown, 1990, U. N.H. Art Gallery, Durham, 1990, 94, Hudson Walker Gallery, Fine Arts Work Ctr., Provincetown, 1991, 92, 93, 94, 95, 96, 97, Creiger-Dane Gallery, Boston, 1996, 97, 98; films and multimedia prodns. include Autobiographical Film, 1969, Bellybutton, 1969, Marianne in Morning, 1970, December Observations, 1971, My Hillside--A Day in June, 1971, A History of American Landscape Photography, 1972, video, 1994, A Nightmare, 1972, Primary, 1973, Annum, 1974; appeared in numerous publs.; paintings in numerous corp. and pvt. collections; writer Art New Eng. Mag., 1994—. Finalist Mass. Artists' Found. fellow Program, 1979, 82; recipient Purchase prize McDonald's Corp. Fine Arts Collection Competition, Oakbrook, Ill., 1984; U. Iowa fellow, 1970-71. Avocations: bicycling, camping, travel, cooking, carpentry. Home: Acton, Mass. Died Dec. 14, 2004.

MCLAIN, THELMA LOUISE, retired librarian; b. Sparks, Okla., Nov. 18, 1918; d. Grant Leroy and Emma Evelyn (Ellington) Spoonemore; m. Bruce McLain, Nov. 27, 1943 (div. June 1948). BA, Tex. Woman's U., Denton, 1940; MLS, U. Tex., 1959. Cert. tchr., Tex. Sch. libr. supr. Works Progress Adminstrn., Waco, Tex., 1940-41; tchr. 5th grade Donna (Tex.) Pub. Schs., 1941-42; h.s. libr. Rosenburg (Tex.) Pub. Schs., 1942-43; bookmobile libr. Houston Pub. Libr., 1943-44; county libr. Morgan County Libr., Versailles, Mo., 1946-49; h.s. libr. Harlingen (Tex.) Pub. Schs., 1950-52; asst. order libr. U. Tex. Libr., Austin, 1953-56; head rsch. and reference Pan Am. U. Libr., Edinburg, Tex., 1957-74; asst. prof. Pan Am. U., Edinburg, 1970-74; co-owner Custom Ladies Dress Designs, McAllen, Tex., 1972-75. Selling arts and crafts, 1975—. Exhibited paintings oil and acrylics spons. by McAllen Art Mus., Hidalgo County Art Legue, McAllen, McAllen Jr. League, Rio Grande Valley Art League, Harlingen, Willacy County Art Legue, Raymondville, Tex., others; author: Long Trail Awinding--My Family's History, 1993. Recipient awards for art. Mem. Order of the Daus. of the King (sec. chpt. 1992—). Episcopalian. Avocations: needlecrafts, especially cloth dolls of original design. Home: La Grange, Tex. Died 2006.

MCLAUGHLIN, EDWARD FRANCIS, JR., lawyer; b. Boston, Aug. 18, 1920; s. Edward Francis and Helen Celia McLaughlin; m. Elizabeth Drake, Apr. 14, 1945; children: Edward F., Patricia A. (dec.), Paul R. (dec.), Robert D., Richard J., Elizabeth A. AB in Bus., Dartmouth Coll., 1942; LLB, Northeastern U., 1949. Bar: Mass. 1949, U.S. Dist. Ct. Mass. 1950, U.S. Ct. Appeals (1st cir.) 1950, U.S. Supreme Ct. 1963. Asst. U.S. atty. U.S. Dept. Justice, Boston, 1950-53; assoc. Sullivan & Worcester, Boston, 1953-61; lt. gov. Commonwealth of Mass., Boston, 1961-63; gen. counsel Metropolitan Transit Authority, Mass. Bay Transportation Authority, Boston, 1962-70; assoc. Herrick & Smith, Boston, 1970, ptnr., Nutter, McClennen & Fish, LLP, Boston, 1986-90, of counsel, 1990-2000; asst. dist. atty. Commonwealth of Mass., Barnstable, Mass., 2000—05. Dir. nat. coun. Northeastern U., Boston, 1979-2005. Councillor Boston City Coun., Mass., 1954—61, pres. Mass., 1959—60; del. Dem. Nat. Conv., L.A., Calif. Lt. USN, 1942—45. Named Outstanding Alumnus Northeastern U., 1974. Fellow Mass. Bar Assn. Roman Catholic. Avocations: sports, political activities, reading. Home: Osterville, Mass. Died Jan. 21, 2005.

MCLAUGHLIN, JOHN RICHARDSON, electric motor company executive; b. New Orleans, Sept. 8, 1929; s. Thomas Phillip and Louise (Fortier) McL.; m. Lorraine Bergstrom, Aug. 9, 1952; children: Elizabeth, Richard, Thomas. BSChemE, Tulane U., 1950, MBA in Mgmt., 1953. Gen. mgr. housewares mfg. dept. GE Co., Bridgeport, Conn., 1953-78; group v.p. Lear Siegler Co., Greenwich, Conn., 1978-85; pres. Electric Indicator Co. Inc., Norwalk, Conn., from 1985. Bd. dirs. Japanese Products Corp., Norwalk. Selectman Town of Easton (Conn.), 1997-99; chmn. ch. coun. Easton Congl. Ch., 2000—. Recipient Official Citation Gen. Assembly State of Conn., 1999. Mem. Easton Exch. Club. Republican. Congregationalist. Avocations: tennis, fishing, chess. Home: Easton, Conn. Died May 22, 2005.

MCLEAN, IAN WILLIAM, ophthalmic pathologist, researcher; b. Durham, N.C., Sept. 21, 1943; s. I. William and Brita (Rosenqvist) McL.; m. Susan R. Gabler, June 14, 1987; children: Elenor Lee, Rebecca Ann, January D. BS, U. Mich., 1965, MD, 1969. Diplomate in anatomic pathology Am. Bd. Pathology. Pathology intern U. Colo. Med. Ctr., Denver, 1969-70, resident in pathology, 1970-73; staff pathologist, dept. ophthalmic pathology Armed Forces Inst. Pathology, Washington, 1973-83, acting chmn. dept. ophthalmic pathology, 1983-86, chmn. dept., from 1986. Contbr. more than 175 articles to sci. jours. Col. U.S. Army, 1973-94. Recipient Gold medal U. Sao Paulo, 1988. Mem. Assn. for Rsch. in Vision and Ophthalmology, Eastern Ophthalmic Pathology Soc., Am. Acad. Ophthalmology, Am. Assn. Ophthalmic Pathologists, Verhoeff-Zimmerman Soc. Home: Bethesda, Md. Died June 15, 2004.

MC LEAN, JACKIE, jazz saxophonist, educator, composer, community activist; b. N.Y.C., May 17, 1932; Doctorate (hon.), Trinity Coll., Hartford, 1999. Bandmaster, counselor N.Y. State Correction Dept.; chmn., prof. Hartt Sch. Music, Hartford, Conn., from 1968; founder Artist Collective, Inc., Hartford, 1970; founder African Am. music program (jazz degree) Hartt sch. music U. Hartford. With Art Blakey's Jazz Messengers, performed with, Charles Mingus; actor: film The Connection; albums include Monuments, New York Calling, Antiquity, Live at Montmarte, Ode To Super, A Ghetto Lullaby, Lights Out, Dr. Jackle, The Meeting, Jack Knife, New and Old Gospel, Let Freedom Ring, Destination Out, One Step Beyond, Grachan Moncur III, (with Jackie McLean Quintet) Dynasty, 1990, Rites of Passage, 1991, Triloka: Rhythm of the Earth, 1992, Jackie MacAttack, 1993, Rhythm of the Earth, 1993, Jackie's Hat Trick, 1995, Swing, Swang, Swingin', 1997, Fire & Love, 1998, Nature Boy, 2000, Blue Note - Fire and Love; guest artist album by Jazz Messengers Midnight Session, 1993; led McLean Jazz Dynasty tour with son Rene in 6 countries in Southern Africa, 1993. Decorated officer of the Arts (France); recipient Bent award U. Hartford, State of Conn. Blue Book Registration Manual award, 1996, Jazz Master award Nat. Endowment for the Arts; named # 1 in Downbeat Mag. Critics Poll, 1993, 94, 95, # 1 in Jazz Times Mag. Readers' Poll, 1993, 94, 95; Jackie McLean Inst. of Jazz named in his honor Music Dept. Hartt Sch. Music. Univ. Hartford, 2000, Beacon award New Sch. Univ., N.Y.C., 2001. Died Mar. 31, 2006.

MCLEAN, MICHAEL LEE, personal manager; b. L.A., Dec. 29, 1941; s. Owen L. and Vivian (Falkner) mcL.; m. Jolie Jones, 1973 (div. 1975); 1 child, Donovan Lee; m. Diane Dimeo, July 4, 1981. Casting dir. 20th Century Fox, Beverly Hills, Calif., 1964-74; TV producer D'Angelo Prodns., Hollywood, Calif., 1974-78; pres. McLean-Ebbins, Inc., Hollywood, 1978-80, Michael McLean & Assocs., Studio City, Calif., from 1980. Casting dir.: (movies) Sound of Music, 1965, Butch Cassidy and the Sundance Kid, 1969, Patton, 1970, Rocky II, 1979; producer, casting dir. Papa and Me, 1975 (Silver Hugo Chgo. Film Festival 1975, Golden Gate award San Francisco Film Festival 1976, Emmy nomination 1975); mgr. Dennis Hopper, 1979-89, Nicole Kidman, 1989—, Armand Assante, 1990—, Pee-wee Herman, 1986—. With USNG Res. Mem. Casting Soc. of Am. (bd. dirs. 1980-86). Died May 14, 2005.

MCLELLAN, JOSEPH DUNCAN, critic, journalist; b. Quincy, Mass., Mar. 27, 1929; s. Malcolm and Elsie May (Turner) McL.; m. Estelle Marie Cajolet, Feb. 3, 1951; children— Joseph, Laura, Andree, Sandra BA, Boston Coll., 1951, MA, 1953. Reporter, columnist The Pilot, Boston, 1953-67; editor fgn. news Religious News Service, NYC, 1967-70; editor mag. AD 1970, South Bend, Ind., 1970; dir. spl. projects N.C. News Svc., Washington, 1970-72; from writer, editor to music critic The Washington Post, Washington, 1972-95; music critic emeritus, 1995—2005. Artistic cons. Alexandria (Va.) Symphony Orch., 1996-98. Mem. Music Critics Assn., Book Critics Circle, Assn. US Chess Journalists Clubs: Mensa (DC). Avocations: chess; computers; video equipment and software; poetry translation. Died Dec. 26, 2005.

MCLEOD, MALCOLM STEWART, financial executive; b. Gloucester, Mass., May 21, 1941; s. Malcolm Stewart and Mary Evelyn (Keane) McL.; m. Stephanie Green, May 29, 1994; children: Karen Rayne, Kristin Sunset. BA, U. Mass., 1966; MA, U. Hawaii, 1968. State trans. economist State of Hawaii, Honolulu, 1975-86; pres. Ctr. for Psycho Social Rsch., Honolulu, 1986-90; v.p. Abel Appraisers and Bus. Valuations, Honolulu, from 1990. Mem. faculty Hawaii Pacific U. Sch. Bus., 19866; mem. adv. com. Royal State Ins. Co., Honolulu. 1986-92; com. mem. Nat. Rsch. Coun., Washington, 1986-95; dir. Investors Fin., 1994. Contbr. articles to profl. jours. Conv. del. Hawaii Govt. Employees Assn., Honolulu, 1987-93. With USAF, 1959-63. Recipient Cert. of Nat. Merit U.S. Dept HUD, 1985. Mem. Am. Econ. Assn., Inst. Bus. Appraisers, Hawaii Yacht Club, Omicron Delta Epsilon. Avocation: yachting. Home: Phoenix, Ariz. Died Aug. 11, 2004.

MCLOUGHLIN, JAMES PATRICK, bishop; b. Galway, Ireland, Apr. 4, 1929; s. Patrick and Winifred (McDermott) McL. BA, St. Patrick's Coll., Maynooth, Ireland, 1950; Higher Diploma in Edn., Univ. Coll., Galway, 1955. Ordained priest Roman Cath. Ch., 1954; ordained bishop, 1993. Prof. St. Mary's Coll., Galway, 1954-65; diocesan sec. Galway (Ireland) Diocese, 1965-83; parish priest Galway (Ireland) Cathedral, 1983-93, bishop, 1993—2005. Home: Galway, Ireland. Died Nov. 25, 2005.

MCMAHON, PAUL EDWARD, chemist, technologist; b. Burlington, Vt., July 2, 1931; s. Walter E. and Madeline O. (LaFlash) McM.; m. Ramona Berard, June 12, 1954 (div. 1970); 1 child, Shelley Kay; m. Eleanora Farano, Feb. 26, 1982. BS in Chemistry, St. Michael's Coll., Winooski, Vt., 1954; MS in Chemistry, U. Vt., 1956; PhD in Chemistry, U. Ill., 1961; MBA, Rutgers U., 1976. Phys. chemist Chemstrand, Raleigh, N.C., 1961-68; from chemist to group leader Hoechst Celanese Corp., Summit, N.J., 1968-80, sr. rsch. assoc., 1980-82, mktg. mgr., 1982-85, tech. mgr., from 1985. Home: Mountainside, NJ. Died Jan. 26, 2004.

MCMAHON, THOMAS FRANCIS, priest, educator; b. Chgo., Sept. 4, 1928; s. Robert and Estelle McM. AB in Philosophy, St. Ambrose Coll., 1950; STD in Moral Theology, U. St. Thomas, 1962; MBA in Mktg., George Washington U., 1970. Ordained priest Roman Cath. Ch., 1954. Prof. moral theology Viatorian Sem., 1957-67, Washington Theol. Coalition, 1968-71; from assoc. prof. bus. law to prof. emeritus Loyola U., Chgo., 1971-99, prof. emeritus, from 1999. Vis. lectr. Cath. U., Washington, 1968-71; vis. prof. St. Mary's of Calif., 1971; cons. Am. Pharmaceutical Assn., Washington, 1965-73, Nat. Conf. Christian Employers and Mgrs., Chgo., 1955-84; com. chmn. advt. review BBB, Chgo., 1985-2000; dir. Loyola Ctr. Values in Bus., Chgo., 1982-95. Author: Transforming Justice, 2000; editor Weekend on Socio-Ethical Values, 1982-93; contbr. articles to profl. jours. Bd. trustees St. Viator H.S., from 2001. Recipient Educator of Yr. award BBB, Chgo., 1980, Chgo. Mayoral Proclamation, 1999. Mem. Soc. Bus. Ethics, Beta Gamma Sigma. Home: Arlington Heights, Ill. Died Nov. 22, 2004.

MCMANUS, FREDERICK RICHARD, priest, educator; b. Lynn, Mass., Feb. 8, 1923; s. Frederick Raymond and Mary Magdalene (Twomey) McM. AB, St. John's Sem., Brighton, Mass., 1947; JCD, Cath. U. Am., 1954; LLD (hon.), St. Anselm's Coll., Manchester, N.H., 1964; SJD (hon.), Coll. of Holy Cross, Worcester, Mass., 1989. Ordained priest Roman Cath. Ch., 1947. Assoc. pastor various chs., Mass., 1947-50; sec. to met. tribunal Archdiocese of Boston, 1950-51; prof. canon law and moral theology St. John's Sem., 1954-58; prof. canon law Cath. U. Am., Washington, 1958—93, vice provost, dean grad. studies, 1974-83; acad. v.p. Cath. Univ. Am., Washington, 1983-85; O'Brien-O'Connor Disting. Prof. of canon law, from 1990. Dir. secretariat Bishop's Com. on Liturgy, Nat. Conf. Cath. Bishops, Washington, 1965-75; pres. Liturgical Conf., 1959-62, 64-65; treas. Internat. Commn. English in Liturgy; bd. dirs. Am. Coun. on Edn.; trustee Mt. St. Mary's Coll., Emmitsburg, Md. Author: Congregation of Sacred Rites, 1954, Rites of Holy Week, 1956, Revival of the Liturgy, 1963, Sacramental Liturgy, 1967, (with Ralph Keifer) The Rite of Penance, 1975, Thirty Years of Liturgical Renewal, 1987, Liturgical Participation: An Ongoing Assessment, 1988; editor: The Jurist, 1959—; contbr. articles to jours. Recipient Pax Christi award St. John's U., Collegeville, Minn., 1964, Michael Mathis award U. Notre Dame, 1978, Presdl. award Nat. Cath. Edn. Assn., 1983. Mem. AAUP, Canon Law Soc. Am. (Role of Law award 1973), Cath. Theol. Soc. Am. (John Courtney Murray award 1990), N.Am. Acad. Liturgy (Berakah award 1979), Cath. Commn. Cultural and Intellectual Affairs, Assn. Cath. Colls. and Univs. (bd. dirs. 1979-80, chmn. 1980-82), Joint Com. Cath. Learned Socs. and Scholars (chmn.). Died Nov. 27, 2005.

MCMILLAN, HUGH HOPKINS, environmental engineer; b. Chgo., Dec. 23, 1936; BSEE, Valparaiso U., 1962. Registered profl. engr., Ill., 1967. Gen. supt. Metro Sanitary Dist., 1962-83; v.p. Paschen Contractors, Chgo., 1983-87, M&O Environ., East Hazel Crest, Ill., 1992-95, Hydrodynamics, Inc., LaGrange, Ill., 1994-95; gen. supt. Metro Water Reclamation Dist., Chgo., 1995—2001; v.p. Consoer Townsend Envirodyne Engineers, 2001—04. Cons. Glenview, Ill., 1987-92. With U.S. Army, 1954-57. Mem. IEEE, WEF, IWEA, Am. Acad. Environ. Engrs., Am. Legion. Avocations: flying, fishing, golf, tennis. Home: Glenview, Ill. Died June 4, 2004.

MCMILLEN, SHANNON M., urologist; b. Ft. Scott, Kans., Apr. 25, 1943; BS, U. Kans., 1966, MD, 1971. Diplomate Nat. Bd. Med. Examiners; lic. physician, Kans., S.C., Oreg. Intern Letterman Gen. Hosp., San Francisco, 1971-76; resident in gen. surgery and urology Madigan Army Med. Ctr., Tacoma, Wash., 1972-76; chief urology svc. Moncrief Army Hosp., Ft. Jackson, S.C., 1976-79; active staff Sacred Heart Gen. Hosp., Eugene, Oreg., from 1979, chief dept. urology, 1985-87. Courtesy staff McKenzie Willamette Hosp., Springfield, Oreg., 1979—, Cottage Grove (Oreg.) Hosp., 1979—; mem. Lane Individual Practice Assn., 1979—, chmn., 1992-93; chmn. Pacific Source Health Plans, Eugene, 1996-97; bd. dirs. Med. and Surg Specialists, chmn., 1997—; bd. dirs. Pacific Dental Plans, PDP Holdings. Contbr. articles and papers to med. jours. Recipient Kimbrough Meml. award, 1975. Mem. Am. Urol. Assn. (mem. Western sect.), Oreg. Med. Assn. (del. 1985-90, chmn. 1987-90), Oregn. Urol. Soc., Soc. Govt. Svc. Urologists, Eugene Surg. Soc. (sec.-treas. 1982-84), Lane County Med. Soc. (chmn. membership com. 1981-83, bd. trustees 1982-90, chmn. mini-internship com. 1984-86, sec.-treas. 1986-87, chmn. OMA del. 1987-90). Home: Eugene, Oreg. Died Mar. 13, 2004.

MCMILLIAN, THEODORE, federal judge; b. St. Louis, Jan. 28, 1919; m. Minnie E. Foster, Dec. 8, 1941. BS, Lincoln U., 1941, HHD (hon.), 1981; LLB, St. Louis U., 1949; HHD (hon.), U. Mo., St. Louis, 1978, Washington U., 2004. Bar: Mo. Mem. Lynch & McMillian, St. Louis, 1949-53; asst. circuit atty. City of St. Louis, 1953-56; judge US Ct. Appeals (8th Cir.), 1987—2003, sr. judge, 2003—06. Judge circuit ct., City of St. Louis, 1956-72, Mo. Ct. Appeals (ea. divsn.), 1972-78; asso. prof. adminstrn. justice U. Mo., St. Louis, 1970—2006; assoc. prof. Webster Coll. Grad. Program, 1977; mem. faculty Nat. Coll. Juvenile Justice, U. Nev., 1972—2006 Served to 1st lt. Signal Corps U.S. Army, 1942-46. Recipient Alumni Merit award St. Louis U., 1965, ACLU Civil Liberties award, 1995, Disting. Lawyer award Bar Assn. Met. St. Louis, 1996, Salute to Excellence Civil Rights award St. Louis Am., 1997, Spirit of Excellence award ABA, 2003; named Disting. Non-Alumnus U. Mo.-Columbia Law Sch., 1999. Mem. Am. Judicature Soc., Am. Bd. Trial Advs. (hon. diplomate), Lawyers Assn. Mo., Mound City Bar Assn., Phi Beta Kappa, Alpha Sigma Nu. Home: Saint Louis, Mo. Died Jan. 18, 2006.

MCNAIR, JOHN FRANKLIN, III, banker; b. Laurinburg, N.C., Apr. 12, 1927; s. John Franklin and Martha (Fairley) McN.; m. Martha Fowler, June 16, 1951; children: John Franklin IV, Elizabeth Fowler. BS, Davidson Coll., 1949; postgrad., U. N.C., 1954-56. Pres. McNair Automotive Co., Inc., Laurinburg, 1949-66, The State Bank, Laurinburg, 1966-68; sr. v.p. Wachovia Bank & Trust, Laurinburg, 1968-70, Raleigh, N.C., 1970-72, exec. v.p. Winston-Salem, N.C., 1972-77, vice chmn., 1977-85, The Wachovia Corp., Winston-Salem, N.C., 1977-87, pres., chief exec. officer, 1987-90, Wachovia Bank & Trust Co, 1987-90, also dir.; exec. v.p. First Wachovia Corp., 1986-90. Bd. dirs., pres. N.C. R.R. Co., 1993-97. Mem. N.C. State Hwy. Commn., Raleigh, 1965-69, Commn. on future N.C., Raleigh, 1981-83; chmn. N.C. Bd. Econ. Devel., 1979-85, N.C. Coun. Econ. Edn., Greensboro, 1980-82, Ind. Coll. Fund N.C., 1989-91, N.C. Citizens for Bus. and Industry, 1988-89; trustee Peace Coll., Raleigh, 1980-89, Davidson Coll., 1985-93, St. Andrews Presbyn. Coll., Laurinburg, N.C., 1968-75; trustee Old Salem, Inc., 1985-98, 1999—2005, treas., 1990-97, chmn., 1997-98; trustee Winston-Salem Found., 1983-91, chmn., 1989-91; co-chmn. gov.'s adv. com. Superconducting Supercollider Project, 1988; trustee, 1986-2003, trustee emeritus, 2003—, mem. exec. com. Rsch. Triangle Found., 1986-99, vice chmn., 1990-93, chmn., 1992-2000; trustee exec. com. Winston-Salem Bus., Inc., 1986-02, chmn., 1990-95, mem. adv. coun., 2002—; mem. govt. performance com. State of N.C., 1991-93; bd. dirs. N.C. Enterprise Corp., 1988-93; bd. dirs. Sr. Svcs., Inc., 1994-2003, exec. com., 1998-2002, chmn., 1999-2000; sr. adv. Park Found., Inc., 1998-2001, sr. trustee, 2000-; chmn. Sr. Svcs. Found., 2002-; chmn. Qual Choice N.C. Inc., 1994-99, bd. dirs., 1994-2002; bd. dirs. N.C. Stroke Assn., 1998-2003, Save Our State, 1998-2003; trustee Park Found., Inc., 2000—. With USN, 1945-46. Recipient Young Man of Yr. award, Laurinburg Jaycees, 1962, Silver Beaver award, Boy Scouts Am., 1967, Disting. Alumni award, Davidson Coll., 1994, citation for disting. citizenship, N.C. Citizens for Bus. and Industry, 2003. Mem. Am. Bankers Assn. (state v.p. 1980-81), Res. City Bankers Assn., N.C. Bankers Assn. (pres. 1976-77), NC Aquarium Soc. (bd. dirs. 2000-), Old Town Club, Piedmont Club, St. Andrews Soc., Rotary. Democrat. Presbyterian. Home: Winston Salem, NC. Died Nov. 3, 2005.

MCNAMEE, WILLIAM LAWRENCE, industrial engineer; b. Pitts., Nov. 10, 1931; s. William Lawrence and Mary Cathrine (Kunkel) McN.; m. Evelyn McSwiggen, Nov. 29, 1952; 1 child, Leisa Jean. BSEE, U. Pitts., 1963. Resident engr. Union Switch & Signal, Swissvale, Pa., 1954-58; elec. technician Mason-Shaver Rhodes, East McKeesport, Pa., 1954-58; shop supr. Westinghouse Atomic, Waltz Mills, Pa., 1958-60; field engr. Martin-Orlando, Oakdale, Pa., 1960-61; sr. elec. engr. U. Pitts. Physics & Astronomy Dept., from 1961. Advisor Electronics Inst., N.Y.C., 1975-81; cons. Extranuclear Labs., Blawnox, Pa., 1980-86, NMR Inst., Pitts., 1987-89. Co-author: Modern Industrial Electronics, 1993; contbr. articles to profl. jours. Served in USCG, 1950-53. Home: Bethel Park, Pa. Died July 9, 2004.

MCNEIL, WILLIAM K., folklorist; b. near Canton, N.C., Aug. 13, 1940; s. William McKinley and Winifred (Rigdon) McN.; m. Grace Joy Taucan Morandarte, July 25, 1994. BA, Carson-Newman Coll., 1962; MA, Okla. State U., 1963, SUNY, Cooperstown, 1967; PhD, Ind. U., 1980. VISTA vol. Office Econ. Opportunity, Barbourville, Ky., 1965-66; historian N.Y. State Dept. Edn., Albany, 1967-70; adminstr., folklorist Smithsonian Inst., Washington, 1975-76; folklorist Ozark Folk Ctr., Mt. View, Ark., from 1976. Pres. Ozark States Folklore Soc., 1980-81. Author: American Proverb Literature, 1971, The Charm is Broken, 1984, Ghost Stories from the American South, 1985, On a Slow Train Through Arkansas, 1985, Southern Folk Ballads, 1987, Appalachian Images in Folk and Popular Culture, 1989, Ozark Mountain Humor, 1989, The Life and Adventures of an Arkansaw Doctor, 1989, Arkansas Folklore Sourcebook, 1992, Southern Mountain Folksongs, 1993, Ozark Country, 1995. Fellow Ind. U., 1970. Fellow Am. Folklore Soc. (book rev. editor 1977-80), Mid-Am. Folklore Soc. (sec., treas. 1987—), N.Y. Folklore Soc., Calif. Folklore Soc., Pa. Folklore Soc. Avocations: reading, swimming, hiking. Home: Mountain View, Ark. Died Apr. 20, 2005.

MCPHEE, RODERICK FULTON, retired school administrator; b. Eau Claire, Wis., Jan. 30, 1929; s. Eugene Roderick and Frances (Fulton) McP.; m. Sharon Sullivan, Aug. 29, 1948; 1 child, Dennis Roderick. BS, U. Wis., 1950, MS, 1953; PhD, U. Chgo., 1959. Secondary sch. tchr. Kohler (Wis.) Pub. Schs., 1950-52; instr. extension div. U. Wis., Madison, 1952-55; field rep. White House Conf. Edn., Washington, 1955-56; staff assoc. Midwest Adminstrn. Ctr., Chgo., 1956-60; assoc. sec. Am. Assn. Sch. Adminstrs., Washington, 1960-61; asst. prof. Grad. Sch. Edn. Harvard U., Cambridge, Mass., 1961-65; supt. of schs. Town of Glencoe, Ill., 1965-68; pres. Punahou Sch., Honolulu, 1968-94. Cons. Arthur D. Little Co., Cambridge, 1967-68; bd. dirs. First Hawaiian Bank, Honolulu, Persis Corp., Honolulu; chmn. Barstow Found., Honolulu; active Cmty. Fedn. Hawaii. Co-author: The Organization and Control of American Schools, 1968; contbr. articles to profl. jours. Named Scot of Yr. Caledonian Soc., Honolulu, 1991, Hawaii Bus. Hall of Fame Laureate, 1993. Mem. Hawaii Assn. Ind. Schs. (pres. 1972, 81, 82), Social Sci. Assn. Honolulu, Oahu Country Club, Waialae Country Club, Rotary (pres. 1975-76), The 200 Club (sec., pres. 1983-84). Avocations: reading, golf, skiing, racquetball. Home: Honolulu, Hawaii. Died Feb. 25, 2005.

MCPHERSON, GAIL SPORY, farmer; b. Johnstown, Pa., Dec. 24, 1945; d. Alfred William and Evelyn (Saylor) Spory; m. Paul McPherson, June 10, 1972; children: Gretchen Sue, Hugh Clark, Sarah Ann. BA in English and Drama, Susquehanna U., 1967; MAT in English, Colgate U., 1971. Tchr. South Eastern Sch. Dist., Fawn Grove, Pa., 1968-73; profl. farmer Maple Lawn Farms, Inc., New Park, Pa., from 1972. Presenter Senate Appropriations Subcom. on Agr., Rural Devel. and Related Agys. for Nat. Peach Coun. on maintaining rsch. funding for fruit, 1979, Sec. of Agr. Bob Bergland, 1980, USDA, 1994, 96, among others. Mem. Centre Presbyn. Ch., New Park, 1971—, sr. h.s. Sunday sch. tchr., 1980-85, jr. h.s. Sunday sch. tchr., 1988-89, jr. Sunday sch. tchr., 1989—, elder, 1989-94, 98—, benevolence treas. 1990—, meml. fund com. chmn. 1990-92, Donegal Presbytery hunger com. 1992, evangelism com., 1993-97; bd. dirs. Pa. Agriculture Awareness Found.; long range planning facilitator Pa. Commodity Round Table. Recipient Spokesman of Yr. for Agr. in the East Cheveon Co. and Farm Chems. Mag., 1976. Mem. York County Farmers Assn. (county newsletter editor 1973-77), Am. Agri-Women (fruit and vegetable program coord. 1976, goal setting and goal-tending chmn. 1977, vital issues chmn. 1978-79, conv. chmn. 1980, 88, bylaws and resolutions com. 1981, policy statements com. 1985, sec. 1989-90, bylaws chmn. 1992—, dir., sec. resource ctr. 1992-96, pres. resource ctr. 1998, dir., bylaws chmn. 1996—, Leaven award 1980, Pres.'s award 1985), Pa. Agri-Women (editor Farm Connection 1980-89, 93—, pres. 1980-84, 97—, creator Penelope, Sweet Pa. Peach 1981, media tng. Sperry New Holland 1981, treas. 1986-90, 95-96, pres. 1997—), Nat. Peach Ptnrs. (asst. coord. 1977-82, conv. publicity chmn. 1978, pres. 1983-87, v.p. 1989—), Pa. Apple Mktg. (bd. dirs. 1991—, sec. 1994, v.p. 1995, chmn. 1997). Home: New Park, Pa. Died July 9, 2005.

MCPHILLEN, BEVERLY LOUISE, registered nurse; b. Perry, Ia., Sept. 18, 1940; d. Victor James and Mildred Isabel (Reynolds) Cornelius; m. Jimmy Lee McPhillen, Dec. 24, 1961 (div. June 20, 1981); children: Michele Ann, Carole Jean; 1 child, Candace Elaine. Diploma computer, DMACC, Ankeny, IA; LPN, RN, DMACC, Boone, IA. Cert. AS 1995; RN 1996. Med. Ass. physician office, Des Moines, Ind.; LPN Nursing Home, Boone, Ind., nursing home, Branson, Mo.; receptionist career ctr., Branson, Mo.; RN nursing home, Branson, Mo., Hollister, Mo. Author: (short stories) campus publications ($250.00, 1993). Mehodist. Avocations: fund raising, walking, teaching handwork, Sunday school classes. Home: Branson, Mo. Died Jan. 16, 2004.

MCWHINEY, GRADY, history professor; b. Sherveport, La., July 15, 1928; s. Henry Grady and Mayme (Holland) McW.; m. Sue B. Baca, Nov. 20, 1947. BS, Centenary Coll. of La., 1950; MA, La. State U., 1951; PhD, Columbia U., 1960. Asst. prof. Troy State U., Ala., 1952-54, Millsaps Coll., Jackson, Miss., 1956-59, Northwestern U., Evanston, Ill., 1960-65; assoc. prof. to prof. U.B. C., Vancouver, Can., 1965-70; vis. prof. U. Calif. - Berkeley, 1959-60, 67-68; prof. Wayne State U., Detroit, 1970-75; vis. prof. Tulane U., New Orleans, summer 1970, U. Mich., Ann Arbor, 1972-73; prof. history, dir. and disting. sr. fellow ctr. for study of so. history and culture U. Ala. University, 1975-83; Lyndon Baines Johnson prof. Am. history Tex. Christian U., Ft. Worth, 1983-96, prof. emeritus, 1996—2006; disting. historian in residence U. So. Miss., Hattiesburg, 1996-97. Mem. NEH Selection Com., 1973, Jefferson Davis Award Com., 1970-72, 75-77; James Murfin Meml. lectr., 1990, Marian Alexander Blake lectr., 1991; Conf. Meml. speaker, 1991; vis. disting. prof. McMurry U., Abilene, Tex., 1997-98; pres. McWhiney Rsch. Found., 1997-2006. Author: Braxton Bragg and Confederate Defeat, Vol. 1, 1969, Southerners and Other Americans, 1973; (with Perry D. Jamieson) Attack and Die: Civil War Military Tactics and the Southern Heritage, 1982, Cracker Culture: Celtic Ways in the Old South, 1988, An American Civil War Primer, 1992, Battle in the Wilderness: Grant Meets Lee, 1994, 2d edit., 1998; editor: (with Sue McWhiney) To Mexico with Taylor and Scott, 1845-1847, 1969, Grant, Lee, Lincoln and the Radicals, 1964; (with Robert Weibe) Historical Vistas, 2 vols., 1963-64, Reconstruction and the Freedmen, 1963, (with Douglas Southall Freeman) Robert E. Lee's Dispatches to Jefferson Davis, 1957, 2d edit., 1994, Confederate Crackers and Cavaliers, 2001 (Fletcher Pratt prize for best Civil War book 2002). With USMC, 1945—47. Recipient Earl A. Davis award, 1996, Frank E. Vandiver award Houston Civil War Round Table, 1993, Charles L. "Pie" Dufour award New Orleans Civil War Round Table, 1994, Outstanding Scholar award U. Ala., 1980, Gallant Svc. award Chgo. Civil War Round Table, 1979, Harry S. Truman award, 1970, Pacific Br. award Am. Hist. Assn., 1969; Huntington Libr. fellow, 1984; recipient Jefferson Davis medal United Daus. of the Confederacy, 1992, Honor award Sons Confederate Vets Tex. Divsn., 1993; rsch.

fellow Mosher Inst. Def. Studies, 1988-2006, 1st recipient Grady McWhiney award, 1998. Fellow St. George Tucker Soc.; mem. Ala. Hist. Assn. (pres. 1978-79), So. Hist. Assn. (exec. council 1976-79), Civil War Round Table U.K. (hon.), Phi Beta Kappa (Disting. Scholar). Home: Abilene, Tex. Died Apr. 18, 2006.

MEAD, CARL DAVID, retired literature educator; b. Cadiz, Ohio, May 4, 1913; s. Carl David and Neva Eloine (Walker) M.; m. Lillian Martha Felton, Apr. 15, 1938; children: Susan, Nancy. Student, Washington and Jefferson Coll., 1932-34; BS, Ohio State U., 1936, MA, 1938, PhD, 1947; degree (hon.), U. Kyukyus. Instr. English Denison U., 1938-39, Ohio State U., 1946-47; faculty Mich. State U., 1948-81, prof. English, 1957-81, head dept., 1959-66; Fulbright lectr. Philippines, 1964. Author: Yankee Eloquence in the Middle West, 1951, (with others) Prentice-Hall Handbook for Writers, 1951, The American Scholar Today, 1970; Adv. editor: Dodd, Mead & Co, 1963-75; editor: Centennial Review, 1966-82. Served with AUS, 1943-46. Decorated Legion of Merit. Mem. MLA, Am. Studies Assn. Home: East Lansing, Mich. Died Aug. 17, 2005.

MEAD, SEDGWICK, physician; b. Guymon, Okla., July 2, 1911; s. Redmond Boyd and Bertha Mabel (Hunter) Corbett; m. Marjorie Frances Chick, Sept. 22, 1940 (dec.); children: Sedgwick Jr., Marshall; m. Mary Adelaide Abbott, May 8, 1995. Student, U. Ariz., 1930-31; SB cum laude, Harvard U., 1934, MD, 1938. Diplomate Am. Bd. Phys. Medicine and Rehab. Baruch fellow Harvard Med. Sch., Boston, 1946-47; assoc. prof. Sch. of Medicine Washington U., St. Louis, 1948-54; med. dir. Kaiser Found. Rehab. Ctr., Vallejo, Calif., 1954-69; ast. clin. prof. Sch. of Medicine Stanford (Calif.) U., 1955-60; clin. prof. U. Calif., Davis, 1969-72; chief neurology Kaiser-Permanente Med. Ctr., Vallejo, 1969-77; med. dir. Easter Seal Rehab. Ctr., Oakland, Calif., 1983-93; intern Mass. Gen. Hosp., 1938-40, resident pathology, 1940-41, resident neurology, 1941-42. Cons. coun. on med. physics AMA, Chgo., 1950-54; pres. Assn. Rehab. Ctrs., 1953, Am. Acad. Cerebral Palsy, Richmond, Va., 1967. Chmn. governing bd. Retired Physicians Assn. Perm Med. Group, Oakland, 1989-90; trustee Costra Costa County Mosquito Abatement Dist., Concord, Calif., 1970-93; mem. White House Conf. on Health, Washington, 1953. With AUS, 1942-45, col. USAR, ret. 1971. Scholar Harvard Coll., 1932. Mem. AMA, World Med. Assn., Mass. Med. Soc., Am. Acad. Neurology, Am. Acad. Cerebral Palsy (pres. 1967), Faculty Club U. Calif. Berkeley, Harvard Club San Francisco. Unitarian Universalist. Avocations: travel, sailing, flying, languages. Home: El Cerrito, Calif. Died Nov. 21, 2004.

MEANS, STEVEN ALLEN, real estate company executive; b. Banana River, Fla., Jan. 5, 1945; s. Bert Leonard and Lottie (Hester) M.; m. Susan Lancaster, Nov. 27, 1971; children: Courtney, Blake, Loren, Sutton, Chandler. BA, So. Meth. U., 1967; MBA, U. Tex., 1972. Ptnr. Lincoln Property Co., Dallas, 1972-79; mng. ptnr. Paragon Group, Inc., Dallas, from 1979. Trustee Dallas Ballet, 1984-85, N. Tex. Commn., 1985—; assoc. Dallas Mus. Art, 1985. Served to capt. USAF, 1969-71, also jet pilot, Tex. Air NG. Mem.: Aerobics Ctr.,"T" Bar "M", Dallas. Republican. Avocations: tennis, skiing, travel. Home: Dallas, Tex. Died Jan. 19, 2005.

MEARS, WILLIAM GEORGE, automotive engineer; b. Petersburg, Va., Nov. 18, 1931; s. Lyman Forbes and Flora Hall M.; m. Georganne Taylor, Feb. 20, 1960 (div. 1974); m. Erica Fitz, July 27, 1975; 1 child, Haley. BSChemE, Worcester Polytech. Inst., 1953. Registered profl. engr., 1977. Jr. technologist to sr. rsch. assoc. Mobil R&D Corp., Paulsboro, N.J., 1953-90; cons. automotive engr. Dynamotive Engring., Inc., Kennett Square, Pa., from 1990. Contbr. articles to profl. jours. Sec. Soc. Hill Civic Assn., Phila., 1965-68. Lt. USN, 1955-58. Mem. NSPE, Soc. of Automotive Engrs. (light duty vehicle performance and economy measurement subcom. 1973-96, Cert. of Appreciation 1983), Internat. Ground Source Heat Pump Assn. Achievements include patents for compression testing method and apparatus, fuel tank vent valve, automatic nozzele-actuated emission valve, method of controlling a dynamometer. Home: Kennet Square, Pa. Died June 24, 2004.

MEDALIE, JACK HARVEY, physician; b. Buhl, Minn., Jan. 8, 1922; married; 3 children. BSc, Witwatersrand U., Johannesburg, 1941, MD, BChir, 1945; MPH cum laude, Harvard U., 1958. Instr. dept. anatomy U. Witwatersrand, 1942—43; resident Johannesburg, 1945—47; rural family physician, 1948—53; sr. lectr. dept. social medicine Hebrew U., Hadassah, Jerusalem, 1962—66; from assoc. prof. to prof., chmn. dept. family medicine Tel Aviv U., 1966—74; chmn. dept. family medicine Case Western Res. U., 1975—87, prof. cmty. health, 1976—87, prof. family medicine, 1976—2006, prof. med. and pediat., 1978—87, prof. emeritus, 1992—2006; med. dir. Family and Cmty. Health Ctr., Jerusalem, 1953—62. Prin. investigator Israel Ischemic Heart Disease Study, 1962—75; co-prin. investigator congenital abnormality study NIH, 1972—74; Robert Wood Johnson Found. fellowship program Case Western Res. U., 1978—88; vis. prof. family medicine and epidemiology U. N.C., Chapel Hill, 1973—74; vis. sr. rsch. scientist Nat. Heart, Blood and Lung Inst., Bethesda, Md., 1974, Bethesda, 1990—91; med. coun. U. Hosps., Cleve., 1975—87; com. impaired physicians U. Hosps., Cleve., 1980—87; med. edn. com. Case Western Res. U., 1980—85, chmn. ambulatory and primary care clerkship com., 1981—83; task force health consequences bereavement NAS, 1982—85, membership com., 1984—88; dir. dept. family practice U. Hosps., Cleve., 1982—87; rsch. cons. Mt. Sinai Med. Ctr., Cleve., 1991—99. Contbr. articles to profl. jours. With U.S. Army, 1942—45, active Israel Def. Force, 1948—49. Recipient Lifetime Achievement award in medicine, Golden Age Ctrs., 1997. Fellow: Royal Soc. Med. Found., Am. Heart Assn., Am. Acad. Family Physicians; mem.: Soc. Behavioral Medicine, Soc. Tchrs. Family Medicine (chmn. task force 1985—87, Curtis Hames Career Rsch. award 1988, Cert. Excellence 1988, Maurice Saltzman award 1988), Inst. Medicine-NAS. Died June 20, 2006.

MEDLAR, DEBORAH STARKEY, history and political science educator; b. Devils Lake, N.D., Sept. 13, 1952; d. Harold Lee and Ruth Adele (Swan) Starkey; m. Richard Lee Medlar, July 21, 1978; children: Noah, Ira. BA cum laude, Jamestown Coll., N.D., 1976. Tchr. Egeland H.S., ND, 1976—77, Dickinson H.S., ND, 1977—79, Trinity H.S., Dickinson, ND, from 1988; adj. lectr. Dickinson State U., ND, from 2001. Tchr. cons. Nat. Geog. Soc. Mem.: APA, N.D. Geog. Alliance, Nat. Coun. for Social Studies. Home: Dickinson, ND. Died July 3, 2004.

MEDLEY, STEVEN PAUL, association executive; b. Palo Alto, Calif., July 11, 1949; s. Robert William and Hermie May (Palmer) M.; m. Jane Rowley, Mar. 12, 1976; children: Charles, Joseph, Andrew. Student, Brown U., 1967-69; BA, Stanford U., 1971; MLS, U. Oreg., 1975; JD, U. Calif., Davis, 1981. Bar: Oreg. 1981. Park ranger, then libr., curator Nat. Park Svc., Yosemite Nat. Park, Calif., 1971-78; ptnr. Schultz, Salisbury, Cauble and Medley, Grants Pass, Oreg., 1981-85; pres. Yosemite Assn., Yosemite Nat. Park, 1985—2006. Author: Complete Guidebook to Yosemite National Park, 1990; co-author: Legends of the Yosemite Miwok, 1993. Home: Oakhurst, Calif. Died Oct. 5, 2006.

MEDLIN, BRAND AARON, construction company owner; b. Great Lakes, Ill., July 19, 1950; s. Edward J. and Georgia G. (Prophitt) M.; m. Ann Carpenter, Nov. 29, 1967; children: Brad Danial, Frank C., Christie Ann. Student, Columbus Vocat. Sch., Ga., 1972. Salesman Coca-Cola Co., Columbus, 1969-71; estimator Columbus Insulating Co., 1971-75, pres., 1975-78, Globe Continental Co., Columbus, 1978-82; project mgr. Centin Corp., Lancaster, Pa., 1982-85; pres. The Medlin Co., Columbus, from 1985. Republican. Baptist. Avocations: hunting, fishing, horseback riding, water-skiing. Died Apr. 14, 2004.

MEEM, JAMES LAWRENCE, JR., nuclear scientist; b. N.Y., Dec. 24, 1915; s. James Lawrence and Phyllis (Deaderick) M.; m. Buena Vista Speake, Sept. 5, 1940; children: James, John. BS, Va. Mil. Inst., 1939; MS, Ind. U., 1947, PhD, 1949. Aero. research sci. NACA, 1940-46; dir. bulk shielding reactor Oak Ridge Nat. Lab., 1950-53, in charge nuclear operation aircraft reactor expt., 1954-55; chief reactor sci. Alco Products, Inc., 1955-57; in charge startup and initial testing Army Package Power Reactor, 1957; prof. nuclear engring. U. Va., Charlottesville, 1957-81, dept. chmn., dir. reactor facility, 1957-77, prof. emeritus, from 1981; cons. U.S. Army Fgn. Sci. and Tech. Ctr., 1981-90. Vis. cons. nuclear fuel cycle programs Sandia Labs., Albuquerque, 1977-78; vis. staff mem. Los Alamos Sci. Lab., 1967-68; mem. U.S.-Japan Seminar Optimization of Nuclear Engring. Edn., Tokai-mura, 1973 Author: Two Group Reactor Theory, 1964. Fellow Am. Nuclear Soc. (sec. reactor ops. div. 1966-68, vice chmn. 1968-70, chmn. 1970-71, Exceptional Service award 1980); mem. Am. Phys. Soc., Am. Soc. Engring. Edn., SAR Home: Charlottesville, Va. Died May 8, 2006.

MEINDL, JAMES RICHARD, psychology educator; b. Naha, Okinawa, Japan, Mar. 16, 1952; came to U.S., 1952; s. John Baptist and Yasuko (Nishimura) M.; m. Roberta Leslie Schatten, June 23, 1980; children: Jeremy Kim, Kevin James. BA in Psychology/Sociology, U. Rochester, 1974; MA in Social Psychology, U. Waterloo, 1978, PhD in Social Psychology, 1981. Postdoctoral fellow, vis. scholar dept. bus. adminstrn. U. Ill., Champaign, 1980-81; asst. prof. orgn. Sch. of Mgmt. SUNY, Buffalo, 1981-87, assoc. prof. orgn. Sch. of Mgmt., 1987-92, prof., dir. PhD program, from 1992. Editor: Advances in Information Processing in Organizations; editorial bd. Adminstrv. Sci. quarterly, 1983-89, Acad. of Mgmt. Jour., 1986-90, Acad. of Mgmt. Rev., 1990—; contbr. articles to profl. jours./publs. Mem. Am. Psychol. Assn., Acad. Mgmt., Soc. for Exptl. Social Psychology. Home: Buffalo, NY. Died July 3, 2004.

MELCONIAN, JERRY OHANES, engineering executive; b. Cairo, Jan. 22, 1934; arrived in U.S., 1967; s. Melik Melconian and Zarouca Papazian; m. Veronique Kocifay, June 12, 1998; 1 child, Terran Kirk. BSc, U. London, 1957. Sect. leader Otis Elevator Co., London, 1957-61, Rolls Royce Ltd., Derby, England, 1961-66; program coord. Textron Lycoming, Stratford, Conn., 1967-74; mgr. TF34 design to cost GE, Lynn, Mass., 1974-77; mgr. mktg. No. Rsch. and Engring. Co., Woburn, Mass., 1977-82; pres. SOL-3 Resources Inc., Reading, Mass., from 1982. Editor: Design and Development of Gas Turbine Combustors, 1980. Mem.: AIAA. Achievements include patents in field. Home: Valrico, Fla. Died June 23, 2005.

MELCZER, ANDREW HENRY, health economist; b. L.A., Dec. 5, 1954; s. Henry Lynn and Revlyn (Kass) M.; m. Susan Woolley, Aug. 28, 1977; children: Alissa, Micah, Jacob. BS, Lewis and Clark Coll., 1976; PhD, Northwestern U., 1982. Sr. economist Ctr. for Health Svcs. and Policy, Northwestern U., Evanston, Ill., 1980-83; healthcare cons. Evanston, from 1983; health economist Ill. State Med. Soc., Chgo., 1984-86, dir. health policy rsch., 1986-94, asst. v.p. health care fin., 1994-95, v.p. health policy rsch., from 1995. Cons. Ill. Dept. Pub. Aid, Springfield, 1981-83, Mass. Med. Soc., Waltham, 1984-88; mem. tech. adv. group Ill. Health Care Cost Containment Coun., Springfield, 1985—, Ill. Dept. Ins. Cost Containment Task Force, 1986-89. Bd. dirs. Beth Emet Synagogue, Evanston, 1985—, treas., 1987-89, exec. com., 1987—, v.p., 1990-91, pres. 1991-95; bd. dirs. Chgo. Fedn., Union Am. Hebrew Congregations, 1991-93; mem. hosp. reimbursement tech. adv. group Ill. Dept. Pub. Aid, 1991-95; bd. dirs. Beth Emet Found., 1993—, pres. 1996—. Home: Evanston, Ill. Died Feb. 8, 2005.

MELICH, GAYLE PETERS, writer; b. Gainsville, Fla., June 10, 1938; d. Carlton Powell and Martha (Watson) Peters; m. Michael Edward Melich, Apr. 25, 1970. BS, Ariz. State U., Tempe, 1961; postgrad., San Diego Coll. Bus., 1971. Employee benefits cons. Gen. AniLine & Film Corp., N.Y.C., 1963-65; transp. mgr. Compton Advt. Inc., N.Y.C., 1966-70; adminstr. Beauvoir, The Nat. Cathedral Elem. Sch., Washington, 1972-74, 79-80; exec. dir. Nat. Women's Polit. Caucus, Washington, 1981-83, 84-85; writer, event mgr. Niceville, Fla., from 1986. Cons Nat. Women's Polit. Caucus Archives Project, Schlesinger Libr., Radcliffe, 1991; charter mem., chair Okaloosa County (Fla.) Commn. on Status of Women, 1995, vice chair, 1999. Editor Procs. Global Summit of Women, 1997, 98. Bd. dirs., pres. Nat. Women's Edn. Fund, Washington, 1979-88; bd. dirs. Child Care Svcs., Inc., Okaloosa County, 1995-96; campaign chair No. to Billboards, Niceville, 1995; co-mgr. Global Summit of Women, London, 1998, event organizer, Miami, Fla., 1997; bd. trustees, pres. Okaloosa County Heritage Mus., Valparaiso, Fla., 1997. Mem. LWV, AAUW, Am. Bus. Women's Assn. (Fla. Women's Hall of Fame chair 1994), Nat. Women's Polit. Caucus Va. (No. Va. chair 1980-81). Avocations: gardening, theater, travel. Home: Niceville, Fla. Died July 19, 2005.

MELLEN, RUTH ELLEN, software engineer; b. Upland, Calif., Sept. 2, 1942; d. William Ernest and Winifred (Greenwood) M.; m. Jonas Martin Frost III, June 28, 1964 (div. Feb. 1967); m. Charles Oakley Kemper, Dec. 31, 1969 (div. Nov. 1976). BS in math., U. Mo., 1964; JD, The George Washington U., 1980. Bar: Va. Statistician, programmer The George Washington U., Washington, 1964-68; programmer, analyst Control Data Corp., Bethesda, Md., 1968-69; analyst The Urban Inst., Washington, 1969-72; info. ctr. dir. Oak Ridge (Tenn.) Nat. Lab., 1972-80; atty. Law Office Ruth Mellen, Fairfax, Va., 1980-85; IV & V analyst Logicon, Inc., Arlington, Va., 1985-93; tech. mgr. CTA Inc., Rockville, Md., from 1993. Tech. usage adv. bd., Montgomery Coun. Pub. Schs., Rockville, 1994—. Contbr. articles to profl. jours. Lobby corps. League of Women Voters, Washington, 1983-92, bd. dirs., 1980-82; adv. bd. The Women's Ctr., Vienna, Va., 1980-85. Mem. Assn. Computing Machinery (chmn. 1993—). Home: Alexandria, Va. Died June 20, 2004.

MELLINK, MACHTELD JOHANNA, archaeologist, educator; b. Amsterdam, Holland, Oct. 26, 1917; came to U.S., 1949; d. Johan and Machteld (Kruyff) M. BA, U. Amsterdam, 1938, MA, 1941; PhD, Utrecht U., Netherlands, 1943; LLD (hon.), U. Pa., 1987, Anatolian U., Turkey, 1990. Faculty Bryn Mawr Coll., 1949-88, prof. classical and Near Eastern archaeology, 1962-88, chmn. dept., 1955-83; staff mem. excavations Tarsus, Turkey, 1947-49, Gordion, Turkey, 1950-74; field dir. excavations Karatas-Semayuk, Lycia, Turkey, 1963—2006; staff mem. Troy, 1988—2006. Rsch. assoc. U. Mus., U. Pa., 1955-82, cons. scholar. Author: Hyakinthos, 1943, A Hittite Cemetery at Gordion, 1956; author: (with Jan Filip) Frühe Stufen der Kunst-Propyläen Kunstgeschichte XIII, 1974; editor: Dark Ages and Nomads c. 1000 B.C., 1964, Troy and the Trojan War, 1986, Elmali-Karatas I, 1992, II, 1994; author: Kizilbel, An Archaic Painted Tomb Chamber in Northern Lycia, 1998; contbr. articles to profl. jours. Recipient Lucy Wharton Drexel medal U. Pa. Mus., 1994. Fellow Am. Acad. Arts and Scis.; mem. Archaeol. Inst. Am. (pres. 1981-84, gold medal 1991), German Archaeol. Inst., Am. Oriental Soc., Am. Philos. Soc.; corr. mem. Royal Netherlands Acad. Scis., Austrian Archaeol. Inst. (corr.), Türk Tarih Kurumu (hon.), Am. Rsch. Inst. Turkey (v.p. 1977-87, pres. 1988-92). Home: Haverford, Pa. Died Feb. 23, 2006.

MELLOW, JUNE, mental health educator; b. Gloucester, Mass., Dec. 19, 1924; d. Joseph E. and Alta M. (Reed) M. Diploma, Salem Hosp., 1946; BS in Psychology, U. Rochester, 1949; MS in Psychiat. Nursing, Boston U., 1953, EdD in Social Founds., 1965. Asst. prof., dir. clin. lab. Doctor of Nursing Sci. program Boston U., 1959-65; dir. staff devel. Nursing Dept. Mass. Mental Health Ctr., Boston, 1966-81; lectr. psychiatric edn. Med. Sch. Harvard U., Boston, 1978-81. Contbr. numerous articles to profl. jours. Nat. League Nursing scholar, 1962-64. Mem. Sigma Theta Tau. Died Oct. 20, 2004.

MELODY, BRIAN JOHN, engineering executive; b. Chgo., Apr. 16, 1952; BS in Chemistry, U. Tenn., 1980. Rsch. chemist Callins Industries, Greenfield, Tenn., 1980-81; sr. engr. Mallory Capacitator, Indpls., 1981-87; dir. rsch. & devel. Alta Group, Fombell, Pa., 1987-88; sr. rsch. & devel. engr. AeroM Corp., Glasgow, Ky., 1988-91; dir. engring. Hilton Industries, Sarasota, Fla., 1991-92; project mgr. Kemet Electronics, Greenville, S.C., from 1992. Cons.

Aerovox Corp., New Bedford, Mass., 1988-91. Mem. Gov.'s Com. on Librs., Bowling Green, Ky., 1990. Mem. Am. Soc. Quality Control, Am. Chem. Soc., Electrochem. Soc. Holder 20 U.S. and fgn. patents. Home: Greenville, SC. Died Mar. 17, 2004.

MELTON, CHARLES ESTEL, retired physicist, educator; b. Fancy Gap, Va., May 18, 1924; s. Charlie Glenn and Ella (Ayers) M.; m. Una Faye Hull, Dec. 7, 1946; 1 child, Wayne. BA, Emory and Henry Coll., 1952, D.Sc., 1967; MS, Vanderbilt U., 1954; PhD, U. Notre Dame, 1964. Physicist Oak Ridge Nat. Lab., 1954-67; prof. chemistry U. Ga., Athens, 1967-97, head dept., 1972-77; now ret. Author: Principles of Mass Spectrometry and Negative Ions, 1970, Ancient Diamond Time Capsules, Secrets of Life and the World, 1985, Primordial Petroleum, 1989; contbr. articles to profl. jours. Served with USNR, 1943-46. Recipient DeFriece medal Emory and Henry Coll., 1959; Nobel Laureate, 2004; recipient numerous research grants. Fellow AAAS; mem. Am. Phys. Soc., Am. Chem. Soc., Ga. Acad. Sci. Achievements include constructing equipment to crush diamonds and identify trapped material which gave the age of 3.1 billion years; showing natural gas and petroleum may have diffused from Earth as evidenced by petroleum deposits found near faults in Earth; calculating the temperature of the Earth at formation and the origin of the atmosphere and oceans; showing that entropy and gravity are equal and opposite force which means the universe is eternal; requiring an eternal universe; showing the origin of the Earth's magnetic field is caused by friction from the moon, explaining the flipping field; showing the theory of organic evolution contradicts physical laws. Home: Hull, Ga. Died Nov. 21, 2005.

MELVILLE, RICHARD ALLEN, investment company executive; b. Springfield, Mass., Sept. 15, 1932; s. Charles Raymond and Vera Alice (Brooks) M.; m. Maria-Angela Garcia-Martinez, June 15, 1963; children: Thomas Alexander, Andrew Michael, Charles Peter. BA, Bates Coll., Lewiston, Maine, 1954; MA, Johns Hopkins U., 1959. Counsel U.S. State Dept., Phnom Penh, Cambodia, 1959-63; v.p. Irving Trust Co., N.Y.C., 1963-70; pres., CEO Allied Bank Group, N.Y.C., 1970-83; dir. Fiduciary Trust Internat., N.Y.C., 1984-87; chmn. bd. Alexander, Andrews & Peters, Hong Kong, 1988—2005. Chief internat. advisor State Commn. for Reform of the Economy, Govt. of People's Republic of China, Beijing, 1993—; cons. Govt. of State of Cambodia, 1991-93. Author: Cambodia: HRAF, 1963, A Northeast Forest, 2000, 2nd edit., 2004, Pseudonovibos spiralis, 2001, P. Spiralis: Epitaph, 2003; editor: Second Chance, 1989; contbr. articles to profl. jours. Pres. Round Top Ctr. for Arts, 2002—; dir. Am. Lighthouse Found.; trustee Johns Hopkins U., Balt., 1979-85, Bates Coll., 1976-90; adv. coun. Hopkins-Nanjing Ctr., China, 1981-90, Nitze Sch. of Advanced Internat. Studies, Washington, 1978-90. With Mil. Dist. of Washington, 1955-56. Mem. Coun. on Fgn. Rels. Republican. Episcopalian. Avocations: bicycling, tennis, writing. Home: Bristol, Maine. Died Jan. 1, 2005.

MELVIN, PEGGY LOUISE, court reporter; b. Tacoma, Wash., Mar. 26, 1950; d. John Douglas and Margaret (Fullinwider) M.; m. Ben Earl McCoy, June 10, 1979. Student, Tacoma Community Coll., 1968-69, Seattle Community Coll., 1969-71. Cert. shorthand reporter, Wash. Legal sec. Office of Pub. Defender, Okanogan, Wash., 1975-77, firm Mansfield & Thomas, Okanogan, Wash., 1977-80, firm Mansfield, Thomas & Reinbold, Okanogan, Wash., 1981-82; legal sec., office mgr. Office of Pub. Defender, Saipan, MP, 1982-95; superior ct. dep. clk. Okanogan County Superior Ct., from 1995. Mem. Wash. Assn. Superior Ct. Adminstrs., Nat. Assn. Ct. Adminstrn. Wash. Shorthand Reporters Assn., ABA, Judicial Assoc. Home: Malott, Wash. Died July 17, 2005.

MENDES DE ALMEIDA, LUCIANO PEDRO, archbishop; b. Rio de Janeiro, Oct. 5, 1930; Auxiliary bishop of Sao Paulo Roman Cath. Ch., 1976—88, archbishop of Mariana Brazil, 1976—2006. Died Aug. 27, 2006.

MENDEZ, C. BEATRIZ, obstetrician, gynecologist, educator, consultant; b. Guatemala, Apr. 21, 1952; d. Jose and Olga (Sobalvarro) M.; m. Mark Parshall, Dec. 12, 1986. BS in Biology and Psychology, Pa. State U., 1974; MD, Milton Hershey Coll. Medicine, 1979. Diplomate Am. Bd. Ob-gyn.; cert. in advanced operative laparoscopy and hysteroscopy Accreditation Coun. for Gynecologic Endoscopy, Inc. Resident in ob-gyn. George Washington U., Washington, 1979-83; pvt. practice Santa Fe, 1985-95, Locum Tenens, 1996; contract physician Lovelace Health Sys., Albuquerque, 1996-98; clin. instr. dept. ob-gyn. U. N.Mex. Sch. Medicine, Albuquerque, 1983—85, 1996—98; pvt. practice anti-aging medicine, 2001—02; cons. to med. facilities; med. dir. The Sterling Inst., 2001—02, Med. Spa Profl. Alliance, from 2002; med. cons. Med. Spa Conf., from 2001. Bd. dirs. Hershey (Pa.) Coll. Medicine, 1977—82; chair perinatal com. St Vincent's Hosp., Santa Fe, 1986—89, mem. quality assurance com., 1986—95, chief ob-gyn., 1992—94; Vol. physician Women's Health Svcs., Santa Fe, 1995—96; clin. instr. dept. ob-gyn. U. N. Mex. Sch. Medicine, Albuquerque, from 1997; med. dir. The Sterling Inst., Santa Fe; med. advisor Med. Spas Conf., from 2001. Med. advisor: MedicalSpa Mag., from 2001. Vol. Women's Health Svcs., Santa Fe, 1985-95. With USPHS, 1983-85. Mosby scholar Mosby-Hersey Med. Sch., Hershey, 1979. Fellow: ACOG (Continuing Edn. award from 1986); mem.: AMA (Physician Recognition award from 1986), Residents Assn. George Washington U. (co-founder 1981—83), Am. Soc. Coloscopy and Cervical Pathology, Am. Fertility Soc., Internat. Soc. Endoscopy, Am. Assn. Gynecol. Laparascopists, Am. Acad. Anti-aging Medicine. Democrat. Home: Santa Fe, N.Mex. Died June 13, 2004.

MENSH, IVAN NORMAN, medical psychology educator; b. Washington DC, Oct. 30, 1915; s. Shea Jacob and Rose (Clayman) M.; m. Frances Levitas. AB, George Washington U., 1940, AM, 1942; PhD, Northwestern U., 1948. Diplomate Am. Bd. Clin. Psychology; lic. psychologist, Calif. Prof., head med. psychology, dept. psychiatry Washington U., St. Louis, 1948-58; prof., head div. med. psychology, dept. psychiatry UCLA, 1958-86, prof. emeritus, from 1986. Author 2 text books; contbr. chpts. to books and numerous articles to profl. jours. Capt. USNR, 1943—. Recipient Certs. of Appreciation, Office Naval Rsch., Am. Bd. Profl. Psychology, Jour. Med. Edn., NIH. Fellow APA (past pres., past sec.); mem. Calif. Psychol. Assn. (past treas., past bd. chair, Silver Psi award), Assn. Am. Med. Colls., Assn. Am. Profs. Med. Psychology, Assn. Behavioral Scis. and Med. Edn., N.Y. Acad. Scis., Western Psychol. Assn. Home: Los Angeles, Calif. Died Apr. 21, 2005.

MENTE, RONALD F., consulting company executive; b. Chgo., Sept. 17, 1941; s. Fred Vincent and Edna Frances Mente; m. Alexandra Georgine Wojtas, Nov. 7, 1969 (div. July 1976). BA, Mont. State U., 1964; MS, DePaul U., 1975; MA, Northeastern Ill. U., 1979; PhD, Vrije U., 1999. Chemist Cities Svc. Oil Co., Cicero, Ill., 1964-67; chief chemist No. Petrochem Mineral Divsn., Lemont, Ill., 1967-69; chemist, chief corp. rsch. chemistry Culligan, Inc., Northbrook, Ill., 1969; rsch. chemist Ctrl. Soya Corp., Chgo., 1970-76; pres. Ronald F. Mente, Cons., St. Petersburg, Fla., from 1976. Contbr. articles to profl. jours. Mem. N.Y. Acad. Scis., Pi Gamma Mu, Delta Upsilon Sigma, Gamma Theta Upsilon, Sigma Psi. Roman Catholic. Achievements include conducting study documenting radioecology of pines in nature. Home: St Petersburg, Fla. Died July 20, 2005.

MENTER, MARTIN, retired lawyer; b. Syracuse, N.Y., July 1, 1915; s. Benjamin and Sarah (Kasmovitch) M.; m. Irene Rothschild, Nov. 10, 1940; children: Toby M. Berger, Joshua Lewis Menter. AB, Syracuse U., 1937, JD, 1939; LLM, George Wash. U., 1949. Bar: N.Y. 1939, U.S. Supreme Ct. 1948, U.S. Dist. Ct. (we. dist.) N.Y. 1939, U.S. Ct. Appeals D.C. 1962, Supreme Ct. Japan 1953. Pvt. practice, Rochester, N.Y., 1939-40, Washington, 1971-88; commd. 2d lt. U.S. Army, 1940-48, USAF, 1948-70, advanced through grades to brig. gen., ret., 1970; writer, speaker, from 1950. Atty., assoc. gen. counsel FAA, Washington, 1959-65; staff judge advocate USAF Far East Air Forces and UN Air Command, Tokyo, 1951-53, USAF Aerospace Def. Command and N.Am. Def. Command, Colorado Springs, 1965-70; speaker in field. Author: Astronautical Law, 1959; contbr. numerous articles to profl. jours., 1955-85. Bd. govs. World Hdqrs. USO, Washington, 1976-88, chair pers. com., mem. exec. com., 1974-78, chair by-laws com., 1983-86; life mem. bd. visitors Coll. of Law, Syracuse U., 1967—; bd. dirs. Nat. Jewish Welfare Bd., N.Y.C., 1970-78; v.p. Internat. Inst. Space Law, 1979-85, hon. dir., 1985—. Decorated D.S.M., Legion of Merit with Oak Leaf Cluster, Bronze Star; recipient Recognition Cert., Air Force Assn., 1969; Disting. Contbn. Internat. Inst. of Space Law, 1990, Lawyers Lawyer award N.Y.C. Assn. of USAFR Judge Advocates, 1964, Inter-Am. Bar Found. Space Law award, 1990. Mem. ABA, Am. Soc. Internat. Law, Am. Astronautical Soc., Fed. Bar Assn., Internat. Acad. Astronautics. Avocations: swimming, walking, reading, writing. Home: Chevy Chase, Md. Died Nov. 24, 2004.

MENZ, FREDRIC CARL, economics professor; b. Cleve., Oct. 10, 1943; s. Paul John and Janet (Rackliffe) M.; m. Eleanor Bell, Jan. 2, 1977; children: Carolyn, Jonathan, Christian. BA, Rockford Coll., 1965; PhD, U. Va., 1970. Asst. prof. Temple U., Phila., 1968-73; prof. Clarkson U., Potsdam, N.Y., from 1979. Dir. Canadian-U.S. Ctr., Clarkson U., 1988—. Author: Economic Opportunities in Freer U.S. Trade with Canada, 1991, (study guide) Economics, 5th to 11th edit., 1978-96. Fulbright scholar, 2001—02, Nonresident scholar, Ctr. Internat. Climate and Environment, from 2003. Home: Colton, NY. Died Apr. 23, 2006.

MERCADO, JOSEPH ZACARIAS, social worker; b. Sacramento, July 7, 1948; s. Jose and Grace (Esparza) M.; m. Sally Boe, Apr. 11, 1970; children: Dawn Marie, Jennifer Lynn, David Anthony, Christopher Ryan, John Andrew. AA in Social Sci., West Valley Coll., 1980; BA in Psychology, San Jose State U., 1983. Counseling intern Inst. for Community as Extended Family, San Jose, Calif., 1985-86; from eligibility worker I to III Santa Clara County Social Service Dept., San Jose, 1975-78, eligibility work supr. I, from 1978. Religious edn. tchr. St. Lucy's Cath. Ch., Campbell, Calif., 1980-84, St. John Vianney, San Jose, 1984-85. Contbr. articles to profl. jour. Recipient Outstanding Vol. Cert. Appreciation Vol. Action Ctr. Jur. League San Jose, 1978, Award of Merit Parent Participation Nursery Sch. Mgmt. Assn., 1985. Mem. Internat. Soc. for Prevention of Child Abuse and Neglect, Am. Profl. Soc. on Abuse of Children, Am. Assn. for Protecting Children, Nat. Assn. Social Workers (cert.), Alpha Gamma Sigma (cert. achievement 1979). Democrat. Avocation: reading. Home: San Jose, Calif. Died June 24, 2004.

MERI, LENNART, former President of Estonia; b. Tallinn, Estonia, Mar. 29, 1929; s. Georg Peeter and Alice Briggita (Engmann) Meri; m. Helle Pihlak; children: Mart, Kristjan, Tuule. Grad. in History, Tartu U., 1953; DLitt (hon.), Helsinki U., 1986, U. Lapland, Finland, 1999, St. Olaf Coll., 2000, Turku U., 2000. Actor Vanemuine Theatre, 1953—55; prof. Tartu Art Sch.; prodr. Estonian Radio, 1955—61; scriptwriter Tallinnfilm, 1963—68, prodr., 1968—71; fgn. rels. sec. Estonian Writers union, 1985—87; prodr. Tallinnfilm, 1986—88; founder, dir. Estonian Inst., 1988—90; min. fgn. affairs Govt. of Estonia, Tallinn, 1990—92, pres., 1992—2001, amb. to Finland Helsinki, 1992. Head manuscript sect. Vanemuine Theatre, 1953—55. Author: (Books) Following the Trails of Cobras and Black Widows, 1959, Shipmates on the Green Ocean, 1961, To the Land of Fiery Mountains, 1964, At the Gate of Northern Lights, 1974, Silverwhite, 1976, Approaching Coasts, 1977, Silverwhiter, 1984, (Book (in Finnish) Coming from the Country Called Estonia, 1995, (Books) Presidential Speeches, 1996, Presidential Speeches II, 2001; co-author: 1940 in Estonia. Documents and Materials, 1989; author: (films) The Waterfowl People, 1970, The Winds of the Milky Way, 1977, The Sounds of Kaleva, 1986, The Sons of Thorum, 1989, Shaman, 1997. Founder and dir. Estonian Inst., 1988—90; mem. internat. coun. Meml. Found. for Victims of Communism, from 1995; active mem. Estonian Popular Front and Nat. Heritage Preservation Assn., 1980—90; mem. Inter-Parliamentary Coun. against Antisemitism. Authority on the history of the Finno-Ugric peoples. Died Mar. 14, 2006.

MERINOFF, HERMAN IRWIN, vintager, wine company executive; b. NYC, Oct. 28, 1928; s. Charles and Gertrude Merinoff; m. Susan Kletz, 1965; children: Charles, Spencer, Linda, Cathy, Barbara. Grad., Syracuse U.; JD, Harvard U. Chmn., pres., CEO Sonoma Vineyards, Healdsburg, Calif.; CEO Charmer Industries Inc., Queens, N.Y. Vintager, wine and spirits executive. Chmn., pres., CEO Sonoma Vineyards, Healdsburg, Calif; CEO, Charmer Industries Inc., Queens, New York. Died June 28, 2006.

MERRIAM, GEORGE RENNELL, JR., ophthalmologist; b. Harrisburg, Pa., May 22, 1913; s. George Rennell and Harriet (Lombard) M.; m. Martha Hildegarde Carlson, Sept. 5, 1936; children: George, John, Charlotte, Susan. AB, Brown U., 1934; MD, Columbia U., 1941. Diplomate Am. Bd. Ophthalmology. Instr. in ophthalmology Coll. of Physician and Surgeons/Columbia U., N.Y.C., 1949-54, assoc. in ophthalmology, 1955-58, asst. prof. of clin. ophthalmology, 1959-63, assoc. prof. clin. ophthalmology, 1964-73, prof. clin. ophthalmology, 1973-78, prof. emeritus, from 1978. Ophthalmologist Francis Delafield Hosp., N.Y.C., 1949-75; dir. surgical svc. Edward S. Harkness Eye Inst., N.Y.C., 1960-78; cons. ophthalmologist, Meml. Hosp., N.Y.C., 1949-69; cons. Harlem Hosp., N.Y.C., 1970-87. Contbr. articles to profl. jours. Capt. Med. Corps, 1942-45, ETO. Mem. AMA, ACS, Am. Ophthal. Soc., Am. Acad. of Ophthalmology, Am. Radium Soc., N.Y. Ophthal. Soc., N.Y. Acad. Medicine. Republican. Presbyterian. Avocations: sailing, photography, travel. Home: Tenafly, NJ. Died Jan. 13, 2004.

MERRIFIELD, BRUCE (ROBERT BRUCE MERRIFIELD), biochemist, educator; b. Ft. Worth, Tex., July 15, 1921; s. George E. and Lorene (Lucas) Merrifield; m. Elizabeth Furlong, June 20, 1949; children: Nancy, James, Betsy, Cathy, Laurie, Sally. BA, UCLA, 1943, PhD, 1949; PhD (hon.), U. Colo., 1969, Uppsala U., 1970, Yale U., 1971, Newark Coll. Engring., 1972, Med. Coll. Ohio, 1977, Colgate U., 1977, Boston Coll., 1984, Fairleigh Dickinson U., 1985, N.J. U. Medicine & Dentistry, 1985, U. Barcelona, 1986, Adelphi U., 1987, U. Montpellier, 1988, Delaware Valley Coll., 1991, Scripps Rsch. Inst., 1998, Rockefeller U., 1998. Chemist Park Research Found., 1943—44; research asst. Med. Sch., UCLA, 1948—49; asst. Rockefeller Inst. for Med. Research, 1949—53, assoc., 1953—57; asst. prof. Rockefeller U., 1957—58, assoc. prof., 1958—66, prof., 1966—92, John D. Rockefeller prof., 1984—92, prof. emwritus, 1992—2006. Nobel Guest Prof. Uppsala U., 1968. Assoc. editor: Internat. Jour. Peptide and Protein Research; contbr. Named one of Top 75 Contbrs. to Chem. Enterprise during past 75 yrs., Chem. & Engring. News, 1998; recipient Lasker award biomed. rsch., 1969, Gairdner award, 1970, Intra-Sci. award, 1970, Nichols medal, 1973, Instrument Specialties Co. Award, U. Nebr., 1977, Alan E. Pierce award, Am. Peptide Symposium, 1979, Nobel prize in chemistry, 1984, UCLA Disting. Svc. medal, 1986, Royal Soc. Chemistry medal, 1987, Rudinger award, European Peptide Soc., 1990, Chem. Pioneer award, Am. Inst. Chemists, 1993, Glenn T. Seaborg medal, 1993, UCLA Alumnus of Yr. award, 1997, award, Assn. Biomolecular Resource Facilities, 1998. Mem.: NAS USA, Am. Soc. Biol. Chemists, Am. Chem. Soc. (award creative work synthetic organic chemistry 1972, Hirschmann award in peptide chemistry 1990, Glenn T. Seaborg award 1993), Alpha Chi Sigma, Phi Lambda Upsilon, Sigma Xi. Achievements include discovery of solid phase peptide synthesis; completed (with B. Gutte) 1st total synthesis of an enzyme, 69. Home: Cresskill, NJ. Died May 14, 2006.

MERRILL, PHILIP, publisher; b. Balt., Apr. 28, 1934; m. Eleanor Merrill; children: Douglas, Catherine, Nancy. BA, Cornell U., 1955; PMD, Harvard Bus. Sch., 1963. Spl. asst. to dep. sec. US Dept. State, Washington, 1961-68; counselor under sec. for policy US Dept. Def., Washington, 1981-83; asst. sec. gen. NATO, Brussels, 1990-92; pub., chmn. Capital-Gazette Communications, Inc., Washingtonian

Mag., Washington, 1968—2006; pres., chmn. US Export-Import Bank, 2002—05. Mem. Def. Policy Bd., US Dept. Def., 1983-90. Del. USA Short Wave Treaty, USA Law of the Sea Treaty; trustee Cornell U., U. Md. Found., Aspen Inst.; bd. dirs. Ctr. Strategic and Internt. Studies, Johns Hopkins Sch. Advanced Internat. Studies; bd. dirs. Johnson Sch. Mgmt. Cornell U., Chesapeake Bay Found., Fed. City Coun., U. Md. Sch. Pub. Policy; mem. Gulf War Air Power Survey, 1991-92. Recipient Disting. Svc. medal U.S. Dept. Def., 1988. Mem. Coun. Fgn. Rels., Inst. Internat. Strategic Studies, Chief Execs. Orgn., World Pres. Orgn. Home: Arnold, Md. Died June 10, 2006.

MERRITT, JOHN HOWARD, secondary school educator; b. Salisbury, Md., May 19, 1948; s. Robert Wilson and Iris Amy (Horsey) M.; m. Carole A. Tramontana; children: Robert W. II, John H. Jr.; 1 stepchild, Stephen A. Capelli Jr. BS, Salisbury State Coll., 1971; MEd, Salisbury State U., 1990. Cert. secondary tchr., Md. Propr. constrn. bus., Salisbury, 1977-86; high sch. math. tchr. Wicomico Count Schs., Salisbury, from 1986. Instr. math. NROTC Prep Sch., San Diego, 1988-91. Capt. USNR, 1970—2003. Mem.: Kappa Delta Pi. Republican. Methodist. Avocations: swimming, gardening, residential real estate investments, commodity futures trading, ocean and river kayaking. Home: Salisbury, Md. Died Mar. 24, 2004.

MESIHA, MOUNIR SOBHY, industrial pharmacy educator; b. Alexandria, Egypt, Feb. 14, 1945; came to U.S., 1985; s. Madiha Sidhom, Sept. 4, 1972; 1 child, Mena. BS in Pharmacy with distinction, Pharmacy Coll., Alexandria, 1967; PhD in Pharmaceutics, Pharmacy Coll., Kharkov, Ukraine, 1977. Lic. pharmacist. Instr. dept. pharms. U. Assiut, 1967-69, instr., 1969-72, sr. instr., 1972-77, asst. prof. indsl. pharmacy, 1978-83, assoc. prof., 1983-85; prof. indsl. pharmacy U. P.R., San Juan, 1985-89, L.I. U., Bklyn., from 1990. Sci. com. Industry U. Rsch. Ctr., P.R., 1988-89. Contbr. articles to Jour. Pharmacy and Pharmacology, Die Pharmazie, Drug Devel. and Indsl. Pharmacy, Internat. Jour. Pharmaceutics, others. Industry U. Rsch. Ctr. grantee, P.R., 1989. Mem. Am. Diabetes Assn., Am. Pharm. Soc., Am. Assn. Colls. Pharmacy, Am. Assn. Pharm. Scientists (charter), Fedn. Internat. Pharmaceutique (assoc.). Christian Orthodox. Achievements include enhancement of gastrointestinal absorption of insulin in fatty acid media; research in interaction and incomplete release of drug substances incorporated with cellulose derivatives, acceleration of solubility of benzodiazepines by controlled crystallization, energy and mass transfer and properties of tablets during microwave drying of granules, directly compressed controlled release medication, computational chemistry and applied database in design of drug delivery systems and molecular Beta cell target delivery systems. Home: Jericho, NY. Died July 2, 2005.

MESIROW, STANLEY M., dermatologist; b. Benton Harbor, Mich., Apr. 11, 1924; s. Manuel and Pearl (Block) M.; m. Frances Leona Falk, Sept. 8, 1949; children: Manuel, Robert, Donna. BA, U. Chgo.; MD, U. Iowa, 1949. Intern Grant Hosp., Chgo.; resident U. Chgo.; dermatologist Benton Harbor, Mich., from 1955. With U.S. Army, 1943-46, 51-54. Mem. Mich. State Med. Soc., Benton Harbor Med. Soc., Chgo. Med. Assn. Democrat. Jewish. Home: Benton Harbor, Mich. Died July 22, 2004.

MESKILL, DAVID THOMAS, retired manufacturer's representative; b. Boston, Aug. 9, 1917; s. David T. and Florence Mary Meskill; m. Adelaide Agnes Meskill, Oct. 17, 1942; children: Kathleen, Timothy, Susan, Patricia, Maureen. BS in Acctg., U. Notre Dame, 1939. From mgr. fan sales to mgr. cen. zone GE distbn. GE Housewares Div., 1939-76; mfr.'s rep., 1976-82. Editor St. Francis Xavier Parish Sunday Bull. Bd. dirs. North Shore Sr. Ctr.; pres. Shore Line Place, Inc.; chmn. Wilmette (Ill.) Sr. Resources Commn.; mem. Wilmette Forum. Lt. comdr. USN, 1942-46. Named Wilmette Sr. Citizen of Yr., 1989. Mem. Chgo. Housewares Club, GE Elfun Soc. (past chmn. Chgo. soc.). Republican. Roman Catholic. Avocations: gardening, model trains, writing, movie photography. Home: Wilmette, Ill. Died Jan. 13, 2004.

MESSERSCHMIDT, JOYCE IRENE, retired elementary school educator; b. LaGrange Twp., Wis. Teaching cert., Racine Kenosha Norman Sch., 1948; BEd, Wis. State Coll., Whitewater, 1957; MS, U. Wis., Whitewater, 1973. Cert. elem. tchr., Wis. 2d grade tchr. Elkhorn (Wis.) Area Schs.; kindergarten and 1st grade tchr. Sharon (Wis.) Community Schs.; rural sch. tchr. Walworth County, Elkhorn; 1st grade tchr. Elkhorn (Wis.) Area Schs.; ret., 1993. Cooperating tchr. for student tchrs. and interns, mentor for 1st yr. tchrs., chmn. kindergarten-3d grade level Elkhorn Area Schs. Commendation cert. Kenosha, Racine and Walworth Counties, 1993. Mem. NEA, Wis. Edn. Assn., Elkhorn Edn. Assn. (mem. coms.), So. Wis. Edn. Assn., Kiwanis (Tchr. of Yr. 1991), Alpha Delta Kappa (past pres., v.p., sec., mem. coms., chair local chpt., state corr. sec.). Home: Elkhorn, Wis. Died Feb. 4, 2005.

MESSMAN, DAVID VERNON, civil engineer; b. Dakota, Ill., Nov. 27, 1908; s. David Frederick and Edith Jane (Hutchison) M.; m. Edith Marie Bear, July 5, 1936; children: Martha, Laurel; m. Lucille Elizabeth Thern, Dec. 21, 1996. BA in Physics, Cornell Coll., 1932; BCE, U. Wis., 1934. Registered profl. engr., Ga., Tenn. Asst. engr. So. R.R. Sys. various locations, 1936-42; from asst. engr. of bridges to engr. of bridges So. R.R. Sys., Knoxville, Tenn., 1947-61, from asst. engr. to asst. chief engr. Washington and Atlanta, 1962-73; from mgr. to sr. engr. Ralph Whitehead Assoc., Atlanta, 1973-96. With French Horn, Knoxville, Tenn. and Charlotte, N.C., 1946-61. Capt. U.S. Army, 1942-46. Mem. ASCE (life), Am. R.R. Bridge Bldg. Assn., Am. Railway Engring. and Maintenance of Way Assn. (hon.). Avocations: music, French horn. Home: Winona, Minn. Died July 5, 2004.

MESSNER, GERALD MICHAEL, English educator, author, editor; b. Yreka, Calif., Mar. 2, 1935; s. Michiel Harris and Adelaide (Wright) M.; m. Nancy Carol Shingler, Aug. 17, 1963; 1 child, Michael Harris. AB, Stanford U., 1956; postgrad., U. Calif., 1956-57, Stanford U., 1957-58; MA, L.A. State U., 1961. Prof. English Am. River Coll., Sacramento, 1961-64, Coll. San Mateo, Calif., 1964-68, Cañada Coll., Redwood City, Calif., from 1968. Dean humanities Cañada Coll., 1974-79. Author: Another View: Black in America, 1970, Collection: Lit. for 70s, 1972, Patterns of Thinking, 1976, Our Indian Heritage, 1977. Mem. Am. Studies Assn., Calif. Community Colls. Acad. Senate, San Francisco Lighthouse for the Blind. Democrat. Roman Catholic. Avocations: films, film history, black history. Home: Los Altos, Calif. Died Mar. 23, 2004.

METTLER, RUBEN FREDERICK, former electronics and engineering company executive; b. Shafter, Calif., Feb. 23, 1924; s. Henry Frederick and Lydia M.; m. Donna Jean Smith, May 1, 1955; children: Matthew F., Daniel F. Student, Stanford U., 1941; BSEE, Calif. Inst. Tech., 1944, MS, 1947, PhD in Elec. and Aero. Engring, 1949; LHD (hon.), Baldwin-Wallace Coll., 1980; LLD, John Carroll U., 1986. Registered profl. engr., Calif. Assoc. div. dir. systems research and devel. Hughes Aircraft Co., 1949-54; spl. cons. to asst. sec. US Dept. Def., 1954-55; asst. gen. mgr. guided missile research div., tech. supr. Atlas, Titan, Thor and Minuteman programs Ramo-Wooldridge Corp., 1955-58; exec. v.p., then pres. TRW Space Tech. Labs. (merger Thompson Products and Ramo-Wooldridge), 1958-65; pres. TRW Systems Group, 1965-68; asst. pres. TRW Inc., 1968-69, pres., chief operating officer, 1969-77, chmn., CEO, 1977-88. Bd. dirs. Goodyear Tire & Rubber Inst. Internat. Econs., Bank Am. Corp., Merck & Co., Japan Soc. Inc.; mem. Pres. Reagan's Commn. Exec. Exchange, Adv. Coun. on Japan-U.S. Econ. Rels., Pres.'s Blue Ribbon Def. Panel, 1969-70; vice chmn. Def. Industry Adv. Coun., 1964-70, chmn. Pres.'s Task Force on Sci. Policy, 1969-70. Author: reports on airborne electronic systems; patentee interceptor fire control systems. Nat. campaign chmn. United Negro Coll. Fund, 1980-81; chmn. Nat. Alliance Bus., 1978-79; co-chmn. 1980 UN Day, Washington; chmn. bd. trustees Calif. Inst. Tech.; trustee Com. Econ. Devel., Cleve. Clinic Found.; bd. dirs. Nat. Action Council for Minorities in Engring. Served with USN, 1942-46. Named one of Outstanding Young Men of Am., U.S. Jr. C. of C., 1955, So. Calif.'s Engr. of Year, 1964; recipient Meritorious Civilian Service award Dept. Def., 1969, Nat. Human Relations award NCCJ, 1979, Excellence in Mgmt. award Industry Week Mag., 1979, Disting. Service award Calif. Inst. Tech., 1966, Automotive Hall of Fame Leadership Award, Nat. Medal Honor (Electric Industries Assn.), Nat. Engring. award Am. Assn. Engring. Socs., 1993. Fellow IEEE, AIAA; mem. Sci. Research Soc. Am., Bus. Roundtable (chmn. 1982-84), Conf. Bd. (trustee 1982—), Bus. Council (vice chmn. 1981-82, chmn. 1986-87), Nat. Acad. Engring. (Arthur M. Bueche award 1992), The Japan Soc. (bd. dirs.), Sigma Xi, Eta Kappa Nu (Nation's Outstanding Young Elec. Engr. 1954), Tau Beta Pi, Theta Xi. Died May 23, 2006.

METZGER, THOMAS ANDREW, mathematics educator; b. Paterson, N.J., July 14, 1944; s. Andrew and Elizabeth Catherine (Boyle) M.; children: Beth Ann, James T., Pamela M., Katie, Bill. BS, Seton Hall U., 1965; MS, Creighton U., 1967; PhD, Purdue U., 1971. Asst. prof. math. Tex. A&M U., College Station, 1971-73; asst. prof. math. and statistics U. Pitts., 1973-80, assoc. prof., 1981—. Author: BMOA on Riemann S., 1987; contbr. articles to profl. jours. Capt. U.S. Army, 1965-73. Mem. Am. Math. Soc., Math. Assn. Am. Home: New Kensington, Pa. Died Feb. 24, 2005.

MEYER, ARMIN HENRY, former ambassador; b. Ft. Wayne, Ind., Jan. 19, 1914; s. Armin Paul and Leona (Buss) M.; m. Alice James, Apr. 23, 1949; 1 dau., Kathleen Alice. Student, Lincoln Coll., Ill., 1931-33; AB, Capital U., 1935, LL.D., 1957; MA, Ohio State U., 1941, LL.D., 1972, Wartburg Coll., S.D. Sch. Mines and Tech., 1972. Faculty Capital U., Columbus, Ohio, 1935-41; staff OWI, Egypt, Iraq, 1942-46; U.S. pub. affairs officer Baghdad, Iraq, 1946-48; pub. affairs adviser U.S. Dept. State, 1948-52; sec. Am. Embassy, Beirut, 1952—55, dep. chief mission Kabul, Afghanistan, 1955—57; dep. dir. Office South Asian Affairs US Dept. State, 1957-58, dep. dir. Office Near Eastern Affairs, 1958-59, dir. Office Near Ea. Affairs, 1959-61, dep. asst. sec. of state for Nr. Ea. and South Asian Affairs, 1961, US amb. to Lebanon Beirut, 1961—65, US amb. to Iran Tehran, 1965—69, US amb. to Japan Tokyo, 1969—72, spl. asst. to sec., chmn. Cabinet Com. to Combat Terrorism, 1972-73. Vis. prof. Am. U., 1974-75; dir. Ferdowsi project Georgetown U., 1975-79, adj. prof. diplomacy, 1975-86; Woodrow Wilson vis. fellow, 1974-2006; cons. internat. bus. and environment, 1975-2006. Author: Assignment Tokyo: An Ambassador's Journal, 1974, Quiet Diplomacy, Fro Cairo to Tokyo in the Twilight of Imperialism, 2003; co-author: Education in Diplomacy, 1987. Hon. mem. Lincoln Sesquicentennial Commn., 1959; bd. dirs. Washington Inst. Fgn. Affairs, 1979-2006, pres., 1988-98. Recipient Meritorious Svc. award Dept. State, 1958, Superior Honor award, 1973; decorated Order of Rising Sun, 1st class (Japan), 1982; inducted into Hall of Excellence Ohio Fedn. Ind. Colls., 1989. Mem. Sigma Psi. Lutheran. Home: Washington, DC. Died Aug. 13, 2006.

MEYER, CHARLES FRANKLIN, electrical engineer; b. El Paso, Tex., Jan. 18, 1922; s. Charles Franklin and Annis Belle (Ford) M.; m. Alice B. Longbottom, Apr. 24, 1942; children: C. Richard, D. Lee, Barbara. BSEE, N.Mex. State U., 1942; MS, U. Ariz., 1955; postgrad., Stanford U., 1956. Engr. Gen. Electric Co., Pa., N.Y., Conn., and N.Mex., 1942-44, 45-49; sr. project leader Motorola Research Lab., Phoenix, 1949-56; engring. specialist and program mgr. Sylvania Electronic Def. Lab., Mountain View, Calif., 1956-63; mem. tech. staff, program mgr. Gen. Electric. Ctr. for Advanced Studies, Santa Barbara, Calif., 1963-81; sr. scientist Kaman Scis. Corp., Santa Barbara, from 1982. Cons. in advanced energy systems, Santa Barbara, 1981-82; cons. electronic warfare specialist, analyst, 1982—. Contbr. articles to profl. jours. Commr. Santa Barbara City Bd. Water Commrs., 1974—. Served with USNR, 1944-45. Mem. IEEE, Am. Geophys. Union, Assn. Old Crows, Winchester Canyon Gun Club (bd. dirs. 1977-83), Nat. Rifle Assn., Sigma Xi, Sigma Tau. Avocations: shooting, photography, computers. Home: Santa Barbara, Calif. Died Oct. 7, 2004.

MEYER, JANE STIRLING, advertising executive; b. New Haven, Conn., Oct. 4, 1949; d. John Stirling and Wendy (Haskell) M.; m. Claude Mundy, Apr. 21, 1990. Student, U. Mich., 1967-68; BFA, Ea. Mich. U., 1972. Art gallery owner Basilisk Gallery, Ann Arbor, Mich., 1972-75; dir. Geotype mktg. Words & Things, Houston, 1975-77; dir. bus. devel. Graphic Support Group, Houston, 1977-80; account mgr. bus. devel. Graphic Designers Group, Houston, 1980-82; cons. bus. devel., account mgr. Piland Goodell Inc., Houston, 1982-85, Hinckley & Slade, Inc., Houston, 1985-88; cons. bus. devel. Internat. Printing & Pub., Houston, 1988-90; v.p. bus. devel. Manlove Advt., Houston, from 1990. Speaker Massey Bus. Coll., U. Houston, 1976, Houston Credit Union Mktg. Round Table, 1991. Painter, artist, sculptor and ceramicist. Mem. Soc. Mktg. Profl. Svcs., Internat. Assn. Bus. Communicators (Excaliber award 1981, various creative awards), Greater Houston Builders Assn. Avocations: aerobics, running, weights, reading. Home: Houston, Tex. Died Apr. 28, 2005.

MEYER, MARTA BOHN, federal agency administrator; BS in Aero. Engring., Rensselaer Poly. Inst., Troy, N.Y. Jr. engr. NASA's Dryden Flight Rsch. Ctr., Edwards, Calif., ops. engr. F-104 aircraft, ops. engr. F-14 variable sweep laminar flow flight experiment, project mgr. F-16XL supersonic laminar flow control project, crew mem. SR-71 aircraft, 1991, aerospace project mgr., dep. dir. aerospace projects, dep. dir. flight ops., dir. Office of Safety and Mission Assurance, 1999—2005. Lectr in field. Avocations: building and flying aerobatic airplanes, running, reading, writing, sewing. Died Sept. 18, 2005.

MEYER, RAYMOND JOSEPH, retired college basketball coach; b. Chgo., Dec. 18, 1913; s. Joseph E. and Barbara (Hummel) M.; m. Margaret Mary Delaney, May 27, 1939 (dec. 1985); children— Barbara (Mrs. Gerald Starzyk), Raymond Thomas, Patricia (Mrs. Thomas Butterfield), Merianne (Mrs. James McGowan; dec. 1997), Joseph, Robert. AB, U. Notre Dame, 1938. Asst. coach U. Notre Dame, 1941-42; basketball coach DePaul U., Chgo., 1942—84, spl. asst. to the pres., 1984—97. Author: How To Play Winning Basketball, 1960, Basketball as Coached by Ray Meyer, 1967, Ray Meyer, 1 Coach, 1980, Coach, 1987. Named Coach of Yr. Chgo. Basketball Writers, 1943, 44, 48, 52, Coach of Yr. Nat. Assn. Basketball Coaches, 1978-79, Sportwriters Coach of Yr., 1978, Salvation Man of Yr., 1990; recipient Marine Corps Sportsman of Yr. award, 1979, Bunn award, 1981, Victor award, 1981, Lincoln Acad. award, 1988, Nat. Basketball Coach's Golden Jubilee award, Notre Dame Lifetime Achievement award 1998; inducted into Basketball Hall of Fame, 1979, Basketball Hall of Fame Chgo., 1981, Basketball Hall of Fame Ill., Golden Anniversay award Nat. Basketball Coaches, 1992, Naismith Found. Good Sportsman's award, 1998. Mem. Nat. Basketball Coaches Assn. Roman Catholic. Died Mar. 17, 2006.

MEYER, SHELDON, publisher; b. Chgo., June 8, 1926; s. Arthur Christof and Hester Truslow (Sheldon) M.; m. Margaret Mary Kirk, July 29, 1964; children: Arabella Christina, Andrew Kirk. AB summa cum laude, Princeton U., 1949; MA (hon.), U. Oxford, 1993. With Funk & Wagnalls Co., 1951—55; assoc. editor Grosset & Dunlap, 1955-56; with Oxford Univ. Press, N.Y.C., 1956-96, editor, 1956-70; exec. editor Trade Books, 1970-82, v.p., 1974-79, sr. v.p., 1982-96, consulting editor, 1997—2006. Recipient The Lawrenceville medal for eminent achievement, The Lawrenceville Sch., 2001. Mem. Am. Assn. Univ. Presses (bd. dirs. 1969-71, 79-82, v.p. 1979-80), Am. Hist. Assn., Orgn. Am. Historians, Inst. Early Am. History and Culture (bd. dirs. 1985-87), Nat. Bd. Rev. Motion Pictures, Century Assn., Phi Beta Kappa. Home: New York, NY. Died Oct. 9, 2006.

MEYER, WARREN GEORGE, vocational educator; b. Plymouth, Wis., May 12, 1910; s. charles Martin and Lillie Margaret (Liese) M.; m. Marion Magdaline Lehmann, June 19, 1939; children: Karen Rhem, Stephen George. BA, U. Wis., 1932; MS, NYU, 1933. Asst. buyer Mandel bros.,

Chgo., 1933-34, The Davis Store, Chgo., 1934-35; divsn. head Sears Roebuck & Co., Lansing, Mich., 1935-36, Detroit, 1936-37; mktg. instr. Vocat. Adult Sch., West Allis, Wis., 1937-38; adult field instr. Wis. Vocat. Schs., 1938-41; state supr. Dept. Vocat. Edn., Topeka, Kans., 1941-46; prof. vocat. edn. U. Minn., Mpls., 1946-76, vocat. prof. emeritus, from 1976. Vocat. edn. cons. U.S. Dept. State, Frankfurt, Germany, 1951; mktg. edn. cons. Va. Poly. Inst. and State U., Blacksburg, 1960-70, U. Mass., Amherst, 1966; adv. coun. mem. Nat. Ctr. for Vocat. Edn., Columbus, Ohio, 1965-75. Lead author: Retail Marketing Principles and Practices, 1964-82 edits.; co-author: Coordination in Cooperative Vocational Education, 1975; lead author: Retail Marketing, 1988; editor: Vocational Education and Nations Economy, 1977. Lt. (s.g.) USNR, 1944-46. Recipient Tchr. Edn. Acad. award Coun. for Distributive Tchr. Edn., 1969, Horace Morse Standard Oil award U. Minn., 1972, John Robert Gregg award Nat. Bus. Edn. Assn., 1973. Mem. Am. Vocat. Assn. (hon. life), Lions (sec. 1980-98), Men of Yorke, Delta Pi Epsilon. Home: Edina, Minn. Died Nov. 27, 2004.

MGRDECHIAN, RAFFEE, electronics company executive; b. N.Y.C., Aug. 4, 1927; s. DeKran and Aznive (Sobajian) M.; m. Zabelle Mesrobian, Jan. 21, 1956; children: Dickran, Joyce Mgrdechian Kechian, Dora Lee Mgrdechian Morris. BEE, CUNY, 1950. Test and design engr. Lewyt Corp., Bklyn., 1950-54; chief engr. Carol Electronics, Martinsburg, W.Va., 1954-56, Keystone Products, Union City, N.J., 1956-58; gen. mgr. magnetics Westbury (N.Y.) Electronics, 1958-60; mgr. ops. INTEC (merger with Westbury Electronics), 1960-61; v.p., gen. mgr. De-Flectronics, Groton, Conn., 1961-63; v.p. R & D, Axel Electronics Inc., Jamaica, N.Y., from 1963. Contbr. articles to symposia. Former Sunday sch. tchr., trustee, chmn. bd. trustees Armenian Ch. of Holy Martyrs, Bayside, N.Y.; cubmaster Boy Scouts Am., 1969-70. Mem. Knights of Vartan (comdr. 1984-85, chmn. Mid-Atlantic 1988). Avocations: swimming, gardening, music, reading, writing. Home: Westbury, NY. Died Mar. 19, 2004.

MICHAEL, HENRY N., retired geography and anthropology educator; b. Pitts., July 14, 1913; s. Anthony M. and Albina (Dubska) M.; m. Ida Nemez, June 18, 1943; children: Susan Shelley, Richard Carleton, Andrew Paul. BA, U. Pa., 1948, MA, 1951, PhD, 1954. Instr. geography U. Pa., 1948-54; faculty Temple U., 1958-80, prof. geography, chmn. dept., 1965-73, prof., 1965-80. Rsch. assoc. Univ. Mus., Phila., 1959-82, sr. fellow; mem. Bi-Nat. Commn. Social Scis. Humanities, Am. Council Learned Socs./Acad. Scis. USSR. Editor: Anthropology of the North, 1959-72; editor, author: Dating Techniques for the Archaeologist, 1971, 73, 82; translator, editor various archaeol. and ethnographic works; mem. adv. publs. com. Mus. Applied Sci. Ctr. for Archaelogy, U. Pa., Anthropology and Archaeology of Eurasia-A Jour. of Transls., Alaska-Siberia Rsch. Ctr.; mem. editorial bd. Expedition-The Univ. Mus. Mag. Archaeology and Anthropology, U. Pa.; contbr. articles to profl. jours. Served to 1st lt. AUS, 1942-45. Decorated Purple Heart; recipient Dir.'s award U. Pa. Mus. Archaeology, Anthropology, 2000. Fellow Am. Anthrop. Assn., Arctic Inst. N.Am.; mem. Phila. Anthrop. Soc. (coun. 1954-90), Delaware Valley Assn. Geographers, Assn. Am. Geographers, Sigma Xi. Home: Ardmore, Pa. Died Feb. 19, 2006.

MICHAEL, JAMES HARRY, JR., federal judge; b. Charlottesville, Va., Oct. 17, 1918; s. James Harry and Reuben (Shelton) m. Barbara E. Puryear, Dec. 18, 1946 (dec. Dec. 2002); children: Jarrett Michael Stephens, Victoria von der Au. BS, U. Va., 1940, LLB, 1942. Bar: Va. 1942. Sole practice, Charlottesville; ptnr. Michael & Musselman, 1946-54, J.H. Michael, Jr., 1954-59, Michael & Dent, 1959-72, Michael, Dent & Brooks Ltd., 1972-74, Michael & Dent, Ltd., 1974-80; assoc. judge Juvenile and Domestic Rels. Ct., Charlottesville, 1954-68; judge U.S. Dist. Ct. (we. dist.) Va., Charlottesville, 1980-95, sr. judge, 1995—2005; mem. Va. State Senate, Richmond, 1968-80. Exec. dir. Inst. Pub. Affairs, U. Va., 1952; chmn. Coun. State Govts., 1975-76, also mem. exec. com.; chmn. So. Legis. Conf., 1974-75. Mem. Charlottesville Sch. Bd., 1951-62; bd. govs. St. Anne-Belfield Sch., 1952-76. Served with USNR, 1942-46; comdr. Res. ret. Wilton Park fellow Wilton Park Conf., Sussex, Eng., 1971 Fellow Am. Bar Found.; mem. ABA, Va. Bar Assn. (v.p. 1956-57), Charlottesville-Albermarle Bar Assn. (pres. 1966-67), Am. Judicature Soc., 4th Jud. Conf., Va. Trial Lawyers Assn. (Va. disting. svc. award 1993), Assn. Trial Lawyers Am., Raven Soc., Sigma Nu Phi, Omicron Delta Kappa. Episcopalian (lay reader). Home: Charlottesville, Va. Died Aug. 29, 2005.

MICHAELS, AGNES ISABELLE, education educator; b. Cooperstown, N.Y., Feb. 3, 1912; d. Howard Nehemiah and Edna Isabelle (Potter) M. BS, SUNY, Cortland, 1936; MA, NYU, 1948; EdD, U. Buffalo, 1954. Tchr. Montour Falls (N.Y.) Pub. Schs., 1936-38; supr. phys. edn. North Tonawanda (N.Y.) Pub. Schs., 1938-41; tchr. phys. edn. Bethlehem Cen. Schs., Delmar, N.Y., 1941-44; club dir. ARC, CBI Theater, 1944-46; dir. phys. edn. St. Mary's Hall, San Antonio, 1946-47; asst. prof. Okla. State U., 1947-48; assoc. prof. dir. women's physical edn., health SUNY, Fredonia, 1948-73, assoc. prof. emeritus, from 1973. Mem. curriculum com. SUNY, Fredonia, 1948-73; mem. Village of Fredonia Parks Commn. 1959-61. Contbr. articles to profl. jours. Golden Eaglet Girl Scout, 1929. Recipient Life Sav. medal ARC, 1929, Presidential citation for meritorius svc., World War II, 1946. Mem. AAUW, Eastern Assn. Phys. Edn. for Coll. Women (emeritus), Vero Beach Art Club, Kappa Delta Pi, Pi Lambda Theta. Methodist. Avocations: photography, jewelry, painting, lapidary. Home: Melbourne, Fla. Died Jan. 13, 2004.

MICHAELSON, GERALD ALLEN, marketing consultant; b. Wausau, Wis., Feb. 23, 1929; s. Alexander Knute and Emilie (Schneider) M.; m. Janice Dawn Uekert, May 21, 1956; children: Steven, Deanne. BBA, U. Wis., 1951. Field service trainer Maytag Corp., Newton, Iowa, 1951-56; field sales mgr. Magnavox Co., Los Angeles, 1957-65, div. mgr. Detroit, 1966-71, v.p. N.Y.C., 1971-74, Ft. Wayne, Ind., 1974-80, N.Am. Philips, Knoxville, Tenn., 1980-84; cons. ABT Assocs., Cambridge, Mass., from 1984, Tenn. Assocs. Internat., from 1987. Bd. dirs. LaCrosse, Wis. Footwear. Author: Winning the Marketing War, 1987; contbr. articles on sales and mktg. to profl. pubs. 2d lt. U.S. Army, 1952-53, Korea. Mem. Am. Mktg. Assn. (v.p. 1987-88), Univ. Wis. Iron Cross Soc. Home: Knoxville, Tenn. Died July 18, 2004.

MICHELE, DIANE, counselor, psychotherapist, educator; b. Pontiac, Mich., Apr. 27, 1954; d. Nick and Elaine A. (Larson) Palmer; m. James Michael Dankovich, May 20, 1989 (div. Apr. 1996); 1 child, Christopher James. AA in Psychology, Oakland C.C., 1978; BA in Psychology, Mercy Coll. Detroit, 1980; MA in Counseling, Oakland U., 1983; M in Metaphysics, U. Metaphysics, 1997, PhD in Metaphysics, 1998. Cert. social worker, Mich.; lic. profl. counselor, Mich.; nat. bd. cert. clin. hypnotherapist; nat. bd. fellow. counselor; diplomate in psychotherapy; ordained min. Internat. Metaphys. Ministry, 1996. Saleswoman Dale Carnegie courses, 1976-79; dir. admissions Hospice of Southeastern Mich., 1980-83; pvt. practice Woodcreek Counseling, 1983-95; grief specialist funeral homes, 1985-95; pvt. practice, cons., spkr., trainer Birmingham, Mich., from 1995. Adj. prof. Siena Heights U., Southfield, Mich., 1988—; co-dir., v.p. Metro Detroit Ctr. for Attitudinal Healing, Royal Oak, Mich., 1992-99; cons., trainer, spkr. Selfridge Air Force Base, 1994—. Acad. chair PTA Pierce Elem., Birmingham, 1997-98. Recipient Spl. Recognition for outstanding merit in area of continuing edn. Nat. Bd. Cert. Counselors. Mem.: ACA, Acad. of Religion and Psychical Rsch., Mich. Assn. for Spiritual, Ethical and Religious Values in Counseling (pres. 2002—04), Assn. for Religious and Spiritual Values in Counseling, Mich. Assn. for Marriage and Family Counseling, Mich. Counseling Assn., Am. Assn. for Marriage and Family Counseling, Internat. Network for Attitudinal Healing (regional steward). Unity. Avocations: scuba diving, flying single engine land airplane, gardening, reading, meditation. Home: Rochester Hills, Mich. Died Apr. 24, 2005.

MICHELIN, EDOUARD, tire company executive; b. Clermont-Ferrand, Puy-de-Dome, France, Aug. 13, 1963; s. Francois Michelin and Bernadette (Montagne); married; 6 children. BS, Ecole Centrale, Paris, 1985. With Compagnie Générale des Etablissements Michelin, France, 1989; plant mgr. Michelin N. Am. ops., 1991—93; mng. ptnr. Compagnie Générale des Etablissements Michelin, Clermont-Ferrand, France, 1991—99; chief exec. Compagnie Général des Établissements Michelin, 1999—2006. Served in French Navy, 1987—89. Avocation: theology. Died May 26, 2006.

MICHELMAN, IRVING SIMON, financial consultant; b. Pittsfield, Mass., Nov. 1, 1917; s. Abraham M. and Rae (Goldstein) M.; m. Shirley Stoloff, Sept. 8, 1940; children: John, Nancy. BS cum laude, Harvard U., 1939. Exec. v.p. Signature Loan Co., Inc., N.Y.C., 1940-58, Budget Industries, Inc., L.A., 1958-72; ind. fin. cons. L.A., from 1973. Adv. com. for truth-in-lending legislation FRS, 1960; mem. Nat. Bus. Coun. Consumer Affairs, U.S. Dept. Commerce, 1962. Author: Business at Bay: Critics and Heretics of American Business, 1965 (Best Non-fiction award Commonwealth Club Calif.), textbooks on bus. adminstrn. With USNR, 1943-45. Mem. Am. Arbitration Assn. Democrat. Jewish. Died May 14, 2005.

MICK, DAVID LEE, agronomist; b. Newton, Iowa, Oct. 25, 1937; s. Clifford Merlyn and Errisje (Kolfschoten) M.; m. Phyllis Lorraine Monsma, June 2, 1959; children: Todd, Krista, Kayla. BS, Iowa State U., 1960, MS, 1961, PhD, 1969. Extension agronomist Iowa State U., Ames, 1962-65, extension entomologist, 1965-69; assoc. prof. preventive medicine and environ. health Coll. Medicine, U. Iowa, Iowa City, 1969-74; dir. Land Quality div. Iowa Dept. Environ. Quality, Des Moines, 1974; entomologist Laverty Sprayers, Inc., Indianola, Iowa, 1974-83; mgr. agronomy Pioneer Hi-Bred Internat., Inc., Liberty, Mo., from 1983. Contbr. articles to profl. and popular publs., 1965—. Mem. Sigma Xi, Gamma Sigma Delta. Presbyterian. Achievements include patent for Log Burning Support. Died Nov. 25, 2004.

MIDDLETON, JOHN CALVIN, biochemistry-toxicology consultant; b. Chgo., Oct. 5, 1922; s. John Calvin and Lydia Mary (Blaha) M.; m. Maxine Belle Rohrer, Jan. 29, 1943; children: John C. III, M. Edward, Tina Katherine. BSc. in Chemistry, Wayne U., 1947, MSc., 1955; postgrad., Johns Hopkins U., 1983-88. Hematologist technician Harper Hosp., Detroit, 1946-48; tchr. Detroit Pub. Schs., 1948-53; lab. mgr. 3M Co-ACS Div., Detroit, L.A., 1953-63; dir. product safety U.S. Borax & Chem. Co., Anaheim, Calif., 1963-89, cons. L.A., from 1989. Contbr. articles to profl. jours., including Jour. Am. Water Works, Chem. Engring., Jour. Forest Prodn. Rsch. Soc., Jour. Dermatology. Mem. sch. bd. Yorba Linda (Calif.) Sch. Dist., 1955-63; adv. com. mem. Fullerton (Calif.) Community Coll., 1957-63; mem. adv. bd. CAL-OSHA, San Francisco, 1990-91; life mem. PTA, Yorba Linda, Calif., 1957. 1st lt. U.S. Army, 1944-46, 50-52. Recipient Allderdice award Chem. Specialties Mfrs. Assn., 1983, Disting. Mem. award, 1989. Mem. Am. Coll. Toxicology, Am. Chem. Soc. (chmn. Orange County, Calif. chpt. 1976), Am. Conf. on Chem. Labeling. Republican. Presbyterian. Achievements include 57 U.S. and fgn. patents. Home: Oxnard, Calif. Died Jan. 11, 2004.

MIDDLETON, MICHAEL CHARLES, electrical engineer; b. Flint, Mich., Oct. 8, 1937; s. Leo C. and Vivian Marie (Peterson) M.; m. Marsha R. Gustafson, June 26, 1960; children: Bonnie, Lisa. BSBA, U. Phoenix, 1982. Electronic technician Gen. Electric, Phoenix, 1965-66, Motorola Corp., Phoenix, 1966-67; sr. elec. engr. Honeywell, Phoenix, 1967-84; elec. engr., chief exec. officer Wirebenders, Phoenix, from 1984. Cons. THESYS Memory Systems, Scottsdale, Ariz., 1983-85. Contbr. articles to profl. mags.; inventor computer sequencing. Served with USAF, 1956-60. Mem. Ariz. Bicycle Club (pres. 1965-75). Republican. Presbyterian. Avocations: backpacking, bicycling. Home: Glendale, Ariz. Died June 1, 2005.

MIGNACCA, EGIDIO CARMEN, retired principal; b. Detroit, May 19, 1931; s. Luigi and Antonietta (Lato) M.; m. Joann Veronica Oddo, July 31, 1965; 1 child, Briana. BS in Edn., Wayne State U., 1957, EdD in Adminstrn., 1988; MA in Edn., U. Detroit, 1962; EdS in Adminstrn., Ea. Mich. U., 1975. Tchr. Detroit Bd. Edn., 1957-68, Warren (Mich.) Consol. Schs., 1968-70, 81-83, 84-86, asst. prin., 1970-75, 83-84, cmty. edn. specialist, 1980-81, prin., 1975-80 and from 86. Instr. U. Detroit, 1975-77. Mem. Optimists (treas. Sterling-Warren, Mich. 1990), Phi Delta Kappa (v.p. 1978-79). Republican. Roman Catholic. Avocations: history, art history, foreign travel, music, walking. Home: Sterling Heights, Mich. Died Mar. 6, 2004.

MIKESELL, RAYMOND FRECH, economics professor; b. Eaton, Ohio, Feb. 13, 1913; s. Otho Francis and Josephine (Frech) M.; m. Desyl DeLauder, 1937 (div.); children: George DeLauder and Norman DeLauder (twins); m. Irene Langdoc, 1957 (dec.); m. Grace Schneiders, 1997. Student, Carnegie Inst. Tech., 1931-33; BA cum laude, Ohio U., 1935, MA, 1935, PhD, 1939. Asst. prof. econ. U. Wash., 1937-41; economist OPA, Washington, 1941-42, U.S. Treasury Dept., 1942-46, rep. Cairo, 1943-44, cons., 1946-47; on Middle East affairs FOA, 1953; chief fgn. minerals div. Pres.'s Materials Policy Commn., 1951-52; mem. staff Fgn. Econ. Policy Com. (Randall Com.), 1953-54; mem. U.S. Currency Mission to Saudi Arabia, 1948; spl. U.S. rep. to Israel, summer 1952; mem. U.S. mission to Israel, Ethiopia, summer 1953; prof. econs. U. Va., 1946-57; W.E. Miner prof. econs. U. Oreg., 1957-87, emeritus prof. econ., from 1987; dir. Inst. Internat. Studies and Overseas Adminstrn., 1958-60; assoc. dir. Inst. Internat. Studies and Overseas Adminstrn. U. Oreg., 1960-68; vis. prof. Grad. Inst. Internat. Studies, Geneva, 1964. Sr. staff mem. Council Econ. Advisers, Exec. Office of Pres., 1955-56, cons. to Council Econ. Advisers, 1956-57; cons. Pan Am. Union, 1954-63, Dept. State, 1947-53, 63-67, 71-83, Ford Found., 1962, Dept. Commerce, 1962-64, ICA, 1952-53, 61-62, OAS, 1963-73, AID, 1964-71; mem. UN Econ. Commn. for Latin Am. working group on regional market, 1958; cons. Senate Fgn. Relations Com., 1962, 67, World Bank, 1968, Inter-Am. Devel. Bank, 1968-75; mem. panel advisers Sec. Treasury, 1965-69; sr. fellow Nat. Bur. Econ. Research, 1972-73 Author: U.S. Economic Policy and International Relations, 1952, Foreign Exchange in the Postwar World, 1954, The Emerging Pattern of International Payments, 1954, Foreign Investments in Latin America, 1955, Promoting United States Private Investments Abroad, 1957, Agricultural Surpluses and Export Policy, 1958, U.S. Private and Government Investment Abroad, 1962, (with M. Trued) Arabian Oil, 1949, (with H. Chenery) Postwar Bilateral Payments Agreements, 1955, (with J. Behrman) Financing Free World Trade with the Sino-Soviet Bloc, 1958, Public International Lending for Development, 1966, (with R.W. Adler) Public External Financing of Developing Banks, 1966, Public Foreign Capital for Private Enterprises in Developing Countries, 1966, The Economics of Foreign Aid, 1968, Financing World Trade, 1969, (with others) Foreign Investment in the Petroleum and Mineral Industries, 1971, (with H. Furth) Foreign Dollar Balances and the International Role of the Dollar, 1974, Foreign Investment in the Copper Industry, 1975, The World Copper Industry, 1979, New Patterns of World Mineral Development, 1979, The Economics of Foreign Aid and Self-Sustaining Development, 1983, Foreign Investment in Mining Projects, 1983, Petroleum Company Operations and Agreements in the Developing Countries, 1984, Stockpiling Strategic Materials, 1986, Nonfuel Minerals: Foreign Dependence and National Security, 1987, (with John W. Whitney) The World Mining Industry: Investment Strategy and Public Policy, 1987, The Global Copper Industry: Problems and Prospects, 1988, (with Lawrence F. Williams) International Banks and the Environment, 1992, Economic Development and the Environment, 1992, The Bretton Woods Debates, 1994, (with Richard Auty) Sustainable Development in Mineral Economies, 1998, Foreign Adventures of an Economist, 2000; mem. editl. adv. bd. Middle East Jour., 1947-58; mem. bd. editors: Am. Econ. Rev., 1953-55. Home: Eugene, Oreg. Died Sept. 12, 2006.

MIKLOZEK, FRANK LOUIS, retired federal agency administrator, consultant, lawyer; b. Terre Haute, Ind., Aug. 22, 1914; s. Stanislaus M. and Nellie Sophia Meyer; m. Louise S. Stoffers, Nov. 29, 1945; children: Candace L.,

Meredith A., Frank L. Jr. BA, Ind. State U., 1936; JD, Ind. U., 1939. Bar: Ind. 1939, U.S. Dist. Ct. (so. dist.) Ind. 1939. Pvt. practice, Terre Haute, Ind., 1939-41; assoc. Beasley, O'Brien & Beasley, Terre Haute, Ind., 1945-50; postmaster sectional ctr. US Postal Svc., Terre Haute, Ind., 1950-74, postmaster, 1972-74; nat. pres. Nat. Assn. Postmasters, Washington, 1972-73; exec. dir. Nat. Assn. Postmaster US, Washington, 1974-86, cons. legis. matters, 1986-95. Asst. city atty. City of Terre Haute, Ind., 1948-50. Contbr. articles to Postmaster's Gazette, 1972-86. Pres. Vigo County Young Democrats, Terre Haute, Ind, 1947-50, Sixth Congressional Dist., Terre Haute, 1948-49. 2nd lt. US Army, 1941-45. Recipient Disting. Alumni Ind. State U., 1974, Cert. of Appreciation for Svc. on Draft Bd. President L.B.J. Johnson, R. Nixon, 1956-72, Order of the Vest Nat. Air Trans. Assn. Mem. Nat. ASsn. Postmasters (life), Ind. U. Alumni Assn. Democrat. Roman Catholic. Avocations: inventing games, civil war, golf, hiking, travel. Home: Gaithersburg, Md. Died July 13, 2004.

MILANO, CECELIA MANCHOR, mental health nurse; b. Pitts., Apr. 19, 1918; d. Joseph and Anna (Plisowski) Manchor; m. Louis J. Milano, Aug. 12, 1946. BSN, Duquesne U., 1945; MS in Adult Psychiat. Nursing, Boston U., 1961; cert. in family therapy, Cambridge Family Inst., 1977; postgrad., Boston U., 1978; cert. in Advanced Grad. Study Spl. Edn., Nova U., 1991, D. in Public Admistrn., 1991. RN, Pa., Fla., Mass. Head nurse med.-surg. unit various hosps., Akron, Ohio, 1945-47; adminstrv. supr. med.-surg. unit Presbyn.-Univ. Hosp., Pitts., 1949-50; asst. prof. psychiat. nursing U. Miami, Fla., 1955-66, U. Pitts., 1966-67, Duquesne U., 1967-68; asst. prof. grad. psychiat. nursing Boston U., 1970-74; nurse psychiat. emergency svcs. Jackson Meml. Hosp., Miami, from 1979. Presenter workshops; speaker at seminars Rep. Pres. Carter's Freedom Forces, spring 1995, Moscow. Fellow Orthopsychiat. Assn.; mem. Alpha Tau Delta. Home: Miami, Fla. Died May 25, 2004.

MILITELLO, SAMUEL PHILIP, lawyer; b. Buffalo, Dec. 16, 1947; s. Samuel Anthony and Katherine (Pesono) M.; m. Anne Little, May 27, 1972, divorced Dec. 26, 2003; children: Matthew Samuel, Rebecca Anne, Caitlin Frances. BA, Canisius Coll., 1969; JD, SUNY, Buffalo, 1972. Bar: NY 1972, US Ct. Mil. Appeals 1973, US Army Ct. of Mil. Rev. 1976, US Ct. Claims 1977, US Supreme Ct. 1977, US Dist. Ct. (we. dist.) NY 1986, US Dist. Ct. (no. dist.) NY 1987, US Dist. Ct. (ea. dist.) NY 1994, US Ct. Appeals (2d cir.), 1990. Assoc. Williams & Katzman, Watertown, NY, 1978-79; legal counsel, mgr. of litigation Parsons Corp., Pasadena, Calif., 1979-84; gen. counsel, sec. Envirogas, Inc., Hamburg, NY, 1984-86; assoc. Bond, Schoeneck & King, Watertown, 1987-88; mng. ptnr. Samuel P. Militello, PC, 1995, Watertown, 1989-1995; counsel Parsons Gilbane, New Orleans, 1979-81; gen. counsel The Stebbins Engring. and Mfg. Co. and subs., 1986—. Capt. JAGC, US Army, 1973-78. Decorated Army Commendation medal with one oak leaf cluster, Meritorious Service medal. Mem. ABA, NY State Bar Assn., Bar Assn. of Erie County (NY), mem. of Bd. of Dir., No. Wy. Builders Exchange, 1989-1995; mem., Bd. of Dir. of Mery Hosp. of watertwon, NY; mem., of Sch. Bd. of Imaculate Heart, Ctrl. HS, 1988-2000; Knights of Columbus, 4th degree; Bar Assn. of Jefferson County (NY), Am. Legion, K.C. (adv. 1978-79). Roman Catholic. Died Oct. 4, 2004.

MILLAR, BARBARA LEE, technical writer, school administrator; b. St. Louis, Feb. 15, 1947; d. Roe Dell and Dorothy Anna (Fuhrmann) Rowland; m. James Watson Millar, June 10, 1980 (div. Sept. 1988); children: James R., Katherine, Matthew, Jack. BA in Math., U. Mo., St. Louis, 1969; MA in Math., So. Ill. U., Edwardsville, 1971; MA in Applied Linguistics, So. Ill. U., Carbondale, 1994. lic. comml. pilot; cert. flight instr. Instr. math. So. Ill. U., Edwardsville, 1969-71; effectivity engr. McDonnell Douglas Aircraft Corp., St. Louis, 1976-81; ops. rsch. analyst Dept. Army, St. Louis, 1981-82; editl. assoc. So. Ill. U., Carbondale, 1991-94; lectr., instr. So. Ill. U. and John A. Logan Coll., Carbondale, 1994-95; tech. writer Millar Writing, Murphysboro, Ill., from 1995; sch. adminstr. Christian Athenaeum, from 1998. Sch. adminstr. Christian Athenaeum. Editl. assoc. Jour. Pidgin and Creole Langs., 1991-94; contbr. poetry to various publs. 1st lt. USAF, 1973-75. Mem. Phi Kappa Phi, Kappa Delta Pi. Lutheran. Avocations: gardening, reading. Died June 7, 2004.

MILLER, CARL VOSBURGH, artist; b. Waterbury, Conn., Feb. 13, 1932; s. Carl Vosburgh Miller; m. Catherine L. Webb, Aug. 22, 1956; children: Craig, Cari. Student, Grand Canyon Coll., Ariz. State Coll. Cert. tchr., Calif. Exhibited watercolor paintings in numerous shows including Adirondacks, N.Y., 1992, West Conn. Watercolor Soc., 1992, Western Colo. Watercolor Soc., 1991, 94, Nat. Watercolor Soc., 1991, Watercolor West, 1986, 87, 88, 90, San Diego Internat., 1988, 90, Rocky Mountain Nat., 1990, many others; contbd. paintings to various books including Painting With the White of Your Paper, 1994, Creative Watercolor, 1995, The Best of Watercolor, 1995. Recipient Pauline Mintz award Audubon Artists, 1989, Gold medal award, 1990, Merit award West Conn. Watercolor Soc., 1992, Mary S. Litt medal Am. Watercolor Soc., 1993, Award of Achievement and Contbns. to Arts Stockton Arts Commn., 1994, award of honor Niagara Frontier Nat. Exhbn., 1996; works included in Creative Watercolor (Mary Ann Beckwith), The Best of Watercolor (Betty Lou Schlemm and Tom Nicholas), Painting with the White of Your Paper (Judi Wagner and Tony Van Hasselt) Mem. Watercolor West, Midwest Watercolor Soc., Am. Watercolor Soc. Avocations: wood carving, block printing, electronics, amateur radio, drawing. Home: Stockton, Calif. Died Aug. 7, 2004.

MILLER, CLARK ALVIN, human resource and organization management consultant; b. Akron, Ohio, Oct. 29, 1934; s. Harold J. and Hallie Mary (Coburn) M.; m. Tanya Bellomo, Dec. 29, 1956 (div. 1975); children: Brian, Bruce, Paul, Timothy, David, Joel; m. Linda Oswald, 1978. BA in Psychology cum laude, U. Buffalo, 1956; grad., Gen. Motors Inst., 1957; MBA, U. Rochester, 1971. Mgr. employment and wage adminstrn. Harrison Radiator div. Gen. Motors, Lockport, N.Y., 1956-64; asst. to pres. U.S. Rubber Reclaiming Corp., Buffalo, 1964-66; div. human resources mgr. Carborundum Co., Niagara Falls, N.Y., 1966-70, group dir. human resources, 1970-78; v.p. human resource Mech. Tech., Inc., Latham, N.Y., 1978-82; pres. BSG Mgmt. Cons., Clifton Park, N.Y., from 1980; v.p. employee rels. Coleco Industries, Inc., Amsterdam, N.Y., 1983-85. Mem. Phi Beta Kappa. Home: Ballston Lake, NY. Died Jan. 21, 2005.

MILLER, DIANE MARIE WYNNE, minister; b. Rochester, Minn., Nov. 27, 1948; d. Ervin William and D. Marie (Wynne) M.; m. Michael D. Durall, May 13, 1979; children: Graham Wynne Durall, Drew McCallum. BA, Macalester Coll., 1972; MDiv, Harvard Div. Sch., 1976. Interim minister Follen Ch., Lexington, Mass., 1975-76; from asst. minister to interim sr. minister The First Unitarian Soc. of San Francisco, 1976-81; sr. minister The First Ch. in Belmont, Mass., from 1981. Del. on ch. staff Fin. Coun., Boston, 1982-85; mem. Melcher Book Award Com., Boston, 1985-87. Co-author: Coming Out of Marriage, 1974; bd. govs. Kairos Jour., 1977-80. Mem. Unitarian Universalist Ministers Assn., Ministerial Sisterhood. Home: Belmont, Mass. Died Nov. 7, 2004.

MILLER, FREDERICK STATEN, music educator, academic administrator; b. Lima, Ohio, Dec. 12, 1930; s. Donald Frederick and Esther Lillian (Moore) Miller; m. Florence Dorothy Mistak, June 20, 1959; children: Jennifer Leigh Greene, John Staten. BA in Music Edn., Northwestern U., 1957, MA in Music, 1958; Ph.D in Music Performance, U. Iowa, 1974. Mem. music faculty U. Ark., Fayetteville, 1958-64; asst. dir. bands Northwestern U., Evanston, Ill., 1964-70, assoc. dean, sch. music, 1970-76; dean, sch. music DePaul U., Chgo., 1976-95, ret., 1995. Bd. dirs., Concertante de Chgo.; accreditation evaluator North Ctrl. Assn., Boulder, Colo., 1982—91, Nat. Assn. Schs. Music, Washington, 1981—91; mem. bd. edn. New Trier H.S., 1997—2001. Composer/arranger numerous pub. works for band; editor music publs. Served with USN, 1948-52. Mem. ASCAP, Nat. Assn. Schs. Music (hon. life, regional chmn. 1982-84, instl. rep., treas. 1984-88, v.p. 1988-91, pres. 1991-94), Pi Kappa Lambda (bd. regents 1970-74), Phi Kappa Phi, Univ. Club (Chgo.) Sheridan Shore Yacht Club (Wilmette, Ill.). Roman Catholic. Avocations: sailing, cooking, jazz performance. Home: Wilmette, Ill. Died Feb. 1, 2006.

MILLER, G. WILLIAM (GEORGE WILLIAM MILLER), merchant banker, former secretary of the treasury; b. Sapulpa, Okla., Mar. 9, 1925; s. James Dick and Hazle Deane (Orrick) M.; m. Ariadna Rogojarsky, Dec. 22, 1946. BS in Marine Engring., US Coast Guard Acad., 1945; JD, U. Calif., Berkeley, 1952; degree (hon.), Babson Coll, Boston U., Brown U., Bryant Coll., Fairfield U., Fla. State U., RI U. Bar: Calif. 1952, NY 1953. Asst. sec. Textron Inc., 1956-57, v.p., 1957-60, pres., 1960-74, COO, 1960-67, CEO, 1967-78; chmn. bd. govs. Fed. Res. Sys., Washington, 1978-79; sec. US Dept. Treasury, Washington, 1979-81; chmn. G. William Miller & Co. Inc., Washington, 1981—2006; chmn., CEO Federated Dept. Stores, Inc., 1990-92; chmn. bd. HomePlace of Am., Inc., 1995-2001, The H. John Heinz III Ctr. Sci., Econ., Environ., 2000—06. Past chmn. adv. coun. Pres.'s Com. EEO, 1963—65; mem. coun. Nat. Found. Humanities, 1966—67; bd. dirs. Washington Opera, USCG Acad. Found., 1969—78, pres., 1973—77, chmn., 1977—78. U. Calif. fellow, Berkeley. Mem. State Bar Calif., Nat. Alliance Businessmen (bd. dirs. 1968-78, chmn. 1977-78), Conf. Bd. (trustee 1972-78, chmn. 1977-78), Bus. Coun., Lyford Cay Club (Nassau), Brook Club (NYC), Burning Tree Club, Chevy Chase Club, Order of Coif, Phi Delta Phi. Home: Washington, DC. Died Mar. 17, 2006.

MILLER, JAMES A., chemist; b. Akron, Oct. 27, 1939; s. Roy Emerson and Marie Wanda (Rohinett) M.; m. Nancy Louise Scott, June 25, 1965; children: Scott E., Mary L., Carol A. BS in Chemistry, U. Akron, 1961. Tech. dir., chemist Morgan Adhesives Co., Stow, Ohio, 1961-86, mgr. advanced tech., 1986-88; tech. dir. Adhesive Cons. Inc., Akron, 1988-92, Chemsultants Internat. Newark, Mentor, Ohio, 1992-95; cons. J. Miller Assocs., Stow, from 1995. Contbr. articles to profl. jours.; 8 patents. Radio officer Emergency Mgmt., Summit County, Ohio, 1985—; emergency coord. Am. Radio Emergency Svc., Summit County, 1978—; pres. Family United Ch. of Christ, 1997—. Recipient Pres. award Bemis Co., Inc., 1979, Vol. of Yr. Am. Diabetes Assn., 1996; named Radio Amateur of Yr. Akron U. Radio Club, 1997. Mem. Am. Chem. Soc., Cleve. Soc. for Cons. Tech. (conf. presenter). Avocations: amateur radio, photography, music, computers, gardening. Home: Stow, Ohio. Died Dec. 30, 2004.

MILLER, JOHN ALBERT, retired musician; b. Black River Falls, Wis., Mar. 20, 1928; s. Albert B. and Mildred V. (Hoyer) M.; m. Aug. 19, 1956, widowed Oct. 22, 1989. BA, U. Minn., Mpls.; M in Music, Northwestern U., Evanston, Ill.; MLS, U. Wis., Madison; EdD, U. Minn., Mpls.; postgrad., U. Iowa, 1982. Cert. dept. edn., Iowa. Music/fine arts chmn. Athens (Ala.) Coll., 1951-53; music instr., choir dir. Huntington (Ind.) Coll., 1953-94; music dept. chmn. Northwest Sch. Agrl., Crookston, Minn., 1954-56; high sch., hosp. choir dir. Nekoosa Northwestern Hosp., Mpls., 1957-61; bd. dirs., asst. prof. Juniata Coll., Huntington, Pa., 1961-63; art and music libr. Pub. Schs. and Librs., Milw., 1967-71; asst. dept. Pub. Edn. NSW Pub. Schs., Newcastle, 1971-74; res. tchr., libr. Jasper/Mahaska/Marion &/Warren Co., Knoxville, Iowa, 1979-89, chmn., from 1989; with Miller Bibliographic Enterprises, Knoxville. Dir. Knoxville (Iowa) LDS Chorus, 1979-82; cellist Ctrl. Coll., Pella, Iowa, 1981-94, Penn Coll., Oskaloosa, Iowa, 1979-81; actor Knoxville Area Cmty. Theater, Des Moines, 1982-87. Music chair Ch. of Jesus Christ of Latter Day Saints, also exec. sec. Cpl. M.C., U.S. Army, 1946-47. Named Most Valuable Musician VFW, Mpls., 1945. Avocations: creative writing, music composition and arrangement. Home: Knoxville, Iowa. Died Apr. 5, 2005.

MILLER, JOHN HAROLD, priest, journal editor; b. New Orleans, Dec. 29, 1925; s. Joseph Thomas and Mary Rose (Unland) M. PhB, Angelicum, Rome, 1948, STB, 1950, STL, 1952; STD, Theol. Faculty, Trier, Fed. Republic Germany, 1955. Joined Order of Holy Cross, 1943; ordained priest Roman Cath. Ch., 1951. Lectr. theology Cath. U. Am., Washington, 1958-60, staff editor New Cath. Ency., 1963-65; asst. prof. U. Notre Dame, South Bend, Ind., 1960-63, assoc. prof., 1963-67, Loyola U., New Orleans, 1965-74; dir. office religious edn. Archdiocese New Orleans, 1975-76; provincial superior So. Province Holy Cross, New Orleans, 1976-80; exec. dir. Ctrl. Bur. Catholic Ctrl. Verein Am., 1986—2006; editor Social Justice Rev., St. Louis, 1986—2006. Author: Fundamentals of Liturgy, 1960, Signs of Transformation in Christ, 1963, Called by Love, Love Responds, 1990. Died Feb. 8, 2006.

MILLER, JOHN NELSON, banker, educator; b. Youngstown, Ohio, Sept. 15, 1948; s. W. Frederic and Julia Elizabeth (Lohman) Miller. MusB in Cello, Westminster Coll., 1970; MBA in Fin., U. Pa., 1974. Asst. br. mgr. Mahoning Nat. Bank, Youngstown, 1970—72; asst. dir. fin. svcs. dept. Mellon Bank N.Am., Pitts., 1974—76; v.p., head cash mgmt. divsn. Md. Nat. Bank, Balt., 1976—79; v.p., mgr. corp. cash mgmt. divsn. N.Y. Bank of Am., N.Y.C., 1978—80; dir. cash mgmt., strategic planning, product mgmt. and tng. Bank of Am. S.F., 1980—81; v.p., global account officer for utilities/telecomm. Bank of Am., N.Y.C., 1981—84, team leader, CFO, corp. payment divsn. large corp. sales, 1984—87, mgr. credit preparation and analysis unit N.Am. divsn., 1987—88; v.p., ea. region mgr. cash mgmt. divsn. Wells Fargo Bank of N.Y., 1988—90, v.p., mgr. Ea., Midwestern, Rocky Mt., Pacific & nat., 1990—93; v.p. and group sales mgr. Bank of Am., NT and SA Fgn. Currency Svcs., San Francisco, 1993—94; v.p., regional sales mgr. Bank of Am. Global Payment Svcs., Bank of Am., 1994—99; sr. v.p. Global Payment Svcs. Bank of Am., 1999—2004. Lectr. Wharton Grad. Sch., U. Pa., Am. Mgmt. Assn. cash mgmt. seminars, Bank Adminstrn. Inst.; spkr. Payment Sys. Inc., Corp. EFT Seminar, Atlanta, Nat. Conf. Treasury Mgmt. Assn.; mem. Corp. Payment Task Force, N.Y.C., Corp. EFT Cost-Benefit Task Force. Chmn. ann. giving program Wharton Grad. Sch., 1977-79; trustee San Francisco Performances, 1993-99; bd. trustees Westminster Coll., New Wilmington, Pa., 2003—; mem. exec. bd. Diablo Silverado coun. Boy Scouts Am. Mem. Wharton Grad. Sch. Alumni Assn., (pres. local club, rep., nat. dir., exec. com.), Bank Adminstrn. Inst. (subcom. interindustry commn.), Am. Nat. Stds. Inst. (subcom. interindustry optical scan stds.) Cash Mgmt. Inst. (dir.), Omicron Delta Kappa, Rotary. Home: Clayton, Calif. Died Oct. 24, 2005.

MILLER, J(OHN) WESLEY, III, lawyer; b. Springfield, Mass., Oct. 3, 1941; s. John Wesley Jr. and Blanche Miller. AB, Colby Coll., 1963; AM, Harvard U., 1964, JD, 1981. Bar: Mass. 1984, U.S. Dist. Ct. Mass. 1984, U.S. Supreme Ct. 1993. Instr. English Heidelberg Coll., Tiffin, Ohio, 1964-69, U. Wis., 1969-77; real estate broker, 1977-84. Founder Miller-Wilson Family Papers, U. Vt., Madison (Wis.) People's Poster and Propaganda Collection, St. Hist. Soc. Wis. Author: History of Buckingham Junior High School, 1956, The Millers of Roxham, 1958, Symphonic Heritage, 1959, Community Guide to Madison Murals, 1977, Aunt Jennie's Poems, 1986, Blanche and John's Fernbank: A Wilbraham Camping Experience, 2001; founding editor: Hein's Poetry and the Law Series, 1985—; editor: Curiosities and Law of Wills, 1989, Lawyers Alcove, 1990, Famous Divorces, 1991, Legal Laughs, 1993, Coke in Verse, 1999, Law and Lawyers Laid Open, 2002; founding editor: Law Libr. Microform Consortium Arts Law Letters Collection, 1991—; exhibitor A Salute to Street Art, State Hist. Soc. Wis., 1974 Recipient Cmty. Activism award Bay State Objectivist, 1993-95; fellow Wisdom Hall of Fame, 2000, Samuel Victor Constant fellow, 2001. Mem. MLA, Am. Philol. Assn., Nat. Leather Assn., Milton Soc., New Eng. Historic Geneal. Soc., Vt. Hist. Soc., Wis. Acad. Scis., Arts and Letters, Pilgrim Soc., Ancient and Hon. Arty. Co., Mayflower Soc., Soc. Colonial Wars, Sons and Daus. of the Victims of Colonial Witch Trials, Mensa, Springfield Renaissance Group, Nat. Leather Assn. Died Sept. 13, 2005.

MILLER, KARL G., broadcast executive, graphic design consultant; b. Phila., July 18, 1959; AS, Bucks County Coll., Newtown, Pa., 1977-79; student, Brevard C.C., Cocoa, Fla., 1979-81. News cameraman TV-One, Inc., Melbourne, Fla., 1980; prodr., dir. Comms. Concepts, Cape Canaveral, Fla., 1981-83; opers. engr. So. Broadcast WMOD-TV, Melbourne, Fla., 1983-84, prodr., dir. Press Broadcast, 1984-88; prodn. mgr. WBSF-TV/Blackstar Comms., Melbourne, Fla., from 1988. Mem. Keep Brevard Beautiful. Recipient Charlie award Am. Advtsg. Fedn. 4th dist., Fla./Caribbean, Crystal Reel award Fla. Motion Picture and T.V. Assn., Addy awards 1988-91, 92-94, 97. Mem. Nat. Assn. Broadcasters, Space Coast Ad Fedn., Nat. Assn. TV Program Execs. Republican. Roman Catholic. Avocations: freelance writing, music composition, sportfishing, champion dog breeding. Home: Palm Bay, Fla. Died Oct. 8, 2004.

MILLER, MARGARET HAIGH, retired librarian; b. Ashton-under-Lyne, Lancashire, Eng., Feb. 26, 1915; came to U.S., 1915, naturalized, 1915; d. Errwood Augustus and Florence (Stockdale) Savage; m. Mervin Homer Miller, June 30, 1940; children: Nancy Elaine Reich, Edward Stockdale, Jane Elizabeth Miller-Dean. BS in Libr. Sci., Millersville U., Pa., 1937; MS in Libr. Sci., U. So. Calif., 1952; postgrad. in supervision, Calif. State U., 1957Northridge, 1957—59. High sch. libr. Phoenixville (Pa.) Sch. Dist., 1937-40; jr. high sch. libr. L.A. Unified Sch. Dist., 1952-55; coord. libr., 1955-62; coll. head libr., 1959-62; sur. libr. svcs., 1962-83; lectr. children's lit. U. So. Calif., L.A., 1959-76; advisor Sch. Libr. and Info. Sci., 1980-83; resource person Nat. Coun. Accreditation Tchr. Edn., Washington, 1976-85; ret., 1985. Cons. Pied Piper Prodns., Glendale, Calif., 1978-80, David Sonnenshein Assocs., L.A., 1983-85, Baker & Taylor Co., Inc., N.Y.C., 1979-83, H.W. Wilson Co., N.Y.C., 1975-82, Mook & Blanchard, La Puente, Calif., 1985—, Enslow Pub., Inc., Hillside, N.J., 1986—. Editor: Book List for Elementary School Libraries, 1966, Books for Elementary School Libraries, 1969, Children's Catalog, 13th edit., 1976, Multicultural Experiences in Children's Literature, Grades K-6, 1978, Periodicals for School Libraries, Grades K-12, 1977, Multicultural Experiences in Literature for Young People, Grades 7-12, 1979, Baker & Taylor School Selection Guide, K-12, 1980, 82, 82,83, Supplement to Multicutlural Experiences in Children's Literature, 1982, Special Books for Special People: A Bibliography about the Handicapped, 1982, Bibliographer: Concepts in Science, Levels 1 through 6 students' edits. (P. Brandwein et al), 1972; columnist, book reviewer L.A. Times, various jours. Mem. L.A. area planning com. Libr. Congress Yr. of the Young Reader, 1989. Recipient Dorothy McKenzie award for disting. contbn. outstanding svc. in field of children's lit., 1992 Mem. L.A. Sch. Libr. Assn. (cons. 1952—), Calif. Assn. Sch. Librarirans (pres. 1977), Assn. Libr. Svc. to Children, Friends Children and Lit. (dir. 1979—, pres. 1987-88), Calif. Media and Libr. Educators Assn. (com. mem. 1977-95), ALA (com. mem.), Young Adult Svcs., Am. Assn. Sch. Librarians, So. Calif. Coun. on Lit. for Children and Young People (dir. 1961—, pres. 1973-74, 1st v.p. 1986, 3rd v.p. 1987-88, awards chair 1989-91), Calif. Sch. Libr. Assn., Calif. Libr. Assn., Young Adult Reviewers Booklist Com. (sec. 1995), Assn. Adminstrs. L.A. Unified Sch. Dist., Women's Nat. Book Assn., Beta Phi Mu (dir. 1977-79, 84-86, pres. 1979-80, Calif. Readers core selection com., bd. dirs. 1996—), Pi Lambda Theta (chpt. pres. 1967-66, 91-92), Delta Kappa Gamma (chpt. sec. 1962-64), Phi Delta Kappa (contest essay judge). Died 2006.

MILLER, PAUL LAWRENCE, JR., beverage company executive; b. Starkville, Miss., May 25, 1942; s. Paul Lawrence Sr. and Alma (Boyd) M.; m. Effie Marie Walker, Nov. 9, 1968; children: Paul III, Stephen, Nicole. SB in Acctg., St. Louis U., 1965; postgrad., Stanford U., 1983; MBA, Washington U., 1985. Sub-contract planner McDonnell-Douglas Corp., St. Louis, 1965; v.p. Miller & Sons, Inc., St. Louis, 1968-85; pres. United Svc. Distbrs., St. Louis, 1978-83, P.L. Miller & Assocs., St. Louis, from 1980, Beverage Concepts, St. Louis, from 1987. Exec. v.p. LeConte Cosmetics, Inc., L.A., 1974-77; dir. Landmark Bank, St. Louis. Trustee Cen. Bapt. Ch., St. Louis, 1986—; bd. dirs. St. Louis Coun. Boy Scouts Am., 1984—, Goodwill Industries, St. Louis, 1984—. Recipient Entrepreneurship award Sentinel Newspaper, 1983; named Bus. Person of Yr. U.S. Dept. of Commerce, 1984. Mem. Am. Mgmt. Assn., Am. Mktg. Assn. Died July 14, 2005.

MILLER, ROBERT RYAL, history educator; b. Lake Andes, S.D., Oct. 3, 1923; s. John Carroll and Hazel C. (Peck) M.; m. Penelope Handsaker, June 12, 1955. AB, U. Calif., Berkeley, 1948, MA, 1951, PhD, 1960. Asst. prof. history U. Southwestern La., Lafayette, 1959-60; asst. to assoc. prof. N.Mex. State U., Las Cruces, 1960-68; prof. history Ind. U. Southeast, New Albany, Ind., 1970, Calif. State U., Hayward, 1970-80, prof. emeritus, from 1980. Vis. prof. San Marcos U., Lima, Peru, 1966. Author: For Science and National Glory, 1968, Mexico: A History, 1985, Shamrock and Sword, 1989, Juan Alvarado, Governor of California, 1836-1842, 1998. Served in U.S. Army Air Corps, 1942-46, Med. Mem. Conf. on Latin Am. History, Calif. Hist. Soc. Home: La Jolla, Calif. Died Aug. 5, 2004.

MILLER, SALLY, retired public relations professional; b. N.Y.C., Dec. 6, 1925; d. Samuel and Marion Levy; m. Merle Roy Miller, Dec. 26, 1946; children: Terry L., Laurie Farr, Deborah Burke, Wendy Miller. MA, SUNY, Stony Brook, 1982. Adminstr., tchr. Dists. 3 and 7, Oyster Bay, Huntington, N.Y., 1957-68; copywriter and Broadway theatre reviewer Sta. WGSM, Huntington, 1968-69; program and publicity coord., dir. pub. rels. Half Hollow Hills Cmty. Library, Dix Hills, N.Y., 1969-81; pub. rels. specialist Sally Miller Enterprises, Huntington, 1981-99; ret. Lectr. C.W. Post Library Sch., 1978, Suffolk Co. Library Assn., 1974, ALA, 1974, Huntington Historical Soc., 1974; producer t.v. comml. Parachute Prodns., 1989; cons. Nassau/Suffolk Library Inst. Editor: DATA, Suffolk Co. Library Assn., 1966-67. Pres. Library Pub. Relations Coun., 1977-78, Suffolk Co. Library Assn., 1980-81; bd. dirs. AIDS Interfaith L.I. Recipient John Cotton Dana award, 1973, Big Apple award Parents F.L.A.G., 1996. Mem. ALA (pub. rels. sect. cert. of recognition 1990). Home: Huntington Station, NY. Died May 21, 2005.

MILLETT, MICHAEL FREDRIC, education educator; b. Portland, Maine, Jan. 19, 1955; s. Myron Anson and Shirley Louise (Cline) M.; m. Elaine Louise Morin, Feb. 18, 1978; children: Andrea, Brandon. BS in Elem. Edn., U. Maine, 1977. Tchr. Ashland (Maine) Cen. Sch., from 1977, elem. basketball coach, baseball coach, 1977-84, head tchr., computer coord., from 1985. Girls' jr. varsity basketball coach Ashland Community High Sch., 1978-84; sch. coord. New Eng. Math. League Contest, 1983—. Bd. dirs. Aroostook Valley Health Ctr., Ashland, 1986-93; sec. Ashland Dem. Party, 1986—. Mem. NEA, Maine Tchrs. Assn., Ashland Area Tchrs. Assn. (pres. 1979-80), Nat. Coun. Tchrs. Math., Assn. Tchrs. Math. in Maine, Maine Sci. Tchrs. Assn., Ashland Rotary Club (pres. 1989-90). Roman Catholic. Avocations: reading, outdoor activities, travel. Home: Ashland, Maine. Died Jan. 3, 2004.

MILLIGAN, GATEWOOD CARLISLE, physician, retired; b. Shannon, Miss., July 23, 1907; s. Martin Gatewood and Johnnie Carlisle (McCown) M.; m. Maxine Louise Redeker, Apr. 1, 1933; children: Jociele Aline Nordwall, Jonanna Lee Dilsaver. Student, Park Coll., 1924-26, Hastings Coll., 1927, U. Wyo., 1927-28; MD, U. Colo., 1929-33. Lic. to practice medicine Colo. 1933, Tex., 1935. Pvt. practice, Denver, 1934-36; partner C.W. Bixler & G.C. Milligan, Erie, Colo., 1935, Drs. Alldredge & Milligan, Englewood, Colo., 1935-46, Drs. Milligan & Hogan, Englewood, 1946-52, Drs. Milligan & Miner, Englewood, 1952-69, Drs. Milligan, Miner & Langstaff, Englewood, 1957-60; ob.-gyn. pvt. practice Englewood, 1969-84. Pres. Arapohoe county Med. Soc., Englewood, 1940-41, Colo. Med. Soc., Denver, 1957-58; pres. med. staff Porter Hosp., Denver, 1944-45, Swedish Hosp., Englewood, 1960-61. Mem. Englewood City Coun., 1954-58, Colo. Commn. on Aging, Denver, 1964-72, Colo. State Bd. Health, Denver, 1977-86, Elsie Malley Sr. Recreation Ctr. Adv. Bd., Englewood, 1975-81; chmn. bd. trustees Malley Trust Fund, Englewood, 1983-95. Recipient Outstanding Svc. award Arapahoe Med. Soc., Englewood, 1973-74, Cert. of Svc. award Colo. Med. Soc., Denver, 1957, 66, 78, Excellence award U. Colo. Med. Alumni, Denver, 1986, Humanitarian award Rocky Mt. Conf. United Meth. Ch., Denver, 1990. Mem. AMA (hon.), Arapahoe County Med. Assn. (hon.), Colo. Med. Assn. (hon.), Englewood Rotary (Compassion award dist. 5450 1992), Englewood United Meth. Ch. Democrat. Methodist. Home: Englewood, Colo. Died Feb. 27, 2004.

MILLS, JOYCE ANN, foundation administrator; b. Pierson, Iowa, Oct. 31, 1940; d. Marion Lewis and Josephine Miriam (Nuhn) Dennis; m. Dwain Emmett Mills, Aug. 22, 1959 (div. Aug. 1975); children: Tauny Lynn Mills Hickman, Derek Dwain (dec.), Jody Ann Mills Cook. BS in Mgmt., Marylhurst Coll., 1987. Real estate agt. Robin Realty, Milwaukie, Oreg., 1978-80; assoc. dir. United Way of Oregon, Portland, 1980-85; exec. dir. Burke County United Way, Morganton, N.C., from 1987. Mem. Pvt. Industry Coun. Morganton, 1989—; bd. dirs. Wachovia Bank, Morganton; presenter chief vol. officer Small Cities Workshops, 1989, 90. Pres. Burke Partnership for Children, Morganton, 1993-95; bd. dirs. Grace Hosp., Morganton, 1994—. Named Woman of Yr. Bus. and Profl. Women, Morganton, 1993. Mem. AAUW (state chair women's issues com. 1990-91, local ednl. equity com. 1992, pres. 1989-93), Morganton C. of C. (chair health affairs), Women's Health Connection, Grace Hosp., Rotary Club (bd. dirs. 1989—, program chair). Avocations: sewing, gardening, crafts, reading. Home: Morganton, NC. Died Nov. 5, 2004.

MILLS, PAUL CHADBOURNE, museum director; b. Seattle, Sept. 24, 1924; Student, Reed Coll., 1945-48; BA, U. Wash., 1953; MA, U. Calif., Berkeley, 1961; PhD (hon.), Calif. Coll. Arts and Crafts, 1971. Reporter Bellevue Am., Wash., 1948-51; asst. curator Henry Gallery, U. Wash., 1952-53; curator art Oakland Mus., Calif., 1953-70; v.p. Western Mus. Conf., 1956, 59; dir. Santa Barbara Mus. Art, 1970-82, New Glory Bicentennial Flag Hist. and Design Project, 1974-77; exec. dir. Santa Barbara Flag Project, from 1977. Bd. dirs. Santa Barbara Trust for Hist. Preservation, 1992—, 1st v.p., 1994. Author: The New Figurative Art of David Park, 1988, David Park Scroll, 1989; art editor: O, California!, 1988, 89; publisher The California Missions of Edwin Deakin, 1966, Colonial and Revolutionary Era Flags, 1975, (with Mark Adams), 1984. Bd. dirs. Santa Barbara Downtown Orgn., 1990—; Air Fair Flags ptnr., Santa Barbara, 1983—. Ford Found. fellow, 1960-61; grantee Spain, 1977-79. Mem. Am. Assn. Mus., Am. Assn. Art Mus. Dirs. (hon. mem., trustee 1971-72, sec. 1973), N.Am. Vexillological Assn., Western Assn. Art Mus. (v.p. 1956-57, treas. 1971-72, trustee 1979), Heraldry Soc., Santa Barbara Hist. Soc., Santa Barbara Geneal. Soc. Home: Santa Barbara, Calif. Died Sept. 17, 2004.

MILLS, RICHARD WARD, JR., physician; b. Chgo., Oct. 5, 1916; s. Richard Ward and Grace Dorothy (Brown) M.; m. Adrian Corder Bond, June 1946 (div. 1949); 1 child, Pamela; m. Nancy Jane Houck, Jan. 6, 1950; children: Jennifer Jane, Richard Lynn. BS, Northwestern U., 1938, B Medicine, 1941, MD, 1942. Diplomate Am. Bd. Internal Medicine. Intern U. Mich. Hosp., Ann Arbor, 1941-42, asst. resident, 1947-48, resident, 1948-49, instr., 1949-50; ptnr. F.C. Smith Clinic, Marion, Ohio, 1950-62; practice medicine specializing in internal medicine Marion, from 1962. Chief staff Marion Gen. Hosp., 1976-78, chmn. dept. medicine, 1969, 72, 73; courtesy staff Ohio State U. Hosp., Columbus, 1950-58; clin. instr. Ohio State U., 1950-58; treas./sec. Compcare, Inc., Marion, 1976-79, also bd. dirs. Bd. dirs., mem. exec. com. Marion Health Found.; bd. dirs. Marion Gen. Hosp., 1976-79, Marion County Tuberculosis and Health Assn., 1957-70, pres., 1964-70. Served to lt. comdr. M.C., U.S. Navy, 1942-47, PTO. Mem. AMA, Ohio State Med. Soc., Marion County Acad. Medicine (pres.), Phi Rho Sigma (pres. 1938), Alpha Omega Alpha. Lodges: Rotary. Republican. Episcopalian. Avocations: flying, boating, photography, scuba diving. Home: Marion, Ohio. Died Feb. 21, 2004.

MILNE, MARGERY JOAN, history professor, consultant, writer; b. NYC, Jan. 18, 1922; d. Samuel and Rebecca Greene; m. Lorus Johnson Milne, 1944. BA, Hunter Coll., 1941; MA, Columbia U., 1942, Radcliffe Coll., 1943, PhD, 1945. Prof. biology U. Vt., Burlington, 1948-49; prof. zoology U. N.H., Durham, 1950-52, lectr., 1952-65, lectr. in writing sci., 1965-75; instr. sci. U. N.H. System, from 1975, instr. nonfiction writing, instr. Elderhostel, from 1980, instr. Sch. for Lifelong Learning, from 1985. Cons. on ecology and zoology Reader's Digest, 1988—; semester at sea lectr. U. Pitts., 1985. Author: (with Lorus J. Milne) The World of Night, 1960, The Senses of Animals and Men, 1962, Water and Life, 1964, North American Birds, 1969, The Nature of Plants, 1971, Invertebrates of North America, 1972, Ecology Out of Joint, 1977, Audubon Society Field Guide to North American Insects and Spiders, 1980, Animal Babies: Behavior and Learning, 1989, Nature in America, 1991, also numerous others; co-author numerous books for juveniles, including Nature's Clean-up Crew (Jr. Lit. Guild award 1982), A Shovelful of Earth, 1987, Understanding Radioactivity, 1989, Insects and Spiders, 1992; author lead rev. Rachel Carson's Silent Spring, N.Y. Times Book Rev., 1962; contbr. over 100 articles to popular mags. Keeper of swans Town of Durham, 1969—. Recipient sci. writing award AAAS, 1949, Eugene Saxton Lit. award Harper & Row Pubs., 1950; grantee Nat. Geog. Soc., 1966; South Africa Leader-Exchange fellow, UN ednl. fellow, N.Z. Fellow Explorers Club; mem. Soc. Women Geographers (hon.), Phi Beta Kappa, Sigma Xi, Phi Sigma, Phi Kappa Phi. Republican. Unitarian Universalist. Avocations: photography, hiking, biking, travel. Home: Durham, NH. Died Feb. 28, 2006.

MILOŠEVIĆ, SLOBODAN, former President of the Federal Republic of Yugoslavia; b. Pozarevac, Serbia, Yugoslavia, Aug. 20, 1941; s. Svetozar and Stanislava Milosevic; m. Mirjana Markovic; children: Marko, Marija. Student, Belgrade (Yugoslavia) U. Adviser on econ. affairs Mayor of Belgrade; head Belgrade City Info. System Svc., 1966-69; dep. dir. Tehnogas, 1969-73, dir.-gen., 1973-78; pres. Beogradska Udružena Banka, 1978-83, Belgrade City Com., League of Communists, 1984-86; mem. presidency League of Communists of Serbia, pres., 1986-88; mem. Fed. Coun.'s Commn. for Long-Term Stblzn. Program; pres. Govt. of Serbia, 1990—2000, Socialist Party of Serbia, 1992—2001, Govt. of Fed. Republic of Yugoslavia, 1997—2000. Decorated Order of Labour with gold wreath, Order of Labour with red flag (Yugoslavia). Died Mar. 11, 2006.

MIMS, MARY CHARLINE, microbiology educator; b. Edmond, Okla., June 13, 1921; d. Charles Leo and Mary (Wantland) McGehee; m. James L. Mims Jr., Dec. 31, 1941; children: James L. III, Charles L., Robert Lee. BA, U. Tex., Austin, 1941; MS, Trinity U., San Antonio, 1961. Cert. med. technologist. Prof. microbiology San Antonio Coll., 1961-86; tchr. microbiology San Antonio Dental Sch., 1978-82; ret., 1986. Mem. Bexar County Med. Soc. Aux. (v.p. 1959), Tex. Jr. Coll. Assn., Phi Beta Kappa, Delta Kappa Gamma. Republican. Methodist. Avocations: gardening, pottery. Home: San Antonio, Tex. Died Mar. 6, 2004.

MINAMI, ROBERT YOSHIO, artist, graphic designer; b. Seattle, May 1, 1919; s. Kichitaro and Suma (Fujita) M.; m. Shizu Tashiro, May 30, 1953; 1 child, Ken. Artist; student, Art Inst., Chgo., 1957, Am. Acad. Art, 1980-81. Graphic artist Filmack Studios, Chgo., 1945-48, S. Taylor & Leavitt Assocs., Chgo., 1949-50; head graphic designer NBC-TV, Chgo., 1950-82; fine artist Robert Minami's Studio, Oceanside, Calif., from 1983. Artist Goodman Theatre Design, Chgo., 1955-56; mem. Oceanside Mus. Art Exhbn. Com.; art instr. Mus. Sch. Art, Oceanside, 1997-2003. Exhibits include Oceanside Mus. Art, 1996, nat. juried show Internat. Soc. Exptl. Art, 2002. Active Supporters for City Couns., Oceanside, 1984—. Recipient Merit award Artist Guild Chgo., 1956, People's Choice award Carlsbad Oceanside Art League, 1986, Dick Blick award, 1992, 1st place award Mixed Media Collage, 1993, Nat. Watercolor award Watercolor West, 1994, Best of Watercolor Painting, Texture award, 1997. Mem. San Diego Watercolor Soc., United Scenic Artists (life), Am. Fine Art Connection, San Diego Art Inst., Nat. Watercolor Soc. (assoc.), Watercolor West Juried Assn., Internat. Soc. Exptl. Art (exptl. art jury exhib.,

2002), San Diego Artists Guild, San Diego Mus. Fine Arts. Avocations: painting, travel, movies, concerts, opera. Home: Oceanside, Calif. Died Aug. 20, 2005.

MINCER, JACOB, economics professor; b. Tomaszow, Poland, July 15, 1922; came to U.S., 1948; s. Isaac and Deborah (Eisen) M.; m. Flora Kaplan, 1951; children: Deborah M., Carolyn F. BA, Emory U., 1950; PhD, Columbia U., 1957; LLD honoris causa, U. Chgo., 1991. Asst. prof. CUNY, 1954-59; assoc. prof. Columbia U., NYC, 1960-62, prof. econs., 1962—91, prof. emeritus, 1991—2006. Mem. research staff Nat. Bur. Econ. Research, N.Y.C. Author: Schooling, Experience and Earnings, 1974, Studies in Human Capital, 1993, Studies in Labor Supply, 1993; author, editor: Economic Forecasts and Expectations, 1969. Contbr. numerous articles to profl. publs. Recipient IZA prize in Labor Econs., 2002; postdoctoral fellow U. Chgo., 1957-58; Guggenheim fellow, N.Y.C., 1971. Fellow Am. Statis. Assn., Econometric Soc., Am. Econ. Assn. (Disting.); mem. NAS, Am. Acad. Arts and Scis., Nat. Acad. Edn. Died Aug. 20, 2006.

MINDIN, VLADIMIR YUDOVICH, information systems specialist, chemist, educator; b. Tbilisi, Georgia, Russia, June 6, 1939; arrived in U.S., 1992, naturalized, 1997; s. Yuda Isaakovich and Sofia Markovna (Ioffe) M.; m. Irina Alexandrovna Pleshivaia, July 1, 1964; children: Liya, Yakov. MS, Georgian Tech. U., Tbilisi, 1961, PhD, 1969. Sr. rsch. scientist Georgian Tech. U., 1970-80, assoc. prof. phys. chemistry, 1980-92; founder, head computational chemistry lab. Georgian Acad. Sci., 1980-92; investigator Beltran Inc., Bklyn., 1993-94, prin. investigator, 1994-95; statistician AFP, Inc., Manhasset, NY, 1995-98, info. systems dir., 1998-2001; prof. dept. computer sys. and math. Globe Inst. Tech., NYC, 2001—04, chair dept. computer sci. and math., from 2004. Cons. DNS Sci., Inc., Bklyn., 1992-97; chief sci. officer BioNova, Inc., Forest Hills, NY, 1997-2001, v.p. info. sys., 2001-03, v.p. tech., 2003-04, v.p. info. and tech., 2004—. Author: (with A.G. Morachevskii and A.S. Avaliany) Liquid Cathodes, 1978, (with A.V. Sarukhanishvily and J.S. Galuashvily) Inorganic Substances Thermodynamic Parameters Calculation on Computers by Landia Method, 1987; (with S.M. Mazmishvily and D.V. Eristavy) Album of Compositions of Condensed and Gaseous Phase of Silica-Carbon System, 1988 (Georgian Chem. soc. award 1989), (with A.V. Sarukhanishvily) Chemical Thermodynamics, 1990; (with D.V. Eristavy) Investigation on Thermodynamics of Interaction in Boron and Silicon Containing Systems By Means of Digital Chemistry Methods, 1994; contbr. articles to profl. jours. Grantee Dept. Def., 1994-95. Mem. Minerals, Metals, Materials Soc., Assn. Engrs. and Scientists for New Ams. (assoc. exec. dir. 1993-94). Achievements include co-development of the first complete phase diagram of the silica-carbon system; patents (with others): method of manganese salt solutions obtaining, method of manufacturing of porous electrodes, method of manganese obtaining, device for electrochemical measurement during electrolysis of melted media, working of sulphur ores, nonferrous metals sulfide ores roasting process, unhydrous manganese chloride producing process, a way of working sulfide ores containing nonferrous metals, furnace charge for silicomanganese obtaining, the batch for the medium carbonic ferromanganese smelting. Home: Brooklyn, NY. Died 2006.

MINKOFF, SANDRA RITA, counseling administrator; b. Chgo., May 21, 1936; d. Edward and Rachel (Bernstein) Cohen; m. Robert Minkoff, June 17, 1956; children: Michael, Eileen. Assocs., Wright Coll., Chgo., 1954-56; BE, Chgo. Tchrs. Coll., 1956-57; postgrad., Inst. Psychoanalysis, 1971-72; MA in Guidance and Counseling, Northeastern Ill. U., 1984. Tel. operator Ill. Bell. Tele., Chgo., 1953-54; group leader Jewish Community Ctr., Chgo., 1954-56; receptionist Dr. Arnold Black, Chgo., 1955-56; kindergarten tchr. Bright and Bradwell Schs., Chgo.; tchr. Beal Sch., Chgo., 1957-58, Kitty Coll., 1966, Stone Sch., Chgo., 1967-82; elem. and kindergarten tchr., reading resource Stone Scholastic Acad., Chgo., 1982-88, counselor, 1988-93, Stockton Sch., Chgo., from 1993. Mem. Saints, orgn. promoting and aiding theatre, Chgo. Mem. PTA, Sch. Counselor Assn. Avocations: reading, dance, extra in movies, exercising, swimming. Home: Skokie, Ill. Died Aug. 11, 2004.

MINNEY, BARBARA ANN, elementary educator and administrator; b. Lancaster, Pa., Oct. 5, 1948; d. Jack K. and Amy Teresa (Luttenberger) Dunlap; m. Michael Jay Minney, June 28, 1975; 1 child, Michael Jayson. BS in Edn., West Chester (Pa.) U., 1969; MEd, Millersville (Pa.) U., 1971, postgrad., 1989, Temple U., 1991. Cert. tchr., supr., prin., Pa. Elem. tchr. Sch. Dist. of Lancaster, 1970-91, adminstrv. asst., 1991-93, elem. prin., 1993—2000, elem. tchr., from 2001. Jury commr. County of Lancaster, 1978-86. Named Outstanding Young Women Am., 1980, Dist. Alumnus, McCaskey High Sch., 2001. Lutheran. Home: Lancaster, Pa. Died Mar. 8, 2004.

MINNICK, ADRIENNE KAVANAGH, management consultant; b. Evanston, Ill., Dec. 9, 1920; d. Clarence Henry and Elizabeth Victoria (Ashenden) Kavanagh; m. R. Donald Minnick, Mar. 7, 1942 (dec. Mar. 1945); 1 child, Richard Donald. BS, Northwestern U., 1949; MS, U. Mich., 1958, PhD, 1972. Exec. dir. Girl Scouts Bartholomew County, Columbus, Ind., 1945-49, Girl Scouts of Sheboygan, Wis., 1949-51; field supr., dir. research Girl Scouts Met. Detroit, 1951-72; research dir., evaluation analyst Girl Scouts U.S.A., N.Y.C., 1972-85; co-owner Organizational Resource Devel. Cons., Houston, Galveston, Tex., from 1986. Bd. dirs. United Way of Westchester and Putman Counties, N.Y., 1985; tchr. Christian edn. program, St. Helen's Ch., Pearland, Tex., 1988. Mem. Country Place Master Community Assn. (sec. 1986-88, treas. 1988, bd. dirs., chairperson rules and deed restrictions com.), Assn. Girl Scout Professional Workers. Republican. Roman Catholic. Avocations: golf, swimming. Home: Dearborn, Mich. Died Feb. 21, 2004.

MINOR, JAMES ERNEST, research executive, chemical engineer; b. Davenport, Wash., Apr. 10, 1919; s. Ernest and Matilda (Hardin) M.; m. Dorothy Ann Sabro, Jan. 28, 1950; children: Ann Louise, James Craig, Carl Steven. BCE, Wash. State U., 1941; PhD in Physical Chemistry, U. Wash., 1950. Registered profl. engr., Wash. Research chemist Proctor and Gamble, Cin., 1950-52; research scientist, sect. mgr. Gen. Electric Co., Richland, Wash., 1952-65; research mgr. Battelle NW, Richland, 1965-88; ret., 1988. Mem. State of Wash. High Tech. Coordinating Bd., 1985-86, West VAlley Tech. Rev. Group, 1988—. Contbr. articles to profl. jours. Mem. Richland City Council, 1956; chmn. Richland Sch. Bd., 1972-74; chmn. bd. trustees Columbia Basin Coll., Pasco, Wash., 1977-82. Served to maj. U.S. Army, 1941-46, ETO. Mem. Am. Soc. for Metals, Sigma Xi, Alpha Chi Sigma. Democrat. Presbyterian. Avocations: reading, fishing. Home: Richland, Wash. Died Nov. 19, 2004.

MINTON, MELANIE SUE, neuroscience nurse; b. Cin., Apr. 3, 1950; d. Lester L. and Wanda (Harman) M. Diploma, The Christ Hosp. Sch. Nursing, 1971; BS in Nursing, Prairie View U. A&M, 1982; MBA in Health Care Mgmt., Our Lady of Lake U., Houston, 1995. RN, Tex.; CNRN, ACLS instr., BCLS instr., bd. cert. neurosci. Staff, charge nurse The Christ Hosp., Cin., 1971—72, Barnes Hosp, St. Louis, 1972; asst. head nurse The Christ Hosp., Cin., 1972—74; relief nurse supr. The Meth. Hosp., Houston, 1975—87, clin. educator, 1989—2000; trauma rehab. nurse Inst. for Rehab. & Rsch., Houston, 1987—89; nurse specialist neurosurg., neurol. and otolaryn. ICUs Meth. Hosp., Houston, 1989—2000; coord. continuing edn. U. Tex. Sch. Nursing, Houston, 2000—03; lead bus. faculty LeTourneau U., Houston, from 1997; critical care educator Bayshore Med. Ctr., Pasadena, Tex., 2001—02; dir. neurosci. nursing Meml. City Hosp., Houston, from 2002. Presenter, speaker in field. Co-editor, contbg. author: Neuroscience Nursing for the New Millennium—Nursing Clinics of North America, 1999. Mem. Am. Assn. Neurosci. Nurses, S.E. Tex. Chpt. Am. Assn. Neurosci. Nurses, World Fedn. Neurosci. Nurses. Home: Cincinnati, Ohio. Died Jan. 30, 2004.

MIRINGOFF, MARC L., educational administrator, educator, researcher; b. N.Y.C., May 29, 1945; s. Hyman and Helen Miringoff; m. Marque-Luisa Wolfson, Sept. 8, 1968. BA, SUNY, Albany, 1967; MSW, Rutgers U., New Brunswick, N.J., 1969; PhD, U. Chgo., 1973. Asst. dir. Office of Policy Rsch. Human Resources Adminstrn., N.Y.C., 1973—75; asst. prof. SUNY, Sch. Social Welfare, Albany, 1976—83; dean Fordham U., Sch. Social Svc., Tarrytown, NY, 1983—92; founder, dir. Fordham Inst. for Innovation in Social Policy, Tarrytown, NY, 1992—2004. Mem. Social Sci. Rsch. Coun., N.Y.C., 1997—2001; mem. pub. issues commn. Ad Coun., N.Y.C., 1997—2004; founding mem. Four Freedoms Roundtable, Hyde Park, NY, 2001—04. Author: Management in Human Service Organizations, 1981, American Social Welfare Policy, 1987, The Social Health of the Nation, 1999. Policy advisor Bradley for President, West Orange, NJ, 2000; policy and strategy advisor Gore for President, Washington, 2000, Edwards for President, Washington, from 2002. Fellow, Harvard Sch. Pub. Health, 1995—96; grantee, Ford Found., 1996—2002, Rockefeller Found., from 1996. Mem.: Nat. Assn. Social Workers (pres. 1983—2004), Coun. of Social Work Edn. (pres. 1983—2004). Avocations: classical and folk guitar, reading, volunteer service work. Home: Poughkeepsie, NY. Died Mar. 4, 2004.

MISCHER, WALTER MAX, diversified company executive, bank holding company executive; b. 1923; married. With Stone & Webster, 1943-46; chmn. bd. Allied Bancshares Inc., Houston, Mischer Corp., Houston, CEO; sr. chmn. bd. First Interstate Bank Tex.; pres. Southern Investors, Houston. Died Dec. 18, 2005.

MITCHELL, CHARLES PETER, library director; b. Bklyn., May 3, 1949; s. Charles S. and Anna B. Mitchell; m. Roberta Downing, Dec. 10, 1977. BA summa cum laude, Pace U., 1971; MLS, Pratt Inst., 1972. Jr./sr./prin. libr. Paterson (N.J.) Pub. Libr., 1972-80; libr. dir. Falmouth (Maine) Meml. Libr., 1980-93, Blue Hill (Maine) Pub. Libr., 1993-95, Millinocket (Maine) Meml. Libr., from 1995. Tchr. adult edn. program Falmouth, Maine, 1992; lectr. Woman's Lit. Union, Westbrook Coll., 1986. Columnist book reviews: Katahdin Times, 1995—, Forecaster, Falmouth, Maine, 1984-92; contbr. articles to profl. jours. Chmn. So. Maine Libr. Dist., Portland, 1983-85, Libr. Prime, 1988-91, treas., 1986-88, 92-93. Recipient Nat. Libr. award, 1989. Mem. Maine Libr. Assn., Richard III Soc. Avocations: classical music, film history. Home: Millinocket, Maine. Died Jan. 25, 2005.

MITCHELL, ELAYNE SUDAK, financial planner; b. Cleve., Sept. 8, 1929; d. Sol and Leona (Simms) Sudak; m. Fred Mitchell, Sept. 11, 1948 (div. 1969); children: Marcy, Ross, Dale, Jonathan; m. Richard W. Voldrich, Nov. 14, 1993. BA, Cleve. Coll., 1950. CFP. Cert. fin. planner Elayne S. Mitchell Agency Inc., 1975-89; securities mgr. TFR, Highland Hghts, Ohio, 1989-96; pvt. practice fin. planner Highland Heights, Ohio, 1996—99; regulatory rep. ISI Corp., from 1999. Fin. counselor Xelan Corp., The Econ. Assn. Health Profls., San Diego, 1998—. Died June 25, 2004.

MITCHELL, JOHN DIETRICH, theatre arts institute executive; b. Rockford, Ill., Nov. 3, 1917; s. John Dennis Royce and Dora Marie (Schroeder) M.; m. Miriam Pitcairn, Aug. 25, 1956; children: John Daniel, Lorenzo Theodore, Barbarina Mitchell Heyerdahl. BSS, Northwestern U., 1939, MA, 1941; EdD, Columbia U., 1956; HHD (hon.), Northwood U., 1986. Dir., producer Am. Broadcasting Co., N.Y.C., 1942-46; assoc. editor Samuel French, Publ., N.Y.C., 1946-48; assoc. prof. Manhattan Coll., N.Y.C., 1948-58; pres. Inst. for Advanced Studies in the Theatre Arts, N.Y.C., 1958-97. Founder, pres. Eaton St. Press, Key West, Fla., 1994, Mitchell Performing Arts Ctr., Campus Acad., Pa., 2001; bd. dirs. Beneficia Found., Jenkintown, Pa. Author: Staging Chekhov, 1990, Actors Talk, 1991, Gift of Apollo, 1992, Staging Japanese Theatre: Noh and Kabuki, 1995, Men Stand on Shoulders, 1996; author: (aka Jack Royce) The Train Stopped at Domodossola, 1993, Murder at the Kabuki, 1994, Dressed to Murder, 1997, Way to the Towers of Silence, 1997, Bewitched by the Stage, 1997, Troubled Paradise, 1998, The Wallpaper Murder, 1998, Death in the Suit of Lights, 1999, Too Beautiful to Live, 2002, The Sleepers, 2003. Trustee emeritus Northwood U., Midland, Mich., 1972-91; patron Met. Opera, N.Y.C.; golden donor Am. Ballet Theatre. Named hon. conch Key West (Fla.) Commrs., 1994; dedication of Mitchell Performing Arts Ctr., Bryn Athyn, Pa., 2001. Mem. Met. Mus., Key West Arts and Hist. Soc., Spencer Family Assn. Mayflower Soc., Key West Literary Seminar (emeritus), Nippon Club N.Y.C. Mem. Community Ch. Avocations: tai chi chuan, swimming, collecting musical recordings, books. Died Feb. 21, 2005.

MITCHELL, MARILYN JUNE, writer, lyricist; d. Francis Vernon Mitchell and Viola Marie Scott Mitchell; m. James Albert Delbridge, June 15, 1947 (dec.); children: Diane Lynn Delbridge, Holly Delbridge, James Michael Delbridge. Student, Duke U., 1944, Miami U., Oxford, Ohio, 1944—47, Santa Barbara City Coll., Calif., 1987—88. Securities lic. N.Y. Stock Exch. Model, advt. and TV, N.Y.C., 1954—70; stockbroker Thomson, McKinnon Securities, Denver, 1970—84; v.p. Thomson McKinnon, Denver, 1984—2000; lyricist Nashville, from 1988. Author: Patterns on the Wall; editor: (anthology) Patchwork, An Uncommon Quilt of Words; author many songs; contbr. Recipient 1st pl., 3d pl., Channel City Camera Club, 1988, cert. of recognition poetry excellence, Office of the Mayor, Nashville, 2003. Mem.: DAR, ASCAP, Wordsmith's Ink, Delta Gamma Frat. Avocations: travel, photography, music, theater, writing. Home: San Jose, Calif. Died July 22, 2005.

MITCHELL, ROBERT DEATRICK, theatrical scene designer, consultant; b. Passaic, N.J., Apr. 14, 1929; s. Roger Irving and Anna Louise Deatrick. BA cum laude, Yale U., 1951. Resident designer Guthrie Theatre, Mpls., 1967-68, Annenberg Ctr. U. Pa., Phila., 1970-73, Nat. Theatre Greece, Salonika, Athens, 1976, 82. Theater cons. Jo Mielziner Studio, N.Y.C., 1963-66, Am. Acad. Dramatic Arts, N.Y.C., 1963, Guthrie Theatre, 1967, CUNY, N.Y.C., 1973, Jules Fisher and Assoc., N.Y.C., 1975-84, Denver Ctr. Performing Arts, 1981. Designer (plays) Harry, Noon and Night, 1965, Tango, 1968 (Emmy nomination 1968), The Screens, 1972 (Obie award 1972), Medea, 1976, Basic Training of Pavlo Hummel, 1977, Oedipus Rex, 1982 (nat. Olympic selection 1982), (ballets) La Peri, 1966, L'Absence, 1970, Cantique des Cantiques, 1973, Under the Sun, 1976, (musical) Bealtemania, 1977. Lt. (j.g.) USNR, 1951-53. Mem. U.S. Inst. Theatre Tech., Phi Beta Kappa. Avocations: travel, collecting, inventing. Died Aug. 18, 2006.

MITCHELL, ROBERT EDGAR, JR., gastroenterologist; b. Oct. 20, 1919; s. Robert Edgar and Julia Gardner (Carlton) M.; m. Mary Elizabeth Hiester, June 26, 1954; children: Robert Edgar III, Clark Carlton, Richard Gardner. AB, Hampden-Sydney Coll., 1940; MD, U.Va., 1950. Instr. in medicine Tulane U. Med. Sch., New Orleans, 1953-54; resident gastroenterology svc. of Dr. Bockus Univ. Pa. Grad. Hosp., Phila.,., 1954-55; chief gastroenterology sect. McGuire VA Hsop., Richmond, Va., 1955-56; clin. prof. medicine Med. Coll. Va. Commonwealth U., Richmond, from 1956. Past pres., chmn. bd. Richmond Acad. Medicine, 1976-79. chief of staff Henrico Doctors' Hosp., Richmond, 1982; chief of medicine Henrico Doctors' Hosp., Richmond Meml. Hosp., Sheltering Arms Hosp. Lt. USNR, 1942-46; capt. Res. ret. Fellow ACP, Am. Coll. Gastroenterology; mem. Med. Soc. Va. (chmn. ethics com. 1990-91, assoc. editor quarterly med. jour.), Bockus Alumni Internat. Soc. Gastroenterology, N.Y. Acad. Sci., Am. Fedn. for Clin. Rsch., Sigma Xi. Avocations: reading, hiking, tennis. Died Jan. 15, 2004.

MITCHELL, SERETTE ELIZABETH, law enforcement official; b. Chgo., July 24, 1953; d. Otis Joseph and Luna Mae (Lucas) M. AA, Compton Community Coll., 1976; BA in Sociology, Calif. State U., L.A., 1980. Cert. motorcycle mechanic. Profl. roller skater Nat. Skating Derby, Hollywood, Calif., 1970-77; mail carrer, clk. U.S. Postal Service, L.A., 1977-78; tutor Compton (Calif.) Community Coll., 1979-80; recreation leader Lynwood (Calif.) Parks & Recreation, 1980-81; sub. tchr. Compton (Calif.) Sch. Dist.,

1981-82; police officer Compton Police Dept., from 1982. Poet. Boxing coach Sheriff's Amateur Athletic League, Lynwood, 1988—; rape/crisis intervention counselor YWCA, Compton, 1989—; guest speaker annual career awareness day, Lynwood Unified Sch. Dist., 1982; speaker career day, L.A. Unified Sch. Dis.t, 1983, Compton Unified Sch. Dist., 1979; social change accessor, Calif. State Coll. Dominguez Hills., City of Lynwood, 1977; Christian Sunday Sch. Tchr. Mem. Compton Police Officers Assn., Peace Officers Rsch. Assn. Calif., Internat. Union Police Assn., Alpha Gamma Sigma Tau (membership chmn. 1975-76), Calif. State U. Giving Club. Democrat. Home: Compton, Calif. Died Sept. 17, 2004.

MITCHELL, WILLIAM ALEXANDER, food consultant; b. Raymond, Minn., Oct. 21, 1911; s. Ernst Michael and Florentina (Fletter) M.; m. Ruth Chilla Cobbey (dec. 1999), Sept. 3, 1938; children: William, Charles, Michael, John Jan, Steven, Cheryl. BA, Nebr. Wesleyan U., 1935; MS, U. Nebr., 1938; DS (hon.), Nebr. Wesleyan U., 1980. High sch. sci. tchr., Belvidere, Nebr., 1935-36; chemist Experimental Sta., Univ. Nebr., Lincoln, 1937-38; organic chemist Eastman Kodak Co., Rochester, N.Y., 1939-41; project leader to rsch. scientist Gen. Foods Corp., Hoboken to Tarrytown, N.J., N.Y., 1941-76; pvt. practice, food cons. Lincoln Park, Shelburne, 1976—2004. Contb. articles to profl. jours.; patentee in field. Sch. bd. to v.p. Lincoln Park, 1953-61. Mem. Am. Chem. Soc., Cereal Chemist. Lutheran. Home: Livermore, Colo. Died July 26, 2004.

MITTELMAN, EUGENE, lawyer; b. Brooklyn, Nov. 23, 1935; s. Irving and Marion (Hassin) M.; m. Frances J. (Paris); children: Karen Sue, Deborah. BA, Bard Coll., 1957; JD, Columbia U., 1961. Bar: N.Y., 1962. Assoc. McGoldrick, Dannett, Horowitz, and Golug, N.Y.C., 1962—67; minority counsel U.S. Senate Com. on Labor and Human Resources, Washington, 1967—74; ptnr. Mittelman and Gordon, Washington, 1975—85, Dreyer and Traub, N.Y.C., 1985—96, Maidman and Mittelman, LLP, N.Y.C., from 1996. Labor arbitrator, 1975-90. Mem. ABA, Assn. of the Bar, City of NY. Republican. Jewish. Home: New York, NY. Died May 19, 2005.

MLOTEK, HERMAN VICTOR, former religious education educator; b. Poland, Apr. 8, 1922; arrived in Can., 1932; came to U.S., 1939, naturalized, 1949; s. Shlomo Zalmen and Rose (Goldkind) M.; m. Estelle Weiss, Nov. 23, 1947; children: David Benjamin, Alan Steven. BS, De Paul U., 1946; postgrad., Hebrew Theol. Coll., Skokie, Ill., 1939-47, Roosevelt U., 1956-57, Nat. Coll. Edn., 1978. Ordained rabbi, 1952; cert. elem., secondary, jr. coll. tchr. and supr., Ill. Prin. Beth Itzchok Sch., Chgo., 1947-62, Albany Park Day Sch., Chgo., 1949-51, Albany Park-Beth Itzchok Sch., Chgo., 1962-64, Lincolnwood (Ill.). Jewish Congregation, 1964-73; tchr. Chgo. Pub. Schs., 1973-92, ret., 1992. Mem. Am. Fedn. Tchrs., Ill. Fedn. Tchrs., Chgo. Tchrs. Union, Religious Zionists Chgo., Agudath Isreal Ill., Associated Talmud Torah Chgo., World Jewish Congress. Avocations: chess, reading, walking. Home: Chicago, Ill. Died July 17, 2005.

MOBURG, KENNETH DEAN, retired health services executive; b. Monmouth, Ill., Aug. 20, 1925; s. Eddie Victor and Julia (Palmer) M.; m. Dorothy Josephine Jackson, June 10, 1950; children: Steven, Donna, Peter, Lucia. BA, Augustana Coll., 1949; MA, Northwestern U., 1951. Adminstrv. resident The Grace Hosp., Detroit, 1950-51; administr. Schoolcraft Meml. Hosp., Manistique, Mich., 1951-54, Bell Meml. Hosp., Ishpeming, Mich., 1954-56, Luth. Hosp., Moline, Ill., 1956-68, pres., 1968-88; pres., CEO Quad Cities Health Care, Moline, 1984-88; pres., chief exec. officer United Health Systems, Moline, 1984-88, vice chmn., 1989-90; ret., 1990. Trustee Augustana Coll., Rock Island, Ill., 1962-68, 1981-89; bd. Black Hawk Coll., Moline, 1970-78 (chmn. 1976-78). With USAF, 1944-46. Luth. Hosp. Assn. bd. has awarded Kenneth D. Moburg award for grad. study since 1986. Fellow Am. Coll. Healthcare Execs. (life); mem. Am. Hosp. Assn., Luth. Hosp. Assn., Moline C. of C., Rotary, ARC. Republican. Lutheran. Avocation: antique automobiles. Home: Appleton, Wis. Died Jan. 17, 2005.

MOCHEL, MYRON GEORGE, mechanical engineer, educator; b. Fremont, Ohio, Oct. 9, 1905; s. Gustave A. and Rose M. (Minich) M.; m. Eunice Katherine Steinicke, Aug. 30, 1930 (dec. Dec. 1982); children: Kenneth R., David G., Virginia June. BSME, Case Western Res. U., 1929; MSME, Yale U., 1930. Registered profl. engr. N.Y., Mass., Pa. Devel. engr. nitrogen div. Allied Chem. Corp., Hopewell, Va., 1930-31; devel. engr. R&D dept. Mobil Corp., Paulsboro, NJ, 1931-37; design and devel. engr. gearing div. Westinghouse Electric Corp., Pitts., 1937-43; rsch. assoc. underwater sound lab. Harvard U., Cambridge, Mass., 1943-45; supr. of tng. steam turbine div. Worthington Corp., Wellsville, NY, 1945-49; prof. mech. engr. Clarkson U., Potsdam, NY, 1949-71, prof. emeritus, from 1971. Lect. U. Pitts., 1938-43, N.Y. State U. Adult Edn., Wellsville, 1946-49, Oswego, 1965, N.Y. State High Sch. Enrichment Program, Potsdam, 1962-71; cons. Designers for Industry, Cleve., 1953, rsch. engr. Morris Machine Works, Baldwinsville, N.Y., 1954, design engr. Racquette River Paper Co., Potsdam, 1955. Author: Fundamentals of Engineering Graphics, 1960, Pre-Engineering and Applied Science Fundamentals, 1962, Fortran Programming, Programs and Schematic Storage Maps, 1971; co-author: (with Eunice S. Mochel) Funds For Fun, 1983, (with Donald H. Purcell) Beyond Expectations, 1985; contbr. articles to profl. jours. and on internet. Officer, vol. St. Lawrence Valley Hospice, 1983; pres. Mayfield Tenants Assn., 1989-91. Mem. ASME, Am. Soc. Engrng. Edn. (advt. mgr. Jour. Engrng. Graphics 1963-66, sec. 1966-67, high schs. laision on engrng. graphics 1962-65, awards com. chmn. 1965-66), Am. Assn. Ret. Persons (founder St. Lawrence County chpt., income tax counselor 1988-89, medicare/medicaid assistance program counselor 1988—, pres. 1989-90). Republican. Mem. Unitarian Universalist Ch. Home: Auburn, NY. Died 2005.

MOCKLER, ADELE, secondary school educator; b. N.Y.C., June 12, 1927; d. Max and Rose (Zipkin) R.; m. Nils E. Mockler, Feb. 26, 1954; children: P. Anna, Michael W. ABD, SUNY, Albany, 1979; BA, Hunter Coll., 1949, MA, 1957. Tchr. Putnam Valley Cmty., Putnam Valley, N.Y., 1963-67, Duanesburg Central, Delanson, N.Y., 1967-79; sales Northwestern Mutual Life, Latham, N.Y., from 1980. Pres. League of Women Voters Putnam Valley, 1966, Hunter Coll. Alumni Assn., Albany, 1990-95; chmn. Cong. Gates of Hearon, 1999—. Mem. CLU. Democart. Jewish. Avocations: book group, torah study. Home: Altamont, NY. Died Nov. 16, 2004.

MOFFO, ANNA, opera singer; b. Wayne, Pa., June 27, 1927; d. Nicholas and Regina (Cinti) Moffo; m. Mario Lafranchi, 1957 (div. 1972); m. Robert Sarnoff, Nov. 14, 1974 (dec. 1997). Grad. with honors, Curtis Inst.; studied, Santa Cecilia Acad., Rome. Appeared (TV Operas) Madame Butterfly, Italy, debut (Operas) Spoleto; singer: (Operas) (opera houses) Paris, London, Salzburg, Vienna, Milan, numerous others abroad; Am. debut (Operas) Lyric Opera Co., Chgo., 1957, debut as Violetta, Met. Opera Co., N.Y.C., 1959, appeared Voice of Firestone telecast, 1957, (films) Lucia, U.S. and Italy, (films Concerto) numerous TV appearances, numerous recordings Emi, Ariola, Angel, Columbia, RCA Victor. Decorated Order of Merit Republic Italy; recipient Liebe Augustin award, Young Artists award Phila. Orch., Silver Griffo award for film Love Story); Fulbright scholar. Died Mar. 9, 2006.

MOGUL, EUGENE, executive search consultant; b. N.Y.C., July 27, 1923; s. Samuel and Tillie (Stern) M.; m. Rhoda Marylyn Blate, Sept. 12, 1948; children: Susan, Mark, Samuel, Kim, Jess, Pamela. BS in Engring., Columbia U., 1943. Pres. Comfax Communications Inc., N.Y.C., 1968-71; gen. mgr. service Savin Bus. Machines, Valhalla, N.Y., 1971-73; pres. Mogul Cons., Inc., Jericho, N.Y., from 1973. Mem. IEEE (sr.). Democrat. Jewish. Home: East Norwich, NY. Died Jan. 25, 2004.

MOLINA, MARIA TERESA, social worker; b. Havana, Cuba, Feb. 26, 1932; came to U.S., 1961, nauturalized, 1970; d. Manuel and Teresa (Fernandez) Rodriguez; m. Rafael E. Molina, Nov. 20, 1955; children: Louis R., Maria T., Manuel E., Rafael E. Jr. BA, MSW, Havana U. Sec., pers. courier for chief Underground in Cuba, 1960; asst. to asst. dir. Catholic nat. Welfare Conf., Cuba, 1962-66; pres. bd. Prestera Ctr. Mental Health Svcs., Inc., Huntington, W.Va., 1981-83, Goodwill Industries, Huntington, W.Va., 1985-86; Spanish translator Cts. of W.Va., from 1988. Founder, past 1st pres. YWCA Internat; past pres. Cabell County Med. Aux.; past mem. citizens adv. com. Bd. Edn., W.Va.; past bd. dirs. Family Svc., Credit Counseling; lt. Huntington Police Res. Unit, 1979-85; mem. human resources com. Black Diamond Girl Scout coun., 1986-87; mem. GOP Exec. Com., Cabell County, 1987-88; chmn. W.Va. Rep. Women Americanism Com., 1990—, W.Va. Rep. Women Mem. Com., 1992—; mem. Rep. Presdl. Task Force, 1980—; active Huntington Cabell Rep. Women, 1990—; regional dir. region II outreach program Nat. Fedn. Rep. Women, 1991-92, co-chair, 1992—. Mem. Rotary Aux. (past pres.), Huntington Women Internat. Club (past pres. coun., chairwoman crime prevention and home safety). Roman Catholic. Avocations: cooking, gardening. Died Jan. 6, 2005.

MONAGHAN, EILEEN See WHITAKER, EILEEN

MONAHAN, MARIE ADORNETTO, law educator; b. Buffalo, Feb. 26, 1951; d. Samuel Adornetto and Josephine Lucci; m. Peter A. Monahan, May 23, 1981; children: Matthew, Joseph. BA, SUNY, Buffalo, 1973; MA, SUNY, 1975; JD, DePaul U., Chgo., 1981; PhD, Northwestern U., 1986. Bar: Ill., U.S. Dist. Ct. (no. dist.) Ill. Instr. Northwestern U., Evanston, Ill., 1975-81; law clk. Ill. Appellate Ct., Chgo., 1981-83; assoc. atty. Baker & McKenzie, Chgo., 1983-88; asst. prof. No. Ill. U. Sch. Law, DeKalb, 1988-89; asst. prof. law John Marshall Law Sch., Chgo., from 1989. Hearing officer Atty. Registration and Disciplinary Commn., Chgo., 1998-9. Co-author casebook; author tng. manual; contbr. articles to legal cjours. Mem. ABA, Chgo. Bar Assn. (investigator, mem. hearing panel jud. evaluation com. 1993-98). Democrat. Roman Catholic. Died Apr. 11, 2004.

MONAHAN, MARIE TERRY, lawyer; b. Milford, Mass., June 26, 1927; d. Francis V. and Marie I. (Casey) Terry; m. John Henry Monahan, Aug. 25, 1951; children: Thomas F., Kathleen J., Patricia M., John Terry, Moira M., Deirdre M. AB, Radcliffe Coll., 1949; JD, New Eng. Sch. Law, 1975. Bar: Mass. 1977, U.S. Dist. Ct. Mass. 1978, U.S. Supreme Ct. 1982. Tchr. French and Spanish Holliston (Mass.) High Sch., 1949-52; pvt. practice Newton, Mass., from 1977. Mem. Mass. Assn. Women Lawyers (pres. 1986). Avocations: reading, travel. Died Feb. 14, 2005.

MONDUZZI, DINO CARDINAL, bishop; b. Brisighella, Italy, Apr. 2, 1922; Attended, Seminary of Faenza, Pontifical Lateran U., Rome. Ordained priest Roman Cath. Ch., 1945; pastoral work Italy, 1945—59; adj. sec. for audiences Office of Master of Chamber, 1959—67; sec., regent Pontifical Household, 1967—86; prefect of Pontifical Household, 1986—98; prefect emeritus, 1998—2006; consecrated bishop, 1987; created cardinal, 1998. Died Oct. 13, 2006.

MONEY, JOHN WILLIAM, retired psychologist, educator; b. Morrinsville, New Zealand, July 8, 1921; came to U.S., 1947, naturalized, 1962; s. Frank and Ruth (Read) M. MA with honors, Victoria U. Coll., New Zealand, 1943; postgrad., U. Pitts., 1947; PhD, Harvard U., 1952; DHL (hon.), Hofstra U., 1992. Jr. lectr. philosophy and psychology U. Otago, New Zealand, 1945-47; part-time vis. lectr. Bryn Mawr Coll., Pa., 1952-53; mem. faculty Johns Hopkins U., Balt., 1951—2005, prof. med. psychology, 1972-86, assoc. prof. pediatrics, 1959-86, prof. emeritus med. psychology and pediatrics, 1986—2006; psychologist Johns Hopkins Hosp., 1955—2005, founder psychohormonal research unit, 1951, founding mem. gender identity com., 1966. Vis. prof. pediats. Albert Einstein Coll. Medicine, 1969, U. Nebr. Coll. Medicine, 1972; vis. prof. endocrinology Harvard U., 1970; vis. prof. ob-gyn. U. Conn., 1975; Rachford lectr. Children's Hosp., Cin., 1969; bd. dirs. Sex Info. and Edn. Coun. U.S., 1965-68, Neighborhood Family Planning Ctr., 1970-82; mem. task force homosexuality NIMH, 1967-69; mem. study sect. devel. and behavioral scis. NIH, 1970-74; mem. task force on nomenclature Am. Psychiat. Assn., 1977-79, 85-87; pres. Am. Found. Gender and Genital Medicine and Sci., 1978-2006; bd. advisors Elysium Inst., 1980-2000; mem. external com. for rev. of Inst. for Sex Rsch., Ind. U., 1980; mem. sci. adv. bd. Kinsey Inst. for Rsch. in Sex, Gender and Reprodn., 1982-97; hon. chmn. internat. adv. bd. Nat. Inst. Rsch. in Sex Edn., Counseling and Therapy, 1991; Kan Tongpo vis. prof. dept. psychiatry U. Hong Kong, 1994. Mem. editl. bd. numerous jours.; field editor Medicine and Law: an Internat. Jour., 1982-95; subject (book) John Money: A Tribute, 1991, (TV documentary) Coming Home, 1999. Recipient Hofheimer prize Am. Psychiat. Assn., 1956, Gold medal Children's Hosp., Phila., 1966, citation Am. Urol. Assn., 1975, Harry Benjamin medal of honor Erickson Ednl. Found., 1976, Outstanding Contbn. award Md. Psychol. Assn., 1976, Lindemann lectr. pediatrics Cornell U., 1983, Bernadine Disting. lectr. U. Mo., 1985, Maurice W. Laufer Meml. lectr. Bradley Hosp. and Brown U., 1986, Disting. Scholar award Harry Benjamin Internat. Gender Dysphoria Assn., 1987, Outstanding Rsch. Accomplishments award Nat. Inst. Child Health and Human Devel., 1987, Gloria Scientae Polish award, 1991, Lifetime Outstanding award for Treatment of Sex Offenders, 1991, Richard J. Cross award Robert Wood Johnson Med. Sch., 1992, Career Achievement award N.Y. Soc. Forensic Scis., 1994, Coun. of Sex Edn. and Parenthood Internat. award, 1994, gold medal for lifetime achievement World Assn. Sexology, 1995, sexology medal Am. Acad. Clin. Sexology, 1996, Magnus Hirschfeld medal for sexual scis., 2002; named Sexologist of Yr. Polish Acad. Sex. Sci., 1988; James McKeen Cattell fellow Am. Psychol. Soc., 1993; Rm. in his name Kinsey Inst., Ind. U., 2003, wing at Ea. Southland Gallery Inc., Gore, New Zealand, 2003. Fellow: AAAS (life), Soc. Sci. Study Sex (charter, pres. 1974—76, award 1976, Past Pres. award 1987, Kinsey award western regional chpt. 1996, John Money award named in his honor 2003), Nat. Inst. Rsch. Sex Edn., Counseling and Therapy (hon.), Harriet Lane Alumni Soc.; mem.: APA (master lectr. 1975, Disting. Sci. award 1985), Nat. Assn. Sexology (chief patron), Internat. Coll. Pediats., Md. Soc. Med. Rsch., N.Y. Acad. Scis., Internat. Soc. Psychoneuroendocrinology, European Soc. Pediat. Endocrinology (corr.), Asian Fedn. for Sexology (hon.), Soc. Andaluza de Sexologia (hon.), Assn. Sexologists (life), Am. Assn. Sex Educators, Counselors and Therapists (hon. awards 1976, 1985), Columbian Sexol. Soc. (hon.), Czechoslovak Sexology Soc. (hon.; internat. adv. bd. 1995), New Zealand Soc. on Sexology (hon.; life), Soc. Brasileira de Sexologia (hon.), Can. Sex Rsch. Forum (hon.), Assn. Especialistas en Sexologia (hon.), Internat. Acad. Sex Rsch. (charter, award 1991), Lawson Wilkins Pediat. Endocrine Soc. (founder), Soc. Pediat. Psychology, Internat. Orgn. Study Human Devel., Deutsche Gesellschaft fur Sexualforschung. Home: Baltimore, Md. Died July 7, 2006.

MONHOLLON, LELAND, lawyer; b. Corbin, Ky., Nov. 8, 1925; s. Lewis Tom and Thelma (Prewitt) M.; m. Gawinna Owens, 1946 (div. 1969); 1 child, Patricia Lynn; m. Alice Faye Burden, July 3, 1970. JD, U. Ky., 1952. Bar: Ky. 1952. Supervising adjustor Travelers Ins. Co., Louisville, 1955-69; pvt. practice law Madisonville, Ky., 1969-97; ret., 1997. With USN, 1943-46, PTO, USNR, 1963-69. Mem. Ky. Bar Assn., Hopkins County Bar Assn., Am. Legion, VFW. Republican. Methodist. Home: Madisonville, Ky. Died June 21, 2005.

MONKS, JOHN, JR., screenwriter, playwright, actor, director; b. Bklyn., June 25, 1910; s. John and Emily Frances Monks; m. Margaret Josephine Jackson, Aug. 24, 1949; 1 child, Sara Elizabeth. BA, Va. Mil. Inst., 1932. Actor various mediums, 1932-36; playwright, screenwriter, 1937—2004. Playwright Brother Rat 1936, screenwriter: (films) The Mad Miss Manton, 1938, Brother Rat, 1938, Brother Rat and a Baby, 1940, Strike up the Band, 1940, We Are the Marines (also dir.), 1942, The House on 92nd Street, 1945, 13 Rue Madeleine, 1947, Wild Harvest, 1947, Knock On Any Door, 1949, The West Point Story, 1950, Dial 1119, 1950, The People Against O'Hara, 1951, About Face, 1952, Where's Charley, 1952, So This Is Love, 1953, No Man Is an Island, (also dir.), 1962; exec. prodr. The Delta Factor,

1970; (TV spls.) A Box of Chocolates, Miracle on 34th Street, The Gioconda Smile, High Tor, Emily, Murder by Fire, Paradise Bay (also creator); (original screenplay) The Battle of Ocean View. Served to maj. USMC, 1942-45, PTO. Mem.: The Players (N.Y.C.). Avocations: fly fishing, fly tying. Died Dec. 10, 2004.

MONROE, HELEN LEOLA, nurse, consultant, educator; b. Alma, Ga., Jan. 30, 1931; d. Silas Leo Monroe and Thelma (Fussell) Smith; 1 child, Reavena M. M. Oliver. BS, Fla. A&M U., 1954; MS, St. John's U., L.I., N.Y., 1959. Staff nurse Vis. Nurse Assn. Duval County, Jacksonville, Fla., 1954-55; instr. sch. nursing Fla. A&M U., Tallahassee, 1955-57, asst. prof., 1959-64; dir. nursing edn. Mississippi Valley State Coll., Itta Bena, Miss., 1964-67; asst. prof. Norfolk State Coll. Va., 1967-68; asst. prof., dir. nursing edn. Lincoln U., Jefferson City, Mo., 1968-80; pvt. practice nursing Jefferson City, 1981-85; pvt. practice achievement cons. Jacksonville, from 1987. Cons. Jacksonville, 1987—; cons. nursing William Woods Coll., Fulton, Mo., 1972-73; established first ednl. program for nonwhites to become RNs in Miss. Sec. Jefferson City chpt. NAACP, 1971-73; chmn. edn. com. Cancer Soc. Cole County, Jefferson City, 1972-74; v.p. Cole County Mental Health Assn., 1973; mem. fin. com. United Way Cole County, 1975. Recipient Outstanding Achievement award Citizens' Com. of Jefferson City, 1970, Woman of Achievement award AAUW, 1974, Permanent Royal Patronage from Principality of the Hutt River Province, 1994. Avocations: gardening, sewing, reading, bicycling, bowling. Home: Jefferson City, Mo. Died Dec. 11, 2004.

MONSEN, RONALD PETER, musician, educator, artist; b. Milw., Sept. 20, 1940; s. Ray Thelmert and Eunice Irene (Friebl) M.; m. Joan Grace Williams, Dec. 21, 1963; children: Dirk Andrew (dec.), Peter Colin, Kirsten Jo. BSc, U. Wis., Milw., 1964; MMus, Northwestern U., Evanston, Ill., 1968; performer's diploma, Royal Acad. Music, London, 1971; D of Mus. Arts, U. Wis., Madison, 1978. Music tchr. Milw. pub. schs., 1964-67; prof. woodwinds Concordia Coll., Moorhead, Minn., 1968-73; prof. clarinet U. Ky., Lexington, from 1980. Clarinet clinican Selmer Co., Elkhart, Ind., 1986—. Clarinet recitalist appearances include Denver, 1983, London, 1984, Seattle, 1986, Cin., 1992; mem. Okla. Clarinet Symphony, 1985. Mem. Internat. Clarinet Assn. (mem. state chair, pres. 1992). Avocations: model railroading, photography, france. Home: Lexington, Ky. Died May 7, 2004.

MONTAG, MILDRED LOUISE, nursing educator; b. Struble, Iowa, Aug. 10, 1908; d. Joseph P. and Louise (Schnell) Montag. BA, Hamline U., 1930; BS, U. Minn., 1983; MA, Columbia U., 1938, EdD, 1950. Instr. U. Minn. Sch. Nursing, 1935-37; instr. Sch. of Nursing St. Lukes Hosp., N.Y.C., 1938-41; staff nurse Nurse Testing divsn. Henry Street Vis. Nurse Svc., N.Y.C., 1941; staff nurse Psychol. Corp., N.Y.C., 1941-42; dir. Sch. Nursing Adelphi U., N.Y.C., 1942-48; prof. Tchr.'s Coll. Columbia U. Tchr.'s Coll., N.Y.C., prof. emerita Tchr.'s Coll., 1972. Mem. ANA, AAUP, AAUW, Nat. League for Nursing, Zonta. Home: Garden City, NY. Died Jan. 21, 2004.

MONTALVO, GABRIEL, archbishop; b. Santafé de Bogota, Colombia, Jan. 27, 1930; D in Canon Law, Lateran U., Rome. Ordained priest Archdiocese of Santafé, Bogota, 1953; recipient Episcopal Ordination by Pope Paul VI, 1974. With Holy See, Bolivia, Argentina and El Salvador, 1957-64, sec. of state sect. Ea. Eurpean Countries, 1964-74; apostolic nuncio Nicaragua and Honduras, 1974; apostolic pro-nuncio Algeria and Tunisia, 1980-86; apostolic del. Lybia, 1980-86; from mem. to head Papal Mediation Office, 1982—84; apostolic pro-nuncio Yugoslavia, 1986-96; 1st apostolic nuncio Belarus, 1993; pres. Pontifical Ecclesiastical Acad., 1993; apostolic nuncio to the US The Vatican, 1998—2005; permanent observer Holy See to Org. of Am. States, 1998—2006. Died Aug. 2, 2006.

MONTGOMERY, FRED, JR., mayor; b. Henning, Tenn., Nov. 22, 1916; s. Fred Sr. and Ionie (Hawkins) M.; m. Mary Earnestine Bonds, Mar. 10, 1935; children: Charles, Marvin, Roy, Fred III, Henry, Jerdine, Ella, Larry, Derik, Sheila. MPA (hon.), Mid. Tenn. State U., 1989. Cert. master plumber and contractor. Alderman Bd. Alderman, Henning, 1971-89; former mayor City of Henning, from 1989. Historian, guide, Haley Mus., Henning, 1971—. Historian, cons. Palmerstown USA, Roots-Mini Series. Recipient Cmty. Svc. award Tenn. State U., 1982, Xi Lamba Omega, 1990, Award of Excellence Kunte Kinte Heritage Group, 1994, Certificate of Merit Tenn. Hist. Soc., 1996, Hon. Citizenship award African Am. Soc., 1994. Mem. Am. Griot Soc. (Certificate of Merit 1995), Nat. Def. Internat. Fellows (hon.), Coun. Mayors Tenn. Methodist. Avocations: fishing, storytelling, singing. Home: Henning, Tenn. Died July 12, 2006.

MONTGOMERY, GILLESPIE V. (SONNY MONTGOMERY), former congressman; b. Meridian, Miss., Aug. 5, 1920; s. Gillespie and Emily (Jones) Montgomery. BS, Miss. State U. Mem. Miss. State Senate, 1956-66, US Congresses from 3rd Miss. Dist., 1967-96; ranking minority mem., 1994-96; mem. vets. affairs com., 1978-96, chmn., 1981-94, select com. on missing persons in southeast Asia, 1975-96; mem. Woodcock Commn., 1977; pres., CEO The Montgomery Group, Alexandria, Va., 1997—2004. Pres. Miss. N.G. Assn., 1959; pres. Miss. Heart Assn., 1967-68. Served with AUS, World War II, Korea, ret. maj. gen. Miss N.G. Decorated Bronze Star medal, Combat Inf. Badge; recipient Miss. Magnolia award, 1966, Lifetime Achievement award, Mil. Educators & Counselors Assn., 1992, Presdl. Medal of Freedom, The White House, 2005. Mem. VFW, Am. Legion 40 and 8, Congl. Prayer Breakfast Group (pres. 1970) Lodges: Masons; Shriners; Scottish Rite. Democrat. Episcopalian. Home: Yazoo City, Miss. Died May 12, 2006.

MONTGOMERY, PHILIP O'BRYAN, JR., pathologist; b. Dallas, Aug. 16, 1921; BS, So. Meth. U., 1942; MD, Columbia U., 1945. Diplomate Am. Bd. Pathology, Am. Bd. Clin. Pathology and Forensic Pathology. Intern Mary Imogene Bassett Hosp., Cooperstown, N.Y., 1945-46; fellow in pathology Southwestern Med. Sch., Dallas, 1950-51, asst. prof. pathology, 1953-55, assoc. prof., 1955-61, prof., 1961—2005, assoc. dean, 1968-70, Ashbel Smith prof. pathology, 1991—2005; rsch. asst. pathology and cancer rsch. Cancer Rsch. Inst. New Eng. Deaconess Hosp., Boston, 1951-52; spl. asst. to chancellor U. Tex. System, 1971-75. Exec. dir. Cancer Ctr. U. Tex. Health Sci. Ctr. Dallas, 1975-89; pathologist Parkland Meml. Hosp., Dallas, 1952—, Dallas City Zoo, 1955-68; med. examiner Dallas-County, 1955-58; cons. Navarro County Meml. Hosp., Corsicana, Tex., 1952-53, McKinney (Tex.) Vets. Hosp., 1952-65, Lisbons Vets. Hosp., Dallas, 1953—, St. Paul Hosp., Dallas, 1958—, Flow Meml. Hosp., Denton, Tex., 1958-65; pathologist Tex. Children's Hosp., Dallas, 1954-55. Contbr. numerous articles to profl. jours., sci. abstracts, jours. Bd. dirs. Planned Parenthood of Dallas, 1958-63, pres., 1958-60; trustee St. Mark's Sch. Tex., 1958—, v.p., chmn. exec. com. bd. trustee, 1966-68, v.p., 1968-69, pres. 1974-76; trustee Lamplighter Sch., 1967-70; chmn. Dallas Area Libr. Planning Coun., 1970-72, Goals for Dallas Health Task Force com., 1975-76, Fleet Adm. Nimitz Mus. commn., 1979-81; mem. adv. bd. Dallas Citizens coun., chmn. health com. 1988-89; bd. dirs. Met. YMCA, 1960-63, Dallas Coun. on World Affairs, 1962-65; pres., bd. dirs. Damon Runyon, Walter Winchell Cancer Fund, 1974-79; cord. Dallas Arts Dist., 1982-95. Fellow Am. Soc. Clin. Pathologists; mem. Am. Assn. Pathologists and Bacteriologists, Am. Assn. Cancer Rsch., Internat. Acad. Pathology, Am. Acad. Forensic Scis., Soc. Exptl. Biology and Medicine, Internat. Soc. Cell Biology, Biophys. Soc., Am. Soc. Cell Biology, Am. soc. Exptl. Pathology, Tissue Culture Assn., Internat. Fedn. Med. Electronics, Profl. Group Med. Electronics of Inst. Radio Engrs., AAAS, Optical Soc. Tex. (founding), Pan-Am. Med. Assn., AMA, So. Med. Assn., Tex. Med. Assn., AAUP. Died Dec. 24, 2005.

MONTGOMERY, ROBERT EARL, physicist, researcher; b. Natchez, Miss., Aug. 31, 1941; s. Earl William and Marjorie Estell (Wilson) M.; m. Valerie Ann Sarkisian, Aug. 16, 1978 (div. Feb. 1990); 1 child, Benjamin Robert. BS, La. State U., 1963, PhD in Physics, 1970. Rsch. assoc. U. Tex., Dallas, 1969-71; asst. prof. physics Austin Coll., Sherman, Tex., 1971-77; cons. Austin, Tex., 1977-80; sr. scientist Tex. Rsch. Inst., Austin, 1980-85; rsch. physicist Naval Rsch. Lab., Orlando, Fla., from 1985. Contbr. articles to profl. jours.; contbr.: Transducers for Sonics and Ultrasonics, 1992. Recipient A. D. Berman Pub. award, 1994; Sml. Bus. Innovative Rsch. grantee NSF, 1984. Mem. Acoustical Soc. Am. Avocations: tennis, fitness exercising, reading. Home: Casselberry, Fla. Died Feb. 6, 2005.

MONTGOMERY-DAVIS, JOSEPH, osteopathic physician; b. Annapolis, Md., Aug. 27, 1940; s. John and Flonila Alice (Sutphin) Swontek. Student, U. Wis., Milw., 1967-70; DO, Chgo. Coll. Osteo. Medicine, 1974. Diplomate Nat. Bd. Examiners for Osteo. Physicians and Surgeons; cert. family practice & osteo. manipulative treatment. Chief technologist nuclear medicine dept. Columbia Hosp., Milw., 1964-70; intern Richmond Heights (Ohio) Gen. Hosp., 1974-75; pvt. practice Raymondville, Tex., from 1975. Mem. med. care adv. com. Tex. Dept. Human Svcs., Austin, 1983—86, Austin, 1990—93, Austin, from 2002, mem. physician payment adv. com., 1991—95, Austin, from 2001; cons. health care issues Tex. Osteo. Med. Assn., from 1991; health officer Willacy County Health Authority, Raymondville, from 1984; mem. med. care adv. com. Tex. Workers Compensation Commn., 1997—2001; clin. assoc. prof. dept. family medicine North Tex. Health Sci. Ctr., Ft. Worth, from 2000. Contbr. articles to profl. jours. With USAF, 1959-63. Mem. Am. Osteo. Assn., Am. Coll. Osteo. Family Physiaicns (spl. Recognition award 1995), Tex. Soc. Am. Coll. Osteo. Family Physicians (pres. 1985-86, Physician of Yr. award 1989, T.R. Sharp Meritorious Svc. award 1999), Tex. Med. Found., Tex. Osteo. Med. Assn. (pres. 1989-90), Tex. Coll. Osteo. Medicine Alumni Assn., Phi Eta Sigma, Sigma Sigma Phi. Home: Raymondville, Tex. Died Jan. 2005.

MONTY, GLORIA, retired television producer, film company executive; b. Union City, N.J. d. Joseph and Concetta M. (Mango) Montemuro; m. Robert Thomas O'Byrne, Jan. 8, 1952 BA, NYU; MA, Columbia U. Dir. New Sch. Social Rsch., N.Y.C., 1952-53; dir. Old Towne Theatres, Smithtown, N.Y., 1952-56, Abbey Theatre Workshop, N.Y.C., 1952-56; chmn. N.J. Motion Picture & TV Commn., Newark. Cons. ABC Dir. numerous TV programs and series, including First Hundred Years, 1950, Secret Storm, 1956-72, The Bright Promise, 1969, Screaming Skull, 1973, Sorority Kill, 1974, The Screaming Skull, 1993 and numerous episodes ABC Wide World Entertainment; exec. prodr. General Hospital, 1978-86, 91-92, The Hamptons, 1983-85; made-for-TV movies, including Confessions of a Married Man, 1982, The Imposter, 1984; exec. prodr. in devel. for primetime TV 20th Century Fox, 1987-90; head cons. daytime TV ABC, 1987-90; prin. Gloria Monty Prodns. for new ABC daytime drama devel.; co-exec. prodr. Remember Me, 1995, While My Pretty One Sleeps, 1997, FAMILY CHANNEL, 1995-97, Let Me Call You Sweetheart, 1997, Moonlight Becomes You, 1998; made-for-TV movies in assn. with Grosso-Jacobson. Chair Film Commn., State of N.J. Recipient Emmy awards, 1982, 84, Am. Soc. Lighting Dirs. award, 1979, Most Successful TV Show in History of TV award ABC, 1982, Spl. Editors award Soap Opera Digest, 1984, numerous others; named Woman of Yr., Paulist Choristers So. Calif., 1986. Mem. Women in Film, Dirs. Guild Am. (mem. exec. com.), Stuntman's Assn. (hon.), Thunderbird Country Club (Rancho Mirage, Calif.), Bel Air Country Club (Calif.), Deal Country Club, Navesink Country Club. Died Mar. 30, 2006.

MONTZ, DWIGHT HAYES, bank executive; b. Monroe, Mich., May 27, 1922; s. Charles and Mary Ethel (Plewes) M.; m. Helen Ada Cronenwett, June 12, 1947; 1 child, Kim I. Montz Diven. BA, Dartmouth Coll., 1946; MBA, U. Toledo, 1965. CPA, Mich. Credit mgr. Monroe Co-Op Oil Co., 1949-55; estimator Consolidated Paper Co., Monroe, 1955-57; acctg. supr. Union-Camp Corp., Monroe, 1957-65; ptnr. Richwine, Newton & Carlton, Monroe, 1965-69; v.p., controller Security Bank Monroe, 1969-77, sr. v.p., cashier, from 1977. Pres. adv. bd. Salvation Army, Monroe, 1977-78; fin. sec. Monroe YMCA, 1979; v.p., bd. dirs. Roselawn Meml. Park, 1980-87; pres. Monroe Council Chs., 1960. Served with USN, 1942-46. Mem. Am. Inst. CPA's, Mich. Assn. CPA's, Bank Adminstrn. Inst. (treas. 1970-71, v.p. 1971-72, pres. 1972-73). Lodges: Kiwanis (treas. North Monroe club 1955-57, sec. Monroe club 1968-70). Republican. Methodist. Home: Monroe, Mich. Died Apr. 25, 2004.

MOORE, JAMES ALFRED, ski company executive, lawyer; b. Madisonville, Ky., Oct. 20, 1915; s. Virgil Yandell and Dorothy Ina (Price) M.; m. Lucile Carpenter, June 29, 1970; children by previous marriage: Marjorie M. Eickel, James Kelly, Kathleen M. Marozzi; m. Judith Gallen, June 10, 1995. AB, U. Ky., 1936; LL.B., Harvard U., 1939. Bar: Pa. 1940, D.C. 1969, Va. 1978. Assoc. firm Pepper, Hamilton & Scheetz, Phila., 1940-51, partner, 1951-69, ptnr. Washington, 1969-77; pres. Camelback Ski Corp., Tannersville, Pa., 1963-86, chmn., 1986-93, chmn. emeritus, 1993—2006. Contbr. articles to various law revs. Bd. dirs. Phila. Soc. for Crippled Children and Adults, 1959-69. Served from ensign to lt. comdr. USNR, 1942-45. Mem. Am. Bar Assn., Am. Law Inst. Republican. Methodist. Home: Tannersville, Pa. Died July 19, 2006.

MOORE, JOHN STERLING, JR., retired minister; b. Memphis, Tenn., Aug. 25, 1918; s. John Sterling and Lorena (Bounds) M.; m. Martha Louise Paulette, July 6, 1944; children: Sterling Hale, John Marshall, Carolyn Paulette. Student, Auburn U., 1936-37; AB, Samford U., 1940; ThM, So. Bapt. Theol. Sem., 1944. Ordained to ministry So. Bapt. Conv., 1942. Pastor chs., Pamplin, Va., 1944-48, Amherst, Va., 1949-57; pastor Manly Meml. Bapt. Ch., Lexington, Va., 1957-84, pastor emeritus, from 1984. Mem. Hist. Commn., So. Bapt. Conv., 1968-75; pres. Va. Bapt. Pastor's Conf., 1963. Author: History of Broad Run Baptist Church, 1762-1987, 1987, The History of Second Baptist Church Richmond Virginia, 1998; co-author: Meaningful Moments in Virginia Baptist Life, 1715-1972, 1973; editor Va. Bapt. Register, 1972-2001; contbr. articles to profl. jours. Chmn. Lexington Mayor's Com. on Race Rels., 1962-65; bd. dirs. Stonewall Jackson Hosp., 1967-72, pres., 1969-71; treas. Rockbridge Mental Health Clinic, 1971-84. Recipient Disting. Svc. award Hist. Commn., So. Bapt. Conv., 1988. Mem. Am. Soc. Ch. History, So. Bapt. Hist. Soc. (bd. dirs. 1972-91, pres. 1975-76, sec. 1977-85), Va. Bapt. Hist. Soc. (exec. com. 1963—, pres. 1984-85), Va. Hist. Soc., Masons. Home: Richmond, Va. Died Jan. 27, 2006.

MOORE, MARGARET ANNE, retired civilian military employee; b. Birmingham, Ala., Nov. 9, 1937; d. Leonard Elgie Turner and Fannie Ellen Black-Turner; m. Robert Eugene Hunter, Jan. 6, 1956 (div. 1967); children: Desiree Hunter, Rita Hunter, Rico Hunter, Rennie Hunter; m. John Moore, Dec. 21, 1968; 1 child, Monica Anne 1 stepchild, Dirk Eugene. A in Procurement and Materials Mgmt., Sinclair C.C., 1982; BA in Mgmt., Antioch U., 1990. Cert. acquisition profl., level I Dept. of Air Force, 1991, acquisition profl., level II Dept. of Air Force, 1992. Clk. typist Def. Electronics Supply Ctr., Dayton, Ohio, 1955—56, 1959—60; clk. stenographer Wright Patterson AFB, Ohio, 1965—66, procurement asst. Ohio, 1966—78; clk. asst. technician Arlington City, Va., 1978—80, Wright Patterson AFB, Ohio, 1985—95, configuration mgr. Ohio, 1985—95, ret., 1995. Watercolor art, one-woman shows include Paul Lawrence Dunbar House, 2001. Corr. sec. Blacks in Govt., Wright Patterson AFB, 1980—90; mem. Fairborn Art Assn. Mem.: Iota Phi Lambda (pres. 1991—93). Baptist. Avocations: art, aerobics. Home: Fairborn, Ohio. Died Nov. 4, 2004.

MOORE, MITCHELL STEVEN, computer consultant; b. Balt., Aug. 5, 1953; s. Donald David and Geraldine Anna (Krish) M.; m. Ann Lucille Cuomo, Aug. 25, 1973 (div. Oct. 1987); children: Michelle Ann, Steven Anthony; m. Lizzy-ann C. Lucena, Nov. 28, 1987; 1 child, Elizabeth Amy Sha'ou. BS in Psychology, Georgetown U., 1975, MS in Pharmacology, 1979. Designer AT&T, Skokie, Ill., 1980-82; regional sales mgr. Siemens Corp., Hauppauge, N.Y., 1982-88; sr. mem. tech. staff Hill Assocs., Inc., Winooski, Vt., 1988-93; pres. MSM Enterprises, Inc., Colchester, Vt., 1993-99; sr. mem. tech. staff Hill Assocs., Inc., Colchester, from 1999. Author: Manager's Guide to Packet Switching, 1988; contbr. articles to profl. jours. Mem. IEEE. Republican. Avocations: reading, music, golf, motorcycling, biking. Home: Colchester, Vt. Died Feb. 7, 2004.

MOORE, OMAR KHAYYAM, experimental sociologist; b. Helper, Utah, Feb. 11, 1920; s. John Gustav and Mary Jo (Crowley) M.; m. Ruth Garnand, Nov. 19, 1942; 1 child, Venn. BA, Doane Coll., 1942; MA, Washington U., St. Louis, 1946, PhD, 1949. Instr. Washington U., St. Louis, 1949-52; teaching assoc. Northwestern U., Evanston, Ill., 1950-51; rsch. asst., prof. sociology Tufts Coll., Medford, Mass., 1952-53; researcher Naval Rsch. Lab., Washington, 1953-54; asst. prof. sociology Yale U., New Haven, 1954-57, assoc. prof. sociology, 1957-63; prof. psychology Rutgers U., New Brunswick, NJ, 1963-65; prof. social psychology, sociology U. Pitts., 1965-71, prof. sociology, 1971-89, prof. emeritus, from 1989; scholar-in-residence Nat. Learning Ctr.'s Capital Children's Mus., Washington, 1989-90. Pres. Responsive Environ. Found., Inc., Estes Park, Colo., 1962—; assessor of rsch. projects The Social Scis. and Humanities Rsch. Coun. Can., 1982—; adj. prof. U. Colo., Boulder, 1992—. Contbg. editor Educational Technology; contbr. numerous articles to profl. jours.; patentee in field; motion picture producer and director. Recipient Award The Nat. Soc. for Programmed Instruction, 1965, Award Doane Coll Builder Award, 1967, Ednl. Award Urban Youth Action, Inc., 1969, Award House of Culture, 1975, Cert. of Appreciation, 1986, Cert. of Appreciation D.C. Pub. Schs., 1987, da Vinci Award Inst. for the Achievement of Human Potential, 1988, Cert. of Appreciation Capital Children's Museum, 1988, award Jack & Jill of America Found., 1988, Cert. of Appreciation U.S. Dept. of Edn., 1988, Cert. of Appreciation D.C. Pub. Schs., 1990, Person of Yr. in Ednl. Tech. award Ednl. Tech. mag., 1990. Mem. AAAS, Am. Math. Soc., Am. Psychol. Assn., Internat. Sociol. Assn., Am. Sociol. Assn., Assn. for Symbolic Logic, Assn. for Anthrop. Study of Play, Philosophy Sci. Assn., Psychonomics Soc., Soc. for Applied Sociology, Soc. for Exact Philosophy, Math. Assn. Am. Republican. Avocation: mountain climbing. Home: Pittsburgh, Pa. Died 2006.

MOORE, RAYBURN SABATZKY, American literature educator; b. Helena, Ark., May 26, 1920; s. Max Sabatzky and Sammie Lou (Rayburn) M.; m. Margaret Elizabeth Bear, Aug. 30, 1947; children: Margaret Elizabeth Moore Kopcinski, Robert Rayburn. AB, Vanderbilt U., 1942, MA, 1947; PhD, Duke U., 1956. Script writer King Biscuit Time, Interstate Grocer Co., KFFA, 1947-50; Vice pres. Interstate Grocer Co., Helena, 1947-50; research and grad. asst. Duke U., 1952-54; asst. prof. English, Hendrix Coll., Conway, Ark., 1954-55, asso. prof., 1955-58, prof., 1958-59; asso. prof. U. Ga., Athens, 1959-65, prof., 1965-90, prof. emeritus, from 1990, chmn. Am. studies program, 1968-90, chmn. div. lang and lit., 1975-90. Vis. scholar Duke U., 1958, 64 Author: Constance Fenimore Woolson, 1963, For the Major and Selected Short Stories of Constance Fenimore Woolson, 1967, Paul Hamilton Hayne, 1972, A Man of Letters in the Nineteenth-Century South: Selected Letters of Paul Hamilton Hayne, 1982; sr. editor: History of Southern Literature, 1985, Selected Letters of Henry James to Edmund Gosse (1882-1915): A Literary Friendship, 1988, The Correspondence of Henry James and the House of Macmillan, 1877-1914: All the Links in the Chain, 1993, The Letters of Alice James to Anne Ashburner, 1873-1878, Resources for American Literary Study, vol. 27 numbers 1 and 2, 2001; mem. editorial bd. U. Ga. Press, 1972-74, Ga. Rev., 1974-82, chmn., 1980-82; contbr. articles, revs. to profl. jours. Adv. bd. Letters of Henry James complete edit., 1995—, editl. bd., 1997—; troop com. Boy Scouts Am., Athens, 1973-75; deacon, elder Presbyterian Ch., 1962—; Lamar Meml. Lectures com. Mercer U., 1984-91. Capt. US Army, 1942-46, PTO. Recipient John Hurt Fisher award South Atlantic Assn. Depts. English, 2000, honoree English Language and Lit., Philoological Assn. of Carolinas, 1990. Mem.: MLA (exec. com. Gen. Topics VI 1972—75), Va. Hist. Soc., Am. Lit. Assn. (chair Simms Soc. Sessions from 1993), South Atlantic MLA (exec. com. 1975—77, nominating com. 1985—87), South Atlantic Grad. English Coop. Group (exec. com. 1969—79, chmn. 1971—72), Soc. Study So. Lit. (exec. com. 1968—69, 1974—79, 1985—88, 1991—94, v.p. 1981—82, pres. 1983—84), Constance Fenimore Woolson Soc., Philol. Assn. Carolinas, William Gilmore Simms Soc. (exec. com. 1993—94, pres.-elect 1993—95), Edgar Allan Poe Soc., Phi Beta Kappa, Blue Key, Sigma Chi. Home: Athens, Ga. Died Feb. 2006.

MOORE, ROBERT BYRON, chemical engineer, consultant; b. Bangkok, Nov. 11, 1929; arrived in U.S., 1930; s. William Robert and Ruth Byron Moore; m. Mary Frances Trager, June 18, 1955; children: Robert Byron, Kathryn Lynn. BSChemE, U. Mich., 1952. EIT Tex., La. Process engr. Phillips Chem. Co., Dumas, Tex., 1952—53, Houston, 1955—59; process mgr. Air Products, West Palm Beach, Fla., 1959—61, ops. supt., 1961—63; project engr. Air Products and Chems., Allentown, Pa., 1963—64, New Orleans, 1965—66, project mgr. Allentown, 1967—73; ret., 1999; chem. engring. cons. Hydrogen Tech., from 2003. Mgr. econ. evaluation Air Products and Chems., Allentown, 1974—99; cons. hydrogen gas Ind. Cons., Allentown, from 2000. Contbr. scientific papers to profl. jours. With U.S. Army, 1953—55. Achievements include patents for hydrogen and chemical production. Avocations: tennis, skiing, golf. Home: Allentown, Pa. Died Mar. 17, 2004.

MOORE, ROBERT EDMUND, materials consultant; b. Orange, N.J., Dec. 11, 1925; s. Edmund James and Helene Mathilde (Meyer) M.; m. Leona Ann Levey, Aug. 30, 1952; 1 child, James Davenport. Student, N.J. Inst. Tech., 1942-44, BS in Chem. Engring., 1948; postgrad., Pa. State U., 1945; MS, Rensselaer Polytech. Inst., 1950. Devel. chemist MacDermid, Inc., Waterbury, Conn., 1950-51, F. Gumm Chem. Co., Kearny, N.J., 1951-54, sales engr., 1954-56; engr. semiconductor dept. Gen. Electric Co., Syracuse, N.Y., 1956-60, cons. engr. semiconductor dept., 1960-66, cons. engr. space div. Valley Forge, Pa., 1966-69, program mgr. ordnance systems Pittsfield, Mass., 1969-83, materials cons., 1983-88; pvt. practice materials cons. Pittsfield, from 1988. Vol. Internat. Exec. Svc. Corps, 1989-. Contbr. articles to profl. jours. Mem. Rep. Party N.J. and N.Y., 1960-64; instr. ARC, Pittsfield, 1975-; various offices and coms. Boy Scouts Am., 1946-86. With U.S. Army, 1944-46. Mem. Internat. Soc. Hybrid Microelectronics, Soc. Sigma Xi, Omicron Delta Kappa, Phi Lambda Upsilon. Episcopalian. Avocation: art conservation. Died July 24, 2004.

MORALES, PAUL TIMOTHY, financial planning executive; b. Riverside, Calif., June 19, 1960; s. John Garcia and Juliette Beatrice (Chavez) M. AB in Philosophy, Harvard U., 1982; MBA, Harvard Bus. Sch., Boston, 1990. Cons. AMS, Washington, 1982-84, Huntington Nat. Bank, Columbus, Ohio, 1984; dir. acquisitions Summit Investments, Acton, Mass., 1985-88; chief operating officer, chief fin. officer MJ Rsch., Inc., Watertown, Mass., from 1990. Home: Valencia, Spain. Died Mar. 3, 2005.

MORALES, XAVIER CHRISTOPHER, elementary school educator; b. San Juan, P.R., July 3, 1947; s. Gonzalo and Ana (Diaz) M.; m. Francine (div. July 1990); 1 child, Mayteana; m. Evelyn Garcia, June 22, 1996; children: Cristina, Richard, Kanere Xavier. BA, Coll. S.I., 1971; MS, L.I. U., 1977; ABD, NYU, 1985. Tchr. Great Neck (N.Y.) Pub. Schs., 1973-74, Hempstead (N.Y.) Pub. Schs., from 1974, acting dir. bilingual English as 2d lang., from 1997. Adj. Coll. William Paterson (N.J.), 1981-84, Boricua Coll., Bklyn., 1981-89, Hofstra U., Hempstead, 1989—, Coll. Old Waterbury (N.Y.), 1990—. Pres. Hempstead PTA, 1983. Mem. NAt. Assn. Bilingual Edn., N.Y. State Assn. Bilingual Edn., United Univ. Profs. Democrat. Roman Catholic. Avocations: writing, racquetball, paddleball, music, dance. Home: Freeport, NY. Died Mar. 26, 2005.

MORAN, JOHN DOUGLAS, investment banker; b. Phila., Oct. 24, 1926; s. William Bailey and Florence Dorothy (Hildenbrand) M.; m. Ann Biddle, Feb. 10, 1960 (div. 1984); children: J. Douglas, James Biddle; m. Barbara T. McNeel, May 13, 1990. BS, U. Pa. Wharton Sch. of Bus., 1951; MA, U. Pa., 1955. Trainee Fed. Res. Bank, Phila., 1951-53; credit analyst Fidelity Bank, Phila., 1953-60; asst. v.p. Indsl. Valley Bank, Phila., 1961-68; v.p. Mgmt. Data Corp., Phila., 1968-74; dir. corp. fin. Suplee-Mosley, Inc., Phila., 1975-76; sr. v.p. Danes, Cooke & Keleher, N.Y.C., 1975-76; sr. ptnr. J.D. Moran Assocs., Phila., 1976-84 and from 86; v.p. Boenning & Scattergood, Phila., 1985. Pres. Windsor Fin. Corp., Flemington, N.J., 1986. With USN, 1944-46, Philippines. Mem. Phila. Cricket Club, Princeton Club of N.Y. Republican. Episcopalian. Avocations: bridge, golf. Home: Philadelphia, Pa. Died May 20, 2005.

MOREHEAD, BRUCE M., insurance agent; b. Falls City, Nebr., Jan. 24, 1952; s. Vincel and Rachel Delta (Williamson) M.; m. Vickie Jean Lippold, Aug. 3, 1973; children: Kristin Nicole, Lucas Michael. BA in Bus., Peru (Nebr.) State Coll., 1974. Cert. independent ins. agent. Security guard Cooper Nuclear Sta., Brownville, Nebr., 1972-73; ins. agent Bankers Life & Casualty, Lincoln, Nebr., 1973-82; ins. agent, branch mgr. Corp. Fin. Svcs., Falls City, Nebr., from 1982. Pres. Falls City, Nebr., 1988-89. With U.S. Army, 1970-72, Res., 1972-79. Mem. Profl. Ins. Agents Am., Nebr. Jaycees (bd. dirs. 1987-88, pres. Falls City area 1988-89, state dir. 1989—), Men's Bowling Assn. (bd. dirs. 1987-88), Elks. Democrat. Lutheran. Avocations: sports, bowling. Home: Falls City, Nebr. Died Feb. 2, 2005.

MORELL, RICHARD LOUIS, electrical engineer; b. Enid, Okla., Mar. 26, 1940; s. Richard Abraham and Meriym Kathryn (Vessels) M.; m. Jill Kathryn Duggin; children: Julie Diane, Jeffrey Brian. BSEE, U. Tex., 1964. Electrician's helper Cen. Power and Light Co., Mission, Tex., 1958-62; rsch. asst. U. Tex., Austin, 1962-64; operation mgr. Indsl. Generating Co., Rockdale, Tex., 1964-69; elec. instrument engr. Ashland Chem. Co., Houston, 1969-71; project elec. engr. Power Systems Engring., Houston, 1971-72; elec. design engr. Brown and Root, Inc., Houston, 1972-74; elec. engring. supr. Bechtel Petroleum Co., Houston, 1974-83; elec./instrumentation mgr. Allstates Design & Devel., Houston, 1984-87; chief elec. engr. Am. Ref-Fuel, Houston, 1987-97; project engring. mgr. Enron Engring. and Constrn., Houston, from 1997. Mem. IEEE, Instrument Soc. Am. Avocation: genealogy. Home: Houston, Tex. Died Jan. 29, 2004.

MORENO, ARMANDO, organization executive; b. Vienna, June 21, 1920; came to U.S., 1985; s. Julius and Sabina (Silberman) M.; m. Angelia Kostic, June 17, 1921 (div. Nov. 1984); children: Dolores, Mario; m. Hilde Kula, Nov. 9, 1987. Prof., U. Sarajevo, Yugoslavia, 1967. Sec. Diplomatic Sch., Belgrade, Yugoslavia, 1945-50; chief staff UNICEF Mission, Belgrade, 1950-53; mgr. Tourist Offices in Scandinavia, Stockholm, Copenhagen, 1953-57, Tourist Offices Dalmatia, Split, Yugoslavia, 1957-75; prof. English, French, German langs. and letters U. Split, 1967-80; sec.-gen. Internat. Fedn. Festival Orgns., L.A., from 1967. Chief press Mediterranean Games, Split, 1979; mem., advisor UNESCO, 1971—. Author: Tourism--The Passport to Peace, 1967, About Information Service and Publicity in Tourism, 1976; contbr. numerous articles to tourism, arts and show bus. mags. Recipient medal for merit Pres. Republic of Yugoslavia. Avocations: music, arts. Died Apr. 4, 2005.

MORET, MARC, retired chemical company executive; b. Ménières, Switzerland, Nov. 15, 1923; married; 3 children. D Pub. Econs., U. Fribourg and Sorbonne, Paris, 1948. With practical indsl. tng. and assignments Swissair, Sulzer Bros., Nestlé S.A.; gen. mgr. Guigoz Internat.; from head of agro sales, to head agro and nutrition divsns. Sandoz Ltd., 1968, head finance dept., 1976, vice chmn., 1980-85, pres., CEO, 1981-94, chmn., 1985—96. Died Mar. 17, 2006.

MORGAN, CLAUDIA BURGHARDT, manufacturing executive; b. Durham, N.C., July 23, 1939; d. William Frankin Burghardt and Mayme Ethel (Spaulding) Carter; m. John Paul Morgan, Sept. 5, 1964; children: Jennifer Lyle, Zachary Ross. BA, Radcliffe Coll., 1961; M of Community Planning, U. Cin., 1965. Cert. in ednl. adminstrn., N.Y. Planner Cin. City Planning Commn., 1963-65; sr. planner Syracuse (N.Y.) City Planning Dept., 1965-66; ednl. planner Rochester (N.Y.) City Sch. Dist., 1974-77; project dir. Settlement Housing Fund, Inc., N.Y.C., 1978-81; gen. mgr. Barrington Structural Frames, Inc., N.Y.C., from 1982. Bd. dirs. Community Chest, Rochester, 1975-77. Planning Commr. Rochester Planning Commn., 1975-77. Mem. Am. Planning Assn., World Future Soc., Panel Am. Women, Alpha Kappa Alpha. Democrat. Unitarian Universalist. Avocation: travel. Home: New York, NY. Died Apr. 14, 2005.

MORGAN, JAMES BURNELL, personnel executive; b. Poughkeepsie, N.Y., Feb. 6, 1936; s. Robert Wilfred and Lucy (Burnell) M.; m. Annette Woodbury, Dec. 22, 1965 (div. 1980). BS, Tufts Coll., 1958; MS, SUNY, Albany, 1962. Mgr. employee devel. IBM, White Plains, N.Y., 1979-82, mgr. community exec. program Armonk, N.Y., 1982-84, sr. personnel advisor, program mgr. Fishkill, N.Y., 1984-87, NDD program mgr. Montvale, N.J., from 1987. Pres. AME Zio Trinity Devel. Fund Co., Poughkeepsie, 1987. Cons. ARC, Washington, 1984, Girl Scouts USA, N.Y.C., 1984, 86, 87; bd. dirs. exec. com. Mid-Hudson Pattern, Newburgh, N.Y., 1979-88; trainer, vol. ARC, 1984; pres. bd. trustees Smith Met. AME Zion Ch., Poughkeepsie, 1986—; bd. dirs. Dutchess Co. Council, Hudson Valley Philharmonic Soc., Inc., 1962-75. Mem. Phi Delta Kappa. Methodist. Home: Hopewell Junction, NY. Died Apr. 16, 2004.

MORGAN, JOHN SMITH, writer; b. Cleve., Mar. 20, 1921; s. Clyde Spencer and Mariem (Smith) M.; m. Virginia Lucille Willis, Feb. 15, 1947; children: Penelope, Patricia M. Berger, Medeleine M. Fackler. BA, Yale U., 1943. Managing editor Steel Mag., Cleve., 1947-64; cons. GE, N.Y.C., 1964-74; dir. employee communication Rockwell Internat. Corp., Pitts., 1974-80; owner Advocacy Communications, Pitts., from 1980. Author: Getting Across to Employees, 1964, Practical Guide to Conference Leadership, 1966, Managing the Young Adults, 1967, Improving Your Creativity on the Job, 1968, Managing Change, 1972, Noah Webster, A Biography, 1975, Robert Fulton, A Biography, 1977, The Wolf Strikes, 1981, How Executives Solve Problems, 1987, Interpersonal Skills for the Manager, 1987, Getting a Job After 50, 1988, Organizational Development To Meet Changing Needs, 1989, Death Begins At 50, 1996, Dishonor Thy Fathers, and others; contbr. articles to profl. jours. Sgt. Med. Dept., 1943-46. Mem. Coun. Communication Mgmt. (bd. dirs. 1970-74), U. Club Pitts. (bd. dirs. 1988-90). Republican. Presbyterian. Avocations: travel, bridge, reading. Home: Los Altos, Calif. Died Oct. 26, 2004.

MORGAN, LARRY GENE, accountant; b. Mo., Mar. 13, 1939; s. Glenn Eugene and Wilma Lorene Morgan; m. Bonnie Kay Barnes, Sept. 2, 1962; children: Douglas Eugene, Denise Kay. BSBA, Cen. Mo. State U., 1963, MBA, 1964. CPA, Mo. Acct., auditor, mgr. Grant Thornton, Kansas City, Mo., 1964-77; acct., auditor, owner Van Quaethem, Morgan & Co., P.C., Blue Springs, Mo., from 1977. Sec., treas. Blue Springs Econ. Devel. Commn., 1987. Served with USNG, 1960-66. Mem. Am. Inst. CPA's, Nat. Assn. Accts., Mo. Soc. CPA's, Blue Springs C. of C. (pres. 1982). Lodges: Rotary (bd. dirs. Blue Springs 1986—), Masons. Methodist. Avocations: fishing, golf. Home: Blue Springs, Mo. Died Feb. 16, 2005.

MORGAN, ROBERT ASHTON, minister, ethics and world religions educator; b. Mpls., May 5, 1929; s. Thomas Ashton and Kathryn (Roberts) M.; m. Honoria Wilson, Jan. 15, 1955 (dec. Mar. 1995); 1 child, Emily Kathryn. BA, Macalester Coll., 1950, DD, 1978; MDiv, Yale U., 1954. Ordained to ministry Presbyn. Ch., 1954. Min. First Presbyn. Ch., Eveleth, Minn., 1954-58; asst. min. Westminster Presbyn. Ch., Mpls., 1958-67, min. Austin, Minn., 1967-92; instr. Riverland C.C., Austin, 1992-99. Bd. dirs. Austin (Minn.) Med. Ctr. Author: Advent Recollections, 1985, Stories Around the Baby, 1991. Bd. dirs. ARC, Mower County, 1967-92, bd. chmn., 1991-92. Mem. Rotary (pres. 1972-73). Presbyterian. Avocations: reading, gardening, travel. Home: Austin, Minn. Died July 16, 2005.

MORITA, (NORIYUKI) PAT, actor, comedian; b. Isleton, Calif., June 28, 1932; m. Yuki Morita, 1970 (div.); 3 children; m. Evelyn Guerrero, Nov. 24, 1993 Former nightclub comedian, Los Angeles. Regular mem. cast: (TV series) The Queen and I, 1969, Sanford and Son, 1974-75, (as Arnold) Happy Days, 1975-76, 82-83, The Mystery Files of Shelby Woo, 1996—99, Adventures with Kanga Roddy, 1998; starring roles: (TV series) Mr. T and Tina, 1976, Blansky's Beauties, 1977, Ohara, 1987-88; TV films include Farewell to Manzanar, 1976, The Vegas Strip War, 1984, Amos, 1985, Babes in Toyland, 1986, Greyhounds, 1994, Singapore Sling: Road to Mandalay, 1995, Hart to Heart: Secrets of the Heart, 1995, Lamb Chop's Special Chanukah, 1995, Reflections on Ice: Michelle Kwan Skates to the Music of Disney's Mulan, 1998, Gone to Maui, 1999; feature films: Thoroughly Modern Millie, 1967, Kill My Wife Please, 1975, Midway, 1976, When Time Ran Out, 1980, Full Moon High, 1981, Savannah Smiles, 1982, Jimmy the Kid, 1982, The Karate Kid, 1984 (Acad. award nomination 1985), The Karate Kid Part II, 1986, Captive Hearts, 1987, Collision Course, 1989, The Karate Kid Part III, 1989, Goodbye Paradise, 1991, Do or Die, 1991, Honeymoon in Vegas, 1992, Miracle Beach, 1992, Even Cowgirls Get the Blues, 1993, Auntie Lee's Meat Pies, 1993, The Next Karate Kid, 1994, The Misery Brothers, 1995, Timemaster, 1995, Deliver Us from Evil, 1995, American Ninja 5, 1995, Bloodsport 2, 1996, Earth Minus Zero, 1996, Reggie's Prayer, 1996, Spy Hard, 1996, Bloodsport 3, 1997, (voice) Mulan, 1998, I'll Remember April, 1999, Los Gringos, 1999, King Cobra, 1999, Hammerlock, 2000, Talk to Taka, 2000, House of Luk, 2001, The Boys of Sunset Ridge, 2001, The Center of the World, 2001, Shadow Fury, 2001, Whasango, 2001, The Stoneman, 2002, The Biggest Fan, 2002, Cats and Mice, 2003, Stuey, 2003, Rice Girl, 2003, Spymate, 2003, 18 Fingers of Death, 2004, Miss Cast Away, 2004, The Karate Dog, 2004, (voice) Mulan II, 2004, Genghis Khan, 2005, Down and Derby, 2005, others; guest appearances (TV series) Green Acres, 1971, Hawaii Five-O, 1973, The Odd Couple, 1972, M*A*S*H, 1973, 74, The Bob Newhart Show, 1972, Kung Fu, 1975, The Incredible Hulk, 1978, Laverne & Shirley, 1980, Fresh Prince of Bel-Air, 1994, Married...With Children, 1996, Boy Meets World, 1996, The Outer Limits, 1998, Family Matters, 1998, Diagnosis Murder, 1998, Caroline in the City, 1999, Baywatch, 2000, 01, Son of the Beach, 2001, Yes, Dear, 2003, (voice) Robot Chicken, 2005, others. Recipient Lifetime Achievement award Assn. Asian/Pacific Am. Artists, 1987. Died Nov. 24, 2005.

MORITZ, CARL A., food company executive; b. Middle Village, N.Y., Oct. 29, 1906; s. John and Anna (Hoerning) M.; m. Frances M. Von Loosen, Oct. 16, 1931 (div. 1961); 1 child, Carol Ann; m. Margaret A. Herrmann, July 26, 1962. Student pub. schs., Englishtown, N.J. Pres. Moritz Plumbing & Heating Co. Inc., Franklin Square, N.Y., 1940-69, Carl A Moritz Fuel Co., Franklin Square, 1946-70; owner, mgr. Carl A. Moritz, Smoked Eels & Fish, Hampton Bays, N.Y., from 1969. Mem. Elks. Republican. Roman Catholic. Avocations: fishing, greenhouse plants and flowers. Died Oct. 30, 2004.

MORRIS, HENRY MADISON, JR., education educator; b. Dallas, Oct. 6, 1918; s. Henry Madison and Ida (Hunter) M.; m. Mary Louise Beach, Jan. 24, 1940; children: Henry Madison III, Kathleen Louise, John David, Andrew Hunter, Mary Ruth, Rebecca Jean. BS with distinction, Rice Inst., 1939; MS, U. Minn., 1948, PhD, 1950; LLD, Bob Jones U., 1966; LittD, Liberty U., 1989. Registered profl. engr., Tex. Jr. engr. Tex. Hwy. Dept., 1938-39; from jr. engr. to asst. engr. Internat. Boundary Commn., El Paso, 1939-42; instr. civil engring. Rice Inst., 1942-46; from instr. to asst. prof. U. Minn., Mpls., also research project leader St. Anthony Falls Hydraulics Lab., 1946-51; prof., head dept. civil engring. Southwestern La. Inst., Lafayette, 1951-57, Va. Poly. Inst., Blacksburg, 1957-70; v.p. acad. affairs Christian Heritage Coll., San Diego, 1970-78, pres., 1978-80; dir. Inst. for Creation Rsch., 1970-80, pres., 1980-96, pres. emeritus, 1996—2006. Author (with Richard Stephens): (report) Report on Rio Grande Cosnervation Investigation, 1942; author: 2d edit That You Might Believe, 1946; author: (with Curtis Larson) (book) Hydraulics of Flow in Culverts, 1948; author: The Bible and Modern Science, 1951, rev. edit, 1968; author: (with John C. Whitcomb) The Genesis Flood, 1961; author: Applied Hydraulics in Engineering, 1963, The Twilight of Evolution, 1964, Science, Scripture and Salvation, 1965, Studies in The Bible and Science, 1966, Evolution and the Modern Christian, 1967, Biblical Cosmology and Modern Science, 1970, The Bible has the Answer, 1971, Science and Creation: A Handbook for Teachers, 1971; author: (with J.M. Wiggert) Applied Hydraulics, 1972; author: A Biblical Manual on Science and Creation, 1972, The Remarkable Birth of Planet Earth, 1973, Many Infallible Proofs, 1974, Scientific Creationism, 1974;: 2d edit, 1985, Troubled Waters of Evolution, 1975, The Genesis Record, 1976, Education for the Real World, 1977, 1991, (book) The Scientific Case for Creation, 1977, The Beginning of the World, 1977, 2d edit, 1991, Sampling the Psalms, 1978, King of Creation, 1980, Men of Science, Men of God, 1982, 2d edit, 1988, Evolution in Turmoil, 1982, The Revelation Record, 1983, History of Modern Creationism, 1984, 2d edit, 1993, The Biblical Basis for Modern Science, 1984, 2002, Creation and the Modern Christian, 1985, Science and the Bible, 1986, Days of Praise, 1986, The God Who is Real, 1988, 2d edit., 2000, The Remarkable Record of Job, 1987; author: (with Martin Clark) The Bible Has the Answer; author: (with Gary E. Parker) What is Creation Science?, 1982; author: 2d edit., 1988, The Long War Against God, 1989; author: (with John D. Morris) Science, Scripture and the Young Earth, 1989; author: The Bible Science and Creation, 1991, Creation and the Second Coming, 1991, Biblical Creationism, 1993, The Defender's Bible, 1995, The Modern Creation Trilogy, 1996, The Heavens Declare the Glory of God, 1997, That Their Words May be Used Against Them, 1998, The Origin of Earth and its People, 1999, Defending the Faith, 1999, Treasures in the Psalms, 2000, Solomon and His Remarkable Wisdom, 2001, God and the Nations, 2002, The Incredible Journey of Jonah, 2003, Miracles, 2004, For Time and Forever, 2004, Days to Remember, 2005, The New Defender's Story Bible, 2006. Fellow AAAS, ASCE, Am. Sci. Affiliation; mem. Am. Soc. Engring. Edn. (sec.-editor civil engring. divsn. 1967-70), Trans-Nat. Assn. Christian Schs. (pres. 1983-95), Creation Rsch. Soc. (pres. 1967-73), Am. Geophys. Union, Geol. Soc. Am., Am. Assn. Petroleum Geologists, Geochem. Soc., Gideons (pres. La. 1954-56), Phi Beta Kappa, Sigma Xi, Chi Epsilon, Tau Beta Pi. Baptist. Home: San Diego, Calif. Died Feb. 25, 2006.

MORRIS, JAMES WILLIAM (BILL MORRIS), retired chemical engineer; b. Clarksville, Tex., June 25, 1918; s. Felix Bailey and Mabel Lucile (Rush) M.; m. Ruth Estelle Price, Sept. 4, 1949; children: James Lee, Hugh Bailey, Anne Estelle. AA, Paris Jr. Coll., 1937; BSChemE, U. Tex., Austin, 1940, MSChemE, 1941, PhD in Chem. Engring., 1944. Sr. supr. EI du Pont de Nemours, Hanford, Wash., 1944-45, rsch. engr. Wilmington, Del., 1945-47, group leader Cleve., 1947-49, process engr. Wilmington, 1949-50, group leader, asst. tech. supt., tech. supt. Newport, Ind., 1950-53, sec. dir. Savannah River Lab. Aiken, S.C., 1953-80, planning engr., 1980-83, ret., 1984. Mem. indsl. adv. bds. coop. edn. Clemson (S.C.) U., 1972-75, mech. engring., 1975-79; coop. edn. Ga. Inst. Tech., Atlanta, 1973-76. Contbr. articles to jour. Indsl. and Engring. Chemistry, Chem. Engring. Progress. Named Paris Jr. Coll. Disting. Alumnus, 1995. Fellow AIChE; mem. Am. Chem. Soc., Am. Nuclear Soc., S.C. Acad. Sci. (pres. 1967), Tau Beta Pi, Sigma Xi, Omega Chi Epsilon, Phi Lambda Upsilon, Phi Theta Kappa. Home: Greenwood, SC. Died Apr. 10, 2005.

MORRIS, JERALD VINSON, minister; b. Cotter, Ark., July 31, 1931; s. James Hubert and Esther Marie (Thrasher) M.; m. Estel Myree Glover, Jan. 10, 1953; children: Jerald Vinson Jr., Denise Myree. Student, So. Calif. Bible Coll., 1959-60, 61-62, Orange Coast Coll., 1960-61; BTh, Internat. Bible Inst. and Sem., 1983, ThM, 1984. Ordained to ministry Assemblies of God, 1969. Pastor Assemblies of God, McDermitt and Yerington, 1963-67, Assembly of God, MacDoel, Calif., 1967-69, Buena Vista, Colo., 1969-73, Bisbee, Ariz., 1973-77, Tolleson, Ariz., 1977-81, North Loma Linda Assembly of God, San Bernardino, Calif., 1982-85; evangelist Assemblies of God, 1985-86; pastor River Chapel Assembly of God, Riviera, Ariz., from 1986. Active ministerial alliance various communities, 1963—; dir. Colo. River Christian Ministerial, 1986-89. Chmn. Are You Interested Drug Prevention Program, Buena Vista, 1970-73; v.p. Ariz. State Teen Challenge Bd. Dirs., Phoenix, 1977-81; vice chmn. Bullhead Against Drugs, Bullhead City, Ariz., 1987-90. With U.S. Army, 1948-52. Mem. Alliance (treas. 1989-90), Ariz. Dist. Coun. Assemblies of God (dist. presbyter 1988—). Republican. Home: Bisbee, Ariz. Died Jan. 5, 2004.

MORRIS, THERESA LINTHICUM, retired medical social worker; b. Wickliffe, Ky., Nov. 27, 1906; d. Charles Presley and Ruby Regal (Ives) Linthicum; m. Harrell H. Morris, Aug. 24, 1932. MSW, Washington U., 1947. Lic. social worker, Okla. Intake worker Okla. Emergency Relief, Oklahoma City, 1934-37; field supr. Works Progress Adminstrn., Oklahoma City, 1937-41; dir. med. social work Okla. Commn. Crippled Children, Oklahoma City, 1937-56, social work cons., 1956-57; med. social worker Okla. Dept. Pub. Welfare, Oklahoma City, 1957-58, Okla. Dept. Health, Oklahoma City, 1958-71; med. social worker otorhinolaryngology dept. U. Okla. Med. Ctr., Oklahoma City, 1971-90; ret., 1990. Past mem. bd. dirs. Salvation Army Sr. Citizens Ctr., Oklahoma City. Recipient spl. recognition U. Okla. Med. Ctr., 1989. Mem. Acad. Cert. Social Workers. Methodist. Home: Oklahoma City, Okla. Died Apr. 16, 2005.

MORRISON, HARVEY LEE, JR., lawyer; b. Hattiesburg, Miss., June 7, 1947; s. Harvey Lee Sr. and Tommye (Walker) M.; m. Norma Hairston, Aug. 21, 1976; 1 child, Harvey Lee III. BBA, U. Miss., 1970, JD, 1972. Bar: Miss. 1972, U.S. Dist. Ct. (no. dist.) Miss. 1982, U.S. Ct. Appeals (5th cir.) 1982. Ptnr. Tubb, Stevens & Morrison, West Point, Miss., from 1972. Mem. ABA, Miss. State Bar Assn., Miss. Def. Lawyers Assn., Clay County Bar Assn. (pres. 1986—). Lodges: Rotary (sec. 1975, v.p. 1976, pres. 1977, dist. gov. Miss. and Tenn. 1984-85, Paul Harris fellow 1985). Presbyterian. Avocations: jogging, tennis. Home: West Point, Miss. Died Apr. 6, 2004.

MORRISON, JAMES HARRIS, psychologist; b. St. Louis, Oct. 29, 1918; s. Carlton Tremont and Nellie (Harris) M.; m. Mary Berthold, Jan. 6, 1942; children: Elaine, Kathleen. BS, Washington U., St. Louis, 1952; MA in Psychology, U. Mo., Kansas City, 1955. Lic. psychologist, Mo. Tng. supr. Gen. Cable Co., St. Louis, 1948-50; tng. specialist Western Auto Supply Co., Kansas City, Mo., 1950-66; v.p., ptnr. Lawrence-Leiter & Co., Kansas City, 1967-85; pres. The Company, Overland Park, Kans., from 1985. Author: The Human Side of Management, 1971; (with others) Practical Transactional Analysis in Management, 1977. Bd. dirs. Kansas City chpt. ARC, 1958. Served with USN, 1944-46. Mem. Am. Psychol. Assn., Soc. Indsl. and Orgn. Psychologists. Avocations: scuba diving, backpacking, cross country skiing. Died June 7, 2004.

MORRISON, JAMES R., retired bank executive; b. Duluth, Minn., May 1, 1924; s. Earl Angus and Jessie (McLean) M.; m. Clarice Mae Wolf, June 5, 1949; children— Kenneth, Alan, Jane, Richard MBA, U. Chgo., 1976. Br. mgr. Parkersburg State Bank, Iowa, 1947-49; asst. cashier Bank of Sparta, Wis., 1949-50; cashier Tobacco Exchange Bank, Edgerton, Wis., 1950-53; sr. v.p. Fed. Res. Bank Chgo., 1953-89, ret. Bd. dirs. Bank of Tokyo-Mitsubishi Chgo., 1994-98; chmn. subcom. on credits and discounts Fed. Res. Sys., Chgo., 1984-86; mem. Mt. Prospect Fin. Commn., 1989-2001. Served with U.S. Army, 1943-46, ETO Home: Rosemount, Minn. Died Jan. 9, 2006.

MORRISSEY, CLARENCE JOSEPH, patent lawyer; b. Chgo., Sept. 2, 1924; s. Thomas Earl and Martha Elizabeth M.; m. Helen Dorothy Niespodziany, Aug. 1952. BS, Northwestern U., Evanston, Ill., 1945, MS, 1948; JD, John Marshall Law Sch., 1963. Bar: Ill. 1963. Chem. engr. Abbott Labs., North Chicago, Ill., 1947-51, Bendix Aviation Co., South Bend, Ind., 1951-52, Sinclair Rsch. Co., Harvey, Ill., 1953-56; tech. staff Hughes Rsch. Labs., Culver City, Calif., 1956-57; patent engr. Standard Oil Co., Chgo., 1958-63; tech. staff Aerojet Gen. Corp., Azusa, Calif., 1963-65; patent atty. Am. Potash and Chem. Co., L.A., 1965-66, Jet Propulsion Labs., Pasadena, Calif., 1966-84, Calif. Inst. Tech., Pasadena, 1984-94. Co-contbr. articles to profl. jours. Mem. L.A. Patent Law Assn. (mem. chem. practice com. 1965-75), Sigma Xi. Home: Glendale, Calif. Died Jan. 13, 2004.

MORROW, ROSANNE SURINA, civil engineer; b. L.A., Aug. 5, 1956; d. Daniel and Marjorie Isabel (Klarich) Surina; m. Paul David Morrow, May 11, 1991. BSCE, Calif. State Poly. U., 1979. From asst. engr. to sr. structural engr. Lockheed Corp., Burbank, Calif., 1979-91; mgr. engring. scis. Nordskog Industries, Inc., Van Nuys, Calif., from 1991. Designated engring. rep. FAA, Long Beach, Calif., 1992. Avocations: ceramics, sewing, dance, bridge, cribbage. Home: Anaheim, Calif. Died May 23, 2005.

MORSE, HELVISE GLESSNER, physical and life sciences educator, geneticist, educator, biophysicist, educator; b. Frederick, Md., Sept. 17, 1925; d. George Edward and Rosa May (Durphy) Glessner; m. Melvin Laurance Morse, Jan. 25, 1949; children: Margaret Louise, Laurance Clinton. BA, Yale U., 1946; MS, U. Ky., 1949, U. Colo., Denver, 1963, PhD, 1966. Supr. cytogenetics lab. Children's Hosp., Denver, 1978-79; postdoctoral fellow U. Colo. Med. Ctr., Denver, 1966-67, rsch. assoc., 1968-73, rsch. cytogeneticist, 1974-78, asst. prof. biochemistry, biophysics and genetics, 1979-88, assoc. prof. biochemistry, from 1988; dir. cytogenetics CORE for Cancer Ctr. U. Colo. Cancer Ctr., Denver, from 1988; Eleanor Roosevelt Inst. Cancer Rsch. fellow U. Colo., Denver, from 1979. Mem. cytogenetics subcom. Nat. Children's Cancer Study Group, U.S.A. and Can., 1980-87. Contbr. articles on gene mapping, cytogenetics and Leukemia research to profl. publs., 1970—. Active So. Poverty Law Ctr. Mem. NAACP, Mortar Bd., Sigma Xi. Democrat. Avocations: photography of wild flowers, attending local symphony orchestra concerts and opera. Home: Denver, Colo. Died Mar. 11, 2005.

MORTENSEN, RICHARD EDGAR, engineering educator; b. Denver, Sept. 29, 1935; s. Edgar Steele and Frieda Amalie (Boecker) M.; m. Sarah Jean Raulston, Oct. 12, 1974 (div. 1978). BSEE, MSEE, MIT, 1958; PhD, U. Calif., Berkeley, 1966. Co-op. engr. GE Co., Schenectady, N.Y., 1955-57; mem. tech. staff Space Tech. Labs., L.A., 1958-61; rsch. asst. U. Calif., Berkeley, 1961-65; prof. engring. UCLA, 1965-91, prof. emeritus, from 1991. Cons. TRW, Inc., Redondo Beach, Calif., 1966-70, Aerojet-Gen. Corp., Azusa, Calif., 1970-72, Applied Sci. Analytics, Inc., Canoga Park, Calif., 1980-82; guest lectr. Indian Inst. Sci., Bangalore, India, 1991. Author: Random Signals and Systems, 1987; contbr. to profl. publs. Team mem. Beyond War, Topanga, Calif., 1986-89; alcoholism counselor. Grantee NSF, 1987-90; named to Alumni Hall of Fame, Lambda Chi Alpha, 1996. Mem. IEEE, Soc. Indsl. and Applied Math., Sigma Xi, Tau Beta Pi, Eta Kappa Nu, Lambda Chi Alpha (Hall of Fame 1996). Avocations: hiking, yoga. Home: Topanga, Calif. Died Oct. 26, 2004.

MORTON, MARK, aeronautical engineering executive; b. Phila., Jan. 1, 1913; s. Samuel and Miriam Morton; m. Ruth Morton, May 29, 1943; children: Stephan Bruce, Kenneth Scott. BSME, NYU Guggenheim Coll. of Aeros., 1934; DEng. (hon.), Rose Poly. Instn., 1971. Registered profl. engr., Pa. Engr. Philco Corp., Phila., 1935-37; aero. engr. Naval Aircraft Factory, Phila., 1937-44; head aircraft design Naval Air Modification unit, Johnsville, Pa., 1944-51; head engring. div. Naval Air Devel. Ctr., Johnsville, Pa., 1951-56; mgr. aerospace GE, Phila., 1956-62, gen. mgr. aerospace Valley Forge, Pa., 1962-68, v.p., 1968-69, sr. v.p., 1969-78, ret., 1978. Bd. dirs. Interspec, Inc., Ambler, Pa.; bd. govs. Aerospace Industries Assn. Am., Washington, 1972-77; mem. nat. indsl. adv. coun. Opportunities Industrialization Ctrs. Am., 1977; cons. in field. Author: (jour.) Progress in Reentry Vehicle Devel., 1961; patentee float-wing aircraft. Bd. govs. Hugh O'Brian Youth Found., 1976; mem. Nat Adv. Com. of Oceans and Atmosphere, Washington, 1971-72. Recipient commendation for outstanding svc. USN, 1946, NASA Pub. Svc. Group Achievement award Apollo Program, 1969, Pathfinder award and top citations Opportunities Industrialization Ctrs. Am., 1969, 73, 76, commendation for equal opportunity leadership Pres. Nixon and Pres. Carter, 1970-76. Fellow AIAA (assoc.). Avocations: acrylic painting, scuba diving, deep sea photography. Home: Coatesville, Pa. Died Apr. 12, 2005.

MOSHER, LOREN RICHARD, psychiatrist; b. Monterey, Calif., Sept. 3, 1933; s. Harold and Anne (O'Brien) M.; m. Irene Carleton, May 26, 1961 (div. 1972); children: Hal, Tim, Missy; m. Judy Schreiber, Apr. 10, 1988. AB, Stanford U., 1956, postgrad., 1956-58; MD, Harvard U., 1961. Diplomate Am. Bd. Psychiatry and Neurology, Nat. Bd. Med. Examiners. Asst. prof. psychiatry Yale U., New Haven, 1967-68; chief Ctr. Studies of Schizophrenia, divsn. extramural rsch. NIMH, Rockville, Md., 1968-80; prof. psychiatry U.S. U. Health Sci., Bethesda, Md., 1981-88, clin. prof., from 1988; clin. dir. mental health svcs. San Diego County, Calif., 1996-98; clin. prof. psychiatry U. Calif., San Diego, 1997—2004. Cons. Swedish, German and Italian Health Depts., 1989-96; chief med. dir. Dept. Health and Human Svcs., County of Montgomery, Rockville, Md., 1988-96. Co-author: Community Mental Health Principles and Practice, 1989, Community Mental Health: a Practical Guide, 1994; editor books; editorial adv. bd. Contemporary Family Therapy, Internat. Jour. Therapeutic Communities, Schizophrenia Bull., Psychosocial Rehab. Jour.; contbr. articles to profl. jours. Capt. USPHS, 1974-88. Mem. APA, Am. Family Therapy Acad., Am. Orthopsychiat. Assn. Avocations: writing, tennis, sailing, travel. Died July 10, 2004.

MOSLEY, SAMUEL ADOLPHUS, retired chemical engineer, consultant; b. Birmingham, Ala., Jan. 9, 1923; s. Alvin Martis and Thyrza Elizabeth (Brown) M.; m. Mary McKinley Howell, June 10, 1946 (div. Jan. 1964); childrn: Samuel Adolphus, Pamela Ann, James Irwin; m. Jean Elizabeth Harper, Oct. 30, 1964; children: Patrick Stephen Andrew, Jennifer Gladys Elizabeth. BS in Chem. Engring., Auburn U., 1946. Cert. bldg. ofcl., code analyst; registered profl. engr., Ala., N.C. Chemist Tenn. Coal, Iron & R.R. Co., Ensley, Ala., 1940-45; instr. math. Auburn (Ala.) U., 1947; chem. engr. Union Carbide Corp., South Charleston, W.Va., 1947-51, Chemstrand Corp., Decatur, Ala., 1951-60, Chemstrand/Monsanto Co., Coleraine, No. Ireland, 1960-63, Israel Chem. Fibers, Tel Aviv, 1963-64, Monsanto co., Decatur, 1964-69, Celulosa y Derivados S.A., Monterrey, Mex., 1969-77, Rust Engring., Birmingham, Ala., 1977-86; chem. engr., instr. code edn. and enforcement So. Bldg. Code Congress, Birmingham, 1986-91; cons. code practice and enforcement So. Bldg. Code Congress, Birmingham, 1991. Cons., expert witness for bldg. constrn. and code enforcement matters. Contbr. articles to profl. jours. Patentee in field. Cpl. USAAF, 1943-45. Mem. Am. Chem. Soc., Ala. Archeol. Soc. (life, sec. 1952-58, v.p. 1959-60). Republican. Methodist. Avocations: photography, hunting, lapidary, golf, collecting (archaeology). Home: Decatur, Ala. Died June 6, 2004.

MOSLEY, THOMAS EDMOND, JR., marketing executive; b. Tinker Air Force Base, Okla., June 12, 1950; s. Thomas Edmond and Winnie B. (Harris) M.; m. Marla R. Gates, Sept. 7, 1974; children: Monica, Valerie, Meredith, Thomas III. Student, U. Okla., 1968-72. Zone-mktg. mgr. Motorola, Inc., Oklahoma City, 1980-84; account mgr. Digital Equipment Corp., Oklahoma City, 1984-87; new product developer Okla. Dept. Commerce, Oklahoma City, 1988-90; pres. Data Search & Retrieval, Inc., Midwest City, Okla., 1985-90, Strategic Mktg. Alliances, Inc., Oklahoma City, from 1990. Cons. Gordon Pub., Oklahoma City, 1989-90. Editor, pub.: Secrets to Buying Diamonds, 1990; author (annual reports to gov.) Inventors' Assistance Program, 1988, 89; editor, pub. (white paper) Blank Check Companies--The Good, the Bad and the Ugly, 1989. Mem. Okla. Venture Investment Corp., pres., 1987-88. Mem. Okla. Venture Forum. Republican. Avocations: tennis, golf, reading. Home: Broken Arrow, Okla. Died Dec. 16, 2004.

MOSS, BARBARA WONG, marketing professional; b. Berkeley, Calif., Apr. 14, 1934; d. Wing and Ruth (Lee) W.; divorced; 1 child, John A. BA, U. Calif., Berkeley, 1955; MBA, Drexel U., 1980. Cert. tchr., Calif., Pa. Tchr. Calif. Schs., 1955-58, Japan, Germany, 1958-60; mgr. planning Bell of Pa., Phila., 1980-83, mgr. mktg., 1983-86, mgr. pub. relations, 1986-88, systems mgr.mktg. network architecture, from 1988. Cons. computers, Phila., 1985—. Pres. LWV, Radnor, Pa., 1974-76; planner Radnor Twp., 1985—; trustee Delaware County Community Coll., Pa. 1980—, chmn. bd. 1986—. Mem. Phi Beta Kappa. Republican. Unitarian Universalist. Avocations: tennis, travel. Home: Wayne, Pa. Died May 13, 2004.

MOSS, MELVIN LIONEL, anatomist, educator; b. N.Y.C., Jan. 3, 1923; s. Maurice and Ethel (Lander) M.; m. Letty Salentijn, Apr. 1970; children (by previous marriage)— Noel Morrow, James Andrew. AB, N.Y. U., 1942; D.D.S., Columbia, 1946, PhD, 1954. Mem. faculty Columbia U., 1954—93, prof., 1967-93, prof. emeritus, 1993—2006; dean Columbia U. Sch. Dental and Oral Surgery.). Recipient Lederle Med. Faculty award, 1954-56 Fellow AAAS, Royal Anthrop. Soc. Gt. Britain; mem. Am. Assn. Anatomists, Am. Assn. Phys. Anthropologists, Internat. Assn. Dental Research (craniofacial biology award), Am. Soc. Zoologists, Sigma Xi, Omicron Kappa Upsilon. Achievements include research, numerous publs. on skeletal growth and application of computer-assisted methods of numerical and graphic analysis of growth. edu. Died June 25, 2006.

MOSTELLER, FREDERICK (CHARLES FREDERICK MOSTELLER), mathematical statistician, educator; b. Clarksburg, W.Va., Dec. 24, 1916; s. William Roy and Helen (Kelley) M.; m. Virginia Gilroy, May 17, 1941; children: William, Gale. ScB, Carnegie Inst. Tech. (now Carnegie-Mellon U.), 1938, MSc, 1939, DSc (hon.), 1974; AM, Princeton U., 1942, PhD, 1946; DSc (hon.), U. Chgo., 1973, Wesleyan U., 1983; D. of Social Scis. (hon.), Yale U., 1981; LLD (hon.), Harvard U., 1991. Research assoc. Office Pub. Opinion Research, 1942-44; spl. cons. research br. War Dept., 1942-43; research mathematician Statis. Research Group, Princeton, applied math. panel Nat. Devel. and Research Council, 1944-46; mem. faculty Harvard U., 1946—87, prof. math. stats., 1951-87, Roger I. Lee prof., 1978-87, prof. emeritus, 1987—2006, chmn. dept. stats., 1957-69, 75-77, chmn. dept. biostats., 1977-81, chmn. dept. health policy and mgmt., 1981-87; dir. Tech. Assessment Group, 1987—2006; dir. Ctr. for Evaluation Am. Acad. Arts and Scis., 1994—2006. Vice chmn. Pres.'s Commn. on Fed. Stats., 1970-71; mem. Nat. Adv. Council Equality of Ednl. Opportunity, 1973-78, Nat. Sci. Bd. Commn. on Pre-coll. Edn. in Math., Sci. and Tech., 1982-83; Fund for Advancement of Edn. fellow, 1954-55; nat. tchr. NBC's Continental Class-room TV course in probability and stats., 1960-61; fellow Center Advanced Study Behavioral Sciences, 1962-63, bd. dirs., 1980-86; Guggenheim fellow, 1969-70; Miller research prof. U. Calif. at Berkeley, 1974-75; Hitchcock Found. lectr. U. Calif., 1985. Co-author: Gauging Public Opinion (editor Hadley Cantril), 1944, Sampling Inspection, 1948, The Pre-election Polls, 1948, 49, Stochastic Models for Learning, 1955, Probability with Statisticial Applications, 1961, Inference and Disputed Authorship, The Federalist, 1964, The National Halothane Study, 1969, Statistics: A Guide to the Unknown, 3d edit., 1988, On Equality of Educational Opportunity, 1972, Sturdy Statistics, 1973, Statistics By Example, 1973, Cost, Risks and Benefits of Surgery, 1977, Data Analysis and Regression, 1977, Statistics and Public Policy, 1977, Data for Decisions, 1982, Understanding Robust and Exploratory Data Analysis, 1983, Biostatistics in Clinical Medicine, 1983, 3d edit., 1994, Beginning Statistics with Data Analysis, 1983, Exploring Data Tables, Trends and Shapes, 1985, Medical Uses of Statistics, 1986, 2d edit., 1992, Quality of Life and Technology Assessment, 1989, Fundamentals of Exploratory Analysis of Variance, 1992, Meta-analysis for Explanation, 1992, Doing More Good Than Harm, 1993, Medicine Worth Paying For, 1995; author articles in field. Trustee Russell Sage Found.; mem. bd. Nat. Opinion Research Center, 1962-66. Recipient Outstanding Statistician award Chgo. chpt. Am. Statis. Assn., 1971, Boston chpt., 1989, named Sports Statistician of 1996; recipient Myrdal prize Evaluation Research Soc., 1978, Paul F. Lazarsfeld prize Council Applied Social Research, 1979, R.A. Fisher award Com. of Pres.'s of Statis. Socs., 1987, Medallion of Ctrs. for Disease Control, 1988. Fellow AAAS (chmn. sect. U 1973, dir. 1974-78, pres. 1980, chmn. bd 1981), Inst. Math. Statistics (pres. 1974-75), Am. Statis. Assn. (v.p. 1962-64, pres. 1967, Samuel S. Wilks medal 1986), Social Sci. Research Council (chmn. bd. dirs. 1966-68), Math. Social Sci. Bd. (acad. governing bd. 1962-67), Am. Acad. Arts and Scis. (council 1986-88), Royal Statis. Soc. (hon.); mem. Am. Philos. Soc. (council 1986-88), Internat. Statis. Inst. (v.p. 1986-88, pres.-elect 1989, pres. 1991-93), Math. Assn. Am., Psychometric Soc. (pres. 1957-58), Inst. Medicine of Nat. Acad. Scis. (council 1978), Nat. Acad. Scis., Biometric Soc. Home: Arlington, Va. Died July 23, 2006.

MOTT, CHARLES DAVIS, civil engineer; b. Phila., Aug. 30, 1914; s. Charles Hillard and Emma (Davis) M.; m. Ellen Mary Hooge, Aug. 13, 1938 (dec.); children: Ellen H., Charles H., Joseph W. H.; m. Helen M. Michaels, 1993. BSc in Civil Engring., U. Pa., Phila., 1932; grad., Army-Navy Guided Missile Sch., Ft. Bliss, Tex., 1951; M Engring. Adminstrn., George Washington U., 1967. Engr. Cruse Kemper Co., Ambler, Pa., 1936-37; flight leader Am. Vol. Group, Burma, China, 1941-45; tech. staff/mgr. Analytic Svcs., Arlington, Va., from 1963. Mem. staff Rsch. and Devel. Bd., Office Sec. of Def., Washington, 1952-55. Pres. Lakevale Ct. Citizens Assn., Vienna, Va., 1972, 87. Capt. USN (aviator), 1937-41, 1946-63. Decorated DFC; recipient Cloud and Banner medal Chinese Air Force, 1958, POW medal USN, 1990. Mem. AIAA (mem. coun. Nat. Capitol sect. 1984-86), Am. Def. Preparedness Assn. Baptist. Achievments include membership in concept formulation team, F-15, Navy Torpedo Programs Review Group and participant in Project Forecast: rsearch in air to surface guided weapons. Home: Vienna, Va. Died July 30, 2004.

MOTT, MICHAEL IRVINE, retired military officer; b. Nashville, Oct. 1, 1949; s. Charles Ransom and Edith (Whitehead) M.; m. Kathy Sue McDonald, July 21, 1973; children— Michael Irvine, Ashley Miriam. B.Engring., Vanderbilt U., 1971; M.S., U. So. Calif., 1981; student U.S. Naval Test Pilot Sch., 1978-79. Commd. 2d lt. U.S. Marine Corps, 1971, advanced through grades to lt. col., 1981, ret. 1991; assigned Marine Fighter/Attack squadrons, 1971-78; test naval flight officer, Strike Aircraft Test Directorate, 1979-82; spl. project officer for chief of Naval Ops., Washington, 1982-83; aviation devel. officer, Yuma, Ariz., 1983-87, exec. officer, 1987-88, commanding officer Marine Aircraft Group 41A, assoc. dep. adminstr., NASA, 1993-98, v.p., gen. mgr. NASA systems, Boeing Co., 2000-05; Decorated Meritorious Service medal, Legion of Merit with gold stars; recipient Test Naval Flight Officer of Yr. award Naval Air Test Center, 1981, Marine Naval Flight Officer of Yr., 1987. Mem. Marine Corps Aviation Assn., Marine Corps Assn., Tailhook Assn., Assn. of Naval Aviation, Assn. of Old Crows, Nat. Eagle Scout Assn., Alpha Phi Omega. Presbyterian. Contbr. articles to profl. publs. Home: Laguna Hills, Calif. Died Nov. 19, 2005.

MOTZ, SIMION, minister; b. Rostoci, Romania, Aug. 4, 1926; came to U.S., 1978; s. George and Agrima (Tomsa) M.; m. Maria Ban, July 10, 1947; children: Dorin, Daniel, Nicoleta, Eugene. Grad., Normal Sch. for Tchrs., Arad, Romania, 1947; diploma, MIU, Saliste, Romania, 1952. Ordained to ministry Ind. Bapt. Ch., 1981. Lay preacher Bapt. chs., Romania; imprisoned for religious activity Gherla, Ostrov, Romania, 1958-62; lay preacher, Sunday sch. tchr. Bapt. chs. Romania, 1963-77; missionary, evangelist, acct. to various Communist countries Glendale, Calif., 1978-88; pres. The Suffering Ch. Ministries, Norcross, Ga., from 1988. Author: On The Way of the Cross In Kings Service, 1982, Clarifications About The Holy Spirit, 1984, Dew Drops: Sermons, Meditations, 1984, The Final Events of the Bible, 1987, The Complete Salvation of God, 1987. Died Aug. 21, 2005.

MOUBRAY, JOHN MITCHELL, engineering company executive; b. Harare, Zimbabwe, Feb. 2, 1949; arrived in U.K., 1986; s. James W. and Dorothy May (Robinson) M.; m. Edith I. Dashorst, Jan. 4, 1976; children: Alastair, Donovan, Cameron. BSc in ME, U. Cape Town, South Africa, 1971. Engr. Metal Box Co., Cape Town, 1971-73; field engr. Mobil Oil, Johannesburg, South Africa, 1973-74; dir. P-E Cons. Svcs., Johannesburg, 1974-86; CEO Aladon LLC, Asheville, N.C., from 1986. Author: Reliability-Centered Maintenance, 1991, 2nd edit. 1997. Mem. Soc. Maintenance and Reliability Profls. Avocation: reading. Died Jan. 15, 2004.

MOUL, DALE ALLEN, research executive; b. Reading, Pa., May 6, 1947; s. W. Wilson Moul and Elizabeth Mae (Naugle) Stump; m. Barbara Jean Kulman, Oct. 25, 1970; children: Steven, Jennifer. BS, Mich. State U., 1969; JD, U. Md., 1979. Bar: Va. 1979. Assoc. NUSAC, Inc., McLean, Va., 1976-79; mgr. security programs Wackenhut Advanced Tech., Reston, Va., 1979-86; assoc. dept. mgr. Battelle Meml. Inst., Columbus, 1986-89, v.p. security tech. and tng., from 1990. Treas. Herndon (Va.) Youth Soccer, 1985-86, div. commr., 1983-84; coach Worthington (Ohio) Boosters Soccer, 1986-88. Capt. U.S. Army, 1970-76. Decorated Army Commendation medal with oak leaf cluster, Meritorious Svc. medal. Mem. Inst. Nuclear Materials Mgmt., Phi Kappa Phi. Republican. Avocations: fishing, golf. Home: Columbus, Ohio. Died Apr. 29, 2004.

MOULE, WILLIAM NELSON, electrical engineer, consultant; b. Highland Park, Mich., Sept. 13, 1924; s. Hollis Creager and Kate DeEtte (Hill) Moule; m. Barbara Ann Bagley, June 27, 1953; children: Janice Louise, Robert Hollis(dec.), Linda Anne, Nancy Lynn Moule Moles. BSEE, Mich. State U., 1949; MSEE, U. Pa., 1957. Reg. profl. engr., N.J. Design engr. Radio Corp. of Am., Camden, NJ, 1949—59, sr. design engr. Moorestown, NJ, 1959—67; sr. engr. Emerson Elec. Co., St. Louis, 1967—70, Emerson Elec. Rantec Divsn., Calabasas, Calif., 1970; sr. staff engr. Raytheon Co., Santa Barbara, Calif., 1970—73, ITT Gilfillan, Van Nuys, Calif., 1973, Jet Propulsion Lab., Pasadena, Calif., 1973—79; sr. rsch devel. engr. Lockheed Advanced Devel. Co., Burbank, Calif., 1979—2000, cons. engr., from 2000. Patentee numerous inventions, from 1956. Dir. nat. alumni bd. Mich. State U., East Lansing, 1984-87; pres. Big Ten Club of So. Calif., L.A., 1992. Staff sgt. USAAF, 1943-46. Mem. IEEE (sr., L.A. chpt. sec., treas. Antennas and Propagation soc. 1987-89, vice chmn. 1989-90, chmn. 1990-91), 305th Bombardment Group Meml. Assn. (life; pres. 2000-2001). Democrat. Presbyterian. Avocations: travel, photography, genealogy. Home: Calabasas, Calif. Died Apr. 27, 2006.

MOULTON, DOROTHY LEE, advertising and marketing executive; b. Newburgh, N.Y., July 29, 1938; d. Edward Chapin and Thelma (Drake) M. BS in Pub. Relations, Boston U., 1966. Sec. Sterling Forest Corp., Tuxedo, N.Y., 1962-64; rep. N.Y. Telephone, Mt. Kisco, 1966-69; employment supr. Westchester and N.Y.C., 1969-73; community relations cons. N.Y.C., 1973-78; mgr.-advt., 1978-81; mgr.-research, 1981-83; mgr.-policies NYNEX Enterprises, N.Y.C., 1983-85, staff dir.-advt., 1985-88, mktg. mgr., from 1988; co-owner Maid of Montauk (N.Y.) Cottages, from 1986; pres. Diana Drake Ltd., N.Y.C., from 1984. Bd. dirs. Queens chpt. ARC, Flushing, N.Y., 1977-78, Flushing Boys Club, 1977-78, Queens Preventive Medicine, 1976-78; mem. Montauk Arts Coun., 1989. Recipient Civic awards Elmhurst Civic Assn., Queens, N.Y., 1977, Flushing Boys Club, Queens, 1977, Carl Whitmore Telephone Pioneer award, 1976. Mem. NAFE, Women in Communications, Am. Women Econ. Devel., Telephone Pioneers Am., Boston U. Alumni Assn. Republican. Episcopalian. Avocations: writing poetry and children's stories, song writing, painting, piano. Home: Oceanside, NY. Died Feb. 12, 2004.

MROZ, MICHAEL BARRY, engineer, consultant; b. Detroit, May 7, 1945; s. Edward Nicholas and Ann (Poniktera) M. Staff engr. The Express Sound Co., Costa Mesa, Calif., 1977-79, Sunset Sound, Hollywood, Calif., 1979-82, The Record Plant, Los Angeles, 1982-84; chief engr. Caribou Ranch, Nederland, Colo., 1984-85, Audio Engring. Assocs., Pasadena, Calif., from 1985. Lectr., cons. Calif. State U., Dominguez Hills, 1986—; lectr. The Grove Sch. Music, Studio City, Calif., 1986—; freelance cons., Los Angeles,

1987—. Served as cpl. USMC, 1963-69, Vietnam. Mem. Audio Engring. Soc. Avocations: camping, hiking, horseback riding, woodcraft. Home: Lebec, Calif. Died Sept. 30, 2004.

MUDICA, ALBERT LEE, mechanical engineer; b. Jackson, Mich., Mar. 13, 1932; s. Albert R. and Dorothy M. (Lee) M.; widowed Feb. 1986; children: Terri L. Ellis, Albert T. BME, Tri-State U., Angola, Ind., 1953. Dir. engring. Weatherite, Los Angeles, 1978-81; gen. mgr. Climate Engring., Belmont, Calif., 1981-82; chief engr. A&A Facilities Systems, San Jose, Calif., 1982-83; mgr. ops. Advanced Mech. Engring., Menlo Park, Calif., 1983; project engr. Cal Air Conditioning, San Jose, from 1984. Served with USAR, 1953-55. Mem. ASHRAE. Republican. Home: Louisville, Ky. Died Nov. 2, 2004.

MUDRICK, DAVID LEWIS, physician; b. Phila., May 14, 1928; s. Harry and Irene (Wax) M.; m. Henrietta Epstein, July 6, 1952; children: Marylyn, Carl, Sharon, Deborah, Franklin. MD, Temple U., 1954. Intern Chester Hosp., 1954-55. Capt. U.S. Army, 1956-57. Mem. AMA, Pa. Med. Soc., Delco County Med. Soc. (pres.), Alpha Omega Alpha. Avocation: tennis. Home: Wallingford, Pa. Died Apr. 4, 2004.

MUIR, HELEN, journalist; b. Yonkers, N.Y., Feb. 9, 1911; d. Emmet A. and Helen T. (Flaherty) Lennehan; m. William Whalley Muir, Jan. 23, 1936; children: Mary Muir Burrell, William Torbert. With Yonkers Herald Statesman, 1929-30, 31-33, N.Y. Evening Post, 1930-31, N.Y. Evening Jour., 1933-34, Carl Byoir & Assocs., N.Y.C., Miami, 1934-35; syndicated columnist Universal Svc., Miami, 1935-38; columnist Miami Herald, 1941-42; children's book editor, 1949-56; women's editor Miami Daily News, 1943-44; freelance mag. writer numerous nat. mags., from 1944. Drama critic Miami News, 1960-65. Author: Miami, U.S.A., 1953, expanded edit., 2000, Biltmore: Beacon for Miami, 1987, 3d rev. edit., 1998, Frost in Florida: A Memoir, 1995. Trustee Coconut Grove Libr. Assn., Friends U. Miami Libr., Friends Miami-Dade Pub. Libr.; vis. com. U. Miami Librs.; bd. dirs. Miami-Dade County Pub. Libr. Sys., chmn. emeritus, 1999. Recipient award Delta Kappa Gamma, 1960, trustees and friends award Fla. Libr. Assn., 1973, award Coun. Fla. Librs., 1990, trustee citation ALA, 1984, spirit of excellence award, 1988; named to Fla. Women's Hall of Fame, 1984, Miami Centennial '96 Women's Hall of Fame; named chmn. emeritus Metro-Dade Libr. Sys., 1999. Mem.: ALA (named leading libr. adv. 20th Century), Authors' Guild, Soc. Women Geographers (meritorious svc. award 1996, Fla. Groups First Woman of World award 2000), Women in Comms. (Cmty. Headliner award 1973), Biscayne Bay Yacht Club, Cosmopolitan Club (N.Y.C.), Fla.Women's Press Club (award 1963). Home: Miami, Fla. Died Feb. 13, 2006.

MULLINS, LESLIE MORRIS, lawyer; b. Coeburn, Va., Apr. 19, 1917; s. George Milburn and Willie Sue (Boyd) M.; m. Dorothy Ann McGlothlin, June 26, 1943; children: Michael, Ann. AB, Emory and Henry U., 1940; LLB, U. Va., 1942, JD, 1970. Bar: Va. 1942, U.S. Dist. Ct. (we. dist.) Va. 1946, U.S. Ct. Appeals (4th cir.) 1960. Ptnr. Mullins, Thomason & Harris, Norton, Va., 1946-93. Pres., bd. dirs. The Kline Found., Norton. Editorial bd.: U. Va. Law Rev., 1942. Lt. USNR, 1943-46. Named Citizen of Yr. Wise County C. of C., 1983. Mem. Va. State Bar Assn. (v.p. 1955-56, coun.), Lonesome Pine Country Club (bd. dirs. 1987), Masons, Kiwanis (pres.). Methodist. Avocations: golf, travel, reading. Home: Tallahassee, Fla. Died Jan. 15, 2004.

MULVIHILL, WILLIAM PATRICK, writer; b. Sag Harbor, N.Y., June 25, 1923; s. Daniel Francis Mulvihill and Anna Christian McDonough; m. Mary Joubert Marceau, June 18, 1946; children: Nancy Jeanne, Mary Ann. BA, Cornell U., 1948; MA, Columbia U., 1951. Author: The Sands of Kalahari, 1960, Serengeti, 1965, Night of the Axe, 1972, Sagaponack, 1995, God is Blind, 1997. With U.S. Army, 1943-45, ETO. Avocations: book collecting, travel. Home: Glen Cove, NY. Died Sept. 17, 2004.

MUMFORD, ROBERT SUTTON, psychiatrist; b. Seattle, July 23, 1918; s. Maurice Clearance and Ione (Sutton) M.; m. Emily Hamilton, July 1950 (div. 1969); m. Beverly Hess Hamilton, 1975; children: Bonnie McIlhenny, Betsy Cohen, Nancy Pierce. MD, McGill U., 1943. Diplomate Am. Bd. Psychiatry and Neurology; cert. Nat. Bd. Medicine. Intern Montreal Gen. Hosp., Can., 1943, L.A. County Hosp., 1944; resident in psychiatry N.Y. Psychiatr. Inst., 1947-48, Bellevue Psychiat. Hosp., 1948-50; pvt. practice N.Y.C., from 1950, Old Greenwich, Conn., from 1975. Assoc. editor N.Y. State Psychiat. Assn. Bull., 1950—; cons. in psychiatry Presbyn. Hosp., N.Y.C. Capt. USAF, 1944-47. Fellow Am. Psychiat. Assn. (life), Am. Coll. Psychiatrists, Am. Coll. Psychoanalysts (pres. 1987), N.Y. Acad. Medicine (life); mem. AMA (life), Univ. Club, Innis Arden Country Club. Republican. Mem. Christian Ch. Avocations: tennis, golf, skiing. Died Feb. 25, 2005.

MUMMERT, THOMAS ALLEN, manufacturing company executive; b. Toledo, Ohio, Dec. 24, 1946; s. James Allen and Betty Alice (Thomas) M.; student U. Toledo, 1965-66; m. Icia Linda Shearer, Dec. 17, 1966; children—Sherry Lynn, Robert Thomas, Michael Allen. Pres., Mummert Electric & Mfg. Co., Inc., Toledo, 1969-70; research engr. Am. Lincoln Corp., Bowling Green, Ohio, 1970-73; test engr. Dura div. Dura Corp., Toledo, 1973-74; research dept. head Jobst Inst., Inc., Toledo, 1975-84, mgr. med. equipment design, 1984—. Served with USN, 1968-69. Mem. AAAS, Laser Inst. Am., Biol. Engring. Soc., Ohio Acad. Sci., N.Y. Acad. Sci., Am. Soc. for Quality Control, Am. Soc. Engring. Edn., Nat. Mgmt. Assn., Assn. for Advancement of Med. Instrumentation, ASTM. Baptist. Inventor sequential dual window operating mechanism, 1974, therapeutic appliance for flexing joints, 1980, sequencing valve mechanism, 1981, electronic circuit for dynamic pressure wave pneumatic control system, 1981, artificial foot, 1981, and others; patentee in field. Home: Coldwater, Mich. Died Feb. 27, 2005.

MUNSON, LEON J., portfolio manager; b. McGill, Nev., Dec. 14, 1939; s. Edward Ivin Munson Sr. and Ella Jean (Jenne) Nagel; m. Gloria Leiko Ursal, Aug. 17, 1989. BS, U. Nev., 1963. Teller, mgmt. trainee 1st Nat. Bank of Nev., Reno, 1963-65, trust investment officer, 1965-71, asst. v.p., head trust, 1971-74; 2nd v.p., investment officer Bishop Trust Co., Ltd., Honolulu, 1974-78; asst. v.p., investment officer 1st Hawaiian Bank, Honolulu, 1978-79, v.p., head trust investment, 1979-85; v.p. portfolio mgr. Cadinha & Co., Honolulu, from 1985, prin., from 1988. Mem. Investment Soc. Hawaii (bd. dirs. 1979-83), Assn. Investment Mgmt. and Rsch., Security Analysis of San Francisco, Internat. Soc. Fin. Analysts, Nat. Assn. Security Dealers (regional arbitrator 1980—). Home: Honolulu, Hawaii. Died July 16, 2004.

MUNSON, RAY EUGENE, judge; b. Leavenworth, Wash., Sept. 10, 1927; s. Will Keller and Jessie May (Tyler) M.; m. Christine A. Parr, Nov. 13, 1954; children: Mark P., Bradley W., Scott E., Cristofer R. BBA, U. Wash., 1952, JD, 1954. Bar: Wash. 1954, U.S. Dist. Ct. (ea. dist.) Wash. 1957. Spl. agt. FBI, 1954-55; dep. pros. atty. Yakima (Wash.) County Pros. Atty. Office, 1956-57, pros. atty., 1957-61; assoc. Halverson, Applegate, McDonald, Yakima, 1962-65; judge Superior Ct. Wash., Yakima, 1965-69, Wash. Ct. Appeals Div. III, Yakima, from 1969, presiding chief judge, 1978, chief judge, 1971-73, 77-79, 83-85, 89. With USN, 1945-48. Avocations: gardening, golf. Home: Yakima, Wash. Died Feb. 22, 2004.

MURK, LYNDON KEITH, minister; b. Amor, Minn., June 12, 1926; s. Gilbert Gabriel and Mabel (Lien) M. BA, Augustana Coll., Rock Island, Ill., 1947; MA, Pacific Luth. U., 1971. Ordained to ministry Luth. Ch., 1951. Pastor Bethel Luth. Ch., Gt. Falls, Mont., 1951-64, Tacoma, from 1964. Chaplain Boy Scouts Am., 1960, 73, 77, Am. Guild Organists, Tacoma, 1979—; pres., dir. Assoc. Ministries, Tacoma, 1974-78. Author: The Influence of Martin Bucer, 1971. Recipient Silver Beaver award Boy Scouts Am., 1960, Vigil Honor Order of Arrow Boy Scouts Am., 1960, Lamb award Luth. Coun. USA, 1975. Mem. Hymn Soc. Am., Soc. for Preservation and Encouragement of Barber Shop Quartet Singing in Am. (treas. Tacoma chpt. 1975—), Kiwanis (dir. Gt. Falls club 1957-61, pres. 1960, dir. Tacoma club 1984—), Order of Runeberg (pres. 1980-82). Home: Tacoma, Wash. Died Oct. 3, 2004.

MURPHY, BARBARA ANN, protective services official; b. Oct. 4, 1922; d. Thomas Henry and Charlotte Ruth (Ticer) Murphy. BS, Jersey City State Coll., 1944; MA, Columbia U., 1949. Ret. educator. Chair child placement rev. bd., Hudson County Superior Court of N.J., Chancery Divsn. Family, 1992—. Pres. bd. trustees Weehawken (N.J.) Libr., 1994—; adv. panel United Water. Recipient Gov.'s Tchr. Recognition Program award, Princeton, N.J., 1989; named to Weehawken H.S. Hall of Fame, Weehawken Bd. Edn., 1992. Mem. AAUW (pres. 1988-91), N.J. Schoolwomen's Club (v.p. 1980), Weehawken Hist. Soc. (life mem.), Weehawken Adult Club (charter), Palisade Gen. Hosp. Vols. Avocations: travel, reading, gardening, piano. Home: Weehawken, NJ. Died June 19, 2004.

MURPHY, LYLE, composer; b. Aug. 19, 1908; s. John Lawrence and Fanny (Lohdefinck) M.; m. Marjory Michael, Dec. 18, 1954. Freelance musician, from 1925. Author: (instruction books) Clarinet-Saxophone, 1939-71; author, instr. 12-volume course in composition, arranging and orchestration, Horizontal Composition Based on Equal Intervals; rec. 15 albums, motion picture scores; arranger: Casa Loma Orch., 1934-36, Benny Goodman Orch., 1935-37, Robbins Music Corp., 1935-39; arranger, composer Columbia Pictures, 1936-49; leader clarinet Lyle Murphy Orch., 1936-40. Served with Merchant Marine, 1942-46. Recipient Resolution and Commendation City Coun. of L.A., 1977, Golden Score Am. Soc. Music Arrangers, 1981; named Jazz Educator of Yr., L.A. Jazz Soc., 1990. Mem. Am. Fedn. Musicians, Am. Soc. Music Arrangers, ASCAP. Avocations: travel, photography, sports. Home: Los Angeles, Calif. Died Aug. 5, 2005.

MURPHY, PETER GREGORY, literature educator, writer; b. Trenton, N.J., June 19, 1957; s. George Joseph and Margaret Ann Murphy. MA in Philosophy, Bowling Green U., 1987; MA in Spanish, U. Ark., 1997, MA in English, 1999, PhD in Comparative Lit., 2000. Cert. secondary tchr. Instr. philosophy Bowling Green (Ohio) State U., 1985—87; English tchr. McCurristin H.S., Trenton, 1987—91, Colegio Internat. de Carbobo, Valencia, Venezuela, 1991—93; Spanish instr. U. Ark., Fayetteville, 1994—97, master lectr., 1997—2000; asst. prof. U. S.C., Union, from 2000. Author essays. V.p. Union County Friends Libr., from 2002. Faculty Devel. grant, U. S.C., 2002—03, Sampa-Ulloa grant, Leonor Ulloa-Radnor, 2003. Mem.: Union Mental Health Assn. (bd. mem. from 2002), Union Libr. Coun. (bd. mem. from 2002), Simms Soc., Caroliniana Soc., Thomas Cooper Soc. Avocations: music, landscaping. Home: Union, SC. Died Dec. 19, 2004.

MURPHY, THOMAS AQUINAS, former automobile manufacturing company executive; b. Hornell, N.Y., Dec. 10, 1915; s. John Joseph and Alma (O'Grady) M.; m. Catherine Rita Maquire, June 7, 1941; children: Catherine, Maureen, Thomas Aquinas. BS, U. Ill., 1938. With Gen. Motors Corp., 1938-88, asst. treas. N.Y.C., 1959, comptroller Detroit, 1967, treas., 1968, v.p. in charge car and truck group, 1970-72, vice chmn., 1972-74, chmn., CEO, 1974-80, dir., 1980-88. Bd. dirs. U. Ill. Found. Served with USNR, 1943-46. Mem. Fin. Execs. Inst., Bus. Coun., Bloomfield Hills (Mich.) Country Club, Delray Dunes (Fla.) Golf Club, Ocean Club (Fla.). Died Jan. 18, 2006.

MURRAY, GEORGE HOPKINS, III, internal auditor, consultant; b. Cambridge, Md., May 9, 1940; s. George Hopkins Jr. and Edna Mildred (Duffy) M.; m. Janette Louise Parmentier, Dec. 29, 1962; children: Kathleen Anne, Kelly Michelle. B in Computer Sci., Benjamin Franklin U., 1976; postgrad., Calif. Coast U., Marymount U. Cert. fraud examiner. Pub. acct. Sinrod & Tash CPAs, Washington, 1970-74; dir. internal auditing Washington-Lee Savings & Loan Assn., Alexandria, Va., 1974-76; bank examiner Fin. Gen. Bankshares Inc., Washington, 1976-78; dir. internal auditing A.G. Van Metre Assocs. Inc., Alexandria, 1978-81; sr. internal auditor UNC Resources, Inc., Falls Church, Va., 1981-83; internal auditor, cons. Computer Scis. Corp., Lanham, Md., from 1985. Author and facilitator various seminars. With USN, 1961-67. Mem. Inst. Internal Auditors (past pres., v.p. No. Va. chpt., bd. dirs., instr., mem. quality assurance rev. team), Cert. Fraud Examiners (bd. dirs. Washington Met. chpt. 1991-92). Methodist. Avocation: leathercraft. Home: Dale City, Va. Died Feb. 21, 2005.

MUSELMAN, JOHN ARTHUR, publishing company executive; b. Decatur, Ind., Sept. 29, 1952; s. Carl Henry and Marilyn Catherine (Smith) M. BS in Gen. Mgmt., Ind. U., 1974. Pres. Lehman Travel Bur., Inc., Berne, Ind., 1974-77; compt. Ho. of White Birches, Inc., Berne, from 1985; v.p. purchasing Economy Printing Concern, Inc., Berne, Ind., from 1970-. Bd. dirs. Berne Tri-Weekly News, Third Muselman Family Found., Berne, Carl H. Muselman Family Found., Berne. Mem. Rotary, Jaycees, Sons of Am. Legion. Democrat. Avocations: snow and water skiing, sailing, travel. Home: Phoenix, Ariz. Died Oct. 5, 2004.

MUSGROVE, ANNABELL HARRIET FEUGE, gerontology nurse; b. Fredericksburg, Tex., Apr. 19, 1934; d. Harry Edward and Lydia Ella (Rusche) Feuge; m. Carl Christopher Musgrove, Dec. 31, 1954 (div. Oct. 1991); children: Carl Christopher II, Charles Clifford. Diploma, Brackenridge Hosp. Sch. of Nursing, 1954; BSN, Northwestern State U., 1982; postgrad., Northwestern State U., Shreveport, La., 1982. RN, Tex., La.; cert. gerontology nurse. Staff nurse obstetrics unit Brackenridge Hosp., Austin, Tex.; staff nurse Hunter AFB, Savannah, Ga.; charge nurse evening shift Schumpert Med. Ctr., Shreveport; staff nurse Overton Brooks VA Med. Ctr., Shreveport. Mem. ANA, ARC. Died May 31, 2004.

MUSLIN, HARVEY PAUL, lawyer; b. Chgo., Jan. 5, 1945; s. Isidore Sam and Margie (Axelrod) M.; m. Adrienne Marilyn Berg, Sept. 5, 1966; children: Ivan Scott, Erica Beth, David Oliver. Student, Kendall Jr. Coll., Evanston, Ill., 1963-64, Bradley U., Peoria, Ill., 1964-65; BSBA, Roosevelt U., Chgo., 1967; JD, John Marshall Law Sch., Chgo., 1971. Bar: Ill. 1971, Fla. 1980, U.S. Dist. Ct. (mid. dist.) Fla. 1981, U.S. Dist. Ct. (no. dist.) Ill. 1971, U.S. Supreme Ct. 1979. Asst. state atty. Cook County, Ill., 1971-74; sole practice, Chgo., 1974-80, Tampa, Fla., from 1981; instr. law Hillsborough Community Coll., Tampa, 1981-82. Mem. Decalogue League Lawyers, Ill. Bar Assn., Chgo. Bar Assn., Fla. Bar Assn., Hillsborough County Bar Assn., Am. Trial Lawyers Assn. Lodges: B'nai B'rith (v.p. 1982-83). Democrat. Jewish. Home: Tampa, Fla. Died Jan. 25, 2004.

MUSSELMAN, NORMAN BURKEY, retired editor; b. Arkansas City, Kans., Mar. 21, 1929; s. Norman Beachy and E. Ruth (Burkey) M.; m. Elizabeth Temple Henry (dec. 2001), Oct. 26, 1957; children: Elizabeth Temple Whitson, Norman Henry, Robert Beachy (dec. 2005). BA, U. Okla., 1951, MA, 1954. Columnist McGraw Hill Pub. Co., Washington, 1954-67; editor Nat. Assn. Electric Cos., Washington, 1967-80; dir. govt. com. Edison Electric Inst., Washington, 1980-94; retired, 1994. Pres. Okla. U. Alumni Club, Washington, 1957-58; pres. men of ch. Presbyn. Meeting House, Alexandria, Va., 1962-63, clk. of session, 1980-82; elder 1st Presbyn. Ch., Glenwood Springs; precinct capt. Rep. Party, Fairfax County, Va., 1968-69; cubmaster, pack chmn., scout com. Boy Scouts, Alexandria, 1970-73, 78-82. 1st lt. U.S. Army, 1951-53. Mem. Soc. for the Preservation and Encouragement of Barber Shop Singing in Am. (pres. Garfield Colo. chpt. 1998, Barbershopper of Yr. 1996), Colo. Archeol. Soc. (Roaring Fork chpt.), Glenwood Springs Lions Club (v.p.), Nat. Press Club, Sigma Delta Chi (pres. Okla. U. chpt. 1953-54). Home: Glenwood Springs, Colo. Died Mar. 10, 2006.

MUSSELMAN, ROBERT METCALFE, lawyer; b. N.Y.C., June 12, 1914; s. Joseph Franklin and Susan M. (Metcalfe) Musselman; m. Lucie Carolyn Clarke, Sept. 6, 1958; 1 child, Susan Carole. BS, U. Va., 1934, MA in Polit. Sci., 1940, LLB, 1945. Bar: Va. 1945, U.S. Dist. Ct. (ea.

dist.) Va. 1948, U.S. Tax Ct. 1948, U.S. Dist. Ct. (we. dist.) Va. 1951, U.S. Ct. Appeals (4th cir.) 1953, U.S. Supreme Ct. 1964, U.S. Claims Ct. 1986, U.S. Ct. Appeals (11th cir.) 1987, U.S. Ct. Appeals (fed. cir.) 1988, U.S. dist. Ct. (ctrl. dist.) Ill. 1994, U.S. Ct. Appeals (7th cir.) 1994. Instr., lectr. U. Va., Charlottesville, 1936-59, chief acct., 1943-46; law clk. to judge U.S. Ct. Appeals (4th cir.), 1945-46; ptnr. Michael and Musselman, Charlottesville, 1946-53, Musselman and Drysdale, Charlottesville, 1953-56; pvt. practice Charlottesville, from 1956. Lectr. in field. Editor-in-chief: Alexander's Federal Tax Handbook, 1955—61, bd. editors: Jour. Taxation, 1954—73. Pres. Charlottesvill-Albemarle Young Dem. Club, 1940—43; mem. Albemarle County Dem. Com., from 1978. Mem.: AICPA, ABA, Va. Soc. CPAs (bd. dirs.), Charlottesville-Albemarle Bar Assn., Va. Bar Assn., Am. Assn. Atty.-CPAs (charter, bd. dirs.), 4th Cir. Jud. Conf., Phi Sigma Kappa. Episcopalian. Home: Charlottesville, Va. Died Nov. 9, 2004.

MUTH, JOHN WILLIAM, economics educator; b. Atlanta, Dec. 20, 1948; s. William Franklin and Edith Maxine (Powell) M. BA summa cum laude, Colo. Coll., Colorado Springs, 1970; MA in Econs., U. Colo., 1974, PhD in Econs., 1978. Staff assoc. Acad. Ind. Scholars, Boulder, Colo., 1980; field coord. Instnl. Devel. and Econ. Affairs Svc., Boulder, 1979; asst. prof. U. Colo., Denver, 1982-83; dir. divsn. bus. Regis U., Denver, 1989—92, 1997—2002, assoc. prof., 1983—2002, prof., from 2002. Vis. lectr. Richmond Coll., London, 1985; cons. Colo. Office Regulatory Reform, Denver, 1985, U.S. Dept. Edn., Washington, 1988—; field evaluator Assn. Collegiate Bus. Schs. and Programs, 1992—; asst. dir. Regis U. Forensics Program, Denver, 1991-97. Editor, co-author: (curriculum guides) Community Social Profiles, 1976-78; author curriculum module econs., internat. trade, 1984-86; co-author, editor profl. exam rev. Micromash CMA Rev., 1992-93; author computer interactive tutorial Friendly Finance, 1996. Pres. bd. dirs. Parkway Towers Condo Assn., Denver, 1991-2000. Mem. Phi Beta Kappa. Avocation: native americans of the southwest studies. Home: Aurora, Colo. Died May 11, 2005.

MYERHOLTZ, RALPH W., JR., retired chemical company executive, chemist, researcher; b. Bucyrus, Ohio, July 29, 1926; s. Ralph W.E. and Vera (Kirkland) M.; m. Lois Ellen Congram, June 24, 1951; children: Carl Alan, Lynne Elaine Myerholtz Patterson. BS, Purdue U., 1950; PhD in Organic Chemistry, Northwestern U., 1954. Project chemist Standard Oil Co. (Ind.), Whiting, Ind., 1954-58; group leader Amoco Chem. Corp., Whiting, 1958-66, rsch. assoc., 1966-69, dir. polymer physics divsn. Naperville, Ill., 1969-86, ret. Contbr. articles to profl. jours.; holder 7 patents. Trustee Greenfield (Ind.) Pub. Libr., 1995-2001; radio officer CD, Naperville, 1971-81; scoutmaster Boy Scouts Am., Hammond, Ind., 1955-59. Sgt. U.S. Army, 1944-46, PTO. Mem. Am. Chem. Soc., Sigma Xi, Pi Kappa Phi, Phi Lambda Upsilon. Avocations: photography, electronics, woodcarving, nature/environment. Home: Greenfield, Ind. Died Feb. 15, 2005.

MYERNICK, GLENN, professional soccer coach; b. Dec. 29, 1954; Student, Hartwick Coll. Profl. soccer player Dallas Tornado, 1977-79, Portland, 1980-82, Tampa Bay, Fla., 1983-84; asst. coach U. Tampa, 1985-86, Hartwick Coll., 1986-89; nat. coaching coord. US Soccer Team, 1989-96; asst. coach US Olympic Team, 1996; head coach Colo. Rapids, Denver, 1997—2001; asst. coach US Men's Nat. Team, 2002—04; head coach US Nat. Under-23 Men's Team, 2004—06. Capt. U.S. Pan Am. Team, 1975, U.S. Olympic Team, 1976. Recipient Hermann Trophy as College Player of the Yr., 1976; named U.S. Soccer Fedn. Coach of the Yr. by U.S. Olympic Com., 1998. Died Oct. 9, 2006.

MYERS, ARNO RHODES, corporate executive; b. Elwood, Ill., Aug. 27, 1907; s. Oscar Rhodes and Nellie Josephine (Gurney) M; m. Elizabeth Nellegar, Aug. 3, 1985. BA in Acctg., U. Wis., 1931. With acctg. dept. G.W. Rossiter, Chgo., 1931-32, Farmess Nat. Grain Corp., Chgo., 1932-39; pres., chmn. bd. Airtex Corp. and subsidiaries, Chgo., from 1939. 1st lt. U.S. Mil., 1932-44. Mem. Coun. on World Affairs (pres. Naples, Fla. chpt. 1987), Internat. Sub-Contractors Assn. (pres. Nat. Assn. 1964), Skokie Country Club, Hole-In-Wall-Golf Club, Royal Porciana Golf Club, Naples Yacht Club. Republican. Avocations: trout fishing, photography, golf. Home: Naples, Fla. Died Apr. 3, 2004.

MYERS, ARTHUR B., journalist; b. Buffalo, Oct. 24, 1917; s. Edward A. and Isabelle (Baker) M.; m. Irma H. Ashley, 1972. BA, Hobart Coll., 1939. Journalist Rochester (N.Y.) Times Union, 1948-52, Washington Post, 1956-57, Berkshire (Mass.) Eagle, 1957-64; contbg. editor Coronet mag., 1965-68; columnist Bergen Record, Hackensack, N.J., 1969-71; exec. editor Berkshire Sampler, Pittsfield, Mass., 1971-77; tchr. writing Mass. U. extension program and Berkshire Community Coll., Pittsfield, 1958-62, Fairleigh Dickinson U., Teaneck, N.J., 1970, Cambridge (Mass.) Coll., 1989. Author: (with J. O'Connell) Safety Last: An Indictment of Auto Industry, 1966, Journalism Careers for the 70's, 1971, Analysis: The Short Story, 1975, Analysis: The Personal Profile Magazine Article, 1976, Kids Do Amazing Things, 1980, The Ghost Hunters, 1980, Sea Creatures Do Amazing Things, 1981; (with Irma Myers) Why You Feel Down and What You Can Do About It, 1982, The Ghostly Register, 1986, Ghosts of the Rich and Famous, 1988, The Ghostly Gazetteer, 1990, Ghost Hunter's Guide, 1993, The Cheyenne, 1992, The Pawnee, 1993, The First Movies, 1993, The First Baseball Game, 1993, The First Football Game, 1993, Drugs and Peer Pressure, 1995, Communicating with Animals, 1997; also short stories, articles. Mem. PEN, Nat. Writers Union, Mensa, Boston Authors Club. Home: Wellesley, Mass. Died Apr. 2006.

MYERS, DEBI LYNN, financial analyst; b. Ft. Harrison, Ind., Feb. 12, 1956; d. Wendell Holmes and Barbara Ann (Johnson) Overton; div. 1986; 1 child, Theresa Elizabeth; m. Cannon Myers. AA, St. Petersburg Jr. Coll., 1976; BA, U. South Fla., 1978. Fin. aid officer Jones Colls., Jacksonville, Fla., 1978-79, Summit Systems Colls. and Schs., Tampa, Fla., 1979-83; cons. J.V. & Assocs., Jacksonville, 1982-85; dir. fin. aid United Schs., Inc., Clearwater, Fla., 1985-88, dir. operational svcs., 1989-90; dir. fin. aid Chgo. State U., 1990-91, Student Loan Mktg. Assn., Tampa, Fla., 1991-93; with Penntrust Mortgage, Atlanta, 1994—95, Fin. Aid Svcs., Atlanta, from 1996. Mem. Nat. Assn. Student Fin. Aid Adminstrs., Fla. Assn. Student Fin. Aid Adminstrs., So. Assn. Student Fin. Aid Adminstrs., Women's Coun. of Realtors. Democrat. Home: Atlanta, Ga. Died June 17, 2004.

MYERS, HOWARD BENJAMAN, corporate lawyer; b. Beaver Falls, Pa., Apr. 11, 1937; s. Edward Isadore and Sayde (Oliker) M.; m. Ruth Adams; children: Kathryn Anne Myers Pittaway, Richard Adams, Edward Isadore, Elizabeth Casey. BA, Cornell U., 1959; LLB, Columbia U., 1962. Atty. Allied Corp., N.Y.C., 1962-66; assoc. gen. counsel Amerada Hess Corp., N.Y.C., 1966-83; gen. counsel, sec. RSR Corp./Bayou Steel Corp., Dallas, from 1983. Founding dir. N.J. Shakespeare Festival, Madison, 1972-78. Mem. ABA, Tex. Bar Assn., Dallas Bar Assn. Home: Plano, Tex. Died Aug. 4, 2004.

MYERS, JULIAN SHERRY, rehabilitation counseling educator; b. Hartford, Conn., Mar. 24, 1918; s. Barney and Fanny (Sherry) M.; m. Mary Helen Scott, Aug. 12, 1960; children: Alan, Andrew, Barry, Melanie, Julie. BA, City Coll. N.Y., 1939; MA, Columbia U., 1946; PhD, NYU, 1953. Lic. psychologist, N.Y., Mass., Ohio; cert. rehabilitation counselor. Psychologist Inst. Phys. Medicine and Rehab., N.Y.C., 1948-51, Burke Found., White Plains, N.Y., 1951-57; assoc. prof. rehabilitation counseling Boston U., 1957-66; founder, dir. U. Cin. Rehab. Ctr., 1969-83; prof. U. Cin., 1966-88, prof. emeritus, from 1988; clin. dir. Ikron Rehab Ctr., from 1993. Vocational cons. Social Security Adminstrn., Boston and Cin., 1957-83; cons. Rehab. Commn., Columbus, 1986. Editor: Orientation to Chronic Disease and Disability, 1965. Served to capt. Med. Specialist Corps, U.S. Army, 1942-46, USAR, 1946-57. U.S. Rehab. Services Adminstrn. fellow, 1973. Mem. Am. Psychol. Assn., Ohio Psychol. Assn., Cin. Psychol. Assn., Cin. Assn. Profl. Psychology, Ohio Assn. for Counselor Edn., Harvard Med. Alumni Assn. (assoc.). Home: Cincinnati, Ohio. Died Apr. 22, 2005.

MYERS, MARGARET ALICE, music educator; b. Des Arc, Ark., Jan. 14, 1937; d. Cecil Ernest and Juneidabeth Letsch Myers. BSE, U. Ark., 1958, MEd, 1963. Cert. tchr. Kans. Music and string tchr. El Dorado (Ark.) Dist. # 15, 1958—77; string tchr. Parsons (Kans.) Schs. Unified Sch. Dist. # 503, from 1977. Viola player South Ark. Symphony, El Dorado, 1958—77, S.E. Kans. Symphony, Pittsburg, from 1979, Labette C.C. Orch., Parsons, from 2000. Recipient commendation, Ark. Senate, 1971. Mem.: Suzuki Assn. Ams., Music Educators Nat. Conf., Ark. Elem. Music Assn. (sec.-treas. 1968—77). Republican. Lutheran. Avocations: cats, knitting, travel. Died Mar. 3, 2006.

MYERS-TURNER, DARAUGH ANNE, architect; b. Lock Haven, Pa., July 16, 1956; d. Marceau Chevalier and Judity May (Kleine) M.; m. William Reynolds Turner, Aug. 8, 1981; 1 child, Ashley Anne. BA, Bucknell U., 1978; MArch, Rice U., 1983. Designer Marks & Salley, Inc., Houston, 1979-81, Thompson-Frater Assocs., Houston, 1985-87, L. Barry Davidson Architects, Houston, 1987-88; owner Design Svcs., Houston, from 1988. Chair cultural arts Harvard Elem. PTA, Houston, 1989-90; vol. Channel 8 Pub. TV. Mem. Proctor Plaza Civic Club. Died Feb. 14, 2005.

MYRONUK, DONALD JOSEPH, consulting mechanical engineer, forensic engineer; b. Kapuskasing, Ont., Can., Apr. 11, 1939; came to U.S., 1964; s. John and Amelia (Yzchstaulyn) M.; m. Barbara Bonch, Aug. 13, 1966; children: Kathryn, Jennifer, Lara. Bc, Queen's U., Kingston, Ont., 1961, MSc, 1965; PhD, U. Ill., 1969. Registered profl. engr., Calif.; lic. pvt. investigator, Calif. Design engr. Atomic Energy Can., Chalk River, Ont., 1961-62, 64; prof. mech. engring. San Jose (Calif.) State U., 1969-92, assoc. dean engring., 1981-86, mem. acad. senate, 1990-92; cons. mech. engr., San Jose, from 1992; chief investigator DJM Investigations, San Jose, from 1992. Rsch. scientist hot surface ignition of aircraft fluids NASA, 1976-81. Bd. dirs. Santa Clara Valley chpt. Am. Lung Assn., 1975-77, Santa Clara Valley Sci. and Engring. Fair Assn., 1976—, San Jose State U. Found., 1982-89. Named Outstanding Prof., San Jose State U. Sch. Engring., 1981, 87. Fellow Am. Acad. Forensic Science (engring. exec. com. 1993—, engring. program chmn. 1993-94, A.H. Payne spl. achievement award 1993); mem. ASME (faculty advisor 1978-91, R. Fitz Leadership award 1992), Soc. Automotive Engrs. (R.R. Teetor award 1973), Nat. Forensic Ctr. Democrat. Evangelical. Avocations: music, painting, native art, fossicking, mining. Died Sept. 10, 2004.

MYSLIWIEC, CHRISTINE ROSE, secondary school educator, educator; b. Rochester, N.Y., Mar. 19, 1950; d. Casmer J. and Virginia M. (Siwicki) M. AA, AS, St. Petersburg (Fla.) Jr. Coll, 1981; BA, U. South Fla., Tampa, 1984. Cert. elem. tchr. Math tchr. Diocese St. Petersburg, 1984-86, Pinellas County Sch. Bd., St. Petersburg, 1986-88, Hillsborough County Sch. Bd., Tampa, from 1988. Mem. Suncoast Assn. Tchr. Tng., Kappa Delta Pi (sec. 1983-86). Home: Saint Petersburg, Fla. Died Dec. 10, 2004.

NADLER, MYRON JAY, lawyer, director; b. Youngstown, Ohio, July 22, 1923; s. Murray A. and Jean (Davis) N.; m. Alice Blue, Nov. 4, 1951; children: Jed M., Wendy D., John M.S. Student, N.Mex. State Coll., 1943-44; BS in Econs. Wharton Sch., U. Pa., 1947; JD with distinction, U. Mich., 1949. Bar: Ohio 1950. Pres., shareholder Nadler, Nadler & Burdman Co., L.P.A., Youngstown, 1950-95, pres., 1950-95; ret., 1996. Asst. editor Mich. Law Rev., 1949; instr. Youngstown U. Law Sch., 1952-59. Author: (with Saul Nadler) Nadler on Bankruptcy, 1965, April's Bankruptcy Forms and Practice, 1964; contbr. articles to profl. jours. Chmn. exec. budget com. United Appeal, Youngstown, 1964-66, v.p., 1967-70; co-chmn. Mayor's Commn. Human Rights, 1957; mem. Mahoning County Planning Commn., 1965-71, Nat. Budget and Consultation Com., 1967-70; trustee Cmty. Corp., Youngstown, v.p., 1977-82, chmn. pers. com., 1974-92; bd. dirs. Ctr. for Learning, Villa Maria, Pa., 1969-95, pres., 1981-89, chmn. bd., 1989-94. With AUS, 1943-45. Decorated Purple Heart with oak leaf cluster, Combat Infantryman's badge. Mem. Fellows of Ohio Bar Assn. Found., ABA, Ohio Bar Assn., Mahoning County Bar Assn., Scribes Assn. Legal Writers, Comml. Law League Am., Squaw Creek Country Club (pres. 1966-68), Hamlet Country Club. Died Sept. 14, 2005.

NADLER, SCOTT FREDERIC, sports medicine educator; b. Bklyn., Sept. 19, 1964; s. Allen and Judith Nadler; m. Jodi Sue Nadler, May 10, 1997; children: Sydni Michelle, Haley Elizabeth. BA, Rutgers U., 1986; DO, U. Med. Dental Sch. N.J., 1990. Intern Kennedy Meml. Hosp., Stratford, N.J., 1990-91; resident and chief resident in rehab. medicine U. Medicine and Dental N.J., Newark, 1991-94, prof. rehab. medicine, from 2003, dir. sports medicine, from 1999; sports medicine fellow Kessler Inst., West Orange, N.J., 1994-95; med. faculty U.S. Figure Skating, from 2000; U.S. team physician 2004 World Figure Skating Championships. Med. dir. Prudential Inst. Co., Roseland, N.J., 1997-99, Horizon Casualty Svcs., Newark, 1997—; cons. Procter & Gamble Co., Cin., 1998—; mem. adv. bd. Elan Pharms., San Francisco, 1998—2002. Contbr. articles to profl. jours. Rsch. grantee Procter & Gamble, 1998, 2001, 03, Elan Pharms., 1999. Fellow Am. Coll. Sports Medicine, Am. Acad. Phys. Medicine and Rehab., Assn. Acad. Physiatrists, Physiat. Assn. Spine Sports Occupational Rehab.; mem. Am. Coll. Occupational/Environ. Medicine, N.Am. Spine Soc. Avocations: fishing, golf, travel, rock/fossil collecting. Home: Randolph, NJ. Died Dec. 26, 2004.

NAFTULIN, ROSE, artist; b. Phila., Aug. 31, 1925; d. Morris and Sara (Goldman) Freedman; m. Morton Naftulin, Mar. 17, 1945 (dec. 1977); children: Louis, Elise, Nancy. Student, Phila. Coll. Art, 1944—45, Barnes Found., 1962—64. Tchr. Cheltenham Art Ctr., Pa., 1961-79, Woodmere Art Mus., Phila., 1977-81; free-lance painter Wyndmoor, Pa., 1961—2005. Represented by Gross McCleaf Gallery, Phila., Kornbluth-Walker Gallery, Fairlawn, N.J. Represented in permanent collections Burlington Industries, Johnson and Johnson Co., Provident Bank, Phila., Shnader, Harrison, SEgal and Lewis, Phila., E.I. DuPont de Nemours and Co., Fed. Nat. Mortgage Assn., Woodmere Art Mus., Prescott Forbes, Butler Inst Art, Ohio, N.J. State Art Mus., Bryn Mawr Coll., Pa.; numerous pvt. collections, U.S., Can. Recipient Cert. Merit Nat. Acad. Design, Purchase prizse Woodmere Art Mus., David Humphreys prize Allied Artists Am. Died Dec. 11, 2005.

NAGATA, GLENN MASAYOSHI, lawyer; b. Tokyo, Jan. 29, 1957; came to U.S., 1965; s. Gilbert Y. and Kimie (Aizawa) N.; m. Sheryl Lee Aruga, Nov. 11, 1985. BA in Econs. and Polit. Sci., U. Hawaii-Manoa, Honolulu, 1979; JD, U. Hawaii-Manoa, 1982. Bar: Hawaii 1982, U.S. Dist. Ct. Hawaii 1982, U.S. Ct. Appeals (9th cir.) 1991. Atty. at law Kuniyuki & Chang, Honolulu, 1982-97. Mem. med. claims conciliation panel Dept. Commerce and Consumer Affairs, Honolulu, 1986—; hearings officer Adminstrn. Driver Lic. Revocation Office, Honolulu, 1992—. Mem. Neighborhood Bd. #5, Honolulu, 1987-88, vol. Hawaii Lawyers Care, 1997—. Mem. ABA, Hawaii State Bar Assn. (treas. young lawyers divsn. 1989-91), Hawaii Inst. CLE 1998—. Home: Honolulu, Hawaii. Died Aug. 25, 2005.

NAGY, ROBERT HENRY, manufacturing executive, real estate developer; b. Milw., Aug. 24, 1937; s. Henry and Marie (Jaeger) N.; m. Dorothy Bonell Clark, June 23, 1961; children: John Robert, Wendy Christine, Daniel Andrew. BA, Ripon Coll., 1959. Salesman Spancrete Industries, Inc., Waukesha, Wis., 1956-63, mktg. mgr., 1960-63, v.p., 1963-68, pres., 1968-86, COO, 1986-91, pres., COO, from 1991. Patentee spancrete machines. Republican. Lutheran. Avocations: hunting, fishing, computers. Home: Hartland, Wis. Died June 6, 2004.

NAHUMCK, NADIA CHILKOVSKY, performer, dance educator, choreographer, author; b. Kiev, Ukraine, Jan. 8, 1908; came to U.S., 1914; d. Moiseiy Nicholas and Bela (Segalova) Chilkovsky; m. Nicholas Nahumck, Mar. 1940 (dec. Nov. 1994). BS in Edn., Temple U., 1928; MusD, Combs Coll. Music, 1971; postgrad., U. Pa., 1973-74; D Dance (hon.), Phila. Coll. Performing Arts, 1979. Founder, dir. Phila. Dance Acad., 1946-77; dean sch. dance Phila. Coll. Performing Arts (now Univ. Arts), 1977-79, dean emeritus, 1979—2006. Instr. Curtis Inst. Music, Phila., 1946-68, Acad. Vocal Arts, Phila., 1958-78; vis. lectr. Temple U., Phila., 1944-45, 67, 69, Swarthmore (Pa.) Coll., 1958-60, Thomas Jefferson U., 1976; lectr. in dance ethnology U. Pa. Mus., 1973-76; vis. rsch. scholar Rhodes U., 1977; founder Performing Arts Sch. for combined arts and acad. edn., 1962. Author: Three R's for Dancing, book I, 1953, book II, 1956, book III, 1960, My First Dance Book, 1954, Isadora Duncan: The Dances, 1994, Ten Dances in Labanotation, 1955, Three R's for Dancing, 1955, 3d edit., 1960, Short Modern Dances in Labanotation, 1957, American Bandstand Dances, 1959, Introduction to Dance Literacy, 1978, Dance Curriculum Resource Guide, 1980, Interpretation of the Labanotated Duncan Dance Scores, 2000; contbr. articles to profl. jours.; choreographer 75 works including 5 with Phila. Orch., 1947-50; prodr. 17 dance films for classroom use. Mary Wigman Profl. Dance Sch./Steinway Hall scholar, 1931-32; grantee U.S. Office of Edn., 1965-67, Wenner-Gren Found., 1965, 73. Fellow Internat. Coun. Kinetography Laban; mem. Internat. Isadora Duncan Inst. Coun., Soc. Ethnomusicology (coun. 1958-63, Svc. award 1976, master notator 1965-2006), Nat. Mus. Women in the Arts (charter mem.). Avocations: language studies, music, gardening, mentoring young students, reading. Home: Seattle, Wash. Died Apr. 23, 2006.

NALAND, PATRICIA MAE, psychotherapist; b. Lincoln, Nebr., Sept. 16, 1937; d. Lester Lavern and Nelda Minneta (Doran) Sherman; m. Paul Robert Naland, Sept. 14, 1958; children: Robert, Randall, Kristina Naland Geer, Katherine, Karen Naland Freeman. B Journalism, U. Mo., 1959; MS in Counseling, U. Wis.-Stout, Menomonie, 1990. Cert. profl. counselor, marriage and family therapist, clin. social worker, Wis. Therapist West Iowa Cmty. Mental Health Ctr., Sac City, Iowa, 1990-91; instr. Iowa Ctrl. C.C., Ft. Dodge, 1991-93; family therapist Quakerdale, Manning, Iowa, 1991-93; therapist Family Support Ctr., Chippewa Falls, Wis., 1994-97; psychotherapist Luth. Social Svcs., Menomonie and Eau Claire, Wis., from 1995. Home: Menomonie, Wis. Died May 16, 2004.

NANASI, MADONNA, reading educator; b. Bogalusa, La., Dec. 26, 1936; d. Maxwell Redus and Elizabeth Ann (Harkins) Pollard; m. Laszlo Nanasi; 1 child, Michael Andras. BA, U. Detroit, 1971; MAT in reading, Oakland U., 1978. Cert. elem. and secondary tchr. Past dist. dir. of compensatory edn./reading specialist Anchor Bay Sch. Dist., New Baltimore, Mich., reading cons., chpt. I instr. tchr. assistance team bldg. coord. Pres. Macomb Reading Coun. 1993-94; adj. prof. U. Detroit; invited U.S./China Joint Conf. Edn., Reading, Beijing, 1992, Oakland U., 1999—; guest presenter Oakland U., 1992; mem. state and local com. for early literacy, participant writing of Mich. Litercy Progress Profile, 1996-2001, trainer, 1998—; trainer tchrs. for Playful Literacy Program for Presch. Educators, 2001—; adj. prof. Oakland U., 1998—. Author: (handbook) Whole Language, Whole Books, Whole Child, 1991; co-author: (curriculum guide) Integrating Language Arts in Science and Math Using Children's Literature, 1994. Mem. Macomb Reading Specialist Com. Mem. Mich. Reading Assn., Internat. Reading Assn., Alpha Delta Kappa (past pres.). Home: Sterling Heights, Mich. Died Mar. 23, 2004.

NANCE, NOLETA, dentist; b. Hindsville, Ark., Sept. 6, 1908; d. Lucy (Eld) Nance. DDS, Washington U., St. Louis, 1942. Pvt. practice, Fayetteville, Ark., from 1942. Mem. Order of Eastern Star. Died Jan. 14, 2004.

NARELL, IRENA, freelance writer, history educator; b. Sanok, Poland, Sept. 17, 1923; came to U.S., 1939; d. Abraham and Antonina Penzik; m. Murray Narell, June 29, 1945 (dec. Jan. 1991); children: Jeff, Andrew. BS, Columbia U., 1969. Asst. to Polish UN Delegation, N.Y.C., 1945-51; owner Art Originals Gallery, N.Y.C., 1961-63, 1964-69; co-mgr. The Steel Bandits—a mus. group. Project dir. San Francisco Jews-Old Traditions on a New Frontier, bicentennial exhibit Judah L. Magnes Mus., Cmty. and Diversity, Bay Area Jewish Families, 1989, Inst. for Hist. Study. Mem. editl. bd.: Western States Jewish History; author: Ashes to the Taste, 1961, The Invisible Passage, 1969, Joshua Fighter for Bar Kochba, 1978 (Nat. Jewish Book award 1979), Our City: The Jews of San Francisco, 1981, History's Choice, 1996; contbr. numerous short stories, revs. and articles to profl. jours. and mags.; translator: Holy Week (Jerzy Andrzejewski) Samson (Kazimierz Brandys), Summer in Nohant (Jaroslaw Iwaszkiewicz), Poetry by Julian Tuwim. Mem. Jewish Arts Cmty. of the Bay, San Francisco, 1975-96. Mem. Inst. Hist. Study. Jewish. Avocations: swimming, collecting art and antiques. Home: Oakland, Calif. Died Mar. 15, 2004.

NARWOLD, LEWIS LAMMERS, JR., paper products manufacturer; b. Cleve., Sept. 4, 1921; s. Lewis Lammers and Dorothy Marie (Andrus) N.; m. Marilyn Ebner, Oct. 26, 1944; 1 dau., Christine. BBA, Western Res. U., 1942; MBA, Harvard, 1947. Salesman Hoerner Boxes, Inc., 1950-54, gen. sales mgr., 1954-57, v.p., gen. mgr., 1957-62; v.p. So. div. Hoerner Waldorf Corp., St. Paul, 1962-70; sr. v.p., container div. Hoerner Waldorf Corp., 1970-72; founder, pres., CEO SouthWest Packaging Inc., Tulsa, 1972—2006. Dir. UNCA Bankshares, Utica Nat. Bank & Trust, Thermo Chem. Corp., Sooner Box Corp., Hoerner Boxes, Inc., So. Mo. Container Corp.; organizer 1st Bank & Trust Co. of Okla. Chmn. United Fund of Sand Springs, Okla.; pres., trustee Tulsa Charity Horse Show.; Trustee Children's Med. Center of Tulsa, Tulsa Psychiat. Clinic, U. of the Ozarks. Capt. USMC, 1943-45. Decorated Purple Hearts; recipient Presdl. Citation. Mem. Sand Springs C. of C. (dir.), Tulsa C. of C. (dir.), N.A.M., Tulsa Mfg. Club, Mason Club, Summit Club (dir. and organizer), So. Hills Country Club, Union League Club (Chgo.), Coves Golf Club. Home: Tulsa, Okla. Died June 19, 2006.

NASH, N. FREDERICK, retired librarian; b. Brockton, Mass., Apr. 18, 1936; s. Norman Blake and Emily Hazel (Dahlborg) N. AB, Harvard U., 1960; M.L.S., Rutgers U., 1964. Asst. reference librarian U. Md., College Park, 1964-67, serials cataloger, 1967; circulation librarian U. Ill.-Urbana, 1967-69, rare book librarian, curator of rare books, 1969—97, assoc. prof. library adminstrn. Author: An American Bookshelf, 1776; (with Marcella Grendler) The Renaissance at Illinois, 1980; contbr. articles on library history and hist. bibliography to profl. publs. Mem. ALA, Bibliog. Soc. Am., Bibliog. Soc. London, Assn. Coll. and Rsch. Librs. (sec. rare books and manuscripts sect. 1975-78, exec. bd. 1980-83). Episcopalian. Avocations: choral singing, book collecting. Home: Urbana, Ill. Died May 29, 2006.

NASH, PAUL, composer, artistic director; b. Bronx, N.Y., Feb. 19, 1948; s. Al and Anne (Gelman) N. BM in Music Composition, Berklee Coll. of Music, 1972; MA in Music Composition, Mills Coll., 1976. Composer-in-residence San Francisco Sch. Dist., 1977-78; dir. Paul Nash Ensemble, San Francisco, 1977-81; artistic dir. Bay Area Jazz Composers Orch., San Francisco, 1987-88, Manhattan New Music Project, N.Y.C., 1989—2005. Dir. Creative Arts Lab., Columbia Tchrs. Coll., 1994-95; cons. in field. Composer classical works, including Sostenuto, 1982, Seven Affections, 1989, Wind Over the Lake, 1989, Synchronicity, 1990, Guitar Etudes, 1995; recordings A Jazz Composers Ensemble, 1979, Second Impression, 1985, Night Language, 1987, Mood Swing, 1993; musical score for Macbeth, 1979; performed with Chambers Symphony San Francisco, 1989, JVC Jazz Festival N.Y., 1997, Musical Elements, 1986, Concordance, 1989. Fellow U. Calif.-Berkeley, 1986, NEA, 1988, 94, Djerassi Found., 1990, MacDowell Colony, 1982, Yaddo, 1992, Banff Centre, 1993; grantee Meet the Composer Calif., 1989, David and Lucile Packard Found., 1987. Mem. Am. Composers Alliance (bd. dirs. 1989-92). Home: New York, NY. Died Jan. 27, 2005.

NASHOFER, RACHELLE LEAH, writer; b. Bklyn., Nov. 23, 1959; d. Bernard Louis and Mildred charlotte (Fenster) N. BS, Yeshiva U., 1981. EDP auditor CCT Kasing, Woodmere, N.Y., 1981-82, Am. Savs. Bank, Manhattan, N.Y., 1982-83; auditor IRS, Manhattan, 1983-84; EDP auditor L.I. Savs. Bank, Centereach, N.Y., 1985-87; programmer/cons. Internat. Paper, Manhattan, 1987-88. Author book, screenplays: The Eyes of Tomorrow, 1986; composer songs: The International Reunion, 1988, The Strenght of a People, Trail of Happiness, 1996—, I'm Walking, My Salvation, My Brother, Resurrection. Mem. EDP Auditors Assn. (cert.). Home: Forest Hills, NY. Died Aug. 18, 2004.

NATALE-HOWARD, ANNE-MARIE, retired secondary school educator, computer scientist; b. Albion, N.Y., Dec. 6, 1952; d. Ralph Patrick and Julie Veronica (Quarantello) Natale; m. Douglas Eldene Howard, Oct. 23, 1982; children: Danielle, Nicholas. BA, St. Bonaventure U., 1975; postgrad., SUNY, Brockport, 1975-78, Ariz. State U., 1978, 90-92; paralegal cert., Sterling Sch., Phoenix, 1982. Tchr. 7th and 8th grades social studies Albion Ctrl. Sch. Dist., 1975-78; tchr. advanced placement govt., free enterprise Apollo High Sch., Glendale Union Dist., Glendale, Ariz., 1978-95, chair social studies dept., 1993-94; tchr. St. Mary's High Sch., Phoenix, 1995—2002, ret., 2002. Chmn. social studies St. Mary's HS, 1997—2000. Com. person Baker Com. for Pres. (Ariz.), Phoenix, 1980. Mem. NEA, Am. Polit. Sci. Assn. Republican. Roman Catholic. Home: Phoenix, Ariz. Died Feb. 5, 2005.

NATHAN, ADELE MARCIA, research director; b. N.Y.C., July 19, 1960; d. M. David and Myra (Lerner) N. Student, Queens Coll., 1978-84, De Anza Coll., 1989, Santa Monica Coll., 1994. Sales asst. Seltel, N.Y.C., 1984-85; buying asst. Botway Libov, N.Y.C., 1985-86; sr. broadcast negiotiator, data syss. coord. Grey Advt., N.Y.C., 1986-89; customer svc. mgr. Mktg. Resources Plus, Palo Alto, Calif., 1989-90; rsch. mgr. Galavision, L.A., 1990-93; rsch. dir. KWHY-TV, L.A., 1993-94. Pres. A.M.N. Graphic Solutions, L.A., 1993—. Mem. Am. women in Radio and Television, Am. Mktg. Assn., L.A. Television Sta. Rsch. Com., Ad-Club L.A., Hollywood Radio and Television Soc. Died Dec. 18, 2004.

NATHAN, MARK RYAN, producer, musician; b. Denver, June 9, 1971; s. Lawrence Alan Nathan and Sheryl Rich (Wolf) Ettinger. Student, U. New Haven, from 1990. Owner, entertainer After Hours Recording, Denver, 1984-90; disc jockey, entertainer Sweetness and Co., Denver, 1987-89; disc jockey New Eng., 1990; salesman Sam Ash, N.Y.C., from 1990. Arranger, writer for E-Street Dancers, 1988. Life mem. B'nai Brith Youth Orgn. Mem. Am. Engineers Soc. Jewish. Avocations: art, music, cartoonist, clay animation, producing/engineering. Died Mar. 20, 2005.

NAUGHTON, MICHAEL ARTHUR, biochemical educator; b. Crewe, Eng., June 23, 1926; came to U.S., 1959; s. Peter and Maude (Boughey) N.; m. Teresa, July 31, 1987; children: Stuart Shaw, Sean Patrick, Kathleen-Mary, Siobhan Michell. BS, U. St. Andrews, Scotland, 1952; PhD, Cambridge U., 1959. Rsch. assoc. MIT, Cambridge, 1959-62; assoc. prof. Johns Hopkins Med. Sch., Balt., 1962-67; sr. prin. rsch. scientist in animal genetics Commonwealth Sci. and Indsl. Rsch. Orgn., Ryde, Australia, 1967-72; prof. ob-gyn Genetics Biochemistry Sci. Ctr., U. Colo. Health Scis. Ctr., Denver, from 1970. Navigator RAF, 1944-48. Democrat. Home: Aurora, Colo. Died Apr. 18, 2004.

NAVICKAS, JOHN, retired fluid dynamics engineer, researcher, consultant; b. Reseiniai, Lithuania, Nov. 26, 1933; came to U.S., 1949; s. John and Ona (Remeikis) N.; m. Marija D. Masionis Navickas, Sept. 1, 1985; children: Rima, Rymante, Tadas, Dalia. BS, UCLA, 1957; MS, 1961. Tech. fellow The Boeing Co., Huntington Beach, Calif., 1957—2003, ret., 2003. Cons. Lloyd's Registry of Shipping, Eng., 1982, Am. Bur. Shipping, 1992, Nippon Kokan, Japan, 1979-82, Lithuania Acad. Sci., 1978, 82. Editor: Conference Proceedings Computational Experiments, 1989; author more than 40 articles on multi-phase fluid dynamics, computational methods and space systems. Com. mem. Lithuanian Childrens Hope, L.A., 1992—. Capt. U.S. Army, 1957-65. Mem. ASME, AIAA. Home: Westlake Village, Calif. Died June 4, 2004.

NAYLOR, CHARLES ROBERT, JR., lawyer; b. Columbia, Ky., May 3, 1944; s. Charles Robert and Virginia Mae (Yarberry) N.; m. Sally Kathryn Schoen, Nov. 7, 1969; 1 child, Richard. BA, Ohio State U., 1966, JD, 1969. Bar: Ohio 1969. Sec., gen. counsel Corco, Inc., Columbus, Ohio, 1972-76; sec., gen. counsel Flavorland Industries, Denver, 1976-78; v.p. labor relations Dubuque (Iowa) Packing Co., 1978-82; v.p., gen. counsel FDL Foods, Inc., Dubuque, from 1982. Bd. dirs. FDL Foods, Inc. Capt. U.S. Army, 1970-72. Mem. ABA, Ohio State Bar Assn., Am. Meat Inst. (legal com.). Democrat. Episcopalian. Avocations: skiing, antiques, travel, cooking. Home: Dubuque, Iowa. Died July 30, 2005.

NEAL, ALBERT HARVEY, retired minister; b. Morganton, Ark., Apr. 4, 1925; s. Albert Wilburn ad Alma Fay (Bittle) N.; m. Barbara Jean Sly, Oct. 28, 1946 (div. Jan. 1984); children: Brenda L. Wood, Linda Caroll, Ronda Jean Easter; m. Betty Lu Dunn Beasley, Sept. 25, 1987. DD (hon.), Sch. Bible Theology, San Jacinto, Calif., 1989. Ordained to ministry Pentecostal Ch. of God, 1950. Pastor, Yreka, Calif., Farmersville, Calif., 1949-55; dir. Indian missions, 1955-65; dist. supt. Pacific NW Dist., 1965-77; world missions field rep., 1977-79; pastor Longview, Wash., 1979-82, Grover City, Calif., Kelseyville, Calif., 1982-90. Area sales dir. Bennie Harris Assocs., 1973-91; asst. gen. supt. Pentecostal Ch. of God, Joplin, Mo., 1973-77. With USN, 1942-46, PTO. Decorated Presdl. Unit Citation, Philippines Liberation with 2 stars, South Pacific ribbon with 9 stars. Republican. Home: Ceres, Calif. Died Oct. 25, 2004.

NEAL, ANITA, artist; b. Glendale, Calif., June 13, 1929; d. Frank Bartholdy and Dora Mae (Jones) Mendelssohn; m. James Truman Dowdle, Jan. 17, 1948 (dec. Nov. 1969); children: Doug Dowdle, Wendy Grobe; m. Albert Dale Neal, July 2, 1971. AA, Golden West Coll., 1981; ind. study art, culture and calligraphy, China, 2000; ind. study, Alphonsa Mucha, Chez Republic, 2002. Lic. real estate agt., Calif.; cert. Coastline C.C. Dist. Tchg. Host Friends of Artists for Cultural Exch., 1988; judge Ms. Sr. Am. Pageant, 1989—91; founder The ANCA Group. Exhibited in group shows New Calif. Mus. of Sci. and Industry, L.A., 1968, New Art in N.Y., N.Y.C., 1985, Laguna Art Mus., Laguna Beach, Calif., 1986, Loyola Marymount U., Orange, Calif., 1986, Bowers Mus., Santa Ana, Calif., 1987, Expo Site Plaza of Nations, Vancouver, 1988, Irvine (Calif.) Fine Arts Ctr., 1989, Chautauqua Invitational Exhibit U. Calif., Irvine, 1989, Berkley (Calif.) U., 1994, U. Calif., Irvine, 1999; artist in charge of Orange County, Calif., children's mural Imagination Celebration, NEA, Washington, 1987-96; performance artist Richard Bennett Gallery, L.A., 1989; prodr.: (shows) Coconut Grove-Calif. Girl, L.A., 1970; prodr., publicist Airport, City of Santa Monica, 1968; featured artist: How to Market Fine Art by Sally Prince Davis. Sponsor 32 artists Anita Neal Contemporary Art, Laguna Beach, 1986-87; mem. artist coun. bd. Laguna Art Mus., Laguna Beach, 1986; mem. allied arts bd. City of Huntington Beach, Calif., 1988; sponsor So. Calif. Artists, Anita Neal Gallery, Fawnskin, Calif., 1994—. Co-winner Mademoiselle mag. writing contest, 1970; recipient LULU award Women in Advt., 1968, New Art in New York (NANY) award, 1985, Golden Web award, 2003—. Mem. Am. Portrait Soc., Artist's Equity Assn. (L.A. chpt.), Orange County Visual Artists, L.A. Inst. Contemporary Art, Nat. Mus. Women in Arts (charter), L.A. Contemporary Art Assocs., Coun. of Arts State of Calif. Artist Registry, Alpha Gamma Sigma (Sigma Pi chpt.). Republican. Avocations: airplane pilot, european museum studies, helping emerging artists, poetry. Home: Huntington Beach, Calif. Died Jan. 30, 2005.

NEAL, SISTER MARIE AUGUSTA, sociology educator; b. Boston, June 22, 1921; d. Thomas Francis and Helen Agnes (Taylor) N. AB, Emmanuel Coll., 1942; MA, Boston Coll., 1953; PhD, Harvard U., 1963; LHD (hon.), The Elms, Chocopee, Mass., 1979, St. Michael's Coll., Winooski, Vt., 1987; LLD (hon.), Notre Dame U., 1985. Joined Sisters of

Notre Dame de Namur, Roman Cath. Ch. High sch. tchr. St. Augustine Sch., South Boston, Mass., 1946-47, St. Mary Lawrence Sch., Lawrence, Mass., 1947-53; tchr. Emmanuel Coll., Boston, 1953-91, emerita, from 1991. Vis. prof. sociology U. Calif., Berkeley, 1969; vis. prof. sociology of religion Harvard U., Cambridge, Mass., 1973-75, vis. lectr. Divinity Sch., 1982-83; dir. rsch. Leadership Conf. Women Religious, Washington, 1966-74, 80, 89, South African Cath. Edn. Study, 1970-71; lectr. in field. Author: Values and Interests in Social Change, 1965, A Sociotheology of Letting Go, 1977, Catholic Sisters in Transition, 1984, Just Demands of the Poor, 1987, From Nuns to Sisters, 1990. Area chair Gov.'s Commn. on Status of Women, Mass., 1964-67; mem. adv. com. ACLU, Mass., 1972-75; bd. dirs. Women's Theol. Ctr., 1980-89, Cath. Com. on Intellectual and Cultural Affairs, 1973-76; bd. advisors U.S. Cath. Conf. of Bishops, 1970-71. Ford Found. faculty fellow, 1974-76; recipient Pope John XXIII award New Rochelle Coll., 1985, Ecumenical award Xavier U., 1988. Fellow Am. Sociol. Assn. (Disting. Tchr. award 1986), Soc. for Sci. Study of Religion (pres. 1982-84); mem. Assn. for Sociology of Religion (pres. 1971-72). Democrat. Avocations: comparing the media, justice and peace edn. Home: Roslindale, Mass. Died Feb. 25, 2004.

NEARY, GERALD CLARKE, lawyer; b. N.Y.C., Dec. 27, 1932; s. Gerald Patrick and Rita Augusta (Cating) N.; m. Mary Alice Gerstell, May 26, 1962 (div. 1972); children: Elizabeth B., Mary Louise. Student Yale U., 1950-52, AB, 1957; LLB, NYU, 1963. Bar: N.Y. 1964, N.J. 1973, U.S. Ct. Appeals (3d cir.). Assoc. Milbank, Tweed, Hadley & McCloy, N.Y.C., 1963-69, 71-72; staff tax atty. Rockefeller Family and Assocs., N.Y.C., 1969-71; ptnr. Pitney, Hardin, Kipp & Szuch, Morristown, N.J., 1972—. Mem. ABA (tax sect.), N.Y. State Bar Assn. (tax sect.), N.J. State Bar Assn. (tax sect., chmn. 1980-81). Republican. Roman Catholic. Home: Belle Mead, NJ. Died Mar. 1, 2005.

NEASE, STEPHEN WESLEY, retired academic administrator; b. Everett, Mass., Jan. 15, 1925; s. Floyd William and Madeline Anzelette (Nostrand) N.; m. Dorothy Christine Hardy, June 17, 1946; children: Linda Carol Nease Scott, Floyd William II, Stephen Wesley Jr., David Wayne, Melissa Jo Nease Wallace. AB, Brown U., 1946; Th.B., Eastern Nazarene Coll., 1947, D.D., 1966; Ed.M., Boston U., 1956; postgrad., Harvard Div. Sch., 1946-48. Ordained to ministry Ch. of the Nazarene, 1951; pastor East Side Ch. of the Nazarene, Newark, Ohio, 1948-50; dean men, instr. religion Ea. Nazarene Coll., Wollaston, Mass., 1950-53, dir. devel., 1953-66, pres. emeritus, 1966—2006; founding pres. Mt. Vernon (Ohio) Nazarene Coll., 1966-72, pres. emeritus, 1972—2006; pres. Bethany (Okla.) Nazarene Coll., 1973-76, Nazarene Theol. Sem., Kansas City, Mo., 1976-80, Eastern Nazarene Coll., Wollaston, Mass., 1981-89; edn. commr. Ch. of the Nazarene, 1989-94; exec. dir. Capital and Endowment Devel., Mt. Vernon, Ohio, from 1994. Served with USNR, 1943-46. Died Apr. 6, 2006.

NEBIKER, JOHN HERBERT, civil engineer; b. Eastport, Maine, May 26, 1936; s. Fred John and Ilse Gertrud (Kündig) N.; m. Ursula Hunter, May 26, 1962; children: David, Steven. BSCE, MIT, 1958; DSc in Tech., Swiss Fed. Poly., Zurich, Switzerland, 1965. Diplomate Am. Acad. Environ. Engrs. Asst. prof. Vanderbilt U., Nashville, 1965-67, U. Mass., Amherst, 1967-69; sr. v.p. Curran Assocs., Inc., Northampton, Mass., 1969-72; sanitary engr. WHO, Geneva, 1972-75; environ. engr. Malcolm Pirnie, Inc., White Plains, N.Y., 1975-79; sanitary engr. World Bank, Washington, 1979-84, procurement advisor, 1984-91, cons. svcs. advisor, 1991-93, procurement policy advisor, from 1993. Mem. ASCE. Avocations: tennis, travel. Died Aug. 21, 2005.

NE'EMAN, YUVAL, Israeli government official, physics educator; b. Tel Aviv, May 14, 1925; s. G'daliyahu and Zipporah Ne'e.; m. Dvora Rubinstein-Schiff, 1951; children: Anath, Tidal. BSME, Technion U., Haifa, Israel, 1945, cert. in ME, 1946; PhD, London U., 1962; DSc (hon.), Israel Inst. Tech., Haifa, 1966, Yeshiva U., 1972, Clausthal Tech. U., 1990. Group leader Israel Soreq Research, Israel, 1961-63; asst. prof. Tel Aviv U., Israel, 1962, prof. physics, 1965, Pollak chair of physics, 1969-76, pres., 1971-75, Wolfson chair extrodinary in theoretical physics, from 1977, dir. Sackler Inst. Advanced Studies, from 1979; research fellow Calif. Inst. Tech., Pasadena, 1963-64, vis. prof., 1964-65; prof. physics U. Tex., Austin, 1968, dir. Ctr. for Particle Theory, 1968; mem. Knesset, Jerusalem, 1981-90; min. sci. and devel. Israeli Cabinet, Jerusalem, 1982-84, min. sci. and tech., min. energy and infrastructure, 1990-92. Mem. Israel AEC, 1965-82, acting chmn., 1982-84, def. chief scientist, 1974-76; chmn. Hatehiya Pty., 1979-92, Israel Space Agy., 1982; assoc. mem. Inst. Strategic Studies, 1959-80. Author: The Eightfold Way, 1964, Algebraic Theory of Particle Physics, 1964, The Past Decade of Particle Theory, 1973, Symmetries, Jauges et Varietes de Groupes, 1979, Group Theoretical Methods in Physics, 1980, To Fulfill a Vision, 1981, The Particle Hunters, 1986 (transl. into Spanish, Italian, Hebrew, German, Japanese), (with Barut and Bohm) Dynamical Groups and Spectrum Generating Algebras, 1989; other lecture series, 1984; contbr. over 300 articles to profl. jours.; reviewer profl. books. Pres. Nat. Assn. for Children with Mental Deficiencies, 1969-75; active Pub. Com. for USSR Jewry, 1971-82; chmn. Scientists Com. for USSR Jewry, 1971-82; bd. govs. Israel Coun. on Fgn. Rels., 1987—. Col. Israeli Def. Forces 1948-60. Named assoc. Internat. Ctr. for Theoretical Physics UN, 1965-68; recipient Weizmann Prize for Exact Scis., 1966, Rothschild Prize, 1968, Israel Prize for the Exact Scis., 1969, Albert Einstein medal and award, 1970, Coll. de France Medal, 1972, Wigner medal, 1982. Fellow Am. Phys. Soc., Inst. Physics and Phys. Soc.; mem. Israel Nat. Acad. Scis. and Humanities, Israel Phys. Soc., Internat. Astron. Union (mem. commn. 47 Cosmology, 48 High Energy Astrophysics), AAAS (fgn. hon. mem.), Nat. Acad. Scis. U.S. (fgn. assoc.), N.Y. Acad. Scis. (hon. life mem.), Imperial Coll. (diploma 1962), Acad. des Scis. Paris (presented 1972). Jewish. Died Apr. 26, 2005.

NEFF, EDWARD JOHN, accountant; b. North Hackensack, N.J., July 1, 1924; s. George Jacob and Anna Gladys (Sindle) N.; m. Francine Irving, July 7, 1948; children: Sindle Neff Tomforde, Edward Vann. BBA, U. N.Mex., 1947. CPA, N.Mex. Founding ptnr. Neff and Co. CPA's, Albuquerque, from 1947; pres. Clifford Corp. Mgmt., Albuquerque, from 1986. Bd. dirs. Albuquerque Community Coun., 1962, Albuquerque Symphony Orch., 1969-72, N.Mex. Neurol. Found., 1968-73, Albuquerque Little Theatre, 1970-72, Friends of Indian Pueblo Cultural Ctr. 2nd lt. U.S. Army, ETO. Mem. N.Mex. Soc. CPA's (pres. 1958-59), N.Mex. Estate Planning Coun. (pres. 1962), Am. Inst. CPA's (coun. mem. at large 1974, com. taxation 1964-67, com. mng. acctg. practice 1971-74), Am. Mgmt. Assn., Phi Delta Theta (treas. 1946-48). Clubs: 4 Hills Country (Albuquerque) (charter, bd. trustees 1958, v.p.). Republican. Episcopalian. Home: Albuquerque, N.Mex. Died Jan. 21, 2005.

NEHER, THOMAS BEERY, sales executive; b. Dayton, Ohio, Sept. 14, 1936; s. Robert Roy and Francis Lucille (Rudy) N.; m. Wendy Rae Woodward, Sept. 13, 1969 (div. Dec. 1975); 1 child, Kimberly Ann. AA, Phoenix Coll., 1958. Sr. buyer Del Mar Engrng., Irving, Calif., 1971-75; sales person Woods Co., Burbank, Calif., 1975-76; buyer Bendix, Sylmar, Calif., 1976-79; sr. buyer CitiCorp/TTI, Santa Monica, Calif., from 1979. Served with U.S. Army, 1955-62. Mem.: Eagles (pres. Lakewood, Calif., 1974-75). Republican. Methodist. Avocations: gardening, musician, bowling. Home: Artesia, Calif. Died Apr. 3, 2004.

NEHRLING, ARNO HERBERT, JR., retired chemical company executive; b. Richmond, Ind., Mar. 5, 1928; s. Arno Herbert and Irene Thelma (Dahlberg) N.; m. Mary Helen Mudd, Jan. 11, 1958; children: Amy Irene Nehrling Belz, Dorothy Louise Nehrling Murphy. BA, Cornell U., 1950; MBA, Harvard U., 1955. Various supervisory and mgmt. positions E.I. DuPont de Nemours & Co., Wilmington, Del., 1955-64, dir. fin. Dusseldorf, Fed. Republic Germany and Mexico City, 1965-71, asst. mgr. credit div., asst. mgr. treasury div., asst. mgr. fgn. and banking div. Wilmington, Del., 1972-76, asst. treas., dir. employee compensation and benefits, from 1977. Former pres. Geriatric Svcs. of Del., Inc.; chmn. Del. Health Info. Network. Mem. Health Resources Bd., Tuition Savings. Bd. Del., Health Care Com. Del. Mem. Fin. Execs. Inst. (past chmn. employee benefits com., past chmn. com. on other post employment benefits), Pension Investment Com. Del. Home: Timonium, Md. Died Aug. 23, 2005.

NEIHARDT, HILDA, foundation administrator, writer, educator, lawyer; b. Bancroft, Nebr., Dec. 6, 1916; d. John Gneisenau and Mona (Martinsen) N.; m. Albert Joseph Petri, Apr. 18, 1942 (div. Oct. 1963); children; Gail Petri Toedebusch, Robin, Coralie Joyce Hughes. AB, U. Nebr., 1937; postgrad., Letitia Barnum Sch. Theatre, Chgo., 1943-44; JD, U. Mo., 1963. Bar: Mo. 1963. Adminstrv. asst. Consulate of Switzerland, St. Louis, 1937-42; pvt. practice Columbia, Mo., 1963-85, Lake Ozark, Mo., 1985-88; pres. John G. Neihardt Found., Bancroft, 1987—2000. Lectr. in field. Author: Black Elk and Flaming Rainbow, 1995, Black Elk Lives, 2000; editor: The Giving Earth, 1991, The End of The Dream, 1991, The Ancient Memory, 1991. Trustee John G. Neihardt Trust, Columbia and Tekamah, Nebr., 1973-99; chmn. bd. dirs. John G. Neihardt Found., 2000-02; with USN, 1944-45. Mem. AAUW, Westerners, Internat. P.E.O. Avocations: boating, camping, horses. Home: Goodyear, Ariz. Died Dec. 2004.

NEIL, HERBERT EDWARD, JR., economist, consultant; b. Bridgeport, Conn., June 14, 1931; s. Herbert Edward and Florence Theresa (Storms) N.; m. Joan Ruth Nelson, May 2, 1953; children: Cynthia Ann, Stephen Bruce, Robert Mark, Marcia Ellen. AB, U. Mich., 1952, MBA, 1953, PhD, 1961. Trainee GE, Louisville, 1953; rsch. asst. Eastman Kodak Co., Rochester, N.Y., 1955-57, U. Mich., Ann Arbor, 1957-59; v.p. Harris Bank, Chgo., 1960-85; pres. Fin. & Econ. Strategies, Chgo., from 1985. Lectr. Roosevelt U., Chgo., 1969-70, U. Ill., Chgo., 1970-71, Lake Forest (Ill.) Sch. Mgmt., 1980, DePaul U., Chgo., 1982-89. Contbr. articles to profl. jours. Bd. dirs. Highland Park (Ill.)-Deerfield High Sch. Dist., 1968-74; precinct chmn. West Deerfield Dem. Com., 1976-84. With U.S. Army, 1953-55. Fellow Ford Found., 1959-60. Mem. Am. Econ. Assn., Am. Statis. Assn. (pres. Chgo. chpt. 1968-69, Crystal Ball Forecasting award 1964, 82), Nat. Assn. Bus. Economists (pres. Chgo. chpt. 1975-76, Forecasting award 1989). Mem. United Ch. of Christ. Avocations: golf, skiing, tennis, hiking, running. Home: Deerfield, Ill. Died July 12, 2005.

NEILSON, SUSAN BIEKE, federal judge; b. Ann Arbor, Mich., Aug. 27, 1956; d. Ronald and Sheila Bieke; m. Jeffrey Neilson; 2 children. AB, U. Mich., 1977; JD, Wayne State U., 1980. Bar: Mich. 1980. Assoc. Dickinson Wright PLLC, 1980—85, ptnr., 1986—91; judge 3d Jud. Ct. Mich., 1991—2005, US Ct. Appeals (6th cir.), 2005—06. Named Internat. Women of Distinction, Soroptimists, 1994. Mem.: State Bar Mich., Irish Am. Lawyers Soc., Women Lawyers Assn. Mich., Soroptimist Internat. Svc. Orgn. (past pres.), Explorer Scouts Detroit. Died Jan. 25, 2006.

NELLSON, JACK EVERETT, state official; b. Kearney, Nebr., June 15, 1934; s. Byron E. and Eleanor P. (Foster) N.; m. Joan Carroll, June 7, 1963; children: Susan, Sally A. AB in Edn., Kearney State Coll., 1956; postgrad., Kearney State U., 1959-63. High sch. prin., counselor Upland (Nebr.) Pub. Schs., 1961-62, Shelton (Nebr.) Pub. Schs., 1964-65; investment banker Van Horne Investments, Omaha, 1964-65; dir. sales tng. Heartland of Am., Omaha, 1965-66; v.p., account exec. Shearson Lehman, Omaha, 1966-79; part owner, compt. Omaha Testing Lab., 1979-81; owner, mgr. Platte Systems, Ashland, Nebr., 1981-85; dir. Nebr. Pub. Employee Retirement Systems, Lincoln, from 1985. Mem. Nat. Pub. Employees Retirement Assn., Nat. Sch. Retirement Assn., Nat. State Investment Officers, Internat. Found. Employee Benefit Plans, Omaha-Lincoln Fin. Assn., Ashland C. of C. (v.p. 1985), Rotary (pres. Ashland 1985), Elks (exalted ruler Omaha 1971). Avocations: hunting, fishing. Home: Ashland, Nebr. Died Aug. 5, 2004.

NELSON, HARRY GLADSTONE, biology educator, researcher; b. Chgo., Feb. 4, 1922; s. Harry Walfred and Nina Elizabeth (Torke) N.; m. Paula Hyland Rosales, July 1, 1944 (div. 1985); children: Susan, Deborah; m. Abbie Lynn Fiterman, July 16, 1986 (div. 1992). SB, U. Chgo., 1945, postgrad., 1947. Instr. Gary (Ind.) Coll., 1947-48; tchr. zoology Herzl Br. Chgo. Jr. Coll., 1948-51; lectr. Roosevelt U., Chgo., 1951-54, asst. prof., 1954-61, assoc. prof., 1961-69, prof. biology, 1969-89, acting chmn., 1965-66, 88, chmn. dept. biology, 1966-72, prof. emeritus, 1989—2006. Summer curator div. insects Field Mus. of Natural History, Chgo., 1958—; editorial cons. biology Compton Ency., 1980. Bd. dirs. Evanston (Ill.) Environ. Control Bd., 1971-81. With USNR, 1943. Mem. AAAS, Am. Entomol. Soc., N.Am. Benthological Soc., Coleopterists Soc. Avocation: gardening. Home: Evanston, Ill. Died Mar. 19, 2006.

NELSON, LINDA BEATRICE D'ANDREA, volunteer worker; b. Waterbury, Conn., Apr. 27, 1926; d. Consalvo August and Margaret Donata (Santoro) D'Andrea; m. Robert Andrew Nelson, June 20, 1949; children: Eric Robert, Forrest Andrew. Grad. high sch., Terryville, Conn. Mem. staff Am. Bd. Anesthesiology, Hartford, Conn., 1958-82. Author: (poetry) Satan's Beat, 1975, Rhyme Remembrances, 1990. Charter mem. Burlington (Conn.) Land Trust, 1989; founder Burlington Concerned Citizens, 1987. Avocations: environmental activist, writing, communications. Home: Burlington, Conn. Died Jan. 20, 2006.

NELSON, WALDEMAR STANLEY, civil engineer, consultant; b. New Orleans, July 8, 1916; s. Bernard Stanley and Mary Lockett (Hutson) N.; widowed; children: Mary Sue Nelson Roniger, Martha Nelson Frost, Charles W., Virginia Nelson Dodge, Kenneth H. BS in Mech. and Elec. Engring., Tulane U., 1936. Registered civil, elec. and mech. engr., 43 states. Jr. engr. A. M. Lockett & Co., 1936-37; civil engr. Jeff. Lake Sulphur Co., Brazoria, Tex., 1937-38; chief survey party N.O. Pub. Belt. R.R., New Orleans, 1938; resident engr. James M. Todd, Buras, La., 1938-39; pvt. practice New Orleans, 1939-40; asst. chief engr. W. Horace Williams Co., Camp Claiborne, La., 1940-41; sr. engr. U.S. Engr. Dept., Camp Claiborne, 1941-44; prin. Waldemar S. Nelson and Co. Inc., New Orleans, 1945—2006, dir. emeritus, 2003—06. Past chmn. La. State Bd. Registration Profl. Engrs. and Land Surveyors; founding mem., past pres. bd. advisors sch. engring. Tulane U. Chmn. Tulane Alumni Fund, Mems' Coun., 1984; mem. bd. visitors Tulane U.; active The Chamber/New Orleans, Boy Scouts Am.; past chmn. Com. of 50; past pres. bd. commrs. New Orleans City Pk. Improvement Assn.; mem. exec. bd. Christmas New Orleans, 1988; past sr. warden of vestry St. Andrew's Episcopal Ch., mem. property com.; past chmn. bd. dirs. St. Andrew's Episcopal Sch.; past pres. bd. trustees St. Martin's Protestant Episcopal Sch.; trustee Tulane Engring. Found.; bd. dirs. River Region, MetroVision. Recipient Outstanding Engring. Alumnus award Tulane U., 1976, Honor award Constrn. Industry Assn. New Orleans, Inc., 1982, Role Model of Yr. award Young Leadership Coun., 1987, Vol. of Yr. award Tulane U. Alumni Affairs, 1992, George Washington Honor medal Freedom's Found. at Valley Forge New Orleans chpt., 1998, Weiss award Nat. Conf. for Cmty. and Justice, 1998, Times-Picayune Loving Cup, 2001. Fellow: NSPE (past. v.p., past chmn. bd. ethical rev.), ASME (life; past. chmn. New Orleans sect.), ASCE (life); mem.: French-Am. C. of C. (pres. La. chpt. 1992—93, chmn. 1994, pres. 1996—97, 1998, named to Bus. Hall of Fame 1997, UNO's First Citizen of the Learning Soc. award 1998), Soc. Tulane Engrs. (past pres.), La. Engring. Found. (trustee 1990, treas. 1991, sec. 1994—95, pres. 1995—96, 1997—99), Soc. Naval Archs. and Marine Engrs., La. Engring. Soc. (hon.; past pres., Charles M. Kerr Pub. Rels. award, Leo M. Odom Profl. Svcs. award, A.B. Paterson medal, Andrew M. Lockett medal), Am. Pub. Works Assn. (life), Soc. Am. Mil. Engrs., Nat. Coun. Engring. Examiners (past treas., Disting. Svc. award), Am. Acad. Environ. Engrs. (diplomate), IEEE, La. Southeast Council, Engrs. Club New Orleans (past pres.), Tulane Alumni Assn. (past. pres.), Boy Scouts of Am. (Disting. Citizen award 2001), Eta Kappa Nu, Pi Tau Sigma, Tau Beta Pi. Avocations: fishing, boating, gardening, shop work, photography. Home: Baton Rouge, La. Died Nov. 15, 2005.

NESTY, GLENN ALBERT, manufacturing executive; b. Muncie, Ind., Dec. 23, 1911; s. William Harry and Esther (Peakman) N.; m. Iona Martha Brooks, July 3, 1936; children: Philip, Gregory. BA, DePauw U., 1934; PhD, U. Ill., 1937. Rsch. chemist Allied Chem. Corp., N.Y.C., 1937-42, group leader, 1942-44, asst. dir. cen. rsch. Morristown, N.J., 1944-46, assoc. dir. cen. rsch., 1946-55, v.p. R & D N.Y.C., 1955-68, bd. dirs., 1957-68; v.p. R & D Internat. Paper Co., N.Y.C., 1968-76, ret., 1976. Cons. Internat. Paper Co., N.Y.C., 1976-85; bd. dirs. Toth Aluminum Corp., Vacherie, La. Patentee in field. Mem. NSF Study of Industry, Govt. and Univs., Republic of China, 1968; chmn. Dirs. of Indsl. Rsch., 1968, Textile Rsch. Inst., 1964; chmn. rsch. and adv. com. Inst. Paper Chemistry, 1972. DePauw U. Rector scholar, 1930-34; Chem. Found. fellow U. Ill., 1937. Fellow N.Y. Acad. Scis.; mem. AAAS, TAPPI, Am. Chem. Soc. Republican. Methodist. Avocations: cabinetry, gardening, lectures. Home: Fullerton, Calif. Died Apr. 21, 2004.

NETTLESHIP, HAROLD R. (HAL RAYMOND), radio announcer; b. Hillsboro, Ill., June 9, 1932; s. Orville Raymond and Tempa Mae (Gerhart) Nettleship; m. Harriet Marie Buffam, Jan. 29, 1960; children: Kevin Raymond, Julie Marie, Kari Sue. BS in Journalism, U. Ill., 1954. Morning announcer Sta. WEEK, Peoria, Ill., 1957-59; mem. prodn. staff, announcer Sta. WIRL, Peoria, 1959; morning announcer Sta. KISN, Portland, Oreg., 1959; announcer Sta. KAYO, Seattle, 1960; program dir. Sta. KBOX, Dallas, 1961, Sta. WDGY, Mpls., 1961-64; morning announcer Sta. KGW, Portland, 1964-69; program dir. Sta. KEX, Portland, 1969-73; announcer Sta. WSBA, York, Pa., 1973-95, Sta. WOYK, York, from 1995. Served with U.S. Army, 1954-56. Democrat. Mem. Soc. Of Friends. Home: York, Pa. Died Aug. 8, 2005.

NEUSTADT, MORRIS, physicist; b. San Francisco, Nov. 21, 1917; s. Julius and Frances (Nathan) N.; m. Joan Raphael, June. 2, 1946; children: Julie Neustadt Heifetz, John Robert. AB in Physics summa cum laude, U. Calif., Berkeley, 1939, MA in Physics, 1942, PhD in Physics, 1943. Prin. engr. Northrop Corp., Hawthorne, Calif., 1956-72; sr. engr. scientist McDonnell Douglas Space Systems Co., Huntington Beach, Calif., from 1972. Tchr. physics and math. various univs. Mem. Sigma Xi, Phi Beta Kappa, Pi Mu Epsilon. Avocations: reading, walking, hiking. Home: Los Angeles, Calif. Died Apr. 30, 2004.

NEVIN, JOHN JOSEPH, former tire and rubber manufacturing executive; b. Jersey City, Feb. 13, 1927; s. Edward Vincent and Anna (Burns) N.; m. Anna Filice, June 16, 1951; children: Stanley James, John Joseph, Richard Charles, Paul Edward, Gerald Patrick, Mary Anne. BS, U. Calif., 1950; MBA, Harvard U., 1952. Various positions fin., product planning and mktg. Ford Motor Co., Dearborn, Mich., 1954-71, v.p. mktg., 1969-71; pres. Zenith Radio Corp., Chgo., 1971-76, chmn., 1976-79; pres. Firestone Tire & Rubber Co., Akron, Ohio, 1979-82, CEO, 1980—88, chmn., 1981—90. Gen. chmn. Summit County United Way, 1983. Served with USNR, 1945-46. Died May 23, 2006.

NEW, CHERYL CARTER, business executive; b. Asheville, N.C., Dec. 13, 1946; d. Lawrence David and Elizabeth Andre (Carter) New; m. James Aaron Quick, Jan. 18, 1991. BA in Edn., Furman U., 1969; postgrad., U. S.C., 1979-80, Clemson U., 1979-80. Tchr. Pub. Sch., Spartanburg, S.C., 1969-73, media reading specialist Martinsville, Va., 1973-74; coord. Headstart Blue Ridge Community Action, Lenoir, N.C., 1975-77; coord. spl. project Greenville (S.C.) Tech. Coll., 1977-78, instr. coll. transfer div., 1978-82; freelance writer Greenville, 1982-84; pres. Polaris Corp., Greenville, from 1984. Nat. speaker on proposal writing and grants acquisition. Author: Grantwriting Fundamentals, Believe in It and Say It Right, 1991, 5th edit., 1994, Grantseeking Fundamentals: Where's the Funding and How to Get It, 1991, 5th edit., 1994; contbr. articles to profl. jours. Pres. Creative Bus. Exchange, Greenville, 1988. Avocations: creative writing, swimming, travel, reading, gardening. Home: Inman, SC. Died Aug. 8, 2004.

NEWCOMER, JAMES HENRY, retired federal agency administrator; b. Waterloo, Iowa, Sept. 11, 1920; s. Henry Raymond and Nettie (Logston) Newcomer; m. Esther Laura Reinhardt, July 29, 1941; children: James Ralph, Edward Reinhardt, Henry Lewis, Carolyn Ruth. Warehouseman Cutler Wholesale Hardware, Waterloo, 1939-42; electrician Cedar Falls (Iowa) Electric & Hardware, 1946-51; quality assurance rep. Def. Contract Adminstrn. Svcs., St. Louis, 1951-78; trail ranger Black Hawk County Conservation Bd., Cedar Falls, 1990-96; tchr. computers Waterloo Sr. Activity Ctr., 1996. Compiler geneology: Newcomer and Related Families. With U.S. Army, 1942—46, ETO. Decorated Purple Heart, Bronze Star; recipient Disting. Career award, Dept. Def., 1978, cert. of Appreciation, Hawkeye Valley Area Agy. Aging, 1996, Gov.'s Vol. award, 1997. Mem.: VFW, DAV, Am. Legion. Republican. Presbyterian. Avocations: photography, boating, woodworking, metalworking, cooking. Home: Waterloo, Iowa. Died Jan. 26, 2005.

NEWMAN, ARNOLD, photographer; b. NYC, Mar. 3, 1918; s. Isidore and Freda (Perell) N.; m. Augusta Rubenstein, Mar. 6, 1949; children— Eric Allan, David Saul. Student, U. Miami, Coral Gables, Fla., 1937-38, DFA (hon.), 1981; DHL (hon.), Art Ctr. Coll. Design, Pasadena, Calif., 1987; doctorate (hon.), U. Bradford, Eng., 1989; DFA (hon.), New Sch. Social Rsch./Parson Sch. Design, 1990; DHL (hon.), Acad. Art Coll., San Francisco, 1996; DFA (hon.), U. Arts, Phila., 1999, Newbury Coll., Brookline, Mass., 1999, Corcoran Coll. Art Design, Washington, 2000, U. Hartford, 2003. Began photography, 1938; exptl. portraiture, 1941; opened N.Y.C. studio, 1946; adj. prof. photography Cooper Union, N.Y.C., NY, 1968—75. Resident dirs. visitor/lectr. Inst. for Advanced Study, Princeton, N.J., 1991; lectr. U.S. and abroad. Exhibited and represented in collections, Mus. Modern Art, NYC, Met. Mus. Art, NYC, Art Inst. Chgo., Smithsonian Instn., Washington, Phila. Mus. Art, Internat. Mus. Photography at George Eastman House, Rochester, NY, Photography Gallery, London, Israel Mus., Jerusalem, Victoria and Albert Mus., London, Moderna Museet, Stockholm, Australia Nat. Gallery, Camberra, Nat. Portrait Gallery, London, Nihon U. Coll. Art, Tokyo, Odakyu Gallery, Tokyo, Japan, Nat. Gallery Can., Ottawa, Tel Aviv Mus., Israel, Stedelijk Mus., Amsterdam, Internat. Ctr. Photography, NYC, Ctr. Creative Photography, Univ. Ariz., Tucson, others; traveling retrospective exhbn., Arnold Newman-Five Decades, Mus. of Photographic Arts, San, Diego, 1986, Art Inst. of Chgo., 1986, Mpls. Inst. Art, 1987, Norton Gallery & Sch. Art, MIT Mus., Cambridge, 1988, Modern Art Mus., Ft. Worth, 1988-89, Cin. Art Mus., 1989, De Nieuwe Kerk, Amsterdam, The Netherlands, 1989, The Joan Miró Fedn., Barcelona, Spain, 1990, Frankfurter Kunstverein, Germany, Musee de l'Elysee, Lausanne, Switzerland, 1992, Mus. Modern Art, Oxford, England, 1992, Arnold Newman's Ams., Nat. Portrait Gallery, Washington, 1992, One World, One People, originated Portland Jewish Mus., 1999, Arnold Newman: Breaking Ground, Internat. Ctr. Photography, NYC, 1999, Mpls. Inst. Art, 2000, Corcoran Gallery, Washington, 2000, Denver Mizel Mus., 2001, Hotel Sully, Paris, 2002, Glerie Chateau Eau, Toulouse, France, 2003, La. Mus. Modern Art, Humlebaek, Denmark, 2003, Jewish Mus. Fla., 2003; author: Bravo Stravinsky, 1967, One Mind's Eye: The Portraits and Other Photographs of Arnold Newman, 1974, Faces USA, 1978, The Great British, 1979, Artists: Portraits from Four Decades, 1980, I Grandi Fotographi Arnold Newman, 1983, Arnold Newman-Five Decades, 1986, Arnold Newman in Florida, 1987, Arnold Newman's Americans, Portrait Gallery, Washington, 1992, Arnold Newman's Americans, 1992; Arnold Newman, 1992, The Detroit Inst. Arts, 1993, LBJ Libr. & Mus., Austin, Tex., 1993, Columbus (Ga.) Mus. Art, 1993-94, Greenville (S.C.) County Mus. Art, 1994, Worcester (Mass.) Art Mus., 1994, Arnold Newman's Gift, George Eastman House, Rochester, N.Y., 1994, Arnold Newman-Selected Photographs, 1999; Arnold Newman, Taschen, 2000, Arnold Newman, French Ministry of Culture, France, 2002, Arnold Newman, La. Mus., Denmark, 2002; contbr. to Travel and Leisure, Life, Look, Holiday, Fortune, Esquire, Town & Country, Vanity Fair, Scientific American, Harper's Bazaar, The New Yorker, 1946—; subject of Nebr. Ednl. TV program The Image Makers: The Environment of Arnold Newman, 1977; invited exhbn. and lecture tour throughout country Czechoslovakian govt., 1989, Mus. Contemporary History, Budapest, Hungary, 1990. Bd. dirs., founder photography dept. Israel Mus., Jerusalem, 1965. Recipient Photokina award, Cologne, Germany 1951, Newhouse citation Syracuse (N.Y.) U. 1961, Gold medal 4th Biennale Internazionale della Fotagrafic, Venice, Italy 1963, Andy award Advt. Club N.Y., 1983, Mo. Honor medal for journalism U. Mo., 1985, Medal of Merit, 1986, Medal of Merit Lotos Club, 1986, Lifetime Achievement in Photography award Photographic Adminstrs., 1988, Joseph Sudek Commemorative medal, 1989, Honor award Am. Soc. Media Photographers, 1996, Master of Photography award Internat. Ctr. Photography, 1999, Master Photography award Internat. Ctr. Photography, 1999, Lifetime Achievement award WPPI, 2000, Profl. Photographers Am., 2002, Nat. Treasure award Seasoned Citizen Theatre Co., 2003, Commandeur Ordre Arts des Lettres award French Min. Culture and Comm., 2003, Lucie Outstanding Achievement Portraiture award, 2004, others; named Hon. Fellow of Israel Mus. of Jerusalem, 1986, Commemorative medal in hon. 150th anniversary photography Ministry of Culture Czechoslovakia, 1989, Disting. Alumnus award U. Miami, 1993; named N.Y. Alumnus of Yr. U. Miami, 1993; World Image award and Arnold Newman Scholarship Fund named in honor Parsons Sch. Design, N.Y.C., 1993. Mem. Bd. of Israel Mus., Jerusalem and Founded Photography Dept., 1965, Photographic Soc. Japan (Years of Photography award 1989), Royal Photographic Soc. (Centenary medal 2004), Am. Soc. Mag. Photographers (Life Achievement in Photography award 1975, honor award 1996), Inst. for Advanced Study (bd. dirs. visitor Princeton chpt. 1991). Home: New York, NY. Died June 6, 2006.

NEWMAN, CHARLES HAMILTON, author, editor, English educator; b. St. Louis, May 27, 1938; s. Charles H. and June (Toney) N. BA summa cum laude, Yale U., 1960; postgrad., Balliol Coll. Oxford (Eng.) U., 1960-62. Instr. English Northwestern U., Evanston, Ill., 1964-65, asst. prof., 1965-68, assoc. prof., 1968-73, prof., 1974-75; prof., chmn. writing seminars Johns Hopkins U., 1975-77; prof. English Washington U., St. Louis, 1985—2006. Dir. coordinating coun. lit. mags. Nat. Endowment for Arts, Washington, 1968-74; dir. PEN; fellow Inst. Humanities U. Mich., Ann Arbor, 1989. Blue Mountain Found., Blue Mountain Lake, N.Y., 1991, Rockefeller Found., Bellagio, Italy, 1992. Author: (novels) New Axis, 1968, The Promisekeeper, 1971, There Must Be More to Love than Death, 1976, White Jazz, 1984; (non-fiction) A Child's History of America, 1973, The Post Modern Aura, 1985; contbr. short stories to various mags. and anthologies including Best American Short Stories of 1971, 1977; also numerous articles; editor: New Writing from East Europe, 1968, New American Writers Under Thirty, 1970, The Art of Sylvia Plath, 1970, Nabokov: Criticism and Reminiscences, Translations and Tributes, 1970, Literature in Revolution, 1972, Prose for Borges, 1974; founder/editor Tri Quar. Rev., 1964-75, adv. editor, 1975-78; contbr. essays to profl. jours. Recipient Disting. Svc. award Midland Authors Soc., 1973, Disting. Svc. award Friends of Lit., 1973, Zabel prize innovative writing Nat. Inst. Arts and Letters, 1975; Woodrow Wilson fellow, 1960-61, Nat. Endowment Creative Writing fellow, 1973, Guggenheim fellow, 1974-75; Fulbright grantee, 1961-62, Rockefeller grantee creative writing, 1967-68, Ingram Merrill grantee creative writing, 1974. Died Mar. 13, 2006.

NEWMAN, GRANT HOWARD, music educator; b. Grand Forks, N.D., Dec. 8, 1931; s. Clark Newman and Dorothy Grant Shroyer; m. Patricia Marie Smith, May 21, 1966; children: Allen Grant, Joseph Clark. BFA, U. S.D., 1954; MS, U. Ill., 1959, EdD, 1966. Band dir. pub. schs., 1956-58, 60-61; asst. prof. Ea. Mont. Coll., 1959-60, 61-63, Winthrop Coll., 1965-66, Ind. State U., 1966-67; assoc. prof. Ea. Ill. U., 1967-69, U. Maine, Portland, 1969-70; prof. music So. Ill. U., Edwardsville, 1970-81, U. Maine, Orono, 1981-84; chmn. div. music edn. Iowa State U., Ames, 1984-94. Author: Teaching Children Music, 1979, 4th edit., 1995; editor: Kodály Envoy, 1995—. 1st lt. U.S. Army, 1954-56. Mem. Music Educators Nat. Conf., Orgn. Am. Kodály Educators, Am. Orff Schulwerk Assn., Midwest Kodály Music Educators of Am. (exec. bd. 1980-82, 85-87), Coll. Music Soc., Iowa Music Educators Assn. Home: Ankeny, Iowa. Died Jan. 30, 2004.

NEWMAN, LAURA EAGER, psychologist, counselor; b. Jacksonville, Fla., Jan. 30, 1928; d. William Goronwy and Eugene (Johnston) Eager; m. E. Gustave Newman, Dec. 29, 1948; children: Lindsay, Richard Ernest, Dana Davidson, Heather. Student, Queens Coll., N.C., 1946; AB, Duke U., 1948; postgrad., U. N.C., 1948-49; MEd, PhD, U. Fla., 1975. Lic. psychologist, Fla. Psychometrist Counseling Assocs., Gainesville, Fla., 1969-71; psychotherapist Consultation & Guidance Svc., Gainesville, 1972-75; psychologist Brevard County Mental Health Ctr., Rockledge, Fla., 1975-76, Gustave Newman, M.D., Largo, Fla., 1976-77; psychologist, co-owner Consultation & Guidance Svc., Gainesville, 1977-81; psychologist, dir. Alternatives Unltd., Gainesville, 1981-88; dir., psychologist Laura E. Newman Assocs. Cons. courtesy faculty dept. psychiatry and medicine, U. Fla., Gainesville, 1977-88, 85—. Contbr. articles to profl. jours. Vol. English in Action, Gainesville, 1966; del. Baha'i Faith Campus Ministries Coop., U. Fla., 1979—. Mem. Am. Psychol. Assn., Am. Mental Health Counselors Assn., Fla. Mental Health Counselors Assn. (pres. 1980-81), Am. Assn. for Marriage and Family Therapy (clin.), Am. Assn. Sex Educators, Counselors and Therapists, Am. Bd. Sexology. Home: Gainesville, Fla. Died Oct. 4, 2004.

NEWMAN, MARTHA SILBERMAN, foundation consultant; b. Kansas City, Aug. 21, 1930; d. J.D. and Irene (Golling) Silberman; m. Jon O. Newman, June 19, 1953; children: Leigh Anne, Scott Allan, David Blair. BA, Mount Holyoke Coll., So. Hadley, Mass., 1952. Exec. dir. Hartford Courant Found., Hartford, Conn., 1980-87, Fisher Found., W. Hartford, Conn., from 1988. Bd. mem. United Way Capitol Region, Hartford, 1987—; coord. Coun. for Found., 1991—; trustee Hartford Courant Found., 1989—. Home: West Hartford, Conn. Died Feb. 8, 2005.

NEWMAN, OSCAR, architect, city planner, sculptor; b. Montreal, Sept. 30, 1935; m. Irene Kopper; children: Paul, Jon, Hinde. BArch, McGill U., Montreal, 1959. Cert. arch., city planner. Assoc. prof. arch., city planning Washington U., St. Louis, 1964-68, Columbia U., N.Y.C., 1968-70, NYU, 1970-72, dir. Inst. Planning and Housing, 1970-72; exec. dir., founder Inst. Cmty. Design Analysis, N.Y.C., from 1972. Keynote spkr. Internat. Crime Prevention Conf., New Zealand, Australia, 2001, Environ. Design Rsch. Conf. Harvard U., 1995; participant numerous confs.; feature writer The Mountain Eagle, 2000; spkr. in field. Author: Defensible Space, 1972, Community of Interest, 1976, Unmasking a King, 1981, Issues in Housing Discrimination, 1985, Creating Defensible Space, 1996, Visualizing Myth, 1999, Secret Stories in the Art of the Northwest Indian, 2003; contbr. articles to profl. jours.; sculptor Native Am. masks, totem poles; work featured in documentary; featured in Nat. Pub. Radio NBC Nightly News, Dateline NBC TV, other radio and tv shows; subject of articles in Miami Herald, Time, U.S. News and World Report, Readers Digest, Chgo. Tribune, N.Y. Times, The Oregonian, Newsweek, San Francisco Examiner, L.A. Times, numerous other publs. Exec. dir. Interdenominational Housing Program, N.Y., 1978—; mem. bd. rev., bd. dirs. Greene Co. Coun. on the Arts, 1998—; fed. ct. master Yonkers (N.Y.) housing discrimination case, 1986-94 Named Man of Yr. Law Enforcement News, 1995; recipient Achievement award Environ. Design Rsch. Conf., 1997, Annual Award of Achievement Environ. Design Rsch. Assn., 1998. Died Apr. 14, 2004.

NEWTON, ELISABETH GUERRY, geologist, consultant; b. Bennettsville, S.C., June 5, 1933; d. Walter Monroe and Annie Elisabeth (Guerry) N. BS in Geology, U. S.C., 1956. Geologist adminstr. U.S. Geol. Survey, Reston, Va., 1975-85; policy advisor U.S. Dept. Interior, Washington, 1985-87; pres. E.G. Newton & Assoc., Washington, 1988-98; cons. Washington, from 1998. Author: Encyclopedia Earth Sciences, 1996. Fellow: Geol. Soc. Am.; mem.: Assn.

of Engring. Geologists, Am. Inst. Profl. Geologists (hon. mem., congl. liaison, Galey award for pub. svc. 1989), Am. Assn. Petroleum Geologists (congl. liaison). Died Mar. 5, 2005.

NICHOLAS, FAYARD ANTONIO, dancer, actor, entertainer; b. Mobile, Ala., Oct. 20, 1914; s. Ulysses Domonick and Viola (Harden) N.; m. Geraldine Pate (div. 1955); children: Anthony Fayard, Paul Didier; m. Barbara January, Sept. 17, 1967. Pvt. ed. in, high sch. and coll. related courses. Owner, dancer Cotton Club, Phila., from 1932. Guest lectr. San Francisco State U., UCLA, U. So. Calif., U. Hawaii. Appeared in films Kid Millions, 1934, The Big Broadcast, 1936, Down Argentine Way, 1940, Tin Pan Alley, 1940, The Great American Broadcast, 1941, Sun Valley Serenade, 1941, Orchestra Wives, 1942, Stormy Weather, 1943, The Pirate, 1948, others; Broadway shows include Ziefgield Follies, 1936, Babes in Arms, 1937, St. Louis Woman, 1946; actor The Liberation of L.B. Jones, 1970; choreographer Broadway musical Black and Blue (Tony award), 1989; starred in ballet Nutcracker, San Diego Ballet Co., 1990; commd. Japan Satellite Broadcasting Co., 1991; performer maj. TV shows; entertainer (with Bob Hope) troops in Vietnam. Supporter numerous charity events including Danny Thomas-St. Jude Hosp., Jerry Lewis Telethon, Negro Coll. Fund, Drug Abuse, Spl. Concern with the Plights of Homeless. With U.S. Army, 1943-44. Recipient Emmy award, 1965, Bumps Blackwell Life Achievement award, 1980, Ellie award Nat. Film Soc., 1984, City of L.A. award, 1984, resolution, 1991, City of Hope award, 1986, Golden Angel award, 1986, Josephine Baker award, 1986, Ebony Life Achievement award, 1987, Jeanne Golden Halo award, 1988, Tony award, 1989, Lafayette Players West award, 1991, Paul Robeson award Black Am. Cinema Soc., 1992, Dance Mag. award, 1995, numerous others; named to Black Filmmakers Hall of Fame, 1989; with brother Harold honored at White House and Kennedy Ctr., 1991; honored TV Documentary, 1992; honored Lincoln Ctr., N.Y.C., 1993. Mem. Acad. Arts and Sci. (life), Dance Gallery, Friars Club (life), San Fernando Valley Art Coun. Home: Woodland Hills, Calif. Died Jan. 24, 2006.

NICHOLL, NOBES EINSEL, JR., business, finance and economics consultant; b. Oklahoma City, Oct. 11, 1936; s. Nobes Einsel and Juanita Joy (Nelson) N.; m. Joan Elaine Warner, Oct. 6, 1972 (div. Dec. 1985); 1 child, Tamara Belaine. BBA in Fin. and Acctg., U. Okla., 1962, MBA in Fin. and Econs., 1963. Fin. and econ. analyst, treas., fin. planning officer Exxon Corp. and field affiliates, N.Y.C., Paris, Houston, 1963-73; sr. fin. advisor corp. treas. dept. Exxon Corp., N.Y.C., 1973-75; dir. internat. fin. Becton, Dickinson & Co., Paramus, N.J., 1975-82; corp. asst. treas., internat. treas. Warner-Lambert Co., Morris Plains, N.J., 1982-87; prin. N.E. Nicholl & Assocs., Hackensack, N.J., from 1987. Mem. faculty World Trade Inst., N.Y.c., 1989-90; adj. prof. corp. fin. and internat. fin. Seton Hall U., 1989—, Fairleigh Dickinson U., 1989-90, Pace U., 1993-94. Contbr. articles to bus. and econs. publs. Mem. Am. Econ. Assn., Am. Mgmt. Assn., World Trade Assn. N.J. Died Apr. 28, 2004.

NICHOLS, DONALD GEORGE, foundation executive; b. Irvington, N.J., Aug. 8, 1943; s. Alfred Boyd and Elizabeth Jane (Titus) N.; m. Marsha Beth Pelley, Nov. 21, 1973; children: Craig, Brian, Tina, Jeffrey, Teri, Hollie. BA in Journalism, U. Ga., 1965; postgrad., U. So. Fla., 1966. Publicist GE Co., Cleve., 1965-69; mgr. corp. communications Gen. Learning Corp. div. GE Co., Morristown, N.J., 1969-71; mgr. advt. and pub. rels. Saga Devel. Corp., Coral Gables, Fla., 1971-72; assoc. dir. devel. Med. Coll. of Ga., Augusta, 1972-78; dir. univ. rels. Univ. Wis., Superior, 1978-81; dir. communications Minn. Med. Found., Mpls., 1981-83; v.p. Medic Alert Found., Turlock, Calif., 1983-93; exec. v.p. Medic Alert Implant Registry, Turlock, 1986-93; dir. devel. Emanuel Med. Ctr., Turlock, from 1993. Bd. mem. Coun. for Advancement and Support of Edn., Region V, Washington, 1979-81, Nat. Voluntary Health Agy., Washington, 1983—, Emanuel Hosp. Community Cabinet, Turlock, 1991—. Contbr. articles to profl. jours. Mem. of vestry St. Francis Episcopal Ch. Named Outstanding PR Program, Coun. for Advancement and Support of Edn., 1980; recipient Touch Tone award Chgo. (Ill.) Publicity Club, 1992, Silver Anvil, Internat. Bus. Communicators, 1992. Mem. Kiwanis Club Turlock. Avocations: baseball umpire, camping, recreational travel. Home: Turlock, Calif. Died Apr. 24, 2005.

NICHOLS, LARANDA C., newspaper reporter; b. Summerville, Ga., July 8, 1949; d. Edward and Betty Jane (Chitwood) Carroll; m. Nick G. Nichols, Jan. 21, 1975; 1 child, Jonathan Alan. BA, U. Ala., 1971. Reporter The Sand Mountain Reporter, Albertville, Ala., 1971-72; news editor The Leader Dispatch, Boaz, Ala., 1972-74; reporter The Huntsville (Ala.) Times, from 1974. Mem. Soc. Profl. Journalists, Press Club of Marshall County (sec.-treas. 1986-96). Home: Albertville, Ala. Died June 11, 2005.

NICHOLS, MARCI LYNNE, gifted education coordinator, educator, consultant; b. Cin., July 7, 1948; m. James G. Nichols, June 19, 1970; children: Lisa, Jeannette. B in Arts and Sci., Miami U., Oxford, Ohio, 1970, MEd, 1990, PhD, 1997. Cert. Secondary English, elem. gifted edn., computer edn., Ohio. Secondary English tchr. West Clermont Local Schs., Cin., 1970-71; coord. gifted edn. and tchr. Batavia (Ohio) Local Schs., from 1981. Spkr., cons. Local Gifted Orgns., Cin., 1988—; vis. instr. dept. ednl. psychology Miami U., Oxford, Ohio, 1991-98, assoc./adj. prof. 1998—; presenter Nat. Rsch. Symposium on Talent Devel., 1991. Author, presenter: (videotape series) Parenting the Gifted Parts I and II, 1992; columnist, contbr. Resources for Everyday Living; contbr. articles to profl. jours; creator attitude assessment instrument. Speaker Christian Women's Club, Ohio, Ind., Ky., W.Va., 1981—; deacon First Presbyn. Ch. of Batavia, Ohio, 1986-88; bd. trustee Super Saturday program gifted edn. com. Miami U., 1995—. Recipient Douglas Miller Rsch. award Miami U., 1991. Mem. ASCD, Am. Ednl. Rsch. Assn. (presenter 1997, 98), Nat. Assn. for Gifted Children, Consortium Ohio Coords. of Gifted, Parents Assn. for Gifted Edn. (trustee 1997), Midwest Ednl. Rsch. Assn. (presenter), Internat. Platform Assn., Mensa (ann. gathering presenter 1998), Phi Kappa Phi. Home: Batavia, Ohio. Died Jan. 29, 2005.

NICHOLS, WILLIAM GEORGE, JR., retired surgeon; b. Atlanta, 1912; s. William George Sr. and Florence Pauline (Driskell) N.; m. Naomi Betsy Berrier, July 3, 1943; children: Anne Driskell Nichols Reynolds, Betsy Berrier Nichols Lowenstein. EdB, Tulane U., 1936, MD, 1942. Diplomate Am Bd. Surgery. Intern Charity Hosp., New Orleans, 1942—43; commd. 1st lt. U.S. Army, 1943, advanced through grades to maj., 1948; advanced through grades to col. USAR, 1957; resident gen. surgery VA Hosp., New Orleans, 1946—51, chief surgery Phila., 1951—57; comdr. U.S. Army Hosp., Gulfport, Miss., 1957—72, Ft. Sam Houston, Tex., 1961; ret. USAR, 1972. Cons. Keesler AFB, Biloxi, Miss., 1957-72. Decorated Legion of Merit. Fellow ACS (life); mem. Phila. Acad. Surgery, Ret. Officers Assn. (life), SAR (pres. Gulfport chpt.). Home: Winter Park, Fla. Died Dec. 23, 2005.

NICKEL, MELVIN EDWIN, metallurgical engineer; b. St. Louis, Aug. 24, 1915; s. Jacob William and Mary Anna Nickel; m. Mary Louise Breuer, Sept. 12, 1942; children: Elizabeth Ann Nickel Overleas, Mary Patricia Nickel Hepburn, Sheila Breuer Nickel Stojak, William Louis. BS in Metall. Engring., U. Mo., Rolla, 1938, degree in metall. engring., 1967. Mgmt. trainee Bethlehem (Pa.) Steel Corp., 1938-39; asst. to supt. blast furnaces Wis. Steel div. Internat. Harvester Co., Chgo., 1939-43, gen. foreman furnaces, blast furnaces, 1943-48, asst. supt. blast furnaces, 1948-49, supt. open hearths, 1949-61, supt. basic oxygen furnaces, mgr. steel prodn., 1961-68, mgr. primary ops., 1968-77; mgr. facilities planning and appropriations, works mgr. Envirodyne Industries, Inc., Wis. Steel Corp., 1977-80; pres. Melvin E. Nickel & Assocs., Inc., Chgo., 1980—2005. Contbr. articles to profl. jours. Trustee Iron and Steel Soc. Found., Warrendale, Pa., 1980—91. Named to Athletic Hall of Fame, Mo. Sch. Mines/U. Mo.-Rolla, 1993; recipient Disting. Merit award, U. Mo.-Rolla, 1960, Benjamin F. Fairless award, Iorn and Steel Soc., 2001. Mem.: AIME (hon.; nat. v.p., dir. 1974—76, Hon. Membership award 1978), Western States Blast Furnaces and Coke Assn., Assn. Iron and Steel Engrs., Metall. Soc. of AIME, Iron and Steel Soc. of AIME (nat. pres. 1974—75, elected disting. mem. 1975), Acad. Sch. Mines and Metallurgy U. Mo.-Rolla, U. Mo. Rolla Alumni Assn., Jackson Hole Wildlife Soc., Beverly Hills Univ. Club, Ridge Country Club Chgo., Triangle Fraternity. Republican. Roman Catholic. Achievements include development of early practices for production of special bar quality and alloy steel in top blown basic oxygen furnace. Avocations: hunting, fishing, carpentry, mineral collecting, boating. Died Sept. 7, 2005.

NIEDERHAUSER, WARREN DEXTER, chemist; b. Akron, Ohio, Jan. 2, 1918; s. Harold Warren and Edna Isabel (Dexter) N.; m. Floris Eldredge (dec. 1996), Dec. 31, 1949; 1 child, Sue Dexter Niederhauser Edmondson. AB, Oberlin Coll., 1939; PhD, U. Wis., 1943. Sr. chemist Rohm and Haas Co., Phila., 1943-55, head chemistry sect. Huntsville, Ala., 1955-59, rsch. supr. Bristol, Pa., 1959-66, asst. dir. rsch., 1966-73, dir. pioneering rsch. Spring House, Pa., 1973-83, former cons. Editor: Legal Rights of Chemists and Engineers, 1977. Mem. Am. Chem. Soc. (nat. pres. 1984, nat. dir. 1976-85, chmn. coun. sci. soc. pres. 1986). Achievements include 54 patents on scientific and commercial developments in the areas of organic chemistry, plastics, surfactants and propellants. Home: Philadelphia, Pa. Died Jan. 23, 2005.

NIEDZIELSKI, EDMUND LUKE, chemist, consultant; b. Bklyn., Nov. 14, 1917; s. Florian S. and Natalie M. (Skalski) N.; m. Isabelle R. Paradis, June 7, 1946; children: M. Suzanne, Denise M., Robert E., Marc P., C. Michele. BS, St. John's Coll., Bklyn., 1938; MS, Fordham U., 1940, PhD, 1943. Sr. rsch. chemist E.I. Du Pont De Nemours & Co., Wilmington, Del., 1946-86; cons. Wilmington, from 1986. Contbr. articles to profl. jours including Jour. Am. Chem. Soc., Jour. Organic Chemistry, Indsl. Engring. Chemistry. Dist. chair New Castle County Dem. Com., Wilmington, 1986-94. Lt. USNR, 1942-46. Fellow Am. Inst. Chemists. Roman Catholic. Achievements include 12 patents for motor fuels, additives, brake fluid, and diffusion processes. Home: Wilmington, Del. Died June 11, 2004.

NIELSEN, NIELS HOEG, management consultant; b. Montreal, Que., Can., Nov. 30, 1930; came to U.S., 1969; s. Niels Christian and Anna (Hoeg) N.; m. Joan Shirley Anderson, May 18, 1957; children: Karen Shirley, Niels Eric, Christine Ellen. BA, McGill U., Montreal, 1951, MA, 1954. Market rsch. asst., fin. control analyst, sr. economist Du Pont of Can., Montreal, 1953-60; human resources specialist, employee benefits mgr., sr. computer systems analyst/Massey Ferguson, Toronto, Ont., Can., 1961-67; mgr. spl. projects, employee and pub. rels., dir. compensation and benefits/Domtar, Montreal, 1967-68; dir. corp. benefits Allis-Chalmers, Milw., 1969-71; dir. corp. compensation and benefits Johnson & Johnson, New Brunswick, N.J., 1971-74; dir. compensation and benefits J. C. Penney, N.Y.C., 1974-78; corp v.p. pers. svcs. ARA Svcs., Phila., 1978-80; pres. Princeton (N.J.) Mgmt. Cons., Inc., from 1980. Author: Human Resources Forms and Reports, 1989; developer computer software Salary Survey Manager, 1991. Vice chmn. Coalition for Nuclear Disarmament, Princeton, 1981—; trustee Westminster Choir Coll., Princeton, 1984—; bd. dirs. Rider Coll. Sch. Bus., Lawrenceville, N.J., 1987-90, Family Svc. Agy., Princeton, 1990—. Mem. Am. Compensation Assn. (Outstanding Article award), Soc. Human Resource Mgmt., Assn. Human Resources Systems Profls. Episcopalian. Avocations: music, theater, art, gardening, travel. Home: Princeton, NJ. Died Apr. 14, 2005.

NIELSEN, WALDEMAR AUGUST, corporate social policy consultant, writer; b. Greensburg, Pa., Mar. 27, 1917; s. Malta August and Mary Pauline (Shaffer) N.; m. Marcia Kaplan, Apr. 22, 1943; 1 child, Signe Barbara. AB in Econ., U. Mo., 1939, BS in Bus., 1939, MA in Polit. Sci., 1940; DPhil (hon.), U. Lagos (Nigeria), 1972. Economist U.S. Govt., Washington, 1940-42, U.S. State Dept., Washington, 1945-46; spl. asst. sec. commerce for Marshall Plan Dept. Commerce, Washington, 1947-48; chief info. divsn. Marshall Plan Hqrs., Paris, 1948-52; officer behavioral scis. program Ford Found., N.Y.C., 1953-54, exec. asst. to pres., 1955-57; officer internat. affairs program, exec. dir. White House Commn. Internat. Affairs, Washington, 1959-60; pres. African Am. Inst., N.Y.C., 1961-68, Waldemar A. Nielsen, Inc., N.Y.C., 1969—2001. Bd. dirs. Home Life Ins., N.Y.C., The Observer, London, Hispanic Policy Devel. Project, N.Y.C.; trustee Nat. Mus. Am. Indians, Washington. Author: Africa, 1965, African Battleline, 1966, The Big Foundations, 1972, The Endangered Sector, 1980, The Golden Donors, 1985; contbr. to nat. publs. Chmn. Internat. Arts Assn., N.Y.C. Lt. USN, 1943-46, PTO. Rhodes scholar, 1939-40; decorated Bronze Star (U.S.), comdr. Legion of Merit (Italy), comdr. Royal Order Phoenix (Greece), Chevalier de l'Ordre de la Valeur Camerounaise, commandeur de l'Ordre National de la Republique du Senegal, officer de l'Ordre National Ivoirien. Sr. fellow Aspen Inst. Humanistic Studies (bd. dirs.); mem. Century Assn., Coun. Fgn. Rels. Democrat. Avocations: golf, chinese art collecting. Home: New York, NY. Died Nov. 2, 2005.

NIELSON, ROBERT DELOYD, retired landsman; b. Ephraim, Utah, Nov. 4, 1908; s. Andrew Christian Nielson and Teckla Pauline Christensen; m. Lenore Lewis Nielson, Dec. 23, 1935 (dec.); children: Joanne Johnson, Carolyn, Sharon Selner, Paula Rochelle. BS in Agronomy & Soil Sci., Utah State U., 1934. Jr. range examiner US Dept. Interior Divsn. Grazing, Salt Lake City, 1935—36; range survey specialist US Dept. Interior Grazing Svc., Albuquerque, 1936—40, dist. grazier Salt Lake City, 1940—43, chief range specialist Billings, Mont., 1943—54; state supr. Mont. Bureau Land Mgmt., 1954—59, asst. chief range mgr. Dept. Interior DC, 1959—61; state dir. Utah US Dept. Interior, Salt Lake City, 1961—73; ret., 1973. Mem. Interstate Power Commn., 1973; chair Land Use Planning Commn., Utah, 1974. Author: Reflections & Recollections, 2001, How the West Was Run During the 20th Century, 2005. Chair, adv. bd. Land Use Planning Com., Salt Lake City, 1973—74; mem. adv. com. Fed./State Alaska Planning Commn., Anchorage, Ala., 1974. Recipient Jim Bridger award, Utah State Forestry Club, 1968. Achievements include the implemention of the Taylor Grazing Act in Utah between 1935-36; surveyed 16 million acres of public land in Arizona and New Mexico; set up Dugway Proving Grounds; inventoried public lands in the Missouri River Basin spanning across seven states between 1947-52; set up the Moab Slick Rock Bike Trail in 1965; established the state/federal boundary of the navigable Great Salt Lake based on the mean water level in 1966; acquired lands for Glacier Nation Park between 1949-52. Avocations: winemaking, wine, history writing. Died Mar. 17, 2006.

NIEMEYER, ANTONIO BILISOLY, JR., school system administrator; b. Norfolk, Va., Apr. 13, 1928; s. Antonio Bilisoly Niemeyer and Lutie Stuart Spotts; m. Alice Virginia Berry, Nov. 20, 1965; children: William Frederic, Frank Berry, John Stuart. BS, Va. Mil. Inst., 1949; MEd, U. Va., 1955; cert. advanced study, Old Dominion U., 1973. Asst. prin. Portsmouth (Va.) Schs., 1966-67, supr. sci., 1967-77, prin. Churchland Jr., 1977-78, prin. Manor H.S., 1978-80, 86-88, dir. secondary edn., 1980-86, dir. personnel, 1988-91. Dir. Va. Jr. Acad. Sci., 1979-81. Cons. Science Far and Near, Tchrs. edit., 1973. Pres. Tidewater Heart Assn., 1968. Recipient Disting. Svc. award Jr. C. of C., 1957; named Sci. Educator of Yr., Tidewater Sci. Congress, 1975; fellow Va. Acad. Sci. Mem. SAR. Episcopalian. Avocation: historical studies. Home: Chesapeake, Va. Died Apr. 28, 2005.

NIGRO, ANN K., geriatrics nurse, educator; b. Omaha, Mar. 22, 1948; d. William L. and Helen M. (Kusek) Skotz; m. Frank S. Nigro, Sept. 13, 1975; children: Stephanie, Vincent, Andrew. BSN, Creighton U., 1970. Staff nurse Douglas County Hosp., Omaha, team leader, asst. head nurse surg. ICU, dir. staff devel. Mem. ANA (cert. in continuing edn. and staff devel. 1990), Nebr. Nurses Assn., Am. Soc. for Healthcare Edn. and Tng., Nat. Nursing Staff Devel. Orgn., Sigma Theta Tau. Home: Omaha, Nebr. Died July 5, 2004.

NIHART, FRANKLIN BROOKE (F. BROOKE NIHART), retired museum administrator, retired military officer; b. L.A., Mar. 16, 1919; s. Claude Eugene and Vera Howard (Brooke) N.; m. Mary Helen Brosius, Feb. 11, 1945; children: Mary Catherine, Virginia Brooke Nihart. BA, Occidental Coll., 1940. Commd. 2nd lt. USMC, 1940, advanced through grades to col., 1957, dep. dir. Marine Corps. History and Mus. Washington, 1973-92; ret., 1992. Fellow, past gov., pres. Co. Mil. Historians, 1967-71; founder Marine Corps Hist. Found., 1979. Decorated Navy Cross, Bronze Star with one gold star; named to Order del Mar Oceano; recipient Disting. Svc. award Co. Mil. Historians, 1982, Disting. Svc. award Marine Corps. Hist. Found., 1992. Mem. Va. Mus. Mil. Vehicles (bd. dirs.), Internat. Assn. Mus. Arms and Mil. History (hon. life), Orgn. Mil. Mus. Can. (hon. life), Washington Naval Corrs. Circle, Army and Navy Club, Mil. Order of Carabao (Disting. Svc. award 1987), Ends of the Earth Club, Order of St. Crispins. Republican. Avocations: history, politics, travel, shooting, writing. Home: Springfield, Va. Died Aug. 30, 2006.

NILSSON, BIRGIT, soprano; b. Karup, Sweden, May 17, 1918; d. Nils P. and Justina (Paulsson) Svensson; m. Bertil Niklasson, Sept. 10, 1948. Student, Royal Musical Acad., Stockholm; MusD (hon.), Amherst U., Mass., Andover U., Manhattan Sch. Music, 1982, Mich. State U., 1982, Sibelius Acad., Helsinki, Finland, 1982. Tchr. master classes Manhattan Sch. Music, N.Y.C., 1983-93. Appeared opera and concert houses in Europe, N.Am., S.Am., Japan and Australia; most famous roles include: Isolde, Brünnhilde, Turandot, Elektra, Dyer's wife, Salome, Fidelio; now ret. Decorated 1st comdr. Order of Vasa (Sweden); comdr. Order of St. Olav 1st class (Norway); comdr. Arts et Lettres (France); recipient Swedish Golden medal Illis Quorum CL.18; Austrian and Bavarian Kammersaengerin; named Swedish Royal Court Singer. Hon. mem. Royal Acad. Music London, Royal Acad. Music Stockholm, Vienna State Opera, Vienna Philharm. Orchestra. Died Jan. 2006.

NISENHOLTZ, FREDERICK, pharmacist; b. Phila., Oct. 20, 1929; s. Samuel and Sophie (Kaprow) N.; m. Rhoda Annette Altus, Apr. 20, 1958; children: Tina F., Hollie S. BS in Pharmacy, Temple U., 1953. Lic. pharmacist, Pa. Pharmacist Sun Ray Drug, Phila., 1955-56, Davis Pharmacy, Elkins Park, Pa., 1956-57, Levin Pharmacy, Phila., 1957-59; pharmacist, owner Nisenholtz Pharmacy, Phila., 1959-92, ret., 1992. With U.S. Army, 1953-55, Korea. Mem. Steuben Lodge 113. Home: Philadelphia, Pa. Died Apr. 11, 2005.

NISSEL, STANLEY N., lawyer; b. N.Y.C., Jan. 13, 1930; s. Samuel and Etta (Ostrie) N.; m. Judith Gorfinkle, Dec. 27, 1953 (dec. June 1990); children: Jonathan R., Susan D.; m. Gertrude Pedersen, Dec. 9, 1995. BS, NYU, 1950; JD, Harvard U., 1953; LLM, Columbia U., 1957. Bar: N.Y. 1954, U.S. Supreme Ct. 1960, Conn. 1989. Atty. Office of Gen. Counsel U.S. Dept. of the Navy, Washington, 1957-65; sr. atty. Office of Gen. Counsel U.S. Dept. of Def., Washington, 1965-74; dep. gen. counsel (logistics) U.S. Dept. of the Army, Washington, 1974-86; assoc. gen. counsel United Techs. Corp., Hartford, Conn., 1986-91; ret., 1991. Recipient Presdl. award Pres. of the U.S., 1982. Mem. ABA, Fed. Bar Assn. Home: Hamden, Conn. Died Aug. 1, 2004.

NOLAN-PITERI, DAWN C., state legislator; b. McKees Rocks, Pa. m. David Piteri; 3 children. Mem. N.H. Ho. of Reps. (dist. 34), Concord, from 1996, mem. local and regulated rev. com., from 1996. Mem. Nashua Rep. City Com., 1996—. Died 2006.

NOLLAU, LEE GORDON, lawyer; b. Balt., Feb. 6, 1950; s. E. Wilson and Carolyn G. (Blass) N.; m. Carol A. Haughney, Aug. 12, 1978; children: Ann G., Catherine E., Margaret C. BA, Juniata Coll., 1972; MAS, Johns Hopkins U., 1975; JD, Dickinson Sch. Law, 1976. Bar: Pa. 1976, U.S. Dist. Ct. (mid. dist.) 1982, U.S. Dist. Ct. (we. dist.) 1988, U.S. Ct. Appeals (3d cir.) 1980, U.S. Supreme Ct. 1982. Instr. Juniata Coll., Huntingdon, Pa., 1976-78; asst. dist. atty. Centre County, Bellefonte, Pa., 1978-80, dist. atty., 1981; assoc. Litke, Lee, Martin, Grine & Green, Bellefonte, 1981-83, Jubelirer & Assocs., State College, Pa., 1983-87; ptnr. Jubelirer, Nollau, Young & Blanarik, Inc., State College, 1988-89, Jubelirer, Rayback, Nollau, Walsh, Young & Blanarik, Inc., State College, 1989-94, Nollau & Young, State College, from 1994. Mental health rev. officer Centre County, Bellefonte, 1982—; instr. Pa. State U. Smeal Coll. Bus., 1995—; lectr., author Pa. Bar Inst., 1995—. Author: Trial Tactics: Direct Examination of Lay Witnesses. Mem. ABA, Pa. Bar Assn., Centre County Bar, Pa. Assn. Criminal Def. Lawyers, Am. Inn. Ct. (pres. 2004—). Presbyterian. Home: Port Matilda, Pa. Died Dec. 7, 2004.

NONKIN, PAUL MARTIN, physician, cardiologist; b. Newark, June 22, 1929; s. Raymond and Leah (Lasser) N.; m. Madeline Lee, Oct. 4, 1953 (div. 1966); m. Ann Marie Helena Vallen, June 7, 1982; children: Lesley Jane, Elizabeth Ann. BA, NYU, 1950; MD, N.Y. Med. Coll., 1954. Diplomate Am. Bd. Internal Medicine, Am. Bd. Anesthesiology. Intern Jackson Meml. Hosp., Miami, Fla., 1954-55; resident in medicine U. Miami Med. Ctr., 1958-60, NIH fellow in cardiology, 1960-61; resident in anesthesiology Columbia-Presbyn. Med. Ctr., N.Y.C., 1966-68; pvt. practice N.Y.C., 1966-90. Mem. med. bd., dir. internal medicine Manhattan Eye, Ear & Throat Hosp., N.Y.C., 1978-90; mem. med. bd. Dr.'s Hosp., N.Y.C., 1987-90. Lt. comdr. USNR, 1955-58. Mem. ACP, AMA, Am. Heart Assn., N.Y. Athletic Club. Republican. Home: Lakeville, Conn. Died Dec. 2, 2004.

NOODLEMAN, JEFFREY SCOTT, radiologist; b. Mpls., May 24, 1953; s. Benny Norman and Esther (Gonor) N. Student with honors, Pasadena City Coll., 1973; BA in Chemistry summa cum laude, BS in Biol. Scis. summa cum laude, U. Calif., Irvine, 1975, MA in Chemistry, 1976; MD, Loyola U., Chgo., 1979. Diplomate Am. Bd. Radiology, Am. Bd. Nuclear Medicine, Am. Bd. Med. Examiners. Intern U. Calif. Irvine Affiliates, 1979-80; resident L.A. County— U. So. Calif. Med. Ctr., L.A., 1980-81, VA West L.A., 1981-86; physician Family Health Plan, Anaheim, Calif., 1986-89, Western Roentgenologic Assocs., Canoga Park, Calif., from 1989. Mem. Am. Coll. Nuclear Physicians, Soc. Nuclear Medicine, Radiol. Soc. N.Am., Am. Roentgen Ray Soc., Phi Beta Kappa. Democrat. Home: Arcadia, Calif. Died Aug. 13, 2005.

NOONAN, MARY GRACE, women's health nurse; b. Pittsfield, Mass., Feb. 19, 1925; d. Thomas John and Mary Florence (Reagan) Maloney; m. John A. Noonan, Sept. 16, 1950; children: John A. Jr., Robert G., Mary K., Michael J., Timothy J. RN, St. Luke's Hosp. Sch. Nursing, 1946; student, Boston Lyin In Hosp., 1948. Night nurse delivery rm. Berkshire Med. Ctr., Pittsfield; supr. delivery rm. St. Luke's Hosp., Pittsfield; pvt. duty night nurse Mrs. Bruce Crane, Dalton, Mass. Vol. in blood pressure program ARC. Recipient Nurse of the Yr. award Berkshire Med. Ctr., 1984. Mem. St. Luke's Hosp. Sch. of Nursing (treas. scholarship fund), Cath. Nurses of Holyoke, Mass. Home: Pittsfield, Mass. Died Sept. 5, 2004.

NOORDA, RAYMOND JOHN, former computer software company executive; b. Ogden, Utah., June 19, 1924; m. Lewena Taylor; children: John, Alan, Andy, Taylor. BSEE, U. Utah, 1949. CEO Novell Inc., 1983—95; chmn. MTI Inc. (now MTI Tech. Corp.), Anaheim, Calif., from 1994; founder The Canopy Group, 1995; co-founder Noorda Family Trust, 1980—92; bd. dirs. Noorda Family Trust Ventures, Caldera Systems. Died Oct. 9, 2006.

NORDLING, BERNARD ERICK, lawyer; b. Nekoma, Kans., June 14, 1921; s. Carl Ruben Ebben and Edith Elveda (Freeburg) N.; m. Barbara Ann Burkholder, Mar. 26, 1949. Student, George Washington U., 1941-43; AB, McPherson Coll., 1947; JD, U. Kans., 1949. Bar: Kans. 1949, U.S. Dist. Ct. Kans. 1949, U.S. Ct. Appeals (10th cir.) 1970. Pvt. practice, Hugoton, Kans., from 1949; ptnr. Kramer, Nordling & Nordling, Hugoton, Kans., 1950-99; mem. Kramer, Nordling & Nordling, LLC, Hugoton, Kans., 1999—2005; city atty. City of Hugoton, 1951-87; county atty. Stevens County, Kans., 1957-63. Kans. mem. legal com. Interstate Oil Compact Commn., 1969-93; mem. supply tech. adv. com. nat. gas survey FPC, 1975-77. Editor: U. Kans. Law Rev., 1949. Mem. Hugoton Sch. Bds., 1954-68, pres. grade sch. bd., 1957-63; trustee McPherson Coll., 1971-81, mem. exec. com., 1975-81; mem. Kans. Energy Adv. Coun., 1975-78, mem. exec. com., 1976-78; bd. trustees Kans. 4-H Found., 1987-2003. With AUS, 1944-46. Recipient Citation of Merit, McPherson Coll., 1987, Disting. Alumnus award, Kans. U. Law Sch., 1993, Lifetime Achievement award, Hugoton Kans. Area C. of C., 1994. Fellow: Am. Bar Found. (Kans.); mem.: ABA, Am. Inn of Ct., S.W. Kans. Royalty Owners Assn. (exec. sec. 1968—94, asst. exec. sec. from 1994), Nat. Assn. Royalty Owners (bd. govs. 1980—99, James L. Stafford Founder's award 2003), City Attys. Assn. Kans. (exec. com. 1975—83, pres. 1982—83), Kans. Bar Assn., Kans. U. Alumni Assn. (bd. dirs. 1992—97, Fred Ellsworth medallion 1997, James Woods Green medallion 2001), Kans. U. Endowment Assn. (trustee from 1987), U. Kans. Law Soc. (bd. govs. 1984—87), Phi Alpha Delta, Order of Coif. Died Aug. 31, 2005.

NORDSTROM, PAUL E., retired academic administrator; b. Fremont, Nebr. m. Lea Nordstrom; children: Kenneth, Steven, Amy. BS in Geology, U. Mont., 1959; MS, Ph.D, U. Mont. State. With SD State Coll., 1972—88; provost, v.p. We. State Coll., Gunnison, Colo., 1988—92; pres. U. Maine, Machias, 1992—99. Died May 15, 2006.

NORRIS, MARILYN RUTH, education educator; b. Bklyn., Mar. 1, 1933; d. Nicholas Frederick and Barbara Elizabeth (Oehl) Sevling; m. Richard Donald Norris, Aug. 9, 1952; children: Richard, Robert, William, Lawrence, Barbara Wiggs, Maureen, Laurel Anne Williams, Patrick. AA with highest honors, Saddleback Community Coll., Mission Viejo, Calif., 1978; BS magna cum laude, U. So. Miss., 1980, MS, 1982. Cert. vocat. home econs. tchr., N.Y. Clothing/textiles supr. Goodwill Industries of Redwood Empire, Santa Rosa, Calif., 1980; nurse asst. instr. Gulfport (Miss.) Job Corps, 1981-82; acad. dir., registrar, instr. Nat. Career Coll., Huntsville, Ala., 1984; edn. specialist U.S. Army Mil. Police Sch., Fort McClellan, Ala., 1985; adj. instr. Am. Lang. Sch., Tangier, Morocco, 1986; edn. specialist U.S. Army Ordnance, Missile, Munitions Ctr. and Sch., Redstone Arsenal, Ala., 1987-88; curriculum devel. specialist J.F. Drake State Tech. Coll., Huntsville, from 1988. Adj. prof. vocat. edn. Athens State U., 1987—. Mem. Am. Vocat. Assn., Am. Soc. Tng. and Devel., Internat. Vocat. Assn., Assn. for Supervision and Curriculum Devel., Kappa Delta Pi. Republican. Roman Catholic. Avocations: computer programming, sewing, embroidery. Died Oct. 7, 2004.

NORRIS, WILLIAM C., engineering executive; b. 1950; m. Jane Norris; 8 children. Grad. with degree in Elect. Engring., U. Nebr., 1932. With Westinghouse Corp.; creator Engring. Rsch. Associates (purchased by Remington Rand in 1951, then Sperry Rand Corp.), St. Paul; chmn., CEO Control Data Corp., 1957-86, emeritus chmn., 1986-92; founder William C. Norris Inst., Bloomington, Minn., chmn. Minn. Dir., chmn. Greater Minn. Corp. With USN. Recipient Nat. medal of Tech., 1986, Founders medal IEEE. Mem. NAE. Died Aug. 21, 2006.

NORRIS, WILLIAM CHARLES, retired computer systems executive; b. Inavale, Nebr., July 14, 1911; s. William H. and Mildred A. (McCall) N.; m. Jane Malley, Sept. 15, 1943; children: W. Charles, George, Daniel, Brian, Constance, Roger, Mary N., David. BS, U. Nebr., 1932. Sales engr. Westinghouse Electric Mfg. Co., Chgo., 1935-41; v.p., gen. mgr. Engring. Research Assocs., 1946-55, Univac (divsn. Sperry Rand Corp.), 1955-57; pres. Control Data Corp., Mpls., 1957-77, past chmn.; chmn. William C. Norris Inst., Bloomington, Minn., 1988—2006. Bd. dirs. N.W. Bank Corp., N.W. Growth Fund, Tronchemics, Inc. Trustee Hill Reference Library; adv. com. White House Conf. on Balanced Nat. Growth and Econ. Devel., 1978—. Served to comdr. USNR, 1941-46. Recipient Nat. Medal Tech., 1986. Died Aug. 21, 2006.

NORTHROP, GAYLORD MARVIN, dean, university official; b. Little Rock, Dec. 15, 1928; s. Guy Santee and Gladys Marie (Hilsmeyer) N.; m. Diane Joslyn Lake, Dec. 8, 1956 (div. 1980); children: Melanie Gay, Dana Rogers; m. Marjorie Joan Dyer, Aug. 8, 1981; stepchildren: Elizabeth, Sandra, Jonathan. BSEE, U. Ark., 1952; MA in Engring., Yale U., 1955, DEng, 1961. Rsch. specialist II N.Am. Aviation, Inc., L.A., 1952-53; engr. Sperry Gyroscope Co., Lake Success, N.Y., 1954; dep. dept. head Raytheon Missile System Div., Bedford, Mass., 1956-57; engr. Hughes Aircraft, Inc., Culver City, Calif., 1958, The RAND Corp., Santa Monica, Calif., 1960-67; v.p. Ctr. for Environment & Man, Inc., Hartford, Conn., 1967-82; assoc. prof. U. Bridgeport, Conn., 1982-86; assoc. prof. electronics and instrumentation dept. U. Ark., Little Rock, 1987-94, dir. Grad. Inst. Tech., from 1988, assoc. dean for rsch. Coll. Sci. and Engring. Tech., from 1990. Dir. Ark. Space Grant Consortium, Little Rock, 1991—; dir. Ark./STRIVE Program, 1993—; mgr. NASA/EPSCoR Program, 1994—. Sgt. USMC, 1946-48. Mem. AIAA, IEEE, Data Processing Mgmt. Assn., Rotary Internat., Tau Beta Pi, Sigma Xi, Sigma Pi Sigma. Avocations: rock climbing, civil war history, video taping, photography, computer programming. Home: North Little Rock, Ark. Died Oct. 1, 2004.

NOURSE, THOMAS MILLER, consulting company executive; b. Greenville, Ohio, Aug. 24, 1922; s. John Darlington and Louise Anderson (Miller) N.; m. Dorothy Ann Beale, Apr. 3, 1945; children: James Gregory, Daniel Miller, William Beale. BSChemE, Purdue U., 1943. Registered profl. engr., N.Y. Sales mgr. Hagan Chems. & Controls, Pitts., 1947-62; mktg. mgr. Daystrom Control Systems Div., La Jolla, Calif., 1962-63, Foxboro-Digital Systems Div., Foxboro, Mass., 1963-65; strategic planning Gen. Electric, Charlottesville, Va., 1965-68; v.p., gen. mgr. Interactive Scis. Corp., Braintree, Mass., 1968-70; pres. Nourse Assocs., Inc., San Diego, Calif., from 1970. Task force mem. Fin. Acctg. Standards Bd.-Cash Flow Reporting, Stamford, Conn., 1985-87. Pres. San Diego Hall of Sci., 1975-78. Lt. USNR, 1943-46. Mem. Instrument Soc. Am., Assn. Iron and Steel Engrs. Republican. Episcopalian. Avocations: swimming, golf, U.S. industry competitiveness. Died July 7, 2004.

NOWACK, WAYNE KENYON, artist; b. Des Moines, May 7, 1923; s. Bernard F. and Bertha A. (Meeker) N.; m. Jean Ann Curtis, Sept. 19, 1952. Student, Drake U., 1943-45; BA summa cum laude, State U. Iowa, 1947, MA, 1948, MFA, 1950. Art therapist Mental Health Inst., Independence, Iowa, 1951-53, Hall-Brooke Sanitarium, Westport, Conn., 1953-56; assoc. prof. art Union Coll., Schenectady, N.Y., 1957-65; freelance artist, from 1965. Solo exhbns. include Des Moines Art Ctr., 1950, 57, Union Coll., 1957, Albany (N.Y.) Inst. History and Art, 1960, Allan Stone Gallery, NYC., 1967, 70, 74; group shows include Gallery Modern Art, Washington, 1963, Whitney Mus. Am. Art, 1969, Minn. Mus. Art, St. Paul, 1977, Upstairs Gallery, Ithaca, N.Y., 1987, Gallery North, Setauket, N.Y., 1990; represented in pvt. and pub. collections including Ft. Worth Mus., Des. Moines Art Ctr., Yale Art Mus., New Haven, Conn., Hirshhorn Mus., Smithsonian Instn., Washington, others. Grantee Danforth Found., 1963, Nat. Endowment for Arts, 1973. Avocations: gardening, photoghraphy. Home: Spencer, NY. Died Aug. 16, 2004.

NOWAK, GERALD L., wholesale grocery executive; b. Alpena, Mich., Dec. 25, 1930; s. Stephen Harry and Celia Regina (Filipiak) N.; m. Gayle Adele Reynolds, July 11, 1953; children: Jay, Ann, Paul, Sue, Jon, Peter. BS in Mktg., Notre Dame, 1952. Exec. v.p. mktg. Alpena (Mich.) Wholesale Grocer Co., from 1954. Trustee Alpena Twp., 1968-82; chmn. Alpena Twp. Zonning Bd. of Appeal, 1970-92; pres. Alpena Twp. Econ. Devel. Co., 1975-92. Sgt. U.S. Army, 1952-54. Avocations: hunting, golf, bowling, fishing. Home: Alpena, Mich. Died Apr. 23, 2004.

NUGENT, BARBARA ANN, medical facility administrator; b. Bklyn., Nov. 25, 1941; d. Joseph William and Catherine Theresa (Bykowska) Vanderbosch; (div.); children: Mary Ann, Joseph. Student, Molloy Coll., Rockville

Centre, N.Y., 1959-61; BS in Nursing, D'Youville Coll., 1963; MPA, Pa. State U., 1988. RN; cert. nursing adminstrn. Nursing supr. USNR, St. Albans, N.Y., 1963-65, Sasebo, Japan, 1965-66; staff nurse VA, Charlestown, S.C., 1970-71; instr. NASSAU Sch., East Meadow, 1971-75; dir., home health agy. Tempo Svcs., Fresh Meadow, N.Y., 1976; instr. Gloria K. Sch., Great Neck, N.Y., 1976; staff nurse, ICU Harrisburg (Pa.) Hosp., 1977; staff nurse, head nurse supr. VA Med. Ctr., Lebanon, Pa., 1977-85, resource allocation, DRG and UR coord., 1985-87, staff asst. to med. ctr. dir., 1987-89, staff asst., dir. Balt., from 1989. Cons. Pa. State U., Harrisburg, 1988-89; dir. VA ea. region, Balt., 1985-89; bd. advisors Susquehanna Health Care, Harrisburg, 1976-82. Author: The Effect of Utilization Review on the VA's Resource Allocation Methodology, 1988. Parish coun. St. Mary's Ch., Lebanon, Pa., 1985-87; multimedia instr. ARC, Lebanon, 1985-86; cons., facilitator Open Encounter, Ephrata, Pa., Canadaigua, N.Y., 1982-84; program devel. Pa. Right to Life, Lebanon, 1982-84; active Friendship Fire Co., Lebanon. Lt. USNR, 1963-66. Recipient Spl. Contribution award, Regional Dir. VA, Durham, 1988, Recognition award Mil. Order of Purple Hearts, Lebanon, 1984. Mem. VA Employees Assn., Am. Legion Aux., Am. Assn. Health Care Execs. (nominee). Roman Catholic. Avocations: reading, travel. Home: Baltimore, Md. Died July 7, 2004.

NUGENT, MAXINE E., bank executive; b. Canton, Tex., Sept. 26, 1931; d. John C. and Ora Frances (Pettit) Gamel; m. Chester L. Nugent, Aug. 4, 1953; children: LeAnne Nugent McClure, Karen F. Student, Longview Comml. Coll., 1951. With Peoples Loan Service, Longview, Tex., 1950-53, 1954-55, Federated Dept. Store, Longview, 1953, AAA Automobile Service, Longview, 1953-54, San Francisco Tex. Consumer Fin. Corp., 1958-65; v.p. Union Modern Mortgage Corp., Longview, from 1973. Tchr. Valley View Bapt. Ch., Longview, 1977—. Mem. Longview Bd. Realtors. Republican. Home: Longview, Tex. Died May 1, 2004.

NUNN, THOMAS CALVIN, school supervisor, retired army officer; b. Weleetka, Okla., Mar. 28, 1928; s. Ernest Howard and Beatrice (Thomas) N.; m. Agnes Ruth Zaletel, Sept. 2, 1950; children: Thomas C. Jr., Pamela, Becky, Marilyn, Linda. BA, Okla. State U., 1952; MA, U.S. Army Command & Gen. Staff Coll., 1967. Cert. sch. supr. Platoon leader 1st armored div. U.S. Army, Ft. Hood, Tex., 1950-52, provost marshal Fairbanks, Alaska, 1953-55, co. comdr. 1st cav. div. Korea, 1960-61, ops. officer Berlin, 1963-65, battalion comdr. 25th infantry div. Vietnam, 1967-68, chief plans and ops. fifth hdqrs. Ft. Sheridan, Ill., 1968-72, dep. comdr. criminal investigation command Heidleberg, Germany, 1972-74; supr. Lafourche Parish Sch. Bd., Thibodaux, La., 1974-95. Dir. army inst. LaFourche Parish Sch. Bd., Thibodaux, 1974-95. Co-chmn. Civic Com., Thibodaux, 1979. Lt. Col. U.S. Army, 1950-74. Decorated Legion of Merit (3 awards), D.F.C., Purple Heart (3 awards), others; named Outstanding La. Educator, State Dept. Edn., Baton Rouge, 1981; recipient Svc. award Citizen of Yr. City Svc. League, Thibodaux, 1990, Outstanding Civilian Svc. medal Dept. of the Army, 1995, Outstanding Vol. Activist award S.E. L.A. Area, 1994. Mem. DAV (life), VFW (life), Purple Heart Assn. (life), Am. Legion (v.p. 1975-79), Gulf South Suprs. Assn., La. Sch. Suprs. Assn., Lions Club (prs. 1978-79, Lion of Yr. 1979-80). Avocations: fishing, golf, gardening. Home: Thibodaux, La. Died Apr. 21, 2005.

NURI, SAYED ABDULLO, Tajikistani government official; b. Oshtien, Tajikistan, Mar. 15, 1947; married; 8 children. Leader Unite Tajik Oppostion, 1993—97; chmn. Nat. Reconciliation Commn., 1997—2000, Islamic Rebirth Party. Organizer Nahzati islomi, Islamic youth grp., 1974. Chief editor Minbari Islom, Qaziyat, Muslim spiritual directorate, 1988—92. Died Aug. 9, 2006.

NUTTER, CORINTHIAN C., school system administrator; b. Forney, TX, Dec. 10, 1906; d. Robert Rafe and Roxie Anna Ricks; m. Austin Kline Nutter, June 2, 1942 (dec.). BS in Adminstrn./Elem. Edn., Kans. State Tchr.'s Coll., 1950, MS in Adminstrn./Elem. Edn. Tchr. Dunbar Sch., Shawnee, Kans., 1938—43, Walker Sch., Merriam, Kans., 1943—49, Lincoln Sch., Olathe, Kans., 1950—54, prin., 1954—58, Westview Sch., Olathe, 1958—72. Former mem. bd. dirs. Cedar House, Inc., Olathe, Kans. Named to Rosa Parks Wall of Tolerance, Montgomery, Ala.; recipient Humanitarian award for Promoting Human and Civil Rights, N.E. Johnson County NAACP, Shawnee, Kans., 2001, Humanitarian and Human Dignity award, Olathe NAACP, 1981. Mem.: AAUW, NAACP (life), Alpha Kappa Alpha. Home: Shawnee Mission, Kans. Died Feb. 11, 2004.

NUTTER, DAVID EDWIN, psychiatrist, researcher; b. Lancaster, Pa., Apr. 3, 1947; s. Phosa David and Laura (Marsh) N.; m. Rita Rafas, July 14, 1973 (div. July 1991); children: David, Aaron; m. Susannah Maria Vail, May 16, 1992. BS, Hampden-Sydney Coll., 1969; MS, Villanova U., 1971; MD, Thomas Jefferson U., Phila., 1976. Diplomate Am. Bd. Psychiatry and Neurology, Am. Bd. Sexology, Nat. Bd. Med. Examiners. Teaching asst. Villanova (Pa.) U., 1969-70; resident in psychiatry Brown U., Providence, 1976-79, chief resident in psychiatry, 1978; fellow in psychopharmacology Hosp. U. Pa., Phila., 1979; clin. supr. Human Sexuality Ctr., Lancaster, Pa., 1980-84; staff psychiatrist St. Joseph Hosp., Lancaster, Pa., from 1980, chmn. dept. psychiatry, 1989-94; pvt. practice Lancaster, Pa., from 1980; med. dir. Samaritan Ctr., Lancaster, Pa., from 1989. Clin. asst. prof. dept. psychiatry and human behavior, Jefferson Med. Coll., Phila., 1981-89; cons. in human sexuality Compuserve-Computer Network, Columbus, Ohio, 1987—; presenter in field. Contbr. articles to profl. jours. Bd. dirs. Lancaster Guidance Ctr., 1984-86. Recipient Achievement award Am. Chem. Soc., 1965, Cert. of Excellence, Forum Mag. of Photography, 1991, 92, 93, 1st Place award New Danville (Pa.) Photo Expo, 1993. Mem. AMA, Pa. Med. Assn., Lancaster County Med. Assn., Soc. Sex Therapy and Rsch., Soc. Sci. Study of Sex (sci. com. ea. region, ea. rep. bd. dirs.), Psi Chi. Presbyterian. Avocation: photography. Home: Lancaster, Pa. Died Sept. 20, 2004.

NYE, CARRIE (CAROLYN NYE MCGEOY), actress; b. Greenwood, Miss., Oct. 14, 1936; m. Dick Cavett, 1964. Student, Stephens Coll.; grad., Yale Sch. of Drama, 1959. Actress: (Broadway debut) A Second String, Eugene O'Neill Theatre, 1960, (stage prodns.) Ondine, 1961, Mary, Mary, 1962, Macbeth, 1961, Troilus and Cresida, 1961, Ghosts, 1961, The Importance of Being Earnest, 1963, The Comedy of Errors, 1963, The Trojan Women, 1963, A Very Rich Woman, 1965, The White Devil, 1965, Home Fires, 1969, After Magritte, 1972, A Streetcar Named Desire, 1973, Platonov, 1977, The Little Foxes, 1977, Children of the Sun, 1979, The Man Who Came to Dinner, 1980, The Wisteria Trees, 1982, Paducah, 1985, The Madwoman of Chaillot, 1986, others, (TV movies) Divorce His/Divorce Hers, 1973, The Users, 1978, (TV mini-series) Moviola: The Scarlett O'Hara War, 1980. Died July 14, 2006.

NYKVIST, SVEN VILHEM, cinematographer; b. Moheda, Sweden, Dec. 3, 1922; s. Gustaf Nathanael and Gerda Emilia (Nilson) N.; 1 son, Carl-Gustaf. Student, Stockholm Photog. Sch.; doctorate (hon.), Am. Film Inst., 1991. Asst. cameraman, Stockholm, 1941-44; co-owner film prodn. co. Josephson-Nykvist, Stockholm. Cinematographer: (films) Sawdust and Tinsel, 1953, The Virgin Spring, 1960, Winter Light, 1962, Karin Mansdotter, The Silence, 1963, Loving Couples, 1964, Persona, 1966, Hour of the Wolf, 1968, One Day in the Life of Ivan Denisovich, 1971, The Dove, 1973, Cries and Whispers (Acad. award for Best Cinematography), 1973, Scenes from a Marriage, 1973, Black Moon, 1975, The Magic Flute, 1975, Face to Face, 1976, The Tenant, 1976, The Serpent's Egg, 1977, Autumn Sonata, 1978, King of the Gypsies, 1978, Pretty Baby, 1978, Hurricane, 1979, Starting Over, 1979, Willie and Phil, 1980, The Postman Always Rings Twice, 1981, Cannery Row, 1982, Fanny and Alexander (Acad. award for Best Cinematography), 1983, Star 80, 1983, Swann in Love, 1984, Agnes of God, 1985, Dream Lover, 1986, The Sacrifice, 1986, The Unbearable Lightness of Being, 1988, Another Women, 1988, Brothers, 1988, New York Stories (Oedipus Wrecks segment), 1988, Crimes and Misdemeanors, 1989, Buster's Bedroom, 1991, The Ox, 1991, Charlie, 1992, Sleepless in Seattle, 1992, Chaplin, 1992, Him, 1993, Gilbert Grape, 1993, Him, 1993, Night Before Christmas, 1993, With Honor, 1994, Only You, 1994, Mixed Nuts, 1994, Something to Talk About, 1995, Kirsten Laviansdatter, 1994, Celebrity, 1998, Curtain Call, 1999; (TV movies) Nobody's Child, 1986 Bergman, 1995 (Golden Eagle 1996), Private Confessions, 1996; dir. (films) The Vine Bridge, 1965; dir., cinematographer (films) Oxen, 1991; author: Resan Till Lambarene. Recipient Caesar French Acad. award, Swedish Acad. award, Doctorate Am. Film Inst., 1991. Mem. Swedish Film Acad., Am. Soc. Cinematographers (Life Achievement award 1996), Svenska Teaterforbundet. Home: Saltsjo-Duvnas, Sweden. Died Sept. 20, 2006.

OAKES, ROBERT GIBSON, retired electronics company executive, management consultant; b. Oyster Bay, N.Y., Mar. 20, 1918; s. George Nettleton and Sarah (Thornton) O.; m. Delores Marie Cook, June 12, 1954 (div. Oct. 1962); 1 child, Robert Jr. BBA, Manhattan Coll., 1941; postgrad., Harvard U., 1942-43; MBA, NYU, 1954; cert. in profl. contracts mgmt., UCLA, 1969. Cert. profl. contracts mgr. Enlisted USN, 1943, advanced through grades to comdr., asst. naval attache Rome, 1949-50, retired, 1965; adminstrv. buyer N. Am. Aviation Co., Downey, Calif., 1966-68; subcontract mgr. Rockwell Internat. Corp., Downey, 1968-72; head cost analysis group Hughes Aircraft Co., El Segundo, Calif., 1973-80, mgr. cost analysis, 1980-85, procurement mgr., spl. projects (Hughes-Gen. Motors), 1986-88; mgmt. cons., from 1988. Pres. Sunset Rep. Club, Sherman Oaks, Calif., 1988-89, 96-97. Fellow Nat. Contract Mgmt. Assn.; mem. Res. Officers Assn. (bd. dirs. chpt. 14, treas. 1996, sec., treas., pres. 1994-95), Ret. Officers Assn. (2nd v.p. San Fernando Valley chpt. 1994, bd. dirs. 1995-97), Am. Legion, Hughes Mgmt. Club (3d v.p. 1998), Mil. Order World Wars, Navy League U.S., KC (mem. coun. 43). Republican. Roman Catholic. Avocations: sailboat racing and cruising, golf, swimming. Died Aug. 23, 2004.

OAKLEY, GORDON SCOTT, engineer, retired, management consultant; b. Portland, Maine, Apr. 20, 1925; s. Ralph Bouidon and Grace Hazel (Scott) O.; m. Ida Faye Crumly; 1 child, Kathy Gail Oakley-Aitken. BS in Computer Sci. with honors, Ala. A&M U. Registered profl. engr., Calif.; lic. flight examiner and check airman. Flight and ground instr. USAF, 1948-53; final assy inspector Lockheed/Ga., Marietta, 1953; assy inspector foreman Hayes Internat., Birmingham, Ala., 1953-56, mgr., shipping and receiving inspector, 1956-58, engring. liaison, 1958-61, mgr. packaging engring. Huntsville, Ala., 1961-64, mgr. quality assurance and reliability, 1964-70, Computer Scis., Huntsville, 1970-74, mgr. engring., 1974-77; supr. logistics USBI/United Techs. Corp., Huntsville, 1977; mgr. range safety USBI/UTC, Huntsville, 1978-79, mgr. SR&QA, 1979-81, mgr. safety, reliability & quality assurance, 1981-85, mgr. space transp. system &advanced solid rocket booster, 1985-87, mgr. advanced ops., 1987-91; ret., 1991; supr. reliability & quality assurance McDonnell/Douglas, Huntsville, 1977-78. Mgmt. cons. in field. Patentee method for making solid rocket propellant. With inf. U.S. Army, 1943-45. Recipient Silver Snoopy award NASA Astronaut Corps, 1985. Republican. Seventh Day Adventist. Home: Huntsville, Ala. Died May 8, 2004.

OAKLEY, RICHARD EMBREY, III, waste services company executive, civil engineer; b. Orlando, Fla., Dec. 15, 1952; s. Richard Embrey Jr. and Bernice Hall (Holton) O.; m. Deborah Ann Scheier, Aug. 29, 1980; children: Lauren Elizabeth, Ryan Embrey. BSCE, U. Fla., 1977, MEng in Civil Engring., 1978. Registered profl. engr., Tex., La. Draftsman, designer Kessler & Wilhelm, Gainesville, Fla., 1974-77; survey crewman Dyer, Riddle, Precourt & Mills, Orlando, 1977; teaching asst. dept. civil engring. U. Fla., Gainesville, 1977-78; project engr. McClelland Engrs., Inc., Houston, 1978-83; project mgr. Browning-Ferris Industries, Houston, 1983-85, divisional v.p. environ. affairs dept., from 1985. Contbr. articles to profl. jours. With U.S. Army, 1972-74. Mem. ASCE (control group environ. concerns in geotech. enring. com. 1989—), ASTM (D34 waste disposal com. 1988—), Internat. Soc. Soil Mechanics and Founds. Engrs. Republican. Mem. Christian Ch. (Disciples Of Christ). Avocation: golf. Home: Houston, Tex. Died Sept. 21, 2004.

OATES, JOHN FRANCIS, classics educator; b. Holyoke, Mass., Aug. 7, 1934; s. William Adrian and Lilian (Woods) O.; m. Rosemary Walsh, June 27, 1957; children: Elizabeth, Emily, John Francis, Sarah. BA, Yale U., 1956, MA, 1958, PhD, 1960; postgrad. (Fulbright fellow), Am. Sch. Classical Studies in Athens, Greece, 1956-57. Instr. classics Yale U., 1960-63, asst. prof., 1963-67; asso. prof. ancient history Duke U., 1967-71, prof., 1971—2002, prof. emeritus, 2002—06, chmn. dept. classical studies, 1971-80, chmn. humanities coun., 1975-80, dir. database of documentary papyri, 1982—2006, dir. papyrus catalog project, 1992-95. Hon. rsch. asst. Univ. Coll. London, 1965—66; vis. prof. Smith Coll., Northampton, Maine, 1967, Northampton, 68; mem. mng. com. Intercollegiate Ctr. Classical Studies in Rome, 1972—77, Am. Sch. Classical Studies in Athens, 1973—2006, mem. com. on coms., 1975—77; mem. Coun. for Internat. Exch. of Scholars, 1974—77; v.p., trustee Triangle Univs. Ctr. for Advanced Study, Inc., 1975—90; trustee Nat. Humanities Ctr., 1977—90, trustee emeritus, 1990—2006; adv. coun. Sch. Classical Studies, Am. Acad. in Rome, 1976—2006; dir. summer seminar Nat. Endowment Humanities, 1978; dir. Nat. Fedn. State Humanities Couns., 1980—83; mem. N.C. Humanities Com., 1977—83, chmn., 1980—82; mem. adv. bd. Greek, Roman and Byzantine Studies, 1977—2006, Humanities Report, 1981—83. Author: The Status Designation, 1963; author: (with A.E. Samuel and C.B. Welles) Yale Papyri in the Beinecke Library, 1967; author: The Basilikos Grammateus, 1995, A Checklist of Papyrological Editions, 2001; author: (with J.D. Sosin) Duke Data Bank of Documentary Papyri; author: (with P.M. Sijpesteijn and A. Kaplony) Checklist of Arabic Papyri. ACLS fellow, 1973-74 Mem. Am. Philol. Assn. (chmn. com. computer activities 1974-75, dir. 1975-78, mem. nominating com. 1980-83), Archaeol. Inst. Am., Am. Hist. Assn., Am. Soc. Papyrologists (v.p. 1971-73, pres. 1976-80, dir.), Assn. Internationale de Papyrologues, Classical Assn. Middle West and South (v.p. 1972-74, pres. So. sect. 1974-76). Home: Durham, NC. Died June 24, 2006.

OBERMAN, HAROLD AUSTEN, physician, educator; b. Chgo., Oct. 21, 1932; s. Isidore Fred and Lillian (Simons) O; m. Marylen S. Oberman, Jan. 25, 1959; children: Michelle, Debra, Jeffrey. AB, U. Omaha, 1952; MD, U. Nebr., 1956. Intern and resident U. Mich. Hosp., Ann Arbor, 1956-61; asst. chief Walter Reed Gen. Hosp., Washington, 1961-63; from asst. prof. to prof. U. Mich., Ann Arbor, from 1963, dir. Blood Bank and Transfusion Svcs., from 1964, head. sect. clin. pathology, 1981-87, co-dir. clin. labs., from 1987. Mem. exam. com. Am. Bd. Pathology, Tampa, Fla., 1984—; cons. blood program ARC, Detroit, 1965—, Washington, 1984-88. Co-author: Tumors of the Breast, 1993; author, editor: Diagnostic Surgical Pathology, 1989; co-editor: Breast Cancer: Collaborative Management, 1988. Capt., U.S. Army, 1961-63. Mem. Am. Soc. Clin. Pathologists (disting. svc. award 1989), Coll. Am. Pathologists, Am. Assn. Blood Banks (bd. dirs. 1971-73, chmn. program com. 1984-87, assoc. editor Transfusion, 1973—; editor standards for blood banks and transfusion svcs. 1969-82), Alpha Omega Alpha. Avocations: tennis, bicycling. Home: Ann Arbor, Mich. Died Oct. 21, 2004.

O'BRIEN, CATHERINE THERESE, nurse; b. N.Y.C., Oct. 5, 1938; d. Patrick and Elizabeth (Henry) McParland; m. Thomas O'Brien, Aug. 8, 1959 (dec.); children: Thomas, Catherine, Nancy, Veronica. Diploma, Westchester Sch. Nursing, 1959; BS in Health Care Adminstrn., St. Joseph's Coll., 1987; MSN, Pace U., 1992. Cert. advanced oncology, med.-surg. nurse. Staff nurse Deepdale Gen. Hosp., Little-neck, N.Y., 1977-89, nurse educator, 1989-90, asst. dir. nursing edn., 1990-94; med. oncology coord. Cancer Inst. Mary Immaculate Hosp., Jamaica, N.Y., 1994-98; oncology clin. nurse specialist Vis. Nurse Svc. of N.Y., from 1999. Mem. Am. Cancer Soc. (exec. bd.), Oncology Nursing Soc.(Survivorship SIG coord., newsletter editor,

L.I./Queens chpt. past pres., chairperson program), N.Y. State Cancer and AIDS Pain Initiative (bd. dirs.), Sigma Theta Tau. Home: Mineola, NY. Died Mar. 18, 2004.

O'BRIEN, MICHAEL F., retail executive; b. Cleve., Apr. 1, 1944; s. James Leo and Donna M. (Frame) O'B.; m. Jean Ellen; children: Jeffrey, Timothy, Patrick. BA, U. Charleston, 1966. Salesman photo div. Honeywell Inc., L.A., 1966-68; pres. Flags Photo Ctrs., Inc., L.A., from 1968. Active arts council Pasadena (Calif.) Jr. Colls. Mem. Pasadena Mental Health Assn., Photo Mktg. Internat. Assn. (Territorial V.p. of Yr. award 1987), So. Calif. Photo Mktg. Assn., University Club, Elks Lodge. Avocations: boating, travel. Home: Pasadena, Calif. Died July 20, 2004.

O'BRIEN, ROBERT THOMAS, investment company executive; b. Phila., Oct. 7, 1941; s. James Francis Sr. and Mildred Anita (Gomez); m. Aurora Carol Forsthoffer, Nov. 7, 1964; 1 child, Michael Joseph. Cert., N.Y. Inst. Fin., 1963; BS, St. Joseph's U., 1971. Securities trader Brown Bros. Harriman, Phila., 1964-69, portfolio mgr., 1969-77, investment officer, 1977-80, asst. mgr., investment adv., 1980-83; v.p. Newbold's Asset Mgmt., Phila., 1983-85, sr. v.p., 1985-93, also bd. dirs., 1990-93; mng. dir. W.H. Newbold's Son & Co., Phila., from 1993. Bd. dirs. Cath. Philopatrian Literary Inst., 1973-76, Mary J. Drexel Home, 1992—, treas. 1992—; mem. fin. and investment com. Neumann Coll., 1990—. Served with USAF and Pa. Air N.G., 1960-67. Mem. Phila. Securities Assn., Air Force Assn. (life), Confederate Air Force (life, wing fin. officer 1992). Clubs: Racquet of Phila., Sailing Assn. (commodore 1980-82); Lewes Yacht, Miles River Yacht, Avalon Yacht, Eastport Yacht, Aronimink Golf, Idle Hour Tennis. Republican. Roman Catholic. Avocations: tennis, squash, sailing, golf. Home: Gladwyne, Pa. Died Aug. 18, 2004.

O'BRIEN, WILLIAM HENRY, civic organization administrator, lawyer; b. Chgo., Feb. 21, 1920; s. William Daniel and Mildred H. (Ferguson) O'B.; m. Patricia Courtney, Aug. 30, 1958; children: Catherine O'Brien McCuish, Mary Alice, William H. Jr. BA, Grinnell (Iowa) Coll., 1949; MPA, U. Mich., 1951; LLB, U. Detroit, 1958. Bar: Mich. 1960. Asst. exec. dir. Civic Searchlight, Inc., Detroit, 1952-57, exec. dir., from 1957. Trustee Nat. Automobile History Collection, 1980—. Editor Civic Searchlight's Voters Guide. V.p. Friends of Detroit Pub. Libr., 1977; pres. Indian Village Assn., Detroit, 1967. With USN, 1942-46, PTO. Mem. Detroit Bar Assn., Mich. Bar Assn. Roman Catholic. Avocations: reading, sailing. Died Apr. 20, 2004.

OCHS, RICHARD WAYNE, artist, art gallery owner; b. Newburgh, N.Y., Dec. 26, 1938; s. Harold John Ochs and Gertrude Adelaid Goetchius; m. Cindy Ochs, Apr. 14, 1968. AB in Econs. and Math., Hamilton Coll., 1960; postgrad., SUNY, New Paltz, 1961-70. Cert. secondary tchr., N.Y. Math. tchr. Newburgh Sch. Dist., 1960-92; artist, owner Richard Ochs Gallery, Newburgh, from 1993. Represented by Art Nook Gallery, Newburgh, 1979-93, Gallery Frame Shop, New Paltz, N.Y., 1996-, Jordane Artworks, Fort Myers Beach, Fla., 1998-2003, Nadeja Gallery, Newport, R.I., 2001—, Watermark Gallery, Tuckerton, NJ, 2003-; mem. Coast Guard Artists' Program. Treas. Newburgh Tchrs.' Assn., 1965; pres. Dutchess County Art Assn., Poughkeepsie, N.Y., 1979, trustee, 1975-76. Staff sgt. N.Y. ARNG, 1963-69. Recipient Grumbacher Gold medal Mt. St. Mary Coll., 1997, 98, George Gray award USCG. Fellow Am. Artist's Profl. League; mem. Artist's Fellowship, Hudson Valley Art Assn. (bd. dirs.), Kent Art Assn. (exec. bd. 1996—, 2d v.p. 1999-2000), North East Watercolor Soc. (treas. 1984-94, 1st v.p. 1995-97, pres. 1997-2002, 1st v.p. 2003-04, pres. 2004-, trustee 2001-2004), Mo. Watercolor Soc. (signature), Cmty. Arts Assn. (exec. bd. 1996—), Soc. Creative Artists of Newtown, Middletown, NY Artist's Group, Watercolor Soc. Ala., Soc. Marine Artists, Artist's Fellowship, Ctrl. NY Watercolor Soc., Morris County Art Assn. (tchg. faculty 2003—), Salmagundi Club Died Jan. 30, 2006.

O'CONNELL, JOSEPH D., lawyer, magistrate; b. Boston, June 4, 1954; s. James S. and Mary A. (Kelly) O'C.; m. Karla F. Huntington, Aug. 13, 1983; children: Connor J., Jordan E. AB cum laude, Boston Coll., 1975; JD cum laude, Suffolk U., 1979. Bar: Mass. 1979, Ariz. 1980, Alaska 1981, U.S. Dist. Ct. Alaska 1981, U.S. Ct. Appeals (9th cir.) 1994. Atty., VISTA vol. So. Ariz. Legal Aid, Tucson, 1979-81; atty. Alaska Legal Svcs. Corp., Anchorage, 1981-85; magistrate, standing master Alaska Ct. System, Palmer, 1985-90, magistrate Anchorage, 1991-93; solo practitioner Anchorage, 1993-97; shareholder Huntington & O'connell, P.C., Anchorage, from 1997. Mem. Amnesty Internat., Anchorage; co-chair Eagle River Optional Sch. Program, 1992-94, steering com., 1994—; mem. Eklutna dist. We. Alaska coun. Boy Scouts Am., 1994—, den leader, 1994-96, chair com., 1996—; bd. dirs. Abused Women's Aid in Crisis, Anchorage, 1982-85. Mem. Alaska Bar Assn. (family law com., presenter Ann. Conv. 1994), Mass. Bar Assn., Ariz. Bar Assn. Democrat. Avocations: history, chess, fishing. Home: Eagle River, Alaska. Died Jan. 7, 2005.

O'CONNELL, WILLIAM BUTLER, trade association executive; b. Chgo., Jan. 28, 1923; s. Thomas Joseph and Catherine Alice (Butler) O'C.; m. Marion Edythe Bissonette (dec. 1992), Oct. 30, 1943; children: William Butler, Robert D., Kevin T. BA, Loyola U., Chgo., 1945; postgrad., Northwestern U., 1947-48. Fin. writer Chgo. Daily News, 1945-48; pub. rels. counsel U.S. League of Savs. Instns., Chgo., 1948-77, sr. pub. affairs advisor, 1977-79, exec. v.p., CEO, 1980-88; pres., CEO, chmn. U.S. League Mgmt. Svcs. Inc., Chgo., 1989-90; vice-chmn. Fin. Instns. Ins. Fund, Inc., Chgo., from 1990. Contbr. articles to profl. jours. With U.S. Army, 1943-45. Recipient Disting. Service award Fed. Savs. and Loan Council, 1979; recipient Leadership award Homer Hoyt Inst., 1983 Mem. Am. Soc. Assn. Execs., Nat. Econ. Commn., Am. Legion, Park Ridge Club, Camelview Golf Club, Scottdale Club. Roman Catholic. Home: Glenview, Ill. Died Jan. 10, 2006.

O'CONNOR, JOEL STURGES, retired ecologist; b. Auburn, N.Y., Mar. 6, 1937; s. Donald James and Audrey (Harkness) O'C.; m. Eleanor Brocia, Jan. 7, 1976. BS, Cornell U., 1958; PhD, U. R.I., 1965. Chief Computer Ops. Br. Atomic Energy Commn., Oak Ridge, Tenn., 1965-68; sr. rsch. assoc. Brookhaven Nat. Lab., Upton, N.Y., 1968-71; from rsch. assoc. to assoc. prof. SUNY, Stony Brook, 1971-73; sr. ecologist Marine Ecosystem Analysis program Nat. Oceanic and Atmospheric Adminstrn., Stony Brook, 1973-85, sr. ecologist ocean assessments div. Rockville, Md., 1985-88; ocean policy coord. EPA, N.Y.C., 1988-99; ret., 1999. Vis. investigator Marine Biol. Lab., Woods Hole, Mass., 1970-74; mem. governing bd. Estuarine Rsch. Fedn., 1972-74; mem. sci. panel Hudson River Found., N.Y.C., 1984-87; chmn. U.S.-Can. Subcom. on Stewardship Indicators for Lake Ontario. Chmn. editl. bd. Marine Ecosystem Analysis N.Y. Bight Atlas Monograph series, 1975-82. Advisor L.I. Environ. Coun., Great Neck, N.Y., 1971-77; chair Head-of-the-Harbor and Nissequogue Joint Coastal Mgmt. Commn., 1997—. Mem. N.Y. Acad. Scis., Ecol. Soc. Am., Internat. Soc. Ecol. Econs., Cosmos Club, Phi Kappa Phi, Sigma Xi. Democrat. Home: Saint James, NY. Died Apr. 27, 2005.

O'CONNOR, THOMAS EDMUND, endowment executive; b. Cleve., Sept. 8, 1941; s. Ernest Edmund and Alice Frederica (Carlson) O'C.; m. Hilkka Helena Kauppinen, July 3, 1976; children: Kelly Alissa, Kara Johanna, Patrick Thomas. BA, Ohio Wesleyan U., 1963; diploma, U. Vienna, 1965; M of Internat. Svc., Am. U., 1967; M of Internat. Pub. Policy, Johns Hopkins U., 1981. Pub. affairs officer U.S. Consulate Gen., Hamburg, Germany, 1970-74; dir. regional resources unit U.S. Embassy, London, Eng., 1974-78; dep. dir. pvt. sector programs U.S. Info. Agy., Washington, 1978-80, exec. asst. to dir., 1981-83; pub. affairs officer U.S. Embassy, Helsinki, Finland, 1983-87, Vienna, Austria, 1987-91; dir. Office of Policy Guidance, Washington, 1991-93; dept. dir. program Nat. Endowment for Democracy, Washington, 1993-94; v.p. Youth for Understanding, Washington, from 1994. Dir. Fulbright Commn., Helsinki, 1984-86, Vienna, 1989-91. Mem. Am. Fgn. Svc. Assn., Nat. Press Club, Psi Chi (chpt. pres. 1962-63), Phi Beta Kappa. Home: Washington, DC. Died Jan. 10, 2004.

ODELL, JERRY A., insurance company executive; b. Phila., Oct. 7, 1926; s. Samuel and Pauline (Finnel) O.; m. Arlene Phylis Diamond, Dec. 26, 1954; children: Steven Andrew, Anne Diamond, Robert David. BS in Econs., U. Pa., 1950. Ins. broker Allman Bros., Phila., 1950-53; ptnr. S. Odell & Son, Phila., 1954-57; v.p. Waber-Odell Co., Phila. and Overbrook Hills, Pa., from 1957, pres. Wynnewood and Bala Cynwyd, Pa., from 1965. Mem. adv. council CNA Ins. Group, Phila., 1981-83, Utica (N.Y.) Mut., 1965-66, Crum & Foster, Phila., 1985—; instr. U. Pa., 1954. Contbr. articles to trade mags. Served to lt. (j.g.) USNR, 1946-53. Mem. Soc. Chartered Property Casualty Agts. (cert.), Profl. Ins. Agts., Nat. Assn. Ins. Agts., Phila. Pres.'s Orgn. (chmn. 1984), Young Pres.'s Orgn., World Bus. Council, Lloyd's Underwriting. Clubs: White Manor Country (Malvern, Pa.) (pres. 1984-86). Republican. Avocations: golf, photography, reading, swimming, walking. Home: Wynnewood, Pa. Died June 21, 2004.

O'DONNELL, MARY MURPHY, retired medical/surgical nurse; b. Lincoln, Ill., Feb. 21, 1918; d. Thomas Edward and Frances Ward (Hayes) Murphy; m. Maurice A. O'Donnell, Jan. 29, 1942. Diploma, St. John's Sch. Nursing, Springfield, Ill., 1939. RN Ill., Fla. Asst. to ear, nose and throat specialist, 1939—42; nurse U.S. Govt. Hosp., 1942—43; asst. to gen. practitioner Springfield, 1943—55; staff nurse City Health Dept., Springfield, 1955—65; dir. tng. and edn. Springfield and Sangamon County Civil Def. Agy., 1965—66; exec., cons. in charge med. self-help Ill. Dept. Pub. Health, 1966—74; nurse epidemiologist St. Joseph Hosp., Port Charlotte, Fla., 1975—91, part-time epidemiologist, 1992—93; ret., 1993. Cons., from 1993. Mem. AIDS task force Charlotte County Dept. Pub. Health, Fla., pres. epidemiology group Fla., 1991; instr. AIDS Program, 1987—93; v.p. S. Ctrl. Area Ill. Women's Civil Def. Coun.; mem. Civic Def. Coun.; chmn. civil def. activities ARC; v.p., mem. health svcs. adv. com. U.S. Civil Def. Coun.; ofcl. vol. rep. Am. Social Health Assn. Recipient Spl. award, State Dept. Am. Legion Aux., 1954, cert. Honor, Mayor of City of Springfield, 1966, Silver Wing bracelet, Ground Observer Corps, 1959, Pfizer award merit, U.S. Civil Def. Coun., 1969, Presdl. citation, 1972. Mem.: S.W. Regional Infection Control, Assn. Practitioners Infection Control, USAF Air Def. Team (hon.). Republican. Roman Catholic. Avocations: boating, swimming, clog dancing, golf, horses. Home: Punta Gorda, Fla. Died June 10, 2005.

O'DONNELL, ROBERT PATRICK, priest; b. Gary, Ind., June 11, 1919; s. Liquori Alphonsus and Carolyn Emily (Senn) O'D. Student, Art Inst., Chgo.; BA, U. Chgo., 1943; MA, Cath. U., 1945; postgrad., Gregorian U., Rome, 1980-81. Ordained priest Roman Cath. Ch., 1949. Asst. Sacred Heart Ch., Russellville, Ky., 1950-52; adminstr. Our Lady of Lourdes Ch., Otway, Ohio, 1953-55; pub. rels. Glenmary Home Missioners, Glendale, Ohio, 1956-60; chaplain Glenmary Sisters, Fayetteville, Ohio, 1960-66; pastor Holy Redeemer Ch., Vancebury, Ky., 1987-94, St. Agnes Ch., Elkton, Ky., 1981-87, St. Mary & St. James Ch., Guthrie, Ky., St. Francis De Sales Ch., Idabel, Okla., 1987-94; with Glenmary Home Missioners, Cincinnati, from 1994. Editor, photographer, illustrator Glenmary's Challenge, Cin., 1952-80; designer/builder seven chs. in Ky., Ohio, N.C., 1952-64. Founder/designer: Appalachian Studios-resident artist, gen. mgr., 1966-80; composer music, producer: (musical) From Sheeba They Came, 1990; producer: (movie) Glenmary Story, 1958; other. With maritime svc. USN, 1943, ATO. Recipient Thomas Jefferson award, U.S. Office of Pres., 1979, Four Chaplains Nat. award Office of Four Chaplains Found., Phila., 1981; Art scholar U. chgo. Mem. Rotary (internat. exc. chmn. 1989-91), Phi Kappa Psi (pres. 1943), AFL CIO, KC. Died July 22, 2004.

OEHLER, RICHARD DALE, lawyer; b. Iowa City, Dec. 9, 1925; s. Harold Lawrence Oehler and Bernito Babb; m. Rosemary Heineman, July 11, 1952, (div.); m. Maria Luisa Holguin-Zea, June 11, 1962; children: Harold D., Richard L. BA in Med. Scis., U. Calif., Berkeley, 1951; JD, Loyola U., L.A., 1961. Bar: Calif. 1962, Fla. 1968. Sales rep. Abbott Labs., Pasadena, Calif., 1951-63; with claims dept. Allstate Ins., Tampa, 1963-70; pvt. practice Tampa, from 1970. Instr. Dale Carnegie Courses West Fla. Inst., Tampa, Scott Hitchcock & Assocs., Tampa, 1969—. Pres. U. South Fla. Parents Assn., Tampa, 1986-87. Mem. Fla. Bar Assn., Hillsborough County Bar Assn., Acad. of Fla. Trial Lawyers, Assn. of Trial Lawyers of Am., Masons (32d degree), Shriners, Phi Beta Kappa. Republican. Presbyterian. Avocations: jogging, road races, target shooting, fishing. Died Dec. 7, 2004.

OESTMANN, MARY JANE, retired health science association administrator; b. Chgo., May 22, 1924; d. Charles Edward and Harriet Evelyn (Stoltenberg) O. BA in Math, Chemistry with honors, Denison U., 1946; MS, U. Wis., 1948, PhD, 1954; DSc (hon.), Denison U., 1975. Research chemist Inst. for Atom Energy, Oslo, 1954—55; vis. scientist AB Atom Energy, Stockholm, 1955—56; vis. prof. chem. dept. U. Iowa, Iowa City, 1957; sr. scientist Battelle Meml. Inst., Columbus, Ohio, 1957—61; assoc. chemist Argonne Nat. Lab, Ill., 1961—71; environ. project mgr. U.S. AEC, Washington, 1971—75; sr. radiation specialist U.S. Nuclear Regulatory Commn., Glen Ellyn, Ill., 1975—87; ret. Bd. dirs. U. Wis.-Madison Alumni Assn. of the So. Lakes, 1992—. Contbr. articles to profl. jours. Planning and zoning commn. Town of Burlington, 1991-2004; bd. trustees Plymouth Congl. UCC Ch. Burlington, 1993-96; mem. Art Inst. Chgo. Recipient UN Internat. Women's Yr. award Nuclear Regulatory Commn., 1975, Dist. Alumni citation Denison U., 1971. Fellow Am. Inst. Chemists, Am. Nuclear Soc. (bd. dirs. 1983-86); mem. Am. Chem. Soc., Inst. Environ. Sci. and Tech. (sr. mem.), Health Physics Soc. (sec.-treas. Midwest chpt. 1978, exec. com. 1983-86), NY Acad. Scis., Wis. Acad. Scis., Arts and Letters, Wis. Fedn. Rep. Women (1st Congl. Dist. 1990-2004), Nat. Parks Conservation Assn., Nat. Conservancy, Nat. Arbor Day Found., Am. Scandinavian Found., Burlington Woman's Club (treas., chair scholarship com. 1993—), Browns Lake Yacht Club (Burlington), Rep. Women Racine County-West Club (v.p. 1992-93, pres. 1994-2005, Anita Hunt award, Bovay award), Sigma Xi, Phi Beta Kappa, Sigma Delta Epsilon, Iota Sigma Pi Home: Burlington, Wis. Died June 17, 2006.

OFVERSTEDT, MARGARET ELISE, music educator, library and information scientist; b. Blue Earth, Minn., Feb. 15, 1933; d. George Adam and Olivia Elizabeth (Bartel) Hartwick; m. Elvir Harry Ofverstedt, Feb. 13, 1954; children: Rose Marie Ofverstedt Vohland, Karen Cowdry, Laurie Jaafar. Grad., U. Mo., Kansas City, 1976. Cert. music, libr. sci., math., English, elem. tchr. Mo. 7th gr. sci. tchr. St. Ann's Parochial, Prairie Village, Kans.; 3d and 4th gr. tchr. Pleasant Green Cmty. Sch., Kansas City, Kans.; sci. tchr. Oxford Park Acad.; tchr. Our Lady of the A, Kansas City; libr. Pleasant Green Cmty. Sch.; sub. tchr. Shawnee Mission and Olathe Pub. Schs., 1988—2001. Mem. Mendlesohn Choir, Kansas City, 1967—71, U. Mo. Kansas City Civic Choir, 1972—2000, Kansas City Mus. Club, 1972—2002; mem. staff Queen's Herald, 1990—2002. Ch. soloist. Home: Overland Park, Kans. Died July 11, 2004.

OGILVIE, ELISABETH MAY, author; b. Boston, May 20, 1917; Author: High Tide at Noon, 1944, Storm Tide, 1945, Honeymoon, 1947, The Ebbing Tide, 1947, Rowan Head, 1949, My World Is an Island, 1950, The Dawning of the Day, 1954, Whistle for a Wind: Maine 1820, 1954, No Evil Angel, 1956, Blueberry Summer, 1956, The Fabulous Year, 1958, The Witch Door, 1959, How Wide the Heart, 1959, The Young Islanders, 1960, Becky's Islands, 1961, Call Home the Heart, 1962, Turn Around Twice, 1962, Ceiling of Amber, 1964, Masquerade at Sea House, 1965, There May Be Heaven, 1966, The Seasons Hereafter, 1966, The Pigeon Pair, 1967, Waters on a Starry Night, 1968, Bellwood, 1968, Come Aboard and Bring Your Dory, 1969, The Face of Innocence, 1970, A Theme for Reason, 1970, Weep and Know Why, 1972, Strawberries in the Sea, 1973, Image of a Lover, 1974, Where the Lost Aprils Are, 1975, The Dreaming Swimmer, 1976, An Answer in the Tide, 1978, A Dancer in Yellow, 1979, The Devil in Tartan, 1980, Beautiful Girl, The Silent Ones, 1981, Too Young to Know, 1983, The Road to Nowhere, 1983, Jennie About to Be,

1984, My Summer Love, The World of Jennie G, 1986, The Summer of the Osprey, 1987, When the Music Stopped, 1989, Jennie Glenroy, 1993, The Day Before Winter, 1997. Died Sept. 9, 2006.

OGWYN, JOHN HARDY, minister; b. Taylor, La., Mar. 29, 1949; s. John Hardy and Trudy B. (Miller) O.; m. Imogene Slotsve, June 6, 1971; children: Charles Ogwyn, David Ogwyn. BA, Ambassador Coll., Pasadena, Calif., 1971. Tchr. Imperial Schs., Pasadena, Calif., 1970-71; ch. pastor Worldwide Ch. of God, Cape Girardeau, Mo., from 1971, Paducah, Ky., 1973-74, Corpus Christi, Tex., 1974-79, Houston, 1979-87, Baton Rouge, La., 1987-93; pastor Global Ch. of God, Baton Rouge, from 1993. Coord. S.E. Tex. dist. Youth Opportunities United, Houston, 1982-84; Worldwide Ch. of God chaplain Tex. Dept. Corrections, Huntsville, 1979-87; pastor South-Cen. U.S.A. region Global Ch. of God. Assoc. editor World Ahead mag.; contbr. articles to profl. jours. Mem. La. Cattleman's Assn., Sons of Confederate Vets. Avocations: reading, hiking, camping, cattleraising. Home: Kilgore, Tex. Died June 14, 2005.

OHANIAN, EDWARD, psychologist; b. Selma, Calif., Nov. 14, 1922; s. Benjamin and Mary (Gorouzian) O.; m. Martha Loraine Taylor, Aug. 17, 1950; chidlren: Valerie Gay, Lee Edward. BA, U. So. Calif., 1947, MA, 1950, PhD, 1952. Lic. psychologist, Calif. Instr. U. Mont., Missoula, 1953-54; asst. prof. Pepperdine U., L.A., 1954-57, assoc. prof., co-dir. psychology-speech clinic, 1958-61; pvt. practice L.A., 1961-67, Carmel, Calif., from 1967. Cons. Freeman Clinic, L.A., 1952-53; vis. prof. U. Calif., L.A., Santa Barbara, Santa Cruz, Riverside, 1956-82; dir. Parent Tng. Ctr., L.A., 1957-59; lectr. Loyola U., L.A., 1961-67. With USNR, 1942-45, PTO. Mem. APA, Wine and Food Soc. Monterey Peninsula (pres. 1973-74), Brotherhood Knights of the Vine (master knight). Avocations: hiking, swimming, ecological environmentalist. Died Mar. 1, 2004.

O'HANLON, JOHN REED, lawyer; b. Council Bluffs, Iowa, Oct. 18, 1946; s. Clark James and Eleanor (Lutz) O'H.; m. Paula Jean Vellucci, June 15, 1968; children: Megan Kelley, Reed Paul. BS, U. Nebr., 1968; JD, Creighton U., 1971. Bar: Nebr. 1972, U.S. Dist. Ct. Nebr. 1972. City atty., Kennard, Blair, Herman, Nebr., 1977-82; city atty. Ft. Calhoun, Nebr., 1977-82; ptnr. O'Hanlon Law Officers, Blair, from 1982; owner, operator Blair Abstract & Title Co., Blair, 1972. Bd. dirs. Thousand Adventures, Inc., Heartland Travel, Inc.; pres. Arch, Inc., Omaha, 1985—. Mem. ABA, Nebr. Bar Assn., Washington County Bar Assn. (pres. 1980), Blair C. of C. (pres. 1976), Phi Alpha Delta. Republican. Roman Catholic. Avocation: golf. Home: Blair, Nebr. Died Sept. 15, 2004.

O'HARA, SUSAN J., secondary school educator; b. Creston, Iowa, July 10, 1946; d. Ervin Adolph and Thelda Irene (Mangels) Queck; m. Dennis Michael O'Hara, Nov. 26, 1971 (div. July 1980). BA in English, Wartburg Coll., 1968; MA in Elem. Edn., Pacific Luth. U., 1970. Cert. tchr. with reading endorsement. Tchr. corps. intern Sumpter (S.C.) Pub. Schs., 1968-69, Tacoma Pub. Schs., 1969-70; tchr. 4th grade South Umpqua Sch Dist., Myrtle Creek, Oreg., 1970-79, tchr. chpt. I, from 1979. Treas. edn. 1st com. Myrtle Creek, 1984—; bd. dirs. People for Improvement in Edn. OEA, Tigard, Oreg., 1984-86,; negotiators cadre Riddle (Oreg.) Edn. Assn., 1985—, Glide Edn. Assn. Contbr. articles to profl. jours. Mem. commn. Douglas County Cen. Com., Roseburg, Oreg., 1984—; del. 4th dist. Dem. Conv., Eugene, Oreg., 1985, Platform Conv., Beaverton, Oreg., 1986. Mem. NEA, Oreg. Edn. Assn. (bd. dirs. 1986—), Internat. Reading. Assn., Umpqua-Rogue UniServe Council, South Umpqua Edn. Assn. (pres. 1981-82, 85-87), Beta Sigma Phi. Democrat. Lutheran. Avocations: reading, sewing, crafts, politics, socializing. Died Aug. 20, 2005.

O'KEEFE, NANCY JEAN, retired real estate company executive; b. Mpls., Minn., Jan. 26, 1926; d. Dana Charles and Bonnie Theresa (Lane) Eckenbeck; m. John Robert O'Keefe, Sept. 11, 1946 (div. June 1977); children: Teresa O'Keefe Ankeny, J. Patrick, Leslie O'Keefe Kelly, Bridget O'Keefe Gidley, Elizabeth, Peter. BS in Social Welfare, U. Minn., 1973. Cert. real estate specialist, Minn., real estate appraiser, Minn.; grad. Real Estate Inst. Sales agt. Harvey Hansen Realty, Edina, Minn., 1976-87; pres., mgr., agt. 1st Mpls. Realty, Edina, 1987-92; agt. Great. Mpls. Real Estate, 1992-99; ret., from 1999. Mem. 5th Dist. Rep. Com., Mpls., 1951-52, Minn. Rep. Ctrl. Com., 1951-52; dist. chmn. fund drive ARC, Mpls., 1956; city chmn. fund drive March of Dimes, Mpls., 1957, 58; bd. dirs. St. Barnabas Hosp., Mpls., 1960-61; pres. Mpls. League Cath. Women, 1974-75. Mem. Minn. Assn. Realtors (bd. dirs. 1990-92), Greater Mpls. Assn. Realtors (bd. dirs. 1986-89, chmn. arbitration bd. 1988, Super Sales Agt. award 1982), Profl. Women's Appraisal Assn., Am. Arbitration Assn. (panel), Pi Beta Phi. Roman Catholic. Avocations: writing, poetry, watercolors, bridge, reading. Home: Minneapolis, Minn. Died Mar. 19, 2004.

OKIN, SUSAN MOLLER, political science educator; b. Auckland, New Zealand, July 19, 1946; came to U.S., 1970; d. Erling Leth and Kathleen Marion (Morton) Moller; m. Robert L. Okin, July 29, 1972; children: Laura, Justin. BA, U. Auckland, New Zealand, 1966; MPhil, Oxford U., Eng., 1970; PhD, Harvard U., 1975; PhD (hon.), Mt. Vernon Coll., 1991. Asst. prof. Brandeis U., Waltham, Mass., 1976-81, assoc. prof., 1981-89, prof., 1989-90; Marta Sutton Weeks prof. of ethics in soc., dir. ethics in soc. program Stanford U., Calif., 1990—2004. Author: Women in Western Political Thought, 1979, Justice, Gender and the Family, 1989; contbr. articles to profl. jours. and chpts. to books. Recipient Bing Tchg. fellowship Stanford U., 1995. Mem. Am. Polit. Sci. Assn. (Victoria Schuck prize 1990), Am. Soc. for Legal and Polit. Philosophy, Conf. for Polit. Thought. Democrat. Avocations: reading, swimming, music, gardening, skiing. Home: Los Altos, Calif. Died Mar. 3, 2004.

OKLAND, STEPHEN DOUGLAS, sales executive; b. Fredrick, Wis., July 3, 1942; s. Elmer Norman and Lorene G. (Johnson) O.; m. Dorothy S. Wray, Jan. 7, 1962; children: Stephen D. Jr., Scott M., Sean D. BA, U. S.C., 1965. Terr. mgr. Baxter/Travenol Labs., Savannah, Ga., 1965-67, med. electronics specialist Atlanta, 1967-70, field asst., dist. mgr. Denver and Dallas, 1970-75, regional mgr. Dallas, 1975-77; nat. sales mgr. Litton Med. Electronics, Dallas, 1977-80; v.p. sales & mktg. Biochem Internat. Inc., Milw., 1980-84; dir. sales & mktg. Nat. Control Systems Inc., Milw. and Dallas, 1984-86; dir. sales Criticare Systems, Dallas, 1986-88, v.p. sales, from 1988. Cons., ptnr. ESM & Assocs., Dallas, 1985—. Bd. dirs. Grapevine (Tex.) Athletic Booster Club, 1987; charter mem. Republican Task Force, Grapevine. Recipient Daniel J. Peterson Meml. award, 1968. Mem. Am. Anthropol. Assn., Am. Soc. Indsl. Security. Clubs: Grapevine High Sch. Booster (bd. dirs. 1987). Republican. Lutheran. Avocations: youth sports, athletics, reading. Home: Southlake, Tex. Died June 5, 2004.

OKOBRICK, MICHAEL EDWARD, marketing executive; b. Bronx, N.Y., Aug. 23, 1939; s. Michael Joseph and Jean Alice (Abramczyk) O.; m. Mary Marguerite Temple, Oct. 15, 1960; children: Theresa, kelly, Heidi. Student, Porter Design Sch., 1966, Worcester Poly. Inst., 1983; BBA, Calif. Coast U., 1987, MBA in Mktg., 1988. Design engr. Gerber Sci. Inst. Co., South Windsor, Conn., 1964-67; product mgr. Iona Mfg. Co., Manchester, Conn., 1967-73; real estate broker Okobrick Realty, Vernon, Conn., 1973-77; sales, mktg. rep. Guest Co., Meriden, Conn., 1977-87; pres., owner Delta Internat. Marine Products, Vernon, from 1987; owner R&S Repair Ctr., Vernon, Conn., from 1990. Cons. in field. Author manual: Customer Service, 1985. With U.S. Army, 1960-64. Mem. Am. Boat and Yacht Council, Nat. Marine Mfrs. Assn., Conn. Marine Trades Assn., Am. Soc. Mfg. Engrs., Brit. Am. Club (Manchester), Polish Am. Club (Vernon). Republican. Roman Catholic. Avocations: racquetball, softball, tennis. Home: Vernon Rockville, Conn. Died Aug. 6, 2004.

O'KONSKI, CHESTER THOMAS, chemistry professor; b. Kewaunee, Wis., May 12, 1921; s. Thomas Michael and Stella (Ratajczak) O'K.; m. A. Hollingsworth, 1948 (div. 1975); children: Holly Ann, Timothy Chester, Mark Steven, Brian Nelson. BS, U. Wis., 1942; MS, Northwestern U., 1946, PhD, 1948. Instr. chemistry dept. U. Calif., Berkeley, 1948-50, asst. prof., 1950-56, assoc. prof., 1956-60, prof., 1960-91, prof. chemistry emeritus, 1991—2006. Mem. faculty grad. biophysics program U. Calif., 1952-91; Knapp lectr. U. Wis., 1958; Miller rsch. prof. U. Calif., Berkeley, 1960; Nobel guest prof. Uppsala U., Spring, 1970, Kerr medal electro-optics, 1991; vis. rsch. prof. U. Erlangen, U. Basel, Weismann Inst., 1978, U. Ill., fall, 1989. Co-author, editor: Molecular Electro-optics, Part I Theory and Methods, 1976, Part 2 Applications to Biopolymers, 1978; contbr. articles to profl. jours. NRC fellow, 1946-48; Guggenheim fellow Leiden U., Netherlands, 1955; NIH spl. fellow Princeton U., Harvard U., 1962-63. Mem. AAAS, Am. Chem. Soc., Am. Phys. Soc., Biophys. Soc., Thomas More and Jacques Maritain Soc., Internat. Com. for Molecular Electro-Optics (hon.), Phi Beta Kappa, Sigma Xi (pres. Bk. chpt. 1976-77), Phi Eta Sigma, Phi Lambda Upsilon, Phi Lambda Mu, Alpha Chi Sigma. Home: Richmond, Calif. Died Aug. 2, 2006.

OLAH, ELSA CRUZ, state government specialist; b. Guaynabo, P.R., Jan. 29, 1942; d. Felix Cruz and Justina (Lopez) Rivera; children: Gizella, Paul. EdM, Rutgers U., 1979. cert. tchr., Mass. Mgr. Alme Corp., Bklyn., 1958-63, Mr. Ephraim, N.Y.C., 1965-70; research asst. Rutgers U., Camden, N.J., 1976-82, teaching asst., 1980-82; trainer counsel Temple U., Phila., 1982-85; program specialist N.J. Dept. Health, Trenton, from 1985. Author Spanish poetry, plays; contbr. articles to profl. jours. Mem. Assn. Female Execs., Rutgers U. Alumni Assn., Sociedad Nacional Hispanica, Museo Del Pueblo, Kappa Delta Pi. Avocations: writing, acting. Died Mar. 1, 2004.

OLBIS, KAREN, elementary education educator, musician, vocalist; b. Freehold, N.J., Oct. 18, 1964; d. John Anthony and Caroline Dorothy (Faber) O. BA, Rutgers U., 1987, M of Ednl. Adminstrn., 1991; postgrad., Juilliard Sch. Music, N.Y.C., 1987-88. Cert. tchr. of nursery sch., elem. sch., English and music, N.J.; cert. paralegal. Pub. sch. tchr., Freehold, n.J., from 1984. Cantor, soloist St. Robert Bellarmine Ch., Freehold, 1982—; voice tchr. in pvt. studio, Freehold, 1990—; free-lance soloist, 1984—. Soloist Orch. St. Peter-by-the-Sea, others. Singer, actress in community theater, 1983—; singer in community and profl. choral orgns., 1983—. Roman Catholic. Avocations: reading, antiques, theater, golf, piano. Home: Freehold, NJ. Died July 23, 2005.

OLDS, GLENN ALVERO, former state official, former academic administrator; b. Sherwood, Oreg., Feb. 28, 1921; s. Glenn Alvero and Hazel (Ross) O.; m. Eva Belle Spelts, June 20, 1944; children— Linda Olds, Glenn Richard. AB magna cum laude, Willamette U., 1942, D.D. (hon.), 1955; B.D. with highest distinction, Garrett Theol. Sem., 1945; MA in Philosophy with honors (Swift Travelling fellow), Northwestern U., 1945; PhD in Philosophy (Robinson fellow), Yale U., 1948; D.Humanics (hon.), Springfield Coll., Mass., 1965; L.H.D., Inter-Am. U. P.R., 1968, Lakeland Coll., 1971; LL.D., Akron U., 1971; L.H.D., Muhlenberg Coll., 1972; LL.D., Central Mich. U., 1976, St. Lawrence U., 1975; D.Litt., Redlands U., 1974, Hon. Academian, China Acad., Taiwan, 1967, Academico Honoris Causa, Mexican Acad. Internat. Law, 1967; D.H.L. (hon.), Chung-Ang U., Korea, 1978; D. Pub. Svc., Nazareth Coll., 1988. Asst. in instruction Yale U., 1947-48; asst. prof. philosophy DePauw U., Greencastle, Ind., 1948; assoc. prof. philosophy and ethics Garrett Theol. Sem., 1948-51; univ. chaplain, prof. U. Denver, 1951-54; dir. united religious work Cornell U., 1954-58; pres. Springfield Coll., 1958-65; exec. dean for internat. studies and world affairs State U. N.Y. System, 1965-68; spl. asst. to Pres. for policy & manpower devel. The White House, Washington, 1968-69; amb. to UN US Dept. State, 1969-71; pres. Kent (Ohio) State U., 1971-77, Alaska Pacific U., Anchorage, 1977-88; mem. council Center for Integrative Edn., 1958-91; commr. commerce and econ,. devel. and internat. trade State of Alaska, Juneau, 1991-92, commr. natural resources. Vis. prof. philosophy Northwestern U., 1948-51; cons. in field; mem. exec. com. internat. edn. Nat. Assn. State Univs. and Land-Grant Colls., 1966-68, mem. com. ednl. opportunities for minority groups; trustee Dag Hammarskjold Coll., 1968— Interfiath Campus Ministry, N.E. Ohio Coll. Medicine, 1974—; bd. dirs. Ednl. Futures Internat., Inst. Noetic Scis., 1974—, Commonwealth North, 1979; founding mem. U.S. Com. for UN Univ., Alaska Aerospace Devel. Corp.; chmn. Consortium for Internat. Energy Research; mem. Commn. Honest Elections Alaska, 1978; del. Global Forum, Moscow, 1990; adj. prof. philosophy culture, U. Alaska, 1991, 92. Author: The Christian Corrective: Christ Transforming Culture: Study Guide for the Conscience of Culture, 1953; contbr. articles to profl. publs. Mem. Ohio Gov's. Adv. Council on Malabar; mem. Met. Akron (Ohio) Jobs Council; bd. dirs. Council Study Mankind; gov. Blossom Festival Soc., Ohio; pres. bd. Design Sci. Inst.; ex-officio trustee Akron Art Inst.; chmn. Alaska State Bond Com., Alaska State Salmon Task Force; vice chmn. Alaska Indsl. and Export Authority, Alaska State Housing Authority; statutory mem. Alaska Amateur Sports Authority, Alaska R.R. Corp., Alaska Energy Authority, Alaska Housing Fin. Corp., Alaska Student Loan Corp., Alaska Coastal Policy Coun., Gov.'s Mini-Cabinets on Rural Econ. Devel. and Natural Resource Devel., Alaska Sci. and Tech. Found.; mem. Am. Coun. for UN U.; founding mem. Denali Found., 1990. Recipient Outstanding Citizen award City of Springfield, 1965, Outstanding Tchr. award U. Denver, 1953, Am. Alliance William H. Anderson award, 1986, Alaska Pacific U. medal, 1986, Disting. Alumni Svc. award Northwestern U., 1981; Nat. Council on Religion in Higher Edn. Nat. fellow, 1946. Mem. Oceanic Soc. (charter), Blue Key, Omicron Delta Kappa, Tau Kappa Alpha, Omicron Delta Sigma, Eta Sigma Gamma (hon.) Home: Falls Church, Va. Died Mar. 11, 2006.

O'LEARY, STEPHEN BARRY, church administrator; b. Mpls., Aug. 31, 1925; s. Stephen Barry and Leola Darwina (Layden) O'L.; m. Shirley Elaine Vinton, Dec. 26, 1947; children: Lesley, Bruce, Daniel. BBA, U. Minn.; MDiv., Seabury-Western Theol. Sem., DD (hon.), 1976. Planning and devel. officer Episcopal Diocese Minn., Mpls., 1969-73, adminstrv. officer, from 1973. Trustee Seabury Western Theol. Sem., 1970-78. Author: Planning for Action, 1970. Served with U.S. Army, 1943-45, ETO. Home: Minneapolis, Minn. Died Mar. 26, 2004.

OLENIK, CAROL STATON, nurse educator; b. Hanover, Pa., Jan. 5, 1945; d. Philip Hartford and Margaret Louise (Brauning) Staton; m. Joseph Olenik, Oct. 29, 1966; 1 child, Christina Lynn. Diploma, Ch. Home and Hosp., 1966; BS, St. Joseph's Coll., 1984. Asst. head nurse U.S. Army Hosp., West Berlin, Germany, 1977-80; head nurse Springfield Hosp. Ctr., Sykesville, Md., 1980-84, nurse instr., from 1984. Recipient United Way Vol. of the Yr. award, 1985, Gov.'s Ounce of Prevention Award, 1990. Mem. Ch. Home Alumni Assn., Md. League for Nurses (bd. dirs. and convention com. chair). Home: Sykesville, Md. Died July 1, 2005.

OLFORD, STEPHEN FREDERICK, religious organization administrator, minister; b. Kalene Hill, Northern Rhodesia, Mar. 29, 1918; came to U.S., 1959; s. Frederick Ernest Samuel and Bessie Rhoden (Santmier) O.; m. B. Heather Brown, June 30, 1948; children: Jonathan MacGregor, David Lindsay. Student, Oxford U., Eng.; Diploma in Theology, St. Luke's Coll. Mildmay, London, 1937; postgrad., Missionary Tng. Colony Upper Norwood, London, 1939; ThD, Luther Rice Sem., 1978; DD (hon.), Dallas Bapt. U., 1983, Wheaton (Ill.) Coll., 1966; LittD (hon.), Houghton Coll., 1966; HHD (hon.), Richmond Coll., Toronto, Ont., Can., 1975. Ordained to ministry Bapt. Ch., 1953. Army chaplain, Newport, South Wales, 1939-45; sr. min. Duke St. Bapt. Ch., Richmond, Surrey, Eng., 1953-59, Calvary Bapt. Ch., N.Y.C., 1959-73; pres. Encounter Ministries, Inc., Memphis, from 1973. Mem. coun. reference Evang. Bible Sem., Republic South Africa, 1986—, Helps Internat. Ministries, Harlem, Ga., 1988—, S.Am. Mission, Lake Worth, Fla., 1989—, Women Alive Ministries, Collingswood, N.J., 1982—, Italy for Christ, Atlanta, 1984—; mem. adv. bd. Internat. Bible Reading Assn., Murfreesboro,

Tenn., 1989—. Author 19 books, 14 booklets; contbr. articles to religious periodicals. Recipient award for 15th yrs. on Sta. WPIX-TV, 1975, Faith and Freedom award Religious Heritage of Am., 1983; Disting. Svc. award Nat. Religious Broadcasters, 1987, honor award So. Cen. chpt., 1991. Fellow Royal Geographic Soc., Philos. Soc. Great Britain (life). Home: Memphis, Tenn. Died Aug. 29, 2004.

OLIGARIO, MAX, retired accountant; b. Port-Au-Prince, Haiti, Sept. 17, 1920; arrived in U.S., 1958; s. Felix and Guillermina (Gonzales) Oligario; m. Gnislaine Romulus; children: Natasha, Sagine, Max Oligario Jr.; m. Fernande St. Leger (div.); 1 child, Carole. AS in Engring. Scis., Nassau C.C., 1965; BBA, Hofstra U., 1969; MS in Pub. Acctg., C.W. Post Coll., 1972. CPA N.Y.; ordained 1999. Mgr. Champs Ednl. Supplies, Mineola, NY, 1958—66; asst. supr. cost acctg. Gt. Lakes Carbon, NY, 1966—69; supr., auditor Sperry/Unisys, Nassau County, NY, 1969—88; pvt. practice Brentwood, NY, 1988—89; ret., 1990. Mem. Rep. Presdl. Task Force Presdl. Commn., Washington, 1986; mem. Presdl. Round Table, Washington, from 1993; life mem. Rep. Presdl. Task Force, Washington, 1989. Named Donor of Yr., Hospitalized Vets., 2002; recipient Order of Merit, Rep. Presdl. Legion of Merit, 1994, Cert. of Appreciation, Nat. Pk. Trust, 1995, Nat. Children's Cancer Soc., 2001, Royal honor, Principality of Hutt River Province, 1996—97. Home: Fort Myers, Fla. Died Apr. 29, 2004.

OLIVER, DANIEL ANTHONY, electrical engineer, company executive; b. Camden, N.J., Sept. 15, 1939; s. James D. and Mary Catherine (Duda) O.; m. Judith Anne Hatch, Oct. 15, 1966; children: Jeanne Marie, James Daniel II, Joseph, J. Andrew, Jerome, Judith, Anne, Justin, Joy, Jackson. BSEE, U. Colo., 1960; MS, BA, Drexel U., 1970. Design engr. def. space and spl. systems group Burroughs Corp., Paoli, Pa., 1963-67; prin. programmer Univac div. Sperry Rand Corp., Blue Bell, Pa., 1967-73; mgr. Can. ops. Fairchild Test Systems Group, San Jose, Calif., 1973-81; pres., founder Dan Oliver & Assocs., Inc., Haddon Heights, N.J., from 1981; prin. Source Sci., Inc., Haddon Heights, from 1988. Contbr. articles to profl. jours. With U.S. Army, 1960-63. Recipient best tech. paper award Hanover (Germany) Fair, 1982. Mem. Assn. Test Engrs. (sr.), Am. Aviation Hist. Soc., U.S. Naval Inst. (life), Assn. Old Crows (adv. bd. 1987—), Am. Legion, Polish Legion Am. Vets. Republican. Roman Catholic. Achievements include patent for design or fixuring for a 50 OHM environment. Home: Haddon Heights, NJ. Died Sept. 15, 2004.

OLIVERA, HERBERT ERNEST, business educator, accountant, consultant; b. N.Y.C., Apr. 6, 1923; s. James Phillip and Francella (Haylett) O.; m. Jewell Hackett, July 4, 1956; children: Herbert Ernest Jr., Angela Dawn; m. Elizabeth Bacon, Dec. 21, 1969. BS, Ky. State U., 1950; MA, NYU, 1953; MBA, U. Oreg., 1961; M in Acctg., U. Ariz., 1969, PhD, 1973. CPA, Ky., Ariz., Ill., Ala., Md. Assoc. prof. Ky. State U., Frankfort, 1955-68; rsch. asst. U. Ariz., Tucson, 1968-70; assoc. prof. Pima (Ariz.) Coll., 1970-73; chmn. acctg. Gov.'s State U., Park Forest, Ill., 1973-77; dean Sch. Bus., Ala. A&M U., Huntsville, 1977-81, Sch. Bus., Morgan State U., Balt., 1981-88; prof. Sch. Bus., Towson (Md.) U., from 1988. Prin. Herbert Olivera & Assocs., Park Forest, 1973-79; cons., co-owner Olivera-Bashty Buckenmeyer, Park Forest, 1975-79. Mem. Pima County Health Planning Commn., Tucson, 1970-73; pres. SCORG/ACE, Huntsville; mem. Xiamen Sister City Com.; mem., chmn. fin. and tax com. Village of Park Forest, 1974-78. Served with USMC, 1944-46. Named Outstanding Tchr., Ky. State U., 1965. Mem. Am. Acctg. Assn., Balt. Engring. Club, Fin. Execs. Inst., Govtl. Acctg. Assn., Am. Taxation Assn., HUB Club (chmn. econ. devel. com. 1984—), Alpha Kappa Mu, Beta Alpha Psi, Beta Gamma Sigma. Democrat. Episcopalian. Home: Belcamp, Md. Died Nov. 1, 2004.

OLKOWSKI, ZBIGNIEW LECH, physician, educator; b. Wilno, Poland, Nov. 24, 1938; came to U.S., 1970; s. Joseph and Jane (Poplawska) O.; m. Krystyna Nardelli, Apr. 15, 1963. MD, Silesian U., Zabrze, Poland, 1963, ScD, 1969. Cert. lab. dir., Ga. Assoc. prof. dept. radiation oncology Emory U. Med. Sch., Atlanta, 1972-75, assoc. prof., from 1975; dir. lab. tumor biology Emory U. Clinic, Atlanta, 1973-85; resident radiation oncology Emory U. Med. Sch., Atlanta, 1976-78, fellow radiation oncology, 1979-80. Mem. spl. study sect. on cancer Nat. Cancer Inst., Bethesda, Md., 1980; mem. senate com. on environ. Emory U., Atlanta, 1992-94. Contbr. over 60 articles on oncology and clin. immunology to nat. and internat. sci. jour., 1970-92, over 10 chpts. to books. Recipient contracts and grants NIH, Bethesda, Md., 1976-85. Fellow Internat. Acad. Cytology, Royal Microscopical Soc.; mem. Brit. Inst. Radiology, Am. Soc. Therapeutic Oncology, Am. Rifle Assn. (life), Nat. Skeet Shooting Assn. (life), Ga. Skeet Shooting Assn. (life). Achievements include discovery of dopamine and serotonine transporters system in human lymphocytes, method of labeling and "education" of human lymphocytes with technesium 99m to make them selectively cytotoxic to human malignant tumor cells, biological role of AP-endonuclease in the protection against oxidative stress in mammalian cells, mutation of AP endonuclease gene in patients with neurodegenerative disorders. Home: Decatur, Ga. Died Mar. 22, 2004.

OLMSTED, ANN GARVER, lawyer; b. Ft. Dodge, Iowa, Dec. 11, 1924; d. H. Woodford and Florence Edna (Hoppe) Garver; m. Donald Warren Olmsted, Sept. 9, 1950; 1 child, Caroline Ellen. BA, U. No. Iowa, Cedar Falls, 1945; PhD, U. Minn., 1954; JD, Mich. State U., 1982. Bar: Mich. 1982. Tchr. pub. schs., Algona, Iowa, 1945-46; teaching asst. U. Minn., Mpls., 1946-49, asst. dir., instr., 1950-55; instr. W.Va. U., Morgantown, 1949-50; rsch. assoc. U. Wis., Madison, 1955-57; from rsch. assoc. to prof. Mich. State U., East Lansing, from 1957, interim dir. med. sch. admissions, 1992-93. Workshop dir. Hunan Med. U., Changsha, Peoples Republic of China, 1991. Contbr. chpts. to books, articles to profl. jours. Bd. dirs., officer Mich. Dyslexia Inst., Lansing, 1980—; bd. dirs. Mich. Lung Assn., Lansing, 1986-92, Mich. Health Data Corp., Lansing, 1984-90, Mich. Peer Rev. Orgn., Plymouth, 1992—. Recipient Lester Evans Disting. Svc. award Coll. Human Medicine/Mich. State U., 1991. Mem. Mich. State Bar Assn., Ingham Bar Assn., Am. Sociol. Assn. Democrat. Congregationalist. Avocations: cooking, reading. Died June 18, 2004.

ONDETTI, MIGUEL ANGEL, chemist, consultant; b. Buenos Aires, May 14, 1930; came to U.S., 1960, naturalized, 1971; s. Emilio Pablo and Sara Cecilia (Cerutti) O.; m. Josephine Elizabeth Garcia, June 6, 1958; children: Giselle Christine, Gabriel Alexander. Licensiate in Chemistry, U. Buenos Aires, 1955, D.Sc., 1957. Prof. chemistry Inst. Tchrs., Buenos Aires, 1957-60; instr. organic chemistry U. Buenos Aires, 1957-60; rsch. scientist Squibb Inst. Med. Rsch., Buenos Aires, 1957-60, rsch. investigator Princeton, NJ, 1960-66, rsch. supr., 1966-73, sect. head, 1973-76, dir. biol. chemistry, 1976-79; assoc. dir. Squibb Inst., 1980-82, v.p. rsch. cardiopulmonary disease, 1982-86, sr. v.p. cardiovascular rsch., 1987-91; pharm. cons., 1991—2004. Ad-hoc cons NIH; mem. adv. com. dept. chemistry Princeton U., 1982-86 Patentee in field (115); contbr. articles to sci. jours. Served with Argentine Army, 1950-51 Recipient Thomas Alva Edison Patent award R&D Coun. N.J., 1983, Ciba award for hypertension rsch. Am. Heart Assn., 1983, Perkins medal Soc. Chemistry Industry, 1991, Warren Alpert Found. award, 1991, Albert Lasker Clinical Med. Research award, 1999; scholar Brit. Coun., 1960, Squibb, 1956. Mem. AAAS, Am. Chem. Soc. (Alfred Burger award 1981, Creative Invention award 1992, Perkin medal 1992), Am. Soc. Biol. Chemists. Died Aug. 23, 2004.

O'NEIL, JOHN JOSEPH, artist, educator; b. N.Y.C., Apr. 20, 1932; s. John Joseph and Betty (Grady) O'N.; m. Iris Bird, Jan. 15, 1956 (dec. Aug. 1975); children: Virginia, John, Thomas; m. Robin Harmon, Dec. 3, 1977; 1 child, Robin Wade. A degree, SUNY, Bklyn., 1953; BS, SUNY, Buffalo, 1959; degree (hon.), U. Florence, Italy, 1960; MA, Columbia U., 1965, EdD, 1972. Graphic designer Mutual Broadcasting, N.Y.C., 1951-52, Stanys Conliam Whitehead, N.Y.C., 1952, B. Altman, L.I., 1955, Givandan Advt., N.Y.C., 1955; tchr. art East Meadow (N.Y.) High Sch., 1950-63; prof. U. S.C., Columbia, 1963-66, assoc. head, 1966-73, chmn. art dept. Sloan Coll., 1973—95. Mem. presdl. bd. to evaluate and upgrade Fed. Graphics; chmn. southeastern region New Art Examiner, Washington. Exhibited in group shows at Florence Mus., S.C., Furman U., Chrysler Mus., Norfolk, Va., Gibbs Gallery, Charleston, S.C., Greenville Mus., Spartenson, S.C., St. Paul's Cathedral Gallery, N.Y.C.; represented by Aronsen Gallery, Atlanta. Bd. dirs. Columbia Mus. Art. With U.S. Army, 1952-55. Mem. Nat. Assn. Art Adminstrs., Guild S.C. Artists (bd. dirs.), S.C. Craftsmen (founder), Artist Guild Columbia (pres.), So. Graphic Coun. (pres.), Art Dirs. Club. Home: Columbia, SC. Died Dec. 12, 2004.

O'NEILL, KEVIN, plastic engineer, consultant; b. Jersey City, Feb. 7, 1933; s. John Joseph and Camille Lois O'Neill; m. Jacqueline Reilly, Sept. 12, 1953 (div. Oct. 1, 1965); children: Patricia, Sean, Moira, Kevin, Deirdre; m. Theresa Ann, Dec. 20, 1997. BS, Seton Hall U., 1955; AA, Newark Coll., 1958; MBA, C.W. Post Coll., 1964. Plastic engring., sales Celanese Corp. Am., N.Y.C., 1955-59; product mgr. cellulose acetate Columbian Carbon Co., N.Y.C., 1959-67; mkt. devel. mgr. Polymer Materials Inc., Farmingdale, N.Y., 1968-79; sales and mktg. mgr. Georgia Pacific Corp., Oak Brook, Ill., 1979-84. Cons. Synergistics Chemicals Ltd., Toronto, Can., 1984-87, Hoechst A.G., Lonstein, Germany, 1989, Erkwepa A.G., Erkrath, Germany, 1990, 9A7 Specialty Chemicals, Wayne, N.J., 1991. Mem. Soc. Plastic Engrs. Assn., Plastic Pioneers Assn., Am. Mgmt. Assn. Avocation: tennis. Died Nov. 16, 2004.

OPLINGER, CLARENCE G., construction company executive; b. Detroit, Apr. 10, 1934; s. Clarence G. and Gay (Wertz) O.; m. Elaine Carol (div.); children: James Joseph, Vicki Lynn; m. Nancy Oplinger. Grad. high sch., Fraser, Mich. Lic. residential/comml. builder, Mich. Apprentice carpenter Ernest Antonis, Fraser, 1952-55; crew chief All-City Plumbing and Excavating, Warren, Mich., 1957-66; carpenter Lee Walters, Inc., Birmingham, Mich., 1967; carpenter foreman All-City Constrn., Warren, 1967-70; owner, pres. Rosebrier Bldg. Co., St. Clair Shores, Mich., 1970-73; owner Oplinger Music, Inc., St. Clair Shores, 1973-78; gen. supt. Macomb Structural Concrete, Rochester, Mich., 1978-79; supt. R.R.C.S., Inc., Southfield, Mich., 1980-81; project supt. Tishman Constrn. Fla., Lake Buena Vista, 1981-84; gen. supt. Carlson S.E., Smyrna, Ga., 1984-85; supt. Barton-Malow, Southfield, 1985-88, McDevitt & Street Co., Macon, Ga., from 1988. V.p. custom costumes Rochester (Minn.) Inc., 1988-89; pres. Act One Costume and Theatrical Rentals, Minn.; owner Platinum Imagineering, Inc., Gary, Ind. Past pres. Mich. Recreation and Parks Assn. With U.S. Army, 1955-57. Mem. VFW, DAV, Bldg. Officials and Code Adminstrs. Internat., Eagles. Avocations: reading, drafting, boating, fishing, exercising. Died Dec. 5, 2004.

ORBAN, KURT, import/export company executive; b. S.I., N.Y., Aug. 6, 1916; s. Kurt and Gertrude (Astfalck) Orbanowski; children: Robert Arnold, Robyn Ann, Kurt-Matthew, Jonathan; m. Catherine Cheng, 2002. Grad. steel fgn. trade course, Stahlunion-Export GmbH, Duesseldorf, Germany, 1938. Fgn. trade corr. Stahlunion, Dusseldorf, 1938, rep., 1939—40, Sofia, Bulgaria, 1940—41; steel export trader Steel Union Sheet Piling Co., N.Y.C., 1941; v.p. North River Steel Co., N.Y.C., 1941; chmn., pres. Kurt Orban Co., Inc., Wayne, NJ, from 1946; now sr. ptnr., chmn./CEO Kurt Orban Ptnrs. LLC. Mem. field hockey games com. U.S. Olympic Com., 1948-61; playing mgr., team capt. U.S. Field Hockey Team., London, Eng., 1948, playing coach, Melbourne, Australia, 1956; U.S. rep. Bur. Internat. Hockey Fedn., Brussels, 1954-62. Served to 1st lt., pilot USAAF, 1943-45. Field Hockey Assn. Am. named its cup for each yrs. men's team competition for him; named one of the Ten Best All-Time (1920-2003) U.S. Field Hockey Players. Mem. Am. Inst. for Internat. Steel (charter; pres. 1966-68, 78-80, bd. dirs. N.Y.C.), Am. Exporters and Importers Assn. (pres. 1972-73, bd. dirs.), Wire Assn. Internat., Am. Wire Prodrs. Assn. (charter). Avocations: tennis, skiing. Died Feb. 8, 2006.

ORINGER, MAURICE JULES, retired oral surgeon; b. N.Y.C., June 18, 1905; s. Louis and Gerturde Cynthia (Trommer) O.; m. Helen Jane Ornstein, Apr. 11, 1953. DDS, NYU Coll. Dentistry, 1928. Diplomate Am. Bd. Oral Electrosurgery. Guest instr. Dept. Continuing Edn. 31 U.S. and Fgn. Dental Schs., 1951-89; profl. lectr. St. Louis U. Dental Sch., 1953-58; pres. Midtown Dental Soc., N.Y.C., 1953; prof. honoraire Ctr. de Perfectionnement en Odonto Stomatologie Cote d'Azur, France, 1966; founder Am. Acad. Dental Electrosurgery, N.Y.C., 1962, pres., 1963-67; cons. oral surgery/diagnosis St. Francis Hosp., Poughkeepsie, N.Y., 1965-71; exec. sec. Am. Acad. Dental Electrosurgery, N.Y.C., from 1968; cons. ADA Coun. Dental Materials and Devices, Chgo., from 1970; chmn. ADA/ANSI Stds. Subcom. for Electrosurgery Device, Chgo., from 1976; adj. prof. Dept. Biomedical Engring. U. Miami, 1976-88. Cons. Coles Electronic Corp., Phila., 1958-70, Ritter Co., Rochester, N.Y., 1973-75, Cavitron Corp., N.Y.C., 1970-72, Siemens, Bensheim, Germany, 1979-81. Author: Electrosurgery In Dentistry, 1962, 2d edit., 1975, Color Atlas of Oral Electrosurgery, 1984; co-editor: Dental Clinics North America, 1969; contbr. articles to profl. jours. Capt. AUS Dental Corps, CBI, 1942-46. Oringer award named in his honor Acad. Dental Electrosurgery. Mem. Am. Dental Assn., Am. Coll. Dentists, Am. Acad. Dental Electrosurgery, Royal Soc. Health. Jewish. Avocations: reading, writing, fishing, gardening, duplicate bridge. Home: New York, NY. Died Nov. 7, 2004.

ORLANDO, C. JANE, medical/surgical nurse, educator; b. Oreg. m. Michael A. Orlando; children: Michael, George, Anthony, Jeffery. Diploma, St. Anthony's Hosp., Pendleton, Oreg. Cert. instr. in med. self-help; cert. in nuclear medicine; cert. flight observer Civil Air Patrol. Vol. tchr., med. aide, Afghanistan, 1985-87, 89-90; staff nurse Carnival Cruise Line, Am. Adventure and Disney Big Red One. Cons. for movies and TV; tchr. of nurses in Iraq and Thailand; nat. lectr. on Afghanistan, 1988-96. Guest appearance on Regis Philbin Show, Gary Collins Hour Mag. Surgical nurse vol. Dominican Republic, 1990-92; hon. mem. Tender Essence, Inc. 2d lt. USAF, 1953. Recipient Cert. of Appreciation, Govt. of Afghanistan, Union of Afghan Mujahid Doctors. Home: Delray Beach, Fla. Died Sept. 28, 2004.

ORLOWSKY, LILLIAN, artist; b. NYC, Oct. 14, 1914; d. Sam and Rose O.; m. William Freed, Jan. 28, 1942 (wid. May 1984). Student, Am. Sch. Fine Arts, N.Y.C., 1935, Hans Hofmann, 1937-47, Am. Artist Sch., N.Y.C., 1935-36, Edn. Alliance Art Sch., NYC, 1932—33; Student, Nat. Acad. Art Design, N.Y.C., 1933-34. Instr. drawing and painting Bronx House, N.Y.C., 1963-77, James Gallery, N.Y.C., 1954-62; textile design N.Y.C., 1949-58; artist WPA Arts Project, N.Y.C., 1937-41, Cape Mus. Fine Arts, Dennis, Mass., 1985, Faces of the Artists, 1980; instr. Provincetown Art, Mass., from 1997. Curator Provincetown (Mass.) Art Assn. and Mus., 1990, 1994—95. One-woman shows include Hans Hofmann 4 Seasons, Hans Hofmann His Studcuts 1935-45; exhibited in group shows at Cherry Stone Gallery, Wellfleet, Mass., 1993, 95, City Gallery, Copenhagen, 1993, Cortland Jessup Galllery, Provincetown, Mass., 1995-97, Cape Mus. of Fine Arts, Dennis, Mass., 1992, Koganei, Japan, 1996, Met. Mus., N.Y.C., 1978, Provincetown Art Assn. and Mus., 1989, 91, Day's Studio, Provincetown, 1977, New Brunswick Coll., N.J., 1989, David Dinkins Office and Gallery, N.Y., 1989, Kenkelebra House, N.Y., 1950-70, 85, HCE Gallery, 1979-82, Sch. House Gallery, Cortland Jessup Gallery, Provincetown, Cherry Stone-Cortland Galleries, Jessup, Mass., 1995, Cotuit C.C., 1998, Va. Poly. Inst. and State U., 1998, Women's Ctr. Va. Tech., Blacksburg, 1998, Acme Gallery, Boston, Mass., 2001-03, Beauregard Gallery, Rearson, N.J., 2001-03, Burton Mass. ACME Gallery, 2001-03, Cherry Stove Gallery, 2002, Wellfleet, Mass., 2003; permanent collections include Cape Mus. Fine Art, Met. Mus. Art, N.Y., Balt. Mus., Provincetown Art Assn. and Mus., Chrysler Mus. of Art, Norfolk, Va., Jerusalem Mus., Israel, Brandeis U. Rose Mus., Waltham, Mass., Met. Mus. Art. Grantee, Robert A. Florsheim Fund, 1992, 1995. Died Aug. 7, 2004.

OROSZ, CHARLES GEORGE, biomedical researcher; b. Cleve., Jan. 9, 1949; s. George John and Mary Helen (Palmer) O.; m. Nancy Marie O'Linn, Aug. 23, 1974;

children: Matthew Michael and Kathleen Elizabeth (twins), Molly Nielan. BS, Cleve. State U., 1971, MS, 1975, PhD, 1978. Postdoctoral fellow U. Wis., Madison, 1978-80; vis. rsch. fellow U. Minn., Mpls., 1980-81, asst. prof. lab. medicine and pathology, 1981-83; asst. prof. surgery Ohio State U., Columbus, 1983-87, dir. therapeutic immunology rsch. labs., from 1981, dir. Clin. Histocompability Testing Lab., from 1981, prof. dept. surgery, pathology-med. microbiology-immunology, from 1995. Mem. study sect., site vis. teams Nat. Cancer Inst.-NIH, mem. subcom. transplantation, 1996. N.Am. editor Transplant Immunology; mem. editl. bd. Jour. Heart Lung Transplantaton, Immunopharmacology, Internat. Jour. Exptl. and Clin. Chemotherapy; contbr. over 150 articles to sci. jours. With USNR, 1967-73. Recipient investigator award NIH, 1982, rsch. award Nat. Kidney Found., 1984, NIH, 1984, 88, 90, 93, 96. Mem. Am. Soc. Histocompatability and Immunology Comprehensive Cancer Care Ctr., Transplantation Soc., Am. Soc. Transplant Physicians and Immunologists, Inter-Am. Soc. for Chemotherapy, Leukemia Soc. Am. (bd. dirs. Ctrl. Ohio chpt. 1984-86, spl. fellow 1982), N.Am. Vascular Biology Orgn. Roman Catholic. Home: Columbus, Ohio. Died Aug. 7, 2005.

ORR, HENRY STEERS, II, finance educator; b. N.Y.C., Oct. 8, 1940; s. John Clifton II and Cora (Legg) O.; m. Nannette Foss, May 29, 1965; children: John Clifton, Nannette Chandlee Gustafson. BA, U. Pa., 1962; MBA, U. New Haven, 1980; grad., Sch. Credit and Fin. Mgmt., 1981. Cert. secondary tchr. Project mgr., salesman Lawrence Investing Co., Inc., Bronxville, N.Y., 1962-68; asst. v.p. Bankers Trust Co., N.Y.C., 1968-71; v.p. relationship mgr. Conn. Bank & Trust Co., Hartford, 1971-91; adj. faculty fin. Mercy Coll., Dobbs Ferry, N.Y., 1991-95; asst. prof. fin., econs., acctg. Housatonic C.C., Bridgeport, Conn., from 1995. Chmn., trustee Indian Brook Assemblage-The Nature Conservancy, Katonah, N.Y., 1976—; allocations com. head United Way North Fairfield County, Danbury, Conn., 1980-90; trustee Fund for Blind, N.Y.C., 1990—. Recipient NISOD award, Cmty. Coll. Leadership Program, 1997, 2000. Avocations: fly fishing, investing, travel, hiking, birding. Home: Katonah, NY. Died Jan. 12, 2004.

ORTINO, HECTOR RUBEN, chemical company executive; b. Buenos Aires, July 23, 1942; came to U.S., 1983; s. Miguel and Maria Julia (Moauro) O.; m. Beatriz Monica Mayantz, Dec. 14, 1972; children: Nicolas Martin, Gabriela Andrea. B in Acctg. and Adminstrn., Buenos Aires U., 1971. Mng. dir. Ferro Argentina, Buenos Aires, 1976-81, also bd. dirs.; mng. dir. Ferro Mexicana, Mexico City, 1982-83, also bd. dirs.; asst. to v.p. fin. Ferro Corp., Cleve., 1983-84, v.p. fin., from 1984, chief fin. officer, 1987-93, exec. v.p., chief fin.-adminstrv. officer, 1993-96; pres. & COO Ferro Corp, Cleve., 1996-99; chmn., CEO Ferro Corp., Cleve., from 1999. Bd. trustees Playhouse Square Found., Musical Arts Assn., United Way. Mem. Fin. Exec. Inst. Clubs: Cleve. Skating, Cleve. Athletic. Roman Catholic. Avocations: tennis, swimming, hunting. Home: Pepper Pike, Ohio. Died Nov. 28, 2005.

OSTERLOH, WELLINGTON FREDERICK, oil company executive, consultant; b. N.Y.C., Oct. 22, 1936; s. Wellington D. and Mary (Bokar) O.; m. Claurice Ruth Eby, Jan. 21, 1960; children: Debbie, Judy, Eric. Student, Bernard Baruch Sch. Bus., CUNY, 1954-56. Pub. relations mgr. Post div. Gen. Foods Corp., White Plains, N.Y., 1962-69; corp. dir. editorial service Martin-Marietta Corp., N.Y.C., 1969-72; corp. dir. pub. relations Union Pacific, N.Y.C., 1972-75, The Coastal Corp., Houston, from 1975. Past v.p., bd. dirs. Oak Creek Village Civic Assn.; mem. pub. relations com. Performing Arts Ctr. Served with U.S. Army, 1960-62. Mem. Pub. Relations Soc. Am. (bd. dirs., pres., Houston chpt.), Profl. Photographers Am., Nat. Coal Assn. (chmn. pub. relations com.), Nat. Investor Relations Inst., Tex. Pub. Relations Assn. (v.p., past pres., bd. dirs., Best of Tex. award 1980), Houston Corp. Relations Roundtable (co-founder). Clubs: Houston City, Houston Press. Republican. Methodist. Died Apr. 6, 2005.

OSTERMAN, MELVIN HOWARD, lawyer, writer; b. N.Y.C., Sept. 26, 1934; s. Melvin Howard and Selma Elsie (Lenz) O.; m. Norma Grace Meacham, May 29, 1982; children: Lawrence, Edith, Jeffrey, Laura, Andrew. AB, Cornell U., 1955, LLB with distinction, 1957. Bar: N.Y. 1957, U.S. Dist. Ct. (so. dist.) N.Y. 1957, U.S. Dist. Ct. (ea. dist.) N.Y. 1957, U.S. Dist. Ct. (no. dist.) N.Y. 1975, U.S. Ct. Appeals (2d cir.) 1958, U.S. Supreme Ct. 1974. Assoc. White & Case, N.Y.C., 1957-58, 59-62; law clk. to justice Charles D. Breitel N.Y. App. Div. 1st Dept., 1958-59; asst. counsel to Gov. Nelson A. Rockefeller Albany, N.Y., 1962-64; counsel for employee relations, 1968-72; assoc. Graubard Moskowitz McGoldrick Dannett & Horowitz, N.Y.C., 1964-65, mem., 1965-72; dir. employee relations State of N.Y., Albany, 1972-75; mem. Whiteman Osterman & Hanna, Albany, 1975—2005. Faculty Sch. Indsl. and Labor Relations, Cornell U., 1974—76, Empire State Coll., SUNY, 1976—77, Grad. Sch. Pub. Affairs, SUNY, Albany, 1979—86, Siena Coll., 2000; pres. Northeastern Living and Learning Ctr., 1981—2005. Author: Productivity Bargaining in New York State, 1975, N.Y. Lawyers Deskbook (Labor Law); contbr. articles to legal publs.; mem. Cornell Law Rev., 1955-57, Labor Rels. in the Pub. Sector, 1999. Cons. on judiciary Temporary State Commn. on Constl. Conv., 1966; spl. cons. on legal svcs. N.Y.C. Bd. Edn., 1967; mem. Temporary State Commn. on Eminent Domain and Real Property Tax Assessment Rev., 1974—75; cons. N.Y. State Sch. Bds. Assn., 1978—86. Mem.: ABA, Saratoga County Bar Assn., Albany County Bar Assn., Assn. of Bar of City of N.Y., N.Y. State Bar Assn. (chmn. com. govt. employee labor rels. 1979—82, exec. com. labor law sect. 1979—82, 1982—84, chmn. com. govt. employee labor rels. 1984—87, exec. com. labor law sect. from 1988,). Home: Delmar, NY. Died Aug. 14, 2005.

OSTERUD, HAROLD TRUMAN, public health and preventive medicine physician, researcher; b. Richmond, Va., May 1, 1923; s. Hjalmer Lauritz Osterud and Zella Surfus; m. Jessie Harrison Binford, Mar. 3, 1949; children: Bruce Harrison, Lauritz Binford, Erin Lee. BS, Randolph-Macon Coll., 1943; MD, Med. Coll. Va., 1947; MOH, U. N.C., 1951. Diplomate Am. Bd. Preventive Medcine. Intern Good Samaritan Hosp., Portland, Oreg., 1947—48; health officer Wasco-Sherman Health Dept., The Dalles, Oreg., 1948—50, Coos County Health Dept., Coquille, Oreg., 1953—55, Lane County Health Dept., Eugene, Oreg., 1956—61; assoc. prof. Oreg. Health Scis. U., Portland, 1961—66, prof., chmn. pub. health, 1967—89, prof. emeritus, from 1990. Cons. Gov., State Legislature, Salem, Oreg., 1958—93; physician, mem. adv. bd. YMCA, Portland, Oreg.; mem. Oreg. State Senate, Salem, 1976—78; mem. preventive medicine and dentistry rev. com. NIH. Author: Parasitic Protocols. Environ. activities Bull Run Heritage Found., Portland, Oreg., 1972—2002. Capt. US Army, 1951—53, Japan & Korea. Decorated Bronze Star; recipient Outstanding Leadership award, Oreg. Pub. Health Assn., 1969, John N. Sippy award, APHA, 1969, 1988. Mem.: Oreg. Med. Assn. (chmn., pn & safety 1981—91, Presdl. Citation 1991), Oreg. Pub. Health Assn. (life; pres. 1948—2002), Portland Art Mus., Alpha Omega Alpha. Presbyterian. Achievements include Oregon's first local medical examiner, Lane County Oregon, 1958-1961. Avocations: music, photography, hiking, building doll houses. Home: Lake Oswego, Oreg. Died Dec. 31, 2004.

OSTERYOUNG, ROBERT ALLEN, chemistry educator; b. Cleve., Jan. 20, 1927; m. Phyllis K. Balderston (div. 1968); children: Katherine, Susan, David; m. Janet Jones, Aug. 17, 1969; children: Anne, Adam. BS, Ohio U., 1949; MS, U. Ill., 1951, PhD, 1954. Chemist Harshaw Chem., Cleve., 1951-52; asst., assoc. prof. Rensselaer Poly., Troy, N.Y., 1954-59; rsch. scientist Atomics Internat. div. Rockwell Internat., L.A., 1954-62; group leader Sci. Ctr. div. Rockwell Internat., L.A., 1962-68; dir. materials process lab. Autonetics div. Rockwell Internat., L.A., 1966-68; vis. assoc. Calif. Inst. Tech., Pasadena, 1962-68; prof., chmn. Colo. State U., Ft. Collins, 1968-79; prof. SUNY, Buffalo, 1979-91; rsch. prof. N.C. State U., Raleigh, from 1991. Assoc. editor Analytical Chemistry, 1988—. With USN, 1944-45. Fellow AAAS, Electrochem. Soc.; mem. Am. Chem. Soc. (Disting. Svc. award 1978, Electrochemistry award 1991). Home: Raleigh, NC. Died Aug. 10, 2004.

OSTOW, MORTIMER, physician; b. N.Y.C., Jan. 8, 1918; s. Kalman Isidore and Gertrude (Liebman) O.; m. Miriam Furst Ostow, May 4, 1942 (dec. 2005); children: Robin, Jeremy, Abigail, Rachel. BA, Columbia Coll., 1937; MA, Columbia U., 1938, MedScD, 1949; MD, NYU, 1941; DLitt (hon.), Jewish Theol. Sem. Am., 1991. Diplomate Am. Bd. Psychiatry and Neurology. Intern Beth Israel Hosp., N.Y.C., 1941-42; resident in psychiatry St. Elizabeths Hosp., Washington, 1942-44; resident in neurology Mt. Sinai Hosp., N.Y.C., 1946-47; instr. in clin. neurology George Washington Univ. Sch. Med., Washington, 1942-44; asst. neurology N.Y.U. Coll. Med., N.Y.C., 1948-49; asst. adj. neurologist Beth Israel Hosp., N.Y.C., 1949, assoc. neuropsychiatrist, 1949-55; assoc. attending psychiatrist Montefiore Hosp., Bronx, N.Y., 1960-80, attending psychiatrist, 1980—90. Sandrow visiting prof. Jewish Theol. Sem. Am., N.Y.C., 1965-90, prof. emeritus, 1990-2006; lectr. in psychiatry Mt. Sinai Med. Sch., N.Y.C., 1969-84; various positions Jewish Theol. Sem. Am., N.Y.C., 1965-2006; pres. Psychoanalytic R & D Fund, Inc., 1980-2006; mem. faculty NYU Psychoanalytic Inst. Author: (with Strauss and Greenstein) Diagnostic Electroencephalography, 1952, (with Scharfstein) The Need to Believe, 1954, Drugs in Psychoanalysis and Psychotherapy, 1962, The Psychology of Melancholy, 1970; editor: (with Winnik and Moses) Psychological Bases of War, 1973, Sexual Deviation/Psychoanalytic Insights, 1974, The Psychodynamic Approach to Drug Therapy, 1979, Judaism and Psychoanalysis, 1982, Myth & Madness: The Psychodynamics of Antisemitism, 1995, Ultimate Intimacy: The Psychodynamics of Jewish Mysticism, 1995, Israel Journal of Psychiatry, 1963-2006; contbg. author to profl. jours. With USPHS, 1944-46. Recipient Maimonides Award of Wisconsin, 1979. Hon. mem. Israel Psychoanalytic Soc.; life fellow Am. Psychiatric Assn.; life mem. Am. Psychoanalytic Assn.; mem. Internat. Psychoanalytic Assn., Bronx County Med. Soc., Phi Beta Kappa, Alpha Omega Alpha, Sigma Xi. Died Sept. 23, 2006.

OTTLEY, WILLIAM HENRY, professional association director, consultant; b. N.Y.C., Mar. 7, 1929; s. James Henry and Margaret (Deeble) O. BA, Yale U., 1950; spl. cert., Georgetown U., 1953; D of Aero. Sci. (hon.), Embry Riddle Aero. U., 1979. Dir. pub. rels. Thomas A. Edison Co., West Orange, NJ, 1953-56; exec. v.p. Career Publs., Inc., N.Y.C., 1956-60; dir. spl. exhibits N.Y. World's Fair, 1960-65; exec. dir. Nat. Pilots Assn., Washington, 1965-77, U.S. Parachute Assn., Washington, 1978-92, Nat. Aero. Assn., Washington, 1992-93; pres. Internat. Gen. Aviation Commn., Paris, 1994-99. V.p. Fedn. Aero. Internat., Paris, 1994-99. Pres. Nat. Skydiving Mus. 1st lt. USAF, 1951—53. Recipient Skydiving Lifetime Achievement award, 1994. Mem. Met. Club Washington, Soc. of Cin. Republican. Episcopalian. Avocations: skydiving, flying, scuba diving, waterskiing, skiing. Died Dec. 1, 2005.

OTTO, EDGAR JOHN, minister; b. Guthrie, Okla., Oct. 7, 1926; s. Edgar and Anna Hattie (Wendel) O.; m. Rosemarie Naig, July 23, 1949; children: Vicki, Deborah, Bunnie, Ole. BA, Macalester Coll., 1947; BTh, Concordia Sem., Springfield, Ill., 1951, BD, 1969, MDiv, 1971; MA in Religion, Concordia Sem., St. Louis, 1973. Ordained to ministry Luth. Ch.-Mo. Synod, 1951. Pastor Grace/Christ Luth. Ch., Pequot Lakes, Minn., 1951-54, Ea. Heights Luth. Ch., St. Paul, 1954-66, Immanuel Luth. Ch., Springfield, 1966-75, St. John's Luth. Ch., East Moline, Ill., 1975-80; adminstrv. asst. mission dept. South Wis. dist. Luth. Ch.-Mo. Synod, Milw., from 1980. Recipient Servus Ecclesiac Christi Concordia Theol. Sem., 1978. Republican. Home: Spirit Lake, Iowa. Died Nov. 15, 2004.

OTTO, INGOLF HELGI ELFRIED, banking institute fellow; b. Duesseldorf, Germany, May 7, 1920; s. Frederick C. and Josephine (Zisenis) O.; m. Carlyle Miller, 1943 (div. 1960); children: George Vincent Edward, Richard Arthur Frederick. A.B., U. Cin., 1941; M.A., George Washington U., 1950, Ph.D., 1959. CPCU. Assoc. prof. fin. NYU, N.Y.C., 1960-62; prof. fin. U. Nuevo Leon, Monterrey, Mexico, 1962-65, U. So. Miss., Hattiesburg, 1965-67, U. So. Ala., Mobile, 1967-81; sr. fellow Inst. Banking and Fin., Mexico City, 1981—. Contbr. articles on fin. to profl. jours. Served to col. U.S. Army, 1941-46. Decorated Legion of Merit, Meritorious Service medal, Purple Heart. Mem. Am. Econ. Assn., N.Am. Econ. and Fin. Assn. Home: Dulles, Va. Died Mar. 17, 2004.

OVARY, ZOLTAN, pathology educator, immunologist; b. Kolozsvar, Hungary, Apr. 13, 1907; came to U.S., 1954; s. Elemer and Olga (Purjesz) O. Degree, Reformed Coll. at Kolozsvar, 1924; MD, U. Paris, 1935. Rsch. fellow in microbiology Med. Sch., Johns Hopkins U., Balt., 1954-59; asst. prof. Sch. Pathology, NYU, N.Y.C., 1959-62, prof., 1964—2005. Author: Souvenirs: Around the World in Ninety Years, 1999; contbr. over 300 articles to sci. jours. Recipient Disting. Svc. award, Internat. Assn. Allergology and Clin. Immunology, 1985. Achievements include first to demonstrate passive cutaneous anaphylaxis, diversity of antibody functions related to isotype bridging or crosslinking as first step of cellular activation. Died June 12, 2005.

OVERHOLSER, PHILLIP IVAN, retired vocational teacher; b. Peyton, Colo., Nov. 23, 1930; s. Daniel Edward, Sr. and Nina Beatrice (Adair) O.; m. Lillian Patrica Hayes, Apr. 18, 1927; 1 child, Diane. Vocat. Tchg. Diploma, Jersey City State Coll., 1972. With Paterson (N.J.) Evening News, N.J., 1956-57; linotype operator Quinn & Boden, Rahway, N.J., 1957-58; with Cranford (N.J.) Citizen and Chronicle, 1958-69; tchr. Bayonne (N.J.) Bd. Edn., 1969-92; with Advanced Printing, Garwood, N.J., 1992-94, Bd. Edn., Westfield, N.J., 1995-97; ret. With USN, 1952-55. Mem. Am. Legion. Democrat. Avocation: sml. train collector. Home: Westfield, NJ. Died Dec. 26, 2004.

OWADES, JOSEPH LAWRENCE, chemist, consultant; b. N.Y.C., July 9, 1919; s. Samuel and Gussie (Horn) O.; m. Ruth Markowitz, Sept. 7, 1969. BS, CCNY, 1939; MS, Poly. Inst. Bklyn., 1944, PhD, 1950. Research chemist Fleischman Labs., N.Y.C., 1948-51; v.p., tech. dir. Rheingold Breweries, N.Y.C., 1951-69; tech. coordinator Anheuser-Busch, St. Louis, 1969-72; v.p. brewing Carling-O'Keefe, Waltham, Mass., 1972-75; dir. Ctr. for Brewing Studies, San Francisco. Contbr. articles on beer and brewing to profl. jours. Fellow Inst. of Brewing, London; mem. N.Y. Acad. Scis., AAAS, Master Brewers Assn. Am., Am. Soc. Brewing Chemists. Avocation: gardening. Home: San Francisco, Calif. Died Dec. 16, 2005.

OWEN, FERRIS SYDNEY, farmer, international development administrator; b. Newark, Ohio, Jan. 25, 1918; s. Wilfred Robert and Maria Emily (Nichol) O.; m. Helen Irene Cavins, Oct. 12, 1940; children: Gwendolyn Rae, Barbara Jean, James Coriner, Susan Carol. BS in Home Econs., Ohio State U., 1940, BS in Aricultural Engring., 1940. Pres., oper. mgr. Owen Potato Farm, Newark, Ohio, 1940-66; dir. internat. programs Coop. League U.S.A., 1966-83, v.p. internat. devel., 1980-83, internat. coop. cons., from 1983. Organizer farm supply and mktg. assn. in western Ukraine for Internat. Exec. Svc. Corps., 1994; bd. dirs. Coop. Devel. Found. Elder Presbyn. ch. Democrat. Avocations: skiing, bridge, dance, motorhome vacations, water sports. Home: Newark, Ohio. Died Aug. 13, 2005.

OWENS, BUCK (ALVIS EDGAR OWENS JR.), singer, musician, songwriter, broadcast executive; b. Sherman, Tex., Aug. 12, 1929; s. Alvis Edgar and Maicie Azel Owens; m. Bonnie (Campbell) Owens, Jan. 13, 1948 (div. 1953); children: Alan Edger (Buddy), Michael Lynn; m. Phyllis Owens (div. 1972); 1 son, Johnny Dale; m. Jennifer, June 21, 1979. Attended pub. schs., Mesa, Ariz. Owner Sta. KNIX-FM, Phoenix, 1968-99. Formed Buck Owens Enterprises, 1965-2005, Buck Owens Studios, 1969; Pres. Buck Owens Prodns., Buck Owens Crystal Palace, 1996-2006; owner stas. KUZZ-FM, KUZZ-AM, KCWR-AM, Bakersfield, Calif., stas. KCWW-AM, KNIX-FM, Phoenix, sta. Bakersfield, Owens Enterprises, Bakersfield, Home Preview and Camera Ads Publs. Rec. artist, Capitol Records, 1958-76, 88-2006, Warner Bros. Records 1976-80; star syndicated TV shows Buck Owens Ranch Show, 1966-73; leader,

Buck Owens' Buckaroos Band, 1960-2006; star of TV show Hee Haw, 1969-86. Records include Second Fiddle, 1959, Under Your Spell Again, 1959, Above and Beyond, Excuse Me (I Think I've Got a Heartache), 1960, Fooling Around, 1961, Act Naturally, 1963, Love's Gonna Live Here, 1963, My Heart Skips a Beat, 1964, Together Again, 1964, I Don't Care(Just as Long as You Love Me), 1964, I've Got a Tiger by the Tail, 1965, Only You (Can Break My Heart), 1965, Under the Influence of Love, Waitin' in the Welfare Line, 1966, Think of Me, 1966, Open Up Your Heart, 1966, Where Does the Good Times Go, 1967, Sam's Place, 1967, Your Tender Loving Care, 1967, It Takes People Like You (To Make People Like Me), 1968, How Long Will My Baby Be Gone, 1968, Sweet Rosie Jones, 1968, Let The World Keep On Turnin, 1968, I've Got You On My Mind, 1968, Tall Dark Stranger, 1969, Who's Gonna Mow the Grass, 1969, The Kansas City Song, 1970, Bridge Over Trouble Waters, 1971, Rollin' in My Sweet Baby's Arms, 1971, Ruby (Are You Mad), 1971, Made In Japan, 1972, Streets of Bakersfield, 1972, Too Old to Cut the Mustard, 1972, Arms Full of Empty, 1973, Big Game Hunter, 1973, On the Cover of the Music City News, 1974, It's A Monster's Holiday, 1974; (albums) include Buck Owens, 1961, Buck Owen Sings Harlan Howard, 1961, You're for Me, 1962, Famous Country Music Sound of Buck Owens, 1962, On the Bandstand, 1963, Buck Ownes Sings Tommy Collins, 1963, I Don't Care, 1964, Christmas With Buck Owens, 1965, Roll Out the Red Carpet, 1966, Dust On My Mother's Bible, 1966, Open Up Your Heart, 1966, Buck Ownes & His Buckaroos in Japan, 1967, Your Tender Loving Care, 1967, America's Most Wanted Band, 1967, A Night On the Town, 1968, Meanwhile Back at the Ranch, 1968, The Buck Owens' Buckaroos Strike Again!, 1968, Buck Ownes in London, 1969, The Guitar Player, 1969, Anywhere U.S.A., 1969, Roll Your Own with Buck Owens' Buckaroos, 1969, Your Mother's Prayer, 1970, Big in Vegas, 1970, A Merry Hee Haw Christmas, 1970, Boot Hill, 1970, Buck Owens, 1970, Kickin In, 1970, Rompin' & Stompin, 1970, The Great White Horse, 1970, I Wouldn't Live In New York City, 1971, Buck Owens' Ruby & Other Bluegrass Specials, 1971, Merry Christmas from Buck and Susan, 1971, Play the Hits, 1971, Ruby & Other Bluegrass Specials, 1971, Buck Owens Live at the Nugget, 1972, Live at the John Ascuga's Nugget, 1972, Live at the White House, 1972, Ain't It Amazing Gracie, 1973, Good Old Days, 1973, In the Palm of Your Hand, 1973, Live at the Sydney Opera House, 1974, Live in Japan, 1974, Live in New Zealand, 1974, 41st Street Lonely Hearts Club, 1975, Buck 'Em, 1976, Hot Dog, 1988, Act Naturally, 1989, Live at Carnegie Hall, 1989, All Time Greatest Hits Vol. 1, 1990, vol. 2, 1992, vol. 3, 1993, The Buck Owens Collection (1959-90), 92, Half A Buck: Buck Owens' Greatest Duets, 1996, In London Live, 2005, and others; co-owner Blue Book Publishing, 1967-80 (sold to Tree) Recipient Instrumental Group of Year award Country Music Assn., 1967-68, pioneer award Acad. Country Music, 1988; named Artist of Decade Capitol Records, Country Artist of Year for 5 consecutive years Billboard, Cash Box and Record World; awarded 28 consecutive No. 1 records; elected to Country Music Hall of Fame, 1996, Nashville Songwriter's Hall of Fame, 1996. Died Mar. 25, 2006.

OWENS, PHILLIP REBER, mechanical engineer; b. Downers Grove, Ill., Sept. 8, 1920; s. Thomas John and Georgia Anna (Snowden) O.; m. Sylvia Elizabeth Tyack-Lovegrove, July 25, 1952; stepchildren: Susan Lovegrove Graziano, Sara C. Lovegrove, Robert E. Lovegrove. BSME, Purdue U., 1943. Registered profl. engr., N.Mex. Design engr. Lockheed Aircraft Co., Burbank, Calif., 1943-44; staff mem. Sandia Corp., Albuquerque, 1946-85; owner, pres. The Vertel Co., Albuquerque, from 1996. Author: A History of the Purdue Club of New Mexico: 1950-1988, 1990, (mag.) New Mexico Professional Engineer, 1982-83, 97. Chmn. Sandia dist. Boy Scouts Am., 1956-59; arch.-engr. selection adv. com. mem. Albuquerque, 1988-91. With U.S. Army, 1944-46, Los Alamos, N.Mex. Recipient Silver Beaver award Boy Scouts Am., 1971. Mem. AIAA, ASME, NSPE (v.p. 1975-76, outstanding svc. award 1976), N.Mex. Soc. Profl. Engrs. (Engr. of Year 1974, pres. 1982-83). Republican. Methodist. Achievements include patent allowed for V/STOL aircraft. Died July 21, 2006.

OWINGS, JOE H., communications administrator; b. Nashville, May 18, 1939; s. Joe H. and Marjorie G. (Johnson) O.; m. Jan H.; childre: Steven, Cheri, Sandi, Carol, Mark, Beth, Lynn. AAS in Law Enforcement, St. Louis C.C.; BS in Adminstrn. of Justice, U. Mo.; MA in Pub. Adminstrn., Webster U. Police officer St. Louis County Police Dept., 1960-76; acct. mgr. A&E Elecs. Corp., St. Louis, 1976-92, comm. svc. mgr., from 1992. Sgt. U.S. Army Res., 1960-66. Mem. IEEE, Assn. Pub. Safety Comm. (Mo. chpt.), Radio Club Am. Avocations: amateur radio, antiques, stamp collecting/philately. Home: Saint Charles, Mo. Died July 24, 2004.

OZAN, GERALD MARTIN, lawyer; b. Cleve., May 16, 1931; s. Philip Ozan and Lillian (Baker) Weissman; m. Joan Sally Blumenthal, June 21, 1953; children: Philip S., Kara E. BBA, Ohio State U., 1953; JD, Cleve. State U., 1960. Bar: Ohio 1960. Agt. IRS, Cleve., 1956-61; ptnr. Steiner, Stern & Ozan, Cleve., 1961-77; sole practice Cleve., from 1977. Cpl., USMC, 1954-56. Mem. Knights of Pythias. Jewish. Avocation: sports. Home: Lyndhurst, Ohio. Died Jan. 31, 2004.

OZELIS, TERRIE FORREST, elementary school educator; b. Tecumseh, Mich., Mar. 5, 1945; d. Kenneth Dennison and Lucy Jane (Adams) McEnroe; m. Daniel Albert Ozelis, Dec. 28, 1968. BA, Ea. Mich. U., 1968; MEd, Nat. Louis U., 1989; EdD, No. Ill. U., 1992. 5th grade tchr. New Boston (Mich.) Pub. Schs., 1968, West Chgo. (Ill.) Pub. Schs., 1969-73, kindergarten tchr., 1973-92; asst. prof. Ga. Southwestern Coll., Americus, from 1992. Univ. resources advisor No. Ill. U., DeKalb, 1990. Pres. Delnor Hosp. Aux., St. Charles, Ill., 1975-77. Recipient scholarship Sage Found., 1964-67. Mem. ASCD, Ga. Assn. Supervision & Curriculum Devel., Mentoring Leadership Network, Phi Delta Kappa, Kappa Delta Pi (scholarship 1991). Avocations: alpine skiing, swimming, sewing. Home: Kennett Square, Pa. Died Jan. 15, 2004.

OZMUN, KENT FREDERICK, lawyer; b. Akron, Ohio, Feb. 17, 1929; s. Sylvester P. and Elizabeth (Bedford) O.; m. Mary Louise Fox, Oct. 8, 1960; children: Janelle, Richard. BA, Baldwin-Wallace Coll., 1951; JD, Ohio State U., 1955. Bar: Ohio 1956. Assoc. Lane, Huggard & Alton, Columbus, Ohio, 1956-58; asst. atty. gen. State of Ohio, Columbus, 1958-59; adminstr. appraisal bur. State of Ohio, Columbus, 1959-63; mgr. Harrisburg Bank, Grove City, Ohio, 1963-65; pvt. practice Grove City, 1965—. Law dir. City of Grove City, 1966-70; mem. Franklin County (Ohio) Bd. Health, 1976—, pres., 1993; lay leader Grove City United Meth. Ch., 1983-84; v.p. govtl. rels. Grove City Area C. of C., 1996-97. Cpl. U.S. Army, 1951-53. Mem. Columbus Bar Assn., Ohio State Bar Assn. Lodge: Kiwanis (pres. Grove City chpt. 1966-67). Died Feb. 4, 2005.

PAASCH, WAYNE CHARLES, bank executive; b. Abington, Pa., July 26, 1951; s. Robert Henry and Ruth Ann (Rosell) P.; m. Wanda Joy Tackett, Apr. 14, 1984; children: Christopher, Stefanie. BSBA in Mgmt., U. Fla., 1973, MBA in Quantitative Mgmt., 1974. Systems analyst Procter & Gamble Co., Cin., 1974-78, Firemans Fund Ins. Co., San Rafael, Calif., 1978; mgr. profit ctr. Informatics Inc., San Francisco, 1978-82; pres. Mgmt. Systems Group, San Francisco, 1982-84; mgr. Wells Fargo Bank, San Francisco, 1984-85; group product mgr. Bank of Am., San Francisco, 1985-86, sr. product mgr., 1987-89, asst. v.p. product mgmt., from 1989. Cons. in field, 1978-84. Author, producer, The IBM PC-A Comprehensive View, 1983. Democrat. Roman Catholic. Avocations: water sports, snow sports. Home: San Rafael, Calif. Died Dec. 23, 2004.

PACKENHAM, RICHARD DANIEL, lawyer; b. Newton, Pa., June 23, 1953; s. John Richard and Mary Margaret (Maroney) P.; m. Susan Patricia Smillie, Aug. 20, 1983. BA, Harvard U., 1975; JD, Boston Coll., 1978; LLM in Taxation, Boston U., 1985. Bar: Mass. 1978, Conn. 1979, U.S. Dist. Ct. Mass. 1979, U.S. Dist. Ct. Conn. 1979, U.S. Ct. Appeals (1st cir.) 1981, U.S. Supreme Ct. 1985. Staff atty. Conn. Superior Ct., 1978-79; ptnr. McGrath & Kane, Boston, 1979-94, Packenham, Schmidt & Federico, Boston, from 1994. Mem. ABA, Mass. Bar Assn., Conn. Bar Assn., Boston Bar Assn., Mass CLE (faculty). Clubs: Harvard (Boston). Democrat. Roman Catholic. Home: Walpole, Mass. Died Oct. 3, 2005.

PACKER, KERRY FRANCIS BULLMORE, media company executive; b. Sydney, Australia, Dec. 17, 1937; s. Sir Frank and Lady Gretel P.; m. Roslyn Weedon, 1963; children: James, Gretel Student, Cranbrook Sch., Geelong Ch. of Eng. Grammar Sch. Chmn. Consol. Press Holdings Ltd., 1974—98; started World Series Cricket, Australia, 1977; owner Channel Nine TV, Australia, 1979—87, 1992—94; founder Publishing and Broadcasting Ltd. (merger of ACP & Channel Nine TV), Australia, 1994—98. Decorated companion Order of Australia. Mem. Royal Sydney Golf Club, Australian Golf Club, Elanora Country Club, Tattersall's Athanaeum (Melbourne) Club. Named one of World's Richest People by Forbes in 1999, 00, 01, 02, 03, 04. Died Dec. 26, 2005.

PALUMBO, LOUISE COREY, fashion and special events administrator; b. Charleston, W.Va., Aug. 19, 1931; d. George N. and Bahia (George) Corey; m. Mario Joseph Palumbo, Apr. 13, 1933; children: Mario Joseph Jr., Corey Lee. BA, Morris Harvey Coll., 1955. Trainee Saks Fifth Ave., N.Y.C., 1956; asst. fashion coord. Ind. Retailers Syndicate, N.Y.C., 1956-59; corp. fashion and spl. events dir. Stone & Thomas, Charleston, W.Va., 1959—2004; ret.; freelance fashion shows. Host TV show Fashion Today. State dir. Friendship Force, W.Va., 1983—; founder, chmn. River Lights, Charleston, 1982—; coord. Uniforms for Spl. Olympics, W.Va., 1992; chmn. Inaugural Balls for Gov. Rockefeller, W.Va., 1983, 87; mem. Preservation of Gov. Mansion, W.Va., 1992—, Women's Arts, W.Va., 1994—, Symphony League for Women, W.Va., 1994—; trustee Sunrise Mus., Charleston, 1983-89; chair Clay Ctr. Art and Sci. Mus. opening. Recipient Mayor's Award for the arts Fund for the Arts, 1992, Creative Achievement award Advt. Club Huntington, 1971, Cert. of Appreciation Nat. Coun. Jewish Women, 1992. Democrat. Ea. Orthodox. Avocations: tennis, skiing. Home: Charleston, W.Va. Died July 3, 2004.

PANITZ, ESTHER LEAH, English language educator; b. N.Y.C., Mar. 9, 1922; d. Robert and Gittel (Halkin) Allentuck; widowed; children: Jonathan A., Raphael, Michael. BA, Hunter Coll., 1942; B of Hebrew Lit., Theol. Sem., 1943; MA in English and Comparative Lit., Columbia U., 1951. Tchr. Syracuse (N.Y.) Pvt. Schs., 1943-51, Washington Secondary Schs., 1959-61; lectr. Bible studies, history Temple Adas Israel, Washington, 1951-59, Temple Emanuel, Paterson, N.J., 1960-86; adj. faculty William Paterson Coll., Wayne, N.J., 1989-95. Adj. faculty Seton Hall, Paramus, N.J., 1972-73, Mercy Coll., Dobbs Ferry, N.Y., 1990-93, 95—; presenter papers to coll. confs. Author: American Jewish Historical Quarterly, 1971, 72, 74, The Alien in Their Midst, 1981, Simon Wolf: Private Conscience and Public Image, 1987, Beyon Cain: A Post-Christian Vision; contbr. revs. to Pioneer Woman, 1946-61; book rev. editor Pioneer Woman Jour., 1951-61; contbr. articles to profl. jours. Vol. tutor John C. Hart Meml. Libr.; trustee Shrub Oak Park Assn., 1993. Charles Dickens fellow. Mem. MLA (mem. religion and lit. commn., speaker conv. 1995), Am. Jewish Hist. Soc., N.J. Coun. Tchrs. English, N.J. English Coll. Tchr.'s Assn., Jewish Theol. Sem. Am. Alumni Assn., Soc. St. Joseph's Hosp., Lupus Found., Brandeis U. Women, Phi Beta Kappa. Avocations: walking, mystery stories, live theatre, transcontinental railroad travel. Home: Shrub Oak, NY. Died Apr. 11, 2004.

PANKAU, EDMUND JOHN, investigation company executive; b. N.Y.C., July 4, 1945; s. Edmund Pankau and Barbara Loud Vail; m. Linda Lindow, June 17, 1987; children: Brian, Anastasia, Eddie. BS in Criminology, Fla. State U., 1972. Cert. legal investigator, cert. fraud examiner, cert. protection profl. Owner E.J. Pankau & Co., Tavernier, Fla., 1966-70; spl. agt. U.S. Treasury/Intelligence, Miami, Fla., 1971-73; pres. Intertect Inc., Houston, from 1973. Bd. dirs. Space Commerce Corp., Houston; instr. Am. Inst. Banking, Dallas, 1987—; dir. Tex. Paralegal Coll., Houston, 1985—. Author: How to Investigate by Computer, 1987, Check It Out, 1990; contbr. articles to profl. jours. Security Coun. dir. U. Houston. Capt. USAR, 1963-85. Named Investigator of the Yr., Am. Inst. Criminology, 1979. Mem. Nat. Assn. Cert. Fraud Examiners (bd. regent), Am. Soc. Indsl. Security, Investigators Online Network (dir. 1988—), Nat. Assn. Legal Investigators (past reg. dir.), Nat. Assn. Investigative Specialists (bd. dirs. 1986—), World Assn. Detectives. Avocations: sailing, fishing, hunting, competition shooting. Home: Katy, Tex. Died Oct. 9, 2004.

PANZER, MITCHELL EMANUEL, lawyer; b. Phila., Aug. 2, 1917; s. Max and Cecelia P.; m. Edith Budin, Apr. 13, 1943; children: Marcy C. Pokotilow, Leslie S. Katz. AB with distinction and 1st honors, Temple U., 1937; JD magna cum laude, U. Pa., 1940; LLD honoris causa, Gratz Coll., 1972. Bar: Pa. 1942, U.S. Dist. Ct. (ea. dist.) Pa. 1948, U.S. Ct. Appeals (3d cir.) 1949, U.S. Supreme Ct. 1961. Gowen Meml. fellow U. Pa. Law Sch., 1940-41; law clk. Phila. Ct. Common Pleas, No. 7, 1941-42; assoc. Wolf, Block, Schorr and Solis-Cohen, Phila., 1946-54, ptnr., 1954-88, of counsel, 1988-2006; spl. adv. counsel Fed. Home Loan Mortgage Corp., Fed. Nat. Mortgage Assn., 1972-82; dir. emeritus, former counsel St. Edmond's Fed. Savs. Bank; former dir. State Chartered Group, Pa. Bldg. and Loan Assn. Treas., Jewish Fedn. Greater Phila., 1981-82, v.p., 1982-86, trustee, 1963-2006, mem. exec. com., 1981-86, hon. life trustee, 1992-2006; trustee emeritus Pa. Land Title Inst., 1992-2006; bd. regents Gratz Coll., 1958-2006, pres., 1962-68. Served to capt. USAF, 1942-46. Decorated Bronze Star medal; recipient Man of Year award Gratz Coll. Alumni Assn., 1964. Mem. Am. Coll. Real Estate Lawyers, ABA (chmn. spl. com. on residential real estate transactions 1972-73), Pa. Bar Assn. (mem. spl. com. on land titles), Phila. Bar Assn. (chmn. com. censors 1966, chmn. bd. govs. 1971, parliamentarian 1965-67, 71, chmn. charter and by-laws com. 1972), Jewish Publ. Soc. (trustee 1966-81, 85-88, v.p. 1972-75, sec. 1975-78), Order of Coif (pres. 1961-63, exec. com.). Jewish. Clubs: 21 Jewel Square (Phila.); Masons. Patentee in field. Home: Merion Station, Pa. Died Jan. 4, 2006.

PAOLINI, MARIE ELAINE, mental health nurse; b. Pen Argyl, Pa., Jan. 14, 1953; d. Nello and Millie (Ronco) P. AAS, Northampton Coll., 1978. Cert. psychiat./mental health nurse. Staff nurse, charge nurse The Easton (Pa.) Home. Home: Wind Gap, Pa. Died June 23, 2005.

PAPALEO, ANTHONY See FRANCIOSA, ANTHONY

PAREDES, ROBERT WESLEY, music educator; b. San Diego, Feb. 10, 1948; s. Fernando Napoleon Paredes and Laureta Gay Williams; m. Melody Noel Scherubel, Nov. 2, 2001. MA, U. of Iowa, 1989, PhD, 1990. Instr. U. of Iowa, 1987—91, vis. asst. prof. & dir. of exptl., sic studios, 1991—93; composer, educator, freelance musician, brass and woodwind instrument repairman Iowa City, 1993—2001; adj. asst. prof., jazz studies U. of Iowa, from 2000. Freelance musician, Melbourne, Australia, 1984—86; artist in residence Festival of Improvised Music/Evos Found., Perth, Australia, 1986, Unit One/Exptl. Sch. of the U. of Ill., Champaign, Urbana, 1989—89; composer-adjudicator for the mcknight prize Minn. Composer's Forum, Mpls., 1992; artist in residence/festival de inverno Universidade Fed., Belo Horizonte, Brazil, 1992; composer in residence Meet the Composer: So. Arts Fedn., Nat. Endowment for the Arts & The Ala. State Coun. of the Arts, Birmingham, Ala., 1993. Author (composer): (text) Open Space Mag., Perspectives of New Music, Empty, 1993, After...In...After, 2003; musician (clarinetist): (jazz recording) Out On the Western Plains, (recording) The Bewitched, 1980; musician: (clarinetist, saxophonist) (jazz recording) Blood and Water:, 2000, PHD, Paredes-Hatwich Duo, 2001; musician: (clarinetist, bass clarinetist) John Rapson's Mallicked Simulacrum, 2002; exhibition, xerox art work, Tex. Musicians in Art, 1987, exhibition, xerox art works, Composition as Eco-Sys., 1990; composer (musician): (recording) (On)e for flute and clarinet, 1985; composer: (musician, clarinetist) Forgetting and Remembering for two-channel tape (a multi-track accumulation of improvisations on clarinet, 1986; composer: (electronic music) Speakers, a series of seventeen tape compositions-as-writings/drawings, 1987—93, (electronic music, recording) #16 (Speakers)/Fiesta, 1992, (electronic music recording) #17 (Speakers)/In Every Moment of Decay), 2-channel tape, 1993, (composition for solo cello, recording) Small Writing, 1994. Henry and Parker Pelzer fellow, 1989—90. Mem.: Pi Kappa Lambda. Buddhist. Home: Coralville, Iowa. Died Aug. 20, 2005.

PARK, ALICE MARY CRANDALL, author, genealogist; b. Loda, Ill., Oct. 4, 1901; d. Frederick Adam and Sarah Elizabeth (Clemens) Crandall; m. Lee I. Park, Aug. 29, 1925 (dec. Aug. 24, 1978); children: Lee Crandall, Nancy Park Kern. BS, U. Chgo., 1924. Tchr. U. Chgo. Lab. Sch., 1924-25; genealogy rschr. Washington, 1925—2006. Author: Park/e/s and Bunch on the Trail West, 1974, rev. edit., 1982, Schenck and Related Families in New Netherland, 1992, One Crandall Family 1651-1996, 1996, supplement, 1999, Our Immigrant Ancestors from Scotland: George Smith and His Wife, Mary Baird and Their Descendants, 2002. Pres. Falls Church (Va.) PTA, 1941-42, LWV, Fairfax County, Va., 1947-48. Mem. DAR, Nat. Soc. Colonial Dames Am., Nat. Soc. Sons and Daughters of Pilgrims, Nat. Soc. Daughters Am. Colonists, Friends Holland Soc., Nat. Huguenot Soc., Nat. Soc. U.S. Daughters 1812, Soc. Daughters Holland Dames: Descs. Ancient and Hon. Families of New Netherland, Chevy Chase Club, Met. Club, Farmington Country Club. Avocations: gardening, travel, cooking, music. Home: Washington, DC. Died May 21, 2006.

PARKER, HARRY JOHN, retired psychologist, educator; b. Sioux City, Iowa, Jan. 18, 1923; AB, Elmhurst Coll., 1947; MA, Northwestern U., 1953, PhD, 1956, postgrad., 1958, Roosevelt U., 1957-58; LittD, Elmhurst Coll., 1990. Lic. psychologist, Okla. Tex.; diplomate bd. cert. in rehab. psychology Am. Bd. Profl. Psychology. Counselor Northwestern U. Counseling Ctr., Chgo., 1952-56, counseling psychologist, 1956-59, asst. dir., 1957-58, dir., 1958-59; pvt. practice counseling psychologist Chgo., 1956-59, Okla., 1959-69, Tex., from 1969; prof. edn. U. Okla., 1959-69; dir. manpower planning, regional med. program and Sch. Health Related Professions U. Okla. Med. Ctr., Oklahoma City, 1967-69, prof. preventive medicine and pub. health, 1966-69, prof. human ecology, 1969; assoc. dean Sch. Allied Health Scis. U. Tex. Southwestern Med. Ctr., Dallas, 1969-74, prof. phys. medicine and rehab. 1969-90, prof. psychiatry, 1969-90, prof. rehab. sci., 1970-90. Adj. prof. rehab. U. N. Tex., 1990; adj. prof. psychology Ill. Inst. Tech., 1990-96, Tex. Woman's U., 1991-99; adj. prof. allied health edn. U. Tex. Southwestern Med. Ctr., Dallas, 1990-98. Contbr. articles to profl. jours. Served with U.S. Army, 1943-46 Fellow Am. Psychol. Assn.; mem. Southwestern Psychol. Assn. (life), Dallas Psychol. Assn., Tex. Psychol. Assn., Sigma Xi, Phi Delta Phi, Alpha Eta. Died Jan. 25, 2006.

PARKER, JAMES FLETCHER, middle school educator; b. Washington, Aug. 13, 1951; s. Clifford Marion and Martha Lois (McPhail) P. Student, Shenandoah Coll., 1969-71; BS, Old Dominion U., 1973. Cert. tech. edn., Va. Tchr. Spratley Jr. High Sch., Hampton, Va., 1974, Lindsey Jr. High Sch., Hampton, 1974, East Suffolk (Va.) Mid. Sch., 1974-79, Driver Intermediate Sch., Suffolk, 1979-90, John Yeates Mid. Sch., Suffolk, from 1990. Contbr.: (state curriculum guide) Introduction to Technology, 1988. Vol. Suffolk Young Dems., 1976-78; mem. Driver Intermediate Sch. PTA, 1979-90, John Yeates Mid. Sch. PTA, Suffolk, 1990—. Mem. ASCD, NEA, Va. Edn. Assn., Edn. Assn. of Suffolk (v.p. 1997—), Am. Vocat. Assn., Va. Vocat. Assn., Internat. Tech. Edn., Assn., Va. Tech. Edn. Assn., Suffolk Tech. Edn. Assn., Edn. Assn. Suffolk (exec. bd. 1996-97), Tech. Student Assn. (chpt. adv. 1979—), Tidewater Tech. Tchrs., Va. Mid. Sch. Assn., Coun. Tech. Tchr. Edn. Avocations: golf, reading, computers. Home: Portsmouth, Va. Died Sept. 18, 2004.

PARKER, JOSEPH SYDNEY, critical care nurse; b. Daytona Beach, Fla., July 11, 1952; s. Robert J. and Ardis M. (McDonald) P.; m. Barabara Lesher, Sept. 4, 1976; children: Daniel, Allison, Keri. ADN, Daytona Beach Community Coll., Fla., 1975; BSN, Ga. State U., 1977. Cert. CNOR, 1980. Clinician, scrub nurse Peachtree Cardiovascular Assn., Atlanta; dir. operating and recovery rooms Doctor's Hosp., Tucker, Ga.; dir. surgical svcs. Meml. Hosp., Chattanooga, Tampa (Fla.) Gen. Hosp. Contbr. articles to profl. jours. Mem. Assn. Operating Room Nurses (chpt. pres. elect, Chattanooga, nat. legislative com.), Fla. Orgn. Nurse Execs., v.p. student nurse assn. Fla. Avocation: Karate (black belt). Home: Jacksonville, Fla. Died Feb. 21, 2005.

PARKER, PATRICIA D., school counselor; b. Shepherd, Tex., Aug. 18, 1934; d. James Eldon and Nolie Agnes parker; m. John Lewis Segrest (div.); children: Pam, Jeanne. BS, Stephen F. Austin State U., 1970, MEd, 1973, MEd, 1983. Lic. sch. counselor, Tex. Tchr. kindergarten and 2d grade Pine Tree Ind. Sch. Dist., Longview, Tex., 1970-77; coord. math. and remedial reading Ore City (Tex.) Ind. Sch. Dist., 1981; tchr. remedial reading Kilgore (Tex.) Ind. Sch. Dist., 1981-88; counselor K-8 Colorado (Tex.) Ind. Sch. Dist., 1988-89; elem. counselor Waxahachie (Tex.) Ind. Sch. Dist., from 1986; dir. Family Therapy Ctr., Waxahachie, from 1994. Lead tchr. grad. equivalency diploma program, Kilgore, 1987-88; dir. aerospace edn. seminars, CAP, Ft. Worth, 1986, Dallas, 1989, dep. chief of staff, 1982-92. Contbr. articles to profl. jours. Chmn. parent edn. com., Ellis Coutny, 1994-96. Mem. Am. Sch. Counselors Assn., Tex. Sch. Counselors Assn. (chmn. com. 1996—), Am. Counselors Assn., Tex. Counselors Assn., Tex. State Tchrs. Assn. (life). Mem. Ch. of Christ. Avocations: skiing, gardening, reading, flying. Died Feb. 28, 2004.

PARKER, SIMON B., theology educator; b. Manchester, Eng., Feb. 23, 1940; came to U.S., 1961; s. Harold William and W.J. Irene (Smith) P.; m. Sonia Margarita Palmer, Aug. 26, 1961; children: Jonathan Aldwin, Jeremy Edmund. BA, U. Manchester, 1960; BD, Asbury Theol. Sem., Wilmore, Ky., 1963; PhD, Johns Hopkins U., 1967. Asst. prof. Reed Coll., Portland, Oreg., 1967-75; vis. asst. prof. U. Oreg., Eugene, 1976-77; asst. to pres. Boston U., 1977-78, asst. provost, 1978-81, assoc. dean Sch. Theology, 1981-88, assoc. prof. Hebrew Bible, Sch. Theology and Grad. Sch., 1988—2006. Author: The Pre-Biblical Narrative Tradition, 1989; assoc. editor Maarav, L.A., 1977-81, co-editor, 1981-85; mem. publ. adv. bd. Writings from the Ancient World, 1986-91, chief editor; contbr. articles to scholarly books and jours. Moderator, Auburndale (Mass.) United Parish, 1992-94. Recipient Graves award Pomona Coll., 1972; NEH grantee, 1988, 92; Fels dissertation fellow, 1966. Mem. Soc. Bibl. Lit. (group chair 1985-87), Am. Oriental Soc., Soc. for O.T. Study, Phi Beta Kappa. Methodist. Avocations: classical music, hiking, piano. Home: Newton, Mass. Died Apr. 29, 2006.

PARKS, GEORGE RICHARD, retired librarian; b. Boston, Apr. 11, 1935; m. Carol A. Richmond; children: Elizabeth, Jennifer, Geoffrey. AB summa cum laude, U. N.H., 1959; MAL.S., U. Mich., 1962; postgrad., Johns Hopkins, 1959-65; EFM cert. Sch. Theology, U. of the South, 1985. Preprofl. young adult librarian Enoch Pratt Free Library, Balt., 1960-61, ctrl., br. librarian, 1962-65, asst. to asst. dir., 1965-66; asst. dir. for adminstrn., libraries U. Rochester, 1966-68, chief adminstrv. officer, 1968-69; dean of libraries U. R.I., 1969-80; univ. librarian Colgate U., 1980-85, U. So. Maine, Portland, 1985-97; ret., 1997. Lectr. in field, cons. libr. bldg.; cons. antique map collection; mem. exec. bd. Greater Portland Theol. Libr., 1986-88, Maine Community Cultural Alliance, 1992-98; mem. exec. bd. So. Maine Libr. Dist., 1990-97, chmn., 1993. Apptd. Maine State Libr. Commn., 1994-98; asst. treas. St. Ann's Episcopal Ch., 1999-2004, lay preacher 2001—. Recipient Margaret Mann award U. Mich., 1962; Phillips Exeter Acad. scholar, 1952-54; U. N.H. scholar, 1955-59; Enoch Pratt Free Library scholar, 1961-62; Woodrow Wilson fellow, 1959-60. Mem. ALA, Assn. Coll. Rsch. Librs. (pres. New Eng. chpt. 1975, chmn. nat. conf. 1978, coll. librs. sect. planning com. 1994-96), Consortium R.I. Acad. Rsch. Librs (chmn. 1972-73), Maine Libr. Assn., New Eng. Libr. Assn. (conf. planning com. 1992-97, v.p./pres. elect 1995-96, pres. 1996-97, exec. bd. 1997-99), Libr. Adminstrn. and Mgmt. Assn. (exec. bd. bldgs. and equipment sect., libr. bldg. awards com. 1983-85), U. So. Maine Retirees Assn. (exec. bd. 2002—), Phi Beta Kappa, Phi Kappa Phi, Beta Phi Mu. Home: Westbrook, Maine. Died Oct. 17, 2005.

PARKS, GORDON ROGER ALEXANDER, film director, photographer, composer; b. Ft. Scott, Kans., Nov. 30, 1912; s. Jackson and Sarah (Ross) P.; m. Sally Alvis, 1933 (div. 1961); m. Elizabeth Campbell, 1962 (div. 1973); m. Genevieve Young, Aug. 26, 1973 (div. 1979); children by previous marriage: Gordon (dec.), Toni Parks Parsons, David, Leslie. Student pub. schs., Fort Scott, St. Paul; DFA (hon.), Md. Inst., 1968, Fairfield U., 1969; D (hon.), Boston U., 1969; LittD (hon.), Kans. State U., 1970; LHD (hon.), St. Olaf Coll., 1973; DFA (hon.), Colby Coll., 1974; DLit (hon.), MacAlester Coll., 1974; D (hon.), Lincoln U., 1975; HHD (hon.), Thiel Coll., 1976; DA (hon.), Columbia Coll., 1977; DFA (hon.), Rutgers U., 1980, Pratt Inst., 1981; LHD (hon.), Suffolk U., 1982; DFA (hon.), Kansas City Art Inst., 1984; LHD (hon.), Art Ctr. Coll. Design, 1986; DA (hon.), Hamline U., 1987; DFA (hon.), Am. Internat. Coll., 1988; HHD (hon.), Savannah Coll. Art and Design, 1988; D (hon.), U. Bradford, Eng., 1989; DFA (hon.), Rochester Inst. Tech., 1989, SUNY, 1990, R.I. Coll., 1990, Parsons Sch. Design, 1991, Manhattanville Coll., 1992, Coll. New Rochelle, 1992, Skidmore Coll., 1993; LittD (hon.), Montclair State U., 1994. Freelance fashion photographer, Mpls., 1937-42; photographer Farm Security Adminstrn., 1942-43, OWI, 1944, Standard Oil Co., NJ, 1945-48, Life mag., 1948-68; ind. photographer, film maker, from 1954. Color and black and white cons. various motion picture prodns., U.S. and Europe, 1954-2006. Writer, producer, dir.: The Learning Tree, 1969; dir.: (films) Shaft, 1972, 2000, Shaft's Big Score, 1972, The Super Cops, 1974, Leadbelly, 1976, Odyssey of Solomon Northup, 1984, Moments Without Proper Names, 1986 (Silver medal Internat. Film Festival 1989); creator, composer, dir. Martin, 1990; TV documentary: Diary of a Harlem Family, 1968 (Emmy award); author: Flash Photography, 1947, Camera Portraits: The Techniques and Principals of Documentary Portraiture, 1948, The Learning Tree, 1963, A Choice of Weapons, 1966 (Notable Book award ALA 1966), Born Black, 1971, Flavio, 1977 (Christopher award 1978), (novel) Shannon, 1981, Voices in the Mirror, 1990; founder, editorial dir. Essence mag., 1970-73; composer Piano Concerto, 1953, Tree Symphony, 1967, 3 piano sonatas, 1956, 58, 60, modern works for piano and wind instruments, (film scores) The Learning Tree (Libr. Congress Nat. Film Registry Classics film honor, 1989), Shaft's Big Score, The Odyssey of Solomon Northup, Moments Without Proper Names; dir., composer (film) Ballet for Martin Luther King, 1991; traveling exhibits in U.S. and abroad, 1990. Bd. dirs. Schomburg Ctr. for Research in Black Culture, Am. Arts. Alliance, W. Eugene Smith Meml. Fund, Black Tennis and Sports Found., Rondo Ave. Inc., St. Paul; Harlem Symphony Orch., N.Y.C.; mem. adv. com. Kans. Ctr. for the Book; bd. advocates Planned Parenthood Fedn. Am. Inc.; patron N.Y. City Housing Authority Symphony; supporter Apple Corps Theatre, N.Y.C., Quindaro Project, Kans., numerous other civic activities. Decorated Comdr. de l'Ordre des Arts et des Lettres (Republique Francaise); recipient Julius Rosenwald award for photography, 1942, award NCCJ, 1964, awards Syracuse U. Sch. Journalism, 1961, Newhouse citation Syracuse U., 1963, awards Phila. Mus. Art, 1964, awards N.Y. Art Dirs. Club, 1964, 68, Frederic W. Brehm award, 1962, Carr Van Anda Journalism award Ohio U., 1970, Carr Van Anda Journalism award U. Miami, 1964, Pres.'s fellow award R.I. Sch. Design, 1984, Am. Soc. Mag. Photographers award, 1985, Nat. Medal Arts award Commonwealth Mass. Communications, 1988, Kans. Gov.'s medal, 1986, Nat. medal of Arts, 1988, World Press Photo award, 1988, N.Y.C. Mayor's award, 1989, Artist of Merit Josef Sudek medal, 1989, award Internat. Ctr. Photography, 1990; named Kansan of Yr. Sons and Daus. Kans., 1985. Mem. Urban League N.Y., ASCAP, Writers Guild, NAACP (Spingarn award 1972, Hall of Fame 1984), Acad. Motion Pictures Arts and Scis., AFTRA, Am. Inst. Pub. Service, Nat. Urban League Guild, Internat. Mark Twain Soc. (hon.), Newspaper Guild, Assn. Composers and Dirs., Dirs. Guild (nat. dir.), Dirs. Guild N.Y., Am. Soc. Mag. Photographers (Photographer of Yr. award 1960, 85), Nat. Assn. for Am. Composers and Condrs., Stylus Soc. (hon.), U.S. Tennis Assn. Inc., Am. Film Inst, Kappa Alpha Mu. Clubs: Pen; Black Tennis and Sports Found. (bd. dirs.). Died Mar. 7, 2006.

PARKS, THOMAS RICHARD, food scientist, consultant; b. Melrose Park, Ill., Mar. 26, 1931; m. Althea Sayward, July 9, 1960; children: Richard, Alison. BS, U. Mass, 1953, MS, 1958. Process engr. Gerber Products Co., Oakland, Calif., 1959-62; mgr. product engring. research StarKist Food, Terminal Island, Calif., 1962-69; mgr. food, agroscis. Stanford Research Inst., Menlo Park, Calif., 1969-79; pres., chmn. bd. Food and AgroSystems Inc., Sunnyvale, Calif., from 1979. Cons. in field. Inventor in field. Served to lt (j.g.) USNR, 1953-57. Mem. Inst. Food Technologists. Republican. Methodist. Avocations: woodcarving, inventing, naval architecture. Home: Sunnyvale, Calif. Died July 10, 2005.

PARMAN, MICHAEL J., publishing executive; b. Reno, Nev., Mar. 8, 1945; s. May Parman; m. Michaela McCulloch; children: Leah, Clark. BA, MA, U. Reno. Exec. editor Press Democrat, Santa Rosa, Calif., 1985—91, pub., 1991—2005. Died July 1, 2006.

PARRISH, CAROLE ANNE, nurse educator; b. Boston, Aug. 24, 1934; d. William A. and Phyllis M. (Atwater) Carr; m. Henry M. Parrish, Dec. 21, 1957; children: Cynthia, Catherine, Cheryl. BSN, U. Miami, 1957; postgrad., U. Pitts., 1957-58; MPH, U. Mo., 1967; EdD, U. S.D., 1973. RN, Fla.; cert. real estate salesperson, Fla. Office nurse, mgr. H.J. Parrish, M.D., Ocala, Fla., from 1973; sch. bd. mem. State Fla. Voters, Ocala, from 1974; instr. Cen. Fla. Community Coll., Ocala, 1974-76; nurse H.J. Parrish, M.D., Ocala. Contbr. articles to profl. jours. Recipient U.S. Pub. Health Traineeship in Nursing U. Pitts., 1958; named to Sigma Xi, Delta Kappa Gamma. Mem. Student Nurses Assn., Spanish Club, Mo. Student Pub. Health Assn., ANA, Am. Pub. Health Assn., Mo. Pub. Health Assn., Mo. Nurses Assn., Ocala Women's Club, Nat. Sch. Bd. Assn., Nat. Assn. for Year-Round Edn., Marion County Med. Assn. Aux., Marion County C. of C., Alpha Delta Pi. Home: Ocala, Fla. Died Jan. 30, 2005.

PARRISH, HARRY JACOB, state legislator; b. Manassas, Va., Feb. 19, 1922; m. Mattie Hooe Cannon; children: Judith R. Ratcliffe, Harry J. II. Student, Wofford Coll., Va. Polytech. Inst. Mem. Va. State Legis., 1982—2006, co-chair fin. com., mem. corps. ins. & banking com., mem. conservation & natural resources com., mem. labor & commerce com., mem. rules com. Republican. Methodist. Died Mar. 28, 2006.

PARSON, SARAH JANE, retired insurance executive; b. Phila., Nov. 11, 1931; d. Harry and Dorothy (Beatty) P. Grad. high sch., Phila., 1949. Typist, clk. Hartford Steam Boiler I & I Co., Phila., 1949-69, underwriter, 1969-86, sr. mktg. exec., 1986-93; acct. exec. Murray Ins. Agy., Scranton, Pa., 1994-95; ret., 1995. Contbr. articles to profl. jours. Recipient Ins. Women of Yr. award Greater Scranton Ins. Women, 1991, Rep. award Ins. Systems Unltd., 1991. Mem. Nat. Assn. Ins. Women, Northeastern Pa. Inst. Assn. (past pres. 1991-92), The Scranton Club, Order Eastern Star (worthy matron 1966-67, 81-82, 90-91). Democrat. Baptist. Avocations: golf, gardening, music, cameras, old movies. Home: Philadelphia, Pa. Died Oct. 18, 2004.

PARSONS, THOMAS WHITNEY, computer science educator, consultant; b. Hartford, Conn., Jan. 1, 1931; s. Thomas Madison and Claire (Trester) P.; m. Patricia Jean Pilliard, Nov. 5, 1963. BA in Greek, U. Wis., 1952; PhD in Elec. Engring., Polytechnic U., 1975. Registered profl. engr., N.Y. Prof. Hofstra U., Hempstead, N.Y., from 1981. Author: Voice and Speech Processing, 1986, (with others) Digital Signal Processing, 1991, Introduction to Compiler Construction, 1992. Mem. IEEE (sr.), Assn. for Computing Machinery, Acoustical Soc. Am., Sigma Xi. Achievements include provision of technical support to court-appointed panel of experts investigating Watergate tapes. Home: Brooklyn, NY. Died Aug. 20, 2004.

PARTRIDGE, LLOYD DONALD, physiologist, educator; b. Cortland, N.Y., Dec. 18, 1922; s. Bert James and Marian (Rice) P.; m. Jean Marie Rutledge, Aug. 6, 1944; children: Lloyd Donald, David Lee, Gayle Ann Partridge Kneller Spence BS, U. Mich., 1948, MS, 1949, PhD, 1953. Instr. U. Mich., Ann Arbor, 1953-56; asst. prof. physiology, research assoc. in neurology Yale U., New Haven, 1956-62; assoc. prof. neurophysiology U. Tenn., Memphis, 1962-70, prof., 1970-94, dep. chmn. physiology, 1965-73. Cons. neurophysiology and bioengring. Conn. State Hosp., 1957-62, Boelter Bioengring. Ctr., UCLA, 1982-87, Acad. Sci. Sofia, Bulgaria, 1981; cons. U. So. Calif., 1992; vis. prof. U. We. Ont., 1981, 82, Med. Coll. Ohio, Toledo, 1985; vis. prof. Memphis State U., 1985, adj. prof. math., 1989-91, adj. prof. biomed. engring., 1993—; adj. prof. biomed. engring. U. Memphis, 1993—; vis. scientist Acad. Sci. USSR, 1987, Pavlov Physiology Soc., USSR, 1989; vis. prof. physiology U. Vt., 1965, 66. Author: The Nervous System, Its Function and Interaction with the World, 1993; assoc. editor: Trans Bio. Med. Engring., 1973-81; assoc. Behavior Brain Rsch., 1981—; sect. editor Annals Biomed. Engring., 1985-94; contbr. chpts. to books, articles to profl. jours. Served with AUS, 1944-46. Mem. Internat. Brain Research Orgn., Am. Acad. Neurology, Am. Physiol. Soc. (editorial bd. 1976-81), Biomed. Engring. Soc. (adminstrn. com. 1977-79), Biophysics Soc., Engring. Medicine and Biology Soc. (bd. dirs. 1985-89), IEEE, Neurosci. Soc., Sigma Xi. Home: Memphis, Tenn. Died Apr. 4, 2005.

PASSERO, JAMES JOSEPH, insurance agent, broker; b. Johnstown, Pa., Oct. 23, 1934; s. Frank and Ann Eve (Fezenko) P.; m. Angeline Catherine Lake, Nov. 27, 1958; 1 child, Mitchell James. BS, St. Francis Coll., 1960; CLU, Am. Coll., 1981. Mgmt. trainee N.Y. Life Ins. Co., N.Y.C., 1960-62; cost acct. Internat. Paper Co., N.Y.C., 1962-64; asst. to contr. Ga. Pacific Co., Stamford, Conn., 1964-65; sr. fin. analyst Olin Corp., N.Y.C., 1965-66; mgr. fin. analysis RCA Random House, N.Y.C., 1966-70; budget dir. Trans Cont. Investing Co., N.Y.C., 1970-71; v.p., contr. Balt. Paint and Chem. Co., 1971-72; cons. various cos., Stamford, 1972-77; agt., broker Equitable Fin. Cos., Stamford, from 1977. With USMC, 1958-64. Mem. Italian Ctr. of Stamford (bd. dirs. 1984—). Republican. Avocations: basketball, Karate. Died June 14, 2004.

PATACSIL, PETER ESPEJO, science administrator; b. Honolulu, Sept. 25, 1937; s. A.N. Patacsil and Donatela Ayson (Espejo) Enrado; m. Julia Lizama Leon-Guerrero, Apr. 16, 1966; children: Peter Kenneth, Matthew Raymond, Catherine Elizabeth. BSCE, U. Hawaii, 1960; MS in Ops. Research, U.S. Naval Postgrad. Sch., 1966; diploma, Air Command and Staff Coll., 1971. Commd. ensign USN, Newport, R.I., 1961, advanced through grades to comdr. Honolulu, 1976, retired San Diego, 1983; sr. analyst Sci. Applications Internat. Corp., San Diego, from 1983. Contbr. reports to tech. pubs. Ex-officio mem. Guam Territorial Bd. Edn., Agana, 1976-78; chmn. Chamorro Dist. Aloha Council Boy Scouts Am., Agana, 1977-78, exec. bd. dirs. 1977-78; chmn. Role Com. Kamahameha Dist. Aloha Council Boy Scouts Am., Aiea, Hawaii, 1975-76; bd. dirs. Jr. Achievement, Agana, 1976-78; mem. Guam Adv. Council on Vocat. Edn., Agana, 1977-78, exec. com. 1st and 2d annual Spl. Olympics, Agana, 1977-78, Guam State Adv. Council for Handicapped, Agana, 1977-78; mem. Guam Eagles chpt. Pop Warner Football Assn. 1977-78; treas. Mira Mesa High Sch. chpt., San Diego, 1983-84; vice-chmn. Agueda Johnston Jr. High Sch. PTA, Chalan Pago, Guam, 1977-78; mem. West Point Parent's Soc., 1985/6. Named to Ancient Order of the Chamorri, Gov. of Guam, Agana, 1978. Mem. Armed Forces Communications and Electronics Assn. Republican. Roman Catholic. Avocation: coin collecting/numismatics. Home: San Diego, Calif. Died Mar. 31, 2005.

PATE, ROGER D., electronics engineer; b. Eva, Ala., July 8, 1946; s. Claude W. Pate and Iris F. (Cahela) England; m. Sandra J. Wright, July 8, 1980; children: Lisa D., William A.L., Dale K. BA in Psychology, Calvary Grace, 1984; consumer electronics cert., Calhoun Coll., 1990. Aviation foreman, missile technician U.S. Army, 1964-87; electronic technician Phase IV Sys., Huntsville, Ala., 1989-94; agr. trapper USDA, Athen, Ala., 1994-96; prodn. mgr. Gamefinder, Huntsville, 1994-95, lead technician phase IV sys., from 1995. Asst. scout master Boy Scouts Am., Falkville, Ala., 1992-98. Mem. AF&AM, Cahaba Shrine. Avocation: amateur radio operator. Home: Tuscaloosa, Ala. Died Jan. 13, 2004.

PATICOFF, HARVEY, lawyer; b. N.Y.C., Dec. 20, 1931; s. Albert Oscar and Mollie (Pomerantz) P.; m. Sheila Ruth Grenard, June 23, 1957; children: Vicki Lynn Latorella, Kim Hali. BA, Bklyn. Coll., CUNY, 1954; JD, Bklyn. Law Sch., 1956. Bar: N.Y. 1956, U.S. Dist. Ct. (so. and ea. dists.) N.Y. 1979. Atty. Aetna Casualty & Surety Co., N.Y.C., 1960-61; ptnr. Tellerman, Paticoff & Greenberg, N.Y.C., from 1961. 1st lt. JAGC, U.S. Army, 1957-59. Mem. ABA, N.Y. State Trial Lawyers Assn., Assn. Trial Lawyers of City of N.Y. (pres. 1993-95), N.Y. County Lawyers Assn. Democrat. Avocations: photography, gardening, bicycling. Home: Jericho, NY. Died July 21, 2004.

PATRICK, JANE AUSTIN, association executive; b. Memphis, May 27, 1930; d. Wilfred Jack and Evelyn Eudora (Branch) Austin; m. William Thomas Spencer, Sept. 11, 1952 (div. Apr. 1970); children: Duke Anthony-Spencer Austin, ToniLee Candice Spencer; m. George Milton Patrick, Oct. 1, 1971 (dec. July 2002). Student, Memphis State U., 1946-47; BSBA, Ohio State U., 1979. Svc. rep. So. Bell Tel. and Tel., Memphis, 1947-52; placement dir. Mgmt. Pers., Memphis, 1965-66; pers. dir. E & E Ins. Co., Columbus, Ohio, 1966-69; Ohio exec. dir. Nat. Soc. for Prevention of Blindness, Columbus, 1969-73; regional dir. Ohio and Ky. CARE and MEDICO, Columbus, 1979-87; v.p. Career Execs. of Columbus, 1987-91; owner, pres. Patricks Distbn., from 1994. Lectr., cons. in field. Author of poetry. Mem. choir 1st Cmty. Ch., Columbus, 1972--, bd. dirs. Ohio State U. Med. Ctr. Svc. Bd.; bd. dirs. Columbus Coun. on World Affairs, 1980-92, sec., 1983-91, chmn. devel. com.; chmn. pers. com. Ohio Hunger Task Force, 1989-90; founder Ctrl. Ohio Lions Eye Bank. Recipient commendation Nat. Soc. Prevention Blindness, commendation Ctrl. Ohio Lions Eye Bank, 1973, Svc. award plaque Upper Arlington Pub. Schs., 1986. Mem. Non-Profit Orgn. Mgmt. Inst. (pres.), Nat. Soc. Fund-Raising Execs. (cert., nat. dir., v.p.), Pub. Rels. Soc. Am. (cert., membership com. chairperson), Ohio State Med. Ctr. Svc. Bd. (bd. dirs.), Ins. Inst. Am. (cert.), Mensa Internat., Columbus Dental Soc. Aux. (historian and publicity chair), Germantown Country Club, Alpha Gamma Delta (undergrad. editor Gamma Zeta chpt.), Epsilon Sigma Alpha (pres.). Home: Memphis, Tenn. Died Mar. 29, 2006.

PATTEN, WILLIAM HAZEL, III, drilling company official; b. Millersburg, Ohio, Mar. 9, 1957; s. William Hazel Jr. and Patricia Ann (Whetsell) P.; m. Teresa Ann Mohr, Mar. 5, 1958 (div. Sept. 1984); children: William Hazel IV, Maynard M. Student, Marietta Coll., 1976. Operator Patten Drilling Co., Inc., Millersburg, 1976-81; field supt. Mac Oil Field Svc., Inc., Millersburg, 1981-83; owner, pres. P&N Exploration/Dig-Me Drilling, Inc., Holmesville, Ohio, 1983-86; driver Mast Trucking, Inc., Millersburg, 1988-90; operator G & H Drilling, Mt. Hope, Ohio, 1986-88 and from 90. Mem. Am. Legion, Eagles. Avocation: snow and water skiing. Home: Millersburg, Ohio. Died Dec. 19, 2004.

PATTERSON, HUGH BASKIN, JR., publishing executive; b. Cotton Plant, Miss., Feb. 8, 1915; s. Hugh Baskin and Martha (Wilson) P.; m. Louise Caroline Heiskell, Mar. 29, 1944 (div. 1988); children: Carrick Heiskell, Ralph Baskin; m. Olivia Owen Nisbet, 1992; stepchildren: A. Wyckliff, Olivia Student, Henderson State Tchrs. Coll., 1933. Sales dept. Smith Printing Co., Pine Bluff, Ark., 1933-36; asst. to sales mgr. Democrat Printing & Lithographing Co., Little Rock, 1936-38, promotion mgr., 1940-42; sales dept. Art Metal Constrn. Co., N.Y.C., 1938-39; planning and prodn. mgr. Rufus H. Darby Co. (printers and pubs.), Washington, 1939-40; pub. Ark. Gazette, 1948—86; pres., treas. Ark. Gazette Co. Pres. Ark. Bldg. Co. Bd. dirs. Fgn. Policy Assn., Inc.; bd. visitors U. Ark. at Little Rock. Served to maj. USAAC, 1942-46. Gazette recipient Pulitzer gold medal for pub. service, 1957, Freedom award Freedom House, 1958 Mem. Am. Newspaper Pubs. Assn., So. Newspaper Pubs. Assn. (pres. 1959-60), Inter Am. Press Assn. (dir.), Council Fgn. Relations, Internat. Press Inst., Sigma Delta Chi. Clubs: Overseas Press, Nat. Press, Little Rock Country. Democrat. Presbyterian. Died May 29, 2006.

PATTERSON, MAURICE LEE, mathematics educator, retired; b. Wurtsboro, N.Y., Oct. 28, 1910; s. Horace Lee and Laura Augusta (Reed) P.; m. Ferne Elizabeth Kitson, June 29, 1940; children: Muriel, Janet, Reed. BS in Sci., Alfred U., 1934; MS in Edn., Cornell U., 1939. Cost acct. GE, Schenectady, N.Y., 1928-30; sci. tchr. Alfred (N.Y.) High Sch., 1934-36, Interlaken (N.Y.) Cen. Sch., 1936-60, dist. prin., 1960-68; supt. of sch. South Seneca Cen. Sch., Interlaken, 1968-70; dir. computer ctr. Bd. of Coop. Edn. Svc., Ithaca, N.Y., 1970-72. Author: (local history) Between the Lakes, 1976, (genealogy) Pioneers of Quarry Hill, 1983; editor: (ch. history) Interlaken Reformed, 1980, Interlaken Hist. Soc. Newsletter, 1975-92; co-editor: (genealogy and history) The Covert Family, 1989. Sec. Interlaken (N.Y.) Firemen's Assn., 1939-44; master Farmerville Masonic Lodge, Interlaken, 1946, sec., 1970-75; pres. Interlaken Pub. Libr., 1960-83, Intrlaken Hist. Soc., 1972-92, Masonic Hall Assn., 1987-91; exec. com. Regional Conf. Hist. Agy., 1980-82; pres. Finger Lakes Libr. System, Ithaca, 1994. Republican. Avocations: woodworking, writing, reading, travel. Home: Interlaken, NY. Died Feb. 18, 2005.

PATTERSON, WILLIAM GLENN, II, military officer; b. Jefferson City, Mo., Jan. 31, 1954; s. William Glenn and Marceline Ann (Bacon) P.; m. Debbie Kay Pirner, Feb. 23, 1974; children: William Glenn III, Nathan Andrew, Morgan B. BA in Bus. Adminstrn., Columbia (Mo.) Coll., 1983. Commd. 2d lt. Mo. Nat. Guard, advanced through grades to maj., 1990, ops. officer Jefferson City, 1979-81, chief SIDPERS br., 1981-88, logistics officer St. Louis, 1988-91, recruiting officer, chief drug demand reduction program Jefferson City, Mo., from 1991. Ambassador U.S. Jr. C. of C., 1990; senator Jr. Chamber Internat., 1990. Mem. SAR, Mo. Nat. Guard Assn., Mil. Order World Wars, Jefferson City Jaycees (membership v.p. 1984), Mo. Jaycees (state editor), Rotary Internat. Roman Catholic. Avocations: rappeling, photography, water-skiing, fishing, exercise. Home: Jefferson City, Mo. Died June 30, 2004.

PATTERSON, WILLIAM HENRY, regional planner, retired army officer; b. Indpls., July 2, 1927; s. William Henry and Pearl Mona (Larlee) P.; m. Joyce Ann Powell, Aug. 19, 1950; children: William H., Catherine E., Carol M., Patricia J., Christopher E., Michael T. BA in Polit. Sci., George Washington U., 1959; MA in Pub. Law and Govt., Columbia U., 1963. Commd. 2d lt. U.S. Army, 1946, advanced through grades to col., 1969; capital outlay com. Brevard County (Fla.) Sch. Dist., 1986-93. Mem. Charter Com., Brevard County, 1993-94; chmn. Brevard County Planning and Zoning Bd. and Local Planning Agy., 1994; chmn. dept. Nat. and Internat. Security Studies, occupant Eisenhower chair U.S. Army War Coll., Carlisle Barracks, Pa., 1976-78. Chmn. Merritt Island (Fla.) Exec. Coun. Homeowner Assns., 1981-82; co-founder Civic Action Coun., Brevard County, 1983; dir. Washington-Moscow Presdn. Hot Line, 1962-63. Decorated Legion of Merit (4), Bronze Star, Air medal. Mem. Ret. Officers Assn., Mil. Order World Wars (chpt. comdr. 1995-96). Republican. Roman Catholic. Avocation: civil war history. Home: Merritt Island, Fla. Died Aug. 19, 2004.

PATTIE, CHARLES CAMERON, marketing manager; b. Huntsville, Tex., June 11, 1946; s. Charles Mack and Ann Eileen (Wilson) P.; m. Barbara Porter, Aug. 28, 1977; children: Caroline Rose, William Wilson. BA, U. North Tex., 1968; MBA, Loyola U., 1988. Clin. tsch. U. Calif., Berkeley, 1978-81; sr. dosimitrist, instr. Med. Coll. Va., Richmond, 1981-83; project mgr. Oldelft, Fairfax, Va., 1988-89, mktg. mgr., from 1989. Home: Arlington, Va. Died Feb. 18, 2004.

PATUREAU, ARTHUR MITCHELL, chemical engineer, consultant; b. Beaumont, Tex., Nov. 22, 1913; m. Clara Davis, Dec. 24, 1934. BSChemE, U. Tex., 1943, postgrad., Pa. State U., 1946. Chief process engr. Gasoline Plant Constrn. Co., Corpus Christi, Tex., 1944-46, McCarthy Chem. Co., Houston, 1946-48; chief application engr. Fisher & Porter Co., Hatboro, Pa., 1948-50; cons. reactor coolant controls Nautilus nuc. submarine Westinghouse Atomic Power Divsn., Pitts., 1950-53; chief application engr. chem. industry Brown Instrument Divsn., Phila., 1953-55; western sales mgr. Barksdale Valves, L.A., 1955-74; western divisional mgr. Pa. Indsl. Chem. Co., L.A., 1974-75; divisional mgr. Hercules, Inc., L.A., 1973-75; cons. to chem. industry Temple, Tex., from 1975; pres. Artgraphics, Inc., from 1975. Editor: (tech. book) Resins in Rubber, 1975; contbg. author to Ency. Chem. Engring.; contbr. articles to profl. jours. Mem. engring. fund adv. coun. U. Tex. Coll. Engring., 1970—75. Mem. AIChE, L.A. Rubber Group, Rotary. Episcopalian. Avocations: art work, camping, travel, computer work. Died Apr. 6, 2005.

PAUL, ALICE, foundation executive; b. N.Y.C., Dec. 18, 1936; d. Lusha and Irene (Seplow) Nelson; m. HenryKurt Paul, June 28, 1956 (div. 1985); children: Karen Diane, Rachel Irene. BA, New Sch. Social Rsch., 1968. Program assoc. Joint Found. Support, N.Y.C., 1970-76; resource and info. coord. Neighborhood Stabilization Program N.Y.C. Commn. on Human Rights, 1976-78; exec. dir. Astella Devel. Corp., Bklyn., 1979-83, Uris Bros. Found., N.Y.C., from 1983. Bd. dirs., v.p. Assn. Neighborhood Housing Devel., N.Y.C., 1981-83; pub. mem. N.Y. State Bd. Architecture, N.Y.C., 1982—; bd. dirs. Bklyn. in Touch, 1986—, Non-Profit Coordinating Com., N.Y.C., 1989—. Coord., Com. on Decent Unbiased Campaign Tactics, N.Y.C., 1984-86; bd. dirs., v.p. N.Y.C. Transit Authority Adv. Coun., 1986—. Mem. Women in Housing and Fin. (bd. dirs.), AIA, City Club N.Y. (trustee, com. chair). Democrat. Jewish. Avocations: architecture, ballet, films, travel. Home: Brooklyn, NY. Died Dec. 20, 2004.

PAULEY, BLAGA SLAVCHEVA, mathematics professor; b. Sofia, Bulgaria, Oct. 5, 1960; arrived in U.S., 1989; d. Slavcho Vassilev and Hristina Diulgerova; children: Thomas, Richard, James. BA in Classical Music and Opera Performance, MA in Classical Music and Opera Performance, Bulgarian State Conservatory, Sofia; AA in Early Childhood Edn., MSJC; BA in Math., MA in Math., Calif. State U., San Bernardino. Opera singer European opera theaters, 1980—89; math. isntr. Mt. San Jacinto (Calif.) Coll., 1998—2001, Crafton Hills Coll., Yucampa, Calif., 1998—2001; asst. prof. math. Riverside (Calif.) C.C., from 2001. Participant summer seminars Nat. Inst. Math., Park City, Utah, 1999—2000; spkr. in field. Active support groups for breast cancer Loma Linda U. Med. Ctr. Named Tchr. of Yr., USTC, 1998, Educator of Yr., Latino Students L.A. County, Riverside C.C., 2003—04, Disting. Tchr., Luth. Students, Riverside C.C., 2004; winner nat. and internat. opera competitions, 1982—89. Russian Orthodox. Avocations: breadmaking, cooking, reading, singing, crocheting. Home: Riverside, Calif. Died May 2, 2005.

PAULUS, ERWIN FERDINAND, JR., forestry company executive; b. Warren, Ark., May 23, 1921; s. Erwin F. and Blanche (Cahill) P.; m. Olive Wise, Sept. 3, 1946; children: Lee Paulus Leming, Tom, Michael. BSBA, U. Ark., 1948. V.p., mgr. Warren Cotton Oil Co., 1948-59; sales mgr. Wilson Oak Flooring Co., Warren, 1960-69; land agt. So. div. Potlatch Corp., Warren, from 1970. Mem. nat. devel. coun. U. Ark., Fayetteville, 1986—; mayor City of Warren, 1960-64; bd. dirs., past pres. S.E. Ark. Concret Assn., 1978—; vice chmn. U. Ark. Found., 1985—. Mem. Ark. Forestry Assn. (bd. dirs. 1973—, Pres.'s award 1981),

Warren Country Club (v.p. 1968), Masons, Rotary (past pres. Warren chpt.), Sigma Alpha Epsilon. Democrat. Presbyterian. Avocations: golf, hunting, fishing. Home: Warren, Ark. Died May 29, 2004.

PAVA, ESTHER SHUB, artist, educator; b. Hartford, Conn., June 29, 1921; d. Jacob H. and Rose (Rietkop) Shub; m. Jacob Pava, June 16, 1946; children: David Lauren, Jonathan Michael, Daniel Seth, Nathaniel Alexander. BFA, R.I. Sch. of Design, 1944; MA, San Francisco State U., 1971. Artist New Eng. Roto Engraving Co., Holyoke, Mass., 1944-46, Wyckoff Advt. Agy., San Francisco, 1947-48; tchr. San Francisco Unified Sch. Dist., 1963-66, Laguna Salada Sch. Dist., Pacifica, Calif., 1966-83; artist, educator Belmont, Calif., from 1983. Tchr. pvt. students. Bd. dirs. Belmont Arts Commn. Recipient numerous awards for artwork. Mem. AAUW, Burlingame Art Soc. (pres. 1983-84), Thirty and One Artists (pres. 1992-93), Soc. Western Artists (signature mem. and juror, 2d v.p. and program chmn. 1997-98, pres. 1999-2001) Calif. Watercolor Assn., Nat. League Am. Pen Women, Belmont Arts. Commn. Avocations: world travel, book discussion groups, sketching on location, painting in studio. Home: Danville, Calif. Died Aug. 25, 2006.

PAVKOV, JANET RUTH, nurse; b. Wadsworth, Ohio, Aug. 7, 1939; d. George and Helen Rose (Pamer) P. RN, Mansfield Gen. Hosp., Ohio, 1960; BS in Tech. Edn., U. Akron, 1972, MA in Family Life, 1976; cert. in nursing home adminstrn., Ohio State U., 1983. Lic. social worker; lic. nursing home adminstr.; cert. activity cons./educator, qualified mental retardation profl. Charge nurse obstet. dept. Mansfield Gen. Hosp., 1960; gen. practice office nurse P.O. Staker, M.D., Mansfield, 1961; operating room nurse Akron (Ohio) Gen. Hosp., 1961-70; charge nurse obstet. dept. Wayne Gen. Hosp., Orrville, Ohio, 1970-71; nursing faculty mem. North Cen. Tech. Coll., Mansfield, 1972-74, asst. chairperson nursing program, 1973-74; instr. St. Thomas Hosp. Sch. Nursing, Akron, 1974-77; nurse epidemiologist Alum Crest Nursing Home, Columbus, 1978-84, nursing supr., 1978-80; nursing home adminstr. Am. Health Care Facilities, Springfield and Canton, Ohio, 1986-89; health facilities standards rep. II dept. health State of Ohio, Akron, 1989-90; mgr. nursing svcs. Columbus Community Mental Health Ctrs., 1990-91; documentation supr. Alum Crest N.H., Columbus, 1991-92; crises svcs. nurse Net-Care Corp., Columbus, from 1992; emergency svcs. nurse North Ctrl. Mental Health, Columbus, from 1992. Vol. nurse and camp counselor Webster Springs (W.Va.) Camp, 1960-75, Palisades Camp, Pacific Palisades, Calif., 1963, Camp Massanetta, Harrisonburg, Va., 1978-79, 86; vol. nurse Prescott (Ariz.) Pines Camp, 1967, Oakwood Camp, Syracuse, Ind., 1968, Presbyn. Camp, Portland, Oreg., 1970; cons. McNeil Pharms., Spring House, Pa., 1982, 84, Assn. Developmentally Disabled Intermediate Care Facility for Mentally Retarded, Columbus, 1983-85, Alum Crest Nursing Home, 1979-85; mem. ARC Vol. Nurse Div., 1958—, Nat. Council Nursing Home Nurses, 1979-84, Nat. Council Family Relations, 1975-84, Retired Sr. Vol. Program adv. council, 1975-77; instr. lic. practical nurse program Warren (Ohio) Pub. Schs., 1972; active Ohio Dist. 6 Mental Health Older Adult Council, 1977-84; staff nurse Eastland Care Ctr., Columbus, 1981-84; adminstr.-on-call nursing services Kimberly Pkwy. Group Home, Columbus, 1983-84, coordinator patient assessment and nursing services, 1983-84; counselor, shift leader emergency services Columbus Area Community Mental Health Ctr., Columbus, 1977-86, coordinator geriatric services, 1977-87, mem. quality assurance and peer rev. com., 1978-87; mem. adv. bd. home health care div. Health Care Personnel Assn., Inc., 1983-86; sec. Specialized Health Adminstrv. Resource Enterprises, 1983-85; chairperson Franklin County Mental Health Bd. Older Adult Task Force, 1984-87; mem. adv. com. Program 60 Ohio State U., 1984-87; workshop and seminar leader; adj. fellow Inst. of Life Span Devel. and Geontology U. Akron, 1988—; lectr. in field. Editor: Ohio Gerontol. Soc. newsletter, 1984-85; mem. editorial adv. bd. Jour. Long Term Care Adminstrn., 1985-87; editorial asst. Ohio chpt. Am. Coll. Health Care Adminstrs. newsletter, 1985-87; contbr. articles to profl. jours. Instr. Sunday sch. Apostolic Christian Ch., 1958-83; mem. exec. com. Internat. Christian Friendship Group, 1965-79, mem. missionary com., 1980-83. Recipient Bronze medal Brit. Med. Soc., 1983, Staff award Franklin County Mental Health Bd., 1985. Mem. Am. Coll. Long Term Care Adminstrs., Am. Home Econs. Assn., Gerontol. Soc. Am., Ohio Gerontol. Assn., Cen. Ohio Geriatric Nurses Assn. (mem. program and planning com. 1979-86, chairperson publicity com. 1980-81, sec. 1979-81, sec.-treas. 1981-84, mem. edn. com. 1983-86), Mansfield Gen. Hosp. Alumnae Assn. (sec. 1960-61). Avocations: photography, travel. Home: Doylestown, Ohio. Died Dec. 26, 2004.

PAVLIK, LYNDA MCELROY, communications consultant; b. Irving, Ill., Feb. 26, 1939; d. Gerald Wilson and Mildred Louise (Lipe) McElroy; m. James Wm. Pavlik, July 18, 1959 (div. May 1985); children: Claire Cook, David James, Anne Louise. Student, Carthage Coll., 1956-59; BA, U. Wisconsin, 1972. Office mgr. WBCR Radio, Blacksburg, Va., 1959-61; tchr. Modern City Acad., Kumasi, Ghana, West Africa, 1961-62; admin. asst. UNESCO, Addis Ababa, Ethiopia, 1968-69; freelance writer Worcester, Mass. and River Falls, Wis., 1970-78; tech. editor Digital Equipment Corp., Marlboro, Mass., 1978-79, prodn. mgr. Bedford, Mass., 1979-85, european pub. mgr. Reading, England, 1985-88, mktg. mgr. electronic pub. techs. Nashua, N.H., 1988-92. Contbr. numerous articles to profl. jour. Unitarian Universalist. Avocations: genealogy, travel, gardening, reading. Home: North Dartmouth, Mass. Died June 4, 2005.

PAYNE, JEAN L., writer; b. Quincy, Mass., Jan. 13, 1932; d. Louis Pierre and Blanche Istella Lemire; m. Gregory D. Payne, June 28, 1954 (dec. Aug. 6, 1968); children: Douglas, Dwight. BA, Bates Coll., Lewiston, ME, 1953; postgrad., U. Maine, 1957. Office worker Oldtown H.S., Old Town, Maine, 1946—49; bus. asst. Morin's, Old Town, 1948—49; speech asst. Bates Coll., Lewiston, 1950—53; ins. writer Aetna Life Ins., Hartford, 1953—54; educator/libr. Lewiston H.S., Lewiston, 1954—55; libr., acquisitions Bates Ladd Libr., Lewiston, 1970—90; writer Free-lance Writer, Lewiston, from 2002. Mem.: Women's Lit. Union (pres. 1967), Art/Lit. Club (pres. 2002), LA Coll. Club (pres. 1956). Independent. Avocation: poetry. Home: Lewiston, Maine. Died July 1, 2005.

PAYNTER, HARRY STRATTAN, II, lawyer; b. New Albany, Ind., Aug. 15, 1926; s. Harry Strattan and Edith (Ryals) P.; m. Martha Jo Averitt, Dec. 28, 1953; children: Lynn K., Harry S. III. AB, Ind. U., 1950; JD, U. Louisville, 1964. Bar: Clark Cir. Ct., U.S. Fed. Ct., Ind. Inspector Clark County Health Dept., Jeffersonville, Ind., 1950-57; adjuster Meridian Mutual Ins., Jeffersonville, Ind., 1957-64; atty. Jeffersonville, Ind., 1964-72; judge Superior Ct., Jeffersonville, Ind., 1972-82; atty. Jeffersonville, Ind., from 1983. Judge Clark Superior Ct., Jeffersonville, Ind., 1972-83. Mem. So. Ind. Health Sys., State Juvenile and Family Judge's Assn. Democrat. Methodist. Avocations: farming, travel, politics. Died Jan. 5, 2005.

PEABODY, WILLIAM TYLER, JR., retired paper manufacturing company executive; b. Melrose, Mass., Mar. 17, 1921; s. William Tyler and Dorothy (Atkinson) P.; m. Florence Marshall, July 27, 1946 (dec. June 18, 1993); children: Carol Peabody Mathews, William Tyler III, Janet Peabody Barrow, Marshall R.; m. Kay Nolan Giffen, Sept. 18, 2000. AB cum laude, Harvard U., 1942, postgrad. Grad. Sch. Arts and Scis., 1946-47, LLB, 1949. Bar: NY 1950. Asso. firm Root, Ballantine, Harlan, Bushby & Palmer, N.Y.C., 1949-54; with law div. Scott Paper Co., Phila., 1954-62, 67-85, asst. to gen. mgr. Everett, Wash., 1962-67, asst. sec., 1965-71, corp. sec., 1971-83, asst. sec., 1983-84, ret., 1985. Pres. Knollwood Terrace Civic Assn., Carle Place, NY, 1952-53; pres. Carle Place Taxpayers Assn., 1953-54; bd. dirs. Nether Providence Cmty. Assocs., Inc., Wallingford, Pa., 1969-75, pres., 1969-70, operator neighborhood social svcs. ctr.; bd. dirs. Ethel Mason Day Care Ctr., Wallingford, 1976-81, pres., 1979-80; vestryman St. Mary's Episc. Ch., Carle Place, NY, 1953-54; vestryman, jr. warden Trinity Episc. Ch., Everett, Wash., 1965-67; chmn. Rose Valley Folk, 1977-78; bd. dirs. Helen Kate Furness Free Libr., Wallingford, 1984-87, v.p., 1986-87; bd. dirs. Chester-Wallingford chpt. ARC, 1991-98, 99-2006, exec. com., 1992-98, 2000-06, 1st vice chmn., 1994-95, chmn., 1995-98, sec., 2000—06; bd. dirs. Everett, Wash. Area C. of C., 1965-67; Snohomish County Family Counseling Svc., Everett, 1962-67, pres., 1965; pres. Wallingford, Pa. Swim Club, 1960-61. Lt. USNR, 1942-46. Mem. ABA, Am. Soc. Corp. Secs. (dir. 1977-81, pres. Middle Atlantic group 1976-77), Harvard Club (Phila., sch. com. 1959-62, 76-90). Home: Wallingford, Pa. Died Jan. 27, 2006.

PEACOCK, DONNA VAN BENTHUYSEN, special education educator; b. Goldsboro, N.C., Oct. 19, 1952; d. Richard and Helen Sauls Van Benthuysen; children: Robin Lear, Haley Van Lauren. AA, Louisburg Jr. Coll., Louisburg, N.C., 1972; BS in Intermediate Edn., Campbell U., 1974. Cert. AG, 1998, svc. and profound. EMD/learning disabled tchr. Wayne County Pub. Schs., Goldsboro, NC, 1975—77, tchr. 5th grade, 1977—96; biology and physical sci. EMD tchr. So. Wayne H.S., Goldsboro, NC, 1996—99, life skills teacher, 1999—2001. Recipient Bright Ideas award, Tri County Electric Corp., 2000, 2002, 2003. Home: Dudley, NC. Died June 14, 2005.

PEARCE, MARY MCCALLUM (MRS. CLARENCE A. PEARCE), artist; b. Hesperia, Mich., Feb. 17, 1906; d. Archibald and Mabel (McNeil) McCallum; m. Clarence A. Pearce, June 30, 1928 (dec.); children: Mary Martha (Mrs. William B. Robinson), Thomas McCallum. AB, Oberlin Coll., 1927; postgrad., John Huntington Inst., 1929-34, Cleve. Inst. Art, 1935-37, 54, Dayton Art Inst., 1946-49. Tchr. art, supr. pub. schs., Mayfield Heights, Ohio, 1927-28, Maple Heights, Ohio, 1928-30. One woman shows include Cleve. Women's city club, 1959, 69, Plymouth Harbor, Sarasota, Fla., 1989, 90, 94, Cleve. Orch., 1967, Cleve. Playhouse Gallery, 1968, 71, 76, 87, Van Wezel Hall, 1979, Sarasota (Fla.) Libr., 1979, Hilton Leech Gallery, Sarasota, 1979, 80, 81, 86, 97, Fed. Bank, sarasota, 1980, Unity Gallery, Sarasota, 1993; group shows include Oberlin art Mus., Smithsonian Inst., Birmingham Mus. Art, Am. watercolor soc., Cleve. Mus. Art, Foster Harmon Galleries, 1986, Fla. Watercolor soc., Ala., 1973, 74, 75, 77, 78, 79, 890, 87, 88, 92, 96, Fla. Artist Group, 1980, 81, 83,85, 90, 94, 95, 96 Southeastern Watercolorists, 1989, Friends of Arts and Scis., 1992, Fla. Watercolor Signature Group, 1992, Hilton Leech Gallery, 1992, Sarasota Ctr. Visula Arts (Best of Show 1994), Ala. Watercolor Soc., Fla. Sumcoast Watercolor (Best of Show 1995-96, 2nd prize 1998), Butler Inst. Am. art, 1998, Lake Point Woods, Sarasota, Fla., 2003, The Fountains, Sarasota, Fla., 2003, many others; represented in pvt. collections. Named Best Woman Artist Ohio Watercolrs Soc., 1955; recipient Bush meml. award Columbus Gallery Fine Arts, 1962, Nat. 1st Prize for Drawing Nat. League Am. Pen Women, 1966, 68, 96; littlehouse award Ala. Watercolor Soc., 1968; Wolfe award Columbus Gallery fine arts, 1971, awards Longboat Key Art Ctr., 1973, 75, 79-86, Equal award Longboat Key, 1993, award Southeastern Art Soc., 1975, 2nd prize Art League Manatee County, 1973, 90, 1st prize, 1988, Merit awards, 1975, 77, 88, 89, 93, 3rd prize Sarasota Visual art Ctr. (formerly Sarasota Art Assn.), 1977, 78, hon. mention, 1989, Merit award, 1981, 85, 90, 91, Best of show, 1994, hon. merit award, 1996, 1st prize Venice (Fla.) Art League, 1979, 81, 82, 83, 86, 87, 2nd prize, 1979, 90, 81, 89, 3rd prize 1978, 92, Merit award, 1985, 89, 92, 1st prize Hilton Leech Gallery, 181, 85, 90, 1st prize Friends of Arts and Scis., 1997, 2nd prize Suncoast Watercolor Soc., 1987, 90, 92, hon. mention Fla. State Merit award, Fla. west Coast Parade of Prize Winners, 1990, 1st award Women's Resource Ctr., 1992, Grumbacher award Fla. Artists Group, 1994 (Pres.'s award 1998). Mem. Nat. League Am. Pen Women (treas. 1962), Am. Watercolor Soc. (assoc.), Fla. Watercolor Soc. (signature), Ala. Watercolor Soc. Republican. Presbyterian. Home: Sarasota, Fla. Died Mar. 22, 2005.

PEARCE, PATSY BEASLEY, elementary school educator; b. Dunn, N.C., Apr. 13, 1945; d. Marvin Franklin and Christine (Bryant) Beasley; m. Robert Michael Cole, Aug. 15, 1970 (div.); 1 child, Matthew Bryant Cole; m. Elwood Glenn Pearce, Mar. 1, 1980. BSEd, E. Caroline U., 1966. Cert. collegiate profl., Va. Primary tchr., 1st and 2d grade Va. Beach (Va.) City Schs., 1966-75; primary tchr., 1st. and 3rd grade Jasper County Schs., Hardeeville, SC, 1976-78; tchr., 4th grade Campbell County Schs., Lynchburg, Va., 1979; kindergarten tchr. Aesop Acad., Portsmouth, Va., 1981-84; primary tchr., 1st grade Chesapeake (Va.) City Schs., 1984—2001; ret., 2001. Mem. social studies adoption com. Chesapeake City Schs., 1996-98, colleague mentor, 1997-98, Pizza Hut Book-It chairperson, 1997-2001; United Way chair, 1995-97; sch. rep. Chesapeake Reading Coun., 1986-95, colleague mentor, 1988-90; equity tutor Camelot Elem. Sch., Chesapeake, 1994, grade level chmn., 1990-95, coop. tchr., 1990-91; mem. tech. tng. Va. Stds. Learning Tng., 1999-2001, 2001. Sunday sch. tchr. Cradock United Meth. Ch., Portsmouth, Va., 1982, worship com. chmn. 1990-91, Acolyte chmn., 1984-89; vacation Bible sch. tchr. Thail United Meth. Ch., Virginia Beach, 1969; com. chmn., treas. Cub Scout Pack 251, Portsmouth, Va., 1980-91; roundtable commr. Merrimac Dist. Boy Scouts Am., Portsmouth, 1989-90, dist. chmn. Scouts Ann. Mall Show and Pinewood Derby Race, 1987-89; children's choir dir. Kempsville Ch. of Christ, Virginia Beach, 1979-80. Named Camelot's Tchr. of Yr., 1995-96. Mem. NEA, Va. Edn. Assn., Chesapeake Edn. Assn., Chesapeake Reading Coun., Internat. Reading Coun., PTA (corr. sec. 1997-98). Avocations: gardening, needlework crafts, travel. Home: Chesapeake, Va. Died Feb. 5, 2004.

PEARLE, FRIEDA, artist; b. N.J., Oct. 30, 1916; d. Hugo and Esther (Haller) Bachenheimer; m. George Pearle, June 26, 1940; children: Harry, Karen, Judith. Student, Nat. Acad. Fine Arts, 1945. Legal sec. B.M. Halpern, Atty., N.Y.C., 1935-40; sec. May Co., N.Y.C., 1940-50, Mus. Modern Art, N.Y.C., 1950-60, Jewish Mus., N.Y.C., 1960-70, Am. Jewish Com., N.Y.C., 1970. One-woman shows in two L.I. Galleries, Flanzer Jewish Cmty. Ctr., Sarasota, Fla.; groups shows in Longboat Key Art Assn., Sarasota, Sarasota Art Assn., 1986-95. Docent Nassau County L.I. Mus., N.Y., 1975-88, Ringling Mus., Sarasota, Fla., 1985-95; mem. B'Nai Brith, Oceanside, N.Y., 1984-95, Hadassah, Sarasota, Fla., 1984-95; mem. choir Temple Emanuel. Mem. L.I. Art Assn., Sarasota (Fla.) Art Assn., Longboat Key (Fla.) Art Assn. Democrat. Jewish. Home: Oakland, Calif. Died June 22, 2005.

PEARLMAN, MEYER, retail executive; b. Detroit, July 24, 1917; s. Abraham and Mary (Kaplan) P.; m. Sarah Ida Stein, Jan. 19, 1941; children: Allan, Mark, Sheldon. Master, Coll Hardknocks, 1939. Sales apprentice Cen. Stores, Detroit, 1935-39; salesman Perfect Appliance, Detroit, 1939-41; from sales mgr. to pres. Canton China and Equipment, Detroit, from 1941-. Pres. Jewish Assn. for Retarded Citizens Southfield, Mich., 1976-77. Sgt. U.S. Army, 1943-45. Mem. Tam O Shauter Country, Bnai Brith. Avocations: golf, travel. Home: Bloomfield Hills, Mich. Died June 5, 2005.

PEARSON, ANDRALL EDWIN, former food service company executive; b. Chgo., June 3, 1925; s. Andrall E. and Dorothy M. (MacDonald) P.; m. Joanne Pope, Mar. 2, 1951; 1 dau., Jill Lee. BS, U. So. Calif., 1944; MBA, Harvard U., 1947. Mktg. mgr. Standard Brands, Inc., N.Y.C., 1948-53; assoc. to prin. McKinsey & Co., Inc., N.Y.C., 1953-70, dir., 1965-70; exec. v.p. PepsiCo, Inc., Purchase, NY, 1970-71, pres., 1971—84; prof. Harvard Bus. Sch., 1985—93; oper. ptnr. Clayton, Dubilier and Rice, 1993—97; CEO, chmn. Tricon Restuarants (now Yum Brands!, Inc.), 1997—2001. Bd. dirs. Pepsi Co., 1971—96; dir., mem. exec. com. May Co. Dept. Stores; bd. dirs. Comml. Credit Corp., Hasbro Inc., Munford Inc., Citigroup. Contbr. articles profl. jour., chpt. in handbook. Trustee Wesleyan U., 1977—83; trustee N.Y.U. Med. Sch., Good Samaritan Med. Ctr., Palm Beach, Fla. Lt. (j.g.) USNR, 1943—46. Mem. Ref. Ch. of Bronxville (elder). Clubs: Harvard Bus. Sch. of N.Y. (N.Y.C.) (dir.), Bronxville Field (N.Y.C.), Blind Brook (N.Y.C.); Longwood Cricket (Boston). Home: Greenwich, Conn. Died Mar. 11, 2006.

PECHOTA, VRATISLAV HENRY, legal scholar; b. Dobruska, Czechoslovakia, July 25, 1928; came to U.S., 1979; s. Vratislav and Emilie (Kristof) P.; m. Vera Lipavska, Dec. 18, 1956; children: Vera, Vratislav III. Law degree, Shevchenko U., Kiev, USSR, 1952; LLD, Charles U., Prague, Czechoslovakia, 1951, PhD, 1962. Mem. legal staff to chief legal advisor Czechoslovak Ministry of Fgn. Affairs, Prague, 1953-68; sr. research fellow UN Inst. for Training and Research, N.Y.C., 1968-71; adj. prof. NYU Sch. of Law, N.Y.C., 1981-84; sr. research scholar and asst. dir. Parker Sch. of Fgn. and Comparative Law, Columbia U., N.Y.C., from 1984. Mng. ptnr. Princeton (N.J.) Internat. Cons., 1980-84; co-editor in chief Am. Rev. Internat. Arbitration, 1990—. Author: Complementary Structures of Third-Party Settlement of International Disputes, 1971, The Quiet Approach: A Study of the Good Offices Exercised by the UN Secretary General, 1972; co-author: The World Arbitration Reporter, 1986-89; contbr. articles to profl. jours. Cons. Amnesty Internat., N.Y.C., 1980; del. 8th to 23rd sessions of the UN Gen. Assembly and in numerous diplomatic confs.; chmn. Legal (6th) Com. at 21st session UN Gen. Assembly, 1966. Mem. Am. Soc. Internat. Law, Internat. Law Assn. Home: New York, NY. Died June 12, 2005.

PEDEN, KATHERINE GRAHAM, industrial consultant; b. Hopkinsville, Ky., Jan. 2, 1926; d. William E. and Mary (Gorin) P. Student pub. schs. Vice pres. radio sta. WHOP-CBS, Hopkinsville, 1944-68; owner sta. WNVL, Nicholsville, Ky., 1961-71; commr. commerce Ky., 1963-67; mem. Gov. Ky. Cabinet, Frankfort, 1963-67; pres., cons. Katherine G. Peden & Assos. Inc., Louisville, indsl. and community developers. Bd. dirs. Westvaco Corp.; mem. adv. bd. Norfolk So. Corp. Chmn. Louisville and Jefferson County Riverport Authority, 1975-80; civilian aide to Sec. of Army, 1978-82; mem. com. Pres.'s Commn. on Status of Women, 1961-62; mem. Pres.'s Commn. on Civil Disorders, 1967; pres. Ky. Derby Festival, 1979-80; Dem. nominee U.S. Senate, 1968; mem. adv. coun. U. Ky. Coll. Bus.; trustee Spalding U., 1980-86. Named Woman of Year Hopkinsville, 1952 Mem. Fedn. Bus., Profl. Women's Clubs (pres. state 1955-56, 1st nat. v.p. 1960-61, nat. pres. 1961-62). Mem. Christian Ch. (deaconess 1956-59, 60-63). Home: Louisville, Ky. Died Jan. 8, 2006.

PEDERSEN, WALTER, minister; b. Bklyn., Apr. 7, 1924; s. Oswald and Inga (Olsen) P.; m. Solveig Dahl, Jan. 19, 1951; children: Russell, Dianne, Dean. Student, CCNY, 1948; BS in Theology, North Cen. Bible Coll., 1953. Ordained to ministry Fellowship of Christian Assemblies, 1953. Pastor Evang. chs., N.Y., N.J., 1953-58; pastor Calvary Gospel Assembly, Estherville, Iowa, 1958-64, Rock Ch., Rockford, Ill., 1964-69, Homewood Full Gospel Ch., Homewood, Ill., from 1969. Pres., bd. dirs. Homewood Full Gospel, 1988—; supt., founder Homewood Christian Acad., 1975—, Homewood Bible Inst., 1986—; bd. dirs. Global PLAN, Inc., Homewood, 1987—; talk show host WYCA Radio, 1987-89; internat. lectr. in field; speaker in field. Contbr. articles to profl. jours. Bd. dirs. South Suburban Hosp., Hazelcrest, Ill., 1986—; com. mem. Mayor Richard Daley Com. for Gospelfest, Chgo., 1990—, Mayor Daley Com. for M.L. King Day, Chgo., 1990—; bd. dirs. GRS Systems Internat., Homewood, 1990—. With USCG, 1942-46. Named Israel Tourism Del., 1983, Fact Finding Mission Del. U.S. Dept. Agriculture, 1987. Mem. Fellowship Christian Assemblies. Home: Homewood, Ill. Died Oct. 15, 2004.

PEIFER, JANET MARIE, minister; b. Manheim, Pa., Apr. 13, 1945; d. Paul Milton and Mabel Kathryn (Myers) Witmer; m. Elvin Herr Peifer, Sept. 4, 1965; children: Loreen Renea, Scott Douglas. BA in Religious/Bibl. Studies, Messiah Coll., 1988; MDiv, Ea. Bapt. Theol. Sem., Phila., from 1988. Lic. to ministry Brethren in Christ Ch., 1990. Interim asst. pastor Refton (Pa.) Brethren in Christ Ch., 1988, pastoral asst. for pastoral care and counseling, from 1989. Dir. music Refton Brethren in Christ Ch., 1988-91, dir. prayer, missions and outreach, 1984-89. Contbr. articles to profl. jours. Mem. Brethren in Christ Hist. Soc., Christians for Bibl. Equality. Republican. Died Nov. 13, 2004.

PELIKAN, JAROSLAV JAN, history professor; b. Akron, Ohio, Dec. 17, 1923; s. Jaroslav Jan and Anna (Buzek) P.; m. Sylvia Burica, June 9, 1946; children: Martin, Michael, Miriam. Grad. summa cum laude, Concordia Jr. Coll., Ft. Wayne, Ind., 1942; BD, Concordia Theol. Sem., St. Louis, 1946; PhD, U. Chgo., 1946; MA (hon.), Yale U., 1961; DD (hon.), Concordia Coll., Moorehead, Minn., 1960, Concordia Sem., 1967, Trinity Coll., Hartford, Conn., 1987, St. Vladimir's Orthodox Theol. Sem., 1988, Victoria U., Toronto, 1989, U. Aberdeen, Scotland, 1995; LittD (hon.), Wittenberg U., 1960, Wheeling Coll., 1966, Gettysburg Coll., 1967, Pacific Luth. U., 1967, Wabash Coll., 1988, Jewish Theol. Sem., 1991; HHD (hon.), Providence Coll., 1966, Moravian Coll., 1986, Jewish Theol. Sem., 1991; LLD (hon.), Keuka Coll., 1967, U. Notre Dame, 1979, Harvard U., 1998, U. Regina, 1998; LHD (hon.), Valparaiso U., 1966, Rockhurst Coll., 1967, Albertus Magnus Coll., 1973, Coe Coll., 1976, Cath. U. Am., 1977, St. Mary's Coll., 1978, St. Anselm Coll., 1983, U. Nebr.-Omaha, 1984, Tulane U., 1986, Assumption Coll., 1986, LaSalle U., 1987, Carthage Coll., 1991, U. Chgo., 1991, So. Meth. U., 1992, SUNY, Albany, 1993, Fla. Internat. U., 1997; LHD (hon.), U. Pa., 2004, St. Tikhan's Orth. Sem., 2004; ThD (hon.), U. Hamburg, 1971, St. Olaf Coll., 1972, Charles U., Prague, 1999; STD, Dickinson Coll., 1986; DSc in Hist., Comenius U., Bratislava, 1992; ScD (hon.), Loyola U., Chgo., 1995. Faculty Valparaiso (Ind.) U., 1946-49, Concordia Sem., St. Louis, 1949-53, U. Chgo., 1953-62; Titus Street prof. eccles. history Yale U., 1962-72, Sterling prof. history, 1972-96, William Clyde DeVane lectr., 1984-86, dir. div. humanities, 1974-75, chmn. Medieval studies, 1974-75, 78-80, dean Grad. Sch., 1973-78; Joseph chair Boston Coll., 1996-97; prof. Annenberg Sch. U. Pa., 1998-2001; Disting. Vis. Scholar Libr. Congress, Washington, 2001—02. Vis. prof. Boston Coll., 1996-97, Annenberg Sch. Comm., U. Pa., 1998-2006; Gray lectr. Duke U., 1960, Ingersoll lectr. Harvard U., 1963, Gauss lectr. Princeton U., 1980, Jefferson lectr. NEH, 1983, Richard lectr. U. Va., 1984, Rauschenbusch lectre. Colgate-Rochester Divinity Sch., 1984, Gilson lectr. U. Toronto, 1985, 98, Hale lectr. Seabury-Western Sem., 1986, Mead-Swing lectr. Oberlin Coll., 1986, Gross lectr. Rutgers U., 1989; adv. bd. Ctr. Theol. Inquiry, 1984-90; mem. coun. The Smithsonian Instn., 1984-90; US chmn. US Czechoslovak Commn. on Humanities and Social Scis., 1987-92; scholarly dir. instns. of democracy project Annenberg Found Trust, Sunnylands, 2002-06. Author: From Luther to Kierkegaard, 1950, Fools for Christ, 1955, The Riddle of Roman Catholicism, 1959 (Abingdon award 1959), Luther the Expositor, 1959, The Shape of Death, 1961, The Light of the World, 1962, Obedient Rebels, 1964, The Finality of Jesus Christ in an Age of Universal History, 1965, The Christian Intellectual, 1966, Spirit Versus Structure, 1968, Development of Doctrine, 1969, Historical Theology, 1971, The Christian Tradition, 5 vols., 1971-89, Scholarship and Its Survival, 1983, The Vindication of Tradition, 1984, Jesus Through the Centuries, 1985, The Mystery of Continuity, 1986, Bach Among the Theologians, 1986, The Excellent Empire, 1987, The Melody of Theology, 1988, Confessor Between East and West, 1990, Imago Dei, 1990, Eternal Feminines, 1990, The Idea of the University: A Reexamination, 1992, Christianity and Classical Culture, 1993, Faust the Theologian, 1995, The Reformation of the Bible/ The Bible of the Reformation, 1996, Mary through the Centuries, 1996, The Illustrated Jesus Through the Centuries, 1997, What Has Athens to do with Jerusalem?, 1997, Divine Rhetoric, 2001, Credo, 2003, Interpreting the Bible and the Constitution, 2004; editor, translator: Luther's Works, 22 vols., 1955-71, The Book of Concord, 1959; editor: Makers of Modern Theology, 5 vols., 1966-68, The Preaching of Chrysostom, 1967, Interpreters of Luther, 1968, Twentieth-Century Theology in the Making, 3 vols., 1969-70, The Preaching of Augustine, 1973, The World Treasury of Modern Religious Thought, 1991, Sacred Writings, 7 vols., 1992, Whose Bible is It?, 2005; (with Valerie Hotchkiss) Creeds and Confessions of Faith in the Christian Tradition, 3 vols., 2003; mem. editl. bd. Collected Works of Erasmus, Classics of Western Spirituality, Evangelisches Kirchenlexikon, Emerson's Nature, 1986, The World Treasury of Modern Religious Thought, 1990; departmental editor Ency. Britannica, 1958-69; adminstrv. bd. Papers of Benjamin Franklin; chmn. publs. com. Yale U. Press, 1979-90, 922006, v.p. bd. govs., 1988-2006; contbr. articles to profl. jours. Pres. 4th Internat. Congress for Luther Research, 1971, New Eng. Congress on Grad. Edn., 1976-77. Recipient Abingdon award, 1959; Pax Christi award St. John's U., Collegeville, Minn., 1966, Colman J. Barry award, 1995; John Gilmary Shea prize Am. Cath. Hist. Assn., 1971, nat. award Slovak World Congress, 1973, religious book award Cath. Press Assn., 1974, Christian Unity award Atonement Friars, 1975, Bicentennial award Czechoslovak Soc. Arts and Scis., 1976, Wilbur Cross medal Yale U. Grad. Sch. Assn., 1979, Profl. Achievement award U. Chgo. Alumni Assn., 1980, Shaw medal Boston Coll., 1984, Comenius medal Moravian Coll., 1986, Alumnus of Yr. award U. Chgo. Div. Sch., 1986, Bicentennial medal Georgetown U., 1989, award for excellence Am. Acad. Religion 1989, Umanità award Newberry Libr., 1990, Jacques Barzun award Am. Acad. for Liberal Edn., 1997, Festschriften: Schools of Thought in the Christian Tradition, 1984, The Unbounded Community, 1996; sr. fellow Carnegie Found. for Advancement Tchg., 1982-83. Fellow Medieval Acad. Am. (councillor, Haskins medal 1985); mem. Am. Hist. Assn., Am. Soc. Ch. History (pres. 1965, Achievement award 1998), Internat. Congress Luther Rsch. (pres. 1971), Am. Acad. Arts and Scis. (v.p. 1976-94, pres. 1994-97), Am. Philos. Soc. (councillor 1984-87, Moe prize 1997), Am. Acad. Polit. and Social Sci. (pres. 2000—), Coun. Scholars of Libr. of Congress (founding chmn. 1980-83), Elizabethan Club, Mory's, Phi Beta Kappa (senator United chpts. 1985-90). Home: Hamden, Conn. Died May 13, 2006.

PENN, CHRISTOPHER, actor; b. LA, Oct. 10, 1965; s. Leo Penn and Eileen Ryan. Film appearances include Charlie and the Talking Buzzard, 1979, Rumble Fish, 1983, All the Right Moves, 1983, Footloose, 1984, The Wild Life, 1984, Pale Rider, 1985, At Close Range, 1986, Made in U.S.A., 1987, Return from the River Kwai, 1989, Best of the Best, 1989, Futurekick, 1991, Mobsters, 1991, Future Kick, 1991, Leather Jackets, 1992, Reservoir Dogs, 1992, Beethoven's 2nd, 1993, Best of the Best II, 1993, Josh and S.A.M., 1993, The Music of Chance, 1993, The Pickle, 1993, Short Cuts, 1993, True Romance, 1993, Imaginary Crimes, 1994, Sacred Cargo, 1995, Fist of the North Star, 1995, To Wung Foo, Thanks for Everything, Julie Newmar, 1995, Under the Hula Moon, 1995, Funeral, 1996, Papertrail, 1996, The Boys Club, 1997, Liar, 1996, Mulholland Falls, 1996, Sacred Cargo, 1995, Cannes Man, 1996, The Boys Club, 1997, Lulu on the Bridge, 1997, Family Attraction, 1998, Flagpole Special, 1998, One Tough Cop, 198, Rush Hour, 1998, The Florentine, 1999, Cement, 1999, Kiss Kiss (Bang Bang), 2000, Corky Romano, 2002, Murder By Numbers, 2002, Redemption, 2002, Stealing Harvard, 2002, Masked and Anonymous, 2002, Shelter Island, 2003, Starsky and Hutch, 2004, After the Sunset, 2004, Holly, 2005, The Darwin Awards, 2006; actor, exec. prodr. (films) Juarez: Stages of Fear, 2005; actor (TV movies) North Beach and Rawhide, 1985; (TV series) (voice only) AFP: American Fighter Pilot, 2002, The Brotherhood of Poland, New Hampshire, 2003; (miniseries) Dead Man's Walk, 1996; TV appearances include Magnum, P.I., 1982, Faerie Tale Theatre, 1987, The Young Riders, 1990, Seinfeld, 1993, Chicago Hope, 1995, CSI: Miami, 2003, Will and Grace, 2003, Law & Order: Criminal Intent, 2005, Everwood, 2005, Entourage, 2005 Died Jan. 24, 2006.

PENNAK, ROBERT WILLIAM, biologist, educator; b. Milw., June 13, 1912; s. William Henry and Ella Sophia (Clemeson) P.; m. Alberta Vivian Pope, Sept. 7, 1935; children: Richard Dean, Cathy Ann. BS, U. Wis., 1934, MS, 1935, PhD, 1938. Instr. biology U. Colo., Boulder, 1938-40, prof. biology, 1941-74, prof. emeritus, from 1974. Cons. numerous nat. and internat. corps. Author: Fresh-water Invertebrates of the U.S., 1953, Collegiate Dictionary of Zoology, 1964; contbr. over 120 articles to profl. jours. Rsch. grantee various orgns. Mem. Am. Microscopical Soc., Am. Benthological Soc. (Excellence in Benthic Sci. award 1991), Am. Soc. Limnology and Oceanography, Am. Soc. Zoologists, Internat. Assn. Meiobenthologists. Avocations: bowling, pocket billiards, trout fishing. Home: Denver, Colo. Died June 23, 2004.

PENRAAT, JAAP, architect; b. Amsterdam, Apr. 11, 1918; came to U.S. 1958; s. Gerrit Johannes and Maria (Leenslag) P.; m. Ottoline Henriette Gerarde Jongejans, Oct. 17, 1950; children: Marjolyn Renee, Mirjam Ruth, Noelle Denise. Grad., Acad. for Art, Amsterdam, 1937. Registered architect, Netherlands, N.Y. Founder Jaap Penraat Assocs., Leeds, N.Y.C., 1958—2006. Lectr. in field. Contbr. articles to profl. jours. Recipient Italian Carrara prize; named Righteous Among the Nations, Israeli Amb., 1997. Mem. Am. Inst. Graphic Arts, Am. Cotton Batting Inst., Package Design Coun. Achievements include 12 patents. Home: Leeds, NY. Died June 25, 2006.

PENZER, MARK, lawyer, writer; b. Bklyn., Nov. 22, 1932; s. Ed and Fay (Weinberg) P.; m. Eileen Malen, Aug. 12, 1962; children: Matthew, Nicole; m. Nydia A. Rey, Nov. 25, 1984. BBA, CCNY; JD, Fordham U. Bar: N.Y. 1968, D.C. 1973, Fla. 1982, U.S. Dist. Ct. (ea. dist.) N.Y. 1976, U.S. Dist. Ct. (so. dist.) Fla. 1991; cert. instr. DMA, 1986. Free-lance writer, 1950-83; editorial asst. Hearst mags., N.Y.C., 1955, asst. editor, 1956, assoc. editor, 1957-66; columnist N.Y. Jour.-Am., 1960-62; editor in chief Rudder mag., 1967-69, editorial dir., 1970-74; editor in chief True, 1970-73, editor at large, 1973-75; pub., editor in chief Jour. Energy Medicine, 1978-81; Medicare hearing officer Miami, Fla., 1981-82; pres. Success Internat., Inc., Coral Gables, Fla., 1984-85; adj. prof. bus. and tech. writing Fla. Internat. U., small bus. mgmt., U. Miami, 1986-89; pres. Heroica, Inc., Miami Lakes, Fla., 1989-90; pvt. practice Law Offices of Mark Penzer, Hialeah and Miami Lakes, Fla., 1991—2006. Tchr. creative writing Dade County Off Campus Edn. Author: The Motorboatman's Bible, 1965, The Powerboatman's Bible, 1977; asst. editor: The Path of Least Resistance, 1989, Do It!, 1991. Served with AUS, 1953-55. Mem.: Miami Lakes Bar Assn., Hialeah-Miami Lakes Bar Assn. (pres. 1990—92), D.C. Bar Assn., N.Y. Bar Assn., Fla. Bar Assn. Died Jan. 3, 2006.

PEPPER, ARNOLD NORMAN, small business owner; b. N.Y.C., Nov. 12, 1925; s. Samuel and Sadie (Bornstein) Pfeferblum. Grad. high sch., N.Y.C., 1942. V.p. E-Lite Co. Inc., N.Y.C., 1952-76; exec. v.p. Satco Products Inc., Brentwood, N.Y., from 1977. Bd. dirs. Am. Home Lighting Inst., Chgo., 1974-76. With USN, 1943-46, PTO, 1950-52. Avocations: art, music, decorating. Home: West Hills, Calif. Died Apr. 23, 2004.

PEPPER, ROLLIN ELMER, microbiology educator, consultant; b. Glens Falls, N.Y., June 8, 1924; s. Henry Orville and Ruby Mae (Tucker) P.; m. Lucille Blackman, May 30, 1953 (dec.); children: Roger R., Barbara Pepper Moquin, Susan Pepper Aisenberg; m. Martha Charles, Mar. 3, 1990. BA, Earlham Coll., 1950; MS, Syracuse U., 1953; PhD, Mich. State U., 1963. Assoc. scientist Ethicon, Inc., Somerville, N.J., 1951-60; rsch. assoc. Mich. State U., East Lansing, 1963-64; prof. biology Elizabethtown Coll., Pa., 1964-90, chmn. dept. Pa., 1967-77, prof. emeritus Pa., from 1990. Vis. prof. biology U. Zambia, Lusaka, 1972-73; microbiology cons. Sporicidin Co., Rockville, Md., 1971-94, Baums Bologna, Elizabethtown, 1976-83; health officer Borough of Elizabethtown, 1981-97. Contbr. chpt. to book, articles to profl. jours.; patentee in field. Pres. Elizabethtown Bd. Health, 1976-77. Mem. Elizabethtown Club, Rotary (pres. 1983-84, dist. youth exch. chmn. 1978-81, Presdl. citation 1984, pres. chpt. Friendship Force 1991-92, Vincent W. O'Connor Cmty. Svc. award 1997), Sigma Xi. Mem. Brethren in Christ Ch. Avocations: travel, camping, photography. Home: Elizabethtown, Pa. Died Nov. 24, 2004.

PERALTA, JOSE RAMON, utilities executive; b. Chaparra, Oriente, Cuba, Nov. 10, 1926; came to U.S., 1960; s. Jose Ramon and Mariana (Rodriguez) P.; m. Mercedes Lloret, Feb. 26, 1949; children: Jose Ramon, Nancy, Mariana. BS in Elec. Engring., U. Havana (Cuba), 1953. Registered profl. engr., Fla. Power plant operator Compania Cubana de Electricidad, Havana, 1945-53, power plant engr., 1953-57, asst. prodn. supr., 1957-60; service engr. Ill. Water Treatment Co., Rockford, 1960-61; tng. and safety dir. C.A. Energia Electricidad de Venezuela, Maracaibo,

1961-65, mgr. commercial dept., 1965-71; ops. mgr. Rex. Utilities, Inc., Miami, Fla., 1972-77; asst. v.p. engring. Gen. Devel. Utilities, Miami, 1977-85, asst. v.p. environ. affairs, from 1985. Mem. Nat. Soc. Profl. Engrs., Am. Water Works Assn., Water Pollution Control Fedn., Fla. Soc. Profl. Engrs. Home: Miami, Fla. Died July 29, 2004.

PERCY, CONSTANCE, statistician; b. N.Y.C., Oct. 20, 1914; d. Harold Arnold and Lucile (Mordecai) Lebair; m. Joseph H. Percy, July 1, 1938; children: Norma Lee Percy, Connie Percy Aaronson. BA, Cornell U., 1936; MSPH, Columbia U., 1937. Jr. statistician Health Dept., N.Y.C., 1936-37; jr. statistician Health Dept., State of N.Y., Albany, 1937-38; statistician Harlem Hosp. Littauer Pneumonia (NYU), N.Y.C., 1938-42, Internat. Ladies Garment Workers Union Health Ctr., N.Y.C., 1943-45, Am. Cancer Soc., N.Y.C., 1947-70; health statistician Nat. Cancer Inst., Bethesda, Md., from 1970. Cons. tumor registries. Editor: International Classification of Diseases for Oncology, 1976, (2d edit.) 1990. Home: Rockville, Md. Died Mar. 24, 2004.

PERDUNN, RICHARD FRANCIS, management consultant; b. Trenton, N.J., Dec. 12, 1915; s. Francis R. and Edith (Nogle) P.; m. Eugenia E. Morel, June 7, 1941; 1 child, Justine Reneau; m. Doris D. Andrus, Jan. 30, 1993. BS, Lehigh U., 1939; postgrad. student, U. Pitts., 1939-40, Johns Hopkins, 1941-42. With U.S. Steel Co., also Glenn L. Martin, 1939-43, supt. machine and assembly, 1941-43; partner Nelson & Perdunn (engrs. and cons., also); v.p. Penco Corp., 1947-49; with Merck & Co., 1949-54, mgr. adminstrn., 1951-54; with Stevenson, Jordan & Harrison (mgmt. engrs.), N.Y.C., 1954-68, exec. v.p., 1962-64, pres., 1964-68; pres., chief exec. officer Bachman-Jacks, Inc., Reading, Pa., 1968-71; sr. v.p. Golightly Internat., N.Y.C., from 1971, also dir. Chmn. Perdunn Assocs., Inc., 1979—, dir. West Point & Annapolis Text Book Pub. Co., 1948—, Indsl. Edn. Films Inc., 1966—, Eldun Corp., 1964—, Security Nat. Bank, Newark, 1964—, Surburban Life Ins. Co., 1966—, Mainstem Inc., 1965—, Greenhouse Decor Inc., 1961—, Neuwirth Mut. Fund Inc., 1975—; Lectr. on finance and mfg. in, U.S., Can., Eng., Sweden. Assoc. editor: Systems and Procedures Quar, 1948-51; Contbr. articles to profl. publs. Bd. dirs. Inst. Better Confs., Internat. Inst. Bus. Devel., Inst. Urban Affairs, People Care, Inc.; dir. finance Assn. Help for Retarded Children. Served with USAAF, 1942-47. Mem. N.Y.C. C. of C., Council Econ. Devel., Am. Mgmt. Assn., AIM (pres.'s council), Newcomen Soc. N.Am., Systems and Procedures Assn. Am., Soc. Advanced Mgmt. Died May 27, 2006.

PEREZ-STABLE, ELISEO, medical educator; b. Cuba; m. Nenita Perez-Stable (dec. 1996); children: Marifeli, Eliseo, Carlos, Alina; m. Maria Elena Perez-Stable, 1997. Doctor, Cuba; lab techician VA Hosp., Pitts., 1961; chief of staff Miami VA Med. Ctr. Co-founder (with Maria Cristina Herrera & Marifeli Perez-Stable) Cuban Com. for Democracy, 1993. First Cuban-Am. physician to earn distinction of master internist by the Am. Coll. Physicians; among first three Cuban doctors to be recertified in Am. Died Aug. 13, 2005.

PEREZ-SUAREZ, ELOISA, retired state official; b. Tampico, Mex., Sept. 28, 1935; came to U.S., 1940; d. Abraham Perez Villareal and Julia Suarez Perez; m. Alan W. Spencer (div.); children: Linda, Eric, Tovi, Lisa. BA in Human Relations, Skidmore Coll., 1980; MPA bilingual/bicultural, Rutgers U., 1990. Bilingual/bicultural adminstrv. asst. SUNY, Dept. Puerto Rican Studies, Albany, 1975-80; bilingual adminstrv. asst. SUNY, Hispanic and Italian Studies Dept., Albany, 1980-81; supr. cert. Gov.'s Office of Minority and Women's Bus. Devel., Albany, 1989-91; supr. intake and records mgmt. div. Minority and Women's Bus. Devel. N.Y. State Dept. Econ. Devel., 1991-95, ret., 1995. Past chair Albany Human Rights Commn., v.p., 1990—. Mem. editl. bd. Fineweed quar. newsletter of Many Walks Coun., 1996—. Past pres., Centro Civico Hispanoamericano, Albany, 1975-89; mem. N.Y. State Employment and Tng. Coun., 1978-82; past chair City of Albany Commn. on Human Rights, Black and Hispanic Polit. Caucus of the Albany Area, Inc.; past mem. Coalition on Minority Employment, Albany Urban League; past elder, choir mem. Unity Ch., Albany, 1995; founder, mem. Mexicans at Heart, 1996; affiliate Good Medicine Soc. With USAF, 1953-56. Recipient YWCA Outstanding Women's award, 1982, No. Region Black & Hispanic Caucus Youth award, 1978, Disting. Svc. award Centro Civico Hispanoamericano, 1978. Home: Albany, NY. Died Apr. 5, 2005.

PERINE, ROBERT HEATH, artist, writer; b. L.A., Nov. 30, 1922; s. Theo Wesley and Irma Barnes (Heath) P.; m. La Dorna Larson, Mar. 12, 1947 (div. Sept. 1970); children: Jorli, Lisa, Terri; m. Blaze Newman, Dec. 31, 1979. Student, U. So. Calif., 1945, 56; cert., Chouinard Art Inst., L.A., 1947-50. Pres. Artra Pub., Inc., Encinitas, Calif., 1985—2004. Author: Chouinard: An Art Vision Betrayed, 1986, The California Romantics, 1987, San Diego Artists, 1988; one-man exhbn. Oceanside (Calif.) Mus. Art, 1999; contbr. articles to Arts Mag., The Publ. Mag., Vintage Guitar Mag., San Diego Mag. With USN, 1942-46. Mem. Nat. Watercolor Soc. (bd. dirs. 1949-51, 71-88, purchase award 1972), Butler Inst. Am. Art (purchase award 1972), Nat. Watercolor Soc. (hon. mention 1973), San Diego Art Inst. (1st pl. award 1974); co-founder, dir.Chovinard Sch. Art., South Pasadena, Calif. Avocation: photography. Died Nov. 6, 2004.

PERKINS, DOLORES ESPINOZA, nurse; b. Johnstown, Pa., Apr. 8, 1928; d. Alphonso P. and Helen M. (Rushnak) Espinoza; m. Albert Perkins, Aug. 28, 1977. Diploma, Windber Hosp. Nursing Sch., Pa., 1948. RN. Head nurse Phila. State Hosp., 1948-49; gen. and pvt. duty nurse Jewish Hosp., Phila., 1952-76. Office mgr. Hans A. Abraham, M.D., Phila., 1949—. Recipient Legion of Honor Chapel of Four Chaplains, Phila., 1979. Mem. Am. Assn. Med. Assts., (Phila. chpt.). Avocations: hypnosis, reading, travel. Home: Philadelphia, Pa. Died Apr. 20, 2005.

PERKINS, MARY KNOTTS, government official; b. Houston, July 17, 1932; d. William Henry and Mary Lois Gilpin Knotts; m. William Drew Perkins, Dec. 18, 1954; children: Holly Knotts Perkins-Meyers, Robin Love Perkins McBride, William Drew Jr., Giles Gilpin. Student, Gulf Park Coll., 1949-50; BA, U. Tex., 1953; MA, Sam Houston State U., 1962. English tchr. Corpus Christi (Tex.) Ind. Sch. Dist., 1953-54, Lufkin (Tex.) Ind. Sch. Dist., 1955-57. Part-time English instr. Angelina Coll., Lufkin, 1997—2001; mem. Lufkin Panel for Edn. of Young Children, 1996—98, Tex. State Bd. Edn., 1989—94; bd. dirs. Rubicon Prodns. Bd. dirs. Deep East Tex. Sch. to Work Partnership; mem. Tex. State Bd. Edn., 1989-94, chair long-range planning com.; mem. bd. edn. Lufkin Ind. Sch. Dist., 1976-87, pres. 1978-79, 85-86; Tex. rep. Nat. State Bds. Task Force on Violence and Crime, Washington, 1993-94; former sec. Tex. Rural Cmtys. Bd.; chair Carnegie grant Tex. Task Force Middle Schs., 1989-90; former pres. W.C. Trout Elem. Sch. PTA, Lufkin City Coun. of PTA, St. Cyprian's Day Sch. Bd. Parents' League; pres. United Meth. Women, chair commn. on stewardship, youth coord., tchr. Wesley class, dir. vacation Bible sch., chair coun. in ministries First United Meth. Ch.; pres. Lufkin Cmty. Concerts Assn.; chair centennial exhibit, docent Mus. East Tex.; mem. Angelina County Grievance Com.; mem. state adv. com. Keep Tex. Beautiful; mem. adv. com. Boy Scouts Am., Girl Scouts USA; bd. sec. Tex. Rural Cmtys., 1996; chair br. adv. coun. Planned Parenthood. Recipient Outstanding Contbn. in Edn. award NAACP, 1982, Pub. Svc. award Speech-Lang.-Hearing Assn., 1995, Disting. Achievement award Tex. Bus./Edn. Coalition, 1996, Woman of Yr. in East Tex., KJCS/KEEE, 1990, Top Six Women of Yr., KJCS/KEEE. Mem.: ASCD, AAUW (hon.), Tex. Mid. Sch. Assn. (Mary Knotts Perkins award named in her honor, Spotlight award 1995), Tex. Coun. Tchrs. English, Tex. Adult Literacy League (life hon. award 1994), Jr. League Lufkin (Sustainer of Yr. 1986), Tex. PTA (life), Kappa Kappa Gamma (50 Yr. Membership award). Democrat. Methodist. Avocations: reading, writing, travel, grandchildren. Home: Lufkin, Tex. Died Aug. 8, 2004.

PERL, HAROLD, business administration educator; b. Jersey City, May 28, 1926; s. Herman and Sadie (Feig) P.; m. Roslyn Minsky, Apr. 16, 1950; children: Ronald, Sander, Susan. BA, NYU, 1949; MA, Montclair State Coll., 1970; EdD, NYU, 1986. Prin. Perl Furniture Co., Passaic, N.J., 1949-75; prof. bus. County Coll. Morris, Randolph, N.J., from 1975, asst. chair dept. bus. adminstrn., 1984-85, chair dept. bus. adminstrn., 1985-91. V.p. retail affairs Passaic Area C. of C., 1963-74; bd. dirs., v.p., chmn. bd. dirs. N.J. Furniture Assn., 1960-74; person-to-person del. U.S./China Joint Session on Industry, Trade and Econ. Devel., Beijing, 1988. Bd. dirs. Passaic area YMCA, 1958-75, v.p., 1973-75; bd. dirs. Salvation Army, Passaic, 1972-75, Dover, N.J., 1988. With USN, 1944-46, PTO. Named N.J. Small Bus. Advocate of Yr. U.S. Small Bus. Adminstrn., 1983. Mem. Assn. Mktg. Educators (past pres.), Am. Mktg. Assn., Am. Mgmt. Assn., N.J. Home Furnishing Assn. (adv. bd.), Am. Vocat. Assn., N.J. Furniture Assn. (hon. life mem.), Masons, Shriners. Avocations: music, golf. Home: Randolph, NJ. Died Aug. 1, 2004.

PERLIK, WILLIAM ROBERT, lawyer; b. Pitts., May 20, 1925; s. Charles A. and Teresa Anna (Kraft) P.; m. Annabel Virginia Shanklin, June 16, 1949; children— Ronald A., Lynn C. BA, Oberlin Coll., 1948; JD, Yale U., 1951; LLD (hon.), Oberlin Coll., 2000. Bar: D.C. 1952, Va. 1955, U.S. Supreme Ct. 1974. Law clk. to judge U.S. Ct. Appeals, Washington, 1951-52; assoc., then ptnr. Cox Langford Stoddard & Cutler, Washington, 1952-62; ptnr., of counsel Wilmer Cutler & Pickering, Washington, 1962-98; adj. prof. politics and econs. Oberlin Coll., Ohio, 1973-1997. Trustee, chmn., mem. exec. com. Oberlin Coll., 1980-2000; pres. Va. Sch. Bd. Assn., 1971-72; mem. and chmn. Fairfax County Sch. Bd., Va., 1964-72; pres. Fairfax County Fedn. Citizens Assns., 1958. Served with U.S. Army, 1943-46; ETO. Recipient Edn. award Fairfax Edn. Assn., 1960; Citizen of Yr. award Washington Evening Star, 1961 Mem. ABA, Phi Beta Kappa. Avocations: music, gardening. Home: Mc Lean, Va. Died June 2, 2006.

PERLMUTTER, FRANK, retired horticulturist; b. Newark, June 2, 1912; s. Harry and Rebecca (Mark) P.; m. Eleanor Leah Lifschutz, Dec. 12, 1942; children: Marion and Jane (identical twins). BS, N.C. State U., 1934; MS, U. Md., 1939, postgrad., 1939-41, Hunter Coll., Lehman Coll., 1964-66, Cornell U., 1974-75. Dist. supr. plant disease USDA, North Wilkesboro, N.C., 1934, horticultural inspector Raleigh, N.C., 1936, rsch. horticulturalist Beltsville, Md., 1938-41, soil conservationist Sanford, N.C., 1941-46, plant quarantine insp. Hoboken, N.J., 1948-60, supr. N.Y.C., 1960-68; horticulturist Caswell Tng. Sch., Kinston, N.C., 1934-36, D.C. Tng. Sch., Laurel, Md., 1936-38; horticulturist br. office Hort. Maintenance br. office VA, N.Y.C., 1946-48; tchr. biology, sci., horticulture N.Y.C. Bd. Edn., 1968-82, per diem tchr., from 1982; docent N.Y. Bot. Garden, Bronx, from 1978. Author: Photoperiod N. Fertilizer on Blueberries, 1942, Raspberry, Blackberry Tetraploids, 1943. Staff sgt. USAAF, 1942-45, ETO. Fellow AAAS; mem. Am. Soc. Hort. Sci., N.Y. Acad. Sci. (life), DAV (life), Am. Inst. Biol. Sci., N.Y. Bot. Garden (achievement award 1986), Insps. Nat. Assn. (exec. chmn. plant quarantine 1958-59, pres. 1959-60), 8th Air Force Hist. Soc., 94th Bomb Group Meml. Assn. (life), Jewish War Vets. of U.S. Avocations: philatelist, plant propagation, swimming, chess, computers. Died Apr. 17, 2004.

PERLMUTTER, JACK, artist; b. NYC, Jan. 23, 1920; s. Morris and Rebecca (Schiffman) P.; children: Judith Faye, Ellen. MA, PhD in Fine Arts. Staff Dickey Gallery, D.C. Tchrs. Coll., 1951-68, dir., 1962-68, prof. art; prof. art, chmn. printmaking dept. Corcoran Gallery Art, Washington, 1960-82; resident artist St. Olaf Coll., Minn., Gibbs Art Gallery, Charleston, SC, Mus. Sch. Art, Greenville, SC. Vis. prof. art U. Costa Rica, San Jose, 1983; Fulbright research prof. painting and printmaking Tokyo U. Arts, 1959-60; art cons. Pres.'s Com. to Hire Handicapped; curator exhibits Cosmos Club, Washington. NASA artist for: 1st Saturn V moon rocket, Apollo 6, Apollo 16, Orbiter Columbia (space shuttle), Voyager II; contbg. editor: Art Voices South, 1979-80, Art Voices, 1980-82; one-man shows include Balt. Mus. Art, Brandeis U., Corcoran Gallery Art, Dintenfass Gallery, NYC, Makler Gallery, Phila., Smithsonian Inst., Yoseido Gallery, Tokyo, C. Troup Gallery, Dallas, Nat. Acad. Scis., 1981, Arts Club Washington, 1981, Annapolis, Md., 1982, galleries in Amsterdam, Rotterdam, The Hague and Costa Rica; exhibited in group shows in U.S., Switzerland, Yugoslavia, Europe, S.Am., Can.; represented in permanent collections Bklyn. Mus., Cin. Mus. Art, Carnegie Inst. Art, Corcoran Gallery Art, Library Congress, Met. Mus. Art, NYC, Nat. Gallery Art, Washington, Phila. Mus. Art, Walker Gallery, Mpls., Nat. Mus. Modern Art, Tokyo, U.S. Embassies in Bucharest, Budapest, Bonn, Dublin, London, Prague, Tokyo, others. Recipient awards for paintings and prints from Balt. Mus. Art, Libr. Congress, Corcoran Gallery Art, Butler Inst. Arts, Smithsonian Inst., Soc. Am. Graphic Artists, First Internat. Exhbn. Fine Arts in Saigon, Mus. Fine Arts in Saigon, Mus. Fine Art, Boston, others. Fellow Internat. Inst. Arts and Letters; mem. Soc. Am. Graphic Artists. Clubs: Cosmos (Washington; curator paintings and prints). Achievements include having prints, drawings and biog. data in Art Archives Am. Died May 4, 2006.

PERLMUTTER, JEROME HERBERT, communications specialist; b. N.Y.C., Oct. 17, 1924; s. Morris and Rebecca (Shiffman) P.; m. Evelyn Lea Friedman, Sept. 19, 1948; children: Diane Muriel, Sandra Pauline, Bruce Steven. AB cum laude, George Washington U., 1949; MA, Am. U., 1957. Chief editor svc., prodn. editor NEA, Washington, 1949-50; editor in chief Jour. AAHPER, Washington, 1950-51; editor Rural Elec. News, REA, USDA, Washington, 1951-53; publ. writer Agrl. Rsch. Svc., 1953-56; chief, editor br. Office Info., 1956-60; sec. Outlook and Situation Bd., 1960-62; chief econ. reports Econ. Rsch. Svc., 1960-62; chief div. pub. and reprodn. svcs. U.S. Dept. State, Washington, 1962-79; pres. Perlmutter Assocs., from 1979. Writing cons. CSC, 1956, World Bank, 1967—; communication cons. European Investment Bank, Can. Internat. Devel. Agy., Inter-Am. Devel. Bank, Internat. Monetary Fund; faculty agr. grad. sch. U. Md., also Fgn. Svc. Inst.; pub. cons. White House Conf. on Children and Youth, 1971. Author: A Practical Guide to Effective Writing, 1965; Contbr. articles profl. jours. Coord. fed. graphics Nat. Endowment for Arts, 1972-79, graphic designer, conv. of maj. polit. com., 1980. With USNR, 1943-46. Recipient award U.S. Jr. C. of C., 1963, Editors Choice award Nat. Libr. Poetry. Mem. Am. Assn. Agr. Coll. Editors, Assn. Editl. Bus. (bd. dirs.), Fed. Editors Assn., Am. Farm Econ. Assn., Soc. Tech. Comm. (bd. dirs.), Md. Literacy Coun., Soc. Profl. Journalists, Phi Beta Kappa, Phi Eta Sigma, Artus. Home: Silver Spring, Md. Died Oct. 6, 2005.

PERRY, NELSON ALLEN, retired radiation safety engineer, radiological consultant; b. Louisville, Mar. 26, 1937; s. Leslie Irvin and Sue Helen (Harris) P.; m. Sarita Sue Cornn, Apr. 28, 1956; children: Melody S. Doyle, Kimberly D. Horne. AS, Campbellsville (Ky.) Coll., 1954; BS, U. Louisville, 1961; MS, U. Okla., 1966. Cert. hazard control mgr., hazart material mgt.; lic. med. physicist, Tex. Assoc. prof. Ind. Christian U., Indpls., 1974-76; asst. prof. Ind. U., Indpls., 1971-75; instr. Ind. Voc. Tech. Coll., Indpls., 1968-76; health physicist Michael Reese Hosp., Chgo., 1966-68; radiation safety officer St. Francis Hosp., Beech Grove, Ind., 1968-76, Ind. U., Indpls., 1971-74, U. South Ala., Mobile, from 1976, assoc. prof., 1981—2001; radiol. cons. Perry Radiol. Cons., Inc., 1974—2001. Radiol. cons., 1974—. Contbr. articles to profl. jours. Named Ky. Col., 1964; USPHS trainee, 1965-66. Mem. Am. Assn. Physicists in Medicine, Health Physics Soc., Ala. Health Physics Soc. (sec. 1977-79, pres. 1980-81). Republican. Baptist. Avocation: collecting miniatures. Died Jan. 29, 2005.

PERRY-WIDNEY, MARILYN (MARILYN PERRY), real estate company executive, television producer, diversified financial services company executive; b. NYC, Feb. 11, 1939; d. Henry William Patrick and Edna May (Bown) Perry; m. Charles Leonidas Widney (dec. Sept. 1981). BA, Mexico City Coll., 1957. Pres. Marilyn Perry TV Prodns., Inc., N.Y.C., from 1970, C.L. Widney Internat., Inc., N.Y.C., from 1977. Mng. dir. Donerail Corp., N.Y.C., 1980-88, Lancer, N.Y.C., 1980-88, Assawata, N.Y.C., 1980-88. Prodr., host TV program Internat. Byline, series of more than 100 documentaries on the UN; host 80 radio and 200 pages on Internet series regarding environ. and devel. issues; author: (reference book) Leaders of the World, 2003; contbr. pages on environ. and devel. issues to radio and Internet sites; internat. byline-mem. nations UN exec. com. HNCA, 1998, PBS, in S.C., N.C., Ga., Tenn. Bd. dirs. UN After Sch. Program; ambassadorial candidate Pres. Bush., 1989. Recipient U.S. Indsl. Film Festival award, CINE Golden Eagle award, Bronze medal Internat. Film & TV Festival of N.Am., Bronzenen Urkinde, Berlin, award for superior quality Intercom-Chgo. Internat. Film Festival, Knights of Malta Trophy award for superior programming from Min. of Tourism, Internationales Tourismus award Film festival, Vienna, Manhattan Cable Ten Year award for continuous programming, citations from former pres. Ford and Carter, King Hussein Jordan, Pres. Clinton, pres. Maumoon Gayoon, Maldives, pres. Jacques Chirac, France. Mem. UN Corrs. Assn., UN After Sch. Programs, Rep. Presdl. Task Force (charter, journalist). Avocations: music, travel, antiques. Home: New York, NY. Died Aug. 2, 2005.

PERSONS, STOW SPAULDING, historian, educator; b. Mt. Carmel, Conn., June 15, 1913; s. Frederick Torrell and Florence Isabel (Cummings) P.; m. Dorothy Mae Reuss, Sept. 4, 1943; 1 dau., Catherine. BA, Yale U., 1936, PhD, 1940. Instr. history Princeton U., 1940-45, asst. prof., 1945-50; prof. history U. Iowa, from 1950, rsch. prof., 1956-57, Carver Disting. prof., 1978-81, prof. emeritus, from 1981, acting dean Grad. Coll., 1960-61; sr. rsch. fellow NEH, 1967-68. Vis. prof. Salzburg (Austria) Seminar, 1955, 61, Stetson U., 1957, San Francisco Coll., 1959, U. Wyo., 1960, U. Colo., 1964 Author: Free Religion, 1947, American Minds, 1958, The Decline of American Gentility, 1973, Ethnic Studies at Chicago, 1987, The University of Iowa in the 20th Century, 1990; editor: Evolutionary Thought in America, 1950, (with D. Egbert and T.D.S. Bassett) Socialism and American Life, 1952, Social Darwinism: Selected Essays of William Graham Sumner, 1963, The Cooperative Commonwealth (Laurence Gronlund); mem. editorial bd. Am. Quar., 1958-61, Mississippi Valley Hist. Rev., 1954-57. Fellow Fund Advancement Edn., 1954-55 Mem. Am. Hist. Assn., Orgn. Am. Historians (exec. com. 1960-63). Home: Iowa City, Iowa. Died Jan. 6, 2006.

PESLAR, NORMAN GEORGE, automotive executive; b. Grosse Pointe, Mich., Jan. 31, 1942; s. Frank Peter and Ruby B. (Smith) P.; m. Rose C. Lewis, Aug. 29, 1970; 1 child, Bethany Rose. BS in Engring., U. Mich., 1964, JD, 1967. Engr. Automotive Moulding, Warren, Mich., 1967-71, chief engr., 1971-72, v.p., 1972-77, pres., from 1977. Chmn. bd. Proto Type Extrusions, Rotterdam, N.Y.; vice chmn. Automotive Moulding de Mexico, Mexico City, 1980—. Editor U. Mich. Law Rev., 1967. Regional chmn. U. Mich. Law Sch. Fund, Ann Arbor; fin. chmn. Frink For Congress, Mt. Clemens, Mich.; exec. bd. mem. Detroit council Boy Scouts of Am. Mem. Young Pres.'s Orgn., Soc. Automotive Engrs. Clubs: Bloomfield Hills Country (Mich.); Grosse Pointe. Roman Catholic. Avocations: golf, boating, skiing, reading. Home: Bloomfield Hills, Mich. Died Aug. 1, 2005.

PETERS, VIRGINIA SWAIN, housing development administrator; b. Durham, N.C., June 25, 1933; d. Herbert Lee Swain and Sallie (McArten) Farrell; m. Charles Alvin Peters, Aug. 9, 1958; children: Alvin Lee, Cynthia Anne, Susan Lynne, Marcia Jeanne. BA, Greensboro Coll., NC, 1955; postgrad., U. NC, 1956, Columbia Tchr.'s Coll., 1957, U. Chgo., 1977. Tchr. Madison (N.J.) Bd. Edn., 1955-58, Arlington (Va.) Bd. Edn., 1958-61; with pub. relations dept. Operation Break-Through, Falls Church, Va., 1973-75; mgmt. asst. Columbus First Housing Assn., London, 1977; exec. dir. Wesley Housing Devel. Corp., Alexandria, Va., from 1977. Advisor South County Housing Coalition, Inc., Alexandria, 1987; mem. Va. Housing Study Commn. Subcom. on Prodn. Affordable Housing, 1987—. Vice pres. precinct ops. Dranesville Dist. Dem. Com., 1976; chmn. Chesterbrook Precinct Dem. Com., 1973-76, 78—; organizer Com. for Responsible Legis. on Firearms, Fairfax County, Va., 1969, Home Visit Prog., Princeton, N.J., 1965; mem. Met. Washington Coun. of Govts. Housing Task Force, 1990—; adv. bd. Fairfax County Affordable Dwelling Unit, 1990—. Recipient Ch. and Soc. award, Va. Ann. Conf. United Meth. Ch., 1986; first recipient Alumni Excellence award, Greensboro (N.C.) Coll., 1990. Mem. Embassy Wives Assn. (speaker's bur. 1969-72, chmn. vol. and ways and means coms.). Avocations: painting, sewing. Home: Mc Lean, Va. Died Mar. 23, 2004.

PETERSDORF, ROBERT GEORGE, physician, educator, academic administrator; b. Berlin, Feb. 14, 1926; s. Hans H. and Sonja P.; m. Patricia Horton Qua, June 2, 1951; children: Stephen Hans, John Eric. BA, Brown U., 1948, DMS (hon.), 1983; MD cum laude, Yale U., 1952; ScD (hon.), Albany Med. Coll., 1979; MA (hon.), Harvard U., 1980; DMS (hon.), Med. Coll. Pa., 1982, Brown U., 1983; DMS, Bowman-Gray Sch. Medicine, 1986; LHD (hon.), N.Y. Med. Coll., 1986; DSc (hon.), SUNY, Bklyn., 1987, Med. Coll. Ohio, 1987, Univ. Health Scis., The Chgo. Med. Sch., 1987; DSc (hon.), St. Louis U., 1988; LHD (hon.), Ea. Va. Med. Sch., 1988; DSc (hon.), Sch. Medicine, Georgetown U., 1991, Emory U., 1992; DSc (hon.), Tufts U., 1993; DSc (hon.), Mt. Sinai Sch. Medicine, 1993, George Washington U., 1994; other hon. degrees. Diplomate Am. Bd. Internal Medicine. Intern, asst. resident Yale U., New Haven, 1952—54; sr. asst. resident Peter Bent Brigham Hosp., Boston, 1954—55; fellow Johns Hopkins Hosp., Balt., 1955—59; chief resident, instr. medicine Yale U., 1957—58; asst. prof. medicine Johns Hopkins U., 1958—60, physician, 1958—60; assoc. prof. medicine U. Wash., Seattle, 1960—62, prof., 1962—79, chmn. dept. medicine, 1964—79; physician-in-chief U. Wash. Hosp., 1964—79; pres. Brigham and Women's Hosp., Boston, 1979—81; prof. medicine Harvard U. Med. Sch., Boston, 1979—81; dean, vice chancellor health scis. U. Calif.-San Diego Sch. Medicine, 1981—86; clin. prof. infectious diseases Sch. Medicine Georgetown U., 1986—94; pres. Assn. Am. Med. Colls., Washington, 1986—94, pres. emeritus, 1994—2006; prof. medicine U. Wash., from 1994, disting. prof., sr. adv. to dean, 1998—2006; disting. physician Vets. Health Adminstrn., Seattle, 1995—98, sr. physician, 1998—2006. Cons. to surgeon gen. USPHS, 1960—79; cons. USPHS Hosp., Seattle, 1962—79; mem. spl. med. adv. group VA, 1987—94. Editor: Harrison's Principles of Internal Medicine, 1968—90; contbr. numerous articles to profl. jours. With USAAF, 1944—46. Named Disting. Internist of 1987, Am. Soc. Internal Medicine; recipient Lilly medal, Royal Coll. Physicians, London, 1978, Wiggers award, Albany Med. Coll., 1979, Robert H. Williams award, Assn. Profs. Medicine, 1983, Keen award, Brown U., 1980, Disting. Svc. award, Baylor Coll. Medicine, 1989, Scroll of Merit, Nat. Med. Assn., 1990, 2d Ann. Founder's award, Assn. Program Dirs. in Internal Medicine, 1991, Flexner award, Assn. Am. Med. Coll., 1994. Master: ACP (pres. 1975—76, Stengel award 1980, Disting. Tchr. award 1993, Laureate award Wash. chpt.); fellow: AAAS, Execs. Assn. (hon.); mem.: Assn. Am. Physicians (pres. 1976—77, Kober medal 1996), Inst. Medicine of NAS (councillor 1977—80), Rainier Club, Cosmos Club. Died Sept. 29, 2006.

PETERSON, CARL WILLIAM, JR., lawyer; b. Utica, N.Y., May 23, 1932; s. Carl William and Anna Mae (Fisher) P.; m. Virginia Lucile Wood, Apr. 20, 1957; children: Carl W. III, David H. AB, Hamilton Coll., 1953; LLB, Cornell U., 1956. Bar: N.Y. 1956, U.S. Dist. Ct. (no. dist.) N.Y. 1971, U.S. Supreme Ct. 1960. Assoc. Estabrook, Burns, Hancock & White, Syracuse, N.Y., 1960-66; 1st asst. corp. counsel City of Syracuse, 1966-68, corp. counsel, 1968-69; ptnr. Hancock & Estabrook, LLP, Syracuse, from 1970. Pres. Vol. Ctr. Onondaga County, N.Y., 1987-88; dir. Metro Water Bd., Onondaga County, N.Y., 1968-69, Onondaga Citizens League, 1991-95, Onondaga Bar Found., 1991-95. Lt. USAF, 1957-60. Mem. N.Y. Bar Assn. (house of dels. 1983-85), Onondaga County Bar Assn. (pres. 1984, chmn. law mentors 1986-95, chmn. 5th jud. dist. grievance com. 1992-95), Hiscock Legal Aid Soc. (pres. 1985-86), Cedar Lake Club. Republican. Episcopalian. Avocations: reading, golf. Home: Clayville, NY. Died Feb. 7, 2005.

PETERSON, DEAN MCCORMACK, mechanical engineer; b. Wessington, S.D., Dec. 12, 1931; s. Walter Henry and Era Faye (McCormack) P.; m. Mary Joan Drake, Oct. 20, 1954; children: Michael Dean, Marshall Drake. BS in Gen. Engring., S.D. Sch. Mines, Rapid City, 1954; MS in Mech. Engring., U. Rochester, 1963. Sr. project engr. Eastman Kodak Co., Rochester, 1954-68; mgr. engr. Honeywell, Inc., Denver, 1968-78, Fisher Price Toys, San Diego, 1978-81; dir. engring. Nimslo Corp., Atlanta, 1981-83, Spin Physics, San Diego, 1983-87, Am. Optical, San Diego, 1987-89, Signet Armorlite, San Marcos, Calif., 1989-90; pvt. engring. cons. Pacific Innovations Co., Escondido, Calif., 1990-91; v.p. engring. Galen Med., Escondido, 1991-94, HPS Musical Inc., Edina, Minn., from 1995. Instr. Rochester Inst. Tech., 1963-68, Arapaho Community Coll., Littleton, Colo., 1972-76. Patentee in field. Election asst. Rep. Party, Escondido, 1985. With U.S. Army, 1954-56. Fellow Soc. Photo Scientists & Engrs.; mem. ASME, Soc. Plastics Engrs., Soc. Photo-Optical Engrs., Triangle, Sigma Tau. Republican. Presbyterian. Avocations: golf, fly fishing, travel, wine tasting. Home: Escondido, Calif. Died June 14, 2004.

PETERSON, HELMER WILLIAM, religious organization executive, clergyman; b. Plainfield, N.J., Apr. 14, 1936; s. Helmer and Karin Augusta (Persson) P.; m. Elizabeth Thorton Myers, Aug. 1, 1959 (dec. Oct. 1990); children: Karin Elizabeth, Michael William, Nils Edward, Katherine McVichie. AB, Centre Coll., Danville, Ky., 1958; MDiv, Louisville Presbyn. Sem., 1961. Ordained to ministry Presbyn. Ch. U.S.A., 1961. Pastor 1st Presbyn. Ch., Springfield, Ky., 1961-66; assoc. dir. youth ministry bd. Christian edn. Presbyn. Ch. in U.S., Richmond, Va., 1966-68, dir. youth ministry, 1968-71; assoc. presbytery exec. Presbytery Western Ky., Hopkinsville, 1971-74, presbytery exec., 1974-85; exec. dir. Mountain Retreat Assn., Montreat (N.C.) Conf. Ctr., from 1985. Cons., designer Community Change Project, Hopkinsville, 1971-75; mem., pres. Pennyroyal Mental Health/Mental Retardation Bd., Hopkinsville, 1978-84, Pennyrile Players, Hopkinsville, 1977-85; originator Arts Alive Program, Montreat, 1986—. Mem. N.Am. Retreat Dirs. Assn., Internat. Assn. Conf. Ctr. Adminstrs., Rotary. Avocations: photography, fishing. Home: Prospect, Ky. Died Aug. 23, 2005.

PETERSON, JOHN EDWARD, artist, consultant; b. San Francisco, May 13, 1948; s. John Alfred and Lois Dorothy (Rima) P.; m. Susan Jane Kaplan, May 1, 1980 (div. May 7, 1987); 1 child, Aaron Charles. Artist, carpenter, Calif., 1970-80; artist, designer Prescott, Ariz., 1980-88; theater carpenter Gaslight Theater, Tucson, 1988-92; exhibits dir. Tucson Children's Mus., 1992-96; artist, designer San Francisco, from 1996. Designer, builder Ecol. Design Earth house, 1980-87, Interactive exhibits recyc led materials, Tucson Children's Mus., 1992-96. V.p. Cmty. Coun., Dewey, Ariz., 1984-85. With U.S. Army, 1996-70. Recipient Best of Show, Southwestern Artists Assn., Ariz., 1986, judges choice, Tucson Home Show, 1995, Tu Ch Mu, Tucson Children's Mus., 1996. Avocations: philosophy, natural medicine. Died June 24, 2005.

PETERSON, JOHN ERIC, physician, educator; b. Norwalk, Ohio, Oct. 26, 1914; s. Charles Augustus and Fannie Helen (Stanford) P.; m. Lodene C. Pruett, Aug. 18, 1938; children— Carol Peterson Haviland, John Eric. Student, Columbia Jr. Coll., 1932-34; MD, Coll. Med. Evangelists, 1938. Diplomate: Nat. Bd. Med. Examiners, Am. Bd. Internal Medicine. Intern Henry Ford Hosp., Detroit, 1938-39, resident, 1939-42; practice medicine specializing in internal medicine Los Angeles, 1942-56, Loma Linda, Calif., from 1956; mem. staff Los Angeles County Hosp., Riverside (Calif.) County Gen. Hosp.; mem. faculty Sch. Medicine, Loma Linda U., from 1942, prof. medicine, 1967-88, prof. medicine emeritus, from 1988, chmn. dept., 1969-80; asso. dean Sch. Medicine, Loma Linda U. (Sch. Medicine), 1965-75; mem. staff Loma Linda U. Hosp., from 1967, chief medicine service, 1969-80. Rsch. assoc. Harvard Med. Sch., 1960-61; cons. to univs. and fgn. govts. Contbr. articles to various publs. Fellow ACP; mem. AMA, Calif. Med. Assn., San Bernardino County Med. Assn., Calif. Soc. Internal Medicine, Inland Soc. Internal. Medicine, Am. Diabetes Assn., Western Soc. Clin. Investigation, Assn. Profs. of Medicine, L.A. Acad. Medicine, Diabetes Assn. So. Calif., Sigma Xi, Alpha Omega Alpha. Home: Loma Linda, Calif. Died Mar. 10, 2005.

PETERSON, JOHN WILLARD, composer, publishing executive; b. Lindsborg, Kans., Nov. 1, 1921; s. Peter Ephraim and Adlina Mary (Nelson) P.; m. Marie Alta Addis (Feb. 11, 1944); children: Sandra Lynn Peterson Catzere, Candace Kay Peterson Strader, Pamela Lee Peterson Cruse. Student, Moody Bible Inst., 1947-48; MusB, Am. Conservatory Music, 1952; MusD (hon.), John Brown U., 1967; DD (hon.), West Bapt. Sem., 1970; DFA (hon.), Grand Canyon U., 1979. Radio broadcaster Sta. WMBI, Chgo., 1950-55; editor in chief, pres. Singspiration, Inc., Grand Rapids, Mich., 1955-71, exec. composer Carefree, Ariz., 1977-83; pres. Good Life Prodns., Scottsdale, Ariz., 1977-83, John W. Peterson Music Co., Scottsdale, 1983-88. Bd. dirs. Gospel Films, Inc., Muskegon, Mich. Co-author: (autobiography) The Miracle Goes On, 1976; composer works include numerous cantatas, musicals, gospel songs, hymns and anthems. 1st lt. USAAF 1942-45, CBI. Decorated Air medal; recipient Sacred Music award Nat. Evang. Film Found., 1966, Music Achievement award Christian Artists, 1985; Honor Cert. Freedoms Found., 1975; winner Internat. Gospel Composition of Yr., Soc. European Stage, Authors and Composers, 1986, Ray DeVries Ch. Music award, 1996; inductee Gospel Music Hall of Fame, 1986. Mem. ASCAP, Hump Pilots Assn. Home: Scottsdale, Ariz. Died Sept. 27, 2006.

PETERSON, PAULETTE ELIZABETH, biochemist; b. Fresno, Calif., June 25, 1957; d. Carl Benjamin and Lila Irene (Orvik) P.; m. Bruce Eric Kirkpatrick, Aug. 9, 1987. BS in Biochemistry, U. Calif., Davis, 1979; postgrad., U. Calif., Santa Clara, 1979-80; MFA, San Jose State U., 1994. Teaching asst., grad. asst. U. Calif., Santa Cruz, 1979-80; rsch. & devel. chemist I, II & III SYVA, Palo Alto, Calif., 1981-86; sr. chemist, project leader Biotrack, Mountain View, Calif., 1986-90; sr. scientist, project mgr. Cholestech, Hayward, Calif., 1990-93; practicing artist, art instr. pvt. practice, Santa Clara, Calif., from 1993. Patentee, inventor in field; contbr. articles to profl. jours. Mem., activist, coord. Com. Against U.S. Intervention in El Salvador, Palo Alto, 1984. Recipient hon. mention Olympiad of the Arts, Los Gatos, Calif., 1994; winner illustration competition Applied Materials Internat., 1992. Avocations: art, cooking, gardening. Home: Santa Clara, Calif. Died Oct. 16, 2004.

PETERSON, WILLIAM ALLEN, lawyer; b. Marshall, Mo., Oct. 1, 1934; s. R.O. and Marjorie E. (Mallot) P.; m. Mary Kay Moore, July 26, 1958; children: Laura, Clayton, Mary M., Sarah. BS, Drury Coll., Springfield, Mo., 1958; JD, Washington U., 1963. Bar: Mo. 1963, U.S. Dist. Ct. (ea. dist.) Mo. 1964, U.S. Dist. Ct. (we. dist.) Mo. 1965, U.S. Supreme Ct. 1967. Assoc. Riddle, O'Herin & Newberry, Malden, Mo., 1963-65; asst. atty. gen. State of Mo., Jefferson City, 1965-70; legislator Mo. Ho. Reps., Jefferson City, 1970-74; pvt. practice Marshall, from 1974. Atty. City of Marshall, 1976-78, City of Slater, Mo., 1988-89; judge mcpl. divsn. State Cir. Ct., Marshall, 1979-80, 2000—, Slater, 1990-94; pros. atty. County of Saline, Marshall, 1979-80, 84-88. With USN, 1954-56. Mem. ABA, Mo. Bar Assn., Assn. Trial Lawyers Am., Am. Legion, VFW. Methodist. Home: Marshall, Mo. Died Oct. 10, 2004.

PETRALIA, ELAINE PHYLLIS, sales executive; b. Albany, N.Y., May 28, 1960; d. Arnold Ross and Phyllis Helme (Conklin) P. BSBA magna cum laude, SUNY, Albany, 1982. Sales rep. One Way Records, Inc., Albany, 1984-88, nat. retail sales rep., 1988, nat. sales mgr., from 1988. Mem. Nat. Assn. Record Merchandisers, Rails to Trails. Avocations: bicycling, skiing, tennis, reading. Home: Albany, NY. Died July 13, 2005.

PETRAUSKAS, HELEN O., automobile manufacturing company executive; b. Lviv, Ukraine, 1944; m. Raymond Petrauskas; 1 child, Laura BS in Math., Wayne State U., 1966, JD, 1971. Chemist, group supr. Sherwin-Williams Co., 1966-71; various positions Ford Motor Co., Dearborn, Mich., 1971-79, asst. dir. emissions and fuel economy cert., 1980-82, exec. dir. environ. and safety engring and rsch.

staff, 1982-83, exec. dir. engring. and tech. staff, 1983, corp. v.p. environ. and safety engring., 1983—2001; ret., 2001. Named one of 50 Women to Watch, Bus. Week mag., 1987. Died Mar. 8, 2006.

PETREK, JEANNE ANN, surgeon, researcher; b. Youngstown, Ohio, Jan. 5, 1948; m. Jeffrey Duban; 2 children. BA, Case Western Res., 1969, MD, 1973. Diplomate Am. Bd. Surgery; lic. physician, N.Y. Intern Peter Bent Brigham Hosp., Boston, 1973-74, resident in gen. surgery, 1974-78; surg. oncology rsch. fellow Meml. Sloan-Kettering Cancer Inst., 1978-80, dir. surgical program, Evelyn H. Lauger Breast Ctr., 1984, asst. attending surgeon breast svc. dept. surgery, 1984, chief breast-cancer surgeon; asst. prof. surgery Emory U. Sch. Medicine, Atlanta, 1980-84, Cornell U. Sch. Medicine, N.Y.C., 1984—2003, prof. surgery, 2003—05; assoc. physician The Rockefeller U., N.Y.C., 1984. Staff mem. Grady Meml. Hosp., 1980-84, Emory U. Hosp., 1980-84, Crawford W. Long Hosp., 1980-84; asst. mem. Meml. Hosp., 1984, surg. quality assurance com. mem., grievance com. mem., surg. day hosp. quality assurance com. mem.; sci. adv. bd. Calcium Info. Ctr.; presenter in field. Co-author (with Carolyn D. Runowicz) Women and Cancer: A Thorough and Compassionate Resource for Patients and Their Families, 1999; contbr. articles to profl. jours. and local newspapers. Recipient Clin. Oncology Career Devel. award Am. Cancer Soc., 1985-88; grantee Am. Cancer Soc., 1987-88, Nat. Cancer Inst., 1988-90. Mem. AMA, Assn. Acad. Surgery, Soc. for Surg. Oncology (local arrangement com. mem.), Soc. for Head and Neck Surgery, Southeastern Surg. Congress, Southern Med. Assn., Am. Med. Womens Assn. (jour. editor), N.Y. Met. Breast Cancer Group. Died Apr. 11, 2005.

PETRIK, ALOIS RICHARD, retired radio station official; b. Sioux City, Iowa, Jan. 15, 1928; s. Alois Robert and Frances (Miller) P.; m. Vivian Irene Latham, Aug. 1, 1953; children: Daniel, Gail, Janna, Maribeth, David. BA in Journalism, U. Iowa, 1951. News dir. Sta. KOEL, Oelwein, Iowa, 1952-93; ret., 1993. Home: Oelwein, Iowa. Died Dec. 29, 2004.

PFNISTER, ALLAN OREL, humanities educator; b. Mason, Ill., July 23, 1925; s. Ardon Orel and Rose Margaret (Sandtner) P.; m. Helen Edith Klobes, Dec. 18, 1948; children: Alicia Ann, Jonathan Karl, Susan Elaine. AB summa cum laude, Augustana Coll., 1945; MDiv summa cum laude, Augustana Theol. Sem., 1949; AM, U. Chgo., 1951, PhD, 1955; LLD (hon.), U. Denver, 1978. Instr. in religion Augustana Coll., 1946-47; instr. in philosophy and German Luther Coll., Wahoo, Nebr., 1949-52, dean, 1953-54; research asst., univ. fellow U. Chgo., 1952-53, instr., 1954-57, asst. prof., 1957-58; dir. research joint bds. parish edn. Lutheran Ch. Am., 1958-59; vis. asso. prof. U. Mich., 1959-62, asso. prof., 1962-63; dean Coll. Liberal Arts, prof. philosophy Wittenberg (Ohio) U., 1963-67, provost, prof., 1967-69, acting pres., 1968-69; prof. higher edn. U. Denver, 1969-77, 78-90, exec. vice chancellor and acting chancellor, 1977-78, vice chancellor acad. affairs, 1984-87, assoc. provost, 1988-89, prof. emeritus, 1990—2005. Dir. study fgn. study programs Fedn. Regional Accrediting Commns. Higher Edn., 1970-72; cons. in field; bd. dirs. Nat. Ctr. for Higher Edn. Mgmt. Systems Mgmt. Svcs.; trustee Capital U., Columbus, Ohio, 1983, vice chmn. bd., 1987-89, 91-94. Author: Teaching Adults, 1967, Trends in Higher Education, 1975, Planning for Higher Education, 1976; contbr. numerous articles on higher edn. to profl. jours. Bd. visitors Air Force Inst. Tech., 1978-83, chmn. bd. visitors, 1981-83. Recipient Outstanding Achievement Alumni award Augustana Coll., 1963, Outstanding Contributions to the Univ. award Univ. Denver, 1995. Mem. Am. Am. Assn. Higher Edn., Assn. for Study Higher Edn., Comparative and Internat. Edn. Soc., Blue Key, Phi Beta Kappa. Democrat. Home: Denver, Colo. Died Oct. 13, 2004.

PHELPS, CAROL JO, neuroendocrinologist; b. Sendai, Japan, Apr. 20, 1948; d. Harry J. and Helen I. (Davies) P.; m. James B. Turpen, June 13, 1969 (div. Apr. 1982); children: J. Matthew Turpen, John A. Turpen; m. David L. Hurley, Oct. 12, 1985. BS in Zoology, U. Denver, 1969; PhD in Anatomy, La. State U. Med. Ctr., 1974. Postdoctoral fellow NIH, U. Rochester, NY, 1974-76; rsch. assoc. Pa. State U., Univ. Park, 1976-77, instr., 1977-80, postdoctoral scholar, 1980-82; asst. prof. neurobiology U. Rochester, 1982-90; assoc. prof. anatomy Tulane U. Sch. Medicine, New Orleans, 1990-94; prof., from 1994. Nat. sci. adv. coun. Am. Fedn. Aging Rsch., N.Y.C., 1988—; rev. coms. Nat. Inst. on Aging, Bethesda, Md., 1993-97; editl. bd. Neuroendocrinology, Paris, 1994-2000, Endocrinology, 1996-2000, Jour. of Andrology, 1996-99. NIH fellow, 1974-76; grantee NIH, 1983—; Burroughs-Wellcome Rsch. Travel grantee, 2001. Mem. Am. Assn. Anatomists, Soc. Exptl. Biology and Medicine, Endocrine Soc., Soc. Neurosci. (chpt. pres. 1995-96). Avocations: antique restoration, photography. Home: New Orleans, La. Died 2005.

PHIFER, (LYNDON) GREGG, communication educator; b. Cin., May 17, 1918; s. Lyndon Burke and Wilma Louise (Young) P.; m. Elizabeth Bowman Flory, June 8, 1956 (dec. Apr. 1978); children: Margie Phifer Tullos, Linda Phifer Rogers, Dorrie Phifer Presson. BA, Coll. of Pacific, 1940; MA, U. Iowa, 1941, PhD, 1949. Cert. master ofcl. USA Track and Field. Asst. prof. speech and English, Baldwin-Wallace Coll., Berea, Ohio, 1946-48; instr. speech U. Iowa, Iowa City, 1948-49; asst. prof., assoc. prof. comm. Fla. State U., Tallahassee, 1949-61, prof., 1961-95, prof. emeritus Tallahassee, from 1995. Parliamentarian Fla. Teaching Profession-Nat. Edn. Assn., 1989-90, Fla. Credit Union League, 1988-90, ALA, 1990-92. Co-author: Salesmanship: Communication, Persuasion, Perception, 1966; editor: Readings in Parliamentary Law, 1992; also numerous articles. Sec. Tallahassee chpt. ACLU, 1989-96; treas. Coun. Neighborhood Assn., Tallahassee, 1990-92. Mem. So. States Comm. Assn. (pres.), Fla. Comm. Assn. (pres.). Democrat. Methodist. Home: Tallahassee, Fla. Died June 2, 2005.

PHILBRICK, DONALD LOCKEY, retired lawyer; b. Portland, Maine, May 3, 1923; s. Donald Ward and Ruth (Lockey) P.; children: Deborah Palmer Peiser, Sarah Peyton Shick; adopted children: Paul Sloat, Mark Whitfield, Andrew Hunter; m. Janet Mitchell Poole, Aug. 7, 1982. AB, Bowdoin Coll., 1944; JD, Harvard U., 1948. Bar: Maine 1948. Pvt. practice, Portland; ptnr. Verrill & Dana, 1951-82. Selectman, Cape Elizabeth, Maine, 1957-63. Served with AUS, 1943-45; with USAF, 1951-53. Mem. Maine Hist. Soc. (past pres.), N.E. Hist. Gen. Soc., Delta Kappa Epsilon. Clubs: Portland Country. Republican. Congregationalist. Home: Scarborough, Maine. Died Sept. 12, 2005.

PHILIPSON, JOSEPH, chemist; b. Chgo., Aug. 30, 1918; s. Isador and Minnie (Haas) P.; m. Amy Goldstein, Apr. 11, 1942 (dec. Oct. 1985); children: David, Alice, Robert, Jean; m. Stella Rudnick, Jan. 14, 1990. BS, U. Wis., 1940; MS, U. Minn., 1941; PhD, U. So. Calif., 1944. Registered profl. engr., Calif. Rsch. chemist Sanitary Dist. Chgo., N.Am. Aviation, Inglewood, Calif., 1945-47, Aerojet Gen. Corp., Azusa, Calif., 1947-52; chief chemist Grand Cen. Rocket Co., Pocoima, Calif., 1952-54; div. dir. Atlantic Rsch. Corp., Pasadena, Calif., 1957-64; cons. chemist, Pasadena, from 1964. Contbr. articles to profl. jours.; patentee in field. Mem. AIAA, Am. Chem. Soc., Soc. Plastic Engrs., Soc. Aerospace Material and Process Engrs., Cons. Chemists Assn. Died May 10, 2004.

PHILLIPS, ALAN GUY, ceramics engineer, artist; b. Colorado Springs, Colo., Apr. 18, 1949; s. Hilda H. (Guy) P. BA in Chemistry, U. Colo., 1971. Chemist Diamond Shamrock, Houston, 1972; with new product R & D Kaman Scis., Colorado Springs, 1973-77, Rockwell Internat. EG&G Rocky Flats, Golden, Colo., from 1978. Owner Alan Phillips, Inc., Arvada, Colo., 1980-85, The Ambrosial Woods Gallery, Arvada, 1990—. Mem. Nature Conservancy, Wilderness Soc., Sierra. Avocations: photography, writing, sculpture, art. Home: Lakewood, Colo. Died July 7, 2004.

PHILLIPS, ALMARIN, economics professor, consultant; b. Port Jervis, N.Y., Mar. 13, 1925; s. Wendell Edgar and Hazel (Billett) P.; m. Dorothy Kathryn Burns, June 14, 1947 (div. 1976); children: Almarin Paul, Frederick Peter, Thomas Rock, David John, Elizabeth Linett, Charles Samuel; m. Carole Cherry Greenberg, Dec. 19, 1976 (dec. 2005); m. Anita S. Behrle, May 20, 2005 BS, U. Pa., 1948, MA, 1949; PhD, Harvard, 1953. Instr. econs. U. Pa., 1948-50, 51-53, asst. prof. econs., 1953-56, prof. econs. and law, 1963-91, prof. emeritus, 1991—2006; Hower prof. pub. policy U. Pa, 1983-91; chmn. dept. econs. U. Pa., 1968-71, 72-73, assoc. dean Wharton Sch., 1973-74, dean Sch. Pub. and Urban Policy, 1974-77, chair faculty senate, 1990-91. Teaching fellow Harvard, 1950-51; assoc. prof. U. Va, 1956-61, prof., 1961-63; vis. prof. U. Hawaii, summer 1968, U. Warwick, London Grad. Sch. Bus. Studies, 1972, Ohio State U., McGill U., 1978, Calif. Inst. Tech, Northwestern U., 1980, Ariz. Coll. Law, 1987, Inst. Europeén d'Adminstrn. des Affairs (INSEAD), France, spring 1990; co-dir. Pres.'s Commn. Fin. Structure and Regulation, 1970-71; mem. Nat. Commn. Electronic Fund Transfers, 1976-77; chmn. bd. Econsult Corp., 1990-96. Author: (with R.W. Cabell) Problems in Basic Operations Research Methods for Management, 1961, Market Structure, Organization and Performance, 1962, Technology and Market Structure: A Study of the Aircraft Industry, 1971, (with P. Phillips and T.R. Phillips) Biz Jets: Technology and Market Structure in the Corporate Jet Aircraft Industry, 1994; Editor: Perspectives on Antitrust Policy, 1965, (with O.E. Williamson) Prices: Issues in Theory, Practice and Policy, 1968, Promoting Competition in Regulated Markets, 1975; editor Jour. Indsl. Econs., 1974-90; Contbr. articles to profl. jours. Served with AUS, 1943-45. Decorated Purple Heart, Bronze Star. Fellow: AAAS, Am. Statis. Assn.; mem.: Internat. Telecomms. Soc. (bd. dirs. 1990—2002), European Econ. Assn., Econometric Soc., Am. Econ. Assn. Home: Wynnewood, Pa. Died Aug. 26, 2006.

PICKER, NELLY, soloist, educator; b. Vienna, Sept. 11, 1916; came to U.S., 1954; d. Anton and Henny Picker; 1 child, Daniela. Student, Vienna Acad., 1935-39; grad., Conservatory G. Verdi, Milan, 1939. Cert. tchr. Singer British Army ENSA, Middle East, 1942-45, PBS (Palestine Broadcasting Svc.) Opera, 1939-52; tchr. Pub. Sch. System, N.Y.C., 1965-67; Hohokus Pub. Schs., 1967-69; tchr. Pub. Sch. System, Kearny, N.J., 1969-81, Studio for the Performer, Arlington, N.J., from 1981. Choral dir. Bel Canto Singers, Arlington, N.J., 1982--. Mem. Nat. Assn. Tchr. of Singing, Am. Choral Dir. Assn., Nat. Piano Tchr. Guild, Nat. Opera Assn. Avocation: languages. Died June 17, 2004.

PICKETT, WILSON, singer; b. Prattville, Ala., Mar. 18, 1941; Singer (albums) In the Midnight Hour, 1965, Wicked Picket, 1966, The Exciting Wilson Pickett, 1966, Great Wilson Pickett Hits, 1967, The Sound of Wilson Pickett, 1967, The Very Best of Wilson Pickett, 1967, Midnight Mover, 1968, I'm in Love, 1968, Hey Jude, 1969, Right On, 1970, Wilson Pickett in Philadelphia, 1970, Engine No. 9, 1971, The Best of Wilson Pickett, Vol. 2, 1971, Don't Knock My Love, 1971, Mr. Magic Man, 1973, Wilson Pickett's Greatest Hits, 1973, Miz Lena's Boy, 1973, Tonight I'm My Biggest Audience, 1974, Pickett in the Pocket, 1974, Live in Japan, 1974, Join Me and Let's Be Free, 1975, Peace Breaker, 1975, Chocolate Mountain, 1976, Star Collection, 1978, A Funky Situation, 1978, I Want You, 1979, The Right Track, 1981, Star Collection, Vol. 2, 1981, Best of Wilson Pickett, 1985, Great Hits, 1987, American Soul Man, 1987, Man and a Half: The Best of Wilson Pickett, 1992, It's Harder Now, 1999; hit singles include In the Midnight Hour, 1965, Land of 1000 Dances, 1966, 634-5789 (Soulsville, U.S.A.), 1966, Mustang Sally, 1966, Everybody Needs Somebody to Love, 1967, Funky Broadway, 1967, She's Lookin' Good, 1968, Hey Jude, 1969, Engine Number 9, 1970, Don't Let the Green Grass Fool You, 1971, Fire and Water, 1972; actor (films) Sgt. Pepper's Lonly Hearts Club Band, 1978, The Committments, 1991, Blues Brothers 2000, 1998 Inducted into Rock and Roll Hall of Fame, 1991, The Ala. Music Hall of Fame, 1999. Home: New York, NY. Died Jan. 19, 2006.

PICKUS, GLORIA B., retired secondary school educator; b. Bluefield, W.Va., Aug. 14, 1933; d. J.V. "Jack" and Tobie Slifkin Blank; children: Kimberly, A. Scott. AA, Stephens Coll., 1952; BS, Ohio State U., 1954; MS, Radford U., 1976. Tchr. McDowell County Schs., Northfork, W.Va., 1955—56, Mercer County Schs., Bluefield, W.Va., 1959—81, ret., 1956. Vol. Am. Cancer Soc., from 1955, Am. Heart Assn., from 1955; vol. bd. mem. Cancer Rsch. Network, Hollywood, Fla., from 1998; assoc. dir. Preliminary Miss Am. Pagent, Bluefield, 1955—63; bd. dirs. Ohio Valley Sch. Dist., 1966—69; v.p., pres. Sisterhood Temple, Bluefield, 1965—67, pres., 1967—69. Mem.: AAUW (vol. fundraiser from 1954, bd. mem.). Avocations: boating, bridge, waterskiing. Home: Simpsonville, SC. Died Jan. 5, 2004.

PIDEL, ANTOINETTE, nurse practitioner; b. N.Y.C., Sept. 18, 1935; d. Joseph and Jennie (Bonsanque) DeMarco; m. Albert Pidel, June 13, 1964; children: Thomas, Jennie, Ann. RN, Cochran Sch. Nursing, 1980; BSN, SUNY, Yonkers, 1984; MEd, Lehman Coll., 1988. Cert. Adult Nurse Practitioner. Public health nurse VNS Home Care, Bronx, N.Y.; nurse practitioner Ruth Taylor Inst., Hawthorne, N.Y. Mem. Coalition of Nurse Practitioners, Bronx Women Against Rape.adr Home: Yonkers, NY. Died May 16, 2004.

PIERCE, DON FREDERICK, country music entrepreneur; b. Seattle, Oct. 10, 1915; s. Frederick and (Bergeron) Picht; m. Vadis Thelma Larrabee; 1 child, Victoria Turner. BA, U. Wash., Seattle, 1938. Underwriter United Pacific Ins. Co., Seattle, 1937-42; capt. U.S. Army, 1943-46; v.p. 4 Star Record Co., Pasadena, Calif., 1946-52; pres. Starday Record Co., Nashville, 1953-70, Cages Bend Developers, Hendersonville, Tenn., from 1970. Creator, selector Master Achievement Awards presented to outstanding country music artists by Reunion of Profl. Entertainers. Founder and chmn., Music City Pro-Celebrity Golf Tournament, Nashville, 1965-67. Named Country Music Man of the Year, Billboard Mag., N.Y., 1970. Founder, bd. dirs. Country Music Assn., Nashville. Avocation: golf. Home: Gallatin, Tenn. Died Apr. 3, 2005.

PIERCE, GLENN PALEN, language educator; b. Sept. 10, 1940; BS, Georgetown U., 1962; PhD, UCLA, 1977. Asst. prof. U. Va., 1976-84; prof. Italian Mo. U., Columbia, from 1985. Home: Columbia, Mo. Died Oct. 5, 2004.

PIERCE, WILLIAM LEE, foundation administrator; b. Arnold, Nebr., June 10, 1936; AB, Benedictine Coll., 1958; PhD, Union Inst., 1978. Pub. info. officer U.S. Office of Econ. Opportunity, Kansas City, Mo., 1966-69; asst. exec. dir. Day Care and Child Devel. Coun. Am., Washington, 1969-70, Child Welfare League Am., Washington, 1970-80; pres. Nat. Coun. for Adoption, Washington, from 1980. Co-author: Encyclopedia of Adoption, 1991; editor: Adoption Factbook I, 1986, II, 1989. Fellow Am. Orthopsychiatric Assn. Democrat. Roman Catholic. Home: Bethesda, Md. Died Jan. 13, 2004.

PINE, PATRICIA PALMER, aging services administrator; b. Portland, Maine, Mar. 14, 1940; d. Maurice George and Elizabeth Wadsworth (Syphers) Palmer; m. James Erlon Hannaford, Oct. 1, 1960 (div. June 1970); children: Paula L., Brenda J.; m. Vanderlyn Russell Pine, Aug. 9, 1974; stepchildren: Gordon K., Brian T., Daniel R. AB, Vassar Coll., 1972; MA, Columbia U., 1975; PhD, SUNY, Albany, 1993. Dir. Dutchess County Office for the Aging, Poughkeepsie, N.Y., 1976-80; assoc. dir. Hudson Valley Health Systems Agy., Tuxedo, N.Y., 1980-83; exec. dir. Hospice Assn. of Ulster County, Kingston, N.Y., 1983-84; assoc. exec. dir. WellCare N.Y., Kingston and Newburgh, 1984-86; dir. Ulster County Office Aging, Kingston, 1986-95; exec. dep. dir. N.Y. State Office For The Aging, Albany, 1995-2001, dir., 2001—03; prof. pub. svc. SUNY Albany Sch. Social Welfare, from 2003. Adj. prof. SUNY, New Paltz, 1973-95, Marist Coll., Poughkeepsie, 1976-79, 95, Adelphi U., L.I. City, 1983; pres. CEO The Gerontol Inst., 1993—; mem. faculty Brookdale Ctr. of Hunter Coll., 2000-03. Pres. United Way of Ulster County, Kingston, 1989-90; mem. N.Y. State Adv. Commn. on Aging-In Initiative, 1991-2003; trustee The Kingston Hosp., 1993-96; co-chair Panel for Elderly Prescription Ins. Program, 2001-03; chair Gov.'s Osteoporosis Edn. and Prevention Com., 2001—. Gerontol. Soc. Am. fellow, 1987, Paul Harris fellow Rotary Internat., 1989; named Vol. of the Yr., United Way of Ulster County,

1990. Fellow Gerontol. Soc. of Am.; mem. NASW, Nat. Coun. on Aging, N.Y. State Assn. Area Agys. on Aging (rec. sec. 1978-80, chair statewide conf. 1980, chair tng. com. 1986-88, pres. 1995). Avocations: travel, reading. Home: New Paltz, NY. Died May 2, 2004.

PIRAINO, THOMAS, writer, retired electrical engineer; b. Syracuse, N.Y., Apr. 22, 1912; s. Paul and Domenica (La Macchia) P.; m. Theodora M. Merzani, July 4, 1937; children: Maria Burnham, Paula Grimes, Joanne Dahlgren, Andrea Stidsen, Thomas A. Assoc. in Liberal Arts, Massasoit C.C., 1988; cert. in elec. engring., MIT, 1938, cert. in mech. engring., 1941. Registered profl. engr., Mass. Elec. engring. draftsman USN-Charlestown Navy Yard, Boston, 1940-42; elec. designer E.B. Badger & Sons, Boston, 1942-45; elec. engr. Jackson & Moreland, Engrs., Boston, 1945-51; sr./project elec. engr. Chas. T. Main, Inc., Boston, 1951-78; freelance writer Braintree, Mass., from 1979. Author: The Sicilian Fisherman's Son, 1992. Vol. radio reader Talking Info. Ctr. Radio Sta. for Visually Impaired, Marshfield, Mass., 1984-89; mem. Rep. Party, 1978—. Mem. IEEE (sr., life mem.), Am. Inst. Elec. Engrs. (sr. mem., chmn. pub. com. 1958-59, gen. meetings com. 1960-62, chmn. Yearbook com. 1962-63). Roman Catholic. Home: Braintree, Mass. Died Apr. 20, 2004.

PIRKLE, ESTUS WASHINGTON, minister, writer; b. Vienna, Ga., Mar. 12, 1930; s. Grover Washington and Bessie Nora (Jones) P.; m. Annie Catherine Gregory, Aug. 18, 1955; children: Letha Dianne, Gregory Don. BA cum laude, Mercer U., 1951; BD, MRE, Southwestern Bapt. Sem., 1956, ThM, 1958; DD, Covington Theol. Sem., 1982. Ordained to ministry So. Bapt. Conv., 1949. Pastor Locust Grove Bapt. Ch., New Albany, Miss. Spkr. Camp Zion, Myrtle, Miss. Author: Wintertime, 1968, Preachers in Space, 1969, Sermon Outlines Book, 1969, Are Horoscopes All Right?, 1971, I Believe God, 1973, Who Will Build Your House?,1978, The 1611 King James Bible: A Study by Dr. Estus Pirkle, 1994; prodr. religious films: If Footmen Tire You, What Will Horses Do?, 1973, The Burning Hell, 1975, Believer's Heaven, 1977, Percy ray - A Ray for God, 1998. Died Mar. 3, 2005.

PISHKIN, VLADIMIR, psychologist, educator; b. Belgrade, Yugoslavia, Mar. 12, 1931; came to U.S., 1946, naturalized, 1951; s. Vasili and Olga (Bartosh) P.; m. Dorothy Louise Martin, Sept. 12, 1953; children— Gayle Ann, Mark Vladimir. BA, Mont. State U., 1951, MA, 1955; PhD, U. Utah, 1958. Dir. neuropsychiat. research labs. VA Hosp., Tomah, Wis., 1959-62; chief research psychologist Behavioral Sci. Labs., Oklahoma City, 1962-75. Prof. psychiatry Coll. Medicine, U. Okla. Health Scis. Ctr., Oklahoma City, 1973-93, prof. emeritus, 1994; chmn. rsch. coun. dept. psychiatry and behavioral scis., 1972-75; bd. dirs. VA Med Ctr., Oklahoma City; dir. clin rsch. Willow View Hosp., Oklahoma City, 1987—. Author: (with Mathis and Pierce) Basic Psychiatry, rev. 3d edit, 1977; editor in chief: Jour. Clin. Psychology, 1974—; contbr. numerous articles to profl. jours. Served with USAF, 1952-54. Recipient Disting. Service award Jr. C. of C. Fellow Am. Psychol. Assn., Am. Psychol. Soc.; mem. Southwestern Psychol. Assn. (pres. 1973-74), Okla. Psychol. Assn.(Disting. Psychologist award 1986), Midwestern Psychol. Assn., AAAS, Psychonomics Soc. Clubs: Masons, Shriners. Home: Oklahoma City, Okla. Died Apr. 8, 2006.

PITTS, GERTRUDE LOUISE, minister; d. Samuel Norris and Myrtle Lewis; m. Robert David Pitts, Aug. 25, 1956 (dec. Mar. 14). Student, Buffalo Bible Inst.; BTh, Am. Bible Inst.; DD, A. E. W. Inst. of Cathedral of the Living Word, Balt., 1986. Apptd. bishop 1996. Nat. pres. Youth Ch. Mt. Calvary Holy Chs. of Am., Inc., 1941—83, nat. missionary pres., dist. mother Wis.-Ohio-Mich. dist.; pastor Mt. Calvary Ch., Milw., from 1957. Active Neighborhood Action Group, 2001. Recipient Cert. Merit and Honor, U. Wis.-Milw. Dept. Edn., Min. of Yr. award, Inner City Travel Svc., Inc., 1984, Black Excellence award, Milw. Times, Econo Print, and Mils. Jour./Sentinel, 1996, citation, Wis. State Assembly, 2001. Pentecostal. Avocations: collecting pigs, reading, listening to music and singing. Home: Milwaukee, Wis. Died Feb. 23, 2005.

PIZZIMENTI, DAVID MICHAEL, minister; b. Chicago Heights, Ill., Mar. 9, 1954; s. Louis John and Carolyn Dean (Morgan) P.; m. Judy Ann Konkol, Apr. 1974 (div. 1980); children: Jessica Marie, Joshua Michael; m. Kelly Elise Burden, Oct. 24, 1981. AA, Enterprise (Ala.) Jr. Coll., 1985. Ordained to ministry, 1986. Founding pastor Glory to Him Fellowship, Inc., Ozark, Ala., from 1987; Ala. dist. dir. Rhema Ministerial Assn., Tulsa, from 1989. With U.S. Army, 1981-86. Home: Ozark, Ala. Died July 7, 2004.

PLATNER, WARREN, architect; b. Balt., June 18, 1919; s. Warren Kelly and Alice Darling (Chapman) P.; m. Joan Payne, 1945; children: Bronson, Joan, Sharon, Madeleine. B.Arch., Cornell U., 1941. Assoc. Eero Saarinen and Assocs. (architects), 1950-65; propr. Warren Platner Assocs. (architects), New Haven, 1965—2006. Vis. lectr. archtl. schs. Prin. works include Kent Meml. Library, Suffield, Conn., 1972, Princeton U. Prospect Center, 1970, MGIC Hdqrs, Milw., 1973, Am. Restaurant, Kansas City, Mo., 1974; malls at Water Tower Pl., Chgo., 1975, Windows on the World, N.Y.C., 1976, Standard Brands Research Center, Wilton, Conn., 1979, Providence Athenaeum, 1980; Sea Containers Hdqrs., London, 1983, Wildflower Restaurant Lodge, Vail, Colo., 1985, Porter, Wright, Morris & Arthur Headqrs., Columbus, Ohio, 1986, Pan Am Bldg. additions, N.Y.C., 1987, ships Fantasia and Fiesta, 1990, Carlyle Hotel additions, 1990, Fain Residence, 1990, Friedman Residence, 1993, The Upstairs at '21', 2002. Recipient Rome prize architecture, 1955; advanced research Fulbright award architecture, 1955; Graham Found. award advanced studies fine arts, 1962; 1st ann. award Designers Lighting Forum, 1975; Pres.'s fellow R.I. Sch. Design, 1980; Interior Design Hall of Fame award, 1985; also several internat. design awards. Fellow AIA, Am. Acad. in Rome. Died Apr. 17, 2006.

PLAUCHÉ, JACK FOGGIN, insurance and investment agent; b. Marietta, Ohio, Nov. 6, 1937; s. LeMoyne E. and Vivian F. Plauché; m. Nancy C. Siferd, Aug. 1959 (div. Aug. 1979); children: Michel, Jacqui, Jon; m. Rosalie A. Chaput, Mar. 21, 1980. BSc, Ohio U., 1959. CLU. Agt. Plauché Ins. Planning, Parkersburg, W.Va., from 1962. Past pres. YMCA, Parkersburg, 1972; past chmn. bd. dirs. Salvation Army, Parkersburg, 1992. Capt. U.S. Army, 1959-62. Fellow Life Underwriters Training Coun.; mem. Life Underwriters Assn., Nat. Quality Award, Million Dollar Round Table. Republican. Roman Catholic. Avocations: boating, travel. Died Dec. 11, 2004.

PLAUT, THOMAS F.A., psychologist; b. NYC, Dec. 29, 1925; s. Alfred and Margaret (Blumenfeld) P.; m. Evelyn Z. McPuroff, Dec. 26, 1950 (div. Sept. 15, 1976); children: Melanie, Anthony, Jeffrey, Daphne, Iris, Roger; m. Bonnie A. Cox, Nov. 27, 1976; stepchildren: Carole, Susan. BA, Swarthmore Coll., 1949; PhD, Harvard U., 1956, MPH, 1957. Dir. alcoholism program State Mass., Boston, 1961-62; rsch. assoc. Stanford (Calif.) Univ., 1963-67; asst. chief Ctr. for Alcoholism NIMH, Bethesda, Md., 1962-69, dir. tng. divsn. Rockville, Md., 1969-71, dep. dir., 1974-79, dir. prevention, 1979-80, assoc. divsn. dir. biometry, 1987-92; pub. health advisor Ctr. Mental Health, Rockville, 1993-95; cons. in field Bethesda, from 1995. Consumer advisor Giant Foods, Landover, Md., 1988-92. Author: Alcohol Problems, 1967; co-author: Personality In Communal Society, 1956, Treatment of Alcoholism, 1967. Served in U.S. Army, 1944-46. Fellow APA, Am. Sociol. Assn.; mem. APHA (life), Phi Beta Kappa, Delta Omega. Democrat. Home: Princeton Junction, NJ. Died Aug. 20, 2004.

PLEXICO, WALTER MOORE, JR., college dean; b. Union, S.C., Mar. 3, 1945; s. Walter Moore and Elizabeth Zena (Hood) P.; m. Donna Cooper, July 8, 1967; children: D. Michelle, Karen E. BA, Wofford Coll., Spartanburg, S.C., 1967; MEd, U. N.C., Charlotte, 1971; MLibrarianship, U. S.C., 1976; EdD, U. Ga., 1980. Counselor, dir. counseling Spartanburg Meth. Coll., 1971-73, dept. chairperson, 1973-75, dir. learning resources, 1975-77; asst. dean instrn. Rockingham Community Coll., Wentworth, N.C., 1980-84; dean of instrn. Haywood Community Coll., Clyde, N.C., from 1984. Grad. Leadership Program, Western N.C.; sec. Pisgah coun. Girl Scouts U.S., 1989-92; mem. Exec. Leadership Mgmt., Raleigh, N.C., 1990—; chair small bus. com. Econ. Adjustment Strategy Effort, Waynesville, N.C., 1990-92; active Haywood County Arts Coun., Waynesville, 1987—, pres., 1987, Tuscola Band Boosters, Waynesville, 1990-91; bd. mem. Western N.C. Associated Cmtys., 1992-94; coord. com. Atlanta Ballet Summer Residency, 1991—. Lt. U.S. Army, 1968-70. Mem. Haywood County C. of C. (bd. dirs. 1991-94), Haywood Rotary Club (pres. 1989-90), Leadership Haywood Alumni (sec., v.p., pres. 1989—), N.C. C.C. Instructional Adminstrs. (sec. 1987-89). Mem. Haywood County C. of C. (bd. dirs. 1991—), Haywood Rotary Club (pres. 1989-90), Leadership Haywood Alumni (sec., v.p., pres. 1989—), N.C. Commun. Coll. Instructional Adminstrs. (sec. 1987-89). Democrat. Methodist. Avocation: model railroading. Home: Waynesville, NC. Died June 14, 2005.

POHL, LEIF ALAN, minister; b. Milw., Sept. 22, 1940; s. Neil Alan and Frieda (Radtke) P.; m. Janice Jean Forsyth, May 28, 1966; children: Eric, Jennifer, Andrew, Thomas. BA, U. Colo., 1962; MDiv, Luth. Sch. Theology Chgo., 1966. Ordained to ministry Luth. Ch. Am., 1966. Campus pastor Ball State U., Muncie, Ind., 1966-69; pastor Holy Trinity Luth. Ch., Muncie, 1966-69, Faith Luth. Ch., Owensboro, Ky., 1969-76, Our Saviour Luth. Ch., Valparaiso, Ind., 1976-85, Grace Luth. Ch., Muscatine, Iowa, from 1985. Pres. Porter County Coun. Luth. Chs., Valparaiso, 1982-84; pastor, supr. Luth. Sch. Theology, Chgo., 1986—; bd. dirs. Porter County Luth. Relief Fund, Portage, Ind. Contbr. articles to ch. publs. Bd. dirs. Muscatine County Commn. on Aging, 1987—. Home: Muscatine, Iowa. Died May 28, 2005.

POLL, HEINZ, choreographer, artistic director; b. Oberhausen, Germany, Mar. 18, 1926; arrived in U.S., 1964, naturalized, 1975; s. Heinrich and Anna Margarete (Winkels) Poll. Dancer Nat. Ballet Chile, 1952—62; co-founder, dir. The Dance Inst., U. Akron, 1967-77; founder, artistic dir., choreographer Ohio Ballet, Akron, 1968-99. Tchr. Chilean Instituto de Extension Musical, 1951—61, N.Y. Nat. Acad., 1965—66. Dancer Göttingen Mcpl. Theatre, 1947—49, Deutsches Theatre Konstanz, 1949—50, East Berlin State Opera, 1950—51, Nat. Ballet Chile, 1964, Ballet de la Jeunesse Musicales de France, 1963—64; guest artist Nat. Ballet Chile, 1964, Am. Dance Festival, 1965; choreographer Nat. Ballet Chile, Paris Festival Ballet, Ballet de la Jeunnesses Musicales de France, Nat. Ballet Can., Pa. Ballet, Ohio Ballet, Limon Dance Co., dancer Ellen Kogan. Recipient Ohio Dance award, 1983, 1988—89, Achievement Dance award, No. Ohio Live Mag., 1985—86, 1988—89, 1993—94, 1994—95, 1996—97, Cleve. Arts prize, 1995, Irma Lazarus Govs. award, 1999; grantee, Endowment for Arts, 1974—75. Mem.: NEA (dance panelist 1987—89, 1992—93). Died Apr. 30, 2006.

POLLAN-COHEN, SHIRLEY, poet, educator; b. N.Y.C., June 6, 1924; d. Benjamin and Anna (Flatow) Pollan; children: Robert, Linda. Student, CUNY, 1967. Editor newsletter Bronx C.C., CUNY, 1974-76, adminstrv. asst., 1980-99. Tutor ESL students, 1993-95; cons. Bronx Coun. on Arts, 1983-90. Performer poetry Bronx Mus. Arts, Acad. Gerontol. Edn. and Devel., Bronx C.C., Coll. of Mt. St. Vincent, Fordham U., Kingsbridge Heights C.C., Hostos C.C., CUNY, Lehman Coll., CUNY, also others; contbr. poetry to Bronx Roots I, II and III, Connections, Grub Street, Jewish Currents, Heiroglyphics Press, Garland, also others. Vol. Share the Gift of Literacy program, Bronx C.C., 1998—; mem. nat. women's com. Brandeis U. Poets and Writers grantee, 1986-89. Mem. Poets and Writers (grantee 1986-91), Bronx Poets and Writers Alliance (bd. dirs. 1983-90), Internat. Women's Writing Guild, Phi Theta Kappa. Avocations: crocheting, making jewelry, walking, reading, attending concerts. Died Apr. 6, 2006.

POLLIS, MARCIA FELDMAN, social worker; b. N.Y.C., July 13, 1937; d. Murray and Eva (Taub) Feldman; m. Merle Robert Pollis, June 10, 1956; children: Gail Rachel Spiro, Andrew Stuart. BA, U. Pitts., 1973; M in Social Service Adminstrn., Case Western Res. U., 1975. Dir. social services Woodruff Hosp., Cleve., 1975-86; pvt. practice clin. social work Shaker Heights, Ohio, from 1978; supr. staff devel. St. Vincent Charity Hosp., Cleve., 1986-89; outpatient therapist Kaiser-Ohio Permanente, Cleve., from 1989. Co-chmn. Peace and Social Welfare Com., Cleve., 1977-78. Fellow Acad. Cert. Social Workers; mem. Orthopsychiat. Assn., Nat. Assn. Social Workers. Avocations: writing, acting. Home: Cleveland, Ohio. Died Apr. 3, 2004.

POMPEDDA, MARIO FRANCESCO CARDINAL, bishop, lawyer; b. Ozieri, Sardinia, Italy, Apr. 18, 1929; Attended, Archiepiscopal Seminary, Sassari, Italy, Reg. Seminary, Cagliari, Pontifical Biblical Inst.; ThD, Pontifical Gregorian U., Rome; D of Canon Law, Pontifical Lateran U.; LLD (hon.), Inst. Catholique, Paris, 1995. Ordained priest Roman Cath. Ch., 1951; pastoral work, 1951—81; tribunal Sacred Roman Rota, 1955—93, dean, 1993; pres. Appellate Ct, Vatican City, 1993—99; consecrated bishop, 1998; Ecclesiastical Counsellor of the Order, 2003—06; prefect Supreme Tribunal of Apostolic Signature, 1999—2004; prefect emeritus, 2004—06; created cardinal, 2001. Faculty canon law Pontifical Gregorian U., Roman Athenaeum of Holy Cross. Died Oct. 18, 2006.

PONCE, ARNOLDO A., financial analyst, poet; b. San Salvador, El Salvador, Ctrl. Am., Dec. 2, 1945; s. Francisco A. and Julia Ponce; m. Thelma D. Ponce, May 25, 1975; children: Julia M., Jorge A. Acct., Escuela Nacional De Comercio, 1964. Mgr. fire ins. dept. Seguros E Inversiones S.a., San Salvador, El Salvador, 1965—74; purchase agt. Mkay Teer Constructors, San Salvador, El Salvador, 1975—78; mgr. claim dept. Aseguradora Popular S. A., San Salvador, El Salvador, 1979—86; pres. Patria S.a. De C.v. Asesores De Seguros, San Salvador, El Salvador, 1986—88; fin. advisor Provident Mut. Life Ins., Terrytown, 1989—93; rsch. analyst Thomson Fin., Northport, NY, from 1993. Claim pres. Asociacion Salvadorena De Aseguradores, San Salvador, 1982—83. Author: (poetry book) Pedazos De Cristal. Vol. Cath. Charities, Huntington, NY, 1992—94. Mem.: Asociacion De Contadores Publicos De El Salvador (assoc.). Democrat-Npl. Roman Catholic. Achievements include design of Forms And Operative Manuals For Claims Insurance. Avocations: travel, camping, poetry. Home: Kings Park, NY. Died Sept. 27, 2004.

PONDER, JERRY WAYNE, historian; b. Doniphan, Mo., Aug. 8, 1937; s. Leonard and Hazel (Keel) P.; m. Janice Ruth Albright, Oct. 11, 1962; 1 child. BBA, SUNY, Albany, 1961. Surveyor Mo. Hwy. Dept., Sikeston, 1956-60; fgn. svc. officer U.S. Dept. State, 1966-79; freelance hist. rschr., Doniphan, Mason, Tex., 1980-90 and from 93; dir., curator Current River Heritage Mus., Doniphan, 1990-93. Mem. Tex. Hist. Commn., 1998—. Author: The 15th Missouri Cavalry Regiment, 1994, The Battle of Chalk Bluff, 1996, The Civil War of Fredericktown, Mo., 1997, Fort Mason, Texas, Training Ground, 1997, Major General John S. Marmaduke, CSA, 1999, General Sterling Price's 1864 Invasion of Missouri, 1999. Pres. Ripley County Water Dist., Doniphan, 1985-91; v.p. Ripley County Hist. Soc., 1990-92; bd. dirs. Doniphan Neighborhood Assistance Program, 1990-93; bd. dirs. Cochise C.C., Sierra Vista, Ariz., 1977-78. Officer U.S. Army, 1960-66. Named Writer of Yr., So. Hist. Writers Assn., 1987, hon. Ky. Col., 1991. Mem. State Hist. Soc. Mo., Ark. Hist. Assn., Tex. Hist. Soc., Libr. Congress Assn., Southwestern Writer's League. Home: Mason, Tex. Died July 16, 2005.

POOLE, ALMA LOUISE, federal agency administrator; b. Kansas City, Mo., Apr. 27, 1939; d. Elder Luther W. and Alma C. (McWilliams) S.; m. George Lee Poole Sr., May 14, 1955; children: George Jr., Angela, Virgil, Terry Poole. BA, Mid Am. Nazarene Coll., 1984. Cert. Air Traffic Controller. Tax examiner IRS, Kansas City, 1968-72; air traffic controller FAA, Burlington, Iowa, 1972-75, Emporia, Kans., 1975-76, Kansas City, 1976-81, equal employment opportunity specialist Olathe, Kans., 1981-85, air traffic control tng. specialist, 1985-86, personnel staffing specialist Kansas City, from 1986, investigator, from 1982. Author One PK's Opinion, 1986. Vol. Planned Parenthood, Kansas

City, 1976-80, United Auto Workers Women Vols., 1979-83, Women United, 1981-84, Big Bros./Big Sisters, Kansas City, 1977-83; sec. A. Philip Randolph Inst., Kansas City, 1983-85. Recipient Spl. Service award Fed. Exec. Bd., Kansas City, 1982, Community Service award So. U., 1984, Mgrs. award Fed. Women Program, Washington, 1985. Mem. Am. Bus. Women (pres. 1982-84), Negro Bus. and Profl. Women (chairperson 1987—). Clubs: We're On Our Way Investment (pres. 1986—). Democrat. Pentecostal. Avocations: sewing, cooking. Died Dec. 7, 2004.

POPE, TONY ALLEN, transportation executive; b. Newton, N.C., June 25, 1944; s. Forrest Eugene and Glenna Mae (Schell) P.; m. Patricia Ann Bumgarner, Oct. 4, 1964; children: John Robert, Tina Lynn. Student, King's Bus. Coll., Charlotte, N.C., 1962-64. Cost dept. mgr. Charles Pindyck Co., Inc., Newton, 1964-67; sec., treas. Catawba Rental Co., Inc., Claremont, N.C., 1967-80, pres., from 1980, Cargo Transporters, Inc., Claremont, from 1983, Freight Connection, Inc., Claremont, from 1984. Chmn. City of Claremont Planning Bd., 1977; pres. St. Mark's Luth. Ch., Claremont, 1979, United Way, Newton, 1980. Served with USNG, 1966-72. Recipient Outstanding Service award St. Mark's Luth. Ch., 1979; named Boss of Yr., Hickory (N.C.) Jaycees, 1984. Mem. Am. Truck Leasing Network (v.p. 1980—), Truck Renting and Leasing Assn. (bd. dirs. 1986—), N.C. Car and Truck Leasing Assn. (bd. dirs. Raleigh chpt. 1972—), N.C. Trucking Assn., Catawba Valley Traffic Club, Catawba County C. of C. (v.p. 1987—), Am. Legion, Delta Nu Alpha Traffic Club. Clubs: Catawba Country. Lodges: Rotary (pres. Newton chpt. 1985-85). Avocaitons: golf, skiing. Died May 31, 2005.

PORTELA, MARY GREEN, primary school educator; b. Jacksonville, Fla., Mar. 22, 1932; d. Silas and Bertha Lee (Teart) Gillard; m. John Green, July 3, 1964 (div. Aug. 1974); children: Carolyn Geniece Franklin, Frederick Virgil Green; m. Saul Portela Rosales, Dec. 18, 1988. AA, Edward Waters Coll., 1952; BS, Oakwood Coll., 1955; MA, Fla. A&M U., 1964; student, Walkers Comml. Bus. Coll., Fla. State U., U.S. Sch. Music, Inst. Children's Lit., from 1990. Cert. elem. tchr., Fla. Tchr. counseling, music, elem. edn. Greenville (Fla.) Tng. Sch., 1957-71; tchr. mental retardation Greenville (Fla.) Primary Sch., 1971-85, tchr. phys. edn., 1985-87, Fla's. model classroom/pre-kindergarten intervention tchr., 1987-90; adult basic edn. tchr. North Fla. Jr. Coll., Madison, Fla., 1975-90. Musician, singer Shiloh Missionary Bapt. Ch., Greenville, 1968-78, and other churches of Madison, Leon and Jefferson County including New Hope Primitive Bapt. Ch., Serman, Fla., Greenville Ch. of God, 1956-90. Author: A Journey To Heaven, 1989, Everybody Has To Cry Sometime, 1988, God's Protection, 1989, The Christmas Child, 1989; (poetry) Everybody Has To Cry Sometimes, 1991; contbr. Glory To God In The Highest. Mem. Bush Task Force and Inner Circle, 1989-90; mem., charter founder The Ronald Reagan Rep. Ctr. and Smithsonian Instn., 1989-90; nursing home and missionary worker, Monticello, Tallahassee, Jacksonville and Madison, 1957-90, also other cities in U.S., Israel, Egypt, Greece and Guatemala, 1985-90. Mem. Habitat for Humanity, Madison County Tchr. Assn. (past v.p.), Higher Dimensions, NEA, Capital Area Progresive Woman's League (reporter 1989-90), Dwight Thompson World Outreach. Seventh Day Adventist. Avocations: singing, playing organ and piano, cooking, collecting, writing poems and short stories. Home: Greenville, Fla. Died Dec. 18, 2004.

PORTER, CHARLES ORLANDO, lawyer, former congressman; b. Klamath Falls, Oreg., Apr. 4, 1919; s. Frank Jason and Ruth (Peterson) P.; m. Priscilla Dean Galassi, Mar. 1, 1943; children: Donald Jason, Christopher Dean, Samuel Curry, Anne Julia. AB, JD, Harvard U., 1947. Bar: Oreg. 1948, U.S. Dist. Ct. Oreg., U.S. Ct. Appeals (9th cir.) 1952, U.S. Claims Ct. 1983, U.S. Supreme Ct. 1955. Law clk. to justice U.S. Ct. Appeals, San Francisco, 1947-48; asst. to survey legal profession dir. ABA, Boston, 1948-51; mem. U.S. Ho. of Reps., Washington, 1957-60; staff mem. The White House, 1961; sole practice Eugene, Oreg., 1951—56, 1961—2005. Author: (with others) The American Lawyer, 1955, The Struggle for Democracy in Latin America, 1961. Mem. Oreg. State Bar Assn. Democrat. Mem. United Ch. of Christ. Avocations: squash, swimming, jogging. Home: Eugene, Oreg. Died Jan. 1, 2006.

PORTER, MICHAEL ARTHUR, chemicals executive; b. W.Va., Sept. 23, 1949; s. Arthur Porter; m. Paula Savoie; 1 child, Michael Jr.; children from previous marriage: Leigh Porter Osborne, Scott. MBA, W.Va., 1971. With contr.'s dept. Union Carbide Corp., Florence, S.C., 1971-75; asst. to v.p. Linde Welding Products, Tarrytown, N.Y., 1976; bus. analyst to pres. Linde. divsn. Union Carbide Corp., Tarrytown, 1977-78, with sales dept. Linde. divsn. Houston, 1978, area sales mgr. state of La., 1979; pres. Mon Arc, Houston, 1980-81; regional mktg. mgr. Gulf Coast, Houston, 1982-83; v.p. sales & mktg. Kaldair divsn. British Petroleum, 1984-85; v.p., gen. mgr. Airco P.S.A., 1985, BOC Internat. P.S.A., 1987; pres., ceo Generon Systems, Houston, from 1988. Pres., bd. dirs. Aquagolf, Houston and Fla. Planary speaker Nat. Innovation Workshop, U. Houston, 1990; chmn.-dir. Doug Sanders Celebrity Classic Sr. PGA Golf Tour. Mem. Internat. Oxygen Mfrs. Assn., N.Am. Membrane Soc., Chem. Mfrs. Soc., Am. Chem. Soc., Am. Welding Soc., Am. Petroleum Inst., Houston N.W. C. of C., Forum Club Houston. Avocations: golf, tennis. Home: Houston, Tex. Died Feb. 10, 2005.

PORTER, WILLIAM ROBERT, academic administrator; b. Bklyn., Nov. 3, 1922; s. William E. and Laura E. (Manger) P.; m. Jeanne Merle Sargent, Oct. 7, 1949. BS, U.S. Naval Acad., 1946; BSEE, Mass. Inst. Tech., 1948; Naval Engr., MIT, 1955; MSEE, Mass. Inst. Tech., 1955; PhD, U. Calif., 1960; MA, U. Md., 1968. Enlisted USN, 1940, commd. ensign, 1946, advance through grades to capt., 1967, retired, 1973; dir. edn. C.S. Draper Lab., Cambridge, Mass., 1973-74; v.p. academic affairs SUNY Maritime Coll., Ft. Schuyler, 1974-92. Died May 28, 2005.

PORTUESI, DONNA RAE, psychotherapist, consultant; b. Easton, Pa., Nov. 19, 1949; d. Peter and Alice Lorraine (Hull) Stagnito; m. Sebastian Portuesi, Jr., Nov. 22, 1972 (div. Sept. 1986); 1 child, Christi Noel Buck. AA, No. Seattle C.C., 1987; BA magna cum laude, Western Wash. U., 1989; MSW cum laude, U. Wash., 1992. Registered counselor, Wash. Sec. for Sen. Harry Byrd, Jr. U.S. Senate, Washington, 1970-72; founder Denver chpt. Nat. Found. for Crohn's and Colitis, 1975-79; counselor Mental Health Svcs., Everett, Wash., 1982-84; co-founder Adoption Search and Counseling Cons., Seattle, 1990-96; psychotherapist, cons. ASCC Svcs., Seattle, from 1992. Press and speech asst. U.S. Senate, Washington, 1970-72; post adoption cons., Seattle, 1992-96; workshop developer, leader Adoption Search and Counseling, Seattle, 1992-96, exec. dir., 1990-96; ind. search cons. Reunite Adoptees and Birth Parents, 1991—. Contbr. articles to profl. jours. Mem. NASW, Am. Counseling Assn., Am. Adoption Congress. Democrat. Avocations: piano, travel, pets, reading, arts and crafts. Died July 13, 2004.

POST, LEO BLAISE, chemical engineer; b. Chgo., Feb. 3, 1918; s. Jacob and Caroline (LaPata) Poskonka; m. Mary A. Biluk; children: Michael J., Elisabeth E., Carole A., Thomas J. BSChE, Ill. Inst. Tech., 1938. Registered profl. engr., Ill. Analytical chemist Victor Chem. Works, Chicago Heights, Ill., 1938-41, chem. engr., 1941-46, group supr. inorganic process devel., 1946-57; asst. mgr. process devel. Victor divsn. Stauffer Chem., Chicago Heights, 1957-62, mgr. process devel., 1962-65; mgr. process devel. ea. rsch. ctr. Stauffer Chem. Co., Dobbs Ferry, N.Y., 1965-80; cons. New City, N.Y., from 1980. Mem. Am. Chem. Soc. (emeritus), AIChE. Achievements include 15 patents. Home: New City, NY. Died Nov. 29, 2004.

POTTS, RAMSAY DOUGLAS, lawyer; b. Memphis, Oct. 24, 1916; s. Ramsay Douglas and Ann Clifton (VanDyke) Potts; m. Veronica Hamilton Raynor, Dec. 22, 1945 (dec. May 1993); children: Ramsay Douglas, David Hamilton, Lesley Ann, Lindsay Veronica. BS, U. N.C., 1941; LL.B., Harvard U., 1948. Bar: Tenn. 1948, DC 1954, U.S. Supreme Ct. 1957. Commd. 2d lt. USAAF, 1941, advanced through grades to maj. gen. Res., 1961; various combat and operational assignments (8th Air Force and Air Force Res.), 1942-60; chmn. Air Force Res. Policy Com., 1967-68; practice law, Washington, from 1955; spl. asst. to chmn. Nat. Security Resources Bd., 1951; pres. Ind. Mil. Air Transport Assn., 1952-55; ptnr. Shaw, Pittman, Potts & Trowbridge, 1956-86; sr. counsel Pillsbury Winthrop Shaw Pittman (formerly Shaw, Pittman, Potts & Trowbridge), Washington, 1986—2006. Pub.: Air Power History, 1989—93; contbr. articles to profl. jours. Mem. State Coun. Higher Edn. Va., 1968—71; trustee Air Force Hist. Found., pres., 1971—75, Washington Area Tennis Patrons Found., 1984—87; trustee emeritus Physicians for Peace, 1989—2006. Decorated DSC, others. Mem.: ABA, DC Bar Assn., Internat. Lawn Tennis Club, Army Navy Country Club (Arlington, Va.), Met. Club (Washington), Phi Beta Kappa. Home: Delray Beach, Fla. Died May 28, 2006.

POTUZNIK, CHARLES LADDY, lawyer; b. Chgo., Feb. 11, 1947; s. Charles William and Laverne Frances (Zdenek) P.; m. Mary Margaret Quady, Jan. 2, 1988; children: Kylie Brommell, Kathryn Mary. BA with high honors, U. Ill., 1969; JD cum laude, Harvard U., 1973. Bar: Minn. 1973. Assoc. Dorsey & Whitney LLP, Mpls., 1973-78, ptnr., corp. group, from 1979, and co-chmn., broker dealer area. Co-head Broker-Dealer and Investment Markets Regulation Practice Group. Mem. Minn. State Bar Assn. (chmn. state securities law subcom. 1987-2000), Hennepin County Bar Assn., Minn. Securities Adv. Com., Phi Beta Kappa. Mem. Evang. Free Ch. Avocations: hunting, fishing, camping, canoeing, foreign travel. Died Mar. 22, 2005.

POUGH, FREDERICK HARVEY, mineralogist; b. Bklyn., June 26, 1906; s. Francis H. and Alice H. (Beckler) P.; m. Eleanor C. Hodge, Oct. 14, 1938 (dec. May 1966); children: Frederick Harvey, Barbara Hodge. SB, Harvard, 1928, PhD, 1935; MS, Washington U., 1932; student, Ruperto Carola, Heidelberg, Germany, 1932-33. Asst. curator mineralogy Am. Mus. Natural History, N.Y.C., 1935-40, acting curator, 1941, curator, 1942-44, curator phys. geology and mineralogy, 1942-52, cons. mineralogist, 1953—64; gem cons. Jewelers Circular-Keystone, 1940-85. Dir. Santa Barbara Mus. Natural History, 1965-66; pres. Mineralogy, Inc., 1978—2006 Author: Jewelers Dictionary, 1945, 50, 76, 96, Field Guide to Rocks and Minerals, 1952, 72, 97, All About Volcanoes and Earthquakes, 1953, Hindi translation, 1958, Persian translation, 1959, Bengali translation, 1959, Italian translation, 1960, Arabic translation, 1962, Portuguese translation, 1964, Our Earth, 1961, The Story of Gems and Semi-Precious Stones, 1967, Guide des Roches et Mineraux, 1969, 79, First Guide to Rocks and Minerals, 1991; contbg. editor: Lapidary jour. Recipient Bronze medal Royal Geol. Soc., Belgium, 1948, Derby medal Brazilian Geol. Survey, Hanneman award for outstanding contbns. in lit. of mineralogy and gemology, 1988, Mineral. award Carnegie Mus. Nat. History, Pitts., 1989, Lifetime Achievement award Accredited Gemologist Assn., 1993; named Mineralogist of Yr., Am. Fedn. Mineral Soc., 1966. Fellow Mineral Soc. Am., Geol. Soc. Am.; mem. Mineral Soc. Gt. Britain., Gemmological Assn. All Japan (Am. rep.). Clubs: Harvard (N.Y.C.); Explorers. Home: Pittsford, NY. Died Apr. 7, 2006.

POUL, FRANKLIN, lawyer; b. Phila., Nov. 6, 1924; s. Boris and Anna P.; m. Shirley Weissman, June 26, 1949; children— Leslie Poul Melman, Alan M., Laurie Price. Student, U. Pa., 1942-43, Haverford Coll., 1943-44; LL.B. cum laude, U. Pa., 1946. Bar: Pa. 1949, U.S. Supreme Ct. 1955. Asso. firm Gray, Anderson, Schaffer & Rome, Phila., 1948-56, Wolf, Block, Schorr and Solis-Cohen, Phila., 1956-60, partner, 1960-93. Bd. dirs. ACLU, Phila., 1955-80, pres., 1975-76. Served with AUS, 1943-46. Mem. ABA, Am. Law Inst., Order of Coif. Home: Wynnewood, Pa. Died Aug. 27, 2006.

POWER, BARBARA LOUISE, artist, educator; b. Niskayuna, N.Y., Jan. 14, 1958; d. Thomas Dunbar and Norma Virginia Power; m. Joshua Arthur Muskin, July 5, 1992; 1 child, Saul E. Muskin. BS, Western Mich. U., Kalamazoo, 1980; MA in Art Edn., R.I. Sch. of Design, Providence, 1985; MFA, Vt. Coll. assoc. with Norwich U., Montpelier, 1998. Cert. tchr. Va., 2001. Adj. instr. Bainbridge Coll., 1992—98, Valdosta (Ga) State U., 1997; pt. time instr. FACE, Tallahassee, 1998; adj. instr. Frederick (Md.) Cmty. Coll., 1999; tchr. Langley HS, McLean, Va., 1999—2002. Summer student Penland Sch., NC, 1989, 95, Fla. State U., Tallahassee, 1993, Anderson Ranch, Snowmass, Colo., 1994; instr. summer Corcoran Sch. of Art, Washington, 1999, Md. Coll. of Art and Design, Silver Spring, 1999. One-woman shows include Cole Pratt Gallery, New Orleans, 1999, Roles and Rels., Divsn. of Cultural Arts, Tallahassee, 1995, Holden Gallery, Warren Wilson Coll., 1999. Chmn. United Way, Tallahassee, 1993—94; tutor Laubach Literacy, Tallahassee, 1992—95. Scholar Grassroots Cultural Program, Bainbridge (Ga.) Coll., 1995; Kast Grant, Germantown Acad., Ft. Wash., Pa., 1995. Mem.: Nat. Mus. of Women in the Arts, Washington Sculpture Group, Capitol Hill Art League. Democrat. Avocations: bicycling, reading, walking, yoga. Home: Silver Spring, Md. Died June 30, 2004.

POWER, NORMA JEAN, hospital dietary administrator; b. Bluffton, Ind., June 22, 1928; d. John Raymond and Nettie May (Gilbert) Young; m. James Burton Power, June 28, 1950; children: Susan, Steven, J. Bradley. BSHE, Purdue U., 1950; MS, Mich. State U., 1976. Registered dietitian Am. Dietetic Assn. Tchr. Bd. of Edn., Saginaw, Mich.; home svc. advisor Consumers Power Co., Saginaw; dietitian Wells County Hosp., Bluffton, Ind.; dir. of dietary Meml. Health Care Ctr., Owosso, Mich.; retired. Mem. AAUW, Dietetic Assn., Am. Soc. Hosp. Food Svc. Dirs., Gen. Fedn. Women's Club, Omicron Nu. Republican. Lutheran. Avocations: entertaining, travel. Home: Dayton, Ohio. Died Jan. 13, 2005.

POWERS, KAREN ELIZABETH, information technology manager; b. Warren, Ohio, Jan. 6, 1955; d. Shannon Curtis and Charlene (MacAtee) P.; 1 child, Elizabeth Sutliffe Grady Powers. BA, Emory U., 1977; MBA, Columbia U., 1980; MA, Boston U., 1995. Asst. treas. The Bank of NY, NYC, 1980-87; rsch. asst. Harvard U. Med. Sch., Boston, 1993-95; project coord. Harvard Sch. Pub. Health, Boston, 1996-98, project mgr. The Coll. Alcohol Study, 1998—2004; project mgr. condo conversions Coleman Realtors, Providence, from 2004. Episcopalian. Home: Barrington, RI. Died June 7, 2005.

POYNOR, DEBORAH ANN, English language educator; b. Chillicothe, Ohio, Dec. 11, 1952; d. Everett Hershall and Virginia Ann (Stanhope) Keller; m. Raymond Walter Poynor, Aug. 9, 1974; children: Dedra Ann, Brad Raymond, Jessica Renee. AS in Computers, Scioto Tech. Coll., 1973; BS, Ohio U., 1991. Cert. English and secondary edn. tchr., Ohio. Computer operator Med. Ctr. Hosp., Chillicothe, 1973-75; clk. Harrison Twp., Chillicothe, 1980-2000; substitute tchr. city and county schs., Chillicothe, 1991-96; dropout recovery specialist PIC 17 Workforce Bd., Chillicothe, from 1996. Honorary mem. Ross County Com. for the Elderly, 1985—, Ross County 4-H, 1983-95; vol. Ross County Adult Basic and Literacy Edn. program, 1994-96. Mem. Ross County Trustees and Clks. Assn., Ross County Homemakers. Avocations: reading, cooking, cross stitching, ceramics. Died June 6, 2005.

PRATER, JAMES FRANKLIN, auditor; b. San Francisco, May 16, 1943; s. Walter Rufus and Edith (Griffin) P. BS, San Jose State U., 1965. Sr. auditor Allstate Ins. Co., Menlo Park, Calif., 1970-72; instr. Hartnell Coll., Salinas, Calif., 1976-79; audit dir. 20th Century Ins. Co., Woodland Hills, Calif., from 1982. Mem. People for Am. Way, Washington, 1982-86. Served to sgt. U.S. Army, 1968-70. Mem. Inst. Internal Auditors (bd. mem., bd. govs., San Fernando Valley chpt. 1984-86, author, editor monthly newsletter), Calif. Real Estate Tchrs. Assn., Real Estate Cert. Inst. Democratic. Avocations: artistry, desert hiking. Home: Studio City, Calif. Died Jan. 6, 2005.

PRATER, RONALD F., retired aerospace engineer, career officer; b. Chgo., Oct. 11, 1934; s. Carroll E. and Selma D. (Funk) P.; m. Ellen Faye Wilson, Aug. 25, 1956; children: Richard E., Elizabeth P. Oligmueller, Ronald C. BA in

Physics, Grinnell Coll., 1956; MS in Applied Physics, UCLA, 1958; PhD in Aerospace Engring., Air Force Inst. Tech., 1970. Engr. Hughes Aircraft Co., Culver City, Calif., 1956-58; commd. 2d lt. USAF, 1956, advanced through grades to col., 1979; ret., 1984; project officer Air Force Weapons Lab. Kirkland AFB, N. Mex., 1958-65; rsch. scientist Air Force Materials Lab. Wright-Patterson AFB, Ohio, 1967-72; br. chief Air Force Weapons Lab. Kirkland AFB, N. Mex., 1972-78; program mgr. Def. Advanced Rsch. Projects Agy., Arlington, Va., 1978-84; ret. USAF, 1984; dir. BDM Internat., Tysons Corner, Va., 1984-85; sr. systems engr. W.J. Schafer Assoc., Inc., Arlington, Va., 1985-92, ret., 1992. Computer instr. United Cmty. Ministries, Alexandria, Va., 1995-97; computer adminstr. Aldersgate United Meth. Ch., Alexandria, 1995—. Mem. SPIE, Optical Soc. Am. (sec. nat. capital sect.), Stratford Landing Citizen's Assn. (treas. 1996—). Methodist. Avocations: tennis, photography, personal computers. Home: Alexandria, Va. Died Nov. 17, 2004.

PRATHER, ROBERT FRANKLIN, not-for-profit fundraiser; b. N.Y.C., Aug. 20, 1935; s. Theodore Roosevelt and Evelyn Trimarco P.; m. Jessie Holtby Prather, Nov. 14, 1959 (dec. Jan. 1989); children: Craig, Keith, Debra Jo, Todd, Adam, Jennifer; m. Monica Marshall Prather, Feb. 10, 1990; children: Kathy, Natalie. BS in Journalism, Ohio U., 1957; MA, Columbia U., 1964, EdD, 1981. Mng. editor Corning (N.Y.) Glass Works, 1964-66; dir. devel. The Coll. of Ins., N.Y.C., 1966-73; v.p. for devel. Mercyhurst Coll., Erie, Pa., 1973-80, Olivet (Mich.) Coll., 1980-82; v.p. univ. rels. Tiffin (Ohio) U., 1984-86; pres. W.Va. Found. for Ind. Colls., Charleston, 1986-93, Tex. Ind. Coll. Fund, Fort Worth, from 1993. Presiding officer Found. for Ind. Higher Edn., Washington, 1998-2001, southwestern regional rep., 1995-98, midwestern regional rep., 1990-93, dir., 1995—. Edn. com. State of W.Va., Charleston, 1990-93, advanced placement adv. com., 1990-93; pres. Erie (Pa.) Playhouse, 1973-80; co-pres. Coun. on Adoptable Children, Erie, 1973-80. Capt. U.S. Army, 1957-59, 61-62. Mem. Fort Worth Rotary, Found. for Ind. Higher Edn. (dir 1995—). Democrat. Avocations: reading, thinking. Died Aug. 5, 2005.

PRATT, HENRY LUCIUS, retired industrial engineer; b. L.I., Oct. 31, 1920; s. henry l. and L.H. (Hindley) P. BS, U. So. Calif., 1950. Mfg. engr. Lockheed Aricraft Co., Burbank, Calif., 1951-58, 1958-66, indsl. engr., 1966-76, ret., 1976. Sgt. Inf., 1944-46. Avocations: creative writing, photography. Home: Chula Vista, Calif. Died Nov. 28, 2004.

PRATT, ROBERT JOHN ALBERT, finance educator, consultant; b. Greensburg, Pa., July 22, 1930; s. Thomas Carden and Alice Ethel (Kepple) P.; m. Laura Lou Bills, June 3, 1955; children: Darcee Seanor Pratt Purvis, Lilas Kinsey Pratt, Sydney Kepple Pratt Girardi. BS, Carnegie Inst. Tech., Pitts., 1958, MS, 1960, postgrad. Lectr. U. Pitts. Grad. Sch. Bus., 1961-82; assoc. prof., dept. head Mgmt. U. Pitts., Greensburg, 1982-99, faculty emeritus, 1999—2004. Bd. dirs. Westmoreland County Humans Opportunities, Greensburg. Editor Pitts. Bus. Rev., 1962-74. Capt. USAF, 1953-57. Ford Found. fellow Carnegie Inst. Tech., 1961-62. Mem. Am. Legion, Lions. Republican. Presbyterian. Avocations: gardening, travel. Home: Ligonier, Pa. Died Aug. 4, 2004.

PRATT, ROSALIE REBOLLO, harpist, educator; b. N.Y.C., Dec. 4, 1933; d. Antonio Ernesto and Eleanor Gertrude (Gibney) Rebollo; m. George H. Mortimer, Esquire, Apr. 22, 1987; children: Francesca Christina Rebollo-Sborgi, Alessandra Maria Pratt Jones. MusB, Manhattanville Coll., 1954; MusM, Pius XII Inst. Fine Arts, Florence, Italy, 1955; EdD, Columbia U., 1976. Prin. harpist N.J. Symphony Orch., 1963-65; soloist Mozart Haydn Festival Avery Fisher Hall, N.Y.C., 1968; tchr. music pub. schs. Bloomfield and Montclair, N.J., 1962-73; mem. faculty Montclair State Coll., 1973-79; prof. Brigham Young U., Provo, Utah, 1984-99, coord. grad. studies dept. music, 1985-87, biofeedback and neurofeedback specialist, from 1993, prof. emeritus, from 1999; dir. R&D Music Health Inst., Provo, from 1999. U.S. chair 1st internat. arts medicine leadership conf., Tokyo Med. Coll., 1993. Author: Hospital Arts, 1997; co-author: Elementary Music for All Learners, 1980; editor Internat. Jour. Arts Medicine, 1991—, (procs.) 2d, 3d, 4th Internat. Symposia Music Edn. for Handicapped, Arts Medicine, 1997; sr. editor Music Medicine 3, 1999, Arts in Healthcare, 2003—; author, sr. editor: The Arts in Healthcare Movement in the U.S., 2003; contbr. articles to profl. jours. Recipient Utah Music Educator of the Yr., Utah Music Educators Assn., 1997; Fulbright grantee, 1979; Myron Taylor scholar, 1954. Mem. Am. Harp Soc. (Outstanding Svc. award 1973), AAUP (co-chmn. legis. rels. com. N.J. 1978-79), Internat. Soc. Music Edn. (chair commn. musicin spl. edn., music therapy, and medicine 1985—), Internat. Soc. Music in Medicine (v.p. 1993—), Internat. Assn. of Music for the Handicapped (co-founder, exec. dir., jour. editor), Coll. Music Soc., Music Educators Nat. Conf., Soc. for Study of Neuronal Regulation, Brigham Young U. Grad. Coun., Phi Kappa Phi, Sigma Alpha Iota. Home: West Plains, Mo. Died Dec. 31, 2005.

PRAUSNITZ, FREDERIK WILLIAM, conductor; b. Cologne, Germany, Aug. 26, 1920; came to U.S., 1937; s. Friedrich Julius and Maja Eleanor (Moritz) P.; m. Margaret Violet Prausnitz; children: Sebastian, Maja. Grad. diploma in conducting, Juilliard Grad. Sch., 1946. Condr., adminstr. Juilliard, N.Y.C., 1946-61; condr. of recs. for Angel Argo Columbia, EMI, Philips; condr. New Eng. Conservatory, Boston, 1961-69; music dir. Syracuse (N.Y.) Symphony Orch., 1971-74; music dir. to dir. of conducting programs Peabody Conservatory of Johns Hopkins U., Balt., 1976-97. Cons. The Lincoln Ctr., N.Y.C., 1963, Oakland U., Sussex (Eng.) U., 1969-71, Libr. of Congress, 2000. Author: Score and Podium: A Complete Guide to Conducting, 1983, Roger Sessions, How a Difficult Composer Got That Way, 2002. Recipient 1st prize for young condrs. Detroit Symphony, 1944, Mahler Medal of Honor Am. Bruckner Soc., 1974; Hon. Fellow Sussex U., Eng., 1969; Condr. Laureate Peabody Orch., Balt., 1982; Rockefeller Found. writing grantee. Mem. Savage Club (London). Home: Lewes, Del. Died Nov. 12, 2004.

PREGALDIN, ANTON JOSEPH, retired lawyer; b. Fieldon, Ill., Apr. 26, 1931; s. Charles Victor and Esther-Irene (Slater) P. AB, St. Louis U., 1953, JD, 1960; MA, U. Chgo., 1954. Bar: Mo. 1960. Assoc. gen. counsel Gen. Am. Life Ins. Co., St. Louis, 1957-92. Bd. dirs. Ctr. for French Colonial Studies, Prairie du Rocher, Ill., 1982-86; treas., v.p., bd. dirs. St. Louis-Lyon Sister Cities Com., 1985—. Woodrow Wilson fellow, 1953-54. Mem. Met. St. Louis Bar Assn., Mo. State Bar Assn., St. Louis County Bar Assn., French Soc. St. Louis (pre., sec., treas. bd. dirs.), Alliance Francaise St. Louis (pres. v.p., treas. bd. dirs.), Media Club, St. Louis Club, St. Louis Westerners Club, Alpha Sigma Nu, Delta Theta Phi. Democrat. Roman Catholic. Avocations: French lang. cultural activities, geneal. rsch., local history. Home: Saint Louis, Mo. Died June 8, 2004.

PREIS, CARL OTTO, company executive, mechanical engineer; b. Bklyn., Jan. 14, 1927; s. Otto and Madeline Adele Preis; m. Vera Marie Mayer, Aug. 2, 1952; children: Carl Ernest, Brenda Marie. Student, Cornell U., 1950-51; BME, Poly. U., Bklyn., 1957. Registered profl. engr., N.Y. WTS engr. Republic Aviation, Farmingdale, N.Y., 1951, missile design engr. Missile divsn. N.Y.C. and Hicksville, N.Y., 1951-58; with Hazeltine Corp., Little Neck, N.Y., 1959, shock and vibration cons. Green Lawn, N.Y., 1959-64; CEO, Preis Mayer Corp., Baldwin, N.Y., 1965-87, Copace Corp., Baldwin, from 1968. Cons. engr., Baldwin, 1955—; operator Timber Hill Farm, Presque Isle, Maine. Editor Atlantic Rock Artisans Newsletter, 1970-80. Night school instr. Baldwin Adult Edn., 1970-80; past pres. Rep. Social Club, Baldwin. With USNR, 1942-46. Mem. Am. Assn. for Artificial Intelligence, N.Y. Soc. Profl. Inventors, Pi Tau Sigma (hon.), Phi Sigma Kappa. Achievements include patent for variable frequency vibration absorber. Died Sept. 23, 2004.

PREISKEL, ROBERT HOWARD, lawyer; b. Passaic, N.J., Mar. 23, 1922; s. Louis and Lottie (Brown) P.; m. Barbara Scott, Oct. 28, 1950; children— John S., Richard A. BA, U. Mich., 1943; LL.B., Yale U., 1948. Bar: N.Y. bar 1948. Assoc. Fried, Frank, Harris, Shriver & Jacobson, N.Y.C., 1948-54, ptnr., 1954-91, of counsel, from 1991. Vis. lectr. Yale U., 1982, 83. Pres. NAACP Legal Def. and Ednl. Fund, Inc., 1984—; bd. dirs. Africa Watch, 1990—. Mem. ABA, N.Y. Bar Assn., Assn. of Bar of City of N.Y. (chmn. tax com. 1974-77), Nat. Assn. for Pub. Interest Law (exec. com., v.p. fellowships). Home: New York, NY. Died Aug. 21, 2006.

PREJEAN, KATTIE CALVIN, educational administrator; b. Rayville, La., July 28, 1939; d. John C. Jr. and Callie (Loche) Calvin; 1 child, Karron Prejean. BS in Elem. Edn., Grambling (La.) U., 1961; MS in Adminstrn., Pepperdine U., 1974; EdD, Nova U., Ft. Lauderdale, Fla., 1984; postgrad., Eubank Conservatory Music, L.A. Cert. gen. tchr., elem. and secondary social studies and English tchr., gen. adminstrn., Calif. Tchr. Ministry Edn., Antigua and Barbuda; vol. Peace Corps, St. Johns, Antigua and Barbuda, 1971-73; elem. sch. prin. L.A. Unified Sch. Dist., from 1985. Condr. staff devel. workshops; adj. prof. Nat. U., 1992-95. Named Mother of Yr., 1981; recipient music award Alpha Kappa Alpha, 1988. Mem. ASCD, Assn. Elem. and Secondary Adminstrs., Coun. Black Adminstrs., Calif. Tchrs. Assn., Nat. Coun. Social Studies, EDUCARE, Phi Delta Kappa. Home: Los Angeles, Calif. Died June 21, 2004.

PRESTON, BILLY (WILLIAM EVERETT PRESTON), musician, vocalist, composer; b. Houston, Sept. 9, 1946; Keyboardist, vocalist solo career, from 1962; keyboardist John Lennon's Plastic Ono Band, 1969-71. Albums include Sixteen Year Old Soul, 1963, Gospel in My Soul, 1964, Most Exciting Organ Ever, 1965, The Wildest Organ in Town, 1967, Thats the Way God Planned It, 1969, Encouraging Words, 1969, The Apple of Their Eye, 1969 I Wrote a Simple Song, 1971, Music Is My Life, 1972, Everybody Likes Some Kind of Music, 1973, The Kids & Me, 1974, It's My Pleasure, 1975, Bill Preston, 1976, A Whole New Thing, 1977, Soul'd Out, 1979, Billy & Syreeta, 1981, Pressin' On, 1982, Minister of Music, 1995, Words and Music, 1996, Ultimate Collection, 2000, Music From My Heart, 2001; singles include That's the Way (God Planned It), 1969, Will It Go Round in Circles, 1973, Outta Space (Grammy award for Best Instrumental Song), 1973, Nothing from Nothing, 1974; (with The Beatles) Let It Be, 1970; (with The Rolling Stones) Sticky Fingers, 1971, Exile on Main Sreet, 1972, Goats Head Soup, 1973, It's Only Rock and Roll, 1974, Love You Live, 1977; backed Little Richard, Mahalia Jackson, Sam Cooke, Ray Charles; Co-writer (songs) (with Bruce Fisher) You Are So Beautiful, 1975; Actor (films) St. Louis Blues, 1958, Sgt. Pepper's Lonely Hearts Club Band, 1978, Blues Brothers 2, 1998, Ticker, 2001, The Derby Stallion, 2005; (TV movies) On Faith Alone: The Jozy Pollock Story, 2003 Died June 6, 2006.

PRESTON, FRANK STEELE, computer engineer; b. Iowa City, July 30, 1918; s. Howard Hall and Lucy Steele Preston; m. Elizabeth Lewis, Aug. 19, 1943; children: Carl, Ralph, Bruce, Glenn. BSEE, U. Wash., 1940; MSEE, MIT, 1950. Registered profl. engr., Conn. Rsch. assoc. MIT, Cambridge, 1941-44; chief engr. Norden Labs. Corp., bombsight co., N.Y.C. and White Plains, N.Y., 1944-58; assoc. tech. dir. Norden divsn. United Aircraft, Norwalk, Conn., 1958-77; lectr. U. N.C., Charlotte, 1977-82; systems engr. Ames Rsch. Ctr., NASA, Mountain View, Calif., 1982-89, sr. computer scientist Langley Rsch. Ctr. Hampton, Va., 1989-99; ret., 1999. Inventor and developer in field; 17 patents in field. With USNR, 1936-40. Recipient Navy Ordnance Devel. award USN, 1944. Fellow The Murphy Inst. (sr.); mem. IEEE (life, chpt. pres. 1950), Sigma Xi, Tau Beta Pi. Avocations: sports, music, reading. Home: North Branford, Conn. Died Mar. 31, 2004.

PRESTON, WILLIAM LEON, family practice; b. Salina, Kans., Nov. 19, 1947; s. Billie Wirth and Mary May Preston; m. Rebecca Cecilia Preston, June 19, 1971; children: William Andrew, Ellen Marie. BA in Physics, Kans. Wesleyan U., 1968; MD, U. Colo., 1972. Diplomate Am. Bd. Family Physicians. Resident West Suburban Family Practice, Oak Park, Ill., 1972-75; assoc. dir. Family Practice Ctr., LaGrange, Ill., 1975-79; med. dir. Wholistic Health Ctr., LaGrange, 1979-80; sr. ptnr. Preston Family Practice, Western Springs, Ill., from 1980. Med. dir. St. Thomas Hospice, Hinsdale, Ill., 1980-00. Lay leader First United Meth. Ch., Western Springs, 1992-1999. Fellow Am. Acad. of Family Physicians; mem. Nat. Hospice Orgn., Am. Coll. of Sports Medicine. Republican. Methodist. Avocations: photography, music, martial arts. Home: La Grange Park, Ill. Died Sept. 3, 2004.

PRESTRIDGE, PAMELA ADAIR, lawyer; b. Delhi, La., Dec. 25, 1945; d. Gerald Wallace Prestridge and Louis Baugh and Peggy Adair (Arender) Martin. BA, La. Poly. U., 1967; M in Edn., La. State u., 1968, JD, 1973. Bar: U.S. Dist. Ct. (mid. dist.) La. 1975, U.S. Dist. Ct. (so. dist.) Tex. 1982, U.S. Ct. Appeals (5th cir.) 1982, U.S. Supreme Ct. 1990. Law clk. to presiding justice La. State Dist. Ct., Baton Rouge, 1973-75; ptnr. Breazeale, Sachse & Wilson, Baton Rouge, 1975-82, Hirsch & Westheimer P.C., Houston, 1982-92; pvt. practice Houston, from 1992. V.p. Atty.-Mediators Coop., 1994. Counselor Big Bros./Big Sisters, Baton Rouge, 1968-70; legal cons., bd. dir. Lupus Found. Am., Houston, 1984-93, Quota Club, Baton Rouge, 1979-82, Speech and Hearing Found., Baton Rouge, 1981-82, The Actors Workshop, Houston, 1988-93, Tex. Satsang Soc., 2000-2004. Recipient Outstanding Woman of Houston award, Fedn. Profl. Women, 1984, Pres.'s award, Lupus Found. Am., 1991, cert. of Appreciation, Assn. Atty. Mediators, 1992, citation Outstanding Members, 1993. Mem. La. Bar Assn., Tex. Bar Assn., Houston Bar Assn., Houston Bar Found., Phi Alpha Delta. Eckankar. Avocations: acting, ultralite flying. Home: Houston, Tex. Died Jan. 29, 2005.

PREVO, RANDALL MURRAY, personnel administrator; b. Casper, Wyo., Oct. 15, 1921; s. William Henry and Florence Jane (Moses) P.; m. Irene Marie Thouvenin, July 14, 1945; children: Martine Jane, Odile L., Ann-Marie, Bernadette Phyllis Kidd. AA, S.J. Jr. Coll., Stockton, Calif., 1949; AB, Coll. of Pacific, Stockton, Calif., 1951; Cert. in Pub. Adminstrn., U. Calif., Alameda, 1963. Registered lobbyist, 1988. Pers. adminstr. City of Stockton, 1952-56; pers. dir. San Joaquin County, Stockton, 1956-68; gen. mgr. Marin County Employees Assn., San Rafael, Calif., 1968-70; pers. officer, dep. adminstr. Napa County, Calif., 1970-71; gen. mgr. Calif. Pub. Employees Fedn., Sacramento, 1971-73, Kern County Employees Assn. Local 700, Bakersfield, Calif., 1973-74, Alameda Employee Assn. Local 616, Oakland, Calif., 1974-76; gen. mgr., rep. San Diego Pub. Employees Assn., 1976-88. Contbr. articles to profl. jours. Trustee exec. com. Coun. 2 of S.E.I.U., San Francisco, 1974-76; bd. dirs. Indsl. Rels. Coun., U. Calif., Alameda, 1974-76; pres. IKE for Pres. Club, Stockton, 1952. With U.S. Army, 1940-45; ETO. Decorated Bronze Star medal; named Sertoman of the Yr., Sertoma Club, 1987-88. Mem. Am. Legion, VFW, K.C. (3d degree), Elks, Pi Gamma Mu, Phi Kappa Phi. Republican. Roman Catholic. Avocations: golf, history, writing, civil war buff. Home: Stockton, Calif. Died July 18, 2004.

PRICE, JAMES TOWNLEY, medical mycologist, lawyer, partner; b. Ft. Bragg, N.C., Feb. 25, 1942; s. George Townley and Florence Alexandra (Stalker) P.; m. Carol Ann Houchin, Sept. 19, 1963 (div. Sept. 1980); children: Laurie Lynn Price Penix, James Trevor (dec.). BS, U. Okla., 1963; MS, U. Okla. Health Sci. Ctr., 1971, PhD, 1973; JD, Tulsa U., 1989. Bar: Okla. 1989, U.S. Dist. Ct. (no. dist.) Okla. 1991, U.S. Dist. Ct. (ea. dist.) Okla. 1993. Asst. prof. pathology U. Okla. Health Sci. Ctr., Oklahoma City, 1973-79; asst. prof. elec. engring. U. Okla., Norman, 1975-76; assoc. prof. pathology Okla. State Coll. Osteo. Medicine, Tulsa, 1979-84; assoc. Frasier & Frasier, Tulsa, 1989-93, ptnr., 1993. Dir. med. microlab Okla. U. Health Sci. Ctr., Oklahoma City, 1973-79. Contbr. articles to Infection and Immunity. Capt. U.S. Army, 1963-67, Viet Nam. Mem. ABA, Sigma Xi. Died Mar. 2, 2005.

PRICE, MARK A., dentist; b. Bernice, La., Nov. 13, 1924; s. Mark A. and Mary (Moore) P.; m. Margie Nell Allen; children: Mary Price Molnar, John M. BS, La. Tech. U., 1948; DDS, Emory U., 1956. Sole practice gen. dentistry and orthodontics, Monroe, La., 1956-89; ret., 1989. Mem. ADA. La. Dental Assn. (pres. 1975), S.W. Soc. Orthodontists (pres. 1978), Am. Assn. Orthodontists, Am. Coll. Dentists, Internat. Coll. Dentists. Lodges: Rotary. Home: Monroe, La. Died Oct. 18, 2004.

PRINCE, JOHN LUTHER, III, engineering educator; b. Austin, Tex., Nov. 13, 1941; s. John Luther and Glynda (Chollett) P.; m. Martha Ann Hight, Mar. 4, 1960; children: Cynthia Kay, John Luther IV, Alan Douglas, David William. BSEE, So. Meth. U., 1965; MEE, N.C. State U., 1968, PhD, 1969. Research engr. RTI, Res. Tri. Park, NC, 1968-70; mem. tech. staff Tex. Instruments, Dallas, 1970-75; from assoc. prof. to prof. Clemson (S.C.) U., 1975-80; dir. R.A. Intermedics, Inc., Freeport, Tex., 1980-83; prof. U. Ariz., Tucson, from 1983. Acting dir. packaging scis. Semiconductor Rsch. Corp., 1991-92; dir. Electronic Packaging Lab., 1984-91, Ctr. for Electronic Packaging Rsch., 1991—, SEMATECH Ctr. of Excellence for Contamination and Defect Control, 1988-90; cons.in field Contbr. articles to profl. jours. Named Ariz. Innovator of the Yr., 1992; NSF fellow, 1965-68. Fellow: IEEE; mem.: Am. Philatelic Soc. Lutheran. Avocations: stamp collecting/philately, classic cars, motorcycles. Home: Tucson, Ariz. Died 2006.

PRINCE, ROBERT GEORGE, retired university administrator; b. Columbus, Ohio, Mar. 3, 1929; s. Richard Baxter and Edna Hazel (Dressler) P.; m. Lewretta Knott, Dec. 31, 1948 (div. 1977); children: Robert George, Patricia, Jody, Joanne, Douglas, Theresa; m. Suzanne Robertson Josey, Sept. 18, 1978. BA, Coll. of William & Mary, Williamsburg, Va., 1952. Asst. dist. mgr. Met. Life Ins. Co., Newport News, 1952-63; spl. agt. FBI, Washington, 1963-83; security rep. Piedmont Airlines, Winston-Salem, N.C., 1983-88; dir. security Wake Forest U., Winston-Salem, N.C., 1988-92, security cons., 1992-93. 2nd lt. U.S. Army, 1947-48. Avocations: boating, golf. Home: Orlando, Fla. Died Nov. 4, 2004.

PRINCEN, HENRICUS MATTHEUS, surface science consultant; b. Eindhoven, Netherlands, Apr. 15, 1937; s. Hermanus Henricus and Engelina Cornelia (Verhoeckx) P.; m. Raphaela Maria van Spaandonk, Aug. 25, 1960 (div. Apr. 1979); children: Anita, Eric; m. Andrea Dancs, June 1, 1991. BS in Chemistry, U. Utrecht, Netherlands, 1956, MS in Chemistry, 1960; postgrad., U. So. Calif., 1960-62, McGill U., 1962-64; PhD in Phys. Chemistry, U. Utrecht, Netherlands, 1965. Rsch. chemist Philips Rsch. Labs., Netherlands, 1960; sr. rsch. assoc. Lever Bros. Co., Edgewater, N.J., 1965-74, mgr. phys. chemistry, 1974-81; rsch. assoc. Exxon Rsch. and Engring. Co., Annandale, N.J., 1981-86; prin. scientist Gen. Foods Corp., Tarrytown, N.Y., 1987-89; scientist Mobil Technology Co., Paulsboro, N.J., 1989-00; ret., 2000. Vis. scientist Coll. de France, Paris, 1986-87; chmn. Gordon Rsch. Confs. on Chemistry at Interfaces, 1974; mem. adv. bd. Jour. of Colloid and Interface Sci., 1973-75, 83-85, Langmuir, 1989-92, Colloids and Surfaces, 1983-91, Jour. Disperson Sci. and Technology, 1983—. Patentee in field; contbr. numerous articles to profl. jours. Mem. Am. Chem. Soc., Divsn. of Colloid and Surface Chemistry (sec. 1970-72, exec. com. 1992-94, La Mer award com. 1988-90). Home: Flemington, NJ. Died Dec. 19, 2004.

PRINCIPE, JOSEPH VINCENT, JR., environmental engineer; b. N.Y.C., Feb. 5, 1946; s. Joseph Vincent and Ruth Marie (Horan) P.; m. Jeanne Gerber, May 9, 1970; children: Benjamin, Matthew. BS, East Stroudsburg U., 1982. Engring. asst. Metro. Edison Co., Reading, Pa., 1975-84; environ. project leader Gen. Battery Corp., Reading, Pa., 1985; power plant supr. Fairchild Republic Co., Farmindale, N.Y., 1985-87; environ. engr. Stone & Webster Engring. Corp., N.Y.C., from 1987. Chmn. Cub Pack 86, Boy Scouts Am., Stroudsburg, 1983-87. With USN, 1967-75. Mem. ASME. Republican. Home: Stroudsburg, Pa. Died Feb. 27, 2004.

PRIORE, ROGER L., biostatistics educator, consultant; b. Buffalo, Apr. 21, 1938; s. Anthony J. and Linda M. (DeMarchi) P.; m. Carol A. Cooper, Sept. 3, 1960; children— Howard W., Susan L., John D. BA, SUNY-Buffalo, 1960, MS, 1962; Sc.D., Johns Hopkins U., 1965. Jr. cancer research scientist Roswell Park Meml. Inst., Buffalo, 1960-65, sr. cancer research scientist, 1965-67, assoc. cancer research scientist, 1967-69, prin. cancer research scientist, 1974-79, dir. computer sci., 1979-83, dir. dept. biomath., 1983-91, dir. mgmt. info. systems, 1988-91; asst. rsch. prof. SUNY, Buffalo, 1966-68, assoc. rsch. prof., 1968-69, rsch. prof., dir. grad. studies in biometry, 1980-91, clin. prof. dept. social and preventive medicine, 1991—2006, clin. prof. dept. statistics, 1995—2006; rsch. prof. Niagara U., 1968-91; cons. in stats. and computing, 1991—2006; pres. Compustat Assocs., Inc., Buffalo, 1993—2006. Cons. Am. Joint Com. on Cancer, 1980-88. Contbr. articles to profl. jours. Mem. Am. Statis. Assn., Soc. for Epidemiol. Rsch., Sigma Xi Died May 21, 2006.

PRITZKER, LEON, statistician, consultant; b. N.Y.C., June 26, 1922; s. Harry and Sophie (Greene) P.; m. Mary Anne Watts; children: William Earl, David Ronald, Paul Mark, Carol Ann, Phillip Joseph. BS, CCNY, 1942; MA, U. Pa., 1947. Statistician U.S. Bur. of Census, Washington, 1947-61, chief response rsch. br., 1961-67; dir. mktg. info. svcs. Anheuser-Busch Cos., St. Louis, 1967-73, dir. mgmt. systems, 1973-84; exec. v.p., staff ops. Campbell Taggart, Inc., Dallas, 1985-90; cons., from 1990. Vis. faculty Case Inst. Tech., Cleve., 1954-55; cons. Cen. Statis. Bur., Govt. Israel, Jerusalem, 1961, Inst. Stats., Govt. Turkey, Ankara, 1967; dir. Med. Alliance, Inc. Contbr. articles to profl. jours. With U.S. Army, 1943-46. Fellow Am. Statis. Assn.; mem. Internat. Assn. Survey Statisticians. Died Nov. 2, 2005.

PROBERT, DOROTHY WITTMAN, retired social worker; b. Ridgeway, Pa. d. William Edward and Marie (Ticknor) W.; m. Lionel W. Probert, June 15, 1946 (wid. June 1993); children: Susan Zaveruha, Sally Caldarazzo, William Probert, Marguerite Moller, Thomas Probert. BA, Pa. State U., 1944; MSW, Fordham Sch. Social Svcs., N.Y.C., 1967. Diplomate, Am. Psychotherapy Assn. Social worker Cath. Family Svcs., 1962-69; sch. social worker Trumbull (Conn.) Bd. Edn., 1969-73, Bridgeport (Conn.) Bd. Edn., 1973-99; ret., 1999. Mem. AARP, NEA, NASW, Acad. Cert. Social Workers, Assn. Ret. Tchrs. Conn., Lic. Clin. Social Workers, Conn. Edn. Assn., Bridgeport Edn. Assn., Greater Bridgeport Ret. Tchrs. Assn., Pa. State Alumni Assn. Roman Catholic. Home: Stratford, Conn. Died May 9, 2004.

PROCTOR, LESTER TALLEY, JR., lawyer, bank consultant; b. Dayton, Ohio, Aug. 18, 1927; s. Lester Talley and Eva (Brackney) P.; m. Carol Gravett, Aug. 13, 1949; children: Carol Jean Proctor Turner, Nancy Jean Proctor Brown, Lester Talley III, Margaret Ann Proctor Schroeder. BS in Commerce, U. Iowa, 1949, JD, 1953. V.p. N.W. Bank Des Moines, N.A., 1953-70, Marine Nat. Exch. Bank, Milw., 1970-79; v.p., then sr. v.p. No. Ind. Bank & Trust Co., Valparaiso, 1979-86; sr. v.p. Gainer Bank, N.A., Gary, Ind., 1986-89; pvt. practice Valparaiso, from 1989. Pres., bd. dirs. Vis. Nurses Assn. Porter County, Valparaiso, 1982—, Home Health Svcs., 1989—. Mem. ABA, Iowa Bar Assn., Ind. Bar Assn., Greater Valparaiso C. of C., Valparaiso Country Club. Republican. Avocations: travel, golf, computers, reading. Home: Valparaiso, Ind. Died July 21, 2005.

PROFFITT, JOHN ROSCOE, JR., carpet manufacturing company executive; b. Tifton, Ga., July 31, 1924; s. John R. and Floried Edre (Adams) P.; m. Syble Joyce Harrison, Mar. 13, 1948; children; John R. III, William T. BA, Emory U., 1944, MA, 1948, PhD, 1950. Rsch. chemist E.I. duPont de Nemours, Waynesboro, Va., 1950-56, rsch. supr., 1956-59; v.p. Proffitt Mfg. Co., Dalton, Ga., 1959-82, pres., from 1982. Dir. emeritus Hardwick Bank & Trust Co., Dalton, 1962—; dir. emeritus Hardwick Holding Co., Dalton, Svc. Corp., Dalton. Contbr. articles to profl. jours.; patentee in field. Mem., vice chmn. Dalton City Bd. Edn., 1963-76; mem., chmn. Whitfield County Bd. Equalization, Dalton, 1977; mem., vice chmn. Whitfield County Bd. Tax Assessors, 1982—; With U.S. Army, 1944-46. Mem. Kiwanis Club (past pres.), Rotary Club (past pres., Paul Harris fellow 1987), Phi Beta Kappa, Sigma Xi. Baptist. Home: Dalton, Ga. Died June 23, 2004.

PROMISEL, NATHAN E., materials scientist, metallurgical engineer; b. Malden, Mass., June 20, 1908; s. Solomon and Lyna (Samwick) P.; m. Evelyn Sarah Davidoff, May, 17, 1931; children: David Mark, Larry Jay. BS, M.I.T., 1929, MS, 1930; postgrad., Yale U., 1932-33; D.Engring. (hon.), Mich. Tech. U., 1978. Asst. dir. lab. Internat. Silver Co. Meriden, Conn., 1930-40; chief materials scientist and engr. Navy Dept., Washington, 1940-66; exec. dir. nat. materials adv. bd. Nat. Acad. Scis., Washington, 1966-74; cons. on materials and policy, internationally, Washington, 1974—2005. Mem., chmn. NATO Aerospace Panel, 1959-71; U.S. rep. (materials) OECD, 1967-70; U.S. chmn. U.S./USSR Sci. Exch. Program (materials), 1973-77); hon. guest USSR Acad. Scis.; permanent hon. pres. Internat. Conf. Materials Behavior; mem. Nat. Materials Adv. Bd.; adv. com. Oak Ridge Nat. Lab., Lehigh U., U. Pa., U.S. Navy Dept. Labs., U.S. Congress Office Tech. Assessment. Contbr. 65 articles to profl. jours.; contbr., editor: Advances in Materials Research, 1963, Science and Technology of Refractory Metals, 1964, Science, Technology and Application of Titanium, 1970, others Named Nat. Capitol Engr. of Yr. Coun. Engring. and Archtl. Socs., 1974; recipient Outstanding Accomplishment awards Navy Dept., 1955-64, Nat. Materials Advancement award, Fedn. Materials Socs., 1994; annual hon. lectr. Electrochem. Soc., 1970. Fellow AIME (hon, ann. disting. lectr. Metall. Soc. 1984), Soc. Advanced Materials and Process Engring. (one of 12 material scientists who contributed most to aerospace in 20th century 2003), Am. Soc. Materials Internat. (hon., pres. 1972, Carnegie lectr. 1967, ann. hon. lectr. 1984), Brit. Inst. Materials; mem. NAE, ASTM (hon., ann. disting. lectr. 1964), Fedn. Materials Soc. (pres. 1972-73, 1st Decennial award 1982), Soc. Automotive Engrs. (chmn. aerospace materials divsn. 1959-74), Alpha Sigma Mu (hon.). Achievements include invention of electroplating, metall. devels. Died Dec. 15, 2005.

PROSSER, WESLEY LEWIS, advertising and public relations executive; b. Dodge City, Kans., Oct. 28, 1938; s. Wesley Lewis and Sarah Arvilla (Ellis) P.; m. Doris Jean Russell, Apr. 29, 1972 (dec. Nov. 1986). BA, Okla. State U., 1959. Advt. coordinator Aero-Commander, Inc., Oklahoma City, 1962-65; copy coordinator Farmland Industries, Inc., Kansas City, Mo., 1965-72; copy supr. Fletcher/Mayo/Assocs. Inc., St. Joseph, Mo., 1972-74; advt. and pub. relations dir. Agchem Abbott Labs., North Chicago, Ill., 1974-76; account exec. Rumrill & Hoyt, Inc., Rochester, N.Y., 1976-77; account rep. Vangard Communications Inc., St. Louis, 1977-78; v.p., client group supr. Bozell & Jacobs, Inc., Chgo., 1978-84; account supr. McKinney/Mid America, Chgo., 1984-85; mgr. advt. and pub. rels. Inter Innovation LeFebure Inc., Cedar Rapids, Iowa, 1986-89; mgr. bus. devel. Fanning Advt. Agy. Inc., Davenport, Iowa, 1989-91; dir. mktg. comm. Farm Bus. Software Sys., Inc., Aledo, Ill., from 1991. Presenter in field. Prodr. interactive promotional presentation on computer diskette; contbr. articles to profl. jours. Vol. Jackson County Rep. Party, Kansas City, Mo., 1969, Salvation Army, Dodge City, Kans., 1997-2000. 1st lt. USAF, 1959-61. Recipient 1st Place award Nat. Premium Execs., 1969, Objectives and Results award Am. Bus. Press, 1980-81, 83, others. Mem. Nat. Agrimarketers Assn. (1st Place Best in Advt. award 1974), Bus. and Profl. Advertisers Assn., Assn. Agrl. Computing Cos., Sports Car Club Am. Methodist. Avocations: aviation, summer water sports, creative writing. Home: Sherrard, Ill. Died 2004.

PROSSER-ARMSTRONG, JUDY ANN, curator, librarian, consultant, historian, researcher; b. Cheyenne, Wyo., May 13, 1954; d. John Clarence and Dorothy Anna Prosser; m. Harley Joe Armstrong, June 25, 1988 (dec. Jan. 20, 2006). BA, U. Wyo., 1976, MA in Am. Studies, 1978; MLS, Emporia State U., Kans., 1996. Cert. archivist. Asst. pub. info. officer Wyo. State Archives, Museums and Hist. Dept. and Wyo. State Libr., Cheyenne, 1978; dir. Saratoga Cultural and Hist. Mus., Saratoga, Wyo., 1979; registrar Mus. of Western Colo., Grand Junction, 1979—80, archivist-registrar, 1980—93, collections and info. mgr., 1993—95, curator of archives and libr., 1995—98, curator of archives, libr. and registrar, from 1998. Newsletter editor Colo.-Wyo. Assn. Mus., Denver, 1978—82, historian, from 1984, also bd. dirs., co-chair, profl. workshops, from 2003; mus. and archives cons. Mus. Western Colo., Grand Junction, from 1979; NW Colo. rep. Colo. Preservation Alliance, Denver, 1992—2004. Grand Junction PAAC coord., from 1982; bd. dirs. Grand Junction Hist. Preservation Bd., from 2003; sec. of vestry Ch. of the Nativity, Grand Junction, 2000—03, newsletter editor, 1998—2003; v.p. of comm. Creative Visions Express Network, Am. Bus. Women, Grand Junction, 2003—05; pres., v.p., sec., newletter editor, orchard mesa rep. Mesa County Hist. Soc., Grand Junction, 1982—2005; pres., v.p Mesa County Geneal. Soc., Grand Junction, 2000—05; program for avocational archaeological cert. Colo. Archaeological Soc., Grand Junction, 2000—05. Named Employee of the Month, Mesa County Employee Assn., 1988, Bus. Assoc. of the Month and Yr., Grand Junction Charter Chpt., Am. Bus. Woman's Assn., 2000, Woman of the Yr., Creative Visions Express Network, Am. Bus. Woman's Assn., 2004. Mem.: Am. Assn. of Museums, Mountain Plains Museums Assn., Soc. of Rocky Mountain Archvists, Soc. of Am. Archivists, DAR. Home: Grand Junction, Colo. Died Jan. 20, 2006.

PROUT, BETTY JEAN, county clerk; b. Coleman, Mich., Sept. 12, 1926; d. Frank Elmer and Tillie (Kunzmann) Lattimer; m. Duane Lavern Prout; children: Larry (dec.), Janet, Mark, Marjorie, Thomas, Dennis, Mary Ellen. Cert. Continuing Edn., Mich. State U., 1994. Clk. Agr. Stabilization and Conservation Svc., Mt. Pleasant, Mich., 1944-45, 67-69; ct. clk. Isabella County, Mt. Pleasant, Mich., 1964-67, circuit ct. clk., 1969-72, Isabella county clk., from 1973. Chmn. PTA, Rosebush, Mich., 1961-63, Summer Flouride Program, Rosebush, 1961-70; mem. Rep. Party, Mt. Pleasant, 1971—; mem., program chmn. Christian Womens Club, Mt. Pleasant, 1990-93. Recipient Clk. of Yr. award Mich. Twp. Assn., 1997. Mem. Mich. Assn. County Clks. (various com. positions 1972—), United County Officers Assn., Mich. Assn. Counties (County Excellence award for Mich. 1995, County Clk. of Yr. 1996). United Methodist. Avocations: gardening, reading, photography, cooking, travel. Home: Mount Pleasant, Mich. Died July 29, 2004.

PROXMIRE, WILLIAM, former senator; b. Lake Forest, Ill., Nov. 11, 1915; s. Theodore Stanley and Adele (Flanigan) P.; m. Ellen Hodges, 1957, 3 children Grad., Hill Sch., 1934; BA, Yale, 1938; MBA, Harvard, 1940, M.P.A. in Pub. Adminstrn, 1948. Assemblyman Wis. Legislature, 1951; nominee gov. Wis., 1952, 54, 56; pres. Artcraft Press, Waterloo, Wis., 1953-57; U.S. senator from Wis., 1957-89; former chmn. Sen. Banking, Housing and Urban Affairs com., Cong. JointEcon. com. Author: Can Small Business Survive?, 1964, Uncle Sam: Last of the Big Time Spenders, 1972, You Can Do It, 1977, The Fleecing of America, 1980, Your Joy Ride to Health, 1993. Democrat. Home: Washington, DC. Died Dec. 15, 2005.

PRUGH, GEORGE SHIPLEY, lawyer; b. Norfolk, Va., June 1, 1920; s. George Shipley and Florence (Hamilton) P.; m. Katherine Buchanan, Sept. 27, 1942; children: Stephanie Dean, Virginia Patton. AB, U. Calif., Berkeley, 1941; JD, U. Calif., San Francisco, 1948; postgrad., Army War Coll., 1961-62; MA, George Washington U., 1963. Bar: Calif. 1949, U.S. Supreme Ct. 1954. Legal advisor U.S. Mil. Assistance Command, Vietnam, 1964-66; legal adviser U.S. European Command, Stuttgart, Ger., 1966-69; Judge Adv., U.S. Army Europe, Heidelberg, Ger., 1969-71; Judge Adv. Gen. Washington, 1971-75; ret., 1975. Prof. law Hastings Coll. Law, U. Calif., San Francisco, 1975-82 Author: (with others) Law at War, 1975; (play) Solferino; contbr. articles to profl. jours. Mem. Sec. Def. Task Force on Racial Discrimination in Adminstrn. Mil. Justice, 1973; mem. U.S. del. Diplomatic Conf. on Law of War, Geneva, 1974, 75. 2d lt. U.S. Army; maj. gen. JAGC, 1971. Decorated D.S.M. with oak leaf cluster, Legion of Merit with oak leaf cluster.

Mem. ABA, Am. Judicature Soc., Internat. Soc. Mil. Law and Law of War (hon. pres.), Civil Affairs Assn. (hon. dir.), Selden Soc., Calif. Bar, Order of Coif, Bohemian Club, Army and Navy Club (Washington), Phi Delta Phi. Episcopalian. Home: Orinda, Calif. Died July 6, 2006.

PRUITT, MARY ANN, chiropractor; b. Glen Rose, Tex., Mar. 2, 1930; d. Sterling Holder Sr. and Oveda Jean (Wade) P.; widowed. DC, Palmer Coll. Chiropractic, 1949; postgrad., Tex. Christian U., 1951, Tex. Wesleyan U., 1952-53. Chiropractor, owner Pruitt Chiropractic Clinic, Ft. Worth, Tex., from 1949. Appointee state peer rev. bd. Tex. Bd. Chiropractic Examiners; appointee Tex. Indsl. Accident Bd., Chiropractic Adv. Com. Precinct chair Dem. Party, Tarrant County, county del. state conv., county del.; mem., base operator Citizens on Patrol, Ft. Worth, 1994-95. Recipient Mabel Palmer award World of Congress of Women Chiropractors, 1993; fellow Palmer Coll. Acad. Fellow Internat. Chiropractors Assn. (mem. legis. com. 1993-94), Palmer Acad. Chiropractic; mem. Chiropractic Soc. Tex. (treas., Sterling Pruitt Humanitarian award 1994), Tex. Coalition for Concerned Chiropractors (treas. 1993), Congress of Ind. Chiropractors, Palmer Alumni Assn. Tex. (regional officer, past bd. dirs.), Assn. for Chiropractic Ednl. Stds. (treas. and sec. 1994-97), Sigma Phi Chi (Hon. Supreme Kiatrus). Methodist. Home: Fort Worth, Tex. Died June 4, 2005.

PRYCE, WILLIAM THORNTON, former ambassador; b. San Diego, July 19, 1932; s. Roland Fremont and Katharine (Hartmann) P.; m. Joan MacClurg, Mar. 22, 1958; children: Kathy Ellen, Jeffrey Fremont, Scott Fisher. BA, Wesleyan U., 1953; MA, Tufts U., 1954. Joined Fgn. Svc., US Dept. State, 1958; spl. asst. to under sec. of state for econ. affairs, asst. sec. for Latin Am. affairs Washington, 1964-65; polit. officer Am. ambassies in Moscow, Panama, Guatemala, 1966-74; dir. Soviet ednl. and cultural programs US Dept. State, Washington, 1974-76; exec. asst. to amb.-at-large Ellsworth Bunker Washington, 1977-78; polit. counselor Am. Embassy, Mexico City, 1978-81, dep. chief of mission La Paz, Bolivia, 1981-82, Panama City, Panama, 1982-86; alt. U.S. rep. to OAS US Dept. State, Washington, 1986-89; spl. asst. to pres. for nat. security affairs NSC, Washington, 1989-92; US amb. to Honduras US Dept. State, Tegucigalpa, 1993-96; v.p. Coun. Ams., Washington, from 1997. Lt. USN, 1955-58. Recipient Meritorious Honor award Dept. State, 1986, Superior Honor award, 1989, Sr. Performance award 1982-87, 89, 90, 92. Mem. Coun. Fgn. Rels., Am. Fgn. Svc. Assn., City Tavern Club. Episcopalian. Died July 11, 2006.

PRYOR, RICHARD (RICHARD FRANKLIN LENNOX THOMAS PRYOR III), actor, writer; b. Peoria, Ill., Dec. 1, 1940; s. LeRoy and Gertrude (Thomas) Pryor; M. Patricia Price (1960-61), Shelly Bonus (1967-69), Deboragh McGuire (1977-79), Flynn BeLaine (1986-87, remarried 1990-91), Jennifer Lee (1981-82, remarried 2001-); children Renee, Richard Jr., Elizabeth, Stephen Michael, Kelsey, Franklin Matthew Mason, Rain. Grad. high sch. Appeared on: Rudy Vallee's On Broadway Tonight, Kraft Summer Music Hall, Ed Sullivan, Merv Griffin and Johnny Carson television shows in 1960s; appeared in motion pictures The Busy Body, 1968, The Green Berets, 1968, Wild In The Streets, 1969, The Phynx, 1970, You've Got to Walk It Like You Talk It or You'll Lose That Beat, 1971, Dynamite Chicken, 1972, Lady Sings the Blues, 1972, Hit!, 1973, Wattstax, 1973, The Mack, 1973, Some Call It Loving, 1973, Uptown Saturday Night, 1974, Adios Amigos, 1976, The Bingo Long Travelling All-Stars and Motor Kings, 1976, Car Wash, 1976, Silver Streak, 1976, Greased Lightning, 1977, Which Way is Up?, 1977, Blue Collar, 1978, California Suite, 1978, The Wiz, 1978, Richard Pryor Live in Concert, 1979, The Muppet Movie, 1979, Wholly Moses!, 1981, In God We Trust, 1980, Stir Crazy, 1980, Bustin' Loose, 1981(also prodr.), Some Kind of Hero, 1982, The Toy, 1982, Superman III, 1983, Richard Pryor Here and Now, 1983, Brewster's Millions, 1985, Critical Condition, 1987, Moving, 1988, See No Evil, Hear No Evil, 1989, Harlem Nights, 1989, Another You, 1991, Lost Highway, 1996, Mad Dog Time, 1996; actor, writer, producer, dir. Jo Jo Dancer Your Life Is Calling, 1985; writer scripts for The Flip Wilson Show, Sanford and Son; co-writer TV spls. for Lily Tomlin, 1973 (Emmy award); writer Richard Pryor: Live on the Sunset Strip, 1982)also prodr.), Here and Now, 1983 (also dir.), Live and Smokin', 1985; host (children's show) Pryor's Place, 1984; host (TV) Saturday Night Live; featured actor A Party for Richard Pryor, 1991; co-writer of screenplay Blazing Saddles, 1973 (Am. Writers Guild award, Am. Acad. Humor award), Lily, 1974 (Am. Acad. Humor award); recorded That Nigger's Crazy, 1974 (Grammy award, certified Gold and Platinum album), Bicentennial Nigger, 1976 (Grammy award); star, exec. prodr. Richard Pryor Show, NBC-TV, 1977; owner Richard Pryor Enterprises, Inc., Los Angeles, 1975-2005; guest appearances (TV) Toast of the Town, 1965-67 (several episodes), Away We Go, 1967, The Mod Squad, 1968, The Partridge Family, 1971, Martin, 1993, Chicago Hope, 1995, Malcom & Eddie, 1996, The Norm Show, 1999; co-author Pryor Convictions: And Other Life Sentences, 1995. Served with U.S. Army, 1958-60. Named one of 100 Greatest Stand-Ups of All Times (chosen #1), Comedy Central, 2004; recipient Grammy award, "...and It's Deep Too!", 2002, Lifetime Achievement Honoree, Am. Comedy Awards, 1992, CableACE Best Entertainment/Cultural Documentary or Internat. Spl., 1993, Hall of Fame award, NAACP, 1996, Mark Twain prize for Am. Humor (first recipient), Kennedy Ctr., 1998. Mem. Nat. Acad. Rec. Arts and Scis., Writers Guild Am. Died Dec. 10, 2005.

PUCKETT, KIRBY, former professional sports team executive, retired professional baseball player; b. Chgo., Mar. 14, 1961; s. Catherine Puckett; m. Tonya Hudson; children: Catherine, Kirby, Jr. Student, Bradley U., Ill., Triton Coll. Baseball player Minn. Twins, Mpls., 1982-96, exec. v.p., 1996—2000. Author: I Love This Game!, 1993, Be The Best You Can Be, 1993. Founder, benefactor Kirby Puckett Eight-Ball Invitational to benefit Children's Heart Fund, United Way. Recipient All-Star Most Valuable Player award, 1993, Gold Glove award, 1986-89, 1991-92, Silver Slugger award, 1986-89, 92, 94, All-Star team, 1986-94; named to Sporting News All-Star Team, 1986-89, 92, 94, Am. League All-Star Team, 1986-89, Am. League Batting Champion, 1989, Minn. Twins Most Valuable Player 1985, 86, 88, 89, 92; named Calif. League Player of the Yr., 1983, Most Valuable Player, Am. League Championship Series, 1991, Best Hitter and Most Exciting Player, Baseball America, 1992; inducted Triton Coll. Hall of Fame, 1993. Mem. Alexis de Tocqueville Soc. Achievements include: led Major League in hits 1988-92, highest batting average among active batters 1988-92, seasons with 200 or more hits: 1986-89, 92, inducted into Major League Baseball Hall of Fame, 2001. Died Mar. 6, 2006.

PUDDY, DONALD RAY, mechanical engineer; b. Ponca City, Okla., May 31, 1937; s. Lester Andrew and Mildred Pearl (Olson) P.; m. Dana C. Timberlake, Sept. 8, 1956; children: Michael R., Douglas A., Glenn L. BSME, U. Okla., 1960; MBA, U. Houston, 1978; postgrad., Harvard U., 1991. Officer USAF, Fort Walton Beach, Fla., 1960-64; flight controller NASA Johnson Space Ctr., Houston, 1964-66, head module systems sec., 1966-69, asst. chief of lunar module systems br., 1969-72, asst. chief of space sci. and tech. br., 1972-74, chief of mission ops. br., 1974-75, flight dir. Apollo, Skylab, ASTP, Shuttle, lead flight dir. for shuttle orbiter programs, 1976-82, chief mission ops. systems div., 1982-85, asst. dir. for systems in mission ops., 1985-86, dir. flight crew ops., 1988-92; acting dep. dir. NASA's Ames Rsch. Ctr., Calif., 1986; asst. assoc. adminstr. spaceflight NASA Hdqs., Washington, 1986-87; asst. to NASA adminstr., 1991; spl. asst. joint U.S./Russian Programs NASA, Houston, 1992-95; cons., 1995—2004. Pres. PTA, Ed White Elem. Sch.; past troop com. chmn. and asst. scoutmaster Boy Scouts Am. Mem. AIAA (mem. coun. 1983-84), Internat. Acad. Astronautics, Pi Tau Sigma, Sigma Tau. Home: Seabrook, Tex. Died Nov. 22, 2004.

PURCELL, DALE, college president, consultant; b. Baxley, Ga., Oct. 20, 1919; s. John Groce and Agnes (Moody) P.; m. Edna Jean Rowell, Aug. 2, 1944; children: David Scott, Steven Dale, Pamela Jean; m. Mary Louise Gerlinger, Aug. 26, 1962; adopted children: Amelia Allerton, Jon Allerton. BA, U. Redlands, 1948, MA, 1949; postgrad., Northwestern U., 1951-52; LL.D., Lindenwood Colls., 1974. Topographer U.S. E.D., 1939; U.S. counter-intelligence agt., 1940-42; assoc. prof. Ottawa U., 1953-54, asst. to pres., 1954-58; gen. sec. Earlham Coll., 1958-61; dir. devel. U. So. Fla., 1961-63; exec. dir. Cancer Research Center, Columbia, Mo., 1963-65; pres. Westminster Coll., Fulton, Mo., 1973-76, Dale Purcell Assocs., 1972-92; a founding dir. Am. Sports Medicine Inst., Birmingham, Ala., 1987-92. Rep. cons. clients Hughston Sports Medicine Found., Columbus, Ga., Berry Coll., Mt. Berry, Ga., Hope Coll., Holland, Mich., William Woods Coll., Fulton, Mo., Eureka (Ill.) Coll., Cranbrook Insts., Bloomfield Hills, Mich., Penrose Hosp., Colorado Springs, Colo., Northwestern Coll., Orange City, Iowa, Centro Medico Docente, Caracas, Venezuela, Wayland Acad., Beaver Dam, Wis., Cen. Coll., Pella, Iowa, U. of Stirling, Scotland, U. Ottawa, Ont., Can., Washington & Lee U., Lexington, Va., Taylor U., Upland, Ind., Menninger Found., Topeka, Kans., Ill. Wesleyan U., Bloomington, Cox Med. Systems, Springfield, Mo., Nat. Council Family Rels. Mpls., Stephens Coll., Columbia, Mo., Hist. Savannah Found., Ga. Bd. visitors Berry Coll. Capt. USMCR, 1942-46, 52-53. Recipient Disting. Achievement award Berry Coll., 1974, medal Pres. of China, 1945, medal Pres. of Korea, 1953. Mem. Pi Kappa Delta (Alpha chpt.). Presbyterian (elder 1964—). Clubs: St. Louis (Clayton), Univ. (St. Louis and N.Y.C.), Litchfield County Ct. Home: Falls Village, Conn. Died Nov. 20, 2005.

PURCELL, STUART MCLEOD, III, financial planner; b. Santa Monica, Calif., Feb. 16, 1944; s. Stuart McLeod Jr. and Carol (Howe) P. AA, Santa Monica City Coll., 1964; BS, Calif. State U., Northridge, 1967; grad., CPA Advanced Personal Fin. Planning Curriculum, San Francisco, 1985. CPA, Calif.; CFP. Sr. acct. Pannell Kerr Forster, San Francisco, 1970-73; fin. cons. Purcell Fin. Services, San Francisco, 1973-74, San Rafael, Calif., 1980-81; controller Decimus Corp., San Francisco, 1974-76, Grubb & Ellis Co., Oakland, Calif., 1976-78, Marwais Steel Co., Richmond, Calif., 1979-80; owner, fin. counselor Purcell Wealth Mgmt., San Rafael, from 1981. Exec. dir. www.norforprofits.com, 2000--; guest lectr. Golden Gate U., San Francisco, 1985—; leader ednl. workshops, Larkspur, Calif., 1984; speaker Commonwealth Club Calif., 1989, 91. Contbr. articles to newspapers and profl. jours. Treas. Salvation Army, San Rafael-San Anselmo-Fairfax, Calif., 1987—; chmn. fin. planners div. United Way Marin County, Calif., 1984; mem. fundraising com. Marin County March of Dimes, 1987—, Marin County Arthritis Found., 1988—; mem. Marin Estate Planning Council. Served to lt. (j.g.) USNR, 1968-76. Named Eagle Scout, 1959, Best Fin. Advisor Marin County Independent-Jour. newspaper, 1987, Top Producer Unimarc, 1986; recipient Outstanding Achievement award United Way, 1984; named to The Registry of Fin. Planning Practitioners, 1987. Mem. AICPA, Calif. Soc. CPAs, Nat. Speakers Assn., Internat. Assn. for Fin. Planners (exec. dir. North Bay chpt., San Francisco 1984), Internat. Soc. Pre-Retired Planners, Soc. CPA-Fin. Planners (dist. membership chmn. San Francisco 1986), Registry Fin. Planning Practitioners, Sigma Alpha Epsilon. Presbyterian. Avocations: travel, auto racing, skiing, gardening. Home: San Rafael, Calif. Died Mar. 20, 2006.

PURDY, CAROL ANN, psychotherapist; b. Long Beach, Calif., Jan. 5, 1943; d. Melvin Boyce and Kathryn Delia (Wilbur) Slaughter; m. John Allen Purdy, June 8, 1963; children: Laura Beth, Mark Robert, Sarah Ruth. BA, Calif. State U., Long Beach, 1964; MSW, Calif. State U., Sacramento, 1990. LCSW; cert. tchr. Calif. Tchr. Orange (Calif.) Unified Sch. Dist., 1964-67; freelance author, from 1977; social worker Tehama County Mental Health, Red Bluff, Calif., 1989-94; therapist in pvt. practice Red Bluff, Calif., 1994-99; conf. coord., play therapy supr. Kid Power Counseling and Tng. Ctr., from 1995, PlayTherapyCentral.com, from 1995. Lectr. in field; founder, trainer Kid Power Program Groups for High Risk Children, Red Bluff, 1989—. Author: Iva Dunnit and the Big Wind, 1985, Least of All, 1987, The Kid Power Program, 1989, Mrs. Merriwether's Musical Cat, 1994, Nesuya's Basket, 1997, Playing with Janet, 1999, Helping Them Heal, 1999. Mem.: Assn. Play Therapy (registered play therapist supr. cert. 2001). Avocations: music, gardening, language study, travel. Died May 14, 2005.

PURPURA, CHARLES GERARD, screenwriter, production company executive; b. N.Y.C., Sept. 14, 1945; s. Charles Carmelo and Jennie (LaMacchia) P.; m. Jennie Simeone, Aug. 22, 1970; children: Simon Henry (dec.), William Charles. Student, N.Y.U. Film Sch., 1975-78. Pres. Bop House Prodns., Los Angeles, from 1982. Screenwriter: (feature films) Heaven Help Us, 1985, Satisfaction, 1988, (TV film) The Day the Senior Class Got Married, 1985 (Emmy award, Humanitas award). Mem. Nat. Acad. TV Arts and Scis., Writers Guild Am. Roman Catholic. Masons. Home: Massapequa, NY. Died Mar. 20, 2005.

PUSATERI, LAWRENCE XAVIER, lawyer; b. Oak Park, Ill., May 25, 1931; s. Lawrence E. and Josephine (Romano) P.; m. Eve M. Graf, July 9, 1956; children: Joanne J. Katsis, Lawrence F., Paul L., Mary Ann, Eva M. Campbell. JD summa cum laude, DePaul U., 1953. Bar: Ill. 1953. Asst. state's atty. Cook County, 1957-59; ptnr. Newton, Wilhelm, Pusateri & Naborowski, Chgo., 1959-77; justice Ill. Appellate Ct., Chgo., 1977-78; ptnr. Peterson, Ross, Schloerb & Seidel, Chgo., 1978-95; of counsel Peterson & Ross, Chgo., 1996—2000. Pres. Conf. Consumer Fin. Law, 1984-92, chmn. gov. com., 1993-99; mem. Ill. Supreme Ct. Com. on Pattern Jury Instrns., 1981-96; mem. adv. bd. Ctr. for Analysis of Alt. and Dispute Resolution, 1999-2005; mem. U.S. Senate Jud. Nominations Commn. State Ill., 1993, 95; exec. dir. State of Ill. Jud. Inquiry Bd., 1995-96; panel chmn. Cook County mandatory arbitration, 1990—, judicate Am. Arbitration; mem. Merit Selection Panel for U.S. Magistrate; lectr. law DePaul U., Chgo., 1962, Columbia U., N.Y.C., 1965, Marquette U., Milw., 1962-82, Northwestern U. Law Sch., Def. Counsel Inst., 1969-70; apptd. by U.S. Senator Paul Simon to Merit Screening Com. Fed. Judges, U.S. Atty. and U.S. Marshal, 1993, others; mem. task force indigent appellate def. Cook County Jud. Adv. Coun., 1992-95; mem. Ill. Gen. Assembly, 1964-68. Contbr. articles to profl. jours. Chmn. Ill. Crime Investigating Commn., 1967-68, chmn. Ill. Parole and Pardon Bd., 1969-70; bd. dirs. Ill. Law Enforcement Commn., 1970-72; chmn. Com. on Correctional Facilities and Svcs.; exec. v.p. and gen. counsel Ill. Fin. Svcs. Assn., 1980-95; chmn. law forum Am. Fin. Svcs. Assn., 1975-76; mem. spl. commn. on adminstrn. of justice in Cook County, Ill. (Greylord Com.) 1984-90, bd. dirs. Chgo. Crime Commn., 1986-91; bd. govs. Cath. Lawyers Guild; mem. Ill. Supreme Ct. Spl. Commn. on the Adminstrn. of Justice, Ill. Supreme Ct. Appointment, 1991; mem. adv. bd. Ctr. for Analysis of Alternative Dispute Resolution Systems, 1998-2005; past pres. Justinian Soc. Lawyers. Served to capt. JAGC, AUS, 1955-58. Named One of Ten Outstanding Young Men in Chgo., Chgo. Jr. Assn. Commerce and Industry, 1960, 65; recipient Outstanding Legislator award Ill. Gen. Assembly, 1966; named Prin. for a Day Big Shoulders Fund. Fellow Am. Coun. Fin. Svcs. Attys.; mem. ABA (com. consumer fin. svcs. 1975-99, ho. dels. 1981-90, jud. adminstrn. divsn. 1980-95, mem. exec. com. lawyer's conf. 1994-95, mem. bench and bar rels. com. 1994-96, mem. adv. com. to Ill. State Del., Jud. Adminstrn. Divsn. in Recognition of Leadership in Improvement of Adminstrn. of Justice award 1993, 50 Yr. award 2003), Ill. State Bar Assn. (pres. 1975-76, com. on fed. jud. and related appointments, mem. adv. com., state del., 1994-99, bd. dirs., co-chmn. joint com. jud. compensation 2002-05, Abraham Lincoln Legal Writing award 1959, Sr. Counsellor award 2003), Chgo. Bar Assn. (bd. mgrs. 1965-66), Fred B. Snite Found. (sec., counsel 1976-90), Gertrude and Walter Swanson Found. (sole trustee 1995-2005), Am. Legion, Mid-Am. Club Chgo. Republican. Roman Catholic. Home: Chicago, Ill. Died Nov. 24, 2005.

QUELLMALZ, FREDERICK, foundation executive, editor; b. N.Y.C., May 24, 1912; s. Frederick and Edith (Grant) Q.; m. Jayne Elizabeth Osten, May 29, 1942; children: Barbara Jayne Coffin, Carol Grant Arran, Patricia Ellen, Sandra Lee Erchinger, Tracy Louise Koziel, Frederick Quellmalz Jr. AB, Princeton U., 1934; grad., Woodrow Wilson Sch. Pub. & Internat. Affairs, 1934; B of Profl. Arts (hon.), Brooks Inst., 1968. Statis. asst. Pepperell Mfg. Co., 1934-40; dir. photographic activities N.Y. World's Fair,

1940; editor PSA Jour., 1939-52; exec. sec. Photographic Soc. Am., Phila., 1940-42; asst. to chief engr. U.S. Naval Ordinance Plant, York, Pa., 1942-45; exec. v.p. Profl. Photographers Am., Des Plaines, Ill., 1952-74; editor, pub. Profl. Photographer mag., 1953-74; exec. dir. Photog. Art and Sci. Found., Oklahoma City, 1965-94, pres., 1988-96; pres. Internat. Photog. Hall of Fame and Mus., Kirkpatrick Ctr., Oklahoma City, 1988-96. Trustee Winona Sch. Profl. Photography, 1953-75; amb. Oakton Community Coll.; mem. Oakton Found. Devel. Coun., 1996—; treas. Des Plaines Spl. Events Commn., 1999—. Named to Hon. Order Ky. Cols.; recipient Father Smyth Humanitarian award City of Des Plaines, Ill., 1991. Fellow Royal Soc. Arts (London); mem. Photo Soc. Am. (hon. mem., assoc.), Profl. Photographers Am. (hon. master of photography, photo craftsman), Cert. Assn. Execs., Am. Soc. Assn. Execs. (bd. dirs. 1963-66), Chgo. Soc. Assn. Execs. (life mem.), Internat. Assn. Exposition Mgrs. (life mem., cert. exposition mgr., bd. dirs. 1959-61), Wis. Soc. Assn. Execs. (sec. 1963, pres. 1965), Am. Soc. Photographers (hon. assoc.), Nat. Press Photographers Assn. (life), Royal Photographic Soc., Am. Society Medalists, Am. Assn. Retired Persons (treas. Des Plaines chpt. 1982, 83, 90, pres. 1984-85, tax-aide coord. 1980-97), Sister Cities Internat. (treas. local chpt. 1980-88, 93—, pres. 1989-93, treas. Ill. state chpt. 1986—), Des Plaines Spl. Events Commn., 1999-2002 (treas. 1999-02, Oakton Found. Devel. Coun., 1996-, CElks, Princeton Club, York Camera Club, Bella Vista Country Club, Kappa Alpha Mu. Died Dec. 29, 2005.

QUIGLEY, NANCY LOUISE, elementary school educator; b. Pontiac, Mich., May 25, 1935; d. Esther E. (Hicks) Q.; 1 child, Deborah L. Roe. BA, U. Mich., 1962. Mem. Trail Blazers, Ann Arbor, 1989-91; vol. Girl Scouts Am., Ypsilanti, Mich., 1990-91, City of Ann Arbor; mem. Dawntreader, Ann Arbor, 1991. Mem. AAUW (vol.). Episcopalian. Avocations: reading, sports, gardening, music. Home: Ann Arbor, Mich. Died May 8, 2004.

QUINN, WILLIAM FRANCIS, lawyer, former governor; b. Rochester, NY, July 13, 1919; s. Charles Alvin and Elizabeth (Dorrity) Q.; m. Nancy Ellen Witbeck, July 11, 1942; children: William Francis, Stephen Desford, Timothy Charles, Christopher Thomas, Ann Cecily, Mary Kaiulani, Gregory Anthony. BS summa cum laude, St. Louis U., 1940; LLB cum laude, Harvard U., 1947. Bar: Hawaii 1948. Ptnr. Robertson, Castle & Anthony, Honolulu, 1947-57; gov. Ter. of Hawaii, Honolulu, 1957-59, State of Hawaii, Honolulu, 1959-62; ptnr. Quinn & Moore, Honolulu, 1962-64; exec. v.p. Dole Co., Honolulu, 1964-65, pres., 1965-72; ptnr. Jenks, Kidwell, Goodsill & Anderson, Honolulu, 1972-73, Goodsill Anderson & Quinn, 1973-82, Goodsill Anderson Quinn & Stifel, 1982-91; ret., 1991. Mem. sr. adv. bd. 9th Cir. Jud. Coun. Served with USN, 1942-45. Decorated knight of Holy Sepulchre Order. Mem. Pacific Club (Honolulu). Republican. Roman Catholic. Home: Honolulu, Hawaii. Died Aug. 28, 2006.

QUINTO, ROCHELLE A., lawyer; b. Long Beach, Calif., Jan. 12, 1954; d. Mario Joseph and Marianne T. Quinto; m. Richard Xavier Menke, Sept. 6, 1990. BS in Animal Sci., U. Conn., 1975; JD, Vt. Law Sch., 1978; D in Sci. of Law, Cornell U., 1985. Bar: N.Y. 1979. Corp. atty. Approved Purification Corp., Stamford, Conn., from 1978. Racehorse atty., Quintus Farms, Interlaken, N.Y. and North Bridgeport, Conn., 1985—; cons. Alexander Group, Interlaken, 1992—. Intercollegiate polo champion, U.S. Polo Assn., 1972, 73, 74. Mem. Internat. Mgmt. Assn. (adv. bd. Ithaca chpt. 1979-90), Tompkins County (N.Y.) Bar Assn. (adv. bd. 1979—), N.Y. Simmental Assn. (pres. 1977-80), Ky. Horse Park, Ithaca Dog Tng. Club, Tompkins County C. of C. Avocations: breeding purebred cattle, horses and dogs, art collecting, internet, coaching polo. Died Dec. 13, 2004.

QURAISHI, MARGHOOB A., management consultant; b. Jaipur, India, July 15, 1931; s. Nazir A. Quraishi and Khudija B. Khan; married; 4 children. B of Commerce, U. Karachi, Pakistan, 1955, postgrad., 1956; cert. in bus. fin., indsl. mgmt. & rels., McGill U., Montreal, Que., 1958; MBA, Stanford U., 1959. Rsch. economist Riches Rsch., Inc., 1960-61; acct., auditor Webb & Webb, CPAs, 1961-62; contr., adminstrv. asst. to pres. Capcom, 1963; v.p., sr. cons. CPM Internat., Inc., 1964-65; mgr., contr. Woodside Homes, 1965-66; founder, pres. Associated Mgmt. Systems, Palo Alto, Calif., from 1966. Guest speaker, tchr. in field. Author numerous publs. in field. Mem. Inst. Mgmt. Cons., Am. Arbitration Assn., Am. Mgmt. Assn., Am. Mktg. Assn., Am. Soc. Appraisers. Died Jan. 26, 2005.

QURESHI, AZAM SAJJAD, manufacturing executive; b. Hyderabad, India, Oct. 18, 1942; came to U.S., 1965; naturalized; s. Khadim Hussain and Rafath Q.; m. Asima Qureshi, Jan. 4, 1969; children: Huma, Huda, Ali. BE in Mech. Engring., Osmania U., India, 1965; MS in Mech. Engring., Okla. State U., 1967; MBA, U. Santa Clara, 1974. Lic. profl. engr., Ont. Engr. rsch. and devel. div. Allis-Chalmers Corp., West Allis, Wis., 1967-69; sr. analytical engr. mobile div. Sperry-Vickers, Troy, Mich., 1969-72; design specialist ground vehicle systems group Lockheed Missiles & Space Co., Sunnyvale, Calif., 1972-75; mgr. engring. Tomco, Inc., Racine, Wis., 1975-77; v.p. engring. and product safety Calavar Corp., Santa Fe Springs, from 1977. Contbr. articles to profl. jours. Patentee in field (Queen's Silver Medal 1983). Mem. Soc. Automotive Engrs., Am. Soc. Safety Engrs., Am. Nat. Standards Inst., Mfr. Elevating Work Platform Council, Mfr. Aerial Devices and Digger Derricks Council. Republican. Islamic. Avocations: bridge, travel. Home: Fullerton, Calif. Died June 1, 2004.

RABE, PAUL ROBERT, marketing executive; b. Napoleon, Ohio, Oct. 3, 1948; s. George Fred and Amanda (Ludemann) R.; m. Karen Sue Behrman, Apr. 25, 1970; children: Kirsten, Brian. BS in Elec. and Computer Engring., Wayne State U., 1976; MS in Elec. and Computer Engring., Mich. State U., 1980. Cert. R.E.T.S., 1968. Research asst. Gen. Motors Research Labs., Detroit, 1968-74, sr. research asst., 1974-77, sr. project engr. diesel equipment Grand Rapids, Mich., 1977-78, supr. test lab., 1978-80, mgr. staff systems Detroit, 198-84; dir. product devel. Cummins Electronics Co., Columbus, Ind., 1984-87, v.p. mktg. and sales, from 1987. Contbr. articles to profl. jours.; patentee if field. Mem. IEEE, Soc. Autmotive Engrs. (vice chmn. 1978-80). Home: Columbus, Ind. Died Nov. 28, 2004.

RABINOWITZ, SAMUEL NATHAN, lawyer; b. Hazleton, Pa., Sept. 16, 1932; s. Morris M. and Bodia (Janowitz) R.; m. Barbara Cohen, Mar. 27, 1955; children— Fredric E., Mark I., Joshua A. BA, Pa. State U., 1955; JD, Temple U., 1959. Bar: D.C. 1959, Pa. 1960. Agt. IRS, Phila., 1956—60; sole practice Phila., 1960—61; ptnr. Blank Rome, LLP, Phila., 1961—2004. Mem. trust com. Continental Bank, Phila., 1983-91; faculty Temple U. Sch. Law Contbr. articles to profl. jours. Active Phila. Friends Boys Town Jerusalem; bd. dirs. Jerusalem Soc. Boys Town, Phila., Friends of Ben Gurion U. the Negev, Jewish Nat. Fund Coun., Phila.; chair, hon. chair Jewish Cmty. Ctr. Greater Phila.; dir. Arts in Edn. Fellow Am. Coll. Trust and Estate Counsel; mem. ABA, Pa. Bar Assn., Phila. Bar Assn. (chmn. probate and trust sect. 1985-86), Green Valley Country Club, Elkview Country Club, Delaire Country Club (Delray Beach, Fla.), Golden Slipper, Maccabi/USA Sports for Israel (exec. com., counsel). Home: Delray Beach, Fla. Died June 8, 2006.

RABINOWITZ, WILBUR MELVIN, manufacturing executive, consultant; b. Bklyn., Feb. 18, 1918; s. Harry A. and Caroline (Simmons) R.; m. Audrey H. Perlmutter, Apr. 30, 1944; 1 child, Michael B. PhB, Dickinson Coll., 1940; JD, Harvard U., 1943. Gen. mgr. J. Rabinowitz & Sons, Inc., Bklyn., 1945-67, pres., 1967-81, pres. emeritus cons., 1981-95. Pres. Met. Glass & Plastic Containers, 1967-81; trustee Mendeleyev U., Moscow, 1991—. Author: Almost Everywhere. Pres. Rabinowitz Found., N.Y.C., 1967—; trustee Dickinson Coll., Carlisle, Pa., 1975—. With AUS, 1943-45, ETO. Mem. Nat. Assn. Container Distbrs. (past pres.), U.S. Power Squadrons (past comdr.), Explorers Club. Home: New York, NY. Died Apr. 29, 2005.

RAFFA, STANLEY WILLIAM, engineer; b. N.Y.C., Sept. 3, 1925; s. Luigi and Flavia Sacca Raffa. Degree, Adelphi U., Poly. Inst. Bklyn., 1949. Tech. writer Am. Bosch Arma, Garden City, NY, site supr. Seattle; site dir. Western Union, Mahwah, NJ, asst. v.p.; ret. Author: Growing Up With the Movies, 1934-1941. Mem.: Alpha Phi Delta (nat. sec., v.p., pres.). Home: Dumont, NJ. Died Sept. 29, 2006.

RAFTERY, WILLIAM JOHN, priest; b. Somerville, Mass., July 16, 1916; s. William Francis and Beatrice Mary (Cody) R. BA, Cath. U., 1945; MA, Villanova U., 1953. Ordained priest Roman Cath. Ch., 1945. Tchr. St. Mary's Prep. Sch., Penndel, Pa., 1945-58; rector, prin. Immaculate Sem., Lafayette, La., 1958-64; rector, pres. Grad. Sch. Notre Dame Sem. Coll., New Orleans, 1964-67; parish priest Diocese Worcester, Mass., from 1968. Chaplain Lafayette Serra Club. Mem. Sch. Prins. Assn., Coll. Pres's. Assn. Died Feb. 8, 2005.

RAINES, IRENE FREEZE, real estate broker; b. Gadsden, Tenn., Nov. 13, 1924; d. Fred Dozier and Donnie May (Flippo) Freeze; m. James Athel Raines, 1944; children: Shirley Carol Canady, Carey Athel, David Anthony. Cert., Memphis Sch. Commerce, 1943; student, Jackson State Community Coll., 1978-84. Grad. Realtors Inst., 1986. Insp. Wayne Knitting Mills, Humboldt, Tenn., 1959-69; legal sec. Emison & Emison, P.C., Alamo, Tenn., 1969-79; affiliate broker Hale Herndon Agy., Humboldt, 1979-84; broker Raines Real Estate Agy., Alamo, from 1984. Clk. Chancellor's Office, Alamo, 1979; mem. Crockett County (Tenn.) Dem. Exec. Com., 1976; tchr. Sunday sch., dir. Women's Missionary Union, Bapt. Ch. Mem. Nat. Assn. Realtors, Tenn. Assn. Realtors (edn. com. 1987-88, chaplain), Crockett County C. of C. (charter mem., membership 1991—). Avocations: reading, crocheting, church work. Home: Bells, Tenn. Died Dec. 29, 2004.

RAINEY, FORD, actor; b. Mountain Home, Idaho, Aug. 8, 1908; s. Archie Coleman and Verna (Kinkade) R.; m. Sheila Mary Hayden, Feb. 4, 1954; children: Robert, James, Kathleen. Student, Centralia Coll., 1929-30, Cornish Sch. Arts, 1931-34, Santa Monica Coll., 1983-85. Actor Broadway prodns. including J.B. (dir. by Elia Kazan), The Posessed, Twelfth Night, Playboy of the Western World; actor off-Broadway prodns. including The Crucible, Richard III, Month in the Country, Death of a Salesman; actor feature films including Parallax View, Sand Pebbles, Kings of the Sun, Two Rode Together; actor TV film My Sweet Charlie; actor numerous TV shows including M*A*S*H*, Rawhide, Perry Mason, St. Elsewhere, General Hospital, Quincy; actor motion picture Bed & Breakfast. Served with USCG, 1942-45, PTO. Recipient Los Angeles Drama Critics award for Home by Pinter, 1980. Avocations: beekeeping, golf. Home: Malibu, Calif. Died July 25, 2005.

RAITT, JOHN EMMETT, singer; b. Santa Ana, Calif., Jan. 29, 1917; s. Archie John and Stella Eulalee (Walton) R.; m. Marjorie Geraldine Haydock, Dec. 28, 1942 (div. 1970); children: Steven James, Bonnie Lynn, David John; m. Kathleen Landry, 1970 (div. 1980); m. Rosemary Kraemer Lokey, Oct. 2, 1981. BA, U. Redlands (Calif.), 1939, D Music, 1957; LLD, Pepperdine U., Malibu, Calif., 1988. Singer appearing in Oklahoma, 1944, Carousel, 1945, Magdalena, 1948, Three Wishes Fortamie, 1951, Carnival in Flanders, 1953, The Pajama Game, 1954-57, Destry, 1960, Carousel, 1963, 65, Annie Get Your Gun, 1957, Zorba, 1970, Shenandoah, 1977-80. Hon. mayor Pacific Palisades (Calif.), 1990-94. Named to Hollywood Walk Fame, 1992, Theatre Walk Fame, 1994. Mem. The Riviera County Club. Avocations: swimming, golf. Home: Pacific Palisades, Calif. Died Feb. 20, 2005.

RALSTON, RACHEL WALTERS, developmental psychologist; b. Max, N.D., June 13, 1915; d. Lewis David and Wilhelmina May Bertha (Freitag) Walters; m. William Clifton Hollowell, May 22, 1944 (div. May 1962); m. John Elvin Ralston, June 24, 1964. AA, Foothill Jr. Coll., 1964; BA, San Francisco State U., 1969; postgrad., Can. Coll., 1975-81. Chair North Fair Oaks Adv. Coun., Redwood City, Calif., 1975-77; initiator Community Concern for Sr. Citizens, Menlo Park and San Mateo County, Calif., 1975-80; organizer, pres. Concerned Srs., Inc., San Mateo County, 1980-86, chair exec. bd. Redwood City, from 1987; peer counselor for the elders Mental Health div. Health Dept., San Mateo County, 1986-94. Mem. Older Adults Com., Mental Health Adv. Bd., 1985—; mem. adv. bd. Emeritus Inst. Coll. of San Mateo, 1987—. Mem. Com. on Aging San Mateo County, 1978-90; del. State House Conf. on Aging, Sacramento, 1980. Recipient Commendation Pvt. Sector Initiative, Washington, D. C., 1986; named Citizen of The Day Sta. KABL, San Francisco, 1985. Mem. AAUW, Am. Soc. on Aging, Am. Assn. Ret. Persons. Republican. Avocations: travel, photography, golf, dance. Home: Redwood City, Calif. Died June 7, 2004.

RALSTON, ROY B., petroleum consultant; b. Monmouth, Ill., June 7, 1917; s. Roy Crews and Helen Ruth (Boggs) R.; m. Catherine Elizabeth Thompson, Aug. 6, 1940; 1 child, John Richard. BA, Cornell Coll., 1939; student, Iowa U., 1938; postgrad., U. Ill., 1940-41. Petroleum cons., Colorado Springs, Colo., 1977-98, Bartlesville, Okla., from 1998; dist. mgr. exploration Skelly Oil Co., Evansville, Ind., 1941-46; div. mgr. exploration and prodn. Ashland Oil Co., Henderson, Ky., 1946-50, mgr. exploration and prodn. Ashland, Ky., 1950-54; div. mgr. exploration Phillips Petroleum Co., Evansville, 1955-58, Amarillo, Tex., 1958-65, Oklahoma City, 1965-69; v.p. exploration and prodn. Phillips Petroleum Can. Ltd., Calgary, Alta., Can., 1969-73; exploraton mgr. North Am. Phillips Petroleum Co., Bartlesville, Okla., 1973-75, regional mgr. exploration and prodn. Denver, 1975-77. Petroleum con. 1st Nat. Bank, Amarillo, Tex., 1977-93, Valley Nat. Bank, Phoenix, 1977-93, 1st Interstate Bank, Phoenix, 1977-86. Youth career dir. Oklahoma City C. of C., 1966-68. Recipient Disting. Svc. award Okla. Petroleum Coun., 1968, Svc. award Land Mgmt. Sch. Okla. U., 1978. Mem. Am. Assn. Petroleum Geologists (publicity dir. nat. conv. Oklahoma City 1968, cert. petroleum geologist), Am. Assn. Petroleum Landmen, Soc. Petroleum Engrs. AIME, Ariz. Geol. Soc., N.Mex. Geol. Soc., Rotary. Republican. Presbyterian. Avocations: hunting, horseback riding, water sports. Home: Bartlesville, Okla. Died Sept. 30, 2004.

RAMIREZ CANCEL, CARLOS MANUEL, psychologist, educator; b. Mayaguez, P.R., Nov. 10, 1944; s. Carlos M. Ramirez-Forestier and Celia Cancel Ramirez; m. Ana Isobel Martinez, Dec. 20, 1969; children: Ana Isabel, Marie Claire, Carlos Javier. BA in Psychology, U. P.R., 1969; MA in Psychology, Inter-Am. U., 1971; PhD in Psychology, Tex. A&M U., 1975. Counselor U. P.R., Mayaguez, 1969-72; teaching asst. Tex. A&M U., College Station, 1972-75; psychologist, assoc. prof. U. P.R., Mayaguez, 1975-86; part-time prof. U. P.R. Med. Sci. Campus, Mayaguez, 1977—2004; psychologist Mental Health Ctr. Hosp., Rincon, PR, 1976—2004; pvt. practice Mayaguez, 1976—2004. Psychologist S.S. Disability Determination Program, San Juan, 1976-2004; evaluations psychologist P.R. Dept. Edn., San Juan, 1976-2004, Dept. Social Svcs., San Juan, 1976-2004. Active mem. Statehood for P.R., 1976-2004, Citizens for Animal Protection, 1976-2004; active PTA, Immaculate Conception Sch., 1989-91; bd. dirs. southwestern Sch., Mayaguez, 1976-78. Mem. APA, Alliance Francaise d'Mayaguez (pres. 1991-2004). Republican. Roman Catholic. Home: Mayaguez, PR. Died July 23, 2004.

RAMSAY, WILLIAM THADDAEUS, retired secondary and college educator; b. Greensboro, N.C., Jan. 22, 1928; s. Douglas Taylor and Mary Ethel (Harrington) R.; m. Kendall Lathrop Durant, Sept. 20, 1952; children: Kathryn Linder, Laird William, Alan Douglas. AB, Atlantic Christian Coll., 1954; MA, East Carolina Coll., 1955. Cert. tchr., N.C. Tchr. Halifax (N.C.) County Schs., 1955-56, Atlantic Christian Coll., Wilson, N.C., 1956-60, Montgomery County Schs., Rockville, Md., 1960-61; tchr., adminstr. Montgomery Coll., Takoma Park, Md., 1961-83; tchr. Martin Community Coll., Williamston, N.C., 1983-84, Martin County Schs., Williamston, 1984-88; adminstr. Camden (N.C.) County Schs., 1988-93; ret. Cons. Oxford Assocs., Washington,

1978-82. Sgt. U.S. Army, 1950-52. Mem. Sigma Phi Epsilon. Democrat. Episcopalian. Avocations: music, reading. Home: Windsor, NC. Died June 22, 2004.

RAMSEY, GEORGE HAMILTON, petroleum engineer; b. Ardmore, Okla., Dec. 31, 1922; s. Ralph Hamilton and Grace (Nelson) R.; m. Merrily Thielecke, Jan. 20, 1946; children: David, Roger, Holly. BS in Mech. Engring., Mo. Sch. Mines, 1948. Rsch. engr. Standard Oil Co., Tulsa, Okla., 1948-52; cons. engr. Ardmore, from 1952. Chmn. bd. Omnia Inc., Ardmore, 1982—. Sgt. USAF, 1943-46. Mem. Soc. Petroleum Engrs., Okla. Soc. Profl. Engrs. (Engr. of Yr. South Cen. chpt. 1981). Presbyterian. Home: Ardmore, Okla. Died Mar. 8, 2004.

RAMSEY, JAMES JAY, real estate company executive, farmer; b. Wichita, Kans., Sept. 21, 1944; s. Jay C. and Margaret (Rapp) R.; m. Lynne L. Summer, Sept. 8, 1973 (div. Oct. 1986); children: Jason, Justin, Jarrod. Student, Ft. Hays State U., 1963-65. Farmer, Valley Center, Kans., 1966-68 and from 73; yellow pages salesman Southwestern Bell, Kansas City, Kans., 1968-73; with sales J.P. Weigand & Sons Inc., Kansas City, from 1983. Sgt. USAF, 1966-70. Mem. Kans. Real Estate Assn. Home: Spicewood, Tex. Died Dec. 12, 2004.

RAND, AUSTIN STANLEY, biologist, researcher; b. Seneca Falls, N.Y., Sept. 29, 1932; s. Austin Loomer and Rheua Vaughn (Medden) R.; m. Patricia Jane Grubbs, June 24, 1961; children: Hugh, Margaret, Katherine. BA, De Pauw U., 1954; PhD, Harvard U., 1961. Biologist Smithsonian Tropical Rsch. Inst., Balboa, Ancon, Rep. of Panama, 1964-97, asst. dir., 1974—79. Cons. Nat. Geog., 1970-2005. Editor: Iguana of the World, 1982; contbr. articles to profl. jours. Served in U.S. Army, 1955—57. Mem. Assn. Tropical Biology, Am. Soc. Icthyologists and Herpetologists, Animal Behavior Soc. Home: Alexandria, Va. Died Nov. 14, 2005.

RANEY, JEAN PUCKETT, art gallery director, artist; b. San Juan, P.R., May 11, 1954; d. Ralph Puckett and Jean Martha Martin; m. Dixon Flanary Raney, Sept. 11, 1982; children: Lauren Flanary, Dixon Flanary, Jr. BA in Polit. Sci. cum laude, U. Ga., 1976. Cert.: Nat. Ctr. for Paralegal Tng. (legal asst.). Legal asst. Webb, Carlock, Atlanta, 1978—86; owner Wedding Wand, Atlanta, 1984—94, Jean Raney Studios, Atlanta, from 1992. Art instr. Jean Raney Studio, Atlanta, from 1995; tchr. art appreciation Austin Elem., Dunwoody, Ga., 1997—99; judge DeKalb County State of Ga. Reflections Contests, Atlanta, 1998, Atlanta, 99, Outstanding Young Artists Competition, Alpharetta, 2002—03. Author: Paralegal Training Manual, 1980, Training and Procedures Manual for DFAA Gallery, 1995; co-author: Art Appreciation for Elementary Schools, 1996. Fundraiser United Way Atlanta, 1981; spl. events chair, fundraiser Ga. Trust for Hist. Preservation, 1979—81; mem., chair coms. Jr. League Atlanta, from 1982; PTA pres., bd. dirs. Austin Elem. Sch., Dunwoody, 1991—99; Vol., creator and chmn. Downtown Night "Mingle, Jingle & Jazz" Egleston Hosp. Festival Trees, 1979—86; mem. young careers and membership dr. High Mus. Art, Atlanta, 1978—81; co-chmn, mem. Dunwoody Twigs, 1989—2001; mem. social com. Wyntercreek Neighborhood1989, 1989—90; Sunday Sch tchr. 5th and 6th grades St. Luke's Presbyn. Ch., Dunwoody, 1991—93; bd. dirs. Neighbors of Wyntercreek, 1999—2001. Named Selected Artist, So. Living Idea House, 2000, Featured Artist, Wesleyan Sch., 2001. Mem.: Ga. Assn. Legal Assts. (newsletter chmn., bd. dirs.), PACESETTERS (bd. dirs., sec., spl. events chmn.), Dunwoody Fine Arts Assn. (gallery dir. 1995—98, bd. dirs., vol.), Wesleyan Arts Alliance (artist market chair from 1999, pres. 2003), Colonial Dames. Methodist. Avocations: painting in Italy, skiing, reading, studying languages, camping. Died June 29, 2004.

RANKIN, JIMMIE R., neuroscience nurse; b. Auburn, Calif., May 22, 1941; s. Gilbert O. and Wilma E. (Robertson) R. MSN, U. Calif., San Francisco, 1989; BSN, SUNY, 1983; BA, U. Calif., Berkeley, 1969; BS in Psychology, ASN, SUNY, Albany, 1977; ThD, St. Thomas Inst., 2001. Staff nurse Neurol. Inst., N.Y.C.; ind. nurse, prin. Dry Bones Nursing BBS, Dry Bones Press, San Francisco; dir. nursing Pacific Coast Hosp., San Francisco. Mem. AANN. Died Aug. 9, 2005.

RANNEY, J. AUSTIN (JOSEPH RANNEY), political science educator; b. Cortland, NY, Sept. 23, 1920; s. Frank Addison and Florence Edith (Ranney) R.; m. Elizabeth Mackay (div. Oct. 1975); m. Nancy Boland; children: Joseph, Douglas, Gordon, David. BS, Northwestern U., 1941, LLD (hon.), 1995; MA, U. Oreg., 1943; PhD, Yale U., 1948, DSS (hon.), 1985; LLD (hon.), SUNY, 1986, Northwestern U., 1995. Statistician Douglas Aircraft Corp., Chgo., 1942-44; instr. Yale U., New Haven, 1945-47; from instr. to prof. U. Ill., Urbana, 1947-63; prof. U. Wis., Madison, 1963-76; resident scholar Am. Enterprise Inst., Washington, 1976-86; prof. U. Calif., Berkeley, 1986-91, prof. emeritus, 1991—2006, chmn. dept. polit. sci., 1987-90. Author: The Doctrine of Responsible Party Government, 1954, Governing, 1958, Curing the Mischiefs of Faction, 1975, Channels of Power, 1983. Mem. Presdl.-Congl. Commn. on Polit. Activity Govtl. Employees, Washington, 1967-68, Dem. Nat. Com. Commn. on Party Structure, Washington, 1969-72, Commn. on Presdl. Debates, Washington, 1980-88; chmn. Gov.'s Commn. on Registration and Voting Participation, Madison, Wis., 1964, social sci. rsch. coun. Com. on Govtl. Processes, 1964-71, coun. on social scis. policy Yale U., 1983-88. Recipient Wilbur Lucius Cross medal Yale U. Grad. Sch., 1977; sr. rsch. fellow NSF, 1970, John Simon Guggenheim fellow, 1974, fellow Ctr. for Advanced Study in Behavioral Scis., 1974. Fellow Brit. Acad. (corr.); mem. Am. Polit. Sci. Assn. (pres. 1975-76), Am. Acad. Arts and Scis. (v.p. 1981-84). Home: Berkeley, Calif. Died July 24, 2006.

RAPP, GERALD DUANE, lawyer, manufacturing executive; b. Berwyn, Nebr., July 19, 1933; s. Kenneth P. and Mildred (Price) R.; children: Gerald Duane Jr., Gregory T., Amy Frances Wanzek. BS, U. Mo., 1955; JD, U. Mich., 1958. Bar: Ohio bar 1959. Practice in, Dayton, from 1960; ptnr. Smith & Schnacke, 1963-70; asst. gen. counsel Mead Corp., Dayton, 1970, v.p. human resources and legal affairs, 1973, v.p., corp. sec., 1975, v.p., gen. counsel, corp. sec., 1976, v.p., gen. counsel, 1979, sr. v.p., gen. counsel, 1981-91, counsel to bd. dirs., 1991-92; of counsel Bieser, Greer & Landis, 1992—2005. Pres. R-J Holding Co., Weber Canyon Ranch, Inc. Sr. editor U. Mich. Law Rev., 1957-58. Past chmn. Oakwood Youth Commn.; past v.p., bd. dirs. Big Bros. Greater Dayton; mem. pres.'s visitors com. U. Mich. Law Sch.; past trustee Urbana Coll.; past pres., trustee Ohio Ctr. Leadership Studies, Robert K. Greenleaf Ctr., Indpls.; past pres. bd. trustees Dayton and Montgomery County Pub. Libr.; past. mem. bd. visitors Law Schs. of Dayton. 1st lt. U.S. Army, 1958-60. Mem. ABA, Ohio Bar Assn., Dayton Bar Assn., Moraine Country Club, Dayton Racquet Club, Dayton Lawyers Club, Met. Club Washington, Phi Kappa Psi, Phi Delta Phi, Beta Gamma Sigma. Presbyterian. Died Nov. 27, 2005.

RASKIN, JEF, computer consultant, writer; b. N.Y.C., Mar. 9, 1943; s. William Benjamin and Frieda (Botfeld) R.; m. Linda Sara Blum, July 27, 1982; children: Aza Benjamin, Aviva Frieda, Aenea Hannah. BS in Math., SUNY, Stony Brook, 1965; MS in Computer Sci., Pa. State U., 1967. Prof. U. Calif. at San Diego, LaJolla, 1969-74; pres. Bannister & Crun, Brisbane, Calif., 1974-78; mgr. advanced systems Apple Computer Inc., Cupertino, Calif., 1978-82; chmn., CEO Info. Appliance Inc., Palo Alto, Calif., 1982-89; cons. Pacifica, Calif., 1989—2005. Cons. Hewlett Packard, IBM, NCR, Fujitsu, Ricoh, McKesson, others; vis. scholar Stanford Artifical Intelligence Lab., Stanford, 1973, Ctr. for Computer Rsch. in Music and Acoustics, 1995; creator Apple's Macintosh Project, 1979-82. Patentee in field; contbr. articles to profl. jours.; contbg. editor Wired Mag; Author: The Humane Interface, 2000 Bd. dirs. Pacifica Land Trust, Chanticleer, San Francisco, 1982-85; mem. San Mateo Regional Planning Commn., Redwood City, Calif., 1975-78. Grantee in thermal scis. NSP, 1962; Acad. Senate Rsch. Com. grantee U. Calif. San Diego, 1971; rsch. grant in computer music Pa. State U., 1966; fellow Creative Arts Inst., 1973. Mem. AAAS, Assn. for Computing Machinery, Acad. of Model Aeronautics, Calif. Acad. of Scis. Avocations: music, archery, model planes, naturalist. Home: Pacifica, Calif. Died Feb. 26, 2005.

RASMUSSEN, GAIL MAUREEN, critical care nurse; b. Can., Feb. 22, 1941; d. Thomas Alfred and Bernice Hilda (Sayler) Salisbury; m. Byron Karl Rasmussen, June 28, 1964; children: Stephen, Carla, Wade, Gregory. AS, Riverside City Coll., 1961; BSN, U. Phoenix, 1987; MS in Health Professions Edn., Western U Health Scis., 1991. RN, Calif.; CCRN. Staff nurse Meml. Med. Ctr., Long Beach, Calif., 1961-63, UCLA Med. Ctr., 1963-64; clin. nurse critical care unit Intercomty. Med. Ctr. (name changed to Citrus Valley Health Ptnrs.- Intercomty. Campus), Covina, Calif., 1964—71, from 1978. Instr. ACLS, Los Angeles County, 1991—. Mem. AACN. Home: Covina, Calif. Died Jan. 10, 2004.

RATHKE, GEORGE EDWARD, manufacturing executive; b. Rockford, Ill., June 2, 1945; s. Alfred G. and Alice D. Rathke; m. Debbie A. Rhodes, Sept., 11, 1965. BS, Rockford Coll., 1973. Mgr. strategic planning Sundstrand Corp., Rockford, 1973-74; dir. European Mktg. Sounstrand Corp., Dijon, France, 1974-75; group v.p., dir. Clausing Corp., Kalamazoo, 1975-81; v.p. sales and mktg. Ex-Cell-O Mfg. System Co., Rockford, 1981-85; v.p. contract services and advanced tech. programs Washington Sci. Ind., Inc., Long Lake, Minn., from 1985. Died June 4, 2004.

RATLIFF, MARTHA DOWDELL, real estate broker; b. Memphis, Jan. 2, 1925; d. David Merrick and Cornelia Adam (Jett) Dowdell; m. George Ernest Ratliff, Aug. 31, 1947; children: George Jr., Connie, David, Thomas. BS in Bus. cum laude, Miss. State Coll. for Women, 1946; postgrad., Wharton Jr. Coll., 1978. Lic. real estate broker. Co-owner, bookkeeper Ratliff Grocery, Cedar Lane, Tex., 1957-78; real estate sales rep. O'Connell & O'Connell Realty, Van Vleck, Tex., 1979-81; real estate broker Ratliff Realty, Cedar Lane, from 1981. Election judge Van Vleck Ind. Sch. Bd. Election, Cedar Lane, 1986-87. Mem. Matagorda County Bd. Realtors (v.p. Bay City, Tex. 1987—), Cedar Lane Extension Homemakers (treas. bldg. fund 1957-87), Bay City C. of C., United Meth. Women. Democrat. Methodist. Avocation: computers. Home: Cedar Lane, Tex. Died Jan. 6, 2005.

RATTIGAN, MARY THERESE, religion educator; b. N.Y.C., May 14, 1933; d. John Vincent and Mary Ellen (Heneghan) R. BA, Caldwell (N.J.) Coll., 1964; MA, Providence Coll., 1965; PhD, Fordham U., 1973. Adj. St. John's U., N.Y.C., 1974-79, asst. prof., 1979-86; assoc. prof. religion Caldwell Coll., from 1987. Contbr. articles to profl. jours. Trustee Kenmare Alt. High Sch., Jersey City, 1984-90, Holy Name Hosp., Teaneck, N.J., 1987—, St. Joseph Sch. for Blind, Jersey City, 1988—. Roman Catholic. Avocations: theater, hiking, travel. Home: Hackensack, NJ. Died July 17, 2005.

RAU, JOHANNES, former President of Germany; b. Wuppertal, Germany, Jan. 16, 1931; s. Ewald and Helene (Hartmann) Rau. Mem. North Rhine-Westphalian Diet, 1958-98; minister-pres. North-Westphalian Land, 1978-98. Chmn. North Rhine-Westphalian Parliamentary Group, Social Democratic Party, 1967—70, mem. exec. bd., 1968—99, chmn. dist. bd., 1977—98, mem. presidence, 1978—98, dep. chmn., 1982—99; pres. Bundesrat, 1982—83, 1994—95; lord mayor City of Wuppertal, 1969—70; min. sci. & rsch. North-Rhine Westphalia, 1970—78; pres. Fed. Republic Germany, Berlin, 1999—2004. Author: Oberstufenreform und Gesamthochschule, 1970, Die Neue Fernuniversitat, 1974, Friede als Ernstfall, 2001, Geschichte in Portraits, 2001. Decorated grand cross Order of Merit (Fed. Republic Germany), numerous others. Died Jan. 27, 2006.

RAUH, THOMAS RICHARD, management consultant, retail consultant; b. Cin., Nov. 10, 1949; s. Richard Frederick and Virginia (Nowak) R.; m. E. Porcher Hester, May 12, 1973; children: Grace, Claire, Elliott. BA, Williams Coll., Williamstown, Mass., 1971; MA, Occidental Coll., Eagle Rock, Calif., 1975; MBA, Stanford U., 1978. Rsch. analyst Office of Sen. Edmund Muskie, Washington, 1971-72; dir. rsch. Congressional Action Fund, Washington, 1972; field dir. Clean Water Action Project, Washington, 1972-73; urban planner Calif. Coastal Commn., San Francisco, 1974-76; mgmt. cons. Touche Ross & Co., San Francisco, 1978-87; pres. chief exec. officer Intermark corp., N.Y.C., 1987-88; mgmt. cons., ptnr. Ernst & Young, N.Y.C., from 1988. Mem. adv. com. Retail Mgmt. Inst., Santa Clara U., Calif., 1986-89. Died May 8, 2005.

RAUTMAN, ARTHUR LOUIS, clinical psychologist; b. Sheboygan County, Wis., Feb. 7, 1910; s. Louis and Louise (Westphal) R.; m. Florence Emily Ward, June 23, 1936; children: Christopher Arthur, Marcus Louis, Alison Eunice Rauk. BS in Chemistry, U. Wis., 1934, M. Philosophy, 1935, PhD, 1938. Diplomate in clin. psychology Am. Bd. Profl. Psychology. Clin. psychologist No. Wis. Colony and Tng. Sch., Chippewa Falls, 1938-42; psychologist, supr. spl. edn. Sioux City (Iowa) Pub. Schs., 1942-45; assoc. prof. Carleton Coll., Northfield, Minn., 1945-48, U. Fla., Gainesville, 1948-49; clin. psychologist U. N.Mex., Albuquerque, 1949-51; chief clin. psychologist U.S. VA Hosp., Bay Pines, Fla., 1951-52, U.S. VA Regional Office, St. Petersburg, Fla., 1952-71; pvt. practice clin. psychologist St. Petersburg, from 1971. Psychol. cons. Fla. Dept. Vocat. Rehab., St. Petersburg, 1955—, Fla. Dept. Health & Rehab. Svcs., St. Petersburg, 1970—, Family Svc. Ctrs., St. Petersburg, 1965—; prof. U. Mich. Rackham Grad. Sch., Ypsilanti, summers 1947, 48. Editorial bd. mem. VOICES: Jour. Am. Acad. Psychotherapists, 1983-89; contbr. numerous articles on psychology and edn. to profl. jours. Committeeman Boy Scouts Am., St. Petersburg, 1958-72, merit badge counselor, 1958—; bd. dirs. Country Day Sch., St. Petersburg, 1959-62; pres. Pinellas Psychol. Assn., St. Petersburg, 1961, 62. Fellow Am. Psychol. Assn. (fellow in clin. psychology, fellow in sch. psychology, div. psychotherapy, Recognition for Disting. Contbns. to the Discipline of Clin. Psychology 1986). Home: Saint Petersburg, Fla. Died Apr. 17, 2004.

RAVENSCROFT, VERNON FRANK, consultant; b. Buhl, Idaho, Jan. 26, 1920; s. William Francis and Fern (Gould) R.; m. Harriett Elnora Burkhard, Dec. 28, 1940; children: Marilyn, Carolyn, Lynell (dec.), Allan, Gordon, Bryan. BS in Forestry, U. Idaho, 1943. Extension forester Idaho Agrl. Extension Svc., Moscow, 1942-51; gen. mgr. Penta Post & Treating Co., Tuttle, Idaho, 1951-73; farming & cons. pvt. practice, Tuttle & Boise, 1973-79; pres. Consulting Assocs. Inc., Boise, from 1979. Contbr. articles to profl. jours. Mem. sch. bd. Hagerman (Idaho) Sch. Dist., 1956-64; state rep. Idaho State Legis., Boise, 1962-74; state party chmn. Idaho Reps., Boise, 1975-77; mem. adv. bd. Sawtooth Nat. Forest, Shoshone Dist. B.L.M., State of Idaho B.L.M. Recipient NAt. Outstanding 4-H Leadership award. Mem. Idaho Pvt. Power Coun. (state chmn. 1982-84), Idaho Ind. Energy Coun. (bd. dirs. 1992). Avocations: hunting, fishing, christmas tree culture. Home: Bliss, Idaho. Died Oct. 29, 2004.

RAVITZ, LEONARD J., JR., physician, scientist, consultant; b. Cuyahoga County, Ohio, Apr. 17; s. Leonard Robert and Esther Evelyn (Skerball) R. BS, Case Western Res. U., 1944; MD, Wayne State U., 1946; MS, Yale U., 1950. Diplomate Am. Bd. Psychiatry and Neurology, 1952, Am. Bd. Forensic Examiners, 1996, Am. Coll. Forensic Examiners; bd. cert. forensic examiner. Rsch. asst. EEG to A.J. Derbyshire, PhD Harper Hosp., Detroit, 1943-46; spl. trainee in hypnosis to Milton H. Erickson, MD Wayne County Gen. Hosp., Eloise, Mich., 1945-46, 46-80; rotating intern St. Elizabeth's Hosp., Washington, 1946-47; jr. asst. resident in psychiatry Yale-New Haven Hosp., 1947-48; asst. in psychiatry and mental hygiene Yale Med. Sch., 1947-48, assoc. in psychiatry and mental hygiene, sr. asst. resident, 1948-49, rsch. fellow to Harold S. Burr, PhD, sect. neuro-anatomy, 1949-50, sr. resident in neuropsychiatry Richard S. Lyman svc., 1950-51; instr. Duke U. Med. Sch., Durham, 1950-51; assoc. to R. Burke Suitt, MD, Pvt. Diagnostic Clinic, Duke Hosp., Durham, 1951-53; assoc. Duke U. Med. Sch., 1951-53; vis. asst. prof. neuropsychiatry and asst. to vis. prof. Richard S. Lyman, MD, Meharry

Med. Ctr., Nashville, 1953; asst. dir. profl. edn. in charge tng. U. Wyo. Nursing Sch. Affiliates; chief rsch. rehab. bldg. Downey VA Hosp. (now called VA Hosp.), N. Chicago, Ill., 1953-54; assoc. psychiatry Sch. Medicine and Hosp., U. Pa., Phila., 1955-58; electromagnetic field measurement project office dep. asst. sec. def. in charge health & med. E.H. Cushing MD Dept. Def., Pentagon, 1958; dir. tng. and rsch. Ea. State Hosp., Williamsburg, Va., 1958-60; pvt. practice neuropsychiatry specializing in hypnosis Norfolk, Va., 1961-69. Psychiatrist, cons. Divsn. Alcohol Studies and Rehab. Va. Dept. Health (later Va. Dept. Mental Health and Mental Retardation), 1961-81; psychiatrist Greenpoint Clinic, Bklyn., 1983-87, 17th St. Clinic, N.Y.C., 1987-92, Downstate Mental Hygiene Assocs., Bklyn., 1983—; sec.-treas. Euclid-97th St. Clinic, Inc., Cleve., 1957-63, pres., 1963-69; spl. tng. in epistemology and methodologic foundations of sci. knowledge F.S.C. Northrop, PhD, 1973-92; electrodynamic field rschr. with Harold S. Burr, PhD, sect. neuro-anatomy Yale Med. Sch., 1948-73; cons. hypnosis with Milton H. Erickson, MD, 1945-80; clin. asst. prof. psychiatry SUNY Health Sci. Ctr. Med. Sch., 1983—; pvt. cons., Cleve., 1961-69, Upper Montclair, N.J., 1982-90; lectr. sociology Old Dominion U., Norfolk, 1961-62, cons. to Ruth Harrell, 1978-90; spl. med. cons. Frederick Mil. Acad., Portsmouth, Va., 1963-71; cons. Tidewater Epilepsy Found., Chesapeake, Va., 1962-68, USPH Hosp. Alcohol Unit, Norfolk, 1980-81, Nat. Inst. Rehab. Therapy, Butler, N.J., 1982-83; participant 5th Internat. Congress for Hypnosis and Psychosomatic Medicine, Gutenburg U., Mainz, Germany, 1970; organizer symposia on hypnosis in psychiatry and medicine, field theory as an integrator of knowledge, hypnosis in gen. practice, history of certain forensic and psychotherapeutic aspects of the study of man, Eastern State Hosp., Coll. William and Mary, James City County Med. Soc., Va. Soc. Clin. Hypnosis, Williamsburg, Va., 1959-60. Author Electrodynamic Man: Electromagnetic Field Measurements in Biology, Medicine, Hypnosis and Psychiatry, 2002; asst. editor Jour. Am. Soc. Psychosomatic Dentistry and Medicine, 1980-83; mem. editorial bd. Internat. Jour. Psychosomatics, 1984—; contbr. sects. to books, articles, book revs., abstracts to profl. publs. Sr. v.p. Willoughby Civic League, 1971-75. ASTP AUS, 1946-48. Lyman Rsch. Fund grantee, 1950-53. Fellow AAAS, Am. Psychiat. Assn. (life), N.Y. Acad. Scis., Am. Soc. Clin. Hypnosis (charter, life, cons. cert. program), Royal Soc. Health (London); mem. Va. Soc. Clin. Hypnosis (founding pres. 1959-60), Norfolk Acad. Medicine, Soc. for Investigation of Recurring Events, Va. Med. Soc., Sigma Xi, Nu Sigma Nu. Achievements include discovery of electromagetic field correlates of hypnosis, emotions, psychiatric/medical disorders, aging, and electrocyclic phenomena in humans which parallel those of other life forms, earth and atmosphere underwriting beginning short- and long-range predictions preceding clinical changes, such seemingly disparate phenomena united under a single regulating principle defined in terms of measurable field intensity and polarity. Died Nov. 21, 2005.

RAWLEY, JAMES ALBERT, history professor; b. Terre Haute, Ind., Nov. 9, 1916; s. Frank S. and Annie B. (Vanes) R.; m. Ann F. Keyser, Apr. 7, 1945; children: John Franklin, James Albert. AB, U. Mich., 1938, A.M., 1939; PhD, Columbia U., 1949. Instr., Columbia U., 1946-48; Instr. N.Y. U., 1946-51, Hunter Coll., 1951-53; asso. prof. to prof. Sweet Briar Coll., 1953-64, chmn. history dept., 1953-57, chmn. div. social studies, 1962-64; prof. U. Nebr., 1964-87, prof. emeritus, 1987—2005, chmn. history dept., 1966-67, 73-82, acting dean univ. libraries, 1984-85, honors MASUA lectr., 1984-85, Carl Happold Disting. prof., 1986-87; resident scholar Rockefeller Study and Conf. Center, Italy, 1977. Vis. prof. U. Hanover, 1990; mem. adv. bd. Salmon P. Chase Papers, Abraham Lincoln Prize. Author: Edwin D. Morgan: Merchant in Politics, 1811-1883, 1955, Turning Points of the Civil War, 1966, Race and Politics, 1969, The Politics of Union, 1974, The Transatlantic Slave Trade, 1981, rev. edit., 2005, Secession: The Disruption of the American Republic, 1844-1861, 1989, Abraham Lincoln and a Nation Worth Fighting For, 1996, 2d edit., 2003, London, Metropolis of the Slave Trade, 2003; editor: The American Civil War: An English View, 1964; editor: Lincoln and Civil War Politics, 1969; contbr.: Essays in American Historiography, 1960. Served to 1st lt. AUS, 1942-46. Recipient Outstanding Research and Creativity award U. Nebr., 1983, George Howard-Louise Pound Disting. Career award U. Nebr., 1991; NEH fellow Huntington Library, 1979 Fellow Royal Hist. Soc., Soc. Am. Historians; mem. Am. Hist. Assn., So. Hist. Assn., Nebr. State Hist. Soc. (past pres.), Orgn. Am. Historians, Abraham Lincoln Assn. (bd. dirs.), Civil War Round Table Nebr. (charter pres. 1989-90), Lincoln Country Club, Phi Beta Kappa. Home: Lincoln, Nebr. Died Nov. 29, 2005.

RAWLINGS, NORBORNE LEWIS, JR., investment company executive; b. Washington, Nov. 19, 1931; s. Norborne Lewis and Lucy (Hix) R.; m. Jane Pierson Watson, Feb. 1, 1958; children: Frances Payne, Jane Pierson. Mng. ptnr. Loomis Sayles & Co., Phila., from 1963. Bd. dir. Castle Energy Corp., Blue Bell, Pa. Trustee Bryn Mawr (Pa.) Hosp., 1983, Dunwoody Home, Newtown Square, Pa., l98l; chmn. bd. Dunwoody Corp., l988—. lst lt. U.S. Army, 1953-55. Mem. Fin. Analysts Phila, Pa. Golf Assn. (pres. 1987). Episcopalian. Home: Devon, Pa. Died Apr. 26, 2004.

RAWLS, LOU, singer; b. Chgo., Dec. 1, 1935; m. Nina Malek Inman, Jan. 1, 2004; children: Louanna, Lou Jr. Former mem. musical group Pilgrim Travelers, solo rec. artist from 1962 (1 platinum, 6 gold albums), albums All Things in Time, Best of Lou Rawls, Classics, Lou Rawls Live, Trying as Hard as I Can, When You Hear Lou, You've Heard it All, At Last, 1989, It's Supposed to be Fun, Stormy Monday, 1990, Greatest Hits, 1991, Portrait of the Blues, 1993, Great Gentlemen of Song: Spotlight on Lou Rawls, 1996, Seasons for You, 1998, Best of Lou Rawls - Volumes 1 & 2, 2000, I'm Blessed, 2001, Rawls Sings Sinatra, 2003; composer: (songs) Natural Man, Love Is a Hurtin' Thing; appeared in motion pictures Angel Angel Down We Go, 1969, Believe in Me, 1971; star (spls. TV series) Soul, 1968, Lou Rawls and the Goldddiggers, 1969, numerous guest appearances (TV series) Uptown-A Tribute to the Apollo Theatre, 1980, nat. spokesman for Budweiser, from 1976, TV Telethon (UNCF), 1991. Hon. chmn. United Negro Coll. Fund. With U.S. Army, 1956—58. Recipient Grammy awards for rhythm and blues recs. Dead End Street, 1967, A Natural Man, 1971, Unmistakably Lou, 1977. Died Jan. 6, 2006.

RAYMOND, HAL See NETTLESHIP, HAROLD R.

RAYMOND, LAWRENCE PAUL, natural resource company executive; b. Pasadena, Calif., Nov. 3, 1944; s. Stanley Walter Raymond and Pauline (Scherer) Johnson. BS, San Diego State Coll., 1968; PhD, U. Calif., Santa Cruz, 1979; MBA, U. Colo., 1986. Research asst. U.S. Bur. Comml. Fisheries, La Jolla, Calif., 1964-69; head environ. analysis and planning Oceanic Found., Waimanalo, Hawaii, 1971-75; cons. biomass prodn. State Dept. Planning and Econ. Devel., Honolulu, 1975-79; research scientist food and agriculture Battelle N.W. Inc., Richland, Wash., 1977-78; mgr. biomass program Solar Energy Research Inst., Golden, Colo., 1979-84; chief exec. officer Internat. Bio-Resources, Golden, from 1983; pres., chief exec. officer, chmn. bd. Inland Mariculture Co., Lakewood, Colo., from 1986. Advisor marine biomass program Gas Research Inst., Chgo., 1980-83; advisor hyacinth project Disney World, Orlando, Fla., 1981-83; advisor Gov.'s Office Marine Affairs, Honolulu, 1975-79; co-chmn. biotech. 1st U.S.-China Tech. Exchange, Beijing, Peoples Republic of China, 1982. Contbr. articles to profl. jours.; patentee in field; inventor in field. Mem. Joint-Interagy. Subcom. on Aquaculture, Washington, 1981-82, Interagy. Subcom. Resource Recovery, Washington, 1979-80. Recipient Letter of Commendation, Garrison Study Commn., Denver, 1985. Mem. Phycol. Soc. Am., Nat. Shellfish Sanitation Conf. (mem. aquaculture com. 1988— Republican. Roman Catholic. Avocations: sailing, swimming, hiking, scuba diving. Home: Austin, Tex. Died July 19, 2004.

RAZOUK, RASHAD ELIAS, retired chemistry professor; b. Dumiat, Egypt, Aug. 22, 1911; arrived in U.S., 1968; s. Elias A. and Martha A. (Israfil) R.; m. Emily S. Habib, Aug. 24, 1946 (dec. Dec. 1988); children: Reda R., Rami R.; m. Henrietta Doche, July 8, 1990. BSc with honors, Cairo U., 1933, MSc, 1936, PhD, 1939. Asst. prof. Cairo U., 1939-46, assoc. prof., 1946-50; prof. chemistry, chmn. dept. Ain Shams U., Cairo, 1950-66; prof. Am. U. Cairo, 1966-68, Calif. State U., L.A., 1968-78, emeritus prof., from 1978; vice dean Faculty Sci. Ain Shams U., Cairo, 1954-60. Acting dir. divsn. surface and coll. chem. Nat. Rsch. Ctr., Cairo, 1954-68; vis. rsch. prof. U. So. Calif., 1965; cons. Lockheed Aircraft Co., L.A., 1971-73. Contbr. articles to profl. jours. Fellow Am. Inst. Chemists (hon.); mem. Am. Chem. Soc. (hon.), Royal Soc. Chemistry. Democrat. Roman Catholic. Achievements include research in adsorption, active solids, wetting and wettability, solid reactions, surface tension, and contact angles. Home: Burbank, Calif. Died Jan. 17, 2005.

READER, ARTHUR MURRAY, chemist; b. Bklyn., May 24, 1930; s. Charles Harry and Susan (Helhor) R.; m. Patricia Mae Silverstein, Dec. 10, 1954; children: Jeffrey Maxwell, Janet Anne Saari, Deborah Lynn, Michael Eugene. AB in Chemistry with distinction, Cornell U., 1952; PhD in Organic Chemistry, U. Tex., 1962. USPHS fellow U. Tex., Austin, 1961-62.; rsch. chemist Esso Rsch. & Engring. Co., Linden, N.J., 1962-63, Celanese Rsch. Co., Summit, N.J., 1964-66; sr. rsch. chemist, group leader Celanese Chem. Co., Corpus Christi, Tex., 1966-68; rsch. mgr. Riegel Textile Corp., Ware Shoals, S.C., 1969-71; product devel. mgr. Thiokol Fibers Div., Waynesboro, Va., 1971-76; dir. quality control E.T. Barwick Industries, Inc., LaFayette, Ga., 1977-79; tech. cons. Carpet & Rug Inst., Dalton, Ga., 1980; tech. dir. Laurkim Internat., Inc., Chattanooga, Tenn., 1981-83; tech. mgr., sr. rsch. chemist BASF Corp., Sylvania, Ga., 1984-89, sr. rsch. chemist II Enka, N.C., from 1990. Teaching asst. U. Tex., Austin, 1958-60; coadjutant instr. chemistry U. Coll., Rutgers U., New Brunswick, N.J., 1964-65; asst. prof. math. Dalton Jr. Coll., 1980. Contbr. articles to profl. jours.; patentee in field. 1st lt. USAF, 1952-58. Mem. Phi Beta Kappa, Sigma Xi. Avocations: travel, languages, computers, swimming. Home: Arden, NC. Died Mar. 18, 2005.

READY, WILLIAM ALVA, III, lawyer; b. Columbia, S.C., Jan. 11, 1955; s. William A. Jr. and Susie Ready; m. Deborah Boyles Gresham, May 21, 1977 (div. Dec. 1990); children: Rebekah Lynn, Deborah Leigh; m. Diana Carol Cook, Sept. 13, 1997. BA, Clemson U., 1977; JD, U. S.C., 1980. Bar: S.C. 1980, U.S. Dist. Ct. S.C. 1984, U.S. Ct. Appeals (4th cir.) 1986. Asst. solicitor Lexington (S.C.) County Solicitor's Office, 1980-84; asst. atty. gen. Office of the Atty. Gen., Columbia, 1984-87; staff counsel S.C. Dept. Health and Environ. Control, Columbia, from 1987. Organizer, dir. S.C. 1st Juvenile Arbitration Program for 1st Offenders, Lexington, 1983-84. Mem. Nat. Assn. Atty. Gens., S.C. Bar Assn., Phi Kappa Phi. Baptist. Avocations: reading, spending time with family, movies, church. Home: Columbia, SC. Died May 29, 2004.

REARDON, DANIEL FRANCIS, priest; b. Chgo., Jan. 24, 1932; s. James Joseph and Ann Valeria Reardon. BS, Loyola U., Chgo., 1954; MS, Marquette U., 1961; MST, Jesuit Sch., Berkeley, Calif., 1981. Cert. secondary sch. tchr., Ill. Instr. Viatorian Schs. Cathedral High Sch., Spalding Inst., St. Viator, Springfield, Peoria, Arlington Heights, Ill., 1954-73; pastor Holy Cross Ch., Morgan city, La., 1974-79; assoc. pastor Maternity B, Bourbonnais, Ill., 1981-83; pastor St. Mary, St. Martin, St. John, Iroquois County, Ill., 1983-89; assoc. pastor St. Viator Ch., Chgo., from 1989. Democrat. Died Oct. 28, 2004.

REARDON, MICHAEL DENNIS, construction executive; b. Millville, N.J., June 25, 1934; s. James Joseph and Lillian Edith (Vail) R.; m. Judith Eunice Schmidt; children: Susan, Kathleen, Maryann, William. Diploma Archtl. Estimate, Temple U., 1956. Bricklayer McCloskey & Co., Phila., 1952-56; v.p. Dan Lepore & Sons, Co., Phila., from 1956. Bd. dirs. therapeutic riding program Pegasus, Phila.; coord. One-Act Plays, Diocese of Phila., 1974—. Commdr. USCG Aux., Phila., 1974—. Republican. Roman Catholic. Avocations: boating, horseback riding, working with disabled children. Home: Philadelphia, Pa. Died Oct. 23, 2004.

REAVES, GIBSON, astronomer, educator; b. Chgo., Dec. 26, 1923; m. Mary Craig Kerr, Apr. 2, 1955; 1 child, Benjamin Kerr. BA in Astronomy, U. Calif., L.A., 1947; PhD in Astronomy, U. Calif., Berkeley, 1952. Mem. faculty U. So. Calif., L.A., 1952-94, prof. astronomy emeritus, 1965-94. With C.E., U.S. Army, 1942-46, PTO. Fellow AAAS, Royal Astron. Soc.; mem. Am. Astron. Soc., Astron. Soc. Pacific, Internat. Astron. Union; assoc. meritus Lowell Observatory. Achievements include research on dwarf galaxies in clusters, rsch. on history of astronomy, asteroid orbits. Home: Palos Verdes Peninsula, Calif. Died Apr. 8, 2005.

RECHTIN, EBERHARDT, retired aerospace transportation executive; b. East Orange, N.J., Jan. 16, 1926; s. Eberhardt Carl and Ida H. (Pfarrer) R.; m. Dorothy Diane Denebrink, June 10, 1951; children: Andrea C., Nina, Julie Anne, Erica, Mark. BS, Calif. Inst. Tech., 1946, PhD cum laude, 1950; D (hon.), U. So. Calif., 2005. Dir. Deep Space Network, 1958-67; asst. dir. Calif. Inst. Tech. Jet Propulsion Lab., 1960-67; dir. Advanced Rsch. Projects Agy., Dept. Def., 1967-70, prin. dep. dir. def. rsch. and engring., 1970-71, asst. sec. def. for telecom., 1972-73; chief engr. Hewlett-Packard Co., Palo Alto, Calif., 1973-77; pres., CEO Aerospace Corp., El Segundo, Calif., 1977-87, pres. emeritus, 1988—2006; prof. U. So. Calif., 1988—96, prof. emeritus, 1994—2006. Author: Systems Architecting. Creating & Building Complex Systems, 1991, The Art of Systems Architecture, 1997, Systems Architecting of Organizations, Why Eagles Can't Swim, 2000. Served to lt. USNR, 1943-56. Recipient maj. awards NASA, Dept. Def., USN, Disting. Alumni award Calif. Inst. Tech., 1984. Fellow AAAS, AIAA (Robert H. Goddard Astronautics award 1991), IEEE (Alexander Graham Bell award 1977), Internat. Coun. Sys. Engrs. (Pioneer award 1999); mem. Nat. Acad. Engring. (C&C prize Japan 1992), Tau Beta Pi, Eta Kappa Nu (eminent mem.). Home: Palos Verdes Peninsula, Calif. Died Apr. 14, 2006.

RECTOR, IRENE, retired elementary school educator; b. Vigo County, Ind., June 6, 1917; d. Warren Ray and Nellie (Davis) Rector. BS, Ind. State U., 1940, MS, 1965. Elem. tchr. Brazil City Schs., 1941—44; tchr. Boone County Schs., Thorntown, Ind., 1944—47; tchr. remedial reading Clay Community Schs., Brazil, Ind., 1947—75; elem. tchr. Marshall County Schs., Argos, Ind., 1941—44; tutor speech therapy and remedial reading, Brazil, 1947—64; coord. spl. reading program Boone County Schs., 1971—76, tchr., 1976—77, ret., 1977. Mem. NEA (coord. spl. reading program), Ind. Tchrs. Assn., Clay Community Classroom Tchrs., IRTA, CCRTA (past treas., sec.). Home: Brazil, Ind. Died June 26, 2005.

RED, JOHN WEST, JR., educational institution executive; b. Chattanooga, Dec. 18, 1920; s. John West and Margaret (Sadd) R.; m. Josephine Moore, May 16, 1945; children: Josephine Stewart, John West III, Margaret Terry. BS in Indsl. Adminstrn., Yale U., 1943. Div. mgr. Canada Dry, Charlotte, N.C. and Washington, 1946-55, asst. nat. sales mgr., 1955-56, v.p., 1956-62, exec. v.p., dir., 1962-68; assoc. James H. Oliphant & Co., N.Y.C., 1968-69; pres. Smith Richardson Found., Greensboro, N.C., 1969-73, Ctr. for Creative Leadership, Greensboro, 1970-81, sr. v.p., chief fin. officer, trustee, from 1981. Chmn. bd. trustees Well-Spring Retirement Community, Greensboro, 1986—. Lt. USNR, 1942-45. Mem. Yale Club N.Y.C., Greensboro Country Club, Rotary (bd. dirs. 1976-79). Episcopalian. Home: Greensboro, NC. Died Mar. 26, 2005.

REDD, VIVIAN CORTEZZA, government agency administrator; b. Harrisonburg, Va., Sept. 18, 1934; d. Manie Minerva Adelia Redd. LLB, LaSalle Ext. U., 1974. Clk. U.S. Patent & Trademark Office, Washington, 1965—66, patent reclassification clk., 1966—67, clk., 1967—72, office copier control clk., 1972, patent classification aid/tech., 1972—77, file integrity tech., 1977—84, sr. documentation projects asst., 1984—86, patent applications asst., from 1986. Avocations: reading, puzzles, crossword puzzles. Home: Arlington, Va. Died May 13, 2005.

REED, KENNETH PAUL, industrial hygienist, consultant; b. Covington, Ky., Aug. 30, 1937; s. George Anderson and Alice Martha (Spritzky) R.; m. Carol Irene Luken, May 21, 1966; children: Ann E., Susan L., Pamela N. AB, Thomas More Coll., 1957; MS, Xavier U., 1959; PhD, La. State U., 1968. Cert. indsl. hygienist Am. Bd. Indsl. Hygiene. Prof. chemistry Thomas More Coll., Ft. Mitchell, Ky., 1959-78, dir. devel., 1975-78, chmn. dept., 1969-75, asst. dean freshman and gen. studies, 1972-75; gen. mgr. Actus Environ. Svc., Florence, Ky., 1978-80; pres., founder Kenneth P. Reed and Assocs., Covington, from 1980. Cons. Nat. Inst. Occupl. Safety and Health, Cin., 1975—, U.S. Geol. Survey, Doraville, Ga., 1980-82, No. Ky. Bd. Health, Covington, 1980—, Hamilton County Bd. Health, 1996—. Author: Venture, 1975, (with others) Quantitative Chemistry, 1965; contbr. articles to profl. jours. NSF fellow, 1966-67. Mem. ASHRAE, NRA (life), Assn. Ofcl. Analytical Chemists, Am. Chem. Soc., Am. Indsl. Hygiene Assn., Am. Conf. Govtl. Indsl. Hygienists, Greater Cin. Area Safety Coun. (founder), Kenton (Ky.) Fish and Game Club, Rotary (bd. dirs. Covington 1982-87, pres. 1986-87). Republican. Roman Catholic. Home: Edgewood, Ky. Died Apr. 5, 2004.

REES, CHARLES H. G., retired finance company executive, investor, consultant; b. Trenton, NJ, Mar. 6, 1922; s. Albert H. and Helen (Gallagher) R.; m. Nancy Thomas, Oct. 30, 1954; children: Liberty, Camilla, Nancy, Hilleary. BA, Princeton U., 1948. Salesman John A. Roebling's Sons Co., Trenton, 1948-50; staff officer CIA, Washington, 1951-54; assoc. J.H. Whitney & Co., N.Y.C., 1954-59; gen. ptnr. Whitcom Investment Co., N.Y.C., 1967-85; with Whitney Comm. Corp., N.Y.C., 1960-85, pres., 1982-85; ret., 1985. Trustee Riverside Rsch. Inst., N.Y.C. With U.S. Army, 1942—46, capt. U.S. Army, 1950—51. Decorated Bronze Star. Mem.: Wadawanuck Yacht Club, Misquamicut Club, Ivy Club, Brook Club, Pilgrims N.Y.C. Home: Mystic, Conn. Died July 12, 2006.

REESE, MADGE ELEANOR READ, elementary school educator; b. North Vernon, Ind., Feb. 26, 1917; d. Parley Garfield and Ella Josephine (Smith) Read; m. Harry Boxell Reese, Aug. 12, 1940 (dec. June 1991); children: Paul David, Patricia Ellen, Michele Annette. BEd, Ball State U., 1955, MEd, 1956. Cert. tchr. Tchr. Muncie (Ind.) Cmty. Sch., 1956-76. Author: Sprial of Life, 1996, Humpback Barn, 1997; contbr. articles to profl. jours. Mem. DAR (chaplain 1993-99). Avocations: music, gardening, knitting. Home: Yorktown, Ind. Died Sept. 16, 2004.

REESER, DONALD M., pastor; b. Orangeville, Ill., Mar. 30, 1931; s. Martin Van Buren and Gladys L. (Schulz) R.; m. Joan Ellen Kurtz, Aug. 27, 1991; stepchildren: Mari Ellen, Renate Anne, Donald Martin. Diploma, Moody Bible Inst., 1954; AB in Psychology and Religion, Greenville (Ill.) Coll., 1956; MRE, No. Bapt. Theol. Sem., 1958; MA in German, So. Ill. U., 1975. Missionary tchr. Greater Europe Mission, Wheaton, Ill., 1960-69; asst. prof. Greenville Coll., 1969-79; pastor Bethany Bapt. Ch., Highland, Ill., from 1983. Vice moderator area V Gt. Rivers region Am. Bapt. Chs., 1991—. Mem. Area V Am. Bapt. Chs. of the Great Rivers Region (vice moderator 1991—). Republican. Home: Greenville, Ill. Died June 27, 2004.

REIBMAN, JEANETTE FICHMAN, retired state senator; b. Ft. Wayne, Ind., Aug. 18, 1915; d. Meir and Pearl (Schwartz) Fichman; m. Nathan L. Reibman (dec. 2005), June 20, 1943; children: Joseph M. Edward D., James E. AB, Hunter Coll., 1937; LLB, U. Ind., 1940; LLD (hon.), Lafayette Coll., 1969; degree (hon.), Wilson Coll., 1974, Cedar Crest Coll., 1977, Lehigh U., 1986, Moravian Coll., 1990. Bar: Ind., 1940, U.S. Supreme Ct. 1944. Pvt. practice law, Ft. Wayne, 1940; atty. U.S. War Dept., Washington, 1940-42, U.S. War Prodn. Bd., Washington, 1942-44; mem. Pa. Ho. of Reps., 1956-66, Pa. State Senate, Harrisburg, 1966-94, chmn. com. on edn., 1971-81, minority chmn., 1981-90, majority caucus adminstr., 1992-94. Mem. Edn. Commn. of the States. Trustee emeritus Lafayette Coll.; bd. mem. Pa. Higher Edn. Assistance Agy., Pa. Coun. on Arts, Camphill Schs. Recipient Disting. Dau. of Pa. award and medal Gov. Pa., 1968, citation on naming of Jeanette F. Reibman Adminstrn. Bldg., East Stroudsburg State Coll., 1972, Early Childhood Learning Ctr. Northampton Community Coll., 1992, Pub. Svc. award Pa. Psychol. Assn., 1977, Jerusalem City of Peace award Govt. Israel, 1977; named to Hunter Coll. Alumni Hall of Fame, 1974; U. Ind. Law Alumni fellow, 1993. Mem. Hadassah (Myrtle Wreath award 1976), Sigma Delta Tau, Delta Kappa Gamma, Phi Delta Kappa, Order Ea. Star. Democrat. Jewish. Home: Bethlehem, Pa. Died Mar. 11, 2006.

REID, ROBERT CLARK, chemical engineering professor; b. Denver, June 11, 1924; s. Frank B. and Florence (Seerley) R.; m. Anna Marie Murphy, Aug. 26, 1950; children: Donald M., Ann Christine. Student, Colo. Sch. Mines, 1946-48; BS, Purdue U., 1950, MS, 1951; ScD, MIT, 1954. Prof. chem. engring. MIT, Cambridge, from 1954, now prof. emeritus chem. engring.; Olaf A. Hougen prof. chem. engring. U. Wis., 1980-81. Author: (with J.M. Prausnitz and B.E. Poling) Properties of Gases and Liquids, 1966, 4th edit., 1987, (with M. Ohara) Modeling Crystal Growth Rates from Solution, 1973, (with M. Modell) Thermodynamics and Its Applications, 1974, 2d edit., 1983; Contbr. articles to profl. jours. Recipient Warren K. Lewis award, 1976; Chem. Engring. award Am. Soc. Engring. Edn., 1977; research fellow Harvard U., 1963-64 Mem. Am. Inst. Chem. Engrs. (Ann. lectr. 1967, council 1969-71, editor jour. 1970-76, Founders award 1986), Nat. Acad. Engring., Blue Key, Sigma Alpha Epsilon, Tau Beta Pi. Home: Lexington, Mass. Died May 18, 2006.

REILLY, ROBERT THOMAS, writer; b. Lowell, Mass., July 21, 1922; s. Joseph Michael and Elizabeth Hildergard (Cull) R.; m. Regina Marie McKenzie, June 9, 1945; children: Kathleen, Eileen, Colleen, Michaela, Christine, Hugh, Moira, Donal, Michael, Pegeen. BA, Suffolk U., 1947; MA, Boston U., 1948, postgrad., 1948-50. Accredited pub. rels. Prodn. mgr. Lawrence Advt. Agy., Boston, 1946-50; pub. rels. dir. Creighton U., Omaha, 1950-66; v.p., ptnr. Holland Dreves Reilly, Inc., Omaha, 1966-74; prof., communications Univ. Nebr., Omaha, 1972-87; writer, self-employed Omaha, from 1954. Pub. rels. cons. Bill Ramsey Assocs., Omaha, 1988—. Author 13 books including: Red Hugh, Prince of Donegal, Public Relations in Action, Irish Saints; author numerous documentary film scripts; contbr. articles to jours. Candidate 2d Dist. Congress, Nebr., 1970; active numerous civic orgns. including Am. Red Cross, Nat. Conf. Christians and Jews, others. 1st lt. infantry, U.S. Army, 1942-46, ETO. Named Boss of Yr., Nebr. Secretaries, 1969, Journalist of Yr., Midland Coll., 1977; recipient Hibernian award Jameson Whiskies, 1981, Fonda/McGuire award Omaha Playhouse, 1954. Mem. Pub. Rels. Soc. Am. (pres. 1988, Profl. of Yr. award 1985), Internat. Assn. Bus. Communicators, Omaha Press Club. Democrat. Roman Catholic. Avocations: photography, reading, travel. Home: Omaha, Nebr. Died Apr. 14, 2004.

REINER, ERICA, language educator; b. Budapest, Hungary; came to U.S., 1952; d. Imre and Clara Reiner Lic., Pazmany Peter U., Budapest, 1948; diploma, Ecole Pratique des Hautes Etudes, Paris, 1951; PhD, U. Chgo., 1955. John A. Wilson Disting. Service prof. Near Eastern languages. Oriental Inst. U. Chgo. Rsch. asst., The Assyrian Dictionary, 1952-56, rsch. assoc., 1956-62, editor, 1962-73, editor-in-charge, 1973-96 Author: A Linguistic Analysis of Akkadian, 1966, (with others) Enuma Anu Enlil: Babylonian Planetary Omens, Part 1, 1975, Part 2, 1981, Part 3, 1998, Part 4, 2005, Your thwarts in pieces, your mooring rope cut, 1985, Letters from Early Mesopotamia, 1993, Astral Magic in Babylonia, 1995, An Adventure of Great Dimension, The Launching of the Chicago Assyrian Dictionary, 2002 Grantee Am. Council Learned Socs., 1961; John Simon Guggenheim Meml. Found. fellow, 1974 Fellow Am. Acad. Arts and Scis.; mem. Am. Philos. Soc., Linguistic Soc. Am., Am. Oriental Soc. (pres. 1983-84) Home: Chicago, Ill. Died Dec. 31, 2005.

REINSEL, GREGORY CHARLES, statistician, educator; b. Wilkinsburg, Pa., Mar. 10, 1948; s. Philip D. and Ann (Popson) R.; m. Sandra Lee Kessock, May 15, 1976; children: Christopher, Sarah. BS, U. Pitts., 1970, MA, 1972, PhD, 1976. Asst. prof., prof. stats. U. Wis., Madison, from 1976, dept. assoc. chmn., 1995-97, dept. chmn., 1997—2001. Author: (book) Elements of Multivariate Time Series Analysis, 1993; co-author: Time Series Analysis: Forecasting and Control, 1994, Multivariate Reduced-Rank Regression, 1998; contbr. articles over 75 to profl. jours. Fellow: Inst. Math Stats, Am. Statistical Assn., Royal Statistical Soc.; mem.: Am. Geophysical Union. Avocations: basketball, hiking, running, music, modeling. Home: Madison, Wis. Died May 5, 2004.

REIS, WALTER J., psychiatrist, psychoanalyst; b. Wurtzberg, Germany, Aug. 5, 1918; married, 1941; children: Judy, Alan, Claude. BS in Chemistry, Gonzaga U., 1947, B in Philosophy, 1947; PhD, Western Res. U., 1951; MD, Emory U., 1956. Med. dir., surgeon U.S. Pub. Health, Norfork, Va., 1955-83; pvt. practice, from 1959. Cons., 1952-73; clin. prof. Western Psychiatric, Pitts., 1959—. Contbr. articles to profl. jours. Clin. psychologist U.S. Air Corps, 1943-46. Fellow Am. Psychiatric Assn. (life); mem. AMA, Am. Psychiatric Assn., Am. Psychoanalytic Assn., Internat. Psychoanalytic Assn., Am. Psychol. Assn., Soc. Projective Techniques; Pa. Med. Soc., Psychiatric Assn., Pitts. Psychoanalytic Soc., Pitts. Psychiatric Soc. Home: Pittsburgh, Pa. Died July 24, 2005.

REITMAN, SANFORD, radiologist; b. Newark, June 12, 1933; BS, Allegheny Coll., U. Pa., 1954; MS in Physiology and Biochemistry, Rutgers U., 1955; MD, U. Ala., 1959. Diplomate Am. Bd. Radiology. Rsch. fellow neuroanatomy Nat. Found., 1956-57; intern radiology Naval Hosp., Phila., 1959-60; resident radiology San Diego Naval Hosp., 1961-64; med. dir. radiology Harris Hosp. NW, Fort Worth; assoc. prof. biomed. engring. U. Tex.; physician group practice Radiology Assocs. Tarrant County, Fort Worth. Chief resident therapy and diagnosis, Regional Naval Med. Ctr., San Diego; chief of radiology Newport Naval Hosp., 1975-85; sr. cons. interventional radiology Meml. Hosp., R.I.; chmn. radiology Arlington Meml. Hosp., 1973-87, Harris Southwest Hosp., 1987-96. State bd. dirs. Am. Cancer Soc., 1972-74, dist. dir. 1972, pres. county chpt. 1970-71. NIH fellow, 1957-58. Fellow Royal Soc. Health; mem. Am. Coll. Radiology, Assn. Mil. Surgeons of the U.S., Am. Nuc. Soc., Biomed. Engring. Soc., Royal Coll. Surgeons (faculty radiologist), Radiol. Soc. N.Am., Am. Assn. Univ. Profs., Tex. Med. Assn., Tex. Radiol. Soc., New Eng. Roentgen Ray Soc., Ala. Acad. Sci. Died Apr. 18, 2006.

REITZ, SPENCER, marine engineering consultant; b. Bklyn., Feb. 22, 1918; s. George Ballantyne and Lillian Spencer (Hegeman) R.; m. Barbara Buford Scott, Dec. 7, 1943; children: Scott Hegeman, Spencer Ballantyne. BS in Engring., U. Mich., 1941; MS, MIT, 1948; cert. in advanced mgmt., U. Pitts., 1960. Registered mechanical engr., Mass. Commd. ensign USN, 1941, advanced through grades to capt., ret., 1969; dir. naval programs Quincy (Mass.) Shipbldg. divsn. Gen. Dynamics, 1969-77; dep. gen. mgr. electric boat divsn. Gen. Dynamics, Groton, Conn., 1977-82; cons. naval architecture and marine engring. Old Lyme, Melbourne, Conn., Fl., from 1982. Alternate mem. Zoning Commn., Old Lyme, 1982-85. Decorated Legion of Merit. Mem. Soc. Naval Architects and Marine Engrs. (life, tech. papers com., awards com. 1941-95), N.Y. Yacht Club, Essex Yacht Club, Chi Psi. Republican. Mem. Dutch Reformed Ch. Avocations: golf, sailing. Home: Melbourne, Fla. Died July 3, 2005.

REMLEY, MARLIN EUGENE, nuclear company executive; b. Walcott, Ark., Apr. 25, 1921; s. Aubrey James and Kate (Clarida) R.; m. Ruth Neoma Evens, Apr. 4, 1943; children: Carol Sue Bothwell, Nancy Ann Hedges, Barbara Jean Taylor. AB, Southeast Mo. State U., 1941; postgrad., Iowa State U., 1941-42; MS, U. Ill., 1948, PhD, 1952. Registered profl. nuclear engr., Calif. Instr. physics and math. Southeast Mo. State U., Cape Girardeau, 1946-47; research asst. U. Ill., 1947-51; with Atomics Internat. div. Rockwell Internat., Canoga Park, Calif., from 1951, dir. reactor devel., 1958-60, dir. reactor physics, instrumentation, 1960-61, dir. health, safety, radiation services, 1961-84, dir. nuclear safety and licensing, from 1984. Lectr. nuclear engring. UCLA extension; exec. dir. Atomic Energy Info. Services. Contbr. articles to profl. jours. Served to capt., Signal Corps U.S. Army, 1942-46. Recipient Southeast Mo. State U. Alumni Merit award, 1973. Fellow Am. Nuclear Soc. (officer reactor ops. div. 1972-76, chmn. 1975-76, mem. nuclear power plant standards com.), Atomic Indsl. Forum (reactor safety com.), Nat. Mgmt. Assn. (pres. Valley chpt. 1969, Silver Knight Mgmt. award 1983), Calif. Mfrs. Assn., Pacific Coast Electric Assn., Chatsworth C. of C. (pres. 1972-78), Sigma Xi, Phi Kappa Phi, Pi Mu Epsilon, Alpha Phi Omega. Republican. Presbyterian. Home: Northridge, Calif. Died June 26, 2005.

REMMERS, MARVIN HENRY, minister; b. Adams, Nebr., June 15, 1935; s. John Benjamin and Grace (Busboom) R.; m. Geraldine Ann Bauer, June 22, 1958; children: John, Julia, Joel. BA, Wartburg Coll., 1957, B of Divinity, 1961, MDiv, 1977. Pastor St. Paul's Evangel. Luth. Ch., Cole Camp, Mo., 1961-65, Evangel. Luth. Ch. of the Cross, Chgo., 1965-71; sr. pastor Am. Luth. Ch., Rantoul, Ill., from 1971. Vice-pres. Ill. Dist. Am. Luth. Ch., Chgo., 1977-81; bd. dirs. Oaks (Okla.)-Cherokee Oaks Indian Mission, 1962-65, nat. stewardship com. Am. Luth. Ch., 1970-71, congregational life com./Evangel. Luth. Ch., 1989—, hospice com. Venany Hosp., Urbana, Ill., 1989—; chaplain Ill. State Senate, 1968; others. Chmn. Human Rels. Com., Rantoul, Ill., 1973-76; bd. dirs. Champaign County Community Svcs., Rantoul, 1973-77; pres. Rantoul Ministerial Assn., 1976, 81. Mem. Exch. Club. Republican. Home: Rantoul, Ill. Died Feb. 1, 2005.

RENAKER, LORETTA ELIZABETH, retired elementary school educator; b. Dayton, Ohio, Oct. 30, 1936; d. August Carl and Margaret B. (Falkner) Hartung; children: Deborah Elizabeth Montgomery, Sharon Linn Helm. BS in Elem. Edn., U. Dayton, 1962; MS in Elem. Edn., Miami U., Oxford, Ohio, 1972. Cert. tchr., Ohio, Ind. 3d grade tchr. Meadowlawn Elem. Sch., Kettering, Ohio, 1957-59, Brookville (Ind.) Elem. Sch., 1964—96. Mem.: NEA-R, Franklin County Ret. Tchrs. Assn. (sec.-treas.), Ind. State Tchrs. Assn., Franklin County Cattlemens Assn., Nat. Angus Assn., Kappa Kappa Kappa, Delta Kappa Gamma. Avocations: sewing, piano, reading, raising aberdeen black angus, travel. Died Jan. 16, 2004.

RENDA, DOMINIC PHILLIP, air transportation executive; b. Steubenville, Ohio, Dec. 25, 1913; s. Joseph J. and Catherine (Roberta) R.; m. Delores E. Noland, July 12, 1980; children: Dominique Patricia, Dominic Phillip, Patrick Blake. BS in Bus. Adminstrn; JD, Ohio State U., 1938. Bar: Ohio 1938. Practice law, Steubenville, 1938-41; adminstrv. asst. to mem. Congress, 1941-42; with Western Air Lines, Inc., Los Angeles, 1946-68, asst. sec., 1947, v.p. legal, 1954-65, sr. v.p. legal, corp. sec., 1958-68; pres. Air Micronesia, Inc., Los Angeles, 1968-73; sr. v.p. internat. and pub. affairs Continental Air Lines, Inc., 1968-73; exec. v.p., dir., mem. exec. com. Western Air Lines, 1973-76, pres., mem. exec. and nominating coms., 1976-81, CEO, mem. mgmt. resources and compensation com., 1979-81, chmn. bd., 1981, chmn. emeritus, 1982-85. Dir. Bank of Montreal, Calif.; Mem. bus. adminstrn. adv. council Coll. Adminstrv. Sci., Ohio State U., 1974-82; bd. councilors Sch. Internat. Relations, U. So. Calif., 1967-82 Trustee Peace Found., Ponape, Caroline Islands, 1976-84; chmn. devel. com. Marymount High Sch., 1977-82. Served to lt. comdr. USNR, 1942-46. Mem. Calif., Ohio state bars, ABA, Los Angeles County Bar Assn. (past trustee), Calif. C. of C. (dir.), Phi Alpha Delta (pres. Los Angeles 1965-66) Clubs: Los Angeles Chancery (pres. 1966-67), Morningside Country Club, Rancho Mirage. Home: Rancho Mirage, Calif. Died Sept. 2, 2006.

RENFREW, GLEN MCGARVIE, former world news service executive; b. Aberdare, New South Wales, Australia, Sept. 15, 1928; s. Robert and Jane Grey (Watson) R.; m. Daphne Ann Hailey, Feb. 20, 1954; children: Barry Glen, Ann Gladys (dec.), Susan Jane, Judith Hailey. BA, Sydney U., Australia, 1949. With Reuters News Service, 1952-91, began in London, Eng., 1952, then served in reporting and mgmt. posts in Africa, Europe and Far East, mgr. computer div., 1964-70, mgr. N.Am., 1971-81; mng. dir., chief exec. officer Reuters Holdings PHC, London, 1981-91; chmn. Reuters N.Am., Inc., 1987-91. Mem. Nat. Press Club, Manhassett Bay Yacht Club. Died June 29, 2006.

RENNINGER, JOHN SNOWDEN, lawyer; b. Philadelphia, Oct. 10, 1924; s. Francis X. and Mary R. (Renninger); m. Katharine (Steele), Nov. 17, 1951; children: Ann, Molly, Sarah, Patrick. BA, Pa. State U., 1948, LLB, 1951. Bar: Pa., 1951; lic. pvt. pilot. Law clk. Ct. of Common Pleas, Phila., 1951-52; atty. Atlantic Refining Co., Phila., 1952-55; assoc. Ross and Smith, Doylestown, Pa., 1955-58; ptnr. Ross, Smith, and Renninger, Doylestown, Pa., 1958-68, Pepper, Hamilton, and Sheetz, Phila., 1968-72, Renninger and Kupits, Doylestown, Pa., 1972—2004, Renninger, Spear, and Myers, Doylestown, Pa., 1987-94. Bd. dir., counsel Bucks Beautiful, Doylestown; pres., bd. dir. The Pennsbury Soc., Morrisville, Pa., 1963-2005; bd. dir. Pearl S. Buck Internat.; bd. dir., chmn. Washington Crossing Reenactment. Mem. Pa. Ho. of Rep., Harrisburg, 1964-76; Sgt., USAF, 1943-46; PTO. Mem. ABA; Pa. Bar Assn.; Phila. Bar Assn.; Bucks County Bar Assn. (sec.); Lawyer Pilots Bar Assn. (bd. dir. 1990-94); Law Rev. Republican. Episcopalian. Avocation: flying. Died Apr. 2, 2005.

RESSNER, PHILIP, editor; b. Bklyn., Oct. 29, 1922; s. Charles and Jane (Kerensky) R.; m. Lydia Ehrlich, Aug. 13, 1957 (dec. Sept. 1975); children: Simon, Alice Joan, Anabel Reine. Student, Columbia U., 1947, U. Chgo., 1949-50; BA, NYU, 1954. Motorman N.Y.C. Transit System, 1948, 50-54; editor Harper & Row (now Harper Collins), N.Y.C., 1958-67, Harcourt Brace Jovanovich, N.Y.C., 1967-81, WH Freeman/Scientific Am. Books, N.Y.C., 1982-85; writer, editor MTA Metro-North R.R., N.Y.C., 1986-98. Author: August Explains, 1965, Dudley Pippin, 1965, At Night, 1967, The Park in the City, 1971, Jerome, 1972, Dudley Pippin's Summer, 1979. Served in U.S. Army, 1942-46. Home: Brooklyn, NY. Died Dec. 27, 2005.

RESTIVO, RICHARD RENE, service company executive; b. Winnipeg, Man., Can., May 30, 1944; s. Sam and Teresa (Berube) R. BA, Calif. State U., Fullerton, 1968. Pres. Relocation Systems (N.Am. Van Lines Moving Co.), City of Industry, Calif., from 1976. Sgt. U.S. Army, 1968-70, Vietnam. Decorated Silver Star, Bronze Star, Purple Heart. Republican. Roman Catholic. Home: West Covina, Calif. Died May 14, 2005.

REVSIN, LESLIE KIM, writer, chef consultant; b. Chgo., Oct. 19, 1944; d. William Revsin and Selma Geraldine (Brous) Weisenborn; m. William Raymond Arp, May 2, 1964 (div. Aug. 1975); 1 child, Rachel; m. Philip Donald Carlson, Aug. 16, 1980. BA magna cum laude, Macalaster Coll., 1966; AAS, N.Y. Tech. Coll., 1973. Chef poissonière and saucière Waldorf Astoria, N.Y.C., 1972-74; head chef P.S. 77 Restaurant, N.Y.C., 1974-76; owner, chef Restaurant Leslie, N.Y.C., 1977-81; exec. chef One Fifth Restaurant, N.Y.C., 1984-85, Inn at Pound Ridge, N.Y., 1990-94; owner Pan Prodns., Bronxville, 1994—2004. Cons. The Rainbow Rm., N.Y.C., Rockrimmon Country Club, R&R Restaurants Ct., 1988-2004; spokesperson Driscoll Strawberries, Watsonville, Calif., 1993-2004; mem. corp., mem. com. Culinary Inst. of Am., Hyde Park, N.Y., 1994-2004. Author: Great Fish, Quick, 1997, Come for Dinner, 2003; on-air talent, guest various TV programs, 1993-2004, including PBS cooking series Master Chefs of N.Y., 1985. Grantee De-Witt Wallace Found., 1965; named to Top Am. Chefs, Food & Wine Mag., 1983; recipient Tribute to Am. Chefs award Ocean Spray Co., 1983. Mem. Women Chefs and Restaurateurs (chair scholarship com. 1996-2004), Internat. Assn. Culinary Profls., Les Dames d'Escoffier (founding mem.). Avocation: gardening. Died Aug. 9, 2004.

REYNOLDS, BETTY JANE, retired nursing administrator and educator; b. Terre Haute, Ind., Dec. 19, 1926; d. George H. and Mary I. (Lambeth) Defel; m. Alex J. Reynolds (dec.); children: Cindy Carley, Elaine Platt. AAS, Mohawk Valley C.C., Utica, N.Y., 1971; BSN, Syracuse U., 1975; MSN, U. Cin., 1977; EdD, U. Rochester, 1984. RN, N.Y., Ohio, N.C. Instr. Syracuse U., 1977-79; asst. prof. SUNY, Utica, 1979-85; assoc. prof. East Carolina U., Greenville, N.C., 1985-90, U. N.C., Wilmington, 1990-92, assoc. dean, 1992-95; ret., 1995. Surveyor N.C. Commn. on Accreditation of Home Care, Raleigh, 1986-94; cons. for nursing Reynolds Consultation, Stokes, N.C., 1985-98. Author chpt. and articles in field. U. Cin. scholar, 1975-77, U. Rochester fellow, 1982-84. Mem. Nat. League for Nursing, Sigma Theta Tau, Kappa Delta Pi. Avocations: gourmet cooking, quilting, walking, swimming, stained glass. Home: Stokes, NC. Died July 2, 2004.

RHEA, MARY ELIZABETH, financial planner; b. Warren, Pa., Nov. 26, 1924; d. Francis H. and Wilma (Burkett) Nelson; m. Charles Otis Rhea, June 2, 1984; children by previous marriage: Susan, Judy, Milt, Betsy. Student, Westmar Coll., 1951-52, Coll. of Desert, 1963, Cypress Coll., 1968-69. CFP. Fin. planner Am. Pacific Securities, San Diego, 1970-89, co-owner, mgr., sec., 1984-88; fin. planner Fin. Network, San Diego, from 1989, mgr., from 1988. Gen. securities prin., 1973-89. Recipient Big Eagle award Am. Pacific Securities, 1983, 84, 86, 87. Mem. Internat. Assn. Fin. Planning, Inst. Cert. Fin. Planners, C. of C., Soroptomists. Home: El Cajon, Calif. Died Jan. 9, 2004.

RHINELANDER, ESTHER RICHARD, secondary school educator; b. Honolulu, Aug. 31, 1940; d. William Wise and Elizabeth (Chilton) Richard; m. Harvey James Rhinelander, July 24, 1965; 1 child, Lori. BEd, U. Hawaii, 1963, profl. cert., 1964. Tchr. music Kamehameha Sch., Honolulu, from 1965, Kamehameha Sch. for Girls, Honolulu, 1964, Waianae High and Intermediate Sch., Honolulu, 1965. Dir. Waiokeola Ch. Choir, Honolulu, 1964-67, Kawaiahao Ch. Choir, Honolulu, 1980-87; judge song contest Kamehameha Schs., 1972, 88; judge choral composition contest Hawaii Found. on Culture and Arts, Honolulu, 1984, 85; pianist Kahikuonalani Ch., Honolulu, 1987—, Ch. Choral Ensemble, 1987—; tchr. Sunday Sch., 1988—. Mem., asst. accompanist Honolulu Opera Guild, 1955-59. Mem. Am. Choral Dirs. Assn., Soc. Gen. Music Tchrs. (sec. 1989-90), Music Educators Nat. Conf., Hawaii Music Educators Assn. Democrat. Mem. United Ch. of Christ. Avocations: reading, gardening, baking. Home: Pearl City, Hawaii. Died Nov. 16, 2004.

RHOADS, NORMAN GLEN, construction company executive; b. Wheeler, Mich., Oct. 12, 1928; s. Cleo Charles and Edith Milisa (Hendricks) R.; m. Viola Mae Weaver, July 24, 1948; children: Bethany Mae Rhoads Barker, Thomas Glen, Brenda Kay (Rhoads) Herivel. Grad. high sch., Burton, Mich. Gen. mgr. James Lumber Co., Flint, Mich., 1946-61; v.p. Case Constrn. Co., Flint, 1961-66; v.p., gen. mgr. Center Constrn. Co., Flint, 1966-69; pres., gen. mgr. Rhoads & Johnson Constrn., Inc., Flint, 1969-82, chmn. bd., from 1982; sec. Rhoads & Johnson, Inc., Prescott, Ariz., from 1985. Ptnr. Silver Lake Centre, Flint, 1975—; mng. ptnr. C.J.R. Co., Flint, 1979—. Bd. dirs. Brookview Found., Inc., Fenton, Mich., 1979-84, pres. 1979-82; bd. dirs. South Flint Ch. of Nazarene, 1951—. Mem. Metal Bldg. Dealers Assn. Lodges: Optimists (pres. Flint chpt. 1970-71). Republican. Avocations: flying, water sports, hunting. Home: Linden, Mich. Died Feb. 18, 2005.

RHODES, RICK, composer; b. L.A., July 28, 1951; s. Milton and Shirley Francis (Pagter) Rothstein; m. Vivian Elaine Weinstein, Sept. 12, 1982; children: Allison Suzanne, Adam Michael. Student, Santa Monica Coll., 1970-71. TV composer, music dir. Santa Barbara (NBC), Burbank, Calif., 1986—92, Family Ties (NBC), L.A., 1987-89, Day By Day (NBC), L.A., 1988-89. Songwriter, musician, L.A., 1971-2005. Composer/music dir.: (TV show) Santa Barbara (Emmy 1988, Emmy nomination 1989, 90). Avocations: swimming, family trips, baseball. Home: Oak Park, Calif. Died Nov. 2, 2005.

RHYNE, CARL EDWARD, small business owner; b. Clinton, Tenn., June 26, 1939; s. Lester Eugene and Maude (Jennings) R.; m. Jean Louise Ault, June 11, 1960; children: Deborah Marie, Duane Keith, Donna Faye. BS, U. Tenn., 1961. Investigator Retail Credit Co., Knoxville, Tenn., 1961-63; acct. Rohm & Haas Co., Knoxville, 1963-75; owner, mgr. Knoxville Tours, Inc., 1974-79, Vol. Tours and Travel, Knoxville, from 1979. Deacon Black Oak Heights Bapt. Ch., 1980—, chmn., 1986. Mem. Assn. Profl. Travel Agys. (treas. 1987—). Lodges: Rotary. Avocations: fishing, weather forecasting. Home: Powell, Tenn. Died Jan. 26, 2004.

RICE, EMILY JOY, retired secondary school and adult educator; b. Terrell, Tex., Aug. 30, 1928; d. Martin Alexander Joy Jr. and Susan Martha (Helen) Ruth Joy; m. LeRoy Noonon Rice Jr., May 30, 1951; children: Edna Anne Rice-Padhi, Margaret Elizabeth (dec.). BS, Tex. Woman's U.; postgrad., U. Tex., Tex. A&I U. Tchr. adult Bible studies First United Meth. Ch., Harlingen and Austin, Tex., Bellaire United Meth. Ch., Houston; instr. Austin C.C., 1982-90; tchr. Austin Ind. Sch. Dist., 1982-92; writer, lectr. Vol. Meth. Hosp., Houston, 1993-2001; mem. scholarship com. U. Tex. Mem. Current Study Club Houston (pres. 2000-2002), Tex. Woman's Univ. Nat. Alumnae Assn. (pres. 2001-2002 Houston chpt.), Delta Kappa Gamma. Home: Houston, Tex. Died Aug. 25, 2004.

RICE, RICHARD FRANCIS, chemical engineer, researcher; b. N.Y.C., May 20, 1957; s. Robert Richard and Frances Kathryn (Luedeke) R. BS, Clarkson Coll., 1978, MS, 1980. Rsch. engr. Allied-Signal/Polypure, Solvay, N.Y., 1980-91; sr. rsch. chem. engr. Am. Cyanamid/Cytec, Stamford, Conn., from 1991. Home: Stamford, Conn. Died Aug. 31, 2004.

RICE, ROBERT RICHARDSON, food products executive; b. Sanford, N.C., Sept. 20, 1955; s. V.L. Rice and Rita Nelmer (Richardson) Sweeney; stepfather George Franklin Sweeney; m. Judy Belle Veal, Aug. 9, 1980; 1 child, Michael Richardson. BS in Maths., U. Ga., 1977, M in Acctg., 1979. CPA, Ga. Sr. mgr. Ernst & Whinney, Atlanta and London, 1979-87; mgr. bus. devel. The Coca-Cola Co., Atlanta, from 1987. Mem. adv. bd. N. Fulton Ctr. for Internat. Studies, Atlanta, 1982-87; treas. Peachtree Park Civic Assn., Atlanta, 1983-86, bd. dirs., 1983-86; devel. chmn. Young Alumni Coun.-U. Ga., Atlanta, 1985-89. Full Academic Found. scholarship U. Ga., 1973-77. Mem. AICPA, Ga. Soc. CPAs, U. Ga. Alumni Soc. (5th dist. v.p. bd. mgrs. 1989—), U. Ga. Honors Program Alumni Assn. (pres. 1989—), Phi Beta Kappa, Phi Kappa Phi, Kappa Sigma (sec. 1977-78). Clubs: Ansley Golf (Atlanta, com. mem. 1989—). Methodist. Avocations: golf, travel, softball, jogging, skiing. Home: Atlanta, Ga. Died Mar. 14, 2005.

RICE-SIMMONS, CATHRYN FATIMA, communications educator; b. Seattle, Aug. 24, 1954; d. Leighton Charles and Marie Anne (Vitalech) Rice; m. Keith Charles Simmons, Dec. 20, 1986. AA, Tacoma (Wash.) Community Coll., 1984; BA in Communications/Theatre Arts (hons), U. Puget Sound, Tacoma, 1986; MA in Communication Studies, U. Calif., Santa Barbara, 1988. Reporter, news editor Collegiate Challenge, Tacoma, 1982-84; teaching asst. I.E.L.I., Pacific Luth. U., Tacoma, 1984; prog. asst. Assoc. Students, U. Puget Sound, 1984-85; editor arts and features The Trail, Tacoma, 1984-85; newswriter pub. rels. U. Puget Sound, 1985-86, teaching asst., 1985-86, U. Calif., Santa Barbara, 1986-88; communications instr. Brooks Inst. Photography, Santa Barbara, 1990; speech comm. instr. Ventura (Calif.) Coll., from 1991. Home: San Diego, Calif. Died Feb. 19, 2004.

RICHARD, WILLIAM, food company executive; b. Oak Park, Ill., Aug. 27, 1937; s. Paul Anthony and Verna Lucretia (Elwood) R.; m. Karen Marie Meyer, June 20, 1959 (div. Oct. 1, 1971); children: Julie E. Carmaniti, Sarah M. Bennett, Beth A.; m. Carol Sue Wills, Mar. 31, 1973; children: Ann Bradley, Michael Richard, Tonya Wallace. BA in Chemistry, Monmouth Coll., 1959; MBA, MIT, 1962. Products rsch. assoc. Procter & Gamble Co., Cin., 1961-63; tech. sales rep. Durkee Foods Div. Glidden Co., Chgo., 1963-66, product market mgr., 1966-69; mgr. comm. devel. Durkee Foods Div. SCM Corp., Cleve., 1969-72, ind. sales mgr. Chgo., 1972-75, regional mgr. Rockville Ctr., N.Y., 1975-80, dir. mktg. Cleve., 1980-88; dir. bus. devel. VandenBergh Foods Co., Cleve., 1988-90, Van den Bergh Foods Co., Chgo., from 1990. Contbr. articles to profl. jours. Dir., treas. Chateau Lorraine Homeowners Assn., Bloomingdale, Ill., 1992-95. Recipient fellowship MIT, 1959. Mem. Inst. Food Tech., Calorie Control Coun., Hon. Kettle Com. Avocations: reading, gardening, tennis, modern jazz. Home: Sarasota, Fla. Died Apr. 25, 2004.

RICHARDS, ANN, actress, educator, poet; b. Sydney; came to U.S., 1942; d. Mortimer Delaforce and Marion Bradshaw (Dive) Richards; m. Edmond J. Angelo, Feb. 4, 1949 (dec. Mar. 1983); children: Christopher E., Mark R., Juliet M.; m. Paul M. Kramer, Feb. 14, 1987 (dec. Aug. 1996). Student, Stotts Coll., 1936-37, Studio Sch. of Drama, 1936-38. Actress Cinesound Studio, Australia, 1936-42, Metro-Goldwyn Mayer, 1942-45, Hall Wallis-Paramount, 1945-47, R.K.O., 1947, Eagle-Lion Studios, 1947-48, Edmond Angelo Prodns., 1953, Anthony Buckley Prodns., Australia, 1995. Poetry reader with Robert Pinsky's nat. program Lib. of Congress Bicentennial Project, 1999. Author: The Grieving Senses, 1971, Odyssey for Edmond, 1996, New Poems-Old Themes, 1997; contbr. poetry to anthology Poetry From the Art, 1999; actress films including An American Romance, Love Letters, The Searching Wind, Badman's Territory, Sorry, Wrong Number, Lost Honeymoon, Breakdown, Don't Call Me Girlie, Celluloid Heroes, 1994-95; appearances TV program, film, and tape maker Australia, Time Life Assocs., 1977. Vice pres. Tchr. Rememberance Day Found., 1952—; internat. chmn. Apple of Gold Edn. awards, 1953—. Recipient meritorious svc. citation Govs. of Great Britain, U.S., New Zealand, Australia, 1939-46, Star Pattern award Inst. Profl. Direction, 1951, Cert. of Appreciation award Literacy is Reading Program, 1997, Edward Dean Mus., 1996. Mem. AAUW, Nat. Mus. Women in Arts, San Gorgonio Poets Soc., San Gorgonio Artists Soc., Zeta Phi Eta (v.p. nat. coun. 1970-73). Home: Hermosa Beach, Calif. Died Aug. 24, 2006.

RICHARDS, ANN WILLIS, former governor; b. Lakeview, Tex., Sept. 1, 1933; d. Cecil and Ona Willis; children: Cecile, Daniel, Clark, Ellen. BA, Baylor U., 1954; postgrad., U. Tex., 1954-55. Cert. tchr. Tex. Tchr. Austin Ind. Sch. Dist., Tex.; mgr. Sarah Weddington Campaign, Austin, Tex., 1972, adminstrv. asst., 1973-74; county commr. Travis County, Austin, 1976-82; treas. State of Tex., Austin, 1983-91, gov., 1991-95; sr. adv. Verner, Liipfert, Bernhard, McPherson & Hand, Austin, 1995—2006, Pub. Strategies Inc., Austin, 2001—06. Chair Dem. Nat. Conv. 1992; Austin Transp. Study, Tex., 1977-82, Capital Indsl. Devel. Corp., Austin, Tex., 1980-81, Spl. Commn. Delivery Human Services in Tex., 1979-81; Dem. com. Southern Governor's Assn. Travis County Dem. com. Author (with Peter Knobler): Straight From the Heart, 1989, (with Richard Levine) I'm Not Slowing Down, 2003. Com. mem. strategic planning Dem. Nat. Com., 1983; keynote speaker Dem. Nat. Conv., 1988. Named Woman of Yr., Tex. Women's Polit. Caucus, 1981, 1983. Mem. Nat. Govs. Assn. Democrat. Died Sept. 13, 2006.

RICHARDS, GLEN ELVIN, industrial education educator; b. Sank, Mo., May 1, 1938; s. Harvey Elvin and Thelma Cecil (Garner) R.; m. Doris Maree Finley, Mar. 7, 1964; children: Elizabeth Maree, Lee Elvin. BA, S.E. Mo. State U., 1964, MA, 1968. Cert. indsl. arts tchr., Mo., vocat. edn. tchr., Mo. Indsl. arts tchr Sikeston (Mo.) Middle Sch., 1964-68; automotive tech. tchr. Sikeston Area Vocat. Sch., 1968-70; v.p. Midwest Tech. Inst., Kansas City, Mo., 1970-75; coord. Liberty (Mo.) High Sch., from 1975. Greeter Grandview (Mo.) Assembly of God, 1970—. With U.S. Army, 1961-63. Mem. NEA, Am. Vocat. Assn., Mo. Vocat. Assn. (bd. dirs., program com. 1992-94), Mktg. and Coop. Edn. Assn. (Mo. coop. insdsl. edn. curriculum team 1986-88, nat. tchrs. exam. validation com. 1990, pres.-elect 1992-93, pres. 1993-94, bd. dirs. 1989—), Coop. Edn. Assn. (pres. elect. 1989-90, pres. 1990-91). Avocation: bass fishing. Home: Kansas City, Mo. Died Mar. 20, 2005.

RICHARDS, LLOYD GEORGE, theater director, academic administrator; b. Toronto, Ont., Can., June 29, 1919; arrived in US, 1923; s. Albert George and Rose Isabelle (Coote) R.; m. Barbara Davenport, Oct. 11, 1957; children: Scott, Thomas. Grad., Wayne U., 1944. Head actor tng.

NYU Sch. Arts, N.Y.C., 1966-72; artistic dir. Nat. Playwrights Conf., Eugene O'Neill Meml. Theatre Ctr., Waterford, Conn., 1969; prof. theatre and cinema Hunter Coll., N.Y.C., 1972-79; dean Yale U. Sch. Drama, New Haven, 1979-91; artistic dir Yale Repertory Theatre, New Haven, 1979-91. Prof. emeritus Sch. Drama, 1991-2006; artistic dir. Yale Repertory Theater, 1979-91; pres. Theater Devel. Fund; head actor tng. Sch. Arts NYU, 1966-72; lectr., cons. in field; bd. dirs. Theatre Comm. Group, U.S. Bicentennial World Theatre Festival; mem. various profl. adv. groups, task forces; mem. playwrights selection com. Rockefeller Found.; mem. new Am. plays program com. Ford Found.; mem. com. on profl. theater tng. Nat. Endowment Arts. Actor on radio, TV and theater, since 1943; including Broadway plays The Egghead, 1957, Freight, 1956; disc jockey, Detroit; dir. for: radio, TV, film and theater, including Broadway plays A Raisin in the Sun, 1958, The Long Dream, 1960, The Moon Besieged, 1962, I Had a Ball, 1964, The Yearling, 1966, Paul Robeson, 1977-78, Ma Rainey's Black Bottom, 1984, Fences, 1987 (Tony award 1987), Joe Turner's Come and Gone, 1986, The Piano Lesson, 1990, Two Trains Running, 1992, 7 Guitars, 1996; and TV prodns. include: segment of Roots: The Next Generation, 1979, Bill Moyers' Jour, 1979, Robeson, 1979, Hallmark Piano Lesson 95. Served with USAAF, 1943—44. Recipient Pioneer award Audience Devel. Co., 1986-87, Frederick Douglas award, 1986-87, Golden Plate award, 1987, Nat. Medal of Arts, 1993, Mr. Abbott award, 1996; Hoffman Eminent scholar Fla. State U., 1997. Mem. Soc. Stage Dirs. and Choreographers (pres.), Actors Equity Assn., AFTRA, Dirs. Guild Am. Died June 29, 2006.

RICHARDS, WALTER DUBOIS, artist, illustrator; b. Penfield, Ohio, Sept. 18, 1907; s. Ralph DuBois and Ruby Mildred (Smith) R.; m. Glenora Case, June 20, 1931; children: Timothy, Henry Tracy. Grad., Cleve. Sch. Art, 1930. With Sundblom Studios, Chgo., 1930-31, Tranquillini Studios, Cleve., 1931-36, Charles E. Cooper Studios, N.Y.C., 1936-50; freelance artist, from 1950. Executed paintings and illustrations for leading indsl. corps., nat. mags.; designed: U.S. postage stamps including Frederick Douglas 25 cent stamp; block of 4 stamps on beautification of Am.; Am. bald eagle-Mus. Natural History with commemorative; Cape Hatteras Nat. Parks Centennial block of four stamps; Paul Lawrence Dunbar Am. Poets commemorative; block of 4 stamps on Am. trees, 1978, blocks of 4 stamps on Am. architecture, 1979-82; co-designer anti-pollution block of four stamps; James Hoban stamp, 1981, Timberline Lodge 50th Anniversary U.S. commerorative stamp, 1987; exhibited, Cleve. Mus. Art, Art Inst., Chgo., Met. Mus., N.Y.C., Pa. Acad. Fine Arts, Bklyn. Mus., N.A.D., Whitney Mus., 200 Years Watercolor Painting, Met. Mus., 1966, 200 Years Am. Illustration, N.Y. Hist. Soc., 1976; represented in permanent collection, Whitney Mus., New Britain Mus. Am. Art, Cleve. Mus. Art, William A. Farnsworth Library and Art Mus., West Point Mus., Worcester (Mass.) Art Mus., Yale U. Art Gallery-New Haven, Conn., Smithsonian, Washington, D.C. Bd. dirs. Rowayton Art Center, Historic New Orleans Collection, 1989. Recipient highest award in lithography Cleve. Mus. Art, ann. 1935-38; Spl. Honor USAF, 1964; ann. Environ. Improvement award, 1983; named to Rocky River (Ohio) High Sch. Hall of Fame, 1991. Mem. Am. Watercolor Soc. (2d v.p. 1965-67), Conn. Watercolor Soc., NAD, 1974- (Academician, 1994-), Soc. of Illustrators, Fairfield Watercolor Group (pres., founder), Westport Artists. Died May 22, 2006.

RICHARDSON, DAVID NEAL, investment advisor; b. Oklahoma City, Sept. 5, 1939; s. David E. and Lera E. (O'Neal) R.; m. Pat M. Richardson; children: Natasha, Jennifer, David M. BS, Okla. State U., 1960; MBA, U. Cin., 1962. CPA, Okla. Sr. trust officer Cen. Trust Co., N.A., Cin., 1962-77; pres. First Ky. Investment Advisors, Inc., Louisville, 1977-81; pres., founder Asset Mgmt. Corp., Louisville, from 1981. Chmn. The Richardson Found., Inc., Louisville, 1987—. Mem. Louisville Soc. Fin. Analysts, N.Y. Soc. Fin. Analysts. Republican. Avocations: archaeology, coin collecting/numismatics, travel. Died Apr. 8, 2005.

RICHARDSON, PAUL RALPH, entertainer; b. Wilmington, Del, Sept. 19, 1932; s. Ralph Lemuel and Hannah Francis (Kehnast) R.; m. Dee Andrews Teitsworth, Nov. 27, 1993; children: Susanne, Jon Paul, Vicki. Student, U. Del., 1954-60, Goldey Bus. Coll., 1955, Beacom Bus. Sch., 1956. Band leader Miami Beach Night Clubs, Fla., 1953-54, Chgo. Music Industries, east coast U.S., 1962-75; dist. sales mgr. Hammond Organ Co., Washington, N.J., Del., Md., 1975-76; concert artist Yamaha Internat., Buena Park, Calif., 1976-87. Organist Phila. Phillies, Major League Baseball, 1970-2005, weekend organist, NY Yankess, 1978-82; mem. music com. Del. Symphony. Featured artist Roland Organ Corp., 1995 Home Organ Festival, Asilomar, Calif., CD: Take Me Out to the Ballgame...at the Phillies, 1995, CD: Paul Richardson at the Roland Organ, 1996. Appeared on front cover: The Organist mag., 1975, Hurdy Gurdy Organists mag., 1980; recipient World Series Ring award Phila. Nat League Baseball Club. Mem. Am. Fedn. Musicians, Del. Realtors Assn., Hammond Organ Soc., (pres. 1956-57), Amateur Organist Assn. Internat. (pres. 1984-85). Avocations: art, photography, amateur film-making. Home: Wilmington, Del. Died Oct. 2, 2006.

RICHENBURG, ROBERT BARTLETT, retired artist, educator; b. Boston, July 14, 1917; s. Frederick Henry and Spray (Bartlett) R.; m. Libby Chic Peltyn, Nov. 11, 1942 (dec. 1977); 1 child, Ronald P.; m. Margaret Kerr, Feb. 9, 1980; stepchildren: William Blakeley Kerr, MD, David Garrett Kerr, Margaret Frances Kerr. Student, Boston U., George Washington U., Corcoran Sch. Art, Art Students League N.Y., Ozenfant Sch. Fine Arts, Hans Hofmann Sch. Art. Tchr. painting Schrivenham Am. U., England, 1945; instr. Coll. City N.Y., 1947-52, Cooper Union, 1954-55; instr., dir. Bklyn.-Queens Central YMCA, 1947-51; instr. NYU, 1960-61, Pratt Inst., Bklyn., 1951-64; assoc. prof. art Cornell U., Ithaca, NY, 1964-67; prof. art Hunter Coll., N.Y.C., 1967-70, Aruba (Netherlands Antiles) Research Center, 1970, Ithaca Coll., 1970-83, mem. council on arts. Panelist in field. One-man shows include Hendler Gallery, Phila., NY Artists Gallery, Tibor DeNagy Gallery, Hansa Gallery, NY, Dwan Gallery, LA, Santa Barbara Mus. (Calif.), Dayton Art Inst., Dana Arts Center Colgate U., Ithaca Coll. Mus. Art, Grad. Sch. Bus. Cornell U., Rose Art Mus., Brandeis U., U. Art Gallery, Staller Ctr., SUNY Stonybrook, Pollock-Krasner House and Study Ctr., East Hampton, N., Arlene Bujese Gallery, East Hampton, Guild Hall Mus., East Hampton, MB Modern Gallery, NY, 2001, Thomas McCormick Gallery, Chgo., 2002, 06, David Findlay Jr. Fine Arts, NY, 2003, 04, 05, others; exhibited in group shows at Mus. Modern Art, Solomon Guggenheim Mus., NYC, Chrysler Art Mus., Yale Art Gallery, Whitney Mus., NYC, Univ. Art Mus., Austin, Tex., Balt. Mus., Cocoran Mus. Art, Washington, Bklyn. Mus., Knox Albright Mus., Buffalo, Larry Aldrich Mus., Seattle Art Mus., Boston Mus. Fine Arts, others; represented in permanent collections Mus. Modern Art, Whitney Mus., Hirschorn Mus., Inst. Valenciano de Arte Moderno, Valencia, Spain, Phila. Mus. Art, Pasadena Mus. Fine Art, U. Art Mus. U. Calif., Berkeley, U. Tex. Art Mus., Austin, Zimmerli Art Mus. Rutgers U., Rose Art Mus. Brandeis U., Coll. William and Mary, Chrysler Mus. Art, Hofstra U. Mus., Johnson Mus. Cornell U., Ithaca Coll. Mus., Parrish Mus. Art, Southampton, Guild Hall Mus., East Hampton, Heckscher Mus. Art, Huntington, NY, others. Served with AUS, 1942-45. Mem. Am. Assn. U. Profs., Coll. Art Assn., Internat. Platform Assn., Art Students League N.Y. (life) Clubs: (N.Y.C.). Home: East Hampton, NY. Died Oct. 10, 2006.

RICHTER, RICHARD PAUL, academic administrator; b. Bryn Mawr, Pa., Mar. 6, 1931; s. Manuel DeWitt and Emma Margaret (Theilacker) R.; m. Margot Denithorne (dec. 2004), Sept. 5, 1953; children: Karen Lee, Kurt Richard. BA, Ursinus Coll., 1953, LLD (hon.), 1976; MA, U. Pa., 1957; cert., Inst. Ednl. Mgmt., Harvard U., 1974; DHL (hon.), Tohoku Gakuin U., Sendai, Japan, 1986, Muhlenberg Coll., 1989. Editor Provident Mut. Life Ins. Co., Phila., 1956-58; supr. employee communications Phila. Gas Works divsn. UGI Corp., 1958-65; alumni dir. Ursinus Coll., Collegeville, Pa., 1965-67, asst. to pres., 1967-69, v.p. adminstrv. affairs, 1969-76, pres., 1976-94, pres. emeritus, 1995—2005, instr. in English, 1965-73, asst. prof. English, 1973-86, prof. of coll. Collegville, Pa., 1986-94. Chmn. Commn. for Ind. Colls. and U. Pa., 1984, Found. for Ind. Colls. of Pa., Harrisburg, 1985; past chmn. Coun. for Higher Edn. United Ch. of Christ. Contbtr. articles, poems to various publs. Recipient Gold Quill award Am. Assn. Indsl. Editors, 1964, Lindback award for excellence in tchg. Ursinus Coll., 1973, Silver Beaver award Boy Scouts Am., 1985, Muhlenberg Leadership award Hist. Soc. Trappe, Pa., 1994, Francis J. Michelini award for outstanding svc. Assn. Ind. Colls. and Univs. of Pa., 1996, Arthur V. Ciervo award Coll. and Univ. Pub. Rels. Assn. of Pa., 1996. Mem. Pa. Assn. Colls. and Univs. (bd. dirs.), Phi Beta Kappa. Home: Frederick, Pa. Died Dec. 16, 2005.

RICKMAN, CLAUDE ROGER, retired college official, clergyman; b. Brevard, N.C., Nov. 10, 1917; s. Andrew Cornelius and Flora Pearl (Powell) R.; m. Evelyn Thornton Tucker, Jan. 1, 1942; children: Claude Merideth, Sharon Carol Rickman Wallace, Bryan Cary. AB, BS, Marion Coll., 1941; MA, U. N.C., 1952, PhD, 1956; LLD (hon.), Central (S.C.) Wesleyan Coll., 1982. Ordained elder Wesleyan Meth. Ch., 1947. Pastor Ragan Wesleyan Ch., Gastonia, N.C., 1946, 48-50; dean Cen. Wesleyan Coll., 1946-68, pres., 1968-79, asst. to pres., 1980-89, dir. Alumni Assn., 1980-88; ret., 1989. Pres. ministerial standing, N.C. dist. Wesleyan Ch., 1946-87, N.C. dist. Wesleyan Youth, Colfax, 1951-56; del. Gen. Conf. Wesleyan Ch., 1956-80, 88; mem. Wesleyan Coun. Edn., 1968-79. Mem. Pickens County (S.C.) Sch. Bd., 1983—; trustee Hephizibah Children's Home, Macon, Ga., 1989—; bd. dirs. Pickens, Oconee, Anderson Mental Health, 1986—. With USNR, 1942-45, lt. comdr. Res. ret. Mem. Lions. Republican. Home: Central, SC. Died Feb. 13, 2004.

RIDDELL, ROBERT MCALPIN, graphic artist, sales promotion executive; b. Hanford Kings County, Calif., June 18, 1919; s. Edwin Belmont and Vesta Mercer (Baker) R.; m. Glengene Samis (div. 1960); children: Gloria Jean, William Bruce, Robert Glen, Edwin Belmont. Grad. high sch., Covina, Calif. Graphic artist pvt. practice, Stockton, Calif., from 1989. Artist: (books) Mosaic of Memory, 1990, Naked Woods, 1990. Mem. alcohol adv. bd. San Joaquin County, 1989—; pres. Alamo Club. Mem. Masons. Died Dec. 21, 2004.

RIDEOUT, PATRICIA IRENE, vocalist; b. St. John, N.B., Can., Mar. 16, 1931; d. Eric Aubrey and Florence May (Chase) R.; m. Rolf Edmund Dissmann, Sept. 3, 1955 (dec. 1975); m. Leonard R. Rosenberg, May 25, 1987. Student, U. Toronto Opera Sch., Royal Conservatory Music, 1952-55. Tchr. voice Queen's U., Kingston, Ont., 1980-86, Royal Conservatory Music, Toronto, 1980-91. Singer Can. Opera Co., Toronto, 1954-85; leading roles in operas, Stratford, Ont., Vancouver, B.C., Guelph, Ont., 1956-85, CBC, 1958-90. Mem.: Actors Equity Assn., Assn. Radio and TV Artists, Toronto Heliconian Club. Unitarian Universalist. Home: Cambridge, Canada. Died Sept. 8, 2006.

RIDER, LESTER LEROY, III, business manager and promoter, photographer; b. Chgo., Aug. 31, 1952; s. Lester Leroy Jr. and Patricia Laverne (Murtaugh) R.; m. Beverly Karen Johnson, Apr. 14, 1973 (div. Jan. 1991); children: Michele Marie, Diane Yvonne; m. Gloria Jean Rider, Jan. 26, 1991. Grad., Greer Tech. Inst., 1971; student, Kankakee Community Coll., 1979-81. Owner Auto Repair Shop, 1973-81, L&B Fotos, 1981-90; subcontractor Artcraft Studio, Kankakee, Ill., 1982; pres., chmn. bd. dirs. Am. Photo/Video, Inc., Chgo., 1990-91; road mgr., promoter Gloria Jean, from 1991. Spl. coorespondent, asst. photographer, reporter Fantasy/Modern Miss Mag. Asst. capt. 12th Ward Dem. Orgn., Chgo., 1975-76. Recipient 1 award Kankakee Community Coll., 1983, 2 photographic awards, Ft. Dearborn Camera Club,1988. Mem. Camera Club Chgo., Internat. Freelance Photographer Orgn., Internat. Freelance Models Orgn., Ft. Dearborn Chgo. Camera Club (studio chmn. 1988). Died Jan. 23, 2005.

RIEDELL, EDWIN HENRY, obstetrician; b. Anamoose, N.D., Mar. 4, 1912; s. Henry Thayer and Christine (Kreiser) R.; widowed; children: Louise, Christine, Nancy, Edwin Jr. D Osteopathy, Coll. Osteopathic Physicians and Surgeons, Los Angeles, 1939; MD, Calif. Coll. Medicine, Los Angeles, 1962. Intern Monte Sano Hosp., Los Angeles, 1939-40, resident physician, 1940-41; resident obstetrician Los Angeles County Maternity Service, 1941; attending surgeon Los Angeles County Hosp. Unit II, 1946-66, chief obstetrical surgeon, 1960-66. Active and cons. surgeon various hosps., 1946-80. Contbr. articles to profl. jours. Fellow Am. Coll. Osteopathic Surgeons. Lodges: Rotary (pres. 1962-63). Republican. Avocations: writing, speaking, inventing, boating, fishing. Home: Brea, Calif. Died May 28, 2005.

RIEDERS, FREDRIC, forensic toxicologist; b. Vienna, July 9, 1922; came to U.S., 1939; s. Kalman and Ethel Julia (Quastler) Rozsa; m. Betty Jean Stockwell, Apr. 28, 1955; children: Eric F., Michael F., Carl W., Julia H. AB, Wash. Sq. Coll., 1948; MS, NYU, 1949; PhD, Thomas Jefferson U., 1952. Diplomate Am. Bd. Forensic Toxicology, Am. Bd. Clin. Chemistry. Jr. toxicologist Office of Chief Med. Examiner, N.Y.C., 1946-49; fellow in indsl. toxicology Jefferson Med. Coll., Thomas Jefferson U., Phila., 1949-52; from instr. to assoc. prof. dept. pharmacol. Jefferson Med. Coll., Phila., 1952-56, former prof. pharmacology and toxicology; chief toxicologist Dept. of Health, Med. Examiner, Phila., 1956-70, dir. poison info., 1956-70; dir. labs. U. Med. Svcs. Inc., King of Prussia, Pa., 1969-70; former lab. dir. Nat. Med. Svcs. Inc., Willow Grove, Pa. Contbr. articles to profl. jours. Cpl. U.S. Army, 1942-46, ETO. Recipient Disting. Alumnus award Thomas Jefferson U. Coll. Grad. Studies, 1992. Fellow Am. Acad. Forensic Scis. (chmn. toxicology sect., A.O. Gettler award 1986), Am. Chem. Soc.; mem. Am. Soc. Pharm. Exptl. Therapeutics, Internat. Assn. Forensic Toxicologists (charter). Republican. Lutheran. Home: Rushland, Pa. Died Nov. 26, 2005.

RIEFF, PHILIP, sociologist; b. Chgo., Dec. 15, 1922; s. Gabriel and Ida (Hurwitz) R.; m. Susan Sontag, 1950 (div. 1958), 1 child, David; m. Alison Douglas Knox, Dec. 31, 1963 BA, U. Chgo., 1946, MA, 1947, PhD, 1954. Teaching fellow U. Chgo., 1946, instr., 1947-52; asst. prof. Brandeis U., Waltham, Mass., 1952-57; fellow Ctr. for Advanced Study in Behavior Scis., Palo Alto, Calif., 1957-58; assoc. prof. sociology U. Calif., Berkeley, 1958-61; prof. U. Pa., Phila., from 1961, Univ. prof. sociology, 1965-67, Benjamin Franklin Prof. Sociology, 1967-93, prof. emeritus, 1993—2006. Chief editorial cons. Beacon Press, Boston, 1952-58; vis. assoc. prof. Harvard U., 1960; vis. fellow Ctr. for Study of Dem. Instns., Santa Barbara, Calif., 1963-64; Gauss lectr. Princeton U., 1975; Terry lectr. Yale U., 1976-77; prof. psychiatry and preventive medicine, Med. Coll. Pa., 1993—; vis. professorial lectr. Naval Acad., 1993. Author: Freud: The Mind of the Moralist, 1959, rev. edit., 1961, The Triumph of the Therapeutic: Uses of Faith After Freud, 1966, Fellow Teachers, 1973, The Feeling Intellect, 1990; editor The Collected Papers of Sigmund Freud (10 vols.), 1961; assoc. editor Am. Sociol. Rev., 1958-61; founding editor Jour. Am. Acad. Arts and Scis., 1956-59, Daedalus. Chief cons. planning dept. Nat. Coun. Chs., 1961-64. Named Fulbright Prof. U. Munich, 1959-60, Guggenheim fellow, 1970, Sometime fellow All Souls Coll., Oxford. Fellow Royal Soc. Arts London; mem. Libr. Co. Phila., Am. Sociol. Assn., Soc. Sci. Study Religion (mem. coun.), Societe Europeene de Culture, Garrick Club of London. Died July 1, 2006.

RIESE, BEATRICE, artist, consultant; b. The Hague, The Netherlands, Sept. 22, 1917; came to U.S., 1940; d. Walther and Hertha (Pataky) R. Grad., Ecole d'Art et de Dessin, Paris, 1940; postgrad., Va. Commonwealth U., 1943-45. Mem., artist Pleiades Gallery, N.Y.C.; former pres. Am. Abstract Artists, N.Y.C. Former mem. adv. coun. Snite Mus. Art, Notre Dame, Ind. Died Apr. 2, 2004.

RIESE, JANE, actress, associate producer; b. L.A., Mar. 1, 1945; d. John Nytar and Rae (Sharp) R. BA in Edn., Seattle U., 1968; postgrad. studies, Cen. Wash. U., 1970-74. Intern copywriter Sta. KAMT-AM, Tacoma, Wash., 1985-86; drama instr. Tacoma Community Coll., 1988; assoc. producer, scriptwriter, actress TCTV Channel 31 Pub. TV, Olympia, Wash., from 1989; actress The Annex Theatre, Seattle, from 1990. Drama tchr. Western State Hosp.,

Tacoma, Wash., 1988-90; model, spokesperson for Avenues Fashion Sta. KIRO-TV, Seattle, 1989, speaker, audition judge, Andersen Model/Talent Agy., Tacoma Wash., 1989—; cons. non-traditional casting Actors' Equity Assn. Actress: (plays) Agnes of God, Dr. Livingtone, 1986, As Is, 1987, (TV dramatic series) Hope and Glory, 1989-90; (TV drama comedy) M.M, Inc., 1990—, (film featured extra) To Cross the Rubicon, 1990; scriptwriter: Hope and Glory (episodes 4-8), M.M, Inc., 1990—. Activist, advocate, Spina Bifida Assn. Am., Tacoma, Wash., 1988—, Citizens Initiative Conf., Women of Vision, Goodwill Games, 1990—. Named Miss Wheelchair Washington, Wash. State Govs. Com. to Employ the Handicapped, Olympia, Wash., 1974; honored by Tacoma City Coun. naming Miss Wheelchair Washington Day, 1974; nominee Best Supporting Actress Tacoma Little Theatre, 1976, nominee Best Actress, 1988. Mem. Am. Film Inst., Media Access Group L.A., The Annex Theatre, Seattle, Women of Vision (del. USSR/USA conf.). Democrat. Avocation: handwriting analysis. Home: Tacoma, Wash. Died Aug. 16, 2004.

RIETVELD, THOMAS ALAN, clergyman; b. Harvey, Ill., Sept. 28, 1951; s. Glenn and Caryl Thelma (Kamstra) R.; m. Diane Wynn Garfield, June 9, 1973; 1 child, Jori Katherine. BA, Wheaton Coll., 1973; MRE, Trinity Evangel. Divinity Sch., 1976. Ordained elder So. Calif. Conf. Free Meth. Ch., 1993. Dir. Christian edn. No. Suburban Evangel. Free Ch., Deerfield, Ill., 1975-78; assoc. pastor Wheaton (Ill.) Bible Ch., 1978-82, Scottsdale (Ariz.) Bible Ch., 1984-88; mng. editor Gospel Light Pub. Co., Ventura, Calif., 1982-84, cons., 1984-88; owner, pres. Diamond Comml. Svcs., Phoenix, 1988-92; sr. pastor Mountain View Free Meth. Ch., Upland, Calif., from 1992. Bd. dirs. Internat. Ctr. for Learning, Ventura, 1983-84, christian edn. South Calif. Free Meth. Ch. 1993—; cons. So. Calif. Free Meth. Conf., Azusa, Calif., 1992—; pastoral adv. Inland Empire Nat. Day of Prayer com., 1994—. Producer, dir. video tng. seminars; editor ch. sch. curriculum Living World Curriculum, 1982, Vanguard newsletter, 1984. Pres. Number 2, Wheaton, 1981; founder, pres. Children's Ministry Fellowship, Phoenix, 1987-88; bd. dirs. Greater Phoenix Sunday Sch. Conv., 1988; mem. Dad's Club of Scottsdale Christian Acad., 1988-90; mem. Better Bus. Bur., hoenix, 1991-92; treas. Upland Community Coord. Coun., 1993. Republican. Avocations: woodworking, golf. Home: Chesterfield, Mo. Died Jan. 24, 2004.

RIFFATERRE, MICHAEL CAMILLE, retired language educator; b. France, Nov. 20, 1924; s. Camille and Marie R.; m. Hermine Bilfeld, May 15, 1965; children: Lee, Jason. Ed., U. Lyons, France, 1941, U. Paris, 1945-50; PhD, Columbia U., 1955. Asst. prof. French Columbia U., N.Y.C., 1955-58, assoc. prof., 1958-64, prof., 1964-75, Univ. prof., 1982—2004, chmn. dept., 1974-83, Blanche W. Knopf prof. French lit., 1975-82. Vis. prof. Johns Hopkins U., Balt., 1980, 89, Coll. de France, Paris, 1981, Yale U., New Haven, 1983, Harvard U., 1985-86, CUNY, 1985, U. Pa., 1989; sr. fellow Dartmouth Coll. Sch. Criticism and Theory, former dir.; vis. sr. fellow St. John's Coll., Oxford, Eng., 1991. Author: Le Style de Gobineau, 1957 (Ansley award), Stylistique Structural, 1971, Semiotics of Poetry, 1978, Text Production, 1983, Litterature et Realité, 1982, Fictional Truth, 1989; gen. editor: Romanic Rev., 1971-2000. Former dir. Reid Hall, Inc. Decorated officer Order Palmes Academiques, France, 1977; recipient U. Helsinki medal, 1994, Columbia Grad. Faculties Alumni award for excellence, 1984; Guggenheim fellow, 1962, 79 Fellow Am. Acad. Arts and Scis.; mem. Am. Assn. Tchrs. of French (pres. chpt. 1962-64), Am. Assn. Study of Dada and Surrealism (pres. 1965-66, 73-79), Acad. Lit. Studies (pres. 1978-79), Semiotic Soc. Am. (pres. 1985-86), Toronto Semiotic Circle (hon.) Home: New York, NY. Died May 27, 2006.

RIFKIN, JOSEPH S., political and business consultant; b. Port Jervis, N.Y., Dec. 6, 1960; s. Robert P. and Marlene Rifkin; 1 child, Jack. BA in Labor Rels., SUNY, Buffalo, 1983, JD, 1986. Bar: N.J. 1987. COO, Marine Equipment Functions, Port Jervis, 1989-91; polit. and bus. cons. JSR Cons., Port Jervis, from 1988. Chmn. Port Jervis Bicentennial of Costn. Com., 1986-87; pres. Port Jervis Coun. for Arts, 1995-2000, Arts Coun. Orange County, Middletown, N.Y. 2000-01. Mem. Port Jervis Country Club (bd. govs. 1999-2002). Democrat. Avocations: wine and jazz enthusiast, drummer, golf. Home: Port Jervis, NY. Died Jan. 5, 2004.

RIGGS, ROBERTA BELL, storage facility owner; b. N.Y.C., Sept. 3, 1930; d. Conrad Jr. and Roberta (Burbridge) Bell; widowed, 1988; children: Margot, Roberta, Isobel Meacham, John Riggs, Elizabeth Riggs. Grad. high sch., Albany, N.Y. Owner, mgr. Mex. House, Inc., La Jolla, Calif., 1970-80, Container Storage, Inc., St. Croix, V.I., from 1983. Mem. St. Croix Yacht Club (rear commodore 1986-88, fleet capt. 1988-90). Democrat. Roman Catholic. Avocation: yachting. Home: Christiansted,. Died June 30, 2004.

RILEY, ELISA ORI, nurse; b. Highland Park, Ill., Apr. 10, 1935; d. Mario and Mary (Ori) O.; m. Michael J. Riley, Sept. 28, 1958 (div. 1973); 1 child, Lisa A. Cert. in nursing, St. Therese Sch. Nursing, 1956; AS, Coll. Lake County, 1985. Nurse Highland Park (Ill.) Hosp., from 1974. Home: Highwood, Ill. Died Aug. 8, 2005.

RINSLAND, ROLAND DELANO, retired academic administrator; s. Charles henry and Lottie Rinsland. AB with distinction, Va. State U.; AM, profl. diploma, EdD, Columbia U. Asst. to dean of men Va. State Coll., Petersburg; asst. purchasing agt. Glyco Products Co., Inc., N.Y.C.; asst. office registrar Tchrs. Coll. Columbia U., N.Y.C., tchr. cert. advisor, registrar, 1966—71, asst. dean student affairs, registrar, dir. doctoral studies, 1971—95; ret., 1995. Mem. Tchrs. Coll. Devel. Coun.; rep., presenter degrees Tchrs. Coll., Japan, 1989, 91, 93, 94. 1st lt. AUS, 1954-56. Mem. AAAS, NEA (Leah B. Sykes award for life), ACA, Am. Coll. Pers. Assn., Nat. Soc. Study Edn., Am. Ednl. Rsch. Assn., Assn. Collegiate Registrars and Admission Officers (inter-assn. rep. to state edn. depts. tchr. cert. 1973-74, com. orgn. and adminstrn. registrars activities 1973, 74-76), Assn. Records Execs. and Adminstrs. (charter, by-laws and program chmn. 1969), Am. Acad. Polit. and Social Sci., Am. Assn. Higher Edn., Assn. Instl. Rsch., Internat. Assn. Applied Psychology, Soc. Applied Anthropology, Assn. Study Higher Edn., Mid. States Assn. Collegiate Registrars and Officers of Admission., N.Y. State Pers. and Guidance Assn., N.Y. Acad. Scis., Scabbard and Blade, Kappa Phi Kappa, Kappa Delta Pi, Phi Delta Kappa (emeritus). Home: Cincinnati, Ohio. Died Nov. 14, 2005.

RITCHEY, JOHN HERBERT, retail executive; b. Augusta, Ga., Feb. 15, 1948; s. Herbert Doyle and Ada Mae (Wessinger) R.; m. Vickey Diane Elliott, Nov. 24, 1973; children: Tara Elizabeth, Samuel Elliott. BS in Bus. Adminstrn., Athens (Ala.) State U., 1971. V.p. Gadsden (Ala.) Printing Co., Inc., 1971-77; owner, pres. Ala. Raiders, Gadsden, from 1989, Ritchey Bus. Ctr., Inc., Gadsden, from 1977. Mem. Etowah County Rep. Exec. Com., Gadsden, 1971—; mem. So. Rep. Exchange, Birmingham, Ala., 1988—; treas. Young Reps., Ala., 1968-84. Mem. Gadsden Rotary. Presbyterian. Avocations: reading, politics, finance. Home: Gadsden, Ala. Died May 9, 2005.

RITTER, HENRY, JR., physician; b. N.Y.C., Apr. 14, 1920; s. Henry and Beatrice Victoria R.; m. Mary Loewe, June 10, 1949; children: Mark, Caroline. BA, Lafayette Coll., 1941; MD, NYU, 1945. Physician pvt. practice, N.Y.C., 1954-55, Redwood, Calif., 1955-94, Palo Alto, Calif., 1955-72, Menlo Park, Calif., 1972-94, Atherton, Calif., from 1994. Treas. Sequia Hosp., Redwood, 1983—, chmn. urology, 1975—, chmn. credit com., 1988. Author: From Man to Man, 1979. Mem. AMA, Am. Coll. Surgeons, Am. Urological Assn. (western sect.), Northwest Med. Assn. (pres. elect 1996, bd. dirs. 1993-96), Calif. Med. Assn. (communication commn.), No. Calif. Urological Soc., N.Y.C. Med. Soc., Rotary. Died Dec. 20, 2004.

RIVERS, RICHARD ROBINSON, lawyer; b. Dallas, June 9, 1942; s. Stewart Robinson and Madge (Fiske) R.; children: Laura Ellen, Jonathan Stewart. BA, Tulane U., 1964; JD, Cath. U. Am., 1974; MA, Johns Hopkins U., 2003. Bar: D.C. 1974. Writer Bauerlein, Inc., New Orleans, 1965-68; staff asst. Office of House Majority Whip, Washington, 1968-70, Office of House Majority Leader, Washington, 1971—72; internat. trade counsel Com. on Fin. U.S. Senate, Washington, 1973-77; gen. counsel Office Spl. Trade Rep., Washington, 1977-79; ptnr. Akin, Gump, Strauss, Hauer & Feld, Washington, 1979-96. Instr. Dalian (Peoples Republic of China) Inst. Tech., 1986. Trustee Am. Indian Coll. Fund. Mem. ABA, D.C. Bar Assn., Coun. Fgn. Rels., Met. Club City of Washington. Democrat. Episcopalian. Home: Washington, DC. Died Apr. 30, 2006.

RIVERS, WILLIAM LEIMOINE, lawyer; b. Hollis, Okla., June 27, 1940; s. A. Garland and L. Olene (West) R.; m. Patricia A. Jacks, May 27, 1956; children: Janis A. Rivers Plequette, L. Michelle Rivers Moore. BBA, West Tex. U., 1971; JD, Tex. Tech U., 1973. Bar: Tex. 1974, U.S. Dist. Ct. (no. dist.) Tex. 1976, U.S. Supreme Ct. 1981. Briefing atty. Ct. Appeals for 7th Dist. Tex., Amarillo, 1973-74; assoc. Lemon, Close, Atkinson & Shearer, Perryton, Tex., 1974-77; county dist. atty. Ochiltree County, Perryton, 1977-81; pvt. practice, Amarillo, from 1981. Home: Amarillo, Tex. Died Dec. 24, 2004.

RIVLIN, RONALD SAMUEL, retired mathematics professor; b. London, May 6, 1915; came to U.S., 1952, naturalized, 1955; s. Raoul and Bertha (Aronsohn) R.; m. Violet Larusso, June 16, 1948; 1 son, John Michael. BA, St. John's Coll., Cambridge U., 1937, MA, 1939, ScD, 1952; D.Sc. h.c., Nat. U. Ireland, 1980, Nottingham U., 1980, Tulane U., 1982; Dr. h.c., Sch. Tech. U. Thessaloniki, 1984. Rsch. physicist GE, Eng., 1937-42; sci. officer Telecom. Rsch. Establishment, Ministry Aircraft Prodn., Eng., 1942-44; rsch. physicist, head phys. rsch., supt. rsch. Brit. Rubber Prodrs. Rsch. Assn., 1944-52; head rsch. group Davy-Faraday Lab., Royal Instn., London, 1948-52; cons. Naval Rsch. Lab., Washington, 1952-53; prof. applied math. Brown U., 1953-63, L. Herbert Ballou U. prof., 1963-67, prof. applied math. and engring sci., 1963-67, chmn. divsn. applied math., 1958-63; professeur associé U. Paris, 1966-67; Centennial U. prof., dir. Ctr. for Application of Math. Lehigh U., Bethlehem, Pa., 1967-80, prof. emeritus, 1980—2005, adj. Univ. prof., 1980-88. Co-chmn. Internat. Congress Rheology, 1963; Russell Severance Springer vis. prof. U. Calif.-Berkeley, 1977; fellow Inst. Advanced Study, Berlin, 1984-85; Disting. vis. prof. U. Del., 1985-86, cons. prof. Stanford U., 2004-05. Contbr. articles profl. publs.; mem. editorial com. Jour. Rational Mechanics and Analysis, 1952-57, Archive for Rational Mechanics and Analysis, 1957-72, Jour. Math. Physics, 1960, Jour. Applied Physics, 1960-63, Rheologica Acta, 1963-2000, Internat. Jour. Biorheology, 1972-74, Mechanics Research Communications, 1974-2002, Jour. Non-Newtonian Fluid Mechanics, 1975-2001, Meccanica, 1975-94, Internat. Jour. Solids and Structures, 1990-95, Zietschrift für Angewandte Mathematik und Mechanik, 1992—; collected papers pub., 1996. Recipient Panetti prize, 1975, von Humboldt Sr. award, 1981, Charles Goodyear medal Am. Chem. Soc., 1992, von Karman medal ASCE, 1993; Guggenheim fellow, 1961-62. Fellow ASME (mem. exec. com. applied mechanics divsn. 1975-80, vice-chmn. and sec. 1978-79, chmn. 1979-80, Timoshenko Medal 1987), Acad. Mechanics, Am. Phys. Soc.; mem. NAE, Soc. Natural Philosophy (chmn. 1963-64), Am. Acad. Arts and Scis., Inst. Physics (gov. 1974-76), Soc. Rheology (exec. com. 1957-59, 71-77, Bingham medal 1958, v.p. 1971-73, pres. 1973-75, nat. com. theoretical and applied mechanics 1973-82, chmn. 1976-78, vice chmn. 1978-80), Internat. Union Theoretical and Applied Mechanics (gen. assembly 1975-82, chmn. U.S. del. 1978), Coun. Sci. Pres. (sec.-treas. 1975, exec. bd. 1975-77), Mex. Soc. Rheology (hon.), Accademia Nazionale dei Lincei (fgn.), Royal Irish Acad. (hon.). Home: Palo Alto, Calif. Died Oct. 4, 2005.

RIZER, DEAN KIRBY, retired internist; b. Anaconda, Mont., May 4, 1912; s. Robert Inskeer and Ruth Muriel (Lackersteen) R.; m. Kathryn Eleanor Waitney, Sept. 4, 1939 (div. 1952); children: Ann, Dean K. Jr. AB cum laude, Princeton U., 1934; MD, Harvard Med. Sch., Boston, 1938. Diplomate Am. Bd. Internal Medicine. Prof. U. Minn., 1938; intern Peter Beut Brigham and Childrens Hosp., 1938-42; pvt. practice Mpls., 1946-86; ret., 1986. From.instr. to clin. prof. medicine U. Minn., Mpls., 1946-80, prof. emeritus, 1980; cons. in field. Bd. dirs. ARC, Mpls., 1950, Viking coun. Boy Scouts Am., Mpls., 1953-58, Minn. Sci. Mus., St. Paul. Maj. M.C., U.S. Army, 1943-46, ETO. Mem. Minn. Med. Soc. (environ. resource com. 1970's). Republican. Avocations: painting, raising orchids, fly fishing. Home: Minneapolis, Minn. Died Feb. 12, 2004.

ROAZEN, PAUL, writer; b. Boston, Aug. 14, 1936; s. Julius and Anna (Lebow) R.; divorced; children: Jules, Daniel. BA, Harvard U., 1958, PhD, 1965. Instr. dept. govt. Harvard U., Cambridge, Mass., 1965-68, asst. prof., 1968-71; assoc. prof. social and polit. sci. York U., Toronto, Ont., Can., 1971-74, prof., 1974-95; ret., 1995. Author: Freud: Political and Social Thought, 1968, Brother Animal: The Story of Freud and Tausk, 1969, Freud and His Followers, 1975, Erik H, Erikson, 1976, Helene Deutsch, 1985, Encountering Freud: The Politics and Histories of Psychoanalysis, 1990, Meeting Freud's Family, 1993, How Freud Worked: First Hand Accounts of Patients, 1995, Canada's King: An Essay in Political Psychology, 1998, Political Theory and the Psychology of the Unconscious, 2000, Oedipus in Britain: Edward Glover and the Struggle Over Klein, 2000, The Historiography of Psychoanalysis, 2001, The Trauma of Freud: Controversies in Psychoanalysis, 2002, Cultural Foundations of Political Psychology, 2003, On the Freud Watch: Public Memoirs, 2003, Edoardo Weiss:The House that Freud Built, 2005. Fellow: Royal Soc. Can.; mem.: Am. Psychoanalytic Assn. (hon.), Phi Beta Kappa. Home: Cambridge, Mass. Died Nov. 3, 2005.

ROBBINS, KENNETH CARL, biochemist; b. Chgo., Sept. 1, 1917; s. Samuel and Mary (Silberbrandt) R.; m. Pearl Podorowsky, Mar. 31, 1946; children: Paula Lange, Shelley R. BS, U. Ill., 1939, MS, 1940, PhD, 1944. Asst. prof. pathology Western Res. U. Sch. Medicine, Cleve., 1947-51; head protein sec. biochemistry rsch. The Armour Labs., Chgo., 1951-58; dir. biochemistry rsch., scientific dir. Michael Reese Rsch. Found., Chgo., 1958-84; prof. medicine and pathology Pritzker Sch. Med./Univ. Chgo., 1970-87, prof. emeritus, from 1987; dir. exptl. pathology Michael Reese Hosp. and Med. Ctr., Chgo., 1984-86; rsch. scientist, prof. hematology and oncology medicine Northwestern Univ. Sch. Medicine, Chgo., 1989-95, ret., 1995, emeritus, from 1997. Mem. hematol. study sect. NIH, Bethesda, Md., 1971-75, 76-80, blood diseases & resources adv. com. Nat. Heart, Lung, and Blood Inst., NIH, 1976-80; chmn. Gordon Conf. Hemostasis, N.H., 1975; mem. Internat. Com. on Thrombosis and Haemostasis, 1980-86, chmn. subcom. on Fibrinolysis, 1980-82; lectr. in field. Mem. editorial bd. Jour. Biol. Chemistry, 1975-80; contbr. articles to profl. jours. Recipient fouth Elwood A. Sharp award Wayne State U. Sch. Medicine, Detroit, 1971, Prix Servier Medal and Prize, Fifth Internal Congress Fibrinolysis, Malmo, Sweden, 1980; grantee NIH, Bethesda, 1960-95. Mem. Am. Assn. Immunologists, Am. Soc. Biochemistry and Molecular Biology, Am. Soc. Hematology, Soc. Exptl. Biology and Medicine. Achievements include 10 patents in field; discovery of fibrin stabilizing factor, pancreatic elastase zymogen-proelastase, mammalian enzymatic omega oxidation of fatty acids system; development of oral thrombolytic therapy, hybrid pasminogen activators. Home: Chicago, Ill. Died Feb. 18, 2005.

ROBERTS, ANITA BAUER, science foundation executive; b. Pitts. m. Robert Roberts; children: Greg, Karl. BA in Chemistry, Oberlin Coll., 1964; PhD in Biochemistry, U. Wis., 1968. Postdoctoral fellow dept. pharmacology NIH, Harvard U. Sch. Medicine, Boston, 1968-69; staff chemist Aerospace Rsch. Applications Ctr., Bloomington, Ind., 1969-72; asst. prof. chemistry Ind. U., Bloomington, 1973-75; staff fellow lab. chemoprevention Nat. Cancer Inst., NIH, Bethesda, Md., 1976-80, rsch. chemist, 1980-90, dep. chief, Lab. Cell Regulation and Carcinogenesis, 1990-95, chief, 1995—2004. Contbr. articles to profl. jours. Recipient Brinker award for Scientific Distinction, Komen Found., 2005, Experimental Biology Award for Excellence in Sci., Fedn. Am. Societies, 2005. Mem.: Am. Acad. Arts & Sciences. Died May 26, 2006.

ROBERTS, ANTHONY HARRIS, insurance broker; b. L.A., June 8, 1943; s. Lewis Joseph and Marcia (Ross) R.; m. Andrea Lucille Dammann, Dec. 28, 1966; children: Cory L., Alexandra N. Grad. high sch., Tucson. Registered health underwriter. Salesman Ram Chem. Co., L.A., 1963-66; ins. agt. Milico/Prin. Mut., L.A., 1966-70; ins. exec. Jacob C. Fruchthendler, Tucson, 1971-79; pres. Anthony H. Roberts Orgn. Inc., Tucson, from 1979. Bd. dirs. Jewish Community Found., Tucson, 1983-85; mem. Tucson Parks Found. Mem. Nat. Assn. Life Underwriters (Agt. of Yr. 1982), Greater Tucson Assn. Life Underwriters, Tucson Conquistadores, Nat. Assn. Health Underwriters, U. Ariz. Wildcat Club, Million Dollar Roundtable (life). Avocations: golf, bicycling, photography. Home: Tucson, Ariz. Died Feb. 24, 2005.

ROBERTS, DORIS EMMA, epidemiologist, consultant, public health nurse; b. Toledo, Dec. 28, 1915; d. Frederic Constable and Emma Selina (Reader) Roberts. Diploma, Peter Bent Brigham Sch. Nursing, Boston, 1938; BS, Geneva Coll., Beaver Falls, Pa., 1944; MPH, U. Minn., 1958; PhD, U. N.C., 1967. RN Mass. Staff nurse Vis. Nurse Assn., New Haven, 1938—40; sr. nurse Neighborhood House, Millburn, NJ, 1942—45; supr. Tb Baltimore County Dept. Health, Towson, Md., 1945—46; Tb cons. Md. State Dept. Health, Balt., 1946—50; cons., chief nurse Tb program USPHS, Washington, 1950—57, cons. divsn. nursing, 1958—63; chief nursing practice br. Health Resources Adminstrn., HEW, Bethesda, Md., 1966—75; adj. prof. U. N.C. Sch. Pub. Health, 1975—92. Cons. WHO, 1961—82. Contbr. articles to profl. jours. Capt. commn. corps USPHS, 1945—2005. Recipient Disting. Alumna award, Geneva Coll., 1971, Disting. Svc. award, USPHS, 1971, Outstanding Achievement award, U. Minn., 1983. Fellow: APHA (v.p. 1978—80, Disting. Svc. award Pub. Health Nursing sect. 1975, Sedgwick Meml. medal 1979), Am. Acad. Nursing (hon.); mem.: Inst. Medicine of NAS, Sigma Theta Tau, Delta Omega. Democrat. Episcopalian. Avocations: needlepoint, gardening, reading, church volunteer work. Home: Bethesda, Md. Died Oct. 22, 2005.

ROBERTS, EARL JOHN, carbohydrate chemist; b. Magee, Miss., May 14, 1913; s. William J. and Mary E. (Kennedy) R.; m. Mary Kirk Lilly, Oct. 28, 1944; children: Mary Karyl, John William. BA, Miss. Coll., 1939; MS, La. State U., 1942. Cert. chemist. Jr. chemist U.S. Dept. Agrl., New Orleans, 1942-44, prin. chemist, 1944-47, sr. chemist, 1948-72; sr. rsch. chemist Sugar Processing Rsch. Inst., New Orleans, from 1972. Contbr. articles to profl. jours. Recipient Sugar Crystal award. Achievements include patents for preparation of glue from peanut protein, recovery of aconitic acid from molasses, preparation of derivatives of cotton cellulose. Home: New Orleans, La. Died Mar. 22, 2004.

ROBERTS, JOHN DOUGLAS, veterinarian, educator; b. Jefferson, Iowa, July 29, 1950; s. Carl and Georgia Elizabeth Roberts; m. Marie Elaine Nelson, May 24, 1974 (div. Aug. 1975); m. Beverly Theresa Malek, Jan. 26, 1978; children: Amy, Nicholas, Lee. DVM, Iowa State U., 1974; PhD, N.C. State U., 1998. Animal practitioner Britt Vet. Clinic, Iowa, 1974—79; owner Prairie Vet. Assocs., Oelwein, 1979—92; mgr. vet. svcs. Seaboard Farms, Buyman, Okla., 1995—99; asst. prof. N.C. State U., Raleigh, from 1999. Mem. ext. engagement com. N.C. State U., from 2000, mem. admissions com, 1999—2003; mem. nat. park coun. edn. Nat. Park Coun., Des Moines, from 2003. Grantee, N.C. State U., 2000, N.C. Park Coun., 2001, 2002. Mem.: N.C. Vet Med. Assn., Am. Assn. Ext. Vets., Am. Assn. Swine Vet., Alpha Zeta. Roman Catholic. Avocations: motocross, martial arts. Home: Apex, NC. Died Feb. 27, 2004.

ROBERTS, MARK (ROBERT ELLIS SCOTT), actor, writer; b. Denver, June 9, 1921; s. Ward Ellis and Daisy (Hobson) Scott; m. Audrey von Clemm (dec.); children: Ward Ellis II, Margot, Jeffrey Frazier. Student, U. Kans., 1940-41; BA, U. Ariz., 1943. Cert. tchr. life, Calif. Ind. TV, stage, film actor, from 1944. Co-founder Kairos Theater, Los Angeles, 1964; dir. Theater Arts Program of Los Angeles, 1975-79. Novelist: The Only Man in Hollywood, 1980; playwright Summer's Welcome, 1954; film actor: (as Robert Scott) Girl in the Case, The Black Arrow (serial), One Mysterious Night, 1944, Ten Cents A Dance, 1945, Prison Ship, 1945, Gilda, 1946, The Unknown, 1946, Shadowed, 1946, Dead Reckoning, 1946, (as Mark Roberts) Taxi, 1950, Onionhead, 1955, The Money Jungle, 1957, Once is Not Enough, 1975, Posse, 1976, For the Boys, 1991, Intersection, 1993; actor: (TV series lead roles) The Front Page, 1950, Miss Susan, 1951, Three Steps to Heaven, 1953, Date With Life, 1955, The Brothers Brannigan, 1959-60, (TV episodes) Kraft Theatre, Philco Playhouse, Studio One, Suspense, Playhouse 90, FBI, Dan August, Perry Mason, Cannon, Highway to Heaven, Who's the Boss, Murder She Wrote, L.A. Law, Murphy Brown, (Broadway prodns.) Stalag 17, 1951, The Sacred Flame, 1952, (Chgo. prodn.) Dial 'M' For Murder, 1953 (Los Angeles prodn.), Garden Dist., 1958-59, Mornings at Seven, 1986, Summer and Smoke, 1991. Mem. Acad. Motion Picture Arts and Scis., Actors Equity Assn., Screen Actors Guild, AFTRA, Writers Guild Am. West, ASCAP, Phi Delta Theta (pres. U. Ariz. chpt. 1942). Democrat. Presbyterian. Avocations: collecting American and early California art, songwriting. Died Jan. 5, 2006.

ROBERTS, MICHAEL STUART, writer, restauranteur; b. Utica, N.Y., June 22, 1949; s. Sidney H. and Lucille P. (Picker) R.; m. Felicity Ann Faulkner, Feb. 2, 1979 (div. 1983). BA, NYU, 1972. Exec. 2d chef 1 Fifth Ave., N.Y.C., 1977-79; chef Le Soir, L.A., 1979-80; chef, owner Trumps Restaurant, West Hollywood, Calif., 1980—92. Cons. Kinco Group, San Francisco, 1987; bd. dirs. Centre Technique Ferrundi, Paris. Author: Secret Ingredients, 1988, Make-Ahead Gourmet, 1990, What's for Dinner, 1992; syndicated columnist L.A. Times Syndicate, 1990. Named Chef of the Yr. So. Calif. Restaurant Writers Assn., 1986, Hon. Roll Am. Chefs Food and Wine Mag., 1982. Mem. Am. Inst. of Wine and Food (L.A. chpt. chmn. 1988), James Beard Found. Avocation: bridge. Home: Philadelphia, Pa. Died Mar. 30, 2005.

ROBERTS, WALLACE ARTHUR, company executive; b. North Adams, Mass., June 3, 1939; s. Wallace Earl and Eleanor (Gelinas) R.; m. Nancy Elizabeth Russ, Aug. 20, 1960 (div. 1984); children: Michael, Mark, Craig, Douglas, Ashley; m. Diane Louise McElligott, Aug. 17, 1985. BSEE, Wentworth Inst., Boston, 1960. Pres., CEO Proteus, Inc., Bellingham, Mass., from 1963; pres. Roberts Inst. Clinics, Brookline, Mass., from 1986; med. electrology program coord. Newbury Coll., Brookline, from 1986. Patentee in field. Mem. Soc. Clin. and Med. Electrologists (pres. 1992—), Internat. Electrology Educators (pres. 1984), Internat. Guild Profl. Electrologists, Franklin, Mass. C. of C. (pres. 1970), Lions (pres. 1973). Avocation: antique automobiles. Home: Bellingham, Mass. Died May 6, 2005.

ROBERTSON, ELIZABETH ANN, nurse; b. Phila., Jan. 21, 1943; d. Joseph Hamilton and Edna Atkinson (Clayton) R. Diploma in Nursing, Presbyn. Sch. Nursing, Phila., 1963; BS in Nursing, Villanova U., 1969, MEd, 1976. RN, Pa. Operating room staff nurse Presbyn.-U. Pa. Med. Ctr., Phila., 1963-66; staff nurse Taylor Hosp., Ridley Park., Pa., 1966-69; mem. nursing faculty Presbyn. Sch. Nursing, Phila., 1969-79; substitute sch. nurse Lower Merion (Pa.) Sch. Dist., 1980-83; nurse counselor Phila. Child Guidance Clinic, 1980-83; staff nurse Haverford Community Hosp., Havertown, Pa., from 1983. Vol. nurse African Evangelical Fellowship Mission, Zambia, 1971. Mem. Pa. Nurses Assn., Presbyn. Sch. Nursing Alumnae Assn. (rec. sec. 1975-79, bd. dirs. 1989-91), DAR. Republican. Avocations: needlepoint, painting, sewing, knitting, travel. Home: Media, Pa. Died July 24, 2005.

ROBERTSON, HUGH DUNBAR, biomedical researcher, consultant; b. Boston, June 12, 1943; s. Randal McGavock and Florence French (Dunbar) R.; m. Janet Abernathy, July 6, 1968; children: Andrew Dunbar, Michael Henry. BA in Life Scis., Harvard U., 1964; PhD in Genetics, Rockefeller U., 1969. Whitney postdoctoral fellow MRC Lab. of Molecular Biology, Cambridge, Eng., 1969-72; asst. prof. genetics Rockefeller U., N.Y.C., 1972-78, assoc. prof. genetics, 1978-88; assoc. prof. biochemistry Med. Coll. Cornell U., N.Y.C., 1989-97, prof. biochemisty Med. Coll., from 1997. Chair sci. adv. bd. Enzo BioChem, Inc., N.Y.C., 1981-87; co-founder, chair sci. adv. bd. Innovir Labs., Inc., N.Y.C., 1989-98; organizer Cold Spring Harbor (N.Y.) RNA meeting, 1983, 84, 86, 93; cons. in field. Mem. editl. bd. Virology, 1982-88, RNA Jour., 1995-99; contbr. more than 115 articles to profl. jours. on RNA rsch. Patentee ribozyme compositions and methods. Bd. dirs. Christodora Charitable Found., N.Y.C., 1984—, v.p., 1995-96; mem. Canterbury Choral Soc., N.Y.C., 1973—, bd. chair, 1989-95, pres., 1988-89. Recipient Rsch. Excellence award McKnight Found., 1983; grantee NIH, 1979—, NSF, 1973-91, USDA, 1978-84, N.Y. State, 1993—, Am. Cancer Soc., 1978-82—. Mem. Am. Soc. Virology (founding mem., 1982—, admission com. 1982-88), RNA Soc. (founding mem. 1993—), Appalachian Mountain Club, Mass. Audubon Soc. Democrat. Episcopalian. Achievements include discovery of first two RNA processing enzymes; replication mode for viroid-like pathogens, including that causing human hepatitis delta; hepatitis C translation start signals. Avocations: choral singing, research on RNA evolution, hiking. Home: New York, NY. Died Aug. 22, 2005.

ROBERTSON, JAMES SYDNOR, retired nuclear medicine physician, government agency official; b. Richmond, Va., Nov. 27, 1920; s. Paul Augustus and Beth O'Ferrall (Whitacre) R.; m. Ruth Elizabeth Henrici, Jan. 15, 1944; children: Kathleen Mary, John Paul, Marion Adelle. BS, U. Minn., 1943, MB, 1944, MD, 1945; PhD in Physiology, U. Calif., Berkeley, 1949. Diplomate Am. Bd. Nuclear Medicine. Head med. physics Brookhaven Nat. Lab., Upton, N.Y., 1950-75; cons. nuclear medicine Mayo Clinic, Rochester, Minn., 1975-84; dir. human health Office Energy Rsch., U.S. Dept. Energy, Washington, D.C., 1984-91. Author, editor: Compartmental Distribution of Radiotracers, 1983; contbr. articles to profl. jours. Served to capt. USNR. Fellow AAAS; mem. Am. Physiol. Soc., Health Physics Soc., Radiation Rsch. Soc., Soc. Nuclear Medicine, Math. Assn. Am., Masons. Democrat. Methodist. Home: Gaithersburg, Md. Died July 10, 2005.

ROBERTSON, RUTH CARLSON, educational administrator; b. Oil City, Pa., Aug. 3, 1940; d. Elmer F. and Elizabeth D. (Anthony) Carlson; m. Amos G. Hollinger, Mar. 23, 1963 (div. Jan. 1980); 1 child, Mark T. Hollinger; m. A. Bruce Robertson, Jan. 2, 1986; 2 children, Mark Robertson, Paul Robertson. BS in Physics, Pa. State U., 1962, PhD in Materials Sci., 1970; postgrad., Johns Hopkins U., 1962-63. Part-time instr., then asst. prof. physics Pa. State U., Altoona, 1968-76, planning analyst University Park, 1976-79; asst. chmn. dept. physics and astronomy Northwestern U., Evanston, Ill., 1979-81; mgr. chemistry dept. Princeton (N.J.) U., 1981-87; acad. planner U. Wis. System, Madison, 1987-91; assoc. vice chancellor acad. affairs U. Md. System, Adelphi, 1991—2005. Mem. Am. Assn. Physics Tchrs. Methodist. Home: Greenbelt, Md. Died Oct. 19, 2005.

ROBINS, BETTY DASHEW, retired small business owner; b. N.Y.C., Feb. 14, 1923; d. Leon and Esther (Turits) Dashew; m. Arthur Joseph Robins, Sept. 26, 1948; children: Lisa Dale, Michael Lee. BA, NYU, 1952. Field staff Pearl Buck Open Door, N.Y.C., 1944-45; dir. MacArthur House, San Francisco, 1945-47, Georgetown House, Washington, 1948-50; asst. curator S. Asian Collection Mus. of Art and Archaeology, U. Mo., Columbia, 1967-68; owner BDR Assocs. Arts and Antiques, Columbia, 1976—2005; ret., 2005. Founding mem., 1st pres. Columbia Art League, 1959-61; gen. chmn. 1st Tenn. Artist Craftsman Fair, Nashville, 1971-72; bd. mem. Mus. Assocs., Mus. Art and Archaeology, U. Mo., 1975-85, Boone County Hist. Soc., 2001—; mem. S. Asian studies com., 1976-85; coord. Festival of India, 1985-86, Festival of China, 1986-87, Peace Through the Arts, 1987-88, yr.-long programs commemorating 50th anniversary India independence, Columbia, 1997; mem. profl. visual arts adv. com. Mo. Arts Coun., 1980-82; cons. Denver Art Mus., 1991-92; advisor India Arts exhibit U. Mo. Mus. Art and Archaeology, 1997; organizer gallery exhibits, such as carved coconut Scrapers of Malaysia, India, Indonesia, Nat. Inst. of Pub. Adminstrn., Kuala Lumpur, 1989, Traditional Arts of India and U.S.A., U. Mo., 1989, Healing Imagery of Malaysia and U.S.A., U. Mo., 1991, Decorative Arts India, Stephens Coll., 1998, Storytelling through the Everyday Art of Mo. and India, Boone County Hist. Mus., 1998. Co-author: Everyday Art of India, 1968; contbr. articles to profl. jours. Bd. dirs. PAST (hist. preservation of Mo.), 1978-79. Named Woman of the Yr., Women in Comms., 1977-78, Vol. of Yr., Vol. Action Coun., 1983; recipient Quiet Hero award Columbia Pub. Schs., 1998. Home: Columbia, Mo. Died Aug. 21, 2005.

ROBINSON, ANNE DURRUM, human resources development consultant; b. Hugo, Okla., May 14, 1913; d. William Landon and Effie Anne (Lear) Durrum; B.J., Tex. Women's U., 1935; M.A., U. Tex., 1960; m. Harold G. Robinson, June 6, 1945; 1 dau., Marye Lear. Staff writer NBC, Hollywood, Cal., 1945; continuity editor KTBC, Austin, 1942-44, KNOW Radio, Austin, 1946-49; KASE, hostess TV program Sta. KTBC-TV, Austin, 1955-56; editor Sta. KASE, Austin, 1959-61; hostess KLRN-TV, Austin, 1961-63, KHFI-TV, Austin, 1966-67; mng. editor jour., writer Travis County Med. Soc., Travis County Med. Soc. Blood Bank and Med. Exchange, Austin, 1961-63; freelance writer, lectr., performer, tchr., 1968; copywriter, office mgr. David G. Benjamin, Inc., 1963-68; asst. dir. curriculum devel. Tex. Dept. Human Services, Austin, 1973-77, edn. dir. mgmt. tng. div., 1977-78; ind. cons. human resource devel. Creativity, Communication, Common Sense, 1978—. Grantee research Women in Comm., Inc., 1959, 71, nat. one-act play prize Hermit Club, Cleve., 1947, 1948, three-act play prize Houston Little Theatre, 1947, song lyrics award Nat. Five Arts awards, 1947, numerous poetry prizes. Mem. AAAS, ASTD, Women in Comm. (chpt. pres. 1952, named Outstanding Woman in Continuing Edn., Austin chpt. 1977, Most Valuable Chpt. Mem. 1989), Intergovtl. Tng. Council (Austin chpt.), Inst. Noetic Scis., Tex. Public Employees Assn., Women's Symphony League, Center Positive Prayer, Global Intuition Network, Herrmann Rsch. & Devel. Network, The Brain Club, Innovative Thinking Network. Author: Symphony for Simple Simon; Never the Twain Shall Eat. Died June 7, 2005.

ROBINSON, CARRIE C., English educator; b. San Angelo, Tex., May 11, 1911; d. James Henry and Fannie (Hulen) R. BA, Fisk U., 1933, MA, 1934; postgrad., U. Wis., 1946. Assoc. prof. English Prairie View (Tex.) A&M U.; chmn. dept. English Miles Coll., Birmingham, Ala.; assoc. prof. English Winston-Salem (N.C.) State U., prof. English, prof. emeritus English. Fisk U. Acad. scholar. Mem. AAUP. Died June 6, 2005.

ROBINSON, COURTLAND NORMAN, polymer engineer; b. Richmond, Va., July 26, 1935; s. Courtland Alexander and Lottie Pearl (Olphin) R.; m. Plugenia Pauline Smith Robinson, July 27, 1956 (div. June 1965); m. Margetta Elose Parker Gardner Robinson, Sept. 16, 1967; children: Rommel Andre, Jarrel Andrew, Douglas James Gardner. BS in Chemistry, Va. Union U., Richmond, 1956; PhD, U. Utah, Salt Lake City, 1973. Scientist, tech. mgr. Atlantic Rsch. Corp., Alexandria, Va., 1956-71; rsch. asst. prof. U. Utah, Salt Lake City, 1971-73; mem. tech. staff, tech. mgr. AT&T Bell Labs., Allentown, Pa., 1973-87, North Andover, Mass., 1987-95; adjunct prof. chemistry Lehigh U., Bethlehem, Pa., 1975-88; mgr. indsl. alliances Sheldahl Inc. Microproducts Divsn., Longmont, Colo., 1995-99, ret., 1999. Cons. Atlantic Rsch.Corp., ALexandria, Va., 1971-73. Author: (book chpt.) Polymer for Electronic and Photonic Applications, 1993; co-author: (book chpt.) Chip on Board Technologies for Multichip Modules, 1994. Mem. news adv. bd. KCPX-TV, Salt Lake City, 1972-73; mem. adv. bd. YM-YWCA, Salt Lake City, 1972-73; mem. bd. dirs. Rotary Internat. Emmaus, Pa., 1980-88, United Way, Lehigh Valley, Pa., 1990-93. Recipient Garnett Rylan award for Chemistry and Physics, Va. Union U., Richmond, Va., 1956, Rsch. award Honor Soc., Salt Lake City, 1973; named Outstanding Grad., Sigma Xi, Salt Lake City. Mem. Internat. Micro Elec. Assembly and Packaging Soc., Internat.

Soc. for Hybrid Microelectronics. Achievements include two patents on inhibitors for solid propellant grains. Home: Longmont, Colo. Died Feb. 9, 2004.

ROBINSON, IMOGENE DECROW, museum director; b. Searsport, Maine, Oct. 4, 1901; d. Frank Porter and Grace (Crockett) Decrow; m. Roger William Robinson, Feb. 25, 1938; 1 child, Roger Lee. Grad., Dean Acad., Franklin, Mass., 1921. Dir. Willard House and Clock Mus., Grafton, Mass., from 1968. Bd. dirs. Bay State Hist. League, Boston. Chair ladies com. Wayside Inn, Sudbury, Mass.; chair Blind Assn. Worcester County; pres. Grafton Garden Club. Fellow Nat. Assn. Watch and Clock Collectors; mem. Grafton Hist. Soc. (v.p.). Republican. Avocation: gardening. Home: Grafton, Mass. Died Feb. 15, 2004.

ROBINSON, LEONARD HARRISON, JR., foundation administrator, former federal agency administrator; b. Winston-Salem, N.C., Apr. 21, 1943; s. Leonard Harrison and Winnie Cornelia (Thomas) R.; children: Kimberly Michelle, Rani Craft. NSF cert., Bennett Coll., Greensboro, N.C., 1959; BA, Ohio State U., 1964; postgrad., SUNY, Binghamton, 1966-67, Am. U., 1982-89, Harvard U., 1991; LLD (hon.), Shaw U., Raleigh, N.C., 1983; LHD (hon.), Huston-Tillotson Coll., 1991. Vol. Peace Corps, Bihar, India, 1964-66, assoc. dir. for India Madras, 1967-70, dir. recruitment Washington, 1970-71; dir. inner-city programs US EPA, Washington, 1971-72; dir. mgmt. Family Planning Internat. Assistance, N.Y.C., 1972-74, Africa dir. Accra, Ghana and Nairobi, Kenya, 1974-77; task force dir. U.S. Ho. Reps., Washington, 1977-78; dir. population Africa AID, Washington, 1978-79; dir. Internat. Devel. Ctr. Battelle Inst., Washington, 1979-83; dep. asst. sec. for African affairs US Dept. State, Washington, 1983-85, 1990-93; pres. African Devel. Found., Washington, 1985-90; founder, pres. LHR Internat. Group, Inc., Washington, from 1993; exec. v.p., then pres., CEO Nat. Summit on Africa Secretariat, Washington, 1997—2000; co-founder, pres., CEO, Africa Soc. Nat Summit Africa, 2001—06; Diplomat scholar in residence U. Va., 2004—06. Cons. area studies U. Mo. Peace Corps, summer 1966; mgmt. analyst ATAC, Washington, 1971; mem. U.S. presdl. del. to Dakar, Senegal, 1987, to Malawi, Mozambique, and Uganda, Sept. 1988, to Mali, Uganda, and Kenya, Dec. 1988, v.p.'s visit to Africa, 1991; hon. consul Govt. Sao Tome and Principe, 1996-2001. Author: monographs Assessment and Analysis of Population Attitudes in Tanzania, 1981, Analyze African Official Attitudes Concerning U.S. Population Assistance in Lesotho, Tanzania, Senegal and Togo, 1981. Adviser Population Resource Ctr., N.Y.C., 1978-82; adviser internat. program for health and tng., U. N.C., Chapel Hill, 1980-84; vice-chmn. New Directions Task Force Rep. Party, Montgomery County (Md.), 1982-83; adv. coun. Nat. Coun. Returned Peace Corps Vols., 1987-2006; bd. dirs. Washington Ballet, 1982-85, 86-91, v.p. bd. dirs. 1988-90; bd. dirs. Friends of Smithsonian Mus. African Art, Washington, 1982-84, Coalition for Equitable Representation in Govt., Montgomery County, Montgomery County Bd. Soc. Svcs., 1986-89, Joint Agrl. Consultative Corp., 1985-86, Alan Gutmacher Inst., 1992-96, Friends of the U. of Natal, South Africa, 1995-2003; trustee U. D.C., 2004-06, vice chmn. bd. trustees, 2006; bd. dirs. UN Devel. Program-US Com., 2005-06. Decorated commandeur de l'Ordre National du Niger, 1989; recipient Africare Disting. Svc. award, 1990, Key to the City of Greensboro, N.C., 1991, Christian D. Maxwell Disting. Svc. award Liberian Com. for Relief, Resettlement and Reconstruction, 1993; hon. counsel for the Govt. of Sao Tome and Principe, Ctrl. Africa; sr. fellow U. Mass. John W. McCormack Inst. Fellow Nat. Acad. Pub. Adminstrn.; mem. Soc. Internat. Devel. (dir. 1982), Am. Pub. Health Assn. (sec. population sect. 1979-81), Coun. on Fgn. Rels., C. of C. of D.C. (dir. 1979-82), City Club Washington, Kappa Alpha Psi, Sigma Pi Phi. Home: Washington, DC. Died July 25, 2006.

ROBINSON, MARSHALL ALAN, economics professor, retired foundation administrator; b. Berkeley, Calif., Feb. 16, 1922; s. Webster Richard and Evelyn (Casey) R.; m. Ynid Douglas Rankin, June 5, 1944 (div. 1973); children: Joan Douglas, Margaret Elaine, Richard Webster; m. Flavia Derossi, Oct. 1974. AB, U. Calif.-Berkeley, 1943; MA, Ohio State U., 1948, PhD, 1950. Instr. econs. Ohio State U., 1948-50; asst. prof. econs. Tulane U., 1951-53; research asso. Nat. Bur. Econ. Research, 1951-52; asst. prof. econs. Dartmouth Coll., 1953-55; sr. staff mem., asst. to pres. Brookings Instn., 1955-60; prof. econs., dean Grad. Sch. Bus., U. Pitts., 1960-63; dir. econ. devel. and adminstrn. program Ford Found., 1964-67, program officer in charge higher edn. and research, 1967-71, dep. v.p. edn. and research, 1971-73, v.p. resources and environ., 1973-79; pres. Russell Sage Found., N.Y.C., 1979-86; vis. prof. Grad. Sch. CUNY, 1986-89; fellow Inst. Social and Policy Studies Yale U., 1989-91; v.p. Daniele Agostino Found., 1992—2005. Author: An Introduction to Economic Reasoning, 1956, 5th edit., 1981, The National Debt Ceiling, 1959. Bd. dirs. Belgium-Am. Ednl. Found., 1981-96; trustee Antioch U., 1987-90. Served to 1st lt. USMCR, 1943-45, PTO. Decorated Royal Order of Leopold, Belgium. Mem. Am. Econs. Assn., N.Y. Sci. Policy Assn., Coun. on Fgn. Rels., Century Assn., Alpha Delta Phi. Home: New York, NY. Died Jan. 7, 2006.

ROBINSON, OLIVIA HARRIS, mental health nurse, administrator; b. Columbia, S.C., Nov. 24, 1950; d. Belton Masion Sr. and Ludelle Olivia (Benson) Harris; m. Edward William Robinson, Apr. 30, 1969; children: Daryll Myron, Christy Dionne, Sandi Denise. ADN, U. S.C., 1977. RN. Staff nurse Providence Hosp., Columbia, S.C., 1977-79, Orangeburg (S.C.) Regional Hosp., 1986-87; clin. nurse Moncrief Army Community Hosp., Ft. Jackson, S.C., 1985-86; nursing supr. S.C. State Hosp., Columbia, 1979-85, Dowdy Gardner Nursing Care Ctr., Columbia, 1987-91; nursing mgr. II SCDMH-Craft Farrow State Hosp., Columbia, from 1992. Home: Columbia, SC. Died June 2, 2004.

ROBINSON, WINDSOR CALVERT, historian, consultant, photographer; b. Gardner, Mass., June 17, 1950; s. Alwynn Glenn and Marguerite Ruth (Allen) R. AS in Gen. Studies, Mt. Wachusett Community Coll., 1973; BA in History, Franklin Pierce Coll., 1977; MEd in History, Worcester State Coll., 1981. Cons. Gardner Heritage State Park Touring Exhibit, 1984-85, Boston Mus. Design Group, Somerville, 1985-86. Photographer: Gardner: A Portrait of Its Past, 1978; editor: The Diary of Aaron Greenwood, Vol. I, 1983, Vol. II, 1984, Vol. III, IV, 1986, Vol. V, VI, 1990, 92, 96; co-author: Images of America, 1996. Mem. Gardner Hist. Commn., 1975-86, treas., 1978-86; mem. Gardner Rep. City Com., 1976-96, precinct warden, 1992-92; mem. Gardner Mus., Inc., 1977-89, trustee, 1982-89; v.p. South Gardner Hist. Soc., 1991-97. Died Dec. 7, 2004.

ROBISON, WILBUR GERALD, JR., research biologist; b. Cheyenne, Wyo., Dec. 27, 1933; s. Wilbur Gerald and Irene (Decker) R.; m. Lucia Maria Panuncio, Sept. 20, 1957; children: Sylvia Lee, Stanley Jay, Nancy Kay, Lydia Joy. BA, Brigham Young U., 1958, MA, 1960; PhD, U. Calif., Berkeley, 1965; postgrad., Harvard U., 1966. Postdoctoral rsch. fellow Harvard Med. Sch., Boston, 1965-66; asst. prof. biology U. Va., Charlottesville, Va., 1966-72; sr. staff fellow Nat. Eye Inst., NIH, Bethesda, Md., 1972-76, geneticist, cell biologist, 1976-83, head exptl. anatomy, 1983-85, head pathophysiology, from 1985, acting head pathology, from 1988. Contbr. articles to profl. publs., chpts. to books. Mem. AAAS, Am. Diabetes Assn., Assn. for Rsch. in Vision and Ophthamology. Mem. Lds Ch. Achievements include development of rat model for diabetic retinopathy and demonstration of prevention with aldose reductase inhibitors. Home: Silver Spring, Md. Died Mar. 18, 2004.

ROBLES, ELIODORO GONZALES, consulting company executive, educator; b. Paniqui, Tarlac, The Philippines, July 3, 1923; s. Mariano Abraham and Lucia (Gonzales) R.; m. Rosario Palaganas Lavitoria, Oct. 30, 1964; children: Michael, Elmer, Eliodoro Jr., Marilou, Jonathan, Jay. BS in Polit. Sci., Far Eastern U., 1953; MA in Internat. Rels., Cornell U., 1954; MA in Polit. Economy, Harvard U., 1955, PhD in Polit. Economy, 1959. Cert. tchr., Calif.; cert. C.C. instr., Calif. C.C.; cert. C.C. supr., Calif. C.C. Instr. Far Eastern U., Manila, 1952-53; tech. cons., staff asst. Embassy of the Rep. of Indonesia in the Philippines, 1950-53; spl. asst. on fgn. econ. policies Program Implementation Office of the Pres. of the Philippines, 1962-64; prof. econs. and polit. sci., dean Grad. Sch. Far Eastern U., Manila, 1959-64; econ. officer, dep. dir. for econ., cultural, social affairs S.E. Asia Treaty Orgn. (SEATO), Bangkok, 1964-74; project dir. San Francisco Unified Sch. Dist., 1975-79; sr. assoc. Devel. Assocs., Inc., Walnut Creek, Calif., from 1979; evaluation specialist including polit. economist USAID, various locations, Calif., 1984-85, ednl. adminstrn. specialist Manila and Islamabad, 1987, tng. specialist, Asia Narcotics Edn. Program, 1988-89, polit. economist, from 1992; project dir. tng. and tech. assistance for Native Am. tribes, 1990—2002. Presenter in field. Author: Economic Analysis, 1966, The Philippines in the Nineteenth Century, 1969. Lt. col. Philippine Army, 1941-46; 1st lt. inf. U.S. Army, 1946-49. Fulbright Assn. scholar, 1954; Telluride fellow Cornell U., 1954, Fletcher fellow Harvard U., 1954-55, Newberry fellow Newberry Libr., 1957-58. Mem. Fulbright Assn., Filipino Am. Tchrs. Assn., Far Eastern U. Alumni Assn. (bd. dirs., adviser 1991—), Harvard Club San Francisco. Democrat. Methodist. Avocations: general gardening, orchid growing, stamp and coin collecting. Home: Richmond, Calif. Died June 20, 2004.

ROBSON, STUART, secondary school educator; b. Springfield, Mass., Mar. 16, 1914; s. Everett Gladstone and Eva (Gordon) R.; m. Charlotte Greenwood Paul, Oct. 7, 1940; children: Stuart Jr., Nancy Louise. BS, Springfield Coll., 1935; MA, Columbia U., 1937; cert. tax assessor, Rutgers U., New Brunswick, N.J., 1967. Tchr. Cathedral Choir Sch., N.Y.C., 1935-40, Princeton (N.J.) Day Sch., 1940-80; antique restorer Early Am. Interiors, Princeton, from 1941. Assessor Princeton Twp., 1954-81, Princeton Borough, 1976-81; appraiser real estate Snowden Inc., Princeton, 1964—; agt. Lord & Burnham Solar Structures, Princeton, 1966—; dir. Westward Ho Princeton Travel, 1937—; lectr. 100% Property Valuation, N.J., 1954—, expert witness State Tax Ct., N.J., 1954— Mem. Mercer County Assessors Assn. (pres. 1960-65), Mcpl. Assessors of N.J., Nassau Club. Republican. Episcopalian. Died Sept. 7, 2004.

ROCHE, GEORGE CHARLES, III, retired academic administrator; b. Denver, May 16, 1935; s. George Charles, Jr. and Margaret (Stewart) R.; children: George Charles, IV, Muriel Eileen, Margaret Clare, Jacob Stewart. BS, Regis Coll., Denver, 1956; MA, U. Colo., 1961, PhD, 1965. Tchr. jr. and sr. high schs., Salida, Colo., 1958-60; mem. faculty U. Colo., 1963-64, Colo. Sch. Mines, 1964-66; pres. Hillsdale (Mich.) Coll., 1971-99. Dir. seminars Found. Econ. Edn., N.Y.C., 1966-71, trustee, 1971-90. Author: Power, 1967, American Federalism, 1967, Education in America, 1969, Legacy of Freedom, 1969, Frederic Bastiat: A Man Alone, 1971, The Bewildered Society, 1972, The Balancing Act: Quota Hiring in Higher Education, 1974, America by the Throat: The Stranglehold of Federal Bureaucracy, 1983, Going Home, 1986, A World Without Heroes, 1987, A Reason for Living, 1989, One By One, 1990, The Fall of the Ivory Tower: Government Funding, Corruption, and the Bankrupting of American Higher Education, 1994, The Book of Heroes: Great Men and Women in American History, 1998; also articles, newspaper column. Chmn. acad. adv. council Charles Edison Meml. Youth Bd., Nat. Council Ednl. Research, 1982-85. Served to 1st lt. USMCR, 1956-58. Recipient Freedom Leadership award Freedoms Found., 1972 Mem. Am. Hist. Assn., Am. Acad. Polit. and Social Sci., Am. Assn. Pres.'s Ind. Colls. and Univs., Mt. Pelerin Soc., Phila. Soc. Home: Hillsdale, Mich. Died May 5, 2006.

ROCHE, SISTER THERESE AQUINAS, philosophy educator; b. Boston, Apr. 12, 1921; d. Edward Stephen and Catherine Elizabeth (Ferris) R. BA, Coll. St. Elizabeth, Convent Station, N.J., 1954; MA, Cath. U. Am., 1955; PhD, St.John's U., 1967. Joined Sisters of Charity of St. Elizabeth, 1937. Elem. sch. tchr. St. Joseph Sch., Oradell, N.J., 1939-54; secondary sch. tchr. St. Patrick Sch., Elizabeth, N.J., 1955-57; from instr. to prof. philosophy Coll. St. Elizabeth, Convent Station, 1957-91, prof., semi-ret., from 1991. Mem. Am. Cath. Philos. Assn., Metaphys. Soc. Am., Hastings Inst. Home: Convent Station, NJ. Died Jan. 10, 2005.

ROCKEFELLER, WINTHROP PAUL, lieutenant governor; b. Sept. 17, 1948; s. Winthrop Rockefeller Sr. and Barbara (Sears); m. Lisenne Rockefeller; eight children. Student, Oxford U.; grad. Ranch Mgmt. Program, Texas Christian U., 1974. Lt. gov. State of Ark., Little Rock, 1996—2006. Chmn. Pres. Coun. on Rural Am., 1991-93, Juvenile Justice Adv. Group; bd. dirs. Ark. Crime Commn., Tex. Christian U.; mem. Ark. State Police Commn., 1981-95; pres. Ark. Cattlemen's Assn., 1976-78. Vice-chmn. Winthrop Rockefeller Found., Ark. Cancer Rsch. Ctr., Ark. Arts Found.; founder, chmn. Brit. Found., U.S. Marshal's Assn.; trustee Winthrop Rockefeller Charitable Trust; mem. nat. bd. dir., Boy Scouts of Am., asst. scoutmaster. Mem. Ducks Unlimited (trustee emeritus). Republican. Died July 16, 2006.

ROCKMAN, ILENE FRANCES, librarian, educator, editor; b. Yonkers, N.Y., Nov. 9, 1950; d. Leon and Margaret (Klein) Rockman; m. Fred Gertler, Mar. 9, 1996. BA, UCLA, 1972; MSLS, U. So. Calif., 1974; MA, Calif. Poly. State U., 1978; PhD, U. Calif. Santa Barbara, 1985. Libr. Wash. State U., Pullman, 1974—75, Calif. Poly. State U., San Luis Obispo, 1975—98, Calif. State U., Hayward, 1998—2001, office of the chancellor, from 2001. Adj. prof. Cuesta Coll., San Luis Obispo, 1982—85; abstracter Women Studies Abstracts, Rush, NY, 1976—91. Contbr. articles to profl. jours.; editor: Reference Svcs. Rev., from 1986, Integrating Information Literacy into the Higher Education Curriculum: Practical Models for Transformation, 2004; co-author: BLISS-Basic Library Information Sources and Svcs., 1991—95; mem. editl. bd.: Libr. Hi Tech., from 1997, Am. Libr., 1997—99, Jour. Acad. Librarianship, 2003. Del. Dem. Nat. Conv., 1984; bd. dirs. Friends of Hayward Pub. Libr., from 2001. Recipient scholarship, Calif. PTA, L.A., 1973, Literati award, MCB Univ. Press, 2001. Mem.: ALA, Total Libr. Exch. (pres. 1979—80), Am. Ednl. Rsch. Assn., Calif. Assn. Rsch. Librs. (exec. bd. 1998—99), Assn. Coll. and Rsch. Librs. (exec. com. edn. and behavioral sci. sect. 1988—90, exec. com. univ. libr. sect. 1999—2002, Disting. Libr. of Yr. Ednl. and Behavioral Sect. 2003, Inst. Libr. of Yr. 2005, Dudley award 2005), Calif. Libr. Assn. (coun. 1983—86), Spl. Libr. Assn., Am. Assn. Higher Edn., Calif. Reading Assn. (Exemplary Svc. award 1992), Libr. Assocs. Calif. Poly. State U. (exec. sec. 1981—83). Home: Hayward, Calif. Died 2005.

RODELL, FRED, company executive; b. Nuremberg, Ger., July 4, 1920; came to U.S. 1938; s. Leopold and Frida (Stein) Rosenfeld; m. Shirley Viola McCormick Rodell, Dec. 27, 1949; 1 child, Leonard Mark. B.Engring., Instututo Radiotecnico, Milan, Italy, 1938. Pres. C.P.C., Houston and Austin, from 1955, Fred Rodell & Assocs., Houston and Austin, from 1949; sr. ptnr. Profl. Investigation Consortium, Houston & Dallas, from 1978. Cons. in field; lectr. in field. Contbr. articles to profl. jours. Reappointed by Pres. Endara as hon. consul for Tex. to Panama, 1990-92. With U.S. Army, WWII. Named Hon. Consul Gen. for Tex., Republic of Panama, 1968; Knight of Merit, Soveriegn Mil. Order St. John of Rhodes and Malta Hospitaller, Orthodox Order of St. Basil The Great; Knight Comdr., Sovereigh Mil. Order St. Stevens the Martyr. Mem. Nat. Mil. Intelligence Assn., Nat. Intelligence Study Ctr., Vets. of OSS, Assn. of Former Intelligence Officers (chpt. pres. 1979-90), Navy League of U.S. Home: Austin, Tex. Died Feb. 19, 2005.

RODRIGUEZ, JOSE FRANCISCO, financial consultant; b. Highland Park, Mich., Mar. 3, 1942; s. Jose Alexander and Elvira Helen (Csillagh) R.; m. Doris Helen Sandoval, July 7, 1977; 1 child, Tamara Sue. BA, Northrop Inst. of Tech., 1967. Prodn. supr. AiResearch div. Garrett Corp., L.A., 1963-69; corp. staff Bestline Products, Inc., San Jose, Calif., 1969-73; dist. mgr. Avis Rent-A-Car, Palm Springs, Calif., 1974-77; owner, operator Giant Rock Airport, Landers, Calif., 1977-80; pres., chief exec. officer Jose Rodriguez & Assocs., Las Vegas, from 1981. Recipient Pres. Award for Edn., Office of the Pres. of U.S., 1967. Mem. United Smokers Assn. (founder, chmn.). Republican. Avocations: flying, photography. Died Jan. 17, 2005.

ROE, EARL DEFOREST, religious organization administrator, minister; b. Endicott, N.Y., Sept. 12, 1918; s. Henry Thurston and Marian Lura (West) R.; m. Eunice Alline Harris, June 2, 1943 (div. 1950); 1 child, Joyce Alline Fishel; m. Thelma Rose Kiser, Sept. 1, 1951. Grad., Missionary Tng. Inst., Nyack, N.Y., 1940. Ordained to ministry Christian and Missionary Alliance, 1943. Asst. pastor Gospel Tabernacle, High Point, N.C., 1940-41; pastor Christian and Missionary Alliance Ch., Lexington, N.C., 1941-42, Madera, Pa., 1942-44, Peckville, Pa., 1944-47, Secretary, Md., 1947-48; bus. mgr. Northport Bapt. Ch., East Northport, N.Y., from 1981. Republican. Home: Commack, NY. Died Sept. 12, 2004.

ROEDER, MORRIS LEE, manufacturing executive; b. Louisville, Feb. 28, 1949; s. Lawrence Roeder and Jean (Ferguson) Ponder; m. Barbara Meyer, Feb. 17, 1973; 1 child, Michael. BA, U. Louisville, 1974, MBA, 1977. Sr. application engr. Carborundum Co., Knoxville, Tenn., 1977-80, regional mgr., 1980-81; successively indsl. mktg. mgr., product mgr., dist. mgr. Fuller Co., Bethlehem, Pa., 1981-88, gen. mgr., from 1988. Pres. Lehigh Valley Comets Youth Hockey, Bethlehem, 1985. Mem. Soc. Plastics Engrs., Conveying Equipment Mfrs. Assn., Soc. Plastics Industry, TAPPI, Air Pollution Control Assn. Republican. Avocations: ice hockey (referee), golf. Home: Bethlehem, Pa. Died Sept. 22, 2004.

ROGERS, ADRIAN PIERCE, minister; b. West Palm Beach, Fla., Sept. 12, 1931; s. Arden and Rose (Purcell) R.; m. Joyce Gentry, Sept. 2, 1951; children: Steve, Janice, David, Gayle. BA, Stetson U., 1954; ThM, New Orleans Bapt. Theol. Sem., 1958; DD (hon.), Trinity Coll., Clearwater, Fla.; LittD (hon.), Calif. Grad. Sch. Theology, Glendale. Ordained to ministry Bapt. Ch., 1951. Pastor First Bapt. Ch., Fellsmere, Fla., 1951-54, Waveland (Miss.) Bapt. Chapel, 1955-58, Parkview Bapt. Ch., Ft. Pierce, Fla., 1958-64, First Bapt. Ch., Merritt Island, Fla., 1964-72, Bellevue Bapt. Ch., Memphis, 1972—2005. Pres. So. Bapt. Conv., 1980, 87, 88, So. Bapt. Pastors' Conf., 1976. Author: The Secret of Supernatural Living, God's Way to Health, Wealth and Happiness, Mastering Your Emotions. Home: Memphis, Tenn. Died Nov. 15, 2005.

ROGERS, ALLEN EUGENE, musician, educator; b. Santa Barbara, Calif., Oct. 29, 1922; s. Allen Eugene and Florence Lorain (Black) R.; m. Margaret Virginia Willoughby, Sept. 10, 1949; children: Suzanne, Jeffrey. MusB, U. So. Calif., Los Angeles, 1950; MA in Music, Calif. State U., Northridge, 1986. Cert. elem., secondary music tchr., Calif. Sideman various bands, Santa Barbara, 1939-42, Los Angeles, 1945-52 and from 54, The I. Newton Perry Orch., Santa Barbara, 1952-54; pvt. music tchr. Los Angeles, from 1965; sideman, leader The Al Rogers Orch., Los Angeles, from 1974; tchr. music Las Virgennes (Calif.) and Los Angeles Sch. Dists., 1976-80, Am. Youth Bands, Los Angeles, 1979-80. Mem. Apt. House Mgr's. Assn., L.A., 1965-66, Industry-Edn. Coun., L.A., 1972-74. Pvt. U.S. Army, 1942-45, PTO. Mem. Musicians Union, Internat. Assn. Jazz Educators, Sinfonia Frat. Am. (sec. 1948-50), U. So. Calif. Inter-Greek Soc. (charter), Phi Kappa Tau (sec. 1947-49). Avocations: spectator sports, reading, gen. constrn., words and their meanings. Died June 7, 2005.

ROGERS, MELVIN F., management consultant, mechanical engineer; b. Deming, N.Mex., Oct. 2, 1931; s. Roy L. and Mary (Christian) R.; m. Jeanne M. Chung, May 24, 1957 (div. Oct. 1985); children: Lisa J., Brian D. BA in Mech. Engring., U. Wash., Seattle, 1962. Project controls mgr. Procon, Inc., Des Plaines, Ill., 1968-72; sr. cost engr. Gen. Atomic, San Diego, 1973-75; tng. mgr. Fluor Utah, San Mateo, Calif., 1975-77; group mgr., project contbr. Austin Industries, Dallas, 1977-78; mgr. constrn. svc. Brown & Root, Inc., Houston, 1978-80; mgmt. specialist WPPSS, Richland, Wash., 1980-85; cons. Mgmt. Analysis Co., San Diego, 1985-86; owner MelCor Assocs., Fremont, Calif., 1986-89, pres. Richmond, from 1990. Mgmt. cons. in field. Foster father Foster Parents. Cpl. U.S. Army, 1955-57, Korea. Republican. Mem. Christian Ch. Avocations: golf, fishing. Died July 16, 2005.

ROGERS, RICHARD EDGAR, tire manufacturing company executive; b. Akron, Ohio, Dec. 8, 1929; s. James Edward and Amy Margaret (Krieger) R.; m. Marcelyn Mae Emerson, Nov. 20, 1954 (div. 1975); children: Cynthia, Randall, Mark; m. Ruth Ann Krause, Apr. 12, 1995. BA, Houghton Coll., N.Y., 1954. Real estate mgr./mgr. properties Goodyear Tire & Rubber Co., Akron, 1963-95; retired, 1995. Home: Akron, Ohio. Died Oct. 7, 2004.

ROGERS, VIVIAN ALICIA, adult counselor, educator; b. New Haven, Sept. 3, 1919; d. Martin Louis and Josephine Regina (Granfield) R.; m. Donald R. McCoy, Sept. 30, 1949 (div. 1980); children: Patricia, Bernard, William. BA in Econs. and Sociology, Albertus Magnus Coll., New Haven, 1941; MA in Internat. Relations, U. Chgo., 1949; MSEd in Guidance and Counseling, U. Kans., 1972; PhD in Adult and Occupational Edn., Kans. State U., 1975; marriage and family cert. prog., Menninger Found., 1984. Registered counselor, N.C. Dir. adult life resource ctr. U. Kans., Lawrence, 1968-81, asst. to dean of continuing edn., 1981-85; vis. prof. dept. coll. student pers. Bowling Green (Ohio) State U., 1985; dir. ctr. for edn. of women U. Mich., Ann Arbor, 1985-87, rsch. scientist, 1987-88; counselor, cons. U. N.C., Wilmington, 1988-92. Vis. scholar U. N.C., Wilmington, 1988—. Author: Career Exploration for Women, 1974, Create: A New Model for Adult Career Change, 1979 (Am. Coll. Testing/Nat. U. Extension Assn. Creative Programming award), The Adult Life Cycle, 1978; editor: A Life Transitions Reader, 1980, Adult Development Through Relationships, 1984; contbr. articles to profl. publs., chpt. to book. Capt. USMC Women's Res., 1943-46. Recipient Alumna of Yr. award Albertus Magnus Coll., 1976; Menninger Found. fellow, 1978-79; grantee Ford Found., 1975-77, HEA, 1977-78, 82-84. Mem. ACA. Avocation: photography. Home: Wilmington, NC. Died June 14, 2004.

ROGNSTAD, ROBERT ALAN, biochemist; b. Mpls., Nov. 15, 1930; s. Joseph Edwin and Lillian Dagmar (Evenson) R.; m. Darlene Krebs, May 29, 1966. BA, Pomona Coll., 1953; PhD, U. So. Calif., 1971. Rsch. biochemist Cedars-Sinai Med. Ctr., L.A., 1963-87, Lemontree Rsch. Inst., L.A., 1987-89, Whittier Inst., La Jolla, Calif., 1989-95, U. Calif.-San Diego, La Jolla, from 1995. Author book chpts.; contbr. numerous articles to profl. jours.; editl. adv. bd. Biochem. Soc., London, 1993-97. With U.S. Army, 1954-56. Rsch. grantee NIH, 1971-97. Mem. Am. Soc. Biochemistry and Molecular Biology, European Assn. Study of Diabetes. Democrat. Achievements include research in futile cycles in metabolism. Home: Pocatello, Idaho. Died May 12, 2004.

ROHRBACH, PETER THOMAS, writer; b. N.Y.C., Feb. 27, 1926; s. James P. and Kathryn Ann (Foley) R.; m. Sheila Sheehan, Sept. 21, 1970; 1 child, Sarah. MA, Cath. U., Washington, 1952. Editl. cons. Harvard U., Urban Inst., Nat. Urban Coalition, HEW, Dept. Transp. Author 16 books including: The Largest Event, 1994, Conversation with Christ, 1994, Journey to Carith, 1966, American Issue, 1984, Stagecoach East, 1983; (booklets) Find, 1985, Many Missions, 1986; Editor: The Wright Brothers, The Jet Age, Prelude to the Space Age, Messerschmitt (winner Prix Aéronautique in France 1981); editor jour. Spiritual Life, Air and Space mag.; writer TV and motion picture scripts for comml. and pub. prodns. including Wally's Workshop and PBS's series on aging; contbr. articles to profl. jours. Mem. Authors Guild, PEN. Died Dec. 10, 2004.

ROJAHN, ELIZABETH J., diplomat; b. Oshkosh, Wis., Sept. 16, 1916; d. Frank and Anna Elizabeth (Mace) R. BS, Wis. State U., Oshkosh, 1938. Tchr. pub.schs., Endeavor, Wis., 1938-39, Oshkosh, 1939-42, Truax Field, Madison, Wis., 1942-43, Scotfield, St. Louis, 1944-45; with Office of Chief of Staff, Pentagon, Washington, 1947; diplomat U.S. Embassies in Japan, Colombia, Greece, Iraq, Lebanon, Can., 1947-67. Recipient award of appreciation Govt. of Iran, 1966. Home: Oshkosh, Wis. Died Feb. 16, 2005.

ROLLIN, BARBARA KLEINBERG, real estate professional; b. N.Y.C., July 18, 1941; d. Lawrence L. and Hermia (Rosen) Hyams; m. David K. Kleinberg, Aug. 22, 1963 (div. Sept. 1980); children: Julie, Michael; m. Dennis S. Rollin, May 13, 1981 (dec. Sept. 1985). BA in English Lit., Queens Coll., 1962; MA in English Lit., Hunter Coll., 1964; postgrad., U. Md., 1965-67. Tchr. English Trumansburg (N.Y.) High Sch., 1963-65; instr. gourmet cooking, creative writing Prince Georges Community Coll., Largo, Md., 1976-78; realtor Century 21 Award Realty, Crofton, Md., 1978-81, Long & Foster Real Estate, Crofton, Md., from 1981; instr. Bowie, Md., 1983; tng. dir. Crofton, 1985-86. Mem. editorial bd. Realtor Mag., Fairfax, Va., 1985-86. Named to Disting. Sales Club, Anne Arundel County, 1980—; U. Md. fellow, 1966. Mem. Anne Arundel County Bd. Realtors, Prince Georges County Bd. Realtors. Democrat. Jewish. Died Dec. 16, 2004.

ROMAN, ROBERT JUSTIN, electrical engineer; b. N.Y.C., Sept. 24, 1923; s. John A. and Lucy N. (Christiano) R.; m. Hilda Bolton, 1948 (dec. 1979); children: Kenneth J., Richard B., William R., James P.; m. Betty Taylor, May 23, 1980. BSEE, Columbia U., 1944; MBA, U. Rochester, 1969. Prog. mgr. Eastman Kodak Co., Rochester, N.Y., 1946-83; sr. ptnr. AEREA Assocs., Salt Lake City, from 1983. Cons. Eastman Kodak Co., Rochester, 1984-86; instr. U.S. Naval Acad., 1945. Patentee in field. Chmn. Greater Rochester Internat. Airport Users Com., 1984-88. With USN, 1943-46; PTO. Mem. IEEE, Indsl. Electronics Soc. (treas.), Hunt Hollow Ski Club, Rochester Pilots Assn. (pres. 1984-87), Tau Beta Pi, Beta Theta Pi, Beta Gamma Sigma. Republican. Presbyterian. Avocations: skiing, flying, art. Died Jan. 9, 2004.

ROMANSKY, MONROE JAMES, internist, educator; b. Hartford, Conn., Mar. 16, 1911; s. Benjamin and Henrietta (Levine) R.; m. Evelyn Muriel Lackman, Jan. 10, 1943; children: Stephen, Gerald, Michael, Richard. AB, U. Maine, 1933; MD, U. Rochester, 1937. Diplomate: Am. Bd. Internal Medicine. Intern Strong Meml. Hosp.-U. Rochester, NY, 1937-38, asst. resident, 1938-39, James Gleason Research fellow studies on relationship of kidneys to hypertension, 1939-40, chief resident, 1940-41, instr. in medicine, 1941-42; investigator Office Sci. Research and Devel., Surgeon Gen. U.S., 1941-42; chief biochemistry and antibiotic research Walter Reed Army Hosp., 1942-46; asso. prof. Sch. Medicine, George Washington U., Washington, from 1946, prof. medicine, 1957—91; dir. George Washington U. med. div. D.C. Gen. Hosp., 1950-69; dir. infectious diseases research lab. and infectious diseases div. D.C. Gen. Hosp., 1950-69. Cons. internal medicine antibiotics Walter Reed Army Hosp., Washington; Cons. internal medicine antibiotics VA Hosp., Washington, 1952—2006, NIH, Bethesda, Md., 1953—2006, Surgeon Gen. USAF, 1966—2006; mem. Asian influenza adv. com. D.C., 1956-61; mem. ad hoc adv. com. Bur. Medicine FDA, 1966-67; examiner Am. Bd. Internal Medicine, 1965, 67, 69 Editorial bd.: Antimicrobial Agts. and Chemotherapy, 1961-72; Contbr. to profl. jours. Trustees council U. Rochester, 1965—2006; Served with USMC., AUS, 1942-46. Decorated Legion of Merit; recipient Founders award Tau Epsilon Phi, Disting. Career award U. Maine. Fellow ACP (adv. bd. to gov. D.C. 1969—2006); mem. Am. Soc. Internal Medicine, Am. Fedn. Clin. Research, Soc. Exptl. Biology and Medicine, Am. Soc. Microbiology, Infectious Diseases Soc. (founding council 1963-66), Soc. Med. Cons. to Armed Forces, Sigma Xi, Alpha Omega Alpha. Clubs: Woodmont Country. Achievements include pioneer work in prolonging action of penicillin, requiring only single daily injection, Romansky Formula, 1944; nutritional studies in obesity as related to weight reduction. Home: Chevy Chase, Md. Died Aug. 12, 2006.

ROMIG, EDGAR DUTCHER, clergyman; b. N.Y.C., July 6, 1921; s. Edgar Franklin and Ella Woodruff (Dutcher) R. BA, Princeton U., 1942; MDiv, Episcopal Theol. Sch., Mass., 1951; DD (hon.), Va. Theol. Sem., 1969. Ordained deacon Episcopal Ch., 1951, priest, 1952. Asst. minister Trinity Ch., Boston, 1951-53; rector Grace Ch., North Attleboro, Mass., 1953-58, St. Stephen's Ch., Lynn, Mass., 1958-64, Ch. of Epiphany, Washington, 1964-92. Dep. Episcopal Gen. Conv., 1973, 76, 79, 82, 85, 88, 91. Author: Trinity Church in the City of Boston, 1953; contbr. articles to various jours. Ambulance driver Am. Field Svc., 1942-43, NATOUSA; with AUS, 1943-45, ETO. Decorated Bronze Star, Purple Heart. Mem. Century Club (N.Y.C.), Princeton Club (N.Y.C.), Met. Club. Democrat. Home: Washington, DC. Died June 13, 2006.

ROMJUE, STEPHEN WALTER, utility company executive, electrical engineer; b. Alton, Ill., Mar. 21, 1940; s. Russell Clark and Georgia Gloria (Elordi) R.; m. Marilyn Kay Dobyns, June 5, 1960; children: Diane Kay, Lisa Marie, Laura Eva. BSEE, Wash. State U., 1967. Registered profl. elec. engr., Wash. Elec. engr. Wash. Water Power Co., Spokane, 1967-71, dist. supr. engring., 1971-74, transmission and distbn. engring. supr., 1974-80, asst. div. mgr., 1980-82, mgr. Spokane div., 1982-88; gen. mgr. PUD #1, Grays Harbon County, Wash., from 1988. Chmn. Southside Cath. Schs., Spokane, 1978; bd. dirs. Campfire Girls Eastern Wash. div., 1979-82, Connoisseur Concerts, Spokane, 1985-88; mem. Cath. Bishop Fin. Council, Spokane, 1985-88. Mem. IEEE (chmn. Spokane chpt. 1978), Power Engring. Soc. (chmn. Spokane chpt. 1975), NW Electric Light and Power Assn. (engring and ops. sect. chmn. 1982). Republican. Avocations: gardening, skiing, running. Home: Jordan Valley, Oreg. Died July 10, 2005.

RONSON, RAOUL R., publishing executive; b. Fiume, Italy, Mar. 22, 1931; came to U.S., 1951; s. Mirko and Margaret (Fischer) Ruzicka; m. Susan Kohn, July 22, 1962; 1 child, Paul. DBA, U. Rome, 1950; MA, New Sch Social Research, 1957; postgrad., Inst. for Advanced Internat. Studies, U. Miami, 1967-68, NYU, 1974. Fgn. corr., freelance writer, 1953-59; treas. Daron Enterprises, Inc., 1959-63; pres. Seesaw Music Corp., N.Y.C., from 1963, Okra Music Corp., N.Y.C., 1963-77, Ulsyra Prodn. Corp., N.Y.C., from 1963. Pres. The Composers Press, 1972-76; acad. lectr. Am., Australian, New Zealand univs. and conservatories; vis. lectr. Youngstown (Ohio) State U., 1985—, Finch Coll., N.Y.C., Eastman Sch. Music, Rochester, N.Y., Wake Forest U., Winston-Salem, N.C. Producer documentary films, 1959—, classical music recs., 1963—, The Dana Recording Project (nominated 2 Grammy awards). Mem. Emergency Control Bd. Office of Mayor, N.Y.C., 1973-82, Fed. Emergency Mgmt. Agy., Washington, 1982-84; rsch. analyst Office of the Sec. Def., Res. Affairs, The Pentagon, Washington, 1984-91; liaison officer U.S. Mil. Acad., West Point, N.Y., 1988-97. With M.I., AUS, 1952-54, USAR, 1955-91, ret. 1991. Decorated Legion of Merit, Def. Superior Svc. medal, Def. Meritorious Svc. medal, Army Meritorious Svc. medal, Army Commendation medal, Def. Identification badge Office Sec., Korean Svc. medal, UN Svc. medal, medal from Korean pres.; recipient numerous other awards and decorations; Grammy award nominee for Classical Prodr. of the Yr., 1993. Mem. Am. Polit. Sci. Assn., Am. Acad. Polit. and Social Sci., Internat. Platform Assn., Civil Affairs Assn., Sibelius Soc. (bd. dirs. 1978-85), Nat. Acad. Rec. Arts and Scis., Masons. Home: New York, NY. Died Oct. 1, 2005.

ROOD, RALPH EDWARD, lawyer; b. Washington, Ga., Nov. 7, 1943; s. Arthur Edward Rood Jr. and Amelia (Golucke) Brooks; m. Linda Kimbrough Beneke, Nov. 20, 1993; children: Virginia Hooper, Amelia Gordon. BBA, U. Ga., 1966; JD, U. Miss., 1972. Bar: Miss. 1972, U.S. Dist. Ct. (no. dist.) Miss. 1972, U.S. Ct. Appeals (5th cir.) 1972, U.S. Supreme Ct. 1977, U.S. Ct. Appeals (6th cir.) 1980. From assoc. to ptnr. Gholson, Hicks & Nichols, Columbus, Miss., from 1971. Research editor Miss. Law Jour., Oxford, 1971-72. Mem. exec. com. Lowndes County Rep. party, Columbus, 1978-82. Lt. USNR, 1966-69. Mem. ABA, Miss. Bar Assn. (mem. ethics com. 1994—), Maritime Law Assn. of U.S. (proctor in admiralty), Miss. Def. Lawyers (com. chmn. 1983), Def. Research Inst., Ducks Unltd. (outstanding sponsor com. 1983, outstanding dist. dir. 1985, sec. Miss. council), Baily Brake Hunting & Fishing Assn. Clubs: Magowah Gun and Country (bd. dirs. 1976-79, 82-85), Bossom Bayou Hunt (Tallahatchie County, Miss.) (pres. 1986). Avocations: reading, hunting, fishing, retriever field trials, running. Home: Columbus, Miss. Died Feb. 20, 2005.

ROOMANN, HUGO, architect; b. Tallinn, Estonia, Mar. 25, 1923; came to U.S., 1951, naturalized, 1957; s. Eduard August and Annette (Kask) R.; m. Raja R. Suursoho, Sept. 15, 1945; children— Katrin-Kaja, Linda-Anu. BS, Inst. Tech. Carolo Wilhelmina, Braunschweig, W. Ger., 1950; M.F.A. in Arch. (scholar 1956-57), Princeton U., 1957. Archtl. engr. Austin Co., Roselle, NJ, 1951-54; archtl. designer Epple & Seaman, Newark, 1954-55, 57-61; propr. Hugo Roomann, Cranford and Elizabeth, NJ, 1961-66; ptnr. A.M. Kinney Assocs. (Architects and Engrs.), Cin., N.Y.C. and Chgo., 1966-89. Dir. architecture, v.p. corp. ops. A.M. Kinney, Inc., Cin., 1967, 77, 89; dir. Walter Kidde Constructors, Inc., 1973, A.M. Kinney, Inc., A.M. Kinney Assocs. Inc., Chgo.; pres. Design Art Corp., 1986. Prin. works include Grad. Rsch. Ctr. for Biol. Scis., Ohio State U., 1970, Lloyd Libr., Cin., 1968, offices, labs. and mfg. facilities, Miles Labs., West Haven, Conn., 1969, Am. Mus. Atomic Energy, Oak Ridge, 1975, Renton K. Brodie Sci. Ctr., U. Cin., 1970, EPA Nat. Labs., Cin., 1975, NALCO Tech. Ctr., Naperville, Ill., 1979, Brown & Williamson Corp. Hdqrs., Louisville, 1983, U. Cin. Kettering Lab., 1989; pub.: Urban Growth and the Development of an Urban Sewer System, City of Cincinnati 1800-1915, 2001. Pres. Citizens League, Elizabeth, N.J., 1966, Estonian Heritage Assn. Cin., 1991-94; bd. dirs., pres. Inter-Ethnic Coun. of Greater Cin., 1992-95. Recipient Top Ten Plant award Factory mag., 1967, Top Ten Plant award Modern Mfg. mag., 1970 Mem. AIA (Ohio chpt. award for Renton K. Brodie Sci. Ctr. 1971, for NALCO Ctr. 1980), Princeton Club. Lutheran. Home: Cincinnati, Ohio. Died Jan. 6, 2006.

ROONEY, GEORGE WILLARD, lawyer; b. Appleton, Wis., Nov. 16, 1915; s. Francis John and Margaret Ellen (O'Connell) R.; m. Doris I. Maxon, Sept. 20, 1941; children: Catherine Ann, Thomas Dudley, George Willard. BS, U. Wis., 1938; JD, Ohio State U., 1948. Bar: Ohio 1949, U.S. Supreme Ct. 1956, U.S. Ct. Appeals 1956. Assoc. Wise, Roetzel, Maxon, Kelly & Andress, Akron, Ohio, 1949-54; ptnr. Roetzel & Andress, and predecessor, Akron, 1954—; dir. Duracote Corp. Nat. bd. govs. ARC, 1972-78; trustee, mem. exec. bd. Summit County chpt. ARC, 1968, 1975—; v.p. Akron coun. Boy Scouts Am., 1975—; pres. Akron Automobile Assn., 1980-83, trustee, 1983—; chmn. bd. Akron Gen. Med. Ctr., 1981-86, trustee, mem. exec. com., 1986—; trustee Mobile Meals Found., Bluecoats, Inc. Maj. USAAF, 1942-46. Decorated D.F.C. with 2 oak leaf clusters, Air medal with 3 oak leaf clusters; recipient Disting. Community Svc. award Akron Labor Coun.; Disting. Svc. award Summit County chpt. ARC, 1978. Mem. ABA, Ohio Bar Assn. Akron Bar Assn. Am. Judicature Soc., Rotary (past pres.), Portage Country Club (past pres.), Cascade Club (past chmn., bd. govs.), KC. Republican. Roman Catholic. Avocations: golf, travel, gardening. Home: Akron, Ohio. Died Apr. 30, 2006.

ROOP, RALPH GOODWIN, retired oil marketing company executive; b. Snowville, Va., June 23, 1915; s. Guy C. and Ora (Goodwin) R.; married; children: Nancie Roop Kennedy, Paterson Roop Webster. BS, Va. Poly. Inst., 1936; MS, Cornell U., 1937. Various positions So. States Coop., Richmond, Va., 1937-66; pres. and/or chmn. bd. Petroleum Marketers, Inc., Richmond, 1954-88. Trustee Va. Wesleyan Coll., Norfolk, 1982—; bd. dirs. Suhor Found., 1988—, Trinity Found., Richmond. Named Oil Man of Yr., Va. Petroleum Jobbers Assn., 1983. Mem. Va. Petroleum Council (chmn. 1964-67), Va. Oil Men's Assn. (pres. 1975-76), Am. Petroleum Inst., Richmond C. of C. (past bd. dirs.). Methodist. Avocations: travel, photography, fishing. Home: Richmond, Va. Died Jan. 21, 2006.

ROOT, JOHN DAVID, history educator; b. Michigan City, Ind., Dec. 20, 1940; s. Joseph McKelvey and Margaret Rose (Biever) R. BA, U. Notre Dame, 1962; MA, Ind. U., 1964, PhD, 1974. Prof. history Ill. Inst. Tech., Chgo., from 1969. Contbr. articles to profl. jours. Capt. U.S. Army, 1966-68, Vietnam. NEH fellow, 1981; grantee Am. Philos. Soc., 1976-79. Mem. Am. Acad. Religion, Am. Soc. for Ch. History, Am. Cath. Hist. Soc. (exec. coun. 1985-87), Am. Hist. Assn. Home: Chicago, Ill. Died Sept. 24, 2004.

ROOT, RICHARD KAY, retired medical educator; b. N.Y.C., Dec. 1, 1937; s. Raymond Willard and Carolyne Mary (Kay) R.; m. Marilyn Parletta, Mar. 19, 1960 (dec. 2001); children: Richard Allen, David Lawrence, Daniel Christopher; m. Rita A. O'Boyle, Sept. 22, 2002. BA, Wesleyan U., 1959; MD, Johns Hopkins U., 1963; MA, U. Pa., 1973, Yale U., 1975. Resident Mass. Gen. Hosp., Boston, 1963-65, U. Wash., Seattle, 1968-69; sr. investigator Nat. Inst. Allergy and Infectious Disease, NIH, Bethesda, Md., 1969-71; asst. to assoc. prof. medicine U. Pa. Sch. Medicine, Phila., 1971-75; prof. medicine Yale U. Sch. Medicine, New Haven, 1975-82, U. Wash. Sch. Medicine, Seattle, 1982—85, 1991—2002, vice-chair medicine, 1991—2002, prof. emeritus, 2002—06; prof. medicine U. Calif., San Francisco, 1985-91. Chief of medicine Seattle (Wash.) VA Med. Ctr., 1982-85, Harborview Med. Ctr., Seattle, 1991; chair of medicine U. Calif. Sch. Medicine, San Francisco, 1985-89, assoc. dean, 1989-91; dir., AIDS Adv. Com., NIH, 1986-91. Editor: (textbook) Harrison's Principles of Internal Medicine, 1990, editor-in-chief (textbook) Clinical Infectious Diseases; contbr. chpts. to books and articles to profl. jours. Mem. med. com., bd. dirs. Yale China Assn., New Haven, 1979-82; bd. dirs. Conn. Hospice, Branford, 1981-82. Comdr. USPHS, 1965-69. Recipient Rsch. Career Devel. award NIH, 1975-78. Fellow ACP, Infectious Diseases Soc. Am.; mem. Am. Fedn. Clin. Rsch. (pres. Ea. sect. 1978-79), Am. Soc. Clin. Investigation, Assn. Am. Physicians, Western Assn. Physicians (councilor 1986-89, pres. 1997), Soc. Gen. Internal Medicine, Alpha Omega Alpha, Phi Beta Kappa. Avocations: guitar, bicycling, kayaking, tennis, reading. Home: Kirkland, Wash. Died Mar. 19, 2006.

ROSATO, FRANCIS ERNEST, retired surgeon; b. Phila., June 2, 1934; s. Ernest Lancelot and Mary Rita (Huggard) R.; m. Gertrude Blount Doman, Oct. 27, 1962; children— Ernest, Ann, Gertrude, Frank, Aimee. Student, St. Joseph's Coll., Phila., 1952-55; MD, Hahnemann Med. Coll., Phila., 1959. Diplomate: Nat. Bd. Med. Examiners. Resident in surgery U. Pa.; mem. faculty to prof. surgery, 1965-74; prof. surgery, chmn. dept. Eastern Va. Med. Sch., Norfolk, 1974-78; prof., chmn. dept. surgery Jefferson Med. Coll. of Thomas Jefferson U., Phila., 1978—2005. Advanced clin. fellow Am. Cancer Soc. Author: Surgery of the Breast, 1986, Atlas of Surgical Technique, 1992; contbg. author: Cameron's Current Surgical Therapy, Ana Sabiston's Text of Surgery; contbr. articles to med. jours. Fellow ACS; mem. Soc. Univ. Surgeons, Am. Surg. Assn., So. Surg. Assn., Halstead Soc., Phila. Country Club, Merion Cricket Club, Union League, Friendly Sons. of St. Patrick. Roman Catholic. Home: Gladwyne, Pa. Died Oct. 18, 2006.

ROSE, JIMY EARLENE BRADY, rancher; b. Ardmore, Okla., Mar. 13, 1929; d. James Roy and Mamie Eaves Brady; m. Eldrige Rose, Dec. 31, 1977; children: Glena Yates, Linda Kay Tiller. Student, Monticello Coll., 1947-49. Owner, mgr. Brandy Ranches, from 1969. Bd. dirs., officer Am. Cattle Assn., 1981-85. Okla. state pres. Epsilon Sigma Alpha, 1970-72; chmn. Ardmore Centennial Commn. Birthday Com., 1984; pres. bd. trustees Carter County Hist. and Geneol. Soc., 1988; chmn. Carter County March of Dimes; past pres. Nat. League Am. Pen Women; fundraiser in cmty. Recipient Cert. of Appreciation, City of Ardmore, 1989, City of Ardmore Cmty. Svc. award, 1990; named Miss Rodeo of Okla., 1949; inductee Am. Cattle Breeders Hal of Fame, 1979. Died Jan. 2, 2004.

ROSE, SHERYL ANN, medical/surgical nurse, mental health nurse; b. Framingham, Mass., Aug. 8, 1963; d. David Nye and Jeanette Lourette (Tessier) Settele; m. James Alan Rose, Jan. 5, 1990. BSN, U. Conn., 1986. RN, Maine, Conn. Primary caseworker, therapist Boston VA Hosp., Jamaica Plains, Mass.; staff nurse psychiat. dept. Nalbrook Hosp., Westport, Conn.; charge nurse med. flr. St. Joseph's Hosp., Bangor, Maine. Recipient 1990 Nurses Day award, St. Joseph's Hosp. Mem. ANA (cert. psychiat. nurse). Home: Bangor, Maine. Died May 24, 2004.

ROSEN, ROBERT THOMAS, analytical and food chemist; b. Concord, N.H., Nov. 5, 1941; s. Maurice J. and Miriam M. (Miller) R.; m. Sharon Lynne Beres, Apr. 23, 1972. BA (cum laude), Nasson Coll.; PhD, Rutgers U. Sr. rsch. scientist Chem. Rsch. and Devel. Ctr., FMC Corp., Princeton, NJ, 1966-84; program dir. analytical support facilities, from 1984; assoc. dir. Ctr. for Advanced Food Technology, Rutgers U., New Brunswick, NJ, from 1993; rsch. prof. food sci. Rutgers U., New Brunswick, from 2000. Contbr. articles and book reviews to profl. jours. Recipient award for best oustanding rsch., Cook Coll./Rutgers U., 2001. Fellow Am. Inst. Chemists, Am. Chem. Soc. (agrl. and food chemistry divsn.); mem. Inst. Food Technologists, Phi Lambda Upsilon (hon.). Achievements include research in gas and liquid chromatography of organic compounds in fruits and vegetables, determination of phytochemicals in food, natural products and the environment by liquid chromatography and mass spectrometry. Home: Monroe Township, NJ. Died May 16, 2005.

ROSEN, S. PETER (SIMON PETER ROSEN), physicist, former dean; b. London, Eng., Aug. 4, 1933; came to U.S., 1957, naturalized, 1973; s. Louis and Annie R.; m. Yvonne A. Marglous, June 4, 1958 (div. Aug. 1985); children: Daniel M., Sarah E.; m. Adrienne Hayes, Oct. 11, 1987; stepchildren: Robert D., Catherine B. Hayes. BA, Merton Coll. Oxford U., 1954, MA, D.Phil., Merton Coll. Oxford U., 1957. Research asso. Washington U., St. Louis, 1957-59; scientist Midwestern U. Research Assn., Madison, Wis., 1959-61; NATO fellow Oxford, 1961-62; mem. faculty Purdue U., 1961—84, asst. prof. physics, 1961, asso. prof., 1962-66, prof., 1966—84; sr. theoretical physicist U.S. Energy Research and Devel. Adminstrn., Washington, 1975-77; program assoc. for theoretical physics NSF, Washington, 1981-83; assoc. leader T-Div. Los Alamos Nat. Lab., 1983-90; dean Coll. Sci., U. Tex. Arlington, 1990—96; assoc. dir, High Energy & Nuclear Sci. divsn., Office Sci. US Dept. Energy, 1997—2003. Cons., lectr., referee for profl. jours.; vis. prof. various univs.; research fellow Sussex U., 1969 Contbr. numerous articles profl. jours. Fellow Am. Phys. Soc., Am. Assn. Advancement Sci.; mem. AAUP (chpt. pres. 1971-72), Sigma Xi, Sigma Pi Sigma. Home: Rockville, Md. Died Oct. 13, 2006.

ROSEN, SUMNER M., social sciences educator; b. Boston, June 17, 1923; m. Judith Davidoff, 1949; children: Max, Rebekah. BS in Econ., 1948; PhD, MIT, 1959. Rsch. dir. New Careers Devel. Ctr. NYU, 1968-70; sr. rsch. scholar Inst. Pub. Adminstrn., 1971-75; prof. social policy Columbia U., 1975-93, sr. scholar Ctr. for Study of Human Rights, 1994-95. Vis. prof. nat. Chengchi U., Taiwan, 1993-94, Cornell U. Sch. Indsl. and Labor Rels., 1996-2005. Contbg. author: Face of the Nation, Vol. 3, Ency. of Social Work, 1987, Jobs For all, 1994; contbr. articles to profl. jours. Vice-chmn. Nat. Jobs for All Coalitio, 1994-2005; bd. dirs. Jews for Racial and Econ. Justice, 1990-96; vice-chmn. Greater N.Y. Labor-Religion Coalition, 1995-2005; bd. dirs. Pub. Health Assn. of N.Y.C., 1994-96, 98-2000; bd. dirs. Five Borough Inst., 1997-2005, others. Fulbright scholar, Taiwan, 1989-90. Died Aug. 17, 2005.

ROSENBERG, CHARLES HARVEY, otorhinolaryngologist; b. N.Y.C., June 10, 1919; s. Morris and Bessie (Greditor) R.; m. Florence Rich, Dec. 27, 1942; children: Kenneth, Ina Garten. BA cum laude, Alfred U., 1941; MD, U. Buffalo, 1944. Intern Jewish Hosp. Bklyn., 1944-45; resident otolaryngology Mt. Sinai Hosp., N.Y.C., 1945-46, 48-50; teaching faculty, sr. clin. asst. Mt. Sinai Hosp. and Med. Sch., N.Y.C., 1950-72; attending surgeon Stamford Hosp., St. Joseph's Hosp., Stamford, Conn., 1953—2000, ret., 2000. Dir. dept. otolaryngology Stamford Hosp. and St. Joseph's Hosp., 1973-79. Campaign chmn. United Jewish Fedn., Stamford, 1978-81, pres., 1981-83, exec. com., 1978—; trustee Alfred (N.Y.) U., 1996-2000. Capt. U.S. Army, 1945-46. Fellow ACS; mem. AMA, Stamford Med. Soc., Fairfield Med. Soc., Conn. State Med. Soc., Am. Bd. Otolaryngology, Am. Acad. Ophthalmology and Otolaryngology. Democrat. Jewish. Home: Stamford, Conn. Died Feb. 17, 2004.

ROSENBERG, JOHN ALAN (JACK ROSENBERG), business owner; b. Milw., Apr. 6, 1920; s. Louis and Mary (Lichtenstein) R.; m. Sue Miller, 1953 (div. 1979); 1 child, John; m. Lorraine Greenberg, 1981 (div. 1982); m. Lucille Barash Glicklich, Aug. 12, 1984. BA, U. Wis., 1941. Pres., owner Lavo Co., Milw., 1948-55, Jax Hi-Fi, Milw., 1958-62, Cen. Parking, Milw., 1960-63, Fox Co., Milw., 1969-75, Milw. Terminal Warehouse, Milw., 1969-70; CEO, co-owner Telechek/Wis., Milw., 1975-95. V.p. Childrens Outing, Milw., 1985—, Milw. Chamber Theatre, 1989—, Cmty. Advs., Milw., 1990—, Next Act Theatre, 1992—, Generations in Jazz, 1992—; bd. dirs., v.p. Wis. ACLU, 1982—; bd. dirs., treas. Transcenter, 1993—; bd. dirs. Jewish Found. Econ. Opportunity, 1997—; vol. SCORE, Milw., 1985-88, Victim Offender Reconcilation, 1990-92; sponsor, dir. The Chosen, 1991—. Mem. Grand Ave. Club (bd. dirs., treas. 1996—). Democrat. Avocations: tennis, reading, theater, concerts, auditing courses. Home: Milwaukee, Wis. Died Jan. 11, 2005.

ROSENBLUM, ARNOLD, manufacturing executive; b. Bklyn., Sept. 10, 1935; s. Israel and Kate (Forman) R.; m. Linda G. Zweibel, Aug. 24, 1985; children: Michael I, Joseph B., Steven A.; stepchildren: Steven L., Jonathan B., Jodi L. AAS in Machine Design, Pratt Inst., Bklyn., 1960; BSME, Fairleigh Dickinson U., 1965. Tech. illustrator, writer Mantek Svcs., Bronx, N.Y., 1956-58, Volt Tech. Svcs., N.Y.C., 1958-60; chief mech. designer Indsl. Test Equipment Co., Port Washington, N.Y., 1960-64; sale application engr. Automatic Switch Co., Florham Park, N.J., 1964-67; sales engr. Tex. Instruments Supply div. Tex. Instruments, Clark, N.J., 1967-69; gen. mgr. Loral Distbr. Products div. Loral, Great Neck, N.Y., 1969-73; v.p., ptnr. Arco Electronics Co., Commack, N.Y., 1973-77, Cole-Flex Corp., West Babylon, N.Y., 1977-86, pres., CEO, owner, from 1986. Bd. dirs., sec. Electronic Industry Show Corp., Chgo., 1991-93, v.p., 1993—. Author: Words of a Different Man, 1978. Cpl. U.S. Army, 1954-56. Named Young Tiger of Yr. Young Tigers of Electronic Industries, Las Vegas, 1988. Mem. Electronic Industries Assn. (chmn. ea. region 1985-93, chmn. components divsn. 1993—, bd. govs. 1989—, distbn. forum chmn. 1989—), Electronic VIP Club (life), Electronics Execs. Club. Republican. Jewish. Avocations: reading, drawing. Home: Boca Raton, Fla. Died Feb. 28, 2005.

ROSENBLUM, VICTOR GREGORY, political science professor; b. NYC, June 2, 1925; s. George and Vera (Minster) R.; m. Louise Rann, Feb. 21, 1946; children: Susan, Ellen, Laura, Keith, Jonathan, Peter, Warren, Joshua. AB, Columbia U., 1945, LL.B., 1948; PhD, U. Calif.-Berkeley, 1953; D.H.L., Hebrew Union Coll., 1970; D.L., Siena Heights Coll., 1982, Wabash Coll., 1998. Bar: Ill., N.Y., U.S. Supreme Ct. Lectr. polit. sci. U. Calif., Berkeley, 1949-52, asst. prof. polit. sci., 1953-57; assoc. prof. polit. sci. Northwestern U., 1958-63, prof. polit. sci. and law, 1963-68, 70-88, Nathaniel L. Nathanson prof., 1988—92; pres. Reed Coll., Portland, Oreg., 1968-70. Sr. legal cons. project on bankruptcy govtl. studies div. Brookings Instn., 1964-69; vis. Fulbright lectr. Sch. Law U. Louvain, Belgium, 1966-67, vis. prof., 1978-79, 91-92; mem. Adminstrv. Conf. U.S., 1982-96. Editor in chief Adminstrv. Law Rev., 1958-62; author: Law As A Political Instrument, 1955, (with A.D. Castberg) Cases on Constitutional Law: Political Roles of the Supreme Court, 1973, (with Frances Zemans) The Making of a Public Profession, 1981; contbr. to law revs., also law and polit. sci. books. Staff assoc. Govtl. Affairs Inst., Washington, 1952-53; cons., assoc. counsel Subcom. on Exec. and Legis. Reorgn., Com. on Govt. Ops., U.S. Ho. of Reps., 1956-57; bd. dirs. Center for Adminstrv. Justice, 1972-78. Mem. ABA (council sect. adminstrv. law 1962-65, 72-75, chmn. 1977-78), Fed. Bar Assn., Am. Polit. Sci. Assn., Law and Soc. Assn. (pres. 1970-72), Am. Judicature Soc. (dir. 1982-90, chmn. bd. 1985-86), Assn. Am. Law Schs. (exec. com. 1984-88, pres. 1987), Consortium of Social Sci. Assns. (pres. 1987-88), Phi Beta Kappa, Pi Sigma Alpha. Democrat. Jewish. Home: Evanston, Ill. Died Mar. 13, 2006.

ROSENFELD, AZRIEL, computer science educator, consultant; b. N.Y.C., Feb. 19, 1931; s. Abraham Hirsh and Ida B. (Chadaby) R.; m. Eve Hertzberg, Mar. 1, 1959; children— Elie, David, Tova BA, Yeshiva U., 1950,

M.H.L., 1953, MS, 1954, D.H.L., 1955; MA, Columbia U., 1951, PhD, 1957; D.Tech. (hon.), Linkoping U., Sweden, 1980; D of Tech. (hon.), Oulu U., Finland, 1994; LHD (hon.), Yeshiva U., 2000. Ordained rabbi, 1952. Physicist Fairchild Controls Corp., N.Y.C., 1954-56; engr. Ford Instrument Co., Long Island City, N.Y., 1956-59; mgr. research electronics div. Budd Co., Long Island City and McLean, Va., 1959-64; prof., dir. Ctr. for Automation Rsch. U. Md., College Park, 1964-2001, Disting. univ. prof., 1995-2001, prof. emeritus, from 2001. Vis. asst. prof. Yeshiva U., N.Y.C., 1957-63; pres. ImTech, Inc., Silver Spring, Md., 1975-92 Author, editor numerous books; editor numerous jours. Recipient Info. Sci. award Assn. for Intelligent Machinery, 1998. Fellow IEEE (Emanuel R. Piore award 1985), IEEE Computer Soc. (Harry Goode Meml. award 1995), IEEE Sys., Man and Cybernetics Soc. (Norbert Wiener award 1995), Washington Acad. Scis. (Sci. Achievement award 1988), Am. Assn. for Artificial Intelligence (founding), Assn. Computing Machinery (founding); mem. Math. Assn. Am., Machine Vision Assn. (bd. dirs. 1984-88, Pres.'s award 1987), Internat. Assn. Pattern Recognition (pres. 1980-82, K.S. Fu award 1988, founding fellow 1994), Assn. Orthodox Jewish Scientists (pres. 1963-65), Nat. Acad. Engring. of Mex. (corr.). Home: Baltimore, Md. Died Feb. 22, 2004.

ROSENFELD, ERVIN, videotape company executive; b. Budapest, Hungary, Mar. 1, 1934; came to U.S., 1949; s. Samuel and Sarolta (Bernstein) R.; m. Arielle Frances, Feb. 6, 1960; children: Michael, David, Elizabeth. BA, Queens Coll., 1959. Film editor Gerald Prodn., N.Y.C., 1959-61; mgr. distbn. Sponsors Film Svc., N.Y.C., 1961-64; exec. v.p. P.A.T. Film Svcs. Inc., N.Y.C., 1964-87, pres., from 1987. Pres. Media 500, N.Y.C., 1970—; treas. Preferred Audio Tapes, N.Y.C., 1970—; sec. Accutreat Films Inc.; treas. Reel Tyme Video Ltd. Treas. Police Boys Club, Syosset, N.Y., 1969-86. Mem.: Knights of Pythias. Avocations: reading, playing bridge, tennis, golf. Home: Delmar, NY. Died Mar. 1, 2004.

ROSENGARTEN, ELLEN, sociology educator; b. Detroit, Aug. 8, 1950; d. Benjamin and Estelle (Binder) Nason; m. Samuel Judah Rosengarten, June 23, 1977; children: Rachel Ariel, Michael Jacob, Caroline Laura. BA, Kent State U., 1972; MA, U. Akron, 1974. Prof. Sinclair C.C., Dayton, Ohio, from 1974. Author: Study Guide for Hess, et al., 1991. Mem. Am. Sociol. Assn. (membership com.), Soc. for Applied Sociology (co-chair membership com. 1992). Home: Fairborn, Ohio. Died Dec. 9, 2004.

ROSENHEIM, EDWARD WEIL, language educator; b. Chgo., May 15, 1918; s. Edward Weil and Fannie (Kohn) R.; m. Margaret Morton Keeney, June 20, 1947; children: Daniel Edward, James Morton, Andrew Keeney. BA, U. Chgo., 1939, MA, 1946, PhD, 1953. Publicity writer Pub. Relations Service, Chgo., 1939-40; instr. Gary (Ind.) Coll., 1946; faculty U. Chgo., from 1947, prof. English, from 1962, David B. and Clara E. Stern prof., 1980—88, prof. emeritus, 1988—2005, assoc. chmn. dept. English, 1967-75, dir. broadcasting for univ., 1954-57; dir. Nat. Humanities Inst., 1977-80. Disting. vis. prof. Pa. State U., 1961; Disting. lectr. Nat. Coun. Tchrs. English, 1967; mem. Ill. Humanities Coun., 1982-2005, pres., 1985-87. Author: What Happens in Literature, 1960, Swift and the Satirist's Art, 1963; editor: Selected Prose and Poetry of Jonathan Swift, 1958, Jour. Gen. Edn., 1954-56; co-editor: Modern Philology, 1968-88. Served to capt. inf. AUS, 1941-46. Recipient Alumni Svc. medal U. Chgo., 1990; Willet Faculty fellow, 1962, Guggenheim Meml. fellow, 1967. Mem. Am. Soc. 18th Century Studies, Johnson Soc. (pres. Ctrl. region 1971) Clubs: Quadrangle, Wayfarers, Caxton. Home: San Francisco, Calif. Died Nov. 28, 2005.

ROSENN, MAX, federal judge; b. Plains, Pa., Feb. 4, 1910; s. Joseph and Jennie (Wohl) Rosenn; m. Tillie R. Hershkowitz, Mar. 18, 1934; children: Keith S., Daniel Wohl. BA, Cornell U., 1929; LLB, U. Pa., 1932. Bar: Pa. 1932, U.S. Supreme Ct. 1955, Cts. of Philippines 1946. Gen. practice, Wilkes-Barre, Pa., 1932—70; spl. counsel Pa. Dept. Justice, 1939; asst. dist. atty. Luzerne County, 1942—44; solicitor various mcpl. boroughs, ptnr. Rosenn, Jenkins & Greenwald, Wilkes-Barre, 1954—70; sec. pub. welfare State of Pa., 1966—67; judge U.S. Ct. Appeals (3rd Cir.), 1970—81, sr. judge, 1981—2006. Criminal procedure rules com. Supreme Ct. Pa., 1958—85; mem. Pa. Commn. to Revise Pub. Employee Laws, 1968—69; Pa. chmn. com. children and youth White House Conf., 1968—70. Contbr. articles to profl. jours. Active Pa. Bd. Pub. Welfare, 1963—66; chmn. study commn. Pa. Gov.'s Coun. for Human Svcs., 1966—67; exec. bd. Commonwealth of Pa., 1966—67; chmn. Commn. Met. Govt., 1957—58, Pa. Human Rels. Commn., 1969—70, Legis.-exec. Task Force Structure for Human Svcs., 1970, Flood Recovery Task Force, 1972; pres. Property Owners Assn. Luzerne County, 1955—57; alt. del. Rep. Nat. Conv., 1964; pres. Wyoming Valley Jewish Com., 1941—42; life trustee Wilkes-Barre Jewish Cmty. Ctr. 1st lt. U.S. Army, 1944—46. Named a U.S. Courthouse in his honor, 1996, libr., U.S. Courthouse at Scranton in his honor, 2002. Fellow: Internat. Acad. Trial Lawyers, Am. Coll. Trial Lawyers; mem.: ABA, Am. Judicature Soc., Am. Soc. Law and Medicine (past assoc. editor), Am. Law Inst., Luzerne County Bar Assn., Pa. Bar Assn., Westmoreland Club, Masons (33rd degree), B'nai B'rith (life; pres. dist. grand lodge 1947—48, bd. govs., chmn. bd. dirs. Anti-Defamation League Pa., W.Va. and Del. 1955—58, nat. commr. from 1964), Alpha Epsilon Pi. Jewish. Home: Kingston, Pa. Died Feb. 7, 2006.

ROSENSTEIN, LEONARD, real estate company executive; b. Phila., Aug. 4, 1922; s. Benjamin and Esther (Zibulski) R.; m. Eleanor M. Peterson, Mar. 11, 1960; children: Elissa L., Risa B., Tedd B. BS in Pharmacy, Temple U., 1943; BS in Pharmacy (hon.), New Orleans. Lic. pharmacist, Pa., N.J. Pres. Lincoln Pharmacy, Atlantic City, N.J., 1947-69, Mercy Ambulance, Las Vegas, Nev., 1971-73, Nev. Devel. and Realty Co., Las Vegas, from 1973, am. Mgmt. Co., Las Vegas, from 1973; chmn. Players Express Travel, Las Vegas, from 1990. Editor: Temple University Apothecary, 1943. Chmn. Downtown Improvement Authority, Atlantic City, N.J., 1982-84; pres. N.J. Pharm. Assn., 1960; chmn., pres. Nat. Assn. Retail Druggists, Washington, 1969; commr. So. Nev. Regional Housing Bd., Las Vegas, 1993-94.; mem. Beth Sholem Congregation, 1971—. Cpl. U.S. Army, 1943-46, ETO. Recipient award Am. Legion, 1940, E.R. Squibb, 1960, Bowl of Hygea, A.H. Robbins, 1965; named Ky. Col., 1965—. Mem. Greater Las Vegas Realtor Assn., Inst. Real Estate Mgmt., Jewish War Vets, Am. Legion, Elks, Alpha Zeta Omega. Avocations: photography, reading. Home: Las Vegas, Nev. Died Nov. 11, 2004.

ROSENSTOCK, ROBERT, diplomat, lawyer; b. N.Y.C., Mar. 1, 1935; s. Jesse Metzger and Edith Baruch Rosenstock; m. Gerda (Michorl) Rosenstock, Aug. 21, 1970; children: Elisabeth, Thomas, Nicholas. BA, Cornell U., 1957; LLB, Columbia U., 1961. Bar: N.Y. Min. counselor U.S. Mission for UN, N.Y.C.; elected mem., 1st v.p. Internat. Law Commn.; alt. U.S. rep. to UN Security Coun. Tchr. internat. law U. Ga., Pace U. Law Sch. Contbr. numerous articles to prof. jours. Recipient Meritorious Exec. award U.S. Pres. Bush. Home: Pelham, NY. Died Sept. 20, 2004.

ROSENTHAL, A.M. (ABRAHAM MICHAEL ROSENTHAL), former newspaper editor, journalist; b. Sault St. Marie, Ont., Can., May 2, 1922; came to U.S., 1926, naturalized, 1951; s. Harry and Sarah (Dickstein) R.; m. Ann Marie Burke, Mar. 12, 1949; children: Jonathan Harry, Daniel Michael, Andrew Mark; m. Shirley Lord, June 10, 1987. BS in Social Sci., CCNY, 1944, LLD (hon.), 1974; degree (hon.), SUNY, 1984. Staff N.Y. Times, 1944-99, UN corr., 1946-54, assigned India, 1954-58, Warsaw, Poland, 1958-59, Geneva, Switzerland, 1960-61, Tokyo, 1961-63, met. editor, 1963-66, asst. mng. editor, 1967-68, asso. mng. editor, 1968-69, mng. editor, 1969-77, exec. editor, 1977-86, assoc. editor and columnist, 1986-87, columnist, 1986-99. Pres. Fgn. Corr. Assn. India, 1957. Author: 38 Witnesses: The Kitty Genovese Case, 1964; co-author: (with Arthur Gelb) One More Victim: The Life and Death of an American Jewish Nazi, 1967; co-editor: The Night the Lights Went Out, 1965, The Pope's Journey to the United States, 1965; contbr.: articles Foreign Affairs. Recipient citation for work in India Overseas Press Club, 1956, for work in India and Poland, 1959, for two fgn. affairs mag. articles, 1965; Pulitzer prize for internat. reporting, 1960; Number One award Overseas Press Club, 1960; George Polk Meml. award, 1960, 65; Page One award Newspaper Guild N.Y., 1960; Hon. award Assn. Indians in Am., 1974; New York County Bar Assn. award, 1978; Nat. Press Found. Award, 1987, Presdl. Medal of Freedom, 2002. Home: New York, NY. Died May 10, 2006.

ROSENTHAL, JOE, retired photographer; b. Washington, Oct. 9, 1911; m. Lee Rosenthal (div.); 1 adopted child, Joseph J. 1 child, Anne. With Newspaper Enterprise Assn., 1930—32; reporter, photographer San Francisco News, 1932; with ACME Newspictures, San Francisco, 1936; San Francisco bur. chief NY Times-Wide World Photos (purchased by AP); photographer, corr. AP; photographer San Francisco Chronicle, 1946—81. Photographer of famous photograph of World War II portrait of American troops raising the flag on Mount Suribachi during the Battle of Iwo Jima on Feb. 23, 1945. This became the model for the Iwo Jima Meml. near Arlington Nat. Cemetery in Va. (officially known as the Marine Corps War Meml.) Applied for military photographer in the Merchant Marines. Recipient Pulitzer prize. Mem.: Bay Area Press Photographers Assn. (former pres.), San Francisco Press Club (former pres.), San Francisco-Oakland Newspaper Guild (pres. 1951). Died Aug. 20, 2006.

ROSENTHAL, WILLIAM EDWARD, lawyer; b. Amityville, N.Y., Jan. 24, 1953; s. Milton and Blanche (Moskowitz) R.; m. Ruby Meryl Leppo, Mar. 25, 1979; children: Erica Lauren, Mark Ryan. BA cum laude, U. Pitts., 1975; JD, John Marshall Law Sch., Chgo., 1978. Bar: N.Y. 1979, Ill. 1981, Ind. 1981, U.S. Dist. Ct. (ea. and so. dists.) N.Y. 1979, U.S. Dist. Ct. (no. dist.) Ind. 1981. Assoc. Semon & Braverman, Jericho, N.Y., 1979-81; assoc. gen. counsel Sullair Corp., Michigan City, Ind., 1981-84; sr. atty. United Techs. Corp.-Elliott, Pitts., 1984-87; counsel United Techs. Corp., Turbo Power and Marine Systems, Farmington, Conn., from 1987. Legal counsel tech. devel. program with Peoples Republic of China, 1986, R&D Programs with industry bodies, Germany, 1987, licensing Japanese corps., 1988. Avocations: bicycling, sailing. Home: West Simsbury, Conn. Died July 27, 2005.

ROSS, CLAUDE GORDON ANTHONY, former ambassador; b. Chgo., Oct. 26, 1917; s. Claude George and Grace Geraldine (Faulkner) R.; m. Antigone Andrea Peterson (dec. 2004), Aug. 3, 1940; children: Christopher, Geoffrey. BS in Fgn. Svc. U., So. Calif., 1939. Entered U.S. Fgn. Svc., 1940, first sec. Beirut, 1955-56, Nat. War Coll., 1956-57; polit. counsellor Cairo, 1957-60; counsellor Conakry, 1960-62, US Dept. State, 1962-63, US amb. to Central African Republic, 1963-67, US amb. to Haiti, 1967-69, US amb. to Tanzania, 1969-72, dep. asst. sec. for African Am. Affairs, 1972-74, sr. fgn. svc. inspector, 1974, cons., 1975-88; pres. DACOR, Inc, 1989—91. Mem. Am. Fgn. Svc. Assn. (life, chmn. edn. com. 1983-88, Fgn. Svc. Cup 1986), Diplomatic and Consular Officers Ret. (life, v.p. 1987-89, pres. 1989-91), Washington Inst. Fgn. Affairs, Sister Cities Internat. (exec. bd.), Mid. East Inst., Phi Beta Kappa, Phi Kappa Phi, Delta Phi Epsilon. Home: Washington, DC. Died Jan. 18, 2006.

ROSS, DONALD PAUL, JR., robotics design executive; b. Pascagoula, Miss., Aug. 21, 1958; s. Donald Paul Sr. and Patricia Ann (Ryals) R.; m. Brenda Joe McClendon, 1976 (div. Apr. 1977); 1 child, Donald Paul III. Pres. Ross Work's Inc., Hurley, Miss., from 1996. Cons. engr. Ross Work's, Pensacola, Fla., 1988-93. Author, editor computer program Don's Glove Machine Program, 1989; inventor tank safety valve. Avocation: computer programming. Died Aug. 16, 2004.

ROSS, GERALDINE M. SCHNEIDER RYHERD, retired special education educator; b. Lacona, Iowa, Mar. 17, 1929; d. Jospeh Mathew and Margaret Dora (Miller) S.; m. Robert Ryherd, May 29, 1950 (dec. Jan. 1980); children: Robert Jr., Billie Ryherd Walker, Margaret Ryherd Brown, Dan, Tim, Tony; m. Laurence Ross, Aug. 2, 1992. BA in Elem. Edn., U. No. Iowa, 1966, MA in Spl. Edn., 1976. Tchr. Iowa Schs., 1949-67; tchr. spl. edn. Waterloo (Iowa) Community Schs., 1967-73; tchr. learning disabilities Clayton County Schs., Elkader, Iowa, 1973-75, MFL Consoldiated Schs., Monona, Iowa, 1975-77; curriculum cons. Keystone Area Edn. Agy., Elkader, 1977-81, work experience coord., 1981-86. Vol. Vols. for Youth, Oelwein, Iowa, 1984—, bd. dirs. 1987—; bd. chmn. Alternative Living Care Review, Oelwein, 1988—; vol. Parent Share and Support, Oelwein, 1989—; county com. Rep. County Orgn., Fayette Co., Iowa, 1984—; mission quilters Sacred Heart Mission Quilters, Oelwein, 1987—; instr. ARC, Oelwein, 1988—; bd. dirs. South Fayette County Red Cross, 1987—; chmn. Care Review Com., 1988—. Recipient Cert. Vols. for Youth, 1985. Mem. AAUW, Cath. Daugs. of the Ams. (pres. 1989—), Oelwein Area Retired Tchrs. (membership chmn. 1989—), Sacred Heart Rosary Soc. Republican. Roman Catholic. Avocations: sewing, gardening, walking, swimming, travel. Home: Oelwein, Iowa. Died Oct. 8, 2004.

ROSS, IRWIN, writer; b. Chgo., Apr. 9, 1919; s. Sol A. and Dora (Brown) R.; m. Patricia Rummel, Dec. 29, 1978. BA, Harvard U., 1940. Editor Threshold mag., N.Y.C., 1941-43; staff writer N.Y. Post, N.Y.C., 1953-61; roving editor Reader's Digest, Pleasantville, N.Y., 1982-85, staff writer, from 1985. Author: Strategy for Liberals, 1949, The Image Merchants, 1959, The Loneliest Campaign, 1968. Staff sgt. U.S. Army, 1945, ETO. Mem. Am. Soc. Journalists and Authors, PEN, Authors Guild, Century Assn. Jewish. Died May 17, 2005.

ROSS, RICHARD LEE, retired lawyer; b. St. Louis, Feb. 26, 1928; s. Julius A. and Minnie B. (Blum) Razovsky; m. Marjorie N. Ross, Apr. 6, 1952; children: Maurice N., Julian E. AB, Washington U., St. Louis, 1948, JD, 1950. Bar: Mo. 1950, U.S. Dist. Ct. (8th cir.) 1950, U.S. Supreme Ct. 1970. V.p., sec. Banner Industries, Inc., St. Louis, 1950-62; ptnr. Slonim & Ross, St. Louis, 1962-77; pvt. practice St. Louis, from 1978. Bd. dirs. MNR Inc. Contbr. articles to profl. jours. Recipient Outstanding Achievement in Labor Relations award, Automotive Workers of Am., St. Louis, 1967. Mem. ABA, Nat. Acad. Arbitrators (mem. various coms.), Mo. Bar Assn. (mem. various coms.), Met. Bar Assn. (mem. various coms.), Meadow Brook Country Club. (bd. dirs.), Shriners (unit pres.). Home: Chesterfield, Mo. Died June 30, 2004.

ROSS, ROBERT, medical association administrator; BA in English Lit., NYU. Dir. pub. info. Muscular Dystrophy Assn., 1955—62, exec. dir., sr. v.p., 1962—73, v.p., 1973—2001, pres., CEO, 2001—06. Died June 5, 2006.

ROSS, ROBERT LEROY, educator; b. Eugene, Oreg., June 7, 1934; s. Raymond Melvin and Harriet Angeline (Howard) R.; m. Anita Ruth Trimmier, Jan. 10, 1965. BA in English, U. Oreg., 1955; MA in English, Tex. Christian U., 1963; PhD in English, U. Tex., 1979. Faculty mem. Clemson (S.C.) U., 1980-81, So. Meth. U., English Dept., Dallas, 1981-87; rsch. assoc. U. Tex., Edward A. Clark Ctr. Australian Studies, Austin, 1988—2005. Author: Australian Literary Criticism, 1989; editor: Antipodes, N.Am. Jour. Australian Lit., 1987-2005, Internat. Lit. in English, 1991; editor: Writing and Rewriting India, 1996; contbr. articles to profl. jours., chpts. to books. Rsch. fellow India So. Meth. U., 1987, fellow Australian Def. Force Acad., 1994. Mem. Am. Assn. Australian Lit. Studies (pres. 1987-91). Democrat. Home: Dallas, Tex. Died May 26, 2005.

ROSS, WILLIAM ROBERT, lawyer; b. Sundance, Wyo., Aug. 10, 1929; s. James Thomas and Kathryn Melvina (Ormsby) R.; m. Dorothy Evelyn Spencer, Mar. 19, 1951 (dec. July 1980); children: James Bradley, Keith Spencer, Rebecca Ann Ross Duncan; m. Kathleen Riggin Worthington, July 30, 1983. BS in Law, U. Nebr., 1958; LLB, U. Md., 1958. Bar: Wyo. 1958, Colo. 1967. Atty., spl. asst. to solicitor U.S. Dept. of Interior, Washington, 1958-61; atty. Am. Sugar Co., N.Y.C., 1961-64; internat. counsel Gates Rubber Co., Denver, 1964-69; pres. Wexco Internat. Corp., Denver, 1969-70; atty., shareholder Lohf & Barnhill, PC, Denver, 1970-87; pres., shareholder Lohf, Shaiman & Ross,

PC, Denver, 1987-93; pvt. practice Littleton, Colo., from 1993. Instr. Law Sch., U. Denver, 1967-73, instr. Bus. Sch., 1970-72. Contbr. articles to profl. law jours. Founding dir., exec. com. World Trade Ctr., Denver, 1989-94. With USAF, 1950-54. Mem. Wyo. State Bar, Colo. Bar Assn., Denver Bar Assn. Home: Littleton, Colo. Died Jan. 5, 2005.

ROSSI, PETER HENRY, sociology educator; b. N.Y.C., Dec. 27, 1921; s. Peter Maxim and Elizabeth (Porcelli) R.; m. Alice Schaerr, Sept. 29, 1951; children: Peter Eric, Kristin Alice, Nina Alexis. BS, CCNY, 1943; PhD, Columbia, 1951. Research asso. Bur. Applied Social Research, Columbia U., 1947- 51; asst. prof. Harvard U., 1951-55; prof. dept. sociology U. Chgo., 1955-67; dir. Nat. Opinion Research Center, 1960-67; prof. dept. social relations Johns Hopkins, 1967-74, chmn. dept., 1967-70; dir. research Center for Met. Planning and Research, 1972-74; prof. sociology, dir. Social and Demographic Research Inst., U. Mass., Amherst, 1974-92, Stuart A. Rice prof. sociology, dir., 1984-92, prof. emeritus, 1992—2006; faculty assoc. Chapin Hall U. Chgo., 1994—2006. Author: Why Families Move, 1956, The Politics of Urban Renewal, 1962, The Education of Catholic Americans, 1966, New Media and Education, 1967, Ghetto Revolts, 1970, Cities Under Siege, 1971, Evaluating Social Programs, 1972, Roots of Urban Discontent, 1974, Reforming Public Welfare, 1976, Prison Reform and State Elites, 1977, Evaluation: A Systematic Approach, 1979, Money, Work & Crime, 1980, After the Clean-up, 1980, Social Science and Natural Hazards, 1981, Measuring Social Judgements, 1982, Natural Hazards and Public Choice, 1982, Under the Gun, 1983, Applied Sociology, 1983, Without Shelter, 1989, Down and Out in America, 1989, Of Human Bonding, 1990, Just Punishments, 1997, Feeding the Poor, 1999; editor: Am. Jour. Sociology, 1957-58; assoc. editor: Am. Sociol. Rev, 1957-60, Am. Sociologist, 1964-66; editor: Social Sci. Research, 1972-89; contbr. articles to profl. and popular jours. Served with AUS, 1942-45. Recipient Alvah and Gunnar Myrdal award for contbns. to evaluation research, 1981; Commonwealth award for contbns. to sociology, 1985; faculty research grantee Social Sci. Research Council, 1959; Carnegie sr. fellow, 1965 Fellow Am. Acad. Arts and Scis.; mem. Am. Sociol. Assn. (sec. 1968-72, pres.-elect 1979-80, pres. 1980-81), Am. Evaluation Assn. Home: Amherst, Mass. Died Oct. 7, 2006.

ROSSNER, JOHN THEODORE, farmer; b. McMinnville, Oreg., Jan. 24, 1944; s. Theodore Bertram and Frances Eleanor (Duerst) R.; m. Astutiningsih Rahayu Rossner, Mar. 9, 1974; children: Madae Frances, Christina Astuti. BS, Oreg. State U., 1966, MS, 1968. Devel. officer Ch. World Svc., Surabaya E. Java, Indonesia, 1969-74; farmer Rossner Farms, McMinnville, Oreg., from 1974. V.p. then pres., bd. dirs. Sheridan Grain Co., Oreg., 1981-88. Elder, Presbyn. Ch., McMinnville, 1976-81, deacon, 1986-89; mem. Rep. Central Com., 1986-88. Named Outstanding Young Farmer, Jaycees, 1979. Mem. West Valley Farmers (v.p., bd. dirs. 1988-90), Oreg. Seed Growers League (v.p., then pres. 1979-81), Oreg. Farm Bur. (2d v.p. 1987—), Yamhill County Farm Bur. (pres. 1982-87), Oreg. Wheat Growers League, Nat. Railway Hist. Soc. Avocation: railroading. Died Mar. 16, 2005.

ROSTENBERG, LEONA, rare book dealer, writer; b. NYC, Dec. 28, 1908; d. Adolph and Louisa (Dreyfus) R. BA, NYU, N.Y.C., 1930; MA, Columbia U., 1933, PhD, 1973. Founder Leona Rostenberg Rare Books, N.Y.C., from 1944; ptnr. Leona Rostenberg & Madeleine Stern Rare Books, N.Y.C., from 1945. Author: English Publishers in the Graphic Arts 1599-1700, 1963, Literary, Political, Scientific, Religious and Legal Publishing, Printing and Bookselling in England, 1551-1700, 2 vols., 1965, The Minority Press and the English Crown: A Study in Repression 1558-1625, 1971, The Library of Robert Hooke: The Scientific Book Trade of Restoration England, 1989, Bibliately: The History of Books on Postage Stamps, 1977; co-author: Bookman's Quintet: Five Catalogues About Books, 1980, Old and Rare: Forty Years in the Book Business, 1974, 1988, Between Boards: New Thoughts on Old Books, 1977, 1983, Quest Book - Guest Book: A Biblio-Folly, 1993, Connections: Our Selves - Our Books, 1994, Old Books in the Old World: Reminiscences of Book Buying Abroad, 1996, Old Books, Rare Friends: Two Literary Sleuths and Their Shared Passion, 1997, New Worlds in Old Books, 1999, Books Have Their Fates, 2000, Bookends, 2001, From Revolution to Revolution: Perspectives on Publishing and Bookselling, 2002; contbr. articles to profl. jours. Recipient Alumni Achievement award NYU, N.Y.C., 1998. Mem. Antiquarian Booksellers Assn. Am. (pres. 1972-74), Am. Printing History Assn. (award 1983), Bibliog. Soc. Am., Manuscript Soc. Democrat. Jewish. Achievements include discovery of Louisa May Alcott pseudonym. Home: New York, NY. Died Mar. 17, 2005.

ROTHER, LORRAINE FLINT, psychiatric clinical nurse specialist; b. Washington, Oct. 13, 1953; d. Thomas Michael and Helen Flora (Loudon) Flint; m. Timothy Scott Rother, Oct. 15, 1977; children: Scott Flint, Amanda Kate. BSN, U. Md., 1975; MSN, U. Calif., 1984. Cert. psychiat. mental health specialist, pub. health nurse, community coll. tchr., Calif. Psychiat. nurse El Camino Hosp., Mountain View, Calif., 1985-91, Good Samaritan Hosp., San Jose, Calif., 1984-91, NIH, Bethesda, Md., 1975-76; psychiat. nurse/rsch. nurse Stanford (Calif.) U. Med. Ctr., 1977-91; nursing instr. various colls., Calif., 1984-91; psychiatric clin. nurse specialist Dept. Veterans Affairs, San Jose, Calif.,

from 1991. Contbr. articles to profl. jours. Grantee NIMN, 1980-82. Mem. ANA (del. conf. 1982), Calif. Nurses Assn. (del. conf. 1981). Home: San Jose, Calif. Died Aug. 22, 2004.

ROTHMANN, BRUCE FRANKLIN, pediatric surgeon; b. Akron, Ohio, July 11, 1924; s. Edwin Franklin Rothmann and Mary Madoline Policy; m. Lola May Secor, June 14, 1947; children: Susan Ann, Pamela Jane, Elizabeth Rothmann Rusnak. Student, Case Western Reserve U., 1942-43, Wesleyan U., 1943-44; MD, NYU, 1948. Diplomate Am. Bd. Surgery. Intern Akron City Hosp., 1948-49, from resident in surgery to chief resident surgeon, 1949-55; from resident pediatric surgeon to chief staff Children's Hosp., Akron, 1953-74; pvt. practice in surgery Akron, 1955; pvt. practice in pediatric surgery, from 1968. Clin. instr. Case Western Reserve U., Cleve. 1962-64, asst. clin prof, 1967-83, assoc. clin. prof. pediatric surgery, 1968-99, assoc. clin. prof. emeritus, 1998—; asst. surgeon Univ. Hosp. Cleve. 1962-98; cons. in pediatric surgery Akron City Hosp.; v.p. Nat. Invention Ctr., Inc., 1990-92. Contbr. med. articles to profl. jours. Dir. Med. Outreach Children Hosp. Med. Ctr. of Akron, 1986-2002; bd. mgmt. Cuyahoga Falls Comty. YMCA, 1957-63; trustee Akron Symphony Orch., 1959-85, Akron Jr. Achievement, 1980-88, 1st Congl. Ch. Akron, 1960-64; mem. adv. bd. Children's Concert Soc., Akron, 1970—; bd. trustees Children's Family Care, 1984-86, Cuyahoga Falls H.S. Found., 1988—; pres., mem. exec. bd. Gt. Trail coun. Boy Scouts Am., coun. pres., 1997-99; mem. Nat. Inventors Hall of Fame, Cleve. Inst. Music, Nat. Inventors Hall of Fame Found., March of Dimes. With USN, 1942-45, 50-52. Home: Cuyahoga Falls, Ohio. Died 2006.

ROTTENBERG, EVERETT NEWTON, physician; b. Detroit, Jan. 22, 1927; s. Joseph and Anna (Shapiro) R.; m. Beatrice Shirley Goldstein, Aug. 17, 1948; children: Mark Fredric, Lisa Ellen Rottenberg Friedman, Joan Marta Rottenberg Lipsitz. BA in Chemistry, U. Mich., 1948, MD, 1952; MS in Medicine, U. Minn., 1957. Diplomate Am. Bd. Internal Medicine. Intern U. Wis. Gen. Hosp., Madison, 1953; fellow Mayo Found., Rochester, Minn., 1953-57; chief rheumatology Sinai Hosp., Detroit, 1957-83, sr. physician, from 1983; staff physician Harper Hosp., Detroit, from 1957-, Physician Rehab. Inst. Detroit, from 1958; pvt. practice Detroit, 1972-78; chief med. services Arthritis Ctr. of Southfield (Mich.), 1978-80, med. dir., from 1980-. Clin. assoc. prof. med. sch. Wayne State U., Detroit, 1981—, clin. asst. prof. prof., 1970-81, clin. instr., 1958-70. Contbr. articles to profl. jours. Pres. Rehab. Inst. Met. Detroit, 1965; active soc. action com. Temple Israel, 1973-75; chmn. bd. dirs. Mich. chpt. Arthritis Found., 1981-83; mem. bd. dirs. Metro Detroit div. Mich. chpt. Arthritis Found., 1986—. Recipient Founder's Soc. award Mich. Arthritis Found., 1986. Fellow Am. Geriatric Soc., Am. Coll. Physicians, Internat. Rehab. Medicine, Am. Rheumatism Assn. (founder), Am. Coll. Rheumatology. Jewish. Avocations: bridge, bowling, walking. Home: West Bloomfield, Mich. Died Apr. 23, 2005.

ROVICK, ALLEN A., physiologist, educator; b. Chgo., Feb. 11, 1928; s. Max Israel and Tillie (Clausman) R.; m. Renah Adar Reinstein, Jan. 30, 1949; children: Sharon, Lynn, Joshua, Jonathan. BS, Roosvelt U., 1951; MS, U. Ill. Med. Ctr., 1954, PhD, 1958. Instr. to assoc. prof. Loyola U. Med. Sch., Chgo., 1957-67; vis. prof. U. Ill. Med. Ctr. Changmai Project, Changmai, Thailand, 1967-68; assoc. prof. U. Ill. Med. Sch., Chgo., 1969-70; exec. sec. cardiovascular study sect. Div. Rsch. Grants, Nat. Inst. Health, Bethesda, Md., 1970-71; chief, cardiac diseases br. Nat. Heart and Lung Inst. Nat. Inst. of Health, Bethesda, 1971-72; assoc. prof. to prof. Rush Med. Coll., Chgo., 1972—2004. Vis. prof. U. Ill. Med. Sch., Chgo. Coll. of Osteopathy, Scholl Coll. of Podiatric Med., Ill. Coll. of Optometry. Author computer teaching programs; contbr. articles to profl. jours. With U.S. Army, 1946-48. Recipient Rsch. grantee NIH, Bethesda, Md., 1960-67, Am. and Chgo. Heart Assns., 1974-79, Office Naval Rsch., 1989—. Mem. AAAS, Am. Physiol. Soc. (councilor, treas. teaching sect.), Sigma Xi. Avocations: painting watercolors, plant raising. Home: Chicago, Ill. Died Dec. 18, 2004.

ROWE, HERMAN F. W., radio station executive; b. Feb. 28, 1943; B of Bus., Northwestern U., 1971. Gen. mgr. Sta. KXRT, Taos, N. Mex.; sales rep. Quaker Oats Co., Chgo., mktg. asst.; account exec. Sta. WGLD, Chgo.; dir. advt. and mktg. MTC Assocs., Chgo.; sr. account exec. Sta. WXRT, Chgo.; gen. sales mgr. Sta. WCEV, Chgo. Died Jan. 29, 2004.

ROWSER, JAMES EDWARD, musician, educator; b. Phila., Apr. 18, 1926; s. Joseph Churchill and Lelia Tom (Coleman) R.; m. Sadye Elizabeth Lewis; children: Sharon, Lorraine. BS magna cum laude, CUNY, 1986; M in Arts and Teaching, Herbert H. Lehman Coll., 1987. Bassist Dinah Washington, N.Y.C., 1956-57, 60-62, Maynard Ferguson, N.Y.C., 1957-58, N.Y. Playboy Club, N.Y.C., 1962-63, Benny Goodmand, N.Y.C., 1963, Frederich Golda, N.Y.C., 1964; free-lance bassist N.Y.C., 1965-68 and from 80; bassist Les McCann, Los Angeles, 1969-79, Bronx Symphony Orch., N.Y.C. from 1986, N.J. Philharmonic, from 1987. Served to cpl. U.S. Army, 1945-47. Democrat. Avocations: tennis, chess. Home: Teaneck, NJ. Died June 24, 2004.

ROY, TAPON, statistician, researcher; b. Chapel Hill, NC, Apr. 3, 1958; s. Samarendra Nath and Bani Sen Roy. AB in Chemistry, U. NC, 1980, MS in Pub. Health Biostatistics, 1982. Statistician Ciba-Geigy, Summit, NJ, 1982—84; sr. statistician Boehringer Ingelheim, Ridgefield, Conn., from 1984. Presenter in field. Contbr. over 25 peer-reviewed articles and notes to profl. jours. including Antimicrobial Agents and Chemotherapy, Biometrics, Jour. Chemometrics, Jour. Math. Chem., Jour. Math. Physics, Jour. Med. Chem., Jour. Pharm. Biomedical Analysis, Jour. Pharm. Sci., Jour. Phys. Chem., Jour. Stat. Comp. Simul.; reviewer: numerous statistical and sci. jours. Fellow: Royal Statis. Soc.; mem: Inst. Math. Stats., Pharm. Rsch. and Mfrs. Assn., Am. Statis. Assn., Biometric Soc. Achievements include research in development and implementation of resampling, robust, and error propagation techniques in biology, chemistry, medicine, pharmaceuticals, and physics. Avocations: reading, theater, photography. Home: Bethel, Conn. Died June 27, 2005.

ROYER, DANIEL KING, construction company executive; b. Labelle, Fla., Jan. 26, 1922; s. Carl Evan and Alice Lorena King; m. Naomi Martha Anderson, June 20, 1943; children: Nana Lorena, Patrick Steven, David Evan, Carl Samuel. B in Civil Engring., U. Fla., 1943, MS in Bldg. Constrn., 1964, MA, 1965, PhD in Bus. Adminstrn., 1966. Registered profl. engr., Fla. Project mgr. El Dorado Engring., San Juan, Puerto Rico, 1976-78, Brown & Root, Houston, 1978; constrn. engr. Rexach Co., Trinidad and Tobago, 1979-81; supervising civil engr. Kuljian Co., Jubail, Arabia, 1981-82; cons. in field St. Augustine, Fla., from 1982. Pres. King Royer, Inc., St. Augustine, 1982—. Author: Applied Field Surveying, 1968, Desk Book for Construction Superintendents, 1969, 2d. edit., 1980, The Construction Manager, 1968, 2d. edit., 1981. Served with USNR, 1943-46. Fellow ASCE (nat. com. 1976-82). Avocations: boating, gardening, horseback riding. Died Mar. 8, 2004.

RUANE, WILLIAM J., lawyer; b. Jersey City, May 14, 1955; s. William J. and Margaret M. (Moran) R.; m. Pamela Ruth Selfridge, May 2, 1987. BA cum laude, NYU, 1977; JD, Fordham U., 1980. Bar: N.Y. 1981, N.J. 1988, U.S. Ct. Appeals (2d, 7th and 8th cirs.), U.S. Dist. Ct. (so. and ea. dists.) N.Y. Assoc. Donovan Leisure Newton & Irvine, N.Y.C., 1980-88; spl. counsel litigation Am. Home Products Corp., N.Y.C., 1989-92, asst. gen. counsel litigation, from 1993. Dir. Lawyers for Civil Justice, Washington, 1992-96. Bd. dirs. Morristown Area Red Cross, 1994-96. Mem. Fed. Bar Coun., Def. Rsch. Inst. (vice chair drug and med. device litigation com. 1994-96). Home: Randolph, NJ. Died Oct. 4, 2005.

RUBENSTEIN, LEONARD SAMUEL, communications executive, ceramist, painter, photographer; b. Rochester, NY, Sept. 22, 1918; s. Jacob S. and Zelda H. (Gordon) R.; m. (dec. 1983); children: Carolinda, Eric, Harley. Student, Case Western Res. U., 1938; BFA cum laude, Alfred U., 1939; postgrad., U. Rochester, 1940-41. Creative dir. Henry Hempstead Advt. Agy., Chgo., 1949-55; v.p., exec. art dir. Clinton E. Frank Advt. Agy., Chgo., 1955-63; v.p., nat. creative dir. Foster & Kleiser divsn. Metromedia, Inc., L.A., 1967-73; ret. Metromedia, Inc. L.A., 1984, v.p. corp. creative cons., 1984-88. Guest lectr. U. Chgo.; instr. Columbia Coll., Chgo., Fashion Inst., L.A.; creator Smithsonian exhibition Images of China: East and West, 1982; lectr. in field. Author: (with Charles Hardison) Outdoor Advertising, 1967; contbr. articles to profl. jours.; one-man show at Calif. Mus. Sci. and Industry, 1970; two-person shows at Palos Verdes Art Ctr., 1987; one-man shows: Palos Verdes Art Ctr., 1998, Distinctive Edge Gallery, San Pedro, Calif., 2003; exhibited in group shows; writer, prodr.: (video) Paul Soldner, Thoughts on Creativity, 1989, High-Tech/Low-Tech: The Sci. and Art of Ceramics, 1994; represented in permenant collections Smithsonian Instn. Renwick Gallery, Am. Ceramic Soc. Ross C. Purdy Ceramic Mus., Internat. Mus. Ceramic Art Alfred U., Laguna Mus. Art, Calif. Past pres. Art Dirs. Club Chgo. Recipient Spl. Citation, Art Dirs. Club Chgo. Mem. Soc. Typog. Arts (past dir.), Am. Ceramic Soc. (bd. dirs. So. Calif. design chpt. 1998), Inst. Outdoor Advt. (past plans bd.), L.A. County Mus. Art, Mus. Contemporary Art L.A. (charter), Palos Verdes (Calif.) Art Ctr., B'nai B'rith, Zeta Beta Tau. Died Sept. 3, 2006.

RUBI, ERNEST PHILIP, retired finance educator, company executive; b. Winslow, Ariz., Oct. 3, 1930; s. Lorenzo Sabastian and Virginia Jean (Lopez) R.; m. Margarita Guerrero, Dec. 27, 1956; children: Ernest Jr., Ramon, Herbert, Fred, Richar, Lucedes Rubi-McBroom. BS Edn., No. Ariz. U., 1956. Tchr. Stockton (Calif.) Unified Sch. Dist., 1956-70; instr. Pima C.C., Tucson, 1970-94; pres. The WAEGS Corp., Tucson, from 1989. Author: Japanese Through Simple Arithmetic, 1991, Prepatory Japanese, 1992; patentee in field of electricity generation. Sgt. USAF, 1954-54, Korea. Avocations: writing, song-writing, investments, golf. Died Mar. 9, 2005.

RUBIN, ALLAN AVROM, lawyer; b. Chgo., Feb. 2, 1916; s. Sol and Sadie (Bloom) R.; m. Harriet Ann Schainis, June 24, 1941; children: Sally Ann Rubin Kovacs, Donald Bruce. AB, U. Mich., 1937, JD, 1939. Bar: Ill. 1939, U.S. Dist. Ct. (no. dist.) Ill. 1939, U.S. Dist. Ct. D.C., U.S. Supreme Ct., Order of Coif. Atty. Randolph Bohrer Law Firm, Chgo., 1939-41; atty., counsel FCC, Washington, 1941-43; chief counsel OPA, Washington, 1943-46, regional counsel Chgo., 1946-50; pvt. practice Chgo. 1950-52; gen. counsel, exec. v.p. U.S. Brewers Assn., Washington, 1952-82; govt.

counsel G. Heileman Brewing Co., Washington, 1982-89; pres. Allan A. Rubin, P.C., Washington, from 1982. Cons., WOC (Pro Bono), Fed. Emergency Mgmt. Agy., Washington, 1968—; mem. Nat. Def. Exec. Res., Washington, 1968—; dir. legal adv. com. Am. Nat. Metric Coun., 1975-82, chmn., 1979-81. Editor Mich. Law Rev., 1938-39. Mem. ABA, FBA, Ill. Bar Assn., Army and Navy Club, Internat. Club, Order of Coif, Nat. Lawyers Club, Officers Clubs of Mil. Dist. of Washington. Died Apr. 1, 2005.

RUBIN, WILLIAM, art curator, historian, educator; b. N.Y.C., Aug. 11, 1927; AB, MA, PhD, Columbia U. Prof. art history Sarah Lawrence Coll., 1952-67; prof. art history Grad. Div., CUNY, 1960-68; adj. prof. art history Inst. Fine Arts, NYU, from 1968; chief curator painting and sculpture Mus. Modern Art, N.Y.C., 1968—88, dir. painting and sculpture, 1973-88; dir. emeritus painting and sculpture Mus. modern Art, N.Y.C., 1988—2006; exhbns. arranged include Dada, Surrealism and their Heritage, 1968, New American Painting and Sculpture, 1969, Stella, 1970, Miro, 1973, Picasso: A Retrospective, 1980, Giorgio DeChirico, 1982, Primitivism in 20th Century Art, 1984, Frank Stella 1970-87, 1987, Picasso and Braque: Pioneering Cubism, 1989, Ad Reinhardt, 1991. Author: Modern Sacred Art and the Church of Assy, 1961, Matta, 1957, Dada, Surrealism and Their Heritage, 1966, Dada and Surrealist Art, 1969, Frank Stella, 1970, Picasso in the Collection of the Museum of Modern Art, 1972, Miró in the Collection of the Museum of Modern Art, 1973, The Paintings of Gerald Murphy, 1974, Anthony Caro, 1975, (with Carolyn Lanchner) André Masson, 1976, Paris-New York: Situation de l'Art, 1978; editor: Cezanne: The Late Work, 1977, Picasso: A Retrospective, 1980; Giorgio DeChirico, 1982; editor: Primitivism in 20th Century Art, 1984, (with Roger Shattuck, Michael Hoog, Henri Behar, and Carolyn Lanchner) Henri Rousseau, 1985; Frank Stella 1970-87, 87; Les Demoiselles d'Avignon, 1988, Picasso and Braque: Pioneering Cubism, 1989, Ad Reinhardt, 1991; Am. editor: Art internat. Mag., 1959-64. Trustee Sarah Lawrence Coll., 1979-86. Named Chevalier of the French Legion of Honor, 1979, Officer, 1991. Died Jan. 22, 2006.

RUBINSTEIN, ELAINE PERLE, technical writer; b. L.A., Dec. 22, 1953; d. William Crandall and Charlotte Rhoda (Streifer) R.; m. Theodore Perle, June 19, 1983. BA cum laude, Yale U., 1976. Editorial asst. Fawcett Publs., N.Y.C., 1973-74; adminstrv. asst. Japan Calif. Bank, L.A., 1977-78; word processing specialist U. Calif., Irvine, 1979-82; jr. tech. writer Burroughs Corp. (name now Unisys), Mission Viejo, Calif., 1982-85; intermediate tech. writer AST Research, Inc., Irvine, 1985-87; sr. tech. writer Emulex Corp., Costa Mesa, Calif., 1987-91, Printronix Corp., Irvine, from 1993. Founder cons. firm P.C. Spectrum Services, Irvine, 1987—. Author computer user and tech. reference manuals, AST Enhanced Graphics Diagnostics Manual, 1986 (Achievement award), Emulex Performance 8000 Ethernet Terminal Server Hardware Installation Manual (Merit award), others; rsch. asst. History of Am. Women Artists, 1984 (ALA award 1982). Mem. NOW, AAUW, Soc. Tech. Communication (Orange County chpt., sec. 1983-84, co-editor newsletter 1984-85, writer 1985—, Disting. Tech. Communication Newsletter award 1985, v.p. membership 1989-90, 90-91), Orange County Yale Club. Democrat. Jewish. Avocations: bicycling, museums, theater. Died Oct. 28, 2004.

RUBY, PATTY KAY, rehabilitation nurse; b. Rawlins, Wyo., June 7, 1943; d. Glen and LaVerne Juanita (Matts) McGeath; m. Richard Paul Ruby, June 28, 1985; children: Kelly Lynn Freeman, Richard Todd Moore, Corey Evan Moore. LVN, Howard County Jr. Coll., Big Spring, Tex., 1971; ADN, Ea. N.Mex. U., Clovis, 1987. Office nurse Pediatric Pulmonary Assocs., Albuquerque; staff nurse West Plaines Med. Ctr., Muleshoe, Tex.; sch. nurse Springlake-Earth Ind. Sch. Dist., Earth, Tex.; charge nurse St. Mary of the Plains, Lubbock, Tex. Mem. peer rev. com. St. Mary of the Plains. Home: Lubbock, Tex. Died June 2, 2005.

RUDIN, DONALD OLIVER, physician, scientist; b. Honolulu, Mar. 31, 1923; married. MD, Harvard U., 1948. Rsch. fellow Harvard U., 1949-51, rsch. assoc. Cambridge, Mass., 1951-56; dir. dept. of molecular biology Ea. Pa. Psychiatric Inst., Phila., 1956-80; scientist, author, from 1980. Mem. psychopharmacological study sect. NIH, 1958-80, grants referee 1958-80. Editl. referee Nature, Sci., Jour. Theoretical Biology, Biochimica Biophysica Acta, IEEE Trans. SCM; contbr. numerous articles to profl. jours. Capt. U.S. Army, 1952-54. Greene Scholarship, 1944-46. Mem.: IEEE (named Disting. Prof. Internat. Inst. Advanced Studies). Achievements include discovery of electrically variable channel-forming peptides, ion selective carrier peptides and syntheis of ion ultraselective bilayer membranes; pioneering patent in ultraselective ion electrodes; discovery of axiomatic world theory. Died Nov. 18, 2005.

RUDOFF, JACQUELINE ANN, interior designer, consultant; b. Milford, Conn., Aug. 7, 1932; d. John Albert and Bertha Elizabeth (Hamm) Rifkin; m. Alex Rudoff, Dec. 28, 1960; children: John A., Alexandra S. BA, Marymount Coll., 1954; postgrad., Valley Coll., San Bernardino, Calif., 1976. Fashion coord. Ed W. Malley Dept. Store, New Haven, Conn., 1954-57; mdse. and promotion asst editor Harper's Bazaar Mag., N.Y.C., 1957-59; sales promotion copywriter Allied Stores, N.Y.C., 1959-61; dir. spl. events May Co., L.A., 1961-64; fashion stylist Bullocks Dept. Store, L.A., 1968-72; interior designer Richardson Interiors, Apple Valley, Calif., 1976-78; prof. interior design Victor Valley Coll., Victorville, Calif., 1977-87; owner Interiors by Jacqueline, Apple Valley, from 1978. Cons. Apple Valley Country Club, 1994. Fund raiser Am. Cancer Soc., Victorville, 1990-93, United Way, Victorville, 1976-90; vol. St. Mary Med. Ctr., Apple Valley, Calif., 1997-2003, exec. sec., 1999, 2000, 2003, pres., 2001. Avocations: painting, sewing, creative crafts, gourmet cooking. Died Oct. 25, 2004.

RUDOLPH, MARK EDWARD, minister; b. Herrin, Ill., July 31, 1921; s. James and Emma Flora (Black) R.; m. Geneva June Purvis, July 3, 1942; children: Marquita Lee Rudolph Sparks, Emma Jean Rudolph Zabel. Grad. high sch., Kokomo, Ind., 1937. Ordained to ministry United Pentecostal Ch. Internat., 1949; cert. ultrasonic insp. Pastor Pentecostal Assembly, Granite City, Ill., 1950-51, 1st United Pentecostal Ch., Peru, Ind., 1958-98, sect. presbyter Ind. dist., 1985-94. With U.S. Army, 1942-45. ETO. Mem. 25 Yr. Club (chaplain 1985-90). Home: Peru, Ind. Died Apr. 14, 2004.

RUELLAN, ANDREE, artist; b. N.Y.C., Apr. 6, 1905; d. André and Louise (Lambert) R.; m. John W. Taylor, May 28, 1929. Student, Art Students League, 1920-22; art schs., France and Italy. Guest instr. Pa. State Coll., summer 1957 One-man shows include Paris, 1925, Weyhe Galleries, N.Y.C., 1928, 31, Maynard Walker Galleries, 1937, 40, Kraushaar Galleries, 1945, 52, 56, 63, 80-81, Phila. Art Alliance, 1955, S.I. Mus., 1958, nat. exhbns., Carnegie Inst., Whitney Mus., Art Inst. Chgo., Corcoran Gallery, Internat. Expn., San Francisco, Artists for Victory Exhbn., N.Y.C., other cities U.S.; retrospective exhbns., Storm King Art Ctr., Mountainville, N.Y., 1966, Lehigh U., 1965, Woodstock Artists Assn., 1977, Ga. Mus. of Art, 1993, Hyde Collection, Glens Falls, N.Y., 1993, Gibbs Mus of Art, Charleston, S.C., 1993, Prints Gallery at Parkbest, Kingston, N.Y., 1995; drawing retrospective Kaushaar Galleries, 1990, 93, Ga. Mus. Art, Athens, 1993, The Hyde Collection, Glen Falls, N.Y., 1993, Gibbs Mus. Art, Charleston, S.C., 1993, Butler Inst., 1996, Grolier Club, 1996-97; executed murals in Emporia, Va., Lawrenceville, Ga.; represented in permanent collections at Met. Mus. Art, Whitney Mus. Am. Art, N.Y.C., Fogg Mus., Harvard U., Phila. Mus., Storm King Art Ctr., William Rockhill Nelson Mus., Kansas City, Mo., Duncan Phillips Gallery, Washington, Springfield Mus., Norton Gallery, Art Mus., New Britain, Conn., Libr. of Congress, Ency. Brit., IBM Collections, Art Inst., Zanesville, Ohio, U. Ga., S.I. Mus., Butler Inst., Pa. State U., Lehigh U., Columbia (S.C.) Mus. Art, The Whatcom Mus., Washington, Springville (Utah) Mus. Art, S.C. State Mus., Wichita Art Mus., Telfair Mus., Savannah, Ga., drawing retrospective Butler Inst. Am. Art, 1996; also numerous pvt. collections. Recipient 3d prize for painting Charleston Worcester Mus. Biennial, Jan. 1938; 1,000 grant in arts Am. Acad. and Inst. Arts and Letters, 1945; Pennell medal Pa. Acad., 1945; medal of Honor and purchase Pepsi-Cola Paintings of Year, 1948; Dawson Meml. medal Pa. Acad., 1950; Purchase award N.Y. State Fair, 1951; Drawing award Ball State Tchrs. Coll.; Guggenheim fellow, 1950-51; recipient Kuniyoshi award, 1994. Mem. Woodstock Artists Assn. (Sally Jacobs award 1981), Art Students League (life), Nat. Mus. Women in Arts Home: Shady, NY. Died July 15, 2006.

RUF, H(AROLD) WILLIAM, JR., retired lawyer; b. Madison, Wis., July 1, 1934; s. Harold W. and Margaret (Dottridge) R.; m. Suzanne Williams, Aug. 25, 1962 (div. Jan. 1978); m. Jocelyn C. Ruf, Nov. 21, 1981; children: David W., Margaret E., Katharine S. BS, U. Wis., 1960, JD, 1962. Bar: Wis. 1962, Ohio 1963. Field atty. N.L.R.B., Cleve., 1962-65; counsel Oglebay Norton Co., Cleve., 1965-74, dir. indsl. rels., 1974-78, v.p., 1978-94; v.p. adminstrn. and legal affairs Oblebay Norton Co., Cleve., 1994-97; ret. Pres. bd. trustees Moreland Ct. Condo. Assn. Mem.: Cleve. Skating Club. Home: Cleveland, Ohio. Died Nov. 24, 2004.

RUGOVA, IBRAHIM, President of Kosovo; b. Crnce, Kosovo, Dec. 2, 1944; m. Fana Rugova; 3 children. Grad., U. Pristina; studied at, Sorbonne, Paris. Founding mem., head Dem. League of Kosovo (LDK); pres. of self-proclaimed Rep. of Kosovo, 1992—2000; pres. Kosovo, 2002—06. Prof. Albanian lit.; corr. mem. Kosovo Acad. Arts and Scis., 1996. Recipient PL-Fonden Prize for Peace and Freedom, 1995, Sakharov Prize for Freedom of Thought, 1998, Homo Homini Award, 1998, Peace and Tolerance Award, 1999. Died Jan. 21, 2006.

RUHL, ROLAND LUTHER, consulting firm executive, engineering educator; b. Chgo., Dec. 13, 1942; s. Roland Andrew and Nancy (Boggs) R.; m. Mary Louise Enstrom, Aug 25, 1965; children: Roland A. II, Andrew Luther, Laura Louise. BME, Cornell U., 1965, MBA, 1966, PhD, 1970. Registered profl. engr. Prof. U. Ill., Urbana, 1970—2006; pres. Ruhl Forensic Inc. (formerly Ruhl and Assocs.), Champaign, Ill., 1979—2006. Contbr. tech. papers to profl. publs. Commr. Water and Sewer Commn. Freeport, Ill., 1990. Mem. ASME, Soc. Automotive Engrs., Am. Soc. Safety Engrs., Soc. Mfg. Engrs. Avocations: automobiles, pvt. pilot. Home: Champaign, Ill. Died Sept. 8, 2006.

RUHRUP, CLIFTON BROWN, sales executive; b. Jacksonville, Fla., Nov. 9, 1916; s. Ernest Alfred and Elizabeth L. (Garrett) R. Student, U. Okla., 1934-35, Oklahoma City U., 1946-48; cert. sales mgmt., U. Okla., 1962. From intern trainee to asst. sales mgr. Dolese Bros. Co., Oklahoma City, 1950-54, gen. sales mgr. aggregate div., 1955-61, gen. sales mgr. aggregate and prestress div., from 1966, asst. sec., from 1971. Chmn. bd. dirs. Cen. YMCA, Oklahoma City, 1973-78, named Outstanding Vol. of Yr., 1978, fellow mem., 1978—; bd. dirs. Better Bus. Bur., 1992—; mem. assoc. bd. Associated Bd. Contractors Okla. S/Sgt. USAAF, 1943-46, PTO. Mem. Oklahoma City C. of C., Toastmasters (pres. 1968), Rotary (editor newspaper 1972-76, contbg. editor 1988—, Paul Harris fellow), Phi Eta Sigma. Republican. Mem. First Christian Ch. Avocations: photography, fishing, travel, real estate. Home: Oklahoma City, Okla. Died June 9, 2004.

RUKEYSER, LOUIS RICHARD, economic commentator, financial advisor; b. N.Y.C., Jan. 30, 1933; s. Merryle Stanley and Berenice Helene (Simon) Rukeyser; m. Alexandra Gill, Mar. 3, 1962; children: Beverley Jane, Susan Athena, Stacy Alexandra. AB, Princeton U., 1954; LittD (hon.), N.H. Coll., 1975; LLD (hon.), Moravian Coll., 1978, Mercy Coll., 1984, Am. U., 1991; DBA (hon.), Southeastern Mass. U., 1979; LHD (hon.), Loyola Coll., 1982, Johns Hopkins U., 1986, Western Md. Coll., 1992; D in Fin. (hon.), Roger Williams U., 1997. Polit. and fgn. corr. Balt. Sun newspapers, 1954—65; chief polit. corr. Evening Sun, 1957—59; chief London bur. The Sun, 1959—63, chief Asian corr., 1963—65; sr. corr., commentator ABC News, 1965—73, Paris corr., 1965—66, chief London bur., 1966—68, nat. econ. commentator, 1968—73; econ. columnist McNaught Syndicate, 1976—86, Tribune Media Services, 1986—93. Internat. lectr. in field. Host (radio program) Rukeyser's World, (TV series) Wall St. Week With Louis Rukeyser, 1970—2002; host: (TV series) Louis Rukeyser's Wall St., 2002—04; author: How to Make Money in Wall Street, 1974 (Lit. Guild selection, 74, 76), 1976, What's Ahead for the Economy: The Challenge and the Chance, 1983 (Lit. Guild selection, 84), 1985, Louis Rukeyser's Bus. Almanac, 1988, 1991, Louis Rukeyser's Book of Lists, 1997, Right on the Money, 1998; editor-in-chief: newsletters Louis Rukeyser's Wall St., 1992—2006, Louis Rukeyser's Mutual Funds, 1994—2006. With U.S. Army, 1954—56. Recipient Overseas Press Club award, 1963, Overseas Press Club citation, 1964, G.M. Loeb award, U. Conn., 1972, Janus award for excellence in fin. news programming, 1975, George Washington Honor medal, Freedoms Found., 1972, 1978, award, N.Y. Fin. Writers Assn., 1980, Free Enterprise Man of the Yr. award, Tex. A&M U. Ctr. for Edn. and Rsch. in Free Enterprise, 1987, Women's Econ. Roundtable award, 1990, 1st Hero of Wall St. award, The Mus. of Am. Fin. History, 1998, Malcolm S. Forbes award for excellence in advancing fin. understanding, Fin. Planning Assn., 2000, Lifetime Achievement Honoree, UCLA Anderson Sch. Mgmt., 2004. Died May 2, 2006.

RUKSTAD, MICHAEL GEORGE, economics educator; b. Watertown, S.D., Aug. 5, 1954; s. Virgil Duane and Georgia Ann (Bauer) R. Student, London Sch. Econs., 1974-75; BA, U. S.D., 1975; MA, U. Calif., Berkeley, 1978, PhD, 1981. Asst. prof. econs. Harvard Bus. Sch., Boston, 1981-87, assoc. prof., 1987—91, sr. rsch. fellow, 1998—2006; pres. Rukstad & Assoc., 1982—2001; founder Peripherals Direct, Inc., 1995—96. Author: Macroeconomic Decision Making in the World Economy, 1986, 2d edit., 1989; contbr. articles to profl. jours. Recipient Outstanding Faculty award for Excellence, U. Va. Darden Sch. Bus., 1997, Faculty Marshall award, Friend of the Students award, Wharton Exec. MBA Outstanding Teaching award, 2001. Died May 17, 2006.

RUPP, ELAINE HELEN, social worker; b. Charter Oak, Iowa, May 28, 1944; d. Ralph Wallace Berg and Helen Mary (Hartigan) Berg Hall; m. Royden Carl Rupp, June 6, 1964; children: Timothy, Christopher, Lynn Arinda. BA in Social Work magna cum laude, Briar Cliff Coll., 1987. Part-time social work monitor Luth. Social Svcs., Sioux City, Iowa, 1986-87; social worker II Iowa Dept. Human Svcs., Cherokee, 1988-93; social worker IV Sioux City (Iowa) Regional Office, from 1993. Bd. dirs. Cherokee (Iowa) Day Care Incorp., 1991. Mem. AAUW (sec. 1991-92), NASW. Avocations: reading, golf, cross-stitch. Home: Cleghorn, Iowa. Died Dec. 2, 2004.

RUPP, ROGER PHILLIP, dentist; b. Hays, Kans., Jan. 22, 1943; s. Ignatius John and Mary Katherine (Wolf) R.; m. Carol Ann Walters, May 22, 1965; children: Amy, Lisa, Suzanne, Sarah. BA, Ft. Hays State U., 1965; DDS, U. Mo., 1969. Dental officer USNR, Camp Pendelton, Calif., 1969-71; pvt. practice dentistry Winfield, Kans., 1971-73; dental assoc. Synder Clinic Assn., Winfield, 1973-78; pvt. practice dentistry Winfield; KS 67156. Cons. Winfield State Hosp. and Tng. Ctr., 1980--, Winfield Child Care Ctr., Winfield, 1980--, Kans. Dept. corrections, 1986-87, Cowley County Devel. Services, Winfield, 1986-87. Contbr. articles to profl. jours. Pres. Cowley Cou Roman Catholic. Avocations: cooking, photography. Home: Winfield, Kans. Died Dec. 26, 2004.

RUPP, SIGRID LORENZEN, architect; b. Bremerhaven, Germany, Germany, Jan. 3, 1943; came to U.S., 1953; d. Harry Wilhelm and Mary Sophie (Gernert) Lorenzen; m. Steven Rupp, June 8, 1963 (div. 1976). BArch, U. Calif., Berkeley, 1966. Registered architect, Calif., Mont., Mass., Colo., Wash., Utah, Ariz., Idaho. Assoc. Spencer Assocs., Palo Alto, Calif., 1971-76; pres. SLR Architects, Palo Alto, from 1976. Mem. Arch. Rev. Bd., Palo Alto, 1971-77, chmn., 1975-77. Trustee Theatre Artaud, 1988—; bd. dirs. Laurence Pech Dance Co., 1996. Mem. AIA (bd. dirs. Santa

Clara Valley chpt.), Constrn. Specification Inst., Calif. Women in Environ. Design (pres. 1992-94), Orgn. Women Architects. Democrat. Home: Palo Alto, Calif. Died May 27, 2004.

RUPP, VIRGIL WILLIAM, journalist, editor; b. Marshall, Minn., Aug. 26, 1929; s. Iliff William and Alice (McLain) R.; m. Rosemary Ann Bracken, Apr. 26, 1929; children: Linda Ann, Eric William. Student, U. Minn., 1947-78, 53-54. Reporter, columnist The Bull., Bend, Oreg., 1955-59; copyeditor, columnist Duluth (Minn.) Herald & News-Tribune, 1959-63; reporter, photographer East Oregonian, Pendleton, Oreg., 1963-83; editor Agri-Times N.W., Pendleton, from 1983. Author: Let'er Buck, 1985, PGG--A History of a Co-op, 1982; contbr. short story to Reader's Digest. Bd. dirs. Am. Heart Assn., Pendleton, 1991-92, Pendleton Friends of Libr., 1992—, Round-Up Hall of Fame, Pendleton, 1992—; mem. N.E. Nev. Hist. Soc., Umatilla County Hist. Soc. Staff sgt. U.S. Army MC, 1951-52, Korea. Avocations: hunting, fishing, geology, photography, antiquarian books. Home: Pendleton, Oreg. Died May 21, 2004.

RUSSELL, PATRICK JAMES, priest; b. Boise, Idaho, May 10, 1959; s. Glenn Edward and Doralea (Trumble) R. BA, Boise U., 1982; MDiv, St. Patrick's Sem., 1986. Ordained priest Roman Catholic Ch., 1986. Assoc. pastor St. Marks Cath. Ch., Boise, 1986-91; chaplain Chateau de Boise, from 1991, Bishop Kelly H.S., from 1993. Active Nat. Cath. Office for Persons With Disabilities, 1991—, Idaho Vocations Bd., 1992-95; founder, dir. Father Russell Charity Golf Scramble for Persons with Chronic Illnesses, 1986—; apptd. tribunal advocate Office of Canonical Affairs, Idaho, 1996—; apptd. priest mem. bioethics com. St. Alphonsus Regional Med. Ctr., 1999. Named Idaho Handicapped Student of Yr., 1974, Best Actor, Boise Little Theatre, 1979-80, Outstanding Young Man of Am., 1983, 84, 86, 87, Outstanding Youth in Achievement, Cambridge, U.K., Internat. Man of Yr., Cambridge, 1995. Mem. Osteogenesis Imperfecta Fdn., Am. Film Inst., Amnesty Internat., Nat. Theatre Comm. Group (charter), Internat. Soc. Poets (life, award), Right to Life/Spl. Olympics, Sigma Phi Epsilon. Democrat. Avocations: writing, painting, music, public speaking, acting. Died Feb. 22, 2004.

RUSSELL, WYLIE HAYDEN, business executive; b. Ft. Worth, Mar. 19, 1920; s. Virgel and Louise (Hayden) R.; m. Louise Milar, Dec. 31, 1945; children: Patricia Louise, Michael Hayden. AB, Oklahoma City U., 1944, EdM, 1948; AM, George Washington U., 1953, EdD, 1958. Various adminstrv. positions Am. U., Nebr. Wesleyan U., Greensboro Coll., Culver-Stockton Coll., Elizabethtown Coll., 1958-70; research adminstr. Cybernetic Research, Inc., Washington, 1970-74; consumer affairs asst. Arlington County, Va., 1974-78; owner The Seacrafter, Southport, N.C., from 1979, Hayden Originals, Southport, N.C., from 1985. Owner Southeastern Editorial and Counseling Services, 1986—. Founder, pres. Save Am. Youth. Mem. Am. Personnel Assn., Personnel and Guidance Assn., NEA, Nat. Tchrs. Assn., Am. Assn. Retired Persons, Brunswick County Artists, Associated Artists of Southport, Modern Bards. Democrat. Methodist. Avocations: art, plant propagation, sr. citizens' interests. Died Aug. 14, 2005.

RUSSO, ANTHONY DANIEL, publishing executive; b. Hartford, Conn., May 12, 1931; s. Donato and Rose (Santoli) R.; m. Mary Lescoe, Aug. 4, 1970. AB in Greek, Fairfield U., 1954; MA, U. Hartford, 1960. Tchr. Wethersfield (Conn.) Pub. Schs., 1960-66; assoc. prof. Hartford State Tchrs. Coll., 1966-87, chmn. dept. humanities, 1975-87; pres., CEO 21st Century Publs., Tolland, Conn., from 1986; owner Tolland Farms, from 1975. Cons. Komputer Svcs., Inc., Plaineville, Conn., 1990-93. Author: Handbook for Human Relations, 1974, Filling Gaps, 1978, 2nd edit. 1980, The Assertive Forumula, 1984, Assertiveness Is..., 1986 and others. Chmn. COPE, Conn., 1979-86. Mem. N.Y. Thoroughbred Breeders, Conn. State Fedn. Tchrs., Conn. State Employees Assn. Home: Tolland, Conn. Died May 6, 2004.

RUTLEDGE, CAROL MARIE BRUNNER, writer, historian; b. Newton, Kans., Mar. 9, 1938; d. Daniel and Alice May (Anderson) Brunner; m. Donavon Roby Rutledge, July 13, 1957; children: Lance D., Daniel E., Doni Marie, Joel Roby. BA cum laude, Wichita (Kans.) State U., 1977. Rsch. asst. Wichita Unified Sch. Dist., 1978-80, rsch. technician, info. dissemination, 1980-86, asst. supr. test editing, 1986-88; exec. dir. Hist. Topeka, Kans., 1989; freelance writer Topeka, from 1989. Author: We Had Feelings, 1979, A Time to Remember, 1981, The Brothers of Ark Valley, 1985, The Story of Wichita, 1986, The Women of Hypatia, 1986; playwright: Threads of My Life, 1981, Trappers and Traders of Plains, 1983, Hidden on the Prairie, 1983, Come to Stay, 1986; contbg. writer ednl. cablevision programs. Mem. Wichita Libr. Bd., 1982-88; producer Summer-Shakespeare in the Park, Wichita, 1982-87; founder Midtown Citizens Assn. for restoration of hist. inner city; past bd. dirs. Work Options for Women, YWCA, Wichita Free U., Vol. Action Agy. Recipient Woman of Yr. Matrix award Women in Communications, 1976, Good Neighbor award Midtown Citizens' Assn., 1977, Liberty Bell award Wichita Bar Assn., 1981. Democrat. Mem. Christian Ch. (Disciples Of Christ). Died Sept. 9, 2004.

RYAN, BRUCE DOUGLAS, botanist; b. L.A., Sept. 13, 1950; s. George Frisbie and Beverly Louise (Riffe) R. BA in Humanities, Wash. State U., 1972; MS in Biology, Western Wash. U., 1981; PhD in Botany, Ariz. State U., 1989. Instr. Ctr. for Continuing Edn. Western Wash. U., Bellingham, 1978-83; faculty rsch. assoc. dept. botany Ariz. State U., Tempe, 1989-91; botanist Fremont Nat. Forest, Bly, Oreg., 1991; postdoctoral fellow Smithsonian Instn., Washington, 1992. Summer intern office pesticide programs EPA, Washington, 1977. Contbr. articles to N.W. Sci., The Bryologist, Cryptogamic Botany, Mycotaxon, Nova Hedwigia. Mem. The Nature Conservatory, Arlington, Va., 1989—, The Wilderness Soc., Washington, 1989—. Rsch. grantee Wash. Native Plant Soc., 1982-83, Ariz. State U. Grad. Student Assn., 1988, Dissertation Improvement grantee NSF, 1986-88, Short-Term Visitor grantee Smithsonian Inst., 1987; scholar Ariz. Fedn. Garden Clubs, 1986. Mem. AAAS, Am. Inst. Biol. Sci., Bot. Soc. Am., Am. Bryological and Lichenological Soc. Achievements include decription of over 5 new species; made 1 new combination; reported over 7 species new to North America. Died Jan. 22, 2004.

RYAN, JAMES FREDERICK, lawyer, educator; b. Boston, Mar. 11, 1928; s. James Denvir and Harriet Chenery (Bonney) R.; m. Dorothea Elizabeth Dydek, Sept. 1, 1958. AB, Harvard U., 1949, LLB, 1952. Bar: Mass. 1952, U.S. Dist. Ct. Mass. 1959, U.S. Ct. Mil. Appeals 1957, U.S. Ct. Appeals (1st cir.) 1979, Supreme Ct. Republic of Korea, 1956, U.S. Supreme Ct. 1957. Teaching fellow in law Harvard U. Law Sch., 1956-57; pvt. practice, Boston, 1958—; lectr. Suffolk Law Sch., 1958—; atty. Mass. Crime Commn., 1963-64; asst. corp. counsel City of Boston, 1968-73. Pres. alumni council Roxbury Latin Sch., 1976-78. Served with JAG Corps, USAF, 1953-56, lt. col. USAFR. Recipient Wellington prize for disting. service Roxbury Latin Sch., 1970. Mem. ABA, Mass. Bar Assn., Boston Bar Assn., Harvard Club. Author: Massachusetts Bar Examination— Questions, Answers, Comments, 1973; contbr. articles to legal jours. Home: Boston, Mass. Died Apr. 3, 2005.

RYAN, MARY A., former federal agency administrator, former ambassador; b. New York, N.Y., Oct. 1, 1940; BA, St. John's Univ., 1963, MA, 1965. With Fgn. Svc., US Dept. State, 1966—2002; consular and adminstrv. officer Naples, Italy, 1966-69; personnel officer Am. Embassy, Tegucigalpa, Honduras, 1970-71; consular officer Am. Consulate Gen., Monterrey, Mexico, 1971-73; adminstrv. officer Bur. of African Affairs, Dept. of State, Washington, 1973-75, post mgmt. officer, 1975-77; career devel. officer Bur. of Personnel, Dept. of State, 1977-80; adminstrv. counselor Abidjan, Ivory Coast, 1980-81, Khartoum, Sudan, 1981-82; inspector, Office of Insp. Gen. US Dept. State, Washington, 1982-83, exec. dir. Bur. of European and Can. Affairs, 1983-85, exec. asst. to Under Sec. of State for Mgmt., 1985-88, US amb. to Swaziland, 1988-90, dep. asst. sec. Washington, 1990; dir. Kuwait task force, 1990-91; ops. dir. UN spl. commn. on elimination of Iraqi weapons, 1991; dep. asst. sec. Bur. European & Can. Affairs US Dept. State, Washington, 1991-93, asst. sec. Bur. of Consular Affairs, 1993—2002. Died Apr. 25, 2006.

RYEN, RICHARD HARLAN, financial consultant; b. Mpls., Mar. 27, 1933; s. Halvor and Elizabeth (Savage) R.; m. Ann A. Smith, Apr. 4, 1953 (div. 1976); children: Dawn, Richard, Rhea, Susan; m. Lillian Kay Rogalski, Oct. 22, 1977; children: Christopher, Daniel, Elizabeth. Student, U. Wis., 1951-52, Am. Coll., Bryn Mawr, Pa., from 1991. CLU, ChFC, cert. fin. planner. Loan analyst Pacific Nat. Bank, Seattle, 1957-63; agt. Equitable of Iowa, Seattle, 1963-67; ins. broker Ins. Svc. Inc., Seattle, 1967-71; mgr. Met. Life, Seattle, 1971-72; agt. Phoenix Mut., Seattle, 1972-74; gen. agt. Nat. Life, Seattle, 1975-90; agt. Nat. Life/Ryen & Assocs., Seattle, from 1990. Pres. Stevens Hosp. Found., Edmonds, Wash., 1990-91; chmn. fin. com. Seattle U. Albers Sch. Bus., Seattle, 1990—; bd. dirs. Vis. Nurse of Wash., Bellingham, 1991—, Am. Heart Assn. Wash., Seattle, 1971-75. Sgt. U.S. Army, 1949-51, Korea. Mem. CLUs (Seattle chpt., profl. mem., pres. 1990-91), Seattle Life Underwriters Assn. (pres. 1974-75, Inspirational award 1975), Res. Officers Assn., Sons of Norway (pres. 1966-68), Rotary. Republican. Roman Catholic. Avocations: boating, skiing. Home: Seattle, Wash. Died Dec. 19, 2004.

RYLE, EDWARD JOSEPH, priest, religious organization administrator; b. Chgo., Dec. 23, 1930; s. John J. and Irene (Evans) R. MSW, Cath. U. Am., 1963, MA, 1974; MDiv, Pontifical Coll. Jesephinum, Columbus, Ohio, 1973. Ordained priest Roman Cath. Ch., 1956. Asst. pastor St. Thomas the Apostle Ch. Roman Cath. Ch., Phoenix, 1956-61; asst. dir., dir. Cath. Charities Ariz., Tucson, 1963-71; dean grad. sch. social work Marywood Coll., Scranton, Pa., 1977-84; exec. dir. Ariz. Cath. Conf., Phoenix, 1984—2003. Mem. social policy com., Cath. Charities USA, Alexandria, Va. Author: (with others) Justice and Health Care, 1985; contbr. articles to jours. in field. Bd. dirs. Phoenix Urban League, 1985-89, Community Coun., Phoenix; mem. Gov.'s Coun. on Children, Phoenix, 1986-87; chmn. Indsl. Commn. Ariz., Phoenix. Recipient Outstanding Achievement in Social Work award Cath. U. Am. Alumni Assn., 1984, Disting. Citizen citation, Phoenix Union High Sch. Dist., 1991. Mem. Cath. Theol. Soc. Am., Am. Pub. Welfare Assn. Died Dec. 28, 2005.

RYLE, HAROLD CHARLES, accountant; b. Charleston, W.Va., Oct. 1, 1925; s. Harold and Marietta (Hayden) R.; m. Alice Ann Akers, Sept. 15, 1950; children: Diana Lynn, Denise Michelle, Keisha Ann. Gen. Acctg. Diploma, Internat. Accts. Soc., Chgo., 1954; RBA, Marshall U., 1992; Cert. Tax Profl., Am. Inst. Tax Studies, Vancouver, Wash., 1992. Clk. W.Va. Water Works, Charleston, 1944-47; adminstrv. asst. W.Va. NG, Charleston, 1947-54; acct., office mgr. Wurts Motor Sales, Ashland, Ky., 1955-57; acct. Kenova, W.Va., 1958-80, Houdaille Industries, Inc., Huntington, W.Va., 1957-80; treas. Ryle & Co., Kenova, from 1980. Chmn. auditing com. Houdaille Credit Union, Huntington, 1963-70. Mem. fin. com. Sacred Heart Ch., Huntington, 1991-92. Mem. Ohio Valley Accts. Assn., Nat. Soc. Pub. Accts., W.Va. Pub. Accts. Assn., Nat. Soc. Tax lProfls., Am. Radio Relay League, River Cities Lions, K.C. (treas. coun. 963). Democrat. Roman Catholic. Avocations: walking, dance, artistic roller skating judge, music. Home: Kenova, W.Va. Died Mar. 11, 2005.

SABLOFF, STEVEN E., film producer; b. Orange, N.J., Jan. 7, 1947; s. Herbert and Kathryn (Blumson) S. BS, U. Md., College Park, 1972, MA, 1983; MFA, U. So. Calif., 1977, PhD, 1980. With Image Makers, N.Y.C., 1973-74; grad. fellow, adj. prof. cinema U. So. Calif., L.A., 1974-79, pres. Cinema Circulus, 1979-84, bd. mem. div. cinema, from 1984. Exec. staff producer Celestial Mechanix Inc.; adj. prof. Loyola Marymount, U. L.A., 1989-90. Dir. film Kids, 1977. Robert Wise Directing fellow U. So. Calif. faculty, 1976, Columbia Broadcasting Co. System fellow; recipient Cine Gold Eagle award, Washington, Spl. Gold Judges award Miamifest-Miami Internat. Film Festival, Clio awards, 1989. Mem. U. So. Calif. Alumni Assn. (bd. mem. 1989—), Am. Soc. Mag. Photographers, Delta Kappa Alpha. Avocations: electric trains, Big Bro. Found., weight lifting. Home: Los Angeles, Calif. Died Aug. 11, 2005.

SACHDEV, SOHINDAR SINGH, mathematics educator; b. Gakhar, Punjab, India, Apr. 1, 1929; came to U.S., 1968; s. Mulkh Singh and Ram (Kaur) S.; m. May 8, 1956; children: Harvindar, Neena, Parmindar, Mina, Davindar. BA in Math., Punjab U., 1949, BTech., 1952, MA in Math., 1956; EdD, Utah State U., 1971. Cert. tchr., N.C. Tchr. sci. D.B. High Sch., Kharkhoda, Punjab, 1952-53; tchr. math. Govt. High Sch., New Delhi, 1953-56, prin., 1959-65; lectr. Delhi (India) Poly., 1956-58; exch. tchr. Cen. High Sch., Springfield, Mo., 1965-66; lectr. math. edn. State Inst. Edn., Delhi, 1966-67; insp. schs. Govt. of Delhi, 1967-68; asst. prof., assoc. prof. Elizzabeth City (N.C.) State U., 1970; prof. Elizabeth City (N.C.) State U., from 1981. Author: Geometry for V Grade, 1964, Arithmetic for VI Grade, 1965, Geometry for High School, 1968. Mem. Nat. Coun. Tchrs. Math., Nat. Assn. Mathematicians, N.C. Coun. Tchrs. Math., Math. Assn. Am., Am. Math. Soc. Home: Alexandria, Va. Died Jan. 6, 2004.

SACHS, MEL A., lawyer; b. Bronx, NY, June 1946; m. Grace Sachs; children: Jaclyn, Harrison. BS, Boston U., 1968; JD, Brooklyn Law Sch., 1971. Bar: NY 1972, US Dist. Ct. (ea. and so. dists.) NY, US Ct. Appeals (2nd and 9th cirs.). Trial atty. Pvt. Practice; gen. counsel Congress of Racial Equality (CORE), Internat. Immigration Found.; counsel NY State Parole Officers' Assn., Port Authority Patrolmans' Benevolent Assn. Lectr. Nat. Inst. Trial Advocacy, Nat. Coll. Criminal Defense; tchr. law Cornell U. Law Sch., Emory U. Law Sch., U. Colo. Law Sch., Hofstra U. Sch. Law; legal analyst Court TV; legal and polit. analyst Fox News Channel. Recipient Lawyer of Yr., Inst. Jewish Humanities. Mem.: Legal Aid Soc. Avocation: magic. Died Aug. 30, 2006.

SACK, JOHN, writer, producer; b. N.Y.C., Mar. 24, 1930; BA, Harvard U., 1951; postgrad., Columbia U., 1963-64. War corr. Stars and Stripes, Korea, 1952-53, United Press, Korea, 1953; contbr. The New Yorker, N.Y.C., 1953-61; writer, producer CBS News, N.Y.C., 1961-66; war corr. Esquire Mag., Vietnam, 1966-67; contbg. editor Esquire mag., N.Y.C., 1968-78, Playboy mag., L.A., 1978-86; writer That's Incredible, L.A., 1981; writer, producer Sta. KCBS-TV, L.A., 1982-84; war corr. Esquire Mag., U.S. Press Pool, Iraq and Kuwait, 1991, Esquire Mag., Bosnia, 1995-96. Author: (books) The Butcher, 1952, From Here to Shimbashi, 1955, Report from Practically Nowhere, 1959, M, 1967, Lieutenant Calley, 1971, The Man-Eating Machine, 1973, Fingerprint, 1983, An Eye for an Eye, 1993, Company C, 1995. Served with U.S. Army, 1952-53, Korea. Mem. AFTRA, PEN, SAG, Writers Guild Am. West. Home: Ketchum, Idaho. Died Mar. 27, 2004.

SACKERSON, ALBERT TIM, training director; b. Iron Mountain, Mich., Oct. 28, 1944; s. Gilbert H. and Gladys M. (Underhill) S.; (div. Jan. 1995); 1 child, Amy Elizabeth. BS in Journalism, Northwestern U., 1966, MS in Journalism, 1967, PhD in Journalism, 1968. Product mgr. The Marmon Group, Chgo., 1967-70; sales mgr. Novo Air Freight, San Francisco, 1970-74; tng. mgr. Fed. Express, Memphis, 1974-87; tng. dir. Burlington Air Express, Irvine, Calif., 1987-94, Grede Foundries, Kingsford, Mich., from 1994. Mem. adv. bd. N.E. Wis. Tech. Coll., Green Bay, 1994—. V.p. Habitat for Humanity, Iron Mountain, 1995—; pres. United Way, Iron Mountain, 1996-97; bd. dirs. The Salvation Army, Iron Mountain, 1997—; bd. govs. Menominee Range Hist. Found., Iron Mountain, 1997—. Named Jaycee of the Yr., U.S. Jaycees, Lake Forest, Ill., 1974. Mem. Kiwanis Internat. (2nd v.p. 1995-96, pres.-elect 1996-97, pres. 1997-98). Avocations: photography, golf. Home: Appleton, Wis. Died May 13, 2004.

SADLER, ALVIN LEWIS, real estate broker; b. Cin., Feb. 7, 1925; s. Lewis LaMont and Corinne Ruth (Schlotman) S.; m. Ruby Fay Smith, June 7, 1948; children: Sandra Fay, Gary Alvin. Student, Purdue U., 1946. Lic. real estate broker, Ohio; cert. residental real estate appraiser. With sales and mktg. depts. Swift & Co., 1948-60; sales mgr. French Bauer, Inc., Cin., 1960-75; corp. mktg. dir. Coca-Cola Bottling Co., Cin., 1977-78; real estate broker Sibcy Cline, Inc., Cin., from 1978. With USN and USMC, 1942-46. Mem. Nat. Residential Appraisers Inst., Rotary (pres. Cin. 1977), Masons. Republican. Presbyterian. Avocations: model railroads, golf, boating, flying, travel. Home: Cincinnati, Ohio. Died Feb. 21, 2005.

SADLER, DOLORES ANN (DEE SADLER), retired clinical social worker, psychotherapist; b. N.Y.C., Feb. 18, 1943; d. Gerard R. and Helen C. (Moran) Endres; m. Charles L. Sadler, May 1962 (div. 1975); children: Lynn, Robert, Kristine; m. John K. Hobbins, Aug., 1976 (div. 1978). AAS, County Coll. of Morris, Randolph, N.J., 1981; BA, Rutgers U., 1983, MSW, 1984. Lic. clin. social worker, N.J. Adminstrv. asst. Morristown (N.J.) Rehab. Ctr., 1972-82; social worker Lyons (N.J.) VA Med. Ctr., 1982-84, Americare Rehab., Englewood, Fla., 1984-85; psychotherapist, clin. social worker Med. Ctr. Hosp. psychiat. ctr., Punta Gorda, Fla., 1985-93; pvt. practice psychotherapy Punta Gorda, 1993-95. Supr. grad. students U. South Fla., 1987-93, Barry U., 1987-90, Nova U., 1991-93. Bd. dirs. Heart and Lung Assn. of Charlotte County, 1985-86, Women's Support Ctr., 1994—; bd. trustees Mt. Olive Assn. Tenants, 1983-84; developer Swim, Inc. (for handicapped), 1975-79; organizer Orgn. Handicapped Students, 1979-81; vol. Morris County Hotline, 1982-83; advocate Arts & Culture Assn., Charlotte County, Fla. Mem. NASW, ACLU, NOW, Acad. Cert. Social Workers (cert.), Amnesty Internat., Alumni Assn. Rutgers U. Democrat. Home: Venice, Fla. Died Mar. 6, 2005.

SADLER, JOHN PETER, mechanical engineering educator; b. Rochester, N.Y., May 29, 1946; s. Joseph Elmer and Eleanor Loretta (Meisenzahl) S.; m. Sharon Anne Canham, Nov. 20, 1965; children: Deborah Lynn, Jennifer Anne, Katherine Jo. BS cum laude, Rensselaer Poly. Inst., 1968, MEngring., 1969, PhD in Engring., 1972. Registered profl. engr., N.D. Asst. prof. SUNY, Buffalo, 1972-75, U. N.D., Grand Forks, 1976-78, assoc. prof., 1978-84, prof. engring., 1984-86; assoc. prof. mech. engring. U. Ky., Lexington, 1986-95, prof. mech. engring., from 1995. Editor for dymanics Jour. Mechanism and Machine Theory, 1989—, assoc. editor, 1982-89; assoc. editor Jour. Mech. Design, 1976-78; author: (with C.E. Wilson and W.J. Michels) Kinematics and Dynamics of Machinery, 1983, (with C.E. Wilson) Kinematics and Dynamics of Machinery, 2d edit., 1993). Fellow NDEA, 1968, Cluett-Peabody Found., 1971. Mem. ASME (various offices), Am. Soc. Engring. Edn. (Dow Outstanding Young Faculty award 1978, N.D. Young Engr. award 1981), Nat. Soc. Profl. Engrs., Soc. Mfg. Engrs., Sigma Xi, Tau Beta Pi, Pi Tau Sigma. Roman Catholic. Home: Lexington, Ky. Died June 19, 2005.

SAGINOR, SIDNEY V., management consultant; b. London, May 28, 1909; s. Phillip Saginor Sr. and Polly Miller; m. Ruth K. Saginor, Dec. 13, 1935; children: Mark L., Gail J. Slater. BSME, Case Res. U., 1933. Registered profl. engr.; lic. real estate broker. Estimator, engr. Johns-Manville Corp., Cleve., 1928-35; mech. engr., heat transfer specialist Carbide & Carbon Chems. Corp., 1935-39; prodn. mgr. Davey Compressor Co., 1939-41, gen. mgr., 1941-46; 1st v.p., dir. Robinson Clay Products Co., Akron, Ohio, 1946-53; v.p. tech. svcs. Gladding, McBean & Co., L.A., 1953-57, v.p. corp. tech. planning & overseas assignments, 1958-61, v.p., gen. mgr. tech. ceramics divsn., 1961-64; exec. v.p., dir. Ilco Corp. (formerly Ind. Lock Co.), Fitchburg, Mass., 1964-67, pres., CEO, 1969-73; mgmt. cons., 1967-69 and from 73. Fin. advisor Federally Registered Investment Advisor, Washington, 1975—; bd. dirs., CFO San Fernando Valley Mental Health Assn., Van Nuys, Calif., 1983-93, advisor, 1983—. Bd. dirs. Fitchburg C. of C., 1964-73; chmn. indsl. comm. Fitchburg Red Cross, 1966. Lt. U.S. Army Corps Engrs., 1939-43. Recipient Cert. Merit, Office Sci. R&D Com., 1945. Mem. ASME (life, award), SAG, Nat. Soc. Profl. Journalists (life), Nat. Soc. Ceramic Engrs., Am. Ceramic Soc. (Emeritus award), Indsl. Rsch. Inst., Inc., Am. Mgmt. Assn., Nat. Clay Pipe Rsch. Corp., Am. Legion, Masons, Rotary, LA Press Club, Jonathan Club, Sigma Delta Chi. Died Dec. 2, 2005.

SAILER, RUTH LUCKENBILL, retired women's health nurse; b. Port Carbon, Pa., Jan. 28, 1925; d. Oscar I. and Kathryn (Sanders) Luckenbill; m. Donald Stanley Sailer, June 21, 1952. Diploma, Reading Hosp. Sch. Nursing, West Reading, Pa., 1946. Asst. head nurse newborn nursery Reading Hosp., 1946-52; obstet. staff nurse Chambersburg (Pa.) Hosp., 1952-61, head nurse labor and delivery, 1961-73, charge nurse labor and delivery, 1973-87; ret., 1987. Mem. Alumni Assn. of Reading Hosp. Sch. Nursing (life), Am. Assn. Ret. Persons. Avocations: horseback riding, reading, crossword puzzles, theater, collecting hummel figurines. Home: Chambersburg, Pa. Died May 17, 2005.

ST. CLAIR SMITH, RICHARD, editor; b. Newton, Iowa, Nov. 16, 1910; d. William Walter and Nelle Grace (Van Dusseldorp) Smith; m. George Charles Richard, Dec. 3, 1933; children: Thomas, Randall, D. du Chane. BS, Columbia U., 1933. Mng. ptnr. Halo House, Larchmont, N.Y., from 1946; journalism instr. Good Counsel Coll., White Plains, N.Y., 1961-64; pub. rels. dir. Westchester Libr. Sys., Mt. Vernon, N.Y., 1966-71; pub. info. officer Westchester Med. Ctr., Valhalla, N.Y., 1974-76; editor Sound View News, Larchmont, N.Y., from 1986. Author: Women in Public Service, 1964. Press sec. Rep. State Com., Albany, 1964-65; mem. pub. rels. com. Westchester Dem. Com., White Plains, 1972-74; campaign dir. Dems., White Plains, 1972-74, Mt. Vernon, 1960, Reps., Mamaroneck, N.Y., 1955-56; active ARC, Mt. Vernon, 1936; exec. dir. Mcpl. Ofcls. Westchester, 1969-89. Mem. Woman's Club of Mamaroneck (v.p. 1998—), Westchester County Fedn. Woman's Club (pres. 1987-89), Delta Gamma. Episcopalian. Died Mar. 5, 2004.

ST. JOHN, SEYMOUR, priest; b. New Haven, Feb. 29, 1912; s. George Clare and Clara Hitchcock (Seymour) St. J.; m. Margaret Gordon Spencer, June 20, 1936 (dec. Oct. 1986); children: Gordon Webb, Margaret Seymour; m. Marie Annette Landry, June 24, 1989; children: Frederick Race, Laura Hasty, Margaret Rogers, Marie Kafus. BA, Yale U., 1935; MA, Columbia U., 1945; postgrad., Va. Theol. Sem., 1940-42; LHD (hon.), Tufts U., 1952; DD (hon.), Va. Theol. Sem., 1967. Ordained priest Episcopal Ch., 1942. Headmaster Choate Sch., Wallingford, Conn., 1947-73; assoc. min. Christ Meml. Chapel, Hobe Sound, Fla. Contbr. articles to religious jours. Trustee, headmaster emeritus Choate Rosemary Hall, Wallingford, 1973-2006. Mem. Jupiter Island Club, Hobe Sound Yacht Club (commodore 1988-90). Home: Hobe Sound, Fla. Died Apr. 17, 2006.

SAKANASHI, MARK TAKESHI, financial consultant; b. Oakland, Calif., Oct. 13, 1952; s. Takeshi Henry and Kay Keiko (Yokoyama) S.; m. Akiko Fukami, June 26, 1977; children: Philip Takeshi, Stephen Hiroski, Kaori Christine, John Kiyoski. BA, Seattle Pacific U., 1974; postgrad., Fuller Sem., 1976-78. CLU, cert. fin. planner. Agt. Penn Mut. Life Ins. Co., Los Angeles, 1978-80, dist. mgr. Anaheim, Calif., 1980-81; prin., owner Mark Sakanashi & Assocs., Los Angeles, 1978-82; pres. Matrix Fin. Ins. Svcs., Inc., Pasadena, Calif., from 1982, Matrix Fin. Cons., Inc., Pasadena, from 1982, Matrix Fin. Corp., Pasadena, from 1988. Bd. dirs. L.A.-Nagoya Sister City Affiliation, 1988—, chmn. 1990; bd. dirs. Pasadena Christian Sch., 1989—. Named Outstanding Young Am. Jaycees, 1981; Seattle Pacific U. fellow, 1986. Mem. Inst. Cert. Fin. Planners, Internat. Assn. Fin. Planning, Nat. Assn. Realtors. Republican. Methodist. Avocation: golf. Home: Altadena, Calif. Died May 19, 2004.

SALEMME, MARTHA ANNE CAROLINE, former nurse, artist; b. Geneva, Ill., Aug. 30, 1912; d. John and Amanda (Carlson) Blomgren; m. Antonio Salemme, Aug. 5, 1941. RN, Augustana Hosp. Sch. Nursing, Chgo., 1934. From staff nurse to spl. duty nurse N.Y. Hosp., 1935, 43-72; painter oil and watercolor paintings, drawings; then nurse/sec. Dr. Mather Cleveland, N.Y.C. Exhibited in group shows at Van Diemen-Lilienfeld Gallery, N.Y.C., 1949, Flamingo Gallery, Falkenburg, Sweden, 1975, Fahlnaes Gallery, Gothenburg, Sweden, 1975, Guild Hall, East Hampton, N.Y., 1958, 59, Ctr. d'Art Contemporain, Paris, 1985, Jersey City Mus., 1959; exhibited in one-woman shows at Sagittarius Gallery, N.Y.C., 1963, Galerie Mouffe, Paris, 1974, Horred (Sweden) Libr. Gallery, 1980, Bach. & Co. Gallery, Emmaus, Pa., 1991, Grace Ehlers Gallery, Easton, Pa., 1992, Town Hall, Bethlehem, Pa., 1995, others. Mem. Artists Equity, Assn. Pour La Promotion Du Patrimoine Artistique Francais. Republican. Died Dec. 6, 2004.

SALES, GRAUMAN GROVER, music educator, writer; b. Louisville, Oct. 26, 1919; s. Grover Grauman and Rosalind Esther (Harris) S.; m. Enid Thompson (div. 1955); m. Georgia Ann Schwartz, Dec. 30, 1972; 1 child, Rachel. Student, Reed Coll., 1946-48; BA, U. Calif., Berkeley, 1949, postgrad., 1949-51. Mem. Critics Circle O'Neill Theater Found., Waterford, Conn., 1967-71; instr. Dominican Coll., San Rafael, Calif., 1982-84; former instr. U. Calif. extension, Berkeley, San Francisco State U., San Francisco Conservatory of Music, Stanford U. Publicist Monterey Jazz Festival, Calif., 1958-65; critic (newsroom) Sta. KQED-TV, San Francisco, 1972-75. Author: John Maher of Delancey Street, 1976, Jazz: America's Classical Music, 1984; (with Georgia Sales), Clay-Pot Cookbook, 1974; columnist Tiburon Ark, Marin County, Calif., 1988—. Served to sgt. USAAF, 1942-46, CBI. Recipient Spl. Mention First Sang prize for drama criticism, 1968, Peabody award for Chevron's Music Makers Series, 1976, nominee Grammy award for Best-Liner Notes Original Cast album and film Amadeus, 1985. Phi Beta Kappa. Democrat. Jewish. Avocations: collecting records, folk art, cooking, photography, jazz. Home: Belvedere Tiburon, Calif. Died Feb. 14, 2004.

SALGO, MICHAEL NICHOLAS, civil engineer, consultant; b. Oradea Mare, Romania, Jan. 17, 1914; came to U.S., 1914; s. Louis and Celia (Kain) S.; m. Ruth Farkas, Aug. 20, 1944; children: Peter Lloyd, Jeffrey Boyd. BS in Engring., Northwestern U., 1938; MS in Civil Engring., Va. Poly. Inst., 1938. Registered profl. engr., S.C., N.Y., N.J., others. Rsch. fellow Va. Poly. Inst., Blacksburg, 1937-38; teaching asst., instr. Ill. Inst. Tech., Chgo., 1938-39; subway rodman City of Chgo., 1939-40; naval architect, structural engr. U.S. Navy-Charleston (S.C.) Navy Yard, 1940-43; structural engr. U.S. Navy-Bur. Yards and Docks, Washington, 1943-46; prin. maintenance engr. U.S. Navy Superintending Civil Engring., N.Y.C., 1946-48; ret. staff civil engr. U.S. Navy-Third Naval Dist., N.Y.C., 1948-57; dir. facilities engring. CBS Inc., N.Y.C., 1957-74; mgr. transp., sr. assoc., dir. engring. various cos., N.Y.C., 1974-90. Author materials in field. Mem. Soc. Profl. Engrs., (life), ASCE (pres. met. sect. 1959-60, dir., v.p. 1963-66, 70-71, treas. 1976-88; elected to hon. membership 1994). Republican. Achievements include working as project director for CBS East Coast Broadcast Center and many other national and international facilities projects. Home: Flushing, NY. Died Dec. 15, 2004.

SALINSKY, CATHY JOAN, social worker; b. Manchester, Conn., Oct. 8, 1953; d. David Theodore and Lillian Mae (Richardson) Robbins; m. Terry Michael Salinsky, July 29, 1972; children: Adam Michael, Destiny Lynn. Student, Willimantic Cosmotology, Conn., 1974; BA in Psychology, Ea. Conn. State U., 1987. Hairdresser, Glastonbury, Conn, 1974-75; mental retardation aide State of Conn., Mansfield, 1977-80; day care provider Coventry, Conn., 1980-84; recreation director Riverside Health Care, E. Hartford, Conn.; social worker Riverside Health Care Ctr., East Hartford, Conn., 1988. Pres. Country Industries, Inc., 1986-87. Mem. Conn. Traumatic Brain Injury, Conn. Assn. Soc. Workers. Congregationalist. Avocations: softball, soccer coaching, reading, singing, volleyball. Home: Coventry, Conn. Died Dec. 17, 2004.

SALTEN, DAVID GEORGE, academic administrator; b. NYC, Aug. 23, 1913; s. Max Elias and Gertrude (Brauer) S.; m. Frances Claire Brown (div. 1983); children: Phoebe, Cynthia, Melissa; m. Adrienne O'Brien, 1989. ScB, Washington Sq. Coll., N.Y.C., 1933; AM, Columbia U., 1939; PhD, NYU, 1944; LLD (hon.), Lynn U., 1976; L.H.D., Nova U., Ft. Lauderdale, Fla., 1983; Sc.D. (hon.), N.Y. Inst. Tech., 1984; LHD (hon.), Hofstra U., 1996. Registered psychologist, N.Y. Chemist Almay Cosmetics, 1934-35, City of New York, 1938-40; tchr., chmn. dept., high sch. prin. N.Y.C. Bd. Edn., 1940-50; assoc. prof. Hunter Coll. Grad. Program, 1947-63; supt. of schs. City of Long Beach, NY, 1950-62, City of New Rochelle, NY, 1962-65; exec. v.p. Fedn. of Jewish Philanthropies, N.Y.C., 1965-69; exec. v.p., provost N.Y. Inst. Tech., Old Westbury, 1969-90; chmn. Nassau County Indsl. Devel. Agy., Mineola, NY, 1985—2002; exec. dir. Nassau County Tax Relief Commn., 1990-93. Mem. White House Conf. on Edn., 1955, White House Conf. on Youth, 1960; U.S. resource person on edn. World Mental Health Congress, Paris, 1961; mem. Bd. Edn., Hawthorne, Cedar Knolls, N.Y., 1963-65; mem. adv. council Columbia U. Sch. of Social Work, 1967-69; chmn. adv. council NYU Sch. Edn., 1963-65; chmn. adv. council to Select Com. on Higher Edn. N.Y. Legislature, 1971-73. Author: Mathematics: A Basic Course, 1957. Editor instructional software. Contbr. articles on edn. and ednl. adminstrn. to profl. publs. Vice chmn. N.Y. State Mental Health Council, Albany, 1965-72; pres. N.Y. State Citizens Council, 1957; pres. Nat. Council on Aging, Washington, 1975-77; chmn. Nassau County Local Devel. Agy., 1982-2006, Nassau County Local Devel. Corp., N.Y., 1982-2006, pres., 1992-2006; chmn. Nassau County Cultural Devel. Bd., 1980—94; bd. dirs. NAACP Legal Def. Fund, 1964-74; chmn. bd. trustees The Hewlett Sch., 1991-2006. Recipient citation U.S. Navy, 1947, Mental Health Assn., Nassau County, N.Y., 1955, Long Beach Edn. Assn., N.Y., 1962, Council of City of New Rochelle, N.Y., 1965, Council of Town of Islip, N.Y., 1982. Fellow AAAS, Am. Orthopsychiat. Assn.; mem. Princeton Club (N.Y.C.). Avocations: opera, ballet, international travel, photography. Home: Port Washington, NY. Died Oct. 1, 2006.

SALTER, (ALICE) LOUISE, English teacher, writer; b. Mar. 28, 1916; d. William Henry Zeigler and Nora Alice; m. Manuel Lee Salter; children: 1 son, 1 daughter, Jean Karen. BA with high honors, Huntington Coll., 1935; MA in English, Ind. U., 1938; postgrad., Columbia U., 1939—41. Tchr. English Jefferson Ctr., Ind., 1935—38; tchr. Taylor U., Ind., 1941—42; speech writer Libr. Congress, 1942—45; tchr. Hampton Bays H.S., 1953-57, Port Jefferson, 1958-60; tchr. 12th grade English Harborfields H.S., 1961-73, ret., 1973; tax acct. H. & R. Block; substitute tchr. New Field High; proofreader Yankee Trader, 1974—83; telephone seller car and ho. ins.; tutor coll. students; bookkeeper, acct., clerk retail stores Crabtree Valley Mall, 1983—88. Author: Gosling Rhymes, My New Family (as seen through the eyes of a German Shepherd), Children of the Sixties, 1966, Blue Flame of Love, 1986, On Wings of Song, 1995, Oh No--What Next, 1998, Songs of Earth and Heaven, 1998, Perils of Nursing Homes, 2000, Millennium Captured in Poetry, 1999-2002. Worked for the disabled. Recipient Poet of Yr. award, 1998, 1999, inducted into the Internat. Hall of Fame, 1997. Mem. Phi Delta Gamma, Internat. Poetry Soc. Presbyterian. Avocations: teaching sunday school, choir, organizing holiday programs, hiking, listening to classical music. Home: Raleigh, NC. Died Aug. 12, 2005.

SALZANO, JOSEPH, business development consultant; b. Aug. 22, 1922; BA, U. of Red Lands, 1951. Analyst USAF, Washington; bus. devel. cons. Washington. Home: Rockville, Md. Died June 23, 2005.

SAMETH, JACK R., television executive producer; b. Bluefield, W.Va., Sept. 16, 1926; s. M. Edwin and Octavia B. (Harris) S. BA, Syracuse U., 1949. Entry level Dumont TV, N.Y.C., 1950; exec. producer ABC TV, N.Y.C., 1950-63, Sta. WNET PBS, N.Y.C., 1963—96. Master sgt. U.S. Army, 1945-47. Recipient Emmy award NATAS, Peabody awards (2), Ohio State award, DuPont/Columbia award. Mem. Dirs. Guild Am. Home: Northport, NY. Died July 4, 2006.

SAMOREK, ALEXANDER HENRY, electrical engineer, mathematics and technology educator; b. Detroit, Feb. 14, 1922; s. Walter and Gladys (Kurys) S.; m. Deloris Gehrig 1944 (dec. Mar. 1948); 1 child, David A.; m. Matilda Louise Dusincki, May 10, 1952 (dec. Dec. 1998). Student, U.

Detroit, 1946-49; BSEE, Detroit Inst. Tech., 1961. Electronics instr. Radio Electronic and TV Sch., Detroit, 1946-49; electronics inspector USAF Procurement Office, Detroit, 1950-53; chief technician Wayne Engring. and Rsch. Inst., Wayne State U., Detroit, 1954-57; elec. engr. Control Engring. Co., Detroit, 1957-60; chief engr., engring. mgr. Weltronic Co. subs. Ransburg Corp., Clare, Mich., 1960-84; electronic instr. Redford High Sch., Redford Twp., Mich., 1966; instr. math. and elec./electronics Mid. Mich. Community Coll., Clare, 1984-95. With USAAF, 1942-46. Mem. (life) IEEE, Soc. Automotive Engrs. Died Sept. 14, 2004.

SAMS, JAMES FARID, real estate development company executive; b. Bay City, Mich., Apr. 21, 1932; s. James and Adele Sams; m. Betty Suham Hamady, Aug. 17, 1957; children: James Karl, Alicia Diane, Victoria Saab. BA, Northwestern U., 1954; JD, U. Mich., 1957; LLM, Harvard U., 1959. Com. counsel ABA spl. com. World Peace/Law, Washington, 1960-63; ptnr. Reeves, Harrison, Sams & Revercomb, Washington, 1964-69, Brown & Sams, Washington, 1969-71, Kirkwood, Kaplan, Russin, Veechi & Sams, Beirut, 1971-74; owner, prin. Am. Devel. Services Corp., Washington, 1978—2005. Rep. U.S. State Dept. Ams. Abroad, Washington, 1965; del. UN Com. on Internat. Trade Law, N.Y.C., 1970; adv. bd Ctr. for Internat. and Comparative Law, U. Mich. Law Sch. Contbr. articles to profl. jours. Co-founder, dir. Am. Near East Refugee Aid, Washington, 1968-92; mem. adv. bd. Georgetown U. Ctr. for Arab Studies; mem. visitors com. U. Mich. Law Sch.; mem. adv. bd. Ctr. Internat. and Comparative Law; former chmn., dir. Grameen Found. USA, Washington. Served to lt. U.S. Army, 1957-58. Mem. ABA, Bar Assn. of Washington, Am. Soc. Internat. Law, Cosmos Club. Home: Bethesda, Md. Died Dec. 21, 2005.

SAMUELS, ABRAM, stage equipment manufacturing company executive; b. Allentown, Pa., Sept. 15, 1920; s. Irving and Ann (Friedman) S.; m. Harriet Ann Goodman, Sept. 1, 1945; children: Margaret A. Samuels Berger, Katherine E., Sally R. Samuels Slifkin, John A., Dorothy M. Samuels Lampl, Caroline J. Samuels Bagli. BS, Lehigh U., 1942; auditor philosophy, Princeton U., 1962-65. Pres. Automatic Devices Co., Allentown, 1946-75, chmn. exec. com., 1987-92, chmn. bd., 1975-87 and from 93, Mchts. Bank, 1981-85, chmn. exec. com., 1985-91. Past guest lectr. Cedar Crest Coll., 1969-71, 84, Muhlenberg Coll., 1977-82, 92. Author: Where the Colleges Rank, 1973. Pres. Samuels Family Found., 1959—; past pres. Pa. Soc. for Crippled Children and Adults, 1957-58; past pres., hon. bd. dirs. Lehigh County Crippled Children's Soc., 1949-51; past pres. Lehigh County Humane Soc., 1960-64, Cedar Crest Coll. Assocs., 1968-70; bd. dirs. Allentown Hosp., 1977-88, chmn. bd., 1987; vice chmn. Allentown Hosp.-Lehigh Valley Hosp. Ctr., 1988; pres. Lehigh County Hist. Soc., 1976-78; past bd. dirs. Nat. Soc. for Crippled Children and Adults, Pa. Mental Health Assn., Merchants Bank, 1965-91, Lehigh County Indsl. Devel. Corp., Pa. Stage Co., 1983-84, Health East, Inc., 1985-91, Nightingale Awards of Pa., 1989-91; trustee St. Augustine's Coll., 1970-77, 92-95, Allentown YWCA, 1977-83, Cedar Crest Coll., 1996—; hon. doctorate, 2003; bd. dirs. Fund to Benefit Children and Youth of Lehigh Valley Inc., 1992-2003, Lehigh County Hist. Soc., 1999-2003. With AUS, 1942-46. Recipient Benjamin Rush award Lehigh County Med. Soc., 1954, Allentown Human Relations award, 1979; named Outstanding Young Man of Year Jr. C. of C., 1954. Mem. Hon. First Defenders, C. of C. (past v.p. 1960), Pa. German Soc., Am. Soc. Psychical Rsch. (trustee 1985-91, treas. 1990), Princeton Club (NYC), Rotary (pres. Allentown club 1955-56, dist. gov. 1964-65). Republican. Died 2006.

SAMUELS, GERALD, artist; b. Bklyn., Nov. 14, 1927; s. Aaron and Anna (Berlinsky) S.; m. Jehan Shahly, 1954; children: Lisa, Heather, Katrina. Student, Contemporary Sch. of Art, Bklyn., 1953, Hans Hofman Sch., N.Y., 1956, NYU, 1960, Pratt Inst., 1973. Advanced painting instr. Pratt Inst., Bklyn., 1967-73, Bklyn. Coll., 1970-78, N.Y. Studio Sch., 1980, NYU, 1979-80, Goddard Coll., Plainfield, Vt., 1980, Art Students League, N.Y.C., 1980-83, Art Ctr. of No. N.J., from 1981; program dir. Sundays At Jasa, N.Y.C., from 1984. One man shows include Landmark Gallery, N.Y.C., 1981, Needham Gallery, Damariscotta, Maine, 1985, No. N.J. Art Gallery, 1991, Calback Gallery, Rockend, Maine, 1991; exhibited in group shows at Bayonne (N.J.) Community Ctr., Artfellow Gallery, Belfast, Maine, Queens Mus. UFO Show, N.Y., Green Mountain Gallery, N.Y.C., Schoelkopf Gallery, N.Y.C., Clarkstown (N.Y.) Town Hall, Riverrun Gallery, Edgartown, Mass.; represented in permanent collections San Francisco Mus. of Art, Ciba Geigy Collection, Weatherspoon Art Gallery, MIT, Corcoran Gallery. With U.S. Army, 1944-47. Home: New York, NY. Died Aug. 22, 2004.

SANAZARO, LEONARD ROCCO, language educator, writer; b. Chgo., Oct. 29, 1949; BA, Lewis U., 1971; MA, U. Nev., 1979. Tchr. St. John the Bapt. Sch., Harvey, Ill., 1972-74; tchr. U. Nev., Reno, 1982-86, City Coll. San Francisco, from 1986. Author: (critical essays) Sylvia Plath: A Reconsideration, 1982; contbr. poetry to Antioch Rev., Seattle Rev., Denver Quar., Art and Understanding. Mem. Nat. Coun. Tchrs. English (com. mem. 1996-98), Acad. Am. Poets. Democrat. Home: San Francisco, Calif. Died Feb. 9, 2004.

SANCHEZ, FRANK PEREZ, elementary school educator; b. Artesia, N.Mex., June 25, 1957; s. Dolores R. and Delia R. (Perez) S.; m. Angi Lynn Rowland, Sept. 24, 1977; children: Jessica Lynn, Joshua Andrew, Jeremy Franklin; 1 foster child, Tiffiny Maree Robinson; 1 adopted child, Christina Yvette Sanchez. AA, N.Mex. State U., Carlsbad, 1989; BS, Ea. N.Mex. U., Portales, 1991. Cert. tchr., N.Mex. Adult basic edn. tchr. N.Mex. State U., Carlsbad, 1991-92; tchr. math., social studies Artesia (N.Mex.) Pub. Schs., from 1992. Roman Catholic. Avocations: camping, guitar, sports, woodworking. Home: Loco Hills, N.Mex. Died May 2, 2005.

SANDBROOK, JOHN RICHARD, environmental advisor; b. Bath, England, Aug. 13, 1946; s. John P. and E. Joan (Sutton) S.; m. Mary Wray, 1970; children: Benjamin M.R., Jeremy M.G. Degree in biol. scis., U. E. Anglia, Norwich, England, 1969. Pres. Student Union, 1968; auditor sr. Arthur Andersen & Co., London, 1969-73; mng. dir. Friends of the Earth, London, 1973-76; from mem. staff to v.p., exec. dir. Internat. Inst. Environ. & Devel., London, 1976—2005. Founder, bd. dirs. U.N.E.P. (U.K.), London, European Environment Bur., Brussels. Bd. dirs. Environ. Liaison Centre, Nairobi, Kenya, 1973-81. Decorated Order of Brit. Empire, 1990; recipient Global 500 award UN, 1989, Blue Planet Prize, Asahi Glass Foundation, 1992. Fellow Inst. Chartered Accts. England Wales, Royal Soc. Arts; mem. Brit. Ecol. Soc. Avocations: sailing, watercolors, fishing, gardening. Home: London, England. Died Dec. 10, 2005.

SANDERS, DAVID MARVIN, personnel executive; b. Norton, Va., Jan. 1, 1953; s. Woodrow and Patricia J. (Hawkins) S.; m. Ketha S. Smith; children: Lori, Benjamin. BA, U. Va., 1976, postgrad. Tchr. USDA Forest Svc., Coeburn, Va., 1977-80, pers. specialist Roanoke, Va., 1980-82, asst. pers. dir., 1982-84; pers. dir. EEOC, Charlotte, N.C., from 1984. Cons. in field. Mem. Charlotte Neighborhood Watch, Charlotte PTA; coach, Charlotte, 1985—. Mem. Internat. Pers. Adminstrs., Position Classification Soc. Democrat. Baptist. Avocations: body building, classic car restorations, poetry, music. Died July 16, 2004.

SANDERS, JACK FORD, physician; b. St. Louis, Mich., July 16, 1918; s. Ford and Viva (Marvin) S.; m. Gretchen A. Jellema, Feb. 2, 1945; children: Karen Jean, Vicki Leigh, Mary Beth, Donald Curtis, Wendy Lynn BS summa cum laude, Alma Coll., Mich., 1939; MD, U. Mich., 1945; LL.D., Northwood U. Diplomate Am. Bd. Internal Medicine; cert. flight instr. aircraft and instruments, airplane single and multi-engine land and sea; flight safety counselor FAA; CAP check pilot; sr. aviation med. examiner. Intern Henry Ford Hosp., 1945-46, resident in internal medicine, 1947-50; practice medicine specializing in internal medicine Alma, Mich.; sr. attending physician internal medicine Butterworth Hosp., Blodgett Hosp., Grand Rapids, Mich.; cons. St. Mary's Hosp., Grand Rapids, Ferguson-Droste-Ferguson Hosp.; med. dir. Mich. Masonic Home, Alma, 1940—91; med. dir. rehab. div., chmn. dept. medicine, chief staff Gratiot Community Hosp.; chmn. dept. medicine Tri-County Hosp., Edmore, Mich.; clin. assoc. prof. medicine Coll. Human Medicine, Mich. State U. Mem. Com. on Aging, Gov's Adv. Coun. on Heart Disease, Cancer and Stroke; del White Ho. Conf. on Aging; bd. dirs. Mich. Masonic Home and Hosp.; chmn. bd. Cen. Mich. Wendy's, Inc.; sec., treas. Gratiot Aviation, Inc. Contbr. articles to profl. jours. Chmn. bd. govs. Mich.; bd. dirs. Northwood U., Gratiot Cmty. Airport Bd. Instr. ACTS, U.S. Air Corps and lt. (j.g.) M.C., USNR, WWII. Fellow ACP, Am. Geriatrics Soc.; mem. AMA, Mich. State Med. Soc., Gratiot Med. Soc., Kent Med. Soc., Gratiot-Isabella-Clare County Med. Soc. (pres. 1965), Am. Diabetes Assn., Am. Heart Assn., Am. Multiple Sclerosis Soc., Mich. Crippled Children and Adults Soc., East Ctrl. Mich. Health Svc. Assn., Mason (33d degree), Rotary, Phi Sigma Pi (hon.). Home: Alma, Mich. Died Apr. 14, 2006.

SANDERS, JAMES WORTHINGTON, lawyer; b. Scranton, Pa., Sept. 30, 1946; s. John H. and Kathryn (Ellis) S.; m. Barbara H., Dec. 18, 1971; children: John H. II, Susan E., Robert H. BA, Baldwin-Wallace Coll., 1968; JD, Cleve. State U., 1973. Bar: Ohio 1973, U.S. Dist. Ct. (no. dist.) Ohio 1974, U.S. Supreme Ct. 1976. Asst. gen. counsel Cleve. Regional Sewer Dist., 1973-76; asst. sec. and counsel Oglebay Norton Co., Cleve., from 1976. Contbg. author: The Encyclopedia of Cleveland History, 1987. Mem. Greater Cleve. Growth Assn. Pub. Affairs Com., 1976—, Citizens League of Cleve., 1983—, bd. edn. St. Thomas Sch., Rocky River, Ohio, 1984—. Mem. Greater Cleve. Bar Assn., Ohio Bar Assn., Jaycees (pres. 1979-80), Rocky River Hist. Soc. (historian), Phi Kappa Tau (Key award 1976). Republican. Lutheran. Home: Penfield, NY. Died Dec. 26, 2004.

SANDFORD, GORDON THOMAS, music educator, musicologist; b. Upland, Calif., Oct. 21, 1929; s. Edward Joseph and Margaret (Swan) S.; m. Marguerite Hynes, Aug. 8, 1952 (div. 1985); children: James W., Claire S. Olander, Paul G.; m. Martha Sandstead, Aug. 31, 1985. AB, San Jose State U., 1951; AM, Redlands U., 1952; PhD, U. So. Calif., 1964. Cert. music tchr., Calif. Prof. U. Colo., Boulder, from 1966. Chair Boulder Faculty Assembly, 1993-94. Music rev. editor: American Recorder, 1987-93. Served to cpl. U.S. Army, 1953-55. Mem. Am. Recorder Soc. (music rev. editor), Early Music Am., Am. Musicol. Soc., Am. Musical Instrument Soc., Viola da Gamba Soc. Am. (v.p. 1984-88, pres. 1988-92, music rev. editor Jour. Viola da Gamba Soc. Am. 1987-97, also mem. jour. editorial bd.), Music Educators Nat. Conf., Pi Kappa Lambda. Avocations: performing early music, mountain climbing. Home: Estes Park, Colo. Died Mar. 3, 2004.

SANDLER, DAVID BRUCE, lawyer; b. Newark, June 27, 1952; s. Maurice David and Leona E. S.; m. Debbie Dargavel, Oct. 6, 1995; children: Shannon, Nick, Corin, Rory. BS, U. Pa., 1974; JD, U. Louisville, 1980. Labr rels. supr. B.f. Goodrich, Louisville, 1975-77; mgr. labor rels. Am. Standard, Louisville, 1977-80; ptnr. Westfall, Talbott & Woods, Louisville, 1981-97; atty. Greenebaum, Doll & McDonald, Louisville, from 1997. Co-author: (chpt.) Kentucky Statutes Affecting Labor and Employment, 1992. Asst. gen. coun. Goodwill Ky., Louisville, 1984-86. Mem. ABA, Ky. Bar Assn., Louisville Bar Assn. Republican. Avocations: triathlons, backgammon, music. Home: Louisville, Ky. Died June 3, 2005.

SANDLIN, WALKER PATTERSON, JR., petroleum consultant; b. Cayce, Miss., Dec. 31, 1919; s. Walker Patterson and Matalena (Bennett) S.; m. Mary E. Broderick, Dec. 29, 1946 (dec. June 1982); children: Teresa Ann Jarrell, Mary Elizabeth Price, Sara Jane Rowe, Matalena Bennett Reiss, Walker Patterson Sandlin III, Jamie Frances Hale. Student, Rhodes Coll., Memphis, 1938-40; BA in Physics and Math, U. Miss., 1942; MS in Mgmt., Ga. Sch. Tech., Atlanta, 1946. Registered profl. engr., Okla., Ky. Prodn. supr. Seagram Distilleries, Louisville, 1947; petroleum engr. Shell Oil Co., Houston, 1948-51; prodn. mgr. Davon Oil Co., Oklahoma City, Okla., 1951-52; consulting petroleum engr. Oklahoma City, from 1952. Mayor Silver Lake Assn., Oklahoma City, 1961, 66. Maj. USAF, 1942-46. Mem. Soc. Ind. Earth Scientists (chmn. Okla. chpt. 1983), Petroleum Club. Republican. Presbyterian. Avocation: flying. Home: Albuquerque, N.Mex. Died Apr. 24, 2005.

SANDOR, GYORGY, pianist; b. Budapest, Hungary; came to U.S., 1938, naturalized, 1943; s. Ignac and Zsenka (Czipszer) S.; 1 child, Michael. Student, Liszt Ferenc Acad., Budapest, 1927-33; studied piano with, Bela Bartok; composition with, Zoltan Kodaly. Mem. piano faculty Juilliard Sch., 1982—2005. Made concert debut, Budapest, 1931; toured, Europe, 1931-38, Am. debut Carnegie Hall, N.Y.C., 1939, touring throughout U.S., Mexico, Can., W.I., North Africa, C.Am., S.Am., Europe, Australia, Far East, New Zealand; rec. with N.Y. Philharm. and Phila. orchs., also solo rec. (Grand Prix du Disque for rec. entire piano repertory of Bela Bartok's works 1964); rec. entire solo piano repertory of Prokofiev, 1967, Kodály, 1973; author: On Piano Playing: Motion, Sound and Expression, 1981; world premiers include Bartok's 3d Piano Concerto, Ormandy and Phila. Orch., 1946, Dance Suite piano version, Carnegie Hall, 1945, Concerto for Orch., piano version by Bartok, 1990, Sony Classical, Vox Candide Turnabout, Columbia Records, Trio, Phillips Records, Brahms 2d Piano Concerto, Chopin 1st Concerto, De Falla Nights in the Gardens of Spain. Named to Order of Arts and Letters, French Govt., 2003. Home: New York, NY. Died Dec. 9, 2005.

SANDOZ, WILLIAM CHARLES, lawyer; b. Opelousas, La., Aug. 23, 1928; s. Lawrence Broussard and Cecelia (Boagni) S.; m. Jane Simmons, Apr. 29, 1950; children: Yvonne Marie, William Simmons, Charles Jeffrey. Student, La. State U., 1945-47, U. Southwestern La., 1945-47; JD, La. State U., 1950. Bar: La. 1950, U.S. Dist. Ct. (we. dist.) 1950, U.S. Dist. Ct. (ea. dist.) La. 1972, U.S. Dist. ct. (mid. dist.) La. 1972, U.S. Ct. Appeals (5th cir.) 1963. Pvt. practice, Opelousas, 1950-54, 83-87; ptnr. Sandoz & Sandoz, Opelousas, 1954-60, Sandoz, Sandoz & Schiff, Opelousas, 1960-83, Law Offices William C. Sandoz and W. Simmons Sandoz, Opelousas, from 1983. Also Alexandria, Baton Rouge, Houma, Lafayette, Lake Charles, Monroe, New Orleans, and Shreveport; bd. dirs. Church Point (La.) Bank & Trust Co.; lectr. profl. assns. Mem. La. Law Rev., 1948. Named to Hall of Fame, La. State U. Law Sch., 1987. Mem. ABA, La. Bar Assn., St. Landry Parish Bar Assn., Assn. Trial Lawyers Am., La. Trial Lawyers Assn., Nat. Assn. Bankruptcy Trustees, Am. Bankruptcy Inst., Comml. Law League Am., KC (re. sec. Opelousas 1950-52) Elks, Order of Coif, Delta Kappa Epsilon, Phi Delta Phi. Republican. Roman Catholic. Died Oct. 4, 2004.

SANDS, DERRICK JUSTIN, microbiologist; b. Santa Barbara, Calif., July 2, 1966; s. Richard Lyle and Jeanette Little S.; m. David Louis Ruch, Mar. 15, 1987 (div. July 1993); 1 stepdaughter, Erin Amelia Ruch. BS in Microbiology, U. Idaho, 1987. Quality control scientist Berkeley (Calif.) Biologicals, 1987-89; quality control mgr. Berkeley (Calif.) Biologicals/Alk-Abello, 1986-89; sr. quality contol microbiologist/supr. quality control Elan Pharms., South San Francisco, Calif., from 1986. Rep. to FDA/Industry Joint Panel. Vol. AIDS/HIV crisis line, San Francisco, 1998—. Mem. Am. Assn. Advancement of Microbiology, Parenteral Drug Assn. Democrat. Buddhist. Avocations: gardening, salt water aquariums, computers. Home: San Francisco, Calif. Died Apr. 24, 2005.

SANDSTRÖM, GEORGE FREDERICK, artist, illustrator, travel agency executive; b. Rosario, Argentina, Apr. 25, 1925; came to U.S., 1950; s. Karl Frederick and Helen Lucy (Minturn) S.; m. Marita Mullan, 1953 (div. 1963); children: Robert, Ronald; m. Leslie Lockhart, 1963 (div. 1973); children: Diana, Cort, Scott; m. Sherry Miller, 1988 (div. 1993). M in Econs., Litoral U., Rosario, 1944. Acct. Swift Co., Rosario, 1945-46; treasury dept. staff F.C.C.A. (English Railroad), Rosario, 1946-50; audit dept. staff Ctrl. Penn Nat. Bank, Phila., 1951-53; artist, from 1954; pres. Planet Tours & Travel, Inc., Longwood, Pa., from 1987. Illustrator: Seashells of the World (trans. 7 langs.), 1962, Minerals of the World, 1973, Seashells of North America, 1968, The

Stream of Life, 1969, Tropical Fish, 1975, Nature's Tiny Maid, 1974, Knight in Crusty Armor, 1974, Edible Seashells (2 book series), 1977, South Pacific Birds, 1976, Woodpeckers of the World, 1982, Starfishes, Seashells & Crabs, 1993, Ranger Rick Mag.; one-man shows include Chadds Ford (Pa.) Gallery, 1983; exhibited in group shows at Brandywine River Mus., Chadds Ford, 1990; commns. include 1st Limited Edit. Print for Brandywine Wildlife Expo, Unionville, Pa., 1986; painting featured on front page of N.Y. Times, 1986; subject numerous newspaper, mag., radio and TV interviews and features. Contbr. art works for auction to Brandywine Hemophiliac Found., Chadds Ford, 1980-2006. Mem. Carpathia Soc. (life), Brandywine River Mus. (assoc.), Highlander Club (life). Home: Cochranville, Pa. Died June 1, 2006.

SANDT, JOHN JOSEPH, psychiatrist, educator; b. N.Y.C., June 29, 1925; s. John Jacob and Victoria Theodora Sandt; m. Mary Cummings Evans, Sept. 14, 1946; children: Christine, Karen, John K., Kurt, Colin, Carol; m. Mary W. Griswold, July 10, 1992 (dec. Dec. 1998). BA, Vanderbilt U., 1948; MA, Yale U., 1951; MD, Vanderbilt U., 1957. Instr. English Vanderbilt U., Nashville, 1951-52, Syracuse (N.Y.) U. Coll., 1960-61; intern SUNY Upstate Med. Ctr., Syracuse, 1957-58, resident, 1958-61; instr. psychiatry Southwestern Med. Sch., Dallas, 1961-63; chief psychiatry VA Med. Ctr., Dallas, 1961-63; chief outpatient clinic Dept. Mental Health, Springfield, Mass., 1963-66; asst. prof. psychiatry U. Rochester (N.Y.) Med. Sch., 1966-75, clin. assoc. prof. psychiatry, 1975-98; chief psychiatry Clifton Springs (N.Y.) Hosp., 1985-88, VA Med. Ctr., Bath, N.Y., 1988-96; pvt. practice Hammondsport, N.Y., from 1996. Cons. psychiatry VA Med. Ctr., Northampton, Mass., 1965-66, Springfield Coll., 1964-66, Brockport (N.Y.) State Coll., 1966-75, Fairport (N.Y.) Bapt. Home, 1966-88; asst. dir. ind. study program U. Rochester Med. Sch., 1971-75. Author: Clinical Supervision of Psychiatric Resident, 1972; contbr. articles to profl. jours. Vestryman All Saints Episcopal Ch., South Hadley, Mass., 1963-66. With USNR 1944-46, PTO. Nathaniel Currier fellow Yale Grad. Sch., 1948-49. Mem. AAAS, Am. Psychiat. Assn. Died May 16, 2004.

SANFORD, WAYNE UNSWORTH, corporate executive; b. Salt Lake City, Jan. 20, 1926; s. Fred Charles and Mary Alice (Unsworth) S.; m. Nadine Todd, Apr. 2, 1946; children: LaRene, Darryl, Gayle, Jolane, Kerry, Ryan. Student, LDS Bus. Coll., Salt Lake City, 1948-49. Salesman Utah Paper Box Co., Salt Lake City, 1948-69, sales mgr., 1970-75, v.p. sales and credit, 1975-84, exec. v.p., from 1984, also bd. dirs., from 1970. Pres. Utah State Umpires Assn., Salt Lake City, 1955-75, NACM Intermountain, Salt Lake City, 1965; bishop Latter-day Saint Mormon Ch., Bountiful, Utah, 1964-69. With USN, 1944-46. Mem. Nat. Assn. Credit Mgmt. Intermountain (dir. 1965-88, Credit Mgr. of Yr. 1988). Mem. Lds Ch. Avocation: athletic dir. of tournaments. Home: Bountiful, Utah. Died Aug. 14, 2004.

SANTAMARIA, PHILLIP, academic administrator, dean; b. Buffalo, Mar. 10, 1943; s. Anthony J. and Carmela (Gugliuzza) S.; m. Linda DeForno, Aug. 24, 1968; children: Michael, Christa. BA, St. Francis Coll., Loretto, Pa., 1966; MA, Niagara U., 1969; PhD, Kent State U., 1977; mgmt. devel. program, Harvard U., 1993. Area dir. Kent (Ohio) State U., 1968-74; asst. dir. career devel. ctr. Baldwin-Wallace Coll., Berea, Ohio, 1975-76, dir. career devel. ctr., 1976-78; v.p. for student affairs Daemen Coll., Amherst, N.Y., 1978-79; assoc. v.p. for student affairs, dean of students SUNY, Buffalo, from 1979. Presenter in field. Author: The Question of Education in the Third Russian Duma, 1990; contbr. articles to profl. jours. Bd. dirs. Puerto Rican Am. Community Assn., Buffalo, 1987—, Western N.Y. Hispanics & Friends Civic Assn., Buffalo, 1989—, Buffalo Ballet Theatre, 1991, United Way of Buffalo and Erie County, 1985—, Hispanic Unidos de Buffalo; Buffalo Coun. on World Affairs (pres., v.p., 1982—). Mem. Coll. Student Pers. Assn. N.Y. State (mem.-at-large 1988-89, membership chair 1989—), Western N.Y.Consortium Higher Edn. (chief student affairs officer coord. 1981—), Nat. Assn. Student Pers. Adminstrs., Ea. Assn. Counselors, Deans and Advisors of Students, Nat. Assn. Intercollegiate Athletics, Coll. Placement Coun., Ohio Assn. Sch., Coll. and Univ. Staffing (sec.-treas. 1977-78), Creative Problem Inst., Adelante Estudeiantes Latinos (advisor), Rotary, Tau Kappa Epsilon. Roman Catholic. Avocations: music, reading, jogging, camping. Home: Buffalo, NY. Died June 29, 2005.

SANTARLASCI, JOSEPH HOWARD, performing arts executive; b. Phila., Mar. 11, 1921; s. Alfred and Mary C. (Murray) S.; m. Rosemary Teresa Donovan, Sept. 18, 1943 (dec. 2005); children: Joseph H., Stephen. Student, Temple U., 1947-51. Asst. mgr. Phila. Orch. Assn., 1951-78, mgr., 1978—85. Served to 1st lt. AUS, 1942-45, ETO. Recipient Louis B. Sudler award Am. Symphony Orch. League, 1985. Mem. Mus. Fund Soc. Democrat. Roman Catholic. Home: Paoli, Pa. Died Nov. 7, 2005.

SAPP, ROY G., clergy man; b. Wills Point, Tex., Sept. 13, 1928; s. Willis R. Sapp and Harriot (Telia) Girdley; m. Irene Odelle Cunningham, Sept. 1, 1948; 1 child, Sharon Diane Seaward. DD, Calif. Grad. Sch. Theology, 1975, BTh, 1982; DHL, So. Calif. Theol. Sem., 1992. Ordained to ministry Assembly of God, 1951. Pastor Ctrl. Assembly of God, Lubbock, Tex., 1948-49; kpastor First Assembly of God, Santa Ana, Calif., 1953-58; presbyter So. Calif. Dist. of Assemblies of God, Pasadena, Calif., 1955-58, youth dir., 1959-62; dir. youth missions Gen. Coun. Assemblies of God., Springfield, Mo., 1962-65; pastor First Assembly of God, Wilmington, Calif., 1965-76; gen. presbyter Gen. Coun. of the Assemblies of God, Springfield, 1969-76; presbyter So. Calif. Dist. Assemblies of God, Pasadena, 1968-76; pastor First Assembly of God, Honolulu, from 1976. Bd. dirs. So. Calif. Coll., Costa Mesa, 1955-58, Bethany Coll., Santa Cruz, Calif., 1980-83, King Manor Hosp., 1970-76, Bethany Retirement Home, Costa Mesa, 1970-76. Home: Aiea, Hawaii. Died May 15, 2004.

SARDI, OTTO, geologist; b. Hungary, Sept. 4, 1932; came to U.S., 1956; s. István and Mária Sardi; m. Henriette Augusta Wimmer, Feb. 27, 1965; children: Monica A. and Nancy M. (twins), Sylvia H. MEd, Eötvös Lóránd U., Budapest, Hungary, 1956; MS, Miami U., Oxford, Ohio, 1962; PhD, Ind. U., 1969. Geology instr. U. Dayton, 1963-66; rsch. assoc. Nat. Lead Co., Cin., 1968-70; prof. geology Cornell U., Ithaca, N.Y., 1970-73, Conn. State U., Willimantic, Conn., 1976-97; rsch. prof. U. Munich, Germany, 1987; ret., 1997. Head basic refractories LECO Corp., St. Joseph, Mich., 1974-75; cons. in field, Benton Harbor, Mich., 1975-76. Author: (rsch. publ.) Crystal Chemistry of Oxides, 1965-66; contbr. articles to profl. jours.; patentee in field. Listed spkr. Willimantic C. of C., 1976-96; mem. Parish Coun., St. Francis of Assisi, Lebanon, Conn., 1976-96; chmn. nominating com. Tchr.'s Corps Cmty. Coun., Willimantic, 1976-96; mem. Dem. Town Com., Columbia, Conn., 1976-96. Predoctoral fellow U.S. Bur. Mines, 1966-68; postdoctoral, Purdue U., NASA, 1973, Mellon, Yale U., 1982-83. Roman Catholic. Avocations: collecting gems and minerals, swimming, chess, travel. Home: Columbia, Conn. Died Feb. 26, 2004.

SARETT, HERBERT PAUL, nutritionist, consultant; b. Bklyn., Feb. 5, 1916; s. Max and Mary (Goodman) Saretsky; m. Helen Deborah Statsinger, Dec. 26, 1948; children: David Charles, Mark Edward, Joshua Daniel. BS, Bklyn. Coll., 1936; MS, Cornell U., 1937; PhD, Duke U., 1942. Instr. biochemistry med. sch. Duke U., Durham, N.C., 1942-43; assoc. prof., research assoc. Oreg. State Coll., Corvallis, 1943-45; research assoc. med. div. Chem. Warfare Svc., U.S. Army, Edgewood, Md., 1945; asst. prof. biochemistry, medicine Tulane U. Med. Sch., New Orleans, 1946-50, assoc. prof. biochemistry, medicine, 1950-51; dir. nutrition & biochemistry research Mead Johnson Research Ctr., Evansville, Ind., 1951-67, v.p. nutritional scis., 1967-71, v.p. nutritional sci. resources, 1971-81; cons. Nutritional Scis., Sarasota, Fla., from 1981. Tech. advisor com. on nutrition Am. Acad. Pediatrics, Evanston, Ill., 1961-81, chmn. 1971-75; com. food standards & fortification policy Food & Nutrition Bd., NAS, Washington, 1970-73; U.S. del. com. on foods for spl. dietary uses, Codex Alimentarius Commn., Bonn, Fed. Republic of Germany, 1971-81. Editorial bd. Jour. of Nutrition, 1967-72; contbr. articles to profl. jours. Tech. advisor Meals on Wheels, Evansville, 1970—; scientific advisor Am. Coun. on Sci. & Health, N.Y.C., 1981—, participant WHO/UNICEF Meeting on Infant & Young Child Feeding, Geneva, 1979, FoodTech & Nutrition for Closed Ecolocigal Life Support Systems, NASA, Washington, 1980. Recipient Disting. Alumnus award Bklyn. Coll., 1959; Centennial scholar Johns Hopkins U., 1975. Fellow Am. Inst. Nutrition (editorial bd. 1967-72, industry liaison com. 1981-85), AAAS, N.Y. Acad. Sci.; mem. Am. Soc. Clin. Nutrition, Am. Chem. Soc. (chmn. Ind.-Ky. sect. 1954-56), Am. Soc. Biologic Chemists, Am. Soc. for Parenteral and Enteral Nutrition, Inst. Food Technologists, Nutrition Soc. (British), Nutrition Today Soc., Soc. for Experimental Bilogy and Medicine, Soc. for Inherited Metabolic Disorders, Soc. for Nutrition Edn., Pan Am. Med. Assn. (Nutrition Coun.), Phi Beta Kappa. Democrat. Jewish. Died Mar. 6, 2004.

SARGENTICH, THOMAS OLIVER, law educator, researcher; b. Los Angeles, May 9, 1950; s. Daniel Milo and Margaret Amelia (Lientz) Sargentich; m. Susan Hazard Farnsworth, Jan. 2, 1981; 1 child, Catherine Victoria. BA magna cum laude, Harvard U., 1972; JD cum laude, 1977; MPhil politics, Magdalen Coll., Oxford U., 1974. Bar: DC 1978, US Supreme Ct. 1981. Law clk. to judge US Ct. Appeals, Phila., 1977—78; atty., advisor Office of Legal Counsel, US Dept. Justice, Washington, 1978—83; lectr. Am. U. Washington, 1981; assoc. prof. law, 1983—86; prof. law, 1986—2005; co-dir. program on law and govt., 1993—2005; dir. LLM program law and govt., 1998—2005; adj. prof. law Georgetown U., Washington, 1982; lectr. on adminstrv. and constl. law to various orgn., 1981—2005; cons. Adminstrv. Conf. US, 1986—88, 1992—94; reporter Task Force Fed. Judicial Selection Citizens Ind. Ct., 1999; Daniel vis. prof. U. Iowa Coll. Law, 1997. Contbr. articles in field to legal jour.; editor: (anthology) An Adminstrv. Law Anthology, 1994; co-editor (assoc.): (law) Major Acts of Congress, 2003. Recipient Outstanding Performance award, US Dept. Justice, 1981, Pauline Ruyle Moore scholar, Am. U., 1989, Elizabeth Payne Cubberly scholar, 1999; fellow John H. Finley fellow, Harvard U., 1972, Eng. Speaking Union fellow, 1973. Mem.: Adminstrv. Law Rev. (chair faculty rev. bd. from 1996), Am. U. (mem. 1983—86, chair appointments com. 1993—94), Washington Coll. Law (admissions com.), Am. U. Fulbright (scholarship com., Washington 1984—94), Phi Beta Kappa. Home: Arlington, Va. Died Apr. 21, 2005.

SARPANEVA, TIMO TAPANI, designer; b. Oct. 31, 1926; s. Akseli Johannes Sarpaneva and Martta Sofia Karimo; m. Ann-Mari Holmberg (div.); m. Marfatta Svennerig; 4 children. Ed. Indsl. Art Inst., Helsinki, Finland; Dr. Design (hon.), Royal Coll. Art, London, 1967. Designer, A. Ahlstrom Oy, Iittala Glassworks, 1950—; tchr. textile printing and design Indsl. Art Inst. Helsinki, 1953-57; artistic dir. Porin Puuvilla Cotton Mill, 1955-66; with AB Kinnasand Textile Mill, Sweden, 1964—2006; designer for Juhava Oy, Jughans AG, W.Ger., Opa Oy, Primo Oy, Rosenlew Oy, Roserthal AG, W.Ger., Villayhnyma; invited by Brazilian govt. to lectr. on and exhibit Finnish art glass, 1958; exhbn. architect for Finnish indsl. art exhbns., Europe, Japan, U.S.; architect Finnish sect. Expo 1967, Montreal, Que., Can.; bd. dirs. State Com. Design, Bd. Inst. Indsl. Design; exhibited in Finland, Sweden, Norway, Denmark, Iceland, Netherlands, Eng., Germany, France, Italy, U.S., Brazil, USSR. Decorated Order of Lion (Finland); recipient numerous awards, including 3 Grand prix Milan Triennali. Mem. Assn. Arts and Crafts (dir.). Died Oct. 2, 2006.

SARSHAR, MIR AHMAD, surgeon; b. Jan. 22, 1932; came to U.S., 1958; s. Seyed Taghi and Robabeh (Hessabi) S.; m. Roslyn Kronenberg, Feb. 27, 1960; children: Maryam, Farah, Kamran. Diploma, Sharaf, Tehran, Iran, 1948; MD, U. Tehran, 1955. Diplomate Am. Bd. Surgery; cert. hand surgeon. Intern South Balt. Gen. Hosp., 1958, resident, 1959-63; pvt. practice Balt., from 1964. 2d lt. M.C. Iranian Imperial Army, 1955-57. Fellow ACS, Southeastern Surg. Congress; mem. Am. Soc. Surgery of Hand, Soc. Surgery Alimentary Tract. Moslem. Avocations: stamp collecting/philately, photography. Home: Lutherville Timonium, Md. Died Nov. 19, 2004.

SASVARI, GEORGE STEVE, structural engineer; b. Budapest, Hungary, Oct. 30, 1924; came to U.S., 1957; s. Joseph and Leonora (Lukardy) S.; m. Kathleen W. Crawley, Jan. 23, 1982; children: Judy, Susy, George, Robert. B in Civil Engring., Tech. U., Budapest, 1956. Registered profl. engr., Fla., Ga. Various positions, Hungary, 1945-56; chief structural engr. Prime Design Inc, Tampa, Fla., from 1957. Republican. Roman Catholic. Home: Palmetto, Fla. Died Mar. 27, 2005.

SATO, KAZUO, marketing educator; b. Sapporo, Hokkaido, Japan, Jan. 5, 1927; came to U.S., 1962; s. Kinzo and Naka (Uchiyama) S.; m. Midori Sasayama, Oct. 11, 1961; children: Kumi, Nina, Gaku. BA, Hokkaido U., 1953; MA, Yale U., 1956, PhD, 1960. Asst. prof. Osaka (Japan) U., 1959-64; econ. affairs officer UN, N.Y.C., 1962-70; prof., leading prof. SUNY, Buffalo, 1970-83; spl. prof. Rutgers U., New Brunswick, N.J., from 1984. Vis. prof. MIT, Cambridge, Mass., 1969-70, Columbia U., N.Y.C., 1982-83, Yale U., New Haven, 1985; sr. rsch. assoc. Columbia U., N.Y.C., 1983—; rsch. assoc. Columbia U. Ctr. on Japanese Economy, 1986—. Author: Productivity Functions on Aggregation, 1975; editor: Industry and Business in Japan, 1980, The Anatomy of Japanese Business, 1984; editor Japanese Econ. Studies, Armonk, N.Y., 1972—; assoc. editor Jour. Asian Econs., 1989—. Grantee Japan Soc. for Preservation of Sci., Osaka, 1987, Japan Econ. Rsch. Found., 1986. Mem. Am. Com. on Am. Econ. Studies (assoc. dir. 1982—). Home: New York, NY. Died Sept. 21, 2004.

SAUER, NORMAN GARDINER, judge, attorney; b. Independence, Iowa, Aug. 28, 1921; s. Olvin Charles and Dorothy (Geiser) S.; m. Irene Manuth, Sept. 14, 1947; children: Georg, James, Vicki, Douglas. BS, U.S. Mil. Acad., 1945; JD, Gonzaga U., Spokane, Wash., 1975. Atty. pvt. practice, Republic, Wash., 1976-77; prosecuting atty. Ferry County, Republic, Wash., 1977-82; atty. pvt. practice, Republic, Wash., 1983-88; dist. court judge Ferry County, Republic, Wash., 1989-94; pvt. practice as atty. Republic, Wash., from 1995. Judge pro tem Ferry County Dist. Ct., Republic, Wash., 1982-88; superior ct. commr. Ferry County Superior Ct., Republic, Wash., 1989-94; mcpl. ct. judge City of Republic, Wash., 1989-92. Chmn. Rep. Ctl. Com., Ferry County, Wash., 1976. Lt. col. USAF, 1964-70. Home: Republic, Wash. Died June 1, 2005.

SAUNDERS, GRADY F., biochemistry and biology educator, researcher; b. Bakersfield, Calif., July 11, 1938; m. Priscilla Saunders; 1 child, Nicole. BS, Oreg. State U., 1960, MS, 1962; PhD, U. Ill., 1965. USPHS postdoctoral fellow Inst. de Biology, Physics-Chemistry, Paris, 1965-66; asst. prof. biochemistry dept. devel. therapeutics U. Tex. Anderson Cancer Ctr., Houston, 1966-72, assoc. prof. biochemistry, 1972-77, dept. biochemistry U. Tex. Anderson Cancer Ctr., Houston, 1977-78, prof., 1978—99, Ashbel Smith prof. biochemistry and molecular biology, 1986-90, Anise J. Sorrell prof., 1990—99. Exchange scientist US-USSR Inst. Molecular Biology Acad. Scis. USSR, Moscow, 1972, '82; acting head dept. biochemistry U. Tex. Med. Dept. Anderscon Cancer Ctr., Houston, 1982-83; vis. prof. pediatrics U. Tex. Med. Sch. at Houston, 1990-99; mem. numerous nat. and local med. coms. Editor Anticancer Rsch., 1990-2005; contbr. over 170 articles to profl. jours., chpts. to 17 books; editor: Cell Differentiation and Neoplasia, 1978, Perspectives on Genes and the Molecular Biology of Cancer, 1983, Yearbook of Cancer 1985, '86, '87, '88. Recipient of many grants for cancer rsch., 1986-2005. Mem. AAAS, Am. Soc. Biol. Chemists, Am. Soc. Cell Biology, Am. Soc. Human Geneticists, Biophys. Soc., Human Genome Orgn., Phi Sigma, Sigma Xi. Achievements include two U.S. patents: probe for detection of specific human leukemia, 1989, defensins, 1991. Home: Houston, Tex. Died Aug. 26, 2005.

SAUNDERS, JOHN WILLIAM, JR., investment company executive; b. Wenatchee, Wash., Jan. 30, 1935; s. John William and Lillian Beatrice (Lee) S.; m. Judith Leslie Watson, Jan. 5, 1957; children: John William III, Leslie Watson. BS, Portland (Oreg.) State U., 1965. Treas. Western Investors Fund, Portland, 1959-61; pres. Saunders Investment Co., San Antonio, 1964-66; computer salesman IBM, San Antonio, 1967-68; asst. personnel dir. USAA, San Antonio, 1961-64, sr. v.p. investments, from 1969. Bd. dirs. USAA Investment Mgmt. Co., San Antonio, USAA Mut. Fund, USAA Tax Exempt Fund, USAA Investment Trust, BHC Securities, Inc., Phila. Vice pres. Fiesta San Antonio Commn., 1989—. Lt. col. USAF, 1953-58, 68-69, mem. Res. ret. Fellow Fin. Analysts Fedn.; mem. Inst. Chartered Fin. Analysts, San Antonio Soc. Fin. Analysts (pres. 1977-78), Tex. Cavaliers (comdr. 1985-86, King Antonio LXV 1987-88), San Antonio Country Club, Order of Alamo. Republican. Episcopalian. Avocations: flying, boating, skiing. Home: San Antonio, Tex. Died May 7, 2004.

SAUNDERS, MARY SUE (SUSIE SAUNDERS), art museum director; b. Kokomo, Ind., Mar. 15, 1943; d. William Kenneth and Clarice Lucille (Tucker) Bache; m. Charles William Saunders, Sept. 1, 1963; children: Beth, Abby, Mark. BS, Murray (Ky.) State U., 1965. Tchr. Ft. Knox (Ky.) High Sch., 1967-68; instr. Ind. Bus. Coll., Columbus, 1988-94; office mgr. C. of C., Columbus, 1988-95; dir. Indpls. Mus. Art, Columbus Gallery, from 1995. Chmn. Young Audiences of Minn., Mpls., 1987-88; bd. dirs. Young Audiences of Ind., Indpls., 1990—; pres. Leadership Barth County Alumni, Columbus, 1990-91; co-chmn. 10th Anniversary Indpls Mus. of Art, Columbus, 1984, sec. Mus. Art., 1993; sec. W&M pub. Columbus Svc. League, 1982-84; treas. Ind. Leadership Assn.; bd. dirs., 1st v.p. Columbus Area Arts Coun.; elder Disciples of Christ Ch. Mem. PEO, Kappa Kappa Gamma (pres. 1983-84), Kappa Kappa Kappa (sec. 1983-85). Republican. Avocations: music, needlecrafts. Home: Columbus, Ind. Died July 29, 2005.

SAVAGE, AUDREY COTTON, psychotherapist; b. Mpls., July 12, 1931; d. Earl Dewey and Leona (Beske) Cotton; m. Frank Roland Savage, Oct. 15, 1954 (div. Feb. 1980) children: Antonia Ellen, Theresa Gail. BS, U. Minn., 1953; MA, DePaul U., 1964; PhD, Northwestern U., 1972. Cert. clin. therapist. Speech pathologist Pub. Schs., Ohio, Mich., and Tenn., 1955-65; dir. speech dept. Mercy Hosp., Chgo., 1965-69; instr., dir. clin. tng. DePaul U., Chgo., 1967-68; instr. Indpls. U. Med. Sch., 1972-74; pvt. practice Indpls., from 1975; dir. tng. Indpls. Gestalt Inst., 1977-83, Sch. of Gestalt and Experiential Teaching, San Francisco, from 1990. Author: The Fourth Woman, 1988 (Honorable Mention 1987), Twice Raped, 1990 (1st prize 1991), The Making of a Man, 1991, The Magical Woman, 2000, Dance of Life Cards: An Intimate Tarot, 2000. Mem. NOW, Am. Assn. Marriage and Family Therapists. Democrat. Avocations: sailing, golf, guitar, drums, dance. Died July 7, 2005.

SAVAGE, TERRY RICHARD, information systems executive; b. St. Louis, Oct. 21, 1930; s. Terry Barco and Ada Vanetta (Cochran) S.; m. Gretchen Susan Wood, Sept. 26, 1964; children: Terry Curtis, Christopher William, Richard Theodore. AB, Washington U., St. Louis, 1951, MA, 1952; PhD, U. Pa., 1954. Mgr. system software IBM Rsch., Yorktown Heights, N.Y., 1956-63; dir. data processing Documentation Inc., Bethesda, Md., 1963-64; mgr. info. systems Control Data Corp., Rockville, Md., 1964-67; dir. rsch. Share Rsch. Corp., Santa Barbara, Calif., 1967-68; computer-aided acquisition and logistic support program mgr. TRW, Redondo Beach, Calif., 1968-92; ret., ind. cons. pvt. practice, from 1992. Expert witness for various coms. U.S. Congress, 1981, 84, 88, 89. Contbr. articles to profl. jours. Bd. dirs. ABC-Clio Press, Santa Barbara, 1970-75, Help the Homeless Help Themselves, Rancho Palos Verdes, Calif., 1988-94, ChorusLiners, Rancho Palos Verdes, 1983—, Savage Info. Svcs., Inc., Torrance, Calif., 1992—. Mem.: Cosmos Club. Died Aug. 16, 2004.

SAWABINI, WADI ISSA, retired dentist, educator; b. Jaffa, Palestine, Jan. 14, 1917; s. Issa J. and Julia C. (Malak) S.; m. Harriet Colgate Abbe Lack, Aug. 6, 1949; children—Wadi' Issa, Frederick Lack, Stuart John, Julia Malak. Student, College des Ecoles Chrétiennes, 1924-32; D.D.S., Am. U. Beirut, 1940. Grad. study Forsyth Dental Infirmary, 1940-41; intern Med. Center Hosp. Vt. (formerly DeGoesbriand Meml. Hosp.), Burlington, 1941-42; attending staff; assoc. pvt. practice Dr. Charles I. Taggart, 1942-51; pvt. practice Burlington, 1951-88, ret.; instr. oral pathology U. Vt., 1951-58; dir. U. Vt. (Sch. Dental Hygiene), 1953-72; asst. prof. oral hygiene U. Vt. (Coll. Medicine), 1958-72; chief dental staff Mary Fletcher Hosp., 1958-68, assoc. prof. dept. allied health scis., 1969-72. Mem. adv. bd. Vt. Pub. Health Dept.; mem. Vt. Bd. Health, 1980-86; v.p. bd. dirs. Overlake Day Sch., 1962-63; mem. Ethan Allen Homestead Fundraising Com., 1990—. Paul Harris fellow Burlington Rotary. Fellow Internat. Coll. Dentists (mem. exec. council 1950-54), Am. Coll. Dentists; mem. Vt. Dental Soc. (pres. 1956-57, mem. bd. rev., Disting. Service award 1972), New Eng. Dental Soc., Champlain Valley Dental Soc., C. of C., ADA, Fedn. Dentaire Internat. Republican. Episcopalian (vestryman). Clubs: Mason (Shriner), Rotary (dir. 1955-56, pres. 1961-62), Ethan Allen (Burlington). Home: Shelburne, Vt. Died Mar. 17, 2006.

SAWIN, CLARK TIMOTHY, endocrinologist; b. Boston, May 23, 1934; s. W. Clark and E. Loretta (Keegan) S.; m. Leslie, Jan. 10, 1982; children: Jennifer, Philip, Kenneth. BA, Brandeis U., Waltham, Mass., 1954; MD, Tufts U., Boston, 1958. Diplomate Am. Bd. Internal Medicine, Endocrinology and Metabolism. Intern U. Ill. Rsch./Ednl. Hosp., 1958-59; fellow endocrinology Tufts-New Eng. Med. Ctr., 1962-63, 65-66, resident internal medicine, 1963-64, Boston VA Hosp., 1964-65; chief endocrine diabetes sect. Boston VA Med. Ctr., 1966—98; prof. medicine Tufts U., Boston, 1981—94, Boston U., 1994—2000; med. inspector Vets. Health Adminstrn., Washington, 2000—04, dir. Office History and Archives, 2003—04. Contbr. over 100 articles to profl. jours. Capt. Med. Corps U.S. Army, 1959-62. Recipient Reynolds award, Am. Physiol. Soc., 1990, Disting. Career Tchg. award Tufts U., 1997. Achievements include definition of changes in thyroid function in older persons. Home: Washington, DC. Died Aug. 11, 2004.

SAWYER, CHARLES HENRY, anatomist, educator; b. Ludlow, Vt., Jan. 24, 1915; s. John Guy and Edith Mabel (Morgan) S.; m. Ruth Eleanor Schaeffer, Aug. 23, 1941; 1 dau., Joan Eleanor. BA, Middlebury Coll., 1937, DSc honoris causa, 1975; student, Cambridge U., Eng., 1937-38; PhD, Yale, 1941. Instr. anatomy Stanford, 1941-44; assoc., asst. prof., assoc. prof., prof. anatomy Duke U., 1944-51; prof. anatomy UCLA, Los Angeles, 1951-85, prof. emeritus, 1985—2006, chmn. dept., 1955-63, acting chmn., 1968-69, faculty research lectr., 1966-67. Editorial bd.: Endocrinology, 1955-59, Proc. Soc. Exptl. Biology and Medicine, 1959-63, Am. Jour. Physiology, 1972-75; Author papers on neuroendocrinology. Mem. Internat. Brain Research Orgn. (council 1964-68), AAAS, Am. Assn. Anatomists (v.p. 1969-70, Henry Gray award 1984), Am. Physiol. Soc., Am. Zool. Soc., Neurosci. Soc., Endocrine Soc. (council 1968-70, Koch award 1973), Am. Acad. Arts and Scis., Nat. Acad. Scis., Soc. Exptl. Biology and Medicine, Soc. Study Reprodn. (dir. 1969-71, Hartman award 1977), Internat. Neuroendocrine Soc. (council 1972-76), Hungarian Soc. Endocrinology and Metabolism (hon.), Japan Endocrin Soc. (hon.), Phi Beta Kappa, Sigma Xi. Home: Los Angeles, Calif. Died June 20, 2006.

SAWYER, JEANNIE LYNN, special education educator; b. Phoenix, Ariz., Mar. 15, 1960; d. Gene Paul Thomé and Sylvia Ann (Bawden) Eastin; m. Bruce Richard Sawyer, June 12, 1982; children: Jared Michael, Lindsay Michele. BS, Eugene Bible Coll., 1982; MS in Edn., Western Oreg. U., 1997. Instrnl. asst. spl. edn. West Linn/Wilsonville (Oreg.) Sch. Dist., 1992-94; learning specialist Beaverton (Oreg.) Sch. Dist., from 1996. Multidisciplinary team coord. Beaverton Sch. Dist., 1996—, parent/family cadré, 1996—, talented and gifted com., 1996—. Mem. Coun. for Exceptional Children. Avocations: taekwon do, gardening, teaching piano, sewing. Home: Chandler, Ariz. Died Dec. 29, 2004.

SAWYER, JOHN MICHAEL, language arts educator; b. Lonsdale, Minn., Aug. 3, 1944; s. Philip H. and Helen (Boyle) S.; m. Marian White, July 19, 1975; children: Benjamin, Anna, Michael. BA, U. Wis., Oshkosh, 1968; MS, U. Wis., Madison, 1978, PhD, 1985. Tchr. English Menasha (Wis.) Sr. High Sch., 1970-74; reading specialist La Grande (Oreg.) Elem. Sch., 1978-80; asst. prof. Ctrl. Wash. U., Ellensburg, 1988-89, Stephen F. Austin U., Nacogdoches, Tex., 1989-90, Montana State U., Bozeman, from 1990. Cons. various sch. dists., Mont., Wis., Wash., Tex., 1980—. Author: Science of Scholarship, 1992; contbr. articles to profl. jours. Mem. Internat. Reading Assn. (editl. adv. bd. 1995—), Kappa Delta Pi, Phi Delta Kappa. Died July 4, 2004.

SAWYER, THEODORE L., neurological surgeon; b. Feb. 11, 1933; BS, Andrews U., 1957; MD, U. Miami, 1963. Diplomate Am. Bd. Forensic Medicine. Intern L.A. County Hosp., 1963-64; resident in neurosurgery U. So. Calif., L.A., 1964-65, Children's Hosp., L.A., 1965-67, Long Beach (Calif.) VA Hosp, 1968-70. Mem. AMA, Calif. Med. Assn., Orange County Med. Assn., Cong. Neurol. Surgeons, Calif. Assn. Neurol. Surgeons, N.Am. Spine Soc. Died Apr. 7, 2005.

SAX, HERBERT, financial planner; b. N.Y.C., Nov. 5, 1929; s. Murray and Rose (Rifkin) S.; m. Carolyn Tambor, Jan. 20, 1952; children: Jeffrey F., Edward J. BA in Psychology, Bklyn. Coll., 1950; postgrad., Bernard Baruch Sch. Bus. Adminstrn., 1953-59, Coll. for Fin. Planning, 1986-88. CPA; cert. fin. planner; registered investment adviser. Asst. office mgr. Arrow Metal Products, N.Y., 1953-54; acct. Samuel Arlow & Co., N.Y., 1954-56, Morris R. Feinsod & Co., N.Y., 1956-60; contr., treas., v.p. fin. Ehrenreich Photo-Optical Industries and Nikon Inc., Garden City, N.Y., 1960-73, pres., chief exec. officer, 1973-84; exec. dir. Coalition to Preserve Integrity Am. Trademarks, Washington, 1984-85; pres. Herbert Sax & Assocs., Woodland Hills, Calif., from 1986. Bd. dir. Internat. Photographic Coun., N.Y. Cpl. U.S. Army, 1951-53. Mem. AICPA, N.Y. State Soc. CPAs, Internat. Bd. Standards and Practices for Cert. Fin. Planners. Home: Mission Viejo, Calif. Died Apr. 12, 2005.

SAXON, DAVID STEPHEN, physics professor, former academic administrator; b. St. Paul, Feb. 8, 1920; s. Ivan and Rebecca (Moss) S.; m. Shirley Goodman, Jan. 6, 1940; children: Margaret Elizabeth, Barbara Susan, Linda Caroline, Catherine Louise, Victoria Jean, Charlotte Mala. BS, MIT, 1941, PhD, 1944; PhD (hon.), Hebrew Union Coll., U. Judaism, U. So. Calif., U. BC, U. Bordeaux, U. Fla., U. Gottingen. Rsch. physicist MIT, 1943-46, Philips Labs., 1946-47; with UCLA, 1947—74, asst. prof. theoretical nuclear physics, chmn. physics dept., 1963-66, dean phys. scis., 1966-68, vice chancellor, 1968-75, emeritus faculty mem. physics and astronomy dept., 1990; provost U. Calif., 1974-75, pres., 1975-83, pres. emeritus, 1983—2005; mem. MIT Corp., 1977-90, chmn. corp., 1983-90, hon. chmn., 1990-95. Vis. scientist Centre d'Etudes Nucléaires, Saclay, France, 1968-69; vis. prof. faculty scis. U. Paris, Orsay, France, 1961-62; cons. to rsch. orgns., 1948—; mem. tech. adv. coun. Ford Motor Co., 1979-94; bd. mem. Eastman Kodak Co., Houghton-Mifflin Co., Am. U. Armenia. Author: Elementary Quantum Mechanics, 1968, (with A.E.S. Green and T. Sawada) The Nuclear Independent Particle Model, 1968, (with Julian Schwinger) Discontinuities in Wave Guides, 1968, (with William B. Fretter) Physics for the Liberal Arts Student, 1971. Mem. Mass. Ctr. Excellence, 1985-91; mem. com. to visit Med. Sch., Sch. Dental Medicine, Harvard U., 1985-90. Decorated Royal Order of No. Star; Guggenheim fellow Niels Bohr Inst. Theoretical Physics, Copenhagen, 1956-57, 61-62; Fulbright grantee, 1961-62 Fellow Am. Phys. Soc., Am. Acad. Arts and Scis., AAAS; mem. Am. Assn. Physics Tchrs., Am. Inst. Physics, Am. Philosophy Soc., Phi Beta Kappa, Sigma Xi, Sigma Pi Sigma. spl. rsch. theoretical physics, nuclear physics, quantum mechanics, electromagnetic theory, scattering theory. Died Dec. 8, 2005.

SAYLOR, DENNIS ELWOOD, hospital chaplain; b. St. Louis, Sept. 22, 1933; s. Clarence Claude and Maggie Dena (Beard) S.; m. Helen Lucile Howe, Aug. 9, 1953; children: Dennis Alan, Douglas Brian. ThB, Calvary Bible Coll., 1954; BA, Taylor U., 1956; MA, Ball State U., 1957; PhD, Clayton U., 1978. Asst. prof. Calvary Bible Coll., St. Louis, 1958-60; pastor 1st Presbyn. Ch., Tilden, Ill., 1960-68; asst. prof. Ill. Coll., Jacksonville, 1968-71; chaplain Passavant Hosp., Jacksonville, 1971-74; dir. chaplaincy Presbyn. Hosp., Albuquerque, 1974-88; dir. pastoral care San Diego Hosp. Assn., from 1988. With adv. coun. Bethel Sem., San Diego, 1989—. Author: And You Visited Me, 1979, Songs in the Night, 1980, A Guide to Hospital Calling, 1983; contbr. 30 articles to jours. Bd. dirs. Consumer Credit Counseling Svc., Albuquerque, 1978-88; mem. profl. edn. com. Am. Cancer Soc., San Diego, 1988—. Recipient Teagle Found. grant, 1985. Fellow Coll. Chaplains Am. Protestant Hosp. Assn. (state rep. 1984-88); mem. Assn. for Clin. Pastoral Edn., Pastoral Care Inst. (exec. dir. 1983-88). Presbyterian. Home: San Diego, Calif. Died Oct. 21, 2004.

SCANLON, PATRICK JOSEPH, cardiologist, educator; b. Cleve., Jan. 30, 1938; m. Marianne McNamara, June 9, 1962; children: John, Susan, Kate, Beth, Margaret. Premedicine, Xavier U., Cin., 1955-58; MD, Loyola U., 1962. Diplomate Am. Bd. Internal Medicine, Am. Bd. Cardiovasc. Disease, Nat. Bd. Med. Examiners. Intern Cook County Hosp., Chgo., 1962-63; fellow in internal medicine Cleve. Clinic, 1963-65, fellow in cardiology, 1965-66; fellow in cardiology, asst. in medicine U. Colo. Med. Ctr., Denver, 1968-70; from asst. prof. to assoc. prof. medicine Loyola U. Med. Ctr., Maywood, Ill., 1970-79, prof., from 1979, dir. cardiopulmonary lab., 1970-78, dir. clin. cardiology, assoc. chief cardiology, 1978-82, chief sect, cardiology, 1982-93, co-dir. cardiovasc. Inst., 1994-97. Hosp. ethics com. Stritch Sch. Medicine, 1983—2001. Contbr. over 300 articles and abstracts to med. jours., chpts. to books. Capt. med. corp. U.S. Army, 1966-68. Fellow Soc. Cardiac Angiography (sec. 1984-87, pres.-elect 1987-88, pres. 1988-89, chmn. nominating com. 1990-91, chmn. govt. rels. com. 1992-95), Am. Coll. Cardiology (gov. state of Ill. 1985-88, govt. rels. com. 1986-92, chmn. bd. govs. nominating com. 1988, database com. 1990-92, bd. trustees 1991-95, asst. sec. 1991-92, sec. 1992-95); mem. Am. Heart Assn. (v.p. Met. Chgo. chpt. 1989-90, pres.-elect 1990-91, pres. 1991-92, nominating and awards com. 1993-95) Avocations: golf, reading, travel. Home: Glen Ellyn, Ill. Died July 14, 2005.

SCARBROUGH, PAMELA LYNN JONES, dietitian; b. Gadsden, Ala., June 20, 1952; d. ArLin David and Irene (Taylor) J.; m. David Edward Scarbrough, June 8, 1991; children: Shane, Rachel, David. BS in Nutrition & Foods, Auburn U., 1974. Student dietitian Opelika (Ala.) Nursing Home, 1973-74; student caterer Auburn (Ala.) U., 1973-74; student dietitian Bapt. Meml. Hosp., Gadsen, Ala., 1972-73, staff dietitian, 1974-78; dietitian, asst. dir. Northeast Ala. Regional Med. Ctr., Anniston, 1978; cons. dietitian Gadsden Health Care Ctr., 1974-91, adminstr., 1979-98; consulting dietitian Collinsville (Ala.) Nursing Home, 1978-99; cons. Beverly Healthcare, 1997-98, dir. dietetics, from 1998. Bd. dirs. Auburn U. Parent's Assn., Blount County R.S.V.P.; mem. Ala. Dem. Exec. Com., Birmingham, 1982-991, Etowah County Dem. Exec. Com., Gadsden, 1982-91; mem. worship com. First United Meth. Ch., Albertville, Ala. Mem. Am. Dietetic Assn., Am. Diabetes Assn., Ala. Dietetic Assn., Gadsden Svc. Guild (chmn. ways and means 1982), Auburn U. Alumni Assn. Democrat. Methodist. Home: Albertville, Ala. Died Oct. 7, 2004.

SCHACHNER, ROBERT WAHL, record producer, author; b. Jersey City, June 20, 1940; s. Samuel and Frieda (Wahl) S.; m. Susan L. Fuller, Nov. 18, 1967 (div. June 1986); children: Alex, Victoria. Student, Carnegie Mellon Inst., 1959-62, Duquesne U., 1962-63. Gen. mgr. Cassette Recording Corp., 1970-71; sales exec. Viewlex, Inc., N.Y.C., 1971-74; designer, owner Sound Book Studios, N.Y.C., 1973; sales rep. ASR Duplicating Corp., 1976; designer, owner Gemcom Recording Studios, Davie, Fla., 1981; pres., chief exec. officer RTV Sales Corp., 1984-88; pres. RTV Comm., Dania, 1989-97; dir. Fla. Keys Jazz and Blues Festival, from 1997. Author: Official Scrabble Word Finder, 1988; co-author: Lost Words of the English Language, 1989, How and When to be Your Own Lawyer, 1992. Mem. USCG Aux., Hallandale, Fla., 1984—. Mem. Nat. Assn. Recording Merchandisers, Am. Mgmt. Assn., French Music Industry Conv., Music Retailers Show, Am. Booksellers Assn. Jewish. Avocations: sailing, photography. Home: Tavernier, Fla. Died Oct. 15, 2004.

SCHAEFER, DANIEL L., former congressman; b. Gutenberg, Iowa, Jan. 25, 1936; s. Alvin L. and Evelyn (Everson) S.; m. Mary Margaret Lenney, 1959; children: Danny, Darren, Joel, Jennifer. BA, Niagara U., 1961, LLD (hon.), 1986; postgrad., Potsdam State U., 1961-64. Pub. rels. cons., 1967-83; mem. Colo. Gen. Assembly, 1977-78, Colo. Senate, 1979-83, pres. pro tem, 1981-82, majority whip, 1983; mem. US Congress from 6th dist. Colo., Washington, 1983—99. Bd. dirs. Gen. Instruments Co-chair Nat. Retail Sales Tax Caucus, Congl. Oil and Gas Forum; mem. Spkrs. Task Force on Environ.; founder Nat. Trails Caucus, House Renewable Energy Caucus; pres. Foothills Recreation Bd., 1973-76; sec. Jefferson County Rep. Party, Colo., 1975-76. With USMCR, 1955-57. Recipient Colo. Park and Recreation citation, 1976; named Elected Ofcl. of Yr., Lakewood/South Jeffco C. of C., 1986, 88, 90, Leadership award U.S. Congl. Adv. Bd., Am. Security Coun. Found., Taxpayers Friend award Nat. Taxpayer's Union, 1985-86, 88, 90, 91, 92, 93, 94, 95, Golden Bulldog award Watchdog of Treasury, 1985-86, 87-88, 88-89, 89-90, 91-92, 93-94, 95-96, Spirit of Enterprise award U.S. C. of C., 1995, Nat. Health award Am. Assn. Nurse Anesthetists, 1996, Nat. Security Scorecare Perfect 100 award Ctr. for Security Policy, 1995, Friend of Taxpayer Perfect 100% award Ams. for Tax Reform, 1996; named Guardian of Small Bus., Nat. Fedn. Ind. Bus., 1996. Mem. C. of C., Rotary, Beta Theta Pi. Roman Catholic. Died Apr. 16, 2006.

SCHAEFER, KATHLEEN NORMA, accountant; b. St. Louis, Oct. 9, 1941; d. Walter Frederick and Lulu Emma (Sides) Kelpe; m. Ruston R. Schaefer, June 9, 1962; children: Teresa Jo, Melinda Joy. AA, St. Louis Community Coll., 1984; BSBA, St. Louis U., 1987. Bookkeeper SE Mo. Hosp., Cape Girardeau, 1961-62; sales clk. J.C. Penney Co., St. Louis, 1972; grader acctg. dept. St. Louis U., 1986; accounts payable clk. City Photo Stockhouse, St. Louis, from 1986; accounts acct. Grace and Co., St. Louis, from 1987. Tchr. sunday sch. Resurrection Luth. Ch., 1970-79; mem. solicitation com. Luth. High Sch. Assn. Auction, St. Louis, 1981-84. Mem. Beta Alpha Psi (v.p. 1986). Avocations: reading, volleyball, stained glass windows. Home: Saint Louis, Mo. Died Aug. 12, 2005.

SCHAEFER, NANCY TURNER, artist, educator; b. Hamilton, Ohio, July 4, 1940; d. Edward and Leota (Taylor) Turner; m. Richard Burton Price, June 16, 1967 (div. July 1970); m. Donald Raymond Schaefer, July 6, 1970 (dec. Nov. 1990). BA in English and Art, Ea. Ky. U., 1965; postgrad., Cin. Art Acad., from 1995. Cert. tchr., Ky., Ohio, Va. Tchr. Boone County Bd. Edn., Florence, Ky., 1965-67, Rockingham County Bd. Edn., Harrisonburg, Va., 1967-69, Hamilton County Bd. Edn., Cin. and Greenhills, Ohio, 1969-86; pvt. tchr. art, instr. cmty. colls., Sarasota and Bradenton, Fla., from 1986. Demonstrator Palm Aire Artists Orgn., Sarasota, 1995; bd. dirs. Art League Manatee County. Works exhibited in two woman show Longboat Key (Fla.) Edn. Ctr., 1996, four woman show Art League of Manatee County, 1995 (Equal Merit award 1995), group shows Hilton Leech Studio, Sarasota, Fla., 1995 (1st honorable mention for mixed media 1995); represented in permanent collections Art League of Manatee County and many pvt. collections. Recipient numerous awards for paintings. Mem. Fla. Suncoast Watercolor Soc., Art League Manatee County (demonstrator 1995), Nat. Mus. Women in Arts (assoc.). Avocations: piano, gourmet cooking, calligraphy, cats, interior decorating. Died Jan. 28, 2005.

SCHAFF, ALFRED, mechanical engineer, consultant; b. Bogas Del Tora, Panama, June 8, 1920; s. Alfred and Juanita (Kragstadt) S.; m. Cecile Becker, 1942 (div. 1949); children: Thomas, Anita; married; 1 child, Edward. BSME, Calif. Inst. Tech., 1941; PhD, Kensington U., 1982. Lic. pilot. Maintenance supt. Pan Am.-Grace Airways, 1941-44, capt., 1946-51; large liquid, rocket test engr. Aerojet Gen., 1951-57, mgr. test and field svc. divsn., 1957-60, mgr. spl. solid rocket projects., 1960-65, engring. mgr. nuclear rocket test facility, 1965-69; v.p., gen. mgr., dir. rsch. and devel. Ametek/Micro Electronics, El Segundo, 1969-87. Contbr. articles to profl. jours.; patents in field. Mem. IEEE, ASTM, SME, ISHM, Assoc. Calif. Inst. Tech., Am. Rocket Soc., Ancient and Secret Order of Quiet Biromen (keyman 1997—), OX-5 Aviation Pioneers, Red Barrows. Republican. Avocation: flying. Home: Playa Del Rey, Calif. Died June 5, 2005.

SCHAGRIN, ELIHU, rabbi; b. Wilmington, Del., June 20, 1918; s. Charles Wolf and Frances (Schwartz) S.; m. Dorothy Wallach, June 17, 1945; children: Gail S. Isaacs, Charles Wolf, Judith Michal. BA, U. Pa., 1940; M. Hebrew Lit., Jewish Inst. Religion, 1946; DD (hon.), Hebrew Union Coll.-Jewish Inst. Religion, 1971. Ordained rabbi, 1946. Rabbi Beth Israel Congregation, Coatesville, Pa., 1945-53, Temple Concord, Binghamton, N.Y., 1953-85, rabbi-emeritus, from 1985; rabbi Norwich (N.Y.) Jewish Ctr., from 1986, Leo Baeck Centre, Melbourne, Australia, 1989-90. Chaplain U.S. Vets. Hosp., Coatesville, 1945-53. Pres. Coatesville Interracial Com., 1949-53; pres. Metro-Interfaith Housing, Inc., Binghamton, 1976-78, 86-89, Family and Children's Svc. Soc., Binghamton, 1961-63; sec. United Way of Broome County, Binghamton, 1976-77. Recipient Broome County Med. Soc., 1967, Man of Yr. award Beth David Orthodox Congregation, 1981, Founder's award Hillel Day Sch., 1987. Mem. Cen. Conf. Am. Rabbis (mem. exec. bd. 1968-70, 80-82, mem. placement commn. 1978-84), Hebrew Union Coll.-Jewish Inst. Religion Alumni Assn. (exec. bd. 1965-68), Rotary (pres. local chpt. 1967-68). Democrat. Home: Sarasota, Fla. Died Dec. 28, 2004.

SCHANTZ, HERBERT FELIX, marketing executive; b. Trenton, N.J., Aug. 7, 1930; s. Herbert Frank and Anna Marie Schantz; m. Letty Louise Moxley, June 9, 1954; children: Louise Anne, Felice Marie. BSME, Drexel U., 1954, MS in Mgmt. Sci., 1968. Registered profl. engr. Md., Tex. Sr. engr. RCA Corp., Moorestown, 1957-62; chief rsch. scientist Black & Decker, Towson, Md., 1962-65; product devel. mgr. Computest Inc., Moorestown, 1965-68; product line gen. mgr. Recognition Equipment, Dallas, 1968-80; v.p. Graham Carlisle, Ft. Worth, 1980-87; pres. HLS Assocs., Southlake, Tex., 1987-88, pres., gen. ptnr. Sterling, Va., from 1988; dir. tech. ops. Fed. Nat. Computer Systems, Washington, 1988-89; sr. assoc. Strategic Mktg. and Communications Inc., Boston, from 1988. V.p., bd. dirs. Edn. Assn. Inc., Southlake, Tex.; bd. dirs. Graham Magnetics Ltd., Graham Japan, Ameritech Corp., Inc., Screening Systems and Svcs., Advanced Corp. Systems, Inc., Le Baron Internat.; presenter, speaker in field. Author: History of OCR, 1980, Optical Imaging Text Systems, 1991; tech. editor OCR Today; mem. editorial adv. bd. ID Systems mag., 1989—; contbr. articles to mags. including ID systems and RTUA-Today; author: Optical Imaging Systems-Theory and Applications; patentee OCR and imaging. Pres. Towson Civic Assn. D.W. Hills, Towson, 1988, elected charter commn. City of Southlake, 1986, mem. Southlake Noise Awareness Commn., Southlake City Zoning Bd. Adjustments. 1st lt. C.E., U.S. Army, 1955-57. Mem. IEEE (sr.), NSPE, Am. Standards Com. for Info. Processing, Assn. Info. Image Mgmt. (bd. dirs. Washington chpt., bd. dirs. Health Care SIG), Data Processing Mgmt. Assn. (cert. data processor), Assn. for Computing Machinery, Dallas Engrs. Club, Internat. Tape Assn., Computer and Communication Industry Assn., Recognition Techs. Users Assn. (v.p, bd. dirs. Tex. chpt. 1979-82, 90—, founding pres. Washington chpt. 1990-91), Drexel Alumni Assn. (chmn. S.W. chpt.), Mensa, K.C., Optimists (bd. dirs. Sterling chpt.), Kiwanis, Lions (pres. Southlake chpt. 1985-88, charter bd. dirs.). Avocations: helping mentally handicapped children, travel, raising dachshunds, gardening. Home: Sterling, Va. Died Nov. 7, 2004.

SCHARLACH, BERNICE SHERMAN, writer, lecturer; b. Bklyn., Nov. 3, 1919; d. Max and Gertrude Helen (Berger) Sherman; m. Arthur Gustav Scharlach, May 19, 1946; children: David, Alan, Gary. BA, U. Calif., Berkeley, 1941. Reporter, columnist C.C. Times, Walnut Creek, Calif., 1960-70; lectr. on San Francisco history, book reviewer, from 1983; freelance writer, contbr. to mags., from 1971. V.p., bd.d irs. Am. Jewish Com., San Francisco, 1976—. Author: House of Harmony, 1983, Big Alma (Spreckels), 1990, Ben Swig; editor Jewish Cmty. Fedn. Greater East Bay, Oakland, Calif., 1971-78; author monographs. Bd. dirs. Evergreen Dem. Party, San Jose, Calif., 1994—. Mem. Women in Comms. (bd. dirs. 1971-80). Jewish. Home: San Jose, Calif. Died Dec. 28, 2004.

SCHATT, PAUL, newspaper editor; b. N.Y.C., Aug. 31, 1945; m. Carol Peden Schatt; children: Suzannah, Andrew; m. Laura Schatt; 2 stepchildren. BA with distinction Polit. Sci., English, Ariz. State U., 1967. Editor Ariz. Republic, 1964-66, reporter, 1965-74, urban affairs editor, 1974-75, asst. city editor, 1975-79, chief asst. city editor, 1979-82, asst. met. editor, 1985-86, met. editor, 1986-88, editor edit. pages, from 1993; asst. editor Ariz. Mag., 1981-82, editor, 1982-85; editor edit. pages Phoenix Gazette, 1988-93, The Ariz. Republic, 1993-97, assoc. editor, 1998—2005. Pres. 1st amendment coalition of Az., 1999; vis. lectr. Pub. Affairs Journalism, Ariz. State U., 1976—2005, instr. Mass. Comm. Dept., 1974-76; dir. Eugene C. Pulliam Fellowship. Phoenix program, 1990—2005; writing coach, 1989; del. Pre White House Conf. Librs., 1991, pres., Arizona Newspapers Assn., 2000—2005. V.p. Crisis Nursery, 1984-87, bd. dirs. 1980-87; exec. bd. Hospice of the Valley, 1980-87; pres. Friends of Phoenix Pub. Libr., 1985-86, bd. dirs. 1986—2005; bd. trustees 1st Amendment Congress, 1989—2005; bd. dirs. Ariz. Humanities Coun., 1999—2005; Dean's adv. bd., Arizona State U. Honors Coll., 1999—2005, adv. bd., Northern Arizona U. Sch. of Communications, 1999—2005, bd. dirs. Camelback Hosps. 1982-89, chmn. bd. dirs. 1986-87, Cactus Pine Coun. Girl Scouts Am., 1988-89, Sun Sounds Inc., 1982-89, Valley Leadership Inc., 1991—2005, alum. assn., 1985-89, Ariz. Zool. Soc., 1991—2005, Barrow Neurol. Found., 1991—2005, Kids Voting, 1991-93, Barry Goldwater Inst., 1991-93, Ariz. Club, 1991—2005. With Ariz. Nat. Guard, 1966-79. Recipient Montgomery award Outstanding Svc. to Community Friends of Phoenix Pub. Libr., 1989; profl. Journalism fellow Stanford U., 1970-71. Mem. Am. Soc. Newspaper Editors, Soc. Profl. Journalists (pres. Valley of Sun chpt. 1974-75, 83-84, exec. bd. 1988-92), Sigma Delta Chi (co-chair nat. convention 1974). Died Nov. 18, 2005.

SCHAUBERGER, AMANDA LOUISE, freelance writer; b. Swea City, Iowa, Feb. 11, 1925; d. William and Catherine (Mathies) S. Student, Hamilton Sch. Commerce, Mason City, Iowa, 1943-44. Assembly worker Gen. Dry Batteries, Dubuque, Iowa, 1945-46; sales David Lionel Press, Chgo., 1946-49; sewing machine operator Workshop for the Blind, Sioux City, Iowa, 1950-53, 57-58; phone solicitor Aetna Roof Svc., San Francisco, 1962-63, Blind and Handicapped Products, San Francisco, 1963-64, Blind Made Products, San Francisco, 1964, Vols. of Am., San Francisco, 1965, DAV Store, Mpls., 1972-92. Contbr. articles to The Ringsted Dispatch, Pack of Fun, numerous others; columnist The Arlington Citizen, 1961-67, Dubuque Leader, 1984—. Vol. disc jockey KFAI-FM, Mpls., 1978-87. Avocation: reading. Home: Des Moines, Iowa. Died Oct. 24, 2004.

SCHEFFCZYK, LEO CARDINAL, cardinal, theologian; b. Beuthen, Germany, Feb. 21, 1920; Grad., U. of Breslau; PhD, Theology, U. of Munich. Ordained minister Roman Cath. Ch., 1947; pastor, 1947—48; subregent Konigstein Seminary, 1948—51, prof., Philosophy, Theology, 1952—62; prof., Theology U. of Tubingen, 1959—65, U. of Munich, 1965—85; mem. Pontifical Council for the Family, 1983—2001; created Cardinal Roman Cath. Ch., 2001. Mem.: Pontifical Roman Theological Academy, Pontifical Internat. Marian Academy, Bavarian Academy of Sciences. Died Dec. 9, 2005.

SCHEID, MARTIN F., physician; b. Jan. 11, 1931; BA, Rice U., 1953; MD, U. Tex., Galveston, 1957. Diplomate Am. Bd. Surgery. Postgrad. tng. Hermann Hosp., Houston, 1957-62; pvt. practice surgery, from 1962; surgeon Houston, 1999—2000; chief surgery Hermann Meml. Hosp., 2000—01. Chair bd. Tex. Med. Liability Trust, Austin, 1993—98. Mem. ACS (examiner). Died Sept. 17, 2004.

SCHELBLE, DANIEL TIMOTHY, emergency medicine physician; b. LaCrosse, Wis., July 9, 1946; s. Robert Martin and Pearl Elizabeth Schelble; m. Susan Jean Sadler, Oct. 27, 1973; children: Anita Marie, Dana Marie. BS in Biology, Loras Coll., Dubuque, Iowa, 1968; MD in Medicine, U. Wis., 1972. Diplomate Am. Bd. Emergency Medicine, recert. Surgery intern Meth. Hosp., Dallas, 1972-73; emergency medicine resident Akron (Ohio) Gen. Med. Ctr., 1975-77, emergency medicine residency dir., 1978-80, emergency medicine dept. chmn., from 1980, emergency medicine svcs. staff, from 1977. Prof. clin. emergency medicine Northeastern Ohio Univ. Coll. Medicine, 1994—. Contbr. numerous articles and chpts. to med. publs. Mem. mayor's adv. com. on emergency med. svcs. City of Akron, 1980—; med. advisor Mogadore (Ohio) Fire Dept., 1991—. Lt. USN M.C., 1973-75. Fellow Am. Coll. Emergency Physicians (mem. Ohio chpt., bd. dirs., mem. reimbursement com. 1977—), Soc. Tchrs. of Emergency Medicine (bd. dirs., pres.-elect, pres., chmn. pub. rels. 1980—), Summit County Med. Soc. Republican. Avocations: exercise, history. Home: Stow, Ohio. Died Nov. 2005.

SCHIAVONE, GEORGE JOSEPH, management science educator; b. Pitts., May 30, 1948; s. George Joseph and Philomena Julia (Marisco) S. BS, U. Pitts., 1969; MS in Physics, Carnegie-Mellon U., 1971, MS in Math., 1972; MS in Engring., Yale U., 1973. Instr. sci. Carlow Coll., Pitts., 1973-77; instr. math. Roxbury Community Coll., Boston, 1979-81, math., scis., bus., tech. div. chmn., 1981-87; instr. mgmt. sci. U. Mass., Boston, from 1987. Adj. instr. mgmt. sci. U. Mass., Boston, 1980-87; lectr. computer sci. Boston Coll., 1989—; dir. mgmt. info. systems Roxbury Community Coll., Boston, 1983, also dir. sch./coll. collaboratives, 1983-85, dir. minority sci. improvement program, 1985-87. Reviewer: N.J. Regents, 1986, 88, MacMillan, Inc., 1987. Grantee Mass. Dept. Edn., 1981-85, U.S. Dept. Edn., 1981-83; Ford Found. fellow U. Pa., 1969. Mem. Am. Math. Soc., Inst. Mgmt. Scis., Data Processing Mgmt. Assn., Soc. for Info. Mgmt. Roman Catholic. Avocations: reading, traveling, jogging, studying langs. and cultures of Spain and Italy. Home: Newbury Port, Mass. Died Jan. 26, 2005.

SCHIEB, DAVID ALLEN, biomechanist, physical therapist, researcher; b. Toledo, Nov. 26, 1951; s. Edwin Leonard and Betty Lou (Merz) S.; m. Debra Mary Hay, Apr. 19, 1951; children: Matthew Geoffrey, Brian Andrew. BA, LeTourneau U., 1974; MA, So. Meth. U., Dallas, 1975; EdD, U. No. Colo., 1982; MS, Tex. Woman's U., 1995. Instr. health and phys. edn. So. Meth. U., Dallas, 1974-79; biomechanics rsch. asst. U. No. Colo., Greeley, 1979-82; asst. prof. Gordon Coll., Wenham, Mass., 1982-83; biomechanist Nike Sport Rsch. Lab., Exeter, N.H., 1984-85; biomechanics product mgr. Kistler Instrument Corp., Amherst, N.Y., 1985-93; adj. asst. prof. SUNY, Buffalo, 1991-93; postdoctoral fellow Tex. Woman's U., Houston, from 1993. Biomechanics researcher Baylor Coll. Medicine, Houston, 1993-96; phys. therapist Southfield Health Care Ctr., 1995—; asst. clin. prof. Tex. Woman's U., Houston, 1996—; cons. in field. Contbr. articles to Posture and Gait: Control Mechanism's, ASTM, Pedestrian Footwear and Surfaces, Physiotherapy Can., Topics in Geriatric Rehab. Recipient Ctr. for Innovative Devel. award N.Y. State Sci. and Tech. Found., 1993; Sigma Xi grantee, 1981. Mem. ASTM, Am. Phys. Therapy Assn., Am. Coll. Sports Medicine, Internat. Soc. Biomechanics. Republican. Baptist. Avocations: running, sports, church, camping. Home: Friendswood, Tex. Died May 2, 2004.

SCHIEFNER, DIETER, test engineer; b. Diez, Hessen, Federal Republic of Germany, Oct. 24, 1939; came to U.S., 1953; s. Alfred Karl and Gertrude Anna-Maria (Neirath) S.; m. Maria Pounaridou, Nov. 21, 1963. BS in Computer Sci., U. Cen. Fla., 1987. Test equipment specialist Fed. Electric Corp./The Bionetics Group, Kennedy Space Ctr., Fla., 1964-87; chief test engr. Serv-Air, Inc. (E-Systems), Lexington, Ky., from 1987. With USAF, 1960-64. Republican. Greek Orthodox. Avocations: music, water-skiing, photography. Home: Lexington, Ky. Died Feb. 26, 2005.

SCHILDKRAUT, JOSEPH JACOB, psychiatrist, educator; b. Bklyn., Jan. 21, 1934; s. Simon and Shirley (Schwartz) S.; m. Elizabeth Rose Beilenson, May 22, 1966; children: Peter Jeremy, Michael John. AB summa cum laude, Harvard U., 1955; MD cum laude, Harvard Med. Sch., 1959. Intern medicine U. Calif. Hosp., San Francisco, 1959-60; resident in psychiatry Mass. Mental Health Center, Boston, 1960-63, dir. neuropsychopharmacology lab., 1967—98, founding dir., 1998—2004, sr. psychiatrist, 1967—2004; rsch. psychiatrist NIMH, Bethesda, Md., 1963—67, cons., 1967-68; asst. prof. psychiatry Harvard Med. Sch., Boston, 1967-70, assoc. prof., 1970-74, prof., 1974—2004, prof. emeritus, 2004—06. Dir. psychiat. chemistry lab. Mass. Mental Health Ctr., 1977—98, founding dir., 1998—2004. Author: over 200 publ. including, Neuorpsychopharmacology and the Affective Disorders, 1970; editor: Depression and the Spiritual in Modern Art: Homage to Miró, 1996, U.S. patent, 2002; editor-in-chief Jour. Psychiat. Rsch., 1982-92; mem. editorial bd. Psychophysiology, 1968-74, Jour. Psychiat. Rsch., 1968-82, Psychopharmacology, 1970-84, Sleep Revs., 1972-79, Communications in Psychopharmacology, 1974-81, Psychotherapy and Psychosomatics, 1974-91, Rsch. Communications in Psychology, Psychiatry and Behavior, 1976—, Jour. Clin. Psychopharmacology, 1980-2006, Integrative Psychiatry, 1982-89, 91-2006, others. Bd. dirs. Med. Found., Boston, 1991-97 chair clin. rsch. com., 1994-96; trustee Mind/Body Med. Inst. Deaconess Hosp., Harvard Med. Sch., Boston, 1988-2002, chair sci. adv. bd., 1988-95. Served as surgeon USPHS, 1963-65. Recipient Anna-Monika Found. prize, 1967, Hofheimer award Am. Psychiat. Assn., 1971, hon. mention award, 1968; McCurdy-Rinkel prize No. New Eng. Dist. br. Am. Psychiat. Assn., 1969; William C. Menninger award ACP, 1978; Neuropsychiatry Classics, 1995; Lifetime Achievement award Soc. of Biological Psychiatry, 1996; Award for Rsch. in Mood Disorders The Am. Coll. of Psychiatrists, 1999. Fellow: Am. Psychiat. Assn. (disting. life), Am. Coll. Neuropsychopharmacology (life; emeritus); mem.: AAAS, Soc. Neurosci., Collegium Internat. Neuropsychopharmacologicum, Assn. Rsch. in Nervous and Mental Disease, Group Without a Name, Am. Soc. Neurochemistry, Am. Soc. Pharmacology and Exptl. Therapeutics, Am. Coll. Psychiatrists, Am. Psychopath. Assn., N.Y. Acad. Scis., Soc. Biol. Psychiatry, Am. Psychosomatic Soc., Psychiat. Rsch. Soc., World Psychiat Assn. (sec. sect. biol. psychiatry 1972—77), Phi Beta Kappa. Achievements include patents in field concerning development of a rapidly acting antidepressant. Died June 26, 2006.

SCHILTZ, JOYCE DOROTHY, word processing company executive; b. New Britain, Conn., Mar. 29, 1949; d. Raymond T. and Teresa D. (Nimro) Anderson; m. Billy L. Schiltz, Sept. 6, 1969 (div. Apr. 1980); 1 child, Trina Kathleen. AA, Strayer Coll., 1969. Licensing asst. Church's Fried Chicken, San Antonio, 1976-79; membership dir. Fair Oaks County Club, San Antonio, 1979; personnel dir. Sosa & Assocs. Advertising, San Antonio, 1980-89; pres., owner NIGHType, San Antonio, from 1989. Legis. asst. Sen. Jacob Javitz, Washington, 1969; vol. Mayor Henry Cisneros Election Campaign, San Antonio, 1984, 86. Mem. Internat. Fund for Animal Welfare, Humane Soc. the U.S., People for the Ethical Treatment Animals, San Antonio Advt. Fedn., Musicians Assn. Avocations: music, travel. Died Feb. 17, 2004.

SCHLATTER, DONALD ALLAN, metal company executive, lawyer; b. Toledo, Ohio, Aug. 25, 1929; s. Ezra Andrew and Alpha Ida (Bornhoft) S.; m. Barbara Louise Reichert, June 18, 1955; children: Louise, Edward, Richard, Ann, Robert, Thomas. SB, MIT, 1951; LLB, M in Indsl. Engring., U. Toledo, 1956. Bar: Ohio, 1956. Priorities dir. Art Iron, Inc., Toledo, 1951-52, asst. prodn. mgr., 1952-54, mgr. sales distbn., 1954-64, mgr. metal services ctr. div., 1964-73, pres., chief exec. officer, from 1973. Mem. exec. com. Steel Svc. Ctr. Inst., Cleve., 1981—, treas., 1983—. Mem. exec. com. YMCA, Toledo, 1979—, v.p., 1981-85; chmn. employee divsn. United Way, Toledo, 1984; exec. com. St. Luke's Hosp., Maumee, 1981—, vice chmn., 1988-90, chmn., 1990-93; exec. com. Ohiocare Health Sys., Inc., 1989—, chmn., 1993. Mem. ABA, Ohio Bar Assn., Toledo Bar Assn., Am. Soc. Metals, Am. Soc. Testing Materials, Soc. Automotive Engrs., Am. Welding Soc. Clubs: Toledo. Lutheran. Home: Sylvania, Ohio. Died July 30, 2005.

SCHMIDT, DARYL DEAN, religious educator; b. Sioux Falls, S.D., Aug. 12, 1944; s. Arnold A. and Jennie Frances (Glanzer) S. BA, Bethel Coll., North Newton, Kans., 1966; MDiv, Assoc. Mennonite Seminaries, Elkhart, Ind., 1970; PhD, Grad. Theol. Union, Berkeley, Calif., 1979. Asst. prof. religion Tex. Christian U., Ft. Worth, 1979—84, assoc. prof. religion, 1984—95, prof. religion, 1995—2006. Vis. prof. Pacific Sch. Religion, Berkeley, Calif., 1991-93 Author: Hellenistic Greek Grammar and Noam Chomsky, 1981, The Gospel of Mark: Scholars Bible 1 with Introduction Notes and Original Text, 1991; contbr. articles and revs. to profl. jours. Recipient Jr. Scholar Rsch. award Southwest Commn. on Religious Studies, 1986, Faculty award for Outstanding Involvement with Student Devel., Tex. Christian U., 1987. Mem. Soc. Bibl. Lit., Studiorum Novi Testamenti Societas. Democrat. Episcopalian. Died Mar. 21, 2006.

SCHMIDT, JOHN RICHARD, agricultural economics professor; b. Madison, Wis., July 3, 1929; s. Oscar John and Alma Theodora (Ula) S.; m. Rosemary Pigorsch, Oct. 7, 1951; children: Janet, Deborah, Allen. BS, U. Wis., 1951, MS, 1953; PhD, U. Minn., 1960. Asst. prof. agr. econs. U. Wis., Madison, 1956-61, assoc. prof., 1961-65, prof., 1965-95, prof. emeritus, 1995—2006, chmn. dept., 1966-70; mng. dir. North Ctrl. Computer Inst., 1981—95; owner, mgr. JRS Computing Svcs., Madison, 1995—2006. Farm mgmt. cons. Am. Farm Bur. Fedn., Chgo., 1962; cons. Banco de Mexico, 1972-84, IBRD (World Bank), 1973-94, Agrl. Devel. Bank Iran, 1974-76; adv. bd. Internat. Devel. Inst., 1983; faculty Salzburg Seminar, 1983, 85. Contbr. articles to profl. jours. Bd. dirs. U. Wis. Credit Union, 1968-77, pres., 1969-75; mem. com. Wis.-Upper Mich. Synod Sem., 1972-75, ch. coun. 1967-69, 72-75, pres. 1974-75. Mem. Rotary (pres. Madison West 1994-95), Delta Theta Sigma (nat. sec. 1962-64), Gamma Sigma Delta (pres. Wis. chpt. 1975). Lutheran. Died Jan. 30, 2006.

SCHMIDT, MARTHA BUBECK, social sciences educator; b. Cadott, Wis., Sept. 28, 1912; d. Karl Christian and Lydia Sarah (Keller) Bubeck; m. Eugene Milton Schmidt, Sept. 11, 1943; children: Eugene Karl, Fredric John. BS, U. Wis., Stout, 1934; MPhil, U. Wis., Madison, 1947, M in Psychology and Behavioral Studies, 1959. Tchr. home econs. Barron (Wis.) High Sch., 1934-37; supr. student teaching U. Wis., Stout, 1937-38; state supr. home econs. edn. Wis. State Bd. Vocat. Edn., Madison, 1938-48; instr. adult evening sch. Madison Area Tech. Coll., 1949-69; guidance counselor Madison Met. Schs., 1959-79; coord. AARP and Wis. Ret. Tchrs. Assn., Madison, 1986-90; state chmn. health/long term care action group AARP, Wis., 1990-99, coord. health advocacy svcs., 1991-2001. Founder Future Homemakers of Am., 1943, past advisor; condr. fgn. study programs, Europe, Asia, Australia, 1971-88. Bd. dirs. Madison Oakwood Retirement Ctr., 1983-89, mem. resident care com., 1992—; com. mem. Wis. Legis. Study Elderly Abuse, 1985-88. Recipient Disting. Educator award, U. Wis., Stout, 1998. Mem.: AAUW, AARP, Mental Health Assn./Wis. Coalition Aging Groups (regional bd.), Valparaiso U. Guild (state pres. 1981—85), Luth. Women Missionary League, Nat. Honor Soc. Home Econs., Wis. Ret. Tchrs. Assn. (rec. sec. 1983—89, bd. dirs. 1990—2002), Madison Civics Club, Rotary (Sr. Svc. award 1998). Lutheran. Avocation: volunteering. Home: Madison, Wis. Died Sept. 5, 2004.

SCHMONES, SHIRLEY See WALLACH, SHIRLEY SCHMONES

SCHMUTZHART, SLAITHONG CHENGTRAKUL, sculptor, educator; b. Bangkok, Jan. 1, 1934; came to U.S., 1960; d. Sunee Chengtrakul; m. Berthold L. Schmutzhart, 1963 (div. 1988). Diploma Ceramics, Corcoran Sch. Art, Washington, 1968, Diploma Sculpture, 1970; BFA in Sculpture, U. D.C., 1977; MFA, George Washington U., 1983. Instr. art The Lab Sch., Washington, 1968-71; instr. sculpture, adult edn. No. Va. C.C., Louson County, Va., 1978-80; lectr. studio art/ceramics Am. U., Washington, 1980-82; lectr. studio art Mtm. Vernon Coll., Washington, 1979-90; asst. prof. sculpture Corcoran Sch. Art, 1981—2002. Exhibited in 7 one-person shows, numerous group shows; about 50 sculptures with pvt. collectors. Ford Found. scholar, 1966. Mem. AAUP, Corcoran Sch. Faculty Assn. Home: Washington, DC. Died Jan. 19, 2006.

SCHNABLE, GEORGE LUTHER, chemist; b. Reading, Pa., Nov. 26, 1927; s. L. Irvin and Laura C. (Albright) S.; m. Peggy Jane Butera, May 4, 1957; children: Lee Ann, Joseph G. BS, Albright Coll., 1950; MS, U. Pa., 1951, PhD, 1953. Project engr. Lansdale (Pa.) Tube Co., 1953-58; engring. specialist Philco Corp., Lansdale, 1958-61; mgr. materials and processes Philco-Ford Corp., Blue Bell, Pa., 1961-71; head process rsch. RCA Labs., Princeton, N.J., 1971-80, head device physics and reliability, 1980-87, David Sarnoff Rsch. Ctr., Princeton, 1987-91; ind. tech. cons. Schnable Assocs., Lansdale, 1991—2005. Author: (with others) Advances in Electronics and Electron Physics, 1971, The Chemistry of the Semiconductor Industry, 1987, Microelectronics Reliability, 1989, Microelectronics Manufacturing Diagnostics Handbook, 1993; editor spl. issue RCA Rev., 1984; divsn. editor Jour. of Electrochem. Soc., 1978-90; contbr. 80 articles to profl. publs. With U.S. Army, 1946-47. Fellow AAAS, Am. Inst. Chemists, Electrochem. Soc. (chm. Phila. sect. 1969-71); mem. IEEE (sr.) (assoc. guest editor Proceedings 1974), Alpha Chi Sigma, Phi Lambda Upsilon, Sigma Xi. Achievements include 39 patents (several with others); contributions to semiconductor device fabrication technology and reliability. Died Aug. 7, 2005.

SCHNEIDER, ERNEST EMIL, consultant, writer, editor; b. Greensboro, N.C., Dec. 2, 1925; s. Rudolph and Edith Marjorie (Kerle) S.; m. Marlene McGregor, May 25, 1932 (div. 1959); children: Anthony, Elliott, Andrew; m. Susanne Mark, Nov. 29, 1943; 1 child, Martin. Fgn. svc. officer U.S. Dept. State, Netherlands, Austria, 1950-55; policy dir. Radio Free Europe, Munich, Fed. Republic Germany, N.Y.C., 1954-70; correspondent Research Inst. Am., Washington, 1971-74; researcher, editor Hudson Inst., Croton on Hudson, N.Y., Indpls., 1974-88; adj. sr. fellow Croton on Hudson, from 1988. Editor: Next 200 Years, 1976, World Economic Development, 1979; co-author: The Future of Austria, 1984; contbr. articles to Policy Rev., 1981, Defense Analysis, 1988. With U.S. Army, 1944-46, ETO. Mem. Yale Club (N.Y.C.), Phi Beta Kappa. Democrat. Died Aug. 14, 2005.

SCHNUDA, DANIEL NASR, internist, pathologist; b. Luxor, Egypt, Dec. 20, 1938; came to U.S., 1961; s. Daniel Schnuda; children: Charles, Peter. MB, MD, Faculty of Medicine, Cairo, 1959; MSc, Ohio State U., 1966. Diplomate Am. Bd. Pathology. Resident in pathology Ohio State U., Columbus, 1963—66, mem. faculty, 1966—67; rsch. fellow immunology Toronto (Can.) Western Hosp., 1967—68; rsch. fellow electron microscope Banting Inst. U. Toronto, 1968—71; asst. prof. pathology Wayne State U., Detroit, 1971—76; chmn. dept. pathology, dir. of labs. Edgewater Hosp. Mazel Med. Ctr., Chgo., 1976—79; assoc. prof. Chgo. Med. Sch., 1977—81; pres. N.W. Internal Medicine S.C., Palatine, Ill., from 1981; attending physician N.W. Cmty. Hosp., Arlington Heights, Ill., from 1983, med. dir., leader, from 1996; courtesy physician Good Shepherd Hosp., Barrington, Ill., from 1989, St. Alexius Hosp., 1981. Pres. Chgo. Internat. Corp. Ltd., 1987—. Contbr. articles in molecular and cellular immunology to nat. and internat. profl. jours.; patentee organic fertilization in desert. CEO Internat. Med. Coun. Ill., 1996—; founder "Crops for the World", 1998; founding bd. dirs. Assn. Am. Physicians and Surgeons, Ill., 1998. Fellow Coll. Am. Pathologists; mem. AMA, ACP, Ill. State Med. Soc. (del. 1988—), Chgo. Med. Soc. (coun. 1988—, v.p. 2001-02, pres. Irving Park and N.W. Suburban br. 2002-2004, trustee 2003-2004). Achievements include work conducting agriculture projects to convert desert land into fertile land, achieved in the Egyptian desert and the Chinese desert using newly invented patented product "fertile desert.". Home: Palatine, Ill. Died July 6, 2004.

SCHOENBERG, BETTY REBECCA, artist; b. N.Y.C., June 13, 1916; d. Abraham and Sonja (Weisband) Cohen; m. Albert Schoenberg, Dec. 26, 1952; children: Steven Mark, Lisa Hillary. Dental hygienist, U. So. Calif., 1948; BA in Art History, Calif. State U., Carson, 1978. Registered dental hygienist, Calif., 1949. Dental hygienist Dr. Mark Shulman, L.A., 1948-88; artist L.A., from 1973. Exhibited at Westwood Ctr. for the Arts, 1980 (1st prize). With U.S. Army, 1943-46. Grantee Women's Bldg. L.A., 1985. Mem. Women's Caucus for Art (bd. dirs., Achievement award 1995), Neighbors United (del. 1991-95), World's Women On-Line, Internet Installation, UN Fourth World Conf. on Women (participant 1995-96). Democrat. Jewish. Avocations: modern dance, reading, poetry, walking, hiking. Home: Los Angeles, Calif. Died Apr. 4, 2004.

SCHOENBRUNN, ERWIN FREDERICK, chemical engineer; b. Newark, N.J., July 15, 1921; s. Erwin O. and Katherine (Stetter) S.; m. Dorothy M. Rinehart, Nov. 21, 1948; children: Carol R., Mary R., Laura R., Frederick R. BS in Engring., Princeton U., 1947; MS in Engring., U. Pa., 1949. Project engr. Sharples Corp., Phila., 1947-51; project mgr. Nat. Rsch. Corp., Cambridge, Mass., 1951-58; dept. head process and exploratory rsch. Escambia Chem. Co., Wilton, Conn., 1958-68; sr. rsch. chem. engr. Am. Cyanamid, Stamford, Conn., 1968-91; cons. Ridgefield, Conn., from 1991. Patentee in field. Sgt. U.S. Army, 1943-46, PTO. Mem. Am. Chem. Soc. (chmn. Southwestern Conn. chpt. 1973-74), Am. Inst. Chem. Engrs. Democrat. Lutheran. Died Jan. 18, 2005.

SCHOENE, KATHLEEN SNYDER, lawyer; b. Glen Ridge, N.J., July 24, 1953; d. John Kent and Margaret Ann (Bronder) Snyder. BA, Grinnell Coll., 1974; MS, So. Conn. State Coll., 1976; JD, Washington U., St. Louis, 1982. Bar: Mo. 1982, Ill. 1983. Head libr. Mo. Hist. Soc., St. Louis, 1976-79; assoc. Peper, Martin, Jensen, Maichel & Hetlage, St. Louis, 1982-88, ptnr., 1989-98, Armstrong Teasdale LLP, St. Louis, from 1998, exec. com., from 2003. Bd. dirs. Legal Svcs. of Eastern Mo. Author: (with others) Missouri Corporation Law and Practice, 1985, Missouri Business Organizations, 1998; contbr. articles to profl. jours. Trustee Grinnell (Iowa) Coll., ex officio voting mem., 1991-93; bd. dirs. Jr. League St. Louis, 1995-96, Leadership Ctr. Greater St. Louis, 1995-96, FOCUS St. Louis, 1996-2001, exec. com., 1997-99; active St. Louis Forum, 1997—, Herbert Hoover Boys and Girls Club, St. Louis, 1999—. Mem. ABA, Nat. Conf. Bar Founds. (trustee 1996-2000, pres. elect 1997-98, pres. 1998-99), The Mo. Bar (bd. govs. 1997-99, chair bus. law com. 2000-02), Ill. State Bar Assn., Bar Assn. Met. St. Louis (treas. 1991-92, sec. 1992-93, v.p. 1993-94, pres.-elect 1994-95, pres. 1995-96, chair small bus. com. 1987-88, exec. com. 1988-96, chair bus. law sect. 1988-89, mem. exec. com. young lawyers sect. 1988-90), St. Louis Bar Found. (bd. dirs. 1994-2000, v.p. 1995-96, pres. 1996-98). Home: Saint Louis, Mo. Died Aug. 2004.

SCHOEPPEL, JOHN FREDERICK, mechanical and electrical engineer, consultant; b. South Bend, Ind., Oct. 25, 1917; s. Frederick Otto and Helen S.; m. Jacqueline Mae Gall, Apr. 17, 1949; children: Pamela Jo, Sonja Lou. BSc, Northwestern U., Evanston, Ill., 1939. Devel. engr. Honeywell, Inc., Mpls., 1939-47; mgr. flight references Lear, Inc., Grand Rapids, Mich., 1947-60; gen. mgr. instrn. and control divsn. Pneumo, Grand Rapids, Mich., 1960-66; dir. new products NWL Corp., Kalamazoo, 1966-71; v.p., gen. mgr. Sundstrand Data Control, Redmond, Wash., 1971-73; exec. v.p. Veriflo Corp., Richmond, Calif., 1974-90, cons. R & D, from 1990. Contbr. articles to profl. jours. Mem. ASTM, Semiconductor Equipment Mfrs. Inst. (com. 1990-92), SEMATECH Standards (com. 1991-93). Republican. Achievements include patents for Autopilots, Gyros, Flight Reference Display, Equipment for Semiconductor Production,

Automatic Autopilot; development of two gyro stable platforms for aircraft outpilot, modern all-attitude flight displays for Airforce and Navy. Home: Jacksonville, Fla. Died Aug. 22, 2004.

SCHOLER, MARGARET D., adult education educator; b. La Habra, Calif., June 14, 1920; d. James Robards Darling and Ula McWhorter; m. Emerson C. Scholar, 1964 (dec.); m. Philip Lynden Evans, 1941 (div. 1960); children: Lynden Anthony Evans, Conrad St. George Evans, Madelon Blythe Evans Mitchell. AB, U. Calif., Berkeley, 1942. Rsch. crew U. Calif., Berkeley, 1942—43; asst. Robert Johnson, Interiors, Oakland, Calif., 1948; libr. asst. Oakland Pub. Libr., 1960—62; asst. mgr. Fairyland Dutchess Caterers, Oakland, 1962—63; mgr. art gallery Bret Harte Board Walk, Oakland, 1962—63; lectr. Am. Antiques Normandale Coll., Mpls., 1969—90, Ohio State U. Continuing Edn., Columbus, 1990—97, Cuesta Coll. Continuing Edn., San Luis Obispo, Calif., 1998—99, Elderhostel, Calif. Poly. U., Cambria Pines, 2000—01. Acquisitions co-chair Godfrey Ho. Mus., Mpls., 1978—90; bd. dirs. decorative arts coun. Mpls. Inst. Arts, 1980—90; lectr., Mpls. and St. Paul, 1970—90. Mem.: AAUW (co-chair programs Morro Bay chpt. 2000—02, garden tour chair 2003). Democrat. Episcopalian. Home: Morro Bay, Calif. Died Jan. 15, 2004.

SCHOLZ, LAWRENCE CHARLES, retired electrical engineer; b. New York, Aug. 8, 1933; s. Lawrence Henry Scholz and Helen Irene (Westervelt) Brodhead; m. Claire Seidner, Jul. 28, 1954; children: Richard, Lawrence, Karen Lisa. BEE, City Coll. N.Y., 1954. Engr. electron tube divsn. RCA, Harrison, N.J., 1954-60; rsch. physicist IIT Rsch. Inst., Chgo., 1960-64; group leader Vitro Labs., West Orange, N.J., 1964-69; dir. sys. analysis Man Tech, Livingston, N.J., 1969-70; sr. engr. astro space RCA, Princeton, N.J., 1970-88; mgr. sys. engr. GE Astro Space, Princeton, 1988-93; divsn. fellow Lockheed Martin Astrospace, Princeton, 1993-98; ret., 1998. Ind. cons., 1998—; mem. com. for earth studies space studies bd. NRC, 1998-2001. Author, editor: Design of Electron Tubes, 1961. Scoutmaster, commr., Boy Scouts Am., Essex County, N.J., 1968-70. Mem. IEEE (sr.), AAAS, AIAA (assoc. fell.). Avocation: bird watching. Home: West Orange, NJ. Died Feb. 17, 2006.

SCHON, ALAN WALLACE, lawyer, actor; b. Mpls., Nov. 27, 1946; s. Hubert Adelbert and Jennie (Jamieson) S.; m. Linda Kay Long, June 14, 1969; 1 child, Cynthia Anne. BA, U. Minn., 1969; JD, William and Mary Coll., 1973; grad. Command & Gen. Staff Coll., U.S. Army, 1984. Bar: Minn. 1973, U.S. Dist. Ct. Minn., Alaska 1986, U.S. Dist. Ct. Alaska, U.S. Ct. Appeals (9th cir.) 1988, Va. 1995. Prin. Schon Law Office, Fairbanks, Alaska, 1986-94; owner, pub. Nordland Pub. Co., Hampton, Va., 1991-94; dep. city atty. mcpl. bonds, environ. law, pub.-pvt. econ. devel. funding environ. law City of Hampton, Va., 1994-99. Nationwide environ. group mgr. Delphi Info. Network, Gen. Videotex Corp., Cambridge, Mass., 1991-94; ind. assoc. Pre-Paid Legal Svcs. Inc., 1999—. Author, pub. EnvironLaw, 1991-94; editor William and Mary Law Rev., 1970-73; stage, film and TV actor; screenwriter: Operation Desert Fire, 1997, Operation Firestorm, 1998. Dir. Alaska State Fair, Fairbanks, 1987-91, Fairbanks Light Opera Theater, Fairbanks, 1991-94, Theatre of Virginia Beach, Va., 2002—; dir., v.p. bus. and fin. Williamsburg (Va.) Players Theater, 2000-01; dir., v.p. for bus. Little Theatre of Virginia Beach, 2002—; dir., sec. Riding for Am., Inc., 1993-97; dir. Interior Alaska Econ. Devel. Ctr., 1993-94. Maj. U.S. Army, 1974-86. Mem. Fairbanks C. of C. (chmn. environ. concerns com. 1992-94). Avocations: outdoor sports, arts. Died Jan. 20, 2005.

SCHONEBAUM, ALFRED, food company executive; b. Dortmund-Horde, Westfalen, Germany, Nov. 27, 1914; came to U.S., 1947; s. Emil and Bertha (Muller) S.; m. Margaret Karliner, July 13, 1939; 1 child, Reuben-Max. Abitur, Real Gymnasium, Dortmund-Horde, 1930. Dept. mgr. Wollwaren House Saxonia, Dresden, Germany, 1934-35, buyer, 1936-38; sales rep. Import Firm, Soerabaia, Java, 1938-40, exec. Semarang, Java, 1940-47; dept. mgr. textile firm N.Y.C., 1948-52; exec. Specialty Food Co., N.Y.C., 1952-80. Cons. in field. Pres. condo bd., Jackson Heights, N.Y., 1986-93; vol. Light House, Rego Park, N.Y., 1980-94. Recipient Mgmt. Achievement award N.Y. Habitat, 1988. Mem. Coun. N.Y. Coops. Democrat. Jewish. Avocations: stamp and coin collecting, travel, photography. Home: San Diego, Calif. Died Feb. 18, 2004.

SCHONTHAL-SECKEL, RUTH E., composer, pianist, music educator; b. Hamburg, Germany, June 27, 1924; came to U.S., 1946; d. Fritz and Ida (Spitz) Schonthal; m. Oscar Ochoa (div.); 1 child, Ben; m. Paul B. Seckel, Feb. 3, 1950; children: Bernhard, Alfred. Student, Conservatorium Stern, Berlin, 1930-37, Royal Acad. Music, Stockholm, 1938-415, Conservatorio Nacional, Mex., 1941-45, Yale U., 1946-48. Adj. faculty NYU, 1974-2006, Westchester U. Conservatory of Music, 1974-2006, SUNY, Purchase, 1980-2006; pvt. music educator, 1950-2006. Compositions include three full-length operas The Courtship of Camilla, 1979-80, Princess Maleen, 1994, and Jocasta, 1996-97; symphonic works include chamber music, 3 string quartets, vocal music, 2 works for solo instruments, harpsichord and organ works, 1940-2006; Archives at Kunst Akademie, Berlin have complete music manuscripts and papers. Recipient awards Meet the Composer, ASCAP, City Opera Competition, Yale U., NYU, 1994, Internat. Heidelberger Kunstlerinnen Preis, 1994. Democrat. Avocations: theater, literature, the arts, psychology, sociology. Home: Scarsdale, NY. Died July 10, 2006.

SCHORR, BRUCE ALAN, gastroenterologist; b. N.Y.C., July 14, 1941; s. Leon William and Natalie (Goldstein) S.; m. Carol Diane Gildersleeve, June 4, 1964; children: David Michael, Natalie Susan. BA, Adelphi U., 1963; MD, Med. Coll. of Va., Richmond, 1967. Diplomate: Am. Bd. Internal Medicine, subspecialty Gastroenterology. Physician, ptnr. Diagnostic Clinic of Largo, Fla., from 1974. Trustee Hosp. Corp. Am. Largo Med. Ctr. Hosp. Co-author articles in profl. jour. Lt. USNR 1968-70 (Viet Nam). Mem. Am. Gastroent. Assn. Republican. Jewish. Avocations: fishing, travel, gourmet foods and wines. Home: Clearwater, Fla. Died Mar. 31, 2004.

SCHOTT, HOWARD MANSFIELD, lawyer, musicologist; b. N.Y.C., June 17, 1923; s. Simon Leopold and Rebecca Louise (Landay) S. BA, Yale U., 1943, JD, 1948; PhD, Oxford (Eng.) U., 1978. Bar: N.Y. 1949, Mass. 1986. Assoc. Fried, Frank, Shriver & Kampelman, Washington, 1948-51; atty. AEC, N.Y.C., 1951-54; ptnr. Duncombe, Oltarsh & Schott, N.Y.C., 1954-60; internat. counsel Schering Corp., Bloomfield, N.J., 1961-67; musicologist Victoria & Albert Mus., London, 1976-81; pvt. practice law and mediation, Boston, from 1981. Cons. Ashmolean Mus., Oxford, 1969-79, Met. Mus. Art, N.Y.C., 1981. Author: Playing the Harpsichord, 1971, 3d edit., 1979, Catalogue of Keyboard Instruments in Victoria and Albert Mus., 1984. Sec., dir. Walter W. Naumburg Found., Inc., N.Y.C., 1961-76; sr. common rm. affiliate Mather House, Harvard U. With U.S. Army, 1943-46, ETO. Mem. Oxford and Cambridge Soc. New Eng. (pres. 1990-92), United Oxford and Cambridge U. Club London, Glyndebourne Sunday Club. Died June 23, 2005.

SCHOW, HORACE, II, lawyer; b. Brownwood, Tex., Nov. 14, 1932; s. Horace and Mary W. (Sears) S.; m. Hildegard Wagner, June 7, 1958; children: Mary W., Peter H., Alice P. BS, U.S. Military Acad., 1955; MS, MIT, 1961; JD, Fla. State U., 1977. Bar: Fla., 1978, U.S. Patent Office, 1979; registered profl. engr., Vt. Commd. 2nd. lt. U.S. Army, 1955, advanced through grades to lt. col., 1969, retired, 1975; officer U.S. Army Corps. of Engrs., svc. includes Korea, Vietnam, France and Germany, 1955-75; asst. atty gen. State of Fla., Tallahassee, 1978-80; atty. div. bond fin. dept. gen. svcs. State of Fla., 1980-84; gen. counsel Fla. State Bd. of Adminstrn., Tallahassee, from 1984. Decorated Legion of Merit with Oak Leaf Cluster. Mem. ABA, Nat. Assn. Bond Lawyers, Nat. Assn. Pub. Pension Attys., West Point Soc. of Tallahassee, Killearn Country Club and Inn. Roman Catholic. Avocations: tennis, horseback riding. Home: Tallahassee, Fla. Died Mar. 29, 2005.

SCHREIBER, SHARRON KAY, child psychologist, nurse specialist; b. Lawton, Okla., Sept. 18, 1951; d. Jack F. and Jerri (Wood) Johns; m. John R. Johnson, Dec. 25, 1971 (div. Apr. 1983); m. Donald C. Schreiber, Aug. 8, 1986; children: Maya S., Asia B. BS, U. Okla., 1974, MS, 1980, PhD, 1988. Lic. psychologist, Ga. Founder, exec. dir. Can. County Parents Assistance Ctr., Yukon, Okla., 1980-83; clin. nurse specialist maternal child nursing Presbyn. Hosp., Oklahoma City, 1980-83; dir. psychology Inner Harbour Hosp., Rockmart, Ga., 1989-90; pvt. practice Psychol. and Counseling Svcs., Douglasville, Ga., from 1990, sr. ptnr., from 1990. Bd. mem. Okla. Statewide Child Abuse Adv. Bd., Oklahoma City, 1982-83; instr. childbirth and parent edn., program dir., founder ABC classes for parents of newborns Presbyn. Hosp., 1980-83; apptd. mem. family and child advocacy case mgmt. team U.S. Army, Ft. Stewart, Ga., 1987-89. Mem. Amnesty Internat., 1990—, Sierra Club, Ga., 1990—, Nat. Wildlife Fedn., 1989—. Capt. U.S. Army, 1986-89. Recipient Ednl. Scholarship award Bur. Indian Affairs, 1970-74, Am. Indian Scholarship award Am. Indian Scholarship, Inc., 1977-80; named Outstanding Am. Indian Women in Am., 1981. Mem. APA, Ga. Psychol. Assn., Ga. Coun. on Child Abuse, Coalition Against Sexual Abuse of Children. Democrat. Avocations: hiking, camping, white water rafting, swimming, reading. Home: Powder Springs, Ga. Died July 13, 2005.

SCHROEDER, FREDERICK WILLIAM, real estate development executive; b. N.Y.C., Aug. 19, 1928; s. Frederick William and Anna Catharine (Dittmar) S.; m. Elizabeth Gail Schroeder, Sept. 23, 1988; children: Frederick W., Craig H., Laura L., Lisa A., Kimberly C., Melissa G. Student, Farleigh Dickinson U., Johns Hopkins U. Dir. prodn. Westinghouse Elec. Co., Pitts., 1953-63; dir. devel. The Rouse Co., Columbia, Mass., 1964-79; pres., chief exec. officer Process Mgmt. Group Inc., Miami, from 1979. Lectr. real estate and constrn., 1988, 90. Avocations: boating, sport fishing. Home: Cape Coral, Fla. Died Aug. 9, 2005.

SCHROEDER, PAUL HERMAN, entomologist; b. Elmer, N.J., Sept. 26, 1930; s. Harry and Emily (Blumke) S.; m. Janet Elma Wiedrich, Feb. 8, 1964; children: Paula, Jana, David, Krista. BS, Rutgers U., 1952, MS, 1960, PhD, 1963. County agrl. agt. Passaic County N.J., Paterson, 1952-57; rsch. asst. Rutgers U., New Brunswick, N.J., 1957-63; biologist entomology and nematology Niagara Chem. Divsn. FMC, Middleport, N.Y., 1963-64, nematologist, 1964-66, mgr. field rsch., 1966-70, mgr. Gasport (N.Y.) Rsch. Field Sta., 1970-71; nematologist Castle & Cook Corp., Dole Divsn., Honolulu and Lanai City, Hawaii, 1971-76; product devel. mgr. Union Carbide Corp., Agrl. Products Divsn., Salinas and Jacksonville, 1976-80; registration specialist US EPA, Washington, 1980-92, efficacy reviewer and registration mgr., from 1992. Mem. Entomol. Soc. Am., Soc. Nematologists, Sigma Xi. Home: Centreville, Va. Died Apr. 14, 2005.

SCHROM, ELIZABETH ANN, retired writer; b. Princeton, Minn, June 7, 1941; d. Raymond Alois and Grace Eleanor (Hayes) S. Student, U. Minn., 1960; BA, St. Scholastica Coll., Duluth, Minn., 1963; postgrad., Princeton U., 1965; MEd, Temple U., 1972; MLS, Drexel U., 1974; postgrad., NYU, 1981, Russian Temple U., 1983. Tchr. Strandquist H.S., Minn., 1963—64, Hutchinson H.S., Minn., 1964—65, Peace Corps, Ankara, Turkey, 1965—67, Phila. Sch. Dist., 1968—80; children's libr. Laurel Pub. Libr., Del., 1983; writer Ortonville Ind. Newspaper, Minn., 1983—2004. Mem. Jewish Com. on Mid. East, Washington, 1988-90, 93, Nat. Coun. Returned Peace Corps. Vol., Washington, 1989-99, Nat. Taxpayers Union, Washington, 1988-92; mem. bd. policy Liberty Lobby, Washington, 1989-2000; mem. Arkadashlar, 2003-05. Populist. Roman Catholic. Avocations: writing, cooking, history, travel, sewing. Home: Ortonville, Minn. Died Sept. 6, 2005.

SCHUBERT, GLENDON, political scientist, educator; b. Oneida, NY, June 7, 1918; s. Glendon Austin and Agnes (Rogers) S.; m. Elizabeth Josephine Neal (dec. 1949); children: Frank, James; m. Elizabeth Harris (div.); children: Susan, Kathleen, Robin; m. Natalie Klavans, 1999. AB, Syracuse U., 1940, PhD, 1948. Mem. faculties Syracuse U., 1946-48, UCLA, 1948-49, Howard U., 1949-50, Rutgers U., 1950-51, Franklin and Marshall Coll., 1951-52, Mich. State U., 1952-67, U. Minn., 1955; William Rand Kenan Jr. prof. polit. sci. U. N.C. at Chapel Hill, 1967-68; prof. York U., 1968-70; prof. polit. sci. U. Hawaii, 1970-2000, prof. emeritus, 2000—06; rsch. prof. polit. sci. So. Ill. U. at Carbondale, 1986-91. Fulbright lectr. U. Oslo, Norway, 1959-60; fellow Center for Advanced Study in Behavioral Scis., 1960-61; sr. scholar in residence Center for Cultural and Tech. Interchange Between East and West, U. Hawaii, 1963-64, 65; Fulbright-Hays research scholar, Netherlands, 1977; NSF faculty fellow U. Groningen, Netherlands, 1977-78; NATO sr. fellow, U.K.; fellow Netherlands Inst. Advanced Study Humanities and Social Sci., Wassenaar, Netherlands, 1978-79 Author 30 books; assoc. editor for biosocial behavior The Behavioral and Brain Sci., 1979-2006; adv. editor Jour. Social and Evolutionary Systems, 1980-2006; assoc. editor Politics and the Life Scis., 1980-90; contbr. articles to profl. jours. in biobehavioral and polit. sci., jud. behavior and politics, and pub. policy. Served with Signal Intelligence U.S. Army, 1942-46. Decorated Bronze Star; recipient Regents' medal and award for excellence in research U. Hawaii, 1975 Mem. Internat. Soc. Polit. Psychology, Am. Polit. Sci. Assn. (past mem. exec. coun., Career Lifetime Achievement award 1999), Assn. Polit. Life Scis. (past pres., Lifetime Career Achievement award 1994), Internat. Soc. Human Ethology, Phi Beta Kappa. Home: Sammamish, Wash. Died Jan. 15, 2006.

SCHUESSLER, MARY ANN PETERY, executive recruiter; b. Portland, Oreg., June 1, 1936; d. Walter Henry and Ida May (Harzell) Bauer; children: Melinda, Lorri. Degree in mgmt., Harvard U., 1977. With Selma Pressure Treating Co., Calif., from 1965; sec./treas. Selma Leasing Co., 1971-77, pres. Calif., 1978-85; recruiter exec. ITT Employer Services, West Los Angeles, 1985-86; pres. Drake & Assocs., Beverly Hills, Calif., from 1986. Cons. SBA; mem. adv. council to chancellor forest products dept. U. Calif.; mem. adv. council Sch. Bus., Calif. State U., Fresno; del. White House Conf. Small Bus.,; del 1980 White House Conf. om Small Bus. Mem. Town Hall, Los Angeles, 1986, Friends Hollywood Bowl, Los Angeles, 1988. Mem. Am. Wood Preservers Assn., Harvard Bus. Sch. Assn., Better Bus. Bur. (dir.), Fresno County Hist. Soc., DAR, Fresno Geaneal. Soc., Am. His. Soc. Germans from Russia, New Eng. Geaneal. Soc. Avocations: weaving, reading, music. Died July 24, 2004.

SCHUETZ, MICHAEL DAVID, communications manager; b. Detroit, Mar. 28, 1959; s. Rudy Ludwig and Shirley Jean (Engel) S.; m. Nancy Brand, Jan. 9, 1984; 1 child, Benjamin Michael. BS in Indsl. Design, U. Cin., 1984. Artist, graphic designer Just Your Type, Upper Saddle River, N.J., 1984-86; art dir. Image Works, Ramsey, N.J., 1986-89; corp. communications mgr. The Texwipe Co., Upper Saddle River, from 1989. Freelance designer MS Design, Allendale, N.J., 1982—. Mem. Am. Ctr. for Design (corp.), Art Dirs. Club N.J. Republican. Methodist. Avocations: photography, illustration, model building, collecting antique toys. Home: Allendale, NJ. Died July 6, 2004.

SCHULTE, GARY RODGER, consumer products company executive; b. Detroit, Feb. 25, 1949; s. Rodger Louis and Helen May (Byrd) S.; m. Felicia Delores Gillish, Sept. 5, 1970; children: Kimberly Kathleen, Keith Daniel. BS in Architecture, Lawrence Technol. U., Southfield, Mich., 1972. Registered architect, Mich. Project engr. Ford Motor Co., Dearborn, Mich., 1972-74, Dow Chem. Co., Midland, Mich., 1974-79, engring. mgr., 1979-84; project mgr. Dow Consumer Products, Bay City, Mich., 1984-86, supt., 1986-88; ops. dir. Dow Brands, Mpls., 1988-93, ops. mgr. Urbana, Ohio, 1993-98; mfg. mgr. S.C. Johnson Wax, Racine, Wis., 1998-2000; ops. improvement mgr. S.C. Johnson Was, Bay City, Mich., from 2000. Bd. dirs. Mid-Mich. Health Care Systems, Midland, 1978-88; vice chmn. bd. Stratford Pines

Nursing Home, Midland, 1984-87; chmn. bd. Gladwin (Mich.) Nursing Home, 1987-88; vice chmn. bldg. com. Midland Hosp. Ctr., 1982-88; elder Midland Reformed Ch., 1986-88, deacon, 1980-83; bd. dirs. Leadership Bay County, 1985-88; loaned exec. United Way, 1979-80. Evangelical Christian. Avocations: coaching sports, orchestra, playing sports of all kinds. Home: Midland, Mich. Died June 18, 2005.

SCHULTZ, CAROLINE REEL, artist; b. Evansville, Ind., July 5, 1936; d. Howard and Helene (Englert) Reel; m. Milton H. Schultz, Feb. 2, 1958; children: Paul, Jim. Student various including, Art Ctr. Coll. of Design, L.A., U. Ill., 1960-62, European Sch. of Art, Mallorca, Spain, 1962; Diploma of Merit (hon.), U. Arts, Parma, Italy, 1970. Dir. Spanish Village Art Ctr., San Diego, 1974; art dir. East African Wildlife Soc., Kenya; African safari organizer various spl. interest groups; art dir. Creative TV Prodns.; pres. Creel Fine Arts, Inc., San Diego, Calif., from 1979; owner African Impressions, San Diego, from 1980; dir. safari U.S. Internat. U., from 1993; owner, dir. Exotic Travel Consultants, from 1995. Lectr. on animal anatomy and art/Africa; participant spl. TV shows; travel writer, others. Major exhibits and one-woman shows include: San Diego Mus. of Art, 1960, Evansville, Ind. Mus. of Art, Exposition of Art, Urbana, Ill., 1960, Art Ctr. Gallery, St. Louis, Springfield, Ill. Art Assn., East African Wildlife Soc. Gallery, Mt. Kenya Safari Club, Nairobi, Kenya, 1991 (one award), Palm Springs Festival of Arts and Music, 1980 (three awards), San Diego County Exposition of Art (award), Whaletail, Nairobi, Kenya, 1991. Recipient Appreciation award Jean-Pierre Hallet/Pygmy Fund, 1980, Oil Painting award Nairobi Kenya Purchase, 1993. Mem. Assn. for Promotion of Tourism to Africa (bd. dirs.), East African Wildlife Soc., Nat. Assn. Scuba Divers, Cen. Ill. Artist League, So. Calif. Presswomen. Home: San Diego, Calif. Died Dec. 30, 2004.

SCHULTZ, EVELYN ECALE, artist; b. Chgo., Nov. 28, 1931; d. George Ecale and Marie Elise Bauermeister; m. Robert Frank Schultz, Dec. 19, 1925; children: Kenneth M., Robin C. Brower, Karen M. Rantis, Jennifer B. Kaiser, Erik K., Steven E., Jason Robert. Attended, U. Ill., 1949-54, Coll. DuPage, Glen Ellyn, Ill., 1995—2002, numerous art workshops. Owner, operator ECALE Studio, Villa Pk., Ill., 1997—2003; represented by Ill. Artisans Shop, Chgo., Wallscapes Gallery, Elmhurst Art. Mus. Gallery, DuPage Art Gallery and Sch., Coll. of DuPage, Glen Ellyn, Ill. Del. W. Suburban Fine Arts Alliance, Oakbrook Terrace, Ill., 1995-97; judge U. Ill., Coop. Ext. Svc., DuPage County, Triton Coll., River Grove, Ill., Naperville Art League, Ill., Henry Hyde Congressional Art Exhbn., Elmurst Art Mus., local guilds and leagues, others. One-woman shows include Loyola Med. Ctr., Maywood, Ill., Navy Pier, Chgo., Hinsdale (Ill.) Libr., DuPage Gallery, Wheaton, Ill., Wallscapes Gallery, Elmhurst, Riverside Art Exhbn., Elmhurst Art Mus., Coll. DuPage, Ill. (2d pl. painting), Firstar Bank, Elmhurst, West Suburban Bank, Villa Park, Villa Park, Bloomingdale Art Mus., Oakbrook Golf & Tennis Club, Elmhurst Garden Club, exhibited in group shows at Chgo. Cultural Ctr., 1999—2003, Elmhurst Art Mus., 1999 (Knudson Meml. award, 1st Pl.), Ill. State Profl. Art Exhbn., Springfield, ICARUS, Nags Head, N.C., St. Charles Art and Music Festival, Ill., Thompson Ctr., Chgo., others, Art Open Chgo. (Profl. Artists Ill. 2nd Pl. award), Bloomingdale Art Mus., 2004, U. Health Scis., Lombard, Ill., 2004, Nat. Watercolor Soc., Phila., 2004, Chgo. Cultural Ctr., 2004, Represented in permanent collections Ray Allen, Oak Brook, Ill., Elkbrook, Northlake, Fra Angelica Sacred Art Exhibit, River Grove, Ill. (3d Pl.), Triton Coll., Women's Works, Woodstock, Ill., Challenge of Champions, Houston, Okla. Art Guild (Excellence award), Neville Mus., Green Bay, Wis., Elmhurst Art Mus., Ill., Beverly Art Ctr. Mus., Chgo., Drury Ln. Theater, Oakbrook, Ill., DuPage County Bar Assn., Wheaton, Pegasus Assocs., Chgo., Elk Grove Village Libr., Villa Park Libr., Elmhurst Mcpl. Bldg., Coll. of DuPage (3d Pl.), Gahlberg Gallery, others, Angelican Riverside, York Theater, Coll. DuPage, Riverside, Elmhurst, Glen Ellyn, Ill.; subject of numerous articles: in newspapers, mags.; curator (EAG) Elmhurst Art Mus. Bd. dirs. Elmhurst Art Mus., 2002—03; v.p. Sr. Art Network Chgo., 2002; exec. bd. Elmhurst Art Mus., 1998—99. Named Best of Show, Beverly Arts Ctr., Chgo., 1999, DuPage Art League and Gallery, Sr. Art Network, Chgo., Bloomingdale Art Mus., Ill., Addison Art Guild, Ill., Elmhurst Artists Guild, 1997; recipient Grumbacher medallion and award of excellence, No. Colo. Art Assn., 1998, Gold medallion award, Merit award, Ill. Watercolor Exhbn., 1999, 1st pl. Christian Art Exhbn., Coll. DuPage, 1997, 1998, 3d pl. award, Grumbacher Gold medallion exhbn. in nat. shows, numerous other nat. and internat. awards excellence in painting, 1st Pl. award, Fra Angelica Found., 2004, 3d place Best of Best, Triton Coll., River Grove, Ill., 2004, Meml. Eng award, Elmhurst Art Mus., 2004. Mem. Water Color Soc. (signature, Midwest, Ga., Mont., Pa., Tex., Ill., Niagara Frontier, We. Colo., La., Okla., Ky.), Taos Soc. Watercolorist (signature), Elmhurst Art Mus. (bd. dirs. 2003—), Watercolor Soc. (assoc., Phila., W. Tex., La., Colo., Ky., Ala.), La. Watercolor Soc. (signature), Art Inst. Chgo., Elmhurst Artists Guild (hon. life, pres. 1995-2000, 3d v.p. 2003—), Addison Art Guild, Chgo. Artists Coalition, Sr. Art Network (v.p. 2002—), DuPage Art League. Roman Catholic. Avocations: opera, German studies, museum studies, travel, books. Home: Elmhurst, Ill. Died Apr. 21, 2005.

SCHULTZ, JOAN (ELIZABETH) LEAGUE, banker; b. Chgo., Aug. 8, 1935; d. Howard Sigsbee and Estelle (McAver) L. m. James J., Aug. 4, 1959 (div. June 1975); Children: James Joseph Jr., Elisabeth Schultz Grenus, Christine Schultz Gustafson, David Howard. BA (Arts), Loyola U., 1957. Loan sec. Union Realty Mortgage Co., Chgo., 1968-71, 1st Federal S & L of Crystal Lake, Ill., 1971-74; loan adminstr. Grayslake Nat. Bank, Ill., 1975-78; mgr. (student loans) No. Trust Bank/Lake Forest, Ill.; prin. Boomer Ball, Grayslake, Ill., from 1985-. Co-chmn. Concerned Canine Owners Coalition, Grayslake Ill. 1987--. Mem. Am. Assoc. of Zoological Parks and Aquariums., Bull Terrier Club of Am., Scottish Terrier Club of Am., Ft. Dearborn Bull Terrier Club (Sec. 1986). Republican. Roman Catholic. Avocation: research. Home: Grayslake, Ill. Died Mar. 29, 2005.

SCHULZ, HELMUT WILHELM, chemical engineer, energy executive; b. Berlin, July 10, 1912; came to U.S., 1924; s. Herman Ludwig Wilhelm and Emilie (Specka) S.; m. Colette Marie Francoise Prieur, Mar. 6, 1954; children: Raymond A., Caroline P., Roland W., Robert B., Thomas F. BS, Columbia U., 1933, ChE, 1934, PhD, 1942. Rsch. engr. to mng. dir. Union Carbide Corp., Charleston, W.Va., 1934-69; spl. asst. to dir. def. rsch. and engring. U.S. Dept. Def., Washington, 1964-67; spl. asst. to U.S. commr. of edn. U.S. Dept. Edn., Washington, 1971; sr. rsch. scientist, adj. prof. chem. engring. Columbia U., N.Y.C., 1972—83; founder, dir. Urban Technology Ctr., Columbia Engring. Sch., N.Y.C., 1972—83; chmn., CEO Dynecology, Inc., Harrison. Contbr. articles to profl. jours. Mem. N.Y.C. Mayor's Sci. and Tech. Adv. Coun., 1973-74; bd. dirs. Charleston Symphony Orch., 1956-62, Am. Cancer Soc., W.Va., 1954-58; chmn. W.Va. Atomic Energy Commn., Charleston, 1962-64. Grantee in field; Egleston medal for disting. engring. achievement Columbia Engring. Sch. alumni assn., 2004. Fellow AIChE; mem. N.Y. Acad. Scis., Am. Chem. Soc. (emeritus), N.Y. Yacht Club, Cosmos Club. Achievements include patents for centrifugation cascade for enrichment of fissionable uranium isotope; high acceleration rocket motor; tar-free, slagging coal/waste gasifier; enhanced oil recovery process; synthesis of ethanol from ethylene and steam; waste-to-energy conservation processes; 60 U.S. and fgn. patents. Home: Harrison, NY. Died Jan. 28, 2006.

SCHUMACHER, ROBERT BOYCE, transit consultant, civil engineer; b. N.Y.C., Feb. 15, 1917; s. Ernest and Graycie (Boyce) S.; m. Eva H. Jasie, Feb. 20, 1948; 1 child, George, 1 stepchild, Edward Jasie. BSCE, Cooper Union, 1942; MSCE, Polytechnic, 1957; MS in Urban Planning, Columbia U., 1967. Registered profl. engr., N.Y. Engr. office design and field supervision heavy indsl. cons. various pvt. cons. firms, 1936-43, 46-56; civil engr., asst. to gen. mgr., asst. supt. structure dept. N.Y.C. Transity Authority, 1956-61; transp. planning engr. N.Y. State Office Transp., 1961-68; supr. inspectors of track & structures r.r. divsn. N.Y. State Pub. Svc. Commn., 1968-69; dir. mass transit planning N.Y.C. Dept. Transp., 1969-87; apptd. MTA Citizens Adv. Coun., from 1985; cons. transp. planning, from 1987. Home: Mount Vernon, NY. Died Aug. 12, 2004.

SCHUNK, WILLIAM ALLEN, military officer; b. Omaha, Sept. 27, 1942; s. Orville Edwin and Beulah Fern (Andersen) S.; m. Diane Adele Brodbeck, July 25, 1964; children: Eric, Kelly, Karen. BA in English, U. Nebr., Omaha, 1964; MA in Police Adminstrn., Troy State U., 1981. Commd. 2d lt. USAF, 1964, dep. dir. tng. disciplinary barracks Ft. Leavenworth, Kans., 1969-72, instr. security police acad. Lackland AFB, Tex., 1972-76, chief security police Yokota AFB, Japan, 1976-79, mgmt. cons. Montgomery, Ala., 1979-82, advanced through grades to lt. col., 1981, chief security police Offutt AFB, Nebr., from 1982. Mem. Internat. Assn. Chiefs of Police, Air Force Soc. Mgmt. Cons., Air Force Assn., Bellevue, Nebr. C.of C. (mil. affairs com. 1982-86, Pres.' special service award 1984, Vol. of Yr. award 1985). Republican. Lutheran. Avocations: golf, bridge, reading. Home: Omaha, Nebr. Died Jan. 8, 2005.

SCHUSTER, STEPHANIE ELLEN, apparel executive; b. N.Y.C., Apr. 13, 1952; d. Harold Jason Schuster and Constance (Cargill) S.; 1 child, Raphael Rosati. BFA, R.I. Sch. Design, Providence, 1975. Free-lance designer, Italy, 1974-84; knitwear designer Jones N.Y., Bristol, Pa., 1984-85, Six Continents, N.Y.C., 1985-86; pres. Stephanie Schuster, N.Y.C., from 1986. Merchandiser, design cons. Cherokee, Children's Pl., N.Y.C. and N.J., 1986-90. Mem. Nat. Assn. Women Bus. Owners. Avocations: skiing, community volunteer work. Home: Flemington, NJ. Died Mar. 13, 2005.

SCHUTTE, HENRY JOHN, accountant; b. Waldwick, N.J., Sept. 8, 1925; s. Arend John and Matilda Christina (Morgan) S.; m. Ruby Gertrude Rice, June 13, 1946 (div., 1969); children: Judith Lynn, Patrick Cole, Rory Don, Tony Gene. Degree in acctg., Bliss Coll., 1951. Enlisted USNR, 1944; advanced through ranks to AK2 rate USN, honorable discharged, 1954. Treas. Franklin County Dem. Party, 1992-93, 94-95; pres. Greater Reynoldsburg Dem. Club, 1992-93; chmn. Reynoldsburg Nonpartisan Polit. Action Com., 1992; recreation commr. Reynoldsburg, Ohio; coach Little League, VFW Baseball; founder, first program dir. Reynoldsburg Youth Football; city auditor City of Reynoldsburg; asst. state auditor State of Ohio; clk.-treas. Jefferson Local Sch. Dist. Named Citizen of Yr., 1963; decorated Am. Theatre medal, Asiatic Pacific medal, Philippine Liberation medal. Mem. Assn. of Govt. Accts., Nat. Soc. Tax Profls., VFW (nat. aide de camp, county commdr., post commdr), Am. Legion, Amvets, Masons. Democrat. Baptist. Died Mar. 3, 2005.

SCHUTTER, MARJORIE LUCILLE, English educator, librarian; b. Tunnel Hill, Ill., May 9, 1921; d. John and Myrtle Alice (Corbit) McHugh; m. Howard Nelson Schutter June 17, 1944 (dec. 1993); children: Annamarie, John. Student, So. Ill. U., 1942-43; BA, We. Mich. U., 1947; MA in Libr. Sci., U. Mich., 1952. Tchr. elem. Mt. Olive Sch., Vienna, Ill., 1940-43; tchr. English, sch. libr. Romulus (Mich.) H.S., 1947-52, Milan (Mich.) H.S., 1954-59; instr. English Huntington (Ind.) Coll., 1953-54; instr. English, libr. U. Wis., Stevens Point, 1959-62; asst. prof. English, libr. sci. Northwestern Coll., Orange City, Iowa, 1964-75; sub. tchr. Williamsburg (Kans.) Schs., 1987-92; tchr. English Williamsburg H.S., 1976-87; tchr. ESL Small World, Lawrence, Kans., from 1994. Lectr. to cmty. groups and chs. Cpl. U.S. Army Air Force, 1943-45. Mem. AAUW (Outstanding Mem. of Yr. 1996), Am. Assn. Ret. Persons, Am. Assn. Ret. Tchrs. (v.p. 1995). Avocations: travel, reading, studying spanish, studying computers, piano. Home: Anchorage, Alaska. Died July 16, 2004.

SCHUTZ, JOHN ADOLPH, historian, educator, former university dean; b. LA, Apr. 10, 1919; s. Adolph J. and Augusta K. (Gluecker) Schutz. AA, Bakersfield Coll., 1940; BA, UCLA, 1942, MA, 1943, PhD, 1945. Asst. prof. history Calif. Inst. Tech., Pasadena, 1945—53; assoc. prof. history Whittier Coll., Calif., 1953—56, prof., 1956—65; prof. Am. history U. So. Calif., L.A., 1965—91, chmn. dept. history, 1974—76, dean social scis. and communication, 1976—82. Author: William Shirley: King's Governor of Massachusetts, 1961, Peter Oliver's Origin and Progress of the American Rebellion, 1967, The Promise of America, 1970, The American Republic, 1978, Dawning of America, 1981, Spur of Fame: Dialogues of John Adams and Benjamin Rush, 1980, 2001, A Noble Pursuit: A Sesquicentennial History of the New England Historic Genealogical Society, 1995, Legislators of the Massachusetts General Court, 1691-1780, 1997; joint editor: Golden State Series; contbg. author: Spain's Colonial Outpost, 1985, Generations and Change: Genealogical Perspectives in Social History, 1986, Making of America: Society and Culture of the United States, 1990, rev. edit., 1992, Encyclopedia Britannica. Trustee Citizens Rsch. Found., 1985—99; mem. Neighborhoodwatch of Victor Heights, L.A., from 1999, v.p., from 2004; officer Neighborhood Coun. L.A., from 2002; mem. Hist. Cultural Neighborhood Coun., from 2002. NEH grantee, 1971; Sr. Faculty grantee, 1971-74; U. Calif. fellow, 1944-45. Mem. Am. Hist. Assn. (pres. Pacific Coast br. 1972-73, sec.-treas. 1951-88, 95-96), Am. Studies Assn. (pres. 1974-75), Mass. Hist. Soc. (corr.), New Eng. Hist. Geneal. Soc. (trustee 1988-2000, trustee emeritus 2001—, editor, author intro. book Boston Merchant Census of 1789, 1989, rec. sec. 1995-96), Colonial Soc. Mass. (corr.) Home: La Habra, Calif. Died Nov. 5, 2005; Los Angeles.

SCHWAB, NELSON, JR., lawyer; b. Cin., July 19, 1918; s. Nelson Sr. and Frances Marie (Carlile) S.; m. Elizabeth Bakhaus (div.); m. Sylvia Lambert; children: Nelson III, Richard O. BA, Yale U., 1940; LLB, Harvard U., 1943. Bar: Ohio 1947. Ptnr. Graydon Head & Ritchey, Cin., 1947-95; sr. counsel, from 1995. Bd. dirs. Rotex, Inc., Ralph J. Stolle co., Security Rug Cleaning Co., Yoder Die Casting Corp. Grants Review Com. The Greater Cin. Found.; mem. Cin. Pub. Schs. Degration Task Force; former chmn. bd. Vol. Lawyers for the Poor Found.; trustee Cin. Scholarship Found., FISC; adv. bd. Cin. Playhouse in the Park;; past mem., sec. Cin. Bus. Com., 1977-88, mm. Schs. Task Force; past mem. Cin. City Mgr.'s Working Rev. Com. 2000 Plan, chmn. Reconstituted 2000 Plan Rev. Com., 1990; pres. Greater Cin. C. of C., 1973; chmn. Greater Cin. Ednl. TV, 1965-70, hon. trustee; chmn. Cincinnati and Hamilton County Am. Red Cross, 1955-57, hon. trustee; incorporator United Appeal, 1955; mem. Cin. Sch. Bd., 1959-64. Honoree Greater Cin. Region NCCJ, 1990; Great Living Cincinnatian Grater Cin. C. of C., 1991 Mem. 6th Cir. Jud. Conf., Cin. Country Club (past bd. dirs., sec.), Commonwealth Club (past pres.), Comml. Club, Recess Club (past pres.), Gyro Club (past pres.), Queen City Club, Queen City Optimists (past pres.), Cin. Yale Club (past pres.), Lincoln's Inn Soc., Delta Kappa Epsilon. Home: Cincinnati, Ohio. Died Apr. 9, 2005.

SCHWAB, PAUL JOSIAH, psychiatrist, educator; b. Waxahachie, Tex., Jan. 14, 1932; s. Paul Josiah and Anna Marie (Baeuerle) Schwab; m. Martha Anne Beed, June 8, 1953; children: Paul Josiah III, John Conrad, Mark Whitney. BA, North Ctrl. Coll., 1953; MD, Baylor U., 1957. Diplomate Am. Bd. Psychiatry and Neurology. Intern Phila. Gen. Hosp., 1957—58; clin. assoc. Nat. Cancer Inst., Bethesda, Md., 1958—60; resident internal medicine U. Chgo., 1960—62, resident psychiatry, 1962—65, chief resident, instr. psychiatry, 1965, lectr. psychiatry, 1968—74, assoc. prof., 1974—79, clin. assoc., 1979—86, clin. assoc. prof., from 1986, dir. residency tng., 1976—79, dir. in-patient unit and day treatment program, 1975—79; pvt. practice Naperville, Ill., 1965—2004; cand. Chgo. Psychoanalytic Inst., 1970—72. Clin. instr. dept. psychiatry U. Ill., Chgo., 1965—66; vis. lectr. in psychology North Ctrl. Coll., 2002—03. Contbr. articles to profl. jours. Pres. North Ctrl. Coll. Alumni Assn., 1979—80; trustee North Ctrl. Coll., chair liaison com., 1983—2004, vice-chmn. acad. and student affairs com., 1983—92, vice chair admissions fin. aid and student devel., 1992—95. Recipient Outstanding

Alumnus, North Ctrl. Coll., 1983, Gael D. Swing award, 2001. Fellow: Am. Psychiat. Assn. (life Nancy C.A. Roeske award 1991); mem.: AMA, Am. Soc. Clin. Psychopharmacology, Alpha Omega Alpha. Democrat. Methodist. Died Oct. 25, 2004.

SCHWAM, MARVIN ALBERT, graphic design company executive; b. Newark, Apr. 18, 1942; s. Meyer and Fannie (Lerman) S.; m. Jeanette Fein, June 13, 1964; children; Frederic, Matthew. BFA, Cooper Union, 1964. Staff artist Domerus & Co., 1964-66; mgr. Flowerental Corp., N.Y.C., 1966-68; pres. M. Schwam Floralart, N.Y.C., 1968-76; exec. v.p., bd. chmn. Florenco Foliate Systems Corp., N.Y.C., 1975-88; pres., chmn. bd. Am. Christmas Decorating Svc., Inc., N.Y.C., 1989—2005. Res. Marc Shaw Graphics, Inc., N.Y.C., Florenco Graphics Systems, Inc.; exec. v.p. Display Arts Worldwide, 1975-88; pres. Creative Animations, Inc., 1988-90; creative dir., v.p. Rennoc Animations, Inc., 1988-90; pres. Almar Comm., Ltd., 1990-94, Sayso Comm., Ltd., 1990-95, Gay Entertainment TV, Inc., 1992-99, Forma Studio Gallery, 1999-2005; chmn. bd., pres. Union Sq. Ceramic Ctr., 2002. Industry chmn. March of Dimes, 1975-78, pres. bd. dirs. Happi Found for Austic People, N.Y.C.; trustee Nat. Found. Jewish Genetic Diseases; patron Young Adult Inst. and Workshop, Inc.; co-chmn. restaurant, hotel and entertainment industry lincheon Boy Scouts Am., 1988-96; chmn. benefit com. Plan Internat. USA, 1991-92; pres. Union Square Ceramic Ctr., 2002-05. Recipient award of merit for svc. to GM Corp., 1978, award for Highlight of Christmas Citibank/Citicorp Ctr., 1978, Disting. Svc. award Coler Hosp., 1982-86, Sr. Citizens of Roosevelt Island. Mem. Mcpl. Art Soc. N.Y., Am. Mus. Natural History, Alumni Assn. Cooper Union (2d Century Soc. fellow), Internat. Platform Assn. Achievements include designer largest artificial Christmas tree in U.S., Radio City Music Hall, N.Y.C., 1979; decorator Pulitzer Fountain, N.Y.C., 1979-80 Christmas season; chief designer Town Sq., New Orleans, Christmas, 1981, Albany Tricentennial, 1986; interior landscape designer La. State Pavillion World's Fair, New Orleans, 1984. Home: New York, NY. Died Dec. 10, 2005.

SCHWARTZ, ARMOND G., lawyer; b. Houston, July 26, 1914; s. Marcus and Jessie Rose (Gluck) S.; m. Jean Carolyn Nussbaum, June 8, 1946; children: Marcus Frank, Armond G. Jr. BA, JD with highest honors, U. Tex., 1938. Bar: Tex. 1937, U.S. Dist. Ct. (so. dist.) Tex. 1939, U.S. Dist. Ct. (we. dist.) Tex. 1941, U.S. Dist. Ct. (no. and ea. dists.) Tex. 1951, U.S. Ct. Appeals (5th cir.) 1951. City atty. City of Hallettsville, Tex., 1939-94. County atty. Lavaca County, Tex., 1950-58; pvt. atty., Tex. Fellow Tex. Bar Found. (life); mem. ABA (former stat chmn. jr. bar conf.), State Bar Tex., Order of Coif, Rotary Club Hallettsville (dir., pres.). Avocations: hunting, fishing. Home: Hallettsville, Tex. Died June 2, 2004.

SCHWARTZ, BARBARA ANN, artist; b. Phila., Aug. 23, 1948; d. Jacob and Esther (Sheffer) S. BFA, Carnegie Mellon U., 1970. Instr. The Sch. of Visual Arts, N.Y.C., 1977-2005, Parsons Sch. of Art and Design, N.Y.C., 1974-76; panelist Nat. Found. for Advancement in Arts, 1990-93; asst. prof. Hunter Coll., N.Y.C., 1988-89; vis. artist The Cooper Union, N.Y.C., 1985-86. One-woman shows include Willard Gallery, N.Y.C., 1993-94, Andre Zarre Gallery, N.Y.C. 1996, 2000, 03, Hirschl & Adler Modern, N.Y.C., 1987, 91, 92, Green Gallery, Miami, Fla., 1990, Koplin Gallery, L.A., 1983, Morris Gallery, Pa. Acad. Fine Arts, Phila., 1988, others; group shows include Whitney Biennials, 1975, 79, others; work represented in numerous pub. collections. Grantee N.Y. State Coun., 1982-83. Home: New York, NY. Died May 8, 2006.

SCHWARTZ, EDWARD LESTER, retired lawyer; b. N.Y.C., July 13, 1910; s. Alexander and Serene (Brown) S.; m. Edna B. Smith, July 31, 1941 (dec.); 1 child, Andrea Helen Saiet. BA, CCNY, 1931; JD, Harvard U., 1934. Bar: N.Y. 1935, Mass. 1939. Pvt. practice, N.Y.C., 1935-39, Boston, 1939-90. Lectr. law Boston U., Northeastern U., Suffolk U., New Eng. Law Inst., Mass. Continuing Legal Edn. Inst.; asst. atty. gen. State of Mass., 1970-75; commr. Nat. Conf. Commrs. on Uniform Laws (life); chmn. spl. com. Uniform Securities Act, spl. com. Landlord/Tenant Relationship Act; Mass. commr. Interstate Coop., 1949-74. Author: Lease Drafting in Massachusetts, 1961, updated 1996; contbr. articles to profl. jours. Mem. ABA, Am. Law Inst. (life), Am. Judicature Soc., Boston Bar Assn., Mass. Bar Assn. (lectr.), Scribes, New Eng. Law Inst. (exec. com.), Mass. Continuing Legal Edn. (bd. dirs.). Home: Weston, Mass. Died May 25, 2004.

SCHWARTZ, HAROLD DANIEL, consulting company executive; b. Chgo., Jan. 4, 1926; s. Irving E. and Belle (Galler) S.; m. Molly Ann Kamin, June 26, 1949 (dec. Dec. 1985); m. Lee Ducat, Apr. 5, 1987; children: Lynn, Susan, Mark. BS in Mktg. and Bus. Adminstrn., U. Ill., 1949. V.p. advt. Neon Products, Inc., Lima, Ohio, 1949-71; v.p. sales and mktg., pres. Chez & Schwartz, Inc., Chgo., from 1972. Bd. dirs. Cobra Electronics Corp. (formerly Dynascan Corp.), Chgo., Ariz. Instrument Corp., DCA Rsch. Found., Inc.; co-chairperson NIH Conf., Bethesda, 1986. Pres. Nat. Kidney Found. of Ill., Chgo., 1963-66; v.p. Nat. Kidney Found., N.Y.C., 1971-72, chmn. 1978-79; adv. coun. Nat. Inst. of Diabetes, Digestive and Kidney Disease, NIH, Bethesda, 1981-90. With USN, 1944-46. Named Man of Yr., Nat. Kidney Found. of Ill., 1986; recipient Gift of Life award, 1987, Vol. Svc. award, 1970, Martin Wagner award, 1975, Nat. Kidney Found., Disting. Svc. award Am. Soc. Nephrology, 1987. Avocations: golf, reading, volunteer work. Home: Chicago, Ill. Died May 8, 2005.

SCHWARTZ, JAMES HARRIS, neurobiologist, educator; b. N.Y.C., Apr. 20, 1932; s. Milton An. and Marjorie A. (Bloom) S.; m. Frances Messik, June 30, 1963 (dec. 1984); children: Peter Joseph, Margaret Clare; m. Catherine Bing Lipkin, 1988; stepchildren Jonathan Lipkin. AB, Columbia U., 1954; MD, NYU, 1959; PhD, Rockefeller U., 1964. Asst. prof. microbiology NYU Sch. Medicine, 1964-67, assoc. prof., 1967-72, prof., 1972-74; assoc. mem. Pub. Health Rsch. Inst. City of N.Y., 1969-74; prof. physiology Columbia U. Coll. Physicians and Surgeons, 1974-76, prof. physiology and cellular biophysics, prof. neurology, 1976—2006, prof. psychiatry, 1992—2006. Investigator Howard Hughes Med. Inst., 1984-92; vis. scholar N.Y. Psycho Analytic Inst., 1990; vis. prof. Weitzmann Inst., 1987, Nat. Inst. Dental Rsch., 1991; cons. Nat. Inst. Neurol. and Communicative Disorders and Stroke; Wesley Spink lectr. in comparative medicine U. Minn., 1989; Janssen disting. lectr. Soc. Neurosurg. Anesthesia and Critical Care, 1981, 89, 91; vis. fellow Oxford U., 1992-93. Co-editor: Principles of Neural Science, 1981; mem. edit. bd. of Brain Rsch., 1975-84, Jour. Neurophysiology, 1980-83, Jour. Neurosci., 1980-86, sect. editor, 1986-92; mem. edit. bd. Molecular Brain Rsch., 1985; contbr. articles to profl. jours. Bd. dirs. Hebrew Free Loan Soc., 1976. Recipient Selman A. Waksman lectureship award Theobald Smith Soc., 1968, Lucy G. Moses prize in basic neurology, 1980, Solomon A. Berson Med. Alumni Achievement award in basic sci. NYU Sch. Medicine, 1988. Fellow Am. Numis. Soc.; mem. AAAS, Am. Soc. Biochemistry and Molecular Biology, Soc. Neurosci., Am. Soc. Neurochemistry, N.Y. Acad. Scis., Harvey Soc., Numismatic Soc. (former trustee), Sigma Xi. Died Mar. 13, 2006.

SCHWARTZ, JOAN LAM, computer graphics consultant, writer, artist; b. Phila., Dec. 19, 1928; d. Alfred C. and Sara (Maybaum) Lam; m. Arthur J. Schwartz, Sept. 17, 1952; children: Charles, Dona. BArch, U. Pa., 1951; MA in Adminstrn., Antioch U., 1983; postgrad., Northrop U., 1984. Cert. community coll. instr., Calif. Archtl. designer Pullinger, Stevens, Bruder and Assocs., Phila., 1951-52; pvt. practice Phila., 1952-75; acct. exec. Fahnestock and Co., N.Y. Stock Exch., Phila., 1975-80; rsch. cons. The Rand Corp., Santa Monica, Calif., 1982-83; rsch. analyst Info. Displays, Inc., L.A., 1984-85, Info. Internat., Inc., Culver City, Calif., 1985; computer graphics cons. L.A., from 1985. One man shows Barzansky Galleries, N.Y.C., 1966, 68; represented in mus. collections; contbr. articles to profl. jours. Recipient nat. 3d prize Beaux Arts Inst. Design, 1949, Benedictine award, 1967, honorable mention Corel Draw Internat. Design Contest, 1991, Excellence award Corel Internat. Design Contest, 1993. Mem.: Siggraph, Assn. Computing Machinery. Democrat. Avocations: golf, photography, bridge, travel. Died Jan. 7, 2004.

SCHWARTZ, LENORA, school nurse; b. Phila., Jan. 15, 1946; m. Allen H. Schwartz; children: Gary, Eric. Diploma in nursing, Thomas Jefferson U., 1966; BS in Edn., Temple U., 1971, MEd, 1974. RN, Pa.; cert. sch. nurse. Instr. nursing Thomas Jefferson U., Phila.; supr. Chandler Hall, Newtown, Pa.; sch. nurse and svcs. coord. Council Rock Sch. Dist., Richboro, Pa. Mem. Bucks County Sch. Nurse Assn. (past pres.), Pa. State Edn. Assn. (pres. dept. pupil svcs. Mideastern region). Home: Richboro, Pa. Died Apr. 18, 2005.

SCHWARTZ, MELVIN, retired physics professor, laboratory administrator; b. NYC, Nov. 2, 1932; s. Harry and Hannah (Shulman) Schwartz; m. Marilyn Fenster, Nov. 25, 1953; children: David N., Diane R.; 1 child, Betty Lynn. AB, Columbia U., 1953, PhD, 1958, DSc (hon.), 1991; DSc, Weizmann Inst. Sci., 1995. Assoc. physicist Brookhaven Nat. Lab., 1956—58; mem. faculty Columbia U., NYC, 1958—66, prof. physics, 1963—66, NYC, 1991—94, I.I. Rabi prof. physics, emeritus, 1994—2006; prof. physics Stanford U., Calif., 1966—83, cons. prof., 1983—91; chmn. Digital Pathways, Inc., Mountain View, Calif., 1970—91; assoc. dir. High Energy and Nuclear Physics Brookhaven Nat. Lab., Upton, NY, 1991—94. Co-discoverer muon neutrino, 1962; author: Principles of Electrodynamics, 1987. Weizmann Inst. Sci. Co-recipient Nobel prize in Physics, 1988; recipient John Jay award, Columbia Coll., 1989, Alexander Hamilton medal, Columbia U., 1995; fellow Guggenheim, 1968. Fellow: Am. Phys. Soc. (Hughes award 1964); mem.: NAS. Died Aug. 28, 2006.

SCHWARTZ, MILTON LEWIS, retired judge; b. Oakland, Calif., Jan. 20, 1920; s. Colman and Selma (Lavenson) S.; m. Barbara Ann Moore, May 15, 1942; children: Dirk L., Tracy Ann, Damon M., Brooke. AB, U. Calif., Berkeley, 1941, JD, 1948. Bar: Calif. bar 1949. Rsch. asst. 3d Dist. Ct. Appeal, Sacramento, 1948; dep. dist. atty., 1949-51; practice in Sacramento, 1951-79; partner McDonough, Holland, Schwartz & Allen, 1953-79; judge U.S. Dist. Ct. (ea. dist.) Calif., 1979-90, sr. judge, 1990—2005. Prof. law McGeorge Coll. Law, Sacramento, 1952-55; mem. Com. Bar Examiners Calif., 1971-75 Pres. Bd. Edn. Sacramento City Sch. Dist., 1961; v.p. Calif. Bd. Edn., 1967-68; trustee Sutterville Heights Sch. Dist. Served to maj. 40th Inf. Divsn. AUS, 1942-46, PTO. Named Sacramento County Judge of Yr., 1990; Milton L. Schwartz Am. Inn of Court named in his honor, Davis, Calif. Fellow Am. Coll. Trial Lawyers; mem. State Bar Calif., Am. Bar Assn., Am. Bd. Trial Advocates, Anthony M. Kennedy Am. Inn of Ct. (pres. 1988-90, pres. emeritus 1990-2005). Died Oct. 3, 2005.

SCHWARTZ, ROBERT J., brokerage house executive; b. N.Y.C., Oct. 2, 1917; s. Joseph and Helen (Morvay) S.; m. Beatrice Shiner, June 27, 1941 (div. 1962); 1 child, Robert J. Jr.; m. Josephine Diaz, Jan. 29, 1967. BS, CCNY, 1940; MA, Columbia U., 1943; PhD in Econs., Am. U., Washington, 1957. Dir. divsn. internat. stats. US Dept. Treasury, Washington, 1941-53; economist Columbia Pictures Corp., N.Y.C., 1953; sr. v.p. Amalgamated Bank of N.Y., N.Y.C., 1954-62; v.p. Israel Discount Bank Ltd., N.Y.C., 1962-66; sr. fund analyst Bache & Co. Inc., N.Y.C., 1966-69; adj. assoc. prof. Baruch Coll., N.Y.C., 1969-89; sr. v.p. Smith Barney Shearson Inc., N.Y.C. Contbr. articles to profl. jours. Bd. dirs. SANE/FREEZE, N.Y.C., Social Investment Forum, Washington; treas. Advocates for Children, N.Y.C.; treas., trustee Economists Allied for Arms Reduction, N.Y.C.; mem. Friends of China. Capt. USMC, 1944-46. Mem. Internat. Assn. Univ. Pres.'s (steering commn.), Nat. Emergency Civil Liberties Union. Avocations: swimming, reading, theater. Home: New York, NY. Died May 9, 2006.

SCHWARTZ, THERESE, freelance/self-employed artist; b. N.Y.C., Dec. 7, 1928; d. David and Rose (Allen) Matt. Student, Bklyn. Mus. Art Sch., 1945-46, Corcoran Mus. Art Sch., 1947-49, Am. U., 1951-53. Freelance artist N.Y.C. One-woman shows include Barnet Aden Gallery, Washington, 1953, Travelling Watercolor Show, 1954, Howard U., Washington, 1952, Hacker Gallery, N.Y.C., 1953, Urban Gallery, N.Y.C., 1955, Parma Gallery, N.Y.C., 1959, 60, 61, East Hampton Gallery, 1965, 66, A.M. Sachs Gallery, N.Y.C., 1969, 70, Rutgers U., N.J., 1973, Angerer Gallery, Kansas City, Mo., 1974, Arnot Art Mus., Elmira, N.Y., 1975, Landmark Gallery, N.Y., 1976, 78, Gloria Cortella, N.Y., 1979, Tallgrass Fine Arts, Kansas City, 1981, Barbara Fiedler Gallery, Washington, 1982, Galerie Fabian Walter, BAsel, Switzerland, 1986, Humphrey Fine Art, N.Y.C., 1989, 92, 95, Duke U. Med. Ctr., 1993, B.F. Goodrich Co., Cleve., 1995; group shows include Grey Gallery, NYU, 1981, Arnot Art Mus., 1981, Freedman Gallery, Albright Coll., Reading, Pa., 1980, Tyler Sch. Art, Phila., 1978, Van Doren Gallery, San Francisco, 1978, Leo Castelli Gallery, N.Y., 1975, Corcoran Gallery Art, Washington 1976; represented in permanent collections Bklyn. Mus., William Rockhill Nelson Gallery Art, Kansas City, Herbert F. Johnson Mus., Cornell U., Ithaca, N.Y., Edwin A. Ulrich Mus., Wichita State U., Ciba-Geigy Corp., Ardsley, N.Y., Corcoran Gallery Art, Smithsonian Inst., Washington, Advanced Elastomer Systems, Akron, Ohio, Howard U. Art Gallery, Washington, Rutgers U. Gallery, New Brunswick, N.J., Arnot Art Mus., Elmira, N.Y., Albright Mus, Freedman Gallery, Reading, Pa., Reading Pub. Mus., Lehigh U. Art Gallery, Bethlehem, Pa., Huntington Mus., Pasadena, Calif., Pepsico Corp., Purchase, N.Y., numerous others; contbr. articles to profl. jours. Home: New York, NY. Died Oct. 6, 2005.

SCHWARZ, ECKHARD CHRISTIAN AUGUST, chemical executive; b. Lubeck, Fed. Rep. of Germany, Nov. 13, 1930; s. Christian and Alwine (von der Heyde) S.; m. Elke Tilgner, July 2, 1960 (div. Dec. 1976), children: Hartmut, Birgit, Roland, Bernhard. Diploma, U. Hamburg, 1956; PhD, McGill U., 1962. Sr. research chemist DuPont & Co., Kinston, N.C., 1962-68, process engr. Uentrupp, Germany, 1972-73; group leader research Kimberly Clark, Neenah, Wis., 1968-72; dir. research and devel. Presto Products, Appleton, Wis., 1973-75; pres. Biax Fiberfilm Corp., Neenah, Wis., from 1975. Patentee in field. Mem. Am. Chem. Soc., Tech. Assn. Pulp and Paper Industry. Republican. Lutheran. Avocations: sailing, flying. Home: Neenah, Wis. Died Aug. 2, 2004.

SCHWARZ, RALPH JACQUES, retired engineering educator; b. Hamburg, Germany, June 13, 1922; naturalized, 1944; s. Simon J. and Anna (Schoendorff) S.; m. Irene Lassally, Sept. 9, 1951; children: Ronald Paul, Sylvia Anne. BS, Columbia U., 1943, MS, 1944, PhD, 1949; postgrad., Poly. Inst. Bklyn., 1944-45, N.Y. U., 1946-47. Registered profl. engr., N.Y. Mem. faculty Columbia U., 1943-92, prof. elec. engring., 1958-92, chmn. dept., 1958-65, 71-72, assoc. dean acad. affairs Faculty Engring. and Applied Sci., 1972-75, acting dean, 1975-76, 80-81, vice dean, Thayer Lindsley prof., 1976-92, Thayer Lindsley prof. emeritus, 1992—2006; cons. systems analysis, communications and noise theory, 1945—2006. Vis. assoc. prof. UCLA, 1956; adviser Inst. Internat. Edn., 1952-65; vis. scientist IBM Research Center, 1969-70 Author: (with M.G. Salvadori) Differential Equations in Engineering Problems, 1954, (with B. Friedland) Linear Systems, 1965. Bd. dirs. Armstrong Meml. Research Found.; trustee Associated Univs., Inc., 1980-92. Fellow: IEEE (chmn. circuit theory group 1963—65, Centennial medal 1984). Home: New Rochelle, NY. Died Jan. 2, 2006.

SCHWARZKOPF, ELISABETH, soprano; b. Jarotschin, Poland, Dec. 9, 1915; m. Walter Legge, 1953 (dec. 1979). Student, Berlin Hochschule für Musik, 1934; pvt. studies with Maria Ivogün; MusD (hon.), Cambridge U. Debut at Berlin Städtische Opera, 1938, U.S. debut at San Francisco, 1955; appearances include Vienna Staatsopera, 1944, Covent Garden, 1947, La Scala Milan, 1953, Chgo. Lyric Opera, 1959, Met. Opera, 1964, Salzburg Festival, 1947-64, many others; numerous recs. Decorated Medal of the Unesco,

1991; named Dame Comdr. of Order of Brit. Empire, 1992; recipient Grosses Verdienst-Kreuz, Germany. Mem. Wiener Staatsoper (hon.), Berliner Staatsoper (hon.). Died Aug. 3, 2006.

SCHWERIN, JULES VICTOR, director, filmmaker, journalist; b. N.Y.C., Feb. 4, 1919; s. Charles Frederic and Jeannette (Solomon) S.; m. Doris Belle Halpern, Mar. 2, 1946; 1 child, Charles Norman. Student, Northwestern U., 1940, The New Bauhaus, 1941. Jr. economist War Prodn. Bd., Washington, 1941-44, Office of War Info., N.Y., 1941-44; ind. filmmaker documentaries, 1948-50; documentary filmmaker The Loves of Franistan, 1948; writer Ben Grauer's Daily program Sta. WNBC, 1950; documentary filmmaker Indian Summer, 1953; supervising producer RKO/Pathe Studios, Culver City, Calif., 1951-52; prod. mgr. ind. film Salt of the Earth, N.Mex., 1952-53; dir. The Morning Show CBS-TV, N.Y.C., 1954; dir., writer Eric Sevareid's The American Week, 1955; dir. Filmways, Inc., N.Y.C., 1955-56; assoc. producer Bell Telephone Hour, N.Y.C., 1957-58; dir. Westinghouse Children's Programs, 1960-61; with post prodn. Judgment at Nuremburg, United Artists, 1963; writer, dir. Fortune and Men's Eyes MGM, Can., 1969-70; freelance journalist Parade, N.Y.C., from 1986. Editor: Encyclopedia Americana, 1960; contbg. editor: Year, 1953, Flight, 1954, The Bulletin, 1974-75, Assn. Photo Journalists Mag. Pub. Jour.; screenwriter, dir., producer Mahalia Jackson--Got to Tell It (Grammy award 1976); dir. (film) A Publisher Is Known By the Company He Keeps (Cine Golden Eagle award); producer (film) Dialogue with Blanche and Alfred A. Knopf, 1960; assoc. producer (TV miniseries) Twist of Fate, 1989; author: The Wedding, 1985, Got To Tell It, 1992 (Deems Taylor award ASCAP 1993), Mahalia Jackson, Queen of Gospel; prodr. (audio cassette) I Sing Because I'm Happy, Mahalia Jackson Speaks For Herself. Named hon. citizen City of Lafayette, La., 1967. Mem. Dirs. Guild Am. Jewish. Avocations: reading, films, gardening. Died Feb. 8, 2004.

SCHWICHTENBERG, DARYL ROBERT, drilling engineer; b. nr. Tulare, S.D., Nov. 8, 1929; s. Robert Carl and Lillian Rose (Hardie) S.; m. Helen M. Spencer, 1955 (div. Jan. 1971); children: Helayne, Randall, Hyalyn, Halcyon, Rustan; m. Helen Elizabeth Doehring, Nov. 11, 1971 (div. May 1982); 1 child, Suzanne. Student, U. Wyo., 1954-55; BSME, S.D. Sch. Mines and Tech., 1957; postgrad., Alexander Hamilton Inst., N.Y.C., 1962-63. Lic. pilot, rated AMEL. Office engr. Ingersoll-Rand Co., Mpls., 1957-58, sub br. mgr. Duluth, Minn., 1959-60, product engr. N.Y.C., 1960-63, devel. engr., 1964, sales mgr. Phillipsburg, N.J., 1965; pres., founder Daryl Drilling Co., Inc., Flagstaff, Ariz., 1965-82; pres. Silent Rose Mining Co., Fallon, Nev., 1982-85; sr. design engr. Nev. Test Site Fenix & Scisson, 1985-90; prin. project engr. Raytheon Svcs. Nev., 1990-95, project mgr. Nev. Test Site, 1995-96; asst.project mgr. Bechtel Nev., Las Vegas, from 1996. Co-owner, mgr. Dead Shot Ranch, Bondurant, Wyo., 1977-82. Inventor electronic subtitling for opera patrons. 1st lt. U.S. Army, 1950-54, Korea. Decorated Bronze Star. Mem. ASME, NRA, VFW, Inst. Shaft Drilling Tech. (speaker, instr. 1986-96), Am. Legion, Mensa, Ducks Unlimited, The Will James Soc. Republican. Avocations: hunting, raising and training horses, flying, prospecting. Home: Great Falls, Mont. Died July 2.

SCOFIELD, RODERICK ARTHUR, meteorologist, researcher, educator; b. Louisville, Dec. 3, 1942; s. Edward Harold and Hortense Alice (Gillespie) S.; m. Eileen Joyce Wiedmar, Aug. 22, 1964; children: Michelle Eileen, Matthew Roderick, Brett Edward. BS in Physics, U. Louisville, 1964; MS in Meteorology, U. St. Louis, 1969, PhD in Meteorology, 1973. Rschr. Nat. Weather Svc., Silver Springs, Md., 1972-74; rschr. flood prediction, precipitation forecaster Nat. Environ. Satellite Data Information Svc., Camp Springs, Md., 1974—2006. Cons. Project Atmosphere, Washington, 1984-2006; tchr. meteorol. enhancement program. Contbr. articles to profl. jours. including Monthly Weather Review, Remote Sensing Review, Bull. Am. Meteorol. Soc., Am. Geophys. Union Newsletter. Recipient bronze medal NOAA, 1989, medal Weather Bureau of Taiwan, 1992, gold medal for outstanding rsch. and leadership in developing flash flood forecasting techniques using satellite data Dept. Commerce, 1999; named U. Louisville Arts and Scis. Alumni Fellow of Yr., 2000; fellow Univ. Louisville Arts and Sci. Alumni, 2000. Fellow: Am. Meteorol. Soc. (Reichelderfer award 1999, bronze awards for edn. and tng. flash flood forecasting techniques 1999, bronze award for edn. and tng. flash flood forecasting techniques 2001); mem.: Am. Geophys. Union, Nat. Weather Assn. (pres.-elect 1999, pres. 2000, outstanding contbns. award 1986), Sigma Xi. Episcopalian. Achievements include the development of a neural network (expert system) algorithm that uses geostationary and polar microwave date for diagnosing flash floods around the world. Home: Pomfret, Md. Died Feb. 25, 2006.

SCOGGINS, ROBERT CONROY, deacon, employee benefits administrator; b. Houston, Apr. 29, 1935; s. Robert Conroy and Gertrude Adelle (Crenshaw) S.; m. Trula Delle Harrison, July 25, 1959; children: Robert C. III, Lynn Ann, Katherine Camille. BS, U. Houston, 1957; postgrad., U. Dallas, 1971-74. Permanent deacon St. Mark Roman Cath. Ch., Plano, Tex., from 1974; mgr. employee benefits Ben E. Keith Co., Dallas, from 1977. Lector, reader St. Francis de Sales Ch., Houston, 1962-67; acolyte St. Mark Roman Cath. Ch., Plano, 1966-67. With USAF, 1958-64. Fellow Inst. Life Ins. Coun.; mem. Am. Coll. Life Underwriters (cert. 1971), K.C. (grand knight 1966-67). Republican. Home: Richardson, Tex. Died Feb. 9, 2004.

SCOTT, CHARLES EDMUND, real estate corporation officer, consultant; b. Balt., Nov. 26, 1933; s. Edmund Champayne and Gladys (Worrell) S., m. Patricia Ann Mettee; children: Richard, Brian A. BS in Bus. Mgmt., U. Balt., 1956. Cert. sr. profl. human resources. Mgr. employee relations Bata Shoe Co., Belcamp, Md., 1956-59; sales mgr. Adm. Constrn. Corp., Balt., 1960-61; employment mgr. A.L. Mathias Co., Balt., 1961-63; personnel mgr. Washington Aluminum Co., Balt., 1963-70; dir. human resources The Sheppard & Enoch Pratt Hosp., Towson, Md., 1970-86; prin. Diversified Human Resources Services, Aberdeen, Md., from 1986. Mem. Civil Services Bd. Harford County, Bel Air, Md., 1970-72; chmn. Personnel Adv. Bd. Harford County, Bel Air, 1972-76, ambulance com. Md. State Firemen's Assn., 1980-85; capt. ambulance and rescue Abingdon (Md.) Fire Co., 1974-80; pres. Personnel Assn. Greater Balt., 1977-78, Sheppard Pratt Fed. Credit Union, Towson, 1985-86; mgr. Churchville Pirates Unltd. Baseball Team. Mem. Am. Soc. Personnel Adminstrn. Republican. Methodist. Bush River Yacht (Abingdon); Old Timers Baseball (Balt.). Home: Abingdon, Md. Died Mar. 24, 2005.

SCOTT, DAVID WILLIAM, financial executive; b. Ellwood City, Pa., Mar. 23, 1950; s. George Alfonso and Lucille Laura (Shoaf) S.; m. Sheila Anne Terrels, Sept. 18, 1971; children: Sean, Ryan. BS in Bus., U. Pitts., 1975, MBA in Fin., 1979. From trainee to acct. to jr. cost acct. Union RR Co., Pitts., 1975-78, cost analyst, 1978-79, sr. cost analyst, 1979; supr./analyst USS Fabrication, Ambridge, Pa., 1979-81; supr. govtl. accounting U.S. Steel, Homestead, Pa., 1981-83; mgr. cost, inventory and payroll Teledyne Rodney Metals, New Bedford, Mass., 1983-86; fin. advisor Teledyne, Inc., Latrobe, Pa., from 1986. Controller CC Industries div. of Teledyne Inc.; asst. sec. Merla Inc. subs. Teledyne Inc. Home: Xenia, Ohio. Died Mar. 13, 2004.

SCOTT, DOROTHY HELEN, organization official, actress; b. Denver, July 24, 1923; d. William Henry and Helen Mae (Foster) Williams; m. William John Scott, Apr. 28, 1943 (dec. Nov. 1985); children: John, Barbara, Robert. Student, U. Denver; BA cum laude, Pasadena (Calif.) Playhouse, 1968; counseling cert., U. So. Calif. With Denver Dist. Engrs., 1941-43; teletype officer So. Pacific R.R., L.A., 1943-45; speech counselor Tierra Del Sol, Sunland, Calif., 1955-62; substance abuse counselor Meml. Hosp., Glendale, Calif., 1977-82; coord., program dir. Elderhostel, Santa Paula, Calif., from 1989; storyteller Reader's Theater, from 1989. Vol. LWV, L.A. and Ventura, 1955—, substance abuse rehab. facilities, Episcopal Ch., L.A.; actress Santa Paula Theater Ctr., Elite Theater, Plaza Players, Ornard Coll., Simi Valley Cultural Ctr., 1988—; reader elem. sch. children Reader's Theater, 1989—. Home: Ventura, Calif. Died Jan. 2, 2004.

SCOTT, EUGENE LYTTON, publisher; b. NYC, Dec. 28; m. Polly Eastman, Dec. 9; children: Lucy, Samuel. BA, Yale U., 1960; JD, U. Va., 1965. Atty. Burke & Burke, NYC, 1966-68; founder, pub., editor Tennis Week, NYC, 1974—2006; tournament dir. Nabisco Masters, NYC, 1986-90; former tournament dir. Kremlin Cup, Moscow. Bd. dirs. Quadrax Corp., Providence. Author: Biorn Borgj, The Tennis Experience; editor: Rallybook, 1995, 96, Slam, 1996. Recipient William Johnston award, 1963, Souders Meml. award, 1983. Died Mar. 20, 2006.

SCOTT, IDA GATLING, retired medical/surgical nurse; b. Conway, N.C., Feb. 1, 1936; d. George W. and Izula (Cumbo) Gatling; m. Melvin V. Scott, June 3, 1966. Diploma, St. philip Sch. Nursing, Richmond, Va., 1958; BA, George Washington U., 1984. Cert. venipuncture specialist. Staff nurse Washington Hosp. Ctr., 1959—62, head nurse, 1962-76, supr. gastrointestinal room, 1980—90, nurse clinician HIV/AIDS nursing, 1992—97; ret., 1997. Lectr. in field. Panelist for consensus conf., NIH, 1989. Recipient Disting. Svc. award D.C. Area Hosp. Assn. Nurse Clinician Infusion Ctr. Home: Washington, DC. Died Aug. 17, 2005.

SCOTT, JOHN WALTER, chemical engineer, consultant; b. Berkeley, Calif., May 27, 1919; s. John Walter and Cora Viola (Wampfler) S.; m. Jane Ellen Newman, June 27, 1942; children— Nancy, Barbara, Charles, James, Richard BS in Chemistry, U. Calif., Berkeley, 1941, MSChemE, 1951. Registered profl. chem. engr., Calif. Process and catalyst research and devel. Chevron Research, Richmond, Calif., 1946-67, v.p., 1967-84, cons., 1985—2006. Contbr. articles to profl. jours.; patentee in field Trustee U. Calif.-Berkeley Found., 1985-91; adv. coun. Lawrence Hall of Sci., 1990-97; mem. coun. Town of Ross, Calif., 1992-96. Capt. U.S. Army, 1941-46. Fellow Am. Inst. Chem. Engrs. (awards com. 1979-84, award 1978), AAAS; mem. Nat. Acad. Engring., Am. Chem. Soc., Am. Petroleum Inst. (chmn. research data info. services 1971-73, 77-80, cert. of appreciation 1983) Avocations: travel, books. Home: Corte Madera, Calif. Died Jan. 3, 2006.

SCOTT, MARJORIE THOMPSON, housekeeping service executive; b. Hanover, N.H., Oct. 9, 1925; d. Charles Edwin and Maude Alice (Stark) Thompson; m. Edwin Lorton Scott, July 15, 1953; children: William, James, Robert, Sue. BEd, Plymouth State Coll., 1947. High sch. tchr. Jaffrey Sch. Dist., East Jaffrey, N.H., 1947-49, Enfield (N.H.) Sch. Dist., 1949-53, Orford (N.H.) Sch. Dist., 1953-54; teaching asst. The Amos Tuck Sch./Dartmouth Coll., Hanover, N.H., 1956-71; adminstrv. asst. Regional Ctr. for Edn. Tng., Hanover, N.H., 1971-81; sec., human resource dir. Dartmouth Printing Co., Hanover, 1981-89; housekeeping supr. Kendal at Hanover, N.H., from 1991. Treas. Hanover and Dresden Sch. Dists., 1960-80, Town of Hanover, 1977-80. Avocation: church organist. Died Mar. 6, 2004.

SCOTT, ROBERT ELLIS See ROBERTS, MARK

SCOTT, ROBERT LEE, JR., retired military officer, writer; b. Macon, Ga., Apr. 12, 1908; s. Robert Lee and Ola (Burckhalter) S.; m. Catharine Rix Green, Sept. 1, 1934; 1 child, Robin Lee Scott Fraser. Student, Mercer U., 1924-25; BS, U.S. Mil. Acad., 1932; grad., Nat. War Coll., 1954. Commd. 2d lt. Air Corps, 1932, advanced through grades to brig. gen., 1955, service in 99th Squadron Mitchel Field, 78th Pursuit Squadron Canal Zone, flying instr. Randolph Field, Tex., 1937-39, commanded Cal-Aero Acad., 1939-41, commanded 23d Fighter Group, 1942-43, fighter comdr. for Gen. Chennault, 1943-45, dep. for ops. 14th Air Force Orlando, Fla., 1945-46, wing comdr. Jet Fighter Sch. Williams Field, Ariz., 1947-49, commanded 36th Fighter Bomber Wing Furstenfeldbruck Air Base, 1950-53; dir. info. services USAF, 1954-56, comdg. gen. 3600 Crew Tng. Wing Luke AFB, Ariz., 1956-57, retired, 1957; pres. Scott Prodns., Inc., from 1957; campaign chmn. Heritage of Eagles Campaign, Mus. Aviation at Robins AFB, Warner Robins, Ga., from 1986. Author: God is My Co-Pilot, 1943, Damned to Glory, 1944, Runway to the Sun, 1945, Between the Elephant's Eyes, 1954, Samburu, 1956, Look of the Eagle, 1957, Flying Tiger, Chennault of China, 1959; Tiger in the Sky, 1959; Boring a Hole in the Sky, 1961, God is STILL My Co-Pilot, 1964, The Day I Owned the Sky, 1988. Decorated Silver Star with oak leaf cluster, D.F.C. with 2 oak leaf clusters, Air Medal with 3 oak leaf clusters, also spl. citation from Chief of Staff, AUS, 1943 (U.S.); Order of Cloud Banner; Yum Hwei, Ten Star Dragon Medal (China); Spl. War Cross form U.D.C.; D.F.C. (Great Brit.). Mem. VFW (Macon chpt.), Air Force Assn., Order of Daedalians, Profl. Hunters Assn. of East Africa, Mil. Order of World Wars, Royal Geographical Soc., Internat. Order Characters, Rotary (life), Am. Legion (Macon chpt.). Clubs: Explorers; Kiwanis (Macon). Republican. Episcopalian. Home: Warner Robins, Ga. Died Feb. 27, 2006.

SCOTT, RUTH LOIS, dental hygiene educator; b. Chanute, Kans., Aug. 28, 1934; d. Walter Roy and Ruth Lois (Cunningham) Harder; m. Charles Calvin Scott, July 3, 1956 (div. July 1963); children: Valerie Elizabeth, Matthew Stuart, David Bruce. BA in Psychology and Theatre with honors, U. Kans., 1958; Cert. in Dental Hygiene, U. Mo.-Kansas City, 1954, MS in Dental Hygiene Edn., 1972. Asst. prof. U. Iowa Coll. Dentistry, 1972—73, instr. to clin. instr. dept. dental hygiene, 1969—71, asst. prof. dept. preventive dentistry, asst. prof. comprehensive dentistry for adults, 1973—77, asst. prof. div. dental hygiene, 1977—81, assoc. prof., 1981—97; prof. emerita U. Mo.-Kansas City Sch. Dentistry, from 1998; pvt. practice dentistry Kans., Mo., from 1954. Small animal vet. cons., 1998—. Contbr. articles to profl. jours. Charter mem. Kansas City chpt. Parents Without Ptnrs. Recipient Dental Hygiene Alumni Svc. award U. Mo.-Kansas City, 1992, Dental Hygiene Alumni Achievement award, 2003; Student Coun. Instr. of Yr. award, 1992. Mem. Am. Dental Hygienists Assn., Mo. Dental Hygienists Assn., Greater Kansas City Dental Hygiene Component Soc., U. Mo.-Kansas City Dental Hygiene Alumni Assn., U. Mo.-Kansas City Alumni Assn., Kansas U. Alumni Assn., Center State Tai Chi ChuanPhi Beta Kappa, Sigma Phi Alpha (exec. sec. 1990-96), Phi Psi, Phi Kappa Phi. Unitarian-Universalist. Home: Shawnee Mission, Kans. Died July 21, 2004.

SCROGGS, ROBIN JEROME, theology educator; b. Raleigh, N.C., Oct. 14, 1930; s. James Wade Scroggs and Lucille Dowd; m. Leah Margaret Self Bennett, June 29, 1954 (div.); 1 child, Mark Wade; m. Marilee Ruth Munger, May 29, 1971; 1 child, Jonathan Paul. AB, U. N.C., 1951, B in Music, 1952; BDiv, Duke U., 1955; PhD, Princeton U., 1962. From instr. to assoc. prof. and chmn. dept. religion Dartmouth Coll., Hanover, N.H., 1959-69; assoc. prof., then prof. Chgo. Theolog. Sem., 1969-86, acting dean, 1974-75; Edward Robinson prof. Biblical theology Union Theolog. Sem., N.Y.C., 1986-97, prof. emeritus, from 1997. Lectr. numerous coll., univs. and chs. throughout U.S., Can. and Germany. Author: The Last Adam, 1967, Paul for a New Day, 1977, the New Testamentand Homosexuality, 1983, Christology in Paul and John, 1988, The Text and the Times, 1993; translator: Glory and the Way of the Cross: The Gospel of Mark, 1972; contbr. numerous articles to jours. Mem. Soc. Biblical Lit., Studiorum Novi testamenti Societas,chgo. Soc. bibllical Rsch. (pres. 1979-80), Cath. Biblical Assn. Avocations: music, keyboarding, choral conductor. Home: Pompton Plains, NJ. Died Apr. 25, 2005.

SCUDDER, CHARLES A., primary and secondary education educator; b. Madison, Ind., Aug. 8, 1916; s. Earl and Laura (Phillips) S.; children: Gary, Sharon, Shirlene. BS, Ctrl. Normal U. Comdr. USN. Mem. Masons. Republican. Baptist. Home: Boulder, Colo. Died Mar. 15, 2005.

SCUDERI, SALVATORE CARMELO, lawyer; b. Springfield, Mass., Jan. 1, 1927; s. Salvatore and Grace (Saccamando) S.; m. Esther Didomenicantonio, Oct. 12, 1963;

children: Jon, Dave. BS in Commerce, U. Notre Dame, 1953; JD, Harvard U., 1956. Bar: Mass. 1956, U.S. Dist. Ct. Mass. 1958, U.S. Supreme Ct. 1961, Fla. 1971, U.S. Dist. Ct. (so. dist.) Fla. 1973, U.S. Dist. Ct. (mid. dist.) Fla. 1978. Ptnr. Scuderi & Conway, West Springfield, Mass., 1956-72, Woodward & Scuderi, Marco Island, Fla., 1972-73; pvt. practice Marco Island, 1973-86; ptnr. Scuderi & Childs, Marco Island, from 1986. Instr. law Western New Eng. Coll. Law, Springfield, 1960-70. Pres. Pelican Bay Improvement Dist., Naples, Fla., 1974-86; chair Marco YMCA, 1977. With USN, 1944-46. Mem. ABA, Collier County Bar Assn., K.C. (grand knight 1977-78). Avocations: tennis, reading. Home: Marco Island, Fla. Died Apr. 7, 2005.

SEABOLT, CLARENCE, management executive; b. Bergoo, W.Va., Oct. 5, 1929; Cert. traffic mgr., Nebr. Mgr. traffic and purchasing Seiberling Rubber Co., Barberton, Ohio, 1954-67; rechr. Ea. Ctrl. Motor Carrier Assn., Akron, Ohio, 1967-72; distbn. mgr. Hedgestrom Corp., Ashland, Ohio, 1972-92; v.p. Logistics Mgmt. Inc., Ashland, Ohio, from 1992. Served to cpl. U.S. Army, 1951-53. Mem. Nat. Indsl. Transp. League, Distbn. and Transp. Assn. (pres. 1980-81, 86-87), Ctrl. Ohio Traffic Club (pres. 1987-88, Hall of Fame 1989). Republican. Avocations: golf, raquetball, swimming, spectator sports. Home: Ashland, Ohio. Died Sept. 16, 2004.

SEABRIGHT, FRANCES, volunteer; b. Laurium, Mich., May 17, 1912; d. Joseph Krausz and Rosa Rosenberg; m. Lawrence H. Seabright (dec.); children: Robert, Carol S. Christensen. BS, Ohio U., 1934; MS, Ohio State U., 1937. Cert. tchr. Ohio. Tchr. Portsmouth Pub. Schs., Ohio, 1934—38; chemist Sears Roebuck, Chgo., 1939—42; asst. prof. Elmhurst Coll., Ill., 1942—44, U. Ill., Chgo., 1953—80. Pk. dist. reporter League Women Voters, Elmhurst, 1988—90; election judge City Elmhurst, from 1980; vol. hist. mus., art gallery. Mem.: AAUW (hon.), Hosp. Guild, Chem. Soc. (com. chmn., pres.), Woman's Club, Travel Club. Democrat. Methodist. Avocations: travel, bridge, flower arranging. Home: Elmhurst, Ill. Died Jan. 27, 2005.

SEAGER, KATHLEEN MULEADY, psychotherapist; b. L.A., Apr. 4, 1950; d. Thomas William and Eileen (Shelley) Muleady; m. Robert Donald Seager, Sept. 9, 1972; children: Danielle Marie, Michael Donald. BA in Cultural Anthropology, U. Calif., Santa Barbera, 1972, BA in History, 1974; postgrad., U. Calif., Berkeley, 1976; MA in Counseling, U. No. Iowa, 1985. Diplomate Am. Bd. Med. Psychotherapy. Counselor CUH, Waterloo, Iowa, 1987-92; coord. grief support svcs. Cedar Valley Hospice, Waterloo, 1992-96, clin. program specialist, from 1996. Author: (tng. manual) Psycho-Social Issues of AIDS, 1987; contb. article to newsletter. Mem. Symphony Guild Waterloo-Cedar Falls Symphony, 1986—. Recipient scholarship Kennedy Found., 1987. Fellow Am. Bd. Med. Psychotherapy. Democrat. Episcopalian. Avocations: music, poetry, arts. Home: Cedar Falls, Iowa. Died May 8, 2004.

SEAGRAVE, JANET LEE, economic developer; b. Okinawa, Japan, Dec. 31, 1951; d. Rodman Gamble and Patricia Jane (McDonald) S. Student, Maple Woods Coll., 1974-78, Del Mar Coll., 1978-79. Cert. econ. developer. Exec. sec. Am. Indsl. Devel. Coun., Kansas City, Mo., 1973-78; dir. western sales Indsl. Properties Report, Corpus Christi, Tex., 1978-79; indsl. devel. location cons. Amarillo (Tex.) Bd. Devel., 1979-81; dir. econ. devel. divsn. Roswell (N.Mex.) C. of C., 1981-86; exec. dir. Sheridan (Wyo.) County Econ. Devel. Coun., 1986-90, High Plains Devel. Authority, Great Falls, Mont., 1990-94, Indsl. Devel. Corp. of Lea County, Hobbs, N.Mex., from 1994. Mem. faculty Ariz. Basic Econ. Devel. course, U. Ariz., Tucson, 1983-94. Bd. regents Am. Indsl. Devel. Coun., 1981-83, bd. dirs., 1984-88; chmn., bd. dirs., mediator, treas. Great Falls Area Labor/Mgmt. Com., 1991-94; mem. Pres.'s coun. Coll. of Great Falls, 1991-94. 9th woman in N.Am. to obtain Cert. Econ. Developer designation, 1982. Mem. Mont. Profl. Econ. Devel. Assn. (bd. dirs. 1993-94), Am. Devel. Coun. (bd. dirs. 1982-86, bd. regents 1982-84), N.Mex. Indsl. Devel. Execs. (bd. dirs. 1994—), N.Mex. Commerce and Industry Assn., Hobbs Rotary, Order of Eastern Star. Republican. Baptist. Avocations: gardening, walking, working with children, church activity. Home: Roswell, N.Mex. Died Aug. 7, 2004.

SEELBACH, CHARLES WILLIAM, retired chemist; b. Buffalo, Dec. 13, 1923; s. Charles George and Marcia (Grimes) S.; AB, Cornell U., 1948; MS, Western Res. U., 1952; PhD, Purdue U., 1955; m. Patricia O'Reilly, July 7, 1946; children: Janet, Jeanne, Paul. Group leader Ohio Rsch., Cleve., 1948-52; asst. sect. head Esso Standard Oil, Baton Rouge, 1956-57; sect. head Esso Rsch. and Engring., Linden, N.J., 1955-56, 58-63; bus. mgr. Esso Chem. Inc., N.Y.C., 1963-67; mgr. devel. USS Chems., Pitts., 1968-83; cons., 1983-89. Elder Presbyn. Ch., Cranford, N.J., also trustee. Served with USMC, 1942-46. Purdue U rsch. fellow, 1953-55. Mem. Am. Chem. Soc., Comml. Devel. Assn., Am. Mgmt. Assn., AAAS, Catalysis Soc., N.Y. Acad. Scis., Am. Oil Chemists Soc., Psi Lambda Upsilon. Patentee in field. Home: Chelsea, Mich. Died Mar. 5, 2005.

SEELEY, JAMES J., lawyer; b. Camden, N.J., July 17, 1945; s. James J. and Phyllis (Herman) S.; m. Alexis M. Popoff, June 6, 1968; children: James IV, Thomas, Elizabeth, Alexis. Student, U. Ga., 1963-64; grad., Rutgers U., 1966; LLB, Duke U., 1969. Bar: N.J. 1969, U.S. Dist. Ct. N.J. 1969, Pa. 1971, U.S. Dist. Ct. (ea. dist.) Pa. 1971, Del. 1974, U.S. Dist. Ct. Del. 1974, U.S. Ct. Appeals (3d cir.), U.S. Supreme Ct. asst. dean, prof. Rutgers U. Law Sch., Camden, N.J., 1969-71; regional counsel U.S. EPA, Phila., 1972-73; assoc. Morris, Nichols, Arsht & Tunnel, Wilmington, Del., 1973-74; ptnr. Stanger & Seeley, Bridgeton, N.J., 1975-83; sole practice Bridgeton, from 1983. Prof. law Rutgers Law Sch., Camden, 1969-79; co-adj. prof. Rutgers U., New Brunswick, N.J., 1980—; spl. counsel N.J. Legislature Judiciary Com., Trenton, 1978-79. Mcpl. atty. Greenwich Twp., 1973—, Hopewell Twp., 1980—, Commercial Twp., 1983—, Lawrence Twp., 1981—. Named One of Outstanding Young Men of Am., U.S. Jaycees, 1977. Mem. N.J. State Bar Assn., N.J. Fedn. Planners, Cumberland County Bar Assn. Died July 13, 2005.

SEFCIK, JOHN KAROL, minister; b. Johnstown, N.Y., Mar. 21, 1922; s. Karol and Johanna (Vach) S.; m. Delphine Marie Covington, July 7, 1954; children: Karolton, John D., Nathan. BA, Park Coll., 1950; BD, Princeton (N.J.) Theol. Sem., 1953, ThM, 1968. Pastor First Presbyn., Mays Landing, Tuckahoe, N.J., 1953-55, Christ Presbyn., Catskill, N.Y., 1955-58, John Hus Presbyn., Binghamton, N.Y., 1959-71; chaplain Broome County Jail, Binghamton, 1960-70; pastor S.W. United Presbyn., Detroit, 1971-87; parish assoc. First Presbyn., Dearborn, Mich., 1987-90, ret. Moderator Susquehanna Valley Presbytery, South Tier, N.Y., 1968; mem. task force on youth Binghamton, 1965, Triple Cities Urban Mission, Binghamton, 1966. Dir. Ecumenical Project SAVE, Detroit, 1978-84; mem. S.W. Detroit Mental Health Com., Detroit, 1973; developer S.W. Detroit Aging Coalition, 1984; dir. S.E. Mich. Food Coalition, 1985. Sgt. U.S. Army, 1942-45. Recipient Svc. to Community award Hubbard Richard Community Coun., 1984, Svc. to Frail Elderly Ecumenical Project SAVE, 1979-85. Mem. Presbytery of Detroit. Died Feb. 9, 2004.

SEGREST, PATRICIA, school system administrator; b. Vicksburg, Miss., July 10, 1946; d. Zellner James and Hazel Brown Anderson; divorced; 1 child, Pamela E. Segrest. BS, Alcorn State U., 1967, MS, 1976; postgrad., Miss. State U., Miss. Coll., U. So. Miss., JSU. Tchr. Vicksburg Warren Schs., Vicksburg, 1967-86, asst. prin., 1986-87, prin., 1987-93, dir. parent ctr./dir. testing, coord. profl. devel., from 1993. Bd. dirs. Hospice, Vicksburg. Named to Hall of Honor, Alcorn State U. Nat. Alumni, 1992. Mem. Les Soeurs Charmantes (pres.), Young Adults for Positive Action (pres., treas.), Alpha Kappa Alpha (pres.), Phi Delta Kappa. Democrat. Baptist. Avocations: sewing, listening to soft music, reading. Home: Vicksburg, Miss. Died May 5, 2004.

SEGURA, JOSEPH WESTON, urologist, educator; b. Little Rock, Mar. 12, 1940; s. H. Weston and Jane Ann (Nadeau) S.; children: Alison, Sarah, Cynthia, Leal, Suzanne. AB, Princeton U., 1961; MD, Northwestern U., Chgo., 1965. Diplomate Am. Bd. Urology. Staff physician Peace Corps, Santiago, Chile, 1966-68; intern Charity Hosp., New Orleans, 1965-66; resident in urology Mayo Clinic, Rochester, Minn., 1968-72, cons., 1972—2006, instr. urology, 1973-74, asst. prof., 1974-78, assoc. prof., 1978-84, prof., 1983—2006, Carl Rosen prof., 1984—2006. Co-editor: Transurethral Surgery, 1979. Fellow ACS; mem. Am. Urol. Assn., Am. Assn. Genitourinary Surgeons, Endourology Soc., Can. Urol. Assn., North Ctrl. Sect. Am. Urol. Assn. Home: Rochester, Minn. Died May 23, 2006.

SEIBERLICH, CARL JOSEPH, retired military officer; b. Jenkintown, Pa., July 4, 1921; s. Charles A. and Helen (Dolan) S.; m. Trudy Germi, May 29, 1952; children: Eric P., Heidi M., Curt A. BS, U.S. Mcht. Marine Acad., 1943; grad., Armed Forces Staff Coll., 1959. Commd. ensign U.S. Navy, 1943, advanced through grades to rear adm., 1971; designated naval aviator, 1947; comdg. officer Airship ZPM-1, 1949—51, Air Anti-Submarine Squadron 26, 1961—62, U.S.S. Salamonie, 1967—68, U.S.S. Hornet, 1969—70; dir. recovery astronauts Apollo 11 and 12 lunar missions, 1969; comdr. anti-submarine warfare group 3 Flagship U.S.S. Ticonderoga, 1971—73; dir. aviation programs, 1973—75; comdr. task force 74 Viet Nam Ops., 1972; asst. dep. chief naval ops. for air warfare Navy Dept., 1975-77; dep. chief naval personnel, 1977-78; comdr. Naval Mil. Personnel Command, 1978-80; with VSE Corp., 1980-82; pres. U.S. Maritime Resource Ctr.; dir. mil. program Am. Pres. Lines, 1983-95, TranSystems Corp., Reston, Va., 1996—2006; chmn. bd., CEO Dellaware River Maritime Enterprise Coun., 2000—01; U.S. rep. intermodal and short sea shipping subcom. Internat. Orgn. for Standardization; ISO del. Internat. Maritime Orgn., maritime safety com. and maritime security working group, 2001—06. Co-chmn. intermodal task force Nat. Rsch. Coun., Transp. Bd.; mem. NAFTA Info. Exch. & Automation working group. Vice pres. Naval Aviation Mus. Found.; active Boy Scouts Am. Decorated Legion of Merit (6), Air medal; recipient Harmon Internat. trophy for devel. 1st variable depth towed sonar, 1951; Vincent T. Hirsch Maritime award Navy League, 1995, Its Am. award for Intermodal Transp. Achievement, 2002. Mem. VFW, AIAA, Am. Soc. Naval Engrs., Soc. Naval Architects and Marine Engrs., Intelligent Transp. Sys. Am., Am. Helicopter Soc., U.S. Naval Inst., U.S. Naval Sailing Assn. (commodore 1979), Am. Angus Assn., Tailhook Assn., Navy Helicopter Assn., Naval Airship Assn., Early and Pioneer Naval Aviators Assn., Nat. Def. Transp. Assn., Navy League U.S. (maritime affairs com.), Propeller Club, Order of Daedalians, U.S. Mcht. Marine Acad. Alumni Assn., Assn. Naval Aviation, Am. Legion, Nat. Space Club, Delta Sigma Pi. Home: Haymarket, Va. Died Mar. 24, 2006.

SEIDEN, PAUL, insurance agent, consultant; b. Rzeszow, Poland, Nov. 16, 1920; came to U.S., 1939, naturalized, 1943; s. Simon and Amalia Grauer S.; m. Ida Perlin, Nov. 27, 1943 (div. 1961); children: Mark D., Henry A.; m. Judith Ellen Barkalow, Jan. 19, 1962; children: Lewis J., Eve M. Student, CUNY, 1939-41; MS in Mgmt., MS in Fin. Svcs., Am. Coll., 1985. Real estate broker Simon J. Boss Realty Co., Bklyn., 1948-51; life ins. agt. Phoenix Mutual Life Ins. Co., N.Y.C., 1952-56; asst. gen. agr. Aetna Life Ins. Co., Miami, 1956-61; gen. agt. Nat. Life Vt., Beverly Hills, Calif., 1962-90, agt. Encino, Calif., from 1991. Cons. mktg., pres. Income Devel. Corp., Encino, 1968—. 1st Lt. U.S. Army, WWII ETO, 1942-46. Mem. Nat. Assn. Life Underwriters, U.S. Army Ret. Officers Assn., West Dade Masonic Lodge # 388, Am. Legion, Kosciuszko Found., Simon Wiesnthal Ctr. Jewish. Avocations: trap and skeet shooting, dance, swimming, history studies, teaching. Home: Calabasas, Calif. Died July 12, 2004.

SEIDLER, HARRY, architect, educator; b. Vienna, Austria, June 25, 1923; s. Max and Rose S.; m. Penelope Evatt, 1958; 2 children. Ed. Cambridge Tech. Sch., B. Architecture, U. Manitoba, Can., 1944, Harvard U.; M.Arch.; studied with Walter Gropius, Harvard U., 1946; student Josef Albers, Black Mountain Coll., 1946; LLD (hon.) U. Manitoba, Canada, 1988, LittD U. Tech., Sydney, 1991, DSc (hon.) U. NSW, 1999, U. Sydney, 2000. Chief asst. Marcel Breuer, N.Y.C., 1946-48; prin. architect Harry Seidler and Assocs., Sydney, Australia, 1948—; Thomas Jefferson prof. architecture U. Va., 1978—; vis. com. Harvard U. grad. Sch. Design, 1995-2001; adj. prof. U. Sydney, 2001; vis. prof. Harvard U., 1976-77, U. New South Wales, 1980, U. Sydney, 1984, 96, E.T.H., Zurich, 1993. Maj. works: housing units in Australia, urban redevel. Australia Sq., Sydney, 1962-66, Commonwealth Trade Office Complex, Canberra, Australia, 1970-72, High Rise Apts., Acapulco, 1970, M.L.C. Ctr., Martin Pl., Sydney, 1972-75, Australian Embassy, Paris, 1974-76, Hong Kong Club and Office Bldg., 1980-84, Grosvenor Place, Sydney, 1982-87, Riverside Ctr., Brisbane, Australia, 1983-86, Capita Ctr., Sydney, 1985-88, Shell Hdqrs., Melbourne, Australia, 1985-88, QVI Tower, Perth, 1987-91, Waverly Art Gallery, Melbourne, 1988, Horizon Apts., Sydney, 1990-98, Wohnpark Neue Donau, Vienna, 1994-2002, Cove Apts., Sydney, 1999-03, N. Apts., Sydney, 2001-03; author: Houses, Interiors and Projects, 1949-54, Harry Seidler, 1955-63, Architecture in the New World, 1974, Australian Embassy, Paris, 1979, Two Towers, Sydney, 1980, Internment 1940-41: The Diaries of Harry Seidler, 1986, Harry Seidler: Four Decades of Architecture, 1992, Harry Seideler: The Master Architect Series III, 1997, Riverside Ctr., 1988, Neue Donau Housing Estate, Vienna, 2003, Houses and Interiors, Vols. 1 & 2, 2003, Grand Tour-Travelling the World with an Architect's Eye, 2003; Decorated Companion of the Companion Order of Australia, 1987, Order Brit. Empire; recipient Wilkinson award, 1965, 66, 67, 99, Sir John Sulman medal, 1951, 67, 81, 83, 91, Civic Design award, 1967, 81, Sir Zelman Cowen Nat. award, 1987, RAIA Lustig and Moar prize, 1989, Gold medal City of Vienna, 1989, RAIA Interior Design award, 1991, RAIA Comml. Arch. award, 1991, 92, 2001, Gold medal City of Vienna, Austria, 1989, Austrian Cross Honor 1st Class Art and Sci., 1995, Royal Gold medal Royal Inst. Brit. Archs., 1996, RAIA Blacket award, 2001; Golden Decoration Svs. to Viennese State, 2002; mem. AIA (hon., Pan Pacific citation 1968), Royal Australian Inst. Architects (life; Gold medal 1976, Old Trienniel Robin Dods medal 1989), Australia Acad. Tech. Scis.; mem. Academie D'Architecture Paris, Academician Internat. Acad. Architecture. E-mail: hsa@seidler.net.au. Home: Killara, Australia. Died Mar. 9, 2006.

SEIDMAN, MARSHALL JACOB, lawyer; b. Pitts., Oct. 20, 1925; s. Jesse I. and Matilda (Amdur) S.; m. June Korson, June 15, 1947 (div. Aug. 1969); m. Cecelia Fox, Sept. 1, 1970; children: Mark, Barbara, Daniel. BS in Econs., U. Pa., 1947; JD, Harvard U., 1950, LLM, 1970. Bar: D.C. 1950, Pa. 1953, Ind. 1970. Atty. NLRB, Washington, 1950-55; dep. atty. gen. Commonwealth of Pa., Harrisburg, 1955-60; pvt. practice Phila., 1960-70; prof., assoc. dean Law Sch. Ind. U., Indpls., 1970-84; pvt. practice Ft. Myers, Fla., from 1985. Author: The Law of Evidence in Indiana, 1975. V.p., chmn. Russian Resettlement Program and Cmty. Rels. Coun., Jewish Fedn. Lee County; treas. Temple Beth El; bd. dirs. Tanglewood Spl. Improvement Dist.; chair Lee County Human Rels. Rev. Bd. Mem. ABA, Nat. Acad. Arbitrators, Harvard Club Lee County (bd. dirs.), Forest Country Club. Republican. Died May 18, 2004.

SEIFRIED, ALLEN CHARLES, elementary school educator; b. Little Falls, N.Y., Dec. 2, 1945; s. Jacob and Armetta (Youker) S.; m. Cheryl Elizabeth Haughton, July 2, 1982; children: Tricia, Nathaniel. BA in Sociology, Syracuse U., 1967; MS in Edn., SUNY, Oneonta, 1971; postgrad., SUNY, Oswego, 1972, Pa. State U., 1979, U. N.C., 1980; Cert. Advanced Study, SUNY, Cortland, 1985; MS in Counseling, Liberty U., 1994. Cert. elem. tchr., N.Y. Tchr. Ilion (N.Y.) Ctrl. Schs., from 1967, coach, from 1967; adminstr. Log Cabin Pre-Sch., Ilion, from 1993. Pres. Ednl. Experiences, Ilion, 1992—; cons. Inst. for Scientific Info., Phila., 1976; presenter Learning Tech. Fair, Albany, 1982, Syracuse, 1983, Herklmer, 1984; instr. Madison Onieda Bd. Cooperative Edn. Svcs., 1983, 85; coord. Barringer Rd. Nature Trail State grant, 1989; ednl., computer cons. Inst. for Sci. Info., 1988. Mem. Am. Counseling Assn., Christian Counselors Assn. Baptist. Avocations: sports, travel. Home: Ilion, NY. Died Jan. 19, 2004.

SEITAN, IULIU AUREL, international global strategic advisor; b. Cluj, Romania, Apr. 21, 1925; came to U.S., 1973; s. Ion and Maria S.; m. Eufrosina Vidrighin, Jan. 15, 1955 (div.); 1 child, Dorin; m. Herlinda Baltazar, Oct. 6, 1977; children: Carmen, Linda. PhD in Civil Engring., U. Dallas, 1974. Registered profl. engr. Sr. engr. C. F. Braun, Alhambra, Calif., 1974-78; resident engr. Ebasco Svcs., Inc., N.Y.C., 1978-80; project mgr. Fluor Engring., Irvine, Calif., 1980-83; sr. project mgr. City of Houston (Tex.) Met. Authority, 1983-90; pres. Roman Corp., Houston, from 1990. Author: (books) A Man Without Youth, 1988, A Dead Man Alive, 1991. Fellow Am. Soc. Civil Engrs.; mem. Nat. Soc. Profl. Engrs., N.Y. Acad. Scis. Home: Houston, Tex. Died July 8, 2005.

SELBY, JANET S. GROSHART, retired elementary educator; b. La Junta, Colo., Mar. 15, 1927; d. Oscar Doyle and Helen Rucker (Gard) Groshart; m. Meredith H. Stice, June 28, 1946 (dec. 1964); children: Barry W., Mitchell R., Tracy S., Meredith G., Aaron M.; m. Andrew G. Sligar, Jan. 2, 1982 (div. 1992). BA in Elem. Edn., U. Ariz., 1965; MA in Early Childhood Edn., U. LaVerne, Calif., 1975, MS in Sch. Counseling, 1983. Cert. in elem. edn., high sch. counseling. Elem. educator Santa Ana (Calif.) Unified Schs., 1966-68, Capistrano Unified Sch. Dist., San Juan Capistrano, Calif., 1968-85. Mem. AAUW (arts chair 1989-90), Women's Nat. Polit. Caucus. Episcopalian. Avocations: painting and drawing, sculpture, swimming, reading, music appreciation. Home: Haiku, Hawaii. Died Oct. 3, 2004.

SELBY, NAOMI ARDEAN, women's health nurse, medical/surgical nurse; b. Duncan, Okla., Jan. 17, 1946; d. Orbie J.N. Sr. and Dorothy Naomi (Foster) S. BSN, Tex. Woman's U., 1969. Staff nurse, head nurse labor and delivery Meth. Med. Ctr., Dallas; cons., staff nurse ob-gyn. Southeastern Meth. Hosp., Dallas, staff nurse, operating room; head nurse ob-gyn. Yukon Delta Regional Hosp./USPHS/Indian Health Svc., Bethel, Alaska; nurse mgr. cen. supply rm./oper. rm., acting interim DON, Yukon Kuskokwim Health Corp. Mem. Assn. Operating Room Nurses. Home: Bethel, Alaska. Died Jan. 27, 2005.

SELF, GARY WAYNE, pharmacist; b. Feb. 26, 1943; BA Comparative Biochemistry/Physiology, Kans. U., 1968; BS in Pharmacy, Southwestern Okla. State U., 1993. Registered pharmacist. Chem. rschr. Okla. U., NOrman, 1974-87; rancher and farmer, 1974-87; analytical chemist Gen. Testing Labs., Kansas City, Mo., 1989-91; pharmacist Walmart, Neosho, Mo., from 1996. Mem. Am. Chem. Soc. Home: Baxter Springs, Kans. Died Mar. 30, 2005.

SELLARDS, LYLE DURKIN, minister; b. Centralia, Wash., Feb. 17, 1929; s. John Harrison and Lura Elizabeth (Cox) S.; m. Geraldine Virginia Updike, July 14, 1951 (div. Dec. 1968); m. Joyce Williams, Oct. 11, 1975; children: Sandra Lynn Riley, Carol Ann Walker, Catherine Marie, Janet Leade, Pamela Lehde, Gretchen Lucas. AA, Centralia Community Coll., 1949; BTh, N.W. Christian Coll., 1951; MDiv, Lexington (Ky.) Theol. Sem., 1955; MTh, Vancouver (B.C., Can.) Sch. Theology, 1981; M in Counseling, Idaho State U., 1981. Ordained to ministry, 1951. Youth pastor Univ. Christian Ch., Seattle, 1951-52; pastor to coll. youth Cen. Christian Ch., Lexington, 1952-55; assoc. pastor Univ. Pl. Ch., Champaign-Urbana, Ill., 1955-59; with United Campus Christian Found., Bellingham, Wash., 1959-68, Idaho State U. Ecumenical Ministry, Inc., Pocatello, 1975-85; pastor Little White Ch. Congl. United Ch. of Christ, Malta, Mont., 1988-90, Orem (Utah) Community Ch., from 1990. Interim pastor First Congl. Ch., Colville, Wash., 1985-86, St. John United Ch. of Christ, Hebron, N.D., 1987-88; clergy Utah Christian Ch. (Disciples of Christ), 1951—. Mem. Am. Assn. Pastoral Counselors, Am. Assn. Marriage and Family Mediators, Interim Ministry, Phillips County Ministerial Assn. (pres. Malta chpt. 1989-90), United Ch. of Christ, Rocky Mountain Conf. United Ch. of Christ, Utah. Home: Kenmore, Wash. Died Aug. 2, 2004.

SELLIN, DAVID, art historian, consultant; b. Phila., Apr. 13, 1930; s. Thorsten and Amy (Anderson) S.; m. Anne Robertson, Nov. 27, 1965. BA, U. Pa., 1952, MA, 1956, PhD, 1968; postgrad., Royal Art Acad., Stockholm, 1952-53. Asst. curator Phila. Mus. Art, 1958-60; dir. art schs. Pa. Acad. Fine Arts, Phila., 1960-62; asst. prof., gallery dir. Colgate U., Hamilton, N.Y., 1963-68; vis. assoc. prof. Tulane U., New Orleans, 1968-69; assoc. prof., gallery dir. Conn. Wesleyan U., Middletown, 1969-72; curator Office of Architect U.S. Capitol, Washington, 1976-80; guest curator Phoenix Art Mus., 1980—83; rsch. fellow Smithsonian Instn., Washington. Vis. prof. U. Mass., Amherst, 1983. Mem. Com. of 100 on Federal City, Washington, Citizens Planning Coalition, Washington, Midway Civic Assn., Washington. Fellow Am. Scandinavian Found., 1952-53, Fulbright fellow, Italy, 1956-68, SMithsonian Inst. Postdoctoral fellow, 1972-73, Pa. Acad. Fine Arts fellow. Mem. Columbia Hist. Soc. (bd. mgrs. 1980-89), Potomac Soc. Stereo Photographers, Phi Beta Kappa. Home: Washington, DC. Died Apr. 11, 2006.

SELM, ROBERT PRICKETT, engineer, consultant; b. Cin., Aug. 9, 1923; s. Frederick Oscar and Margery Marie (Prickett) S.; m. Rowena Imogene Brown, Nov. 25, 1945 (div. Jan. 1975); children: Rosalie C. Selm Pace, Linda R. Selm Partridge, Robert F., Michael E.; m. Janis Claire Broman, June 24, 1977. BSChemE, U. Cin., 1949. Registered profl. engr. Enlisted U.S. Army, 1943, advanced through grades to sgt. CBI Marianas, 1943-46, commd. capt., 1949, resigned, 1954; design engr. Wilson & Co., Salina, Kans., 1954-67, gen. ptnr., 1967-81, sr. ptnr., 1981-89; ptnr. in charge Wilson Labs., Salina, Kans., 1956-88, chmn. bd. dirs.; dir. Upper Eagle Valley Water Authority, Avon, Colo., from 1994; ind. investor Salina, Kans., from 1989. Contbr. articles to profl. jours.; patentee in field. Mem. Gov.'s Adv. Commn. on Health and Environ. Named Engr. of Yr. Kans. Engring. Soc., Topeka, 1986. Fellow AIChE; mem. NSPE (state chmn. environ. resource com., nat. legis. and govt. affairs com. 1988-91), Am. Chem. Soc., Am. Water Works Assn., Water Pollution Control Fedn., Am. Acad. Environ. Engrs. (diplomate), Petroleum Club, Salina Country Club (pres. 1986), Elks, Shriners. Republican. Episcopalian. Avocations: golf, lapidary arts. Home: Salina, Kans. Died June 16, 2005.

SEMOS, CHRIS VICTOR, county commissioner; b. Dallas, June 2, 1936; s. Victor H. and Evelyn (Tassos) S.; m. Anastasia Kontos, Feb. 25, 1967; children: Mary Katherine, Victoria Evelyn, Kristina Anastasia. BBA, So. Meth. U., 1962; postgrad., Anglo-Am. Sch., Athens, Greece, 1952-54, Ecole Hotelier, Lausanne, Switzerland, 1954-55; LLD (hon.), Northwood Inst., Cedar Hill, Tex., 1985. Co-owner, mgr. Torch Restaurant, Dallas, 1948-85; mem. Commrs. Ct. Dallas County, Dallas, 1983—95. Anchorman A Touch of Old Athens, Sta. KSKY, 1956-60; mem. faculty, lectr. Robert A. Taft Inst. Govt., U. Tex., Arlington, 1973-78. Mem. Tex. Ho. of Reps., 1967-83; trustee, mem. exec. com. United Way Tex.; bd. dirs., mem. exec. com. United Way Met. Dallas; nat. trustee NCCJ; chmn., trustee, mem. exec. com. Baylor Coll. Dentistry; chmn. bd. govs. Dallas Family Hosp.; trustee Dallas Hist. Soc.; mem. adv. bd. Dallas Boys Choir, Love for Kids, Irving Aid, Inc.; mem. exec. com., bd. dirs. Dallas Coun. on World Affairs; mem. adv. coun. Inst. Texan Cultures, U. Tex., San Antonio; numerous others. Recipient Humanitarian award NCCJ, 1980, Man of Yr. award Oak Cliff Tribune, Dallas, 1980, Father of Sesquicentennial award Office of Gov., State of Tex., 1986, award of excellence Dallas County Hist. Soc., 1986. Mem. Am. Hellenic Ednl. and Progressive Assn., Lions, Masons (33d deg.), Shriners, Order of Eastern Star. Democrat. Greek Orthodox. Avocation: travel. Home: Dallas, Tex. Died June 15, 2004.

SENER, JOSEPH WARD, JR., security firm executive, director; b. Balt., June 30, 1926; s. Joseph Ward and Clara (Hodshon) S.; m. Ann Clark TenEyck, May 3, 1952 (dec. Oct. 1967); children: J. TenEyck, Beverley T., Joseph Ward III; m. Jean Eisenbrandt-Johnston, Feb. 6, 1971. AB, Haverford Coll., Pa., 1950; diploma, Inst. Investment Banking, U. Pa., 1954. With John C. Legg & Co., Balt., 1950-70, gen. partner, 1961-70; exec. v.p., dir. Legg, Mason & Co., Inc., Balt., 1970-72; vice chmn. bd. dirs., chief adminstrv. officer Legg Mason Wood Walker, Inc., Balt., 1976-80; dir. Legg Mason, Inc., 1982-96. Bd. dirs. Chesapeake Bank and Trust, Chestertown, Md., 1986-96, chmn., 1992-96; bd. visitors and govs. Washington Coll. Trustee emeritus Boys' Latin Sch., Balt., pres. bd. trustees, 1980-82; chmn. emeritus bd. govs. Chesapeake Bay Maritime Mus. Served with USAAF, 1944-46. Mem. Nat. Assn. Securities Dealers (past dist. chmn.), Balt. Security Analysts Soc. (past pres.), Md. Club (Balt.). Republican. Episcopalian. Home: Church Hill, Md. Died Sept. 4, 2006.

SENTANY, MARKI SUWITA, plastic surgoen; b. Bandung, Indonesia, May 28, 1939; MD, Pajajaran U., Bandung, 1965. Diplomate Am. Bd. Plastic Surgery. Intern Marion County Gen. Hosp., Indpls., 1969-70, resident in gen. surgery, 1970-74; resident in plastic surgery Ind. U. Med. Ctr., Indpls., 1974-76; practice medicine specializing in plastic surgery Indpls., from 1976. Fellow ACS; mem. AMA, Am. Soc. Plastic and Reconstructive Surgeons. Home: Indianapolis, Ind. Died May 16, 2004.

SERETAN, EDWARD LLOYD, retired ophthalmologist; b. N.Y.C., Apr. 23, 1916; s. Charles and Mollie (Abramowitz) S.; m. Enid S. Seretan, Aug. 31, 1947 (dec. Oct. 1982); children: Douglas Hartley, Clifford Stewart; m. Cynthia Advocat, Aug. 12, 1984. BS, N.Y. U., 1936; MD, St. Louis U., 1940. Diplomate Am. Bd. Ophthalmology, Nat. Bd. Med. Examiners. Intern Walter Reed Gen. Hosp., Washington, 1940-41; resident ophthalmology Valley Forge Gen. Hosp., Phoenixville, Pa., 1945-46, Percy Jones Gen. Hosp., Battle Creek, Mich., 1946-47, Oliver Gen. Hosp., Augusta, Ga., 1947-48, Mt. Sinai Hosp., N.Y.C., 1948-50; clin. asst. prof. ophthalmology SUNY, Stony Brook, from 1970; pvt. practice ophthalmology Forest Hills, N.Y., from 1950, New Hyde Park, N.Y., from 1976. Instr. ocular pathology North Shore Hosp.; assoc. examiner Am. Bd. Ophthalmology. Lt. col. U.S. Army, 1940-48, PTO. Fellow ACS, Am. Acad. Ophthalmology, N.Y. Acad. Medicine, Nassau Acad. Ophthalmology (chmn. sect. ophthalmology 1973-74); mem. L.I. Ophthal. Soc. (pres. 1972-73), Alpha Omega Alpha. Democrat. Jewish. Home: Huntington, NY. Died Jan. 31, 2004.

SERGI, ARTURO, tenor, music educator, academic administrator; b. N.Y.C., Nov. 8, 1925; s. Maxwell and Sophie Kagan; m. Leonore Glickman, Apr. 29, 1959; children: Arturo, David. Student, Manhattan Sch. of Music, 1947—48, Conservatorio Giuseppe Verdi, Milan, Italy, 1948—51, Conservatorio Santa Cecelia, Rome, 1951—54; pvt. study, Maestro Sergi Nazor, Italy and Germany, 1954—69. Leading tenor Städtische Bühnen, Wuppertal, Germany, 1954—57, Frankfurt, Germany, 1957—60, Staatsoper, Hamburg, Germany, 1958—62, Met. Opera Assn., N.Y.C., 1962—67, 1979—84; assoc. prof. voice U. Tex., Austin, Tex., 1971—77; cantor Congregation Beth Israel, Houston, 1972—85; leading tenor, concert artist various opera cos. and symphony orchs., 1980—90; founding pres. East-West Internat. Music Acad., Altenburg, Germany, from 1990. With U.S. Army, 1946—47, U.S. and Japan. Recipient Kulturpreis der Stadt Altenburg, City of Altenburg, Germany, 1998, Fed. Republic of Germany Friendship award, German Amb. to U.S., 2003; grantee, U.S. State Dept., 1992—2002. Mem.: Coll. Music Soc. (life), Rotary (hon.). Democrat. Jewish. Avocations: swimming, exercise. Died 2006.

SERRILL, THEODORE ANDREW, publications consultant; b. Phila., Apr. 16, 1911; s. John Burtus and Mary (Lenahan) S.; B.A., Pa. State U., 1932; m. Alice Marguerite Ferner, Oct. 27, 1933 (dec. 1986); children— Theodore Michael, James Alan; m. Patricia W. Schaffer, Feb. 21, 1987. Mem. staff Washington News, 1933-37, Charlotte (N.C.) News, 1937-38, Easton (Pa.) Express, 1938-42; dep. dir. War Loans Region III, 1942-44; asso. mgr. to gen. mgr. Pa. Newspaper Pubs. Assn., 1945-56; exec. dir. Washington Pubs. Assn., 1956-60; employee relations dir. Grocery Mfrs. Am., 1960-61; exec. v.p. Nat. Newspaper Assn., 1961-76; publs. cons. 1976-94; dir. Daily Record Co., Balt., 1982-86, also pres., pub. Pinellas County Rev., St. Petersburg, Fla., 1976—; Bd. govs. USO, 1975-82; exec. res. U.S. Dept. Commerce, 1969-91; mem. coms. Bur. Labor Stats.; mem. U.S. Postal Adv. Council, Clearwater (Fla.) Library Bd., 1985-90, Clearwater Spouse Abuse Program, 1986-92; mem. pub. relations com. Am. Revolution Bicentennial. Recipient service award Pa. Soc. Newspaper Editors, 1956. Mem. Nat. Assn. Execs. Club, Am. Soc. Assn. Execs. (Key award 1974), Nat. Newspaper Assn. (Presdl. award 1958, 76), Am. Ct. and Comml. Newspapers, Suncoast Penn State Club (pres. 1984-87), Sigma Delta Chi, Alpha Delta Sigma, Phi Kappa Theta. Republican. Roman Catholic. Clubs: Rotary (Seminole, Fla.), Torch (pres. 1973-74) (Washington), Clearwater. Columnist Assn. Trends, Washington, 1979—; editor, pub. Pubs. Aux., 1961-76 (Amos award Nat. Newspaper Assn. 1991). Home: Seminole, Fla. Died Jan. 1, 2005.

SETTIPANE, GUY ANTHONY, allergist, medical educator; b. Middletown, Conn., July 19, 1930; AB in Biology, Brown U., 1953; MD, N.Y. Med. Coll., 1957. Diplomate Am. Bd. Allergy and Immunology, Nat. Bd. Med. Examiners. Resident U.S. Naval Hosp., Newport, R.I., 1957-58, resident in internal medicine Portsmouth, Va., 1958-59; fellow in allergy R.I. Hosp., Providence, 1962-63, dir. adult allergy divsn., from 1973, co-dir. allergy/immunology tng. program, from 1979; fellow in allergy Roosevelt Hosp., N.Y.C., 1963-64; dir. adult allergy divsn. St. Joseph's & Fatima Hosp., Providence, 1966; clin. prof. of medicine Brown U., Providence, clin. assoc. prof. medicine, 1979-90, clin. prof. medicine, from 1990. Allergy cons. U.S. Naval Hosp., Quonset, R.I.; mem. med. staff R.I. Hosp., Miriam Hosp., St. Joseph's Hosp., Pawtucket Meml. Hosp., Roger Williams Gen. Hosp.; mem. cons. staff Miriam Hosp., Providence; presenter in field. Editor-in-chief jour. Allergy Procs., 1980-92; editor: Rhinitis, 2d edit., Nasal Manifestations of Systemic Diseases, H1 and H3 Histamine Receptors, Current Treatment of Ambulatory Asthma; contbr. column to Health Care Profl.; mem. editorial bd. R.I. Med. Foun., 1970-76, Challenges in Dermatology Jour., 1978—, Jour. Geriatric Drug Allergy, Perspective in Immunology, 1986&; cons. editor Am. Jour. Rhinology, 1987—; contbr. articles to profl. publs.; referee jours. in field. Bd. dirs. R.I. Civic Choral, 1971; mem. ho. dels. R.I. Med. Soc., 1972-80. Officer USN, 1957-62. Grantee Am. Cancer Soc., 1967-77; recipient Physician's Recognition award AMA, 1969. Fellow Am. Acad. Allergy (chmn. com. on cutaneous allergy 1971-73): mem. ACP, Am. Acad. Allergy and Immunology (mem. exec. com. 1988—), Assn. R.I. Med. Malpractice Ins. (bd. dirs. joint underwriting), Am. Coll. Allergy, New Eng. Soc. Allergy (sec. 1974-76, pres. 1980, program com. 1970), Am. Soc. Clin. Immunology and Allergy, R.I. Soc. Internal Medicine, Am. Thoracic Soc., Am. Coll. Chest Physicians. Died Aug. 21, 2004.

SEVERINO, CHARLES L., financial planner; b. Copaigue, N.Y., July 29, 1955; s. Charles C. Severino and Rose Marie (Rossi) Martin; m. Tina Marie Brooks (div.); 1 child, Paul Stephen; m. Vonni Diane Hartley, Aug. 4, 1979; 1 child, Charles Taylor. CLU, Am. Coll., 1982, ChFC, 1986; fellow, Life Underwriting Tng. Coun., Washington, 1987; CFP, Coll. for Fin. Planning, Denver, 1991. CFP. Agt. Mony, Albuquerque, 1976-79; assoc., account rep. Resources Fin., Albuquerque, 1979-83; pres. Charles Stephen and Co., Inc., Albuquerque, from 1983. Advanced underwriting adv. coun., Security Mut. Life, Binghamton, N.Y., 1990-94; mem. Leaders Round Table, Lincoln Nat. Life, Ft. Wayne, Ind., 1979-94; regional mktg. cons. Fin. Profiles, Carlsbad, Calif., 1994. Newspaper columnist, 1991-93. Mem. Am. Soc. CLU and ChFC, Nat. Assn. Life Underwriters, Million Dollar Round Table, Inst. Cert. Fin. Planners. Home: Corrales, N.Mex. Died May 13, 2004.

SEWARD, DORIS KLUGE, service executive, consultant; b. Washington, Dec. 12, 1920; d. Russell O. and Edna Ashford Kluge; m. Robert F. Seward, June 18, 1947. BA, Tex. U., 1943; MS in Edn., U. So. Calif., 1968, M in Pub. Adminstrn., 1972, D in Pub. Adminstrn., 1974. Mgmt. analyst U.S. Dept. Air Force, Columbus AFB, Miss., 1959-62; tng. asst. Los Angeles City Schs., 1963-66; tng. officer Los Angeles County, 1967-79, personnel mgmt. specialist, 1979-84; pres. Pub. Adminstrn. Research and Edn., Whittier, Calif., from 1981, Temporary Tng. Skills, Whittier, from 1984. Instr. UCLA extension, Los Angeles, 1973—,

Calif. State U., Long Beach, 1975—, Northrop Corp., Hawthorne, Calif., 1984—; lectr. Calif. State Poly. U., Pomona, 1987—; cons. Exec. Service Corps So. Calif., 1984—. Mem. Los Angeles County Grand Jury, 1986-87; chmn. Editorial, Continuity Com., Govt. Ops. and Audit Com.; mem. Los Angeles County Economy and Efficiency Commn., 1987—. Recipient Research award Western Govt. Research Assn., 1974, Henry Reining Jr. award U. So. Calif., 1975. Mem. Am. Soc. Pub. Adminstrn. (exec. council mem. Los Angeles Met. chpt., 1974-76, membership chmn. 1974-76), Women's Equity Action League (nat. pres. 1974-75), Am. Soc. Tng. and Devel. (exec. council mem., dir. programming Los Angeles chpt., 1976), Internat. Personnel Mgmt. Assn., So. Calif. Personnel Mgmt. Assn. (life, hon.), Los Angeles County Mgmt. Council (chmn. mgmt. devel. com.,1972, editor jour. 1972-75, chmn. program com. for mgmt. conf., 1976, mem. edn. and tng. com. 1980-84). Clubs: Whittier Women's, Soroptimist. Republican. Methodist. Avocations: aerobic dancing, raising cocker spaniels. Died June 20, 2005.

SEXTON, CLARENCE DANIEL, JR., construction company executive; b. Columbia, S.C., Feb. 5, 1927; s. Clarence Daniel and Ada (Smith) S.; m. Irene Tenk (dec. July 1976); children: Margaret Sexton Johnson, Mary Louise, Jennifer Danelle, Teresa Jeanne, Elizabeth Ann; m. Martha Cross, July 1, 1978; stepchildren: Elaine Marr, Richard Marr. BCE, U. S.C., 1948. Registered profl. engr., S.C., land surveyor. Supervising engr. Standard Oil of N.J., Aruba, The Netherlands and West Indies, 1948-56; v.p. Republic Contracting Corp., Columbia, from 1956. Chmn. adv. com. S.C. Water Quality, Columbia. Mem. S.C. Election Commn., fin. com. S.C. State Dem. Orgn., past treas.; vice chmn. Riverbanks Zool. Commn., Columbia. Named to Order of Palmetto, State of S.C. Mem. ASCE (senior), Assoc. Gen. Contractors (past chmn. utilities div.). Clubs: Woodmen of the World (Columbia). Lodges: Lions. Avocations: book collecting, hiking, tennis, gardening. Home: Cincinnati, Ohio. Died Sept. 18, 2004.

SEYLER, WILLIAM C., retired university official; b. Kittanning, Pa., Nov. 27, 1921; s. Harry J. and Blanche M. (McPherson) S.; m. Isobel Opel Seyler, July 4, 1942; children: Carol, Kathryn, William C. Jr. BA, U. Pitts., 1942, MA, 1948; PhD, Duke U., 1952. Dir. practical polit. edn. U. Pitts., 1952-55; dir. prog. and policy rsch. Gov.'s Office, Commonwealth of Pa., Harrisburg, 1955; dep. sec. Dept. Internal Affairs, Commonwealth of Pa., Harrisburg, 1955-67; asst. to pres. Temple U., Phila., 1967-68, asst. v.p. and sec., 1969-82, univ. and bd. sec., 1982-92; ret., 1992. Committeeman, Dem. Party, Camp Hill, 1960-66. With U.S. Army, 1943-46; ETO. Duke U. fellow, 1950-51; recipient Thomas C. Freeman award, E. Abington (Pa.) Little League, 1975. Mem. AAUP, Am. Polit. Sci. Assn., Am. Soc. for Pub. Adminstrn. (chpt. pres. 1959-60), Omicron Delta Kappa, Phi Beta Kappa. Avocations: sports, walking. Home: Elkins Park, Pa. Died Dec. 19, 2004.

SEYMOUR, FREDERICK PRESCOTT, JR., industrial engineer, consultant; b. Oak Park, Ill., June 19, 1924; s. Frederick Prescott and Ivy Louise (Horder) S.; m. Janet Mary Stocking, Oct. 15, 1960; children: Robert Prescott, Bruce Stocking, Mary Janet. BS, Cornell U., 1948; MS in Commerce, U. Ill., 1951; MBA, U. Chgo., 1957. Indsl. engr., dir. planning, exec. salesman R.R. Donnelley and Sons Co./Lakeside Press, Chgo., 1951-72; regional dir. U.S. Postal Svc., Chgo., 1972-76; dir. advt. Spiegel, Inc., Chgo., 1976-80; pres. Frederick P. Seymour and Assocs., Inc., Winnetka, Ill., from 1980. Pres. Cornell Univ. Club. Chgo., 1960-61, Exec. Program Club, Chgo., 1972-73; mem. Postmaster Gen.'s tech. adv. com., Washington, 1973—. Contbg. editor: Gravure mag., 1982—; contbr. articles to profl. jours. Precinct capt. New Trier Rep. Orgn., Winnetka, 1970-72. With USN, 1944-46, PTO. Mem. ASME (life), Cornell Soc. Engrs., Graphic Comms. Assn. (Innovator award 1988), Gravure Assn. Am., Graphic Arts Industry Rsch. and Engring. Coun. (Non Pareil Soc. award 1990), Assn. Postal Commerce (bd. dirs. 2003), Econ. Club Chgo. (life). Died Aug. 20, 2004.

SHACKELFORD, ALPHONSO LEON, pharmacist, medical writer; b. Grapevine, Tex., June 4, 1920; s. Alphonso Lee and Ida May (Marriott) S.; m. Frances Chapman, June 30, 1945; children: Alan Eugene, Anne Marr, Sally Sue. BS, Coll. of Ozarks, 1949, DPharm, 1981. Registered pharmacist, Tex. Asst. chief pharmacy service Meth. Hosp., Dallas, 1949-51; pharmacist Myers and Rosser Prescription Pharmacy, Dallas, 1951-52; owner, operator Shackelford Prescription Pharmacy, Dallas, 1952-58; staff pharmacist Nix Meml. Hosp., San Antonio, 1958-60; pharmacy mgr. Sommers Drug Store, San Antonio, 1960-73; owner, cons. Alchem Assocs., San Antonio, 1973-83; staff pharmacist S.W. Gen. Hosp., San Antonio, 1983-87. Columnist Flying Rev., 1985—, news editor, 1986—; mem. edit. bd. Med. Communications. Vol. story teller Inst. Texan Culture, 1986. Served as sgt. USAAF, 1942-45. Mem. Am. Med. Writers Assn. (pres. S.W. chpt. 1979-82), U.S. Pilots Assn., Tex. Pilots Assn. Republican. Episcopalian. Avocation: flying. Died Sept. 11, 2004.

SHACKLETON, SIR NICHOLAS JOHN, science researcher; b. London, June 23, 1937; s. Robert Milner and Gwen (Harland) S.; m. Judith Carola Murray, 1967 (div. 1975) m. Vivien Anne Law (dec. 2002), 1986. BA, Cambridge (Eng.) U., 1961, PhD, 1967, ScD, 1984. Sr. rsch. assoc. Lamont-Doherty; ofcl. fellow Clare Hall, Cambridge; reader U. Cambridge, 1987-91; ad hominen prof. Godwin Inst. for Quarternary Rsch., U. Cambridge, 1991—2004, dir., 1995—2004. Vis. prof. Cath. U. Louvain-La-Neuve, 1994-95, ETH, Zurich, 1979; sr. vis. rsch. fellow Lamont-Doherty Geol. Obs., Columbia, 1974-75; rsch. fellow Clare Hall, Cambridge, 1974-81; asst. dir. rsch. sub-dept. quaternary rsch., Cambridge, 1972-85. Contbr. numerous sci. rsch. articles to profl. jours. Recipient Lyell medal Geol. Soc. London, Carus medal Leopoldina, Halle, Crafoord Prize, Royal Swedish Acad. of Science, 1995. Fellow Royal Soc. London (Royal medal, 2003) Avocation: playing and researching clarinet. Home: Cambridge, England. Died Jan. 24, 2006.

SHAFER, PAUL TERRELL, biophysicist; b. San Francisco, Nov. 23, 1938; s. Eugene Wesley and Margaret Negley (Hare) S. PhD in Biophysics, U. Calif., Berkeley, 1972. Postdoctoral fellow, rsch. physicist U. Kans. Med. Ctr./Kansas City VA Hosp., 1972-77; asst. prof. U. Kans., Kansas City, 1977-85; sr. scientist Sensor Diagnostics Corp., Irvine, Calif., 1986-88; founding biophysicist, prototype group leader Biocircuits Corp., Burlingame, Calif., from 1989. Contbr. articles to profl. publs. Capt. U.S. Army, 1961-63. Mem. AAAS, Soc. Plastics Engrs. Achievements include patent for medical diagnostic cassette; discovery of first known site for prostaglandin binding; discovery of action of endonucleases against lipid bilayers. Home: Burlingame, Calif. Died May 7, 2004.

SHAFFER, IDA FAY, retired elementary school educator; b. Portsmouth, Ohio, Oct. 20, 1929; d. Lewis Daniel and Laura Bell (Adkins) Artis; m. Ellis L. Shaffer, June 6, 1951; children: Laurel, Mark, Holly. BS in Edn., Ohio U., 1951. Elem. resource tchr. Volusia County Sch. Bd., Deland, Fla., from 1965. Mem. Fla. Textbook Com., Volusia County, 1971—; team mem. So. Assn. Colls., Volusia County, 1989-90; mem. adv. com. Volusia County Sch. Improvement Com., 1993—; pres. Panhellenic Coun., New Smyrna Beach, Fla., 1968-69. Pres. Oceanside Woman's Club, New Smyrna Beach, Fla., 1972. Named Tchr. of Yr., Edgewater Sch., 1987. Mem. AAUW, Alpha Delta Kappa (sec. New Smyrna Beach 1969-70, treas. 1996—), Beta Sigma Phi (pres. New Smyrna Beach 1973, Woman of Yr. award 1974), Zeta Tau Alpha. Republican. Methodist. Avocations: bridge, reading. Home: New Smyrna Beach, Fla. Died Feb. 29, 2004.

SHALLECK, ALAN JAY, video producer; b. N.Y.C., Nov. 14, 1929; s. Max and Dora (Fried) S.; children: David, Adam. BS, Syracuse U., 1950. Mem. staff Sta. WCAU-TV, Phila., Sta. CFCF-TV, Montreal, Que., Can., Sta. CFTO-TV, Toronto, Ont., Can.; assoc. dir., stage mgr. CBS-TV, N.Y.C.; ind. video producer N.Y.C.; pres. A.J. Shalleck Prodns. Producer, dir. numerous indsl., comml. promotional and feature videos including A Tribute to Lynrd Skynrd, (short tag-on film) Grease (Oscar nomination), (ednl. video series) Curious George, (political videos) Abe Beame, Ralph Caso, (TV med. spl.) To Your Health, TV pub. health spots, tng. films. Served as cpl. U.S. Army, 1951-53. Democrat. Jewish. Died Feb. 8, 2006.

SHANET, HOWARD STEPHEN, conductor, educator; b. N.Y.C., Nov. 9, 1918; s. Eugene Joseph and Jennie (Diesenhouse) S.; m. Bernice Grafstein, Oct. 10, 1963; 1 son, Laurence Paul. AB with honors in Music (Pulitzer scholar), Columbia U., 1939, A.M. in Musicology (William Mitchell Honor fellow), 1941. Instr. Hunter Coll., 1941-42, 46-53; asst. prof. music Columbia U., 1953-59, assoc. prof., 1959-69, prof., 1969—2006, chmn. dept. music, 1972-78, dir. music performance, 1978—2006, condr. univ. orch., 1953—2006. Mem. nat. conducting screening com. Fulbright Awards, 1967-72, 76-77, 81-82, judge various music competitions, 1966—2006; mem. advisory bd. Sta. WNCN, 1976—2006 Asst. condr., N.Y. City Symphony Orch., 1947-48, to Serge Koussevitzky on, internat. tour, 1949-50; condr., Berkshire Music Center, Tanglewood, Mass., 1949-52, Huntington (W.Va.) Symphony Orch., 1951-53, Music-in-the-Making, N.Y.C., 1958-61, String Revival, N.Y.C., 1975—2006; author, participant: TV series Learn to Read Music, 1962, 63; condr., guest condr. orchs., U.S. and abroad, including premieres of many Am. and European works.; Author: Learn to Read Music, 1956 (also Brit., Norwegian, Italian, Spanish edits.), Philharmonic, A History of New York's Orchestra, 1975; editor: Early Histories of the New York Philharmonic, 1979; contbr.: articles to N.Y.C. Symphony and N.Y. Philharmonic program notes; mus. compositions include Variations on a Bizarre Theme for orch.; also works for mil. band, piano, chamber ensembles. Served with U.S. Army, 1942-46, Iwo Jima. Decorated Bronze Service Star; recipient Presdl. citation Nat. Fedn. Music Clubs, 1977; certificate of distinguished service Inst. Internat. Edn., 1977; MacDowell Colony fellow, 1953, 63; Huntington Hartford Found. fellow, 1954; Martha Baird Rockefeller grantee, 1962-63 Mem. Coll. Music Soc., Am. Musicol. Soc., Sonneck Soc., Sibelius Soc. Home: New York, NY. Died June 19, 2006.

SHANNON, AMELIA RUSSELL, volunteer; b. Memphis, May 24, 1927; d. Edward Percy and Carroll (Johnston) Russell; m. Jack Thomas Shannon, June 15, 1950 (dec. Mar. 1985); children: Jack Thomas, Carroll S. Nenon, Richard Lee. Stewardess Chgo. and So. Airline, Memphis, 1949-50; vol. Memphis Cotton Carnival Assn., 1947-49, 63-75. Trustee Dixon Gallery and Gardens, Memphis, 1988-90; treas. Jr. League Memphis, 1964-65. Mem. Colonial Dames Am. (project chmn. Tenn. chpt. 1986-88), Memphis Garden Club (pres. 1988-90), Memphis Botanic Gardens (dir. 1972-73). Home: Memphis, Tenn. Died Nov. 19, 2004.

SHANNON, RICHARD STOLL, III, financial executive; b. N.Y.C., Mar. 22, 1943; s. Richard Stoll Jr. and Margaret (Cather) S.; m. Ann Wright Schmidt, June 14, 1965; children: Clea Cather, Kathryne Baltzelle, Arianna Wright. BA, Stanford U., 1966, MA, 1969; PhD, Harvard U., 1973. Asst. prof. U. Mich., Ann Arbor, 1973-78; mgr., trustee, gen. ptnr. various family trusts, partnerships and corps. Englewood, Colo., 1978-84; pres. Shannon Mgmt. Corp., Englewood, from 1985. Author: The Arms of Achilles, 1975; editor (with others) Oral Literature and The Formula, 1976. Bd. dirs. Cherryvale Sanitation Dist., Englewood, 1984—, pres., 1986-93; regional chmn. Stanford Ann. Fund/Keystone Project, 1985-98; mem. Rackham Advancement Coun., U. Mich., 1992-97. Teaching fellow Harvard U., 1970-73. Mem. Cherry Hills Country Club, Phi Beta Kappa. Avocations: golf, fishing, reading, research. Home: Englewood, Colo. Died Feb. 14, 2004.

SHAO, MARIE SHENG, corporate secretary; b. Shanghai, Peoples Republic of China, Oct. 21, 1928; came to U.S., 1946; d. Chenhua Herbert and Dora (Shen) Sheng; m. Otis Hung-i Shao, Apr. 2, 1955. BA, Greensboro Coll., 1950; MA, Columbia U., 1951. Instr. art St. Petersburg (Fla.) Jr. Coll., 1963-66; instr. Fla. Presby. Coll., St. Petersburg, 1966-68; assoc. prof. Callison Coll., Stockton, Calif., 1969-76; corp. sec. Sheng Shao Enterprises of Calif., Gualala, from 1984, also bd. dirs. Cons. Gen. Arts and Crafts Corp., Beijing, Peoples Republic of China; v.p. Pacific-Asia Mus., Pasadena, Calif., 1976-78. Contbr. articles to profl. jours.; judge art shows, 1963-66. V.p. Pacific-Asia Mus., Pasadena, Calif., 1976-78, coordinator Han and Tang Mural Exhibition, 1977; designer Exhibition of Festival of Plants from the Book of Songs, Kaneohe, Hawaii, 1981. Democrat. Presbyterian. Avocation: internat. travel. Home: The Sea Ranch, Calif. Died Apr. 8, 2004.

SHAPERO, PAUL DAVID, lawyer; b. N.Y.C., Mar. 13, 1920; s. William and Rose C. (Cantor) S.; m. Amy Miller, Jan. 11, 1948; children: David, Elisabeth M. AB, Brown U., 1941; LLB, Columbia U., 1951. Assoc. Spelke & Zone, Stamford, Conn., 1951-52, Spelke & Weil, Stamford, Conn., 1952-57; ptnr. Shapero & Cuching, Stamford, Conn., 1957-59, Shapero & Bingham, Stamford, Conn., 1959-83; atty. pvt. practice, Stamford, Conn., from 1983. Mem. exec. com. Conn. Probate Assembly, 1983. Mem. Bd. Reps., Stamford, 1960-64; rep. State of Conn., 1967; corp. counsel City of Stamford, 1967-69, 90-91; founder, dir. Liberty Nat. Bank, Stamford, 1971; pres. United Way, Stamford, 1977-79, Child Guidance CLinic, Stamford, 1979-84; mem. adv. coun. Children & Youth Svcs., Conn.; judge Stamford Probate Ct., 1983-90. Capt. U.S. Army, 1946. Mem. Conn. Bar Assn., Stamford Regional Bar Assn. Democrat. Jewish. Home: Eagle Bridge, NY. Died Feb. 6, 2005.

SHAPIRO, GAIL GREENBERG, pediatric allergy educator; b. NYC, Jan. 11, 1947; d. Jay and Roberta (Falk) Greenberg; m. Peter Shapiro, July 13, 1967; children: Jessica, Evan. BA, Brown U., 1967; MD, Johns Hopkins U., 1970. Diplomate Am. Bd. Pediatrics, Am. Bd. Allergy and Immunology (editorial bd. 1987-2006), Nat. Bd. Med. Examiners. Intern Johns Hopkins Hosp., Balt., 1970-71; resident in pediatrics U. Wash. and Children's Orthopedic Hosp. and Med. Ctr., Seattle, 1971-72, fellow in allergy and clin. immunology, 1972-74; clin. instr. pediatrics U. Wash., Seattle, 1974-75, clin. asst. prof., 1975-77, clin. assoc. prof., 1977-83, clin. prof., 1983—2006; clin. prof. allergy div. Children's Hosp. and Med. Ctr., Seattle, 1988-89. Vis. prof. Mayo Clinic, August, 1983, Nat. Jewish Hosp., Feb., 1984, Oakland Children's Hosp., June, 1988, Children's Meml. Hosp., Sept., 1989; mem. pulmonary and allergy adv. panel FDA, 1988-2006. Author: (with others) Current Therapy, 1975, Muscular Exercise and the Lung, 1977, The Critically Ill Child, 1977, Allergic Diseases of Infancy, Childhood and Adolescence, 1980, Practice of Pediatrics, 1980, A Differential Diagnosis of Pediatric Allergy, 1981, The Allergy Encyclopedia;, 1981, Allergy and Immunology, 1984, Recent Advances in Otitis Media with Effusion, 1984, The Critically Ill Child, 1985, Childhood Asthma Pathophysiology and Treatment, 1987, Current Therapy, 1988, Conn's Current Therapy, 1988; contbr. numerous articles to profl. jours. Fellow Am. Acad. Pediatrics (chmn. 1982-84, chmn. sect. allergy and program 1981-82, mem. exec. com. 1980-86), Am. Acad. Allergy and Immunology (chmn. continuing med. edn. com. 1988-2006, chmn. pub. edn. and info. on accepted med. practices subcom. 1989-2006, bd. dir., 1992-97, med. editor acad. news, 2003-04); mem. AMA, Am. Bd. Allergy and Immunology (bd. dirs. 1984-89, chmn. bd. dirs. 1987-88, chmn. exam. com. 1986-87), Wash. State Soc. Allergy and Immunology (past pres.), Wash. State Pediatric Soc., Wash. Lung Assn., Puget Sound Allergy Soc. (past pres.), King County Med. Soc., Wash. State Med. Soc., King County Med. Svc. Bur., Western Soc. Allergy amd Immunology. Home: Seattle, Wash. Died Aug. 25, 2006.

SHAPIRO, HAROLD DAVID, lawyer, educator; b. Chgo., Apr. 15, 1927; s. Charles B. and Celia (Nierenberg) S.; m. Beatrice Cahn, June 6, 1950; children: Matthew D., Michal Ann, Nicholas J. BS, Northwestern U., Chgo., 1949, JD, 1952. Adminstrv. asst. State of Ill. Dept. Fin., Springfield, 1952; assoc. Sonnenschein Nath & Rosenthal LLP, Chgo., 1953-59, ptnr., 1959—2005, chmn., 1985—90; Edward A. Harriman adj. prof. law Northwestern U., Chgo., 1970—2005. Sec., bd. dirs. West Side Affordable Housing, Inc., West Side Village, Inc. Trustee, mem. exec. com., sec. Jr. Achievement of Chgo.; bd. dirs. Schwab Rehab. Ctr., Chgo.; pres. Homan & Arthington Found., 1995—96; trustee The Ringer Found., 2000—05, The Guthman

Found., 2003—05; pres. Northwestern U. Law Sch. Alumni Assn., Chgo., 1984—85, chmn. dean's adv. coun., 1997—99. With Seabees USNR, 1945—50, PTO. Recipient Merit award Northwestern U., 1988. Mem. Ill. Bar Assn., ABA, Chgo. Bar Assn., Chgo. Council Lawyers, Legal Club of Chgo. (pres.), Law Club of Chgo., Order of Coif, Wigmore Key, Standard Club, Met. Club, Cliff Dwellers, Chicago Club, Lake Shore Country Club. Democrat. Jewish. Home: Wilmette, Ill. Died Dec. 1, 2005.

SHAPIRO, LUDMILLA NIKOLAEVNA, lecturer, photographer, journalist; b. Moscow, June 11, 1913; came to U.S., 1954; d. Nikolai Pavlovich and Alexandra Vladimirovna (Zhdanovskaya) Nikitin; m. Henry Shapiro Dec. 3, 1933 (dec. Apr. 1991); 1 child, Irina H. Corten. Diploma, Inst. Fgn. Langs., Moscow, 1932, Gorkiy Lit. Inst., 1939. Cert. interpreter in English, French and German, USSR. Translator, lectr., photographer Moscow Bur., UPI and N.Y. Herald Tribune, New York Times, 1935-73; corr. Moscow Bur., Religious News Svc., 1957-59, London Observer, 1960-61; rschr. Russian Rsch. Ctr., Harvard U., Cambridge, Mass., 1957; photographer Moscow Bur. Magnum Photos, 1958-60; Moscow rep. of Sol Hurok, impresario, 1965-68; lectr., cons. on Russia, U. Wis., Madison, from 1973. Author: How Russians Laugh at Themselves, 1975, (booklet) What the Russians Read, 1976; contbg. author: Anthology of 18th Century English and American Writers, 1938. Mem. AAUW, Harvard Dames. Avocation: collecting russian art (donated major collection of russian porcelain to cooper-hewitt museum). Home: Madison, Wis. Died May 8, 2005.

SHAPIRO, PETER EFIMOVICH, sculptor; b. Moscow, Jan. 17, 1933; came to U.S., 1994; s. Efim Semionovich Shapiro and Nina Isaak Hollender; m. Anjelika Plavan, Feb. 7, 1960. BS, Surikov Inst. Sch. of Art, Moscow, 1954; postgrad., Sculptor Studio of M. Olenin, Moscow, 1954-55. Sculptor, Moscow, from 1955. Prin. works include Mus. Art, Moscow, 1977, Mus. Art, Reykjavik, Iceland, 1992, Libr. Congress, Washington, 1994, Aleichem Pl., N.Y.C., 1997, Nat. Portrait Gallery, Washington, 1998. Bd. dirs. USSR - Great Britain Soc., Moscow, 1975-79. Semi-finalist Meml. Bust Competition, Denver Cultural Coun., Denver, 1994; recipient 1st place project "Decembrist", USSR Ministry of Culture, Moscow, 1985, Sculpture of L. Van Beethoven, Bolshoy Theater, Moscow, 1967, Sculpture of Leo Tolstoy, Leo Tolstoy Mus., Yasnaya, Poliana, USSR, 1953. Fellow World Acad. Art and Sci.; mem. Nat. Sculpture Soc. Avocation: music. Home: Rockville, Md. Died Oct. 16, 2004.

SHAPIRO, RAQUEL, counseling administrator, educator; b. Havana, Cuba; came to U.S., 1941; d. Morris and Ida (Antosvilsky) Rebe; m. Nathan Shapiro, Jan. 11, 1948; 1 child, Ronald. BS, R.I. Coll., 1960, MEd, 1966, CAGS, 1972; EdD, Boston U., 1985. Cert. sch. counselor, sch. psychologist, tchr., R.I. Prin., psychologist, counselor, tchr. Providence Sch. Dept., 1960—73; psychologist, counselor, prof. R.I. Coll., Providence, from 1973. Mem. Nat. Assn. Sch. Psychologists, Nat. Assn. Lab. Schs., Ea. Psychol. Assn., New Eng. Psychol. Assn., R.I. Sch. Psychologists. Assn., Pi Lamdba Theta, Delta Kappa Gamma (pres. 1990). Avocations: photography, music, theater. Home: Providence, RI. Died June 19, 2006.

SHAPIRO, ROBERT SIDNEY, psychiatrist, consultant; b. N.Y.C., Feb. 17, 1927; AB, Washington U., 1948, MD, 1952; cert. psychoanalysis, Columbia U., 1962. Pvt. practice psychiatrist and psychoanalyst, N.Y.C., from 1956. Cons. Jewish Home and Hosp. for Aged, Bronx, N.Y., 1956—, Isabella Geriatric Soc., N.Y.C., 1977—. With USN, 1945-46. Died July 5, 2005.

SHARPE, RONALD MORGAN, state police commissioner; b. Phila., Apr. 16, 1940; s. Cornelius Wendell and Elizabeth (Morgan) S.; m. Jessie L. Sowell, May 1, 1965; children: Martin, Tracey, Jennifer. Grad. police adminstrn., Northwestern U., 1968; BA, Elizabethtown Coll., 1975; MA, St. Francis Coll., Loretto, Pa., 1978; postgrad. in edn., Temple U., 1983-85. Patrolman, cpt., sgt. Pa. State Police, 1962-77, lt. Lancaster, 1977-85, capt. Milesburg, 1985-86, maj. Harrisburg, 1986-87, dep. commr., 1987, commr., from 1987. Former adj. prof. Shippensburg (Pa.) U.; chmn. Mcpl. Police Officers' Edn. and Tng. Commn. Trustee Bethel A.M.E. Ch., Harrisburg. Recipient Law Enforcement Oscar, Phila. Housing Police and Internat. Union Police Assns., achievement awards Optimist Club, Lions Club, Outstanding Achievement award 5th Masonic Dist., lllth Tactical Air Support Group, Outstanding Svc. award Elks of World, spl. recognition award Men and Women for Justice, numerous othrs. Mem. Nat. Orgn. Black Law Enforcement Execs., Internat. Assn. Chiefs Police, Pa. Chiefs Police Assn., Dauphin County Chiefs Police Assn., Northwestern U. Traffic Inst. Alumni Assn., NAACP (life, spl. recognition award), Alpha Phi Alpha (Outstanding Pub. Svc. award). Democrat. Avocations: reading, basketball, football, tennis, golf. Home: Hershey, Pa. Died Dec. 21, 2004.

SHATTUCK, ROGER WHITNEY, author, educator; b. NYC, Aug. 20, 1923; s. Howard Francis and Elizabeth (Colt) S.; m. Nora Ewing White, Aug. 20, 1949; children—Tari Elizabeth, Marc Ewing, Patricia Colt, Eileen Shepard. Grad., St. Paul's Sch., Concord, N.H., 1941; BA, Yale U., 1947; DHC (hon.), U. Orléans, France, 1990, Univ. of the South, 2003, St. Michael's Coll., Burlington, Vt., 2003. Information officer UNESCO, Paris, 1947-48; asst. editor Harcourt, Brace & Co., 1949-50; mem. Soc. Fellows, Harvard, 1950-53, instr. French, 1953-56; faculty U. Tex., Austin, 1956-71, prof. English, French, 1968-71, chmn. dept. French and Italian, 1968-71; Commonwealth prof. French U. Va., Charlottesville, 1974-88; prof. modern fgn. languages Boston U., 1988-97. Mem. adv. bd. Nat. Translation Center, 1964-69, chmn., 1966-69; provediteur gen. Coll. de Pataphysique, Paris, 1961-2005; Fulbright prof. U. Dakar, Senegal, 1984-85, elected bd. mem. Mt. Abraham Union H.S., 2000-04. Author: The Banquet Years, 1958; poems Half Tame, 1964, Proust's Binoculars, 1963, Marcel Proust, 1974 (Nat. Book award 1975), The Forbidden Experiment, 1980, The Innocent Eye, 1984, Forbidden Knowledge, 1996, Candor and Perversion, 1999, Proust's Way, 2000; editor or co-editor: Selected Writings of Guillaume Apollinaire, 1950, Mount Analogue, (René Daumal), 1959, The Craft and Context of Translation (with William Arrowsmith), 1961, Selected works of Alfred Jarry, 1965, Occasions by Paul Valèry, 1970, The Story of My Life and The World I Live In (by Helen Keller), 2003; mem. editl. bd. PMLA, 1977-78. Capt. USAAF, 1942-45. Decorated Ordre Palmes Academiques (France).; Guggenheim fellow, 1958-59; Fulbright rsch. fellow, 1958-59; ACLS rsch. fellow, 1969-70. Fellow AAAS; mem. Assn. Literary Scholars and Critics (pres. 1995-96). Died Dec. 8, 2005.

SHAUGHNESSY, EDWARD LAWRENCE, English educator; b. Indpls., June 14, 1932; s. Edward Lawrence and Kathleen Josephine (Walsh) S.; m. Janet Maddox, Nov. 28, 1957; children: Margaret, Katharine Anne McManus (dec.), Mary M., Kevin C. (dec.). AB in English, Butler U., 1958, MA in English, 1963; PhD in English, Ind. U., 1972. Instr. Park Sch. for Boys, Indpls., 1957-65; asst. prof. English Butler U., Indpls., 1970-75, assoc. prof. English, 1975-82, prof. English, 1982-92, Edna R. Cooper prof. English, 1987-92, Edna R. Cooper prof. English emeritus, from 1993. Author: Eugene O'Neill in Ireland: The Critical Reception, 1988, Down the Nights and Down the Days: Eugene O'Neill's Catholic Sensibility, 1996, The Benedictine Oblates of Saint Meinrad Archabbey: A Brief History, 1879-1999, 2000; contbr. articles to profl. jours, chpts. to books. Founder, 1st pres. Forest Manor Neighborhod Assn., Indpls., 1966-67; adv. bd. Repertory Theatre, Christian Theol. Sem., 1974-79. With U.S. Army, 1954-55. Recipient 2nd prize for Essay Arts Ind., 1991, Hibernian Rsch. award, 1994; The Edward L. Shaughnessy prize in Irish Lit. established in his honor, 1993. Mem. AAUP (pres. Butler U. Chpt. 1976-77), MLA, The Eugene O'Neill Soc. (founding mem. 1978), Ind. Tchrs. of Writing, Am. Irish Hist. Soc., Am. Conf. Irish Studies, Santayana Soc., Indpls. Literary Club. Democrat. Roman Catholic. Home: Indianapolis, Ind. Died Jan. 22, 2005.

SHAW, HERBERT JOHN, physics professor; b. Seattle, June 2, 1918; s. Herbert John and Nell Grace (Cayley) S.; m. Francel Harper, Apr. 25, 1943; children: John Joseph, Kathleen, Karen. BA, U. Wash., 1941; MS, Stanford U., 1943, PhD, 1948. Test engr. GE, Schenectady, 1940-41; rsch. assoc. elec. engring. dept. Stanford (Calif.) U., 1948-50, rsch. assoc. Microwave Lab., 1950-57, sr. rsch. assoc., 1957-74, assoc. dir., 1968-77, adj. prof., 1974-83, rsch. prof. applied physics dept., 1983-88, prof. emeritus, 1989—2006. Liaison scientist U.S. Office Naval Rsch., London, 1968-69; cons. to numerous electronics and optics cos. and govt. agys., 1950-2006. Fellow IEEE (Morris N. Liebmann Meml. award 1976, achievement award group on sonics and ultrasonics 1981); mem. NAE, Tau Beta Pi. Home: Menlo Park, Calif. Died Jan. 19, 2006.

SHAW, WILLIAM, diversified telecommunications company executive; b. 1924; married. BS, Bklyn. Coll. Mgr. Remington Rand Co., Inc., 1945-48; with Nat. Lead Industries, 1948-50; chmn. bd., pres., chief exec. officer Volt Info. Scis., Inc., N.Y.C., 1950—2006. Died Mar. 9, 2006.

SHEA, FREDERICKA PALMER, nursing educator; b. Pittsfield, Mass., June 13, 1940; d. Michael J. and Fredericka Zilpha (Palmer) S. BS, Boston U., 1962, MS, 1963; PhD, U. Mich., 1986. Staff nurse Berkshire Med. Ctr., Pittsfield, Mass., 1963-64; pub. health nurse Peace Corps., Togo, West Africa, 1964-66; ICU-CCU nurse Wayne State U. Coll. Nursing, Detroit, 1967-72; asst. prof. Wayne State U. Ctr. Health Rsch., Detroit, 1969-73; assoc. prof. Wayne State U. Coll. Nursing, Detroit, from 1972. Bd. dirs. Wayne State U. Ctr. Health Rsch., 1986—. Contbr. articles to profl. jours. Adv. com. Crockett Vocat. Sch., Detroit Public Schs., 1989—; AIDS educator Mich. Dept. Pub. Health, Lansing, 1988—. Grantee NIH. Mem. ANA, Midwest Nursing Rsch. Soc., Mich. Nurses Assn. (AIDS task force, 1986), Detroit Nurses Assn. Home: Detroit, Mich. Died Sept. 1, 2004.

SHEARER, ERIC BERTHOLD, agricultural economist; b. Berlin, Jan. 27, 1922; came to U.S., 1938; s. Henry and Kate (Nathan) S.; m. Marion Steinberg, Jan. 27, 1946 (div. 1971); children: Evelyn, Robert Henry; m. Maria Adela Mendez, Dec. 30, 1974. BS, MS, U. Ill., 1947; postgrad., NYU, 1947-48, N.Y. State Sch. Agr., 1939-41. Agrl. economist U.S. Dept. Agr., Washington, 1948-49, 55-57; asst. agrl. attache Am. Embassy, Rome, 1949-54, econ. officer Madrid, 1957-61; agrl. officer, vice consul Am. Consulate Gen., Bombay, India, 1954-55; agrl. planning adviser UN FAO, Bogota, Colombia, 1961-63, regional liaison officer Rome, 1963-66; coordinator agrarian reform studies Interam. Com. for Agrl. Devel., Washington, 1966-69; chief agr. US AID Missions, Panama and Santo Domingo, 1974-79; free lance cons. Chevy Chase, Md., from 1980. Sr. agrl. economist Rsch. Triangle Inst., Research Triangle Park, N.C., 1981-84. Co-author: Land Tenure and Socio-Economic Development in Colombia, n1965; contbr. articles to profl. jours. With U.S. Army, 1942-45. Mem. Internat. Assn. Agrl. Economists. Democrat. Avocation: environmental concerns. Died Mar. 31, 2005.

SHEARER, STEVE LANCE, management company executive; b. Portland, Oreg., Feb. 11, 1947; s. Helmer Rasmus and Wilda Marie (Farmer) Johnson; m. Rose Marie Molling, July 15, 1965 (div. Nov. 1969); 1 child, Tammy Michelle; m. Vickie Lynn Bilton, Nov. 29, 1969; children: Sean Lance, Ryan Eugene, Dana Lynn. Student, San Jose State U., 1962-63, Harper Coll., 1972-73. Customer engr. Xerox Corp., Santa Monica, Calif., 1972-80, mgr. field service, 1980-83, system support engr., 1983-84; br. mgr. Wang Labs., Anaheim, Calif., 1984-85; gen. mgr. field ops. Advanced Image Systems, Glendale, Calif., 1985-86; western dist. mgr. ModComp, La Palma, Calif., from 1986. Instr. CPR ARC, Copley, Ohio, 1977. Served with USN, 1965-69. Mem. Mchts. and Mfrs. Assn. Republican. Baptist. Avocation: woodworking. Home: Upland, Calif. Died July 19, 2005.

SHECHTMAN, HARRY, retired judge, law educator; b. Paris, Aug. 19, 1912; arrived in U.S., 1915; s. Solomon and Rose Shechtman; m. Betty Goodman, Nov. 20, 1940 (dec.). BS, L.I. U., 1933, LLD (hon.), 1999; JD, Columbia U., 1938. Bar: N.Y. 1938. Pvt. practice, N.Y.C., 1938—78; adminstrv. law judge N.Y. State Health Dept., N.Y.C., 1978—95. Adj. prof. Fla. Atlantic U., 1995—99; pres. Adminstrv. Law Judge Assn., N.Y.C., 1980—81. Pres. B'nai B'rith Met. Coun., N.Y.C., 1959—61; bd. trustees L.I. U., 1972—83. Mem.: B'nai B'rith, A.J.M. Schwartz Coll. Health Scis., Jewish Nat. Fund. Democrat. Jewish. Died Apr. 13, 2005.

SHEINGORN, LARRY A., ophthalmologist; b. Washington, Sept. 11, 1952; s. Abe and Helen Sheingorn. Undergraduate, Northwestern U., Chgo. Diplomate Am. Bd. of Opthalmology. Pvt. practice, Rockville, Md., from 1982. Developer numerous computer programs for office mgmt. and medically related fields; prodr. dance, music, comedy and med. TV programs. Mem. Montgomery County Med. Soc. Avocation: electronics. Home: Gaithersburg, Md. Died May 6, 2005.

SHELBY, MICHAEL TAYLOR, lawyer, former prosecutor; b. Luling, Tex., Nov. 1958; m. Diana Shelby; children: Elizabeth, Sarah. BS, Tex. A&M U., 1981; JD, U. Tex., 1984. Asst. U.S. atty. (So. Dist.) Tex. US Dept. Justice, 1989—91, asst. U.S. atty. (so. Dist.) Tex., 1992—97, asst. U.S. atty. Dist. Ariz., 1997—2001, U.S. atty. (so. Dist.) Tex., 2002—05; ptnr. Fulbright & Jaworski LLP, Houston, 2005—06. Mem. Pres. Corp. Fraud Task Force, 2002. Comdr. SEAL Team Five USNR. Named a "Texas Superlawyer", 2003, 2004; recipient Director's award, US Dept. Justice. Died July 19, 2006.

SHELLY, JAMES HAROLD, educator, computer engineer, applied mathematician; b. Nov. 28, 1932; Mem. IEEE, Assn. for Computing Machinery, Computer Soc. of IEEE, Sigma Xi. Home: Raleigh, NC. Died June 23, 2005.

SHELTON, MURIEL MOORE, retired religious education administrator; b. Freeport, N.Y., May 29, 1921; d. Samuel Talbott and Agnes Jerolean (Trigg) Payne; m. Ernest William Moore, May 29, 1944 (dec. Apr. 2, 1978); children: Diana Moore Williams, David E. Moore, Cathi Moore Mount, Douglas L. Moore; m. Malcolm Wendell Shelton, Aug. 9, 1987 (dec. March 6, 1997). AB, Eastern Nazarene Coll., 1942; MusM, U. Tex., 1966. Cert. educator gen. and choral music, English, Tex., Tenn., Ark., Kans. Music dir. Coll. Ave. United Meth. Ch., Manhattan, Kans., 1969-71, Cen. United Meth. Ch., Lawrence, Kans., 1971-75, First United Meth. Ch., Horton, Kans., 1975-78; dir. Christian edn. St. Mark's United Meth. Ch., Bethany, Okla., 1980-97; ret., 1997. Chmn. bd. dirs. Northwest Food Pantry, Oklahoma City, 1987-88; rep. St. mark's United Meth. Ch. Labor Link Ctr., 1989—; lectr. in field. Contbr. articles to quar. mags.; author: Song of Joy, 1985, Promises of Good, 1989, Healing in His Wings, 1992. Mem. Christian Educators' Fellowship. Home: Bethany, Okla. Died July 28, 2005.

SHELTON, STEPHEN RALPH, association manager; b. Las Vegas, Nev., Nov. 16, 1937; s. Ralph Verl and Virginia (Golden) S.; m. Sally Anne Long, Dec. 4, 1977 (div. Apr. 1983). BS, Brigham Young U., 1961. Prodn. control mgr. Hercules Powder Co., Bacchus, Utah, 1961-63; mktg. rep. Sinclair Refining Co., Salt Lake City, 1963-66, Shell Oil Co., Santa Monica, Calif., 1966-70; exec. dir. So. Calif. Service Station Assn., Irvine, from 1970. Cons. and guest lectr. U. So. Calif., Calif. Poly. Inst. and Japanese Gasoline Retailers, 1975—; pres. Pro-Calif. Inc., Irvine, 1980—. Author: Energy Crisis Reports, 1974; writer: (TV series) Family Devel., 1972; contbr. articles to profl. jours. Com. person Transportation Adv., Orange City, Calif., 1980, Fuel Shortage Contingency, Orange City, 1981. Served to sgt. U.S. Army, 1957-63. Mem. Am. Soc. Assn. Execs. Democrat. Avocations: scuba diving, travel. Home: San Juan Capistrano, Calif. Died Mar. 3, 2005.

SHEN, CHUNG Y., chemical engineer, consultant; b. Peking, China, Dec. 15, 1921; came to U.S., 1949; s. Chia I. and Yi (Ting) S.; m. Colleen Yu, June 10, 1954; children: Sheldon, Vincent, Anthony. BS, S.W. Assoc. U., Kunming, China, 1942; MSChemE, U. Louisville, 1950; PhD, U. Ill., 1954. Sect. leader Ctrl. Chem. Works, Shang, China, 1948-49; sr. engr. Inst. Ind. Rsch., Louisvllle, 1949-52; rsch.

fellow U. Ill., Urbana, 1952-54; sr. fellow Monsanto Co., St. Louis, 1954-86; founder Shen & Shen, Inc., St. Louis, from 1986. Contbr. more than 20 articles to profl. jours. Fellow AIChE; mem. Orgn. Chinese Ams. (pres. 1976). Achievements include invention of phoscheck fire retardants and fluff detergent process; 67 patents in field. Died Mar. 4, 2005.

SHEN, YING, chemist, educator; b. Changshu, Jiangsu Province, China, Sept. 14, 1924; d. Tung Wu Shen and Yun Quei. BS in Chemistry, Tsing Hua U., Peking, China, 1947; MA in Sci., Peabody Coll., 1959; MS in Chemistry, Ohio State U., 1972; postgrad., Standford U., 1963, U. Okla., from 1980. Tchr., Taipei, Puli, Taiwan, 1947—60; asst. to UNESCO expert UNESCO, Taipei, 1960—62; grad. tchg. asst./assoc. Ohio State U.; lectr. Cen. State U., Edmonds, Okla., 1978—79; lab. scientist/chemist Okla. Dept. Environ. Quality, Oklahoma City, from 1980. Seminar lectr. Beijing Meteorol. Coll., 1999. Sec. Chinese Assn. Greater Oklahoma City, 1982—83. Scholar, Internat. Coop. Adminstrn., 1958—59, Fulbright schol, U.S Dept. State, 1962, Ford Found. scholar, Ford Found./Stanford U., 1963. Mem.: Asia Assn. Okla., Pi Lambda Theta. Democrat. Avocations: music, sports, reading. Home: Fremont, Calif. Died Apr. 16, 2004.

SHEN, YONGRONG, research scientist; b. Hefei, Anhui, China, Sept. 23, 1952; s. Guangbing Shen and Shihua Hu; m. Liyun Cao, May 14, 1980; 1 child, Tao. MS, Chanhchun Inst. Physics, Chinese Acad. Scis., People's Republic of China, 1983, U. Paderborn (Nordrhein-Westfalen, Germany), 1990, PhD, 1994. Rsch. asst. Changchun (Jilin, People's Republic of China) Inst. Physics, Chinese Acad. Scis., 1977-83, rsch. assoc., 1983-88; rsch. asst. U. Paderborn (Nordrhein-Westfalen, Germany), 1988-94, rsch. assoc., 1994-95, U. Wis., Madison, 1995-97, Wash. State U., Pullman, 1998, sr. rsch. assoc., from 1998. Vis. rsch. advisor Lab. Excited State Processes, Chinese Acad. Scis., Changchun, Jilin, 1995-96; referee Jour. Physics, 1997—. Mem. Am. Soc. Physics, German Soc. Physics. Home: Pullman, Wash. Died Sept. 12, 2004.

SHEPHERD, ELIZABETH POOLE, health science facility administrator; b. Bulape, Kasai, Congo, Mar. 16, 1937; (parents Am. citizens); d. Mark Keller and Sara Amelia (Day) Poole; m. Donald Ray Shepherd, June 6, 1958; children: Lisa, Stephanie, Leslie, Don Poole. BA magna cum laude, Austin Coll., 1958. Cert. secondary and elem. tchr., Tex. Tchr. Thomas Jefferson High Sch., Dallas, 1958, Edward H. Cary Jr. High Sch., Dallas, 1959-60; bus. mgr. Donald R. Shepherd, M.D., P.A., Conroe, Tex., 1972-96; bus. mgr., co-owner Profl. Labs, Inc., Houston, 1975-82; bus. mgr. Profl. Pathology Labs., Ltd., Conroe, 1997-2000, ret., 2000. Brownie leader Girl Scouts Am., 1967-69; dist. chmn. San Jacinto council Boy Scouts Am., Conroe, 1977; pres. Women of Ch. First Presbyn. Ch., Conroe, 1973-74, Montgomery County Med. Soc. Aux., Conroe, 1974-75; bd. dirs. ARC, Conroe, 1970-80; bd. dirs., officer Med. Ctr. Hosp. Vols., Conroe, 1978-81. Mem.: AAUW, Llano Women's Culture Club (pres. 2003—04), Alpha Delta, Alpha Chi. Republican. Presbyterian. Avocations: gardening, reading. Died Mar. 9, 2005.

SHEPPARD, HOWARD REECE, accountant; b. Monmouth, Ill., Mar. 1, 1926; s. Loren Ernest and Ruby Pearl (Magee) S.; m. Mary Kathryn Hofstetter, June 8, 1951 (div.); children: Stephen, Peter, Jean Elizabeth; m. Maxine Dolores Johnson, Nov. 28, 1974. BSBA, Northwestern U., Evanston, Ill., 1946. CPA, Calif. Chief cost acct. Sunkist Growers Plant, Corona, Calif., 1946-52; fiscal officer U.S. Guided Missle Test Ctr., Pt. Mugu, Calif., 1952-54; internal auditor Sunkist Growers Plant, Corona, Calif., 1954-58; auditor Eadie & Payne CPAs, San Bernardino, Calif., 1958-61; pvt. practice Corona, 1961-63 and from 87; ptnr. Sheppard, Reynolds & Sholl, Corona, 1963-85, Sheppard, Reynolds & Green, Corona, 1985-87. Faculty expert Hastings Law Sch., U. Calif., San Francisco, 1986-98; lectr. Dept. Water and Power, L.A., 1986. Author: Litigation Services Resource Directory, 1989, 5th edit., 1994; co-author: Litigation Services Handbook, 1990, 3d edit., 2001. Lt. USNR. Mem. AICPA, Calif. Soc. CPAs. Avocation: sailing. Home: Riverside, Calif. Died Aug. 26, 2004.

SHERMAN, BURTON STUART, medical educator, researcher, consultant; b. Bklyn., Nov. 12, 1930; s. Samuel and Mary (Bloom) S.; m. Eileen Iris Chanin, Aug. 30, 1952; children: Steven, Lisa, Cari, Keith. BA, NYU, 1951, MS, 1956; PhD, SUNY, Bklyn., 1960. Rsch. asst. Sloan-Kettering Inst., N.Y.C., 1951-52; rsch. chemist Jewish Hosp. of Bklyn., 1952-56, rsch. assoc., 1959-60; from instr. to assoc. prof. SUNY-Downstate Med. Ctr., N.Y.C., 1960-85, assoc. prof. emeritus, from 1986; prof., dean Sch. Health Scis. Touro Coll., Dix hills, N.Y., 1986-89, prof., dean emeritus, from 1989. Cons. Tobacco Chem. Corp., Wilmington, Del., 1967-74, Hoffman-LaRoche Inc., Basel, Switzerland, 1968-71; vis. scientist, Strangeways Rsch. Lab., Cambridge, Eng., 1964-65; exec. dir., N.Y. Biomed. Cons. Co., Valley Stream, N.Y., 1978—. Co-author: Techniques of Medication, 1969; contbr. articles to profl. jours. Trustee Congregation Beth Emeth, Hewlett, N.Y., 1969—, pres., chmn. bd. trustees, 1971-73. Mem. AAAS, Am. Assn. Anatomists, Am. Assn. Clin. Anatomists, Soc. Sigma Xi. Avocations: langs., reading, sports. Home: Valley Stream, NY. Died Jan. 3, 2005.

SHERMAN, HELEN WILSON, artist; b. Providence, R.I., June 2, 1913; d. Ellery Lewis and Fanny (Hunt) W. Grad., R.I. Sch. Design, 1935, BFA (hon.), 1990. One woman shows include Doll & Richards Gallery, Providence Art Club, Newport Art Assn., Mint Mus., Copley Soc., Boston, James Hunt Galleries, Nantucket, Mass., Attleboro Art Mus., Wildside Galleries, Phoenix, Crossroads of Sport, Inc., N.Y., New England Field Trial Assn., Silvermine Guild Artists. Recipient Ribbons Vistas show, 1982-89, Ribbon Sailor's Valentine Gallery, 1989. Mem. Providence Art Club (life). Republican. Avocation: writing. Died June 7, 2005.

SHERMAN, MARTIN, entomologist, educator; b. Newark, Nov. 21, 1920; s. Louis and Anna (Norkin) S.; m. Ruth Goldsmith, Sept. 25, 1943 (div. Nov. 1975); children: Laurel Deborah Sherman Englehart, Susan Leslie Sherman Kitakis. BS, Rutgers U., 1941, MS, 1943; PhD, Cornell U., 1948. Research fellow in entomology Rutgers U., 1941-43; research asst. Cornell U., 1945-48; entomologist Beech-Nut Packing Co., Rochester, N.Y., 1948-49; mem. faculty U. Hawaii, Honolulu, from 1949, prof. entomology, 1958-86, prof. emeritus entomology, from 1986. Fulbright scholar U. Tokyo, 1956-57, Royal Vet. and Agrl. Coll. of Denmark, 1966; vis. prof. Rutgers U., 1973 Editorial bd.: Pacific Sci, 1962-66, Jour. Med. Entomology, 1968-72. Served to 1st lt. USAAF, 1943-45. Fellow: Am. Inst. Chemists; mem.: Internat. Soc. for Study Xenobiotics, Hawaiian Entomology Soc. (pres. 1969—70), Japanese Soc. Applied Entomology and Zoology, Am. Registry Profl. Entomologists, Soc. Environ. Toxicology and Chemistry, Soc. Toxicology, Am. Chem. Soc., Entomol. Soc. Am. (gov. bd. 1974—77, pres. Pacific br. 1970), Torch Club, Jewish War Vets. U.S.A., Am. Legion, VFW, Sigma Xi, Gamma Sigma Delta, Phi Kappa Phi, Delta Phi Alpha. Died Mar. 16, 2005.

SHERMAN, PAUL JACK, lawyer; b. N.Y.C., May 17, 1922; s. Louis and Freda (Shapiro) S.; m. Judity Jocelyn Broido, Aug. 7, 1949; children: Scott Leigh, Karen Elise Sherman-Schwebel. BA, Columbia U., 1943; JD, Yale U., 1948; MLS, NYU, 1951. Bar: N.Y. 1948. Law sec. Judge Thomas E. Swan, 1948-49; asst. counsel ASCAP, N.Y.C., 1949-55; legal staff mem. Music Corp. Am., N.Y.C., 1955-61; ptnr. Sherman, Barovick & Konecky, N.Y.C., 1961-62; resident counsel, exec. v.p. Gen. Artists Corp., N.Y.C., 1962-63; ptnr. Pryor, Cashman, Sherman & Flynn, N.Y.C., from 1963. Bd. dirs. Montefiore Cemetary Corp. & Springfield, L.I. Cemetary Soc., Beth Moses and Wellwood Cemetery Assn. Editor-in-chief Columbia Daily Spectator, 1943; bd. editors Yale Law Jour., 1948; contbr. articles to profl. jours. Lt. (j.g.) U.S. Navy, 1943-46, PTO. Mem. ABA, N.Y.C. Bar Assn. Avocations: sculpture, photography, skiing, tennis. Home: New Rochelle, NY. Died Dec. 13, 2004.

SHERMAN, SUSAN ROTH, social welfare educator; b. N.Y.C., Oct. 5, 1939; d. Lester and Louise (Klein) Roth; m. Malcolm J. Sherman, Sept. 8, 1963; children: Barbara, Michael. AB, U. Chgo., 1960; PhD, U. Calif., Berkeley, 1964. Asst. prof. Sch. Pub. Health UCLA, 1965-68; assoc. and sr. rsch. scientist N.Y. State Dept. Mental Hygiene, Albany, 1969-75; from lectr. to disting. svc. prof. Sch. Social Welfare U. Albany, 1974. Mem. rsch. rev. com. N.Y. State Health Planning Commn., Albany, 1982-87; mem. adv. bd. Health Systems Agy., Albany, 1979-82; cons. N.Y. State Office for Aging, Albany, 1973-74, 79-80, 87; vis. scholar Columbia U., 1986. Co-author: Foster Families for Adults, 1988, Environment for Aging, 1988; contbr. articles to profl. jours. Bd. dirs. Sr. Svc. Ctr., Albany, 1980-86, B'nai B'rith Parkview Sr. Apts., Albany, 1988-98; mem. Jewish Student Svcs. Com., 1987-96. Grantee SUNY, N.Y. State Health Rsch. Coun., NIMH, AOA, Andrus Fedn., 1975-88. Fellow Gerontol. Soc. Am. (mem.-at-large of sect. exec. com. 1980-82); mem. Assn. for Gerontology in Higher Edn. (pres. 1989-90, treas. 1981-83, chair nominations com., long-range planning com., pers. com., program evaluation com., regional fac. devel. 1979-94), State Soc. on Aging (pres. 1979-80, Beattie award 1990). Home: Albany, NY. Died June 3, 2004.

SHERO, JOHN PAUL, JR., minister; b. Dallas, Oct. 14, 1929; s. John Paul and Alberta Elizabeth (King) S.; m. Jeam Haris Thompson, Jan. 20, 1947 (wid. Nov. 1985); children: John Paul III, Michael Lee, David Wayne, James Arthur; m. Elsie Mae Carl, Sept. 3, 1990; children: Leah Rae Honza, Kathy Smith, Tony Honza, Eddy Kay Skinner, Mark Wayne Honza. Student, Abilene (Tex.) Christian U., 1957-72. Lic. child care adminstr., Tex. Ceramic tile setter J.P. Shero Tile Co., Dallas, 1947-53; min. Lilley's Chapel Ch. of Christ, Daingerfield, Tex., 1953-57, Russell Ave. Ch. of Christ, Abilene, 1957-64, Baker Heights Ch. of Christ, Abilene, 1964-82, Austin Ave. Ch. of Christ, Brownwood, Tex., 1972-82, Weshill Ch. of Christ, Corsicana, Tex., 1982-90, Cen. Ch. of Christ, Victoria, Tex., from 1990. Bd. dir., pres. Cherokee (Tex.) Home for Children, 1964-82; coord. Monterrey (Mex.) Sch. of Preaching, 1975-82; bd. dir. Boles Children's Home, Quinlan, Tex., 1987—; dir., founder Austin Ave Sch. Bibl. Studies, Brownwood, 1976-82; speaker Ablene Christian U. Elders Workshop, 1981, 85, Lubbock Christian U. Lectureship, 1984, Okla. Christian Coll. Lectureship, Oklahoma City, 1980. Author (video series) Concepts of Leadership, 1986; contbr. articles to Christian Bible Tchr., Firm Found., 20th Century; co-host Mediterranean Holy Land Lectureship Cruise, 1978-79; announcer radio programs. Bd. dir. Navarro Coll. Found., Corsicana, 1987-90. Mem. NRA, Safari Club Internat., Lions (Riley club), Rotary (S.W. Abilene, Brownswood and Corsicana chpts.). Avocations: hunting, travel, photography. Home: San Saba, Tex. Died Oct. 21, 2004.

SHERRICK, CARL EDWIN, research psychologist, consultant; b. Carnegie, Pa., Oct. 28, 1924; s. Carl Edwin and Ruth Hunter (Clark) S.; m. Patricia Ames Daily, Oct. 15, 1954; children: Kathleen, Diana, Molly Clark. BS in Chemistry, Carnegie-Mellon U., 1948; MA in Psychology, U. Va., 1950, PhD in Psychology, 1952. Asst. prof. psychology Washington U., St. Louis, 1953-59; rsch. assoc. Cen. Inst. for Deaf, St. Louis, 1959-61, U. Va., Charlottesville, 1961-62; rsch. psychologist Princeton (N.J.) U., 1962-70, sr. rsch. psychologist, from 1970. Mem. communicative scis. study sect. NIH, Bethesda, Md., 1967-71, mem. adv. coun. Nat. Adv. Neurol. and Communicative Disorders and Stroke, 1985-89, Nat. Inst. on Deafness and Other Communication Disorders, 1989-91. Contbr. articles and revs. to sci. jours. Sgt. AUS, 1944-46. Rsch. grantee NIH, 1972-91. Fellow APA, Am. Psychol. Soc., Acoustical Soc. Am.; mem. Psychonomic Soc., Raven Soc., Sigma Xi. Unitarian Universalist. Avocations: computer telecommunications, human factors. Home: Princeton, NJ. Died June 14, 2005.

SHERWIN, JOHN MARTIN, orthopaedic surgeon; b. White Plains, N.Y., July 2, 1929; s. Martin Hutchinson and Barbara (Laimbeer) S.; m. Marjorie Richardson, Feb. 23, 1952; children: Elizabeth, James, Jane. BA, Colgate U., 1951; student, Union Theol. Sem., 1951; MD, Albany Med. Coll., 1960. Intern Hartford (Conn.) Hosp., 1960-61, resident in surgery, 1961-62; resident in orthopaedic surgery Newington Children's Hosp., 1963, Yale-New Haven Med. Ctr., 1963-65; resident Yale U., New Haven, 1965; pvt. practice orthopaedic surgery Manchester, N.H., from 1965. Pres. med. staff Elliot Hosp., Manchester, 1975; del. to AMA, Chgo., 1984-95. Inventor Sherwin knee retractor, 1971. Capt. USMCR, 1951-56. Fellow ACS, Am. Acad. Orthopaedic Surgeons; mem. AMA, N.H. Med. Soc. (pres. exec. com. 1982), Hillsborough County Med. Soc. Republican. Presbyterian. Avocation: flying. Died Feb. 11, 2004.

SHERWOOD, LEONA, artist; b. N.Y.C., May 20, 1914; d. William and Caroline (Maile) Herrmann; m. Joseph S. Keiper, Aug. 11, 1940 (div. 1948); m. William C. Sherwood, Sept. 17, 1961 (dec. 1978). Pvt. studies with John Chetcuti, N.Y.C.; pvt. critiques with Robert Gelinas, U. South Fla.; pvt. critiques with Philip Hicken, Nantucket, Mass.; student workshop, Mint Mus., Charlotte, N.C. Exec. sec. fund raising and promotions Nat. Council Episcopal Ch., N.Y.C., 1940-48; asst. to religious dir. Crusade for Freedom, N.Y.C., 1951-53; exec. sec. collegiate sch. liaison West End Collegiate Ch., N.Y.C., 1954-61; instr. painting, drawing Longboat Key (Fla.) Art Ctr., from 1969, Manatee Art League, Bradenton, Fla., 1974-89. Instr., France, 1986—87, 1989, 91, 93, Portugal, 87, Greece, 89, Ireland, 90, Madeira, 90, Malta, 92, Wales, 92. Represented in permanent collections Longboat Key Art Ctr., one-woman shows include Hickory Mus. Fine Art, N.C., 1979, Edison Coll., Ft. Myers, Fla., 1964, Venice Art League, Fla., 1969, S. Fla. Mus., Bradenton, 1971, Nat. League Am. Penwomen State, Tampa, Fla., 1972, Fla. Watercolor Soc., Boca Raton, 1984, numerous others with various awards and placings. Mem. Longboat Key Art Ctr. Mem.: N.Y.C. Artists Fellowship, Fla. Suncoast Watercolor Soc., Nat. League of Am. Penwomen (Bienniale Washington, D.C. "best of show" 1992), Fla. Watercolor Soc. (Alan Chiara award 2001), Fla. Artist Group, Longboat Key Art Ctr. (best of show 1994). Democrat. Avocations: theater, walking, reading, crossword puzzles. Home: Longboat Key, Fla. Died Oct. 24, 2004.

SHIELDS, ALAN J., artist; b. Lost Springs, Kans., Feb. 4, 1944; s. Donald Chester and Arvis Ione (Long) S.; m. Maria Rosiaria Loconsolo, July 8, 1978; children: Jason Loconsolo, Victoria Moon. Student, Kans. State U., 1962-67; student, U. Maine, 1968-69. One-man shows include Contemporary Paula Cooper Gallery, N.Y., 1991, Art Gallery, Ahmedabad, India, 1989, Paula Cooper Gallery, N.Y., 1988, Lakeside Gallery, Richland Community Coll., Dallas, 1988, Visual Arts Gallery, SUNY, Purchase, 1987, Leidy Gallery, Guild Hall Mus., E. Hampton, N.Y., 1987, Cleve. Ctr. Contemporary Art, 1986, Williams Coll. Mus. Art, Williamstown, Mass., 1981, Mus. Contemporary Art, Chgo., 1973; exhibited in group shows Walker Art Ctr., Mpls., 1989, Kalamazoo Inst. Arts, 1988, Galerie Albrecht, Munich, 1988-89, Phila. Mus. Art, 1986, Mus. Modern Art, N.Y., 1986. Guggenheim fellow, 1973. Mem. Ducks Unlimited Club, Nature Conservancy (Shelter Island, N.Y.). Died Dec. 20, 2005.

SHIELDS, JAMES RICHARD, alcohol and drug counselor, consultant; b. Milw., Mar. 1, 1935; s. Edmund and Louise S.; m. Marlene Brietkreutz, Nov. 20, 1957. Grad. high sch., Hartford, Wis. Cert. alcohol and drug counselor, Wis.; nat. cert. addiction counselor, alcohol and drug counselor; cert. employee asst. profl.; cert. addictions specialist. Cons. Wis. Energy Corp., Milw., from 1979. With U.S. Army, 1959-66. Mem. Occupational Programing Cons. Assn., Employee Assistance Soc. N.Am., Employee Assistance Program Assn. (cert.). Home: Hartford, Wis. Died Feb. 14, 2005.

SHINEVAR, PETER O'NEIL, lawyer; b. Jackson, Mich., Oct. 3, 1955; m. Karen Kay Coats, Aug. 25, 1979. AB with high distinction, U. Mich., 1977, JD summa cum laude, 1980, postgrad., 1978-81. Bar: D.C. 1982, N.Y. 1994. Law clk. U.S. Ct. Appeals (D.C. cir.), Washington, 1981-82; assoc. Bredhoff & Kaiser, Washington, 1982-88, ptnr., 1989-92; assoc. dir. rsch. The Segal Co., 1992-95; spl. counsel O'Melveny & Myers LLP, 1995-2000, ptnr., from 2000. Mem. ABA (sec. labor and employment law employee benefits com., mgmt. co-chair, subcom. on welfare plans, sec. taxation, employee benefits com.), Order of the Coif, Phi Beta Kappa. Democrat. Home: Oradell, NJ. Died Feb. 19, 2004.

SHIPLEY, JOYCE DEBORAH, psychologist; b. Boston, Sept. 6, 1956; d. Kenneth Saul and Elinor Miriam (Godes) Wolfson; m. Anthony Alfred Shipley, Sept. 1, 1985; 1 child, Justin John. BA, U. So. Calif., L.A., 1978; PhD, Calif. Sch. Profl. Psychology, 1984. Psychiat. aide North Hollywood Community Hosp., Hollywood, Calif., 1979-80; psychol. asst. Arroyo Counseling Svcs., Pasadena, Calif., 1983-84; program dir. The Psychol. Ctr., Lawrence, Mass., 1984-85; clin. psychologist Chelmsford (Mass.) Med. Assocs., 1984-86; co-dir. Chelmsford Family Counseling Ctr., from 1986. Tutor Elmira (N.Y.) Correctional Facility, 1974-75; community cons. Lowell High Sch., 1988—; supr. Boston Coll. Interns, Chelmsford, 1986—; co-dir., co-founder Chelmsford Family Counseling Ctr., 1987—. Mem. Am. Psychol. Assn., Mass. Psychol. Assn., Amnesty Internat. Democrat. Jewish. Avocations: running, skiing, weight training. Home: Chelmsford, Mass. Died Feb. 20, 2004.

SHIPP, JACQUELYN ADAMS, retired school district administrator; b. Minden, La., May 17, 1931; d. Gordon Earl and Lorene (Sanders) Adams; m. William Carl Shipp (div.); children: Gordon Carl, Carolyn Shipp Calloway. Student, La. Tech. U., 1947-49; BA, Northeast La. U., 1955, MEd, 1962. Cert. tchr., La. Elem. tchr. Franklin Parish Sch. System, Gilbert and Wisner, La., 1955-68, guidance counselor Winnsboro, 1968-70, elem. sch. supr., 1970-87, sch. supt., 1987-94; ret., 1994. Del. La. Dem. Conf., Monroe, 1972; bicentennial chmn. Franklin Parish, 1975-76; mem. Task Force Gov.'s Priorities of Future of La., 1978, Gov.'s Conf. on Tourism, 1978; bd. dirs. Franklin Parish Coun. on Aging, 1982-87. Named Disting. Alumnus Coll. Edn. N.E. La. U., 1987. Mem. La. Assn. Sch. Supts., La. Assn. Sch. Execs., Franklin Parish Northeast La. U. Alumni (pres. 1972-73), Phi Delta Kappa, Delta Kappa Gamma (state and local officer 1975-89). Methodist. Home: Winnsboro, La. Died Apr. 7, 2005.

SHIRAI, REYNOLD S., physician; b. Honolulu, May 29, 1930; m. Edna T. Kozuma, Aug. 22, 1953; 4 children. MD, Creighton U., 1954. Diplomate Am. Bd. Pediatrics. Pvt. practice pediatrics, Honolulu, from 1960. Capt. U.S. Army, 1961-63. Fellow Am. Acad. Pediatrics; mem. AMA, Hawaii Med. Assn. Republican. Roman Catholic. Avocations: woodworking, gardening, mutual fund watching. Died July 15, 2005.

SHIREY, MARGARET (PEGGY SHIREY), elementary school educator; b. Sussex, N.J., Nov. 24, 1950; d. Steve and Grace (McGlew) Piniaha; children: Todd, Jessica. BS, Marymount Coll., Salina, Kans., 1972; M Elem. Edn., Ctrl. State U., 1985. Cert. elem. tchr., Okla. Tchr. Putnam City Sch. Dist., Oklahoma City, from 1980. Active Putnam City Reading Coun.; bargaining mem. Putnam City, 1993-95. Recipient Excellent Educator award; named One of Okla.'s Best Tchrs. Channel 5 Alive, Oklahoma City, 1991, Tchr. of the Yr. Harvest Hills Elem., 1998, 2002. Mem. NEA, ASCD, Okla. Edn. Assn., Putnam City Assn. Classroom Tchrs. (bldg. rep. 1983-86, legis. chairperson 1989-92). Democrat. Avocations: writing, reading, walking. Home: Oklahoma City, Okla. Died Apr. 1, 2005.

SHIROTANI, KYOKO YUYUU, artist; b. Hawaii, May 20, 1940; BA in Art, Kohnan U., Japan, 1968. Actor: (book) Greater Love, 1995. Bd. dirs. Nika, Japan, 1970—71; pastor Interface Christ Ch., Calif., 1990—95. Avocation: horticulture, exploring. Died Jan. 28, 2005.

SHMUKLER, STANFORD, lawyer; b. Phila., June 16, 1930; s. Samuel and Tessye (Dounne) S.; m. Anita Golove, Mar. 21, 1951; children: Jodie Lynne Shmukler Girsh, Joel Mark, Steven David. BS in Econs., U. Pa., 1951, JD, 1954. Bar: D.C. 1954, Pa. 1955, U.S. Ct. Appeals (2d cir.) 1959, U.S. Supreme Ct. 1959, U.S. Ct. Appeals (3d cir.) 1960, U.S. Ct. Mil. Appeals 1966. Atty. U.S. Bur. Pub. Roads, 1954-55, cons., 1955-57; sole practice Phila., from 1955. Lectr. Temple U. Law Sch., 1975-78; mem., past sec., exec. dir. crminal procedural rules com. Pa. Supreme Ct., 1971-87; mem. lawyers adv. com. Ct. Appeals for 3d cir., 1977-80, selection com. Criminal Justice Act Panel, 1979-84; chmn. selection com. Phila. Bar Ct. Appointments, 1988-91. Contbr. articles to profl. jours. Bd. dirs. Ecumenical Halfway House, 1967-71; bd. mgrs. Alumni Assn., Ctrl. High Sch., Phila. Served to col. JAGC, USAR, from 1955 (ret.). Recipient Phila. Bar Assn. Criminal Justice Sect. award, 1977, Justice Thurgood Marshall award, 1992; Legion of Honor, Chapel of the Four Chaplains, 1983. Mem. ABA, Pa. Bar Assn., Phila. Bar Assn. (bd. govs. 1971-73, past chmn. criminal justice com. and mil. justice com.), Fed. Bar Assn. (past chmn. criminal law com. adminstrn. justice sect., co-chmn. criminal law com. Phila. chpt., Leadership award Phila. 1991, 94), Pa. Assn. Criminal Def. Lawyers, Nat. Assn. Criminal Def. Lawyers. Democrat. Jewish. Deceased.

SHOCKEY, THOMAS EDWARD, real estate company executive, engineer; b. Aug. 17, 1926; s. Verlie Draper and Margaret Ruth (Shuford) S.; m. Jacqueline McPherson, June 4, 1949; children: Cheryl Ann, Jocelyn Marie, Valerie Jean. BS, Tex. A&M U., 1950; postgrad., St. Mary's U., 1964, San Antonio Coll., 1972, Pacific Western U., 1981. With Petty Geophys. Survey, 1947-49, J.E. Ingram Equipment Co., 1950-51; co-owner, archtl. engr., realtor Moffett Lumber Co., Inc., San Antonio, 1952-76; cons. gen. contracting, gen. real estate, from 1944; retailer wholesale bldg. material, from 1951; v.p., from 1959. Real estate counselor, appraiser, 1972—; real estate appraiser Gill Appraisal Svc., San Antonio, 1977—; comml. loan appraiser, underwriter, analyst Gill Savs. Assn., Gill Cos., San Antonio, 1979; chief appraiser, underwriter, architect, engr., insp. Gill Cos., 1981, v.p., 1981-87, ret., 1987; v.p. La Hacienda Savs. Assn., 1988-91, ret., 1991. Fire chief Mico Vol. Fire Dept., 1993—95, tng. officer, 1996—2000. With inf. Signal Corps U.S. Army, 1944—46, ETO. Davidson fellow Tau Beta Pi. Mem. San Antonio C. of C., Nat. Lumber Dealers, Nat. Home Builders, Nat. Real Estate Bd., Nat. Inst. Real Estate Brokers, Internat. Soc. Real Estate Appraisers, Tex. Assn. Real Estate Insps., Real Estate Appraisers Tex., Nat. Assn. Rev. Appraisers and Mortgage Underwriters, Internat. Inst. Valuers, Internat. Platform Assn., State Firemen's and Fire Marshal's Assn. of Tex. Home: Mico, Tex. Died June 26, 2006.

SHOCKLEY, JAMES THOMAS, retired physics professor; b. Topaz, Mo., Sept. 16, 1925; s. William Ervin and Minnie Catherine (Turnbull) S.; m. Joan Elsie Griess, June 17, 1950 (div. Aug. 1968); 1 child, John William; m. Betty Jean Truitt, July 28, 1989. BA, Calif. State U., Fresno, 1951, MA, 1953; postgrad., Claremont Grad. Sch., 1955; PhD, U. So. Calif., 1961. Cert. secondary tchr., Calif.; cert. community coll. tchr., Calif. Aerodynamicist N.Am. Aviation, Los Angeles, 1953; instr. Calif. State U., Fresno, 1954-55, asst. prof. physics, 1956-63, instr. workshop in phys. sci. for elem. tchrs., 1961, credential advisor, supr. student teaching, 1956-86, assoc. prof., 1963-68, prof., 1968-90, prof. emeritus physics, from 1990. Cons. Fresno County Schs., 1971, USAF, Fresno, 1971, 72; validity cons. Commn. Tchr. Preparation and Licensing, San Francisco, 1977; instr. NSF Inst. for high sch. physics tchrs., 1962-63. Author: Physics and Astronomy for Liberal Arts Students, 1970; creator 7 Univ. Courses, 1958-85; textbook reviewer, 1965-77. Active mem. Civil Def., Fresno, 1952; mem. City-Univ. Edn. Liaison Com., Fresno, 1963-64; judge Bullard High Sch. Sci. Fair, Fresno, 1964-66; sponser Physics Club, Fresno, 1953-55. Recipient I Dare You award Danforth Found., Sanger, Calif., 1944, Tchr. grant Danforth Found., Fresno, 1958; Congress of Parents and Tchrs. scholar, San Diego, 1960. Mem. Am. Inst. Physics, Planetary Soc., Astron. Soc. Pacific, Aero Club, Phi Delta Kappa. Mem. Christian Ch. Avocations: flying, reading, photography, international travel, painting. Home: Oakhurst, Calif. Died Sept. 23, 2005.

SHOEMAKER, ROBERT GARDNER, philosopher educator; b. Long Branch, N.J., Sept. 26, 1941; s. Harold Gardner and Isabel Mae (Hiester) S.; m. Nancy Elise Matheny, July 6, 1963 (div. 1982); children: David Gardner, Catherine Denise; m. Nell Doyle, July 27, 1991. Student, Emory U., 1959-60; BA, Millsaps Coll., 1963; PhD, U. Tex., 1967. Prof. philosophy Hendrix Coll., Conway, Ark., 1966-87, prof. emeritus philosophy, from 1987. Vis. lectr. Millsaps Coll., Jackson, Mis., 1968, 70; vis. scholar U. Ark., Fayetteville, 1978, Vanderbilt U., Nashville, 1978-79 Author philos. books and articles, revs., papers, novels and short stories. Various posts Boy Scouts Am., Conway, 1978-81; actor, singer Conway Community Arts Assn., 1970-87; sec., pres. other offices Human Rels. Coun., Conway, 1968-72; pres. other offices Hendrix Coll. AAUP, Conway, 1970-87; chmn. Ark. Humanities Com., 1975-77. Nat. Merit scholar, 1959-60; Woodrow Wilson fellow, 1963-64. Mem. Ark. Philos. Assn. (pres. other offices 1969-89), Miss. Philos. Assn., Am. Philos. Assn. Avocations: fishing, painting, bridge, singing. Home: Conway, Ark. Died Oct. 8, 2004.

SHOFFNER, CLARENCE LORENZO, dentist; b. Greensboro, N.C., Dec. 13, 1921; s. Ira Benjamin and Lelia (Hairston) S.; m. Carrie Carter, Nov. 13, 1943; children: Selia Lorene, Annah Yvonne. BS, A&T State U., 1942; DDS, Howard U., 1951. Lic. dentist, Md., N.C., N.Y. Dental surgeon Dept. Pub. Health, Raleigh, N.C., 1951-52; sole practice dental surgeon Weldon, N.C., from 1952. Com. mem. Dental Indsl. commn., N.C., 1973-74; dep. dental examiner N.C. State Bd. Dental Examiners, Raleigh, 1980-83. Bd. Trustees N.C. Community Coll., 1987—; mem. Bd. Edn. Weldon City Sch. System, 1987—. Served with USAF, 1942-45. Recipient award Howard U. Alumni Coll. Dentistry, Washington, 1974, 20th Yr. Appreciation award N.C. Human Relations Council, 1983. Mem. ADA, Acad. Dentistry Internat., Acad. Gen. Dentistry, Am. Coll. Dentistry, N.C. Dental Soc. (com. mem. oral cancer 1972-73), Omega Psi Phi (recipient 40 Yr. Service award 1982). Clubs: Nat. Guardsmen, Inc., H-M of Am. Lodges: KC. Democrat. Roman Catholic. Avocations: golf, swimming. Home: Weldon, NC. Died Mar. 6, 2004.

SHORT, FORREST EDWIN, lawyer; b. Ft. Scott, Kans., Aug. 3, 1928; s. Forrest Edwin Sr. and Laura Elizabeth Short; m. Sharon Lynn Miller, May 1, 1955; children: Stacey Lynn, Laurie Leigh. JD, U. Ala., Tuscaloosa, 1953. Bar: Kans. 1955, U.S. Dist. Ct. Kans. 1956, U.S. Dist. Ct. (so. dist.) Ala. 1953, U.S. Ct. Appeals (10th cir.) 1975, U.S. Supreme Ct. 1976. Sole practitioner, Ft. Scott, 1954-66; ptnr. Short & Short, Ft. Scott, 1966-77, Short & Gentry, Ft. Scott, 1977-83, Short, Gentry & Bishop, Ft. Scott, 1983-93; pres. Short, Gentry & Bishop, P.A., Ft. Scott, from 1993. Contbr. articles to profl. jours. 1st lt. JAG, U.S. Army, 1953-54. Mem. ABA, Kans. Bar Assn., Bourbon County Bar Assn., Ft. Scott Rotary Club (pres. 1996-97). Republican. Methodist. Avocations: golf, gardening. Died May 3, 2004.

SHORT, PHILLIP DEAN, banker; b. Lawrence, Kans., Apr. 7, 1945; BSBA, U. Colo., 1968. CFP. Sr. acct. Arthur Andersen & Co., Chgo., 1968-71; pres., chief exec. officer First Chicago Bank of Mount Prospect, Ill., 1971-88, Burling Bank, Chgo., from 1989. Chmn. suburban fin. instns. sect. Met. United Way/Crusade of Mercy, Chgo., 1986; bd. dirs. Rainbows for All God's Children, Des Plaines, Ill., 1988. Mem. Bankers Club of Chgo., Internat. Assn. Fin. Planners, Exec. Club of Chgo., Rolling Green Country Club, The Meadow Club, Rotary (pres. Mt. Prospect chpt. 1979). Avocations: golf, travel. Died May 18, 2005.

SHORTER, DANIEL ALBERT, retired biology professor; b. Goltry, Okla., May 20, 1927; s. Wily Brink and Edna Isabella (Mason) S.; m. Margery Jean Peck, Jan. 13, 1946; children: Cynthia, Edana, Terry, Sherry. BS in Biology Edn., N.W. Okla. State U., 1949; MS in Natural Sci., Okla. State U., 1960, PhD in Entomology, 1965. Cert. secondary tchr., Okla., Kans. Instr. in math. Anthony (Kans.) Pub. Schs., 1949-58; from asst. prof. to prof. biology N.W. Okla. State U., Alva, 1960-87, dir. admissions, 1972-75, prof. emeritus, from 1987. V.p. Okla. Ornithol. Soc., 1967. Mem. Local Vocat. Tech. Bd. Edn., Alva, 1974—; chmn. Alva Hosp. Authority, 1991-95, mem., 1995—. Named Outstanding Conservation Educator, Okla. Soc. Soil Conservation Dists., 1985. Mem. Am. Legion, Ducks Unltd. (zone chmn. 1984—, Outstanding Zone Chmn. award 1989, 90), Kiwanis (pres. 1956, 82, Kiwanian of Yr. 1992, lt. gov. Divsn. 16 1994-95, 95-96), Masons. Democrat. Methodist. Avocations: riding highwheeled bicycles, collecting belt buckles. Home: Alva, Okla. Died Aug. 2, 2005.

SHOWALTER, DENISE M., communications marketing administrator; b. Bridgeport, Conn., June 26, 1946; d. Paul J. and Magdalena D. (Feske) Amato; m. George W. Showalter, Aug. 26, 1967; children: Anthony (dec.), Kristen. BS in Bus. Adminstrn., U. Redlands, 1985; MS in Sys. Mgmt., U. Denver, 1991. Cert. sys. profl. Mktg. rep. Pacific Telephone Co., L.A., 1967-69; real estate sales Whitehead Realtors, Rockford, Ill., 1972-77; mktg. mgmt. Pacific Bell, Orange/San Ramon, Calif., from 1977. Bd. dirs. Switched Digital Svcs. Applications Forum, 1996—. Avocations: model railroading, golf. Died Aug. 22, 2005.

SHRIEVES, SANDRA KAY, business educator; b. Athens, Ohio, Oct. 20, 1943; d. John William and Mildred Holland (Gulley) Grubb; m. Kenneth McLain, Dec. 8, 1961 (div. 1974); children: Tammy Dee McLain Carsey, Connie Lee McLain Wallace; m. John Robert Shrieves, June 25, 1983; stepchildren: Kelly, Susan. BS in Edn., Ohio U., 1985, postgrad., 1989-95. Bookkeeper McLain Plumbing, Athens, 1965-74; sec. Bur. Vocat. Rehab., Athens, 1972-77; clerical supr. Ohio U., Athens, 1977-79; asst. dir. Athens County Comprehensive Employment and Tng. Act, 1979; bus. adminstr. HAVAR, Inc., 1979-81; bus. instr. Tri-County Adult Edn., Nelsonville, Ohio, 1981-90; placement coord. Tri-County Vocat. Sch. and Adult Ctr., Nelsonville, Ohio, 1985-89; computerized acctg. instr. Tri-County Vocat. High Sch., Nelsonville, from 1989. Co-chmn. S.E. Ohio Placement Network, Athens, 1988-89; evaluator So. Ohio Mgmt. Team, Athens, 1980. Mem. fin. com. Ohio Pvt. Residential Assn., Columbus, 1981; treas. Athens County Community Svcs. Coun., 1989; treas. for campaign for candidate for County Auditor, Athens, 1986. Mem. Am. Vocat. Assn., Ohio Vocat. Assn., Ohio Manpower Assn., Bus. Profls. of Am. (advisor), Athens C. of C. (edn. com. 1988-89). Avocations: reading, fishing, walking. Home: The Plains, Ohio. Died Aug. 29, 2005.

SHRIVER, ELIZABETH, computer scientist, researcher; b. L.A., Nov. 12, 1966; d. Bruce and Beverly Shriver; m. Tom Swartz. PhD, NYU, 1997. Mem. tech. staff Lucent Techs., Murray Hill, NJ, 1997—2002. Died Jan. 15, 2004.

SHRIVER, JOYCE ELIZABETH, anatomy educator; b. Quincy, Ill., Sept. 14, 1937; d. Victor Henry and Alma Freida (Henerhoff) S. BA magna cum laude, William Jewell Coll., Liberty, Mo., 1959; PhD, U. Kans., 1965. Fellow coll. physicians and surgeons Columbia U., N.Y.C., 1964-67, spl. fellow, 1967-68; asst. prof. Mount Sinai Sch. Medicine, N.Y.C., 1968-71, assoc. prof., from 1971, asst. dean for student affairs, 1976-81, assoc. dean for student affairs, from 1981. Contbr. articles to profl. jours.; author of numerous videorecordings. Vol. Community Soup Kitchen, N.Y.C., 1986—. Recipient citation for achievement William Jewell Coll., 1990; Nat. Inst. Neurol. Disorders grantee, 1969-72. Mem. Soc. for Neuroscience, Am. Assn. Anatomists, Am. Soc. Zoologists, Assn. for Rsch. in Nervous and Mental Disease, N.Y. Acad. Sci., Harvey Soc., CCNY Acad. for Humanities and Scis. (bd. dirs. 1988—), Sigma Xi. Mem. Christian Ch. Avocations: travel, volunteer work, theater, current affairs, reading. Died Oct. 27, 2004.

SHUBART, DOROTHY LOUISE TEPFER, artist, educator; b. Ft. Collins, Colo, Mar. 1, 1923; d. Adam Christian and Rose Virginia (Ayers) Tepfer; m. Robert Franz Shubart, Apr. 22, 1950; children: Richard, Lorenne. AA, Colo. Women's Coll., 1944; grad., Cleve. Inst. Art, 1946; student, Western Res. U., 1947—48; BA, St. Thomas Aquinas Coll., 1974; MA, Coll. New Rochelle, 1978; student, Santa Fe C.C., 2001—03. Art tchr. Denver Mus., 1944—50; portrait painter, 1947—50; art tchr. adults and children Cleve. Recreation Dept., 1950—60; adult edn. art tchr. Nanuet Pub. Sch., NY, 1950-65, Pearl River Adult Edn., 1960—75. Rec. sec. Van Houten Fields Assn., West Nyack, NY, 1964—66. Exhibited in group shows at Hopper House, Rockland Ctr Arts, CWC, Cleve. Inst. Arts, Coll. New Rochelle, Rockland County Ann. Art Fair, Gonzalez Sr. Ctr.; co-author: (book and brochure) Van Houten Fields 1937-87, 1987; co-author, photographer: Windmills & Dreams, 1997; group show, Watercolor show, Santa Fe Cmty. Coll., 2003, exhibited in group shows at Santa Fe C.C. Leader 4-H Club, Nanuet, 1960—80, Girl Scouts US, 1961—68; mem. scholarship com., gen. com. PTA, 1964—68; rec. sec. Van Houten Fields Assn., West Nyack, NY, 1960—74; com. mem. Environ. Def. Fund, Union Concerned Scientists, Nat. Com. to Preserve Social Security and Medicare; capt., organizer Neighborhood Watch; campaign vol. Jim Baca for Gov., N.Mex., 1996, Gore for Pres., Santa Fe, 2000; bd. mem., mailings Friends of Santa Fe Libr., from 2003; vol. Santa Fe Libr., from 1998; com. mem. Eldorado Cmty. Improvement Assn.-Arterial Rd. Planning Com., 1992—94; campaign vol. Tom Udall for Congress, 1999—2003, 2003; mem. Eldorado Hist. Com., 1995—97; vol. Eldorado's Vista Grande Libr., 2001—03; mem. Eldorado chpt. Security Com., Eldorado Conservation Greenbelt Com., 1996—97, Shakespeare in Santa Fe Guild, 1998, Mil. Hist. Found., from 2000; vol. Cerro Grande Food Bank, from 1998. Gund traveling scholar, Cleve. Inst. Arts, 1946. Mem.: NOW, AAUW, Audubon Soc., Action on Smoking and Health, Union Concerned Scientists, Am. Dem. Action, Environ. Def. Fund, Wilderness Club, Phi Delta Kappa, Delta Tau Kappa. Democrat. Avocations: books, gardening, photography, bicycling, writing. Home: Cambridge, Mass. Died Feb. 28, 2004.

SHUEY, RICHARD LYMAN, engineering educator, consultant; b. Chgo., May 7, 1920; s. Ralph Clement and Abbie Miriam (Strong) S.; m. Frances Barbara Fortier, Sept. 22, 1944; children: Roy Fortier, Marie Frances. BS in Engring., U. Mich., 1942, BSE in Math., 1942; PhD in Elec. Engring., U. Calif., Berkeley, 1950. Registered profl. engr., NY, Calif. Engr. U. Calif. Radiation Lab., Berkeley, 1946-50; rsch. staff, br. mgr. GE Rsch. Lab., Schenectady, N.Y., 1950-84; adj. prof. Rensselaer Polytech. Inst., Troy, N.Y., from 1985; cons. Schenectady, from 1985. Author: The Architecture of Distributed Computer Systems, 1997; contbr. articles to profl. jours. Bd. dirs. Self Help for Hard of Hearing N.Y. Assn., 1996-2001. Sr. mem. IEEE (various coms., offices 1952-87, Donald McLellan Cmty. Svc. award, 3d Millennium medal), AAAS, Am. Auditory Soc., Soc. Mfg. Engrs., Assn. Computing Machines, Sigma Xi, Tau Beta Pi. Avocations: golf, bridge, photography. Home: Schenectady, NY. Died Sept. 11, 2006.

SHUMWAY, NORMAN EDWARD, surgeon, educator; b. Kalamazoo, Mich., Feb. 9, 1923; m. Mary Lou Stuurmans (dec.); children: Michael, Amy, Lisa, Sara. MD, Vanderbilt U., 1949; PhD in Surgery, U. Minn., 1956; degrees (hon.). Diplomate: Am. Bd. Surgery, Am. Bd. Thoracic Surgery. Intern U. Minn. Hosps., 1949-50, med. fellow surgery, 1950-51, 53-54, Nat. Heart Inst. research fellow, 1954-56, Nat. Heart Inst. spl. trainee, 1956-57; mem. surg. staff Stanford U. Hosps., 1958, asst. prof. surgery, 1959-61, assoc. prof., 1961-65, prof., 1965—93, head div. cardiovascular surgery Sch. Medicine, 1974—93; Frances and Charles D. Field prof. Stanford U., 1976-2000, prof. emeritus, 2000—06. Served to capt. USAF, 1951-53. Recipient Scientific Achievement award, AMA, 1987. Mem. AMA, Soc. Univ. Surgeons, Am. Assn. Thoracic Surgery, Am. Coll. Cardiology, Transplantation Soc., Samson Thoracic Surg. Soc., Soc. for Vascular Surgery, Alpha Omega Alpha Achievements include being the first surgeon to perform a heart transplant operation in the United States, Jan. 6, 1968. Died Feb. 10, 2006.

SHYMAN, CARL SANFORD, manufacturing company executive; b. Seattle, Dec. 31, 1925; s. Irving and Vivian (Lurie) S.; B.S. in Elec. Engring., U. Wash., 1948; M.S. in Elec. Engring., Stanford U., 1949; m. Heloise J. Sarchin, Dec. 17, 1950; children— Carol, William, Steven. With North Am. Aviation, Downey, Calif., 1949-55, Boeing Co., Seattle, 1955-64; gen. mgr. avionics div. Westinghouse Electric Corp., Balt., 1964-88. Served with USMCR, 1943-46. Mem. Am. Security Council, Am. Def. Preparedness Assn. Home: Silver Spring, Md. Died Jan. 5, 2004.

SIDEY, HUGH SWANSON, correspondent; b. Greenfield, Iowa, Sept. 3, 1927; s. Kenneth H. and Alice Margaret (Swanson) S.; m. Alice Anne Trowbridge, Dec. 5, 1953; children: Cynthia Anne, Sandra, Bettina, Edwin. BS, Iowa State U., 1950. Reporter Adair County (Iowa) Free Press, 1950, The Nonpariel, Council Bluffs, Iowa, 1950-51, Omaha World-Herald, 1951-55; reporter Life mag., 1955-58; corr. Time mag., 1958-96; columnist The Presidency, Time mag., Life mag., 1966—96; chief Washington Bur., Time mag., 1969-78, Washington contbg. editor, 1978-96; narrator & interviewer, Am. Pres. series PBS, 2000. Contbr. Time mag., 1996—2005. Author: John F. Kennedy, President, 1963, A Very Personal Presidency, Lyndon Johnson in the White House, 1966, These United States, 1975, Portrait of a President, 1975, The Presidency, 1991, Portraits of the Presidents, 2000; co-author: 1,000 Ideas for Better News Pictures, 1956, The Memories, 1961—JFK—1963, 1973, Hugh Sidey's Portraits of the Presidents, 2004; contbr.: The Kennedy Circle, Prelude to Leadership, European Diary of John F. Kennedy, Summer 1945, 1995, Remembering Jack, 2003. Served with AUS, 1945-46. Mem. White House Hist. Assn. (chmn. 2000-03). Died Nov. 21, 2005.

SIEBEL, MATHIAS PAUL, mechanical engineer, consultant; b. Witten, Germany, Mar. 6, 1924; arrived in U.S., 1957, naturalized, 1962; s. Franz and Marie-Luise Siebel; m. Katherine Elizabeth Jente, May 27, 1960. BSME, U. Bristol, Eng., 1949; PhD, U. Bristol, 1952. From R&D engr. to asst. plant mgr. Tube Investments Ltd., Birmingham, England, 1952-57; rsch. assoc. Columbia U., N.Y.C., 1958-59; mgr. pressure equipment Pall Corp., Glen Cove, NY, 1959-64; v.p. ops. RDI Co., Westbury, NY, 1964-65; dir. mfg. engring. lab., then mem. sci. staff Marshall Space Flight Center, NASA, Huntsville, Ala., 1965-79; mgr. NASA Michoud Assembly Facility, New Orleans, 1979-87, cons., from 1987. Assoc. dean Coll. Engring. U. New Orleans, 1989—92, adj. prof. mech. engring., 1993—2001. Achievements include patents in field. Home: Kenner, La. Died June 8, 2006.

SIEGAN, BERNARD HERBERT, lawyer, educator; b. Chgo., July 28, 1924; s. David and Jeannette Siegan; m. Sharon Goldberg, June 15, 1952 (dec. Feb. 1985); m. Shelley Zifferblatt, Nov. 19, 1995. AA, Herzl. Jr. Coll., Chgo., 1943, 46; Student, Roosevelt Coll., Chgo., 1946-47; JD, U. Chgo., 1949. Bar: Ill. 1950. Practiced in, Chgo.; ptnr. Siegan & Karlin, 1952-73; pres., sec. various small corps. and gen. partner in partnerships engaged in real estate ownership and devel., 1955-70; weekly columnist Freedom newspaper chain, other papers, 1974-79. Cons. law and econs. program U. Chgo. Law Sch., 1970-73; adj. prof. law U. San Diego Law Sch., 1973-74, Disting. prof., 1975-2006; adj. scholar Cato Inst., Washington, 1991-2006, Heritage Found., 1992-2006; cons. windfalls and wipeouts project HUD, 1973-74; cons. FTC, 1985-86, US Dept. Justice, dir. constl. bibliog. project, 1986-88; keynote speaker 5th Internat. Conf. on Urbanism, Porto Alegre, Brazil, 1989; nominated by Pres. Reagan to U.S. Ct. Appeals (9th cir.) Feb. 2, 1987, confirmation denied July 14, 1988 by party line vote Senate Judiciary Com. Author: Land Use Without Zoning, 1972, Spanish edit., 1995, Other People's Property, 1976, Economic Liberties and the Constitution, 1980, The Supreme Court's Constitution: An Inquiry Into Judicial Review and Its Impact on Society, 1987, Drafting a Constitution for a Nation or Republic Emerging into Freedom, 1992, 2d edit., 1994, Portuguese, Ukrainian, Polish and Spanish edits., 1993, Property and Freedom: The Constitution, Supreme Court and Land Use Regulation, 1997, Adapting a Constitution to Protect Freedom and Provide Abundance (in Bulgarian), 1998, Property Rights: From Magna Carta to the Fourteenth Amendment, 2001, Economic Liberties and the Constitution, rev. edit., 2005; editor: Planning without Prices, 1977, The Interaction of Economics and the Law, 1977, Regulation, Economics and the Law, 1979, Government, Regulation and the Economy, 1980. Mem. pres.-elect's Task Force on Housing, 1980-81; mem. Pres.'s Commn. on Housing, 1981-82; mem. Nat. Commn. on bicentennial of U.S. Constn., 1985-91; chmn. adv. com. Affordable Housing Conf., San Diego, 1985, Rights of Regulated Conf., Coronado, Calif., 1976; chmn. Conf. on the Taking Issue, 1976; mem. Houston Regional Urban Design Team, Study of Houston, 1990; mem. U.S. team Bulgarian Econ. Growth and Transition Project, 1990; mem. devel. bd. Mingei Internat. Mus. World Folk Art, 1981-84. Served with AUS, 1943-46. Research fellow law and econs. U. Chgo. Law Sch., 1968-69; Urban Land Inst. research fellow, 1976-86; recipient Leander J. Monks Meml. Fund award Inst. Humane Studies, 1972, George Washington medal Freedom Founds. at Valley Forge, 1981, Spl. award Liberal Inst. of Rio Grande do Sul, Porto Alegre, Brazil, 1989, Thorsnes award for outstanding legal scholarship, 1998; named Univ. Prof., U. San Diego, 1997-98. Died Mar. 27, 2006.

SIEGEL, ARTHUR BERNARD, lawyer; b. Bklyn., Mar. 22, 1932; s. Abraham and Sarah (Hecht) S.; m. Miriam Ann Barck, Dec. 22, 1963; children: Hugh David, Susan Barck. BA, Syracuse U., 1954; M in Indsl. and Labor Relations, Cornell U., 1958; JD, Columbia U., 1971. Bar: Pa. 1972, U.S. Dist. (mid. dist.) Pa. 1979. Ptnr. Finan, Beecher, Wagner & Rose, P.A., Milford, Pa., 1972-79, Beecher, Wagner, Rose, Siegel & Klemeyer, Milford, 1979; pvt. practice, Milford, from 1979. Pub. defender Pike County (Pa.), Milford, 1980-82; former solicitor Pa. County, Pike County Office on Aging; solicitor Pike County Recorder of Deeds and Register of Wills. Pub. Pike County Courier; contbr. articles Pike County Dispatch. Treas. Pike County Rep. com., Milford, 1982-84. Served to 1st. lt. USAF, 1955-57, served to capt. USAFR, 1967. Recipient Cmty. Svc. award Pike County C. of C., 2000. Mem. ABA, Pa. Bar Assn., Pike County Bar Assn., Columbia U. Law Sch. Alumni Assn., Pike County Legal Aid Soc. (founder 1979), Phi Beta Kappa, Phi Kappa Phi, Sigma Delta Chi. Jewish. Avocations: photography, music, collecting memorabilia, travel. Home: Milford, Pa. Died June 9, 2005.

SIEGEL, JEROME SAMUEL, trucking company executive; b. Newark, Dec. 16, 1944; s. Harry Charles and Pauline Ruth (Schwartz) S.;m. Janet Iris Lukes, Oct. 18, 1975; children: Laura Anne, Jason Henry. BS in Hotel Adminstrn., Cornell U., 1967; MS in Bus., Am. U., Washington, 1971. Co-owner Whitby's Restaurant, Washington, 1969-73; v.p. Siegel & Cohen Express, Newark, 1973-78; co-owner Halo Optical Products, Inc., Johnstown, N.Y., 1978-84; owner, founder SLA Transport, Inc., Gloversville, N.Y., from 1981. Bd. dirs. Jewish Community Ctr., Gloversville, 1982—, Promote Gloversville Devel. Corp., 1986—. Mem. Fulton County C. of C. (dir. 1983—, pres. 1992—), Eccentric Club. Republican. Jewish. Avocations: skiing, swimming, tennis, travel. Home: Gloversville, NY. Died Mar. 12, 2004.

SIERACKI, ALOYSIUS ALFRED, religious organization administrator; b. Chgo., Nov. 5, 1929; s. Peter Paul and Mary Ann (Kroll) S. BS in Chem. Engring., Ill. Inst. Tech., 1951; cert. in theology, Whitefriars Hall, Washington, 1960; MS in Math., U. Notre Dame, 1962. Ordained priest Roman Cath. Ch., 1959. Secondary sch. tchr. Mt. Carmel High Sch., Chgo., 1960-67; instr. chemistry and math. Mt. Carmel Coll., Niagara Falls, Ont., Can., 1967-68; instr. math. Marquette U., Milw., 1968-75; assoc. pastor St. Agnes Parish, Phoenix, 1975-81; provincial dir. lay Carmelites in U.S. and Can. Aylesford Carmelite Ctr., Darien, Ill., from 1981. Chmn. Lay Carmelite Commn., 1987—. Author: Songs for God, 1990; editor: Carmel's Call, 10th edit., 1991; editor Aylesford Carmelite Newsletter, 1984—; contbr. articles to profl. jours. With U.S. Army, 1951-53. Democrat. Avocations: walking, poetry. Home: Darien, Ill. Died Feb. 17, 2005.

SIEWICKI, BRENDA JOYCE, healthcare executive; b. Mt. Airy, Md., Aug. 21, 1949; d. Rudolph M. and Olga M. (Sofinowski) S. BS in Nursing, U. Md., 1971; M in Nursing, U. Wash., 1975. Clin. specialist United Gen. Hosp., Sedro Wolley, Wash., 1975-76; tchr., practictioner Rush-Presbyn. St. Luke's Med. Ctr., Chgo., 1976-79; v.p. Medicus Systems Corp., Evanston, Ill., 1978-79; healthcare cons. IBM Corp., Atlanta, from 1989. Contbr. chpt. to books and articles to profl. jours. Chmn. teen support group St. Philips Luth. Ch., Glenview, Ill., 1987-88; bd. dirs. Oak Park Townhome Assn., Atlanta, 1989. Mem. Am. Nurses Assn., Chgo. Coun. Fgn. Relations, Sigma Theta Tau. Home: Boston, Mass. Died Feb. 9, 2005.

SIGLER, KATHERINE, social planning professional; b. Fernandina Beach, Fla., Mar. 7, 1948; d. George J. and Elizabeth Wye (Pearson) Arfaras; m. Richard E. Sigler, Sept. 19, 1970; children: Richard E. Jr., Faith Elizabeth. Student, Fla. State U. Mem. catalog staff Sears Roebuck & Co., Tallahassee; mem. svc. staff Diner's Club, Miami, Fla.; dept. mgr. rsch. IRS, Atlanta; prin. Sigler Enterprises/Anchor Rental Party Prodns., Ft. Pierce, Fla. Mem. St. Lucie Rep. Exec. Com.; mem. County Arts Appropriation Com.; chmn. various civic groups. Mem. Advt. Fedn., St. Lucie Coun. Arts, Am. Bus. Women's Assn. (past pres.). Anglican. Home: Fort Pierce, Fla. Died May 19, 2004.

SIKOV, MELVIN RICHARD, toxicologist; b. Detroit, July 8, 1928; s. Paul Merrill and Emma (Perlman) S.; m. Shirley Dressler, June 1, 1952; children: Peter H., Stacy J., Thomas R. BS, Wayne U., 1951; PhD, U. Rochester, 1955. Asst. prof. Wayne State U., Detroit, 1955-60, assoc. prof., 1961-65; sr. research scientist Battelle N.W., Richland, Wash., 1965-68, research assoc., 1968-78, mgr. devel. toxicology, 1978-81, sr. staff scientist, from 1981. Contbr. numerous publs. to sci. jours. Served with U.S. Army, 1946-47, ATO. Fellow Am. Inst. Ultrasound in Medicine; mem. Am. Assn. Pathologists, Health Physics Soc., Radiation Research Soc., Teratology Soc., Soc. Toxicology. Home: Richland, Wash. Died Aug. 4, 2005.

SILBERMAN, LOU HACKETT, literature educator emeritus, rabbi; b. San Francisco, June 23, 1914; s. Lou Harry and Myrtle (Mueller) S.; m. Helen Sue Epstein, June 14, 1942 (dec. 1979); children: Syrl Augusta, Deborah (Mrs. Alan Cohn). Student, UCLA, 1931—33; AB, U. Calif., Berkeley, 1934, postgrad., 1935; BHL, Hebrew Union Coll., Cin., 1939, MHL, 1941, DHL, 1943; postgrad., U. Basel, 1959. Rabbi, 1941; instr. medieval Bibl. exegesis Hebrew Union Coll., 1941-43; asst. rabbi Temple Emanuel, Dallas, 1943-45; rabbi Temple Israel, Omaha, 1945-52; asso. prof. Jewish lit. and thought Vanderbilt U., 1952-55, Hillel prof. Jewish lit. and thought, 1955-80, prof. emeritus, 1980—2006. Dir. grad. studies Bibl. field, 1960-65, 67-69, acting chmn. grad. dept. religion, 1960-61, chmn. dept. religious studies, 1970-77; vis. prof. Oriental Inst., U. Vienna, 1965-66, Carleton Coll., 1972, Emory U., 1973; Rosenstiel fellow Notre Dame U., 1972; Touhy lectr. interreligious studies John Carroll U., 1973; vis. prof. U. Chgo. Divinity Sch., 1978; vis. scholar Postgrad. Center Hebrew Studies Oxford, 1978; vis. prof. Toronto Sch. Theology, 1980, Duke U., 1988; vis. prof. U. Ariz., 1981-85, adj. prof., 1985—. Editor: Semeia Studies, 1981-87; editorial adviser: Ency. Internat; contbr.: Ency. Judaica, Ency. Britannica; editorial adviser Dictionary Bibl. Interpretation; author studies dealing with Dead Sea Scrolls, rabbinic lit., contemporary theology. Chmn. community relations com. Nashville Jewish Community Council, 1956-61; vice chmn. Nat. Jewish Community Relations Adv. Council, 1964-70. Mem. Soc. Bibl. Lit. and Exegesis (pres. So. sect. 1959-60, pres.-elect 1981, pres. 1982), Am. Acad. Religion, Central Conf. Am. Rabbis, Am. Soc. Study Religion, Assn. for Jewish Studies, Am. Theol. Soc., Studiorum Novi Testamenti Societas. Clubs: Shamus (Nashville). Home: Tucson, Ariz. Died June 6, 2006.

SILBERMAN, REBECCA LOUISE, psychologist; b. L.A., Apr. 15, 1957; d. Max and Mildred (Lapidus) S. BA, U. Calif., Santa Cruz, 1979; MA, Duquesne U., 1980, PhD, 1989. Lic. psychologist, Pa. Mental health counselor YWCA, Pitts., 1983-86; psychologist in pvt. practice Pitts., from 1990; clin. therapist Western Psychiat. Inst. and Clinic, Pitts., from 1986. Mem. APA, Pa. Psychol. Assn. Home: Pittsburgh, Pa. Died Feb. 23, 2005.

SILIPIGNI, ALFREDO, opera conductor; b. Atlantic City, Apr. 9, 1931; s. Alfredo and Elisabeth (Calhoun) S.; m. Gloria Rose DiBenedetto, Apr. 11, 1953; children: Marisa, Elisabetta Luisa, Afredo Roberto. Student, Westminster Choir Coll., 1948, Juilliard Sch. Music, 1953; HHD (hon.), Kean Coll. N.J., 1978. Prin. condr., gen. dir., artistic dir. N.J. State Opera, Newark, 1965—2006, founder Young Artist Program, 1969—2006. Guest lectr. Glassboro (N.J.) State Coll.; music dir. Teatro Grattacielo, NY. Carnegie Hall debut with Symphony of the Air, 1956; condr. NBC Symphony, Boston, Bklyn. and Conn. operas, Newark Symphony, Teatro Grattacielo, Lincoln Ctr. Performances of Verissimo Operas; guest condr. Vienna State Opera, 1976, Grand Liceo di Barcelona, Spain, 1976, London, 1977, also numerous cos. Eng., Venezuela, France, Italy, Mex. and Can. with frequent appearances at L'Opera de Montreal; made recs. of Zaza by Leoncavallo, "Adriana Lecouvrer" by Cilea; prin. guest condr. and advisor Bellas Artes, Mex., 1993-94; guest condr. Opera Colo., 1997-98, largest prodn. Aida anywhere in world, Shanghai, 2000. Decorated cavaliere Order of Merit (Italy); recipient Centennial medal St. Peter's Coll., 1972, Disting. Svc. to Culture award City of San Remo, Columbia Found. award, Boys Town of Italy award, Music award N.J. Edn. Assn., 1988. Died Mar. 25, 2006.

SILLS, NANCY MINTZ, lawyer; b. N.Y.C., Nov. 3, 1941; d. Samuel and Selma (Kahn) Mintz; m. Stephen J. Sills, Apr. 17, 1966; children: Eric Howard, Ronnie Lynne Sills Lindberg. BA, U. Wis., 1962; JD cum laude, Albany Law Sch. Union U., 1976. Bar: N.Y. 1977, U.S. Dist. Ct. (no. dist.) N.Y. 1977, U.S. Tax Ct. 1984. Asst. editor fin. news Newsweek mag., N.Y.C., 1962-65; staff writer, reporter Forbes mag., N.Y.C., 1965; rsch. assoc. pub. rels. Ea. Airlines, N.Y.C., 1965-67; asst. editor Harper & Row, N.Y.C., 1968-69; freelance writer, editor N.Y.C., Albany, 1967-70; confidential law sec. N.Y. State Supreme Ct., Albany, 1976-79; assoc. Whiteman, Osterman & Hanna, Albany, 1979-81, Martin, Noonan, Hislop, Troue & Shudt, Albany, 1981-83; ptnr. Martin, Shudt, Wallace & Sills, Albany, 1984; of counsel Krolick and DeGraff, Albany, 1984-89; ptnr. Hodgson, Russ, Andrews, Woods & Goodyear, Albany, 1990-91; pvt. practice Albany, 1991—2001; of counsel Lemery & Reid, Albany and Glens Falls, NY, 1993—94, O'Connell and Aronowitz, Albany, NY, from 2002. Asst. counsel N.Y. State Senate, 1983-88; cons. The Ayco Corp., 1975; jud. screening com. Third Jud. Dept., 1997—. Editor: Reforming American Education, 1969, Up From Poverty, 1968; rschr.: The Negro Revolution in America, 1963; contbr. articles to mags. Bd. dirs. Jewish Philanthropies Endowment, 1983-86, United Jewish Fedn. N.E. N.Y. Endowment Fund, 1992-96, Daus. Sarah Found., 1994-97, Albany Jewish Cmty. Ctr., 1984-87; mem. Guilderland (N.Y.) Conservation Adv. Coun., 1993-96; mem. planned giving tech. adv. com. Albany Law Sch., Union U., 1991-95, chmn., 1992-95; mem. regional cabinet State of Israel Bonds Devel. Corp. for Israel, 1991-92; surrogate decision making com. N.Y. State Commn. Quality of Care for Mentally Disabled. Mem. ABA, N.Y. State Bar Assn., Albany County Bar Assn., N.Y. Criminal and Civil Cts. Bar Assn. (dir. 2000-), Estate Planning Coun. Ea. N.Y., Aux. Albany County Med. Soc., Capital Dist. Trial Lawyers Assn., Capital Dist. Women's Bar Assn., Phi Beta Kappa, Sigma Epsilon Sigma. Republican. Home: Guilderland, NY. Died 2005.

SILVA, ELAINE ANN, art director, photographer; b. New Bedford, Mass., Nov. 29, 1947; d. Alfred Seraphin and Mary Cornell (Lewis) S.; m. Roy Leo Masse, July 1, 1978. BFA, Southeastern Mass. U., 1969; postgrad., Boston U., 1974-76. Advt. designer New Bedford Standard-Times, 1969-74; art dir. Basics, Inc., Hingham, Mass., 1976-78; asst. art dir. Allied Advt., Inc., Boston, 1978-80; art dir. New Bedford mag., 1980-81; owner, art dir. Design/Illustration, New Bedford, from 1981; sr. graphic designer Knapp Shoe, Inc., Brockton, Mass., from 1988. Publicity chairperson, photographer The Spouters, New Bedford, 1969-74. Producer, designer Citizens Ride Whaling City Program, New Bedford, 1985-88. Mem. Steamship Hist. Soc. Am., Charles River Wheelmen, Narragansett Bay Wheelmen. Avocation: bicycling. Home: Fairhaven, Mass. Died May 11, 2005.

SILVERMAN, MARTIN ISAAC, rabbi; b. Bklyn., Jan. 9, 1927; s. Edmund George and Anna Lucille (Dorn) S.; m. Phyllis Olshin, July 6, 1952; children: Sara Lee, Amy Cohen, Ethan David. BA, Yale U., 1948; MHL, Hebrew Union, Cin., 1953; DDiv, Hebrew Union Coll., N.Y.C., 1978. Ordained rabbi. Rabbi Levittown (N.Y.) Reform Congregation, 1953-55; asst. rabbi Temple Ahavath Sholom, Bklyn., 1955-60; rabbi Temple Israel, Monroe, La., 1960-64, Temple Mizpah, Chgo., 1964-72, Congregation Beth Emeth, Albany, N.Y., from 1973. Exec. com. Cen. Conf. Am. Rabbis, N.Y.C., 1989-91; pres. Capital Dist. Bd. Rabbis, Albany, 1976-78m, N.E. Region Cen. Conf. Am. Rabbis, 1987-89. Pres. United Jewish Fedn. N.E. N.Y., latham, 1989-91; chmn. Human Rights Commn., Albany, 1985—; mem. Community-Police Rev. Bd., Albany, 1987—; v.p. Planned Parenthood, 1985-87. With U.S. Army, 1945-46. Recipient Carlyle Adams Ecumenical award, Capital Area Coun. Chs., 1959, DeWitt Clinton Masonic award, 1990. Mem. Cen. Conf. Am. Rabbis, N.Y. Bd. Rabbis (exec. com. 1988—). Home: Albany, NY. Died Mar. 25, 2004.

SILVERMAN, SIDNEY WILLIAM, electrical engineer; b. N.Y.C., Aug. 27, 1918; s. Max and Eva (Kalfus) S.; m. Charlotte Helen Kant, Sept. 7, 1947; children: Susan Marti, Barbara Ann. BEE, CUNY, 1947; MSEE, U. Mich., 1949. Draftsman Cert. Gauge Co., Long Island City, N.Y., 1934-43; engr. Boeing Co., Seattle, 1949-59; engring. mgr. Boeing Aerospace Co., Seattle, from 1959. Mem. adv. com. NASA, Washington, 1983-85. Contbr. articles to profl. jours. Served to 1st lt., 1943-46. Mem. IEEE (chmn. power system com. 1976—), AIAA (chmn. power systems com. 1980-84). Avocations: stamp collecting/philately, photography, leatherwork, skiing, hiking. Home: Seattle, Wash. Died May 3, 2005.

SILVERSTEIN, MARTIN ELLIOT, retired surgeon, consultant, writer; b. NYC, Sept. 6, 1922; s. Louis and Ethel (Statman) S.; m. Mabelle A. Cremer, Dec. 10, 1962. AB cum laude, Columbia U., 1945; MD, N.Y. Med. Coll., 1948; D of Mil. Medicine and Surgery (hon.), Uniformed Svcs. U. for Health Scis., 2003. Instr. bacteriology N.Y. Med. Coll., 1953-57, asst. to dean for clin. scis., 1953-58, instr. surgery, 1953-55, asst. dean, 1958, assoc. dean, 1959—62; asst. vis. surgeon Bird S. Coler Hosp., N.Y.C., 1953-57, assoc. vis. surgeon, 1957-60; asst. vis. surgeon Met. Hosp., N.Y.C., 1953-57, assoc. vis. surgeon, 1957-60; asst. attending surgeon Flower and 5th Ave. Hosps., N.Y.C., 1953-57; asst. attending surgeon Monorah Med. Ctr. U. Kans. Sch. Medicine, N.Y.C., 1963-65, exec. dir. Monorah Med. Ctr. Kansas City, 1963-65, exec. dir. Danciger Inst. for Health Scis., 1963-66, chmn. dept. exptl. surgery Danciger Inst. for Health Scis., 1963-66; chmn. dept. Surgery Menorah Med. Ctr. U. Kans. Sch. Medicine Affiliate, Kansas City, 1963-66; assoc. clin. prof. surgery U. Kans. Sch. Medicine, Kansas City, 1966-67; surgeon courtesy staff N.Y. Infirmary, 1969; surgeon Grand Canyon Med. Group and Hosp., 1969-70; chief sect. on surgery of trauma, dept. surgery U. Ariz. Coll. Med., Tucson, 1974-80, adj. assoc. prof. optical scis., 1979-83, assoc. prof. surgery, 1974-83, dir. quality assurance Univ. Hosp., 1983-84, rsch. prof. family and community medicine, internat. medicine, 1984-85, rsch. prof. surgical biology, 1984-85; sr. fellow in sci. and tch. Ctr. for Strategic and Internat. Studies Georgetown U., Washington, 1983-87; ret., 1987; cons., from 1992. Pres. Claude Gips Found. Inc., N.Y.C., 1967-93; disting. vis. prof. Uniformed Svcs. U. Health Scis., 1984, adj. prof. surgery, 1999—; clin. prof. surgery F. Edward Hebert Sch. Medicine, 1984-99; disting. vis. prof. Tulane U. Med. Sch., 1984; mem. internat. adv. bd. Univ. Microfilms Internat. Collections on Terrorism, 1987—; internat. cons. Disaster Mgmt. and Disaster Medicine, Australia, India, others, 1983—; gov. emeritus Internat. Coun. for Computer Comm., 1996—, exec. com., v.p., 1972-92; bd. rep. Am. Coll. Nuclear Med., 2001— Author: Disaster: Your Right to Survive, 1991; mem. editorial bd. Terrorism, 1976—, Prehosp. and Disaster Medicine, 1989—; assoc. editor Jour. Prehosp. Care, 1984-85; contbr. articles to profl. jours. With U.S. Army, 1943-45; lt. (j.g.) USNR, 1946-53. Fgn. fellow NSF, 1974. Fellow ACS (chmn. Ariz. State com. on trauma 1979-84), Am. Assn. for Surgery of Trauma, Am. Coll. Emergency Physicians, Am. Coll. Gastroenterology, Am. Coll. Nuc. Medicine (bd. reps. 2001—); mem. World Assn. for Emergency and Disaster Medicine (exec. com. 1987-92), Critical Care Soc., Internat. Coun. Computer Comm. (co-founder). Died Feb. 10, 2006.

SIMMONS, CLEDA-MARIE, artist; b. Douglas, Wyo., June 24, 1927; d. Neil and Hulda Louise (Anderson) Diehl; m. Alfred Allen Simmons, May 9, 1951 (dec. Dec. 1987); children: Alfred Allen Jr., Barry Neal, Nina Marie. Student, Casper (Wyo.) Jr. Coll., 1946-47, U. N.Mex., Albuquerque, 1947-51. Painter, illustrator, muralist, graphic artist, Vista, Calif., from 1978; graphic artist Epsilon Sigma Alpha Women Internat., Ft. Collins, Colo., 1969-70; art editor ESA Women Int., Ft. Collins, Colo., 1970-73, art dir., 1973-77. Artistic dir. Vista Iniatitive for Visual Arts, 1990-94, bd. dirs.; artistic dir. Murals of Vista, 1994-96. Illustrator Our Government, 1969, Beneath the Peaks, 1973; co-author: Art of Editorship, 1972; author: Design and Your World, 1995; one-woman shows include Ateneo de Belles Artes, Madrid, 1955-90 (Purchase award 1955), Art Ways-Design Ctr., San Diego, 1991, Creative Art Ctr., Burbank, Calif., 1986, Mark Reuben Gallery, San Francisco, 1985, Gallery of World Art, Newton Upper Falls, Mass., 1982, Ahmed's Gallery Lounge, Cambridge, Mass., 1981, The Catseye, Wellesley, Mass., 1979, Loveland (Colo.) Mus., 1978, The Art of Mixing Colors, 2005, and numerous others 1954—. Exhbn. dir. Women's Caucus for the Arts, L.A., 1985, Women Exhbns. in Boston, 1980-83. Avocations: tennis, yoga, hiking. Died Mar. 25, 2005.

SIMMONS, TED CONRAD, writer; b. Seattle, Sept. 1, 1916; s. Conrad and Clara Evelyn (Beaudry) S.; m. Dorothy Pauline Maltese, June 1, 1942; children: Lynn, Juliet. Student, U. Wash., 1938-41, UCLA and L.A. State U., 1952-54, Oxford U., Eng., 1980. Drama critic Seattle Daily Times, 1942; indsl. writer, reporter-editor L.A. Daily News, 1948-51; contbr. Steel, Western Metals, Western Industry, from 1951. Past poetry dir. Watts Writers Workshop; instr. Westside Poetry Center; asst. dir. Pacific Coast Writers Conf, Calif. State Coll. Los Angeles. Author: (poetry) Deadended, 1966; (novel) Middlearth, 1975; (drama) Greenhouse, 1977, Durable Chaucer, 1978, Rabelais and other plays, 1980, Dickeybird, 1981 (nominated TCG Plays-in-Progress award 1985), Alice and Eve, 1983, Deja Vu, Deja Vu, 1986, The Box, 1987, Ingrid Superstar, 1988, Three Quarks for Mr. Marks, 1989, Ingrid: Skier on the Slopes of Stromboli, 1990, A Midsummer's Hamlet, 1991, Hamlet Nintendo, After Hours, Dueling Banjoes, Viva el Presidente, Climate of the Sun, 1992, Nude Descending Jacob's Ladder, 1993, Almost an Opera, 1994, Landscape with Inverted Tree and Fred Astaire Dancing, 1995, O.J. Othello, Fast Track, Searching for Alice Liddell, Mr. Blue of Freaky Animals, Inc., 1997, Rosenstern & Guildencrantz II, 1997, Rosa/Rosa of the Centuries/Rosa of the Thorns, 1997, Joyce, 1997, Joyce-After Hours, 1997, Amadeus & da Cultchur Club, 1997, Wonderland: Alice's New Adventures, 1998, The Brilliant Life of an Intelligent Orchid-A Play About Ingrid Bergman, 1998, Chekhov Off-Broadway, The Premiere, Good Night Sweet Prince, The Scare, 1999, 18 Mini-Micro Dramas, BloomsDay, The Scream, The Bird, 2000, Will, Jean "n" Jim— A Play, 2001; writer short story, radio verse; book reviewer Los Angeles Times; contbr. poetry to the Am. Poet, Prairie Wings, Antioch Rev., Year Two Anthology; editor: Venice Poetry Company Presents, 1972. Served with USAAF, 1942-46. Grantee Art Commn. King County, 1993. Died Jan. 19, 2006.

SIMON, GERALD AUSTIN, management consultant; b. N.Y.C., Aug. 19, 1927; s. William and Ray (Goldberg) S.; m. Margaret Cornwall, Dec. 1979; 1 son by previous marriage, Dana Alexander; 6 stepchildren. BBA, CCNY, 1950; MBA, Harvard U., 1956, postgrad. rsch. fellow, 1956-58. With various advt. firms, Phila., N.Y.C., Providence, 1950-54; rsch. asst., Ford Found. doctoral rsch. fellow Bus. Sch. Harvard U., 1956-58; vis. lectr. Northwestern U., Evanston, Ill., 1958-59; mng. dir. Cambridge Rsch. Inst., 1959-79; pres. Gerald Simon & Assocs., Berkeley, Calif., 1979—. Co-editor: Chief Executives Handbook, 1976; chmn. editorial bd. Jour. Mgmt. Cons. Pres. Humane Soc. East Bay. Served with USNR, 1945-46. Fellow Cert. Mgmt. Cons., mem. Inst. Mgmt. Cons. (founding mem., past dir.); mem. Assn. Cons. Mgmt. Engrs. (past dir.), Harvard U. Bus. Sch. Assn. (exec. coun., past dir.), Harvard Univ. Alumni Assn. (past dir.), Assn. Corp. Growth, Harvard Club (N.Y.C.), Harvard U. Faculty Club, U. Calif. at Berkeley Faculty Club. Died Apr. 28, 2005.

SIMON, JACK AARON, retired geologist; b. Champaign, Ill., June 17, 1919; s. Abraham and Lenore (Levy) S. BA, U. Ill., 1941, MS, 1946; postgrad., Northwestern U., 1947-49, D.Sc. (hon.), 1981. Tech. and research asst. Ill. State Geol. Survey, Urbana, 1937-42, asst. to assoc. geologist, 1945-53, geologist, head, coal sect., 1953-67, prin. geologist, 1967-74, asst. chief, 1973-74, chief, 1974-81, prin. scientist, 1981-83, ret., 1983. Assoc. prof. dept. metallurgy and mining engring. U. Ill., 1967-74, prof., 1974-77, 80-85, adj. prof. dept. geology, 1979-86; cons. in field. Served with F.A. AUS, 1942-43, F.A., USAAF, 1943-45. Decorated Air Medal with 4 oak leaf clusters; recipient Disting. Svc. award So. Ill. U., Edwardsville, 1982, Coal Day award So. Ill. U., Carbondale, 1982, Alumni Achievement award U. Ill. dept. geology, 1994. Fellow AAAS (sect. E chmn. 1980), Geol. Soc. Am. (chmn. coal geology div. 1962-63, Gilbert H. Cady award 1975, coun.l and exec. com. 1979-81); mem. Am. Assn. Petroleum Geologists (ea. sect. Gordon M. Wood Jr. Meml. award 1991), AIME (chmn. Midwest coal sect. 1966, Percy W. Nicholls award 1981), Am. Inst. Profl. Geologists (v.p. 1973), Am. Mining Congress, Assn. Am. State Geologists (hon., Disting. Svc. award, 2004), Ill. Mining Inst. (hon. life; exec. sec.-treas. 1963-68, v.p. 1980-81, pres. 1981-82), Ill. Soc. Coal Preparation Engrs. and Chemists, Ill. Geol. Soc., Ill. Acad. Sci., Soc. Econ. Geologists (councillor 1982-84), B'nai Brith, Sigma Xi. Clubs: Exchange (Urbana) (pres. 1969). Died Dec. 17, 2005.

SIMON, SEYMOUR, lawyer, former state supreme court justice; b. Chgo., Aug. 10, 1915; s. Ben and Gertrude (Rusky) S.; m. Roslyn Schultz Biel, May 26, 1954; children: John B., Nancy Simon Cooper, Anthony Biel. BS, Northwestern U., 1935, JD, 1938; LLD (hon.), John Marshall Law Sch., 1982, North Park Coll., 1986, Northwestern U., 1987. Bar: Ill. 1938. Spl. atty. Dept. Justice, 1938-42; practice law Chgo., 1946-74; judge Ill. Appellate Ct., Chgo., 1974-80; presiding justice Ill. Appellate Ct. (1st Dist., 3d Div.), 1977, 79; justice Ill. Supreme Ct., 1980-88; ptnr. DLA Piper Rudnick Gray Cary, Chgo., 1988—2006. Former chmn. Ill. Low-Level Radioactive Waste Disposal Facility Siting Commn.; former dir. Nat. Gen. Corp., Bantam Books, Grosset & Dunlap, Inc., Gt. Am. Ins. Corp. Contbr. articles to profl. jours. Mem. Cook County Bd. Commrs., 1961-66, pres., 1962-66; pres. Cook County Forest Preserve Dist., 1962-66; mem. Pub. Bldg. Commn., City Chgo., 1962-67; Alderman 40th ward, Chgo., 1955-61, 67-74; Democratic ward committeeman, 1960-74; bd. dirs. Schwab Rehab. Hosp., 1961-71, Swedish Covenant Hosp., 1969-75. With USNR, 1942-45. Decorated Legion of Merit; recipient Pub. Svc. award Tau Epsilon Rho, 1963, Northwestern U. Sch. of Law, 2006, Hubert L. Will award Am. Vets. Com., 1983, award of merit Decalogue Soc. Lawyers, 1986, Judge Learned Hand award Am. Jewish Com., 1994, Frances Feinberg Meml. Crown award Associated Talmud Torahs of Chgo., 1995, Bill of Rights in Action award Constl. Rights Found., 1997, Chgo. Coun. Lawyers and the Appleseed Fund Justice Commitment to Justice award, 1998, Civic Contbn. award LWV Chgo., 2000, Lifetime Achievement award Ill. Judges Assn., 2002, Justice award Jewish Judges Assn. Ill., 2003, John Peter Altgeld Freedom of Speech award Newberry Libr. Bughouse Sq. Debate Com., 2005; named to Sr. Citizen's Hall of Fame, City of Chgo., 1989, Hall of Fame Jewish Cmty. Ctrs. Chgo., 1989, Laureate Lincoln Acad. Ill., 1997. Mem. ABA, Ill. Bar Assn., Ill. Judges Assn., Chgo. Bar Assn. (Justice John Paul Stevens award 2004, Abraham Lincoln Marovitz Lena a Hand award

2006), Chgo. Hist. Soc., Decalogue Soc. Lawyers (Merit award 1986), Izaak Walton League, Am. Legion, VFW, Jewish War Vets., Chgo. Hort. Soc., Comml. Club Chgo., Std. Club, Variety Club, Order of Coif, Phi Beta Kappa, Phi Beta Kappa Assocs. Home: Chicago, Ill. Died Sept. 26, 2006.

SIMONDS, JOHN ORMSBEE, landscape architect; b. Jamestown, N.D., Mar. 11, 1913; s. Guy Wallace and Marguerite Lois (Ormsbee) S.; m. Marjorie C. Todd, May 1, 1943; children: Taye Anne, John Todd, Polly Jean, Leslie Brook. BS, Mich. State U., 1935, DSc hon.; MLandscape Architecture (Eugene Dodd medal), Harvard U., 1939. Landscape architect Mich. Dept. Parks, 1935-36; ptnr. Simonds and Simonds, Pitts., 1939-70, Collins, Simonds and Simonds, Washington, 1952-70, The Environ. Planning and Design Partnership, Pitts., also Miami Lakes, 1970-82, emeritus, from 1983. Cons. Dept. Pks., Collier County, Fla., 1986-90, Land and Nature Trust, Lexington, Ky., 1987-92, SW Fla. Water Mgmt. Dist., 1987-89; lectr., vis. critic urban and regional planning Carnegie-Mellon U., 1955-67; vis. critic Grad. Sch. Planning, also Sch. Architecture, Yale, 1961-62; Cons. Chgo. Cen. Area Com., 1962, Allegheny County Dept. Regional Pks., 1961-74; U.S. cons. community planning Inter-Am. Housing and Planning Ctr., Bogota, Colombia, 1960-61; mem. jury Am. Acad. Rome, 1963, 65, 66, 69; mem. jury projected pilgrim's reception Cultural Ctr., Mecca, 1995; mem. Nat. Adv. Com. on Hwy. Beautification; chmn. panel on pks. and open space White House Conf. on Natural Beauty; mem. Interprofl. Commn. on Environ. Design; mem. and report editor urban hwy. adv. bd. U.S. Bur. Pub. Rds., 1965-68; mem. landscape architecture adv. panel U.S. C.E., 1968-71, Pres.'s Task Force on Resources and Environ., 1968-70; mem. design adv. panel Operation Breakthrough, HUD, 1970-71; mem. Mid-Atlantic regional adv. bd. Nat. Park Svc., 1976-78; assoc. trustee U. Pa., 1962-66, mem. bd. fine arts, 1962-66; chmn. joint com. planning Carnegie-Mellon U. and U. Pitts., 1959-60; overseer's vis. com. Harvard Grad. Sch. Design, 1962-68, exec. coun. alumni assn., 1960-63; adv. com. Sch. Design, N.C. State U., 1965-67; mem. Fla. Gov.'s Task Force on Natural Resources, 1979-80, Chgo. Bot. Garden 25th Anniversary, 1991, keynote address, 1991, Internat. Fedn. Landscape Architects, Seoul, Korea, 1992; speaker keynote address Internat. Congress Urban Green, Geneva, 1986. Author: Landscape Architecture, the Shaping of Man's Natural Environment, 1961, 2d rev. edit., 1997, Earthscape, a Manual of Environmental Planning, 1978, revised edit. 1986, Garden Cities 21, Creating a Livable Urban Environment, 1994, Lessons, 1999; editor: Virginia's Common Wealth, 1965, The Freeway in the City, 1968, The Freeway in the City for Urban Advisors; contbr. sect. on urban design Ency. Architecture, 1990, sect. on landscape architecture Ency. Urban Planning, 1980, Lessons, 1999. Maj. works (with others) include master plans for Chgo. Bot. Garden, Mellon Sq., Pitts., Equitable Plaza, (Miami Lakes New Town, Va. I-66 Corridor, Fairfax and Arlington counties, Va., Pelican Bay Community, Fla., Weston New Town, Fla. Bd. dirs. Hubbard Ednl. Trust, 1974—. Recipient citation Top Men of Year Engring. News-Record, 1973, Sigma Lambda Alpha award Coun. Educators in Landscape Architecture, 1979, Charles L. Hutchinson medal Chgo. Hort. Soc., John R. Bracken medal Dept. Landscape Architecture, Pa. State U., 1985, Landscape Design award Am. Hort. Soc., 2004. Fellow Am. Soc. Landscape Architects (mem. exec. com. 1959-67, pres. 1963-65, pres. Found. 1966-68, recipient medal 1973, Centennial Pres.'s medal 1999), Royal Soc. Arts (Gt. Britain); mem. Nat. Acad. (US), Archtl. League N.Y., Royal Town Planning Inst. (hon. corr.), Landscape Arch. Found., Am. Soc. Landscape Archs., Am. Hort. Soc. (Landscape Design award 2004), AIA (hon. assoc. Pa. chpt.), Harvard-Yale-Princeton Club. Presbyterian (ruling elder). Home: Pittsburgh, Pa. Died May 26, 2005.

SIMONS, KENETH ALDEN, consultant; b. Phila., Mar. 10, 1913; s. Samuel and Gertrude Winifred (Alden) S.; m. Reta Evens (dec. 1973); children: Kurt Alden, Andri Muth, Dona Vigo; m. Mary Kerr Richey (dec. 1986). BSc in Elec. Engring. with distinction, U. Pa., 1938. Radar-TV field engr. RCA, Camden, N.J., 1938-46; gen. engr. WCAU, Phila., 1941; chief TV instr. Ctrl. Radio Sch., Kansas City, Mo., 1946-49; TV advanced devel. Sylvania, Buffalo, 1950; cons., then chief engr., then v.p. R&D Jerrold Electronics, 1951-76; cons. U. Pa., Phila., from 1990. Author U.S. Navy SYNCHRCS, Technical Handbook for CATV; holder Brit., Can. and U.S. patents; author some 20 tech. mag. articles. Chmn. panel 1 CTAC, Washington, 1973-75. Named CATV Engr. of Yr. NCTA, 1965. Fellow Brit. Soc. Cable Engrs.; mem. IEEE (life), Soc. Cable and TV Engrs. Avocation: skin diving. Home: Lenhartsville, Pa. Died June 2004.

SINCLAIR, ELDRIDGE, management consultant; b. Portland, Dec. 12, 1912; s. John William Eldridge and Una Dell S.; m. Muriel Meyer, June 30, 1946 (div. June 1955); m. Joan Gillison, June 11, 1956; children: Nancy, Adelaide, Wayne, Annie Laurie. BBA, U. Wash., 1934; MBA, Harvard U., 1936. Adminstrv. officer Rural Electrification, Washington, 1936-39; mgmt. specialist Bonneville Power, Portland, 1939-42, 45-53; utility cons. Zinder & Assocs., San Francisco, 1955-63; asst. to utilities dir. Pub. Utilities Dept., Riverside, Calif., 1963-77, utilities dir. Banning, Calif., 1981-87. Legis. chair Am. Assn. Retired Persons, Riverside, 1988—, Retired Pub. Employees Assn., Riverside, 1998—. 2d lt. U.S. Army, 1942-45. Democrat. Avocations: golf, tennis. Home: Riverside, Calif. Died 2005.

SINGER, KURT DEUTSCH, commentator, writer; b. Vienna, Aug. 10, 1911; came to U.S., 1940, naturalized, 1951; s. Ignaz Deutsch and Irene (Singer) S.; m. Hilda Tradelius, Dec. 23, 1932 (div. 1954); children: Marian Alice Birgit, Kenneth Walt; m. Jane Sherrod, Apr. 9, 1955 (dec. Jan. 1985); m. Katherine Han, Apr. 8, 1989. Student, U. Zürich, Switzerland, 1930, Labor Coll., Stockholm, 1936; PhD, Div. Coll. Metaphysics, Indpls., 1951. Escaped to, Sweden, 1934; founder Ossietzky Com. (successful in release Ossietzky from concentration camp); corr. Swedish mag. Folket i Bild, 1935-40; founder Niemöller Com.; pub. biography Göring in Eng. (confiscated in Sweden), 1940; co-founder pro-Allied newspaper Trots Allt, 1939; corr. Swedish newspapers in, 1940; editor News Background, 1942; lectr. U. Minn., U. Kans., U. Wis., 1945-49; radio commentator Sta. WKAT, 1950; corr. N.Am. Newspaper Alliance, N.Y.C., 1953—2005; pres. Singer Media Corp., 1987—99. Dir. Oceanic Press Svc., San Clemente, Calif. Author, editor: underground weekly Mitteilungsblätter, Berlin, Germany, 1933; author: The Coming War, 1934, (biog.) Carl von Ossietzky, 1936 (Nobel Peace prize), Germany's Secret Service in Central America, 1943, Spies and Saboteurs in Argentina, 1943, Duel for the Northland: The War of Eneny Agents in Scandinavia, 1943, White Book of the Church of Norway, 1940, Spies and Traitors of World War II, 1945, Who are the Communists in America, 1948, 3000 Years of Espionage, 1951, World's Greatest Women Spies, 1952, (juvenile) Kippie the Cow, 1952, Polgar the Hypnotist, 1953, Gentlemen Spies, 1953, The Man in the Trojan Horse, 1954, World's Best Spy Stories, 1954, Charles Laughton Story; adapted TV, motion pictures, 1954, Spies Over Asia, 1955, More Spy Stories, 1955, My Greatest Crime Story, 1956, My Most Famous Case, 1957, The Danny Kaye Saga; My Strangest Case, 1958, Spy Omnibus, 1959, Spies for Democracy, 1960, Crime Omnibus Spies Who Changed History, 1961, Hemmingway-Life and Death of a Giant, 1961, True Adventures in Crime, Dr. Albert Schweitzer, Medical Missionary, 1962, Lyndon Baines Johnson-Man of Reason, 1964, Ho-i-man; juveniles, 1965; Kurt Singer's Ghost Omnibus, 1965; juvenile Kurt Singer's Horror Omnibus; The World's Greatest Stories of the Occult, The Unearthly, 1965, Mata Hari-Goddess of Sin, 1965, Daughter of Mata Hari, 1965, Lyndon Johnson-From Kennedy to Vietnam, 1966, Weird Tales Anthology, 1966, I Can't Sleep at Night, 1966, Weird Tales of Supernatural, 1967, Tales of Terror, 1967, Famous Short Stories, 1967, Folktales of the South Pacific, 1967, Tales of The Uncanny, 1968, Gothic Reader, 1968, Bloch and Bradbury, 1969, Folktales of Mexico, 1969, Tales of the Unknown, 1970, The House in the Valley, 1970, Hablan Los Artistas, 1970, Tales of the Macabre, 1971, Three Thousand Years of Espionage, 1971, El Mundo de Hoy, 1971, Cuentos Fantasticos del Mas, 1971, Aldous Huxley, El Camino al Infierno, 1971, Ghouls and Ghosts, 1972, The Unearthly, 1972, The Gothic Reader, 1972, Satanic Omnibus, 1973, The Plague of the Living Dead, 1973, Gothic Horror Omnibus, 1974, Dictionary of Household Hints and Help, 1974, Supernatural, 1974, They are Possessed, 1976, True Adventures into the Unknown, 1980, I Spied-And Survived, 1980, Great Adventures in Crime, 1982, The Oblong Box, 1982, Shriek, 1984, First Target Book of Horror, 1984, 2d, 1984, 3d, 1985, 4th, 1985, Solve A Crime, 1994, The Ultimate Quiz Book, 1994, The Complete Guide to Career Advancement, 1994, The Sex Quiz Book, 1994, The Marriage Quiz Book, The Psychology Quiz Book, The Teenage Quiz Book, Success Secrets, 1995, Conozcase Mejor y Triunfe, 1995, The Joy of Practical Parenting, 1995, Der Deutsche Widerstand gegen Hitlers Krieg - 1939-45, 2002; editor: UN Calendar, 1959-58; fgn. corres. German mags., 1996-2000; contbr. articles to newspapers, popular mags., U.S., fgn. countries, all his books and papers in Boston U. Libr.-Spl. Collections, Danish Peace Acad., 2001, Gandhi Centre Berlin, 2003, Awd Literatur Haus, Vienna, Austria. Mem. UN Speakers Rsch. Com., UN Children's Emergency Fund, Menninger Found. Mem. Nat. Geog. Soc., Smithsonian Assos., Internat. Platform Assn. (v.p.), United Sch. Assemblies (pres.), Danish Peace Acad. Died Dec. 9, 2005.

SINGER, RONALD, anatomist, educator; b. Cape Town, South Africa, Aug. 12, 1924; s. Solomon Charles and Sonia (Swirsky) S.; m. Shirley Bernice Gersohn, Dec. 10, 1950; children— Hazel Lynn, Eric Gersohn, Sonia Esther, Charles Malcolm. M.B., Ch.B., U. Capetown, 1947, D.Sc., 1962. Resident med. officer Kimberley Hosp., South Africa, 1947-48; govt. med. officer, supt. Gwelo Native Hosp., Rhodesia, 1948-49; faculty U. Capetown, 1949-62, asso. prof., 1960-62; vis. prof. anatomy U. Ill., 1959-60; prof. anatomy U. Chgo., 1962—2006, dept. chmn., prof. anatomy and anthropology, 1963—2006, Robert R. Bensley prof. biology and med. scis., 1973—2006. Contbr. articles to profl. jours. Recipient Americanism medal DAR, 1979; Rotary Found. fellow Carnegie Instn. Washington Embryology Labs., Johns Hopkins, 1951-52 Fellow Royal Soc. So. Africa, Royal Anthrop. Inst.; mem. Am. Assn. Anatomists, Am. Assn. Phys. Anthropologists, Anat. Soc. Gt. Britain and Ireland, Soc. Study Human Biology, A.A.A.S., Sigma Xi. Home: Chicago, Ill. Died Apr. 17, 2006.

SINGLEHURST, DONA GEISENHEYNER, horse farm owner; b. Tacoma, June 19, 1928; d. Herbert Russell and Rose Evelyn (Rubish) Geisenheyner; m. Thomas G. Singlehurst, May 16, 1959 (dec.); 1 child, Suanna Singlehurst. BA in Psychology, Whitman Coll., 1950. With pub. rels. and advt. staff Lane Wells, L.A., 1950-52; staff mem. in charge new bus. Bishop Trust Co., Honolulu, 1953-58; mgr. Town & Country Stables, Honolulu, 1958-62; co-owner, v.p. pub. rels. Carol & Mary, Ltd., Honolulu, 1964-84; owner Stanhope Farms, Waialua, Hawaii, 1969—2006. Internat. dressage judge, sport horse breeding judge US Equestrian; sr. judge Can. Dressage Fedn. Chmn. ways and means com. The Outdoor Cir., Hawaii, 1958-64, life mem.; pres. emeritus Morris Animal Found., Englewood, Colo., 1988—, pres., 1984-88; bd. dirs., pres. Delta Soc., Renton, Wash., 1994-97, chmn. emeritus 1998—, N.Y.C.; mem. Jr. League of Honolulu; mem. devel. com. Honolulu Symphony. Recipient Best Friends award Honolulu Vet. Soc., 1986, Spl. Recognition award Am. Animal Hosp. Assn., 1988, Recognition award Am. Vet. Med. Assn. Mem. NAFE, AAUW, Hawaii Horse Show Assn. (Harry Hutaff award 1985, past pres., bd. dirs.), Hawaii Combined Tng. Assn. (past pres. bd. dirs.), Calif. Dressage Soc., U.S. Dressage Fedn., U.S. Equestrian Team (area chmn. 1981-85), Hawaiian Humane Soc. (life), U.S. Pony Clubs (dist. commr. 1970-75, nat. examiner 1970-75), Pacific Club, Outrigger Canoe Club. Republican. Episcopalian. Avocations: music, travel. Died May 1, 2006.

SINHA, SURYA PRAKASH, law educator; b. Poona, Maharashtr, India, July 29, 1937; came to U.S., 1959; s. Jagannath Prasad and Paj Pyari (Srivastava) S.; m. Jessica Feinberg; 1 child, Sonya Shanti. B of Commerce, U. Poona, 1956; LLB, U. Bombay, India, 1958; MS, U. Ariz., 1962; LLM, U. Ill., 1964; cert. Am. Summer Course, U. Paris, 1967; diploma, Inst. of Cost and Works Accts., Calcutta, India, 1957; JSD, U. Ill., 1966; cert., Iowa Writer's Workshop, U. Iowa, 1988. Bar: Ontario, Can., 1973. Cost acct. Mahindra-Owen Pvt. Ltd., Poona, 1958-59; trust officer Stewart Title and Trust, Inc., Tucson, 1960-62; spl. asst. to v.p. A.O. Smith Internat., S.A., Milw., 1963; research asst. Bur. Instl. Research, Urbana, Ill., 1964-65; researcher Am. Bar Found., Chgo., 1964-65; asst. and assoc. prof. law U. S.D. Sch. Law, Vermillion, 1965-69; vis. scholar Columbia U., N.Y.C., 1969-70, 74-75; assoc. prof., prof. law U. Western Ontario Faculty of Law, London, 1970-74; vis. prof. law Villanova (Pa.) U. Sch. Law, 1975-76; prof. law Seton Hall U. Sch. Law, Newark, 1976-79, Pace U. Sch. Law, White Plains, N.Y., from 1979. Assoc. U. Seminar on the Problem of Peace Columbia U., 1969—; founder, advisor Pace Yearbook of Internat. Law, White Plains, N.Y., 1987—. Author: New Nations and the Law of Nations, 1967, Asylum and International Law, 1971, What is Law?, 1989, Jurisprudence: Legal Philosophy in a Nutshell, 1993, Legal Polycentricity and International Law, 1995; contbr. articles to profl. jours. Bd. dirs. Alam Sch. of Indian Classical Music, N.Y.C., 1977-82. Recipient Honorary Citizenship of the City of Tucson, 1960. Mem. Internat. Law Assn. (human rights com.), Am. Soc. Internat. Law. Hindu. Avocations: writing novels, play indian classical music on sitar. Home: Norwalk, Conn. Died July 30, 2005.

SISKE, ROGER CHARLES, lawyer; b. Starkville, Miss., Mar. 2, 1944; s. Lester L. and Helen S.; m. Regina Markunas, May 31, 1969; children: Kelly, Jennifer, Kimberly. BS in Fin. with honors, Ohio State U., 1966; JD magna cum laude, U. Mich., 1969. Bar: Ill. 1969. Assoc. Sonnenschein Nath & Rosenthal LLP, Chgo., 1969—78, ptnr., 1978—2006. Served to capt. U.S. Army, 1970—71. Decorated Bronze Star. Fellow Am. Coll. Employee Benefits Counsel (charter); mem. ABA (past chmn. tax sect. employee benefits com., past chmn. joint com. on employee benefits and exec. compensation and bus. law sect., employee benefits and exec. compensation com., conf. chmn. various confs.), Chgo. Bar Assn. (past chmn. employee benefits com., mem. exec. coun. of tax com.), past chmn. employee benefits coun. ISBA, Order of Coif (editor law review), Phi Alpha Kappa. Republican. Died Jan. 4, 2006.

SKAUEN, DONALD MATTHEW, retired pharmaceutical educator; b. Newton, Mass., May 14, 1916; s. Marcus and Mary A. (Duncan) S.; m. Rachel M. Burns, Oct. 25, 1942; children: Deborah Skauen Hinchcliffe, Bruce. BS, Mass. Coll. Pharmacy, 1938, MS, 1942; PhD, Purdue U., 1949. Dir. pharm. svc. Children's Hosp. Med. Ctr., Boston, 1940-46; teaching asst. Purdue U., West Lafayette, Ind., 1946-48; asst. prof. pharmaceutics U. Conn., Storrs, 1948-53, assoc. prof., 1953-59, prof., 1959-79, prof. emeritus, 1979—2006. Mem. del. of med. scientists to discuss biol. and pharm. uses of ultrasound Nat. Coun. U.S.-China Trade, People's Republic China, 1979. Co-author: American Pharmacy, 4th edit., 1955, 5th edit., 1961, 6th edit., 1966, Husa's Pharmaceutical Dispensing, 1959, 2d edit., 1966, Radioecology, 1963; contbr. numerous articles to Sci., Nature, Jour. Am. Pharm. Assn. Mem. Am. Pharm. Assn., Am. Soc. Hosp. Pharmacists, Sigma Xi. Achievements include research on effects of ultrasound on pharmaceutical and biological systems; radioecology, including gross beta levels in oysters and other organisms in Thames River, Connecticut, and zinc-65 levels in oysters. Home: Storrs Mansfield, Conn. Died Apr. 13, 2006.

SKLAR, LOUISE MARGARET, computer company executive; b. L.A., Aug. 12, 1934; d. Samuel Baldwin Smith and Judith LeRoy (Boughton) Nelson; m. Edwynn Edgar Schroeder, Mar. 20, 1955 (div. July 1975); children: Neil Nelson Schroeder, Leslie Louise Schroeder Grandclaudon, Samuel George Schroeder; m. Martin Sklar, Oct. 17, 1983. Student, U. So. Calif., 1952-54, UCLA, 1977-79. Acct. Valentine Assocs., Northridge, Calif., 1976-78, programmer, 1978-79; contr. Western Monetary, Encino, Calif., 1979-81; pres. Automatic Computer Composition, Reno, from 1984. Mem.: DAR, New England Hist. Genealogical Soc., So. Calif. Assistance League, Conn. Soc. Genealogists, Greater L.A. Zoo. Assn., Am. Contract Bridge League (bd. govs. 1993—99, mem. nat. charity com. from 1982, mem. nat. goodwill com. from 1994), Assn. Los Angeles

County Bridge Units (bd. dirs. 1990—2000, sec. 1984—86), Ky. Hist. Soc., Safari Club Internat., Zeta Tau Alpha. Republican. Avocations: tournament bridge, travel. Home: Reno, Nev. Died July 21, 2005.

SKOLER, CELIA REBECCA, retired art gallery director; b. Sioux City, Iowa, Apr. 7, 1931; d. Jacob and Flora (Gorchow) Stern; m. Louis Skoler, Aug. 24, 1952; children: Elisa Anne, Harry Jay. BFA in Art and Music magna cum laude, Syracuse U., 1976. Fin. planner Architects' Partnership, Syracuse, NY, 1969-71; bus. mgr. Skoler & Lee Architects P.C., Syracuse, 1971-89; owner, dir. New Acquisitions Gallery, Syracuse, 1981-95, 1995—2003; ptnr. Gallery Metro, Syracuse, 1991-93, mng. ptnr., 1992-93; contbg. writer Syracuse Herald and Syracuse Newtimes, Syracuse, 1989-91; ret., 2003. Art cons. Costello, Cooney & Fearon, Syracuse, 1981—83, IBM Hdqs., Syracuse, NY, 1983, Rochester, NY, 84, Albany, NY, 86, Menter, Rudin & Trivelpiece, Syracuse, 1987—88, Blue Cross/Blue Shield, Ctrl. N.Y., Syracuse, 1990, Syracuse Newspapers, 1992—94, GTE Svcs. Corp., Syracuse, 1995; gallery supr. of sudent interns Syracuse U., 1981—93; dir. mayoral portrait City of Syracuse, 1983; dir. Gelling Meml. portrait U. Coll., 1984; dir. Levine Meml. Commn. Temple Concord, 1984; TV producer Syracuse U. Friends of Art, 1979—80; panelist for art critique Everson Mus. Art, Syracuse, 1989; lectr. on gallery mgmt. Syracuse U. Sch. of Art, 1989; juror fine art N.Y. State Fair, 1982, 89; panelist Cultural Resources Coun., Onondaga County, NY, from 2001. One-man shows include Camillus Plaza, 1972, The Associated Artists Gallery, Syracuse, 1973, Libr. Fayetteville, N.Y., 1974; exhibited in group shows at N.Y. State Fair (1st prize 1974), U. Coll, 1967, 69, 71, Rochester Meml. Gallery, 1969-72, 74, The Associated Artists, 1971-72, Cen. N.Y. Art Open, 1970, 71, (Purchase prize 1970, 71), Munson Williams Protor Inst, Utica, N.Y., 1971, 72, Cayuga Mus., Auburn, N.Y., 1972, Oneida (N.Y.) Art Festival, 1969, (1st prize), Jewish Community Ctr., Syracuse, 1968 (1st prize 1969), St. David's Invitational, Dewitt, N.Y., 1970-75, Cooperstown Art Inst., Nat. Show, 1973, 74, Arena Nat. Show, Binghamton, N.Y., 1975 (Purchase prize 1975); prodr.: (autobiographical CD-ROM) In Rehearsal, 1997; represented in permanent collection at Savannah (Ga.) Coll. Art and Design & Syracuse U. Peer counselor Univ. Coll., Syracuse, 1980-85; Tel-auc auctioneer Sta. WCNY-TV, Liverpool, N.Y., 1982; mem. steering and implementation com. Gelling Meml. Lounge U. Coll., 1984-85; exec. bd. Syracuse U. Friends of Art, 1977-80; fine art juror Downtown Com., Syracuse, 1982, Oswego (N.Y.) Art Guild, 1984. Recipient Purchase prize Marine Midland Bank, 1974, Crouse-Irving Hosp., 1971, 1974; named to Sioux City Ctrl. High Roster Hall of Fame, 1998. Mem. Everson Mus. Art (corp.) mem. Phi Kappa Phi, Alpha Sigma Lambda (pres. 1980-81). Died Apr. 23, 2006.

SKOLNICK, SHERMAN HERBERT, media host/producer, researcher, court reformer; b. Chgo., July 13, 1930; s. Max and Pauline (Lubelsky) S. Grad., DePaul U.; student, John Marshall Sch. Law. Legal rschr., Chgo., 1958—2006; founder, chmn. Citizens Com. to Clean Up the Cts., Chgo., 1963—2006. Instr., civic investigation Columbia Coll., 1969-70. Author: Secret History of Airplane Sabotage, 1973; radio talk show guest, 1967-2006, moderator, 1973-75; condr. univ. seminars in field; editor Hotline News, 1971-2006; prodr./panelist weekly pub. access Cable TV shows, Chgo., suburbs, 1991—, prodr., host, 1995—; writer Internet categories, websites, 1994-2006; writer/rsch. Japan Times Weekly, Tokyo, 1995. Died May 21, 2006.

SLADE, JOANN KAYE, retired educator; b. Billings, Mont., Dec. 10, 1933; d. Joseph Frank and Erma Mae (Giltner) S. BA, St. Mary Coll., Xavier, Kas., 1956; MA, Ariz. State U., 1968; postgrad., U. Nev., Las Vegas, from 1965, U. Va. in Washington, 1980. Cert. art specialist. Tchr. art Lewiston (Mont.) Jr. High Sch., 1957-58, McCormic Jr. High Sch., Cheyenne, Wyo., 1958-62; camp dir., counselor Cen. Mont. Girl Scouts U.S., Lewistown, 1958-63; tchr. art, English Wheelus High Sch. USAF Base, Tripoli, Libya, 1962-63, Toul-Rosier (France) USAF Base, 1963-64, Western High Sch., Las Vegas, from 1964. Past pres. Clark County Art. Edn., Las Vegas, (Publicity chmn. 1980-87). Work exhibited Portfolio Inc. Art Gallery, 1985-88, Clark County Library Dist. Show, 1986. Active Cen. Com. Rep. Party, Las Vegas; del. Edinburgh Soc., 1985. Recipient Gov.'s Art award Nev. Council Arts, 1988, Experience Tchr. Scholarship Ariz. State U., 1968, Fed. Forum fellowship Fed. Forum, 1980; fellow Victorian art and lit. U. Nev. Las Vegas, 1989. Mem. Nat. Art Edn. Assn. Clark County Classroom Tchrs. Assn., Nev. State Edn. Assn.(chairperson faculty coun. 1980, 90, Tchr. of Yr. 1990), Art Alliance Nev., Inst. Contemporary Art, Allied Art Soc. Democrat. Avocation: travel. Home: Las Vegas, Nev. Died Nov. 15, 2004.

SLAGLEY, CHARLES AARON, JR., high school principal; b. Alton, Ill., Oct. 16, 1948; s. Charles Aaron and Wanda (Jones) S.; m. Glenda Gwyn, Jan. 29, 1967; children: Charles III, David, Jeremy. BS in Edn., No. Ill. U., 1970; MS in Secondary Edn., So. Ill. U., 1974, Specialist in Ednl. Adminstrn., 1988. Tchr., coach Alton Community Unit Dist. No. 11, 1970-79; asst. prin. Marissa (Ill.) Community Unit Dist. No. 43, 1979-80, jr. high prin., 1980-84, jr.-sr. high prin., 1984-87, supt., 1986-89; high sch. prin. Galena (Ill.) Unit Dist. No. 120, from 1989. Mem. ASCD, Nat. Assn. Secondary Sch. Prins., Ill. Assn. Supervision and Curriculum Devel., Ill. Prin. Assn., Masons, Scottish Rite, Elks. Home: Galena, Ill. Died Jan. 16, 2005.

SLEWETT, ROBERT DAVID, lawyer; b. N.Y.C., June 4, 1945; s. Nathan and Evelyn (Miller) S.; m. Sheila Faith Winkler, Jan. 27, 1973; children: Gregory, Danielle. BA in Pub. Affairs, George Washington U., 1967; JD, Cornell U., 1970. Bar: Fla. 1970. Mem. Smith and Mandler, Miami Beach, Fla., 1970-73; with Robert D. Slewett, Atty. at Law, Miami Beach, 1973-87; ptnr. Steinberg, Slewett & Yaffe, Miami Beach, 1987-98, Robert D. Slewett, P.A., Miami Beach, from 1998. Lectr. in probate and medicaid field. Exec. v.p., gen. counsel Nat. Parkinson Found., Miami, Fla., 1993—; bd. dirs., legal counsel Boystown of Jerusalem Found. Am., N.Y.C., 1993—; mem. Dade County Estate Planning Coun., Heritage Soc. Miami Jewish Home and Hosp. Named One of Leading Fla. Attys. in Field of Trusts and Estates. Mem. Nat. Acad. Elder Lawyers, Fla. Bar Assn. (probate litigation com., probate rules com. 2000—), Dade County Bar Assn. (chmn. spl. needs trust com., Pro Bono award 2002), Estate Planning Coun. Dade County. Home: Miami, Fla. Died Sept. 13, 2004.

SLIDER, MARGARET ELIZABETH, elementary school educator; b. Spanish Fork, Utah, Nov. 27, 1945; d. Ira Elmo and Aurelia May (Peterson) Johnson; m. Richard Keith Slider, Oct. 25, 1968; children: Thomas Richard, Christopher Alan. AA, Chaffey Coll., 1966; BA, Calif. State U., San Bernardino, 1968, MEd in English as Second Lang., 1993. Cert. elem. tchr., Calif. Tchr. Colton (Calif.) Unified Sch. Dist., from 1968; lead sci. tchr. McKinley Sch., 1994-96; mem. sci. steering com. Colton Joint Unified Sch. Dist., from 1996. Mem. kindergarten assessment com. Colton Joint Unified Sch. Dist., Colton, 1988-90, dist. math. curriculum com., 1992-94; trainer Calif. State Dept. Edn. Early Intervention for Sch. Success, 1993—, demonstrator on-site classroom, 1994. Treas. McKinley Sch. PTA, Colton, 1989-91. Mem. NEA, ASCD, AAUW, Calif. Tchrs. Assn., Calif. Elem. Edn. Assn., Calif. Assn. of Tchrs. of English to Students of Other Langs., Calif. Mathematics Coun., Assn. Colton Educators, Pi Lambda Theta. Avocations: needlecrafts, reading, bicycling. Home: Redlands, Calif. Died July 29, 2005.

SLOAN, ALBERT J., II, academic administrator; b. Atlanta, Sept. 24, 1942; s. Albert John Hicks and Addie Cannon S.; m. Emma Lillian Lee, Aug. 29, 1970; children: Ashaki Nicole, Ashante Denise, Alescia Alexandria. BA, Albany State U., 1965; MDiv, Interdenominational Theol., Ctr., Atlanta, 1968; JD, Miles Law Sch., 1982; DDiv, Faith Grant Coll., 1998; LLD, Tex. Coll., 1999. Counselor Upward Bound Program/Ala. State U., Montgomery, 1969-71; team tchr. Huntsville (Ala.) Space Ctr., 1974-75; prof. religion and philosophy Miles Coll., Fairfield, 1972-89, asst. to the pres., 1972-73, dean of chapel, 1971-89, dean of students, 1987-89, pres., 1989—2005. Pres. Fairfield Bd. Edn., 1978-93, Birmingham Civil Rights Inst.; mem. Jud. Coun. C.M.E. Ch., Birmingham; assoc. justice C.M.E. Ch. Religious editor: Atlanta Enquirer, 1969-70; contbr. articles to religious publs. Mem. Birmingham Personnel Bd., Leadership Birmingham, Fairfield C. of C. Recipient Nat. Hist. Preservation award Ala. Hist. Commn., 1994. Mem. Nat. Bar Assn., Omega Psi Phi, Phi Delta Kappa, Delta Theta Pi. Avocations: swimming, singing, public speaking. Home: Fairfield, Ala. Died Nov. 25, 2005.

SMIRNOV, DIANA, music educator; b. St. Petersburg, Russia, Nov. 9, 1955; d. Vladimir and Faina (Bryanskaya) Frumkin; m. Alexander Joseph Smirnov, July 14, 1975 (div. Oct. 1992); 1 child, Anya; m. Andrew Maratovich Krichak, May 11, 1996. MusB, Specialized Music Sch., St. Petersburg, Russia, 1974; MusM, St. Petersburg Conservatory, 1978, New England Conservatory, 1982. Instr. piano, accompanist Music Sch., St. Petersburg, Russia, 1974-78, Wheaton Coll., Norton, Mass., 1983-87; organist, choir dir. Providence Presbyn. Ch., 1984-94; instr. piano Providence Coll., from 1986; free-lance musician U.S., Can., Italy, Russia, from 1978. Author: Musictionary, pt. 1, 2002, pt. 2, 2003; numerous TV and radio appearances, U.S., Can., Russia. Recipient 3d prize Joanna Hodges Internat. Piano Competition, Palm Desert, Calif., 1984. Mem. Music Tchrs. Nat. Assn. (corr. sec. 1995-97, ind. music tchrs. forum 1997-2002), RI Music Tchrs. Assn. (1st v.p.). Avocations: ping-pong, swimming, reading, jazz, languages. Home: Warwick, RI. Died Jan. 23, 2004.

SMITH, ALAN BRONSON, JR., military officer, farm executive; b. Milw., Aug. 7, 1917; s. Alan Bronson and Claire Christie (Lund) S.; m. Harriett Ellen Rittenour, July 10, 1943; children: Alan Bronson III, Christie, Kyle, Kerry. BA, Ohio Wesleyan U., 1940; grad., Air Command and Staff Coll., Maxwell AFB, Ala., 1951, Naval War Coll., Newport, R.I., 1963; MBA, George Washington U., 1959. Commd. 2d lt. USAF, 1940, advanced through grades to col., 1962; ret., 1969; assoc. dir. Grant Hosp., Columbus, Ohio, 1969-74; owner, producer Meadowbrook Farms, Circleville, Ohio, 1974-91. Researcher in low cholestrol, low-fat beef and pork. Decorated DFC, Air medal with 3 oakleaf clusters, Legion of Merit; recipient Pub. Rels. award Am. Hosp. Assn., 1970, 73; named Eagle Scout Boy Scouts of Am., 1934. Mem. Air Force Assn. (life), Navy League U.S. (life; bd. dirs. Columbus coun. 1969-76), Ret. Officers Assn. (life), Rotary (com. chmn. Columbus 1982-98), Sigma Alpha Epsilon. Republican. Methodist. Avocations: sailing, gardening, photography, travel, aerobics. Died June 14, 2005.

SMITH, ALBERT CARL, physician, scientist; b. LA, Sept. 13, 1934; s. Salmon and Sadie (Lewis) S.; m. Mary Ellen Reeley Dec. 31, 1997; children: Connie Powell, Shana Smith, John Reeley, Christopher Reeley, Chelsea Smith. BA in Zoology, UCLA, 1956; PhD in Biol. Scis., U. Calif., Irvine, 1967; MD, U. Hawaii, 1975. Diplomate Nat. Bd. Med. Examiners; cert. in clin. pathology, Am. Bd. Pathology. Rsch. assoc., instr. dept. population and environ. biology U. Calif., Irvine, 1966-67; assoc. prof. biology U. Hawaii, Hilo, 1967-73, rsch. fellow, 1975-76, resident in clin. pathology, 1975-79; chief cons. Hawaii Biomarine, Honolulu, 1973—80; dir. Med. Labs. Hawaii, Honolulu, 1979—80; sr. scientist Oceanic Inst., Waimanalo, Hawaii, 1973—79; chief clin. lab. VA Med. Ctr., Gainesville, Fla., 1980—85; clin. pathology cons. Sunland Ctr., Gainesville, 1985; chief clin. pathology VA Med. Ctr., Bay Pines, Fla., 1985—91; asst. prof. pathology Coll. Medicine U. Fla., Gainesville, 1980-85, adj. prof. divsn. comparative medicine Coll. Vet. Medicine, from 1982; courtesy prof. Coll. Marine Sci. U. South Fla., St. Petersburg, from 1987; pvt. practice Panama City, Fla., from 1993; courtesy prof. dept. oceanography Fla. State U., Tallahassee, from 1998; prof. dept. sci. Barry U., Tallahassee Ctr., Panama City, from 2001. Dean of basic sci. Saba U. Sch. Medicine, Dutch Netherland Antilles, 1999-2000; site team mem. NIH. Author: Treasures From the Sea for Medicine, 2000, The Aquatic Roots of Human Pathology, 2002; contbr. chpts. to books, more than 90 articles to profl. jours. Fellow Coll. Am. Pathologists; mem. Internat. Soc. Aquatic Medicine (hon.), Soc. for Invertebrate Pathology (charter), Am. Longevity Soc. (hon.), AAAS, Internat. Soc. Devel. and Comparative Immunology, Fla. Med. Assn., Bays Med. Soc., Saba Marine Biology Rsch. Found., Island Saba (chmn. bd. 1999-2000). Avocations: scuba diving, saxophone playing. Died July 16, 2004.

SMITH, ALBERT LEE, oil company executive; b. Bainville, Mont., Nov. 14, 1914; s. Charles Edward and Ruth Hattie (Leeson) S.; m. Edel Petersen, Dec. 31, 1941; children: Gary Lee, Debra Ann. Grad. high sch., Farmer, Mont. and Bainville. Grain supr. Triple A Farm Program, Great Falls, Mont., 1941-46; ptnr. Edmonson-Smith Real Estate, Great Falls, 1946-48; owner, operator Smith Agy., Great Falls, 1948-53; pres. Cloverleaf Petroleum, Great Falls, 1949-55; owner Al Smith Drilling, Newcastle, Wyo., 1956-70; pres. Accidental Oil Co. Inc., Newcastle, from 1967. Wyo. dir. Old West Trail Found., 1982—; exec. sec. Wyo. D&K Tourist, Newcastle, 1977—. Mem. Rotary, Kiwanis, Toastmasters (dist. gov. 1948). Republican. Methodist. Avocation: woodworking. Home: Newcastle, Wyo. Died Mar. 13, 2005.

SMITH, ANITA BINGHAM, accountant, tax preparer; b. Charlotte, N.C., July 11, 1919; d. Irving Westerman and Lula Vernon (McGregor) Bingham; m. Charles Marsden Smith Sr., Sept. 9, 1944; children: Anita Dempsey, Thomas, Charles M. Jr., Martha. Cert., Queens Coll., 1936. Lic. tax preparer, Calif. Acct. B. R. Sharp & Co., Riverside, Calif., 1953-59; asst. office mgr. Crail Fuller Co., Vandenberg AFB, Calif., 1959-61; tchr. Govt. Guam (Mich.), 1961-62; pvt. practice acct. and tax preparer Riverside, from 1965. Treas. Riverside County Rep. Ctrl. Com., 1975-83; v.p. and pres. Rubidoux Cmty. Svcs. Dist., Riverside, 1978—; treas. Riverside Art Mus., 1980-84; pres. Riverside Art Alliance, 1986-87; treas. Legislator and Senator, Calif. State Legislature, Riverside, 1987—; chairperson and vice chairperson bd. dirs. Calif. State Water, Riverside, 1983-95 Anita B. Smith Treatment Facility named in her honor Rubidoux Cmty. Svcs. Dist., 1995; floral design chosen for floral arrangement calender Nat. Coun. State Garden Clubs Inc., 1997. Presbyterian. Avocations: orhid hobbyist, floral arranger, political activist, community service. Home: Riverside, Calif. Died Mar. 6, 2004.

SMITH, ANN WEBSTER, historic preservationist, consultant; b. Dallas; d. Robert King and Sarah Carroll (Harrison) Webster; m. Byron Arnold Smith III, (div.); 1 child, Richard Blackmer Smith II. BA, U. N.C.; student, Sorbonne, 1975-76. Dep. to sec. gen. Internat. Council on Monuments & Sites, Paris, 1975-79, advisor, 1991-93, v.p., 1981—90, 1996—2002, pres. U.S. Com. Washington, 1995—2002; hist. preservation cons., 1991—2006; dep. commr. N.Y. State Parks, Albany, 1979-83; v.p. Hist. Annapolis (Md.), Inc., 1983-85; dir. Friends of English Heritage, Washington, 1987-91. Trustee Hist. Hudson Valley, Tarrytown, N.Y., 1980-95, Canterbury Cathedral Trust, Washington, 1981-97, Tudor Place Found., Washington, 1995-2002. Recipient Gazzola prize for Contributions to Internat. Hist. Preservation., Internat. Coun. on Monuments and Sites, 2005. Democrat. Episcopalian. Home: Washington, DC. Died Apr. 20, 2006.

SMITH, CARL HERBERT, computer science educator; b. Burlington, Vt., Apr. 25, 1950; s. Seymour S. and Annette C. (Cohen) S.; m. Patricia E. Gibbs, Feb. 4, 1972; 1 child, Austin. BS, U. Vt., 1972; MS, SUNY, Buffalo, 1975, PhD, 1979; Habil., U. Latvia, 1993. Teaching asst. computer sci. dept. SUNY, Buffalo, 1973-76, rsch. asst. computer sci. dept., 1976-78; asst. prof. computer sci. dept. Purdue U., 1978-82, U. Md., College Park, 1982-87, assoc. prof. computer sci. dept., 1987-96, prof. computer sci. dept., from 1996. Programmer Nanodata Corp., Buffalo, 1974, Roswell Park Meml. Inst., Buffalo, 1975; cons. divsn. math. and computer sci. NSF, Washington, 1982-84; rsch. computer scientist Nat. Inst. Standards and Tech., Nat. Computer Systems Lab., Advanced Systems Divsn., 1985-90; program dir. computer and computation theory Divsn. Computer and Computation Rsch., Directorate for Computer and Info. Sci. and Engring., NSF, 1987-88; speaker and presenter in field. Editor Internat. Jour. Founds. of Computer Sci., Jour.

Computer and Sys. Scis., Fundamenta Informatical, Theoretical Computer Sci.; referee Jour. ACM, 1987—, IEEE Trans. on Software Engring., 1988, SIAM Jour. on Computing, 1991—, Jour. Exptl. and Theoretical Artificial Intelligence, 1992—, ACM Trans. on Software Engring. and Methodology, 1992—, New Generation Computing, 1993—, many others; reviewer jours. Stichting Informatica-Onderzoek in Nederland, 1993—, Internat. Sci. Found., 1993—, numerous others; contbr. chpts. to books and articles to profl. jours. Bd. mem. Takoma Park Boys and Girls Club, 1985-92; mem. City of Takoma Park Block Grant com., 1989, City of Takoma Park Citizens Com. to Select a New City Adminstr., 1991, Tacoma Park Nuclear Free Zone Com., 1994—. Grantee NSF, 1979-81, 81-82, 83-85, 84-85, 87-90, 88-90, 91-93, 92, 91-94, 92—, 93, 94—, Nat. Security Agy., 1984-86, Office of Naval Rsch., 1992-93; recipient Internat. Travel award NSF, 1983, Outstanding Performance award, 1988; Fulbright scholar, Germany, 1997. Avocations: racquetball, beer tasting. Home: Takoma Park, Md. Died July 24, 2004.

SMITH, CHARLES EDWARD, electrical engineering educator; b. June 8, 1934; s. Roy L. and Emma E. (Boyd) S.; m. Evelyn Juanita Blow, July 1, 1960; children: Charles E. Jr., Steven A., Gary L. BEE with honors, Auburn U., 1959, MS, 1963, PhD, 1968. Rsch. engr. Auburn U., Ala., 1959—68; from asst. prof. dept. elec. engring. to assoc. prof. U. Miss., University, 1968—76, chmn. dept. elec. engring., 1975—2002, prof., 1977—2002, prof. emeritus, 2002—05. Contbr. articles to profl. jours. With USAR, 1953-65. Named Outstanding Engring. Tchr., U. Miss. Alumni Engring., 1970-71, Outstanding Faculty Mem., 1980-81, 87-88, 93-94, 99-2000, Burlington No. Faculty Achievement award outstanding tchg. and scholarship, 1993. Mem. IEEE (sr., life), Am. Soc. Engring. Edn., Kiwanis (v.p., pres. 1975-77), Sigma Xi (pres. U. Miss. chpt. 1976-77), Tau Beta Pi, Eta Kappa Nu, Phi Kappa Phi (exec. com. U. Miss. chpt. 1985). Baptist. Died May 12, 2005.

SMITH, CLIFFORD WALTER, III, music educator, musician; b. Chgo., Ill., Nov. 13, 1951; s. Clifford Walter Smith, Jr. and Shirley Jean Smith; m. Clodagh Marie Casey, Mar. 5, 1988; children: Bridget Jean, Clifford Walter IV. BMusEd, Bradley U., Peoria, Ill., 1973, MMusEd, 1976. Asst. dir. bands Limestone H.S., Bartonville, Ill., 1974—76; asst. dir. bands and dir. jazz studies Bradley U., Peoria, 1976—79; dir. bands Peoria Heights Sch. Dist., 1977—79; sales Sam Ash Music Co., N.Y.C., 1979—86, Baldwin Piano Co., Matteson, Ill., 1986—89; tchr. music Glenwood Sch. Boys, 1989—90; dir. bands St. Anne Grade Sch., from 1990. Trumpet Swing Kings Big Band, Kankakee, Ill., from 1992. Mem.: NEA, Music Educators Nat. Conf., Ill. Edn. Assn., Phi Mu Alpha. Avocations: golf, reading. Home: Bourbonnais, Ill. Died July 12, 2005.

SMITH, DAVID ALLEN, insurance company executive; b. Hunstsville, Ala., Aug. 1, 1943; s. Clarence Theodore and Bernice (Snell) Smith; m. Michelle Haviland McCaffrey, June 1, 1964; 1 child, Eric Michael. BA, Calif. State U., L.A., 1969. Mgr. Allstate Ins. Co., L.A., 1969-81; v.p. Nat. Am. Ins. Co., Long Beach, Calif., 1982-86, First Calif. Property & Casualty Ins., Calabasas, Calif., 1987-89; sr. v.p. Sterling Casualty Ins. Co., Van Nuys, Calif., from 1989. Cons. various ins. cos. and law firms. Contbr. numerous environmental and outdoor articles. Vice chmn. Boy Scouts Am., L.A.; instr. ARC, Pasadena; vol. U.S. Forest Service, Angeles Nat. Forest, L.A. Recipient Silver Beaver award, Boy Scouts Am., L.A., 1986, award of merit, 1983, vigil honor, 1980; Vol. Service award, U.S. Forest Service, 1987. Mem. Blue Goose Internat., High Adventure Team. Republican. Presbyterian. Avocations: photography, cross country skiing, rock climbing. Home: Van Nuys, Calif. Died Apr. 23, 2004.

SMITH, DENNIS ROBERT, lawyer; b. Newton, Mass., Mar. 19, 1946; s. Elmer Hunt and Jessie Susan (Millar) S.; m. Janette Evelyn Scandale, Aug. 10, 1968; children: Alexander Duncan, Amanda Jill. BA magna cum laude, Wesleyan U., 1967; JD cum laude, Harvard U., 1970. Bar: Mass.1970. Assoc. Pollock, O'Connor et al, Waltham, Mass., 1970-71; pres. D.R. Smith & Assocs., Waltham, 1971-72; assoc. Csaplar and Bok, Boston, 1972-76; assoc. gen. counsel, sec. Comml. Union Ins. Cos., Boston, from 1977. Contbr. articles to profl. jours. Mem. ABA, Mass. Bar Assn., Boston Bar Assn., Nat. Assn. Securities Dealers (gen. securities prin.), Phi Beta Kappa. Home: Sudbury, Mass. Died Jan. 31, 2005.

SMITH, FRANCES MAY, special education teacher; b. Silsbee, Tex., Dec. 22, 1922; d. Charles Calvin and Fannie Irene (Rawlinson) Rhymes; m. Henry Lester Smith, Jan. 20, 1946; children: Sharon Elizabeth Smith Burum, Pamela Sue. BS, Stephen F. Austin U., 1944; cert. tchr. mentally retarded, Tex. Tech U., 1969; cert. tchr. learning disabilities, Tex. Women's U., 1972. Asst. auditor USN, Washington, 1944-45; bookkeeper Crawford Lumber Co., Nacogdoches, Tex., 1945-46; tchr. of bus. A&M Consol. High Sch., College Station, Tex., 1946-48; elem. tchr. Brazosport ISD, Freeport, Tex., 1950-51; tchr. spl. edn. Levelland (Tex.) ISD, 1967-69, Grand Prairie (Tex.) ISD, 1969-79, vocat. adjustment coordinator, chmn. spl. edn. dept., from 1979. Rep. Dallas Tchr. Credit Union, 1984-87. Named Outstanding Tchr., Lee Jr. High, Grand Prairie, 1976, Tchr. of Yr., Grand Prairie C. of C., 1983. Mem. Nat. Assn. Vocat. Spl. Needs Persons, Tex. Classroom Tchrs. Assn. (rep. 1984-87), Tex. Vocat. Adjustment Coordinators (v.p. 1983-85, sec. 1985-86), Am. Assn. Univ. Women (ednl. chmn. 1984-87). Avocations: bridge, square dancing, golf. Home: Grand Prairie, Tex. Died Apr. 27, 2005.

SMITH, FREDERICK THEODORE, lawyer, educator; b. Jersey City, Apr. 7, 1956; s. George Gilbert and Caroline (Jeter) S. BA, Harvard Coll., 1978; BA, MA, Oxford (Eng.) U., 1980; JD, Harvard U., 1985; MPA, J.F. Kennedy Sch., 1985. Bar: N.J. 1987, U.S. Dist. N.J. 1990, U.S. Supreme Ct. 1996. Summer assoc. Lowenstein, Sandler, Kohl, Fisher & Boylan, Newark, 1982, Manatt, Phelps, Rothenberg & Tunney, L.A., 1983; intern Office of N.J. Pub. Adv., spring 1985; summer assoc. Kaye, Scholer, Fierman, Hays & Handler, Washington, 1985; jud. clerkship to Hon. David Nelson Fed. Dist. Ct., Boston, 1985-86; assoc. Shearman & Sterling, N.Y.C., 1984, 86-87, McCarter & English, Newark, 1987-93, ptnr., from 1993. N.J. Bd. Law Examiners, 1990—; hearing officer Essex County, N.J., 1988-91; adj. prof. Seton Hall Law Sch., N.J., 1994—. Editor: New Jersey Law of Product Liability, 1994; mem. editl. bd. N.J. Lawyer, 1993-95. Bd. overseers Gov.'s Schs. N.J., 1994—; trustee St. Peter's Prep. Sch., Jersey City, 1993—; bd. dirs. Newark YMCA, 1996—. Recipient Rhodes scholarship Oxford U./Rhodes Trust, Eng., 1978-80, Earl Warren scholarship NAACP Legal Def. Fund, 1981. Mem. Harvard Club N.J. (exec. com. 1990—). Home: Newark, NJ. Died Apr. 4, 2005.

SMITH, GARRY LEE, marketing manager; b. Waterville, Kans., Apr. 20, 1944; s. Adolph Clifton Smith and Mabelle Josephine Kalous; m. Nancy Carol Grey, July 20, 1968 (div. Aug. 1986); children: Andrea, Eric. BS, Kans. State U., 1967; MBA, William and Mary U., 1970. Fin. mgr. Ford Assn., Kansas City, Mo., 1967; sales rep., field mgr. Am. Hosp. Supply, Chgo., 1970-86, Baxter Internat., Chgo., from 1986. V.p. mktg. S&T Health Modulars, Phoenix. Writer, pub.: (nonfiction) Yuppies Lifestyle, 1987. Pres. Gov. Recall, Ariz., 1987, organizer 50 + 1 Constnl. Reform, Ariz., 1988; bd. dirs. King of Glory Luth., Tempe, Ariz., 1985-86. 1st lt. U.S. Army, 1967-69; bd. dirs. Windsor Sq. Homeowners Assn., 1994—; mem. Team Ariz., pres., 1990-91. Recipient Bell of Freedom award Martin Luther King Holiday Com., 1990. Mem. Leading Edge Club (chair 1997—), Sierra Club, Mountain Preserve Club. Avocations: hiking, skiing, writing, home renovation, travel. Home: Phoenix, Ariz. Died July 30, 2004.

SMITH, GEORGE E., chemical company executive; m. Mary Pollock; children: John, Michael, Mark. Former pres., CEO Alco Industries Inc., Valley Forge, Pa. Died June 16, 2006.

SMITH, GEORGE LARRY, analytical and environmental chemist; b. Beloit, Kans., Oct. 11, 1951; s. Richard Bailey and Vonda Ellene (Cox) S.; m. Charlene Janell Musgrove, Sept. 4, 1973; 1 child, Brian Lawrence. BA, Augustana Coll., 1973. Lab. technician Sanitary Dist. of Hammond, Ind., 1973; chemist Federated Metals Corp., Whiting, Ind., 1973-77; rsch. technician Air Pollution Tech., Inc., San Diego, 1978-80, environ. chemist, 1980-81, sr. tech. asst., 1981; staff chemist I Occidental Rsch. Corp., Irvine, Calif., 1981-82, receiving chemist, 1982-84; processing chemist Chem. Waste Mgmt., Inc., Kettleman City, Calif., 1984-87, analytical chemist, 1987-89, wet analytical chemistry group leader, 1989-90, inorganic lab. supr., 1990-94, quality assurance/quality control specialist, 1994-96; lab. mgr. Bolsa Rsch. Assocs., Inc., Hollister, Calif., from 1996; lab. mgr., chemist Tri Cal-Bolsa Rsch. Assocs., Inc., Hollister, Calif., from 1999. Lab. analyst for published article in environ. sci. and tech., 1981. Bd. dirs. Apostolic Christian Missions, Inc., San Diego, 1978—82. Mem.: Analytical Lab. Mgrs. Assn., Assn. Ofcl. Analytical Chemists Internat., Nat. Geog. Soc., Am. Chem. Soc., Planetary Soc., Sierra Club. Avocations: coin collecting/numismatics, drawing, photography, reading about science, history and religion. Home: Hollister, Calif. Died Oct. 27, 2004.

SMITH, JACQUELINE, critical care nurse; b. Kilgore, Tex., June 7, 1950; d. Horace and Pearline (Miller) Jackson; m. Henry Earl Smith, Oct. 24, 1973; children: Errick J., Brandon D. BS, Tex. Woman's U., 1970; AD, Kilgore Jr. Coll. Sch. Nursing, 1972. Cert. intensive care unit, CCU, stress test cons. Intensive care unit supr. Mother Frances Hosp., Tyler, Tex., head nurse med.-surg.; head nurse Med. Ctr. Hosp., Tyler. Author: A Guide for Pt's and Family. Home: Arp, Tex. Died June 8, 2005.

SMITH, JAMES EVERETT, minister; b. Winnipeg, Mo., May 6, 1927; s. Clarence Everett and Myrtle Frances (Woody) S.; m. Virginia Juanita Jones, June 14, 1953; children: Karen, Melinda. BA, Tex. Christian U., 1962; MDiv, Brite Sch. Div., 1962, D Ministry, 1980. Ordained to ministry Christian Ch. (Disciples of Christ), 1961. Min. 1st Christian Ch., Howe, Tex., 1953-54, Cen. Christian Ch., Stamford, Tex., 1954-61, Urbandale Christian Ch., Dallas, 1962-71; sr. min. 1st Christian Ch., Duncan, Okla., from 1972. Mem. nat. gen. bd. Christian Ch. (Disciples of Christ), 1980-84; mem. com. on ministry, Okla. Disciples of Christ, 1982-84, moderator, 1986-88, regional exec. com., 1988-90; tour condr. Faith Roots Tour of Middle East, 1972, 75, 78, 84, tour Far East, 1973; moderator dist. Author: Standing on Holy Ground: An Ecumenical Study of Significant Biblical Sites, 1980. Pres. Duncan Community Residence, 1975-77, Duncan Sr. Citizens, 1976, Stephens County Mental Health Assn., 1976; v.p. Duncan United Way, 1979. Recipient Liberty Bell award Stephens County Bar Assn., 1980. Mem. Duncan Ministerial Alliance (pres. 1976), Rotary (pres. Duncan club 1988-89). Home: Oklahoma City, Okla. Died Mar. 18, 2005.

SMITH, JENNIFER COCKERILL, artist; b. North Hollywood, Calif., July 25, 1957; d. Dean Brownell and Jean Wayne (Morse) Cockerill; m. Lon Meredith Smith, Dec. 1, 1984. BA, Calif. Luth. Coll., Thousand Oaks, 1979. Apprentice Rex Irvine Graphics, Inc., Westlake, Calif., 1977-79; pasteup printer Star Printing & Graphics, Palm Springs, Calif., 1979-80; advt. artist Desert Sun Newspaper, Palm Springs, 1980-81; freelance artist Palm Springs, 1981-83; owner Cockerill Gallery & Custom Framing, Palm Desert, Calif., 1983-84; fine artist L & J Designs, Whittier, N.C., from 1984. Artist decorative map, Native Am. Tribes, 1987; 2 person show includes Living Desert Res., 1985, Palm Springs Aerial Tramway, 1985, Marriot's Rancho Las Palmas Hotel, Rancho Mirage, Calif., 1985, Old Grist Mill, St. Augustine, Fla., 1985; group shows includes Palm Springs Desert Mus., 1982, Grand Prix of Art, Monaco,1983; represent in premanent collections Mus. of the Cherokee (N.C.) Indian, N.C., Catalina (Calif.) Yacht Club. Recipient Pica award of excellence, 1988. Republican. Presbyterian. Avocation: airbrush art. Died Feb. 6, 2005.

SMITH, JOHN JOSEPH, JR., lawyer; b. Birmingham, Ala., Sept. 28, 1945; s. John Joseph and Ruth Lee (Snavely) S.; m. Sandra Ann Prater, May 25, 1975; 1 dau., Leigh Galbraith, B.A. in English, Vanderbilt U., 1967; J.D., U. Ala.-Tuscaloosa, 1970, LL.M. in Taxation cum laude, 1979. Bar: Ala. 1970, U.S. Dist. Ct. (no. dist.) Ala. 1970, U.S. Ct. Appeals (5th cir.) 1976, U.S. Ct. Appeals (11th cir.) 1982, U.S. Tax Ct. 1973, U.S. Supreme Ct. 1977. Ptnr. Smith & Smith, Birmingham, 1970—. Served to sgt. USNG, 1968-74. Mem. ABA, Assn. Trial Lawyers Am., Ala. Bar Assn., Ala. Trial Lawyers Assn., Ala. Criminal Def. Attys. Assn., Birmingham Bar Assn. (chmn. grievance com. 1982-83, mem. speakers bur. 1981-83, exec. com. 1985-87), Nat. Legal Aid and Defender Assn., Bench and Bar, Birmingham Estate Planning Council, Birmingham Tax Club, Birmingham C. of C. Democrat. Methodist. Clubs: Santa Rosa (Fla.) Golf and Beach, Downtown Democratic, Kiwanis (dir. club), Birmingham Tip-Off, Altadena Valley Country, Relay House, Birmingham Venture (Birmingham). Lodge: Masons. Home: Birmingham, Ala. Died Mar. 13, 2005.

SMITH, LELAND D., JR., management consultant; b. Houston, June 7, 1931; s. Leland D. and Julia Elizabeth (Branard) S.; m. Betty L. Laws, Apr. 16, 1955; children: Leland D. III, Bradley L., Linda D. Smith Davis. BBA in Bldg. Products Mktg., Tex. A&M U., 1954. Project purchasing agt. Brown and Root, Inc., Houston, 1957-60; sales rep. Corey Supply Co., Houston, 1960-62; from sales rep. to v.p. so. regiona Lafarge Corp., various locations, 1962-92; mgmt. cons., v.p. Denaux Corp., Atlanta, from 1993; exec. v.p. World Thrust, Inc., from 1994. Active numerous civic orgns. 1st lt. U.S. Army, 1955-57. Mem. Portland Cement Assn. Presbyterian. Avocations: golf, church activities. Home: Atlanta, Ga. Died Nov. 11, 2004.

SMITH, MELVIN SYLVAN, insurance company executive; b. Brookline, Mass., Sept. 15, 1927; s. Samuel and Marion (Scovell) Sm.; m. Marcia Kotzen, June 8, 1952; children: David L., Michael A., Robert J. JD, Northeastern U., Boston, 1952. CLU; registered health underwriter; ChFC. Atty. Strathcona Realty Corp., Cambridge, Mass., 1952-56; cons. Conn. Gen. Life Ins. Co., Boston, 1956-59, sr. cons. N.Y.C., 1959-60; pres. The Smith Agys., N.Y.C., from 1960. With USNR, 1944-47. Mem. CLU and ChFC, Inc. (pres. N.Y. chpt. 1974-75, Man of Yr. 1980), N.Y. Ctr. for Fin. Studies (pres. 1980-81), Gen. Agts. and Mgrs. Assn. of Greater N.Y. (pres. 1985-86), Life Suprs. Assn. of N.Y., Life Underwriters Assn. of N.Y.C. (bd. dirs. 1976-77) B'nai Brith (pres. L.I. chpt. 1965-67), Nat. Coun. Northeastern U. (dir. 1975—). Avocations: tennis, boating. Home: New York, NY. Died Feb. 15, 2004.

SMITH, MITCHELL BRIAN, financial officer; b. Queens, N.Y., May 13, 1955; s. David and Sonya (Feinstien) S. BS, Cornell U., 1977, MBA, 1979. Assoc. dir. arts svc. orgn. dept. N.Y. State Coun. on the Arts, N.Y.C., 1979-81; dir. fin. and adminstrn. Cultural Coun. Found., N.Y.C., 1981-83; CFO The Ehrenkrantz Group, P.C., N.Y.C., 1983-87, VVKR, Inc., Alexandria, Va., 1987-89; assoc. The LePatner Mgmt. Group, Washington, 1989-91; CFO, exec. dir. Studios Arch., Inc., Washington, 1992-97; COO Environ Internat. Corp., from 1998. Treas. Fund for Architecture and the Environment, N.Y.C., 1985-87, Dan Wagoner Dance Co., N.Y.C., 1981-83; vol. Bus. Vols. for the Arts, Washington, 1990—. Mem. AIA, Nat. Assn. Acct., Am. Mgmt. Assn. Home: Alexandria, Va. Died Sept. 7, 2004.

SMITH, ROBIN JEAN, health services professional; b. Pitts., Nov. 30, 1953; BSFR, W.Va. U., 1976. Cert. pesticide applicator, W.Va.; cert. life safety code surveyor, health surveyor Health Care Fin. Adminstrn. Environ. health specialist Allegheny County, Pitts., 1977-79; supr. food svc. W.Va. U. Med. Ctr., Morgantown, 1979-80; sanitarian Brooke County Health Dept., Wellsburg, W.Va., 1980-83; sanitarian health div. State of W.Va., Charleston, 1983-98; sanitarian Berkeley County Health Dept., Martinsburg, W.Va., 1998-2000; WIC nutritionist MOVHD WIC Program, Parkersburg, W.Va., from 2002. Home: Charles Town, W.Va. Died July 23, 2004.

SMITH, RUTH HALL, journalist; b. Chgo., May 31, 1918; d. Albert Neely and Bertha (Cassidy) Hall; m. Robert James Smith; children: Gregory Hall, Gerald Edward, Marilyn Smith Lovett, Brian Woodley. Student, U. Ill., 1937-40, Northwestern U., Evanston, Ill., 1945. Sec.-treas., designer, editor Craft Patterna Co. & Craft Products Co., Elmhurst and St. Charles, Ill., 1941-84; pres. Craft Products Miniatures, Elmhurst and St. Charles, 1975-84, Decorator Crafts, Sanibel, Fla., 1989-94. Author: Home Handicraft for Girls, 1941 (Book of the Month Club award 1941). Mem. Pottawatomie Garden (horticulture chmn. 1985-89), Alpha Xi Delta. Republican. Methodist. Avocations: photography, gardening, crafts. Died Sept. 18, 2004.

SMITH, TED JAY, III, mass communications educator; b. Dobbs Ferry, NY, Sept. 14, 1945; s. Ted Jay Jr. and Marie Glencora (Hershey) S.; m. Rosemary Tibbe, June 12, 1971. Student, U. Pitts., 1963-64; Student, U. So. Miss., 1968-69; BA with high honors, Mich. State U., 1971, MA, 1972, PhD, 1978. Commd. 2nd lt. USAF, 1971, advanced through grades to 1st lt., 1973, from electronics technician to electronics instr., 1965-70, airman edn. & commissioning program student E. Lansing, Mich., 1970-71, info officer, 1971-74, resigned, 1974; grad. teaching/rsch. asst. Mich. State U., E. Lansing, 1974-77; asst. prof. SUNY, Albany, 1977-79; lectr. I, Warrnambool Inst. Advanced Edn., Warrnambool, Australia, 1979-82; asst. prof. U. Va., Charlottesville, 1982-87, dir. grad. studies, 1984-87; assoc. prof. Va. Commonwealth U., Richmond, from 1987, dir. grad. studies, 1990-94; sr. rsch. fellow Ctr. for Media & Pub. Affairs, from 1996. Bradley resident scholar Heritage Found., Washington, 1992-93; pres. Applied Anaytics, Inc., Richmond, Va., 1986—; sr. analyst Rowan & Blewitt, Inc., Washington, 1986-90; co-founder, sr. rsch. fellow Ctr. for Comm. Rsch., Warrnambool, 1982—; mem. policy adv. coun. VA Inst. for Pub. Policy, 1996—; mem. nat. adv. bd. Comm. Rsch. Corp., Washington, 1986-95, nat. adv. coun. The Media Inst., Washington, 1987—; faculty adviser FBI Nat. Acad., Quantico, Va., 1983-87; bd. dirs. Nat. Assn. Scholars, 1990—; mem. Main St. Commn., Rockford Inst., 1992—; educators adv. bd. Inst. for Pub. Rels. Rsch. & Edn., 1992—; co-founder Statis. Assessment Svc., 1993. Author: The Vanishing Economy, 1988, Moscow Meets Main Street, 1988; co-author: What Do the People Want From the Press?, 1997; editor: Communication in Australia, 1983, Propaganda: A Pluralistic Perspective, 1989, Steps Toward the Restoration of Our World, 1998, In Defense of Tradition, 2000; co-editor: Communication and Government, 1986; co-editor human communication book series SUNY Press, Albany, 1987—; contbr. articles to profl. jours. Mem. The Nature Conservancy, Albany, 1977-79, Charlottesville, 1982—, Accuracy in Media, Washington, 1982—; contbg. mem. Va. Mus. Fine Arts, Richmond, 1987—. Grantee FBI, U. Va., Warrnambool Inst., Bradley Found., Raldolph Found., Scaife Found., Earhart Found. Mem. Am. Assn. for Pub. Opinion Rsch., Assn. for Edn. in Journalism and Mass Communication, Australian Communication Assn. (founding), Internat. Communication Assn., Anglican Guild of Scholars, Nat. Assn. Scholars (bd. dirs. 1990—), Pub. Rels. Soc. Am., Phila. Soc., Va. Assn. Scholars (founding bd. dirs., pres. 1990—), So. Speech Communication Assn., St. George Tucker Soc., Southern League, Va. Speech Communication Assn. (chair theory divsn. 1986-91, 1st v.p. 1991-94), Phi Kappa Phi, Kappa Tau Alpha. Republican. Anglican Catholic. Avocations: nature study, fine arts and crafts, classical music. Home: Richmond, Va. Died Jan. 4, 2004.

SMITH, VIRGINIA DODD (MRS. HAVEN SMITH), former congresswoman; b. Randolph, Iowa, June 30, 1911; d. Clifton Clark and Erville (Reeves) Dodd; m. Haven N. Smith (dec. 1997), Aug. 27, 1931. AB, U. Nebr., 1936; degree (hon.), Nebr. U., 1987, Chadron State Coll., 1988. Nat. pres. Am. Country Life Assn., 1951-54; nat. chmn. Am. Farm Bur. Women, 1954-74; dir. Am. Farm Bur. Fedn., 1954-74, Country Women's Council; world dep. pres. Asso. Country Women of World, 1962-68; mem. Dept. Agr. Nat. Home Econs. Research Adv. Com., 1960-65, 94th-101st Congresses from 3rd Nebr. dist., 1975—91. Bd. dirs. Norwest Bank Cmty. Bd., Property Owners and Residents Bd., Sun Health Corp. Bd., Recreation Ctrs. Sun City West, sec., mem. gov. bd.; bd. dirs. Del Webb Hosp. Mem. Crusade for Freedom European inspection tour, 1958; del. Republican Nat. Conv., 1956, 72; bd. govs. Agrl. Hall of Fame; mem. Nat. Livestock and Meat Bd., 1955-58, Nat. Commn. Community Health Services, 1963-66; adv. mem. Nebr. Sch. Bds. Assns., 1949; mem. Nebr. Territorial Centennial Commn., 1953, Gov.'s Commn. Status of Women, 1964-66; chmn. Presdl. Task Force on Rural Devel., 1969-70; mem. appropriations com., ranking minority mem. agrl. appropriations subcom., appropriations subcom. on energy and water devel. 94th-101st Congresses from 3d dist. Nebr.; v.p. Farm Film Found., 1964-74, Good Will ambassador to Switzerland, 1950. Apptd. adm. Nebr. Navy; bd. dirs. Shepherd of the Hills Meth. Ch. Recipient award of Merit, DAR, 1956; Disting. Service award U. Nebr., 1956, 60; award for best pub. address on freedom Freedom Found., 1966; Eyes on Nebr. award Nebr. Optometric Assn., 1970; Internat. Service award Midwest Conf. World Affairs, 1970; Woman of Achievement award Nebr. Bus. and Profl. Women, 1971; selected as 1 of 6 U.S. women Govt. France for 3 week goodwill mission to France, 1969; Outstanding 4H Alumni award Iowa State U., 1973, 74; Watchdog of Treasury award, 1976, 78, 80, 82, 83, 84, 86, 88; Guardian of Small Bus. award, 1976, 78, 80, 82, 84, 86, 88; Nebr. Ak-Sar-Ben award, 1983, Agrl. Achievement, Nebr. U., 1987; named Favorite Community Leader, Sun City West, 1994. Mem. AAUW, Delta Kappa Gamma (state hon. mem.), Beta Sigma Phi (internat. hon. mem.), Chi Omega, PEO (past pres.), Eastern Star. Clubs: Business and Professional Women. Methodist. Died Jan. 23, 2006.

SMITHER, THOMAS DAILEY, SR., sales and marketing executive; b. Sullivan, Ind., Sept. 26, 1944; s. Albert Arnold and Martha Caroline (Lester) S.; m. Virginia Ann Burton, July 29, 1967; children: Tamara S., Thomas Dailey Jr. From various sales positions to regional mgr. IBM, 1964-83; dir. distbn. Raytheon Data Systems, Norwood, Mass., 1983-84; dir. fed. govt. ops. Harris Corp., McLean, Va., 1984-87; v.p. sales Alcatel, Tempe, Ariz., 1987-88, Cognos, Burlington, Mass., 1988-90; v.p. sales and mktg. Ontologic, Inc., Burlington, from 1990. Avocations: tennis, racquetball, reading. Home: Louisville, Ky. Died July 21, 2005.

SMOLA, CYNTHIA JANE, mental health nurse; b. Denver, June 12, 1946; d. Franklin B. and Virginia L. (Landrum) Sipes; m. Emery Smola, Dec. 26, 1965. ADN, Cen. Meth. Coll., 1981. RN, Mo. Clin. nurse Fulton (Mo.) State Hosp., 1981-84, nursing supr. psychiat. area, 1984-86, assoc. dir. psychiat. nursing div., 1986-87, unit DON adult psychiat. svcs., 1987-90, dir. nursing edn., from 1994; unit DON Biggs Forensic Ctr., 1991-94;, from 1994. Mem. ANA (cert. mental health nurse). Home: Fulton, Mo. Died Apr. 7, 2005.

SMOLEY, MELVIN, family physician; b. N.Y.C., June 23, 1917; s. Philip and Fanny (Garn) S.; m. Renee Lucille Smoley. AB, NYU, 1940, postgrad., 1946; MB, Chgo. Med. Sch., 1943, MD, 1945. Diplomate Am. Bd. Family Practice. Extern, asst. physician Cook County Jail Hosp., Chgo., 1941-42; intern Beth El Hosp., Bklyn., 1944-45; pvt. practice Rego Park, N.Y., 1946-49, Levittown, N.Y., 1949-73; resident in psychiatry Kings Park State Hosp., 1949; pvt. practice as family physician Sunrise, Fla., from 1973. Attending physician Manhattan Gen. Hosp., N.Y., 1946-49, Horace Harding Hosp., Queens, N.Y., 1946-49, Nassau County Med. Ctr., Meadowbrook Hosp., East Meadow, N.Y., 1960-73, Ctrl. Gen. Hosp., Plainview, N.Y., 1960-73; examining physician, phlebotomist blood bank Postgrad. Hosp., N.Y., 1946-49; dir. Levittown Blood Bank, 1949-68; fire surgeon Levittown Fire Dept., 1950-73; chmn. Emergency Med. Svc., Levittown, 1950-60; sch. physician Island Trees Pub. Schs., Levittown, 1950-73; drug abuse cons. Levittown High Sch.; mem. exec. com. Hempstead Gen. Hosp. and Nursing Home, 1958-73; 1st chief of staff Lauderdale Lakes Gen. Hosp., Fla. Med. Ctr. Hosp., 1973-74; chief family medicine Fla. Med. Ctr. Hosp., 1974; vol. preceptor, faculty-clin. assoc. coll. medicine U. Fla., 1977-91; police surgeon City of Sunrise, 1977-84; chmn. instl. rev. Humana Hosp. Bennett, Plantation, Fla., 1977-79; med. examiner FAA, 1979-80; house physician Sunrise Mus. Theatre, 1979—; clin. instr. dept. medicine U. Miami, 1980-91; med. advisor prison health svcs. State of Fla. Med. Peer Rev.; mem. Fla. State Family Practice Postgrad. Edn. Com.; lectr. in field. Mem. Broward County Environ. Control Bd., Fla. Lt. (s.g.), sr. med. officer USPHS, 1945-46, capt. M.C., USAFR. Fla. Med. Ctr. Hosp. Teaching Auditorium dedicated in his honor, 1974. Fellow Am. Acad. Family Physicians (charter), Am. Coll. Allergy (assoc.); mem. AMA (Physician Recognition award), Am. Acad. Family Practice, Family Practice Soc. (hon.), Am. Med. Polit. Action Com., Acad. Psychosomatic Medicine, Fla. State Med. Soc., N.Y. State Med. Soc., Nassau County Med. Soc. (mem. editorial bd. drug and alcoholism com.), Broward County Med. Soc., West Broward C. of C. (chmn. emergency med. svc.), Tau Delta Phi, Phi Lambda Kappa. Avocations: photography, painting, boating. Died Dec. 4, 2004.

SMYSER, RICHARD DAVID, retired newspaper editor, retired secondary education educator; b. York, Pa., Aug. 19, 1923; s. Adam Milton and Miriam Olivia (Stein) S.; m. Mary Cochran Pigford, May 12, 1950; children: Lucy Pigford Smyser Tashman, Katherine Mary Smyser McAleer. BA, Pa. State Coll., 1944. Reporter Chester Pa. Times, 1946-49; mng. editor The Oak Ridger, Oak Ridge, Tenn., 1949-68, editor, 1968-88, founding editor, 1988—93; Atwood prof. journalism U. Alaska, Anchorage, 1986-87; editor in residence, vis. prof. journalism U. Nebr., Lincoln, 1988-89; Meeman disting. prof. of journalism U. Tenn., Knoxville, 1991-93. Vis. prof. journalism Pa. State U., State College, 1989-91; bd. dirs. Coun. for Advancement of Sci. Writing, 1982—, Scientist Inst. for Pub. Information, 1985-93. Author: Oak Ridge: A Commemorative Portrait, 1992, (with others) Journalism Stories from the Real World, 1995, The Newspaper, 1981, Read All About It - 50 Years of Am. Soc. Newspaper Editors, 1974; contbr. articles to profl. jours. Bd. dirs. Friends of Oak Ridge Nat. Laboratory. With US Army, 1943-45. Recipient Kilgore Counselor award DePauw U., Greencastle, Ind., 1973, Carol Burnett Lecture on Journalism Ethics award U. Hawaii, Honolulu, 1985, dist. alumnus Pa. State U., 1985. Mem. AP Mng. Editors Assn. (pres. 1973-74), Am. Soc. of Newspaper Editors (pres. 1984-85), Rotary Club (hon., vocational svcs. award Oak Ridge Rotary, 1988). Unitarian Universalist. Avocations: theater, music, swimming, hiking. Home: Oak Ridge, Tenn. Died Mar. 14, 2005.

SMYTHE-HAITH, MABEL MURPHY, former ambassador, former federal agency administrator; b. Montgomery, Ala., Apr. 3, 1918; m. Hugh H. Smythe, June 22, 1939 (dec. 1977); 1 child, Karen Pamela; m. Robert Haith, Jr., Oct. 18, 1985 Student, Spelman Coll., 1933-36, LLD (hon.), 1980; BA, Mt. Holyoke Coll., 1937, LHD (hon.), 1977; MA, Northwestern U., 1940; PhD, U. Wis., 1942, LLD (hon.), 1991; LHD (hon.), U. Mass., 1979. Asst. prof. Lincoln U., Mo., 1942-45; prof. Tenn. A. and I. U., 1945-46, Bklyn. Coll., 1946-47; vis. prof. Shiga U., Japan, 1951-53; dep. dir. rsch. for sch. segregation cases NAACP Legal Def. and Edn. Fund, 1953; tchr., prin. New Lincoln High Sch., N.Y.C., 1954-69; with Phelps-Stokes Fund, 1970-77, dir. research and publs., 1970-72, v.p., 1972-77; U.S. amb. to United Republic of Cameroon, US Dept. State, Yaounde, 1977-80, U.S. amb. to Equatorial Guinea, 1979-80, dep. asst. sec. for African Affairs, 1980-81; Melville J. Herskovits prof. African studies Northwestern U., Evanston, Ill., 1981-83, disting. prof., 1983-85, prof. emeritus, 1985—2006, co-dir. internat. internship program, 1983-85, co-dir. African seminar, 1985. Mem. Adv. Com. on Ednl. Exchange U.S. Dept. State, 1961-62, Adv. Commn. on Internat. Ednl. and Cultural Affairs, 1962-65; mem. Dept. State adv. coun. on African Affairs, 1962-65; U.S. del. 13th gen. conf. UNESCO, 1964; trustee Conn. Coll., 1964-65, 69-77, Mt. Holyoke Coll., 1971-76, vice chmn., 1975-76, trustee fellow, Spelman Coll., 1980-89, life trustee, 1991—, Hampshire Coll., 1971-77, 85-88, vice chair, 1975-76; mem. U.S. Nat. Com. for UNESCO, 1965-70, Nat. Adv. rev. Bd., 1974-77; co-dir. African seminar for pres. black colls., 1971; bd. dirs. Nat. Corp. for Housing Partnerships, 1972-77; scholar-in-residence U.S. Commn. on Civil Rights, 1973-74; U.S. del. Internat. Conf. for Assistance to Refugees in Africa, Geneva, 1981, So. African Devel. Coordination Conf. II, 1980; guest scholar Woodrow Wilson Internat. Ctr. for Scholars, Smithsonian Instn., Washington, 1982; mem. Aspen Inst. Humanistic Studies Exec. Seminar, 1983; mem. study mission to Japan with Assn. Black Am. Ambassadors, 1984, 85; mem. com. on policy for racial justice Joint Ctr. for Polit. and Econ. Studies, 1983-92; co-leader: Md. Consortium to Togo, Sierra Leone, Senegal, Liberia and Cameroon from 1970; co-dir. Mission to Malawi Women's Commn. on Refugee Women and Children, Malawi, 1989; adv. commn. Howard Univ. Patricia Roberts Harris Public Affairs Program; adv. bd. Lincoln Univ. (Pa.) Ctr. for Public Policy and Diplomacy; bd. dirs. Ralph Bunche Inst. on UN, CUNY, 1986-94; co-chair African-Am. Inst. Del. to observe presdl. elections, Madagascar, Feb., 1993. Author introduction: A Slaver's Log Book or 20 Years Residence in Africa, 1976; co-author: The New Nigerian Elite, 3d edit, 1971, Intensive English Conversation, Vol. I, 1953, Vol. II, 1954; editor: The Black American Reference Book, 1976; co-editor: Curriculum for Understanding, 1965; contbr. chpts. to coop. books, articles to profl. jours. Bd. dirs. Refugee Policy Group, 1983-89, adv. coun.; cons. African Devel. Found.; mem. Friends Inst. for Democracy in South Africa (formerly Inst. for a Democratic Alternative in South Africa). Decorated grand officer Order of Valor (Cameroon); Grand Dama D'Inore, Order of Royal Crown of Crete (Malta); recipient Top Hat award Pitts. Courier, 1979, Mary McLeod Bethune award, 1981, Decade of Service award Phelps-Stokes Fund, 1982, Ella T. Grasso award Mt. Holyoke Coll., 1982, Northwestern U. Alumna of Year award, 1983, Disting. Service award Nat. Coalition of 100 Black Women, 1984, Disting. Service award USIA, 1986, Am. Bicentennial Presdl. Inaugural award, 1989, Black History Makers award Associated Black Charities, 1990, Hugh H. and Mabel M. Smythe Internat. Svc. citation award InterFuture, Inc. Mem. Coun. Fgn. Rels., Nat. Coun. Women U.S., Coun. Am. Ambassadors, Assn. Black Am. Ambassadors (exec. com.). Died Feb. 7, 2006.

SNEED, ALBERTA NEAL, retired elementary education educator; b. Tipton County, Tenn., Jan. 13, 1926; d. Robert and Mary Lou (Wilks) Neal; m. Sollie Jr. Sneed, Jan. 26, 1968; 1 child, Hortense Yolanda Johnson Jeans. BS, Lane Coll., 1949; MEd, Memphis State U., 1975, postgrad., 1982. Cert. elem. and secondary tchr., Tenn., supr. and adminstr. Tchr. Ouachita Parish Sch. Bd., Monroe, La., Covington (Tenn.) City Bd. Edn., ret.; cons. Tipton County Bd. Edn., Covington. Mem. ASCD, NEA, Tenn. Assn. Supervision and Curriculum Devel., Tenn. Edn. Assn, TCEA, WTEA, Delta Sigma Theta. Home: Millington, Tenn. Died Aug. 27, 2004.

SNIBBE, ROBERT MCCAWLEY, association executive, public relations consultant; b. Catonsville, Md., Apr. 28, 1913; s. George W. and Mildred (Robinson) S.; m. Ellen Hynes Heavey; children: Robert, John Stewart (dec.), Ellen Lansdell. BA, St. John's Coll., Annapolis, Md., 1937. Dir. svcs. Standard & Poor's Corp., N.Y.C., 1938-42; bus. mgr. Bur. Nat. Affairs-U.S. News, Washington, 1942-43, 46-52; dir. press rels. Com. for Econ. Devel., N.Y.C., 1949-52; exec. v.p. Good Reading Rack Svc., N.Y.C., 1952-55; founder, pres. Employee Rels., Inc., N.Y.C., 1955-63, Snibbe Publs., Inc., Clearwater, Fla., 1963-79, Napoleonic Assn. Inc., Clearwater, from 1983. Commr. Town of Bellair, 1982-88. Lt. (s.g.) USN, 1943-46, PTO. Recipient honor medal Freedom Found., Valley Forge, Pa., 1957; named knight cmdr. Sovereign Greek Order St. Dennis de Zante, 1993. Mem. Belleair Country Club, Carlouel Yacht Club (Clearwater), Kappa Alpha. Republican. Avocations: golf, beekeeping. Home: Clearwater, Fla. Died June 8, 2004.

SNIDER, HARLAN TANNER, former manufacturing company executive; b. Owensboro, Ky., July 20, 1926; s. George William and Lydia (Tanner) S.; m. Helen Boswell, Mar. 7, 1953; children— William Jeffrey, Katherine Snider. BA, Transylvania U., 1949. Territory salesman Sunray DX Corp., Owensboro, 1950-57, dist. sales mgr. Ind., 1958-63, div. mgr. Iowa, 1963-65, dir. mktg. services Tulsa, 1965-67; pres. Red Barn Chems., Tulsa, 1967-69; dir. petrochems. Sun Oil Co., Phila., 1969-71, v.p. mktg., 1973-75; pres. Sunmark Industries, Phila., 1975-79; sr. v.p., external affairs Sun Co., Inc., Radnor, Pa., 1980-84, sr. v.p. planning pub.

affairs, 1984-88; ret., 1988. Served with USAF, 1944-46. Mem. Am. Petroleum Industry, 25 Yr. Club Petroleum Industry. Clubs: Union League (Phila.), Aronimink Golf (Newtown Square, Pa.), Mariner Sands Golf Club (Stuart, Fla.). Home: Bryn Mawr, Pa. Died Mar. 9, 2006.

SNIDER, PATRICIA ANN, college counselor; b. Fremont, Ohio, Sept. 7, 1937; d. Millard Alfred and Mary (Danchisen) Snider. B.S. in Edn., Bowling Green State U., 1959; M.Ed., Ohio U., 1963. Instr. St. Joseph Coll., Emmitsburg, Md., 1959-61; grad. asst. tchr. Ohio U. Athens, 1961-63; head resident advisor Western Ill. U., Macomb, Ill., 1963-67; counselor Morton Coll., Cicero, Ill., 1967—. Author: (with others) Community College Career Alternatives Handbook, 1979; Women on their Way-A Guide for Women Returning to School, 1984. Contbr. articles to profl. jours. Bd. dirs. Cicero chpt. Am. Cancer Soc.; flotilla vice comdr. U.S. Coast Guard Aux., 1969-82. Recipient Faculty Mem. of Yr. award Morton Coll. Endowment Found., 1982. Mem. Am. Assn. for Counseling and Devel., Nat. Acad. Advisors Assn., Nat. Assn. for Women Deans, Adminstrs. and Counselors, Ill. Assn. for Counseling and Devel., Nat. Coll. Personnel Assn., Ill. Coll. Personnel Assn. Roman Catholic. Avocations: reading; fishing. Home: Chicago, Ill. Died Oct. 25, 2004.

SNOW, CINDY (CYNTHIA DAWN SNOW), manufacturing executive; b. Carlsbad, N.M, Apr. 24, 1957; d. Amos Austen Snow; m. Steven W. Hallock, Jan. 19, 1984. Student, Pitzer Coll., Claremont, Calif., 1975, U. Calif., Berkeley, 1977, U. Calif., Santa Cruz, 1980. Export affairs advisor Taifung Flexible Tubing, Taipei, Rep. of China, 1980-82; v.p. Airmax Inc., Gilmer, Tex., 1983-87, pres., 1989-92; owner, mgr. Applecart Enterprises, Inc., Mineola, 1989-91; exec. v.p. Snowmax, 1991-92, pres., from 1992. Organizer YWCA Big Sisters Am., Monrovia, Calif., 1977; counselor YMCA, L.A., 1977. Mem. NAFE, Air Conditioning and Refrigeration Inst., Air Conditioning and Refrigeration Wholesalers Assn. Avocations: pottery, music, sewing, gardening. Home: Lindale, Tex. Died July 19, 2004.

SNYDER, EARL ALBIN, financial planner and consultant; b. Kokomo, Ind., Feb. 17, 1918; s. Earl A. and Fanny E. (Ford) S. AB, Ind. U., 1942, JD, 1947; LLM, Cath. U., 1953. Bar: Ind. 1947, Eng. 1958, D.C. 1961,; cert. fin. planner; chartered fin. cons.; CLU; real property appraiser. Pvt. practice, Crawfordsville, Ind., 1947-50; commd. lt. USAF, 1939, advanced though ranks to maj., 1948, judge adv., 1950-65, ret., 1965; prof. law Howard U., Washington, 1965-66; legis. asst. U.S. Ho. of Reps., Washington, 1966-68; pres., owner Earl Snyder Assocs., Laurel, Md., from 1968. Adj. faculty mem. Ind. U., 1947-50, U. Md., 1955-76, Coll. for Fin. Planning, Denver, 1986-89, The Am. Coll., Bryn Mawr, Pa., 1987—, Inst. Fin. Edn., Chgo., 1987—, Soc. of Real Estate Appraisers, Chgo., 1980-89. Author: General Leemy's Circus, 1955, Every Serviceman's Lawyer, 1960, Before You Invest, 1981. Chmn. Midwest Young Reps., 1947. Mem. D.C. Bar Assn., Balt. Assn. for Fin. Planning (bd. dirs. 1986-90), Soc. Profl. Journalists of D.C. (bd. dirs. 1986-89), Nat. Assn. Realtors Am. Soc. CLUs and Chartered Fin. Cons., Fin. Analysts Fedn., Nat. Lawyers Club (founder 1962—). Died Jan. 11, 2004.

SNYDER, ESTHER L., food service executive; b. Sorrento, Ill. m. Harry Snyder, 1948 (dec. 1976); children: Guy (dec. 1999), Rich (dec. 1993). BS in Zoology, Seattle Pacific U., 1947. Co-founder, pres. In-N-Out Burger, Baldwin Park, Calif., 1948—2006. Co-founder In & Out Burger Found. (formerly Child Abuse Found.), 1984. Died Aug. 6, 2006.

SOBIESZEK, ROBERT A., photographer, educator; b. Chgo., Mar. 11, 1943; Student, Ill. Inst. Tech., 1961-63; BFA with honors, U. Ill., 1965; MA in Art History, Stanford U., 1969; MPhil in Art History, Columbia U., 1981. From assoc. lectr. to asst. prof. art history U. Rochester, 1971-76; assoc. curator George Eastman House, 1971-72, assoc. curator, dir. rsch. ctr., 1972-75, dir. photog. collections, 1981-90; lectr. photography Rochester Inst. Tech., 1977-90; curator of photography Los Angeles County Mus. Art, 1990—2005, chair com. on mus. ethics, 1994, curatorial co-chair, 1997—2005. Vis. faculty in art history U. So. Calif., L.A., 1994, 96, 97, 98; cons. Hollywood Photographers Archives, L.A., 1984-86, Nat. Gallery of Art, 1988; lectr. in field. Dir. numerous exhbns. Recipient numerous awards; grantee NEA, 1971-72, Kress Found., 1968-69, Carnegie Corp. N.Y., 1967-68, others; Woodrow Wilson Nat. fellow, 1965-66. Home: Los Angeles, Calif. Died July 15, 2005.

SODEN, RUTH M., geriatrics nurse, educator; b. Tipton, Iowa, Nov. 29, 1940; d. Tony and Clarissa Arlene (Beall) Koreman; m. James D. Soden; children: Shannon, Scott, Suzan, Staci. AA, Highline Community Coll., Midway, Wash. Cert. in intravenous therapy. Charge nurse Wildwood Health Care Ctr., Puyallup, Wash.; admissions coord. Forestglen Nursing Ctr., Seattle, staff devel. dir.; charge nurse Green River Terrace Nursing Ctr., Auburn, Wash., Discovery Care Ctr., Hamilton, Mont.; nurse mgr. Tacoma Luth. Home; charge nurse and minimum data set coord. Discovery Care Ctr., Hamilton. Mem. Clover Park Tech. Coll., Tacoma. Mem. Nat. Gerontol. Nursing Assn. (practical nurse program adv. com.), Wash. State Nurses Assn., Assn. for Practitioners in Infection Control, Nat. Coun. on Family Rels., Phi Theta Kappa. Home: Hamilton, Mont. Died Aug. 8, 2004.

SOHN, LOUIS BRUNO, lawyer, educator; b. Lwów, Poland, Mar. 1, 1914; came to U.S., 1939, naturalized, 1943; s. Joseph and Fryderyka (Hescheles) S.; m. Elizabeth Mayo. LLM, Diplomatic ScM, John Casimir U., 1935; LLM, Harvard U., 1940, SJD, 1958; LLD (hon.), Free U. Brussels, 1990, George Washington U., 2000. Asst. to Judge M. O. Hudson, 1941-48; John Harvey Gregory teaching fellow Harvard Law Sch., 1946-47, lectr. law, 1947-51, asst. prof. law, 1951-53, John Harvey Gregory lectr. in world orgn., 1951-81, prof. law, 1953-61, Bemis prof. internat. law, 1961-81; Woodruff prof. internat. law U. Ga., 1981-91; vis. Congl. prof. George Washignton U. Law Sch., 1991-92; Disting. rsch. prof. and dir. rsch. and studies Internat. Rule of Law Ctr., George Washington U. Law Sch., 1992—2006. Disting. fellow Jennings Randolph program U.S. Inst. Peace, 1991-92; cons. U.S. ACDA, 1960-70, Office Internat. Security Affairs, US Dept. Def., 1963-70; rsch. asst. joint project for internat. law of future ABA and Can. Bar Assn., 1943-44; asst. to del. Permanent Ct. Internat. Justice, San Francisco Conf. UN, 1945; exec. sec. legal subcom. on atomic energy Carnegie Endowment for Internat. Peace, 1946; asst. reporter on progressive devel. internat. law Am. and Canadian bar assns., 1947-48; cons. UN secretariat, 1948, 69, legal officer, 1950-51; counselor internat. law, US Dept. State, 1970-71, cons., 1982-2006; U.S. counsel Internat. Ct. Justice, 1971, 84; U.S. del. to UN Law of Sea Conf., 1974-82; U.S. del. head Athens Conf. on Settlement Internat. Disputes, 1984. Author: Cases on World Law, 1950, Cases on United Nations Law, 1956, 2d edit., 1967, (with G. Clark) World Peace Through World Law, 1958, 3d edit., 1966, Basic Documents of African Regional Organizations, 4 vols, 1971-72, (with T. Buergenthal) International Protection of Human Rights, 1973, (with K. Gustafson) The Law of the Sea in a Nutshell, 1984, International Organization and Integration: student edit. 1986, (with T. Buergenthal) The Movement of Persons Across Borders, 1992, Rights in Conflict: The United Nations v. South Africa, 1994; also articles on internat. legal subjects; editor devel. internat. law: Am. Bar Assn. Jour, 1947-50; editorial bd.: Am. Jour. Internat. Law, 1958—2006. Recipient World Peace Hero award World Federalists of Can., 1974, Grenville Clark award, 1984, William A. Owens award for creative rsch. in social and behavioral scis. U. Ga., 1985, Harry Leroy Jones award Washington Fgn. Law Soc., 1993, Internat. Human Rights award UN Assn. Nat. Capital Area, 1997, Internat.Environ. Law award, Ctr. for Internat. Environ. Law, 2003 Mem. ABA (hon., co-rapporteur joint working group with Can. Bar Assn. on peaceful settlement of disputes 1976-2006, vice chmn. internat. law and practice sect. 1983-91, chmn. 1992-93, mem. coun. 1993-97, councillor 1997-2006, Leonard J. Theberge award 1992), Am. Soc. Internat. Law (mem. exec. coun. 1954-57, v.p. 1965-66, hon. v.p. 1980-87, 90-2006, pres. 1988-90, Manley O. Hudson medal 1996), World Parliament Assn. (legal advisor 1954-64), Internat. Law Assn. (v.p. Am. br.), Am. Law Inst. (assoc. reporter Fgn. Rels. Law 1978-87), Inst. Internat. Law (Geneva) (reporter on consensus in internat. law 1997-99), Fedn. Am. Scientists (vice chmn. 1963, mem. coun. 1964-65, 68-69), Commn. Study Orgn. Peace (chmn. 1986-98). Home: Arlington, Va. Died June 7, 2006.

SOLOMON, ELAINE DEBORAH, school administrator; b. N.Y.C., Dec. 8, 1938; d. Abraham and Mimi (Moskowitz) S. BS in Edn., CCNY, 1959; MA in Edn., NYU, 1962, MA in Guidance, 1966. Cert. tchr., guidance counselor, prin., guidance dir. Tchr. Pub. Sch. 119, Bronx, N.Y., 1959-64, tchr. of gifted, 1964-65; guidance counselor Pub. Sch. 100, Bronx, 1965-69; asst. prin. Pub. Sch. 64, Bronx, 1969-71, prin., 1971-74, Midland Sch., Paramus, N.J., 1974-79; curriculum coordinator Paramus Pub. Schs., 1974-79; prin. Demarest (N.J.) Pub. Schs., 1979-81; prin., dir. elem. edn. Pequannock Pub. Schs., Pompton Plains, N.J., from 1981. Adminstr. Community Progress Ctrs., Bronx, 1969; dir. headstart N.Y.C. Bd. Edn., Bronx, 1970-71; evening guidance counselor title I N.Y.C. Bd. Edn., 1971-75; adj. prof. dept. edn. Kean Coll., Union, N.J., 1987-88. Merck Pharm. Inst. for Research fellow, 1986—. Mem. Internat. Reading Assn., Assn. Adminstrs. and Suprs., Prins. Suprs. Assn. N.J., Pequannock Adminstrs. and Suprs. Assn. Clubs: Bergen County Recorder. Avocations: backgammon, music, photography, reading, tennis. Home: New York, NY. Died Aug. 24, 2005.

SOLSO, ROBERT L., psychology educator; b. Sioux City, Iowa, June 22, 1933; s. F.I. and Elizabeth (Pressly) S.; children: Anne, Laird, Robert. BA, Hastings Coll., 1957; MA, U. Nebr., 1959; PhD, St. Louis U., 1967. Prof., dept. chmn. Moorhead (Minn.) State U., 1957-68; prof. Loyola U., Chgo., 1968-74; postdoctoral rschr. Stanford (Calif.) U., 1974-75; prof., chmn. U. Idaho, Moscow, 1975-81; prof., chmn. dept. psychology U. Nev., Reno, 1982—2004. Vis. prof. Stanford (Calif.) U., 1975-81, Oxford (Eng.) U., 1980, Moscow State U., 1980-81; world lectr. tours, 1981, 97. Author: Cognition and the Visual Arts, 1996, Cognitive Psychology, 2001, The Psychology of Art and the Evolution of the Conscious Brain, 2003; editor: The Science of the Mind, 1995, Mind and Brain Sciences, 1997, Show, The Nat. Portrait Gallery, London, 1999. Bd. dirs. Nev. Opera Bd., Reno, 1986-92. Served U.S. Army, 1953—55. Mem. Western Psychol. Assn. (pres. 1997, dir. Pan Pacific program 2000). Died Jan. 16, 2005.

SOMERS, SARAH PRUYN, retired elementary school educator; b. Albany, N.Y., Oct. 15, 1936; d. Howard Sewall and Carolyn (Decker) Pruyn; m. Richard Moss Somers Jr., Aug. 15, 1959 (dec. Jan. 1986); children: Sewall Wendy Somers Hautzinger, Sarah Louise. BS in Edn., Wheelock Coll., 1958. Cert. elem. tchr., Mass., N.J. Elem. tchr. Madison (N.J.) Pub. Schs., 1960-63, 76-99; ret., from 1999. Group chmn., student tchr. sponsor Madison Pub. Schs., 1980-99, rep. roundtable, 1988-99; reading vol. Cold Spring Elem. Sch., Doylestown, 2000—. Vol. libr. Torey J. Sabatini Sch., Madison, 1970-76, room mother, 1970-81; room mother Kings Rd. Sch., 1976-77, Madison High Sch., 1976-81, The Gill/St. Bernards Sch., Bernardsville, N.J., 1977-82, The Morristown Beard Sch., 1982-86; vol. Cold Spring Elem. Sch. Doylestown, Pa., 2000—; chaperone, coach YMCA Nat. Swim Meet, 1979-81; mem. aquatic com. YMCA, Madison, 1973-80; mem. Jr. League Boston, Morristown; mem. Madison Hist. Soc., 1988-99; chaperone Madison Teen Ctr., 1991-99. Recipient Govs. Tchr. Recognition award, 1988. Fellow NEA (ret.); mem. N.J. Edn. Assn. (ret.), Morris County Edn. Assn. (ret.), Madison Edn. Assn. (rep. coun. 1992—), Bucks County Hist. Soc. Republican. Episcopalian. Avocations: reading, active sports, tennis, walking, tv. Home: Doylestown, Pa. Died Oct. 1, 2004.

SONNENBLICK, HARVEY IRWIN, psychiatrist; b. N.Y.C., June 3, 1936; s. Paul and Adele (Newman) S.; children: Lissa, Jordan. BA, U. Va., 1958; MD, NYU, 1962. Diplomate Am. Bd. Psychiatry and Neurology. Intern Kings County Hosp., Bklyn., 1962-63, resident, 1963-65; resident, fellow S.I. (N.Y.) Mental Health Soc., 1965-67; staff psychiatrist Seamen's Soc. for Children and Families, S.I., from 1978, Jewish Bd. Family & Children's Svcs., S.I. and Bklyn., from 1981. Vis. psychiatrist Sea View Hosp. Rehab. Ctr. and Home, S.I., 1966—. Maj. U.S. Army, 1968-70. Mem. AMA, Am. Psychiat. Assn., Phi Beta Kappa. Avocation: basketball. Home: Staten Island, NY. Died Feb. 11, 2005.

SORENSEN, JEAN, artist; b. San Diego, Nov. 18, 1920; d. William James and Hallie (Moran) Hart; m. Ralph James Sorensen, Sept. 1, 1939; children: Ellen Marie Pacchetti, Ann Christine Coons, James Christian. Student, San Jose State U., 1938-39, U. Calif., Santa Cruz, from 1972. Tchr. watercolor workshop DeAnza State Coll., Cupertino, Calif., 1984, Santa Clara Valley Watercolor Soc., Yosemite Nat. Park, 1984; tchr. botany Stanford U., 1985; ptnr. View Points Art Gallery, Los Altos, Calif., 1972-92; pres. View Prints Art Gallery, Los Altos, Calif., 1988-90. Exhibitor at Palazzo Veccico, Florence, Italy, 1972, Soc. Western Arts, DeYoung Mus., San Francisco, 1970-75; guest exhibiter biennial Kofu Watercolor Exhibit, Japan, 1983; commd. painting City of Syktyvhear, Russia, 1990, Tait Mus. Art, Los Gatos, Calif., 1997, Rose Shensen Gallery, Triton Mus., Santa Clara, Calif., 2001. Vol. docent Mid-Peninsula Regional Park Open Space Dist., San Mateo and Santa Clara counties, Calif., 1977-91. Mem. Nat. Assn. Women Artists, Soc. Western Artists, Allied Artists West (pres. 1990-92), Santa Clara Valley Watercolor Soc., Monterey County Watercolor Soc., Calif. Native Plant Soc. Avocations: genealogy, botany. Home: San Jose, Calif. Died May 11, 2005.

SORRENTINO, GILBERT, literature and language professor, novelist, poet; b. Bklyn., Apr. 27, 1929; s. August E. and Ann Marie (Davis) S.; m. Victoria Ortiz; children: Jesse, Delia, Christopher. Student, Bklyn. Coll., 1950—51, student, 1954—55. In various positions, 1947-70; including reins. clk. Fidelity and Casualty Co., N.Y.C., 1947-48; freight checker Ace Assembly Agy., N.Y.C., 1954-56; packer Bennett Bros. Inc., N.Y.C., 1956-57; messenger Am. Houses, Inc., N.Y.C., 1948-49; shipping-room supr. Thermo-fax Sales, Inc., Queens, NY, 1957-60; editor Grove Press, NY, 1965-70; tchr. Columbia U., 1966, Aspen Writers Workshop, 1967, Sarah Lawrence Coll., 1972, The New Sch. for Social Rsch., 1976—81; NEH chairperson in lit. U. Scranton, 1979; prof. English Stanford U., Calif., 1982—99, prof. emeritus, 1999—2006. Editorial cons. Contemporary Lit., 1989-97. Author: The Darkness Surrounds Us, 1960, Black and White, 1964, The Sky Changes, 1966, The Perfect Fiction, 1968, Steelwork, 1970, Imaginative Qualities of Actual Things, 1971, Corrosive Sublimate, 1971, Splendide-Hotel, 1972, Flawless Play Restored, 1974, A Dozen Oranges, 1976, White Sail, 1977, Sulpiciae Elegidia/Elegiacs of Sulpicia, 1977, The Orangery, 1978, Mulligan Stew, 1979, Aberration of Starlight, 1980, Selected Poems, 1958-80, 1981, Crystal Vision, 1981, Blue Pastoral, 1983, Something Said: Essays, 1984, Odd Number, 1985, Rose Theatre, 1987, Misterioso, 1989, Under the Shadow, 1991, Red the Fiend, 1995, Pack of Lies: A Trilogy, 1997, Gold Fools, 2001, Little Casino, 2002, The Moon in Its Flight, 2004, New and Selected Poems, 1958-1998, 2004, Lunar Follies, 2005. With U.S. Army, 1951—53. Recipient Samuel Fels award in fiction Coord. Coun. Lit. Mags., 1974, John Dos Passos prize, 1981, Am. Acad. and Inst. Arts and Letters award in lit., 1985, Lannan Lit. Fiction award 1992, Lannan Lifetime Achievement award 2005; John Simon Guggenheim Meml. fellow, 1973-74, 87-88; grantee Creative Artists Pub. Svc. Program, 1974-75, NEA, 1974-75, 78-79, 83-84. Mem. PEN Am. Ctr. Home: Brooklyn, NY. Died May 18, 2006.

SOSNICK, FAY MAXINE, retired healthcare executive, volunteer; b. N.Y.C., June 25, 1914; d. Philip and Gussie (Cohen) Shapiro; m. Max Sosnick, Dec. 25, 1937 (dec. Sept. 1989); children: Renee Beth Bain, Janet Ruth Hughes. BA in Chemistry, Math. and Sci., Hunter Coll., 1934; MEd in Math., Fairleigh Dickinson U., 1964; AAS in Philosophy, Brookdale C.C., N.J., 1984; student, Rutgers U., from 2002. Auditor U.S. Fin. Office, 1943-46; acctg., analyst and payroll staff Quindar Electronics, NJ, 1965—68; exec. Inglemoor Nursing Homes, 1969-74; ret., 1974. Creator, organizer Home Owners Assn., The Guardian-Newspaper

Pub. Condo. Assn., 1973-76; creator, liaison Self-Help Groups in Arthritis, Fitness, Svcs. to Hosp., Freehold Boro Hosp., 1974—, ombudsmen's team; vol. govtl. svc. Sr. Health Ins. N.J. State, 1976-80; with Brookdale C.C. Alumni Assn., N.J., 1983-87; mem. juvenile conf. com. Superior Ct. Chancery Divsn., N.J., 1985-89; creator patient support group St. Peters U. Hosp., Circle of Friends, Cmty. Sr. Ctr.; resident, program chmn. Sr. Homes, Temple; mem. staff Bill of Rights Sr. Facility; pastoral mentor St. Peter's U. Hosp., 1997—, Recipient Svc. award, Bikur Choleem. Achievements include being the creator of ombudsmen's team for redress of grievances plans to create a community at own residence; working with governor and legislative bodies to create a community of residents of senior living facilities. Died May 1, 2006.

SOUTH, LEONARD J., cinematographer; b. LI, NY, 1913; Cinematographer (films) I Sailed to Tahiti with an All Girl Crew, 1968, Hang 'Em High, 1968, Frenzy, 1972, Family Plot, 1976, Herbie Goes to Monte Carlo, 1977, The North Avenue Irregulars, 1979, Amy, 1981; (TV films) Night Gallery, 1970, Me and the Chimp, 1972, Home for the Holidays, 1972, The Chill Factor, 1973, Snatched, 1973, The Letters, 1973, Linda, 1973, Screaming Pretty Peggy, 1973, Hitchhike!, 1974, Satan's Triangle, 1975, Death Stalk, 1975, You Lie So Deep, My Love, 1975, Terraces, 1978, The Jordan Chance, 1978, The North Avenue Irregulars, 1979, Father Murphy, 1981; (TV series) Me and the Chimp, 1968, The Rockford Files, 1974, The Associates, 1979, 9 to 5, 1982, Foley Square, 1985, Designing Women, 1986, Coach, 1989 Mem.: Am. Soc. Cinematographers (pres. 1989—90). Died Jan. 6, 2006.

SOUTHARD, RUTH AUDREY, medical/surgical nurse; b. Kearny, N.J., Aug. 17, 1923; d. Robert James and Edna Leola Zerbe; m. Carl B. Southard, Dec. 17, 1983 (dec. Mar. 1989). Diploma, Muhlenberg Hosp. Sch. Nursing, Plainfield, N.J., 1944; BSN, Seton U., 1953; MA in Pub. Health Nursing, N.Y. U., 1968. Dir. svc. MCOSS Family Health and Nursing Svc., Red Bank, NJ, 1945—72; asst. prof., sr. coord. Mankato State U., Minn., 1972—74; coord. sr. level cmty. health nursing, asst. prof. U. R.I., 1974—75; coord. ambulatory care svcs. Jersey City Med. Ctr., 1977—78; adminstrv./supr. nurse Jewish Child Care Assn. N.Y., 1978—79; primary nurse Loeb Ctr. Nursing and Rehab., Montefiore Hosp., Bronx, NY, 1980; with employee health dept. J.P. Morgan Trust Co., NY, 1980; nurse crisis intervention unit Hahneman U. Hosp., Phila., 1982—83; nurse psychiat. unit John F. Kennedy Hosp., Cherry Hill, NJ, 1983—84. Contbr. articles to profl. jours. Mem. N.J. Libr-.for Blind and Disabled, Defenders of Wildlife. Capt. U.S. Army Nuse Corps, 1945—58. Mem.: ANA, Am. Nurses Found., N.J. Sate Nurses Assn., Gloucester County Stamp Club, AARP, Sierra Club, Century Club. Protestant. Home: Pennsauken, NJ. Died July 20, 2004.

SOUTHWELL, SAMUEL BEALL, English educator; b. Lockhart, Tex., Jan. 15, 1922; s. George Thomas Jr. and Lucile Mariam (Beall) S.; m. Mary Jane Bamford, Dec. 16, 1944; children: Michael Beall, Teresa Bamford. BJ, U. Tex., 1947, MA, 1948, PhD, 1955; D (hon.), U. Autonoma de Guadalajara, Mex., 1965. Assoc. prof. Tex. A&M U., College Station, 1950-58; ednl. exch. officer USIA, Mexico City, 1959-60, U.S. Consul, Guadalajara, 1961-65; assoc. prof. U. Houston, 1965-69, chmn. dept. English, 1969-73, prof., 1970-95, ret., 1995, prof. emeritus, from 1996. Author: (novel) If All the Rebels Die, 1966, Quest for Eros: Browning and "Fifine", 1980, Kenneth Burke and Martin Heidegger: With a Note on Deconstructionism, 1987, Crossing the Wasteland: An Intellectual Quest for God, 2002, Consciousness Reclaimed: The Human Commingling of Sound and Light, 2003. Lt. (j.g.) USN, 1944-45, Pacific Fleet. Democrat. Roman Catholic. Avocations: reading, bicycle riding, walking. Home: Houston, Tex. Died Mar. 22, 2004.

SOWELL, WILLIAM RAYMOND, entrepreneur; b. Maud, Okla., Mar. 11, 1928; s. William Thomas Sowell and Blanche Hardaway; m. Helen LaDawn Hilton, Dec. 24, 1950; 1 child, William Hilton. BSME, Okla. Baptist U., 1950; BSAE, Calif. Aero Tech. Inst., Glendale, 1952; M Engring., U. So. Calif., 1958; M Ocean Engring., UCLA, 1966. Program mgr. Rockwell Internat., L.A., 1952-70; v.p. Ocean Environments, Inc., St. Thomas, Virgin Islands, 1970-73; v.p., dir. Royal Industries, Thompson Div., Carson, Calif., 1973-75; cons. Intercontinental Mgmt., Inc., Torrance, Calif., 1976-79; gen. mgr. Nat. Engring. Svcs. and Mktg., Jeddah, Saudi Arabia, 1980-84; dir. contracts Murdock, Inc., Compton, Calif., 1984-89; chmn. Soule Internat., Palos Verdes Estates, from 1989; pres. The World of Nicholas and Ashlee, from 1989, Profl. Image, from 1989, The Third Dimension Internat., from 1989. Author technical papers. With USMC, 1946-47, PTO, China. Recipient Menta Martin award, Inst. Aeronautical Scis., L.A., 1952. Mem. Nat. Contract Mgmt. Assn. (bd. dirs. 1987-88). Republican. Covenant Ch. Avocations: scuba, photography/video, fgn. travel, archaeology. Home: Palos Verdes Peninsula, Calif. Died June 5, 2004.

SPALDING, EDWARD WYMAN, retired secondary school educator; b. N.Y.C., June 8, 1918; s. Henry Boardman and Geraldine (Wyman) S.; divorced; children: Wilda, Simon, David. BA, UCLA, 1948. Cert. gen. edn., Calif. Stage mgr. Berkeley (Calif.) Festival Assn., 1941; plans and mgmt. office, 6th Army Hdqrs., The Presidio U.S. Army, San Francisco, 1955-60; tchr., drama dir. A.P. Giannini Jr. High Sch., San Francisco, 1962-84; dep. cmdr. Ctr. for Mil. History No. Calif. Br., San Francisco, Sacramento, from 1987; vol. guide Presidio Army Mus. and Ft. Point Historic Site, San Francisco, from 1987. Capt. USAAF, 1941-45. Mem. Co. Mil. Historians, E Clampus Vitus, Civil War Round Table (past pres.). Home: Santa Paula, Calif. Died Dec. 3, 2004.

SPAMER, JAMES SLOAN, civil engineer; b. Balt., Mar. 14, 1925; s. William A. and Martha May (Hughes) S.; m. Lilly A., Aug. 25, 1945; children: James S., Lilly A. BS, U. Ill., 1945, U. Md., 1946, MS, 1948. Instr. civil engring. U. Md., College Park, 1946-48; engr. Dept. Pub. Works, Balt., 1948-50; chief utilities engr. A.E. Pohmer Co., Balt., 1950-52; owner, chief engr. J.S. Spamer & Assocs., Towson, Md., 1953-82; chief engr. J. Harms & Assocs., Pasadena, Md., 1982-84; cons., from 1985. Fellow Am. Soc. Civil Engrs; mem. Md. Soc. Profl. Engrs. (pres. 1997), Engring. Soc. Balt. (pres. 1982), H.L. Mencken Soc., Masons. Democrat. Avocation: world travel. Home: Jensen Beach, Fla. Died Jan. 26, 2005.

SPANGLER, KENNETH LEE, lawyer; b. Joliet, Ill., Nov. 15, 1940; s. Kenneth Alexander and Alice Laura (Phelps) S.; m. Colleen Renee Blaisdell, Aug. 28, 1965; children: Heather, Brooke, Kenneth, Jr. BA, U. Ill., 1962; JD, U. Mich., 1965. Bar: N.Y. 1966, Pa. 1986; U.S. Dist. Ct. (so. and ea. dists.) N.Y. 1975; U.S. Ct. Appeals (2d cir.) 1975; U.S. Supreme Ct. 1975. Assoc. Chadbourne, Parke, Whiteside & Wolff, N.Y.C., 1965-66, 69-74; assoc. gen. counsel Sperry Corp., N.Y.C., 1974-86; ptnr. Windels, Marx, Davies & Ives, N.Y.C., 1986-1991; sr. v.p., gen. counsel Blount, Inc, Mongomery, Al, 1991-93; sr. v.p. law Nat. Westminster Bancorp, Inc., N.Y.C., from 1993. Adj. prof. Lubin Grad. Sch. Bus., Pace U., N.Y.C., 1989-92. Author: International Joint Ventures, 1990, 92; co-author: Negotiating the Bank Merger Process, 1994. Capt. Ambulance Corps, Larchmont, 1983. 1st lt. inf. U.S. Army, 1966-69, Vietnam. Decorated Bronze Star. Mem. ABA, Assn. Bar City N.Y., Am. Corp. Counsel Asn., Larchmont Yacht Club. Republican. Episcopalian. Avocations: sailing, tennis, jogging, reading. Died Jan. 28, 2004.

SPARK, DAME MURIEL SARAH, writer; b. Edinburgh, Scotland, Feb. 1, 1918; d. Bernard and Sarah Elizabeth Maud (Uezzell) Camberg; m. S.O. Spark, (marriage dissolved); 1 son. Student James Gillespie Sch., Heriot Watt Coll., Edinburgh; DLitt (hon.), Strathclyde U., 1971, U. Edinburgh, 1989; CLitt, Royal Soc. Lit., 1991; DLitt (hon.), Aberdeen U., 1995, U. Oxford, 1999; DUniv. (hon.), Heriot-Watt U., 1995; DLitt (hon.), U. St. Andrews, 1998. Gen. sec. Poetry Soc., 1947-49; editor Poetry Rev., 1947-49. Author: (non-fiction) Child of Light: A Reassessment of Mary Wollstonecraft Shelley, 1951 (rev. as Mary Shelley, 1987), Emily Brontë: Her Life and Work, 1953, John Masefield, 1953, revised, 1992, The Essence of the Brontës, 1993; (poetry) The Fanfarlo and Other Verse, 1952, Collected Poems I, 1967, Going Up to Sotheby's and Other Poems, 1982; (autobiography) Curriculum Vitae, 1992; (fiction) The Comforters, 1957, Robinson, 1958, The Go-Away Bird and Other Stories, 1958, Memento Mori, 1959, The Ballad of Peckham Rye, 1960, The Bachelors, 1960, Voices at Play, 1961, The Prime of Miss Jean Brodie, 1961, The Girls of Slender Means, 1963, The Mandelbaum Gate, 1965 (James Tait Black Meml. prize 1966, Yorkshire Post Book of Yr. award 1965), Collected Stories I, 1968, The Public Image, 1968, (juvenile) The Very Fine Clock, 1968, The Driver's Seat, 1970, Not to Disturb, 1971, The Hothouse by the East River, 1973, The Abbess of Crewe, 1974, The Takeover, 1976, Territorial Rights, 1979, Loitering with Intent, 1981, Bang-Bang You're Dead and Other Stories, 1982, The Only Problem, 1984, The Stories of Muriel Spark, 1985, A Far Cry from Kensington, 1988, Symposium, 1990, Reality and Dreams, 1996, The French Window and the Small Telephone, 1993, Aiding and Abetting, 2000, All the Stories of Muriel Spark, 2001; (play) The Doctors of Philosophy, 1962; (radio plays) The Party Through the Wall, 1957, The Interview, 1958, The Dry River Bed, 1959, The Ballad of Peckham Rye, 1960 (Prix Italia 1962), The Danger Zone, 1961; editor: Selected Poems of Emily Brontë, 1952. Decorated Officier de l'Ordre des Arts et des Lettres (France), 1988, Comdr., 1996; Officer,1967, Dame Order Brit. Empire, 1993; recipient Observer short story prize, 1951, Ingersoll T.S. Eliot award, 1992, The David Cohen Brit. Lit. prize, 1997, Gold Pen award Internat. P.E.N., 1998. Fellow Royal Soc. Edinburgh; mem. AAAL (hon. 1978). Died Apr. 13, 2006; Civitella della Chiana, Italy.

SPECTOR, JOEL MATHEW, rare book conservator; b. Cleve., Oct. 23, 1949; s. Sam and Dorothea Spector. BA, Goodard Coll., 1972; MFA, Columbia U., 1981; MLS, U. Wis. Madison, 1992; cert. apprentice, U. Iowa, 1997. Restorer stained glass Newe Daisterre, Cleveland Heights, Ohio, 1977—84; apprentice, asst. adj. prof. U. Iowa Libr., Iowa City, 1993—97; proprietor, owner Cold Hill Bindery, Iowa City, 1997—99, Hollow Woods Bindery, Peacham, Vt., from 1999. Apprentice Mellon Found., 1993—97. Translator (poetry): Peter Huchel Wilson Quar., 1994, Ivan Goll Agni, 1989; author (poem): Slant Rev., 2002. Fellow, Kress Found., 1998, Folger Shakespeare Libr., 1999. Mem.: Guild of Book Workers, Am. Inst. for Conservation, Beta Phi Mu. Home: Portland, Maine. Died June 4, 2005.

SPELLER, ROBERT ERNEST BLAKEFIELD, publishing executive; b. Chgo., Jan. 19, 1908; s. John Ernest and Florence (Larson) S.; m. Flora Maxine Elliott Watkins (dec. May 1997); children: Robert Ernest Blakefield, Jon Patterson. Student, Columbia U., 1929. Mng. editor Fgn. Press Svc., 1930-31; pres. Mohawk Press, 1931-32, Robert Speller Pub. Corp., 1934-52, Record Concerts Corp., 1940-53, Robert Speller & Sons, Pubs., inc., from 1955, Norellyn Press, Inc., 1960-83, Transglobal News Svc., Inc., from 1960. Corresp. Raleigh News & Observer, 1949-53; pub. Hough's Ency. Am. Woods, 1957—, mng. editor 1964-75; chmn. bd., pres., chief exec. officer Nat. Resources Publs., Inc., 1968-84; pres., dir. Transglobal Resources Devel. Corp., 1983—; owner, operator, prodr. Concert Theatre, N.Y.C., 1939-43, mgr. Otto Klemperer, Leon Barzin, Margaret Speaks, others; pub. East Europe Mag., 1970-; sec., dir. Encoder Research & Devel. Corp., 1971—, Pecos Internat., Inc., 1974-77; v.p., dir. Pecos Western Corp. of Del., 1973-83; dir. Gen. Research Corp., Fashion Form Mfg. Corp. Mem. founding bd. USO Trustee Philippa Schuyler Meml. Found. With Signal Corps U.S. Army, 1944—45. Mem. Gourmet Soc. (founder), Am. Legion, Local 38 Musicians Assn. AFL, Westchester Country Club, Columbia U. Club (N.Y.C.), PGA Tour Ptnrs. Club, Delta Chi. Episcopalian. Died Mar. 9, 2006.

SPELLING, AARON, film and television producer, writer, actor; b. Dallas, Apr. 22, 1923; s. David and Pearl (Wall) Spelling; m. Carolyn Jones, Apr. 10, 1953 (div. 1964); m. Carol Jean Marer, Nov. 23, 1968; children: Victoria Davey, Randall Gene. Student, Sorbonne, U. Paris, France, 1945-46; BA, So. Meth. U., 1945. Actor Thomas-Spelling Prodn., LA, 1953-69; screenwriter Zane Grey Series, LA, 1972-76; prodr. Zane Grey Theater, LA, 1977-86, The Dick Powell Show, LA, 1961—63; co-owner with Danny Thomas Thomas-Spelling Prodn., LA, 1969-72; co-pres. Spelling-Goldberg Prodn., LA, 1972-76; pres. Aaron Spelling Prodn., Inc., LA, 1977-86, chmn., CEO, 1986—2006. Exec. prodr.: Pair of Boots, 1962, My Daddy Can Lick Your Daddy, 1962, Honey West, 1966, Crickets on the Hearth, 1967, Off to See the Wizard, 1967, The Over-the-Hill Gang, 1969, Wake Me When the War is Over, 1969, The Pigeon, 1969, How Awful About Allan, 1970, The Old Man Who Cried Wolf, 1970, Wild Women, 1970, The Over-the-Hill Gang Rides Again, 1970, Crowhaven Farm, 1970, Love Hate Love, 1971, River of Gold, 1971, Five Desperate Women, 1971, The Last Child, 1971, In Broad Daylight, 1971, The Reluctant Heros, 1971, If Tomorrow Comes, 1971, Two for the Money, 1972, The Daughters of Joshua Cabe, 1972, Rolling Man, 1972, Home for the Holidays, 1972, Every Man Needs One, 1972, The Chill Factor, 1973, The Great American Beauty Contest, 1973, The Letters, 1973, The Bait, 1973; exec. prodr.: The Affair, 1973; exec. prodr.: California Split, 1974, Only With Married Men, 1974, The Daughters of Joshua Cabe Return, 1975, The Fireman's Ball, 1975, Murder on Flight 502, 1975, One of My Wives Is Missing, 1976, The New Daughters of Joshua Cabe, 1976, Death at Love House, 1976, The Boy in the Plastic Bubble, 1976, Little Ladies of the Night, 1977, The San Pedro Bums, 1977, Wild and Wooly, 1978, Kate Bliss and the Ticker Tape Kid, 1978, The Users, 1978, Beach Patrol, 1979, The Power Within, 1979, Return of the Mod Squad, 1979, Love's Savage Fury, 1979, Waikiki, 1980, Murder Can Hurt You, 1980, Casino, 1980, The Best Little Girl in the World, 1981, Sizzle, 1981, Massarati and the Brain, 1982, The Wild Women of Chastity Gulch, 1982, Don't Go to Sleep, 1982, Shooting Stars, 1983, Making of a Male Model, 1983, Dark Mirror, 1984, A Season in Purgatory, 1996, After Jimmy, 1996, International Airport, 1985, Mr. and Mrs. Ryan, 1986, Dark Mansions, 1986, Cracked Up, 1987, Three O'Clock High, 1987, Divided We Stand, 1988, Day One, 1989, Rich Men, Single Women, 1990, The Love Boat: A Valentine Voyage, 1990, Jailbirds, 1991, Back to the Streets of San Francisco, 1992, Grass Roots, 1992, And the Band Played On, 1993, A Stranger in the Mirror, 1993, Jane's House, 1994, Love On the Run, 1994, Cross Town Traffic, 1995, Satan's School for Girls, 2000, Home of the Braves, 2002, Hotel, 2003, The Law and Mr. Lee, 2003, Silver Lake, 2004, Summerland, 2004, Bounty Hunters, 2005, Wanted, 2005; exec. prodr.: (TV series) Daniel Boone, 1964; exec. prodr.: (TV series) The Most Deadly Game, 1970, The Young Rebels, 1970, Chopper One, 1974, Firehouse, 1974, S.W.A.T., 1975, Starsky and Hutch, 1975, Family, 1976, Charlie's Angel, 1976, The Love Boat, 1977, Fantasy Island, 1978, Return to Fantasy Island, 1978, Vega$, 1978, Friends, 1979, B.A.D. Cats, 1980, T.J. Hooker, 1982, Hotel, 1983, Beverly Hills 90210, 1990—2000, Savannah, 1996, Kindred: The Embraced, 1996, 7th Heaven, 1996, The Colbys, 1985, Life with Lucy, 1986, Melrose Place, 1992, 2000 Malibu Road, 1992, The Heights, 1992, The Round Table, 1992, Models Inc., 1994, Malibu Shores, 1996, Pacific Palisades, 1997, The Love Boat: The Next Wave, 1998, Buddy Faro, 1998, Rescue 77, 1999, Safe Harbor, 1999, Titans, 2000, All Souls, 2001, Deep Cover, 2002, Queens Supreme, 2003, 10-8: Officers on Duty, 2003, Clubhouse, 2004, Charmed, 1998—2006; exec. prodr., prodr. (TV series) Dynasty, 1981; exec. prodr.: (TV series) Hart to Hart, 1979, Hart to Hart Returns, 1993; (TV films) Hart to Hart (various titles), 1994—95; (TV miniseries) The French Atlantic Affair, 1979, Hollywood Wives, 1985, Crossings, 1986, Kingpin, 2003; (films) Mr. Mom, 1983, The Mod Squad, 1999, Charlie's Angels, 2000; prodr.: Soapdish, 1991, The Dick Powell Show, 1962, The Love War, 1970, But I Don't Want to Get Married, 1970, The House That Would Not Die, 1970, Run, Simon, Run, 1970, Yuma, 1971, Congratulations, It's a Boy!, 1971, A Taste of Evil, 1971, The Death of Me Yet, 1971, No Place to Run, 1972, Say Goodbye, Maggie Cole, 1972, The Bounty Man, 1972, Snatched, 1973, Satan's School for Girls, 1973, Hijack, 1973, Letters from Three Lovers, 1973, The Death Squad, 1974, The Girl Who Came Gift-Wrapped, 1974, Cry Panic, 1974, Savages, 1974, Death Sentence, 1974, Hit Lady, 1974, Death Cruise, 1974, The Legend of Valentino, 1975, Baby Blue Marine,

1976, Fantasy Island, 1977, Cruise Into Terror, 1978, Velvet, 1984, Finder of Lost Loves, 1984, Night, Mother, 1986, Surrender, 1987, Satisfaction, 1988, Loose Cannons, 1990, Green Dolphin Beat, 1994, Odd Jobs, 1997, Stop at Nothing, 2001; (TV series) The Mod Squad, 1968, The New People, 1969, Strike Force, 1981, At Ease, 1983, Glitter, 1984, Nightingales, 1989, Robin's Hoods, 1994, University Hospital, 1995, Sunset Beach, 1997; exec. prodr., prodr. The Monk, 1969, The Ballad of Andy Crocker, 1969, The Trackers, 1971, Gulf City, 1993; dir.: Wagon Train, 1959; assoc. prodr. Cross My Heart, 1987; actor: (films) Vicki, 1953, Three Young Texans, 1954, Alaska Seas, 1954, Black Widow, 1954, Mad at the World, 1955, Target Zero, 1955, Barbara Stanwyck: Straight Down the Line, 1997; (TV films) Treasury Men in Action, 1954; (TV series) I Love Lucy, 1995, Soldiers of Fortune, 1955, Dragnet, 1953—54, Alfred Hitchcock Presents, 1955, Crusader, 1956, Gunsmoke, 1956, The Millionaire, 1956; actor, prodr. (TV series) Burke's Law, 1963, guest appearance Studio 57, 1956—57, writer (episodes) Jane Wyman Presents The Fireside Theatre, 1957, Wagon Train, 1957, Playhouse 90, 1958, Westinghouse Desilu Playhouse, 1958, Dante, 1960, The Dick Powell Show, 1961, writer, exec. prodr., prodr. The Rookies, 1974—75, writer, prodr. Zane Grey Theater, 1958—61, Johnny Ringo, 1959, (films) Guns of Timberland, 1960, writer One Foot in Hell, 1960, creator, prodr. (TV series) The Guns of Will Sonnett, 1967, written by, exec. prodr., prodr. (TV films) Carter's Army, 1970; author: Aaron Spelling-A Prime Time Life, 1996. Bd. dirs. Am. Film Inst. With USAF, 1942—45. Decorated Bronze Star medal, Purple Heart with oak leaf cluster; named Man of Yr., Publicists Guild Am., 1971, Man of Yr. B'nai B'rith, Beverly Hills chpt., 1972, 1985, NAACP Humanitarian of Yr., 1983, Man of Yr. Scopus award, Am. Friends of Hebrew U., 1993; named to TV Acad.'s Hall of Fame; recipient Eugene O'Neill awards, 1947, 1948, NAACP Image awards, 1970, 1971, 1973, 1975, Winston Churchil medal of Wisdom, 1988, Lifetime Achievement award, People's Choice Awards, 1996, Courage to Dream award, Fulfillment Fund, 1996, GLADD award, 1st prodr. honored by Mus. of Broadcasting, honored for contbns. to victims' rights by City of Las Vegas. Mem.: Acad. Motion Picture Arts and Scis., Writers and Dirs., The Caucus of Prodrs., Prodrs. Guild Am., Writers Guild Am. (award 1962), Hollywood TV Acad. Arts and Scis., Hollywood Radio and TV Soc., Big Brothers of Am., Friars. Democrat. Jewish. Died June 23, 2006.

SPENCER, LEWIS VANCLIEF, retired physicist; b. Hillsdale, Mich., Nov. 29, 1924; s. William Gear and Dorothy (Burns) S.; m. Elizabeth Williams, Sept. 20, 1948; children: Dorothy Spencer Wagener, Betty Spencer Schiele, Carl, Mary Ellen Spencer Goree, Robert. BA, Franklin Coll., 1945; PhD, Northwestern U., 1948. Rschr. radiation transport Nat. Bur. of Standards, Washington, 1948-57, cons. Gaithersburg, Md., 1957-68, sect. chief radiation physics Washington, 1960-61, rsch. radiation shielding Gaithersburg, 1969-84, ret., 1984. Asst. prof. physics and math. Ottawa (Kans.) U., 1957-60, prof. physics and math., 1961-68; adj. prof. physics Hopkinsville C.C. of U. Ky.; mem. adv. com. NAS-NRC, 1966-70; mem. com. SC-63 NCRP, 1981-84. Author: Structure Shielding Against Fallout Gamma Rays from Nuclear Detonations, 1980; contbr. numerous articles to profl. jours. Mem. Gov.'s Nuclear Energy Adv. Coun., Kans., 1964-69, chmn. civil def. subcom., 1967. Recipient Meritorious Svc. award U.S. Dept. Commerce, 1952, 62, 72, Disting. Svc. award U.S. Office Civil and Def. Mobilization, 1960, L.H. Gray medal for outstanding contbn. to radiation sci. Internat. Commn. on Radiation Units and Measurements, 1969, Disting. Jayhawker award Kans., 1964, Community Svc. award C. of C., 1964. Mem. AAAS. Baptist. Achievements include research in penetration and diffusion of x-rays, theory of electron penetration, theory of cavity ionization. Home: Hopkinsville, Ky. Died Nov. 11, 2005.

SPENCER, PRISCILLA JAMES, physical education educator; b. Boston, Aug. 21, 1960; d. Richard P. and Gwendolyn (Williams) S. BA in Psychology, Bates Coll., Lewiston, Maine, 1983; MS in Phys. Edn. Recreation, So. Conn. State U., 1990; PhD in Phys. Edn., Temple U., 1999. Cert. educator in phys. edn. and health, Conn. Counselor Youth and Family Svcs., Westfield, Mass., 1983-85; phys. edn. tchr. Pleasant Valley Elem. Sch., South Winds, Conn., 1989-93; instr. kinesiology Pa. State U., from 1998. Cons. Pub. Schs., Conn., 1991—. Co-author: Popcorn's Travels Across America, 1992; author: Gymnastics for All, 1994. Named Outstanding Elem. Phys. Edn. Program Conn. Assn. Health, Phys. Edn. and Recreation, 1991; recipient Celebration of Excellence award State Conn. Dept. Edn., 1992; Fels Found. grantee, 1995; Pa. State Dept. Health cmty. grantee, 1999. Mem. AAHPERD, Inst. Manchester Cmty. Coll. Home: Hartford, Conn. Died June 10, 2005.

SPENCER, WILLIAM COURTNEY, foundation executive, international business executive; b. Uniontown, Pa., Sept. 15, 1919; m. Evelyn Van Cleve Bailey, Aug. 6, 1942; children: Courtney Lloyd, Henry Bailey, Edward Ashley. AB, Drew U., 1941; AM, Columbia U., 1946, EdD, 1952. Tchr. Scarsdale (N.Y.) Pub. Schs., 1946-49; dir. Univ. Sch. Columbia, 1949-52; prof. edn. and adminstrn. U. Del., 1952-55; prof., dir. grad. program tchr. edn. NYU, 1955-59, prof. higher edn. and internat. affairs, 1960-61; prof. adminstrn. U. Chile, Santiago, 1959-60; dir. Interam. affairs Inst. Internat. Edn. and asst. sec. gen. Coun. Higher Edn. in Am. Republics, 1961-65; assoc. dean Grad. Sch. Bus. Columbia U., 1965-67, spl. asst. to pres., 1967-69; pres. Western Coll., Oxford, Ohio, 1969-74, The Lindenwood Colls., 1974-79; v.p. Trans Internat. Mgmt. Corp., 1979-88; spl. adviser Fund for Higher Edn., 1979-82, pres., 1982-86; spl. asst. to pres. Internat. Exec. Svc. Corps, Stamford, Conn., 1988; dir. internat. devel. svcs. Nippon Manpower Ltd, Tokyo, 1988-91; pres. Trans Internat Exec. Svcs., 1988—95. Cons. UNESCO Latin Am. major project in edn., Chile, 1959-60, project edn. and econ. planning, India, 1962; cons. Am. Coun. Edn., 1960-61; del. Pan-Am Assembly on Population, 1965; mem. standing com. on internat. edn. Coll. Entrance Exam. Bd., 1972-74; cons. Am. Med. Internat. Inc., 1980, McGraw Hill Internat. Book Co., 1981, AID, Indonesia, 1982, Thermo-Electron Corp., China, 1984, Internat. Exec. Svc. Corps, Jamaica, 1989, Costa Rica, 1991, 93, Hungary, 1991. Author: Education and World Responsibility, 1965, also articles; editor: Art and the University, 1964, University and National Development, 1965, Agriculture and the University, 1965. Bd. dirs. Internat. Sch. Svc., 1963-69, chmn., 1967-69; mem. Mo. master planning com. Coordinating Bd. Higher Edn., 1975-79; pres. Ind. Colls. and Univs. of Mo., 1977-79; bd. dirs. St. Louis Coun. on World Affairs, 1977-79; mem. scholarship bd. Timken Co. Ednl. Fund, 1971-76; bd. dirs. Internat. Inst. Energy Conservation, 1984-89, Conn. River Mus., 1988-2002. Lt. comdr. USNR, 1942-46. Decorated Purple Heart; commendation medals from Royal Navy, U.S. Navy. Mem. Coun. Fgn. Relations, N.Y. Yacht Club, Essex (Conn.) Yacht Club, North Cove Yacht Club. Died Nov. 2, 2005.

SPIELMAN, BARBARA HELEN NEW, retired editor; b. Canton, Ohio, June 28, 1929; d. Arthur Daniel and Helen Barbara (Rickenmann) New; m. David Vernon Spielman, Nov. 24, 1956; children: Daniel Bruce, Linda Barbara. BS in English and History Edn. cum laude, Miami U., Oxford, Ohio, 1951. Cert. tchr. Ohio, Tex. Tchr. Canton Pub. Schs., 1951-53; vets. aide U. Tex., Austin, 1954-57; copy editor, mng. editor U. Tex. Press, Austin, 1964-91; ret., 1991. Editl. cons. Amon Carter Mus., Ft. Worth, from 1970, Ctr. Mex. Am. Studies, Austin, 1980, Jack S. Blanton Mus. Art (formerly Archer M. Huntington Art Gallery), Austin, from 1975; mem. search com. for dir. U. Tex. Press, Austin, 1991. Editl. cons. Chicago Manual of Style, 13th edit., 1975. Officer PTA, Austin, 1964—73; troop leader Girl Scouts U.S., Austin, 1970—73; editl. cons. 64 Beds Project Homeless and Hungry, Austin, from 1989. Mem.: Seton Med. Ctr. Aux., Althenoi, Smithsonian Instn., Nat. Geog. Soc., Phi Beta Kappa, Sigma Sigma Sigma, Kappa Delta Pi. Democrat. Presbyterian. Avocations: reading, gardening, piano, painting, drawing. Home: Austin, Tex. Died Apr. 11, 2006.

SPIERS, FINN ROBERT CAMILLO, eye surgeon; b. Thisted, Denmark, Sept. 6, 1931; came to U.S., 1983; s. Robert M.T.R. and Nancy A.H. (Auerbach) S.; m. Hanna Kragballe, May 19, 1956; children: Mette, Pernille, Soren, Malene. AB, Aarhus Kathedralschool, Aarhus, Denmark, 1950; MD, U. Aarhus, 1960. Intern Centralsygehuset, Nykoebing F., Denmark, 1960-61, resident gen. surgery and internal medicine, 1961-62, ophthalmology Nykoebling F., Denmark, 1963-64; with Righospitalet, Copenhagen, 1964-65; neurosugery Bisebjerg Hosp., Copenhagen, 1965; 2d chief of staff ophthalmology Rigshospitalet, Copenhagen, 1965-66; pvt. practice Silkeborg, Denmark, 1966-83; dir. rsch. and office mgr. Eye Surgeons and Physicians of Ft. Lauderdale (Fla.), 1983-89; ophthalmologist Hertzler Clinic, Halstead, Kans., 1989-97. Presenter and lectr. in field; tchr. nurse edn. Centralsygehuset, Nykoebing F., Rigshospitalet, Copenhagen; tchr. nurse edn., affiliate Centralsygehuset, Silkeborg; affiliate Centralsygehuset, Viborg, Denmark, Braedstrup Sygehus, Denmark, Kjellerup Sygehus, Denmark, Statshospitalet, Viborg, Skanderborg Sygehus, Denmark, Halstead Hosp., Attica Dist. Hosp. Contbr. articles to profl. jours. Mem. City Coun. of Silkeborg, 1978-82. Surgeon lt. Royal Danish Navy, 1962-63. Republican. Lutheran. Avocations: golf, gastronomy, genealogy, stamp collecting/philately. Home: West Palm Bch, Fla. Died Oct. 19, 2004.

SPIESS, FRED NOEL, oceanographer, educator; b. Oakland, Calif., Dec. 25, 1919; s. Fred Henry and Elva Josephine (Monck) S.; m. Sarah Scott Whitton, July 25, 1942 (dec. Sept. 2002); children: Katherine Spiess Dallaire, Mary Elizabeth Spiess DeJong, John Morgen Frederick, Helen Spiess Shamble, Margaret Josephine Deligio-Spiess. AB, U. Calif., Berkeley, 1941, PhD, 1951; MS, Harvard U., 1946. With Marine Phys. Lab., U. Calif., San Diego, from 1952, dir., 1958-80, U. Calif. Inst. Marine Resources, 1980-88, Scripps Inst. Oceanography, La Jolla, 1964-65, prof. oceanography, 1961-90, prof. emeritus, rsch. prof., 1990—2006; chair U. Calif. Acad. Coun. and Assembly U. Calif. Bd. Regents, 1988-90. Mem. Naval Rsch. Adv. Commn., 1978-81; mem. com. on geodesy Nat. Acad. Scis., 1980-84, mem. ocean studies bd., 2003-05; mem. Def. Sci. Bd., 1976-79; chair Acad. Senate Task Force U. Calif., Merced, 1999-2001. Capt. USNR, 1941-79. Decorated Silver Star medal, Bronze Star medal; recipient John Price Wetherill medal Franklin Inst., 1965; Compass Disting. Scientist award Marine Technol. Soc., 1971; Robert Dexter Conrad award U.S. Sec. of Navy, 1974, Navy Disting. Pub. Svc. award, 1990; Newcomb Cleveland prize AAAS, 1981 Fellow Acoustical Soc. Am. (Pioneers of Underwater Acoustics medal 1985), Am. Geophys. Union (Maurice Ewing award 1983), Marine Tech. Soc. (Lockheed award 1985); mem. Nat. Acad. Engring., Phi Beta Kappa, Sigma Xi. Home: La Jolla, Calif. Died Sept. 8, 2006.

SPIESS, LEONA LOUISE, nurse; b. Odessa, Mo., Mar. 27, 1929; d. Horace Helm and Bessie Marie (Willard) Bell; m. LeRoy Ralph Spiess Sr., Mar. 30, 1946; children: LeRoy Ralph Jr., Leona Marie, Robin Lee, Jerry Dean, Larry Eugene, Beverly Renea. Lic. practical nurse, Area Vocat. Sch., 1978; AA with honors, Kansas City Community Coll., Kans., 1982. Sr. staff nurse Providence St. Margarets Health Ctr., Kansas City, Kans. Adv. bd. Area Vocat. Sch. Mem. AACCN, Phi Theta Kappa. Home: Kansas City, Kans. Died Dec. 1, 2004.

SPILLANE, MICKEY (FRANK MORRISON SPILLANE), author; b. Bklyn., Mar. 9, 1918; s. John Joseph and Catherine Anne S.; m. Mary Ann Pearce, 1945 (div.) children, Kathy, Ward, Mike, Carolyn; m. Sherri Malinou, Nov. 1964 (div.); m. Jane Rodgers Johnson, Oct. 1983. Attended, Kans. State Coll. Scripter, asst. editor Funnies, Inc., in 1940's; co-founder Spillane-Fellows Prodns., Nashville, 1969. Author: (mystery-suspense novels) I, the Jury, 1947, Vengeance is Mine!, 1950, My Gun Is Quick, 1950, The Big Kill, 1951, One Lonely Night, 1951, The Long Wait, 1951, Kiss Me, Deadly, 1952, Tough Guys, 1960, The Deep, 1961, The Girl Hunters, 1962, Day of the Guns, 1964, The Snake, 1964, Bloody Sunrise, 1965, The Death Dealers, 1965, The Twisted Thing, 1966, The By-Pass Control, 1967, The Delta Factor, 1967, Body Lovers, 1967, Killer Mine, 1968, Me. Hood!, 1969, Survival: Zero, 1970, Tough Guys, 1970, The Erection Set, 1972, The Last Cop Out, 1973, The Flier, 1973, Tomorrow I Die, 1984, The Killing Man, 1989, Black Alley, 1996, Something's Down There, 2004; (children's books) The Day the Sea Rolled Back, 1979 (Junior Literary Guild award 1979), The Ship That Never Was, 1982; screenwriter, actor: (films) The Girl Hunters, 1963; creator: (TV series) Mike Hammer, 1984-87; editor: Murder Is My Business, 1994, (with Max Collins) Vengeance is Hers, 1997, Golden Age of Marvel Comics, 1998, Private Eyes, 1998, Century of Noir, 2002; appeared in Miller Lite Beer commls. Served to capt. USAAF, World War II. Named Grand Master, Mystery Writers Am., 1995. Died July 17, 2006.

SPILLAR, PAUL VICTOR, marketing consultant; b. Prague, Czechoslovakia, Jan. 30, 1932; came to U.S., 1941; s. Charles V. and Margaret M. (Mandler) S.; m. Anne C. Stephenson, Oct. 29, 1960 (div. 1974); children: Charles, Catherine. BSE, U. Pa., 1953, MBA, 1954. Dir. advt. and pub. relations Baldwin-Lima-Hamilton, N.Y.C., 1957-63; copywriter Marschall, N.Y.C., 1963-64, Doyle Dane Bernbach, N.Y.C., 1964-65; group creative dir. Cunningham & Walsh Inc. subs. Newcourt Industries Inc., N.Y.C., 1965-67; asst. to pres. internat. group Ted Bates Worldwide Inc., N.Y.C., 1967-70; creative dir. Grey Advt., San Francisco, 1970-72; exec. v.p. Sharp Communications, San Francisco, 1972-79; mng. dir. Export Import Mktg., Burlingame, Calif., from 1979. Served with U.S. Army, 1955-57. Mem. Am. Mktg. Soc. (local bd. dirs. 1972—), World Future Soc., Aviation/Space Writers Assn, Soc. Profl. Mgmt. Conss. (bd. dirs. 1975-85). Clubs: Wharton (San Francisco). Avocations: music, art, travel. Home: Ross, Calif. Died Dec. 2, 2004.

SPITZER, WALTER OSWALD, epidemiologist, educator; b. Asuncion, Paraguay, Feb. 19, 1937; Canadian citizen; MD, U. Toronto, 1962; MHA, U. Mich., 1966; MPH, Yale U., 1970. Gen. dir. Internat. Christian Med. Soc., 1966-69; asst. prof. clin. epidemiology McMaster U., Hamilton, Ont., Can., 1969-73, assoc. prof., 1973-75; prof. epidemiology McGill U., Montreal, 1975-95, prof. medicine, 1983-95, Strathcona prof., chmn. dept. epidemiology and biostats., 1984-93, prof. emeritus, 1996—2006; pres. Methods in Epidemiology, Inc., 1997—2006; clin. prof. medicine Stanford U., 1996—2006. Cons. PanAm. Health Orgn., Washington, 1975, 77, Aga Khan Found., Geneva, 1983-84. Editor Jour. Clin. Epidemiology, 1981-95; contbr. articles to biomed. jours. Named Nat. Health Scientist of Can., 1981 Fellow Royal Coll. Physicians and Surgeons Can., Am. Coll. Epidemiology, Faculty of Pharm. Medicine of the Royal Colls. of Phys. of the U.K.; mem. Inst. Medicine of Nat. Acad. Scis. (U.S.). Avocations: music, sailing, photography. Home: Bath, Canada. Died Apr. 27, 2006.

SPRAGUE, CHARLES CAMERON, medical foundation president; b. Dallas, Nov. 14, 1916; s. George Able and Minna (Schwartz) Sprague; m. Margaret Frederica Dickson, Sept. 7, 1943; 1 child, Cynthia Cameron; m. Alayne W. Nelson, June 12, 1992. BBA, BS, DSc, So. Meth. U.; MD, U. Tex. Med. Branch, Galveston, 1943; DSc (hon.), U. Dallas, 1983, Tulane U., 1991. Diplomate Am. Bd. Internal Medicine. Intern U.S. Naval Med. Center, Bethesda, Md., 1943—44; resident Charity Hosp., New Orleans, 1947—48, Tulane U. Med. Sch., 1948—50; Commonwealth research fellow in hematology Washington U. Sch. Medicine, St. Louis, also Oxford (Eng.) U., 1950—52; mem. faculty Med. Sch. Tulane U., 1952—67, prof. medicine, 1959—67; dean Med. Sch. Tulane U. (Sch. Medicine), 1963—67; prof., dean U. Tex. Southwestern Med. Sch., Dallas, 1967—72; pres. U. Tex. Health Sci. Center, Dallas, 1972—86, SW Med. Found., 1987—88, chmn. bd., CEO, 1988—95; pres. emeritus U. Tex. SW Med. Ctr., 1988—95; chmn. emeritus SW Med. Found., 1995—2005. Mem. Nat. Adv. Coun., 1966—70; mem. adv. coun. to dir. NIH, from 1973; chmn. Gov.'s Task Force Health Manpower, 1981; mem. Gov.'s Med. Edn. Mgmt. Effectiveness Com.; chmn. allied health adv. com., coordinating bd. Tex. Coll. And Univ. Sys.; mem. coordinating bd. Tex. Higher Edn., 1989—95, vice chmn., 1990—96; mem. adv. com. Ctr. Sci. and Soc. U. Tex., Dallas, from 1991. With USNR, 1943—47. Recipient Ashbel Smith Disting. Alumnus award, U. Tex. Med. Br., 1967, Disting. Alumnus award, So. Meth. U., 1965, Sports Illustrated Silver Anniversary award, 1963. Mem.: Assn. Acad. Health Ctrs. (bd. dirs. 1982—2005, chmn. bd. 1985—86), Am. Soc. Hematology (pres. 1966), Assn. Am. Med. Colls. (chmn. coun. deans 1970, chmn. exec. coun. and assembly 1972—73). Home: Dallas, Tex. Died Sept. 17, 2005.

SPRAKER, HAROLD STEPHEN, mathematics and computer science educator; b. Cedar Bluff, Va., May 13, 1929; s. Stephen M. and Cynthia Polly (Cook) S.; m. Betty Jean Conley, Oct. 2, 1954; children: John Stephen, Mark Conley. BS, Roanoke Coll., 1950; EdM, U. Va., 1955, cert. of advanced grad. study, 1959, EdD, 1960. Asst. prin., tchr. math. Richlands High Sch., Va., 1953-57; rsch. asst., assoc. U. Va., Charlottesville, 1958-60, instr. extension div., 1959-60; prof. math. Middle Tenn. State U., Murfreesboro, 1960-67, chmn. dept. math., stats., 1967-92; prof. emeritus of math., 1992—. Served with U.S. Army, 1951-53. Recipient Outstanding Tchr. award Middle Tenn. State U., 1967; NSF grantee, 1957-58. Mem. Nat. Council Tchrs. Math., Tenn. Math. Tchrs. Assn. (statistician), Math. Assn. Am., Pi Mu Epsilon. Lutheran. Avocations: camping, photography, gardening, traveling, reading. Home: Murfreesboro, Tenn. Died Apr. 29, 2005.

SPRATT, GEORGIA A. POTTERTON, children's educational director, parish administrator; b. Manchester, Conn., May 29, 1940; d. George Arthur and Barbara Fenn (Isham) Potterton; m. Edward N. "Jack" Spratt; children: John, Janina, Stephen. BS, U. Conn., 1962, MA in Edn., 1969. Cert. secondary tchr., Conn. Tchr. Bassick H.S., Bridgeport, Conn., 1962; tchr., head home econs. dept. Eastern Jr. H.S., Greenwich, Conn., 1962-71; home econs. instr. Mattatuck C.C., Waterbury, Conn., 1972-76; adminstrv. dir. Garden Edn. Ctr., Cos Cob, Conn., 1982-85, shop mgr., 1985-89, dir. children's programs, from 1993. Lectr. in field. Parish adminstr. St. Saviour's Episcopal Ch., Old Greenwich, Conn., 1989—; vol. Greenwich chpt. ARC Blood Program. Mem. AAUW, DAR (vice regent, local, state, and nat. chpts., past regent Putnam Hill chpt., state chaplain, state membership chmn., recording sec., mem. bd. dirs. Ellsworth Meml. Assn., nat. speaker's staff), Am. Assn. Family and Consumer Svcs. (life), Conn. Home Econs. Assn. (past pres.), Garden Club of Old Greewich (rec. sec., past pres.), Fedrated Garden Clubs of Conn. (life), Navy League of U.S., Nat. Maritime Hist. Soc., Scott Family Assn., U. Conn. Alumni Assn. (life), Old Greenwich Yacht Club (life), State Officers' and Regents' Club (rec. sec., chaplain 1996—). Republican. Avocations: golf, travel, crafts, gardening, reading. Home: Old Greenwich, Conn. Died May 13, 2004.

SPRECHER, DREXEL ANDREAS, retired lawyer, writer; b. Independence, Wis., Mar. 25, 1913; s. Walter Edmund Sprecher and Florence LaVerne Maloy; m. Eleanor Rust Peirce, 1941 (div. 1946); m. Virginia Lee Sprecher, Sept. 24, 1949; children: Drexel A. Jr., Jenna Garman, Karen Maloy. Student, North Ctrl. Coll., Naperville, Ill., 1930—31; BA, U. Wis., 1934; JD, Harvard U., 1938. Bar: Wis. 1938, U.S. Supreme Ct. 1957. Trial atty. Nat. Labor Rels. Bd., Washington, 1938—42; from sgt. to capt. U.S. Army, 1942—46; asst. prosecutor Chief of Counsel for War Crimes, Nuremberg, Germany, 1945—49; asst. adminstr. Small Def. Plants Adminstrn., Washington, 1950—51; writer Chevy Chase, Md., 1972—2006. Pres. Potomac Constrn. Co., Chevy Chase, 1957-59; co-owner Ridgeland Farm Estates, Potomac, Md., 1957-65; pres., v.p. Leadership Resources, Inc., Washington, 1960-72. Author: Inside the Nuremberg Trial: A Prosecutor's Comprehensive Account, 1998 (Ann. List Acad. Titles, Choice Mag. 1999); chief editor: Trials of War Criminals Before the Nuremberg Military Tribunals, 15 vols., 1948-51. Pres. Potomac Dem. Club, 1955-56; dep. chmn. Nat. Dem. Com., Washington, 1957-60. Unitarian Universalist. Avocations: gymnasium exercise, walking. Died Mar. 18, 2006.

SQUIRE, JUDITH MAUREEN, aviation company executive; b. Hollywood, Calif., Nov. 21, 1942; d. James Francis and Virginia E. (Joham) Power; m. Dennis Davis, May 30, 1969 (div. Dec. 1970); m. Robert George Squire, Feb. 10, 1978. AA, Pierce Coll., 1962; BA, Valley State U., 1964. Cert. paralegal. Mgr. Dow Jones & Co., L.A., 1965-70, Power & Assocs., Colorado Springs, Colo., 1970-71; sec., paralegal, mgr. Sklar, Coben, Stashower, L.A., 1971-78; owner Judy's Secretarial Svcs., Ennis, Mont., 1978-89; paralegal, mgr. Ben Johnson Properties, Ennis, 1979-87; ptnr., mgr. Bob's Aircraft, Ennis, 1979-88, Squire Aircraft, Inc., Buhl, Idaho, from 1988, also bd. dirs. Cons. Madison Valley Land Mgmt., Ennis, 1980-88. Mem. Buhl Econ. Coun., 1992. Mem. 20th Century Club (pres. 1991-93, bd. dirs. 1989-94), Idaho Fedn. Women Clubs (scholarship chmn. 1992—, 1st v,o, dist. II 1992-94, pres.-elect dist. II 1994-96, rec. sec. 1994-96), Buhl C. of C. Avocations: reading, gardening, travel. Home: Buhl, Idaho. Died Aug. 20, 2005.

SRINIVASAN, SAMUEL, physiatrist; b. Pasumalai, India, July 17, 1936; s. Appasrinivasan and Ruby Jemima Vethanayagam; m. Victoria Sathianathan, June 8, 1960; children: Reuben, David. MBBS, U. Madras, 1960; FRCS, Royal Coll. Surgeons, 1968. Diplomate Am. Bd. Phys. Medicine and Rehab. Registrar orthopaedic surgery Royal Lancaster (Eng.) Infirmary, 1966-68; surgeon Kalyani Hosp., Madras, 1969-70; orthopaedic surgeon Queen Victoria Hosp., Morecambe, Eng., 1970-73; resident U. Mich. Med. Ctr., Ann Arbor, 1976-79; dir. rehab. R.I. Hosp., Providence, 1979-84; practice medicine specializing in rehab. medicine Saginaw, Mich., from 1984. Asst. prof. Brown U., Providence, 1979-84; chmn. Bd. Physical Therapy, State of R.I., 1981-84. Fellow Am. Acad. Physical Medicine and Rehab.; mem. AMA, Am. Acad. Thermology, Am. Soc., Clin. Evoked Potentials, Am. Assn. Electrodiagnosis and Electromyography, N.Y. Acad. Scis., Internat. Platform Assn. Clubs: Saginaw Country, Centurian. Republican. Episcopalian. Avocations: music, travel, tennis, golf. Home: Saginaw, Mich. Died Aug. 26, 2004.

STAFFORD, MARY ELLEN, university administrator; b. Providence, July 1, 1933; d. Gordon Charles and Clarion Helen (Bachmann) Mackie; m. Rick Stafford, June 16, 1951; children: Charity, Felicity, Christopher. AB, Harvard U., 1971; MA, Met. U., Boston, 1976. Animal caretaker Mass. Gen. Hosp., Boston, 1950-53; clk. N.E. Credit Bur., Boston, 1957-59; dietician Franklin Park Childrens Zoo, Boston, 1961-65; sales clk. Lambert Co., Boston, 1967-69; mem. radiation safety staff Harvard Biology Labs., Cambridge, Mass., 1969-71; rsch. immunologist Boston U. Sch. Medicine, 1971-76, surgery office mgr., 1976-78, adminstrv. coord. surg. residency, 1978-83, admisntrv. coord. surg. edn., from 1983. Owner Marrick Graphics, Allston, Mass.; co-owner Yankee Sarpint. Mem. Country Dance Soc. Boston Centre (pres. 1982), New Eng. Herpetol. Soc. (sec. 1989-90). Avocations: wildlife rehab., quilting, country dancing. Home: Allston, Mass. Died July 6, 2005.

STAGE, RICHARD LEE, consultant, retired utilities executive; b. Byesville, Ohio, Nov. 5, 1936; s. Clifford Earl Stage and Evelyn Virginia (Nunley) Rolston; m. Joan Eleanor Bednarz, Feb. 1, 1958; 1 child, Julie Marie. B in Mgmt., Malone Coll., 1987. Fleet office supr. Ohio Power Co., Canton, 1954-77; supr. automotive acctg. and leasing Am. Electric Power, Canton, 1977-83, dir. fleet mgmt. Columbus, 1983-95; fleet mgmt. cons., Canton, from 1995. Mem. Soc. Automotive Engrs. (chmn. utilities com. 1988-89, exec. com.), Edison Electric Inst. (fleet mgmt. com. 1983-95), Masons. Republican. Avocations: golf, woodworking. Died Jan. 4, 2004.

STAHL, CLARENCE LARRY, researcher; b. Alta., Can., Jan. 19, 1932; came to U.S., 1961; s. Jacob and Emma (Plitt) S.; m. Jean Carolina Carlson, July 24, 1954; children: Sharon F., G. Elaine. BA, Calif. State U., L.A., 1964, MA, 1967. Tchr. English Glendora (Calif.) H.S., 1965-66, Red Bluff (Calif.) H.S., 1967-73. Author: Inherit a Star, 1988. Home: Salem, Oreg. Died Aug. 5, 2005.

STANSFIELD, ROGER ELLIS, chemistry educator; b. Sanford, Maine, July 16, 1926; s. Ernest and Eva (Ellis) S.; m. Audrey May Hasselbacher, Jan. 9, 1929; children: Samuel, Harold. BS, Northwestern U., 1950; MS, Carnegie Tech., 1953, PhD, 1955. Postdoctoral researcher Duke U., Durham, N.C., 1954-56; mem. faculty chemistry dept. Forman Christian Coll., Lahore, Pakistan, 1964-66; prof. chemistry Baldwin-Wallace Coll., Berea, Ohio, 1956—2004, chmn. dept., 1972-90. Moderator Presbytery of Western Reserve, Cleve., 1987. With USN, 1944-46, PTO. Mem. Am. Chem. Soc. (chair Cleve. sect. 1973), AAAS, Ohio Acad. Sci., AAUP. Democrat. Home: Acton, Maine. Died Oct. 17, 2004.

STANTON, SHERRY FRANCES, dermatologist; b. New Haven, Apr. 23, 1950; d. Henry Leopold and Irene Mary (Townsend) Stanton. BA, Wellesley Coll., 1968-72; MD, N.Y. Med. Coll., 1975. Diplomate Am. Bd. Dermatology. Intern medicine Albany (N.Y.) Med. Ctr., 1975-76; resident in dermatology Brown U., Providence, R.I., 1976-79; pvt. practice N.Y.C., from 1979. Fellow Am. Acad. Dermatology; mem. Dermatologic Soc. Greater N.Y., N.Y. State Dermatologic Soc., N.Y. State Med. Soc., Internat. Soc. Dermatology, Women's Dermatologic Soc. Home: New York, NY. Died Dec. 29, 2004.

STAPLETON, MAUREEN, actress; b. Troy, N.Y., June 21, 1925; d. John P. and Irene (Walsh) S.; m. Max Allentuck, July 1949 (div. Feb. 1959); children: Daniel, Katharine; m. David Rayfiel, July, 1963 (div. June 1966). Student, Siena Coll, 1943. Debut in Playboy of the Western World, 1946; toured with Barretts of Wimpole Street, 1947; plays include Anthony and Cleopatra, 1947, Detective Story, The Bird Cage, Rose Tattoo, 1950-51 (Tony award for Best Supporting Actress), The Sea Gull, Orpheus Descending, The Cold Wind and the Warm, 1959, Toys in the Attic, 1960-61, Plaza Suite, 1969, The Gingerbread Lady, 1970 (Tony award for Best Actress), 27 Wagons Full of Cotton, Country Girl, 1972, Secret Affairs of Mildred Wild, 1972, The Gin Game, 1977-78, The Little Foxes, 1981; film appearances include Lonely Hearts, 1959, The Fugitive Kind, 1960, A View from the Bridge, 1962, Bye Bye Birdie, 1963, Trilogy, 1969, Airport, 1970, Summer of '42 (voice only), 1971, Plaza Suite, 1971, Dig, 1972, Voyage to Next (voice only), 1974, Interiors, 1978, The Runner Stumbles, 1979, Lost and Found, 1979, Reds, 1981 (Acad. award for Best Supporting Actress), The Fan, 1981, On the Right Track, 1981, Mother's Day, 1984, Johnny Dangerously, 1984, Cocoon, 1985, Money Pit, 1986, The Cosmic Eye (voice only), 1986, Heartburn, 1986, Sweet Lorraine, Made in Heaven, 1987, Nuts, 1987, Doin' Time on Planet Earth, 1988, Cocoon: The Return, 1988, Passed Away, 1992, Trading Mom, 1994, The Last Good Time, 1995, My Universe Inside Out (voice only), 1996, Addicted to Love, 1997, Wilbur Falls, 1998, Living and Dining, 2003; (TV films) All the King's Men, 1958, For Whom the Bell Tolls, 1959, Save Me a Place at Forest Lawn, 1966, Mirror, Mirror, Off the Wall, 1969, Tell Me Where It Hurts, 1974, Queen of the Stardust Ballroom, 1975, Cat On a Hot Tin Roof, 1976, The Gathering, 1977, The Gathering, Part II, 1979, Letters From Frank, 1979, The Electric Grandmother, 1982, Little Gloria...Happy at Last, 1982, Alice in Wonderland, 1983, Family Secrets, 1984, Sentimental Journey, 1984, Private Sessions, 1985, Liberace: Behind the Music, 1988, Last Wish, 1992, Miss Rose White, 1992; (TV series) The Thorns, 1988; (TV appearances) Curtain Call, 1952, Goodyear Television Playhouse, 1953, Star Tonight, 1955, The Philco Television Playhouse, 1955, Justice, 1955, Armstrong Circle Theatre, 1955, The Alcoa Hour, 1956, Studio One, 1956, Kraft Television Theatre, 1958, Playhouse 90, 1959, Playhouse 90, 1959, Play of the Week, 1961, Car 54, Where Are You?, 1961, Naked City, 1962, The DuPont Show of the Week, 1962, East Side/West Side, 1964, B.L. Stryker, 1989, The Equalizer, 1989, Road to Avonlea, 1995; Author: A Hell of a Life: An Autobiography, 1995 Recipient Nat. Inst. Arts and Letters award, 1969, Actors Studio award, 1980; Named to Theatre Hall of Fame, 1981 Died Mar. 13, 2006.

STARK, NORMAN, secondary school educator; b. Bronx, N.Y., Sept. 15, 1940; s. Martin and Margaret (Neuman) S.; m. Betty Joanne Kelton, Sept. 4, 1994 (dec. May 1998); 1 child, Michelle Allison; m. Lois Marie Ricketson, Dec. 25, 2001. Student, Newark State Coll., Union, 1963-69. Creative writing tchr., acting tchr., singles forum tchr., film tchr. Plantation (Fla.) High Sch., 1988; Hoover Mid. Sch. and Palm Bay H.S., Melbourne, Fla., 1995. Editor West Palm Beach News, 1979; screenplay writer, actor. With U.S. Army, 1963—69. Avocations: reading, puzzles, movies. Died Jan. 31, 2005.

STARR, WANDA MAE, corporate risk manager; b. Spokane, Wash., Aug. 21, 1942; d. Raymond Francis and Helen Mae (Staggs) Conboy; m. James F. Starr, Jan. 26, 1970 (div. Mar. 1986); children: Brian L., Sandra A. Natasha J.L. AA, Wash. State Coll., 1978; student in fin. statement analysis, Inst. of Fin. Edn., Phoenix, 1990-91; student in internat. bus. mgmt., Pima Coll., from 1991. CPCU. Asminstrv. asst. Internat. Sales Div. GTE Corp., Spokane, 1975-79; owner, founder Comml. Group Svcs., Spokane, 1979-86; comml. mktg. mgr. Great Am. Fin. Svcs., Phoenix, 1986-88; risk mgr. Pima Fed. Savings and Loan, Phoenix, 1988-91; pres. Pima Ins. Agy., Phoenix, 1989-91; risk mgr. Burr-Brown Corp, Tucson, from 1991. Dir. CPCU of Ariz., Phoneix, 1990-91; cons. Risk Mgmt. Cons., Phoenix, 1990-91. Com. mem. Cystic Fibrosis Found., Phoenix, 1988-90; rep. com. mem. Nat. Coalition of Ins. Legislators, Phoenix, 1991. Mem. Nat. CPCU (risk mgmt., sect. mem. 1990—), Risk and Ins. Mgmt. Soc. of Ariz. (v.p. 1989-90, pres. 1990-91, Ariz. State Rep. western regional confs. 1989-90), CPCU (Central Ariz. chpt. membership chmn. 1989-90, dir. 1990-91, leadership conf. rep. 1991), Assn. Risk Mgmt. Democrat. Episcopalian. Avocations: photography, interior decorating. Home: Scottsdale, Ariz. Died Apr. 19, 2004.

STASCH, ANN RITA, nutrition educator; b. St. Petersburg, Fla., Sept. 18, 1927; d. E. Robert and Irene M. Stasch. BS, Fla. State U., 1948; MS, U. Fla., 1952, PhD, 1956. Asst. chemist Ga. Experiment (Ga.) Sta., 1956-59; assoc. dir. Home Econs. Rsch., State College, Miss., 1959-62; assoc. prof. N.Mex. State U., Las Cruces, 1962-70; cons. Albuquerque, 1970-73; rsch. assoc. Tex. A&M U., College Station, 1973-74; prof. nutrition Calif. State U., Northridge, from 1974. Coord. grad. programs Home Econ. Dept., Calif. State U., 1978—. Contbr. articles to profl. jours. Fellow AAAS; mem. Am. Chem. Soc., Am. Home Econs. Assn., Inst. Food Technologists. Republican. Home: Reseda, Calif. Died Nov. 22, 2004.

STAVRO, STEVE A., professional hockey team executive; b. Gavro, Greece, Sept. 27, 1927; m. Sally Stavro; 4 children. Chmn., CEO Toronto Maple Leafs, Ont., Canada; founder Toronto City Soccer Club, 1961—66. Decorated Knight Comdr. Knights of Malta; named to Canadian Soccer Hall of Fame, 2005; recipient Ellis I. award, 1991, Order of Canada, 1992, Sovereign award, 1992. Died Apr. 24, 2006.

STEAR, RICHARD LEE, educational administrator; b. Rochester, N.Y., Dec. 6, 1941; s. Robert George and Jean Phyllis (Bentley) S.; m. Sharon Marie Morehouse (div. May 1981); children: Jennifer Lee, Benjamin Preston; m. Kathleen Anne Kubarycz, Aug. 15, 1981; 1 child, Kimberly Anne. AB, U. Rochester, 1963, AM, 1965. Cert. tchr. English 7-12, sch. adminstr., N.Y. Asst. to assoc. dir. residence hall U. Rochester, 1964-65; English master Govt. Coll. Keffi, N. Nigeria, 1965-68; English tchr. Rochester City Sch. Dist., 1968-84, dept. head English, fgn. langs., English as second lang., 1984-90, dir. English and writing, from 1990. Author: (computer programs) CAW: Computer Assisted Writing, 1986, Analyzing and Writing About Literature, 1986, Apply Yourself: Job and College Application Assistance, 1986; contbr. articles to profl. jours. Bd. dirs. Ctr. for Ednl. Devel., Rochester, 1987-91; div. leader United Way, Rochester, 1987—; mem. adv. com. U. Rochester, 1988—. Recipient Excellence in Teaching award N.Y. State English Coun., 1982. Mem. Rochester Tchrs. Assn. (sec. 1979-81, v.p. 1981-83, Exemplary Svc. award 1982), Assn. Suprs. and Adminstrs. of Rochester (pres. 1987—), Sch. Adminstrs. Assn. of N.Y. State (bd. dirs. 1988—), ASCD, Nat. Coun. Tchrs. English. Democrat. Avocations: reading science fiction, magic. Home: Penfield, NY. Died Nov. 8, 2004.

STECKER, THEODORE FRANCIS, radio consultant; b. Castroville, Tex., Jan. 10, 1949; s. Theodore Joseph and Frances (Biery) S.; m. Deborah Pingenot, Sept. 1973 (div. 1980); m. Doris Leone Thompson, Sept. 19, 1981. AA, San Antonio Coll., 1970. Program dir. various radio stations in San Antonio, 1968-77, Sta. WNDU-U. Notre Dame, Ind., 1978, Stas. KHYS-KPAC, Port Arthur, Tex., 1979-80, Sta. WPKX, Washington, 1980-81; ops. mgr. Sta. WKHX, Atlanta, 1981-82; cons., pres. Stecker-Thompson Assocs., Cin., 1982-84, San Antonio, from 1985; ops. mgr. Stas. WBAP, KSCS, Dallas and Ft. Worth, from 1988. Republican. Roman Catholic. Avocations: running, reading. Died Apr. 27, 2004.

STEELE, CAROLYN ANN, secondary school educator; b. Libertyville, Ill., Feb. 1, 1946; d. Charles Allen and Marion Elsing (Decker) Hudson; m. James Howard Steele, June 27, 1970. BS, Bradley U., Peoria, Ill., 1968; MA, Bradley U., 1975; postgrad., Ill. State U., So. Ill. U. Tchr. Bolin Elementary Sch., East Peoria, Ill., 1969-70, Neil Armstrong-Oakview Sch., East Peoria, 1971-85, Lincoln Elementary Sch., East Peoria, 1986-88, Cen. Jr. High Sch., East Peoria, from 1989. Lobbyist, Peoria Coalition; coach Intramural Basketball, East Peoria. Bradley U. grad. assistantship, 1969. Mem. AAUW, NEA, Ill. Edn. Assn., Cen. Ill. Bradley Alumni Assn., E. Peoria Elementary Edn. Assn., Delta Kappa Gamma, Beta Sigma Phi (Woman of the Yr.). Methodist. Avocations: cooking, reading, basketball. Home: East Peoria, Ill. Died Nov. 25, 2004.

STEELE, DIANA MARIE, nurse; b. Branson, Mo., Sept. 24, 1960; d. Benton Leon and Dorothy Mae (Selsor) Craig; divorced; children: Brian, Adam. AS, Penn Valley Community Coll., Kansas City, Mo., 1983. Nurse ICU, gynecol. North Kansas City (Mo.) Meml. Hosp., 1983-84; nurse ICU, shock trauma Suburban Hosp., Bethesda, Md., 1984-85; nurse ICU Potomac Hosp., Woodbridge, Va., 1985-86; nurse ICU and critical care, clin. preceptor Holy Cross Hosp., Silver Spring, Md., 1986-87; nurse ICU Stat Nurse, Silver Spring, from 1988; pub. rels. profl. Regional Computer Svcs. Author publs. in field. Past sec. County Geneal. Soc.; guest speaker and insvc. coord. genealogists; vice-chmn. Colonial Cape Found.; bd. dirs. Women In Need. Mem. Am. Assn. Critical Care Nurses, Phi Beta Kappa (pres. nursing sch. class Kansas City chpt. 1981-83). Avocation: genealogy. Home: Cape Girardeau, Mo. Died May 12, 2004.

STEFANO, JOSEPH WILLIAM, film and television producer, writer; b. Phila., May 5, 1922; s. Dominic and Josephine (Vottima) S.; m. Marilyn Epstein, Dec. 5, 1953; 1 son, Andrew Dominic. Student pub. schs. Pres. Villa di Stefano Prodns., from 1962. Toured as song and dance man in Student Prince, 1945, Merry Widow, 1946; composer music and lyrics popular songs, night club revues, indsl. shows, others, 1946-57; author screenplays The Black Orchid, 1958, The Naked Edge, 1960, Psycho, 1960, Anna di Brooklyn, 1962, Eye of the Cat, 1969, Futz, 1970, The Kindred, 1986, Blackout, 1989, Psycho IV: The Beginning, 1990, Two Bits, 1995, Psycho, 1998; TV drama Made in Japan, 1959, movies for TV, 1970-78; prodr., author TV series The Outer Limits, 1963-64, Swamp Thing, 1990; exec. con. The Outer Limits, 1995—. Recipient Robert E. Sherwood award for Made in Japan, Fund for Republic, 1959, Edgar Allen Poe award for Psycho, Mystery Writers Am., 1960, Columbia award Federated Italo-Ams. Calif., 1964, Pres.'s award Acad. Sci.-Fiction Fantasy and Horror Films, 1987, Movieguide commendation for Two Bits, One of Ten Best Films of 1995; inducted into Cultural Hall of Fame, South Phila. H.S. Mem. ASCAP, Writers Guild Am., Dirs. Guild Am., Producers Guild Am., Acad. Motion Pictures Arts and Scis., Mystery Writers Am. Home: Beverly Hills, Calif. Died Aug. 25, 2006.

STEFFEY, RICHARD DUDLEY, former land use consultant; b. Plymouth, Ind., Apr. 13, 1929; s. Albert Otto and Ethel (Williams) S.; m. Evelyn Jean Brunn, Apr. 5, 1952 (div. Nov. 4, 1985); children: Janet, Diane, Steffey-Smith, Kay; m. Barbara Mae Clark, Nov. 28, 1985. Student, Northwestern U., 1949-51. Mgmt. trainee, mgr. Lockheed Aircraft Corp., Burbank, Calif., 1953-59; asst. mgr., registered rep. Schwabacher & Co., Palo Alto, Calif., 1959-63; v.p. Colby's, Northbrook, Ill., 1963-67; pres. Steffey Fruit Ranch, Temecula, Calif., 1967-85. Dir., pres. Rancho Calif. Water Dist., Temecula, 1974-79, 85— (Distinguished Svc. award 1979); dir. Elsinore Murrieta Anza Resource Conservation Dist., Temecula, 1977-81, 86-90; commr., chmn. Riverside (Calif.) County Planning Commn., 1980-85 (Distinguished Svc. award 1985); commr. Local Agy. Formation Comm., Riverside, 1986—, chmn., 1992. With USAF, 1951-53. Avocations: gardening, hunting, golf. Died Feb. 28, 2005.

STEGER, WILLIAM MERRITT, federal judge; b. Dallas, Aug. 22, 1920; s. Merritt and Lottie (Reese) S.; m. Ann Hollandsworth, Feb. 14, 1948; 1 son, Merritt Reed (dec.). Student, Baylor U., 1938-41; LL.B., So. Meth. U., 1950. Bar: Tex. 1951. Pvt. practice, Longview, 1951-53; US atty. (ea dist.) Tex. US Dept. Justice, 1953-59; mem. firm Wilson, Miller, Spivey & Steger, Tyler, Tex., 1959-70; judge U.S. Dist. Ct. (ea. dist.) Tex., Tyler, Tex., 1970—87, sr. judge, 1987—2006. Republican candidate for gov. of Tex., 1960; for U.S. Ho. of Reps., 1962; mem. Tex. State Republican Exec. Com., 1966-69; chmn. Tex. State Republican Party, 1969-70. Pilot with ranks 2d lt. to capt. USAAF, 1942-47. Mem. State Bar Tex., Masons (32 degree, Shriner). Home: Tyler, Tex. Died June 4, 2006.

STEHLE, JOHN JOSEPH, mechanical engineer; b. Chgo., June 6, 1935; s. Andrew Joseph and Anna Katherine (Springer) S.; children: Thomas Edward, Timothy John. AA, U. Wis., 1957. Sr. devel. engr. R.C. Can Co., Elk Grove Village, Ill., 1963-69; chief engr. Design & Build Co., Palatine, Ill., 1969-72; owner, pres. Best Barricade Co. Inc., Palatine, 1072-74; sr. design engr. Scholin, Inc. Automation, Harwood Heights, Ill., 1974-76; v.p. engring. Chgo. plant Lydall, Inc., Hartford, Conn., 1976-82; sr. applications engr. Westech Automation, Buffalo Grove, Ill., 1982-84; project cons. Tandy/Bell & Howell Video, Northbrook, Ill., 1984-86; pres., owner Mech. Design & Devel. Cons., Elmhurst, Ill., 1986-94; plant mgr., chief engr. Better Bilt Products Inc., Addison, Ill., 1993-94. Patentee in field. With USNR, 1953-58. Recipient Best Energy Conservation Project award ASHRE, 1980. Mem. Soc. Mfg. Engrs. (sr.), Mensa. Avocations: automobile racing, sports cars, stock cars, photography, nature. Home: Hillside, Ill. Died Mar. 24, 2004.

STEIDLEY, ROY BURKE, packaging company executive; b. Oakland, Calif., Oct. 4, 1937; s. Burke Frandsen and Elva Elena (Morales) S.; m. Nov. 28, 1957 (div. 1967); children: Douglas Dayton, Shari Lynn Steidley Stover; m. Elizabeth Ann Rounthwaite, Dec. 5, 1970. BSME cum laude, Calif. State U., Long Beach, 1967. Engring positions Calif. manufacturers, 1958-68; owner, opertor ICN Engrs. & Cons., Long Beach, Calif., 1968-70; v.p. engring. RDW Industries, Irvine, Calif., 1970-71; sr. project engr. McGaw Labs., Inc., Glendale, Calif., 1971-73; project mgr. Springborn Labs. Inc., Enfield, Conn., 1973-80; mfg., engring. mgr. Spaulding, Chicopee, Mass., 1980-81; devel. dir. Ball Plastics Div., Evansville, Ind., 1981-83; dir. of Rsch. & Devel. Ball Corp., Muncie, Ind., 1983-85; gen. mgr. Genesis Packaging Systems, Charleroi, Pa., from 1986. Patentee: 8 patents plastic med. devices, applications, plastic flotation devices, 1960-73. Big brother, Enfield Conn., 1973-81; host family Rotary Club exchange student program, Oakmont, Pa., 1987-88, Am. Field Svc. exchange student program, Oakmont, 1989—. Mem. Soc. Plastic Engrs., Tau Beta Pi. Republican. Avocation: sailing. Home: Reno, Nev. Died July 3, 2005.

STEILING, DANIEL PAUL, retired railroad conductor, writer, geographer, educator; b. San Jose, Calif., June 28, 1944; s. Paul Henry and Lois Kathryn (Barton) Steiling; m. Mary Ellen Scioneaux, Apr. 30, 2004. Right of way agt. Caltrans - Calif. State Dept. Transp., San Francisco, 1969-70; owner Dan's Bicycle Shop, Santa Cruz, Calif., 1970-83; soil inspector Soil Svcs. Inc., San Jose, 1983-84; sr. mfg. specialist disk products divsn. IBM, San Jose, 1984-92; R.R. condr. Amtrak, San Jose, 1993-97; ret., 1997. Substitute tchr. history, geography, sci. Murrieta Valley Unified Sch. Dist., 1999—2001; instr. geography Riverside CC, from 2001. Author: Operation and Maintenance of TRACOR Thickness Measuring Gage (Liquid Nitrogen Cooled), 1987. With USAF, 1966—68. Mem.: Assn. Am. Geographers, Early Ford V8 Club Am., Ford Falcon Club Am., Falbrook Vintage Car Club, Antique Auto Club Am. Avocations: bicycling, photography, auto restoration. Home: Temecula, Calif. Died Dec. 22, 2004.

STEIN, CONSTANCE K., cytogeneticist, educator; b. Berea, Ohio; m. William E. Stein, Jr. BA, U. Calif., Riverside, 1973; MS, U. Mich., 1978, PhD, 1984. Diplomate Am. Bd. Med. Genetics (cert. clin. cytogenetics and clin. molecular genetics). Lectr., course coord. U. Mich., Ann Arbor, 1985, rsch. assoc., 1985-89; dir. cytogenetics, asst. prof. pathology and pediatrics SUNY Health Scis. Ctr., Syracuse, N.Y., from 1989. Fellow Am. Coll. Molecular Genetics (founding); mem. Am. Soc. Human Genetics, Assn. Cytogenetic Technologists, Cancer and Leukemia Group B. Died Oct. 2005.

STEIN, FREDRICK MICHAEL, retired chemistry and physics educator; b. Boston, Mar. 15, 1942; s. Sigmund Magnus and Blanche (Tarlin) S.; m. Claudia Schalm, Jan. 30, 1965; children: Mishele, Lisa. BA in Chemistry, U. Colo., 1964; PhD in Chem. Physics, Ind. U., 1971. With Peace Corps, 1965-67; prof. chemistry Western State Coll., Gunnison, Colo., 1971-81, 83-85, dean, 1985-87; prof. Amherst Coll., Mass., 1981-83; dir. Phila. Renaissance in Sci. and Maths., 1988-91; dir. Ctr. for Sci., Math., Tech. Edn., prof. chemistry Colo. State U., Ft. Collins, 1991-99; dir. edn. and outreach Am. Phys. Soc., Washington, 1999—2004; ret., 2004. Elected fellow of Am. Phys. Soc.; vis. prof. U. Colo., summers 1978-87, U. N.Mex., summer 1982. Author jour. Chem. Physics, 1983, Am. Jour. Physics, 1985, 87, 89, Physics Edn., 2000. Mem. Am. Chem. Soc., Am. Phys. Soc., Philosophy of Sci. Assn., Sigma Xi. Avocations: history and philosophy of science, skiing, sailing. Home: Dillon, Colo. Died Oct. 2005.

STEINER, DANIEL, academic administrator; b. Mt. Vernon, NY; m. Prudence Steiner; children: Elizabeth, Joshua. Grad., Harvard Coll.; JD, Harvard Law Sch. Sec. U. com. governance Harvard U., 1969, gen. counsel. then v.p., 1970—92; adj. lectr. public policy John F. Kennedy Sch. Govt., 1993—96; trustee New England Conservatory, Boston, acting pres., 1999—2000, pres., 2000—06. Died June 11, 2006.

STEINER, GILBERT YALE, political scientist; b. Bklyn., May 11, 1924; s. Isidor Aaron and Fannie (Gelbtrunk) S.; m. Louise King, July 27, 1950; children: Charles King, Daniel Tod, Paula Amy. AB, Columbia U., 1945; A.M., 1948; PhD, U. Ill., 1950. Faculty U. Ill., Urbana, 1950-66, prof. govt., pub. affairs, 1959-66; asst. dean U. Ill. (Grad. Coll.), 1956-58; dir. Inst. Govt. and Pub. Affairs, 1958-66; sr. fellow Brookings Instn., Washington, 1966—89, sr. fellow emeritus, 1989—2006, dir. govtl. studies, 1968-76, acting pres., 1976-77. Staff dir. Chgo. Home Rule Commn., 1954-55; research dir. Northeastern Ill. Local Govt. Area Commn., 1957-63; vis. prof. polit. sci. U. Calif.-Berkeley, 1964-65; Kimball lectr. Brigham Young U., 1985; study dir. Commn. to Recommend Plan for Pub. Higher Edn. in, Ill., 1960; spl. asst. to gov., Ill., 1961-63; cons. Bush Found., Edna McConnell Clark Found. Author: The Congressional Conference Committee, 1951, Legislation by Collective Bargaining, 1951, (with others) Chicago's Government, 1954, (with S.K. Gove) Legislative Politics in Illinois, 1960, Social Insecurity, 1966, The State of Welfare, 1971, The Children's Cause, 1976, The Futility of Family Policy, 1981, Constitutional Inequality, 1985; editor: The Abortion Dispute and the American System, 1983. Bd. dirs. Found. for Child Devel., Manpower Demonstration and Research Corp., Governance Inst. Served with AUS, 1943-46. Social Sci. Research Council fellow, 1957; Ford Found. fellow, 1961-62 Home: Chevy Chase, Md. Died Mar. 1, 2006.

STEINKULLER, JOAN SOMMERS, physician, educator; b. Weymouth, Mass., July 21, 1942; d. Waldo Stepler and Cordelia Lucille (Schmidt) Sommers; m. Paul G. Steinkuller, May 7, 1966; children: Anne-Marie, Paul, John. BA, George Washington U., 1964, MD, 1967. Diplomate Am. Bd. Pediats., Pediat. Emergency Medicine. Attending physician Student Health Ctr. George Washington U., Washington, 1976-77; staff physician USPHS, Galveston, Tex., 1977-80; med. dir. East Africa Women's League Immunization Team, Kenya, 1982-83; cons. Adventist Mission Hosp., Malawi, Africa, 1985-86; instr. pediatrics Baylor Coll. Medicine, Houston, 1987-88, asst. prof. pediatrics, from 1988. Cons. Criss Cole Childrens Fund, Houston, 1993; med. cons. First Bapt. Ch., Houston. Editor: Pediatric Ambulatory Care Handbook, 1991, 95, 98. Ch. nursery dir. First Bapt. Ch., Houston. Recipient Active Tchr. award Baylor Family Practice, 1990, Outstanding Tchr. award Baylor Coll. Medicine, 1992, 95. Mem. Christian Med. and Dental Soc., Alpha Omega Alpha. Avocations: cooking, reading. Died June 15, 2004.

STELLE, LYNN DOUGLAS, travel industry executive; b. Springfield, Ill., Aug. 3, 1949; s. Russell Thompson and Norma Jane (Donelan) S.; m. Peggy Ann Werblin, June 26, 1973; children: Andrew, Benjamin, Michael. BBA, George Washington U., 1971, postgrad., from 1971. Asst. to dir. of Price Commn. Cost of Living Coun., Exec. Office of the Pres., Washington, 1971-74; exec. v.p. Statewide Consumer Corp., Phila., 1974-79; CEO specialized travel divsn. Thomson Travel Inc., Phila., 1979-86; v.p. ops. Apple Vacations, Phila.; founder Stratvis Co.; cons. Pa. Gaming Control Bd., 2003—06. Cons. Thomson Travel Inc., 1978-79; mem. Worldspan-Iris adv. group, Kansas City; bd. dirs. Airport Broadcasting Network, Phila. Producer, dir. (music mktg. video) Music Scene, 1978. Recipient award Music Retailer mag., 1978. Avocations: sailing, antique autos, golf. Home: Media, Pa. Died July 27, 2006.

STENACK, RICHARD JOHN, psychologist; b. Allentown, Pa., Nov. 13, 1945; s. Richard John and Doris May (Dvorshak) S.; m. Elli Elisabeth Smolka, July 10, 1968. BS in Psychology, U. Md., 1975; MA in Psychology, Ball State U., 1976; PhD, Purdue U., 1980. Lic. psychologist, Ohio. Psychologist Lin Ctr., Norwalk, Ohio, 1980-82, clin. dir., 1982-86, dir., 1986-88; pvt. practice Norwalk, from 1982. Mem. staff Fisher-Titus Med. Ctr., Norwalk, 1982—, Firelands Community Hosp., Sandusky, Ohio, 1985—; cons. Catholic Charities, Norwalk, 1988—. Sgt. USAF, 1963-67. Mem. Am. Counseling Assn. Republican. Home: Norwalk, Ohio. Died Apr. 9, 2005.

STENGER, MARTIN LANE, financial planner; b. Dallas, Jan. 13, 1949; s. Tressie Marie (Merritt) S.; m. Miriam Rose Yant, Mar. 5, 1972; children: Jason Alexander, Michael Lawrence, Amanda Marie. AA, Riverside Community Coll., 1969; BA, Calif. State U., 1972. V.p. United Calif. Bus. & Estate, Riverside, 1975-80; prin. Perkins, Stenger, Baird & Staffieri, San Bernardino, Calif., 1980-83; pres. Consol. Westchester Fin., Riverside, from 1983. Contbr. articles to profl. jours. Bd. dirs. Estate Planning Coun., Riverside, 1983—. Mem. Am. Soc. Pension Actuaries, Internat. Assn. Registered Fin. Planners, Internat. Assn. Fin. Planners, Life Underwriters Assn. (pres. 1981). Republican. Mem. Lds Ch. Avocations: stamp collecting/philately, sports card collecting, bowling, golf. Home: Riverside, Calif. Died May 18, 2004.

STENGER, VERNON ARTHUR, analytical chemist, consultant; b. Mpls., June 11, 1908; s. Laurence Arthur and Effie Harriet (Dahlberg) S.; m. Ruth Luella Day, Aug. 2, 1933 (dec. Oct. 1994); children: Robert, Emilie, Alan, Gordon, David; m. Eleanor Miller, Sept. 19, 1996. BS, U. Denver, 1929, MS, 1930; PhD, U. Minn., 1933; DSc (hon.), U. Denver, 1971. Chemist Eastman Kodak Co., Rochester, N.Y., 1929-30, N.W. Rsch. Inst., U. Minn., Mpls., 1933-35, Dow Chem. Co., Midland, Mich., 1935-40, tech. expert, 1940-53, asst. lab. dir., 1954-61, rsch. scientist, 1961-73, cons., from 1973. Chmn. subcom. on magnesium alloy analysis ASTM, Phila., 1941-54. Author: (with I.M. Kolthoff) Volumetric Analysis, Vol. I, 1942, Vol. II, 1947, (with Kolthoff and R. Belcher) Volumetric Analysis, Vol. III, 1957; contbr. 10 encyclopedia articles, 6 chpts. to books and articles to profl. jours. Bd. mem. Midland Symphony Orch., hon. mem. 1990—. Recipient Anachem award Soc. Analytical Chemists, Detroit, 1970. Fellow Am. Inst. Chemists,

N.Y. Acad. Scis.; mem. Am. Chem. Soc. (chmn. com. on analytical reagts. 1967-73, mem. adv. bd. Analytical Chemistry 1953-56, Midland sect. award 1979), Geochem. Soc., Sigma Xi. Baptist. Achievements include patent for apparatus for instrumental determination of total organic carbon (TOC), widely used in water analysis, various analytical methods in industry. Home: Midland, Mich. Died June 21, 2005.

STEPHAN, ROBERT CONRAD, consultant; b. Lancaster, Pa., Feb. 2, 1952; s. Stanley Standish and Ethel Elizabeth (Heinaman) S.; m. Candace Carlyle; children: Kristen Ann, Haley Carlyle, Tara Brooks. BS, Bucknell U., 1974; MBA, U. Pa., 1977. Cert. fin. analyst; registered securities rep. Asst. mgr. Armstrong Cork Co., Lancaster, Pa., 1974-76; mgr. mktg. and planning Conn. Gen., Bloomfield, Conn., 1978-81; v.p. corp. devel. Fidelity Bank, Phila., 1982-84; pres. Corp. Investment Co., West Chester, Pa., 1984-85; v.p. mktg. Firstrust Savs. Bank, Phila., 1986-93; pres. Carlyle Brooks & Co., from 1994. Speaker Am. Mktg. Assn., Washington, DISC Nat. Cash Mgmt., Kansas City, Kans., Bank Securities Assn. Mem. Bank Mktg. Assn., Wharton Alumni Club, Bucknell U. Alumni Assn. (pres. 1976-77), Delta Mu Delta, Omicron Delta Kappa. Republican. Lutheran. Avocations: golf, skiing, triathlons, woodworking, swimming. Died Apr. 16, 2004.

STEPHENSON, BARBERA WERTZ, lawyer; b. Bryan, Ohio, Dec. 10, 1938; d. Emerson D. and Beryl B. (Barber) Wertz; m. Gerard J. Stephenson Jr., June 25, 1960; 1 child, Thomas. Student, Smith Coll., 1956-57; BSEE, MIT, 1961; JD, U. N.Mex., 1981. Bar: N.Mex. 1981. Electronic engr. Digital Equipment Corp., Maynard, Mass., 1960-66; logic analyst Librascope, Glendale, Calif., 1966; electronic engr. Md. Dept. of Def., Ft. Meade, 1966-68; mem. tech. staff Xerox Data Systems, Rockville, Md., 1968; pvt. practice cons., Silver Spring, Md., 1969-78; pvt. practice law, Albuquerque, 1981—2000; ret., 2000. Author: Financing Your Home Purchase in New Mexico, 1992; patentee analog to digital converter, kitchen calculator. Mem. N.Mex. Bar Assn. Home: Albuquerque, N.Mex. Died Oct. 4, 2005.

STEPHENSON, LEONARD MERRIMAN, academic administrator, research chemist; b. Wilmington, N.C., Sept. 6, 1942; s. Leonard Merriman and June (Bryan) S.; m. Mary Jo Grdina, Oct. 27, 1943; 1 child, Lara Marie. BS, U. N.C., 1964; PhD, Calif. Inst. Tech., 1967. Research fellow Harvard U., Cambridge, Mass., 1967-68; asst. prof. chemistry Stanford U., Palo Alto, Calif., 1968-75; assoc. prof., prof. Case-Western Res. U., Cleve., 1975-78, prof., 1978-82; founder, exec. dir. Hydrocarbon Rsch. Inst., 1983; v.p. research and devel. Sybron Chem. Co., Birmingham, N.J., 1983-86; dir. research and devel. Fisher Scientific, Fairlawn, N.J., 1986-87; exec. dir. Camille and Henry Deryfus Found., N.Y.C., 1987—88; founder Biotherm Corp., Fairfax, Va., 1988—95; dir. Commn. on Sci. & Tech. State of NJ, 1994—96; dir. patents & licensing U. Medicine & Dentistry NJ, Piscataway, 1996—2001; vice provost for rsch. & graduate policy Drexel U., 2001—06. Cons. Goodyear Tire and Rubber Co., Akron, Ohio, 1977-82, U. Petroleum and Minerals, Dharan, Saudi Arabia, 1978-79. Contbr. numerous articles to jours. Dreyfus Tchr. scholar, 1974; Sloan fellow, 1975 Mem. Am. Chem. Soc., AAAS Home: West Milford, NJ. Died Aug. 26, 2006.

STEPHENSON, SAMUEL EDWARD, JR., retired surgeon; b. Bristol, Tenn., May 16, 1926; s. Samuel Edward and Hazel Beatrice (Walters) S.; m. Janet Sue Spotts, May 16, 1970; children: Samuel Edward III, William Douglas, Dorothea Louise, Judith Maria. BS, U. S.C., 1946; MD, Vanderbilt U., 1950. Intern Butterworth Hosp., Grand Rapids, Mich., 1950-51; instr. to asso. prof. surgery Vanderbilt U., 1955-67; prof. surgery U. Fla., 1967-95, emeritus prof. clin. surgery, from 1995. Chmn. dept. surgery Univ. Hosp., Jacksonville, 1967-78 Asst. editor So. Med. Jour., 1968-88; contbr. articles to profl. jours. Co-chmn. Fla. Burn and Trauma Registry, 1974-77. Served with USNR, 1944-45. Fellow ACS; mem. So. Surg. Assn., Masons. Home: Jacksonville, Fla. Died May 14, 2006.

STERN, GAIL FRIEDA, professional society administrator; b. Atlantic City, May 18, 1950; d. Herbert and Faith (Beldegreen) Stern; m. Irwin Allen Popowsky (div.); m. Shawn Paul Aubitz (div.); 1 child, Jonathan. Student, Brown U., 1972; postgrad., U. Pa., 1973. Asst. in decorative arts Phila. Mus. Art, 1972—75; asst. curator Wheaton Mus. Glass, Millville, NJ, 1973—74; assoc. dir. Pa. Humanities Coun., Phila., 1976—79; mus. curator The Balch Inst. for Ethnic Studies, Phila., 1979—83, mus. dir., 1984—93; dir. Hist. Soc. Princeton, NJ, 1993—2006. Chair Pa. Task Force on Folk Arts and Culture, 1981-82; vice chmn. crafts panel Pa. Coun. on the Arts, Harrisburg, 1988-89; chair cultural conservation com., Pa. Heritage Affairs Commn., Harrisburg, 1990-92; participant Internat. Partnership in Mus., Singapore, 1991. Recipient pub. programming award, NJ Coun. Humanities, 1996, award for outstanding contbns. to NJ history, NJ Hist. Commn., 1999. Mem. Mus. Coun. Phila. (v.p. 1982-83), Am. Assn. Mus./Internat. Coun. Mus. (bd. dirs. 1991-97), N.J. Mus. Assn. (bd. dirs., sec. 1993-98, John Cotton Dana award 2000), Am. Assn. for State and Local History Awards (N.J. chair 1994-95, 2002-05), Mid-Atlantic Assn. Mus. (bd. dirs. 1997-98). Home: Hopewell, NJ. Died Mar. 20, 2006.

STERN, RUDI, artist; b. New Haven, Nov. 30, 1936; s. Kurt Guenter and Else Emily (Jacobi) S.; m. MOira North (div.); m.Raffaella Trivi, 1 child, Stella; B.A., Bard Coll., 1958; M.A., U. Iowa, 1960. Kinetic light artist, 1964-2006; co-founder, 1969, co-dir. Global Village Video Resource Center, Inc., video documentaries, cons., programs, N.Y.C.; neon artist in sculpture, environments, gallery and workshops, 1972; tchr. neon art Let There Be Neon Workshop, N.Y.C.; tchr. exptl. video New Sch., 1971-73; mus. exhbns. include Lights in Orbit, Milw. and Mpls., 1967, Vibrations, Archtl. League N.Y., 1967-68, Options, Inst. Contemporary Art, Chgo., 1968, Expts. in Art and Tech., Bklyn. Mus., 1968, Theater of Light, Austin Art Center, Hartford, Conn., 1968, Vision and TV, Brandeis U., 1970, Contemplation Environments, Mus. Contemporary Crafts, N.Y.C., 1970, Light/Motion/Sound, Hudson River Mus., 1970, Light Sculpture, U. N.C., 1975; gallery exhbns. include Lights in Orbit, Howard Wise Gallery, 1966, also Festival of Light, 1967; The Visionaries, Easthampton Gallery, N.Y.C., 1967; Art Today, N.Y. State Fair Syracuse, summer, 1967; Fun on 57th St., Howard Wise Gallery, N.Y.C., 1967; Let There Be Neon, 1972; Neon, Hallmark Gallery, 1973; dir. (films) Haiti: Killing the Dream, 1992; also lectr., demonstrations and environments in kinetic light and neon; commd. sculpture for Malcolm Forbes collection, 1968. Grantee Rockefeller Found., 1971, 72, 76, John D. Rockefeller III Fund, 1971, N.Y. State Council Arts, 1970, 71, 72, 75, 76, Nat. Endowment Arts, 1971, 74, 76. Author: Let There Be Neon, 1979, The New Let There Be Neon, 1988. Home: New York, NY. Died Aug. 15, 2006.

STETTLER, JOHN EVERETT, pension fund administrator; b. Ashland, Ky., Dec. 7, 1942; s. Lloyd Everett and Alma Carolyn (Moritz) S.; m. Patricia Alice Frazier, Dec. 31, 1964; children: James Everett, Rebecca Ann, Joel Evan. BBA, Ea. Ky. U., 1967; MBA, U. Ky., 1969. Adminstrv. asst. Ashland Oil, Inc., Russell, Ky., 1969-72, asst. treas., 1973-75, asst. treas./mgr. pension fund investments, 1975-84; dir. employee benefit investments Ga.-Pacific Corp., Atlanta, 1984-85, dir. benefit investments/risk mgmt., 1986-95, sr. dir. benefit investments, 1995-97, v.p. benefit investments, from 1998. Mem. So. Employee Benefits Conf. Republican. Mem. Ch. of Christ. Home: Marietta, Ga. Died Sept. 13, 2004.

STEUBER, GARY LEE, chiropractor; b. Erlanger, Ky., May 23, 1963; s. James Phillip and Virginia Mary (Hoffman) S. AA in Sci., Broward C.C., 1988; D Chiropractic, Life Chiropractic Coll., 1993. Chiropractor Chiro-Care Ctrs., Plantation, Fla., from 1993. Recipient Presdl. Leadership award Phi Theta Kappa, 1988. Mem. Am. Chiropractic Assn., Fla. Chiropractic Assn., Fla. Chiropractic Soc. Avocations: competitive softball, rollerblading, golf, travel. Died Aug. 31, 2004.

STEVENS, JUDY CAROLYN, adult nurse practitioner; b. Tupelo, Miss., Sept. 11, 1949; d. Austin Hollis and Anna Carrie (Clayton) Mask; m. Jerry D. Stevens, Mar. 2, 1969; children: Rhonda, Dale. ADN, Itawamba Community Coll., 1985; BSN, Miss. U. for Women, 1990, postgrad., 1990-91, MSN, 1991. Nurse practitioner Evergreen Clinic, Nettleton, Miss. Mem. Sigma Theta Tau. Home: Nettleton, Miss. Died Nov. 23, 2004.

STEVENS, LARRY LYNN, securities broker; b. Columbus, Kans., June 27, 1944; s. Ransome Edward and Ida Chrystine (Lasater) S.; m. Patricia Sue Kannady, Dec. 27, 1966 (div. Mar. 1986); children: Timothy Wayne, Mark Aaron, Jonathan, Andrew. BA, Okla. Bapt. U., 1966; MDiv, Southwestern Bapt. Theol. Sem., 1969. Ordained to ministry Bapt. Ch., 1968. Pastor Antioch Bapt. Ch., Lebanon, Mo., 1969-72, Mt. Sinai Ch., Clever, Mo., 1972-76, 1st Bapt. Ch., Centerton, Ark., 1976-81, Dora, N.Mex., 1985; receiving mgr. Wal-Mart Stores, Yukon, Okla., 1981-82; chaplain Bapt. Med. Ctr., Oklahoma City, 1982-83; staff chaplain High Plains Bapt. Hosp., Amarillo, Tex., 1984; securities broker Penrod & Co., Nixa, Mo., from 1986. Contbr. articles to profl. jours. Bd. dirs. Ark. Bapt. State Conv., Little Rock, 1979-81. Mem. Assn. Clin. Pastoral Edn., Optimist Club (community chmn. Nixa chpt.). Avocations: fishing, swimming, tennis, gardening, collecting od books. Died Aug. 30, 2004.

STEVENS, MICHAEL JOHN, school system administrator; b. Schenectady, N.Y., Apr. 4, 1949; s. Frank C. and Marilyn E. (Spellman) S.; m. Jean C. Morris, Jan. 22, 1972; children: Todd, Kimberly. AAS in Liberal Arts, Hudson Valley Community Coll., 1969; BS in Elem. and Early Secondary Edn., SUNY, Oneonta, 1971, MS in Edn.Reading and Elem. Edn., 1987; MS in Ednl. Adminstrn., Coll. St. Rose, Albany, N.Y., 1987; postgrad., U. Albany, from 1987. Cert. sch. dist. adminstr., N.Y. Tchr. 5th grade Stamford (N.Y.) Cen. Sch., 1971-74; tchr. 6th grade Shenendehowa Cen. Sch., Clifton Park, N.Y., 1974-84, tchr. gifted and talented, 1984-85, dir. instructional computer svcs. and gifted edn., 1985-89; elem. prin. Stillwater (N.Y.) Cen. Sch. Dist., 1989-93; dir. instrnl. svcs. Shenendehowa Cen. Sch. Dist., Clifton Park, from 1993. Contbr. articles to profl. jours. Life mem. N.Y. PTA. Mem. NAESP, ASCD, Adv. for Gifted and Talented N.Y. State, Sch. Adminstrn. Assn. N.Y. State, Ednl. Adminstrn. Assn., Phi Delta Kappa, Kappa Delta Pi. Home: Clifton Park, NY. Died Oct. 30, 2004.

STEWARD, LYLE MERIDA, II, human resource director; b. Coffeeville, Kans., Oct. 23, 1949; s. Lyle Merida Steward and Marthalin Elizabeth Lowe; m. Auburn Jane Foote, May 21, 1972; children: Douglas Merida, Eric Craig. AB in Edn., Drury Coll., 1971; MA in Interpersonal and Orgnl. Comm., U. Ark., 1984. Tchr. Norfolk (Ark.) Pub. Schs., 1971-73; mgr. Fox's Den, Mountain Home, Little Rock, Ark., 1973-75; cons. 1st Property Mgmt., Little Rock, 1976; mgr. Sports Mart, Little Rock, 1977, Spencer Gifts, Little Rock, 1977-80; instr. Bapt. Med. System, Little Rock, 1980-83, dir., from 1984. Adj. faculty Webster U., Little Rock, 1984—. Cubmaster, com. mem. Boy Scouts, Little Rock, 1986—. Mem. ASTD (treas. 1985-86 Ark. chpt., dir.-at-large Ark. chpt. 1989-92). Avocations: computers, camping, hunting, fishing. Home: Little Rock, Ark. Died Apr. 16, 2005.

STEWART, DONALD BRUCE, actor, singer; b. Staten Island, NY, Nov. 14, 1935; s. George and Marian Stewart; m. Susan Tremble (div.); children: Heather Michelle, Genevra; m. Carol Gemberling, 2005. Student, Hastings Coll., 1953-55, Fla. State U. extension. Tester radio equipment Cessna Aircraft Co. Broadway appearances in Camelot, 1961-62, The Fantasticks, 1962, Student Gypsy, 1963, Anyone Can Whistle, 1965; off Broadway roles in Jo, 1964, Babes in the Woods, 1965, Midsummer Night's Dream; appeared as Sgt. Toomey in Biloxi Blues (Nat. Theater award); starred in The Music Man, Jones Beach Theater, 1979; dir. I Do, I Do, Savoy Dinner Theatre, 1990; film appearances include Where Trail Ends, 1942, Wild Horse Stampede, 1943, Arizona Whirwind, 1944, Carnival Magic, 1981, Lost, 1983, American Ninja, 1985, Future Zone, 1990, Rover Dangerfield (voice only), 1991, Listen, 1996; (TV films) The Doomsday Flight, 1966, Valley of Mystery, 1967, Prescription Murder, 1968, The Betty Ford Story, 1987; (TV series) Guiding Light, 1968-84, 1997; TV appearances The Alfred Hitchcock Hour, Dragnet, The Virginian,1965, 67, Adam-12, 1968, Pros & Cons, Remington Steele, 1985, Santa Barbara, 1985, Our House, 1986, L.A. Law, 1988, Highway to Heaven, 1989, Hardball, 1990, Knots Landing, 1990, Life Goes On, 1990, Beverly Hills, 90210, 1996, The X-Files, 1996, Two, 1996, Profiler, 1997, The Young and the Restless, 1998, JAG, 2001; (mini-series) War and Remembrance, 1988; appeared in numerous concerts with major symphony orchs. including N.C. and Ft. Lauderdale; appeared at Kennedy Ctr.+ Host telethons for Cerebral Palsy, Easter Seals, March of Dimes; also benefit performances Am. Cancer Soc., Fight for Sight, United Jewish Appeal. Served as comdr., SAC USAF, 1956-61; Served as comdr. USNR, 1968-81; ret. comdr. Recipient Disting. Alumnus award Hasting Coll., 1984, Nat. Theater award. Mem. Screen Actors Guild, Actors Equity, AFTRA. Winner TV audience poll as best actor on daytime TV. Home: Santa Barbara, Calif. Died Jan. 9, 2006.

STEWART, NANCY SUE SPURLOCK, education educator; b. Phoenix, Dec. 31, 1933; d. Ernest Neal and Ethel Ora (Boothe) Spurlock; m. Biven Stewart, Dec. 31, 1953 (div. 1962); 1 child, Sally K. BA in Edn., Ariz. State U., 1961, MA in Edn., 1968, Reading Specialist Cert., 1970. Cert. tchr. 1-12, Ariz. Elem. tchr., reading specialist Chandler (Ariz.) Pub. Schs. Dist. 80, 1961-92; instr. Greater Phoenix Area Writing Project Ariz. State U. and Chandler Unified Sch. Dist. 80, from 1983. Mem. AAUW, NEA, Chandler Edn. Assn., Ariz. Edn. Assn., Delta Kappa Gamma Soc. Internat., Kappa Delta. Mem. Ch. of Christ. Avocations: crafts, reading. Home: Phoenix, Ariz. Died Feb. 14, 2005.

STEWART, ROBERT GORDON, former museum curator; b. Balt., Mar. 5, 1931; s. Kenneth Elsworth and Ruth (Chambers) S. Student, Gilman Sch., 1946-49; B.F.A., U. Pa., 1954. Architect Ind. Nat. Hist. Park, Phila., 1954, Nat. Park Service, Phila., 1956-57; architect, curator Jefferson Barracks Hist. Park, St. Louis, 1958-61; dir. properties Nat. Trust for Historic Preservation, Washington, 1961-64; sr. curator Nat. Portrait Gallery, Smithsonian Instn., Washington, 1964-94, sr. curator emeritus, 1994—2005. Cons. Loyalist Homestead, St. John's, N.B., Can., 1960; vis. lectr. George Washington U., 1967-70 Author: Nucleus for a National Collection, 1965, Recent Acquisitions, 1966, A Nineteeth-Century Gallery of Distinguished Americans, 1969, Henry Benbridge (1743-1812): American Portrait Painter, 1971, Robert Edge Pine, A British Artist in America 1784-1788, 1979. Dir. Landmarks of St. Louis, 1959-61; adjudicator Jamaican Nat. Art Competition, 1971; cons. The Papers of George Washington, 1990-98; bd. dirs. Washington Studio Sch., 1997-99. Served with U.S. Army, 1954-56. Mem. Md., Dorchester County, Lewes hist. socs., Walpole Soc., Assn. of Historians of Am. Art, Zeta Psi. Episcopalian. Home: Washington, DC. Died Nov. 17, 2005.

STEWART, THOMAS JAMES, JR., baritone; b. San Saba, Tex., Aug. 29, 1928; s. Thomas James and Gladys Naomi (Reavis) S.; m. Evelyn Lear, Jan. 8, 1955; children: Jan Lear, Bonni Lear. Mus.B., Baylor U., 1953; postgrad., Juilliard Sch. Music, 1953-54, Berlin Hochschule for Music, 1957-58. Appeared with, Met. Opera, Chgo. Opera, San Francisco Opera, Bayreuth Festival, Salzburg Festival, Vienna State Opera, Royal Opera Covent Garden, Grand Opera Paris, Deutsche Oper Berlin, La Scala, Milan, Budapest Opera, Prague Opera, 1960—2006, also major orchs., throughout the world. Mem. hon. coun. IVS S'hertogenbosch, The Netherlands, 1996; artistic advisor Vocal Arts Soc., Washington, 1995; mem. hon. adv. bd. George London Found. for Singers, N.Y.C., 1994. Served with USAF, 1945-49. Recipient Kammersaenger of Berlin, 1964; Richard Wagner medal, 1965; San Francisco Opera medal, 1985, Am. Artist citation N.Y. Singing Tchrs. Assn., 1995; Fulbright grantee, 1957-58. Died Sept. 24, 2006.

STIGLITZ, BEATRICE, French and Italian languages educator; b. Sverdlovsk, USSR, Apr. 24, 1945; came to U.S., 1964; d. Herman and Frieda (Fischelsohn) S. BA, Hunter Coll., 1970; MA, Sorbonne, Paris, 1971; MPH, CUNY, 1978, PhD, 1981. Lectr. Ort Sch., N.Y., 1978; instr. U. Vt., 1979; assoc. prof. French and Italian Univ. Charleston, S.C., from 1979. Translator, interpreter Family Ct., N.Y., 1975-79, U.S. State Dept., 1979, Profl. and Bus. Community Charleston, 1980—; cons. radio and local press; faculty advisor for Model Internat. Leagues/UN Security Coun., Arab League, 1989—. Editor: (French) Annals of Scholarship, 1978-87; contbr. articles to profl. jours. Cons. Spoleto festival Charleston Trident C. of C.; exec. officer Alliance Française Charleston; programming dir., Christian-Jewish Coun. Charleston, 1999-2003. Fellow faculty CUNY, 1973, 76-77; grantee Bd. Higher Edn., 1975-77, Provost Rsch., 1984; faculty scholar NYU, 1970-71; recipient Helen Rubinstein award, 1977, Honors Program award U. Charleston, 1983, 88, 92, 93, Jewish Studies Rsch. award, 1993, Faculty Rsch. and Devel. award 1993, Dept. Rsch. award, 1993, 94, 96, 2000, 02, Honors Program award, 1983, 88, 92, 93, 99, 2002. Mem. MLA, Philol. Assn. of Carolinas, Coun. Liberal Learning, S.C. Com. Humanities, Am. Assn. Tchrs. Italian, Am. Assn. Tchrs. French (cert. of Merit 1967, Disting. Tchg. award 1992), South Atlantic MLA, Malraux Internat. Soc., S.C. Jewish Hist. Soc., Platform Assn., Pi Delta Phi, Sigma Iota Rho, Phi Kappa Phi. Avocations: films, dance, international travel, literature and politics. Home: Charleston, SC. Died Dec. 17, 2004.

STILLMAN, MARTHA, interior designer; b. Chgo., Nov. 8, 1924; d. Frederick Arthur and Eva Mable (Ihle) Niestadt; m. Charles Harvey Stillman, Sept. 6, 1947; 1 child, Ann Elizabeth. Student, Beloit (Wis.) Coll., 1943-45; BS in Interior Design/Architecture, Northwestern U., 1947. Interior designer Interiors - Martha Stillman, New Canaan, Conn., from 1961. Cons. in field. Pres. Wilmette Jrs. Infant Welfare Soc., 1953-60; mem. women's bd. Chgo. Infant Welfare Soc., 1957-60, Women's Rep.; advisor Girl Scouts U.S.A. Mem. Assn. Interior Designers (sec., bd. govs. 1964-75), Am. Soc. Interior Designers, Phi Beta Phi. Republican. Mem. United Ch. of Christ. Clubs: Woodway Country (Darien, Conn.); Skytop (Pa.). Avocations: tennis, golf, fishing. Died Sept. 25, 2004.

STIMSON, RICHARD ALDEN, writer; b. Hamden, Conn., Jan. 18, 1923; s. Frank Giles and Susie Alden (Brown) S.; m. Joan D. Crabb, Apr. 19, 1947; 1 child, Richard Edgar Frank. BA, Yale U., 1943. Chief computer ops. U.S. Naval Hosp., Groton, Conn., 1985-90; asst. prof. fin. Conn. State U., Willmantic and Danbury, 1980-85; assoc. prof. U. New Haven (Conn.), 1980-82; nat. coord. U.S.A., Internat. Simultaneous Policy Orgn., from 2001. Author: Playing with the Numbers: How So-called Experts Mislead Us About the Economy, 1999, (e-book) Thirteen Generations in the New World: Life Styles of the Less Rich and Famous, 2001; co-editor Global Solutions: An Internet Community Takes on Globalization, 2003. Sgt. U.S. Army, 1943—46, maj. Res. ret. Home: High Point, NC. Died Nov. 10, 2004.

STINSON, LAJLA JANE, retired teacher; b. Fergus Falls, Minn., Feb. 26, 1928; d. Charles Gerlinger and Lajla Marie Dale; m. Irvine Cohen, Oct. 7, 1951 (div. 1970); children: Mary Ann, Emily, Lajla; m. Robert Stinson, July 19, 1992. MA, L.I. U., N.Y.C., 1969; BA, Macalester Coll., St. Paul, 1950. Prog. asst. sec. Sloane House YMCA, N.Y.C., 1950-51; rsch. writing Inst. Internat. Edn., N.Y.C., 1951-56; tchr. Shepaug Valley Regional Sch. Dist., Wash., 1969-92. Author: Cat and Dog Series, 1980, The Other Dance, 1988, January Visit, 1989. Pres., Washington-Warren VNA, 1974-78; mem. Litchfield Hist. Soc., Conn., 1987—, Wilderness Soc., Nat. Orgn., 1985—. Mem. Washington Art Assn., Am. Indian Archeol. Inst. Democrat. Avocations: music, hiking, travel. Died Feb. 22, 2004.

STLUKA, EUGENE FRANKLIN, equipment manufacturing executive; b. La Crosse, Wis., May 8, 1938; s. Emil Thomas and Mildred Josephine (Haugen) S.; m. Carol Louise Spicer, Sept. 6, 1958; children: Mary, Frederick, Regina, Thomas, Frank, Jeffrey, Christopher, Monica. BME, Ohio State U., 1963. Mgr. mfg. engring. aircraft engine group General Electric Corp., Cin., 1972-73, mgr. A300 engine program aircraft engine group, 1973-75, mgr. wind energy space systems div. Phila., 1975-77, mgr. mfg. space systems div., 1977-82; v.p., gen. mgr. Florig Equipment Co., Conshohocken, Pa., from 1982. Served to lt. cpl. USMCR, 1956-64. Republican. Roman Catholic. Avocations: real estate investment, sailing, running, personal computing. Home: Annapolis, Md. Died May 12, 2005.

STOBER, MASON FREDERICK, JR., retired air traffic control educator; b. Washington, Mar. 8, 1929; s. Mason Frederick and Georgiana Butler (Joyes) S.; m. Dolores Sylvia Determan, Apr. 18, 1950; children: Mason Frederick III, Mary Catherine. BBS, N.H. Coll., 1968. Lic. air traffic controller, FAA. Enlisted USAF, 1947, advanced through grades to major; grad. to 2d lt. Officer Candidate Sch., 1956; navigator, bombardier B-52D USAF, 1956-70, ret., 1970; air traffic controller Boston Air Route Traffic Control Ctr., Nashua, N.H., 1970-87; instr. Seattle Air Rt. Traffic Control Ctr., Auburn, Wash., 1987-94. Decorated DFC, Air medal with nine oak leaf clusters. Mem. Res. Officers Assn. (life, past pres. Nashua chpt.), Nat. Geog. Soc., Alaska Geog. Soc., Am. Legion, VFW, Mil. Order of World Wars, Air Force Assn., Air Force Hist. Soc., U.S. Curling Assn. (Granite Curling Club), AARP, KC (Grand Knight Nashua coun. 5472, 1972-73, 82-83, coun. activity dir. N.H. state coun. 1974-76, state program dir. 1976-78, cmty. activity dir. 1979-81, state program dir. N.H.), Kiwanis (past pres. Greater Fed. Way chpt. 1993-94), Smokey's. Avocations: golf, curling, fishing, model railroading. Died Nov. 17, 2004.

STOCKEL, IVAR HOWARD, paper industry consultant; b. Minneapolis, Apr. 30, 1927; s. Ivar Hjalmar and Helena Cousland (Mickey) S.; m. Virginia May Vickers, June 23, 1951; children: Anna Christine, Mary Cousland, Margaret Elizabeth. BSME, MSME, MIT, 1950, ScDME, 1959. Asst. prof. U.S. Naval Postgrad. Sch., Monterey, Calif., 1950-54; inst. U.S. Naval Acad., Annapolis, Md., 1954-56; engr. and group leader St. Regis Paper Co., Providence, R.I., 1956-61, mgr. rsch. West Nyack, N.Y., 1961-67, mgr. devel., 1967-68, dir. rsch. and devel., 1968-81; prof. and chmn. chem. engring. U. Maine, Orono, 1981-90; pres. Stockel Cons., Inc., Naples, Fla., from 1981; v.p. Recycle Processes Inc., Naples, Fla., from 1988. Dir. Ind. Rsch. Int., N.Y.C. 1976-78; cons. in field, 1981—. Author numerous tech. articles; inventor several inventions. 2d v.p. Myack Hosp. Bd. Trustees, Nyack, 1977. Lt. Comdr. USNR, 1954-56, ret. Fellow Tech. Assn. Pulp and Paper Ind. (com. chmn. 1980); mem. Tau Beta Pi, Sigma Xi. Republican. Episcopalian. Avocation: sailing. Died May 20, 2005.

STOCKTON, ROBERT STANDEFORD, writer, real estate development, construction, sales and management consultant; b. St. Louis, Aug. 20, 1939; s. George Oliver and Naomi Fleeta (Standeford) S.; m. Sharon Laurise Smith, Oct. 28, 1961 (div.); children: Debra Dianne, Virginia Kathleen; m. Bonnie Le Blanc, July 6, 1974 (div.); 1 child, Katharine Elizabeth. AA, Hannibal (Mo.) LaGrange Coll., 1959; BS, Mo. U., 1961; grad. with distinction, USAF Squadron Officer Sch., 1967, USAF Air Command and Staff Coll., 1976; MA, Cen. Mo. U., 1969; grad., Nat. Def. U., 1980. Commd. 2d lt. USAF, 1961, advanced through grades to lt. col., 1978, mem. Minuteman Missile Intercontinental Ballistic Missile combat crew, 1963-72, comdr., vice comdr. RAF bases, 1979-83; mem. resident faculty USAF Command and Staff Coll., 1976-79; ret. USAF, 1982; asst. prof. Pan Am U., Edinburg, Tex., 1972-75; dir. conf. ctr. U. S.W. La., Lafayette, 1983-85; owner Stockton Homes, Lafayette, 1987-92, Stockton Real Estate, Inc., Lafayette, 1987-92, also bd. dirs. Bd. dirs. Stockton Homes, Lafayette; cons. Mgmt. Concepts, Lafayette, 1983-92. Author: Countdown II: Hiroshima. Pres. La. Jr. Miss, Inc., Lafayette, 1984-85, dir. emeritus, 1983-84. Recipient Community Rels. award U.S. Amb. to Eng., 1980, Lifesaving Recognition award House of Commons/Eng. Ministry of Def., 1982. Mem. Nat. Assn. Realtors, La. Assn. Realtors, Ret. Officers Assn., DAV, Lafayette C. of C. (pres.'s club 1984-85). Republican. Roman Catholic. Avocations: computers, writing, real estate devel. projects. Died May 14, 2004.

STOKES, ELIZABETH HENDON, retired psychology educator; b. Richland, Tex., June 5, 1922; d. Walter Lee and Gertrude Arvette (McCord) Hendon; m. William Glenn Stokes. BS, Sam Houston State Coll., 1942, MA, 1947; Ed.S., George Peabody Coll., 1956; EdD, North Tex. State U., 1960. Lic. psychologist, Tenn.; nat. cert. sch. psychologist; cert. sch. psychologist, Tenn. Field worker Tex. State Dept. Pub. Welfare, Huntsville, Jacksonville, 1942-44; tchr. Richland Pub. Schs., 1945-46, 51-53; appraiser VA Guidance Ctr., Navarro Jr. Coll., Corsicana, Tex., 1949-50; sch. psychologist Clarksville (Tenn.) City Schs., 1955-57; asst. prof. psychology Northwest State Coll., Natchitoches, La., 1957-58; instr. psychology North Tex. State U., Denton, 1959-60; assoc. prof. psychology Austin Peay State U., Clarksville, 1960-63, prof. psychology, 1963-87, pvt. practice psychologist, 1960-87. Pres. Tenn. Assn. of Counselor Educators, 1966-67. Contbr. articles to profl. jours. Organizer, sponsor Saturday Recreation Program for Retarded, Clarksville, 1962-87; chmn. Human Rels. Coun., Clarksville, 1969-71; bd. dirs. Day Care Ctr., Clarksville, 1983-86; mem., officer Montgomery County Coun. for Retarded Citizens, Clarksville, 1960-87; vol. Austin (Tex.) Police Crisis Ctr., 1988-89. vol. instrn. parenting classes for low-income parents, Austin, 1988-91. Named Educator of Yr. Tenn. Assn. Retarded Citizens, 1975-76, Outstanding Retiring Educator, Phi Delta Kappa, Austin Peay Ch., 1986-87; recipient Award for Disting. Community Svc., Clarksville C. of C., 1986. Mem. APA, Nat. Assn. Sch. Psychologists (newsletter editor, v.p. 1975-85, bd. dirs., pres., 1978-79, ann. Beth Stokes award for Outstanding Sch. Psychology 1987—). Avocations: travel, bridge, gardening. Home: Austin, Tex. Died Dec. 11, 2004.

STOLBA, K. MARIE, music educator; d. John Nickalos and Elsie Helena Marie Stolba. BA magna cum laude, Monmouth Coll., 1944, DHL (hon.), 1990; MA, U. No. Colo., 1952; PhD, U. Iowa, 1965. Cert. tchr. Iowa. H.S. tchr. Sperry (Iowa) Consol. Schs., 1946—48; H.S. and music tchr. West Burlington (Iowa) Pub. Schs., 1948—64; asst. prof. music Kellogg C.C., Battle Creek, Mich., 1965—67, Ft. Hays (Kans.) State Coll., 1967—71; music tchr. Grace Coll. and Word, Inc., Winona Lake, Ind., 1972—73; full prof. Ind.-Purdue U., Ft. Wayne, 1973—89; vis. prof. Colo. Christian U., Lakewood, from 1990. Permissions/royalties Rodeheaver Co./Word Music, Inc., Winona Lake, Ind., 1972—78; music dir. North Highlands Presbyn. Ch., Ft. Wayne, 1989—96, Grace Presbyn. Ch., Ft. Wayne, 1996—2004; lectr. in field. Author: A History of the Violin Etude, 1967, 1978, Bruni: Caprices & Airs Varies and Cinquante Etudes, 1982, Facsimile of Manscript of J.S. Bach's Sonaten und Partiten fur Violine Allein, 1982, Development of Western Music: History, 1990, 1994, 1998, Development of Western Music: An Anthology, 1990, 1994, 1998, Sigma Alpha Iota (Centenial History), 2003; contbr. articles to profl. jours. Mem.: PEO (pres.), Bach Collegium-Ft. Wayne (bd. dirs., pres. from 2002), Sigma Alpha Iota, Pi Kappa Lambda. Presbyterian. Avocation: violin. Home: Fort Wayne, Ind. Died May 18, 2005.

STOLBERG, ERNEST MILTON, retired environmental engineer, consultant; b. Balt., Aug. 7, 1913; s. Edward B. and Marie S. Stolberg; m. Doris Pearl Goodman, June 1, 1947; children: Barbara, Arnold. B of Engring., Johns Hopkins U., 1937, M in Environ Engring., 1969. Registered profl. engr., Pa., Ohio, Md. Engr., draftsman U.S. Army, Aberdeen, Md., 1939-42; chief mech. engr. Housing Authority Balt., 1947-56; chief plant engr. long range planning Westinghouse Electric Corp., Pitts., 1957-59; chief plant engr. Comml. Shearing Co., Youngstown, Ohio, 1959-67; mech. engr. U.S. Army, Odenton, Md., 1967-72, Exxon, Odenton, 1972-76; chief mech. engr. Washington Govt., 1976-77; environ engr. value analysis U.S. VA, Washington, 1977-85; environ and energy cons. rsch. divsn. dept. legis. reference Md. State Legislature, Annapolis, 1987-90. Contbr. articles to profl. jours. Lt. comdr. USNR, 1942-46, ETO, PTO, NATOUSA. Named Distinguished Toastmaster, Toastmasters Internat., 1983. Mem. ASME (life, chmn. 1975-76, cert. of appreciation 1977), Am. Inst. Plant Engrs. (chmn. 1962), Nat. Wildlife Fedn., Nat. Geog. Soc., Md. Soc. Profl. Engrs. (chmn. 1972, Outstanding Svc. award 1983), Cousteau Soc., People for Am. Way, Nat. Assn. Ret. Fed. Employees (chmn. Randallstown, Md. chpt.), Common Cause, Sierra Club. Democrat. Jewish. Achievements include invention promoting boiler burner safety. Home: Chicago, Ill. Died July 13, 2005.

STONE, DUANE SNYDER, school psychologist, clergyman; b. Turon, Kans., Nov. 10, 1935; s. Herman and Neva F. (Snyder) S.; m. Nancy R. Castillo, July 12, 1958; children: Patricia L. Stone Davis, Christopher D. AA, Graceland Coll., 1953; BA, San Jose State U., 1959, MA, 1961; EdS, Wichita State U., 1985. Ordained to ministry Reorganized LDS Ch., 1951. Tchr., adminstr., supt. Santa Clara County Schs., San Jose, Calif., 1959-63; commd. 2d lt. USAF, 1963, advanced through grades to maj., 1974, security police officer Altus AFB, Okla., 1963-66, instr. Officer Tng. Sch. Lackland AFB, Tex., 1966-69, base def. officer 35 TRW Phan Rang Air Base, Vietnam, 1969-70; asst. prof. aerospace sci. Memphis State U. AFROTC, 1970-73; comdr. security police squadron USAF, Minot AFB, ND, 1973-76; clin. psychologist 91st Regional Hosp. USAF, Minot AFB, 1976-83; ret., 1983; sch. psychologist Wichita (Kans.) Pub. Schs., 1985-86, Butler County Sch. Bd., El Dorado, Kans., from 1986. Pres. Reality Theapy Assocs., Wichita, 1983—. Author: The Ministry of Health and Healing, 1986, Ministry to Persons with Debilitating Lifestyles, 1988. Treas. Springhaven, Andover, Kans., 1955—. Recipient award Reorganized LDS Ch., 1995. Mem. NASP (cert.), DAV, NRA, Ret. Officers Assn. Avocations: flying, photography. Home: Wichita, Kans. Died Jan. 11, 2006.

STORY, MONTE ROBERT, lawyer; b. Edmore, Mich., May 18, 1931; s. Charles and Helen R. (Brown) S.; m. Barbara Brooks, June 27, 1953; children: Julie Kay Story-Wood, Bret C. BA, Mich. State U., 1953; JD, Detroit Coll. Law, 1970. Bar: Mich. 1970, U.S. Tax Ct. 1971. Ptnr. Lyle D. Hepfer & Co., CPA's, Lansing, Mich., 1953-64, Danielson, Story, Lake & Schultz, Lansing, 1964-71; chmn. bd. dirs. Farhat & Story PC, East Lansing, Mich., from 1971. Capt. USAFR, 1954-66. Mem. ABA, Am. Inst. CPA's, Mich. Assn. CPA's, Mich. State Bar Assn., Ingham County Bar Assn. Republican. Lutheran. Home: Haslett, Mich. Died Aug. 6, 2005.

STOUT, LINDA KAY, elementary school educator; b. Marshall, Mo., Sept. 6, 1944; d. David Fowler and May Marchess (Neff) S. BS in Edn., Ohio State U., 1966; MEd, Bowling Green State U., 1977; postgrad., U. Toledo, from 1995. Tchr. 5th grade Battle Creek (Mich.) Pub. Schs., 1966-67; tchr. 4th grade Sylvania (Ohio) Schs., 1967-79, tchr. 5th grade, from 1979. Peer leader, instr. Summer Inst. Reading Intervention, Ohio, 2001—03; tchr. edn. adv. com. Bowling Green State U., Ohio, from 1980; presenter in field. Past advisor 4-H, Toledo; written composition coord. Sylvania Schs., 1997-98; regional problem capt. and trainer for spontaneous Odyessy of the Mind, 1995-98. Jennings scholar, 1988—89. Mem. IRA, Nat. Coun. Tchrs. English, Ohio Coun. Tchrs. English Lang. Arts, Ohio Coun. IRA (chmn. mid. sch. literacy com., conf. com. 2003), Toledo Coun. IRA (past treas., past pres.) Home: Sylvania, Ohio. Died May 4, 2005.

STOUT, LOWELL, lawyer; b. Tamaha, Okla., July 23, 1928; s. Charles W. and Rosetta (Easley) S.; m. Liliane Josue, Nov. 29, 1952; children: Georgianna, Mark Lowell. Student, Northeastern State Coll., Tahlequah, Okla., 1946-49, U. Okla., 1949-51; LLB, U. N.Mex., 1952. Bar: N.Mex. 1952. Ptnr. Easley, Quinn & Stout, Hobbs, N.Mex., 1954-58, Girand & Stout, Hobbs, 1958-60; pvt. practice Hobbs, 1960-80; ptnr. Stout & Stout, Hobbs, from 1980. With U.S. Army, 1952-54. Perenially listed in Best Lawyers in America; named to Roehl Circle of Honor, 2002. Fellow Am. Coll. Trial Lawyers; mem. Assn. Trial Lawyers Am., State Bar N.Mex., N.Mex. Trial Lawyers Assn., Lea County Bar Assn. Home: Hobbs, N.Mex. Died Apr. 18, 2005.

STOUT, WAYNE EVERETT, minister; b. Indpls., Sept. 1, 1930; s. Everett and Mable (Grove) S.; m. Patricia Ann Mauler, Sept. 2, 1948; children: Timothy, Cynthia. BTh, Berean Bible Coll., 1960. Ordained to ministry Ch. of God (Anderson, Ind.), 1960. Pastor 1st Ch. of God, Greenfield, Ind., 1960-72, Portageville, Mo., 1972-79, Norfolk, Va., from 1979. Chmn. Mo. Assembly, Ch. of God, 1978-79, Va. Assembly, Wise, 1986-88, 89-90; chmn. adminstrv. com. Ch. of God Bd. Pensions, Anderson, 1979-90. Bd. dirs. Boys Club Am., Greenfield, 1969-72; mem. adv. bd. Lifenet, Virginia Beach, Va., 1990. Home: Olathe, Kans. Died Mar. 24, 2005.

STOWE, ROBERT ALLEN, catalytic and chemical technology consultant; b. Kalamazoo, July 26, 1924; s. Allen Byron Stowe and Doris Alfreda (Wood) Stowe Weber; m. Dorothea May Davis, Aug. 23, 1947 (div. 1973); children: Michael, Randall, Catherine, Robert; m. Marion June Smith, Oct. 20, 1973 (div. 1980). AB, Kalamazoo Coll., 1948; PhD, Brown U., 1953. Phys. chemist Dow Chem. Co., Midland, Mich., 1952-58, rsch. chemist Ludington, Mich., 1958-64, sr. rsch. chemist, 1964-69, Midland, 1969-72, assoc. scientist, 1972-88; ret., 1988; pres. Bobcat Techs. Ltd., Cross Village, Mich., from 1988; sr. consulting assoc. Omnitech Internat. Ltd., Midland, from 1989; bd. dirs., mem. oper. bd., chief scientist Van Tek Corp. (formerly VF Sales), Midland, from 1990; v.p. tech. Van Tek Corp., Midland, Mich., from 1999. Chief exec. scientist Environ. Assessments Ltd., Midland, 1990—. Contbr. articles to sci. jours.; numerous patents in U.S. and fgn. countries. Treas. Ludington Bd. Edn., 1960-63, pres., 1963-68. With USAAF, 1943-45; mem. Nat. Ski Patrol. Recipient Victor J. Azbe award Nat. Lime Assn., 1964. Fellow Am. Inst. Chemists (cert. profl. chemist); mem. Am. Chem. Soc. (program sec. divsn. indsl. and engring. chemistry 1972-82, chmn. 1982-83, councilor 1986—, sec. gen. Catalysis Secretariat 1990, 94, Joseph P. Stewart award 1984), N.Am. Catalysis Soc., N.Am. Thermal Analysis Soc., Mich. Catalysis Soc. (sec.-treas. 1987-88, pres. 1988-89, Guisseppe Parravano Meml. award 2000). Avocations: tennis, skiing, sailing. Died Sept. 9, 2004.

STOWELL, JAY LEROY, communications specialist; b. Spokane, Wash., Nov. 29, 1940; s. David Jay and Roberta Grace (Edson) S.; m. Martha Jo Spurlin, June 30, 1973. BA, Eastern Wash. State U., 1963; student, U.S. Army Security Agy., Fort Devens, Mass., 1964, Western Coll. of Electronics, 1968, Miami Bible Coll., 1969, John O'Connell Sch., San Francisco, 1972-73, Computer Learning Ctr., 1984-85. Resident engr. Blue Ridge Broadcasting, Black Mountain, N.C., 1970-72; mgr. WLTR FM S.C. Ednl. TV, Columbia, 1973-77; asst. chief engr., announcer Sta. KRDU, Sta. KLTA-FM, Dinuba, Calif., 1977-82; mgr. trainee Radio Shack, Alameda, Calif., 1983-84; communications specialist NASA, Moffett Field, Calif., from 1984. Served with U.S. Army, 1964-67. Recipient cash prize Army Security Agy. Incentive Award Com., Taiwan. Mem.: Ames Amateur Radio, Moffett Field. Baptist. Avocation: amateur radio. Home: Lacey, Wash. Died July 17, 2005.

STOYANOFF, EDWARD MICHAEL, college administrator; b. Gary, Ind., Sept. 14, 1939; s. Nicholas and Sonia (Druinsky) S.; children: Michael Edward, Steven B., Jeffrey Alan. Student, North Cen. Coll., Naperville, Ill., 1958-59; B in Journalism, U. Mo., 1961; MAT, Northwestern U., 1963, postgrad., 1974, No. Ill. U., 1966, Rockford (Ill.) Coll., 1966-71. Sports editor Suburban Life Newspaper, LaGrange Park, Ill., 1961-62; tchr. English and journalism Highland Park (Ill.) High Sch., 1963-64, Niles West High Sch., Skokie, Ill., 1964-66; assoc. prof. English, asst. dean community svcs. Rock Valley Community Coll., Rockford, 1966-74; dir. univ. rels. U. Minn., Crookston, 1974-81; dir. info. svcs. Kishwaukee Community Coll., Malta, Ill., from 1983. City news reporter Rockford Morning Star, 1968; ptnr. in cons. Bus.-Industry -Edn. Cons., Rockford, 1969-71; editor, evaluator Dissertation Rev. Svcs., Rockford, 1982—. Contbr. numerous articles to mags. and newspapers. Trustee Polk County Pub. Libr. Bd., Crookston, 1978-81; active in several polit. campaigns, Rockford; chmn. edn. task force Forward Rockford, 1970-73; pres. Kishwaukee Coll. Senate, 1989-90. Mem. Nat. Coun. Mktg. and Pub. Rels., Phi Kappa Alpha, Sigma Rho Sigma, Phi Delta Kappa (founding pres. Rockford chpt. 1969, life). Unitarian Universalist. Avocations: tournament duplicate bridge, golf, travel. Home: Rockford, Ill. Died Oct. 6, 2004.

STRATTON, JULIUS AUGUSTUS, psychologist, consultant; b. Norfolk, Va., July 9, 1924; s. Julius Augustus and Annie (Thornton) S. BS, Hampton U., Va., 1947; MEd, Cornell U., 1957; postgrad., Harvard U., 1966-67, U. Chgo., 1965. Instr., chmn. dept. counseling Roosevelt High Sch., Gary, Ind., 1952-68; assoc. faculty Ind. U. N.W., Gary, 1971-74; research dir. Gary Sch. Corp., 1968-76; v.p. Cornell Urban Cons., Chgo., from 1976. Author: Nonintellectual Factors Associated with Academic Achievement, 1957; contbr. articles to profl. jours. Mem. Nat. Coun. Tchrs. of Math., Assn. for Measurement and Evaluation in Counseling & Devel., Alpha Phi Alpha, Phi Delta Kappa, Sigma Gamma Mu. Democrat. Episcopalian. Avocations: opera, art, computer telecommunications. Home: Gary, Ind. Died Aug. 11, 2005.

STRAUSS, HERBERT ARTHUR, foundation administrator, history educator; b. Würzburg, Germany, June 1, 1918; came to U.S., 1946, naturalized, 1952; s. Benno and Magdalena (Hinterneder) S.; m. Lotte F. Schloss, Mar. 24, 1944; 1 child, Jane Helen. Grad., Hochsch Wissenschaft des Judentums, Berlin, 1942; PhD in European History summa cum laude, U. Berne, Switzerland, 1946; postgrad., Columbia U., 1949-51. Rsch. fellow Commn. European Jewish Reconstruction, 1946-48; tchr. religion sch. Congregation Habonim, 1946-48; lectr., instr. CUNY, 1948-54, asst., then assoc. prof. history dept., 1960-71, prof., 1971-82, prof. emeritus, from 1982; asst., then assoc. prof. acad. dept Juilliard Sch., N.Y.C., 1954-60; dir. Zentrum für Antisemitismusforschung, prof. Technische U., Berlin, 1982-90, prof. emeritus, 1990. Fellow grad. faculty New Sch. for Social Rsch., N.Y.C., 1949-51; hon. mem. Technische U., Berlin, 1990. Editor: Jewish Immigrants of the Nazi Period in the U.S.A., 8 vols., 1978-92, A.F.J.C.E. Lerntag series; co-editor: Jubilee Volume Dedicated to Curt S. Silberman, 1969, Gegenwat im Rückblick: Festgabe für die Jüdische Gemeinde zu Berlin, 1970, International Biographical Dictionary of Central European Emigres, 1933-1945, 3 vols., 1980-83, Current Research on Autisemitism, 1987—, 4 vols.; contbr. numerous articles in field; appeared in Bavarian T.V. film Herbert Strauss, Flüchtling (Am. title We Were German Jews). Exec. v.p. Am. Fedn. Jews from Ctrl. Europe, N.Y.C., 1964-86; founder, sec., rsch. coord., dir. Rsch. Found. Jewish Immigration, 1972—; sec. Jewish Philanthropic Fund of 1933, 1970—; bd. dirs. N.Y. Found. Nursing Homes, 1975-91, M. Tietz Ctr. Nursing Care, Selfhelp, Blue Card, United Help; mem. presidium Coun. Jews from Germany; rep. of Jewish refugees, Berne, 1944-46; alt. mem. Jewish del. to Flüchtlingsvertretung der Schweiz, 1945-46; mem. Swiss del. to conf. World Union for Progressive Judaism, London, 1946. Fellow and grantee Meml. Found. Jewish Culture, 1956, 60, 63, Am. Coun. Learned Socs., 1963, SOc. Sci. Rsch. Coun., 1963; fellow USPHS, 1949-51. Fellow Leo Baeck Inst. (bd. dirs. 1965-92). Home: New York, NY. Died Mar. 11, 2005.

STRAWSER, NEIL EDWARD, broadcasting news reporter; b. Rittman, Ohio, Aug. 16, 1927; s. Joseph E. and Mamie Rice Christian S.; m. Salea Atwell, 1982; children—Neil Edward, Chris, Jay, Stuart, Clara. BA, Oberlin Coll., 1951; MA in History, George Washington U., 1958. Disc jockey, announcer local news radio sta. WEOL, Elyria, Ohio, 1950-51, radio sta. WATG, Ashland, Ohio, 1951-52; editorial research asst. CBS News, Washington, 1952-56, corr., 1956—86; press officer Ho. Budget Com., Washington, 1987—94. Served with USNR, 1945-48. Mem.: Congressional Country, Washington Press. Home: Washington, DC. Died Dec. 31, 2005.

STRAWSON, SIR PETER FREDERICK, philosophy educator; b. London, Nov. 23, 1919; s. Cyril Walter and Nellie Dora (Jewell) S.; m. Grace Hall Martin, Oct. 27, 1945; children: Julia Katharine, Galen John, Robert Neville, Virginia Ann. MA, Oxford U., 1940; Dr. (hon.), Munich U., 1998; Dr. (hon.), Sofia U., 2003. Lectr. Univ. Coll. N. Wales, Bangor, 1946-47, Univ. Coll., Oxford, 1947-48, fellow, 1948-68; prof. metaphysics Magdalen Coll., Oxford U., 1968-87, prof. emeritus, from 1987. Lectr., vis. prof. in many countries, including U.S.A., Can., Argentina, Mex., India, Israel, Yugoslavia, France, Fed. Republic Germany, Belgium, Spain, China, Czech Republic, Bulgaria. Author: Introduction to Logical Theory, 1952, Individuals, 1959, The Bounds of Sense, 1966, Logico-Linguistic Papers, 1971, Freedom and Resentment, 1974, Subject and Predicate in Logic and Grammar, 1974, Scepticism and Naturalism: Some Varieties, 1985, Analyse et Mètaphysique, 1985, Analysis and Metaphysics, 1992, Entity and Indentity, 1997, Autobiography and Replies to Critics in the Philosophy of P.F. Strawson, 1998. Served as capt. Brit. Army, 1940-46, U.K., Italy, Austria. Created knight bachelor, 1977; scholar St. John's Coll., Oxford, 1937-40. Fellow Brit. Acad.; mem. Am. Acad. Arts and Scis. (fgn. hon.), Acad. Europaea, Mind Assn., Aristotelian Soc. (pres. 1969-70), Athenaeum Club (London, Internat. Kant prize Berlin, 2000). Avocations: walking, travel, reading. Home: Oxford, England. Died Feb. 13, 2006.

STREETON, JACQUI, portrait artist, medical illustrator; b. Columbus, Ohio, Oct. 29, 1943; divorced; 1 child, Lisa Maria. Surg. technician cert., Erlanger Hosp., 1967; AA, Cleveland Community Coll., 1986, AS in Pre-Medicine, 1986. Tchr. art George R. Stuart Elem. Sch., Cleveland, Tenn., 1970-73; med. educator, artist Epilepsy Found. Chattanooga, from 1989. Portrait commns. include Dr. Christian Beard, 1982, Rex Dockery memoria portrait, 1985, Ronald Reagan, 1986, Nina Craigmiles, 1991. Avocations: volunteer for epilepsy foundation, writing, painting flowers, travel, ti chi chaun. Died July 15, 2005.

STREETT, JAMES KENNETH, small business owner; b. Balt., July 31, 1927; s. Marshall Bernard and Mabel Victoria (Hollins) S.; m. Jean Elizabeth Potter, June 6, 1952 (dec. July 1965); children: Suzanne Whitmore, Carol Nabakowski, David, Nancy Cackling; m. Shirley Anne McCraven, Aug. 20, 1966; 1 child, Matthew. BS, U.S. Naval Acad., 1952; MS in Aero. Engring., U. Mich., Ann Arbor, 1958, MS in Instrumentation Engring., 1958. Commd. 2d. lt. USAF, 1952, advanced through ranks to col., 1972, electronic engr., electronic systems div., 1966-67; asst. ops. officer 21st Helicopter Squadron USAF, Nakhon Phanom, Thailand, 1967-68; chief, office of engring. Def. Contract Adminstrv. Region USAF, N.Y.C., 1968-71; chief, aircraft engring. div. Hdqrs. SAC, Offutt AFB, Nebr., 1972-82; retired USAF, 1982; owner, mgr. Bellevue (Nebr.) Solar, from 1982. Craftsman, artist constrn. of high altar at St. Martin of Tours Episc. Ch., Omaha, Nebr., 1985. Mem. dept. missions Episc. Diocese of Nebr., 1984—; acolyte warden Episc. Ch. of the Holy Spirit, Bellvue, 1980—. Named to Legion of Merit USAF. Mem. Kiwanis Club. Republican. Avocation: church activities. Died Aug. 28, 2004.

STREIDL, ISABELLE ROBERTS SMILEY, economist; b. Glen Ridge, N.J., Nov. 7, 1913; d. Orton Ray and Louise Roberts (Speer) Smiley; m. Edward G. Streidl, Apr. 8, 1939 (dec. Sept. 1983); children: Nancy Louise, Linda Jeanne. BA cum laude, Mt. Holyoke Coll., 1935. Clk. VA, Washington, 1936; statis. clk. bur. of labor stats. U.S. Dept. Labor, Washington, 1936-39, sr. examining clk. children's bur., 1939-42, asst. child labor report analyst, 1942-45, child labor report analyst, 1945-46, labor economist women's bur., 1962-65, chief br. labor force rsch. women's bur., 1965-67, chief divsn. econ. status and opportunities, 1967-74. Mem. AAUW. Avocations: bridge, sewing, knitting. Home: Carlisle, Pa. Died Apr. 12, 2005.

STRINGFELLOW, DALE A., virologist; b. Centerville, Utah, Sept. 13, 1944; s. Paul Bennion and Jean (Barton) S.; m. Jean Racker, June 17, 1965; children: Jennifer, Wendy, Ashley. BS, U. Utah, 1967, MS, 1970, PhD, 1972. Instr. U. Utah, Salt Lake City, 1972-73; rsch. head virology and cancer rsch. The Upjohn Co., Kalamazoo, 1973-82; v.p. cancer rsch. Bristol-Myers Corp., Wallingford, Conn., 1982-88; v.p. R & D, Collagen Corp., Palo Alto, Calif., 1988-90; pres., CEO Celtrix Pharm., Santa Clara, Calif., 1990-95, Borlex Bioscis., Richmond, Calif., 1995-2000, Berley Labs., Montville, N.J., from 2000; dir. Myriad Genetics, Salt Lake City, from 1991, Collateral Therapeutics, San Diego, 1999—2001. Vis. prof. SUNY Upstate Med. Ctr., Syracuse, 1982-86; adj. prof. U. Conn., Storrs, 1986-88; mem. contract-grant rev. com. NIH-Nat. Cancer Inst., Bethesda, 1982-86; bd. dirs. Myriad Genetics, Cognetix Pharm., Collateral Therapeutics; scientific advisory bd. Gladstone Inst. UCSF, 2002—. Editor: Virology A Scope Monograph, 1979, Interferon and Interferon Inducers, 1980, Clinical Applications: Inferferon and Inducers, 1982; sect. editor Jour. Interferon Rsch., 1980-89; contbr. over 100 articles to sci. jours. Biotech. adv. bd. U. Conn., 1986-88; advisor Ariz. Infectious Disease Panel, Tucson, 1988-89. Postdoctoral fellow NIH, 1972-73. Mem. Internat. Soc. for Interferon Rsch., Internat. Soc. for Antiviral Rsch., Am. Assn. for Cancer Rsch., Am. Soc. for Microbiology, Biomaterials Rsch. Soc., Biotechnology Industry Orgn., Parenteral Drug Assn., Sigma Xi, Phi Kappa Phi Achievements include 11 patents on interferon inducers, regulation of immune response to viral infections, treatment of cancers, antiviral agents, prostaglandins; regulation of cellular function; development of drugs including pryrimidones, platinol analogs, etoposide, etoposide analogs, and cytokines including transforming growth factor beta and beta interferon. Home: Alamo, Calif. Died Mar. 18, 2005.

STROCK, HERBERT LEONARD, film producer, director, editor, scriptwriter; b. Boston, Jan. 13, 1918; s. Maurice and Charlotte Ruth (Nesselroth) S.; m. Geraldine Polinger, Dec. 25, 1941; children: Leslie Carol, Genoa Ellen, Candice Dell. BA, U. So. Calif., 1941, MA, 1942. Asst. editor Metro-Goldwyn-Mayer, Culver City, Calif., 1941-42; prodr., dir. IMPPRO, Culver City, 1946-51; dir., film editor Hal Roach Studios, Culver City, 1951-53, Ivan Tors Prodns., Culver City, 1951-58; prodr., dir. ZIV Prodns., Hollywood, Calif., 1956-61; dir. Warner Bros., Burbank, Calif., 1958-63; ind. dir., pres. Herbert L. Strock Prodns., Hollywood, Calif., 1963—2005. Pres., chmn. bd. Hollywood World Films Inc., lectr. U. So. Calif. Producer, dir.: I Led Three Lives, Mr. District Attorney, Favorite Story, Corliss Archer, Science Fiction Theater, Highway Patrol, Dr. Christian, Man Called X, Harbor Command, 1954; dir. Battle Taxi; assoc. producer, dir.: Tom Swift series,(TV shows) Mann of Action, Red Light and Siren Sky King; Maverick, Alaskans, Colt 45, Bronco, Cheyenne, 77 Sunset Strip, Bonanza, Hans Brinker Spl., Decisions-Decisions, (feature pictures) Perfect World of Rodney Brewster, I Was a Teenage Frankenstein, Blood of Dracula, How to Make a Monster, Rider on a Dead Horse, Strike Me Deadly, Search the Wild Wind, Magnetic Monster, Riders to the Stars, Gog - Storm Over Tibet; editor, dir.: The Crawling Hand, One Hour of Hell; editorial supr. Shark; writer, dir. Brother on the Run; editor: So Evil My Sister, Chamber-Mades; coproducer Small Miracle; editor, dir. (documentary) They Search for Survival; supervising film editor Hunger Telethon; editor (spl.) The Making of America, co-writer, film editor Hurray for Betty Boop; dir., chief prodn. coordinator for Miss World, 1976; editor (documentary) UFO Journals, UFO Syndrome, Legends, all 1979, Neighborhood Watch; co-dir., film editor Witches Brew, 1979; writer, film editor (TV series) Flipper, 1981. Editor post prodn. services: China--Mao to Now, Eucatastrophe, Tibet, El Papa, Night Screams, King Kung Fu; dir., editor Deadly Presence; producer, writer, dir. (med. documentary) A New Lease on Life; editor Snooze You Lose, Olympic Legacy, Water You Can Trust, Distance, Fish Outta Water; dir., editor Gramma's Gold; co-editor Infinity, Peaceful Sabbath; producer, writer, dir. (fund raising documentary) Combined Federal Campaign; co-dir., editor Detour; editor (experimental film) This Old Man..., Sidewalk Motel; author: Picture Perfect, 2000. Served with U.S. Army, 1940-41. Mem. Acad. Motion Picture Arts and Scis., Dirs. Guild Am., Am. Cinema Editors (dir., bd. mem. 1984-85), Motion Picture Editors Guild, Delta Kappa Alpha (pres. 1941-65), Editors Guild. Democrat. Avocation: photography. Died Nov. 30, 2005.

STROESSNER, ALFREDO, former President of Paraguay; b. Encarnación, Paraguay, Nov. 3, 1912; s. Hugo Stroessner. Student, Mil. Coll., Asunción; Grad., Superior War Coll., 1945. Chief of staff Paraguayan Army. Took over govtl. authority in Paraguay upon resignation in May 1954, of Frederico Chavez who had been pres. since 1949; assumed office of pres., Aug. 15, 1954, pres. for life, 1977-89. Recipient Collar of the Nile prize, United Arab Emirates, 1958, Civil medal, Inter-Am. Press Assn., 1961. Died Aug. 16, 2006.

STROUD, FRANK BERRY, farm management executive; b. Plain Dealing, La., June 18, 1930; s. Benjamin Franklin and Mary Avis (Berry) S.; m. Watha Jo Henderson, Aug. 11, 1962; children: Keith Henderson and Kenneth Berry (twins). BS, Tex. A&M U., 1951, MS, 1955. Bank mgmt. trainee Tex. Bank & Trust, Dallas, 1955-59; sales engr. S.W. Equipment Co., Dallas, 1959-61; ins. agt. N.Y. Life Ins. Co., Dallas, 1961-62; farm mgmt. supr. Farmers Home Adminstrn. USDA, Clarksville, Tex., from 1962. Capt. U.S. Army, 1951-53. Decorated Civilian Svc. medal in Vietnam Dept. State, 1962. Mem. Nat. Assn. County Suprs., Tex. Assn. County Suprs., Kiwanis (Clarksville). Mehodist. Avocation: small cattle farm. Home: Clarksville, Tex. Died June 1, 2004.

STRZELCZYK, ROBERT EDWARD, health care administrator; b. Milw., Jan. 25, 1920; s. Frank John Strzelczyk and Rose Brozyczkowski; m. Patricia Gregory (div.); m. Dorothy Alice Bleyer, Aug. 31, 1956; children: Robert R., Judith A., Mary S., Edward J., Elizabeth. Cert. phys. therapist, Mayo Clinic, 1942; BS, U. Wis., La Crosse, 1954. Registered phys. therapist, nursing home adminstr., Wis. Chief phys. reconditioning VA, Dayton, Ohio, 1951-52, chief phys. therapy Outwood, Ky., 1952-53, supr. chest svc. Wood, Wis., 1953-56; phys. therapist Washington Orthopedic Sch., Madison, Wis., 1956-59; chief phys. therapist St. Nicholas Hosp., Sheboygan, Wis., 1959-62; adminstr. Anna Reiss Nursing Home, Sheboygan, 1962-64; phys. therapist Gaensan Orthopedic Sch., Milw., 1964-66; adminstr. Hearthside Nursing Home, Milw., 1966-69; pres. Rehab Assocs., Therapy Assocs., Mequon, 1969-87. Bd. dirs. T A of Wis., Mequon; bd. dirs., pres. Polish Cultural Ctr. of S.W. Fla., 1995; lectr. in field. Usher St. James Ch., 1966-83, Ch. of the Ascension, 199091. Maj. U.S. Army, 1942-46; U.S. Army Res., 1946-66, Ret. Fellow Am. Coll. Health Care Adminstrs. (treas. Wis. chpt. 1972-73, chmn. peer rev. com. 1972-73); mem. Am. PHys. Therapy Assn. (program chmn. 1981-83, other offices), Wis. Coun. Hosp. and Homes Serving the Aged (bd. dirs. 1962-68), Southeast Wis. Health Planning Agy., Coalition of Health Profls. (treas. 1974), Wis. Assn. Rehab. Ags. (pres. 1980-83), Nat. Assn. Rehab. Agys. (founding com. 1980), Phi Epsilon Kappa, Alpha Psi Omega, other. Roman Catholic. Avocations: bird photography, hunting elk, publishing genealogy. Home: Bonita Springs, Fla. Died Sept. 6, 2004.

STUART, LYLE, publishing company executive; b. NYC, Aug. 11, 1922; s. Alfred and Theresa (Cohen) Stuart; m. Mary Louise Strawn, Sept. 26, 1946; children: Sandra Lee Strawn, Rory John Strawn; m. Carole Livingston, Feb. 4, 1982; 1 child, Jennifer Susan. Student pub. schs., N.Y.C.; PhD (hon.), State of Calif. Reporter Internat. News Service, 1945, Variety, 1945-46; script writer Dept. State, Voice of Am., 1946; editor Music Bus. mag., 1946-48; founder Expose, 1951; pub. The Independent, 1951-75; bus. mgr. MAD mag., 1952-54; pres. Citadel Press, 1970-89; founder Lyle Stuart, Inc., 1956; pres. University Books, Inc., 1983—2006, Hot News, 1983, Barricade Books, 1990—2006. Founder North Bergen (N.J.) Pub. Library. Prodr. Chinese Festival of Music, 1952-62; author: God Wears A Bowtie, 1949, The Secret Life of Walter Winchell, 1953, Mary Louise, 1970, Casino Gambling for the Winner, 1978, Lyle Stuart on Baccarat, 1983, 2d edit., 1997, Winning at Casino Gambling, 1995. Served with AUS, 1942-44. Mem.: Silurians, Nat. Acad. TV Arts and Scis., Soc. Ky. Cols., NY Zool. Soc. Home: Fort Lee, NJ. Died June 24, 2006.

STUBBINS, HUGH ASHER, JR., architect; b. Birmingham, Ala., Jan. 11, 1912; s. Hugh Asher and Lucile (Matthews) S.; m. Diana Hamilton Moore, Mar. 3, 1938 (div. 1960); children: Patricia, Peter, Hugh Asher III, Michael; m. Colette Fadeuilhe, Sept. 1960 (dec. 1992); m. June M. Kootz, 1994 (dec. July, 2001). BS in Architecture, Ga. Inst. Tech., 1933; MArch, Harvard U., 1935. Pvt. practice, Boston, 1935-38 and from 41; formed partnership, 1938-40; pvt. practice Birmingham, 1940; assoc. prof. Grad. Sch. Design Harvard U., 1946-52, chmn. dept. architecture, 1953, mem. vis. com. Grad. Sch. Design, 1958-72; pres. Hugh Stubbins & Assocs., Inc., 1957-83, chmn., 1983-92. Vis. critic-in-residence, Yale U., 1948-49, U. Oreg., 1950; sec. Rotch travelling Scholarship, 1971-80; Thomas Jefferson prof. architecture U. Va., 1979; mem. adv. coun. Sch. Architecture, Princeton U., 1962-65; mem. Harleston Parker Medal Com., 1973. Designer Berlin Congress Hall, 1957, Countway Libr. Medicine, Harvard U., Fed. Res. Bank, Boston, U. Va. Law Sch., Citicorp Ctr., N.Y.C., St. Peter's Ch., N.Y.C., Fifth Ave. Pl., Pitts., 1988, Bank One, Indpls., 1989, Landmark Tower, Minoto-Mirai 21, Yokohama, Japan, 1989, Ronald Reagan Presdl. Libr., 1990, numerous other bldgs.; exec. architect Phila. Stadium; one-man show Norton Sculpture Gallery, West Palm Beach, 1997-98. Hon. mem. Boston Archtl. Ctr.; chmn. design adv. com. Boston Redevel. Authority, 1964-76; mem. design rev. panel Worcester Redevel. Authority, 1966-70; mem. adv. com. Office Fgn. Bldgs. Ops., U.S. Dept. State, 1979-82; bd. dirs. Benjamin Franklin Found.; mem. arts and archtl. com. Kennedy Meml. Libr.; mem. Fgn. Bus. Coun., Commonwealth of Mass., 1978-79; mem. nat. adv. bd. Ga. Inst. Tech., 1978-81; trustee Tabor Acad., 1974-78; mem. adv. bd. Whitney Libr. Design, 1976-78. Recipient Alpha Rho Chi medal, 1933, 3d prize at competition Nat. Smithsonian Gallery of Art, 1939, Progressive Architecture 1st Design award, 1954, Arcadia Achievement award, 1957, Rodgers and Hammerstein award, 1961, award Am. Inst. Steel Constrn., 1970, award Archtl. Record, 1971, award Prestressed Concrete Inst., 1971, award of merit Inst. So. Affairs and So. Acad. Letters, Am. Acad. Arts and Scis., 1973, citation Am. Assn. Sch. Adminstrs., 1974, award for environ. design, 1975, award of merit Libr. Bldgs. award for Nathan Marsh Pusey Libr., Harvard U./AIA/ALA, 1976, Spl. Energy award for Shiraz Tech. Inst., Am. Assn. Sch. Adminstrs./AIA, N.E. Regional Coun. award Fed. Res. Bank, 1979, Thomas Jefferson Meml. medal U. Va., 1979, R.S. Reynolds Meml. award Citicorp, 1981, numerous other awards. Fellow AIA (v.p. 1964-65, jury fellows 1974-75, chmn. Nat. Honor award com. 1966, 79-80, Merit award 1970, Honor award 1979, Firm award 1967), Mexican Soc. Archs. (hon.), AAAS; mem. NAD (academician, 1994-), Mass. Assn. Archs., Boston Soc. Archs. (pres. 1969-70, Honor award 1988), Archl. League NY (Silver medal 1958), Harvard Club, Laurel Brook Club, Malapan Yacht Club, The Little Club (Gulf Stream, Fla.), Century Club (NYC), Delray Beach Yacht Club, Beta Theta Pi, Omicron Delta Kappa. Home: Boynton Beach, Fla. Died July 5, 2006.

STUCKEY, HELENJEAN LAUTERBACH, counselor educator; b. Bushnell, Ill., May 17, 1929; d. Edward George and Frances Helen (Simpson) Lauterbach; m. James Dale Stuckey, Sept. 30, 1951; children: Randy Lee, Charles Edward, Beth Ellen. BFA, Ill. Wesleyan U., 1951; MEd, U. Ill., 1969. Cert. art tchr., guidance, psychology instr.; lic. clin. profl. counselor, Ill. Display designer Saks Fifth Ave., Chgo., 1951; interior designer Piper City, Ill., 1953-63; tchr. art Forrest (Ill.)-Strawn-Wing Schs., 1967-68; tchr., counselor Piper City Schs., 1969-74; counselor, tchr. art Ford Cen. Schs., Piper City, 1974-85; psychiat. counselor Community Resource Counseling Ctr., Ford County, Ill., 1985-87; tchr. history, counselor Iroquois West H.S., Gilman, Ill., 1987-88; spl. needs coord. Livingston County Vocat., Pontiac, Ill., 1988-93; ret., 1993; clin. profl. counselor, pvt. practice Piper City, from 1995. Substitute tchr., 1993—. Mem. ACA, Ill. Counseling Assn., Ill. Mental Health Counselors Assn., Ill. Ret. Tchrs. (membership chmn.), Delta Kappa Gamma (v.p., sec., program chmn., pres.). Presbyterian. Avocations: skiing, reading, travel, sewing, playing flute. Died June 29, 2004.

STUDDS, GERRY EASTMAN, former congressman; b. Mineola, N.Y., May 12, 1937; s. Eastman and Beatrice (Murphy) S. BA, Yale U., 1959, MAT., 1961. Fgn. service officer US Dept. State, Washington, 1961-63; exec. asst. to presdl. cons. for a nat. service corps The White House, 1963; legis. asst. to Sen. Harrison Williams U.S. Senate, 1964; tchr. St. Paul's Sch., Concord, N.H., 1965-69; mem. US Congress from 12th Mass. dist., 1973-83, US Congress from 10th Mass. dist., 1983—97. Chmn. com. Merchant Marine and Fisheries, 1993; mem. commerce com., resources com., ranking minority of Fisheries, Wildlife and Oceans subcomm. Candidate for U.S. Congress from 12th Dist. Mass., 1970; del. Democratic Nat. Conv., 1968 Home: Boston, Mass. Died Oct. 14, 2006.

STUKEY, VIRGINIA MARGARET, artist; b. N.Y.C. d. Richard Charles and Madeline Theresa (Barton) Gramlich; m. John Henry Stukey, Nov. 12, 1949 (dec.); children: Erin, John Henry, Richard Howe. Student, Columbia U., 1949-51. Tchr. painting various orgns., N.Y.C. and N.J., 1960-75; instr. Riverside Ch. Arts and Crafts Dept., N.Y.C., 1965-75; artist Keane Mason, N.Y.C., 1984-87, Salon des Artists Art Gallery, N.Y.C., 1987-89. Solo exhbns. include Rural Life Ctr., Hinton, N.C., 1967, 68, Pietrantonnio Gallery, N.Y.C., 1972; invitational group shows include Studio 54, N.Y.C., 1982, N.Y. Acad. Scis., 1991, Interfaith Ctr., N.Y.C., 1989, Bergen Mus., 1985-90, Marbella Gallery, N.Y.C., 1989, 100 Years 100 Women, 1990-91, ARC Gallery, Chgo., 1992, Athens, 1996; represented in permanent collections including Riverside Ch., N.Y.C. Mem. Am. Soc. Contemporary Artists, Nat. Assn. Women Artists (pres. 1995-97, permanent advisor), Painting Affiliates Art Ctr. N.J., N.Y. Artists Equity. Avocations: music, poetry, bird watching. Home: Murfreesboro, Tenn. Died May 10, 2006.

STUPSKER, CHARLES A., lawyer; b. Toledo, May 1, 1940; s. Harry and Jeannette (Karp) S.; m. Sandra Stupsker, Aug. 22, 1965 (div. 1992); children: Julie, Laura, Hallie; m. Susan M., Nov. 26, 1993. BA, U. Mich., 1962; LLB, JD, Ohio State U., 1965. Bar: Ohio 1965. Asst. dir. law City of Toledo, 1967-75, chief prosecutor, 1971-75; atty. pvt. practice, Toledo, from 1965. Zoning commn. Sylvania Twp., Lucas County, Ohio, 1981-2000. Fellow Toledo Bar Assn. (pres. 1997); mem. ABA, Ohio State Bar Assn., Lucas County Bar Assn. (pres. 1983). Republican. Avocations: coin collecting/numismatics, bridge, jogging. Home: Toledo, Ohio. Died June 21, 2005.

SUDARSHAN, ARVIND JEWETT, lawyer, principal; b. Rochester, N.Y., Mar. 22, 1962; s. George and Lalita Sudarshan. AB, Harvard U., 1983; JD, U. Tex., Austin, 1986. Assoc. McGinnis, Lochridge & Kilgore, Austin, 1983-87, ptnr., 1988-92; prin. Arvind J. Sudarshan, Atty. at Law, Austin, 1992. Home: Taos, N.Mex. Died June 13, 2004.

SUIT, NANCY E., real estate agent; b. Vancouver, Wash., Jan. 30, 1942; d. William Bender and L. June (Tower) Edmiston; m. Robert Wade Suit, Sept. 1, 1967 (dec. June 1997); 1 child, Justin Robert. BA, La. State U., 1964. Intelligence analyst and linguist CIA, Washington, 1964-66; office mgr. Connecti Mut. Ins. Co., New Orleans, 1967-68; pub. rels. asst. Touro Infirmary, New Orleans, 1968-70; engring. aide Boeing Co., New Orleans, 1968-70; freelance musician and music tchr. Virginia Beach, Va., 1972-89; realtor Realty Execs., Virginia Beach, Va., from 1993. Realtor, 1986-93. Organist, choir dir., 1979-94; violinist, mem. Virginia Beach Pops Orch., 1974-82. Mem. Nat. Assn. Realtors (lic.), Va. Assn. Realtors, Tidewater Assn. Realtors (Sales Achievement award 1995, 96), Realty Execs. Southeast (Achievers Sales award 1996). Republican. Methodist. Avocations: gardening, reading, playing piano. Home: Virginia Beach, Va. Died Nov. 24, 2004.

SUKENICK, RONALD, author, English educator; b. Bklyn., July 14, 1932; m. Lynn Luria, 1961 (div. 1984), Julia B. Frey, 1992. BA, Cornell U., 1955; PhD, Brandeis U., 1962. Instr. Hofstra U., 1961—62; asst. prof. CUNY, 1966—67, Sarah Lawrence Coll., 1968—69; writer-in-residence Cornell U., 1969—70, U. Calif, Irvine, 1970—72; prof. English U. Colo., Boulder, 1974—2002, dir. creative writing, 1974—77, dir. publications ctr., 1986—99. Dir. FC2/Black Ice Books, Normal, Ill., 1985-2004. Author: Wallace Stevens: Missing the Obscure, 1967, Up, 1968, The Death of the Novel and Other Stories, 1969, Out, 1973, 98.6, 1975, Long Talking Bad Conditions Blues, 1979, In Form: Digressions on the Art of Fiction, 1985, The Endless Short Story, 1986, Blown Away, 1986, Down and In: Life in the Underground, 1987, Doggy Bag: Hyperfictions, 1994, Mosaic Man, 1999, Narralogues, 2000, Cows, 2002; former co-pub. Am. Book Rev.; pub. Black Ice mag., 1987. Died July 22, 2004.

SULEIMAN, SAMI KHALIL, financial planner, accountant; b. Palestine, Palestine, Mar. 27, 1947; came to U.S., 1969; s. Khalil A. and Hasna (Khatib) S.; m. Penelope Mitchell, Jan. 26, 1984; children: Nura, Ramzy. BS in Econs., U. Jordan, 1969; MBA in Internat. Fin., Stanford U., 1979. Sr. cons. Arthur Young and Co., N.Y.C., 1979-80; chief fin. officer Internat. Food Policy Inst., Washington, 1980-83; pres. Internat. Fin. Services, Washington, from 1983; fin. planner Home Life Ins. Co., N.Y.C., from 1987. Rockefeller Found. scholar, 1977. Mem. Nat. Soc. Pub. Accts., Nat. Assn. Security Dealers, Nat. Assn. Life Underwriters, Stanford Bus. Sch. Alumni Assn. (treas. 1985—), Assn. Arab-Am. Univ. Grads. (pres. 1983). Avocation: swimming. Home: Bethesda, Md. Died June 23, 2005.

SULLIVAN, WALTER LAURENCE, writer, educator; b. Nashville, Jan. 4, 1924; s. Walter Laurence and Aline (Armstrong) S.; m. Jane Harrison, Aug. 30, 1947; children: Pamela Sullivan Chenery, Walter Laurence, John Harrison. BA, Vanderbilt U., 1947; MFA, U. Iowa, 1949; Litt.D., Episc. Theol. Sem., Lexington, Ky., 1973. Instr. dept. English Vanderbilt U., Nashville, 1949-52, asst. prof., 1952-57, assoc. prof., 1957-63, prof., 1963—2001, prof. emeritus, 2001—06. Lectr. on pub. TV. Author: Sojourn of a Stranger, 1957, The Long, Long Love, 1959, Death by Melancholy: Essays on Modern Southern Fiction, 1972, A Requiem for the Renascence: The State of Fiction in the Modern South, 1976, In Praise of Blood Sports and Other Essays, 1990, Allen Tate: A Recollection, 1988, A Time to Dance, 1995, The War the Women Lived, 1995, Nothing Gold Can Stay: A Memoir, 2006; co-author: Southern Fiction Today: Renascence and Beyond, 1969, Southern Literary Study: Problems and Possibilities, 1975, Writing From the Inside, 1983; writer, narrator film for pub. TV; contbr. articles to publs. 1st lt. USMC, 1943-46. Ford Found. fiction fellow, 1951-52; Rockefeller Found. fiction fellow, 1957-58. Mem. Fellowship of So. Writers. (vice chancellor 1997-99, chancellor, 1999-2006). Roman Catholic. Home: Nashville, Tenn. Died Aug. 15, 2006.

SULLIVAN, WHITNEY BRAYTON, municipal court judge; b. Pueblo, Colo., Jan. 6, 1922; s. Clyde A. Sullivan and Lucy Estelle (Patch) Johnson; m. Virginia Ruth Lower, July 27, 1946; children: Kerry Jay, Carol Anne, Brian Gordon. BBA, U. N.Mex., 1948; grad., Air War Coll., 1968; postgrad., Nat. Jud. Coll., Reno, Nev., 1976-87, Am. Acad. Jud. Edn., Boulder, Colo., 1981. Appointed county ct. judge Gov. Lamm Colo. State Jud. Dept., 1976. Commd. 2d lt. USAAF, 1943; advanced through grades to lt. col. USAF, 1965, served in CBI, ETO, 1943-46, officer, pilot various locations including Korea, 1946-53, officer, sr. pilot U. Utah ROTC, 1953-56, command pilot SAC, 1956-72, ret., 1972; county ct. judge Colo. State Jud. Dept., Westcliffe, 1977-92; mcpl. ct. judge Towns of Westcliffe and Silver Cliff, Colo., 1984-87 and from 89. Jud. planning com. Colo. State Jud. Dept., Denver, 1985-87; faculty adviser Nat. Jud. Coll., 1987-89; 1st pres. Custer County Airport Authority; founder Custer County Credit Union. Editor: The Gavel, 1982-83; contbr. to profl. publs. Pres. Wet Mountain Valley Rotary Club, Westcliffe, 1974-75; chmn. County Centennial/Bicentennial Com., Westcliffe, 1975-76. Recipient 7 decorations, 17 medals USAF, pilot wings RAF, 1943. Mem. Nat. Judges Assn. (exec. dir., pres. 1982-83, McEachern Meml. award for Outstanding Non-Atty. Judge in U.S. 1987), Colo. Assn. County Judges (pres. 1984-85), Westcliffe Ctr. for Arts (pres. 1990-91), Masons (past master). Republican. Methodist. Avocations: painting, singing, golf, reading, band music. Home: Pueblo West, Colo. Died Apr. 7, 2004.

SULZER, ALEXANDER JACKSON, retired research microbiologist, educator; b. Emett, Ark., Feb. 13, 1922; s. Eugene August and Edna Jerita (Weaver) Sulzer; m. Faye Katherine Ross, Oct. 4, 1942; children: Dan L., Harry E. BA, Hardin-Simmons U., 1946—49; MS, Emory U., 1960—61, PhD, 1961—63; DHC, Univ. Peruana Cayetano Heredia, 1977. Rsch. microbiologist Ctr. Disease Control, Atlanta, 1951—90, med. parasitologist, 1952—62, rsch. parasitologist Atlanta, 1962—74; ret., 1990. Adj. prof. U. N.C., Chapel Hill, 1979—82; maleria cons. Pan Am. Health Org., 1980—90, World Health Org., 1980—90. Author: (book chpt.) Manual of Clinical Microbiology, 1995. Tech-5, medic U.S. Army, 1942—43, U.S. Recipient Sci. award, Bausch & Lomb, 1940, hon. lifetime mem., Peruvian Soc. Microbiology, 1979, 1st place, med. rsch., Inst. Hipolito Unanue, 1981; fellow rsch., Atomic Energy Commn., 1950—51, CDC-rsch., Emory U., 1959—60, Nat. Inst. Health, 1960—62. Fellow: Indian Soc. Malaria and Communicable Diseases (hon. lifetime fellow 1958—59); mem.: Nat. Registry Microbiology (life), Am. Soc. Parasitology (life), Royal Soc. Trop. Med. & Hyg. (life lifetime fellow 1957), Am. Soc. Paraistology (life), Am. Soc. Tropical Med. (life), Am. Acad. Microbiology (life lifetime fellow 1958). Achievements include discovery of similiar internal morphology of Toxoplasma gondii and Besnoitia jellisoni with silver protein stain, 1957; reproduction of Toxoplasma gondii by internal budding (endodiogeny), 1958; antipenic cross-reactions between Babesia argentina and Plasmodium vivax and Plasmodium falciparum, 1972; maleria and antibody patterns in primitive population in South America, 1980; indirect immunofluorescence test for human Babesia microti infections, 1986; development of thick smear antigen for maleria IFA tests, 1969. Home: Bowdon, Ga. Died July 4, 2005.

SUN, YUN-SUAN, former Taiwanese government official; b. Penglai, Shantung, China, Nov. 11, 1913; B.S., Harbin Poly. Inst., 1934; m. Yu Hui-hsuan, 1947; children— Yi-ho, Lu-hsi, Lu-yun, Yi-hung. Engr., Nat. Resource Commn., 1937-40; supt. Tienshui Electric Power Plant, 1940-43; engr.-in-tng. TVA, 1943-45; from head engr. elec. and mech. dept. to pres. Taiwan Power Co., 1946-64; chief exec. officer, gen. mgr. Electricity Corp. Nigeria, 1964-67; minister of communications, 1967-69, of econ. affairs, 1969-78; premier Republic of China, 1978-84; sr. advisor to the Pres.; Mem. central standing com. Kuomintang. Decorated cravat Order Brilliant Star, 1952; recipient Engring. award Chinese Inst. Engrs., 1954. Fellow Internat. Acad. Mgmt. Died Feb. 15, 2006.

SUPLINSKAS, RAYMOND JOSEPH, materials scientist; b. Hartford, Conn., Aug. 29, 1939; s. Paul Peter and Delina Alice (Vallieres) S.; m. Janet Hazel Mainello, Aug. 29, 1959; children: Paul, Deborah, Michael. BS, Yale U., 1961; PhD in Chemistry, Brown U., 1965. Mem. tech. staff Bell Labs., Murray Hill, N.J., 1964-65; assoc. prof. chemistry Yale U., New Haven, 1965-72; chmn. dept. chemistry Swarthmore (Pa.) Coll., 1972-77; prin. staff scientist Textron Splty. Materials, Lowell, Mass., 1977—2001; chief scientist Splty. Materials, Lowell, Mass., from 2002. Contbr. articles to Jour. Chem. Physics. Grantee NSF, 1965-72. Achievements include research in development of refractory reinforcing filaments (including SCS-6), metal matrix composites, and carbon/carbon composites; patents in field. Home: Haverhill, Mass. Died June 10, 2005.

SUTHERLAND, RAYMOND ELWOOD, plastics company executive; b. McComas, W.Va., Aug. 10, 1937; s. Raymond Clarence Sutherland and Mavis Ruth (Sanders) Kahle; m. Billie June Beaman, Nov. 22, 1958; children: Raymond David, Judith Ann, William Thomas. BS in Chemistry, Concord Coll., 1959; MS in Chemistry, U. Tenn., 1962. Chemist R&D Eastman Chem. Products, Kingsport, Tenn., 1962-69; engring. mgr. United Carr div. TRW, Knoxville, Tenn., 1969-74; plant mgr., v.p., gen. mgr. Emconite div. Amerace Corp., Indpls., Denton, Tex., 1974-80; v.p. Leon Plastics div. U.S. Industries, Grand Rapids, Mich., 1980-82; pres. Mich. Plastic Products Co., Grand Haven, Mich., from 1982. Mem. econ. devel. div. ACI Grand Haven, 1983—, also past pres.; bd. dirs. Ottawa County Am. Cancer Soc., Holland, Mich., 1986-90, Coalition for Excellence and Tech., Grand Haven Pub. Schs., 1986—. Rsch. grantee NSF U. Tenn., 1960-62. Mem. Soc. Plastics Industry (chpt. bd. dirs. 1988—, nat. bd. dirs. 1989—), Soc. Plastics Engrs., Assn. Commerce and Industry (past pres.), Rotary, Spring Lake Country Club (bd. dirs. 1989—). Republican. Avocations: flying, boating, golf. Home: Spring Lake, Mich. Died May 27, 2005.

SÜTÖ, ANDRAS, writer; b. Pusztakamarás, Romania, June 17, 1927; s. András and Berta (Székely) S.; m. Éva Szabó. 1949; children: András Jr., Agnes. Student, Ref. Coll., Cluj, Romania, 1945-48. Journalist, reporter Világosság, daily, Cluj, 1946-48; editor, then editor-in-chief Falavak Népe, weekly, Cluj, 1948-54; dep. chief editor Igaz Szó, lit. monthly, Tirgu Mures, Romania, 1955-57; editor-in-chief Uj élet, pictorial bi-monthly, Tirgu Mures, 1958-89. Author: People are Starting, 1953, Salamon, the Uncompanionable, 1956, Quiet Dreams Promised by My Mother, 1970, Gods and Little Rocking Horses, 1973, Years Haunting like Ghosts, 1980, Close Grasp of the Present, 1984, Following the Wounded Bird, 1988, Diary-notes, 1990, Eye for Words, 1993, Herode's Age, 1994, Wedding of the Wild Peafowl, 1994; (dramatic trilogy) Palm Sunday of a Horse Dealer, Star at the Stake, Cain and Abel, 1978, (plays) The Wedding of Susa, 1979, Advent in the Hargita Mountains, 1985, The Dream Collecting Commando, 1987, The Barking Bird, 1993, Plays, 1989, 2nd vol., 1992, Holders of the Falling Heavens, 1990, A Dragon is Sleeping in Your Bed, 1991, Waking Up of the Sleeping Beauty, 1993, Let Words Come to Me, 1994, Tales, 1994. Recipient state prize for lit. in Romania, 1953, 54, Herder prize, Vienna, Austria, 1979, Kossuth prize for lit., Hungary, 1992. Mem. Writers Fedn. Socialist Republic Romania (v.p. 1973-81), PEN Club Hungarian Writers from Romania. Home: Tirgu Mures, Romania. Died Sept. 30, 2006.

SUTTON, JESSE NOEL, minister; b. Gilmer, Tex., Jan. 18, 1926; s. Rufus Noel and Jessie Lola (Parnell) S.; m. Norma Dell Beard, Dec. 24, 1948; children: Rhonda Cheryl Sutton Stege, Lola Celeste Sutton Bailey, Andrea Gay Sutton Holcek. Student, Hardin-Simmons U., 1946-48; cert., So. Tech. Inst., Dallas, 1950; B Sacred Music, So. Bapt. Theol. Sem., Ft. Worth, 1957. Ordained to ministry So. Bapt. Conv., 1979. Min. music, edn. and youth Hilltop Drive Bapt. Ch., Irving, Tex., 1955-56, 1st Bapt. Ch., Ranger, Tex., 1957-58, Freeport, Tex., 1958-65, Canyon, Tex., 1965-67, Trinity Bapt. Ch., Amarillo, Tex., 1967-74; min. music and edn. 1st Bapt. Ch., Van Buren, Ark., 1974-78, min. music Delhi, La., 1978-95; interim min. Holly Brook Bapt. Ch., Hawkins, Tex., 1995—2002. 2d v.p. Ark. Bapt. Religious Edn. Conf., 1975-76, 1st v.p., 1976-77, pres., 1977-78. Mem. Singing Men of Ark., 1974-78. With AUS, 1944-46, ETO, PTO. Mem. La. Singing Mins., Lions (pres. Delhi 1984-85). Republican. Baptist. Home: Quitman, Tex. Died Nov. 15, 2005.

SUTTON, RONALD G., data processing executive; b. Kansas City, Kans., Oct. 12, 1941; s. Charles Franklin and Virginia Ethel (Akers) S. BS in Math., Kans. State U., 1964; BA in Theology, Roosevelt U., 1965, PhD in Theology, 1972. Systems dir. Butler Mfg. Co., Kansas City, Mo., 1965-69; pastor Ch. of the Holy Spirit, Brooksville, Fla., 1974-76; v.p. data processing Murry's Inc., Forestville, Md., from 1977. Cons. German Armed Forces Adminstrn., Washington, 1984-85, Howard Way Assoc., Washington, 1983-84; lectr. George Washington U., Washington, 1983-86. Contbr. articles to profl. jours. Mem. Am. Mgmt. Assn. (chmn. 1987), The Inst. Mgmt. Scis. (asst. dir. 1984). Clubs: Andrews Officer (Washington). Republican. Methodist. Avocations: bridge, writing, gourmet cooking. Home: Jupiter, Fla. Died July 2, 2005.

SVOBODA, GEORGE JIRI, historian, librarian; b. Bratislava, Slovak Republic, Mar. 28, 1933; s. Vaclav and Marie Svoboda; m. Yanna A. Verunacova, Dec. 21, 1963; 1 child, John. PhD, Charles U., Prague, 1956. Asst. prof. Charles U., Prague, 1957-68; head Slavic libr. U. Calif., Berkeley, 1980-93, cons., 1993-94. Sec. Czechoslovak Hist. Conf., 1986-90. Author: Social Movements in Bohemia in the 18th Century, 1967. Avocation: travel. Home: Richmond, Calif. Died Sept. 5, 2004.

SWARVAR, LARRY CARL, snack food company executive; b. Muskegon, Mich., May 24, 1949; s. Ralph M. and Florence Augusta (Pierson) S.; m. Karen Sue Plemmons, Apr. 9, 1988; children: Lara, Brian, Eric. AS, Muskegon C. C., 1972; BSME cum laude, Western Mich. U., 1975; MBA, U. Dallas, 1987. Registered profl. engr., Mich., Pa. Draftsman Blu-Surf Thermo Engring., Muskegon, 1967-69; chief draftsman Campbell Grinder Co., Muskegon, 1969-73; design engr. Kellogg Inc., Battle Creek, Mich., 1975-77, equip. devel. engr., 1977-78, internat. engr. Bogota, Colombia, 1978-80; sr. project engr. Frito-Lay Inc., Irving, Tex., from 1981. Mem. ASME. Avocations: pool, reading. Home: Dallas, Tex. Died May 30, 2005.

SWATOSH, ROBERT BERYL, retired army officer, nuclear physicist; b. Sheldon, Iowa, Oct. 11, 1916; s. Edward Alfred and Nina Beryl (Stake) S.; m. Sandra Melida Peters, June 25, 1988; children: Audren, Sharon, Stuart, Shawn. BS in Journalism and Chemistry, Iowa State Coll., 1939; advanced mil. degree, U.S. Command & Gen. Staff, Ft. Leavenworth, Kans., 1955, advanced student nuc. physics, 1956. Advt. mgr. Knoxville (Iowa) Jour., 1939-40; commd. 2d lt. U.S. Army, 1940, advanced through grades to lt. col., 1940-60; ret., 1960; rsch. specialist Lockheed Missile & Space, Sunnyvale, Calif., 1960-70; broker, owner Swat Realty, Inc., Clearlake Oaks, Calif., 1970-80; ret., 1980. Pres., CEO Pacific Far East Salvage, Japan, 1951-54. Author: Wings, Wars & Life, 1996, Live 120 Healthy, Happy Years, 1997, Gung Ho Marines, 2000. Decorated Bronze Star with V, Purple Heart (2). Mem. Am. Legion (dept. comdr. Panama, Costa Rica, 1990-91), Lions Club (pres. Sun City Ctr., Fla., chpt. 1996-97), Masons. Republican. Roman Catholic. Avocations: flying, boating, fishing. Home: Sun City Center, Fla. Died Nov. 15, 2004.

SWEETMAN, JOHN STUART, JR., funeral director; b. Chgo., Mar. 9, 1939; s. John S. and Grayce E. (Gibboney) W.; m. Kathleen Conrath, Sept. 10, 1960; children: Kathleen Brady, Charmaine Moore, Kelly Gleason, Wendy. Student, Loyola U., 1957-59; BS, Worsham Coll., 1960. Mgr. Weinstein Bros. Funeral Homes, Chgo., from 1989; sec. Umpire Protective Assn., Chgo., from 1990. Dir. Rogers Park C. of C., Chgo., 1992—. Mem. Ill. Funeral Dirs. Assn., Nat. Assn. Sports Ofcls., Umpires Protective Assn., Am. Cancer Soc. (dir., sec. 1992—). Roman Catholic. Avocation: baseball card collection. Died Mar. 22, 2005.

SWENSON, ANN-MARIE, education educator; b. Ogden, Iowa, Dec. 30, 1921; d. Algot Valentine and Ruth Polly (Jacobson) Christofferson; m. John Hilbert Swenson, July 4, 1942; children: John H. Jr., Frederick Lawrence, Sonja Christine. Student, Bethany Coll., Lindsborg, Kans., 1939-40, Augustina Coll., Rock Island, Ill., 1942; BA in Elem. Edn., U. Denver, 1960, MA in Spl. Edn., 1975; postgrad., U. Lund, Sweden, 1972. Tchr. Sapinero Rural Sch., Gunnison County, Colo., 1949-50, Brighton-Whittier Sch., 1954-55, Westlake Sch. Adams Dist., Thornton, Colo., 1961, Pocatello Idaho Elem., 1961-62, Boulder (Colo.) Valley Schs., 1962-74; resource tchr. Walden (Colo.) Jr. Sr. H.S., 1974-83; tchr. Tempe (Ariz.) Elem. Sch., 1983-86, Tempe (Ariz.) Union H.S. Dist., 1986-90. Pres. North Parks Schs. Edn. Assn., 1982-83; parent and child advocacy, Ariz. Edn. Dept., Phoenix, 1987-89. Mem. State Commn. Profl. Rights and Responsibilities, Boulder, Colo., 1966-68. Recipient Tuition scholarship Climax Molibdenum Co., Leadville County, Colo., 1975. Mem. NEA, Colo. Edn. Assn., Boulder Valley Edn. Assn., Ariz. Edn. Assn. Democrat. Avocations: reading, hiking, walking, sewing, volunteering. Home: Boulder, Colo. Died June 7, 2005.

SWINEHART, TIMOTHY E., music educator; b. Coshocton, Ohio, Dec. 12, 1950; s. James Edward and Willanna Fay Swinehart; m. Pauline Sue Toy, July 15, 1972; children: Shad J., Jason E. MusB, Capital U., 1972; MusM, Wichita State U., 1976; PhD, Ohio State U., 1994. Tchr. Berne Union HS, Sugar Grove, Ohio, 1972—75, Wichita State U., Kans., 1975—76, Lexington HS, Ohio, 1976—78, U. Dayton, Ohio, 1978—83, Capital U., Columbus, Ohio, from 1983. Clinician, adjudicator Ohio Music Edn. Assn., Columbus, from 1980; bd. of dir. Bexley Music Assn., Ohio, from 1984. Author: A Parents Guide to Musical Instruments, 1987; composer: (musical score) Fantasies, 1992; author: (articles) various profl. jours., 1998. Fundraiser Bexley Meadow Music Assn., from 1984; series admin. Ctrl. Coll. Concert Series, Westerville, Ohio, from 1999. Recipient Mayor's Cmty. Svc. citation, City of Bexley, 2002. Mem.: Ohio Music Edn. Assn. (conf. chair from 1972, 25 Year award 1998), Phi Beta Mu (Honorary) (pres. from 1985, Golden Baton award 2001). Achievements include founder of the Ohio Music Edn. Assn. Marching Band Competitions; co-founder of "NOW" Music Festival, Ohio. Avocations: woodworking, swimming, automobile detailing, furniture design. Home: Westerville, Ohio. Died June 25, 2005.

SWORDS, BETTY EDGEMOND, cartoonist; b. Gilroy, Calif., Aug. 17, 1917; d. John William and Gertrude Catherine (Gahr) Edgemond; m. Henry Leonard Swords, Dec. 12, 1941; children: Richard Allen, Stephen John. BA, U. Calif., Berkeley, 1938; postgrad., Acad. Advt. Art, San Francisco, 1938-39, Fresno State Coll., 1942. Fashion illustrator The Fair, Breuners, Eastern, Sacramento, 1943. Instr. U. Denver, 1976, Met. State Coll., Denver, 1977, Arapaho C.C., Littleton,Colo., 1977, U. Colo., Denver, 1985; humor book reviewr Denver Post and KBDI-TV, 1972-85; guest lectr. Nat. Confs. on Violence, Denver, 1975, 76, Federally Employed Women, San Francisco, Denver, 1975, acad., profl., social groups, radio and TV, Denver, 1970—; presenter papers on humor's power internat. confs., 1983, 85. Free lance cartoonist Saturday Evening Post, Look, Redbook, Changing Times, Good Housekeeping, Ladies' Home Jour., 1955-74; humor/feature writer McCall's, Christian Sci. Monitor, Denver Post, others, 1960—; illustrator: Making the Most of Every Move, 1957; cartoonist: (Bigelow ads) The New Yorker, 1969; (calendar) Male Chauvinist Pig Calendar, 1974, 1973; author: (chpt.) New Perspectives on Women and Comedy, 1992. Precinct committeewoman Dem. Party, Denver, 1973. Mem. NOW (v.p. 1970, head media, speaker's bur. 1971-76), Colo. Women's Polit. Caucus, Denver Woman's Press Club (awards 1964-90), Colo. Author's League (v.p. 1969, awards 1964—). Avocations: doing comedy improvisation, dress design, embroidery, travel, reading. Home: Denver, Colo. Died Aug. 14, 2005.

SWORTZELL, LOWELL STANLEY, theater educator; b. Washington, Aug. 5, 1930; s. Stanley and Ora (Van Pelt) S.; m. Nancy Ellen Foell, Sept. 6, 1959. PhD, NYU, 1964. Asst. in playwriting Drama Sch. Yale U., New Haven, 1958-59; asst. prof. drama NYU, N.Y.C., 1964-5; assoc. prof. theatre U. Wis., Madison, 1965-66; former prof. edn. theatre NYU, N.Y.C. Author, editor, playwright, researcher, book reviewer, play reviewer, former dir., workshop leader NYU, N.Y.C. Author: Here Come the Clowns, 1978; editor: All the Worlds's a Stage, 1972 (Outstanding Book of Yr. N.Y. Times Book Rev., 1972), (reference book) International Guide to Childrne's Theatre and Educational Theatre, 1990 (Am. Alliance for Theatre & Edn. Disting. Book of Yr. 1990); author (play) Little Humpback Horse, 1984, 12 plays for young people. Home: New York, NY. Died Aug. 9, 2004.

SWOYER, JAMES FREDERICK, JR., lawyer; b. Lawrence, Kans., Feb. 19, 1923; s. James Frederick Sr. and Hazel Ann (Baker) S.; m. Martha Ann Truman; 1 child, Karl Frederick. AB, U. Kans., 1949, LLB, 1952. Bar: Kans. 1952. Pvt. practice, Oskaloosa, Kans., from 1960. Mayor City of Oskaloosa. Mem. Masons. Republican. Home: Oskaloosa, Kans. Died Aug. 29, 2004.

SYKES, DONALD JOSEPH, plastic company executive; b. Buffalo, Mar. 16, 1936; s. Joseph John and Josephine Mary (Zielinski) S.; m. Suzanne Kay Marble, May 28, 1960; children: Kathryn, Jeffrey. BS, Rochester (N.Y.) Inst. Tech., 1958. Dir. Cormac Chem. Corp., N.Y.C., 1959-63; from rsch. mgr. to sr. v.p. Hunt Chem. Co. (now Olin Hunt Specialty Co.), Palisades Park, N.J., 1963-83; dir. Marpac Industries, Inc., Waldwick, N.J., 1983-88, chmn. of bd., from 1988. Contbr. articles and papers to field; patentee;

holds over 20 U.S. patents. With U.S. Army Reserve, 1958-62. Mem. Am. Soc. Quality Control, Soc. Plastics Engrs., Am. Chem. Soc. Home: Saddle River, NJ. Died Aug. 10, 2004.

SYKES, GREGORY EDWARD, insurance company executive, writer; s. Felix John and Grace Forster Sykes; m. Claudia Lee Gloe, July 28, 1973; children: Gregory E. II, Joshua D., Meridith L., Michael A. BS, Kans. State U., 1974; MS, U. Okla., 1984. Cert. EMT Kans.; police office Okla., Kans. Police officer Plainville (Kans.) Police Dept.; casuality claims examiner Am. Family Ins., Salina, Kans.; police sgt. Lindsborg (Kans.) Police Dept.; claims examiner Columbia Ins. Group, Salina, Am. States Ins., St. Louis; supr. spl. investigations Ohio Casualty Group, Fairfield. Dept. tng. officer Lindsborg Dept. Pub. Safety, 1990—97; radio show host Sta. KJLS-AM, Creve Coeur, Mo., 1998—99. Author: Thou Shalt Not Steal, 2003, Mice in the Pantry, 2003, Grim Corporate Fairy Tales, 2004; contbr. articles to profl. jours.; author: Martin Luther-Private Dectective, Knockout-A Novel of Terrorism, The Fireants-A Novel of Terrorism. Bd. dirs. Parks and Recreation Commn., St. Peters, Mo., 1998—2001; candidate for sheriff Rep. Party, Saline County, Kans., 1996; bd. dirs. Sanford-Fritch (Tex.) Sch., 1983. Capt. USAFA, 1998—2002. Recipient Silver Star for Bravery, Am. Polic Hall of Fame, 1995, Nat. Commendation, Coun. Law Enforcement Accreditation, Kans., 1996. Mem.: Assn. Cert. Fraud Examiners, Internat. Assn. Arson Investigators, Internat. Assn. Spl. Investigation (bd. dirs. from 2004). Died July 2, 2005.

SYKES, RICHARD MACRAE, manufacturing executive; b. Flushing, N.Y., Feb. 7, 1940; s. Macrae and Jean (George) S.; m. Gillian Gray, June 11, 1965 (div. 1985); m. Jane Stebbins, Nov. 29, 1985; children: Alexandra M., Colin M. BA, Williams Coll., 1961; MBA, Columbia U., 1963. CPA, N.Y. Audit mgr. Ernst & Young, N.Y.C., 1964-73; v.p. fin., treas. Teleprompter Corp., N.Y.C., 1973-83, DNA Plant Tech. Corp., Cinnaminson, N.J., from 1983. Served with U.S. Army, 1963-64. Mem. AICPA, N.Y. State Soc. CPA's, Seawanhaka Corinthian Yacht Club, N.Y. Yacht Club, Piping Rock Club. Avocation: sailing. Died Aug. 19, 2004.

SYKES, SUSAN HUGGARD PARKER, public relations executive; b. N.Y.C., July 29, 1939; d. Bill C.W. and Margaret (Effinger) Huggard; m. Edward Parker, 1979 (div.); children: Julie Parker Marini, Cindy Parker, Debbie; m. Charles Jeremy Sykes, Feb. 7, 1989. BA in English, U. Mich., 1961; MA in Media, Fairfield U., 1980. Lic. tchr. English. High sch. drama dir. Stamford (Conn.) Cath. High Sch., 1971-72; contbg. editor Stratford (Conn.) News, 1976-77; high sch. drama dir. Joel Barlow High Sch., Redding, Conn., 1978-80; tech. coord. Nat. CSS, Wilton, Conn., 1981-82; pub. rels. mgr. Intec Corp., Trumbull, Conn., 1982-83, Creative Output, Inc., Milford, Conn., 1983-84, Decision Resources, Inc., Westport, Conn., 1985-86; v.p. Inter Active Software, N.Y.C., 1988-90; owner, pres. Market Makers Pub. Rels., Glen Cove, N.Y., 1987-92; v.p., mgr. tech. div. Howard Blankman Inc., Jericho, N.Y., 1992-93; adminstr. Sm. Bus. Coun. L.I. Assn., from 1994. Mem. Pub. Rels. Soc. Am., Nat. Assn. Women Bus. Owners (L.I. chpt., chmn. membership 1989-92, v.p. 1990-91, pres. 1991-92), Gamma Phi Beta. Unitarian Universalist. Avocations: writing, svc. to others, sailing, teaching. Home: Huntington, NY. Died Oct. 25, 2004.

SYLVIA, CONSTANCE MIRIAM, family nurse practitioner, clinical specialist; b. Brockton, Mass., Oct. 29, 1934; d. W. Earle and Bernice M. (Hood) Dougherty; m. Charles S. Sylvia, Sept. 17, 1983; children: Phoebe Coggins, Eric, Edward. Diploma in nursing, New Eng. Deaconess Hosp., Boston, 1955; BSN, Boston U., 1958; postgrad., U. N.C., 1959-60, Boston U., 1964-65, 82-83; MA in Psychology, Bridgewater State Coll., 1988; cert. FNP, Worcester Hahnemann Hosp., 1977. RN, Mass.; cert. clin. nurse specialist, psychiat. mental health nurse. Pub. health nurse Town of Middleborough, Mass., 1971-74; continuing care nurse Lakeville (Mass.) Hosp., 1974-75; pub. health clinic nurse handicapped children's svcs. Mass. Dept. Pub. Health, Lakeville, Mass., 1975-79; family nurse practitioner Wrentham (Mass.) State Sch., Children's Hosp., 1979-82; head nurse psychiatric unit New Eng. Deaconess Hosp., 1982-83; head nurse psychiat. crisis stblzn. unit Brockton (Mass.) Multi-Svc. Ctr., 1983-85; nurse practitioner Taunton (Mass.) State Hosp., 1985-87, Cape and Islands Mental Health, Pocasset, Mass., 1987-92; indepentent therapy practice, from 1992. Nurse therapist Middleboro (Mass.)-Lakeville Cmty. Counseling Ctr., 1978-79, sec., 1993-95, sec. bd. dirs., 1995-98; bd. dirs. Cmty. Care Svcs., 1999—. Vice chmn. Middleborough Conservation Commn., 1970-74; leader Ranger Rick Nature Club, 1972-73; pres., organizer for women's health Taunton and Middleborough area NOW, 1974-76; bd. dirs. Mental Health Assn., 1971-80, vice chmn., 1974-80; mem. Coun. on Aging; bd. dirs. Am. Cancer Soc., 1973, ComCare-Clerk, 1995-96, Cmty. Care Svc., Taunton, Mass., 1998—; supr., facilitator breast cancer support groups, 1993—; area mem. Region V Comprehensive Health Planning, 1972-82; resource person, tchr. Sunday sch. Unitarian Universalist Ch., 1980—, co-leader youth group, 1987-89; instr. hunter edn. Mass. Dept. Natural Resources, 1983-99. Katherine Delano Grant scholar New Eng. Deaconess Hosp., 1952-55. Mem. ANA (cert. family nurse practitioner), Mass. Nurses Assn., Mass. Pub. Health Assn., Mass. Coalition of Nurse Practitioners. Died Apr. 27, 2005.

SZABLYA, JOHN FRANCIS, electrical engineer, consultant; b. Budapest, Hungary, June 25, 1924; came to U.S., 1963, naturalized, 1979; s. John and Alexandra (Huszar) S.; m. Helen Bartha-Kovacs, June 12, 1951; children: Helen A., Janos L., Louis J., Stephen J.P., Alexandra H.R., Rita H.C., Dominique-Mary H. Diploma engring., Jozsef Nador U., Budapest, 1947, diploma edn., 1948, D in Econs., 1948. Registered profl. engr., Wash., Mont., Alaska, Wyo., Oreg., Colo., Idaho, B.C. and Ont., Can. Design engr. Ganz Elec. Works, Budapest, 1947-56; assoc. prof. Tech. U. Budapest, 1951-56, U. B.C., Vancouver, Canada, 1957-63; prof. elec. engring. Wash. State U., Pullman, 1963-82, now prof. emeritus; mgr. elec., instrumentation and control engring. EBASCO Svcs., Inc., Bellevue, Wash., 1981-90; ret., 1990; cons. engr., v.p. Szablya Cons., Inc., Kirkland, Wash., from 1990. Vis. prof. Technische Universitat Braunschweig, 1973-74, U. W.I., St. Augustine, Trinidad and Tobago, 1983-2001, U. Wash., Seattle, 1985—, Seattle U., 1987. Contbr. numerous articles to profl. jours. Recipient Zipernowszky medal Hungarian Inst. Elec. Engrs., 1954, diploma of recognition, 1998, Arpad Academia Gold medal, 1990. Fellow IEEE, Instn. Elec. Engrs. (London); mem. Hungarian Acad. Scis., Sigma Xi. Roman Catholic. Home: Kirkland, Wash. Died Oct. 29, 2005.

TABRAH, RUTH MILANDER, minister, writer; b. Buffalo, N.Y., Feb. 28, 1921; d. Henry Milander and Ruth Harwood; m. Frank L. Tabrah, May 8, 1943 (div. Aug. 1970); children: Joseph, Thomas. BA, SUNY, Buffalo, 1941. Minister Honpa Hongwanji Mission of Hawaii, Honolulu, Hawaii, from 1983. Lectr. in field. Author: Pulaski Place, 1949, Voices of Others, 1959, Emily's Hawaii, 1967, Hawaii Nel, 1967, The Red Shark, 1980, Buddhism, A Modern Way of Life and Thought, 1970, Lanai, Biography of an Island, 1976, Hawaii, a History, 1982, Niihau: The Last Hawaiian Island, 1987, Ajatasatu, The Story of Who We Are, 1988, Shin Sutras to Live By, 1991, The Monk Who Dared, 1995, The Natural Way of Shin Buddhism, 1994, Maui The Romantic Island, 1991-92, Kauai The Unconquerable Island, 1991-92, Golden Children of Hawaii, 1989; editor, text adaptor 9 titles Island Heritage Folktales and Legends, 1973-78; editor Buddhist Study Ctr. Press, 1979—; contbr. articles to jours. Founder Buddhist Study Ctr. Press, Honolulu, 1979; mem. Hawaii State Bd. Edn., Honolulu, 1966-78; chmn. Hawaii County Dem. Com., Hilo, 1979-80. Mem. Internat. Assn. Shin Buddhist Studies. Home: Honolulu, Hawaii. Died Apr. 8, 2004.

TAFT, JOHN JOSEPH, counselor; b. Bklyn., Dec. 5, 1946; s. John Taft and Marie Eva Martineau; m. Susan M. Alfin (div. Nov. 1984); 1 child, Donna L.; m. Linda L. Bleecker, May 25, 1987. BS, C.W. Post Coll., 1993. Sr. dispatcher Village of Hempstead, N.Y., 1972-85; vets. counselor Nassau County, Plainview, N.Y., from 1985. Sgt. USMC, 1965-71. Decorated Purple Heart. Mem. VFW, DAV, Am. Legion, First Marine Divsn. Assn., Marine Corps League (past area vice commandant L.I. chpt., nat. chmn.), Mil. Order Devil Dogs (past pack leader, past pound keeper), Mil. Order Purple Heart, Nat. Amputation Found., Second Marine Divsn. Assn., Third Marine Divsn. Assn., Vets. Vietnam War, Vietnam Dog Handler Assn. (past nat. v.p.). Home: North Merrick, NY. Died Apr. 30, 2004.

TAFT, NATHANIEL BELMONT, lawyer; b. Tarrytown, N.Y., Aug. 12, 1919; s. Louis Eugene and Etta Minnie (Spivak) Tepp; m. Norma Rosalind Pike, May 22, 1943 (dec. Dec. 1997); children: Charles Eliot, Stephen Pike. BS in Econs., Fordham U., 1940; JD, Harvard U., 1948. Bar: N.Y. 1949. Asst. to gen. counsel N.Y. State Ins. Dept., Albany, 1948-50; law dept. N.Y. Life Ins. Co., N.Y.C., 1951-65, group dept., 1965-84, ret. as group v.p., 1984; sole practice law White Plains, N.Y., from 1985. Lectr., author on healthcare reform, 1992—. Contbr. articles to profl. jours.; author monographs on group ins. regulation. Bd. dirs. Westchester Philharm., 1991-2002, pres., 2001-02. Mem. ABA, N.Y. State Bar Assn., Nat. Assn. Physicians (sec.-treas. 1991—). Republican. Jewish. Avocation: writing. Died Jan. 11, 2004.

TAGLLACOZZO, DAISY MARGOT, sociology educator; b. Berlin, Mar. 26, 1923; came to U.S., 1946, naturalized, 1951; d. Botho and Luise (Meinecke) Lilienthal; m. Luigi Tagliacozzo, May 12, 1955. BA, Boston U., 1950; PhD, U. Chgo., 1956. Tchr. Wright Jr. Coll., Chgo., 1956-59; lectr. adult edn. U. Chgo. and U. Ill., 1959-61; assoc. prof. sociology Ill. Inst. Tech., Chgo., 1961-66, prof., 1966-71, chmn. dept. polit. and social sci., 1964-66; prof. sociology U. Mass., Boston, 1971-88, dean coll., 1971-75, prof. emeritus, 1988—2006. Dir. NSF Acad. Year Inst. in Sociology, 1965-71; prin. investigator NIH grant nurse-patient edn. and patterns of compliance, 1966-71; mem. nat. bd. cons. NIH, 1975-82; mem. Social Sci. Edn. Consortium, 1978-79 Mem. Am. Sociol. Assn. Home: Brookline, Mass. Died July 20, 2006.

TALIAFERRO, HENRY BEAUFORD, JR., retired lawyer; b. Shawnee, Okla., Jan. 12, 1932; s. Henry Beauford Sr. and Laudys L. (Anthony) T.; m. Janet Stewart Myers, Nov. 23, 1955 (div. Feb. 1985); children: Sarah Stewart T. deLeon, Henry B. III, William N.; m. Patricia Ann Shoemaker, May 16, 1987. BA, U. Okla., 1954, JD, 1956. Bar: Okla. 1956, U.S. Supreme Ct. 1966, D.C. 1969, U.S. Claims Ct. 1970. Assoc. Monnet, Hayes & Bullis, Oklahoma City, 1956-59, ptnr., 1959-66; exec. dir. O.E.O. legal svcs. program Oklahoma County, 1966-67; dir. congl. rels., acting exec. dir. Pres.'s Nat. Adv. Commn. on Civil Disorders, Washington, 1967-68; assoc. solicitor for Indian Affairs Dept. of the Interior, Washington, 1968-69; pvt. practice Washington, 1969-70; ptnr. Casey, Lane & Mittendorf, Washington, 1970-80; exec. v.p., gen. counsel The GHK Cos., Oklahoma City, 1980-83; of counsel Kerr, Irvine & Rhodes, Oklahoma City, 1987—2002; ret., 2002. Cons. Gas Pipeline Acquisitions & Mgmt., Oklahoma City, 1983-87; mem. Interstate Oil and Gas Compact Commn., 1980—, Okla. Commn. on Nat. Gas Policy, 1991-99, Okla. Energy Resources Bd., 1994—, vice-chair, 1996-97, chair, 1997-99. Author: (with others) Report of Presidents National Advisory Commission on Civil Disorders, 1968; contbr. articles to profl. jours. Candidate 5th dist. U.S. Ho. of Reps., Okla., 1966; mem. planning commn. Fairfax County, Va., 1973, platform com. Dem. Nat. Conv., San Francisco, 1984. Mem. ABA, Okla. Bar Assn., D.C. Bar Assn., Oklahoma City Golf and Country Club. Democrat. Episcopalian. Avocations: fishing, golf. Home: Oklahoma City, Okla. Died Aug. 4, 2004.

TALLEY, CLARENCE HOLLIS, minister; b. Winters, Tex., Oct. 28, 1945; s. William Clarence and Mattie Lucille (Hoover) T.; m. Kathleen Louise Bahlman, Dec. 29, 1967; children: William Thomas, Holly Dorinda, Mary Anna, Tiffany Renee. Ordained to ministry Ch. of Christ, 1967. Missionary Ch. of Christ, Battle Creek, Mich., 1967-68, minister L.A., 1968-73, Abilene, Tex., from 1973. Adv. bd. John Abraham Meml. Christian Relief, Amarillo, Tex., 1974—, Berean Family Home, Albany, La., 1981—, San Angelo (Tex.) Bible Inst., 1985—, India Missions, El Dorado, Ark., 1990—. Mem. adv. coun. Mental Health Mental Retardation, Abilene, Tex., 1975-77; mem. parents adv. coun. Wylie Ind. Sch. Dist., Abilene, 1989—. Home: Abilene, Tex. Died July 16, 2005.

TANG, YOUSIN, electrical engineer, consultant; b. Shanghai, June 20, 1951; came to US, 1983; s. Xinguo Tang and Liyin Chen; m. Tina Y. Zhu, Sept. 23, 1952; 1 child, Lisa. Diploma, Anhui (China) B. T. U., 1982; BS magna cum laude, Norfolk State U., 1985; MS, U. New Orleans, 1987; PhD, Ga. Inst. Tech., 1995. Registered profl. engr., Ga. Asst. elec. engr. Shucai Co., Maanshan, China, 1979-83; asst. prof. Ft. Valley (Ga.) State U., 1987-90; researcher Ga. Tech., Atlanta, 1990-95; elec. engr. Global Engring. Co., Roswell, Ga., 1995-98; ceo, cons. Acutech Computing Co., Duluth, Ga., from 1998. Contbr. articles to profl. jours. Achievements include development of new computer analysis model for power system reliability study. Home: Duluth, Ga. Died Jan. 3, 2004.

TANGOREN, GULEN F., retired anesthesiologist, pain management specialist; b. Istanbul, Turkey, July 7, 1934; came to U.S., 1959; d. Ahmet Hamdi Iyigun and Hasene Kant; married; 5 children. MD, U. Istanbul, 1957. Diplomate Am. Bd. Pain Mgmt. Formerly in pvt. practice; formerly sec., treas. dept. anesthesia Sibley Meml. Hosp.; now ret. Founding mem. Muslim Cmty. Ctr.; active Simon Wiesenthal Ctr. Fellow Am. Coll. Anesthesiologists; mem. AMA, Am. Soc. Anesthesiologists, Md., D.C. Soc. Anesthesia, Internat. Anesthesia Soc. Republican. Moslem. Home: Rockville, Md. Died July 17, 2005.

TANIS, JANET ELEANOR, museum administrator, retired elementary school educator; b. Elizabeth, N.J., Oct. 24, 1921; d. Jacob Tanis and Hazel Cecilia Pellens; m. Layton Wolfram, Dec. 26, 1943 (dec.); m. Edwin Geckeler, Feb. 26, 1961 (dec.). BS, Douglass Coll., 1943; EdM, Rutgers U., 1957; postgrad., Drew U., 1963, Fairleigh Dickinson U., 1963—64, Rutgers U., 1963, U. Colo., 1968, postgrad., 1974, Kean Coll. of N.J., 1972—78, Chaminade U. of Honolulu, 1978. Cert. tchr. sci., phys. sci., secondary, home econs. 5-12, elem. K-8 N.J., supr. gen. and supr. sci. N.J., tchr., elem., 1-6, sci., 7-9, 9-12; home econs, 7-12 Fla. Tchr. home econs. 7-12 Roselle (N.J.) H.S., 1943—44; clk. Calco Chem. Corp., Bound Brook, NJ, 1944; substitute tchr. Hampton (N.J.) Pub. Sch., 1944—45; clk.-typist Somerville (N.J.) Quartermaster Depot, 1945; asst. hostess Woodlawn, Douglass Coll. Alumnae Ho., New Brunswick, NJ, 1945—48; home econs. advisor Pub. Svc. Electric and Gas Co., Plainfield and New Brunswick, NJ, 1948—53; asst. foods editor Woman's Home Companion mag., N.Y.C., 1953—54; tchr. Aldene Sch., Roselle Park, NJ, 1954—57, Washington Sch., Summit, NJ, 1957—58; elem. sch. sci. coord. Summit, 1958—62; sci. coord. K-9, 1962—75; tchr. grade 6 Lincoln Sch., Summit, 1975—76; tchr. earth sci. Summit Jr. H.S., 1976—79; tchr. sci. grades 8 and 9 Benjamin Sch., North Palm Beach, Fla., 1980—81; substitute tchr. Palm Beach County Pub. Schs., 1981—82; salesperson Harold Grant, North Palm Beach, 1984—89; asst., dir., dir. edn. Hibel Mus. Art, Palm Beach and Jupiter, Fla., from 1987. Tchr. Rutgers Grad. Sch. Edn., 1958, 59, 60, 1961—65, 1964; sci. writer, curriculum developer, substitute tchr. The Sch. Bd. of Palm Beach County, 1982—84; tchr. Fairleigh Dickinson U., Madison, NJ, 1972—73; instr. Nova U., Ft. Lauderdale, Fla., 1984; del. to U. Bristol (Eng.) Nat. Sci. Tchrs. Assn., 1968—69. Author: The Festival of Animals Coloring Book, 1991. Rep. for Hibel Mus. Art Palm Beach Cultural Coun., from 1989, Palm Beach County Attractions Assn., from 1989; vol. Am. Cancer Soc., West Palm Beach, 1985; sec., mem. Friends of the Lake Park (Fla.) Libr., 1986. Recipient Disting. Svcv. award, N.J. Sci. Suprs. Assn., 1982; grantee, IBM Corp., 1968—69. Fellow: N.J. Sci. Tchrs. Assn.; mem.: Mus. Educators of S.E. Fla., Nat. Sci. Tchrs. Assn. (life Fellowhip award 1978), Rutgers Alumni Assn., Douglass Coll. Alumnae Assn., Kappa Delta Pi. Republican. Episcopalian. Avocations: reading, research, photography, painting, cooking. Home: North Palm Beach, Fla. Died Oct. 21, 2004.

TANKARD, JAMES WILLIAM, JR., retired journalism educator, writer; b. Newport News, Va., June 20, 1941; s. James William and Eileen (Looney) T.; m. Sara Elaine Fuller, July 21, 1973; children: Amy Elizabeth, Jessica Hope, Margaret Elaine. BS, Va. Poly. Inst., 1963; MA, U. N.C., 1965; PhD, Stanford U., 1970. Newswriter AP, Charlotte, N.C., 1965; reporter The Raleigh (N.C.) Times, 1965-66; vis. asst. prof. U. Tex., Austin, 1970, U. Wis., Madison, 1970-71; asst. prof. Temple U., Phila., 1971-72, U. Tex., Austin, 1972-76, assoc. prof., 1976-82, prof., 1982—2004, Jesse H. Jones prof. in journalism, 1989—2004, prof. emeritus, from 2004. Author: The Statistical Pioneers, 1984; co-author: Basic News Reporting, 1977, Communication Theories, 1979, 5th edit., 2001, Mass Media in the Information Age, 1990; How to Build Social Science Theories, 2004, Writing for Print and Digital Media, 2005; editor Journalism Monographs, 1988-94. Mem. AAUP, Assn. for Edn. in Journalism and Mass Communication (chair rsch. com. 1987-88), Internat. Communication Assn., Soc. Profl. Journalists. Avocations: hiking, bicycling, songwriting. Home: Austin, Tex. Died Aug. 12, 2005.

TANNER, JACK EDWARD, federal judge; b. 1919; m. Glenda M. Martin; children: Maryetta J. Greaves, Donnetta M. Gillum. Sole practice, Tacoma, 1955-78; judge U.S. Dist. Ct. (we. dist.) Wash., Tacoma, 1978—91, sr. judge, 1991—2006. Mem. Nat. Bar Assn. Died Jan. 10, 2006.

TAOFINU'U, PIO CARDINAL, retired archbishop; b. Falealupo, Samoa, Dec. 8, 1923; Ordained priest Roman Catholic Ch., 1954, joined Soc. of Mary, 1962, consecrated bishop, 1968. Bishop of Apia, Samoa and Tokelau, 1968-73; elected to Coll. Cardinals, 1973; archbishop of Samoa-Apia and Tokelau, 1982—2002. Mem. Congregation Causes of Saints Died Jan. 19, 2006.

TATE, MANFORD BEN, guided missile scientist, investor; b. Okolona, Ark., Aug. 3, 1916; s. Ernest and Mabel (Burley) T.; m. Marjorie Belle Stone, Sept. 9, 1942; children: Howard Ernest, Virginia Louise (Gina) Tate Smythe, Barbara Anne. Student, Cen. Coll. Liberal Arts, 1935-37; BSCE, U. Mo., 1940, MSCE, 1942; PhD in Theoretical and Applied Mechanics, Iowa State U., 1949. Grad. fellow, instr., asst. prof., assoc. prof. U. Mo., Columbia, 1940-51; lectr, engring. mechanics U. Va., Hampton, 1944-45; grad. fellow, instr. Iowa State U., Ames, 1946-47; engr. U.S. Naval Ordnance Lab., White Oak, Md., 1950-56; lectr., advisor U. Md., White Oak, 1950-56; guided missile rsch. scientist Johns Hopkins U. Applied Physics Lab., Laurel, Md., 1956-78, prof. missile structures, 1958-64; pres., gen. ptnr. Tate Ptnrs., Silver Spring, Md., from 1968. Concrete inspector Mo. Hwy. Dept., 1940; vis. prof. Cath. U. Am., Washington, 1956-58; aeronautical rsch. Nat. Adv. Com. Aeronautics, Langley Field, Va., 1944-45; cons. in field. Bridge designer Bur. of Bridges, 1941; Crane designer Dravo Corp. Pitts.; co-inventor Tomahawk Cruise Missile (patentee 1971); derived theoretical solution for shock strength of the Fat Man Atom Bomb; author: (with others) Selected Problems in Materials Testing, 1943; contbr. more than 400 articles to profl. jours./publs. Cub scouts chmn., cubmaster Boy Scouts Am., 1956-61, chmn. rev. bd., 1962-65; ciCD chmn. PTA, 1961-63; hon. coun. mem. Lakota Sioux Indian Tribe, Chamberlain, S.D., Ogalala Sioux Indian Tribe, Rapid City, S.D. Recipient Disting. Svc. Gold medal in Engring. award U. Mo., 1995. Mem. ASCE, ASTM, ASME, Am. Soc. Engring Edn., Am. Soc. Ordnance Engrs., Soc. Exptl. Stress Analysis, Sigma Xi, Phi Kappa Phi, Chi Epsilon. Democrat. Methodist. Achievements include patents on the Tomahawk Cruise Missile; first investigator in world to derive theoretical solution for air oscillations in ducted missiles/derived theoretical solution for shock strength of the Fat Man atom bomb. Died Mar. 17, 2004.

TATNALL, GEORGE JACOB, aeronautical engineer; b. Cin., Aug. 9, 1923; s. George Henry and Ida Mae (Hazelbaker) T.; m. G. Virginia Morgan, Feb. 5, 1949; children: Robert, William, Jeffrey, Thomas, Jane. BSME in Aeronautics, U. Pitts., 1949. Devel. engr. Naval Air Devel. Ctr., Warminster, Pa., 1949-57, supr. electro-mech. design br., supr. radome antenna sect., 1957-62, 63-78; engring. group leader Corning (N.Y.) Glass Works, 1962-63; cons. Semcor, Inc., Warminster, 1979-81; cons. pvt. practice Warminster, 1982-84; cons. Rome Rsch. Corp., New Hartford, N.Y., 1993-95. Tech. advisor Seventh Fleet USN, S.E. Asia, during Vietnam War, 1971. Contbr. to sci. papers presented at confs. (many also pub. in proceedings); author: (with others) chpt. in book Environmental Simulation and Test Data; author: manuals and documentation aircraft equipment. With US Army AF, 1943-45, China. Mem. AIAA (pres. U. Pitts. chpt. 1948), VFW, Flying Tiger U.S. 14th Air Force Assn. Achievements include patents for Speed Brake Retarding Mechanism for an Air Dropped Store, Air Dropped Minature Sonobuoy, Rotatable and Tiltable Radome with ind. scan and tilt antenna; developed low noise coupling through laminar boundary layer for acoustic homing missile, test facilities for supersonic rain erosion of aircraft materials. Home: Warminster, Pa. Died Dec. 19, 2004.

TAUBE, HENRY, chemistry professor; b. Sask., Can., Nov. 30, 1915; arrived in U.S., 1937, naturalized, 1942; s. Samuel and Albertina (Tiledetski) Taube; m. Mary Alice Wesche, Nov. 27, 1952; children: Linda, Marianna, Heinrich, Karl. BS, U. Sask., 1935, MS, 1937, LLD, 1973; PhD, U. Calif., 1940; PhD (hon.), Hebrew U. of Jerusalem, 1979; DSc

(hon.), U. Chgo., 1983, Poly. Inst., N.Y., 1984, SUNY, 1985, U. Guelph, 1987, Seton Hall U., 1988, Lajos Kossuth U. Debrecen, Hungary, 1988; DSc, Northwestern U., 1990; DSc (hon.), U. Athens, 1993. Instr. U. Calif., Berkeley, 1940—41; instr., asst. prof. Cornell U., 1941—46; faculty U. Chgo., 1946—62, prof., 1952—62, chmn. dept. chemistry, 1955—59; prof. chemistry Stanford U., 1962—86, chmn. dept. chemistry, 1972—74, 1978—79, Marguerite Blake Wilbur prof., 1976; prof. emeritus Stanford U, 1986—2005. Baker lectr. Cornell U., 1965; cons. Catalytica Assocs., Inc., Mountain View, Calif. Contbr. articles to profl. jours. Recipient Chandler medal, Columbia U., 1964, F. P. Dwyer medal, U. NSW, 1973, Nat. medal of sci., 1976—77, Excellence in Grad. Tchg. and Innovative Sci. award, Allied Chem., 1979, Nobel prize in chemistry, 1983, Bailar medal, U. Ill., 1983, award in chemistry, Robert A. Welch Found., 1983, Disting. Achievement award, Internat. Precious Metals Inst., 1986, Merit award, Brazilian Order of Sci., 1994; fellow, Guggenheim, 1949, 1955. Fellow: Royal Soc. Can. (hon.), Indian Chem. Soc. (hon.), Royal Soc. Chemistry (hon.); mem.: NAS (award in chem. scis. 1983), Engring. Acad. Japan (fgn. assoc.), Royal Soc. (fgn. mem.), Royal Danish Acad. Scis. and Letters, Finnish Acad. Sci. and Letters (fgn. mem.), Am. Philos. Soc., Royal Physiographical Soc. of Lund, Am. Chem. Soc. (award for nuclear applications in chemistry 1955, Harrison Howe award, Rochester sect. 1960, John Gamble Kirkwood award, New Haven sect. 1966, Disting. Svc. in Advancement Inorganic Chemistry award 1967, Nichols medal 1971, Willard Gibbs medal, Chgo. sect. 1971, T.W. Richards medal, Northeastern sect. 1980—81, Monsanto Co. award in inorganic chemistry 1981, Linus Pauling award, Puget Sound sect. 1981, Priestley medal 1985, Oesper award, Cinn. sect. 1986, G.M. Kosolapoff award, Auburn sect. 1990), Australian Acad. Scis. (corr.), Brazilian Acad. Scis. (corr.), Am. Acad. Arts and Scis. (PR) (corr.), Chem. Soc. Japan (hon.), Hungarian Acad. Scis. (hon.), Can. Soc. Chemistry (hon.), Coll. Chemists of Catalonia and Beleares (hon.), Sigma Xi, Phi Beta Kappa, Phi Lambda Upsilon (hon.). Died Nov. 16, 2005.

TAYBACK, MATTHEW L., medical scientist, consultant, educator; b. Tarrytown, N.Y., July 30, 1919; s. Arnold and Ann (Link) T.; m. Anita Mary Moffat, June 6, 1945; children: Robert Moffat, Matthew Gordon, Sheila Leatherman. AB, Harvard U., 1939; AM, Columbia U., 1940; ScD, Johns Hopkins U., 1953. Dep. commr. of health City of Balt., 1960-69; asst. sec. of health State of Md., 1969-73, state dir. of aging, 1974-83; coord. Ctr. on Aging Johns Hopkins U., Balt., from 1983, adj. prof. health, from 1983. Hon. prof. Pahlavi U., Shiraz, Iran, 1975-78; vis. prof. Jordan U. Faculty of Medicine, Amman, 1988-95; vice chmn. City of Balt. Com. on Aging, 1995. Elder Govans Presbyn. Ch. Lt. col. U.S. Army, 1942-45, ETO. Decorated Bronze Star; recipient Disting. Citizen award State of Md., 1983. Democrat. Home: Baltimore, Md. Died Sept. 19, 2004.

TAYLOR, CLARENCE ALBERT, JR., housing coordinator, drug counselor; b. Charlottesville, Va., Nov. 23, 1950; s. Clarence A. and Mary E. (Washington) T. BS, Wilberforce (Ohio) U., 1974. G.E.D. instr. Dept. Labor Svcs., Topeka, 1978-80; youth svc. worker Youth Ctr., Topeka, 1981-86; coord. transitional living-employment Breakthrough House, Inc., Topeka, 1982-86; program mgr. N. W. Mental Health Ctr., Phila., 1986-89; employment counselor Offender Aid and Restoration, Charlottesville, Va., 1989; housing coord. Greene Co. Community Devel., Stanardsville, Va., 1991-94; housing coord., EEO officer Skyline Cmty. Action Program, Inc., Stanardsville, from 1994. Trainee Horizon House, Phila., 1987-88, Med. Coll. of Pa., Phila., 1988. Named Outstanding Young Man Am., Jaycees of Am., 1978; first black hired in middle level mgmt. position in history of Greene County govt. Democrat. Baptist. Avocations: music appreciation, reading, community volunteer work, sporting events spectator. Home: Quinque, Va. Died Mar. 24, 2005.

TAYLOR, JAMES MARION, II, automotive wholesale executive; b. Andalusia, Ala., Jan. 20, 1926; s. Marion Doby and Catherine (Hill) T.; m. Abbie Chapman Henderson, Mar. 22, 1947; children: Cathy, James III, Merrily, Abbie, John. Student, U.S. Merchant Marine Acad., 1944-46, Auburn U., 1946-47. Salesman Taylor Parts, Inc., Andalusia, 1947-49, salesman, dir., 1950, v.p., sales mgr., 1950-61, v.p., gen. mgr., 1961-62, pres., 1962-88, chmn., chief exec. officer, 1988-92. Bd. dirs. Covington County Bank, Andalusia; chmn. Southern Nat., Andalusia, 1986—; mem. adv. bd. Shatterproof Glass Co., Detroit, 1968, AC-Delco, Detroit, 1966-67, Walker (Tenneco) Racine, Wis., 1985. Bd. dirs. Ala. Wildlife Fedn., Montgomery, 1974-77, pres., 1977-78; bd. dirs. Lurleen B. Wallace Jr. Coll. Found., Andalusia, 1986-89, Covington County Bd. Edn., Andalusia, 1960-74, City of Andalusia Downtown Devel. Authority, 1989-96, City of Andalusia Indsl. Devel. Bd., 1969-71. Mem. Nat. Assn. Wholesalers (bd. dirs. and 1st vice chmn. 1988-90, chmn.-elect 1991, chmn. 1992, treas. 1993-94), Automotive Hall of Fame (Midland, Mich. bd. dirs. 1986-94), Automotive Info. Coun. (bd. dirs. 1987-92), Andalusia C. of C. (bd. dirs. 1960-62, 89-92), Auburn Alumni Assn. (life), Kiwanis (pres. Andalusia club 1969-70), Am. Legion. Republican. Baptist. Avocations: hunting, fishing, gun collecting. Home: Andalusia, Ala. Died Aug. 11, 2005.

TAYLOR, JOHN FORREST, retail executive; b. Chillicothe, Mo., Feb. 13, 1935; s. Jonathon Edward Taylor and Iona Berniece (Ingman) Walters; m. Shirley Ann Schlichtmann, June 5, 1955; children: Sharon, John, Susan, James.

Student, Valparaiso U., 1953-55. Mgr. Nat. Tea Co., Chgo., 1954-59, Joe Tittle & Sons Inc., Gary, Ind., 1959-65; owner Taylors Food Ctr., Valparaiso, Ind., 1965-69; v.p. sales R.W. Pool Co. Inc., Valparaiso, 1969-86; owner, franchisee Snappy Tomato Pizza, N.W. Ind., 1986-88; v.p. gen. mgr. Time Low Corp., Valparaiso, from 1987. Bd. govs. Shrine Hosps., Chgo., 1989—; lay minister Evang. Luth. Ch., 1971—; pres., bd. dirs. Porter County Crimestoppers, Valparaiso, 1988—. Mem. Nat. Assn. Convenience Stores, Ind. Assn. Convenience Stores, Valparaiso C. of C., Shriners (past potentate Michigan City, Inc.). Democrat. Avocation: reading. Home: Valparaiso, Ind. Died Mar. 9, 2004.

TAYLOR, PATRICK FRANKLIN, energy company executive; b. Beaumont, Tex., June 12, 1937; s. Sibyl Partin Gayman; m. Phyllis Diane Miller Taylor, Dec. 16, 1966. BS in Petroleum Engring., La. State U., 1959; ScD (hon.), U. New Orleans, 1988. Petroleum engr. John W. Mecom, Sr., New Orleans, 1957-66; pres. T.N.T., Inc., New Orleans, 1967-79, Circle Bar Drilling Co., New Orleans, 1976-80; chmn. bd., chief exec. officer Taylor Energy Co., New Orleans, from 1979. Cons. in field. Bd. dirs. U.S. Coast Guard Found., New Orleans, 1988, La. Assn. Bus. & Industry, 1989—, Jr. Achievemetn of S.E. La., New Orleans, 1987-88; chmn. Greater New Orleans Conv. Fund, 1988; fin. chmn. Rep. Nat. Conv., New Orleans, 1988; bd. dirs. Inst. for Human Understanding, New Orleans, 1987-88; chmn. March of Dimes "TeamWalk", New Orleans, 1985-88, others; established "Taylor's Kids" prog. for scholarship, New Orleans, 1988—, Taylor Plan, 1989—. With USMCR, 1957-59. Recipient 1988 Weiss Brotherhood award NCCJ, 1988, 1988 Altruism award Black Orgn. of Police, 1988, 1988 Disting. Svc. award Miss. State U. Alumni Assn., 1989, Outstanding Bus. Leader award Northwood Inst., 1989, Beta Gamma Sigma medallion for entrepreneurship, 1989, Freedoms Found. award, 1990; named Man of the Yr., NAACP, 1990. Mem. Soc. Petroleum Engrs., AIME, Am. Petroleum Inst., New Orleans C. of C., Internat. Trade Mart, Nat. Ocean Ind. Assn., La. State U. Ports and Waterway Inst. (adv. council), YMCA Century Club, New Orleans Petroleum Club, Navy League of U.S., Bus. Council New Orleans and River Region, Metairie Country Club, Plimsoll Club, City Club of New Orleans, others. Republican. Baptist. Avocations: game ranching, skeet, hunting, reading, power boat racing, weapons. Home: New Orleans, La. Died Nov. 5, 2004.

TAYLOR, T. RABER, lawyer; b. Colorado Springs, Colo., Dec. 31, 1910; s. Ralph Franklin and Mary Catherine (Burns) T.; m. Josephine Loretto Reddin, Sept. 20, 1938; children: Mary Therese, Carol Anne, Margaret Claire, Josephine R., Rae Marie, Kathleen Mae, Anne Marie. BA magna cum laude, Regis Coll., 1933; JD, Harvard U., 1937. Bar: Colo. 1937, U.S. Dist. Ct. Colo. 1937, U.S. Tax Ct. 1938, U.S. Ct. Appeals (10th cir.) 1940, U.S. Supreme Ct. 1950. Pvt. practice law, Denver, from 1937. Bd. dirs. Denver Cath. Charities, 1946-71; v.p. Nat. Conf. Cath. Charities, 1956-57, 69-75; mem. gov.'s com., White House Conf. on Children and Youth, 1971. Lt. comdr. USNR, 1943-45, NATOUSA, ETO. Knight Order St. Gregory, 1971, Equestrian Order of Holy Sepulchre of Jerusalem, 1973; recipient St. Vincent de Paul medal St. John's U., Jamaica, N.Y., 1971, St. Thomas More award Cath. Lawyers Guild Denver, 1981. Fellow Am. Coll. Probate Counsel; mem. ABA, Colo. Bar Assn., Denver Bar Assn., Denver Estate Planning Coun. (pres. 1962-63), Greater Denver Tax Counsel Assn., Serra Club Denver. Home: Denver, Colo. Died Mar. 31, 2004.

TEAGUE, WALTER DORWIN, JR., industrial designer, consultant; b. N.Y.C., July 2, 1910; s. Walter Dorwin and Cecilia (Fehon) T.; m. Rita Lynn (div. 1938); children: Walter Dorwin III, Lewis; m. Harriette Barnard (dec. 1998), Dec. 29, 1939; 1 child, Harry. Student, MIT, 1931. Dir. prodn. design Walter Dorwin Teague Assocs., N.Y.C., 1935-42; head of rsch., engring. dept. Bendix Aviation Corp., Teterboro, N.J., 1942-52; ptnr. Walter Dorwin Teague Assocs., N.Y.C., 1952-67; former pres. Dorwin Teague Inc., Nyack. Patentee in field; contbr. articles to profl. jours; Author: Industrial Designer: The Artist as Engineer, 1998. Recipient Best Design of Yr. award, Indsl. Design Inst., 1960, Best Product Design of Yr. award, Am. Iron and Steel Inst., 1969. Fellow AIAA (assoc., Pioneer award 1981); mem. Amateur Yacht Rsch. Soc. (U.S. organizer 1965-74), N.Y. Yacht Club, Cruising Club Am., Classic Car Club Am. (hon.), Marmon Automobile Club (hon.). Avocations: sailing, skiing, birding, hiking. Died Sept. 16, 2004.

TEAT, HERBERT LEROY, retired music educator; b. El Paso, Tex., May 14, 1923; s. Herbert Leroy Teat and Martha Motee Shannon; m. Angelien Francis, Aug. 4, 1951 (div. Jan. 1975); children: Herbert L. III, James Stephen, Adonna Mary; m. Sue Ellen French, Dec. 17, 1976 (div.); 1 child, Timothy Shannon. MusB, North Tex. State Tchrs. Coll., 1948; MusM, Westminster Choir Coll., 1954. Cert. music tchr., Tex., Ala. Band dir., music dir. Rusk (Tex.) Sch. Dist., 1948-52; choral dir., music dir. Longview (Tex.) Sch. Dist., 1954-69, Tarleton State U., Stephenville, Tex., 1969-83, U. North Ala., Florence, 1984-86; ret. Cons. choral music edn. Contbr. articles to profl. jours.; mem. editl. bd. Southwestern Musician mag., 1958-62; author workbook: EEV Music Reader, 1968. Chmn. campaign March of Dimes, Cherokee County, Tex., 1950; charter mem., v.p. Tex. Choral Dirs. Assn., 1955; state v.p. Music Educators Assn., 1958-60, state pres. 1960-62, mem. state pres. assembly nat. conf.,

Washington, 1962. Mem. San Gabriel Writers League, Tex. Music Educators (hon. life mem.), Congress of Parent-Tchrs. (hon. life mem.). Methodist. Home: Georgetown, Tex. Died July 23, 2004.

TEDFORD, TERRELL LAWRENCE, building automation company executive; b. Atlanta, Jan. 27, 1949; s. Bennie Lawrence Jr. and Dara Louise (Grainger) T.; m. Pamela Jane Hunnicutt, Mar. 19, 1971 (div. Sept. 1986); children: Brad T., Ryan T.; m. Anita Sue Gentry, Nov. 27, 1988; children: Cheryl Eden, Jennifer Eden. BEE, Ga. Inst. Tech., 1971; MBA, U. Okla., 1975. Elec. constrn. estimator State Electric Co., Atlanta, 1969-71; sales mgr. Johnson Controls, Atlanta, 1975-81; gen. mgr. Landis & Gyr Powers Inc., Atlanta, from 1981. Sunday sch. leader and tchr. Eastside Bapt. Ch., Ga., Meadowood Bapt. Ch., Okla., 1973-88; mem. Citizens for Responsible Growth, Gwinnett County, Ga., 1992-93. Capt. USAF, 1971-75. Mem. ASHRAE, Assn. Energy Engrs. (sr.), Ga. Inst. Tech. Alumni Assn. (mentor 1990—, chmn. scholarship com. 1991—). Republican. Avocations: tennis, golf, racquetball, reading, jogging. Home: Alpharetta, Ga. Died Apr. 1, 2005.

TEEL, RAYMOND FRANK, landscape engineer and designer, artist; b. Sudan, Tex., July 19, 1929; s. John Hugh and Grace Arizone (Branscum) T.; m. Ruth Ann Gilbert, Mar. 1972 (div. Jan. 1977). Grad. high sch. Real estate developer, Los Angeles, 1962-66; prin. Teel Landscape Co., San Pedro, Calif., from 1972; artist, proprietor, distbr. ltd. edition art Teel Gallery, Los Angeles, from 1969. Republican. Avocation: art shows. Died Mar. 6, 2005.

TEEL, ROBERT LEE, retail company executive; b. Kansas City, Mo., Mar. 7, 1925; s. William Henry and Mary Ophelia (Biddlecome) T.; m. Sue Newcomer, Oct. 3, 1952; children: Leslie Sue, Robert Lee II. BA in Econs., U. Kans., 1950. Owner Unfinished Shop, Fairway, Kans., 1955-81, Kansas City, 1958-80, Woodcraft Products, Kansas City, 1963-84; co-founder, exec. dir. Integratism Found., Kansas City, 1985-87, chmn., bd. trustees, from 1987. Active mem. U.S. Olympic Swimming Com., 1972-76; bd. dirs. Homes Assn. of Country Club Dist., Prairie Village, Kans., 1975-77. With USNR, 1943-46, 50-54. Mem. Amateur Athletic Union U.S. (regional chmn. 1969-70, nat. chmn. age group swimming com. 1970-72, pres. Mo. Valley Assn. 1971-72), Mchts. Assn. Fairway (pres. 1955-65), Mensa, Phi Kappa Psi. Avocations: trap and skeet gun, western riding, golf, astronomy, yachting. Home: Shawnee Mission, Kans. Died May 6, 2004.

TELLIER, RICHARD DALE, retail company executive; b. Williamson, N.Y., Apr. 9, 1933; s. Abram Michael and Susan Bush (Johnville) T. AA, Rochester Inst. Tech., 1953; BS, U. Miami, 1958. Buyer The Denver (Colo.), 1959-61, home furnishings coord., 1962-64; market rep. Associated Merchanding Corp., N.Y.C., 1965-67, worldwide home furnishings devel., 1968-75; v.p. merchandising May Dept. Stores, N.Y.C., 1975-82; v.p. Wedgwood USA, N.Y.C., 1982-86, Waterford/Wedgwood USA, N.Y.C., from 1986. Active N.Y.C. Dem. Club, 1978; coord. Victorian Soc., N.Y.C., 1985. 1st Lt. U.S. Army, 1954-56. Recipient Designer award, German Glass Fedn., Manien, Germany, 1977, Yugoslavian Rogaska Crystal award, Belgrade, 1980. Mem. Nat. Tabletop Assn. (v.p. 1988—), Internat. Tabletop Assn. (dir. 1983—), 200 Club (v.p. N.Y.C. 1971-80). Democrat. Episcopalian. Died Jan. 28, 2004.

TELLO, RICHARD J., radiologist, researcher; b. Mexico City, Dec. 24, 1960; s. Mona Joan Lener; m. Jeanette M. Pratt, Dec. 27, 1983; 1 child, Rebecca. BS in Math., MIT, 1982, BSE in Mech. Engring., 1982, MSME, 1983, postgrad., from 1984; MD, Stanford U., 1989; MPH, Harvard U., 1998; PhD in Med. Imaging, U. Melbourne, 2003. Diplomate Am. Bd. Med. Examiners, Am. Coll. Radiology; certificate Diagnostic Radiology 1994, Special Competence Nuclear Medicine 1995. Rsch. asst. The Kidney Ctr., Boston, 1979, Beth Israel Hosp., Boston, 1980-81; rsch. engr. Extracorporeal Med. Specialties, King of Prussia, Pa., 1980; engr. IBM, Boulder, Colo., 1981-82, researcher, engr. Palo Alto, Calif., 1982-83; internal med. intern St. Mary's Hosp., San Francisco, 1989-90; radiology resident New England Deaconess Hosp., Boston, 1990-94; fellow nuclear medicine Harvard U., Boston, 1993-94; fellow MRI Brigham & Women's Hosp., Boston, 1994-95; dir. clin. MRI rsch. U. Melbourne, Australia, 1995-96; assoc. radiologist Alfred Hosp., Melbourne, Australia, 1996; assoc. prof. radiology Boston U., from 1996, assoc. prof. of epidemiology and biostats., from 1999, dir. cardiac MRI, radiology rsch., from 2000, prof., dir. MRI, from 2001, prof. radiology, epidemiology and biostats., from 2001. Adv. bd. Magnetic Resonance Imaging & Single Photon Emission Computed Tomography St. Mary's Hosp., 1990, Digital Radiology New England Deacness Hosp., 1991, Internet Tech. and Care, Boston U.; admissions panel Stanford Med. Sch., 1983; tchr., lectr. and presenter in field. Editor-in-chief: Internat. Jour. Radiology; author: tech. reports and conf. proceedings; contbr. articles to profl. jours. Nat. Hispanic Scholarship Fund scholar, 1979-88, Leopold Schepp Found. scholar, 1979-84, 1987-89, Nat. Med. Found. scholar 1983-84, Paul W. Mayer scholar Alliance for Engring. in Med. and Biology, 1986; Recipient Clapp and Poliak Eng. and Design award, 1980, Luis de Flores award MIT, 1982, special projects award and Rolex award for Innovation, 1993; MIT rsch. fellow 1983, MIT-Harvard HST/Whitaker Found. fellow 1984-87; grantee Sigma Xi, 1981, Hearst Found., 1985-87. Mem. ASME, Internat. Soc. Magnetic Resonance in Medicine, Radiological Soc. of No. Am. (rsch. resident award 1992), N.Y. Acad. Sci. (Otto P. Bergdorf honor 1978), Am. Roentgen Ray Soc. (New England chpt., pres. award 1994, Exec. Coun. award 2001), Internat. Soc. of Magnetic Resonance in Medicine, Pi Tau Sigma, Sigma Xi. Achievements include patents in field of biomedical extracorporeal blood perfusion and filtration with additional work on continuous monitoring of blood pressure via development of new instrumentation; notable work in image analysis with emphasis on three dimensional anatomic reconstruction, on biomedical flow analysis with emphasis on cardiac and kidney function. Home: Wellesley, Mass. Died Mar. 8, 2005.

TEMKO, ALLAN BERNARD, writer; b. NYC, Feb. 4, 1924; s. Emanuel and Betty (Alderman) T.; m. Elizabeth Ostroff, July 1, 1950 (dec. Aug. 1996); children: Susannah, Alexander. AB, Columbia U., 1947; postgrad, U. Calif., Berkeley, 1949-51, Sorbonne, 1948-49, 51-52. Lectr. Sorbonne, 1953-54, Ecole des Arts et Metiers, Paris, 1954-55; asst. prof. journalism U. Calif., Berkeley, 1956-62, lectr. in city planning and social scis., 1966-70, lectr. Grad. Sch. Journalism, 1991; lectr. art Stanford U., 1981, 82; architecture critic San Francisco Chronicle, 1961-93, art editor, 1979-82. Archtl. planning cons.; chmn. Yosemite Falls Design Workshop, 1992; Pulitzer Prize juror, 1991-92; architecture advisor Roman Cath. Cathedral, Oakland, Calif., 2000-06. Author: Notre Dame of Paris, 1955, Eero Saarinen, 1962, No Way To Build a Ballpark and Other Irreverent Essays on Architecture, 1993; contbr. articles to U.S. and fgn. mags. and newspapers; West Coast editor, Archtl. Forum, 1959-62. Served with USNR, 1943-46. Recipient Gold medal Commonwealth Club Calif., 1956, Silver medal, 1994, Journalism award AIA, 1961, Silver Spur award San Francisco Planning and Urban Renewal Assn., 1985, AIA Inst. Honor award, 1991, Nathaniel A. Owings award AIA Calif. Coun., 1995, 1st prize in archtl. criticism Mfrs. Hanover/Art World, 1986, Critic's award Mfrs. Hanover/Art World, 1987, Profl. Achievement award Soc. Profl. Journalists, 1988, Pulitzer Prize for criticism, 1990; grantee Rockefeller Found., 1962-63, 20th Century Fund, 1963-66, NEA, 1988, Graham Found., 1990; Guggenheim fellow, 1956-57. Home: Berkeley, Calif. Died Jan. 25, 2006.

TEMPLE, ARTHUR, III, investment company executive; b. Texarkana, Ark., Apr. 8, 1920; s. Arthur and Katherine (Sage) T.; m. Mary MacQuiston (div. 1963); children: Arthur III, Charlotte; m. Charlotte Dean, Sept. 4, 1963. Student, U. Tex.-Austin, 1937-38; LLD (hon.), Pepperdine U., 1982. Bookkeeper, asst. mgr. retail yard Temple Lumber Yard, Lufkin, Tex., 1938-48; pres., chmn. bd. Temple Assocs., Inc., Diboll, Tex., 1941-70; exec. v.p. Temple Industries, Inc., Diboll, Tex., 1948-51, pres., CEO, 1951-75, chmn. bd., 1972-73; bd. dirs. Temple-Eastex Inc., Diboll, Tex., from 1973—, chmn. bd., 1975-83; chmn. planning and devel. com. Time Inc., Diboll, Tex., 1973-81, group v.p., 1973-78, vice chmn., 1978-83; chmn. bd. Exeter Investment Co., Lufkin, Tex., 1982-83, Temple-Inland Inc., Lufkin, Tex., 1984—91, chmn. emeritus, 1991—94; chmn. bd. First Bank and Trust Ea. Tex., Diboll. Bd. dirs. Contractor's Supplies, Lufkin, Lufkin Block, Lumberman's Investment Corp., Austin, Sunbelt Ins. Co., Austin, Gt. Am. Res. Ins. Co., Dallas, Temple-Inland Fin. Svcs. Inc., Temple Inland Properties Inc., Austin Crest Hotel Inc.; chmn. bd. T&T Corp., Lufkin, Pineland State Bank; ltd. ptnr. Dallas Cowboys. Football Club; pres., bd. dirs. Tex. Southeastern R.R. (bd. dirs.). Pes. Angelina County C. of C., 1950; active State Bd. Edn., 1949; bd. regents Lamar Tech. U., 1957; trustee Duke U., 1983, John E. Gray Inst., T.L.L. Temple Founds.; bd. dirs. St. Michael Hosp. Found., Texarkana, Nat. Park Found., 1984—. Recipient 1 0f 5 Outstanding Young Men in Tex. award Tex. Jr. C. of C., 1948, Conservationist of Yr. award, 1977, East Texan of Yr. award Deep East Tex. Coun. Govts., 1983, Conservationist of Yr. award Safari Club Internat., 1983; named to Tex. Bus. Hall of Fame, 1983. Mem. Nat. Forest Product Assn (past chmn., pres., bd. dirs.), Nat. Assn. Mfrs (bd. dirs.), So. Forest Products Assn. (past chmn., pres.), Lumbermen's Assn. Tex. (past chmn., pres.), Am. Forest Products Assn. (trustee), Crown Colony Club (bd. dirs.), Delta Kappa Epsilon. Died Apr. 12, 2006.

TEMPLE, CARROLL GLENN, JR., medicinal chemist; b. Hickory, N.C., Mar. 7, 1932; s. Carroll Glenn Sr. and Cora Melissa (Stephens) T.; m. Leone Felton Newell, Apr. 21, 1956; children: Laura Felton, Sara Lisa. BS in Chemistry, Lenoir Rhyne Coll., 1954; MS in Chemistry, Birmingham-So. Coll., 1958; PhD in Organic Chemistry, U. N.C., 1962. Rsch. asst. dept. chemistry U. N.C., Chapel Hill, 1954, So. Rsch. Inst., Birmingham, Ala., 1955-59; mem. faculty U. Ala., Birmingham, 1962, Birmingham-So. Coll., 1964; head drug synthesis sect. organic chemistry dept. So. Rsch. Inst., Birmingham, 1966-80, head pharm. chemistry divsn., 1980-94, dir. organic chemistry dept., 1991-94, Disting. scientist, from 1994. Formal presentations various meetings. Contbr. articles to profl. jours.; patentee in field. Ad hoc mem. Am. Cancer Soc., 1981, Nat. Cancer Inst., NIH, 1987. Recipient Disting. Alumnus award Lenoir-Rhyne Coll., 1983. Mem. Am. Chem. Soc. (chmn. Ala. sect. 1975, congl. counselor 1976-78, 78-80). Died Aug. 14, 2005.

TEN EYCK, ROBERT LANCASTER, JR., psychologist; b. Hartford, Conn., Nov. 13, 1944; s. Robert Lancaster Sr. and Anne Laurie (Van Hook) Ten E.; m. Hannah Jo Hofherr, Aug. 12, 1967; children: Peter, Nicholas. BA, DePauw U., 1966; MS, Fla. State U., 1968, PhD, 1970. Registered health service provider. Dir. internship program Larue Carter Meml. Hosp., Indpls., 1973-79, chief psychologist children's dept., from 1970; instr. Ind. U. Sch. Medicine, Indpls., 1970-73, asst. prof., from 1973. Dir. psychol. services Humana Women's Hosp., Indpls., 1988—; cons. psychologist Marion Superior and Cir. Cts., Indpls., 1976—, Raines Pastural Counseling Ctr., Indpls., 1970-86. Contbr. articles to profl. jours. Pres. Raines Pastural Counseling Ctr., Indpls., 1975, v.p., 1976-86; bd. dirs. Ind. Prevention of Child Abuse Assn., 1985-88; mem. adv. commn. State Ind Commn. for the Handicapped, 1985—. USPHS Pre Doctoral Research fellow NIMH, 1968. Mem. Am. Psychol. Assn. (council of reps. 1987, Ind. Psychol. Assn. (pres. div. profl. psychol. 1977-78, pres. 1985-86, council reps. 1987—), Sigma Xi. Home: Indianapolis, Ind. Died June 26, 2004.

TENNENT, VALENTINE LESLIE, accountant; b. Apia, Western Samoa, Apr. 5, 1919; came to U.S., 1922; s. Hugh Cowper and Madge Grace (Cook) T.; m. Jeanne Marie Elder, Dec. 10, 1941; children: Madeline Jeanne Walls, Hugh Cowper II, Michael Waller, Val Leslie, Paul Anthony. Student, U. Calif., Berkeley, 1938-40. CPA, Hawaii, La. Mgr. Tennent & Greaney, CPAs, Hilo, Hawaii, 1945-50; ptnr. Cameron, Tennent & Dunn, CPAs, Honolulu, 1950-56, KPMG LLP, Honolulu, 1956-79, cons., 1979-84. Ind. rschr. pub. fin. and banking, polit. economy, moral philosophy, San Diego, 1984-2000. Founding trustee, pres., treas. Tennent Art Found., Honolulu, 1955-77; trustee, treas. Watumull Found., Honolulu, 1963-90; bd. dirs. Iolani Sch., Inst. for Human Svcs., Honolulu, Lyman Mus., Hilo. Capt. USAF, 1941-45. Recipient Bishop's Cross for disting. svc. Protestant Episcopal Ch., Dist. Hawaii, 1965, G.J. Watumull award for disting. achievement Watumull Found., Honolulu, 1982. Mem. AICPA (governing coun. 1961-64), Hawaii Soc. CPAs (pres. 1960). Episcopalian. Avocations: swimming, fine arts, music, literature. Died June 7, 2005.

TERREBONNE, RAY ANTOINE, secondary school educator; b. Golden Meadow, La., Jan. 12, 1945; s. Clifton J. and Rosie M. (Galliano) T.; m. Carol Lou Pitre, Nov. 22, 1969. BA, Nicholls State U., 1969, BA in Med. Tech. and Elem. Edn., 1988, MEd in Elem. Counseling, 1991. Lab. technician Touro Infirmary, New Orleans, 1968-69; tchr. elem. Holy Rosary Sch., Larose, La., 1982-87, LaFourche Parish Schs., Thibodaux, La., from 1987. Yearbook editor Holy Rosary Sch., 1984-87, active computer dept., 1986-87; with Golden Meadow Lower Sch., 1988—. With USN, 1969-71. Mem. Am. Assn. for Counseling and Devel., Am. Soc. Clin. Pathologists, Am. Legion, Lions (sec. Golden Meadow chpt. 1982-84), Fleet Res. Assn., DAV. Avocations: reading, travel, jigsaw and crossword puzzles. Home: Galliano, La. Died Mar. 7, 2005.

TERRY, NANCY A., medical record director; b. Heafer, Ark., Feb. 26, 1940; d. John Hall and Maryella M. (Tisher) Butler; m. Allen W. Scefcyk, Apr. 2, 1983 (div. 1986); children: Richard A., David P. Asst. dir. med. records Crittenden Meml. Hosp., W. Memphis, Ark., 1974-79; dir. med. records Victoria Hosp., Miami, Fla., 1979-84; dir. med. records Hollywood Med. Ctr. Nat. Med. Enterprises, Hollywood, Fla., from 1984. Contbr. articles to profl. jours. Mem. Am. Med. Records Assn. (accredited records technician), Ark. Med. Records Assn., Fla. Med. Records Assn. Republican. Methodist. Avocations: study of psychology, helping emotionally ill and homeless children. Home: Memphis, Tenn. Died Nov. 27, 2004.

THAXTON, EVERETTE FREDERICK, lawyer; b. Charleston, W.Va., Jan. 11, 1938; s. Wilbur and Mildred F. (Gerwig) T.; m. Karen Caldwell, Dec. 29, 1967; children: James, LeeAnn, Emily. BA, U. Charleston, 1967; JD, W.Va. U., 1970. Bar: W.Va. 1970, Va. 1981, U.S. Ct. Appeals (fourth cir.) 1983. Cartographer, hwy. design technician W.Va. Dept. of Hwy., Charleston, 1961-63; dir. tax mapping W.Va. Tax Dept., Charleston, 1963-65; ptnr. Thaxton & Daniels, Charleston, from 1970. Co-author: Construction Law in West Virginia, 1990. Served with USAF, 1955-61. Mem. ABA (various coms.), W.Va. Bar Assn., Assn. Trial Lawyers Am., W.VA. Trial Lawyers Assn., Am. Arbitration Assn. (panel arbitrators), Pi Gamma Mu. Avocations: flying, sports cars, constrn. machinery and equipment. Home: Charleston, W.Va. Died Sept. 7, 2004.

THAYER, STUART WALLACE, shipping company executive; b. North Oxford, Mass., Apr. 27, 1924; s. Walter E. and Helen Margaret (Riedel) T.; m. Marilyn Iris Rossbach, Nov. 22, 1950; children: David Ross, Dana Helen. BS in Marine Transp., MIT, 1948. Marine engr. Lykes Bros. Steamship Co., Inc., New Orleans, 1948-51, mgr. new constrn., 1954-70, v.p. engring., from 1970. Contbr. articles to profl. jours. Mem. La. Export Council, 1984-85. Served to comdr. USNR, 1943-47, 51-54. Named La. Maritime Man of Yr., Propeller Club, New Orleans, 1973. Mem. Soc. Naval Architects and Marine Engrs. (v.p. 1985—). Clubs: Marine (New Orleans). Republican. Baptist. Avocation: computers. Home: New Orleans, La. Died May 22, 2005.

THEIS, JAMES EDWARD, pastry chef, interior designer; b. Bellville, Ill., May 23, 1963; s. Clement John and Alice Florence (Schoeppner) T. AA, Crafton Hills Coll., 1983; BS in Wildlife Mgmt., Humboldt State U., 1987; A of Occupational Sci. in Culinary Arts, Calif. Culinary Acad., San Francisco, 1994. Wild animal trainer San Diego Zoo, 1983-84, Wild Animal Tng. Ctr., Riverside, Calif., 1980-85; jewelry salesperson J.C. Penney's, West Covina, Calif., 1987-88; display supr. Sherwood Mgmt., Inc., Bell Gardens, Calif., 1989-90; counselor State of Calif. Sch. for Deaf,

Riverside, from 1990; mgr. fine jewelry Finlay Fine Jewelry Corp, Monclair, Calif., 1990; interior designer Theis Interiors, Calimesa, Calif., 1990-93; asst. banquet chef Ritz Carlton Hotel, Rancho Mirage, Calif., 1994-95; chef tournat Elcaris Restaurant, Palm Springs, Calif., 1995-97; exec. chef Cottage Garden Restaurant, Palm Springs, 1996—97; pastry chef Wolfgang Puck's Cafe, San Diego, 1997-99; chef Roppongi, San Diego, 2000—02. Scoutmaster Boy Scouts Am., Athens, Greece, 1985-86; fundraiser Desert AIDS Project. Sgt. USAF, 1985-86. Named to Outstanding Young Men Am., 1986. Republican. Roman Catholic. Avocations: water-skiing, skiing, rock and ice climbing, hiking, outdoor activities. Died May 15, 2005.

THEIS, PAUL ANTHONY, publishing executive; b. Ft. Wayne, Ind., Feb. 14, 1923; s. Albert Peter and Josephine Mary (Kinn) T.; m. Nancy Ann Wilbur, Aug. 21, 1971; children: Mitchell A. BA in Journalism, U. Notre Dame, Ind., 1948; BS in Fgn. Svc., Georgetown U., 1949; postgrad., Am U., 1949-52. Reporter Army Times & Fairchild Pubs., Washington, 1950-53; corres. Newsweek Mag., Washington, 1953-54; adminstrv. asst. to U.S. Congressman, Washington, 1955-57; radio-TV dir. Nat. Rep. Congl. Com., Washington, 1957-60, dir. pub. rels., 1960-74; exec. editor to Pres. The White House, 1974-76; dep. undersec. Dept. Agr., Washington, 1976-77; staff cons. U.S. Ho. of Reps., Washington, 1977-81; pres. Headliner Editorial Svc., Washington, from 1981. Pub. rels. officer Pres. Eisenhower's Inaugural, Washington, 1957; vice chmn. publicity Pres. Nixon's Inaugural Com., 1969. Co-author: All About Politics, 1972; author: Devil in the House, 2004; co-inventor game Hat in the Ring, 1965; co-editor Who's Who in Am. Politics, 1965-75. Alt. del. rep. Nat. Conv., Dallas, 1984, del., New Orleans, 1988, Houston, 1992; mem. D.C. Rep. Com., 1980-99. With U.S. Army Air Corps, 1943-46, ETO; maj. USAFR, Ret. Mem. Nat. Press Club, Capitol Hill Club, Cosmos Club. Roman Catholic. Home: Washington, DC. Died Mar. 24, 2004.

THEISEN, GEORGE I., manufacturing executive; b. N.Y.C., May 22, 1926; s. Svend I. and Olga (Sorensen) T.; m. Joan Lucille Gerold, Sept. 20, 1947; children: Claude, Lisbeth, Clifford, Susan, Eva-Marie. Student, NYU, 1942-43, 46, Pace Inst., 1947, 48. Founder, pres. T&S Brass & Bronze Works, Inc., N.Y.C., 1947-78, Greenville, S.C., from 1978; pres. GIT, Inc., Greenville, from 1988. Pres. PTA, East Norwich, N.Y., 1960; bd. dirs. Jr. Achievement, L.I., N.Y., 1974-76, Greenville, S.C., 1988, Greenville Tech. Found. Cpl. USMC, 1944-46, World War II. Decorated Purple Heart, Iwo Jima; recipient Humanitarian award Am. Jewish Com., 1976, 77. Mem. Am. Soc. Plumbing Engrs., Am. Soc. Sanitary Engrs., Nat. Assn. Food Equipment Mfrs., Plumbing Mfrs. Inst. (pres. 1976-78), Green Valley C. of C., Greenville C. of C. (pres. 1987-88). Republican. Methodist. Avocations: golf, bridge. Home: Johns Island, SC. Died Nov. 16, 2004.

THERRIEN, ROBERT WILFRID, contracting company executive; b. Manchester, N.H., Oct. 31, 1929; s. Alfred Wilfrid and Fedora Alma (Morin) T.; m. Beverly G. Ferron, Aug. 15, 1954; children: Robert Wilfrid, Clara Elena, David, Mary. BA, St. Anselm's Coll., Manchester, 1952; postgrad., Boston Coll., 1953. Pres. Al Melanson Co., Inc., Keene, N.H., from 1953, R&M Realty, Inc., Keene and Rutland, Vt., from 1961, Vt. Roofing Co., Inc., Rutlandand Bennington, from 1962, Tri-State Acoustical, Inc., Keene and Rutland, from 1987, N.E. Roofing Cons., Inc., Keene, from 1980, A.C. Hathorne Co., Inc., Burlington, Vt., from 1983. Bd. dirs. Monadnock Humane Soc., Keene, YMCA, Keene, Monadnock United Way; trustee N.H. Cath. Charities; mem. exec. bd. Daniel Webster council Boy Scouts Am., 1963 (recipient Silver Beaver award 1963). Mem. Nat. Roofing Contractors Assn. (nat. bd. dirs. 1980—), N.E. Roofing Contractors Assn. (bd. dirs. 1976—, pres. 1982-84, Clarence Carr award 1985), St. Anselm's Coll. Alumni Assn. (bd. dirs.), Rotary, Elks, Moose. Home: Swanzey Center, NH. Died July 20, 2005.

THIBO, GARY LYNN, real estate executive, consultant; b. Shelbyville, Ind., Jan. 6, 1945; s. Lowell Robert and Rita Ann (Fischer) T.; m. Kathryn L. Thibo, Nov. 8, 1988; children: Brian M., Christine L., Jason Robert. BS in Acctg., U. Dayton, 1966, MBA, 1968. CPA, Ohio. Acct. Ernst & Young, Dayton, Ohio, 1966-72; exec. v.p. and treas. C.H. Huber Enterprises, Dayton, Ohio, 1972-89; pres. Deluxe Homes, Dayton, Ohio, 1989-91; exec. v.p. L.K. Snell Builder/Developer, Dayton, Ohio, from 1991. Mem. com. St. Charles Cath. Ch., Dayton, 1980—. With U.S. Army, 1966-68. Mem. AICPA, Ohio Soc. CPAs (bd. dirs. 1980-85), Ohio Home Builders Assn. (pres. Miami Valley chpt. 1991), Nat. Home Builders Assn. (bd. dirs. 1988—), Dayton C. of C., Jaycees (steering com. Dayton chpt. 1980—). Avocation: part-time educator. Home: Dayton, Ohio. Died May 1, 2005.

THIEL, REBECCA BALDWIN, community activist; b. Monroe, N.C., June 24, 1947; d. Jesse Alfred and Jane Boone (Ridenhour) Baldwin; m. Gerald Edward Thiel, May 4, 1983. BA, Emory and Henry Coll., 1969. Tchr. elem. sch., Lynchburg, Va., 1969-70; flight svc. Am. Airlines, Dallas-Ft. Worth, 1970-78; food svc. design, 1978-90; computer system design Am. Airlines, Dallas, Ft. Worth, 1990-91. Author: (brochures) Japanese Dining, 1986, Mayor's Award for Urban Design, 1992, Arlington Cares, 1993. Pres. Pkwy. Ctrl. Neighborhood Orgn., Arlington, Tex., 1992; chairperson Urban Design Award Com., 1992—. Recipient Mercuary award Internat. Food Catering Assn., London, 1988, Arlington Good Neighbor award. Avocations: writing, gardening, horseback riding. Home: Arlington, Tex. Died Oct. 31, 2004.

THIERRY, JOHN ADAMS, heavy machinery manufacturing company executive, lawyer; b. Watertown, Mass., May 8, 1913; s. Louis Sidney and Adelaide (Hamlin) T.; m. Mary Mills Hatch, June 6, 1953 (div.); 1 child, Charles Adams; m. Silvie Marie Frère, Dec. 1977. AB summa cum laude, Harvard U., 1935, A.M., 1936, JD, 1940; postgrad. (Sheldon traveling fellow Harvard), U. Cambridge, Eng., 1936-37. Bar: Wis. 1941. With Bucyrus-Erie Co., South Milwaukee, Wis., 1940-82, sec., 1958-77, gen. atty., 1958-76, v.p., 1960-77, sr. v.p., 1977-78, dir., 1961-79, mem. exec. com., 1967-78; v.p., dir. Bucyrus Erie Co. Can., Ltd., 1959-78; dir. Ruston-Bucyrus, Ltd., Lincoln, Eng., 1964-79, Komatsu-Bucyrus K.K., Japan, 1971-81; former dir. Bucyrus (Australia) Pty. Ltd., Bucyrus Internat., Inc., Brad Foot Gear Works, Inc., Pitts. Gear Co., South Milw. Marine Bank, Atlas Chain & Precision. Dir. Wis. Pub. Expenditure Survey, 1954-78; v.p., bd. dirs. Bucyrus-Erie Found., 1963-78; bd. dirs. Pub. Expenditure Research Found., 1964-78, YMCA, Milw., 1973-78, Milw. Symphony Orch., 1974-78; trustee Wis. Conservatory Music, 1969-78, S.E. Asia Art Found., 1977—; pres. United Performing Arts Fund, Milw., 1969; mem. adv. council Coll. Engring. U. Wis.-Milw., 1975-78, mem. adv. council Sch. Bus., 1975-78; mem. council Med. Coll. Wis., 1975-78; pres. Milw. Patent Law Assn., 1961-62. Served to capt., C.E. AUS, 1942-46. Recipient Granite State award U. N.H., 1986 Mem. Cambridge Union Soc., Harvard Club (Boston and N.Y.C.), Phi Beta Kappa. Episcopalian. Home: Hill, NH. Died Feb. 1, 2006.

THOM, LESLIE MCCASEY, nursing educator; b. Springfield, Ill., Jan. 23, 1945; d. Frank Leslie and Virginia Leigh (Bales) McCasey; m. James Joseph Thom; Aug. 20, 1966; children: Kelly Denise Thom Wendlandt, Deborah Maureen. BSN, U. Iowa, 1966; MS in Community Health Nursing, No. Ill. U., 1977; EdD, Ill. State U., 1986. Staff devel. coord. Dodge County Asylum, Juneau, Wis., Union Hosp., New Ulm, Minn.; instr. Sch. Nursing Michael Reese Hosp. and Med. Ctr., Chgo.; coord. grad. program, dept. nursing Bradley U., Peoria, Ill. Contbr. articles to profl. jours. Mem. Am. Assn. for History of Nursing, Sigma Theta Tau. Home: Peoria, Ill. Died Sept. 9, 2004.

THOMAS, ANN BOLTON, educator; b. Rich Square, N.C., Dec. 17, 1935; d. Aubrey Albert and Frances (Parker) Bolton; m. Charles Broughton Thomas, Aug. 10, 1958 (dec. Feb. 1987); children: Christopher, Mary. AA, Mars Hill Coll., 1956; BA in Sociology, Wake Forest U., 1958; MA in Internat. Trade Law, Antioch U. Sch. Law, 1984. Cert. tchr. Tchr. Wake County Pub. Schs., Garner, N.C., 1959-63, Leonardtown (Md.) Mid. Sch., 1963-84, Great Mills (Md.) High Sch., 1984-86, Leonardtown High Sch., from 1986; instr. Charles County Community Coll., La Plata, Md., from 1989. Author: From a Poor Circle to a Rich Square, 1991. Chmn. March of Dimes, St. Mary's County, Md., 1967; pres. Woman's Soc. St. Paul's Meth. Ch., Leonardtown, 1969; mem., vol. Project HOPE, Lexington Park, Md., 1989—. Selected to be Md. exchange tchr. to Japan, 1992-93. Mem. Nat. Coun. Social Studies, NEA, Nat. Capitol Hist. Assn., Md. State Tchrs. Assn. Democrat. Methodist. Avocations: water colors, writing, backpacking, travel. Home: Leonardtown, Md. Died Dec. 28, 2004.

THOMAS, BERTRAM DAVID, retired chemical engineer; b. Renton, Wash., May 5, 1903; s. David and Minnie Belle (Custer) T.; m. Dorothy Glorian Butler, Dec. 21, 1928 (dec. 1986); children: Preston David, Nancy Glorian, Lawrence Eldon. BS, U. Wash., 1929, PhD in Chemistry, 1933. Registered profl. engr., Ohio. Rsch. engr. Battelle Meml. Inst., Columbus, Ohio, 1934-40, asst. dir., 1940-56, pres., 1956-68; ret. Mem. adv. com. on environment, Santa Barbara, Calif., 1970-73. Patentee ore dressing and coal preparation methods; contbr. articles to sci. publs. Trustee Columbus Mus. Art, 1962-67, Ohio State U., Columbus, 1965-68, Santa Barbara Mus. Art, 1973—; trustee, pres. Santa Barbara Botanic Garden, 1974-82. Recipient Order Civil Merit 1st Class, Republic of Korea, 1965; DEng. (hon.), Mich. Coll. Mining and Tech., 1957; DSci (hon.) Ohio State U., 1963, Otterbein Coll., Westerville, Ohio, 1965, Cleve. State U., 1968. Fellow AAAS; mem. Chemists Club N.Y., Am. Che. Soc., Sigma Xi. Home: Santa Barbara, Calif. Died Feb. 15, 2004.

THOMAS, DAVID EDWIN, marketing executive; b. Phoenix, Apr. 17, 1935; s. Albion Clarence and Lucille (Nichols) T.; m. Mildred Reese, Aug. 18, 1958 (div. Feb. 1977); children: Brian, Bruce; m. Patricia Pauline Fallmer, Apr. 23, 1977; children: Todd, Shawnell. BS in Econs., U. Redlands, 1957. V.p. Haskell-Thomas, Inc., Phoenix, 1960-68; pres. Zesbaugh-Thomas, Inc., Seattle, 1968-77, Thomas Archtl. Products, Inc., Seattle, 1977-87; mktg. mgr. Constrn. Specialties, Inc., Mill Creek, Wash., from 1987. V.p. Constrn. Specifications Inst., 1987-88. Lt. U.S. Navy, 1957-60. Fellow The Constrn. Specifications Inst., Mill Creek Country. Republican. Methodist. Avocations: golf, reading, public speaking. Died Jan. 23, 2004.

THOMAS, DWIGHT, investigator; b. Arbyrd, Mo., Mar. 28, 1932; s. Emmett George and Minnie Lee (Hays) T.; m. Nancy Thomas; children: Farley D., Clay E., Lisa F. MS, Nova U., Ft. Lauderdale, Fla., 1979. State trooper Mo. State Patrol, Jefferson City, 1955-61; spl. investigator U.S. Treasury Dept. ATF, Washington, 1961-82, U.S. Customs, Washington, 1992-94, U.S. Dept. Def., Washington, 1992-94; nat. dir. Intercon Investigative Svc., Sikeston, Mo., from 1986. Pres. Fed. Criminal Investigators Assn., Omaha, 1975; spl. instr. Internat. Police Acad., Washington, 1974-75; parliamentarian FCIA, Golden Isles, St. Simon, Ga., 1976; sr. instr. U.S. Treasury Law Enforcement Officers Tng. Sch., Glenco, Ga., 1975-77; cert. instr. Dept. Pub. Safety, Jefferson City, Mo., 1984—. Author: Explosive Investigation, U.S. Treasury ATF Lab. Paper, 1972, Jail Article The National Sheriff Magazine, 1986. Lecturing Knight Elks Club, Sikeston, Mo., 1991. Cpl. U.S. Army Airborne Spl. Troops, 1952-54. Named Nat. Police Officer Master Detective Mag., N.Y.C., 1970, Best Investigations List Investigators On Line, Phoenix, 1993. Mem. A,. Soc. Indsl. Security, Internat. Assn. Bomb and Arson Technicians and Investigators, Nat. Sheriff's Assn., Fed. Criminal Investigations Assn., Nat. Assn. Treasury Agts., Internat. Intelligence and Organized Crime Investigators Assn. Avocations: skydiving, swimming, boxing, hunting, fishing. Died Sept. 10, 2004.

THOMAS, FRANKLIN ROSBOROUGH, retired animator; b. Santa Monica, Calif., Sept. 5, 1912; s. Frank Waters and Ina Marcella (Gregg) T.; m. Jeanette Armentrout, Feb. 16, 1946; children: Ann Winfield, Gregg Franklin, Theodore William, Douglas Craig. Student, Fresno State Coll., 1929-31; AB magna cum laude, Stanford U., 1933; postgrad., Chouinard Art Sch., 1933-34, Walt Disney Studio, 1934. Directing animator Walt Disney Co., Burbank, Calif., 1934-78; ret., 1978. Lectr., spkr. in field; chmn. jury NY Internat. Animated Film Festival, 1975. Animator for numerous films, including Show White and the Seven Dwarfs, 1937, Pinocchio, 1940, Bambi, 1942, The Three Caballeros, 1945, The Many Adventures of Winnie the Pooh, 1977; directing animator The Adventures of Ichabod and Mr. Toad, 1949, Cinderella, 1950, Alice in Wonderland, 1951, Peter Pan, 1953, Lady and the Tramp, 1955, Sleeping Beauty, 1959, 101 Dalmatians, 1961, Sword in the Stone, 1963, Mary Poppins, 1964, The Jungle Book, 1967, The Aristocats, 1970, Robin Hood, 1973, The Rescuers, 1977; supervising animator: The Fox and the Hound, 1981; also animator for numerous shorts; co-author: Disney Animation: The Illusion of Life, 1981, Too Funny for Words, 1987, Bambi-The Story and the Film, 1990, Jungle Book Portfolio, 1993, Disney Villains, English edit., 1993, French edit., 1995; contbr. editor to sketch book series; Dixieland jazz pianist Firehouse Five Plus 2, 1949-68, appearing on radio and TV programs The Bing Crosby Show, The Milton Berle Show, Ed Wynn TV Shows, others; subject of documentary Frank and Ollie, 1995; exhibited drawings in Whitney Mus., NYC, 1981. Guest spkr. Russian Govt. and Soyuzmultfilm and other East European countries, 1976, U.S. Info. Agy. Cultural Exch. Program, 1986. With USAF, 1942-45. Recipient numerous awards, including Annie award Internat. Animated Film Soc., 9 Old Men award Hon. Cinema Soc. Mem. Phi Beta Kappa. Died Sept. 8, 2004.

THOMAS, JASMINE K., medical/surgical nurse, educator; b. Jamaica, W.I., Oct. 14, 1939; d. Jonathan and Ivy; m. Edward Thomas, May 7, 1960; children: Caroline, Ann Marie, Bently, Clare, Edward. Diploma, Kingston Sch. Nursing, Jamaica, 1961; BSc, St. Josephs Coll., Bklyn., 1983; MPA, L.I. U., 1994; cert. in family nurse practitioner, U. W.I., Jamaica; cert. in midwifery, Victoria Jubilee Hosp., Kingston, Jamaica, W.I. Nurse entrepreneur Alt. Licensed Home Care Svcs. Staff nurse Actg. wd. sister Chapelton Hosp., Jamaica, 1961-68; clinician Bird and Coler Hosp., Health and Hosp. Corp., N.Y.C., 1968-70; nurse practitioner Clarendon Health Dept., Jamaica, 1970-79; asst. H/N Coney Island Hosp., Jamaica, 1979-84; supr., clinician Queens Hosp. Ctr., Jamaica, from 1984. Contbr. (book) International Nursing. Mem. N.Y. State Nurses Assn. (chmn. recruitment and retention com., nurse distinction 1994). Home: Jamaica, NY. Died Apr. 3, 2005.

THOMAS, JOHN HANSFORD, JR., physician, farmer; b. Greenville, Va., June 19, 1909; s. John Hansford and Ella Blanche (Burnett) T.; m. Mary Johnston Lasley, June 19, 1941; children: Gail McCormick Thomas Zug, Sarah Doak Thomas Guerry, Mary Lasley Thomas Burleson, John Hansford III, Thomas Randall. Student, Washington and Lee Univ., 1927-30; MD, U. Va., 1934. Intern Balt. city hosps., 1934-35; pvt. practice Greenville, from 1935. Mem. AMA, Augusta Med. Soc. (pres. 1944), Augusta Hosp. Corp. (pres. 1960), Med. Soc. Va., So. Med. Assn., World Med. Assn, Greencroft Club. Presbyterian. Avocations: yachting, travel. Died Apr. 1, 2005.

THOMAS, LLOYD EDWARD, agricultural engineer, consultant; b. Colver, Pa., Feb. 15, 1939; s. John Leonard and Maude Ellen (Lloyd) T.; m. Shirley Lou Simons, July 18, 1964; children: Terri Lynn Thomas Ruch, Christopher David. BS in Agrl. Engring., Pa. State U., 1961. Registered profl. engr., Pa. Agt. USDA Soil Conservation Svc., Harrisburg, more Pa twns., 1964-76, Syracuse, N.Y., 1976-80, Chester, Pa., 1980-94. Mem. agrl. adv. coun. Pa. State U., University Park, 1986—. With U.S. Army, 1962-64. Named Outstanding Engr. Alumnus Pa. State U. Coll. Engring., Univ. Park, 1992 Mem. Am. Soc. Agrl. Engrs., Nat. Soc. Agrl. Engrs., Rotary Club (v.p. Newfoundland, Pa., 1998). Republican. Methodist. Avocations: farming, golf. Home: Newfoundland, Pa. Died Oct. 1, 2004.

THOMAS, TAMARA BYRD, art consultant, public art advisor; b. Oakland, Calif., July 24, 1940; d. Bruce Everman and Elaine (Hudspeth) Eldridge; m. Hardy L. Thomas; children: Kirk, Tara. Student, U. Calif., Berkeley, 1957-61,

U. Geneva, 1961. Former pres. Fine Arts Svcs., Inc., L.A.; former mng. ptnr. Fine Arts Assocs., Ltd., L.A. Mem. Assn. Profl. Art Advisors (founding mem.), Art Table. Died Apr. 2, 2004.

THOMPSON, CARLTON FREDERICK, lawyer; b. Syracuse, N.Y., Aug. 18, 1924; s. Fredrick and Dorothy (Nielsen) T.; m. Betty Sue, June 18, 1949; children: C. Kendall, Gail. AB magna cum laude, Syracuse U., 1948, JD cum laude, 1950. Bar: N.Y. 1950, U.S. Dist. Ct. (no. dist.) N.Y., U.S. Dist. Ct. (we. dist.) N.Y., U.S. Dist. Ct. Vt. Assoc. Levene and Gouldin, Binghamton, NY, 1950—53; ptnr. Levene, Gouldin & Thompson, Binghamton, NY, 1953—2005. 1st lt. U.S. Army, 1943-46. Fellow Am. Coll. Trial Lawyers; mem. N.Y. State Bar Assn. (chmn. trial lawyers sect. 1982-83), Broome County Bar Assn. (pres. 1966-67), Phi Beta Kappa. Home: Binghamton, NY. Died Sept. 4, 2005.

THOMPSON, GARFIELD, congressman; b. Fort Worth, June 29, 1916; s. Ernest Sidney Jr. and Mallener (Cox) T.; m. Dorothy Ruth Thompson, 1942; children: Fannie Louise Gibson, Willie Ruth Jones, Ruby Denise Grant, Ida Lorraine Bridgwater, Ernest Sidney. Grad. high sch., Fort Worth. With Burlington-Rock Island R.R.; county courthouse custodian; mem. Tex. Ho. of Reps., 1984—94. Chmn. budget and oversight liquor regulation com. Tex. Ho. of Reps., mem. appropriations com., local and consent calendars com., select com. on child abuse and pornography, vice chmn. budget and oversight com. on transportation, vice chmn. liquor regulation com., interim com. on petroleum, oil and gas regulations, transportation standing com., licensing and adminstrv. procedures standing com.; pres. Tarrant County Employees Union; manpower rep. AFL-CIO. Mem. exec. com. Tex. Area 5 Health Systems Agy.; pres. Tarrant County Precinct Workers Coun.; chmn. Neighborhood Action, Inc.; mem. zoning commn. City of Fort Worth, mem. employment com. human rels. commn.; mem. Manpower Planning Coun., Fort Worth; mem. adv. com. on adult edn. Fort Worth Ind. Sch. Dist.; chmn. deacon bd. St. Peter Presbyn. Ch., pres. Presbyn. Men. With U.S. Army, 1942-45. Mem. Am. Legion. Democrat. Died Dec. 8, 2005.

THOMPSON, HAROLD LEROY, electricity educator; b. Mineville, N.Y., Nov. 5, 1923; s. Harold Benjamin and Grace Mae (Spring) T.; m. Marietta Rachele Corbo, Aug. 15, 1948; children: Sandra Mary, Rosemary Grace, Howard Stanley, Harold Leroy, John Francis. Cert. safety profl. Elec. apprentice Republic Steel Corp., Mineville, 1941-42; signalman 2d class U.S. Navy, Washington, 1943-46; from electrician standard to asst. maintenance supt. Republic Steel Corp., Mineville, Cleve., 1946-72; instr. John W. Harrold Edn. Ctr., Pitts., from 1973. Federal mine inspector U.S. Bur. Mines, Pitts., 1974-78; subdist. mgr. Mine Safety & Health Adminstrn., Albany, N.Y., 1978-89; safety & health cons. Skyway Roofing, Inc., Albany, 1989—. Pres. Mineville Bd. Edn., 1951-53. Served in U.S. Navy, 1943-46, South Pacific. Mem. VFW (cmdr. 1972-73), Am. Legion, U.S. Navy WWII Vets., U.S. Naval Armed Guard WWII (sec. 1991), Elks (treas. Niskayuna lodge 1989-91, grand auditor Clifton Park lodge 1993). Democrat. Roman Catholic. Avocations: fishing, hunting, photography, sports, wildlife management. Home: Clifton Park, NY. Died June 3, 2004.

THOMPSON, JANN MARIE, secondary school educator; b. Marshalltown, Iowa, July 12, 1953; d. Thomas Ronald and Evelyn Marie (Muckler) Thompson; m. Michael Alden Knight, Sept. 2, 1972 (div. July 1994); children: Amy Susanne, Kelly Michael, Aaron. BA, U. Iowa, 1975; MA in Edn., U. No. Iowa, 1992. Cert. reading specialist K-12, cert. secondary tchr., English and ESL. English tchr. Charles City (Iowa) Jr. H.S., 1990-92, ESL tchr., 1991-92, reading specialist, 1992-93; coord., CLHS Carrie Lane H.S., Charles City, from 1992, grant coord., 1994-96; instr. developmental studies Hawkeye C.C., Waterloo, Iowa, from 1996. Adj. prof. U. No. Iowa, Charles City, 1992—; adv. coun. mem. Workstart Adv. Coun., Des Moines, 1991-94; adv. com. Workstart Consortium Adv. Com., Marshalltown, Iowa; grand coord. Reading Connections Literacy Project, Charles City, 1994—. Grantee ComServ Iowa, 1994, Iowa Dept. of Health, 1995. Mem. ASCD, Iowa Assn. of Alternative Educators, Internat. Reading Assn., Alpha Upsilon Alpha, Phi Delta Kappa. Republican. Methodist. Avocations: photography, travel, antiques, gardening. Died Jan. 3, 2005.

THOMPSON, JOHN MORGAN, neurological surgeon, educator; b. Tampa, Fla., Feb. 14, 1924; s. Robert Hamilton and Nannie Lee (Clewis) T.; m. Dorothy Georgene Kinne, June 21,1947; children: Lauralee Ann, John Tilynn. BS, Tulane U., 1946; MD, Johns Hopkins U., 1948. Diplomate Am. Bd. Neurol. Surgery. NRC fellow in neurophysiology John Hopkins U., Balt., 1948, 49; intern U. Mich. Hosp., Ann Arbor, 1949-50, resident, 1950-55; faculty dept. neurosurgery U. Mich. Med. Sch., Ann Arbor, 1955-56; practice neurosurgery Bayfront Med. Ctr./St. Anthony's Hosp., St. Petersburg, Fla., from 1956, All Children's Hosp., St. Petersburg, from 1956; mem. faculty U. So. Fla. Med. Sch., Tampa, from 1971, clin. prof. neurol. surgery, from 1986. Cons. neurol. surgery U.S. VA Hosp., Tampa, 1975—. Editor: History Congress of Neurological Surgeons 1951-1991, 1991. Served to lt. M.C., USNR, 1950-52, Korea. Recipient Borden Rsch. award Johns Hopkins U., 1948; Henry Dennison fellow, 1946-48, NRC fellow, 1948-59. Mem. AMA, Congress Neurol. Surgeons (pres. 1969-70), Am. Assn. Neurol. Surgeons, Fla. Neurosrug. Soc., Pinellas County Med. Soc. (v.p. 1988-89), Phi Beta Kappa, Sigma Xi, Alpha Omega Alpha. Avocations: art, photography, travel. Home: Saint Petersburg, Fla. Died July 21, 2005.

THOMPSON, LEAH D. EMBRY, tax lawyer; b. Pitts., Sept. 24, 1952; d. Lee Arthur Sr. and Lula Mae (Smith) Embry (div. 1981); 1 child, Kulika Penda. AA, Prince George's Community Coll, Largo, Md., 1979; BA, Am. U., 1983; JD, George Washington U., 1986. Bar: Md. 1986. Assoc. John Wesley Days, P.C., Silver Spring, Md., 1986-87; tax law specialist IRS, Washington, from 1987. Sgt. USAF, 1972-76. Earl Warren Legal Tng. scholar, 1983-86, Jones scholar, 1982. Mem. ABA, Prince George's Bar Assn., Md. State Bar Assn., Alpha Phi Sigma, Phi Kappa Phi. Democrat. Avocations: reading, weight training, charitable activities. Home: Upper Marlboro, Md. Died July 16, 2004.

THOMPSON, MALACHI RICHARD, musician; b. Princeton, Ky., Aug. 21, 1949; s. Harvey McCormick and Anna Louise Thompson; children: Terrence Mansa, Dhyia Malika. AA, Malcolm X Coll., Chgo., 1972; BA in Music Compostion, Governors State U., Park Forest, Ill., 1974. Cert. arts edn. Urban Gateways, 1995. Jazz musician, trumpeter, composer; jazz historian. Founder Sutherland Cmty. Arts Initiative, 1991, Hyde Park/Kenwood JAAZ Festival, 1991; founder and editor Creativity Mag.; condr. master classes and jazz workshops; lectr. in field. Composer: (recordings) Seventh Son; composer and performer: recordings Buddy Bolden's Rag (Chgo. Tribune Jazz Record of Yr., 1995), Time Line, Blue Jazz (Chgo. Tribune Jazz Record of Yr., 2003), I Only Have Eyes For You (German Grammy winner, 1985), Legends and Heroes, Spirit, New Standards (Top Ten jazz radio charts, 1994), 47th Street (Chgo. Sun Times Record of Yr., 1997), Freebop Now! (Chgo. Tribune Record of Yr., 1998), Rising DayStar (Top Ten jazz radio charts, 1999), Lift Every Voice (Chgo. Tribune Record of Yr., 1993), prodr. and composer: recordings Talking Horns; performer (with Lester Bowie): Avant Pop, Twilight Dreams; performer: (with Quincy Jones) Save The Children; performer: Ram's Run, Attica Blues Big Band, The Jazz Life (Top Ten jazz radio charts, 1992); author: (essays) Historic Trends in African American Music, Sonic Warfare, The New Renaissance, What Happened To Chicago Jazz?, The Mystery of Jazz, Jazz Oppression, Talking Horns: The Rumor of Jazz's Demise Is Greatly Exaggerated, The Coltrane Sound, Innovation In Jazz: Cross Parallels Between Jazz and Scientific Paradigms, 2004, The Evolution of Jazz and the Survival of Our Democratic Society, Cultural Ground Zero, Understanding Ethnocide, Up From 47th Street: The Cultural Redevelopment of Bronzeville, Hip Hop Science, The Evolution of Jazz and the Survival of Our Democratic Society, 2004. Vol. SCLC, Chgo. Named Arts Midwest Jazz Master, Arts Midwest, 1995, Chicagoan of Yr., Chgo. Tribune, 1996; recipient Meritorious award, SCLC, 1972, Presdl. cert. Merit, Pres. Jimmy Carter, 1977, Arts Activism award, Chgo. Endowment for the Arts, 1997, Original Music award, Jefferson Award Com., 1998, cert. Appreciation, Florence B. Price Sch., 1999, Hidden Jewel in the Cmty. award, Jewel-Osco, 2022; fellow, Ky. Coun. Arts, 1985, Ill. Arts Coun., 1987; grantee, Nat. Endowment Arts, 1972, 1976, 1981, Music Composition Commn. Meet The Composer Inc., 2000, Aaron Copeland Fund, 2002, New Works Creation, Chamber Music Am., 2002. Home: Chicago, Ill. Died July 16, 2006.

THOMPSON, MARTTIE LOUIS, lawyer; b. Meridian, Miss., July 5, 1930; s. Samuel L. and Rosie (Young) T.; m. Cornelia Gaines, Apr. 2, 1966; 1 child, Sandra M. Ruffin. BS, U. Toledo, 1954; postgrad., St. John's U., 1955-57, Columbia U., 1977. Bar: N.Y. 1963, D.C. 1980, U.S. Dist. Ct. (so. and ea. dists.) N.Y. 1966, U.S. Ct. Appeals (2d cir.) 1966, U.S. Supreme Ct. 1971. Atty. Wolf, Popper, Ross, Wolf and Jones, N.Y.C., 1963-65; assoc. William C. Chance, Jr., N.Y.C., 1965-66; house counsel Ft. Greene Cmty. Corp., Bklyn., 1966-68; mng. atty. MFY Legal Svcs., Inc., N.Y.C., 1968-70. Gen. counsel and exec. dir. Cmty. Action, N.Y.C., 1971-77; regional dir. Legal Svcs. Corp., Phila., 1977-84; adj. prof. Seton Hall Law Ctr., 1979-80; chmn. Nat. Employment Law Project. Contbr. articles to profl. jours. Pres., Stockton Civic Assn., 1978; mem. East Orange Planning Bd. and Citizens Union, 1976; bd. dirs. Nat. Legal Aid and Defenders Assn., 1980. Sgt. USAF, 1946-49. Recipient William Nelson Cromwell award, 1991. Fellow Am. Bar Foun., N.Y. State Bar (ho. of dels.); mem. ABA, Assn. Bar City N.Y., N.Y. County Lawyers Assn. (past chmn. legal aid com., bd. dirs., past chmn. com. on minorities, vice chmn. Ams. for Dem. Action), D.C. Bar, Nat. Bar Assn. Democrat. Episcopalian. Home: East Orange, NJ. Died Mar. 19, 2005.

THOMPSON, PAMELA J., nurse; b. Hutchinson, Minn., Feb. 5, 1959; d. James Sidney and Frances Helen (Boller) Orloff; m. Philip Ernest Thompson, July 5, 1979 (div. Apr. 1993); 1 child, Amber, Renee. Student, Kans. State U., 1991-94; BSN magna cum laude, Washburn U., 1996. RN Kans. Mech. welding inspector Daniel Internat. Corp., Burlington, Kans., 1981-84, Braidwood, Ill., 1984-85; quality specialist Eval. Rsch. Corp., Glen Rose, Tex., 1985-87; multi disciplinary quality inspector Fluor Daniel, Mineral, Va., 1988-89, Surry, Va., 1989-90, quality engr. Boss, Mo., 1990-91; nurse asst. Manor Care Health Svc., Topeka, 1995-96, charge nurse, 1997-98, asst. dir. nurses, from 1998. Vol. Sr. Ctr., Topeka, 1996, Rescue Mission, Topeka, 1995, ARC, 1989—. Mem. ANA, Phi Kappa Phi, Sigma Theta Tau. Republican. Avocations: crochet, history, reading, embroidery, cooking. Died Jan. 16, 2005.

THOMPSON, PAUL BROWER, lawyer; b. East Orange, N.J., Feb. 15, 1922; s. Harvey Brower and Agnes (Norman) T.; m. Audrey Hyde, Aug. 17, 1952; 1 child, Paul Brower Jr. BA, Colgate U., 1943; JD, Harvard U., 1948. Bar: N.J. 1949, U.S. Ct. Appeals (3d cir.) 1949, U.S. Dist. Ct. N.J. 1949. Assoc. Markley & Broadhurst, Jersey City, N.J., 1949-55, Lamb Langan & Blake, Jersey City, N.J., 1955-59; ptnr. Lamb Blake Thompson & Chappell, Jersey City, N.J., 1959-74; judge Esssex County Ct., Newark, 1975-79, Superior Ct. N.J., Newark, 1979-85, presiding judge, civil divsn., 1985-91; of counsel Tompkins McGuire Wachenfeld & Barry, Newark, from 1991. Editor (compendium) Traps for the Unwary, 1997. With USAF, 1942-46. Fellow Am. Bar Found.; mem. ABA, N.J. Bar Assn., Essex County Bar Assn., Montclair Hist. Soc. (pres. 1980), Harvard Law Sch. Assn. N.J. (pres. 1985), Retired Judges Assn. (pres. 2000—). Republican. Congregationalist. Avocations: golf, gardening. Home: Chester, NJ. Died June 27, 2005.

THOMPSON, ROBERT J., state senator; b. West Chester, Pa., Nov. 30, 1937; m. Nancy Blackman. BA, Pa. State U., 1959. Mem. Pa. State Senate, 1995—2006. Mem. United Way of Chester County; elder First Presbyterian Ch. of West Chester; exec. dir. C. of C.; vice chmn. to chmn. SEPTA. Recipient Legion of Honor award, Chapel of the Four Chaplains. Mem.: Westtown-Goshen Rotary (pres.). Republican. Died Jan. 28, 2006.

THOMPSON, RONALD F., marketing professional; b. Akron, Ohio, Mar. 22, 1945; s. Ronald Wilmer and Kathryn Jane (Lantz) T.; m. Karyn S. Wellendorf, Spet. 17, 1970 (div. May 1980); 1 child, Daniel Joshua; m. Nancy Biles, June 27, 1984; children: Hollya, Suzanne. BA, Balddwin Wallace, 1976; postgrad., Kent State U., 1980. Office mgr. Rentco, Cleve., 1970-73, branch mgr., 1973-76, regional mgr. Oakland, Calif., 1976-78, Detroit, 1978-79, nat. acct. mgr., 1979-81, gen. sales mgr., 1981-83; sales Fruehauf, El Paso, Tex., 1983-86, Trailmobile, Atlanta, 1986-89; regional sales Benton-CMC, Atlanta, from 1989. Contbr. articles to profl. jours. Recipient Disting. Svc. award Jaycees, 1975-76. Mem. N.W. Ga. TFC Club, Atlanta Traffic Club, N.Ga. Transp. Assn. Jaycees (dir. 1973-76). Republican. Avocation: golf. Home: Orange Park, Fla. Died Sept. 11, 2004.

THOMPSON, RONALD MACKINNON, former family physician, artist, writer; b. N.Y.C., Oct. 19, 1916; s. George Harold and Pearl Anita (Hatfield) T.; m. Ethel Joyce Chastant, June 30, 1950; children: Phyllis Anita, Walter MacKinnon, Charles Chastant, Richard Douglas. BS, U. Chgo., 1947, MS, 1948, MD, 1949. Diplomate Am. Bd. Family Practice. Intern U. Mich., Ann Arbor, 1950-51; resident in psychiatry U. Tex., Galveston, 1951-52; pvt. practice, family and internal medicine South Dixie Med. Ctr., West Palm Beach, Fla., 1952-85; ret., 1985. Instr. Anatomy, U. Chgo., 1946-47, Pharmacology, 1948-49. Contbr. more than 300 poems and short stories to lit. mags., also articles to med. jours.; 7 one-man shows (over 30 awards for painting in regional and nat. shows); represented in permanent collections at 6 mus. Former mem. bd. dirs. Norton Mus. of Art, West Palm Beach. With Fla. N.G., 1936-40; cadet USAAF, Force, 1943-44. Over thirty awards for painting in juried regional and nat. shows. Fellow Am. Acad. Family Physicians; mem. AMA, Fla. Med. Assn., Fla. Acad. of Family Physicians, Palm Beach County Med. Soc., Nat. Watercolor Soc., Ariz. Watercolor Soc. Republican. Episcopalian. Avocations: chess, writing, square and round dancing. Home: Mesa, Ariz. Died May 7, 2005.

THOMSON, KENNETH R. (LORD THOMSON OF FLEET), publishing executive; b. Toronto, Sept. 1, 1923; s. Lord Thomson of Fleet; m. Nora Marilyn Lavis, June 1956; children: David Kenneth Roy, Peter John, Taylor Lynne. Student, Upper Can. Coll., Toronto; BA, MA, U. Cambridge, Eng., 1947. With editl. dept. Timmins Daily Press, Ont., 1947; with advt. dept. Cambridge (Galt) Reporter, 1948-50, gen. mgr., 1950-53; chmn. The Thomson Corp., 1976—2002. Chmn., bd. dirs. The Woodbridge Co. Ltd.; pres., bd. dirs. Thomson Works of Art Ltd. With RCAF, World War II. Named one of Top 200 Collectors, ARTnews Mag., 2004. Mem. Granite Club, Hunt Club, Toronto Club, York Club. Avocation: collecting Medieval and Renaissance art and Canadian paintings. Home: Toronto, Canada. Died June 12, 2006.

THORN, EMILY LENORE LUCH, educational consultant; b. Bethlehem, Pa., Aug. 25, 1915; d. Myron Jacob and Martha Eliza (Harlacher) Luch; m. Ernest Welsey Thorn, Sept. 10, 1938; children: Geoffrey Myron, Harry Wesley, Philip Andrew. BA, Smith Coll., 1936; MEd, S.C. Univ., 1960; postgrad., W.Va. U., U. Vt. Cert. Adlerian family counselor. Instr. English and journalism Briarcliff Coll., Briarcliff Manor, N.Y., 1936-38; staff dir. Del. Coop. Prschs. Assn., Wilmington, 1951-55; dir. religious edn. First Unitarian Ch. Sch., Wilmington, 1955-75; ednl. cons. pub. and pvts. schs. New Castle County, Del., from 1978, Delaware County, Pa., from 1978; nat. religious edn. cons. Am. Ethical Union, N.Y.C., 1976-84. Course instr. Family Edn. Ctr. Del., 1972—; continuing edn. instr. U. Del., 1985-88; instr. tchr. in-svc. programs, Delaware County, 1975-82. Author: Relation of Other Elizabethan Literature to Shakespeare's Plays, 1936, History of Preschool Education in Delaware, 1958, Understanding and Helping Children's Behavior, 1972, Teaching for Optimum Human Development, 1976; contbr. articles and poetry to profl. jours. Pres. Family Edn. Ctr. Del., 1980-82. Recipient Best Hymn award Unitarian Universalist Assn., 1972, Project Head Start Svc. award, Wilmington, 1970; grantee Vassar Euthenics Inst., Del. Presch. Assn., Wilmington, 1951, Del. Agy. to Reduce Crime, 1976-78 Mem. NOW, LWV, ACLU, DAR, AAUW (life), UN Assn., Common Cause, N.Am. Soc. Adlerian Psychology (corr. Edn. Sect. Newsletter), Liberal Religious Educators Assn. (life, pres. 1961-63), Am. Ethical Union (life mem. at large),, Am. Humanist Assn., Am. Humanist Assn., World Federalists, Smith Coll. Alumnae Assn. (life), Smith Coll. Club Del. (pres. 1965-68), Phi Beta Kappa. Republican. Unitarian-Universalist. Avocations: fine arts practitioner, travel, camping. Home: Wilmington, Del. Died Nov. 5, 2004.

THORN, ROBERT JEROME, chemist; b. Constantine, Mich., Dec. 1, 1914; s. Edward R. and Gladys R. (Hassinger) T.; m. Mary C. Craig, Aug. 15, 1942 (dec. July 1992); children: Craig E., Susan J. (dec.). BS, Alma Coll., 1938; PhD, U. Ill., 1942. Chemist U.S. Rubber Co., Detroit, 1942-46, Argonne (Ill.) Nat. Lab., 1946-48, assoc. chemist, 1948-58, sr. chemist, 1958-84, rsch. assoc., from 1984. Vis. prof. U. Kans., Lawrence, 1967-68; cons. Internat. Atomic Energy Agy., Vienna, Austria, 1961-65; chmn. Gordon Rsch Conf. on High Temperature Chemistry, 1970. Contbr. over 80 articles to profl. publs., 5 chpts. to books. Fellow AAAS; mem. Am. Chem. Soc. (emeritus), Sigma Xi. Achievements include rsch. on correlation of energy and entropy, nonstorichiometry in oxides, conductivity of normal state of oxide and organic superconductors. Home: Downers Grove, Ill. Died Oct. 25, 2004.

THORNDIKE, JOSEPH JACOBS, JR., editor; b. Peabody, Mass., July 29, 1913; s. Joseph Jacobs and Susan Ellison (Farnham) T.; m. Virginia Lemont, Sept. 7, 1940; children— John, Alan; m. Margery Darrell, Oct. 3, 1963; 1 son, Joseph Jacobs III. AB, Harvard, 1934. Asst. editor Time Mag., 1934-36; assoc. editor Life Mag., 1936-46; mng. editor Life, 1946-49. Pres. Thorndike, Jensen & Parton, Inc.; co-founder, contbg. editor Am. Heritage Pub. Co. Author: The Very Rich, 1976, The Magnificent Builders, 1978, The Coast, 1993; editor: Seafaring America, 1974, Mysteries of the Past, 1977, Discovery of Lost Worlds, 1979, Mysteries of the Deep, 1980, Three Centuries of American Architects, 1981. Mem.: Harvard (N.Y.C.). Unitarian Universalist. Home: Harwich, Mass. Died Nov. 22, 2005.

THORNE, ALISON COMISH, women's studies educator, economist; b. Chgo., May 9, 1914; d. Newel Howland and Louise (Larson) Comish; m. David Wynne Thorne, Aug. 3, 1937 (dec. Feb. 1979); children: Kip Stephen, Barrie, Sandra, Avril, Lance Gaylord. BS in Econs., Brigham Young U., 1934; MS in Econs., Iowa State U., 1935; PhD in Econs., 1938; postgrad., U. Chgo., 1935-36. Instr. consumer econs. Colo. State U., Ft. Collins, 1936; instr. econs. Iowa State U., Ames, 1937; lectr. sociology, home econs., women's studies Utah State U., Logan, 1964-85; prof. emeritus, from 1985. Mem. Gov.'s Com. on Status of Women in Utah, Salt Lake City, 1964-69, chair, 1968-69. Author: Leave the Dishes in the Sink: Memoirs of a Liberal in Conservative Utah, 1997; editor parent's page Gifted Child Quarterly, 1964-68. Mem. Logan City (Utah) Bd. Edn., 1959-71, chair; mem. Utah State Bldg. Bd., Salt Lake City, 1965-77; mem. adv. coun. State Dept. Employment Sec., Salt Lake City, 1966-82, chair, 1975-82; mem. No. Utah Cmty. Action Program, Logan, 1966-71, chair, 1971. Recipient Disting. Svc. award Utah Sch. Bds. Assn., 1965, Vol. Svc. award Gov. Utah, 1980. Mem. Am. Econs. Assn. (mem. com. status of women in econ. profession), Nat. Women's Studies Assn., Internat. Assn. Feminist Econs. Democrat. Avocations: community work, writing. Home: Logan, Utah. Died Oct. 23, 2004.

THORNTON, ROBERT LEE, education educator, consultant; b. Orrville, Ohio, June 8, 1917; s. Lee Edwin and Fannie Oresta Thornton; m. Mary Elizabeth Kelly, Dec. 6, 1941; children: Mary Elizabeth, Alix Lee, John Kelly, Sally. BS, U. Akron, Ohio, 1939; MBA, U. Mich., 1951, PhD, 1969. Commd. 2d lt. USAF, 1941, advanced through grades to col., 1965, ret., 1965; from asst. to assoc. prof. Fla. State U., Tallahassee, 1968-75; prof. Miami U., Oxford, Ohio, from 1975. Logistics planner USAF, 1941-65. Decorated Bronze Star, D.S.M. Mem. Oxford Country Club (sec. bd. dirs. 1979-82). Home: Oxford, Ohio. Died July 10, 2005.

THRANE, JUDITH M., nursing educator; b. Chgo., Dec. 7, 1932; Diploma, Ill. Masonic Hosp., Chgo., 1954; BSN, Washington U., St. Louis, 1958, MS in Nursing, 1960; PhD in Nursing, Tex. Woman's U., 1980. Clin. nurse specialist Michael Reese Med. Ctr., Chgo.; supr. nursing Flow Meml. Hosp., Denton, Tex., Jo Ellen Smith Med. Ctr., New Orleans; assoc. prof. grad. program coll. nursing U. Wis., Oshkosh; assoc. prof. grad. program nursing svc. adminstrn. sch. nurs La. State U. Med. Ctr., New Orleans. Contbr. articles to profl. jours. Faculty devel. bd. grantee, U. Wis., Oshkosh, 1985. Mem. ANA, La. State Nurses Assn., New Orleans Dist. Nurses Assn., Washington U. Alumnae Assn., Sigma Theta Tau. Home: Metairie, La. Died Feb. 1, 2005.

THRIFT, SYDNOR W., JR., former professional sports team executive; b. Feb. 25, 1929; m. Dolly; children: Jim, Mark. BA, Randolph-Macon Coll., Va. Baseball player N.Y. Yankees minor league teams, 1949-51; player, mgr. U.S. Army baseball team, Ft. Eustis, Va., 1951-52; high sch. tchr., coach, part-time scout N.Y. Yankees and Pitts. Pirates, 1953-56; scouting supr. Pitts. Pirates, 1957-67; scouting dir. Kans. City Royals, 1967-74; with Oakland A's, 1975-76; realtor, Fairfax, Va., 1976—85; pres., CEO Syd Thrift and Assocs. Inc. Realtors; sr. v.p., gen. mgr. for baseball ops. Pitts. Pirates, 1985-88; sr. v.p. baseball ops. NY Yankees, 1989; asst. gen. mgr. Chgo. Cubs, 1991—94; various exec. position Baltimore Orioles, 1994—99, v.p. baseball ops., 1999—2002; cons. Tampa Bay Devil Rays, 2002—04. Author: The Game According to Syd: The Theories and Teachings of Baseball's Leading Innovator, 1990. Died Sept. 18, 2006.

THULL, SUZANNE WHITE, writer, retired cultural organization administrator; b. Orange, NJ, Aug. 24, 1921; d. Gordon Stowe and Lillian (Siegling) White; m. George I. Hull, Feb. 20, 1943 (dec. Mar. 1990); children: George Gordon Hull, James Rutledge Hull, Anne Elizabeth Hull Sheldon. BA with honors, Swarthmore Coll., 1943; MSLS, U. So. Calif., 1967. Mem. staff Huntington Libr., Art Gallery and Bot. Gardens, San Marino, Calif., 1969-86, dir. adminstrn. and pub. svcs., 1972-86, also prin. officer. Cons. Women Writers Project, Brown U., 1989-2001. Author: Chaste, Silent and Obedient, English Books for Women, 1475-1640, 1982, 88, Women According to Men: The World of Tudor-Stuart Women, 1996, Japanese edit., 2003, Mara Haviland, 2005; editor: State of the Art in Women's Studies, 1986. Charter pres. Portola Jr. HS PTA, LA, 1960-62; pres. Children's Svc. League, 1963-64, YWCA, LA, 1967-69; alumni coun. Swarthmore Coll., 1959-62, 83-86, mem.-at-large, 1986-89; adv. bd. Hagley Mus. and Libr., Wilmington, Del., 1983-86, Betty Friedan Think Tank, U. So. Calif., 1985-93, Early Modern Englishwoman: A Facsimile Libr. Essential Works, 1995-2001; hon. life mem. Calif. Congress Parents and Tchrs.; bd. dirs. Pasadena Planned Parenthood Assn., 1978-83, adv. com., 1983-2004; founder-chmn. Swarthmore-LA Connection, 1984-85, bd. dirs., 1985-92; founder Huntington Women's Studies Seminar, 1984, steering com., 1984-91, adv. bd., 1991-96; organizing com. Soc. for Study of Early Modern Women, 1993-94; hon. mem. Huntington Women's Com. Mem. Monumental Brass Soc. (U.K.), Renaissance Soc., Brit. Studies Conf., Western Assn. Women Historians, Soc. Study of Early Modern Women, Authors Guild, Beta Phi Mu (chpt. dir. 1981-84). Died May 8, 2006.

THURMAN, HERMAN ROBERT, JR., retired structural engineer; b. Louisville, Apr. 7, 1926; s. Herman R. and Frieda L. Abratis T.; m. Elsie Evaline Graves, Aug. 11, 1951; children: Robert C., Eileen, David J. Civil Engr. degree, U. Cin., 1949; MS in Civil Engring., Lehigh U., 1950. Registered profl. engr., Del. Engr., structural steel design F.H.McGraw for Armco, Middletown, Ohio, 1950-51; trainee constrn. divsn. E.I. DuPont Co., Seaford, Del., 1951-52, structural designer for Savannah River Plant Wilmington and Newark, 1952-57, engr. comml. plants Newark, 1957-60, structural design engr. internat. dept., 1960-62, engr. stress analysis, explosions analysis, 1962-65; lead designer, mech. and structural engr. Textile Fiber Plants, Newark, 1965-70; mech. cons. Stress Analysis/Explosion Analysis and Reconstrn., Newark, 1970-77; project engr. AEC Work/E.I. DuPont Co., Newark, 1977-86; part-time structural engr. Cons. Design at First Contact Design, Hockessine, Del., from 1986. Cpl. Signal Corps, U.S. Army, 1944-46. Univ. scholarship, Lehigh U., 1950. Mem. ASCE (v.p. 1981, pres. 1982). Home: Wilmington, Del. Died Mar. 10, 2005.

THURSTON, ETHEL HOLBROOKE, retired music educator, foundation executive; b. Mpls, Minn, Oct. 30, 1911; d. Edward Sampson and Florence Chapman (Holbrooke) T. BA, Vassar Coll., 1933; diploma in organ, Fontainebleau Music Sch., France, 1930, 38; diploma in Gregorian chant, Pius X Sch., N.Y.C., 1945; PhD, NYU, 1954. Lectr. Coll. St. Catherine, St. Paul, 1945-46; prof. Hunter Coll., NYC, 1953-59, St. John's U., Jamaica, NY, 1959-66; chmn. music history Manhattan Sch. Music, NYC, 1966-81; ret., 1981. Editor facsimile edition The Music in the St. Victor Manuscript, 1959; editor music and text: The Works of Perotin, 1970, The Conductus Collections in Ms. Wolfenbuttel 1099 (3 vols.), 1980; contbr. articles on 13th century polyphony and manuscript transcription to various publ. Chair Beauty Without Cruelty USA, NYC, 1972— Mem. Am. Musicological Assn., Music Libr. Assn., Internat. Musicological Assn., Phi Beta Kappa, Mu Phi Epsilon, Mu Sigma. Home: New York, NY. Died Jan. 4, 2006.

THURSTON, JOHN THOMAS, retired academic administrator; b. Lockport, N.Y., Oct. 24, 1948; s. John Henry and Helen Lenore (Schaffert) Mahar. BA in English and Journalism, So. Ark. U., 1971. Writer ednl. affairs SUNY, Buffalo, 1972—74, sci. editor, 1974—76, news editor, 1976—77, assoc. dir. Univ. New Burs., 1977—78, dir., 1979—83, assoc. dir. pub. affairs, 1983—86, staff assoc. Univ. Rels. Buffalo, 1987—92, officer budget and pers. dept. Univ. Advancement and Devel., 1992—99, grant writer, from 2000; ret., 2000. Comm. instr., freelance writer, cons. Hockey coach, ofcl., youth baseball, basketball and football, pres. We. N.Y. H.S. Club, 1983-85; pres. Lockport Tigers Youth Hockey Assn., 1996—. Recipient nat. award Coun. Advancement and Support of Edn., 1975, 78; named Lockport Sportsman of Yr., 1984. Mem. Coun. Advancement and Support Higher Edn., Nat. Assn. Sci. Writers, Constrn. Writers Am., Pub. Rels. Soc. Am., USA Hockey, Prof. Com. We. N.Y. Republican. Roman Catholic. Home: Lockport, NY. Died June 6, 2005.

TIBBALS, DAVID LESTER, risk management consultant; b. Chgo., Nov. 29, 1945; BA, Rutgers U., 1969, MBA, 1976; postgrad., U. Chgo., 1975-76. Asst. v.p. Alexander & Alexander, N.Y.C. and Chgo., 1971-78; cons. Betterley Cons. Group, Boston, 1978-81; v.p. Tillinghast, Nelson & Warren, Inc., Boston and Atlanta, 1981-87; pres. D.L. Tibbals Risk Mgmt. Cons., Atlanta, from 1987. Mem. Soc. Risk Mgmt. Cons. (bd. dirs. 1988—, pres. 1993-94). Died June 8, 2005.

TIBBS, ROBERT CLINTON, II, pediatrician; b. Miss., Sept. 16, 1931; s. Eugene Clinton Tibbs and Laverne Katherine Fell; m. Patricia Lynn Tibbs, Aug. 3, 1962; four children. BS in Physics and Chemsitry, Delta State U., 1953; MD, U. Tenn., Memphis, 1956. Diplomate Am. Bd. Pediat. Active staff Bolivan Med. Ctr., Cleve., from 1965. Achievements include 8 patents in propulsion systems, injection device, energy transfer rotational device, lift surface. Died July 25, 2005.

TILLMAN, JUNE TORRISON, musician; b. Mpls., June 11, 1917; d. Odvin Olai and Anne Johanne (Andersen) Torrison; m. Jean Paul Tillman, July 19, 1941; 1 child, Paula Jeanne Tillman Morrow. BA, Macalester Coll., 1940; postgrad., MacPhail Coll Music, 1952-55, U. Minn., 1944-45; student, Dr. Hoch's Konservatorium, Frankfurt am Main, 1956-57. Cert. piano tchr., Fla., Mo. Clk. auditing dept. The Dayton Co., Mpls., summer 1935; tchr., libr. Howard Lake H.S., Minn., 1941; prin. clk. Army Office Chief of Fin., Washington, 1942-43; gold acct. Gen. Refineries, Inc., Mpls., 1944-45; asst. acct. First Acceptance Corp., Mpls., 1946-47, 51; property acct. clk. Army Quartermaster Commissary, Camp Wolters, Tex., 1959-61; music tchr. various orgns., from 1953. Nat. com. chmn. Music Tchrs. Nat. Assn., Ind. Music Tchrs. Forum Studio Policies, 1975-77; state conv. chmn. Fla. State Music Tchrs., Ft. Lauderdale, 1978; auditions ctr. chmn. Nat. Guild Piano Tchrs., Ft. Lauderdale, 1975-87; sponsor, tchr. Mus. Arts Jr. Club of Fla. Fedn. Music Clubs, Wilton Manors, 1976-87, Springfield, Mo., 1988-91, sr. club mem., 1987, pres., 1990-92, state conv. accompanist, 1988-90, v.p. S.W. region of Mo., 1989-91; organist, choir dir. various mil. chapels and civilian chs., U.S., Germany and Japan, 1935-65. Composer numerous works, 1958-87; reviewer (books, records, choral arrangements) 1978-86; editor Fla. Fedn. Music Clubs Publs., 1975-77, 81-84; music editor 12 Choral Octavos, 1981; composer, panelist state convention Minn. Fedn. Music Clubs, Bloomington, 1984; Soprano, Alto, Tenor, Bass, Organ anthem performed by Moramus Chorale at Moravian Music Festival, Winston-Salem, N.C., 1978; prodr., dir., accompanied Menotti's The Old Maid and the Thief, 1965, Argento's The Boor, 1966. Chmn. 10-piano concerts Broward County Music Tchrs., Plantation, Fla., 1969, 71;life mem. Women's Div. Boys Clubs of Broward, Fla., Ft. Lauderdale Symphony Soc.; organist, choir dir. Coral Ridge Moravian Ch., Ft. Lauderdale, 1966-85. Mem. Music Tchrs. Nat. Assn., Nat. Fedn. of Music Clubs (life, dist. pres. 1983-85, young artists auditions com. 1993-97), Morning Musicale of Ft. Lauderdale, Inc. (hon., life, pres. 1970-72), Am. Guild Organists (treas. 1967), Phi Beta (founder, pres. Pi Alpha Rho chpt., life, honor bracelet, scrolls 1971, 76, 83, citations 1988), Order Ea. Star (Richfield, Minn. chpt.), Masons (Fla. Grand chpt. Cmty. Svc. award 1987), Springfield Piano Tchrs. Forum, Toastmasters (gov. S.W. Mo. area 1988-89). Avocations: reading (especially biographies), crossword puzzles, langs. Died Sept. 3, 2006.

TILLMAN, ROBERT ERWIN, ecologist; b. Hammondsport, N.Y., June 29, 1937; s. Erwin George and Mary Lola (Sullivan) T.; m. Elfriede Wirth, Aug. 20, 1960 (div. 1986); children: Henry Charles, Franz Robert; m. Marie Edward Tillman, May 31, 1986. BA, SUNY, Albany, 1959; MA, SUNY, 1961; PhD, Cornell U., 1972. Assoc. prof. biology Dutchess Community Coll., Poughkeepsie, N.Y., 1966-69, chmn. dept. natural resources, 1971-72; wildlife resources staff N.Y. Bot. Garden, Millbrook, N.Y., 1973-75, chmn. envirfon. assessment, 1975-82; human settlements officer UN Centre for Human Settlements, Nairobi, Kenya, 1982-84; environ. advisor USAID/Peru, Lima, 1984-85; sr. environ. scientist Assocs. in Rural Devel., Burlington, Vt., 1985-89; environ. specialist World Bank, Washington, from 1989. Cons. in field. Contbr. articles to profl. jours. Chmn. N.Y. State Forest Practice Bd., 1980-83. Mem. Soc. Am. Foresters, Internat. Soc. Tropical Foresters, Wildlife Soc. Avocations: bird watching, gardening. Home: Rock Stream, NY. Died May 31, 2005.

TILTON, JAMES JOSEPH, research librarian; b. Sioux City, Iowa, Oct. 1, 1942; s. Jesse Verner and Antoinette Marie (Seek) T.; m. Doreen Carole Buck, Apr. 7, 1973; 1 child, James Joseph. BA in History, U. Va., 1968; MLS, U. Md., 1970. Libr. Defense Tech. Info. Ctr., Alexandria, Va., 1970-72; sr. reference libr. U.S. Dept. Housing & Urban Devel., Washington, 1972-78; program mgr. Bibliographical Ctr. for Rsch., Denver, 1978-80; mktg. mgr. Sorities Group, Inc., Springfield, Va., 1980-81; mktg. mgr. southeast region N.Y. Times Info. Svcs., Arlington, Va., 1982-83; libr., asst. libr. Inst. Def. Analyses, Alexandria, 1984-90; sr. libr. IIT Rsch. Inst., Lanham, Md., from 1990; libr. mgr. BMD Tech. Info. Ctr., Arlington, from 1994. Cons. in field. V.p. Civic Assn., Annandale, Va., 1976-77, co-block capt., Springfield, 1990-92; vol. Fairfax County Pub. Schs., Springfield, 1980-88. With USAF, 1962-66. Independent. Achievements include planning of first DOD automated information center at DTIC; intra-automated database services as a research tool at HUD library; establishment of the Strategic Defense Initiative library at the Inst. Defense Analyses. Home: Springfield, Va. Died May 20, 2004.

TINDEL, JOHN CURTIS, lawyer; b. Cabool, Mo., Nov. 19, 1935; s. Curtis Jordan and Nell Catherine (Johnson) T.; m. Shirley A. Haynes, Sept. 13, 1954; children: John M., Curtis J., Jeanne. BA, U. Mo., Columbia, 1956, MA, 1957; JD, U. Mo., 1963. Bar: Mo. 1963, Mich. 1977, U.S. Supreme Ct. 1980. Ptnr. Kennedy & Tindel, Nevada, Mo., 1963-68; real estate atty. Monsanto Co., 1968-75; asst. gen. counsel St. Paul Title Ins. Corp., 1975-76; pvt. practice Cabool, 1976-82; ptnr. Tindel & Ellsworth, Cabool, 1982-83; pres. Hiett Abstract Co., Houston, Mo., from 1980; pvt. practice Cabool, Houston, Mountain Grove, from 1983; pres. Wright County Title Co., Cabool, from 1989. Mem. adj. faculty Drury Coll.; judge Mountain Grove and Licking mcpl. divsn. Tex. County Cir. Ct., 1979—. Author: (with others) Missouri Family Law, 1967. Pres., bd. dirs. Legal Aid Soc. S.W. Mo., 1991-93; parliamentarian Mo. Bapt. Conv. Mem. ABA, Mo. Bar, Mich. Bar, Mo. Assn. Assoc. and Mcpl. Ct. Judges, Bar Assn. Met. St. Louis, Texas County Bar Assn. Republican. Home: Cabool, Mo. Died Dec. 2004.

TIRNAUER, LAWRENCE THEODORE, psychologist, psychotherapist; b. N.Y.C., Apr. 15, 1933; s. Samuel and Rose Tirnauer; m. Sandra Smathers (div.); children: Jennifer, Karen, Diana, Eric. BA, Otterbein Coll., 1954; MS, Pa. State U., 1955, PhD, 1959. Lic. psychologist, Washington. Staff psychologist St. Elizabeth's Hosp., Washington, 1959-60; psychologist Child Guidance Clinic D.C. Health Dept., Washington, 1960-63, chief psychologist children's program area C, 1963-64, chief psychologist adolescent program area C, 1964-65; chief psychologist Bur. Infant and Maternal Care, Washington, 1965-68; pvt. practice psychology and psychotherapy Washington, from 1968. Cons. McFarland Child Guidance Clinic, Washington, 1965-68, Washington Free Clinic, 1970-75, Pastoral Counseling Ctrs., 1965-85; supervisory cons. in psychotherapy Affiliated Cmty. Counselors, Rockville, 1998—. Mem. editl. bd. Voices: The Art and Sci. of Psychotherapy, 1977—, poetry editor, 1996—; assoc. editor The Psychotherpay Patient, 1984—; contbr. articles on psychotherapy to profl. jours., chpts. to books. Mem. APA, Am. Acad. Psychotherapists (pres. 1986-88, chair rsch. com. 1992-98), Am. Group Psychotherapy Assn., D.C. Psychol. Assn. Avocations: painting, tennis, fishing, creative writing. Home: Bethesda, Md. Died Mar. 21, 2004.

TISCH, ROBERT (PRESTON ROBERT TISCH), corporate financial executive, sports association executive; b. Bklyn., Apr. 29, 1926; s. Abraham Solomon and Sayde (Brenner) T.; m. Joan Hyman, Mar. 14, 1948; children: Steven E., Laurie M., Jonathan M. Student, Bucknell U., 1943—44; BA, U. Mich., 1948. Chmn. bd. dir. Loews Corp., N.Y.C., 1960—2005; postmaster gen. U.S. Postal Svc., Washington, 1986—88; chmn., co-CEO, half owner N.Y. Football Giants, 1991—2005. Bd. dirs. CNA Fin. Corp., Bulova Watch Co. Chmn. emeritus N.Y. Conf. and Visitors Bur., Nat. Dem. Conv., 1976, 80; chmn. Citymeals on Wheels, 1993-2002, chmn. emeritus, 2003-05; trustee NYU; mem. Quadrennial Commn. on Exec., Legis. and Jud. Salaries, 1988; mem. Gov.'s Bus. Adv. Coun. for N.Y. State; founder, chmn. Take the Field (rebuilding N.Y.C. sch. athletic facilities). With AUS, 1943-44. Mem. Century Country Club, Sigma Alpha Mu; Fellow Am. Acad. Arts and Sciences. Died Nov. 16, 2005.

TISDALE, PATRICIA CLAIRE, lawyer; b. Detroit, Sept. 7, 1951; d. Joseph Terrence Jr. and Patricia Ann (Cottrell) Brennan; m. Douglas Michael Tisdale, Dec. 29, 1972; children: Douglas M., Sara E., Margaret P., Victoria C. BA, U. Detroit, 1971; JD, U. Denver, 1979. Bar: Colo. 1979, U.S. Dist. Ct. Colo. 1979. Dep. city atty. City of Arvada, Colo., 1979-90; spl. counsel Holme Roberts & Owen, Denver, from 1990. Mem. ABA, Colo. Bar Assn. (conv. com. chmn. 1984-86), Denver Bar Assn., Metro City Attys. Assn., Phi Alpha Delta. Republican. Roman Catholic. Avocations: skiing, golf, reading. Home: Englewood, Colo. Died Jan. 6, 2004.

TODD, R(ICHARD) PAUL, academic dean; b. Harrisonville, Mo., Dec. 14, 1939; s. George W. and Iva M. (Bills) T.; m. Alice I. Clavin, June 3, 1961; children: Diana, Marcia, Elaina. BSBA, Rockhurst Coll., 1970; MBA, Cen. Mo. State U., 1973; PhD, Columbia Pacific U., 1985. Cert. supr. adult vocat. edn. Printer Kansas City (Mo.) Star Co., 1967-70; plant mgr. Kansas City Cen. Paper Box Co., 1970-71; supt. St. Regis Paper Co., Dubuque, Iowa, 1971-73; instr. printing Kansas City Tech. Edn. Ctr., 1973-75; plant mgr. Interstate Book Mfrs., Olathe, Kans., 1975-76; dir. Adult Vocation Edn., Kansas City, 1976-79, Kansas City Skill Ctr., 1979-80; pres. T.D.Q. Inc., Kansas City, 1980-86; acad. dean Nat. Coll., Kansas City, from 1986. Cons. printing various cos., 1976—. Author: Basic Auctioneering, 1985. Comdr. Aquarian Div. U.S. Naval Sea Cadet Corps, Kansas City, 1987—. With USAR, 1956-81. Mem. Navy League. Democrat. Roman Catholic. Avocation: auctioneer. Home: Kansas City, Mo. Died Feb. 4, 2004.

TOLL, CHARLES HULBERT, construction executive; b. Los Angeles, June 30, 1931; s. Charles Hulbert Sr. and Kathryn (Burrows) T.; m. Barbara Jean Tressler, Mar. 5, 1955; 1 child, Wendy Warren Toll Greene. Grad. high sch., North Hollywood, Calif. Various positions The Flinkote Co., Blue Diamond, Nev., 1955-67, works mgr., 1967-75; v.p. The Grail Co., Santa Ana, Calif., 1975-78, H.G. Toll Co., El Segundo, Calif., 1978-80, pres. Scottsdale, Ariz., 1980-89, Toll Constrn., Scottsdale, Ariz., from 1989. Republican. Episcopalian. Home: Scottsdale, Ariz. Died Aug. 3, 2004.

TOM, CLARENCE YUNG CHEN, retired city and county official; b. Honolulu, Jan. 25, 1927; s. John Chong and Dorothy Oi Fook (Ing) T.; m. Vivian Kam Oi Lum, July 19, 1969; children: Claire-Anne, Karen-Anne, Patricia-Anne. BS in Chem. Engring., Purdue U., 1947, MS in Chem. Engring., 1957; M City Planning, Harvard U., 1959. Chem. engr. Libby, McNeill & Libby, Honolulu, 1947-50, 52-54; planner City and County Honolulu, 1958-89, chief environ. and plans assessment br. dept. gen. planning, 1960-88. Mem. Hawaii Census Tract Com., 1960-89. Jr. warden St. Mary's Ch., Honolulu, 1970-82; vestryman Ch. Holy Nativity, Honolulu, 1984-86. Served with U.S. Army, 1950-52, Korea. Mem. Hawaii Govt. Employees Assn. (steward 1971-72, 81-82, alt. steward 1988). Democrat. Home: Honolulu, Hawaii. Died July 8, 2004.

TOMIKAWA, SOJI, educational institute administrator; b. Nagoya, Aichi-Ken, Japan, July 13, 1918; came to U.S., 1953; s. Tatsujiro and Yuki (Kojima) T. Law degree, Tohoku U., Sendai, Japan, 1942; MA in pub. adminstrn., Syracuse U., 1955, PhD in polit. sci., 1966. Mem. facilities subcom. Admin. Agreement U.S.-Japan Security Treaty Prime Minister's Office Japanese Govt., Tokyo, 1950-53; chief procurement officer UN Hdqs., N.Y.C., 1960-80; officer-in-charge UN Peace Keeping Emergency Force Middle East, Jerusalem, 1973-74; exec. sec. Japanese Edn. Inst. N.Y., N.Y.C., 1982-90, spl. adv. coun. for founding Greenwich Japanese Sch. Greenwich, Conn., from 1990. 1st lt. Japanese Navy, 1942-46. Decorated Order of Rising Sun, Gold and Silver Rays, H.M. Emperor Hirohito of Japan, 1994; recipient Fulbright Exchange Program scholarship, 1953-57, 46th Yomiuri Shimbun Press cert. of excellence in edn., 1997, 23rd Internat. Contribution award Kokokai exclusive cultural soc. Gtr. Nagoya Area Japan, 2000. Mem. U.S.-Japan Fulbright Alumni Assn. N.Y.C., Japan Soc. Fairfield County (Conn., chair adv. bd.), Nippon Club N.Y.C. (bd. dirs.), The Japanese Am. Assn. N.Y. Avocations: golf, swimming, hiking. Home: Flushing, NY. Died Mar. 12, 2004.

TOMKO, REGINA JACQUELINE, nurse practitioner; b. Detroit, Oct. 31, 1940; d. Chester and Genevieve (Kanafol) Chilinski; m. Robert F. Tomko, Sept. 10, 1966; 1 child, Jennifer A. RN, Providence Hosp., Detroit, 1961; BA, U. Detroit, 1976; MSN, Wayne State U., 1981. Cert. nurse practitioner, ANA. Mgr., nurse practitioner Detroit Osteopathic Hosp., Highland Park, Mich., 1982-84; nurse practitioner in employee health Kaiser Permanente Reg. Hdqrs., Pasadena; nurse practitioner Kaiser Permanent, Granada Hills, Calif., 1985-94, Woodland Hills, Calif., 1994—99, Lancaster, from 1999. 1st lt. USAF, 1962-66. Mem. Calif. Coalition of Nurse Practitioners. Home: North Hills, Calif. Died Apr. 12, 2004.

TONN, MARTIN HELMUTH, retired special education educator; b. Sioux Center, Iowa, Apr. 11, 1921; s. William F. and Dora (Brunquell) T.; m. Phyllis Ann Tonn, June 7, 1952; children: Laura Beth, Martha Louise. BA, U. Iowa, 1949, MA, 1950, PhD, 1964. Speech and hearing cons. Dept. Pub. Instrn., Des Moines, 1950-51; speech therapist Carroll County (Iowa) Sch. System, 1951-55, dir. spl. edn., 1955-57; assoc. prof. Moorhead (Minn.) State U., 1957-82. Author: Animal Adventures, 1953, Adventures Around Town, 1954; contbr. articles to profl. jours. Chmn. Clay-Wilkin Opportunity Coun., Moorhead, 1967. Staff sgt. U.S. Army, 1942-46. Spl. edn. fellow U.S. Office Edn., 1963-64. Mem. NEA (life), Am. Speech, Lang. and Hearing Assn. (life, pres. Iowa chpt. 1956). Democrat. Lutheran. Avocations: writing, reading. Home: Moorhead, Minn. Died Feb. 8, 2005.

TOOKER, ELISABETH JANE, anthropologist, educator; b. Bklyn., Aug. 2, 1927; d. Clyde and Amy (Luce) T. BA, Radcliffe Coll., 1949, PhD, 1958; MA, U. Ariz., 1953. Instr. anthropology U. Buffalo, 1957-60; asst. prof. Mt. Holyoke Coll., South Hadley, Mass., 1961-65, Temple U., Phila., 1965-67, assoc. prof., 1967-77, prof., 1977-92, prof. emeritus, from 1992. Author: An Ethnography of the Huron Indians, 1964, The Iroquois Ceremonial of Midwinter, 1970; editor: Native American Spirituality of the Eastern Woodlands, 1979, An Iroquois Source Book, 1985-86; editor Am. Ethnol. Soc. jour. 1978-82. NEH fellow, 1981-82, Smithsonian Instn. fellow, 1989-90; recipient Cornplanter medal Cayuga County Hist. Soc., 1986. Mem. Am. Anthrop. Assn., Am. Soc. for Ethnohistory (pres. 1981-82). Home: Philadelphia, Pa. Died Jan. 13, 2005.

TOOLE, BRUCE RYAN, retired lawyer; b. Missoula, Mont., June 21, 1924; s. John Howard and Marjorie Lee (Ross) T.; m. Loris Knoll, Sept. 29, 1951; children: Marjorie, Ryan, Allan. JD, U. Mont., 1949. Bar: Mont., U.S. Ct. Appeals (9th & Fed. cirs.), U.S. Supreme Ct., U.S. Claims Ct. Sole practice, Missoula, 1950; dep. county atty. Missoula County, 1951; ptnr. Crowley Law Firm, Billings, Mont., 1951-92, of counsel, from 1992; ret. Editor Mont. Lawyer, 1979-83. Mem. Mont. Com. for Humanities, Missoula; v.p. Billings Preservation Soc.; precinctman Yellowstone County Reps. With U.S. Army, 1944-45, ETO. Fellowship grantee NEH, Harvard U., 1980. Fellow Am. Coll. Trial Lawyers, Am. Bar Found.; mem. Am. Bd. Trial Advs., State Bar Mont. (pres. 1977-78), Yellowstone County Bar (pres. 1973, chmn. com. on mediation 1992), Internat. Assn. Def. Counsel. Avocations: politics, history, photography, metal work. Home: Billings, Mont. Died Sept. 16, 2005.

TOOMIM, MARJORIE K., psychologist, biofeedback therapist; b. L.A., Feb. 25, 1923; d. Elias Victor and Mildred (Firth) Rosenkranz; m. Morris Kawin, Sept. 14, 1942 (div. Sept. 1959); children: Bruce, Elise Kawin Osner, Pamela Kawin Smith. AA in Sociology, Pomona Coll., 1942; BA in Sociology and Psychology, U. So. Calif., 1945, PhD in Clin. Psychology, 1966. Lic. psychologist, Calif.; cert. Biofeedback Inst. Am. Staff psychologist L.A. Psychiat. Svcs., 1966-67; pvt. practice, L.A.; dir. Biofeedback Inst. L.A. (formerly New Health Insts.), Culver City, Calif., from 1973. Dir. mental health cons. svcs. to project Head Start Los Angeles County Soc. Clin. Psycologists Psychol. Ctr., L.A., 1967-68; dir. Assoc. Counseling Svcs., L.A., 1968-74; co-dir. Biocomp. Rsch. Inst., Culver City, 1970—; paper presenter in field. Contbg. author: Therapeutic Needs of the Family, 1984; editor: The Comprehensive Biofeedback Manual: A Book of Readings in Clinical Biofeedback, 1983; contbr. articles to profl. jours. Mem. APA, Assn. Applied Psychophysiology and Biofeedback, Soc. for Study Neuronal Regulaton, Calif. Psychol. Assn., Biofeedback Soc. Calif., Los Angeles County Psychol. Assn., Phi Beta Kappa, Phi Kappa Phi, Alpha Kappa Delta. Died Jan. 18, 2005.

TORDA, T. PAUL, retired educator; b. Budapest, Hungary, Sept. 22, 1911; came to U.S., 1946; s. Joseph and Ilona (Varga) T.; m. Florence Juran, 1954; children: Phyllis, Roger. Dipl.Ing., Tech. U. Berlin, 1936; PhD, Polytech. Inst., Bklyn., 1949. Naval architect Ganz & Co., Budapest, 1936-38; mech. engr. Melbourne, Australia, 1939; aircraft design engr. Commonwealth Aircraft Corp., Melbourne, 1939-44; prodn. mgr. Winton Mfg. Co., Melbourne, 1944-45; chief engr. Tecalemit A'Asia, Ltd., Melbourne, 1945-46; rsch. assoc. sr. grade Polytech. Inst., Bklyn., 1946-49; assoc. prof. aeronautical engring. U. Ill., Urbana, 1949-50, prof., 1950-55; prof. mech. engring. Polytech. Inst., Bklyn., 1955-59; dir. rsch. Armour Rsch. Found., Chgo., 1959-62; prof. mechanics, mech. and aerospace engring. Ill. Inst. Tech., Chgo., 1962-77, emeritus prof. mechanics, mech. and aerospace engring., 1977—2004; sr. sci. adviser Triodyne, Inc., Niles, Ill., 1979-81. Cons. to fed. govt. and pvt. industry, 1946—; dir. Edn. and Experience in Engring. Program, 1971-77; pres. Thorae Corp., Washington, 1986—; mem. sci. and engring. adv. bd. Emeritus Found., 1990-95. Bd. dirs. Joint Bd. on Sci. and Engring. Edn., Washington, 1986-90. Fellow ASME (co-founder tech. and soc. divsn., chmn. edn. in transition com. 1973—), AIAA (assoc.); mem. Sr. Scientists and Engrs./AAAS (vice chmn. edn. 1990-94, mem. edn. com. 1994—), Combustion Inst. (founder Ctrl. State sect. 1966), Sigma Xi. Died Mar. 24, 2004.

TOSHEFF, JULIJ GOSPODINOFF, psychiatrist; b. Svishtov, Bulgaria, July 3, 1925; came to U.S., 1968; s. Gospodin P. and Mara A. (Karaivanova) T.; m. Finnie I. Kancheva, Feb. 10, 1927; 1 child, Deana. MD, Higher Med. Inst., Sofia, Bulgaria, 1952. Resident Higher Inst. Specialization of Physicians, Sofia, Bulgaria, 1953-56, 59-62, staff physician, 1957-59, staff psychiatrist clinic psychiatry, 1962-67; staff internist Gen. City Hosp., Tetovo, Yugoslavia, 1967; rsch. assoc. dept. psychiatry Johns Hopkins U. Sch. Medicine, Balt., 1968-69, instr. behavioral biology, dept. psychiatry, 1969-72; intern South Baltimore Gen. Hosp., 1972-73; resident L.I. Jewish Med. Ctr., Hillside Hosp., Glen Oaks, NY, 1973-76, staff psychiatrist, from 1976. Contbr. articles to profl. jours. Lt. Bulgarian Army. Mem. APA. Avocations: classical music, opera, reading. Home: Manhasset, NY. Died Dec. 24, 2005.

TOUBY, RICHARD, lawyer; b. Sioux City, Iowa, Nov. 17, 1924; s. Louis and Rebecca (Keck) T.; m. Marion Lascher, Aug. 6, 1949; children: Jill Diane, Kim Paula. LLB, U. Miami, 1948; LLM, Duke U., 1950. Bar: Fla. 1948. Faculty U. Miami, Coral Gables, Fla., 1948-63; mem. 8th Air Force Meml. Assn., 305 Bomb Group (H) Assn., from 1994. 1st Lt. USAF, 1943-45. Home: Miami, Fla. Died May 16, 2004.

TOUCHSTONE, FRANK VIRGIL, psychologist; b. London, Ky., July 11, 1927; s. Cary and Mabel Ellen (Thomas) T.; m. Dorothy Viola Anderson, Nov. 10, 1961; 1 child, Ellen E. BA, So. Meth. U., 1950; MS in Psychology, Purdue U., 1952, PhD in Psychology, 1957. Lic. psychologist, Ky., Nebr. Counseling psychologist VA, Marion, Ind., 1956-60, clin. and counseling psychologist Shreveport, La., 1960-63; assoc. prof. psychology Centenary Coll., Shreveport, 1963-67; assoc. prof. edn. Pa. State U., State College, 1967-70; chief psychologist Mental Health Ctr., Hazard, Ky., 1970-74; dir. psychology Hastings (Nebr.) Regional Ctr., from 1974. Vocat. specialist, cons. U.S. Social Security Adminstrn., 1967—. Editor Rehab. Counseling Bull., 1966-70. Served as sgt. USAF, 1946-49. Mem. Am. Psychol. Assn., Am. Assn. for Counseling and Devel. (chmn. com. 1983-84), Am. Rehab. Counseling Assn. (pres. 1978-79, Superior Service award 1976). Presbyterian. Home: Hastings, Nebr. Died Mar. 22, 2005.

TOUPIN, EDWARD BERNARD, engineer, mathematician and computer scientist; b. Houma, La., Mar. 2, 1964; s. Bernard Ovid and Edna Mae (Pennison) T. AAS, North Harris County Coll., Houston, 1986; BS in Math. and Computer Sci., Met. State Coll. of Denver, 1992. Bench tech. R&D Instrument Svcs., Inc., Houston, 1984-85; owner, technician Hi Res. Technologies, Houston, 1985-88; programmer/analyst Johnson & Higgins of Tex., Houston,

1988-89; programmer/analyst cons. Edward B. Toupin, Houston and Denver, from 1988; automation engr. Texaco Trading and Transp., Inc., Denver, 1990-96, tech. analyst, software engr., from 1996; tech. editor, author QED/John Wiley & Sons, Denver, 1993-94, Macmillan Pub., Indianapolis and Denver, 1993-95; cons. RTX, Inc., Denver and Loveland, Colo., 1994-95; contract developer Mabry Software, Inc., Seattle and Denver, 1995-96. Condr. seminars in field; designer/developer comms. classes various software packages. Author: The Windows Expert System v1.01, 1992, Network Programming under VMS/DECNet Phases IV and V, 1993, Easy Programming with C, 1994, Easy Programming with Visual BASIC 4.0, 1995, Mabry Software's Internet Pack, 1996; lead author Special Edition, Using Turbo C++ 4.5 for Windows, 1995; contbg. author Visual BASIC 4.0 Expert Solutions, 1995, Building OCXs, 1995, Visual Basic 4 Unleashed, 1995, Visual Basic 4 Multimedia Adventure Set, 1995, Ultimate VB 4 Controls Sourcebook, 1995, Building Internet Applications with Visual C++, 1995, Visual Basic Internet Programming, 1996, Windows Development Exchange, 1996, Developing Visual Basic 4 Communications Applications, 1996, Windows 95 Power Toolkit, 1996; tech. editor Visual C++ 1.5 by Example, 1994, Spl. Edition, Using C++ 2.0, 1994, Insider's Guide to Windows 95 Programming, 1995, VBA Database Solutions, 1996; inventor in field. Vol. toys for Denver Children's Hosp., 1993, 94. With USAF. Met. State Coll. Colo. Scholars awardee, 1991, 92. Mem. ACM, Microsoft Developers Network (Level 2), AI-CD Network, Am. Assn. Artificial Intelligence, Math. Assn. Am., The Internet Soc., Colo. Advanced Software Inst., Rocky Mountain Windows NT Users Group, U.S. Powerlifting Fedn., Gulf Coast Sailing Assn., Gulf Coast Cycling Assn., Golden Key. Roman Catholic. Avocations: power lifting, writing, sailing, hiking, travel. Home: Las Vegas, Nev. Died Feb. 2, 2005.

TOWNSEND, KENNETH ROSS, retired priest; b. Holly Grove, Ala., Oct. 31, 1927; s. James Ernest and Mary H. (Jordan) T.; m. Irene Fogleman, Mar. 18, 1951; children: Marietta, Martha, Kenneth Ross, Elizabeth. AB, Birmingham South Coll., 1956; postgrad., Union Theol. Sem., 1960-63; MDiv, Va. Theol. Sem., 1964. Ordained priest Episcopal Ch., 1965. Pastor meth. chs. N.C. and Va. Confs., 1954-63; priest Bath Priest Parish, Dinwiddie, Va., 1964-69, St. Paul's Ch., Vanceboro, N.C., 1969-89; ret., 1989. Lectr. philosophy Richard Bland Coll. of Coll. William and Mary, Williamsburg, Va., 1966-68; del. to synod Province IV, 1973; mem. liturgical com. Episcopal Diocese of East Carolina, Wilmington, N.C., 1971-82, mem. prison commn., 1984; resident priest Olivet Ch., Franconia, Va., 1995—. Writer, painter With USNR, 1945-46. Mem.: VFW, Delta Sigma Phi. Home: Woodbridge, Va. Died May 9, 2004.

TOWNZEN, JACK EDWARD, JR., dancer; b. Odessa, Tex., Nov. 5, 1954; s. Jack Edward and Mary Ruth (Garren) T. Student, Odessa Coll., 1973-74, North Tex. State U., 1974-75, Dallas Ballet, Los Angeles Ballet, Bolshoi Ballet Co., Joffrey Ballet and Sch.; studies with, Gus Giordano, Joe Tremain, Choo San Goh, George Skibine, Marjorie Tallchief. Freelance singer, dancer, from 1977. Choreographer, prin. guest artist, tchr., asst. to artistic producer Las Vegas Civic Ballet, 1985—, artistic dir., 1995; ind. choreographer and dir. Producer, choreographer, coordinator (fundraising benefit for persons living with HIV/AIDS) Golden Rainbow Show, 1987, Golden Rainbow presents A Toast to Broadway, 1988, Golden Rainbow: A Salute to the Musicals, 1989, Golden Rainbow: Showstoppers, 1990, Golden Rainbow: Ribbon of Life Shows, 1991-96; dancer, singer Shennandoah, 1977, Nutcracker, 1977-78, Fiddler on the Roof, 1978, Manon (with Dallas Civic Opera), 1978, Homage to Diagalev (with Rudolf Nureyev and the Joffrey Ballet), 1979, Romeo and Juliet (with Bolshoi Ballet), 1979, Kansas City Ballet, 1979-80, Brigadoon, Little Me, 1980, T. Finnans World of Entertainment, 1981, Lisbon, Portugal, Le Hot Las Vegas Show, Seoul, Korea, 1981-82, Allez Lido, Lido de Paris, Stardust, 1984-86, An Evening at La Cage-Riviera, 1986, City Lites; choreographer, asst. prodr., Flamingo Hilton, 1986-94; guest student, performer Bolshoi Ballet, 1979. Artistic dir. Golden Rainbow 10th Anniversary Prodn. Ribbon of Life Show, Las Vegas, Nev., 1987—, also 11th Ann. Show. Avocations: collecting old movies, travel. Died Sept. 3, 2004.

TRACY, DENNIE MATISOFF, controller; b. Phila., Nov. 3, 1932; d. Nathaniel Alexander and Beatrice (Lees) Matisoff; m. Thomas E. Tracy, Apr. 26, 1975; children: Shari Lee Whitlock, Scott Andrew Mazur, Steven Yale Mazur; 1 stepchild, Thomas C. Tracy. BS, La Salle U., 1983. Contr. Plastics Devel. Corp. Am., Phila., 1970-76, Towa Corp., Morrisville, Pa., 1977-80; corp. contr. Talco Metals Co., Phila., 1983-91, Enterprise Mfg. Co., Phila., from 1991. Staffer Rice for Pa. Senate, 1990. Mem. Am. Soc. Women Accts. Avocations: mural painting, child care. Home: Philadelphia, Pa. Died Sept. 7, 2004.

TRAPOLIN, FRANK WINTER, retired insurance executive; b. New Orleans, Jan. 29, 1913; s. John Baptiste and Florence Bertha (Winter) T.; m. Thelma Mae Mouledoux, Oct. 27, 1937; children: Timothy, Patricia Couret, Jane Oaksmith, Anne Britt. BS in Econs., Loyola U., New Orleans. cert. ofcl. U.S.A. Track and Field. Agt. Godchaux & Mayer, New Orleans, 1935-42m 46-51; pres. Trapolin-Couret Ins. Agy., Inc., New Orleans, 1953-92; v.p. Gillis, Ellis & Baker, Inc., New Orleans, 1993-94; ret., 1994. Mem. faculty Loyola U., 1938-40; TV lectr., instr. seamanship USCG Aux., New Orleans. Former pres. Cath. Human Rels. Commn. Greater New Orleans, Associated Cath. Charities, Maryland Drive Homeowners Assn., Loyola U. Alumni Assn; former chmn. adv. bd. Ursuline Nuns New Orleans, New Orleans Juvenile Cts.; past scoutmaster Boy Scouts Am., former chmn. troop com.; former v.p. Cmty. Rels. Coun. Greater New Orleans, New Orleans Jr. C. of C.; former v.p. La. Interch. Conf., now treas. emeritus; former trustee United Fund Greater New Orleans Area; dir. emeritus Cath. Book Store Found.; tng. officer 8th USCG Aux.; former mem. adv. bd. Coll. Bus. Adminstrn., Loyola U., Mother-house Sisters of Holy Family, Immaculate Conception Cath. Ch.; group capt. Manresa Retreats, 1947-97; former bd. dirs. St. John Berchman Orphanage, New Orleans Interfaith Conffn.; St. Elizabeth's Home for Girls, Manresa Retreat House; mem. adv. bd. New Orleans Track Club; founder Serra Run for Vocations; bd. dirs. Aubudon Blvd. Assn.; participant U.S. Sr. Olympics, 1997; lector Cath. Ch., 1964-87, eucharist min., 1986-2001. With USN, 1942-46, 51-53; capt. USNR ret. Decorated Order of St. Louis; recipient merit cert. City of New Orleans, 1972; winner 80 and over category La. Sr. Olympics 5000 meter walk, 1995, 96. Mem. La. Assn. Ins. Agts., Nat. Assn. Ins. Agts., New Orleans Ins. Exch., Navy League, Mil. Order World Wars, Greater New Orleans Execs. Assn. (hon. life, pres. 1985, Exec. of Yr. award 1985), New Orleans Photog. Soc., New Orleans Runners Assn., World Trade Ctr. New Orleans (hon.), Serra Club (pres. New Orleans 1973-74), Sertoma Club (pres. New Orleans 1955-56), Internat. House, New Orleans Track Club, New Orleans Yacht Club, Pass Christian Yacht Club, KC (4th degree), Blue Key. Democrat. Achievements include patents for gunnery, training and machinery devices for US Navy. Home: New Orleans, La. Died Aug. 28, 2005.

TRAUTH, PAUL AUGUST, JR., sales and marketing executive; b. St. Louis, June 12, 1950; s. Paul August Sr. and Lucille Clara (Purzner) T.; m. Carol Ann Vehlewald, Sept. 5, 1970; children: Dawn Marie, Jeffrey Allen, Karen Beth. BS, George Washington U., 1970; BS in Pharmacy, U. Mo., 1974; MPH, Lindenwood Coll. and U. Mo., 1977. Surg. cons. U.S. Surg. Corp., Norwalk, Conn., 1978-89; sr. cons. ophthalmic systems IOLAB Corp. Johnson & Johnson, Claremont, Calif., 1982-88; exec. dir. Comprehensive Vision Care, Inc., St. Louis, from 1988; dir. profl. svcs.dept. ophthalmology Bethesda Eye Inst., St. Louis U., from 1988. Bd. dirs. MTF Med. Assocs. Inc., Fairview Heights Inc.; pres., advt. and mktg. communications cons. Smart Solutions Inc., St. Louis, 1987—. Served with USN, 1968-72. U.S. Surg. Corp. fellow U. Pitts., 1979. Fellow Am. Acad. Physicians Assts. (state dir. 1974-80), Greater St. Louis Soc. Health Edn. and Tng.; mem. Am. Pub. Health Assn., Lions (pres. St. Louis Harmony chpt. 1980, bd. dirs. 1981—). Democrat. Lutheran. Avocations: swimming, outdoor activities. Died Apr. 17, 2004.

TREAT, ASHER EUGENE, retired biology educator; b. Antigo, Wis., July 6, 1907; s. Asher Robbins and Pearl Eugenia (Barnes) T.; m. Joy Gilder, Oct. 7, 1939 (dec. Sept. 1987); 1 child, Bryan G. PhD, Columbia U., 1941. Fellow dept. biology CUNY, 1930-31, tutor, 1931-41, instr., 1941-48, asst. prof., 1948-57, assoc. prof., 1957-64, prof., 1964-66, prof. emeritus, from 1966. Rsch. assoc. Am. Mus. Natural History, N.Y.C., 1970-83. Author: Mites of Moths and Butterflies, 1975. With USAAF, 1942-46. Fellow AAAS; mem. ACLU, Entomol. Soc. Am., Acarological Soc. Am., N.Y. Entomol. Soc. Democrat. Avocation: music. Home: Tyringham, Mass. Died June 8, 2004.

TRENCHARD, KENNETH ROBERT, auditor; b. Dearborn, Mich., Oct. 31, 1929; s. Robert and Lillian (Livingstone) T.; married, 1955; children: Kenneth Jr., Holly, Randall. BS, Temple U., 1958. CPA, Pa. Acct. Tait, Weller & Baker CPA, Phila., 1958-62; pvt. practice in acctg. Willow Grove, Pa., 1962-64; auditor/regional contr. ARA Svcs., Phila., 1965-84; treas., bd. dirs. Leona's Restaurants, Chgo. Co-trustee Jay Frank Parmly Trust, Chgo., 1977—. With U.S. Army, 1947-52. Mem. DAV, Am. Legion, Ill. Retaurant Risk Mgmt. Assn. Avocation: tennis. Home: Valparaiso, Ind. Died July 25, 2005.

TRESELER, KATHLEEN MORRISON, retired nursing educator; b. Tacoma, Wash., Apr. 28, 1925; d. Charles T. and Elizabeth M. (McDermott) Morrison; m. Donald K. Treseler, July, 1949; children: Michael S., C. Maureen Treadwell, Patrick A. BS, Seattle Coll., 1946; M in Nursing, U. Wash., 1966. Prof. Seattle U. Sch. Nursing, 1968-91, prof. emeritus, from 1991. Author: Clinical Laboratory and Diagnostic Tests, 1982, 3d edit., 1995. Home: Seattle, Wash. Died Dec. 6, 2004.

TREVANIAN, (RODNEY WILLIAM WHITAKER), author; b. Tokyo, Jan. 12, 1925; m. Diane Brandon Whitaker; children: Lance, Christian, Alexandra, Tomasin. BA in Drama, U. Wash., 1959, MA in Drama, 1960; PhD in Comm., Northwester U., 1966. Formerly prof. U. Tex. Author: The Language of Film, 1970; (as Trevanian) Eiger Sanction, 1972, The Loo Sanction, 1973, Apology for a Peddeler, 1975, The Main, 1976, Shibumi, 1979, The Summer of Katya, 1983, Incident at Twenty-Mile, 1998, Hot Night in the City and Other Stories, 2000, Crazyladies of Pearl Street, 2005; (as Nicholas Seare) 1339 or So...Being an Apology for a Pedlar, 1975, Rude Tales and Glorious: The Account of Diverse Feats of Brawn and Bawd Performed by King Arthur and His Kights of the Round Table, 1983 Served in USN, 1949—53. Died Dec. 14, 2005.

TREVER, JOHN CECIL, religion educator; b. Milw., Nov. 26, 1915; s. John Henry and Hilda Amanda (Carpenter) T.; m. Ellizabeth Signe Burman, Aug. 29, 1937; children: John Paul, James Edgar. AB magna cum laude, U. So. Calif., 1937; BD, Yale Div. Sch., 1940; PhD, Yale U., 1943. Ordained to ministry United Meth. Ch., 1943. Assoc. min. 1st Meth. Ch., Santa Monica, Calif., 1942-44; assoc. prof. Drake U., Des Moines, 1944-47; exec. dir. dept. English Bible Nat. Coun. Chs., 1948-53; prof. religion Morris Harvey Coll., Charleston, W.Va., 1953-59, Baldwin-Wallace Coll., Berea, Ohio, 1960-75; prof. Sch. Theology at Claremont, Calif., 1975-80, dir. Dead Sea Scrolls Project Calif., 1975—2006. Author: The Cradle of Our Faith, 1954, The Untold Story of Qumran, 1965, Scrolls from Qumrân Cave I, 1972, The Dead Sea Scrolls: A Personal Account, 1977. Two Bros. fellow Yale U., 1940. Mem. Phi Beta Kappa. Home: Lake Forest, Calif. Died Apr. 29, 2006.

TRIPLETT, ERIC, fashion coordinator; b. Detroit, July 18, 1960; s. Ulysses and Anna Lenova (Jackson) T. AA, Wayne County C.C., Detroit, 1979; MA in Merchandising, Fashion Inst., L.A., 1981; cert. fashion coord., Paris (France) Fashion Inst., 1981. Chmn. Triplett Corps., Detroit, from 1972; window dresser Himelhochs, Southfield, Mich., 1976; sales assoc. J.L. Hudson, Southfield, 1976; dept. mgr. The Broadway, Culver City, Calif., 1978; intern in merchandising J.W. Robinsons, L.A., 1979; fashion model Kleine-Kinsler, L.A., 1981; presse attache May Co., L.A., 1981; fashion developer Bullocks, Sherman Oaks, Calif., 1980. Owner Eric Triplett Inc., Detroit, 1982-83. Paris Fashion Inst. scholar, 1981. Avocations: swimming, fashion modeling, tourism, shopping, directing movies. Home: Detroit, Mich. Died Jan. 22, 2005.

TRIPLETT, WILLIAM CARRYL, physician, researcher; b. St. Marys, W.Va., May 9, 1915; s. Harry Carryl and Glenna Olive (Dotson) T.; m. Jane Dinsmoor, June 11, 1940 (div. 1961); children: William C. II, Jan Frances; m. Josephine Vann (div.); children: Harriett, Amber, Charles; m. Kathleen Quigley. BA, W.Va. U., 1936; MD, U. Md., 1940. Intern Ohio Valley Gen. Hosp., Wheeling, W.Va., 1940; resident in internal medicine Berkley County Meml. Hosp., 1941-42; med. dir. Camp Wood (Tex.) Convalescent Ctr.; pvt. practice Corpus Christi, Tex., 1946-68, 72-88; dir. rsch. TRIAD Assocs. Inc., from 1947, ENA, 1968-92, Intercontinental Cardiac Rsch., 1984-92; dir. pub. health Real County, Tex., from 1989; med. dir. Cedar Hills Geriatric Ctr., Camp Wood, Tex., from 2003. Inventor and patentee in field. Bayfront adv. com. Corpus Christi, 1950-55; bay drilling com. Corpus Christi, 1954-56; environ. com., Tex., 1968-72; assoc. dir. Tex. Mil. Inst. Capt. USCG Aux., 1952-56. Named Man of Yr. Camp Wood/Nucces Canyon C. of C., 1990; 18 awards as editor Costal Bd. Medicine, Corpus Christi. Mem. AMA, Tex. Med. Assn., Corpus Christi Yacht Club (comdr. 1953). Anglican. Avocations: hunting, fishing, yachting, hydroplane racing. Died Mar. 4, 2004.

TRIPP, RAYMOND PLUMMER, JR., English literature educator; b. Acushnet, Mass., Dec. 15, 1932; s. Raymond Plummer and Mildred Evelyn (Willis) T.; m. Susan Jane Scofield, June 6, 1959. BA, U. Mass., 1960; MA, U. Toronto, Ont., 1963; PhD, Union Grad. Sch., 1971. Asst. prof. Clarion (Pa.) State Coll., 1964-67; prof. U. Denver, from 1968. Vis. prof. Hirosaki Coll., Japan, 1980-81. Author: Reflections on Walden, 1972, Beyond Canterbury, 1977 (Acad. Book of Yr.), More About the Fight with the Dragon: The Dragon in Beowulf, 1983, The Mysterious Kingdom of Emily Dickinson's Poetry, 1988, Literary Essays on Beowulf, 1992. Pres. Univ. Profs. for Acad. Order, Washington, 1989-90. With U.S. Army, 1954-57. Mem. Soc. for New Lang. Study (founder 1972). Western Rite Orthodox. Home: Concord, Vt. Died Feb. 1, 2005.

TROPF, CHERYL GRIFFITHS, accountant, mathematician; b. Newark, Oct. 15, 1946; d. Frank R. and Shirley J. (Magnusson) Griffiths; m. William Jacob Tropf, III, Aug. 31, 1968; 1 child, Andrew Zachary. BS, Coll. William and Mary, 1968; MS in Acctg., Georgetown U., 1983; MAM, U. Va., 1972, Ph.D., 1973. CPA, Md. Sr. math. physicist Johns Hopkins Applied Physics Lab., Laurel, Md., 1973-80; congl. sci. fellow U.S. Senate Commerce Com., Washington, 1980-81; program mgr. U.S. Nuclear Regulatory Commn., Washington, 1981-82; asst. prof. U. Balt. Sch. Bus., 1983-85; pvt. practice acctg., Columbia, Md., 1984-2004. Vice chmn. Howard County Commn. for Women, 1983-84, chmn., 1984-85; vice chmn. United Way, 1985, Landlord/Tenant Rels. Task Force, 1986. Congl. Sci. fellow, 1980-81; named Outstanding Bus. Woman Howard County C. of C., 1986. Mem. AICPA, Md. Assn. CPAs, Soc. Indsl. and Applied Math., Phi Beta Kappa, Sigma Xi. Avocation: stocks. Home: Highland, Md. Died Apr. 8, 2004.

TROUT, CHARLES HATHAWAY, academic administrator, historian, educator; b. Seattle, Nov. 3, 1935; s. Charles Whyron and Elizabeth (Hathaway) T.; m. Margot Stevens, Dec. 30, 1961 (div. 1983); children: Nicholas H., Benjamin C.; m. Katherine Taylor Griffiths, Oct. 6, 1984. BA, Amherst Coll., 1957; MA, Columbia U., 1961, PhD, 1972. History instr. Hill Sch., Pottstown, Pa., 1958-59, Philips Exeter Acad., (N.H.), 1960-69; prof. history Mt. Holyoke Coll., South Hadley, Mass., 1969-80; provost, dean faculty Colgate U., Hamilton, N.Y., 1980-90; pres. Washington Coll., Chestertown, Md., 1990-95; tchr. Tchr. for Africa, Korongoi, Litein, Kenya, 1996-97; interim pres. Harcum Coll., Bryn Mawr, Pa., 2002—03, pres., 2003—06. Vis. prof. U. Mass. Labor Rels. and Rsch. Ctr., 1974-80 Author:

Boston, The Great Depression, and the New Deal, 1977. Chmn. bd. World Edn. Inc.; trustee Sultana Projects, Inc. Columbia U. Pres.'s scholar, 1959-60; NEH rsch. fellow, 1975-76; Charles Warren fellow Harvard U., 1978-79. Democrat. Episcopalian. Home: Chestertown, Md. Died Sept. 27, 2006.

TROWBRIDGE, ALEXANDER BUEL, JR., business consultant, former secretary of commerce; b. Englewood, N.J., Dec. 12, 1929; s. Alexander Buel and Julie (Chamberlain) T.; m. Eleanor Hutzler, Apr. 18, 1981; children by previous marriage: Stephen C., Corrin S., Kimberly. Grad., Phillips Acad., Andover, Mass., 1947; AB cum laude, Princeton U., 1951; LLD (hon.), D'Youville Coll., 1967, Hofstra U., 1968, Hobart Coll., William Smith Coll., 1975. With Calif. Tex. Oil Co., 1954-59; ops. mgr. Esso Standard Oil S.A. Ltd., Panama C.Z., 1959-61, div. mgr. El Salvador, 1961-63; pres. Esso Standard Oil Co., P.R., 1963-65; asst. sec. for domestic & internat. bus. US Dept. Commerce, Washington, 1965-67, sec., 1967-68; pres. Am. Mgmt. Assn., N.Y.C., 1968-70, The Conf. Bd., Inc., N.Y.C., 1970-76; vice chmn. bd. Allied Chem. Corp., 1976-80; pres. NAM, Washington, 1980-90; founder Trowbridge Partners, 1990—2004. Bd. dirs. NAM, 1978—2006. Mem. Pres.'s Task Force on Pvt. Sector Initiatives, Nat. Commn. on Social Security Reform, 1982; mem. Nat. Commn. on Exec., Legis. and Jud. Salaries, 1985, Nat. Commn. on Pub. Svcs.; mem. Competitiveness Policy Coun., 1991. With USMCR, 1951-53, maj. Res. Decorated Bronze Star with combat V; recipient Arthur Flemming award, 1966, Pres.'s E cert. for export service, 1968, Bryce Harlow award for Bus.-Govt. Rels., 1988. Mem. Coun. Fgn. Rels., Met. Club, Georgetown Club, Univ. Club. Home: Washington, DC. Died Apr. 27, 2006.

TROXEL, JOHN MILTON, physician; b. Missoula, Mont., Jan. 14, 1960; s. George Owen and Christina M. (Long) T.; m. Sarah C. Burrell, Jan. 14, 1989. BS, Stanford (Calif.) U., 1982, MD, 1986. Intern in surgery U. Calif., San Francisco, 1986-87; resident in otolaryngology Stanford Med. Ctr., 1987-90, chief resident in otolaryngology, 1990-91, resident plastic surgery, 1991-92; chief resident plastic surgery, 1993-94. Mem. AMA, N.Y. Acad. Scis., Alaska Med. Assn. Avocations: snow and water skiing, biking, hiking, fishing. Died June 16, 2005.

TRUESDELL, WALTER GEORGE, minister, librarian; b. N.Y.C., Oct. 22, 1919; s. George Anson and Hattie (Evans) T.; m. Mary Schurok, June 10, 1944; children: Walter George, Susan Hattie. AB, Columbia U. Columbia Coll., 1941; MDiv, Theol. Sem. of the Ref. Episcopal Ch., Phila., 1944; BLS, Pratt Inst., 1950; MA, Columbia U. Tchrs. Coll., 1975; DD (hon.), Cummins Theol. Sem. Reformed Episcopal, Summerville, S.C., 2002. Ordained to ministry Ref. Episcopal Ch., 1944. Asst. min. First Ref. Episcopal Ch., N.Y.C., 1944-54, sr. assoc. min., from 1989; rector Ch. of the Redemption, Bklyn., from 1956; lectr. apologetics and English Bible Theol. Sem. Ref. Episcopal Ch., Phila., 1945-48, libr. Phila. (relocated to Blue Bell, Pa., Sept. 2000), 1964-93, Shelton Coll., 1951-69; libr. Cummins Theol. Sem. Reformed Episcopal, Summerville, SC, 1996—2002. Chmn. com. on state of ch. Ref. Episcopal Ch., 1960-87, mem., 1987-96, mem. gen. com. 1978-96; real estate broker, 1979—. Editor Episcopal Recorder, 1980-90. Mem. ALA (life), Pa. Libr. Assn., Assn. Statisticians Am. Religious Bodies. Died July 22, 2006.

TRUOG, DEAN-DANIEL WESLEY, counselor, educator; b. Denver, Apr. 1, 1938; s. George Calvin and Zelma Elizabeth (Bennett) T.; m. Dorothy Anne Harding, May 31, 1961; children: David Robert, Denise Dawne. Student, Bethel Coll., 1960-61, L'Abri Fellowship Found., Switzerland, 1967-68; diploma in Bible and Leadership Devel., The Navigators Internat. Tng. Inst., 1968; BA in History, U. Colo., 1971; Diploma in Gen. Univ. Studies in French Civilization, U. Strasbourg, France, 1977; MA in Liberal Edn., St. John's Coll., 1986; M of Liberal Arts in History of Sci., Harvard U., 1987; postgrad., Boston U., 1987-93. Sr. resident adv. U. Colo., Boulder, 1964-65; rep., tutor, lectr. biblical studies and practical christianity The Navigators, 1965-93; rep. for greater Washington area, 1965-67; training asst. The Navigators, Colorado Springs, Colo., 1968, rep. at U. Colo. Boulder, 1968-70, No. Colo. dir., 1970-71, spl. adv. Birmingham, Eng., 1971-72, rep. at large Boulder, Colo., 1979-80; founding dir., pres. Les Navigateurs, France, 1972-84, v.p., 1984-85, rep. to U. Strasbourg, 1973-79, rep. to U. Grenoble, 1980-85; sr. teaching fellow in non-deptmental studies Harvard U., Cambridge, Mass., 1987-90; founding pres., life mgmt. cons./counselor Cornerstone Inst. for Values and Relationships, from 1990; v.p. U.S.-Bulgaria Inst., Cambridge, from 1991; spl. cons. to mems. U.S. Congress, from 1993. Tutor North House, Harvard U., 1987-91; founding chmn. Harvard Christian Assocs., 1987-92; spkr., tchr. profl. confs.; designer, dir. leadership devel. programs, Boston, Washington, Colo., Austria, France, Switzerland. With USN, 1958-59. Mem. AAAS, History of Sci. Soc., Am. Sci. Affiliation, Soc. Christian Philosophers, Assn. for Religion and Intellectual Llife, Inst. on Religion in Age of Sci., Ctr. for Theology and Natural Scis., Nat. Assn. Scholars, Rotary. Presbyterian. Avocations: bicycling, gardening, skiing, tennis, swimming. Died Oct. 27, 2004.

TRUSTY, DIRK ELVIN, SR., real estate executive; b. New Hampton, Iowa, Dec. 31, 1932; s. Elvin Lester and Geraldine (Burns) T.; m. Myrl Thomas, Jan. 9, 1958 (div. 1976); children: Dirk Elvin II, Veri Marie; m. Jane Rosner, Aug. 24, 1978; 1 child, Sydnie Leigh. BBA, U. Miami, 1954. Asst. mgr. Jacksonville Paper Co., Mobile, Ala., 1957-60; salesman Pope & Quint Real Estate, Mobile, 1960-65; sales mgr. Pope & Quint, Inc., Mobile, 1965-70, v.p., 1970-75, exec. v.p., 1975-81; owner, pres. Pope, Quint & Trusty, Inc., Mobile, from 1981. Bd. advisors Real Estate Leaders Am., Atlanta, 1981—; bd. dirs. Altus Bank, Mobile. Pres. South Ala. Arthritis Found., Mobile, 1987; treas. Jr. Achievement, Mobile, 1987; v.p. Better Bus. Bur., Mobile, 1988. Served as sgt. U.S. Army, 1954-56. Mem. Ala. Assn. Realtors (bd. dirs. 1977-79, 87—), Mobile County Bd. Realtors (pres. 1977, bd. dirs. 1988—, Realtor of Yr. 1978), Sales and Mktg. Execs. Mobile (pres. 1980), Grad. Realtors Inst., Assn. Cert. Residential Specialist (cert., regional v.p. 1985-86). Clubs: Country of Mobile. Lodges: Kiwanis. Republican. Avocations: reading, gardening. Died Feb. 3, 2004.

TRUSTY, RICHARD VINCENT, JR., recording industry executive, musician; b. Phoenix, Ariz., Dec. 18, 1955; s. Richard Vincent and Charlotte Willie (Diggs) T. Grad. high sch., Hayden, Ariz., 1973; student in voice tng., Ariz. State U., 1974. Drummer, percussionist, vocalist, guitarist, from 1966; owner, performer Rico Prodns., Lafayette, Ind., from 1989; prin. Jumpin' Bones Music, B.M.I., Lafayette, from 1988. Prin. works include 14 musical/lyrical songs, (album) Sweet Inspiration, 1979. Entertainer Lafayette Environ. Coun., 1989, Tippecanoe Arts Fedn., Lafayette, 1987-89. Avocations: camping, skiing, boating. Died Apr. 21, 2004.

TSANG, TUNG, physics educator, researcher; b. Shanghai, Aug. 17, 1932; s. Ngeu F Tsang and Ying W Liu; m. Dolly M Wong, Oct. 12, 1957; 1 child, Susan M Persons. BS, Ta-Tung U., Shanghai, China, 1949; MS, U. Minn., Minneapolis, MN, 1952; PhD, U. Chgo., Chicago, IL, 1960. Phys. chemist Honeywell Inc, Minneapolis, Minn., 1952—56, Argonne Nat. Lab., Argonne, Ill., 1960—67, Nat. Bur. Standards, Washington, 1967—69; physics prof. Howard U., Washington, from 1969. Author: (book) Classical Electrodynamics, Statistical Mechanics. Home: Rockville, Md. Died Jan. 1, 2005.

TUCKER, MARCIA, museum director, curator; b. N.Y.C., Apr. 11, 1940; d. Emanuel and Dorothy (Wald) Silverman. Student, Ecole du Louvre, Paris, 1959-60; BA, Conn. Coll., New London, 1961; MA, Inst. Fine Arts, NYU, 1969; doctorate (hon.), San Francisco Art Inst. Curator Willian N. Copley Collection, N.Y.C., 1963-66; editl. assoc. Art News mag., N.Y.C., 1965-69; collections cataloger Alfred H. Barr, Jr., N.Y.C., 1966-67; catalog raisonée Howald Collection Am. Art, Ford Found. Columbus (Ohio) Gallery Fine Arts, 1966-69; curator painting and drawing Whitney Mus. Am. Art, N.Y.C., 1969-77; dir., founder The New Mus., N.Y.C., 1977-99. Faculty U. R.I., Kingston, 1966-68, City U. N.Y., 1967-68, Sch. Visual Arts, 1969-73, Columbia U. Sch. Arts and Scis., N.Y.C., 1977; guest lectr. San Francisco Art Inst., Yale U., Balt. Mus. Art, Art Inst. Chgo., Smithsonian Instn., Princeton U.; U.S. commr. 1984 Venice Biennale Mem. Coll. Art Assn., Assn. Art Mus. Dirs., Am. Assn. Mus., Phi Beta Kappa. Author: Anti-Illusion: Procedures/Materials, 1969, Catalog of Ferdinand Howald Collection, 1969, Robert Morris, 1970, The Structure of Color, 1971, James Rosenquist, 1972, Bruce Nauman, 1973, Al Held, 1974, Richard Tuttle, 1975, Early Work by 5 Contemporary Artists, 1977, Bad Painting, 1978, Barry Le Va, 1979, John Baldessari, 1981, Not Just For Laughs: The Art of Subversion, 1981, Earl Staley: 1973-83, 1984, Paradise Lost/Paradise Regained catalog for Am. exhbn. at Venice Biennale, commr., 1984; series editor: Art After Modernism: Rethinking Representation, 1984, Choices: Making An Art Out of Everyday Life, 1986, Pat Steir, Self Portrait: An Installation, 1987, Blasted Allegories: An Anthology of Writings by Contemporary Artists, 1987, Markus Raetz: In the Realm of the Possible, 1988, Out There: Marginalization & Contemporary Cultures, 1990, Discourse: Conversations in Postmodern Art & Culture, 1992, Bad Girls, 1994, A Labor of Love, 1996, The Time of Our Lives, 1999, Documentary Sources in Contemporary Art, Vols. I-V; catalog for Am. exhbn. at Venice Biennale; also articles. Home: Santa Barbara, Calif. Died Oct. 17, 2006.

TU'IPELEHAKE, PRINCE FATAFEHI, Tongan government official; b. Nuku' alofa, Tonga, Jan. 7, 1922; s. Vilame Tungi and Salote Tupou III; m. Princess Melenaite Tupou Moheofo; children: Mele Siuilikutapu Kalanivalu-Fotofili, Elisiva Fusipala Hahano Vahái, Sione Ngu Uluvalu Takeivulai Tukuaho, Lavinia Mataotaone Maafu, Ofeina'e he Langi Tuku' aho, Viliami Tupoumalohi Mailefihi Tuku' aho. Student, Newington Coll., Sydney, Australia, Catton Agr. Coll., Queensland, Australia. Vis. agrl. officer 1944-49, 1944—49; No.1 nobles' rep. for Ha'apai Legis. Assembly, Tonga, 1999—2005, No. 3 nobles' rep. for Tongatapu, from 2005. Gov. Vava'u, 1949-55, Ha' apai, 1955; minister of lands, 1953; former prime minister of Tonga, also minister for agr., min. of marine affairs; chmn. Tonga Commodities Bd.; chmn. com. of the whole, Legis. Assembly, Tonga, 1999-2005, mem. legis. com., 1999-2005. Decorated comdr. Order Brit. Empire. Died July 7, 2006.

TULCHIN, STANLEY (TED TULCHIN), bank executive, educator, credit manager, theater producer; m. Pat Reyburn Tulchin; 3 children. Founder, chmn. bd. STA Internat. (formerly Stanley Tulchin Associates), Westbury, NY, 1955—95; founder, chmn. Continental Bank, Garden City, NY. Bd. dirs. NY Inst. Credit, Topps Corp., Lawyers Reinsurance Co., from 2003; founder, chmn. Reprise Capital Corp. Prodr.: (Broadway plays) Taller Than a Dwarf, 2000, Fortune's Fool, 2002, Vincent in Brixton, 2003; co-prodr.: Sweeney Todd, 2005; prodr.: (off-Broadway plays) The Unexpected Man, 2000, Thunder Knocking on the Door, Trying, Our Lady of Sligo, Rounding Third, Madame Melville; (plays) Dinner With Friends, 2000; (plays, London theatre) Guys and Dolls, Whose Life Is It Anyway?, Hitchcock Blonde, 2003. Bd. dirs. Playwrights Horizons, WLIW, NYC. Recipient Leadership in Credit Edn. award, NY Inst. Credit, 1990. Mem.: Am. Acad. Dramatic Arts (treas., bd. dirs.), Nat. Assn. Credit Mgmt., Comml. Law League Am. (President's Cup award 1975). Died Dec. 18, 2005.

TULIPANA, GEORGE PAUL, transportation company executive; b. Kansas City, Mo., July 13, 1944; s. George Paul and Helen Louise (Mudd) T.; m. Rena Margaret Guzel, June 14, 1968; children: Steven Michael, George Paul, Kevin Frank, Sean David. BS, Ctrl. Mo. State U., 1972. Trainee B&H Freight Line, Harrisonville, Mo., 1962-64; transp. specialist Western Electric, Lee's Summit, Mo., 1964-67, various positions, 1969-73; v.p. Am. Ctrl Transport Inc., Joliet, Ill., 1973-78; regional mgr. Ringsby Truck Lines, Denver, 1978-81; exec. v.p./COO Am. Ctrl. Transport Inc., Joliet, from 1981. Ptnr. Prospectus Group, Kansas City, 1989—; bd. dirs. Am. Ctr. Transp. Inc., T&C Acres, Liberty, Mo. With U.S. Army, 1967-69, Vietnam. Mem. VFW, Rotary Internat., Traffic Transp. Club, Delta Nu Alpha (v.p. 1985-86). Democrat. Roman Catholic. Avocations: reading, golf, walking. Home: Liberty, Mo. Died Feb. 13, 2005.

TUNG, FONG-CHUNG (FANG ZHONG DONG), surgery educator; b. Hankow, Hubei, China, Feb. 1, 1915; s. Yen-Sun and Chi-Yuen (Sun) T.; m. Xing-Fang Li, July 22, 1944; children: Nai-Guang, Nai-Ming. MD, St. John's Med. Sch., Shanghai, People's Republic of China, 1941; M in Surgery, U. Pa., 1947. Chmn. dept. surgery Lester's Hosp., Shanghai, 1947-57; prof., chmn. dept. surgery Rui Jin Hosp., Shanghai, from 1957; med. advisor Shanghai Second Med. U., from 1983. Contbr. articles to profl. publs. Mem. Nat. Polit. Cons. Conf., Beijing, 1982—; pres. Tung Fong-chung Found., Shanghai, 1986; bd. dirs. Red Cross, Shanghai, 1982. Recipient 1st Degree Distinction award Chinese Ministry of Health, 1964. Fellow Internat. Coll. Surgeons (hon.) Home: Little Falls, NJ. Died Apr. 23, 2005.

TUPOU, HIS MAJESTY TAUFA'AHAU, IV, King of Tonga; b. July 4, 1918; eldest son of Viliami Tungi and Queen Salote Tupou III; m. Princess Mata'aho, 1947; children: Tupouto'a, Pilolevu, 'Alaivahamama'o, 'Aho'eitu. Student, Newington Coll., Sydney U., BA, LL.B., 1942. Former min. of edn., 1943. Min. health, 1944-49, premier of Tonga, Fgn. Affairs, minister of Agr., 1949-65; king of Tonga, 1965-2006; revised Tongan Alphabet, 1949, established teacher's tng. coll., 1944, high sch., 1947, broadcasting sta., 1961, govt. newspaper, 1964. First Chancellor U. South Pacific, 1970-73. Decorated knight Order Brit. Empire, Kreuzes Des Vedienstordens, Fed. Republic of Germany, 1979, Comdr. Brit. Empire, 1952, Knight Comdr. St. Michael and St. George, 1968, Grand Cross Victorian Order, 1970, Grand Cross St. Micheal and St. George. Died Sept. 10, 2006.

TURNBULL, MIRIAM DOROTHY, social worker; b. Waterloo, Iowa, June 20, 1920; d. Joseph and Bessie (Abelson) Lederman; m. James Gordon Turnbull, Aug. 27, 1945; children: Toni Jane, Thomas Roger, George Robert. BA, U. No. Iowa, 1942; MSW, U. Iowa, 1971. Tchr. Martelle (Iowa) Sch., 1942-43; fingerprint expert FBI, Washington, 1943-44; social worker Cook County Pub. Aid, Chgo., 1944-45; pub. welfare worker Johnson County, Iowa City, 1945-47, Story County, Ames, Iowa, 1947-48; pub. welfare worker, probation officer Black Hawk County, Waterloo, Iowa, 1963-69; social worker Polk County, Des Moines, 1971-88; supr. Black Hawk County Bd. Supervision, Waterloo, from 1993. Grantee U.S. Dept. Human Svcs., 1973. Mem. NASW (Waterloo br., cert.). Democrat. Avocations: reading, walking, country skiing, sewing. Home: Cedar Falls, Iowa. Died Aug. 23, 2005.

TURNER, HARRY EDWARD, lawyer; b. Mt. Vernon, Ohio, Dec. 25, 1927; s. Paul Hamilton and Harriett (Krafft) T.; m. Shirley Marilyn Eggert, July 8, 1950; children: Harry Edward, Thomas Frederick (dec. Mar. 1995). BA, Baldwin Wallace Coll., 1951; JD, Ohio No. U., 1954. Bar: Ohio 1954, U.S. Supreme Ct. 1966. Practice in Mt. Vernon, from 1954; state rep. Ohio Gen. Assembly, 1973-85; solicitor Mt. Vernon, 1958-62. Prosecutor Mt. Vernon Municipal Ct., 1955-58 Mem. Mt. Vernon City Sch. Bd., 1964-70, pres., 1965-70; trustee Ohio Sch. Bd. Assn., 1968-70, Hannah Browning Home, 1987-2001, Sta. Break/Commn. on Planning Svcs., 1989-95; mem. Knox County Pub. Defender Commn., 1987-91. With USN, 1946-47. Mem. Ohio State Bar Assn., Knox County Bar Assn. (pres. 1970), Alpha Sigma Phi, Sigma Delta Kappa. Republican. Lutheran. Died July 27, 2004.

TURNER, LARRY WILLIAM, agricultural engineer, educator; b. Cin., Dec. 18, 1954; s. Roy Obertate and Martha Lucille (McNeely) T.; m. Lois V. Lynch, Oct. 23, 1976; children: Molly Elizabeth, Amy Rebekah, Clay Matthew. BS, Purdue U., 1976, MS in Agrl. Engring., 1978; PhD, U. Ky., 1984. Lic. profl. engr., 1980. Grad. instr. Purdue U., West Lafayette, Ind., 1976-78; cons. engr. Turner Engring., Rising Sun, Ind., 1980-81; extension agrl. engr. U. Ky., Lexington, 1978-80, rsch. specialist, 1981-84, asst. extension prof., 1984-89, assoc. extension prof., 1989-94, extension prof., 1994—99, chair Dept. Biosystems & Agrl. Engring., 1999—2001, assoc. dean for extension, 2002—06, dir. Ky. Cooperative Extension Svc., 2002—06. Vis. scientist Silsoe Rsch. Inst., England, 1992-93; cons. Smith Constrn., State of Ky. Contbr. articles to profl. jours. Chmn. bd. Christ United Meth. Ch., Lexington, 1980, lay leader, 1983; evangelism chmn. St. Andrew's United Meth. Ch., 1989-90, chmn. bd., 1990-91. Mem. Am. Soc. of Agrl. Engrs., Am. Soc. of Heating, Refrigerating and Air Conditioning Engrs., Tau Beta Pi, Alpha Epsilon, Phi Kappa Phi, Gamma Sigma Delta. Republican. Methodist. Avocations: painting, drawing, fishing, basketball. Home: Lexington, Ky. Died Aug. 27, 2006.

TURNER, MABEL CROUGHAN, retired microbiologist; b. Macomb, Ill., Jan. 13, 1920; d. Walter Wilson and Mary Frances (Miner) Wilson-Johnson; m. Claire Malloy Croughan, July 18, 1940 (dec.); children: Jack, Caitlin, Shelley Booth, Timothy, Mary Minihane-Croughan, Matthew; m. Hubert Edwards Turner, Jan. 16, 1996. AA, UCLA, 1939; B Arts and Sci., U. Calif., Berkeley, 1940. Cert. pub. health lab. technician, pub. health bacteriologist, clin. lab. technician, clin. lab. technologist, Dept. Health, State Calif.; cert. approval dairy bacteriology Dept. Agr., State Calif. Lab. dir. Santa Cruz (Calif.) County Hosp., 1945-46, Campbells Clin. Lab., Santa Cruz, 1946-50; clin. technologist Marin Med. Lab., San Rafael, Calif., 1954-55, 1961-66; lab. dir. Ross Gen. Hosp. Lab., Kentfield, Calif., 1955-56, Ross Valley Doctors Lab., Kentfield, 1956-57, Doctors Clin. Lab., El Dorado, Kans., 1958-61, Pub. Health Lab. Marin County, San Rafael, 1966-88; ret. Trustee Novato Unified Sch. Dist., 1973-90; cook, hostess, supr. Homeless Shelter, Presbyn. Ch., Novato, 1980; state com. on tchr. credentials State of Calif., Sacramento, 1987-89; elder, mem. nominating com. for pastor Novato Presbyn. Ch., 1992-95; liason com. Cmty. Buck Ctr. on Aging, Novato, 1994—; active Commn. on Aging, County of Marin, San Rafael, 1995-96. Named Life Member PTA and Outstanding Parent, 1954, 65, Woman of the Yr. and Woman of Distinction, Soroptomist Club, 1983, 95, Sr. Citizen of Yr., Calif. State Senate and Assembly, 1993. Achievements include co-discovery of new virus "Marin Agent" which causes diarrhea and vomiting in patients. Home: Novato, Calif. Died Nov. 9, 2004.

TURNER, MARY JANE, educational association administrator; b. Colorado Springs, Colo., June 1, 1923; d. David Edward and Ina Mabel (Campbell) Nickelson; m. Harold Adair Turner, Feb. 15, 1945 (dec.); children: Mary Ann, Harold Adair III. BA in Polit. Sci., U. Colo., 1947, MPA in Pub. Adminstrn., 1968, PhD in Polit. Sci., 1978. Secondary tchr. Canon City (Colo.) Sch. Dist., 1950-53; tchr. assoc. in polit. sci. U. Colo., Denver, 1968-70, Boulder, 1970-71; rsch. asst. Social Sci. Edn. Consortium, Boulder, 1971, staff assoc., 1972-77; dir. Colo. Legal Edn. Program, Boulder, 1977-84; assoc. dir. Ctr. for Civic Edn., Calabasas, Calif., 1984-88; dir. Close Up Found., Alexandria, Va., 1988-92, sr. edn. advisor Arlington, Va., from 1992. Author: Political Science in the New Social Studies, 1972; co-author: American Government: Principles and Practices, 1983, 4th edit., 1996, Law in the Classroom, 1984, Civics: Citizens in Action, 1986, 2d edit., 1991, U.S. Government Resource Book, 1989; contbg. author: Internat. Ency. Dictionary of Edn., 2000. Chair curriculum com. Idaho State Bar Found., from 2000. Recipient Isadore Starr award for spl. achievement in law-related edn. ABA, 1997. Mem. Nat. Coun. for Social Studies (chair nominations 1983-84, chair bicentennial com. 1986), Social Sci. Edn. Consortium (pres. 1986-87, bd. dirs. 1984-87, 99—), Pi Lambda Theta, Pi Sigma Alpha. Democrat. Presbyterian. Home: Post Falls, Idaho. Died Apr. 23, 2004.

TURNER, MORTIMER DARLING, research geologist; b. Greeley, Colo., Oct. 24, 1920; s. Clarence Earnest and Satia May (Darling) T.; m. Laura Mercedes Perez-Mendez, Jan. 25, 1945 (dec. Mar. 1965); children: Satia Elisa, Ylla Sofia, Robert Stuart; m. Joanne Kay Church, Dec. 5, 1965; 1 stepchild, Christopher Scott Dort. BS, U. Calif., Berkeley, 1943; student, Va. Polytechnic Inst., 1943-44; MS, U. Calif., Berkeley, 1954; PhD, U. Kans., 1972. Registered geologist and engring. geologist, Calif. Asst. mining geologist Calif. Div. Mines and Geology, San Francisco, 1949-54; state geologist P.R. Econ. Devel. Adminstrn., Santurce, 1954-59; phys. sci. adminstr. NSF, Washington, 1959-61, program mgr. polar earth scis., 1965-85; rsch. assoc. U. Kans., Lawrence, 1962-65, Tex. Tech U., Lubbock, 1985; sr. rsch. assoc. emeritus U. Colo., Boulder, 1988—2004. Former cons., ptnr. JCT Enterprises, Boulder; assoc. professorial lectr. George Washington U., Washington, 1972-88, U. Colo., Denver; adj. prof. Quaternary studies U. Maine, Orono, 1985-94; chmn. sci. coun. Ctr. for Study of First Ams., Orono, 1989-91, Corvallis, Oreg.; lectr. Antarctica Expdn. Cruises, Seattle, 1990. Editor: Clays and Clay Technology, 1957, Geology of Central Transantarctic Mountains, 1987; contbr. articles to profl. jours. With U.S. Army, 1943-46. Recipient Presdl. award for mgmt. improvement, White House, 1975; Fellow Shell Oil, 1964. Fellow Geol. Soc. Am.; mem. Internat. Geol. Congress (v.p. 1956), Antarctican Soc. (dir., pres. 1959-68), numerous other sci. and engring. socs. Democrat. Avocations: stamp collecting/philately, mountain hiking. Home: Boulder, Colo. Died May 1, 2004.

TURNER, NANCY ELAINE, writer; b. Dallas, Nov. 20, 1953; d. Stanley Edward and Wahnemia Jo (Belcher) Groves; m. John Charles Turner; children: April E. Bracht, John Sterling. BFA, U. Ariz., 1999. Instr. fiction writing Pima C.C., Tucson, 2001. Author: These Is My Words, 1998 (Ariz. Adult Author of Yr., Ariz. Libr. Assn., 1999, nominated Pulitzer prize, 1998), The Water and the Blood, 2001. Avocations: piano, ceramics, painting. Died Jan. 2, 2005.

TURNER, PREWITT BATES, JR., insurance company executive; b. Kansas City, Mo., Oct. 12, 1932; s. Prewitt Bates and Mary Belle (Mundy) T.; m. Karen Van Voorst, Dec. 12, 1957; children: Rebecca, Jennifer, Prewitt III. AB, Princeton U., 1954. Sr. v.p. Marsh & McLennan, Kansas City, 1980; chmn. Agri.-Risk Services, Inc., Kansas City, 1980-88; also bd. dirs. Agri-Risk Services, Kansas City; chmn. Bates Turner, Inc., Kansas City, 1982-86; also bd. dirs. Bates Turner, Kansas City; chmn. Turner Farms, Glasgow, Mo., from 1972. 1st lt. USAF, 1954-57. Mem.: Kansas City Country, River (Kansas City). Republican. Episcopalian. Home: Shawnee Mission, Kans. Died Feb. 14, 2005.

TUTT, DAVID EMMETT, minister, translator; b. St. Paul, Mar. 8, 1925; s. David Henry and Emily Bertha (Carrell) T.; m. Goldie Mae Seifert, Dec. 25, 1954; children: Tricia, Tim, Tom, Ted. BA, Bethel Coll., 1949; MDiv, Asbury Sem., 1966. Bus driver, Seattle, 1953-54; missionary Meth. Mission, Farmington, N.Mex., 1954-68. Adv. bd. Navajo Missions Inc., 1990-99. Transl. (Navajo bible) Diyin God Bizaad, 1985, rev. edit, 2000. Quartermaster USN, 1943-46. Republican. Methodist. Avocations: hiking, travel. Home: Farmington, N.Mex. Died Feb. 17, 2005.

TUTTLE, EDWIN ELLSWORTH, chemical company executive; b. Syracuse, N.Y., Apr. 24, 1927; s. John Ross and Celia (Boyington) T. BS, Haverford Coll., 1949; MBA, Harvard U., 1951. With Pennwalt Corp., Phila., 1951-90; chmn., CEO Pennwalt Corp. (merger Elf Aquitaine), Phila., 1978-89; vice. chmn. Atochem N. Am. (subs. Societe Nat. Elf Aquitaine., France), Phila., 1990, ret. Bd. dirs. CoreStates Bank, N.A., Westmoreland Coal, Gen. Accident Ins. Co. Am., Fidelity Mut. Life Ins. Co. Bd. dirs. Met. Phila. Family YMCAs; chmn. Pa. Ballet, 1983-90, chmn. emeritus, 1990-2006; bd. mgrs. Haverford Coll. Home: Ventnor City, NJ. Died May 19, 2006.

TWILLEY, JOSHUA MARION, lawyer; b. Dover, Del., Mar. 23, 1928; s. Joshua Marion and Alice Hunn (Dunn) T.; m. Rebecca Jane Buchanan, Dec. 27, 1952; children: Stephanie, Jeffrey, Linda, Edgar, Joshua; m. Rosemary Miller, Dec. 1, 1972. BA cum laude, Harvard U., 1950, JD, 1953. Bar: Del. 1953, U.S. Dist. Ct. Del. 1960, U.S. Supreme Ct. 1976. Pvt. practice, Dover, 1955-72; sr. ptnr. Twilley, Jones & Feliceangeli, Dover, 1972-88, Twilley, Street & Braverman, Dover, 1988-95, Twilley & Street, Dover, from 1995. Pres. Del. Indsl. Enterprises, Inc.; chmn. Incorporating Svcs. Ltd., Del. Incorporating Svcs. Ltd.; bd. dirs. 1st Nat. Bank Wyo.; sec. Sunshine Builders, Inc. mem. Del. Pub. Svc. Commn., 1975—, vice chmn. 1995—; pres. Kent County Levy Ct., 1970-75. Mem. exec. com. Del. Dem. Com., 1970-93; pres. Elizabeth Murphey Sch., 1957—. With U.S. Army, 1953-55. Mem ABA, Del. Bar Assn., Kent County Bar Assn. Democrat. Lutheran. Avocations: gardening, landscape architecture. Home: Dover, Del. Died June 25, 2005.

TWITCHETT, DENIS CRISPIN, historian; b. London, Sept. 23, 1925; came to U.S., 1980; m. Umeko Ichikawa, Feb. 18, 1956; m. Umeko Ichikawa (dec. 1993), children: Peter, Nicholas. BA, Cambridge U., Eng., 1949, MA, 1950; PhD, Cambridge U., 1955. Lectr. Far Eastern History London U., 1954-56; lectr. classical Chinese Cambridge U., Eng., 1956-60; prof. Chinese London U., 1960-68, Cambridge U., 1968-80; Gordon Wu prof. Chinese Studies Princeton U., N.J., 1980-94, prof. emeritus, 1994—2006. Author: Financial Administration Under the Tang Dynasty, 1970, Perspectives on the Tang, 1973, The Birth of Chinese Meritocracy: Bureaucrats and Examinations in Tang China, 1976, Printing and Publishing in Medieval China, 1983, The Cambridge History of China, 1986, The Writing of Official History under the Tang, 1992. Fellow Brit. Acad. Home: Cambridge, England. Died Feb. 24, 2006.

UBBELOHDE, CARL WILLIAM, history educator; b. Waldo, Wis., Nov. 4, 1924; s. Carl William and Carrie (Stratton) U.; m. Mary Jean Tipler, May 31, 1952 (div. 1990); children: Susan, Nell, Libby, Katherine. BS, State Tchrs. Coll., Oskosh, Wis., 1948; MS, U. Wis., 1950, PhD, 1954. From instr. to assoc. prof. U. Colo., Boulder, 1954-65; from assoc. prof. to Henry Eldridge Bourne prof. Case Western Res. U., Cleve., 1965-93, prof. emeritus, from 1994. Vis. prof. U. Wis., 1961, U. Tex., 1964, U. Vt. 1966, 67, U. Pa., 1968. Author: Vice Admiralty Courts, 1960, A Colorado History, 7th edit., 1995, The American Colonies, 1968; co-author: Clio's Servant, 1967. Mem. Charter Rev. Commn., Cleve. Hts., Ohio, 1982, Landmark Commn., 1982-87. Recipient Herfurth award U. Wis., 1955. Mem. ACLU (bd. dirs. 1970-73), Am. Hist. Assn., Orgn. Am. Historians, Ohio Acad. History (pres. 1990-91), Ohio Hist. Soc., Western Res. Hist. Soc. Democrat. Unitarian Universalist. Home: Cleveland Hts, Ohio. Died Dec. 9, 2004.

ULITIN, VLADIMIR GREGOR, retired Russian language and literature educator; b. Kamensk, Russia, Sept. 29, 1908; came to U.S., 1949; s. Gregory Anton and Taisiya Alexandra (Dubovskaya); m. Helen Sawa, Nov. 20, 1958 (div. 1968); m. Sophia Gregor Kishkovsky, Fev. 2, 1969; 1 child, Leonid. Student, Robert Coll., Istanbul, Turkey, 1924-28; BS, U. Belgrade, Yugoslavia, 1932; BA, Pomona Coll., 1968. Civil engr. Austrian firm, Yugoslavia, Austria, Poland, Italy, 1932-45; social worker, dir. refugee children UNRRA, Austria, 1945-49; dir. refugee pr. Am. Friends Svc. Com., Pasadena, Calif., 1950-57; instr. Russian, Calif. Inst. Tech., Pasadena, 1957-61, Pasadena City Coll., 1957-61, U. Calif., Riverside, 1960-61; asst. prof. Russian lang. and lit. Pomona Coll., Claremont, Calif., 1960-64, assoc. prof., 1964-74, disting. prof., 1968-74, prof. emeritus, from 1974. Editor Vestnik jour., 1961-70; contbr. articles to mags. Mem. Congress Russian-Ams. (So. Calif. rep.), Claremont Univ. Club (hon.). Russian Orthodox. Avocations: gardening, roses, sports. Home: Claremont, Calif. Died Oct. 21, 2004.

UMAN, FRANK LEWIS, retired lawyer; b. Springfield, Mass., June 19, 1916; m. Shirley E. Baron. LLB, Boston U., 1940, JD, 1990. Bar: Mass. Pvt. practice, Springfield, Mass., 1940-93; of counsel Santanello, Posnik & Basile, Springfield, 1994-98; ret., 1998. V.p. Mass. Bar Assn. 1976-78; many coms., offices, including pres. Hampden County Bar Assn., 1959-85. Lt. cmdr. USNR, 1941-44 PTO. Home: Springfield, Mass. Died Feb. 28, 2004.

UMBEHOCKER, KENNETH SHELDON, priest; b. Mpls., Sept. 23, 1934; s. Kenneth and Mildred Adeline (Johnson) U. BA, Vanderbilt U., 1956; MDiv, Seabury-Western, Evanston, Ill., 1959, 2000; M Mgmt., U. Ga., 1974. Ordained to ministry Episcopal Ch., 1959. Priest-in-charge St. John's Ch., Hallock, Minn., 1959-62; rector St. Paul's Ch., Virginia, Minn., 1962-67; priest-in-charge Emmanuel Ch., Rushford, Minn., 1968-74; asst. to dean Gethsemane Cathedral, Fargo, N.D., 1974-86; priest-in-charge St. Peter's Ch., Warroad, Minn., 1986-90; rector Ch. of the Good Shepherd, Windom, Minn., 1990-94, St. John's by the Lake, Worthington, Minn., 1990-94, Holy Trinity, Luverne, Minn., 1990-94, Episcopal Parish of St. Mark and St. John, Jim Thorpe, Pa., 1995—2004. Community developer, 1968-86; trustee Episcopal Diocese of Minn., Mpls., 1987-90, coun. mem., 1980-94; mem. standing com. Diocese of Bethlehem, 1998-2005. Field rep. Am. Cancer Soc., Mpls., 1965-67; dept. mgr. Rochester (Minn.) Area C. of C., 1967-74; exec. dir. Fargo Parking Authority and Downtown Assn., 1974-86. Seabury fellow Seabury-Western Sem., 1980; named Young Man of Yr. Rochester Jaycees, 1970; recipient Order of Purple Cross, York Rite Coll. North Am., 1988; Canterbury scholar Canterbury Cathedral of Canterbury, Eng., 1996. Mem. Am. Acad. Parish Clergy, Am. C. of C. Execs., Nat. Parking Assn. (v.p. 1983-86, Disting. Svc. award 1985), Union League Phila., Knights Templar (grand comdr. N.D. club 1985-86), Masons (grand chaplain Minn. club 1994), Seven Continents Club, Rotary Internat. Home: Jim Thorpe, Pa. Died Jan. 19, 2005.

UNDERHILL, DAVID EARL, postal clerk, body shop owner; b. Leitchfield, Ky., July 22, 1948; s. Lloyd Earl Underhill and Nova (Tilford) Woosley; m. Carolyn Shartzer, Dec. 28, 1979 (div. Aug. 1990). Diploma, Grayson County VA Sch. Auto body man Duvall Buick Inc., Leitchfield, 1970-79; owner Northside Body Shop, Leitchfield, 1979-86, Discount Auto Body, Leitchfield, 1986-92; window clk. U.S. Post Office, Leitchfield, from 1992. With U.S. Army, 1968-70, Vietnam. Mem. Am. Legion (bd. dirs. 1994-95), VFW (Post 1495 comdr. 1995-96). Democrat. Baptist. Home: Leitchfield, Ky. Died Dec. 12, 2004.

UNDERWOOD, WALLACE ALBERT, retired industrial designer; b. Worcester, Mass., May 18, 1920; s. Earle Alden and Miriam Katherine (Wallace) U.; m. Nancy Grinnell Sayre, Dec. 1946 (div. Mar. 1958); children: Nancy Elizabeth, Peter Grinnell, Michael Alden; m. Joanne Dunn Woolner, Aug. 1959 (div. Apr. 1968); m. Judith Pond Sterne, May 1973 (div. 1992). BFA, RISD, 1955. Indsl. designer refrigerator divsn. Westinghouse Elec. Corp., Mansfield, Ohio, 1949-50; indsl. designer, prodn. mgr. Clark-Babbitt Industries, New Bedford, Mass., 1950-52; indsl. designer, treas. Samuel Ayres Assoc. Inc., Boston, 1952-63; mgr. product planning Van Dyck Corp., Westport, Conn., 1963; project mgr. product devel. Am. Can. Co., Union, N.J., 1964-66, asst. dir. R&D plastics Batavia, Ill., 1966-71; sales and gen. mgr. Marshall Marine Corp., South Dartmouth, Mass., 1972-75; designer Pylon Corp., North Attleboro, Mass., 1977-80, Sippican Corp., Marion, Mass., 1981-82, J&J Profl., New Bedford, Mass., 1982-90; ret., 1990. Spkr. in field. Chmn. Advanced Grades U.S. Power Squadron, Mattapoisett, Mass., 1971-90. Lt. (j.g.) USNR, 1942-46. Avocations: sailing, skiing, writing books. Home: New Bedford, Mass. Died Nov. 14, 2004.

UNGER, LEONARD HOWARD, literature educator; b. N.Y.C., July 26, 1916; s. Joseph and Sadie (Friedman) U.; m. Sherley Glasscock, July 3, 1946; children: Anne Elizabeth, Thomas Michael, Amy Catherine. BA, Vanderbilt U., 1937; MA, La. State U., 1938, postgrad., 1938-39; PhD, State U. Iowa, 1941. English instr. Bemidji (Minn.) State Coll., 1941, Bard Coll., 1946-47; mem. faculty U. Minn., Mpls., from 1947, prof. English, 1956-86, prof. emeritus, 1986—2006, co-editor pamphlets on Am. writers. Fulbright lectr. Am. lit. U. Rome, U. Florence, Italy, 1957-58, U. Athens, 1963-64 Author: Donne's Poetry and Modern Criticism, 1950, The Man in the Name: Essays on the Experience of Poetry, 1956; pamphlet T.S. Eliot, 1961; T.S. Eliot: Moments and Patterns, 1966, Eliot's Compound Ghost: Influence and Confluence, 1981; also essays, poems.; Editor: T.S. Eliot: A Selected Critique, 1948; editor: (with W.V. O'Connor) Poems for Study, 1953; Editor: Seven Modern American Poets, 1967. Served with USAAF, 1942-

45. Guggenheim fellow, 1953; Ind. Sch. Letters fellow, summers 1957, 67 Mem. Phi Beta Kappa. Home: Saint Paul, Minn. Died Feb. 23, 2006.

UNVERFERTH, RICHARD ARTHUR, farm equipment manufacturing company executive; b. Kalida, Ohio, Sept. 4, 1923; s. Lawrence G. and Lorreta (Quinn) U.; m. Glaydy Marie Pugh, July 7, 1951; children: Steven, Joseph, James, Mark, Jeffrey, Lawrence, David, Chad. Grad., Kalida High Sch. Ptnr. Unverferth Mfg. Co., Kalida, 1948-60, owner, 1960-64, pres., from 1964, Unverferth Farms Inc., Kalida, from 1964. Pres. Unferferth Leasing, Inc., 1964—, Hammer & Gump Corp., Kalida, 1966—, McCordy Mfg. Co., Ada, Ohio, 1971-86; pres., chmn. Health Care Facilities, Inc., Lima, Ohio, 1969—; bd. dirs. BankOne Lima, Health Care Riet, Toledo. Pres. Kalida Athletic Assn., 1951-52; chmn. St. Michael Fin. Com., Kalida, 1971-81; bd. dirs. St. Rita Hosp., Lima. Served with USN, 1943-48, PTO. Mem. Farm Equipment Mfrs. Assn. (pres. 1987—), Shawnee Country Club, Country Acres Kalida Club, Elks, Lions. Roman Catholic. Avocation: golf. Home: Kalida, Ohio. Died Feb. 24, 2004.

UOTILA, URHO ANTTI KALEVI, engineering educator; b. Pöytyä, Finland, Feb. 22, 1923; came to U.S., 1951, naturalized, 1957; s. Antti Samuli and Vera Justina (Kyto) U.; m. Helena Vanhakartano, Aug. 6, 1949; children: Heidi, Kirsi, Elizabeth, Julie, Trina, Caroline. BS, Finland's Inst. Tech., 1946, MS, 1949; PhD, Ohio State U., 1959. Surveyor, geodesist Finnish Govt., 1944-46, 46-51; geodesist Swedish Govt., 1946; research asst. Ohio State U., 1952-53, research assoc., 1953-58, research supr., 1959-88, lectr. in geodesy, 1955-57, asst. prof., 1959-62, assoc. prof., 1962-65, chmn. dept. geodetic sci., 1964-84, prof., 1965-89, chmn., prof. emeritus, from 1989. Mem. Solar Eclipse Expdn. to Greenland, 1954; Mem. adv. panel on geodesy U.S. Coast and Geodetic Survey, Nat. Acad. Sci., 1964-66; mem. geodesy and cartography working group, space sci. steering com. NASA, 1965-67, mem. geodesy/cartography working group, summer conf. lunar exploration and sci., 1965, mem. geodesy and cartography adv. subcom., 1967-72; mem. ad hoc com. on N.Am. datum div. earth scis. Nat. Acad. Scis.-N.A.E., 1968-70; bd. dirs. Internat. Gravity Bur., France, 1975-83; mem. com. on geodesy Nat. Acad. Scis., 1975-78 Mem. editorial adv. com.: Advances in Geophysics, 1968-77; Contbr. articles to profl. jours., encys. Served with Finnish Army, 1942-44. Recipient Kaarina and W.A. Heiskanen award, 1962, Apollo Achievement award NASA, 1969, Disting. Svc. award Surveyor's Inst. Sri Lanka, Earle J. Fennell award Am. Congress on Surveying and Mapping, 1989. Fellow Am. Geophys. Union (v.p. geodesy sect. 1964-68, pres. 1968-70), Am. Congress Surveying and Mapping (nat. dir. 1970-73, 2d v.p. 1977-78, pres.-elect 1978-79, pres. 1979-80), Internat. Assn. Geodesy (pres. spl. study group 5.30 1967-71, pres. sect. V 1971-75, exec. com. 1971-79); mem. Am. Assn. Geodetic Surveying (pres. 1984-86), Am. Soc. Photogrammetry, Can. Inst. Surveying, Univs. Space Research Assn. (trustee 1973-75), Finnish Nat. Acad. Scis (fgn.), Profl. Land Surveyors Ohio (hon.), Ala. Soc. Profl. Land Surveyors (hon.), Tenn. Assn. Profl. Surveyors (hon.) Achievements include: research in geometric geodesy, phys. geodesy and statis. analysis of data. Home: Columbus, Ohio. Died Mar. 2006.

URICCHIO, WILLIAM ANDREW, biology educator; b. Hartford, Conn., Apr. 21, 1924; s. William and Mary (Donadio) U.; m. Velma Mathias, June 12, 1950; children: William, MaryLynn, Barbara, Robert, Michael. AB, Cath. U. Am., 1949, MS, 1951, PhD, 1953. From asst. to assoc. prof. Carlow Coll., Pitts., 1953-61, prof., 1961-94, prof. emeritus, from 1994. Chmn. dept. biology Carlow Coll., Pitts., 1953-87, chmn. divsn. natural sci., 1987—; cons. edn. divsn. Xerox, Pitts., 1967-75; assoc. program dir. NSF, Washington, 1967-68. Author: Microbiology for Nurses, 1966, Independent Research in the Sciences, 1975; editor: Nat. Family Planning Proc., 1973, Pa. Acad. Sci. jour., 1963-67. Bd. dirs. Duquesne U., Pitts., 1973—, McGuire Meml., Pitts., 1972—, Human Life Found., Washington, 1968-80. With U.S. Army, 1943-46. Named Knight of St. Gregory, Pope Paul VI, 1967; recipient Pa. Sci. Edn. award Pa. Jr. Acad. Sci., 1976. Fellow AAAS; mem. Pa. Acad. Sci. (editor, pres. 1970-72), Am. Grad. and Profl. Com. (pres. 1970-74), Internat. Fedn. for Family Promotion (hon., bd. dirs. 1978—), Serra Club (pres. 1970-71), Delta Epsilon Sigma (nat. lectr. 1985, pres. 1960-82). Roman Catholic. Home: Pittsburgh, Pa. Died July 12, 2005.

URRY, GRANT WAYNE, retired chemistry professor; b. Salt Lake City, Mar. 12, 1926; s. Herbert William and Emma (Swanner) U.; m. Lillian Alibertini, Sept. 4, 1946; children— Lisa, Claudia, Serena, Anthony. SB, U. Chgo., 1947, PhD, 1953. Research asst., then research assoc. U. Chgo., 1949-53, research assoc., asst. prof., 1954-55; asst. prof. Washington U., St. Louis, 1955-58; assoc. prof. Purdue U., Lafayette, Ind., 1958-64, prof., 1964-68; prof. chemistry Tufts U., Medford, Mass., 1968-92, Robinson prof. chemistry, 1970-92, chmn. dept., 1968-73, Robinson prof. emeritus chemistry, from 1992. Alfred P. Sloan fellow, 1956-58 Fellow N.Y. Acad. Scis., Am. Inst. Chemists, AAAS; mem. Am. Chem. Soc., Am. Soc. Sci. Glassblowers, Fedn. Am. Scientists, Sigma Xi, Phi Lambda Upsilon. Home: Winchester, Mass. Died Jan. 4, 2006.

URSREY, LAWTON RANDALL, college administrator; b. Hazlehurst, Ga., Aug. 17, 1940; s. Lawton Randall and Geraldine (Quinn) U.; m. Marilyn Linda Carter, Mar. 19, 1972; children: Caroline, Randy. BA, U. Ga., 1962; MEd, Ga. So. Coll., 1971; PhD, Fla. State U., 1981. Tchr. Jeff Davis County High Sch., Hazlehurst, Ga., 1966-70; instr., counselor Mid. Ga. Coll., Cochran, 1971-75, asst. prof., counselor, 1975-79, assoc. prof., counselor, 1979-81, assoc. prof., assoc. dean students, 1981-85, assoc. prof., dean students, 1985-90, v.p. student affairs, from 1990. Mem. exec. bd. Parents and Tchrs. Orgn., Cochran, 1982; co-chair Am. Heart Assn. Fund Dr., Cochran, 1985-86; bd. dirs. Bleckley County unit Am. Cancer Soc., Cochran, 1979. Mem. APA, AACD, NEA, Nat. Assn. Coll. Pers. Adminstrs., Ga. Assn. Higher Edn. (pres. 1978-79), Cochran Rotary Club Internat., Kiwanis Club Cochran (pres. 1985-86), Cochran/Bleckley C. of C. (bd. dirs. 1990-91). Baptist. Home: Cochran, Ga. Died June 29, 2005.

USTAYEV, RAKHIM, psychologist; b. Kirki, Turkmenistan, Sept. 10, 1910; came to U.S., 1981:; s. Ephraim and Balur (Ustozodayev) U.; m. Sipora Ustayev, Nov. 22, 1938; children: Efrem, Istam, Svetlana, Mikhail, David, Maria, Rubin. MS in Psychology, Pedag. Inst., Dushanbe, Tajikistan, 1939; Candidate Sci. in Psychology, Baku (Azerbajan) Pedagogic Inst., 1973. Tchr. Pedagogic Sch., Kurgan-Tube, Tajikistan, 1939-40, Pub. Sch., Dushanbe, Tajikistan, 1943-53; prof. psychology Dushanbe Pedagogic Inst., 1953-81. Author: Thinkers of the Ancient East, 1992, Thinkers About Spiritual Life, 1994, Thinkers About Perconal Psychology, 1997, Chosen Psychology, 1999. Lt. Soviet Army, 1940-43. Mem. N.Y. Acad. Scis. Jewish. Home: Forest Hills, NY. Died Sept. 10, 2005.

UTTERBACK, BETTY HARRIS, writer; b. Coalmont, Ind., July 30; d. Earl Daniel and Esther Jane (Bosley) Harris; student in journalism Ind. U., 1945-47; BA in Cultural Studies, Empire State Coll., 1988; m. Max Gene Utterback, Aug. 10, 1947 (dec.); children: Pamela Kim Utterback Tyminski, Max Andrew. Pub. relations ofcl. Purdue U., 1947-50; free lance writer, 1950-69, 84—; with Gannett Rochester (N.Y.) Newspapers, 1969-84, TV editor, 1973-80, feature writer, 1980-84, columnist Gannett News Service, 1973-80. Co-author: (with John Robertson) Suddenly Single, 1986. Bd. dirs. Literacy Vols. Am., Rochester, 1984-87. Recipient 1st prize for feature N.Y. State AP, 1977. Independent. Presbyterian. Home: Pittsford, NY. Died Dec. 13, 2005.

UTZ, JOHN PHILIP, physician, educator; b. Rochester, Minn., June 9, 1922; s. Gilbert C. and Marion H. (Hoy) U.; m. Dorothy Mary Griffin, July 2, 1947; children: Jane Hamilton, Christopher, Charles, Jonathan, Stephen. Student, Notre Dame U., 1940-42; BS, Northwestern U., 1943, MD, 1946; MS, Georgetown U., 1949. Diplomate: Am. Bd. Internal Medicine. Intern Mass. Meml. Hosp., 1946-47; researcher Lab. Infectious Diseases, 1947-49; chief infectious disease service Lab. Clin. Investigation, Nat. Inst. Allergy and Infectious Diseases, NIH, Bethesda, Md., 1952-65; prof. medicine, chmn. div. immunology and infectious disease Med. Coll. Va., Richmond, 1963—73; instr. Sch. Medicine, Georgetown U., Washington, 1952-56, asst. prof. medicine, 1956-62, assoc. prof., 1962-65, dean Sch. Medicine, 1973-78, prof., 1973—95. Lectr. dept. preventive medicine Howard U., 1960-73; fellow Mayo Found., Rochester, Minn., 1949-52; vis. investigator, prof. Pasteur Inst., Paris, France, 1962-63, 82; cons. U.S. Dept. State, El Salvador, 1953, Costa Rica, 1954; cons. Hoffmann-La Roche Co., Nutley, N.J., 1965-78, Clin. Center, NIH, Bethesda, 1965-85, VA, 1965—85; 32d ann. Howard Lilienthal Meml. lectr., 1982 Co-author: Medical Mycology, 1st, 2d, 3d edits; Bd. editors: Jour. Infectious Diseases, Antimicrobial Agents and Chemotherapy. Founder, Nat. Found. Infectious Diseases, 1973, pres. 91-94, also bd. dir.; trustee Am. Type Culture Collection, 1978-86, vice chmn., 1980-81, chmn., 1981-83; mem. sci. adv. bd. Leonard Wood Found., 1980-83. Served with AUS, 1943-45. Recipient Ruth Gray award, 1973; Disting. Alumnus award Northwestern U., 1977, Disting. Alumnus award Mayo Found., 1989; Armine T. Wilson lectr. Wilmington, 1982. Mem. Am. Fedn. Clin. Research, A.C.P., Am. Coll. Chest Physicians (gov. D.C. chpt. 1978-84), Am. Clin. and Climatol. Assn., Soc. Exptl. Biology and Medicine, Am. Thoracic Soc., Am. Assn. Immunologists, So. Soc. Clin. Investigation, Infectious Disease Soc. Am., Am. Soc. Microbiology, Am. Coll. Clin. Pharmacology and Chem. Therapy, Internat. Soc. Human and Animal Mycology, Soc. Clin. Investigation, Assn. Am. Physicians, Med. Mycol. Soc. Am. (council, pres. 1974-75), Academie Royale des Sciences D'Outre Mer (Belgium), Academie Nat. de Medecine (France), Alpha Omega Alpha. Died Apr. 4, 2006.

VAIL, PATRICK VIRGIL, laboratory administrator, entomologist, researcher; b. Pasadena, Calif., Nov. 16, 1937; s. Virgil Parks and Mary Theresa McGuire V.; m. Susan Saroyan; children: Kimberly Ann, Patricia Lynn, Stacey Marie. BA, Calif. State U., Fresno, 1960, MA, 1962; PhD, U. Calif., Riverside, 1967. Cert. entomologist in insect ecology and biol. control. Research entomologist, Agrl. Research Service USDA, Riverside and Fresno, 1962-69, 1978-86, research leader, Agrl. Research Service Phoenix, 1969-75, lab. dir. Agrl. Research Service Fresno, from 1982; sect. head Insect and Pest Control sect. Internat. Atomic Energy Agy. UN, Vienna, Austria, 1975-78. Cons. numerous state, fed., sci. and internat. orgns. Editor: Baculoviruses, 1975; contbr. over 80 articles to profl. jours. Mem. Soc. Invertebrate Pathology, Entomol. Soc. Am. (chair internat. affairs com. 1979-84), AAAS (steering com. consortium of affiliates for internat. programs), Internat. Plastic Modelers Assn. Clubs: Tempe Racquet (Ariz.) (bd. dirs. 1972-74). Roman Catholic. Avocations: tennis, squash, fishing, scale-model aircraft. Home: Fresno, Calif. Died Feb. 8, 2004.

VALENTINE, CAROL ANN, educational program director, consultant; b. Mt. Clemens, Mich., Dec. 5, 1942; d. Joseph Eldon and Erna Fredericka (Brandt) V.; married; children: Christopher, David. BA, U. Mich., 1964, MA, 1965; PhD, Pa. State U., 1971. Tchr. Oak Park (Ill.)-River Forest High Sch., 1965-67; research assoc. U. Md., College Park, 1967; dir. grants Pa. State U., State College, 1967-78; asst. prof. Oreg. State U., Corvallis, 1970-74; vis. prof. U. Oreg., Eugene, 1974-75; assoc. prof. Ariz. State U., Tempe, 1975-85, assoc. dir. women's studies, from 1975. Cons. Tempe, 1975—. Author: First Impressions, 1980, Women and Communicative Power, 1988. Bd. dirs. Tempe Pub. Library, 1984—. Named Outstanding Woman of Phoenix, 1987. Mem. Zeta Phi Eta. Democrat. Presbyterian. Home: Tempe, Ariz. Died May 4, 2004.

VALENTINE, JOHN HENRY, JR., foundation president, secondary education educator; b. West Point, NY, May 28, 1930; s. John Henry and Thelma (Turner) V.; m. Ruth Mae McAdams, May 26, 1956. AES in Gen. Edn., Galveston (Tex.) Coll., 1980. Cert. security officer, Tex.; notary pub., Tex. Sgt. USAF, Germany, 1951-54; mgr. radio sta., Galveston, 1954-65; owner, pub. newspaper, Galveston, 1965-75; owner Valentine's Video, Galveston, 1976-85; supr. med. records John Sealy Hosp., Galveston, 1987; exec. dir. Galveston Ch. Directory, 1987-89; founder, pres. Jack A. Johnson Found. Inc., Galveston, 1989-98; security officer Master Sgt., Galveston, 1990-98; sub-tchr. Galveston Sch. Dist., 1991-98; pres. John Valentine's Promotions, Galveston, Tex.; sr. security officer Silverlief Seaside Resort, Galveston, from 2001. First Black Heavyweight World Champion. Mem. mayor's aid to srs. com., Galveston; mem. 9th Congl. Dist. U.S. Svc. Selection Bd.; pub. rels. ofcl., sr. aides program, Galveston County Commr.'s Ct. Died Dec. 23, 2005.

VALETTI, LEOTA MAY, artist; b. St. Clair Shores, Mich., Oct. 14, 1926; d. Leo Clyde Williams and Jane Domenica Deldin; m. John Valetti (dec.); m. Earl Laws (div.); children: Eileen Joanne Cromer, Nancy Jane Laws. Grad. H.S., St. Clair Shores; grad., Famous Artists Schs., 1965. Avocations: art, piano, stamp collecting/philately, writing, reading. Home: Saint Clair Shores, Mich. Died Aug. 4, 2005.

VALLAT, LOUISE MARIE, elementary school educator, poet; b. Bklyn., Jan. 13, 1945; d. Joseph Anthony and Marie (Curcio) DeRiggi; m. Bruce Robert Vallat, Sept. 3, 1966; children: Anthony Joseph, Deborah Maria. BA, CUNY-Queens Coll., 1976, MS in Elem. Edn., 1991. Cert. elem. tchr., elem. English tchr., N.Y. Tchr. Bd. Edn., N.Y.C. Pub. Schs., Bklyn., from 1990. Author: (poetry) From Kindergarten to Graduate School, 1992; contbr. poetry to Am. Poetry Anthologies, 1990. Named Poet of Merit, finalist Poet of Yr. contest Am. Poetry Assn., Santa Cruz, Calif., 1990; recipient Editor's Choice award Nat. Libr. Congress, 1993. Mem. Nat. Writing Project. Avocations: writing, painting, organ and guitar, storytelling, poetry. Home: Lancaster, Pa. Died June 12, 2004.

VALSAMIS, MARIUS PETER, neuropathologist, educator; b. N.Y.C., Feb. 23, 1932; s. Peter Christ and Anna (Demetrokopoulos) V.; m. Nancy Weems, June 16, 1957; children: Helen Anna, Demetrios Peter, Ariadne Irene. AB, Columbia Coll., 1953; MD, SUNY, Bklyn., 1957. Intern Hosp. St. Raphael, New Haven, 1957-58; resident physician King's County Hosp., Bklyn., 1958-59; NIH tng. fellow SUNY Downstate Med. Ctr., Bklyn., 1959-63, clin. asst. prof. pathology, neuropathology, 1967-69; surgeon Off. Surg. Gen. USPHS, Bethesda, Md., 1963-65; instr. Neurology, Pathology Jefferson Med. Coll., Phila., 1965-69; chief of labs. Bklyn. State Hosp., 1967-69; assoc. prof. pathology (neuropathology) Albert Einstein Med. Coll., The Bronx, N.Y., 1969-74; prof. neuropathology, dir. pathophysiology course N.Y. Med. Coll., Valhalla, N.Y., 1974-91, prof. neurology, 1994-97, prof. emeritus pathology, 1997—2004; former cons. neuropathology Lincoln Hosp., Bronx; cons. neuropathology Med. Examiners Office of Westchester County, 1992-94. Former cons. Anatomic Pathology Cert. Nat. Cancer Inst., Bethesda, Md., former Clin. Ctr. Nat. Inst. Health, Bethesda; vol. faculty neuropathology NYU Coll. Medicine, 1997; vis. prof., cons. in neuropathology U. Thessalomike, Greece, 1999. Author (with others) AIDS (chapt. on neuropathology); contbr. articles sci. jours. Chmn. Med. Commn. U.S. Fencing Assn., Colorado Springs, Colo., 1972-84, 87-92, hon. chmn.; mgr. Pan Am. Olympic Fencing Team, Colorado Springs, 1975, 79, U.S. Olympic Fencing Team, 1976, 80; mem. Commn. Medicale Fed. Internat. d'Escrime, Paris. Fellow AAAS, N.Y. Acad. Scis.; mem. Am. Assn. Neuropathologists (past archivist), Internat. Soc. Greek Neuroscientists (pres. 1995-96), The Fencers' Club (bd. dirs. N.Y. 1969-91). Avocation: fencing. Died Jan. 6, 2004.

VALTMAN, EDMUND S., editorial cartoonist; b. Tallinn, Estonia, May 31, 1914; came to U.S., 1949, naturalized, 1959; s. Johannes and Pauline Elisabet (Kukk) V.; m. Helmi Grunberg, July 17, 1943. Student, Art and Applied Art Sch., Estonia, 1942-44, Hartford Art Sch. Conn., 1953-57. Freelance cartoonist and comml. artist, Tallinn, 1936-42; editorial cartoonist Eesti Sona, Tallinn, 1942-44, Eesti Post, Geislingen, Germany, 1945-49, Hartford (Conn.) Times, 1951-75; freelance cartoonist, grapic artist Hartford, 1975—2005. Author: Valtman, 1991, The Editorial Cartoons of Edmund S. Valtman, 1961-91; exhbns. include The Great Challenge, Washington, London, Tokyo, 1958-59, Politics 1960, Columbia U., 1960, Internat. Salon Cartoons, Montreal, 1968-71, World Cartoon Festival, Belgium, 1971; exhibited paintings Wadworth Atheneum, Hartford, Silvermine Guild, Norwalk, New Britain Mus., Slater Meml. Mus., Norwich, Green Gallery, Guilford, Conn., Shepee Gallery, N.Y.C.; exhibited cartoons Libr. Congress Thomas Jefferson Bldg., 2003, Internet presentation. Recipient Pulitzer prize for cartooning, 1962, Leadership medal Greater Hartford C. of C., 1962, Gannett Newspaper Frank Tripp award, 1963, Pub. Interest award Nat. Safety Coun., 1958, Graphic award Old Lyme Art Works, 1985. Mem. Assn. Am. Editorial Cartoonists, Nat. Cartoonists Soc. (Silver Plaque on T-Square 1962, graphic arts awards 1982, 84, painting award 1991), Conn. Acad. Fine Arts, Canton Artists Guild, West Hartford Art League. Died Jan. 12, 2005.

VAN ALLEN, JAMES ALFRED, physicist, researcher; b. Mt. Pleasant, Iowa, Sept. 7, 1914; s. Alfred Morris and Alma E. (Olney) Van A.; m. Abigail Fithian Halsey, Oct. 13, 1945; children: Cynthia Schaffner, Margot Cairns, Sarah Trimble, Thomas, Peter. BS, Iowa Wesleyan Coll., 1935; MS, U. Iowa, 1936, PhD, 1939; ScD (hon.), Iowa Wesleyan Coll., 1951, Grinnell Coll., 1957, Coe Coll., 1958, Cornell Coll., Mt. Vernon, Iowa, 1959, U. Dubuque, 1960, U. Mich., 1961, Northwestern U., 1961, Ill. Coll., 1963, Butler U., 1966, Boston Coll., 1966, Southampton Coll., 1967, Augustana Coll., 1969, St. Ambrose Coll., 1982, U. Bridgeport, 1987; DHL (hon.), Johns Hopkins U., 1999. Rsch. fellow, physicist dept. terrestial magnetism Carnegie Instn., Washington, 1939-42; physicist, group and unit supr. applied physics lab. Johns Hopkins U., 1942, 46-50; organizer, leader sci. expdns. study cosmic radiation Peru, 1949, Gulf of Alaska, 1950, Arctic, 1952, 57, Antarctic, 1957; prof. physics, head dept. U. Iowa, Iowa City, 1951-85, Carver prof. physics, 1989-92, Regent disting. prof., 1992—2006. Rsch. assoc. Princeton U., 1953-54; mem. devel. group radio proximity fuze Nat. Def. Rsch. Coun., OSRD; regents fellow Smithsonian Instn., 1981; pioneer high attitude rsch. with rockets, satellites and space probes. Author: Origins of Magnetospheric Physics, 1983, First to Jupiter, Saturn and Beyond, 1981; 924 Elementary Problems and Answers in Solar System Astronomy, 1993; contbg. author: Physics and Medicine of Upper Atmosphere, 1952, Rocket Exploration of the Upper Atmosphere; editor: Scientific Uses of Earth Satellites, 1956, Cosmic Rays, the Sun, and Geomagnetism: The Works of Scott E. Forbush, 1993; acting editor Jour. Geophys. Rsch.-Space Physics, 1991-92; contbr. articles to profl. jours. Lt. comdr. USNR, 1942-46, ordnance and gunnery specialist, combat observer. Recipient Physics award Washington Acad. Sci., 1949, Space Flight award Am. Astronautical Soc., 1958, Louis W. Hill Space Transp. award Inst. Aero. Scis., 1959, Elliot Cresson medal Franklin Inst., 1961, Golden Omega award Elec. Insulation Conf., 1963, Iowa Broadcasters Assn. award, 1964, Fellows award of merit Am. Cons. Engrs. Coun., 1978, Nat. Medal of Sci., 1987, Crafford prize, Royal Sweden Acad. Scis., 1989, Nansen award and prize, Norwegian Acad. Sci. and Letters, 1990, Vannevar Bush award NSF, 1991, Gerard P. Kuiper prize Am. Astron. Soc. 1994; named comdr. Order du Merit Pour la Recherche et l'Invention, 1964; Guggenheim Found. rsch. fellow, 1951. Fellow Am. Rocket Soc. (C.N. Hickman medal devel. Aerobee rocket 1949), IEEE, Am. Phys. Soc., Am. Geophys. Union (pres. 1982-84, John A. Fleming award 1963, William Bowie medal 1977); mem. NAS, AAAS (Abelson prize 1986), Iowa Acad. Sci., Internat. Acad. Astronautics (founding), Am. Philos. Soc., Am. Astron. Soc., Royal Astron. Soc. U.K. (Gold medal 1978), Royal Swedish Acad. Sci. (Crafoord prize 1989), Am. Acad. Arts and Scis., Cosmos Club, Sigma Xi (Procter prize 1987), Gamma Alpha. Presybterian. Achievements include discovery of radiation belts (now named the Van Allen belts) around earth in 1958 with satellite missions Explorer I and Explorer III. Died Aug. 9, 2006.

VAN ANDEL, BETTY JEAN, retired direct selling company executive; b. Mich., Dec. 14, 1921; d. Anthony and Daisy (Van Dyk) Hoekstra; m. Jay Van Andel, Aug. 16, 1952; children: Nan Elizabeth, Stephen Alan, David Lee, Barbara Ann. AB, Calvin Coll., 1943. Elem. sch. tchr., Grand Rapids, Mich., 1943-45; svc. rep. and supr. Mich. Bell Telephone Co., Grand Rapids, 1945-52; bd. dirs. Amway Corp., Grand Rapids, from 1972. Treas. LWV, 1957-60; pres. Eagle Forum, Mich., 1972-92; co-chmn. Mich. Botanic Garden Capital Campaign; former trustee Christian Sch. Internat. Found., Grand Rapids Opera, excec. com.; trustee Pine Rest Christian Hosp., 1981-90; past pres. La Grave Ave. Reformed Ch. Svc. Guild. Mem. Nat. Fedn. Women, Nat. Trust Hist. Preservation, Smithsonian Assns., Gerald R. Ford Rep. Women's Club. Home: Grand Rapids, Mich. Died Jan. 18, 2004.

VANARSDEL, THOMAS PAUL, architect, consultant; b. Phila., July 7, 1923; s. William Campbell and Mabel Elizabeth V.; m. Carolyn Jean Beall; children: Thomas II, Peter Roland, Carolyn Sue, Richard, Kathryn Jean (dec.). BS in Sci., Purdue U., 1948; degree in Elec. Engring., U.S. Army, 1944; JD cum laude, Bernadean U., 1983. Registered profl. engr., Ind., Ohio, Miss.; registered architect, Ohio. Chief structural engr. Fanning and Howey, Celina, Ohio, 1968-74; dir. pipeline safety divsn. Pub. Svc. Commn. State of Ind., Indpls., 1976-87; engr. Rundell-Ernstberger, Muncie, Ind., 1987-97; arch. City of Fortville, Ind., 1997; pvt. practice architect, engr. Fortville, from 1997. Patentee in field; expert witness in Mich., Ohio, Ind., 1987-99. World record holder Sr. Masters Divsn. 220# class bench press competition Mem. AAAS, AIA, Nat. Soc. Profl. Engrs., Bldg. Officials Code Adminstrs. Internat., Indpls. Scientific and Engring. Found. (chmn. of ops. com.), N.Y. Acad. Scis., Indpls. Scientech. Club, Scottish Rite Mason, Murat Shrine. Died Jan. 14, 2005.

VANBURKALOW, ANASTASIA, retired geography educator; b. Buchanan, N.Y., Mar. 16, 1911; d. James Turley and Mabel Ritchie (Ramsay) VanB. BA, Hunter Coll., 1931; MA, Columbia U., 1933, PhD, 1944; DSc with honors, Hunter Coll., 1996. Rsch. asst. in geomorphology Columbia U., N.Y.C., 1934-37; from tutor to prof. geography Hunter Coll. CUNY, 1938-45, 48-75; rsch. and editorial asst. Am. Geog. Soc., N.Y.C., 1945-48; prof. Hunter Coll. CUNY, 1961-75, prof. emeritus Hunter Coll., from 1975. Cons. geologist E.I. DuPont deNemours & Co., Wilmington, Del., 1945-59. Editor: Megalopolis (Jean Gottman), 1961, Geol. Edn., 1954-56; contbg. editor Geog. Rev., 1949-72; contbr. articles to profl. jours.; composer hymns. Bd. dirs. United Meth. City Soc., N.Y.C., 1972—, Bethany Deaconess Soc., 1982—, N.Y. Deaconess Assn., 1984—, Five Points Mission, N.Y.C., 1979-89; trustee John Street United Meth. Ch., N.Y.C., 1972-84. Kemp fellow, 1937-38. Fellow AAAS, N.Y. Acad. Scis. (sec. geology sect. 1957-58), Geol. Soc. Am., Hymn Soc. of Am. (recording sec. 1974-80); mem. Assn. Am. Geographers, Am. Geophys. Union, Am. Guild Organists, Soc. Woman Geographers (mem. exec. com. 1978-80, 83-85), Phi Beta Kappa, Sigma Xi. Died Jan. 14, 2004.

VANCE, DOROTHY SAUNDERS, real estate consultant; b. Ogden, Utah, Jan. 16, 1944; d. Heber Clyde Saunders and Norma Leone (Phillips) Devorss; m. John T. Ferrier, Mar. 8, 1962 (div. 1970); 1 child, John T. Ferrier. m. Kimball Roland Vance, July 17, 1976 (dec. Oct. 1991); children: Amanda Keturah, Richard James. Student, Pacific State Hosp., Pomona, Calif., 1970, Weber State U., Ogden, Ut., 1974-75, Lumbleau Coll., Salt Lake City, 1978. Lic. Real estate. Dispatcher Pomona (Calif.) Police Dept., 1968; psychiatric tech. Pacific State Hosp., Pomona, Calif., 1970-71; real estate cons. Motel Hotel Sales and Mgmt., Salt Lake City, from 1981; v.p. Worldwide Inst. Mktg., Salt Lake City; owner, mgr. Macks Inn (Ida.) Resort, 1982. Hotel cons. Motel Hotel Sales and Mgmt., Salt Lake City. Author: Vance Family Genealogy. Mem. Utah Alliance for Mentally Ill, Salt Lake City; worker Rep. Group, 1989—; vol. Utah State Prison, 1981-89, Head Start, 1989. Mem. Relief Soc., Bd. Realtors. Avocations: skiing, tennis, swimming, world travelling. Home: Salt Lake City, Utah. Died Sept. 10, 2004.

VANCE, WILLIAM L., television news director; b. Oak Park, Ill., Oct. 14, 1932; s. William L. and Lillian (Teich) V.; m. Margaret Ann Beckett, Dec. 30, 1956; children: Thomas, Suellen. BS in Polit. Sci., Knox Coll., 1954; MS in Journalism, Northwestern U., 1958. Writer, producer, reporter WOOD AM and TV, Grand Rapids, Mich., 1958-61, WLS-TV, Chgo., 1961-67; city editor, assignment editor WBBM-TV, Chgo., 1967-70; asst. news dir. KYW-TV, Phila., 1970-73; news dir. WJAR AM & TV, Providence, R.I., 1973-74, WBNS-TV, Columbus, Ohio, 1974-79, dir. news ops., from 1986; news dir. KXAS-TV, Ft. Worth, 1979-83, WJBK-TV, Detroit, 1983-86. Recipient variety of awards for news leadership and programs 1975— including 2 Emmy awards NATAS, 1975. Mem. Press Club of Ohio (v.p. 1990—). Died Jan. 9, 2005.

VANDERPOOL, WARD MELVIN, management and marketing consultant; b. Oakland, Mo., Jan. 20, 1918; s. Oscar B. and Clara (McGuire) V.; m. Lee Kendall, July 7, 1939. MEE, Tulane U. V.p. charge sales Van Lang Brokerage, Los Angeles, 1934-38; mgr. agrl. div. Dayton Rubber Co., Chgo., 1939-48; pres., gen. mgr. Vee Mac Co., Rockford, Ill., from 1948; pres., dir. Zipout, Inc., Rockford, from 1951, Wife Saver Products, Inc., from 1959. Chmn. bd. Zipout Internat., Kenvan Inc., 1952—, Shevan Corp., 1951—, Atlas Internat. Corp.; pres. Global Enterprises Ltd., Global Assocs. Ltd.; chmn. bd. dirs. Am. Atlas Corp., Atlas Chem. Corp., Merzat Industries Ltd.; trustee Ice Crafter Trust, 1949—; bd. dirs. Atlas Chem. Internat. Ltd., Kenlee Internat., Ltd., Shrimp Tool Internat. Ltd.; mem. Toronto Bd. Trade; chmn. bd. dirs. Am. Atlas Corp., Am. Packaging Corp. Mem. adv. bd. Nat. Security Council, congl. adv. com. Heritage Found.; mem. Rep. Nat. Com., Presdl. Task Force, Congrl. Adv. Com. Hon. mem. Internat. Swimming Hall of Fame. Mem. Nat. (dir. at large), Rock River (past pres.), sales execs., Sales and Mktg. Execs. Internat. (dir.), Am. Mgmt. Assn., Rockford Engring. Soc., Am. Tool Engrs., Internat. Acad. Aquatic Art (dir.), Am. Inst. Mgmt. (pres. council), Am. Ordnance Assn., Internat. Platform Assn., Heritage Found., Ill. C. of C., Jesters Club, IAA Swim Club, Elmcrest Country Club, Pyramid Club, Dolphin Club, Marlin Club, Univ. Club, Athletic Club, Oxford Club, Masons (consistory), Shriners, Elks. Home: Cedar Rapids, Iowa. Died May 27, 2004.

VANDERSPEK, PETER GEORGE, management consultant, writer; b. The Hague, Netherlands, Dec. 15, 1925; came to U.S., 1945; s. Pieter and Catherine Johanna (Rolf) V.; m. Charlotte Louise Branch, Aug. 18, 1957. Student, Tilburg (Netherlands) U., 1944; MA in Econs., Fordham U., 1950, PhD in Econs., 1954; postgrad., George Washington U., 1967-68. Internat. economist Mobil Oil Corp., N.Y.C., 1956-59; mgr. internat. market rsch. Celanese Corp., N.Y.C., 1959-63; internat. economist Bethlehem (Pa.) Steel Corp., 1964-65; sr. tech. adviser Battelle Meml. Inst., Washington, 1965-66; indsl. adviser Inter-Am. Devel. Bank, Washington, 1967-69; economist Fed. Res. Bank, N.Y.C., 1970-72; mgr. internat. market rsch. Brunswick Corp., Skokie, Ill., 1973-76; mgr. advanced planning Sverdrup Corp., St. Louis, 1979-87, cons., 1988-90; pres. OBEX, Inc., San Luis Obispo, Calif., from 1988. Author: Planning for Factory Automation, 1993; contbr. to profl. jours. Thomas J. Watson fellow, IBM-Fordham U., 1945-49. Mem. Mensa. Avocations: travel, writing. Died July 22, 2004.

VAN DE WALLE, ETIENNE, demography professor; b. Namur, Belgium, Apr. 29, 1932; came to U.S., 1961; s. Arnould and Yolande (Blommaert) Van De W.; m. Francine Robyns de Schneidauer, Aug. 24, 1955; children: Dominique, Nicolas, Jean-Francois, Patrice. Dr. in Law, U. Louvain, Belgium, 1956, MA in Econs., 1957, PhD in Demography, 1973. Researcher Irsac, Rwanda, Burundi, 1957-61; rsch. assoc. Princeton (N.J.) U., 1962-64, rsch. staff, 1964-67, rsch. demographer, 1967-72; vis. lectr. U. Calif., Berkeley, 1971-72; prof. deomgraphy U. Penn., Phila., 1972—2001, prof. emeritus, 2001—06. Dir. Population Studies Ctr., U. Pa., 1976-82; sr. assoc. The Population Coun., Bamako, Mali, 1982. Author: The Female Population of France, 1974; co-author: The Demography of Tropical Africa, 1968. Fellowship Woodrow Wilson Ctr. for Scholars, 1976. Mem. Internat. Union for Scientific Study of Population, Population Assn. of Am. (pres. 1992). Home: Merion Station, Pa. Died Mar. 21, 2006.

VANDIVIERE, H. MAC, medical educator; b. Ga., Mar. 26, 1921; s. Augustus Vandiviere and Luna Castlebury; m. Margaret Reynolds, (dec. Feb. 1967); children: Christopher, Martin; m. Irene G. Melvin, March 23, 1968. AB, Mercer Coll., 1943, MS, 1944; MD, U. N.C., 1960. Intern St. Antoine's Hosp., Jeremie, Haiti, 1961—66; dir. spl. svc. unit Ga. Dept. Health, Rome, 1948—51; rsch. bacteriologist N.C. Sanatorium Sys., McCain, 1951—53, dir. clin. lab., 1953—67; from asst. prof. to prof. emeritus U. Ky., Lexington, 1967-91, prof. emeritus, from 1991; pvt. practice Lancaster, Ky., from 1991. Dir. TB control and remedial svcs. Ky. Dept. Health, Frankfort, 1971-76; cons. Southeastern Consortium for Internat. Devel., Lexington, Ky., Chapel Hill, N.C., 1988-89. Contbr. articles to profl. jours. Pres. com. Hospice of Lexington, 1980-81; chmn. program planning and evaluation Bluegrass Mental Health, Mental Retardation Bd., Lexington, 1983-85, 90-99; pres., co-chmn. Am. Lung Assn. of Ky., Louisville, 1971-97. Fellow Am. Soc. Geriatrics, Am. Pub. Health Soc.; mem. Am. Ky. Med. Soc., So. Assn. Geriatric Medicine, So. Assn. Family Practice, So. Med. Assn. (Disting. Svc. award 1999). Republican. Episcopalian. Home: Lancaster, Ky. Died Mar. 1, 2004.

VANDRY, BRET EDWARD, manufacturing company executive; b. Jackson, Mich., Jan. 22, 1948; s. Inman Edward and Mary Jane (Wood) V.; m. susanne Lee Woods, June 12, 1976; children: Christine Lee, Jennifer Lynn. BS, Mich. State U., 1971. With mktg. dept. GE, Bloomington, Ill., 1972-78, with sales dept. Flint, Mich., 1978-80, sales mgr. Inpls., 1980-84, dist. mgr. St. Louis, 1984-86, Phila., 1986-89, nat. svc. mgr. Charlotte, N.C., from 1989. Participant video on self-direction, 1991. Avocations: jogging, swimming, tennis. Died June 8, 2004.

VAN HORN, RICHARD, geologist; b. San Diego, Feb. 22, 1920; s. Charles William and Charlotte Caroline (Schmidt) Van H.; m. Alice Marion Byrne, Oct. 20, 1942; children: Michael, Patricia, James, Ted, Kathleen. Degree in geol. engring., Colo. Sch. Mines, 1947. Geologist U.S. Geol. Survey, Denver, from 1947. Scout and cub master Boy Scouts Am., Golden, Colo.; instr. swimming ARC, Golden; speaker and field trip leader on geology for schs. and civic groups. Capt. Corps of Engrs., U.S. Army, 1942-45. Avocations: skiing, golf, canoeing, sailing. Home: Golden, Colo. Died June 30, 2005.

VAN INGEN, HUBERT ANTHONY, linguistics educator; b. Amsterdam, Oct. 24, 1931; came to U.S., 1953; s. Bernardus Gerrit and Neeltje (DeVries) Van Ingen Schenau; m. Elizabeth Clark Gibbons, Feb. 7, 1960; children: Caroline, Linda, Marianne. Student, U. Akron, Ohio, 1953-54, 57-58. Export trainee Firestone Tire & Rubber Co., Akron, 1953-54, 57-58; sales rep. Firestone Internat. Co., Teheran, Iran, 1958-62; pres., gen. mgr. Societe Anonyme De Pneumatiques Firestone, Casablanca, Morocco, 1962-66; sales mgr. Firestone South Africa Proprietary, Ltd., Port Elizabeth, Republic of South Africa, 1967-74; dir. sales Asia div. Bandag, Inc., Muscatine, Iowa, 1974-76, v.p., 1976-89, tech. instr., from 1990. Pres. Churchill Club, Casablanca, 1964-65. With U.S. Army, 1955-56, Korea. Mem. Am. Bus. Assn. (pres. Teheran chpt. 1961-62), Am. Legion, Geneva Golf and Country Club. Republican. Avocations: languages, history. Home: Muscatine, Iowa. Died June 28, 2005.

VAN ORDEN, STUART COPELAND, artist; b. Buffalo, Dec. 8, 1918; s. George Harrison and Mildred Amy (Copeland) Van O.; m. Marie Evans, Sept. 13, 1948; children: Stuart D., Charles H. BA, Southwestern U., Tex., 1948; MFA, Cornell U., 1950; PhD, Syracuse U., 1972. Sgt. U.S. Army, 1942-46. Unitarian Universalist. Home: Perkins, Okla. Died Feb. 25, 2005.

VAN TIL, WILLIAM, retired education educator, writer; b. Corona, NY, Jan. 8, 1911; s. William Joseph and Florence Alberta (MacLean) Van Til; m. Beatrice Barbara Blaha, Aug. 24, 1935; children: Jon, Barbara, Roy. BA, Columbia U., 1933; MA, Tchrs. Coll., 1935; PhD, Ohio State U., 1946. Tchr. N.Y. State Tng. Sch. for Boys, 1933-34; instr. dept.

univ. schs. Coll. Edn., Ohio State U., 1934-36, asst. prof., 1936-43, on leave, 1943-45; researchist, writer Consumer Edn. Study NEA, 1943-44; dir. learning materials Bur. Intercultural Edn., 1944-47; prof. edn. U. Ill., 1947-51; prof. edn., chmn. div. curriculum and teaching George Peabody Coll. Tchrs., Nashville, 1951-57; prof. edn., chmn. dept. secondary edn. N.Y. U., 1957-66, head div. secondary and higher edn., 1966-67; Coffman disting. prof. edn. Ind. State U., Terre Haute, 1967-77, prof. emeritus, 1977; dir. univ. workshops Writing for Profl. Publs., 1978—2006; founder Lake Lure Press, 1983. Author: The Danube Flows Through Fascism, Economic Roads for American Democracy, The Making of a Modern Educator, Modern Education for the Junior High School Years, The Year 2000: Teacher Education, One Way of Looking At It, Education: A Beginning, Another Way of Looking At It, Van Til on Education, Secondary Education: School and Community, Writing for Professional Publication, rev., 1986; autobiography My Way of Looking At It, 1983, expanded 2d edit., 1996; Sketches, 1989, Admonitions and Challenges, 2002; editor: Forces Affecting American Education, Curriculum: Quest for Relevance, ASCD in Retrospect, 1986, Critique on Work Teaching Education, 1993; author: Teachers and Mentors: Profiles of Distinguished Twentieth Century Professors of Education, 1996, U. S.C. dissertation, William Van Til: Pub. Intellectual, 2002; co-editor: Democratic Human Relations, Intercultural Attitudes in the Making, Education in American Life; adv. editor Houghton Mifflin, 1964-70; interviewed in Social Education, 1989, Preface to the Eight Year Study Revisited, 1998; contbr. articles to profl. jours., popular mags. including Saturday Rev., Woman's Day, Parents; columnist: Ednl. Leadership, Contemporary Edn., Kappan; adv. bd. Profl. Educator, 1984-95. Mem. Ill. Interracial Commn., 1949-51; moderator Nashville Sch. desegregation meetings, 1955-57; mem. adv. bd. Jour. Tchr. Edn., 1956-59; co-organizer Nashville Community Rels. Conf., 1956; cons. Phelps-Stokes Fund project, 1958-62; mem. staff P.R. Edn. Survey, 1958-59, Iran Tchr. Edn. Survey, 1962, V.I. Edn. Survey, 1964; lectr. abroad, 1974; mem. staff U. Ind. Phi Delta Kappa Inst., 1984-90; 1st Ann. Van Til lectr. Ind. State U., 1989. Recipient Centennial Achievement award, Ohio State U., 1970; awards N.J. Collegiate Press Assn., 1962; N.J. Assn. Tchrs. English, 1962; named to Edn. Hall of Fame, Ohio State U., 1989; Annual Van Til Lectr. Series, Ind. State U., est. 1989, est. Annual Van Til Writing award, 1989, award of recognition Spring conf., 1999. Mem. John Dewey Soc. (v.p. 1957-60, acting pres. 1958-59, pres. 1964-66, award 1977, 86, Outstanding Achievement award 1991), Assn. Supervision and Curriculum Devel. (dir. 1951-54, 57-60, pres. 1961-62, chmn. rev. council 1972-73, resolutions com. 1982-85), United Educators (chmn. bd. educators 1969-77), Nat. Soc. Coll. Tchrs. Edn. (pres. 1967-68), Am. Edn. Studies Assn. (editorial bd. 1970-77), Asso. Orgn. Tchr. Edn. (adv. council 1967-73, chmn. issues tchr. edn. 1972-73), Nat. Soc. Study Edn. (editor Yearbook Issues in Secondary Edn. 1976), Kappa Delta Pi (laureate 1980—, chmn. book-of-yr. com. 1984-86, contbr. Honor in Teaching Reflections 1990, Experiencing Dewey 2005). Home: Terre Haute, Ind. Died May 24, 2006.

VAN VLISSINGEN, PAUL FENTENER, retired gas, oil industry executive; b. 1941; With SHV Holdings N.V., Utrecht, 1960—2005, chief exec., 1984—97, chmn. supervisory bd., 1997—2005. Founder Van Vlissingen Cancer Fund. Died Aug. 21, 2006.

VANWARMER, RANDY, composer; b. Denver, Mar. 30, 1955; s. Roger and Elizabeth (Harry) VanWormer; m. Suzi Brockhaus Blosser, Mar. 23, 1988. Composer Terraform Music, Kingston, N.Y., 1980-85, VanWarmer Music, Brentwood, Tenn., from 1985. Composer popular songs including Just When I Needed You Most (Gold Record 1980), I Guess It Never Hurts to Hurt Sometimes, I Will Whisper Your Name, I'm In a Hurry (and don't know why); composer/artist (album) Warmer (Gold Record). Mem. ASCAP (song writing award 1984, 88, 94), Nat. Songwriters Assn. Internat. (former mem. bd. dirs., song writing award 19180), NARAS, Acad. Country Music, Country Music Assn. Home: Brentwood, Tenn. Died Jan. 12, 2004.

VAN WART, THOMAS, librarian; b. Bay Shore, N.Y., Aug. 15, 1949; s. Harold Edgar and Anna Theresa (Prygocki) Van W.; m. Louise Ellen Cummings, Dec. 27, 1972; children: Scott, Audra, Rebecca. BA, SUNY, Oswego, 1971; cert. in linguistics, Def. Lang. Inst., 1973; MLS, SUNY, Albany, 1976. Cert. pub. librarian, N.Y. Instr. Persian lang. Lang. Tng. Facility, Ft. Hood, Tex., 1973-75; librarian N.Y. State Library, Albany, 1976-77; chief tech. library U.S. Army Corps Engrs., Buffalo, from 1977. Library cons. Ctr. for Aging, Buffalo, 1979-80; course coordinator U.S. Army Corps Engrs., Huntsville, Ala., 1984, automation instr., 1987—. Served with U.S. Army, 1972-75. Mem. Spl. Libraries Assn., Soc. Am. Mil. Engrs., Western N.Y. Library Resources Council. Republican. Roman Catholic. Home: Lockport, NY. Died Mar. 30, 2005.

VARGA, NICHOLAS, historian, archivist, retired educator; b. Elizabeth, N.J., Sept. 13, 1925; s. Joseph and Anna (Buchko) V.; m. Margaret Joan Skinner, Sept. 8, 1951; children: Deidre Kayne, Damian Guy, Colin Piere. BS cum laude, Boston Coll., Chestnut Hill, Mass., 1951, MA, 1952; PhD with honors, Fordham U., 1960. Instr. history Loyola Coll., Balt., 1955-59, asst. prof., 1959-62, assoc. prof., 1962-66, prof., 1966-92, chmn. dept., 1964-68, prof. emeritus, from 1992, coll. archivist, from 1976. Author: Baltimore's Loyola, 1990. Advisor Jo Tydings Election Campaign, Balt., 1964, 70; bd. dirs. UN Assn. Md., Balt., 1966-70; pres. Woodbourne Sch. PTA, Balt., 1967-68; mem. Howard County Bicentennial Com., Ellicott City, Md., 1974-77. Publ. grantee Md. Hist. Soc., 1989. Mem. AAUP (founder, pres. Loyola Coll. chpt. 1966-69), Am. Hist. Assn. (interviewer Cate report 1966), Am. Cath. Hist. Assn. (nominating com. 1975-78), Soc. Am. Archivists, Mid-Atlantic Region Archivists Conf., Alpha Sigma Nu (hon.). Democrat. Byzantine Catholic. Home: Baltimore, Md. Died Jan. 18, 2005; Balt.

VASSAR, WILLIAM GERALD, gifted and talented education educator; b. Springfield, Mass., Oct. 5, 1925; s. William Walter and Mary Ellen (Burns) V.; m. Barbara Ellen Benhard, June 21, 1952; children: William G., James P., Richard G., Carol A. Vassar Pettit. BA in History magna cum laude, Am. Internat. Coll., Springfield, 1950; MEd, Springfield Coll., 1951; cert. of advanced grad. study, U. Mass., 1967, postgrad., 1962-70. Elem. tchr. West Springfield (Mass.) Pub. Schs., 1950-53, jr. high tchr., 1953-55, secondary sch. prin., 1955-65, dir. program for gifted, 1955-65; sr. supr. academically talented Mass. State Dept. Edn., Boston, 1965-66; state dir. programs for gifted and talented Conn. State Dept. Edn., Hartford, 1966-86; coord. gifted edn., dept. spl. edn. Cen. Conn. State U., New Britain, 1968-86, asst. to dean Sch. Edn., 1986-88; spl. cons. advanced placement program The Coll. Bd., N.Y.C., 1986—2000; prodr. interactive satellite confs. on Advanced Placement, 1992—2000. Coord. White House Task Force Gifted and Talented, Washington, 1967-68, U.S. Dept. Edn. Congl. Study Gifted and Talented, Washington, 1969-71, Capitol Region Edn. Coun. Info. and Resource Ctr., Windsor, Conn., 1992—; cons. gifted and talented U.S. Dept. Edn., 1967-85, Nat. Assn. State Bds. Edn., 1978-84, George Washington U. Edn. Policy Fellowship Program, 1978-84; spl. cons. gifted and talented legislation Staff of Senate subcom. on Edn., 1967-85; vis. lectr. U. Conn., 1966-83, So. Conn. State U., 1970-84, Sacred Heart U., 1986-92, others. Contbg. editor The Gifted Child Quar., Jour. Talented and Gifted; author monographs; contbr. numerous articles to profl. jours. Mem. exec. bd. Mass. Commn. on Children and Youth, Boston, 1959-65, Nat. Commn. Orgn. and Children and Youth, Washington, 1964-68; mem. Conn. Commn. on Youth Svcs., Hartford, 1966-70; mem. Mass. Hwy. Safety Commn., Boston, 1957-63; baseball scout San Francisco Giants, 1957-70. With USN, 1943-46, PTO. Named Disting. Educator U.S. Dept. Edn. Office Gifted, Washington, 1974, Disting. Educator, Conn. State Legislature, Hartford, 1986; recipient Disting. Svc. award Mass. Commn. on Children and Youth, Boston, 1966, Gold Pass award Mass. Baseball Umpires Assn., 1997. Mem. ASCD, Internat. Coun. Exceptional Children (pres. Assn. Gifted divsn. 1970-71, chmn. regionals 1969-78, Disting. Svc. award 1972), Nat. Assn. Gifted Children (life, pres. 1965-68, bd. dirs. 1960-68, Disting. Svc. award 1974, Pres.'s award for lifetime significant contbn. 1998), Coun. State Dirs. Gifted (pres. 1977-80), Conn. Assn. Gifted, Conn. Assn. Pub. Sch. Supts. (ret.), Nat. Football Hall of Fame Found., Eastern Assn. Intercollegiate Football Ofcls., Indian Hill Country Club, Eastern Coll. Athletic Conf., Phi Delta Kappa. Democrat. Roman Catholic. Avocations: reading, golf, football. Home: Newington, Conn. Died Nov. 28, 2004.

VAUGHN, JAMES LLOYD, retired microbiologist, researcher; b. Marshfield, Wis., Mar. 2, 1934; s. Lloyd Robert and Irene (Tague) V.; m. Jeanette Darlene Lustig, June 11, 1955 (div. 1988); children: Susan, Katherine, Michael, David.; m. Carol Schiller, June 23, 1989. BS, U. Wis., 1957, MS, 1959, PhD, 1962. Rsch. officer Insect Pathology Inst., Sault Ste. Marie, Ont., Can., 1961-65; rsch. microbiologist Agrl. Rsch. Svc. USDA, Beltsville, Md., 1965-79, rsch. leader, 1979-95, rsch. microbiologist, 1995-99; ret. Adv. bd. Agr. Rsch. Svc. USDA. Mem. Am. Soc. Microbiology, Soc. for In-vitro Biology. Home: Tulsa, Okla. Died July 22, 2005.

VAUSHER, ABRAHAM LUKE, safety engineer; b. Mehalla-el-Koubra, Egypt, July 28, 1928; came to U.S., 1969—. s. Naguib and Labieba Ibrahim; m. Afeefa Marie Vausher, July 24, 1954; children: Alexander, George, Phoebe. BS, U. Cairo, 1949; MA in Chemistry, Mankato State U., 1971; MPH, U. Minn., 1972. Assoc. chemist Midwest Research Inst., Hopkins, Minn., 1974-78; application engr. Gen. Resource Corp., Hopkins, 1978-81; staff chemist Goodyear Atomic Corp., Piketon, Ohio, 1981-85; engr. scientist McDonnell Douglas Astronautic Corp., Huntington Beach, Calif., from 1986. Contbr. articles to profl. jours. Mem. Am. Inst. Chem. Engrs., Am. Chem. Soc. Home: Chino, Calif. Died Jan. 4, 2004.

VAYHINGER, JOHN MONROE, psychotherapist, minister; b. Upland, Ind., Jan. 27, 1916; s. Paul Johnson and Harriet Estelle (Palmer) V.; m. Ruth Imler, Sept. 17, 1939; children: John Earl, Karen Lynn Vayhinger Childs. AB, Taylor U., 1937; grad., Asbury Theol. Sem., Wilmore, Ky., 1937-39; BD, MA, Drew U., 1940, 51; MA, PhD, Columbia U., 1948, 56. Diplomate Am. Bd. Psychology; ordained Meth. Ch. as pastor. Pastor United Meth. Ch., Conn., Ind., N.Y., Colo., 1938-68, ret.85; assoc. prof., head dept. W.Va. Wesleyan U., Buckhannon, 1949-51; chief clin. psychologist Mental Health Clin., South Bend, Ind., 1951-58; lectr. Ind. U., South Bend, 1953-58; prof. psychology and pastoral counseling Garrett Theol. Sem. Northwestern U., Evanston, Ill., 1958-64; prof. psychology of religion and pastoral counseling Iliff Sch. Theology U. Denver, 1964-67; prof. psychology and pastoral counseling Anderson (Ind.) U. Sch. Theology, 1968-81, Asbury Theol. Sem., Wilmore, Ky., 1981-84, ret.84; pvt. practice Ky., Ind., Ill, Colo., from 1958, Colorado Springs, Colo., from 1984. Dir. inst. ministries Ind. Coun. Chs., Indpls., 1968-81; chairperson Pastoral Counseling Inst., Atlanta, 1985—. Author: Before Divorce, 1972, (with Newman Cryer), Casebook of Pastoral Counseling, 1962; contbr. 12 chpts. edited books. Tchr. police schs., South Bend, Ind., Anderson, Ind., Denver. Capt. AUS, 1944-47, PTO. Fellow Am. Orthopsychiatric Assn., Am. Assn. Sci. Study of Religion, Christian Assn. Psychol. Studies, Am. Assn. Clin. Sexiologists, Am. Assn. Christian Counselors; mem. Am. Assn. Pastoral Counselors (diplomate), Soc. Psychol. in Pvt. Practice, Am. Psychol. Assn., AAUP, AAAS, Colo. Psychol. Assn., Ind. Psychol. Assn., Am. Assn. Marital and Family Therapists (clin.), Religious Rsch. Assn., Am. Assn. Sex Educators, Counselors and Therapists, Nat. Coun. Family Relations, Assn. Clin. Pastoral Edn., Nat. Congress Parents and Tchrs. (life), USN Inst., and more. Republican. Home: Colorado Springs, Colo. Died June 11, 2006.

VEMURI, SARMA LAKSHMINARAYANA, mathematics educator; b. Vaddadi, Andhra, India, July 1, 1928; came to U.S., 1985; s. Someswara Rao and Sita (Tenneti) V.; m. Lalita Cherukuri, June 17, 1953; children: Sita, Yasodhara, Ramamohan, Narasimha Murti, Murali Krishna. BS, Andhra U., Waltair, India, 1946; MS, Banaras Hindu U., Varanasi, India, 1948; PhD, U. Rochester, 1962. Research asst. Banaras Hindu U., Varanasi, India, 1948-50, lectr., 1950-64, reader, 1964-85, prof., 1985; assoc. prof. SUNY, Buffalo, 1967-68, Union Coll., Schenectady, N.Y., 1982-84, Ohio U., Athens, 1984-85, Allegheny Coll., Meadville, Pa., 1986-88, St. Lawrence U., Canton, N.Y., 1988-89; assoc. prof. math. Hampton (Va.) U., from 1989. Contbr. various articles to profl. jours. Recipient Fulbright Travel Grant, 1958. Mem. Am. Math. Soc., Math. Assn. Am., Indian Math. Soc. Hindu. Avocations: indian music, sanskrit language. Died Apr. 17, 2005.

VENDLER, ZENO, retired philosophy educator; b. Devecser, Hungary, Dec. 22, 1921; came to U.S., 1953; s. Zeno Miklós Vendler and Vilma Gubás; m. Helen Hennessy, May 21, 1960 (div. May 1964); 1 child, David; m. Semiramis da Silva, May 28, 1964; 1 child, Alexander. Sacrae Theologiae Licentia, Canisianum, Maastricht, The Netherlands, 1952; PhD, Harvard U., 1959. Asst. prof. Cornell U., Ithaca, N.Y., 1960-64; assoc. prof. Bklyn. Coll., 1964-65; prof. philosophy U. Calgary, Can., 1965-73, Rice U., Houston, 1973-75, U. Calif., San Diego, 1975-88, prof. emeritus, from 1988. Panelist Can. Coun., Ottawa, 1965-73, NEH, Washington, 1973-82. Author: Linguistics in Philosophy, 1967, Adjectives, 1968, Res Cogitans, 1972, Matter of Minds, 1984. Avocations: travel, geography. Died Jan. 13, 2004.

VERCESI, HAYDÉE MARGARITA CHACHA, biomedical scientist; b. Bahia Blanca, Argentina, Sept. 24, 1959; arrived in U.S., 1988; d. Hector Vercesi and Elisa Martinez; m. Frederick Chanyapate Lahser, May 13, 1995; 1 child, Christopher Arthur Lahser-Vercesi. Vet. physician degree, U. Nacional del Centro, Argentina, 1983; MSc, Tex. A&M U., 1994. Technician Tex. A&M U., College Station, 1988-90, tchg. asst., 1990-94; rsch. technician Ctr. Behavioral Neurosci., SUNY, Stony Brook, 1995-97; rsch. coord. Mt. Sinai Med. Ctr., N.Y.C., 1997-99; assoc. scientist Schering Plough Rsch. Inst., Kenilworth, N.J., from 1999. Campaign coord. Amnesty Internat., 1991—, Ronkonkoma, N.Y., 1998. Avocations: flag collecting, writing, music, reading, human rights activist. Home: Springfield, NJ. Died Jan. 10, 2004.

VERGARI, CARL ANTHONY, lawyer, former prosecutor; b. Yonkers, N.Y., Dec. 7, 1921; s. Frank and Teresa (Molinari) V.; m. Genevieve Louise Lindermann, June 21, 1922; children— Bohn C., Jeanne Vergari Martinelli. Student Fordham U., 1938-40; LL.B., St. John's U., 1948; LL.M., N.Y. U., 1952. Bar: N.Y. 1948, U.S. Supreme Ct. Asst. dist. atty. N.Y. County, 1948-58; chief counsel N.Y. State Commn. of Investigation, 1958-68; dist. atty. Westchester County, White Plains, N.Y., 1968-94; of counsel David E. Worby PC; mem. joint strike force council on organized crime US Dept. Justice, mem. exec. working group for fed.-state prosecutorial relations; Bd. dirs. Am. Com. on Italian Migration, 1976—; bd. dirs. Enrico Fermi Ednl. Fund of Yonkers, pres., 1973-75, mem. adv. bd. Nat. Obscenity Law Center; mem. Westchester County Youth Services Adv. Com., Westchester County Exec.'s Adv. Com. on Narcotics, 1968—. Served to capt. USMCR, 1941-45. Mem. Nat. Dist. Attys. Assn. (v.p. 1968, chmn. commn. on victim/witness assistance 1973-77, chmn. task force on ofcl. corruption 1978-80), N.Y. State Dist. Attys. Assn. (exec. com. 1968, pres. 1973-74), ABA, Westchester Bar Assn., Guild Cath. Lawyers. Died Oct. 15, 2006.

VICKERY, EUGENE BENTON, JR., lawyer; b. New Orleans, Nov. 23, 1936; s. Eugene Benton and Esther (Cleveland) V.; m. Anne Saunders Porteous, Aug. 25, 1961; children: Eugene Benton III, Saunders P., Ninette C., William A. AB, Williams Coll., 1962; JD, Loyola U., New Orleans, 1967. Bar: La. 1967, U.S. Dist. Ct. (ea. and we. dists.) La. 1967, U.S. Ct. Appeals (5th cir.) 1967. Supr. computer sys., sr. tech. programmer Shell Oil Co., New Orleans Data Ctr., 1962-67; jr. ptnr. Porteous, Toledano, Hainkel & Johnson, New Orleans, 1968-73; ptnr. Sutterfield & Vickery, New Orleans, 1974-82; sole practice New Orleans, from 1982. Procurator-adv. Met. Tribunal for Archdiocese of New Orleans. Trustee St. George's Epis. Sch., 1975-83, chmn., 1978-79; mem. La. Landmarks Soc., Met. Crime Commn., Uptown Neighborhood Improvement

Awsn., New Orleans and River Region C. of C. Served with U.S., 1956-59. Mem. ABA, La. Bar Assn., New Orleans Bar Assn., La. Assn. Def. Counsel, New Orleans Assn. Def. Counsel, Def. Rsch. Inst., Am. Judicature Soc., Am. Arbitration Assn. (panel of arbitrators 1968—), Notaries Assn. New Orleans, Boston Club, La. Club, Williams Club (N.Y.C.), Delta Phi. Republican. Roman Catholic. Died Apr. 29, 2004.

VIERECK, PETER R., poet, historian, educator; b. N.Y.C., Aug. 5, 1916; s. George S. and Margaret (Hein) V.; m. Anya de (Markov), June 1945 (div. May 1970); children: John-Alexis, Valerie Edwina Gibbs; m. Betty Martin (Falkenberg), Aug. 30, 1972. BS summa cum laude (hon.), Harvard U., 1937, MA, 1939; Henry fellow Christ Ch., Oxford U., Eng., 1937—38; PhD, Harvard U., 1942; LHD (hon.), Olivet Coll., 1959. Tchg. asst. Harvard U., 1941—42, instr. German lit., tutor history and lit. dept., 1946—47; instr. history U.S. Army U., Florence, Italy, 1945; asst. prof. history Smith Coll., 1947—48, vis. lectr. Russian history, 1948—49; assoc. prof. Modern European, Russian history Mt. Holyoke Coll., 1948—55, prof., 1955. Vis. lectr. Am. Culture Oxford U., 1953; Whittal lectr. in poetry Libr. of Congress, 1954, 63, 79; Fulbright prof. Am. poetry and civilization U. Florence, Italy, 1954-56; Elliston chair poetry lectr. U. Cin., 1956; vis. lectr. U. Calif., Berkeley, 1957; Disting. William R. Kenan prof. Mt. Holyoke Coll., 1979; charter mem. Council Basic Edn.; vis. poet Russian Am. cultural exchange program Dept. State, USSR, 1961; vis. rsch. scholar 20th Century Fund, USSR, 1962-63; vis. scholar Rockefeller Study Ctr., Bellagio, Italy, 1977; vis. artist and scholar Am. Acad., Rome, 1949-50, 78; dir. poetry workshop N.Y. Writers Conf., 1965-67; rsch. fellow Huntington Library, San Marino, Calif., 1978. Author: Metapolitics: From the Romantics to Hitler, 1941 Swedish edit., 1942, Italian, 1948, rev. edit., 2003, Terror and Decorum, poems, 1948, reprinted, 1972, Who Killed the Universe, novelette included in anthology New Directions Ten, 1948, Conservatism Revisited: The Revolt Against Revolt 1815-1949, (English edit, 1950), Strike Through the Mask, New Lyrical Poems, 1950, Towards a World Cmty., 1950, Mid-century Am. Poets, 1950, Arts in Renewal, 1951, reprinted, 1972, The New American Right, 1955, Edn. in a Free Soc., 1958, The Radical Right, 1962, Soviet Policy Making, 1967, Outside Looking In, 1972, The First Morning: New Poems, 1952, reprinted, 1972, Shame and Glory of the Intellectuals, 1953, rev. edit., 1965, reprinted 1978, Dream and Responsibility, The Tension Between Poetry and Society, 1953, The Unadjusted Man; a New Hero for Americans, 1956, reprinted, 1973, revised expanded edit, Conservatism: From John Adams to Churchill, 1956, reprinted, 1978, The Persimmon Tree, poems, 1956, Inner Liberty, The Stubborn Grit in the Machine, 1957, The Tree Witch: A Verse Drama, 1961, reprinted, 1973, Meta-politics, The Roots of the Nazi Mind, 1961, rev. expanded edit. 1965, Conservatism Revisited and The New Conservatives: What Went Wrong; rev. paperback edits., 1962, 65, reprinted hardcover, 1978, New and Selected Poems, 1932-67, 1967, A Question of Quality, 1976, Archer in the Marrow: The Applewood Poetry Cycles of 1967-87, 1987, The So. Calif. Anthology, 1987, rev. editions, 1987, 89, Decade: New Letters Anthology of the 80's, 1990, Tide and Continuities: Last and First Poems, 1995, Meta-politics: From Wagner and the German Romantics to Hitler, 2003, expanded edit., Unadjusted Man in an Overadjusted Age, 2004, Conservatism Revisited, 2004, expanded edit., Strict Wildness, 2005, Doorlast Poems, 2005, Conservative Thinkers: From John Adams to Churchill, 2005, Shames and Glory of the Intellectuals, 2006; contbg. essays and poems to popular magazines, and profl. journals, monograph on Conservatism in Ency. Brit., 1974. Sgt. U.S. Army, 1943-45, served in Africa and Italy. Decorated 2 battle stars; awarded Tietjens prize for poetry, 1948, Pulitzer prize for poetry, 1949; recipient Most Disting. Alumnus Award Horace Mann School for Boys, 1958, Poetry Translation Award Translation Center, Columbia U., 1978, Sadin poetry prize N.Y. Quar., 1977, Golden Rose Award New Eng. Poetry Club, 1981, Varoujan prize, 1983, New Eng. Poetry Club prize, 1998, Anne Sexton prize Agni mag., 1999; Guggenheim fellow, Rome, 1949-50; Rockefeller Found. rschr. in history Germany, summer 1958; NEH sr. rsch. fellow USSR, 1969; Mass. Artists Found. fellow, 1978. Mem. Am. Hist. Assn., Oxford Soc., Poetry Soc. Am., P.E.N., Phi Beta Kappa. Clubs: Harvard, N.Y.C. and London; Bryce, Oxford, Eng. Home: South Hadley, Mass. Died May 13, 2006.

VIGNALI, CARL LOUIS, avionics company executive; b. Merrill, Wis., July 10, 1934; s. Claude Fortineau and Irma Irene (Cottrell) V.; m. Virginia Clyde Richardson, July 9, 1955; children: Rosemary Vignali Woodhouse, Linda Vignali Guevares, Carl Renfroe. BS, Aurora (Ill.) U., 1956; MS, Auburn U., 1958. Physicist U.S. Costal Systems Ctr., 1958-60; tech. devel. staff Honeywell, 1960-66; space engr. IBM Fed. Systems, Apollo prog., 1966-69; tech. mgmt. staff Honeywell, 1969-72, 1974-83; with Med. Sci. Internat. Hosp. Automation, 1972-74; gen. mgr. Space and Strategic Avionics div. Honeywell Co., Clearwater, Fla., 1983-87; group v.p. Honeywell Space Systems, Clearwater, from 1987. Mem. Fla. High Tech. Industry Coun., Tallahassee, 1984—; vice chmn. Pinellas Edn. Found., Clearwater, 1987. Mem. AIAA, IEEE, Nature Conservancy, Fla. Wildlife Fedn. Republican. Adventist. Avocation: conservation. Home: Panama City, Fla. Died Jan. 3, 2005.

VIGRAN, STANLEY LOUIS, investment executive; b. Richmond, Ind., Mar. 9, 1926; s. Harry and Rose (Dobrow) V.; m. Joan Belle Hays, June 5, 1960; children: Gary Hays, Brad Steven, Richard Thomas, Ross Dobrow. BS, Miami U., Oxford, Ohio, 1947. Owner Harry Vigran & Sons, Richmond, from 1947. Bd. dirs. Bank One, Richmond, Ross Realty, Richmond, Md. Corp., Richmond, Northview, Inc., Richmond.; dir. Atlantis Submarine Hawaii L.P. Bd. dirs. Richmond Parks and Recreation, 1956-78, Young Mens Christian Assn., Richmond, 1977, Reid Hosp. Found., Wayne County Found., Wayne County Small Bus. Devel. Corp., Econ. Growth and Devel. Bd. Jewish. Died Dec. 3, 2004.

VILTER, RICHARD WILLIAM, SR., retired internist, educator; b. Cin., Mar. 21, 1911; s. William Frederick and Clara (Bieler) V.; m. Sue Potter, Aug. 17, 1935 (dec. Aug. 2003); 1 son, Richard William, Jr. (dec.). AB, Harvard U., 1933, MD, 1937. Diplomate Am. Bd. Internal Medicine. Intern, resident internal medicine Cin. Gen. Hosp., 1937-42, founding dir. divsn. hematology/oncology, 1945-56, asst. dir. dept. internal medicine, 1953-56, dir., 1956-78; assoc. prof. medicine U. Cin. Coll. Medicine, 1948-56, Gordon and Helen Hughes Taylor prof., 1956-78, prof. medicine on spl. assignment, 1978-81, prof. medicine emeritus, from 1981, asst. dean, 1945-51; ret., 1981. Cons. VA, 1947—; cons. hematology Good Samaritan Hosp., Cin.; cons. physician Christ, Drake hosps., Cin.; mem. sci adv. bd. Nat. Vitamin Found., 1953-56; spl. cons. nutritional anemias in Egypt WHO, 1954; cons. Pan Am. Sanitary Bur. Anemias of Kashiorkor in Guatemala and Panama, 1955; mem. Am. Cancer Soc. Com. on Investigation and Therapy of Cancer, 1960-64, chmn. 1964; chmn. hematology sect. NIH, 1965-69, chmn. nat. adv. com. anemia malnutrition Rsch. Ctr. Chiengmai, Thailand, 1967-75. Assoc. editor Jour. Clin. Investigation, 1951-52; contbr. to profl. publs. Recipient Joseph Goldberger award AMA, 1960, Daniel Drake medal U. Cin., 1985, Golden Apple award U. Cin., 1985, award for excellence U. Cin., 1990, Daniel Drake Humanitarian award Acad. Medicine, Cin., 1991, 1st recipient U. Cin. Coll. Medicine Lifetime Tchg. award, 1995, Great Living Cin. award Cin. C. of C., 2005; Richard W. and Sue P. Vilter endowed professorship U. Cin. Coll. Medicine est. and funded 1999. Master ACP (past gov. Ohio bd. regents, sec. gen. 1973-78, pres.-elect 1978-79, pres. 1979-80, pres. emeritus 1984, Laureat award Ohio chpt. 2002); mem. Federated Coun. for Internal Medicine (chmn. 1979-80), Clin. and Climatol. Assn. (v.p. 1982-83), Assn. Am. Physicians, Am. Soc. Clin. Nutrition (pres. 1960-61), Am. Soc. Clin. Investigation, Ctrl. Soc. Clin. Rsch. (coun. mem. 1957-60), Am. Soc. Hematology, Am. Bd. Nutrition, Internat. Soc. Hematology, Cin. Lit. Club (pres. 1990-91), Phi Beta Kappa, Alpha Omega Alpha, Nu Sigma Nu. Home: Cincinnati, Ohio. Died 2006.

VINCENT, AMOS JOSEPH, JR., priest; b. Lake Charles, La., Mar. 22, 1923; s. Amos Joseph and Rosa Felicia (Grove) V. BA in Philosophy, Notre Dame Sem., New Orleans, 1946; B Canon Law, Cath. U. Am., Washington, 1954; MA in Psychology, North Tex. State U., Denton, 1973; PhD in Clin. Psychology, U. Ottawa, Ont., Can., 1975. Ordained priest Roman Cath. Ch., 1949. Assoc. pastor St. John Cathedral Parish, Lafayette, La., 1949-53; vice chancellor, bishop's sec. Diocese of Lafayette, 1954-67, presiding judge on ch. ct. annulments, 1954-67. Mem. S.W. La. Mental Health Adv. Bd., La. State Office Mental Health, Lake Charles, 1981-95. Author: A Perceptual Approach to the Rorschach Shading Responses, 1981. Bd. dirs. Samaritan Counseling Ctr., Lake Charles, 1987-94; knight comdr. Equestrian Order of Holy Sepulchre of Jerusalem, Vatican City, 1981; knight of grace Constantinian Order of St. George of Royal House of Borbon-Two Sicilies, Naples, Italy, 1994. Named Papal Chamberlain, The Holy See, Vatican City, 1961, Hon. Prelate, 1966, Protonotary Apostolic, 1998. Mem. AAAS, Canon Law Soc. Am. Avocations: arranging music, heraldry design, reading history of central and eastern europe, researching family genealogy. Home: New Iberia, La. Died July 18, 2005.

VIZCAINO, HENRY P., mining engineer, consultant; b. Hurley, N.Mex., Aug. 28, 1918; s. Emilio D. and Petra (Perea) V.; m. Esther B. Lopez, Sept. 16, 1941; children: Maria Elena, Rick, Arthur, Carlos. BS in Engring., Nat. U., Mexico City, 1941; geology student, U. N.Mex., 1951-54. Registered profl. engr. With Financiera Minera S.A., Mexico City, 1942-47; gen. mgr. Minas Mexicanas S.A., Torreon, Mex., 1947-51; exploration engr. Kerr McGee Corp., Okla., 1955-69; cons. Albuquerque, 1969-75 and from 84; regional geologist Bendix Field Engring., Austin, Tex., 1976-79, staff geo-scientist Grand Junction, Colo., 1979-81; sr. geologist Hunt Oil Co., Dallas, 1981-84. Contbr. articles to profl. publs. Mem. AIME, Internat. Platform Assn., Aircraft Owners and Pilots Assn., Rotary, Elks. Republican. Congregationalist. Died Jan. 31, 2004.

VLISSIDES, JOHN MATTHEW, computer scientist; b. Washington, Aug. 2, 1961; s. Matthew John and Sophia (Drakoulis) V.; m. Dru Ann Miller, Nov. 14, 1992; children: Matthew, Helen (dec.), Mark, Robert BSEE, U. Va., 1983; MSEE, Stanford U., 1985, PhD in Elec. Engring., 1990. Post-doctoral scholar Stanford (Calif.) U., 1990-91; rsch. staff mem. IBM Rsch., Hawthorne, 1991—2005. Cons. Fujitsu Inc., San Jose, Calif., 1988-91, Hewlett-Packard, Sunnyvale, Calif., 1990-91, ABB, Mannheim, Germany, 1991; mem. industry adv. bd. IBM, Snoqualmie Falls, Wash., 1994. Co-author: Design Patterns, 1995, Object Oriented App Frameworks, 1995; columnist C++ Report. Named to The IBM Acad. Tech., 1998; recipient Chairperson's prize, U. Va., 1983, IBM Tech. Achievement award, 1996. Mem. Tau Beta Pi, Eta Kappa Nu. Avocations: music, cooking, creative writing. Home: Mohegan Lake, NY. Died Nov. 24, 2005.

VODERBERG, KURT ERNEST, machinery sales company executive; b. Rendsburg, Germany, Apr. 8, 1921; s. Max Henry and Margarethe (Siedel) V.; m. Louise Collier, May 21, 1948 (div. 1969); children: Paul, John, Mary Beth, Jill; m. 2d, Sophie Dufft, Sept. 5, 1969. B.S. in M.E., Ill. Inst. Tech., 1943; postgrad. Northwestern U., 1944-45. Registered profl. engr., Ill. Asst. master mechanic Danly Machine Co., Cicero, Ill., 1943-47; pres. Dynamic Machine Co., Chgo., 1947-75, pres. Dynamic Machinery Sales, Inc., Chgo., 1975-90, chmn. bd. dirs., 1990—. Mem. Ill. Soc. Profl. Engrs., Soc. Mfg. Engrs., Tooling & Mfg. Assn. Presbyterian. Clubs: Michigan Shores, American Turners, Glenbrook Shrine. Lodge: Masons. Patentee in field. Home: Wilmette, Ill. Died Apr. 19, 2004.

VOEGE, JEAN, nursing educator; b. Carroll, Iowa, Aug. 14, 1960; d. Harold Otto and Phyllis Elaine (Mueller) Voege; m. David Salisbury, May 30, 1987 (div.). Diploma, Bishop Clarkson Sch. Nursing, Omaha, 1981; BSN, Bishop Clarkson Coll., 1984; MSN, Clarkson Coll., Omaha, 1995. Cert. in med.-surg. nursing. Critical care staff nurse Bishop Clarkson Hosp., Omaha, 1981—82, Bergan Mercy Hosp., Omaha, 1982—86, Immanuel Med. Ctr., Omaha, 1986—88; program devel. specialist profl. devel. div. Clarkson Coll., Omaha, 1988—94; faculty Met. C.C., Omaha, 1994—95, N.W. Coll., Powell, Wyo., 1995—2001, Lane C.C., Eugene, Oreg., from 2001. Bd. dirs. Lions Eye Bank of Nebr. Coord. community wide critical care awareness health fair, 1989. Mem. ANA, AACN, Nebr. Nurses Assn. Home: Springfield, Oreg. Died Feb. 14, 2006.

VOGEL, RICHARD WIEDEMANN, business owner, ichthyodynamicist, educator; b. N.Y.C., Apr. 12, 1950; s. Jack and Edna Jeanne (Wiedemann) V.; m. Pamela Jane Gordon, Aug. 7, 1974; children: Amy Jane, Katy Lynn, Gina Marie, Krista Jeanne. Postgrad. Owner, operator ichthyol. rsch. and comml. fishing vessel, Santa Barbara, Calif., 1973-88; designer advanced hydrodynamic curvature Clark Foam Factory, Laguna Beach, Calif., from 1994. Lectr. Surfrider Found. Conf., U. Calif., San Diego, 1994. Inventor in field. Episcopalian. Avocations: music, athletic tng. and fitness. Home: Princeville, Hawaii. Died May 2, 2005.

VOGELEY, CLYDE EICHER, JR., engineering educator, artist, consultant; b. Pitts., Oct. 19, 1917; s. Clyde Eicher and Eva May (Reynolds) V.; m. Blanche Wormington Peters, Dec. 15, 1947; children: Eva Anne, Susan Elizabeth Steele. BFA in Art Edn., Carnegie Mellon U., 1940; BS in Engring. Physics, U. Pitts., 1944, PhD in Math., 1949. Art supr. Pub. Sch. Sys., Spingdale, Pa., 1940—41; rsch. engr. Westinghouse Rsch. Labs., East Pittsburgh, Pa., 1944—54; adj. prof. math. U. Pitts., 1954—64; sr. scientist Bettis Atomic Power Lab., West Mifflin, Pa., 1956—59, supr. tech. tng., 1959—71; mgr. Bettis Reactor Engring. Sch., West Mifflin, 1971—77, dir., 1977—92; cons. U.S. Dept. Energy, Washington, 1992—95. Cons. Bettis Atomic Power Lab., W. Mifflin, 1954-56; U.S. Navy Nuclear Power Schs., Mare Island, Calif., Bainbridge, Md., 1959-69. Author: (grad. sch. course) Non-linear Differential Equations, 1954; (rev. text) Ordinary Differential Equations, Rev. edit. 5, Shock and Vibration Problems, Rev. Edit. 6, 1991; rsch. report distributed to Brit., Can. and U.S. Govts. for use in design of airborne radar systems, 1944; oil painting represented in permanent Latrobe collection; acrylics, water colors and Christmas card designs in several pvt. collections; oil painting included in Barbara H. Nakle's A Unique Vision of Art, 1997, water color included in collection Superior Ct. of Pa. 1999. Pres., trustee Whitehall (Pa.) Pub. Libr., 1985. Recipient letter of commendation naval reactors br. USN, 1992. Mem. IEEE (life), Am. Phys. Soc., Assoc. Artists Pitts. (hon.), Pitts. Watercolor Soc., Sigma Xi, Sigma Pi Sigma, Sigma Tau. Presbyterian. Achievements include patents for Automatic Continuous Wave Radar Tracking System, Modulating Signals Passing Along Ridged Waveguides, Ridged Waveguide Matching Device, Method for Joining Several Ridged Waveguides, Antenna Feed Modulation Unit, others. Home: Beaver, Pa. Died Feb. 23, 2006.

VOLPE, KENNETH RALPH, accountant; b. Millville, N.J., Feb. 17, 1945; s. James Romeo and Angeline (Delbuono) V.; m. Rita Mary Badame, May 16, 1970; 1 child, Jamie Marie. BS in Econs., Villanova U., 1967. CPA, Pa., N.J. Sr. acct. Haskins & Sells, CPAs, Phila., 1967-70, Cherry Hill, N.J., 1970-76; pvt. practice Vineland, N.J., from 1976; v.p. fin. Friedrich & Dimmock, Inc., Millville, N.J., from 1991. Pres. Jaycees, Newfield, N.J., 1975. Mem. AICPA, Nat. Model Railroad Assn., Pa. Inst. CPAs, N.J. Soc. CPAs. Avocations: model railroading, railroad history, boating, classic autos. Home: Vineland, NJ. Died Mar. 27, 2005.

VONDERSMITH, BERNARD JOSEPH, association executive; b. Balt., Dec. 4, 1943; s. Thomas L. Sr. and Margaret A. (Ritmiller) V.; m. Mary Jo Matricciani, June 18, 1966; children: Laurie Anne, Amy Lynne, Bridget Mary. AB in English, Loyola Coll., Balt., 1965; MA in English, Duquesne U., 1967, PhD English Renaissance, 1971. Prof. English Ind. State U., Terre Haute, 1968-79; asst. to commr. State Bd. for Higher Edn., Annapolis, Md., 1980-83; exec. dir. Associated Utility Contractors Md., Inc., Balt., 1981-89;

exec. v.p. Mech. Contractors Assn. Md., Inc., Towson, Md., from 1983; exec. dir. Masonry Inst. Md., Inc., Balt., from 1985. Co-editor: Contemporary Thought on Edmund Spenser, 1975; co-author: A Reference Guide to Edmund Spenser, 1984. Trustee Community Coll. Balt., 1985-88; chmn. annual giving, Towson State U., 1987-89. Mem. Am. Soc. Assn. Execs., Engring. Soc. Balt., AIA, Internat. Found. Employee Benefit Programs, Spenser Soc., Mencken Soc. Republican. Home: Timonium, Md. Died Aug. 12, 2005.

VON MEHREN, ARTHUR TAYLOR, lawyer, educator; b. Albert Lea, Minn., Aug. 10, 1922; s. Sigurd Anders and Eulalia Marion (Anderson) von M.; m. Joan Elizabeth Moore, Oct. 11, 1947; children: George Moore, Peter Anders, Philip Taylor. S.B., Harvard U., 1942, LL.B., 1945, PhD, 1946; Faculty of Law, U. Zurich, 1946-47; Faculte de Droit, U. Paris, 1948-49; Doctor iuris (h.c.), Katholieke U., Leuven, 1985, U. Pantheon-Assas, Paris, 2000. Bar: Mass. 1950, U.S. Dist. Ct. Mass. 1980. Law clk. U.S. Ct. Appeals (1st cir.), 1945-46; acting chief legislation br., legal div. Occupation Mil. Govt. U.S.,Germany, 1947-48, cons. legal div., 1949; asst. prof. law Harvard U., 1946-53, prof., 1953-76, Story prof., 1976-93, prof. emeritus, 1993—2006, dir. East Asian legal studies program, 1981-83. Tchr. Salzburg Seminar in Am. Studies, summers 1953, 54; Fulbright rsch. prof. U. Tokyo, Japan, 1956-57, Rome, Italy, 1968-69; cons. legal studies Ford Found., New Delhi, 1962-63; vis. prof. U. Frankfurt, summer 1967, City Univ. Hong Kong, 1995; Ford vis. prof. Inst. Advanced Legal Studies, U. London, 1976; assoc. prof. U. Paris, 1977; Goodhart prof. legal sci. U. Cambridge, 1983-84, fellow Downing Coll., 1983-84, hon. fellow, 1984-2006; fellow Wissenschaftskolleg zu Berlin, 1990-91. Author: The Civil Law System: An Introduction to the Comparative Study of Law, 1957, 2d edit. (with J. Gordley), 1977, Law in the United States: A General and Comparative View, 1988, (with D.T. Trautman) The Law of Multistate Problems: Cases and Materials on the Conflict of Laws, 1965, (with S. Symeonides and W. Perdue) Conflict of Laws: American, Comparative, International, 1998, 2d edit., 2003, (with T. Varady, J. Barcelo) International Commercial Arbitration, 1999, 2d edit., 2002, Theory and Practice of Adjudicatory Authority in Private International Law: A Comparative Study of the Doctrine, Policies and Practices of Common- and Civil-Law Systems, 2002 (Canada Prize Internat. Acad. Comparative Law), Hague Academy of International Law, Collected Courses, Vol. 295; mem. editl. bd. Am. Jour. Comparative Law, 1952-86; contbr. articles to profl. jours.; editor: Law in Japan-The Legal Order in a Changing Soc., 1963; mem. editl. com. Internat. Ency. Comparative Law, 1969-2006. Mem. U.S. Del. Hague Conf. pvt. internat. law, 1966, 68, 76, 80, 85, 93, 96, 2001. Decorated Order of the Rising Sun with golden rays (Japan); Guggenheim fellow, 1968-69; inst. fellow Sackler Inst. Advanced Studies, 1986-87. Mem. ABA (Leonard J. Theberge Award for Pvt. Internat. Law 1997, Sect. of Internat. Law and Practice), Am. Acad. Arts and Scis., Institut de Droit Internat., Japanese Am. Soc. Legal Studies, Am. Soc. Comparative Law (bd. dirs., former pres.), Am. Soc. Polit. and Legal Philosophy, Phi Beta Kappa. Home: Cambridge, Mass. Died Jan. 16, 2006.

VON MOLTKE, KONRAD, environmental policy educator; b. Kreisau, Schweidnitz, Germany, Sept. 23, 1941; came to U.S, 1984; s. Helmuth James and Freya V. M.; children: Johannes, Dorothea, Daniel, Jakob. BA, Dartmouth Coll., 1964; PhD, U. Göttingen, 1970. Asst. prof. history SUNY Buffalo, 1968-72, assoc. prof. history, 1972-74; dir. Inst. European Environ. Policy, Bonn, Paris, London, 1970-84; sr. fellow World Wildlife Found., Washington, 1984-99, Internat. Inst. Sustainable Devel., Winnipeg, Man., Can., from 1994. Dir. collegiate assembly SUNY Buffalo, 1970-72; adj. prof. environ. studies Dartmouth Coll., Hanover, N.H., 1984—; vis. prof. Inst. Environ. Studies, Free U., Amsterdam, 1996—. Author: Leopold von Ranke: The Theory of Practice of History, 1973, Bausteincurriculum Amerikakunde, A modular curriculum for teaching American Studies in German high schools, 1974-76, Arbeitsbuch Amerikakunde, 1976, Educational Leave for Employees, European Experience, 1977, The Maastricht Treaty and the Winnipeg Principles on Trade and Sustainable Development, 1994, International Environmental Management, Trade Regimes and Sustainability, 1995; co-author: Public Policy for Chemicals. National and International Issues, 1980, Global Product Chains: Northern Consumers, Southern Producers, and Sustainability, 1998; rapporteur O.E.C.D. Revs. Nat. Policies Edn.: Norway, 1976; examiner O.E.C.D. Revs. Nat. Policies Edn.: Austria, 1975; prin. drafter The World Trade Orgn. and Sustainable Devel.: An Ind. Assessment, 1996; writer numerous tech. reports; contbr. numerous articles to profl. jours.; book reviewer medieval history and environ. policy. Home: Norwich, Vt. Died May 19, 2005.

VON SCHMIDT, KATHERINE BARNES HORNBOGEN, mental health counselor, psychotherapist; b. Marquette, Mich., Aug. 21, 1928; d. Daniel Powell and Katherine Alison (Barnes) Hornbogen; children: Katherine Barnes Carlson, Georgiana Lee Paul. Student, U. Mich., 1946-49; BA, U. Miami, 1951; MA, U. So. Fla., 1975. Diplomate Nat. Bd. Cert. Counselors. Tchr. pvt. sch., Miami, Fla., 1955-57; rsch. asst. Cape Haze Marine Lab., Sarasota, Fla., 1963-69; cons., lectr. natural scis. Sarasota, 1968-75; pvt. practice, from 1975. Co-author Bull. Marine Sci., 1965; contbr. articles to profl. jours. Fellow Am. Orthopsychiat. Assn.; mem. AACD, Am. Mental Health Counseling Assn. Avocations: research in women's history, music, art, her grandchildren. Home: Sarasota, Fla. Died Nov. 16, 2004.

VOREACOS, SALLY A., social worker; b. Cleveland, Ohio, Feb. 16, 1929; d. William Ambrose Cahill and Laura Rebecca Bell; m. Paul Howard Voreacos, Dec. 15, 1951; children: Susan Ellicott, David Paul. BA cum laude, Radcliffe Coll., 1950; MSW, U. Md., 1968. LCSW Md., ACSW, NASW. Social worker VA Hosp., Balt., 1969—71; sr. social worker Johns Hopkins Hosp., Balt., 1975—90. Home: Lutherville Timonium, Md. Died May 8, 2005.

VORHOFF, GILBERT HAROLD, banker, consultant; b. New Orleans, Jan. 22, 1919; s. James Conrad and Lillie (Morosini) V.; m. Nadine Esther Robbert, June 10, 1942 (dec. Aug., 1974); children: Gilbert H. Jr., Robbert W., Gregory R., David C.; m. Brenda S. Braun, Aug. 24, 1984. BA in Econs., Tulane U., 1939, MA in Econs, 1941; cert. in Petroleum Engring., MIT, 1952. Export mgr. Internat. Lubricant Corp., New Orleans, 1942-48; v.p. petroleum divsn. Hemisphere Internat. Corp., New Orleans, 1948-57, pres., CEO, dir., 1957-65; chmn., CEO, owner Hemisphere Internat., New Orleans, from 1989; v.p. internat. divsn. Hibernia Nat. Bank, New Orleans, 1965-70, sr. v.p., 1970-89. Bd, commrs. New Orleans Pub. Belt R.R., 1974—, chmn. pres. 1980-82; pres., chmn. bd. dirs. New Orleans Bd. of Trade, Ltd., 1975—; mem. pres.'s coun. Tulane U., 1977-78; chmn. Mayor's Bus. Devel. Coun., New Orleans, 1978-84. Contbr. articles to profl. jours. and mags. Chmn., mem. Regional Export Expansion Coun., New Orleans, 1967-90; mem. Nat. Export Coun., 1969-71, New Orleans Food Ctr. Authority, 1978-85; mem. bd. vis. Tulane U., New Orleans, 1977-78; treas. La. Superport Authority, 1979-87; mem. long range planning coun. Tulane U., New Orleans. Mem. World Trade Club of New Orleans (Outstanding Mem. 1961, Hon. Life Mem. 1977), Tulane Alumni Assn. (past. pres. Hon. Life Mem. Bd. Dirs.), New Orleans-Brazil C. of C. (founder, first pres.), Japan-La. Assn. New Orleans (founder, first pres.), Phi Beta Kappa, Kappa Delta Pi (founder, first pres. Tulane chpt.). Presbyterian. Avocations: golf, travel, genealogy. Home: New Orleans, La. Died Dec. 24, 2004.

VOSBURGH, WILLIAM GEORGE, hobby and craft shop owner; b. Flint, Mich., May 30, 1925; s. Merle Joseph and Eda (Morgen) V.; m. June 15, 1946 (dec. Sept. 1987); children: William George Jr., Robert, Susan, Bruce, John, Nancy. PhD in Organic Chemistry, U. Del., 1956. Chemist E.I. Du Pont de Nemours and Co., Wilmington, Del., 1950-51, rsch. chemist, 1951-71, sr. rsch. chemist, 1971-82; owner, mgr. Vosburgh's Hobby and Craft Shops, West Chester, Pa., 1959-86, V.H.C. Corp., West Chester, Pa., 1986—2006. With AUS, 1943-48, PTO. Home: West Chester, Pa. Died Sept. 21, 2006.

VYBORNY, CARL JOSEPH, radiologist; b. Oak Park, Ill., Nov. 23, 1950; s. Ernest Joseph and Praxedes Felicia (Nowinski) V.; m. Terrieann Susin, Nov. 28, 1975; 1 child, Margaret. BS with highest distinc., U. Ill., Chgo., 1972; MS, U. Ill., Urbana, 1973; PhD, U. Chgo., 1976, MD with hons., 1980. Diplomate Am. Bd. Radiology. Fellow dept. physics U. Ill., Urbana, 1972-73; fellow dept. radiology U. Chgo., 1973-76, resident in radiology, 1980-84, asst. prof. radiology, 1984-85, clin. assoc. prof. radiology, 1985-2000, clin. prof. radiology, 2001—04; attending radiologist LaGrange (Ill.) Meml. Hosp., 1985—2002, former mem. bd. physicians practice group. Former mem. institutional rev. bd. LaGrange Meml. Hosp.; chmn. mammography com. Ill. Radiol. Soc.; former mem. early detection com. Am. Cancer Soc., Ill.; former mem. clin. rev. tng. com. Ctr. for Disease Control/Am. Coll. Radiology; spl. reviewer diagnostic radiology study sect. NIH, 1993; bd. dirs. Acad. of Radiology Rsch.; radiation protection adv. coun. State of Ill.; chmn. report com. on chest radiography Internat. Commn. Radiation Units and Measures. Contbr. articles to profl. jours. Recipient Eastman Kodak Sci. award, 1976, Itek award, Soc. Photographic Scientists and Engrs., 1979, Nels Stranford Meml. award, U. Chgo., 1980; Andrew W. Mellon Found. fellow, 1984. Fellow Soc. for Breast Imaging, Am. Coll. Radiology (mem. mammography accrditation com.), Am. Assn. Physicists in Medicine; mem. AMA, Radiol. Soc. N.Am., Chgo. Radiol. Soc. (resident sect. 1983-84, pres. 2000). Roman Catholic. Avocations: tennis, golf, astronomy. Home: Riverside, Ill. Died Mar. 20, 2004.

WADE, FAIRES PELTON, lawyer; b. Rockwall, Tex., Oct. 11, 1916; s. Henry M. and Lula Ellen (Michie) W.; m. Katherine Norrid, May 29, 1943; children: Julie Wade Greeley, Ellen Kay, Jennifer. LLB, SJD, Tex. U., 1940. Bar: Tex. 1939, U.S. Ct. Appeals (Fed. cir.) 1946. Dist. atty. Rockwall County, Tex., 1941-42; pvt. practice Nueces County, Corpus Christi, Tex., 1946 and from 52, asst. county atty., 1947-52. Capt. U.S. Army, 1942-46, ETO. Decorated Purple Heart, Prisoner of War medal. Mem. ABA, Nueces County Bar Assn., Corpus Christi Country Club. Democrat. Methodist. Avocations: golf, raising bird dogs, bird hunting. Died Sept. 30, 2004.

WADE, MALCOLM SMITH, chemist, chemical engineer; b. Owensville, Ind., June 3, 1923; s. Frank Eliot and Margaret (Smith) W.; m. Mary Lou Gurley, May 17, 1958; 1 child, Marvin Lee. AB in Chemistry, Ind. U., 1949, BS in Edn., 1950, AB in Social Sci., 1950; postgrad., U. Kans., 1960. Project chemist Gulf Oil Corp. AG Div., Pittsburg, Kans., 1959-66; start-up advising engr. Kuwait Chem. Fertilizer Co., Pittsburg, 1966; chief chemist, fin. mgr. Chinhae Chemn. Co., Chinhae, Korea, 1966-69; sr. project chemist Gulf Oil Corp., Shuiba, Kuwait, 1969-70; start-up chief chemist and engr. PIC, Gulf Oil Corp., Shuiba, 1970-72; tech. dept. mgr. Fertilizer Co. of Saudi Arabia, Dammam, 1973-76; LNG storage and sect. head ops. R.M. Huffington, Bontang, Indonesia, 1976-78; advisor, trainer P.T. Arun (Mobil Oil assignment), Lhukseu, Indonesia, 1978-83, engr. for LNG expansion, 1983-84, spl. project engr., 1984-86. Deacon Grace Presbyn. Ch., Jackson, Tenn. Home: Cedar Hill, Tex. Died May 31, 2004.

WAGENER, HOBART D., retired architect; b. Sioux Falls, S.D., May 10, 1921; s. Frank Samuel and Beatrice (Hobart) W.; m. Violet LaVaughn, Dec. 16, 1944; children: Diane Kay Wagener, Jeffrey Scott, Shaw Bradley. BArch, U. Mich., 1944. Registered architect, Colo. Draftsman Eggers & Higgins, Architects, N.Y.C., 1946-47, Pietro Belluschi, Architect, Portland, Oreg., 1947-50; designer James Hunter, Architect, Boulder, Colo., 1950-53; prin. Hobart D. Wagener Assocs., Boulder, 1953-77; prin. ptnr. Wagener Vander-Vorste, Architects, Boulder, 1977-86; ret., 1986. Mem. selection com. Colo. Supreme Ct., Denver, 1968-72. Co-author: The School Library, 1962; work pub. in Archtl. Record, Sunset mag., N.Y. Times, House Beautiful, 25 Years of Record Houses. Chmn. Boulder Planning Commn., 1966; pres. Boulder C. of C., 1971. Lt. (j.g.) USN, 1944-46, PTO. Named Outstanding Designer for past 50 yrs. Hist. Boulder, 1983; also numerous nat. and regional design awards. Fellow AIA (pres. Colo. 1973, Colo. Architect of Yr. award 1985, pres. award N. chpt. 1998), Lions (pres. Boulder 1965). Avocations: travel, golf. Died Sept. 30, 2005.

WAGNER, RICHARD (DICK WAGNER), retired professional sports team executive, athletics consultant; b. Central City, Nebr., Oct. 19, 1927; s. John Howard and Esther Marie (Wolken) W.; m. Gloria Jean Larsen, May 10, 1950; children— Randolph G., Cynthia Kaye. Student, pub. schs., Central City. Gen. mgr. Lincoln (Nebr.) Baseball Club, 1955-58; mgr. Pershing Mcpl. Auditorium, Lincoln, 1958-61; exec. staff Ice Capades, Inc., Hollywood, Calif., 1961-63; gen. mgr. Sta. KSAL, Salina, Kans., 1963-65; dir. promotion and sales St. Louis Nat. Baseball Club, 1965-66; gen. mgr. Forum, Inglewood, Calif., 1966-67; asst. to exec. v.p. Cin. Reds, 1967-70, asst. to pres., 1970-74, v.p. adminstrn., 1975, exec. v.p., 1975-78, gen. mgr., 1977-83, pres., 1978-83, Houston Astros, 1985-87; spl. asst. Office of Baseball Commr., 1988-93; asst. to chmn. Major League Exec. Coun., 1993-94. Pres. RGW Enterprises, Inc., Phoenix, 1978-97. Served with USNR, 1945-47, 50-52. Named Exec. of Yr., Minor League Baseball, Sporting News, 1958. Republican. Methodist. Died Oct. 5, 2006.

WAGNER, ROBERT PHILIP, geneticist, educator; b. Bronx, N.Y., May 11, 1918; s. Philip Joseph and Annette Victoria (Pavelka) Wagner; m. Margaret Lillian Campbell, June 12, 1947 (dec. Sept. 1987); children: Philip Campbell, James Robert, Ruth Annette. BSc, City Coll. N.Y., 1940; PhD, U. Tex., 1943. Tchg. fellow zoology U. Tex., 1940—43, instr. zoology, 1944, asst. prof. zoology, 1945—50, assoc. prof. zoology, 1950—56, prof. zoology, 1956—77, prof. emeritus zoology, 1977—99, emeritus prof. molecular genetics and microbiology, from 1999. Vis. prof. zoology dept. Ind. U., 1962; rsch. assoc. Calif. Inst. Tech., 1948, 51, 53, Nat. Cotton Coun., 1944—45; occasional lectr., vis. prof. U. Tex. Med. Br., 1977—82; vis. scientist Los Alamos Nat. Lab., 1975—76, cons. life scis. divsn., 1977—99; lectr. in field. Author: Genes and Proteins, 1975; author: (with HK Mitchell) Genetics and Metabolism, 1955, 1964; author: (with B. Judd, B. Sanders, and R. Richardson) An Introduction to Modern Genetics, 1980; author: (with H.E. Sutton) Genetics, A Human Concern, 1985; author: (with M. Maguire and R. Stallings) Chromosomes: A Synthesis, 1993; co-editor: (jours.) Biochem. Genetics, 1969—79; contbr. articles to profl. jours. Mem. panel on genetic biology NSF, 1961—64; mem. pre and post doctoral com. Nat. Rsch. Coun., 1962—63. Recipient Career award, NIH, 1962—77; fellow Nat. Rsch. Coun. fellow, Calif. Inst. Tech., 1946—47, Guggenheim fellow, U. Calif. Dept. Biochemistry, 1957—58. Fellow: AAAS; mem.: Tex. Genetics Soc. (Disting. Svc. award 1984), Am. Genetics Assn., Am. Soc. Biochemistry and Molecular Biology, Am. Soc. Naturalists, Soc. Study of Evolution, Genetics Soc. Am. (mem. Mendel centennial com. 1965, sec. 1965—67, v.p. 1970, pres. 1971, organizer, chmn. standing com. for maintenance of genetic stocks 1958—64). Achievements include research in linkage conservation in vertebrates; vertebrate evolution; genome and chromosome structure, function, and evolution. Home: Santa Fe, N.Mex. Died Mar. 3, 2004.

WAKEFIELD, ERNEST HENRY, research scientist; b. Vermilion, Ohio, Feb. 11, 1915; BS, U. Mich., 1938, MS, 1939, PhD, 1952. Instr. elec. engring. U. Tenn., 1939-42; assoc. physicist Mass. Inst. Tech., 1942, Manhattan Project/Univ. Chgo., 1943-46; pres. RCL Inc., 1946-62, RCL Calif. Inc., 1956-62, Linear Alpha Inc., 1962-78, Imported Interiors Inc., 1965-70; chmn. 3d World Energy Inst. Internat., from 1978, Internat. Inst. Mgmt. & Appropriate Tech. Emerging Nations, from 1981, Honors Press, Inc., from 1986; hon. prof. Cen. U. Ecuador, 1958. Dir., Atomic Industrial Forum, 1960-62; pres., Evanston Bd. Edn., 1966-67. Author: The Mystery of Fisherman's Reef, 1953, Nuclear Reactors for Industry and Universities, 1954, The Consumer's Electric Car, 1977, The Battle of Mobile Bay, 1987, The Lighthouse that Wanted to Stay Lit, 1992,

History of the Electric Automobile, Vol. 1, 1993. Sgt. U.S. Army, 1942-46. Avocations: reading, writing. Home: Evanston, Ill. Died Mar. 25, 2005.

WAKEMAN, FREDERIC EVANS, JR., historian, educator; b. Kansas City, Kans., Dec. 12, 1937; s. Frederic Evans and Margaret Ruth (Keyes) Wakeman; m. He Lea Liang; children: Frederic Evans III, Matthew Clark, Sarah Elizabeth. BA, Harvard Coll., 1959; postgrad., Institut d'Etudes Politiques, U. Paris, 1959-60; MA, U. Calif., Berkeley, 1962, PhD, 1965. Asst. prof. history U. Calif., Berkeley, 1965-67, assoc. prof., 1968-70, prof., 1970-89, Haas prof. Asian Studies, 1989—2006, dir. Ctr. Chinese Studies, 1972-79; humanities research prof., vis. scholar Corpus Christi Coll., U. Cambridge, Eng., 1976-77, Beijing U., 1980-81, 85. Acad. adviser U.S. Ednl. Del. for Study in China; chmn. Joint Com. Chinese Studies Am. Coun. Learned Socs./Social Sci. Rsch. Coun.; sr. adviser Beijing office NAS; pres. Social Sci. Rsch. Coun., 1986-89, chmn. com. on scholarly comm. with China, 1995-2000; dir. Inst. East Asian Studies, Berkeley, 1990-2001; vis. prof. U. Heidelberg, Germany, 2000; hon. prof. China People's U. Author: Strangers at the Gate, 1966, History and Will, 1973, The Fall of Imperial China, 1975, Conflict and Control in Late Imperial China, 1976, Ming and Qing Historical Studies in the People's Republic of China, 1981, The Great Enterprise: The Manchu Reconstruction of Imperial Order in 17th Century China, 1986, Shanghai Sojourners, 1992, Policing Shanghai, 1927-37, 1995, Shanghai Badlands, 1996, China's Quest for Modernization, 1997, Reappraising Republican China, 2000, Spymaster: Dai Li and the Chinese Secret Service, 2003. Harvard Nat. scholar, 1955-59; Tower fellow, 1959-60; Fgn. Area fellow, 1963-65; Am. Coun. Learned Socs. fellow, 1967-68; Guggenheim fellow, 1973-74; NRC fellow, 1985. Fellow: Am. Acad. Berlin; mem.: Shanghai Acad. Social Scis. (fgn.), Am. Philos. Soc., Am. Hist. Assn. (pres.), Am. Acad. Arts and Scis. Home: Lake Oswego, Oreg. Died Sept. 14, 2006.

WAKSBERG, JOSEPH, statistical company executive, researcher; b. Kielce, Poland, Sept. 20, 1915; s. Harry and Anna (Kalichstein) W.; m. Roslyn Karr, Dec. 25, 1941; children: Arlene, Mark. BS, CCNY, 1936; postgrad., NYU, 1936-37, Am. U., 1941-43. Project dir. WPA, Phila., 1938-40; assoc. dir. stats. U.S. Bur. Census, Washington, 1940-73; chmn. Westat, Inc., Rockville, Md. Tchr. U. Mich., Ann Arbor, 1968-75; statis. cons. CBS, N.Y.C., 1967-90, UN, 1975-81, Voter News Svc., N.Y.C., 1992-96. Editor: Telephone Survey Methodology, 1988; assoc. editor Survey Methodology; contbr. articles to profl. jours. Mem. tech. adv. com. United Jewish Communities, N.Y.C. Recipient Gold medal U.S. Dept. Commerce, 1965. Fellow Am. Statis. Assn. (bd. dirs., chair several sects.); mem. Internat. Statis. Inst., Internat. Assn. Survey Statisticians (mem. coun. 1975-77). Home: Bethesda, Md. Died Jan. 10, 2006.

WALBRIDGE, WILLARD EUGENE, broadcasting executive; b. Republic, Pa., Mar. 11, 1913; s. Peter D. and Anna (Higbee) W.; m. Marietta H. Arner, Nov. 15, 1941; 1 child, Peter F. AB, U. Mich., 1936. Salesman, Sta. WWJ, Detroit, 1939-43; mgr. Sta. WWJ-TV, Detroit, 1946-53; exec. v.p., gen. mgr. Sta. WJIM AM-TV, Lansing, Mich., 1953-54, Sta. KTRK-TV, Houston, 1954-70; sr. v.p. corp. affairs Capital Cities Communications, Inc., 1970-78, cons., 1978-81; sr. cons. Hill & Knowlton, Inc., Houston, 1987—2006. Dir. Houston Lighting & Power Co., Houston Industries, Inc., 1975-83, Internat. Systems & Controls, Inc., Tex. Commerce Med. Bank. Pres., Greater Houston Community Found.; bd. dirs. Salvation Army, Houston Area council Boy Scouts Am., Houston Grand Opera Assn.; mem. nat. bd. govs. ARC, 1974-80, also bd. dirs. Houston chpt., 1965-83, chmn. Houston chpt., 1972-75; chmn. bd. TV Info. Office, N.Y.C., 1965-70; trustee Mus. Broadcasting, 1978-82. Served from ensign to lt. USNR, 1943-46. Decorated Silver Star. Mem. Maximum Service Telecasters (dir. 1971-81), Houston Assn. Community TV (dir. 1972-82), Internat. Radio and TV Fedn. (dir. 1969-76), Nat. Assn. Broadcasters (dir. 1965-70, chmn. bd. 1970-71), U.S. C. of C. (dir. 1975-81), Houston C. of C. (dir. 1971-83, chmn. bd. 1975-76), Houston Council Fgn. Relations (chmn. 1977-78) Died Mar. 3, 2006.

WALDEN, PHILIP MICHAEL, recording industry executive; b. Greenville, S.C., Jan. 11, 1940; s. Clemiel Barton and Carolyn Hayes (McClendon) W.; m. Peggy Hackett, Sept. 13, 1969; children: Philip Michael, Amantha Starr. AB in Econs., Mercer U., 1962. Pres. Phil Walden & Assocs., 1961, Capricorn Records, Inc., 1969—2006. Campaign chmn. Macon Muscular Dystrophy Assn., 1975; chmn. Macon Heritage Found.; mem. In-Town Macon Neighborhood Assn.; Mem. nat. finance com. Jimmy Carter for Pres.; mem. Com. for Preservation of the White House; mem. nat. adv. bd. NORML; bd. dirs. Brandywine Conservancy; mem. Presdl. Inaugural Com., 1977; trustee Ga. Trust for Historic Preservation., Mercer Univ. Press, Otis Redding Meml. Found.; founder Otis Redding Scholarship Fund, Mercer U., Phil Walden scholarship; bd. dirs. Atlanta Preservation Ctr., Otis Redding Found. Served to 1st lt. Adj. Gen. Corps AUS, 1963-65. Recipient Gold and Platinum Record awards, pub. awards; Big Bear award Mercer U., 1975; Martin Luther King, Jr. Humanitarian award, 1977; Human Relations award Am. Jewish Com., 1978 Mem. Common Cause, Middle Ga. Hist. Soc., Nat. Assn. Rec. Arts and Scis., Rec. Industry Assn. Am. (dir.), Nat. Assn. Rec. Merchandisers, Phi Delta Theta Alumni Assn., Atlanta Coll. of Art, Camp Sunshine, Ga. Trust for Historic Preservation, Capitol City Club. Home: Atlanta, Ga. Died Apr. 23, 2006.

WALDER, EUGENE, psychologist; b. Bronx, N.Y., Aug. 29, 1930; s. Max Benjamin and Shirley (Goldstone) W.; m. Loretta Berkowitz, June, 1954 (div. June 1975); children: Brian, Noeleen; m. Marjorie Jackson, Oct. 26, 1983. BBA, CCNY, 1952; MA, Columbia U., 1953, PhD, 1958. Lic. psychologist, N.Y. Psychologist Hofstra Coll., Hempstead, N.Y., 1958-60, Roslyn (N.Y.) Pub. Schs., 1960-62; chief clin. psychologist Civic Ctr. Clinic, Bklyn., 1962-69; pvt. practice N.Y.C., from 1960. Founder, dir. Psychotherapies Selection Svc., N.Y.C., Inst. for Integrated Tng. in Psychotherapy, N.Y.C., 1989-92; instr. Columbia U., N.Y.C., 1958-60, Fairfield (Conn.) U., 1973-75; cons. Hartford (Conn.) Parole Dist., 1974-75. Contbr. articles to profl. jours. Mem. Beta Gamma Sigma, Kappa Delta Pi. Jewish. Avocations: Karate, Aikido. Home: New York, NY. Died Sept. 26, 2004.

WALDMAN, NAHUM MAYER, Bible and Hebrew literature educator; b. Boston, July 6, 1931; s. Irving B. and Rose L. (Tucker) W.; m. Saula Rubenz, Dec. 27, 1957; children: Oren, Ethan, Ilana, Iscah. BA, Harvard U., 1952; MA, Jewish Theol. Sem., N.Y.C., 1957, PhD (hon.), 1987; PhD, Dropsie Coll., Phila., 1972. Ordained rabbi, 1957. Prof. Bible and Hebrew lit. Gratz Coll., Phila., from 1968. Rabbi various congregations, Phila., 1957—. Author: The Recent Study of Hebrew, 1989; editor: Community and Culture. Mem. internal rev. bd. Einstein Med. Ctr., 1980-95. Mem. Rabbinical Assembly Am., Bd. Rabbis. Jewish. Avocation: music. Home: Philadelphia, Pa. Died Mar. 17, 2004.

WALDRON, CLARENCE RAYMOND, JR., microbiologist, statistician, clergyman; b. Trenton, N.J., Jan. 27, 1940; s. Clarence Raymond and Hilda Gertrude (Dean) W.; m. Joan Lynn Grau, Jan. 6, 1968; children: Kathleen Marie, John David. AB, Rutgers U., 1961; MDiv, Phila. Div. Sch., 1964; MS, Rutgers U., 1971, PhD, 1985. Ordained priest Episcopal Ch. Rector St. John's Ch., Gibbsboro, N.J., 1964-72, St. James Ch., Edison, N.J., 1972-78; rsch. instr. Rutgers U., New Brunswick, N.J., 1980-83; rsch. microbiologist Campbell Soup Co., Napoleon, Ohio, 1983-86; mgr. sys. devel., safety, environ. issues and biometrics Campbell's Fresh, Inc. (formerly CAMSCO Produce Co., Inc.) div. Campbell Soup Co., Napoleon, 1986-91; dir. safety Campbell's Fresh, Inc. (formerly CAMSCO Produce Co., Inc.), Napoleon, 1991-93, dir. safety/tech./rsch. svcs., 1993-95; pres., dir. Claw Botanical Specialties. Contbr. articles to profl. jours. Pres. Gibbsboro Bd. Health, 1966-70; chmn. Juvenile Conf. Com., Gibbsboro, 1966-70; vicar St. Luke's Episcopal Ch., Van Wert, Ohio, 1985—; chaplin Starr Commonwealth Schs., 1993-98. Mem. Soc. Indsl. Microbiologists, Am. Soc. for Quality Control, N.J. Acad. Sci., Area Coun. for Tech. of N.W. Ohio (bd. dirs. 1986-88, co-dir. rsch. apprenticeships in sci. 1987-91), Fellowship of Ordained Scientists, Interdenominational Roundtable on Sci. and Religion, Sigma Xi. Achievements include patentee in cellulose degrading enzymes from thermophilic actinomycetes. Home: Albany, Ohio. Died Oct. 19, 2004.

WALKER, BILLY M., singer; b. Ralls, Tex., Jan. 14, 1929; s. Herbert Green and Baby Ruth (Dyess) W.; m. Bettie E. Crook, Feb. 6, 1978; children from previous marriage: Judy, Deana, Tina, Julie. Grad., Ralls H.S. Featured artist Big D Jamboree, Shreveport, 1949-51, Louisiana Hayride, Shreveport, 1952-55, Ozark Jubilee, Springfield, Mo., 1955-58, Grand Ole Opry, Nashville, from 1960; host Country Carnival TV Show, Nashville, 1968-70. Appeared on TV in Am. Swingaround, Dick Clarks's Am. Bandstand, Fandango, Jimmy Dean Show, Ozark Jubilee, Backstage At the Opry, Porter Wagoner Show, Prime Time Country, numerous others; Top Ten hits include Funny How Time Slips Away, Charlie's Shoes, Cross The Brazos at Waco, A Million and One, When A Man Loves A Woman, Sing Me A Love Song To Baby, Anything Your Heart Desires, Thank You For Calling, I've Got You On My Mind Again, Adam's Side The Wedding Song. Voted among Top 20 Most Played Artists for 20 Years, Billboard Mag. Died May 21, 2006.

WALKER, CORA THOMESINA, lawyer; b. Charlotte, N.C., June 20, 1926; d. William H. and Benetta (Jones) W.; m. Lawrence Randolph Bailey Sr., June 28, 1948 (div.); children: Lawrence Randolph Jr., Bruce Elliott. BS in Econs., Acctg., St. John's U., 1944, JD, 1946. Bar: N.Y. 1947, U.S. Dist. Ct. (so. dist.) N.Y. 1950, U.S. Dist. Ct. (ea. dist.) N.Y. 1951, U.S. Ct. Appeals (2nd cir.) 1976, U.S. Ct. Appeals (D.C. cir.) 1980. Pvt. practice, N.Y.C., 1954; mem. Doles, Sandifer & Walker, N.Y.C., 1954-58; ptnr. Doles & Walker, N.Y.C., 1958-60; gen. counsel Harlem River Consumers Coop., Inc., N.Y.C., 1969-76; sr. ptnr. Walker & Bailey, N.Y., 1976—99. Spl. counsel to joint subcom. on pub. welfare N.Y. State Legis., 1960-61; spl. dep. to Atty. Gen. N.Y. State. Gen. counsel Nat. Polit. Congress of Black Women, African Stock Exch. and Devel. Corp., Coalition of 100 Black Women, Inc., Assn. of Black Charities; mem. exec. com., gen. counsel to the Edler G. Hawkins Found.; bd. mem. TheaterWorks USA; mem. Citizen's Union; coord. Harlem Improvement Program; sec., treas. Mid-Eastern Co-ops., Inc., 1962-69; bd. dirs. Harlem YMCA, N.Y. State Polit. Workshops, Inc.; trustee UN Internat. Sch., vice-chmn., 1952-56. Recipient Outstanding Community Svc. award Women for Achievement, Hall of Fame Alumni award James Monroe High Sch., 1967, N.Y. Club Profl. award, 1969;, Malcolm X award, 1969, Gertrude Rush award Jud. Friends award. Mem. ABA, Nat. Bar Assn. (bd. of govs.), Nat. Bar. Assn., City Bar Assn. (mem. commn. on minorities), Nat. Assn. of RR Trail Counsels, Assn. of Bar of City of N.Y. (co-chmn. of gen. practice, sect. sub-com. on comml. law), N.Y State Bar Assn. (Ho. of Dels.), N.Y. County Lawyers Assn., Harlem Lawyers Assn. (past pres.). Home: New York, NY. Died July 13, 2006.

WALKER, JAMES E., academic administrator, educator; b. Phenix City, Ala. s. Curtis and Mamie (Milner) W.; m. Gwendolyn Pompey, Dec. 22, 1968; children: Jamell E., Jabrina E. BS, Ala. State U., 1963; MA, Atlanta U., 1967; EdD, Pa. State U., 1972; LhD, Mt. St. Mary's Coll., 1991. Chmn., tchr. Parks Jr. High Sch., Atlanta, 1967-69; instr. Western Mich. U., Kalamazoo, 1971; asst. prof. spl. edn. So. Ill. U., Edwardsville, 1972-74; exec. asst. to supt. Bryce Hosp., Tuscaloosa, Ala., 1975-77; chmn. spl. edn. Ill. State U., Normal, 1977-80; dean edn. Calif. State U., Hayward, 1980-87; v.p. provost U. No. Colo., Greeley, 1987-91; pres. Mid. Tenn. State U., Murfreesboro, 1991—2000, So. Ill. U., 2000—05. Adj. prof. U. Ala., Tuscaloosa, 1975-77; presenter in field. Author: Behavior Management: A Practical Approach for Educators, 1987, 5th edit., 1992. Commr. Boy Scouts Am., Nashville, 1992—; mem. Black Health Care Task Force, Nashville, 1992—. USDE/BEH fellow Pa. State U., 1969-72, State of Ga. Dept. Edn. fellow, 1966-67; recipient Outstanding Alumni award Ala. State U., 1986, Coll. Edn. Alumni award Pa. State U., 1988. Mem. AAUW, Am. Assn. Higher Edn., Rotary. Democrat. Roman Catholic. Avocations: reading, travel, golf. Home: Johnson City, Tenn. Died Feb. 5, 2006.

WALKER, JOHN SAMUEL, retired pediatrician; b. Brevard, N.C., June 25, 1921; s. Hugh Raven and Mary Jane (King) W.; m. Jean Lane Davis, June 9, 1945 (div. Mar. 1986); children: Virginia Davis, Hugh Raven, Samuel Vivian, Joseph Andrew, Jean Lane; m. Chieko Akahori, May 31, 1986; 1 child, Mary Jane Haruko Walker. BS, Wake Forest U., 1943; MD, Jefferson Med. Coll., 1946. Diplomate Am. Bd. Pediatrics. Resident in pediatrics Crawford W. Long Meml. Hosp., Atlanta, 1950-51, Children's Hosp., Cin., 1951-52; pvt. practice pediatrics Children's Med. Group, Atlanta, 1952-61; mgr. clin. rsch. Upjohn Co., Kalamazoo, Mich., 1961-67; v.p. med. affairs Riker Labs., Northridge, Calif., 1967-69; dir., sr. dir. clin. rsch. Merck Rsch. Labs., West Point, Pa., 1969-77, sr. dir. regulatory affairs, 1977-92; ret., 1992. Lt. (j.g.) Med. Corps USN, 1946-49. Fellow Am. Acad. Pediatrics, Am. soc. for Clin. Pharmacology and Therapeutics, Royal Soc. Medicine; mem. AMA. Republican. Episcopalian. Avocations: study of japanese language, collecting models of turtles and tortoises, walking. Home: Winston Salem, NC. Died Mar. 15, 2005.

WALL, MARK HENRY, surgeon; b. Superior, Wis., June 2, 1932; s. Mark Henry and Anna Stephana (Sokolnikoff) W.; m. Mary Thomasine Micetich, Dec. 26, 1954; children: Yvonne, Linda, Mark Jr., Stephen, Scott, Thomasine Ann. BS, U. Wis., 1954; MD, U. So. Calif., 1958. Diplomate Am. Bd. Surgery, Am. Bd. Thoracic Surgery. Intern L.A. County Hosp., L.A., 1958-59; resident in gen. surgery Harbor Gen. Hosp., Torrance, Calif., 1959-63; resident in thoracic surgery City of Hope Med. Ctr., Duarte, Calif., 1965-67; pvt. practice as thoracic surgeon Santa Barbara, Calif., 1967-73, Santa Fe, N.Mex., 1973-79, Auburn, N.Y., 1979-87, Cleve., 1989-91. Contbr. articles to profl. jours. Fellow ACS, Am. Coll. Chest Physicians; mem. Soc. Thoracic Surgeons, Soc. Clin. Vascular Surgery. Avocations: mountain climbing, skiing, bicycling, hiking, diving. Died July 20, 2005.

WALLACE, PAUL VINCENT, JR., hospital administrator; b. N.Y.C., Jan. 3, 1934; s. Paul Vincent and Rosemary (Zimmer) W.; m. Joan Pinette (div. Apr. 1965); 1 child, Laura; m. Sharon Hull (div. Aug. 1980); children: Frank Randall, Stephanie Diane, Paul Vincent III. BA, Columbia Coll., 1956; PA, U. Md., 1960. V.p. Cook-Ft. Worth Children's Med. Ctr., from 1963. Adv. bd. Community Outreach Ctr., Ft. Worth, 1989-91. Bd. dirs. Camp Sanguinity, Ft. Worth, 1981-91; bd. dirs. N.E. chpt. Cystic Fibrosis Found., 1981-91, McDonald House, 1981-91. Staff sgt. USAF, 1956-60. Recipient Pres. award Cystic Fibrosis Found., Dallas, 1988, Angie Surina award, Ft. Worth, 1989. Mem. Frog Club. Democrat. Roman Catholic. Avocations: opera, gardening. Home: Fort Worth, Tex. Died May 11, 2005.

WALLACE, ROBERT BRUCE, minister; b. Phoenix, Aug. 28, 1933; s. Samuel S. and Mildred (Butterbaugh) W.; m. Donna J. Sutton, June 28, 1957 (div. May 1980); m. Peggy Ruth Riggins, June 19, 1981; children: Lynn, Bonnie, David, Richard. BA, U. Redlands, 1955; MDiv, Am. Bapt. Seminary, Berkeley, Calif., 1958; STD, San Francisco Theol. Seminary, 1978. Ordained to ministry Bapt. Ch., 1958. Assoc. min. 1st Bapt. Ch., L.A., 1958-61; campus min. Ariz. State U., Tempe, 1961-65; min., univ. pastor University Bapt., State College, Pa., 1965-73; sr. min. 1st Bapt. Ch., Redlands, Calif., 1973-83, Ann Arbor, Mich., 1984-91, Melrose, Mass., from 1991. Chmn. Interfaith Counseling Svc., Ann Arbor, 1985-90, East Valley Area Health Coun., Redlands, 1980-82, Div. Christian Higher Edn., East Lansing, Mich., 1985-90; bd. dirs. North Am. Bapt. Peace Fellowship. Chmn. Housing Commn., Redland, 1982-83, Shelter Assn., Ann Arbor, 1988, Fair Housing, 1997, Am.-Bapt. Elder Ministries, 1998; active Housing Policy Bd., Ann Arbor, 1990-91, Human Rights Commn., Melrose, Mass. Recipient Citizen of Yr. award Social Workers Assn., Ann Arbor, 1987. Mem. Am. Bapt. Mins. Coun., Bapt. Joint Com. on Pub. Affairs, Am. Bapt. Campus Ministry Assn., Rotary. Democrat. Home: Worcester, Mass. Died June 7, 2004.

WALLACH, SHIRLEY SCHMONES (SHIRLEY SCHMONES), physician; b. N.Y.C., Nov. 29, 1920; d. Benjamin and Gertrude (Schwartz) Schmones; m. Morton B. Wallach, June 11, 1944 (div. 1971); children: Joelle Marsha, Lee Ann Wallach Saltzman. BA magna cum laude, NYU, 1941, MD, 1943; postgrad., Dartmouth Med. Sch., Taylor Manor Hosp., Mt. Sinai Sch. Medicine, So. Conn. State U. Diplomate Am. Bd. Psychiatry and Neurology, Am. Bd. Child Psychiatry. Intern The Jewish Hosp. of Bklyn., 1944; resident in internal medicine NYU, 1945-46; resident in psychiatry Hillside Hosp., Queens, N.Y., 1959-61; fellow in child psychiatry Mt. Sinai Hosp., N.Y.C., 1961-62, Albert Einstein Coll. Medicine, Bronx, N.Y., 1962-63; dep. unit chief Harlem Valley Psychiat. Ctr., N.Y., 1981-82; psychiatrist Queens Children's Hosp. Ctr., 1982-85; psychiatrist II Creedmoor State Hosp., 1985-86; sch. psychiatrist City of N.Y. Bd. Edn.; pvt. practice N.Y.C. and Forest Hills, N.Y., 1946-86. Attending physician NYU-Bellevue Hosp., N.Y.C., 1946—, Beth Israel Hosp., N.Y.C., 1948, Mt. Sinai Hosp., N.Y.C., 1968; cons. psychiatrist Menorah Hosp., Ottilie Home for Children, 1963-64, Child Devel. Ctr.; supervising psychiatrist S.I. Children's Hosp.; dir. adolescent unit Fair Oaks Hosp., Summit, N.J., 1977-78; coord. resident tng. program dept. psychiatry divsn. child psychiatry Mt. Sinai Hosp., N.Y.C., 1963-77, Elmhurst Hosp., N.Y.C.; instr. Hunter Coll., N.Y.C., 1949-52; cardiac cons. N.Y.C. Dept. Health; asst. clin. prof. dept. psychiatry Mt. Sinai Sch. Medicine Appointment, 1969. Contbr. articles to profl. jours. Fellow Am. Psychiat. Assn., Am. Acad. Child Psychiatry, Acad. Psychosomatic Medicine, Am. Geriatrics Soc.; mem. AMA, Am. Med. Writers' Assn., Am. Assn. Psychiat. Clinics for Children, N.Y. Acad. Scis., Hastings Inst. Soc., Ethics and Life Scis. Died Dec. 10, 2004.

WALLIS, THOMAS LEE, librarian; b. Baldwyn, Miss., Feb. 7, 1942; s. William Isom and Mary Irene (Snell) W. AS, N.E. Miss. Jr. Coll., Booneville, 1963; BA, William Carey Coll., 1965; MEd, U. Miss., 1978; postgrad., U. So. Miss., 1992. Cert. tchr., sch. adminstr., libr. Tchr. Cherokee County Schs., Woodstock, Ga., 1965-67, Douglas County Schs., Douglasville, Ga., 1967-71, Prentiss County Schs., Booneville, Miss., 1971-73, Union County Schs., New Albany, Miss., 1973-75; adminstrv. staff N.E. Miss. C.C., Booneville, 1975-82, instr., 1982-91, libr., from 1991. Editor: Prentiss County History, 1984; author: The History of Mt. Olive Baptist Church, 1993; contbr. Union County History, 1991; contbr. articles to profl. jours. Mem. Miss. Libr. Assn., Miss. C.C. Faculty Assn., Nat. Soc. SAR (Liberty medal 1991), Nat. Soc. Sons Confederate Vets., Nat. Congress Patriotic Orgns., Clan Stewart Soc. Am., Inc. Republican. Baptist. Avocations: travel, genealogy, antiques. Home: Baldwyn, Miss. Died Aug. 30, 2004.

WALLS, CHARLES GREY, oil company executive; b. Ft. Worth, Tex., Apr. 8, 1946; s. Charles Reinhart and Sara Louise (Fishback) W.; m. Linda Rose Turo, June 15, 1968; children: Geoffrey, Christopher. BS in Chemistry, Tex. Christian U., Ft. Worth, 1968; MS in Mgmt., U. So. Calif., L.A., 1973. Chemist Shell Oil-Deer Park Complex, Houston, 1968-69, sr. environ. engr., 1973-78, process mgr. lubes, 1978-80; mgr. quality assurance and environ. control Shell Oil - Wood River (Ill.) Complex, 1980-83; mgr. tng and adminstrn. Saudi Petrochem., Houston, Al-Jubail, 1983-84; environ. support mgr. Shell Oil Co., Houston, 1984-87, mgr. pub. affairs mfg., 1987-91, mgr. compliance assessment, health, safety and environ., from 1992. Capt. USAF, 1969-73. Mem. Environ. Auditing Roundtable, Chem. Mfg. Assn. (chmn. crisis mgmt. 1991—, com. pubished guidelines Crisis Mgmt.). Republican. Methodist. Avocation: golf. Home: Houston, Tex. Died Jan. 20, 2004.

WALSH, MICHAEL JOSEPH, marketing research executive; b. Phila., Oct. 11, 1935; s. Michael Joseph and Katherine Theresa (Maguire) W.; m. Neva E. Menear, Mar. 2, 1962; children: Laura, Kathryn, Michael, Patricia, Caroline. BS in Econs., Villanova U., 1957. Account exec. Rambo, Close & Kerner, Phila., 1959-67, Suplee Mosley, Inc., Phila., 1967-69, asst. sales mgr., 1969-75; v.p., sales mgr. Boenning & Scattergood, Inc., Phila., 1975-78, v.p., dir. research and mktg., from 1978. Contbr. articles on stock market to newspapers and radio commentary. Bd. dirs. Radnor Twp. Mcpl. Authority, Wayne, Pa., 1986, Bryn Mawr (Pa.) Fire Co., 1986. Served as cpl. USMCR, 1957-58. Mem. Securities Industry Assn. (sales mktg. com.), Phila. Securities Com. (bd. dirs. 1986). Clubs: Aronomink Golf (Newton Sq., Pa.) (bd. dirs. 1981—); Bachelors Barge (Phila.). Lodges: Kiwanis (pres. Bryn Mawr chpt. 1972, lt. gov. 21st dist., Pa., 1975). Republican. Roman Catholic. Avocations: golf, writing. Home: Villanova, Pa. Died Dec. 31, 2005.

WALSH, STEVEN M., lawyer, municipal official; b. New Bedford, Mass., June 4, 1960; s. Thomas P. and Patricia A. W.; m. Mariann, May 5, 1984; children: Kate Angela, Brendan Daniel. BS, Bridgewater State Coll., 1983; JD, New Eng. Sch. Law, 1989. Bar: U.S. Dist. Ct. Mass. 1990, U.S. Ct. Appeals 1995, U.S. Supreme Ct. 1998. Corrections officer Plymouth County Sheriff's Dept., Plymouth, Mass., 1983-89, asst. dep. supt., 1990-94, gen. counsel Mass., from 1994; city councilor City of Fall River (Mass.), from 1996. Paralegal instr. Kinton-Campbell Bus. Sch., Brockton, Mass., 1990-96; police acad. instr. Mass. Criminal Justice Tng. Coun., Plymouth, 1990—; law instr. Mass. Sheriff's Assn. Contbr. articles to The Warrant newspaper. Vol. Michael's Fund, Fall River, 1997—, Thomas Guinta Meml. 5K Road Race, Fall River, 1997—; bd. dirs. Walsh Cup, 1991—; chmn. Econ. Devel. and Tourism Com., 1998—; mem. Pub. Safety, Legislation, Fin. Coms. Mem. Am. Correctional Assn., Nat. Sheriff's Assn., Southeastern Mass. Prosecutor's Assn., Irish Cultural Soc., Friendly Sons of St. Patrick. Avocations: rugby refereeing, ice hockey. Home: Fall River, Mass. Died Jan. 20, 2004.

WALSH, THOMAS JOSEPH, lawyer; b. Kansas City, Mo., Oct. 3, 1932; s. Thomas E. and Clare E. (O'Leary) W.; m. Ellen B. Butler; children: Carolyn, David, Kathy. AB, U. Mo., 1953; JD, Georgetown U., 1958. Bar: D.C. 1958, Mo. 1958. Sole practice, Lee's Summit, Mo., from 1958. Mem. 4th Congl. Dist. Youth Coun., 1985-92; vice chmn. Mo. Coun. on Criminal Justice, 1977-80, chmn., 1977-80; atty. to Jackson County Sheriff's Dept., 1967-72; sec. Jackson County Bd. Election Commrs., 1993-96, chmn. 1997-2001. Served to 1st lt. U.S. Army, 1953-55. Mem. Mo. Bar Assn., Assn. Trial Lawyers Am., Met. Kansas City Bar Assn., Knights of Columbus. Lodges: Optimists (lt. gov. 1963-64, pres. 1960-61). Democrat. Roman Catholic. Home: Lees Summit, Mo. Died July 1, 2005.

WALTERS, CANDACE REBECCA, counselor, educator; b. Suffolk, Va., Feb. 20, 1947; d. John Derward and Eula (Farrar) W. BA in History, Fisk U., 1968; MEd in Elem. Edn., U. Va., 1970; MEd in Counseling, Regent U., 1989. Aide Head Start, Suffolk, summer 1967, 68; tchr. Suffolk Pub. Schs., 1970-71, Fairfax (Va.) County Pub. Schs., 1971-92, counselor, from 1992. Singles leader United Pentecostal Ch. Arlington, 1992—. Home: Virginia Bch, Va. Died Mar. 20, 2005.

WALTERS, STEVEN CRAIG, school administrator; b. Burbank, Ariz., May 6, 1949; s. John Harrison Walters and Vivian (Organ) Mills; m. Ann Constance Thomas, Dec. 20, 1981; children: Daniel, John. BA, Occidental Coll., 1971; MS, Ariz. State U., 1983, EdD, 1985. Math. tchr. Willow Run Jr. High Sch., Ypsilanti, Mich., 1973-74; elem. tchr. Montrose Elem. Sch., Glendale, Calif., 1974-77; tchr. specialist Glendale Schs., 1977-79; math. tchr. Canyon High Sch., Newhall, Calif., 1979-81, Tempe (Ariz.) High Sch., 1981-87; math. coord. Paradise Valley Schs., Phoenix, 1987-88; elem. prin. Village Vista Elem. Sch., Phoenix, 1988-90; tchr. edn. coord. Prescott (Ariz.) Coll., from 1990. Mem. ASCD, Phi Delta Kappa (chpt. v.p. 1991-92). Home: Prescott, Ariz. Died Oct. 29, 2004.

WALTHER, JOSEPH EDWARD, health facility administrator, retired internist; b. Indpls., Nov. 24, 1912; s. Joseph Edward and Winona (McCampbell) W.; m. Mary Margaret Ruddell, July 11, 1945 (dec. July 1983); children: Mary Ann Margolis, Karl, Joanne Landman, Suzanne Conran, Diane Paczesny, Kurt. BS, MD, Ind. U., 1936; postgrad., U. Chgo., Harvard U., U. Minn., 1945-47; DSc (hon.), Ind. U., 1997, Purdue U., 1998. Diplomate Nat. Bd. Med. Examiners, Am. Bd. Internal Medicine, Am. Bd. Gastroenterology. Intern Meth. Hosp. and St. Vincent Hosp. of Indpls., 1936-37; physician, surgeon U.S. Engrs./Pan Am. Airways, Midway Island, 1937-38; chief resident, med. dir. Wilcox Meml. Hosp., Lihue, Kauai, 1938-39; internist, gastroenterologist Meml. Clinic Indpls., 1947-83, med. dir., pres., CEO, 1947—2005; founder, pres. Doctors' Offices Inc., Indpls., 1947—2005; founder, pres., CEO Winona Meml. Found. and Hosp. (now Walther Cancer Inst.), Indpls., 1956—2005. Clinical asst. prof. medicine Ind. U. Sch. Medicine, Indpls., 1948-93, clin. asst. prof. emeritus, 1993—. Author: (with others) Current Therapy, 1965; mem. edit. rsch. bd. Postgrad. Medicine, 1982-83; contbr. articles to profl. jours. Bd. dirs. March of Dimes, Marion County div., 1962-66, Am. Cancer Soc., Ind. div., 1983-92. Col. USAAF, 1941-47, PTO. Decorated Bronze Star, Silver Star, Air medal; named to Pres.'s Cir., Ind. U., 1999; recipient Disting. Alumni Svc. award, 2001, Sing the Heroes award, Ind. U. Sch. Medicine, 2001, Healthcare Heroes Award for Corp. Achievement in healthcare, 2002, Living Legend award, Ind. Hist. Soc., 2003. Mem.: AMA (del. 1970—76), Hoosier Hundred, Marion County Med. Assn., Ind. Med. Assn., Soc. Cons. to Armed Forces, Am. Coll. Gastroenterology (pres. 1970—71, master and charter, Weiss award 1988), Ind. U. Alumni Assn. (life), 702 Club, Indpls. Athletic Club, Waikoloa Golf and Country Club (Hawaii), Highland Golf and Country Club (hon.). Republican. Home: Indianapolis, Ind. Died Dec. 10, 2005.

WALTHER, RICHARD ERNEST, psychology educator, library administrator; b. Des Moines, Nov. 12, 1921; s. Rudolph Herman and Ruth Viola (Leekley) W.; m. Viola Eugenia Godwin, May 4, 1951; children: Mark Edward, Diane Elaine. Student, U. Ill., 1941-42; BA, Tex. Christian U., 1949-50, MA, 1950-52; EdD, North Tex. State U., Denton, 1954-62. Cert. Lifetime Teaching Credentials, Tex. Supt. Dallas Juvenile Home, 1951-61; v.p. rsch and devel. U.S. Industries, Ednl., N.Y.C., 1961-69; pres. Walther & Assoc., Silver Springs, Md., 1969-72; dir. of libr. Ambassador U., Pasadena, Calif., 1972-90, dir., instl. rsch. Big Sandy, Tex., 1990-92, assoc. dir. Coll. Libr., prof. psychology, 1992-96; prof. emeritus, from 1996. V.p. rsch. Humane Soc. of the U.S., Washington, 1968-70; tng. cons. Bell Telephone Labs., Piscataway, N.J., 1968-72. Author: Handling Behavior Problems, 1959. Mem. APA, Am. Ednl. Rsch. Assn. Avocations: photography, writing, research. Died Apr. 18, 2005.

WALTON, DAVID LEE, JR., automotive company official; b. Ironton, Mo., Aug. 26, 1953; s. David L. and Norma Ruth (McConnell) W.; m. Nancy Jane Berg, July 1, 1978; children: Brooke R., James R. BA, Drury Coll., 1975; postgrad., U. Mo., Kansas City, 1981-82. Counterman, bookkeeper A-1 Auto Parts, Springfield, Mo., 1975-76; computer coord. Genuine Parts Co. div. NAPA, Kansas City, Kans., 1976-78, field salesman, 1978-80, purchasing mgr., 1980-84, ops. mgr. St. Louis, 1984-87, Reliable Automotive Kans., Lenexa, 1987-89; div. mgr. ops. Relco Corp., Dallas, 1989-92; mgr. customer svc. Lincoln A Pentair Co., St. Loiuis, from 1993. Mem. adminstrv. and fin. coms. Park Hill Bapt. Ch., Kansas City, Mo., 1979-83, 87-89, mem. fin. com., Sunday sch. tchr. Matthew Rd. Bapt. Ch., Dallas, 1990-92. Mem. Internat. Material Mgmt. Soc., Motor Equipment Mfrs. Assn. (data processing com.), Automotive Wholesalers Assn. (data processing com., young exec. com.). Avocations: computers, reading, gardening, walking. Home: Saint Charles, Mo. Died Dec. 18, 2004.

WALTON, EDWARD HAZEN, academic administrator; b. Easton, Pa., Apr. 21, 1931; s. Edward Hazen and Nina Virginia (Kellam) W. m. Ruth E. Dow, Apr. 23, 1955; children: William E., Susan L. BS, U. Conn., 1953. Asst. office svcs. chief Bridgeport (Conn.) Brass Co., 1955-60; chief office svcs. Columbia Records div. CBS, Bridgeport, 1960-65; registrar U. Bridgeport, 1965-70, dir. personnel, 1970-80, dir. adminstrv. svcs., 1980—2004. Historian Boston Red Sox., 1984—; columnist Coman Publ., Durham, N.C., 1982-95. Author: This Date in Boston Red Sox History, 1979, Red Sox Triumphs and Tragedies, 1980, The Rookies, 1981; contbr. Boston Red Sox Mag., 1978—. Mem. selection com. Boston Red Sox Hall of Fame, 1995—. Served in U.S. Army, 1953-55. Recipient merit award Adminstrv. Mgmt. Soc., 1979, diamond merit award, 1981. Mem. Soc. for Am. Baseball Rsch., Boston Braves Hist. Assn. Avocations: baseball, model railroading. Died Nov. 14, 2005.

WANG, NIAN TZU, economist, educator; Student, U. London; AB in Econs., Columbia U.; AM in Econs., PhD in Econs., Harvard U. Adj. prof., dir. China-Internat. Bus. Project Grad. Sch. Bus. & Sch. Internat. & Pub. Affairs Columbia U., N.Y.C.; sr. rsch. scholar East Asian Inst., Columbia U., N.Y.C. Mem. disting. scholar exch. program, com. on scholarly comm. with Peoples Republic of China, Chinese Acad. Social Scis.; dir. info. analysis divsn. UN Ctr. on Transnat. Corps.; chief econ. survey sect. UN Secretariat; vis. prof. Pitts. U., Nankai U., Nat. Chengchi U., CUNY, Chinese U. Hong Kong; assoc. project on Chinese Studies Harvard U.; instr. Columbia Coll., Columbia U.; cons. World Bank, UN, Internat. Fin. Corp., major cos.; lectr. univs. and ednl. instns. N.Am., S.Am., Asia and Africa; guest prof. Tianjin U. Fin. and Econs. Editor: Taxation and Development, 1976, Business With China: An International Assessment, 1980, Taiwan's Enterprises in Global Perspective, 1992; author: China's Modernization and Transnational Corporations, 1984, Chinese Legal Framework for Foreign Investment and Its Implications, 1986; (with Teng Weizao) Transnational Corporations and China's Open Door Policy, 1988; How to Penetrate the World Market by Chinese Enterprises, 1995, My Nine Lives, 2001; dir., prin. author Multinational Corporations in World Development, 1973, A Reexamination, 1978; contbr. articles to profl. jours. Univ. fellow Harvard U.; Austin scholar; recipient N.Y. Gov. Outstanding Asian-Am. award; named Hon. Prof. Shanghai U. Fin. and Econs., U. Internat. Bus. and Econs., Beijing, Beijing Inst. Chem. Engring. Mgmt., East China U. Chem. Tech., Shanghai, Guangzhou U., Guangdong Inst. Commerce, Nankai U., Shandong Inst. Econs., Hefei U. Tech., Yunnan Inst. Fin. and Econs. Fellow Internat. Acad. Mgmt., Phi Beta Kappa. Home: Larchmont, NY. Died Aug. 26, 2004.

WANGAARD, FREDERICK F., science educator, consultant; b. Mpls., Jan. 3, 1911; s. Christian and Hanna Marie Wangaard; m. Lorraine M. Crouch, 1936; children: Frederick F. Jr., Walter C., David B. BS, U. Minn., 1933; MS, SUNY, Syracuse, 1935, PhD, 1939. Instr. U. Wash., Seattle, 1936—39, asst. prof., 1939—42; technologist Forest Products Lab., Madison, Wis., 1942—45; asst. to assoc. prof. Yale U., New Haven, 1945—52, prof., 1952—67; dept. head for sci. Colo. State U., Ft. Collins, Colo., 1967—76, prof. emeritus, 1976; spl. master N.Mex. State Ct., 1976—79. FAO UN advisor Forest Products Rsch. Inst., Los Banos, Philippines, 1957; coord. clark heritage workshop Forest Products Lab., Madison, 1979. Author: (textbook) Mechanical Properties of Wood. Recipient Borden Chem. award, Forest Products Rsch. Soc., 1973, Outstanding Achievement award, U. Minn., 1975, Hon. Alumnus award, U. Wash., 1999; Fulbright Rsch. scholar, Norsk Treteknisk Inst., 1958. Fellow: Internat. Acad. Wood Sci.; mem.: Soc. Am. Foresters (Golden award 1984), Soc. Wood Sci. and Tech. (assoc.; pres. 1964—65, Disting Svc. award 1983), Forest Products Soc. (assoc.; pres. 1975—76, Disting Svc. award 1976). Presbyterian. Home: Fort Collins, Colo. Died Apr. 10, 2005.

WANGLER, KENNETH JOHN, utility executive; b. Bayonne, N.J., Feb. 14, 1948; s. Kenneth Jacob and Margaret (Bezek) W.; m. Stella Candiloros, Oct. 24, 1971; children: Stephanie, Gregory. BA, Fairleigh Dickenson U., 1970, MBA in Fin., 1982. Payroll examiner Pub. Svc. Electric & Gas Co., Newark, 1970-75, plant acct., 1975-77, fin. analyst, 1977-80, adminstr. cash ops., from 1980. Mem. zoning bd. of adjustment Greenbrook Twp. Fairleigh Dickinson U. athletic scholar, 1965. Mem. N.J. Cash Mgmt. Assn. (alt.). Republican. Greek Orthodox. Avocations: collecting U.S. coins and stamps, baseball cards. Home: Green Brook, NJ. Died Sept. 12, 2004.

WARD, DAVID ALOYSIUS, consulting engineer; b. Joliet, Ill., Nov. 13, 1930; s. Aloysius and Flora May (Picton) W.; m. Diana Nainis, July 4, 1953; children: Rebecca, David Jr., Thomas, Kathleen, Eileen, Mary, Christopher, Jonathan, Matthew. BS in Mech. Engring., U. Ill., 1953. Engr. E.I. DuPont De Nemours, Alken, S.C., 1953-67, engring. mgr., 1967-89; consulting engr. David Ward Assocs., Inc., North Augusta, S.C., from 1989. Mem., chmn. Adv. Com. Reactor Safeguards, Washington, 1980-92. Chmn. parish sch. bd. Our Lady of Peace Sch., North Augusta, 1972-78. Recipient Disting. Svc. award U.S. Nuclear Regulatory Commn., Washington, 1992. Mem. NSPE, Am. Nuclear Soc., Inst. Nuclear Power Ops. (mem. nat. nuclear accediting bd. 1993—). Republican. Roman Catholic. Home: North Augusta, SC. Died July 8, 2005.

WARD, SHEILA DANEEN, secondary school educator; b. Ottawa, Kans., Oct. 13, 1935; d. James Delridge and Halbur Gertrude (Bartlett) Dye; m. William Gordon Ward, Nov. 7, 1964 (dec. May 1984); 1 child, Dana Carolyn. AB in Home Econs. and Spanish, U. Kans., 1957; MS in Nutrition, U. Iowa, 1959; DMSc, Ind. U., 1978. Dietetic intern nutrition dept. U. Iowa Hosps. & Clinics, Iowa City, 1957-58; rsch. dietitian Med. Sch. Harvard U., Cambridge, Mass., 1959-62; rsch. dietitian, asst. prof. Sch. of Medicine Ind. U., Indpls., 1962-67, 79-90; nutrition counselor, cons. Tavel, Lamkin & Gabovitch, MDs, Indpls., 1967-70; lectr. in nutrition Marian Coll., Indpls., 1974; sch. lunch dir. St. Luke's Cath. Sch., Indpls., 1973-76, postdoctoral fellow dept. med. genetics Sch. Medicine, 1978-79, dietetic internship dir., asst. prof., assoc. dir., 1979-90; ret., 1990. Mem. Pan-Hellenic Coun., Indpls., 1972-75; vol. United Way, Indpls., 1970-72, 87-89, Am. Heart Assn., Indpls., 1980-90; precinct vice chair Marion County Reps., Indpls., 1966-67; bd. dirs. Ind. Arthritis Found., Indpls., 1972-80. Mem. Ind. Dietetic Assn. (speaker 1979), Ind. Nutrition Coun., Cen. Ind. Dietetic Assn. (pres. 1968-69), Am. Dietetic Assn. (coun. on edn. 1985—, bd. editors Jour. 1980-88), Indpls. Alumni Assn., Sigma Xi, Alpha Omicron Pi (pres. 1970-72). Episcopalian. Avocations: sewing, reading, swimming, gardening. Home: Carmel, Ind. Died Dec. 26, 2004.

WARDEN, JACK, actor; b. Newark, Sept. 18, 1920; s. Jack Warden and Laura M. (Costello) Lebzelter; m. W. Dupree, 1958; 1 son, Christopher. Student, pub. schs., Newark; acting classes, N.Y.C. Appeared in repertory Margo Jones Theatre, Dallas, 1947-51; (Broadway plays) The Man In The Glass Booth, 1969; Actor (films) You're in the Navy Now, 1951, The Frogmen, 1951, Man with My Face, 1951, Red Ball Express, 1952, From Here to Eternity, 1953, Edge of the City, 1957, The Bachelor Party, 1957, Twelve Angry Men, 1957, Run Silent, Run Deep, 1958, Darby's Rangers, 1958, That Kind of Women, 1959, The Sound and the Fury, 1959, The Lawbreakers, 1960, Wake Me When Its Over, 1960, Donovan's Reef, 1962, Escape from Zahrain, 1962, The Thin Red Line, 1964, Blindfold, 1965, Bye Bye Braverman, 1968, The Sporting Club, 1971, Summertree, 1971, Who Is Harry Kellerman and Why Is He Saying Those Terrible Things About Me?, 1971, Welcome to the Club, 1971, Dig, 1972, The Man Who Loved Cat Dancing, 1973, The Apprenticeship of Duddy Kravitz, 1974, Billy Two Hats, 1974, Shampoo, 1975, All the President's Men, 1976, The White Buffalo, 1977, Heaven Can Wait, 1978, Death on the Nile, 1978, The Champ, 1979, Dreamer, 1979, Beyong the Posiedon Adventure, 1979,...And Justice for All, 1979, Being There, 1979, Used Cars, 1980, The Great Muppet Caper, 1981, Carbon Copy, 1981, Chu Chu and the Philly Flash, 1981, So Fine, 1981, The Verdict, 1982, Crackers, 1984, The Aviator, 1985, (voice only) The Cosmic Eye, 1986, September, 1987, The Presidio, 1988, Everybody Wins, 1990, Problem Child, 1990, Problem Child 2, 1991, Passed Away, 1992, Night and the City, 1992, Toys, 1992, Guilty as Sin, 1993, Beyond Innocence, 1993, Bullets Over Broadway, 1994, While You Were Sleeping, 1995, Things to Do in Denver When You're Dead, 1995, Mighty Aphrodite, 1995, Ed, 1996, The Volunteers, 1997, The Island on Bird Street, 1997, Chairman of the Board, 1998, Bulworth, 1998, Dirty Work, 1998, A Dog of Flanders, 1999, The Replacements, 2000; (TV series) Mr. Peepers, 1952-55, Norby, 1955, The Asphalt Jungle, 1961, The Wackiest Ship in the Army, 1965-66, N.Y.P.D., 1967-69, Jigsaw John, 1976, The Bad News Bears, 1979-80, Crazy Like a Fox, 1984-86, Knight & Day, 1989; (TV mini-series) Robert Kennedy & His Times, 1985, A.D., 1985; (TV movies) The Face of Fear, 1971, Brian's Song, 1971, What's a Nice Girl Like You...?, 1971, Mon on a String, 1972, Lieutenant Schuster's Wife, 1972, Wheeler and Myrdoch, 1973, Remember When, 1974, A Memory of Two Mondays, 1974, The Godchild, 1974, Journey from Darkness, 1975, They Only Come out at Night, 1975, The Raid on Entebbe, 1977, Topper, 1979, A Private Battle, 1980, Hobson's Choice, 1983, Helen Keller: The Miracle Continues, 1984, Alice in Wonderland, 1985, The Three Kings, 1987, Three Wishes for Jamie, 1987, Still Crazy Like a Fox, 1987, Hoover v. the Kennedys: The Second Civil War, 1987, Dead Solid Perfect, 1988, Police Story: The Watch Commander, 1988, Judgment, 1990, Problem Child 3: Junior in Love; (TV appearances) Tales of Tomorrow, 1952, The Man Behind the Badge, 1953, Campbell Playhouse, 1953, Center Stage, 1954, Justice, 1955, Producer's Showcase, 1955, Danger, 1955, Kraft Televisoion Theater, 1955, Studio One, 1955, Philco Television Playhouse, 1956, The Alcoa Hour, 1956, Climax!, 1956, The Kaiser Aluminum Hour, 1956, Hallmark Hall of Fame, 1957, The United States Steel Hour, 1957, Suspicion, 1957, The Lawless Years, 1959, Five Fingers, 1959, Bonanza, 1959, Playhouse 90, 1959, The Twilight Zone, 1959, Westinghouse Desilu Playhouse, 1960, Stagecoach, 1960, Outlaws, 1960, The

Untouchables, 1960, Checkmate, 1961, Bus Stop, 1961, Tales of Wells Fargo, 1962, Traget: The Corruptors, 1962, Alcoa Premiere, 1962, Ben Casey, 1962, Naked City, 1963, 77 Sunset Strip, 1963, The Virgininan, 1962, Wagon Train, 1962, Route 66, 1963, Breaking Point, 1964, The Great Adventure, 1964, Kraft Suspense Theater, 1964, Bewitched, 1964, Bob Hope Presents the Chrysler Theater, 1964, Slattery's People, 1964, The Adventure of Gallagher, 1965, Disneyland, 1965, Dr. Kildare, 1965, The Fugitive, 1967, The Invaders, 1967, N.Y.P.D., 1967 The Norm Show, 1999, Ink, 1999; Recipient Obie award, 1963, Emmy award, 1972. Served with USN, 1938-41, U.S. Maritime Service, 1941-42, U.S. Army, 1942-46, ETO. Mem. SAG, AFTRA, Actors Equity Democrat. Home: Malibu, Calif. Died July 19, 2006.

WARE, BARBARA ANN SCOTT, construction company executive; b. Bklyn., Feb. 17, 1955; d. Dudley and Marian (James) Scott; m. Morris Ware Sr. May 11, 1974; children: Michele, Morris, Jr. Grad. high sch., Roosevelt, N.Y. cert. energy auditor, N.Y. Community aide Roosevelt (N.Y.) Schs., 1974-76; tchrs. aid Salvation Army, Hempstead, N.Y., 1976-78; asst. dir. NOW, Mineola, N.Y., 1978-80; co-owner JOW, Hempstead, N.Y., from 1980. Lectr. Nelson A. Rockefeller Inst., Albany, N.Y., 1987. Bd. dirs. Long Island Women's Equal Opportunity Council, 1981—; mem. adv. bd. N.Y. State Dept. of Social Services, 1986; chair Long Island Affirmative Action Program, Inc., 1986. Mem. Assn. Minority Entrepreneurs. Home: Roosevelt, NY. Died Feb. 2, 2004.

WARE, DOLLIE, retired nursing educator; b. Bklyn., Apr. 1, 1947; d. Solomon Henry and Lucille (Reel) Antley; m. Jim Ware. Dec. 27, 1969; children: Athena, Christopher, Monica, Jeremy. Nursing diploma, Kings County Hosp. Sch Nursing, Bklyn., 1967; BA in Health Care Psychology, Graceland Coll., Lamoni, Iowa, 1991. RN; cert. psychiat. and mental health nurse, chem. dependency nurse, addiction specialist, BCLS instr., cert. instr. Nat. Crisis Prevention Inst. Staff nurse Kings County Hosp., Bklyn., 1967-68; asst. clin. instr. Kings County Hosp. Sch. Nursing, Bklyn., 1968-73; inservice instr. Kings County Hosp. Ctr., Bklyn., 1975-89, supr., instr. continuing edn. psychiatry-addiction, 1989—97; ret., 1997. Mem. Drug and Alcohol Nurses Assn., Nat. Consortium Chem. Dependency Nurses, Am. Psychiat. Nurses Assn., Regional Emergency Med. Svcs. Coun. N.Y.C. Inc. Avocations: reading, continuing education, walking, computer. Died June 12, 2004.

WARE, ELIZABETH FISHER, chemistry educator; b. Rezina, Bessarabia, Romania, Oct. 31, 1915; came to U.S., 1923; d. Hillel and Bella (Gichko) Fisher; m. Lawrence L. Ware Jr., Jan. 27, 1946; children: David A., Kenneth R., Barbara Ware Mankuta. BS, U. Pitts., 1938; MS, Ariz. State U., 1964; cert. in advanced chemistry, Am. U., Washington, 1976. Cert. secondary tchr., Ariz. Rsch. chemist Johnson & Johnson, New Brunswick, N.J., 1942-44; asst. chief analytical chemistry U.S. Army Quartermaster Lab., Chgo., 1944-46; chief chemist James Labs., Chgo., 1947-51; instr. chemistry West High Sch., Phoenix, 1961-62; prof. chemistry Phoenix Coll., 1963-66, North Va. C.C., Annandale, 1966-86, prof. emerits, from 1987. Patentee in field. Bd. dirs. Am. Cancer Soc., Fairfax, Va., 1970-73. Mem. AAUP, Am. Chem. Soc. (sr., chair social com. 1942—, faculty advisor 1970-76), Ariz. Acad. Sci., Va. Acad. Sci., Women Engrs. Phoenix (charter). Avocations: photography, travel, engineering design chemical laboratories, environment. Died Aug. 20, 2005.

WARENSKI, MARILYN LISTON, writer; b. Salt Lake City, May 9, 1931; d. Charles Russell and Vaughn (Tuttle) Liston; m. James Carl Warenski, Sept. 9, 1953; children: Lisa, Jane, James, Paul. BA, U. Utah, 1952; design degree, N.Y. Sch. Interior Design, 1962; MFA in Writing, Vt. Coll., 1988. Tchr. pub. sch. sys., Salt Lake City, 1952-53; tchr. pub. sch. Teaneck, N.J., 1953-55; tchr. U. Utah, Salt Lake City, 1969-72. Freelance interior designer, Salt Lake City, 1962-75; pub. spkr. in field, we. U.S., 1978-84. Author: (book) Patriarchs and Politics: The Plight of the Mormon Woman, 1978 (ERA Alice Paul award 1984). Vol. Jr. League Salt Lake City, 1963-71; bd. dirs. Chamber Music Soc., Salt Lake City, 1986-90. Recipient Nat. Best Dressed Table Design award Gorham Co., 1971, Utah Women's Polit. Caucus award 1983, ERA Alice Paul award, 1984. Democrat. Avocations: travel, tennis, cooking, reading. Home: Salt Lake City, Utah. Died June 8, 2004.

WARFEL, JOHN HIATT, retired medical educator; b. Marion, Ind., Mar. 3, 1916; s. Robert A. and Mary (Hiatt) W.; m. Marjorie Jane Wolfe, Oct. 28, 1942; children: Barbara, Susan, David. BS, Capital U., 1938; MS, Ohio State U., 1941; PhD, Case Western Res. U., 1948. Assoc. prof. anatomy SUNY, Buffalo, 1949-86; ret., 1986. Author: The Extremities, 6th edit., 1993, The Head, Neck and Trunk, 6th edit., 1993. Lt. (s.g.) USNR, 1942-46. Mem. Am. Assn. Anatomists, Mason, Sigma Xi. Methodist. Died May 6, 2005.

WARN, GRACE HELEN, city official; b. Chgo., Feb. 5, 1922; d. Fred Albert and Sophie (Kozakiewicz) Miller; m. Raymond B. Stosik, May 7, 1949 (div. Oct. 1968); children: Michael, Raymond, Patricia, Susan, David, Grace, James, Paul. Grad. high sch., Chgo. Cert. pub. housing mgr., Mich. Exec. dir. Alpena (Mich.) Housing Commn., from 1952. With WAC, 1943-45, PTO. Mem. Mich. Housing Dirs. Assn., Alpena Assn. for Retarded, VFW, DAV, Am. Assn.

Ret. Persons, Am. Diabetes Assn., Elks. Roman Catholic. Avocations: bowling, health club, walking, Bingo. Home: Alpena, Mich. Died Dec. 7, 2004.

WARNER, LEE MICHAEL, food products executive; b. Cleve., Oct. 10, 1917; s. Ray I. and Ann (Goldber) W.; m. Janet Hoffman, Aug. 3, 1941 (dec. 1961); m. Hope Landis, Mar. 1, 1963; 1 child, Christopher Arthur. BSc, Ohio State U., 1939. Pres., chief executive officer Laurbank Sales Corp., L.A., 1947-53, Pacific Fruit Processing, Beverly Hills, Calif., 1960-78, CENSA, Beverly Hills, 1967-78, Santa Fe Driscoll, Beverly Hills, 1952-78; chmn. Pacific Fruit Processing Inc., South Gate, Calif., from 1978. Chmn. State of Calif. Strawberry Adv. Bd., Sacramento, 1963-65; pres. Warner Investment Co., Santa Monica. Bd. mem. Andrus Sch. Gerentology, L.A., 1987—. Capt. U.S. Army, 1942-46. Died Jan. 16, 2005.

WARNER, LINDA PAMELA, music educator; b. Passaic, N.J., July 22, 1947; d. Leonard and Lillian (Sabanosh) Warner; m. Frederick G. Pfarrius (div.); 1 child, Frederick James Pfarrius. BA, William Paterson U., Wayne, N.J., 1965—69; pvt. piano study, Nina Svetlanova, N.Y.C., 1974—79; MMus, Columbia U., N.Y.C., 1986—89; pvt. voice study, Dino Anagnost, Columbia U., N.Y.C., 1990—97. Cons. Teaneck Bd. Edn., NJ, 1969—72; tchr. Hollingsworth Sch. for Gifted, N.Y.C., 1986—88; chair, music dept. Holy Angels Acad., Demarest, NJ, 1989—99; tchr. Bergen Acad. Gifted, Hackensack, NJ, 1995—2000, Rolling Hills Sch., Vernon, NJ, from 2000. Bd. trustees Classical Music Outreach, N.Y.C., 1990—92; spl. area rep. N.J. Edn. Assn., 2002—04. Composer: (musical) Let's Build a Church, 1986. Bd. trustees Columbia/Anagnost Orgn., N.Y.C., 1988—2003; choir, music dir. Holy Counselor Lutheran Ch., Vernon, NJ, 2002—04. Mem.: NJ Nat. Educators Assn., N.J. Music Educators, Music Educators Nat. Conf. Democrat. Lutheran. Home: Staten Island, NY. Died Aug. 30, 2005.

WARREN, PATRICIA ANN, government official; b. Dayton, Ohio, Nov. 8, 1940; d. Kenneth Willis and Ola Mary (Colvin) Pfaff; m. Jefferson Donald Vallance, May 14, 1960 (div. Jan. 1965); children: Donald Jeffery, Daniel Craig; m. Edward Lynn Warren, Dec. 10, 1966. Student, Wright State U., Fairborn, Ohio, 1980, East Sinclair Community Coll., Dayton, 1980-87. Ops. mgr. O.D.H. Inc., investment advisors, L.A., 1970-74; space mgmt. facilities mgr. Air Force Systems Command, Dayton, 1977-80; space mgr. Air Force Logistics Command, Wright-Patterson AFB, Ohio, 1980-83; realty officer, from 1983. Treas. Whispering Oaks Homeowners Assn., Centerville, Ohio, 1988-89. Mem. Soc. Am. Mil. Engrs. Republican. Avocations: tennis, skiing, bridge. Home: Murrieta, Calif. Died Sept. 18, 2004.

WASHINGTON, FLOYD, JR., land development executive; b. Shreveport, La., June 6, 1943; s. Floyd Sr. and Rosa (Thomas) W.; m. Juanita Allen, June 19, 1969; children: Floyd III, Rosalind Lou. BS, Grambling State U., 1965; MBA, U. Chgo., 1967. Lic. real estate broker, Mich. Market rsch. analyst Spiegel Inc., Chgo., 1965-67; fin. analyst Ford Motor Parent Co., Dearborn, Mich., 1967-73; from fin. analyst to fin. mgr. Ford Motor Land Devel. Corp., Dearborn, Mich from 1973; pres. Joint Fraternal Devel. Corp., Detroit, 1991; v.p. Alpha Woodward Restoration, Inc., Detroit, 1991. Bd. dirs. Detroit Econ. Devel. Corp., 1992-93; v.p. Alpha Woodward Restoration, Inc., Detroit, 1991. Bd. mem. Mus. of African Am. History, Detroit, 1987; adv. com. Wayne County Community Coll., Detroit, 1988. Recipient Pres. citation, Outstanding Alumni of Grambling State U., Nat. Assn. for Equal Opportunity in Higher Edn., Washington, 1983; named Outstanding Young Man Am., The Outstanding Am. Found., 1970; fellow U. Chgo., 1965. Mem. Black MBA Assn., Grambling State U. Alumni Assn. (pres. 1975-77), Phi Beta Lambda (pres. 1963-65), Kappa Delta Pi, Alpha Kappa Mu, Sigma Rho Sigma, Alpha Phi Alpha. Democrat. Baptist. Home: Southfield, Mich. Died Apr. 11, 2005.

WASSERMAN, JEFFREY ANDREW, artist; b. Mt. Vernon, N.Y., July 21, 1946; s. Arthur Jay and Lenore (Robinson) W.; m. Anne Colby Newburg, Jan. 2, 1990, children, Jane, Hugo BFA, Temple U., 1968; postgrad., Royal Coll. Art, London, 1968-69. Sr. lectr. painting Phila. Coll. Arts, 1988. Solo exhbns. include Mcpl. Theatre, Caen, France, 1980, Red Bar, N.Y.C., 1982, Virtual Garrison, N.Y.C., 1984, Daniel Newburg Gallery, N.Y.C., Philippe Briet Gallery, N.Y.C., 1988, Nina Freudenheim Gallery, Buffalo, 1991; group shows include Charles More Gallery, Phila., 1984, Ted Greenwald Gallery, N.Y.C., 1985, Rosa Esman Gallery, N.Y.C., 1986, Daniel Newburg Gallery, 1987, Scott Hanson Gallery, N.Y.C., 1988, 89, 90, Fay Gold Gallery, Atlanta, 1991; represented in permanent collections. Died July 2, 2006.

WASSERMAN, SYLVIA KATZ, lawyer; b. Milw., Mar. 30, 1916; d. Abraham and Anna Esther Katz; m. Eugene Wasserman (dec. Mar. 1970); children: Barbara Wasserman Vinson, Louis. BA, U. Ill., 1937; B of Law, Northwestern U., 1939, JD, 1970. Lawyer Office of Daniel D. Carmell, Chgo., Legal Br. N.Y. Ordnance Dist., N.Y.C.; lawyer, brief editor Bala Cynwyd, Pa.; lawyer Sheboygan, Wis., from 1951. Commr. Sheboygan Police and Fire Commn., 1980-93; bd. dirs. Friendship House, Sheboygan, 1974-96. Recipient Commendation award Friendship House, 1986. Mem. ABA, Ill. Bar Assn., Wis. Bar Assn., Sheboygan Bar Assn. Democrat. Jewish. Home: Northbrook, Ill. Died May 19, 2004.

WASSERSTEIN, WENDY, playwright, author; b. Bklyn., Oct. 18, 1950; d. Morris and Lola Wasserstein; 1 child, Lucy Jane. BA, Mt. Holyoke Coll., 1971; MA, CCNY, 1973; MFA, Yale Drama Sch., 1976. Author: (plays) Any Woman Can't, 1973, Happy Birthday, Montpelier Pizz-zazz, 1974, (with Christopher Durang) When Dinah Shore Ruled the Earth, 1975, Uncommon Women and Others, 1975, Isn't It Romantic, 1981, Tender Offer, 1983, The Man in a Case, Miami, 1986, The Heidi Chronicles, 1988 (Pulitzer prize for drama, 1989, Outer Critics Cir. award for best play, 1989, N.Y. Drama Critics Cir. award, 1989, Susan Smith Blackburn prize, 1989), The Sisters Rosensweig, 1991 (Outer Critics Cir. award, 1993), An American Daughter, 1997, Old Money, 2000, (screenplays) Uncommon Women and Others, 1978, The Sorrows of Gin, 1979, (with Durang) House of Husbands, Isn't It Romantic, The Heidi Chronicles, (children's book) Pamela's First Musical, 1995; actress (plays) An American Daughter, Life with Mikey; author: (essays) Bachelor Girls, 1990, Shiksa Goddess, 2003, (books) Sloth, 2005. Recipient Hale Matthews Found. award; grantee Am. Playwrights Project, 1988, Commissioning Program Phoenix Theater; Guggenheim fellow, 1983. Mem.: bd. Channel Thirteen, McDowell Colony, WNET, British Am. Arts Assoc., Dramatists Guild for Young Playwrights, artistic bd. Playwrights Horizons, Coun. Dramatists Guild. Home: New York, NY. Died Jan. 30, 2006.

WASSON, DAVID WESLEY, educational service agency director; b. Whitefish, Mont., Dec. 15, 1942; s. Lewis Henry and Betty F. (Bahm) Larter; m. Sue Caroll Gentry, Aug. 25, 1964; children: Wesley, Tammy, Bonnie, Kimberly. AA, York Coll., Nebr., 1962; BSE, Abilene Christian U., Tex., 1965; MA, No. Ariz. U., 1971. Cert. tchr. Ariz., Tex. (life), Calif. (life). Tchr., dept. head Needles (Calif.) High Sch., 1965-73; curriculum specialist Mohave County Career Edn., Kingman, Ariz., 1973-76; exec. dir. Mohave Ednl. Services, Kingman, Ariz., from 1976. Res. instr. San Bernadino Valley Coll., Needles, 1966-73, Mohave County Community Coll., Kingman, 1973—, No. Ariz. U., Kingman, 1976—; cons. office career edn. U.S. Office Edn., Washington, 1978-80; bd. dirs. Harper & Wasson Pubs., Inc., Kingman, 1984—. Author, dir. (TV spl.) Sky-12 Visits Ariz., 1984; producer: (videotape) How to Speak Indian Sign Language, 1984, Wovoka and the Ghost Dance, 1985; author: The Silent Language of the Plains, 1986, Youth Awareness: A Drug Prevention Program, 1987, Teen Awareness: A Drug Awareness Program, 1987, Geography Basics, USA, 1988. Bd. dirs. Mohave Mus. History and Arts, Kingman, 1979-82; mem. exec. bd. Kingman Centennial Commn., Kingman, 1979-83, vocat. edn. task force Ariz. Dept. Edn., 1980-86. TIPS fellow U. Colo., 1971, COE fellow Pepperdine U., 1972. Mem. Ariz. Assn. Career Edn. Clubs: Toastmasters. Republican. Avocations: stamp collecting/philately, photography, freelance writing. Home: Kingman, Ariz. Died Sept. 20, 2004.

WATERS, CURTIS JEFFERSON, retired minister, evangelist; b. Spartanburg, S.C., Apr. 8, 1929; s. Leroy Belton and Lillian Isola (Tucker) W.; m. Nancy Carol Taylor, Oct. 25, 1947; children: Curtis Michael, Ronald Stephen, Gloria Lynn. BA, North Greenville Coll., Tigerville, S.C., 1953; BD, Luther Rice Sem., Jacksonville, Fla., 1973; DD (hon.), North Fla. Bapt. Theol. Sem., 1988, ThD, 1991. Ordained to ministry So. Bapt. Conv., 1950; lic. real estate broker, N.C. Pastor Gap Creek Bapt. Ch., Marietta, S.C., 1950-51, Fairmont (S.C.) Bapt. Ch., 1951-55, Francis Bapt. Ch., Palatka, Fla., 1955-60, Double Springs Bapt. Ch., Greer, S.C., 1960-63, Churchwell Avenue Bapt. Ch., Knoxville, Tenn., 1963-71, Tuxedo (N.C.) 1st Bapt. Ch., 1971-75, City View 1st Bapt. Ch., Greenville, S.C., 1975-93; retired, 1993; chmn. bd. dirs. Champions for Christ Found. City View 1st Bapt. Ch., Greenville, S.C., 1987-93; ret., 1993; evangelist, from 1993. Dir. E.J. Daniels Crusade, Palatka, Fla.; evangelist 9 states and Jamaica; sem. commencement speaker North Fla. Bapt. Theol. Sem., 1989-90, 90-91; speaker Bible confs. Bd. dirs. Jacksonville (Fla.) Bapt. Theol. Sem., The Last Days Generation, Jacksonville, Fla. Republican. Home: Greenville, SC. Died July 27, 2005.

WATERS, ED (EDWARD SARSFIELD WATERS), screenwriter, television producer, writer; b. N.Y.C., Sept. 23, 1930; s. Edward Sarsfield and Winifred Cunningham (O'Brien) W.; m. Diane Ernestene Garrett, Oct. 23, 1965; 1 child, Peter Gregory. BA magna cum laude, U. Notre Dame, 1952. Freelance film and TV writer various studios, Los Angeles, 1956-73, 78-83; exec. story editor Kung Fu Warner Bros., Burbank, Calif., 1973-75, producer The Mississippi, 1983-84; exec. story cons. Police Story Columbia, Burbank, 1975-77; supervising producer Baretta Universal, Universal City, Calif., 1977-78, supervising producer Miami Vice, 1985-86, co-exec. producer The Equalizer, 1986-88; exec. producer Jake and the Fat Man, 1988-89; ind. screenwriter, TV series creator Calif., 1989—2004. Writer numerous films, dramatic episodes, TV films and pilots; frequently cited in Tom Stempel's "Storytellers to the Nation" - A History of American Television Writing. Recipient Golden Reel award Miami Vice TV episode, 1985, Emmy award for Police Story, Acad. TV Arts and Scis., 1977. Mem. Writers Guild Am. West. Roman Catholic. Home: Malibu, Calif. Died Nov. 9, 2004.

WATSON, JANE WERNER, writer; b. Fond du Lac, Wis., July 11, 1915; d. Henry Charles and Elsa Elizabeth (Nast) W; m. Earnest C. Watson (dec. 1954). BA, U. Wis., 1936, DHL (hon.). Editor Western Printing & Pub. Co., Racine, Wis., 1938-42, N.Y.C., 1942-46, Beverly Hills, Calif., 1946-47, N.Y.C., 1947-54; freelance writer Pasadena, 1954-60, New Delhi, 1960-62, Santa Barbara, Calif., from 1962. Part-time tchr. writing Santa Barbara City Coll. Adult Edn., 1963-93. Author: A Woods Story, 1945, Walt Disney's Vanishing Prairie, 1946, Walt Disney's Living Desert, 1954, A Farm Story, 1955, The World of Science, 1958 (L.A. Times Woman of the Yr. for Lit. 1959), Ethiopia: Mountain Kingdom, 1966, India: Old Land, New Nation, 1966, Iran: Crossroads of Caravans, 1966, Thailand: Rice Bown of Asia, 1966, Egypt: Child of the Nile, 1967, Greece: Land of Golden Light, 1967, Nigeria: Republic of a Hundred Kings, 1967, Peru: Land Astride the Andes, 1967, Canada: Giant Nation of the North, 1968, Mexico: Land of the Plumed Serpent, 1968, Finland: Champion of Independence, 1969, The Indus, 1970, Castles in Spain, 1971, The Mysterious Gold and Purple Box, 1972, Rama of the Golden Age, 1972, The Volga, 1972, Soviet Union: Land of Many Peoples, 1973, Dance to a Happy Song, 1973, Tanya and the Geese, 1974, India Celebrates, 1974, Parade of Soviet Holidays, 1974, Living Together in Tomorrow's World, 1976; (with David Todd) Rescue!, 1976; The Case of the Semi-Human Beans, 1979, Which is the Witch?, 1979, Alternate Energy Sources, 1979, The First Americans, 1980, Case of the Vanishing Space Ship, 1982, World in Danger: Too Many People, Conservation of Energy. Hon. bd. dirs. Planned Parenthood of Santa Barbara, 1994—. Mem. Santa Barbara Mus. of Art (hon. bd. dirs. 1995—), Channel City Club (former bd. dirs.), Little Town Club (former bd. dirs., sec. 1989-95). Democrat. Avocations: travel, photography. Home: Santa Barbara, Calif. Died Apr. 9, 2004.

WATTENBARGER, JAMES LORENZO, higher education educator; b. Cleveland, Tenn., May 2, 1922; s. James Claude and Lura G. (Hambright) W.; m. Marion Swanson, June 11, 1947; children: J. Frank, Carl E., Robert D. BA in Edn. with high honors, U. Fla., 1943, MA in Edn., 1947, EdD, 1950. Tchr. Palm Beach H.S., West Palm Beach, Fla., 1946-47; asst. prin. P.K. Yonge U. Fla., Gainesville, Fla., 1948-49; asst. prof. Coll. of Edn., UF, Gainesville, 1950-54, asoc. prof., 1954-55; dir. Cmty. Coll. Coun., Tallahassee, 1955-57; exec. dir. State Dept. of Edn. Cmty. Colls., Tallahassee, 1957-68; prof., chair dept. edn. adminstrn. U. Fla., Gainesville, 1968-84, prof., dir. Inst. Higher Edn., 1968-92, disting. svc. prof. Inst. Higher Edn., 1990-92, disting. svc prof. emeritus, 1992—2006. Author: Financing Community Colleges, 1990; co-author: America's Community Colleges: The First Century, 1994; editor Visions, 1995-2006. Capt. USAAC, 1943-45. Mem. Assn. for Study of Higher Edn., Am. Assn. Cmty. Colls., Am. Assn. Higher Edn., Fla. Assn. Cmty. Colls., Delta Tau Delta (pres. house corp. Gainesville chpt. 1970-2006). Democrat. Episcopalian. Avocations: philately (covers), jogging. Home: Gainesville, Fla. Died Aug. 14, 2006.

WATTENMAKER, DIANE M., mental health nurse; b. West Hartford, Oct. 20, 1937; d. Francis and Dorothy (Peterson) Nelson; m. Richard Wattenmaker, Mar. 14, 1976; children: Karen de Sola, David de Sola, Benjamen Wattenmaker. Diploma, Hartford Hosp. Sch. Nursing, 1958; BS, Tchr. Coll. N.Y., 1965, MEd, 1975. Cert. advanced nurse adminstr., clin. specialist, advanced cognitive therapist, APRN. Clin. specialist psychiatry St. Luke's Hosp., N.Y.C., 1978; assoc. v.p. nursing Stamford (Conn.) Hosp., 1978-82; dir. nursing N.Y. State Psychiat. Inst., N.Y.C., 1982-87; clin. practice dir. psychiat. nursing Norwalk (Conn.) Hosp., 1987-95; dir. Cognitive Therapy Ctr. of Conn., Norwalk, from 1992. Mem. ANA, Conn. Nurses Assn., Conn. Soc. for Nurse Psychotherapists, Hartford Hosp. Alumni Assn., Sigma Theta Tau. Home: Wilton, Conn. Died Mar. 21, 2005.

WATTS, MALCOLM S(TUART) M(CNEAL), retired internist, medical educator; b. N.Y.C., Apr. 30, 1915; s. Malcolm S.M. and Elizabeth (Forbes) W.; m. Genevieve Moffitt, July 12, 1947; children: Pauline, Elizabeth, Malcolm, James. AB, Harvard U., 1937, MD, 1941. Diplomate: Pan Am. Med. Assn. Group practice internal medicine, San Francisco, 1948-76; clin. prof. medicine U. Calif. Sch. Medicine, 1972-89, assoc. dean, 1966-89, clin. prof. medicine emeritus, 1989—2006, dir. Extended Programs in Med. Edn., 1973-82; dir. Calif. Statewide Area Health Edn. System, 1979-89. Chmn. bd. trustees San Francisco Consortium, 1968-74, trustee, 1974-80, exec. dir., 1981-94; dir. Soc. Med. Coll. Dirs. Continuing Med. Edn., 1975-82, pres., 1980-81; trustee Hospice of San Francisco, v.p., 1979-85; pres. Alliance Continuing Med. Edn., 1979-81. Editor Western Jour. Medicine, 1968-90, Jour. Continuing Edn. in the Health Professions, 1988-91. Served to capt. M.C. AUS, 1942-46. Recipient Outstanding Community Funds and Councils Am., 1964, U. Calif. San Francisco medal, 1983, Disting. Svc. award Alliance for Continuing Med. Edn., 1990, Disting. Svc. award soc. Med. Coll. Dirs. of Continuing Med. Edn., 1991. Master ACP (pres. emeritus, 2005); fellow Am. Coll. Health Care Execs. (hon.); mem. AMA, AAAS, Calif. Acad. Scis., Calif. Acad. Medicine, Am. Med. Writers Assn. (John T. McGovern award 1986), San Francisco Med. Soc. (pres. 1961), Am. Soc. Internal Medicine (pres. 1964-65), Calif. Med. Assn. (bd. dirs. 1962-90), Nat. Inst. Medicine, Soc. Med. Friends Wine, Acad. Mexicana Ciencias Mexicano de Cultura (corr.). Home: San Francisco, Calif. Died June 6, 2006.

WEAR, ROBERT JOSEPH, educational consultant; b. Hazleton, Pa., Dec. 25, 1917; s. Joseph Carter and Bertha Mary (Fox) W.; m. Marion Virginia Beam, Sept. 7, 1946. BS in Indsl. Engring., Fairleigh Dickinson U., 1961; MA, NYU, 1964. With Acad. Aeronautics, Flushing, N.Y., 1942-54, adminstrv. dean, 1970-86, cons. edn., from 1986. Mem. Bd. Adjustment, Denville, N.J., 1988—. Mem. Soc. for Automotive Engrs., AIAA, Am. Soc. for Engring. Edn. (James H. McGraw award 1979), Accreditation Bd. for Engring. Techs. Home: Denville, NJ. Died Jan. 3, 2004.

WEAVER, DENNIS, actor; b. Joplin, Mo., June 4, 1924; s. Walter and Lenna Weaver; m. Gerry Stowell, Oct. 20, 1945; children: Rick, Robby, Rusty. BFA, U. Okla., 1948. Appeared on N.Y. stage, 1948-52; appeared in Streetcar Named Desire, Hollywood, Calif., 1953; under contract to Universal Internat., Hollywood, 1952-53, freelance actor, Hollywood, 1953-55; appeared on: TV series Gunsmoke, 1955-64, Kentucky Jones, 1964-65, Gentle Ben, 1967-69, McCloud, 1970-77, Stone, 1980, Buck James, 1985-87, Lonesome Dove, 1994; also TV movies: Duel, 1971, Forgotten Man, 1971, Rolling Man, 1973, Terror on the Beach, 1973, Female Artillery, 1973, Patty Hearst, 1979, Stolen Women-Captured Hearts, 1997, Seduction in a Small Town, 1997, The Virginian, 2000; spls. Intimate Strangers, 1977, Police Story-A Cry for Justice, 1977, Pearl, 1978, Ishi, 1978, Islander, 1978, Centennial-The Longhorns, 1978, Amber Waves, 1979, The Ordeal of Dr. Mud, 1979, The Day the Loving Stopped, 1981, Don't Go to Sleep, 1982, Cocaine: One Man's Seduction, 1983, Winners Never Quit, 1986, Bluffing It, 1987, Disaster at Silo 7, 1988, The Return of Sam McCloud, 1989, Mastergate, 1991, (pilot) Greyhounds, 1993, "Buffalo Bill" in Lonesome Dove, the series, 1994-95, (pilot) called "The Wolfe Pack" for CBS, 1996—, (cable movie) Escape from Wildcat Canyon, 1997-98, The Virginian, 1999, High Noon, 2000. Mem. SAG (pres. 1973-75), AFTRA, Dirs. Guild. Died Feb. 27, 2006.

WEAVER, GAIL ELAINE, religious organization administrator, tax specialist, consultant; b. Detroit, July 20, 1954; d. Columbus and Mable Weaver. AA in Acctg., Jimmy Swaggart Bible Coll., 1987; BA in Religious Edn., Cornerstone Theol. Sem., 1990; D (hon.), Urban Bible Inst., 1996. Cert. tax cons., H & R Block, 1989; ordained Nat. Assn. Women Ministry, Detroit, 1990. CEO, prin. Ameri-Tax, from 1987; pres. Nat. Assn. Women Ministry, Detroit, from 1990. Author: My Praise To Thee, Eschewance Of Evil, Psalms. 1981, Lady Weaver, (children books) My House, Mister Sun, Father's Riches; composer: (songs) Saturday Afternoon. Independent. Achievements include design of Christian American Flag. Avocations: travel, bowling, piano, writing. Home: Detroit, Mich. Died May 19, 2005.

WEAVER, MICHAEL ANTHONY, mining engineer, consultant; b. Pitts., Aug. 25, 1948; s. James S. and Ellen W.; m. Patricia L. Barry; children: Scott-Patrick, Dulany. BSCE, U. Pitts., 1976, MS in Mining Engring., 1979, MBA, 1980. Registered profl. engr. Asst. project engr. John T. Boyd Co., Pitts., 1973-75; rsch. mining engr. U.S. Bur. Mines, Pitts., 1975-79, mining engr., 1979-80; chief mining engr. Colo.-Ute Elec. Assn., Montrose, 1980-82; asst. prof. Pa. State U., State College, 1982-88; prin. mining engr., sr. mining engr. Indpls. Power & Light, from 1989. Mem. fossil and synthetic fuel sect. Edison Electric Inst., Washington. Mem. Soc. Mining Engrs. Died June 21, 2005.

WEBB ANDERSON, JOANN MARIE, retired lawyer, advocate; b. St. Louis, Nov. 19, 1942; d. Jeff and Nancy Mae (Harris) Webb; m. Clifton Earl Anderson, Dec. 30, 1966; children: Ronald James Anderson, Nancy D. Anderson Tayborn. Student, U. Mo., Columbia and St. Louis, 1960-62; BA in History, St. Louis U., 1967, JD, 1978; grad., Ind. U., 1974-75. Bar: Mo. 1979, U.S. Dist. Ct. U.S. V.I. 1981, U.S. Dist. Ct. (ea. dist.) Mo. 1979, U.S. Ct. Appeals (8th cir.) 1979, U.S. Ct. Appeals (3d cir.) 1982. Staff atty. Legal Svcs. Ea. Mo., St. Louis, 1979-80; staff atty., mng. atty. Legal Svcs. V.I., Christiansted, Frederiksted, 1980-81; asst. atty. gen. Govt. of V.I., St. Croix, 1981-83; supervising atty. civil divsn. Dept. of Justice, Office of Atty. Gen., St. Croix, 1984-85, acting chief, supervising atty., 1985-87; exec.dir. Navy Relief Soc./Japan Aux., Yokusuka, 1988-89; sole practitioner St. Louis, 1997—2002; ptnr. Anderson and Webb Anderson, LLP, 2002—04. Music arranger, exec. dir. St. Croix Inspirational Singers, 1983-85. Bd. dirs. Archway Cmtys., Inc., St. Louis, 1998-2001, Child Ctr. of Our Lady, 2001—; polit. action com. Coalition of 100 Black Women, St. Louis, 1990; planning and focus group Hyde Park Neighbors/Trinity Sq., St. Louis, 1990—; cmty. adv. panel bd. Mallinkrodt Chemical Co., 1998—. Mem. Bar Assn. Met. St. Louis (econ. devel. com.), Jr. League of St. Louis, Caths. Against Capital Punishment, Blacks for Life/Mo. Right to Life, Lawyers for Life (bd. dirs. St. Louis chot.), Zeta Phi Beta. Roman Catholic. Avocations: neighborhood development, historical preservation, reading, international travel. Home: Saint Louis, Mo. Died Apr. 8, 2005.

WEBBER, WILLIAM ALEXANDER, academic administrator, physician; b. Nfld., Can., Apr. 8, 1934; s. William Grant and Hester Mary (Constable) W.; m. Marilyn Joan Robson, May 17, 1958; children— Susan Joyce, Eric Michael, George David. MD, U. B.C., Can., Vancouver, 1958; LLD, U. B.C., 2000. Intern Vancouver Gen. Hosp., 1958-59; fellow Cornell U. Med. Coll., N.Y.C., 1959-61; asst. prof. medicine U. B.C., 1961-66, assoc. prof., 1966-69, prof., 1969—99, dean faculty medicine, 1977-90, assoc. v.p. acad., 1990-96, dean emeritus, from 1999. Mem. B.C. Med. Assn., Can. Assn. Anatomists, Am. Assn. Anatomists. Achievements include research on renal structure and function. Home: Vancouver, Canada. Died Jan. 24, 2006.

WEBSTER, ORRIN JOHN, agronomist; b. Arkansas City, Kans., June 26, 1913; s. Milo Edwin and Mary Gertrude (Witters) W.; m. LeVenia Hile, May 31, 1936; children:

Dean G., Thomas J., Jean M. BS, U. Nebr., 1934, MS, 1940; PhD, U. Minn., 1950. With Soil Conservation Service, 1935-36, USDA, 1936-75, agronomist Africa, 1951, 63-71, P.R., 1971-75. Adj. prof. U. Ariz., Tucson, 1975—. Contbr. articles to profl. jours. Mem. Am. Soc. Agronomy, Am. Genetics Soc., Sigma Xi, Gamma Sigma Delta, Alpha Zeta. Rebublican. Methodist. Home: Tucson, Ariz. Died Feb. 26, 2004.

WEGHER, PEARL ELLA, retired special education educator; b. Newcastle, Wyo., Jan. 7, 1911; d. Solon Henry and Nina Ethel (Furman) Dewey; m. Arthur Florian Wegher, May 17, 1936; children: Carol, Roland, Rosemary, A. Gene, Marise, Joanne. BA, U. Wyo., 1931; MA, U. No. Colo., 1966. Cert. tchr., remedial reading tchr., spl. edn. tchr. Tchr. Sch. Dist. One, Newcastle, 1928-29, 31-36, 1945-49; remedial reading tchr. Sch. Dist. Seven, Kersey, Colo., 1957-62; spl. edn. tchr. Weld Bd. Coop. Ednl. Svcs., Weld County, Colo., 1962-76. Vol. tchr. Right to Read, Greeley, 1978-93. Frequent election judge Weld County and City of Greeley, 1980-92; active Ch. Women United, 1982-93; vol. tax aid. Recipient Honor scholarship U. Wyo., 1926. Republican. Roman Catholic. Avocations: esperanto, reading, puzzles, house plants. Home: Greeley, Colo. Died July 17, 2005.

WEGMAN, ROBERT B., food service executive; b. Rochester, NY, Oct. 14, 1918; m. Peggy Wegman; children: Daniel, Joan Profeta, Gail Tobin, Marie Kenton. BBA, Niagara Univ., 1947; degree (hon.), St. John Fisher Coll., Rochester, 1986; LHD (hon.), SUNY, Genesco, 1994. With Wegman's Food Markets, Inc., Rochester, 1936—42, store mgr., 1947—49, pres., 1949—76, CEO, 1969—2005, chmn., 1969—2006. Pres. Super Market Inst. (now Food Mktg. Inst.), 1967—69; chmn. pub. policy sub. com. for Grocery Industry Devel. of Universal Prod. Code, 1970—74. With USMC, 1942-46. Named one of 50 Industry Visionaries, Supermarket News, 2002; named to Nat. Bus. Hall of Fame, Phila. Jr. Achievement, 2004; recipient Sidney Rabb Award, Food Mktg. Inst., 1981, VandenBrul Entrepreneurial Award, Rochester Inst. Tech., 1991, Civic Medal Award, Rochester C. of C., 1994, Corning Award, Bus. Coun. N.Y. State, 1998, Edn.l Achievement award, SUNY Coun. for Univ. Affairs and Develop., 2002. Avocations: harmonica, golf, baseball. Died Apr. 20, 2006.

WEHR, WESLEY CONRAD, museum curator; b. Everett, Wash., Apr. 17, 1929; s. Conrad John and Ingeborg (Hall) W. BA, U. Washington, 1951, MA, 1953. Affiliate curator paleontology Burke Mus. U. Wash., Seattle, from 1976. Cons. Stonerose Interpretive Ctr., Republic, Wash., 1990—; guest curator Cheney Cowles Mus., Spokane, 1987, 88, State Capitol Mus., Olympia, Wash., 1986, Frye Art Mus., Seattle, 1984. Mem. Internat. Soc. Paleontology, Botanical Soc. Am., U. Wash. Pres. Club, U. Wash. Deans Club. Democrat. Home: Seattle, Wash. Died Apr. 12, 2004.

WEIGLEY, RUSSELL FRANK, history educator; b. Reading, Pa., July 2, 1930; s. Frank Francis and Meta Beulah (Rohrbach) W.; m. Emma Eleanor Seifrit, July 27, 1963; children: Jared Francis Guldin, Catherine Emma Rohrbach. BA, Albright Coll., 1952; MA, U. Pa., 1953, PhD, 1956; HLD (hon.), Albright Coll., 1978. Instr. history U. Pa., Phila., 1956-58; asst. prof. Drexel Inst. Tech., Phila., 1958-60, assoc. prof., 1960-62, Temple U., Phila., 1962-64, prof. history, 1964-85, Disting. Univ. prof., 1985-98, prof. emeritus, 1998—2004. Vis. prof. Dartmouth Coll., Hanover, N.H., 1967-68; U.S. Army vis. prof. mil. history rsch. U.S. Army War Coll., U.S. Army Mil. History Rsch. Collection, Carlisle Barracks, Pa., 1973-74; pres. Am. Mil. Inst., Washington, 1975-76. Author: Quartermaster General of the Union Army: A Biography of M.C. Meigs, 1959, Towards an American Army: Military Thought from Washington to Marshall, 1962, History of the United States Army, 1967, 84, The Partisan War: The South Carolina Campaign of 1780-82, 1970, The American Way of War, 1973, Eisenhower's Lieutenants, 1981 (Atheneum of Phila. Spl. award for Nonfiction by a Phila. Author, 1983), The Age of Battles: The Quest for Decisive Warfare from Breitenfeld to Waterloo, 1991, A Great Civil War: A Military and Political History, 1862-1865, 2000 (Lincoln prize 2001); editor: The American Military: Readings in the History of the Military in American Society, 1969, New Dimensions in Military History, 1976, Philadelphia: A 300-Year History, 1982. Mem. hist. adv. commn. Dept. of Army, Washington, 1976-79, 88—92, 2003-04, Pa. Hist. Records Adv. Com., Harrisburg, 1977-79; bd. dirs. Masonic Libr., Mus. of Pa., The Grand Lodge of Masons of Pa., Phila., 1990-95, 1997-2003. Penrose Fund grantee Am. Philos. Soc., 1958; fellow John Simon Guggenheim Meml. Found., 1969-70; recipient Samuel Eliot Morison prize Am. Mil. Inst., 1989, Lincoln prize, 2001. Mem. Hist. Soc. Pa. (vice chmn. 1989-93, councilor 1983-89, 92-98, emeritus 1998-2004), Pa. Hist. Assn. (pres. 1975-78, v.p. 1967-75, coun. 1967-2004, editor jour. 1962-67), Am. Hist. Assn., Orgn. Am. Historians, Soc. Mil. Hist. (Disting. Book award 1992), So. Hist. Assn., Soc. Am. Historians Inc., Interuniv. Seminar on Armed Forces and Soc., Am. Philos. Soc., Masons (33d degree, Scottish rite supreme coun. no. Masonic jurisdiction 1999). Democrat. Unitarian Universalist. Home: Philadelphia, Pa. Died Mar. 3, 2004.

WEIL, DANIEL WILKUS, lawyer; b. Chgo., Nov. 17, 1940; s. Myron F. and Virginia (Wilkus) W. Student, London Sch. Econs., 1961; BS, U. Wis., 1962; JD, Northwestern U., 1965. Bar: Ill. 1965, N.D. 1975, U.S. Supreme Ct. 1969. Contractor Agy. for Internat. Devel., San Jose, Costa Rica, 1966; asst. state's atty. Cook County, Chgo., 1967-70; exec. dir. Cook County Dept. Corrections, Chgo., 1970, warden, 1970-73; asst. U.S. atty. (No. dist.) Ill. US Dept. Justice, Chgo., 1973-75; chmn. Ill. Law Enforcement Commn., Chgo., 1977-83; ptnr. Winston & Strawn, Chgo., 1975—89; commr. bldgs. City of Chgo., 1989—94. Vice chmn. RC Cola Bottling Co., Inc., Chgo. Chmn. Ill. Juvenile Justice Adv. Com., Chgo., 1980-82, Cook County Criminal Justice Adv. Commn., Chgo., 1980-83. Russell Sage fellow in Legal Anthropology, 1966. Mem. Fgn. Policy Research (bd. dirs.), Chgo. Bar Assn., Old Town C. of C. (bd. dirs.). Avocations: fgn. policy, government, politics, law enforcement. Home: Chicago, Ill. Died May 30, 2006.

WEIL, ROBERT IRVING, lawyer, retired judge; b. NYC, Apr. 6, 1922; s. Irving Julius and Esther (Aisenstein) W.; m. Carol Ethel Tannenbaum, Nov. 6, 1946 (div. 1953); children: David Irving, Timothy Robert; m. Dorothy Granet Kornhandler, Sept. 12, 1958. AB, UCLA, 1943; MS in Journalism, Columbia U., 1944; JD, U. So. Calif., L.A., 1951. Bar: Calif. 1951, U.S. Dist. Ct. (cen. dist.) Calif. 1951, U.S. Supreme Ct. 1961. Assoc. Pacht, Tannenbaum & Ross, L.A., 1951-54; ptnr. Tannenbaum, Steinberg & Shearer, Beverly Hills, Calif., 1954-58, Aaronson, Weil & Friedman, L.A., 1958-75; judge Calif. County Superior Ct., L.A., 1975-90; pvt. practice L.A., 1990—2005. V.p. L.A. Police Commn., 1973-75; chmn. Calif. Ctr. for Jud. Edn. and Rsch., Emoryville, 1989-90; lectr., seminar leader Calif. Jud. Coll., Berkeley, 1981-2005, The Rutter Group, L.A., 1981-2005. Co-author: California Practice Guide: Civil Procedure Before Trial, 1983; contbr. articles to profl. jours. Mem. ABA, Am. Judges Assn., Calif. Judges Assn. (pres. 1985-86, v.p. 1993-94), Pres.'s award 1987, v.p. 1993, Edn. award 1997), L.A. County Bar Assn., L.A. Copyright Soc., Beverly Hills Bar Assn. Avocations: writing, reading, travel, theater. Died Aug. 13, 2005.

WEILER, HAROLD EDWARD, municipal executive, military officer; b. Medford, Wis., Feb. 9, 1934; s. Nicholas Theodore and Elsa Elizabeth (Bartelt) W.; m. Dolores Elizabeth Easton, June 15, 1963; children: Drew, Deborah, Richard. BS, U. Alaska, 1955; MS, Shippensburg (Pa.) U., 1975. Commd.2d lt. U.S. Army, 1955, advanced through grades to col., 1977, advisor to N.G., 1975-77; comdr. Support Ctr., Frankfurt, Germany, 1977-79; ret. U.S. Army, 1979; asst. city mgr. City of Harken Heights, Tex., 1979-84, city mgr. Tex., 1984-92, City of Bridgeport, W.Va., from 1994. Advisor Area Emergency Med. Svc. Dirs., Killeen, Tex., 1990-92. Dir. Sch. Improvement Coun., Bridgeport, 1994-96. Decorated Legion of Merit (3), Bronze Star (3). Mem. Internat. City Mgrs. Assn., W.Va. City Mgrs. Assn., VFW, Am. Legion, Kiwanis Internat. (dir. 1979-92). Avocations: golf, fishing. Home: Bridgeport, W.Va. Died Jan. 27, 2004.

WEINBERG, ALVIN MARTIN, physicist; b. Chgo., Apr. 20, 1915; s. J.L. and Emma (Levinson) W.; m. Margaret Despres, June 14, 1940 (dec. 1969); children: David, Richard; m. Gene K. DePersio, Sept. 20, 1974 (dec. 2004). AB, U. Chgo., 1935, A.M., 1936, PhD, 1939; LL.D., U. Chattanooga, Alfred U.; D.Sc., U. Pacific, Denison U., Wake Forest U., Kenyon Coll., Worcester Poly. Inst., U. Rochester, Stevens Inst. Tech., Butler U., U. Louisville, U. Bridgeport. Research assoc. math. biophysics U. Chgo., 1939-41, Metall. Lab., 1941-45; joined Oak Ridge Nat. Lab., 1945, dir. physics div., 1947-48, research dir. lab., 1948-55, dir. lab., 1955-74; dir. Office Energy R&D, Fed. Energy Adminstrn., 1974, Inst. Energy Analysis, Oak Ridge, 1975-85; disting. fellow Oak Ridge Associated Univs., 1985—2006. Mem. Pres.'s Sci. Adv. Com., 1960-62, Pres.'s Medal of Sci. Com. Author: Reflections on Big Science, (with E.P. Wigner) Physical Theory of Neutron Chain Reactors, 1958, Continuing the Nuclear Dialogue, 1985, Nuclear Reactions: Science and Trans-Science, 1992, The First Nuclear Era: The Life and Times of a Technological Fixer, 1994; co-author: The Second Nuclear Era, 1985; co-editor: The Nuclear Connection, 1985, Strategic Defenses and Arms Control, 1987; editor: Eugene Wigner's Collected Works on Nuclear Energy. Recipient Atoms for Peace award, 1960, E.O. Lawrence award, 1960, U. Chgo. Alumni medal, 1966, Heinrich Hertz award, 1975, N.Y. Acad. Scis. award, 1976, Enrico Fermi award, 1980, Harvey prize, 1982, Eugene Wigner award in reactor physics, 1992. Mem. Nat. Acad. Scis. (applied sci. sect.), Am. Nuclear Soc. (pres. 1959-60, Alvin M. Weinberg award 1996), Nat. Acad. Engring., Am. Acad. Arts and Scis., Am. Philos. Soc., Royal Netherlands Acad. Sci. (fgn. asso.) Home: Oak Ridge, Tenn. Died Oct. 18, 2006.

WEINBERG, JOHN LIVINGSTON, retired diversified financial services company executive; b. N.Y.C., Jan. 5, 1925; s. Sidney James and Helen (Livingston) W.; m. Sue Ann Gotshal, Dec. 6, 1952; children: Ann K. (dec.), John, Jean. AB cum laude, Princeton U., 1947; MBA, Harvard U., 1950. With Goldman, Sachs & Co., N.Y.C., 1950—2001, ptnr., 1956-76, sr. ptnr., 1976-90, co-chmn. mgmt. com., 1976-84, sr. ptnr., chmn. mgmt. com., 1984-90, sr. chmn., 1990-2001. Sr. chmn. The Goldman Sachs Group, Inc., 2001-06; mem. Conf. Bd.; hon. chmn. John L. Weinberg Ctr. Corp. Governance, U. Del. Dir. emeritus N.Y. and Presbyn. Hosps. 2d lt. USMCR, 1942-46, capt., 1951-52. Fellow AAAS; mem. Coun. on Fgn. Rels., Bus. Coun. Home: Greenwich, Conn. Died Aug. 7, 2006.

WEINBERGER, CASPAR WILLARD, publishing executive, former secretary of defense; b. San Francisco, Aug. 18, 1917; s. Herman and Cerise Carpenter (Hampson) W.; m. Jane Dalton, Aug. 16, 1942; children: Arlin Cerise, Caspar Willard. AB magna cum laude, Harvard U., 1938, LLB, 1941; LLD (hon.), U. Leeds, Eng., 1989; LittD (hon.), U. Buckingham, 1995, Rennselear Poly., U. San Francisco. Bar: Calif., 1941, U.S. Ct. Appeals (DC cir.) 1990. Law clk. to Hon. William E. Orr US Ct. Appeals (9th cir.), San Francisco, 1945-47; atty. Heller, Ehrman, White & McAuliffe, 1947-69, ptnr., 1959-69; mem. Calif. State Assembly from 21st Dist., 1952-58; vice chmn. Calif. Rep. Ctrl. Com., 1960-62, chmn., 1962-64, Com. Calif. Govt. Orgn. and Econs., 1967-68; dir. fin. State of Calif., 1968-69; chmn. FTC, Washington, 1970; dep. dir. Office Mgmt. & Budget Exec. Office of the Pres., Washington, 1970-72, dir., 1972-73; counsellor to the Pres. The White House, Washington, 1973; sec. US Dept. Health, Edn. & Welfare, Washington, 1973-75; gen. counsel, v.p., dir. Bechtel Power Corp., San Francisco, 1975-80, Bechtel, Inc., 1975-80, Bechtel Corp., 1975-80; sec. U.S. Dept. Def., Washington, 1981-87; counsel Rogers & Wells LLP, Washington and NYC, 1988-94; pub. Forbes mag., NYC, 1989—93; chmn. Forbes Inc., NYC, 1993—2006. Formerly staff book reviewer San Francisco Chronicle; moderator weekly TV program Profile, Bay Area, sta. KQED, San Francisco, 1959-68; Frank Nelson Doubleday lectr., 1974; co-host World Bus. Review, 1996-99 Author: Fighting for Peace: Seven Critical Years in the Pentagon, 1990; co-author (with Peter Schweizer): The Next War, 1996, Chain of Command, 2005; co-author: (with Gretchen Roberts) In the Arena: A Memoir of the 20th Century, 2001; co-author: (with Wynton C. Hall) Home of the Brave: Honoring the Unsung Heroes in the War on Terror, 2006. Chmn. Pres.'s Com. on Mental Retardation, 1973-75; mem. Pres. Fgn. Intelligence Adv. Bd., 1987-88; former mem. Trilaterial Commn.; former mem. adv. coun. Am. Ditchley Found.; former bd. dirs. Yosemite Inst.; former trustee St. Luke's Hosp., San Francisco, Mechanics Inst.; former chmn. nat. bd. trustees Nat. Symphony, Washington; former bd. govs. San Francisco Symphony; chmn. bd. USA-ROC Econ. Coun., 1991-94; co-chmn. Winston Churchill Travelling Fellowships Found., 1989-99; trustee Winston Churchill Meml. Trust; bd. dirs. Chatham House Found., Inc.; mem. coun. on fgn. rels; served as Capt., AUS, 1941-45; PTO. Decorated Bronze Star, Grand Cordon of Order of the Rising Sun (Japan), Hon. Knight Grand Cross Civil Div. Order of Brit. Empire, Order of Brillians Star with Grand Cordon, Taiwan; recipient Presdl. medal Freedom with distinction, 1987, Merite First Class, Mex., 1987, George Catlet Marshall medal, 1988, Civil award Hilal-i-Pakistan, 1989. Mem. ABA, State Bar Calif., D.C. Ct. Appeals, Century Club (N.Y.), Bohemian Club (San Francisco), Pacific Union Club (San Francisco), Harvard Club (Washington). Episcopalian (former treas. Diocese of Calif.). Home: Mount Desert, Maine. Died Mar. 28, 2006.

WEINDRUCH, LINDA SUE, lawyer; b. Davenport, Iowa, June 4, 1956; d. Ira and Donna (Friedman) W. BA in Psychology and Sociology, St. Ambrose Coll., Davenport, 1980; postgrad. in Internat. Studies, London Sch. Econs., 1982; JD with honors, Drake U., 1983; LLM in Taxation, NYU, 1988. Bar: Iowa, U.S. Tax Ct. 1984. Rsch. asst. Drake Law Sch., Des Moines, 1982-83; tax specialist Peat Marwick Mitchell & Co., Des Moines, 1984; assoc. Belin Harris Helmick, P.C., Des Moines, 1984-87; ptnr. Dickinson, Mackaman, Tyler & Hagen, P.C., Des Moines, from 1988. Mem. ABA (state and local tax com.), Iowa Bar Assn. (chair taxation sect. 1993-94), Polk County Bar Assn., Nat. Assn. Bond Lawyers, Order of Coif. Died Oct. 5, 2004.

WEINER, CHARLES R., federal judge; b. Phila., June 27, 1922; s. Max and Bessie (Chairney) W.; m. Edna Gerber, Aug. 24, 1947; children: William, Carole, Harvey. Grad., U. Pa., 1947, MA, 1967, PhD, 1972; LL.B., Temple U., 1950. Bar: Pa. bar 1951. Asst. dist. atty. Philadelphia County, 1952-53; mem. Pa. Senate from Phila. County, 1952-67, minority floor leader, 1959-60, 63-64, majority floor leader, 1961-62; judge Ea. Dist. Pa., 1967—88, sr. judge, 1988—2005. Mem. Phila. County Bd. Law Examiners Mem. Pres.'s Adv. Commn. Inter-Govtl. Rels., Phila., Pub. Policy Com., Phila. Crime Prevention Assn., Big Bros. Assn.; mem. Pa. Bd. Arts and Scis.; trustee, exec. com. Fedn. Jewish Philanthropies of Phila., Allied Jewish Appeal of Phila.; bd. dirs. Mental Health Assn. of Pa., Phila. Psychiat. Ctr., Phila. Tribune Charities, Phila. Wharton Ctr. Parkside YMCA, Jewish Publ. Soc. Am., The Athenaeum, and others. With USN, 1942—46. Recipient Phila. Fellowship award; Founder's Day award Temple U.; Alumni award U. Pa.; Founder's award Berean Inst.; others. Mem. ABA, Pa. Bar Assn., Phila. Bar Assn., Am. Law Inst. Died Nov. 9, 2005.

WEINER, MERVYN LESTER, international consultant; b. Montreal, Que., Can., Oct. 30, 1922; came to U.S., 1948; s. Louis and Beatrice (Feinstein) W.; m. Shirley Reva Hurwitz, Aug. 26, 1951; children: Risa Ellen Weiner Selig, Lewis Richard. BCom, McGill U., 1943; MPhil, Oxford U., 1948. With World Bank, Washington, 1951-84, econ. advisor, chief economist for Western Hemisphere, 1965-69, dir. pub. utility projects, 1969-72, dir. Asia region projects, 1972-74, v.p. South Asia region, 1974-75, dir.-gen. ops. evaluation, 1975-84; internat. cons. Chevy Chase, Md., from 1984. Capt. arty. Royal Can. Army, 1943-46. Rhodes scholar, 1946. Died Mar. 12, 2005.

WEINER, MURRAY, medical educator, pharmaceutical researcher; b. N.Y.C., Apr. 18, 1919; s. Samuel O. and Gussie (Begun) W.; m. Marilyn R. Greenberg, Jan. 14, 1951 (dec. 1973); children: Eve Gail Weiner Shauer, George Jay, Joan Sally Weiner Tarasar; m. Barbara Samuelson, Oct. 17, 1990. BS, CCNY, 1939; MS in Biochemistry, MD, NYU,

1943. Diplomate Am. Bd. Internal Medicine. Intern Sinai Hosp., Balt., 1944; resident, fellow NYU/Goldwater Meml. Hosp., N.Y.C., 1946-49, clin. researcher, 1946-70; from instr. to prof. NYU, N.Y.C., 1946-70; dept. head, v.p. Geigy Pharms., Ardsly, N.Y., 1956-70; v.p. rsch. Merrell-Nat. Labs., Cin., 1970-80; prof. medicine U. Cin., from 1970. Pvt. practice, N.Y.C. and Plainveiw, N.Y., 1949-70; pres. Weiner Cons., Inc., Cin., 1980—; cons. in field. Author: The Medicine Makers, 1979, Nicotinic Acid, 1983, Side Effects to Exipients, 1989; editor: Clinical Pharmacology, 17 vols., 1986-91. Chmn. Cin. chpt. Project Hope, 1978-82. Capt. U.S. Army, 1944-46. Achievements include patent for Method of Drug Incorporation into Red Blood Cells, others; research in coagulation and pharmacodynamics. Home: Cincinnati, Ohio. Died Aug. 25, 2004.

WEINER, SEYMOUR SIDNEY, French language educator; b. N.Y.C., Sept. 4, 1917; s. Morris and Jennie (Ostashinski) W.; m. Bobbie West; children: Anthony (dec.), Marc, Paula. Diplomas, Institut de Touraine, France, 1937, U. de Dijon, 1937, 38; BA, CCNY, 1940; MA, U. Calif., Berkeley, 1941; PhD, Columbia U., 1950, MSLS, 1952. Bibliographer U. Ill. Libr., Champaign, 1952-53; asst. to assoc. prof. U. Wash., Seattle, 1953-63; assoc. prof. French SUNY, Stony Brook, 1963-64; prof. French U. Mass., Amherst, 1964-89, dir. grad. studies, 1965-75, prof. emeritus, from 1989. Mng. editor French Rev., 1965-68; editor-in-chief Critical Bibliography of French Literature, 1965-75; author: Francis Carco, 1952; contbr. 50 articles to profl. jours. U. Wash. grantee, 1954-62; Knight, Order of Merit of the Acad. Palms, France, 1970; recipient medallion Cath. U. of the West, Angers, France, 1987. Mem. ALA, MLA, Am. Assn. Tchrs. French (exec. coun. 1965-68, chpt. pres. 1984-85), Societe des Lettres, Sciences et Arts de l' Aveyron, Societe des Professeurs Francais et Francophones en Amerique. Democrat. Jewish. Avocations: book collecting, travel, opera. Home: Tucson, Ariz. Died Aug. 2, 2005.

WEINGARTEN, SAUL MYER, lawyer; b. L.A., Dec. 19, 1921; s. Louis and Lillian Dorothy (Alter) W.; children: David, Steven, Lawrence, Bruce. AA, Antelope Valley Coll., 1940; AB, UCLA, 1942; cert., Cornell U., 1943; JD, U. Southern Calif., 1949. Bar: Calif. 1950, U.S. Supreme Ct., 1960, Calif. Supreme Ct., 1950, Fed. Dist. Ct., 1950, U.S. Ct. of Mil. Appeals, 1951, U.S. Supreme Ct., 1961. Prin. Saul M. Weingarten Assocs., Seaside, Calif., from 1954. Atty. City of Gonzales, Calif., 1954-74, City of Seaside, 1955-70; gen. counsel Redevel. Agy., Seaside, 1955-76, Security Nat. Bank, Monterey, Calif., 1968-74; bd. dirs., exec. com. Frontier Bank, Cheyenne, Wyo., 1984-99; pres. Quaestor, Inc., 1991-98. Author: Practice Compendium, 1950; contbr. articles to profl. jours. Del. Internat. Union of Local Authorities, Brussels, Belgium, 1963, 73; candidate state legislature Dem. Com., Monterey County, 1958; counsel Monterey Peninsula Mus. of Art, Inc., 1972-80; gen. counsel Monterey County Symphony Assn., Carmel, Calif., 1974-98, Mountain Plains Edn. Project, Glasgow, Mont., 1975-81; chmn. fund raising ARC, Monterey, 1964; chmn., bd. dirs. fund raising United Way, Monterey, 1962-63; pres., bd. dirs. Alliance on Aging, Monterey, 1968-82; bd. dirs. Family Svc. Agy., Monterey, 1958-66, Monterey County Cultural Coun., 1986-94, Clark Found., 1982—; dir., mem. exec. com. Monterey Bay Performing Arts Ctr., 1990. Served to commdr. USN, 1942-46, 50-54, Korea. Grad. fellow Coro Found., 1949-50. Mem. Calif. Bar Assn., Monterey County Bar Assn., Monterey County Trial Lawyers Assn., Rotary (pres. 1970-71, 82-83), Commonwealth Club, Meadowbrook Club. Jewish. Avocation: travel. Home: Pebble Beach, Calif. Died Feb. 18, 2004.

WEINSTOCK, GRACE EVANGELINE, librarian, retired educator; b. Currie, Minn., Dec. 16, 1904; d. Charles Clementine and Lydia Hannah (Halland) O'Neill; m. Joseph Marshall Weinstock, Sept. 1, 1945 (dec. July 1973). BA, Hamline U., 1925; AAS in Libr. Sci. Tech., Coll. Lake County, 1988. High sch. tchr. Latin, history, phys. edn. Bd. Edn., Grafton, N.D., 1925-27, high sch. tchr. Latin, history, phys. edn. Norwood, Minn., 1928-32, high sch. tchr. Latin, English, libr. Wells, Minn., 1932-38; interviewer I Minn. State Employment Svc., Redwood Falls, Minn., 1938-45; interviewer II U.S. Employment Svc., Mpls., 1938-45; substitute tchr. English and bus. depts. North Chicago (Ill.) High Sch. Dist. 123, 1956-72; contractual employment instr. typing U.S. Dept. Army 5th U.S. Army Edn. Ctr., Ft. Sheridan, Ill., 1959-71; mil. personnel clk. Dept. Def., USN, Great Lakes, Ill., 1972-86; part-time libr. Outboard Marine Corp., Waukegan, Ill., 1988-90; part-time clerical worker Highland Park (Ill.) Hosp., 1990-91. Bd. dirs. Lake County Community Concert Orgn., Waukegan, 1990. Grantee Waukegan br. Ednl. Found., 1993. Mem. AAUW (program chmn. Waukegan br. 1960), Navy League U.S., Phi Theta Kappa, Alpha Kappa Delta, Pi Gamma Mu. Avocations: cooking, english smocking, quilting, reading. Home: Lake Bluff, Ill. Died Mar. 7, 2004.

WEISER, NORMAN MYRON, retail executive; b. Cin., July 10, 1931; s. Isadore and Helen (Rubinowitz) W.; m. Margo Groetzinger, Feb. 28, 1954; children: Jeffrey, Cynthia. BBA, U. Cin., 1954. Mgr. systems and programming Shillito's div. Federated Dept. Stores, Cin., 1964-68, corp. v.p. systems R & D, 1978-83; v.p. M.I.S., Cin., 1969-72, v.p., treas., 1972-78; asst. contr. Abercrombie & Fitch, N.Y.C., 1968-69; v.p. M.I.S., Morse Shoe Inc., Canton, Mass., from 1983. Cons. in field. Author: Information Week, 1987, Retail Control, 1986. V.p. ops., bd. dirs. Old Colony Coun. Boy Scouts Am., 1984—. With U.S. Army, 1954-56. Recipient Silver Beaver award Boy Scouts Am., 1974. Mem. Nat. Retail Merchants Assn. (bd. dirs. 1981-88, 1st v.p. systems div. 1986-88). Republican. Jewish. Avocation: model railroading. Home: Loveland, Ohio. Died Nov. 23, 2004.

WEISHAAR, SANDRA JEAN, manufacturing company official; b. Indpls., Aug. 14, 1947; d. Edward Ferguson and Marian Ann (Fehrman) Deeter; m. Donald E. Weishaar, July 15, 1972. Student, Ind. U., 1991; grad., Inst. Children's Lit., 1967. Cert. tng. cons. Customer ops. mgr. Wavetek RF Products, Inc., Indpls., 1980-84, export compliance mgr., 1984-91; traffic mgr. Endress & Hauser, Greenwood, Ind., 1993-97; internat. sales coord. CRC Products, Inc., Indpls., 1997-99. Instr. Internat. Adv. Svcs., Indpls., 1989-97, Internat. Trade Inst., Dayton, Ohio, 1991—; cons. mgmt. and tng. svc. Bedford, Ind., 1991-92. Vol. VISTA, 1965-66; assoc. Indpls. 500 Festival, 1992—; instr. Jr. Achievement, 1985-89. Mem. Nat. Notary Assn., World Trade Club Ind. (bd. dirs. 1987-95, pres. 1993-94), Nat. Authors Registry. Home: Indianapolis, Ind. Died Nov. 14, 2004.

WEISL, EDWIN LOUIS, JR., foundation executive, lawyer; b. NYC, Oct. 17, 1929; s. Edwin L. and Alice (Todriff) W.; m. Barbara Butler, June 12, 1974 (dec.); 1 child, by previous marriage, Angela Jane. AB, Yale, 1951; LL.B., Columbia, 1956. Bar: N.Y. 1956, D.C. 1968. Assoc. Simpson Thacher & Bartlett, N.Y.C., 1956-64, mem. firm, 1964-65, 69-73; adminstr. parks, recreation and cultural affairs, commr. parks City of N.Y., 1973-75; asst. atty. gen. of U.S. in charge of land and natural resources division, 1965-67; asst. atty. gen. in charge civil div., 1967-69; asst. spl. counsel, preparedness investigating com. U.S. Senate, 1957-58; former pres. Internat. Found. for Art Research. Dir. N.Y. State Dem. campaign, 1964; mem. The 1001, World Wildlife Fund; mem. vis. com. dept. European paintings Met. Mus. Art; bd. dirs. Robert Lehman Found.; mem. corp. Presbyn. Hosp., N.Y.C.; bd. dirs. Old Master Exhbn. Soc. N.Y.; mem. Villa I Tatti Coun, Harvard Ctr. for Renaissance Studies. Lt. (j.g.) U.S. Navy, 1951-53. Mem. Explorers Club, Warrenton Hunt Club, Century Assn., Fauquier Club. Died Oct. 27, 2005.

WEISNER, MAURICE FRANKLIN, retired military officer; b. Knoxville, Tenn., Nov. 20, 1917; s. Clinton Hall and Adra Inez (Ogg) W.; m. Norma Holland Smith, May 30, 1942; children: Maurice Hall, Franklin Lee, Stewart Holland. BS, U.S. Naval Acad., 1941; aviation tng., 1943; grad., Nat. War Coll., 1959. Commd. ensign USN, 1941, advanced through grades to adm., 1972, ret.; assigned U.S.S. Wasp, 1941-42; various aircraft squadrons in PTO, 1942-46, (U.S.S. Badoeng Strait), 1947-48; comdr. Patrol Squadron 46, 1949-51; assigned Office Chief Naval Ops., 1951-53; comdr. Fighter Squadron 193, 1954-55; assigned air striking forces study sect. Office Chief Naval Ops., 1955-58; comdr. Fighter Squadron 101, 1959-60, U.S.S. Guadalupe, 1960-61, U.S.S. Coral Sea, 1961-62; assigned Bur. Naval Personnel, 1962-64; dir. air weapons systems analysis staff Office Chief Naval Ops., 1964-65; comdr. Carrier Div. 1, 1965-67; dep. chief naval personnel USN, 1967-69; comdr. Attack Carrier Striking Force 7th Fleet, 1969-70, 7th Fleet, 1970-71; dep. chief naval ops. (air warfare) USN, 1971-72, vice chief naval ops., 1972-73; comdr. in chief U.S. Pacific Fleet, 1973-76, Unified Pacific, 1976-79. Decorated Def. D.S.M., Navy D.S.M. with 4 gold stars, Army D.S.M., Air Force D.S.M.; Legion of Merit with gold star; D.F.C. with gold star; Air medal with 5 gold stars; Navy Commendation medal. Home: Pensacola, Fla. Died Oct. 15, 2006.

WEISS, CHARLES FREDERICK, pharmacologist, pediatrician, retired air force officer; b. Cohoctah, Mich., Apr. 2, 1921; s. Frederick William and Claudius Beehan (Stanard) W.; m. Bernice Pearigen, Aug. 9, 1947; children: Charles S., Paul Frederick, Thomas Barton. BA, U. Mich., 1942; MD, Vanderbilt U., 1949; grad., USAF Sch. Aerospace Medicine, 1952, Indsl. Coll. Armed Forces, 1973. Diplomate Am. Bd. Pediatrics. Commd. 2d lt. USAF, advanced through grades to col.; intern Harper Hosp., Detroit, 1950; resident in pediatrics Children's Hosp. Mich., 1950-52; mini-resident in occupational medicine U. Cin., 1982; pvt. practice in pediatrics Grosse Pointe, Mich., 1953-58; assoc. dir. Parke, Davis and Co., Ann Arbor, Mich., 1958-69; clin. asst. prof. pediatrics/communicable disease U. Mich., 1962-68; assoc. prof. pediatrics, pharmacology, Coll. Pharmacy U. Fla. Coll. Medicine, 1969-73; chief of staff, interin adminstr. Hope Haven Children's Hosp., Jacksonville, Fla., 1974-76; spl. asst., cons. pediatrics, adviser manpower affairs, oversight mgr. drug testing program Office of the Surgeon Gen., USAF, Washington, 1976-83; ret. USAF, 1983; exec. dir. Sunland Ctr., Orlando, Fla., 1984; v.p. med. affairs, chmn. bd. sci. advisors hiMedics, Inc., Hollywood, Fla., 1985-88; dir. planning and devel. Dakle, Inc., Staunton, Va., 1989-92; cons. Siesta Key, Fla., from 1989; clin. assoc. prof. pediatrics U. South Fla. Coll. Medicine, from 1992. Cons. SYVA Corp., 1984-85, Key Pharm., Inc., 1983-84, Fla. Dept. HRS, 1984-87, ELAN Pharm. Rsch. Corp., 1991-92; presenter in field; mem. site visit team mental retardation and metabolic diseases NIH, 1970-72. Editor: Pharmacology for the pediatrician, 1971-75; reviewer Military Medicine, 1974—, Pediatrics, 1975—; contbr. articles and abstracts to profl. publs. Med. dir. Fla. Spl. Olympics, 1973, v.p., 1975, med. dir., v.p. 1976, bd. dirs. 1977; bd. dirs. Duval Assn. for Retarded Children, 1973-76; bd. dirs. Pastoral Counseling Ctr., Presbyn. Synod of Suwanee, 1973-76, treas., 1975-76; bd. dirs. Gainesville Open House, 1972-73; ruling elder 1st Presbyn. Ch., Ann Arbor, 1962-65, 67-73, various other coms., Ann Arbor and Gainesville; bd. ushers Nat. Presbyn. Ch., Washington, 1977-84, vice chmn., trustee 1981-84; ordained, ruling elder Clk. of Session, Siesta Key Chapel, Presbyn., 1998—. Col. USAF, 1972-83. Decorated Legion of Merit, 1983. Mem. AMA (Physicians Recognition award), Am. Acad. Pediatrics (chpt. chmn. Uniformed Svcs. Chpt. 1980-83, com. on sci. mtgs. 1987—, chmn. environ. health com. Fla. chpt. 1990—, Outstanding Svc. award 1986, Pres.' award 1984), Fla. Med. Assn., Fla. Pediatric Soc., Sarasota County Med. Soc., Am. Soc. Clin. Pharmacology and Therapeutics, Soc. Med. Cons. to Armed Svcs., Res. Officers Assn., Ret. Officers Assn., Air Force Assn., Meninak Club Jacksonville, Army and Navy Club, Marine Meml. Club, Order of the Arrow, Rho Chi. Republican. Died Jan. 13, 2004.

WEISS, DAVID JOHN, film and television producer, director, writer; b. Kansas City, Mo., Feb. 22, 1941; s. Ned and Rose (Bernstein) W.; m. Margaret Nikoloric, June 10, 1970 (div. 1975). BA, U. Mo., Kansas City, 1963; MA, U. Mo., 1966. Writer, producer Westinghouse Broadcasting, N.Y.C., 1967-68; producer, dir. Group W TV, San Francisco, 1968-69; freelance writer San Francisco, Los Angeles, 1970-73; writer, producer KCET-TV, Los Angeles, 1973-75; free-lance writer, producer, dir. Los Angeles, 1978-79; news editor Apparel News Group, Los Angeles, 1981-82; exec. producer Redken Labs., Canoga Park, Calif., 1982-85; pres. Beachfront Prodns., Marina Del Rey, Calif., from 1985. Cons. indsl., informational and mktg. communications. Writer, producer, dir. (TV special) Gene Autry: American Hero, 1980 (nominated for Emmy award); contbr. articles to profl. jours. Active Mus. Contemporary Art, Los Angeles. Pilot/planning grantee Nat. Endowment Humanities, Los Angeles, 1974. Mem. Assn. Free-lance Profls. (charter). Democrat. Jewish. Avocations: sailing, bridge, walking. Died Mar. 9, 2004.

WEISS, ERNEST, federal agency administrator; b. Detroit, Oct. 28, 1918; s. Louis and Eugenie (Glick) W.; m. Gloria Caroline Hacker, Feb. 21, 1942; children: Lynn Carol, Gail Corynn. BBA, CUNY, 1942; postgrad., Am. U., 1948-54. With Gen. Svc. Adminstrn. VA, 1946-52, ICC, Washington, 1952-67, asst. to mng. dir., 1955-63, asst. mng. dir., 1963-67; exec. dir. Nat. Transp. Safety Bd., Washington, 1967-72; sr. staff scientist George Washington U., Washington, 1973-78; commr. Montgomery County (Md.) Commn. on Health, 1990-96. Recipient Meritorious Achievement award Transp. Dept., 1968. Mem. Phi Sigma Alpha. Home: Chevy Chase, Md. Died Dec. 17, 2004.

WEISS, MADELINE, artist; b. N.Y.C., July 5, 1926; d. Max and Esther (Reiter) Stern; m. Philip Weiss, Mar. 2, 1946; children: Mark Ira, Joseph. Studied with, Lillian Orlowsky and William, Freed (proteges of Hans Hofmann), N.Y.C. Founder, pres. Nat. Assn. Women Artists Fla. chpt. Contbr. to Who's Who in Am. Art, Kravis Ctr. for Performing Art, Palm Beach Jewish Times, Culture Mag., Images Mag., News/Sun-Sentinel (Palm Beach), 1995, Ice Mag., 1994, N.Y. Times, Art in America, Artspeak Mag., 1988, numerous others; works in pub. collections/commns. include Tustin Rehab. Ctr., Santa Ana, Calif., Good Samaritan Hosp., West Palm Beach, Fla., J.F.K. Med. Ctr., Edison, N.J., Gen. Instrument Corp., N.Y., Transamerica Devel. Corp., N.Y.C., The Palm Beach County Home, Matson, Driscoll and Damico, N.Y.C., The State of Fla., Cocoa; one-woman shows include: The Hodgell Gallery, Sarasota, Fla., 1995, Studio 412, West Palm Beach, 1994, Jewish Community Ctr., West Palm Beach, 1993, Riverside Comm. Ctr., Palm Beach Gardens, Fla., 1993, Northwood Inst., West Palm Beach, 1992—, Deanna Harris Gallery, Lake Worth, Fla., 1991, United Technologies, Palm Beach Gardens, 1990, Governors Club, 1989, others; group shows include Northwood Univ. Gallery, West Palm Beach, 1995—, Royal Palm Beach Cultural Ctr., 1995—, Norton Mus. of Art, West Palm Beach, 1994, numerous others; creator of Tubular Constrns. and Geometric Abstracts. Nominated to Fla. Artists Hall of Fame, 1995, Channel 20/Artist Scene, 1992, Channel 2/PBS, 1986. Avocations: word games, classical music concerts, opera. Home: West Palm Bch, Fla. Died Feb. 2, 2005.

WEISS, MAX TIBOR, retired aerospace transportation executive; b. Hajduananas, Hungary, Dec. 29, 1922; came to U.S., 1929, naturalized, 1936; s. Samuel and Anna (Hornstein) W.; m. Melitta Newman, June 28, 1953; children: Samuel Harvey, Herschel William, David Nathaniel, Deborah Beth. BEE, CCNY, 1943; MS, MIT, 1947, PhD, 1950. Rsch. assoc. MIT, 1946-50; mem. tech. staff Bell Tel. Labs., Holmdel, NJ, 1950-59; assoc. head applied physics lab. Hughes Aircraft Co., Culver City, Calif., 1959-60; dir. electronics rsch. lab. The Aerospace Corp., L.A., 1961-63, gen. mgr. labs. div., 1963-67, gen. mgr. electronics and optics div., 1968-78, v.p., gen. mgr. lab. ops., 1978-81, v.p. engring. group, 1981-86; v.p. tech. and electronics system group Northrop Corp., L.A., 1986-91, v.p., gen. mgr. electronics systems div. Hawthorne, Calif., 1991-94; corp. v.p., dep. gen. mgr. electronics/systems integration Northrop Grumman Corp., Bethpage, NY, 1994-96, corp. v.p., 1996. Asst. mgr. engring. ops. TRW Systems, Redondo Beach, Calif., 1967-68; mem. sci. adv. bd. USAF; bd. dirs. Concorde Solutions, Inc., Concord, Calif. Contbr. articles to profl. jours. With USNR, 1944-45. Fellow Am. Phys. Soc., IEEE (Centennial medal, 1983, Fredrik Philips award, 1993), AIAA, AAAS; mem. NAE, Sigma Xi. Achievements include patents for electronics and communications. Home: Los Angeles, Calif. Died June 10, 2006.

WEITZEL, RONALD L., secondary school educator; b. Monroe, Mich., July 9, 1942; s. Ralph C. and Mary M. Weitzel; children: Derek, Jamie. BA, U. Calif., Davis, 1967, MA, 1969. Social studies tchr. Page Sch. Ho. of Representatives, Washington, 1983—2006. Home: Washington, DC. Died July 13, 2006.

WEITZMAN, ROBERT HAROLD, investment company executive; b. Chgo., July 15, 1937; s. Nathan and Selma Weitzman; m. Marilynn Beth Felzer (dec. 2003), Sept. 5, 1965; children— Joshua C., Eliza S. BA in Bus., Econs., Grinnell Coll., 1959; JD, DePaul U., 1963. Bar: Ill 1963. Vice pres. Weitzman Enterprises, Chgo., 1955-63; assoc. Lissner, Rothenberg, Reif & Barth, Chgo., 1963-68; real estate counsel Continental Ill. Nat. Bank and Trust Co., Chgo., 1968-74; v.p., group head Continental Ill. Investment Trust, Chgo., 1974-76; founding ptnr. Group One Investments, Chgo., 1977—2006. Founding sponsor DePaul U. Real Estate Ctr., 2002-06; lectr. in field Editor: Real Estate Finance Handbook, 1979. Contbr. articles to profl. jours Trustee, advisor Weitzman Found., 1963-77, mng. trustee, 1978—2006; cons., advisor Ill. chpt. Big Bros. Am. Orgn., 1969-72; trustee The Wis. Real Estate Investment Trust, 1980, 81. Recipient Outstanding Young Man Am. award U.S. Jaycees, 1973 Mem. Ill. Bar Assn., Chgo. Bar Assn., Nat. Assn. Rev. Appraisers and Mortgage Underwriters (charter mem. cert. rev. appraiser designation, cert valuation cons.), Real Estate Securities and Syndication Inst. (bd. dirs. Ill. chpt. 1982-90, pres. 1984, regional v. p. 1988, specialist in real estate securities designation 1988, chmn. nat. com. on continuing edn. 1989, 90). Real Estate Investment Assn. (founding mem., Nat. bd. dirs. 1990-2006, exec. com. nat assn. and Ill. chpt. 1990-2006, chmn. nat. com. for advanced edn., 1990-95, nat. pres. 1996-98, nat. chmn. 1999-2006, specialist in real estate investment designation 1990), Am. Inst. Banking, Internat. Coll. Real Estate Cons. Profls., Internat. Real Estate Bd Home: Deerfield, Ill. Died Apr. 1, 2006.

WELCH, CARLOS HARLAN, lay minister; b. Brotherton, Tenn., Sept. 7, 1939; s. Henry Norris and Cornelia (Dishman) W.; m. Phillis Elaine Dement, May 27, 1967; 1 child, Kellie. BA in Edn., Harding U., 1965. Cert. elem. and secondary tchr., Mo. Elem. tchr. Bunker (Mo.) R-3 Sch., from 1979; lay min. Centerville (Mo.) Ch. of Christ, from 1982. Song dir. Harmony Ch. of Christ, Searcy, Ark., 1961-65 Democrat. Home: Centerville, Mo. Died Feb. 26, 2004.

WELCH-BOWLING, PATRICIA, retired nursing educator, not-for-profit developer; b. Middlesboro, Ky., Oct. 10, 1922; d. Charles William and Charlotte Paulina (Willis) W.; m. Charles E. Bowling, July 20, 2004. Diploma in nursing, U. Tenn., Knoxville, 1943. RN, Ky. Commd. ens. USN, 1944, advanced through grades to lt. comdr., with nurse corps, 1944-70, ret., 1970; nursing educator Appalachian Regional Healthcare, Middlesboro, 1970-88; exec. dir. United Way, Middlesboro, from 1995. City councilor City of Middlesboro, 1992—, mem. hist. commn., 1990—; mem. adv. bd. Salvation Army, Middlesboro, 1972—, Boys' Group Home, Middlesboro, 1985—. Recipient Humanitarian Hist. Women Yr., Bell County Ky. C. of C., 2005. Mem. Bell County C. of C. (bd. dirs. 1997—), Middlesboro Garden Club (pres. 1994), Bus. and Profl. Women's Club (pres. 1972-99, Woman of Yr., Woman of Achievement), Kiwanis. Republican. Baptist. Avocations: community service, travel, reading. Home: Middlesboro, Ky. Died Mar. 18, 2005.

WELLISCH, HANS HERBERT, library science educator; b. Vienna, Apr. 25, 1920; came to U.S., 1969; s. Fritz and Marianne (Fischer) W.; m. Shulamith B. Oberlander, Feb. 5, 1946; children: Tamar, Ilana, Yuval. MLS, U. Md., 1972, PhD, 1975. Head documentation ctr. Tahal Cons. Engrs., Tel Aviv, 1956-69; head libr. svcs. Ctr. of Scientific & Technol. Info., Tel Aviv, 1966-67; vis. lectr. Coll. of Libr. & Info. Svcs., U. Md., College Park, 1969-75, prof., 1976-87, prof. emeritus, 1988—2004. Bd. dirs. U.S. Info. Ctr. for the Universal Decimal Classification, College Park. Author: The Conversion of Scripts, 1978 (award 1979), Abstracting and Indexing: An International Bibliography, 1980, 84, Indexing From A to Z, 1991; contbr. articles to profl. jours. Mem. Am. Soc. Indexers (pres. 1984-85), Nat. Info. Standards Orgn. (mem. several coms.), Israel Soc. of Spl. Librs. and Info. Ctrs. (founding mem.). Jewish. Avocations: travel, photography, classical music. Home: Bethesda, Md. Died Feb. 6, 2004.

WELLNER, ROBERT FRANCIS, civil engineer; b. St. Clair, Pa., July 28, 1928; s. Leo Francis and Marcella Frances (Monahan) W.; m. Mary Elizabeth Scanlan, Dec. 27, 1952; children: Teresa M., Mary Louise, Robert L., Maureen E. BSCE, U. S.C., 1951. Registered profl. engr., Pa., N.C., S.C., Fla. Design engr. Bethlehem (Pa.) Steel Corp., 1954-59, devel. engr., 1959-60, sales engr., 1960-67, dist. coord., 1967-69, mgr. constrn. mktg., 1969-83; v.p. Figg Engring. Group, Alexandria, Va., 1983-88, sr. v.p., 1988—2005. Bd. dirs. YMCA, Bethlehem, 1975-81, chmn. bldg. com., 1981-82. Lt. USN, 1951-54. Mem. ASCE (sect. pres. 1972-73), Engring. Soc. West Pa., Am. Road and Transp. Builders Assn. (pres. material svc. div. 1974-75, bd. dirs. 1974-77, dir. planning and design div.), Saucon Valley Country Club, Pinehurst Country Club. Republican. Roman Catholic. Home: Bethlehem, Pa. Died Feb. 9, 2005.

WELLS, BETTY CALHOUN, elementary school educator; b. Haywood County, N.C., Feb. 28, 1938; d. Fred Herbert and Agnes Lee Calhoun; m. Keller Wells, June 15, 1956; children: Cynthia Lee Register, Jeffrey Lane Wells. BS in Elem. Edn., Bob Jones U., Greenville, S.C., 1961; MRE, Bethany Theol. Sem., Dothan, Ala., 1989; postgrad., U. S.C. Cert. elem. tchr. N.C., S.C., Fla. First grade tchr. Greenville County Sch. Dist., S.C., 1961-71, Providence Christian Sch., Riverview, Fla., 1971-80, pre-sch. dir., 1980-91, elem. supr., from 1991. Leader Girl Scouts of Am., Greenville, 1961-65; appointee Child Care Facilities Adv. Bd., 1996; mem. various Bapt. Ch. orgns. Recipient awards for profl. and ch. activities. Mem. Fla. Assn. of Christian Schs. Avocations: knitting, reading, crossword puzzles, handcrafts. Home: Seffner, Fla. Died Apr. 10, 2005.

WELLS, KATHERIN MALISSA, elementary school educator; b. Afton, Mich., Oct. 25, 1931; d. LeRoy John and Dessie Marie (Soules) Ormsbee; m. Wallace Edward Prall, June 7, 1951, (div. 1957); children: Cynthia, Daniel, Julie; m. Howard Dewayne Wells, June 30, 1962 (dec. 1985); children: Penny, Dale. BS, Western Mich. U., 1969. Cert. elem. tchr. Tchr. Bethany Sch., St. Louis, Mich., 1959-60, Needham Sch., Burr Oak, Mich., 1960-62, Colon (Mich.) Elem. Sch., 1962-63, Bronson (Mich.) Elem. Sch., from 1967. Chairperson Burr Oak Twp. Zoning Bd., 1955—; dir. women's, music and christian edn. depts. Reogranized LDS Ch. Mem. NEA, Mich. Edn. Assn., Bronson Edn. Assn. (treas. 1962—), Burr Oak Grange. Avocations: handcrafts, music, reading, travel, collecting bells. Home: Burr Oak, Mich. Died July 15, 2005.

WELLS, LYNN WINHAM, nursing administraotr; b. Texarkana, Ark., June 29, 1930; d. G. Daniel and Teo (Tinker) Winham; m. Bobby R. Wells, Feb. 3, 1951; children: Jo Lynn, Edward Ellis, Bobby Rose. Diploma, T.E. Schumpert, 1951; postgrad., Texarkana Community Coll. Cert. in clin. pastoral ministry. Mycology researcher Commonwealth of Ky., Paris, Ky., 1972-79; asst. dir. nursing svc. Ky. Respiratory Disease Hosp., Paris, 1983-88; dir. critical care St. Michael Hosp., Texarkana, Ark., dir. home health, asst. dir. nursing, 1981-83. Mem. Ark. League for Nursing, Ark. Orgn. Nurse Execs., Ark. Assn. Home Health Agencies. Home: Texarkana, Ark. Died July 11, 2005.

WELLS, MICHAEL TREVOR, communications consultant; b. London, Apr. 6, 1928; came to U.S., 1959; s. George and Lilian Grace (Williams) W.; m. Mary Farkass, July 16, 1960 (div. May 1984); children: Lilian Grace, Michael Anthony; m. Soontree Dulyapitak, 1985. Student, Eng. CPA, Conn.; FCA in U.K. Sr. auditor Haskins and Sells, Paris, 1952-55; audit mgr. Price Waterhouse, Sao Paulo, Brazil, 1956-59; with ITT, 1959-82, gen. mgr. Brazil, 1960-66, area gen. mgr. S.Am. Buenos Aires, 1967-75; exec. dir. external relations ITT World Communications Inc., N.Y.C., 1976-82; exec. v.p. Cable and Wireless N.Am., N.Y.C., 1983-89; mgmt. cons. Argyll Corp., Stamford, Conn., from 1990. Contbr. articles and papers to profl. lit. Served with Royal Arty., 1946-48. Fellow Inst. Chartered Accts.; mem. Can. Inst. Chartered Accts., Assn. Cert. Accts. Clubs: Royal Auto (London); Met. (N.Y.C.); Jockey Argentino (Buenos Aires); Jockey Brasileiro (Rio de Janeiro). Episcopalian. Home: Greenwich, Conn. Died Mar. 28, 2004.

WELLS, MILTON THOMAS, association executive; b. Richmond, Va., Oct. 12, 1948; s. Thomas Milton and Mozelle (Cannon) W.; m. Susan Lee Wooten. BA, Randolph-Macon Coll., 1971; postgrad., U. Va., 1971-73, George Wash. U., 1973-76. Revenue officer IRS, Washington, 1971-77; legis. analyst U.S. Treasury/IRS, Washington, 1977-88; legis. fellow Senator Max Baucus, Washington, 1987-88; v.p. Liz Robbins Assocs., Washington, 1988-89; dir. fed. relations Nat. Assn. of State Treas., Washington, from 1989. Flying col. Delta Air Lines, 1981—. Member Fairfax County Rep. Com., Washington, Congress, Washington, 1988. Recipient Pub. Svc. award U.S. Dept. Transp.-Fed. Hwy. Administrn., 1986. Mem. Am. Soc. Assn. Execs., Greater Washington Soc. Assn. Execs., The Road Gang, Assn. Insiders, Am. Coun. on Capitol Formation, Tax Coun., Kiwanis, Capitol Hill Club, Ky. Col., Ark. Traveler, Sigma Alpha Epsilon. Home: Mc Lean, Va. Died Aug. 26, 2004.

WELSH, SUE C., law librarian; b. Denver, Mar. 5, 1943; d. William Glenn and Viola West Calhoun; m. Neal W. Welsh, Oct. 5, 1968; children: Erick, Ethan. BA, Colo. State U., 1965; MS in Libr. Sci., Cath. U. Am., 1978. Info. specialist U.S. Fed. Jud. Ctr., Washington, 1972—81; deputy cir. libr. U.S. Ct. Appeals (9th cir.), San Francisco, 1981—90; head elec. info. U. Pacific, McGeorge Sch. Law, Sacramento, from 1990. Mem.: Western Pacific Chpt. Law Librs., No. Calif. Assn. Law Librs. (pres. 2001—02), Am. Assn. Law Librs., Kappa Delta. Home: Acampo, Calif. Died June 28, 2004.

WENDEL, JOSEPH ARTHUR, retired secondary education educator; b. Somerville, N.J., Mar. 19, 1926; s. Peter Fred and Lillian Stewart Wendel. BA, Kenyon Coll., 1950; MA in English, U. Iowa, 1967. Tchr. Malcolm Gordon Sch., Garrison, N.Y., 1952-54, St. Bernard's Sch., Gladstone, N.J., 1954-56, Princess Elizabeth Sch., St. John, N.B., Can., 1957-60, Fay Sch., Southborough, Mass., 1960-63; tchr., adminstr. Kingsbrook Acad., Mendham, N.J., 1972-74; asst. headmaster, tchr. St. Paul's Sch., Garden City, N.Y., 1974-83; tchr. Arlington Christian Sch., Fairburn, Ga., 1985-95. Tchr., area rep. U.S. Peace Corps, Asella, Ethiopia, 1963-65; tchr., asst. prof. Haile Selassie I. U., Addis Ababa, Ethiopia, 1967-71; tchr. Tex. Mil. Inst., San Antonio, 1983-84; instr. English Davis & Elkins Coll., Elkins, W.Va., 1984-85. Tutor Literacy Vols. Ea. Panhandle, Martinsburg, W.Va., 1995—; vol. Berkeley County Schs., Martinsburg, 1995—. Quartermaster 3/C USN, 1944-46, PTO. Home: Martinsburg, W.Va. Died Mar. 4, 2005.

WENTZEL, ALAN RAYMOND, lawyer; b. Melrose, Mass., Mar. 6, 1939; s. Raymond E. and Edna R. (Woods) W.; m. Barbara L. Hanson, Aug. 27, 1961; children: Jennifer L., Jeffrey W., Mary E., Stephen C. BA, Amherst Coll., 1960; LLB, Yale U., 1963. Ptnr. Windels Marx Lane & Mittendorf LLP, N.Y.C., from 1970; village justice Justice Ct., Bronxville, N.Y., from 1988. Bd. dirs. Can. Life Ins. Co. N.Y. Village trustee Village of Bronxville, 1983-88. Republican. Home: Bronxville, NY. Died Apr. 30, 2004.

WEPFER, JULIA M., psychologist; b. El Dorado, Ark., May 12, 1936; d. Joseph Gottlieb and Julia Witherspoon (Fletcher) W.; m. Harry Ames Metcalf, June 1, 1957 (div.); 1 child, Holly Kinyon. BS in Bus. Adminstrn., U. Ark., 1958, MA in Psychology, 1965; PsyD, Fla. Inst. Tech., 1980. Lic. psychologist, Ark. Market analyst Am. Investment Advisors, Little Rock, 1958; office mgr. to orthodontist Little Rock, 1958-60; office mgr. to psychiatrist, 1961-64; psycholog. examiner U. Ark. for Med. Scis. Dept. Psychiatry, Little Rock, 1966-67, tchg. asst., 1967-69, instr., 1969-75, asst. prof., 1975-85; pvt. practice Little Rock, from 1985. Mem. Ark. Bd. Examiners in Psychology, Little Rock, 1973-78. Ark. coord. Deaf-Blind Project, Little Rock, 1971—72; mem. Regional AIDS Interfaith Network Care Team, Little Rock, 1992—97; mem. commn. on ministry Episcopal Diocese of Ark., Little Rock, from 1994; pres. bd. dirs. Columbia Land & Timber Co., Beauregard Parish, La. Fellow Ark. Psychol. Assn. (pres. 1982-83); Chi Omega (Psi chpt.). Democrat. Avocations: water aerobics, gardening, computers, scuba diving, weaving. Died June 16, 2005.

WERBOW, STANLEY NEWMAN, language educator; b. Phila., Apr. 19, 1922; s. Morris and Sadie (Newman) W.; m. Naomi Esther Ecker, June 1, 1952; children: Susan Linda, Emily Frances, Carol Martha. BA, George Washington U., 1946; postgrad., Middlebury Coll., 1946, 47, U. Mich., 1948; PhD, Johns Hopkins, 1953. Tchr. Ea. High Sch., Washington, 1946-47; research analyst specialist U.S. Dept. Def., Washington, 1952-53; mem. faculty U. Tex., Austin, 1953—2006, prof., 1965-69, 78-97, chmn. dept. Germanic langs., 1969-71, dean Coll. Humanities, 1971-78, acting dean Coll. Fine Arts, 1980-81, prof. emeritus, 1997—2006. Vis. prof. U. Marburg, 1963, U. N.Mex. German Summer Sch., 1984, 87, 89. Author: Martin von Amberg, 1957, (with Lehmann, Rehder, Shaw) Review and Progress in German, 1959; Editor: Formal Aspects of Medieval German Poetry, 1970. Served with Signal Corps AUS, 1943-45. Decorated Bronze Star medal; Bundesverdienstkreuz erster klasse W. Ger.; recipient Fulbright award to Netherlands, 1950-51; Guggenheim fellow, 1960; Fulbright research scholar Germany, 1960-61 Mem. Modern Lang. Assn. (pres. South Central assn. 1976—2006), Medieval Acad., Internat. Assn. Germanists, Phi Beta Kappa, Phi Kappa Phi, Delta Phi Alpha. Home: Austin, Tex. Died Oct. 9, 2005.

WERNER, BURTON KREADY, insurance company executive; b. St. Louis, Apr. 24, 1933; s. Elmer L. and Helen (Kready) W.; m. Joanna Catherine Hill, Oct. 17, 1959; children: Lisa Anne, Cynthia Catherine, Bradford Kready. AB cum laude, Amherst Coll., 1954; MBA, U. Pa., 1958. CPCU. Sec. Insurers Svc. Corp., St. Louis, 1958-65, exec. v.p., 1965-75, pres., also bd. dirs., 1975-88; v.p., bd. dirs. Safety Mut. Casualty Corp., St. Louis, 1958-76, pres., 1976-87, chmn., 1987-91; also bd. dirs.; chmn. Safety Nat. Casualty Corp., St. Louis, 1991-99, chmn. emeritus, from 1999. Chmn. SIG Holdings, Inc., St. Louis, 1991-96, Delphi Fin. Group, Inc., bd. dirs.; originator unemployment compensation reinsurance for non-profit orgns. under pub. law 91-373. Guarantor St. Louis Mcpl. Opera; trustee Churchill Sch., St. Louis Country Day Sch.; mem. Humane Soc. Mo., Arts and Edn. Coun. St. Louis, Associated Industries Mo., Mo. Bot. Garden, Mo. Hist. Soc., St. Louis Symphony Soc., City Art Mus., St. Louis Landmark Assn, Maui Meml. Med. Ctr. Found., Inc., Hui No'Eau Visual Arts Ctr., Maui Arts and Cultural Ctr. Capt. USAF, 1954—56. Named to Hon. Order Ky. Cols. Fellow: Truman Libr.; mem.: Better Bus. Bur. St. Louis, Am. Soc. CPCU, Nat. Assn. Safety and Claims Orgns., St. Louis McDonnell Planetarium, St. Louis Zoo Assn., Wailea Golf Club, Casa y Pesca Las Cruces Club, Windfall Club, Univ. Club, Racquet Club, Napili Kai Beach Club, Boone Valley Golf Club, Jupiter Hills Club, Delta Kappa Epsilon. Episcopalian. Died Feb. 28, 2005.

WERNICK, JACK HARRY, chemist; b. St. Paul, May 19, 1923; s. Joseph and Eva (Legan) W.; B.Met.E., U. Minn., 1947, M.S., 1948; Ph.D., Pa. State U., 1954; m. Sylvia Katz, Dec. 20, 1947 (dec.); children— Phyllis Roberta Wernick Lauer, Rosanne Pauline; m. 2d, Charlotte Adler, 1983. Staff, Manhattan Project, Los Alamos, 1944-46; mem. staff Bell Labs., Murray Hill, N.J., 1954-84, head solid state chemistry research dept., 1963-81, head device materials research dept., 1981-83; div. mgr. Bell Comm. Rsch., 1983-92; cons. U.S. Office Sci. and Tech., Nat. Bur. Standards, NSF; mem. steering com. div. nuclear fusion ERDA, 1977-79; mem. Gov.'s Roundtable on Superconductivity, N.J., 1989-90. Served in U.S. Army, 1944-46. Fellow N.Y. Acad. Scis., Am. Phys. Soc., AIME, Am. Soc. Metals (McFarland award 1969); mem. Nat. Acad. Engring., AAAS, IEEE, Electrochem. Soc., Sigma Xi, Phi Lambda Upsilon. Jewish. Author: (with E.A. Nesbitt) Rare Earth Permanent Magnets,

1973, (with J.L. Shay) Chalcopyrite Crystals, 1975; editor: Materials and Energy: Selected Topics, 1977; Materials Letters; contbr. articles to profl. jours. Home: Millburn, NJ. Died 2006.

WERSHALS, PAUL LEONARD, lawyer; b. Bklyn., July 10, 1942; AA in Bus. Adminstrn., Midwest Inst. Bus. Adminstrn., 1963; BS in Bus. Adminstrn., Babson Coll., 1965; JD, Suffolk U., 1969; LLM, NYU, 1975. Bar: N.Y. 1974, U.S. Supreme Ct. 1974; cert. comml. mediator Nassau Co. Supreme Ct., 2002. Mem. Nassau County Assigned Counsel Defender Plan; mem. legal com., citizens adv. com. for cablevision Town of North Heampstead, N.Y., 1976-97. Mem. Sen. Michael J. Tully's legis. adv. com., 1982-97; dir. Great Neck (N.Y.) Sr. Citizens Ctr., Inc., Town of North Hempstead, 1985-89. Mem. Am. Judges Assn., N.Y. State Trial Lawyers Assn., Nassau County Bar Assn. (arbitrator 1981—, mem. arbitration tribunal panel 1984—), Great Neck (N.Y.) Lawyers Assn. (bd. dirs. 1973—, sec. 1981-84,pres. 1985, chmn. bd. dirs. 1986-87), Phi Alpha Delta (mem. moot ct.). Died May 16, 2004.

WEST, DAVID EUGENE, director, producer; b. Springfield, Ohio, Jan. 17, 1954; s. William F. and Joan Ann (Nicholson) Pieffer. Student, Jacksonville U., 1972-73, Burlington County Coll., 1973-75, U. West Fla., 1976-78, Columbia Coll., 1979-81, Am. Film Inst., 1984, UCLA, 1988. Audio-visual dir., theater mgr. Holiday Inn, Navarre Beach, Fla., 1974-79; dir. distbn., stage mgr. Western Instructional TV, Inc., Hollywood, Calif., 1979-80; cameraman, mgr. broadcast rentals Video Systems Network, Inc., Los Angeles, 1980-83; producer, cameraman Pacific Video Prodns., Inc., Anaheim, Calif., 1983-84, Am. Videogram, Inc., Los Angeles, 1984-86; producer, dir., cameraman Armour Prodns., Orange, Calif., from 1986. Still photographer, cons. Tishman Constrn. Co., Los Angeles, 1983-86; film/TV cons. Bell and Roberts Advt., Huntington Beach, Calif., 1984—; dir., videographer for Burnett/Ehline Devel. Co., Anaheim, 1987—, Ryder Systems, Miami, Fla., 1987—. Cameraman, assoc. producer (TV segment) The Ultimate Challenge, 1984; dir. photography (TV spl.) Cancer Today, 1985; cameraman (TV spl.) Pat Sajak Live, 1987; producer, dir. photography (indsl. film) Gridlock, 1987. Cameraman for Am. Cancer Soc., Los Angeles, 1985, Hands Across Am./USA for Africa, Hollywood, 1986, Earth Run, Los Angeles, 1986, Cowboys for Indians, Beverly Hills, Calif., 1987. Recipient Outstanding Service award The Ad Club, 1985, 86, Bronze and Silver awards Houston Internat. Film Festival, 1986, Moto award Automobile Jour. Conf., 1988. Mem. Am. Film Inst., U.S. Tennis Assn. Clubs: So. Calif. Tennis (North Hollywood). Republican. Episcopalian. Avocations: playing tennis (open and a tournaments), diving, surfing, water and snow skiing. Died Mar. 27, 2005.

WEST, JAMES E., former mayor; b. Salem, Oreg., Mar. 28, 1951; s. Jack Elton and Claire Louise (Bartlett) West. Student, U. Nev., Reno, Spokane C.C., Spokane Falls C.C.; BA, Gonzaga U. Former police officer, dep. sheriff; mem. Wash. State Ho. Reps., Olympia, 1983—87; senator Wash. State Senate, Olympia, 1987—2003, mem. labor, commerce and fin. instns. com., rules com., mem. small bus. improvement coun., mem. state horse racing commn.; mem. K-20 ednl. network bd. Inst. Pub. Policy; mayor City of Spokane, 2004—05. Bd. dirs. Morning Star Boys Ranch, State Investment Bd. With U.S. Army, 82d Airborne Divsn. Recipient Outstanding Young Citizen of Spokane award Jaycees, 1982. Mem. Rotary Club, Spokane city coun., 1979-82. Republican. Died July 22, 2006.

WEST, LINDA KAY, lawyer, novelist; b. Hamilton, Tex., Nov. 5, 1937; d. William Lee West and Mildred B. (Martin) Grudzien. BA, U. Tex., 1959; LLB, So. Meth. U., 1965. Bar: Tex. 1965, La. 1978. Spl. litigation asst. IRS Dist. Counsel, New Orleans, from 1980. Author (romance novels): Honeymoon Suite, 1995 (Nat. Readers Choice award finalist 1995), The Husband Hunt, 1996, Cowboy Seeks Perfect Wife, 1997. Mem. Novelists, Inc., Romance Writers of Am., Sisters in Crime, Crescent City Writers. Democrat. Episcopalian. Home: Mandeville, La. Died Mar. 1, 2004.

WEST, MARIA MCDONALD, social worker; b. Faunsdale, Ala., Aug. 16, 1923; d. John W. and Maria Newill (Brown) McDonald; m. Herbert B. West, Nov. 29, 1946; children: Newill, Herbert, McDonald, Selden, Jane. BA, Judson Coll., 1945; MSW, Yeshiva U., 1975. Bd. cert. diplomate, Cert. Ind. Social Worker. Caseworker Family and Children's Aid, Norwalk, Conn., 1974-81; family counselor Epsic. Social Svc., Bridgeport, Conn., 1981-82; pvt. practice Darien, Conn., from 1980. Mem. NRHCPCSW, NASW, Conn. Soc. Clin. Soc. Work. Home: Darien, Conn. Died Mar. 8, 2004.

WEST, ROBERTA BERTHA, writer; b. Saline County, Mo, Sept. 7, 1904; d. Robert and Amanda Melvina (Driver) Baur; m. Harold Clinton West, Aug. 27, 1932; children: Arle Faith W. Lohof, Lydia Ann (Lyda) F H. Hyde, Danna Rose F H. Burns. AB, William Jewell Coll., 1928; AM, U. Mo., 1930. Cert. tchr., Mo., Mont. Elem. and secondary sch. tchr. Mo. and Mont. Sch., 1922-47; supt. sch. Hogeland Sch., Mont., 1947-48, 55; prof. fgn. lang. Will Mayfield Coll., Marble Hill, Mo., 1930; columnist Quad County Star, Viburnum, Mo., from 1982; writer and rschr. ch. history, 1964-91. Cons. hist. com. Yellowstone Conf. Meth. Ch., 1971-84; compiler Mont. list of Meth. Mins. 1784-1984. Author: Northern Montana Methodist History, 3 vols., 1974, Faith, Hope and Love in the West, 1971; editor: Brother Van by Those Who Knew Him, 1975, reprinted, 1989,; also contbr. articles. Recipient 1st John M. Templeton prize, 1959, Wedgwood Jasper Plate 70th Anniversary of Class of 1927 Wm. Jewell Coll., 1997. Mem. Alpha Zeta Pi. Democrat. Achievements include first to At age 98, still writing weekly for the Star. Avocation: crocheting. Home: Viburnum, Mo. Died Oct. 20, 2004.

WESTERHAUS, CATHERINE K., social worker; b. Corydon, Ind., Oct. 13, 1910; d. Anthony Joseph and Permelia Ann (Mathes) Kannapel; m. George Henry Westerhaus, Apr. 15, 1950. BEd in Music, Kans. U., 1934; MSW, Loyola U., Chgo., 1949. Cert. Acad. Cert. Social Workers. Clin. social worker Friendly Acres Home of Aged, Newton, Kans.; county welfare dir., state adult svcs. supr. Newton-Harvey County, State of Kans.; vol. cert. social worker Newton. Project dir.: Memories of War Years, 1995, The War Years Including Veterans of Harvey County, Kansas, 1995; contbr. articles to profl. jours. Vol. to veterans, home-bound and disabled people, residents in nursing homes, patients in hospitals. With USNR, 1945-46. Named Kans. Social Worker of Yr., 1975, Kans. 5th Dist. Legionnaire of Yr., 1998. Mem. NASW (cert.), Kans. Soc. Cert. Social Work, Am. Legion (comdr. Wayne G. Austin post 1981-82, del Nat. Conv. 1997, Legionnaire of Yr. Dept. Kans. 1998). Died Jan. 1, 2004.

WESTERVELT, VIRGINIA VEEDER, writer; b. Schenectady, N.Y., Sept. 19, 1914; d. Eugene W. and Millicent Freelove Veeder; m. Ralph Vincent Westervelt, Sept. 1, 1936 (dec. 1993); children: Dirck, Deidre Westervelt Meehan. BA in English, Wellesley Coll., 1935; MA in Journalism, Syracuse U., 1961. Tchr. English New Hartford (N.Y.) High Sch., 1958-66; instr. English dept. U. Redlands (Calif.), 1967-75, Hong Kong Bapt. Coll., 1975. Spkr. in field. Author: Getting Along in the Teenage World, 1957, Choosing A Career in a Changing World, 1959, The World Was His Laboratory, 1964, Incredible Man Of Science, 1968: Irving Langmuir, Pearl Buck, 1979, Here Comes Eleanor (Roosevelt), 1998, Guns On The Heights, 1976, Silent Songs, 2002; contbr. articles, stories to nat. mag. Mem. organizing com. A.K. Smiley Friends Libr., Redlands, Calif.; bd. mem. Friends of the Libr., Symphony Guild, Redlands; moderator Cmty. Svc. award tv series on youth, N.Y.; charter mem. Redlands Hist. Mus. Recipient Hon. Name Grant, AAUW, 1985. Mem. Nat. League Am. Pen Women (pres. San Bernardino br., Woman of Achievement 1970, 82, 98), Soc. Children's Book Writers and Illustrators, W.Va. Poetry Soc., Mountain Valley Writers, Toastmasters. Avocations: reading, music, golf, public speaking, travel. Home: Franklin Lakes, NJ. Died Aug. 12, 2005.

WESTHEIMER, DAVID KAPLAN, novelist; b. Houston, Apr. 11, 1917; s. Adolf and Esther (Kaplan) W.; m. Doris Gertrude Rothstein, Oct. 9, 1945; children: Fred, Eric. BA, Rice Inst., Houston, 1937. Successively asst. amusement editor, radio editor, mag. editor, TV editor Houston Post, 1939-41, 45-46, 50, 53-60, columnist, 1984-88. Columnist: SeniorWomen Web (seniorwomen.com); author: Summer on the Water, 1948, The Magic Fallacy, 1950, Watching Out for Dulie, 1960, Von Ryan's Express, 1964, My Sweet Charlie, 1965, Song of the Young Sentry, 1968, Lighter Than a Feather, 1971, Over the Edge, 1972, Going Public, 1973, Tha Avila Gold, 1974, The Olmec Head, 1974, Rider on the Wind, 1979, Von Ryan's Return, 1980, The Great Wounded Bird, and other poems, 2000, (with John Sherlock) The Amindra Gamble, 1982, Sitting It Out, 1992, Death Is Lighter Than a Feather, 1995, Delay En Route, 2002, (with Karen Westheimer) LoneStar Zodiac, 1995, (play) My Sweet Charlie, 1966, (TV films) Trouble Comes to Town, 1972, A Killer Among Us, 1990. Served to capt. USAAF, 1941-45, ETO; served to capt. USAF, 1950-53; lt. col. USAF; ret. Decorated Air medal, D.F.C.; Recipient Tex. Review Poetry prize, 2000 Mem. ACLU, Writer's Guild Am. West, Ret. Officers Assn., Calif. Writers Club. Democrat. Avocation: reading. Died Nov. 8, 2005.

WESTIE, FRANK ROBERT, social sciences educator; b. Houghton, Mich., Mar. 9, 1921; s. Elmer Westie and Anna Sandell; m. Margaret Louise Blum, July 1, 1944; children: Katharine, Kurt, Anne. PhD, Ohio State U., 1951. Pres. Glen Arbor Enterprises, Mich., 1989—2002; adj. prof. Ariz. State U., Tempe, Ariz., 1982—2000; pres. Inverness Woods, Inc., Bloomington, Ind., 1964—82; prof. Ind. U., Bloomington, 1949—82. Faculty grants chmn. Soc. Sci. Rsch. Coun., N.Y.C., 1970—76; pres. North Ctrl. Sociol. Assn., 1970; mem. bd. Fulbright Com., Wash., DC, 1972—76; mem. coun. Am. Sociol. Soc., Wash., DC, 1950. Author: (novels) Ash Wednesday '45, 1996; contbr. articles to profl. jours. 1st lt. USAF, ETO, WWII. Mem.: Author's Guild. Avocation: musical composition. Home: Glen Arbor, Mich. Died Mar. 5, 2004.

WESTON, ROY B., anesthesiologist; b. Port-of-Spain, Trinidad, May 9, 1929; came to U.S., 1977; s. Bertrand H. and Doris (Pantin) W.; m. Elizabeth C. McLaughlin, Oct. 7, 1961; children: Shiobhan R., Brian R. MB, nat. U. Ireland, Dublin, 1956. Cert. anesthesiologist, Fellow Royal Can. Physicians, 1966. Staff anesthesiologist Humber Meml. Hosp., Weston, Ont., Can., 1962-77, Park City Hosp., Bridgeport, Conn., 1977-88; chief anesthesiology Huntington (Ind.) Meml. Hosp., 1988-98. Fellow Am. Coll. Anesthesiologists; mem. Am. Soc. Anesthesiologists, Royal Soc. Medicine, Ind. Med. Assn., Ind. State Soc. Anesthesiologists, Acad. Medicine, Am. Soc. Regional Anesthesia. Roman Catholic. Avocations: gardening, travel. Died Apr. 23, 2004.

WESTWATER, JAMES WILLIAM, chemical engineering educator; b. Danville, Ill., Nov. 24, 1919; s. John and Lois (Maxwell) W.; m. Elizabeth Jean Keener, June 9, 1942; children: Barbara, Judith, David, Beverly. BS, U. Ill., 1941; PhD, U. Del., 1948. Mem. faculty U. Ill., Urbana, 1948—88, prof. chem. engring., 1962—88, head dept., 1962-80, prof. emeritus, 1988—2006. Papers chmn. 5th Nat. Heat Transfer Conf., Buffalo, 1960; chmn. 3d Internat. Heat Transfer Conf., Chgo., 1966; Reilly lectr. Notre Dame U., 1958; Donald L. Katz lectr. U. Mich., 1978 Contbr. articles profl. jours. Recipient Conf. award 8th Nat. Heat Transfer Conf., 1965. Fellow AIChe (dir., past divsn. chmn., inst. lectr. 1964, named eminent chem. engr., William H. Walker award 1966, Max Jakob award with ASME 1972, Founders award 1984, heat transfer and energy conversion award 1989, Ernest Thiele award 1994); mem. ASME, NAE, Am. Chem. Soc., Am. Soc. Engring. Edn. (Vincent Bendix award 1974). Home: Champaign, Ill. Died Mar. 31, 2006.

WETHERILL, GEORGE WEST, geophysicist; b. Phila., Aug. 12, 1925; s. George West and Leah Victoria (Hardwick) Wetherill; m. Phylllis May Steiss, June 17, 1950 (dec. 1995); children: Rachel, George, Sarah; m. Mary Bailey, 1998. PhB, U. Chgo., 1948, SB in Physics, 1949, SM, 1951, PhD in Physics, 1953. Mem. staff dept. terrestrial magnetism Carnegie Inst., Washington, 1953—60; prof. geophysics and geology UCLA, 1960—75, chmn. dept. planetary and space sci., 1968—72; dir. dept. terrestrial magnetism Carnegie Inst., Washington, 1975—91, mem. sci. staff, 1991—2001, dir. emeritus, 2001—06. V.p. Snickersville Gen. Store, Inc., Bluemont, Va., 1976—80; cons. NASA, NSF, NAS. Editor Ann. Rev. of Earth and Planetary Sci., 1981—96, assoc. editor, 1972—80, Meteoritics and Planetary Sci., Icarus; contbr. articles to profl. jours. With USN, 1943—46. Recipient G.K. Gilbert award, Geol. Soc. Am., 1984, Profl. Achievement citation, U. Chgo. Alumni Assn., 1985, Nat. medal of Sci., 1997. Fellow: Meteoritical Soc. (v.p. 1971—74, 1981—83, pres. 1983—85, Leonard medal 1981), Am. Geophys. Union (pres. planetology sect. 1970—72, H.H. Hess medal 1991), Am. Acad. Arts and Scis.; mem.: NAS (J. Lawrence Smith award 2000), Am. Astron. Soc. (Henry Norris Russell Lectureship 2003), Am. Astron. Soc. Divsn. Planetary Scis. and Dynamic Astronomy (Russell lectr. 2003, G.P. Kuiper prize 1986), Internat. Astron. Union, Internat. Assn. Geochemistry and Cosmochemistry (pres. 1977—80), Geochem. Soc. (v.p. 1973—74, pres. 1974—75), Am. Philos. Soc., Internat. Soc. Study of Origin of Life, Religious Soc. Free Quakers. Episcopalian. Home: Washington, DC. Died July 19, 2006.

WHALEN, RICHARD BRADFORD, consulting engineer executive, electrical engineer; b. Belfast, Maine, July 23, 1927; s. Raleigh Arthur and Ola Belle (Redman) W.; m. Arlene Louise White, June 25, 1950; children: Sharon Ann, Patrick W., Rebecca R. BSEE, U. Maine, 1950. Asst. supr. Boston & Maine R.R., Dover, N.H., 1950-56, asst. signal engr. Boston, 1956-57, field engr. signals, 1957-71; engr. signals Thomas K. Dyer, Inc., Lexington, Mass., 1971-74, v.p., 1975-80, sr. v.p., 1980-86, exec. v.p., 1986-87; chief exec. officer R.B. Whalen Co., Danvers, Mass., from 1987. Author: Elements of Electricity applied to Railroad Signal and Train Control Systems, 1977. Served with USN, 1945-46, PTO. Mem. IEEE, Am. Assn. R.R.'s Communications and Signal Div. (chmn. communications div. 1971). Republican. Died Sept. 14, 2004.

WHALLON, WILLIAM, humanities educator; b. Richmond, Ind., Sept. 24, 1928; s. Arthur J. and Adelaide (Wheeler) Whallon; m. Joanne Holland; children: Andrew, Nicholas. BA, McGill U., 1950; PhD, Yale U., 1957. Prof. Mich. State U., East Lansing, 1963—2006. Author: Formula, Character, and Context, 1969, Problem and Spectacle, 1980, Inconsistencies, 1983, A Book of Time, 1990, The Oresteia/Apollo & Bacchus, 1997, The Jesus Rule, 2002. Home: East Lansing, Mich. Died Jan. 5, 2006.

WHARTON, DAVID C., data processing administrator; b. Caldwell, Ohio, Aug. 2, 1945; s. Clyde W. and Margaret (Fetkovich) W.; m. Maria E. Avelino, June 5, 1965 (div. Sept. 1990); 1 child, Theresa; m. Beryle I. Matsumura, Oct. 12, 1990; children: Nathan, Evan, Megan. BA in Bus. Adminstrn., Otterbein Coll., Westerville, Ohio, 1984; Cert. in Pub. Adminstrn., U. Hawaii, 1990. Systems analyst Miles Labs., Inc., Worthington, Ohio, 1968-72, Drs. Hosp., Columbus, Ohio, 1972-74; sr. systems analyst Hughes Helicopters, L.A., 1978-79, NCR, Inc., Cambridge, Ohio, 1974-78, 79-80; project mgr. Gold Circle Stores, Worthington, 1980-83; quality assurance analyst BancOhio Nat. Bank, Columbus, 1983; project mgr. Online Computer Libr. Ctr., Dublin, Ohio, 1983-85; mgmt. analyst Hawaii Med. Svc. Assocs., Honolulu, 1985-87; mgr. data processing Dept. Land and Natural Resources, Honolulu, from 1987. Served with U.S. Army, 1963-68, Vietnam. Avocation: music. Home: Princeville, Hawaii. Died Feb. 14, 2005.

WHARTON, HUGH DAVIS, III, lawyer, judge; b. Buffalo, June 1, 1940; s. Hugh Davis and Helen Bricka (McAuliffe) W.; m. Patricia Granville Ditton, June 20, 1964 (div. Apr. 1982); children: Jennifer Wharton, Gregory Paul, Michael David. BA, Princeton U., 1961; JD, Yale U., 1964. Bar: Alaska 1965, Colo. 1965, Calif. 1969. Asst. atty. gen. State of Alaska, Juneau, 1964-65; chief law clk. to Judge Doyle, U.S. Dist. Ct., Denver, 1965-66; field rep. U.S. OEO, Office of Pres., Kansas City, Mo., 1966-67, San Francisco, 1967-69, dep. regional atty. Western region, 1969-71, regional atty., 1971-73; city atty. City of Livermore, Calif.,

1973-74; regional atty. Western region U.S. Dept. Energy, San Francisco, 1974-80; pvt. practice San Francisco, Santa Rosa, from 1980; adminstrv. law judge City and County of San Francisco, 1984-01; judge pro tem Superior Ct., from 1990. Pres. Golden Gate Bus. Assn., San Francisco, 1989-92; mem. bd. dirs. United Way of the Bay Area, 1989-2001; candidate for supr. City and County of San Francisco, 1982, 84, candidate for muni judge, 1988; mem. vol. bd. dirs. San Francisco Gen. Hosp., 1983-88; pres. Diamond Hts. Cmty. Assn., San Francisco, 1987-90. Recipient John W. Gardner Disting. Leadership award United Way, 1992. Mem. State Bar of Calif., Bay Area Lawyers for Individual Freedom. Democrat. Episcopalian. Avocations: politics, travel, exercise, classic cars, thai culture. Died Jan. 9, 2004.

WHEELER, C. HERBERT, architect, consultant, educator; b. Merchantville, NJ, June 6, 1915; s. Clarence Herbert and Louise Emma (Pennell) W.; m. Cicely Pointer, Aug. 29, 1940; children: Pamela, Janet, Betsy. BArch, U. Pa., 1937; MArch, MIT, 1940, postgrad., 1953, postgrad., 1956, Alexander Hamilton Inst., 1947. Registered architect N.Y., N.J., Pa., Mich.; cert. Nat. Council Archtl. Registration Bds. Archtl. designer Austin Co., N.Y.C., 1938-41; from architect to chief architect J.G. White Engring. Co., N.Y.C., 1941-55; mgr. engring. Stran Steel Corp., Detroit, 1955-58; mgr. environ. sys. Curtiss-Wright Corp., Quehanna, Pa., 1958-64; prof. archtl. engring. Pa. State U., University Park, 1964-80, prof. emeritus, 1980—2006. Author: Public Organizations and Public Architecture, 1987; co-author: Emerging Techniques of Architectural Practice, 1966, Emerging Techniques of Architectural Programming, 1969. Served to maj. C.E., U.S. Army, 1942-46. Decorated Commendation Ribbon U.S. Army CE, 1945. Fellow AIA (emeritus, internat. rels. com. 1981-84, v.p. Central Pa. chpt. 1984), Union Internat. des Architects Paris (permanent sec. profl. devel. work group 1980-85, coll. dels. 1981-85); mem. Am. Soc. Engring. Edn. (emeritus, chmn. archtl. engring. divsn. 1970), constrn. Specifications Inst., Ret. Officers Assn., Theta Xi (v.p. St. Louis chpt. 1953-54) Republican. Episcopalian/Methodist. Avocations: travel, stamp collecting/philately, geography, literature. Home: State College, Pa. Died Jan. 7, 2006.

WHELAN, JAMES MICHAEL, consultant; b. Joliet, Ill., Feb. 15, 1925; s. James M. and Ellena (Johnson) W.; m. Mary Rockett, June 14, 1952; 1 child, Deirdre (dec.). BS, U. Ill., 1948; PhD, U. Calif., Berkeley, 1952. Mem. tech. staff Calif. Rsch. Corp., Richmond, Calif., 1951-53; supr. Bell Telephone Labs., Inc., Murray Hill, N.J., 1953-64; prof. materials sci., elec. engring., chem. engring. U. So. Calif., L.A., 1964-87; pres. Fugacity, Inc., Wilmington, Calif., from 1987. Cons. Hughes Aircraft Co., Torrence, Carlsbad, Calif., 1970—. Contbr. articles to profl. jours.; patentee in field. With U.S. Army, 1944-46. Democrat. Roman Catholic. Avocation: sailing. Home: Olympia, Wash. Died June 17, 2004.

WHILLOCK, CARL SIMPSON, electric cooperative executive, former academic administrator; b. Scotland, Ark., May 7, 1926; s. Joe and Johnnie (Simpson) W.; m. Margaret Moore Carter; children and stepchildren: Timothy, Tom, Sally Whillock Conduff, Susan Whillock Lipe, Sallie Overbey, Jenny Dakil, Melissa Campbell, Larry, Brennam, Benjamin. BS in Social Welfare, U. Ark., 1948, MA in History and Polit. Sci., 1951; JD, George Washington U., 1960. High sch. tchr., 1946-47; in family bus. livestock feeds, wholesale petroleum co., 1949-55; exec. asst. to Congressman J.W. Trimble, Berryville, Ark., 1955-63; pvt. practice law Clinton, Ark., 1963-66; pros. atty. 14th Jud. Dist., Ark., 1965-66; asst. to pres., dir. univ. rels., part-time instr. polit. sci. U. Ark., Fayetteville, 1966-71, v.p. govtl. rels. and pub. affairs, 1975-78; pres. Ark. State U., Jonesboro, 1978-80, Ark. Electric Coop. Corp., 1980—97; spl. asst. to Pres. for agrl. & trade The White House, Washington, 1997—2001. Bd. dirs. 1st Comml. Bank, Little Rock; campaign mgr. David Pryor for Gov. of Ark. Campaign, 1974-75; exec. sec. Gov. of Ark., 1975, mem., bd. of trustees Univ. of Ark. Mem. Ark. Ho. of Reps., two terms, 1953-56; chmn. Ark. Tax Reform Commn., 1987-88, mem. Pres.'s Ark. Adv. Coun. for Winrock, mem. bd. dirs. Winrock Internat. Inst. for Agrl. Devel. Democrat. Home: Little Rock, Ark. Died Nov. 7, 2005.

WHIMBEY, ARTHUR EMIL, writer; b. New York, Sept. 18, 1940; BA in Psychology, U. Miami, 1961; PhD, Purdue U., 1964. Asst. prof. psychology U. Ill., Urbana, 1965-67; from asst. to assoc. prof. psychology Calif. State U., Hayward, 1967-71; sr. postdoctoral fellow NIMH Inst. Human Learning, Berkeley, Calif., 1971-72; assoc. prof. psychology Dillard U., 1974-75; dir. rsch. CUE project Bowling Green State U., 1976-77, coord. math. and comm. labs. devel. edn. program, 1977-78; acad. support specialist Bethune-Cookman Coll., 1983; reading specialist Miami-Dade Pub. Schs., 1988. Adj. prof. math. CCNY, fall, 1978; vis. prof. math. dept. Xavier U., spring, 1979; cons. Ventures in Edn., Coll. Bd., N.J. State Dept. Edn.; dir. TRAC Inst.; assoc. editor On TRAC Text Reconstrn. Across the Curriculum Newsletter, 1993—; speaker in field. Author: Intelligence Can Be Taught, 1973, Analytical Reading and Reasoning, 2d edit., 1989; (with M.J. Linden) Analytical Writing and Thinking: Facing the Tests, 1990; (with J. Lochhead) Problem Solving & Comprehension, 1991; (with others) Thinking Through Math Word Problems, 1990, Keys to Quick Writing Skills: Sentence Combining and Text Reconstruction, 1992, Blueprint for Educational Change: Improving Reasoning, Literacies, and Science Achievement, 1993; contbr. articles to profl. jours. Resident scholar CCNY, 1978, Clark Coll., 1980-82. Died Aug. 19, 2004.

WHITAKER, EILEEN MONAGHAN (EILEEN MONAGHAN), artist; b. Holyoke, Mass., Nov. 22, 1911; d. Thomas F. and Mary (Doona) Monaghan; m. Frederic Whitaker (dec. 1980). Student, Mass. Coll. Art, Boston. Annual exhibits in nat. and regional juried shows; represented in permanent collections, Frye Mus., Seattle, Hispanic Soc., N.Y.C., High Mus. Art, Norfolk, Va., Mus. Fine Arts, Springfield, Mass., Reading (Pa.) Art Mus., Okla. Mus. Art, St. Lawrence U., Wichita State U., NAD, N.Y.C., San Diego Mus. Art, Retrospective show, Founders Gallery U. San Diego, 1988, invitational one-person show Frye Art Mus., 1990; included in pvt. collections; featured in cover article of American Artist mag., Mar. 1987, in article Art of Calif. mag., July 1991; invitational Am. Realism Exhbn. Cir. Gallery, San Diego, 1992, Challenging Tradition: Women of the Academy, 1826-2003 Exhbn., 2003; author: Eileen Monaghan Whitaker Paints San Diego, 1986. Recipient numerous major awards, including Allied Artists Am., Am. Watercolor Soc., 1st prize Providence Water Color Club, Wong award Calif. Watercolor Soc., De Young award Soc. Western Artists, 1st award Springville (Utah) Mus., Ranger Fund purchase prize, Orbrig prize NA, Walter Biggs Meml. award, 1987; silver medal Am. Watercolor Soc., Watercolor West; fellow Huntington Hartford Found., 1964. Mem. Nat. Acad. Design (Academician, 1978-, William P. and Gertrude Schweitzer prize for excellence in watercolor 171st Annual Exbhn. 1996); mem. Am. Watercolor Soc. (Dolphin fellow), Watercolor West (hon.), San Diego Watercolor Soc. (hon.), Providence Watercolor Club (award), Phila. Watercolor Club. Home: La Jolla, Calif. Died Sept. 28, 2005.

WHITAKER, KATHLEEN K., gifted education facilitator; b. Kansas City, Mo., Mar. 26, 1940; d. Richard Ingram and Rosemary (Frost) Kidd; m. William P. Whitaker, Feb. 24, 1962 (div. 1971); children: Lorie Beth, Minda Corinne. BA, U. Mo., 1962; MS, Kans. U., 1982. Cert. learning disabilities, gifted edn. and social studies tchr.; cert. psychol. examiner. Tchr. learning disabilities Wyandotte County Spl. Edn. Coop., Kansas City, Kans., 1980-84; learning specialist diagnostic team Children's Rehab. Unit Kans. U. Med. Ctr., 1984-85; tchr. learning disabilities Turner Sch. Dist., Kansas City, Kans., 1985-89, tchr. gifted edn., 1988-89 and from 94; facilitator underachieving gifted edn. Shawnee Mission (Kans.) Schs., from 1989; tchr. of gifted, from 1994. Presenter, staff mem. Rimm Underachievement Inst., 1992; presenter, developer larning materials in field; tchr., designer materials for parenting classes. Chmn. worship com. Shawnee Mission Unitarian Soc., 1991, trustee, 1992-93; adv. bd. Saramis Teddy Bear Comfort. Mem. Assn. for Edn. Gifted Underachieving Students, Kans. Assn. for Gifted, Talented and Creative, Phi Delta Kappa. Avocations: bicycling, bridge. Home: Shawnee Mission, Kans. Died Oct. 14, 2004.

WHITAKER, RODNEY WILLIAM See TREVANIAN

WHITE, DAVID ARCHER, petroleum geologist; b. Phila., Jan. 22, 1927; s. Alfred Gary and Enid (Saecker) W.; m. Hester Ann Wolfe, Sept. 6, 1952; children: Jonathan, Daniel, Jennifer. BA, Dartmouth Coll., 1950; MS, U. Minn., 1951, PhD, 1954. Geologist Minn. Geol. Survey, Mpls., 1951-53; sr. rsch. advisor Exxon Prodn. Rsch. Co., Houston, 1954-86; cons., tchr. Oil & Gas Cons. Internat., Austin, Tex., 1987-94. Com. mem. Nat. Petroleum Coun., 1980-81, 85-86. Author: Mesabi Range, Minnesota, 1954; contbr. articles to profl. jours. Served to sgt. U.S. Army, 1945-46, Okinawa. Fellow Geol. Soc. Am.; mem. Am. Assn. Petroleum Geologists, Soc. Ind. Profl. Earth Scientists, Western History Assn. Avocation: writing history of U.S. West. Home: Austin, Tex. Died Nov. 23, 2004.

WHITE, DOROTHY M., pediatrics nurse, administrator; b. Elizabeth, N.J., Dec. 7, 1932; d. William F. and Marie (Beam) Faser; m. Edwin S. White, May 24, 1958; children: Joseph, Paul, Matthew, Mary, William, Kathryn. Diploma, Jersey City Hosp., 1953; BA, Trenton (N.J.) State Coll., 1980. Cert. in adolescent and pediatric nursing. Pediatric staff nurse St. Peter's Med. Ctr., New Brunswick, N.J.; pediatric head nurse Robert Wood Johnson U. Hosp., New Brunswick, pediatrics staff nurse, pediatric asst head nurse. Mem. Orgn. Nurse Execs. N.J. Home: Sicklerville, NJ. Died Feb. 11, 2004.

WHITE, GILBERT F. (GILBERT FOWLER WHITE), geographer, educator; b. Chgo., Nov. 26, 1911; s. Arthur E. and Mary (Guthrie) W.; m. Anne Elizabeth Underwood, Apr. 28, 1944; children: William D., Mary, Frances; m. Claire Sheridan, July 18, 2003. BS, U. Chgo., 1932, SM, 1934, PhD, 1942; LLD (hon.), Hamilton Coll., 1951; ScD (hon.), Haverford Coll., 1955; LLD (hon.), Swarthmore Coll., Earlham Coll., Mich. State U., Northland Coll.; degree (hon.), U. Ariz., 2002; LLD (hon.), Augustana Coll., 2003. Geographer Miss. Valley Com. of P.W.A., 1934, Nat. Resources Bd., 1934-35; sec. land and water com. Nat. Resources Com. and Nat. Resources Planning Bd., 1935-40; with Exec. Office Pres., Bur. Budget, 1941-42; asst. exec. sec. Am. Friends Service Com., 1945-46; relief adminstr. in France, 1942-43; interned Baden-Baden, 1943-44; sec. Am. Relief for India, 1945-46; pres. Haverford Coll., 1946-55; prof. geography U. Chgo., 1956-69; prof. geography, dir. Inst. Behavioral Sci., U. Colo., Boulder, 1970-78, Gustavson disting. prof. emeritus, 1979—2006; dir. Natural Hazards Info. Ctr., 1978-84, 92-94; exec. editor Environment mag., 1983-93. Vis. prof. Oxford U., 1962-63; cons. Investigations Lower Mekong Basin, 1961-62, 70; U.S. mem. UNESCO adv. com. on arid zone research, 1954-55; mem. mission Am. Vol. Agys. Relief Germany, 1946; vice chmn. Pres.'s Water Resources Policy Commn., 1950; mem. com. natural resources Hoover Commn., 1948; chmn. UN Panel Integrated River Basin Devel., 1956-57; chmn. Task Force Fed. Flood Control Policy, 1965-66; sci. adv. to adminstr. UN Devel. Program, 1966-71; chmn. adv. bd. Energy Policy Project, 1972-74; chmn. Am. Friends Service Com., 1963-69; chmn. com. on man and environment IGU, 1969-76; chmn. steering com. High Sch. Geography com., 1964-70; mem. Tech. Assessment Adv. Council, 1974-76; chmn. environ. studies bd. NRC, 1975-77; pres. Sci. Com. on Problems of Environment, 1976-82; chmn. bd. Resources for Future, 1973-79; co-chmn. U.S.-Egypt Joint Consultative Com. on Sci. and Tech., 1981-86; mem. adv. group on greenhouse gases World Meteorol. Orgn., Internat. Council of Scientific Unions, UN Environ. Program., 1986-90; chmn. tech. rev. com. Nev. Nuclear Waste Project, 1987-93; mem. adv. group on water UN Environ. Program, 1989-93, working group for Action Plan for Aral Sea Basin, USSR, 1990-93; chmn. nat. rev. com. Status U.S. Floodplain Mgmt., 1989; bd. dirs. Am. Soc. Flood Plain Mgrs. Found., 1996-2006. Author: Human Adjustment to Floods, 1942, Science and Future of Arid Lands, 1960, Social and Economic Aspects of Natural Resources, 1962, Choice of Adjustment to Floods, 1964, Strategies of American Water Management, 1969; co-author: Drawers of Water, 1972, Assessment of Research on Natural Hazards, 1975, Flood Hazard in the United States, 1975, The Environment as Hazard, 1978, Water and Life: Water Management and Environmental Policy, 2003; editor: Natural Hazards: Local, National and Global, 1974, Environmental Aspects of Complex River Development, 1977; co-editor: Environmental Issues, 1977, The World Environment, 1972-1982, 1982, Environmental Effects of Nuclear War, 1983, Water for Life, 2003. Reicpient Daly medal Am. Geog. Soc., 1971, Eben award Am. Water Resources Assn., 1972, Caulfield medal, 1989, Alumni medal U. Chgo., 1979, Outstanding Achievement award Nat. Coun. for Geog. Edn., 1981, Sasakawa UN Evniron. prize, 1985, Tyler prize, 1987, Laureat d'Honneur award Internat. Geog. Union, 1988, Vautrin Lud Internat. Geog. prize, 1992, Hubbard medal Nat. Geog. Soc., 1994, Volvo Environment prize, 1995. Mem. AAAS, NAS (commn. on natural resources 1973-80, chmn. 1977-80, chmn. com. on water 1964-68, chmn. com. on sustainable water supplies of Middle East 1996-99, Environ. award 1980, Pub. Welfare medal 2000), Assn. Am. Geographers (pres. 1962, Outstanding Achievement award 1955, 74, Anderson medal 1986, US Nat. Medal Sci 2000, Lifetime Achievement award 2002), Internat. Coun. Sci. Unions (steering com. on study of environ. consequences of nuclear war 1983-87, adv. com. on environ. 1990-96), Internat. Water Resources Assn. (Millenium award 2000), Russian Geog. Soc. (hon.), Royal Geog. Soc. (hon.), Ann. Am. State Flood Plain Mgrs. (nat. flood forum 2004-06), Russian Acad. Scis. (fgn.), Am. Philos. Soc., Cosmos Club (Washington, award 1993), Sigma Xi. Mem. Soc. Friends. Home: Boulder, Colo. Died Oct. 5, 2006.

WHITE, JOAN MICHELSON, artist; b. Hartford, Conn., Jan. 4, 1936; d. William Allen and Mitzi (Lurie) Michelson; m. Harvey Marshall White, June 28, 1958; children: Randi Lynn, Andrew Steven. BA, Ctrl. Conn. State U., 1958; postgrad., Wesleyan U., 1980. Cert. tchr., Conn. Mem. Hartford Art Sch. Aux.; mem. adv. bd. U. Hartford Joseloff Gallery; docent Wadsworth Atheneum, Hartford, 1998— One-woman shows include Canton (Conn.) Gallery on the Green, 1977, Saltbox Gallery, West Hartford, Conn., 1986, Key Gallery N.Y.C., 1982, Hartford Jewish Cmty. Ctr., 1980; group shows include Silvermine Guild New Eng. Exhbn., 1977, 79, Springfield (Mass.) Art League Nat. Exhbn., 1980, 83, 86, The Galleries, Wellesley, Mass., 1983, Stephen Haller Fine Arts, N.Y.C., 1987, 88, Penrose Gallery, Nantucket, Mass., 1984, Conn. Artists Showcase, Conn. Commn. on Arts, Hartford, 1986, Provincetown (Mass.) Art Assn. and Mus., 1986, Old Lyme (Conn.) Art Works, 1985, Greene Gallery, Guilford, Conn., 1986, Signature Gallery, West Hartford, 1986-94, Allan Stone Gallery, N.Y.C., 1984, Shippee Gallery, N.Y.C., 1984, Heritage State Park Mus., Holyoke, Mass., 1988, So. Conn. State U., New Haven, 1989, Farmington Valley Arts Ctr., Avon, Conn., 1992, John Slade Ely House, New Haven, 1993, Ute Stebich Gallery, Lenox, Mass., 1994, North Coast Collage Soc., Seattle, 1994, Small Walls Gallery, Hartford, 1998-99 Mem. Conn. Watercolor Soc. (bd. dirs. 1980-82), West Hartford Ctr. for Visual Arts, Conn. Women Artists, Conn. Acad. Fine Arts. Home: West Hartford, Conn. Died Oct. 20, 2005; Simsbury, Conn.

WHITE, RAYMOND EDWIN, JR., astronomer, educator, researcher; b. Freeport, Ill., May 6, 1933; s. Raymond Edwin White and Beatrice Ellen (Rahn) Stone; m. Ruby Elaine Fisk, Oct. 16, 1956; children: Raymond Edwin III, Kathleen M., Kevin D. BS, U. Ill., 1955, PhD in Astronomy, 1967. Instr. astronomy U. Ariz., Tucson, 1964-65, asst. prof. astronomy, 1965-71, lectr. astronomy, 1972-81, assoc. prof. astronomy, 1981-93, prof. astronomy, from 1993, disting. prof., from 1995; program officer astronomy NSF, Washington, 1971-72; astronomer Dunsink Observatory, Dublin, Ireland, 1996-97. Vis. lectr. Trinity Coll., Dublin, 1996-97. Editor: Observational Astrophysics, 1992; editor Astronomy Quar. jour., 1989-91; North Am. editor Vistas in Astronomy jour., 1992-97. 1st lt. U.S. Army, 1955-58. Fulbright scholar Dublin Inst., 1996-97. Fellow AAAS, Royal Astron. Soc.; mem. Am. Astron. Soc., Am. Assn. Physics Tchrs., Math

Assn. Am., Internat. Astron. Union, Sigma Xi. Home: Tucson, Ariz. Died Oct. 12, 2004.

WHITE, ROBERT ROY, retired chemical engineer; b. Bklyn., Mar. 1, 1916; s. Laurance S. and Grace A. (Diffin) W.; m. Elizabeth R. Clark, July 2, 1940; children: Robert Roy, William Wesley, Elizabeth Ann, Margaret. BS, Cooper Union Inst. Tech., 1936; postgrad., Bklyn. Poly. Inst., 1936-37; MS (Horace H. Rackham predoctoral fellow 1938), U. Mich., 1938; PhD, 1941; postgrad., DePaul U. Law Sch., 1940-41, MIT, 1962. Jr. chem. engr. Calco Chem. Co., Bound Brook, NJ, 1936-37; rsch. chem. engr. Dow Chem. Co., 1937-38; chem. engr. Stnd. Oil Co. Calif., 1940, Universal Oil Products Co., 1940-42; faculty U. Mich., 1942-60, prof. chem. engring., 1945-60, assoc. dean Horace H. Rackham Sch. Grad. Studies, 1958-60; assoc. dean U. Mich. Coll. Engring., 1958-60; dir. U. Mich. Inst. Sci. and Tech., 1959-60; v.p., gen. mgr. R & D Atlantic Refining Co., Phila., 1960-62; sr. staff mgmt. svc. divsn. Arthur D. Little, Inc., 1962; v.p. devel. Champion Papers, Inc., Hamilton, Ohio, 1962-66; pres. rsch. divsn. W.R. Grace & Co., 1966-67; dean Sch. Mgmt., Case Western Res. U., Cleve., 1967-71; mng. dir. Karl Kroyer S.A., Denmark, 1970; spl. asst. to pres., dir. forum Nat. Acad. Sci., Washington, 1971-1981. Adj. prof. chem. engring. U. Md., 1982-85, Cath. U. Am., Am. U.; v.p. JC Tech.; cons. in field. Author: (with others) Unit Operations, 1950; Contbr. articles to profl. jours. Recipient Henry Russell award U. Mich., 1945; teaching award Phi Lambda Upsilon chpt. U. Mich., 1949; sesquicentennial award U. Mich., 1967; prof. award Cooper Union Inst., 1975; McCormack-Freud hon. lectr. Ill. Inst. Tech. Mem.: SAR, AIChE (Jr. award 1945, Presentation award 1951, Profl. Progress award 1956), AAAS, Am. Soc. Engring. Edn. (George Westinghouse award 1955), Am. Chem. Soc., Founders and Patriots Soc., Order Crown of Charlemagne, St. Andrews Soc., Baron Magna Charta, Nat. Yacht Club, Cosmos Club, Iota Alpha, Tau Beta Pi, Phi Kappa Phi, Phi Lambda Upsilon, Alpha Chi Sigma, Sigma Xi. Died Jan. 22, 2006.

WHITE, RUTH MOORE, foundation administrator; b. Homestead, Pa., Jan. 25, 1918; d. William H. and Mary Ellen (Hunter) Goode; m. Ralph W. White, Jan. 24, 1941 (div. May 1956); children: Stephanie D. Phillips, Rosalind W.; m. Thomas E. Bembry, Oct. 15, 1983. Bachelor's, W.Va. State Inst., 1938; M in Social Work, U. Pitts., 1969. Mgr. Goode Pharmacy, Pitts., 1946-55; case worker Dept. Welfare, Pitts., 1957-62, N.Y.C. Dept. Welfare, 1962-63; case worker, supr. Child Welfare Services, Pitts., 1963-69; dir. social service McKeeport (Pa.) Area Sch. Dist., 1969-72; exec. dir. Pa. Sickle Cell Soc., Pitts., from 1973. Cons. Boone Young Assocs., N.Y.C., 1983-84. Trustee Second Baptist Ch., Homestead, 1977—. Named Woman of Yr., Iota Phi Lambda, 1975, Pitts., Woman of Yr. Pitts. Courier/Greyhound, 1975. Mem. NAACP, Nat. Sickle Cell Clinic Found. (pres. 1982-85), Nat. Council Negro Women. Democrat. Avocation: reading. Home: Pittsburgh, Pa. Died Sept. 2, 2004.

WHITE, WARREN TRAVIS, educational consultant firm executive; b. Thrift, Tex., Apr. 28, 1926; s. Warren Travis and Leika (Clark) W.; m. Genevieve Greer; children: Warren Travis, Grady Spruce, Robert Coulter, Carroll Greer; m. Elizabeth Jean Dinkmeyer, June 12, 1964; children: Naomi Kimberly, Stacey Michèle. BA, U. Tex., 1949, MA, 1955; EdD, Vanderbilt U., 1968. Cert. pub. sch. teaching and adminstrn., Tex. Tchr. Ft. Worth (Tex.) Ind. Sch. Dist., 1952-56, adminstr., 1971-89; prin. Midland (Tex.) Sch. Dist., 1956-61, Riverview Gardens Sch. Dist., St. Louis, 1963-64; adminstr. Richmond (Va.) Pub. Schs., 1964-68; supt. Caesar Rodney Sch. Dist., Camden, Del., 1968-71; v.p. White and White, Ft. Worth, from 1989. Cons. Office of Indian Edn., Region VI; adj. prof. U. Va., 1964-68, U. Del., 1968-71. Contbr. articles to profl. jours. Mem. ushers com. Univ. Christian Ch.; mem. steering com. Ft. Worth Mayor's Adv. Com. on Energy Conservation; trustee Masonic Temple Assn., Ft. Worth Masonic Libr. and Mus., Ft. Worth Scottish Rite Found., Inc.; bd. dirs. Knights Templar Edn. Found. With U.S. Army, 1944-46, ATO. Mem. NRA, Tex. Assn. Sch. Adminstrs. (chmn. Tex. Pub. Schs. Week com.), Masons (chmn. pub. edn. com. Grand Lodge of Tex., past master Ft. Worth lodge 148, past high priest Ft. Worth chpt. 58, past master Ft. Worth coun. 42), Order of DeMolay (dist. gov., Legion of Honor), Knights Templar (past comdr. Worth Commandery 19), Shriners, Scottish Rite (33-Degree IGH). Avocations: travel, camping, hunting, reading. Home: Fort Worth, Tex. Died Feb. 25, 2005.

WHITEHAIR, LEO ANTHONY, health scientist, administrator; b. Abilene, Kans., June 13, 1929; s. John Leo and Mary Agnes (Morgan) W.; m. Gloria Mary Vezza, Aug. 9, 1958; children: Kirsten, Robert, Courtney. BS and DVM, Kans. State U., 1953; MS, U. Wis., 1954, PhD, 1962. Diplomate Am. Coll. Vet. Preventive Medicine, Am. Coll. Lab. Animal Medicine (hon.). Commd. 1st lt. USAF, 1954, advanced through grades to lt. col.; vet. officer Aeromed. Lab. Wright-Patterson AFB, Dayton, Ohio, 1954-58; vet. officer nutrition br. Food Inst. of Armed Forces, Chgo., 1961-62; vet. officer, divsn. biology and medicine USAEC, Germantown, Md., 1962-67; health scientist adminstr. animal resources br. div. rsch. resources NIH, Bethesda, Md., 1968-75, dir. regional primate rsch. ctrs. program, 1975-85; adminstr. biomed. rsch. lab. ARC, Rockville, Md., 1985-87; dir. comparative med. program Nat. Ctr. for Rsch. Resources, NIH, Bethesda, 1989-99; ret., 1999. Contbr. articles to profl. jours. Capt. USPHS, 1967-85. Recipient Helwig-Jennings award Am. Coll. Vet. Preventive Medicine, 1981, Disting. Svc. award Am. Soc. Primatologists, 1994, Charles A. Griffin award Am. Assn. Lab. Animal Sci., 1995; Alumni fellow Kans. State U., 1995. Mem. AVMA, D.C. Vet. Medicine Assn. (pres. 1992). Home: Rockville, Md. Died Nov. 2, 2004.

WHITEHEAD, TOM SIMMONS, JR., broadcast executive; b. Midland, Tex., July 18, 1928; s. Tom Simmons and Edythe (Kerley) W.; m. Bonnie Dee Thomas, May 23, 1953; children: Tom Dee, Mark Kerley, Robert Clyde. BJ, U. Tex., 1949. Reporter, copy editor Austin (Tex.) Am. Statesman, 1949-51; editor Brenham (Tex.) Banner Press, 1953-62; pres., gen. mgr. Stas. KTTX-FM/KWHI-AM, Brenham, 1962-88; pres., chief exec. officer Stas. KTTX/KWHI-FM, Brenham, from 1988; pres., gen. mgr. TV Cable of Brenham, 1970-87. Dir. Brenham Indsl. Found., 1985-92, pres., 1991; chmn. bd. First Christian Ch. (Disciples of Christ), 1983-84. With U.S. Army, 1951-53. Mem. Nat. Cable TV Assn. (dir. ind. operators bd. 1982-87), Tex. Assn. Broadcasters (pres. 1972, Pioneer Broadcaster of Yr. award 1987), Tex. Cable TV Assn. (pres. 1986, immediate past pres. 1986-87), Am. Legion (comdr. Post #48 1955), Lions (pres. Brenham club 1965). Avocations: tennis, golf. Home: Brenham, Tex. Died Nov. 5, 2004.

WHITLEY, GARY LEE HAYDON, graphics executive; b. Washington, May 5, 1950; s. Elwood Hampdon Whitley and Luella Catherine (Haydon) Estep; m. Johanne H. Guerette, July 29, 1976 (div. Mar. 1979); 1 child, Derek Jason. AA, Chowan Coll., Murfreesboro, N.C., 1970; BS, Ark. State U., 1972. Asst. prodn. mgr. Fairfield Press, Inc., Little Rock, 1972-73; sales mgr. Sir Speedy Print Shops, Denver, 1973-74; quality control Riedel Lithography, Denver, 1974; estimator Eastwood Printing, Denver, 1974-75; prodn. mgr. Mutual Graphics, Inc., Denver, 1975-76; pres. Type-Smith of Colo., Denver, from 1976. Editor Better Times News, 1970-72; editor, pub. Jonesboro Gazette, 1972; pub. Ark. Edn. Bureau Gazette, 1972-73. Served with USCG Aux. Democrat. Methodist. Home: Aurora, Colo. Died Apr. 20, 2004.

WHITLOCK, JAMES KENNETH, JR., city manager; b. Hopewell, Va., Oct. 15, 1941; s. James Kenneth and Anne (Baker) W.; m. Susan Janette Hutchison, Jan. 21, 1966; children: James, Steven, Robert, Paul. BA, Lamar U., 1963; M in Pub. Adminstrn., Kans. U., 1966. Adminstrv. asst., Orange, Tex., 1962-63; budget and research asst. McAlester, Okla., 1964-66; city adminstr. Newburn, Tenn., 1966-67; asst. city mgr. Del City, Okla., 1967-69; city mgr. Henryetta, Okla., 1969-71, Del City, 1971-75, Broken Arrow, Okla., from 1975. Chmn. Regional Met. Utility Authority, Tulsa, 1985; mem. bd. trustees Okla. Mcpl. Retirement Fund, 1987—. Named Com. Chmn. of Yr., Broken Arrow C. of C., 1982. Mem. City Mgmt. Assn. Okla. (pres. 1974), Internat. City Mgmt. Assn., Am. Soc. Pub. Adminstrn. (pres. Northeast Okla. chpt. 1985), Am. Pub. Works Assn. Republican. Roman Catholic. Avocations: fishing, reading. Home: Broken Arrow, Okla. Died Mar. 28, 2005.

WHITTINGHAM, MARY CATHERINE, retired special education educator; b. Louisville, Dec. 6, 1929; d. Charles James and Mary Elizabeth (Nielander) W. BS, Spalding U., 1954; MEd, U. Louisville, 1961, postgrad., 1973. Cert. bus. edn., hearing impaired and educable mentally handicapped tchr., Ky. Tchr. physically handicapped and other health impaired Cath. Sch. Bd. of Louisville, Ky., 1954-67; tchr. hearing impaired students Ky. Easter Seal Speech and Hearing Clinic, Louisville, summer 1959; office mgr. Ky. Easter Seal Camp Kysoc, summer 1962, 63; tchr. educable mentally handicapped and multiple handicapped Jefferson County Pub. Schs., Louisville, 1967. Mem. NEA, Ky. Tchrs. Assn., Jefferson County Tchrs. Assn., Coun. for Exceptional Children (corr. sec. 1968-72, chairperson membership com. 1972-76, co-chairperson scholarship com., del. 1975-76, N.Y.C. 1974, Chgo. chpt. 1976, Atlanta chpt. 1977, Kansas City chpt. 1978). Democrat. Roman Catholic. Avocations: music, drama. Home: Louisville, Ky. Died Dec. 30, 2004.

WHITTINGTON, MAY RINGOLD, historic preservationist, state representative; b. Winona, Miss., Nov. 16, 1942; d. Rupert Marion and May (Spencer) Ringold; 1 child, Joshua Spencer Glazer; m. C. Aven Whittington Jr., May 24, 1983; 1 stepchild, Aven III. BA in Psychology, Oglethorpe U., Atlanta, 1967; MEd, Delta State U., Cleveland, Miss., 1991. Lic. profl. counselor, nat. cert. counselor. Rsch. asst. Emory U., NIH, Atlanta, 1967-71; owner, mgr. Bottom of the Barrel, Atlanta, 1967-71; clin. therapist Life Help, Greenwood, Miss., 1991-93; owner, therapist, mediator Whittington Counseling, Schlater, Miss., 1993-96. Cert. local govt. contact Historic Preservation Commn., Greenwood; rennovator historic endangered bridge Miss. Dept. Transp., 1999. Mem. dist. 34 Mo. Ho. Reps., Dem. Party, 1999—; mem. adv. bd. ARC; bd. dirs. Main St. Greenwood, 1995—, Enterprie Cmty., 1994-98; bd. mem. Greenwood Little Theatre, 1995-97. Recipient 8 awards, 6 grants Main St. Greenwood, 1996-99. Mem. C. of C. (mem. coms.), Rotary, Chi Sigma Iota (life). Episcopalian. Avocations: walking, photography, hiking, biking, swimming. Home: Schlater, Miss. Died July 12, 2006.

WIDELL, LILLIAN WILHELMINA, artist; b. Hartford, Conn., Sept. 30, 1909; d. Nathaniel Frederick Widell and Ellen Wilhelmina Molin. Grad. H.S., Hartford; student, Hartford Art Sch., Fed. Art Sch. Key punch operator Conn. Gen. Life Ins. Co., Hartford, 1925—32, Importers and Exporters Fire Ins. Co., N.Y.C., 1932—34; with acctg. dept. Internat. Paper Co., N.Y.C., 1934—66; freelance artist various dress mfrs., N.Y.C., 1936—64. Exhibitions include Bklyn. YWCA. Avocation: sculpting. Home: Queens Village, NY. Died Mar. 12, 2004.

WIDENER, EDWARD LADD, mechanical technology educator, consultant; b. Madison, S.D., Dec. 23, 1926; s. Homer Williams and Marjorie O'Dell (Ladd) W.; m. Martha Antoinette Born W., Sept. 6, 1952; children: Marjorie, Edward, William, Cora. BS in Physics, Purdue U., 1949, BSME, 1951; MS in Engring. Mechanics, U. Kans., 1962. Registered profl. engr., Ind., N.Y. Fuel engr. U.S. Steel Corp., Gary, Ind., 1951-53; jr. design engr. Union Carbide Corp., Niagara Falls, N.Y., 1953-60; process engr. E.I. du Pont Corp., Richmond, Va., 1962-67; project leader Kimberly Clark Corp., Memphis, 1967-74; process engr. Baker, McHenry & Welch Co., Indpls., 1974-76; mech. project engr. Continental Group, Danville, Ill., 1976-78; assoc. prof. Purdue U., West Lafayette, Ind., 1978—2004. Program evaluator Accreditation Bd., N.Y.C., 1986-2004; grants reviewer NSF, Washington, 1990-91; metals instr. in Malaysia, 1995-96. Mem. Bach Chorale Singers, West Lafayette, 1986-2004. With USN, 1944-46. Mem. Am. Soc. Engring. Educators, ASM, ASME, Gideons Internat. Republican. Mem. Community Reformed Ch. Home: Lafayette, Ind. Died July 4, 2005.

WIECHMANN, HELMUT HENRY, minister; b. Lacrescent, Minn., Aug. 5, 1909; s. Frederick August and Bertha Ann (Stuemke) W.; m. Ruth Louise Krahn, Oct. 4, 1931 (dec. 1979); children: Gerald H., Ralph E., Ruthmary North. BD, Concordia Sem., Springfield, Ill., 1930. Ordained to ministry, Luth. Ch.-Mo. Synod. Missoin developer Killitas County, Ellensburg, Wash., 1930-43; pastor edn. St. Paul Luth. Ch., Olive, Calif., 1943-49; pastor Trinity Luth. Ch., Mequon, Wis., 1949-60, Faith Luth. Ch., Hialeah, Fla., 1960-73; assoc. pastor Prince of Peace Luth. Ch., Springfield, Va., from 1973. Chmn. estate planning S.E. Dist. Luth. Ch.-Mo. Synod, 1974-80, others in past. Recipient Servus Ecclesiae Christi award, Concordia Sem, Ft. Wayne, 1978, Award of Achievement, 1980. Mem. Exchange Club (bull. editor). Republican. Home: Springfield, Va. Died June 29, 2004.

WIEGENSTEIN, JOHN GERALD, retired physician; b. Fredericktown, Mo., June 22, 1930; s. John Joseph and Dorothy Faye (Mulkey) W.; m. Dorothy Iris Scifers, Dec. 27, 1952; children: Mark, Barbara, Paula, Cynthia. BS, U. Mich., 1956, MD, 1960. Intern Tripler Army Gen. Hosp., Honolulu, 1960-61; chmn. Emergency Medicine Ingham Regional Med. Ctr., Lansing, 1975-95; pres. profl. staff Mich. Capital Med. Ctr., Lansing, 1996-98; prof. emergency medicine Mich. State U., 1982-97, prof. emeritus, from 1997; founder Internat. Rsch. Inst. for Emergency Medicine, pres., 1983-85; v.p. occupl. health Emergency Cons., Inc., 1997-99, pres.; ret. Founder Am. Bd. Emergency Medicine, 1976, bd. dirs., 1976-86, pres., 1982-83; pres. Physician Assocs., P.C., 1976-96; chmn. bd. Occupl. Medicine Assocs., P.C., 1989-98; owner Health Care Info. Svcs., Inc., 1989-97. With USAF, 1951-53; M.C., U.S. Army, 1960-63. Recipient Disting. Achievement award, U. Mich. Med. Ctr. Alumni Assn., 2003. Mem. AMA (Disting. Svc. award 2001), Am. Coll. Emergency Physicians (founder, pres., chmn. bd. 1968-71, bd. dirs. 1968-76, John G. Wiegenstein Leadership award named in his honor), Mich. State Med. Soc. (award 1971, 82), Ingham County Med. Soc., Galens Hon. Med. Soc., Soc. Acad. Emergency Medicine (hon.). Died Oct. 28, 2004.

WIEMER, LOYAL HULBERT, minister; b. Syracuse, N.Y., Oct. 28, 1914; s. Bernhard A. and Bertha A. (Hulbert) W.; m. Lola Myrtle Horton, May 28, 1938; children: Douglas Loyal, Carol Jane. AB, Wheaton Coll., Ill., 1937; BD, Ea. Bapt. Theol. Sem., Phila., 1941. Ordained to ministry Am. Bapt. Chs. in U.S.A., 1941. Pastor various chs., N.Y., 1941-43, 48-53; dir. USO, Mass., Maine, R.I., 1943-47; dir. camping Detroit, 1954-59, Mass. Bapt. Conv., Groton, Mass., 1959-62; pastor Clarklake (Mich.) Community Ch., 1963-79; min. at large Am. Bapt. Chs. in U.S.A., from 1979. Exec. dir. Jackson County Interfaith Coun., 1974—; bd. dirs. exec. com. Mich. Bapt. Chs., 1978-90, del. constn. revision com., 1968; pres. Mich. sect. Am. Camping Assn., 1964-68, chmn. standards com. Mich. sect/. 1963-73; chaplain Internat. Order Foresters-Rebekah Homes, 1963-79; chmn. caring ministries Mich.-Am. Bapts. Chs., 1984-90. Author: Flight of the Snow Goose, 1947. Bd. dirs., chmn. budget com. United Way Jackson County, 1969-79; bd. dirs. Jackson Osteo. Hosp., 1969—, United Way Mich., 1973-87, Land O'Lakes coun. Boy Scouts Am.; mem. Jackson Bd. Commrs., 1981-87, vice chmn., 1985—; chair Jackson Transit Authority, 1985. Mem. Am. Bapt. Chs., U.S.A. Mins. Assn., Mich Bapt. Mins. Died June 8, 2004.

WIENER, MAX, mechanical engineer, consultant; b. Newark, Oct. 25, 1918; s. Louis and Rose (Feldmann) Haronsky; m. Laura Wiener, June 30, 1943; children: Saundra Lynn, Joan Carol, Rochelle Iris. BSME, N.J. Inst. Tech., 1942; MSME, Yale U., 1943. Registered profl. engr., N.J., N.Y., Pa., Ga. Sr. engr. Wright Aero. Corp., Wood Ridge, N.J., 1945-48; design engr. Babcock & Wilcox, N.Y.C., 1948-50; project engr. Wigton-Abbott Corp., Plainfield, N.J., 1950-65; sr. project engr. Am. Can Co., Fairlawn, N.J., 1965-82, Alcan Powders & Pigments Co., Union, N.J., from 1982. Cons. engr. M. Wiener & Assocs., Ford, N.J., 1970-80, Englishtown, N.J., 1980—. 2d lt. USAAF, 1943-45. Mem. ASME (life), Nat. Soc. Profl. Engrs. (life), Jewish War Vets. Republican. Died Jan. 4, 2005.

WIGGINS, PATTI S., music educator; b. Mpls., Aug. 14, 1925; d. Wilfred W. and Georgia (Slater) Wiggins; children: Georgia Daniels, Debra Lang, Jim Schliestett, Tom. MusB, West Chester U., 1947; MusM, Occidental Coll., LA, 1950. Music supr. Whittier (Calif.) City Schs., 1950—57, LA City Schs., 1960—2002; pvt. piano tchr. Glendale, Calif., from 1950. Prof. emerita Calif. State U., LA. Author: The Joy of Music, Today's Creative Children. Mem.: Los Angeles County Music Educators Assn., Calif. State Tchrs. Assn., Music Educator's Nat. Conf. Home: Glendale, Calif. Died Jan. 29, 2006.

WILCOXSON, JOAN ELIZABETH, special education educator; b. Portsmouth, Ohio, Feb. 17, 1940; d. Robert Lewis and Bonnie Jeannette (Borders) Stearnes; m. George P. Boss, June 23, 1968 (div. Aug. 1978); children: Catherine Clark, Donna Jean Clark West, Carol Clark, Donald William Clark, Jr. B in Secondary Edn., Ohio U., 1972; M in Spl. Edn., Trenton State Tchrs. Coll., 1976. Cert. supr. spl. edn., elem. prin., secondary prin. Tchr. Lucasville (Ohio) Sch. Sys., 1966-69, Gallia (Ohio) Acad. H.S., 1969-71, Bristol Twp. Sch. Sys., Levittown, Pa., from 1972; chair dept. spl. edn. Armstrong Jr. H.S., Fairless Hills, Pa., from 1992. Author: A Hot Body in a Cool Society, 1980. Mem. NEA, Pa. Ednl. Assn., Bristol Twp. Tchrs. Assn. (bldg. rep.). Home: Portsmouth, Ohio. Died Apr. 18, 2004.

WILD, ALYS TRUITT, writer; b. Pitts., Aug. 19, 1924; d. William and Alice (McGinty) Truitt; m. Walter R. Golubic (dec. 1968); m. William A. Ingram (dec. 1973); 1 child, Clarke Walter Ingram; m. Joseph John Wild, Dec. 27, 1977. Student, U. Pitts., 1947-51. Clk. typist U.S. Bur. Mines, Pitts., 1943-57, 75-84. Author: Someday, 1945, Illusions, 1970, That Precious Moment, 1973, Thoughts for Any Day, 1991, Afterthoughts, 1994, Above and Beyond, 1996, The Winds Within, 1996, Another Version, 1997, (poems) Through the Years, Vol. I and II, 1997. Mem. Pittsburgh Progressive Artists. Democrat. Avocations: writing, painting, swimming. Home: Pittsburgh, Pa. Died Dec. 21, 2004.

WILDE, JOHN, artist, educator; b. Milw., Dec. 12, 1919; s. Emil F. and Mathilda (Lotz) W.; m. Helen Ashman, July 1943 (dec. Dec. 1966); children: Jonathan, Phoebe; m. Shirley Miller, 1969. BS, U. Wis., 1942, MS, 1948. Mem. faculty U. Wis., from 1948, prof. art, from 1960, chmn. dept. art, 1960-62, Alfred Sessler Distinguished prof. art, 1969-82, prof. emeritus, 1982—2006. Elected mem. Nat. Acad. Design, 1994. Works exhibited Met. Mus. Art, Mus. Modern Art, Whitney Mus. Am. Art, Corcoran Mus. Art, Mpls. Art Mus., San Francisco Mus. Art, Whitney Mus. Am. Art, 1978-80, Nat. Portrait Gallery, Smithsonian Instn., 1980, Nat. Gallery, Washington, 1988; drawing retrospective Elvehjem Mus. Art, U. Wis., 1984-85; 3-man retrospective (with Curry and Bohrod), Milw. Art Mus., 1982, 55 Yr. Retrospective Eluehjem Mus. of Art, U. Wis., Madison drawings and paintings, 1999-2000, others; represented in permanent collections, Pa. Acad. Art, Detroit Inst. Fine Art, Worcester Art Mus., Wadsworth Atheneum, Whitney Mus. Am. Art, Carnegie Inst., Nat. Collection Art, Smithsonian Instn., Yale U. Art Gallery, Butler Inst. Am. Art, Art Inst. Chgo., Sheldon Meml. Art Gallery, U. Nebr., Zimmerli Mus. Art, Rutgers U., N. Brunswick, N.J., Mus. Contemporary Art, Chgo., others, also extensive exhbns. abroad; subject of book WildeWorld, The Art of John Wilde, 1999. Recipient numerous awards for painting and drawing in regional and nat. exhbns. including, Childe Hassam purchase award Am. Acad. and Inst. Arts and Letters, 1968, 81, 87, Richard Florsheim Art Purchase award, 1994, Henry LeGrand Cannon prize Nat. Acad. Design, 2001, Sidney Laufman prize, Nat. Acad. Design, 2005; E.D. Found. grantee, 1995. Home: Evansville, Wis. Died Mar. 9, 2006.

WILDER, CAROL LYNN, visual artist, educator; b. Dallas, Dec. 6, 1949; d. Alvin Young and Jo Nell (McCabe) W.; m. Daniel Eugene Jennings, Dec., 1969 (div. 1972); 1 child, Trevor; m. Larry Gene Enge, Dec. 19, 1981; children: Amelia, Jora. BFA, East Tex. State U., 1977; MA, U. Dallas, 1980, MFA, 1981; student, Kent State U., summer 1977. Artist/supr. Neighborhood Walls Unltd., Dallas, 1979; instr.art sr. citizens' ctr., Irving, Tex., 1980; grad. asst., art history slide libr. U. Dallas, Irving, 1980-81; instr. art Children's Art and Ideas Found., Dallas, summers 1982,84; adj. art faculty Richland Coll., Dallas, 1982-85, North Lake Coll., Irving, from 1989. Mural artist Dallas Can! Acad., 1995; vis. artist East Tex.State U. Commerce, 1977; guest curator N. Lake Coll. Gallery, Irving, 1997. One-woman shows include Carol Wilder/Larry Enge Recent Work, Studio Gallery, Dallas, 2003, Collaboration of Souls, Blossom St. Gallery, Houston, Tex., 2001, Seen & Unseen, Bath House Cultural Ctr., 2001, Myths, Legends, Stories & Tales, Art Mus. of South Tex., Corpus Cristi, Tex., 2000, Wilder/Enge Collaborations, Gavleston Aats Ctr., Tex., 2000, Cpllaborations, McMurray Univ., Abilene, Tex., 1998, Introductions '98, Cmty. Artists' Collective, Houston, Tex., 1998, Mayor's Office, City Hall, Dallas, Tex., 1998, many others, exhibited in group shows at A Presensce Seen, Haggerty Gallery, Univ. Dallas, Tex., 2001, Habeas Corpus, Upper Gallery, Univ. Dallas, Dallas, Tex., 2001, EL Corazon 2000, Bath House Cultural Ctr., 2000, Art in the Metroplex, Templton Art Ctr., Fort Worth, Tex., 1999, North Texas Collaborations, Cmty. Artists' Collective, Houston, Tex., 1998, 52nd Ann. Art Competition, Art Mus. of Abilenne, Tex., 1986, Texas Visions, Art Leaugue of Houston, 1986, many others. Facilitator racial reconciliation seminar Bridging the Gap, Dallas, 1994. Recipient Painting award African-Am. Mus., Dallas, 1995; pub. commn. William Grant Still Found., 1996. Mem. Alpha Chi (Tex. Lambda chpt.)(life), Christians in Visual Arts. Avocations: travel, baroque and jazz music, art films, african american history and literature. Home: Dallas, Tex. Died Feb. 11, 2004.

WILDHABER, MICHAEL RENE, accountant; b. Jefferson City, Mo., Aug. 4, 1952; s. Rainey A. and Velma W.; m. Paula M. Wildhaber, Sept. 28, 1974; 1 child, Wendy. AA, Florissant Valley Coll., 1972; BS, U. Mo., 1974. CPA, Mo.; cert. info. sys. auditor, cert. internal auditor, cert. tax preparer, assoc. ins. acctg. and fin., enrolled agt. Sr. auditor, enrolled agt. I.T.T. Fin., St. Louis, 1974-79; audit mgr. Navco, St. Louis, 1980-85; contr. Millers mutual, Alton, Ill., 1985-88; pres. R&M Tax and Acctg., St. Louis, from 1988. Tchr. Jr. Achievement, St. Louis, 1993-94; vol. Olympic Festival, St. Louis, 1994, 100 Neediest Cases, St. Louis, 1990-94, Old News Boy, St. Louis, 1992-94. Mem. AICPA, Mo. Soc. CPAs, Inst. Internal Auditors, Habitat for Humanity (pres.). Home: Festus, Mo. Died May 2, 2005.

WILFLEY, GEORGE MERRITT, manufacturing company executive; b. Denver, May 23, 1924; s. Elmer R. and Margaret W., B.A. U. Colo., 1950, postgrad., 1977; m. Eleanore Breitenstein; children— George Michael, John Frederick. With A.R. Wilfley & Sons, Inc., Denver, 1950—, pres., 1958—, also dir.; pres., dir. Western Foundries, Inc.; dir. First Interstate Bank of Denver. hon. trustee, chmn. bd. Boys Club of Denver, Inc. Served with F.A., AUS, 1943-46. Mem. AIME, Nat. Assn. Corrosion Engrs., Colo. Mining Assn., NAM (dir.). Denver Country Club (past pres.), University Club (past treas.), Alto Lakes Club, Castle Pines Club (charter). Republican. Episcopalian. Avocations: wine and art collecting, golf, fishing, hunting. Home: Denver, Colo. Died Oct. 21, 2004.

WILLEBRANDS, JOHANNES GERARDUS MARIA CARDINAL, archbishop emeritus; b. Bovenkarspel, Netherlands, Sept. 4, 1909; s. Herman and Aafje (Kok) W. PhD, U. Rome, 1937; DLitt (hon.), St. Louis U., 1968; D of Rights (hon.), U. Notre Dame, 1970; ThD (hon.), Cath. U, Louvain, Belgium, 1971, Theol. Acad. Leningrad, USSR, 1973; D of Rights (hon.) Cath. U. Am., 1974; DLitt (hon.), St. Olaf Coll., 1976, Coll. St. Thomas, St. Paul, 1979, Assumption Coll., 1980; ThD (hon.) Cath. U., Lublin, Poland, 1985, U. Oxford, Eng., 1987, Cath. U. Munich, 1987; LHD (hon.), Bellarmine Coll., 1987, Seton Hall U., 1987; ThD (hon.), Hellenic Coll./Holy Cross Greek Orthodox Sch. Theology, Brookline, Mass., 1989; DD (hon.), St. Michael's Coll., Toronto, Can., 1990. Ordained priest, Roman Cath. Ch., 1934, bishop, 1964, created cardinal, 1969; chaplain, Amsterdam, Netherlands, 1937-40; prof. philosophy Filosoficum of diocese Haarlem (Netherlands), 1940-60, dir. Filosoficum, 1945-60; sec. Secretariat for Promoting Christian Unity, Rome, 1960, pres., 1969-89, pres. emeritus of Pontifical Coun. for Promoting Christian Unity, 1989; archbishop of Utrecht (Netherlands), 1975-83; archbishop emeritus 1983-2006. Died Aug. 2, 2006.

WILLER, CHARLES FRANKLIN, producer, entertainer, clown; b. Ft. Wayne, Ind., Sept. 8, 1954; s. Paul Franklin and Dorothy Jean (Andrew) W.; m. Kathy Ann Ramsey; children: Elizabeth Robin, Katrina Joy. Student, Purdue U., 1972-77. Air personality Sta. WLKI, Angola, Ind., 1974-76, Sta. WHFD, Archbold, Ohio, 1976-77; audio producer Creative Info. Assn., Ft. Wayne, 1977-79; announcer, operator Sta. WEZV, Ft. Wayne, 1979-80; air personality Sta. WLYV, Ft. Wayne, 1980-82; owner, operator Audio Architect (formerly Willer Prodns.), Ft. Wayne, from 1979; entertainer Chuckles the Clown & Co., Ft. Wayne, from 1980. With pub. rels. dept. Little River R.R., Angola, 1975—; disc jockey, producer sta. WZRQ, Ft. Wayne, 1986-88; writer, actor, sound effects specialist Renaissance Radio Theater, Ft. Wayne, 1986—; tech. producer Renaissance Radio Network, Ft. Wayne, 1988-89; on-air personality sta. WAJI and WLDE, 1989—; on-camera talent for Chef's Fest-Juggling; chef Bobick's Golf-Juggling; Glenbrook Dodge, Snowflake The Ice Sprite, Lincoln Nat.-Dodger Hubert, among others. Inventor: (magic illusion) Linking Rings: Chair II, 1975; writer, producer numerous TV and radio spots, 1982—, original comedy music broadcast on Doctor Demento show, 1991. Profl. railway historian, 1990—; co-founder, charter mem. 3 Rivers on Heritage Coun. and Heartland Railways Mus., 1994—. Recipient Addy awards, 1981-97, Best-of-Decade award, "Deccy", 1989. Mem. Jugglers Anonymous (founder 1980, coordinator 1980-90). Libertarian. Unitarian Universalist. Avocations: railroads, composing music, amateur radio, disney comics, cartoons. Home: Fort Wayne, Ind. Died Jan. 27, 2004.

WILLIAMS, ASHTON STEELE, financial consultant, business broker; b. Abington, Pa., Sept. 14, 1960; s. Frank Barbar Williams and Alice Randle (Steele) Semke; m. Amy Delone, Nov. 17, 1984. Student, Roanoke Coll., 1979-80. Equity and options broker Janney Montgomery Scott, Phila., 1982-87; ptnr., pres. Wings Fin. Assn. Ltd., Phila., 1986-89; pres. ASW Enterprises Inc., Chadds Ford, Pa., from 1989. Active Gulph Mills (Pa.) Civic Assn., 1985—. Mem. Aircraft Owners and Pilots Assn. Republican. Episcopalian. Avocations: flying, restoring cars, duck hunting, dirt bike riding, cooking. Home: Tucson, Ariz. Died June 26, 2005.

WILLIAMS, BARBARA LOU, library director; b. Seattle, Aug. 20, 1927; d. Lawrence Earl and LouElla Barbara (Eubank) W.; children: Chrstine Mikel, Patricia Hannum, Kathryn McLane, Douglas Alan Hannum. BA, U. Colo., 1948; MEd, U. Ariz., 1963, ednl. specialist, 1976; MLS, U. Okla., 1975. Tchr. Indian Oasis High Sch., Sells, Ariz., 1959-61, Sahuarita Sch., Tucson, 1961-62; elem. libr. Tucson Sch. Dist., 1963-65, high sch. libr., 1965-77; dir. libr. Ariz. Western Coll., Yuma, 1977-82, Tarrant County Jr. Coll. Dist., Ft. Worth, from 1982. Co-author: History of Sheridan, Wyoming, 1956; editor: Directory of Libraries in Southern Arizona, 1972; contbr. to Nobel Prize Winners, 1987. Mem. ALA, Assn. Ednl. Communication and Tech., Tex. Libr. Assn., Tex. Assn. Ednl. Tech., Tex. Jr. Coll. Tchrs. Assn., Librs. Tarrant County (pres. 1990-91), Trinity Valley Quilters Guild, Ft. Worth Opera Guild. Avocations: travel, needlecrafts, arts. Home: Tucson, Ariz. Died Jan. 25, 2005.

WILLIAMS, CARROLL WARNER, film center administrator, cinematographer; b. Chgo., Apr. 15, 1931; s. Charles Warner Williams and Grace Athena (Newman) Conwell; m. Dorothea Rockburne, Apr. 15, 1952; m. Joan Swayze, Apr. 26, 1966; children: Carisa, Carolyn; m. Ginger John; children: Caitlan, Cian. Tchr. graphic arts Black Mountain (N.C.) Coll., 1951-54; designer, engr. Geodesics, Inc., Cambridge, Mass., 1956-57; with record prodn. Ultra Hi-Fi Hdqrs., N.Y.C., 1957-58; freelance filmmaker N.Y.C., 1959-68; dir. Anthropology Film Ctr., Santa Fe, from 1965, co-dir., tchr., from 1966. Pres. Zia Cine, Inc., Santa Fe, 1959—; instr. film and culture U N.Mex., 1989—; cons. various univs. and film prodn. cos., 1954—. Media chmn. N.Mex. State Arts Commn., 1969-76, chmn. City of Santa Fe Art Commn., 1982-88; bd. dirs. Santa Fe Canyon Assn., Nat. Anthropology Film Ctr. of Smithsonian Inst, S.W. Found. for Audio-Visual Resources, 1974-85. Mem. AAAS, Am. Anthrop. Assn. (pres.), Soc. Motion Picture and TV Engrs., Anthropology Film Research Inst. Democrat. Episcopalian. Avocations: computer sci., motorcycling, backpacking, arts and crafts, languages. Died Mar. 30, 2005.

WILLIAMS, CURTIS ALVIN, JR., biology educator, researcher; b. Moorestown, N.J., June 26, 1927; s. Curtis Alvin and Nola (Johnson) W.; m. Marjorie King, Jan. 22, 1960; children: Jennifer, Scott, Elisabeth. BS, Pa. State U., 1950; PhD, Rutgers U., 1954. Predoctoral fellow Waksman Found. Pasteur Inst., Paris, 1952-53, postdoctoral fellow USPHS, 1953-54, Carlsberg Lab., Copenhagen, 1954-55; successively rsch. assoc., asst. prof., assoc. prof. Rockefeller U., N.Y.C., 1955-70; scientist NIH, Bethesda, Md., 1957-60; prof. in biology SUNY, Purchase, 1970-94; prof. emeritus, from 1994; also dean div. Natural Scis. SUNY, Purchase, 1970-80. Adj. prof. Rockefeller U., N.Y.C., 1970-78, NYU Sch. Medicine, N.Y.C., 1976-88; vis. prof. Univ. Coll., London, 1978-79, U. So. Calif., L.A., 1985-86. Editor: Methods in Immunology and Immunochemistry Vols. I through V, 1967-76; contbr. more than 100 articles, reports and revs. to profl. jours. Dir. Friends Neuberger Mus. Art, Purchase, 1986—; trustee Wenner-Gren Found., N.Y.C., 1991—. With USNR, 1945. Recipient Founders award Internat. Electrophoresis Soc., 1982; named NSF fellow, 1978-79; grantee NIH, NSF and other orgns., 1959—. Avocations: sailing, painting. Home: White Plains, NY. Died Oct. 18, 2004.

WILLIAMS, DEBRA DENISE, computer specialist; b. Phila., Aug. 20, 1959; d. John Luther and Dorothy Gertrude (Simmons) W. BA in Social Welfare, Pa. State U., 1979; MS in Tech. Mgmt., Am. U., 1985; MS in Telecomms. Mgmt., U. Md., 1995. Computer sys. programmer Bur. of the Census, Washington, 1980-87, computer programmer, analyst, 1987-90, computer specialist, from 1990. Mem. Delta Sigma Theta. Avocations: tennis, music, weightlifting. Home: Bowie, Md. Died Aug. 14, 2004.

WILLIAMS, DOROTHY S., consultant nurse; b. New Orleans, La., July 17, 1951; d. Daniel Joseph and Bertha Ella Smith; children: Dwaine LeRoi Smith, Andre' LaRay. BS, Coll. Bibl. Studies, 2003. RN Bd.Nurse Examiners, Tex., 1981; Ordained minister Hope of Glory Ministry, Houston, 2001. Nurse Kelsey-Seybold Clinic, Houston, from 1997. Author: (book) Let Go & Let God, 2002. Chaplain intern St. Lukes Episcopal Hosp., Houston, 1999—2000; vol. Kelsey-Rsch. Found., Houston, 2002, Susan G. Komen Breast Cancer Found., Houston, 1999. Home: Houston, Tex. Died Aug. 27, 2004.

WILLIAMS, EVAN THOMAS, college dean, chemistry educator; b. N.Y.C., May 17, 1936; s. Clarke and Margaret (Button) W.; m. Lise Reinholdt Jacobsen, Sept. 19, 1959; children: Elisabeth Clarke, John Reinholdt. AB, Williams Coll., 1958; PhD, MIT, 1963. Rsch. assoc. Rsch. Establishment Risø, Roskilde, Denmark, 1963-65; asst. prof. dept. chemistry Bklyn. Coll., CUNY, 1965-71, assoc. prof., 1971-75, prof., 1976-92, chmn. dept., 1981-84, dean undergrad. studies, 1989-92; dean, v.p. acad. affairs Lewis & Clark Coll., Portland, Oreg., 1992-95, prof. chemistry, from 1992, asst. to pres., 1995-97, chmn. environ. studies program, from 1997. Cons. Geos Corp., Mt. Vernon, N.Y. Contbr. over 40 rsch. articles to sci. jours. Pres. Cobble Hill Assn., Bklyn., 1972-73; mem. Bklyn. Solid-Waste Adv. Bd., 1981-92; trustee Packer Collegiate Inst., Bklyn., 1978-87; mem. exec. com. Edn. for Sustainablity-We. Network, 2002—. Mem. AAAS, Am. Chem. Soc., Am. Phys. Soc., Phi Beta Kappa, Sigma Xi. Home: Lake Oswego, Oreg. Died May 24, 2004.

WILLIAMS, FREDRICK ELBERT, logistics engineer; b. Miami, Mar. 9, 1939; s. John Samual and Lucille (Melton) W. Student, No. Va. Community Coll., Woodbridge, 1978-79, Hartnell Coll., 1980-81. Enlisted USMC, 1957, advanced through grades to master sgt., 1975, ret.,

1978; logistical engr. Vitro Labs., Silver Springs, Md., 1978-79; mgr. configuration Sterling System, Inc., Salinas, Calif., 1979-80, Planning Research Corp., Jacksonville, Fla., 1980-82; product assurance mgr. CACI, Inc.-Fed., Jacksonville, 1982-87; project mgr. Cap Gemini Am., Atlanta, 1987-89; logistical engr. Logistics Svcs. Internat., Orange Park, Fla., from 1989. Mem.: Masons. Republican. Baptist. Home: Milwaukie, Oreg. Died Aug. 21, 2004.

WILLIAMS, GEORGE FRANKLIN, consultant, educator, businessman, researcher; b. Jacksonville, Ala., Oct. 30, 1940; s. Jerret Jr. and Lucille (Franklin) W.; m. Willhammer Hollis, Aug. 31, 1968; children: Darla Denise, Derell Jacinto, Damian Franklin, Derrek Demetri. BS, Friends U., 1968; MEd, Wichita State U., 1971, EdS, 1973; EdD, U. Kans., 1981. cert. suprintendent adminstrv. Ill. Asst. prin. Curtis Jr. H.S., Wichita, Kans., 1980-81, Truesdell Jr. H.S., Wichita, Kans., 1981-83, Wilbur Jr. H.S., Wichita, Kans., 1983-86, Wichita Heights H.S., Wichita, Kans., from 1986-. Team leader Performance Contracting, Wichita, 1970-71; bd. dirs. Adminstrv. Leadership Ctr., Wichita, 1986--. Author The Adventures of Who Me, 1988. Exec. bd. Wichita Edn. Mgmt. Assn., 1985-86; planning com mem. Internat. Assn. Human Rights Organ., 1973-74; participant First Internat. Conf. Innovation Spl. Edn., 1986-87. With ASAF, 1962-66. Mem. Optimists (named student of the year, 1981-82, recipient Spark Plug Award, 1983, pres. 1971), Kans. Assn. Spl. Edn. Adminstrn., Nat. Alliance Black Sch. Educators, Phi Delta Kappa, Alpha Phi Alpha (pres. 1969), Sigma Pi Phi. Democrat. Avocations: reading, writing, computers, swimming, salesmanship. Home: Wichita, Kans. Died Jan. 1, 2005.

WILLIAMS, JOAN, writer; b. Memphis, Tenn., Sept. 26, 1928; BA, Bard Coll., 1950; MA, Fairfield U., 1986. Tchr. Farifield U., Norwalk Cmty. Coll., 1982, Rhodes Coll., 1982, Memphis State U. Author: (novels) Pay The Piper, 1988, County Woman, 1982, The Wintering, 1971, The Powder man, 1967, The Morning and the Evening, 1961. Home: Alpharetta, Ga. Died Apr. 11, 2004.

WILLIAMS, JOHN FREDERICK, chemist, laboratory director; b. York, S.C., May 14, 1923; s. Eddie Meek and Laura Isabella (Pegram) W.; m. Billie Margaret Lowry, Nov. 9, 1945 (dec. Feb. 8, 1970); children: John Franklin, Frederick Lowry; m. Katherine Dabney Coleman, Aug. 29, 1970. BSChemE, U. S.C., 1944; MS in Chemistry, Clemson Coll., 1951; PhD in Analytical Chemistry, U. Va., 1954. Sr. scientist Liggett and Myers Tobacco Co., Durham, N.C., 1954-60, supr. analytical chemistry, 1960-80; div. dir. Ga. Dept. Agr., Atlanta, from 1980. Dir. Williams Realty, Inc., York, S.C., 1964—. Contbr. articles to profl. jours. Lt. (j.g.) USNR, 1943-47. Mem. Am. Chem. Soc., Assn. Ofcl. Analytical Chemists, Assn. Food and Drug Ofcls., Assn. Fertilizer, Food, Pesticides Control Ofcls., Assn. Food and Drug Ofcls. of the So. States. Democrat. Presbyterian. Avocations: golf, bridge. Home: Decatur, Ga. Died Mar. 4, 2004.

WILLIAMS, JOHN PERSHING, industrial relations consultant, retired manufacturing and mining company executive; b. Bluefield, W.Va., July 25, 1919; s. Deck Christopher and Zeora Monte (Brocklehurst) W.; m. Ruth Elizabeth Jones, Sept. 10, 1947; 1 child, Jeanne Lynn. BS, U. Mich., 1951. Mem. indsl. rels. staff King-Seeley Thermos Co., Ann Arbor, Mich., 1950-63; personnel mgr., then indsl. rels. mgr. Butler Mfg. Co., Kansas City, Mo., 1963-66; dir. indsl. rels. Mueller Brass Co., Port Huron, Mich., 1966-69, v.p. indsl. rels., 1969-78; dir. indsl. rels. U.S. Smelting, Refining & Mining, N.Y.C., 1966-78; indsl. rels. cons. UV Industries, N.Y.C., 1969-78; dir. indsl. rels. Fed. Pacific Electric Co., Newark, 1970-76; dir. labor rels. Anamax Mining Co., Sahuarita, Ariz., 1978-85; pres. Alert Consulting Corp., Tucson, from 1985. Co-author: Collective Bargaining, 1985, Strike Planning, 1985. Pres., Perry Nursery Sch., Ann Arbor, Mich., 1957; rd. commr., Scio Twp., Ann Arbor, 1961; del. State Rep. Conv., Detroit, 1961; mem. parents coun., Adrian (Mich.) Coll., 1973-74; bd. dirs., Blue Cross-Blue Shield Mich., Detroit, 1971-77. Mem. Masons. Methodist. Avocation: traditional dixieland jazz. Died Jan. 13, 2005.

WILLIAMS, L. STANTON, glass and chemical manufacturing executive; b. Honolulu, Oct. 7, 1919; s. Urban and Amelia (Olson) W.; m. Dorothy Webster Reed, June 12, 1943; children: Eric Reed, Timothy Howell, Steven Neil, Deborah Williams Sawin. AB, Amherst Coll., 1941, LLD, 1981; MBA, Harvard U., 1943; DHL, Thiel Coll., 1985. With PPG Industries (formerly Pitts. Plate Glass Co.), 1946-84, various acctg. positions, 1946-56, contr., 1956—63, v.p. fin., 1963-75, dir., 1975-90, exec. v.p., 1975-76, vice chmn., 1976-78, chmn., CEO, 1979-84. Chmn. Fed. Home Loan Bank, Pitts., 1971-73; bd. dirs. Duplate Can., 1976-84, Rubbermaid Inc., 1977-90, Dravo Corp., 1978-91, Prudential Ins. Co. Am., 1981-89, Mellon Bank Corp, 1981-92, Texaco Inc., 1988-92. Trustee Family and Children's Service, Pitts., 1955-61; bd. dirs. YMCA, Pitts., 1959-93, pres., 1975-77, mem. YMCA nat. bd., 1973-88, chmn., 1983-85; trustee YMCA Retirement Fund, 1989-94; pres. exec. com. Allegheny Conf. on Community Devel., 1982-83, chmn., 1983-85; bd. dirs. Pa. Economy League, 1978-83, Community Chest Allegheny County, 1961-67, Pitts. Symphony Soc., 1978-90; chmn. United Way Campaign of Southwestern Pa., 1981; bd. dirs. United Way of Allegheny County, 1978-86, pres., 1984-86; trustee St. Margaret's Meml. Hosp., Pitts., 1969-83, Carnegie-Mellon U., 1978-95, Carnegie Inst., 1977-95, Com. Econ. Devel., 1981-84, Tax Found., 1980-84, Pitts. Cultural Trust, 1984-93. Lt. USNR, 1943-46. Mem. Financial Execs. Inst. (pres. Pitts. 1965-66, nat. dir. 1968-73, nat. v.p. 1972-73), Bus. Roundtable (Policy Com. 1982-84), Duquesne Club, Fox Chapel Golf Club (Pitts.), Rolling Rock Club (Ligonier, Pa.), Iron City Fishing Club (Can.), John's Island Club, Bent Pine Golf Club (Fla.), Phi Beta Kappa. Presbyterian. Home: Verona, Pa. Died Nov. 27, 2005.

WILLIAMS, LOUISE RAE, artist, educator; b. Phoenix, Mar. 7, 1947; d. Walter Landon and Lillian Grace (Snowdon) Lyons; m. Robert Alan Williams, Apr. 1, 1967 (div. Apr. 1982); children: Michael Scott, Lisa Beth; m. Thomas James Lineham, Aug. 4, 1990. BA with honors, San Jose State U., 1969; BA, The Evergreen Coll., 1979; MFA, Ctrl. Wash. U., 1985. Asst. to dir. Indochinese refugee program Centralia Coll., Olympia, Wash., 1980-81, adj. instr., 1992; grad. asst. Ctrl. Wash. U., Ellensburg, 1982-85; instr. Yakima (Wash.) Valley C.C., 1984; vis. faculty The Evergreen State Coll., Olympia, 1988, 91, 93-97 and from 97; asst. prof. Webster U., St. Louis, 1989-90. Adj. instr. South Puget Sound C.C., Olympia, 1988-89, Centralia Coll., winter 1992. Solo exhibit King Art Gallery, 1994; represented in pub. collections Wash. State Art In Pub. Places Collection, Tacoma Housing Authority. Sec. Alliance for the Mentally Ill, Thurston/Mason County, Washington, 1998. Artist in Residence, Ucross Found., 1987, Centrum Found., 1995. Mem. Coll. Art Assn. Home: Olympia, Wash. Died Mar. 9, 2004.

WILLIAMS, MARVIN, management consultant, consultant; b. St. Petersburg, Fla., May 23, 1944; s. Early and Valeria Lee (Wilcox) W.; m. Margaret Davis, May 12, 1944 (div. June 1974); m. Rena Joseph, Dec. 23, 1949; children: Tracey Yvette, Courtney Berrien J., Yolan Yasmin J. BS in Comml. Industries, Tuskegee U., 1967. Assemblyman E-A Indsl. Corp., Atlanta, 1970-72; system engr. devel. Electronic Data Systems Corp., Atlanta, 1972-74; shop mgr. H. Salt Fish and Chips, Atlanta, 1974-75; data preparation mgr. Electronic Data Systems Ga., 1975-76; claims processing mgr. Title XIX pharm. program Electronic Data Systems N.C., 1976-77, provider svc. mgr. Title XIX Medicaid program, 1977-78, adminstrn. dir. Title XIX Medicaid program, 1978-79; systems engr., indsl. engr. Electronic Data Systems Corp., Dallas, 1979-83, indsl. engring. mgr., cons. Plano, 1983-96; v.p., gen. mgr. WFS Fin., Irvine, from 1996. With U.S. Army, 1967-70, Vietnam. Decorated Bronze Star. Democrat. Baptist. Home: Allen, Tex. Died July 14, 2005.

WILLIAMS, RICHARD KENNON, ophthalmologist; b. Richmond, Va., Dec. 8, 1923; s. Carter Nelson Jr. and Hattie Maclin (Lifsey) W.; m. Ann Hughes Preston, Nov. 12, 1948 (div. June 1968); children: Elizabeth Kennon, Anna Strudwick, Richard Kennon Jr.; m. Yvonne Kay Hynes, May 1, 1993. BS, U. Richmond, 1943; MD, Med. Coll. Va., 1946. Diplomate Am. Bd. Ophthamology. Physician staff Richmond EENT Hosp., 1950-93; asst. prof. ophthalmologist clin. M.C.V., Richmond, 1950-65; physician staff St. Marys Hosp., Richmond, 1987-93, Henrico Drs. Hosp., Richmond, 1987-93, Rappahanock Gen. Hosp., Kilmarnock, Va., from 1993. Lt. (j.g.) USN, 1947-50. Fellow ACS. Avocations: travel, fishing, boating, swimming. Died May 22, 2004.

WILLIAMS, ROBIN MURPHY, JR., sociology educator; b. Hillsborough, N.C., Oct. 11, 1914; s. Robin Murphy and Mabel Claire (Strayhorn) W.; m. Marguerite York, July 29, 1939; children: Robin Murphy III, Nancy, Susan. BS, N.C. State Coll., 1933, MS, 1935; postgrad., Cornell U., 1935-36; PhD (Austin fellow, 1938-39), Harvard U., 1943; D.Sc. (hon.), U. N.C., Greensboro, 1989. Various research positions govtl. agys., 1933-37; asst. rural sociologist N.C. Agrl. Expt. Sta., 1936-38; instr., research asst. U. Ky., 1939-42; research analyst and statistician, research br. U.S. War Dept., 1942-45; prof. sociology Cornell U., Ithaca, N.Y., 1946-67, Henry Scarborough prof. social sci., 1967-85, prof. emeritus, 1985—2006, chmn. dept. sociology and anthropology, 1956-61; dir. Soc. Sci. Research Center, 1949-54. Cons. Nat. Inst. Mental Health, 1949-67; mem. sci. adv. bd. USAF, 1950-54; adv. com. for social scis. NSF, 1967-69; com. on life sci. and social policy NRC, 1968-74; vis. scholar Russell Sage Found., 1968-69; vis. fellow Center for Creative Leadership, 1974-75; Center for Advanced Study Behavioral Scis. fellow, 1961-62, NSF Sr. postdoctoral fellow; chmn. NRC Com. on Status of Black Ams., 1985-89. Author: The Reduction of Intergroup Tension, 1947, (with others) The American Soldier, vols. I and II, 1949, American Society, 1951, 60, 70, What College Students Think, 1960, Strangers Next Door, 1964, Mutual Accomodation, 1977; editor: (with Margaret W. Ryan) Schools in Transition, 1954, Sociol. Forum, 1984-92, (with Gerald David Jaynes) A Common Destiny, 1989. Mem. Am. Sociol. Soc. (council, 1st v.p. 1956, pres. 1958, sec. 1965-68), Eastern Sociol Soc. (pres. 1966), Am. Philos. Soc., Am. Acad. Arts Scis., Nat. Acad. Scis., Sociol. Research Assn. (pres. 1958), Rural Sociol. Soc. Am. Died June 3, 2006.

WILLIAMS, THEODORE EARLE, retired industrial distribution company executive; b. Cleve., May 9, 1920; s. Stanley S. and Blanche (Albaum) W.; m. Rita Cohen, Aug. 28, 1952; children: Lezlie, Richard Atlas, Shelley, William Atlas, Wayne, Marsha, Patti Blake, Jeff Blake. Student, Wayne U., 1937-38; BS in Engring, U. Mich., 1942, postgrad. in bus. adminstrn, 1942. Pres. Wayne Products Co., Detroit, 1942-43, L.A., 1947-49; pres. Williams Metal Products Co., Inglewood, Calif., 1950-69; CEO, chmn. Bell Industries, L.A., 1970-2000; ret., 2000. Instr. U. Mich., 1942 Patentee in field. Chmn. Calif. Clean Money Campaign. Served to 1st lt. AUS, 1943-46. Recipient Humanitarian award City of L.A., 1977. Democrat. Home: Los Angeles, Calif. Died Sept. 18, 2006.

WILLIAMSON, DOROTHY DALE, mathematics educator; b. Enid, Okla., Feb. 8, 1921; d. Homer and Bertha (Maynard) Dale; m. Kenneth Dale Williamson, Sept. 7, 1946; children: Dale Aden, Kent Alan, Lance Maynard. BS in Chemistry, U. Okla., 1947; M in Guidance Counseling, Marshall U., 1971. Cert. math. tchr. 7-12, phys. sci./gen. sci. tchr., guidance counselor. Chemist E.I. duPont, Pryor, Okla., 1941-43; sec. Phillips Petroleum Co., Bartlesville, Okla., 1948-50; tchr., math. Kanawha County Schs., Charleston, W.Va., 1967-86; instr., bus. dept. W.Va. State Coll., Institute, 1986-89, ret., 1989. Instr., math. Governor's Honors Acad., Buchanan, W.Va., W.Va. Wesleyan, 1986, Shepherd Coll., Shepherdstown, W.Va., 1987. Chmn. LWV, St. Albans, W.Va., 1970-71; mem. Human Rights Commn., St. Albans, 1982-87. Recipient Presdl. award for Math., NSF, Washington, 1984. Mem. W.Va. Edn. Assn., W.Va. Coun. Tchrs. of Math, Nat. Coun. Tchrs. of Math., Kanawha County Coun. Tchrs. of Math. (pres. 1983-84), Kappa Delta Pi. Republican. Christian Science. Home: Saint Albans, W.Va. Died Feb. 8, 2004.

WILLIAMSON, DOROTHY JUNE, art consultant, artist, educator, writer; b. Mpls., June 13, 1929; d. Louis William and Hazel Irene (Johnson) W BA, Asbury Coll., 1951; MA, U. Minn., 1963, postgrad., 1969—71. Cert. edn. Tchr. art Hopkins Pub. Schs., Minn., 1952—53; art cons. Owatonna Pub. Schs., Minn., 1953—54; tchr. art Richfield Pub. Schs., Mpls., 1954—86; art educator, fine arts educator, lectr. Augsburg Coll., Mpls., 1970—91; art cons. Mpls., from 1990. Mem. com. art edn. Mpls. Soc. Fine Art, 1956; grants reader, evaluator U.S. Office of Edn., Washington, 1969—70; sole art del. U.S. Office of Edn.-Ednl. Profl. Devel. Program, Washington, 1971; participant, seminar leader discipline based art edn. Getty Found., Phoenix, 1985; sole art del.-global edn. Minn. State Dept. Edn., St. Paul, 1990—91; spkr. many confs. in field; judge art shows; participant Owatonna Art Project. Contbg. author: Discover Art Series, 1986—; exhibitor Minn. State Arts Exhibit; also in pvt. collections Bd. mem. Women's Aux. Minn. Hist. Soc., 1988—94, chair pub. rels., 1994—96; mem. sch. arts bd., 1976—80; outreach bd. Colonial Ch. of Edina, 1992—95, mem. mission bd., 1996—99, sr. min., 1994—96, mem. search com. Mem.: Internat. Soc. Edn. Art, U.S. Soc. Art, Art Edn. Minn. (pres. 1966—69), Nat. Art Edn. Assn. (regional v.p. 1969—71, chair summer confs., del. rep. search com., exec. sec. 1971—72, chmn. nat. membership 1976—78), Christians in Visual Arts (founder). Congregationalist. Avocations: photography, swimming, travel, printmaking, ceramics. Home: Minneapolis, Minn. Died Apr. 29, 2006.

WILLIAMSON, JOHN ALEXANDER, data processing executive; b. Birmingham, Ala., Feb. 5, 1918; s. John Kelly and Mary (Lee) W.; m. Jean Cochran, Feb. 14, 1948; children: John A. Jr., Wendy Martin, Maggie Brooke. BS, Birmingham So. Coll., 1935, M in Math, 1939; LLD (hon.), Birmingman So. Coll., 1991. Enlisted USN, 1940, advanced through grades to capt., 1946, ret., 1954; dist. mgr. motor div. Chevrolet, Mobile, Ala., 1946-47; sales mgr. Drennen Motor Co., Birmingham, 1952-56; pres., chmn. Cons. Co., Birmingham, 1956-84, Key Royal Auto Co., Birmingham, 1964-88, Dyatron Corp., Birmingham, from 1965, also bd. dirs., 1965-89; pres., chmn. Sungard Corp., Birmingham, from 1989. Cons. in field. Bd. dirs. Birmingham Boys Club, 1961-, Boy Scouts Am., 1984-; Rep. state fin. chmn. senatorial race, 1982-83; pres. Re-Entry Ministries, 1988-. Decorated Silver Star, Legion of Merit; recipient Disting. Alumni award Birmingham So. Coll., 1982, Silver Beaver award Boy Scouts Am., 1991. Mem. Shoal Creek Club, Birmingham Country Club. Avocations: sailing, golf. Home: Birmingham, Ala. Died May 2, 2004.

WILLIAMSON, JOHN RUSSELL, mechanical engineer; b. Michigan City, Ind., Jan. 13, 1924; s. J. Russell and Blanche (Kaser) W.; m. Mary Anne Baird, Mar. 1, 1948; children: Susan, Doug, Nanci. BME, Purdue U., 1951. Project engr. prodn. div. Bendix Corp., South Bend, Ind., 1951-65; staff engr. Garrett Engine Co., Phoenix, 1965-89. Patentee aerospace devices. Sgt. U.S. Army, 1942-46, ETO. Avocations: illustrating aircraft, sports, wildlife. Home: Paradise Vly, Ariz. Died June 5, 2005.

WILLIAMSON, SAMUEL JOHNS, physicist, researcher; b. West Reading, Pa., Nov. 6, 1939; s. Max Miller and Ellen Louisa (Reinhart) W.; m. Joan Brockman, June 16, 1966. SB, MIT, 1961, ScD, 1965; ScD (hon.), N.J. Inst. Tech., 1985; D Tech. (hon.), Helsinki U. Tech., 1994; D Tech. Mem. rsch. staff Francis Bitter Nat. Magnet Lab., MIT, Cambridge, Mass., 1965-66; NAS-Nat. Rsch. Coun. postdoctoral fellow U. Paris, Orsay, France, 1966-67; mem. tech. staff N.Am. Rockwell Sci. Ctr., Thousand Oaks, Calif., 1967-70; lectr. U. Calif., Santa Barbara, 1970-71; assoc. prof. of physics NYU, N.Y.C., 1971-77, prof., 1977—2005, prof. neural sci., 1988—2005; adj. prof. physiology and neurosci. NYU Med. Sch., N.Y.C., 1984—2005, Univ. prof., 1990—2005. Co-dir. NATO Advanced Sci. Inst. on Biomagnetism, Grottaferrata, Italy, 1982; co-chair Internat. Conf. on Biomagnetism, Rome, 1982, N.Y.C., 1989. Author: Fundamentals of Air Pollution, 1973, (with H.Z. Cummins) Light and Color in Nature and Art, 1983; co-editor: Biomagnetism: An Interdisciplinary Approach, 1983, Advances in Biomagnetism, 1989. Chmn. Venture County Citizens

Com. for Clear Air, Calif., 1969-70. Fulbright sr. rsch. scholar, U. Paris, 1979-80; NSF grad. fellow, 1961-65, Danforth grad. fellow, 1961-65. Fellow Am. Phys. Soc., Sigma Xi (pres. NYU chpt.). Achievements include patent (with others) for apparatus for process for making biomagnetic measurements. Home: New York, NY. Died Apr. 25, 2005.

WILLIS, CLIFFORD LEON, geologist; b. Chanute, Kans., Feb. 20, 1913; s. Arthur Edward and Flossie Duckworth (Fouts) W.; m. Serreta Margaret Thiel, Aug. 21, 1947 (dec.); 1 child, David Gerard. BS in Mining Engring., U. Kans., 1939; PhD, U. Wash., 1950. Geophysicist The Carter Oil Co. (Exxon), Tulsa, 1939-42; instr. U. Wash., Seattle, 1946-50, asst. prof., 1950-54; cons. geologist Harza Engring. Co., Chgo., 1952-54, 80-82, chief geologist, 1954-57, assoc. and chief geologist, 1957-67, v.p., chief geologist, 1967-80; pvt. practice cons. geologist Tucson, Ariz., from 1982. Cons. on major dam projects in Iran, Iraq, Pakistan, Greece, Turkey, Ethiopia, Argentina, Venezuela, Colombia, Honduras, El Salvador, Iceland, U.S. Lt. USCG, 1942-46. Recipient Haworth Disting. Alumnus award U. Kans., 1963. Fellow Geol. Soc. Am., Geol. Soc. London; mem. Am. Assn. Petroleum Geologists, Soc. Mining, Metallurgy and Exploration Inc., Assn. Engring. Geologists, Sigma Xi, Tau Beta Pi, Sigma Tau, Theta Tau. Republican. Roman Catholic. Avocations: travel, reading. Home: Alexandria, Va. Died Apr. 30, 2005.

WILLIS, DOYLE HENRY, retired state legislator, lawyer; b. Kaufman, Tex., Aug. 18, 1907; s. Alvin and Eliza Jane (Phillips) W.; m. Evelyn McDavid, 1942; children: Doyle Jr., Dan, Dina, Dale. BS, BA, U. Tex., 1934; LLB, Georgetown U., 1938. Bar: D.C. 1937, Tex. 1938, U.S. Supreme Ct. 1942. Mem. coun. City of Fort Worth, 1963-64; mem. Tex. Ho. of Reps., Austin, 1946-52, 69-96, Tex. State Senate, Austin, 1952-62. Tex. state comdr. VFW, 1958-59. Maj. USAF, 1941-46, PTO. Decorated Bronze Star, 4 battle stars, USAF; named Tex. Vet. of Yr., 1999. Mem. KP (life), Masons (life), Shriners (life), Ind. Order Odd Fellows., Lions Club, Sons Republic of Tex. Knights of the Order of San Jacinto. Democrat. Methodist. Avocations: golf, fishing, reading. Home: Fort Worth, Tex. Died June 22, 2006.

WILLIS, STANLEY EARL, II, retired psychiatrist, municipal government official; b. Hoisington, Kans., July 9, 1923; s. Stanley Earl and Leota Pearl (Brewer) W.; m. Edith Clark Blair, June 23, 1945 (dec.); 1 child: Alan Matson. BA, Stanford U., 1944; MD, McGill U., 1948; JD, U. San Diego, 1968. Diplomate Am. Bd. Psychiatry and Neurology. Commd. lt. USN, 1948, advanced through grades to comdr.; pres. Park Manor Hotel, Inc., San Diego, 1978-80; mng. ptnr. Willis & Willis, San Diego, from 1980, The Centre Assocs.; pres. Gentry Farm Enterprises, Inc., 1988-89; commr. civil service City of San Diego, 1986-91; mng. ptnr. Park Manor Hotel Gentry Assocs. Pvt. practice psychiatry, San Diego, 1957; bd. dirs. Crest Internat. Corp.; cons. Calif. State Bd. Med. Quality Assurance. Author: Understanding and Counseling Male Homosexual, 1967; co-author: New Dimensions in Psychosomatic Medicine; contbr. articles profl. jours. Bd. dirs. San Diego Civic Light Opera Assn., 1959-61; pres. La Jolla (Calif.) Stage Co., 1983-85. Fellow Am. Psychiat. Assn. (life), Am. Psychoanalytic Physicians; mem. AMA, Calif. Med. Assn., San Diego Yacht Club. Republican. Episcopalian. Avocations: sailing, writing. Home: San Diego, Calif. Died Apr. 17, 2004.

WILLMES, FRANCIS EDWIN, general merchandise and health and beauty aids marketing consultant; b. Hancock, Mich., Jan. 12, 1929; s. Elmer Francis and Hilda Elvira (Erickson) W.; m. Carol Lois Lauffer, May 26, 1961; Karen Leigh, Gary Francis, David Eric. BBA, U. Detroit, 1960. Dir. purchasing Mchts. Wholesale Service Co., Detroit, 1950-63; mdse. mgr. Herst -Allen Co., Chgo., 1963-65; v.p. Spartan Stores, Inc., Grand Rapids, Mich., 1965-88; pres. Willmes Mktg. Service, Grand Rapids, from 1988. Pres. G.M.D.C., Colo. Springs, Colo., 1971-78. Served with U.S. Army, 1951-53, Korea. Decorated Korean Service medal with three bronze stars, U.S. Army, 1952. Mem. Gen. Mdse. Distbrs. Council (pres. 1971, 78). Lodges: Masons. Republican. Presbyterian. Avocations: hunting, fishing, skiing, water-skiing. Home: Grand Rapids, Mich. Died Oct. 26, 2004.

WILLNER, LARRY ELLIOTT, telecommunications company executive, consultant; s. Abraham Louis and Ann (Kaye) W.; m. Inga Katz, Oct. 28, 1956; children: Allan, Susan. BS in Engring., U.S. Mil. Acad., 1954; MBA in Fin., Stanford U., 1964; diploma with distinction, Nat. Def. U., 1975. Commd. 2d lt. U.S. Army, 1954, advanced through grades to Col., ret., 1980; from dir. to v.p., gen. mgr. Govt. Systems Divsn. Western Union Corp., McLean, Va., 1981-86; sr. v.p. Govt. Networks Divsn. Contel Corp., McLean, 1986-87; group v.p. Info. Systems and Networks Inc., Bethesda, Md., 1988-89; exec. v.p. INTACT Inc., Chantilly, Va., 1989-97; v.p. Sherikon Corp., 1997-99. Chmn. bd. dirs. Western Union Hawaii, Honolulu, 1985-86; cons. Identity Rsch. Inc., McLean, 1981-92, U.S. Sprint Corp., Herndon, Va., 1989-97, Ops. Rsch. Corp., Arlington, Va., 1981, GTE Corp., McLean, 1990-91, Computer Scis. Corp., Falls Church, Va., 1991-97, ARINC, Inc., 1991-92, Boeing Computer Svcs., 1992-94, Harris Corp., 1992, Grumman Corp., 1992, GSI/Infonet, 1993-95, Boeing Info. Svcs., 1994-95, AT&T, 1994-96, Andrulis Rsch. Corp., 1993-94, SRC Corp., 1994, DC Net, Inc., 1993-95, UNITEL Communication Corp., 1993-96, AT&T Canada, 1997, A.T. Kearney Corp., 1995-97, Sherikon Corp., 1996-97, 99-2000, Cable and Wireless Corp., 1997, USAA Ednl. Found., 1999-2000; apptd. commr. Fairfax County Consumer Protection Commn., 2003—. Contbr. articles on telecommunications, fgn. policy, weapons systems acquisition, etc. to profl. jours. Decorated Disting. Svc. medal, Legion of Merit, Bronze Star; Disting. Rsch. fellow Nat. Def. U., 1975; named Hon. Prof. systems acquisitions Def. Systems Mgmt. Coll., 1974. Mem. IEEE, Armed Forces Communications-Electronics Assn. (internat. bd. 1986-90), Nat. Def. Exec. Res., Fed. Communications Commn. Nat. Industry Adv. Com., Stanford Grad. Sch. Bus. Alumni Assn. (chpt. bd. dirs. 1980-83), Masons, Scottish Rite. Republican. Jewish. Avocations: fishing, photography, collecting cameras. Home: Annandale, Va. Died Jan. 2004.

WILLOUGHBY, JAMES RUSSELL, artist, writer; b. Toronto, Ohio, Apr. 22, 1928; s. Russell Lee and Edna Gertrude (McKeown) Willoughby; m. Dorothy M. Ponder, Sept. 12, 1952 (div. 1958); children: Jim Jr., David; m. Susan N. Boettjer, Nov. 28, 1980. AA, Pasadena City Coll., 1951; postgrad., Art Ctr. Sch. Mem. staff Chrysler Corp., Maywood, Calif., 1951-57; adminstrv. asst., tech. artist Ramo-Wooldridge, El Segundo, Calif., 1957-59; adminstr. asst. Space Tech. Labs., El Segundo, 1959-61; intelligence analyst Aerospace Corp., El Segundo, 1961-65; freelancer Calif., 1965-72, Ariz., 1982—92, Filmation Studios, Reseda, Calif., 1972-82. Storyboard designer Hanna-Barbera, Disney Studios, 1987—90. Author, illustrator (book) Cowboy Country Cartoons, 1988, Birds of the Southwest, 1997, Do you Pray, Duke?, 1999, 2d edit., 2001, co-author, illustrator Cowboy Cartoon Cookbook, 1990, Cactus County, 1992, Sharlot Hall Coloring Book, 1994, Cowboy Cartoons: Quick on the Draw, 1996, A Dude's Guide to the West, 1996; Arizona Humoresque, 1992, Cowpies Ain't No Dish you Take to the County Fair, 1997, Sometimes the Bull Wins, 2002, Prescott Daily Courier. Recipient Disting. Alumnus award, Toronto HS, 1999. Mem.: Nat. Cartoonist Soc., Prescott Corral, Westerners Internat. Avocation: hiking. Home: Prescott, Ariz. Died Dec. 11, 2004.

WILMER, HARRY ARON, psychiatrist, educator; b. New Orleans, Mar. 5, 1917; s. Harry Aron and Leona (Schlenker) W.; m. Jane Harris, Oct. 31, 1944; children: Harry, John, Thomas, James, Mary. BS, U. Minn., 1938, MB, MS, U. Minn., 1940, MD, 1941, PhD, 1944. Intern Gorgas Hosp., Ancon, C.Z., 1940-41; resident in neurology and psychiatry Mayo Clin., Rochester, Minn., 1945-49, cons. in psychiatry, 1957-58; physician Palo Alto (Calif.) Clinic, 1949-51; pvt. practice medicine, Palo Alto, 1951-55, 58-64; prof. psychiatry U. Calif. Med. Sch., San Francisco, 1964-69; sr. psychiatrist Scott & White Clin., Temple, Tex., 1969-74; emeritus prof. psychiatry U. Tex. Health Sci. Ctr., San Antonio, 1974-87; staff mem.(part-time) Audie Murphy VA Hosp., San Antonio, 1974-82; founder, dir. Internat. Film Festivals on Culture and Psychiatry, U. Tex. Health and Sci. Ctr., 1972-80; founder, emeritus pres., dir. Inst. Humanities, Salado, TX, from 1980; pvt. practice, Salado, from 1980. Author: Huber the Tuber, 1942, Corky the Killer, 1945, This is Your World, 1952, Social Psychiatry in Action, 1958, First Book for the Mind, 1963, Vietnam in remission, 1985, Practical Jung, 1987, Closeness: A Dictionary of Ideas, Vol. I, 1989, Father Mother, 1989; (film) People Need People, 1961, Facing Evil, 1988, Evil, 1989, Creativity, 1990, Creativity Paradoxes and Reflections, 1991, Closeness: Personal and Professional Relations, 1992, Understandable Jung, 1994, How Dreams Help, 1999, Quest for Silence, 2000. Served to capt. M.C., USNR, 1955-57; Guggenheim fell., Zurich, 1969-70; NRC fell., Johns Hopkins Hosp., 1944-45. Fell. Am. Pscyhiatry Assn. (life, emeritus), Am. Coll. Psychiatrists, Am. Acad. Psychoanalysis; mem. AAAS, Internat. Assn. Analytical Pscyhology. Home: Salado, Tex. Died Mar. 17, 2005.

WILSON, BRUCE ROY, marketing communications executive; b. Cleve., Sept. 30, 1943; s. Donald Kersey and Mary (Cushing) W.; m. Darlene Rhinehart, Nov. 23, 1964 (div. June 1967); 1 child, Kimberley; m. Patricia C. Crinnion, Oct. 14, 1967; children: Scott, Jennifer. BA, U. Va., 1965. Network TV buyer J. Walter Thompson, N.Y.C., 1965-68; broadcast specialist Eastman Kodak Co., Rochester, N.Y., 1972-79, dir. mktg. communications instant products, 1979-83, dir. mktg. communications film products, 1983-86, dir. mktg. communications & support svcs., consumer products, U.S.A., Latin Am., Can., 1986-89, dir. corp. advt., from 1989. Author: Rochester From A to Z, 1975, Surprising Rochester, 1976. Area coordinator Rep. Com. Brighton, N.Y., 1975-77; v.p. Navy League, Rochester, 1975-78; pres. Victor (N.Y.) Community Baseball, 1985. Served to lt. USNR, 1968-72. Recipient Robert Kent Gooch award U. Va., 1965. Mem. Advt. Council N.Y. (nat. vol. coordinator ARC campaign 1986—). Avocations: golf, tennis, reading, coaching baseball. Home: Victor, NY. Died Sept. 8, 2004.

WILSON, CHRISTINE SHEARER, nutritional anthropologist, consultant, editor; b. Orleans, Mass. d. James and Christina (Smith) W. BA cum laude, Brown U., 1950; postgrad., Harvard U., 1951-56, Vanderbilt U., 1958-59; PhD, U. Calif., Berkeley, 1970. Asst. editor Nutrition Revs., Boston, 1951-56; nutrition analyst USDA, Washington, 1957-58; publ. editor, writer Interdepartmental Com. on Nutrition for Nat. Def., USPHS, Bethesda, Md., 1959-66; asst. rsch. nutritionist, lectr. Univ. Calif., San Francisco, 1970-71, 74-78, 1980-83; rsch. nutritionist Stanford Univ.-Food Rsch. Inst., Palo Alto, Calif., 1971; sr. nutritional scientist Resources Devel. Assocs., Los Altos, Calif., 1974-75; vis. prof. Univ. Guelph, Ont., 1978; asst. prof. San Francisco (Calif.) State Univ., 1979; editor Ecology of Food and Nutrition, N.Y.C. and Annapolis, N.Y., Md., from 1977. Cons., project dir. Soc. for Nutrition Edn., Berkeley, 1971-72, 73-74, 81; peer reviewer grants NSF, Washington, USDA Human Nutrition, Washington, 1979; faculty summer workshop U. Calif. Food Policy, Berkeley, 1978-79; vis. prof. St. George's U. Med. Sch., Georgetown, Grenada, 1982; vis. scientist Fedn. Am. Scientists for Exptl. Biology Program for Minor Inst., No. Ariz. U., 1983; cons. U.S. Agy. for Internat. Devel., Indonesia, 1996. Editor: Manual for Nutrition Surveys, 2d edit., 1963; co-editor: Culture and Ecology of Food and Nutrition, 1992—; contbr. chpts. to books and articles to profl. jours. Mem. Alliance for Md. Forests, Annapolis, 1990-2005; bd. dirs. Econ. Opportunity Com., Anne Arundel County, Md., 1991-95. Spl. Rsch. fellow Nat. Inst. Gen. Med. Scis., U. Calif., Berkeley, 1966-69, Nat. Inst. Digestive Diseases, U. Calif., San Francisco, 1972-73. Fellow Am. Anthrop. Assn.; mem. Am. Inst. Nutrition, Coun. on Nutritional Anthropology (v.p. 1978, pres. 1979-80), Soc. for Internat. Nutrition Rsch. (charter), Soc. for Med. Anthropology, Assn. for Asian Studies (exec. com. women in Asian studies 1984-85), Assn. for Study Food in Soc. (bd. dirs. 1988-90), Soc. for Nutrition Edn., LWV (bd. dirs. 1987-91). Avocations: art, history, music, travel. Home: Annapolis, Md. Died May 31, 2005.

WILSON, KATHY, principal; b. East Providence, R.I., Aug. 10, 1951; d. Marion A. and Rita (Castergine) Higdon; m. Paul O. Wilson, Dec. 21, 1974; children: Casey Rose, Fletcher Todd. BS in Edn., U. Mo., 1973, MA in Edn., 1976. Cert. in tchg., Mo. Social sci. rsch. analyst Dept. Labor, Washington, 1977-80; nat. pres. Nat. Women's Polit. Caucus, Washington, 1981-85; substitute tchr. Alexandria (Va.) City Pub. Schs., 1989-91; tchr. Resurrection Children's Ctr., Alexandria, Va., 1991-93; dir. Abracadabra Child Care & Devel. Ctr., Alexandria, Va., 1993—2005. Model tchr. The Danny Chitwood Early Learning Ctr., Alexandria, Va., 1993, The Danny Chitwood Early Learning Inst. Family Child Care, Alexandria, 1992-93; jr. gt. books tchr. Maury & Lykes Crouch Elem. Schs., 1986-89. Contbr. articles to newspapers. Youth Soccer Coach Alexandria Soccer Assn., 1989-90; recording sec. PTA, gift wrap chmn.; chmn. All Night Grad. Party, T.C. William H.S., 1995-2005; mem. adv. bd. Nat. Womens Polit. Caucus; founder, bd. dirs. Nat. Rep. Coalition for Choice, Washington, 1989-91. Received award for one of Washington's Most Influential Washington Mag., 1985; named one of Am.'s 100 Most Important Women Ladies Home Jour. editl. bd., 1983. Mem. Nat. Assn. for the Edn. of Young Children, Alexandria Child Care Dirs. Assn. (co-chmn. 1995-2005). Republican. Baptist. Avocations: reading, writing, soccer, politics. Home: Alexandria, Va. Died Sept. 1, 2005.

WILSON, MARION LOY, nurse midwife; b. Westmoreland, Jamaica, Feb. 24, 1949; d. Johnaton and Annette Myrtle Wilson; 1 child, Elizabeth Wilson Strudwick. RN, U. Hospital of West Indies, 1968—71. Cert. state cert.nurse, Good Hope Maternity Hosp., 1978, midwifery tutor diploma, Royal Coll. Midwives, 1980, cert. nurse midwife, N.Y., 1995. Nurse midwife Downtown Bronx Med., from 1996; registered nurse Lincoln Hosp., Bronx, Met. Hosp.; life underwriter Mutual Life, Kingston, Jamaica; lectr. Excelsior Cmty. Coll., Kingston, Jamaica; registered nurse U. Hosp. of W.I., Kingston, Jamaica; tchr. Bethel Town Primary Sch., Westmoreland, Jamaica. Curriculum develop. com. Excelsior Coll. Cmty., Kingston, Jamaica, 1983—85. Contbr. articles. Disaster preparedness com. Excelsior Cmty. Coll., 1983—85. Avocations: reading, dance, writing, music, aerobics. Died July 29, 2005.

WILSON, MARK WAYNE, optical and laser physicist, physics instructor; b. Chgo., Sept. 14, 1955; s. William O. and Mary E. (Carroll) W.; m. Michele Maria Marcheschi, Aug. 1977; children: Jennifer A., Matthew C., Rebecca A., Adam J. BS in Physics, Math., Psychology, Ill. Benedictine Coll., 1977; MS in Physics, U. Ill., Chgo., 1979, PhD, 1982. Research asst. U. Ill., Chgo., 1979-82; research physicist SRI Internat., Menlo Park, Calif., 1982-86; program mgr. Sci. Applications Internat. Corp., Los Altos, Calif., 1986-88; sr. staff scientist Westinghouse Idaho Nuclear Co., Inc., Livermore, Calif., from 1988. Instr. Triton Coll., River Grove, Ill., 1981-82, Calif. State U., Hayward, 1986-87. Contbr. articles to sci. jours. Mem. IEEE, Optical Soc. Am., Soc. Photo-optical Engrs., Sigma Pi Sigma. Died Mar. 13, 2005.

WILSON, PAUL WAYNE, retired real estate developer; b. Kokomo, Ind., June 13, 1933; s. Floyd Wayne Wilson and Stella (Dugan) Emry; m. Dixie Lee Cooprider, Feb. 23, 1952; children: Michael Wayne, Susan Jo Wilson-Broadus, Marci Ann, Paul Wayne II. Student, Ind. Bus. Coll., 1957-59. Cert. environ. inspector, environ. specialist,. constrn. inspector. Salesperson Kothe, Wells & Bauer, Indpls., 1956-60; owner, founder Pickin Chicken, Kokomo, 1958-60; broker Wayne Wilson Realty, Inc., Kokomo, 1963-98; owner Wayne Wilson Constrn. Co., Kokomo, 1960-78; apt. developer, 1998-2000; ret., 2000. V.p. Pyramid Inc., Kokomo, 1967-72, Mi-Su-Mar, Inc., Kokomo, 1967-78; founder, pres. Able Alarm Co., Inc., Kokomo, 1976-83; mgr. Honeywell Protection Svcs., Kokomo, 1983-97, ret.; pres., founder Midwest Organics, Inc., Kokomo, 1989-93. Sch. bd. Taylor Community Schs., Center, Ind., 1963-73, pres., 1971; del. Dem. State Conv., Indpls., 1972; pres. Ind. Burglar & Fire Alarm Assn., 1982. Staff sgt. USAF, 1951-

55. Recipient Beautification award Kokomo C. of C., 1979. Mem. Elks, Rotary. Roman Catholic. Avocations: flying, organic gardening. Home: Kokomo, Ind. Died Feb. 25, 2005.

WILSON, WANDA MAE FRENCH, animal association administrator; b. Cin., Ohio, Nov. 20, 1936; d. William Riley French and Grace Mae Walker; m. David William Jordan; children: Melinda, Wendy, Sandra. Student, Nat-.Coll., Kans. City, Mo., 1954—55, Shippensburg U., Cumberland County, Pa., 1972—73, Harisburg Area C.C., Harrisburg, Pa., 1973—75. Employment Interviewer Pa. Dept. Labor and Industry, Harrisburg, Pa., 1970—76, emplyer rels. rep. Lebanon, Pa., 1976—94; founder Little Mouse Club of the Western Hemisphere, New Cumberland, Pa., from 1994. Founder, partner designer custom Jewelery and repair Wilson Jordan Enterprises, Harrisburg, Pa., from 1973. Contbr. articles to profl. jours. and mags. Pres. women's assn. Unitarian-Universalist Women's Assn., Harrisburg, 1979—80; ch. sch. tchr. Unitarian Churches, Indpls., Detroit, Cin., Harrisburg, 1962—74; edn. com. Unitarian Ch., Harrisburg, Pa., 1969—72; charter member National Mus. for Women in the Arts, Washington, 1987—pres; charter mem. Nat. Women's History Mus.; Co organizer, finance committee officer First Feminist Credit Union, Harrisburg, 1973—74; organizer, founder Harrisburg chpt.NOW, Harrisburg, 1972—75; leader Girl Scouts of Am., Indianapolis, Detroit, Cincinnati, 1962—69; union chpt. treas., shop steward Svc. Employee Internat. Union, Harrisburg. Mem.: Unitarian Universalist Women's Assn., Harrisbug Astron. Soc. (trustee 1975—81, v.p. 1980), Mensa (editor 1980—85), N.Am. Rat and Mouse Club Internat. (editor 1994—97, Named Most Valuable mem. 1994), Little Mouse Club (head facilitator, chief info. officer from 1997). Unitarian. Avocations: total solar eclipse chasing, reading, minatures, archaeology. Home: New Cumberland, Pa. Died Feb. 5, 2005.

WILSON, WAYNE ROBERT, communications executive; b. Clawson, Mich., Aug. 3, 1940; s. Robert Grant and Marguerite Isabella (Kohen) W.; divorced; children: Christopher Wayne, Roberta Marie, Cheryl Marguerite, Rebecca Lyn. Student, Elmhurst Coll., 1983-85; BSBA, U. Phoenix, 1986, MBA, 1988. Engr. GTE, Northlake, Ill., 1966-77, mgr. customer support, 1977-84, mgr. tech. assistance ctr. Northlake and Phoenix, 1984-85, mgr. research and devel. Phoenix, 1985-86, dir. research and devel., from 1986; dir. tech. service Siemens Transmission Systems, Inc., from 1987. Adult leader Boy Scouts Am., Ill., Wis., 1966-77; mem. exec. com. Community Chest, Glendale Heights, Ill., 1966-70. Served with U.S. Army, 1961-64. Mem. Salem (Wis.) Jaycees (sec. 1972-74). Home: Phoenix, Ariz. Died Aug. 9, 2005.

WILSON, WILLIAM ANDREW, lawyer; b. N.Y.C., Jan. 3, 1934; s. Robert Blakeley and Sarah (Cruise) W.; children: Robert Ramson, William Andrew Jr., Rebecca Allbright. BA, Syracuse U., 1960; JD, Boston U., 1965. Bar: Colo. 1965, Maine 1965, U.S. Dist. Ct. Colo. 1965, U.S. Ct. Appeals (10th cir.) 1966, U.S. Supreme Ct. 1970. Assoc. Isaacson, Rosenbaum, Goldberg & Miller, Denver, 1965-66; sole practice Denver, from 1966. Dir., legal counsel Citizen's Scholarship Found., Denver, 1967-71. Served with USAF, 1952-56. Mem. ABA, Colo. Bar Assn., Denver Bar Assn. Avocations: mountain climbing, skiing, running, hist. studies. Home: Denver, Colo. Died Aug. 10, 2005.

WILTZ, HECTOR RAFAEL, psychiatrist; b. Havana, Cuba, Oct. 24, 1926; came to U.S., 1969; s. Hector M. and Asuncion (Lancis) W.; m. Maria Wiltz, Aug. 15, 1951; chidlren: Magdalena, Hector, Rafael. MD, Sch. Medicine, Havana, 1951. Practice medicine specializing in psychiatry. V.p. PACHA, MIami, Fla., 1997—. Mem. AMA, Am. Psychiat. Assn., Cuban Med. Assn. in Exile. Republican. Avocations: travel, music, reading. Home: Miami, Fla. Died Jan. 1, 2004.

WINGERTER, JOHN PARKER, artist, photographer; b. N.Y.C., July 27, 1940; s. William and Catherine (Parker) W. Student, Columbia U., 1958-61; LLB, LaSalle U., 1968; postgrad., Arts Student League, 1970-72. Dir. Noho Gallery, N.Y.C., 1982-84. One man shows include Nomo Gallery, 1978-88; exhibitions in group shows at Adelphi U., 1983, LeSalon Des Nations Centre for Contemporary Arts, 1984, Smithtownship Arts Coun. Artist Forum-Mill Pond House, 1996-97, North Shore of L.I. Black Ch., 2000, Town Hall and Huntington Enrichment Ctr., N.Y. Grantee Suffolk County Decentralization, 1999, Spl. Opportunity Stipend grant East End Arts coun., 2000; recipient Proclamation for quality of work Huntington Town Hall. Home: Northport, NY. Died Feb. 29, 2004.

WINKELMAYER, RICHARD, psychiatrist; b. Vienna, Mar. 4, 1930; s. Franz and Maria (Perschinka) W.; m. Patricia Anne Schles, July 28, 1962; children: Richard Jr., Elizabeth Karen, Mark Lawrence. MD, U. Vienna, 1954. Cert. in psychiatry Am. Bd. Psychiatry and Neurology. Intern Elizabeth (N.J.) Gen. Hosp., 1956-57; resident N.J. State Hosp., Marlboro, 1959-62; dir. psychiat. rsch. and edn. Del. State Hosp., New Castle, 1966-84; dir. edn. dept. psychiatry Jefferson Med. Coll., 1971-74; asst. supt. Del. State Hosp., New Castle, 1973-75; clin. prof. Jefferson Med. Coll., Phila., from 1978; dir. rsch. and edn. div. mental health State of Del., 1977-85; psychiat. cons. Wilmington (Del.) VA Med. Ctr., from 1980; med. dir. Del. State Hosp., New Castle, from 1984. Mem. adv. bd.-spl. project NIMH, Bethesda, Md., 1978-80. Author: (with others) Music Therapy, 1968; contbr. articles to Psychiat. Quar., Del. Med. Jour., Pediatrics, Am. Jour. Psychiatry. Bd. dirs. Del. Coun. on Crime, Wilmington, 1984-90. Fellow Am. Psychiat. Assn. (del. 1977—, cert. com. on cert. of mental hosp. adminstrs.); mem. Del. Psychiat. Soc. (del., pres. 1971-72, 85-86, Disting. Svc. 1982), AAAS, Sigma Xi. Democrat. Unitarian Universalist. Home: New Castle, Del. Died Nov. 6, 2004.

WINN, SUZANNE BARBARA, marketing professional; b. Passaic, N.J., Feb. 11, 1957; d. Roger Emmett and Claire Louise (Nicholson) Behre; m. Mitchell D. Winn, May 13, 1978; children: Casey Anne, Amanda Christine. BS in Communications, U. Idaho, 1992; postgrad. in sports mgmt., from 1995. Asst. mgr. Jay Jacobs Clothing, Moscow, Idaho, 1980, Small World Toys and Pets, Moscow, 1980-81; mgr. Fitness Unlimited, Moscow, 1983-87; office mgr., exec. asst. Moscow C. of C., 1987-89; sales mgr. Creative Workshops, Moscow, 1992-93; telecomms. specialist athletic dept. U. Idaho, Moscow, 1993-94, compliance/programs asst. athletic dept., 1994-95; athletic ticket mgr., 1995. Bd. dirs. Moscow Mardi Gras, 1989, Deary Latchkey Program, 1994. Mem. Moscow C. of C. (tourism com. 1988-89, retail com. 1988-89, chair awards banquet 1989, bd. dirs. Latah County Vandal Boosters 1995—). Died July 16, 2004.

WINN, WILLIAM VINCENT, retail executive; b. St. Louis, Jan. 18, 1932; s. James and Mildred (Crume) W.; m. Rubia La Pearl, May 1965 (dec. May 1983); m. Katharine Menardi Stieglitz, June 15, 1984. Cert. data processing, NYU, IBM, UNIVAC, Gen. Electric, and Burroughs. V.p. data processing DiamonData, Chgo., 1969-75; data processing mgr. Trinair Industries, Lomita, Calif., 1975-79, Chase-Revel Co., Los Angeles, 1980-82; system coordinator Mattel Electronics Corp., Hawthorne, Calif., 1982-83; dir. data processing Judy's Merchandise Inc., Van Nuys, Calif., from 1983. V.p., treas. Data Processing Mgmt. Assn., Chgo., 1970, 73, 74; active Common, Hawthorne, Calif., 1983. Contbr. articles on computers to mags. Home: Saint Louis, Mo. Died Apr. 21, 2005.

WINTER, NATHAN HAROLD, religion educator; b. N.Y.C., Mar. 20, 1926; s. Sol Winter and Fannie Sacks; m. Magda Markowitz, Feb. 5, 1949; children: Steven, Elaine, Jonathan. BA, NYU, 1949, MA, PhD, NYU, 1955; B. Religious Edn., Jewish Theol. Sem., N.Y.C., 1951; JD, Bklyn. Law Sch., 1954; D Pedagogy (hon.), Jewish Theol. Sem., 1977. Prof. dept. Hebrew and Judaic studies NYU, N.Y.C., from 1968, Ethel and Irvin prof. of Hebrew and Judaic studies, from 1980. Edn. cons. United Synagogue of Am., N.J., 1954-80; dir. tng. for communal edn. Am. Assn. for Jewish Edn., N.Y.C., 1976-84; lectr. in edn. Rabbinical Sch., Jewish Theol. Sem., N.Y.C., 1972-76. Author: Jewish Education in a Pluralist Society, 1960, Jewish Education in America, The Jewish Experience, 1977, The Bible World, 1980. Sgt. U.S. Army, 1943-46. Mem. Jewish Educators Assembly (hon. pres. 1978—), Assn. for Jewish Studies, World Coun. of Jewish Studies, Coun. of Jewish Edn. (v.p. 1978-84), Nat. Assn. Profs. of Hebrew (mem. editorial bd. 1970-82). Home: Maplewood, NJ. Died Jan. 13, 2004.

WINTERS, SHELLEY (SHIRLEY SCHRIFT), actress; b. St. Louis, Aug. 18, 1922; d. Jonas and Rose Schrift; m. Paul Meyer, Oct. 1943 (div. 1946); m. Vittorio Gassman Apr. 28, 1952 (div. 1954); 1 child, Vittoria; m. Anthony Franciosa, May 4, 1957 (div. Nov. 1960). Student, Wayne U. Began acting career in vaudeville, later played roles on legitimate stage; film appearances include The Diary of Anne Frank, 1958 (Acad. award best supporting actress), Odds Against Tomorrow, Let No Man Write My Epitaph, Matter of Convictions, Lolita, 1962, Wives and Lovers, 1963, The Balcony, 1964, A House Is Not a Home, 1964, Patch of Blue, 1966 (Acad. award Best Supporting Actress), Time of Indifference, 1965, Alfie, 1965, The Moving Target, 1965, Harper, 1966, Enter Laughing, 1967, The Scalp Hunters, 1968, Buona Sera Mrs. Campbell, 1968, Wild in the Streets, 1968, The Mad Room, 1969, How Do I Love Thee, 1971, What's the Matter with Helen, 1971, The Poseidon Adventure, 1972 (Golden Globe award), Blume in Love, 1973, Cleopatra Jones, 1973, Something to Hide, 1973, Diamonds, 1975, Next Stop Greenwich Village, 1976, The Tenant, 1976, An Average Man, 1977, Tentacles, 1977, Pete's Dragon, 1977, King of the Gypsies, 1978, The Visitor, 1980, Looping, 1981, S.O.B., 1981, My Mother, My Daughter, 1981, Over the Brooklyn Bridge, Ellie, Deja Vu, 1985, The Delta Force, 1986, Marilyn Monroe: Beyond the Legend, 1987, Purple People Eater, 1988, An Unremarkable Life, 1989, Touch of a Stranger, 1990, Stepping Out, 1991, The Pickle, 1993, Raging Angels, 1995, Mrs. Munck, 1995, Jury Duty, 1995, Heavy, 1995, Backfire, 1995, The Portrait of a Lady, 1996; Gideon's Webb, 1998, La Bamba, 1999; appeared in: TV films Revenge!, 1971, The Devil's Daughter, 1973, Double Indemnity, 1974, The Sex Symbol, 1974, Elvis, 1978, Alice in Wonderland; plays A Hatfull of Rain, 1955, Girls of Summer, 1957, Night of the Iguana, Cages, Who's Afraid of Virginia Wolf?, Minnie's Boys, Marlon Brando: The Wild One, 1996; (TV miniseries) The French Atlantic Affair, 1979; Author: play One Night Stands of a Noisy Passenger, 1971; (autobiography) Shelley: Also Known As Shirley, 1980, Shelley II: The Middle of My Century, 1989. Recipient Emmy award Best Actress, 1964, Monte Carlo Golden Nymph award, 1964, Internat. TV award as best actress Cannes Festival, 1965 Died Jan. 14, 2006.

WINTHROP, SHERMAN, lawyer; b. Duluth, Minn., Feb. 3, 1931; s. George E. and Mary (Tesler) W.; m. Barbara Cowan, Dec. 16, 1956; children: Susan Winthrop Crist, Bradley T., Douglas A. BBA, U. Minn., 1952; JD, Harvard U., 1955. Bar: Minn. 1955, U.S. Dist. Ct. Minn. 1955, U.S. Tax Ct. Law clk. to chief justice Minn. Supreme Ct., St. Paul, 1955-56; ptnr. Oppenheimer, Wolff & Donnelly, St. Paul, 1956-79; shareholder Winthrop & Weinstine P.A., St. Paul, from 1979. Bd. dirs. Bremer Fin. Corp., St. Paul, Minn., Capital City Partnership; bd. dirs., sec. St. Paul Progress Corp. Mem. ABA, Minn. Bar Assn. (chair exec. coun., bus. law sect. 1992-93), Ramsey County Bar Assn. Avocations: tennis, travel. Died June 6, 2005.

WISHART, JOYCE, marketing professional; b. Cin., Mar. 21, 1942; d. Robert H. and Thelma (Haar) K. Student, Ohio State U., 1983-87, Old Dominican Coll., Columbus, Ohio, 1987-92. Mem. mktg., advt. staff ChemLawn Corp., Columbus, 1980-84, corp. communications coord., 1984-87, residential mktg. and sales coord., 1987-88, mktg. mgr., 1988-89, CheckFree Corp., Westerville, Ohio, 1989-90; owner Carousel Mktg. Svcs., Columbus, Ohio, from 1990. Recipient Echo award Direct Mktg. Assn., 1988, 89, award Ohio Tng. Resource Showcase, 1991, 92. Mem. ASTD, Am. Mktg. Assn., Am. Mgmt. Assn. Home: Sarasota, Fla. Died Jan. 21, 2004.

WITKIN, ISAAC, sculptor; b. Johannesburg, May 10, 1936; children: Tamar, Nadine. Student, St. Martin's Sch. Art, London, 1957-60. Asst. to Henry Moore, 1961-63; tchr. St. Martin's Sch. Art, London, 1963-65; artist in residence Bennington Coll., Vt., 1965-79; tchr. Parson's Sch. Design, N.Y.C., 1975-78; vis. prof. Middlebury Coll., Vt., 1981; prof. sculpture Phila. Coll. Art, 1990—92, Burlington County CC, NJ, 2001—02. Mem. Yale U. Adv. Com. to the Art Sch., 1987-90; mem. Bennington Coll. Art Collection Com., 1987-91, Royal Soc. British Sculptors, 1998-2002; bd. mem. Internat. Sculpture Ctr., 1990—2002. One-person shows include Hamilton Gallery Contemporary Art, N.Y.C., 1981, Mattingly Baker Gallery, Dallas, 1982, McIntosh/Drysdale Gallery, Washington, 1982, 1986, Hirschl & Adler Modern, N.Y.C., 1985, 1988, Jan Turner Gallery, L.A., Patricia Hamilton, N.Y.C., Locks Gallery, Phila., 1991, 93, Walker Hill Art Ctr., Seoul, Korea, 1992, others; exhibited in group shows at Hamilton Gallery, N.Y.C., 1981, Freeman Gallery, Albright Coll., 1982, Fuller Goldeen Gallery, San Francisco, 1982, The Berkshire Mus., Pittsfield, Mass., 1982, Washington Square Plaza, Washington, 1983, Wave Hill, Bronx, N.Y., 1983, Pratt Inst. Gallery, N.Y.C., 1984, Sonoma State U., Calif., 1984, N.J. State Mus., Trenton, 1984, Number One Penn Plaza, N.Y.C., 1984, Williams Coll. Mus. Art, Williamstown, Mass., 1984, N.J. Ctr. for the Visual Arts, Summit, 1987, Zone Arts Ctr., Springfield, Mass., 1988, James A. Michener Fine Arts Ctr., Doylestown, Pa., 1989, Robeson Ctr. Gallery, Rutgers U., Trenton, 1989, Locks Gallery, Phila., 1990-91, Robert Morrison Gallery, N.Y.C., 1993, Marc de Montebello Gallery, N.Y.C., 1995, Atlantic Found., Hamilton, N.J., 1995, Hunterdon Art Ctr., Clinton, N.J., 1995, others; represented in permanent collections Alcoa Co., Pitts., Am. Rep. Ins. Co., Des Moines, Arts Coun. Gt. Brit., London, Atlantic Found., Princeton, Carnegie Inst., Pitts., Chase Manhattan Bank, N.Y.C., CIGNA Corp., Phila., Columbus (Ohio) Mus. Fine Art, Denver (Colo.) Mus. Art, Fine Arts Mus., U. Sydney, Australia, MIT, Boston, Nat. Mus. Am. Art, Washington, numerous others. Recipient First prize Paris Biennale, 1965, Guggenheim fellowship, 1981; grantee N.J. State Coun. on the Arts, 1985, Adolph and Esther Gottlieb Found., 1994. Mem.: NAD (academician from 1996). Died Apr. 23, 2006.

WITKOSKI, JOHN MICHAEL, public relations executive; b. Beaufort, S.C., July 1, 1951; married; children: Patrick, Nicholas, Andrew, Dana. BA in English, U. S.C., 1972, MA in English, 1977, PhD in Linguistics, 1982. Caseworker S.C. Dept. Social Svcs., Beaufort County, 1973-74; from programs officer to dir. planning & programs Midlands Human Resources Devel. Commn., Columbia, 1979-83; rsch. asst. S.C. Ho. of Reps., Columbia, 1983-87, dir. rsch. med., mil., pub. and mcpl. affairs com., 1987-90; v.p. Ferillo & Assocs., Columbia, from 1990. Instr. Beaufort Tech. Coll., 1974-75; grad. tchg. asst. English dept. U. S.C., 1975-76, instr. ESL, 1976-77, continuing edn. dept., 1985—; edtl. asst. Studies in Scottish Lit., 1976-78, Bibliography of Scottish Poetry, 1976-78, Linguistic Atlas of the Middle and South Atlantic States, 1978-79. Recipient Havilah Babcock creative writing award, 1972, awards Acad. Am. Poets, 1976, 78, Frank Durham creative writing award, 1977. Mem. Phi Beta Kappa. Home: Columbia, SC. Died Feb. 25, 2004.

WITTENBERG, MERLE EUGENE, management consultant; b. LaCrosse, Wis., Feb. 3, 1929; s. Roy and Gertrude (Renner) W.; m. Joan McHaffey, Apr. 20, 1952; children: Roy, Heidi, Lisa, Kurt. Sales rep. Container Corp. Am., Chgo., 1954-58; rsch. assoc. Northwestern U., Evanston, Ill., 1958-61; project dir. Kielty, Dechert & Hampe, Chgo., 1961-65; v.p. Beldo & Willmarth, Chgo., 1965-69; chmn. Dechert-Hampe & Co., Northbrook, Ill., 1969-95. Author: The Lifeline of America: A History of the Food Industry, 1965, How Salesman Are Compensated, 1964, SalesExpense Practices, 1967. Cpl. U.S. Army, 1951-53. Home: Whitewater, Wis. Died Jan. 15, 2005.

WITTING, CHRIS J., electrical manufacturing executive; b. Cranford, N.J., Apr. 7, 1915; s. Nicholas and Anne (Begasse) W.; B.S., N.Y. U., 1941; grad. Am. Inst. Banking;

student Fordham Law Sch.; D.Eng. (hon.), Clarkson Coll. Tech.; m. Grace Orrok, Oct. 8, 1938 (dec. 1993); children—Leland James, Anne Kristin, Nancy Jane, Chris J.; m. Marshia K. Pullman, Nov. 15, 1997. Exec. asst. Guaranty Trust Co., 1933-36, N.Y. Trust Co., 1936-39; mgr. Price Waterhouse & Co., 1939-41; comptroller, treas. U.S.O. Camp Shows, Inc., 1941-46; mng. dir. Allen B. DuMont Labs., Inc., 1946-53; pres. Westinghouse Broadcasting Co., 1953-54, group v.p. and gen. mgr. consumer products group, Westinghouse Electric Corp., 1954-64; v.p. exec. asst. to chmn. and pres. Internat. Tel.& Tel. Corp., 1964-65; pres., chief exec. officer, dir. Crouse-Hinds Co., Syracuse, N.Y., 1965-75, chmn., chief exec. officer, 1975-82; vice chmn. bd. Cooper Industries Inc., Houston. Chmn. Pub. Auditorium Authority of Pitts. and Allegheny County, 1963-64; chmn. bd. trustees Syracuse U., 1975-93. Mem. Nat. Electric Mfrs. Assn. (chmn. bd. govs., bd. dirs.), Electronic Industries Assn. (bd. govs. 1961-62, dir. 1960-63), Nat. Planning Assn. (nat. council), Am. Mgmt. Assn. (mem. mktg. planning council), Elec. Mfrs. Club, Met. Devel. Assn. Syracuse and Onondaga County, N.Y. (dir.). Clubs: Athletic, Union League, Century, Onondaga Country, Athletic (Syracuse). Home: Syracuse, NY. Died Dec. 19, 2005.

WITZMAN, AUDREY LORAINE, retired state education official, nursery school owner, educational consultant; b. Galva, Ill., July 22, 1937; d. Clarence Gilbert and Gladys Bernice (Westlin) Peterson; m. Thomas A. Witzman, Aug. 10, 1958; children: Johanna Marie Schroeder, Jocelyn Anne Hibshman. BA, Eureka Coll., 1958; MEd, Nat. Coll. Edn., 1962; PhD, Northwestern U., 1976. Pub. sch. tchr., Ill., 1958—67; asst. prof. early childhood edn. Northeastern Ill. U., Chgo., 1968—71; developer, owner, dir. Country Woods Nursery Sch. and Day Camp, Valparaiso, Ind., 1971—96. Prof. early childhood edn. Govs. State U., University Park, Ill., 1979—87; field assoc. doctoral programs Nova Southeastern U., Ft. Lauderdale, Fla., 1984—2006; cons. birth to spl. edn. programs Ill. State Bd. Edn., 1987—2004; mem. Fed. Interagy. Coord. Coun., 1992. Chmn. Porter County (Ind.) Child Protection Team, Ind., 1980, Ind., 1986; bd. dirs. Family House, Valparaiso, Ind., 1981—87. Mem.: Midwest Assn. Edn. Young Children (co-coord. conf. Indpls. 1982, Ind. rep. to bd. 1981—83, program chair 1993), Ind. Assn. for Edn. Young Children, Nat. Assn. for Edn. Young Children. Methodist. Home: Valparaiso, Ind. Died Feb. 9, 2006.

WOGE, MAIRY JAYN, reporter; b. Sharon, Pa., Mar. 9, 1925; d. George Frederick and Marie Springer Clementson Von Strohe; m. James Henry Woge, Mar. 12, 1947; children: James Henry, Edward George, John Peter, Timothy Christian. Student, U. Pitts. Reporter Sharon (Pa.) Herald, 1961-67, Youngstown (Ohio) Vindicator, 1967-71, Cleve. Plain Dealer, 1971-90. Mem. adv. com. Pa. State U., Shenango Campus, 1964-73; founding mem. Hermitage (Pa.) Hist. Soc., 1977, sec., 1997—; mem. civil svc. bd. Hermitage City, 1992—; mem., writer Mercer County Hist. Soc., 1949—; deacon First Presbyn. Ch., 1999—. Mem. Soc. Profl. Journalists, Cleve. Press Club. Republican. Avocations: writing, library volunteer, research. Died Jan. 8, 2005.

WOJTAS, THOMAS GERARD, art historian, consultant; b. Detroit, Nov. 7, 1955; BA, Wayne State U., 1979; MA, U. Mich., 1984; MPhil, CUNY, 1988, postgrad., from 1988. Rschr. dept. European art Detroit (Mich.) Inst. Arts, 1977-79, cons. to dir., 1980-84; rsch. fellow art history CUNY, N.Y.C., 1985-90; asst. dir. Barbara Fendrick Gallery, N.Y.C., 1989-90; cons. art appraiser O'Toole-Edwald Art Assocs., N.Y.C., 1991-93; ind. art historian/cons. Detroit and N.Y.C., from 1993. Bd. dirs. Detroit Focus Gallery. Contbg. author: Gods, Saints, Heros: Painting in the Age of Rembrandt, 1981; copy editor Detroit Focus Quar., 1993—; contbr. articles to profl. jours. Presdl. merit scholar Wyne State U., 1974-79, GM scholar Wayne State U., 1984-89; Art History Dept. Travel grantee U. Mich., 1983; Art History Dissertation fellow CUNY, 1989. Mem. Am. Assn. Mus., Coll. Art Assn. Am., Founders Soc. Died Apr. 5, 2004.

WOLBERG, RUTH A., critical care nurse; b. Seymour, Wis., Feb. 2, 1947; d. Norman and Eleanor Wolberg. BSN, U. Wis., Milw., 1978; BS in Bacteriology, U. Wis., Madison, 1969; A. in Respiratory Therapy, Milw. Area Tech. Coll., 1975. Staff nurse Sacred Heart Rehab. Hosp., Milw.; respiratory therapist Milw. County Reg. Med. Ctr.; staff nurse Theda Clark Reg. Med. Ctr., Neenah, Wis. Mem. Am. Assn. Critical Care Nurses (v.p.). Home: Seymour, Wis. Died July 31, 2004.

WOLF, BENJAMIN, soil chemist, consultant; b. Deerfield, N.J., Dec. 2, 1913; s. Abraham and Molly (Yankelovitz) W.; m. Esther Lourie, Dec. 22, 1940 (dec. Jan. 1960); children: Andrea Joan Wolf Miller, Marsha Susan Wolf Beidler; m. Margaret Schwartz, Sept. 15, 1960. BS, Rutgers U., 1935, MS, 1938, PhD, 1940. Jr. soil classifier N.J. Agrl. Expt. Sta., New Brunswick, 1936-40; asst., soils dept. Rutgers U., New Brunswick, 1940-41; soil chemist Seabrook Farms Co., Bridgeton, N.J., 1941-49, Dr. Wolf's Agrl. Labs., Ft. Lauderdale, Fla., from 1949. Co-author: Fluid Fertilizer Manual, 1985, Plant Analysis Handbook, 1991; cons. editor Communications Soil Sci. and Plant Analysis Journal, 1970—; contbr. articles to profl. jours. Fellow AAAS; mem. emeritus Am. Chem. Soc., Am. Soc. Hort. Sci. (nutrition chmn. 1964), Am. Soc. Agronomy, Soil Sci. Soc. Am. Achievements include invention of rapid soil and plant analysis methods, standards for leaf analyses for several vegetable crops, foliage plants and flowers; discovery that cause of poor quality of carnations coming from Colombia due to excess ethylene, thereby giving impetus to establishment of floral industry in that country, that cause of poor quality melons coming from Central America was mainly due to lack of potassium and calcium; research on need of boron by radish cauliflower, importance of micronutrients for vegetables, fruits and flowers grown in coastal plains soils of N.J., Del., Md., Va. and Fla. Died Dec. 11, 2004.

WOLF, HARRY FRANCES SCHLESINGER, electrical engineer; b. Atlanta, May 12, 1919; d. Joseph Alfred and Rival (Breslav) Schlesinger; children: Susan Dudley, Ellen Kaplan, Michael Wolf. Designer Bendix Radio; engr. Glen L. Martin Co.; field engr. Westinghouse Elec. Corp. Contbr. articles to profl. jours. Mem. Md. Gov.'s Conf. on Safety and Health; mem. Mayor's Task Force on Safety in the Inner Harbor, Balt.; active ARC, Meals on Wheels; leader Girl Scouts U.S., others; 1st woman candidate Mayor of City of Balt. Recipientg Army-Navy award for excellence; named Woman Engr. of the Yr., IEEE; Westinghouse Engring. Achievement awardee, others. Mem. IEEE (past nat. publicity chmn.), Soc. Am. Value Engrs., Soc. Tech. Comm. (past. chmn. Ea. Md. sect.), Soc. Women Engrs., Md. Acad. Scis. Home: Baltimore, Md. Died Feb. 6, 2004.

WOLF, SEYMOUR DAVID, corporate professional; b. Fallsburg, N.Y., July 26, 1921; s. Abraham and Dora (Herzer) W.; m. Barbara Krupsaw, Oct. 24, 1943; children: Douglas, Beth W. Rosenbloom, Deborah W. Shoham. BS in Engring., U. Md., 1942; MBA, Am. U., 1964. Jr. chem. engr. U.S. Bur. of Mines, Coll. Park, Md., 1942-43; indsl. engr. AW Industries, Inc., Landover, Md., 1946-51, div. mgr., 1951-60, pres., chmn., chief exec. officer, from 1960. Mem. adv. bd. Liberty Mut. Ins. Co. Pres. Better Bus. Bur., Washington, 1966-68, Interracial Council for Bus. Opportunity, Washington, 1966-73; chmn. bus. unit Nat. Symphony Orch., Washington, 1968; bd. trustees U. Md. Found., Jewish Publ. Soc. Am.; bd. of visitors Sch. Bus. U. Md., U. Md. Ctr. Environ. and Estuarine Studies. Served to lt. USN, 1943-46. Recipient Disting. Service award Nat. Assn. Bedding Mfrs., 1971, Alumni award Am. U., 1969, Bedlock Humanitarian award Jewish War Vets. 1971, U. Md. Gottwal award, 1988; named Potomacland Ambassador Bd. of Trade, 1960. Mem. Alumni Internat. U. Md. (trustee, chmn. 1980-82). Democrat. Avocations: sailing, travel. Home: Annapolis, Md. Died Apr. 27, 2005.

WOLF, STEPHEN NICHOLAS, school administrator; b. Kansas City, Mo., Nov. 11, 1955; s. Earl Clifford and Mildred Edith (Nicholas) W.; m. Colleen Elizabeth Belle, June 30, 1979; children: Carson, Collin, Caitlin, Cameron. BA, Ea. Nazarene Coll., Wollaston, Mass., 1978; M, U. Mich., 1979. Lic. tchr., Kans.; cert. adminstr. Assn. Christian Schs. Internat. Tchr. Olathe (Kans.) Pub. Schs., 1979-83; adminstr. Fawn Grove (Pa.) Christian Acad., 1984-85; tchr. Syracuse (N.Y.) Pub. Schs., 1985-95; adminstr. Cornerstone Christian Sch., Manchester, Conn., 1995—98; prof. Ea. Nazarene Coll., 1998—2004. Instr. Cazenovia (N.Y.) Coll., 1986-95; lectr. in field. Avocations: coaching baseball and basketball, photography. Died Aug. 26, 2004.

WOLF, STEWART GEORGE, JR., physician, educator; b. Balt., Jan. 12, 1914; s. Stewart George and Angeline (Griffing) W.; m. Virginia Danforth, Aug. 1, 1942; children: Stewart George III, Angeline Griffing, Thomas Danforth. Student, Phillips Acad., 1927-31, Yale U., 1931-33; AB, Johns Hopkins U., 1934, MD, 1938; MD (hon.), U. Göteborg, Sweden, 1968. Intern N.Y. Hosp., 1938-39, resident medicine, 1939-42, NRC fellow, 1941-42; rsch. fellow Bellevue Hosp., 1939-42, clin. assoc. vis. neuropsychiatrist, 1946-52; rsch. head injury and motion sickness Harvard neurol. unit Boston City Hosp., 1942-43; asst., then assoc. prof. medicine Cornell U., 1946-52; prof., head dept. medicine U. Okla., 1952-67, Regents prof. medicine, psychiatry and behavioral scis., from 1967, prof. physiology, 1967-69; dir. Marine Biomed. Inst., U. Tex. Med. Br., Galveston, 1969-78, dir. emeritus, from 1978, prof. medicine univ., also prof. internal medicine and physiology med. br., 1970-77; prof. medicine Temple U., Phila., from 1977. V.p. med. affairs St. Luke's Hosp., Bethlehem, Pa., 1977-82; dir. Totts Gap Inst., Bangor, Pa., 1958—; supr. clin. activities Okla. Med. Rsch. Found., 1953-55, head psychosomatic and neuromuscular sect., 1952-67, head neuroscis. sect., 1967-69; adv. com. Space Medicine and Behavioral Scis., NASA, 1960-61; cons. internal medicine VA Hosp., Oklahoma City, 1952-69; cons. (European Office), Paris, Office Internat. Rsch., NIH, 1963-64; mem. edn. and supply panel Nat. Adv. Commn. on Health Manpower, 1966-67; mem. Nat. Adv. Heart Coun., 1961-65, U.S. Phamacopeia Scope Panel on Gastroenterology, Regent Nat. Libr. Medicine, 1965-69; chmn., 1968-69; mem. Nat. Adv. Environ. Health Scis. Coun., 1978-82; exec. v.p. Frontiers Sci. Found., 1967-69; mem. sci. adv. bd. Muscular Dystrophy Assns. Am., Inc., 1974-91, chmn., 1980-89; mem. gastrointestinal drug adv. com. FDA, 1974-77; bd. Internat. Cardiology Fedn.; mem. bd. visitors dept. biology Boston U., 1978-88; mem. vis. com. Ctr. for Social Rsch., Lehigh U., 1980-90; chmn. adv. com. Wood Inst. on History of Medicine, Coll. Physicians, Phila., 1980-90, mem. program com. Coll. Physicians, 1990-91; dir. Inst. for Advanced Studies in Immunology and Aging, 1988—. Author: Human Gastric Function, 1943, The Stomach, 1965, Social Environment and Health, 1981, others; adv. editor Internat. Dictionary Biology and Medicine, 1978—; editor in chief Integrative Physiol & Behavioral Sci.: The Official Jour. of Pavlovian Soc., 1990—. Pres. Okla. City Symphony Soc., 1956-61; mem. Okla. Sch. of Sci. and Math. Found., 1961—. Recipient Disting. Svc. Citation U. Okla., 1968, Dean's award for disting. med. svc., 1992; Horsley Gantt medal Pavlovian Soc., 1987, Hans Selye award Am. Inst. Stress, 1988, Rsch. award Carolinska Inst., Stockholm, 1994, Wilém Laufberger medal Acad. Scis. of Czech Republic, Citation for sci. and humanitarian achievement The J.E. Purkyně Bohemian Med. Assn. Fellow Am. Psychiat. Assn. (disting., trustee 1992—, Hofheimer prize for rsch. 1952); mem. AMA (coun. mental health 1960-64), Am. Soc. Clin. Investigation, Am. Clin. and Climatol. Assn. (pres. 1975-76), Assn. Am. Physicians, Am. Psychosomatic Soc. (pres. 1961-62), Am. Gastroent. Assn. (rsch. award 1943, pres. 1969-70), Am. Heart Assn. (chmn. com. profl. edn., com. internat. program, awards), Romanian Acad. Med. Sci. (hon.), Coll. Physicians Phila., Collegium Internat. Activitas Nervosae Superioris (exec. com. 1992—, pres. 1994), Philos. Soc. Tex., Sigma Xi, Alpha Omega Alpha, Omicron Delta Kappa. Clubs: Cosmos (Washington). Home: Bangor, Pa. Died Sept. 24, 2005.

WOLFE, BERNARD MITCHELL, lawyer, real estate developer; b. Winnipeg, Man., Can., May 31, 1917; s. Nathan and Augusta Estelle (Mitchell) W.; m. Beverly Alberta Gantz, June 16,1940; children: Douglas Randall, Patricia Louise. Student, UCLA, 1933; BS, U.S. Naval Acad., 1938, Cert. Naval Arch., 1941; JD, LLB, Stanford U., 1962. Lic. gen. contractor, Calif.; registered profl. engr., Calif. Asst. supr. shipbuilding N.Y. Ship, Camden, N.J., 1940-41; docking officer, asst. shop supt. Mare Is. Navy Yard, Hunters Point, 1941-45; planning officer Suisun Bay, 1941-45; with bur. ships, design sect., in charge of constrn. Presdl. Yacht Williamsburg, Washington, 1945-46; pres. Manning Mitchell, Inc. Paint Mfg. Co., 1946-55; real estate developer Hillsborough Polo Field, restaurants, office bldgs., condos, Oreg. and, Calif., from 1947; lawyer, pvt. practice San Mateo, Calif., from 1962. Comdr. USNR, 1934-46. Mem. Nat. Bd. Field Advs. Democrat. Jewish. Home: Hillsborough, Calif. Died Aug. 12, 2004.

WOLFERTH, CHARLES CHRISTIAN, surgeon, educator; b. Phila., July 31, 1928; s. Charles Christian and Mary (Comber) W.; m. Mary Fances Halsey; children: Mary, Charles III, John, Catherine. Student, Yale U., 1945-47, St. Joseph's U., 1947-48; MD, U. Pa., 1954. Intern Hosp. U. Pa., 1954-55, resident, 1955-60; adj. prof. surgery Hahnemann U. Hosp., Phila., 1988—98; Emilie and Roland T. deHellebranth prof. surgery U. Pa., Phila., 1989—98; surgeon-in-chief, chmn. The Grad. Hosp., Phila., 1989—98. Surg. resident program dir. Grad. Hosp., Phila., 1989-98. Co-author: Advances in Trauma, Vols. I thru X, 1986-96. Recipient Proclamation/Appreciation award Bd. Suprs. San Diego, 1987. Fellow ACS (bd. govs. 1988-91, trauma achievement award 1988, outstanding leadership in hosp. categorizaiton Ea. States Com. on Trauma 1988); mem. Am. Trauma Soc. (bd. dirs. 1985-90), Am. Assn. Surg. Trauma, Ea. Surg. Soc., Del. Valley Vascular Soc. (pres. 1979-82), Phila. Acad. Surgery (pres. 1984-85), Internat. Cardiovascular Soc., Soc. Vascular Surgery, Soc. Surgery Alimentary Tract, Soc. Internationale de Chirugie, Phila. Country Club, Merion Golf Club. Avocations: golf, tennis, skeet shooting. Home: Bryn Mawr, Pa. Died Nov. 15, 2005.

WOLFSKILL, MARY MARGARET, archivist; b. Ft. Benning, Ga., June 10, 1946; d. Clifford Lawrence and Margaret W. BS in History, Radford Coll., 1968; MA in Mgmt., Ctrl. Mich. U., 1979; MS in Women's Studies, George Washington U., 1980. Cert. archivist. Reference libr. Manuscript Divsn. Libr. of Congress, Washington, 1968-70, archivist, presdl. papers, 1970-71, archives specialist preparation sect., 1971-84, asst. head reference libr., 1984-88, head reference svcs., from 1988. Mem. Soc. Am. Archivists, Mid-Atlantic Regional Archives Conf. Democrat. Roman Catholic. Home: Washington, DC. Died May 23, 2005.

WOLFSON, SUSAN WARTUR, retired lawyer; b. Bklyn., May 2, 1938; d. Marcus Harry and Bertha (Stern) Wartur; m. Steven Wolfson, April 10, 1960; children: Ellen Paula, Roger Samuel. BA, Barnard Coll., 1959; JD, U. Conn., 1976. Bar: Conn. 1976, U.S. Dist. Ct. Conn. 1977. Assoc. Lieberman & Segaloff, New Haven, 1976-80; ptnr. Lieberman, Segaloff & Wolfson, New Haven, 1980-87, Susman, Duffy & Segaloff, P.C., New Haven, 1987—2004; ret. Pres. Statewide Legal Svcs., 1996-98. Mem. editl. bd. Conn. Law Tribune, 1998—. Bd. dirs. Legal Assistance Assn. of New Haven, 1982-93. Fellow Conn. Bar Found. (bd. dirs. 1992—); mem. ABA (ho. of dels. 1989-93, chair alimony com. family law sect. 1992-2004), Conn. Bar Assn. (ho. of dels. 1983-87, counsel of pres. 1983-84, bd. govs. 1983-87, sec. 1987-89, v.p. 1989-90, pres. 1991-92), New Haven County Bar Assn. (exec. bd. 1978-88, pres. 1983-84). Home: West Haven, Conn. Died June 14, 2005.

WOLINSKY, JUDITH, film producer; Film prodr. Rainbow Releasing, L.A. Prodr. Always, 1985, Someone To Love, 1987, New Year's Day, 1989, Eating, 1990, Venice/Venice, 1992, Babyfever, 1994, Last Summer In The Hamptons, 1995. Died June 13, 2006.

WOLIS, KENNETH ARNOLD, lawyer; b. N.Y.C., July 3, 1931; s. Sol and Esther (Wolis) W.; m. Nizha Arbib, Feb. 9, 1963; 1 child, Robert. BA, NYU, 1953; JD, U. Miami, 1958. Bar: Fla. 1958, U.S. Dist. Ct. (so. dist.) Fla. 1959, U.S. Ct. Appeals (11th cir.) 1959, U.S. Supreme Ct. 1971. Atty. Von Zamft & Kravitz, Miami, Fla., 1958-59, Meltzer & Nesbitt, Miami, 1960; sole practitioner North Miami, Fla., 1960-64, Miami, 1964-70, Hollywood, Fla., from 1971. Atty. Apt. and Hotel Assn. Hollywood, 1973-97,

Ravenswood Mgmt. Assn., Ft. Lauderdale, Fla., 1990-97, Three Horizons East Condominium, North Miami, 1988-97. Mem. Zoning Bd., Town of Surfside, Fla., 1961-63; treas. Emerald Hills Homeowners Assn., 1999. With U.S. Army, 1954-56. Mem. Masons (chaplain 1988), Shriners, Scottish Rite (pres. 1992), Hollywood Lions Club (pres. 1993-94, Melvin Jones fellow 1994), Allapattah Lions Club (pres. 1969-70). Avocations: reading, walking. Home: Fort Lauderdale, Fla. Died Oct. 15, 2004.

WOLVINGTON, WINSTON WARREN, retired judge; b. Denver, July 10, 1923; s. William Thomas and Bessie Maude (Roberts) W.; m. Shirley Anne Vail, Sept. 9, 1944; children: Gloria, Judith, Donald, Glenn. JD, U. Mich., 1948; BA, Oberlin (Ohio) Coll., 1949. Bar: Colo. 1949. Assoc. Wolvington & Wormwood, Denver, 1949-54, ptnr., 1954-73; dist. judge State of Colo., Golden, 1973-89, sr. judge, 1989-94; retired, 1994. Mem. ABA, Am. Judicature Soc., Colo. Bar Assn., Colo. Judicature Soc., 1st Judicial Bar Assn. (pres., v.p.). Democrat. Avocations: woodworking, genealogy, history, skiing, hiking, camping. Home: Golden, Colo. Died Jan. 14, 2005.

WOO, WILLIAM FRANKLIN, newspaper editor; b. Shanghai, Oct. 4, 1936; came to U.S., 1946; s. Kyatang and Elizabeth Louise (Hart) W.; m. Patricia Ernst, Dec. 18, 1964 (div. June 1980); m. Martha Richards Shirk, Sept. 15, 1981; children— Thomas Shenton, Bennett Richards, Peter Snowdon. BA, U. Kans., 1960. Reporter Kansas City Star, Mo., 1957-62; feature writer St. Louis Post-Dispatch, 1962-68, editorial writer, 1968-73, asst. editor, 1973-74, editorial page editor, 1974-86, editor, 1986-96; Lorry I. Lokey Vis. Prof. of Profl. Journalism, dept. of comm. Stanford U., 1997—2006. Served to staff sgt. USAFR, 1962. Nieman fellow Harvard U., 1966-67. Mem. Am. Soc. Newspaper Editors (bd. dirs. 1993-2006), Am. Press Inst. (bd. dirs. 1995). Died Apr. 12, 2006.

WOOD, ARTHUR MACDOUGALL, retired retail executive; b. Chgo., Jan. 27, 1913; s. R. Arthur and Emily (Smith) W.; m. Pauline Palmer (dec. 1984), Nov. 17, 1945; children: Pauline, Arthur MacDougall Jr. AB, Princeton U., 1934, LLD (hon.), 1976; LLB, Harvard U., 1937; LHD (hon.), DePaul U., 1977; D in Humanics (hon., Springfield Coll., 1978; HHD (hon.), Beloit Coll., 1981. Bar: Ill. 1937. Atty. Bell, Boyd & Marshall, Chgo., 1937-40, Sears, Roebuck & Co., 1946-52, sec., 1952-59, v.p., 1956-68, dir., 1959-83, comptroller, 1960-62, v.p. charge Pacific Coast ter., 1962-67, v.p. midwestern ter., 1967, pres., 1968-72, chmn., CEO, 1973-77. Gen. chmn. United Crusade, Los Angeles County, 1966; co-founder Chgo. United, 1975; gov. United Way Am., 1977; trustee Art Inst. Chgo., chmn., 1978-80; life trustee Rush-Presbyn.-St. Luke's Med. Ctr., Chgo.; former trustee Calif. Inst. Tech., U. Chgo.; mem. Chgo. Hort. Soc., trustee, 1992-93; mem. Pres. Nixon's Labor-Mgmt. Com., 1975, Coun. Minority Bus. Enterprises, 1970-74; bd. dirs. AICPA, 1978-83. With F.A. AUS; lt. col. USAAF, 1941-45. Decorated Legion of Merit. Mem. Bus. Coun. Home: Lake Forest, Ill. Died June 18, 2006.

WOOD, CHARLES EARL, obstetrician, gynecologist; b. Sterling, Colo., Oct. 4, 1930; s. Walter Earl and Dorothy Nancy (Long) W.; m. Patricia Taylor, Nov. 1, 1960; children: Lecia, Spencer, Christine. BA, Phillips U., 1959; MD, U. Colo., 1963. Diplomate Am. Bd. Obstetrics and Gynecology. Intern Denver Gen. Hosp., 1963-64, resident in ob-gyn, 1964-67, mem. staff, 1967-73; practice medicine specializing in ob-gyn Casper, Wyo., 1967-86; mem. staff Skaggs Cmty. Hosp., Branson, Mo., 1986—90; locum tenens, from 1990. Mem. staff Natrona County Meml. Hosp., Casper, 1967-84, chief of obstetrics, 1975, chmn. staff, 1981-83; mem. staff Converse County Hosp., Douglas, Wyo. 1967-85, Carbon County Hosp., Rawline, Wyo., 1968-75; mem. Wyo. Family Practice Residency program, 1978-83; clin. assoc. prof. family practice (ob-gyn) Univ. Hosp. of Wyo. Coll. Human Medicine, 1982-83. Mem. Natrona County Sch. Bd., 1974-80, vice chmn., 1976-77, chmn., 1978-79; pres. Casper YMCA, 1974-76, gen. chmn. fundraising campaign, 1976-77, mem. bldg. com. 1976-78; mem. Blue Envelope, 1970-84; pres., charter mem. Wyo. Right to Life, 1970-75; T-Bird booster Casper Coll., 1970-82; assoc. Sch. of the Ozarks, Pt. Lookout, Mo., 1985—. Served with USN, 1949-50, 52-53. Mem. Am. Coll. Obstetricians and Gynecologists, Am. Fertility Soc. (charter), Wyo. Med. Soc., Denver Med. Soc., Natrona County Med. Soc. (pres. 1979-80), Audubon Soc., Casper Air Modelers Assn. (charter, pres. 1969-76), Wyo. Handball Assn., Wyo. Arabian Horse Assn., Am. Hereford Assn., Irish Wolfhound Club Am., Wyo. Farm Bur., Elks. Home: Rogers, Ark. Died Oct. 28, 2004.

WOOD, JEANNE CLARKE, charitable organization executive; b. Pitts., Dec. 21, 1916; d. Joseph Calvitt and Helen Caroline (Mattson) Clarke; m. Herman Eugene Wood, Jr., May 6, 1936 (dec.); children: Helen Hamilton (Mrs. John Harry Mortenson), Herman Eugene III. Student, Collegiate Sch. for Girls, Richmond, Va., 1932-33. Asst. to Dr. and Mrs. J. Calvitt Clarke, Christian Children's Fund, Inc., Richmond, 1938-64; founder Children, Inc., Richmond, 1964, pres., internat. dir., from 2005. Author: (with Helen C. Clarke) In Appreciation: A Story in Pictures of the World-Wide Family of Christian Children's Fund, Inc, 1958, Children's Christmastime Around the World, 1962, Children's Games Around the World, 1962, Children-Hope of the World-Their Needs, 1965, Children-Hope of the World-Their Friends, 1966; Editor: CI News, 1964. Recipient citation Eastern Council Navajo Tribe, 1970, citations Mayor of Pusan (Korea), 1971, citations Mayor of Seoul, 1971, citations Gov. of Kanagawa Prefecture (Japan), 1972, commendation Pres. of U.S., 1972, citation Stephen Philibosian Found., 1975, citation Santa Ana (El Salvador) Dept. Edn., 1975, citation Nat. Sch. for Blind, Dominican Republic, 1982, citation Navajo Tribal Council of Navajo Nation, Window Rock, Ariz., 1982 Died Jan. 25, 2006.

WOOD, JOHN THURSTON, cartographer, jazz musician; b. Chgo., Apr. 29, 1928; s. Clarence Leo and Hilda Bernice (Miller) W.; m. Erma Louise Vogt, July 3, 1957; children: John Thurston Jr., Holly Lynn, Joseph Miller II. BS, Iowa State U., 1952; postgrad., Ohio State U., 1962-64, Indsl. Coll. Armed Forces, Washington, 1974, Fed. Exec. Inst., Charlottesville, Va., 1985. Commd. 2d lt. USAF, 1952, advanced through grades to lt. col., 1968; combat airlift pilot 535th Troop Carrier Squadron, Vung Tau, Vietnam, 1966-67; comdr. USAF Operational Evaluation Detachment, Topeka, 1967-70; aerial and ground survey officer Def. Intelligence Agy., Washington (D.C.), Def. Mapping Agy., Washington (D.C.), Va., 1972-76; ret., 1976; chief user svcs. Nat. Cartographic Info. Ctr. U.S. Geol. Survey, Reston, 1976-83, dep. chief, 1983-85, chief, 1985-89, 1985-89; chief Earth Sci. Info. Office U. S. Geol. Survey, Reston, 1989-95. Tuba player Buck Creek Jazz Band, 1977—. Decorated Air medal with four oak leaf clusters. Mem. Masons, Shriners. Home: Annandale, Va. Died Jan. 2004.

WOOD, MARGARET GRAY, dermatologist, educator; b. Jamaica, N.Y., May 23, 1918; d. C.W. Bromley and B. Eleanor (Niblack) Gray; m. Alfred Conard Wood (dec. 1986), Mar. 24, 1950; children: M. Diana Wood, Deirdre Wood-Harper, Moira Dorothy Wood. BA, U. ALa., Tuscaloosa, 1941; MD, Woman's Med. Coll. Pa., 1948; D in Med. Scis. (hon.), Med. Coll. Pa., 1990, emeritus prof. medicine, 1993. Diplomate Am. Bd. Dermatology, Am. Bd. Dermatopathology. Intern Phila. Gen. Hosp., 1948-50; resident U. Pa. Hosp., 1950-53; instr. dept. dermatology U. Pa. Sch. Medicine, Phila., 1952-53, assoc., 1953-67, asst. prof., 1967-71, assoc. prof., 1971-75, clin. prof., 1975-80, prof. and chmn. dept. dermatology, 1980-82, prof., 1988-92, prof. emeritus, 1989—2006. Assoc. prof. grad. Sch. Medicine U. Pa., Phila., 1957-71, cons. Sch. Dental Medicine, Sch. Vet. Medicine U. Pa., Phila.; asst. prof. Med. Coll. Pa., Phila., 1957-93, prof. emeritus, 1993-2006, vice chmn. bd. dirs. 1984-88; vice chmn. bd. dirs. Med. Coll. Hosps., Phila., Hahnemann U. Hosp.; mem. exec. com. Am. Med. Women's Hosp. Svc. Com., Washington; dir. Alleghany Health Systems, Pitts., 1987-91, Alleghany Health Edn. and Rsch. Found., 1991-94; bd. dirs. St. Christophers Hosp. for Children, Alleghany U. Pitts., Alleghany Hosp. Systems. Author (with others) 4 books; contbr. numerous articles to med. jours. Recipient Rose Hershfeld award Women's Dermatology Soc., 1989. Mem. AMA, Internat. Dermatology Assn., Internat. Dermatopathology Assn., Phila. Dermatology Soc. (pres. 1978-79), Alpha Omega Alpha. Republican. Episcopalian. Avocations: gardening, medical research. Died Feb. 9, 2006.

WOOD, MARION LONGMORE, educator, nurse; b. New Bedford, Mass., May 16, 1927; d. Harold Thomas and Martha Longmore; m. Floyd T. Wood (dec.); 1 child, Monica. BSN magna cum laude, Adelphi U., Garden City, N.Y., 1948; BS in Edn., Rutgers U., 1960; postgrad., NYU, 1960. Sch. nurse, Levittown, N.Y., 1952-58; tchr. Edison (N.J.) Sch. Sys., 1958, Dade County, Miami, Fla., from 1963. Named Tchr. of Yr., Dade County Sch. Sys., 1994. Mem. Delta Gamma. Avocations: reading, travel. Home: Miami, Fla. Died Feb. 22, 2005.

WOOD, ROBERT HENRY, state legislator; b. Rutland, Va., Apr. 7, 1931; m. Sally Ann Gowdy; 2 children. BS in Agr. cum laude, U. Vt., 1960. Farmer and builder, Brandon, Vt. Dir. 1st Brandon Nat. Bank; mem. Vt. Ednl. TV Bd., Brandon Zoning Bd., Brandon Town Sch. Bd., Otter Valley Union H.S. Bd., chmn.; trustee U. Vt. Mem. Small Fruit and Vegetable Growers Assn. (founding, pres.), Masons, Alpha Zeta Ag. Died Sept. 7, 2005.

WOOD, STUART KEE, retired engineering manager; b. Dallas, Mar. 8, 1925; s. William Henry and Harriet (Kee) Wood; m. Loris V. Poock, May 17, 1951 (dec. June 1990); children: Linda S. Kuehl, Thomas N., Richard D.; m. Lois H. Morton, Nov. 25, 1994. BS in Aero. Engring., Tex. A&M U., 1949. Aircraft sheet metal worker USAF SAC, Kelly Field, San Antonio, Tex., 1942-45; structural design engr. B-52, 367-80, KC-135, 707 Airplanes Boeing, Seattle and Renton, Wash., 1949-55, thrust reverser design engr. 707 and 747 Airplanes Renton, 1955-66, supr. thrust reverser group 747 Airplane Everett, Wash., 1966-69; supr. rsch. basic engine noise 727 airplane FAA, NASA, 1969-74; supr. jetfoil propulsion Jetfoil Hydrofoil Boeing, Renton, 1974-75; supr. rsch. basic engine performance loss JT9D Pratt & Whitney, 1975-79; supr. propulsion systems 757 Airplane Boeing, Renton, 1979-90, supr., propulsion systems thrust reverser 737, 747, 757, 767 Kent, Wash., 1990-94, ret., 1994. Patentee in field. Recipient Ed Wells award AIAA, N.W. chpt., Bellevue, Wash., 1992. Republican. Presbyterian. Avocations: photography, computers, travel. Home: Seattle, Wash. Died Dec. 13, 2004.

WOODBURN, ROBERT JAMES, speech educator; b. Farmville, Va., Jan. 7, 1929; s. Lewis Eugene and Ruby Ann (Young) W.; m. JoAnn Belcher, June, 1952 (dec. Nov. 1963); children: Robert J. II, Tammy Lee; m. Mary Stuart Jenkins, June 4, 1967; children: Robert Stuart. BS in English, Concord Coll., 1960; MA in Speech, Marshall U., 1966; EdD, U. Va., 1979. Announcer Radio Sta. WLOG, Logan, W.Va., 1953-56; announcer, program dir. WLOH, Princeton, W.Va., 1956-60; announcer Sta. WHIS-TV, Bluefield, W.Va., 1960-61; tchr. English Fairview Jr. High Sch., Bluefield, 1960-61; announcer Radio Sta. WFLO, Farmville, Va., 1963-64; speech educator Longwood Coll., Farmville, from 1964. Faculty advisor Longwood Coll., 1964—, Honor Bd., Farmville, 1986-88. Contbr. articles to profl. publs. 1st lt. U.S. Army, 1951-54. Longwood Coll. grantee, 1972-73. Mem. Speech and Hearing Assn. Va., Va. Speech Communication Assn., Lions (sec., 3d v.p., 2d v.p., 1st. v.p. 1976—, pres. 1989-90, zone chair 1990-91, region chair 1991-92), Sports Club. Republican. Methodist. Avocations: photography, sports, reading, do-it-yourself repairs. Home: Chesterfield, Va. Died Aug. 20, 2004.

WOODIN, MARTIN DWIGHT, retired academic administrator; b. Sicily Island, La., July 7, 1915; s. Dwight E. and Gladys Ann (Martin) W.; m. Virginia Johnson, Sept. 7, 1939 (dec.); children: Rebecca Woodin Johnson, Pamela Woodin Fry, Linda Woodin Middleton; m. Elisabeth Wachalik, Oct. 5, 1968. BS, La. State U., 1936; MS, Cornell U., 1939, PhD, 1941; L.H.D. (hon.), U. New Orleans, 1985. Faculty La. State U., 1941-85, prof. agrl. econs., head dept., 1957-59; dir. resident instrn. Coll. Agr., 1959-60; dean La. State U. at Alexandria, 1960-62; exec. v.p. La. State U. System, Baton Rouge, 1962-72, pres., 1972-85. Cons. agr. and planning, Nicaragua, Taiwan, Thailand. Contbr. articles to profl. jours. Dep. dir. La. Civil Def. Agy., 1961-72; v.p., exec. com. United Givers Baton Rouge; sec. La. State U. Found., 1962-72; mem. La. Constn. Revision Commn., Arts and Humanities Coun. of Greater Baton Rouge; mem. pres.'s coun. Nat. Assn. State Univs., 1972-85; mem. coun. trustees Gulf South Rsch. Inst., 1972-85; pres. Coun. So. Univs., 1975-76. With USNR, 1942-46, PTO. Named Alumnus of Yr., La. State U., 1985; named to Order of Jose Cecilio Del Valle, Republic of Honduras, 1985. Mem. Am. Agrl. Econ. Assn., Am. Mktg. Assn., VFW, Am. Legion (post comdr.), Internat. House, So. Assn. Land Grant Colls. and State Univs. (pres. 1977-78, 83-84), Elks, Rotary, Sigma Xi, Omicron Delta Kappa, Phi Kappa Phi (pres.), Beta Gamma Sigma, Phi Eta Sigma, Gamma Sigma Delta, Alpha Zeta, Pi Gamma Mu, Acacia. Presbyterian. Home: Baton Rouge, La. Died Apr. 18, 2006.

WOODING, WILLIAM MINOR, statistics consultant; b. Waterbury, Conn, Aug. 24, 1917; s. George Lee and Ella Elizabeth (Asher) W.; m. Nina C. Peaslee, May 30, 1940; children: Barbara Lee Wooding Bose, Elizabeth Ann. B Chem. Engring. cum laude, Poly. Inst. Bklyn., 1953. Lab. asst. Am. Cyanamid Co., Stamford, Conn., 1941-44, chemist, 1945-50, rsch. chemist, 1950-56, rsch. adminstrv. svc. coord., 1956-57; asst. chief chemist Revlon Rsch. Ctr., NYC, 1957-60, assoc. rsch. dir., 1960-65, Carter-Wallace, Inc., Cranbury, NJ, 1965-67, dir. tech. svcs., 1967-75; dir. statis. svcs. Carter-Wallace, Inc. and Wallace Labs., Cranbury, NJ, 1975-82; cons. med. statis. and clin. trials BioStatistics, Swanton, Vt., from 1982. Instr. Stat-a-Natrix Inst., Edison, N.J., 1983-86. Author: Planning Pharmaceutical Clinical Trials, 1994; contbr. over 20 articles to profl. jours. Died Nov. 2004.

WOODMAN, WALTER JAMES, lawyer; b. Talara, Peru, Jan. 21, 1941; s. Walter James and Nora Carmen (Wensjoe) W.; m. Ruth Meyer, Dec. 19, 1970; children: Justin Meyer, Jessica Hilary. BA, U. Miami, 1964; JD, So. Meth. U., 1967. Bar: Tex. 1967, La. 1980, U.S. Dist. Ct. (no. dist.) Tex. 1967, U.S. Ct. Appeals (5th cir.) 1981, U.S. Supreme Ct. 1971, U.S. Dist. Ct. (we. dist.) La. 1980, U.S. Dist. Ct. (ea. dist.) Tex. 1983, U.S. Dist. Ct. (mid. dist.) La. 1988, U.S. Dist. Ct. (ea. dist.) La. 1989. Pvt. practice, Dallas, 1967-72, Waxahachie, Tex., 1972-79, Shreveport, La., from 1979. Bd. dirs. N.W. La. Legal Svcs., Shreveport, 1993-96. Contbr. articles to profl. jours. Candidate Tex. Ho. of Reps., 1972; bd. dirs. Gov.'s Pan Am. Commn., Baton Rouge, 1993-96. Home: Shreveport, La. Died July 7, 2005.

WOODS, JOHN WILLIAM, retired lawyer, judge; b. Ft. Worth, Dec. 10, 1912; s. John George and Eugenia (Smith) W.; m. Gertie Leona Parker, Apr. 15, 1954. BS, North Tex. State U., 1951, MEd, 1952; JD, St. Mary's U., San Antonio, 1967; postgrad., Fresno State Coll., 1952, West Tex. State U., 1959. Bar: Tex. bar 1966. Tchr., Corcoran, Calif., 1952-53, Pampa (Tex.) Ind. Sch. Dist., 1953-63, Harlandale Sch. Dist., San Antonio, 1963-67; practicing atty. Amarillo, Tex., 1967-68; county atty. Sherman County, Tex., 1969-72; county judge, 1988; ret., 1988; justice of peace, 1975-88; pvt. practice, Stratford, Tex., 1968-95; ret., 1995. Served to ensign USN, 1930-47, ETO. Mem. Tex. Bar Assn., Am. Legion, Masons, Shriners, Scottish Rite, York Rite. Democrat. Mem. Christian Ch. (Disciples Of Christ). Home: Amarillo, Tex. Died Jan. 31, 2006.

WOODSIDE, LYNDON, choral music director; b. Florence, S.C., Mar. 23, 1935; s. Hubert Freneau and Lucia Verlie (Bauknight) W.; m. Jane Marie Wilke, Mar. 12, 1955; children: Curtis Lyndon, Kimberly Ann. MusB, Cleve. Inst. Music, 1957; MS, Juilliard Sch., 1963; Mus D (hon.), Cleve. Inst. Music, 1991. Organist, choir dir. Park Ave. United Meth. Ch., N.Y.C., 1967—2005; organist, music dir. Temple Emanu-El, Yonkers, 1969—2005. Head judge solo competition, Oratorio Soc. N.Y., N.Y.C., 1975-2005, judge Opera Index Awards, N.Y.C., 1993-2005. Guest conductor numerous orchs. in U.S. and Europe, 1971-2005, including Prague (Czech Republic) Symphony Orch., 1994, Orch. Pasdeloup, Paris, 1995, Orch. Symphonique, Tours, France, 1995, I

Solisti di Roma, 1996, English Chamber Orch., London, 1997. Recipient Grammy award, 1977; named Alumnus of Yr., Cleve. Inst. music, 1991. Home: Leonia, NJ. Died Aug. 23, 2005.

WOODWARD, JAMES KENNETH, retired pharmacologist; b. Anderson, Mo., Feb. 5, 1938; s. Audley J. and Doris Evelyn (Fields) W.; m. Kathleen Ruth Winget, June 25, 1960 (div. Nov. 1994); children: Audley J., Kimie Connette; m. Lisa Marie Stuart, Feb. 28, 1996. AB in Chemistry, S.W. Mo. State Coll., BS in Biology, 1960; postgrad., U. Kans., 1960-62; PhD (USPHS fellow), U. Pa. Sch. Medicine, 1967. Pharmacologist Stine Lab., Newark, Del., 1963-65, rsch. pharmacologist, 1967-71; sr. rsch. pharmacologist Merrell-Nat. Labs., Cin., 1972-73, sect. head, 1973-74, head dept. pharmacology, 1974-78; head dept. pre-clin. pharmacology Merrell Rsch. Ctr. Merrell Dow Pharms., Inc., 1978-83; assoc. dir. research adminstrn. Merrell Dow Rsch. Inst., 1983-88, dir. biol. devel., 1988-90, dir. int. reg. affairs, 1990-93; dir. clin. cand. prep. Marion Merrell Dow, 1993; ret., 1993; cons., 1993. Patentee in field. Pres. Golf Manor Recreation Commn., Cin., 1973-75. USPHS post-doctoral fellow U. Pa., 1967. Mem. AAAS, Phila. Physiol. Soc. Democrat. Baptist. Home: Lancaster, Ohio. Died July 16, 2006.

WOOLDRIDGE, DEAN EVERETT, retired engineering executive, scientist; b. Chickasha, Okla., May 30, 1913; s. Auttie Noonan and Irene Amanda (Kerr) W.; m. Helene Detweiler, Sept. 1936; children— Dean Edgar, Anna Lou, James Allan. AB, U. Okla., 1932, MS, 1933; PhD, Calif. Inst. Tech., 1936. Mem. tech. staff Bell Telephone Labs., N.Y.C., 1936-46; co-dir. research and devel. labs Hughes Aircraft Co., Culver City, Calif., 1946-52, v.p. research and devel., 1952-53; pres., dir. Ramo-Wooldridge Corp., Los Angeles, 1953-58, Thompson Ramo Wooldridge, Inc., Los Angeles, also Cleve., 1958-62; research assoc. Calif. Inst. Tech., 1962-79. Author: The Machinery of the Brain, 1963, The Machinery of Life, 1966, Mechanical Man, 1968, Sensory Processing in the Brain, 1979, also articles. Recipient Citation of Honor Air Force Assn., 1950, Raymond E. Hackett award, 1955, Westinghouse Sci. Writing award AAAS, 1963, Disting. Svc. Citation U. Okla, Disting. Alumnus award Calif. Inst. Tech., 1983. Fellow AAAS, Am. Acad. Arts and Sci., Am. Phys. Soc., IEEE, AIAA; mem. Nat. Acad. Scis., Nat. Acad. Engring., Calif. Inst. Assos., Am. Inst. Physics, Phi Beta Kappa, Sigma Xi, Tau Beta Pi, Phi Eta Sigma, Eta Kappa Nu. Died Sept. 20, 2006.

WOOLLEY, ALMA SCHELLE, nursing educator; b. NYC, Oct. 3, 1931; d. Max Carl and Matilda Louise Schelle; m. Arthur E. Woolley Jr., Sept. 11, 1954; children: Mariel Therese, Mark Stephen, Peter James, Jane Frances. Student, CUNY, 1949—51; BSN, Cornell U., 1954; MSN, U. Pa., 1965, EdD, 1980. Instr. sch. nursing U. Pa., Phila., 1965-69; asst. prof. nursing Atlantic Community Coll., Mays Landing, N.J., 1969-74; coord. nursing program Stockton State Coll., Pomona, N.J., 1974-81; dir., Carolyn F. Rupert prof. nursing Sch. of Nursing, Ill. Wesleyan U., Bloomington, 1981-86; dean Sch. Nursing Georgetown U., Washington, 1986-92, prof., 1992-96, prof. emeritus, from 1996. Vis. prof. U. Md., 1996—2000; adj. prof. Uniformed Svcs. U. Health Scis., from 1997. Author: History of Georgetown University School of Nursing, 1903-2000, 2001; mem. editl. bd.: Nurse Educator; editor: Bull. of Am. Assn. for History of Nursing; contbr. articles to profl. jours. Recipient Dist. Alumni award Cornell U. Sch. Nursing, 1989. Mem. ANA, Am. Assn. Colls. of Nursing (bd. dirs. 1988-90), Nat. League for Nursing (bd. of rev.), Am. Assn. for History of Nursing, Cosmos Club, Sigma Theta Tau, Phi Delta Kappa. Episcopalian. Died Dec. 17, 2005.

WOOLUMS, MARGARET CARMICHAEL, thoroughbred bloodline researcher; b. Charleston, W.Va., Aug. 8, 1935; d. H. St. G.T. Jr. and Margaret Lyle (MacCorkle) Carmichael; m. Dan Dudley Gravitt (div. 1956); 1 child Margaret Alexander Lyle; m. William Howard Woolums Jr. (dec. 1992); 1 child, Anna Hetzel Woolums Carney. BBA, U. Ky., 1960. Statistician Blood-Horse Mag., Lexington, Ky., 1954-66; adminstrv. asst., stats. bur. The Jockey Club, Lexington, 1966-69; sec., treas. Pedigree Assocs., Inc., Lexington, 1970-82, pres., 1982-96; v.p. info. Racing Corp. of Am., Inc. div. Ky. Horse Ctr., 1990-91; pres. Pedigree Prodns., Inc., Lexington, from 1990; breeder thoroughbred horses, from 1988. Adviser Internat. Cataloguing Stds., London, 1982—; editor, owner South Am. Thoroughbred Qtr. mag., 1990-92; divsn. dir. Ky. Racing Commn., 1992-93; prin. asst. Ky. Pub. Svc. Commn., 1993-95; coord. internat. info. Jockey Club Racing Svcs., Inc., 1995-2001. Editor Racing Update, Inc., 1993-95; contbr. articles to topical publs. Mem. Thoroughbred Club Am., Cen. Ky. Riding for Handicapped (bd. dirs. 1986-91), Va. Horse Ctr. (bd. dirs. 1985-91), Shoemaker Found. (host com. 1995-99). Democrat. Episcopalian. Home: Lexington, Ky. Died Feb. 28, 2004.

WORDEN, GRETCHEN, medical museum director; b. Shanghai, Sept. 26, 1947; came to U.S., 1948; d. Warren Lester and Mildred Elise (Boericke) W. AA, Urbana Coll., 1967; BA, Temple U., 1970. Asst. to curator Mutter Museum, Coll. Physicians of Phila., 1975-80, acting curator, 1980-82, curator, 1982-88, dir., 1988—2004. Bd. advisor CADUCEUS, Mus. Quar. for the Health Scis., Springfield, Ill., 1989-2004; instl. cons. Internat. Soc. Physician Historians, N.Y.C., 1983-2004; advisor Edward Hand Med. Heritage Mus., Lancaster, Pa., 1989-2004; bd. dirs. Walt Whitman Assn., Camden, N.J., Nat. Mus. Civil War Medicine. Contbr. articles to profl. jours. Co-chmn. Ea. State Penitentiary Task Force, Phila., 1988-90, chmn., 1990-2004. Mem. Am. Assn. Museums, Mus. Coun. Phila. and Del. Valley (pres. 1989-91, bd. dirs. 1991-2004), Med. Mus. Assn., European Assn. Museums of History of Med. Sci. (exec. coun. 1988-2004), West Phila. Shakespeare Club II (pres. 1983-85). Republican. Swedenborgian. Avocations: gardening, architecture, collecting cow creamers. Home: Philadelphia, Pa. Died Aug. 2, 2004.

WORGUL, BASIL VLADIMIR, radiation scientist; b. N.Y.C., June 30, 1947; s. John and Stephanie (Litwin) W.; m. Kathleen R. Hennessey, June 14, 1969; children: Ronald Adam, Suzanne Kathleen. BS, U. Miami, Fla., 1969; PhD, U. Vt., 1974. Rsch. assoc. Columbia U., N.Y.C., 1975-78, asst. prof., 1979-84, assoc. prof., 1984-90, dir. Eye Radiation & Environ. Rsch. Lab., 1984—2006, prof., 1990—2006. Cons. Nat. Coun. on Radiation Protection, Washington, 1988—, Internat. Com. on Radiation Protection, 1988-2006, NASA, 1990-92; dir. Residents Basic Sci., Dept. Ophthalmology, Columbia U., 1983-92; Am. dir. Ukranian Am. Chernobyl Ocular Study, 1992-2006. Mem. editl. bd. Radiation and Environ. Biophysics Jour., 1997-2006, Pharm. Toxicology, 1999-2006, Opthalmology Rsch., 2000-2006. Co-organizer Citizens to Preserve Warwick, N.Y., 1986. Grantee NIH, 1977-2006, NASA, 1987-2006, US Dept. Energy, 1990-2006, DNA, 1992-2006; Robert McCormick Rsch. scholar, 1987-88. Mem. AAAS, Assn. for Rsch. in Vision and Ophthalmology, Radiation Rsch. Soc., Acad. Scis. Ukraine (fgn.), N.Y. Acad. Scis., Soc. Gen. Physiologists, Am. Soc. for Cell Biology, Internat. Soc. Ocular Toxicology (sec., treas. 2000-06). Achievements include definition of the mechanism of radiation cataract development; discovery of Terminal Body-a cellular organelle; description of the preferred dynamic reorientation of the mitotic spindle in an adult epithelium. Died Jan. 19, 2006.

WORTMAN, MAX (JR.) SIDONES, engineering educator, consultant; s. Max Sidence and Pearl May Wortman; m. Cora Ann Reed, Oct. 3, 1959; children: Kirk Bradley, Sara Elizabeth. Student in pre-Engineering, St. Ambrose U., Davenport, Iowa, 1951—53; BS in Civil Engring., Iowa State U., 1956; PhD in Bus. Adminstrn., U. Minn., 1962. Cert. mgr. Inst. of Cert. Profl. Bus. Mgrs., Va., 1981. Instr. engring. Iowa State U., Ames, 1956—57; instr. engring. and bus. U. Minn., Mpls., 1957—61; assoc. prof. of mgmt. U. Iowa, Iowa City, 1961—68; prof. of mgmt. U. Mass., Amherst, 1968—77, Va. Poly. and State U., Blacksburg, 1977—81; Wm. B. Stokely prof. in mgmt. U. Tenn., Knoxville, 1981—88; pioneer hi-bred internat. chair in agribusiness Iowa State U., Ames, 1988—2001, disting. prof. of mgmt. and agribusiness, from 1994. Cons. NOBL Labs., Sioux Center, Iowa, 1991—91, MassMutual Family Bus. Rsch. Program, Washington, 1994—95, U. Mass., Dartmouth, 1997. Author: (book chapter) Foundations of Rural Economic Development Policy. Rsch. adv. com. U.S. EEOC, Washington, 1966—66; vice-chair Mass. State Manpower Svcs. Coun., Boston, 1974; chair Ames Human Rels. Commn., Iowa, 1991—95. Fellow: Internat. Food and Agribusiness Assn. (bd. dirs. 1990—2000), Decision Scis. Assn. (program com. 1986—98), U.S. Assn. of Small Bus. and Entrepreneurship (pres. 1986—87), Acad. of Mgmt. (pres. 1981—82). R-Liberal. Presbyterian. Home: Ames, Iowa. Died Mar. 25, 2005.

WRIGHT, CALVIN PERSINGER, businessman; b. Rochester, Pa., Dec. 17, 1928; s. Jesse A. and Clara R. (Persinger) W. m. Anne Graham Lacy, Nov. 14, 1970; children: Calvin Jr., Jacob; children by previous marriage: Cynthia Wright Kern, Sally Wright Hawkins, Lauren Wright Haynes. Pres., Wright Edsel Sales, Covington, 1957-59, Allegheny Motor Corp., 1959-81, Downtown Autowash, 1972—, Riverside Spraywash, 1975-82, Sta. WXCF, 1972-79, The Stable Wash, 1983—; Stablewash Too, 1989—; animal breeder, antique auto dealer; dir. State Bank Alleghenies. Pres. High Acres Village, Va., 1965—. Active, Alleghany Hist. Soc.; dir. Persinger Meml. Cemetery. Presbyterian. Died July 2, 2005.

WRIGHT, DORIS ERLEANE, retail executive; b. Warsaw, Ind., Oct. 26, 1920; d. Ray M. and Gladys M. (Miller) Pletcher; m. Dale W. Wright, July 3, 1940; children: Janet Leifer, Clinda Conne, Hal. Grad. high sch., Warsaw, Ind. Sec. Lessig Engring., Warsaw, Ind., 1938-40, Playtime Products, Warsaw, 1941-42; v.p. W.R. Thomas $.05 to $1.00 Stores, Warsaw, from 1958. Vice chmn. Dem. County Assn., Warsaw, Mem. Warsaw Ladies Bowling Assn., Lambda Chi Omega, Tippecanoe Lake Country Club, Stonehedge Golf Club. Methodist. Avocations: bowling, golf. Home: Pierceton, Ind. Died Oct. 9, 2004.

WRIGHT, IRENE, artist; b. Detroit, May 1, 1926; d. Joseph and Esther (Hydu) Mrazik; m. C. Russell Wright, Sept. 16, 1950; children: James Joseph, Cinthia Jean, Richard Russell. Student, Ind. U. of Pa., 1976-78. One-woman shows include Nat. Bank of the Commonwealth, 1993, 96. Mem. Ind. Area Art Assn., Ford City (Pa.) Art Assn. (pres. 1972-74). Home: Ford City, Pa. Died Aug. 1, 2005.

WRIGHT, JAMES THOMAS, SR., education educator; b. Montgomery County, Ark., July 17, 1925; s. Joel Schooley and Loretta Cornelia (Grant) W.; m. Pauline A. Williams, Dec. 19, 1959; 1 child, James Thomas Jr. BA in Bus. Adminstrn./Phys. Edn., Ouachita Bapt. Coll., Arkadelphia, Ark., 1950; MS in Secondary Edn., U. Ark., 1957, EdD in Elem. Edn., 1965. Secondary tchr., coach pub. schs., Ark., 1950-55; elem. tchr., prin. pub. schs., Elida and Carlsbad, N.Mex., 1955—61; grad. asst. U. Ark., Fayetteville, 1961-62; head elem. edn. dept., prof. Wayland Bapt. Coll., Plainview, Tex., 1962-64; chmn. elem. edn., dir. student teaching Sul Ross State Coll., Alpine, Tex., 1964-67; assoc. prof. edn. Ouachita Bapt. Coll., Arkadelphia, 1967-68; prof., chmn. elem., early childhood and spl. edn. Henderson State U., Arkadelphia, 1968-90, adj. faculty, 1990—2002. Adv. coun. Bapt. Student Union, Henderson State U., Arkadelphia, 1990-2004, pres., 1994-2004. Mem. exec. bd. Ouachita Area Coun. Boy Scouts Am., Hot Springs, Ark., 1973-2004; mem. bd. Ione Bynum Childcare Ctr., Arkadelphia; mem. Comprehensive Outcomes Evaluation teams schs. in S.W. Ark., 1992-2004; mem. Gov.'s Task Force on Early Childhood Edn. Gov. of Ark. Recipient Silver Beaver and Dist. Award of Merit Ouachita Area Coun. Boy Scouts Am., Hot Springs, Vigil Honors and Founders award Order of Arrow, Boy Scouts Am., H. award Henderson State U. Alumni Assn., Arkadelphia, 1994. Mem. Am. Assn. Ret. Persons (del. White House Conf. on Aging 1995, mem. state legis. com. 1993-2004), Ark. Silver Haired Legislature, Assn. Bapt. for Scouting, Phi Delta Kappa. Baptist. Died Feb. 1, 2004; Hot Springs, Ark.

WRIGHT, NATHALIA, retired English educator; b. Athens, Ga., Mar. 29, 1913; d. Hilliard Carlisle and Elizabeth (MacNeal) W. BA, Maryville Coll., 1933; MA, Yale U., 1938, PhD, 1949. Instr. Maryville Coll., 1934-35, 41-47, libr. asst., 1940-43, asst. libr., 1943-48; asst. prof. English, U. Tenn., Knoxville, 1949-55, assoc. prof., 1955-62, prof., 1962-81, Alumni disting. svc. prof., 1974-81, prof. emerita, from 1981. Author: The Inner Room, 1938, Melville's Use of the Bible, 1949, 2d edit., 1969, Horation Greenough, First American Sculptor, 1963, American Novelists in Italy; the Discoverers, 1965, (with Harold Orton) Questionnaire for the Investigation of American English, 1972, A Word Geography of England, 1974; editor: Mardi (Herman Melville), 1990, Autobiographical Works of Washington Allston, 1991, The Illustrated Marble Faun (Hawthorne), 1991, The Correspondence of Washington Allston, 1993; mem. editl. bd. MLA, 1970-75; contbr. intros. to numerous books; contbr. articles to profl. jours. Grantee Am. Philos. Soc., 1952; Guggenheim fellow, 1953. Mem. MLA (adv. coun. Am. lit. sect. 1973, Jay B. Hubbell medal 1989), Am. Coun. Learned Socs. (bd. dirs. 1971-79), Melville Soc. (pres. 1956, 72), Internat. Acad. Siculo-Normanno, Soc. Storico Catania, Phi Beta Kappa, Phi Kappa Phi. Home: Maryville, Tenn. Died Nov. 22, 2004.

WRIGHT, REBECCA DIANE, program director; b. Springfield, Ohio, Dec. 5, 1947; d. Earl William and Diane Adele W.; m. Charles Spaeth, Nov. 15, 1974 (div. April 1977); m. George De La Pena, Nov. 2, 1984; children: Matthew, Alexander. Grad. h.s., 1966. Ballerina Joffrey Ballet, N.Y.C., 1966-75, Am. Ballet Theatre, N.Y.C., 1975-82; ballet mistress Twyla Tharp, N.Y.C., 1983; prof. Calif. State U., Long Beach, 1986—93; dir. dance program Adelphi U., Garden City, N.Y., 1997-99; dir. Wright Moves, Inc., Garden City, NY, 1998; dir. summer intensives Am. Ballet Theatre, 1997—2004; dir. dance program St. Paul's Sch., 1999—2004; dir. Wash. Sch. of Ballet, Washington, 2004—06. Vis. prof. UCLA, 1993—97; mem. steering com. Fosse Scholarship Awards, 1996—98; panelist LA Arts Coun., 1998—99; site visitor NEA. Starring role: Broadway Musical Merlin, N.Y.C., 1982-83, Broadway Musical On Your Toes, L.A. and N.Y.C., 1983, Merlin, 2003 (Drama Desk nomination 2003). Ford Found. scholar, 1964. Mem. Am. Coll. Dance Assn. (bd. dirs.). Avocations: cooking, reading, writing. Home: Concord, NH. Died Jan. 29, 2006.

WRIGHT, ROBERT ROSS, III, law educator; b. Ft. Worth, Nov. 20, 1931; m. Susan Webber; children: Robert Ross IV, John, David, Robin. BA cum laude, U. Ark., 1953, JD, 1956; MA (grad. fellow), Duke U., 1954; SJD (law fellow), U. Wis., 1967. Bar: Ark. 1956, U.S. Supreme Ct. 1968, Okla. 1970. Instr. polit. sci. U. Ark., 1955-56; mem. firm Forrest City, Ark., 1956-58; ptnr. Norton, Norton & Wright, Forrest City, 1959; asst. gen. counsel, asst. sec. Crossett Co., Ark.; atty. Crossett divsn. Ga.-Pacific Corp., 1960-63; asst. sec. Pub. Utilities Co., Crossett, Triangle Bag Co., Covington, Ky., 1960-62; faculty U. Ark. Law Sch., 1963-70; asst. prof., dir. continuing legal edn. and rsch., then asst. dean U. Ark., Little Rock, 1965-66, prof. law, 1967-70; prof. U. Okla., 1970-77; dean U. Okla. Coll. Law; dir. U. Okla. Law Ctr., 1970-76; vis. prof. U. Ark., Little Rock, 1976-77; Donaghey Disting. prof. U. Ark, 1977-99, Donaghey Disting. prof. emeritus, from 1999. Vis. disting. prof. U. Cin., 1983; vis. prof. law U. Iowa, 1969-70; vis. prof. U. Ark., Little Rock, 1976-77; Ark. commr. Nat. Conf. Commrs. Uniform State Laws, 1967-70; past chmn. Com. Uniform Eminent Domain Code; past mem. Com. Uniform Probate Code, Ark. Gov.'s Ins. Study Commn.; chmn. Gov. Commn. on Uniform Probate Code; chmn. task force joint devel. Hwy. Research Bd.; vice chmn. Okla. Jud. Council, 1970-72, chmn., 1972-75; chmn. Okla. Center Criminal Justice, 1971-76 Author: Arkansas Eminent Domain Digest, 1964, Arkansas Probate Practice System, 1965, The Law of Airspace, 1968, Emerging Concepts in the Law of Airspace, 1969, Cases and Materials on Land Use, 3d edit., 1982, supplement, 1987, 6th edit., 2003, Uniform Probate Code Practice Manual, 1972, Model Airspace Code, 1973, Land Use in a Nutshell, 1978, 4th edit., 2000, The Arkansas Form Book, 1979, 2d edit., 1988, Zoning Law in Arkansas: A Comparative Analysis, 1980, Old Seeds in the New Land: A History and Reminiscences of the Bar of Arkansas, 2001; contbr. articles to profl. jours. Mem. Little Rock Planning

Commn., 1978-82, chmn., 1982. Named Ark. Man of Year, Kappa Sigma, 1958. Fellow: Am. Coll. Trust and Estate Counsel (acad.), Am. Law Inst.; mem.: ABA (ho. of dels. 1994—2000, standing com. fed. jud. improvements 1998—2000, past chmn., exec. coun. gen. practice, solo and small firm sect., former chmn. new pubs. editl. bd., sect. officers conf.), Pulaski County Bar Assn., Ark. Bar Assn. (life; exec. coun. 1985—88, ho. of dels., chmn. eminent domain code com., past mem. com. new bar ctr., past chmn. preceptorship com., exec. com. young laywers sect.), Okla. Bar Assn. (past vice-chmn. legal internship com., former vice-chmn. gen. practice sect.), U. Ark. Alumni Assn., U. Wis. Alumni Assn., Duke U. Alumni Assn., Omicron Delta Kappa, Phi Alpha Delta, Phi Beta Kappa, Order of Coif. Episcopalian. Home: Little Rock, Ark. Died June 4, 2006.

WRIGHT, THOMAS WILLIAM DUNSTAN, architect; b. Rome, Jan. 12, 1919; s. Charles Will and Helen Bree (Dunstan) W.; m. Penelope Ladd, Aug. 6, 1942 (dec. June 1988); children: Peter W.D., Felicity Wright Evans, Allegra; m. Anita Robbins Gordon, Dec. 30, 1995. AB, Harvard U., 1941, MArch, 1950. Designer Joseph Saunders (architect), Alexandria, Va., 1950; assoc. Leon Brown (architect), Washington, 1950-53; ptnr. firm Brown and Wright, Washington, 1953-80; sole propr. Thomas W. D. Wright, FAIA, Architects, from 1980; pres. Wright & Rubin Architects, P.C., 1985-89, Wright & Heyne Architects, 1990-91; prin. Thomas W.D. Wright, FAIA, Washington, 1991—2001. Past mem. Old Georgetown bd. U.S. Commn. Fine Arts; past 1st v.p. D.C. Commn. Arts; past mem. D.C. Commrs. Planning and Urban Renewal Adv. Council; arbitrator Am. Arbitration Assn. Served to lt. comdr. USNR, 1941-46. Am. Sabre Fencing champion, gold medallist sr. age group (70-74); mem. U.S. Sr. Fencing Team, gold medallist sabre 70+, 1995. Fellow AIA (past pres. Washington Met. chpt., past nat. chmn. com. on Nat. Capital City, past mem. com. on design, com. on housing); mem. Soc. Archtl. Historians, Nat. Assn. Intergroup Relations Ofcls., Nat. Assn. Housing and Redevel. Ofcls., Nat. Com. against Discrimination in Housing, ACLU. Clubs: Cosmos (Washington), Harvard (Washington). Democrat. Died Feb. 18, 2006.

WRIGHT, WILLIAM WYNN, chemist; b. Balt., Aug. 13, 1923; s. Andrew Wynn and Margaret Mary (Peters) W.; m. Mary Theresa Mead, Feb. 10, 1945; children: Ann Wynn, Jane Frances, Stephen William, Kathleen Theresa, Drew Edward. BS magna cum laude, Loyola Coll., Balt., 1944; MS, Georgetown U., 1946, PhD, 1948. Rsch. fellow Georgetown U. Grad. Sch., Washington, 1944; chemist Nat. Bur. Stds., Washington, 1945, FDA, Washington, 1945-79; sr. scientist U.S. Pharmacopeia, Rockville, Md., 1979—2004. Cons., advisor WHO, Geneva, 1960-2000. Recipient Superior Svc. award U.S. Dept. Health, Edn. and Welfare, Washington, 1964, USPHS, Washington, 1979, Lifetime Achievement award Indian Drug Mfrs. Assn., 2004; hon. mem. U.S. Pharmacopial Conv., 2005. Fellow AAAS (life), Assn. Ofcl. Analytical Chemists (pres. 1967); mem. Am. Chem. Soc., N.Y. Acad. Sci. (life), Sigma Xi. Roman Catholic. Achievements include development of numerous chemical analytical methods for antibiotics and pharmaceuticals; studies into absorption and excretion of antibiotics; standardization of antibiotic susceptibility discs and of their use in clinical laboratories. Home: Silver Spring, Md. Died July 15, 2006.

WROBLOWA, HALINA STEFANIA, electrochemist; b. Gdansk, Poland, July 5, 1925; arrived in U.S., 1959, naturalized, 1973; 1 child: Krystyna Wrobel-Knight, grandson Christopher E. Knight. MSc, U. Lodz, Poland, 1949; PhD, Warsaw Inst. Tech., 1958. Chmn. dept. prep. studies U. Lodz, 1950-53; adj. Inst. for Phys., Chemistry Acad. Scis., Warsaw, Poland, 1958-60; dept. dir. electrochemistry lab. energy inst. U. Pa., Phila., 1960-67; dir. electrochemistry lab., 1968-75; prin. research scientist Ford Motor Co., Dearborn, Mich., 1976-91; pvt. practice cons., 1991. Chmn. Gordon Rsch. Coun. on Electrochemistry, 1983. Contbr. chpts. to books, articles to profl. jours., patent lit. With Polish Underground Army, 1943—45. Decorated Mil. Silver Cross of Merit with Swords Polish Underground Army. Mem.: Internat. Electrochem. Soc., Electrochem. Soc., Mensa, Sigma Xi. Home: Newtown Square, Pa. Died Aug. 29, 2006.

WRONOSKI, JAMES JOHN, author, musician; b. Bryn Mawr, Pa., June 27, 1964; s. Walter John and Louise Suzanne W.; m. Heather Dunne Wronoski, Jan. 31, 1998. BS, Drexel U., Phila., 1987; MA, Brown U., Providence, R.I., 1995; student, U. Va. Sch. Law, Charlottsville, 1998, U. Mont. Sch. Law, Missoula, 1995. Civil engr., project mgr. Morehall Constrn., Malvern, Pa., 1987-88; civil engr. Buckley/Driscoll, Phila., 1988-90; prof. creative writing Brown U., Providence, R.I., 1993-94; author Pa., 1992-01; pres. Merwood Books and Records, Ardmore, Pa., 1995-01, Fair Heather Music, Ardmore, Pa., 1995-01; singer, songwriter, musician, bandleader, prodr. The Missionaries, Phila., from 1981. Mem. Am. Soc. Civil Engrs., Phila., 1983-90, Assn. Gen. Contractors, Phila., 1984-90, Union Carpenters Am., Phila., 1988-93, Small Publishers, Paradise, Calif., 1995-01. Author: Knaves in Boyland, 1996, The Thaw and Other Stories, 1999, Anniversary Songs, 2000; composer Compact Disc, What's The Damage, Nick Nack?, 2001. Vol. Wellness Cmty. Cancer patient Support, Phila., 1995-01. Recipient NBC Award of Excellence in Dramatic Writing, 1982, Scarsfield Law Scholarship U. Mont. Sch. Law, 1994-95, Full Scholarship Teaching Asst., Brown U., 1992-94, Pirate's Alley William Faulkner Poetry award, William Faulner Pirate's Alley Assn., 1999. Home: Huntington Valley, Pa. Died Aug. 7, 2004.

WUELLNER, WILHELM HERMANN, religion educator; b. Bochum, Fed. Republic of Germany, Feb. 21, 1927; came to U.S., 1954; s. Wilhelm Georg and Emma Henriette (Beckmann) W.; m. Flora May Slosson, May 28, 1954; children: Christine Collins, Virginia Henriette, Lucy Elizabeth. PhD, U. Chgo., 1958. Asst. prof. Mission House Theol. Seminary, Sheboygan, Wis., 1957-58, Grinnell (Iowa) Coll., 1958-60; assoc. prof. Hartford (Conn.) Seminary Found., 1960-65; prof. New Testament Pacific Sch. Religion and Grad. Theol. Union, Berkeley, Calif., from 1965. Mission developer Luth. Bd. Home Mission, Amana Colony, Iowa, 1958-60; coll. chaplain Grinnell Coll., 1958-60. Author: Meaning of Fishers of Men, 1967, (with R. Leslie) The Surprising Gospel, 1984, (with H. Perelmuter) Paul the Jew, 1990; editor: Colloquies of Center for Hermenentical Studies, 1970-83. Am. Assn. Theol. Schs. fellow, 1970-71, NEH fellow, 1977-78, Luth. Brotherhood fellow, 1984-85. Mem. Soc. Bibl. Lit. (pres. Pacific Coast sect. 1968-69), Cath. Bibl. Assn., Studiorum Novi Testamenti Societas, Dolger Inst. für Antike und Christentum, Internat. Soc. for History Rhetoric. Home: Fair Oaks, Calif. Died Feb. 14, 2004.

WYON, JOHN BENJAMIN, public health physician, scientist, consultant; b. London, May 3, 1918; s. Guy Alfred and Emma Mildred (Hitchock) W.; m. Elizabeth Glynne Granmer, JUly 10, 1946 (dec. 1989); children: Rachel Margaret, Thomas Cranmer; m. Joan Litchard Kittredge, Feb. 15, 1992. BA, Cambridge U., 1940, MB, BChir, Cambridge U., 1942; MPH, Harvard U., 1953. Med. officer Friends Ambulance Unit, Adua, Ethiopia, 1943-45; med. missionary Ch. Missionary Soc., U.P., India, 1947-52; field dir. Harvard U. Population Study, Punjab, India, 1953-60; from lectr. to sr. lectr. Harvard Sch. Pub. Health Dept. Population Scis., Boston, 1960-88. Cons. Andean Rural Health Care, Lake Junaluska, N.C., Sarvodaya Shramadana Movement, Moratuwa Sri Lanka, 1978-89. Author: The Khanna Study, 1971. Mem. Am. Pub. Health Assn., Royal Coll. Physicians. Episcopalian. Home: Chestnut Hill, Mass. Died May 31, 2004.

WYSE, WILLIAM WALKER, lawyer, real estate company executive; b. Spokane, Wash., July 20, 1919; s. James and Hattie (Walker) W.; m. Janet E. Oswalt, Jan. 30, 1944; children: Wendy L., Scott C., Duncan E. AB, U. Wash., 1941; JD, Harvard U., 1948. Bar: Oreg. 1948. Pvt. practice, Portland; ptnr. Stoel, Rives, Boley, Jones & Gray, 1953-88; chmn Wyse Investment Svcs., 1988—2005. Past trustee, sec. Pacific Realty Trust; past trustee Holladay Park Plaza. Chmn. ctrl. budget com. United Fund, 1958—60; 1st v.p. United Good Neighbors; chmn. bd. dirs. Portland Sch. Bd., 1959—66; pres. Tri-County Cmty. Coun., 1970—71; bd. dirs., sec. Oreg. Parks Found.; bd. dirs. Cmty. Child Guidance Clinic, 1950—57, pres., 1956—57; bd. dirs. Oreg. Symphony Soc., 1965—74, 1993—99, pres., 1968; bd. dirs. Loaves and Fishes Ctrs., Inc., 1997—2003. Mem. ABA, Oreg. Bar Assn., Multnomah County Bar Assn., Am. Coll. Real Estate Lawyers, Univ. Club, Arlington Club, Portland City Club (past gov.), Wauna Lake Club, Delta Upsilon. Republican. Presbyterian. Died Dec. 11, 2005.

YADAV, RAM LAKHAN SINGH, Indian government official; b. 1919; Leader Bihar, 1991; Minister of Chemicals and Fertilizers Govt. of India, from 1994. Died 2006.

YANCEY, JIMMIE ISAAC, marketing professional; b. Ripley, Miss., Dec. 11, 1935; s. Charlie Edward and Overa (Wilbanks) Y.; m. Jonell Smith, Mar. 1, 1958; children: Angela Jo, Jamie Lorraine, Cynthia Overa, Melanie Ann. BS, Miss. State U., 1963, MBA, 1966. Editor univ. rels. Miss. State. U., Starkville, 1963-65, editor coll. bus., 1965-66; editor Miss. Extension Svc., Starkville, 1966-67, Nat. Cotton Coun., Memphis, 1967-71; pub. rels. dir. Cotton Inc., Raleigh, N.C., 1971, Am. Soybean Assn., Hudson, Iowa, 1971-78; gen. mgr. Prog. Farmer Network, Starkville, 1978-86; owner, mgr. Yancey Agrl. Network, Starkville, from 1986. Mktg. cons. Wyffel's Hybrids, Inc., Atkinson, Ill., 1987-93. Bd. dirs. Agri-Bus. Edn. Found.; sr. adv. com. Coll. Bus. and Industry, Miss. State U. Mem. Nat. Agrl. Mktg. Assn., (pres. 1986-87, Meritorious Svc. award 1986), Nat. Assn. Farm Broadcasters, Am. Advt. Fedn., Starkville C. of C. (venture capital com. 1990), Am. Soybean Assn. (Mertorious Svc. award 1974, Broadcaster of Yr. 1984), Hudson C. of C. (pres. 1972, Iowa chpt.), Nat. Alliance of Ind. Corp. Cons., Miss. Rotary, Pres.'s Club. Presbyterian. Avocations: gardening, fishing. Home: Daytona Beach, Fla. Died Feb. 22, 2004.

YANKOV, LUBEN KRASTANOV, chemist, educator, researcher; b. Sofia, Bulgaria, Apr. 5, 1930; came to U.S., 1993; s. Krastan Yankov and Eugeni Krastanova (Stoycheva) Georgieva; m. Maria Vladimirova Bostanova, Nov. 13, 1955; 1 child, Christian. BS MS in Chem. Tech. and Chem. Engring., Higher Inst. Chem. Tech., Sofia, 1954, PhD in Natural Products, 1964. Head dept. sci. investigation and devel. State Corp. Pharm., Sofia, 1956-59; asst. prof., lectr. organic chemistry Higher Inst. Chem. Tech., Sofia, 1959-72, assoc. prof., 1972-80, prof. organic chemistry, 1980-93, head dept. organic chemistry, 1984-93, v.p. R&D, 1985-89; v.p. State Corp. Heavy Chem. Industry, Sofia, 1972-76; disting. sr. scientist XECHEM, Inc., New Brunswick, N.J., from 1993; pres. Ctrl. Sci. Inst. Chem. Tech., Bulgaria, 1972-79. Main sci. adviser State Ministry Chem. Industry, Sofia, 1979-81; mem. and pres. sci. coun. Higher Inst. Chem. Tech., Sofia, 1976-92; mem. sci. coun. Bulgarian Acad. Scis., Sofia, 1976-89. Author, co-author 7 books and handbooks in the field of organic chemistry; contbr. more than 140 articles to profl. jours. Recipient Hon. Order as Inventor in Chemistry and Chem. Tech., State Com. of Sci. and Tech. Devel. (Bulgaria), 1986, High Achievement in Sci. and Tech. awards, 1976, 77, Spl. Merit and Svc. in Edn., Sci. and Chem. Tech. award Nat. Assembly (Bulgaria), 1986. Mem. Am. Chem. Soc., Am. Soc. Pharmacology, Union Bulgarian Chemists, Union Sci. Workers. Achievements include 55 international patents for synthesis or isolation and production of several synthetic and natural products, including new methods for production of anticancer drugs (Paclitaxel) and synthesis of new active Taxane analogs. Home: Edison, NJ. Died Jan. 10, 2005.

YARBOROUGH, WILLIAM PELHAM, writer, lecturer, retired military officer; b. Seattle, May 12, 1912; s. Leroy W. and Addessia (Hooker) Y.; m. Norma Mae Tuttle, Dec. 26, 1936 (dec.); children: Norma Kay (dec.), William Lee, Patricia Mae Reed. BS, U.S. Mil. Acad., 1936; grad., Command and Gen. Staff Coll., 1944, Brit. Staff Coll., 1950, Army War Coll., 1953. Commd. 2nd lt. U.S. Army, 1936, advanced through grades to lt. gen., 1968, ret., 1971, various assignments U.S., Philippines and ETO, 1936-42; exec. officer Paratroop Task Force, North Africa, 1942; comdr. 2d Bn., 504th Par. Inf. Regt., 82d Airborne Div., Sicily invasion, 1943, 509th Parachute Inf., Italy and France, 1943-44; comdg. officer 473 Inf., Italy, 1945; provost marshal 15th Army Group, ETO, 1945, Vienna Area Command and U.S. Forces, Austria, 1945-47; mem. staff, faculty U.S. Army Info. Sch., 1948-49; operations officer, gen. staff Joint Mil. Assistance Adv. Group, London, Eng., 1951-52; mem. faculty Army War Coll., 1953-56, 57; dep. chief Mil. Assistance and Adv. Group, Cambodia, 1956-57; comdg. officer 66th CIC Group, Stuttgart, Germany, 1958-60, 66th M.I. Group, Stuttgart, 1960; comdg. gen. U.S.A. Spl. Warfare Ctr., 1961; also comdt. U.S. Army Spl. Warfare Sch., Ft. Bragg, 1961-65; sr. mem. UN Command Mil. Armistice Commn., Korea, 1965; asst. dep. chief staff DCSOPS for spl. operations Dept. Army, Washington; chmn. U.S. delegation Inter-Am. Def. Bd., Joint Brazil U.S. Def. Commn., Joint Mexican-U.S. Def. Commn.; Army mem. U.S. sect. permanent Joint Bd. on Def., Can.-U.S. Def. Commn., Washington, 1965; asst. chief of staff intelligence Dept. Army Washington, 1966-68; comdg. gen. I Corps Group, Korea, 1968-69; chief staff, also dep. comdr.-in-chief U.S. Army, Pacific, Hawaii, 1969-71. Contbr. Internat. Mil. and Def. Ency., 1993, MacMillan Ency. of the Am. Mil., 1994; William P. Yarborough collection papers and artifacts donated to Mugar Meml. Libr., Boston U. Decorated Disting. Svc. medal with three oak leaf clusters, Silver Star, Legion of Merit with three oak leaf clusters, Bronze Star, Joint Svc. Commendation medal with oak leaf clusters, Croix de Guerre with Palm (France), Cross for Valor and Diploma (Italy), Order of Merit Second Class (Korea), Order of Ulchi (Korea). Fellow Co. Mil. Historians; mem. Kiwanis Club. Home: Southern Pines, NC. Died Dec. 6, 2005.

YARGER, SAMUEL JACOB, dean, educator; b. Pontiac, Mich., Oct. 8, 1937; s. Ralph And Eva L. (Little) Y.; m. Gwen Polk (div. 1982); 1 child, Mark Alan; m. Sally K. Mertens. BS in Elem. Edn., Eastern Mich. U., 1959; MA in Sch. Psychology, U. Mich., 1962; PhD in Ednl. Psychology, Wayne State U., 1968. Elementary tchr. Pontiac Schools, Mich., 1959—61; psychol. intern. Oakland County, Mich., 1961—62; sch. psychologist Royal Oak Schools, Mich., 1962—65, elementary prin. Mich., 1965—66; tchg. fellow Wayne State U., 1966—67; asst. prof. Oakland CC, Mich., 1967-68, U. Toldeo, 1968-71; assoc. prof. Syracuse U., NY, 1971-77, prof. NY, 1977-84, assoc. dean NY, 1980-84; dean, prof. U. Wis., Milw., 1984-92; dean Sch. Edn. U. Miami, Fla., 1992—2005, prof. Dept. Teaching and Learning, 1992—2005. Rschr. Assessment Pre-Vocat. Skills Mentally Retarded Youth, 1964-65, Tchr. Attitude Change in Rels. to Program Input, 1968, Leader Behavior in a Task Oriented Setting in Relation to Group Activity, 1968, Attitudes Inner-City Residents Toward Ednl. Programs and Tchrs., 1970, Dimensions Tchr. Ctr. Movement in Am. Edn., 1972-75, Dimensions Field Derived Content in Tchr. Edn. Programs, 1973-75, Nat. Study Inservice Edn., 1976-77, Nat. Study Preservice Edn., 1976-77, Nat. Study Preservice Edn., 1976-77, Nat. Study Federally-Funded Tchr. Ctr., 1979-82, Nat. Study Tchr. Edn., 1985-94; developer, dir. tchr. edn. programs, various U.S. locations; mem., chmn. various univs. coms.; cons., spkr. in field. Author: Improving Teacher Education, 1978, Documenting Success-A Guidebook for Teacher Centers, 1979, Inservice Teacher Education, 1980, monographs; contbr. articles to profl. jour., chapters to books. Mem.: Am. Assn. Colleges for Tchr. Edn. (bd. dir. 1984—87, exec. com. 1985—87, chair rsch. and info. com.), Am. Ednl. Rsch. Assn. (assoc. editor. 1983—85, chair elect Orgn. Instl. Affiliates 1994—95). Died Nov. 14, 2005.

YARIGER, GEORGIA LOUISE, executive secretary, real estate executive; b. Nappanee, Ind., Oct. 10, 1926; d. John E. and Nora (Howard) Symonds; m. Arthur Vernon Yariger, Aug. 24, 1948 (dec.); children: Liza Tanzawa, Rebel V. (dec.). Student, Victoria Coll., 1961. Cashier, bookkeeper Bunte Show Salin, South Bend, Ind., 1945-48; exec. sec. Aluminum Co. Am., Point Comfort, Tex., 1949-72; owner real estate Victoria, Tex., from 1989. Mem. Dem. Nat. Com., Washington, 1995—, Dem. Club Victoria, 1995, Dem. Congrl. Campaign Com., Washington, 1995. Recipient Silver, Gold and Pearl medals Women's Christian Temperance Union. Mem. Victoria Preservation, Inc., Victoria Symphony League, Bach Festival, Azelea Garden Club, Victoria Music Club, Sierra Club. Democrat. Avocations: reading, music, collecting clowns, coin collecting/numismatics, collecting norman rockwell figurines. Home: Victoria, Tex. Died Mar. 1, 2004.

YARRINGTON, GEORGE A., retired public relations executive, advertising executive, writer; b. Springfield, Mass., Oct. 20, 1906; s. George Timberlake and Jennie Elizabeth Yarrington; m. Katherine Peter Yarrington, Apr. 15, 1944. BA, Comml. Sci., Northeastern Univ., Boston, MA, 1930—34. Free-lance writer Self Employed, Belleville, Ill., 1972—2002; pub. rels. dir. Builders Assn., Boston, 1968—72; exec. dir. Quincy Taxpayers Assn., Quincy, 1953—68; instr. Burdette Coll., Boston, 1946—53; electronics instr. USAF, Scott Field, 1942—46; radio advt. writer CBS Sta. WMAS, Inc., Springfield, 1940—42; owner-mgr. Yarrington's Ser. Sta., Melrose, 1930—40; dept. store buyer Forbes & Wallace, Inc., Springfield, 1925—30. Pub. speaking instr. Dale Carnegie Inst., New York, NY, 1946—48; chmn. Old Colony Area Transp. Comm., Boston, 1958—60; chmn. adv. bd. News-Dem., Belleville, Ill., 1984—85. Author: (book) Tales of the 20th Century, More Tales of the 20th Century, 2004. Campaign mgr. Ronald Reagan for Pres., North Conway, NH, 1972; admin. asst. to Gov. Foster Furcolo, Mass., 1958—60; bd. dirs. Citizens for Modern Transit, St. Louis, 1982—92. Sargeant USAF, 1942—46, Scott Field, IL. Home: Millstadt, Ill. Died Dec. 11, 2005.

YATES, SHIRLEY JEAN, educator; b. St. Louis, Oct. 3, 1949; d. Norman William and Wilma (Bratton) M.; m. Joseph Hans Sturm, June 24, 1972 (div. June 1980); m. Robert A. Yates, June 2, 1984 (dec. 1993). BA, Harris Tchrs. Coll., 1970; M in Bus. Mgmt., Webster U., 1981. Cert. adminstrv. specialist; cert. gifted tchr. Educator St. Louis Pub. Schs., from 1970; tchr. gifted lang. arts McKinley Classical Jr. Acad., St. Louis, Mo. Vol. abused neglected infants Salvation Army, St. Louis, 1986-92; mem. Dem. Nat. Com., Washington, 1993—, St. Clair NOW, Belleville, Ill., 1991—. Scholarship Parson's Blewett, 1981, 86, 94; recipient Pub. Svc. award Dept. of Justice, 1991, 92. Mem. NOW. Democrat. Roman Catholic. Avocations: bowling, golf, gardening, reading. Home: Saint Louis, Mo. Died Nov. 18, 2004.

YEAGER, HUBERT M., JR., retired automobile accessory company executive; b. Atlanta, Apr. 6, 1923; s. Hubert Sr. and Lucille Elliott Yeager; children: Donald, Wayne, Mark. Sales staff GM, Atlanta, Atlanta Sport Car; owner, salesman Accessory Distbn. Co., Inc., East Point, Ga. With U.S. Army, 1942-46. Baptist. Home: Douglasville, Ga. Died Feb. 7, 2005.

YEAGER, LILLIAN ELIZABETH, dean, nursing educator; b. Bainbridge, Ga., Dec. 23, 1943; d. Earnest and Lottie (Brown) Martin; m. Thomas Stephen Yeager, May 26, 1973 (dec. Oct. 1993); 1 child, Michelle. BSN, Tuskegee U., 1964; MSN, Wayne State U., 1972. RN, Ky., Ind., Mich. Staff/charge nurse John Andrew Hosp., Tuskegee Institute, Ala., 1964-65; instr. nursing Tuskegee U., 1965-69; sr. instr. Harper Hosp. Sch. Nursing, Detroit, 1969-73; staff nurse Met. Hosp., Detroit, 1970-72; asst. prof. nursing Ind. U. Southeast, New Albany, 1973-79, assoc. prof. nursing, 1979—2006, acting asst. dean Sch. of Nursing, 1990-91, dean, 2002—06. Cons. nursing process VA Med. Ctr., Louisville, Ky., 1987-88; cons. clin. recognition Floyd Meml. Hosp., New Albany, 1989-90. Prodr., presenter (video) Patient Education, 1993. Mem. fertilization overview com. Alliant Hosps., Louisville, 1982-95; bd. dirs. Frazier Rehab. Ctr., Louisville, 1981-2006; mem. Louisville Urban League, 1992-2006; mem. dept. evangelism Dicoese of Ky.-Episcopal, Louisville, 1992-2006 Recipient VA Appreciation award VA Med. Ctr., Louisville, 1986, FACET Excellence in Teaching award Office of Pres., Ind. U., 1990, Outstanding Contbns. to Nursing award Jefferson C.C., Louisville, 1992, Univ. Svc. award Coun. Nursing Faculty Ind. U. Sch. Nursing, 1993. Mem. ANA, Ind. State Nurses Assn. (1st v.p. 1986-88, 95-2006, treas. 1988-92), N.Am. Nursing Diagnosis Assn., Kyanna Black Nurses Assn., Sigma Theta Tau, Chi Eta Phi, Delta Sigma Theta. Democrat. Home: Louisville, Ky. Died May 23, 2006.

YEISER, CHARLES WILLIAM, JR., artist, art dealer; b. Womelsdorf, Pa., Nov. 20, 1925; s. Charles William Sr. and Edith Irene (Hoffa) Y.; m. Adele Ann Simola, June 9, 1951; children: Elizabeth Ann, Charles William III. Student, Kutztown (Pa.) State Coll., 1943; cert., Pratt Inst., 1949; BA, NYU, 1951. Asst. dir. Far Gallery, N.Y.C., 1951-71, dir., owner, 1971-80. One man shows include Impressions Gallery, N.Y.C., 1981, 82, Hull Gallery, Washington, 1982, Victoria Munroe Gallery, N.Y.C., 1984, Westmoreland Mus. of Art, Greensburg, Pa., 1984, Country Art Gallery, Locust Valley, N.Y., 1987, Joseph Keiffer Gallery of N.Y., N.Y.C., 1988, 91, L'Atelier Gallery, Piermont, N.Y., 1991; exhbns. in group shows at Hopper House, 1976, Westmoreland Mus. of Art, 1980, 82, Montgomery Gallery, 1985, Joseph Keiffer Gallery, 1990, Louis Stern Galleries, 1991. Bd. dirs. Dessoff Choirs, N.Y.C., 1952-53, Hopper House, Nyack, N.Y., 1975-78, Rockland Ctr. for The Arts, West Nyack, 1989—. Recipient 1st prize Rahway Library, 1949. Mem. Rockland Ctr. for the Arts (bd. dirs. 1988-98). Republican. Avocations: music, gardening, cooking, travel. Home: West Nyack, NY. Died Aug. 28, 2005.

YEN, YEN-CHEN, chemical engineer, consultant; b. Shanghai, Peoples Republic of China, June 21, 1912; came to U.S., 1964; s. Chin-Chuen Yen and Pei Y.; m. Er-Ying, Sept. 9, 1939; children: Martha Meng, Madeline Chu, Rosa Chin, Margaret Chu, Benedict Tien-Sze. Diploma Engring., Tech. Hochschule, Berlin, 1937. Prof. various U.'s, Peoples Republic of China; v.p. Taiwan (Republic of China) Fertilizer Co., 1950-53; commr. Indsl. Devel. Committee, Taiwan, 1953-59; cons. Singapore and Taiwan, Republic of China, 1960-64; sr. chem. engr. SRI Internat., Menlo Park, Calif., 1965-81, cons., from 1981. Contbr. articles to profl. jours. Mem. Am. Chem. Soc., Am. Electrochem. Soc., Am. Inst. Chem. Engring. Home: Palo Alto, Calif. Died Jan. 6, 2004.

YOLTON, JOHN WILLIAM, philosopher, educator; b. Birmingham, Ala., Nov. 10, 1921; s. Robert Elgene and Ella Maude (Holmes) Y.; m. Jean Sebastian, Sept. 5, 1945; children: Karin Frances Yolton Griffith, Pamela Holmes Yolton Smith. BA with honors, U. Cin., 1945, MA, 1946; postgrad., U. Calif., Berkeley, 1946-50; DPhil (Fulbright fellow), Balliol Coll., Oxford, Eng., 1952; LL.D. (hon.), York U., 1974; D.Litt. (hon.), McMaster U., 1976. Vis. lectr. philosophy Johns Hopkins U., 1952-53; asst. prof. Princeton U., 1953-57; assoc. prof. Kenyon Coll., 1957-61; prof. U. Md., 1961-63; prof. philosophy York U., Toronto, 1963-78, chmn. dept., 1963-73, acting dean grad. studies, 1967-68, acting pres., 1973-74; prof. philosophy Rutgers U., New Brunswick, N.J., from 1978, dean Rutgers Coll., 1978-85, John Locke prof. history of philosophy, 1989-92, prof. emeritus philosophy, from 1992. Cons. Bertrand Russell Archives, McMaster U., 1973-86. Author: John Locke and the Way of Ideas, 1956, Metaphysical Analysis, 1967, Locke and the Compass of Human Understanding, 1970, Thinking Matter, 1983, Perceptual Acquaintance from Descartes to Reid, 1984, Locke and French Materialism, 1991, Perception and Reality, 1996, Realism and Appearances, 2000, The Two Intellectual Worlds of JOhn Locke, 2004, other books; gen. editor Clarendon Edit. of Works of John Locke, Oxford U. Press, 1984-92, Blackwell's Companion to the Enlightenment, 1992, Locke Dictionary (Blackwell), 1993, Library of the History of Ideas, 5 books in field; mem. editl. bd. jours. in field; editor (with Jean S. Yolton) Some Thoughts Concerning Education, by Locke, 1989; v.p., bd. dirs. Jour. of the History of Ideas, 1991-98; contbr. articles to profl. jours. Mem. N.J. Com. for Humanities, 1978-85, treas., 1980-85. Am. Coun. Learned Socs. fellow, 1960-61; Can. Coun. fellow, 1968-69. Mem.: Hume Soc., Am. Soc. for 18th Century Studies, Can. Philos. Assn., Mind Assn., Am. Philos. Assn. Home: Piscataway, NJ. Died Nov. 3, 2005.

YOON, JI-WON, virology, immunology and diabetes educator, director; b. Kang-Jin, Chonnam, Korea, Mar. 28, 1939; came to U.S., 1965; s. Baek-In and Duck-Soon (Lee) Y.; m. Chungja Rhim, Aug. 17, 1968; children: John W., James W. BS and MS in Biochemistry, Chosun U., 1961; MS in Genetics and Cell Biology, U. Conn., 1971, PhD in Virology and Immunology, 1973. Postdoctoral fellow in pathobiology Sloan-Kettering Inst. for Cancer Rsch., 1973—74; staff fellow NIH, Bethesda, Md., 1974—76, sr. staff fellow, 1976—78, sr. investigator, 1978—84; prof., chief div. virology U. Calgary, Canada, 1984—90, assoc. dir. Diabetes Rsch. Ctr. Alta., 1985—90, dir. Alta., 1990—99, Julia McFarlane prof., Diabetes Rsch. Ctr. Alta., 1990—2004, dir. Lab. Viral and Immunopathogenesis of Diabetes Alta., 1999—2004, Can. Rsch. Chair Diabetes Alta., 2001—04; prof. microbiology and immunology Rosalind Franklin U. of Medicine and Sci., Chgo. Med. Sch., from 2003, dir., Immunologic Rsch., from 2003, dir. Rosalind Franklin Diabetes Ctr., from 2004; dir. grad. edn., dept. patholgy Chgo. Med. Sch., from 2004. Vis. prof. Diabetes Endocrinology Rsch. Ctr., Yale U., New Haven, from 1997, Can. rsch. chair in diabetes, 2001—03; prof. Yonsei U. Coll. Medicine, from 1999. Contbr. articles to New England Jour. Medicine, Jour. Virology, Sci., Nature, The Lancet, Jour. Diabetes, Jour. Immunology, Jour. Biochemistry, Jour. Exptl. Medicine; Mem. editl. bd. Diabetologia, 1977, Ann. Rev. Advances Present Rsch. Animal Diabetes, 1990—, Diabetes Rsch. Clin. Practice, 1989—, Jour. Biomed. Rsch., 1992—, Jour. Exptl. Molecular Medicine, 1996—; mem. editl. adv. bd. Jour. Diabetologia, 1996—99, Internat. Jour. Exptl. Diabetic Rsch. and Autoimmunity. Recipient NIH Dir. award, 1984, Heritage Med. Scientist award, Alberta Heritage Found. Med. Rsch., 1984, Lectrship. award, 3d Asian Symposium Childhood Diabetes, 1989, 8th Annual Meeting Childhood Diabetes, Osaka, Japan, 1990, 9th Korean/Can. Heritage award, 1989, 1st Compatriot award Fedn. Korean-Can. Assn., 1996, 2000, Korean Broadcasting Sys. Compatriot award, 1998, Lectureship award New England Biosci. Soc., 1998, Ho-Am prize in Medicine, Ho-Am Found., 2000, Disting. Lectureship award Soc. Biomed. Rsch., 2004. Mem. Am. Soc. Immunologists, Am. Diabetes Assn., Am. Soc. Microbiology, N.Y. Acad. Sci., Soc. Virology, Internat. Diabetes Fedn. Baptist. Achievements include first isolation of diabetogenic virus from patients with recent onset of IDDM; first demonstration of prevention of virus-induced diabetes by vaccination with nondiabetogenic virus in animals; discovery that autoimmune IDDM can be prevented by depletion of macrophages in autoimmune diabetic NOD mice, certain viral glycoproteins (rubella virus E2 glycoprotein) can induce organ-specific autoimmune disease; research on molecular identification of diabetogenic viral gene in animal models, discovery of a nontoxic organic compound with no side effects that completely prevents type I diabetes in NOD mice, discovery that bacterial superantigens such as staphylococcal enterotozins (SEC1, SEC3) can prevent autoimmune type I diabetes by activation of CD4+ suppressor T cells in NOD mice; research on the role of cloned T-Cells in the pathogenesis of autoimmune Type I Diabetes at cellular and molecular level, molecular role TGFB in prevention of Autoimmune IDDM, molecular role of macrophages in pathogenesis of virus-induced diabetes; developed the method for prevention of autoimmune type 1 diabetes in diabetic mice by immunogene therapy; developed a new method for prevention of autoimmune diabetes in mice by control of the finely tuned immune balance by treatment with human choriogonadotropin; developed an insulin gene therapy for the cure of autoimmune diabetes by the expression of insulin in hepatocytes under the control of glucose-sensitive synthetic promoter; developed a stem cell gene therapy for the possible cure of type 1 diabetes by regeneration of beta cells in pancreas using betacellulin with the albumin leader sequence for its secretion. Died 2006.

YORK, EVERETT HAYS, corporate executive; b. Johnson, Nebr., Apr. 27, 1912; s. Robert Levi and Tacie Lenore (Hays) Y.; m. Helen Lucille Ackerson, June 1, 1940; 1 child: Carol Jean. Student, Gen. Motors Inst. Tech., Mich., 1944, Naval Engring. Officers Tng., 1944. Regional mgr. (West coast) The Buda Co., Harvey, Ill., 1946-51, sales mgr., 1951-55; prin. Everett H. York Co., Long Beach, Calif., from 1955; pres., chief exec. officer Oildex Corp., Long Beach, Calif., from 1970. Mem. Nat. Adv. Bd. of Nat. Security Council; bd. dirs. Signal Hill, Calif. C. of C., 1967-84, pres., 1983. Served with USNR, 1942-45. Recipient Proclamation from Gov. George Deukmejian (Calif.), 1984, Resolution from State of Calif., 1984, Proclamation of Commendation from the Mayor of City of Signal Hill, 1984. Mem. Nat. Security Council (nat. adv. bd.), Nat. Rifle Assn. Avocations: fishing, travel. Died July 6, 2004.

YOUNG, CHARLES ALBERT, JR., transportation analyst; b. Monroe, La., Sept. 28, 1952; s. Charles Albert and Charlesetta (Richardson) Y.; m. Geraldine Ramey, July 2, 1990; children: April Noel, Ericka Nicole. BS in Social Sci. Edn., Grambling State U., 1978; MA in Tech. and Human Affairs, Washington U., St. Louis, 1990. Tchr. Rapides Parish Sch. Bd., Alexandria, La., 1978-79; traffic analyst Traffic Engring., City of Shreveport, La., 1980-85, 87; transp. analyst East-West Gateway Coord. Coun., St. Louis, from 1988. Pres. Boss Ave Neighborhood Watch Group, Shreveport, 1984-85; human resources com. City of Shreveport, 1983. With U.S. Army, 1971-73. Mem. Optimist, Pi Gamma Mu, Kappa Delta Pi. Methodist. Avocations: plants, potpourri, entrepreneurship. Home: Saint Louis, Mo. Died Dec. 13, 2004.

YOUNG, CHARLES ALEXANDER, artist, educator; b. N.Y.C., Nov. 17, 1930; s. Charles and Mary (Rodgers) Y.; m. Elizabeth Bell, Nov. 1968; children: Paula, Denise. BS, Hampton Inst., 1953; MA, NYU, 1959; postgrad., Cath. U., Washington, 1964, Bowie State U., 1975. Tchr. Dayton St. Pub. Sch., Newark, 1958-60; art instr. Fayetteville (N.C.) State U., 1960-63; asst. prof. Tenn. A&I State U., Nashville, 1963-68; prof., chmn. of art Fed. City Coll., Washington, 1968-78, U. D.C., 1978-84, prof., 1984-90, chmn. dept. art, 1990—2005. Artist-in-residence Va. Ctr. Creative Arts, 1989. One-man shows include Smith-Mason Gallery, Washington, 1969, The Centre d'Art, Port Au Prince, Haiti, 1982, Hampton (Va.) Mus., 1989; exhibited in group shows at N.J. State Mus., Trenton, 1972, Corcoran Gallery of Art, Washington, 1982, U. of D.C. Art Gallery, 1988, Mus. of Modern Art, Gibellina, Italy, 1989. 1st Lt. U.S. Army, 1953-55. Recipient D.C. Commn. of Arts plaque Mayor of D.C., 1979, Phelps-Stokes travel grantee, 1975. Mem. NAACP, Nat. Edn. Assn., AAUP, Nat. Art Edn. Assn., Nat. Conf. Artists, Coll. Art Assn. Democrat. Baptist. Avocations: bike riding, reading. Home: Washington, DC. Died June 5, 2005.

YOUNG, EVERETT CLAIR, industrial designer; b. Bondville, Ill., Sept. 21, 1922; s. George Henry and Iva Belle (Mitchell) Y.; children by previous marriage: Jerry, Kerry, Jan, Sandra, Cindy, Rennie, Glen. BA in Indsl. Design, U. Ill., 1947; MA in Vocational Edn., No. Ariz. U., 1985. Indsl. designer New Metal Crafts, Chgo., 1947-50, Van Esso Inc., Chgo., 1950-52, Phil R. Hinkley, Cleve., 1953-54; design cons. Young Enterprises, Cleve., 1955-65; free-lance designer U. Ill and Ariz. State U., 1966-78; dir. research Intergalactic, Inc., Flagstaff, Ariz., from 1983, pres., researcher, from 1983. Author: History's Greatest Epochal Lie, 1977; inventor, patentee heat shields and housing structures used in Gemini and Apollo spacecraft; other patents in field. Served with USAAF. Recipient Spirit of Arizona award Ariz. State. Senate, 1985. Avocation: all sports. Died Jan. 2, 2004.

YOUNG, FRANCIS ALLAN, psychologist; b. Utica, N.Y., Dec. 29, 1918; s. Frank Allan and Julia Mae (McOwen) Y.; m. Judith Wadsworth Wright, Dec. 21, 1945; children—Francis Allan, Thomas Robert. BS, U. Tampa, 1941; MA, Western Res. U., 1945; PhD, Ohio State U., 1949. Instr. Wash. State U., Pullman, 1948-50, asst. prof., 1950-56, assoc. prof., 1956-61, prof. psychology, 1961-88, dir. primate rsch. ctr., 1957-88, prof., dir. emeritus, from 1988. Vis. prof. ophthalmology U. Oreg., Portland, 1964; asst. dir. U. Wash. Regional Primate Ctr., dir. primate field sta., 1966-68; vis. prof. pharmacology U. Uppsala (Sweden) Med. Sch., 1971; vis. prof. optometry U. Houston, 1979-80 Editor: (with Donald B. Lindsley) Early Experience and Visual Information Processing in Perceptual and Reading Disorders, 1970; contbr. chpts. to books, numerous articles to profl. jours. Named Disting. Psychologist State of Wash., Wash. Psychol. Assn., 1973; recipient Paul Yarwood Meml.

award Calif. Optometric Assn., 1978; Apollo award Am. Optometric Assn., 1980; Nat. Acad. Sci.-NRC sr. postdoctoral fellow in physiol. psychology U. Wash., 1956-57; research grantee NSF, 1950-53; research grantee USAF, 1965-72; research grantee NIH, 1960-78 Home: Pullman, Wash. Died May 24, 2006.

YOUNG, GLENNA ASCHE, elementary school educator; b. Lodi, Ohio, Apr. 14, 1955; d. Virgil Eugene and B. Lucille (Johnson) Asche; m. William Young, Aug. 6, 1983. BS, Ohio State U., 1977, cert. learning-behavioral disorders, 1981; MS, Ashland Coll., Columbus Ohio, 1988. Cert. K-12 phys. edn. tchr., Ohio. Kindergarten and elem. phys. edn. tchr. West Jefferson (Ohio) Local Schs., 1979-82; high sch. tchr. severe behavioral handicapped Madison County Schs., London, Ohio, 1982-86; elem. tchr. learning disabled SW Licking Local Schs., Etna, Ohio, 1986-88, tchr. elem. phys. edn., from 1988. Treas. Etna Sch. PTO, 1989-91. Recipient Golden Apple award Ashland Oil Co. Mem. West Jefferson Edn. Assn. (Disting. Svc. award, President's award), SW Licking Local Edn. Assn. (bldg. rep. 1989-92, sec. 2002—). Home: Pickerington, Ohio. Died Sept. 15, 2004.

YOUNG, JAMES HARVEY, historian, educator; b. Bklyn., Sept. 8, 1915; s. W. Harvey and Blanche (DeBra) Y.; m. Myrna Goode, Aug. 25, 1940 (dec. Oct. 2000); children: Harvey Galen, James Walter. BA, Knox Coll., 1937, D.H.L., 1971; MA, U. Ill., 1938, PhD, 1941; D.Sc., Rush U., 1976. Mem. faculty Emory U., 1941-84, prof. history, 1958-80, Charles Howard Candler prof. Am. social history, 1980-84, prof. emeritus, 1984—2006, chmn. dept., 1958-66. Vis. assoc. prof. Columbia U., 1949-50; mem. nat. adv. food and drug council FDA, 1964-67; mem. Consumers Task Force, White House Conf. on Food, Nutrition and Health, 1969; mem. history life scis. study sect. NIH, 1970-73, 79-80, 91-93, chmn., 1992-93; vis. lectr. Am. Assn. Colls. Pharmacy Vis. Lectrs. Program, 1970-73; cons.-panelist NEH, 1970-83; cons. in history Centers for Disease Control; advisor Am. Coun. Sci. and Health; Logan Clendening lectr. U. Kans. Med. Ctr., 1973; Samuel X. Radbill lectr. Phila. Coll. Physicians, 1978; Beaumont lectr. Yale U., 1980; vis. hist. scholar Nat. Library Medicine, 1986; Harold J. Lawn lectr. U. Minn., 1990; David L. Cowen lectr. Rutgers U., 1990; James Campbell lectr. Rush U., 1992; Waring lectr. Med. U. S.C., 1993; Charles Jackson lectr. U. Tenn., 2001, Cavulier Club lectr., 2002. Author: The Toadstool Millionaires, 1961, The Medical Messiahs, 1967, expanded edit., 1992, American Self-Dosage Medicines, An Historical Perspective, 1974, Pure Food: Securing the Federal Food and Drugs Act of 1906, 1989, American Health Quackery: Collected Essays, 1992; editor: (with W.A. Beardslee and T.J.J. Altizer) Truth, Myth and Symbol, 1962, (with T.L. Savitt) Disease and Distinctiveness in the American South, 1988. Served with AUS, 1943-45. Recipient Arts and Scis. award of distinction Emory U., 1999; FDA rsch. appointee, 1977-85; Carnegie rsch. grantee, 1947, USPHS grantee, 1960-65, Nat. Libr. Medicine grantee, 1990-94; Faculty fellow Fund Advancement Edn., 1954-55, Social Sci. Rsch. Coun. fellow, 1960-61, Guggenheim fellow, 1966-67. Mem. Am. Hist. Assn., So. Hist. Assn. (pres. 1982), Orgn. Am. Historians, Soc. Am. Historians, Am. Assn. History of Medicine (coun., Fielding H. Garrison lectr. 1979, William H. Welch medal 1982, Continuing Lifetime Achievement award 1992), Am. Inst. History of Pharmacy (coun., hon. pres. 1993-95, Edward Kremers award 1962), Phi Beta Kappa, Sigma Xi, Phi Kappa Phi, Omicron Delta Kappa, Phi Alpha Theta. Congregationalist. Died July 29, 2006.

YOUNG, LEO, electrical engineer; b. Vienna, Aug. 18, 1926; came to U.S., 1953, naturalized, 1958; s. Samuel and Marie Y.; m. Fay Merskey, Jan. 4, 1953 (dec. May 1981); children— Philip Michael, Sarah Anne, Joseph David; m. Ruth Breslow, Jan. 2, 1983 (dec. Nov. 1996); m. Jo-Ellen Turner, July 9, 1999. BA, Cambridge U., 1946, MA, 1950; MS, Johns Hopkins U., 1956, D.Engring. (Westinghouse-B.G. Lamme grad. scholar), 1959, D.H.L. (hon.), 1989. Mgr. lab. Decca Radar, Ltd., Surbiton, England, 1951—53; adv. engr. Westinghouse Electric Corp., Balt., 1953—60; staff scientist, program mgr. Stanford Rsch. Inst., Menlo Park, Calif., 1960—73; staff cons., assoc. supt. Naval Rsch. Lab., Washington, 1973—81; dir. rsch. Office Under sec. Def. Rsch. and Engring. US Dept. Def., 1981—94, cons. to dir. def. rsch. and engring., 1994—2002; bd. dirs. Filtronic-Comtek, England. Mem. NSF delegation to Japan, 1995, 99; chair NSF Rev. Panel on Critical Techs., 1997; chair adv. com. dept. elec. and computer engring. Johns Hopkins U., 2003; taught Leeds U., Israel Inst. Tech., Marconi Inst. at Bologna U.; founding mem. NAS/NAE Govt.-Univ.-Industry Rsch. Roundtable. Author: Microwave Filters, 1964, Systems of Units in Electricity and Magnetism, 1969, Advances in Microwaves, Vols. 1-8, 1966-74, Everything You Should Know About Pensions Plans, 1976; also articles; patentee in field. Recipient Woodrow Wilson award for Disting. Govt. Svc., 2001, Outstanding Performance award, Naval Rsch. Lab., Letter of Appreciation, Sect. Def. Casper Weinberger. Fellow: IEEE (pres. 1980, Microwave prize 1963, Disting. Contbns. to Engring. Professionalism award 1993, Pinnacle award 1995, Centennial award, Citation of Honor, Microwave Career award 1988), AAAS; mem.: NAE (Athur M. Bueche award 2005), Am. Assn. Engring. Societies (bd. gov.), Electromagnetics Acad., Royal Acad. Engring. U.K., Microwave Soc. (life; pres. 1969), Sigma Xi. Died Sept. 14, 2006.

YOUNG, MARGARET ALETHA MCMULLEN (MRS. HERBERT WILSON YOUNG), social worker; b. Vossburg, Miss., June 13, 1916; d. Grady Garland and Virgie Aletha (Moore) McMullen; m. Herbert Wilson Young, Aug. 19, 1959. BA cum laude, Columbia Bible Coll., 1949; grad., Massey Bus. Coll., 1958; MSW, Fla. State U., 1965; postgrad., Jacksonville U., 1961-62; MA in Old Testament, Tulane U., 1967, Columbia Internat. U., 1992. Dir. Christian edn. Eau Claire Presbyn. Ch., Columbia, S.C., 1946-51; tchr. Massey Bus. Coll., Jacksonville, Fla., 1954-57, office mgr., 1957-59; social worker, unit supr. Fla. divsn. Family Svcs., St. Petersburg, 1960-66, dist. casework supr., 1966-71; social worker, project supr., program supr. Project Playpen, Inc., 1971-81, pres. bd., 1982-83, cons., 1986-89; pvt. practice family counselor, from 1982. Mem. coun. Child Devel. Ctr., 1983-89; mem. transitional housing com. Religious Cmty. Svcs., 1984-90. Mem. Acad. Cert. Social Workers, Nat. Assn. Social Workers (pres. Tampa Bay chpt. 1973-74), Fla. Assn. for Health and Social Svcs. (pres. chpt. 1971), Nature Conservancy, Rotary Ann (pres. 1970-71), Eta Beta Rho. Democrat. Presbyterian. Home: Summerville, SC. Died Apr. 7, 2006.

YOUNG, RAYMOND H(INCHCLIFFE), JR., chemist; b. Penusauken, N.J., Nov. 22, 1928; s. Raymond Hinchcliffe and Elisabeth Delores (Hand) Y.; m. Nancy Lee Totten, June 20, 1953 (div. 1975); children: JoAnne, Raymond, Michael, Janet; m. Carol Ann Smith, Dec. 5, 1975; children: Warren, Kimberly. BS, Pa. Mil. Coll., 1953; MS, U. Maine, 1955, PhD, 1961. Specialist Monsanto Co., Springfield, Mass., 1960-70; rsch. chemist Freeport Kaolin Co., Gordon, Ga., 1970-84; sr. devel. assoc. Engelhard Corp., Gordon, 1984-99; retired, 1999. Contbr. articles to profl. publs. Cpl. USMC, 1946-48. Mem. Am. Chem. Soc. (Arthur K. Doolittle award coatings and plastics div. 1972), Clay Minerals Soc., Soc. for Mining, Metallurgy and Experimentation, Sigma Xi (rsch. award 1955). Achievements include 8 patents for polymeric UV stabilizers, 7 patents for beneficiations process for kaolin clay. Home: Macon, Ga. Died July 14, 2005.

YOUNG, ROBERT WILLIAM, tool distribution executive, orthodontist; b. Wood-Ridge, N.J., Feb. 23, 1920; s. Isaac Varian and Jeannette G. (Schmidt) Y.; m. Helen Elizabeth Harbour, Mar. 2, 1946; children: Lorna B. Truck, Robert W. Jr., Joann Louise, Kenneth Harbour. Student, NYU, 1937-38; DDS, U. Pa., 1942; AB in Gen. Sci., Drake U., 1963, MDiv, 1968; D Ministries, St. Paul Sch. Theology, 1989; cert. orthodontics, Columbia U., 1954. Pvt. practice gen. dentistry, Hasbrouck Heights, N.J., 1946-52; pvt. practice orthodontics Des Moines, 1954-84; min. various United. Meth. chs. Iowa conf., 1968-70; owner 3 camera stores, Des Moines, 1964-73; distbr. Ace Air Tools, Inc., Des Moines, from 1974. Co-author: Movement in Devitalized Teeth, 1955. Maj. U.S. Army, 1942-46. Mem. Am. Orthodontic Soc. (conv. demonstrator 1970), Grand Lodge Iowa, Kiwanis (officer 1958—). Republican. Avocation: rebuilding antique automobiles. Home: West Des Moines, Iowa. Died Jan. 19, 2004.

YOUNG, THOMAS J., mortgage company executive; b. Midland, S.D., June 12, 1949; s. R.H. and Gwen (Jones) Y.; divorced 1976; children: Susan, Mike, Mark (twins); m. Joyce Young, Aug. 25, 1979. BS in Bus. Adm., St. Joseph Coll., Phila., 1972; postgrad., John Marshall Law Sch., Atlanta, 1977-78. Br. mgr. Borg Warner Acceptance Corp., Cocoa, Fla., 1973-77; regional credit mgr. Comml. Credit Equipment Corp., Atlanta, 1977-79; div. credit mgr. GEICO, Atlanta, 1979-82; account exec. Bank Am., Atlanta, 1982-83; regional V.P. Security Pacific Nat. Bank, Atlanta, 1983-86; v.p. Consol. Capital Co., Atlanta, 1986-88; pres., chief exec. officer Tha Wall St. Mortage Co., Atlanta, from 1988. Bd. dirs. TJY & Assoc., The Crogan Corp. (chmn.) Lawrenceville, Ga.; cons. Small Bus. Assn., Atlanta; faculty speaker at Ga. Tech. Bd. dirs., v.p. Pop Warner Youth Football Assn., Doraville, Ga., 1977-79; chmn. Sch. Adv. Com. Lawrenceville, 1985; commr. Lawrenceville Housing Authority, 1986—; high sch. football referee. Recipient Task Force award Rep. Party, Washington, 1985. Mem. Am. Arbitration Assn., Mortgage Banker Assn., Crittendon Research Group (natl. speaker). Baptist. Avocations: boating, golf. Home: Lawrenceville, Ga. Died Aug. 13, 2004.

YOUNG, WARREN HAROLD, savings and loan executive; b. Bklyn., Aug. 22, 1923; s. Harold and Mary (White) Y.; m. W. Katherine Wagner; children: Genevieve, Sally. Grad. cum laude, NYU, 1953, MBA, 1955. Various personnel, indsl. engring., data processing and prodn. mgmt. positions Sperry Gyroscope Corp. and Bulova Watch Co.; pres., chmn. bd. Yorkville Fed. Savs. and Loan, Bronx, N.Y., from 1959. Former N.Y. state rep. for Nat. Assn. State Savs. and Loan Suprs. Mem. Nat. Assn. Rev. Appraisers, Rev. Mortgage Underwriters, Westchester League of Savs. Instns. (pres.), Soc. Advancement Mgmt. (charter L.I. chpt.), Pres.'s Assn. Home: Youngsville, NC. Died July 4, 2004.

YOUNG, WILLIAM HURLBURT, JR., psychiatrist; b. Newton, Mass., June 1, 1920; s. William Hurlburt and Martha (Booth) Y.; m. Annette Jackson, Mar. 12, 1949; children: Arianne, Kevin, Michael, Lorraine. BS, Harvard U., 1942; MD, U. Mich., 1945. Diplomate Am. Bd. Psychiatry and Neurology. Resident in psychiatry St. Elizabeths Hosp., Washington, 1948-50; fellow in psychiatry Austen Riggs Ctr., Stockbridge, Mass., 1950-51; dir. Alexandria (Va.) Mental Health Clinic, 1951-56; pvt. practice Alexandria, Va., 1951-74; Culpeper, Va., 1974-81; pvt. practice Washington, Va., from 1981; chmn. dept. psychiatry Alexandria Hosp., 1961-67; asst. clin. prof. George Washington U. Sch. Medicine, Washington, 1960-74; faculty Washington Sch. of Psychiatry, 1961-70; med. dir. Rappahannock-Rapidan Mental Health Ctr., Culpeper, 1974-81; physician Comp Health, Salt Lake City, from 1990. Bd. dirs. Hospice of Rapidan, Culpeper; cons. Garrison Counseling, Front Royal, Va., 1988—, Warren Meml. Hosp., Front Royal, 1980—; asst. clin. prof. U. Va. Sch. Medicine, Chalottesville, 1974—; chmn. child mental health study commn. Dept. Mental Health and Retardation, 1975-80; chmn. govs. mental health adv. coun., 1971-76, investigation Anafranil Investigative New Drug humanitarian protocol, 1987-91 Contbr. articles to profl. jours. Chmn. bd. trustees Rappahannock County Pub. Libr., 1985—; chmn. film com. Rappahannock Assn. for the Arts and Comty., Washington, 1983; chmn., mem. civic orgns., 1951—. Capt. U.S. Army, 1946-48. Fellow Am. Psychiat. Assn. (life); mem. AMA, Am. Soc. Adolescent Psychiatry (v.p. 1977), Va. Neuropsychiat. Soc., Washington Psychiat. Soc. (treas. exec. com. D.C. 1960's, chmn. N. Va. chpt. 1960's), Piedmont Environ. Coun. Avocations: photography, gardening, reading, movies, classical music. Home: Washington, Va. Died Jan. 8, 2004.

ZABRISKIE, GEORGE ALBERT, film, video maker; b. Evanston, Oct. 24, 1926; s. George Albert and Dorothy Joyce (Yonkers) Z.; m. Virginia Marshall, June, 1953 (div. Dec. 1961); m. Sherry LaFollette, Feb. 10, 1962; children: Oliver, Tavia LaFollette. BA in History, Princeton U., 1948. USN-V12 Yale U., New Haven, 1944-46; film assoc. Internat. Film Found., N.Y.C., 1949-52; 2d lt. writer Signal Corps ASPC, N.Y.C., 1952-54, U.S. Army civilian writer, 1954-56; film maker Zabriskie Prodns., N.Y.C., 1956-68, Buenos Aires, 1968-71, Ackworth, N.H., 1971-73, Salisbury, Conn., 1973-83, Bklyn. Heights, N.Y., from 1983. Writer, producer over 23 films including Summerdog, 1977, various books and videos; author (e-book) Basic Wine Smarts, 2001. Campaign film Steven Minot/Congrl., Conn., 1962; pres. N.Y. State United World Federalists, N.Y.C., 1960-62; campaign comml. producer Former Congressman Paul McCloskey's Presdl. Quest, N.H., 1972; fund raising chmn.-films-Dem. Town Com., Salisbury, Conn., 1976-78. Blue Ribbon winner Am. Film Festival, 1960, Golden Eagle winner Coun. for Internat./Short, 1964; grantee The Josephine Bay Paul/C. Michael Paul Found., 1988. Mem. Authors Guild. Democrat. Avocations: travel, walking, museums, theater, books, gardening. Home: Brooklyn, NY. Died July 4, 2005.

ZAHN, CLIFFORD JAMES, accountant, consultant; b. Wausau, Wis., June 1, 1932; s. Harry D. and Elsie L. (Krueger) Z.; m. Victoria M. Tewes, Aug. 23, 1958; children: Jonathan C., Christopher J., Tonja V. BBA, Marquette U., 1959; MBA, U. Wis., Milw., 1966. CPA, Wis. Ptnr. Peat, Marwick, Mitchell & Co., Milw., 1959-82; pvt. practice small bus. investment, mgmt. cons., acctg. Milw., from 1982. Cons. in field; bd. dirs. Allied Computer Group, Milw., Badger Case, Inc., Milw. Chmn. bd. fin. St. John's Luth. Ch., 1980-84. Served with U.S. Army, 1952-54. Mem. Nat. Assn. CPA's (local pres. 1977-78), Am. Inst. CPA's, Wis. Inst. CPA's, Inst. of Internal Auditors. Clubs: Wisconsin, North Shore Athletic, Concordia Coll. Century (Milw.) (bd. dirs. treas. 1985—). Republican. Lutheran. Home: Milwaukee, Wis. Died July 28, 2005.

ZAK, BENNIE, pathology educator; b. Detroit, Sept. 29, 1919; s. Morris and Lena (Snyder) Z.; m. Doris Kitty Selby; children: Steven Dennis, Deborah Lise Zak Tataranowicz, Marsha Gale. BS, Wayne State U., 1948, PhD, 1952. Jr. assoc. pathology Detroit Receiving Hosp., 1951-59; asst. prof. clin. chemistry in pathology Wayne State U., Detroit, 1957, from asst. prof. to assoc. prof., 1961-63, prof., 1965-91, prof. emeritus, from 1991. Cons. in field. Contbr. articles to profl. jours. Served to 1st lt. USAF, 1941-45. Recipient Faculty Rsch. award Wayne State U., 1973, Disting. Svc. award, 1983; Benedetti-Pichlr award Am. Microchem. Soc., 1984. Fellow Nat. Acad. Clin. Biochemists; mem. Am. Chem. Soc., Am. Assn. Clin. Chemistry (Ames award 1974, gen. diagnostics lectr. 1981). Avocation: writing. Died July 29, 2005.

ZAMOLSKY, GERALDINE FLORENCE, nurse administrator; b. Bklyn., May 12, 1939; d. Jack and Florence (Masamino) Cardullo; m. Lawrence Zamolsky, Oct. 16, 1999. AA in Nursing, Fairleigh Dickinson U., 1960; BS, Mercy Coll., 1986. Cert. nursing adminstr. Staff nurse Mount Sinai Hosp., N.Y.C., 1960-61, Englewood (N.J.) Hosp., 1961-64; asst. head nurse N.J. Coll. Medicine, Jersey City, 1964-66; head nurse, acting supr. Mt. Sinai Hosp., N.Y.C., 1966-68; sr. adminstrv. supr. Phelps Meml. Hosp., North Tarrytown, N.Y., 1969-85; asst. dir. field ops. Rain Home Attendant, Bronx, N.Y., 1985-86; dir. br. svcs. U.S. Home Care, Bronx, 1986-87; dir. clin. svcs. Kimberly Quality Care, New Rochelle, N.Y., 1987-92; corp. dir. nursing Unltd. Care Inc., White Plains, N.Y., 1992-94; co-owner, founder, adminstr. Forget-Me-Not Tng., Inc., White Plains, N.Y., 1994-2001; RN instrn. Allen Health Care, Bronx, from 2001. Recipient Amita Nursing award, 1969, Nurse award N.Y. State Legislature, 1992; named Dir. Clin. Svcs. of Yr. Lower N.Y. Region, 1990. Mem. N.Y. State Nurses Assn. Home: Cortlandt Mnr, NY. Died July 5, 2005.

ZANELLA, JOHN ANTHONY, JR., tile company executive; b. Grand Rapids, Mich., Aug. 22, 1943; s. John Anthony and Virginia T. (Young) Z.; m. Gwen Rose Dowling, June 25, 1966; children: Rosemary, John Carl, Patrick, Mollie Jo. Student, Davenport Coll., 1962-63, Ferris State Coll., 1964-65. Vice-pres. Grand Rapids Tile and Mosaic Co., 1981-85, pres., from 1985. Mem. Beaver Island (Mich.) Planning Commn., 1978. With U.S. Army, 1966-69. Mem. Alto Businessmen's Assn. (v.p. 1975-76), Grand Rapids Lions Club. Roman Catholic. Avocations: farming, hunting, fishing, boating, travel. Died Dec. 12, 2004.

ZAPRUDER, HENRY GEORGE, lawyer; b. N.Y.C., Mar. 28, 1938; s. Abraham and Lillian Zapruder; m. Marjorie Seiger, Oct. 31, 1963; children: Matthew, Michael, Alexandra. BBA, Okla. U., 1959; LLB, Harvard U., 1962; post-doctoral, Oxford U. Bar: Tex. 1962, D.C. 1967, U.S. Ct. Appeals (D.C. cir.). Atty. tax divsn. U.S. Dept. Justice, Washington, 1963-67; atty., advisor Office Tax Legis. Counsel U.S. Dept. Trasury, Washington, 1967-69; ptnr. Cohen & Uretz, Washington, 1969-85, Morgan, Lewis & Bockius, Washington, 1985—89; founding ptnr. Zapruder & Odell, Washington, 1989—98; sr. ptnr. Baker & Hostetler LLP, Washington, 1998—2006. Home: Bethesda, Md. Died Jan. 24, 2006.

ZEIDLER, FRANK P., former association administrator, former mayor; b. Milw., Sept. 20, 1912; s. Michael and Clara (Nitschke) Z.; m. Agnes Reinke; children: Clara, Dorothy, Michael, Anita, Mary, Jeannette. Student, Marquette U., 1930, U. Wis. Extension Div., 1930-70, U. Chgo., 1937; LLD (hon.), U. Wis., 1958, St. Olaf Coll., 1988; LHD (hon.), Carthage Coll., 1983, Mt. Mary Coll., 1993, U. Wis.-Milw., 1990. Dir. Milw. Pub. Schs., 1941-48; mayor City of Milw., 1948-60; dir. Wis. Dept. Resource Devel., 1963-64. Sec. emeritus Pub. Enterprise Com.; mem. U.S. nat. commn. UNESCO, 1953, 56, 59. Author: A Liberal in City Government, 1962 Pres. Ctrl. North Cmty. Coun.; pres. Greater Milw. UN Assn., pres.; nat. chmn. Socialist Party U.S.A., 1973-83; Socialist Party candidate for Pres. U.S., 1976; convenor Dem. Socialist Conf.; past pres. Luth. Social Action Conf.; bd. dirs. Goethe House, Milw., Milw. Theol. Inst.; mem. exec. coun. Luth. Ch. Am., 1980-82; hon. mem. cabinet Interfaith Conf. Greater Milw.; chmn. Norman Thomas Inst. for Peace and Social Justice. Named One of 10 Outstanding Young Men, Nat. Jr. C. of C., 1949; recipient Eugene V. Debs award, 1977. Mem. Milw. World Federalist Assn. (bd. dirs.), Nat. Model R.R. Assn. (founder). Home: Milwaukee, Wis. Died July 7, 2006.

ZEIGEN, SPENCER STEVEN, architect, consultant; b. Bklyn., Oct. 11, 1924; s. David and Ehtel (Katz) Zeigen; m. Mildred Weinman, Dec. 27, 1952 (dec. Sept. 1992); children: Steven, Scott; m. Lillian Glogau, Oct. 10, 1993; children: Jordan, Laurence, Alexander. BFA summa cum laude, U. Pa., 1952. Registered arch., N.J. Arch. Leo Fischer Arch., South Orange, N.J., 1952-54, Frank Grad Sons Arch., Newark, 1954-64; staff arch. Rutgers State U., New Brunswick, NJ, 1964-74; pvt. practice Highland Park, NJ, 1974-78, Jamesburg, NJ, 1978—2004; arch. Collins, Uhl, Hoisington, Anderson Arch., Princeton, NJ, 1978-80; dir. of arch. Brown Hale Arch., Newark, 1980-82, Brown & Mathews, Fords, NJ, 1982-86. Lectr. Rutgers U., 1961—65; instr. arch. Newark Coll. Engring., 1963—69; litig. expert witness, from 1980; cons. roofing expert, litig. expert witness Kipcon, Inc., North Brunswick, NJ, from 1980, bldg. materials analyst, from 1988; bd. arch. High Rise Condominiums, Fort Lee, NJ, 1982—89. Prin. works include N.J. Divsn. Motor Vehicles Testing Facilities, N.J. Cultural Ctr., Rutgers U. Ednl. Facilities. Bd. dirs. Whittingham Homeowners Assn., Monroe Township, NJ, 1990—93. Sgt. USAF, 1942—46. Mem.: Am. Soc. Planners, Am. Soc. Arch. Democrat. Jewish. Avocations: bridge, tennis, Bocce, reading, drawing. Died Mar. 22, 2004.

ZIEGLER, DANIEL MARTIN, chemistry professor; b. Quinter, Kans., July 6, 1927; s. Anton T. and Clara (Weissbeck) Z.; m. Mary Alice Weir, Aug. 19, 1952; children: Daniel L., Paul W., Mary Claire, James M. BS in Chemistry, St. Benedicts Coll., 1949; PhD in Chemistry, Loyola U., 1955; postdoctoral, U. Wis., 1955-58; DSc (hon.), Benedictine Coll., 2001. Asst. prof. Inst. Enzyme Rsch. U. Wis., Madison, 1958-61; asst. prof. chemistry U. Tex., Austin, 1961-62, assoc. prof. chemistry, 1962-69, prof. chemistry, 1969-97, Roger J. Williams Centennial prof. in biochemistry, 1990-97, prof. emeritus, from 1997. Editor jour. Biol. Chemistry, 1979-83, 85-90, 93-98; mem. editl. bd. Analyt. Biochemistry, 1989-91, Arch. Biochem. Biophys., 1966-71; contbr. articles to profl. jours. Recipient Bernard B. Brodie award Am. Soc. Pharmacol. Exptl. Therapeutics, 1990, Alexander von Humboldt award, Germany, 1991; estab. investigator Am. Heart Assn., 1960-65. Mem. Internat. Soc. for the Study of Xenobiotics (hon. life). Home: Austin, Tex. Died Nov. 9, 2005.

ZIEGLER, ROBERT F., cardiologist; b. Detroit, Mar. 30, 1916; s. Gustave Adolph and Clara Louise (Niepoth) Z.; m. Grace Charlotte Eberle, Apr. 10, 1951; children: Sally, David, James, Michael. BA, Wayne State U., 1937; MD, U. Mich., 1941. Diplomate Am. Bd. Internal Medicine, Am. Bd. Cardiovascular Disease, Am. Bd. Cardiology, Am. Bd. Pediatric Cardiology. Intern Henry Ford Hosp., Detroit, 1941-42, resident in medicine, 1942-43, resident in cardiovascular disease, 1943-46; resident pediat. cardiology Johns Hopkins Hosp., Balt., 1946-47; adj. prof. biol. sci. Mich. Tech. U., Houghton, 1970-85. Author: EKG Studies in Normal Infants and Chilren, 1951, Cardiac Evaluation in Normal Infants, 1965; contbr. chpts. to books and articles to profl. jours. Pres. Aid Assn. Lutherans, Hancock, 1993-95; bd. dirs. Habitat for Humanity, Hancock, 1996-97, chair ch. rels. com., 1997-2001. Mem. Am. Coll. Cardiology, Am. Coll. Chest Physicians, Am. Heart Assn., Keweenaw Kiwanis. Died Jan. 24, 2006.

ZIEGLER, WILLIAM JOHN, JR., retired podiatrist; b. Phila., July 19, 1922; s. William John and Louisa S. Ziegler; m. Marion Edythe Dotter, Sept. 8, 1943. D of Podiatric Medicine, Temple U., 1948; D of Humane Letters, Pa. Coll. Podiatric Medicine, 1988. Instr. anatomy dept. Temple U., Podiatry Sch., Phila., 1948-60; assoc. med. staff Am. Oncological Hosp., Phila., 1972-88; assoc. profl. staff Jeanes Hosp., Phila., 1964-88, chief podiatry sect., 1980-88; ret., from 1988. Sr. mem. bd. trustees Pa. Coll. Podiatric Medicine, Phila., 1960—; pres. podiatric alumni assn. Temple U., Phila., 1953-55. With U.S. Army Med. Corps, 1943-45. Recipient British Soc. Chiropodists hon. fellowship degree, 1991. Fellow Am. Assn. Hosp. Podiatrist, Am. Assn. Podiatric Radiologists; mem. Am. Podiatric Med. Assn., Pa. Podiatric Med. Assn., Bucks-Montgomery Podiatric Med. Assn. (past pres. 1951), Masons (32 Degree). Republican. Lutheran. Avocations: gradening, volunteer archivist. Home: Philadelphia, Pa. Died June 5, 2005.

ZIEVE, MORTON, advertising executive; b. Detroit, Apr. 18, 1927; s. Benjamin E. and Frieda (Lieberman) Z.; m. Mary Lou Simons, June 1, 1958; children: Rob, Melissa Zieve Miller. BA summa cum laude, Wayne State U., 1948; MA, Stanford U., 1950. Producer dir. ABC TV, Detroit, 1950-60; ptnr. Simons Michelson, Inc., Troy, Mich., 1960-77; chmn. Simons Michielson Zieve, Inc., Troy, from 1977. Composer (musical scores) Who Calls It War?, 1948, How Many Minutes to Midnight, 1984. Bd. dirs., trustee Mich. Opera Theatre, Detroit. Recipient Humanity in Arts award Wayne State U., 1984. Mem. Dirs. Guild Am., Intermarket Assn. Advt. Agys., Adcraft Club Detroit. Avocations: composing music, tennis, travel. Home: Bloomfield Hills, Mich. Died Aug. 8, 2005.

ZIFF, WILLIAM BERNARD, JR., retired publishing executive; b. June 24, 1930; s. William B. and Amelia (Morton) Z.; m. Tamsen Ann Kojis, 1987; children from previous marriage: Dirk Edward, Robert David, Daniel Morton. BA, Rutgers U., 1951; postgrad., Heidelberg U., 1952-53, U. Madrid, 1952-53. Ptnr., then owner and chmn. Ziff Davis Pub. Co., N.Y.C., until 1984; chmn., CEO Ziff Communication Co., N.Y.C., 1953—94; ret., 1993. Died Sept. 9, 2006.

ZILZ, MELVIN LEONARD, pastor, ministry educator; b. Detroit, Apr. 15, 1932; s. Charles William and Merle Martha (Yaeger) Z.; m. Carole Jean Brandt, Aug. 17, 1957; children: Karen, Kathryn, Paul. BS, Concordia U., River Forest, Ill., 1953; MS, MA, U. Mich., 1964; PhD, Wayne State U., 1970; colloquy diploma, Concordia Theol. Sem., Ft. Wayne, Ind., 1978. Ordained to ministry Luth. Ch., 1978. Instr. Concordia Luth. Sch., Chgo., 1953-57, Luth. High Sch. East, Detroit, 1957-65; asst. prof. biology Concordia Sr. Coll., Ft. Wayne, 1965-72, assoc. prof., 1972-76, chmn. dept. biology, 1971-72, registrar, 1972-77; assoc. prof. pastoral ministry Concordia Theol. Sem., 1976-78, prof., from 1978, asst. to pres., 1976-78, assoc. acad. dean, 1977-78, dean of adminstrn., 1978-83; pastor Clear Lake Luth. Ch., Fremont, Ind., 1983-84, Bethlehem Luth. Ch., Ossian, Ind., 1987-88, New Hope Luth. Ch., Ossian, 1988, Zion Luth. Ch., Columbia City, Ind., 1988-91. Foster parent Luth. Social Svcs., Ft. Wayne. NSF study fellow, 1960-64, 65-67. Avocations: classical music, travel, cooking, photography, fishing. Home: Fort Wayne, Ind. Died Apr. 5, 2005.

ZIMM, BRUNO HASBROUCK, physical chemistry educator; b. Woodstock, N.Y., Oct. 31, 1920; s. Bruno L. and Louise S. (Hasbrouck) Z.; m. Georgianna S. Grevatt, June 17, 1944; children: Louis H., Carl B. AB, Columbia U., 1941, MS, 1943, PhD, 1944. Research assoc. Columbia U., 1944; research assoc., instr. Polytech. Inst. Bklyn., 1944-46; instr. chemistry U. Calif. at Berkeley, 1946-47, asst. prof., 1947-50, assoc. prof., 1950-51; vis. lectr. Harvard U., 1950-51; research assoc. research lab. Gen. Electric Co., 1951-60; prof. chemistry U. Calif., San Diego, 1960-91, prof. emeritus, 1991—2005. Assoc. editor: Jour. Chem. Physics, 1947-49; adv. bd.: Jour. Polymer Sci., 1953-62, Jour. Bio-Rheology, 1962-73, Jour. Biopolymers, 1963-2005, Jour. Phys. Chemistry, 1963-68, Jour. Biophys. Chemistry, 1973-2005. Recipient Bingham Medal Soc. Rheology, 1960, High Polymer Physics prize Am. Phys. Soc., 1963; Kirkwood medal Yale U., 1982 Mem. Biophys. Soc., Am. Soc. Biol. Chemists and Molecular Biologists, Am. Chem. Soc. (Baekeland award 1957), Nat. Acad. Scis. (award in Chem. Scis. 1981), Am. Acad. Arts and Scis., Am. Phys. Soc. Home: La Jolla, Calif. Died Nov. 26, 2005.

ZIMMERMAN, MARGARET HANSON, accountant, educator; b. Phila., June 27, 1928; d. Edwin M.T. and Ednamay (LaChappele) Hanson; m. Albright G. Zimmerman. BS in Commerce, Drexel U., 1950; MBA, Temple U., 1958. CPA, Pa. Prin. Margaret H. Zimmerman, CPA, Yardley, Pa., from 1962; prof. Rider Coll., Lawrenceville, N.J., 1955-60; vis. lectr. Drexel U., Phila., 1960-61; adj. faculty Trenton (N.J.) State Coll., 1963-65; prof. Bucks County Community Coll., Newton, Pa., 1965-88, prof. emeritus, from 1988. Com. mem. Pa. Inst. CPA's; past prof. Drexel U., Phila., Trenton (N.J.) State Coll., Bucks County Community Coll., Newton, Pa. Auditor Twp. of Lower Makefield, Phila., 1963-81. Recipient Outstanding Alumnae Chpt. award Gamma Sigma Sigma; named to Temple U. Acctg. Hall of Fame, 1987. Mem. AICPA, Pa. Inst. CPA's, Am. Women Soc. CPA's. Died Apr. 6, 2005.

ZION, LEELA CLARICE, retired physical education educator; b. San Francisco, Nov. 4, 1929; d. Edwin Ray and Clarice Leela (Davis) Z. AA, San Mateo Jr. Coll., 1948; BA, Chico State Coll., 1950; MA, Stanford U., 1951; postgrad., UCLA, 1958; EdD, U. Calif., Berkeley, 1963. Tchr. San Juan Union High Sch., Fair Oaks, Calif., 1951-53, Cen. Washington Coll., Ellensburg, 1953-55; service club dir. U.S. Govt., Laon, France, 1955-58; lectr. Mills Coll., 1958-59; prof. health and phys. edn. and women's studies. Humboldt State U., Arcata, Calif., 1959-93. Author: The Physical Side of Learning, 1994; co-author: The Physical Side of Thinking, 1986; producer film Love All, 1970; contbr. article and poetry to profl. publs. Mem. AAHPERD, Internat. Soc. for Gen. Semantics, Am. Badminton Assn., Human Psychology Assn., Greenpeace. Democrat. Avocations: badminton, fiction writing, camping. Home: Bayside, Calif. Died July 21, 2004.

ZOGLIN, MARY LOU, retired college dean, city official; b. York, Pa., Sept. 30, 1928; d. Stuart Edward and Ruth Louise (Strickhouser) Glatfelter; m. Stanton Francis Zoglin, Feb. 14, 1953 (dec. 1976); children: John, Kathryn, William. BA, Radcliffe Coll., Cambridge, Mass., 1949; MA, Vanderbilt U., 1955; PhD, U. Calif., Berkeley, 1979. Editor The Rockefeller Found., N.Y.C., 1952-53; instr. French Vanderbilt U., Nashville, 1953-55; tchr. history Lincoln High Sch., Seattle, 1955-56; mem. bd. trustees Foothill-DeAnza Community Coll. Dist., Los Altos Hills, Calif., 1961-74; bd. govs. Calif. Community Colls., Sacramento, 1974-78; asst. dir. Calif. Community Coll. Assn., Sacramento, 1978-81; assoc. dean Coastline Community Coll., Fountain Valley, Calif., 1981-85, dean of instrn., 1985-91, v.p. instrn., 1991-92; mem. Mountain View (Calif.) City Coun., from 1997; vice mayor City of Mountain View, 1998. Cons. in field. Author: Power and Politics in Community Colleges, 1976; editor: Who Shapes the Curriculum?, 1988; contbr. articles to profl. jours. Chmn. Newport Beach (Calif.) Environ. Com., 1987, S. Coast Inst. for Gerontology, Costa Mesa, Calif., 1989. Fulbright scholar, U. Brussells, (1950), Korea (1986), Germany (1989); Carnegie fellow, 1954; named Citizen of the Yr., Los Altos Bd. Realtors, 1969, Educator of the Yr., Cypress Coll., 1978. Mem. Assn. Calif. Community Coll. Adminstrs., Calif. Elected Women (sec. 1990), Rotary. United Ch. of christ. Avocations: reading, travel, tennis, hiking. Home: Mountain View, Calif. Died Mar. 11, 2005.

ZORN, JAY DANIEL, music educator, writer; b. N.Y.C., Mar. 23, 1931; s. Leo and Sophia (Douglas) Z.; m. June C. August; children: Miriam, Marc, Lisa. MusB, Oberlin (Ohio) Conservatory Music, 1953; MA, Columbia U., 1958; MusEdD, Ind. U., 1969. Dir. bands Mammoneck (N.Y.) High Sch., 1958-68; 1st trumpeter Westchester Philharm. Orch., White Plains, N.Y., 1958-68; dir. bands Muskingum Coll. and Conservatory, New Concord, Ohio, 1968-72; prof. music U. So. Calif., Los Angeles, 1972—2006. Author: Exploring Trumpet's Upper Register, 1975, Brass Ensemble Method, 1978, Fundamentals of Music Theory, 1987, Music Listeners Companion, 1988. Served with USAF, 1953-57. Mem. Music Educators Nat. Conf. (former chmn. chamber music com.). Home: La Crescenta, Calif. Died July 31, 2006.

ZUCCA, GEORGE ROBERT, lawyer; b. Jersey City, June 7, 1943; s. George Anthony and Elizabeth (Masset) Z.; m. Lucy Picardi, May 11, 1980; 3 children. BA, Wagner Coll., 1966; JD, N.Y. Law Sch., 1969. Bar: N.J. 1969, U.S. Dist. Ct. N.J. 1969, U.S. Supreme Ct. 1974. Bond claim atty. USF&G, N.Y.C., 1969-70; staff atty. Calhoun & Reidy, Newark, 1971-72; trial atty. Stevens & Mathias, Newark, 1972-74; assoc. De Seur, Cerutti & Lombardi, Jersey City, 1974-89; assoc. counsel Farabaugh, Frieland, Smith & Hillmann, Lynnhurst, N.J., from 1989. Automobile arbitrator State of N.J., Jersey City, 1986—. Mem. ABA, Am. Arbitration Assn. (arbitrator 1980—). Home: Bayonne, NJ. Died Apr. 22, 2004.

ZUCKER, WILLIAM, retired business educator; b. Bridgeport, Conn., July 21, 1917; s. Meyer and Ida Lena (Elovitz) Z.; m. Kathlyn Saltman, Jan. 16, 1944; children—Peter Bayard, Alison Beth, Jeremy Michael, David Laurence AB, Johns Hopkins U., 1938; AM, Harvard U., 1940, PhD, 1951. Sec. Commerce and Industry Assn. of N.Y., N.Y.C., 1944-59; v.p. Downtown Lower Manhattan Assn., N.Y.C., 1959-64; pres. Southeastern Pa. Econ. Devel. Corp., Phila., 1964-73; adj. prof. Wharton Sch. U. Pa., Phila., 1972-83, assoc. dir. Entrepreneurial Ctr., Wharton Sch., 1973-83, dir. exec. edn. Wharton Sch., 1977-83, dir. Wharton Real Estate Ctr., 1983-88, Meshulam Riklis prof. creative mgmt. Wharton Sch., 1983-88, prof. emeritus, 1988—2006; pres. Adviserv Co., Phila., 1993-94. Lectr. CCNY, 1956-58; vis. prof. Columbia U. Grad. Sch. Bus., N.Y.C., 1988-91; adj. prof. Drexel U., Phila., 1997-2006. Author: Local Development Corporations, 1980, REITS, 1975; editor Real Estate Fin. Jour., 1985-98; contbr. articles to profl. jours. Mem. New Canaan Bd. Edn., Conn., 1961-64, New Canaan Bd. Fin., 1958-61 Democrat. Jewish. Home: Philadelphia, Pa. Died May 13, 2006.

ZUNDE, PRANAS, information science educator, researcher; b. Kaunas, Lithuania, Nov. 26, 1923; came to U.S., 1960, naturalized, 1964; s. Pranas and Elzbieta (Lisajevic) Z.; m. Alge R. Bizauskas, May 29, 1945; children:

Alge R., Audronis K., Aurelia R., Aidis L., Gytis J. Dipl. Ing., Hannover Inst. Tech., 1947; MS, George Washington U., 1965; PhD, Ga. Inst. Tech., 1968. Dir. project Documentation Inc., Bethesda, Md., 1961-64, mgr. mgmt. info. system, 1964-65; sr. research scientist Ga. Inst. Tech., Atlanta, 1965-68, assoc. prof., 1968-72, prof. dept. computer sci., 1973-91, prof. emeritus, from 1991. Cons. UNESCO, Caracas, Venezuela, 1970-72, Esquela Polit. Nacional, Quito, Ecuador, 1974-75, State of Ga., Atlanta, 1976-78, Royal Sch. Librarianship, Copenhagen, 1985-87, Clemson (N.C.) U., 1987—, N.Y. State Dept. Edn., 1993; vis. prof. Simon Bolivar U., Caracas, 1976, J. Kepler U., Austria, 1981; vis. scientist Riso Nat. Lab., Roskilde, Denmark, 1983, Lithuanian Acad. Scis., Vilnius, 1988-89. Author: Agriculture in Soviet Lithuania, 1962, National Science Information Systems in Eastern Europe, 1972; editor: Procs. Info. Utilities, 1974, Procs. Fouds. of Info. and Software Sci., 1983-90; contbr. articles to tech. and sci. jours. Mem. senate Vitoldus Magnus U., Kaunas, Lithuania, 1990—. NSF grantee; Fulbright prof. NAS, 1975. Mem. Am. Soc. Info. Sci., Semiotic Soc. Am., Soc. Sigma Xi. Roman Catholic. Home: Alexandria, Va. Died Dec. 30, 2004.

ZWANG, SHIRLEY SHAPIRO, artist; b. N.Y.C., Apr. 28, 1924; d. Benjamin and Lana Shapiro; widowed; children: David, Robert, Jonathan. Grad. in Illustration, Pratt Inst., 1945; B of Profl. Studies in Studio Art, SUNY, Purchase, 1979. Artist, Danbury, Conn., from 1974. Represented in permanent collections Temple Emanu-El, Temple Beth El, Spring Valley, N.Y., Maimonides Acad., Danbury, Conn., Jewish Fedn. Danbury, Temple Israel, N.Y.C., U.A.H.C., Cystic Fibrosis Found., and pvt. collections; exhibited in group shows at Brookfield (Conn.) Craft Ctr. Gallery, 1974, Ridgefield Guild of Artist Ctr., Westchester Art Assn., White Plains, N.Y., 1976, B'nai B'rith Klutznick Mus., Washington, 1977, 82, Skirball Mus., L.A., 1977, Jewish Fedn. Exhibit, Nashville, 1978, Yeshiva U. Mus., 1978, 79, SUNY, 1979, 80, Mamaroneck, N.Y. Artist Guild Show, 1980, Nat. Coun. Art in Jewish Life, N.Y.C., 1983, Am. Jewish Congress, 1985, Jewish Community Ctr., Tampa, 1986, U.A.H.C. Biennial Conv., Chgo., 1987, Jewish Community Ctr., Richmond, Va., 1988, Klutznik Mus., Ariz., 2000. Bd. dirs. Jewish Fedn. Greater Danbury, 1992—. Mem.: Synagogue Artists and Craftsmen of Union of Am. Hebrew Congregations. Avocations: golf, travel. Home: Danbury, Conn. Died July 9, 2004.